T·H·E
AMERICAN
HERITAGE

LAROUSSE
SPANISH
DICTIONARY

BERKLEY BOOKS, NEW YORK

Based on the hardcover
THE AMERICAN HERITAGE
LAROUSSE SPANISH DICTIONARY

THE AMERICAN HERITAGE LAROUSSE SPANISH DICTIONARY

A Berkley Book / published by arrangement with
Houghton Mifflin Company

PRINTING HISTORY
Berkley edition / August 1987

ISBN: 0-425-10397-8

A BERKLEY BOOK ® TM 757,375
Berkley Books are published by The Berkley Publishing Group,
200 Madison Avenue, New York, New York 10016.
The name "BERKLEY" and the "B" logo
are trademarks belonging to Berkley Publishing Corporation.
PRINTED IN THE UNITED STATES OF AMERICA

10   9   8   7   6   5   4

STAFF

Françoise Dubois-Charlier • *Project Editor, Larousse*

David R. Pritchard • *Editor, Houghton Mifflin*

Diane Traynor Senerth • *Editor*
J. Mauricio Sola • *Editor*

Contributing Editors

Lois Grossman — David Weeks

Ida Calero Fernández — Craig A. Lapine
Hélène Houssemaine-Florent — Grisel Lozano-Garcini
David A. Jost — Fernando A. Pfannl

Proofreading
Thelma Prince

Database Manager
Christopher Leonesio

Production Coordinator
Donna L. Muise

Editorial Production Assistants
Patricia McTiernan
Margaret Anne Miles

Composition Keyboarding
Brenda Bregoli-Sturtevant — Ron Perkins
Celester Jackson — Tracy Weiner

CONTENTS / ÍNDICE

PREFACE

This Dictionary is based on *The American Heritage Larousse Spanish Dictionary*, a major new bilingual work published jointly by Houghton Mifflin Company and Librairie Larousse in 1986. The vocabulary in this condensed version has been selected for its practicality and up-to-dateness, including such terms as **AIDS**, **microchip**, and **videocassette**. The English usage and spelling is that of the United States, with British variants clearly marked, while the Spanish represents both "pan-Hispanic" usage and the diverse special forms and senses found throughout Latin America. Many of the special features of the larger work have been retained. The various meanings of a word are identified by synonyms and labels, with clear typographic distinctions observed throughout the entry, enabling the user to quickly locate a precise equivalent for the particular sense that is wanted. Idioms, phrases, and example sentences have been kept in generous numbers, offering invaluable help in the idiomatic use of both languages.

GUIDE TO THE DICTIONARY

Entry words All entry words are divided into syllables. Words that are identical in spelling but that constitute separate entries are entered with superscript numbers (**haber¹, haber²**).

Inflected entry words Nouns and adjectives that inflect for gender are entered under the masculine form. The feminine ending is separated from the masculine form by a comma (**ca·i·do, a**). When the feminine form contains a syllable break that is different from the masculine, the break is indicated (**cal·cu·la·dor, ·ra**), as is any change in the written accent (**ca·be·zón, o·na**).

Variants Variant spellings of an entry word are indicated with parentheses or with a bold slash (**fe·mi·n(e)i·dad; gla·dia·dor/tor**). Syllable breaks and gender differences are fully shown (**gla·dí·o·lo/dio·lo; ba·rran·co** m./ca f.; **gen·ti·li·dad** f./**lis·mo** m.). The form to the left of the slash always represents a complete word, though an inflected feminine ending after the slash applies to both the entry word and its variant (**gaz·mo·ñe·ro/ño, a**). When the inflected ending applies only to the main entry and not to the variant, it is placed before the slash (**gor·je·a·dor, ·ra/je·an·te**).

Cross-references When a variant form of an entry word does not occur close enough to the main entry to be combined in a single entry, a cross-reference is given (**sicología** f. var. of **psicología**). Feminine nouns that are semantically related to a masculine form are treated under the masculine entry. When a feminine noun falls more than five lines away from its masculine entry in alphabetical order, a cross-reference is given (**justa** f. see **justo, a**).

Irregular verbs All irregular verbs are referenced to the Spanish Verb Table with a boldface section number (**dar §20**). The number corresponds to the appropriate model verb in the Table. Common irregular verb forms are entered in the Dictionary along with cross-references to their infinitives (**estuviera, vo** see **estar**).

Organization of entries Equivalents of the entry word are given in roman type. Synonymous equivalents are separated by commas. Different senses are separated by semicolons. The various senses of an entry word are distinguished by either of two features: (i) a synonym or phrase in the language of the entry word, given in italic type within parentheses, or (ii) a field label printed in small capital letters (CHEM., ECON.). When the first equivalent of an entry word is the most frequent translation or an obvious cognate, no discrimination is given for that sense.

Labels are also used to indicate levels of appropriate usage (COLL., SL.) or restriction to a geographic region (AMER., MEX.). Regional meanings are placed after all other senses for a particular part of speech and are grouped by general region first, then specific countries. Example phrases are enclosed within angle brackets following the sense to which they apply. Note that when the entry word is used within the entry with no change in spelling, it is abbreviated to its initial letter.

Idioms, phrases, and plurals Common idioms and phrases are listed as run-on entries at the appropriate part of speech. The first run-on is introduced by a bold diamond (♦). Additional items follow in alphabetical order and are separated by bold bullets (•). Equivalents or idioms involving the plural usage of the entry word are grouped after a bold diamond followed by the plural label (♦ pl.) Plurals that follow the diamond are abbreviated to their initial letter.

PREFACIO

Este diccionario está basado en *The American Heritage Larousse Spanish Dictionary*, importante y nueva obra bilingüe publicada en conjunto por las editoriales Houghton Mifflin y Librairie Larousse. El vocabulario que presentamos en esta obra condensada es el más práctico y moderno que se pueda encontrar hoy en día, incluyendo términos como **SIDA**, **microplaqueta**, y **videocasete**. El uso del inglés y su ortografía son los correspondientes al inglés de los Estados Unidos, mientras que las variaciones británicas aparecen claramente identifica-das. El castellano representado en este diccionario incluye las diversas formas y acepciones que pueden encontrarse en el habla de Latinoamérica. En la diagramación de esta obra condensada hemos conservado muchas de las características del diccionario original. Los artículos han sido organizados con el fin de ofrecer al lector el equivalente preciso de la palabra o frase que necesita encontrar. Los modismos, frases y ejemplos abundan en esta obra, ofreciendo al lector una ayuda invaluable en el uso idiomático de ambas lenguas.

GUÍA PARA EL USO DE ESTE DICCIONARIO

Vocablos Todos los vocablos han sido silabeados. Las palabras cuya ortografía es idéntica pero cuyos significados son diferentes se incluyen en forma separada, acompañadas de un índice sobrescrito (**like¹**, **like²**).

Fonética La guía para la pronunciación de los vocablos ha sido basada en el sistema usado por *The American Heritage Dictionary*. (Véase la Guía para la Pronunciación Inglesa.) En este sistema los acentos tónicos primarios (´), secundarios (ʹ) y la indicación de una sílaba no acentuada (-) aparecen a continuación de la sílaba que modifican: **generosity** (jĕnʹə-rŏsʹ-ĭ-tē). En esta obra hemos utilizado estos símbolos no sólo para indicar la acentuación sino también para reemplazar las sílabas que se repiten en las palabras derivadas. Por ejemplo, dada la pronunciación del vocablo **humid** (hyōōʹmĭd), hemos abreviado la pronunciación de **humidifier** de esta forma: (-ʹə-fīʹər), en donde (-) reemplaza a la sílaba no acentuada (hyōō-) y (ʹ) reemplaza a la sílaba acentuada (mĭdʹ). De haberse escrito en su totalidad, **humidifier** se transcribiría (hyōō-mĭdʹə-fīʹər). La sílaba o la combinación de sílabas que se pronuncia igual que el vocablo que las precede han sido abreviadas con el símbolo (:). En el caso del vocablo **humidify** (:ə-fī), el símbolo (:) reemplaza a (-ʹ) de la palabra que antecede. De haberse escrito en su totalidad, **humidify** se transcribiría (hyōō-mĭdʹə-fī).

Variantes Las variaciones ortográficas de un vocablo aparecen entre paréntesis o separadas por una vírgula en negrilla (**adz(e)**; **con·vey·er/or**). Los cambios en el silabeo se indican con claridad (**con·vert·er/·tor**), así como el cambio en la pronunciación de una variante (véase **coupe/**-pé). No ofrecemos, en cambio, la pronunciación de las variaciones en los casos se muestran de adjetivos con terminación **-ic/i-cal** (-ĭk/ĭ-kəl) o sustantivos con terminación **-ence/en·cy** o **-ance/an·cy** (-əns/ən-sē) ya que se consideran variaciones regulares.

Formas irregulares Cuando el vocablo inglés tiene una irregularidad, ésta se indica en letra negrilla. Las formas comparativas y superlativas de los adjetivos se muestran de la siguiente manera: 1) **big** adj. **-gg-**, para indicar **bigger**, **biggest**; 2) **happy** adj. **-i-**, para indicar **happier**, **happiest**; 3) **ample** adj. **-er**, **-est**, para indicar **ampler**, **amplest**. No hemos indicado la irregularidad de los adjetivos de una sola sílaba que terminan en consonante (como **hard**, **low**) ya que usualmente forman su comparativo y superlativo agregándosele **-er** y **-est**. La información referente a la formación de plurales irregulares aparece en corchetes (**knife** [pl. **-ves**]).

En cuanto a los verbos, las formas irregulares del pretérito y del participio pasado se indican en la siguiente forma: **sing** intr. **sang**, **sung** (el gerundio se incluye solamente en los casos en que se repite la última consonante). Nótese que cuando el pretérito y el participio pasado coinciden en forma, la forma irregular aparece solamente una vez (**make** tr. **made**). En otros casos indicamos solamente la irregularidad ortográfica, evitando así la repetición: 1) **step** intr. **-pp-**, para indicar **stepped**, **stepped**, **stepping**; 2) **hew** tr. **-ed**, **-ed** o **-n**, para indicar **hewed**, **hewed** o **hewn**; 3) **mimic** tr. **-ck-**, para indicar **mimicked**, **mimicked**, **mimicking**. Los verbos cuya terminación y cambia por *i* se consideran regulares y no aparecen en el artículo (**try**, **tried**, **tried**, **trying**).

Organización de los artículos Los equivalentes del vocablo a definirse y sus sinónimos aparecen en letra redonda y están separados por una coma. Las diferentes acepciones del vocablo aparecen separadas por un punto y coma. Las distintas acepciones de cada palabra se han diferenciado por medio de (i) un sinónimo o frase escrita en el idioma del vocablo, en cursiva y entre paréntesis, o, (ii) un rótulo impreso en letras mayúsculas pequeñas (ECON., QUÍM.). Estas convenciones no han sido utilizadas cuando el primer equivalente del vocablo es de uso muy frecuente o cuando su traducción es un cognado directo.

Los rótulos se usan frecuentemente para indicar el uso apropiado del vocablo (FAM., JER.) o para circunscribir su uso a un país determinado (E.U., G.B.). Los ejemplos aparecen entre corchetes angulares, inmediatamente después de la acepción que ilustran. Nótese que el vocablo inglés se abrevia cuando aparece en el ejemplo exactamente como cuando encabeza el artículo.

Modismos, locuciones y formas plurales Los modismos de interés general y las locuciones aparecen en la parte de la oración a la que corresponden, precedidos por un rombo en negrilla (♦), y separados en forma alfabética por el símbolo (•). Ciertos equivalentes y locuciones que demandan el uso del vocablo en su forma plural han sido agrupados en forma similar (♦ pl.). Las formas plurales que se ofrecen en esta sección se abrevian con la inicial del vocablo que encabeza el artículo.

ABBREVIATIONS / ABREVIATURAS

abbr.	abbreviation	CIENC. FIC.	ciencia ficción
abr.	abreviatura	CIENT.	científico
ACC.	accounting	CINEM.	cinema/cinematografía
ACOUS.	acoustics	CIR.	cirugía
ACÚS.	acústica	COLL.	colloquial
adj.	adjective/adjetivo	COM.	commerce/comercio
adv.	adverb/adverbio	comp.	comparative/comparativo
AER.	aeronautics/aeronáutica	COMPUT.	computers/computadoras
AGR.	agriculture/agricultura	conj.	conjunction/conjunción
ANAT.	anatomy/anatomía	CONSTR.	construction/construcción
ANT.	antiguo	contr.	contraction/contracción
ANTHR.	anthropology	COST.	costura
ANTROP.	antropología	CRIMIN.	criminology/criminología
ARCH.	archaic	CUL.	culinary/culinario
ARCHEOL.	archeology	def.	definite/definido
ARCHIT.	architecture	dem.	demonstrative/demostrativo
ARM.	arms/armas	DENT.	dentistry
ARQ.	arquitectura	DEP.	deportes
ARQUEOL.	arqueología	DER.	derecho
art.	article/artículo	DEROG.	derogatory
ARTE.	bellas artes	DESPEC.	despectivo
ARTIL.	artillery	DIAL.	dialect/dialecto
ARTS	fine arts	DIB.	dibujo
ASTROL.	astrology/astrología	DIPL.	diplomacy/diplomacia
ASTRON.	astronomy/astronomía	ECOL.	ecology/ecología
ASTRONAUT.	astronautical	ECON.	economics/economía
ASTRONÁUT.	astronáutica	EDUC.	education/educación
AUTO.	automobile/automovilismo	ELEC.	electricity/electricidad
aux.	auxiliary/auxiliar	ELECTRON.	electronics
AVIA.	aviation/aviación	ELECTRÓN.	electrónica
BIBL.	Bible	ENGIN.	engineering
BÍBL.	bíblico	ENTOM.	entomology/entomología
BIOCHEM.	biochemistry	EQUIT.	equitation/equitación
BIOL.	biology/biología	ESCULT.	escultura
BIOQUÍM.	bioquímica	esp.	especially/especialmente
BKB.	bookbinding	EUFEM.	eufemismo
BOT.	botany/botánica	EUPH.	euphemism
CARP.	carpentry/carpintería	f.	feminine/femenino
CERAM.	ceramics	FAM.	familiar
CERÁM.	cerámica	FARM.	farmacia
cf.	consulte	F.C.	ferrocarril
CHEM.	chemistry	FIG.	figurative/figurado

FILOS.	filosofía	PALEON.	paleontology/paleontología
FIN.	finance/finanzas	part.	participle/participio
FÍS.	física	PERIOD.	periodismo
FISIOL.	fisiología	pers.	person, personal/personal
FONÉT.	fonética	PHARM.	pharmaceutics
FOR.	forense	PHILOS.	philosophy
FORT.	fortificación	PHONET.	phonetics
FOTOG.	fotografía	PHOTO.	photography
GEOF.	geofísica	PHYS.	physics
GEOG.	geography/geografía	PHYSIOL.	physiology
GEOL.	geology/geología	PINT.	pintura
GEOM.	geometry/geometría	pl.	plural/plural
GEOFI.	geophysics	POET.	poetry, poetic
GRAM.	grammar/gramática	POÉT.	poética
HER.	heraldry/heráldica	POL.	politics/política
HIST.	history/historia	pos.	posesivo
HORT.	horticulture/horticultura	poss.	possessive
HUM.	humorous/humorístico	prep.	preposition/preposición
ICHTH.	ichthyology	pres.	present/presente
ICT.	ictiología	pret.	preterite/pretérito
IMPR.	imprenta	PRINT.	printing
indef.	indefinite/indefinido	pron.	pronoun/pronombre
INDUS.	industry/industria	PSIC.	psicología
ING.	ingeniería	PSYCH.	psychology
interj.	interjection/interjección	QUÍM.	química
interrog.	interrogative/interrogativo	RAD.	radio/radio
intr.	intransitive/intransitivo	RAIL.	railway
inv.	invariable/invariable	reflex.	reflexive/reflexivo
IRÓN.	irónico	REG.	regional/regional
JER.	jerga	rel.	relative/relativo
JEWEL.	jewelry	RELIG.	religion/religión
JOURN.	journalism	RET.	retórica
JOY.	joyería	RHET.	rhetoric
LAW	law	s.	sustantivo
LIT.	literature/literatura	SCI.	science
LOG.	logic	SCULP.	sculpture
LÓG.	lógica	SEW.	sewing
m.	masculine/masculino	sing., sg.	singular/singular
MACH.	machinery	SL.	slang
MAQ.	maquinaria	SOCIOL.	sociology/sociología
MARIT.	maritime	SPORT.	sports
MARÍT.	marítimo	subj.	subjunctive/subjuntivo
MAS.	masonry	superl.	superlative/superlativo
MAT.	matemáticas	SURG.	surgery
MATH.	mathematics	SURV.	surveying
MEC.	mecánica	TAUR.	bullfighting/tauromaquia
MECH.	mechanics	TEAT.	teatro
MED.	medicine/medicina	TEC.	tecnología
METAL.	metallurgy/metalurgia	TECH.	technical
METEOROL.	meteorology/meteorología	TEJ.	tejeduría
MIL.	military/militar	TEL.	telecomunicaciones
MIN.	mineralogy/mineralogía	TELEC.	telecommunications
MITOL.	mitología	TELEV.	television/televisión
MUS.	music	TEN.	teneduría de libros
MÚS.	música	TEO.	teología
MYTH.	mythology	TEX.	textiles
NUMIS.	numismatics/numismática	THEAT.	theater
ODONT.	odontología	THEOL.	theology
OFTAL.	oftalmología	TIP.	tipografía
OPHTHAL.	ophthalmology	TOP.	topography/topografía
OPT.	optics	tr.	transitive/transitivo
ÓPT.	óptica	v.	verbo
ORNIT.	ornitología	var.	variant/variante
ORNITH.	ornithology	VET.	veterinary/veterinaria
p.	past/pasado	ZOOL.	zoology/zoología
PAINT.	painting		

SPANISH PRONUNCIATION GUIDE

Letter	Spanish Example	English Example	Description
a	pata	father	
b	boca	bib	At the beginning of a word
	cabo		Between vowels, closer to *v*
c	calco	cat	Before *a, o, u,* like *k*
	cedro	cedar	Before *e, i* like *s*; in much of Spain pronounced like *th* of *thick*
ch	chiste	church	
d	dar	die	At the beginning of a word
	cada		Between vowels, like *th* of *rather*
e	leche	café	
f	fácil	fat	
g	gente		Before *e, i,* like *h* of *ha*!
	guerra	guide	With *u* before *e, i,* a hard *g*
	gato	got	Before *a, o, u,* a hard *g*
h	honor		Always silent
i	silla	machine	
j	jugo		Like *h* in *ha*!
k	kilo	kite	
l	listo	list	
ll	llama		In Spain, like *lli* of *million*; elsewhere like Spanish consonant *y* (see below)
m	mamá	mum	
n	nona	none	
ñ	año		Like *ny* of *canyon*
o	solo	so	
p	papa	pipe	
q	quita	raquet	
r	caro		Like *dd* of *ladder*
rr	carro		Strongly trilled
s	soso	sass	
t	tonto	tight	
u	luto	lute	
	agüero	anguish	
v	vino		Identical to initial Spanish *b*
	lava		Identical to intervocalic Spanish *b*
w	wat		Pronounced either like English *v* or *w*
x	éxito	exit	Exception: in "México" *x* is like Spanish *j*
	mixto		Before a consonant, may be pronounced *s*
y	y		Like *i* of *machine*
	yeso	yes	In River Plate, like *s* of *vision*
z	zona		Like *s* in *sass*; in much of Spain, like *th* of *thick*

GUÍA PARA LA PRONUNCIACIÓN INGLESA

Símbolo	Ejemplo inglés	Ejemplo español	Sonido aproximado
ă	pat	—	entre la *a* y la *e*
ā	pay, mate	rey	
âr	care, hair	—	parecido a *ea* en *brea* (con la *r*)
ä	father	año	
b	bib	boca	
ch	church	chico	
d	deed, milled	dar	
ĕ	pet, feather	el	
ē	bee, me, piece	mil	
f	fife, phase, rough	fama	
g	gag	gato	
h	hat	joya	
hw	which	juez	
ĭ	pit	—	entre la *i* y la *e*
ī	pie, by	aire	
îr	pier, dear, mere	—	entre *ía* en *día* e *íe* en *fíe* (con la *r*)
j	judge	—	entre la *y* inicial y la *ch*
k	kick, cat, pique	casa	
kw	quick	cuan	
l	lid, needle	luz	
m	mum	muy	
n	no, sudden	no	
ng	thing	inglés	
ŏ	pot, swat	la	
ō	toe, go, boat	solo	
ô	caught, paw, for	corre	
oi	noise, boy	oigo	
ŏŏ	took	—	parecido a la *u* en *yogur*, más breve
ōō	boot, suit	uno	
ou	out, cow	auto	
p	pop	pan	
r	roar	—	una *ere* con la lengua curvada hacia atrás
s	sauce	sapo	
sh	ship, dish	—	una *che* suavizada, más como la *ese*
t	tight, stopped	tu	
th	thin, path	—	parecido a la *ce* de Castilla
th	this, bathe	cada	
ŭ	cut, rough	—	parecido a una *o* que tira a la *a*
yoo	use, few	ciudad	
ûr	urge, term, firm	—	parecido a una *e* que tira a la *o* (con la *r*)
v	valve	—	una *efe* sonora
w	with	cual	
y	yes	yo	
z	zebra, xylem	mismo	
zh	vision, pleasure	—	parecido a la *ll* de Argentina
ə	about, item, edible, gallop, circus	—	parecido a una *e* muy breve que tira a la *i*

SPANISH VERB TABLE

The following Table presents model conjugations for all regular and irregular Spanish verbs. These models include only those tenses in which an irregular conjugation occurs. All irregular forms are printed in bold type.

§01 REGULAR VERB CONJUGATIONS:

-AR Verbs: AMAR	-ER Verbs: VENDER	-IR Verbs: PARTIR
Present		
AM-o	VEND-o	PART-o
-as	-es	-es
-a	-e	-e
-amos	-emos	-imos
-áis	-éis	-ís
-an	-en	-en
Imperfect		
AM-aba	VEND-ía	PART-ía
-abas	-ías	-ías
-aba	-ía	-ía
-ábamos	-íamos	-íamos
-abais	-íais	-íais
-aban	-ían	-ían
Preterit		
AM-é	VEND-í	PART-í
-aste	-iste	-iste
-ó	-ió	-ió
-amos	-imos	-imos
-asteis	-isteis	-isteis
-aron	-ieron	-ieron
Present Subjunctive		
AM-e	VEND-a	PART-a
-es	-as	-as
-e	-a	-a
-emos	-amos	-amos
-éis	-áis	-áis
-en	-an	-an
Imperfect Subjunctive		
AM-ara/ase	VEND-iera/iese	PART-iera/iese
-aras/ases	-ieras/ieses	-ieras/ieses
-ara/ase	-iera/iese	-iera/iese
-áramos/ásemos	-iéramos/iésemos	-iéramos/iésemos
-arais/aseis	-ierais/ieseis	-ierais/ieseis
-aran/asen	-ieran/iesen	-ieran/iesen
Future/Conditional		
AMAR-é/ía	VENDER-é/ía	PARTIR-é/ía
-ás/ías	-ás/ías	-ás/ías
-á/ía	-á/ía	-á/ía
-emos/íamos	-emos/íamos	-emos/íamos
-éis/íais	-éis/íais	-éis/íais
-án/ían	-án/ían	-án/ían
Imperative		
ama/amad	vende/vended	parte/partid
Present Participle		
amando	vendiendo	partiendo
Past Participle		
amado	vendido	partido

§02 ADQUIRIR

Pres.	adquiero	adquirimos
	adquieres	adquirís
	adquiere	adquieren

Pres.	adquiera	adquiramos
Subj.	adquieras	adquiráis
	adquiera	adquieran

§03 AGORAR

Pres.	agüero	agoramos
	agüeras	agoráis
	agüera	agüeran

Pres.	agüere	agoremos
Subj.	agüeres	agoréis
	agüere	agüeren

§04 ALZAR

Pret. alcé, alzaste, etc.
Pres. Subj. alce, etc.

§05 ANDAR

Pret.	anduve	anduvimos
	aduviste	anduvisteis
	anduvo	anduvieron

Imp. Subj. anduviera/iese, etc.

§06 ARCAIZAR

Pres.	arcaízo	arcaizamos
	arcaízas	arcaizáis
	arcaíza	arcaízan

Pret. arcaicé, arcaizaste, etc.

Pres.	arcaíce	arcaicemos
Subj.	arcaíces	arcaicéis
	arcaíce	arcaícen

§07 ARGÜIR

Pres.	arguyo	argüimos
	arguyes	argüís
	arguye	arguyen

Pret.	argüí	argüimos
	argüiste	argüisteis
	arguyó	arguyeron

Pres. Subj. arguya, etc.
Imp. Subj. arguyera/iese, etc.
Pres. Part. arguyendo

§08 ASIR

Pres. asgo, ases, etc.
Pres. Subj. asga, etc.

§09 AVERGONZAR

Pres.	avergüenzo	avergonzamos
	avergüenzas	avergonzáis
	avergüenza	avergüenzan

Pret. avergoncé, avergonzaste, etc.

Pres.	avergüence	avergoncemos
Subj.	avergüences	avergoncéis
	avergüence	avergüencen

§10 AVERIGUAR

Pret. averigüé, averiguaste, etc.
Pres. Subj. averigüe, etc.

§11 BENDECIR like DECIR in all
forms *except* Fut./Cond.:
bendeciré/bendeciría, etc.

§12 BRUÑIR

Pret.	bruñí	bruñimos
	bruñiste	bruñisteis
	bruñó	bruñeron

Imp. Subj. bruñera/ese, etc.
Pres. Part. bruñendo

§13 BULLIR

Pret.	bullí	bullimos
	bulliste	bullisteis
	bulló	bulleron

Imp. Subj. bullera/ese, etc.
Pres. Part. bullendo

§14 CABER

Pres. quepo, cabes, etc.

Pret.	cupe	cupimos
	cupiste	cupisteis
	cupo	cupieron

Pres. Subj. quepa, etc.
Imp. Subj. cupiera/iese, etc.
Fut./Cond. cabré/cabría, etc.

§15 CAER

Pres. caigo, caes etc.

Pret.	caí	caímos
	caíste	caísteis
	cayó	cayeron

Pres. Subj. caiga, etc.
Imp. Subj. cayera/ese, etc.
Pres. Part. cayendo
Past Part. caído

§16 COLGAR

Pres.	cuelgo	colgamos
	cuelgas	colgáis
	cuelga	cuelgan

Pret. colgué, colgaste, etc.

Pres.	cuelgue	colguemos
Subj.	cuelgues	colguéis
	cuelgue	cuelguen

§17 CONOCER

Pres. conozco, conoces, etc.
Pres. Subj. conozca, etc.

§18 CONSTRUIR

Pres.	construyo	construimos
	construyes	construís
	construye	construyen

Pret.	construí	contruimos
	construiste	construisteis
	construyó	construyeron

Pres. Subj. construya, etc.
Imp. Subj. construyera/ese, etc.
Pres. Part. construyendo

§19 CONTAR

Pres.	cuento	contamos
	cuentas	contáis
	cuenta	cuentan

Pres.	cuente	contemos
Subj.	cuentes	contéis
	cuente	cuenten

§20 DAR
Pres. **doy,** das, etc.

Pret.	**di**	**dimos**
	diste	**disteis**
	dio	**dieron**

Pres.	**dé**	demos
Subj.	des	deis
	dé	den

Imp. Subj. **diera/iese,** etc.

§21 DECIR

Pres.	**digo**	decimos
	dices	decís
	dice	**dicen**

Pres. Subj. **diga,** etc.
Imp. Subj. **dijera/ese,** etc.
Fut./Cond. **diré/diría,** etc.
Imperative **di,** decid
Pres. Part. **diciendo**
Past Part. **dicho**

§22 DEDUCIR
Pres. **deduzco,** deduces, etc.

Pret.	**deduje**	**dedujimos**
	dedujiste	**dedujisteis**
	dedujo	**dedujeron**

Pres. Subj. **deduzca,** etc.
Imp. Subj. **dedujera/ese,** etc.

§23 DELINQUIR
Pres. **delinco,** delinques, etc.
Pres. Subj. **delinca,** etc.

§24 DESOSAR

Pres.	**deshueso**	desosamos
	deshuesas	desosáis
	deshuesa	**deshuesan**

Pres.	**deshuese**	desosemos
Subj.	**deshueses**	desoséis
	deshuese	**deshuesen**

§25 DISCERNIR

Pres.	**discierno**	discernimos
	disciernes	discernís
	discierne	**disciernen**

Pres.	**discierna**	discernamos
Subj.	**disciernas**	discernáis
	discierna	**disciernan**

§26 DISTINGUIR
Pres. **distingo,** distingues, etc.
Pres. Subj. **distinga,** etc.

§27 DORMIR

Pres.	**duermo**	dormimos
	duermes	dormís
	duerme	**duermen**

Pret.	dormí	dormimos
	dormiste	dormisteis
	durmió	**durmieron**

Pres.	**duerma**	**durmamos**
Subj.	**duermas**	**durmáis**
	duerma	**duerman**

Imp. Subj. **durmiera/iese,** etc.
Pres. Part. **durmiendo**

xii

§28 EMPELLER

Pret.	empellí	empellimos
	empelliste	empellisteis
	empelló	**empellieron**

Imp. Subj. **empellera/ese,** etc.
Pres. Part. **empellendo**

§29 EMPEZAR

Pres.	**empiezo**	empezamos
	empiezas	empazáis
	empieza	**empiezan**

Pret. **empecé,** empezaste, etc.

Pres.	**empiece**	**empecemos**
Subj.	**empieces**	**empecéis**
	empiece	**empiecen**

§30 ENVIAR

Pres.	**envío**	enviamos
	envías	enviáis
	envía	**envían**

Pres.	**envíe**	enviemos
Subj.	**envíes**	enviéis
	envíe	**envíen**

§31 ERGUIR

Pres.	**irgo***	erguimos
	irgues*	erguís
	irgue*	**irguen***

*[alternate forms: **yergo,** etc.]

Pret.	erguí	erguimos
	erguiste	erguisteis
	irguió	**irguieron**

Pres. Subj. **irga/yerga,** etc.
Imp. Subj. **irguiera/iese,** etc.
Pres. Part. **irguiendo**

§32 ERIGIR
Pres. **erijo,** eriges, etc.
Pres. Subj. **erija,** etc.

§33 ERRAR

Pres.	**yerro**	erramos
	yerras	erráis
	yerra	**yerran**

Pres.	**yerre**	erremos
Subj.	**yerres**	erréis
	yerre	**yerren**

§34 ESCOGER
Pres. **escojo,** escoges, etc.
Pres. Subj. **escoja,** etc.

§35 ESPARCIR
Pres. **esparzo,** esparces, etc.
Pres. Subj. **esparza,** etc.

§36 ESTAR

Pres.	**estoy**	estamos
	estás	estáis
	está	**están**

Pret.	**estuve**	**estuvimos**
	estuviste	**estuvisteis**
	estuvo	**estuvieron**

Pres.	**esté**	estemos
Subj.	**estés**	estéis
	esté	**estén**

Imp. Subj. **estuviera/iese**, etc.

§37 FORZAR

Pres.	**fuerzo**	forzamos
	fuerzas	forzáis
	fuerza	**fuerzan**

Pret. **forcé**, forzaste, etc.

Pres.	**fuerce**	**forcemos**
Subj.	**fuerces**	**forcéis**
	fuerce	**fuercen**

§38 GARANTIR [defective]

| *Pres.* | --- | garantimos |
| | --- | garantís |

Pres. Subj. ---
Imperative ---, garantid

§39 HABER

Pres.	**he**	**hemos**
	has	habéis
	ha	**han**
Pret.	**hube**	**hubimos**
	hubiste	**hubisteis**
	hubo	**hubieron**

Pres. Subj. **haya**, etc.
Imp. Subj. **hubiera/iese**, etc.
Fut./Cond. **habré/habría**, etc.
Imperative hé, habed

§40 HACER

Pres. **hago**, haces, etc.

Pret.	**hice**	**hicimos**
	hiciste	**hicisteis**
	hizo	**hicieron**

Pres. Subj. **haga**, etc.
Imp. Subj. **hiciera/iese**, etc.
Fut./Cond. **haré/haría**, etc.
Imperative **haz**, haced
Past Part. **hecho**

§41 IR

Pres.	**voy**	**vamos**
	vas	**vais**
	va	**van**

Imperfect **iba**, etc.

Pret.	**fui**	**fuimos**
	fuiste	**fuisteis**
	fue	**fueron**

Imp. Subj. **fuera/ese**, etc.
Imperative **vo**, id
Pres. Part. **yendo**

§42 JUGAR

Pres.	**juego**	jugamos
	juegas	jugáis
	juega	**juegan**

Pret. **jugué**, jugaste, etc.

Pres.	**juegue**	**juguemos**
Subj.	**juegues**	**juguéis**
	juegue	**jueguen**

§43 LEER

Pret.	**leí**	**leímos**
	leíste	**leísteis**
	leyó	**leyeron**

Imp. Subj. **leyera/ese**, etc.
Pres. Part. **leyendo**

§44 LUCIR

Pres. **luzco**, luces, etc.
Pres. Subj. **luzca**, etc.

§45 OÍR

Pres.	**oigo**	**oímos**
	oyes	**oís**
	oye	**oyen**
Pret.	**oí**	**oímos**
	oíste	**oísteis**
	oyó	**oyeron**

Pres. Subj. **oiga**, etc.
Imp. Subj. **oyera/ese**, etc.
Pres. Part. **oyendo**
Past Part. **oído**

§46 OLER

Pres.	**huelo**	olemos
	hueles	oléis
	huele	**huelen**
Pres.	**huela**	olamos
Subj.	**huelas**	oláis
	huela	**huelan**

§47 PAGAR

Pret. **pagué**, pagaste, etc.
Pres. Subj. **pagues**, etc.

§48 PEDIR

Pres.	**pido**	pedimos
	pides	pedís
	pide	**piden**
Pret.	**pedí**	pedimos
	pediste	pedisteis
	pidió	**pidieron**

Pres. Subj. **pida**, etc.
Imp. Subj. **pidiera/iese**, etc.
Pres. Part. **pidiendo**

§49 PENSAR

Pres.	**pienso**	pensamos
	piensas	pensáis
	piensa	**piensan**
Pres.	**piense**	pensemos
Subj.	**pienses**	penséis
	piense	**piensen**

§50 PERDER

Pres.	**pierdo**	perdemos
	pierdes	perdéis
	pierde	**pierden**
Pres.	**pierda**	perdamos
Subj.	**pierdas**	perdáis
	pierda	**pierdan**

§51 PLACER

Pres. **plazco**, places, etc.

Pret.	**plací**	placimos
	placiste	placisteis
	plació*	**placieron***

*[alternate forms: **plugo**, **plugieron**]
Pres. Subj. **plazca**, etc.
Imp. Subj. **placiera/iese***, etc.
*[alternate form: **plugiera/iese**]

§52 PLEGAR

Pres. **pliego**	plegamos
pliegas	plegáis
pliega	**pliegan**
Pret. **plegué**, plegaste, etc.	
Pres. **pliegue**	**pleguemos**
Subj. **pliegues**	**pleguéis**
pliegue	**plieguen**

§53 PODER

Pres. **puedo**	podemos
puedes	podéis
puede	**pueden**
Pret. **pude**	**pudimos**
pudiste	**pudisteis**
pudo	**pudieron**
Pres. **pueda**	podamos
Subj. **puedas**	podáis
pueda	**puedan**
Imp. Subj. **pudiera/iese**, etc.	
Fut./Cond. **podré/podría**, etc.	
Pres. Part. **pudiendo**	

§54 PONER

Pres. **pongo**, pones, etc.	
Pret. **puse**	**pusimos**
pusiste	**pusisteis**
puso	**pusieron**
Pres. Subj. **ponga**, etc.	
Imp. Subj. **pusiera/iese**, etc.	
Fut./Cond. **pondré/pondría**, etc.	
Imperative **pon**, poned	
Past Part. **puesto**	

§55 QUERER

Pres. **quiero**	queremos
quieres	queréis
quiere	**quieren**
Pret. **quise**	**quisimos**
quisiste	**quisisteis**
quiso	**quisieron**
Pres. **quiera**	queramos
Subj. **quieras**	queráis
quiera	**quieran**
Imp. Subj. **quisiera/iese**, etc.	
Fut./Cond. **querré/querría**, etc.	

§56 RAER

Pres. **raigo***	raemos
raes	raéis
rae	raen

*[alternate form: **rayo**]

Pret. **raí**	**raímos**
raíste	**raísteis**
rayó	**rayeron**
Pres. Subj. **raiga***, etc.	

*[alternate form: **raya**]

Imp. Subj. **rayera/ese**, etc.
Pres. Part. **rayendo**
Past Part. **raído**

§57 REGIR

Pres. **rijo**	regimos
riges	regís
rige	**rigen**
Pret. **regí**	regimos
registe	registeis
rigió	**rigieron**
Pres. Subj. **rija**, etc.	
Imp. Subj. **rigiera/iese**, etc.	
Pres. Part. **rigiendo**	

§58 REÍR

Pres. **río**	**reímos**
ríes	reís
ríe	**ríen**
Pret. **reí**	**reímos**
reíste	**reísteis**
rió	**rieron**
Pres. Subj. **ría**, etc.	
Imp. Subj. **riera/iese**, etc.	
Pres. Part. **riendo**	
Past Part. **reído**	

§59 REÑIR

Pres. **riño**	reñimos
riñes	reñís
riñe	**riñen**
Pret. **reñí**	reñimos
reñiste	reñisteis
riñó	**riñeron**
Pres. Subj. **riña**, etc.	
Imp. Subj. **riñera/ese**, etc.	
Pres. Part. **riñendo**	

§60 REUNIR

Pres. **reúno**	reunimos
reúnes	reunís
reúne	**reúnen**
Pres. **reúna**	reunamos
Subj. **reúnas**	reunáis
reúna	**reúnan**

§61 ROER

Pres. **roo***	roemos
roes	roéis
roe	roen

*[alternate forms: **roigo** or **royo**]

Pret. **roí**	**roímos**
roíste	**roísteis**
royó	**royeron**
Pres. Subj. **roa***, etc.	

*[alternate forms: **roiga** or **roya**]

Imp. Subj. **royera/ese**, etc.
Pres. Part. **royendo**
Past Part. **roído**

§62 SABER

Pres. **sé**, sabes, etc.

Pret. **supe**	**supimos**
supiste	**supisteis**
supo	**supieron**
Pres. Subj. **sepa**, etc.	
Imp. Subj. **supiera/iese**, etc.	
Fut./Cond. **sabré/sabría**, etc.	

§63 SALIR

Pres. **salgo**, sales, etc.
Pres. Subj. **salga**, etc.
Fut./Cond. **saldré/saldría**, etc.
Imperative **sal**, salid

§64 SEGUIR

Pres.	**sigo**	seguimos
	sigues	seguís
	sigue	**siguen**
Pret.	seguí	seguimos
	seguiste	seguisteis
	siguió	**siguieron**

Pres. Subj. **siga**, etc.
Imp. Subj. **siguiera/iese**, etc.
Pres. Part. **siguiendo**

§65 SENTIR

Pres.	**siento**	sentimos
	sientes	sentís
	siente	**sienten**
Pret.	sentí	sentimos
	sentiste	sentisteis
	sintió	**sintieron**
Pres.	**sienta**	**sintamos**
Subj.	**sientas**	**sintáis**
	sienta	**sientan**

Imp. Subj. **sintiera/iese**, etc.
Pres. Part. **sintiendo**

§66 SER

Pres.	**soy**	**somos**
	eres	**sois**
	es	**son**

Imperfect **era**, etc.

Pret.	**fui**	**fuimos**
	fuiste	**fuisteis**
	fue	**fueron**

Pres. Subj. **sea**, etc.
Imp. Subj. **fuera/ese**, etc.
Imperative **sé**, sed

§67 SITUAR

Pres.	**sitúo**	situamos
	sitúas	situáis
	sitúa	**sitúan**
Pres.	**sitúe**	situemos
Subj.	**sitúes**	situéis
	sitúe	**sitúen**

§68 TAÑER

Pret.	tañí	tañimos
	tañiste	tañisteis
	tañó	**tañeron**

Imp. Subj. **tañera/ese**, etc.
Pres. Part. **tañendo**

§69 TENER

Pres.	**tengo**	tenemos
	tienes	tenéis
	tiene	**tienen**
Pret.	**tuve**	**tuvimos**
	tuviste	**tuvisteis**
	tuvo	**tuvieron**

Pres. Subj. **tenga**, etc.
Imp. Subj. **tuviera/iese**, etc.
Fut./Cond. **tendré/tendría**, etc.
Imperative **ten**, tened

§70 TOCAR

Pret. **toqué**, tocaste, etc.
Pres. Subj. **toque**, etc.

§71 TORCER

Pres.	**tuerzo**	torcemos
	tuerces	torcéis
	tuerce	**tuercen**
Pres.	**tuerza**	**torzamos**
Subj.	**tuerzas**	**torzáis**
	tuerza	**tuerzan**

§72 TRAER

Pres. **traigo**, traes, etc.

Pret.	**traje**	**trajimos**
	trajiste	**trajisteis**
	trajo	**trajeron**

Pres. Subj. **traiga**, etc.
Imp. Subj. **trajera/ese**, etc.
Pres. Part. **trayendo**
Past Part. **traído**

§73 TROCAR

Pres.	**trueco**	trocamos
	truecas	trocáis
	trueca	**truecan**

Pret. **troqué**, trocaste, etc.

Pres.	**trueque**	**troquemos**
Subj.	**trueques**	**troquéis**
	trueque	**truequen**

§74 VALER

Pres. **valgo**, vales, etc.
Pres. Subj. **valga**, etc.
Fut./Cond. **valdrá/valdría**, etc.

§75 VENCER

Pres. **venzo**, vences, etc.
Pres. Subj. **venza**, etc.

§76 VENIR

Pres.	**vengo**	venimos
	vienes	venís
	viene	**vienen**
Pret.	**vine**	**vinimos**
	viniste	**vinisteis**
	vino	**vinieron**

Pres. Subj. **venga**, etc.
Imp. Subj. **viniera/iese**, etc.
Fut./Cond. **vendrá/vendría**, etc.
Imperative **ven**, venid
Pres. Part. **viniendo**

§77 VER

Pres. **veo**, ves, etc.
Imperfect **veía**, etc.

Pret.	**vi**	vimos
	viste	visteis
	vio	vieron

Pres. Subj. **vea**, etc.
Past Part. **visto**

§78 VOLVER

Pres.	**vuelvo**	volvemos
	vuelves	volvéis
	vuelve	**vuelven**
Pres.	**vuelva**	volvamos
Subj.	**vuelvas**	volváis
	vuelva	**vuelvan**

§79 YACER

Pres. **yazco***, yaces, etc.
*[alternate forms: **yazgo** *or* **yago**]
Pres. Subj. **yazca***, etc.
*[alternate forms: **yazga** *or* **yaga**]
Imperative **yaz** *or* yace, yaced

§80 IRREGULAR PAST PARTICIPLES

In addition to verbs already mentioned in this section, the following verbs and their compounds have irregular past participles.

abrir	**abierto**
cubrir	**cubierto**
escribir	**escrito**
freír	**frito**
imprimir	**impreso**
romper	**roto**

VERBOS IRREGULARES DEL INGLÉS

La siguiente lista de verbos da el infinitivo, el pretérito y el participio pasivo de los verbos irregulares del inglés. No se incluyen las formas compuestas con los prefijos be-, for-, mis-, over-, out-, re-, with-, un-, under-, que tienen la misma conjugación.

abide abided *o* abode, abided *o* abode
arise arose, arisen
awake awoke, awaked
be was, been
bear bore, born *o* borne
beat beat, beaten *o* beat
begin began, begun
bend bent, bent
beseech besought *o* beseeched, besought *o* beseeched
bet bet *o* betted, bet *o* betted
bid bade *o* bid, bidden *o* bid
bide bided *o* bode, bided
bind bound, bound
bite bit, bitten
bleed bled, bled
blend blended *o* blent, blended *o* blent
bless blessed *o* blest, blessed *o* blest
blow blew, blown
break broke, broken
breed bred, bred
bring brought, brought
build built, built
burn burned *o* burnt, burned *o* burnt
buy bought, bought
cast cast, cast
catch caught, caught
chide chided *o* chid, chided *o* chid
choose chose, chosen
cleave cleft *o* cleaved, cleft *o* cleaved
cling clung, clung
clothe clothed *o* clad, clothed *o* clad
come came, come
cost cost, cost
creep crept, crept
crow crowed *o* crew, crowed
curse cursed *o* curst, cursed *o* curst
cut cut, cut
deal dealt, dealt
dig dug, dug
dive dived *o* dove, dived

do did, done
draw drew, drawn
dream dreamed *o* dreamt, dreamed *o* dreamt
drink drank, drunk
drive drove, driven
dwell dwelled *o* dwelt, dwelled *o* dwelt
eat ate, eaten
fall fell, fallen
feed fed, fed
feel felt, felt
fight fought, fought
find found, found
flee fled, fled
fling flung, flung
fly flew, flown
forsake forsook, forsaken
freeze froze, frozen
get got, got *o* gotten
gild gilded *o* gilt, gilded *o* gilt
gird girded *o* girt, girded *o* girt
give gave, given
go went, gone
grind ground, ground
grow grew, grown
hang hung, hung
have had, had
hear heard, heard
hew hewed, hewed *o* hewn
hide hid, hidden *o* hid
hit hit, hit
hold held, held
hurt hurt, hurt
keep kept, kept
kneel knelt *o* kneeled, knelt *o* kneeled
knit knit *o* knitted, knit *o* knitted
know knew, known
lade laded, laded *o* laden
lay laid, laid
lead led, led
lean leaned *o* leant, leaned *o* leant
leap leaped *o* leapt, leaped *o* leapt
learn learned *o* learnt, learned *o* learnt
leave left, left
lend lent, lent
let let, let
lie lay, lain
light lighted *o* lit, lighted *o* lit

lose lost, lost	spend spent, spent
make made, made	spill spilled *o* spilt, spilled *o* spilt
mean meant, meant	spit spat *o* spit, spat *o* spit
meet met, met	spin spun, spun
mow mowed, mowed *o* mown	split split, split
pay paid, paid	spoil spoiled *o* spoilt, spoiled *o* spoilt
prove proved, proved *o* proven	spread spread, spread
put put, put	spring sprang *o* sprung, sprung
quit quit *o* quitted, quit *o* quitted	stand stood, stood
read read, read	stave staved *o* stove, stuved *o* stove
rend rended *o* rent, rended *o* rent	steal stole, stolen
rid rid *o* ridded, rid *o* ridded	stick stuck, stuck
ride rode, ridden	sting stung, stung
ring rang, rung	stink stank *o* stunk, stunk
rise rose, risen	strew strewed, strewed *o* strewn
run ran, run	stride strode, stridden
saw sawed, sawed *o* sawn	strike struck, struck *o* stricken
say said, said	string strung, strung
see saw, seen	strive strove *o* strived, striven *o* strived
seek sought, sought	swear swore, sworn
sell sold, sold	sweat sweat *o* sweated, sweat *o* sweated
send sent, sent	sweep swept, swept
set set, set	swell swelled, swelled *o* swollen
sew sewed, sewn *o* sewed	swim swam, swum
shake shook, shaken	swing swung, swung
shave shaved, shaved *o* shaven	take took, taken
shear sheared, sheared *o* shorn	teach taught, taught
shed shed, shed	tear tore, torn
shine shone *o* shined, shone *o* shined	tell told, told
shoe shod, shod *o* shodden	think thought, thought
shoot shot, shot	thrive throve *o* thrived, thrived *o* thriven
show showed, shown *o* showed	throw threw, thrown
shrink shrank *o* shrunk, shrunk *o* shrunken	thrust thrust, thrust
shut shut, shut	tread trod, trodden *o* trod
sing sang, sung	wake woke *o* waked, waked *o* woken
sink sank *o* sunk, sunk	wear wore, worn
sit sat, sat	weave wove *o* weaved, woven *o* weaved
slay slew, slain	wed wedded, wed *o* wedded
sleep slept, slept	weep wept, wept
slide slid, slid	wet wet *o* wetted, wet *o* wetted
sling slung, slung	win won, won
slink slunk, slunk	wind wound, wound
slit slit, slit	wrap wrapt *o* wrapped, wrapt *o* wrapped
smell smelled *o* smelt, smelled *o* smelt	wring wrung, wrung
smite smote, smitten *o* smote	write wrote, written
sow sowed, sown *o* sowed	
speak spoke, spoken	
speed sped *o* speeded, sped *o* speeded	

PLACES, PEOPLES, AND LANGUAGES

♦ (of) place, people, nationality   ◊ language

A·dri·at·ic Sea Mar Adriático	Al·ge·ri·a Argelia
Ae·ge·an Sea Mar Egeo	♦ Al·ge·ri·an argelino
Af·ghan·i·stan Afganistán	Al·giers Argel
♦ Af·ghan afgano	Alps Alpes
Af·ri·ca África	Am·a·zon Amazonas
♦ Af·ri·can africano	A·mer·i·ca América; *(U.S.A.)* Estados
Af·ro-A·mer·i·can afroamericano	Unidos
Al·ba·ni·a Albania	♦ A·mer·i·can americano; *(of U.S.A.)*
♦ ◊ Al·ba·ni·an albanés	estadounidense, norteamericano

xvii

American Indian   indio americano
Am·er·ind/in·di·an   amerindio
An·da·lu·sia   Andalucía
  ♦ An·da·lu·sian   andaluz
An·des   Andes
  ♦ An·de·an   andino
An·glo   angloamericano
An·glo-A·mer·i·can   angloamericano
Ant·arc·ti·ca   Antártida
  ♦ Ant·arc·tic   antártico
Ar·ab   árabe
A·ra·bia   Arabia
  ♦ A·ra·bi·an   árabe
Ar·a·bic   arábigo, árabe
Arc·tic Ocean   océano Ártico
Ar·gen·ti·na   Argentina
  ♦ Ar·gen·tine, Ar·gen·tin·i·an
argentino
A·sia   Asia
  ♦ A·sian   asiático
At·lan·tic Ocean   océano Atlántico
Aus·tral·a·sia   Australasia
Aus·tra·lia   Australia
  ♦ Aus·tra·lian   australiano
Aus·tri·a   Austria
  ♦ Aus·tri·an   austríaco
A·zores   Azores
Az·tec   azteca
Bal·e·ar·ic Islands   Islas Baleares
Bal·kans   Balcanes
  ♦ Bal·kan   balcánico
Bal·tic Sea   Mar Báltico
  ♦ Baltic   báltico
Ban·gla·desh   Bangladesh
Basque   vasco
Bed·ou·in   beduino
Bel·gium   Bélgica
  ♦ Bel·gian   belga
Be·lize   Belice
Beth·le·hem   Belén
Bo·he·mi·an   bohemio
Bo·liv·i·a   Bolivia
  ♦ Bo·liv·i·an   boliviano
Bra·zil   Brasil
  ♦ Bra·zil·ian   brasileño
Brit·ain   Gran Bretaña
  ♦ Brit·ish   británico
  ♦ Brit·on   británico
British Isles   Islas Británicas
Brit·ta·ny   Bretaña
  ♦ ◊ Bret·on   bretón
Bul·gar·i·a   Bulgaria
  ♦ ◊ Bul·gar·i·an   búlgaro
Cam·bo·di·a   Camboya
  ♦ Cam·bo·di·an   camboyano
Ca·na·da   Canadá
  ♦ Ca·na·di·an   canadiense
Ca·nar·y Islands   Islas Canarias
Car·ib   caribe
Car·ib·be·an Sea   Mar Caribe
  ♦ Caribbean   caribe
Cas·tile   Castilla
  ♦ Cas·til·ian   castellano
Cat·a·lo·nia   Cataluña
  ♦ Cat·a·lo·nian   ♦ ◊ Cat·a·lan   catalán

Celt   celta
  ♦ ◊ Celt·ic   ♦ céltico   ◊ celta
Central America   América Central
  ♦ Central American   centroamericano
Chi·ca·no   chicano
Chil·e   Chile
  ♦ Chil·e·an   chileno
Chi·na   China
  ♦ ◊ Chi·nese   chino
China, People's Republic of   República
  Popular de China
China, Republic of   República de China
Co·lom·bi·a   Colombia
  ♦ Co·lom·bi·an   colombiano
Cos·ta Ri·ca   Costa Rica
  ♦ Cos·ta Ri·can   costarriqueño,
  costarricense
Cu·ba   Cuba
  ♦ Cu·ban   cubano
Cy·prus   Chipre
  ♦ Cyp·ri·an   chipriota
Czech·o·slo·va·ki·a   Checoslovaquia
  ♦ Czech·o·slo·va·ki·an   checoslovaco
  ♦ ◊ Czech   checo
Dan·ube   Danubio
Den·mark   Dinamarca
  ♦ Dane   ♦ ◊ Dan·ish   dinamarqués,
  danés
Do·min·i·can Republic   República
  Dominicana
  ♦ Dominican   dominicano
Dutch   holandés
East Germany   Alemania Oriental
East Indies   Indias Orientales
Ec·ua·dor   Ecuador
  ♦ Ec·ua·dor·ian   ecuatoriano
E·gypt   Egipto
  ♦ E·gyp·tian   egipcio
El Sal·va·dor   El Salvador
  ♦ Sal·va·do·ran/ri·an   salvadoreño
Eng·land   Inglaterra
  ♦ ◊ Eng·lish   inglés
English Channel   Canal de la Mancha
Eur·a·sian   eurasiático
Eu·rope   Europa
  ♦ Eu·ro·pe·an   europeo
Fi·li·pi·no   filipino
Fin·land   Finlandia
  ♦ Finn   finlandés
  ♦ ◊ Finn·ish   finlandés
France   Francia
  ♦ ◊ French   francés
Gael·ic   gaélico
Ga·li·cia   Galicia
  ♦ Ga·li·cian   gallego
German Democratic Republic
  República Democrática Alemana
  (Alemania Oriental)
Ger·ma·ny   Alemania
  ♦ ◊ Ger·man   alemán
Germany, Federal Republic of
  República Federal de Alemania
  (Alemania Occidental)
Goth·ic   gótico
Great Britain   Gran Bretaña

Greece   Grecia
   ♦ ◊ Greek   griego
Gua·te·ma·la   Guatemala
   ♦ Gua·te·ma·lan   guatemalteco
Gui·a·na   Guayana
Guy·a·na   Guyana
   ♦ Guy·a·nese   guyanés
Gyp·sy   gitano
Hague, The   La Haya
Hai·ti   Haiti
   ♦ Hai·tian   haitiano
Ha·van·a   La Habana
   ♦ Ha·van·an   habanero
He·brew   hebreo
Hel·len·ic   helénico
Hin·di   hindi
Hol·land   Holanda
   ♦ ◊ Dutch   holandés
Hon·du·ras   Honduras
   ♦ Hon·du·ran   hondureño
Hun·ga·ry   Hungaria
   ♦ ◊ Hun·gar·i·an   húngaro
I·be·ri·a   Iberia
   ♦ I·be·ri·an   ibérico
Ice·land   Islandia
   ♦ Ice·land·er ♦ ◊ Ice·land·ic   islandés
In·ca   inca
   ♦ In·can   incaico
In·di·a   India
   ♦ In·di·an   indio, hindú
Indian Ocean   océano Índico
In·dies   Indias
In·do·chi·na   Indochina
In·do·ne·sia   Indonesia
   ♦ ◊ In·do·ne·sian   indonesio
I·ran   Irán
   ♦ I·ran·i·an   iraní
I·raq   Iraq
   ♦ I·raq·i   iraquí
Ire·land   Irlanda
   ♦ ◊ I·rish   irlandés
Is·ra·el   Israel
   ♦ Is·rae·li   israelí, israelita
It·a·ly   Italia
   ♦ ◊ I·tal·ian   italiano
Ja·mai·ca   Jamaica
   ♦ Ja·mai·can   jamaiquino, jamaicano
Ja·pan   Japan
   ♦ ◊ Jap·a·nese   japonés
Je·ru·sa·lem   Jerusalén
Jor·dan   Jordania
   ♦ Jor·da·ni·an   jordano
Ken·ya   Kenya
   ♦ Ken·yan   keniano
Ko·re·a   Corea
   ♦ ◊ Ko·re·an   coreano
Korea, Democratic People's Republic
   of   República Popular Democrática de
   Corea
Korea, Republic of   República de Corea
La·os   Laos
   ♦ ◊ La·o·tian   laosiano
Lat·in ♦ latino ◊ latín
Latin America   América Latina,
   Latinoamérica

♦ Latin American   latinoamericano
Leb·a·non   Líbano
   ♦ Leb·a·nese   libanés
Lib·y·a   Libia
   ♦ Lib·y·an   libio
Lon·don   Londres
   ♦ Lon·don·er   Londinense
Lux·em·bourg   Luxemburgo
   ♦ Lux·em·bourg·i·an   luxemburgués
Ma·drid   Madrid
Ma·gel·lan, Strait of   Estrecho de
   Magallanes
Ma·jor·ca   Mallorca
Ma·lay·sia   Malasia
   ♦ Ma·lay·sian   malasio
Ma·ya, Ma·yan   maya
Med·i·ter·ra·ne·an Sea   Mar
   Mediterráneo
   ♦ Mediterranean   mediterráneo
Mex·i·co   México
   ♦ Mex·i·can   mexicano
Mi·nor·ca   Menorca
Mon·go·li·a   Mongolia
   ♦ ◊ Mon·gol, Mon·go·li·an   mongol
Mo·roc·co   Marruecos
   ♦ Mo·roc·can   marroquí
Neth·er·lands   Países Bajos
New World   Nuevo Mundo, América
New York   Nueva York
   ♦ New York·er   neoyorquino
New Zea·land   Nueva Zelandia
   ♦ New Zea·land·er   neozelandés
Nic·a·ra·gua   Nicaragua
   ♦ Nic·a·ra·guan   nicaragüense
Ni·ge·ri·a   Nigeria
   ♦ Ni·ge·ri·an   nigeriano
Nile   Nilo
North America   América del Norte,
   Norteamérica
   ♦ North American   norteamericano
North Pole   Polo Norte
Nor·way   Noruega
   ♦ ◊ Nor·we·gian   noruego
Oc·ci·dent   Occidente
Old World   Viejo Mundo
O·ri·ent   Oriente
Pa·cif·ic Ocean   océano Pacífico
Pak·i·stan   Pakistán
   ♦ Pak·i·stan·i   pakistaní
Pal·es·tine   Palestina
   ♦ Pal·es·tin·i·an   palestino
Pan·a·ma   Panamá
   ♦ Pan·a·ma·ni·an   panameño
Par·a·guay   Paraguay
   ♦ Par·a·guay·an   paraguayo
Par·is   París
   ♦ Pa·ri·sian   parisiense
Per·sian ♦ pérsico ◊ persa
Persian Gulf   Golfo Pérsico
Pe·ru   Perú
   ♦ Pe·ru·vi·an   peruano
Phil·ip·pines   Filipinas
   ♦ Phil·ip·pine   filipino
   ♦ ◊ Fil·i·pi·no   filipino
Po·land   Polonia

♦ Pole ♦◊ Po·lish polaco
Pol·y·ne·sia Polinesia
♦ Pol·y·ne·sian polinesio
Por·tu·gal Portugal
♦◊ Por·tu·guese portugués
Puer·to Ri·co Puerto Rico
♦ Puer·to Ri·can puertorriqueño
Pyr·e·nees Pirineos
Quech·ua quechua
Rocky Mountains Montañas Rocosas
Rome Roma
♦ Ro·man romano
Ru·ma·ni·a o Ro·ma·nia Rumania
♦◊ Ru·ma·ni·an o Ro·ma·nian rumano
Rus·sia Rusia
♦◊ Rus·sian ruso
Sal·va·do·ran, Sal·va·do·ri·an
salvadoreño
Sau·di Arabia Arabia Saudita
♦ Saudi, Saudi Arabian árabe saudita
Scan·di·na·vi·a Escandinavia
♦ Scan·di·na·vi·an escandinavo
Scot·land Escocia
♦ Scot, Scotch, Scot·tish escocés
Sem·ite semita
♦ Se·mit·ic semítico, semita
Ser·bo-Cro·a·tian serbocroata
Slav·ic eslavo
South Africa África del Sur
♦ South African sudafricano
South America América del Sur,
Sudamérica
♦ South American sudamericano
South Pole Polo Sur
So·vi·et Socialist Republics, Union of
Unión de Repúblicas Socialistas
Soviéticas
Soviet Union Unión Soviética
♦ Soviet soviético
Spain España
♦ Span·iard español
♦◊ Span·ish español
Spanish America Hispanoamérica
♦ Span·ish-A·mer·ic·an
hispanoamericano
Su·ri·nam Suriname
♦ Su·ri·na·mese surinamés

Swe·den Suecia
♦ Swede sueco
♦◊ Swed·ish sueco
Swit·zer·land Suiza
♦ Swiss suizo
Syr·i·a Siria
♦ Syr·i·an sirio
Tai·wan Taiwán
♦ Tai·wan·ese taiwanés
Thai·land Tailandia
♦◊ Thai tailandés
To·ky·o Tokio
Tol·tec tolteca
tropic of Can·cer trópico de Cáncer
tropic of Cap·ri·corn trópico de
Capricornio
Troy Troya
♦ Tro·jan troyano
Tur·key Turquía
♦ Turk turco
♦◊ Turk·ish turco
U·ru·guay Uruguay
♦ U·ru·guay·an uruguayo
U.S.A EE. UU., E.U.
U.S.S.R U.R.S.S
United Arab E·mir·ates Emiratos
Árabes Unidos
United Kingdom Reino Unido
United States of America Estados
Unidos de América
Vat·i·can Vaticano
Ven·e·zue·la Venezuela
♦ Ven·e·zue·lan venezolano
Viet·nam Viet Nam
♦◊ Viet·nam·ese vietnamita
Wales Gales
♦◊ Welsh galés
West Germany Alemania Occidental
West Indies Indias Occidentales,
Antillas
♦ West Indian antillano
Yid·dish yiddish
Yu·go·sla·vi·a Yugoslavia
♦ Yu·go·sla·vi·an, Yu·go·slav
yugoslavo
Zaire Zaire
♦ Zair·i·an zairense

LUGARES, PUEBLOS E IDIOMAS

♦ (de) lugar, pueblo, nacionalidad   ◊ idioma

A·driá·ti·co, Mar Adriatic Sea
Af·ga·nis·tán Afghanistan
♦ af·ga·no Afghan
Á·fri·ca Africa
♦ a·fri·ca·no African
África del Sur South Africa
♦ su·da·fri·ca·no South African
a·fro·a·me·ri·ca·no Afro-American
Al·ba·nia Albania
♦◊ al·ba·nés Albanian
A·le·ma·na, República Democrática
German Democratic Republic (East
Germany)
A·le·ma·nia Germany
♦◊ a·le·mán German

Alemania Occidental West Germany
Alemania Oriental East Germany
Alemania, República Federal de
Federal Republic of Germany (West
Germany)
Al·pes Alps
A·ma·zo·nas Amazon
A·mé·ri·ca America
♦ a·me·ri·ca·no American
América Central Central America
América del Norte North America;
(E.U.) United States
América del Sur South America
América Latina Latin America
a·me·rin·dio Amerind, Amerindian

An·da·lu·cí·a Andalusia
◆ an·da·luz Andalusian
An·des Andes
◆ an·di·no Andean
an·glo·a·me·ri·ca·no Anglo-American
An·tár·ti·da Antarctica
◆ an·tár·ti·co Antarctic
An·ti·llas West Indies
◆ an·ti·lla·no West Indian
A·ra·bia Arabia
◆ ◊ á·ra·be ◆ Arab, Arabian
◆ ◊ Arabic
A·ra·bia Sau·di·ta Saudi Arabia
◆ á·ra·be sau·di·ta Saudi Arabian, Saudi
a·rá·bi·co/go ◆ Arabian ◆ ◊ Arabic
Ar·gel Algiers
Ar·ge·lia Algeria
◆ ar·ge·li·no Algerian
Ar·gen·ti·na Argentina
◆ ar·gen·ti·no Argentine, Argentinian
Ár·ti·co, océano Arctic Ocean
A·sia Asia
◆ a·siá·ti·co Asian
At·lán·ti·co, océano Atlantic Ocean
Aus·tra·la·sia Australasia
Aus·tra·lia Australia
◆ aus·tra·lia·no Australian
Aus·tria Austria
◆ aus·trí·a·co Austrian
A·zo·res Azores
az·te·ca Aztec
Bal·ca·nes Balkans
◆ bal·cá·ni·co Balkan
Ba·le·a·res, Islas Balearic Islands
Bál·ti·co, Mar Baltic Sea
◆ báltico Baltic
Ban·gla·desh Bangladesh
be·dul·no Bedouin
De·lén Bethlehem
Bél·gi·ca Belgium
◆ bel·ga Belgian
Be·li·ce Belize
bo·he·mio Bohemian
Bo·li·via Bolivia
◆ bo·li·via·no Bolivian
Bra·sil Brazil
◆ bra·si·le·ño Brazilian
Bre·ta·ña Brittany
◆ ◊ bre·tón Breton
Bri·tá·ni·cas, Islas British Isles
◆ bri·tá·ni·co British, Briton
Bul·ga·ria Bulgaria
◆ ◊ búl·ga·ro Bulgarian
Cam·bo·ya Cambodia
◆ cam·bo·ya·no Cambodian
Ca·na·dá Canada
◆ ca·na·dien·se Canadian
Ca·nal de la Man·cha English Channel
Ca·na·rias Canary Islands
Ca·ri·be, Mar Caribbean Sea
◆ caribe Carib, Caribbean
Cas·ti·lla Castile
◆ cas·te·lla·no Castilian
Ca·ta·lu·ña Catalonia
◆ ◊ ca·ta·lán ◆ Catalonian ◆ ◊ Catalan
cel·ta ◆ Celt ◊ Celtic

cen·tro·a·me·ri·ca·no Central American
Co·lom·bia Colombia
◆ co·lom·bia·no Colombian
Co·re·a Korea
◆ ◊ co·re·a·no Korean
Corea, República de Republic of Korea (South Korea)
Corea, República Popular Democrática de Democratic People's Republic of Korea (North Korea)
Cos·ta Ri·ca Costa Rica
◆ cos·ta·rri·cen·se/que·ño Costa Rican
Cu·ba Cuba
◆ cu·ba·ño Cuban
Che·cos·lo·va·quia Czechoslovakia
◆ che·cos·lo·va·co Czech, Czechoslovak, Czechoslovakian
◆ ◊ che·co ◆ Czechoslovak ◆ ◊ Czech
chi·ca·no Chicano
Chi·le Chile
◆ chi·le·no Chilean
Chi·na China
◆ ◊ chi·no Chinese
China, República de Republic of China
China, República Popular de People's Republic of China
Chi·pre Cyprus
◆ chipriota Cypriot
Da·nu·bio Danube
Di·na·mar·ca Denmark
◆ ◊ da·nés, di·na·mar·qués ◆ Dane
◆ ◊ Danish
do·mi·ni·ca·no Dominican
E·cua·dor Ecuador
◆ e·cua·to·ria·no Ecuadorian
EE. UU., E.U. U.S.A.
E·ge·o, Mar Aegean Sea
E·gip·to Egypt
◆ e·gip·cio Egyptian
El Sal·va·dor El Salvador
◆ sal·va·do·re·ño Salvadoran, Salvadorian
E·mi·ra·tos Á·ra·bes U·ni·dos United Arab Emirates
Es·can·di·na·via Scandinavia
◆ es·can·di·na·vo Scandinavian
Es·co·cia Scotland
◆ es·co·cés Scot, Scotch, Scottish
es·la·vo Slavic
Es·pa·ña Spain
◆ ◊ es·pa·ñol ◆ Spaniard ◆ ◊ Spanish
Es·ta·dos U·ni·dos United States
Estados Unidos de América United States of America
◆ es·ta·dou·ni·den·se American, of the United States of America
eu·ra·siá·ti·co Eurasian
Eu·ro·pa Europe
◆ eu·ro·pe·o European
Fi·li·pi·nas Philippines
◆ ◊ fi·li·pi·no ◆ Philippine ◆ ◊ Filipino
Fin·lan·dia Finland
◆ ◊ fin·lan·dés ◆ Finn ◆ ◊ Finnish
Fran·cia France
◆ fran·cés French
ga·é·li·co Gaelic

Ga·les Wales
    ♦ ◊ ga·lés Welsh
Ga·li·cia Galicia
    ♦ ga·lle·go Galician
gi·ta·no Gypsy
gó·ti·co Gothic
Gran Bre·ta·ña Great Britain, Britain
Gre·cia Greece
    ♦ ◊ grie·go Greek
Gua·te·ma·la Guatemala
    ♦ gua·te·mal·te·co Guatemalan
Gua·ya·na Guiana
Gu·ya·na Guyana
    ♦ guyanés Guyanese
Ha·ba·na, La Havana
    ♦ ha·ba·ne·ro Havanan
Hai·tí Haiti
    ♦ hai·tia·no Haitian
Ha·ya, La The Hague
he·bre·o Hebrew
he·lé·ni·co Hellenic
hin·di Hindi
His·pa·no·a·mé·ri·ca Spanish America
    ♦ his·pa·no·a·me·ri·ca·no Spanish-American
Ho·lan·da Holland
    ♦ ◊ ho·lan·dés Dutch
Hon·du·ras Honduras
    ♦ hon·du·re·ño Honduran
Hun·ga·ria Hungary
    ♦ ◊ hún·ga·ro Hungarian
I·be·ria Iberia
    ♦ i·bé·ri·co Iberian
in·ca Inca, Incan
In·dia India
    ♦ in·dio Indian
In·dias Indies
Indias Occidentales West Indies
Indias Orientales East Indies
Ín·di·co, océano Indian Ocean
in·dio Indian
indio americano American Indian
In·do·chi·na Indochina
In·do·ne·sia Indonesia
    ♦ in·do·ne·sio Indonesian
In·gla·te·rra England
    ♦ ◊ in·glés English
I·rán Iran
    ♦ i·ra·ní Iranian
I·raq Iraq
    ♦ i·ra·qí Iraqi
Ir·lan·da Ireland
    ♦ ◊ ir·lan·dés Irish
Is·lan·dia Iceland
    ♦ ◊ is·lan·dés ♦ Icelander ♦ ◊ Icelandic
Is·ra·el Israel
    ♦ is·ra·e·lí/li·ta Israeli
I·ta·lia Italy
    ♦ ◊ i·ta·lia·no Italian
Ja·mai·ca Jamaica
    ♦ ja·mai·qui·no/ca·no Jamaican
Ja·pón Japan
    ♦ ◊ ja·po·nés Japanese
Je·ru·sa·lén Jerusalem

Jor·da·nia Jordan
    ♦ jor·da·no Jordanian
Ken·ya Kenya
    ♦ ke·nia·no Kenyan
La·os Laos
    ♦ ◊ la·o·sia·no Laotian, Lao
la·tín Latin
la·ti·no Latin
La·ti·no·a·mé·ri·ca Latin America
    ♦ la·ti·no·a·me·ri·ca·no Latin-American, Latin American
Lí·ba·no Lebanon
    ♦ li·ba·nés Lebanese
Li·bia Libya
    ♦ li·bio Libyan
Lon·dres London
Lu·xem·bur·go Luxembourg
    ♦ lu·xem·bur·gués Luxembourgian
Ma·drid Madrid
    ♦ ma·dri·le·ño of Madrid
Ma·ga·lla·nes, Estrecho de Strait of Magellan
Ma·la·sia Malasia
    ♦ ma·la·sio Malaysian
Ma·llor·ca Majorca
Ma·rrue·cos Morocco
    ♦ ma·rro·quí Moroccan
ma·ya Mayan, Maya
Me·di·te·rrá·ne·o, Mar Mediterranean Sea
    ♦ mediterráneo Mediterranean
Me·nor·ca Minorca
Mé·xi·co Mexico
    ♦ me·xi·ca·no Mexican
Mon·go·lia Mongolia
    ♦ ◊ mon·gol Mongol, Mongolian
Ni·ca·ra·gua Nicaragua
    ♦ ni·ca·ra·güen·se Nicaraguan
Ni·ge·ria Nigeria
    ♦ ni·ge·ria·no Nigerian
Ni·lo Nile
Nor·te·a·mé·ri·ca North America
    ♦ nor·te·a·me·ri·ca·no American, North American
No·rue·ga Norway
    ♦ ◊ no·rue·go Norwegian
Nueva York New York
    ♦ ne·o·yor·qui·no New Yorker
Nueva Ze·lan·dia New Zealand
    ♦ ne·o·ze·lan·dés New Zealander
Nuevo Mundo New World, America
Oc·ci·den·te Occident, West
O·rien·te Orient, East
Pa·cí·fi·co, océano Pacific Ocean
Pa·kis·tán Pakistan
    ♦ pa·kis·ta·ní Pakistani
Pa·les·ti·na Palestine
    ♦ pa·les·ti·no Palestinian
Pa·na·má Panama
    ♦ pa·na·me·ño Panamanian
Pa·í·ses Ba·jos Netherlands
Pa·ra·guay Paraguay
    ♦ pa·ra·gua·yo Paraguayan
Pa·rís Paris
    ♦ pa·ri·sien·se Parisian

per·sa Persian
Pér·si·co, Gol·fo Persian Gulf
Pe·rú Peru
♦ pe·rua·no Peruvian
Pi·ri·ne·os Pyrenees
Po·li·ne·sia Polynesia
♦ po·li·ne·sio Polynesian
Po·lo·nia Poland
♦◊ po·la·co ♦ Pole ♦◊ Polish
Po·lo Norte North Pole
Polo Sur South Pole
Por·tu·gal Portugal
♦◊ por·tu·gués Portuguese
Puer·to Ri·co Puerto Rico
♦ puer·to·rri·que·ño Puerto Rican
que·chua Quechua
Rei·no U·ni·do United Kingdom
Re·pú·bli·ca Do·mi·ni·ca·na Dominican
Republic
♦ do·mi·ni·ca·no Dominican
Ro·co·sas, Mon·ta·ñas Rocky
Mountains
Ro·ma Rome
♦ ro·ma·no Roman
Ru·ma·nia Rumania or Romania
♦◊ ru·ma·no Rumanian or Romanian
Ru·sia Russia
♦◊ ru·so Russian
sal·va·do·re·ño Salvadoran
se·mi·ta Semite
♦ se·mí·ti·co/mi·ta Semitic
ser·bo·cro·a·ta Serbo-Croatian
Si·ria Syria
♦ si·rio Syrian
so·vié·ti·co Soviet
Su·da·mé·ri·ca South America
♦ su·da·me·ri·ca·no South American
Sue·cia Sweden

♦◊ sue·co ♦ Swede ♦◊ Swedish
Sui·za Switzerland
♦ sui·zo Swiss
Su·ri·na·me Surinam
♦ su·ri·na·més Surinamese
Tai·lan·dia Thailand
♦◊ tai·lan·dés Thai
Tai·wán Taiwan
♦ tai·wa·nés Taiwanese
To·kio Tokyo
tol·te·ca Toltec
trópico de Cán·cer Tropic of Cancer
trópico de Cap·ri·cor·nio Tropic of
Capricorn
Tro·ya Troy
♦ tro·ya·no Trojan
Tur·quí·a Turkey
♦◊ tur·co ♦ Turk ♦◊ Turkish
U.R.S.S. U.S.S.R.
U·nión de Re·pú·bli·cas So·cia·lis·tas
So·vié·ti·cas Union of Soviet Socialist
Republics
Unión So·vié·ti·ca Soviet Union
♦ so·vié·ti·co Soviet
U·ru·guay Uruguay
♦ u·ru·gua·yo Uruguayan
vas·co Basque
Va·ti·ca·no Vatican
Ve·ne·zue·la Venezuela
♦ ve·ne·zo·la·no Venezuelan
Viejo Mundo Old World
Viet Nam Vietnam
♦◊ viet·na·mi·ta Vietnamese
yid·dish Yiddish
Yu·gos·la·via Yugoslavia
♦ yu·gos·la·vo Yugoslavian, Yugoslav
Zai·re Zaire
♦ zai·ren·se Zairian

Geographic Labels / Rótulos Geográficos

AMER.	America/América	G.B.	Great Britain/Gran Bretaña
ARG.	Argentina	GUAT.	Guatemala
BOL.	Bolivia	MEX.	Mexico/México
C. AMER.	Central America/América Central	NIC.	Nicaragua
		PAN.	Panama/Panamá
CARIB.	Caribbean/Caribe	PAR.	Paraguay
CHILE	Chile	PERU	Peru/Perú
COL.	Colombia	P. RICO	Puerto Rico
C. RICA	Costa Rica	R.P.	River Plate/Río de la Plata
CUBA	Cuba	SALV.	El Salvador
DOM. REP.	Dominican Republic/ República Dominicana	S. AMER.	South America/Sudamérica
		SP.	Spain/España
ECUAD.	Ecuador	URUG.	Uruguay
E.U.	Estados Unidos	U.S.	United States
		VEN.	Venezuela

Spanish/English

A

a, A f. first letter of the Spanish alphabet.
a prep. (dirección) to, into, forward; (destino) in, at; (lugar) at, on, to; (distancia) to, up to; (hora) at, in; (método) on, in, by, with, according to; (tasa) at, per, a, by.
á·ba·co m. abacus.
a·bad m. abbot.
a·ba·de·sa f. abbess.
a·ba·dí·a f. abbey.
a·ba·jo I. adv. down; (en una casa) downstairs; (posición) below, underneath ♦ **echar a.** to demolish; POL. to overthrow • **hacia a.** downward(s) II. interj. down with <¡a. el rey! down with the king!>
a·ba·lan·zar §04 tr. & reflex. to fling, hurl (oneself).
a·ba·li·zar §04 tr. to mark with buoys.
a·ba·lo·rio m. glass bead(s).
a·ban·de·ra·do m. standard-bearer.
a·ban·de·ra·mien·to m. registration (of a ship); POL. joining a cause.
a·ban·de·rar tr. to register (a ship); POL. to join (a cause).
a·ban·de·ri·zar §04 tr. to divide into factions —reflex. AMER. to join (a cause).
a·ban·do·na·do, a adj. abandoned; (descuidado) careless; (desaliñado) slovenly.
a·ban·do·nar tr. to abandon, desert; (desertar) to leave; (renunciar) to give up; (descuidar) to neglect —reflex. (entregarse a) to abandon oneself to; (descuidarse) to become slovenly.
a·ban·do·no m. abandonment; (descuido) neglect; (desenfrenamiento) abandon.
a·ba·ni·car §70 tr. & reflex. to fan (oneself).
a·ba·ni·co m. fan; MARIT. winch.
a·ba·ra·jar tr. R.P. (parar) to block, parry (a blow); (agarrar) to catch (in flight).
a·ba·ra·tar tr. to reduce (prices) —reflex. to become cheaper.
a·bar·car §70 tr. (contener) to embrace, cover; (abrazar) to embrace; (divisar) to take in; AMER. to stockpile.
a·ba·rra·mien·to m. (lanzamiento) hurling, hurtling; (sacudimiento) shaking.
a·ba·rran·car §70 tr. to form ditches in —intr. to run aground —reflex. (caerse) to fall into a ditch; (atascarse) to get into a fix.
a·ba·rro·ta·do, a adj. full, crowded.
a·ba·rro·tar tr. (fortalecer) to bar up; (llenar) to fill up; (exceso) to overstock; AMER. (acaparar) to stockpile.
a·ba·rro·te m. bundle ♦ pl. AMER. (comestibles) groceries; (tienda) grocery store.
a·ba·rro·te·rí·a f. C. AMER. hardware store.
a·ba·rro·te·ro, a m.f. AMER. hardware storekeeper.
a·bas·tar·dar tr. to bastardize —intr. to degenerate.

a·bas·te·ce·dor, ·ra m.f. supplier.
a·bas·te·cer §17 tr. to supply, provide (de with).
a·bas·te·ci·mien·to m. (provisión) supply; (aprovisionamiento) supplying.
a·bas·to m. supplying ♦ **dar a.** to produce to capacity • **no dar a. (a)** not to be able to keep up (with) ♦ pl. supplies, provisions.
a·ba·ta·tar·se reflex. AMER. to become embarrassed.
a·ba·ti·ble adj. collapsible, folding.
a·ba·ti·da·men·te adv. despondently.
a·ba·ti·do, a adj. despondent.
a·ba·ti·mien·to m. low spirits.
a·ba·tir tr. (derribar) to knock down, demolish; (desanimar) to depress, discourage —reflex. (desanimarse) to become discouraged; (aves) to swoop.
ab·di·ca·ción f. abdication.
ab·di·car §70 tr. & intr. (resignar) to abdicate.
ab·do·men m. abdomen.
ab·do·mi·nal adj. abdominal.
ab·duc·ción f. abduction.
ab·duc·tor I. adj. abducent II. m. abductor.
a·be·cé m. alphabet; (rudimentos) rudiments.
a·be·ce·da·rio m. alphabet.
a·be·dul m. birch.
a·be·ja f. bee.
a·be·jar m. apiary, beehive.
a·be·jo·rro m. bumblebee; (pesado) pest.
a·be·rra·ción f. aberration.
a·ber·tu·ra f. opening; (hendidura) crack, fissure; (franqueza) frankness; PHOTOG. aperture.
a·be·to m. fir.
a·be·tu·nar tr. (embrear) to tar; (los zapatos) to polish.
a·bier·to, a I. see abrir II. adj. open; (raso) open, clear; (franco) candid; (sincero) sincere; S. AMER. generous.
a·bi·ga·rra·do, a adj. variegated, multicolored.
a·bi·ga·rrar tr. to mottle, variegate.
a·bi·sa·grar tr. to hinge.
a·bi·se·lar tr. to bevel.
a·bis·mal adj. abysmal.
a·bis·mar tr. to overwhelm, depress —reflex. to yield, give oneself up (en to).
a·bis·mo m. abyss ♦ **estar al borde del a.** to be on the brink of disaster.
ab·ju·ra·ción f. abjuration, renunciation.
ab·ju·rar tr. to abjure, renounce.
a·bian·da·bre·vas m.f.inv. COLL. good-for-nothing.
a·blan·da·mien·to m. softening.
a·blan·dar tr. to soften; (suavizar) to mollify; (mitigar) to mitigate —intr. (el viento) to calm down; (la nieve) to thaw —reflex. to soften; (calmarse) to calm down.
a·blan·de m. AMER., AUTO. break-in (period).
a·blan·de·cer §17 tr. to soften.
a·bla·ti·vo m. ablative.
a·blu·ción f. ablution, washing.

ab·ne·ga·ción f. abnegation.

ab·ne·ga·do, a adj. unselfish.

ab·ne·gar §52 tr. to abnegate, renounce —reflex. to deny oneself.

a·bo·ca·do, a adj. involved, engaged (*a* in); (*vino*) mild, smooth.

a·bo·ca·mien·to m. (*acción*) biting; (*acercamiento*) approaching; (*reunión*) meeting.

a·bo·car §70 tr. (*asir*) to bite; (*escanciar*) to decant; (*acercar*) to bring near —intr. MARIT. to enter a channel —reflex. (*aproximarse*) to approach; ARG. to engage (*a* in).

a·bo·car·dar tr. to widen, ream.

a·bo·chor·na·do, a adj. suffocating; (*avergonzado*) ashamed.

a·bo·chor·nar tr. to suffocate; (*avergonzar*) to embarrass; (*hacer sonrojar*) to make blush —reflex. (*avergonzarse*) to become embarrassed; (*sonrojarse*) to blush; AGR. to parch.

a·bo·fe·te·ar tr. to slap.

a·bo·ga·cí·a f. law (profession).

a·bo·ga·do, a m.f. lawyer, attorney ♦ **a. del diablo** devil's advocate.

a·bo·gar §47 intr. (*defender*) to advocate, plead; (*interceder*) to intercede.

a·bo·len·go m. ancestry, lineage; (*patrimonio*) patrimony.

a·bo·li·ción f. abolition, repeal.

a·bo·li·cio·nis·ta m.f. abolitionist.

a·bo·lir §38 tr. to abolish, repeal.

a·bol·sar·se reflex. (*la ropa*) to become baggy; (*la piel*) to sag.

a·bo·lla·do, a adj. dented; AMER., COLL. (*sin dinero*) penniless, broke.

a·bo·lla·du·ra f. dent.

a·bo·llar tr. to dent —reflex. to become dented.

a·bom·ba·do, a adj. convex; AMER. (*aturdido*) stupefied; (*comida*) bad, spoiled.

a·bom·bar tr. to make convex; AMER. (*aturdir*) to stupefy —reflex. AMER. to go bad.

a·bo·mi·na·ble adj. abominable, detestable; (*desagradable*) abominable, disagreeable.

a·bo·mi·na·ción f. abomination.

a·bo·mi·nar tr. to abominate, detest.

a·bo·na·ble adj. payable, due.

a·bo·na·do, a m.f. subscriber, season ticket holder; (*viajero*) commuter.

a·bo·nar tr. (*acreditar*) to vouch for, guarantee; AGR. to fertilize; (*subscribir*) to subscribe to; (*pagar*) to pay ♦ **a cuenta** to pay in installments —reflex. to subscribe.

a·bo·no m. (*estiércol*) fertilizer; (*billete*) subscription; AMER. payment, installment.

a·bor·dar tr. MARIT. to board; (*acercar*) to approach; (*emprender*) to tackle (a problem) —intr. MARIT. to dock.

a·bo·ri·gen adj. & m.f. aboriginal.

a·bo·rre·cer §17 tr. to hate, abhor.

a·bo·rre·ci·ble adj. hateful, abhorrent, loathsome.

a·bo·rre·ci·mien·to m. hatred, loathing.

a·bor·tar tr. & intr. to abort.

a·bor·to m. abortion; FIG. failure; COLL. (*feo*) ugly person.

a·bo·to·nar tr. & reflex. to button (up) —intr. to bud.

a·bo·ve·da·do m. ARCHIT. vaulting.

a·bo·ve·dar tr. to arch, vault.

a·bo·za·lar tr. to muzzle, put a muzzle on.

a·bra·ca·da·bra m. abracadabra.

a·bra·sa·dor, ·ra/san·te adj. burning, scorching.

a·bra·sar tr. (*quemar*) to burn; (*calentar*) to overheat. —intr. & reflex. to burn up.

a·bra·za·de·ra f. (*zuncho*) clamp, bracket; PRINT. bracket.

a·bra·zar §04 tr. to embrace, hug; (*ceñir*) to clasp; (*adoptar*) to adopt, embrace —reflex. to embrace (each other).

a·bra·zo m. embrace, hug.

a·bre·bo·ca m.f. ARG. absent-minded person, featherbrain.

a·bre·car·tas m.inv. letter opener.

a·bre·la·tas m.inv. can opener.

a·bre·va·de·ro m. watering hole *or* trough.

a·bre·var tr. to water (livestock); (*mojar*) to wet, soak.

a·bre·via·ción f. abbreviation, shortening; (*libros*) abridgement.

a·bre·via·do, a adj. (*breve*) brief, short; (*libros*) abridged, shortened.

a·bre·viar tr. (*reducir*) to abbreviate; (*libros*) to abridge; (*acelerar*) to shorten, hasten.

a·bre·via·tu·ra f. abbreviation; (*compendio*) compendium, résumé.

a·bri·dor, ·ra I. adj. opening II. m. (*abrelatas*) can opener; AGR. grafting knife.

a·bri·gar §47 tr. (*proteger*) to shelter; (*cubrir*) to keep warm; (*sospechas*) to harbor —reflex. to wrap oneself up.

a·bri·go m. (*protección*) shelter, cover; (*sobretodo*) overcoat; MARIT. harbor ♦ **al a. de** protected by.

a·bril m. April.

a·bri·llan·tar tr. AMER. to glaze (fruit).

a·brir §80 tr. to open; (*desplegar*) to spread out; (*empezar*) to open, begin; (*encabezar*) to lead, head; (*horadar*) to dig ♦ **a. el apetito** to whet the appetite • **a. la mano** to extend one's hand • **a. paso** to make way • **en un a. y cerrar de ojos** in the twinkling of an eye —reflex. to open; (*aclarar*) to clear up (weather); (*florecer*) to blossom; (*hender*) to split, crack; (*desviarse*) to swerve ♦ **a. con** to confide in, open up to.

a·bro·cha·dor m. (*abotonador*) buttonhook; S. AMER. stapler.

a·bro·char tr. (*con botones*) to button (up); (*con broches*) to fasten; (*zapatos*) to lace, tie; S. AMER. to staple.

a·bro·gar §47 tr. to abrogate, repeal.

a·bro·jo m. thistle, caltrop.

a·bro·que·lar tr. & reflex. to protect (oneself).

a·bru·ma·do, a adj. overwhelmed.

a·bru·ma·dor, ·ra I. adj. overwhelming, oppressive II. m.f. oppressor.

a·bru·mar tr. to overwhelm, oppress —reflex. to become foggy.

a·brup·to, a adj. abrupt; (*escarpado*) craggy, rugged.

abs·ce·so m. abscess.

ab·sen·tis·mo m. absenteeism.

ab·so·lu·ción f. absolution.

ab·so·lu·to, a I. adj. absolute; (*sin mezcla*) pure (alcohol) ♦ **en a.** absolutely not, not at all • **lo a.** the absolute II. f. (*proposición*) dogmatic assertion; MIL. discharge.

ab·sol·ver §78 tr. to absolve; LAW to acquit.

ab·sor·ben·te adj. absorbent; (*cautivante*) absorbing.

ab·sor·ber tr. to absorb —reflex. to become absorbed *or* engrossed.

ab·sor·ción f. absorption.

ab·sor·to, a I. see absorber II. adj. engrossed, entranced.

abs·te·mio, a I. adj. abstemious, teetotaling II. m.f. teetotaler, non-drinker.

abs·ten·ción f. abstention.

abs·te·ner·se §69 reflex. to abstain, refrain.

abs·ti·nen·cia f. abstinence.

abs·trac·ción f. abstraction; (preocupación) preoccupation.

abs·trac·to, a adj. & m. abstract ♦ en a. in the abstract.

abs·tra·er §72 tr. to abstract —reflex. to become withdrawn or lost in thought.

abs·tra·í·do, a I. see abstraer II. adj. (distraído) absorbed; (retirado) withdrawn.

abs·tu·vie·ra, vo see abstenerse.

ab·suel·to, va, ve see absolver.

ab·sur·di·dad f. absurdity.

ab·sur·do, a I. adj. absurd, ridiculous II. m. absurdity.

a·bu·che·ar tr. to boo, hiss.

a·bue·la f. grandmother.

a·bue·lo m. grandfather; (viejo) old man ♦ pl. grandparents.

a·bu·lia f. abulia, lack of will power.

a·bul·ta·do, a adj. large, bulky.

a·bul·ta·mien·to m. (aumento) increase; (hinchazón) swelling.

a·bul·tar tr. (engrosar) to enlarge; (hinchar) to swell — intr. to be bulky

a·bun·dan·cia f. abundance.

a·bun·dan·te adj. abundant, plentiful.

a·bun·dar intr. to abound.

a·bur·gue·sar·se reflex. to become bourgeois.

a·bu·rri·do, a adj. (cansado) bored; (tedioso) boring, tiresome.

a·bu·rri·dor, ·ra adj. boring, tedious.

a·bu·rri·mien·to m. boredom, tedium.

a·bu·rrir tr. to bore —reflex. to become bored.

a·bu·sa·dor, ·ra adj. AMER. abusive.

a·bu·sar intr. to go too far, exceed ♦ a. de to abuse, misuse.

a·bu·so m. excess; (injusticia) injustice.

ab·yec·to, a adj. abject, low.

a·cá adv. here, over here ♦ a. y allá here and there, everywhere • más a. closer.

a·ca·ba·do, a I. adj. finished; (perfecto) complete, consummate; (arruinado) ruined II. m. finish.

a·ca·bar tr. to finish, complete; (perfeccionar) to put the finishing touches on; (pulir) to give a finish to; (consumir) to use up —intr. to end, stop; (morir) to die ♦ ¡acabáramos! finally!, at last! • a. con to put an end to, destroy • a. de to have just • a. por to end up —reflex. to end, terminate; to run out of <se me acabó el tiempo I ran out of time> ♦ ¡se acabó! that's the end of that!

a·ca·cia f. acacia.

a·ca·che·te·ar tr. to slap, hit.

a·ca·de·mia f. academy.

a·ca·dé·mi·co, a I. adj. academic II. m.f. academician.

a·ca·de·mis·ta m.f. academician.

a·ca·e·cer §17 intr. to happen, occur.

a·ca·e·ci·mien·to m. happening, occurrence.

a·ca·lam·brar·se reflex. to get cramps.

a·ca·lo·ra·do, a adj. heated, warm; (enardecido) heated, animated.

a·ca·lo·ra·mien·to m. (ardor) ardor, heat; (entusiasmo) vehemence, passion.

a·ca·lo·rar tr. to warm up; (alentar) to encourage —reflex. to heat up; (hacerse vivo) to get heated; (irritarse) to get excited.

a·ca·lo·ro m. var. of acaloramiento.

a·ca·llar tr. to hush, quiet; FIG. to placate.

a·cam·pa·mien·to m. (acción) camping; (lugar) camp, encampment.

a·cam·pa·na·do, a adj. bell-shaped.

a·cam·pa·nar tr. to shape like a bell.

a·cam·par tr., intr., & reflex. to camp.

a·ca·na·la·do, a adj. fluted, striated.

a·ca·na·lar tr. to striate, flute.

a·can·ti·la·do, a I. adj. (abrupto) steep; (escalonado) shelved (coastline) II. m. cliff.

a·ca·pa·ra·dor, ·ra I. adj. hoarding II. m.f. (acumulador) stockpiler, hoarder; (monopolizador) monopolizer.

a·ca·pa·ra·mien·to m. (acumulación) hoarding; (monopolio) monopoly.

a·ca·pa·rar tr. (acumular) to stockpile, hoard; (monopolizar) to monopolize.

a·cá·pi·te m. S. AMER. (párrafo) paragraph; (subtítulo) subheading.

a·ca·ra·me·la·do, a adj. (bañado) caramelized; (color) caramel-colored; (melifluo) sweet.

a·ca·ra·me·lar tr. to caramelize —reflex. to be or become extremely sweet.

a·ca·ri·ciar tr. to caress; (abrigar) to cherish, hold dear.

a·ca·rre·ar tr. (transportar) to cart, transport; (ocasionar) to occasion, cause.

a·ca·rre·o m. cartage, transportation.

a·ca·so I. m. chance, accident II. adv. perhaps, maybe ♦ por si a. just in case.

a·ca·ta·mien·to m. respect, reverence.

a·ca·tar tr. (respetar) to respect; (obedecer) to observe, comply with.

a·ca·ta·rrar·se reflex. to catch a cold.

a·cau·da·la·do, a adj. wealthy, rich.

a·cau·da·lar tr. to accumulate, amass.

ac·ce·der intr. (consentir) to agree, consent, (al trono) to accede.

ac·ce·si·ble adj. accessible.

ac·ce·so m. (entrada) access, entry, (accesibilidad) accessibility; (arrebato) outburst, fit; MED. attack, fit.

ac·ce·so·rio, a adj. & m. accessory.

ac·ci·den·ta·do, a I. adj. rough, uneven II. m.f. accident victim.

ac·ci·den·tal adj. accidental.

ac·ci·den·tar·se reflex. to have an accident.

ac·ci·den·te m. accident; (del terreno) roughness, unevenness; MED. fit, spell ♦ por a. by chance.

ac·ción f. action; (hecho) act, deed; (efecto) effect; (judicial) legal action, lawsuit; MIL. battle; COM. share (of stock); LIT., THEAT. action, plot; THEAT. gesture ♦ a. de gracias thanksgiving • a. ordinaria COM. common stock.

ac·cio·nar tr. to work, operate —intr. to gesticulate.

ac·cio·nis·ta m.f. shareholder, stockholder.

a·ce·ci·nar tr. to cure (meat).

a·ce·char tr. to watch, spy on.

a·ce·cho m. watching, spying.

a·ce·dar tr. to make sour.

a·cé·fa·lo, a adj. acephalous; FIG. leaderless.

a·cei·tar tr. to oil, lubricate.

a·cei·te m. oil ♦ a. combustible or de quemar fuel oil • a. de hígado de bacalao cod-liver oil • a. de ricino castor oil • a. de linaza linseed oil.

a·cei·te·ro, a I. f. AMER. oil cruet II. adj. oil III. m.f. oil vendor.

a·cei·to·so, a adj. oily.

a·cei·tu·na f. olive.

a·cei·tu·na·do, a adj. olive-green.

a·cei·tu·no, a I. m. olive tree II. adj. olive.

a·ce·le·ra·ción f. acceleration.

a·ce·le·ra·da f. acceleration.

a·ce·le·ra·dor m. accelerator.

a·ce·le·rar tr. to speed up; (facilitar) to expedite —intr. to hurry; (motores) to race.

a·cel·ga f. chard, beet.

a·cen·to m. accent; (signo) accent mark; (tono) tone ♦ a. ortográfico written accent.

a·cen·tua·ción f. accentuation.

a·cen·tua·do, a adj. accented.

a·cen·tuar §67 tr. to accent; (hacer resaltar) to accentuate —reflex. to stand out.

a·cep·ción f. meaning.

a·cep·ta·ción f. acceptance; (aprobación) approval.

a·cep·tar tr. to accept; (admitir) to believe in; (aprobar) to approve of.

a·ce·quia f. irrigation ditch.

a·ce·quiar intr. to dig irrigation ditches.

a·ce·ra f. sidewalk.

a·ce·ra·do, a adj. steel, steely.

a·ce·rar tr. (cubrir) to cover with steel; (aceras) to pave; (fortalecer) to strengthen.

a·cer·bi·dad f. (sabor) sourness; (severidad) harshness.

a·cer·bo, a adj. (agrio) sour; (severo) harsh.

a·cer·ca de prep. about, concerning.

a·cer·ca·mien·to m. approach.

a·cer·car §70 tr. to bring near —reflex. to approach, draw near.

a·ce·rí·a f. steel mill.

a·ce·ri·co m. (almohada) small pillow, cushion; (alfiletero) pincushion.

a·ce·ro m. steel; (arma) blade, sword ♦ a. fundido cast steel.

a·ce·ro·la f. BOT. haw (fruit).

a·cé·rri·mo, a adj. staunch, stalwart.

a·ce·rro·jar tr. to bolt, lock.

a·cer·ta·do, a adj. correct, accurate.

a·cer·tar §49 tr. (adivinar) to guess correctly; (encontrar) to find, hit upon —intr. (tener razón) to hit the mark, be correct; (lograr) to succeed ♦ a. a to happen to • a. con to come upon or across.

a·cer·ti·jo m. riddle.

a·cer·vo m. (montón) pile, heap; (patrimonio) common property.

a·ce·ta·to m. acetate.

a·ce·ti·le·no m. acetylene.

a·ce·to·na f. acetone.

a·ce·tre m. (caldero) water bucket; RELIG. font.

a·cia·go, a adj. fateful, unlucky.

a·ci·ca·la·do, a adj. spruced up.

a·ci·ca·lar tr. & reflex. to dress or spruce up.

a·ci·ca·te m. (espuela) spur; (incentivo) spur, incentive.

a·ci·ca·te·ar tr. to spur, incite.

a·ci·dez f. acidity.

á·ci·do, a I. adj. acid; (agrio) sour, tart II. m. acid; COLL. L.S.D.

a·ci·du·lo, a adj. acidulous, sour.

a·cier·te, to see acertar.

a·cier·to m. (logro) good shot, hit; (éxito) success; (cordura) good sense; (habilidad) skill, dexterity, knack ♦ con a. (con éxito) successfully; (con destreza) skillfully.

a·cla·ma·ción f. acclamation, acclaim.

a·cla·mar tr. to acclaim, hail.

a·cla·ra·ción f. clarification, explanation.

a·cla·ra·do m. rinse, rinsing.

a·cla·rar tr. to clarify; (explicar) to explain; (aguar) to thin; (enjuagar) to rinse —intr. (clarear) to clear up; (amanecer) to dawn —reflex. (hacerse inteligible) to become clear; (clarear) to clear up ♦ a. la voz to clear one's throat.

a·cla·ra·to·rio, a adj. clarifying, explanatory.

a·cla·re·cer §17 var. of aclarar.

a·cli·ma·tar tr. to acclimatize, acclimate —reflex. to become acclimatized or acclimated.

ac·né f. acne.

a·co·bar·da·mien·to m. cowardliness.

a·co·bar·dar tr. to intimidate —reflex. to become intimidated.

a·co·ce·ar tr. to kick.

a·co·dar tr. (apoyar) to rest; CARP. to square —reflex. to lean or rest one's elbows on.

a·co·ge·di·zo, a adj. easily adaptable.

a·co·ge·dor, ·ra adj. (cordial) welcoming; (cómodo) inviting, cozy.

a·co·ger §34 tr. (dar bienvenida) to welcome; (amparar) to shelter; (aceptar) to accept —reflex. (refugiarse) to take refuge ♦ a. a to have recourse in, resort to.

a·co·gi·da f. (recibimiento) reception, welcome; (amparo) shelter, refuge ♦ tener buena a. to be well received.

a·co·go·tar tr. COLL. to knock down (with a blow to the back of the head).

a·col·cha·do, a I. adj. padded, quilted II. m. (relleno) padding; ARG. bedspread.

a·col·char tr. (rellenar) to quilt; (muebles) to upholster.

a·có·li·to m. RELIG. acolyte; (monaguillo) altar boy; (discípulo) disciple, follower.

a·co·me·ter tr. to attack; (intentar) to undertake; (dominar) to overcome.

a·co·me·ti·da f. attack, assault.

a·co·mo·da·do, a adj. (rico) well-off; (moderado) reasonable.

a·co·mo·da·dor, ·ra m.f. usher.

a·co·mo·dar tr. (arreglar) to arrange, put in order; (adaptar) to adapt; (colocar) to accommodate —intr. to suit, be suitable —reflex. AMER. to set oneself up.

a·co·mo·da·ti·cio, a adj. (acomodadizo) accommodating, obliging; (conveniente) suitable.

a·co·mo·do m. (empleo) job; (alojamiento) lodgings; AMER. connections.

a·com·pa·ña·mien·to m. accompaniment; (comitiva) retinue.

a·com·pa·ñan·te, a I. adj. accompanying II. m.f. companion; MUS. accompanist —m. escort —f. chaperon.

a·com·pa·ñar tr. to accompany; (escoltar) to escort; (agregar) to enclose ♦ a. en el sentimiento to express one's condolences • a. con or en MUS. to accompany oneself on.

a·com·pa·sa·do, a adj. (rítmico) rhythmic; (pausado) slow-paced.

a·com·pa·sar tr. to give rhythm to.

a·com·ple·ja·do, a I. adj. suffering from a complex II. m.f. person who suffers from a complex.

a·com·ple·jar tr. to give a complex to —reflex. to get a complex.

a·co·mu·nar·se reflex. to unite, join forces.

a·con·di·cio·na·do, a adj. conditioned ♦ aire

a. air-conditioning • **bien, mal a.** in good, bad condition.

a·con·di·cio·na·dor m. conditioner ♦ **a. de aire** air conditioner.

a·con·di·cio·na·mien·to m. conditioning.

a·con·di·cio·nar tr. *(disponer)* to prepare; *(reparar)* to repair; *(el aire)* to air-condition.

a·con·go·jar tr. to distress —reflex. to be distressed.

a·con·se·ja·do, a adj. sensible, prudent.

a·con·se·jar tr. to advise, counsel —reflex. ♦ **a. con** *or* **de** to consult with, get advice from.

a·con·te·cer §17 intr. to happen, occur.

a·con·te·ci·mien·to m. event, occurrence.

a·co·pia·dor, ·ra I. adj. gathering, collecting II. m.f. gatherer, collector.

a·co·piar tr. to gather, collect.

a·co·pio m. gathering; *(provisiones)* stock; AMER. *(abundancia)* abundance.

a·co·pla·do m. AMER. trailer.

a·co·pla·mien·to m. coupling, joint.

a·co·plar tr. *(unir)* to couple, join; *(aparear)* to mate; *(conciliar)* to reconcile —reflex. to mate.

a·co·ra·za·do, a I. adj. *(blindado)* armored, armor-plated; *(endurecido)* hardened, inured II. m. battleship.

a·co·ra·zar §04 tr. to armor (oneself).

a·cor·da·do, a adj. agreed (upon).

a·cor·dar §19 tr. *(concordar)* to agree; *(decidir)* to decide; *(conciliar)* to reconcile; *(recordar)* to remind; AMER. to grant, accord —intr. to harmonize, go together —reflex. *(recordar)* to remember; *(convenir)* to agree, come to an agreement ♦ **si mal no me acuerdo** if my memory serves me right.

a·cor·de I. adj. *(conforme)* in agreement; *(con armonía)* harmonious II. m. chord.

a·cor·de·ón m. accordion.

a·cor·do·nar tr. *(rodear)* to cordon off, surround; *(atar)* to tie or lace (up).

a·co·rra·lar tr. *(encerrar)* to pen; *(atrapar)* to corner; *(intimidar)* to scare.

a·cor·tar tr. to shorten, reduce —reflex. to become shorter.

a·co·sa·mien·to m. harassment.

a·co·sar tr. *(perseguir)* to harass; *(un caballo)* to spur.

a·cos·ta·do, a adj. in bed, lying down.

a·cos·tar §19 tr. to put to bed, MARIT. to bring alongside —intr. to reach shore —reflex. to go to bed; *(inclinarse)* to list; MARIT. to go alongside ♦ **a. con** COLL. to sleep with • **a. con las gallinas** COLL. to go to bed early.

a·cos·tum·bra·do, a adj. *(habituado)* accustomed or used to; *(habitual)* customary.

a·cos·tum·brar tr. & reflex. to accustom (oneself) —intr. to be accustomed to.

a·co·ta·ción f. *(comentario)* remark; THEAT. stage direction; TOP. elevation mark ♦ **a. al margen** marginal note.

a·co·tar tr. *(amojonar)* to stake out; *(fijar)* to set limits on; *(anotar)* to annotate; *(notar)* to remark; *(admitir)* to admit; TOP. to indicate elevations on.

a·cre¹ m. acre.

a·cre² adj. acrid.

a·cre·cen·ta·mien·to m. increase, growth.

a·cre·cen·tar §49 tr. *(aumentar)* to increase; *(avanzar)* to promote —reflex. to increase, grow.

a·cre·di·ta·ción f. accreditation.

a·cre·di·ta·do, a adj. accredited; *(ilustre)* reputable.

a·cre·di·tar tr. *(embajador)* to accredit; *(afamar)* to make famous; *(asegurar)* guarantee, vouch for; COM. to credit —reflex. **a. de** to develop a reputation as.

a·cree·dor, ·ra I. adj. worthy, deserving II. m.f. creditor.

a·cri·bi·llar tr. *(agujerear)* to riddle (a with); *(molestar)* to hound.

a·crí·li·co, a I. adj. & m.f. acrylic.

a·cri·so·lar tr. *(aclarar)* to clarify; METAL. to refine, purify.

a·cro·ba·cia f. acrobatics.

a·cró·ba·ta m.f. acrobat.

a·crós·ti·co, a adj. & m. acrostic.

ac·ta f. *(informe)* record; *(minutas)* minutes; *(certificado)* certificate ♦ **a. notarial** affidavit • **levantar un a.** to draw up a certificate.

ac·ti·nio m. actinium.

ac·ti·tud f. attitude.

ac·ti·va·ción f. activation.

ac·ti·va·dor m. activator.

ac·ti·var tr. to activate; *(acelerar)* to expedite —reflex. to become activated.

ac·ti·vi·dad f. activity ♦ **en (plena) a.** in (full) operation.

ac·ti·vis·ta adj. & m.f. activist.

ac·ti·vo, a I. adj. active II. m. COM. assets.

ac·to m. act ♦ **a. seguido** immediately after • **a. de presencia** token appearance • **a. reflejo** reflex action • **en el a.** at once.

ac·tor, ·ra I. m. actor —m.f. LAW plaintiff II. adj. acting.

ac·triz f. actress.

ac·tua·ción f. performance; *(acción)* action ♦ pl. LAW proceedings.

ac·tual adj. present-day, current.

ac·tua·li·dad f. *(ahora)* present (time); *(estado)* current situation ♦ **en la a.** nowadays ♦ pl. news, current events.

ac·tua·li·zar §04 tr. to modernize.

ac·tual·men·te adv. at present, nowadays.

ac·tuar §67 tr. to actuate —intr. *(obrar)* to act; THEAT. to perform ♦ **a. de** to act as.

a·cua·re·la f. water color.

a·cua·re·lis·ta m.f. water colorist.

a·cua·rio m. aquarium.

a·cuar·te·lar tr. MIL. to quarter, billet.

a·cuá·ti·co, a/til adj. aquatic.

a·cua·ti·za·je m. AMER. landing on water.

a·cua·ti·zar §04 intr. AMER. to land on water.

a·cu·ciar tr. to hasten, goad.

a·cu·cli·llar·se reflex. to squat, crouch down.

a·cu·chi·lla·mien·to m. *(apuñalamiento)* stabbing, slashing; CARP. surfacing (of wood).

a·cu·chi·llar tr. *(apuñalar)* to slash, cut; *(herir)* to knife, stab; CARP. to plane, scrape.

a·cu·dir intr. *(presentarse)* to go, come; *(valerse)* to appeal, to have recourse; *(asistir)* to attend, show up ♦ **a. a** to turn to • **a. en ayuda de** to go to the aid of.

a·cue·duc·to m. aqueduct.

a·cuer·de, do see **acordar**.

a·cuer·do m. *(convenio)* agreement, accord; *(dictamen)* opinion, ruling ♦ **de a. con** in agreement *or* accordance with • **de** *or* **por común a.** of common accord • **vivir en perfecto a.** to live in absolute harmony.

a·cues·te, to see **acostar**.

a·cui·dad f. acuity, sharpness.

a·cu·llá adv. (over) there, yonder.

a·cu·mu·la·ción f./mien·to m. accumulation, gathering.

a·cu·mu·la·dor, ·ra I. adj. accumulative II. m. storage battery.

a·cu·mu·lar tr. to accumulate, gather.

a·cu·mu·la·ti·vo, a adj. accumulative.

a·cu·nar tr. to rock, cradle.

a·cu·ñar tr. (monedas) to coin, mint; (meter cuñas) to wedge, key.

a·cuo·so, a adj. watery, aqueous.

a·cu·pun·tu·ra f. acupuncture.

a·cu·rru·car·se §70 reflex. to curl up; FIG. to crouch.

a·cu·sa·ción f. accusation, charge.

a·cu·sa·do, a adj. & m.f. accused.

a·cu·sa·dor, ·ra I. adj. accusing II. m.f. accuser.

a·cu·sar tr. to accuse; (denunciar) to give away; (indicar) to acknowledge —reflex. to confess.

a·cu·sa·ti·vo m. accusative.

a·cu·sa·to·rio, a adj. accusatory, accusing.

a·cu·se m. acknowledgment ♦ a. de recibo acknowledgment of receipt.

a·cús·ti·co, a I. adj. acoustic, acoustical II. f. acoustics.

a·cha·car §70 tr. to attribute, to impute.

a·cha·co·so, a adj. sickly, frail.

a·cha·pa·rra·do, a adj. stocky, stubby.

a·cha·que m. ailment, illness ♦ pl. C. AMER. morning sickness • a. de la edad ailments of old age.

a·cha·ro·la·do, a adj. resembling patent leather.

a·cha·ro·lar tr. to varnish, enamel.

a·cha·ta·do, a adj. flat, flattened.

a·cha·tar tr. to flatten, squash —reflex. to become flat.

a·chi·ca·du·ra f./mien·to m. (disminución) reduction; MARIT. bailing.

a·chi·car §70 tr. (disminuir) to reduce; (humillar) to humiliate; (ropa) to take in; MARIT. to bail out —reflex. (disminuirse) to get smaller, shrink; (acobardarse) to shrink back.

a·chi·co·ria f. chicory.

a·chi·cha·rran·te adj. (quemante) scorching; (bochornoso) sweltering.

a·chi·cha·rrar tr. to scorch —reflex. (quemarse) to burn; (calentarse demasiado) to get overheated.

a·chis·pa·do, a adj. tipsy, slightly drunk.

a·chis·par tr. COLL. to make tipsy —reflex. to get tipsy.

a·cho·char·se reflex. to become senile.

a·cho·la·do, a adj. AMER. (mestizo) half-Indian; (avergonzado) red in the face.

a·cho·lar AMER. tr. to embarrass —reflex. (acriollarse) to adopt mestizo ways; (avergonzarse) to be ashamed.

a·chu·bas·car·se §70 reflex. to become threatening or overcast (the sky).

a·chu·ra f. AMER. offal.

a·chu·rar/re·ar tr. AMER. to gut, disembowel; COLL. (matar) to stab to death.

a·da·gio m. (refrán) adage; MUS. adagio.

a·da·lid m. MIL. military leader, commander; FIG. (jefe) leader, head (of a party).

a·dán m. FIG., COLL. ragamuffin, scruffy fellow ♦ A. Adam • ir en traje de A. to be naked.

a·dap·ta·bi·li·dad f. adaptability.

a·dap·ta·ción f. adaptation, adjustment.

a·dap·ta·dor m. MECH. adapter.

a·dap·tar tr. & reflex. to adapt, adjust (oneself).

a·de·ce·nar tr. to divide into groups of ten.

a·de·cua·ción f. fitting, adjustment.

a·de·cua·do, a adj. (apropiado) appropriate, suitable; (suficiente) adequate, sufficient.

a·de·cuar tr. to make suitable, adapt.

a·de·fe·sio m. COLL. (persona) mess; (traje) ridiculous or gaudy outfit.

a·de·lan·ta·do, a adj. (precoz) precocious, advanced; (reloj) fast ♦ por a. in advance.

a·de·lan·tar tr. (avanzar) to move forward; (acelerar) to speed up; (anticipar) to advance; (aventajar) to surpass; AUTO. to overtake, pass; (relojes) to set ahead or forward —intr. (avanzar) to advance, go forward; (relojes) to be fast; FIG. (progresar) to make progress —reflex. to get ahead ♦ a. a to get ahead of.

a·de·lan·te adv. forward, ahead ♦ ¡a.! come in! • de aquí en a. from now on • más a. farther on.

a·de·lan·to m. (de paga) advance; (progreso) progress.

a·del·ga·zar §04 tr. to make slim or thin —intr. to lose weight, become slim.

a·de·mán m. gesture ♦ en a. de as if about to • hacer a. de to make a move to ♦ pl. manners.

a·de·más adv. besides, in addition.

a·den·tro I. adv. within, inside ♦ ser de tierra a. AMER. to be from the interior II. m.pl. the innermost self.

a·dep·to, a I. adj. supportive II. m.f. follower.

a·de·re·zar §04 tr. (condimentar) to season; (adornar) to adorn; (arreglar) to prepare, get ready; TEX. to treat.

a·de·re·zo m. (condimento) seasoning; (adorno) adornment; (arreglo) preparation; TEX. starch, gum.

a·deu·dar tr. (deber) to owe; ACC., COM. to debit —reflex. to get into debt.

ad·he·ren·cia f. adherence, adhesion.

ad·he·ren·te adj. & m.f. adherent.

ad·he·rir §65 tr. to affix, stick on —intr. & reflex. (pegarse) to stick, adhere; (consentir) to support, adhere.

ad·he·sión f. adhesion, adherence.

ad·he·si·vo, a adj. & m. adhesive.

a·di·ción f. addition; AMER. bill, check.

a·di·cio·nal adj. additional, added.

a·di·cio·nar tr. to add (to).

a·dic·to, a I. adj. addicted; (dedicado) fond, attached II. m.f. addict; (partidario) follower.

a·dies·tra·do, a adj. trained.

a·dies·tra·dor, ·ra m.f. trainer, coach.

a·dies·tra·mien·to m. training.

a·dies·trar tr. (instruir) to train, coach; (guiar) to guide, lead —reflex. to teach or coach oneself.

a·di·ne·ra·do, a adj. wealthy, affluent.

a·diós interj. & m. good-by.

a·di·po·so, a adj. adipose, fatty.

a·di·ta·men·to m. (añadidura) addition; (accesorio) attachment ♦ por a. in addition.

a·di·ti·vo, a adj. & m. additive.

a·di·vi·na·ción f. prediction; (conjetura) guessing ♦ a. del pensamiento mind reading.

a·di·vi·na·dor, ·ra adj. & m.f. diviner.

a·di·vi·nan·za f. riddle, puzzle.

a·di·vi·nar tr. (predecir) to predict; (conjeturar) to guess; (el pensamiento) to read; (resolver) to solve ♦ dejar a. algo to hint at something.

a·di·vi·no, a m.f. fortuneteller.

ad·je·ti·var tr. *(poner adjetivos)* to qualify; *(usar como adjetivo)* to use as an adjective —reflex. to be used as an adjective.

ad·je·ti·vo, a I. adj. adjectival II. m. adjective.

ad·ju·di·ca·ción f. adjudication, awarding.

ad·ju·di·ca·dor, ·ra m.f. awarder.

ad·ju·di·car §70 tr. to award —reflex. to appropriate (for oneself).

ad·ju·di·ca·ta·rio, a m.f. awardee.

ad·jun·tar tr. to attach, enclose.

ad·jun·to, a I. adj. attached, enclosed; *(persona)* assistant, adjunct II. m.f. associate.

ad·mi·ní·cu·lo m. instrument, gadget ♦ pl. emergency equipment.

ad·mi·nis·tra·ción f. *(dirección)* administration, management; *(oficina)* headquarters.

ad·mi·nis·tra·dor, ·ra I. adj. administrative II. m.f. administrator, manager.

ad·mi·nis·trar tr. *(dirigir)* to manage; *(conferir)* to administer, give.

ad·mi·nis·tra·ti·vo, a adj. administrative.

ad·mi·ra·ción f. admiration; *(sorpresa)* surprise, wonder; GRAM. exclamation point.

ad·mi·ra·dor, ·ra m.f. admirer.

ad·mi·rar tr. to admire; *(sorprender)* to surprise, amaze —reflex. to marvel at.

ad·mi·si·ble adj. admissible.

ad·mi·sión f. *(acción)* admission; *(aceptación)* acceptance; ENGIN. intake.

ad·mi·tir tr. *(entrada)* to admit; *(aceptar)* to accept; *(reconocer)* to acknowledge; *(tener cabida)* to hold ♦ **admitamos que** supposing.

ad·mo·ni·ción f. admonition, warning.

ad·mo·ni·to·rio, a adj. warning.

a·do·ba·do m. marinated meat.

a·do·bar tr. *(aderezar)* to marinate; *(preservar)* to pickle; *(pieles)* to tan.

a·do·be m. *(ladrillo)* adobe.

a·do·bo m. *(salsa)* marinade; *(de pieles)* tanning.

a·doc·tri·na·mien·to m. indoctrination.

a·doc·tri·nar tr. to indoctrinate, instruct.

a·do·le·cer §17 intr. to fall ill ♦ **a. de** to suffer from, have.

a·do·les·cen·cia f. adolescence, youth.

a·do·les·cen·te adj. & m.f. adolescent, youth.

a·don·de conj. where.

a·dón·de adv. & conj. where.

a·don·de·quie·ra adv. wherever, anywhere.

a·dop·ción f. adoption.

a·dop·tar tr. to adopt.

a·dop·ti·vo, a adj. adoptive, adopted.

a·do·quín m. paving stone; FIG., COLL. dunce, idiot.

a·do·qui·na·do m. *(pavimento)* pavement; *(acción)* paving.

a·do·qui·nar tr. to pave.

a·do·ra·ción f. adoration, worship.

a·do·rar tr. & intr. to adore, worship.

a·dor·me·cer §17 tr. to put to sleep —reflex. to doze off, get sleepy.

a·dor·me·ci·do, a adj. *(soñoliento)* sleepy, drowsy; *(un miembro)* numb, asleep.

a·dor·me·ci·mien·to m. *(acción)* dozing off; *(sueño)* sleepiness; *(modorra)* drowsiness.

a·dor·mi·lar·se/tar·se reflex. to doze, drowse.

a·dor·nar tr. to adorn; SEW. to trim; CUL. to garnish; FIG. to embellish.

a·dor·no m. adornment; SEW. trimming; CUL. garnish ♦ **de a.** decorative.

a·do·sar tr. to place *or* lean against; *(unir)* to join; AMER. *(agregar)* to attach.

ad·qui·ri·do, a adj. acquired ♦ **mal a.** ill-gotten.

ad·qui·ri·dor, ·ra m.f. acquirer, buyer.

ad·qui·rir §02 tr. to acquire, buy.

ad·qui·si·ción f. acquisition, purchase.

ad·qui·si·ti·vo, a adj. acquisitive, purchasing.

a·dre·de adv. on purpose, deliberately.

a·dre·na·lí·na f. adrenaline.

ads·cri·bir §80 tr. *(atribuir)* to attribute, ascribe; *(designar)* to assign.

ads·cri(p)·to, a I. see **adscribir** II. adj. *(atribuido)* ascribed; *(designado)* assigned.

a·dua·na f. customs.

a·dua·ne·ro, a I. adj. customs II. m. customs officer.

a·du·cir §22 tr. to adduce, cite.

a·due·ñar·se reflex. to take over *or* possession.

a·du·la·ción f. adulation, flattery.

a·du·la·dor, ·ra I. adj. adulating, flattering II. m.f. adulator, flatterer.

a·du·lar tr. to adulate, flatter.

a·du·lón, ·o·na COLL. I. adj. fawning, flattering II. m.f. flatterer, fawner.

a·dul·te·ra·ción f. adulteration.

a·dul·te·ra·dor, ·ra I. adj. adulterating II. m.f. adulterator.

a·dul·te·rar tr. to adulterate —intr. to commit adultery.

a·dul·te·rio m. adultery.

a·dúl·te·ro, a I. adj. *(infiel)* adulterous; *(corrompido)* corrupt II. m. adulterer f. adulteress.

a·dul·to, a adj. & m.f. adult.

a·dul·zar §04 tr. to sweeten; METAL. to soften.

a·dus·tez f. austerity, harshness.

a·dus·to, a adj. *(austero)* austere, severe; *(quemado)* scorching, burning hot.

ad·ve·ne·di·zo, a I. adj. foreign, alien II. m.f. *(extranjero)* immigrant, foreigner; *(nuevo rico)* parvenu.

ad·ve·ni·mien·to m. *(llegada)* advent, arrival; *(accesión)* accession.

ad·ve·nir §76 intr. to come, arrive.

ad·ven·ti·cio, a adj. adventitious.

ad·ven·tis·ta adj. & m.f. Adventist.

ad·ver·bio m. adverb.

ad·ver·sa·rio, a m.f. adversary, opponent.

ad·ver·si·dad f. adversity, misfortune.

ad·ver·so, a adj. *(desfavorable)* adverse, unfavorable; *(opuesto)* opposite.

ad·ver·ten·cia f. *(admonición)* warning; *(consejo)* advice; *(noticia)* notice; *(prefacio)* preface, foreword.

ad·ver·ti·do, a adj. *(avisado)* informed, warned; *(capaz)* capable, skillful.

ad·ver·tir §65 tr. *(fijar)* to notice; *(avisar)* to warn; *(aconsejar)* to advise —intr. to notice.

ad·vi·nie·ra, no see **advenir**.

ad·ya·cen·cia f. adjacency, contiguity.

ad·ya·cen·te adj. adjacent.

a·é·re·o, a adj. air, aerial; *(leve)* light.

a·e·ro·bús m. airbus.

a·e·ro·di·ná·mi·co, a I. adj. aerodynamic, aerodynamical II. f. aerodynamics.

a·e·ro·di·na·mis·mo m. aerodynamism.

a·e·ro·dro·mo m. airdrome, aerodrome (G.B.).

a·e·ro·fo·to·gra·fí·a f. *(técnica)* aerial photography; *(foto)* aerial photograph.

a·e·ro·gra·ma f. aerogram, air letter.

a·e·ro·lí·ne·a f. airline.

a·e·ro·li·to m. aerolite, meteorite.

a·e·ro·mo·de·lis·mo m. airplane modeling.

a·e·ro·mo·zo, a m.f. flight attendant —m. steward —f. stewardess.

a·e·ro·nau·ta m.f. aeronaut.

a·e·ro·náu·ti·co, a I. adj. aeronautic, aeronautical II. f. aeronautics.

a·e·ro·na·ve f. airship.

a·e·ro·pla·no m. airplane.

a·e·ro·pos·tal adj. airmail.

a·e·ro·puer·to m. airport.

a·e·ro·sol m. aerosol.

a·e·ros·pa·cial adj. aerospace.

a·e·ros·tá·ti·co, a I. adj. aerostatic, aerostatical II. f. aerostatics.

a·e·ro·te·rres·tre adj. air-land, air-to-ground.

a·fa·bi·li·dad f. affability, geniality.

a·fa·ble adj. affable, genial.

a·fa·ma·do, a adj. famous, renowned.

a·fán m. (fervor) eagerness, zeal; (anhelo) urge, desire.

a·fa·nar·se reflex. strive, toil.

a·fa·no·so, a adj. (fervoroso) eager, zealous; (trabajador) hard-working, diligent; (agitado) hectic, feverish.

a·fe·ar tr. to make ugly, deform.

a·fec·ción f. affection.

a·fec·ta·ción f. affectation.

a·fec·ta·do, a adj. affected; (fingido) feigned.

a·fec·tar tr. to affect; (impresionar) to move; (influir) to influence; (dañar) to afflict —reflex. (impresionarse) to be moved or affected.

a·fec·to, a I. adj. (cariñoso) affectionate; (que gusta) fond (a of) II. m. affection, fondness.

a·fec·tuo·si·dad f. affection.

a·fec·tuo·so, a adj. affectionate, loving.

a·fei·ta·da f. shave, shaving.

a·fei·ta·do·ra f. electric razor or shaver.

a·fei·tar tr. & reflex. to shave (oneself).

a·fei·te m. make-up, cosmetics.

a·fel·pa·do, a I. adj. plush II. m. doormat.

a·fe·mi·na·do, a adj. effeminate.

a·fe·mi·nar tr. to make effeminate —reflex. to become effeminate.

a·fe·rra·mien·to m. (asimiento) grasping; (insistencia) insistence.

a·fe·rrar §49 tr. (asir) to grasp; (agarrar) to hook; (amarrar) to moor —reflex. to cling (a to); (insistir) to persist (a in).

a·fian·za·mien·to m. securing, strengthening.

a·fian·zar §04 tr. (garantizar) to guarantee; (asegurar) to secure —reflex. (asegurarse) to steady oneself; (establecerse) to establish oneself.

a·fi·ción f. (inclinación) inclination, liking (a for); (aficionados) fans, enthusiasts.

a·fi·cio·na·do, a I. adj. fond (a of); (novicio) amateur II. m.f. (diletante) fan, enthusiast; (novicio) amateur.

a·fi·cio·nar tr. to inspire a fondness (a for); —reflex. to become fond (a of).

a·fie·bra·do, a adj. feverish.

a·fie·brar·se reflex. AMER. to become feverish.

a·fie·rra, rro see aferrar.

a·fi·la·do, a adj. sharp.

a·fi·la·dor, ·ra I. adj. sharpening II. m. (persona) sharpener; (máquina) sharpening machine.

a·fi·la·lá·pi·ces m.inv. pencil sharpener.

a·fi·lar tr. to sharpen; AMER., COLL. to woo —reflex. to grow or become thin.

a·fi·lia·ción f. affiliation.

a·fi·lia·do, a m.f. affiliate, member.

a·fi·liar tr. to affiliate —reflex. to become affiliated, join (a with).

a·fín adj. (próximo) adjacent; (parecido) similar.

a·fi·na·dor, ·ra m.f. tuner —m. tuning key.

a·fi·nar tr. (perfeccionar) to refine; (purificar) to refine; MUS. to tune —intr. (cantar) to sing in tune; (tocar) to play in tune.

a·fin·car §70 intr. to acquire real estate —reflex. to establish oneself.

a·fi·ni·dad f. affinity.

a·fir·ma·ción f. affirmation.

a·fir·ma·do m. roadbed.

a·fir·mar tr. (declarar) to affirm; (afianzar) to secure —reflex. to steady oneself.

a·fir·ma·ti·vo, a I. adj. affirmative II. f. affirmative answer or statement.

a·flau·ta·do, a adj. high-pitched.

a·flic·ción f. affliction.

a·fli·gi·do, a adj. distressed; (por muerte) bereaved.

a·fli·gir §32 tr. (apenar) to cause pain; (pesar) to trouble, distress —reflex. to be troubled or distressed (con, de, por by).

a·flo·jar tr. to loosen, slacken; (entregar) to give up —intr. (disminuir) to diminish; (decaer) to grow lax, slack —reflex. to become loose or slack.

a·flo·ra·mien·to m. emergence.

a·flo·rar intr. (aparecer) to emerge; GEOL. to outcrop.

a·fluen·cia f. (de gente) crowding; (abundancia) affluence; (facundia) fluency; (de sangre) flow.

a·fluir §18 intr. (manar) to flow; (acudir) to flock.

a·fo·far·se reflex. to become soft or fluffy.

a·fo·ní·a f. aphonia (loss of voice).

a·tó·ni·co, a or á·fo·no, a adj. aphonic, hoarse; PHONET. voiceless, silent.

a·fo·rar §19 tr. to measure, gauge; COM. to appraise, assess.

a·fo·ris·mo m. aphorism.

a·fo·ro m. measurement; COM. appraisal.

a·for·tu·na·do, a adj. fortunate, lucky; (feliz) happy.

a·fre·cho m. bran.

a·fren·ta f. affront.

a·fren·tar tr. to affront.

a·fren·to·so, a adj. insolent, offensive.

a·fro·di·sía·co, a adj. & m. aphrodisiac.

a·fron·ta·mien·to m. confrontation.

a·fron·tar tr. to face (up) to, confront.

a·fue·ra I. adv. out, outside; (en público) in public II. interj. scram!, get out of here! III. f.pl. outskirts.

a·fue·re, ro see aforar.

a·ga·cha·da f. stooping, crouching.

a·ga·char tr. to bow, bend ♦ a. las orejas to hang one's head, be crestfallen —reflex. to crouch, squat.

a·ga·lla f. ICHTH. gill; BOT. nutgall ♦ pl. FIG., COLL. guts, courage.

á·ga·pe m. banquet.

a·ga·rra·de·ra f. AMER. handle, holder.

a·ga·rra·do, a I. adj. COLL. (mezquino) stingy; (en los bailes) cheek-to-cheek II. m.f. COLL. cheapskate —f. COLL. quarrel.

a·ga·rrar tr. (asir) to grab, grasp; COLL. (enfermedad) to get, catch; (conseguir) to get, wangle; AMER. (vehículo) take —intr. (pegarse) to take hold, stick; (arraigar) to take root ♦ a.

para S. AMER. to head for —reflex. *(asirse)* to cling, hold on; *(pelearse)* to grapple, come to blows.

a·ga·rre m. grabbing; FIG. *(valor)* guts; AMER., COLL. influence.

a·ga·rro·ta·do, a adj. stiff, tense.

a·ga·rro·tar tr. *(estrangular)* to garrote; *(atar)* to bind tightly —reflex. to become stiff.

a·ga·sa·ja·dor, ra adj. *(acogedor)* welcoming; *(obsequiante)* attentive.

a·ga·sa·jar tr. *(festejar)* to entertain; *(regalar)* to lavish gifts on.

a·ga·sa·jo m. *(festejo)* entertainment; *(regalo)* present.

a·ga·za·par·se reflex. *(agacharse)* to squat; *(esconderse)* to hide out.

a·gen·cia f. agency; *(oficina)* bureau.

a·gen·ciar tr. & reflex. to manage, obtain.

a·gen·cio·so, a adj. diligent, industrious.

a·gen·da f. notebook.

a·gen·te m. agent ♦ **a. de bolsa** stockbroker, broker • **a. de policía** policeman.

á·gil adj. agile, nimble.

a·gi·li·dad f. agility, nimbleness.

a·gi·li·tar tr. *(hacer ágil)* to render agile or nimble; AMER. to activate, hasten.

a·gi·li·zar §04 tr. to make agile or nimble.

u·gi·u m. spcculut.iun.

a·gi·ta·ción f. agitation; *(alboroto)* excitement.

a·gi·ta·dor, ra I. adj. agitating II. m.f. *(provocador)* agitator —m. stirring rod.

a·gi·tar tr. to shake; *(alborotar)* to excite —reflex. to wave, flutter; *(perturbarse)* to be agitated; MARIT. to get rough or choppy.

a·glo·me·ra·ción f. agglomeration; *(gentío)* crowd.

a·glo·me·ra·do m. agglomerate; *(combustible)* coal briquette.

a·glo·me·rar tr. to agglomerate —reflex. to be amassed or heaped together; *(apiñarse)* to crowd.

a·glu·ti·na·ción f. agglutination.

a·glu·ti·nan·te adj. & m. agglutinant.

a·glu·ti·nar tr. to agglutinate, bind.

ag·nós·ti·co, a adj. & m.f. agnostic.

a·go·bia·do, a adj. *(cargado de espaldas)* bent over, stooped; *(fatigado)* exhausted, weary.

a·go·bia·dor, ra adj. *(sofocante)* stifling; *(agotador)* backbreaking; *(abrumador)* overwhelming.

a·go·bian·te adj. *(sofocante)* stifling *(agotador)* backbreaking.

a·go·biar tr. *(cargar)* to weigh down; *(cansar)* to weary; *(deprimir)* to depress —reflex. to bend, stoop.

a·go·bio m. *(carga)* burden; *(fatiga)* fatigue.

a·gol·pa·mien·to m. *(cúmulo)* pile; *(gentío)* crowd, crowding.

a·gol·par·se reflex. *(apiñarse)* to flock; *(venirse encima)* to come all at once.

a·go·ní·a f. agony, anguish.

a·gó·ni·co, a adj. dying; *(angustiado)* in agony.

a·go·ni·zan·te adj. dying.

a·go·ni·zar §04 intr. to be at death's door; *(sufrir)* to be in agony; *(extinguirse)* to fade.

a·go·re·ro, a I. m.f. *(adivino)* soothsayer; *(profeta)* prophet of doom II. adj. ominous, foreboding.

a·gor·go·jar·se reflex. to become infested with weevils.

a·gos·tar tr. to parch; *(arar)* to plow in the summer —intr. to graze in the summer.

a·gos·to m. August; *(cosecha)* harvest ♦ **hacer su a.** FIG., COLL. to feather one's nest.

a·go·ta·do, a adj. exhausted; *(libros)* out-of-print; COM. sold-out; AMER. dead (battery).

a·go·ta·dor, ra adj. exhausting, tiring.

a·go·ta·mien·to m. *(abatimiento)* exhaustion; *(disminución)* depletion.

a·go·tar tr. to exhaust —reflex. to be used up or depleted; *(cansarse)* to be exhausted; *(libros)* to be out of print.

a·gra·cia·do, a adj. good looking, attractive.

a·gra·ciar tr. *(embellecer)* to embellish; *(favorecer)* to grace; *(premiar)* to award.

a·gra·da·ble adj. agreeable, pleasant.

a·gra·dar tr. & intr. to please —reflex. to like one another.

a·gra·de·cer §17 tr. to thank; *(sentir gratitud)* to be grateful for.

a·gra·de·ci·do, a adj. & m.f. grateful, thankful (person) ♦ **muy a.** much obliged.

a·gra·de·ci·mien·to m. gratitude, thanks.

a·gra·do m. *(placer)* pleasure; *(gusto)* taste, liking.

a·gran·dar tr. to enlarge; *(exagerar)* to exaggerate —reflex. to grow larger.

u·gru·rloj u·ruj1. ug1uriun, ugricultural.

a·gra·va·ción f./**mien·to** m. aggravation, worsening.

a·gra·van·te I. adj. aggravating II. m. aggravating circumstance.

a·gra·var tr. & reflex. to worsen.

a·gra·via·dor, ra/vian·te I. adj. insulting, offensive II. m.f. offender.

a·gra·viar tr. to offend; *(perjudicar)* to harm —reflex. to take offense.

a·gra·vio m. offense; *(perjuicio)* injury.

a·gra·vio·so, a adj. insulting, offensive.

a·gre·dir §38 tr. to attack, assault.

a·gre·ga·do, a I. adj. aggregate II. m. aggregate; *(añadidura)* addition; P. RICO day laborer ♦ **a. militar** military attaché.

a·gre·gar §47 tr. *(añadir)* to add, attach; *(unir)* to gather, collect —reflex. to join.

a·gre·miar intr. to form a union, unionize.

a·gre·sión f. aggression.

a·gre·si·vi·dad f. aggressiveness.

a·gre·si·vo, a adj. aggressive.

a·gre·sor, ra I. m.f. aggressor II. adj. aggressive.

a·gres·te adj. rustic; FIG. uncouth.

a·griar tr. to (make) sour; *(amargar)* to embitter; *(irritar)* to annoy —reflex. to become sour.

a·grí·co·la or **a·gri·cul·tor, ra** I. adj. agricultural, farming II. m.f. agriculturist, farmer.

a·gri·cul·tu·ra f. agriculture, farming.

a·gri·dul·ce adj. bittersweet.

a·grie·ta·mien·to m. cracking; GEOL. crack.

a·grie·tar tr. & reflex. to crack, split.

a·gri·men·sor, ra m.f. surveyor.

a·gri·men·su·ra f. surveying.

a·grio, a I. adj. sour; *(áspero)* rude, disagreeable II. m. sourness, acidity.

a·gro m. agriculture, farming.

a·gro·no·mí·a f. agronomy, agronomics.

a·gro·nó·mi·co, a adj. agronomical.

a·gró·no·mo, a I. adj. agronomical II. m. agronomist.

a·gro·pe·cua·rio, a adj. ♦ la industria a. agriculture and livestock industry.

a·gru·mar tr. & reflex. to curdle, clot.

a·gru·pa·ción f./mien·to m. (grupo) group; (asociación) association, union.

a·gru·par tr. & reflex. to group, cluster (together).

a·gua f. water; (lluvia) rain; ARCHIT. slope ♦ a. corriente running water • a. de borrajas trifle, nothing • a. de colonia toilet water • a. nieve sleet • a. oxigenada CHEM. hydrogen peroxide • a. salobre or salada salt water • claro como a. crystal-clear • con el a. al cuello in trouble • hacer a. to leak • hacerse a. en la boca to melt in one's mouth • hacérsele a. la boca to make one's mouth water • sin decir a. va ni a. viene suddenly, unexpectedly ♦ pl. (reflejos) wavy pattern; (destellos) sparkle; (orina) urine • a. abajo, arriba downstream, upstream • entre dos a. undecided.

a·gua·cal m. whitewash.

a·gua·ca·te m. avocado.

a·gua·ce·ro m. downpour.

a·gua·cil m. var. of alguacil.

a·gua·chen·to, a adj. AMER. thin.

a·gua·de·ro, a I. adj. waterproof II. m. watering trough or hole.

a·gua·do, a adj. diluted, watered-down; (abstemio) abstemious.

a·gua·fies·tas m.f.inv. killjoy.

a·gua·fuer·te m.f. etching (print or plate).

a·gua·ma·ri·na f. aquamarine.

a·gua·nie·ve f. sleet ♦ pl. wagtail.

a·guan·ta·dor, ·ra adj. AMER., COLL. patient.

a·guan·tar tr. to endure, tolerate; (sostener) to hold up; (contener) to hold, retain —reflex. to control or contain oneself.

a·guan·te m. (paciencia) tolerance; (fuerza) endurance.

a·guar §10 tr. to water down; (malograr) to spoil, mar —reflex. to become watery; (arruinarse) to be spoiled.

a·guar·dar tr. to wait for, await —intr. to wait.

a·gua·rrás m. turpentine oil.

a·gua·te·ro m. AMER. water carrier.

a·gu·de·za f. sharpness; (ingenio) wit.

a·gu·di·za·ción f. (agravación) worsening; (aumento) intensification.

a·gu·di·zar §04 tr. to sharpen; (empeorar) to worsen —reflex. to become serious.

a·gu·do, a adj. sharp, pointed; (chillón) shrill; (perspicaz) keen; MUS. high-pitched; GEOM., GRAM. acute.

a·güe·ro m. prediction; (señal) omen.

a·gue·rri·do, a adj. experienced, seasoned.

a·gue·rrir §38 tr. to accustom to war.

a·gui·jar tr. to goad.

a·gui·jón m. ENTOM. sting; BOT. thorn; (punta) goad; (estímulo) spur.

a·gui·jo·na·zo m. sting, prick.

a·gui·jo·ne·ar tr. to sting; (estimular) to goad.

á·gui·la f. eagle; (condecoración) emblem; (persona) wizard, whiz.

a·gui·le·ño, a adj. aquiline, hook-nosed.

a·gui·lón m. MECH. jib; ARCHIT. gable; (caño) clay drainpipe; (teja) beveled tile.

a·gui·nal·do m. Christmas bonus.

a·gu·ja f. needle; (de sombrero) hatpin; (del reloj) hand; ARCHIT. steeple ♦ a. de gancho crochet hook • a. magnética compass.

a·gu·je·rar/re·ar tr. to pierce, perforate —reflex. to be pierced or perforated.

a·gu·je·ro m. hole.

a·gu·je·ta f. (cinta) lace ♦ pl. MED. soreness.

a·guo·so, a adj. watery, aqueous.

a·gu·sa·nar·se reflex. to get wormy.

a·gu·za·do, a adj. sharpened.

a·gu·zar §04 tr. to sharpen ♦ a. los dientes or el apetito to whet one's appetite • a. el ingenio to sharpen one's wit • a. las orejas or los oídos to prick up one's ears.

¡ah! interj. ah!, ha!

a·he·cha·du·ras f.pl. chaff, siftings.

a·he·char tr. to sift, winnow.

a·he·cho m. sifting, winnowing.

a·he·rrum·brar tr. & reflex. to rust.

a·hí adv. there ♦ a. no más right over there • de a. que hence • por a. thereabouts.

a·hi·ja·do, a m.f. godchild —m. godson —f. goddaughter.

a·hi·jar tr. to adopt; (imputar) to attribute to.

a·hi·la·do, a adj. (suave) gentle, soft; (tenue) faint.

a·hi·lar tr. to line up —intr. to go in single file —reflex. (desmayarse) to faint; (adelgazar) to become thin; BOT. to grow tall and slender.

a·hin·ca·do, a adj. earnest, zealous.

a·hin·car §70 intr. to urge, press —reflex. to hurry, rush.

a·hín·co m. eagerness, zeal.

a·hí·to, a adj. stuffed.

a·ho·ga·do, a I. adj. stifling II. m.f. drowned person.

a·ho·gan·te adj. stifling.

a·ho·gar §47 tr. to drown; (sofocar) to choke; (oprimir) to oppress; AGR. to drown, soak (plants) —reflex. to drown; (sentir sofocación) to choke ♦ a. en un vaso de agua to make a mountain out of a molehill.

a·ho·go m. (en el pecho) shortness of breath; (angustia) anguish.

a·hon·dar tr. to go deeper into —intr. to go deep.

a·ho·ra I. adv. now; (pronto) soon; (hace poco) just now, a few moments ago ♦ a. bien or pues well, now then • a. mismo right now • hasta a. until now • por a. for the time being II. conj. now then, well then.

a·hor·ca·do, a m.f. hanged person.

a·hor·ca·jar·se reflex. to sit astride, straddle.

a·hor·car §70 tr. & reflex. to hang (oneself).

a·ho·ri·ta adv. COLL. right now, this minute.

a·hor·mar tr. to mold, fit.

a·hor·nar tr. to put in the oven —reflex. to bake or burn on the outside only.

a·hor·qui·llar tr. to shape like a fork; AGR. to prop up.

a·ho·rra·dor, ·ra m.f. economizer, saver.

a·ho·rrar tr. to save; (evitar) to spare —reflex. to save or spare oneself.

a·ho·rra·ti·vo, a adj. thrifty.

a·ho·rro m. saving ♦ pl. savings.

a·hu·cha·dor, ·ra m.f. hoarder.

a·hue·ca·do, a adj. hollow.

a·hue·ca·mien·to m. hollowing-out.

a·hue·car §70 tr. to hollow out; (mullir) to fluff up; (la voz) to make deep —intr. ♦ a. el ala COLL. to beat it, split.

a·hue·va·do, a adj. egg-shaped.

a·hu·ma·do, a I. adj. CUL. smoked, cured; (con humo) smoky; (color) smoke-colored II. m. CUL. smoking, curing.

a·hu·mar tr. CUL. to smoke, cure; *(con humo)* to fill with smoke —intr. to be smoky —reflex. *(ennegrecerse)* to be blackened by smoke.

a·hu·yen·tar tr. to drive *or* scare away; *(desechar)* to dismiss —reflex. to flee, run away.

ain·dia·do, a adj. Indian-like.

ai·ra·do, a adj. angry, irate; *(licencioso)* licentious.

ai·rar tr. to anger, annoy.

ai·re m. air; *(viento)* wind; *(apariencia)* air, appearance; *(gracia)* grace; MUS. air, tune; MED., COLL. trick, stiff neck ♦ **a. acondicionado** air conditioning • **al a. libre** in the open air • **darse aires** to put on airs • **estar en el a.** RAD., TELEV. to be on the air; FIG. to be up in the air • **tener un a. con** to resemble.

ai·re·a·ción f. ventilation, air circulation.

ai·re·a·do, a adj. ventilated, aired out.

ai·re·ar tr. to ventilate, aerate; *(discutir)* to discuss, air out —reflex. to take in the air.

ai·re·o m. airing, ventilation.

ai·ro·si·dad f. grace, elegance.

ai·ro·so, a adj. gallant.

ais·la·cio·nis·ta adj. & m.f. isolationist.

ais·la·do, a adj. isolated; *(solo)* alone; *(apartado)* remote; ELEC. insulated.

ais·la·dor, ·ra m. ELEC. insulator.

ais·la·mien·to m. isolation; *(retiro)* seclusion; ELEC. insulation.

ais·lan·te adj. insulating.

ais·lar tr. to isolate; *(retirar)* to seclude; ELEC. to insulate —reflex. to withdraw.

¡a·já! interj. *(aprobación)* sure!; *(sorpresa)* aha!

a·jar tr. to crumple, wrinkle —reflex. to get crumpled *or* wrinkled; BOT. to wither.

a·je·dre·cis·ta m.f. chess player.

a·je·drez m. chess; *(piezas)* chess set.

a·jen·jo m. absinthe.

a·je·no, a adj. another's, someone else's; *(libre)* free, devoid; *(impropio)* inappropriate ♦ **a. de sí** detached, aloof.

a·je·tre·ar tr. & reflex. *(apresurar)* to rush, hurry; *(fatigar)* to tire.

a·je·tre·o m. bustle, rush.

a·jí m. [pl. **-íes**] red *or* green pepper.

a·jo m. garlic; *(diente)* garlic clove.

a·jon·jo·lí m. [pl. **-íes**] sesame.

a·juar m. trousseau.

a·jui·ciar tr. *(hacer juicioso)* to bring to one's senses; *(enjuiciar)* to judge.

a·jus·ta·do, a adj. tight.

a·jus·tar tr. to adjust, adapt; *(modificar)* to alter, fit; *(reconciliar)* to reconcile; *(apretar)* to tighten; *(precios)* to fix; *(contratar)* to hire; COM. to settle; MECH. to fit —intr. to fit —reflex. *(acomodarse)* to adjust, conform; *(acordarse)* to come to an agreement.

a·jus·te m. adjustment; *(modificación)* alteration, fitting; *(arreglo)* arrangement; COM. settlement; MECH. fitting.

a·jus·ti·cia·do, a m.f. executed criminal.

a·jus·ti·cia·mien·to m. execution.

a·jus·ti·ciar tr. to execute.

al contr. of **a** and **el**.

a·la f. wing; *(del sombrero)* brim; *(de la hélice)* blade; ARCHIT. eave; MARIT. sail ♦ **cortarle las alas a** to clip someone's wings • **dar alas a** to encourage.

a·la·ba·dor, ·ra adj. praising, laudatory.

a·la·ban·za f. praise.

a·la·bar tr. to praise, laud —reflex. to boast, brag.

a·la·bas·tro m. alabaster.

a·la·ce·na f. cupboard, closet.

a·la·crán m. scorpion.

a·la·cri·dad f. alacrity, eagerness.

a·la·do, a adj. winged.

a·lam·bi·que m. still, alembic.

a·lam·bra·da f. wire netting.

a·lam·bra·do m. chicken wire fence.

a·lam·brar tr. to fence in with wires.

a·lam·bre m. wire ♦ **a. de púas** barbed wire.

a·lam·bris·ta m.f. tightrope walker.

a·la·me·da f. poplar grove; *(paseo)* boulevard.

á·la·mo m. poplar.

a·lar·de m. show, display.

a·lar·de·ar intr. to boast, brag.

a·lar·de·o m. boasting, bragging.

a·lar·gar §47 tr. to lengthen; *(extender)* to extend, prolong; *(estirar)* to stretch (out); *(cuerda)* to play out —reflex. to get longer; DEROG. to drag out.

a·la·ri·do m. yell, howl.

a·lar·ma f. alarm; *(inquietud)* anxiety ♦ **a. aérea** air-raid warning • **dar la a.** to sound the alarm.

a·lar·ma·dor, ·ra/man·te adj. alarming.

a·lar·mar tr. to alarm; *(asustar)* to scare —reflex. to become alarmed.

a·lar·mis·ta adj. & m.f. alarmist.

a·la·zán, a·na adj. & m.f. sorrel, chestnut.

al·ba f. dawn, daybreak; RELIG. alb ♦ **al a.** at dawn • **al romper el a.** at dawn.

al·ba·ce·a m. executor —f. executrix.

al·ba·ñal m. sewer, drain.

al·ba·ñil m. bricklayer, mason.

al·ba·ñi·le·rí·a f. masonry.

al·ba·ri·co·que m. apricot.

al·ba·yal·de m. white lead.

al·be·drí·o m. free will, *(capricho)* whim, fancy.

al·ber·ca f. *(tanque)* reservoir, tank; MEX. swimming pool.

al·ber·gar §47 tr. to lodge, house; *(una esperanza)* to cherish; *(una duda)* to harbor —intr. & reflex. to stay, take lodgings; *(refugiarse)* to take shelter.

al·ber·gue m. *(alojamiento)* lodging; *(refugio)* shelter, refuge; *(cubil)* den, lair.

al·bi·no, a adj. & m.f. albino.

al·bo, a adj. POET. white.

al·bón·di·ga f. meatball.

al·bor m. whiteness; *(alba)* dawn.

al·bo·ra·da f. dawn; *(toque)* reveille.

al·bo·re·ar intr. to dawn.

al·bor·noz m. *(capa)* burnoose; *(bata)* bathrobe.

al·bo·ro·ta·do, a adj. *(agitado)* excited; *(ruidoso)* rowdy; *(atolondrado)* rash; *(el mar)* rough.

al·bo·ro·ta·dor, ·ra m.f. troublemaker; *(niño)* unruly child.

al·bo·ro·tar tr. *(agitar)* to agitate; *(incitar)* to incite; *(excitar)* to excite —intr. to make a racket —reflex. to get excited *or* agitated; *(el mar)* to become rough.

al·bo·ro·to m. *(jaleo)* uproar; *(ruido)* racket; *(motín)* riot; MEX. *(alegría)* joy.

al·bo·ro·za·do, a adj. jubilant, overjoyed.

al·bo·ro·zar §04 tr. to delight —reflex. to be elated, rejoice.

al·bo·ro·zo m. joy, jubilation.

al·bri·cias interj. great!, congratulations!

al·bur m. risk, hazard ♦ **jugar** or **correr un a.** to take a risk.

al·ca·cho·fa f. artichoke.

al·ca·hue·te, a m.f. COLL. gossip; AMER. squealer —m. pimp —f. madam.

al·ca·hue·te·ar tr. to procure —intr. (ser alcahuete) to pimp; COLL. (chismear) to gossip; (soplar) to squeal.

al·ca·hue·te·rí·a f. pimping ♦ pl. **andar con a.** COLL. to squeal on people.

al·cal·de m. mayor.

al·cal·dí·a f. (cargo) mayoralty; (oficina) mayor's office.

al·ca·li·no, a adj. alkaline.

al·ca·loi·de m. alkaloid.

al·can·ce m. (distancia) reach; (extensión) range, scope; (talento) talent ♦ a al. accessible, within reach (de to, of) ♦ **al a. del oído** within earshot • **dar a. a** to catch up with • **de gran a.** FIG. far-reaching.

al·can·cí·a f. piggy bank.

al·can·for m. camphor.

al·can·fo·rar tr. to camphorate.

al·can·ta·ri·lla f. (cloaca) sewer, drain; (en un camino) culvert.

al·can·ta·ri·lla·do m. sewers, drains.

al·can·ta·ri·llar tr. to lay sewers in.

al·can·zar §04 tr. to reach (up to); (tomar) to catch; (conseguir) to attain; (comprender) to grasp; (igualar) to catch up with; AMER. to pass, hand over —intr. to reach; (durar) to be sufficient or enough ♦ **a. a** to manage to, be able to.

al·ca·pa·rra f. caper.

al·cau·cil m. artichoke.

al·cá·zar m. castle, fortress.

al·ce m. elk, moose.

al·cis·ta FIN. I. m.f. bull II. adj. bullish ♦ **mercado a.** bull market.

al·co·ba f. bedroom.

al·co·hol m. alcohol.

al·co·hó·li·co, a adj. & m.f. alcoholic.

al·co·ho·lí·me·tro m. alcoholometer.

al·co·ho·lis·mo m. alcoholism.

al·co·ho·li·zar §04 tr. to alcoholize.

al·cor·no·que m. cork oak; FIG. blockhead.

al·cor·zar §04 tr. to frost, ice (a cake).

al·cur·nia f. ancestry, lineage ♦ **de noble a.** of noble birth.

al·cu·za f. cruet.

al·da·ba f. (picaporte) (door) knocker; (barra) crossbar, bolt; (de caballería) hitching ring.

al·da·ba·da f. knock.

al·da·be·ar intr. to knock at or on the door.

al·da·be·o m. knocking, rapping.

al·da·bo·na·zo m. loud knock (on a door).

al·de·a f. village, hamlet.

al·de·a·no, a I. adj. village; (campesino) rustic II. m.f. peasant.

¡a·le! interj. come on!, let's go!

a·le·a·ción f. alloy.

a·le·ar[1] intr. to flap, flutter; FIG. to get better.

a·le·ar[2] tr. to alloy.

a·le·a·to·rio, a adj. aleatory, uncertain.

a·lec·cio·nar tr. (enseñar) to instruct, teach; (amaestrar) to train.

a·le·da·ño, a I. adj. bordering, adjoining II. m. boundary, border ♦ pl. outskirts.

a·le·ga·ción f. allegation; AMER. argument.

a·le·gar §47 tr. to allege; (aseverar) to claim —intr. to argue.

a·le·ga·to m. allegation; AMER. argument.

a·le·go·rí·a f. allegory.

a·le·gó·ri·co, a adj. allegorical, allegoric.

a·le·grar tr. to cheer; (avivar) to enliven —reflex. to rejoice, be happy; (achisparse) to get tipsy.

a·le·gre adj. happy, glad; (jovial) cheerful, sunny; (brillante) lively, bright; (achispado) tipsy.

a·le·grí·a f. happiness, joy.

a·le·grón m. COLL. joy.

a·le·ja·do, a adj. distant, remote.

a·le·ja·mien·to m. removal, withdrawal; (enajenación) estrangement; (distancia) distance.

a·le·jan·dri·no adj. & m. POET. alexandrine.

a·le·jar tr. to put farther away; (enajenar) to estrange —reflex. to move away, withdraw.

a·le·la·do, a adj. stupefied, bewildered.

a·le·lar tr. to stupefy, bewilder —reflex. to be stupefied or bewildered.

¡a·le·lu·ya! interj. alleluia!, hallelujah!

a·len·ta·dor, ·ra adj. encouraging.

a·len·tar §49 intr. to breathe —tr. to encourage, inspire —reflex. to cheer up.

a·ler·gia f. allergy.

a·lér·gi·co, a I. adj. allergic ♦ **ser a. a** to be allergic to II. m.f. allergy sufferer.

a·le·ro m. eaves.

a·le·rón m. aileron.

a·ler·ta I. adv. on the alert ♦ **¡a.!** watch out! II. m. alert, warning.

a·ler·tar tr. to alert, warn.

a·ler·to, a adj. watchful, vigilant.

a·le·ta f. ICHTH. fin; (hélice) blade; MECH. leaf; ANAT., ARCHIT. wing.

a·le·tar·ga·mien·to m. lethargy.

a·le·tar·gar §47 tr. to make drowsy.

a·le·te·ar intr. to flutter, flap.

a·le·te·o m. fluttering, flapping.

a·le·vo·sí·a f. treachery, perfidy.

al·fa·bé·ti·co, a adj. alphabetical.

al·fa·be·ti·za·ción f. alphabetization; EDUC. literacy instruction.

al·fa·be·ti·zar §04 tr. to alphabetize; EDUC. to make literate, teach literacy skills to.

al·fa·be·to m. alphabet ♦ **a. Morse** Morse code.

al·fa·nu·mé·ri·co, a adj. alphanumeric.

al·fa·re·rí·a f. pottery.

al·fa·re·ro, a m.f. potter, ceramist.

al·féi·zar m. window sill.

al·fe·ñi·que m. sweetened almond paste; (persona) weakling.

al·fé·rez m. second lieutenant.

al·fil m. bishop (in chess).

al·fi·ler m. pin ♦ **a. de gancho** AMER. safety pin • **no caber un a.** COLL. to be filled to the brim • **pegado** or **prendido con alfileres** COLL. shaky.

al·fi·le·rar tr. to pin.

al·fi·le·ra·zo m. pinprick; FIG. dig, gibe.

al·fi·le·te·ro m. pincushion.

al·fom·bra f. carpet; (tapete) rug, mat.

al·fom·bra·do m. carpets, carpeting.

al·fom·brar tr. to carpet.

al·for·ja f. knapsack; (provisión) supplies.

al·for·za f. pleat, tuck.

al·for·zar §04 tr. to pleat, tuck.

al·ga f. alga, seaweed.

al·ga·ra·bí·a f. uproar, din.

al·ga·rro·ba f. BOT. (planta) vetch; (fruto) carob bean.

ál·ge·bra f. algebra.

al·ge·brai·co, a adj. algebraic.

ál·gi·do, a adj. icy, cold.

al·go I. indef. pron. something; *(en negaciones e interrogaciones)* anything; *(cantidad)* some ♦ **a. es a.** something is better than nothing • **por a.** for some reason **II.** adv. somewhat, a little.

al·go·dón m. cotton ♦ **a. de azúcar** cotton candy • **a. en rama** raw cotton • **a. hidrófilo** absorbent cotton.

al·go·do·nal m. cotton plantation *or* field.

al·go·do·ne·ro, a I. adj. cotton **II.** m. cotton plant.

al·go·rít·mi·co adj. ♦ **lenguaje a.** ALGOL.

al·go·rit·mo m. algorithm.

al·gua·cil m. sheriff; R.P. dragonfly.

al·guien indef. pron. someone, somebody; *(en negaciones e interrogaciones)* anyone, anybody.

al·gún adj. some —see **alguno.**

al·gu·no, a I. adj. some; *(en negaciones e interrogaciones)* any ♦ **a. vez** sometime **II.** indef. pron. someone ♦ **a. que otro** a few, one or two ♦ **pl.** some.

al·ha·ja f. jewel, gem.

al·ha·jar tr. to bedeck with jewels; *(amueblar)* to furnish.

al·ha·je·ra f./o m. AMER. jewelry box.

al·ha·ra·ca f. fuss, ado.

al·he·lí m. [pl. -**íes**] BOT. wallflower, stock.

al·he·ña f. henna.

al·hu·ce·ma f. lavender.

a·lia·do, a I. m.f. ally ♦ **los Aliados** the Allies **II.** adj. allied, confederate.

a·lian·za f. *(unión)* alliance; *(anillo)* wedding ring; BIBL. covenant.

a·liar §30 tr. to ally, join —reflex. to become allies.

a·lias adv. & m. alias.

a·li·bí m. alibi.

a·li·ca·í·do, a adj. *(débil)* haggard; *(deprimido)* depressed.

a·li·ca·tes m.pl. pliers, pincers ♦ **a. de uñas** nail clippers.

a·li·cien·te m. incentive.

a·lie·na·ble adj. alienable.

a·lie·na·ción f. alienation.

a·lie·na·do, a adj. & m.f. insane, mentally deranged (person).

a·lie·nar tr. to alienate.

a·lien·te tr. to see **alentar.**

a·lien·to m. breath; *(valor)* courage ♦ **dar a.** to encourage • **cobrar a.** to take heart • **sin a.** breathless.

a·li·ge·rar tr. to lighten; *(acelerar)* to quicken.

al·i·ma·ña f. pest, vermin.

a·li·men·ta·ción f. *(acción)* feeding; *(comida)* food; *(manutención)* support ♦ **a. deficiente** malnutrition.

a·li·men·tar tr. to feed, nourish; *(mantener)* to support; *(fomentar)* to nurture —reflex. to take nourishment ♦ **a. con** to feed on.

a·li·men·ta·rio, a adj. alimentary, nutritional.

a·li·men·ti·cio, a adj. nourishing, nutritious.

a·li·men·to m. food, nourishment ♦ **pl.** alimony, support.

a·lin·dar tr. to set boundaries to —intr. to be contiguous *or* adjacent.

a·li·ne·a·ción f. *(línea)* alignment; *(colocación)* aligning; SPORT. lineup.

a·li·ne·a·do, a adj. aligned ♦ **no a.** POL. nonaligned.

a·li·ne·ar tr. & reflex. to align, line up.

a·li·ñar tr. to straighten, tidy; CUL. to season.

a·li·ño m. tidiness; CUL. seasoning.

a·li·sar tr. to smooth; *(el pelo)* to slick.

a·li·sios adj. trade <*vientos a.* trade winds>.

a·lis·ta·mien·to m. listing; MIL. recruitment.

a·lis·tar tr. to list; MIL. to recruit —reflex. to enlist; AMER. to get ready.

a·li·te·ra·ción f. alliteration.

a·li·viar tr. to alleviate, ease; *(aligerar)* to lighten; *(acelerar)* to quicken —reflex. to get better.

a·li·vio m. alleviation, easing; *(aligeramiento)* lightening; *(cese)* relief.

al·ji·be m. cistern.

al·ma f. soul; *(individuo)* human being, soul; *(centro)* crux; TECH. core; CONSTR. web; ARTIL. bore ♦ **a. de Dios** COLL. good soul • **a. mía** dearest, darling • **caérsele el a. a los pies** to be disheartened • **con toda el a.** with all one's heart • **no tener a.** to be heartless • **partir el a.** to break someone's heart • **tener el a. en un hilo** to have one's heart in one's mouth.

al·ma·cén m. store; *(depósito)* warehouse; ARTIL. magazine; S. AMER. grocery store.

al·ma·ce·na·je m. *(costo)* storage charge; *(almacenamiento)* storage ♦ **a. frigorífico** cold storage.

al·ma·ce·na·mien·to m. storage.

al·ma·ce·nar tr. to store, warehouse; FIG. to stock up (with).

al·ma·ce·ne·ro m. warehouseman; S. AMER. grocer.

al·má·ci·ga f. *(resina)* mastic; *(semillero)* nursery, seedbed.

al·má·ci·go m. mastic tree; *(semilla)* nursery seed; *(semillero)* nursery, seedbed.

al·ma·na·que m. calendar.

al·ma·za·ra f. oil mill.

al·me·ja f. clam.

al·men·dra f. almond ♦ **a. garrapiñada** praline.

al·men·dra·do, a I. adj. almond-shaped **II.** m. *(pasta)* almond paste; *(macarrón)* macaroon —f. almond milk.

al·men·dro m. almond tree.

al·mí·bar m. syrup.

al·mi·ba·ra·do, a adj. syrupy.

al·mi·ba·rar tr. to candy; FIG. to sweet-talk.

al·mi·dón m. starch ♦ **dar a.** to starch.

al·mi·do·na·do, a I. adj. starched; FIG. smart, dapper **II.** m. starching.

al·mi·do·nar tr. to starch.

al·mi·ran·te m. admiral.

al·miz·cle m. musk.

al·mo·ha·da f. pillow ♦ **consultar con la a.** to sleep on it.

al·mo·ha·di·lla f. *(cojincillo)* small cushion; *(para sellos)* inkpad; AMER. pincushion.

al·mo·ha·di·llar tr. to pad, stuff.

al·mo·ha·dón m. cushion.

al·mo·rra·nas f.pl. hemorrhoids, piles.

al·mor·zar §37 intr. to eat lunch, lunch —tr. to eat for lunch, lunch on.

al·muer·zo m. lunch.

a·lo·ca·do, a adj. thoughtless, crazy.

a·lo·car §70 tr. to drive crazy *or* insane.

a·lo·cu·ción f. allocution, address.

a·ló·ge·no, a adj. of a different race.

a·lo·ja·mien·to m. lodging(s); *(vivienda)* housing.

a·lo·jar tr. to lodge; *(albergar)* to house —reflex. to lodge, stay.

a·lo·jo m. AMER. var. of **alojamiento.**

a·lon·dra f. lark.

a·lon·gar §16 tr. to lengthen, stretch.

a·lo·pa·tí·a f. allopathy.

al·pa·ca f. alpaca.

al·par·ga·ta f. rope-soled sandal.

al·pi·nis·ta m.f. mountain climber.

al·pi·no, a adj. alpine.

al·pis·te m. birdseed; FIG., COLL. alcohol.

al·qui·lar tr. to rent, lease; *(personas)* to hire —reflex. to be for hire ♦ **se alquila** to let, for hire.

al·qui·ler m. *(acción)* renting, hiring; *(renta)* rent ♦ **a. de coches** car-rental service • **de a.** for hire, for rent.

al·qui·mia f. alchemy.

al·qui·mis·ta m. alchemist.

al·qui·trán m. tar, pitch.

al·qui·tra·na·do, a I. adj. tarred II. m. MARIT. tarpaulin.

al·qui·tra·nar tr. to tar, cover with tar.

al·re·de·dor I. adv. *(en torno)* around; *(cerca de)* about, approximately II. m.pl. *(cercanías)* surroundings; *(afueras)* outskirts.

al·ta f. see **alto, a.**

al·ta·men·te adv. highly, extremely.

al·ta·ne·rí·a f. arrogance, haughtiness.

al·ta·ne·ro, a adj. high-flying; FIG. arrogant, haughty.

al·tar m. altar.

al·ta·voz m. loudspeaker.

al·te·ra·ción f. alteration; *(alboroto)* disturbance; *(disputa)* altercation; *(del pulso)* irregularity.

al·te·ra·do, a adj. altered; *(perturbado)* upset; *(enfadado)* angry.

al·te·rar tr. to alter; *(perturbar)* to upset; *(enfadar)* to annoy —reflex. to change; *(perturbarse)* to get upset.

al·ter·ca·ción f./do m. altercation, argument.

al·ter·ca·do, ·ra adj. & m.f. argumentative.

al·ter·car §70 intr. to argue, quarrel.

al·ter·na·do, a adj. alternate.

al·ter·nan·te adj. alternating.

al·ter·nar tr. & intr. to alternate ♦ **a. con** to mix.

al·ter·na·ti·va f. alternative, choice ♦ **tomar una a.** to make a decision.

al·ter·na·ti·vo, a adj. alternating, alternate.

al·ter·no, a adj. alternating; BOT., GEOM. alternate.

al·te·za f. Highness; *(altura)* height.

al·ti·ba·jos m.pl. ups and downs.

al·ti·llo m. *(colina)* hillock; S. AMER. *(desván)* attic.

al·ti·me·trí·a f. altimetry.

al·tí·me·tro m. altimeter.

al·ti·pla·ni·cie f. high plateau, altiplano.

al·tí·si·mo, a adj. very high, most high ♦ **El A.** God, the Almighty.

al·ti·tud f. altitude, height.

al·ti·vez/ve·za f. haughtiness, pride.

al·ti·vo, a adj. haughty, proud.

al·to, a I. adj. high; *(estatura)* tall; *(piso)* upper; *(voz)* loud; *(crecido)* swollen; *(ideales)* lofty; *(traición)* high, serious; *(precio)* high ♦ **a. costura** haute couture • **a. fidelidad, frecuencia** high fidelity, frequency • **a. horno** blast furnace • **altas horas** late hours • **en a.** on high II. m. height, elevation; MUS. alto; MIL. halt, stop; AMER. pile, heap ♦ **de a. high • de lo a.** from on high, from above • **hacer a.** to stop, come to a stop ♦ pl. AMER. upper floors

—f. MED. discharge; *(ingreso)* entry ♦ **dar de a.** MIL. to admit; MED. to discharge III. adv. *(arriba)* up high, above; *(en voz fuerte)* aloud, loudly ♦ **pasar por a.** to overlook, omit IV. interj. halt!, stop! ♦ **¡a. al fuego!** cease fire!

al·to·cú·mu·lo m. altocumulus.

al·to·par·lan·te m. loudspeaker.

al·truis·ta I. adj. altruistic II. m.f. altruist.

al·tu·ra f. height; *(altitud)* altitude; *(nivel)* level; FIG. loftiness ♦ **estar a la a. de las circunstancias** to be worthy of the occasion ♦ pl. the heavens • **a estas a.** at this point *or* stage.

a·lu·bia f. French *or* kidney bean.

a·lu·ci·na·ción f. hallucination.

a·lu·ci·na·dor, ·ra I. adj. hallucinatory II. m. hallucinogen.

a·lu·ci·na·mien·to m. hallucination.

a·lu·ci·nan·te adj. hallucinating; *(extraordinario)* extraordinary.

a·lu·ci·nar tr. & intr. to hallucinate.

a·lu·ci·na·to·rio, a adj. hallucinatory.

a·lu·ci·no·gé·ni·co, a adj. hallucinogenic.

a·lud m. avalanche.

a·lu·di·do, a adj. abovementioned, referred to.

a·lu·dir intr. to allude, refer *(a* to).

a·lum·bra·do, a I. adj. lighted, lit II. m. lighting.

a·lum·bra·mien·to m. lighting; *(parto)* childbirth.

a·lum·brar tr. to light (up), illuminate; FIG. to enlighten, illuminate —intr. to give light; *(dar a luz)* to give birth.

a·lum·bre m. alum.

a·lu·mi·nio m. aluminum, aluminium (G.B.).

a·lum·na·do m. student body.

a·lum·no, a m.f. pupil, student.

a·lu·na·do, a adj. R.P., COLL. grouchy.

a·lu·na·ra·do, a adj. spotted, dotted.

a·lu·nar·se reflex. AMER. *(herida)* to fester; R.P., COLL. to get grouchy.

a·lu·ni·za·je m. lunar landing.

a·lu·ni·zar §04 intr. to land on the moon.

a·lu·sión f. allusion.

a·lu·vión m. flood; *(sedimento)* sediment; FIG. flood.

al·ver·ja f. vetch; AMER. pea.

al·ver·ji·lla f. sweet pea.

al·za f. rise, increase; ARTIL. backsight ♦ **en a.** on the rise.

al·za·do, a I. adj. raised, elevated; *(en celo)* in heat; *(rebelde)* mutinous II. f. height.

al·za·mien·to m. POL. uprising.

al·zar §04 tr. to raise, lift (up); *(recoger)* to gather; MARIT. to hoist ♦ **a. cabeza** COLL. to get back on one's feet • **a. el codo** COLL. to have a lot to drink —reflex. to rise, get up; POL. to rebel, rise ♦ **a. con** COLL. to make off with, steal.

a·llá adv. there, over there; *(en tiempo remoto)* way back ♦ **a. tú** that's your business, it's up to you • **más a.** farther • **más a. de** beyond • **por a.** over there.

a·lla·na·mien·to m. raid ♦ **a. de morada** search of premises.

a·lla·nar tr. *(nivelar)* to flatten; *(invadir)* to raid; *(superar)* to overcome.

a·lle·ga·do, a I. adj. *(cercano)* near, close; *(emparentado)* related II. m.f. *(pariente)* relative, relation; *(partidario)* supporter, adherent.

a·lle·gar §47 tr. to place near, gather —reflex. to approach.

a·llen·de POET. I. adv. beyond II. prep. on the other side of.

a·llí adv. there ◆ por a. (sitio) over there; (camino) that way.

a·ma f. (señora) lady of the house, mistress; (dueña) proprietress ◆ a. de casa housewife • a. de cría or de leche wet nurse • a. de llaves housekeeper.

a·ma·bi·li·dad f. kindness.

a·ma·ble adj. kind

a·ma·do, a adj. & m.f. beloved, dear (one).

a·ma·dri·nar tr. (uncir) to couple; AMER. to train (horses) to follow the lead.

a·ma·es·tra·dor, ·ra m.f. trainer.

a·ma·es·tra·mien·to m. training.

a·ma·es·trar tr. to train.

a·ma·gar §47 tr. (amenazar) to threaten (a, con to); (fingir) to feign.

a·ma·go m. (amenaza) threat; (señal) sign; MIL. mock attack.

a·mai·nar tr. MARIT. to lower —intr. to die down, let up.

a·mal·ga·mar tr. & reflex. to amalgamate, mix.

a·ma·man·ta·mien·to m. suckling, nursing.

a·ma·man·tar tr. to suckle, nurse.

a·ma·ne·cer §17 I. intr. to dawn; (despertar) to wake up, to start the day II. m. dawn, daybreak ◆ al a. at dawn or daybreak.

a·ma·ne·ci·da f. dawn, daybreak.

a·ma·ne·ra·do, a adj. mannered, affected.

a·ma·ne·ra·mien·to m. affectation.

a·ma·ne·rar·se reflex. to become affected.

a·man·sa·dor, ·ra m.f. AMER. horsebreaker —f. R.P. a long wait.

a·man·sa·mien·to m. breaking, taming.

a·man·sar tr. (un animal) to tame; (un caballo) to break; FIG. to soothe —reflex. to calm down.

a·man·te I. adj. fond, loving II. m.f. lover.

a·ma·nuen·se m.f. amanuensis.

a·ma·ña·do, a adj. (falsificado) fixed, falsified; (diestro) clever, skillful.

a·ma·ñar tr. DEROG. to fix, falsify —reflex. to manage.

a·ma·ño m. (maña) skill; (arreglo) scheme.

a·ma·po·la f. poppy.

a·mar tr. to love.

a·mar·fi·la·do, a adj. ivory-like.

a·mar·ga·do, a adj. bitter, embittered.

a·mar·ga·men·te adv. bitterly.

a·mar·gar §47 tr. FIG. to make bitter —intr. & reflex. to become bitter or embittered.

a·mar·go, a I. adj. bitter; FIG. painful II. m. bitterness; AMER. sugarless maté.

a·mar·gor m. bitterness; FIG. pain.

a·mar·gu·ra f. bitterness; FIG. sorrow ◆ ¡qué a.! what a pity!

a·ma·ri·lle·ar intr. to yellow, turn yellow.

a·ma·ri·llen·to, a adj. yellowish; (de tez) sallow.

a·ma·ri·llo, a adj. & m. yellow.

a·ma·rra·de·ro m. (poste) hitching post; MARIT. (poste) bollard; (sitio) mooring.

a·ma·rrar tr. to tie (up), fasten; MARIT. to moor.

a·ma·rre m. tying; MARIT. mooring.

a·ma·rre·te adj. ARG., PERU stingy.

a·mar·ti·llar tr. to hammer; (un arma) to cock.

a·ma·sar tr. to knead; FIG. to amass.

a·ma·si·jo m. CUL. dough; (tarea) task; ARG., COLL. thrashing, beating.

a·ma·teur adj. & m.f. amateur.

a·ma·tis·ta f. MIN. amethyst.

a·ma·to·rio, a adj. amatory, love.

a·ma·zo·na f. MYTH. Amazon; FIG. (mujer varonil) amazon; (caballista) horsewoman.

a·ma·zó·ni·co, a adj. Amazonian.

am·ba·ges m.pl. circumlocution ◆ hablar sin a. not to beat around the bush.

ám·bar m. amber ◆ a. gris ambergris.

am·ba·ri·no, a adj. amber.

am·bi·ción f. ambition.

am·bi·cio·nar tr. to aspire to, strive for.

am·bi·cio·so, a adj. & m.f. ambitious.

am·bi·dex·tro/dies·tro, a adj. ambidextrous.

am·bien·ta·ción f. atmosphere; LIT. setting.

am·bien·tar tr. to give atmosphere to; LIT. to set —reflex. to adjust oneself.

am·bien·te I. adj. surrounding, ambient ◆ el medio a. the environment II. m. atmosphere; FIG. ambiance; R.P. room.

am·bi·güe·dad f. ambiguity.

am·bi·guo, a adj. ambiguous.

ám·bi·to m. (perímetro) boundary, limit; (campo) field.

am·bi·va·len·cia f. ambivalence.

am·bos, as adj. & indef. pron. both.

am·bu·lan·cia f. ambulance.

am·bu·lan·te I. adj. traveling, itinerant II. m. AMER. peddler; MEX. ambulatde driver.

am·bu·lar intr. to ambulate, amble.

am·bu·la·to·rio, a adj. ambulatory.

a·me·ba f. amoeba.

a·me·dren·tar tr. to scare, frighten —reflex. to become scared or frightened.

a·mén I. m. amen ◆ en un decir a. FIG. in an instant II. adv. ◆ a. de besides, in addition to.

a·me·na·za f. threat, menace.

a·me·na·za·dor, ·ra/zan·te adj. threatening.

a·me·na·zar §04 tr. to threaten, menace —intr. to threaten, be imminent.

a·men·guar §10 tr. to diminish

a·me·ni·dad f. amenity, pleasantness.

a·me·ni·zar §04 tr. to make pleasant; FIG. to enliven.

a·me·no, a adj. pleasant, agreeable.

a·me·ri·ca·nis·mo m. Spanish-American word, custom or trait.

a·me·ri·ca·ni·zar §04 tr. to Americanize —reflex. to become Americanized.

a·me·ri·ca·no, a adj. & m.f. American —f. jacket.

a·me·tra·lla·do·ra f. machine gun.

a·me·tra·llar tr. to machine-gun.

a·mian·to m. amianthus, asbestos.

a·mi·ga·ble adj. amicable; FIG. harmonious.

a·mi·gar §47 tr. (amistar) to bring together; (reconciliar) to reconcile —reflex. (amistarse) to become friendly; (reconciliarse) to make up.

a·mi·ga·zo, a COLL. I. adj. close (friend) II. m.f. buddy, pal.

a·míg·da·la f. tonsil, amygdala.

a·mig·da·li·tis f.inv. tonsilitis.

a·mi·go, a I. m.f. friend ◆ a. íntimo or del alma close friend, bosom buddy • a. de lo ajeno COLL. thief • hacerse a. de to make friends with • hacerse amigos to become friends II. adj. friendly; FIG. fond of.

a·mi·go·te m.f. COLL. great friend, pal.

a·mi·gui·si·mo, a adj. very friendly.

a·mi·la·na·do, a adj. intimidated.

a·mi·la·nar tr. to frighten, intimidate; FIG. to dishearten, discourage —reflex. to become frightened or intimidated; FIG. to become disheartened or discouraged.

a·mi·no·á·ci·do m. amino acid.

a·mi·no·rar tr. to reduce, diminish ♦ a. el paso to walk more slowly.

a·mis·tad f. friendship ♦ trabar or estrechar a. to make friends ♦ pl. friends, acquaintances • hacer las a. to reconcile, make up • romper las a. to quarrel.

a·mis·tar tr. to make friends with; (reconciliar) to reconcile —reflex. to become friends; (reconciliarse) to make up.

a·mis·to·so, a adj. amicable, friendly.

am·né·si·co, a adj. & m.f. MED. amnesiac, amnesic.

am·nis·tí·a f. amnesty.

am·nis·tiar §30 tr. to grant amnesty to.

a·mo m. master; (dueño) owner, proprietor.

a·mo·blar §19 tr. var. of amueblar.

a·mo·do·rra·mien·to m. sleepiness.

a·mo·la·dor m. AMER. grinder, sharpener.

a·mo·lar §19 tr. to grind, sharpen; FIG. to irritate, annoy.

a·mol·da·mien·to m. fitting; FIG. adaptation.

a·mol·dar tr. to mold, model; FIG. to adapt, adjust —reflex. to adapt oneself.

a·mo·nes·ta·ción f. (represión) reprimand; (advertencia) warning.

a·mo·nes·tar tr. (reprender) to reprimand; (advertir) to warn.

a·mo·ní·a·co/ní·a·co m. (gas) ammonia; (goma) gum resin.

a·mon·to·na·mien·to m. (acción) heaping, piling up; (montón) accumulation; (de gente) crowding.

a·mon·to·nar tr. (apilar) to heap or pile (up); (acumular) to accumulate, gather; (riquezas) to hoard —reflex. (apilarse) to pile up; (acumularse) to crowd (together).

a·mor m. love; (afecto) affection; (querido) darling, beloved ♦ a. propio pride • hacer el a. to make love • ¡por a. a Dios! for goodness sake! • sin a. loveless ♦ pl. (amoríos) love affairs, romances; (requiebros) endearments • de mil a. COLL. gladly, with pleasure.

a·mo·ra·li·dad f. amorality.

a·mo·ra·ta·do, a adj. purplish; AMER. black-and-blue, bruised ♦ a. de frío blue with cold.

a·mo·ra·tar tr. to make blue or purple; AMER. to bruise —reflex. to turn blue or purple; (magullarse) to bruise, turn black-and-blue.

a·mor·da·zar §04 tr. (una persona) to gag; (un perro) to muzzle; FIG. to silence, gag.

a·mor·fo, a adj. amorphous, shapeless.

a·mo·rí·o m. fling, love affair.

a·mo·ro·so, a adj. loving, affectionate; (enamoradizo) amorous; AMER. charming.

a·mor·ta·jar tr. to shroud; TECH. to mortise.

a·mor·te·cer §17 tr. (golpes) to cushion; (ruidos) to muffle; (luces) to dim; (colores, música) to soften.

a·mor·ti·gua·ción f. var. of amortiguamiento.

a·mor·ti·gua·dor, ·ra I. adj. (de golpes) cushioning; (de ruidos) muffling; (de luces) dimming; (de colores, música) softening II. m. AUTO. (dispositivo) shock absorber; (parachoques) bumper ♦ a. de luz dimmer • a. de ruido muffler.

a·mor·ti·gua·mien·to m. (de golpes) cushioning; (de ruidos) muffling; (de luces) dimming; (de colores, música) toning down.

a·mor·ti·guar §10 tr. (golpes) to absorb; (rui-

dos) to muffle; (luces) to dim; (colores, música) to tone down; FIG. to alleviate.

a·mor·ti·za·ción f. LAW amortization; (de un bono) redemption; (de una deuda) repayment.

a·mor·ti·zar §04 tr. LAW to amortize; (un bono) to redeem; (una deuda) to repay, pay off.

a·mos·car·se §70 reflex. COLL. to get angry.

a·mo·ti·na·do, a I. adj. rebellious; MIL. mutinous II. m.f. rebel; MIL. mutineer.

a·mo·ti·na·mien·to m. uprising; MIL. mutiny.

a·mo·ti·nar tr. to incite to riot —reflex. to rebel; MIL. to mutiny.

am·pa·rar tr. to protect; (defender) to defend —reflex. to protect oneself; (acogerse) to seek protection.

am·pa·ro m. protection; (defensa) aid.

am·pe·ra·je m. amperage.

am·pe·rí·me·tro m. ammeter, amperemeter.

am·pe·rio m. ampere ♦ a. hora ampere-hour.

am·plia·ción f. (extensión) extension, expansion; PHOTOG. enlargement.

am·pliar §30 tr. to expand; (desarrollar) to elaborate on; (aumentar) to increase; (ensanchar) to widen; PHOTOG. to enlarge.

am·pli·fi·ca·ción f. (aumento) amplification, magnification; PHOTOG. enlargement.

am·pli·fi·ca·dor, ·ra I. adj. amplifying II. m. ELEC., RAD. amplifier; (altavoz) loudspeaker.

am·pli·fi·car §70 tr. (aumentar) to amplify; (con microscopio) to magnify; PHOTOG. to enlarge.

am·plio, a adj. (espacioso) spacious, roomy; (extenso) ample, broad; (ancho) full, wide.

am·pli·tud f. (anchura) fullness; (extensión) extent ♦ a. de miras broad-mindedness • de gran a. far-reaching, of large scope.

am·po·lla f. blister; MED. ampoule.

am·po·llar tr. & reflex. to blister.

am·po·lle·ta f. hourglass.

am·pu·lo·si·dad f. pomposity.

am·pu·lo·so, a adj. pompous, bombastic.

am·pu·ta·ción f. amputation.

am·pu·ta·do, a m.f. amputee.

am·pu·tar tr. to amputate, cut off.

a·mue·blar tr. to furnish.

a·mue·ble, blo see amoblar.

a·mu·je·ra·do, a adj. effeminate, womanish.

a·mu·le·to m. amulet, charm.

a·mu·ra·lla·do, a adj. walled.

a·mu·ra·llar tr. to wall, fortify with walls.

a·mus·tiar tr. & reflex. to wither.

a·na·bap·tis·ta adj. & m.f. Anabaptist.

a·na·ca·ra·do, a adj. pearly, mother-of-pearl.

a·na·car·do m. cashew.

a·na·cro·nis·mo m. anachronism.

á·na·de m.f. duck.

a·na·de·ar intr. to waddle.

a·ná·fo·ra f. anaphora, repetition.

a·na·gra·ma m. anagram.

a·na·les m.pl. annals.

a·nal·fa·be·to, a adj. & m.f. illiterate.

a·nal·gé·si·co, a adj. & m. analgesic.

a·ná·li·sis m.inv. analysis ♦ a. de orina urinalysis • a. de sangre blood test.

a·na·lis·ta m.f. analyst; (historiador) annalist.

a·na·lí·ti·co, a I. adj. analytical II. f. analytics.

a·na·li·zar §04 tr. to analyze, examine.

a·na·lo·gí·a f. analogy ♦ por a. by analogy.

a·ná·lo·go, a adj. analogous, similar.

a·na·ná(s) m. [pl. -na(s)es] pineapple.

a·na·quel m. shelf.

a·na·ran·ja·do, a adj. & m. orange.

a·nar·quí·a f. anarchy.

a·nár·qui·co, a adj. anarchic, anarchical.

a·nar·quis·ta I. m.f. anarchist II. adj. anarchistic.

a·nar·qui·zar §04 tr. to make anarchic —intr. to propagate anarchism.

a·na·te·ma m. anathema.

a·na·te·ma·ti·zar §04 tr. to anathematize, excommunicate; (maldecir) to curse, condemn.

a·na·tó·mi·co, a adj. anatomic, anatomical.

a·na·to·mí·a f. anatomy.

a·na·to·mi·zar §04 tr. ARTS. to delineate.

an·ca f. (grupa) croup, rump; (nalga) rump, buttock.

an·cia·ni·dad f. old age.

an·cia·no, a I. adj. old, elderly II. m. old or elderly man; RELIG. elder —f. old or elderly woman.

an·cla f. anchor.

an·clar/co·rar intr. to anchor, drop or cast anchor.

an·char tr. & intr. to widen, broaden.

an·cho, a I. adj. wide, broad; (holgado) loose, full ♦ **de a.** wide ♦ **estar** or **ponerse muy a.** COLL. to boast ♦ **quedarse tan a.** to remain unworried II. m. width, breadth ♦ **a sus anchas** as one pleases.

an·cho·a f. anchovy.

an·chu·ra f. width, breadth; (amplitud) fullness.

an·da·da f. (pan) thin, crisp bread; (caminata) long walk ♦ **volver a las andadas** FIG., COLL. to be up to one's old tricks.

an·da·dor, ·ra I. adj. (veloz) fast-walking; (andariego) wandering II. m.f. (caminante) walker (person); (andariego) wanderer ♦ pl. straps (to support an infant learning to walk).

an·da·du·ra f. (acción) walking; (manera) gait.

an·da·mio m. scaffold; (tablado) platform.

an·da·na·da f. MARIT. broadside; (graderría) covered grandstand ♦ **soltar una a.** FIG., COLL. to scold, reprimand.

an·dan·te I. adj. walking, traveling ♦ **caballero a.** knight errant II. m. & adv. MUS. andante.

an·dan·za m. (suceso) occurrence, event; (aventura) adventure ♦ **volver a las andanzas** to be up to one's old tricks.

an·dar¹ §05 intr. to walk; (marchar) to go, move; (funcionar) to work, function; (transcurrir) to go by, elapse; (estar) to be; (sentirse) to be, feel ♦ ¡anda! (como exhortación) get going!, move along!; (expresando admiración) no kidding! • ¡ándale! COLL. hurry up! • **a. con cuidado** or **con pies de plomo** to be careful, tread cautiously • **a. de broma** to be joking • **a. en** (envolverse) to be mixed up or engaged in; (escudriñar) rummage through, search; (en edad) to be going on, be about • **a. por las nubes** to be absent-minded • **a. tras** to go after, pursue • ¿cómo andas de salud? how is your health? —tr. to travel, go —reflex. to leave, go away ♦ **a. en** to be mixed up in • **a. por las ramas** to beat around the bush.

an·dar² m. pace, gait ♦ **a todo a.** at full speed.

an·da·rie·go, a I. adj. wandering, roving II. m.f. wanderer, rover.

an·da·ri·vel m. (balsa) cable ferry; (maroma) ferry cable; MARIT. lifeline, safety ropes.

an·dén m. station or railway platform; (parapeto) parapet, railing.

an·di·nis·ta m.f. mountain climber.

an·dra·jo m. tatter, rag; DEROG. wretch.

an·dra·jo·so, a adj. tattered, ragged.

an·dro·ce·o m. androecium.

an·dró·gi·no, a I. adj. androgynous, hermaphroditic II. m.f. androgyne, hermaphrodite.

an·droi·de m. android.

an·du·vie·ra, vo see andar¹.

a·néc·do·ta f. anecdote.

a·nec·dó·ti·co, a adj. anecdotal.

a·nec·do·tis·ta m.f. anecdotist.

a·ne·ga·ble adj. floodable, subject to flooding.

a·ne·ga·ción f. flooding.

a·ne·ga·di·zo, a adj. subject to flooding.

a·ne·ga·mien·to m. flooding.

a·ne·gar §47 tr. to flood, inundate —reflex. be inundated; MARIT. to sink ♦ **a. en llanto** to dissolve into tears.

a·ne·jar tr. to join, attach.

a·ne·jo, a I. adj. attached, annexed II. m. annex; LIT. appendix.

a·né·mi·co, a adj. & m.f. anemic.

a·nes·te·sia f. anesthesia.

a·nes·te·siar tr. to anesthetize.

a·nes·té·si·co, a adj. & m. anesthetic.

a·nes·te·sió·lo·go, a m.f. anesthesiologist.

a·nes·te·sis·ta m.f. anesthetist.

a·ne·xar tr. to join; (documentos) to enclose.

a·ne·xo, a I. adj. joined; (documento) enclosed II. m. (suplemento) annex; (apéndice) enclosure.

an·fe·ta·mi·na f. amphetamine.

an·fi·bio, a I. adj. amphibious, amphibian II. m. ZOOL. amphibian.

an·fi·bo·lo·gí·a f. amphibology, amphiboly.

an·fi·tea·tro m. amphitheater.

an·fi·trión, o·na m. host —f. hostess.

án·fo·ra f. amphora.

an·ga·ri·llas f.pl. (andas) stretcher; (camilla) packsaddle with panniers.

án·gel m. angel ♦ **a. custodio** or **de la guardia** guardian angel • **tener a.** to have grace or charm.

an·gé·li·co, a/cal adj. angelic, angelical.

an·ge·li·to m. (ángel) little angel, cherub; (niño) cherub, small child.

an·ge·lo·te m. (niño) chubby child; ICHTH. angelfish.

an·gli·ca·no, a adj. & m.f. Anglican.

an·gli·cis·ta m.f. Anglicist.

an·glo·fo·bia f. Anglophobia.

an·glo·par·lan·te adj. English-speaking.

an·glo·sa·jón, o·na adj. & m.f. Anglo-Saxon —m. (idioma) Anglo-Saxon.

an·go·ra adj. & m. Angora, angora.

an·gos·tar tr., intr., & reflex. to narrow.

an·gos·to, a adj. narrow, tight.

an·gos·tu·ra f. narrowness; (paso estrecho) narrow passage or place; MARIT. narrows, strait; BOT., CUL. angostura.

an·gui·la f. eel.

án·gu·lo m. angle; (esquina) corner, angle ♦ **de á. ancho** PHOTOG. wide-angle • **en á.** at an angle.

an·gu·lo·si·dad f. angularity.

an·gu·lo·so, a adj. angular, sharp.

an·gu·rria f. AMER. (hambre) hunger; (avaricia) greed.

an·gu·rrien·to, a AMER. adj. (avaro) greedy; (hambriento) starved.

an·gus·tia f. anguish.

an·gus·tia·do, a adj. anguished.

an·gus·tiar tr. to anguish, cause anguish —reflex. to become anguished or distressed.

an·gus·tio·so, a adj. anguished; *(penoso)* distressing.

an·he·lan·te adj. *(ansioso)* yearning; *(jadeante)* gasping, panting.

an·he·lar intr. to yearn or long to; *(jadear)* to gasp, pant —tr. to yearn or long for.

an·he·lo m. yearning, longing.

an·he·lo·so, a adj. longing.

an·hí·dri·do m. anhydride ♦ **a. carbónico** carbon dioxide • **a. nítrico** nitric oxide • **a. sulfúrico** sulfur dioxide.

a·ni·dar intr. to nest; *(habitar)* to live —tr. to shelter —reflex. to nest.

a·ni·llar tr. *(dar forma)* to shape into a ring; *(sujetar)* to fasten with rings.

a·ni·llo m. ring; ZOOL., ANAT. annulus, ring ♦ **a. pastoral** bishop's ring • **caer** or **venir como a. al dedo** COLL. to be just right.

á·ni·ma f. soul, spirit; *(de las armas)* bore.

a·ni·ma·ción f. *(viveza)* liveliness; *(movimiento)* animation.

a·ni·ma·do, a adj. *(vivo)* lively; *(activo)* bustling; *(movido)* motivated; ZOOL. animate; AMER. better (of health).

a·ni·ma·dor, ·ra I. adj. *(excitador)* enlivening; *(alentador)* inspiring II. m.f. *(de ceremonias)* master of ceremonies; *(artista)* entertainer.

a·ni·mad·ver·sión f. animadversion.

a·ni·mal I. adj. animal II. m. animal; FIG. beast.

a·ni·ma·la·da f. COLL. foolish or silly thing.

a·ni·ma·lu·cho m. ugly beast.

a·ni·mar tr. *(dar vida a)* to give life to; *(avivar)* to enliven; *(estimular)* to stimulate; *(alentar)* to encourage —reflex. *(avivarse)* to become animated or lively; *(atreverse)* to feel encouraged ♦ **a. a** to decide to, get in the mood to.

á·ni·mo m. spirit; *(energía)* energy, vitality ♦ **¡a.!** courage! • **caerse los ánimos** to lose heart • **dar á. a** to encourage • **estar** or **tener ánimos para** to be in the mood to.

a·ni·mo·si·dad f. animosity, enmity.

a·ni·mo·so, a adj. spirited, courageous.

a·ni·ña·do, a adj. *(pueril)* childlike; *(infantil)* childish.

a·ni·ñar·se reflex. to be childish.

a·ni·qui·la·ción f. annihilation, destruction.

a·ni·qui·la·mien·to m. var. of **aniquilación**.

a·ni·qui·lar tr. to annihilate, destroy —reflex. to be annihilated or destroyed.

a·nís m. anise; *(grano)* aniseed; *(licor)* anisette.

a·ni·sa·do m. anisette.

a·ni·ver·sa·rio, a adj. & m. anniversary.

a·no m. anus.

a·no·che adv. last night, yesterday evening.

a·no·che·cer §17 I. intr. to get dark, fall (night); *(llegar)* to arrive at nightfall II. m. nightfall, dusk.

a·no·che·ci·da f. nightfall, dusk.

a·no·ma·lí·a f. anomaly.

a·nó·ma·lo, a adj. anomalous.

a·no·na·da·ción f. depression, dejection.

a·no·na·dar tr. to overwhelm, dishearten —reflex. to be overwhelmed or disheartened.

a·no·ni·ma·to m. anonymity.

a·nó·ni·mo, a I. adj. anonymous II. m. *(anonimato)* anonymity; *(carta)* anonymous letter.

a·nor·mal adj. abnormal.

a·nor·ma·li·dad f. abnormality.

a·no·ta·ción f. *(acción)* noting; *(nota)* note.

a·no·ta·dor, ·ra I. adj. annotating, noting II. m.f. annotator.

a·no·tar tr. *(poner notas)* to annotate; *(apuntar)* to make note of.

an·qui·lo·sa·mien·to m. MED. stiffening; FIG. paralysis.

an·qui·lo·sar tr. MED. to stiffen —reflex. to become stiff; FIG. *(paralizarse)* to be paralyzed.

án·sar m. goose.

an·sia f. *(inquietud)* anxiety; *(angustia)* anguish; *(anhelo)* yearning.

an·siar §30 tr. to yearn or long for.

an·sie·dad f. anxiety.

an·sio·so, a adj. *(preocupado)* anxious; *(deseoso)* eager.

an·ta·gó·ni·co, a adj. antagonistic.

an·ta·go·nis·ta I. adj. antagonist, antagonistic II. m.f. antagonist, rival.

an·ta·ño adv. in days gone by.

an·te[1] m. ZOOL. elk.

an·te[2] prep. *(delante de)* before, in front of; *(considerando)* in view of, regarding.

an·te·a·no·che adv. the night before last.

an·te·a·yer adv. the day before yesterday.

an·te·bra·zo m. forearm.

an·te·cá·ma·ra f. antechamber, anteroom.

an·te·ce·den·te I. adj. preceding II. m. antecedent ♦ pl. background.

an·te·ce·der tr. & intr. to precede, antecede.

an·te·ce·sor, ·ra I. adj. former II. m.f. *(predecesor)* predecessor; *(antepasado)* ancestor.

an·te·da·tar tr. to antedate, backdate.

an·te·de·cir §11 tr. to foretell, predict.

an·te·di·cho, a adj. aforesaid, aforementioned.

an·te·di·lu·via·no, a adj. antediluvian.

an·te·la·ción f. ♦ **con a.** in advance • **con a. a** prior to.

an·te·ma·no adv. ♦ **de a.** in advance.

an·te·na f. ZOOL. antenna; RAD., TELEV. antenna, aerial; MARIT. lateen yard.

an·te·no·che adv. var. of **anteanoche**.

an·te·o·je·ra f. ♦ pl. blinders.

an·te·o·jo m. telescope ♦ **a. de larga vista** binoculars • pl. *(gafas)* eyeglasses; *(anteojeras)* blinders; INDUS., SPORT. goggles.

an·te·pa·sa·do, a I. adj. before last II. m.f. ancestor.

an·te·pe·cho m. *(baranda)* rail, railing; *(alféizar)* window sill.

an·te·pe·núl·ti·mo, a adj. antepenultimate.

an·te·po·ner §54 tr. *(poner delante)* to place in front; FIG. to put before.

an·te·pro·yec·to m. draft, blueprint ♦ **a. de ley** draft bill.

an·te·pues·to, ta, pusiera, puso see **anteponer**.

an·te·rior adj. previous, before *(a to)*; ANAT., ZOOL. front, fore.

an·te·rio·ri·dad f. ♦ **con a.** beforehand, in advance • **con a. a** prior to.

an·te·rior·men·te adv. previously, before; *(con antelación)* beforehand, in advance.

an·tes I. adj. & adv. before; *(antiguamente)* previously, formerly; *(más bien)* rather, sooner ♦ **a. de** before, prior to • **a. de ayer** the day before yesterday • **a. que** before; *(en vez de)* rather than II. conj. rather, on the contrary.

an·te·sa·la f. anteroom ♦ **hacer a.** to cool one's heels.

an·te·úl·ti·mo, a adj. penultimate.

an·te·vís·pe·ra f. the day before yesterday.

an·ti·á·ci·do, a adj. & m. antacid.

an·ti·a·é·re·o, a adj. antiaircraft.
an·tia·me·ri·ca·no, a adj. & m.f. anti-American.
an·tia·tó·mi·co, a adj. antinuclear.
an·ti·bi·ó·ti·co, a adj. & m. antibiotic.
an·ti·can·ce·ro·so, a adj. anticarcinogenic.
an·ti·ci·pa·ción f. anticipation ♦ con a. in advance.
an·ti·ci·pa·da·men·te adv. in advance.
an·ti·ci·pa·do, a adj. advance, advanced ♦ por a. in advance.
an·ti·ci·pa·dor, ·ra adj. anticipatory.
an·ti·ci·par tr. to advance, move forward; (prestar) to advance; S. AMER. to foresee, anticipate —reflex. to be or arrive early ♦ a. a to get ahead of.
an·ti·ci·po m. anticipation; (dinero) advance (payment).
an·ti·cle·ri·cal adj. & m.f. anticlerical.
an·ti·co·a·gu·lan·te adj. & m. anticoagulant.
an·ti·com·bus·ti·ble adj. & m. noncombustible.
an·ti·co·mu·nis·ta adj. & m.f. anticommunist.
an·ti·con·cep·ti·vo, a adj. & m. contraceptive.
an·ti·con·ge·lan·te I. adj antifreezing II. m. antifreeze.
an·ti·cua·do, a adj. (en desuso) antiquated; (pasado de moda) old-fashioned.
an·ti·cua·rio, a I. adj. antiquarian II. m. antique dealer.
an·ti·cuer·po m. antibody.
an·ti·de·mo·crá·ti·co, a adj. undemocratic.
an·ti·de·pre·si·vo, a adj. & m. antidepressant.
an·ti·di·lu·via·no, a adj. var. of antediluviano.
an·tí·do·to m. antidote.
an·tie·co·nó·mi·co, a adj. uneconomical.
an·ties·té·ti·co, a adj. unaesthetic, unsightly.
an·ti·faz m. mask.
an·ti·gás adj. (against) gas.
an·ti·gua·lla f. COLL. relic, old-fashioned item.
an·ti·gua·men·te adv. (antes) formerly, once; (en tiempos remotos) in ancient times.
an·ti·guar §10 intr. to acquire seniority —reflex. to become old-fashioned.
an·ti·güe·dad f. (vejez) old age; (época) ancient times; (en el empleo) seniority ♦ pl. antiques.
an·ti·guo, a adj. (viejo) ancient, old; (anterior) former ♦ a la a. in the old-fashioned way II. m. old-timer ♦ los antiguos the ancients.
an·ti·hi·gié·ni·co, a adj. unsanitary.
an·ti·in·fla·cio·nis·ta adj. anti-inflationary.
an·tí·lo·pe m. antelope.
an·ti·lla f. moth killer.
an·ti·rrá·bi·co, a adj. antirabies, antirabic.
an·ti·rra·cis·ta adj. & m.f. antiracist.
an·ti·se·mi·ta I. adj. anti-Semitic II. m.f. anti-Semite.
an·ti·se·mí·ti·co, a adj. anti-Semitic.
an·ti·sép·ti·co, a adj. & m. antiseptic.
an·ti·so·cia·ble adj. antisocial, unsociable.
an·ti·so·cial adj. antisocial.
an·ti·sub·ma·ri·no, a adj. antisubmarine.

an·ti·su·do·ral adj. & m. deodorant, antiperspirant.
an·ti·te·rro·ris·mo m. antiterrorism.
an·tí·te·sis f.inv. antithesis.
an·ti·té·ti·co, a adj. antithetical, antithetic.
an·ti·tó·xi·co, a adj. antitoxic.
an·ti·to·xi·na f. antitoxin, antibody.
an·to·ja·di·zo, a adj. capricious.
an·to·jar·se reflex. (gustar) to fancy, feel like; (parecer) to seem.
an·to·jo m. (capricho) whim; (de comida) craving; (lunar) birthmark ♦ a su a. as one pleases.
an·to·lo·gí·a f. anthology ♦ de a. COLL. great.
an·to·ló·gi·co, a adj. anthological.
an·to·ni·mia f. antonymy.
an·tó·ni·mo, a I. m. antonym II. adj. antonymous.
an·to·no·ma·sia f. antonomasia.
an·tor·cha f. torch; FIG. guide ♦ a. a soplete blowtorch.
an·tra·ci·ta f. anthracite, hard coal.
an·tro m. grotto; FIG. den, lair ♦ a. de corrupción den of iniquity.
an·tro·pó·fa·go, a I. adj. anthropophagous II. m.f. cannibal.
an·tro·po·gra·fí·a f. anthropography.
an·tro·poi·de adj. & m. anthropoid.
an·tro·po·lo·gí·a f. anthropology.
an·tro·po·ló·gi·co, a adj. anthropological.
an·tro·pó·lo·go, a m.f. anthropologist.
an·tro·po·me·trí·a f. anthropometry.
an·tro·po·mór·fi·co, a adj. anthropomorphic.
an·tro·po·mor·fo, a adj. anthropomorphous.
a·nual adj. annual, yearly.
a·nua·li·dad f. annual payment.
a·nua·rio m. yearbook, annual.
a·nu·ba·rra·do, a adj. cloudy, overcast.
a·nu·blar tr. to cloud; FIG. to darken, tarnish —reflex. to become cloudy or overcast; FIG. to be tarnished.
a·nu·dar tr. (hacer nudos) to tie in knots; (atar) to tie together —reflex. to become stunted ♦ a. la lengua FIG. to become tongue-tied.
a·nu·la·ción f. annulment, nullification ♦ a. del juicio LAW mistrial.
a·nu·lar[1] I. adj. annular, ring-shaped II. m. ring finger.
a·nu·lar[2] tr. to annul; (desautorizar) to remove from power.
a·nun·cia·ción f. announcement.
a·nun·cia·dor, ·ra I. adj. (declarativo) announcing; (publicitario) advertising II. m.f. (persona) announcer; (empresa) advertiser.
a·nun·cian·te I. adj. advertising II. m.f. advertiser.
a·nun·ciar tr. to announce; (publicar) to advertise; (presagiar) to foreshadow.
a·nun·cio m. announcement; (cartel) poster; (señal) sign; COM. advertisement ♦ anuncios clasificados classified advertisements.
an·ver·so m. obverse.
an·zue·lo m. fishhook; FIG. lure ♦ tragarse el a. COLL. to swallow the bait.
a·ña·di·do m. addition.
a·ña·di·du·ra f. addition ♦ de a. for good measure • por a. besides.
a·ña·dir tr. to add; (aumentar) to increase; (conferir) to lend.
a·ñe·ja·mien·to m. aging, maturing.
a·ñe·jar tr. & reflex. to age, mature.
a·ñe·jo, a adj. aged, mature.

a·ñi·cos m.pl. bits, pieces ♦ **hacerse a.** to break into pieces.

a·ñil I. m. BOT. indigo; *(para lavado)* bluing II. adj. indigo, blue.

a·ñi·lar tr. to dye indigo *or* blue.

a·ñi·nos m.pl. *(piel)* lambskins; *(lana)* lambswool.

a·ño m. year ♦ **a. bisiesto** leap year • **a. económico** fiscal year • **a. lectivo** school year • **a. en curso** current year • **a. luz** light-year • **el a. verde** COLL. never • **en el a. de la nana** COLL. way back • **entrado en años** advanced in years • **tener ... años** to be ... years old.

a·ño·ran·za f. nostalgia.

a·ño·rar tr. & intr. to long, yearn (for).

a·o·jar tr. to give the evil eye to, jinx.

a·o·jo m. evil eye, jinx.

a·o·va·do, a adj. oval; BOT. ovate.

a·o·var intr. to lay eggs.

a·o·vi·llar·se reflex. to roll up into a ball.

a·pa·bu·lla·mien·to m. var. of **apabullo**.

a·pa·bu·llar tr. to crush, squash.

a·pa·bu·llo m. COLL. crushing.

a·pa·cen·ta·de·ro m. pasture.

a·pa·cen·ta·dor, ·ra I. adj. grazing II. m. shepherd —f. shepherdess.

a·pa·cen·ta·mien·to m. *(acción)* grazing, pasturing; *(pasto)* pasture, grass.

a·pa·cen·tar §49 tr. & reflex. to graze, pasture.

a·pa·ci·bi·li·dad f. calmness, gentleness.

a·pa·ci·ble adj. calm, gentle.

a·pa·ci·gua·dor, ·ra I. adj. appeasing, pacifying II. m.f. appeaser, pacifier.

a·pa·ci·gua·mien·to m. appeasement, pacifying.

a·pa·ci·guar §10 tr. *(sosegar)* to appease; *(un dolor)* to relieve —reflex. to calm down.

a·pa·che m.f. Apache; FIG. *(malhechor)* thug, bandit —m. MEX. raincoat.

a·pa·dri·nar tr. *(patrocinar)* to sponsor; *(apoyar)* to support; *(a un niño)* to be godfather to; *(en una boda)* to be best man for; *(en un desafío)* to act as second for.

a·pa·ga·do, a adj. *(extinguido)* extinguished; *(apocado)* shy; FIG. dull, subdued.

a·pa·gar §47 tr. *(el fuego)* to put out; *(la luz)* to turn out; *(la cal)* to slake; *(el ruido)* to silence; *(el color)* to tone down —reflex. to fade.

a·pa·ga·ve·las m.inv. candle snuffer.

a·pa·gón m. blackout, power failure.

a·pa·la·brar tr. to agree to.

a·pa·le·ar tr. to thrash; AGR. to winnow.

a·pa·le·o m. thrashing; AGR. winnowing.

a·pan·di·llar tr. to form into a gang —reflex. to band together.

a·pa·ñar tr. *(asir)* to grasp; *(apoderarse)* to seize; COLL. *(abrigar)* to wrap up; *(reparar)* to repair, mend; ARG., PERU to cover up for, protect; MEX. to excuse, forgive —reflex. *(darse maña)* to manage.

a·pa·ño m. *(acción)* grasping; COLL. *(remiendo)* patch; *(habilidad)* knack; *(lío)* mess, trouble; *(amante)* lover.

a·pa·ra·dor m. *(armario)* sideboard, cupboard; *(taller)* studio; *(escaparate)* window.

a·pa·ra·to m. apparatus, device; FIG. pomp, show; ANAT., ZOOL. system; MED. bandage ♦ **a. de televisión, de radio** television, radio set • **aparatos de mando** controls.

a·pa·ra·to·si·dad f. showiness, ostentation.

a·pa·ra·to·so, a adj. pompous, ostentatious.

a·par·ca·mien·to m. *(acción)* parking; *(garaje)* parking lot, garage.

a·par·car §70 tr. *(estacionar)* to park; MIL. to deposit (arms).

a·par·ce·rí·a f. sharecropping.

a·par·ce·ro, a m.f. sharecropper; AMER. comrade.

a·pa·re·ar tr. to match up, pair off; ZOOL. to mate, breed.

a·pa·re·cer §17 intr. & reflex. to appear; *(mostrarse)* to show up, turn up.

a·pa·re·ci·do m. ghost, phantom.

a·pa·re·ci·mien·to m. appearance.

a·pa·re·ja·do, a adj. apt, fit ♦ **ir a. con** to go hand in hand with • **traer a.** to mean, involve.

a·pa·re·jar tr. to prepare, make ready; *(los caballos)* to harness; MARIT. to rig —reflex. to get ready.

a·pa·re·jo m. preparation; *(arreo)* harness; *(poleas)* derrick; MARIT. rigging; PAINT. priming; CONST. bonding; AMER. saddle.

a·pa·ren·tar tr. *(fingir)* to pretend, feign; *(parecer)* to seem, look.

a·pa·ren·te adj. *(presumible)* apparent, seeming; *(visible)* apparent, visible.

a·pa·ri·ción f. *(acción)* appearance; *(fantasma)* apparition, specter.

a·pa·rien·cia f. appearance ♦ **en a.** apparently • **salvar las apariencias** to keep up appearances, save face.

a·par·ta·de·ro m. sidetrack, siding.

a·par·ta·do, a I. adj. remote, isolated II. m. *(casilla postal)* post office box; *(párrafo)* paragraph, section.

a·par·ta·men·to m. apartment, flat (G.B.).

a·par·ta·mien·to m. *(separación)* separation; *(aislamiento)* isolation.

a·par·tar tr. *(separar)* to separate; *(llevar aparte)* to take aside; *(alejar)* to put aside —reflex. to withdraw, move away.

a·par·te I. adv. *(por separado)* apart, separate; *(a un lado)* aside, to one side ♦ **a. de** besides, apart from II. m. paragraph; THEAT. aside.

a·par·theid m. apartheid.

a·pa·sio·na·do, a adj. enthusiastic, intense.

a·pa·sio·nan·te adj. exciting, thrilling.

a·pa·sio·nar tr. to enthuse, excite —reflex. to become enthused *or* excited.

a·pa·tí·a f. apathy, indifference.

a·pá·ti·co, a adj. apathetic, indifferent.

a·pá·tri·da I. adj. stateless, without a country II. m.f. stateless person, one without a country.

a·pe·a·de·ro m. *(poyo)* mounting block; *(fonda)* inn; RAIL. way station.

a·pe·a·mien·to m. *(de un caballo)* dismounting; *(de un vehículo)* getting out; ARCHIT. bracing; SURV. surveying.

a·pe·ar tr. *(bajar)* to lower; *(árbol)* to fell; *(caballo)* to fetter; *(rueda)* to chock; *(tierras)* to survey; ARCHIT. to prop up —reflex. *(de un caballo)* to dismount; *(de un vehículo)* to get out of; AMER. to stay, lodge.

a·pe·chu·gar §47 intr. ♦ **a. con** COLL. to put up with, face.

a·pe·dre·ar tr. *(lanzar)* to hurl stones at; *(matar)* to stone to death —intr. to hail —reflex. to suffer damage from hail.

a·pe·gar·se §47 reflex. to become attached *or* fond *(a to, of)*.

a·pe·go m. FIG. attachment, fondness ♦ **cobrar a.** to become attached to *or* fond of.

a·pe·la·ble adj. appealable.

a·pe·la·ción f. LAW appeal; *(recurso)* recourse ♦ **interponer a.** to (file an) appeal.

a·pe·lar intr. to appeal ♦ **a. a** *or* **ante** to appeal to.

a·pe·la·ti·vo, a I. adj. appellative II. m. AMER., COLL. last name, surname.

a·pel·ma·za·do, a adj. compact, compressed; FIG. dull, stodgy.

a·pel·ma·zar §04 tr. to compress, compact.

a·pe·lo·to·nar tr. to form into balls *or* tufts —reflex. *(hacerse bolitas)* to form balls *or* tufts; FIG. *(apiñarse)* to cluster, throng.

a·pe·lli·dar tr. to call, name —reflex. to be called *or* named.

a·pe·lli·do m. last name, surname; *(apodo)* nickname ♦ **a. de soltera** maiden name.

a·pe·nar tr. to grieve, pain —reflex. to be grieved *or* pained.

a·pe·nas adv. *(casi no)* scarcely, hardly; *(con dificultad)* hardly, with difficulty; *(enseguida que)* as soon as.

a·pen·dec·to·mí·a f. appendectomy.

a·pén·di·ce m. appendage; ANAT. appendix.

a·pen·di·ci·tis f. inv. appendicitis.

a·per·ci·bir tr. *(disponer)* to make ready; *(advertir)* to warn —reflex. to prepare oneself.

a·per·ga·mi·na·do, a adj. parchment-like; FIG. dried-up.

a·per·ga·mi·nar·se reflex. COLL. to become wizened, dry up.

a·pe·ri·ti·vo, a I. adj. CUL. appetizing; MED. aperitive II. m. CUL. apéritif, appetizer; MED. aperitive.

a·pe·ro m. *(utensilios)* equipment, gear; AGR. draft animals; AMER. riding gear.

a·per·so·nar·se reflex. to present oneself.

a·per·tu·ra f. *(principio)* opening, commencement; *(de un testamento)* reading; *(ajedrez)* opening move; POL. opening.

a·pe·sa·dum·brar tr. to grieve, distress —reflex. to be grieved *or* distressed *(de, por* by).

a·pes·tar tr. *(contaminar)* to infect (with the plague); COLL. *(fastidiar)* to annoy —intr. to stink *(ser contaminado)* to be infected with the plague.

a·pes·to·so, a adj. *(fétido)* stinking; COLL. *(fastidioso)* annoying.

a·pe·te·ce·dor, ·ra adj. appetizing, tempting.

a·pe·te·cer §17 tr. *(ansiar)* to long for, crave; FIG. to desire —intr. to be appealing *or* attractive.

a·pe·te·ci·ble adj. appealing, appetizing.

a·pe·ten·cia f. *(hambre)* appetite; *(deseo)* desire.

a·pe·ti·to m. appetite ♦ **abrir, dar** *or* **despertar el a.** to whet one's appetite

a·pe·ti·to·so, a adj. appetizing, delicious.

a·pia·dar tr. to move to pity —reflex. to (have) pity ♦ **a. de** to take pity on.

á·pi·ce m. *(cima)* apex, top, pinnacle; FIG. *(nonada)* iota, whit ♦ **no ceder un a.** not to give an inch.

a·pi·cul·tor, ·ra m.f. beekeeper, apiculturist.

a·pi·cul·tu·ra f. beekeeping, apiculture.

a·pi·lar tr. to pile *or* heap.

a·pim·po·llar·se reflex. to bud, sprout.

a·pi·ña·do, a adj. *(cónico)* conical; *(apretado)* crammed *or* packed together.

a·pi·ña·mien·to m. *(acción)* crowding; *(aprieto)* crush.

a·pi·ñar tr. & reflex. to cram, jam.

a·pio m. celery.

a·pi·so·na·do·ra f. *(aplastadora)* flattener; *(de carretera)* steamroller.

a·pi·so·na·mien·to m. *(acción)* flattening; *(de carretera)* steamrolling.

a·pi·so·nar tr. *(tierra)* to pack down; *(carretera)* to steamroller.

a·pla·ca·mien·to m. appeasement, placation.

a·pla·car §70 tr. to appease, placate.

a·pla·na·dor, ·ra I. adj. flattening II. f. steamroller.

a·pla·na·mien·to m. leveling, flattening.

a·pla·nar tr. *(allanar)* to level, flatten; COLL. *(pasmar)* to stun —reflex. *(venirse abajo)* to collapse; FIG. to lose heart.

a·plas·tan·te adj. *(agobiador)* overwhelming; *(cansador)* exhausting.

a·plas·tar tr. *(estrujar)* to crush; *(vencer)* to overwhelm; COLL. *(apabullar)* to stun —reflex. AMER. *(desanimarse)* to become discouraged; *(cansarse)* to get tired.

a·plau·dir tr. to applaud; FIG. to applaud, commend.

a·plau·so m. *(palmas)* applause, clapping; FIG. applause, praise.

a·pla·za·mien·to m. postponement.

a·pla·zar §04 tr. *(diferir)* to postpone, put off; AMER. to flunk.

a·pli·ca·ble adj. applicable.

a·pli·ca·ción f. application; *(adorno)* appliqué; *(esmero)* diligence.

a·pli·ca·do, a adj. diligent.

a·pli·car §70 tr. *(poner)* to apply, put on; *(designar)* to assign; *(usar)* to use, employ —reflex. to apply oneself.

a·pli·que m. light fixture.

a·plo·ma·do, a adj. poised.

a·plo·mo m. aplomb; *(verticalidad)* vertical alignment.

a·po·ca·do, a adj. diffident, timid.

a·po·ca·líp·ti·co, a adj. apocalyptic.

a·po·co·par tr. to apocopate, elide.

a·pó·co·pe f. apocope, elision.

a·pó·cri·fo, a adj. apocryphal.

a·po·dar tr. to nickname.

a·po·de·ra·do, a I. adj. empowered, authorized II. m.f. *(poderhabiente)* attorney, proxy; *(empresario)* manager, agent

a·po·de·ra·mien·to m. *(autorización)* authorization; *(apropiación)* seizure.

a·po·de·rar tr. to grant power of attorney to —reflex. ♦ **a. de** *(apropiar)* to take possession of; *(dominar)* to overwhelm.

a·po·do m. nickname.

a·po·ge·o m. ASTRON. apogee; FIG. height.

a·po·li·llar·se reflex. to be moth-eaten; AMER., COLL. to snooze, doze.

a·po·lí·ti·co, a adj. & m.f. apolitical (person).

a·po·lo·gis·ta m.f. apologist, defender.

a·pol·tro·nar·se reflex. to get lazy.

a·por·car §73 tr. to hill, earth up (plants).

a·po·rrar intr. COLL. to be left speechless.

a·po·rre·a·do m. CUBA beef stew.

a·po·rre·ar tr. *(golpear)* to beat; *(instrumento)* to bang on; *(insistir)* to harp on —reflex. FIG. to break one's back.

a·por·tar intr. MARIT. to arrive; *(llegar por casualidad)* to arrive *or* end up by chance —tr. *(traer)* to bring; *(contribuir)* to contribute.

a·por·te m. AMER. contribution, donation.

a·po·sen·tar tr. & reflex. to lodge.

a·po·sen·to m. *(habitación)* room; *(hospedaje)* lodging.

a·po·si·ción f. apposition.

a·pos·tar §19 tr. *(jugar)* to wager; *(colocar)* to post —reflex. to position oneself.

a·pos·ta·tar intr. to apostatize.

a·pos·ti·lla f. marginal note, annotation.

a·pos·to·la·do m. apostolate.

a·pós·tol m. apostle.

a·pos·tó·li·co, a adj. *(de los apóstoles)* apostolic; *(del papa)* papal, pontific.

a·pós·tro·fe m. *or* f. RHET. apostrophe.

a·pós·tro·fo m. GRAM. apostrophe.

a·po·te·ca·rio m. apothecary.

a·po·teg·ma m. apothegm, maxim.

a·po·te·ó·si·co, a adj. *(glorificador)* deifying; *(glorioso)* magnificent.

a·po·te·o·sis f.inv. apotheosis; FIG. glorification.

a·po·te·ó·ti·co, a adj. magnificent.

a·po·yar tr. *(estribar)* to lean, rest; *(ayudar)* to aid, support; *(confirmar)* to uphold; MIL. to reinforce —intr. to lean, rest —reflex. to lean, rest; FIG. to rely on.

a·po·yo m. *(soporte)* support; *(fundamento)* basis; *(protección)* aid.

a·pre·cia·ción f. *(valorización)* appraisal; *(aprecio)* appreciation.

a·pre·ciar tr. to appraise; *(estimar)* to appreciate; *(considerar)* to consider.

a·pre·cia·ti·vo, a adj. appraising.

a·pre·cio m. COM. appraisal; *(estima)* esteem; MEX. attention ♦ **no hacer a. a** MEX. not to pay attention to.

a·pre·hen·der tr. *(apresar)* to apprehend; *(confiscar)* to seize; *(concebir)* to apprehend.

a·pre·hen·sión f. *(apresamiento)* apprehension; *(embargo)* seizure; *(comprensión)* comprehension.

a·pre·hen·si·vo, a adj. apprehensive.

a·pre·mian·te adj. pressing, urgent.

a·pre·miar tr. *(acelerar)* to press; *(oprimir)* to oppress; LAW to compel.

a·pre·mio m. *(urgencia)* urgency; LAW judicial order.

a·pren·der tr. to learn *(a* to*).*

a·pren·diz, ·za m.f. apprentice.

a·pren·di·za·je m. apprenticeship.

a·pren·sión f. *(miedo)* apprehension; *(sospecha)* suspicion.

a·pren·si·vo, a adj. apprehensive.

a·pre·sar tr. *(aprisionar)* to capture; ZOOL. to grasp; MARIT. to capture.

a·pres·tar tr. *(preparar)* to make ready; TEX. to size —reflex. to prepare oneself.

a·pres·to m. *(preparación)* making ready; TEX. sizing.

a·pre·su·ra·mien·to m. hurry, haste.

a·pre·su·rar tr. to hurry, hasten —reflex. to hurry, make haste *(a, por* to*).*

a·pre·ta·do, a adj. *(comprimido)* cramped, tight; COLL. *(arduo)* difficult; *(mezquino)* stingy ♦ **estar muy a.** COLL. *(problemas)* to be in a jam; *(dinero)* to be short of money • **estar a. de trabajo** to be up to one's neck in work.

a·pre·ta·mien·to m. var. of **aprieto**.

a·pre·tar §49 tr. *(nudo)* to tighten; *(estrujar)* to squeeze; *(comprimir)* to compress; *(abrazar)* to hug; *(apremiar)* to urge ♦ **a. la mano** to shake hands • **a. los dientes** to grit *or* clench one's teeth —intr. *(los zapatos)* to pinch; *(la ropa)* to be too tight; *(empeorar)* to worsen, get worse.

a·pre·tón m. grip, squeeze ♦ **a. de manos** handshake.

a·pre·tu·jar tr. *(apretar)* to squeeze; *(apiñar)* to cram.

a·prie·te, to see **apretar**.

a·prie·to m. jam, fix ♦ **poner a alguien en un a.** to put someone on the spot.

a·pri·sa adv. quickly, swiftly.

a·pri·sio·nar tr. to bind.

a·pro·ba·ción f. approval; LAW ratification.

a·pro·ba·do, a I. adj. approved II. m. passing grade.

a·pro·bar §19 tr. *(consentir)* to approve of; *(examen)* to pass; LAW to ratify —intr. to pass an examination.

a·pro·ba·to·rio, a adj. approving.

a·pron·tar tr. *(disponer)* to have ready; *(entregar)* to deliver at once.

a·pron·te m. R.P. *(de caballos)* trial (race); FIG. dry run.

a·pro·pia·ción f. appropriation.

a·pro·pia·do, a adj. appropriate, suitable.

a·pro·piar tr. AMER., FIN. to earmark —reflex. to take possession *(de* of*).*

a·pro·pin·cuar·se reflex. to draw near.

a·pro·ve·cha·dor, ·ra I. adj. opportunistic II. m.f. opportunist.

a·pro·ve·cha·mien·to m. use, utilization.

a·pro·ve·char intr. to be useful —tr. to make good use of —reflex. *(de* to take advantage of*).*

a·pro·vi·sio·na·mien·to m. *(acción)* supplying; *(provisiones)* supplies.

a·pro·vi·sio·nar tr. to supply, provision.

a·pro·xi·ma·ción f. *(proximidad)* nearness; *(estimación)* approximation.

a·pro·xi·ma·da·men·te adv. approximately, about.

a·pro·xi·mar tr. to bring near —reflex. to draw near.

a·prue·be, bo see **aprobar**.

ap·ti·tud f. aptitude ♦ pl. gift, talent.

ap·to, a adj. *(hábil)* competent; *(conveniente)* fit.

a·pues·te, to see **apostar**.

a·pues·to, a I. adj. elegant II. f. bet, wager.

a·pu·nar·se reflex. AMER. to be overcome by altitude sickness.

a·pun·ta·dor, ·ra I. adj. observing, noting II. m.f. THEAT. prompter; MIL. pointer, gunner.

a·pun·ta·la·mien·to m. propping, shoring.

a·pun·ta·lar tr. to prop up, shore up.

a·pun·tar tr. *(arma)* to aim, point; *(señalar)* to point to *or* at, indicate; *(tomar nota)* to make a note of; *(sugerir)* to cue, clue; *(insinuar)* to hint at, suggest; THEAT. to prompt —intr. to begin to show —reflex. to begin to turn sour.

a·pun·te m. *(nota)* note, notation; THEAT. prompter ♦ **llevar el a.** R.P., COLL. *(escuchar)* to pay attention; *(en el galanteo)* to accept someone's attentions.

a·pu·ña·lar tr. to stab, knife ♦ **a. a alguien con la mirada** to look daggers at someone.

apu·ñar tr. to seize in one's fist.

a·pu·ñe·(te·)ar tr. COLL. to punch.

a·pu·ra·do, a adj. AMER. in a hurry.

a·pu·rar tr. AMER. to hurry, press; *(purificar)* to refine; *(agotar)* to use *or* finish up; *(enfadar)* to annoy —reflex. AMER. to hurry.

a·pu·ro m. hurry ♦ **estar en apuros** *(dificultades)* to be in a jam; *(dinero)* to be hard up (for money).

a·que·jar tr. to afflict, distress.

a·quel, ·lla dem. adj. [pl. **-llos, -llas**] that (. . . over there) ♦ pl. those.

a·quél, ·lla dem. pron. [pl. **-llos, -llas**] that one (over there); *(el primero)* the former ♦ pl. those.

a·que·llo neut. dem. pron. that, that matter ♦ **a. de** that business about.

a·que·ren·cia·do, a adj. MEX. in love, enamored.

a·que·ren·ciar·se reflex. ♦ **a. a** to become fond of or attached to.

a·quí adv. *(en este lugar)* here; *(ahora)* now; *(entonces)* then, at that point ♦ **de a. en adelante** from now on, from here on in • **por a.** *(alrededor)* around here; *(por este lado)* this way.

a·quie·tar tr. to calm, soothe —reflex. to calm down, become calm.

a·qui·la·tar tr. JEWEL. to appraise; FIG. to appreciate.

a·ra f. *(altar)* (sacrificial) altar; *(piedra)* altar stone —m. macaw ♦ **en aras de** for the sake of.

a·rá·bi·co/go, a adj. ♦ **número a.** Arabic numeral.

a·rác·ni·dos m.pl. arachnids.

a·ra·da f. *(hecho)* plowing; *(tierra)* plowed land; *(labranza)* farming.

a·ra·do m. *(máquina)* plow; *(acción)* plowing.

a·ran·cel m. tariff, duty.

a·ran·de·la f. MECH. washer; AMER. frills, flounce.

a·ra·ña f. spider; *(candelabro)* chandelier ♦ **a. de mar** spider crab.

a·ra·ñar tr. *(rasgar)* to scratch, scrape; COLL. *(recoger)* to scrape together.

a·ra·ña·zo m. scratch.

a·rar tr. to plow.

a·rau·ca·no, a adj. & m.f. Araucanian

ar·bi·tra·je m. arbitration; COM. arbitrage.

ar·bi·trar tr. to arbitrate; SPORT. to referee, umpire; *(proceder libremente)* to act freely —intr. to arbitrate.

ar·bi·tra·rie·dad f. arbitrariness.

ar·bi·tra·rio, a adj. arbitrary.

ar·bi·trio m. *(voluntad)* will; *(recurso)* means; *(juicio)* judgment.

ár·bi·tro m. arbiter, arbitrator; SPORT. referee.

ár·bol m. tree; MECH. axle; MARIT. mast; ARCHIT. crown post ♦ **á. de levas** camshaft • **á. motor** drive shaft.

ar·bo·la·do, a I. adj. wooded II. m. grove.

ar·bo·lar tr. MARIT. to rig; *(poner derecho)* to set upright —reflex. to rear (a horse).

ar·bo·le·da f. grove, wood.

ar·bo·re·to m. arboretum.

ar·bo·ri·cul·tu·ra f. arboriculture.

ar·bo·ri·zar §04 tr. to forest, plant with trees.

ar·bus·to m. bush, shrub.

ar·ca f. *(cofre)* chest ♦ **a. de agua** reservoir • **a. de la Alianza** BIBL. Ark of the Covenant • **a. de Noé** BIBL. Noah's Ark ♦ pl. coffers.

ar·ca·buz m. *(arma)* harquebus; *(arcabucero)* harquebusier.

ar·ca·da f. ARCHIT. arcade; *(de un puente)* span; *(basca)* retch.

ar·cai·co, a adj. archaic, old-fashioned.

ar·ca·ís·ta m.f. archaist.

ar·cán·gel m. archangel.

ar·ca·no, a I. adj. arcane II. m. mystery.

ar·ce m. maple (tree).

ar·ci·lla f. clay ♦ **a. figulina** potter's clay.

ar·ci·llo·so, a adj. clay-like, clayey.

ar·co m. GEOM. arc; ARCHIT., ANAT. arch; ARM., MUS. bow; SPORT. goal ♦ **a. iris** rainbow • **a. voltaico** ELEC. arc lamp.

ar·chi·du·que m. archduke.

ar·chi·du·que·sa f. archduchess.

ar·chi·mi·llo·na·rio, a m.f. multimillionaire.

ar·chi·pié·la·go m. archipelago.

ar·chi·va·dor, ·ra m.f. filing clerk —m. filing cabinet.

ar·chi·var tr. *(clasificar)* to file, put into a file; FIG. to shelve.

ar·chi·ve·ro, a/vis·ta m.f. archivist.

ar·chi·vo m. archives; *(de oficina)* files.

ar·der intr. to burn; FIG. to glow, blaze ♦ **a. de** or **en** FIG. to rage or be ablaze with.

ar·did m. ruse, scheme.

ar·dien·te adj. *(quemante)* burning; *(al rojo)* glowing; FIG. ardent.

ar·di·lla f. squirrel ♦ **a. listada** chipmunk.

ar·di·te m. old Spanish coin of little value ♦ **no valer un a.** COLL. not to be worth a cent.

ar·dor m. heat; FIG. zeal.

ar·do·ro·so, a adj. hot; FIG. ardent.

ar·duo, a adj. arduous, difficult.

á·re·a f. area.

a·re·na f. sand; *(redondel)* ring; *(campo de batalla)* battlefield ♦ **arenas movedizas** quicksand.

a·re·nal m. *(terreno arenoso)* sandy ground; *(arena movediza)* quicksand.

a·re·nar tr. *(enarenar)* to cover with sand; *(frotar)* to sand.

a·re·ne·ro, a m.f. *(vendedor)* sand merchant —m. RAIL. sandbox.

a·ren·ga f. harangue; FIG. sermon.

a·ren·gar §47 tr. & intr. to harangue.

a·re·ni·lla f. *(calculus; (polvo)* blotting powder.

a·re·nis·co, a I. adj. sandy II. f. sandstone.

a·re·no·so, a adj. sandy.

a·ren·que m. herring.

a·re·te m. *(aro)* hoop, ring; *(pendiente)* earring.

ar·ga·ma·sa f. mortar, plaster.

ar·ga·ma·sar intr. to mix mortar —tr. to mortar, plaster.

ar·gen·ta·do, a adj. *(bañado)* silvered, silver-plated; *(color)* silver, silvery.

ar·gen·tar tr. to silver, silver-plate.

ar·gen·ta·rio m. silversmith.

ar·gén·te·o, a adj. *(de plata)* silver; FIG. silvery.

ar·gen·te·rí·a f. gold or silver embroidery.

ar·gen·ti·nis·mo m. Argentine word or expression.

ar·gen·to m. POET. silver ♦ **a. vivo** quicksilver.

ar·go·lla f. ring; S. AMER. *(anillo)* wedding or engagement ring; MEX., COLL. luck.

ar·go·nau·ta m. MYTH. Argonaut; ICHTH. argonaut, paper nautilus.

ar·got m. slang, jargon.

ar·gu·cia f. subtlety.

ar·güir §07 intr. to argue —tr. *(deducir)* to deduce; *(probar)* to prove.

ar·gu·men·ta·ción f. *(acción)* arguing; *(argumento)* argument.

ar·gu·men·ta·ti·vo, a adj. argumentative.

ar·gu·men·tar intr. to argue.

ar·gu·men·tis·ta m.f. CINEM. script writer.

ar·gu·men·to m. *(razonamiento)* line of reasoning; *(trama)* plot; *(summary)* summary.

ar·gu·ya, yo, yera, yó *see* **argüir**.

a·ria f. aria.

a·ri·dez f. aridity, aridness.

á·ri·do, a I. adj. arid, dry; FIG. dry, dull II. m.pl. dry goods.

a·rie·te m. MIL., HIST. battering ram.

a·rio, a adj. & m.f. Aryan.

a·ris·co, a adj. (desabrido) unfriendly; (salvaje) wild.

a·ris·ta f. GEOM. edge; BOT. beard, awn; ARCHIT. arris.

a·ris·ta·do, a adj. BOT. bearded; (con borde) with edges.

a·ris·to·cra·cia f. aristocracy.

a·ris·tó·cra·ta m.f. aristocrat.

a·ris·to·crá·ti·co, a adj. (noble) aristocratic; (distinguido) distinguished.

a·ris·to·té·li·co, a adj. & m.f. Aristotelian.

a·rit·mé·ti·co, a I. adj. arithmetical, arithmetic II. m.f. arithmetician —f. arithmetic; (libro) arithmetic book.

ar·le·quín m. harlequin, clown.

ar·ma f. weapon, arm ♦ a. blanca bladed weapon • a. de fuego firearm ♦ pl. (instrumentos) arms, weapons; (ejército) troops, army; FIG. (medios) means • ¡a las a.! to arms! • alzarse en a. to rise up in arms • parar por las a. to shoot • presentar a. to present arms.

ar·ma·do, a I. adj. armed; CONSTR. reinforced II. f. armada, (naval) fleet.

ar·ma·du·ra f. MIL. armor; (armazón) frame, framework; ELEC. armature; MUS. key signature.

ar·ma·men·tis·ta adj. arms, armaments.

ar·ma·men·to m. (acción) armament; (armas) weapons.

ar·mar tr. (dar armas) to arm; (aprestar) to prime; (montar) to assemble; (dar fuerza) to reinforce; MARIT. to equip; FIG. to create ♦ armarla to cause a scandal —reflex. to arm oneself; S. AMER. to strike it rich, get lucky.

ar·ma·rio m. closet, wardrobe.

ar·ma·tos·te m. (algo tosco) monstrosity; (palurdo) hulk.

ar·ma·zón m. or f. framework, frame.

ar·me·lla f. eyebolt.

ar·me·rí·a f. (museo) military museum; (tienda) gunsmith's shop; (fabricación) gunsmithing.

ar·mi·ño m. ermine.

ar·mis·ti·cio m. armistice.

ar·mo·ní·a f. harmony.

ar·mó·ni·ca·men·te adv. harmonically, harmoniously.

ar·mó·ni·co, a I. adj. harmonic, harmonious II. m. harmonic —f. harmonica.

ar·mo·nio m. harmonium.

ar·mo·nio·so, a adj. harmonious.

ar·mo·ni·za·ción f. MUS. harmonizing; (reconciliación) reconciliation; (de colores) coordinating.

ar·mo·ni·zar §04 tr. & intr. to harmonize.

ar·nés m. armor ♦ pl. harness.

a·ro m. (círculo) hoop, ring; R.P. earring; BOT. arum ♦ entra por el a. COLL. to yield unwillingly.

a·ro·ma m. aroma, scent; (del vino) bouquet.

a·ro·mar tr. to perfume, scent.

a·ro·má·ti·co, a adj. aromatic.

a·ro·ma·ti·za·ción f. perfuming, scenting.

a·ro·ma·ti·za·dor m. AMER. atomizer.

a·ro·ma·ti·zar tr. perfuming.

a·ro·ma·ti·zar §04 tr. to perfume; CUL. to flavor.

a·ro·mo·so, a adj. aromatic, fragrant.

ar·pa f. harp ♦ a. eolia Aeolian harp.

ar·pí·a f. harpy; COLL. shrew, hag.

ar·pi·lle·ra f. burlap, sackcloth.

ar·pis·ta m.f. harpist.

ar·pón m. harpoon; ARCHIT. clamp.

ar·po·nar/ne·ar tr. to harpoon.

ar·que·a·da f. MUS. bowing.

ar·que·ar tr. (curvar) to curve; MARIT. to gauge —intr. AMER. to audit —reflex. to curve.

ar·que·o m. (acción) curve; MARIT. gauging; COM. audit.

ar·que·o·lo·gí·a f. archaeology.

ar·que·o·ló·gi·co, a adj. archaeological.

ar·que·ó·lo·go, a m.f. archaeologist.

ar·que·ro m. (soldado) archer; (tonelero) cooper; SPORT. goalie.

ar·que·ti·po m. archetype.

ar·qui·dió·ce·sis f.inv. archdiocese.

ar·qui·tec·to, a m.f. architect.

ar·qui·tec·tó·ni·co, a adj. architectural.

ar·qui·tec·tu·ra f. architecture.

ar·qui·tec·tu·ral adj. architectural.

a·rra·bal m. slum ♦ pl. outskirts.

a·rra·ba·le·ro, a I. m.f. COLL. common, coarse person II. adj. COLL. coarse, common.

a·rra·ci·ma·do, a adj. clustered, bunched.

a·rra·ci·mar·se reflex. to form a bunch.

a·rrai·gar §47 intr. BOT. to take root —tr. AMER., LAW to limit or restrict movement —reflex. BOT. to take root; (establecerse) to establish oneself; (vicio, virtud) to become deeply rooted.

a·rrai·go m. BOT. rooting ♦ tener a. to have a sense of belonging.

a·rram·blar tr. (cubrir de arena) to cover with sand (receding waters); (arrastrar) to sweep away; COLL. (arrebatar) to make off with.

a·rran·ca·cla·vos m.inv. claw (of a hammer).

a·rran·ca·da f. sudden start.

a·rran·ca·dor, ·ra I. adj. starting II. m. AUTO. starter —f. AGR. lifter, picker.

a·rran·ca·du·ra f. (desarraigo) uprooting; (extracción) extraction.

a·rran·car §70 tr. (de raíz) to pull up; (con violencia) to pull out; (conseguir) to obtain, seize —intr. (salir) to get started; (provenir) to stem (de from); AUTO. to start (up); RAIL. to pull out.

a·rran·que m. (acción) uprooting; (toma) seizure; (principio) outset; (arrebato) outburst; (ocurrencia) witty remark; AUTO. starter.

a·rra·sa·do, a adj. satiny, satin-like.

a·rra·sa·du·ra f. leveling, smoothing.

a·rra·sar tr. (allanar) to level; (arruinar) to destroy —intr. & reflex. to clear (the sky) ♦ a. en or de lágrimas to fill with tears.

a·rras·tra·di·zo, a adj. (a rastras) trailing; (trillado) frequented.

a·rras·tra·do, a I. adj. wretched II. m.f. rogue.

a·rras·trar tr. to pull, drag; (los pies) to drag, shuffle; (atraer) to attract —intr. to crawl; (colgar) to hang down —reflex. to crawl, grovel.

a·rras·tre m. dragging; FIG. influence, pull.

a·rra·yán m. myrtle.

a·rre·ar tr. (ganado) to herd; (estimular) to urge on; (poner arreos) to harness; AMER. to steal —intr. to move along.

a·rre·ba·ta·di·zo, a adj. excitable, impetuous.

a·rre·ba·ta·do, a adj. (impetuoso) impetuous; (sonrojado) flushed.

a·rre·ba·ta·dor, ·ra adj. (cautivante) charming; (excitante) exciting.

a·rre·ba·tar tr. (arrancar) to snatch; FIG. (con-

mover) to move, stir; AGR. to parch, dry up —reflex. FIG. (*enfurecerse*) to get carried away; AGR. to become parched *or* dry; CUL. to burn.

a·rre·ba·to m. (*arranque*) fit; (*furor*) rage; (*éxtasis*) ecstasy.

a·rre·bol m. (*color*) red glow; (*afeite*) rouge.

a·rre·bo·lar tr. to make red —reflex. to turn red.

a·rre·ciar intr. (*empeorarse*) to worsen; (*el tiempo*) to blow *or* rain harder.

a·rre·ci·fe m. reef.

a·rre·drar tr. to scare *or* frighten away —reflex. to be scared *or* frightened.

a·rre·gla·do, a adj. orderly, neat.

a·rre·glar tr. (*ordenar*) to put in order; (*acomodar*) to tidy up; (*ajustar*) to fix up; (*reparar*) to repair; (*solucionar*) to resolve; MUS. to arrange; ARG., MEX. to settle (a debt) ♦ **¡ya te arreglaré yo!** I'll fix you! —reflex. (*conformarse*) to adjust; (*ataviarse*) to get dressed (up) ♦ **arreglárselas** COLL. to manage.

a·rre·glo m. (*acción*) arrangement; (*orden*) order; (*convenio*) understanding; (*compostura*) repair; MUS. arrangement ♦ **con a.** in accordance with.

a·rre·lla·nar·se reflex. to lounge.

a·rre·man·gado, a adj. turned up

a·rre·man·gar §47 tr. (*levantar*) to lift *or* tuck up; (*las mangas*) to roll up —reflex. COLL. to become determined.

a·rre·me·dar tr. to imitate, copy.

a·rre·me·te·dor, ra adj. & m.f. COLL. determined, resolute (person).

a·rre·me·ter tr. (*atacar*) to attack; COLL. (*emprender*) to go at.

a·rre·me·ti·da f. (*ataque*) assault; (*empujón*) shove.

a·rre·mo·li·nar·se reflex. (*apiñarse*) to crowd about; (*el agua*) to swirl.

a·rren·da·dor, ra m.f. (*propietario*) landlord; (*inquilino*) tenant.

a·rren·da·mien·to m. (*acción*) rental; (*alquiler*) rent.

a·rren·dar §49 tr. (*alquilar*) to rent; (*atar*) to tie up, hitch (horses).

a·rren·da·ta·rio, a I. adj. renting II. m.f. tenant.

a·rre·o m. AMER. herd, drove ♦ pl. harness.

a·rre·pen·ti·mien·to m. repentance.

a·rre·pen·tir·se §65 reflex. to repent; FIG. to regret.

a·rres·ta·do, a adj. arrested.

a·rres·tar tr. to arrest, place under arrest.

a·rres·to m. (*detención*) arrest; (*reclusión*) imprisonment; (*audacia*) boldness.

a·rriar §30 tr. MARIT. to lower; (*aflojar*) to slacken.

a·rri·ba adv. above; (*en una casa*) upstairs; (*en lo alto*) overhead ♦ **¡a.!** (*para animar*) get up!, come on!; (*para victorear*) hurrah for ...! ♦ **a. citado** abovementioned • **de a.** from above; AMER., COLL. free, gratis • **de a. abajo** COLL. (*de cabo a rabo*) from top to bottom; (*desde el principio al fin*) from beginning to end; (*completamente*) from head to foot • **más a.** higher *or* farther up • **para a.** upwards, up.

a·rri·bar intr. to arrive ♦ **a.** to a manage to.

a·rri·be·ño, a AMER. I. adj. highland II. m.f. highlander.

a·rri·bis·ta I. adj. social-climbing II. m.f. social climber.

a·rri·bo m. arrival.

a·rrien·de, do see **arrendar.**

a·rrien·do m. (*acción*) renting; (*precio*) rent; (*contrato*) lease.

a·rrie·ro m. muleteer.

a·rries·ga·do, a adj. (*peligroso*) risky; (*audaz*) daring.

a·rries·gar §47 tr. to risk, venture ♦ **a. el pellejo** to risk one's neck —reflex. to risk.

a·rri·mar tr. to bring *or* draw near; (*arrinconar*) to ignore ♦ **a. el hombro** to lend a hand —reflex. to lean; (*juntarse*) to join together; COLL. (*vivir juntos*) to shack up ♦ **a. al sol que más calienta** COLL. to know which side one's bread is buttered on.

a·rri·mo m. (*sostén*) support; (*pared*) partition.

a·rrin·co·na·do, a adj. (*apartado*) distant; (*desatendido*) neglected.

a·rrin·co·nar tr. (*en un rincón*) to put in a corner; (*acorralar*) to corner; (*abandonar*) to neglect —reflex. to withdraw.

a·rris·ca·mien·to m. daring, boldness.

a·rris·car §70 AMER. tr. to turn up, fold up —reflex. to dress up.

a·rrit·mia f. lack of rhythm; MED. arrhythmia.

a·rro·ba·do, a adj. enraptured.

a·rro·ba·mien·to m. ecstasy, rapture.

a·rro·bar tr. to enrapture —reflex. (*extasiarse*) to be enraptured.

a·rro·ce·ro, a I. adj. rice II. m.f. rice grower.

a·rro·di·llar tr. to make (someone) kneel —reflex. to kneel (down).

a·rro·gan·cia f. arrogance.

a·rro·gan·te adj. arrogant.

a·rro·gar §47 tr. (*atribuir*) to arrogate; (*adoptar*) to adopt —reflex. to arrogate to oneself.

a·rro·ja·do, a adj. (*atrevido*) bold; (*resuelto*) resolute.

a·rro·jar tr. to hurl, fling; (*emitir*) to emit; (*vomitar*) to throw up; COM. to show —reflex. to throw *or* hurl oneself; (*resolverse*) to rush ♦ **a. sobre** to rush at, attack.

a·rro·jo m. (*atrevimiento*) boldness; (*resolución*) resoluteness.

a·rro·lla·dor, ra adj. overwhelming.

a·rro·llar tr. (*envolver*) to roll up; (*llevar*) to sweep *or* carry away <*el agua arrolla la arena* the water sweeps away the sand>; (*atropellar*) to trample; (*derrotar*) to crush.

a·rro·par tr. (*cubrir*) to wrap with clothes; (*acostar*) to tuck in (to bed) —reflex. (*cubrirse*) to wrap up *or* clothe oneself; (*acostarse*) to tuck oneself in.

a·rro·rró/ú m. AMER., COLL. lullaby.

a·rros·trar tr. & reflex. to face (up to).

a·rro·yo m. brook; (*cuneta*) gutter.

a·rroz m. rice ♦ **a. con leche** rice pudding.

a·rro·zal m. rice field *or* paddy.

a·rru·ga f. (*en la piel*) wrinkle, line; (*en la ropa*) wrinkle, crease; GEOL. ruga, fold.

a·rru·ga·do, a adj. wrinkled.

a·rru·gar §47 tr. (*fruncir*) to wrinkle; (*hacer arrugas*) to wrinkle, crease; (*papel*) to crumple ♦ **a. el entrecejo** to frown —reflex. to wrinkle, become wrinkled; (*plegarse*) to become wrinkled *or* creased; (*apañuscarse*) to become crumpled (up).

a·rrui·nar tr. to ruin; FIG. to destroy —reflex. to fall into ruin.

a·rru·lla·dor, ra adj. soothing.

a·rru·llar tr. to coo; (*adormecer*) to lull *or* sing to sleep; (*enamorar*) to woo.

a·rru·llo m. ORNITH. cooing; MUS. lullaby.

a·rru·ma·co m. *(abrazo)* caress; *(zalamería)* flattery ♦ pl. endearments • **andar con a.** to flatter.

a·rrum·bar tr. *(desechar)* to cast or put aside; *(arrinconar)* to neglect.

a·rru·rruz m. arrowroot.

ar·se·nal m. *(astillero)* shipyard; MIL. arsenal; *(depósito)* storehouse.

ar·sé·ni·co m. arsenic.

ar·te m. or f. art; *(habilidad)* art, skill ♦ **bellas artes** fine arts • **con a.** skillfully, cleverly • **no tener ni a. ni parte** to have nothing to do with • **por amor al a.** for free • **por a. de magia** as if by magic.

ar·te·fac·to m. *(aparato)* appliance; ARCHEOL. artifact.

ar·te·ria f. artery.

ar·te·rial adj. arterial.

ar·te·rios·cle·ro·sis f. arteriosclerosis.

ar·te·ro, a adj. cunning, sly.

ar·te·sa·na·do m. *(artesanos)* craftsmen; *(arte)* artisanship.

ar·te·sa·nal adj. artisan, pertaining to craftsmen or artisans.

ar·te·sa·ní·a f. *(habilidad)* craftsmanship; *(producto)* crafts.

ar·te·sa·no, a m.f. artisan, craftsman —f. craftswoman.

ar·te·sia·no, a adj. artesian.

ár·ti·co, a adj. & m. Arctic.

ar·ti·cu·la·ción f. ANAT., MECH. joint; *(pronunciación)* enunciation ♦ **a. esférica** ball-and-socket joint • **a. giratoria** swivel joint.

ar·ti·cu·la·do, a I. adj. articulate II. m. articles.

ar·ti·cu·lar[1] adj. ANAT. articular, of the joints.

ar·ti·cu·lar[2] tr. *(pronunciar)* to enunciate; *(dividir)* to divide into articles; MECH. to join.

ar·tí·cu·lo m. article; *(cosa)* item, thing; *(escrito)* essay; *(en un diccionario)* entry; GRAM. article; ANAT. joint; LAW section ♦ **a. de fondo** JOURN. editorial • **a. de primera necesidad** basic commodity ♦ pl. goods • **a. de consumo** consumer goods • **a. de tocador** toiletries.

ar·tí·fi·ce m.f. artisan; FIG. architect.

ar·ti·fi·cial adj. artificial.

ar·ti·fi·cia·li·dad f. artificiality.

ar·ti·fi·cio m. *(habilidad)* ability; *(aparato)* device; *(ardid)* trick.

ar·ti·fi·cio·so, a adj. ingenious; FIG. cunning.

ar·ti·lu·gio m. *(aparato)* contraption; *(trampa)* gimmick.

ar·ti·lle·rí·a f. artillery.

ar·ti·lle·ro m. artillery soldier.

ar·ti·ma·ña f. *(trampa)* trick; *(astucia)* cunning.

ar·tis·ta m.f. artist; *(actor, actriz)* actor, actress ♦ **a. invitado** guest artist.

ar·tís·ti·co, a adj. artistic.

ar·trí·ti·co, a adj. & m.f. arthritic.

ar·tri·tis f. MED. arthritis.

ar·ve·ja f. *(algarroba)* (spring) vetch, tare; AMER. green pea.

ar·zo·bis·po m. archbishop.

as m. ace.

a·sa f. handle ♦ **en asas** akimbo.

a·sa·do m. *(carne)* roasted meat; AMER. barbecued meat; *(comida)* cookout, barbecue.

a·sa·dor m. *(varilla)* spit; *(aparato)* grill.

a·sa·la·ria·do, a I. adj. salaried II. m.f. salaried worker.

a·sa·la·riar tr. to set a salary for.

a·sal·ta·dor, **·ra/tan·te** m.f. assailant.

a·sal·tar tr. *(atacar)* to assault; *(sobrevenir)* to overtake.

a·sal·to m. *(ataque)* assault; *(fiesta)* surprise party; *(en el boxeo)* round; *(en la esgrima)* bout.

a·sam·ble·a f. *(reunión)* meeting; *(congreso)* conference.

a·sam·ble·ís·ta m.f. member of an assembly.

a·sar tr. to roast ♦ **a. al horno** to bake • **a. a la parrilla** to broil —reflex. FIG. to roast.

as·cen·den·cia f. ancestry.

as·cen·den·te I. adj. ascending, upward II. m. ASTROL. ascendant.

as·cen·der §50 intr. to rise; *(de categoría)* to be promoted ♦ **a.** to amount to, reach —tr. to promote.

as·cen·dien·te I. adj. ascending II. m.f. ancestor —m. influence.

as·cen·sión f. ascension, rise.

as·cen·so m. *(adelanto)* promotion; *(subida)* ascent, rise.

as·cen·sor m. elevator, lift (G.B.) ♦ **a. de carga** freight elevator.

as·cen·so·ris·ta m.f. elevator operator.

as·ce·ta m.f. ascetic.

as·cé·ti·co, a I. adj. ascetic II. f. asceticism.

as·cien·da, do see **ascender**.

as·co m. disgust, revulsion ♦ **dar a.** COLL. to sicken or disgust • **estar hecho un a.** COLL. to be filthy • **ser un a.** COLL. to be disgusting or worthless.

as·cua f. ember ♦ **estar en ascuas** COLL. to be on edge.

a·se·a·do, a adj. *(limpio)* clean; *(ordenado)* neat, tidy.

a·se·ar tr. *(lavar)* to wash; *(limpiar)* to clean; *(ordenar)* to tidy (up) —reflex. *(lavarse)* to wash (up); *(limpiarse)* to clean (up); *(ordenarse)* to tidy (up).

a·se·char tr. to trap, snare.

a·se·diar tr. *(sitiar)* to besiege; *(importunar)* to pester.

a·se·dio m. siege.

a·se·gu·ra·do, a I. adj. insured II. m.f. insured (person), policyholder.

a·se·gu·ra·dor, **·ra** I. adj. insuring, assuring II. m. insurance company —m.f. insurance agent.

a·se·gu·rar tr. *(afirmar)* to secure; *(garantizar)* to guarantee; *(tranquilizar)* to assure; COM. to insure —reflex. *(cerciorarse)* to make sure; COM. to take out insurance.

a·se·me·jar tr. *(hacer semejante)* to make alike or similar; *(comparar)* to compare —reflex. to resemble.

a·sen·ta·de·ras f.pl. COLL. behind, buttocks.

a·sen·ta·do, a adj. *(juicioso)* judicious; *(estable)* stable.

a·sen·tar §49 tr. *(anotar)* to record; *(fundar)* to found; *(colocar)* to place; *(afirmar)* to affirm; *(aplanar)* to level; COM. to enter; MEX. to sadden; ARG. to iron —intr. to suit —reflex. *(establecerse)* to establish oneself; *(las aves)* to perch; *(los líquidos)* to settle; ARCHIT. to settle.

a·sen·ti·mien·to m. consent, assent.

a·sen·tir §65 intr. to assent, agree ♦ **a. con la cabeza** to nod (one's approval).

a·se·o m. *(limpieza)* cleanliness; *(orden)* neatness, tidiness.

a·se·qui·ble adj. *(accesible)* accessible; *(posible)* feasible; *(comprensible)* understandable.

a·ser·ción f. assertion, affirmation.

a·se·rra·de·ro m. sawmill.

a·se·rra·do, a I. adj. serrated II. m. sawing.

a·se·rrar §49 tr. to saw.

a·se·rrín m. sawdust.

a·se·si·nar tr. to murder; POL. to assassinate.

a·se·si·na·to m. murder; POL. assassination.

a·se·si·no, a I. adj. murderous II. m.f. killer, murderer; POL. assassin.

a·se·sor, ·ra I. adj. advising, advisory II. m.f. adviser, counselor.

a·se·so·ra·mien·to m. *(acción)* advising; *(consejo)* advice.

a·se·so·rar tr. to advise —reflex. to seek advice.

a·se·so·rí·a f. consultant's office.

a·ses·tar tr. *(arma)* to aim; *(balazo)* to fire; *(golpe)* to deal.

a·se·ve·ra·ción f. asseveration, assertion.

a·se·ve·rar tr. to asseverate, assert.

a·se·ve·ra·ti·vo, a adj. assertive, affirmative.

a·se·xua·do, a/xual adj. asexual.

as·fal·ta·do, a I. adj. paved II. m. asphalt.

as·fal·tar tr. to asphalt.

as·fal·to m. asphalt.

as·fi·xia f. asphyxia, suffocation.

as·fi·xiar tr. to asphyxiate —reflex. to suffocate.

as·ga, go see **asir**.

a·sí I. adv. *(de esta manera)* so, this way; *(de esa manera)* that way, like that; *(tanto)* so, in such a way • **a.** a. so-so, fair • **a. como** as soon as • **a. de (grande)** so (big) • **a. no más** just like that • **a. sea** so be it • **a. y todo** even so, just the same • **o algo a.** or thereabouts, or something like that • **y a.** thus, and so • **y a. sucesivamente** and so on, and so forth II. conj. *(en consecuencia)* therefore, thus; *(aunque)* even if, even though • **a. pues** therefore, and so III. adj. such.

a·si·de·ro m. *(asa)* handle; ARG. basis.

a·si·dui·dad f. assiduousness.

a·si·duo, a adj. *(persistente)* assiduous; *(frecuente)* frequent.

a·sien·ta, te, to see **asentar** or **asentir**.

a·sien·to m. seat; *(silla)* chair; *(sitio)* site; *(poso)* sediment; *(empacho)* indigestion; *(trasero)* behind; *(estabilidad)* stability; ARCHIT. settling; COM. entry.

a·sie·rre, rro see **aserrar**.

a·sig·na·ción f. *(distribución)* allotment; *(cita)* appointment; *(salario)* salary.

a·sig·nar tr. *(señalar)* to assign; *(nombrar)* to appoint.

a·sig·na·tu·ra f. subject, course (in school) • **aprobar una a.** to pass a course.

a·si·lar tr. *(albergar)* to place in an asylum; *(refugiar)* to give shelter; POL. to give political asylum —reflex. *(albergarse)* to enter an asylum; *(refugiarse)* to take refuge; POL. to seek political asylum.

a·si·lo m. asylum; *(establecimiento)* home; *(refugio)* shelter • **a. de ancianos** old folks' home • **a. de huérfanos** orphanage • **a. de locos** insane asylum • **a. de pobres** poorhouse • **dar a.** to shelter.

a·si·mé·tri·co, a adj. asymmetric.

a·si·mi·la·ción f. assimilation.

a·si·mi·lar tr. to assimilate —reflex. to be similar.

a·si·mis·mo adj. *(igualmente)* likewise, in like manner; *(también)* also, too.

a·sin·tie·ra, tió see **asentir**.

a·sir §08 tr. & intr. to grasp —reflex. • **a. de** to avail oneself of.

a·sis·ten·cia f. *(concurrencia)* attendance; *(ayuda)* aid; MEX. parlor • **a. pública** AMER. health clinic.

a·sis·ten·cial adj. assisting, relief.

a·sis·ten·te, a I. adj. assisting II. m.f. *(ayudante)* assistant —m. MIL. aide.

a·sis·tir intr. to attend —tr. *(acompañar)* to accompany; *(ayudar)* to aid; *(cuidar)* to nurse.

as·ma f. asthma.

as·má·ti·co, a adj. & m.f. asthmatic.

as·na·da f. COLL. stupidity.

as·no m. donkey; FIG. jackass.

a·so·cia·ción f. association • **a. gremial** trade union • **a. sindical** labor union.

a·so·cia·do, a I. adj. associated II. m.f. associate.

a·so·ciar tr. *(ligar)* to connect; *(combinar)* to combine —reflex. to become partners • **a. a** or **con** to join.

a·so·la·dor, ·ra adj. ravaging.

a·so·lar[1] tr. AGR. to scorch, parch.

a·so·lar[2] §19 tr. to ravage —reflex. CHEM. to settle.

a·so·le·a·mien·to m. sunstroke.

a·so·le·ar tr. to put out in the sun —reflex. *(tomar el sol)* to sun oneself; *(tostarse)* to become tanned; *(sofocarse)* to suffer heat suffocation.

a·so·ma·da f. *(aparición)* brief appearance; *(atalaya)* vantage point.

a·so·mar intr. to appear —tr. to show —reflex. *(mostrarse)* to show oneself, appear; *(una ventana)* to look or lean out.

a·som·bra·dor, ·ra adj. amazing, astonishing.

a·som·brar tr. *(sorprender)* to amaze, astonish; *(oscurecer)* to darken, make darker (colors) —reflex. to be amazed or astonished.

a·som·bro m. *(sorpresa)* amazement; *(maravilla)* marvel.

a·som·bro·so, a adj. amazing, astonishing.

a·so·mo m. *(mirada)* look; *(señal)* hint • **ni un a. de** not the least bit of • **ni por a.** no way.

a·so·nan·cia f. POET., RHET. assonance; PHONET. consonance.

as·pa f. *(cruz)* X-shaped cross; *(devanadera)* spool; *(de molinos)* blade.

as·par tr. *(hilo)* to reel; *(crucificar)* to crucify.

as·pa·ven·tar §49 tr. to frighten, scare.

as·pa·ven·te·ro/to·so, a adj. effusive, theatrical.

as·pa·vien·tar·se reflex. C. AMER. to become frightened or alarmed.

as·pa·vien·to m. exaggerated behavior, theatricality • **hacer aspavientos** to make a fuss.

as·pec·to m. aspect.

as·pe·re·za f. *(escabrosidad)* ruggedness; *(brusquedad)* gruffness.

ás·pe·ro, a adj. *(rugoso)* rough; *(escabroso)* rugged; *(brusco)* gruff.

as·per·sión f. sprinkling • **sistema de a. automática** (automatic) sprinkling system.

as·pi·ra·ción f. PHYSIOL. inhalation; *(anhelo)* aspiration; *(succión)* suction; PHONET. aspiration.

as·pi·ra·do, a adj. PHONET. aspirated.

as·pi·ra·dor, ·ra I. adj. aspirating; MECH. sucking **II.** m. MECH., MED. aspirator; MECH. suction pump —f. vacuum cleaner.

as·pi·ran·te m.f. candidate.

as·pi·rar tr. to inhale; MECH. *(atraer)* to suck, draw in; PHONET. *(pronunciar)* to aspirate ♦ **a. a** to aspire to.

as·pi·ri·na f. aspirin.

as·que·ar tr. to disgust —intr. to be disgusting.

as·que·ro·si·dad f. *(suciedad)* filth; *(vileza)* vileness.

as·que·ro·so, a adj. *(repugnante)* repulsive; *(sucio)* filthy.

as·ta f. *(lanza)* spear; *(de lanza)* shaft; *(de bandera)* flagpole; *(mango)* handle; *(cuerno)* horn, antler ♦ **a media a.** at half-staff.

as·te·ris·co m. asterisk.

as·te·roi·de I. m. asteroid **II.** adj. asteroidal.

as·tig·má·ti·co, a adj. astigmatic.

as·tig·ma·tis·mo m. astigmatism.

as·ti·lla f. splinter ♦ **hacer astillas** to splinter.

as·ti·llar tr. to chip, splinter.

as·ti·lle·ro m. MARIT. shipyard; COM. lumberyard.

as·tra·cán m. astrakhan, astrachan.

as·trin·gen·cia f. astringency.

as·trin·gen·te adj. & m. astringent.

as·trin·gir §32 tr. to astringe, contract.

as·tro. m. star.

as·tro·fí·si·co, a I. adj. astrophysical **II.** m.f. astrophysicist —f. astrophysics.

as·tro·lo·gí·a f. astrology.

as·tro·ló·gi·co, a adj. astrological.

as·tró·lo·go, a I. m.f. astrologist **II.** adj. astrological.

as·tro·nau·ta m.f. astronaut, cosmonaut.

as·tro·náu·ti·ca f. astronautics.

as·tro·na·ve f. spaceship, spacecraft.

as·tro·no·mí·a f. astronomy.

as·tro·nó·mi·co, a adj. astronomic; FIG. astronomical.

as·tró·no·mo, a m.f. astronomer.

as·tu·cia f. *(listeza)* astuteness; *(ardid)* trick.

as·tu·to, a adj. *(listo)* astute, clever; *(mañoso)* crafty, shrewd.

a·sue·le, lo see **asolar²**.

a·sue·to m. holiday ♦ **día de a.** day off, holiday.

a·su·mir tr. to assume, take on.

a·sun·ción f. assumption.

a·sun·tar intr. DOM. REP. to pay attention; C. AMER. to investigate, pry.

a·sun·to m. *(tópico)* topic; *(tema)* subject matter; *(argumento)* plot; COLL. *(amorío)* love affair ♦ **a. pendiente** unresolved matter • **el a. es que...** the fact is that... ♦ **ir al a.** to get down to business ♦ pl. business • **tener muchos a. entre manos** to have many matters to deal with.

a·sus·ta·dizo, a adj. easily frightened, skittish.

a·sus·tar tr. to frighten, scare —reflex. to be frightened *or* scared *(de, por, con* by).

a·ta·ba·ca·do, a adj. tobacco-colored.

a·ta·be m. pipe vent.

a·ta·blar tr. AGR. to level.

a·ta·ca·dor, ·ra/can·te I. adj. attacking, assaulting **II.** m.f. attacker.

a·ta·ca·du·ra f./**mien·to** m. fastening.

a·ta·car §70 tr. to attack; *(abrochar)* to fasten; *(criticar)* to criticize; *(iniciar)* to start work on; ARM. to pack *or* tamp down; CHEM. to corrode.

a·ta·de·ras f.pl. COLL. garters.

a·ta·de·ro m. tie, fastener; *(aro)* loop.

a·ta·do, a I. adj. timid **II.** m. *(manojo)* bundle; ARG. cigarette pack.

a·ta·du·ra f. *(acción)* tying; *(cuerda)* cord; *(traba)* restriction.

a·ta·ja·da f. AMER., SPORT. catch.

a·ta·jar tr. *(detener)* to intercept; *(impedir)* to halt; *(interrumpir)* to interrupt, cut off; *(contener)* to stop; AMER. *(tomar)* to catch (in midair) ♦ **a. un golpe** AMER. to parry a blow —intr. to take a short cut.

a·ta·jo m. short cut.

a·ta·la·ya f. *(torre)* observation tower; *(altura)* vantage point —m. guard.

a·ta·ñer §68 intr. to concern, pertain.

a·ta·que m. attack ♦ **a. aéreo** air raid.

a·tar tr. to tie, fasten ♦ **a. cabos** to put two and two together.

a·tar·de·cer §17 **I.** intr. to get dark **II.** m. late afternoon, dusk ♦ **al a.** at dusk.

a·ta·re·ar tr. to assign work to —reflex. to busy *or* occupy oneself.

a·ta·ru·gar §47 tr. *(asegurar)* to pin; *(tapar)* to plug —reflex. COLL. to stuff oneself.

a·ta·sa·jar tr. to jerk (beef).

a·tas·ca·de·ro m. bog; FIG. stumbling block.

a·tas·ca·mien·to m. obstruction; FIG. obstacle.

a·tas·car §70 tr. *(obstruir)* to clog; *(impedir)* to hamper —reflex. *(estancarse)* to get stuck *or* clogged.

a·tas·co m. obstruction; FIG. obstacle.

a·ta·úd m. coffin, casket.

a·ta·viar §30 tr. to adorn, deck out.

a·tá·vi·co, a adj. atavistic.

a·ta·ví·o m. *(adorno)* decoration; *(vestido)* attire ♦ pl. finery, trappings.

a·ta·vis·mo m. atavism, intermittent heredity.

a·ta·xia f. ataxia, ataxy.

a·te·mo·ri·zar §04 tr. to frighten —reflex. to be frightened *(de, por* by).

a·tem·pe·ra·ción f. tempering.

a·tem·pe·rar tr. *(moderar)* to temper; *(adecuar)* to adjust.

a·te·na·ce·ar/zar §04 tr. to torture by tearing off the flesh with pincers; FIG. to torture.

a·ten·ción f. attention ♦ **llamar la a.** *(atraer)* to catch the eye; *(reprender)* to reprimand • **prestar a.** to pay attention ♦ pl. courtesies.

a·ten·der §50 tr. *(hacer caso de)* to pay attention to; *(tener en cuenta)* keep in mind; *(cuidar)* to take care of; *(obedecer)* to heed; COM. to wait on —intr. to pay attention.

a·te·ne·o m. athenaeum.

a·te·ner·se §69 reflex. ♦ **a. a** *(adherirse a)* to rely on; *(sujetarse)* to abide by ♦ **no saber a qué a.** FIG. not to know which way to turn.

a·ten·ta·do m. *(crimen)* crime; *(ataque)* attempt.

a·ten·tar §49 tr. to attempt to commit —intr. to make an attempt.

a·ten·to, a I. see **atender II.** adj. *(observador)* attentive; *(cortés)* considerate ♦ **a. a** in view of.

a·te·nua·ción f. attenuation.

a·te·nuan·te adj. attenuating; LAW extenuating.

a·te·nuar §67 tr. to attenuate; LAW to extenuate.

a·te·o, a I. adj. atheistic **II.** m.f. atheist.

a·ter·cio·pe·la·do, a adj. velvety.

a·te·ri·do, a adj. numb with cold.

a·te·rir·se §38 reflex. to be numb with cold.

a·te·rra·dor, ·ra adj. terrifying.

a·te·rrar[1] §49 tr. (echar por tierra) to knock down; (derribar) to destroy, demolish —intr. AVIA. to land; MARIT. to stand inshore.

a·te·rrar[2] tr. to terrify.

a·te·rri·za·je m. landing ♦ a. a ciegas blind landing ♦ a. forzoso emergency landing.

a·te·rri·zar §04 intr. to land.

a·te·rro·ri·za·dor, ·ra adj. terrifying.

a·te·rro·ri·zar §04 tr. to terrorize.

a·te·so·ra·mien·to m. hoarding.

a·te·so·rar tr. to store up; FIG. to possess.

a·tes·ta·ción f. affidavit, deposition.

a·tes·ta·do, a adj. full to the rim.

a·tes·ta·du·ra f./mien·to m. cramming.

a·tes·tar[1] §49 tr. to stuff.

a·tes·tar[2] tr. to attest, witness.

a·tes·ti·gua·ción f./mien·to m. attestation.

a·tes·ti·guar §10 tr. to attest.

a·te·za·do, a adj. (bronceado) suntanned; (negro) black.

a·te·zar §04 tr. & reflex. to tan.

a·ti·bo·rra·mien·to m. cramming.

a·ti·bo·rrar tr. to cram —reflex. COLL. to stuff oneself.

á·ti·co, a I. adj. HIST., LIT. Attic II. m.f. HIST. (persona) Attic —m. (idioma) Attic; ARCHIT. Attic.

a·tien·da, do see atender.

a·tie·ne see atenerse.

a·tien·te, to see atentar.

a·tie·sar tr. to stiffen, harden.

a·ties·te, to see atestar[1].

a·ti·gra·do, a adj. tiger-striped.

a·til·da·do, a adj. neat.

a·til·da·du·ra f./mien·to m. neatness.

a·til·dar tr. & reflex. to spruce up.

a·ti·nar tr. (encontrar) to find; (acertar) to hit upon ♦ a. a to manage to, succeed in.

a·ti·ran·tar tr. to make taut.

a·tis·bar tr. to watch.

a·tis·bo m. (acecho) watching; (indicio) glimmer.

a·ti·za·dor m. poker (tool).

a·ti·zar §04 tr. (el fuego) to poke; (avivar) to arouse; COLL. (pegar) to strike.

a·ti·zo·nar tr. (un muro) to bond; (un madero) to embed.

at·las m.inv. atlas.

at·le·ta m.f. athlete.

at·lé·ti·co, a adj. athletic.

at·mós·fe·ra f. atmosphere.

at·mos·fé·ri·co, a adj. atmospheric.

a·to·ci·nar tr. (un cerdo) to cut up; (tocino) to make into bacon; COLL. (asesinar) to murder.

a·to·char tr. (de esparto) to fill with esparto; (rellenar) to stuff.

a·to·lon·dra·do, a adj. (impulsivo) reckless; (turbado) bewildered.

a·to·lon·dra·mien·to m. (irreflexión) recklessness; (aturdimiento) bewilderment.

a·to·lon·drar tr. to bewilder —reflex. to be bewildered.

a·to·lla·de·ro m. bog; FIG. obstruction ♦ estar en un a. to be in a fix or jam.

a·to·llar intr. to get stuck in the mud —reflex. COLL. to be stuck in a situation.

a·tó·mi·co, a adj. atomic.

a·to·mis·ta m.f. PHILOS. atomist.

a·to·mi·za·dor m. atomizer, sprayer.

a·to·mi·zar §04 tr. to atomize, pulverize.

á·to·mo m. atom; FIG. iota ♦ á. fisionado split atom.

a·to·nal adj. atonal.

a·to·na·li·dad f. atonality, tonelessness.

a·to·ní·a f. atony.

a·tó·ni·to, a adj. astonished, amazed.

á·to·no, a adj. atonic.

a·ton·ta·mien·to m. (embrutecimiento) stupefaction; (aturdimiento) confusion.

a·ton·tar tr. (embrutecer) to stun; (aturdir) to confuse.

a·to·ra·mien·to m. obstruction, blockage.

a·to·rar tr. to clog —reflex. to choke.

a·tor·men·ta·dor, ·ra adj. (afligente) tormenting; (preocupante) worrisome.

a·tor·men·tar tr. to torment; (torturar) to torture —reflex. to worry.

a·tor·ni·llar tr. to screw in or on.

a·to·ro m. blockage, obstruction.

a·to·rran·te m. R.P., COLL. bum.

a·tor·to·lar tr. COLL. to confuse —reflex. ARG. to fall in love.

a·to·si·ga·dor, ·ra adj. poisonous, toxic.

a·to·si·ga·mien·to m. poisoning; FIG. pressing.

a·to·si·gar §47 tr. to poison; FIG. to press —reflex. to get flustered.

a·tó·xi·co, a adj. nontoxic.

a·tra·bi·lis f.inv. black bile; FIG. bad temper.

a·tra·ca·de·ro m. pier, dock.

a·tra·car §70 tr. (asaltar) to hold up; COLL. (hartar) to stuff; MARIT. to bring alongside —intr. MARIT. to dock —reflex. to stuff oneself.

a·trac·ción f. attraction ♦ sentir a. por to feel attracted to.

a·tra·co m. holdup, robbery.

a·tra·cón m. COLL. (comida) big feed; AMER. brawl.

a·trac·ti·vo, a I. adj. attractive II. m. (encanto) charm; (aliciente) attraction.

a·tra·er §72 tr. to attract.

a·tra·gan·ta·mien·to m. choking, gagging.

a·tra·gan·tar·se reflex. COLL. to get tongue-tied ♦ a. con to choke on.

a·trai·ga, go see atraer.

a·trai·llar tr. to leash; FIG. to hold in check.

a·trai·mien·to m. attraction.

a·tra·je·ra, jo see atraer.

a·tran·car §70 tr. (cerrar) to bolt; (obstruir) to block —reflex. MEX. to be stubborn.

a·tran·co/que m. obstruction; FIG. jam.

a·tra·pa·mos·cas f.inv. Venus's-flytrap.

a·tra·par tr. COLL. (apresar) to catch; (conseguir) to land; (engañar) to take in.

a·tra·que m. MARIT. mooring; ASTRONAUT. docking, link-up; ARM. packing.

a·trás adv. back, behind; (antes) back, ago ♦ ¡a! get back! • dar marcha a. AUTO. to back up • ir hacia a. to go backward.

a·tra·sa·do, a adj. (reloj) slow; (persona) late; (cuenta) in arrears; (revista) back; (país) underdeveloped ♦ a. de noticias behind the times.

a·tra·sar tr. (retardar) to delay; (reloj) to set back —intr. to be slow —reflex. to be late.

a·tra·so m. delay; (retraso) tardiness ♦ a. mental mental retardation ♦ pl. arrears.

a·tra·ve·sa·do, a adj. (bizco) cross-eyed; (confuso) incongruous; ZOOL. crossbred.

a·tra·ve·sar §49 tr. (pasar) to cross (over); (poner oblicuo) to put or lay across; (traspasar) to pierce —reflex. *(obstruir)* to block; *(reñir)* to quarrel.

a·tra·yen·do see **atraer.**

a·tra·yen·te adj. attractive.

a·tre·guar §10 tr. to grant (a truce).

a·tre·ver·se reflex. to dare ♦ **a. a** to dare to • **a. con** *or* **contra** *(descararse)* to be disrespectful to; *(retar)* to take on.

a·tre·vi·do, a I. see **atreverse** II. adj. *(osado)* bold; *(descarado)* impudent III. m.f. *(temerario)* bold person; *(caradura)* insolent person.

a·tre·vi·mien·to m. *(osadía)* boldness; *(insolencia)* rudeness.

a·tri·bu·ción f. attribution; *(función)* duty ♦ pl. authority.

a·tri·bui·ble adj. attributable.

a·tri·buir §18 tr. *(otorgar)* to credit; *(imputar)* to grant —reflex. to take credit for.

a·tri·bu·lar tr. to distress, afflict —reflex. to become distressed.

a·tri·bu·ti·vo, a adj. attributive.

a·tri·bu·to m. attribute; *(símbolo)* symbol; GRAM., LOG. *(predicado)* predicate.

a·tri·bu·ya, ye·ra, yo, yó see **atribuir.**

a·tril m. lectern.

a·trin·che·rar tr. to surround with trenches —reflex. to entrench oneself, dig in.

a·trio m. *(patio)* atrium; *(andén)* portico; *(entrada)* vestibule.

a·tri·to, a adj. THEOL. repentant.

a·tro·ci·dad f. atrocity; FIG. enormity.

a·tro·fia f. atrophy.

a·tro·fia·do, a adj. atrophied, atrophic.

a·tro·fiar tr. & reflex. to atrophy.

a·tro·na·do, a adj. hasty, reckless.

a·tro·na·dor, ra adj. deafening.

a·tro·nar §19 tr. *(asordar)* to deafen; *(aturdir)* to stun.

a·tro·pe·lla·do, a adj. hasty, hurried.

a·tro·pe·lla·dor, ra I. adj. trampling II. m.f. trampler.

a·tro·pe·lla·mien·to m. var. of **atropello.**

a·tro·pe·llar tr. *(pisotear)* to trample (on); *(derribar)* to run over; *(agraviar)* to bully; *(hacer precipitadamente)* to do hurriedly, rush through; *(agobiar)* to overwhelm, oppress —reflex. to act hastily.

a·tro·pe·llo m. assault; FIG. abuse.

a·troz adj. atrocious; FIG. enormous.

a·true·ne see **atronar.**

a·tuen·do m. attire.

a·tu·far tr. to annoy —reflex. *(oler mal)* to smell bad; *(enfadarse)* to get angry.

a·tún m. tuna (fish), tunny (G.B.).

a·tur·di·do, a adj. *(estupefacto)* stunned; *(turbado)* confused.

a·tur·di·mien·to m. *(choque)* shock; *(turbación)* confusion.

a·tur·dir tr. *(atontar)* to stun; *(turbar)* to confuse.

a·tur·que·sa·do, a adj. turquoise (blue).

a·tu·rru·llar tr. COLL. to baffle —reflex. to become flustered.

a·tu·sar tr. *(recortar)* to trim; *(alisar)* to slick back —reflex. FIG. to spruce up.

a·tu·vie·ra, vo see **atenerse**

au·da·cia f. audacity.

au·daz I. adj. audacious II. m.f. audacious *or* bold person.

au·di·ción f. *(facultad)* hearing; *(programa)* program; THEAT. audition.

au·dien·cia f. audience.

au·dí·fo·no m. *(aparato)* hearing aid; *(auricular)* earphone.

au·dió·me·tro m. audiometer.

au·dio·vi·sual adj. audio-visual.

au·di·ti·vo, a adj. auditive, auditory.

au·di·tor, ra m.f. counselor; COM. auditor.

au·di·to·rí·a f. ACC. *(cargo)* auditorship; *(oficio)* auditing; LAW *(cargo)* office of judge advocate; *(tribunal)* judge advocate's court.

au·di·to·rio m. *(público)* audience; *(sala)* auditorium.

au·ge m. *(apogeo)* peak; COM. boom; ASTRON. apogee.

au·gu·rar tr. to augur, predict.

au·gu·rio m. augury, omen.

au·gus·to, a adj. august.

au·la f. classroom, lecture hall.

au·lla·dor, ra I. adj. howling II. m. ZOOL. howler monkey.

au·llar intr. to howl, wail.

au·lli·do *or* **a·ú·llo** m. howl, wail ♦ **dar aullidos** to howl, wail.

au·men·tar tr. to increase; OPT. to magnify; PHOTOG. to enlarge; RAD. to amplify; *(salario)* to raise —intr. to increase.

au·men·ta·ti·vo, a adj. & m. augmentative.

au·men·to m. increase; OPT. magnification; PHOTOG. enlargement; RAD. amplification; *(de sueldo)* raise ♦ **ir en a.** to be on the increase.

aun adv. even ♦ **a. así** even so • **a. cuando** although, even though.

a·ún adv. still, yet ♦ **a. no** not yet • **más a.** furthermore.

au·nar tr. & reflex. to join, unite.

aun·que conj. *(si bien)* although, even though; *(a pesar de)* even if ♦ **a. más** no matter how much.

au·ra f. aura; *(brisa)* gentle breeze.

áu·re·o, a adj. *(de oro)* gold; *(dorado)* golden.

au·re·o·la f. RELIG. halo; ASTRON. aureole.

au·re·o·la·do, a adj. haloed.

au·re·o·lar tr. to halo; FIG. to exalt.

au·rí·cu·la f. auricle.

au·ri·cu·lar I. adj. auricular II. m. TELEC. earpiece ♦ pl. earphones.

au·rí·fe·ro, a adj. auriferous, gold-bearing.

au·ro·ra f. dawn; FIG. beginning; BOT. sagebrush ♦ **a. austral** southern lights • **a. boreal** northern lights.

aus·cul·ta·ción f. auscultation.

aus·cul·tar tr. to ausculate, diagnose by sound.

au·sen·cia f. absence ♦ **brillar uno por su a.** to be conspicuous by one's absence.

au·sen·tar tr. to send away —reflex. *(alejarse)* to leave.

au·sen·te I. adj. absent; FIG. absent-minded II. m.f. absentee.

au·sen·tis·mo m. absenteeism.

aus·pi·ciar tr. AMER. to sponsor.

aus·pi·cio m. auspice ♦ pl. auspices.

aus·pi·cio·so, a adj. AMER. auspicious.

aus·te·ri·dad f. austerity.

aus·te·ro, a adj. austere.

aus·tral adj. austral, southern.

au·tar·quí·a f. autarchy, autarky.

au·tár·qui·co, a adj. autarchic, autarkic.

au·ten·ti·ca·ción f. authentication.

au·tén·ti·ca·men·te adv. authentically.

au·ten·ti·car §70 tr. to authenticate.

au·ten·ti·ci·dad f. authenticity, genuineness.

au·tén·ti·co, a adj. authentic, genuine.

au·tis·ta adj. autistic.

au·to¹ m. LAW judicial decree *or* ruling; THEAT. short play ♦ pl. LAW case file.

au·to² m. COLL. car, auto.

au·to·ad·he·si·vo, a adj. self-adhesive.

au·to·bio·gra·fí·a f. autobiography.

au·to·bio·grá·fi·co, a adj. autobiographical.

au·to·bús m. bus.

au·to·ca·mión m. truck.

au·to·car m. bus, motorcoach.

au·to·cla·ve f. autoclave.

au·to·cra·cia f. autocracy.

au·tó·cra·ta m.f. autocrat.

au·to·crá·ti·co, a adj. autocratic.

au·to·crí·ti·ca f. self-criticism.

au·tóc·to·no, a adj. & m.f. native.

au·to·des·truc·ción f. self-destruction.

au·to·de·ter·mi·na·ción f. self-determination.

au·to·di·dac·to, a adj. & m.f. self-taught (person).

au·tó·dro·mo m. automobile racetrack.

au·to·en·cen·di·do m. self-ignition.

au·to·fe·cun·da·ción f. BOT. self-fertilization.

au·tó·ge·no, a adj. autogenous.

au·to·gi·ro m. autogiro, autogyro.

au·tó·gra·fo, a I. adj. autographic. II. m. autograph.

au·to·in·duc·ción f. self-induction.

au·to·ma·ción f. automation.

au·tó·ma·ta m. automaton; FIG. robot.

au·to·má·ti·co, a I. adj. automatic II. m. (corchete) snap.

au·to·ma·tis·mo m. automatism.

au·to·ma·ti·za·ción f. automatization.

au·to·ma·ti·zar §04 tr. to automate.

au·to·me·di·car·se §70 reflex. to self-medicate.

au·to·mo·tor, triz adj. automotive.

au·to·mó·vil I. adj. self-propelled II. m. automobile, car ♦ a. de carreras racing car.

au·to·mo·vi·lis·mo m. motoring, (industria) automobile industry ♦ a. deportivo car racing.

au·to·mo·vi·lis·ta m.f. driver, motorist.

au·to·mo·vi·lís·ti·co, a adj. automobile.

au·to·no·mí·a f. autonomy.

au·tó·no·mo, a adj. autonomous.

au·to·pis·ta f. expressway, superhighway.

au·to·pro·pul·sa·do, a adj. self-propelled.

au·to·pro·pul·sión f. self-propulsion.

au·top·sia f. autopsy.

au·tor, ·ra m.f. author; (escritor) writer; (originador) creator; LAW perpetrator —f. authoress.

au·to·ri·dad f. authority; (oficial) official; (experto) expert ♦ con a. authoritatively.

au·to·ri·ta·rio, a adj. (dictatorial) authoritarian; (imperioso) imperious.

au·to·ri·za·ción f. authorization.

au·to·ri·za·do, a adj. (digno de respeto) authoritative; (oficial) authorized.

au·to·ri·zar §04 tr. to authorize; (dar permiso) to permit; (legalizar) to legalize.

au·to·rre·gu·la·ción f. self-regulation.

au·to·rre·tra·to m. self-portrait.

au·to·ser·vi·cio m. self-service.

au·to·stop m. hitchhiking ♦ hacer a. to hitchhike.

au·to·su·fi·cien·cia f. self-sufficiency.

au·to·su·ges·tión f. self-suggestion.

au·to·su·ges·tio·nar·se reflex. to induce in one's own thought.

au·xi·lia·dor, ·ra I. adj. helping II. m.f. helper.

au·xi·liar¹ I. adj. auxiliary II. m.f. (subalterno) assistant; (maestro) assistant teacher —m. GRAM. auxiliary.

au·xi·liar² tr. to assist, aid.

au·xi·lio m. assistance, aid ♦ primeros auxilios first aid.

a·val m. COM. endorsement; (garantía) guarantee ♦ por a. as a guarantee.

a·va·lan·cha f. avalanche.

a·va·lar tr. COM. to endorse; (garantizar) to be the guarantor of.

a·va·lo·rar tr. to appraise; FIG. to encourage.

a·va·luar §67 tr. to appraise.

a·va·lú·o m. appraisal, valuation.

a·van·ce¹ m. advance; COM. balance sheet; MECH. feed; CUBA vomit; MEX. looting.

a·van·ce² m. preview.

a·van·za·do, a adj. advanced.

a·van·zar §04 tr. to advance; CUBA to vomit; MEX. to loot —intr. & reflex. to advance.

a·van·zo m. (balance) balance sheet; (presupuesto) estimate.

a·va·ri·cia f. avarice, greed.

a·va·ri·cio·so/rien·to, a I. adj. (tacaño) avaricious, miserly; (codicioso) greedy II. m.f. (tacaño) miser; (codicioso) greedy person.

a·va·ro, a I. adj. (tacaño) miserly; (codicioso) greedy II. m.f. (tacaño) miser; (codicioso) greedy person.

a·va·sa·lla·dor, ·ra I. adj. subjugating II. m.f. subjugator.

a·va·sa·lla·mien·to m. subjugation.

a·va·sa·llar tr. to subjugate.

a·ve f. bird ♦ a. cantora songbird · a. de corral barnyard fowl · a. de paso wanderer · a. de rapiña bird of prey.

a·ve·cin·dar tr. to domicile; reflex. to settle.

a·ve·jen·tar tr. & reflex. to age prematurely.

a·ve·ji·gar §47 tr. to blister.

a·ve·lla·no, a I. adj. hazel II. m. hazel (tree) f. hazelnut

a·ve·ma·rí·a f. (oración) Hail Mary; (del rosario) small rosary bead ♦ en un a. COLL. in a flash.

¡A·ve Ma·rí·a! interj. good heavens!

a·ve·na f. oat, oats.

a·ve·nen·cia f. (acuerdo) agreement; (arreglo) compromise.

a·ve·ni·ble adj. reconciliable.

a·ve·ni·do, a I. adj. ♦ bien a. in agreement · mal a. in disagreement II.f. (calle) avenue; (desbordamiento) flood.

a·ve·ni·mien·to m. reconciliation.

a·ve·nir §76 tr. to reconcile, conciliate —intr. to happen, occur —reflex. (entenderse) to come to an agreement; (armonizar) to go together.

a·ven·ta·ja·do, a adj. (notable) outstanding, (ventajoso) advantageous.

a·ven·ta·jar tr. (superar) to surpass; (ganar) to beat; (llevar ventaja) to be ahead of.

a·ven·ta·mien·to m. winnowing.

a·ven·tar §49 tr. (echar al aire) to cast to the winds; to winnow (grain); CUBA, MEX., AGR. to dry in the sun.

a·ven·tu·ra f. adventure; (riesgo) risk.

a·ven·tu·ra·do, a adj. adventurous.

a·ven·tu·rar tr. (arriesgar) to risk; (proponer) to venture —reflex. to take a risk.

a·ven·tu·re·ro, a I. adj. adventurous II. m. adventurer —f. adventuress.

a·ver·gon·zar §00 tr. to shame —reflex. to be ashamed (de to, por of).

a·ve·rí·a f. *(daño)* damage; *(rotura)* breakdown.

a·ve·ria·do, a adj. *(estropeado)* damaged; *(echado a perder)* spoiled; *(roto)* broken.

a·ve·riar §30 tr. *(estropear)* to damage; *(echar a perder)* to spoil; *(romper)* to break —reflex. *(estropearse)* to become damaged; *(arruinarse)* to spoil; *(descomponerse)* to break (down).

a·ve·ri·gua·ción f. *(investigación)* investigation; *(verificación)* verification.

a·ve·ri·guar §10 tr. *(comprobar)* to ascertain; *(investigar)* to investigate; *(verificar)* to verify.

a·ve·rru·ga·do, a adj. warty.

a·ve·rru·gar·se §47 reflex. to become warty.

a·ver·sión f. aversion ♦ cobrar *or* coger una a. to develop an aversion to.

a·ves·truz m. ostrich.

a·via·ción f. aviation; MIL. air force.

a·via·dor, ·ra m. pilot, aviator —f. pilot, aviatrix.

a·ví·co·la adj. poultry-breeding.

a·vi·cul·tor, ·ra m.f. chicken farmer.

a·vi·cul·tu·ra f. poultry breeding.

a·vi·dez f. *(ansia)* avidity; *(codicia)* greed ♦ con a. *(ansiosamente)* eagerly; *(avariciosamente)* greedily.

á·vi·do, a adj. *(ansioso)* avid; *(codicioso)* greedy.

a·vien·te, to see aventar.

a·vie·so, a adj. twisted; FIG. perverse.

a·vi·na·gra·do, a adj. sour.

a·vi·na·grar tr. to make sour —reflex. to turn sour; FIG. to become sour.

a·vi·nie·ra, no see avenir.

a·ví·o m. *(provisiones)* provisions; AMER. loan ♦ pl. equipment, materials • a. de pesca fishing tackle.

a·vión m. airplane, plane ♦ a. de caza fighter plane • a. de bombardeo bomber • a. a chorro *or* de reacción jet plane • por a. by air mail.

a·vio·ne·ta f. light airplane.

a·vi·sar tr. *(informar)* to inform; *(advertir)* to warn.

a·vi·so m. *(notificación)* notice; *(advertencia)* warning; *(anuncio)* advertisement; MARIT. dispatch boat ♦ estar sobre a. to be on the alert.

a·vis·pa f. wasp.

a·vis·pa·do, a adj. COLL. clever.

a·vis·par tr. to whip —reflex. COLL. to become quick-witted.

a·vis·pe·ro m. *(panal)* honeycomb; *(nido)* wasps' nest ♦ meterse en un a. to get into a big mess.

a·vis·pón m. hornet.

a·vis·tar tr. to sight.

a·vi·tua·lla·mien·to m. provisioning.

a·vi·tua·llar tr. to provision, supply with food.

a·vi·va·dor, ·ra I adj. livening, reviving II. m. ARCHIT. quirk; CARP. rabbet plane.

a·vi·va·mien·to m. *(animación)* enlivening; *(de colores)* brightening; *(renacimiento)* revival; *(de un fuego)* stoking.

a·vi·var tr. *(animar)* to spur on; *(colores)* to brighten; *(un fuego)* to stoke; *(encender)* to arouse —intr. & reflex. to revive, liven up.

a·vi·zor, ·ra I. adj. watchful ♦ estar ojo a. to keep one's eyes open II. m.f. watcher.

a·vi·zo·rar tr. to watch, spy on.

a·xi·a(l) adj. axial, axal.

a·xi·la f. BOT. axil; ANAT. axilla, armpit.

a·xio·ma m. axiom.

a·xio·má·ti·co, a adj. axiomatic.

¡ay! I. interj. *(dolor)* ow!, ouch!; *(aflicción)* oh dear!, alas!; *(admiración)* oh!, wow! ♦ ¡a. de mí! woe is me! II. m. sigh, moan.

a·yer I. adv. yesterday; *(en el pasado)* formerly, in the past ♦ a. no más only yesterday • de a. a hoy recently II. m. yesterday, past.

a·yo, a m.f. tutor —f. governess.

a·yu·da f. *(auxilio)* help, aid; *(dinero)* financial aid; *(jeringa)* syringe; *(lavativa)* enema; EDUC. partial scholarship; EQUIT. spur ♦ a. de cámara valet.

a·yu·dan·te, a m.f. assistant, aide; MIL. adjutant ♦ a. de campo aide-de-camp.

a·yu·dan·tí·a f. assistantship; MIL. adjutancy.

a·yu·dar tr. to help, aid ♦ a. a to help to.

a·yu·nar intr. to fast.

a·yu·no, a I. adj. fasting; FIG. uninformed ♦ en a. *or* ayunas *(sin comer)* fasting; *(sin desayunar)* before breakfast; *(sin saber)* in the dark, all at sea • quedarse en ayunas FIG. to be completely in the dark II. m. fast, fasting.

a·yun·ta·mien·to m. *(reunión)* meeting; *(corporación)* city council; *(edificio)* city hall; *(coito)* sexual intercourse.

a·za·ba·che m. MIN. jet; ORNITH. titmouse.

a·za·da f. hoe.

a·za·dón m. large hoe.

a·za·do·nar tr. to hoe.

a·za·fai·fa f. jujube.

a·za·fa·ta f. AVIA. stewardess; *(criada)* lady-in-waiting.

a·za·frán m. saffron.

a·za·har m. orange, lemon *or* citron blossom.

a·zar m. *(casualidad)* chance; *(desgracia)* misfortune ♦ al a. at random • por a. by chance.

a·za·ran·dar tr. to strain, sieve.

a·za·ro·so, a adj. *(arriesgado)* risky; *(desgraciado)* unlucky.

á·zi·mo adj. unleavened.

a·zo·ga·do, a adj. silvered.

a·zo·gar §47 tr. to silver —reflex to get mercury poisoning; *(inquietarse)* to be restless.

a·zo·gue m. quicksilver.

a·zo·ra·mien·to m. *(sobresalto)* alarm; *(turbación)* fluster.

a·zo·ran·te adj. *(sobresaltante)* alarming; *(desconcertante)* confusing.

a·zo·rar tr. *(sobresaltar)* to alarm; *(confundir)* to confuse —reflex. *(sobresaltarse)* to be alarmed *or* startled; *(confundirse)* to become confused *or* bewildered.

a·zo·rra·do, a adj. foxy.

a·zo·ta·do, a adj. multicolored, motley.

a·zo·tai·na f. COLL. flogging.

a·zo·ta·mien·to m. flogging.

a·zo·tar tr. to flog; FIG. to beat upon.

a·zo·ta·zo m. *(whip)lash;* COLL. spank, swat.

a·zo·te m. *(látigo)* whip; *(golpe)* lash; *(zurra)* spanking; *(embate)* beating.

a·zo·te·a f. *(tejado)* terraced roof; COLL. *(cabeza)* head.

a·zo·ti·na f. COLL. drubbing, thrashing.

a·zú·car m. *or* f. sugar ♦ a. candi rock candy • a. de caña cane sugar • a. en terrones lump sugar • a. en polvo powdered sugar • a. moreno *or* negro brown sugar.

a·zu·ca·ra·do, a adj. sweet.

a·zu·ca·rar tr. *(endulzar)* to sugar-coat; COLL. *(suavizar)* to sweeten —reflex. *(almibarar)* to become sugary; AMER. *(cristalizar)* to become crystallized.

a·zu·ca·re·ro, a I. adj. sugar II. f. *(recipiente)* sugar bowl; *(fábrica)* sugar factory.

a·zu·ce·na f. white *or* Madonna lily.

a·zu·fai·fa f. jujube.

a·zu·fra·do, a I. adj. sulfurous; *(color)* sulfur-colored II. m. sulfurization.

a·zu·frar tr. *(impregnar)* to sulfur; *(sahumar)* to fumigate with sulfur.

a·zu·fre m. sulfur, sulphur.

a·zul I. adj. blue II. m. *(color)* blue; *(azulete)* bluing ♦ a. celeste sky blue • a. marino navy blue • a. turquí indigo.

a·zu·la·do, a adj. bluish.

a·zu·lar tr. to blue, dye *or* color blue.

a·zu·le·jo m. *(baldosa)* glazed tile.

a·zu·li·no, a adj. bluish.

a·zu·zar §04 tr. to set the dogs on; FIG. to stir.

B

b, B f. second letter of the Spanish alphabet.

ba·ba f. spittle ♦ caérsele a uno la b. to drool • echar b. to drool.

ba·bar·se tr. to dribble.

ba·ba·za f. slime; ZOOL. slug.

ba·be·ar intr. to drool.

ba·bel m.f. COLL. babel.

ba·be·ra f. beaver of a helmet; *(hahero)* bib.

ba·be·ro m. bib; *(guardapolvos)* dust cover.

ba·bie·ca COLL. adj. & m.f. simple (person).

ba·bor m. port.

ba·bo·se·ar intr. & tr. to drool (over).

ba·bo·se·o m. dribbling.

ba·bo·so, a I. adj. drooling; FIG. mushy; C. AMER. foolish II. m.f. drooler; FIG. immature person —f. ZOOL. slug.

ba·bu·cha f. slipper ♦ a la b. ARG. piggyback.

ba·ca·la·o m. codfish ♦ cortar el b. COLL. to be in charge.

ba·cán m. AMER. *(amante)* sugar daddy; R.P. *(holgazán)* loafer.

ba·ca·nal f. orgy.

ba·can·te f. FIG. loud drunken woman.

ba·ce·ta f. widow (cards).

ba·ci·lo m. bacillus.

ba·cín m. *(orinal grande)* large chamber pot; *(de mendigo)* beggar's bowl.

ba·ci·ne·te m. *(armadura)* basinet (helmet); *(soldado)* cuirassier; ANAT. pelvis.

ba·ci·ni·ca/lla f. *(de mendigo)* beggar's bowl; *(orinal)* chamber pot.

bac·te·ria f.inv. bacterium.

bac·te·rio·lo·gí·a f. bacteriology.

bac·te·rio·ló·gi·co, a adj. bacteriological.

bac·te·rió·lo·go, a m.f. bacteriologist.

bá·cu·lo m. *(cayado)* staff; FIG. *(apoyo)* support; *(alivio)* relief.

ba·che m. pothole; AER. air pocket; FIG. rough spot.

ba·chi·ller m.f. student ready for admission into an advanced university program.

ba·chi·lle·rar tr. to confer a bachelor's degree on —reflex. to be graduated as a bachelor.

ba·chi·lle·ra·to m. studies which enable a student to enter an advanced university program.

ba·da·jo m. bell clapper; FIG. chatterbox.

ba·de·a f. *(cosa)* tasteless thing; *(fruta)* insipid melon *or* cucumber; *(persona)* dull person.

ba·du·la·que adj. & m. foolish (person).

ba·du·la·que·ar intr. S. AMER. *(engañar)* to cheat; *(ser terco)* to be stubborn.

ba·ga·je m. MIL. equipment; *(acémila)* beast of burden; *(caudal)* stock of knowledge; S. AMER. luggage.

ba·ga·te·la f. trifle.

ba·ga·zo m. bagasse; C. AMER. creep.

ba·gre m. catfish; S. AMER. hag.

¡bah! interj. bah!

ba·hí·a f. bay.

bai·la·dor, ·ra I. adj. dancing II. m.f. dancer.

bai·lar intr. to dance; *(girar)* to spin (tops); *(retozar)* to romp ♦ b. al son que tocan FIG. to adapt to the circumstances —tr. to dance.

bai·la·rín, i·na I. adj. dancing II. m.f. dancer —f. ballerina.

bai·le[1] m. dance; THEAT. ballet ♦ b. de más-caras *or* disfraces costume *or* masked ball.

bai·le[2] m. ARCH. alderman.

bai·lí·a f. bailiwick.

bai·lon·go m. AMER. public *or* village dance.

bai·lo·te·ar intr. *(bailar mucho)* to dance a lot; *(bailar sin esmero)* to dance clumsily.

bai·lo·te·o m. dancing about.

bai·vel m. bevel *or* miter square.

ba·ja f. *(disminución)* drop; MIL. loss; COM. rebate ♦ dar de b. to expel; MIL. to discharge • darse de b. to drop out • estar en b. *or* ir de b. to lose value.

ba·já m. pasha.

ba·ja·da f. drop; *(camino)* sloped path ♦ b. de aguas downspout.

ba·ja·mar f. low tide.

ba·jan·te f. AMER. low tide.

ba·jar intr. to descend; *(apearse)* to get off; *(disminuir)* to drop —tr. to lower; *(llevar abajo)* to bring *or* take down; *(ir abajo)* to go down; *(disminuir)* to lower; *(inclinar)* to bow; *(apear)* to help down; *(humillar)* to humble —reflex. to go down; *(apearse)* to get down *or* off; *(agacharse)* to bend down.

ba·je·za f. lowliness; *(villanía)* baseness ♦ b. de ánimo timidity.

ba·jí·o m. *(banco de arena)* sandbank; *(terreno bajo)* low-lying ground.

ba·jis·ta m.f. bear (in stock market).

ba·jo I. m. *(tierra)* lowland; *(bajío)* shoal; *(voz)* bass; *(violoncelo)* cello ♦ pl. *(piso)* ground floor; *(enaguas)* underskirt; *(barrio)* slums II. adv. *(abajo)* below; *(en voz baja)* low ♦ por lo b. secretly III. prep. under ♦ b. llave under lock and key • b. palabra *on* parole • b. pena de under penalty of.

ba·jo, a adj. *(poco elevado)* low; *(de estatura)* short; *(inclinado)* downcast; *(poco vivo)* pale *(sonido)* low; *(vulgar)* vulgar; *(abyecto)* abject; *(humilde)* humble; *(barato)* cheap ♦ b. de ley METAL. base • b. relieve ARTS bas-relief.

ba·jón[1] m. MUS. bassoon.

ba·jón[2] m. drop.

ba·jo·nis·ta m.f. bassoonist.

ba·la f. *(proyectil)* bullet; *(de cañón)* cannon-ball; *(de carabina)* shot; *(fardo)* bale ♦ b. fría spent bullet • b. perdida stray bullet • como una b. FIG., COLL. like a shot.

ba·la·da f. ballad(ry).

ba·la·dí adj. [pl. -íes] trivial.

ba·la·dro m. *(grito)* shout; *(chillido)* shriek.

ba·la·drón, o·na I. adj. boasting II. m.f. braggart.

ba·la·dro·na·da f. boast.

ba·la·dro·ne·ar intr. to boast, brag.

bá·la·go m. *(de cereal)* grain stalk; *(de jabón)* soapsuds.

ba·la·lai·ca f. balalaika.

ba·lan·ce m. *(vacilación)* vacillation; *(resultado)* balance; COM. balance ♦ **b. comercial** balance of trade • **b. pendiente** balance due.

ba·lan·ce·ar intr. to rock; FIG. to vacillate, waver —tr. to balance —reflex. to rock.

ba·lan·ce·o m. rocking.

ba·lan·cín m. *(contrapeso)* acrobat's balancing pole; *(volante)* minting mill; *(juguete)* seesaw; *(mecedora)* rocking chair ♦ pl. MARIT. sheets.

ba·lan·dra f. MARIT. sloop.

ba·lan·drán m. monk's cassock.

ba·lan·dro m. small sloop.

bá·la·no or **ba·la·no** m. glans penis.

ba·lan·za f. scales; FIG. comparison; AMER. acrobat's balancing pole ♦ **b. comercial** or **mercantil** ECON. balance of trade.

ba·lar intr. to bleat.

ba·las·tar tr. to ballast.

ba·las·to m. ballast.

ba·laus·tra·da f. balustrade.

ba·laus·trar tr. to build a balustrade on.

ba·la·zo m. *(golpe)* shot; *(herida)* bullet wound.

bal·bo·a PAN., FIN. balboa.

bal·bu·ce·ar intr. var. of **balbucir**.

bal·bu·ce·o m. stammering.

bal·bu·cien·te adj. stammering.

bal·bu·cir §38 intr. to stammer.

bal·cón m. balcony; FIG. vantage or observation point.

bal·dar tr. *(lisiar)* to cripple; *(en los naipes)* to trump; *(molestar)* to inconvenience —reflex. *(lisiarse)* to become crippled; COLL. *(cansarse)* to become exhausted.

bal·de[1] m. pail ♦ **como un b. de agua fría** like a ton of bricks.

bal·de[2] adv. ♦ **de b.** *(gratuitamente)* free; *(sin motivo)* without reason • **en b.** in vain • **estar de b.** to be in excess.

bal·de·ar tr. *(regar)* to wash down; *(achicar)* to bail out.

bal·dí·o, a I. adj. AGR. uncultivated; *(vano)* useless; *(vagabundo)* vagrant II. m. uncultivated land.

bal·do·sa f. floor tile.

ba·le·ar tr. AMER. to shoot (at); C. AMER. to swindle —reflex. to shoot at one another.

ba·le·ro m. bullet mold; AMER. cup and ball.

ba·li·do m. bleating.

ba·lín m. pellet ♦ pl. buckshot.

ba·lís·ti·co, a I. adj. ballistic II. f. ballistics.

ba·li·za f. MARIT. buoy; AVIA. beacon.

ba·li·zar §04 tr. MARIT. to mark with buoys.

bal·ne·a·rio, a I. adj. bathing II. m. bathing resort; *(medicinal)* spa.

ba·lom·pié m. soccer.

ba·lón m. *(pelota)* football; *(fardo)* bale; *(recipiente)* glass flask; *(globo)* balloon.

ba·lon·ces·to m. basketball.

ba·lon·ma·no m. handball.

ba·lon·vo·le·a m. volleyball.

ba·lo·ta f. ballot.

ba·lo·ta·je m. AMER. balloting.

bal·sa f. *(charca)* pool; *(embarcación)* raft; BOT. balsa ♦ **b. de aceite** tranquil place.

bal·sá·mi·co, a adj. balsamic.

bál·sa·mo m. balsam.

bal·se·ro m. ferryman.

ba·luar·te m. bulwark.

ba·lle·na f. whale; *(de un corsé)* stay.

ba·lle·na·to m. whale calf.

ba·lle·ne·ro, a I. adj. whaling II. m. whaler.

ba·lles·ta f. crossbow; MECH. spring.

ba·lles·te·ar tr. to shoot (with a crossbow).

ba·lles·te·ra f. loophole for crossbows.

ba·lles·te·rí·a f. *(deporte)* archery; *(ballesteros)* crossbowmen.

ba·lles·te·ro m. crossbowman.

ba·lles·ti·lla f. small whiffletree.

ba·llet m. [pl. s] ballet.

bam·ba·le·ar intr. to sway.

bam·ba·li·na f. THEAT. top curtain ♦ **tras bambalinas** FIG. behind the scenes.

bam·bo·le·ar intr. & reflex. to wobble.

bam·bo·le·o m. wobble.

bam·bo·lla f. COLL. ostentation.

bam·bo·lle·ro, a adj. COLL. showy.

bam·bú m. [pl. -úes] bamboo.

ba·nal adj. banal.

ba·na·na f./no m. banana.

ba·na·nal/nar m. banana grove or plantation.

ba·na·ne·ro, a adj. & m. banana (tree).

ban·ca f. *(asiento)* bench; *(puesto)* stall; COM. banking; *(juego)* baccarat ♦ **hacer saltar la b.** to break the bank • **tener b.** R.P. to have influence.

ban·ca·da f. *(asiento)* stone bench; *(mesa)* large table.

ban·ca·rio, a adj. bank.

ban·ca·rro·ta f. bankruptcy.

ban·co m. bench; *(caballete)* workbench; COM. bank; MAS. row of bricks; MARIT. bank; *(cardumen)* school ♦ **b. de ahorros** savings bank • **b. de arena** sandbar • **b. de datos** data bank • **b. de liquidación** clearing house • **b. de nieve** snowbank • **b. de pruebas** TECH. testing bench.

ban·da[1] f. *(faja)* band; *(cinta)* ribbon; *(lado)* side ♦ **b. sonora** or **de sonido** soundtrack • **b. transportadora** conveyor belt • **cerrarse en b.** FIG. to stick to one's guns.

ban·da[2] f. MIL. band; *(pandilla)* gang; *(partido)* faction; *(bandada)* flock; MUS. band.

ban·da·da f. *(grupo)* group; *(de aves)* flock; *(de peces)* school.

ban·da·zo m. lurch (of a boat); *(paseo)* stroll; *(tumbo)* fall.

ban·de·ja f. tray.

ban·de·ra f. *(pabellón)* flag; *(estandarte)* banner ♦ **a banderas desplegadas** openly • **b. de parlamento** or **de paz** white flag • **con banderas desplegadas** with flying colors • **de b.** COLL. terrific • **jurar la b.** to pledge allegiance.

ban·de·ri·lla f. TAUR. banderilla; AMER. swindle.

ban·de·rín m. pennant; *(soldado)* infantry guide.

ban·de·ri·zar §04 tr. to divide into bands.

ban·de·ro·la f. pennant.

ban·di·da·je m. banditry.

ban·di·do m. bandit; COLL. rascal.

ban·do m. *(edicto)* edict; *(facción)* faction; *(de peces)* school; *(de aves)* flock ♦ pl. marriage banns.

ban·do·le·ra f. bandoleer.

ban·do·le·ris·mo m. banditry.

ban·do·le·ro m. bandit.

ban·do·ne·ón m. concertina.

ban·jo m. banjo.

ban·que·ro m. banker.

ban·que·ta f. stool; *(para los pies)* footstool; MIL. banquette.

ban·que·te m. banquet.

ban·qui·llo m. stool; *(para los pies)* footstool; *(del acusado)* defendant's seat.

ba·ña·de·ra f. AMER. bathtub.

ba·ña·do m. AMER. swamp.

ba·ña·dor, -ra I. adj. bathing II. m.f. AMER. *(persona)* bather; *(traje de baño)* bathing suit

ba·ñar tr. to bathe; *(sumergir)* to immerse; *(cubrir)* to coat; *(tocar)* to lap; *(llenar)* to flood —reflex. to bathe.

ba·ñe·ra f. bathtub.

ba·ñe·ro m. bathhouse owner.

ba·ñis·ta m.f. swimmer.

ba·ño m. *(ducha)* bath; *(bañera)* bathtub; *(cuarto de baño)* bathroom; *(capa)* coat ♦ **b. de María** CUL. double boiler ♦ pl spa.

bap·tis·te·rio m. baptistry.

ba·que·li·ta f. bakelite.

ba·que·ta f. MIL. ramrod; *(castigo)* gauntlet.

ba·que·ta·zo m. blow with a ramrod; COLL. fall.

ba·que·te·a·do, -a adj. *(endurecido)* hardened; *(experimentado)* experienced.

ba·que·te·ar tr. *(ejercitar)* to exercise; *(tratar mal)* to mistreat; *(castigar)* to force to run the gauntlet; FIG. to harass.

ba·que·te·o m. *(molestia)* burden; *(cansancio)* exhaustion.

ba·quia·no, -a adj. & m.f. S. AMER. expert.

bar¹ m. barroom.

bar² m. PHYS. bar.

ba·ra·hún·da f. uproar.

ba·ra·ja f. *(naipes)* deck (of cards); AMER. playing card ♦ **entrarse en b.** to give up • **jugar con dos barajas** to double-deal.

ba·ra·jar tr. *(los naipes)* to shuffle; *(mezclar)* to jumble; *(cifras)* to juggle —intr. to fight, quarrel —reflex. to get mixed up.

ba·ran·da f. banister; *(de billar)* cushion.

ba·ran·di·lla f. banister, handrail; *(balaustrada)* railing.

ba·ra·te·ar tr. to sell at a discount, sell cheap.

ba·ra·ti·ja f. trinket, bauble ♦ pl. junk.

ba·ra·ti·llo m. *(mercancías)* secondhand goods; *(tienda)* junk shop; *(venta)* bargain sale.

ba·ra·to, -a I. adj. & adv. cheap(ly), inexpensive(ly) ♦ **de b.** for free, gratis II. m. bargain sale —f. *(trueque)* barter; COL., MEX. bargain sale; CHILE, PERU cockroach.

ba·ra·ún·da f. var. of **barahúnda**.

bar·ba f. *(barbilla)* chin; *(pelo)* beard; ORNITH. wattle, gill; BOT. beard ♦ **barbas de chivo** goatee • **en las barbas de uno** under one's nose • **hacer la b. a** to shave, give a shave to; FIG. *(adular)* to flatter, fawn over; *(fastidiar)* to annoy, pester • **mentir por la b.** to tell a barefaced lie ♦ pl. whiskers.

bar·ba·co·a f. barbecue; AMER. makeshift cot.

bar·bar intr. to grow a beard.

bar·bá·ri·co, -a adj. barbaric, barbarian.

bar·ba·ri·dad f. barbarity; *(necedad)* foolish act, nonsense; COLL. an enormous amount ♦ **¡qué b.!** how awful!

bar·ba·rie f. barbarousness, barbarity.

bar·ba·ris·mo m. barbarism.

bar·ba·ri·zar §04 tr. to make barbarous —intr. to talk nonsense.

bár·ba·ro, -a I. adj. barbaric, barbarous; *(temerario)* bold, reckless; *(inculto)* barbarian; COLL. *(espléndido)* tremendous, terrific; *(grande)* huge II. m.f. barbarian.

bar·be·rí·a f. barbershop.

bar·be·ro, -a m. barber.

bar·bi·lla f. chin; ICHTH. barb, barbel; CARP. tenon, rabbet.

bar·bi·tú·ri·co, -a adj. & m. barbituric (acid).

bar·bo·tar/te·ar tr. & intr. to mutter, mumble.

bar·bo·te·o m. murmuring.

bar·bu·do, -a adj. heavily bearded.

bar·bu·lla f. COLL. jabbering, chatter.

bar·bu·llar intr. COLL. to jabber, chatter.

bar·bu·llón, -o·na I. adj. jabbering, chattering II. m.f. jabberer, chatterer.

bar·ca f. small boat ♦ **b. de pasaje** ferryboat.

bar·ca·da f. *(carga)* boatload; *(viaje)* crossing.

bar·ca·za f. launch.

bar·cia f. chaff.

bar·ci·no, -a adj. roan, brindled.

bar·co m. boat, ship; *(barranco)* shallow ravine ♦ **b. de carga** freighter • **como b. sin timón** FIG. aimlessly.

bar·da f. bard, armor for a horse; METEOROL. thundercloud.

bar·da·gue·ra f. willow.

ba·rio m. barium.

ba·rí·to·no m. baritone.

bar·lo·ven·te·ar intr. *(navegar)* to tack to windward; *(vagabundear)* to wander, meander.

bar·lo·ven·to m. windward.

bar·niz m. varnish, lacquer; *(maquillaje)* make-up, cosmetics; FIG. veneer, thin coat.

bar·ni·za·do·m *(en varnish(ing)*, lacquer(ing).

bar·ni·zar §04 tr. to varnish, lacquer.

ba·ro·mé·tri·co, -a adj. barometric.

ba·ró·me·tro m. barometer.

ba·rón m. baron.

ba·ro·ne·sa f. baroness.

bar·que·ar tr. & intr. to go across *or* about in a boat.

bar·que·ro m. boatman; ENTOM. water bug.

bar·qui·lla f. small boat.

bar·qui·llo m. cone.

bar·quín m. large bellows.

bar·qui·na·zo m. COLL. bump, jolt; *(vuelco)* rollover, roll.

ba·rra f. bar; *(barandilla)* railing; *(mostrador)* counter, bar; *(de arena)* sandbar, sandbank; MECH. rod, lever; AMER. public, spectators ♦ **b. de labios** lipstick • **barras paralelas** SPORT. parallel bars • **sin pararse en barras** to stop at nothing.

ba·rra·bás m. [pl. **-ases**] scoundrel, rascal.

ba·rra·ba·sa·da f. COLL. dirty *or* mean trick.

ba·rra·ca f. hut, cabin; AMER. warehouse.

ba·rra·cón m. stall, booth.

ba·rra·cu·da f. barracuda.

ba·rran·co m. /ca f. ravine, gorge; FIG. *(obstáculo)* obstacle, difficulty.

ba·rran·cón m. gully, ravine.

ba·rran·co·so, -a adj. full of ravines.

ba·rra·que·ro, -a m.f. builder of a cottage; AMER. warehouse owner.

ba·rre·ar tr. *(fortificar)* to barricade, close (up); *(barretear)* to bar, fasten with bars.

ba·rre·de·ra f. street sweeper.

ba·rre·de·ro, -a I. adj. dragging, sweeping II. f. street sweeper.

ba·rre·dor, -ra I. adj. sweeping II. m.f. sweeper ♦ **b. eléctrica** vacuum cleaner.

ba·rre·du·ra f. sweeping ♦ pl. refuse, residue.

ba·rre·na f. *(instrumento)* drill, gimlet; *(barra)* (drill) bit; AVIA. spin <**b. picada** tailspin>.

ba·rre·nar tr. MECH. to drill, bore; MARIT. to scuttle; FIG. *(desbaratar)* to foil, undermine;

ba·rren·de·ro, a m.f. street sweeper.
ba·rre·ne·ro m. driller, borer.
ba·rre·no m. *(instrumento)* large drill, auger; *(agujero)* bore, drill hole; MIN. blasting hole.
ba·rrer tr. to sweep; *(rozar)* to graze, touch lightly —intr. to sweep ♦ **b. con todo** COLL. to make a clean sweep • **b. hacia adentro** to look out for number one.
ba·rre·ra f. barrier; FIG. obstacle, hindrance ♦ **b. de peaje** tollgate.
ba·rre·ra² f. *(sitio)* clay pit; *(alacena)* crockery cupboard.
ba·rria·da f. neighborhood, district.
ba·rrial m. *(gredal)* clay pit; AMER. *(barrizal)* bog.
ba·rri·ca f. medium-sized barrel or cask.
ba·rri·ca·da f. barricade, barrier.
ba·rri·do, a m. sweep, sweeping —f. S. AMER. sweep, police raid.
ba·rri·ga f. abdomen, stomach; COLL. paunch, belly; *(de una vasija, pared)* bulge ♦ **rascarse la b.** COLL. to twiddle one's thumbs.
ba·rri·gón, o·na/gu·do, a adj. COLL. potbellied.
ba·rril m. *(tonel)* barrel, keg; *(jarro)* jug.
ba·rri·llo m. blackhead, pimple.
ba·rrio n. neighborhood ♦ **barrios bajos** slums • **el otro b.** COLL. the other world.
ba·rris·ta m.f. gymnast on the horizontal bars.
ba·rro m. *(lodo)* mud; *(arcilla)* clay; *(vaso)* earthenware vessel; *(granillo)* blackhead.
ba·rro·co, a adj. baroque; *(extravagante)* ornate, elaborate.
ba·rro·te m. *(barra)* heavy bar, rail; *(sostén)* rung; CARP. crosspiece.
ba·rrun·tar tr. to suspect, guess.
ba·rrun·te/to m. *(sospecha)* feeling, suspicion; *(indicio)* sign, clue.
bar·to·la ♦ a la b. without a care in the world, nonchalantly • **echarse a la b.** to let oneself go.
bár·tu·los m.pl. household goods, belongings; MECH. equipment, gear.
ba·ru·llo m. COLL. racket, rowdiness.
ba·sa f. base; FIG. basis, foundation.
ba·sal·to m. basalt.
ba·sa·men·to m. base of a column.
ba·sar tr. to build on a base; FIG. to base, support —reflex. to be based.
bas·ca f. nausea, queasiness.
bás·cu·la f. TECH. bascule; *(balanza)* platform scale, balance.
ba·se f. base; FIG. *(fundamento)* basis, foundation ♦ **a b. de** with • **b. imponible** tax base • **en b. a** on the basis of.
bá·si·co, a adj. basic.
ba·sí·li·co, a I f. basilica II. adj. basilic.
ba·si·lis·co m. basilisk ♦ **estar hecho un b.** COLL. to be furious or enraged.
bas·ta f. see **basto, a.**
bas·tan·te I. adj. enough, sufficient II. adv. enough, sufficiently; *(muy)* rather, quite.
bas·tar intr. to suffice ♦ **¡basta!** that's enough of that! —reflex. to be self-sufficient.
bas·tar·de·ar intr. to degenerate, decline —tr. to bastardize, adulterate.
bas·tar·dí·a f. bastardy, illegitimacy; FIG. nasty remark or action.
bas·tar·di·llo, a adj. & f. italic(s).
bas·tar·do, a I. m.f. bastard; *(mezcla)* crossbreed, hybrid —m. ZOOL. boa II. adj. bastard, illegitimate; BOT., ZOOL. hybrid.

bas·te m. basting, tacking.
bas·te·ar tr. SEW. to baste, tack.
bas·ti·dor m. *(armazón)* frame, framework; THEAT. flat, wing; AUTO. chassis ♦ **entre bastidores** FIG. behind the scenes; THEAT. off-stage.
bas·ti·lla f. hem.
bas·tión m. bastion.
bas·to, a I. adj. coarse, rough II. m. *(albarda)* packsaddle —f. SEW. basting, tacking.
bas·tón m. cane, walking stick; *(vara)* truncheon, staff; FIG. authority, command.
bas·to·na·da f./**na·zo** m. blow with a cane.
bas·to·ne·ar tr. to cane, beat with a stick.
bas·to·ne·ra f. umbrella stand.
ba·su·ra f. *(desperdicio)* garbage, trash; *(estiércol)* dung, horse manure.
ba·su·ral m. AMER. (garbage) dump.
ba·su·re·ar tr. ARG., COLL. to sling mud on.
ba·su·re·ro m. garbage collector; *(cubo)* garbage or trash can; *(basural)* dump.
ba·ta f. housecoat; *(de trabajo)* frock, smock.
ba·ta·ca·zo m. bump, thud.
ba·ta·ho·la f. COLL. rumpus, ruckus.
ba·ta·lla f. battle ♦ **b. campal** pitched battle • **dar** or **librar b.** to do battle • **de b.** ordinary, everyday.
ba·ta·lla·dor, ·ra I. adj. battling, fighting II. m. battler, fighter.
ba·ta·llar intr. to battle, fight; *(disputar)* to dispute, argue; *(vacilar)* to vacillate.
ba·ta·llón m. battalion.
ba·ta·ta f. sweet potato, yam
ba·ta·ta·zo m. AMER. lucky shot, fluke ♦ **dar b.** *(ganar los caballos)* to win by an upset; *(tener chiripa)* to make a lucky shot.
ba·te m. SPORT. bat; CUBA. busybody.
ba·te·a f. *(bandeja)* wicker tray; *(artesilla)* deep trough; MARIT. scow, punt; RAIL. flatcar.
ba·te·a·dor, ·ra m.f. SPORT. batter, hitter.
ba·te·ar tr. SPORT. to bat, hit.
ba·te·rí·a f. battery; *(bombardeo)* battering; THEAT. footlights; MUS. drums, percussion ♦ **b. de cocina** kitchen utensils.
ba·ti·do, a I. adj. beaten, well-trodden II. m. *(acción)* beating; CUL. batter; *(bebida)* shake <**b. de leche** milkshake> —f. *(cacería)* beat, beating; *(registro)* search; *(de policía)* police raid.
ba·ti·dor, ·ra I. adj. beating II. m. CUL. beater; MIL. scout —f. AMER. mixing bowl.
ba·tien·te I. adj. beating II. m. CONSTR. *(marco)* jamb; *(de puerta)* leaf.
ba·ti·fon·do m. ARG. rumpus, uproar.
ba·tin·tín m. gong.
ba·tir tr. to beat, hit; *(derribar)* to demolish, knock down; *(martillar)* to hammer; *(revolver)* to beat, mix; *(agitar)* to beat, flap; *(peinar)* to comb, tease; *(registrar)* to scour, search; *(vencer)* to beat, defeat; *(superar)* to beat, outdo; NUMIS. to mint; AMER. to rinse ♦ **b. el vuelo** FIG. to scram, beat it • **b. palmas** to clap hands • **b. tiendas** MIL. to break camp —intr. to beat violently, pound —reflex. to fight ♦ **b. en retirada** to beat a retreat.
ba·tís·ca·fo m. bathyscaph.
ba·tis·ta f. batiste, fine cambric.
ba·to·lo·gí·a f. RHET. needless repetition.
ba·tra·cio, a adj. & m. batrachian.
ba·tu·que·ar tr. AMER. to shake, shake up.
ba·tu·ta f. MUS. baton ♦ **llevar la b.** COLL. to be the boss.
ba·úl m. trunk; *(cofre)* coffer, chest.

bau·tis·mal adj. baptismal.
bau·tis·mo m. baptism, christening; *(iniciación)* baptism, initiation.
bau·tis·ta m.f. baptizer; RELIG. Baptist.
bau·tis·te·rio m. baptistry, baptistery.
bau·ti·zar §04 tr. to baptize, christen; *(nombrar)* to name, call; *(apodar)* to nickname; *(mezclar con agua)* to water (down), dilute.
bau·ti·zo m. baptism, christening.
bau·xi·ta f. bauxite.
ba·yo, **a** adj. & m. bay.
ba·yo·ne·ta f. bayonet; AMER. yucca.
ba·zar m. bazaar, marketplace.
ba·zo, **a** I. adj. yellowish-brown II. m. ANAT. spleen —f. *(en los naipes)* trick (in cards); *(oportunidad)* stroke of luck ♦ **meter b.** COLL. to butt in.
ba·zo·fia f. *(sobras)* leftovers, table scraps; *(comida)* slop, swill; *(suciedad)* filth, rubbish.
ba·zu·ca m. bazooka.
be·a·gle m. beagle.
be·a·te·rí·a f. sanctimoniousness, false piety.
be·a·ti·fi·ca·ción f. beatification.
be·a·ti·fi·car §70 tr. to beatify, bless.
be·a·tí·fi·co, **a** adj. beatific, beatifical.
be·a·ti·tud f. beatitude; *(alegría)* bliss.
be·a·to, **a** I. adj. *(feliz)* blissful; *(beatificado)* beatified; *(piadoso)* pious; *(santurrón)* prudish II. m.f. *(religioso)* lay brother or sister; *(piadoso)* devout person; *(santurrón)* prude.
be·bé m. *(nene)* baby; SL. babe, doll.
be·be·de·ro, **a** I. adj. drinkable, potable II. m. watering place or trough; *(de aves)* birdbath; *(pico de vasija)* lip, spout.
be·be·dor, **·ra** I. adj. drinking II. m.f. drinker; *(borracho)* heavy drinker, boozer.
be·ber tr. to drink; *(absorber)* to drink in, imbibe ♦ **b. a sorbos** to sip ♦ **b. a tragos** to gulp (down) ♦ **b. los vientos por** to long for —intr. to drink booze ♦ **b. como una cuba** or **esponja** to drink like a fish.
be·bi·do, **a** I. adj. tipsy, drunk II. f. drink, beverage; *(vicio)* drink, drinking.
be·ca f. *(embozo)* sash, hood; *(colegiatura)* grant, scholarship; *(pensión)* room and board.
be·ca·rio, **a** m.f. scholarship student, fellow.
be·ce·rro, **a** m. yearling bull ♦ **b. marino** ZOOL. seal ♦ **b. de oro** golden calf —f. ZOOL. yearling calf; BOT. snapdragon.
be·cua·dro m. MUS. natural sign.
be·cha·mel f. white or béchamel sauce.
be·del m. EDUC. proctor.
be·go·nia f. begonia.
béis·bol m. baseball.
be·ju·co m. rattan.
bel·dad f. beauty.
be·lén m. crèche, nativity scene; *(confusión)* confusion, bedlam ♦ **meterse en belenes** COLL. to get mixed up in trouble.
be·li·cis·mo m. warmongering, militarism.
be·li·cis·ta adj. & m.f. militarist(ic).
bé·li·co, **a** adj. bellicose, warlike.
be·li·co·si·dad f. bellicosity.
be·li·co·so, **a** adj. bellicose.
be·li·ge·ran·cia f. belligerency.
be·li·ge·ran·te adj. & m. belligerent.
be·lio m. bel.
be·lla·co, **a** I. adj. *(astuto)* sly, cunning; *(pícaro)* knavish, roguish II. m.f. rascal, rogue.
be·lla·que·rí·a f. *(astucia)* slyness, cunning; *(maldad)* roguishness; *(trampa)* sly trick.
be·lle·za f. beauty.

be·llo, **a** adj. beautiful, lovely; *(bueno)* fine, noble ♦ **bellas artes** fine arts.
be·llo·ta f. acorn; *(clavel)* carnation bud; *(borla)* tassel, pompom.
bem·ba f./bo m. AMER. muzzle, snout.
bem·bón, **o·na/bu·do**, **a** adj. AMER., DEROG. thick-lipped.
be·mol m. & adj. MUS. flat.
ben·ci·na f. benzin(e).
ben·de·cir §11 tr. to bless; *(consagrar)* to consecrate; *(alabar)* to praise, extol; *(agradecer)* to bless, thank.
ben·di·ción f. blessing; RELIG. benediction ♦ **b. de la mesa** grace ♦ **bendiciones nupciales** wedding ceremony ♦ **echar la b. a** to give one's blessing to.
ben·di·ga, **go**, **jera**, **jo** see **bendecir**.
ben·di·to, **a** I. see **bendecir** II. adj. *(santo)* holy, blessed; *(dichoso)* fortunate, lucky; *(tonto)* simple, simple-minded ♦ **como el pan b.** like hot cakes III. m.f. *(santo)* saint; *(bonachón)* good soul; *(tonto)* simpleton —m. *(oración)* prayer; AMER. *(nicho)* niche.
be·ne·dic·ti·no, **a** adj. & m.f. Benedictine.
be·ne·fac·tor m. benefactor.
be·ne·fi·cen·cia f. benevolence; *(asistencia)* welfare, public assistance.
be·ne·fi·cia·do, **a** m.f. beneficiary.
be·ne·fi·ciar tr. to benefit; AGR. *(mejorar)* to cultivate; MIN. to develop or work; *(tratar)* to smelt, treat; COM. to sell at a discount; AMER. to slaughter —intr. to be of benefit —reflex. to profit *(de by, from)*.
be·ne·fi·cia·rio, **a** m.f. beneficiary ♦ **b. de cheque** COM. payee ♦ **b. de patente** COM. patentee.
be·ne·fi·cio m. benefit, advantage; *(ganancia)* profit, gain; AGR. cultivation; MIN. working; *(tratamiento)* smelting, treatment; THEAT. benefit (performance); RELIG. benefice; AMER. slaughter; C. AMER. processing plant, refinery ♦ **a b. de** for the benefit of • **no tener oficio ni b.** to be without means.
be·ne·fi·cio·so, **a** adj. beneficial.
be·né·fi·co, **a** adj. *(caritativo)* beneficent, charitable; *(provechoso)* beneficial.
be·ne·mé·ri·to, **a** adj. meritorious, worthy.
be·ne·plá·ci·to m. approval, consent.
be·ne·vo·len·cia f. benevolence, kindness.
be·né·vo·lo, **a** adj. benevolent, kind.
be·nig·no, **a** adj. benign.
ben·ja·mín m. baby of the family.
ben·juí m. benzoin, benjamin.
ben·zo·a·to m. benzoate.
be·o·dez f. drunkenness.
be·o·do, **a** adj. & m.f. drunk.
ber·be·re·cho m. cockle.
be·ren·je·na f. eggplant.
ber·ga·mo·ta f. bergamot.
ber·gan·te m. COLL. scoundrel, rascal.
ber·gan·tín m. brig.
be·ri·lio m. beryllium.
ber·ke·lio m. berkelium.
ber·lin·ga f. SP. clothesline pole.
ber·me·jo, **a** adj. bright red.
ber·me·llón m. vermilion.
ber·mu·da f. Bermuda grass ♦ **pl.** Bermuda shorts.
be·rra f. watercress.
be·rre·ar intr. *(balar)* to bleat; *(gritar)* to howl.
be·rre·o m. temper tantrum, rage.
be·rri·do m. *(balido)* bleat; *(chillido)* shriek.

be·rrin·che m. COLL. rage, tantrum.
be·rro m. watercress.
be·rrue·co m. granite rock.
ber·za f. cabbage.
be·sar tr. to kiss; *(rozar)* to graze, touch —reflex. to kiss one another.
be·so m. kiss; *(roce)* brush, glance.
bes·tia I. f. beast, animal —m.f. COLL. *(bruto)* beast, brute; *(imbécil)* idiot, blockhead ♦ **b. de albarda** pack animal • **b. de carga** beast of burden II. adj. stupid, ignorant.
bes·tia·je m. beasts of burden.
bes·tial adj. bestial, beastly; COLL. *(magnífico)* fabulous; *(enorme)* gigantic.
bes·tia·li·dad f. beastliness, bestiality; *(estupidez)* stupidity, foolishness; *(gran cantidad)* a lot ♦ **¡qué b.!** how awful!
bes·tia·li·zar §04 tr. to bestialize, brutalize —reflex. to become bestialized.
be·su·ca·dor, ·ra COLL. I. adj. fond of kissing II. m.f. kisser.
be·su·car §70 tr. var. of **besuquear**.
be·su·cón, o·na adj. & m.f. var. of **besucador**.
be·su·go m. sea bream; FIG., COLL. *(idiota)* idiot, twerp.
be·su·que·ar tr. COLL. to smooch, lavish kisses.
be·su·que·o m. COLL. smooching.
be·ta·rra·ga/ta f. beet.
be·tún m. shoe polish.
be·tu·nar/ne·ar tr. CUBA, ECUAD. *(pulir)* to shine, polish; *(asfaltar)* to tar, asphalt.
bian·gu·lar adj. biangular.
bia·tó·mi·co, a adj. diatomic.
bi·be·rón m. baby bottle.
bi·blia f. bible ♦ **B.** Bible.
bí·bli·co, a adj. Biblical, biblical.
bi·blió·fi·lo, a m.f. bibliophile, booklover.
bi·blio·gra·fí·a f. bibliography.
bi·blio·grá·fi·co, a adj. bibliographic(al).
bi·bli·ó·gra·fo, a m.f. bibliographer.
bi·blio·lo·gí·a f. bibliology.
bi·blio·te·ca f. library; AMER. bookcase.
bi·blio·te·ca·rio, a m.f. librarian.
bi·car·bo·na·ta·do, a adj. bicarbonate.
bi·car·bo·na·to m. bicarbonate ♦ **b. de sodio** or **de sosa** bicarbonate of soda; CUL. baking soda.
bi·cé·fa·lo, a adj. bicephalic, bicephalous.
bi·cen·te·na·rio m. bicentennial, bicentenary.
bí·ceps m.inv. biceps.
bi·ci f. COLL. bike.
bi·ci·cle·ta f. bicycle.
bi·ci·clo m. velocipede.
bi·co·ca f. trifle, trinket; *(ganga)* bargain.
bi·co·lor adj. bicolor, two-tone.
bi·cón·ca·vo, a adj. biconcave.
bi·con·ve·xo, a adj. biconvex.
bi·cro·má·ti·co, a adj. dichromatic, two-color.
bi·cús·pi·de adj. bicuspid.
bi·cho m. bug, insect; *(animal)* beast, animal; *(toro)* bull; *(fenómeno)* freak, odd person ♦ **todo b. viviente** COLL. everyone.
bi·dé m. bidet.
bi·dón m. large can, drum.
bie·la f. connecting rod, pitman.
bien I. m. good, goodness; *(provecho)* good, benefit ♦ **en b.** to be for the good of • **hacer (el) b.** to do good ♦ pl. property, goods • **b. dotales** dowry • **b. gananciales** community property • **b. inmuebles** or **raíces** real estate • **b. muebles** chattels, personal property • **b. patri-**

moniales capital assets • **b. relictos** estate, inheritance II. adv. well; *(justamente)* right, correctly; *(con éxito)* successfully; *(de buena gana)* willingly, readily; *(sin dificultad)* easily; *(bastante)* quite, very; *(si)* okay ♦ **de b. en mejor** better and better • **más b.** rather • **no b.** just as, as soon as • **o b.** or else, otherwise • **por b.** willingly • **pues b.** then, well now • **y b.** well then III. adj. well-to-do.
bie·nal adj. & f. biennial.
bie·na·ven·tu·ra·do, a adj. & m.f. *(afortunado)* fortunate, lucky (person); *(inocente)* simple, naive (person); RELIG. blessed (person).
bie·na·ven·tu·ran·za f. happiness, well-being.
bie·nes·tar m. well-being, comfort.
bien·ha·bla·do, a adj. well-spoken, courteous.
bien·he·chor, ·ra I. adj. beneficent, beneficial II. m. benefactor —f. benefactress.
bie·nin·ten·cio·na·do, a adj. & m.f. well-meaning (person).
bie·nio m. biennium.
bien·ve·ni·da f. safe arrival; *(salutación)* welcome, greeting.
biés m. bias.
bi·fe m. AMER. steak, beefsteak; R.P. slap.
bi·fo·cal adj. bifocal.
bi·for·me adj. biform.
bif·tec m. [pl. **s**] steak, beefsteak.
bi·fur·ca·ción f. bifurcation, branch; *(de un camino)* fork; *(en ferrocarriles)* junction.
bi·fur·ca·do, a adj. forked, bifurcate.
bi·fur·car·se §70 reflex. to bifurcate, branch (off); *(dividirse un camino)* to fork.
bi·ga·mia f. bigamy.
bí·ga·mo, a I. adj. bigamous II. m.f. bigamist.
bi·ga·rra·do, a adj. multicolored, motley.
bi·gor·nia f. two-beaked anvil.
bi·go·te m. mustache; MIN. slag tap ♦ pl. whiskers • **tener b.** or **ser hombre de b.** COLL. to be firm or stern.
bi·go·te·ra f. mustache cover; FIG. mustache (after drinking).
bi·go·tu·do, a adj. mustached, mustachioed.
bi·gu·dí m. hair curler.
bi·ki·ni m. bikini.
bi·la·bia·do, a adj. bilabiate.
bi·la·bial adj. & f. bilabial.
bi·la·te·ral adj. bilateral.
bi·liar or **bi·lia·rio, a** adj. biliary.
bi·lin·güe adj. bilingual.
bi·lio·so, a adj. bilious.
bi·lis f.inv. bile ♦ **descargar la b.** to vent one's spleen • **exaltársele a uno la b.** to get angry.
bi·lo·bu·la·do, a adj. bilobate.
bi·lo·ca·ción f. bilocation.
bi·llar m. *(juego)* billiards; *(mesa)* billiard table; *(lugar)* billiard room • **b. automático** or **romano** pinball • **b. ruso** snooker.
bi·lle·te m. ticket; *(de lotería)* lottery ticket; *(papel moneda)* bill; *(carta)* note, short letter.
bi·lle·te·ra f./ro m. wallet, billfold.
bi·llón m. trillion (U.S.), billion (G.B.).
bi·llo·né·si·mo, a adj. & m. trillionth (U.S.), billionth (G.B.).
bi·men·sual adj. bimonthly, twice a month.
bi·mes·tral adj. bimonthly, bimestrial.
bi·mes·tre adj. & m. bimonthly (payment).
bi·me·ta·lis·mo m. bimetallism.
bi·mo·tor adj. & m. twin-engine (plane).
bi·na·dor, ·ra m.f. plower.
bi·na·rio, a adj. binary.
bi·no·cu·lar adj. binocular.

bi·nó·cu·lo m. pince-nez.

bi·no·mio m. binomial.

bio·di·ná·mi·ca f. biodynamics.

bio·fí·si·ca f. biophysics.

bio·gra·fí·a f. biography.

bio·gra·fiar §30 tr. to write a biography of.

bio·grá·fi·co, a adj. biographic(al).

bió·gra·fo, a m.f. biographer.

bio·lo·gí·a f. biology.

bio·ló·gi·co, a adj. biologic(al).

bió·lo·go, a m.f. biologist.

biom·bo m. folding screen.

bio·me·cá·ni·ca f. biomechanics.

biop·sia f. biopsy.

bio·quí·mi·co, a I. adj. biochemical II. m.f. biochemist —f. biochemistry.

bios·fe·ra f. biosphere.

bió·xi·do m. dioxide.

bi·par·ti·dis·mo m. two-party system.

bi·par·ti·dis·ta adj. bipartisan, two-party.

bi·par·ti·to/do, a adj. bipartite.

bí·pe·de/do, a adj. & m. biped.

bi·pla·no m. AVIA. biplane.

bir·lar tr. (derribar) to kill or knock down with one blow; (robar) to steal, swipe.

bir·lo·cha f. kite (toy).

bi·rre·te m. RELIG. biretta; (bonete) cap.

bis adv. bis, again.

bi·sa·bue·lo, a m.f. great-grandparent.

bi·sa·gra f. hinge.

bi·se·car §70 tr. to bisect.

bi·sec·tor, triz I. adj. bisecting II. f. bisector.

bi·sel m. bevel, beveled edge.

bi·se·la·do m. beveling.

bi·se·lar tr. to bevel.

bi·se·ma·nal adj. biweekly, semiweekly.

bi·se·xual adj. & m.f. bisexual.

bi·sies·to adj. & m. leap (year).

bi·sí·la·bo/si·lá·bi·co, a adj. bisyllabic.

bis·mu·to m. bismuth.

bis·nie·to, a m.f. great-grandchild.

bi·son·te m. bison.

bi·so·ña·da/ñe·rí·a f. blunder.

bi·so·ñé m. toupee, hairpiece.

bi·so·ño, a adj. & m.f. inexperienced (person).

bis·té/tec m. beefsteak.

bi·su·te·rí·a f. costume jewelry, paste.

bi·tá·co·ra f. binnacle.

bi·tio m. bit.

bi·tu·mi·no·so, a adj. bituminous.

bi·va·len·te adj. bivalent.

bi·zan·ti·no, a I. adj. Byzantine; FIG. intricate; decadent II. m.f. Byzantine.

bi·za·rrí·a f. (valor) bravery, courage; (generosidad) generosity, magnanimity.

bi·za·rro, a adj. (valiente) brave, gallant; (generoso) generous, magnanimous.

bi·za·za f. saddlebag.

biz·car §70 intr. to squint, be cross-eyed —tr. to wink at.

biz·co, a adj. & m.f. cross-eyed (person) ♦ dejar a uno b. to dumbfound, flabbergast.

biz·co·cho m. sponge cake; MARIT. hardtack; CERAM. bisque, biscuit.

biz·ma f. MED. poultice.

biz·nie·to, a m. var. of bisnieto.

biz·que·ar intr. COLL. to squint.

biz·que·ra f. strabismus.

blan·ca f. MUS. half note ♦ estar sin b. COLL. to be broke.

blan·co, a I. adj. white; (claro) fair, light; (cobarde) yellow, chicken ♦ más b. que el papel as white as a sheet II. m.f. white (person); (cobarde) coward, chicken —m. white; (tiro) target; (centro) center; (espacio) blank space, blank; (fin) goal, aim ♦ calentar al b. to make white-hot • dar en el b. to hit the nail on the head • pasar una noche en b. to spend a sleepless night • quedarse en b. to draw a blank.

blan·cu·ra f./ cor m. whiteness.

blan·cuz·co, a adj. whitish.

blan·dir tr. to brandish, wave —intr. to quiver, shake.

blan·do, a adj. soft; (tierno) tender; (fláccido) flabby; (amable) gentle, kind; (cobarde) cowardly ♦ b. de carácter weak-willed.

blan·du·ra f. softness; (ternura) tenderness; (flaccidez) flabbiness; (amabilidad) gentleness, kindness; (cobardía) cowardice, weakness; (lisonja) flattery; (emplasto) poultice, plaster.

blan·duz·co, a adj. softish.

blan·que·a·do m. (acción) whitening; (encalado) whitewashing; (decoloración) bleaching.

blan·que·a·dor, ra I. adj. whitening II. m. or f. whitener; (cal) whitewash; (decoloración) bleach.

blan·que·a·du·ra f. var. of blanqueo.

blan·que·ar tr. to whiten; (dar cal) to whitewash; (lavar) to bleach (clothes) —intr. to turn white or whitish.

blan·que·ci·no, a adj. whitish.

blan·que·o m. whitening; (encalado) whitewashing; (decoloración) bleaching.

blas·fe·mar intr. to blaspheme.

blas·fe·mia f. blasphemy.

blas·fe·mo, a I. adj. blasphemous II. m.f. blasphemer.

bla·són m. heraldry; (escudo) coat of arms, escutcheon; (honor) honor, glory.

bla·so·nar tr. to emblazon —intr. to boast.

bla·so·ne·rí·a f. braggadocio, boasting.

ble·do m. ♦ no importarle un b. not to give a darn or hoot about • no valer un b. not to be worth two cents.

blin·da·do, a armored, armor-plated.

blin·da·je m. armor, armor plate.

blin·dar tr. to armor, cover with armor plate.

bloc m. writing pad or tablet.

blo·que m. block; (grupo) bloc, coalition; (papel) pad, notepad.

blo·que·ar tr. MIL. to blockade; (impedir) to block, obstruct; (frenar) to brake; (obstruir) to jam, block; COM. to freeze (assets).

blo·que·o m. MIL. blockade; (obstáculo) block, obstacle; COM. freeze.

blu·sa f. blouse.

blu·són m. long blouse, smock.

bo·a f. ZOOL. boa (constrictor) —m. (adorno) boa.

bo·ar·di·lla f. attic, garret.

bo·a·to m. show, ostentation.

bo·ba·da f. foolish act or remark.

bo·ba·li·cón, o·na adj. & m.f. silly (person).

bo·be·ar intr. to do or say silly things.

bo·be·ra/rí·a f. foolish act or remark.

bo·bi·na f. spool, reel; SEW. bobbin; ELEC. coil.

bo·bo, a I. adj. (tonto) silly, foolish; (cándido) gullible, naive II. m.f. (tonto) idiot, fool —m. (gracioso) clown, jester.

bo·ca f. mouth; ZOOL. pincer; GEOG. mouth; FIG. entrance, opening; (persona) mouth, person; (filo) cutting edge; (sabor) flavor, bouquet (wine) ♦ a b. de costal freely, abundantly • a b. de jarro FIG. pointblank, at close range • andar de b. en b. FIG. to be the subject of gossip • **b. abajo, arriba** face down, up • **b. de agua** or **de riego** hydrant • **b. de dragón** BOT. snapdragon • **b. de fuego** firearm • **buscar a uno la b.** to draw someone out, pump someone • **¡cállate la b.!** COLL. be quiet! shut up! • **no decir esta b. es mía** COLL. not to open one's mouth • **quedarse con la b. abierta** to be astonished or amazed.

bo·ca·ca·lle f. intersection.

bo·ca·cha f. bigmouth, blabbermouth.

bo·ca·di·llo m. (comida ligera) snack, tidbit; (emparedado) sandwich.

bo·ca·do m. mouthful, bite; EQUIT. bridle, bit • **b. de Adán** Adam's apple • **b. de cardenal** choice morsel • **b. sin hueso** COLL. cushy job.

bo·ca·ja·rro adv. ♦ **a b.** (a quemarropa) point-blank; (de improviso) unexpectedly.

bo·ca·lla·ve f. keyhole.

bo·ca·man·ga f. cuff, wristband.

bo·ca·na·da f. swallow, swig; (de humo) puff; (de aire) gust, rush; (de gente) throng.

bo·ca·za m.f. COLL. bigmouth, blabbermouth.

bo·ce·lar tr. to emboss.

bo·ce·tar tr. to sketch, draft.

bo·ce·to m. sketch, draft.

bo·ci·na f. horn; MARIT. foghorn; MUS. trumpet, horn; (megáfono) megaphone; (caracol) conch shell; TELEC. mouthpiece.

bo·ci·nar intr. to play a horn.

bo·ci·na·zo m. COLL. honk, toot.

bo·cio m. goiter.

bo·cha f. wooden ball.

bo·char tr. AMER. to reject, rebuff; ARG. to fail, flunk.

bo·che m. hole in the ground; COLL. (repulsa) rebuff, slight.

bo·chin·che m. COLL. uproar, commotion; (taberna) dive, low-class bar.

bo·chin·che·ar intr. AMER. to cause an uproar.

bo·chin·che·ro, a adj. & m.f. COLL. rowdy.

bo·chor·no m. (vergüenza) embarrassment, shame; (sonrojo) flush, blush; (calor) suffocating heat.

bo·chor·no·so, a adj. shameful, embarrassing; (sofocante) suffocating, stifling.

bo·da f. wedding, marriage ♦ **bodas de Camacho** feast, banquet.

bo·de·ga f. wine cellar; (despensa) pantry; MARIT. hold; AGR. granary; (taberna) tavern, bar; (depósito) warehouse; AMER. grocery store.

bo·de·gón m. COLL. cheap restaurant, dive; (taberna) tavern, bar; ARTS still life.

bo·de·gue·ro, a m.f. keeper of a wine cellar; AMER. grocer.

bo·drio m. AMER., COLL. muddle, confusion.

bo·fe m. lung ♦ **echar los bofes** to break one's back • **ser un b.** to be a bore.

bo·fe·ta·da f. slap; (afrenta) insult.

bo·ga f. rowing; (moda) fashion, vogue —m.f. (bogador) rower.

bo·gar §47 tr. & intr. to row; (navegar) to sail.

bo·he·mio, a adj. & m.f. bohemian.

bo·hí·o m. AMER. hut, shack.

boi·co·te·ar tr. to boycott.

boi·co·te·o m. boycott, boycotting.

boi·na f. beret, cap.

boi·te f. nightclub.

boj or **bo·je** m. box tree, boxwood.

bo·la f. ball; (canica) marble; (betún) shoe polish; (mentira) lie, fib; CHILE kite; CUBA rumor, gossip; MEX. (tumulto) tumult, uproar ♦ **b. del mundo** globe • **b. de nieve** snowball •

dejar rodar la b. to let (something) ride, let things take their course • **no dar pie con b.** to miss the mark.

bo·la·da f. stroke, billiard shot; AMER. opportunity, lucky break; (mentira) lie, fib.

bo·la·zo m. blow with a ball; (mentira) lie, fib; ARG. (disparate) silly or foolish remark ♦ **de b.** hurriedly, carelessly.

bo·le·a·do·ras f.pl. R.P. bolas.

bo·le·ar tr. AMER. to entangle, entrap —intr. (jugar) to play (billiards) for fun; COLL. (mentir) to fib, lie —reflex. AMER. ro rear and fall, roll over (horses); (ruborizarse) to get flustered; R.P. (tropezar) to stumble, falter.

bo·le·o m. bowling; (sitio) bowling alley.

bo·le·ro, a I. adj. (truhán) truant; (mentiroso) lying, fibbing **II.** m.f. (novillero) truant; (mentiroso) liar, fibber —m. MUS. bolero —f. bowling alley.

bo·le·ta f. admission ticket; MIL. billet; (vale) voucher; AMER. ballot.

bo·le·te·rí·a f. AMER. ticket office, box office.

bo·le·te·ro, a m.f. AMER. ticket seller.

bo·le·tín m. bulletin; (billete) ticket.

bo·le·to m. AMER. ticket.

bo·li·che m. (bolín) jack; (juego) bowling, ninepins; AMER., COLL. (almacén) small store; (taberna) dive, cheap restaurant.

bó·li·do m. fireball, meteorite; FIG. bullet.

bo·lí·gra·fo m. ballpoint pen.

bo·li·llo m. bobbin ♦ pl. S. AMER. drumsticks.

bo·lí·var VEN., FIN. bolivar.

bo·lo m. (palo) pin, ninepin; (tonto) dunce, dummy; ARCHIT. newel post ♦ pl. bowling, ninepins • **echar a rodar los b.** COLL. to stir up trouble.

bol·sa f. (saco) sack, bag; (bolso) purse, pocketbook; ANAT. pocket, sac; MIN. pocket, lode; FIN. stock market; FIG. wealth, money; SPORT. purse, prize money ♦ **aflojar la b.** COLL. to loosen the pursestrings • **b. alcista, bajista** FIN. bull, bear market • **b. de comercio** commodity exchange • **b. negra** black market • **hacer bolsas** to bag, sag.

bol·si·llo m. pocket; (dinero) purse, money.

bol·sis·ta m.f. stockbroker; AMER. pickpocket.

bol·so m. purse, pocketbook.

bol·són m. large purse or handbag; AMER. school bag.

bo·llo m. bun, roll; (hueco) dent; (plegado) fold, crease; (chichón) lump, bump; (lío) fuss, to-do ♦ **armar un b.** to kick up a fuss.

bo·llón m. (clavo) boss, stud; (pendiente) button earring, stud.

bo·llo·na·do, a adj. studded, embossed.

bom·ba f. MIL. bomb, shell; TECH. pump; (sorpresa) bombshell, stunning news; AMER. (mentira) lie, fib; (borrachera) drinking bout ♦ **a prueba de bombas** bombproof • **b. aspirante** suction pump • **b. de mano** TECH. hand pump; MIL. grenade • **caer como una b.** to hit like a bombshell • **estar echando bombas** COLL. to be boiling hot • **estar en b.** AMER. to be drunk • **pasarlo b.** to have a ball.

bom·ba·cha(s) f.(pl.) R.P. baggy trousers.

bom·bar·de·ar tr. to bomb, bombard.

bom·bar·de·o m. bombardment, bombing ♦ **b. en picado** dive bombing.

bom·bar·de·ro, a I. m. (avión) bomber; (soldado) bombardier **II.** adj. bombing.

bom·bar·di·no m. saxhorn.

bom·ba·sí m. bombazine, fustian.

bom·bás·ti·co, a adj. bombastic.
bom·ba·zo m. bomb explosion; *(daño)* damage.
bom·be·ar tr. to bomb, shell; *(sacar)* to pump; *(abombar)* to make convex; *(dar bombo a)* to make a fuss over.
bom·be·ro m. fireman, firefighter.
bom·bi·lla f. light bulb; MARIT. lantern.
bom·bín m. COLL. bowler, derby; *(inflador)* bicycle pump.
bom·bo, a I. adj. COLL. *(atónito)* dazed, dumbfounded; *(tibio)* lukewarm II. m. *(tambor)* bass drum; *(músico)* bass drummer; *(barco)* barge; *(publicidad)* fanfare, buildup ♦ **dar b. a** COLL. to make a fuss over.
bom·bón m. bonbon, chocolate; COLL. *(persona)* gem, peach.
bom·bo·ne·ra f. COLL. cute place, cozy cottage.
bo·na·chón, o·na adj. & m.f. COLL. *(bueno)* good-natured (person); *(crédulo)* gullible (person).
bo·nan·za f. bonanza ♦ **ir en b.** to be fortunate.
bon·dad f. goodness, kindness ♦ **tener la b. de** to be so kind as to.
bon·da·do·so, a adj. good, kind.
bo·ne·te m. bonnet, cap; RELIG. biretta; *(dulcera)* candy dish; *(fortificación)* bonnet.
bo·ne·te·rí·a f. AMER. notions shop.
bo·nia·to m. sweet potato.
bo·ni·fi·ca·ción f. improvement; *(rebaja)* discount, reduction.
bo·ni·fi·car §70 tr. to improve, ameliorate; *(rebajar)* to discount, reduce the price of.
bo·ni·to, a I. adj. *(lindo)* pretty, nice-looking; *(bueno)* good, satisfactory II. m. tuna.
bo·no m. *(vale)* voucher, certificate; COM. *(fianza)* bond.
bo·que·a·da f. gasp.
bo·que·ar intr. *(jadear)* to gasp, *(morirse)* to be at death's door —tr. to mouth, utter.
bo·que·ra f. sluice; MED. lip sore, mouth ulcer.
bo·que·rón m. large aperture or hole; *(bocaza)* big mouth.
bo·que·te m. narrow entrance; *(agujero)* hole.
bo·quia·bier·to, a adj. open-mouthed, gaping; *(atónito)* amazed, astonished.
bo·qui·lla f. MUS. mouthpiece; *(del cigarillo)* cigarette holder; *(filtro)* filter tip; *(mechero)* nozzle; *(de pantalones)* pant leg opening.
bo·ra·ci·ta f. boracite.
bo·ra·to m. borate.
bó·rax m. borax.
bor·bo·llar/lle·ar intr. to bubble, boil; *(tartamudear)* to stutter, stammer.
bor·bo·lleo m. bubbling, boiling.
bor·bo·tar/te·ar intr. to boil, bubble.
bor·bo·te·o m. boiling, bubbling.
bor·bo·tón m. boiling, bubbling.
bor·da f. MARIT. gunwale; *(choza)* hut, cabin.
bor·da·do m. embroidery, embroidering.
bor·da·dor, ·ra m.f. embroiderer.
bor·dar tr. to embroider; FIG. to embellish.
bor·de m. border, edge; *(canto)* brim, rim; MARIT. board, side.
bor·de·ar tr. to border; *(ir por el borde)* to skirt, go around; *(aproximarse)* to approach.
bor·di·llo m. curb.
bor·do m. MARIT. board, shipboard; *(bordada)* tack.
bor·dón m. *(bastón)* staff; *(estribillo)* refrain;

(frase repetida) pet phrase; *(guía)* helping hand, guide.
bo·re·al adj. boreal, northern.
bor·go·ña m. Burgundy (wine).
bó·ri·co adj. boric.
bor·la f. *(hebras)* tassel; *(de polvera)* powder puff.
bor·lar·se reflex. AMER. to get one's doctorate.
bor·ne m. point, tip; ELEC. terminal.
bor·ne·ar tr. to twist, bend; *(guiñar)* to squint one's eyes —reflex. to warp, become warped.
bor·ne·o m. twisting, bending, *(del cuerpo)* swinging, turning.
bo·ro m. boron.
bo·rra f. *(del café)* coffee grounds; *(sedimento)* dregs; *(relleno)* flock, stuffing.
bo·rra·che·ar intr. COLL. to booze.
bo·rra·che·ra f. *(ebriedad)* drunkenness; *(parranda)* binge, spree; *(exaltación)* ecstasy, exultation.
bo·rra·chín m. COLL. drunkard, sot.
bo·rra·cho, a I. adj. *(ebrio)* drunk; *(alcoholizado)* drunken, alcoholic; *(morado)* violet, purple; *(de ron)* rum-soaked; *(dominado)* blind, wild ♦ **b. como una cuba** COLL. drunk as a skunk II. m.f. drunken person; *(alcohólico)* drunkard, alcoholic.
bo·rra·dor m. *(escrito)* rough draft; *(papel)* scratch pad; COM. daybook; *(de borrar)* eraser.
bo·rra·du·ra f. erasure, deletion.
bo·rra·jo m. ember, cinder.
bo·rrar tr. to erase.
bo·rras·ca f. *(tempestad)* storm, tempest; *(riesgo)* hazard, danger.
bo·rras·co·so, a adj. *(tempestuoso)* stormy, tempestuous; *(desordenado)* rowdy.
bo·rre·ga·da f. flock (of lambs).
bo·rre·go, a m.f. lamb; FIG. simpleton, fool.
bo·rri·ca f. she-ass; FIG. stupid woman.
bo·rri·ca·da f. donkey ride; *(necedad)* foolish remark or act.
bo·rri·co m. ass, donkey; *(de carpintero)* sawhorse; *(idiota)* ass, dimwit.
bo·rri·que·te m. sawhorse.
bo·rro m. yearling lamb.
bo·rrón m. *(mancha)* ink blot, smudge; *(borrador)* rough draft; FIG. blemish ♦ **b. y cuenta nueva** FIG., COLL. clean slate ♦ pl. jottings, scribbling.
bo·rro·ne·ar tr. *(escribir)* to scribble, scrawl; *(esbozar)* to outline.
bo·rro·si·dad f. blurriness, fuzziness.
bo·rro·so, a adj. blurred, fuzzy.
bos·ca·je m. thicket, copse; *(pintura)* landscape.
bos·co·so, a adj. wooded, woody.
bós·fo·ro m. strait.
bos·que m. woods, forest; FIG. confusion.
bos·que·jar tr. to sketch, outline.
bos·que·jo m. sketch, outline, draft.
bos·ta f. manure.
bos·te·zar §04 intr. to yawn.
bos·te·zo m. yawn.
bo·ta f. boot; *(odre)* wineskin; *(tonel)* wooden cask ♦ **estar con las botas puestas** to be ready to go • **ponerse las botas** to strike it rich.
bo·ta·do, a AMER. I. adj. *(expulsado)* fired, kicked out; *(barato)* cheap II. m.f. foundling.
bo·tá·ni·co, a I. adj. botanical II. m.f. botanist —f. botany.
bo·ta·nis·ta m.f. botanist.
bo·tar tr. to fling, hurl; COLL. *(despedir)* to dis-

miss, fire; MARIT. to turn; *(lanzar al agua)* to launch; *(tirar)* to throw away; *(malgastar)* to waste, squander —intr. to bounce.

bo·ta·ra·te m. *(tonto)* fool, idiot; AMER. spendthrift, squanderer.

bo·ta·va·ra f. gaffsail.

bo·te m. *(golpe)* thrust, blow; *(brinco)* prance, caper; *(rebote)* bounce; *(pote)* pot, jar; *(lata)* tin can; *(barco)* rowboat ♦ **de b. y voleo** immediately, instantly • **de b. en b.** full, jammed.

bo·te·lla f. bottle.

bo·ti·ca f. pharmacy, drugstore.

bo·ti·ca·rio, a m.f. pharmacist, druggist.

bo·ti·ja f. earthenware jar; C. AMER. buried treasure ♦ **estar hecho una b.** to be very fat.

bo·ti·jo m. earthenware jug; *(persona gorda)* chubby person.

bo·tín[1] m. *(bota)* ankle boot, half boot.

bo·tín[2] m. *(presa)* booty, spoils.

bo·ti·ne·ri·a f. boot *or* shoe store.

bo·ti·ne·ro, a m.f. *(persona que hace botines)* bootmaker, cobbler; *(vendedor)* boot seller.

bo·ti·quín m. medicine chest *or* cabinet; *(estuche)* first-aid kit.

bo·tón m. button; *(llamador)* doorbell, buzzer; BOT. bud ♦ **al b.** AMER. in vain • **b. de arranque** AUTO. starter • **b. de oro** BOT. buttercup.

bo·to·na·du·ra f. buttons, set of buttons.

bo·to·nes m.pl. bellboy, bellhop.

bo·tu·lis·mo m. botulism.

bó·ve·da f. vault; *(techo)* dome, cupola; *(cripta)* crypt; *(caverna)* cave, cavern ♦ **b. celeste** firmament, heavens • **b. palatina** palate, roof of the mouth.

bo·vi·no, a adj. bovine.

bo·xe·a·dor m. boxer.

bo·xe·ar intr. to box.

bo·xe·o m. boxing.

bo·ya f. buoy.

bo·yar intr. to float, to buoy.

bo·zal I. m. muzzle; AMER. halter, headstall —m.f. *(idiota)* simpleton, fool; *(novato)* novice II. adj. *(tonto)* ignorant; *(novato)* raw, green; *(salvaje)* wild, untamed.

bo·zo m. down, fuzz (on upper lip); *(boca)* mouth; *(cabestro)* halter.

bra·ce·ar intr. to flail one's arms; *(nadar)* to swim; *(esforzarse)* to struggle, strive.

bra·ce·o m. waving of the arms; *(natación)* stroke.

bra·ce·ro, a I. adj. throwing II. m. laborer, worker.

bra·co, a adj. & m.f. pug-nosed (person).

bra·ga f. *(cuerda)* sling, rope; *(pañal)* diapers; *(calzón femenino)* panties.

bra·ga·do, a adj. resolute, firm.

bra·ga·du·ra f. crotch.

bra·ga·zas m.inv. henpecked husband.

bra·gue·ro m. MED. truss.

bra·gue·ta f. fly (of pants).

bra·mar intr. to roar, bellow; FIG. to howl.

bra·mi·do m. roar, bellow.

bran·ca·da f. trammel net.

bran·dal m. backstay.

bran·quia f. branchia, gill.

bra·quial adj. brachial, of the arm.

bra·sa f. live *or* hot coal.

bras·ca f. fettling.

bra·se·ro m. brazier.

bra·sil m. brazilwood.

bra·va·ta f. *(reto)* dare, threat; *(jactancia)* boast, brag.

bra·ve·ar intr. *(jactarse)* to boast, bluster; *(aplaudir)* to cheer, shout bravo!

bra·ví·o, a I. adj. *(feroz)* wild, untamed; *(silvestre)* wild, uncultivated; *(rústico)* uncouth, coarse II. m. fierceness, ferocity.

bra·vo, a adj. brave, valiant; *(excelente)* excellent, great; *(feroz)* ferocious, wild; *(áspero)* craggy, rugged; *(valentón)* boastful, swaggering; *(enojado)* angry, furious ♦ **¡b.!** bravo!, well done!

bra·vu·cón, o·na adj. & m.f. boastful (person).

bra·vu·co·ne·ar intr. to boast, swagger.

bra·vu·ra f. bravery, courage; *(fiereza)* fierceness, ferocity; *(bravata)* bluster, bravado.

bra·za f. MARIT. fathom; *(modo de nadar)* breaststroke.

bra·za·da f. extension of the arms; AMER. fathom ♦ **b. de espaldas** backstroke • **b. de pecho** breaststroke.

bra·zal m. armband.

bra·za·le·te m. bracelet.

bra·zo m. arm; ZOOL. foreleg; *(de balanza)* arm, crosspiece; *(fuerza)* power, strength ♦ **a b. partido** *(sin armas)* bare-fisted; FIG. fast and furiously • **asidos** *or* **cogidos de b.** arm in arm ♦ pl. *(jornaleros)* hands, laborers; *(valedores)* backers, supporters.

bre·a f. tar, pitch; *(lienzo)* tarpaulin ♦ **b. seca** rosin.

bre·ar tr. COLL. *(maltratar)* to abuse, ill-treat; *(chasquear)* to make fun of, tease ♦ **b. de golpes** to beat up.

bre·ba·je m. unpalatable concoction *or* brew.

bré·col m./**co·les** m.pl. broccoli.

bre·cha f. MIL. breach; *(abertura)* gap, opening; FIG. impression.

bre·ga f. *(pelea)* fight, scrap; *(trabajo)* hard work, task; *(burla)* practical joke, trick.

bre·gar §47 intr. *(pelear)* to fight, scrap; *(trabajar)* to toil, slave away; *(esforzarse)* to struggle, fight.

bren·ca f. sluice post.

bre·ñal m. brambly, rugged ground.

bre·te m. *(grillete)* shackle, fetter; *(aprieto)* jam, tight spot; BOT. betel.

bre·va f. *(higo)* early fig; *(ventaja)* windfall, piece of luck.

bre·ve adj. brief, short ♦ **en b.** *(pronto)* shortly, soon; *(con brevedad)* in brief.

bre·ve·dad f. briefness, brevity.

bre·via·rio m. breviary; *(compendio)* compendium, abstract.

bri·bón, o·na adj. & m.f. *(perezoso)* lazy (person); *(pícaro)* roguish (person).

bri·bo·na·da f. roguishness.

bri·bo·ne·ar intr. *(holgazanear)* to loaf, bum around; *(hacer bribonadas)* to play tricks.

bri·da f. bridle ♦ **a toda b.** at full gallop; FIG. at full speed.

bridge m. bridge; DENT. bridge, bridgework.

bri·ga·da f. brigade; *(división)* squad, unit; *(de bestias)* team, train; *(de máquinas)* fleet; *(equipo)* gang, team.

bri·ga·dier m. brigadier general.

bri·llan·te adj. brilliant.

bri·llan·tez f. brilliance, brightness.

bri·llan·ti·na f. brilliantine.

bri·llar intr. to shine.

bri·llo m. *(lustre)* brilliance, shine; *(gloria)* distinction, glory ♦ **dar** *or* **sacar b. a** to shine, polish.

brin·car §70 intr. to jump, leap about; *(retozar)*

to frolic, gambol; *(enfadarse)* to get angry, flare up —tr. to bounce.

brin·co m. jump, hop ♦ **en** *or* **de un b.** in a jiffy.

brin·dar intr. to toast, drink a toast —tr. *(ofrecer)* to offer; *(convidar)* to invite —reflex. to offer, volunteer.

brin·dis m. toast.

brí·o m. strength, vigor; *(garbo)* grace, charm.

brio·so, a adj. *(enérgico)* vigorous; *(determinado)* determined, resolute; *(animoso)* fiery, spirited; *(garboso)* graceful, charming.

bri·que·ta f. charcoal briquette.

bri·sa f. breeze, light wind; AGR. bagasse.

briz·na f. bit, piece.

bro·ca f. SEW. reel; MECH. drill, bit.

bro·ca·do, a adj. & m. brocade.

bro·ce·o m. MIN. depletion (of a mine).

bró·cu·li m. broccoli.

bro·cha f. paintbrush; *(de afeitar)* shaving brush; *(dado)* loaded die.

bro·cha·da f. brush stroke.

bro·cha·zo m. brush stroke.

bro·che m. clasp, hook and eye; *(prendedor)* brooch; AMER. paper clip ♦ **b. de oro** crowning glory ♦ pl. AMER. cuff links.

bro·che·ta f. brochette, skewer.

bro·ma f. joke, prank; *(diversión)* fun, jest ♦ **b. pesada** practical joke, prank · **gastar** *or* **hacer una b. a** to play a joke on • **ni en b.** not on your life.

bro·ma·to m. bromate.

bro·me·ar intr. to joke, jest.

bro·mis·ta I. adj. joking II. m.f. joker.

bro·mo m. CHEM. bromine; BOT. brome grass.

bro·mu·ro m. bromide.

bron·ca f. see **bronco, a.**

bron·ce m. bronze.

bron·ce·a·do, a I. adj. *(color)* bronze, bronze-colored; *(tostado)* tanned, bronzed II. m. bronzing; *(piel tostada)* suntan.

bron·ce·ar tr. to bronze; *(piel)* to tan, suntan —reflex. to get a tan, suntan.

bron·co, a I. adj. *(tosco)* rough, coarse; *(desapacible)* harsh, gruff II. f. row, quarrel ♦ **armar b.** to kick up a rumpus, start a row.

bron·co·neu·mo·ní·a f. bronchopneumonia.

bron·que·dad/ra f. *(tosquedad)* coarseness, roughness; *(aspereza)* harshness, gruffness.

bron·quial adj. bronchial.

bron·quio m. bronchus, bronchial tube.

bron·quio·lo m. bronchiole.

bron·qui·tis f. bronchitis.

bro·quel m. buckler, small shield; *(amparo)* shield, protection.

bro·que·lar·se reflex. to shield oneself.

bro·que·ta f. brochette, skewer.

bro·ta·du·ra f. sprouting, budding.

bro·tar intr. BOT. to bud, sprout; *(agua)* to spring, flow; *(estallar)* to break out, spring up —tr. BOT. to sprout.

bro·te m. bud, sprout; *(estallido)* outbreak, rash; *(comienzo)* origin, germ.

bru·ces ♦ **a** *or* **de b.** adv. face down, on one's face • **caer de b.** to fall flat on one's face.

bru·ja f. witch, sorceress.

bru·je·rí·a f. witchcraft, sorcery.

bru·jo m. *(adivino)* sorcerer, wizard; *(de una tribu)* witch doctor, medicine man.

brú·ju·la f. compass; *(norma)* standard, norm.

bru·lo·te m. fire ship; AMER. *(palabrota)* swear word; *(escrito)* satiric article.

bru·ma f. fog, mist.

bru·mo m. refined wax, pure wax.

bru·mo·so, a adj. foggy, misty.

bru·no, a adj. dark-colored, black.

bru·ñi·do, a I. m. burnishing, polishing; *(brillo)* shine, gloss II. adj. burnished, polished.

bru·ñi·du·ra f. polishing, burnishing.

bru·ñir §12 tr. to burnish, polish; AMER. to annoy, pester —reflex. to put on make-up.

brus·co, a adj. brusque.

brus·que·dad f. brusqueness.

bru·tal I. adj. brutal, *(formidable)* terrific, tremendous II. m. brute, beast.

bru·ta·li·dad f. brutality; *(incapacidad)* stupidity, foolishness; *(gran cantidad)* loads, slew.

bru·ta·li·zar §04 tr. to brutalize, maltreat —reflex. to be brutalized.

bru·te·za f. brutishness, boorishness.

bru·to, a I. adj. brutish, boorish; *(necio)* stupid, ignorant; *(diamante)* rough, uncut; *(enorme)* huge, enormous; COM. gross II. m. *(persona)* brute; *(animal)* beast, animal.

bru·za f. scrubbing brush.

bu m. bogeyman.

bu·ba f. pustule, small tumor.

bu·bón m. large tumor *or* swelling.

bu·bó·ni·co, a adj. bubonic.

bu·cal adj. buccal, oral.

bu·ca·ro m. *(arcilla)* fragrant clay; *(botijo)* clay water jug; *(florero)* ceramic flower vase.

bu·ce·ar intr. to swim under water; *(oficio)* to work as a diver; *(explorar)* to delve into.

bu·ce·o m. *(natación)* underwater swimming; *(exploración)* exploration, searching.

bu·cle m. ringlet, curl; AVIA. spin, loop.

bu·có·li·co, a adj. & f. bucolic *or* pastoral (poem).

bu·che m. ORNITH. crop, craw; ZOOL. maw; *(porción)* mouthful, swallow; *(pliegue)* sag, pucker; *(estómago)* belly, gut; *(pecho)* chest, bosom.

bu·dín m. pudding.

buen adj. contr. of **bueno.**

bue·na·ven·tu·ra f. *(suerte)* good fortune, luck; *(adivinación)* fortune.

bue·no, a I. adj. good; *(bondadoso)* kind, benevolent; *(útil)* fit, appropriate; *(sano)* well, healthy; *(agradable)* nice, polite; *(grande)* considerable, goodly; *(bonachón)* innocent, naive ♦ **a** *or* **por las buenas** willingly • **a la b. de Dios** carelessly, any old way • **buenas noches, tardes** good night, afternoon • **buenos días** morning • **de buenas a primeras** all of a sudden • **estar de buenas** to be in a good mood II. adv. all right, okay III. m. good.

buey m. ox, bullock ♦ **trabajar como un b.** COLL. to work like a dog.

bú·fa·lo, a m.f. *(buey salvaje)* buffalo; *(bisonte)* bison.

bu·fan·da f. scarf, muffler.

bu·far intr. *(resoplar)* to snort; *(enojarse)* to snort, puff.

bu·fe·te m. *(escritorio)* writing desk *or* table; *(despacho)* lawyer's office; *(clientela)* lawyer's clientele, practice.

bu·fi·do m. bellow, snort.

bu·fo, a I. adj. comic, farcical II. m. clown, buffoon.

bu·fón, o·na adj. & m. buffoon(ish).

bu·fo·na·da/ne·rí·a f. buffoonery; *(sarcasmo)* sarcastic joke *or* remark.

bu·fo·ni·zar §04 intr. to joke, jest.

bu·har·da/di·lla f. *(ventana)* dormer; *(desván)* attic, garret.

bú·ho m. horned owl; *(recluso)* hermit.

bu·ho·ne·ro m. peddler, hawker.

bui·tre m. vulture.

bu·je m. axle box, bushing.

bu·jí·a f. *(vela)* candle; *(candelero)* candlestick; PHYS. candle, candlepower; ELEC. spark plug.

bu·la f. metal seal, bulla; RELIG. papal bull.

bul·bo m. bulb.

bul(l)·dog m. bulldog.

bu·le·var m. boulevard.

bu·li·mia f. bulimia.

bul·to m. *(tamaño)* bulk, size; *(forma)* form, shape; *(fardo)* package, bundle; MED. swelling, lump; ARTS bust, statue; AMER. briefcase, satchel ♦ **a b.** broadly; COM. wholesale • **de b.** important • **escurrir el b.** to duck, dodge • **hacer b.** to take up space.

bu·lla f. *(ruido)* noise, racket; *(muchedumbre)* crowd, mob; *(prisa)* bustling, rush; AMER. argument, row.

bu·lli·cio m. bustle, hubbub.

bu·lli·cio·so, a adj. *(animado)* bustling; *(alborotador)* riotous, tumultuous.

bu·llir §13 intr. to boil; *(moverse)* to bustle about; ZOOL. to swarm —tr. to move —reflex. to budge, stir

bu·me·rán/ang m. boomerang.

bu·ñue·lo m. fried dough, fritter; COLL. mess, bungle.

bu·que m. ship, vessel; *(casco)* hull ♦ **b. almirante** flagship • **b. tanque** tanker • **b. velero** or **de vela** sailboat, sailing ship.

bu·qué m. bouquet.

bur·bu·ja f. bubble.

bur·bu·je·ar intr. to bubble.

bur·del I. adj. lustful, licentious II. m. brothel.

bur·de·os adj. maroon, deep red.

bur·do, a adj. coarse, rough.

bur·gués, e·sa adj. & m.f. bourgeois.

bur·gue·sí·a f. bourgeoisie, middle class.

bu·ril m. burin, graver.

bu·ri·lar tr. to engrave.

bur·la f. *(mofa)* jeer, taunt; *(chanza)* joke, jest; *(engaño)* trick, hoax ♦ **de burlas** in fun, for fun • **hacer b. de** to make fun of, mock.

bur·lar tr. to make fun of; *(frustrar)* to frustrate, thwart —reflex. to make fun, joke ♦ **b. de** to make fun of, ridicule.

bur·les·co, a adj. burlesque.

bur·le·te m. weather stripping.

bur·lón, o·na I. adj. jeering, joking II.m.f. *(mofador)* jeerer, mocker; *(bromista)* joker, jokester.

bu·ro·cra·cia f. bureaucracy.

bu·ró·cra·ta m.f. bureaucrat.

bu·ro·crá·ti·co, a adj. bureaucratic.

bu·rra f. she-ass, jenny; COLL. *(ignorante)* stupid woman, dunce; *(trabajadora)* hard worker, slave.

bu·rre·ro m. donkey driver.

bu·rro m. donkey, jackass; *(caballete)* sawhorse, sawbuck; *(rueda)* cogwheel; *(borrico)* ass, dunce ♦ **b. de carga** COLL. hard worker, drudge.

bur·sá·til adj. stock, stock market.

bu·ru·jo m. *(bulto)* lump; *(nudo)* tangle, knot.

bus·ca f. search ♦ **ir en** or **a la b. de** to go in search of.

bus·ca·pié m. feeler, insinuation.

bus·ca·piés m.inv. firecracker, squib.

bus·car §70 tr. to search or look for, seek; COLL. *(provocar)* to provoke —reflex. ♦ **buscársela** *(ingeniarse)* to get by, manage; *(provocar)* to look for trouble.

bus·ca·vi·das m.f.inv. *(entremetido)* snoop, busybody; *(ambicioso)* go-getter.

bu·si·lis m.inv. *(clave)* crux of a matter; *(dificultad)* hitch, snag.

bús·que·da f. search.

bus·to m. ANAT. chest, bust; SCULP. bust.

bu·ta·ca f. armchair, easy chair; THEAT. orchestra or box seat.

bu·ta·no m. butane.

bu·ti·le·no m. butylene.

bu·zo m. (deep-sea) diver.

bu·zón m. mailbox, letter box; *(conducto)* sluice, canal; *(tapón)* stopper, plug.

C

c, C f. third letter of the Spanish alphabet.

ca·bal adj. *(exacto)* precise, fair; *(completo)* complete ♦ FIG. **no estar en sus cabales** not to be in one's right mind.

cá·ba·la f. RELIG. cabala.

ca·bal·gar §47 intr. to ride horseback.

ca·ba·lla f. mackerel.

ca·ba·lla·da f. herd of horses; AMER. asinine remark or action.

ca·ba·lle·res·co adj.–knightly; FIG. gentlemanly.

ca·ba·lle·rí·a f. *(animal)* mount, steed; MIL. cavalry.

ca·ba·lle·ri·za f. stable; *(criados)* stablehands.

ca·ba·lle·ri·zo m. stableman.

ca·ba·lle·ro, a I. m. *(noble)* nobleman; *(persona condecorada)* knight; *(señor)* gentleman; *(como cortesía)* sir ♦ **armar c. a** to knight • **c. andante** knight-errant II. adj. riding.

ca·ba·lle·ro·si·dad f. gentlemanliness.

ca·ba·lle·te m. *(soporte)* sawhorse; *(trípode)* easel; AGR. ridge; ANAT. bridge (of the nose).

ca·ba·lli·to m. pony; *(juguete)* hobbyhorse ♦ **c. del diablo** dragonfly • **c. de mar** sea horse.

ca·ba·llo m. horse; *(en ajedrez)* knight; COLL. *(bestia)* beast; CARP. sawhorse ♦ **a c.** on horseback • **a c. de** astride • **c. de batalla** FIG. forte • **c. de carga** packhorse • **c. de carrera** racehorse • **c. de fuerza** MECH. horsepower • **c. de montar** or **de silla** saddle horse • **c. de tiro** draft horse • **c. hora** MECH. horsepower-hour • **como c. desbocado** hastily • **montar a c.** to go horseback riding ♦ pl. horsepower.

ca·ba·ña f. hut, cabin.

ca·ba·ret m. night club, cabaret.

ca·be·ce·ar intr. *(el caballo)* to toss the head; *(negar)* to shake one's head; *(de sueño)* to nod (sleepily); AVIA., MARIT. to pitch —tr. SPORT. to head (a ball).

ca·be·ce·ra f. *(lugar principal)* head <la c. de la mesa the head of the table>; *(de una cama)* headboard ♦ **médico de c.** attending physician.

ca·be·ci·lla m. ringleader.

ca·be·lle·ra f. head of hair; ASTRON. tail (of a comet).

ca·be·llo m. hair ♦ **asirse de un c.** FIG., COLL. to grasp at straws ♦ pl. hair • **ponérsele a uno los c. de punta** COLL. to make one's hair stand on end • **traer (una cosa) por los c.** COLL. to be irrelevant.

ca·ber §14 intr. (*tener lugar*) to fit; (*corresponder*) to fall to; (*ser posible*) to be possible ♦ **cabe decir** one might say • **no cabe duda** there is no doubt • **no cabe más** FIG. that's the limit • **no c. en sí** to be beside oneself • **no c. un alfiler** to be full • **¡no me cabe en la cabeza!** it's beyond me!

ca·bes·tri·llo m. MED. sling.

ca·bes·tro m. halter.

ca·be·za f. head; (*cráneo*) skull; (*jefe*) chief; (*juicio*) judgment; (*capital*) seat ♦ **a la c. de** (*delante*) at the head of; (*en control*) in charge of • **alzar** *o* **levantar c.** COLL. to get back on one's feet • **doblar la c.** COLL. to give in • **c. de ajo** garlic bulb • **c. de chorlito** COLL. featherbrain • **c. de partido** POL. district seat • **c. de puente** MIL. bridgehead • **c. de turco** COLL. scapegoat • **de la c. de uno** of one's own invention • **estar metido de c. con** to be head over heels in love with • **hacer c.** to lead • **írsele de la c.** to go out of one's mind • **írsele la c.** COLL. to feel dizzy • **jugarse la c.** COLL. to risk one's life • **meterse de c. en** COLL. to plunge into • **metérsele en la c.** COLL. to take it into one's head • **pasarle a uno por la c.** COLL. to occur to one • **romperse la c.** COLL. to rack one's brains • **sentar la c.** COLL. to settle down • **subírse a uno a la c.** to go to one's head • **tocado de la c.** COLL. touched in the head.

ca·be·za·da f. (*con la cabeza*) butt; (*en la cabeza*) blow to the head; (*inclinación*) nod.

ca·be·za·zo m. (*golpe*) butt; SPORT. header.

ca·be·zón, o·na adj. COLL. (*terco*) pigheaded; (*cabezudo*) bigheaded.

ca·be·zo·ta m.f. COLL. mule.

ca·be·zu·do, a adj. bigheaded; FIG. pigheaded.

ca·bi·da f. (*capacidad*) room, capacity; (*alcance*) extent ♦ **tener c. en** FIG. to have a place in.

ca·bil·do m. town council.

ca·bi·na f. booth; MARIT. cabin; AVIA. cockpit; AUTO. cab; CINEM. projection booth.

ca·biz·ba·jo, a adj. crestfallen, downhearted.

ca·ble m. cable ♦ **c. aéreo** overhead cable • **c. de remolque** towline.

ca·ble·gra·fiar §30 tr. & intr. to cable.

ca·ble·gra·ma m. cable, cablegram.

ca·ble·vi·sión f. cable television.

ca·bo m. end; (*pedazo*) stub, bit; (*mango*) handle; GEOG. cape; MARIT. cable; MIL. corporal ♦ **al c. de** at the end of • **al fin y al c.** after all • **atar cabos** to put two and two together • **dar c. a** to put the finishing touches on • **de c. a rabo** COLL. from start to finish • **llevar a c.** to carry out.

ca·bo·ta·je m. COM. coastal trading.

ca·bra f. goat ♦ **c. montés** mountain goat • **estar loco como una c.** to be crazy as a loon • **la c. siempre tira al monte** a leopard never changes its spots.

ca·bre·ro, a I. m.f. goatherd II. adj. R.P., COLL. hot-tempered.

ca·bri·lle·ar intr. to form whitecaps.

ca·brio·la f. (*salto*) jump; (*voltereta*) somersault.

ca·brio·lar intr. to jump; (*voltear*) to tumble.

ca·brio·lé m. (*carruaje*) cabriolet; (*coche*) convertible.

ca·bri·ti·lla f. lambskin, kid.

ca·bri·to m. kid, young goat.

ca·brón m. goat; SL. (*cornudo*) cuckold; (*cretino*) bastard.

ca·bro·na·da f. COLL. dirty *or* nasty trick.

ca·bru·no, a adj. of goats, goatlike.

ca·bu·jón/chón m. (*piedra*) cabochon.

ca·ca·hue·te m. peanut.

ca·ca·o m. cacao; CUL. cocoa.

ca·ca·re·a·dor, ·ra adj. cackling; FIG. boasting.

ca·ca·re·ar intr. to cackle —tr. FIG. to boast.

ca·ca·re·o m. cackling; FIG. boasting.

ca·ca·tú·a f. cockatoo.

ca·ce·rí·a f. (*caza*) hunting; (*partida*) hunting party; (*animales*) game bagged ♦ **ir de c.** to go hunting.

ca·ce·ro·la f. casserole, pot.

ca·ci·que m. (*indio*) Indian chief; COLL. (*jefe*) political boss; (*déspota*) tyrant.

ca·ci·que·ar intr. COLL. to boss people around.

ca·co m. (*ladrón*) burglar; (*cobarde*) chicken.

ca·co·fo·ní·a f. cacophony.

cac·to/tus m. cactus.

ca·cu·men m. COLL. acumen, astuteness.

ca·cha f. (*de mango*) handle plate; AMER. (*engaño*) trick, deceit.

ca·cha·da f. R.P. joke.

ca·cha·lo·te m. sperm whale.

ca·char tr. (*astillar*) to chip; (*aserrar*) to split; R.P. (*la he.*) to tease; (*agarrar*) to nab, (*sorprender*) to catch; (*robar*) to rob, steal.

ca·cha·rre·ro, a m.f. pottery vendor.

ca·cha·rro m. (*vasija*) crock; (*pedazo*) shard; COLL. (*trasto*) piece of junk; (*máquina*) wreck; (*coche*) jalopy; AMER. jail, prison ♦ pl. (*trastos*) junk; (*utensilios*) tools.

ca·cha·za f. (*lentitud*) sluggishness; (*aguardiente*) cheap rum.

ca·cha·zu·do, a I. adj. sluggish II. m.f. slowpoke.

ca·che·ar tr. to search, frisk.

ca·che·mi·ra f./**mir** m. cashmere.

ca·che·ta·da f. AMER. slap.

ca·che·te m. (*mejilla*) cheek; (*cachetada*) slap.

ca·che·te·ar tr. AMER. to slap.

ca·che·ti·na f. fist fight.

ca·che·tu·do, a adj. chubby-cheeked, plumpcheeked.

ca·chi·po·rra f. club, bludgeon.

ca·chi·po·rra·zo m. blow with a club.

ca·chi·va·che m. piece of junk; FIG. good-for-nothing ♦ pl. COLL. (*utensilios*) pots and pans; (*cacharros*) junk.

ca·cho m. (*pedazo*) piece; AMER. (*cuerno*) horn; R.P. (*plátanos*) bunch of bananas ♦ **un c.** SL. a bit.

ca·chon·de·ar·se reflex. COLL. ♦ **c. de** to tease.

ca·chon·de·o m. COLL. teasing.

ca·chon·dez f. (*celo*) heat; (*lujuria*) lust.

ca·chon·do, a adj. (*en celo*) in heat; (*libidinoso*) lustful.

ca·cho·rro, a m.f. (*perro*) puppy; (*de otros mamíferos*) cub.

ca·chu·che·ar tr. (*mimar*) to spoil; (*adular*) to flatter.

ca·chue·la f. (*guisado*) stew; (*rápido*) rapids.

ca·da adj. each, every ♦ **c. cual** *or* **uno** each one, everyone • **¿c. cuánto?** how often? • **c. vez más** more and more • **c. vez menos** less and less • **c. vez peor** worse and worse • **c. vez que** whenever.

ca·dal·so m. (*tablado*) platform; (*horca*) gallows.

ca·dá·ver m. corpse, cadaver.
ca·da·vé·ri·co, a adj. cadaverous; FIG. deathly pale.
ca·de·na f. chain ♦ c. de emisoras network • c. de fabricación or de montaje assembly line • c. de montañas mountain range • c. perpetua life imprisonment • reacción en c. chain reaction.
ca·den·cia f. cadence, rhythm.
ca·de·ne·ro m. SURV. chainman; AMER. (caballo) workhorse.
ca·de·ni·lla f. small ornamental chain.
ca·de·ra f. hip, hip joint.
ca·de·te m. MIL. cadet.
cad·mio m. cadmium.
ca·du·car §70 intr. (expirar) to lapse, expire; LAW to be invalid.
ca·du·ci·dad f. caducity.
ca·du·co, a adj. (extinguido) lapsed, expired; LAW canceled; (senil) senile, decrepit.
ca·er §15 intr. to fall; (de rodillas) to drop; (derrumbarse) to fall down, collapse; (el cabello, telas) to hang down; (mala fortuna) to befall; (buena fortuna) to get, receive; (los precios, intereses) to drop; (el sol) to set; (morir) to die; (comprender) to see ♦ al c. la noche at nightfall • c. bien (prenda) to suit; (persona) to make a good impression on; (alimento) to agree with • c. de pie to land on one's feet • c. de plano to fall flat • c. en to fall on or into • c. de espaldas to fall on one's back; FIG. to be stunned • c. enfermo or en cama to fall ill • c. en gracia to make a good impression on • c. en la cuenta to realize • c. mal (prenda) to fit poorly; (persona) to displease; (alimento) to upset one's stomach • c. parado COLL. to be a nuisance • c. por su propio peso to be self-evident • estar al c. to be about to arrive —reflex. to fall; (de las manos) to drop <se me cayó el libro I dropped the book>; (cabello) to fall out • c. de espaldas to fall on one's back; FIG. to be stunned • c. de sí mismo to be obvious • caérsele el alma a los pies COLL. to become disheartened • c. muerto to drop dead • c. redondo to collapse • no tener dónde c. muerto to be destitute —tr. ♦ hacer c. to knock down.
ca·fé m. coffee; (establecimiento) café, coffee shop; S. AMER., COLL. scolding ♦ c. negro or solo black coffee • c. tostado roasted coffee.
ca·fe·í·na f. caffeine.
ca·fe·tal m. coffee plantation.
ca·fe·ta·le·ro, a I. adj. coffee II. m. coffee grower.
ca·fe·te·rí·a f. coffee shop, cafè.
ca·fe·te·ro, a I. adj. coffee II. m.f. (comerciante) coffee merchant; (dueño) café owner —f. CUL. coffeepot ♦ c. de filtro percolator.
ca·fe·tín m. small café.
ca·í·do, a I. see caer II. adj. weak; FIG. downhearted ♦ andar de capa c. COLL. to suffer a setback • c. del cielo out of the blue • c. de un nido COLL. naive • c. en desuso obsolete, outmoded III. f. fall, falling; (tumbo) tumble; (declive) slope; (de tela) hang; (de temperatura, precios) drop; (ruina) downfall; GEOL. dip ♦ a la c. de la tarde at dusk.
cai·ga, go see caer.
cai·mán m. alligator.
cai·rel m. (peluca) hairpiece; (fleco) fringe.
ca·ja f. box; (de madera) chest; (ataúd) coffin; (ventanilla) cashier's window; (tambor) drum; (armazón) cabinet; ARM. gun stock; ARCHIT.

shaft; PRINT. type case; THEAT. wings ♦ c. chica COM. petty cash • c. de ahorros savings bank • c. de cambios or velocidades AUTO. transmission • c. de colores paint box • c. de conexiones ELEC. junction box • c. de fusibles ELEC. fuse box • c. de herramientas toolbox • c. de hierro AMER. safe • c. de jubilaciones pension fund • c. de música music box • c. de reclutamiento MIL. recruiting office • c. de seguridad safe-deposit box • c. de sorpresa jack-in-the-box • c. efectivo COM. cash on hand • c. fuerte safe • c. registradora cash register • c. torácica chest • echar a alguien con cajas destempladas COLL. to send someone packing.
ca·je·ro m. teller, cashier.
ca·je·ti·lla f. (paquete) pack —m. R.P., COLL. dandy.
ca·jis·ta m.f. PRINT. typesetter, compositor.
ca·jón m. (caja grande) case; (gaveta) drawer; S. AMER. (ataúd) coffin ♦ de c. COLL. customary.
ca·jo·ne·rí·a f. set of drawers.
cal f. MIN. lime ♦ c. apagada slaked lime • c. viva quicklime.
ca·la f. GEOG. cove; (trozo) sample; BOT. calla lily.
ca·la·ba·za f. squash; COLL. (tonto) blockhead ♦ dar calabazas a COLL. to jilt.
ca·la·bo·zo m. (cárcel) underground prison; (celda) jail cell.
ca·la·do m. SEW. drawnwork; MARIT. depth.
ca·la·dor m. MECH. driller; AMER. (sonda) probe.
ca·la·fa·te·ar tr. to caulk.
ca·la·mar m. squid.
ca·lam·bre m. cramp.
ca·la·mi·dad f. (desastre) misfortune; COLL. (persona) disgrace.
ca·la·mi·to·so, a adj. calamitous.
ca·lan·drar tr. to calender (paper, cloth).
ca·lan·dria f. ORNITH. type of lark; MECH., TEX. calender.
ca·la·ña f. nature, character.
ca·lar tr. (mojar) to drench; (penetrar) to penetrate; COLL. (descubrir) to see through; (cortar) to cut a sample of; MARIT. to draw; MIL. to fix, aim (weapons); R.P. to stare at —reflex. (mojarse) to get drenched; (ponerse) to put on ♦ c. hasta los huesos to get soaked to the skin.
ca·la·ve·ra f. skull —m. reveler.
ca·la·ve·ra·da f. reckless escapade, tomfoolery.
ca·la·ve·re·ar intr. to have a wild time.
cal·ca·ñal/ñar m. heel, heel bone.
cal·car §70 tr. to trace; FIG. to copy.
cal·cá·re·o, a adj. calcareous, limy.
cal·ce m. (llanta) steel rim or tire; (cuña) wedge.
cal·ce·ta f. knee-high sock or stocking ♦ hacer c. to knit (socks).
cal·ce·tín m. sock.
cal·ci·fi·ca·ción f. calcification.
cal·ci·fi·car §70 tr. to calcify.
cal·ci·nar tr. to calcine; FIG. to burn.
cal·cio m. calcium.
cal·co m. tracing; FIG. copy.
cal·co·ma·ní·a f. decal, transfer.
cal·cu·la·ble adj. calculable.
cal·cu·la·dor, ra I. f. (máquina de calcular) calculator; (electrónica) computer ♦ c. electrónica computer —m.f. calculator II. adj. calculating.
cal·cu·lar tr. (computar) to calculate; (proyec-

tar) to estimate.

cal·cu·lis·ta m.f. calculator, planner.

cál·cu·lo m. *(proceso)* calculation; *(suposición)* estimate; MED. stone, calculus; MATH. calculus ♦ **c. biliar** MED. gallstone • **c. mental** mental arithmetic • **c. renal** MED. kidney stone • **obrar con mucho c.** to act shrewdly.

cal·de·ar tr. to heat *or* warm (up); FIG. to enliven.

cal·de·ra f. caldron; MECH. boiler; MIN. sump ♦ **c. de vapor** steam boiler.

cal·de·ro m. small caldron.

cal·de·rón m. large caldron; *(párrafo)* paragraph mark; MUS. pause sign.

cal·do m. *(consomé)* broth; *(jugo)* juice ♦ **c. de cultivo** BIOL. culture medium • **hacer a uno el c. gordo** to play into someone's hands.

ca·le·fac·ción f. heat, heating.

ca·le·fac·tor m. heater.

ca·len·da·rio m. calendar; *(programa)* schedule ♦ **c. judicial** court calendar.

ca·lén·du·la f. calendula, pot marigold.

ca·len·ta·dor, ·ra I. adj. heating, warming II. m. heater; *(para agua)* water heater; *(de cama)* bed warmer.

ca·len·tar §49 tr. to warm *or* heat (up); *(azotar)* to beat, thrash ♦ **c. al blanco** to make white-hot • **c. al rojo** to make red-hot • **c. las orejas** a COLL. *(chismear)* to gossip • **c. la sangre** a to make (someone's) blood boil • **c. la silla** FIG. to overstay one's welcome —reflex. to warm oneself up; ZOOL. to be in heat; COLL. *(alterarse)* to get excited; AMER. to get angry.

ca·len·tu·ra f. fever.

ca·len·tu·rien·to, ·a adj. feverish.

ca·le·ra f. *(cantera)* limestone quarry; *(horno)* limekiln.

ca·le·sa f. calash, calèche (light carriage).

ca·li·bra·ción f. calibration.

ca·li·bra·dor m. calibrator, calipers.

ca·li·brar tr. *(medir)* to gauge; *(graduar)* to calibrate.

ca·li·bre m. ARM. caliber; TECH. *(tubo)* diameter; *(alambre)* thickness; *(importancia)* importance.

ca·li·can·to m. stone masonry.

ca·li·có m. calico.

ca·li·dad f. quality; *(clase)* class; *(capacidad)* position; *(índole)* nature ♦ **a c. de que** on the condition that • **en c. de** as.

cá·li·do, ·a adj. warm.

ca·l(e)i·dos·co·pio m. kaleidoscope.

ca·lien·ta·piés m. foot warmer.

ca·lien·ta·pla·tos m. plate warmer, hot plate.

ca·lien·te adj. hot; FIG. *(acalorado)* angry ♦ **c. de cascos** hot-tempered • **estar c.** *(animal)* to be in heat.

ca·li·fa m. caliph.

ca·li·fi·ca·ción f. *(clasificación)* classification; *(nota)* grade.

ca·li·fi·ca·do, ·a adj. *(capaz)* qualified; *(eminente)* eminent; *(probado)* proven.

ca·li·fi·ca·dor, ·ra I. adj. examining II. m.f. assessor; *(clasificador)* classifier.

ca·li·fi·car §70 tr. *(clasificar)* to classify; *(dar una nota a)* to grade; *(tratar)* to call <*me calificó de estúpido* she called me stupid>.

ca·li·fi·ca·ti·vo, ·a I. adj. qualifying II. m. qualifier.

ca·li·for·nio m. californium.

ca·li·gra·fí·a f. calligraphy.

ca·lí·gra·fo, ·a m.f. calligrapher ♦ **c. perito**

handwriting expert.

ca·lis·te·nia f. calisthenics.

cá·liz m. chalice; POET. cup; BOT. calyx.

ca·li·zo, ·a I. adj. calcareous, limy II. f. limestone.

cal·man·te I. adj. calming; MED. sedative II. m. sedative.

cal·mar tr. to soothe, calm (down) —intr. to calm (down), abate —reflex. to calm down.

cal·mo, ·a I. adj. calm II. f. *(tranquilidad)* calm; *(serenidad)* calmness; COLL. *(pachorra)* sluggishness ♦ **con c.** calmly • **en c.** calm; COM. in a slack period • **perder la c.** to lose one's composure.

ca·ló m. gypsy dialect.

ca·lo·frí·o m. chill, shiver.

ca·lor m. warmth, heat; *(pasión)* ardor; *(de la batalla)* thick ♦ **dar c.** a to encourage • **entrar en c.** to get warm • **hacer c.** *(tiempo)* to be hot *or* warm • **tener c.** *(persona)* to be hot *or* warm.

ca·lo·rí·a f. calorie.

ca·lo·rí·fe·ro, ·a I. adj. heat-producing II. m. heater ♦ **c. de aire** air heater.

ca·lo·rí·fu·go, ·a adj. heat-resistant.

ca·lo·rí·me·tro m. calorimeter.

ca·lum·nia f. calumny, slander.

ca·lum·nia·dor, ·ra I. adj. slanderous II. m.f. slanderer.

ca·lum·niar tr. to calumniate, slander.

ca·lu·ro·so, ·a adj. warm, hot; FIG. warm, enthusiastic.

cal·va·rio m. calvary; RELIG. Calvary.

cal·vez/vi·cie f. baldness.

cal·vo, ·a I. adj. bald ♦ **quedarse c.** to go bald II. m.f. bald person —f. bald spot.

cal·za f. *(cuña)* wedge; COLL. *(media)* stocking ♦ pl. breeches.

cal·za·da f. highway, road.

cal·za·do m. footwear ♦ **tienda de c.** shoe store.

cal·za·dor m. shoehorn.

cal·zar §04 tr. to put shoes on; *(poner calces)* to wedge; COLL. *(comprender)* to grasp, understand ♦ **¿qué número calza?** what size do you take? —reflex. to put on shoes.

cal·zón m. *(pantalones)* pants, trousers; R.P. panties; MEX. chaps ♦ **a c. quitado** COLL. boldly ♦ pl. pants, trousers • **tener bien puestos los c.** COLL. to be quite a man.

cal·zon·ci·llos m.pl. underwear, shorts.

ca·lla·do, ·a I. adj. *(silencioso)* silent; *(reservado)* reserved II. f. silence.

ca·llar intr. to be or become silent —tr. *(silenciar)* to silence; *(guardar secreto)* to keep secret; *(no mencionar)* not to mention —reflex. *(guardar silencio)* to be quiet *or* silent; *(quedarse callado)* to keep quiet ♦ **¡calla!** be quiet! • **¡cállate la boca!** COLL. shut up!

ca·lle f. street ♦ **echar a la c.** COLL. to throw out of the house • **echarse a la c.** COLL. to take to the streets • **poner en la c.** to put out on the street.

ca·lle·je·ar intr. to wander *or* walk the streets.

ca·lle·je·o m. roaming about.

ca·lle·je·ro, ·a adj. fond of wandering the streets ♦ **perro c.** stray dog.

ca·lle·jón m. alley ♦ **c. sin salida** blind alley; FIG. deadlock.

ca·llo m. corn ♦ pl. tripe.

ca·llo·si·dad f. callosity, callus.

ca·ma f. bed; *(armazón)* bedstead; *(guarida)* lair; *(de paja)* straw bed; CUL. layer ♦ **caer en**

c. to fall ill • c. gemela twin bed **• c. matrimonial** double bed **•** guardar c. *or* estar en c. to stay in bed.

ca·ma·da f. ZOOL. litter; ORNITH. brood; *(capa)* layer.

ca·ma·fe·o m. cameo.

ca·ma·le·ón m. chameleon.

ca·man·du·le·ar intr. R.P., COLL. to be hypocritical, intrigue.

ca·man·du·le·ro, a R.P., COLL. I. adj. sly, cunning II. m.f. hypocrite.

cá·ma·ra f. *(sala)* hall; *(junta)* chamber; AGR. granary; AUTO. inner tube; POL. house; MARIT. cabin; ARM. chamber; PHOTOG. camera ♦ **c. cinematográfica** movie camera **• c. de compensación** COM. clearing house **• c. de oxígeno** oxygen tent **• c. de televisión** television *or* video camera **• c. frigorífica** cold storage chamber **• c. lenta** slow motion **• c. mortuoria** funeral chamber.

ca·ma·ra·da m.f. comrade.

ca·ma·ra·de·rí·a f. camaraderie, comradeship.

ca·ma·re·ro, a m.f. waiter, waitress; MARIT. steward, stewardess.

ca·ma·ri·lla f. clique, coterie.

ca·ma·rín m. RELIG. niche; THEAT. dressing room.

ca·ma·rón m. shrimp, prawn.

ca·ma·ro·te m. MARIT. cabin, berth.

ca·mas·tro m. COLL. makeshift bed; MIL. cot.

cam·ba·la·che m. COLL. *(trueque)* swap; R.P. secondhand store.

cam·ba·la·che·ar tr. COLL. to swap, trade.

cam·ba·la·che·ro, a I. adj. swapping, trading II. m.f. swapper, trader; R.P. owner of a secondhand store.

cam·bia·ble adj. *(que se puede alterar)* changeable; *(por otra cosa)* exchangeable.

cam·bia·di·zo, a adj. changeable, variable.

cam·bia·dor, ·ra m.f. moneychanger —CHILE, MEX., RAIL. switchman ♦ **c. automático** *or* **de discos** record changer.

cam·biar tr. to change; *(alterar)* to alter; *(reemplazar)* to replace; *(trocar)* to exchange; COM. to exchange, change —intr. to change; METEOROL. to shift ♦ **c. de casa** to move **• c. de color** to change color **• c. de dueño** to change hands **• c. de parecer** to change one's mind **• c. de ropa** to change clothes —reflex. to change.

cam·bia·ví·a m. RAIL. switch; AMER. switchman.

cam·bio m. change; *(alteración)* alteration; *(trueque)* exchange; COM. *(tipo de cambio)* rate of exchange; RAIL. switch; AUTO. transmission ♦ **a c. de** in exchange for **• a la primera de c.** COLL. before you know it **• c. automático** AUTO. automatic transmission **• c. de marchas** *or* **velocidades** AUTO. gearshift **• casa de c.** foreign exchange office **• en c.** *(en vez de)* instead; *(por otra parte)* on the other hand.

cam·bis·ta m.f. moneychanger, broker —R.P. switchman.

ca·me·lar tr. COLL. *(halagar)* to flatter; *(enamorar)* to woo; *(engañar)* to deceive; MEX. to watch.

ca·me·le·ar tr. COLL. to deceive.

ca·me·le·o m. COLL. flattery, wheedling.

ca·me·lia f. camellia.

ca·me·lo m. COLL. wooing ♦ **dar c. a** to tease.

ca·me·llo m. camel.

ca·me·ri·no m. THEAT. dressing room.

ca·me·ro, a adj. *(de camas)* double.

ca·mi·lla f. MED. stretcher.

ca·mi·lle·ro m. stretcher-bearer.

ca·mi·nar intr. to walk; *(viajar)* to travel; FIG. to move along ♦ **c. derecho** to behave properly —tr. to walk.

ca·mi·na·ta f. walk, hike.

ca·mi·no m. road; *(senda)* path, trail; *(vía)* route; *(viaje)* trip; FIG. means ♦ **abrir c.** to make way **• allanar el c.** COLL. to smooth the way **• a medio c.** halfway **• c. a** towards **• c. trillado** FIG. beaten path **• en c.** on the way **• en c. de** FIG. on the way to **• ponerse en c.** to get started **• por buen c.** FIG. on the right track.

ca·mión m. truck, lorry (G.B.); MEX. bus ♦ **c. de bomberos** fire engine **• c. de mudanzas** moving van.

ca·mio·ne·ro, a m.f. truck driver.

ca·mio·ne·ta f. van.

ca·mi·sa f. shirt; *(envoltura)* jacket; MECH. casing ♦ **c. de dormir** nightshirt **• c. de fuerza** straitjacket **• dejar sin c. a** COLL. to leave penniless **• en mangas de c.** in shirtsleeves **• perder hasta la c.** COLL. to lose the shirt off one's back.

ca·mi·se·ta f. T-shirt; *(ropa interior)* undershirt; SPORT. jersey.

ca·mi·so·la f. camisole.

ca·mi·són m. nightgown.

ca·mo·mi·la f. camomile, chamomile.

ca·mo·rra f. COLL. squabble ♦ **armar c.** to pick a fight **• buscar c.** to go looking for trouble.

ca·mo·rre·ar intr. COLL. to squabble, quarrel.

ca·mo·rris·ta adj. & m.f. quarrelsome (person).

ca·mo·te m. AMER. m. *(batata)* sweet potato; COLL. *(enamoramiento)* infatuation ♦ **tener un c.** AMER. to be infatuated.

cam·pa·men·to m. camp ♦ **c. de verano** summer camp.

cam·pa·na f. bell; R.P. lookout ♦ **tañer** *or* **tocar las campanas** to ring the bells.

cam·pa·na·da f. stroke, ring (of a bell).

cam·pa·na·rio m. bell tower, belfry.

cam·pa·ne·ar intr. to ring the bells; R.P. *(mirar)* to be the lookout.

cam·pa·ni·lla f. *(campana)* hand bell; *(timbre)* doorbell; ANAT. uvula; BOT. bellflower.

cam·pan·te adj. unruffled, relaxed.

cam·pa·ña f. plain; MIL., POL. campaign; AMER. countryside ♦ **hacer c.** to campaign **• tienda de c.** tent.

cam·pe·cha·no, a adj. COLL. good-natured.

cam·pe·ón, o·na m.f. champion.

cam·pe·o·na·to m. championship.

cam·pe·si·na·do m. peasantry.

cam·pe·si·no, a I. adj. rustic II. m.f. peasant.

cam·pes·tre adj. rural.

cam·pi·ña f. large field.

cam·po m. country, countryside; *(plantío)* field; MIL., SPORT. field ♦ **a c. traviesa** cross-country **• casa de c.** country house **• c. de batalla** battlefield **• c. de deportes** athletic field **• c. de juego** playground **• c. de tiro** firing range **• c. magnético** PHYS. magnetic field **• c. petrolífero** oil field **• c. raso** open country **• c. visual** field of vision **• dar c.** a FIG. to give ground to **• trabajo de c.** field work.

cam·po·san·to m. cemetery, graveyard.

ca·mu·fla·je m. camouflage.

ca·mu·flar tr. to camouflage.

can m. *(perro)* dog; *(gatillo)* trigger.

ca·na f. see **cano, a.**

ca·nal m. canal; *(estrecho)* strait, channel; *(de puerto)* navigation channel; *(tubo)* pipe, conduit, tube; ANAT. tract; ARCHIT. gutter; RAD., TELEV. channel.

ca·na·le·ta f. conduit; R.P. gutter.

ca·na·li·za·ción f. canalization; TECH. piping; ELEC. wiring.

ca·na·li·zar §04 tr. *(abrir canales)* to canalize; *(controlar aguas)* to channel; *(por tuberías)* to pipe; FIG. to channel.

ca·na·lón m. gutter, drainpipe.

ca·na·lla COLL. m. scoundrel —f. riffraff.

ca·na·lla·da f. dirty trick.

ca·na·lles·co, a adj. low, despicable.

ca·na·pé m. *(sofá)* sofa; CUL. canapé.

ca·nas·ta f. basket; *(naipes)* canasta.

ca·nas·ti·lla f. *(canasta pequeña)* small basket; *(de bebé)* layette; AMER. trousseau.

ca·nas·to m. basket.

can·cel m. *(puerta)* storm door; *(mampara)* partition.

can·ce·la f. iron gate.

can·ce·lar tr. to cancel; *(saldar)* to pay off; FIG. to wipe out.

cán·cer m. cancer.

can·cer·be·ro m. severe doorman.

can·ce·ró·lo·go, a m.f. cancer specialist.

can·ce·ro·so, a adj. cancerous.

can·ci·ller m. chancellor.

can·ci·lle·rí·a f. chancellery.

can·ción f. song ♦ **c. de cuna** lullaby.

can·cio·ne·ro m. MUS. songbook.

can·cio·nis·ta m.f. *(compositor)* songwriter; *(cantante)* singer.

can·cro m. MED. cancer; BOT. canker.

can·cha f. *(campo)* field; *(de tenis)* court ♦ **dar c. a** ARG., CHILE, C. RICA to give the advantage to • **estar uno en su c.** R.P., COLL. to be in one's element ♦ **tener c.** R.P., COLL. to be experienced.

can·che·ro, a I.m.f. R.P. expert; AMER. groundskeeper II. adj. R.P. expert, skilled.

can·da·do m. padlock.

can·de·al I. adj. ♦ **pan c.** white bread II. m. ARG., CHILE, PERU hot beverage made with cognac, milk and eggs.

can·de·la f. *(vela)* candle; COLL. *(lumbre)* heat; *(fire)* light.

can·de·la·bro m. candelabrum; ARG. cactus.

can·de·la·ria f. Candlemas; BOT. great mullein.

can·de·le·ro m. candlestick; *(velón)* oil lamp; MARIT. stanchion ♦ **estar en el c.** to be at the top.

can·den·te adj. *(incandescente)* white-hot; *(ardiente)* burning; FIG. *(cargado)* charged; *(grave)* burning, important.

can·di·da·to, a m.f. candidate.

can·di·da·tu·ra f. candidacy.

can·di·dez f. candor; FIG. naiveté.

cán·di·do, a adj. candid; FIG. naive.

can·dil m. oil lamp.

can·di·le·ja f. oil reservoir ♦ pl. footlights.

can·dom·be m. AMER. dance of South American blacks.

can·dor m. candor; *(ingenuidad)* naiveté.

can·do·ro·so, a adj. candid; *(ingenuo)* naive.

ca·ne·ar intr. to grow gray-haired.

ca·ne·la f. cinnamon.

ca·ne·lón m. *(cañería)* roof gutter; *(carámbano)* icicle; *(labor)* tubular braid.

ca·ne·lo·nes m.pl. cannelloni (pasta).

ca·ne·sú m. *(de camisa)* yoke; *(de vestido)* bodice.

can·gre·jo m. crab ♦ **c. de mar** crab • **c. de río** crayfish.

can·gre·na f. var. of **gangrena.**

can·gu·ro m. kangaroo.

ca·ní·bal I. adj. cannibalistic II. m.f. cannibal.

ca·ni·ca f. marble ♦ pl. (game of) marbles.

ca·ni·cie f. grayness (of hair).

ca·ní·cu·la f. dog days; midsummer heat.

ca·ni·lla f. ANAT. shinbone; *(carretillo)* spool; AMER. *(del agua)* tap; MEX., FIG. *(fuerza)* strength; AMER., COLL. *(pierna)* skinny leg.

ca·ni·lli·ta m. S. AMER. newspaper boy.

ca·ni·no, a adj. & m. canine.

can·je m. exchange, trade.

can·je·a·ble adj. exchangeable.

can·je·ar tr. to exchange, trade.

ca·no, a I. adj. gray-haired; FIG. old II. f. *(cabello)* white *or* gray hair; AMER., COLL. jail ♦ **echar una c. al aire** to have fun ♦ pl. gray hair(s).

ca·no·a f. canoe; *(bote)* rowboat.

ca·non m. canon.

ca·nó·ni·co, a adj. canonical, canonic.

ca·nó·ni·go m. canon, prebendary.

ca·no·ni·za·ción f. canonization.

ca·no·ni·zar §04 tr. to canonize.

ca·no·ro, a adj. melodious ♦ **ave c.** songbird.

ca·no·so, a adj. gray-haired.

can·sa·do, a adj. *(fatigado)* tired; *(agotado)* worn-out ♦ **a las cansadas** R.P. after much delay.

can·san·cio m. tiredness ♦ **muerto de c.** dog-tired.

can·sar tr. to tire, make tired; *(aburrir)* to bore; *(fastidiar)* to annoy ♦ **o. la vista** to strain one's eyes —reflex. to become *or* get tired —intr. to be tiring; *(aburrir)* to be boring.

can·tan·te I. adj. singing ♦ **llevar la voz o.** to be in charge II. m.f. singer, vocalist.

can·tar¹ m. song, folk song ♦ **eso es otro c.** COLL. that's another matter.

can·tar² tr. & intr. to sing, FIG. to confess ♦ **en menos de lo que canta un gallo** COLL. in a jiffy.

cán·ta·ro m. jug ♦ **llover a cántaros** COLL. to rain cats and dogs.

can·te·ra f. quarry, pit.

can·te·ro m. *(pedrero)* stonemason; R.P. flowerbed.

cán·ti·co m. canticle; FIG. song.

can·ti·dad f. quantity; *(suma)* sum.

can·ti·le·na f. MUS. cantilena; FIG. same old story.

can·tim·plo·ra f. canteen.

can·ti·na f. canteen; AMER. saloon.

can·ti·ne·la f. var. of **cantilena.**

can·ti·ne·ro, a m.f. saloonkeeper.

can·to¹ m. *(canción)* song; *(arte)* singing; *(monótono)* chant; *(poema)* heroic poem.

can·to² m. *(extremo)* edge; *(borde)* border; *(de cuchillo)* blunt edge; *(de un libro)* front edge; *(guijarro)* pebble ♦ **c. rodado** boulder • **de c.** *(de lado)* on end, on edge; *(grueso)* thick.

can·tor, ·ra I. adj. singing II. m.f. singer.

can·tu·rre·ar/rriar intr. COLL. to sing softly.

cá·nu·la f. thin reed; MED. cannula.

ca·nu·to m. tube.

ca·ña f. reed; *(de azúcar)* cane; *(tallo)* stalk; *(de una bota)* leg; ANAT. long bone; ZOOL. shank; ARCHIT. shaft of a column ♦ **c. de pes-**

car fishing rod • **c. dulce** sugar cane.

ca·ña·da f. ravine; AMER. stream.

ca·ña·dón m. AMER. *(barranca)* ravine; *(arroyo profundo)* deep stream.

ca·ñal m. cane thicket.

ca·ña·ma·zo m. canvas.

ca·ña·miel f. sugar cane.

ca·ña·mo m. hemp.

ca·ña·ve·ra f. reed-grass.

ca·ña·ve·ral m. cane thicket; *(plantación)* sugar-cane plantation.

ca·ñe·rí·a f. *(tubo)* pipe; *(tubería)* pipeline.

ca·ñe·ro m. sugarcane vendor.

ca·ño m. *(tubo)* pipe; *(albañal)* sewer; MARIT. narrow channel; MIN. gallery.

ca·ñón m. MIL. cannon; ARM. barrel; GEOG. canyon, gorge; *(de chimenea)* flue ♦ **c. antiaéreo** antiaircraft gun • **c. antitanque** antitank gun.

ca·ño·na·zo m. *(tiro)* cannon shot; COLL. *(noticia)* bombshell; SPORT. shot.

ca·ño·ne·ar tr. to cannonade, shell.

ca·ño·ne·o m. cannonade, shelling.

ca·ño·ne·ro, a adj. armed with cannons.

ca·ñu·ti·llo m. bead.

ca·o·ba f. mahogany.

ca·os m. chaos.

ca·ó·ti·co, a adj. chaotic.

ca·pa f. *(manto)* cape; *(de pintura)* coat; *(cubierta)* covering; GEOL. layer; ZOOL. coat ♦ **c. y espada** through thick and thin • **andar** or **ir de c. caída** COLL. *(decaer)* to be in rough shape; *(estar triste)* to be depressed.

ca·pa·ci·dad f. capacity; *(espacio)* room; *(talento)* ability; LAW capacity ♦ **c. adquisitiva** purchasing power • **c. de ganancia** earning power.

ca·pa·ci·tar tr. *(instruir)* to train; *(calificar)* to qualify; *(autorizar)* to empower —reflex. to become qualified.

ca·pa·che·ro m. porter.

ca·par tr. to castrate.

ca·pa·ra·zón m. shell, carapace.

ca·pa·taz m. foreman.

ca·paz adj. capable.

cap·cio·so, a adj. deceitful ♦ **pregunta c.** tricky question.

ca·pe·ar tr. COLL. *(engañar)* to fool; *(eludir)* to dodge; MARIT. to weather.

ca·pe·llán m. chaplain.

ca·pe·ru·za f. *(gorro)* hood; *(de pluma)* cap.

ca·pi·cú·a f. palindrome.

ca·pi·lar adj. & m. capillary.

ca·pi·la·ri·dad f. capillarity.

ca·pi·lla f. chapel; *(camarilla)* clan; TECH. hood ♦ **c. ardiente** funeral chapel • **estar en c.** to be on tenterhooks.

ca·pi·llo m. *(de niño)* baby bonnet; *(de bautizo)* baptismal cape; *(del calzado)* toe lining; *(capullo)* silk cocoon.

ca·pi·ro·ta·zo m. fillip, flick (with a finger).

ca·pi·ro·te m. hood ♦ **tonto de c.** fool.

ca·pi·ru·cho m. COLL. hood, cap.

ca·pi·tal I. adj. capital; *(esencial)* vital <*de importancia c.* of vital importance> II. m. capital; *(el que produce intereses)* principal ♦ **c. activo** working capital • **c. circulante** working capital • **c. de inversión** investment capital • **c. disponible** available funds • **c. en giro** operating capital • **c. fijo** fixed capital • **c. líquido** net worth • **c. social** capital stock —f. capital, capital city.

ca·pi·ta·li·no, a I. adj. of the capital II. m.f native or inhabitant of the capital.

ca·pi·ta·lis·ta I. adj. capitalist, capitalistic II. m.f. capitalist.

ca·pi·ta·li·za·ción f. capitalization.

ca·pi·ta·li·zar §04 tr. to capitalize; *(interés)* to compound.

ca·pi·tán, a·na m. captain; FIG. leader ♦ **c. de corbeta** lieutenant commander • **c. de fragata** commander —m.f. SPORT. team captain.

ca·pi·ta·ne·ar tr. to captain; FIG. to command.

ca·pi·ta·ní·a f. *(cargo)* captainship; *(de tropas)* company.

ca·pi·tel m. capital (of a column).

ca·pi·tu·la·ción f. capitulation.

ca·pi·tu·lar intr. to capitulate.

ca·pí·tu·lo m. chapter; *(reunión)* assembly; ANAT., BOT. capitulum.

ca·pó m. AUTO. hood, bonnet (G.B.).

ca·pón I. adj. castrated II. m. capon; R.P. castrated sheep.

ca·po·ral m. foreman; FIG. boss.

ca·po·ta f. *(de mujer)* bonnet; *(de coche)* hood, bonnet (G.B.); *(capa corta)* short cape; AUTO. folding top of a convertible.

ca·po·tar intr. to turn over, roll over.

ca·po·te m. cape ♦ **c. de montar** riding cape • **c. de monte** poncho.

ca·pri·cho m. whim; *(antojo)* fancy; MUS. caprice ♦ **tener c. por** to fancy.

ca·pri·cho·so, a adj. whimsical; *(inconstante)* fickle.

cáp·su·la f. capsule; ARM. cartridge shell.

cap·tar tr. *(atraer)* to attract, win; *(aprehender)* to grasp.

cap·tu·ra f. capture, apprehension.

cap·tu·rar tr. to capture, apprehend.

ca·pu·cha f. hood; PRINT. circumflex accent.

ca·pu·chi·no, a adj. & m.f. RELIG. Capuchin.

ca·pu·llo m. *(brote)* bud; *(de larva)* cocoon; *(de bellota)* cup ♦ **c. de rosa** rosebud.

ca·qui m. BOT. kaki; *(tela y color)* khaki.

ca·ra I. f. face; *(semblante)* look; *(superficie)* surface; *(frente)* front; *(aspecto)* appearance; COLL. *(descaro)* nerve; GEOM. plane; *(anverso)* heads ♦ **asomar la c.** to show one's face • **caérsele la c. de vergüenza** COLL. to blush with shame • **c. a c.** face to face • **c. de pascua** COLL. happy face • **c. de pocos amigos** COLL. unfriendly face • **c. de viernes** COLL. long face • **c. dura** narrow, cheek • **c. o cruz** heads or tails • **cruzar la c. a** to slap • **dar c. a** to face • **dar la c.** to face the consequences • **de dos caras** two-faced • **echar la c. o cruz** to toss a coin • **echar en c.** to reproach • **hacer c. a** to confront • **sacar la c. por** COLL. to stick up for • **saltar a la c.** FIG. to hit the eye immediately • **tener c. de** COLL. to look like • **tener c. para** COLL. to have the nerve to II. adv. ♦ **c. a** or **de c.** facing.

ca·ra·be·la f. caravel.

ca·ra·bi·na f. carbine.

ca·ra·col m. snail; *(concha)* conch; *(espiral)* spiral; *(rizo)* curl; ANAT. cochlea ♦ **¡caracoles!** my goodness! • **escalera de c.** spiral staircase.

ca·ra·co·la f. conch.

ca·rác·ter m. character; *(indole)* nature; *(rasgo)* trait; *(capacidad)* capacity; *(de letra)* handwriting; *(estilo)* style; *(entereza)* moral character ♦ **c. de imprenta** typeface.

ca·rac·te·rís·ti·co, a I. adj. characteristic

II. m. THEAT. character actor —f. (*rasgo*) characteristic; THEAT. character actress; MATH. characteristic; ARG. telephone exchange.

ca·rac·te·ri·za·do, a adj. distinguished.

ca·rac·te·ri·za·dor, ·ra adj. distinguishing.

ca·rac·te·ri·zar §04 tr. to characterize; THEAT. to portray (a role) expressively —reflex. to be characterized; THEAT. to make up.

ca·ra·cú m. AMER. bone marrow.

ca·ra·cul m. karakul.

ca·ra·du·ra adj. & m.f. shameless (person).

¡ca·ram·ba! interj. (*asombro*) good heavens!; (*enfado*) damn it!

ca·rám·ba·no m. icicle.

ca·ram·bo·la f. carom (in billiards); COLL. (*doble resultado*) killing two birds with one stone; (*casualidad*) chance.

ca·ra·me·li·zar §04 tr. (*bañar*) to cover with caramel; (*convertir*) to caramelize.

ca·ra·me·lo m. caramel; (*dulce*) candy.

ca·ran·cho m. AMER. carrion hawk.

ca·rá·tu·la f. (*careta*) mask; AMER. title page.

ca·ra·va·na f. caravan.

¡ca·ray! interj. damn!

car·bo·hi·dra·to m. carbohydrate.

car·bón m. coal; (*de leña*) charcoal; (*lápiz*) carbon pencil; (*papel*) carbon (paper); ELEC. carbon ♦ c. animal boneblack ♦ negro como el c. black as the ace of spades.

car·bo·nar tr. to char, make into charcoal —reflex. to become carbonized *or* charred.

car·bo·na·to m. carbonate.

car·bon·ci·llo m. ARTS charcoal pencil; (*carbonilla*) small coal.

car·bo·ne·rí·a f. coal shop.

car·bo·ne·ro, a I. adj. charcoal II. m. coal supplier; MARIT. coal miner —f. (*pila de leña*) charcoal pile; (*depósito*) coal bin.

car·bo·ní·fe·ro, a adj. & m. carboniferous.

car·bo·ni·lla f. coal dust; (*de la locomotora*) soot; ARG. charcoal pencil.

car·bo·ni·zar §04 tr. to carbonize, char.

car·bo·no m. carbon.

car·bo·run·do m. carborundum.

car·bun·clo m. MIN. carbuncle.

car·bún·cu·lo m. carbuncle, ruby.

car·bu·ra·dor m. carburetor.

car·bu·ran·te I. m. fuel II. adj. containing a hydrocarbon.

car·bu·rar tr. to carburize —intr. COLL. to run, go.

car·bu·ro m. carbide.

car·ca·ja·da f. loud laughter ♦ reír a carcajadas to split one's sides laughing.

car·ca·mán m. MARIT. old ship; AMER. pretentious person; CUBA low-class foreigner.

car·ca·za f. quiver.

cár·cel f. (*prisión*) jail; TECH. clamp.

car·ce·le·ro, a I. m.f. jailer II. adj. jail.

car·ci·no·ma f. carcinoma, cancer.

car·co·mer tr. to eat away, gnaw —reflex. to rot, decay.

car·da·dor, ·ra m.f. TEX. carder —f. carding machine.

car·dán m. cardan *or* universal joint.

car·dar tr. TEX. to card, comb.

car·de·nal m. cardinal; COLL. (*mancha*) bruise.

cár·de·no, a adj. purple.

car·dia·co/dí·a·co, a I. adj. cardiac II. m.f. cardiac ♦ ataque c. heart attack.

car·di·nal adj. cardinal.

car·dió·gra·fo, a m.f. cardiologist —m. electrocardiograph.

car·dio·gra·ma m. electrocardiogram.

car·dio·lo·gí·a f. cardiology.

car·dió·lo·go, a m.f. cardiologist.

car·do m. thistle.

car·du·me(n) m. school (of fish).

ca·re·ar tr. (*confrontar*) to bring face to face; (*cotejar*) to compare.

ca·re·cer §17 intr. ♦ c. de to lack.

ca·ren·cia f. lack; MED. deficiency.

ca·ren·te adj. lacking (in), devoid of.

ca·re·o m. (*confrontación*) confrontation; (*cotejo*) comparison.

ca·re·ro, a adj. expensive (a shopkeeper).

ca·res·tí·a f. scarcity; COM. high prices ♦ c. de la vida high cost of living.

ca·re·ta f. mask ♦ c. antigás gas mask • quitarle a uno la c. to unmask someone.

ca·rey m. sea turtle; (*caparazón*) tortoiseshell.

car·ga f. load; (*acción*) loading; (*flete*) cargo; (*peso*) burden; (*obligación*) duty; (*responsabilidad*) onus; (*impuesto*) tax, duty; MIL. attack; (*de armas*) charge; ELEC. charge ♦ c. bruta gross tonnage • c. personal personal obligation • c. útil payload • llevar la c. de to be responsible for • tomar c. to take on cargo • volver a la c. to persist.

car·ga·de·ro m. loading platform.

car·ga·do, a I. adj. laden; (*sabor*) strong; (*atmósfera*) heavy; ELEC. charged ♦ c. de años old, ancient • c. de espaldas round-shouldered II. f. MEX. loading; R.P. practical joke.

car·ga·men·to m. load, cargo.

car·gan·te adj. tiresome, burdensome.

car·gar §47 tr. to load; (*llenar*) to fill; (*imputar*) to ascribe; (*con obligaciones*) to burden; (*con impuestos*) to impose; COLL. (*importunar*) to pester; ELEC., MIL. to charge, COM. to debit; AMER. to carry ♦ c. la mano a FIG. (*exigir mucho*) to be exacting; (*apremiar*) to press • c. en cuenta COM. to charge to one's account —intr. to load; ARCHIT. to rest ♦ c. con to carry; FIG. to shoulder —reflex. COLL. (*molestarse*) to become annoyed; METEOROL. to become cloudy ♦ c. de to have a lot of • c. de años old, getting along (in years).

car·go m. (*peso*) load; (*dignidad*) position; (*dirección*) direction; (*obligación*) obligation; (*acusación*) charge; COM. debit ♦ a c. de in charge of • c. de conciencia remorse • hacer c. a uno de to hold someone responsible for • hacerse c. de to take charge of.

car·go·se·ar tr. AMER. to pester, bother.

car·go·so, a adj. AMER. bothersome, tiresome.

car·gue·ro, a I. adj. freight II. m. MARIT. freighter.

ca·ria·con·te·ci·do, a adj. COLL. glum.

ca·ria·do, a adj. decayed.

ca·riar tr. & reflex. to decay.

ca·ri·be m. ICHTH. caribe, piranha.

ca·ri·ca·tu·ra f. caricature.

ca·ri·ca·tu·rar tr. to caricature.

ca·ri·ca·tu·ris·ta m.f. caricaturist.

ca·ri·ca·tu·ri·zar §04 tr. to caricature.

ca·ri·cia f. caress ♦ hacer caricias a to caress.

ca·ri·dad f. charity ♦ ¡por c.! for pity's sake! • la c. bien entendida empieza por casa charity begins at home.

ca·ries f.inv. MED. caries, decay.

ca·ri·lla f. page, side.

ca·ri·llón m. carillon.

ca·ri·ño m. *(afecto)* affection; *(amor)* love; *(caricia)* caress; *(esmero)* care ♦ **sentir c. por** or **tener c. a** to be fond of • **tomar c. a** to take a liking to ♦ pl. love (in a letter).

ca·ri·ño·so, a adj. affectionate, loving.

ca·ris·ma m. charisma.

ca·ris·má·ti·co, a adj. charismatic.

ca·ri·ta·ti·vo, a adj. charitable.

ca·riz m. COLL. prospects, outlook.

car·me·li·ta I. adj. Carmelite; AMER. brown II. m.f. Carmelite —f. nasturtium flower.

car·me·sí [pl. **-íes**] adj. & m. crimson.

car·mín I. adj. crimson II. m. *(color)* crimson; *(tinta)* carmine; *(rosal)* mallow rose ♦ **c. de labios** lipstick.

car·na·da f. *(cebo)* bait; *(trampa)* trap, snare.

car·nal adj. carnal; *(sensual)* lustful; *(hermano)* full.

car·na·li·dad f. carnality, lust.

car·na·val m. carnival.

car·ne f. flesh; CUL. meat; BOT. pulp ♦ **c. asada al horno** roast (of meat) • **c. asada a la parrilla** broiled meat • **c. de carnero** mutton • **c. de cerdo** or **de puerco** pork • **c. de cordero** or **de oveja** lamb • **c. de gallina** COLL. goose bumps • **c. de ternera** veal • **c. de vaca** beef • **c. picada** chopped meat • **en c. viva** raw • **ser c. y uña** to be very close.

car·ne·ar tr. AMER. to slaughter.

car·ne·ro m. sheep; *(macho)* ram; CUL. mutton; R.P. scab.

car·net/né m. [pl. **-nés**] card.

car·ni·ce·rí·a f. butcher shop; FIG. carnage.

car·ni·ce·ro, a I. adj. *(carnívoro)* carnivorous; *(cruel)* savage II. m.f. butcher.

car·ní·vo·ro, a I. adj. carnivorous II. m. carnivore.

car·no·so/nu·do, a adj. meaty.

ca·ro, a I. adj. *(costoso)* expensive; *(amado)* dear II. adv. at a high price.

ca·ro·ti·na f. carotene.

ca·ro·zo m. stone, pit.

car·pa¹ f. carp ♦ **c. dorada** goldfish.

car·pa² f. AMER. *(tienda)* tent; *(toldo)* awning.

car·pe·ta f. *(cubierta)* folder; *(tapete)* table cover.

car·pin·cho m. AMER., ZOOL. capybara.

car·pin·te·rí·a f. *(oficio)* carpentry; *(taller)* carpenter shop.

car·pin·te·ro m. carpenter; ORNITH. woodpecker.

ca·rras·pe·ar intr. to clear one's throat.

ca·rras·pe·o m./**pe·ra** f. hoarseness.

ca·rre·ra f. *(espacio recorrido)* run; *(competencia)* race; *(pista)* racetrack; *(profesión)* career; *(hilera)* row; ARCHIT. beam; MUS. run ♦ **a la c. running** • **c. a pie** footrace • **c. de armamentos** MIL. arms race • **c. de fondo** long-distance race • **c. de obstáculos** steeplechase • **c. de relevos** relay race ♦ pl. races.

ca·rre·ris·ta m.f. racing fan.

ca·rre·ta f. wagon ♦ **c. de bueyes** oxcart • **c. de mano** wheelbarrow • **andar como una c.** to go at a snail's pace.

ca·rre·te m. *(bobina)* bobbin; *(de la caña de pescar)* reel.

ca·rre·te·ar tr. to cart; AER. to taxi —intr. AER. to taxi.

ca·rre·tel m. AMER. spool.

ca·rre·te·ra f. highway, road ♦ **c. de circunvalación** bypass • **c. de cuatro vías** four-lane highway • **c. de vía libre** expressway.

ca·rre·ti·lla f. *(carro pequeño)* cart; *(de una rueda)* wheelbarrow; *(del niño)* baby walker; R.P. jaw.

ca·rri·co·che m. *(carro cubierto)* covered wagon; DEROG. decrepit car, jalopy.

ca·rril *(surco)* groove; AGR. furrow; *(de tránsito)* lane; RAIL. rail ♦ **c. americano** trail • **c. conductor** contact rail • **c. de cambio** or **de aguja** switch rail.

ca·rri·llo m. jowl; *(garrucha)* pulley ♦ **comer a dos carrillos** to stuff oneself.

ca·rro m. *(vehículo)* cart; AMER. *(automóvil)* car; *(contenido)* cartload; *(de máquina)* carriage; MIL. tank ♦ **c. alegórico** parade float • **c. blindado** armored car • **c. de asalto** MIL. heavy tank.

ca·rro·ce·rí·a f. AUTO. body.

ca·rro·ma·to m. covered wagon.

ca·rro·ño, a I. adj. rotten II. f. carrion; FIG. trash.

ca·rro·za f. carriage; *(de desfile)* float; AMER. hearse.

ca·rrua·je m. carriage.

ca·rru·sel m. carousel, merry-go-round.

car·ta f. letter; *(naipe)* playing card; *(de derechos)* charter; *(documento)* document; *(mapa)* map ♦ **c. cabal** in every respect • **a la c. a la carte** • **c. aérea** airmail letter • **c. blanca** carte blanche • **c. de porte** COM. bill of lading • **echar una c. al correo** to mail a letter • **poner las cartas sobre la mesa** to put one's cards on the table • **tomar cartas** COLL. to intervene.

car·ta·pa·cio m. *(cuaderno)* notebook; AMER. portfolio.

car·te·ar·se reflex. to write to each other.

car·tel m. poster; FIN. cartel ♦ **prohibido fijar carteles** post no bills.

car·te·le·ra f. billboard; *(de un periódico)* entertainment section.

car·te·o m. exchange of letters.

cár·ter m. MECH. casing ♦ **c. del cigüeñal** crankcase • **c. de engranajes** gearbox.

car·te·ra f. *(de hombre)* wallet; *(de mujer)* pocketbook; *(portadocumentos)* briefcase; *(de bolsillo)* pocket flap; *(ministerio)* cabinet post; COM., FIN. portfolio ♦ **tener en c.** to be planning.

car·te·ris·ta m. pickpocket.

car·te·ro m. mailman, postman.

car·tí·la·go m. cartilage.

car·ti·lla f. *(abecedario)* primer; *(folleto)* booklet.

car·to·gra·fí·a f. cartography, mapmaking.

car·tó·gra·fo, a m.f. cartographer, mapmaker.

car·to·man·cia f. cartomancy.

car·tón m. *(papel)* cardboard; *(caja)* cardboard box; *(de cigarrillos)* carton; *(boceto)* sketch; *(de un libro)* board ♦ **c. piedra** papier-mâché • **c. yeso** plasterboard.

car·tu·che·ra f. cartridge box.

car·tu·cho m. MIL. cartridge; *(cono)* paper cone; *(bolsa)* paper bag ♦ **c. de dinamita** dynamite stick • **c. de fogueo** blank cartridge • **quemar el último c.** to play one's last card.

car·tu·li·na f. pasteboard, fine cardboard.

ca·sa f. house; *(residencia)* home; *(nobleza)* house; *(establecimiento)* firm ♦ **caérsele la c. encima** COLL. to be overwhelmed • **c. de altos** R.P. multistory building • **c. de beneficencia** or **de caridad** poorhouse • **c. de citas** house of assignation • **c. de cuna** foundling home • **c. de departamentos** S. AMER. apartment house •

c. de empeños pawnshop • **c. de expósitos** orphanage • **c. de la moneda** mint • **c. editorial** publishing house • **c. matriz** headquarters • **c. mortuoria** funeral home • **como Pedro por su c.** COLL. right at home • **echar la c. por la ventana** COLL. to go all out • **empezar la c. por el tejado** to put the cart before the horse • **en c.** at home, in • **estar de c.** to be casually dressed • **estar fuera de c.** to be out • **sentirse como en la c. de uno** to feel at home.

ca·sa·ca f. dress coat.

ca·sa·de·ro, a adj. of marrying age.

ca·sa·do, a I. adj. married • **recién casados** newlyweds **II.** m. PRINT. imposition.

ca·sa·mien·to m. marriage, wedding ♦ **c. a la fuerza** shotgun wedding.

ca·sar intr. to marry —tr. to marry (off); PRINT. to impose —reflex. to get married ♦ **c. con** to get married to • **c. en segundas nupcias** to remarry • **c. por interés** to marry for money • **c. por detrás de la iglesia** to live together • **c. por poderes** to marry by proxy • **no c. con nadie** COLL. to maintain one's independence.

cas·ca·bel m. small bell ♦ **poner el c. al gato** to bell the cat, stick one's neck out • **ser alegre como un c.** to be as happy as a lark • **serpiente de c.** rattlesnake.

~~ca·sa·ba la la nr jingle, tinkle.~~

cas·ca·do, a adj. **I.** cracked; COLL. decrepit **II.** f. waterfall.

cas·ca·jo m. (guijo) gravel; (nuez) nut; (trasto) rubbish; (fragmento) shard ♦ **estar hecho un c.** COLL. to be a wreck.

cas·ca·nue·ces m.inv. nutcracker.

cas·car §70 tr. (quebrar) to crack; COLL. (pegar) to beat —intr. COLL. to kick the bucket —reflex. to crack.

cás·ca·ra f. shell; (de fruta) skin; (de queso, fruta) rind; (de cereal) husk.

cas·ca·ri·lla I. f. (de cacao) cacao leaf tea; (de metal) foil; AMER. quick-tempered person **II.** adj. AMER. quick-tempered.

cas·ca·rón m. (cáscara) thick peel or rind; (de huevo) eggshell ♦ **no haber salido aún del c.** to be inexperienced.

cas·ca·rra·bias m.f.inv. COLL. grouch.

cas·co m. MIL. helmet; (tonel) barrel; MARIT. hull; ZOOL. hoof; MECH. casing; COLL. (head) skull; (fragmento) shard ♦ **c. de buzo** diver's helmet • pl. **ligero de c.** COLL. (persona) scatterbrained; (mujer) easy.

cas·co·te m. rubble, debris.

ca·se·rí·o m. (pueblo) hamlet; (cortijo) country house or estate.

ca·se·ro, a I. adj. (de la casa) domestic; (de la familia) family <una reunión c. a family gathering>; (hecho en casa) homemade; (hogareño) home-loving ♦ **cocina c.** home cooking **II.** f. (dueño) owner, landlord; (administrador) caretaker —f. landlady.

ca·se·rón m. COLL. large dilapidated house.

ca·se·ta f. (casa) cottage; (casilla) booth.

ca·se·te m. or f. cassette, tape cartridge.

ca·si adv. almost, nearly ♦ **c. c.** COLL. very nearly • **c. nada** next to nothing • **c. nunca** hardly ever.

ca·si·lla f. (casa pequeña) cabin; (caseta) watchman's hut; (del mercado) stall; AMER. post-office box • **c. telefónica** AMER. telephone booth • pl. **sacar a uno de sus c.** COLL. to infuriate • **salir uno de sus c.** COLL. to lose

one's temper, fly off the handle.

ca·si·lle·ro m. filing cabinet with pigeonholes.

ca·si·no m. casino.

ca·so m. case; (acontecimiento) event; (circunstancia) circumstance ♦ **c. fortuito** unexpected event; LAW act of God • **c. perdido** lost cause • **el c. es que** that fact is that • **en c. de** in the event of • **en c. de que** in case • **en el mejor de los casos** at best • **en el peor de los casos** at worst • **en todo c.** in any case • **en último c.** as a last resort • **hablar al c.** to speak to the question • **hacer** or **venir al c.** COLL. to be relevant • **hacer c. a** to heed • **hacer c. de** to pay attention to • **hacer c. omiso de** to ignore • **no hacer** or **venir al c.** COLL. to be beside the point • **poner por c.** to take as an example • **verse en el c. de** to be compelled to.

ca·són m./**so·na** f. large house, mansion.

cas·pa f. dandruff

¡cás·pi·ta! interj. COLL. gosh!, holy cow!

cas·que·te m. MIL. helmet; RELIG. skullcap; (de mujer) toque; MECH. cap ♦ **c. glaciar** ice cap.

cas·qui·va·no, a adj. COLL. featherbrained.

cas·set·te m. or f. cassette.

cas·ta·ña f. see castaño, a.

cas·ta·ña·zo m. COLL. punch, sock.

cas·ta·ñe·ta f. (chasquido) snap of the fingers; (instrumento) castanet.

cas·ta·ñe·te·ar tr. to play on the castanets; (los dedos) to snap —intr. to chatter.

cas·ta·ñe·te·o m. (de las castañuelas) clacking; (de los dedos) snapping; (de los dientes) chattering.

cas·ta·ño, a I. adj. chestnut, brown **II.** m. chestnut ♦ **pasar algo de c. obscuro** COLL. to go too far —f. BOT. chestnut; (puñetazo) punch • **c. del Brasil** or **de Pará** Brazil nut • **sacar las castañas del fuego** COLL. to have to face the music on behalf of someone else.

cas·ta·ñue·la f. castanet ♦ **estar como unas castañuelas** COLL. to be in a jolly mood.

cas·te·lla·ni·zar §04 tr. to make Spanish.

cas·te·lla·no m. Spanish; (señor) lord of a castle.

cas·ti·dad f. chastity.

cas·ti·gar §47 tr. to punish; (mortificar) to discipline; SPORT. to penalize.

cas·ti·go m. punishment; (mortificación) self-denial; SPORT. penalty ♦ **levantar el c.** to withdraw the sentence or penalty.

cas·ti·llo m. castle; MARIT. forecastle ♦ **c. de naipes** house of cards.

cas·ti·zo, a I. adj. (verdadero) genuine; (típico) typical; LIT. pure **II.** m.f. AMER. quadroon (offspring of a mestizo and a Spaniard).

cas·to, a I. adj. chaste **II.** f. (de personas) lineage; (de la sociedad) caste; ZOOL. breed ♦ **de c.** (animales) purebred; (personas) of breeding; (auténtico) genuine • **le viene de c.** it runs in the family.

cas·tor m. beaver.

cas·tra·ción f. castration.

cas·tra·do I. adj. castrated **II.** m. (hombre) eunuch; (caballo) gelding.

cas·trar tr. to castrate.

cas·tren·se adj. military.

ca·sual adj. chance, coincidental.

ca·sua·li·dad f. chance ♦ **dar la c. que** to just so happen that • **de c.** by chance • **por c.** by any chance.

ca·sual·men·te adv. by chance or accident.

ca·su·lla f. chasuble.
ca·ta·clis·mo m. cataclysm; FIG. upheaval.
ca·ta·cum·bas f.pl. catacombs.
ca·ta·lejo, **·ra** m.f. taster, sampler.
ca·ta·le·jo m. spyglass, small telescope.
ca·ta·lép·ti·co, a adj. & m.f. cataleptic.
ca·tá·li·sis f.inv. catalysis.
ca·ta·li·za·dor m. catalyst.
ca·ta·lo·ga·dor, ·ra I. adj. cataloguing II. m.f. cataloguer.
ca·ta·lo·gar §47 tr. to catalogue, list.
ca·tá·lo·go m. catalogue.
ca·ta·plas·ma f. poultice; FIG. bore.
¡ca·ta·plum!/plún! interj. crash!, bang!
ca·ta·pul·tar tr. to catapult.
ca·tar tr. to sample, taste
ca·ta·ra·ta f. waterfall; MED. cataract ♦ **las cataratas del Niágara** Niagara Falls.
ca·ta·rro m. cold, catarrh.
ca·tar·sis f.inv. catharsis.
ca·tár·ti·co, a adj. cathartic.
ca·tas·tro m. cadaster, official land register.
ca·tás·tro·fe f. catastrophe.
ca·tas·tró·fi·co, a adj. catastrophic.
ca·te·cis·mo m. catechism (book).
cá·te·dra f. (rango) professorship; (asiento) professor's chair; (aula) classroom; (asignatura) subject.
ca·te·dral f. cathedral.
ca·te·drá·ti·co m. university professor.
ca·te·go·rí·a f. category; (clase) type; FIG. standing ♦ **de c. important ♦ de primera c.** first-rate ♦ **de segunda c.** second-rate.
ca·te·gó·ri·co, a adj. categorical.
ca·te·que·sis f./**quis·mo** m. catechism.
ca·te·qui·zar §04 tr. to catechize; FIG. to convince.
ca·ter·va f. band, gang
ca·té·ter m. catheter.
ca·te·to m. leg of a right triangle.
ca·tin·ga f. AMER. foul smell, body odor.
ca·tó·li·co, a adj. & m.f. Catholic ♦ **no ser muy c.** to be or look suspicious.
ca·to·li·zar §04 tr. to catholicize.
ca·tor·ce adj. & m. fourteen(th).
ca·tre m. cot ♦ **c. de tijera** folding canvas cot.
cau·ce m. (lecho) riverbed; (acequia) ditch.
cau·ción f. (precaución) caution; (advertencia) warning; (fianza) bail ♦ **bajo c.** on bail.
cau·cho m. (goma) rubber; (planta) rubber plant or tree.
cau·dal I. adj. ZOOL. caudal; (caudaloso) carrying a lot of water II. m. (riqueza) wealth; (de agua) volume; (abundancia) abundance.
cau·da·lo·so, a adj. (río) deep; (persona) wealthy.
cau·di·llo m. leader; AMER. political boss.
cau·sa f. cause; (motivo) reason; LAW lawsuit ♦ **a or por c. de** because of.
cau·sal I. adj. causative II. f. reason.
cau·sa·li·dad f. causation; (origen) cause.
cau·san·te I. adj. causative II. m.f. originator; LAW person from whom a right is derived.
cau·sar tr. to cause; (ira) to provoke.
cau·sa·ti·vo, a adj. causative.
caus·ti·ci·dad f. causticity; FIG. sarcasm.
cáus·ti·co, a adj. caustic; FIG. scathing.
cau·ta·men·te adv. cautiously.
cau·te·la f. caution.
cau·te·lo·so, a adj. cautious.
cau·te·rio m. (cauterización) cauterization; (instrumento) cauterizer.

cau·te·ri·za·dor, ·ra I. adj. cauterizing II. m.f. cauterizer.
cau·te·ri·zar §04 tr. to cauterize.
cau·ti·van·te adj. captivating.
cau·ti·var tr. (aprisionar) to capture; FIG. (interés, atención) to capture; (fascinar) to captivate.
cau·ti·ve·rio m./**vi·dad** f. captivity.
cau·ti·vo, a adj. & m.f. captive.
cau·to, a adj. cautious.
ca·va·dor, ·ra m.f. digger.
ca·var tr. to dig —intr. to delve into.
ca·ver·na f. cavern, cave; MED. cavity.
ca·ver·no·so, a adj. cavernous; FIG. deep, low.
ca·vial/viar m. caviar.
ca·vi·dad f. cavity.
ca·vi·la·ción f. pondering, rumination.
ca·vi·lar intr. to ponder, ruminate.
ca·vi·lo·so, a adj. COLL. mistrustful.
ca·ye·ra, yó see **caer.**
ca·yo m. MARIT. key, islet.
ca·za f. (cacería) hunt; (animales) game ♦ **andar or ir a c. de** COLL. to be on the lookout for ♦ **dar c.** to give chase ♦ **dar c. a** to hunt down ♦ **ir de c.** to go hunting —m. AVIA. fighter plane, fighter.
ca·za·be m. AMER., CUL. cassava bread.
ca·za·dor, ·ra I. adj. hunting; ZOOL. predatory II. m. hunter, huntsman ♦ **c. de alforja or de pieles** trapper ♦ **c. de cabezas** head-hunter —f. (mujer) hunter, huntress; (chaqueta) hunting jacket.
ca·zar §04 tr. to hunt; (coger) to catch; (conseguir) to land ♦ **c. al vuelo** COLL. to catch on quickly.
ca·zo m. CUL. (cucharón) ladle; (cacerola) saucepan; CARP. gluepot.
ca·zo·le·ta f. ARTIL. pan (of a musket); (de espada) hand guard; (de pipa) bowl.
ca·zón m. dogfish, small shark.
ca·zue·la f. casserole; (guisado) stew; THEAT. gallery.
ca·zu·rro, a adj. & m.f. reserved (person).
ce·ba·de·ra f. nose bag; MARIT. spritsail.
ce·ba·do, a I. adj. AMER., ZOOL. fattened II. f. BOT. barley ♦ **c. perlada** pearl barley.
ce·bar tr. (engordar) to fatten; (un fuego) to stoke; (un anzuelo) to bait; (fomentar) to fuel; ARM. to prime; MECH. to start up; R.P. to brew (maté) —reflex. (excitarse) to become excited; (entregarse) to devote oneself.
ce·bi·che m. AMER. marinated raw fish.
ce·bo m. (alimento) feed; (detonador) charge; (del anzuelo) bait; (aliciente) enticement; ARM. primer.
ce·bo·lla f. onion; (bulbo) bulb.
ce·bo·lle·ta f. BOT. chive.
ce·bo·lli·no m. (sementero) onion seed; BOT., CUL. chive(s).
ce·bra f. zebra.
ce·bú m. [pl. **-úes**] zebu, Asiatic ox.
ce·ca f. royal mint.
ce·ce·ar intr. to lisp.
ce·ce·o m. lisp.
ce·ci·na f. cured meat; ARG. jerky, charqui.
ce·ci·nar tr. to cure (meat).
ce·da·zo m. sieve ♦ **pasar por c.** to sift.
ce·der tr. to cede; (transferir) to transfer; SPORT. to pass —intr. to cede; (rendirse) to yield, give in or up; (disminuirse) to abate.
ce·di·lla f. cedilla.
ce·dro m. cedar.

cé·du·la f. document ♦ **c. de identidad** identification card *or* papers.

cé·fi·ro m. zephyr.

ce·gar §52 tr. to blind; *(tapar)* to clog —reflex. FIG. to be blinded.

ce·ga·to, a COLL. adj. & m.f. nearsighted (person).

ce·gue·dad/ra f. blindness.

ce·ja f. eyebrow; *(saliente)* projection; *(borde)* border; METEOROL. cloud cover; MUS. bridge ♦ **fruncir las cejas** to frown • **meterse algo entre c. y c.** COLL. to get something into one's head.

ce·jar intr. to back up; FIG. to slacken.

ce·la·da f. ambush; FIG. trap.

ce·la·dor, ·ra I. adj. watchful, vigilant II. m.f. *(en la escuela)* monitor; *(de prisión)* guard.

ce·lar tr. to comply with ♦ **c. por** *or* **sobre** to watch out for.

cel·da f. cell.

ce·le·bra·ción f. celebration; *(aclamación)* praise.

ce·le·bran·te adj. I. celebrating II. m. celebrant.

ce·le·brar tr. to celebrate; *(alabar)* to praise; *(venerar)* to venerate; *(una reunión)* to hold; *(un acuerdo)* to reach —reflex. *(cumpleaños)* to be *or* fall on; *(una reunión)* to take place.

cé·le·bre adj. celebrated, famous.

ce·le·bri·dad f. celebrity.

ce·le·ri·dad f. speed ♦ **con toda c.** as quickly as possible.

ce·les·te I. adj. sky-blue ♦ **cuerpo c.** heavenly body II. m. sky blue.

ce·les·tial adj. heavenly.

ce·les·ti·na f. procuress, madam.

ce·li·ba·to m. celibacy.

cé·li·be adj. & m.f. celibate.

ce·lo m. *(actividad)* diligence; *(entusiasmo)* zeal; *(envidia)* jealousy ♦ **estar en c.** to be in heat • pl. jealousy ♦ **dar c.** to make jealous • **tener c.** to be jealous.

ce·lo·fán m. cellophane.

ce·lo·sí·a f. *(ventana)* lattice window; *(enrejado)* latticework.

ce·lo·so, a adj. *(con celos)* jealous; *(suspicaz)* suspicious; *(consciente)* zealous.

cé·lu·la f. cell.

ce·lu·li·tis f. cellulitis.

ce·lu·loi·de m. celluloid.

ce·lu·lo·so, a I. adj. cellulous, cellular II. f. cellulose.

ce·llis·ca f. sleet (storm).

ce·men·te·rio m. cemetery.

ce·men·to m. cement; *(hormigón)* concrete ♦ **c. armado** reinforced concrete.

ce·na f. dinner, supper ♦ **la santa** *or* **última C.** the Last Supper.

ce·na·gal m. swamp.

ce·nar intr. to have dinner *or* supper —tr. to have for dinner *or* supper.

cen·ce·rre·ar intr. *(sonar)* to clang bells; COLL. *(tocar mal)* to play out of tune; *(chirriar)* to squeak.

cen·ce·rro m. cowbell, bell.

ce·ni·ce·ro m. ashtray.

ce·ni·cien·to, a adj. ashen, ash-gray.

ce·nit m. zenith.

ce·ni·zo, a I. adj. ashen II. m. BOT. goosefoot; *(persona)* jinx ♦ **tener el c.** COLL. to have bad luck, be jinxed —f. *(polvo)* ash, ashes; *(restos)* ashes.

cen·so m. census; *(lista)* roll; *(arrendamiento)* rental ♦ **levantar el c.** to take a census.

cen·sor m. censor.

cen·su·ra f. censure; *(de expresión, arte)* censorship.

cen·su·rar tr. to censor; *(criticar)* to criticize.

cen·tau·ro m. centaur.

cen·ta·vo, a I. adj. hundredth II. m. AMER. cent.

cen·te·lla f. *(rayo)* flash; *(chispa)* spark.

cen·te·lle·an·te adj. sparkling.

cen·te·lle·ar/llar intr. *(fulgurar)* to sparkle; *(destellar)* to twinkle; *(chispear)* to flicker.

cen·te·na f. (one) hundred.

cen·te·nar m. (one) hundred ♦ **a centenares** by the hundreds.

cen·te·na·rio, a I. adj. *(viejo)* centenarian; *(aniversario)* centennial II. m.f. centenarian —m. centennial.

cen·te·no m. rye.

cen·té·si·mo, a I. adj. hundredth II. m. hundredth; PAN., URUG. centesimo (coin).

cen·tí·gra·do, a adj. centigrade.

cen·ti·gra·mo m. centigram.

cen·ti·li·tro m. centiliter.

cen·tí·me·tro m. centimeter.

cén·ti·mo, a I. adj. hundredth II. m. cent.

cen·ti·ne·la m.f. sentinel, sentry; FIG. lookout.

cen·to·lla f. spider crab.

cén·tra·do, a adj. centered; FIG. balanced.

cen·tral I. adj. central II. f. *(oficina)* headquarters ♦ **c. de correos** main post office.

cen·tra·li·za·ción f. centralization.

cen·tra·li·zar §04 tr. to centralize —reflex. to be *or* become centralized.

cen·trar tr. to center; *(determinar)* to find the center of; *(enfocar)* to focus; FIG. to aim.

cén·tri·co, a adj. central, centric.

cen·tri·fu·gar §47 tr. to centrifuge.

cen·trí·fu·go, a adj. centrifugal.

cen·trí·pe·to, a adj. centripetal.

cen·tro m. center; *(medio)* middle; *(núcleo)* core; *(ciudad)* downtown ♦ **c. comercial** shopping center • **c. de mesa** centerpiece • **c. turístico** tourist center

cén·tu·plo, a adj. & m. hundredfold.

ce·ñir §59 tr. *(atar)* to bind; *(ropa)* to be tight on; *(abreviar)* to condense —reflex. *(moderarse)* to limit oneself; *(ajustarse)* to adjust.

ce·ño m. frown ♦ **arrugar** *or* **fruncir el o.** to frown.

ce·pa f. *(tronco)* stump; *(de la vid)* rootstalk; *(vid)* vine ♦ **de buena c.** of good stock • **de pura c.** genuine.

ce·pi·llar tr. *(limpiar)* to brush; CARP. to planc.

ce·pi·llo m. brush; CARP. plane ♦ **c. de dientes** toothbrush • **c. para el pelo** hairbrush • **c. para el suelo** scrub brush • **c. para las uñas** nailbrush.

ce·po m. *(rama)* bough; *(del reo)* pillory ♦ **caer en el c.** to fall into the trap.

ce·ra f. wax; *(de los oídos)* earwax; *(de lustrar)* polish.

ce·rá·mi·co, a I. adj. ceramic II. f. ceramics.

cer·ba·ta·na f. blowpipe, blowgun.

cer·ca I. adv. nearby, close by ♦ **c. de** *(cercano a)* near, close to; *(alrededor de)* about • **de c.** closely II. f. fence ♦ **c. alambrada** wire fence • **c. viva** hedge.

cer·ca·do m. *(huerto)* garden; *(valla)* fence.

cer·ca·ní·a f. nearness, proximity ♦ pl. outskirts.

cer·ca·no, a adj. *(próximo)* close; *(vecino)*

neighboring; FIG. impending.

cer·car §70 tr. *(con cerco)* to fence in; *(rodear)* to surround; MIL. to besiege.

cer·ce·nar tr. *(cortar)* to cut; *(disminuir)* to cut down.

cer·cio·rar tr. to assure —reflex. to make sure.

cer·co m. *(círculo)* circle; *(borde)* edge; *(seto)* hedge; *(cercado)* enclosure; *(de un tonel)* hoop; TECH. rim; MIL. siege; ASTRON. corona.

cer·da f. bristle; ZOOL. sow.

cer·da·da f. COLL. dirty *or* lousy trick.

cer·do m. pig ♦ **carne de c.** pork.

ce·re·al adj. & m. cereal ♦ pl. cereals, grain.

ce·re·be·lo m. cerebellum.

ce·re·bro m. brain; FIG. brains.

ce·re·mo·nia f. ceremony; *(cumplido)* affected compliment ♦ **con c.** ceremoniously.

ce·re·mo·nial adj. & m. ceremonial.

ce·re·mo·nio·so, a adj. ceremonious.

ce·re·za f. cherry (fruit).

ce·re·zo m. cherry (tree).

ce·ri·lla f. *(vela)* wax taper; *(fósforo)* match; *(de los oídos)* earwax.

ce·rio m. cerium.

cer·ner §50 tr. to sift, sieve; FIG. to scan —reflex. FIG. to loom.

cer·ni·do m. *(acción)* sifting; *(harina)* sifted flour.

cer·ni·dor m. sieve.

cer·nir §25 tr. to sift, sieve.

ce·ro m. zero ♦ **ser un c. a la izquierda** COLL. to be totally useless.

ce·ro·te m. *(de zapatero)* cobbler's wax; COLL. *(miedo)* fear.

cer·qui·llo m. tonsure.

ce·rra·do, a adj. closed; *(nublado)* overcast; *(espeso)* thick; R.P. stubborn ♦ **a puerta c.** behind closed doors • **c. de mollera** AMER., COLL. dense.

ce·rra·du·ra f. lock.

ce·rra·je·rí·a f. *(oficio)* locksmith's trade; *(taller)* locksmith shop.

ce·rra·je·ro m. locksmith.

ce·rrar §49 tr. to close (up), shut; *(con cerrojo)* to bolt; *(cercar)* to enclose; *(paquete, abertura)* to seal (up); *(negocio, fábrica)* to close down; *(llave, canilla)* to turn off; *(camino, acceso)* to block off; *(debate, polémica)* to conclude; *(cuenta bancaria)* to close out ♦ **c. con llave** to lock • **c. los oídos a** to turn a deaf ear to • **c. los ojos** to die • **c. los puños** to clench one's fists —intr. to close, shut; *(la noche)* to fall —reflex. to close, shut; *(insistir)* to persist; MED. to close up; METEOROL. to cloud over.

ce·rra·zón f. *(cielo)* dark *or* overcast sky; *(torpeza)* denseness.

ce·rro m. hill; ZOOL. *(cuello)* neck; *(espinazo)* backbone.

ce·rro·jo m. bolt, latch.

cer·ta·men m. contest, competition.

cer·te·ro, a adj. accurate, skillful.

cer·te·za/ti·dum·bre f. certainty, certitude.

cer·ti·fi·ca·ción f. certification; *(certificado)* certificate.

cer·ti·fi·ca·do, a I. adj. certified; *(cartas)* registered II. m. certificate ♦ **c. de acciones** COM. stock certificate • **c. de defunción** death certificate.

cer·ti·fi·car §70 tr. *(verificar)* to certify; *(cartas)* to register.

cer·ti·tud f. certainty, certitude.

ce·ru·men m. earwax.

cer·ve·ce·rí·a f. *(fábrica)* brewery; *(taberna)* bar, pub.

cer·ve·za f. beer, ale ♦ **c. de barril** draft beer • **c. negra** dark beer.

cer·vi·cal adj. cervical.

cer·viz f. cervix ♦ **de dura c.** stubborn • **doblar** *or* **bajar la c.** to humble oneself.

ce·sa·ción f. cessation, discontinuance.

ce·san·te adj. & m.f. unemployed (person) ♦ **dejar c.** to dismiss.

ce·san·tí·a f. suspension; *(desempleo)* unemployment.

ce·sar intr. to end, stop ♦ **sin c.** unceasingly.

ce·sá·re·a adj. & f. Caesarean section.

ce·se m. *(suspensión)* cessation; *(revocación)* dismissal ♦ **c. de fuego** *or* **de hostilidades** cease-fire.

ce·sio m. cesium.

ce·sión f. cession.

ce·sio·na·rio, a m.f. cessionary, transferee.

ce·sio·nis·ta m.f. transferor, assignor.

cés·ped m. *(prado)* lawn, grass; *(gallón)* sod; SPORT. field.

ces·ta f. basket; *(cestada)* basketful; *(cochecillo)* wicker cart; *(pala)* jai alai racket; *(baloncesto)* basket ♦ **c. de costura** sewing basket • **c. para papeles** wastepaper basket.

ces·to m. basket ♦ **c. de** *or* **para papeles** wastepaper basket.

ce·tá·ce·o, a adj. & m. cetacean.

ce·tri·no, a adj. sallow, olive.

ce·tro m. scepter; RELIG. staff.

cia·nu·ro m. cyanide.

ciá·ti·co, a I. adj. sciatic II. f. sciatica, lumbago.

ci·be·li·na f. sable.

ci·ber·né·ti·ca f. cybernetics.

ci·bo·lo m. bison.

ci·ca·triz f. scar.

ci·ca·tri·za·ción f. healing.

ci·ca·tri·zar §04 tr. & intr. to heal.

ci·ce·ro·ne m. guide, cicerone.

cí·cli·co, a adj. cyclical, cyclic.

ci·clis·ta I. adj. cycling, cycle II. m.f. cyclist.

ci·clo m. cycle.

ci·clo·mo·tor m. moped, motorbike.

ci·clón m. cyclone ♦ **entrar como un c.** to burst in.

ci·cu·ta f. hemlock.

cid m. FIG. brave *or* valiant man.

cie·go, a adj. & m.f. blind (person) ♦ **c. como un topo** blind as a bat • **quedar c.** to go blind ♦ pl. **a c.** blindly; FIG. *(sin reflexión)* thoughtlessly, carelessly • **andar a c.** to grope one's way.

cie·go, gue see **cegar**.

cie·lo m. sky; *(atmósfera)* atmosphere; *(paraíso)* heaven; *(la providencia)* Heaven; COLL. *(querido)* darling ♦ **c. abierto** *or* **raso** in the open air • **caído** *or* **llovido del c.** COLL. heaven-sent • **cerrarse el c.** to cloud up • **c. raso** ceiling • **escupir al c.** to spit into the wind • **venirse el c. abajo** COLL. to rain cats and dogs ♦ pl. **¡c.!** good heavens! • **poner por los c.** to praise to the skies.

ciem·piés m.inv. centipede.

cien adj. contr. of **ciento**.

cié·na·ga f. swamp, marsh.

cien·cia f. science; *(erudición)* knowledge; *(habilidad)* skill ♦ **a** *or* **de c. cierta** for certain.

cie·no m. muck.

cien·tí·fi·co, a I. adj. scientific II. m.f. scien-

tist.
cien·to adj. & m. one hundred, a hundred ♦ **c. por c.** one hundred per cent • **por c.** per cent.

cier·na, no see cerner or cernir.

cier·ne m. ♦ **en c.** in blossom; FIG. just beginning.

cie·rre m. *(acción)* closing; *(clausura)* shut down; *(cremallera)* zipper; JOURN. deadline ♦ **c. de cremallera** zipper • **c. patronal** R.P. lockout • **o. relámpago** zipper.

cie·rre, rro see cerrar.

cier·to, a I. adj. certain; *(determinado)* definite; *(verdadero)* true; *(alguno)* some II. adv. certainly ♦ **de c.** certainly • **estar en lo c.** to be right • **io c. es que** the fact is that • **por c.** *(a propósito)* incidentally; *(ciertamente)* certainly • **por c. que** of course.

cier·vo m. deer, stag.

ci·fra f. *(número)* digit; *(cantidad)* quantity; *(total)* sum (total); *(clave)* cipher; *(monograma)* monogram; *(síntesis)* synthesis.

ci·frar tr. to encode ♦ **c. en** FIG. to place in.

ci·ga·rra f. cicada.

ci·ga·rre·ra f. cigar box or case.

ci·ga·rre·rí·a f. AMER. tobacco or smoke shop.

ci·ga·rri·llo m. cigarette.

ci·ga·rro m. cigar.

ci·go·to m. zygote, fertilized egg.

ci·güe·ña f. stork.

ci·güe·ñal m. winch; *(de motor)* crankshaft.

ci·lan·tro m. coriander.

ci·lin·drar tr. *(comprimir)* to calender; *(carreteras)* to steamroller.

ci·lín·dri·co, a adj. cylindrical, cylindric.

ci·lin·dro m. cylinder; *(rodillo)* roller.

ci·ma f. *(cumbre)* summit; FIG. pinnacle.

cim·ba·le·ro/lis·ta m. cymbalist.

cím·ba·los m.pl. cymbals.

cim·brar/bre·ar tr. & intr. to vibrate.

ci·men·tar §49 tr. CONSTR. to lay the foundation of; *(afirmar)* to consolidate; METAL. to refine.

ci·mien·to m. CONSTR. foundation; FIG. basis ♦ **echar los cimientos** to lay the foundation.

ci·mi·ta·rra f. scimitar.

cinc m. zinc.

cin·cel m. chisel.

cin·ce·lar tr. to chisel, carve (with a chisel).

cin·co I. adj. five; *(quinto)* fifth ♦ **las c.** five o'clock II. m. five; *(guitarra)* five-string guitar; *(moneda)* five-cent piece ♦ **estar sin un c.** to be broke.

cin·cuen·ta I. adj. fifty; *(quincuagésimo)* fiftieth II. m. fifty.

cin·cuen·ta·vo, a adj. & m.f. fiftieth.

cin·cuen·te·na·rio m. fiftieth anniversary.

cin·cuen·te·na f. group of fifty.

cin·cuen·tón, o·na adj. & m.f. fifty-year-old (person).

cin·cha f. girth, cinch ♦ **a revienta cinchas** *(de mala gana)* unwillingly; *(rápido)* at breakneck speed.

cin·char tr. EQUIT. to girth, cinch.

cin·cho m. *(faja)* belt; *(zuncho)* metal hoop; *(de rueda)* iron rim; ARCHIT. projecting rib of an arch; AMER. girth.

ci·ne m. cinema; PHOTOG., TECH. cinematography; COLL. *(espectáculo)* movies; *(teatro)* movie theater ♦ **c. de estreno** first-run movie theater • **c. mudo** silent films • **c. parlante** or **sonoro** talking pictures.

ci·ne·as·ta m.f. *(director)* filmmaker; *(productor)* film producer.

ci·ne·mas·co·pe m. cinemascope.

ci·ne·ma·te·ca f. film library or archive.

ci·ne·ma·to·gra·fí·a f. cinematography.

ci·ne·ma·to·gra·fiar §30 tr. to film, shoot.

ci·ne·ma·to·grá·fi·co, a adj. cinematographic.

ci·ne·ma·tó·gra·fo m. *(proyector)* (film) projector; *(teatro)* movie theater.

ci·né·ti·co, a I. adj. kinetic II. f. kinetics.

cín·ga·ro, a adj. & m.f. gypsy.

cí·ni·co, a I. adj. cynical II. m.f. cynic.

cin·ls·mo m. cynicism.

cin·ta f. ribbon; *(película)* film ♦ **c. adhesiva** adhesive tape • **c. de freno** brake lining • **c. de medir** measuring tape • **c. de teletipo** ticker tape • **c. magnetofónica** recording tape • **o. métrica** tape measure • **c. transportadora** conveyor belt.

cin·ti·lar tr. to sparkle, twinkle.

cin·to m. *(ceñidor)* belt; *(cintura)* waist.

cin·tu·ra f. waist, waistline ♦ **c. pelviana** pelvic girdle.

cin·tu·rón m. belt ♦ **apretarse el c.** to tighten one's belt • **c. de castidad** chastity belt • **c. de seguridad** seat or safety belt • **c. salvavidas** life preserver.

ci·ña, ño, ñera, ñó see ceñir.

ci·prés m. cypress.

cir·cen·se adj. circus.

cir·co m. circus; GEOL. cirque.

cir·cón m. zircon.

cir·co·nio m. zirconium.

cir·cui·to m. circuit; *(circunferencia)* circumference; *(de carreteras)* network ♦ **corto c.** short circuit.

cir·cu·la·ción f. circulation; *(transmisión)* dissemination; *(tráfico)* traffic ♦ **poner en c.** to put into circulation.

cir·cu·lar¹ I. adj. circular II. f. circular, flier.

cir·cu·lar² intr. & tr. to circulate.

cir·cu·la·to·rio, a adj. ANAT. circulatory; AUTO. traffic.

cír·cu·lo m. circle; *(circunferencia)* circumference ♦ **c. vicioso** vicious circle, circular argument.

cir·cun·ci·dar tr. to circumcise.

cir·cun·ci·sión f. circumcision.

cir·cun·dar tr. to surround, encircle.

cir·cun·fe·ren·cia f. circumference.

cir·cun·fle·jo, a adj. & m. circumflex.

cir·cun·lo·cu·ción f./**lo·quio** m. circumlocution.

cir·cun·na·ve·ga·ción f. circumnavigation.

cir·cuns·cri·bir §80 tr. to circumscribe —reflex. to restrict or limit oneself.

cir·cuns·pec·ción f. circumspection; *(prudencia)* caution, prudence.

cir·cuns·pec·to, a adj. circumspect.

cir·cuns·tan·cia f. circumstance ♦ **en las circunstancias actuales** under the present circumstances.

cir·cuns·tan·cial adj. circumstantial; GRAM. adverbial.

cir·cun·va·la·ción f. MIL. circumvallation ♦ **línea de c.** AUTO. loop.

cir·cun·va·lar tr. to surround, encircle.

cir·cun·vo·lu·ción f. circumvolution ♦ **c. cerebral** cerebral convolution.

ci·rio m. church candle.

ci·rro m. cirrus; MED. scirrhus (tumor).

ci·rro·sis f. cirrhosis.

ci·rue·la f. plum; *(pasa)* prune ♦ **c. pasa**

prune.
ci·rue·lo m. plum tree.
ci·ru·gí·a f. surgery ♦ **c. plástica** or **estética** plastic or cosmetic surgery • **c. mayor** major surgery • **c. menor** minor surgery.
ci·ru·ja·no, a m.f. surgeon.
ci·sión f. incision.
cis·ma m. schism; (discordia) discord.
cis·ne m. swan; R.P. powder puff.
cis·ter·na f. cistern, reservoir.
cis·ti·tis f. cystitis.
ci·su·ra f. scission, fissure.
ci·ta f. (entrevista) appointment, meeting; (con novio, amigo) date; (referencia) quote ♦ **darse c.** to set up a meeting or date with someone.
ci·ta·ción f. subpoena ♦ **c. de remate** notice of public sale.
ci·tar tr. (convocar) to make an appointment or date with; (referirse) to cite; LAW to summon.
cí·ta·ra f. zither, zithern.
ci·to·lo·gí·a f. cytology.
ci·to·plas·ma m. cytoplasm.
cí·tri·co, a I. adj. citric II. m.pl. citrus fruits.
ciu·dad f. city.
ciu·da·da·ní·a f. (derecho) citizenship; (población) citizenry.
ciu·da·da·no, a I. adj. civic, city II. m.f. citizen.
ciu·da·de·la f. citadel, fortress.
cí·vi·co, a adj. civic.
ci·vil I. adj. civil II. m.f. civilian.
ci·vi·li·dad f. civility.
ci·vi·li·za·ción f. civilization.
ci·vi·li·za·do, a adj. civilized, refined.
ci·vi·li·zar §04 tr. to civilize —reflex. to become civilized.
ci·vis·mo m. civic-mindedness.
ci·za·ña f. BOT. (bearded) darnel; (vicio) evil; (disensión) discord ♦ **meter** or **sembrar c.** to cause trouble.
ci·za·ñar tr. to cause or make trouble for.
ci·za·ñe·ro, a I. adj. troublemaking II. m.f. troublemaker.
cla·mar intr. to clamor; FIG. to demand —tr. to cry out for.
cla·mor m. clamor, outcry.
cla·mo·re·ar intr. & tr. to cry out (for).
cla·mo·re·o m. clamoring.
cla·mo·ro·so, a adj. clamorous ♦ **éxito c.** resounding success.
clan m. clan.
clan·des·ti·no, a adj. clandestine.
cla·ra f. see **claro, a.**
cla·ra·bo·ya f. skylight.
cla·re·ar tr. & intr. to dawn ♦ **al c. el día** at the break of dawn.
cla·re·cer §17 intr. to dawn.
cla·re·te adj. & m. claret (wine).
cla·ri·dad f. clarity; (luz) brightness; (nitidez) clearness ♦ **con c.** clearly.
cla·ri·fi·ca·ción f. clarification.
cla·ri·fi·car §70 tr. to clarify.
cla·rín m. clarion; (músico) trumpet player.
cla·ri·ne·te m. clarinet; (músico) clarinetist.
cla·ri·ne·tis·ta m.f. clarinetist.
cla·ri·vi·den·cia f. clairvoyance.
cla·ri·vi·den·te m.f. clairvoyant.
cla·ro, a I. adj. clear; (luminoso) bright; (despejado) cloudless; (cristalino) transparent; (aguado) thin; (obvio) obvious; (inteligible) in telligible; (sin ambages) straightforward ♦ **a las**

claras openly • **c. como el agua** as plain as the nose on your face II. adv. plainly ♦ **¡c.!** or **¡c. que sí!** of course!, sure! III. m. (abertura) gap; (espacio) clearing ♦ **c. de luna** moonlight • **poner** or **sacar en c.** to clarify, explain —f. white (of egg).
cla·ros·cu·ro m. chiaroscuro.
cla·se f. class; (lección) lesson; (aula) classroom ♦ **c. turista** coach • **de c.** of distinction • **toda c.** de all kinds of.
cla·si·cis·ta adj. & m.f. classicist.
clá·si·co, a I. adj. classic, classical; (notable) outstanding II. m.f. (autor) classic author; (clasicista) classicist.
cla·si·fi·ca·ción f. classification.
cla·si·fi·car §70 tr. to classify; (archivar) to file —reflex. SPORT. to qualify.
clau·di·ca·ción f. backing down.
clau·di·car §70 intr. to back down.
claus·tro m. cloister; EDUC. faculty ♦ **c. materno** womb.
claus·tro·fo·bia f. claustrophobia.
cláu·su·la f. clause ♦ **c. absoluta** GRAM. (latín) ablative absolute; (inglés) absolute construction • **c. simple** simple sentence.
clau·su·ra f. (abadía) cloister; (estado) monastic life; (conclusión) closing ceremony; AMER. (cierre) closing; EDUC. commencement.
clau·su·rar tr. (terminar) to bring to a close; (cerrar) to close, shut.
cla·va·do, a adj. (con claves) nail-studded; (en punto) sharp, on the dot.
cla·var tr. to nail; (hincar) to thrust, drive; FIG. (fijar) to fix or rivet on; COLL. (engañar) to cheat.
cla·ve I. f. (cifra) code; (esencia) key; ARCHIT. keystone; MUS. clef ♦ **c. de do** tenor or alto clef • **c. de fa** base clef • **c. de sol** treble clef —m. clavichord II. adj. key.
cla·ve·cín m. harpsichord.
cla·vel m. carnation.
cla·ve·te·ar tr. to stud.
cla·vi·cém·ba·lo m. harpsichord.
cla·vi·cor·dio m. clavichord.
cla·ví·cu·la f. clavicle, collarbone.
cla·vi·ja f. (clavo) peg, pin; CARP. peg, dowel; ELEC. plug; MUS. peg ♦ **ajustarle** or **apretarle a uno las clavijas** COLL. to put the screws on or to someone.
cla·vo m. nail; BOT. clove; R.P. (mercadería) white elephant; (perjuicio) nasty business ♦ **dar en el c.** COLL. to hit the nail on the head.
cle·men·cia f. clemency.
clep·to·ma·ní·a f. kleptomania.
clep·tó·ma·no, a adj. & m.f. kleptomaniac.
clé·ri·go m. clergyman.
cle·ro m. clergy.
cli·ché m. cliché; PRINT. (plancha) cliché, (stereotype) plate; (negativo) negative.
clien·te m.f. COM. client, customer; DENT., MED. patient; LAW client.
clien·te·la f. COM. customers, clientele; DENT., MED. practice, patients; LAW clients.
cli·ma m. climate; FIG. atmosphere.
cli·má·ti·co, a adj. climatic.
cli·ma·ti·za·ción f. air conditioning.
cli·ma·ti·zar §04 tr. to air-condition.
cli·max m.inv. climax.
clí·ni·co, a I. adj. clinical II. m. clinician —f. private hospital.
clip m. (sujetapapeles) paper clip; (aro) earring.
clí·per m. AVIA., MARIT. clipper.

cli·sé m. see **cliché**.
clí·to·ris m. clitoris.
clo·a·ca f. sewer.
clo·car §73 intr. to cluck, cackle.
clon m. clone.
clo·que·ar intr. to cluck, cackle.
clo·que·ra f. brooding, broodiness.
clo·ra·to m. chlorate.
clor·hi·dra·to m. hydrochloride.
clor·hí·dri·co, a adj. hydrochloric.
cló·ri·co, a adj. chloric.
clo·ro m. chlorine.
clo·ro·fi·la f. chlorophyll.
clo·ro·for·mo m. chloroform.
clo·ru·ro m. chloride.
club m. [pl. (e)s] club.
clue·co, a I. adj. broody; COLL. *(decrépito)* feeble II. f. brooder.
clue·que see **clocar**.
co·ac·ción f. coercion; LAW duress.
co·ac·cio·nar tr. to coerce.
co·a·cre·e·dor, ·ra m.f. joint creditor.
co·a·cu·sa·do, a m.f. codefendant.
co·ad·qui·ri·dor, ·ra m.f. LAW joint purchaser.
co·ad·yu·var tr. & intr. to help.
co·a·gen·te m.f. coagent.
co·a·gu·lan·te adj. coagulant, coagulative.
co·a·gu·lar tr. & reflex. to coagulate; *(leche)* to curdle.
co·á·gu·lo m. clot; *(leche)* curd.
co·a·li·ción f. coalition.
co·ar·ta·da f. alibi ♦ **presentar una c.** to provide an alibi.
co·ar·tar tr. to hinder.
co·au·tor, ·ra m.f. co-author.
co·a·xial adj. coaxial.
co·bal·to m. cobalt.
co·bar·de I. adj. cowardly II. m.f. coward.
co·bar·dí·a f. cowardice, cowardliness.
co·ber·ti·zo m. *(protección)* shelter; *(barraca)* shed; *(cochera)* garage.
co·ber·tor m. *(colcha)* bedspread; *(de plumas)* comforter; *(manta)* blanket.
co·ber·tu·ra f. cover, covering.
co·bi·ja f. *(cubierta)* cover, covering; *(teja)* ridge tile; ORNITH. covert; AMER. blanket; MEX. *(chal)* short shawl, wrap.
co·bi·jar tr. to cover (up); FIG. to harbor.
co·bra f. cobra.
co·bra·dor, ·ra m.f. *(recaudador)* bill *or* tax collector; *(perro)* retriever.
co·bran·za f. collection; *(recuperación)* retrieval; *(de un cheque)* cashing; *(pago)* payment.
co·brar tr. *(recibir)* to collect; *(recuperar)* to retrieve; *(precios)* to charge; *(un cheque)* to cash ♦ **c. afecto** *or* **cariño a** to take a liking to • **c. ánimo** to take heart • **c. fama de** to get a reputation for being • **c. fuerza** to gather strength • **c. valor** to muster courage —reflex. to recoup one's losses.
co·bre m. copper; MUS. brass instrument; AMER. cent ♦ **quedarse sin un c.** to be broke.
co·bri·zo, a adj. copper, copper-colored.
co·bro m. collection, collecting; *(de un cheque)* cashing ♦ **c. a la entrega** collect on delivery • **presentar al c.** to present for cashing.
co·ca f. coca; PHARM. cocaine.
co·ca·í·na f. cocaine.
coc·ción f. cooking; *(hervor)* boiling; *(en un horno)* baking.

cóc·cix m.inv. coccyx.
co·ce·ar intr. to kick.
co·cer §71 tr. to cook; *(hervir)* to boil; *(en un horno)* to bake —intr. *(hervir)* to boil; *(fermentar)* to ferment.
co·cien·te m. quotient.
co·ci·mien·to m. cooking; *(al horno)* baking; *(de hierbas)* medicinal extraction.
co·ci·na f. *(cuarto)* kitchen; *(aparato)* stove, range; *(estilo)* cuisine ♦ **de c.** kitchen.
co·ci·nar tr. & intr. to cook.
co·ci·ne·ro, a m.f. cook, chef.
co·co m. coconut; COLL. *(cabeza)* noggin.
co·co·dri·lo m. crocodile.
co·co·ro·có m. cock-a-doodle-doo.
co·co·tal m. coconut grove.
co·co·te·ro m. coconut palm.
cóc·tel m. *(bebida)* cocktail; *(reunión)* cocktail party.
coc·te·le·ra f. cocktail shaker.
co·che m. *(carruaje)* carriage; *(automóvil)* car ♦ **c. blindado** armored car • **c. cama** sleeper, sleeping car • **c. comedor** dining car • **c. de alquiler** *(taxi)* taxi, cab; *(alquilado)* rental car • **c. de carreras** sports car • **c. fúnebre** hearse.
co·che·ra f. garage.
co·che·ro m. coachman.
co·chi·na·da/ne·rí·a f. COLL. *(suciedad)* dirt, filth; *(palabrota)* dirty word; *(trato)* dirty trick ♦ pl. **decir c.** to use foul language.
co·chi·ne·ar intr. COLL. to act like a pig.
co·chi·ni·llo m. piglet, suckling pig.
co·chi·no, a I. m.f. pig; COLL. *(persona)* swine II. adj. *(sucio)* filthy; COLL. *(ruin)* rotten.
co·chi·tril m. COLL. pigsty.
co·da f. coda.
co·da·zo m. jab, poke (with one's elbow) ♦ **dar un c.** to jab ♦ pl. **abrirse paso a c.** to elbow one's way through.
co·de·ar intr. to elbow —reflex. COLL. to rub elbows with.
co·de·í·na f. codeine.
co·de·ra f. elbow patch.
co·deu·dor, ·ra m.f. codebtor, joint debtor.
có·di·ce m. codex, manuscript.
co·di·cia f. *(avaricia)* greed; *(envidia)* envy; FIG. thirst.
co·di·ciar tr. to covet, desire.
co·di·cio·so, a adj. & m.f. greedy (person) ♦ **ser c. de** to covet.
co·di·fi·ca·ción f. encoding; LAW codification.
co·di·fi·ca·dor, ·ra I. adj. codifying II. m.f. codifier.
co·di·fi·car §70 tr. to encode; LAW to codify.
có·di·go m. code ♦ **c. de edificación** building code • **c. de leyes** legal code • **c. fiscal** tax code • **c. postal** zip code.
co·do m. elbow; FIG. bend ♦ **alzar** *or* **empinar el c.** to have a lot to drink • **c. con c.** neck and neck ♦ pl. **hablar por los c.** to be a chatterbox.
co·e·fi·cien·te adj. & m. coefficient.
co·er·ción f. coercion.
co·er·ci·ti·vo, a adj. coercive, restrictive.
co·e·tá·ne·o, a adj. & m.f. contemporary.
co·e·xis·ten·cia f. coexistence.
co·e·xis·ten·te adj. coexistent.
co·e·xis·tir intr. to coexist.
co·fia f. *(red)* hair net; *(gorro)* bonnet.
co·fra·de m.f. member.
co·fra·dí·a f. *(de hombres)* brotherhood; *(de mujeres)* sisterhood; *(gremio)* guild.
co·fre m. *(arca)* chest; *(caja)* box.

co·ger §34 tr. to grab, grasp; *(recoger)* to gather up; *(apresar)* to capture; *(ocupar)* to take up; *(absorber)* to absorb; *(alcanzar)* to catch up with; *(encontrar)* to find; *(sorprender)* to catch by surprise; *(enfermedad)* to catch; *(entender)* to understand.

co·gi·do m. SEW. pleat, fold.

cog·na·do, a m.f. cognate.

cog·ni·ción f. cognition.

cog·nos·ci·ti·vo, a adj. cognitive.

co·go·llo m. heart (of vegetables).

co·go·te m. back of the neck ♦ **tieso de c.** arrogant.

co·go·tu·do, a AMER., COLL. m.f. & adj. *(rico)* wealthy *or* influential (person); *(orgulloso)* arrogant (person).

co·ha·bi·tar intr. to live together, cohabit.

co·he·cho m. bribe, bribery.

co·he·ren·cia f. coherence; PHYS. cohesion.

co·he·ren·te adj. coherent.

co·he·sión f. cohesion.

co·he·si·vo, a adj. cohesive.

co·he·te m. rocket ♦ **al c.** ARG., BOL., COLL. in vain • **c. balístico** ballistic missile • **c. de señales** flare • **salir como un c.** COLL. to be off like a shot.

co·hi·bi·ción f. inhibition.

co·hi·bir tr. *(inhibir)* to inhibit; *(desasosegar)* to make uneasy —reflex. to be *or* feel inhibited.

co·hor·te f. cohort.

coi·ma f. AMER. bribe, payola.

co·in·ci·den·cia f. coincidence.

co·in·ci·den·te adj. coincidental, coincident.

co·in·ci·dir intr. to coincide; *(concordar)* to agree.

co·in·qui·li·no, a m.f. joint tenant.

coi·to m. coitus, sexual intercourse.

co·je·ar intr. to limp; *(una mesa)* to wobble.

co·je·ra f. limp, lameness.

co·jín m. cushion.

co·ji·ne·te m. small cushion; RAIL. socket; MECH. bearing; PRINT. roller clamp ♦ **c. de bolas** ball bearing ♦ pl. COL., MEX., VEN. saddlebags.

co·jo, a I. adj. *(tullido)* crippled; *(un mueble)* wobbly ♦ **no ser c. ni manco** COLL. to be all there **II.** m.f. cripple.

col f. cabbage ♦ **c. de Bruselas** Brussels sprouts.

co·la[1] f. tail; *(de vestido)* train; *(fila)* queue; *(parte final)* rear ♦ **a la c.** last • **c. de caballo** BOT. horsetail; *(pelo)* ponytail ♦ **hacer c.** to line up • **piano de c.** grand piano • **tener** *or* **traer c.** to have serious consequences.

co·la[2] f. glue, gum ♦ **eso no pega ni con c.** COLL. that's nonsense.

co·la·bo·ra·ción f. collaboration.

co·la·bo·ra·cio·nis·ta m.f. collaborationist.

co·la·bo·ra·dor, ·ra I. adj. *(cooperador)* collaborating; LIT. contributing **II.** m.f. *(cooperador)* collaborator; LIT. contributor.

co·la·bo·rar intr. to collaborate; LIT. to contribute.

co·la·ción f. *(merienda)* snack; RELIG. collation ♦ **sacar** *or* **traer a c.** to bring up.

co·la·da f. *(blanqueo)* whitening; *(cañada)* cattle trail; METAL. tap (on a furnace).

co·la·de·ro m. *(cedazo)* strainer; *(camino)* narrow trail; *(examen)* lenient examination.

co·la·do, a adj. cast ♦ **hierro c.** cast iron.

co·la·dor m. strainer; RELIG. collator.

co·lap·so m. collapse ♦ **c. nervioso** nervous breakdown.

co·lar §19 tr. to strain; *(blanquear)* to bleach; COLL. to pass *or* foist (off); METAL. to cast —intr. to squeeze through —reflex. to sneak in.

co·la·te·ral adj. & m.f. collateral.

col·cha f. bedspread.

col·cha·do, a I. adj. quilted **II.** m. quilting.

col·chón m. mattress ♦ **c. de aire** air cushion • **c. de muelles** spring mattress • **c. de plumas** feather bed.

col·cho·ne·ro, a I. adj. SEW. tufting **II.** m.f. *(fabricante)* mattress manufacturer; *(vendedor)* mattress seller.

col·cho·ne·ta f. light mattress.

co·le·a·da f. flick (of the tail); *(de un perro)* wag (of the tail).

co·lec·ción f. collection; LIT. anthology.

co·lec·cio·na·dor, ra m.f. collector.

co·lec·cio·nar tr. to collect.

co·lec·cio·nis·ta m.f. collector.

co·lec·ta f. collection.

co·lec·tar tr. to collect.

co·lec·ti·vi·dad f. community.

co·lec·ti·vis·ta I. adj. collectivistic **II.** m.f. collectivist.

co·lec·ti·vi·za·ción f. collectivization.

co·lec·ti·vo, a I. adj. collective; *(mutuo)* joint **II.** m. GRAM. collective (noun); ARG., BOL., PERU small bus.

co·lec·tor m. collector ♦ **c. de aceite** AUTO. drip pan.

co·le·ga m. colleague, associate.

co·le·gia·do, a adj. collegiate.

co·le·gial adj. school.

co·le·gial, ·la m.f. schoolboy, schoolgirl.

co·le·gio m. *(primario)* elementary school; *(secundario)* high school; *(asociación)* college, association <**c. de abogados** bar association> ♦ **c. de internos** boarding school • **c. de párvulos** nursery school • **c. electoral** electoral college.

co·le·gir §57 tr. to infer, gather.

co·le·óp·te·ro I. adj. coleopteral **II.** m. coleopteran.

có·le·ra f. choler; FIG. anger ♦ **dar c.** to infuriate • **descargar la c. en** to vent one's anger on • **montar en c.** to get angry —m. MED. cholera.

co·lé·ri·co, a I. adj. suffering from cholera; FIG. choleric, irascible **II.** m.f. cholera patient; FIG. irascible person.

co·les·te·rol m./**ri·na** f. cholesterol.

co·le·ta f. *(pelo)* pigtail; FIG., COLL. *(adición escrita)* postscript; AMER. *(lona)* coarse canvas.

co·le·ta·zo m. blow with the tail; AUTO. sway.

co·le·to m. jerkin ♦ **decir para su c.** to say to oneself.

col·ga·do, a adj. let down ♦ **dejar c. a** to let down.

col·ga·jo m. *(jirón)* tatter; *(racimo)* bunch.

col·gan·te I. adj. hanging ♦ **puente c.** suspension bridge **II.** m. pendant.

col·gar §16 tr. to hang (up); *(adornar)* to drape with hangings; *(reprobar)* to flunk ♦ **c. los hábitos** to give up the cloth; FIG. to give up an action or profession —intr. to hang; *(caer)* to hang down.

co·li·brí m. [pl. **-íes**] hummingbird.

có·li·co, a I. adj. colonic **II.** m. colic.

co·li·flor f. cauliflower.

co·li·gar·se §47 reflex. to ally, unite.

co·li·ge, ja, jo see **colegir.**
co·li·lla f. cigarette butt.
co·li·na f. hill.
co·lin·dan·te adj. adjacent, adjoining.
co·lin·dar intr. to be adjacent, adjoin.
co·li·ne·al adj. collinear.
co·li·rio m. collyrium, eyewash.
co·li·se·o m. coliseum, colosseum.
co·li·sión f. collision; FIG. conflict.
co·li·tis f. colitis, colonitis.
col·ma·do, a I. adj. *(lleno)* full, filled; *(cucharada)* heaping II. m. *(café)* café; *(almacén)* grocery store.
col·mar tr. *(llenar)* to fill (up), fill to the brim; FIG. to shower; *(satisfacer)* to fulfill, satisfy ♦ **¡eso colma la medida!** that's the last straw!
col·me·na f. beehive, hive.
col·me·nar m. apiary.
col·me·ne·ro, a m.f. beekeeper, apiarist —m. honey bear.
col·mi·llo m. canine tooth, eyetooth; ZOOL. *(del elefante)* tusk; *(del perro)* fang ♦ pl. **enseñar los c.** COLL. to show one's teeth.
col·mo m. *(exceso)* overflow; *(cumbre)* height; *(límite)* limit ♦ **para c. de desgracias** to make matters worse.
co·lo·ca·ción f. *(acción)* placing; *(lugar)* place; *(empleo)* position.
co·lo·car §70 tr. to place, position; *(dinero)* to invest.
co·lo·fón m. colophon.
co·lo·fo·nia f. rosin.
co·loi·dal/de·o, a adj. colloidal.
co·loi·de m. colloid.
co·lom·bó·fi·lo, a I. adj. pigeon-breeding II. m.f. pigeon breeder.
co·lon m. ANAT. colon.
co·lo·nia f. colony; *(perfume)* cologne ♦ **c. penitenciaria** prison camp.
co·lo·nial adj. colonial.
co·lo·nia·lis·ta adj. & m.f. colonialist.
co·lo·ni·za·ción f. colonization.
co·lo·ni·za·dor, ra I. adj. colonizing, settling II. m.f. colonizer, settler.
co·lo·ni·zar §04 tr. to colonize, settle.
co·lo·no m. settler; AGR. tenant farmer.
co·lo·quio m. *(conversación)* talk; *(conferencia)* seminar.
co·lor m. color; *(colorante)* tint; *(aspecto)* aspect ♦ **a c.** in color • **c. elemental** primary color • **c. firme** fast color • **c. vivo** bright color • **de c.** colored • **mudar de c.** COLL. *(sonrojarse)* to blush; *(palidecer)* to turn pale • **subido de c.** off-color • **ver las cosas de c. de rosa** COLL. to see things through rose-colored glasses ♦ pl. **ponerse de mil c.** COLL. to flush.
co·lo·ra·ción f. coloring ♦ **c. defensiva** BIOL. protective markings.
co·lo·ra·do, a I. adj. *(que tiene color)* colored; *(rojizo)* red, reddish ♦ **ponerse c.** to blush II. m. red.
co·lo·ra·do·te, a adj. COLL. ruddy, red-faced.
co·lo·ran·te I. adj. coloring II. m. colorant.
co·lo·rar tr. *(dar color)* to color; *(teñir)* to dye; *(pintar)* to paint.
co·lo·re·ar tr. *(dar color)* to color —intr. to turn red.
co·lo·re·te m. rouge.
co·lo·ri·do m. *(acción)* coloring; *(colores)* coloration; *(color)* color, FIG. style.
co·lo·rin·che m. R.P. gaudy combination of colors.
co·lo·sal adj. colossal.
co·lo·so m. *(estatua)* colossus; *(gigante)* giant.
co·lum·na f. column, pillar ♦ **c. de dirección** AUTO. steering column • **c. vertebral** spine, spinal column.
co·lum·na·ta f. colonnade.
co·lum·nis·ta m.f. columnist.
co·lum·piar tr. to swing —reflex. *(mecerse)* to swing; COLL. *(contonearse)* to sway.
co·lum·pio m. swing.
co·lu·sión f. collusion.
co·lu·to·rio m. mouthwash, gargle.
co·lla·do m. *(cerro)* hill; *(entre montañas)* mountain pass.
co·llar m. *(adorno)* necklace; *(cadena)* chain; *(de animal)* collar; MECH. ring, collar; ORNITH., ZOOL. collar, ruff.
co·lla·rín m. *(collar)* small collar; RELIG. collar.
co·ma¹ f. comma ♦ **sin faltar una c.** in the minutest detail.
co·ma² m. coma.
co·ma·dre f. godmother; *(relación)* mother of the child (in relation to the godmother); *(partera)* midwife.
co·ma·dre·ar intr. COLL. to gossip.
co·ma·dre·ja f. weasel; ARG. opossum.
co·ma·dro·na f. midwife.
co·man·dan·cia f. *(grado)* command; *(distrito)* district; *(edificio)* headquarters.
co·man·dan·te m. commanding officer; *(grado)* major ♦ **c. de armas** commandant • **c. de barco** commander • **c. en jefe** or **general** commander-in-chief.
co·man·dar tr. MIL. to command, lead.
co·man·di·ta f. ♦ **sociedad en c.** silent partnership.
co·man·di·ta·rio, a I. COM. I. adj. silent II. m.f. silent partner.
co·man·do m. MIL. commando; *(mando)* command; TECH. control ♦ **c. a distancia** remote control.
co·mar·ca f. region, district.
co·mar·car §70 intr. to border on, adjoin —tr. to plant trees in straight lines.
co·ma·to·so, a adj. comatose.
com·ba f. see **combo, a.**
com·ba·du·ra f. bending, curving.
com·bar tr. & reflex. *(encorvar)* to bend, curve; *(alabear)* to warp.
com·ba·te m. combat; FIG. conflict; SPORT. contest ♦ **c. naval** naval *or* sea battle • **c. nulo** draw • **fuera de c.** out of action • **ganar por fuera de c.** SPORT. to win by a knockout.
com·ba·tien·te I. adj. fighting II. m. combatant, fighter; MIL. soldier.
com·ba·tir intr. to battle —tr. *(luchar contra)* to fight; *(acometer)* to attack; *(impugnar)* to oppose; FIG. to beat upon —reflex. to fight, struggle.
com·ba·ti·vo, a adj. combative.
com·bi·na·ción f. combination; *(prenda)* slip; *(plan)* plan; CHEM. compound; RAIL. connection; MATH. permutation.
com·bi·na·do m. stereo; CHEM. compound.
com·bi·nar tr. to combine; *(arreglar)* to work out <c. ideas to work out ideas> —reflex. to combine.
com·bo, a I. adj. bent, curved II. m. *(asiento)*

stand on which wine casks are placed; ARG., CHILE *(martilla)* sledge hammer; CHILE *(puñetazo)* punch, blow —f. *(convexidad)* bend, curve; *(alabeo)* warp; *(juego y cuerda)* skipping rope.

com·bus·ti·ble I. adj. combustible II. m. fuel.

com·bus·tión f. combustion.

co·me·de·ro m. *(recipiente)* feeding trough; *(lugar)* manger.

co·me·dia f. comedy; *(obra)* play; *(edificio)* theater; *(fingimiento)* farce ♦ **c. de capa y espada** cloak-and-dagger play • **c. de costumbres** comedy of manners • **c. en un acto** one-act play • **hacer la c.** COLL. to pretend.

co·me·dian·te, a m. *(comic)* actor —f. *(comic)* actress —m.f. COLL. hypocrite.

co·me·di·do, a adj. *(cortés)* courteous; *(reservado)* reserved; S. AMER. obliging.

co·me·dir·se §48 reflex. to restrain oneself.

co·me·dor, ·ra I. adj. gluttonous II. m.f. big eater —m. *(cuarto)* dining room; *(muebles)* dining room suite ♦ **coche c.** dining car.

co·men·da·dor m. knight commander.

co·men·da·do·ra f. mother superior.

co·men·sal m.f. mealtime companion.

co·men·ta·dor, ·ra m.f. commentator.

co·men·tar tr. to comment on.

co·men·ta·rio m. commentary ♦ **sin c.** no comment ♦ pl. *(memorias históricas)* commentaries, historical memoirs; *(chisme)* gossip.

co·men·ta·ris·ta m.f. commentator.

co·men·zar §29 tr. & intr. to begin, start ♦ **c. a** to begin to • **c. con** to begin with • **c. por** to begin with *or* by.

co·mer tr. to eat; *(roer)* to corrode; *(consumir)* to consume; *(en los juegos)* to take (a piece in chess or checkers) ♦ **sin comerlo ni beberlo** COLL. without having had anything to do with it —intr. to eat • **c. y callar** COLL. beggars can't be choosers • **dar de c.** to feed • **ser de buen c.** COLL. to have a healthy appetite • **tener qué c.** to have enough to live on —reflex. to eat up *<me lo comí todo* I ate it all up>; *(disipar)* to squander; *(pasar)* to skip over.

co·mer·cial I. adj. commercial, business ♦ **centro c.** shopping center II. m. AMER. commercial, advertisement.

co·mer·cia·li·za·ción f. commercialization.

co·mer·cia·li·zar §04 tr. to commercialize.

co·mer·cian·te m.f. merchant —m. businessman, shopkeeper —f. businesswoman ♦ **c. al por mayor** wholesaler • **c. al por menor** retailer.

co·mer·ciar intr. to trade, deal.

co·mer·cio m. *(negocio)* business; *(tienda)* store ♦ **c. exterior** foreign trade • **c. interior** domestic trade.

co·mes·ti·ble I. adj. edible II. m. foodstuff ♦ pl. groceries.

co·me·ta m. comet —f. *(juguete)* kite.

co·me·ter tr. *(encargar)* to charge with; *(un crimen)* to commit; *(un error)* to make.

co·me·ti·do m. assignment.

co·me·zón f. itch.

co·mi·ble adj. COLL. edible.

co·mi·cas·tro m. second-rate actor.

co·mi·ci·dad f. comedy, humor.

co·mi·cio m. elections.

có·mi·co, a I. adj. comical, funny II. m. comic actor —f. comic actress.

co·mi·da f. *(almuerzo, cena)* food, meal; *(almuerzo)* lunch.

co·mi·di·lla f. COLL. talk.

co·mi·do, a adj. fed, having eaten ♦ **c. de gusanos** worm-eaten • **c. y bebido** COLL. supported, kept • **estar c.** to have eaten • **sin haberlo c. ni bebido** for no apparent reason.

co·mien·ce, zo see **comenzar**.

co·mien·zo m. beginning, start; MED. onset ♦ **al c.** at first • **dar c.** to begin, start.

co·mi·lón, o·na I. adj. gluttonous II. m.f. glutton —f. COLL. feast, spread ♦ **darse una c.** to have a feast.

co·mi·llas f.pl. quotation marks ♦ **abrir, cerrar c.** to open, close quotation marks • **entre c.** in quotes.

co·mi·no m. cumin ♦ **no importarle a uno un c.** COLL. not to give a damn about • **no valer un c.** COLL. to be worthless.

co·mi·sar tr. to seize, confiscate.

co·mi·sa·rí·a f. /ria·to m. *(cargo)* commissariat; *(oficina)* office of a commissioner; AMER. police station.

co·mi·sa·rio m. commissioner.

co·mi·sión f. commission; *(encargo)* assignment ♦ **a c.** on a commission basis • **c. mixta** joint committee • **c. permanente** standing committee • **c. planificadora** planning board.

co·mi·sio·na·do, a I. adj. commissioned, authorized II. m.f. *(comisario)* commissioner; FIN., POL. committee or board member.

co·mi·sio·nar tr. to commission, authorize.

co·mi·sio·nis·ta m.f. COM. commission merchant.

co·mi·so m. *(confiscación)* confiscation; *(objeto)* confiscated goods.

co·mi·su·ra f. ANAT. commissure, corner.

co·mi·té m. committee.

co·mi·ti·va f. retinue, party ♦ **c. fúnebre** funeral procession.

co·mo I. adv. *(lo mismo que)* as; *(de tal modo)* like; *(en calidad de)* as, in the capacity of; *(casi)* about, approximately; *(según)* as ♦ **c. quiera que** no matter how • **c. sea** one way or the other II. conj. *(puesto que)* as, since; *(si)* if; *(así que)* as; *(por ejemplo)* such as, like ♦ **así c.** as soon as • **c. que** as if • **c. quien dice** so to speak • **c. si** as if • **hacer c. si** to pretend.

có·mo adv. *(en qué condiciones)* how; *(por qué)* why, how come ♦ **¿a c.?** how much? • **¡c. no!** AMER. of course!

có·mo·da f. chest of drawers, bureau.

có·mo·da·men·te adv. *(confortablemente)* comfortably; *(convenientemente)* conveniently.

co·mo·di·dad f. *(confort)* comfortableness; *(conveniencia)* convenience; *(ventaja)* advantage ♦ pl. comforts.

co·mo·dín m. AMER. comfort lover; *(naipes)* wild card.

có·mo·do, a adj. *(confortable)* comfortable; *(útil)* convenient.

co·mo·do·ro m. commodore.

co·mo·quie·ra adv. anyway, anyhow.

com·pac·tar tr. to compact, compress.

com·pac·to, a adj. *(apretado)* compact; *(denso)* tight.

com·pa·de·cer §17 tr. & reflex. to sympathize (with), feel sorry (for).

com·pa·dre m. godfather; *(relación)* father of the child (in relation to the godfather); COLL. pal.

com·pa·dre·ar intr. *(ser amigos)* to be friends; R.P., COLL. *(jactarse)* to brag.

com·pa·gi·na·ción f. *(ordenamiento)* arranging, putting in order; PRINT. page make-up.

com·pa·gi·na·dor, ·ra m.f. PRINT. pager; *(ordenador)* arranger.

com·pa·gi·nar tr. *(arreglar)* to put in order; *(acordar)* to agree; PRINT. to make up —reflex. to be compatible.

com·pa·ñe·ris·mo m. camaraderie.

com·pa·ñe·ro, a m.f. companion; *(colega)* colleague; *(de una pareja)* mate ♦ **c. de armas** comrade in arms • **c. de clase** classmate • **c. de colegio** schoolmate • **c. de cuarto** roommate • **c. de trabajo** fellow worker • **c. de viaje** traveling companion.

com·pa·ñí·a f. company ♦ **c. anónima** stock company • **c. comanditaria** silent partnership • **c. de seguros** insurance company • **c. tenedora** holding company • **hacer c. a alguien** to keep someone company.

com·pa·ra·ción f. comparison; LIT. simile ♦ **en c. con** in comparison with *or* to • **sin c.** beyond comparison.

com·pa·rar tr. *(relacionar)* to compare; *(cotejar)* to collate, check.

com·pa·ra·ti·vo, a adj. & m. comparative.

com·pa·re·cen·cia f. LAW appearance ♦ **orden de c.** summons.

com·pa·re·cer §17 intr. LAW to appear.

com·pa·re·cien·te m.f. LAW person appearing *(in court).*

com·pa·ren·do m. summons, subpoena.

com·par·sa m.f. THEAT. extra —f. THEAT. chorus; *(banda)* masquerade.

com·par·ti·m(i)en·to m. *(división)* division; *(departamento)* compartment ♦ **c. estanco** watertight compartment.

com·par·tir tr. *(repartir)* to divide (up); *(participar)* to share.

com·pás m. MATH. compass, compasses; MARIT. compass; MUS. *(ritmo)* rhythm; *(unidad métrica)* measure ♦ **al c. de** in step with • **c. binario** MUS. double time • **fuera de c.** out of step • **llevar el c.** MUS. to keep time • **perder el c.** MUS. to lose the beat.

com·pa·sión f. compassion, pity ♦ **¡por c.!** for pity's sake! • **sin c.** merciless • **tener c. de** to feel sorry for.

com·pa·si·vo, a adj. compassionate.

com·pa·ti·ble adj. compatible.

com·pa·trio·ta m.f. compatriot.

com·pe·ler tr. to compel, force.

com·pen·diar tr. to summarize, abridge.

com·pen·dio m. summary, abridgment.

com·pe·ne·tra·ción f. *(interpenetración)* interpenetration; *(afinidad)* mutual understanding.

com·pe·ne·trar·se reflex. to interpenetrate; *(tener afinidad)* to understand each other.

com·pen·sa·ción f. compensation; LAW recompense, redress ♦ **en c.** in exchange *or* return.

com·pen·sa·dor, ·ra I. adj. compensating, compensatory II. m. compensator.

com·pen·sar tr. to compensate; *(recompensar)* to indemnify.

com·pen·sa·to·rio, a adj. compensatory.

com·pe·ten·cia f. competition; *(rivalidad)* rivalry; *(incumbencia)* responsibility; *(aptitud)* competence; *(campo)* field <no es de mi c. it's outside my field>; LAW jurisdiction ♦ **hacer la c. a** to compete with *or* against.

com·pe·ten·te adj. *(adecuado)* suitable; *(apto)* competent; LAW competent.

com·pe·ter intr. *(pertenecer)* to be one's business *or* concern; *(incumbir)* to be up to someone.

com·pe·ti·ción f. competition; *(rivalidad)* rivalry.

com·pe·ti·dor, ·ra I. adj. competing, rival II. m.f. competitor.

com·pe·tir §48 intr. *(contender)* to compete; *(igualar)* to be on a par.

com·pe·ti·ti·vo, a adj. competitive.

com·pi·la·ción f. compilation.

com·pi·la·dor, ·ra I. adj. compiling II. m.f. compiler.

com·pi·lar tr. to compile.

com·pi·ta, to, tiera, tió see **competir.**

com·pla·cen·cia f. complacency; *(tolerancia)* tolerance.

com·pla·cer §51 tr. to please, gratify —reflex. ♦ **c. en** *or* **de** to delight in, take pleasure in.

com·pla·ci·do, a adj. satisfied, content ♦ **c. de sí** self-satisfied.

com·pla·cien·te adj. *(satisfecho)* satisfied; *(obsequio·so)* complaisant.

com·ple·ji·dad f. complexity.

com·ple·jo, a I. adj. *(complicado)* complex, complicated; GRAM. complex; MATH. complex; compound II. m. INDUS., PSYCH. complex.

com·ple·men·tar tr. & reflex. to complement *(each other).*

com·ple·men·ta·rio, a adj. complementary.

com·ple·men·to m. complement; GRAM. object.

com·ple·tar tr. to complete; *(acabar)* to finish.

com·ple·to, a adj. complete; *(acabado)* finished; *(lleno)* full ♦ **por c.** completely.

com·ple·xión f. constitution.

com·pli·ca·ción f. complication.

com·pli·ca·do, a adj. complicated; *(intricado)* complex; FIG. difficult.

com·pli·car §70 tr. to complicate; *(embrollar)* to entangle —reflex. to become complicated; *(embrollarse)* to become involved.

cóm·pli·ce m.f. accomplice.

com·plot m. plot; *(intriga)* scheme.

com·plo·tar intr. to plot, conspire.

com·po·nen·te adj. & m. component.

com·po·ner §54 tr. to compose; *(reparar)* to fix; *(adornar)* to decorate; *(reconciliar)* to reconcile; *(arreglar)* to arrange; COLL. *(calmar)* to settle; S. AMER., MED. to set *(bones)* —intr. to compose —reflex. to be composed *or* made up *(de of)*; *(calmarse)* to compose oneself ♦ **componérselas** COLL. to fend for oneself.

com·pon·ga, go see **componer.**

com·por·ta·mien·to m. behavior, conduct.

com·por·tar tr. to entail —reflex. to behave ♦ **c. mal** to misbehave.

com·po·si·ción f. composition ♦ **hacer c. de lugar** to size up the situation.

com·po·si·tor, ·ra m.f. MUS. composer; PRINT. compositor.

com·pos·tu·ra f. *(reparación)* repair; *(aseo)* neatness; *(decoro)* decorum; *(calma)* composure ♦ **en c.** under repair.

com·po·ta f. compote, stewed fruit.

com·po·te·ra f. compote bowl *or* dish.

com·pra f. *(acción)* purchasing; *(adquisición)* purchase ♦ **c. al contado** cash purchase • **c. a plazos** credit purchase ♦ pl. shopping • **ir de c.** to go shopping.

com·pra·dor, ·ra I. adj. purchasing II. m.f. *(adquiridor)* purchaser; *(cliente)* customer.

com·prar tr. to buy, purchase; *(sobornar)* to

bribe ♦ **c. al contado** to pay cash for • **c. al por mayor** to buy wholesale • **c. al por menor** to purchase at retail • **c. a plazos** or **fiado** to buy on credit.

com·pra·ven·ta f. buying and selling ♦ **boleto de c.** purchase and sale agreement.

com·pren·de·dor, ·ra adj. understanding.

com·pren·der tr. to understand; (contener) to include.

com·pren·si·ble adj. comprehensible.

com·pren·sión f. understanding.

com·pren·si·vo, a adj. comprehensive.

com·pre·sa f. compress ♦ **c. fría** cold pack.

com·pre·si·ble adj. compressible.

com·pre·sión f. compression; GRAM. syneresis.

com·pre·so, a see **comprimir**.

com·pre·sor, ·ra I. adj. compressing, compressive **II.** m. MECH. compressor.

com·pri·mi·do, a I. adj. compressed; FIG. repressed **II.** m. tablet, pill.

com·pri·mir tr. to compress; FIG. to repress.

com·pro·ba·ción f. (verificación) verification; (prueba) proof.

com·pro·ban·te m. proof; COM. voucher ♦ **c. de venta** sales slip.

com·pro·bar §19 tr. (cotejar) to check; (verificar) to verify.

com·pro·ba·to·rio, a adj. confirming.

com·pro·me·te·dor, ·ra adj. compromising.

com·pro·me·ter tr. (poner en peligro) to endanger; (poner en apuros) to compromise; (la salud) to impair; (obligar) to oblige —reflex. (obligarse) to commit oneself; (ponerse en peligro) to compromise oneself; (novios) to get engaged ♦ **c. a** to undertake to.

com·pro·me·ti·do, a adj. (envuelto) implicated; (embarazoso) compromising; (escritor) committed; (novios) engaged; (busy) tied up.

com·pro·mi·so m. (obligación) obligation; (apuro) jam; (convenio) agreement; (novios) engagement ♦ **c. a** without obligation.

com·prue·be, bo see **comprobar**.

com·puer·ta f. (esclusa) floodgate; (puerta) hatch.

com·pues·to, a I. see **componer II.** adj. compound; (arreglado) decked out; (mesurado) calm **III.** m. compound, composite.

com·pul·sar tr. LAW to compare.

com·pul·sión f. LAW compulsion, duress.

com·pun·ción f. compunction, remorse.

com·pun·gir §32 tr. to move to compunction —reflex. to feel compunction ♦ **c. por** to grieve at.

com·pu·sie·ra, so see **componer**.

com·pu·ta·ción f. computation, calculation.

com·pu·ta·do·ra f. computer.

com·pu·tar tr. to compute, calculate.

com·pu·ta·ri·zar/te·ri·zar §04 tr. to computerize.

cóm·pu·to m. computation, calculation.

co·mul·gar §47 tr. to administer communion to —intr. to take communion; FIG. to commune.

co·mún I. adj. common; (usual) customary, usual; (compartido) shared, joint; (vulgar) common, vulgar; FIN. common, public ♦ **por lo c.** commonly, generally **II.** m. general public or population ♦ **el c. de las gentes** most people.

co·mu·na f. commune; AMER. municipality.

co·mu·nal adj. communal.

co·mu·ni·ca·ble adj. (transmisible) communi-

cable; (sociable) sociable.

co·mu·ni·ca·ción f. communication; TELEC. connection ♦ **estar en c. con** to be in touch with.

co·mu·ni·ca·do m. communiqué ♦ **c. de prensa** press release.

co·mu·ni·car §70 tr. to communicate; (transmitir) to transmit; (propagar) to spread —intr. (tener paso) to adjoin; (tratar) to communicate —reflex. to communicate; (tener paso) to be connected.

co·mu·ni·ca·ti·vo, a adj. communicative.

co·mu·ni·dad f. community.

co·mu·nión f. communion; (comunicación) fellowship; (sacramento) (Holy) Communion.

co·mu·nis·ta m.f. communist.

co·mún·men·te adv. commonly, generally; (usualmente) usually.

con prep. with; (a pesar de) in spite of, despite; (hacia) to, towards ♦ **c. ira** in anger • **c. que** so then • **c. tal (de) que** provided that • **c. todo** nevertheless.

co·na·to m. attempt.

con·ca·de·nar tr. to link (up), concatenate.

con·ca·te·na·ción f. concatenation.

con·ca·vi·dad f. (calidad) hollowness; (hueco) hollow.

cón·ca·vo, a adj. concave, hollow.

con·ce·bi·ble adj. conceivable, imaginable.

con·ce·bir §48 tr. (imaginar) to imagine; (comprender) to understand; (engendrar) to conceive —intr. to conceive.

con·ce·der tr. (otorgar) to grant; (admitir) to concede.

con·ce·jal, ·la m.f. (town) councilor —m. councilman —f. councilwoman.

con·cen·tra·ción f. concentration.

con·cen·tra·do, a adj. (centrado) centered; (condensado) concentrated.

con·cen·trar tr. & reflex. to concentrate.

con·cén·tri·co, a adj. concentric.

con·cep·ción f. conception.

con·cep·to m. concept; (idea) idea; (juicio) opinion ♦ **bajo ningún c.** under no circumstances • **en** or **por c. de** as, by way of • **tener buen c. de** or **tener en buen c. a** to think highly of.

con·cep·tual adj. conceptual.

con·cep·tuar §67 tr. to consider, judge.

con·cer·nien·te adj. concerning, regarding ♦ **en lo c. a** as for, with regard to.

con·cer·nir §25 tr. to concern, be pertinent to —intr. to be pertinent or related.

con·cer·tar §49 tr. (coordinar) to arrange, coordinate —intr. to agree.

con·cer·tis·ta m.f. concert performer, soloist.

con·ce·sión f. concession.

con·ce·sio·na·rio, a I. adj. concessionary **II.** m.f. concessionaire, licensee.

con·ci·ba, bo, biera, bió see **concebir**.

con·cien·cia f. conscience; (integridad) conscientiousness; (conocimiento) consciousness ♦ **a c.** conscientiously • **en c.** in good conscience or faith • **remorderle a uno la c.** to have a guilty conscience • **sin c.** unscrupulous • **tener** or **tomar c.** to be or become aware of.

con·cien·zu·do, a adj. conscientious.

con·cier·na, ne see **concernir**.

con·cier·te, to see **concertar**.

con·cier·to m. concert; (ajuste) agreement; MUS. harmony; (obra) concerto.

con·ci·lia·ble adj. conciliable, reconcilable.

con·ci·liá·bu·lo m. secret meeting.

con·ci·lia·ción f. conciliation, reconciliation.

con·ci·lia·dor, ·ra adj. conciliatory.

con·ci·liar tr. to conciliate, reconcile ♦ c. el sueño to get to sleep —reflex. to win, gain.

con·ci·lia·ti·vo/to·rio, a adj. conciliatory.

con·ci·lio m. council.

con·ci·so, a adj. concise, succinct.

con·ciu·da·da·no, a m.f. fellow citizen.

cón·cla·ve or con·cla·ve m. conclave.

con·cluir §18 tr. to conclude, finish; (deducir) to deduce; LAW to sum up —intr. to finish, end ♦ c. con or en to end with or in • c. por to end up —reflex. to finish, end.

con·clu·sión f. conclusion, end; (deducción) deduction; (decisión) decision; LAW summary ♦ en c. in conclusion, finally • llegar a una c. to come to a conclusion.

con·clu·si·vo, a adj. conclusive, final.

con·clu·ya, yo, yera, yó see concluir.

con·clu·yen·te adj. conclusive, decisive.

con·co·mi·tan·cia f. concomitance.

con·co·mi·tan·te adj. concomitant.

con·cor·dan·cia f. agreement; MUS. harmony.

con·cor·dar §19 tr. to bring into agreement; GRAM. to make agree —intr. to agree.

con·cor·de adj. in accord, in agreement.

con·cor·dia f. (armonía) concord; (ajuste) agreement.

con·cre·tar tr. (resumir) to summarize; (precisar) to specify —reflex. to limit or confine oneself; (tomar forma) to take shape.

con·cre·ti·zar §04 tr. to materialize.

con·cre·to, a I. adj. concrete; (definido) specific, definite ♦ en c. in short II. m. AMER. concrete.

con·cu·bi·na f. concubine.

con·cu·bi·na·to m. common-law marriage.

con·cuer·do, do see concordar.

con·cu·ña·do, a m. husband of one's sister-in-law —f. wife of one's brother-in-law.

con·cu·pis·cen·cia f. (lascivia) concupiscence; (codicia) greed.

con·cu·pis·cen·te adj. (lascivo) concupiscent; (avaro) greedy.

con·cu·rren·cia f. audience, crowd; (simultaneidad) concurrence.

con·cu·rren·te I. adj. (coincidente) coinciding; (presente) in attendance II. m.f. person in attendance.

con·cu·rri·do, a adj. (animado) busy, crowded; (popular) well-attended; (frecuentado) frequented.

con·cu·rrir intr. (convenir) to concur, agree; (converger) to converge; (presenciar) to attend; (coincidir) to coincide; (contribuir) to contribute ♦ c. en to agree or concur with.

con·cur·san·te m.f. competitor, contestant.

con·cur·so m. competition, contest ♦ c. hípico horse show • fuera de c. out of the running.

con·cha f. ZOOL. shell; (molusco) shellfish, mollusk; (carey) tortoise shell.

con·cha·bar tr. (unir) to join; (mezclar) to mix; AMER. to hire on —reflex. COLL. to band together.

con·da·do m. (dignidad) earldom; (territorio) county.

con·de m. count, earl.

con·de·co·ra·ción f. (insignia) medal; (ceremonia) award ceremony.

con·de·co·rar tr. to decorate, award.

con·de·na f. (juicio) sentence; (declaración) conviction; (extensión) term ♦ c. condicional suspended sentence • c. perpetua life sentence • cumplir una c. to serve a sentence.

con·de·na·do, a I. adj. (culpable) convicted; (réprobo) reprobate II. m.f. (prisionero) convict; (réprobo) reprobate; COLL. (desgraciado) wretch.

con·de·nar tr. (castigar) to condemn, sentence; (declarar culpable) to convict; (reprobar) to censure; (desaprobar) to disapprove of; (cerrar) to board up.

con·de·na·to·rio, a adj. LAW condemnatory.

con·den·sa·ble adj. condensable.

con·den·sa·ción f. condensation.

con·den·sa·dor, ·ra I. adj. condensing II. m. condenser.

con·den·sar tr. (reducir) to condense; (abreviar) to shorten.

con·de·sa f. countess.

con·des·cen·den·cia f. acquiescence.

con·des·cen·der §50 intr. to acquiesce ♦ c. a to be gracious enough to

con·des·cen·dien·te adj. agreeable, obliging.

con·di·ción f. condition; (estado) state; (clase) status; (cláusula) stipulation; (calidad) capacity ♦ a c. de que on the condition that • pl. (aptitud) talent; (circunstancias) circumstances ♦ c. convenidas COM. terms agreed upon • c. de pago COM. terms of payment • c. de vida living conditions • estar en c. de to be fit for • poner en c. to get ready • sin c. unconditionally.

con·di·cio·na·do, a adj. (acondicionado) conditioned; (condicional) conditional ♦ c. a dependent upon.

con·di·cio·nal adj. conditional.

con·di·cio·nar intr. to agree —tr. ♦ c. a to make (something) conditional on

con·di·men·tar tr. to season, flavor.

con·di·men·to m. condiment, seasoning.

con·dis·cí·pu·lo, a m.f. classmate.

con·do·len·cia f. condolence, sympathy.

con·do·ler·se §78 reflex. to sympathize (de, por with).

con·do·mi·nio m. condominium.

con·dón m. condom.

con·do·na·ción f. (acción) pardoning; (resultado) pardon.

cón·dor m. condor.

con·duc·ción f. (transporte) transportation; (cañería) piping; AUTO. driving; PHYS. conduction.

con·du·cen·te adj. conducive.

con·du·cir §22 tr. (guiar) to lead; (dirigir) to manage; (llevar) to transport; AUTO. to drive —intr. to lead; AUTO. to drive —reflex. to conduct oneself.

con·duc·ta f. conduct ♦ mala c. misconduct.

con·duc·ti·vo, a adj. conductive.

con·duc·to m. conduit; ANAT. duct ♦ por c. de by means of, through • por c. regular through regular channels.

con·duc·tor, ·ra I. adj. conducting; PHYS. conductive II. m.f. AUTO. driver; PHYS. conductor.

con·due·la, lo see condolerse.

con·due·ño, a m.f. joint owner, co-owner.

con·du·je·ra, jo, zca, zco see conducir.

co·nec·tar tr. to connect; (acoplar) to hook up; (enchufar) to plug in; (relacionar) to put in touch with.

co·ne·ja f. doe rabbit ♦ ser una c. COLL. to have a lot of children.

co·ne·je·ro, a m.f. *(criador)* rabbit breeder; *(vendedor)* rabbit seller —f. rabbit burrow.

co·ne·ji·llo m. bunny ♦ **c. de Indias** guinea pig.

co·ne·jo m. rabbit.

co·ne·xión f. connection.

co·ne·xo, a adj. connected, related.

con·fa·bu·la·ción f. plot, conspiracy.

con·fa·bu·la·dor, ·ra m.f. schemer, plotter.

con·fa·bu·lar tr. to discuss —reflex. to plot.

con·fec·ción f. *(fabricación)* manufacture; *(ropa hecha)* ready-to-wear clothing.

con·fec·cio·nar tr. to make, manufacture.

con·fe·de·ra·ción f. confederation; *(liga)* league.

con·fe·de·ra·do, a I. adj. confederated, allied II. m.f. confederate, ally.

con·fe·de·rar tr. & reflex. to confederate.

con·fe·ren·cia f. conference; *(discusión)* discussion; *(discurso)* lecture ♦ **c. de prensa** press conference • **c. de alto nivel** summit conference.

con·fe·ren·cian·te m.f. lecturer, speaker.

con·fe·ren·ciar intr. to confer.

con·fe·ren·cis·ta m.f. lecturer, speaker.

con·fe·rir §65 tr. to confer, bestow.

con·fe·sar §49 tr. to confess; *(admitir)* to admit; *(proclamar)* to proclaim ♦ **c. de plano** to make a clean breast of —reflex. to confess.

con·fe·sión f. confession; *(admisión)* admission; *(del reo)* testimony.

con·fe·sor m. confessor.

con·fia·do, a adj. *(en sí mismo)* confident; *(en los demás)* trusting; *(crédulo)* gullible.

con·fian·za f. confidence; *(seguridad)* self-confidence; *(familiaridad)* closeness ♦ **con toda c.** in all confidence • **de c.** *(confiable)* reliable; *(íntimo)* close • **defraudar la c. de alguien** to let someone down • **en c.** confidentially • **tener c. con alguien** to be on close terms with someone • **tratar a alguien con c.** to treat someone informally.

con·fian·zu·do, a adj. COLL. bold, fresh.

con·fiar §30 intr. to trust, feel confident; *(contar con)* to count on ♦ **c. a la memoria** to commit to memory —tr. *(encargar)* to entrust; *(un secreto)* to confide —reflex. to trust, have faith.

con·fi·den·cia f. *(confianza)* confidence; *(secreto)* secret.

con·fi·den·cial adj. confidential.

con·fi·den·te m.f. *(consejero)* confidant; *(informante)* informant —m. *(canapé)* love seat.

con·fie·ra, ro see **conferir.**

con·fie·se, so see **confesar.**

con·fi·gu·rar tr. to shape, form.

con·fín I. adj. bordering II. m. border ♦ pl. confines.

con·fi·na·mien·to m. confinement; *(destierro)* exile.

con·fi·nar intr. to border —tr. *(encarcelar)* to confine; *(desterrar)* to exile.

con·fi·rie·ra, rió see **conferir.**

con·fir·ma·ción f. confirmation.

con·fir·mar tr. to confirm; *(corroborar)* to endorse.

con·fis·ca·ción f. confiscation, appropriation.

con·fis·car §70 tr. to confiscate, appropriate.

con·fi·ta·do, a adj. candied, sugar-coated.

con·fi·tar tr. to candy.

con·fi·te m. candy, sweet.

con·fi·te·rí·a f. candy shop; AMER. tearoom, café.

con·fi·tu·ra f. confiture, preserve.

con·fla·gra·ción f. conflagration.

con·flic·ti·vo, a adj. conflicting.

con·flic·to m. conflict; *(lucha)* struggle; *(choque)* clash; *(apuro)* quandary; *(angustia)* agony.

con·fluen·cia f. confluence.

con·fluir §18 intr. to converge.

con·for·mar tr. *(adaptar)* to conform, adapt; *(dar forma)* to shape, fashion —intr. to agree *(con, en* with, on); *(satisfacer)* to please —reflex. to resign oneself.

con·for·me I. adj. • **c. a** consistent with • **c. con** resigned to • **c. en** in agreement on II. adv. as soon as ♦ **c. a** in accordance with III. m. approval.

con·for·mi·dad f. *(concordancia)* agreement; *(asentimiento)* consent; *(resignación)* resignation ♦ **de c.** in agreement.

con·for·mis·ta adj. & m.f. conformist.

con·fort m. comfort.

con·for·ta·ble adj. comfortable.

con·for·tan·te adj. comforting, consoling.

con·for·tar tr. *(consolar)* to console; *(dar vigor)* to invigorate; *(animar)* to cheer.

con·fra·ter·ni·dad f. fraternity, fellowship.

con·fra·ter·ni·zar §04 intr. to fraternize.

con·fron·ta·ción f. confrontation; *(comparación)* comparison.

con·fron·tar tr. to confront; *(comparar)* to compare.

con·fun·di·do, a adj. confused.

con·fun·dir tr. to confuse; *(desordenar)* to mix up; *(desconcertar)* to perplex —reflex. *(mezclarse)* to be mixed up; *(en una multitud)* to mingle; *(equivocarse)* to get mixed up; *(turbarse)* to be confused or perplexed.

con·fu·sa·men·te adv. *(con turbación)* confusedly; *(en desorden)* in confusion or disorder.

con·fu·sión f. confusion.

con·fu·so, a I. see **confundir** II. adj. *(mezclado)* mixed up; *(no claro)* unclear; *(desconcertado)* perplexed.

con·ga f. AMER., MUS. conga.

con·ge·la·ble adj. *(que se puede congelar)* freezable; *(que se puede cuajar)* congealable.

con·ge·la·ción f. freezing, congealing.

con·ge·la·dor m. freezer.

con·ge·la·mien·to m. var. of **congelación.**

con·ge·lar tr. to freeze —reflex. to become frozen.

con·gé·ne·re m. fellow.

con·ge·nial adj. congenial.

con·ge·niar intr. to be compatible, get along.

con·gé·ni·to, a adj. congenital.

con·ges·tión f. congestion ♦ **c. cerebral** stroke • **c. pulmonar** pneumonia.

con·ges·tio·nar tr. to congest —reflex. to become or be congested.

con·glo·me·ra·ción f. conglomeration.

con·glo·me·ra·do, a I. adj. conglomerate II. m. conglomerate; FIG. conglomeration.

con·glo·me·rar tr. & reflex. to conglomerate.

con·go·ja f. *(angustia)* anguish; *(pena)* grief.

con·go·jar tr. to distress, cause anguish.

con·gra·ciar tr. to win over —reflex. to ingratiate oneself.

con·gra·tu·la·ción f. congratulation.

con·gra·tu·lar tr. to congratulate.

con·gra·tu·la·to·rio, a adj. congratulatory.

con·gre·ga·ción f. congregation.

con·gre·gar §47 tr. & reflex. to congregate.

con·gre·sal/sis·ta m.f. AMER. congressman/woman, delegate.

con·gre·so m. *(reunión)* congress, meeting; POL. Congress (of the United States).

con·grio m. conger eel.

con·gruen·cia f. congruity; MATH. congruence.

con·gruen·te f. fitting; MATH. congruent.

có·ni·co, a adj. conic, conical.

co·ní·fe·ro, a I. adj. coniferous II. f. conifer.

co·ni·for·me adj. coniform, cone-shaped.

con·je·tu·ra f. conjecture, guess.

con·je·tu·rar tr. to conjecture, guess.

con·ju·ga·ción f. conjugation.

con·ju·gar §47 tr. to combine; GRAM. to conjugate.

con·jun·ción f. conjunction.

con·jun·ta·men·te adv. jointly, together.

con·jun·ti·vi·tis f. conjunctivitis.

con·jun·ti·vo, a I. adj. conjunctive II. f. ANAT. conjunctiva.

con·jun·to m. *(totalidad)* whole; *(agregado)* collection; *(vestido)* outfit; *(de muebles)* suite (of furniture); MECH. unit; MUS. band ♦ **c. motriz** ARG. power plant • **en c.** altogether.

con·ju·rar tr. *(exorcizar)* to exorcise; *(alejar)* to ward off —intr. & reflex. to conspire.

con·ju·ro m. exorcism; *(sortilegio)* spell.

con·me·mo·ra·ción f. commemoration.

con·me·mo·rar tr. to commemorate, celebrate.

con·me·mo·ra·ti·vo, a adj. commemorative.

con·men·su·rar tr. to make commensurate.

con·mi·go pron. with me ♦ **c. mismo** with myself.

con·mi·na·ción f. threat, menace.

con·mi·nar tr. to threaten, menace.

con·mi·se·ra·ción f. commiseration.

con·mi·se·rar·se reflex. to commiserate.

con·mo·ción f. commotion; *(sacudimiento)* shock; *(tumulto)* upheaval ♦ **c. cerebral** concussion.

con·mo·ve·dor, ·ra adj. moving, touching.

con·mo·ver §78 tr. *(emocionar)* to move, touch; *(sacudir)* to shake —reflex. to be moved or touched.

con·mu·ta·ble adj. commutable.

con·mu·ta·ción f. commutation.

con·mu·tar tr. to trade; LAW to commute.

con·no·ta·ción f. connotation.

con·no·tar tr. to connote, imply.

con·nu·bio m. matrimony, marriage.

co·no m. cone.

co·no·ce·dor, ·ra I. adj. knowledgeable, informed II. m.f. connoisseur.

co·no·cer §17 tr. to know; *(tener contacto)* to meet; *(reconocer)* to recognize ♦ **c. de nombre** to know by name • **c. de vista** to know by sight —intr. ♦ **c. de** to know about.

co·no·ci·ble adj. knowable.

co·no·ci·do, a I. adj. well-known, famous II. m.f. acquaintance.

co·no·ci·mien·to m. knowledge; *(entendimiento)* understanding; MED. consciousness ♦ **con c. de causa** with full knowledge of the facts • **c. de embarque** COM. bill of lading • **perder el c.** to lose consciousness • **poner en c. de** to inform, notify.

con·que conj. (and) so.

con·quis·ta f. conquest.

con·quis·ta·ble adj. *(que se puede conquistar)* conquerable; *(fácil de conseguir)* attainable.

con·quis·ta·dor, ·ra I. adj. conquering II. m.f. conqueror; FIG. Don Juan.

con·quis·tar tr. to conquer; *(conseguir)* to win; *(cautivar)* to win over.

con·sa·bi·do, a adj. *(tradicional)* usual; *(muy conocido)* well known.

con·sa·gra·ción f. consecration.

con·sa·gra·do, a adj. *(sagrado)* consecrated; *(dedicado)* devoted; *(confirmado)* time-honored.

con·sa·grar tr. RELIG. to consecrate; *(dedicar)* to devote; *(confirmar)* to establish —reflex. *(dedicarse)* to devote or dedicate oneself (a to); *(adquirir fama)* to establish oneself.

con·sa·gra·to·rio, a adj. consecratory, consecrative.

con·san·guí·ne·o, a I. adj. consanguineous II. m.f. blood relation.

con·san·gui·ni·dad f. blood relationship.

cons·cien·cia f. var. of **conciencia**.

cons·cien·te adj. *(enterado)* aware; MED. conscious; *(responsable)* conscientious.

cons·cien·te·men·te adv. knowingly.

cons·crip·ción f. AMER. conscription.

cons·crip·to m. AMER. conscript, draftee.

con·se·cuen·cia f. consequence; *(deducción)* deduction; *(resultado)* outcome ♦ **a or como c. de or a result or consequence of • de c.** of consequence or importance • **en c.** accordingly • **por c.** consequently, therefore • **sacar en c.** to conclude • **traer como c.** to result in.

con·se·cuen·te adj. & m. consequent.

con·se·cuen·te·men·te adv. consequently, therefore.

con·se·cu·ti·vo, a adj. consecutive.

con·se·guir §64 tr. *(obtener)* to obtain; *(llegar a hacer)* to attain; *(lograr)* to manage.

con·se·je·ro, a m.f. *(guía)* counselor; *(de un consejo)* councilor.

con·se·jo m. advice; POL. council ♦ **c. de guerra** court-martial • **c. de ministros** cabinet.

con·sen·so m. consensus.

con·sen·ti·do, a adj. spoiled, pampered.

con·sen·ti·mien·to m. consent.

con·sen·tir §65 tr. *(autorizar)* to consent; *(permitir)* to allow; *(mimar)* to spoil, pamper, *(soportar)* to bear ♦ **c. a** or **con** to be indulgent with.

con·ser·je m. *(custodio)* concierge; *(portero)* porter.

con·ser·je·rí·a f. concierge's office; *(de un hotel)* reception desk.

con·ser·va f. *(confitura)* preserve; *(alimentos)* preserved food ♦ **conservas alimenticias** canned goods • **en c.** canned.

con·ser·va·ción f. conservation; *(cuidado)* up-keep.

con·ser·va·dor, ·ra I. adj. *(preservativo)* conserving; POL. conservative; *(prudente)* prudent II. m.f. POL. conservative; *(oficio)* conservator.

con·ser·var tr. to conserve; *(preservar)* preserve; *(guardar)* to keep; *(cuidar)* to keep up; *(mantener)* to keep; CUL. to can —reflex. *(permanecer)* to survive; *(cuidarse)* to take care of oneself; *(guardar para sí)* to keep for oneself; CUL. to keep, stay fresh.

con·ser·va·to·rio, a I. adj. conservatory, preservative II. m. conservatory.

con·si·de·ra·ble adj. considerable; *(poderoso)* powerful; *(importante)* important.

con·si·de·ra·ción f. consideration; *(atención)* attention; *(importancia)* importance; *(respeto)* regard ♦ **bajo** or **en c.** under consideration • **de c.** considerable • **en c. a** considering in consideration of • **por c.** out of consideration • **tomar en c.** to take into consideration.

con·si·de·ra·do, a adj. *(respetuoso)* considerate; *(respetado)* respected.

con·si·de·ran·do m. LAW whereas.

con·si·de·rar tr. to consider; *(reflexionar)* to take into consideration; *(estimar)* to regard —reflex. to be considered; *(a sí mismo)* to consider oneself.

con·sien·ta, to see **consentir.**

con·si·ga, go see **conseguir.**

con·sig·na f. *(órdenes)* orders; *(slogan)* watchword; *(depósito)* checkroom.

con·sig·na·ción f. COM. consignment; FIN. *(depósito)* deposit.

con·sig·na·dor m.f. consignor.

con·sig·nar tr. to consign; *(depositar)* to deposit; *(citar)* to note down; *(asignar)* to allocate.

con·sig·na·ta·rio m. COM. consignee; LAW assignee.

con·si·go pron. with him, her, them, you ♦ **c. mismo** with himself, oneself, yourself • **c. misma** with herself, yourself • **c. mismos** or **mismas** with themselves, yourselves.

con·si·guien·te adj. consequent, resulting ♦ **por c.** consequently, therefore.

con·si·guie·ra, guió see **conseguir.**

con·sin·tie·ra, tió see **consentir.**

con·sis·ten·cia f. consistency; *(estabilidad)* stability; *(coherencia)* coherence ♦ **sin c.** insubstantial; CUL. thin.

con·sis·ten·te adj. consistent.

con·sis·tir intr. to consist *(en* of, in).

con·so·la f. console table.

con·so·la·ción f. consolation.

con·so·lar §19 tr. & reflex. to console (oneself).

con·so·li·da·ción f. consolidation.

con·so·li·dar tr. to consolidate; *(asegurar)* to strengthen —reflex. to consolidate.

con·so·mé m. consommé.

con·so·nan·cia f. consonance.

con·so·nan·te adj. & f. consonant.

con·sor·cio m. consortium; *(de circunstancias)* conjunction.

con·sor·te m.f. consort ♦ **pl.** LAW joint litigants.

cons·pi·cuo, a adj. famous, eminent.

cons·pi·ra·ción f. conspiracy.

cons·pi·ra·dor, ra m.f. conspirator.

cons·pi·rar intr. to conspire.

cons·tan·cia f. constancy; *(perseverancia)* perseverance; *(evidencia)* record; AMER. proof.

cons·tan·te I. adj. constant; *(perseverante)* persevering II. f. constant.

cons·tar intr. *(ser cierto)* to be clear or evident; *(quedar registrado)* to be on record; *(consistir)* to consist *(de* of) ♦ **hacer c.** to point out • **hacer c. por escrito** to put on record • **que conste que** let it be clearly known that.

cons·ta·tar tr. to verify, confirm.

cons·te·la·ción f. constellation.

cons·ter·na·ción f. consternation.

cons·ter·nar tr. to consternate —reflex. to be dismayed.

cons·ti·pa·do m. cold, head cold.

cons·ti·par tr. to give a cold to —reflex. to catch a cold.

cons·ti·tu·ción f. constitution; *(composición)*

composition.

cons·ti·tuir §18 tr. to constitute; *(ser)* to be; *(establecer)* to establish —reflex. to be established ♦ **c. en** to assume the position of • **c. en fiador de** to answer for • **c. prisionero** to give oneself up.

cons·ti·tu·ti·vo, a/yen·te adj. & m. component.

cons·tre·ñi·mien·to m. compulsion.

cons·tre·ñir §59 tr. *(compeler)* to compel; *(apretar)* to constrict; *(estreñir)* to constipate.

cons·tric·ción f. constriction.

cons·tric·ti·vo, a adj. constraining.

cons·tri·ña, ñera, ño, ñó see **constreñir.**

cons·truc·ción f. construction; *(edificio)* building ♦ **c. de buques** shipbuilding • **en** or **en vías de c.** under construction.

cons·truc·ti·vo, a adj. constructive.

cons·truc·tor, ra I. adj. construction II. m.f. constructor ♦ **c. naval** shipbuilder.

cons·truir §18 tr. to construct, build; *(fabricar)* to manufacture.

con·sue·gro, a m.f. father/mother-in-law of one's son or daughter (in relation to oneself).

con·sue·le, lo see **consolar.**

con·sue·lo m. *(alivio)* consolation, solace; *(alegría)* joy, delight ♦ **sin c.** inconsolable.

con·sue·tu·di·na·rio, a adj. *(habitual)* customary; *(empedernido)* confirmed.

cón·sul m. consul ♦ **c. general** consul general.

con·su·la·do m. consulate.

con·sul·ta f. consultation; *(opinión)* opinion, advice ♦ **c. a domicilio** house call.

con·sul·tar intr. to consult (with), get advice (from) ♦ **c. con la almohada** to sleep on it —tr. to consult; *(verificar)* to check; *(discutir)* to discuss.

con·sul·tor, ra I. adj. advisory II. m. advisor.

con·sul·to·rio m. *(oficina)* office; MED. doctor's office.

con·su·ma·ción f. consummation; *(fin)* end.

con·su·ma·do, a adj. consummate ♦ **hecho c.** accomplished fact.

con·su·mar tr. to consummate.

con·su·mi·ción f. consumption; *(bebida)* drink ♦ **c. mínima** cover charge.

con·su·mi·do, a adj. thin, emaciated.

con·su·mi·dor, ra I. adj. consuming II. m.f. consumer.

con·su·mir tr. to consume; *(gastar)* use up; *(destruir)* to destroy; *(malgastar)* to waste; *(evaporar)* to evaporate; *(afligir)* to consume —reflex. to be consumed or used up); *(destruirse)* to be destroyed; *(malgastarse)* to waste away; *(evaporarse)* to evaporate; *(afligirse)* to be consumed.

con·su·mo m. consumption ♦ **bienes de c.** consumer goods.

con·ta·bi·li·dad f. *(teneduría de libros)* bookkeeping; *(profesión)* accountancy.

con·ta·bi·li·zar §04 tr. COM. to enter, record.

con·ta·ble I. adj. countable, computable; *(relatable)* relatable II. m.f. accountant.

con·tac·to m. contact ♦ **lentes** or **lentillas de c.** contact lenses • **ponerse en c.** to get in touch.

con·ta·do, a adj. rare ♦ **al c.** (in) cash.

con·ta·dor, ra I. adj. counting II. m.f. *(de libros)* accountant; *(administrador)* auditor —m. *(aparato)* counting device; TECH. meter ♦ **c. público nacional** certified public accountant.

con·ta·du·rí·a f. *(estudio)* accounting; *(oficio)*

accountancy; *(oficina)* accounting office.

con·ta·giar tr. MED. to contaminate; FIG. to corrupt —reflex. MED. to become infected; FIG. to become corrupt.

con·ta·gio m. MED. contagion; FIG. contamination.

con·ta·gio·so, a adj. MED. contagious; FIG. catching.

con·ta·mi·na·ción f. contamination; *(corrupción)* corruption; *(del aire, agua)* pollution.

con·ta·mi·nar tr. to contaminate; *(aire, agua)* to pollute; *(corromper)* to corrupt —reflex. to be contaminated; *(corromperse)* to be corrupted.

con·tan·te adj. ♦ **dinero c. y sonante** cash.

con·tar §19 tr. to count (up); *(referir)* to tell —intr. to count ♦ **c. con** *(confiar)* to count or rely on; *(tener en cuenta)* to figure on • **¿qué cuentas?** what's up?

con·tem·pla·ción f. contemplation.

con·tem·plar tr. & intr. to contemplate.

con·tem·po·ra·nei·dad f. contemporaneity.

con·tem·po·rá·ne·o, a adj. & m.f. contemporary.

con·tem·po·ri·za·ción f. compromise.

con·tem·po·ri·zar §04 intr. to compromise.

con·tén see **contener**.

con·ten·ción f. containment; *(contienda)* competition; LAW dispute.

con·ten·cio·so, a adj. contentious.

con·ten·der §50 intr. to contend; *(competir)* to compete; *(disputar)* to dispute.

con·ten·dien·te I. adj. contending, opposing II. m.f. contender, competitor.

con·te·ner §69 tr. to contain; *(impedir)* to hold back —reflex. to contain or control oneself.

con·te·ni·do, a I. adj. contained, controlled II. m. content(s).

con·ten·ti·zo, a adj. easily satisfied.

con·ten·tar tr. to content —reflex. to be content.

con·ten·to, a I. adj. *(alegre)* happy, pleased; *(satisfecho)* satisfied, content II. m. *(alegría)* happiness; *(satisfacción)* contentment.

con·tes·ta·ción f. answer.

con·tes·tar tr. to answer; LAW. to corroborate —intr. to answer.

con·tex·to m. context.

con·tien·da f. *(pelea)* battle; *(disputa)* argument; *(competencia)* contest.

con·tien·da, do see **contender**.

con·tie·ne see **contener**.

con·ti·go pron. with you ♦ **c. mismo** with yourself.

con·ti·guo, a adj. contiguous, adjacent.

con·ti·nen·cia f. continence, abstinence.

con·ti·nen·te adj. & m. continent.

con·tin·gen·cia f. contingency.

con·tin·gen·te adj. & m. contingent.

con·ti·nua·ción f. continuation; *(prolongación)* continuance ♦ **a c.** next, following.

con·ti·nuar §67 tr. to continue (on) —intr. to continue, go on.

con·ti·nuo, a I. adj. continuous; *(constante)* constant ♦ **de c.** continually II. m. continuum III. adv. continually.

con·to·ne·ar·se reflex. to sway one's hips.

con·to·ne·o m. swaying of the hips.

con·tor·cer·se §71 reflex. to contort oneself.

con·tor·ción f. contortion.

con·tor·no m. contour, outline; *(perímetro*

perimeter ♦ pl. surroundings.

con·tor·sión f. contortion; *(mueca)* grimace.

con·tor·sio·nis·ta m.f. contortionist.

con·tra I. prep. against ♦ **c. viento y marea** against all odds • **en c. de** against II. m. con —f. ♦ **llevar la c.** to oppose • **hacerle** or **llevarle la c. (a alguien)** to contradict (someone).

con·tra·al·mi·ran·te m. MARIT. rear admiral.

con·tra·a·ta·que m. counterattack.

con·tra·ban·de·ar intr. to smuggle.

con·tra·ban·dis·ta m.f. smuggler.

con·tra·ban·do m. *(mercancía)* contraband; *(acción)* smuggling.

con·trac·ción f. contraction.

con·tra·cep·ción f. contraception.

con·tra·cep·ti·vo, a adj. & m. contraceptive.

con·trac·tual adj. contractual.

con·tra·cul·tu·ra f. counterculture.

con·tra·cha·pa·do, a adj. & m. plywood.

con·tra·de·cir §11 tr. to contradict —reflex. to contradict oneself.

con·tra·dic·ción f. contradiction.

con·tra·dic·to·rio, a adj. contradictory.

con·tra·er §72 tr. to contract; *(reducir)* to shorten; *(deudas)* to incur; *(enfermedad)* to catch; *(vicio)* to pick up ♦ **c. la frente** to wrinkle one's brow • **c. matrimonio** to get married.

con·tra·es·pio·na·je m. counterespionage.

con·tra·faz f. reverse, other side.

con·tra·he·cho, a adj. deformed, hunchbacked.

con·trai·ga, go see **contraer**.

con·tra·in·di·ca·ción f. contraindication.

con·tra·in·di·car §70 tr. to contraindicate.

con·trai·je·ra, jo see **contraer**.

con·trai·mi·ran·te m. var. of **contraalmirante**.

con·tra·lor m. comptroller, inspector.

con·tra·ma·es·tre m. *(en un taller)* foreman; MARIT. boatswain.

con·tra·ma·no adv. ♦ **a c.** the wrong way.

con·tra·mar·cha f. countermarch; AUTO. reverse.

con·tra·o·fen·si·va f. counteroffensive.

con·tra·par·ti·da f. COM. cross entry.

con·tra·pe·lo adv. ♦ **a c.** against the grain; FIG. contrary to normal practice.

con·tra·pe·sar tr. to counterbalance.

con·tra·pe·so m. counterbalance.

con·tra·po·ner §54 tr. *(oponer)* to oppose; *(comparar)* to contrast —reflex. to set oneself against.

con·tra·po·si·ción f. *(oposición)* opposition; *(comparación)* comparison; *(contraste)* contrast.

con·tra·pro·du·cen·te adj. counterproductive.

con·tra·pro·po·si·ción f. counterproposal.

con·tra·pues·to, a see **contraponer**.

con·tra·pun·to m. counterpoint.

con·tra·pu·sie·ra, so see **contraponer**.

con·tra·ria f. see **contrario, a**.

con·tra·riar §30 tr. *(oponer)* to oppose; *(contradecir)* to contradict; *(enfadar)* to vex.

con·tra·rie·dad f. *(obstáculo)* obstacle; *(desazón)* annoyance; *(contratiempo)* setback; *(percance)* mishap.

con·tra·rio, a I. adj. opposite; *(adverso)* adverse ♦ **al c.** to the contrary • **al c. de** contrary to • **por el c.** on the contrary • **todo lo c.** quite the opposite II. m.f. opponent, adversary —f. ♦ **llevar la c.** COLL. to contradict.

con·tra·rres·tar tr. to offset; *(resistir)* to resist.

con·tra·rre·vo·lu·ción f. counterrevolution.

con·tra·sen·ti·do m. *(contradicción)* contradiction; *(disparate)* absurdity.

con·tra·se·ña f. password ♦ c. de salida readmission ticket.

con·tras·tar intr. to contrast —tr. to verify; METAL. to assay and hallmark.

con·tras·te m. contrast; *(oposición)* opposition; METAL. *(control)* assay; *(marcador)* assayer ♦ en c. con in contrast to • hacer c. con to contrast to or with • por c. in contrast.

con·tra·tar tr. to contract for; *(emplear)* to hire.

con·tra·tiem·po m. setback; MUS. syncopation.

con·tra·tis·ta m.f. contractor ♦ c. de obras building contractor.

con·tra·to m. contract ♦ c. colectivo de trabajo labor contract • c. de administración management contract • c. de locación lease • c. de compraventa purchase agreement • c. de fideicomiso deed of trust • c. de palabra verbal contract • c. de prenda collateral contract • c. de trabajo employment contract • c. matrimonial marriage contract.

con·tra·ven·ción f. contravention.

con·tra·ve·nir §76 intr. LAW to contravene.

con·tra·ven·ta·na f. *(puertaventana)* storm window; *(postigo)* shutter.

con·tra·ven·tor, ·ra I. adj. violating II. m.f. violator.

con·tri·bu·ción f. contribution; *(impuesto)* tax ♦ c. territorial land tax • c. urbana property or real estate tax.

con·tri·bui·dor, ·ra I. adj. contributory, contributing II. m.f. contributor.

con·tri·buir §18 tr. & intr. to contribute.

con·tri·bu·yen·te I. adj. *(que contribuye)* contributing; *(que paga impuestos)* taxpaying II. m.f. *(que contribuye)* contributor; *(que paga impuestos)* taxpayer.

con·tri·ción f. contrition, repentance.

con·trin·can·te m. rival, opponent.

con·tri·to, a adj. contrite, repentant.

con·trol m. control; *(inspección)* inspection; *(comprobación)* check; *(lugar)* checkpoint; *(examen)* examination; COM. audit ♦ c. de frontera border checkpoint • c. de la natalidad birth control • c. sobre sí mismo self-control.

con·tro·lar tr. to control; *(inspeccionar)* to inspect; *(comprobar)* to check; COM. to audit.

con·tro·ver·sia f. controversy, dispute.

con·tro·ver·ti·ble adj. controvertible.

con·tu·maz adj. obstinate; LAW in default ♦ condenar por c. to convict by default.

con·tun·den·te adj. overwhelming.

con·tu·sión f. bruise, contusion.

con·tu·so, a adj. & m.f. bruised (person).

con·tu·vie·ra, vo see contener.

con·va·le·cen·cia f. convalescence.

con·va·le·cer §17 intr. to convalesce.

con·va·le·cien·te adj. & m.f. convalescent (patient).

con·va·li·dar tr. to confirm, ratify.

con·ven·cer §75 tr. to convince —reflex. to be or become convinced.

con·ven·ci·ble adj. convincible.

con·ven·ci·mien·to m. conviction.

con·ven·ción f. convention.

con·ven·drá, dría, ga, go see convenir.

con·ve·ni·ble adj. *(dócil)* easy-going; *(precio)* fair.

con·ve·ni·do adv. agreed.

con·ve·nien·cia f. *(provecho)* advantage; *(co-*

modidad) convenience ♦ ser de la c. de uno to be convenient for someone.

con·ve·nien·te adj. convenient; *(oportuno)* suitable; *(aconsejable)* advisable; *(provechoso)* advantageous ♦ creer or juzgar c. to think or see fit.

con·ve·nio m. agreement; *(pacto)* pact; COM. settlement ♦ c. comercial trade agreement • llegar a un c. to reach an agreement.

con·ve·nir §76 intr. *(acordar)* to concur; *(corresponder)* to be fitting; *(venir bien)* to suit; *(ser aconsejable)* to be advisable.

con·ven·ti·lle·ro, a m.f. R.P. gossip, meddler.

con·ven·ti·llo m. AMER. tenement house.

con·ven·to m. convent; *(monasterio)* monastery.

con·ver·gen·cia f. convergence.

con·ver·gen·te adj. convergent, converging.

con·ver·ger §34/gir §32 intr. to converge; *(concurrir)* to concur.

con·ver·sa f. COLL. talk, chat.

con·ver·sa·ción f. conversation ♦ cambiar de c. to change the subject • dar c. to make conversation • dirigir la c. a uno to address someone • trabar c. to strike up a conversation.

con·ver·sa·dor, ·ra adj. & m.f. talkative (person).

con·ver·sar intr. to converse, talk.

con·ver·sión f. conversion.

con·ver·ti·ble I. adj. convertible, changeable II. m. AUTO. convertible.

con·ver·ti·dor m. ELEC., METAL. converter.

con·ver·tir §65 tr. *(cambiar)* to change, turn; *(persuadir)* to convert; COM., FIN. to exchange —reflex. to convert, be converted ♦ c. en to turn into.

con·ve·xo, a adj. convex.

con·vic·ción f. conviction.

con·vic·to, a I. see convencer II. adj. convicted III. m.f. convict.

con·vi·da·do, a m.f. guest.

con·vi·dar tr. to invite ♦ c. a uno con to treat someone to.

con·vie·ne see convenir.

con·vier·ta, to see convertir.

con·vin·cen·te adj. convincing.

con·vi·nie·ra, no see convenir.

con·vir·tie·ra, tió see convertir.

con·vi·te m. *(invitación)* invitation; *(banquete)* banquet, feast.

con·vi·ven·cia f. living together; *(coexistencia)* coexistence.

con·vi·vir intr. to live together.

con·vo·ca·ción f. convocation.

con·vo·car §70 tr. to convoke, summon.

con·vo·ca·to·ria f. summons, notice.

con·voy m. convoy; *(escolta)* escort; *(vinagreras)* cruet; *(tren)* train; *(séquito)* retinue.

con·vul·sión f. convulsion; *(trastorno)* upheaval; *(temblor)* tremor.

con·vul·sio·nar tr. to convulse; FIG. to agitate.

con·vul·si·vo, a adj. convulsive ♦ tos c. whooping cough.

con·yu·gal adj. conjugal, connubial.

cón·yu·ge m.f. spouse ♦ pl. husband and wife.

co·ñac m. [pl. s] cognac, brandy.

co·o·pe·ra·ción f. cooperation.

co·o·pe·rar intr. to cooperate.

co·o·pe·ra·ti·vo, a adj. & f. cooperative.

co·or·de·na·da f. MATH. coordinate.

co·or·di·na·ción f. coordination.

co·or·di·na·dor, ·ra I. adj. coordinating

II. m.f. coordinator.

co·or·di·nar tr. to coordinate.

co·pa f. glass, goblet; (*contenido*) glassful; (*trago*) drink; (*de árbol*) treetop; (*de sombrero*) crown; SPORT. cup ♦ **tomarse una c.** to have a drink *or* cocktail.

co·par tr. (*en un juego*) to cover *or* wager (the bank); POL. to win, sweep (an election).

co·par·ti·ci·pe m.f. copartner.

co·pe·te m. (*mechón*) tuft (of hair); ZOOL. forelock; ORNITH. crest; (*cima*) summit, top ♦ **de alto c.** high-class • **tener mucho c.** to be arrogant.

co·pe·tín m. AMER., COLL. drink, cocktail.

co·pia f. copy; (*duplicado*) duplicate; (*imagen*) image; (*imitación*) imitation; ARTS reproduction; CINEM., PHOTOG. print ♦ **c. fotostática** photostat • **sacar una c.** to make a copy.

co·pia·dor, ·ra I. adj. copying II. m.f. copyist —m. COM. letter book —f. photocopier.

co·piar tr. to copy; (*hacer una copia*) to make a copy of; (*apuntar*) to copy down.

co·pi·lo·to m. copilot.

co·pio·si·dad f. copiousness, abundance.

co·pio·so, a adj. copious, abundant.

co·pla f. (*canción*) ballad; (*estrofa*) stanza ♦ pl. COLL. verses, poetry.

co·po m. (*de nieve*) snowflake; TEX. (*mechón*) bundle (of flax) ♦ **c. de algodón** cotton ball.

co·po·se·sión f. co-ownership.

co·pro·duc·ción f. coproduction.

co·pro·pie·dad f. joint ownership.

co·pro·pie·ta·rio, a m.f. co-owner.

có·pu·la f. (*unión*) coupling; (*coito*) copulation; GRAM. copula.

co·pu·la·ti·vo, a adj. copulative.

co·que·te·ar intr. to flirt.

co·que·te·o m. flirtation.

co·que·te·rí·a f. flirtatiousness.

co·que·to, a I. adj. (*agradable*) charming; (*mujer*) flirtatious II. f. flirt.

co·que·tón, ·ona COLL. adj. (*agradable*) charming; (*mujer*) flirtatious.

co·ra·je m. (*valor*) courage; (*ira*) anger ♦ **dar c.** a to make angry.

co·ral[1] m. coral —f. coral snake.

co·ral[2] I. adj. choral II. m. chorale.

co·ra·za f. (*armadura*) cuirass; FIG. armor; ZOOL. shell.

co·ra·zón m. heart; (*valor*) spirit; (*amor*) love ♦ **blando de c.** softhearted • **con el c. en la mano** frankly, openly • **de c.** sincerely • **duro de c.** hardhearted • **encogérsele a uno el c.** to be moved with pity • **helársele a uno el c.** to be stunned • **no caberle el c. en el pecho** to be bursting (with joy) • **no tener c.** to be heartless • **ojos que no ven, c. que no siente** out of sight, out of mind.

co·ra·zo·na·da f. (*impulso*) impulse; (*presentimiento*) premonition.

cor·ba·ta f. tie, necktie ♦ **con c.** wearing a tie • **c. de lazo** bow tie.

cor·cel m. steed, charger.

cor·co·ve·ar intr. to buck; FIG. to grumble.

cor·che·a f. eighth note, quaver (G.B.) ♦ **doble c.** sixteenth note, semiquaver (G.B.).

cor·che·te m. (*broche*) hook and eye, clasp; (*macho del broche*) hook (of clasp); PRINT. (*llave*) bracket.

cor·cho m. cork; (*de la pesca*) float ♦ **sacar el c.** to uncork.

¡cór·cho·lis! interj. good heavens!, gracious!

cor·del m. cord, thin rope.

cor·de·ro m. lamb; (*piel*) lambskin.

cor·dial I. adj. (*afectuoso*) cordial, warm; (*reconfortante*) tonic ♦ **saludos cordiales** cordially yours II. m. tonic.

cor·dia·li·dad f. cordiality, warmth.

cor·di·lle·ra f. chain of mountains, cordillera.

cor·di·lle·ra·no, a adj. & m.f. Andean.

cór·do·ba m. NIC., FIN. cordoba.

cor·dón m. (*cuerda*) cord; (*cinta*) cordon, braid; ANAT., ELEC. CORD.

cor·don·ci·llo m. (*de tela*) rib; (*de una moneda*) milling.

cor·du·ra f. prudence, wisdom.

co·re·o·gra·fía f. choreography.

co·re·ó·gra·fo m. choreographer.

co·ris·ta m.f. MUS. chorus singer; RELIG. chorister; THEAT. member of the chorus.

cor·na·da f. (*golpe*) butt (with a horn); (*herida*) goring ♦ **dar una c.** to gore.

cor·na·men·ta f. horns; (*de ciervo*) antlers.

cór·ne·a f. cornea.

cor·ne·ta f. bugle; (*de caza*) hunting horn; MIL. cornet —m. bugler.

cor·ne·tín m. cornet; (*persona*) cornetist; MIL. bugle.

cor·ni·sa f. cornice.

cor·no m. horn.

cor·nu·co·pia f. cornucopia.

cor·nu·do, a I. adj. horned; COLL. cuckolded ♦ **tras c., apaleado** COLL. adding insult to injury II. m. COLL. cuckold.

co·ro m. chorus, choir ♦ **a c.** in unison.

co·ro·la f. BOT. corolla.

co·ro·la·rio m. corollary.

co·ro·na f. crown; (*de laureles*) wreath; (*aureola*) halo; ARCHIT., ASTRON. corona ♦ **ceñirse la c.** to assume the crown *or* throne.

co·ro·na·ción f. crowning, coronation.

co·ro·nar tr. to crown; (*en ajedrez*) to queen.

co·ro·nel m. colonel.

co·ro·ni·lla f. crown ♦ **estar hasta la c.** COLL. to be fed up.

cor·pa(n)·chón m. COLL. big *or* bulky body.

cor·pi·ño m. (*jubón*) sleeveless bodice; R.P. bra, brassiere.

cor·po·ra·ción f. corporation.

cor·po·rei·dad f. corporeity, corporeality.

cor·pó·re·o, a adj. (*material*) corporeal; (*corporal*) corporal.

cor·pu·len·cia f. corpulence.

cor·pús·cu·lo m. corpuscle.

co·rral m. corral; (*redil*) pen.

co·rra·lón m. (*de animales*) large corral; (*de madera*) lumberyard.

co·rre·a f. (*de cuero*) strap; (*cinturón*) belt; TECH. belt.

co·rre·a·je m. straps, belts.

co·rre·a·zo m. blow with a leather strap.

co·rrec·ción f. (*modificación*) adjustment; (*urbanidad*) propriety ♦ **c. de pruebas** proofreading.

co·rrec·cio·nal I. adj. corrective II. m. reformatory, prison.

co·rrec·to, a I. see **corregir** II. adj. correct.

co·rrec·tor, ·ra I. adj. corrective II. m.f. corrector; PRINT. proofreader.

co·rre·de·ra f. (*carril*) track; (*de molino*) upper millstone; MECH. slide valve.

co·rre·di·zo, a adj. (*puerta*) sliding; (*nudo*) slip.

co·rre·dor, ·ra I. adj. running II. m.f. runner

—m. (pasillo) corridor; (galería) gallery; COM. agent ♦ c. de apuestas bookmaker • c. de cambios stockbroker • c. de seguros insurance agent.

co·rre·gir §57 tr. (enmendar) to correct; (castigar) to chastise; PRINT. to proofread —reflex. to mend one's ways.

co·rre·la·ción f. correlation.

co·rre·la·cio·nar tr. to correlate, relate.

co·rre·la·ti·vo, a adj. & m. correlative.

co·rre·li·gio·na·rio, a m.f. FIG. colleague.

co·rren·ta·da f. AMER. strong current.

co·rre·o m. mail; (mensajero) messenger; (buzón) mailbox; (oficina) post office ♦ a vuelta de c. by return mail • c. aéreo air mail • c. certificado registered mail • echar al c. to mail • por c. by mail ♦ pl. (servicio) mail service; (oficina) post office.

co·rrer intr. to run; (en una carrera) to race; (aguas) to flow; (viento) to blow; (camino) to run; (horas) to pass; (la moneda) to be valid; (rumor) to circulate ♦ a todo c. at full speed • c. a to hurry to • c. con to be responsible for • c. la voz to be said • c. por cuenta de or a cargo de to be the responsibility of —tr. to race; (riesgo) to run; (mundo) to cover; (persona) to chase; (muebles) to move; (balanza) to tip; (cortinas) to draw; (cerrojo) to slide; (nudo) to slip; (aventuras) to meet with; AMER. to throw (someone) out ♦ correría COLL. to live it up —reflex. (deslizarse) to slide; (moverse) to slide over.

co·rre·rí·a f. excursion; MIL. foray.

co·rres·pon·den·cia f. (relación) relationship; (conformidad) agreement; (cartas) correspondence, mail.

co·rres·pon·der intr. (ser igual a) to correspond, match; (tener proporción con) to fit or go with; (reciprocar) to return; (incumbir) to fall to; (tocar) to be one's turn to; (pertenecer) to belong; (ser la proporción) to be the share of —reflex. (escribir) to correspond; (amarse) to love each other.

co·rres·pon·dien·te I. adj. corresponding II. m.f. correspondent.

co·rres·pon·sal adj. & m.f. correspondent.

co·rre·ta·je m. (oficio) brokerage; (comisión) broker's fee.

co·rre·te·ar intr. (vagar) to wander the streets; (retozar) to frolic —tr. (perseguir) to chase; C. AMER. (despedir) to dismiss.

co·rre·ve(i)·di·le m.f. COLL. gossipmonger.

co·rri·da f. race, run ♦ c. de toros bullfight • dar una c. to make a dash • de c. quickly • en una c. in a flash.

co·rri·do, a I. adj. (excedido) full; (consecutivo) straight; (experimentado) worldly ♦ de c. (con fluidez) fluently; (rápido) quickly II. m. ballad.

co·rrien·te I. adj. (que corre) running; (actual) current; (sabido) well-known; (usual) usual; (ordinario) ordinary; (moderno) up-to-date ♦ al c. up-to-date • poner al c. to bring up-to-date • tener al c. to keep informed II. f. current; FIG. trend <una nueva c. a new trend> ♦ c. alterna alternating current • c. continua or directa direct current • dejarse llevar por la c. or ir con la c. to go along with the crowd • llevarle or seguirle la c. a (alguien) to humor (someone).

co·rrien·te·men·te adv. (actualmente) currently; (comúnmente) usually.

co·rri·ja, jo see corregir.

co·rri·llo m. small circle or group, clique.

co·rro m. (de personas) circle of talkers; (espacio) ring.

co·rro·bo·ra·ción f. corroboration.

co·rro·bo·rar tr. to corroborate.

co·rro·bo·ra·ti·vo, a adj. corroborative.

co·rro·er §61 tr. (carcomer) to corrode; GEOL. to erode; FIG. to eat away at.

co·rrom·per tr. to corrupt; (pervertir) to pervert; (seducir) to seduce; (sobornar) to bribe; (pudrir) to decay —reflex. (pervertirse) to become corrupt; (degenerar) to degenerate.

co·rro·sión f. corrosion.

co·rro·si·vo, a adj. corrosive.

co·rro·ya, yera, yó see corroer.

co·rrup·ción f. corruption.

co·rrup·ti·ble adj. corruptible.

co·rrup·to, a I. see corromper II. adj. corrupt, corrupted.

co·rrup·tor, ·ra I. adj. corrupting II. m.f. corrupter.

cor·sa·rio m. corsair.

cor·sé m. corset, corselet.

cor·ta·cés·ped m. lawnmower.

cor·ta·cir·cui·tos m.inv. circuit breaker.

cor·ta·co·rrien·te m. current breaker, switch.

cor·ta·do, a I. adj. (estilo) disjointed; COLL. (sin palabras) speechless; AMER. (sin dinero) broke II. m. coffee with milk —f. AMER. cut, gash.

cor·ta·dor, ·ra I. adj. cutting II. m. (el que corta) cutter; (carnicero) butcher —f. cutter.

cor·ta·du·ra f. (acción) cutting; (incisión) cut; GEOG. mountain pass ♦ pl. scraps.

cor·tan·te adj. cutting, sharp.

cor·ta·pa·pel/pe·les m. letter opener.

cor·ta·plu·mas m.inv. pocketknife.

cor·tar tr. to cut; (recortar) to trim; (carne, aves) to carve; (en porciones) to cut up; (separar) to cut off; (un árbol) to cut down, fell; (con un molde) to cut out; (atravesar) to cut through; (diluir) to dilute; (omitir) to cut out; (suspender) to discontinue; (interrumpir) to cut off; (acortar) to cut short, criticize; R.P. (ahorrar camino) to cut (through or across) ♦ c. por la mitad to cut in half —intr. to cut; (el frío) to be cutting • c. por lo sano to take drastic measures —reflex. (turbarse) to become flustered; (la piel) to chap; (la leche) to curdle.

cor·ta·ú·ñas m.inv. nail clipper.

cor·te[1] m. (acción) cutting; (filo) (cutting) edge; SEW. cutting (out); (de tela) length; (estilo) cut; TECH. section ♦ c. de pelo haircut • c. y confección dressmaking • darse c. COLL. to put on airs.

cor·te[2] f. (residencia) (royal) court; (comitiva) retinue; AMER. court of law ♦ hacer la c. a to court.

cor·te·jar tr. (galantear) to woo; (halagar) to court.

cor·te·jo m. (galanteo) courting; (séquito) entourage ♦ c. fúnebre funeral cortege.

cor·tés adj. courteous, polite.

cor·te·sa·no, a I. adj. courtly II. m. courtier —f. courtesan.

cor·te·sí·a f. courtesy; (galantería) charm.

cor·te·za f. (de árbol) bark; (de fruta) peel; (del pan) crust; (de queso, tocino) rind; ANAT., BOT. cortex.

cor·ti·jo m. farm, grange.

cor·ti·na f. curtain; FIG. screen ♦ c. de fuego barrage of fire • c. de hierro Iron Curtain.

cor·to, a adj. short; *(breve)* brief; *(escaso)* short; *(tímido)* shy ♦ **a la c. o a la larga** sooner or later • **c. de vista** shortsighted • **ni c. ni perezoso** without thinking twice • **quedarse c.** to fall short.

cor·to·cir·cui·to m. short circuit.

cor·va·du·ra f. curvature; ARCHIT. curve.

cor·var tr. to curve, bend.

co·sa f. thing; *(algo)* something; *(en negaciones)* anything; *(asunto)* business ♦ **como c. tuya** as if it came from you • **como quien no quiere la c.** offhandedly • **como si tal c.** COLL. as if such a thing had never happened • **c. del otro mundo** COLL. extraordinary thing • **c. de ver** something worth seeing • **c. nunca vista** COLL. something unheard of • **cosas de la vida** ups and downs • **c. seria** serious matter • **ni c. que lo parezca** nor anything of the kind • **no es gran c.** it's nothing great • **no hay tal c.** there's no such thing • **no sea c. que** lest • **¿qué c.?** COLL. what did you say?

cos·co·rrón m. knock on the head.

co·se·cha f. harvest; *(temporada)* harvest time; FIG. crop ♦ **de su propia c.** of one's own invention.

co·se·cha·do·ra f. combine.

co·se·char tr. to harvest; *(frutas, flores)* to pick —intr. to harvest.

co·se·no m. cosine.

co·ser tr. to sew ♦ **c. a puñaladas** to stab repeatedly —intr. to sew.

cos·mé·ti·co, a adj. & m. cosmetic.

cós·mi·co, a adj. cosmic.

cos·mo·gó·ni·co, a adj. cosmogonic.

cos·mo·gra·fí·a f. cosmography.

cos·mo·lo·gí·a f. cosmology.

cos·mo·ló·gi·co, a adj. cosmological.

cos·mo·nau·ta m.f. cosmonaut, astronaut.

cos·mo·po·li·ta adj. & m.f. cosmopolitan (person).

cos·mos m.inv. cosmos, universe.

cos·qui·llas f.pl. ticklishness ♦ **hacer c.** to tickle • **tener c.** to be ticklish.

cos·qui·lle·ar tr. to tickle.

cos·ta f. *(costo)* cost; *(orilla)* shore ♦ **a c. ajena** at someone else's expense • **a c. de** at the expense of • **a toda c.** at all costs ♦ pl. LAW fees, costs.

cos·ta·do m. side; MIL. flank ♦ **de c.** sideways • **por los cuatro costados** through and through • **tenderse de c.** to lie on one's side.

cos·tal m. sack ♦ **ser harina de otro c.** COLL. to be another story.

cos·ta·ne·ro, a adj. coastal; *(inclinado)* sloping.

cos·tar §19 intr. to cost; FIG. *(ser difícil)* to find it difficult to ♦ **c. barato** to be cheap or inexpensive • **c. caro** to be expensive • **c. trabajo** to take a lot to • **c. un ojo de la cara** COLL. to cost a fortune • **cueste lo que cueste** at all costs.

cos·te m. cost.

cos·te·ar tr. to finance; MARIT. to coast —reflex. R.P. to arrive with difficulty.

cos·te·ro, a I. adj. coastal II. f. *(cuesta)* slope; *(costa)* shore; MARIT. fishing season.

cos·ti·lla f. ANAT. rib; *(chuleta)* cutlet, chop; *(de una silla)* rung; *(de un barril)* stave ♦ pl. COLL. back • **a las c. de** at the expense of.

cos·ti·llar m. ribs.

cos·to m. cost ♦ **al c.** at cost • **c. de la vida** cost of living • **c. efectivo** actual cost.

cos·to·so, a adj. *(caro)* costly; *(grave)* grievous.

cos·tra f. crust; MED. scab.

cos·tum·bre f. custom; *(hábito)* habit; *(práctica)* practice ♦ **de c.** *(usual)* usual; *(usualmente)* usually • **novela de costumbres** novel of manners • **por c.** out of habit • **tener por c.** to be in the habit of.

cos·tu·ra f. needlework; *(unión)* seam; MARIT. seam, splice; MED. scar ♦ **alta c.** high fashion • **sin c.** seamless.

cos·tu·re·ra f. seamstress.

cos·tu·re·ro m. sewing basket.

co·ta f. coat of arms ♦ **c. de malla** coat of mail.

co·te·jar tr. to compare.

co·te·jo m. comparison.

co·te·rrá·ne·o, a adj. of the same country or region.

co·ti·dia·no, a adj. daily, everyday.

co·ti·le·dón m. cotyledon, seed leaf.

co·ti·llo m. head (of a hammer).

co·ti·llón m. cotillion (dance).

co·ti·za·ción f. COM. quotation.

co·ti·zar §04 tr. COM. to quote; *(valorar)* to price.

co·to m. *(terreno)* reserved area; *(mojón)* boundary marker; *(población)* small village in an estate ♦ **c. de caza** game preserve • **poner c.** a to put a stop to.

co·to·rra f. *(loro)* parakeet; *(urraca)* magpie; COLL. chatterbox.

co·to·rre·ar intr. COLL. to chatter, babble.

co·to·rre·o m. COLL. chatter, babbling.

co·tu·fa f. Jerusalem artichoke.

co·va·cha f. *(cueva)* small cave; AMER. *(vivienda)* shack.

co·xis m.inv. coccyx.

co·yo·te m. coyote.

co·yun·tu·ra f. ANAT. joint; *(oportunidad)* chance; *(circunstancias)* circumstance.

coz f. kick; ARM., recoil ♦ **dar** or **pegar coces** to kick.

cra·ne·al/a·ne·o, a adj. cranial.

crá·ne·o m. cranium, skull.

cra·so, a adj. crass, gross.

crá·ter m. crater.

cre·a·ción f. creation.

cre·a·dor, ·ra I. adj. creative II. m.f. creator.

cre·ar tr. to create; *(fundar)* to found; *(establecer)* to establish; *(inventar)* to invent.

cre·cer §17 intr. to grow; *(aumentar)* to increase; *(la luna)* to wax; *(un río)* to swell ♦ **c. como la cizaña** to grow like weeds • **dejarse c. la barba** to grow a beard.

cre·ces f.pl. ♦ **con c.** amply.

cre·ci·do, a I. adj. *(grande)* large; *(adulto)* grown • **estar c.** *(un río)* to be in flood II. f. spate.

cre·cien·te I. adj. *(que crece)* growing; *(que aumenta)* increasing; *(la luna)* crescent II. m. HER. crescent —f. *(luna)* crescent moon; *(marea)* flood tide.

cre·ci·mien·to m. *(acción)* growth; *(aumento)* increase; *(de la luna)* waxing; *(de un río)* swelling.

cre·den·cial I. adj. accrediting II. f. credential.

cré·di·to m. *(aceptación)* credence; *(reputación)* reputation; COM. credit ♦ **abrir** or **dar c.** a to give or extend credit to • **a c.** on credit.

cre·do m. creed; *(doctrina)* credo.

cré·du·lo, a adj. credulous, gullible.

cre·en·cia f. *(convicción)* belief; *(fe)* faith.

cre·er §43 tr. to believe; *(imaginar)* to think; *(estimar)* to consider ♦ **c. a ciencia cierta** to be convinced of • **c. a pie juntillas** to believe blindly • **c. que sí** to think so • **según creo** to the best of my knowledge • **¡ya lo creo!** COLL. I should say so! —intr. to believe ♦ **ver es c.** seeing is believing —reflex. to consider *or* regard oneself ♦ **¿qué se cree?** who does he think he is?

cre·í·ble adj. credible, believable.

cre·í·do, a I. see **creer** II. adj. *(confiado)* credulous; *(vanidoso)* conceited.

cre·ma f. cream; *(natillas)* custard; *(cosmética)* cold cream; *(lo mejor)* cream of the crop ♦ **c. batida** whipped cream • **c. de afeitar** shaving cream.

cre·ma·ción f. cremation.

cre·ma·lle·ra f. MECH. toothed bar; *(cierre)* zipper.

cre·ma·to·rio, a adj. & m. crematory.

cre·mo·so, a adj. creamy.

cren·cha f. *(raya)* part (of hair); *(parte)* each side of parted hair.

cre·o·so·ta f. creosote.

cre·pé m. *(tela fina)* crepe, crèpe; *(caucho)* crepe rubber.

cre·pi·tar intr. to crackle.

cre·pus·cu·lar adj. twilight.

cre·pús·cu·lo m. twilight.

cres·po, a adj. *(cabello)* kinky; *(hoja)* curly.

cres·ta f. crest; *(copete)* tuft; *(cima)* summit ♦ **c. de gallo** cockscomb • **alzar** *or* **levantar la c.** COLL. to show arrogance • **dar en la c. a uno** COLL. to cut someone down to size.

cre·ta f. chalk.

cre·tá·ce·o, a adj. cretaceous.

cre·ti·nis·mo m. cretinism.

cre·ti·no, a I. adj. cretinous; FIG. stupid II. m.f. cretin.

cre·yen·te I. adj. believing II. m.f. believer.

cre·ye·ra, yó see **creer**.

crí·a f. raising; *(animal)* offspring; *(camada)* litter.

cria·de·ro, a m. BOT. nursery; ZOOL. breeding place ♦ **c. de ostras** oyster bed.

cria·di·lla f. testicle (of an animal).

cria·do, a I. adj. bred, brought up II. m. servant —f. maid.

cria·dor, ·ra m.f. breeder.

crian·za f. nurturing; ZOOL. raising; *(lactancia)* lactation; *(cortesía)* manners ♦ **dar c.** to bring up.

criar §30 tr. *(nutrir)* to nurse; *(animales)* to raise; *(niños)* to bring up ♦ **c. carnes** COLL. to put on weight —intr. to reproduce, have young —reflex. to be brought up; *(crecer)* to grow.

cria·tu·ra f. *(niño)* infant; *(cosa creada)* creature.

cri·ba f. screen, sieve.

cri·bar tr. to sift, screen.

cric m. MECH. jack.

cri·men m. crime; FIG. shame.

cri·mi·nal adj. & m.f. criminal.

cri·mi·na·li·dad f. *(calidad)* criminality; *(índice)* crime rate.

cri·mi·na·lis·ta m.f. criminologist; *(abogado)* criminal lawyer.

cri·mi·no·lo·gí·a f. criminology.

cri·mi·nó·lo·go m. criminologist.

crin f. horsehair.

crí·o m. COLL. *(de pecho)* infant; *(niño)* kid.

crio·llo, a adj. & m.f. native.

crip·ta f. crypt.

cri·sá·li·da f. chrysalis, pupa.

cri·san·te·mo m./ma f. chrysanthemum.

cri·sis f.inv. crisis; *(escasez)* shortage ♦ **c. ministerial** cabinet crisis • **c. nerviosa** nervous breakdown • **hacer c.** to reach crisis point.

cris·ma f. COLL. head ♦ **romperle la c. a alguien** COLL. to bash in someone's head.

cri·sol m. crucible.

cris·par tr. ANAT. to contract; FIG. to irritate —reflex. ANAT. to twitch; FIG. to become irritated.

cris·tal m. crystal; *(vidrio)* glass; *(hoja de vidrio)* pane of glass; *(espejo)* mirror ♦ **c. ahumado** smoked glass • **c. de roca** rock crystal • **c. hilado** fiber glass • **c. inastillable** splinter-proof glass • **c. irrompible** shatterproof glass • **c. tallado** cut glass • **de c.** glass.

cris·ta·le·rí·a f. glasswork(s); *(tienda)* crystal shop; *(juego)* crystal service; *(objetos)* glassware.

cris·ta·li·no, a I. adj. *(de cristal)* crystalline; *(diáfano)* crystal clear II. m. crystalline lens.

cris·ta·li·zar §04 tr., intr. & reflex. to crystallize.

cris·tian·dad f. Christendom.

cris·tia·nis·mo m. Christianity.

cris·tia·ni·zar §04 tr. to convert to Christianity.

cris·tia·no, a I. adj. Christian II. m.f. Christian; COLL. *(español)* plain Spanish; *(alguien)* living soul.

Cris·to m. Christ.

cri·te·rio m. *(regla)* criterion; *(juicio)* judgment; *(opinión)* opinion.

cri·ti·car §70 tr. to criticize; *(murmurar)* to gossip about.

crí·ti·co, a I. adj. critical; *(crucial)* crucial II. m.f. critic, reviewer —f. criticism; *(reseña)* review; *(murmuración)* gossip.

cri·ti·cón, ·na I. adj. faultfinding II. m.f. faultfinder.

cro·ar intr. to croak.

cro·chet m. crochet.

cro·ma·do m. chromium plating, chroming.

cro·mar tr. to chrome.

cro·má·ti·co, a adj. chromatic.

cro·mo·so·ma m. chromosome.

cró·ni·co, a I. adj. chronic; *(inveterado)* inveterate II. f. *(historia)* chronicle; *(artículo)* article.

cro·nis·ta m.f. *(historiador)* chronicler; *(periodista)* reporter.

cro·nó·gra·fo m. *(persona)* chronologist; *(aparato)* chronograph.

cro·no·lo·gí·a f. chronology.

cro·no·ló·gi·co, a adj. chronologic, chronological.

cro·no·me·trar tr. to time with a chronometer.

cro·nó·me·tro m. chronometer.

cro·que·ta f. CUL. croquette.

cro·quis m.inv. sketch.

crou·pier m.f. croupier.

cru·ce m. *(acción)* crossing; *(punto)* intersection; RAIL. crossing; BIOL. crossbreeding; *(híbrido)* cross, hybrid ♦ **c. a nivel** grade *or* level crossing • **c. de peatones** pedestrian crossing.

cru·ce·ro m. cruise; ARCHIT. transept; PRINT. crossbar (of a chase).

cru·cial adj. crucial.

cru·ci·fi·car §70 tr. to crucify.
cru·ci·fi·jo m. crucifix.
cru·ci·fi·xión f. crucifixion.
cru·ci·gra·ma m. crossword puzzle.
cru·de·za f. *(estado)* rawness; *(rudeza)* harshness ♦ **con c.** harshly.
cru·do, a I. adj. raw; *(verde)* green; *(amarillento)* yellowish; *(seda)* raw; *(petróleo)* crude; *(clima)* harsh; FIG. cruel II. m. crude oil.
cruel adj. cruel; *(despiadado)* merciless; *(fiero)* savage, *(severo)* severe.
cruel·dad f. cruelty; *(inhumanidad)* inhumanity; *(ferocidad)* savagery; *(severidad)* severity.
cruen·to, a adj. bloody.
cru·ji·do m. *(de hoja, tela)* rustling; *(de puerta)* creaking; *(de dientes)* rattling; *(de huesos)* cracking.
cru·jir intr. *(hoja, tela)* to rustle; *(puerta, madera)* to creak; *(dientes)* to rattle, chatter; *(huesos)* to crack; *(grava)* to crunch.
crus·tá·ce·o, a adj. & m. crustacean.
cruz f. cross; *(reverso)* tails; FIG. cross; PRINT. dagger; MARIT. crown ♦ **en c.** cross-shaped.
cru·za·do, a I. adj. crossed; BIOL., ZOOL. hybrid II. m. crusader —f. HIST. Crusade; FIG. crusade.
cru·za·mien·to m. *(acción)* crossing; *(animales)* crossbreeding.
cru·zar §04 tr. to cross ♦ **cruzarle a uno la cara** FIG. to slap someone across the face —reflex. to cross one another *<las líneas se cruzan the lines cross one another>*; *(pasarse)* to pass ♦ **c. de brazos** to do nothing.
cua·der·no m. notebook.
cua·dra f. stable; *(de casas)* block.
cua·dra·di·llo m. *(regla)* ruler; *(de camisa)* gusset.
cua·dra·do, a adj. & m. square.
cua·dra·ge·na·rio, a adj. & m.f. quadragenarian.
cua·dra·gé·si·mo, a adj. & m. fortieth.
cua·dran·gu·lar adj. quadrangular.
cua·drán·gu·lo, a I. adj. quadrangular II. m. quadrangle.
cua·dran·te m. MARIT., MATH. quadrant; *(reloj)* sundial; *(de reloj)* face.
cua·drar tr. to square —intr. *(conformar)* to square, agree; COM. to balance —reflex. MIL. to stand at attention.
cua·drí·cu·la f. grid.
cua·dri·cu·lar[1] adj. squared.
cua·dri·cu·lar[2] tr. to divide into squares, square (paper).
cua·drie·nio m. quadrennium.
cua·dril m. *(hueso)* hipbone; *(anca)* rump.
cua·dri·lá·te·ro, a adj. & m. quadrilateral.
cua·dri·lla f. *(de obreros)* crew; *(de malhechores)* gang; *(baile)* quadrille; TAUR. team assisting a bullfighter.
cua·dri·pli·car §70 tr. to quadruplicate.
cua·dro m. square; ARTS painting; *(descripción)* description; *(espectáculo)* spectacle; THEAT. scene; *(conjunto de oficiales)* cadre; SPORT. team ♦ **a cuadros** checkered • **c. al óleo** oil painting • **c. vivo** tableau vivant • **en c.** square.
cua·drú·ma·no, a I. adj. quadrumanous II. m.f. quadrumane.
cua·drú·pe·do, a I. adj. quadrupedal II. m.f. quadruped.
cuá·dru·ple adj. quadruple, fourfold.
cua·dru·pli·car §70 tr. & intr. to quadruple.

cuá·drup·lo, a adj. & m. quadruple.
cua·ja·do, a I. adj. ♦ **c. de** full of II. f. curd (of milk).
cua·jar tr. to coagulate, congeal; *(leche)* to curdle; *(adornar)* to cover —intr. COLL. *(tener éxito)* to turn out well —reflex. to coagulate, congeal; *(leche)* to curdle.
cua·jo m. rennet ♦ **de c.** by the roots.
cual I. rel. pron. ♦ **al c.** *(persona)* to whom; *(cosa)* to which • **cada c.** each one, every one • **con lo c.** whereupon, upon which • **del c.** of which • **el c.** *(persona)* who; *(cosa)* which • **por lo c.** whereby, because of which II. adv. like, as ♦ **c. . . . tal** like . . . like • **c. si** as if • **quedarse tal c.** COLL. to be cool as a cucumber.
cuál I. adj. which II. rel. pron. which *(one)* III. indef. pron. some IV. adv. how.
cua·les·quier see cualquier.
cua·les·quie·ra see cualquiera.
oua·li·dad f. quality, characteristic.
cua·li·fi·car §70 tr. to qualify, characterize.
cua·li·ta·ti·vo, a adj. qualitative.
cual·quier adj. [pl. **cuales-**] contr. of **cualquiera** used before nouns.
cual·quie·ra [pl. **cuales-**] I. adj. *(just)* any, any ordinary II. indef. pron. any(one), anybody ♦ **un (hombre) c.** a nobody III. rel. pron. *(persona)* whoever; *(cosa)* whatever; *(nadie)* nobody.
cuan adv. as.
cuán adv. how.
cuan·do I. adv. when, since ♦ **c. más** *or* **mucho** at the most • **c. menos** at least • **de c. en c.** from time to time II. conj. when; *(aunque)* although, even if; *(puesto que)* since; *(si)* if ♦ **aun c.** even though, although • **c. no** if not, otherwise • **c. quiera** whenever III. prep. *(durante)* at the time of; as *<c. niño as a child>*.
cuán·do adv. when.
cuan·tí·a f. *(cantidad)* amount, *(importancia)* importance.
cuan·ti·más adv. COLL. all the more.
cuan·tio·so, a adj. *(grande)* large; *(abundante)* abundant; *(numeroso)* numerous.
cuan·ti·ta·ti·vo, a adj. quantitative.
cuan·to[1] m. quantum.
cuan·to[2] I. adv. *(todo lo que)* as much as; *(todo el tiempo que)* as long as ♦ **c. antes** as soon as possible • **c. más** even more so • **en c.** as soon as • **en c. a** as to, as for • **por c.** insofar as, inasmuch as II. adj. & pron. see **cuanto, a.**
cuán·to I. adv. how ♦ **¡c. me alegro!** how happy I am! • **¡c. cuesta la carne!** how expensive beef is! • **¡c. dura esta película!** how long this movie is! II. adj. & pron. see **cuánto, ta.**
cuan·to, a I. adj. as much as ♦ **c. más. . .** *(tanto)* más the more . . . the more • **c. menos** the less • **cuantos as many** • **unos cuantos** a few, some II. pron. all that, everything, as much as ♦ **unos cuantos** some, a few.
cuán·to, a I. adj. how much ♦ **¿cada c. tiempo?** how often? • **cuántos, cuántas** how many II. pron. how much ♦ **¿cuántos estamos hoy?** what is today's date? • **¿c. cuesta. . .?** how much is. . .? • **cuántos, cuántas** how many.
cua·ren·ta adj. & m. forty; *(cuadragésimo)* fortieth ♦ **cantarle las c. a alguien** COLL. to give someone a piece of one's mind.
cua·ren·ta·vo, a adj. fortieth.
cua·ren·te·na f. *(conjunto)* group of forty; MED. quarantine; COLL. *(aislamiento)* isolation.

cua·ren·tón, o·na adj. & m.f. forty-year-old.
cua·res·ma f. Lent.
cuar·ta f. *(medida)* span (of the hand); ASTRON. quadrant ♦ **andar de la c. al pértigo** R.P., COLL. to live from hand to mouth.
cuar·te·ar tr. *(dividir)* to quarter; *(descuartizar)* to cut up; *(fragmentar)* to crack —reflex. to crack.
cuar·tel m. MIL. barracks ♦ **c. de bomberos** firehouse • **no dar c. a** to show no mercy to • **sin c.** merciless.
cuar·to, a I. adj. fourth II. m. *(habitación)* room; *(cantidad)* fourth, quarter ♦ **c. creciente** first quarter (of the moon) • **c. de baño** bathroom • **c. de dormir** bedroom • **c. de estar** living room • **c. delantero** forequarter • **c. menguante** third quarter (of the moon) • **c. trasero** hindquarter • **c. y comida** room and board.
cuar·zo m. quartz.
cua·si adv. almost, quasi.
cua·te, a AMER. I. adj. *(gemelo)* twin; *(semejante)* similar, alike II. m.f. *(gemelo)* twin; *(amigo)* buddy, pal.
cua·tre·re·ar tr. R.P. to steal, rustle (cattle).
cua·tre·ro, a I. adj. *(de caballos)* pertaining to horse thievery; *(de vacas)* cattle-rustling; MEX., COLL. joking II. m.f. *(de caballos)* horse thief; AMER. *(de vacas)* cattle rustler; MEX., COLL. joker.
cua·tri·lli·zo, a m.f. quadruplet.
cua·tri·mo·tor m. four-engine plane.
cua·tro I. adj. four; *(cuarto)* fourth ♦ **las c.** four o'clock • **c. gatos locos** COLL. a mere handful of people II. m. four; S. AMER. four-string guitar ♦ **más de c.** COLL. quite a few.
cua·tro·cien·tos, as adj. & m. four hundred.
cu·ba f. *(tonel)* cask; *(tina)* vat ♦ **beber como una c.** COLL. to drink like a fish • **estar hecho una c.** COLL. to be plastered.
cu·be·ta f. *(cubo)* bucket; *(tina)* small vat; CHEM., PHOTOG. tray.
cú·bi·co, a adj. GEOM. cubic; MATH. cube (root).
cu·bier·to, a I. see **cubrir** II. m. *(de mesa)* table setting; *(abrigo)* shelter; *(comida)* meal (at a fixed price) ♦ **a c. de** under the protection of • **bajo c.** under cover • **poner los cubiertos** to set the table • **ponerse a c.** to take cover —f. *(cobertura)* cover; *(sobre)* envelope; *(envoltura)* wrapping; MARIT. deck; AUTO. tire.
cu·bil m. lair, den.
cu·bi·le·te m. *(vaso)* tumbler; *(de dados)* dicebox; *(molde)* mold.
cu·bis·ta adj. & m.f. ARTS cubist.
cú·bi·to m. ulna, cubit.
cu·bo m. cube; *(balde)* bucket; *(tina)* vat; *(de rueda)* hub; *(estanque)* millpond ♦ **a cubos** abundantly • **elevar al c.** MATH. to cube.
cu·bre·ca·de·na m. bicycle chainguard.
cu·bre·ca·ma m. bedcover, bedspread.
cu·brir §80 tr. to cover (up); *(proteger)* to protect; *(esconder)* to conceal; *(con honores, atenciones)* to shower —reflex. *(ponerse ropa)* to cover oneself; *(protegerse)* to protect oneself; COM. to cover a debt.
cu·ca·ra·cha f. cockroach.
cu·cli·llas adv. ♦ **en c.** squatting, crouching • **ponerse** or **sentarse en c.** to squat, crouch.
cu·co, a I. adj. COLL. *(bonito)* cute; *(astuto)* crafty II. m.f. clever person —m. ENTOM. caterpillar; ORNITH. cuckoo; *(fantasma)* ghost.

cu·cú m. cuckoo (call of the cuckoo).
cu·cha·ra f. spoon; *(cucharada)* spoonful; TECH. scoop ♦ **c. de albañil** trowel • **c. de postre** dessert spoon • **c. sopera** soupspoon • **meter la c.** COLL. to meddle.
cu·cha·ra·da f. spoonful.
cu·cha·rón m. *(cazo)* ladle; TECH. scoop.
cu·che·ta f. AMER. cabin, berth.
cu·chi·che·ar intr. to whisper.
cu·chi·che·o m. whisper, whispering.
cu·chi·lla f. *(cuchillo)* knife; *(hoja)* blade; *(de afeitar)* razor blade.
cu·chi·lla·da f./**zo** m. *(golpe)* stab; *(herida)* stab wound.
cu·chi·lle·rí·a f. cutler's shop.
cu·chi·llo m. knife ♦ **c. de cocina** kitchen knife • **pasar a c.** COLL. to kill.
cu·chi·tril m. COLL. pigsty.
cue·ce see **cocer**.
cue·le, lo see **colar**.
cuel·ga, gue see **colgar**.
cue·llo m. neck; *(tira de tela)* collar; BOT. stalk ♦ **alargar el c.** to stretch or crane one's neck • **c. alto** turtleneck • **c. de palomita** wing collar • **c. de pico** V-neck • **c. duro** stiff collar • **c. postizo** detachable collar.
cuen·ca f. ANAT. eye socket; GEOG. valley.
cuen·co m. earthenware bowl.
cuen·ta f. *(de restaurante)* check; *(cálculo)* calculation; *(acción de contar)* counting; *(bolita)* bead; COM. account; *(explicación)* account; *(cargo)* responsibility ♦ **abonar en c.** to credit an account • **a c.** on account • **caer en la c.** COLL. to realize • **cargar en c.** to debit an account • **c. acreedora** credit account • **c. bancaria** or **de banco** bank account • **c. corriente** checking account • **c. de ahorros** savings account • **c. de gastos** expense account • **dar c. de** *(contar)* to give an account of; COLL. *(gastar)* to use up • **darse c. de** to realize • **más de la c.** too much • **perder la c. de** to lose track of • **por c. de** on behalf of • **por su propia c.** for oneself • **por c. y riesgo de uno** at one's own risk • **tener en c.** to bear in mind • **tomar en c.** to take into account • **trabajar por su c.** to be self-employed ♦ pl. accounts • **a fin de c.** in the final analysis • **ajustar c.** COLL. to settle up • **en resumidas c.** in short • **llevar las c.** to keep the books • **pedir c. a** to call to account • **rendir c. de** to give an account of.
cuen·ta·go·tas m.inv. dropper, eyedropper ♦ **dar con c.** to give little by little.
cuen·ta·ki·ló·me·tros m.inv. odometer.
cuen·ta·rre·vo·lu·cio·nes m.inv. tachometer.
cuen·te, to see **contar**.
cuen·te·ro, a I. adj. gossipy II. m.f. gossipmonger.
cuen·tis·ta m.f. LIT. short-story writer; COLL. *(chismoso)* gossipmonger.
cuen·to m. story, tale; LIT. short story; *(chisme)* gossip; *(embuste)* hoax ♦ **c. de hadas** fairy tale • **c. del tío** con game • **c. de nunca acabar** endless story • **c. de viejas** COLL. old wives' tale • **¡puro c.!** all lies! • **traer a c.** COLL. to bring up • **venir a c.** to be to the point • **vivir del c.** COLL. to live by one's wits.
cuer·da f. *(cordón)* cord, string; *(del reloj)* watch spring; MUS. string ♦ **aflojar la c.** COLL. to ease up • **andar en la c. floja** COLL. to walk a tightrope • **bajo c.** underhandedly • **c. floja** tightrope • **dar c. a uno** COLL. to get someone

started on a topic • **dar c. a un reloj** to wind a watch ♦ pl. **c. vocales** ANAT. vocal cords.

cuer·do, a adj. & m.f. sane, sensible (person).

cue·re·ar tr. AMER. *(desollar)* to skin; R.P. *(criticar)* to slander.

cuer·no m. horn ♦ **c. de la abundancia** horn of plenty • **¡vete al c.!** go to hell! ♦ pl. **¡c.!** MEX. fat chance! • **poner los c. a** to cuckold.

cue·ro m. *(piel)* hide; *(de zapatos)* leather; *(odre)* wineskin • **c. cabelludo** scalp • **c. charolado** patent leather • **en cueros** naked.

cuer·pe·ar intr. AMER. to dodge.

cuer·po m. body; *(torso)* torso; *(figura)* figure; *(largo)* length; *(cadáver)* corpse; *(corpiño)* bodice; *(espesor)* thickness; *(parte)* component; GEOM. three-dimensional figure ♦ **a c. de rey** like a king • **c. a c.** hand-to-hand (combat) • **c. celeste** heavenly body • **c. de baile** dance company • **c. del delito** LAW corpus delicti • **c. diplomático** diplomatic corps • **dar con el c. en la tierra** to fall down • **dar c. a** to thicken • **de c. entero** full-length; FIG. real, true • **estar de c. presente** to lie in state • **ir de c.** COLL. to relieve oneself • **tomar c.** to take shape.

cuer·vo m. crow, raven.

cues·ta f. slope, hill ♦ **a cuestas** on one's shoulders; FIG. upon oneself • **c. abajo** downhill • **c. arriba** uphill • **hacérsele a uno arriba** COLL. to find it hard to.

cues·ta, te see **costar**.

cues·tión f. *(asunto)* question, matter <*es una c. de fe* it is a matter of faith>; *(duda)* dispute ♦ **en c. de** in the matter of.

cues·tio·na·ble adj. questionable, debatable.

cues·tio·nar tr. to discuss, debate.

cues·tio·na·rio m. *(encuesta)* questionnaire; *(examen)* test questions.

cue·va f. cave ♦ **c. de ladrones** COLL. den of thieves.

cueza, zo see **cocer**.

cui·da·do m. care; *(cautela)* caution; *(miedo)* concern ♦ **con c.** *(con esmero)* carefully; *(con cautela)* cautiously • **¡c.!** be careful!, watch out! • **c. con** beware of • **perder c.** not to worry • **poner c. en** to take care in • **sin c.** carelessly • **tener c.** to be careful.

cui·da·dor, ·ra I. adj. caretaking II. m.f. caretaker.

cui·da·do·so, a adj. *(cauteloso)* careful; *(atento)* attentive.

cui·dar tr. & intr. ♦ **c. de** to take care of —reflex. to take care of oneself ♦ **c. de** *(preocuparse)* to care about; *(protegerse)* to be careful about.

cui·ta f. grief.

cu·lan·tro m. coriander.

cu·la·ta f. *(del caballo)* croup; *(del arma)* butt; *(del cañón)* breech ♦ **salir el tiro por la c.** to backfire.

cu·la·ta·zo m. *(golpe)* blow with a gun butt; ARM. recoil.

cu·le·bra f. snake.

cu·le·bri·lla f. MED. ringworm.

cu·li·na·rio, a adj. culinary.

cul·mi·na·ción f. culmination.

cul·mi·nan·te adj. culminating.

cul·mi·nar intr. to culminate.

cul·pa f. blame, guilt; *(falta)* fault ♦ **por c. de** through the fault of • **echar la c. a uno** to blame someone • **tener la c.** to be to blame, be guilty.

cul·pa·bi·li·dad f. guilt.

cul·pa·ble I. adj. guilty; *(acusado)* accused ♦ **confesarse c.** to plead guilty • **declarar c.** to find guilty II. m.f. *(reo)* culprit; *(acusado)* accused (party).

cul·pa·do, a I. adj. guilty; *(acusado)* accused II. m.f. *(reo)* culprit; *(acusado)* accused (party).

cul·par tr. *(acusar)* to accuse; *(censurar)* to criticize.

cul·ti·va·ción f. cultivation.

cul·ti·va·dor, ·ra I. adj. cultivating II. m.f. cultivator.

cul·ti·var tr. to cultivate; *(arar)* to farm; *(plantar)* to grow; BIOL. to culture.

cul·ti·vo m. *(labor)* cultivation; *(cosecha)* crop; BIOL. culture ♦ **caldo de c.** culture fluid.

cul·to, a I. adj. *(civilizado)* cultured; *(instruido)* learned II. m. *(secta)* cult, religion; *(homenaje)* worship; *(rito)* ritual ♦ **rendir c. a** *(venerar)* to worship; *(homenajear)* to pay tribute to.

cul·tu·ra f. culture; *(educación)* refinement.

cul·tu·ral adj. cultural.

cum·bre m. summit; FIG. pinnacle.

cum·ple·a·ños m.inv. birthday.

cum·pli·do, a I. adj. *(completo)* complete; *(perfecto)* perfect; *(cortés)* courteous II. m. *(cortesía)* polite gesture; *(piropo)* compliment.

cum·pli·dor, ·ra I. adj. trustworthy, reliable II. m.f. reliable person.

cum·pli·men·tar tr. *(felicitar)* to congratulate; *(visitar)* to pay one's respects to; *(ejecutar)* to carry out.

cum·pli·mien·to m. fulfillment; *(cortesía)* polite gesture.

cum·plir tr. *(llevar a cabo)* to carry out; *(la palabra)* to keep; *(los años)* to be; *(la ley)* to obey; *(una condena)* to serve —intr. ♦ **c. con** *(promesa)* to fulfill; *(obligaciones)* to fulfill one's obligations • **por c.** as a formality —reflex. *(realizarse)* to be fulfilled; COM. to fall due.

cú·mu·lo m. pile; *(nube)* cumulus.

cu·na f. *(cama)* cradle; *(origen)* stock; *(lugar de nacimiento)* birthplace ♦ **canción de c.** lullaby.

cun·dir intr. *(extenderse)* to spread; *(inflar)* to expand ♦ **cunde la voz que** rumor has it that.

cu·nei·for·me adj. cuneiform; BOT. cuneate.

cu·ne·ta f. *(de un foso)* ditch; *(de una calle)* gutter.

cu·ña f. wedge; ANAT. tarsal bone; PRINT. quoin ♦ **meter c.** to sow discord • **tener cuñas** R.P. to have pull or influence.

cu·ña·do, a m.f. brother/sister-in-law.

cu·ño m. *(troquel)* die; *(impresión)* impression; FIG. mark ♦ **de nuevo c.** new.

cuo·ta f. *(parte)* quota, share; *(pago)* fee, dues ♦ **c. de admisión** admission fee.

cu·pé m. coupé.

cu·pie·ra, po see **caber**.

cu·plé m. popular song, variety song.

cu·po m. quota.

cu·pón m. coupon.

cú·pu·la f. dome, cupola.

cu·ra¹ m. RELIG. priest.

cu·ra² f. *(curación)* cure; *(apósito)* dressing ♦ **no tener c.** COLL. to be incorrigible.

cu·ra·ble adj. curable.

cu·ra·ción f. cure, treatment.

cu·ra·do, a adj. *(endurecido)* inured; *(curtido)* tanned ♦ **estoy c. de espanto** nothing can shock me anymore.

cu·ran·de·ro, a m.f. quack.
cu·rar intr. ♦ **c. de** MED. to recover from —tr. MED. *(sanar)* to cure; *(tratar)* to treat; FIG. to soothe; *(cueros)* to tan; *(madera)* to season; *(carnes)* to cure ♦ **c. al humo** to smoke —reflex. *(recobrarse)* to get well; *(sanarse)* to heal.
cu·ra·re m. curare.
cu·ra·ti·vo, a adj. & f. curative.
cur·da COLL. m. *(persona)* drunk —f. *(borrachera)* drunkenness ♦ **agarrarse una c.** COLL. to get drunk.
cu·ria f. *(tribunal)* court; LAW bar.
cu·rio m. curium.
cu·rio·se·ar intr. to snoop, pry.
cu·rio·si·dad f. curiosity; *(cosa curiosa)* curio.
cu·rio·so, a I. adj. curious; *(limpio)* neat; *(cuidadoso)* careful; *(excepcional)* odd II. m.f. curious person; *(entremetido)* busybody.
cu·rrí·cu·lum vi·tae m. resumé.
cur·sar tr. *(estudiar)* to study; *(dar curso a)* to attend to.
cur·si adj. *(presumido)* pretentious; *(de mal gusto)* tasteless.
cur·si·le·rí·a s. pretentiousness, snobbery.
cur·si·llo m. *(curso)* short course; *(conferencias)* series of lectures.
cur·si·vo, a I. adj. cursive; PRINT. italic II. f. cursive script; PRINT. italics.
cur·so m. course; FIN. circulation ♦ **c. acelerado** crash course • **c. por correspondencia** correspondence course • **dar libre c. a** to give free rein to ♦ **en c.** under way • **tener c. legal** to be legal tender.
cur·ti·do m. tanning ♦ **pl.** tanned leather.
cur·ti·dor m. tanner.
cur·tiem·bre m. *(proceso)* tanning; *(factory)* tannery.
cur·ti·mien·to m. tanning.
cur·tir tr. *(adobar)* to tan; *(acostumbrar)* to inure —reflex. *(por la intemperie)* to become weather-beaten; *(acostumbrarse)* to become inured.
cur·va f. curve; *(recodo)* curve, bend ♦ **c. cerrada** sharp curve.
cur·va·do, a adj. curved, bent.
cur·var tr. to curve, bend.
cur·va·tu·ra f. *(recodo)* curvature; *(acción)* curving.
cur·ve·ar intr. to curve.
cur·vi·lí·ne·o, a adj. curvilinear.
cur·vo, a adj. curved, bent.
cús·pi·de f. summit; FIG. pinnacle; ANAT., BOT. cusp.
cus·to·dia f. *(vigilia)* custody; *(cuidado)* care; *(persona)* custodian.
cus·to·diar tr. *(cuidar)* to take care of; *(vigilar)* to watch over; *(proteger)* to protect.
cus·to·dio adj. & m. guardian.
cu·tá·ne·o, a adj. cutaneous, skin.
cu·tí·cu·la f. cuticle.
cu·tis m.inv. skin, complexion.
cu·yo, a a rel. pron. whose; *(personas)* of whom; *(cosas)* of which.

CH

ch, Ch f. fourth letter of the Spanish alphabet.
cha·ba·ca·ne·ar intr. AMER. to behave in a coarse or crude way.
cha·ba·ca·ne·rí·a f. *(falta de gusto)* tastelessness; *(grosería)* crude thing.
cha·ba·ca·no, a adj. *(sin gusto)* tasteless; *(grosero)* crude; *(mal hecho)* shoddy.
cha·cal m. jackal.
cha·ca·re·ro, a m.f. AMER. farmer, peasant —f. R.P. peasant dance.
cha·co·ta f. *(bulla)* merriment, fun; *(burla)* ridicule, making fun ♦ **estar de ch.** to be in a joking mood • **hacer ch. de** to ridicule • **tomar a ch.** *(burlarse de)* to make fun of; *(tomar a broma)* to take as a joke.
cha·co·te·ar intr. to kid.
cha·co·te·o m. joking, kidding.
cha·co·te·ro, a m.f. kidder.
cha·cra f. AMER. farm.
chá·cha·ra f. COLL. chatter ♦ **estar de ch.** to make small talk.
cha·cha·re·ar intr. COLL. *(charlar)* to chatter.
cha·fa·lo·ní·a f. scrap silver or gold.
chai·ra f. shoemaker's knife.
cha·já m. ARG. crested screamer.
chal m. shawl.
cha·la f. AMER. corn husk or shuck.
cha·lán, a·na I. adj. horse-trading II. m.f. *(comerciante)* horse dealer or trader —m. AMER. horse trainer —f. barge, flat-bottomed boat.
cha·lar tr. to drive mad or crazy —reflex. to fall head over heels in love.
cha·le·co m. vest ♦ **ch. de fuerza** AMER. straitjacket • **ch. salvavidas** life jacket.
cha·let m. [pl. **s**] chalet; *(de playa)* beach house; *(de lujo)* villa.
cha·li·na f. *(corbata)* cravat; AMER. *(chal)* narrow shawl.
cha·lo·te m. shallot.
cha·lu·pa f. boat; AMER. small canoe.
cha·ma·co, a m.f. CARIB., MEX. kid.
cham·be·lán m. chamberlain.
cham·ber·go m. AMER. broad-brimmed soft hat.
cham·be·ro, a m.f. MEX. itinerant worker.
cham·bón, o·na COLL. I. adj. clumsy II. m.f. bungler.
cham·bo·na·da f. AMER. bungle.
cham·bo·ne·ar intr. AMER. to bungle.
cha·mi·za f. BOT. chamiso; *(leña)* brushwood.
cha·mi·zar §04 tr. AMER. to thatch (with chamiso).
cha·mi·zo m. *(leño quemado)* half-burnt log; *(choza)* thatched hut; COLL. *(garito)* joint.
cha·mo·rro, a adj. shorn, clipped.
cham·pán/pa·ña m. champagne.
cham·pi·ñón m. mushroom, champignon.
cham·pú m. [pl. **(e)s**] shampoo.
cham·pu·rra·do m. AMER. hodgepodge, mess.
cham·pu·rrar tr. COLL. to mix (drinks).
cham·pu·rro m. COLL. mixed drink.
cha·mu·llar intr. AMER., SL. to talk, speak.
cha·mus·car §70 tr. *(quemar)* to scorch; MEX. to sell cheaply —reflex. *(quemarse)* to get singed or scorched.
cha·mus·qui·na f. *(acción)* scorching; *(riña)* quarrel ♦ **oler a ch.** to look like trouble.
chan·ca·do·ra f. AMER., MIN. crusher, grinder.
chan·car §70 tr. AMER. to crush, grind.
chan·ce m. chance.
chan·ce·ar intr. & reflex. to joke.
chan·ci·ller m. var. of **canciller.**
chan·ci·lle·rí·a f. chancery.
chan·cle·ta f. COLL. *(zapatilla)* slipper; AMER., COLL. baby girl ♦ **largar la ch.** COLL. to let one's hair down.

chan·cle·ta·zo m. blow with a slipper.

chan·cle·te·ar intr. to drag around (in slippers).

chan·cle·te·o m. shuffle of slippers.

chan·clo m. (zueco) clog; (zapato) galosh.

chan·cro m. chancre.

chan·cha·da f. AMER., COLL. dirty trick; (porquería) mess.

chan·cho, a I. adj. AMER. dirty, filthy II. m. pig, hog ♦ **hacerse un ch. rengo** AMER. to pretend not to notice • **quedar como ch.** AMER. to let someone down • **ser como chanchos** AMER. to be close friends —f. AMER. sow.

chan·chu·lle·ro, a m.f. crook, swindler.

chan·chu·llo m. COLL. crooked deal ♦ pl. **andar en ch.** to be involved in swindles.

chan·ga·dor m. ARG., BOL. porter.

chan·gar §47 intr. AMER. (picholear) to do odd jobs; ARG., BOL. to work as a porter.

chan·go, a I. adj. CARIB., MEX. playful II. m.f. CARIB., MEX. (bromista) prankster; MEX. youngster —m. R.P. youngster.

chan·ta·je m. blackmail.

chan·ta·jis·ta m.f. blackmailer.

chan·tar tr. (clavar) to drive in; COLL. (cantárselas) to tell to someone's face.

chan·ti·llí m. whipped cream.

chan·za f. jeke, jest ♦ **de o en ch.** in fun • **estar de ch.** to be joking • ♦ pl. **entre ch. y veras** half in fun and half in earnest • **gastar ch.** to crack jokes.

cha·pa f. (de metal, madera) sheet; AMER., AUTO. license plate ♦ **ch. de estarcir** stencil • **ch. metálica** sheet metal.

cha·pa·do, a adj. (de metal) plated; (de madera) veneered ♦ **ch. a la antigua** old-fashioned.

cha·pe·le·ar tr. to splash.

cha·pa·le·o m. splash; (acción) splashing.

cha·pa·po·te m. asphalt.

cha·par tr. (con metal) to plate; (con madera) to veneer; (encajar) to come out with; AMER., SL. (agarrar) to grasp; (apresar) to catch.

cha·pa·rral m. thicket, chaparral.

cha·pa·rro, a I. adj. short and thick II. m. dwarf or scrub oak; (persona) short and chubby man; MEX. (niño) kid.

cha·pa·rrón m. downpour; FIG. shower.

cha·pe·ar tr. (con metal) to plate; (con madera) to veneer; AMER. to clear (the land).

cha·pis·ta m. sheet-metal worker; AUTO. body repairman.

cha·po·dar tr. to prune; FIG. to trim.

cha·po·te·ar tr. to dampen —intr. to splash.

cha·po·te·o m. splash.

cha·pu·ce·ar tr. COLL. (chafallar) to botch, bungle; MEX. (engañar) to deceive.

cha·pu·ce·rí·a f. COLL. sloppy job.

cha·pu·ce·ro, a I. adj. COLL. sloppy II. m.f. careless worker.

cha·puz m. (obra) odd job; (acción) ducking; (chapucería) botched job.

cha·pu·za f. COLL. botched job.

cha·pu·zón m. dive ♦ **darse un ch.** to go for a swim.

cha·qué/quet m. morning coat.

cha·que·ta f. jacket ♦ **ch. de fumar** smoking jacket • **ch. salvavidas** life jacket.

cha·que·ti·lla f. short jacket, bolero.

cha·que·tón m. overcoat.

cha·ra·da f. charade.

cha·ra·mus·ca f. MEX. candy twist; AMER.

(leña) brushwood; CUBA, P. RICO noise.

cha·ran·ga f. brass band.

cha·ran·go m. AMER. small five-stringed Andean guitar.

cha·ra·pe m. MEX. spicy fermented beverage.

char·ca f. pond, pool.

char·co m. puddle, pool.

char·la f. (conversación) chat; (conferencia) talk.

char·la·dor, ·ra I. adj. talkative II. m.f. chatterbox.

char·lar intr. COLL. (parlotear) to chatter; (hablar) to chat.

char·la·tán, a·na I. adj. (parlanchín) talkative, (chismoso) gossipy II. m.f. (parlanchín) chatterbox; (murmurador) gossip; (curandero) quack.

char·la·ta·ne·ar intr. to chatter.

char·la·ta·ne·rí·a f. talkativeness.

char·lis·ta m.f. lecturer.

char·lo·te·ar intr. COLL. to chatter.

cha·rol m. (barniz) lacquer; (cuero) patent leather; AMER. (bandeja) tray.

cha·ro·la·do, a adj. (barnizado) varnished; (lustroso) shiny.

cha·ro·lar tr. to lacquer.

char·que m. AMER., MEX. jerky.

char·que·ar tr. AMER. to dry, cure.

char·qui m. AMER. jerky.

cha·rre·te·ra f. epaulet(te).

cha·rro, a I. adj. (tosco) unsophisticated; COLL. (de mal gusto) gaudy; AMER. (diestro) skilled in horsemanship; MEX. (pintoresco) picturesque II. m. MEX. cowboy.

cha·rrú·a f. small tugboat.

¡chas! interj. pow!, wham!

ohas·ca f. kindling.

chas·car §70 intr. (la madera) to crack; (la lengua) to click —tr. to crunch.

chas·co m. (burla) trick; (decepción) disappointment.

cha·sis m.inv. chassis.

chas·que·ar¹ tr. (burlarse) to play a joke on; (decepcionar) to disappoint.

chas·que·ar² tr. (látigo) to crack; (dedos) to snap —intr. to crackle.

chas·qui m. AMER. (mensajero) messenger; (correo) mail.

chas·qui·do m. crack, snap.

cha·ta·rra f. scrap iron.

cha·ta·rre·rí·a f. junk yard.

cha·to, a I. adj. (de nariz) flat-nosed; (la nariz) flat; (bajo) low; (llano) shallow; AMER., COLL. ordinary ♦ **dejar ch.** AMER. to defeat; MEX. to swindle • **quedarse ch.** AMER. to fail II. m. (querido) darling; (vaso) small wine glass —f. (embarcación) barge; (bacín) bedpan; AMER. (carro) flatcar; COLL. (querida) darling.

cha·tu·ra f. flatness.

¡chau! interj. AMER. goodbye, ciao.

chau·cha f. S. AMER. (patata) new potato; (dinero) money; ARG. (judía) string bean.

chau·vi·nis·ta I. adj. chauvinistic II. m.f. chauvinist.

cha·val, ·la I. adj. young II. m. youngster —f. young girl.

cha·ve·ta f. (clavija) key; COLL. (chiflado) nut ♦ **perder la ch.** COLL. to go off one's rocker.

¡che! interj. AMER. hey!, listen!

che·lo m. I. m. cello II. adj. MEX. blond.

che·que m. check, cheque (G.B.) ♦ **ch. de viajero** travelers check.

che·que·ar tr. AMER. *(inspeccionar)* to check, inspect; *(cotejar)* to compare; MED. to give a checkup to.

che·que·o m. AMER. check; MED. checkup.

che·que·ra f./ro m. checkbook.

chi·bo·lo m. AMER. swelling, bump.

chic adj. chic, stylish.

chi·ca·na f. AMER. chicanery, trickery.

chi·ca·ne·ar intr. AMER. to engage in chicanery.

chi·ca·no, a adj. & m.f. Chicano, Mexican-American.

chi·cle m. *(de mascar)* chewing gum; *(gomorresina)* chicle; MEX. *(suciedad)* filth.

chi·co, a I. adj. small, little II. m. boy —f. girl; *(criada)* maid.

chi·co·ria f. chicory.

chi·co·ta·zo m. AMER. whiplash.

chi·co·te m. AMER. whip; MARIT. end of a rope; COLL. *(cigarro)* cigar.

chi·cha f. *(bebida)* chicha; COLL. *(carne)* meat ♦ **estar ch.** MEX. to be pleasant *or* amusing.

chí·cha·ro m. pea; COL., COLL. bad cigar.

chi·cha·rra f. cicada; COLL. *(persona)* chatterbox; SP. nuisance ♦ **hablar como una ch.** to be a real chatterbox.

chi·cha·rre·ro m. hot place, oven.

chi·cha·rro m. ICHTH. horse mackerel; *(chicharrón)* fried pork rind.

chi·cha·rrón m. *(cerdo)* crisp pork rind; FIG. overcooked *or* burned food; COLL. *(persona)* very tanned person.

chi·che I. m. AMER. *(persona)* elegant person; *(lugar)* well-decorated place; ARG. *(juguete)* toy; ARG., CHILE *(alhaja)* trinket, bauble; MEX. *(nodriza)* wet nurse II. adj. C. AMER. easy, comfortable.

chi·chón m. bump (on the head).

chi·cho·ne·ar intr. S. AMER., COLL. to make *or* play jokes.

chi·cho·ta f. AMER. bump; *(legumbre)* chickpea.

chi·fla f. *(acción)* whistling; *(silbato)* whistle; *(cuchillo)* paring knife; MEX. bad mood.

chi·fla·do, a adj. COLL. *(loco)* nuts; *(enamorado)* in love.

chi·fla·du·ra f. COLL. *(locura)* craziness; *(silbido)* whistling.

chi·flar intr. to whistle; MEX., ORNITH. to sing —tr. to boo —reflex. *(volverse loco)* to go crazy; *(enamorarse)* to fall in love; COLL. *(gustar)* to be crazy about.

chi·fle m. *(silbato)* whistle; *(reclamo)* bird call; *(para la pólvora)* powder horn.

chi·fli·do m. whistle.

chi·hua·hua m. chihuahua.

chi·le m. AMER. pepper, chili; C. AMER. *(patraña)* hoax.

chi·lla·do m. CARP. roof made of laths and shingles.

chi·lla·dor, ·ra I. adj. screaming, shrieking II. m.f. screamer.

chi·llar intr. *(gritar)* to shriek; *(chirriar)* to squeak; *(destacarse)* to be loud —reflex. AMER. to take offense.

chi·lli·do m. *(grito)* shriek; *(chirrido)* squeak.

chi·llón, o·na I. adj. COLL. *(gritón)* shrieking; *(estridente)* loud II. m.f. screamer.

chi·me·ne·a f. chimney; *(hogar)* fireplace, hearth; INDUS. smokestack; MARIT. stack ♦ **caerle a uno una cosa por la ch.** COLL. to receive a windfall ♦ **ch. de aire** air shaft.

chim·pan·cé m. chimpanzee.

chi·na f. see **chino, a.**

chi·nam·pa f. MEX. floating garden near Mexico City.

chin·char tr. *(molestar)* to pester; *(causar molestia)* to bother —reflex. to get upset.

chin·che f. bedbug; *(clavito)* thumbtack ♦ **morir como chinches** to drop like flies —m.f. COLL. boring person.

chin·che·ta f. thumbtack.

chin·chi·lla f. chinchilla.

chin·cho·rro m. *(red)* sweep net; *(bote de remos)* dinghy; MEX. small herd.

chin·chu·do, a adj. ARG. hot-tempered.

chi·ne·la f. *(babucha)* slipper; *(chanclo)* clog.

chin·ga f. AMER. *(barato)* fee paid by gamblers; ZOOL. skunk; C. AMER. cigar butt.

chin·gar §47 tr. C. RICA to cut the tail off of; MEX., SALV. to harass —reflex. AMER. *(fracasar)* to be a flop.

chin·go, a adj. AMER. *(corto)* ill-fitting; *(desnudo)* without a stitch; *(rabón)* tailless; C. AMER. *(mocho)* blunt.

chi·no, a I. adj. AMER. of mixed ancestry; MEX. kinky, curly II. m.f. AMER. *(mestizo)* person of mixed ancestry; *(niño)* kid; *(criado)* servant; *(cariño)* honey; *(campesino)* peasant ♦ **trabajar como un ch.** COLL. to work like a slave —f. *(india)* Indian woman; *(sirvienta)* maid; *(niñera)* nanny; *(tejido)* Chinese silk.

chi·que·ro m. *(pocilga)* pigsty; TAUR. bullpen.

chi·qui·lín m. AMER., COLL. small boy.

chi·qui·lla·da f. childish act.

chi·qui·llo, a I. adj. small II. m.f. child.

chi·qui·tín, i·na I. adj. tiny II. m.f. tot.

chi·qui·to, a I. adj. tiny II. m.f. *(niño)* child —m. R.P. ♦ **esperar un ch.** COLL. to wait just a minute.

chi·ri·bi·ta f. spark ♦ pl. spots before the eyes ♦ **echar ch.** COLL. to be fuming.

chi·ri·bi·til m. *(desván)* garret, attic; COLL. *(cuarto)* tiny room.

chi·ri·go·ta f. COLL. joke, quip.

chi·ri·go·te·ar intr. COLL. to joke, banter.

chi·ri·go·te·ro, a I. adj. joking, bantering II. m.f. joker.

chi·rim·bo·lo m. COLL. gadget ♦ pl. COLL. gear.

chi·ri·mo·ya f. cherimoya.

chi·ri·mo·yo m. cherimoya tree.

chi·ri·pa f. stroke of luck ♦ **de** *or* **por ch.** COLL. by a fluke.

chi·ri·pá m. R.P. gaucho's trousers.

chir·lar intr. COLL. to chatter, jabber.

chir·le I. adj. COLL. tasteless II. m. dung.

chir·lo m. *(herida)* gash (on face); *(cicatriz)* scar.

chi·ro·la f. AMER. *(moneda)* coin of little value; *(cárcel)* slammer.

chi·rre·ar intr. var. of **chirriar.**

chi·rria·dor, ·ra/rrian·te adj. *(un gozne)* creaking; *(al freír)* sizzling; *(un pájaro)* chirping; COLL. *(una voz)* shrill.

chi·rriar §30 intr. *(rechinar)* to squeak; *(al freír)* to sizzle; ORNITH. to screech; COLL. *(cantar)* to sing out of tune.

chi·rri·do m. *(ruido)* screeching; COLL. *(grito)* shriek; *(al freír)* sizzle.

¡chis! interj. sh!, hush!

chis·ca·rra f. soft crumbly limestone.

chis·cón m. SL. garret, closet (small room).

chis·chás m. clash (of swords).

chis·ga·ra·bís m. COLL. busybody, meddler.

chis·gue·te m. COLL. *(trago)* swig, drink; *(chorro)* jet, spurt; AMER., BOT. rubber tree.

chis·mar intr. var. of chismear.

chis·me m. *(murmuración)* gossip; COLL. *(baratija)* trinket.

chis·me·ar intr. to gossip.

chis·me·rí·a f. gossip.

chis·me·ro, a I. adj. gossiping, tattling II. m.f. gossipmonger.

chis·mo·gra·fí·a f. COLL. *(afición)* fondness for gossip; *(cuento)* gossiping.

chis·mo·rre·ar intr. to gossip.

chis·mo·so, a I. adj. gossipy II. m.f. gossipmonger.

chis·pa I. f. *(chiribita)* spark; *(relámpago)* flash; *(poquito)* little bit; *(de lluvia)* sprinkle; *(viveza)* wit; COLL. *(borrachera)* drunkenness ♦ **ser una ch.** or **tener mucha ch.** to be a live wire ♦ pl. **dar ch.** to be bright • **echar ch.** to fume (with anger) • **ni ch.** not the least bit II. adj. MEX. amusing, funny.

chis·par tr. MEX. to take out —reflex. COLL. to get drunk or tipsy.

chis·pa·zo m. spark.

chis·pe·ar intr. *(destellar)* to spark; *(relucir)* to sparkle; *(lloviznar)* to drizzle; *(brillar)* to be brilliant —unipers. AMER. to get tipsy.

chis·po·rro·te·ar intr. to spark, crackle.

chis·po·rro·te·o m. COLL. *(del aceite)* sizzling; *(de la leña)* crackling.

¡chist! interj. sh!, hush!

chis·tar intr. to speak ♦ **sin ch.** COLL. without a word.

chis·te m. *(cuento)* joke; *(prank)* broma ♦ **caer en el ch.** COLL. to get the joke • **ch. verde** dirty or off-color joke • **dar en el ch.** to guess the trouble • **hacer ch. de** to make a joke of.

chis·te·ra f. *(de pescador)* fisherman's basket; COLL. *(sombrero)* top hat.

chis·ti·do m. whistle.

chis·to·so, a adj. funny.

chi·ta f. ANAT. anklebone; *(juego)* game of throwing stones at an upright bone ♦ **a la ch. callando** on the quiet or sly • **dar en la ch.** to hit the nail on the head.

chi·tar intr. var. of chistar.

¡chi·to! interj. hush!, sh!

¡chi·tón! interj. COLL. hush!, quiet!

chi·va f. AMER. *(barba)* goatee; C. AMER. *(manta)* blanket ♦ pl. MEX. odds and ends.

chi·var tr. COLL. *(fastidiar)* to annoy; *(delatar)* to denounce —reflex. COLL. to get annoyed.

chi·va·te·o m. COLL. *(delación)* informing; AMER. *(gritería)* shouting.

chi·va·to, a m.f. ZOOL. kid; COLL. *(delator)* informer, stool pigeon.

chi·vo, a m.f. ZOOL. kid ♦ **ch. expiatorio** scapegoat.

cho·can·te adj. *(desagradable)* offensive; MEX. annoying.

cho·car §70 intr. *(topar)* to crash; *(pelear)* to clash; COLL. *(disgustar)* to offend ♦ **ch. los cinco** COLL. to shake hands • **ch. de frente** to hit head on.

cho·ca·rre·ar intr. to tell dirty jokes.

cho·ca·rre·rí·a f. dirty joke.

cho·ca·rre·ro, a I. adj. coarse II. m.f. teller of dirty jokes.

cho·clo m. *(chanclo)* clog; AMER. *(maíz)* ear of corn; *(carga)* burden; PERU *(conjunto)* bunch, group; ARG. *(dificultad)* difficulty ♦ **meter el**

ch. MEX. to make a mistake.

cho·co I. m. small cuttlefish; CHILE, PERU spaniel; AMER. disabled person; AUTO. brake shoe II. adj. AMER. disabled.

cho·co·la·te I. adj. chocolate II. m. chocolate; *(bebida)* hot chocolate, cocoa.

cho·co·la·te·rí·a f. *(fábrica)* chocolate factory; *(tienda)* chocolate shop.

cho·co·la·te·ro, a I. m.f. *(fabricante)* chocolate maker; *(vendedor)* chocolate seller II. adj. fond of chocolate.

cho·cha·per·diz f. woodcock.

cho·che·ar/char intr. to be senile.

cho·che·ra/chez f. *(senilidad)* senility; COLL. *(admiración)* fondness, doting.

cho·cho, a adj. *(caduco)* senile; COLL. *(lelo)* doting.

chó·fer or **cho·fer** m. chauffeur.

cho·lo, a adj. & m.f. half-breed, mestizo.

chom·ba/pa f. jersey, sweater.

chon·go m. GUAT. curl, lock (of hair); MEX. *(moño)* bun, chignon; *(dulce)* sweet, dessert; COLL. *(broma)* joke; PERU *(querido)* darling.

cho·po m. black poplar; COLL. *(fusil)* rifle, gun.

cho·que m. *(colisión)* collision; *(impacto)* impact; *(pelea)* clash; *(disputa)* dispute; ELEC., MED. shock ♦ **ch. de frente** head-on collision

cho·ri·ce·rí·a f. sausage shop.

cho·ri·ce·ro, a m.f. *(fabricante)* sausage maker; *(vendedor)* sausage seller; SP. frontier dweller.

cho·ri·zo m. sausage.

chor·li·to m. plover, *(tonto)* scatterbrain.

cho·rre·a·du·ra f. *(chorrea)* dripping; *(mancha)* stain.

cho·rre·ar intr. *(fluir)* to gush; *(gotear)* to trickle —tr. *(derramar)* to pour; R.P. to steal —reflex. to steal.

cho·rre·ra f. *(canal)* gully; *(serie)* string.

cho·rro m. *(de líquido)* spout; *(de luz)* flood; R.P., COLL. thief ♦ pl. **a ch.** abundantly • **llo·ver a ch.** to rain cats and dogs • **salir a ch.** to gush out.

cho·ta·ca·bras m.pl. nightjar, goatsucker.

cho·tis m. schottische (dance).

cho·to, a m.f. *(cabrito)* kid; *(ternero)* calf.

cho·va f. chough, jackdaw.

cho·za f. hut, shack.

chu·bas·co m. *(lluvia)* downpour; *(contratiempo)* setback.

chú·ca·ro, a adj. AMER. *(salvaje)* wild; *(huraño)* shy.

chu·ce·ar tr. AMER. to wound with a pike or lance.

chu·che·ar intr. *(cazar)* to trap, snare; *(cuchichear)* to whisper.

chu·che·rí·a f. trinket.

chu·cho, a m. COLL. *(perro)* dog; AMER. *(escalofrío)* shivers; ARG. *(susto)* fright —f. body odor.

chue·co, a adj. *(patizambo)* bowlegged; *(torcido)* crooked.

chu·la·da f. *(acción)* coarse action; COLL. *(gracia)* self-assurance; *(jactancia)* showing off.

chu·le·ar tr. MEX. to court, flirt with; COLL. to play a joke on —reflex. *(burlarse)* to make fun of, tease; COLL. *(presumir)* to show off.

chu·le·rí·a f. COLL. wit, verve.

chu·le·ta f. *(carne)* cutlet; COLL. *(de estudiantes)* cheat sheet, crib.

chu·lo, a I. adj. *(picaresco)* roguish; *(chulesco)* showy; *(descarado)* impudent II. m.f. SP.

lower-class Madrilenian —m. *(rufián)* rascal; *(alcahuete)* pimp.

chum·bar tr. R.P. to bark.

chu·ño m. AMER. potato starch.

chu·pa·ci·rios m.inv. COLL. sanctimonious person.

chu·pa·do, a I. adj. COLL. emaciated; ARG., CHILE, CUBA drunk II. f. sucking.

chu·pa·dor, ·ra I. adj. sucking II. m. *(chupete)* pacifier; *(de biberón)* nipple —m.f. boozer.

chu·par tr. to suck; *(absorber)* to soak up; AMER. *(fumar)* to smoke; COLL. *(extraer)* to bleed —intr. to suck; AMER. *(beber)* to drink —reflex. to become emaciated, waste away ♦ **ch. el dedo** COLL. to be naive • **ch. los dedos** COLL. to lick one's fingers ♦ **¡chúpate esa!** COLL. take that!

chu·pa·tin·tas m.inv. COLL. pencil-pusher.

chu·pe·te m. *(de niños)* pacifier; *(de mamadera)* nipple; AMER. *(dulce)* lollipop.

chu·pe·te·ar intr. to suck, take little licks.

chu·pón, o·na I. adj. sucking II. m.f leech —m. COLL. *(beso)* hickey; MIN. piston, plunger; AMER. *(biberón)* baby bottle; *(chupete)* pacifier; *(de mamadera)* nipple.

chur·dón m. raspberry jam.

chu·rras·co m. AMER. grilled or broiled steak.

chu·rras·que·ar intr. AMER. to have a barbecue.

chu·rre m. *(pringue)* thick grease or fat; COLL. *(suciedad)* filth.

chu·rre·ro, a m.f. *(fabricante)* fritter maker; *(vendedor)* fritter seller.

chu·rre·te m. stain.

chu·rrien·to, a adj. grimy.

chu·rro, a I. adj. coarse II. m. CUL. fritter; COLL. *(chapuza)* botch.

chu·rru·lle·ro, a adj. & m.f. talkative (person).

chu·rrus·car·se §70 reflex. to start to burn.

chu·rrus·co m. burnt toast.

chu·rum·bel m. COLL. kid, youngster.

chu·ru·mo m. COLL. juice.

chus·ca·da f. joke, witticism.

chus·ma f. *(galeotes)* crew of galley slaves; *(gentuza)* riffraff; COLL. *(multitud)* crowd.

chu·zo m. *(bastón)* stick; AMER. *(látigo)* horsewhip; *(aguijada)* goad; *(pica)* pike.

D

d, D f. fifth letter of the Spanish alphabet.

da·ble adj. possible, feasible.

dac·ti·lo·gra·fí·a f. typewriting, typing.

dac·ti·ló·gra·fo m.f. typist.

dá·di·va f. present, gift.

da·di·vo·si·dad f. generosity, liberality.

da·di·vo·so, a adj. generous, lavish.

da·do, a I. adj. given II. m. die ♦ **correr el d.** COLL. to be in luck ♦ pl. dice • **cargar los d.** to load the dice.

da·dor, ·ra I. adj. giving II. m.f. donor.

da·ga f. dagger; AMER. machete.

da·gue·rro·ti·po m. daguerreotype.

da·lia f. dahlia.

dal·to·nis·mo m. colorblindness.

da·ma f. lady; *(de la reina)* lady-in-waiting; *(manceba)* mistress, concubine; *(actriz)* actress; *(en damas)* king; *(en ajedrez, naipes)* queen ♦ **d. de honor** maid of honor ♦ pl. checkers, draughts (G.B.)

da·ma·jua·na f. demijohn.

da·mas·co m. damask.

da·mi·se·la f. damsel; *(cortesana)* courtesan.

dam·ni·fi·car §70 tr. to damage, harm.

dam·ni·fi·ca·do, a I. adj. damaged, harmed; II. m.f. victim.

dan·ta f. *(anta)* elk; *(tapir)* tapir.

dan·za f. dance; COLL. shady business deal; *(riña)* quarrel ♦ **andar** or **estar en la d.** COLL. to be mixed up in a shady deal • **d. de figuras** square dance.

dan·za·dor, ·ra I. adj. dancing II. m.f. dancer.

dan·zan·te I. adj. dancing II. m.f. dancer; *(estafador)* hustler; *(cabeza de chorlito)* scatterbrain; *(entremetido)* busybody.

dan·zar §04 tr. to dance —intr. *(bailar)* to dance; *(temblar)* to dance, bob up and down; COLL. *(entremeterse)* to get mixed up or involved.

dan·za·rín, i·na m.f. dancer.

da·ña·do, a adj. evil, wicked; *(perjudicado)* damaged.

da·ñar tr. to damage, harm —reflex. to become damaged; *(echarse a perder)* to spoil, go bad.

da·ñi·no, a adj. damaging, harmful.

da·ño m. damage, harm ♦ **hacer d.** *(doler)* to hurt; *(perjudicar)* to harm, injure.

dar §20 tr. to give; *(conferir)* to grant; *(proponer)* to propose, offer; *(sacrificar)* to give up; *(repartir)* to deal; *(producir)* to produce, bear; *(soltar)* to give off, emit; *(propinar)* to deal <*el ladrón le dio un tremendo golpe* the thief dealt him a tremendous blow>; *(imponer)* to impose; *(sonar)* to strike <*el reloj dio las dos* the clock struck two>; THEAT. to show; *(aplicar)* to apply, put on; *(comunicar)* to express, convey ♦ **d. a conocer** to make known • **d. a luz** to give birth; FIG. to publish, print • **d. aviso** to give notice • **d. cabezadas** to nod, doze • **d. como** *(considerar)* to regard, consider; *(producir)* to produce • **d. cuenta de** to report on, account for • **d. cuerda a** to wind (clocks); FIG. *(alargar)* to prolong; *(animar)* to encourage, get (someone) started • **d. de lado** to shun, ignore • **d. diente con diente** to shiver • **d. el pésame** to express condolences • **d. el sí** to assent • **d. en cara** to reproach, scold • **d. en prenda** *(prometer)* to pledge; *(empeñar)* to hock, pawn • **d. fe** to certify • **d. fiado** COM. to give credit • **d. fianza** to post bail, bail out • **d. fin a** to complete, finish • **d. frente a** to face, be facing • **darle ganas de** to feel like, have a mind to • **d. gusto a** to please, make happy • **d. la bienvenida** to welcome • **d. la casualidad que** to just so happen that • **d. la lata** COLL. to pester • **d. la razón a** to agree with, support • **d. las espaldas** to turn one's back on • **d. los buenos días** to greet, say good morning • **d. margen** to afford an opportunity • **d. muerte a** to kill • **d. pábulo a** FIG. to feed, foster • **d. palmadas** *(aplaudir)* to applaud, clap hands; *(pegar)* to spank • **d. por** to consider, regard • **d. prestado** to lend • **d. punto final** to conclude • **d. un abrazo** to hug • **d. una vuelta, paseo** to take a stroll, walk • **no d. un bledo** COLL. not to give a hoot —intr. *(tener vista de)* to overlook, face; *(ocurrir)* to arise, occur; *(sobrevenir)* to come over, set in ♦ **¡dale!** COLL. *(¡apúrate!)* hurry up!; *(¡adelante!)* keep it up! • **d. con** *(encontrar)* to find, hit on; *(encontrarse)* to meet, run into;

(chocar) to hit, bang • **d. de** to fall on • **d. en** *(cuer)* to fall; *(empeñarse)* to be bent on; *(acertar)* to catch on to, get • **d. en el clavo** FIG. to hit the nail on the head • **d. igual** or **lo mismo** to be all the same • **darle por** to take it into one's head • **d. sobre** to look out on • **d. tras** to chase, pursue —reflex. to give oneself up, surrender; *(suceder)* to arise, occur; *(dedicarse)* to devote oneself; *(tomar el hábito de)* to take to, give in to • **d. a conocer** to introduce oneself • **d. a entender** to make oneself understood; *(ser evidente)* to become evident or clear • **d. con** or **contra** to hit, bump against • **d. cuenta de** to realize • **dárselas de** to consider oneself, to act like • **d. las manos** or **la mano** to shake hands • **dárselas a uno** to care about • **dársele bien** to be lucky • **d. por** to consider oneself • **d. prisa** to hurry • **d. tono** to put on airs.

dar·do m. dart, arrow; FIG. cutting remark, barb.

dár·se·na f. inner harbor, dock.

da·ta f. date; COM. data, items.

da·tar tr. to date; COM. to enter, credit —intr. to date, begin • **d. de** to date from.

da·ti·vo, a adj. & m. dative.

da·to m. fact, datum; *(documento)* document • pl. data, information.

de prep. *(posesión)* of, -'s, -s'; *(asunto)* of, about, on; *(contenido)* of; *(origen)* from, according to; *(distancia)* from; *(manera)* in, with, on, as; *(hora)* in, at, by, from; *(causa)* from, with, out of, if; *(comparación)* than, of, in.

dé see **dar**.

de·am·bu·lar intr. to wander or roam around.

de·án m. RELIG. dean.

de·ba·jo adv. underneath, below • **d. de** underneath, below • **por d.** underneath, below.

de·ba·te m. debate, discussion.

de·ba·tir tr. to debate, discuss; *(combatir)* to fight, struggle.

de·be m. COM. debit.

de·ber[1] tr. to owe; *(hay que)* to ought to • **d. de** to be probable —reflex. to be due to.

de·ber[2] m. duty, obligation; *(faena)* chore; *(deuda)* debt • pl. AMER. homework.

de·bi·da·men·te adv. properly, duly.

de·bi·do, a adj. due; *(apropiado)* proper, fitting.

dé·bil I. adj. weak; *(marchito)* faint, faded II. m.f. weakling.

de·bi·li·dad f. weakness.

de·bi·li·ta·ción f. debilitation.

de·bi·li·tar tr. & reflex. to weaken.

dé·bi·to m. *(deuda)* debt; COM. debit.

de·but m. debut, opening.

de·bu·tan·te I. adj. beginning II. m.f. beginner, newcomer —f. debutante.

de·bu·tar intr. to begin; THEAT. to debut.

dé·ca·da f. decade.

de·ca·den·cia f. decadence, decline.

de·ca·den·te adj. & m.f. decadent.

de·ca·er §15 intr. to decline, fall.

de·caí·do, a I. see **decaer** II. adj. *(débil)* weak, run-down; *(deprimido)* depressed, discouraged.

de·cai·mien·to m. *(decadencia)* decadence, decline; *(debilidad)* weakness, feebleness; *(desaliento)* discouragement, dejection.

de·ca·no m.f. EDUC. dean; *(viejo)* doyen.

de·can·ta·ción f. decanting, pouring off.

de·can·tar tr. to decant, pour off; *(engrande-*

cer) to exaggerate, aggrandize.

de·ca·pi·tar tr. to decapitate, behead.

de·cat·lón m. decathlon.

de·ca·ye·ra, yó see **decaer**.

de·ce·na f. group of ten; MUS. tenth.

de·cen·cia f. decency.

de·cen·te adj. decent.

de·cep·ción f. deception; *(desengaño)* disenchantment, disappointment.

de·cep·cio·nar tr. to disenchant, disappoint.

de·ce·so m. decease, death.

de·ci·bel/be·lio m. decibel.

de·ci·di·do, a adj. determined, resolute.

de·ci·dir tr. to decide, resolve; *(persuadir)* to persuade, convince —intr. to decide —reflex. to decide, make up one's mind.

de·ci·mal adj. & m. decimal.

de·cí·me·tro m. decimeter.

dé·ci·mo, a adj. & m. tenth.

de·ci·mo·oc·ta·vo, a adj. eighteenth.

de·ci·mo·cuar·to, a adj. fourteenth.

de·ci·mo·no·no/no·ve·no, a adj. nineteenth.

de·ci·mo·quin·to, a adj. fifteenth.

de·ci·mo·sép·ti·mo, a adj. seventeenth.

de·ci·mo·sex·to, a adj. sixteenth.

de·ci·mo·ter·ce·ro, a adj. thirteenth.

de·cir[1] m. *(refrán)* saying; *(ocurrencia)* witty remark; *(locución)* figure of speech.

de·cir[2] §21 tr. to say; *(relatar, divulgar)* to tell; *(hablar)* to talk, speak; *(ordenar)* to tell, order; *(mostrar)* to show, reveal; *(nombrar)* to call, name • **como quien dice** or **como si dijéramos** COLL. so to speak • **d. entre** or **para sí** to say to oneself • **d. por d.** to talk for the sake of talking • **¡diga!** hello! • **el qué dirán** what people may say • **es d.** that is (to say) • **¡no me digas!** you don't say!, really! • **querer d.** to mean • **según el d. general** by all accounts.

de·ci·sión f. decision; *(firmeza)* determination, resoluteness; *(sentencia)* verdict, ruling.

de·ci·si·vo, a adj. decisive, conclusive.

de·cla·mar tr. & intr. to declaim, recite.

de·cla·ra·ción f. declaration, statement; LAW deposition, evidence; *(de cartas)* bid, call.

de·cla·ra·da·men·te adv. manifestly, openly.

de·cla·ran·te I. adj. declaring II. m.f. LAW declarant, witness.

de·cla·rar tr. to declare; *(en los juegos de cartas)* to bid, declare; LAW to find, pronounce —intr. to declare; LAW to testify, give evidence —reflex. to declare oneself.

de·cli·na·ción f. decline; GRAM. declension, ASTRON. declination.

de·cli·nar intr. to decline; *(ir hacia su fin)* to wane, draw to a close —tr. to decline, refuse; GRAM. to decline.

de·cli·ve m. slope, incline; *(decadencia)* decadence, decline.

de·co·lo·ra·ción f. discoloration, fading; *(del pelo)* bleaching.

de·co·lo·ran·te m. decolorant.

de·co·lo·rar tr. to discolor, fade.

de·co·mi·sar tr. to confiscate, seize.

de·co·mi·so m. confiscation, seizure.

de·co·ra·ción f. decoration; THEAT. scenery.

de·co·ra·do m. THEAT. scenery, set; *(acción)* decoration.

de·co·ra·dor, ra I. adj. decorative, ornamental II. m.f. decorator.

de·co·rar tr. to decorate; *(memorizar)* to memorize, learn by heart.

de·co·ra·ti·vo, a adj. decorative, ornamental.

de·co·ro m. respect, honor; *(recato)* decorum, propriety.

de·co·ro·so, a adj. decorous, decent; *(digno)* respectable, honorable.

de·cre·cer §17 intr. to decrease, diminish.

de·cre·ci·mien·to m. decrease, diminution.

de·cré·pi·to, a adj. decrepit, aged.

de·cre·pi·tud f. decrepitude, old age.

de·cre·tar tr. to decree, order.

de·cre·to m. decree, order.

de·cha·do m. model, perfect example; SEW. sampler.

de·dal m. thimble.

de·di·ca·ción f. dedication.

de·di·car §70 tr. & reflex. to dedicate (oneself).

de·di·ca·to·rio, a I. adj. dedicatory, dedicative II. f. dedication, inscription.

de·di·llo m. little finger, pinky ♦ **al d.** COLL. perfectly, thoroughly • **saber al d.** to know by heart.

de·do m. *(de la mano)* finger; *(del pie)* toe; *(porción)* bit, smidgen ♦ **a dos dedos de** FIG., COLL. within an inch of • **cogerse los dedos** to get caught • **chuparse los dedos** to smack one's lips • **d. anular** ring finger • **d. cordial** or **del corazón** middle finger • **d. índice** index finger, forefinger • **d. meñique** little finger, pinky • **d. pulgar** or **gordo** *(de la mano)* thumb; *(del pie)* big toe • **morderse los dedos** to bite one's nails; COLL. *(arrepentirse)* to regret.

de·duc·ción f. deduction; LOG. inference.

de·du·cir §22 tr. to deduce, conclude; *(rebajar)* to deduct, subtract.

de·duc·ti·vo, a adj. deductive.

de·fal·car §70 tr. *(rebajar)* to deduct; *(robar)* to embezzle.

de·fe·ca·ción f. defecation.

de·fe·car §70 tr. & intr. to defecate.

de·fec·ción f. defection, desertion.

de·fec·ti·vo, a adj. defective.

de·fec·to m. defect, flaw; *(falta)* absence, lack ♦ **en d. de** in the absence of, for want of.

de·fec·tuo·so, a adj. defective, faulty.

de·fen·der §50 tr. to defend —intr. & reflex. to defend or protect oneself; *(arreglárselas)* to manage, get by.

de·fen·di·do, a I. adj. defended II. m.f. LAW defendant.

de·fen·sa f. defense ♦ **d. propia** or **legítima** self-defense.

de·fen·si·vo, a I. adj. defensive II. m. defense, safeguard ♦ **d.** defensive.

de·fen·sor, o·ra I. adj. defending, protecting II. m.f. defender, protector —m. LAW defense counsel.

de·fe·ren·cia f. deference.

de·fe·rir §65 intr. to defer —tr. to refer, delegate.

de·fi·cien·cia f. deficiency, lack.

de·fi·cien·te adj. deficient, lacking; *(defectuoso)* defective, poor.

dé·fi·cit m. [pl. **s**] COM. deficit; FIG. *(carencia)* shortage, lack.

de·fien·da, do see **defender**.

de·fie·ra, ro see **deferir**.

de·fi·ni·ción f. definition; *(determinación)* determination, decision.

de·fi·ni·do, a I. adj. defined; GRAM. definite II. m. definition.

de·fi·nir tr. to define; *(determinar)* to determine, decide.

de·fi·ni·ti·vo, a adj. definitive, final ♦ **en defi-**

ni·ti·va *(por fin)* once and for all, finally; *(de verdad)* really, exactly; *(en resumen)* in short.

de·fi·rie·ra, rió see **deferir**.

de·for·ma·ción f. deformation; RAD. distortion; MECH. strain; *(alabeo)* warp.

de·for·mar tr. to deform —reflex. to be or become deformed.

de·for·me adj. deformed, misshapen.

de·for·mi·dad f. deformity.

de·frau·da·ción f. fraud, cheating; *(decepción)* disappointment.

de·frau·dar tr. to defraud, cheat; *(decepcionar)* to disappoint; *(frustrar)* to dash, thwart (hopes); *(turbar)* to disturb, spoil.

de·fun·ción f. demise, death.

de·ge·ne·ra·ción f. degeneration; *(de moral)* degeneracy.

de·ge·ne·ra·do, a adj. & m.f. degenerate.

de·ge·ne·rar intr. to degenerate; *(perder mérito)* to decline, decay.

de·go·lla·de·ro m. throat, windpipe; *(del vestido)* neckline; *(matadero)* slaughterhouse; *(cadalso)* scaffold, block.

de·go·llar §19 tr. *(guillotinar)* to cut or slit the throat of; *(decapitar)* to behead, decapitate; *(masacrar)* to massacre, slaughter; *(destruir)* to destroy, ruin; COLL. *(aburrir)* to bore to death.

de·gra·da·ción f. degradation, debasement.

de·gra·dan·te adj. degrading, debasing.

de·gra·dar tr. & reflex. to degrade or debase (oneself).

de·güe·lle, llo see **degollar**.

de·güe·llo m. throat-cutting; *(decapitación)* beheading, decapitation; *(matanza)* massacre, slaughter ♦ **entrar a d.** to massacre • **tirar a d.** to harm.

de·gus·ta·ción f. tasting, sampling.

dei·dad f. deity, divinity.

dei·fi·car §70 tr. to deify; *(ensalzar)* to glorify.

de·ja·dez f. carelessness, negligence; *(desaliño)* slovenliness, untidiness; *(pereza)* laziness.

de·ja·do, a adj. careless, negligent; *(desaliñado)* slovenly, untidy; *(perezoso)* lazy; *(deprimido)* depressed, dejected.

de·jar tr. to leave; *(consentir)* to let, allow; *(producir)* to yield, produce; *(desamparar)* to abandon, desert; *(nombrar)* to name, designate; *(cesar)* to stop, quit; *(prestar)* to lend, loan ♦ **¡deja!** or **¡déjalo!** never mind! • **d. caer** to drop, let go of • **d. el paso libre** to let pass • **d. en blanco** to leave blank • **d. fresco a** COLL. to baffle, perplex • **d. mal** to let down • **d. plantado** COLL. to leave in the lurch, stand up —intr. ♦ **d. de** to stop, leave off • **d. de existir** to die • **no d. de** not to neglect, not to fail to —reflex. *(descuidarse)* to let oneself go, become sloppy; *(abandonarse)* to give oneself up to, abandon oneself to; *(permitirse)* to allow oneself to be ♦ **d. caer** *(caerse)* to fall, flop; COLL. *(insinuar)* to drop a hint, insinuate; *(presentarse)* to drop in unexpectedly • **d. de** to stop • **d. decir** to let slip, let out • **d. de rodeos** to stop beating around the bush, come to the point • **d. llevar de** to get carried away with • **d. ver** *(aparecer)* to show; *(presentarse)* to show up.

de·jo m. *(dejación)* abandonment, relinquishment; *(fin)* end, termination; *(acento)* accent, lilt; *(inflexión)* drop (in voice); *(gusto)* aftertaste; *(flojedad)* neglect, indolence; FIG. aftertaste.

del contr. of **de** and **el**.

de·lan·tal m. *(sin peto)* apron; *(con peto)* pinafore.

de·lan·te adv. *(con prioridad)* in front, ahead; *(enfrente)* facing, opposite ♦ d. de in front of.

de·lan·te·ro, a I. adj. front, fore II. m. *(de un vestido)* front; SPORT. forward —f. *(frente)* front, front part; *(ventaja)* advantage, lead ♦ coger *or* tomar la d. to take the lead • llevar la d. to lead, be in the lead ♦ pl. overalls.

de·la·tar tr. to denounce, inform on; *(revelar)* to reveal, expose.

de·le·ga·ción f. delegation; *(cargo y oficina)* office; *(sucursal)* branch.

de·le·ga·do, a I. adj. delegated II. m.f. delegate, representative.

de·le·gar §47 tr. to delegate.

de·lei·ta·ble adj. delightful, enjoyable.

de·lei·tar tr. to delight, please —reflex. ♦ d. con *or* en to take pleasure in, delight in.

de·lei·te m. delight, pleasure.

de·le·tre·ar tr. *(pronunciar)* to spell (out); FIG. *(descifrar)* to decipher, interpret.

de·le·tre·o m. spelling; *(desciframiento)* deciphering.

de·lez·na·ble adj. *(que se rompe fácilmente)* crumbly; *(resbaladizo)* slippery; *(quebradizo)* brittle, fragile; FIG. frail, weak.

del·fín m. dolphin; *(príncipe)* dauphin.

del·ga·do, a I. adj. *(esbelto)* slender, slim; *(flaco)* thin; *(tenue)* tenuous, delicate; *(agudo)* sharp, clever ♦ hilar d. COLL. to split hairs • ponerse d. to lose weight II. m.pl. flanks (of animals).

de·li·be·ra·do, a adj. deliberate, intentional.

de·li·be·rar intr. to deliberate, ponder —tr. to decide, resolve.

de·li·ca·de·za f. delicacy; *(discreción)* tactfulness, discretion; *(debilidad)* weakness, frailty ♦ tener la d. de to be thoughtful enough to.

de·li·ca·do, a adj. delicate, *(difícil)* difficult, delicate; *(exigente)* demanding, exacting; *(quebradizo)* fragile, delicate; *(enfermizo)* frail, delicate.

de·li·cia f. delight, pleasure.

de·li·cio·so, a adj. *(agradable)* delightful; *(sabroso)* delicious.

de·li·mi·tar tr. to delimit.

de·lin·ca, co see delinquir.

de·lin·cuen·cia f. delinquency.

de·lin·cuen·te adj. & m.f. delinquent.

de·li·ne·a·mi(en·to m. delineation.

de·li·ne·ar tr. to delineate, outline.

de·lin·quir §23 intr. to break the law.

de·li·ran·te adj. delirious.

de·li·rar intr. to be delirious; *(decir tonterías)* to rave, talk nonsense.

de·li·rio m. delirium; *(manía)* mania, frenzy; *(disparate)* raving ♦ d. de grandeza delusions of grandeur • tener d. por to be crazy about.

de·li·to m. offense, crime ♦ d. de mayor cuantía felony • d. de menor cuantía misdemeanor.

del·ta m. delta.

de·ma·cra·do, a adj. emaciated, wasted away.

de·ma·crar·se reflex. to become emaciated.

de·ma·go·gia f. demagogy, demagoguery.

de·ma·gó·gi·co, a adj. demagogic.

de·ma·go·go, a m.f. demagogue.

de·man·da f. demand; *(petición)* appeal, request; *(limosna)* alms; *(pregunta)* question, inquiry; *(empresa)* enterprise; *(empeño)* perseverance; COM. demand; *(pedido)* order; ELEC. load; LAW *(escrito)* writ; *(acción)* law-

suit, action; THEAT. call ♦ demandas y respuestas haggling • ir en d. de to go in search of • salir uno a la d. to defend.

de·man·da·do, a m.f. defendant.

de·man·dan·te m.f. plaintiff.

de·man·dar tr. *(pedir)* to request, ask for; LAW to sue, file suit against.

de·mar·car §70 tr. to demarcate, delimit.

de·más I. adj. other, rest of the ♦ lo d. the rest • por d. *(en demasía)* excessively, too much; *(inútilmente)* in vain • por lo d. otherwise, other than that • todo lo d. everything else • y d. etcetera, and so on; *(y los otros)* and the others II. adv. moreover, besides.

de·ma·sí·a f. excess, surplus; *(abuso)* disregard, abuse; *(insolencia)* insolence, audacity ♦ en d. excessively.

de·ma·sia·do, a I. adj. too much *or* many, excessive II. adv. too, too much.

de·men·cia f. madness, insanity; MED. dementia.

de·men·te I. adj. insane, demented II. m.f. insane person, lunatic.

de·mo·cra·cia f. democracy.

de·mó·cra·ta I. adj. democratic II. m.f. democrat.

de·mo·crá·ti·co, a adj. democratic.

de·mo·gra·fi·ar §04 tr. to make democratic.

de·mo·grá·fi·co, a adj. demographic.

de·mo·le·dor, ·ra I. adj. demolishing, destructive; *(arruinador)* devastating II. m.f. demolisher, wrecker.

de·mo·ler §78 tr. to demolish, destroy.

de·mo·li·ción f. demolition, destruction.

de·mo·nio m. *(diablo)* demon, devil; *(genio)* evil spirit; COLL. *(travieso)* rascal, mischievous person ♦ como el d. like the devil, like hell • ¡que me lleve el d! I'll be damned! ♦ pl. ¿cómo d.? how in the hell... ? • ¡qd.! hell!, damn! • de mil d. *or* todos los d. a hell of a.

de·mo·ra f. delay, wait.

de·mo·rar tr. to delay, hold up —intr. to linger, stay —reflex. to take a long time, delay.

de·mos·tra·ción f. demonstration; *(ostentación)* show, display; *(prueba)* proof.

de·mos·trar §19 tr. to demonstrate, show.

de·mos·tra·ti·vo, a adj. & m. demonstrative.

de·mu·dar tr. to change, turn pale —reflex. to change, turn pale; *(alterarse)* to become upset suddenly.

de·mue·la, lo see demoler.

de·mues·tre, tro see demostrar.

de·ne·gar §52 tr. *(rechazar)* to refuse, reject; *(negar)* to deny.

de·nie·go, gue see denegar.

de·ni·gra·ción f. denigration, disparagement.

de·ni·gra·dor, ·ra/gran·te I. adj. denigrating, disparaging II. m.f. denigrator, disparager.

de·ni·grar tr. *(desacreditar)* to denigrate, disparage; *(injuriar)* to insult.

de·no·da·do, a adj. bold, intrepid.

de·no·mi·na·ción f. denomination.

de·no·mi·na·dor, ·ra I. adj. denominating, denominative II. m.f. denominator.

de·no·mi·nar tr. to denominate, name.

de·nos·tar §19 tr. to abuse, insult.

de·no·tar tr. to denote.

den·si·dad f. density.

den·so, a adj. dense, thick; *(sólido)* heavy, solid; *(oscuro)* dark, black.

den·ta·do, a adj. dentate, toothed II. m. perforation —f. AMER. bite.

den·ta·du·ra f. (set of) teeth.
den·tal adj. dental.
den·tar §49 tr. to tooth, put teeth in; *(endentecer)* to serrate.
den·te·lla·do, a I. adj. dentate, toothed II. f. *(movimiento)* snap of the jaws; *(mordisco)* bite; *(señal)* tooth mark.
den·te·llar intr. to chatter (teeth).
den·te·lle·ar tr. to nibble, bite.
den·te·ra f. *(envidia)* envy, jealousy; *(deseo intenso)* vehement desire, longing ♦ **dar a alguien d.** *(incomodar)* to set someone's teeth on edge; *(dar envidia)* to make someone jealous.
den·ti·frí·co m. toothpaste.
den·tis·ta m.f. dentist.
den·tro adv. inside, within; *(de un edificio)* inside, indoors ♦ **d. de poco** shortly, soon • **de or desde d.** from (the) inside • **por d.** inwardly, (on the) inside.
de·nue·do m. bravery, courage.
de·nues·te, to see **denostar**.
de·nues·to m. insult, affront.
de·nun·cia f. accusation, denunciation; *(declaración)* declaration, report.
de·nun·cia·dor, ra/cian·te I. adj. denouncing II. m.f. denouncer.
de·nun·ciar tr. to accuse, denounce; *(pronosticar)* to foretell, prophesy; *(declarar)* to declare, announce; *(indicar)* to indicate, reveal; *(delatar)* to denounce, censure.
de·pa·rar tr. to supply, provide.
de·par·ta·men·to m. department, section; *(distrito)* province, district; *(compartimiento)* compartment; *(piso)* apartment, flat (G.B.).
de·par·tir intr. to talk, converse.
de·pen·den·cia f. dependence, reliance; *(parentesco)* relationship, kinship; *(amistad)* friendship, relationship; *(sucursal)* branch (office); *(negocio)* business, agency; *(empleados)* employees, subordinates ♦ pl. accessories.
de·pen·der intr. to depend (**de** on).
de·pen·dien·te, a I. adj. dependent, subordinate II. m.f. *(empleado)* employee; *(de tienda)* clerk, salesperson.
de·pi·la·ción f. depilation.
de·pi·lar tr. to depilate, remove hair from.
de·plo·rar tr. to deplore, lament.
de·po·ner §54 tr. *(apartar)* to lay or put aside; *(privar)* to depose; LAW to testify, provide testimony for; *(bajar)* to lower, bring or take down —intr. *(defecar)* to defecate, move the bowels; *(dar testimonio)* to testify, make a deposition.
de·por·ta·ción f. deportation.
de·por·tar tr. to deport, exile.
de·por·te m. sport.
de·por·tis·ta I. adj. sporting, sporty; COLL. *(aficionado)* fond of sports II. m.f. sports fan, sportsman/woman.
de·por·ti·vo, a adj. sporting, sports; *(aficionado)* sportive, fond of sports.
de·po·si·ción f. deposition; LAW deposition, testimony; PHYSIOL. bowel movement.
de·po·si·tan·te I. adj. depositing II. m.f. depositor.
de·po·si·tar tr. to deposit; *(encomendar)* to place —reflex. to settle.
de·po·si·ta·rio m.f. depositary, trustee —m. *(cajero)* cashier; *(tesorero)* treasurer.
de·pó·si·to m. deposit; *(almacén)* warehouse, storehouse; *(cisterna)* cistern, tank; *(desembolso inicial)* deposit, down payment; CHEM., GEOL., MIN. deposit; MIL. depot, dump.

de·pra·va·ción f. corruption, depravity; *(alteración)* alteration.
de·pra·va·do, a I. adj. depraved, corrupted II. m.f. depraved person, degenerate.
de·pra·var tr. to deprave, corrupt; *(echar a perder)* to harm, damage.
de·pre·car §70 tr. to beg, implore.
de·pre·ca·to·rio, a adj. imploring.
de·pre·cia·ción f. depreciation.
de·pre·ciar tr. to depreciate.
de·pre·dar tr. to plunder, pillage.
de·pre·sión f. depression; *(humillación)* humiliation, embarrassment.
de·pre·si·vo, a adj. MED. depressive; *(deprimente)* depressing.
de·pri·men·te adj. depressing.
de·pri·mi·do, a adj. depressed.
de·pri·mir tr. to depress; *(humillar)* to humiliate, embarrass —reflex. to get depressed.
de·pu·ra·ción f. depuration, purification; POL. purge, purging.
de·pu·rar tr. to depurate, purify; POL. to purge.
de·pu·sie·ra, so see **deponer**.
de·re·chis·ta adj. & m.f. rightist.
de·re·cho, a I. adj. right; right-hand <*el margen d.* the right-hand margin>; *(vertical)* upright, erect; *(recto)* straight, even; AMER. lucky, fortunate ♦ **a derechas** right, properly II. f. *(lado derecho)* right side, right-hand side; *(diestra)* right hand; POL. right, right wing ♦ **a la d.** to or on the right • **¡d!** MIL. right face! —m. right, authority; *(privilegio)* right, privilege; *(conjunto de leyes)* law; *(justicia)* justice; *(estudio)* law ♦ **de d.** LAW de jure, by right • **d. consuetudinario** common law • **d. de paso** right of way • **d. escrito or positivo** statute law • **d. mercantil** business law • **d. penal** criminal law • **hecho y d.** complete, full • **tener d. a** to have a right to ♦ pl. *(impuestos)* duties, taxes; *(honorarios)* fees, charges • **d. de autor** royalties • **d. de entrada** import duties • **hacer valer sus d.** to exercise one's rights III. adv. straight, right; COLL. right, honestly ♦ **todo d.** straight ahead.
de·ri·va f. drift, deviation ♦ **ir a la d.** to drift.
de·ri·va·ción f. derivation; ELEC. *(pérdida)* loss of current; *(circuito)* by-pass, shunt.
de·ri·va·do, a I. adj. derived, derivative II. m. derivative —f. MATH. derivative.
de·ri·var tr. to derive; *(dirigir)* to lead, direct —intr. to derive, be derived; AVIA., MARIT. to drift, go off course —reflex. to be derived or come from.
der·ma·to·lo·gí·a f. dermatology.
der·ma·tó·lo·go, a m.f. dermatologist.
der·mis f. derma, dermis.
de·ro·ga·ción f. LAW derogation, repeal; *(disminución)* decrease, deterioration.
de·ro·gar §47 tr. LAW to derogate, repeal; *(destruir)* to destroy, abolish.
de·rra·ma·mien·to m. spilling; *(rebosamiento)* overflowing; *(dispersión)* dispersion, scattering; *(despilfarro)* squandering, wasting ♦ **d. de sangre** bloodshed, spilling of blood.
de·rra·mar tr. *(verter)* to spill, pour out; *(sangre)* to spill, shed; *(lágrimas)* to shed; *(dispersar)* to scatter, spread; *(diseminar)* to spread, make known; *(impuestos)* to apportion (taxes) —reflex. to overflow, spill over.
de·rra·me m. *(derramamiento)* spilling, pouring out; *(sangre)* spilling, shedding; *(lágrimas)* shedding; *(dispersión)* scattering, spreading;

(diseminación) spreading, dissemination; *(pérdida)* leakage, waste; *(rebosamiento)* overflow; *(declive)* slope, incline ♦ **d. cerebral** cerebral hemorrhage • **d. sinovial** MED. water on the knee.

de·rre·dor m. periphery, circumference ♦ **al** *or* **en d.** around • **por todo el d.** all around.

de·rre·tir §48 tr. to liquefy, dissolve; *(hielo)* to melt, thaw; *(consumir)* to squander, waste —reflex. COLL. *(enamorarse)* to fall madly in love; *(inquietarse)* to worry, fret; *(impacientarse)* to be impatient.

de·rri·bar tr. to knock down; *(subvertir)* to overthrow, topple; MIL. to shoot down; *(humillar)* to humiliate, prostrate —reflex. to fall to the ground.

de·rri·ta, to, tiera, tió see **derretir.**

de·rro·car §70 tr. *(despeñar)* to hurl *or* throw down; *(arruinar)* to demolish, knock down; *(subvertir)* to oust, overthrow.

de·rro·cha·dor, ·ra I. adj. wasteful, squandering II. m.f. spendthrift, squanderer.

de·rro·char tr. to squander, waste.

de·rro·che m. squandering, waste.

de·rro·ta f. MIL. defeat, rout; *(camino)* route, path; MARIT. ship's course, course; *(desorden)* disorder, shambles.

de·rro·tar tr. to defeat, beat, *(arruinar)* to ruin, spoil; *(echar a perder)* to waste, squander —reflex. MARIT. to drift *or* be driven off course.

de·rro·te·ro m. *(rumbo)* course, tack; *(modo de obrar)* course, plan of action; *(tesoro)* hidden *or* buried treasure.

de·rro·tis·ta adj. & m.f. defeatist.

de·rruir §18 tr. to knock down, demolish.

de·rrum·ba·mien·to m. *(caída)* plunge, headlong fall; *(demolición)* demolition; *(desplome)* collapse, falling down; *(ruina)* collapse, fall; *(derrocamiento)* overthrow, MIN. cave-in ♦ **d. de tierra** landslide.

de·rrum·bar tr. *(despeñar)* to hurl *or* cast down; *(demoler)* to knock down, demolish —reflex. *(caerse)* to collapse, fall; *(tirarse)* to throw oneself headfirst; MIN. to cave in, collapse; AMER. to fail.

de·rrum·be/bo m. *(despeñadero)* precipice, cliff; *(socavón)* cave-in; *(de tierra)* landslide; *(demolición)* demolition, knocking down; *(desplome)* falling down, collapse.

de·rru·ya, yera, yo, yó scc **derruir.**

de·sa·bo·to·nar tr. to unbutton, undo —intr. BOT. to blossom, bloom —reflex. to come unbuttoned.

de·sa·bri·do, a adj. *(de poco sabor)* tasteless, insipid; *(de mal sabor)* bad-tasting, unsavory; METEOROL. inclement, unpleasant; FIG. gruff, surly.

de·sa·bri·gar §47 tr. to uncover; *(quitar la ropa)* to undress; *(desamparar)* to deprive of shelter *or* protection.

de·sa·bro·char tr. to undo, unfasten; FIG. to open, uncover —reflex. to undo *or* unfasten one's clothing; *(confiarse)* to unburden oneself, confide.

de·sa·ca·tar tr. to show disrespect for —reflex. to behave disrespectfully.

de·sa·ca·to m. disrespect, irreverence; LAW contempt.

de·sa·cer·ta·do, a adj. mistaken, misguided.

de·sa·cier·to m. error, mistake.

de·sa·co·mo·dar tr. to inconvenience, bother; *(despedir)* to discharge, dismiss —reflex. to

lose one's job.

de·sa·co·plar tr. to uncouple, disconnect.

de·sa·cor·de adj. discordant.

de·sa·cos·tum·bra·do, a adj. unusual, uncommon.

de·sa·cos·tum·brar tr. & reflex. to break (oneself) of the habit (of).

de·sa·cre·di·ta·do, a adj. discredited, disgraced.

de·sa·cre·di·tar tr. to discredit, disgrace.

de·sac·ti·var tr. to deactivate.

de·sa·cuer·do m. disagreement, discord; *(error)* error, mistake; *(olvido)* forgetfulness, loss of memory.

de·sa·fia·dor, ·ra I. adj. defying, challenging II. m.f. challenger.

de·sa·fiar §30 tr. to challenge, dare; *(competir)* to oppose, compete with.

de·sa·fi·lar tr. to blunt, dull.

de·sa·fi·nar intr. MUS. to be out of tune; *(tocar)* to play out of tune; *(cantar)* to sing out of tune; COLL. to speak out of turn —reflex. MUS. to get out of tune.

de·sa·fí·o m. *(reto)* challenge, defiance; *(duelo)* duel; *(competencia)* competition, rivalry.

de·sa·fo·ra·do, a adj. huge; *(sin límite)* boundless; *(contra fuero)* illegal, unlawful.

de·sa·fo·rar §19 tr. to violate (a person's) rights —reflex. to lose control, fly off the handle.

de·sa·for·tu·na·do, a adj. unfortunate.

de·sa·fue·ro m. infringement; *(abuso)* outrage, excess.

de·sa·gra·da·ble adj. disagreeable.

de·sa·gra·dar tr. to displease, offend.

de·sa·gra·de·cer §17 tr. to be ungrateful.

de·sa·gra·de·ci·do, a adj. & m.f. ungrateful (person).

de·sa·gra·do m. displeasure, discontent ♦ **con d.** ungraciously, reluctantly.

de·sa·gra·vio m. compensation, amends ♦ **en d. de** in amends for.

de·sa·gua·de·ro m. drain, outlet.

de·sa·guar §10 tr. to drain, empty (of water); *(malgastar)* to waste, consume —intr. to empty *or* flow into the sea —reflex. *(vomitar)* to vomit; *(defecar)* to defecate.

de·sa·güe m. *(avenamiento)* draining, drainage; *(desaguadero)* drain, outlet.

de·sa·ho·ga·do, a adj. *(descarado)* brazen, fresh; *(despejado)* clear, open; *(espacioso)* roomy, spacious; *(acomodado)* relaxing, easy.

de·sa·ho·gar §47 tr. *(aliviar)* to alleviate, ease; *(dar rienda suelta)* to vent, give rein to —reflex. *(dar rienda suelta)* to let off steam; *(confiarse)* to confide; *(descansar)* to relax, take it easy; *(recobrarse)* to recover, feel better; *(desempeñarse)* to extricate oneself from difficulty.

de·sa·ho·go m. *(alivio)* relief, alleviation; *(descanso)* rest, respite; *(expansión)* space, room; *(libertad)* freedom; *(comodidad)* comfort, ease; *(descaro)* impudence; *(salida)* outlet.

de·sa·hu·ciar tr. *(quitar toda esperanza)* to remove all hope from; *(desesperar)* to lose hope for; *(un inquilino)* to evict.

de·sai·rar tr. to reject, rebuff; *(desestimar)* to underestimate.

de·sai·re m. *(falta de gracia)* gracelessness, lack of charm; *(desprecio)* slight, snub; *(rechazo)* rebuff.

de·sa·jus·tar tr. to disturb, put out of order; *(estropear)* to spoil, upset —reflex. to go wrong, get out of order; *(compromiso)* to break.

de·sa·jus·te m. *(mal ajuste)* maladjustment; *(avería)* breakdown, failure; *(ruptura)* breaking.

de·sa·len·tar §49 tr. to leave breathless, put out of breath; *(desanimar)* to discourage, dishearten —reflex. to become discouraged *or* disheartened.

de·sa·lien·to m. discouragement.

de·sa·li·ña·do, a adj. *(desaseado)* slovenly, untidy; *(descuidado)* careless, neglectful.

de·sa·li·ñar tr. to disarrange, make untidy; *(arrugar)* to crease —reflex. to become disarranged *or* untidy.

de·sa·li·ño m. *(descompostura)* slovenliness, untidiness; *(descuido)* carelessness, neglect.

de·sal·ma·do, a adj. heartless, cruel.

de·sa·lo·jar tr. *(sacar)* to remove, expel; *(desplazar)* to dislodge, displace; *(abandonar)* to abandon, evacuate —intr. to leave.

de·sa·lo·jo m. removal, expulsion; *(desplazamiento)* dislodgement, displacement; *(abandonamiento)* abandonment, evacuation.

de·sal·qui·lar tr. *(dejar de tener alquilado)* to stop renting; *(mudarse)* to vacate —reflex. to become vacant.

de·sa·mor m. indifference, lack of affection; *(antipatía)* enmity, dislike.

de·sam·pa·rar tr. to forsake, abandon.

de·sam·pa·ro m. helplessness, abandonment.

de·san·dar §05 tr. to retrace (one's steps), go back.

de·san·grar tr. to bleed; *(vaciar)* to drain, empty; *(empobrecer)* to impoverish, bleed dry —reflex. to bleed profusely; *(morir)* to bleed to death.

de·sa·ni·ma·do, a adj. downhearted, discouraged; *(poco animado)* dull, lifeless.

de·sa·ni·mar tr. to discourage, depress —reflex. to become discouraged *or* depressed.

de·sá·ni·mo m. discouragement, dejection.

de·sa·nu·dar/ñu·dar tr. to untie, unknot; *(desenmarañar)* to straighten out, clarify.

de·sa·pa·ci·ble adj. unpleasant, disagreeable.

de·sa·pa·re·cer §17 tr. to make disappear, cause to vanish —intr. & reflex. to disappear, vanish; *(disipar)* to wear off.

de·sa·pa·ri·ción f. disappearance, vanishing.

de·sa·pa·sio·na·do, a adj. dispassionate.

de·sa·pe·gar §47 tr. to unstick; *(desaficionar)* to estrange, alienate —reflex. to come unstuck; *(desaficionarse)* to become estranged *or* alienated.

de·sa·pe·go m. indifference, estrangement; *(imparcialidad)* impartiality.

de·sa·per·ci·bi·do, a adj. unprepared, unready; *(inadvertido)* unnoticed, unseen.

de·sa·pli·ca·do, a I. adj. lazy, idle **II.** m.f. lazybones, idler.

de·sa·pre·ciar tr. to underestimate.

de·sa·pren·si·vo, a adj. unscrupulous.

de·sa·pro·ba·ción f. disapproval.

de·sa·pro·bar §19 tr. to disapprove (of).

de·sa·pro·ve·char tr. to waste, misuse —intr. to lose ground, go backwards.

de·sa·prue·be, be see **desaprobar**.

de·sar·ma·do, a adj. *(desprovisto)* unarmed; *(desmontado)* in pieces, dismantled.

de·sar·mar tr. to disarm; *(desmontar)* to take apart, dismantle; *(templar)* to calm, appease; *(encantar)* to disarm, charm —intr. & reflex. to disarm; *(desmontar)* to fall apart *or* to

pieces.

de·sar·me m. disarmament; *(desmontaje)* dismantling.

de·sa·rrai·ga·do, a adj. uprooted, rootless.

de·sa·rrai·gar §47 tr. to uproot, dig up; *(extirpar)* to extirpate, eradicate; *(desterrar)* to banish, expel —reflex. to become uprooted.

de·sa·rrai·go m. uprooting; *(extirpación)* extirpation, eradication; *(destierro)* banishment, expulsion.

de·sa·rre·gla·do, a adj. untidy, disorderly; *(roto)* out of order, broken (down).

de·sa·rre·glar tr. to make untidy, mess (up); *(estropear)* to spoil, upset; *(quebrar)* to put out of order, break —reflex. to become untidy *or* messy; *(quebrar)* to get out of order, break (down).

de·sa·rre·glo m. untidiness, disorder; *(de un mecanismo)* breakdown, trouble.

de·sa·rro·lla·do, a adj. developed.

de·sa·rro·llar tr. *(deshacer)* to unroll, unfold; *(extender)* to develop, expand; *(explicar)* to expound, elaborate —reflex. *(deshacerse)* to unroll, unfold; *(extenderse)* to develop, expand; *(tener lugar)* to take place.

de·sa·rro·llo m. *(despliegue)* unrolling, unfolding; *(extensión)* development, expansion; *(explicación)* exposition, elaboration; *(de los sucesos)* development, course.

de·sa·rru·gar §47 tr. to unwrinkle, smooth the wrinkles from —reflex. to become unwrinkled.

de·sar·ti·cu·lar tr. to dislocate, throw out of joint; *(desmontar)* to disassemble, take apart —reflex. to become dislocated *or* out of joint.

de·sa·se·a·do, a adj. & m.f. *(sucio)* dirty (person); *(desarreglado)* messy (person).

de·sa·se·ar tr. *(ensuciar)* to dirty, soil; *(poner en desorden)* to mess up, disorder.

de·sa·se·o m. *(suciedad)* dirtiness, uncleanliness; *(desarreglo)* untidiness, messiness.

de·sa·sir §08 tr. to release, let go —reflex. to yield, give up.

de·sa·so·ciar tr. to dissociate, separate.

de·sa·so·se·gar §52 tr. to make uneasy, disturb —reflex. to become uneasy *or* disturbed.

de·sa·so·sie·go m. uneasiness, restlessness.

de·sas·tre m. disaster, catastrophe.

de·sas·tro·so, a adj. disastrous, catastrophic.

de·sa·tar tr. to untie, undo; *(soltar)* to unleash, let go; *(aclarar)* to unravel, solve —reflex. to come untied *or* undone; *(soltarse)* to break away *or* loose; *(hablar)* to chatter, babble; *(descomedirse)* to be rude, let oneself go; *(perder el encogimiento)* to loosen up ◊ **d. de** to get out of, rid oneself of.

de·sa·tas·car §70 tr. to pull out of the mud; *(desatrancar)* to clear, unblock; *(ayudar)* to get someone out of a jam —reflex. to get out of the mud.

de·sa·ten·der §50 tr. *(no hacer caso)* to neglect; *(no prestar atención)* to ignore, disregard.

de·sa·ten·to, a I. adj. inattentive; *(descortés)* discourteous, impolite **II.** m.f. impolite person.

de·sa·ti·na·do, a I. adj. foolish, silly; *(imprudente)* rash, reckless **II.** m.f. fool.

de·sa·ti·nar tr. to exasperate, bewilder; *(atolondrar)* to make lose one's head —intr. *(cometer desaciertos)* to make blunders; *(disparatar)* to rave, talk nonsense.

de·sa·ti·no m. nonsense, foolishness; *(acción)* silly *or* foolish act.

de·sa·tran·car §70 tr. *(la puerta)* to unbar, unbolt; *(desatrampar)* to clear, unblock.

de·sau·to·ri·za·do, a adj. unauthorized.

de·sau·to·ri·zar §04 tr. to deprive of authority; *(desmentir)* to deny; *(prohibir)* to prohibit.

de·sa·ve·nen·cia f. discord, enmity.

de·sa·ve·nir §76 tr. to cause discord between —reflex. to disagree, quarrel.

de·sa·yu·nar intr. to have breakfast, breakfast —reflex. to have breakfast, breakfast; FIG. to receive the first news of —tr. to breakfast on, have for breakfast.

de·sa·yu·no m. breakfast.

de·sa·zón f. tastelessness, insipidity; *(disgusto)* annoyance, irritation; *(desasosiego)* anxiety, uneasiness; MED. upset, discomfort.

des·ban·car §70 tr. to break the bank; FIG. to supplant, replace.

des·ban·dar·se reflex. to disband; *(dispersarse)* to disperse, scatter.

des·ba·ra·jus·te m. confusion, disorder.

des·ba·ra·ta·do, a I. adj. *(desordenado)* wild, unruly; *(roto)* wrecked, broken down II. m.f. ruin, wreck; COLL. libertine, debauchee.

des·ba·ra·tar tr. to ruin, wreck; *(malgastar)* to squander, waste; *(estorbar)* to hinder, frustrate; MECH. to break, put out of order; MIL. to rout, throw into confusion, into to talk or act wildly —reflex. to talk or act wildly; MECH. to break down, fall apart.

des·bo·ca·do, a I. adj. *(roto)* chipped; *(mellado)* nicked, damaged; *(malhablado)* foulmouthed; S. AMER. overflowing II. m.f. COLL. foul mouth.

des·bo·ca·mien·to m. bolting (of a horse); *(injurias)* insults, abuse.

des·bo·car §70 tr. *(astillar)* to chip; *(mellar)* to nick —intr. *(dirigir a)* to lead or open into; *(desembocar)* to flow or empty into —reflex. EQUIT. to bolt, run away; *(injuriar)* to start to swear.

des·bor·da·mien·to m. *(inundación)* overflowing, running over; *(de cólera)* outburst.

des·bor·dar intr. *(derramarse)* to overflow, run over; *(rebosar)* to burst or brim with —reflex. *(derramarse)* to overflow, run over; *(rebosar)* to burst or brim with; *(desmandarse)* to lose one's self-control —tr. to pass, go beyond.

des·bro·zar §04 tr. to clear of rubbish or undergrowth.

des·bro·zo m. clearing away of rubbish or undergrowth; *(basura)* rubbish; *(maleza)* undergrowth.

des·ca·be·lla·do, a adj. wild, crazy.

des·ca·be·zar §04 tr. *(decapitar)* to behead, decapitate; *(desmochar)* to top, cut the top of; *(vencer)* to get over the worst of, surmount ♦ d. el sueño to take a nap, doze —intr. to abut, border on —reflex. COLL. to rack one's brains.

des·ca·fei·na·do, a adj. & m. decaffeinated (coffee).

des·ca·la·bra·do, a I. adj. wounded in the head; *(que pierde)* losing, unsuccessful II. m.f. loser.

des·ca·la·brar tr. to injure, wound; COLL. to damage, harm —reflex. to injure one's head.

des·ca·la·bro m. setback, misfortune; MIL. defeat.

des·ca·li·fi·ca·ción f. disqualification; *(descrédito)* discredit.

des·ca·li·fi·car §70 tr. to disqualify.

des·cal·zar §04 tr. to take off; *(quitar un calzo)*

to remove a wedge or block from; *(socavar)* to dig under, undermine —reflex. to take off shoes; *(un caballo)* to lose a shoe.

des·cal·zo, a adj. barefoot(ed), shoeless; *(pobre)* destitute, poor.

des·cam·pa·do, a I. adj. open, clear II. m. open field ♦ en d. in the open country.

des·cam·par intr. to clear up (weather).

des·can·sa·do, a adj. *(tranquilo)* restful, tranquil; *(refrescado)* rested, relaxed.

des·can·sar intr. to rest, take a rest; *(calmarse)* to relax; *(reposar)* to repose, lie down; *(yacer)* to rely on; *(basarse)* to be based on; *(apoyarse)* to rest or lean on; *(yacer)* to lie, rest —tr. to rest, give rest to; *(ayudar)* to help, aid; *(apoyar)* to rest or lean (something) on —reflex. to rest, take a rest ♦ d. en to rely on, have trust in.

des·can·so m. rest, repose; *(alivio)* relief; *(período)* break; *(licencia)* leave; SPORT. half time; THEAT. intermission; ARCHIT. landing.

des·ca·po·ta·ble adj. & m. convertible.

des·ca·ra·do, a adj. & m.f. shameless (person).

des·car·ga f. unloading; ARM. discharge, firing; ELEC. discharge.

des·car·ga·de·ro m. pier, unloading dock.

des·car·gar §47 tr. to unload; *(disparar)* to discharge, shoot; *(extraer la carga de)* to unload, disarm; ELEC. to discharge; *(golpear)* to deal; *(liberar)* to release, free; *(aliviar)* to ease, relieve; *(absolver)* to acquit, clear —intr. to flow, empty —reflex. *(dimitir)* to resign, quit; *(eximirse)* to unburden oneself; *(exonerarse)* to clear oneself.

des·car·go m. unloading; COM. entry; *(excusa)* excuse; *(dispensa)* release.

des·ca·ri·ñar·se reflex. to lose one's affection or love for.

des·car·nar tr. DENT. to scrape flesh from; *(desmoronar)* to wear or eat away; *(desapegar)* to disembody —reflex. to wear away, be eaten away.

des·ca·ro m. shamelessness, brazenness.

des·ca·rriar §30 tr. to misdirect, send the wrong way; *(un animal)* to separate from the herd; *(apartar de la razón)* to lead astray —reflex. *(desviarse)* to stray, get lost; *(apartarse de la razón)* to err, go astray.

des·ca·rri·la·mien·to m. RAIL. derailment; *(descarrío)* act of going astray.

des·ca·rri·lar intr. to be derailed, jump the track; *(una persona)* to get off the track.

des·car·tar tr. to discard, put aside —reflex. to discard ♦ d. de to excuse oneself from.

des·car·te m. discard; *(excusa)* excuse.

des·cas·ca·rar tr. & reflex. to peel.

des·cas·ca·ri·llar tr. to peel, husk.

des·cen·den·cia f. *(hijos)* descendants, offspring; *(linaje)* descent, origin.

des·cen·der §50 intr. to descend, go down; *(proceder)* to descend or be descended from; *(un líquido)* to run or flow down; *(de nivel)* to drop, fall; *(derivar)* to derive or come from —tr. *(bajar)* to descend, go down; *(bajar una cosa)* to lower, bring down.

des·cen·dien·te I. adj. descending II. m.f. descendant, offspring.

des·cen·so m. descent, going down; *(de nivel)* fall, drop; *(degradación)* demotion; *(decaimiento)* drop, decline.

des·cen·tra·do, a adj. off-center.

des·cen·tra·li·za·ción f. decentralization.

des·cen·trar tr. to put off center, uncenter

—reflex. to become off center.

des·ce·rra·jar tr. to force, break open; (descargar) to fire, discharge.

des·cien·da, do see **descender**.

des·ci·frar tr. to decipher; (con clave) to decode; (aclarar) to make out.

des·co·ca·do, a adj. & m.f. brazen, forward (person).

des·co·car §70 reflex. to be impudent or brazen.

des·co·di·fi·car §70 tr. to decode.

des·col·gar §16 tr. (quitar) to take down; (bajar) to lower, let down; (teléfono) to pick up —reflex. (caer) to come or fall down; (bajarse) to climb or come down; (presentarse) to show up, drop in ♦ **d. con** to come up with.

des·co·lo·rar tr. to discolor; (desteñir) to fade; (blanquear) to bleach —reflex. to be discolored; (desteñirse) to become faded; (quedar blanco) to be bleached; (el pelo) to bleach.

des·co·lo·ri·do, a adj. discolored; (pálido) pallid, colorless; (desteñido) faded; (blanqueado) whitened, bleached.

des·co·lo·rir §38 tr. to fade, discolor.

des·co·llar §19 intr. to stand out, be outstanding.

des·com·pa·sar tr. to go too far —reflex. to be rude, be impolite.

des·com·po·ner §54 tr. (desordenar) to disarrange, mess up; (podrir) to decompose, cause to rot; MECH. to break, put out of order; (trastornar) to upset, disturb —reflex. (corromperse) to rot, decompose; MECH. to break down; (indisponerse) to feel sick; (irritarse) to become disturbed, get upset.

des·com·po·si·ción f. decomposition, decay; (desarreglo) disorder, disarrangement.

des·com·pos·tu·ra f. disorder, disarrangement; (desaseo) slovenliness, messiness; (descaro) impudence, rudeness; MECH. breakdown.

des·com·pre·sión f. decompression.

des·com·pri·mir tr. to decompress.

des·com·pues·to, a I. see **descomponer** II. adj. decomposed, rotten; (desarreglado) slovenly, messy; MECH. out of order, broken; (perturbado) upset; (descarado) impudent, rude; S. AMER. tipsy.

des·com·pu·sie·ra, so see **descomponer**.

des·co·mu·nal adj. (enorme) enormous, huge; (extraordinario) extraordinary.

des·co·mu·nal·men·te adv. excessively.

des·con·cer·tan·te adj. disconcerting.

des·con·cer·tar §49 tr. to disconcert, upset; (descomponer) to put out of order; (desordenar) to disarrange, disrupt; MED. to dislocate —reflex. to be disconcerted; (descomponer) to get out of order; (desavenirse) to fall out, disagree; (descomedirse) to go off the deep end; MED. to become dislocated.

des·co·nec·tar tr. to disconnect —reflex. to become disconnected.

des·con·fia·do, a adj. & m.f. distrustful, suspicious (person).

des·con·fian·za f. distrust, mistrust.

des·con·fiar §30 intr. to distrust, mistrust.

des·con·ge·lar tr. (deshelar) to thaw; (la nevera) to defrost; COM. to unfreeze.

des·con·ges·tio·nar tr. to clear.

des·co·no·cer §17 tr. not to know; (no recordar) not to remember; (no reconocer) not to recognize; (negar) to deny, disavow; (desentenderse) to pretend not to know, ignore.

des·co·no·ci·do, a I. adj. unknown; (desagradecido) ungrateful; (muy cambiado) unrecognizable; (extraño) strange, unfamiliar II. m.f. (extraño) stranger; (recién llegado) newcomer.

des·co·no·ci·mien·to m. ignorance; (despreocupación) disregard; (ingratitud) ingratitude; (olvido) forgetfulness.

des·con·si·de·ra·ción f. thoughtlessness.

des·con·si·de·ra·do, a adj. & m.f. inconsiderate, thoughtless (person).

des·con·so·la·do, a adj. disconsolate, sad; (el estómago) empty, starved.

des·con·so·lar §19 tr. to distress, grieve —reflex. to lose heart, become distressed.

des·con·sue·lo m. grief, distress; (del estómago) empty feeling.

des·con·ta·mi·nar tr. to decontaminate.

des·con·tar §19 tr. (quitar) to deduct, take away; (rebajar) to disregard, discount; (dar por cierto) to take for granted, assume; COM. to discount.

des·con·ten·tar tr. to discontent, displease —reflex. to become discontented or displeased.

des·con·ten·to, a I. adj. discontented, dissatisfied II. m. discontent, dissatisfaction.

des·co·ra·zo·nar tr. to tear out the heart of; FIG. to discourage, dishearten —reflex. to lose heart, become discouraged.

des·cor·char tr. to uncork.

des·co·rrer tr. to run back over (ground already covered); (cortinas) to draw back, open —intr. & reflex. to flow.

des·cor·tés adj. & m.f. discourteous, rude (person).

des·cor·te·sí·a f. discourtesy, rudeness.

des·cor·te·zar §04 tr. to strip the bark from, decorticate; (el pan) to remove the crust from; (la fruta) to peel; (desbastar) to refine, knock the rough edges off.

des·co·ser tr. SEW. to unstitch, rip —reflex. SEW. to come unstitched, rip ♦ **no d. los labios** to keep one's lips sealed.

des·co·si·do, a adj. SEW. unstitched, ripped; (indiscreto) indiscreet, talkative; (desordenado) disorderly, chaotic; (excesivo) immoderate, excessive.

des·co·te m. low-cut neckline, décolletage.

des·co·yun·tar tr. MED. to dislocate; FIG. to bother, annoy —reflex. MED. to become dislocated.

des·cré·di·to m. discredit, disrepute.

des·cre·í·do, a I. adj. disbelieving, incredulous II. m.f. disbeliever; RELIG. nonbeliever, infidel.

des·cri·bir §80 tr. to describe; (trazar) to trace, describe.

des·crip·ción f. description.

des·cri(p)·to, a see **describir**.

des·cuar·ti·zar §04 tr. to quarter, cut up.

des·cu·bier·to, a I. see **descubrir** II. adj. uncovered, exposed; (yermo) bare, barren; (sin sombrero) bareheaded, without a hat ♦ **a d.** uncovered; COM. unbacked ♦ **al d.** COM. short; FIG. openly, in the open • **estar en d.** COM. to be overdrawn; FIG. to be at a loss for words • **girar en d.** COM. overdraw III. m. COM. deficit, shortage.

des·cu·bri·dor, ·ra I. adj. discovering, exploring II. m.f. (explorador) discoverer, explorer —m. MIL. scout.

des·cu·bri·mien·to m. discovery; (revelación) disclosure, revelation.

des·cu·brir §80 tr. to discover; (revelar) to reveal, uncover; *(alcanzar a ver)* to be able to see, make out; *(enterarse)* to find out; MIL. to reconnoiter —reflex. *(el sombrero)* to take off or remove one's hat; *(dejarse ver)* to reveal oneself, show oneself.

des·cuel·go, gue see **descolgar.**

des·cue·lle, llo see **descollar.**

des·cuen·te, to see **descontar.**

des·cuen·to m. discount, reduction; *(acción de descontar)* deduction.

des·cue·rar tr. AMER. to skin, flay; *(criticar)* to criticize, tear apart.

des·cui·da·do, a I. adj. *(negligente)* careless; *(desaliñado)* untidy, slovenly; *(desprevenido)* unprepared, off guard; *(abandonado)* neglected, abandoned; *(despreocupado)* carefree, easygoing II. m.f. *(negligente)* careless person; *(desaliñado)* sloppy person, slob.

des·cui·dar tr. *(libertar)* to relieve, free of an obligation; *(no cuidar)* to neglect, forget; *(distraer)* to distract —intr. to be careless —reflex. to be careless; *(desaliñarse)* to neglect oneself, not take care of oneself.

des·cui·do m. carelessness, negligence; *(olvido)* forgetfulness; *(desaliño)* untidiness, slovenliness, *(desatención)* slip, oversight; *(falta)* error, mistake ◆ **al d.** nonchalantly, casually • **en un d.** AMER. when least expected.

des·cha·ve·ta·do, a adj. AMER. crazy, loony.

des·de prep. from, since ◆ **d. hace** for <*no lo hemos visto d. hace un año* we have not seen him for a year> • **d. luego** of course • **d. que** since • **d. ya** AMER. right now.

des·de·cir §11 intr. ◆ **d. de** not to live up to, to fall short of; *(venir a menos)* to degenerate, decline —reflex. ◆ **d. de** to retract, withdraw.

des·dén m. disdain, scorn ◆ **al d.** nonchalantly.

des·de·ña·ble adj. despicable, contemptible.

des·de·ñar tr. to disdain, scorn —reflex. to be disdainful ◆ **d.** not to deign to.

des·di·bu·jar·se reflex. to become blurred.

des·di·ce see **desdecir.**

des·di·cha f. *(desgracia)* misfortune; *(pobreza)* poverty, misery ◆ **por d.** unfortunately.

des·di·cha·do, a I. adj. *(desgraciado)* unfortunate, pitiful; *(infeliz)* unhappy, wretched II. m.f. wretch.

des·di·ga, go, jera, jo see **desdecir.**

des·do·bla·mien·to m. *(extensión)* unfolding, spreading out; *(fraccionamiento)* splitting, breaking down; *(aclaración)* explanation, elucidation ◆ **d. de la personalidad** split personality.

des·do·blar tr. *(extender)* to unfold, spread out; *(separar)* to split, break down.

de·se·ar tr. to wish, desire.

de·se·car §70 tr. to dry, desiccate; *(volver insensible)* to dry up, harden.

de·se·char tr. *(rechazar)* to reject, decline; *(renunciar)* to refuse, turn down; *(apartar)* to cast aside, get rid of; *(menospreciar)* to underrate, undervalue; *(despreciar)* to scorn.

de·se·cho m. residue; *(desperdicio)* waste, rubbish; *(lo peor)* scum, dregs; *(metal)* scrap; *(desprecio)* scorn, contempt.

de·sem·ba·lar tr. to unpack.

de·sem·ba·ra·za·do, a adj. free, clear; *(desenvuelto)* free and easy.

de·sem·ba·ra·zar §04 tr. to clear, rid of obstacles, AMER. to give birth to —reflex. to free oneself, get rid (of).

de·sem·bar·ca·de·ro m. pier, wharf.

de·sem·bar·car §70 tr. to disembark, unload —intr. to disembark, go ashore.

de·sem·bar·co m. landing, disembarkation; MIL. landing; *(escalera)* landing.

de·sem·bar·gar §47 tr. to clear, remove obstacles from.

de·sem·bar·que m. *(de mercancías)* debarkation, unloading; *(de pasajeros)* disembarkation, landing.

de·sem·bo·ca·du·ra f. outlet.

de·sem·bo·car §70 intr. *(río)* to flow, run; *(calle)* to lead to, run.

de·sem·bol·sar tr. to take out of a purse or bag; *(pagar)* to disburse, pay.

de·sem·bol·so m. *(pago)* disbursement, payment; *(gasto)* expenditure, outlay.

de·sem·bo·zar §04 tr. & reflex. to unmask (oneself).

de·sem·bra·gar §47 tr. MECH. to disengage (gears).

de·sem·bria·gar §47 tr. to sober up.

de·sem·bro·llar tr. to unravel, untangle.

de·sem·bu·char tr. ORNITH. to disgorge; COLL. *(revelar)* tell, reveal.

de·sem·pa·car §70 tr. to unpack, unwrap.

de·sem·pa·cho m. ease, self-confidence.

de·sem·pa·ñar tr. *(un cristal)* to clean, polish; *(un niño)* to unswaddle.

de·sem·pa·pe·lar tr. to remove paper from; *(desenvolver)* to unwrap.

de·sem·pa·que m. unpacking.

de·sem·pa·que·tar tr. to unpack, unwrap.

de·sem·pa·tar tr. to break a tie between.

de·sem·pe·ñar tr. *(rescatar)* to recover, redeem; *(pagar)* to get out of debt; *(cumplir)* to fulfill, carry out; *(sacar de apuro)* to get (someone) out of trouble; THEAT. to play (a part) —reflex. *(pagar)* to get oneself out of debt; *(sacarse de apuro)* to get oneself out of trouble.

de·sem·pe·ño m. *(rescate)* redemption; *(de deudas)* freeing from debt; *(cumplimiento)* fulfillment; THEAT. performance.

de·sem·ple·a·do, a adj. & m.f. unemployed (person).

de·sem·ple·o m. unemployment.

de·sen·ca·de·na·mien·to m. unchaining; *(de sucesos)* unfolding.

de·sen·ca·de·nar tr. to unchain, unfetter; *(liberar)* to free, unleash; *(incitar)* to start, incite —reflex. to break loose; *(sucesos)* to unfold.

de·sen·ca·jar tr. MED. to dislocate; *(desconectar)* to disconnect; *(sacar)* to remove, take out —reflex. to become distorted or contorted; *(deshacerse)* to fall apart, become disconnected.

de·sen·ca·mi·nar tr. to lead astray, misdirect.

de·sen·can·tar tr. to disenchant, disillusion.

de·sen·can·to m. disenchantment.

de·sen·ce·rrar §49 tr. *(sacar del encierro)* to free (from confinement); *(abrir)* to open, unlock; *(descubrir)* to bring to light, reveal.

de·sen·cla·vi·jar tr. to disconnect, loosen.

de·sen·co·ger §34 tr. *(extender)* to stretch or spread out; *(desdoblar)* to unfold —reflex. to come out of one's shell.

de·sen·co·le·ri·zar §04 tr. to calm, pacify.

de·sen·co·nar tr. MED. to relieve the inflammation of; *(desahogar)* to soothe, pacify —reflex. to calm down, cool off.

de·sen·co·no m. MED. relief of inflammation;

(apaciguamiento) calming, pacification.

de·sen·chu·far tr. to unplug, disconnect.

de·sen·fa·da·do, a adj. *(desenvuelto)* confident, self-assured; *(despreocupado)* carefree, uninhibited; *(espacioso)* spacious, ample.

de·sen·fa·dar tr. to soothe, pacify —reflex. to calm down, cool off.

de·sen·fa·do m. *(desenvoltura)* confidence, self-assurance; *(facilidad)* ease, naturalness.

de·sen·fre·nar tr. to unbridle —reflex. to surrender oneself, give oneself over; *(las pasiones)* to break loose, be unleashed; *(una tempestad)* to break, burst.

de·sen·fre·no m. wantonness, licentiousness.

de·sen·fun·dar tr. to unsheath.

de·sen·gan·char tr. to unhook, unfasten; *(caballerías)* to unhitch, unharness.

de·sen·ga·ña·do, a adj. disillusioned.

de·sen·ga·ñar tr. to disillusion —reflex. to become disillusioned.

de·sen·ga·ño m. disillusionment; *(comprensión)* enlightenment.

de·sen·gra·nar tr. MECH. to disengage.

de·sen·gra·sar tr. to remove the grease from —intr. *(enflaquecer)* to lose weight, grow slim; *(variar el trabajo)* to change jobs.

de·sen·la·ce m. untying, unfastening; LIT. denouement, ending; *(resultado)* result, outcome.

de·sen·la·zar §04 tr. to unfasten, untie; *(resolver)* to clear up, resolve; LIT. to unravel —reflex. to become untied *or* loose; LIT. to reach a denouement.

de·sen·ma·ra·ñar tr. to untangle, unravel.

des·en·mas·ca·rar tr. *(quitar la máscara)* to unmask; *(descubrir)* to reveal, expose.

de·sen·mu·de·cer §17 tr. & intr. to rid (oneself) of a speech impediment; *(hablar)* to break a long silence.

de·se·no·jo m. calm, calmness (after anger).

de·sen·re·dar tr. to disentangle, unravel; *(poner en orden)* to put in order, straighten out —reflex. to extricate oneself.

de·sen·re·do m. disentangling, disentanglement; *(aclaración)* putting in order, straightening out; LIT. denouement, ending.

de·sen·ro·llar tr. to unroll, unwind.

de·sen·sam·blar tr. to disassemble.

de·sen·si·bi·li·zar §04 tr. to desensitize.

de·sen·si·llar tr. to unsaddle.

de·sen·ta·blar tr. *(desarreglar)* to disarrange, disturb; *(deshacer)* to break up.

de·sen·ten·der·se §50 reflex. to feign ignorance, pretend not to know ♦ **d. de** to take no part in, have nothing to do with.

de·sen·te·rrar §49 tr. to unearth, dig up; COLL. to dig up, recall.

de·sen·to·nar tr. to humiliate, humble —intr. MUS. to be out of tune; FIG. to clash, not to match —reflex. to be rude *or* insolent.

de·sen·to·no m. MUS. dissonance; FIG. rude *or* insolent tone of voice.

de·sen·tra·ñar tr. to eviscerate, disembowel; *(solucionar)* to get to the bottom of —reflex. to give one's all.

de·sen·tu·me·cer §17 tr. to rid of numbness.

de·sen·vai·nar tr. *(un sable)* to draw, unsheathe; *(las uñas)* to bare (claws); COLL. *(sacar a relucir)* to uncover, expose.

de·sen·vol·tu·ra f. *(confianza)* naturalness, confidence; *(elocuencia)* eloquence, facility; *(desvergüenza)* forwardness, brazenness.

de·sen·vol·ver §78 tr. to unroll, unwrap; *(ex-*

plicar) to develop, expand; *(aclarar)* to unravel, disentangle —reflex. to come unrolled *or* unwrapped; *(desempacharse)* to become self-assured; *(desenredarse)* to get oneself out of trouble.

de·sen·vol·vi·mien·to m. unrolling, unwrapping; *(explicación)* development, expansion; *(desenredo)* way out, escape.

de·sen·vuel·to, a I. see **desenvolver II.** adj. *(confiado)* natural, confident; *(elocuente)* eloquent, fluent; *(desvergonzado)* forward, brazen.

de·se·o m. desire, wish.

de·se·o·so, a adj. desirous, anxious.

de·se·qui·li·bra·do, a adj. & m.f. unbalanced (person).

de·se·qui·li·brar tr. to throw off balance —reflex. to lose one's balance; *(dementarse)* to become mentally unbalanced.

de·se·qui·li·brio m. lack of equilibrium, imbalance; *(de la mente)* derangement.

de·ser·ción f. desertion, abandonment; MIL. desertion.

de·ser·tar tr., intr. & reflex. to desert.

de·sér·ti·co, a adj. desert-like, barren; *(sin habitantes)* deserted, unpopulated.

de·ser·tor, ·ra m.f. deserter.

de·ses·pe·ra·ción f. despair, desperation; *(cólera)* anger, exasperation.

de·ses·pe·ra·do, a adj. & m.f. hopeless, desperate (person) ♦ **a la d.** in desperation, as a last hope.

de·ses·pe·ran·te adj. *(que impacienta)* exasperating, infuriating; *(descorazonador)* discouraging, causing despair.

de·ses·pe·ran·za f. despair, hopelessness.

de·ses·pe·ran·zar §04 tr. to deprive of hope, discourage —intr. & reflex. to despair, lose hope.

de·ses·pe·rar tr. to drive to despair, discourage; *(irritar)* to exasperate —intr. & reflex. to lose hope, despair.

de·ses·ti·mar tr. to hold in low esteem.

des·fa·cha·ta·do, a adj. cheeky, insolent.

des·fa·cha·tez f. cheek, nerve.

des·fal·car §70 tr. to remove part of; *(robar)* to embezzle, defalcate.

des·fal·co m. embezzlement, defalcation.

des·fa·lle·cer §17 tr. to weaken, debilitate —intr. to weaken; *(desmayarse)* to faint, pass out.

des·fa·lle·ci·do, a adj. faint, dizzy.

des·fa·lle·ci·mien·to m. weakness, debilitation; MED. fainting, swooning.

des·fa·sa·do, a adj. out of phase.

des·fa·vo·ra·ble adj. unfavorable, adverse.

des·fa·vo·re·cer §17 tr. to disfavor; *(oponer)* to oppose, contradict.

des·fi·gu·ra·ción f./**mien·to** m. disfiguring, disfigurement; *(objeto)* defacement; *(hecho)* distortion, misrepresentation; *(disfraz)* disguise, camouflage.

des·fi·gu·rar tr. *(afear)* to disfigure, mar; *(deformar)* to deform, misshape; *(disfrazar)* to disguise, camouflage; *(desvirtuar)* to distort, misrepresent —reflex. to be disfigured.

des·fi·la·de·ro m. defile, narrow pass.

des·fi·lar intr. to parade, march.

des·fi·le m. march, procession; MIL. parade.

des·flo·ra·ción f./**mien·to** m. deflowering.

des·flo·rar tr. to strip the flowers from; *(ajar)* to tarnish, spoil; *(desvirgar)* to deflower.

des·fo·gar §47 tr. to vent; *(apagar)* to slake;

(soltar) to vent, give vent to —reflex. to vent one's anger, let off steam.

des·fo·gue m. *(agujero)* vent; *(desahogo)* letting off steam, venting.

des·fon·dar tr. to knock the bottom out of —reflex. to have the bottom fall out; *(agotarse)* to wear oneself out, exhaust oneself.

des·for·mar tr. to deform, disfigure.

des·ga·jar tr. to rip *or* tear off —reflex. to come *or* break off.

des·ga·na f. lack of appetite; *(renuencia)* reluctance, unwillingness.

des·ga·na·do, a adj. without appetite, not hungry; *(sin entusiasmo)* indifferent, unenthusiastic.

des·ga·nar tr. to take away (a person's) desire *or* interest —reflex. to lose one's appetite; FIG. *(cansarse)* to get bored, lose interest.

des·ga·no m. var. of **desgana.**

des·ga·ñi·tar·se reflex. to scream loudly.

des·gar·ba·do, a adj. awkward, ungainly.

des·ga·rra·do, a adj. torn, ripped; COLL. impudent, shameless.

des·ga·rra·dor, ·ra adj. *(que da miedo)* bloodcurdling; AMER. heartbreaking, heartrending.

des·ga·rra·mien·to m. ripping, tearing.

des·ga·rrar tr. to rip, tear; *(expectorar)* to spit, empectorate —reflex. to rip, tear, *(apartarse)* to break away, go off by oneself.

des·gas·tar tr. to wear away *or* down; *(debilitar)* to weaken —reflex. *(perder fuerza)* to become weak *or* feeble; *(agotarse)* to wear oneself out.

des·gas·te m. erosion; *(daño)* damage, wear; *(debilitación)* weakening, debilitation.

des·glo·se m. breakdown; CINEM. cutting, editing.

des·gra·cia f. misfortune, adversity; *(accidente)* mishap, setback; *(pérdida de favor)* disgrace, disfavor; *(desgracia) displeasure; (falta de gracia)* gracelessness, clumsiness ♦ **por d.** unfortunately.

des·gra·cia·da·men·te adv. unfortunately.

des·gra·cia·do, a adj. & m.f. unfortunate, unlucky (person); *(infeliz)* unhappy (person); *(desagradable)* unpleasant, disagreeable (person); *(sinvergüenza)* wretched, despicable (person).

des·gra·ciar tr. to displease, annoy; *(estropear)* to ruin, spoil; AMER. *(seducir)* to seduce —reflex. *(perder favor)* to lose favor; *(estropearse)* to be ruined *or* spoiled; *(malograrse)* to fail, fall through.

des·gra·na·dor, ·ra I. adj. threshing, shelling II. m.f. thresher, sheller —f. threshing machine.

des·gra·nar tr. to thresh, shell.

des·gra·sar tr. to remove grease from.

des·gra·var tr. *(rebajar)* to reduce taxes *or* duties; *(eximir)* to exempt from taxes *or* duties; *(aligerar)* to lighten.

des·gre·ñar tr. to dishevel, tousle —reflex. to become disheveled *or* tousled; *(reñir)* to have a heated argument.

des·guar·ne·cer §17 tr. to remove the trimmings; *(desarmar)* to dismantle.

des·ha·bi·ta·do, a adj. uninhabited.

des·ha·bi·tar tr. to vacate, leave; *(despoblar)* to depopulate, leave without inhabitants.

des·ha·bi·tuar §67 tr. & reflex. to break of a habit.

des·ha·cer §40 tr. to undo; *(destruir)* to destroy, ruin; *(desgastar)* to wear out; *(dividir)* to

cut up; *(desarmar)* to take apart; *(disolver)* to melt, dissolve; *(desconcertar)* to break —reflex. *(descomponerse)* to fall apart, break; *(disolverse)* to melt, dissolve; *(desaparecer)* to vanish, disappear; *(inquietarse)* to go to pieces, get worked up; *(desvivirse)* to go out of one's way; *(extenuarse)* to weaken, become weak ♦ **d. de** to get rid of ● **d. en** to dissolve into.

des·he·cho, a I. see **deshacer** II. adj. undone; *(cansado)* tired, worn out.

des·he·lar §49 tr. & reflex. to melt, thaw.

des·he·re·da·do, a adj. & m.f. disinherited (person); *(pobre)* poor, underprivileged (person).

des·he·re·dar tr. to disinherit.

des·he·rrar §49 tr. to unshackle, unchain —reflex. to free oneself from shackles *or* chains; *(un caballo)* to lose a shoe.

des·hi·cie·ra, hice see **deshacer.**

des·hi·dra·ta·ción f. dehydration.

des·hi·dra·tar tr. to dehydrate —reflex. to become dehydrated.

des·hie·le see **deshelar.**

des·hie·lo m. thawing, defrosting.

des·hie·rre, rro see **desherrar.**

des·hi·la·char tr. to ravel, remove threads from —reflex. to fray, become frayed.

des·hi·lar tr. to undo, unravel, FIG. to cut to ribbons *or* pieces —intr. to get *or* grow thin —reflex. to become frayed.

des·hil·va·na·do, a adj. disjointed, disconnected.

des·hil·va·nar tr. to remove tacking *or* basting from.

des·hin·char tr. to reduce the swelling of; *(un balón)* to deflate; *(la cólera)* to give vent to —reflex. to go down; COLL. to be taken down a peg or two.

des·hi·zo see **deshacer.**

des·ho·ja·du·ra f./**mien·to** m. defoliation.

des·ho·jar tr. to defoliate —reflex. to lose leaves.

des·ho·je m. falling of leaves.

des·ho·lli·na·dor, ·ra I. adj. nosy, inquisitive II. m.f. *(persona que deshollina)* chimney sweep; *(escudriñador)* busybody, snoop.

des·ho·lli·nar tr. to sweep chimneys; *(escudriñar)* to scrutinize, examine closely.

des·ho·nes·ti·dad f. dishonesty; *(indecencia)* indecency, impropriety.

des·ho·nes·to, a adj. dishonest; *(indecente)* indecent, improper.

des·ho·nor m. dishonor; *(afrenta)* insult, affront.

des·hon·ra f. dishonor.

des·hon·rar tr. to dishonor, disgrace; *(afrentar)* to insult, affront.

des·hon·ro·so, a adj. dishonorable.

des·ho·ra f. inconvenient time.

des·hue·sar tr. *(carne)* to debone; *(fruta)* to remove the pit from.

des·hu·ma·ni·za·ción f. dehumanization.

des·hu·ma·ni·zar §04 tr. to dehumanize.

des·hu·me·de·cer §17 tr. & reflex. to dry out.

de·si·dia f. negligence, carelessness; *(pereza)* laziness, indolence.

de·sier·to, a I. adj. deserted, uninhabited; *(desolado)* desolate, bleak II. m. desert.

de·sig·na·ción f. designation.

de·sig·nar tr. to design, plan; *(nombrar)* to designate, appoint; *(señalar)* to point out; *(fijar)* to decide on, fix.

de·sig·nio m. design, plan.

de·si·gual adj. unequal; *(quebrado)* uneven; *(diferente)* different; *(injusto)* unfair, inequitable; *(arduo)* arduous, difficult; *(inconstante)* changeable, inconstant.

de·si·gual·dad f. inequality, disparity; *(aspereza)* roughness, ruggedness; *(inconstancia)* inconstancy, changeableness.

de·si·lu·sión f. disillusionment.

de·si·lu·sio·nar tr. to disillusion —reflex. to become disillusioned.

de·si·man·tar tr. to demagnetize.

de·sin·cor·po·rar tr. to dissolve, break up.

de·sin·fec·ción f. disinfection.

de·sin·fec·tan·te adj. & m. disinfectant.

de·sin·fec·tar tr. to disinfect.

de·sin·fla·mar tr. to reduce inflammation in.

de·sin·flar tr. to deflate, let air out of —reflex. to deflate, collapse; COLL. to lose one's nerve.

de·sin·te·gra·ción f. disintegration.

de·sin·te·grar tr. *(disociar)* to disintegrate, break up; PHYS. to split.

de·sin·te·rés m. unselfishness.

de·sin·te·re·sa·do, a adj. disinterested, impartial; *(generoso)* altruistic, unselfish.

de·sin·te·re·sar·se reflex. to lose interest, take no interest in.

de·sin·to·xi·ca·ción f. detoxification.

de·sin·to·xi·car §70 intr. to detoxify.

de·sis·tir intr. to desist; *(de un derecho)* to waive.

des·jui·cia·do, a adj. injudicious.

des·jun·tar tr. & reflex. to separate, divide.

des·la·bo·nar tr. to unlink, disconnect the links of; *(desconcertar)* to upset; *(deshacer)* to ruin, destroy —reflex. to come apart, become disconnected; *(deshacerse)* to fail, fall apart; *(apartarse)* to break away, withdraw.

des·la·zar §04 tr. to unlace, untie.

des·le·al I. adj. disloyal, traitorous II. m.f. traitor.

des·le·al·tad f. disloyalty, treachery.

des·le·ír §58 tr. to dissolve, liquefy; *(un discurso)* to dilute, weaken —reflex. to dissolve.

des·len·gua·do, a adj. *(grosero)* foul-mouthed, coarse; *(descarado)* rude, insolent.

des·len·guar §10 tr. to remove the tongue from —reflex. *(descararse)* to be insolent; *(hablar groseramente)* to use foul language, swear.

des·li·a lío, liera, lió see **desleír**.

des·liar §30 tr. *(desatar)* to untie, undo; *(desenvolver)* to unwrap.

des·li·gar §47 tr. *(desatar)* to untie, unfasten; *(desenredar)* to untangle, unravel; *(dispensar)* to dispense, administer; *(absolver)* to absolve, exonerate; MUS. to pick —reflex. *(desatarse)* to become untied *or* unfastened; *(librarse)* to extricate oneself, break away.

des·lin·dar tr. to delimit, mark the boundaries of; *(aclarar)* to clarify, elucidate.

des·liz m. slip.

des·li·za·mien·to m. *(desliz)* slipping, sliding ♦ **d. de tierra** landslide.

des·li·zar §04 tr. to slip, slide; *(decir por descuido)* to let slip —intr. to slide, slip —reflex. to slide, slip; *(sobre el agua)* to glide; *(escaparse)* to slip away, escape; COLL. *(caerse)* to slip; *(meter la pata)* to slip up.

des·lo·mar tr. to break the back of; *(cansar)* to exhaust, wear out —reflex. to exhaust oneself, wear oneself out.

des·lu·ci·do, a adj. *(sin brillo)* tarnished, dull; *(sin vida)* lackluster, mediocre.

des·lu·cir §44 tr. *(estropear)* to spoil, ruin; *(quitar el brillo a)* to dull, tarnish; *(desacreditar)* to discredit —reflex. *(perder el brillo)* to become dull *or* tarnished; *(desacreditarse)* to become discredited.

des·lum·bra·dor, ·ra/bran·te adj. *(brillante)* dazzling, brilliant; *(asombrante)* overwhelming.

des·lum·bra·mien·to m. *(ceguera)* dazzling, dazzle; *(confusión)* confusion, bewilderment.

des·lum·brar tr. *(cegar)* to dazzle, blind; *(confundir)* to overwhelm, bewilder.

des·lus·tre m. *(falta de brillo)* dullness, lack of shine; *(empañadura)* tarnishing, dulling; *(deshonra)* dishonor, disgrace.

des·ma·de·jar tr. to weaken, enervate.

des·ma·le·zar §04 tr. AMER. to weed.

des·mán m. *(ultraje)* outrage, abuse; *(desgracia)* misfortune, mishap; ZOOL. muskrat.

des·man·da·do, a adj. disobedient.

des·man·dar I. tr. to countermand, rescind II. reflex. to go too far, get out of hand.

des·ma·no adv. ♦ **a d.** out of reach.

des·man·te·la·do, a adj. dismantled, disassembled; *(mal cuidado)* dilapidated, run-down.

des·man·te·lar tr. *(derribar)* to knock down, dismantle; *(una casa)* to vacate, abandon.

des·ma·ña f./ño m. clumsiness, awkwardness.

des·ma·ña·do, a adj. & m.f. clumsy (person).

des·ma·ra·ñar tr. to disentangle, unravel.

des·ma·ya·do, a adj. unconscious; *(un color)* dull, wan; *(desanimado)* discouraged, disheartened; *(agotado)* weak, worn-out.

des·ma·yar tr. to make faint, cause to faint —intr. to lose heart, be discouraged —reflex. to faint, swoon.

des·ma·yo m. *(síncope)* faint, swoon; *(estado)* unconsciousness; *(desánimo)* depression, downheartedness; BOT. weeping willow.

des·me·di·do, a adj. *(excesivo)* excessive, immoderate; *(sin límite)* boundless, limitless.

des·me·dro m. decline, deterioration.

des·me·jo·rar tr. to impair, damage —intr. & reflex. to deteriorate, get worse.

des·mem·bra·ción f./mien·to m. dismemberment; *(división)* division, breaking up.

des·mem·brar tr. to dismember.

des·me·mo·ria·do, a adj. & m.f. forgetful, absent-minded (person).

des·me·mo·riar·se reflex. to become forgetful, lose one's memory.

des·men·ti·da f. *(negación)* denial; *(contradicción)* contradiction.

des·men·tir §65 tr. to contradict; *(refutar)* to refute, disprove; *(proceder contrariamente)* to go against —intr. to deviate, go out of line —reflex. to contradict oneself.

des·me·nu·zar §04 tr. to crumble, break into pieces; *(examinar)* to examine closely, scrutinize.

des·me·re·cer §17 tr. to be unworthy *or* undeserving of —intr. *(decaer)* to deteriorate; *(ser inferior)* to be inferior, compare unfavorably.

des·me·re·ci·mien·to m. demerit, unworthiness.

des·me·su·ra·do, a adj. *(desmedido)* excessive, inordinate; *(sin límite)* boundless, limitless; *(insolente)* insolent, impudent.

des·me·su·rar tr. *(desordenar)* to put in disorder; *(descomponer)* to disturb, upset —reflex. to go too far, forget oneself.

des·mien·ta, te see **desmentir**.

des·mi·gar §47 tr. to crumble (bread).

des·mi·ne·ra·li·za·ción f. demineralization.

des·min·tie·ra, tió see **desmentir.**

des·mo·char tr. *(un árbol)* to top; *(una obra)* to cut.

des·mol·dar tr. to unmold.

des·mon·ta·ble I. adj. detachable II. m. tire iron.

des·mon·tar tr. to dismantle, disassemble; *(bajar)* to dismount; *(árboles)* to fell, cut down; *(terreno)* to level; *(arma de fuego)* to uncock —intr. & reflex. to dismount.

des·mo·ra·li·za·ción f. demoralization.

des·mo·ra·li·za·dor, ·ra I. adj. demoralizing II. m.f. demoralizer.

des·mo·ra·li·zar §04 tr. to demoralize; *(corromper)* to corrupt —reflex. to become demoralized; *(corromperse)* to become corrupt or depraved.

des·mo·ro·na·mien·to m. decay, crumbling.

des·mo·ro·nar tr. to wear away, erode —reflex. to crumble, fall to pieces.

des·mo·ta·dor, ·ra m.f. burler —f. cotton gin.

des·mo·tar tr. to burl.

des·mo·vi·li·za·ción f. demobilization.

des·mo·vi·li·zar §04 tr. to demobilize.

des·na·ta·do·ra f. cream separator, skimmer.

des·na·tar tr. to skim the cream off; *(sacar lo mejor)* to take the cream or the best of.

des·na·tu·ra·li·za·do, a adj. denaturalized; *(corrompido)* perverted, corrupted; *(malo)* cruel, unnatural; CHEM. denatured.

des·na·tu·ra·li·zar §04 tr. to denaturalize; *(corromper)* to pervert, corrupt; CHEM. to denature —reflex. to become denaturalized.

des·ni·vel m. unevenness; *(depresión)* depression, drop; *(diferencia)* difference, disparity.

des·ni·ve·lar tr. to make uneven; *(desequilibrar)* to throw out of balance, unbalance; *(una balanza)* to tip, tilt.

des·nu·car §70 tr. to break the neck of —reflex. to break one's neck.

des·nu·dar tr. to strip, undress; *(descubrir)* to lay bare, uncover; ARM. to bare, draw; *(en el juego)* to fleece, clean out ♦ **d. un santo para vestir a otro** COLL. to rob Peter to pay Paul —reflex. to get undressed, strip ♦ **d. de** to free or rid oneself of.

des·nu·dez f. nudity, nakedness.

des·nu·dis·ta adj. & m.f. nudist.

des·nu·do, a I. adj. undressed; *(en cueros)* naked, nude; *(despojado)* stripped, bare; *(pobre)* dispossessed, destitute; *(patente)* clear, naked ♦ **d. de** devoid of, lacking II. m. ARTS nude.

des·nu·tri·ción f. malnutrition.

de·so·be·de·cer §17 tr. to disobey.

de·so·be·dien·cia f. disobedience.

de·so·be·dien·te adj. & m.f. disobedient (person).

de·so·cu·pa·ción f. *(desempleo)* unemployment; *(ociosidad)* idleness.

de·so·cu·pa·do, a I. adj. unemployed; *(sitio)* vacant II. m.f. *(ocioso)* idler; *(sin empleo)* unemployed person.

de·so·cu·par tr. *(una casa)* to vacate, move out of; *(una vasija)* to empty —reflex. to leave, quit.

de·so·do·ran·te I. adj. deodorizing II. m. deodorant.

de·so·do·ri·zar §04 tr. to deodorize.

de·so·ír §45 tr. to ignore, pay no attention to.

de·so·la·ción f. desolation.

de·so·lar §19 tr. to desolate —reflex. to be grieved, be distressed.

de·so·llar §19 tr. to skin, flay; *(dañar)* to harm, injure; *(hacer pagar mucho)* to skin, fleece; *(criticar)* to flay, criticize; *(murmurar de)* to slander.

de·sor·bi·tar tr. to exaggerate, carry to extremes —reflex. *(los ojos)* to bulge; *(descomedirse)* to go to extremes, lose one's sense of proportion.

de·sor·den m. disorder, disarray; *(lío)* muddle, mess; *(conducta)* disorderliness, unruliness; MED. upset, disorder; *(exceso)* excess, license.

de·sor·de·na·do, a adj. disorderly; *(falta de aseo)* slovenly, untidy; *(excesivo)* excessive, inordinate; *(conducta)* unruly, wild.

de·sor·de·nar tr. to disorder; *(causar confusión)* to throw into confusion; *(desasear)* to make untidy or messy —reflex. to become disorderly; *(salirse de la regla)* to get out of order or out of control.

de·sor·ga·ni·za·ción f. disorganization.

de·sor·ga·ni·zar §04 tr. to disorganize.

de·so·rien·ta·ción f. disorientation.

de·so·rien·tar tr. to disorient; *(confundir)* to confuse —reflex. to be disoriented; *(confundirse)* to become confused.

de·so·vi·llar tr. to unravel; *(dar ánimo)* to encourage.

de·so·ye·ra, yó see **desoír.**

des·pa·bi·la·do, a adj. *(despierto)* alert, wide-awake; *(listo)* clever, sharp.

des·pa·bi·la·dor m. candle snuffer.

des·pa·bi·lar tr. *(apagar)* to snuff; *(robar)* to steal, pinch; *(avivar)* to liven up, stimulate; *(malgastar)* to squander; *(despachar)* to finish quickly; *(matar)* to kill, snuff out —reflex. *(despertarse)* to wake up; *(avivarse)* to liven up; AMER. to leave, disappear.

des·pa·cio I. adv. slow, slowly; *(poco a poco)* little by little, gradually; AMER. in a low voice, quietly II. interj. easy does it!, take it easy!

des·pa·chan·te m. ARG. clerk, employee.

des·pa·char tr. to complete, conclude; *(resolver)* to resolve, settle; *(enviar)* to dispatch, send; *(despedir)* to fire, dismiss; *(vender)* to sell; *(expedir)* to expedite, hurry along; COLL. *(acabar con)* to polish or knock off; *(matar)* to kill, knock off —intr. *(darse prisa)* to hurry up; *(hablar)* to speak one's mind; COM. to do business —reflex. AMER. *(darse prisa)* to hurry up ♦ **d. de** to get rid of.

des·pa·cho m. *(envío)* dispatch, sending; *(oficina)* office, bureau; *(estudio)* study, office; *(tienda)* store, shop; *(venta)* sale; *(comunicación)* dispatch, message; *(resolución)* efficiency; *(cédula)* commission ♦ **tener buen d.** to be efficient.

des·pa·chu·rrar tr. *(aplastar)* to crush, squash; *(una cuenta)* to confuse, mix up; *(una persona)* to silence, squelch.

des·pam·pa·nan·te adj. COLL. astounding, stunning.

des·pan·zu·rrar/chu·rrar tr. COLL. to rip open the belly of, disembowel.

des·pa·re·jo, a adj. *(dispar)* odd; *(sin alineación)* not matching; *(no parejo)* uneven.

des·par·pa·jo m. *(desenvoltura)* ease, confidence; *(descaro)* pertness, freshness.

des·pa·rra·mar tr. to spread; *(derramar)* to

spill, splash; *(malgastar)* to squander —reflex. to scatter, spread; *(divertirse)* to let one's hair down.

des·pa·ta·rrar tr. to astonish, flabbergast —reflex. *(abrirse de piernas)* to open one's legs wide; *(caerse)* to fall with legs apart; *(aturdirse)* to be astonished or flabbergasted.

des·pa·vo·ri·do, a adj. terrified, afraid.

des·pa·vo·rir §38 intr. & reflex. to be terrified.

des·pec·ti·vo, a adj. disparaging, pejorative.

des·pe·char tr. *(enojar)* to anger; *(causar disgusto a)* to displease, disgust; *(irritar)* to vex, peeve; *(destetar)* to wean —reflex. to become angry.

des·pe·cho m. *(ira)* spite, wrath; *(descontento)* displeasure, disgust; *(desesperación)* despair, dejection ◆ a d. de in spite of, in defiance of • por d. out of spite.

des·pe·da·za·mien·to m. breaking or tearing to pieces; *(ruina)* ruin, destruction.

des·pe·da·zar §04 tr. to break or tear to pieces —reflex. *(caerse)* to fall or break into pieces; *(arruinarse)* to be ruined, be destroyed.

des·pe·di·da f. *(adiós)* good-bye, farewell; *(despacho)* dismissal, firing.

des·pe·dir §48 tr. *(soltar)* to throw (out), eject; *(decir adiós)* to say good-bye; *(despachar)* to dismiss, fire; *(deshacerse de)* to get rid of, throw out; *(emitir)* to emit, give off —reflex. to say good-bye *(de* to).

des·pe·ga·ble adj. detachable.

des·pe·gar §47 tr. to unstick, unglue; *(separar)* to detach, separate; *(quitar)* to remove, take off —intr. AVIA. to take off —reflex. to become unstuck or unglued; *(separarse)* to become detached or separated; *(desapegarse)* to grow indifferent.

des·pe·gue m. takeoff.

des·pei·nar tr. to disarrange the hair of.

des·pe·ja·do, a adj. confident, sure of oneself; *(listo)* clever, bright; METEOROL. clear, cloudless; *(sin impedimento)* clear, open; *(espacioso)* spacious, wide.

des·pe·jar tr. to clear; *(quitar)* to get rid of, remove; *(aclarar)* to clear up, sort out —reflex. to become self-confident; METEOROL. to clear up; *(divertirse)* to enjoy oneself; MED. to go down.

des·pe·lu·zar §04 tr. *(desmelenar)* to dishevel, muss; *(erizar)* to make (someone's hair) stand on end —reflex. to be frightened.

des·pe·lle·jar tr. *(desollar)* to skin, flay; *(criticar)* to flay, criticize.

des·pen·sa f. *(lugar)* larder, pantry; *(provisiones)* provisions, supplies; *(oficio)* stewardship.

des·pe·ña·de·ro, a I. adj. steep, precipitous **II.** m. precipice, cliff; *(peligro)* danger, risk.

des·pe·ñar tr. to hurl, throw —reflex. *(precipitarse)* to hurl or throw oneself; *(entregarse)* to give oneself up.

des·pe·pi·tar tr. to remove pits or seeds from —reflex. to shout, rant; *(proceder descomedidamente)* to act rashly, forget oneself ◆ d. por algo to be dying for something.

des·per·di·cia·do, a adj. wasted, squandered.

des·per·di·ciar tr. to waste, squander; *(no aprovecharse de)* not to take advantage of, miss.

des·per·di·cio m. waste, squandering; *(residuo)* waste, remains.

des·per·di·gar §47 tr. to scatter, disperse —reflex. to become scattered or dispersed.

des·pe·re·zar·se §04 reflex. to stretch.

des·pe·re·zo m. stretching, stretch; *(despertamiento)* waking up, shaking off sleep.

des·per·fec·to m. flaw, blemish; *(deterioro)* wear and tear.

des·per·ta·dor, ·ra I. adj. awakening, arousing **II.** m.f. alarm clock; *(aviso)* warning.

des·per·tar §49 tr. to wake up, awaken; *(resucitar)* to revive, resuscitate; *(suscitar)* to awaken, revive; *(excitar)* to whet, excite —intr. to wake up, awaken; *(ser más listo)* to wise up —reflex. to wake up, awaken.

des·pia·da·do, a adj. pitiless, merciless.

des·pi·da, do, diera, dió see **despedir**.

des·pi·do m. dismissal, firing.

des·pier·to, a I. see **despertar II.** adj. awake; *(despabilado)* alert, wide-awake; *(listo)* clever, sharp.

des·pil·fa·rra·dor, ·ra adj. & m.f. spendthrift.

des·pil·fa·rrar tr. to squander, waste —reflex. to squander a fortune.

des·pil·fa·rro m. waste, extravagance; *(destrozo)* spoiling, ruining.

des·pio·jar tr. *(espulgar)* to delouse; COLL. *(sacar de miseria)* to free from poverty.

des·pis·ta·do, a adj. & m.f. absent-minded (person).

des·pis·tar tr. to lead astray —reflex. to be disoriented, lose one's bearings.

des·pis·te m. confusion, bewilderment.

des·plan·te m. arrogant remark or action.

des·pla·za·mien·to m. displacement; *(traslado)* moving, shifting.

des·pla·zar §04 tr. to displace; *(trasladar)* to move, shift.

des·ple·gar §52 tr. to unfold, spread out; *(aclarar)* to explain, unfold; *(mostrar)* to display, show —reflex. to unfold, spread out.

des·plie·gue m. unfolding, spreading out; *(muestra)* display, show.

des·plo·mar tr. to put or throw out of a plumb —reflex. *(inclinarse)* to lean, get out of plumb; *(caerse)* to fall down, collapse; *(desmayarse)* to faint, collapse; ECON. to plummet, drop.

des·plo·me m. *(inclinación)* leaning, getting out of plumb; *(caída)* collapse, fall; ARCHIT. overhang; *(desmayo)* fainting, collapsing.

des·plu·mar tr. to pluck, remove the feathers from; COLL. to fleece, skin.

des·po·bla·do m. wilderness.

des·po·blar §19 tr. to depopulate; *(despojar)* to clear, strip; *(devastar)* to lay waste, ravage —reflex. to become depopulated or deserted.

des·po·jar tr. to deprive, dispossess; *(quitar)* to strip; *(robar)* to rob —reflex. *(desnudarse)* to undress, strip; *(renunciar)* to give up, relinquish.

des·po·jo m. depriving, dispossession; *(botín)* loot, plunder; ZOOL. offal; ORNITH. giblets; *(víctima)* prey, victim ◆ pl. scrap, usable rubble; *(restos mortales)* remains, corpse; *(sobras)* leftovers • d. de hierro scrap iron.

des·po·sa·do, a I. adj. newly wed; *(aprisionado)* handcuffed **II.** m.f. newlywed; *(aprisionado)* person in handcuffs.

des·po·sar tr. to marry, perform a marriage ceremony for —reflex. *(contraer esponsales)* to get engaged; *(contraer matrimonio)* to marry, wed.

des·po·se·er §43 tr. to dispossess, divest —reflex. to renounce, give up.

des·po·sei·mien·to m. dispossession.

dés·po·ta m.f. despot, tyrant.

des·pó·ti·co, a adj. despotic, tyrannical.

des·po·tri·car §70 intr. to rant, rave.

des·pre·cia·ble adj. abject, despicable.

des·pre·ciar tr. to disdain, look down on; *(desairar)* to slight, snub —reflex. to disdain, not to deign.

des·pre·cia·ti·vo, a adj. scornful.

des·pre·cio m. disdain, scorn; *(desaire)* slight, snub.

des·pren·der tr. to unfasten, detach; *(soltar)* to loosen; *(emitir)* to emit, give off —reflex. to come undone, become detached; *(ser emitido)* to issue, emanate; *(proceder)* to be inferred, follow; MED. to be detached ♦ **d. de** to give up, part with.

des·pren·di·do, a adj. detached, loose; *(generoso)* generous, unselfish; *(desinteresado)* disinterested, detached; MED. detached.

des·pren·di·mien·to m. detachment; *(emisión)* emission, release; *(caída de tierra)* landslide; *(generosidad)* generosity, largesse; *(desapego)* disinterest, detachment; MED. detachment.

des·pre·o·cu·pa·ción f. nonchalance; *(imparcialidad)* impartiality, open-mindedness; *(falta de conformidad)* unconventionality; *(descuido)* carelessness, negligence.

des·pre·o·cu·pa·do, a adj. unconcerned, nonchalant; *(imparcial)* impartial, open-minded; *(descuidado)* untidy, sloppy; *(que no conforma)* unconventional.

des·pre·o·cu·par·se reflex. to stop worrying; *(descuidarse)* to become negligent or careless ♦ **d. de** *(olvidarse de)* to forget, neglect; *(no hacer caso de)* not to care about, to disregard.

des·pres·ti·giar tr. to ruin (someone's) reputation; *(desacreditar)* to discredit, disparage —reflex. to lose one's prestige.

des·pres·ti·gio m. loss of prestige.

des·pre·ve·ni·do, a adj. unprepared, off guard.

des·pro·por·ción f. disproportion.

des·pro·por·cio·nar tr. to disproportion.

des·pue·ble, blo see **despoblar.**

des·pués adv. *(más tarde)* afterward, later; *(entonces)* next, then ♦ **d. de (que)** after.

des·pun·tar tr. to break off or dull the point of; MARIT. to sail around, round —intr. *(el día)* to begin, break; *(manifestar agudeza)* to show wit or intelligence; *(sobresalir)* to excel, stand out; BOT. to bud, sprout —reflex. to break its point.

des·qui·cia·dor, ·ra adj. unhinging; *(que turba)* disturbing, disruptive.

des·qui·cia·mien·to m. unhinging; *(perturbación)* perturbation, mental unrest; *(trastorno)* disturbance, disruption.

des·qui·ciar tr. to unhinge; *(desconectar)* to loosen, disconnect; *(descomponer)* to unsettle, undermine; *(quitar la confianza)* to unseat —reflex. to become unhinged; *(desconectarse)* to come loose, become disconnected; *(descomponerse)* to become unsettled; *(trastornarse)* to become upset.

des·qui·tar tr. to compensate —reflex. ♦ **d. de** *(resarcirse de)* to recoup, win back; *(tomar satisfacción)* to get even with.

des·qui·te m. *(de pérdida)* recovery, recouping; *(compensación)* compensation, restitution; *(venganza)* revenge, retaliation.

des·ta·ca·men·to m. MIL. detachment, detail; *(lugar)* post, station.

des·ta·car §70 tr. to emphasize, highlight; MIL. to detail, assign —intr. to stand out, be outstanding —reflex. to stand out, be outstanding; *(aventajarse)* to break away, draw ahead.

des·ta·jo m. *(trabajo)* piecework; *(tarea)* job, stint ♦ **a d.** by the piece; AMER., COLL. at a guess, roughly • **hablar a d.** to chatter, talk excessively.

des·ta·par tr. to open, uncover; *(una botella)* to uncork, uncap; *(descubrir)* to reveal, discover —reflex. to show one's true colors; *(desahogarse)* to unburden oneself, open one's heart; *(desnudarse)* to take off one's clothes.

des·ta·pe m. uncovering, revealing; *(desnudo)* nude.

des·ta·po·nar tr. to unplug, unstop; *(una botella)* to uncork.

des·tar·ta·la·do, a adj. ramshackle, dilapidated.

des·te·char tr. to remove the roof from.

des·te·jer tr. to unweave, unravel; *(desbaratar)* to upset, disrupt.

des·te·llar tr. to flash —intr. to flash; *(centellar)* to sparkle, glitter.

des·te·llo m. flash (of light); *(centelleo)* sparkle, glitter ♦ pl. signs, indications.

des·tem·pla·do, a adj. immoderate, intemperate; *(desigual)* uneven, irregular; METAL. untempered; MUS. out of tune; MED. irregular; *(indispuesto)* indisposed, feverish.

des·tem·plan·za f. intemperance, lack of moderation; *(inclemencia)* inclemency, harshness; MED. irregularity; *(desazón)* indisposition.

des·tem·plar tr. to disturb the order of; *(poner en infusión)* to steep, infuse; METAL. to untemper; MUS. to put out of tune —reflex. *(descomponerse)* to get upset or worked up; METAL. to lose temper; MUS. to get out of tune; MED. to have a slight fever; *(el pulso)* to become irregular; AMER. to have one's teeth on edge.

des·te·ñir §59 tr. & intr. to fade, discolor.

des·ter·ni·llar·se reflex. to tear a cartilage ♦ **d. de risa** to split one's sides laughing.

des·te·rrar §49 tr. to exile, banish —reflex. to go into exile.

des·te·tar tr. to wean —reflex. to be weaned; *(deshabituarse)* to break a habit.

des·tiem·po adv. ♦ **a d.** inopportunely.

des·tie·rre, rro see **desterrar.**

des·tie·rro m. exile, banishment; *(lugar apartado)* remote place.

des·ti·la·ción f. distillation, filtration.

des·ti·lar tr. to distill; *(filtrar)* to filter; *(exudar)* to exude, ooze —intr. *(gotear)* to drip, trickle; *(exudar)* to exude, ooze.

des·ti·le·rí·a f. distillery.

des·ti·na·ción f. destination.

des·ti·nar tr. to destine, intend; *(asignar)* to assign, appoint; *(mandar)* to send; COM. to allot, earmark —reflex. to intend to go into.

des·ti·na·ta·rio, a m.f. *(de una carta)* addressee; *(de un giro)* payee.

des·ti·no m. destiny, fate; *(destinación)* destination; *(empleo)* job, position; *(uso)* use, function ♦ **con d. a** bound for.

des·ti·ña, ñera, ño, ñó see **desteñir.**

des·ti·tu·ción f. dismissal.

des·ti·tuir §18 tr. *(revocar)* to dismiss; *(privar)* to deprive.

des·tor·ni·lla·dor m. screwdriver.

des·tor·ni·llar tr. to unscrew —reflex. to come unscrewed; *(perder el juicio)* to go crazy.

des·tra·bar tr. to untie, unfetter; *(desprender)* to separate, disconnect.

des·tren·zar §04 tr. to unbraid, unplait.

des·tre·za f. skill, dexterity.

des·tri·par tr. to gut, disembowel; *(sacar lo interior)* to remove the stuffing from; *(despachurrar)* to crush, squash.

des·tri·zar §04 tr. *(hacer trizas)* to tear into strips; *(desmenuzar)* to crumble, shred —reflex. to be heartbroken, overcome with grief.

des·tro·na·mien·to m. dethronement; *(derrocamiento)* overthrow.

des·tro·nar tr. to dethrone; *(desposeer)* to overthrow, bring down.

des·tron·car §70 tr. to cut down, fell; *(interrumpir)* to cut off, interrupt; *(descoyuntar)* to dislocate; *(mutilar)* to maim, mutilate; *(cansar)* to exhaust, tire out; *(arruinar)* to ruin.

des·tro·za·dor, ·ra I. adj. destructive **II.** m.f. destroyer, wrecker.

des·tro·zar §04 tr. to smash, break into pieces; *(arruinar)* to destroy, ruin; *(estropear)* to spoil, shatter —reflex. to smash, break into pieces.

des·tro·zo m. *(daño)* damage, *(destrucción)* destruction, ruin; MIL. defeat.

des·truc·ción f. destruction.

des·truc·ti·vo, a adj. destructive.

des·truc·tor, ·ra I. adj. destructive **II.** m.f. destructive person —m. MARIT. destroyer.

des·truir §18 tr. to destroy, ruin; *(malgastar)* to squander, waste; *(deshacer)* to shatter, dash.

de·sue·le llo see **desolar.**

de·sue·lle, llo see **desollar.**

de·su·nir tr. to disunite, separate; *(enemistar)* to cause discord; TECH. to disconnect, disengage —reflex. to smash, break apart.

de·su·sa·do, a adj. *(fuera de uso)* obsolete, out of date; *(poco usado)* uncommon, rare.

de·su·sar tr. to stop using —reflex. to become obsolete.

de·su·so m. disuse, obsolescence.

des·vá·li·do, a adj. & m.f. needy, destitute (person).

des·va·li·jar tr. to rob, plunder.

des·va·lo·rar tr. to depreciate; *(una moneda)* to devalue, devaluate; *(despreciar)* to disdain.

des·va·lo·ri·za·ción f. depreciation; *(de una moneda)* devaluation.

des·va·lo·ri·zar §04 tr. to devalue —reflex. to depreciate, lose value.

des·va·lua·ción f. devaluation, depreciation.

des·ván m. attic, garret.

des·va·ne·cer §17 tr. to make vanish or disappear; *(envanecer)* to make vain or presumptuous; *(hacer desmayar)* to make dizzy; *(disipar)* to remove, dispel —reflex. to vanish, disappear; *(envanecerse)* to become vain; *(evaporarse)* to evaporate; *(desmayarse)* to become dizzy, faint.

des·va·ne·ci·mien·to m. disappearance; *(desmayo)* dizziness, faintness; *(evaporación)* evaporation; *(altanería)* arrogance, haughtiness.

des·va·riar §30 intr. to be delirious.

des·va·rí·o m. delirium, madness; *(disparate)* raving, nonsense; *(capricho)* whim; *(monstruosidad)* monstrosity.

des·ve·lar tr. to keep awake —reflex. to stay awake, go without sleep; *(dedicarse)* to devote or dedicate oneself ♦ **d. por** to be watchful for, take great care over.

des·ve·lo m. sleeplessness, insomnia; *(esfuerzo)* effort; *(esmero)* watchfulness, care; *(devoción)* devotion, dedication ♦ pl. trouble.

des·ven·ci·jar tr. *(aflojar)* to loosen, weaken;

(estropear) to ruin; *(romper)* to break; *(agotar)* to exhaust —reflex. *(romperse)* to break, come apart; COLL. *(estar agotado)* to be exhausted; MED. to rupture oneself.

des·ven·ta·ja f. disadvantage, drawback.

des·ven·ta·jo·so, a adj. disadvantageous.

des·ven·tu·ra f. misfortune, bad luck.

des·ver·gon·za·do, a adj. & m.f. impudent, shameless (person).

des·ver·güen·za f. shamelessness, brazenness; *(insolencia)* insolence.

des·ves·tir §48 tr. & reflex. to undress.

des·via·ción f. *(rodeo)* detour, diversion; *(de un golpe)* deflection; *(de una norma)* deviation, departure.

des·viar §30 tr. *(extraviar)* to divert, deflect; *(disuadir)* to dissuade —reflex. to turn off; *(perder la ruta)* to go off course; *(mudar de dirección)* to change direction; *(hacer un rodeo)* to take a detour; *(apartarse)* to deviate.

des·vin·cu·lar tr. to separate from, break ties with —reflex. ♦ **d. de** or **con** to break contact with, dissociate oneself from.

des·ví·o m. *(rodeo)* detour, diversion; *(desapego)* indifference, coolness; *(desagrado)* aversion, displeasure; PHYS. deviation, deflection; RAIL. siding.

des·vir·gar §47 tr. to deflower.

des·vir·tuar §67 tr. *(echar a perder)* to spoil, impair —reflex. to spoil, go bad.

des·vis·ta, to, tiera, tió see **desvestir.**

des·vi·vir·se reflex. *(mostrar interés)* to be eager, show a great desire; *(estar enamorado)* to be madly in love; *(esforzarse)* to strive, do one's utmost; *(dedicarse)* to dedicate or devote oneself.

de·ta·lla·da·men·te adv. in detail.

de·ta·llar tr. to detail, relate in detail; *(especificar)* to specify, itemize; COM. to sell retail.

de·ta·lle m. detail; *(gesto)* gesture, kind thought.

de·ta·llis·ta I. adj. retail **II.** m.f. COM. retailer; *(considerado)* thoughtful person.

de·tec·tar tr. to detect.

de·tec·ti·ve m. detective.

de·tec·tor, ·ra I. m. detector **II.** adj. detecting.

de·tén see **detener.**

de·ten·ción f. stopping, halting; *(estado)* stoppage, standstill; *(retraso)* delay; *(arresto)* arrest; *(prisión)* detention; *(cuidado)* care, thoroughness.

de·te·ner §69 tr. to stop, halt; *(retrasar)* to delay, detain; *(arrestar)* to arrest; *(retener)* to keep, retain —reflex. to stop; *(retardarse)* to linger, tarry.

de·te·ni·do, a I. adj. *(cuidadoso)* thorough, close; *(tímido)* timid, fainthearted; *(escaso)* sparing; *(preso)* detained, in custody **II.** m.f. person under arrest.

de·te·ni·mien·to m. var. of **detención.**

de·ter·gen·te adj. & m. detergent.

de·te·rio·ra·ción f. deterioration; *(daño)* damage, harm; *(con el uso)* wear and tear.

de·te·rio·rar tr. to deteriorate; *(estropear)* to damage, spoil; *(desgastar)* to wear (out) —reflex. *(dañarse)* to damage, harm; *(desgastarse)* to wear out.

de·te·rio·ro m. deterioration; *(daño)* harm, damage.

de·ter·mi·na·ción f. *(decisión)* decision; *(resolución)* determination, resolve.

de·ter·mi·na·do, a adj. determined, resolute;

(preciso) specific, particular.

de·ter·mi·nar tr. to determine; *(convencer)* to convince, decide; *(fijar)* to specify, fix; *(causar)* to cause, bring about; *(distinguir)* to distinguish, discern; *(estipular)* to stipulate, specify —reflex. to decide, make up one's mind.

de·ter·mi·nis·ta I. adj. deterministic II. m.f. determinist.

de·tes·ta·ble adj. detestable, hateful.

de·tes·tar tr. to detest, hate.

de·tie·ne see **detener**.

de·to·na·ción f. detonation, explosion; *(ruido)* report, blast.

de·to·na·dor m. detonator.

de·to·nan·te I. adj. detonating, explosive II. m. explosive.

de·to·nar intr. to detonate, explode.

de·trac·ción f. denigration, disparagement; *(retiro)* withdrawal.

de·trac·tar tr. to denigrate, disparage.

de·trac·tor, ·ra I. adj. detracting, defamatory II. m.f. detractor, defamer.

de·trás adv. behind ♦ **d. de** behind, in back of • **por d.** behind one's back.

de·tri·men·to m. detriment, damage.

de·tu·vie·ra, vo see **detener**.

deu·da f. debt.

deu·do, a m.f. relative.

deu·dor, ·ra I. adj. debit; *(que debe)* indebted II. m.f. debtor.

de·va·lua·ción f. devaluation.

de·va·luar §67 tr. to devaluate.

de·va·nar tr. to reel, wind.

de·vas·ta·ción f. devastation.

de·vas·tar tr. to devastate, destroy.

de·ve·lar tr. to reveal.

de·ven·gar §47 tr. to be owed; *(interés)* to earn.

de·ve·nir §76 intr. *(suceder)* to happen, come about; *(llegar a ser)* to become, evolve into.

de·vo·ción f. devotion, *(piedad)* devoutness, piety; *(afición)* affection, attachment.

de·vo·lu·ción f. return; *(restauración)* restoration; COM. refund.

de·vol·ver §78 tr. to return, give back; *(corresponder)* to return; *(restaurar)* to restore; *(vomitar)* to throw up, vomit; COM. to refund —reflex. AMER. to return.

de·vo·rar tr. to devour, eat up; *(disipar)* to squander, waste; *(arruinar)* to ruin, destroy.

de·vo·to, a I. adj. devout, pious; *(venerable)* venerable, revered; *(aficionado)* devoted, attached II. m.f. devout person; *(aficionado)* devotee, enthusiast.

de·vuel·va, vo see **devolver**.

dex·te·ri·dad f. dexterity, skillfulness.

dex·tro·sa f. dextrose.

di see **dar** or **decir²**.

dí·a m. day; *(tiempo de claridad)* daytime, daylight; *(tiempo)* weather ♦ **al d.** per day, a day; *(al corriente)* up to date • **al otro d.** on the following day, the next day • **de d.** by day • **d. de fiesta** holiday • **d. entre semana** weekday • **d. señalado** red-letter day • **hoy (en) d.** nowadays, these days • **todo el santo d.** all day long, all the livelong day ♦ pl. **¡buenos d.!** good morning • **de d.** old • **ocho d.** a week • **quince d.** two weeks, fortnight • **todos los d.** every day, daily.

dia·bé·ti·co, a adj. & m.f. diabetic.

dia·blo m. devil, demon; *(travieso)* scamp, devil; *(requetefeo)* monster, ugly person ♦ **al d. or**

como el d. COLL. like the devil, a hell of a lot • **darse al d.** to get angry • **¡diablo(s)!** COLL. wow! • **¡qué diablos!** what the hell!

dia·blu·ra f. deviltry, prank.

dia·bó·li·co, a adj. diabolical, devilish.

dia·co·ni·sa f. deaconess.

diá·co·no m. deacon.

dia·de·ma f. diadem, crown.

diá·fa·no, a adj. diaphanous, transparent.

dia·frag·ma m. diaphragm.

diag·no·sis f. diagnosis.

diag·nos·ti·car §70 tr. to diagnose.

diag·nós·ti·co, a I. adj. diagnostic II. m. diagnosis.

dia·go·nal adj. & f. diagonal.

dia·gra·ma m. diagram.

dia·léc·ti·co, a I. adj. dialectical II. m.f. dialectician —f. dialectics.

dia·lec·to m. dialect.

diá·lo·go m. dialogue.

dia·man·te m. diamond.

dia·man·ti·no, a adj. diamantine.

dia·me·tral adj. diametric, diametrical.

diá·me·tro m. diameter.

dia·pa·són m. diapason, tuning fork.

dia·po·si·ti·va f. slide, transparency.

dia·ria·men·te adv. daily, every day.

dia·rio, a I. adj. daily II. m. daily (paper); *(relación)* diary, journal; *(gasto)* daily expenses; COM. journal, daybook III. adv. daily ♦ **a d.** daily, every day • **de d.** *(diariamente)* daily, every day; *(ordinario)* everyday.

dia·rre·a f. diarrhea.

di·bu·jan·te I. adj. drawing, sketching II. m. drawer, sketcher; *(de dibujos animados)* cartoonist; TECH. draftsman.

di·bu·jar tr. to draw, sketch; *(describir)* to describe, depict —reflex. *(delinearse)* to be outlined, stand out; *(aparecer)* to appear.

di·bu·jo m. drawing, sketch; *(descripción)* description, depiction ♦ pl. **d. animados** cartoons.

dic·ción f. diction.

dic·cio·na·rio m. dictionary.

di·ce see **decir²**.

di·ciem·bre m. December.

di·co·to·mí·a f. dichotomy.

dic·ta·do m. title; *(acción)* dictation ♦ pl. dictates.

dic·ta·dor m. dictator.

dic·ta·du·ra f. dictatorship.

dic·tá·fo·no m. dictaphone.

dic·ta·men m. *(juicio)* opinion, judgment; *(consejo)* advice; *(informe)* report.

dic·ta·mi·nar intr. to express an opinion.

dic·tar tr. to dictate; *(sentencia)* to pronounce, pass; *(inspirar)* to dictate, direct; AMER. *(una conferencia)* to give, deliver; AMER. *(una clase)* to give, teach.

di·cha f. *(felicidad)* happiness; *(suerte)* good fortune ♦ **a o por d.** fortunately, happily.

di·cha·ra·che·ro, a COLL. I. adj. *(gracioso)* witty, racy; *(hablador)* talkative II. m.f. *(gracioso)* joker; *(hablador)* chatterbox.

di·cho, a I. see **decir²** II. adj. said, aforementioned ♦ **d. y hecho** no sooner said than done • **¡haberlo d.!** you should have said so! • **mejor d.** rather, more accurately III. m. *(refrán)* saying, proverb; *(ocurrencia)* witticism, witty remark; COLL. *(expresión insultante)* insulting remark; LAW statement, deposition ♦ **d. de las gentes** gossip, talk ♦ pl. marriage vows.

di·cho·so, a adj. *(feliz)* happy, contented; *(afortunado)* lucky, fortunate; COLL. *(enfadoso)* blasted.

di·dác·ti·co, a I. adj. didactic, pedagogical II. f. didactics.

die·ci·nue·ve adj. & m. nineteen(th).

die·ci·o·cho adj. & m. eighteen(th).

die·ci·séis adj. & m. sixteen(th).

die·ci·sie·te adj. & m. seventeen(th).

dien·te m. tooth; ZOOL. fang; *(de una rueda)* cog; *(de una sierra)* tooth; *(de un tenedor)* prong; BOT. clove ♦ **aguzarse** or **afilarse los dientes** to whet one's appetite • **dar d. con d.** to chatter (teeth) • **d. de león** dandelion • **dientes postizos** false teeth • **estar a d.** to be famished or ravenous • **hablar entre dientes** to mumble, mutter.

die·ra, ron see dar.

dies·tro, a I. adj. deft, dexterous; *(derecho)* right; *(astuto)* shrewd, astute II. right hand ♦ **a d. y siniestra** all over, right and left.

die·ta f. diet.

die·té·ti·co, a I. adj. dietetic, dietary II. m.f. dietician — f. dietetics.

diez I. adj. ten; *(décimo)* tenth ♦ **las d.** ten o'clock II. m. ten ♦ **d. y** var. of **dieci-**.

diez·mar tr. to decimate.

diez·mo m. tithe.

di·fa·ma·ción f. defamation.

di·fa·mar tr. to defame, slander.

di·fe·ren·cia f. difference ♦ **a d. de** unlike, in contrast to • **hacer d. entre** to make or draw a distinction between.

di·fe·ren·cia·ción f. differentiation.

di·fe·ren·ciar tr. to differentiate, distinguish; *(variar)* to vary, change —intr. to differ, disagree —reflex. to distinguish oneself; *(ser diferente)* to differ, be different.

di·fe·ren·te I. adj. different ♦ **diferentes** various, several II. adv. differently.

di·fe·rir §65 tr. to defer, postpone —intr. to differ, be different.

di·fí·cil adj. difficult.

di·fí·cil·men·te adv. difficultly, with difficulty.

di·fi·cul·tad f. difficulty, obstacle; *(objeción)* objection, doubt.

di·fi·cul·tar tr. to make difficult, complicate.

di·fi·cul·to·so, a adj. difficult; *(feo)* ugly, unpleasant.

di·fi·den·cia f. mistrust, diffidence.

di·fie·ra, ro, firiera, firió see diferir.

dif·te·ria f. diphtheria.

di·fun·dir tr. to diffuse; *(derramar)* to spread, scatter; *(divulgar)* to divulge, make known; *(diseminar)* to disseminate, propagate —reflex. to spread, be diffused.

di·fun·to, a I. adj. deceased, dead II. m.f. dead person; *(cadáver)* corpse, cadaver.

di·fu·sión f. diffusion; *(radio)* broadcasting.

di·fu·so, a I. see difundir II. adj. diffuse, wordy; *(ancho)* wide, extended; *(vago)* vague, hazy.

di·fu·sor, ·ra I. adj. diffusing II. f. broadcasting station.

di·ga, go see decir².

di·ge·rir §65 tr. to digest; *(sufrir)* to suffer, endure.

di·ges·tión f. digestion.

di·gi·to m. digit.

dig·nar·se reflex. to deign, condescend.

dig·na·ta·rio m. dignitary.

dig·ni·dad f. dignity; *(cargo)* post, rank.

dig·no, a adj. *(merecedor)* worthy; *(apropiado)* proper, fitting; *(mesurado)* dignified.

di·gre·sión f. digression, deviation.

di·je m. *(adorno)* trinket, charm; COLL. *(persona)* jewel, gem ♦ pl. boasting, bravado.

di·je, jo, jera, jeron see decir².

di·la·ción f. delay, delaying.

di·la·pi·dar tr. to waste, squander.

di·la·ta·ción f. dilation, expansion; *(desahogo)* serenity, calmness.

di·la·tar tr. to dilate, expand; *(retrasar)* to postpone, delay; *(propagar)* to spread —reflex. to dilate, expand; *(propagarse)* to extend, stretch.

di·la·to·ria I. f. delay II. adj. dilatory.

di·lec·to, a adj. beloved, loved.

di·le·ma m. dilemma.

di·le(t)·tan·te m.f. dilettante.

di·li·gen·cia f. diligence, care; *(prisa)* speed, briskness; *(recado)* errand, task; LAW proceeding.

di·li·gen·ciar tr. to take the necessary steps to obtain.

di·li·gen·te adj. diligent; *(rápido)* speedy, quick.

di·lu·ci·da·ción f. elucidation, explanation.

di·lu·ci·dar tr. to elucidate, explain.

di·luir §18 tr. to dilute; *(disolver)* to dissolve; *(debilitar)* to water down, weaken.

di·lu·viar intr. to pour down, rain hard.

di·lu·vio m. flood.

di·men·sión f. dimension.

di·mi·nu·ción f. diminution, lessening.

di·mi·nuir §18 tr. to diminish, lessen.

di·mi·nu·ti·vo, a adj. & m. diminutive.

di·mi·nu·to, a adj. diminutive, little.

di·mi·sión f. resignation (from office).

di·mi·ten·te I. adj. resigning II. m.f. resigner.

di·mi·tir intr. & tr. to resign, relinquish.

di·mos see dar.

di·ná·mi·co, a I. adj. dynamic II. f. dynamics.

di·na·mis·mo m. dynamism.

di·na·mi·ta f. dynamite.

di·na·mi·tar tr. to dynamite, blast.

di·na·mo or **di·na·mo** f. dynamo.

di·nas·tí·a f. dynasty.

di·ne·ra·da f./**ral** m. fortune.

di·ne·ro m. money; *(caudal)* wealth, fortune ♦ **d. al contado** or **al contante** ready cash • **d. suelto** loose change.

di·no·sau·rio m. dinosaur.

din·tel m. lintel.

dio see dar.

dios m. god ♦ **D.** God • **D. mediante** God willing • **¡D. mío!** my God!, oh my! • **por D.** for God's sake • **¡válgame D.!** goodness gracious!

dio·sa f. goddess.

di·plo·ma m. diploma, certificate.

di·plo·ma·cia f. diplomacy.

di·plo·ma·do, a I. adj. having a diploma II. m.f. graduate.

di·plo·mar tr. & reflex. to graduate.

di·plo·má·ti·co, a I. adj. diplomatic II. m.f. diplomat —f. diplomacy.

dip·só·ma·no, a adj. & m.f. dipsomaniac.

dip·ton·go m. diphthong.

di·pu·ta·do, a m.f. delegate, representative.

di·que m. dike, sea wall; *(restricción)* check, restriction ♦ **d. de carena** or **seco** dry dock • **d. de contención** dam.

di·rá, ría see decir².

di·rec·ción f. direction; *(junta)* board of directors, executive board; *(cargo)* directorship, managership; *(señas)* address; AUTO., TECH. steering ♦ **d. general** headquarters, head office.

di·rec·ti·vo, a I. adj. directing II. m.f. director —f. *(orden)* directive, instruction; *(junta)* board of directors.

di·rec·to, a I. adj. direct; *(derecho)* straight II. f. AUTO. high gear.

di·rec·tor, ·ra I. adj. directing II. m.f. director, manager; *(de escuela)* principal, headmaster; MUS. conductor.

di·rec·to·rio, a I. adj. directory II. m. *(instrucción)* manual, directory; *(junta)* directorate.

di·ri·gen·te m.f. leader, director.

di·ri·gir §32 tr. to direct; *(administrar)* to manage; *(una carta)* to address; *(guiar)* to guide; *(dedicar)* to dedicate; AUTO. to drive, steer; MUS. to conduct; CINEM., THEAT. to direct —reflex. to go, make one's way; *(hablar)* to address, speak.

dis·cer·ni·mien·to m. discernment.

dis·cer·nir §25 tr. to discern, distinguish.

dis·ci·pli·na f. discipline; *(doctrina)* doctrine; *(azote)* whip.

dis·ci·pli·nar tr. to discipline; *(enseñar)* to teach, instruct; *(azotar)* to whip, scourge —reflex. to discipline oneself.

dis·cí·pu·lo, a m.f. disciple, follower; *(alumno)* student, pupil.

dis·co m. disk, disc; *(para escuchar)* record; *(para el tránsito)* traffic signal; SPORT. discus; COMPUT. diskette ♦ **d. rayado** COLL. broken record.

dis·co·lo, a adj. wayward, intractable.

dis·con·for·me adj. disagreeing, differing.

dis·con·for·mi·dad f. difference.

dis·con·ti·nuar §67 tr. to discontinue.

dis·con·ti·nui·dad f. discontinuity.

dis·cor·dan·cia f. discordance, disagreement.

dis·cor·dar §11 intr. to differ, disagree; MUS. to be out of tune or dissonant.

dis·cor·de adj. disagreeing, discordant; MUS. discordant, dissonant.

dis·cor·dia f. discord, disagreement.

dis·co·te·ca f. record collection; *(salón de baile)* discotheque.

dis·cre·ción f. discretion, tact; *(astucia)* wisdom, shrewdness.

dis·cre·pan·cia f. discrepancy; *(desacuerdo)* disagreement, dissent.

dis·cre·par intr. to differ, disagree.

dis·cre·to, a adj. discreet; *(ingenioso)* witty, clever; MATH., MED., PHYS. discrete.

dis·cri·mi·nar tr. to discriminate.

dis·cuer·de, de to see discordar.

dis·cul·pa f. *(por una ofensa)* apology; *(excusa)* excuse.

dis·cul·par tr. to excuse, pardon —reflex. to apologize *(con to, de, por for).*

dis·cu·rrir intr. to roam, wander; *(reflexionar)* to reflect, ponder; *(hablar)* to speak, discourse; *(fluir)* to flow, run; *(el tiempo)* to pass —tr. to invent, think up.

dis·cur·sar/se·ar intr. to discourse or lecture on.

dis·cur·so m. speech, discourse; *(facultad)* reasoning, ratiocination; *(transcurso)* passage, course.

dis·cu·sión f. discussion; *(disputa)* dispute, argument.

dis·cu·ti·ble adj. debatable, disputable.

dis·cu·tir tr. to discuss, debate —intr. *(debatir)* to discuss, talk about; *(disputar)* to argue.

di·se·car §70 tr. to dissect; *(conservar)* to stuff, mount.

di·sec·ción f. dissection.

di·se·mi·na·ción f. dissemination, spreading.

di·se·mi·nar tr. to disseminate, spread —reflex. to become disseminated, spread.

di·sen·sión f. dissension, strife.

di·sen·te·rí·a f. dysentery.

di·sen·tir §65 intr. to dissent, differ.

di·se·ñar tr. to design; *(dibujar)* to draw, sketch.

di·se·ño m. design; *(dibujo)* drawing, sketch.

di·ser·ta·ción f. dissertation, discourse.

di·ser·tar intr. to discourse, expound.

dis·fraz m. disguise; *(máscara)* mask; *(pretexto)* pretext, excuse.

dis·fra·zar §04 tr. & reflex. to disguise (oneself).

dis·fru·tar tr. *(gozar)* to enjoy; *(aprovechar)* to make the most of —intr. to enjoy.

dis·fru·te m. *(gozo)* enjoyment; *(provecho)* benefit; *(uso)* use.

dis·gus·ta·do, a adj. annoyed, displeased.

dis·gus·tar tr. to annoy, displease —reflex. *(desagradarse)* to be annoyed or displeased; *(desazonarse)* to fall out.

dis·gus·to m. *(desagrado)* annoyance, displeasure; *(contienda)* quarrel, disagreement ♦ **a d.** unwillingly.

di·si·den·cia f. dissidence, disagreement.

di·si·den·te adj. & m.f. dissident.

di·si·dir intr. to dissent.

di·sien·ta, to see disentir.

di·sí·mil adj. dissimilar, unlike.

di·si·mu·la·ción f. *(simulación)* dissimulation, dissembling; *(encubrimiento)* concealment, hiding; *(tolerancia)* tolerance.

di·si·mu·la·do, a I. adj. *(simulado)* dissimulating, dissembling; *(encubierto)* concealed, hidden II. m.f. dissimulator, dissembler ♦ **hacerse el d.** to act dumb, feign ignorance.

di·si·mu·lar tr. to dissimulate, dissemble; *(encubrir)* to conceal, hide; *(fingir)* to feign, pretend; *(tolerar)* to tolerate, overlook —intr. to dissimulate, dissemble.

di·si·mu·lo m. var. of disimulación.

di·sin·tie·ra, tió see disentir.

di·si·pa·ción f. dissipation; *(derroche)* squandering, wasting.

di·si·pa·do, a I. adj. *(disipado)* dissipated; *(libertino)* dissolute; *(derrochador)* wasteful II. m.f. *(libertino)* dissolute person; *(derrochador)* squanderer, wasteful person.

di·si·par tr. to dissipate; *(derrochar)* to squander, waste; *(una duda)* to dispel —reflex. *(desaparecer)* to disappear, vanish; *(dispersarse)* to disperse, scatter.

dis·lo·ca·ción f. dislocation.

dis·lo·car §70 tr. & reflex. to dislocate.

dis·mi·nu·ción f. diminution.

dis·mi·nuir §18 tr., intr. & reflex. to diminish.

di·so·cia·ción f. dissociation, separation.

di·so·ciar tr. & reflex. to dissociate (oneself).

di·so·lu·ción f. dissolution; *(libertinaje)* dissoluteness, dissipation; *(ruptura)* breakup; COM. liquidation; CHEM. solution.

di·so·lu·to, a adj. & m.f. dissolute (person).

di·sol·ver §78 tr. to dissolve; *(dispersar)* to break up; *(anular)* to annul; COM. to liquidate —reflex. to dissolve.

di·so·nan·cia f. MUS. dissonance.

dis·par adj. unequal; *(diferente)* different.

dis·pa·ra·dor, ·ra m.f. shooter, firer —m. trigger; PHOTOG. shutter release.

dis·pa·rar tr. to fire, shoot; *(echar)* to throw, hurl; SPORT. to shoot —intr. to fire, shoot; *(disparatar)* to act foolishly —reflex. ARM. to go off; *(enfurecerse)* to lose one's patience; AMER. *(irse corriendo)* to rush or dash off.

dis·pa·ra·ta·do, a adj. absurd, nonsensical; COLL. excessive, enormous.

dis·pa·ra·tar intr. to talk or act foolishly.

dis·pa·ra·te m. absurd or nonsensical thing; COLL. enormous amount ♦ pl. nonsense.

dis·pa·ri·dad f. disparity, dissimilarity.

dis·pa·ro m. firing, shooting; *(tiro)* shot; MECH. release, trip.

dis·pen·sar tr. to dispense, give out; *(eximir)* to exempt; *(perdonar)* to forgive, excuse —reflex. to excuse oneself.

dis·pen·sa·rio m. dispensary, clinic ♦ **d. de alimentos** soup kitchen.

dis·pep·sia f. dyspepsia, indigestion.

dis·per·sar tr. & reflex. to disperse, scatter; *(dividir)* to divide.

dis·per·sión f. dispersion, dispersal.

dis·pli·cen·cia f. indifference, coolness.

dis·pli·cen·te adj. disagreeable, unpleasant; *(indiferente)* indifferent, cool.

dis·po·ner §54 tr. *(colocar)* to arrange, place; *(preparar)* to prepare, get ready; *(ordenar)* to order —intr. ♦ **d. de** *(poseer)* to have, have at one's disposal; *(utilizar)* to make use of; *(deshacerse de)* to dispose of —reflex. to prepare, get ready; *(prepararse a morir)* to prepare to die, make one's will.

dis·po·ni·bi·li·dad f. availability.

dis·po·ni·ble adj. available, on hand.

dis·po·si·ción f. disposition; *(posesión)* disposal; *(aptitud)* aptitude, talent; LAW *(precepto)* provision; *(orden)* decree, order ♦ **estar en d. de** to be ready to, be in a position to • **última d.** last will and testament ♦ pl. measures.

dis·po·si·ti·vo, a I. adj. dispositive II. m. device, mechanism.

dis·pues·to, a I. see **disponer** II. adj. good-looking, elegant; *(hábil)* clever, capable ♦ **bien d.** well-disposed; *(saludable)* well, not sick • **estar d. a** to be prepared or willing to • **estar poco d. a** to be reluctant to • **mal d.** ill-disposed; *(enfermo)* ill, indisposed.

dis·pu·sie·ra, so see **disponer**.

dis·pu·ta f. dispute.

dis·pu·ta·ble adj. disputable, debatable.

dis·pu·tar tr. to dispute —intr. to argue, quarrel —reflex. to be disputed.

dis·qui·si·ción f. disgression.

dis·tan·cia f. distance; *(diferencia)* difference ♦ **a (la) d.** at or from a distance • **a larga d.** long-distance.

dis·tan·ciar tr. to separate, space out; *(alejar)* to place at a distance; *(dejar atrás)* to outdistance —reflex. to become separated; *(enajenarse)* to become estranged, drift away.

dis·tan·te adj. distant.

dis·tar intr. to be a certain distance from; *(diferenciarse)* to be different or far from.

dis·te see **dar**.

dis·ten·der §50 tr. to distend —intr. to become distended.

dis·tin·ción f. distinction; *(trato)* respect, deference; *(claridad)* distinctness ♦ **a d. de** as distinct from, in contrast to.

dis·tin·gui·do, a adj. distinguished.

dis·tin·guir §26 tr. to distinguish; *(preferir)* to favor, show preference for; *(honrar)* to pay tribute to, honor —intr. to distinguish, discriminate —reflex. *(ser distinto)* to be distinguished, differ; *(sobresalir)* to distinguish oneself, excel.

dis·tin·ti·vo, a I. adj. distinctive II. m. badge, emblem; FIG. distinguishing mark.

dis·tin·to, a adj. distinct.

dis·tor·sio·nar tr. to distort.

dis·trac·ción f. distraction; *(libertinaje)* dissoluteness; *(error)* slip, oversight; FIN. embezzlement, misappropriation.

dis·tra·er §72 tr. to distract; *(descaminar)* to lead astray; *(entretener)* to amuse, entertain; FIN. to embezzle, misappropriate —intr. to be entertaining —reflex. *(entretenerse)* to amuse oneself; *(descuidarse)* to be distracted.

dis·tra·í·do, a I. see **distraer** II. adj. *(divertido)* amusing, entertaining; *(desatento)* inattentive, absent-minded; *(libertino)* dissolute, libertine.

dis·trai·ga, go see **distraer**.

dis·trai·mien·to m. var. of **distracción**.

dis·tra·je·ra, jo see **distraer**.

dis·tri·bu·ción f. distribution.

dis·tri·bui·dor, ·ra I. adj. distributing, distributive II. m.f. distributor —m. AUTO., TELEC. distributor ♦ **d. automático** vending machine.

dis·tri·buir §18 tr. to distribute.

dis·tri·to m. district, zone.

dis·tur·bar tr. to disturb.

dis·tur·bio m. disturbance, trouble.

di·sua·dir tr. to dissuade, discourage.

di·sua·sión f. dissuasion.

dis·suel·to, ta, va, vo see **disolver**.

dis·yun·ti·vo, a adj. & f. disjunctive.

diu·ré·ti·co, a adj. & m. diuretic.

diur·no adj. & m. diurnal.

di·va·ga·ción f. digression, rambling.

di·va·gar §47 intr. *(errar)* to digress, ramble; *(vagar)* to wander, roam.

di·ván m. divan, couch.

di·ver·gen·cia f. divergence.

di·ver·gir §32 intr. to diverge, differ.

di·ver·si·dad f. diversity.

di·ver·si·fi·ca·ción f. diversification.

di·ver·si·fi·car §70 tr. to diversify.

di·ver·sión f. diversion.

di·ver·so, a adj. diverse ♦ pl. several, various.

di·ver·ti·do, a adj. amusing, entertaining; AMER. drunk.

di·ver·tir §65 tr. *(entretener)* to amuse, entertain; *(distraer)* to divert, distract —reflex. to amuse oneself, have a good time; *(distraerse)* to be distracted.

di·vi·den·do m. dividend.

di·vi·dir tr. to divide —reflex. to divide; *(separarse)* to separate.

di·vier·ta, to see **divertir**.

di·vi·na·to·rio, a adj. divinatory.

di·vi·ni·dad f. divinity; *(belleza)* beauty.

di·vi·no, a adj. divine.

di·vir·tie·ra, tió see **divertir**.

di·vi·sa f. emblem, insignia; COM. currency.

di·vi·sar tr. to discern, make out.

di·vi·sión f. division.

di·vi·sor, ·ra I. adj. dividing II. m. divider; MATH. divisor, denominator.

di·vi·so·rio, a I. adj. dividing; *(divisivo)* divisive II. f. dividing line; GEOL. divide.

di·vo, a m.f. opera star —f. FIG. prima donna.

di·vor·cia·do, a I. adj. divorced II. m. divorcé —f. divorcée.

di·vor·ciar tr. to divorce; *(separar)* to separate, divide —reflex. to divorce, get divorced.

di·vor·cio m. divorce, *(separación)* separation, division.

di·vul·ga·ción f. *(revelación)* disclosure, revelation; *(popularización)* popularization.

di·vul·gar §47 tr. to divulge, disclose; *(popularizar)* to popularize —reflex. to be divulged.

do m. MUS. do, C; COLL. supreme effort.

do·bla·di·llo m. hem.

do·bla·du·ra f. fold, crease.

do·blar tr. to double; *(encorvar)* to bend; to turn, round *<d. la esquina* to turn the corner>; CINEM. to dub —intr. to toll, ring; THEAT. to double, stand in —*(plegarse)* to fold; *(encorvarse)* to double over; *(ceder)* to yield, give in.

do·ble I. adj. double; *(grueso)* thick, heavy; *(disimulado)* two-faced II. m. double; *(pliegue)* fold, crease; *(toque)* death knell; *(copia)* copy, reproduction; COM. margin ♦ **al d.** doubly —m.f. double, stand-in III. adv. doubly.

do·ble·gar §47 tr. to fold, crease; *(curvar)* to bend, flex; *(blandir)* to brandish; *(hacer ceder)* to force someone to give in —reflex. to fold, crease; *(encorvarse)* to bend, flex; *(ceder)* to yield, give in.

do·ble·men·te adv. doubly; *(maliciosamente)* falsely, deceitfully.

do·blez m.f. duplicity, two-facedness —m. *(pliegue)* fold, crease; *(dobladillo)* hem.

do·ce I. adj. twelve; *(duodécimo)* twelfth ♦ **las d.** twelve o'clock II. m. twelve.

do·ce·na f. dozen.

do·cen·te adj. teaching, educational.

dó·cil adj. docile; *(dúctil)* ductile.

doc·to, a adj. & m.f. learned (person).

doc·tor, ·ra m.f. doctor; *(maestro)* teacher, professor; COLL. doctor, physician.

doc·to·ra·do m. doctorate.

doc·to·rar tr. to confer a doctor's degree —reflex. to get a doctor's degree.

doc·tri·na f. doctrine, teaching; *(conocimiento)* knowledge, learning.

doc·tri·na·rio m. adj. & m.f. doctrinaire.

do·cu·men·ta·ción f. documentation.

do·cu·men·ta·do, a adj. documented; *(informado)* well-informed, well-read.

do·cu·men·tal adj. & m. documentary.

do·cu·men·tar tr. to document; *(educar)* to educate —reflex. to research, investigate.

do·cu·men·to m. document; *(prueba)* proof, evidence ♦ **d. a la vista** sight bill, draft • **d.** justificativo voucher, certificate.

do·gal m. *(de caballo)* halter; *(para ahorcar)* noose, hangman's rope ♦ **estar con el d. al cuello** or **a la garganta** COLL. to be in a tight spot.

dog·ma m. dogma.

dog·má·ti·co, a I. adj. dogmatic II. m.f. dogmatist —f. dogmatics.

do·go, a m.f. bulldog.

dó·lar m. dollar.

do·len·cia f. illness, ailment.

do·ler §78 intr. to hurt —reflex. *(arrepentirse)* to repent; *(sentir)* to regret; *(compadecerse)* to sympathize, be sorry; *(quejarse)* to complain

do·lo m. fraud.

do·lor m. pain, ache; *(congoja)* sorrow, distress; *(arrepentimiento)* repentance, regret.

do·lo·ri·do, a adj. sore, aching; *(desconsolado)* pained, distressed.

do·lo·ro·so, a adj. *(lastimoso)* pitiful, distressing; *(sensible)* painful.

do·ma f. taming.

do·ma·dor, ·ra m.f. *(de fieras)* tamer, trainer; *(de caballos)* horsebreaker, broncobuster.

do·mar tr. to tame, domesticate; *(vencer)* to subdue, master.

do·mes·ti·car §70 tr. to tame, domesticate; *(vencer)* to subdue, conquer; *(educar)* to educate, refine.

do·més·ti·co, a I. adj. domestic II. m.f. domestic, household servant.

do·mi·ci·liar tr. to domicile, establish in a residence —reflex. to settle, take up residence ♦ **¿en dónde se domicilia usted?** where do you live?

do·mi·ci·lio m. domicile, residence ♦ **adquirir** or **elegir d.** to settle, take up residence • **d. social** head office, corporate headquarters.

do·mi·na·ción f. domination; *(señorío)* rule, dominion; MIL. high ground.

do·mi·na·dor, ·ra I. adj. dominating; *(avasallador)* domineering, overbearing II. m.f. dominator; *(avasallador)* domineering person.

do·mi·nan·te I. adj. dominant; *(avasallador)* domineering, overbearing II. f. dominant.

do·mi·nar tr. to dominate; *(someter)* to subdue, control; *(saber a fondo)* to know well, master —intr. to dominate, stand out —reflex. to control or restrain oneself.

do·min·go m. Sunday.

do·mi·nio m. dominion, power; *(superioridad)* dominance, supremacy; *(maestría)* mastery, command; *(tierra)* domain, dominion.

do·mi·nó m. dominoes.

don¹ m. *(regalo)* gift, present; *(gracia)* gift, talent, knack ♦ **d. de acertar** or **errar** knack for doing the right or wrong thing • **d. de gentes** personal charm.

don² m. Don (title of respect used before a man's first name).

do·na·ción f. donation, contribution; *(regalo)* gift, present.

do·nai·re m. *(gracia)* grace, gentility; *(agudeza)* witticism, quip.

do·nar tr. to donate, give.

do·na·ti·vo m. donation, gift.

don·cel I. m. young nobleman II. adj. mellow, mild.

don·ce·lla f. maiden, young maid; *(criada)* maid, housemaid.

don·de I. adv. where ♦ **d. no** otherwise • **en d.** in which • **por d.** whereby II. prep. S. AMER. to or at the house of.

dón·de adv. where ♦ **¿a d.?** where? • **¿de d.?** from where? • **¿por d.?** why?

don·de·quie·ra adv. anywhere ♦ **d. que** wherever • **por d.** everywhere, all over the place.

do·no·so, a adj. *(gracioso)* witty, funny; *(elegante)* elegant, poised.

do·no·su·ra f. *(gracia)* grace, gentility; *(agudeza)* witticism, quip.

do·ña f. Mrs., Madame.

do·quier/do·quie·ra adv. var. of **dondequiera.**

do·ra·do, a I. adj. golden; *(cubierto de oro)* gilt, gilded II. m. gilding.

do·ra·dor, ·ra m.f. gilder.

do·rar tr. to gild, cover with gold; METAL. to

gold-plate; *(paliar)* to palliate, minimize —reflex. to become golden *or* gilded.

dor·mi·lón, o·na I. adj. sleepy II. m.f. sleepyhead —f. easy chair.

dor·mir §27 intr. to sleep; *(pernoctar)* to spend the night; *(sosegarse)* to grow calm, subside ♦ **d. de un tirón** *or* **a pierna suelta** to sleep soundly —reflex. to fall asleep; MARIT. to heel, list ♦ **d. en los laureles** to rest on one's laurels —tr. to put to sleep ♦ **d. la mona** to sleep it off ♦ **d. la siesta** to take a nap.

dor·mi·tar intr. to doze, snooze.

dor·mi·to·rio m. bedroom; *(residencia)* dormitory.

dor·so m. back.

dos I. adj. two; *(segundo)* second ♦ **las d.** two o'clock II. m. two; *(naipe)* deuce ♦ **cada d. por tres** frequently ● **en un d. por tres** in a jiffy ● **los** *or* **las d.** both.

dós·cien·tos, as adj. & m. two hundred.

do·si·fi·ca·ción f. dosage.

do·si·fi·car §70 tr. to dose, give in doses.

do·sis f. dose; FIG. portion, quantity.

do·ta·ción f. endowment, bequest; *(dote)* dowry; MARIT. crew; *(personal)* personnel.

do·tar tr. to endow, provide; *(bodas)* to give a dowry; *(testamento)* to bequeath, leave; *(personal)* to man, staff.

do·te m. *or* f. dowry —f. endowment; *(habilidad)* talent, ability.

doy see **dar**.

do·za·vo, a adj. & m.f. twelfth.

drac·ma m.f. FIN. drachma; *(peso)* dram.

dra·ga f. dredge.

dra·gar §47 tr. to dredge, drag.

dra·gón m. dragon; BOT. snapdragon; MIL. dragoon.

dra·ma m. drama.

dra·má·ti·co, a I. adj. dramatic II. m.f. dramatist, playwright —m. actor —f. *(actriz)* actress; *(arte dramático)* drama.

dra·ma·ti·zar §04 tr. to dramatize.

dra·ma·tur·gia f. dramaturgy, dramatic art.

dra·ma·tur·go, a m.f. playwright, dramatist.

drás·ti·co, a adj. drastic.

dre·na·je m. drainage.

dre·nar tr. to drain.

dro·ga f. drug; *(embuste)* fib, lie; *(trampa)* trick; *(molestia)* nuisance; AMER. bad debt.

dro·ga·dic·ción f. drug addiction.

dro·ga·dic·to, a m.f. drug addict.

dro·ga·do, a I. adj. drugged, doped II. m.f. drug addict —m. drugging, doping.

dro·gar §47 tr. to drug, dope.

dro·gue·rí·a f. drugstore, pharmacy; *(comercio)* drug trade.

dro·me·da·rio m. dromedary.

dua·li·dad f. duality.

du·bi·ta·ti·vo, a adj. doubtful.

du·ca·do m. dukedom; NUMIS. ducat.

dúc·til adj. ductile; FIG. pliant, docile.

du·cha f. *(baño)* shower; MED. douche, irrigation.

du·char tr. & reflex. to shower; MED. to douche.

du·cho, a adj. skillful, expert.

du·da f. doubt, uncertainty ♦ **no cabe** *or* **no hay d.** there (is) no doubt ● **poner en d.** to question, doubt ● **sin sombra de d.** beyond the shadow of a doubt.

du·dar tr. to doubt, question —intr. to doubt; *(vacilar)* to vacillate, waver.

du·do·so, a adj. doubtful, uncertain; *(sospechoso)* dubious; *(vacilante)* hesitant, wavering.

due·la, lo see **doler**.

due·lo¹ m. duel.

due·lo² m. *(dolor)* grief, sorrow; *(luto)* mourning, bereavement; *(los afligidos)* mourners ♦ **estar de d.** to be in mourning ● **sin d.** unrestrainedly ♦ pl. troubles.

duen·de m. goblin, ghost; FIG. enchanting quality, magic; TEX. gold *or* silver cloth.

due·ña f. owner; *(ama)* lady of the house; *(señora)* lady, matron.

due·ño m. owner; *(amo)* master (of a house) ♦ **ser d. de sí mismo** to have self-control.

duer·ma, mo see **dormir**.

dul·ce I. adj. sweet; *(dúctil)* soft, ductile; *(agua)* fresh II. m. candy, sweet III. adv. gently, softly.

dul·ce·ro, a I. adj. fond of sweets, sweet-toothed II. m.f. confectioner —f. candy dish.

dul·zu·ra f. sweetness; *(mansedumbre)* mildness, gentleness; *(verbal)* endearment, sweet nothing.

du·na f. dune.

dú·o m. duet, duo.

duo·dé·ci·mo, a adj. & m. twelfth.

du·plex m. duplex, split-level (apartment).

du·pli·ca·ción f. duplication, doubling.

du·pli·ca·do m. copy, duplicate.

du·pli·ca·dor, ·ra I. adj. duplicating, copying; *(que dobla)* doubling II. m. copier, copying machine.

du·pli·car §70 tr. to duplicate, copy; *(doblar)* to double.

du·plo, a adj. & m. double, twofold.

du·que m. duke.

du·que·sa f. duchess.

du·ra·ción f. duration.

du·ra·de·ro, a adj. durable, lasting.

du·ran·te prep. during.

du·rar intr. to last, endure; *(quedar)* to remain.

du·raz·ne·ro m. peach tree.

du·raz·no m. peach.

du·re·za f. hardness; *(fuerza)* strength, toughness; *(dificultad)* difficulty; *(severidad)* severity, harshness; *(obstinación)* obstinacy, stubbornness; *(indiferencia)* indifference.

dur·mien·te I. adj. asleep, sleeping; *(inactivo)* dormant, inactive II. m.f. sleeper —m. RAIL. sleeper, crosstie; CARP. girder, rafter.

dur·mie·ra, mió see **dormir**.

du·ro, a I. adj. hard; *(fuerte)* tough, strong; *(resistente)* resistent, resilient; *(cruel)* callous, cruel; *(obstinado)* stubborn, obstinate; *(terco)* mean, stingy; *(áspero)* harsh ♦ **a duras penas** with difficulty II. adv. hard.

E

e, E f. sixth letter of the Spanish alphabet.

e conj. and.

e·ba·nis·ta m. cabinetmaker, woodworker.

é·ba·no m. ebony.

e·brie·dad f. inebriation, intoxication.

e·brio, a I. adj. inebriated, drunk II. m.f. drunk, drunkard.

e·bu·lli·ción f. boiling; *(efervescencia)* ebullience.

e·cléc·ti·co, a adj. & m.f. eclectic.

e·cle·siás·ti·co, a adj. & m. ecclesiastic.

e·clip·sar tr. to eclipse —reflex. to be eclipsed; (desaparecer) to disappear, vanish.
e·clip·se m. eclipse.
e·co m. echo; (noticia) news; (acogida) response, reception ♦ **hacerse e.** de to repeat, spread • **tener e.** to catch on, be popular.
e·co·lo·gí·a f. ecology.
e·co·no·mí·a f. economy; (ciencia) economics; (parsimonia) thrift, frugality; (escasez) scantiness, scarcity; (miseria) poverty, want ♦ **e. doméstica** home economics • **hacer economías** to economize, save.
e·co·nó·mi·co, a adj. economic; (ahorrador) economical.
e·co·no·mis·ta m.f. economist.
e·co·no·mi·zar §04 tr. to economize on.
e·co·sis·te·ma m. ecosystem.
e·cua·ción f. equation.
e·cua·dor m. equator.
e·cuá·ni·me adj. even-tempered, levelheaded; (imparcial) impartial.
e·cua·ni·mi·dad f. equanimity, levelheadedness; (imparcialidad) impartiality.
e·cua·to·rial adj. equatorial.
e·cues·tre adj. equestrian.
e·cu·mé·ni·co, a adj. ecumenical, universal.
e·cu·me·nis·mo m. ecumenism.
ec·ze·ma m. eczema.
e·char tr. (arrojar) to throw, cast, toss; (expulsar) to throw out, expel; (destituir) to dismiss, fire; (desechar) to throw out or away; (derramar) to shed; (emitir) to emit, give off; (verter) to pour; (añadir) to add, put in; BOT. to sprout, begin to grow; (los dientes) to cut; (tomar) to take; (aplicar) to put on, apply; (imponer) to impose, give; (condenar) to condemn, sentence; (las cartas) to deal; (apostar) to wager, gamble; (llave) to turn; (cerrojo) to shoot; (publicar) to publish, issue; (representar) to put on, present; (pronunciar) to give, deliver; (presentar) to bring, present; (conjeturar) to attribute, guess to be; (adquirir) to develop, get; ZOOL. to mate, couple ♦ **e. a perder** (arruinar) to spoil, ruin; (pervertir) to corrupt; (malograr) to waste • **e. a pique** to sink • **e. de menos a** to miss; (descuidar) to neglect • **e. de ver** to notice, observe • **echarla de** to pose as, pretend to be • **e. mano a** to grab, get a hold of • **e. suertes** to draw lots • **e. tierra a** FIG. to hush or cover up —intr. to grow, sprout ♦ **e. a** to begin, start; (romper) to burst out • **e. por** (una carrera) to choose, go into; (ir) to go —reflex. to throw oneself; (tenderse) to lie down, stretch out ♦ **e. a** to begin, start • **echárselas de** to pose as, pretend to be • **e. una siesta** to take a nap.
e·char·pe m. stole, shawl.
e·dad f. age; (período) time; (época) era, epoch ♦ **e. crítica** menopause, change of life • **E. Media** Middle Ages • **e. viril** prime of life • **mayor de e.** of age • **menor de e.** underage • **¿qué e. tienes?** how old are you?
e·di·ción f. publication; (conjunto de libros o periódicos) edition; (conjunto de revistas) issue ♦ **segunda e.** COLL. spitting image, carbon copy.
e·dic·to m. edict, proclamation.
e·di·fi·car §70 tr. to build, construct; (establecer) to establish, form; (mejorar) to edify, enlighten.
e·di·fi·cio m. building, edifice; FIG. structure, fabric.

e·di·tar tr. to publish.
e·di·tor, ·ra I. adj. publishing II. m.f. publisher; (redactor) editor.
e·di·to·rial I. adj. publishing II. m. editorial —f. publishing house.
e·du·ca·ción f. education, training.
e·du·ca·do, a adj. educated, trained; (cortés) well-mannered, polite.
e·du·car §70 tr. to educate, teach; (criar) to raise, bring up; (desarrollar) to develop, train.
e·fe·bo m. youth, adolescent.
e·fec·ti·va·men·te adv. (en realidad) really, in fact; (por supuesto) indeed, certainly.
e·fec·ti·vi·dad f. effectiveness; MIL. nominal rank.
e·fec·ti·vo, a I. adj. effective; (verdadero) real, actual; (permanente) permanent II. m. (dinero) (hard) cash; (número total) total number.
e·fec·to m. effect, result; (fin) end, purpose; (impresión) impression, impact; (rotación) spin; COM. commercial paper ♦ **a efectos de** for the purpose of • **con** or **en e.** (efectivamente) in effect, in fact; (en conclusión) indeed, precisely • **dar e.** to produce sound effects • **efectos de resultado** or **de residuo** COMPUT. output • **e. útil** MECH. output • **hacer e.** to have an effect • **llevar a** or **poner en e.** to put into effect, implement • **surtir e.** to have the desired effect, work • **tener e.** (efectuarse) to take effect; (ocurrir) to take place ♦ pl. effects, property, (mercancía) goods, merchandise; FIN. bills, securities.
e·fec·tuar §67 tr. to effect, bring about —reflex. to take effect.
e·fer·ves·cen·cia f. effervescence; FIG. excitement, vivacity.
e·fi·ca·cia f. efficacy, effectiveness.
e·fi·caz adj. efficacious, effective.
e·fi·cien·cia f. efficiency.
e·fi·cien·te adj. efficient, effective.
e·fi·gie f. effigy.
e·fí·me·ro, a adj. ephemeral.
e·flu·vio m. effluvium; FIG. vibration, aura.
e·fu·sión f. effusion; FIG. effusiveness, intensity.
e·fu·si·vo, a adj. effusive.
é·gi·da f. aegis, protection.
e·go m. ego, the self.
e·go·cén·tri·co, a adj. egocentric.
e·go·ís·ta adj. & m.f. egoistic (person).
e·go·la·trí·a f. self-worship, narcissism.
e·go·tie·ta I. adj. egotistic, egotistical II. m.f. egotist.
e·gre·sa·do, a AMER. adj. & m.f. graduate.
e·gre·sar intr. AMER. to graduate.
¡eh! interj. hey!; (para confirmar) all right?, okay?
e·je m. axis; FIG. crux, main point; MECH., TECH. shaft, axle.
e·je·cu·ción f. execution, realization; CRIMIN. execution; MUS. performance, rendition.
e·je·cu·tar tr. to execute, carry out; CRIMIN. to execute, put to death; MUS. to perform, play.
e·je·cu·ti·vo, a adj. & m. executive.
e·je·cu·tor, ·ra I. adj. executing; MUS. performing II. m.f. executor ♦ **e. de la justicia** executioner • **e. testamentaria** executrix • **e. testamentario** executor.
e·jem·plar I. adj. exemplary II. m. example; PRINT. copy; (número) number, issue; (precedente) precedent; SCI. specimen ♦ **e. de regalo** complimentary copy • **sin e.** unprecedented,

unique.

e·jem·pli·fi·car §70 tr. to exemplify, illustrate.

e·jem·plo m. example ♦ **dar e.** to set an example • **por e.** for example, for instance • **sin e.** unprecedented.

e·jer·cer §75 tr. to exercise; *(desempeñar)* to practice —intr. to be in practice, practice a profession.

e·jer·ci·cio m. exercise; *(desempeño)* practice; *(tarea)* exercise, drill; *(prueba)* examination; MIL. exercise, drill; POL. tenure ♦ **e. económico** fiscal year.

e·jer·ci·tar tr. *(desempeñar)* to practice; *(adiestrar)* to train, drill —reflex. to train, drill.

e·jér·ci·to m. MIL. army; FIG. army, flock.

el I. def. art. the II. pron. the one ♦ **el que** the one that; *(él)* he who.

él pron. [pl. **e·llos**] he; him *<para él for him>*; it *<tomó el lápiz y escribió con él* she took the pencil and wrote with it> ♦ **de él** his • **él mismo** he himself ♦ pl. they, them • **de ellos** theirs • **ellos mismos** they themselves.

e·la·bo·rar tr. *(fabricar)* to manufacture, produce; *(crear)* to make, create; *(labrar)* to work; *(preparar)* to prepare, work out.

e·lan m. elan, zest.

e·las·ti·ci·dad f. elasticity; FIG. flexibility.

e·lás·ti·co, a I. adj. elastic; *(flexible)* flexible II. m. elastic, elastic band ♦ pl. suspenders —f. AMER. undershirt, T-shirt.

e·lec·ción f. election; *(selección)* selection, choice.

e·lec·to, a adj. & m.f. elect, chosen (person).

e·lec·tor, ·ra I. adj. electing II. m.f. elector, voter.

e·lec·to·ra·do m. electorate.

e·lec·tri·ci·dad f. electricity.

e·lec·tri·cis·ta I. adj. electrical II. m.f. electrician.

e·léc·tri·co, a adj. electric(al); FIG. lightning-fast.

e·lec·tri·fi·car §70 tr. to electrify.

e·lec·tri·zan·te adj. electrifying.

e·lec·tri·zar §04 tr. to electrify.

e·lec·tro·car·dio·gra·ma m. electrocardiogram.

e·lec·tro·cu·ción f. electrocution.

e·lec·tro·cu·tar tr. to electrocute.

e·lec·tro·en·ce·fa·lo·gra·ma m. electroencephalogram.

e·lec·troi·mán m. electromagnet.

e·lec·tro·mag·ne·tis·mo m. electromagnetism.

e·lec·tro·mo·tor, ra I. adj. electromotive II. m. electromotor.

e·lec·trón m. electron.

e·lec·tró·ni·co, a I. adj. electronic II. f. electronics.

e·lec·tro·tec·nia f. electrical engineering.

e·le·fan·te m. elephant.

e·le·gan·cia f. elegance, polish.

e·le·gan·te adj. elegant.

e·le·gí·a f. elegy.

e·le·gir §57 tr. to choose, select; POL. to elect.

e·le·men·tal adj. elemental; *(obvio)* elementary, obvious; *(fundamental)* fundamental, essential.

e·le·men·to m. element; *(miembro)* member; ELEC. cell; AMER. dimwit, blockhead ♦ pl. rudiments, basic principles; *(recursos)* resources, means; *(condiciones atmosféricas)* elements.

e·len·co m. THEAT. company, cast.

e·le·va·ción f. elevation; *(construcción)* erection, building; FIG. promotion; *(enajenamiento)* rapture, ecstasy; MATH. raising.

e·le·va·do, a adj. tall, high; *(sublime)* elevated, lofty.

e·le·va·dor m. AMER. elevator.

e·le·va·mien·to m. var. of **elevación**.

e·le·var tr. to elevate; *(ennoblecer)* to ennoble; MATH. to raise.

e·li·gie·ra, gió, ja, Jo see **elegir**.

e·li·mi·nar tr. to eliminate.

e·li·mi·na·to·rio, a I. adj. eliminatory II. f. SPORT. preliminary, preliminary round.

e·lip·se f. ellipse.

e·lip·sis f. ellipsis.

e·líp·ti·co, a adj. elliptic(al).

e·li·tis·ta adj. elitist.

e·li·xir m. elixir.

e·lo·cu·ción f. elocution.

e·lo·cuen·cia f. eloquence.

e·lo·cuen·te adj. eloquent.

e·lo·giar tr. to eulogize, praise.

e·lo·gio m. eulogy, praise.

e·lu·ci·dar tr. to elucidate, explain.

e·lu·dir tr. to elude, avoid.

e·lu·si·vo, a adj. elusive, evasive.

e·lla pron. she; her *<para e. for her>*; it *<tomó la gorra y se fue con e.* he picked up his cap and left with it> ♦ **de e.** hers • **e. misma** she herself ♦ pl. they, them • **de e.** theirs • **e. mismas** they themselves.

e·llo pron. it.

e·llos, e·llas pron. see **él, ella.**

e·ma·na·ción f. emanation, efflux.

e·ma·nar intr. to emanate, flow.

e·man·ci·pa·ción f. emancipation, liberation.

e·man·ci·par tr. to emancipate, liberate —reflex. to become emancipated *or* liberated.

e·mas·cu·lar tr. to emasculate, castrate.

em·ba·dur·nar tr. to smear, daub.

em·ba·ja·da f. embassy; *(cargo)* ambassadorship; COLL. impertinent proposition.

em·ba·ja·dor, ·ra m.f. ambassador.

em·ba·la·dor m. packer.

em·ba·la·je m. packing, crating; *(materia)* packing material.

em·ba·lar tr. to pack, crate; *(acelerar)* to rev —intr. to race, sprint —reflex. AUTO. to rev; FIG. to be carried away.

em·bal·do·sa·do m. tiling; *(suelo)* tiled floor.

em·bal·do·sar tr. to tile.

em·bal·sa·mar tr. to embalm; *(perfumar)* to perfume, scent.

em·bal·sar tr. to dam up, dam —reflex. to be dammed up.

em·bal·se m. dam.

em·ban·de·rar tr. to decorate with flags.

em·ba·ra·za·da·men·te adv. with embarrassment; *(con dificultad)* with difficulty.

em·ba·ra·za·do, a I. adj. *(preñado)* pregnant; *(molesto)* troubled, bothered II. f. pregnant woman, expectant mother.

em·ba·ra·zar §04 tr. to hinder, impede; *(preñar)* to impregnate, make pregnant; *(molestar)* to bother, embarrass —reflex. to be hindered; *(preñarse)* to become pregnant.

em·ba·ra·zo m. *(preñez)* pregnancy; *(dificultad)* difficulty; *(timidez)* embarrassment.

em·ba·ra·zo·so, a adj. troublesome.

em·bar·ca·ción f. boat, vessel; *(embarco)* embarkation; *(viaje)* voyage.

em·bar·ca·de·ro m. landing stage, pier;

(muelle) wharf, dock; AMER. loading platform.

em·bar·car §70 tr. *(embarcar)* to embark; *(poner a bordo)* to load, ship aboard; *(incluir)* to involve; AMER. to deceive —reflex. to embark; *(enredarse)* to get involved in, engage in.

em·bar·co m. embarkation.

em·bar·gar §47 tr. *(estorbar)* to impede, hamper; LAW to lay an embargo on, distrain; FIG. to overcome.

em·bar·go m. MARIT. embargo; LAW seizure, distraint; MED. indigestion ♦ sin e. however, nevertheless.

em·bar·ni·zar §04 tr. to varnish.

em·bar·que m. loading, shipment.

em·ba·rrar tr. to splash with mud; *(manchar)* to stain; AMER. to annoy, irritate —reflex. to become covered with mud.

em·ba·ru·llar tr. COLL. *(mezclar)* to muddle, mix up; *(chapucear)* to bungle, botch.

em·bas·tar tr. *(un colchón)* to quilt; *(hilvanar)* to baste, tack.

em·ba·te m. dashing, pounding; *(viento)* sea breeze; *(acometida)* sudden attack.

em·bau·ca·dor, ·ra I. adj. deceiving, swindling II. m.f. deceiver, swindler.

em·bau·car §70 tr. to deceive, swindle.

em·be·ber tr. to absorb, soak up; *(empapar)* to soak, wet; *(contener)* to contain, enclose; *(ropa)* to take in —intr. to shrink —reflex. to be absorbed or engrossed.

em·be·le·sar tr. to enthrall, fascinate —reflex. to be enthralled or fascinated.

em·be·le·so m. delight, enchantment.

em·be·lle·ce·dor, ·ra I. adj. beautifying, embellishing II. m. AUTO. hubcap.

em·be·lle·cer §17 tr. to beautify, embellish.

em·bes·ti·da f. attack, onslaught.

em·bes·tir §48 tr. & intr. to attack.

em·be·tu·nar tr. to polish; *(asfaltar)* to cover with pitch or tar.

em·blan·de·cer §17 tr. & intr. to soften.

em·blan·que·cer §17 tr. to whiten, bleach —reflex. to become whitened or bleached.

em·ble·ma m. emblem, symbol.

em·bo·bar tr. to stupefy, fascinate —reflex. to be stupefied or fascinated.

em·bo·ca·du·ra f. MUS. mouthpiece; *(del caballo)* bit; *(desembocadura)* mouth (of a river); *(sabor)* taste.

em·bo·car §70 tr. to put in the mouth; *(engañar)* to make someone swallow; COLL. *(engullir)* to gorge, gulp down; *(comenzar)* to begin, undertake —reflex. to enter, go into.

em·bo·chin·char tr. AMER. to raise a ruckus.

em·bo·lia f. embolism, clot.

ém·bo·lo m. piston.

em·bol·sar tr. to pocket, collect.

em·bo·que m. passage through a narrow place; COLL. trick, hoax.

em·bo·rra·char tr. to intoxicate; *(adormecer)* to make drowsy —reflex. to get drunk.

em·bo·rras·car §70 tr. to irritate, annoy —reflex. to become stormy; *(irritarse)* to become irritated or annoyed; *(fracasar)* to fail, go wrong.

em·bo·rro·nar tr. to cover with smudges or blots; *(escribir)* to scribble.

em·bos·ca·da f. ambush.

em·bos·car §70 tr. to ambush —reflex. to ambush, lie in ambush; COLL. to find an easy way out.

em·bo·ta·du·ra f. bluntness, dullness.

em·bo·ta·mien·to m. blunting, dulling.

em·bo·tar tr. to blunt, dull —reflex. to become blunt or dull.

em·bo·te·lla·mien·to m. bottling; *(de la circulación)* traffic jam, bottleneck.

em·bo·te·llar tr. to bottle; *(obstruir)* to jam, block; *(memorizar)* to learn by heart, memorize.

em·bra·gar §47 tr. to connect, engage.

em·bra·gue m. AUTO. clutch.

em·bra·ve·cer §17 tr. to irritate, infuriate —intr. to flourish, thrive —reflex. to become irritated; *(el mar)* to become choppy.

em·bre·ar tr. to cover with tar or pitch.

em·bria·ga·dor, ·ra/gan·te adj. intoxicating.

em·bria·gar §47 tr. to intoxicate —reflex. to get drunk.

em·bria·guez f. intoxication.

em·brión m. embryo.

em·bro·lla·dor, ·ra I. adj. confusing, embroiling II. m.f. troublemaker.

em·bro·llar tr. to confuse, embroil.

em·bro·llo m. confusion, tangle; *(embuste)* trick, fraud.

em·bro·llón, o·na I. adj. confusing, embroiling II. m.f. troublemaker.

em·bro·mar tr. *(burlarse de)* to make fun of, tease; *(engañar)* to cheat, hoodwink; AMER. *(fastidiar)* to annoy —reflex. AMER. to get annoyed.

em·bru·jar tr. to bewitch, cast a spell on.

em·bru·jo m. spell, charm.

em·bru·te·cer §04 tr. to brutalize.

em·bu·char tr. COLL. *(tragar)* to gulp down, wolf down; *(hacer creer)* to try to make (someone) swallow (something).

em·bu·do m. funnel; *(trampa)* trick, fraud.

em·bus·te m. hoax, fraud; *(mentira)* lie, fib.

em·bus·te·ro, a I. adj. lying, deceitful II. m.f. liar, cheat.

em·bu·ti·do m. inlay, marquetry; CUL. sausage.

em·bu·tir tr. to stuff, cram; *(taracear)* to inlay; *(tragar)* to swallow —reflex. COLL. to stuff oneself, gorge.

e·mer·gen·cia f. *(surgimiento)* emergence; *(accidente)* emergency.

e·mer·ger §34 intr. to emerge.

e·mi·gra·do, a m.f. emigrant, émigré.

e·mi·gran·te I. adj. emigrating, migrating II. m.f. emigrant, émigré.

e·mi·grar intr. to emigrate; ZOOL. to migrate.

e·mi·nen·cia f. eminence.

e·mi·nen·te adj. *(elevado)* high, lofty; *(distinguido)* eminent, distinguished.

e·mi·sa·rio, a m.f. emissary, secret agent.

e·mi·sión f. emission; TELEC. transmission, broadcast; COM. issuance, issue.

e·mi·sor, ·ra I. adj. emitting; TELEC. broadcasting; COM. issuing II. m.f. issuer; TELEC. *(aparato)* transmitter; *(estación)* broadcasting station.

e·mi·tir tr. to emit, throw off; *(poner en circulación)* to issue; *(expresar)* to utter, express —intr. to broadcast, transmit.

e·mo·ción f. emotion, feeling.

e·mo·cio·nan·te adj. moving, thrilling.

e·mo·cio·na·do, a adj. *(conmovido)* moved, touched; *(perturbado)* upset, distressed.

e·mo·cio·nar tr. to move, affect —reflex. to be moved or affected.

e·mo·lu·men·to m. emolument, wage.

e·mo·ti·vo, a adj. emotive, emotional.

em·pa·car §70 tr. to pack, bale; AMER. to annoy, anger —intr. to pack —reflex. to be stubborn; *(turbarse)* to be flustered.

em·pa·char tr. to give indigestion to; *(estorbar)* to obstruct, hinder; *(hacer pasar un apuro)* to embarrass —reflex. to have indigestion.

em·pa·cho m. indigestion; *(apuro)* embarrassment, shame.

em·pa·dro·na·mien·to m. census.

em·pa·dro·nar tr. to take a census of.

em·pa·la·gar §47 tr. to cloy, surfeit; *(fastidiar)* to annoy, tire —intr. to be boring, be tiresome —reflex. to be annoyed (with), be tired (of).

em·pa·la·go m. surfeit, excess; *(molestia)* annoyance, irritation.

em·pa·la·go·so, a I. adj. cloying, sickening; *(fastidioso)* annoying, tiresome. II. m.f. pest, nuisance.

em·pa·li·za·da f. MIL. palisade, stockade.

em·pa·li·zar §04 tr. MIL. to palisade, stockade.

em·pal·mar tr. *(unir)* to connect, join; CARP. to join; PHOTOG. to splice; *(combinar)* to link (up), combine —intr. & reflex. to meet, join; RAIL. to connect, join ♦ **e. con** to follow.

em·pal·me m. join, joint; RAIL., AUTO. junction; PHOTOG. splice.

em·pa·na·do, a I. adj. CUL. breaded II. f. CUL. turnover.

em·pa·nar tr. to bread.

em·pa·ñar tr. *(con pañales)* to diaper, swaddle; *(obscurecer)* to blur, mist; *(manchar)* to tarnish, blemish.

em·pa·par tr. to soak; *(absorber)* to absorb, soak up —reflex. to get soaked; *(imbuirse)* to become inspired; *(ahitarse)* to stuff oneself, gorge oneself.

em·pa·pe·la·do m. papering, lining; *(papel)* wrapping or lining paper.

em·pa·pe·lar tr. *(envolver en papel)* to wrap in paper; *(forrar)* to line, line with paper; *(cubrir paredes)* to wallpaper.

em·pa·que·tar tr. to pack, wrap; *(muchas personas)* to stuff, pack; *(emperejilar)* to dress up.

em·pa·re·da·do, a I. adj. imprisoned, confined; *(retirado)* reclusive II.m.f. prisoner, captive; *(hermitaño)* recluse, hermit —m. sandwich.

em·pa·re·jar tr. to match, pair (off); *(poner a nivel)* to (make) level, level off —intr. *(alcanzar)* to catch up, draw abreast; *(ser pareja)* to match —reflex. to form pairs, pair off.

em·pa·ren·tar §49 intr. to become related by marriage.

em·pas·tar tr. to cover with paste; BKB. to bind; DENT. to fill.

em·pas·te m. DENT. (tooth) filling; BKB. bookbinding.

em·pa·tar tr. *(igualar)* to tie, equal; *(estorbar)* to impede, hold up; AMER. to couple, join —intr. to tie, be equal —reflex. to result in a tie or draw ♦ **empatársela a uno** *(igualarle)* to be a match for someone.

em·pa·te m. tie, draw; AMER. *(estorbo)* obstacle, impediment; *(unión)* joint, connection.

em·pe·ci·na·do, a adj. stubborn, obstinate.

em·pe·ci·na·mien·to m. stubbornness, obstinacy.

em·pe·ci·nar tr. to be stubborn or obstinate.

em·pe·der·ni·do, a adj. hardhearted, insensitive; *(inveterado)* hardened, inveterate.

em·pe·dra·do, a I. adj. dappled, spotted

II. m. cobblestones.

em·pe·drar §49 tr. to pave (with stones); *(cubrir)* to strew, scatter.

em·pei·ne m. *(del vientre)* groin; *(del pie)* instep; MED. impetigo.

em·pe·lo·tar tr. COLL. to wrap up —reflex. *(reñir)* to get into a row, quarrel ♦ **e. con** or por AMER., COLL. to fall madly in love with.

em·pe·llar tr. to push, shove.

em·pe·llón m. push, shove ♦ **a empellones** roughly, violently.

em·pe·ñar tr. to pawn; *(obligar)* to oblige, compel; MIL. to engage in, begin; *(enredar)* to embroil, involve —reflex. *(entramparse)* to go into debt; *(insistir)* to insist, persist ♦ **e. en** to be bent on or determined to ♦ **e. por** or **con** to intercede or mediate on behalf of.

em·pe·ño m. pawn, pledge; *(deudor)* debtor; *(constancia)* insistence, tenacity; *(protector)* patron, supporter ♦ **poner** or **tomar e. en** to take great pains in ♦ **tener e.** to be eager.

em·pe·o·rar tr. to make worse —intr. & reflex. to worsen, deteriorate.

em·pe·que·ñe·cer §17 tr. to diminish, make small; *(desprestigiar)* to belittle, disparage.

em·pe·ra·dor m. emperor.

em·pe·ra·triz f. empress.

em·pe·re·ji·lar/ri·fo·llar tr. COLL. to dress up, doll up —reflex. to get all dressed up.

em·pe·ro conj. but, however.

em·pe·rrar·se reflex. *(encolerizarse)* to flare up, lose one's temper; *(obstinarse)* to be dead set, be determined.

em·pe·zar §29 tr. & intr. to begin (*a* to, *por* by) ♦ **al e.** at the beginning or start ♦ **para e.** to begin with, first.

em·pie·zo see **empezar**.

em·pi·na·do, a adj. very high, lofty; FIG. proud, haughty.

em·pi·nar tr. to stand (up), set straight; *(elevar)* to raise, lift ♦ **e. el codo** COLL. to drink heavily —reflex. *(un caballo)* to rear; *(una persona)* to stand on tiptoe; *(una estructura)* to tower.

em·pí·ri·co, a I. adj. empirical II. m.f. empiricist.

em·pi·za·rrar tr. to cover or roof with slate.

em·plas·tar tr. to plaster; *(maquillar)* apply cosmetics to; *(detener)* to hamper, hold up —reflex. *(ensuciarse)* to become smeared or covered; *(maquillarse)* to make up.

em·plas·to m. plaster, poultice; COLL. *(enfermizo)* weakling, sickly person.

em·pla·zar §04 tr. to call together, convene; LAW to summon to appear in court.

em·ple·a·do, a m.f. employee.

em·ple·a·dor, ·ra I. adj. employing II. m.f. employer.

em·ple·ar tr. to employ; *(invertir)* to invest —reflex. to get a job, become employed ♦ **empleársele bien a uno** to get what one deserves, get one's just deserts.

em·ple·o m. job, occupation; *(uso)* use, utilization; MIL. rank, position; *(inversión)* investment.

em·plo·mar tr. to cover or line with lead; *(poner sellos)* to seal with lead; *(diente)* to fill.

em·plu·mar tr. to feather; *(castigar)* to tar and feather —intr. ORNITH. to fledge, grow feathers; AMER. to flee, take flight.

em·po·bre·cer §17 tr. to impoverish —intr. & reflex. to become poor or impoverished.

em·po·bre·ci·do, a adj. impoverished.

em·po·bre·ci·mien·to m. impoverishment.
em·pol·var tr. to powder; *(ensuciar)* to cover with dust —reflex. to powder (oneself); *(ensuciarse)* to get dusty.
em·po·llar tr. to hatch, brood; *(estudiar mucho)* to bone up on; *(meditar)* to brood or dwell on —intr. to breed, brood; *(estudiar mucho)* to grind, cram.
em·pon·zo·ñar tr. to poison.
em·por·car §73 tr. to soil, dirty —reflex. to become soiled or dirty.
em·po·rio m. emporium, market; *(lugar famoso)* capital, center; AMER. department store.
em·po·trar tr. to embed.
em·pren·de·dor, ·ra adj. enterprising.
em·pren·der tr. to begin, set about ♦ **emprenderla con** to quarrel or wrangle with.
em·pre·sa f. enterprise, undertaking; *(sociedad)* company, firm; *(dirección)* management; *(lema)* emblem, legend.
em·pre·sa·rial adj. managerial, management.
em·pre·sa·rio, a m.f. manager, director; THEAT. impresario.
em·prés·ti·to m. loan.
em·puer·que, co see emporcar.
em·pu·jar tr. to push; *(despedir)* to oust; *(hacer presión)* to pressure.
em·pu·je m. push, shove; *(presión)* pressure; *(energía)* energy, drive.
em·pu·jón m. push, shove ♦ **a empujones** roughly, brusquely.
em·pu·ña·du·ra f. *(de espada)* hilt; *(de paraguas)* handle; COLL. beginning of a story.
em·pu·ñar tr. to seize, grasp.
e·mu·la·ción f. emulation.
e·mu·lar tr. to emulate, rival.
e·mul·sión f. emulsion.
en prep. *(location)* in, into, at, on, upon; *(time)* in, at, as soon as; *(manner)* in, by, at, for, if, into.
e·na·guas f.pl. petticoat, underskirt.
e·na·je·na·ble adj. alienable.
e·na·je·na·ción f. alienation; *(distracción)* distraction, absent-mindedness ♦ **e. mental** madness.
e·na·je·nar tr. to alienate; *(turbar)* to drive crazy, drive to distraction —reflex. to become alienated or estranged.
e·nal·te·ce·dor, ·ra adj. extolling, praising.
e·nal·te·cer §17 tr. to extol, praise.
e·na·mo·ra·di·zo, a adj. easily infatuated.
e·na·mo·ra·do, a I. adj. enamored, in love *(de with, of)*; *(enamoradizo)* easily infatuated, always falling in love II. m.f. lover.
e·na·mo·ra·mien·to m. falling in love.
e·na·mo·rar tr. to enamor, inspire love; *(cortejar)* to court, woo —reflex. to fall in love *(de with)*; *(aficionarse)* to become enamored *(de of)*.
e·na·no, a I. adj. small, minute II. m.f. dwarf.
e·nar·bo·lar tr. to raise, hoist —reflex. to rear up; *(enfadarse)* to be angry.
e·nar·car §70 tr. to bend, arch; *(barriles)* to hoop ♦ **e. las cejas** to raise one's eyebrows —reflex. to bend, arch.
e·nar·de·ce·dor, ·ra adj. fiery, inflammatory.
e·nar·de·cer §17 tr. to ignite, set aflame —reflex. to be ignited.
e·na·re·nar tr. to cover with sand —reflex. MARIT. to run aground.
en·ca·bes·trar tr. to put a halter on, *(atraer)* to attract, seduce.

en·ca·be·za·mien·to m. *(titular)* caption, headline; *(de una carta)* heading; *(registro)* census list or register; *(impuestos)* tax roll.
en·ca·be·zar §04 tr. to head; *(registrar)* to register, enroll —reflex. to agree, come to terms.
en·ca·bri·tar·se reflex. *(un caballo)* to rear up; *(un vehículo)* to pitch upwards; COLL. to get angry.
en·ca·de·na·ción/na·du·ra f./**na·mien·to** m. enchainment; *(eslabón)* connection.
en·ca·de·nar tr. to chain; *(conectar)* to connect, link.
en·ca·jar tr. to fit, insert; *(ajustar)* to force; COLL. *(engañar)* to pass off; *(golpe)* to deal, land —intr. to fit (well) —reflex. to squeeze in.
en·ca·je m. lace; *(inserción)* insertion, inserting; *(unión)* joining, fitting; TECH. inlay.
en·ca·jo·nar tr. to box, crate; *(estrechar)* to squeeze in.
en·ca·lar tr. to whitewash.
en·ca·lla·de·ro m. shoal, sandbank; *(atascadero)* obstruction, stumbling block.
en·ca·llar intr. MARIT. to run aground; FIG. to founder, bog down.
en·ca·lle·cer §17 intr. & reflex. to develop corns, become callused, FIG. to harden, become callous.
en·ca·lle·ci·do, a adj. hardened, calloused.
en·ca·mar·se reflex. COLL. to stay in bed.
en·ca·mi·nar tr. to direct, guide —reflex. to make for, set out for.
en·ca·mi·sar tr. to put a shirt on; *(enfundar)* to put a cover on; *(envolver)* to wrap; MECH. to reline.
en·ca·mo·ta·do, a adj. AMER. in love.
en·ca·mo·tar·se reflex. AMER. to fall in love.
en·ca·na·lar tr. to channel through pipes.
en·ca·na·li·zar §04 tr. var. of encanalar.
en·can·di·la·do, a adj. COLL. erect, tall.
en·can·di·lar tr. *(deslumbrar)* to dazzle; *(avivar la lumbre)* to stir, rake; *(excitar)* to kindle, excite —reflex. to light up.
en·ca·ne·cer §17 intr. & reflex. to go gray; FIG. to age, grow old; *(ponerse mohoso)* to become moldy —tr. to age.
en·can·ta·ción f. var. of encantamiento.
en·can·ta·do, a adj. delighted, charmed; *(distraído)* absent-minded, distracted; *(casa)* haunted.
en·can·ta·dor, ·ra I. adj. enchanting, charming II. m.f. charmer —m. magician, sorcerer —f. sorceress.
en·can·ta·mien·to m. enchantment; *(hechizo)* bewitchment, spell.
en·can·tar tr. to enchant, charm; *(hechizar)* to bewitch, cast a spell on.
en·can·to m. enchantment, bewitchment; *(magia)* magic ♦ pl. charms.
en·ca·ño·nar tr. to channel, pipe; *(apuntar)* to take aim at; *(encanillar)* to wind on a spool or bobbin.
en·ca·po·ta·do, a adj. overcast, cloudy.
en·ca·po·tar tr. to cloak —reflex. *(poner rostro ceñudo)* to frown; *(nublarse)* to become cloudy or overcast.
en·ca·pri·char·se reflex. to take it into one's head, take a fancy *(por, con* to).
en·ca·pu·char tr. to hood, cover with a hood.
en·ca·ra·mar tr. *(levantar)* to lift, raise; *(a un puesto elevado)* to elevate, promote; *(elogiar)*

to extol, praise —reflex. to climb up; AMER. to blush.

en·ca·rar intr. & reflex. to face, confront —tr. *(apuntar)* to take aim at; *(confrontar)* to confront, face.

en·car·ce·lar tr. to incarcerate, imprison; CARP. to clamp.

en·ca·re·cer §17 tr. to raise the price of; *(elogiar)* to extol, praise; *(recomendar)* to recommend, urge —intr. & reflex. to become more expensive.

en·ca·re·ci·da·men·te adv. earnestly.

en·car·ga·do, a I. adj. in charge II. m.f. person in charge ♦ **e. de negocios** chargé d'affaires.

en·car·gar §47 tr. to entrust, put in charge; *(pedir)* to advise, recommend; *(ordenar)* to order, request —reflex. to take charge or responsibility.

en·car·go m. *(recado)* errand, task; *(trabajo)* assignment, job; *(empleo)* post ♦ **hecho de e.** made to order.

en·ca·ri·ñar tr. to make fond of, endear —reflex. to become fond *(con* of).

en·car·na·ción f. incarnation.

en·car·na·do, a I. adj. *(de color de carne)* flesh-colored; *(colorado)* red; *(personificado)* incarnate II. m. flesh color; *(rojo)* red.

en·car·nar intr. to become incarnate; *(cicatrizar)* to heal, close up; *(herir)* to penetrate the flesh or skin; FIG. to make a great impression —tr. to personify, embody —reflex. to mix, join.

en·car·ni·za·do, a adj. *(ensangrentado)* bloodshot; *(sangriento)* bloody; *(intenso)* fierce.

en·car·ni·za·mien·to m. bloodthirstiness.

en·car·ni·zar §04 tr. to make cruel, brutalize —reflex. *(encrudecerse)* to become cruel or brutal; *(pelear)* to fight fiercely.

en·ca·rri·l(l)ar tr. to direct, guide; *(colocar sobre rieles)* to put on tracks; *(dar buena orientación)* to put on the right track.

en·cas·co·tar tr. to fill with debris or rubble.

en·ca·si·llar tr. to pigeonhole; *(clasificar)* to classify, class.

en·cas·que·tar tr. to pull on, put on; *(meter en la cabeza)* to put into someone's head —reflex. to pull on; *(obstinarse)* to take it into one's head.

en·cau·sar tr. to prosecute, sue.

en·cau·zar §04 tr. to channel, direct.

en·ce·fa·li·tis f. encephalitis.

en·ce·fa·lo·gra·ma m. encephalogram.

en·cel·dar tr. to put in a cell, incarcerate.

en·cen·de·dor m. lighter.

en·cen·der §50 tr. to light; *(pegar fuego)* to ignite; *(incendiar)* to set on fire; *(luz)* to turn on; *(excitar)* to arouse, excite; *(causar)* to spark, start —reflex. to light; *(incendiarse)* to catch on fire; *(excitarse)* to get excited; *(estallar)* to break out; *(ruborizarse)* to blush.

en·cen·di·do, a I. adj. lit, switched on; *(hecho ascua)* red, red-hot; *(inflamado)* inflamed, red II. m. AUTO. ignition.

en·ce·ra·do, a I. adj. wax-colored; *(pulido)* waxed, polished II. m. wax; *(pizarra)* blackboard; *(tela)* oilcloth, oilskin; MARIT. tarpaulin.

en·ce·ra·dor, ·ra m.f. floor polisher or waxer.

en·ce·rar tr. to wax, polish —intr. & reflex. to turn yellow, ripen.

en·ce·rrar §49 tr. to enclose, confine; *(incluir)* to hold; *(implicar)* to involve, entail

—reflex. to go into seclusion.

en·cí·a f. gum, gingiva.

en·cí·cli·ca f. encyclical (letter).

en·ci·clo·pe·dia f. encyclop(a)edia.

en·cien·da, do see **encender.**

en·cie·rre, rro see **encerrar.**

en·cie·rro m. *(acción)* shutting, closing; *(recinto)* enclosure; *(clausura)* seclusion; *(retiro)* retirement.

en·ci·ma adv. *(sobre)* on top; *(además)* in addition, besides ♦ **e. de** above • **por e.** superficially • **por e. de** in spite of.

en·cin·ta adj. pregnant, with child.

en·cin·tar tr. to beribbon, adorn with ribbon.

en·claus·trar tr. to put in a cloister; *(esconder)* to hide, conceal.

en·cla·var tr. CARP. to nail (down); *(traspasar)* to pierce, transfix; *(ubicar)* to locate, situate; *(engañar)* to trick, dupe.

en·cla·ve m. enclave.

en·clen·que adj. & m.f. weak, sickly (person).

en·co·co·rar tr. COLL. to annoy, vex —reflex. to be annoyed or vexed.

en·co·frar tr. to plank, timber.

en·co·ger §34 tr. *(reducir)* to shrink, make smaller —intr. & reflex. to contract; *(reducirse)* to shrink, become smaller ♦ **e. de hombros** to shrug one's shoulders.

en·co·gi·do, a adj. & m.f. *(tímido)* shy or bashful (person); *(pusilánime)* faint-hearted or cowardly (person).

en·co·gi·mien·to m. contraction, constriction; *(reducción)* shrinkage, dimunition.

en·co·ja, jo see **encoger.**

en·co·lar tr. to glue, stick.

en·co·le·ri·zar §04 tr. to anger, enrage —reflex. to become angry or enraged.

en·co·men·dar §49 tr. to entrust, commend —reflex. to entrust or commend oneself; *(enviar recuerdos)* to send one's regards.

en·co·miar tr. to praise, extol.

en·co·mien·da f. *(encargo)* commission, task; *(recomendación)* praise, commendation; *(amparo)* care, protection; AMER. postal parcel or package ♦ pl. regards, compliments.

en·co·mien·de, do see **encomendar.**

en·co·mio m. encomium, eulogy.

en·co·nar tr. MED. to inflame, irritate; *(enfadar)* to anger, irritate —reflex. MED. to become inflamed or irritated; *(enfadarse)* to become angry or irritated.

en·co·no m. rancor, ill will; MED. inflammation.

en·con·trar §19 tr. to find; *(topar)* to meet, encounter —intr. to meet —reflex. to meet; *(chocar)* to clash, differ; *(enemistarse)* to have a falling out, become enemies; *(estar)* to be, be located; *(sentirse)* to find oneself ♦ **e. con** *(hallar)* to find, run across; *(topar)* to meet, run into.

en·con·trón/tro·na·zo m. crash, collision; *(riña)* quarrel, dispute.

en·co·pe·tar tr. to raise high —reflex. to put on airs, be conceited.

en·cor·do·nar tr. to bind with cord.

en·co·rra·lar tr. to corral, pen.

en·cor·ti·nar tr. to provide with curtains.

en·cor·va·du·ra f./**mien·to** m. bend, curve.

en·cor·var tr. to bend, curve —reflex. to stoop, bend down; *(inclinarse)* to lean toward, be partial to.

en·cos·trar tr. to cover with a crust —intr. &

reflex. to form a crust.

en·cres·par tr. to curl; (erizar) to make (one's hair) stand on end —reflex. to curl; (erizarse) to stand on end; (enredarse) to become complicated; (enardecerse) to become agitated.

en·cru·ci·ja·da f. crossroads, intersection; (emboscada) ambush, snare.

en·cua·der·na·ción f. bookbinding; (taller) bindery.

en·cua·der·na·dor, ·ra m.f. bookbinder.

en·cua·der·nar tr. to bind.

en·cua·drar tr. to frame; (encajar) to fit in, insert; (rodear) to surround, enclose.

en·cu·bier·to, a I. see **encubrir II.** adj. hidden, concealed.

en·cu·bri·dor, ·ra m.f. accessory after the fact.

en·cu·brir §80 tr. to hide, conceal; (amparar un criminal) to harbor.

en·cuen·tre, tro see **encontrar.**

en·cuen·tro m. meeting, encounter; (choque) crash, collision, (oposición) clash, conflict; (hallazgo) find, discovery; SPORT. match, game; ARCHIT. joint ♦ salir al e. de (recibir) to go out to meet; (oponer) to oppose, confront.

en·cues·ta f. investigation, inquiry; (sondeo) survey, poll.

en·cum·bra·do, a adj. high, lofty.

en·cum·brar tr. to raise, lift; FIG. to exalt, honor —reflex. to put on airs, become haughty; (elevarse mucho) to tower, rise.

en·cur·de·lar·se reflex. COLL. to get drunk.

en·cur·ti·do m. pickled fruit or vegetable.

en·cur·tir tr. to pickle, preserve.

en·cha·pa·do m. veneer, overlay; (acción) veneering, plating.

en·cha·par tr. to veneer, overlay.

en·char·car §70 tr. to flood —reflex. to become flooded, become swamped; (encenagarse) to wallow.

en·chi·la·da f. enchilada.

en·chi·la·do, a adj. AMER. seasoned with chilli, (rojo) (bright) red, vermillion.

en·chi·lar·se reflex. AMER. to fly into a rage.

en·chu·far tr. ELEC. to connect, plug in; (acoplar tubos) to fit together, couple; COM. to combine, merge; (ejercer influencia) to pull strings for —reflex. to land a job through connections.

en·chu·fe m. ELEC., TECH. connection; (hembra) socket; (macho) plug; COLL. (puesto) cushy job, sinecure; (relaciones) contacts, pull.

en·de adv. ♦ por e. therefore, consequently.

en·de·ble adj. weak, flimsy.

en·dé·mi·co, a adj. endemic.

en·de·mo·nia·do, a I. adj. possessed; FIG. devilish, fiendish II. m.f. person possessed.

en·den·te·cer §17 intr. to teethe, cut teeth.

en·de·re·zar §04 tr. to straighten; (poner vertical) to set or stand up straight; (encaminar) to direct, guide; (enmendar) to correct, rectify —intr. to go straight to —reflex. to become straight; (ponerse vertical) to stand up straight.

en·deu·dar·se reflex. to fall into debt, become indebted.

en·dia·bla·do, a adj. devilish, diabolical; (feísimo) hideous, repulsive.

en·di·bia f. endive.

en·dil·gar §47 tr. COLL. to send off, dispatch; (encajar) to foist or palm off.

en·dio·sar tr. to deify —reflex. to become vain; (enajenarse) to become preoccupied.

en·do·min·gar·se §47 reflex. to dress up.

en·do·sa·ble adj. endorsable.

en·do·san·te m.f. endorser.

en·do·sar tr. to endorse; (encajar) to palm off.

en·do·so m. endorsement.

en·do·ve·no·so, a adj. intravenous.

en·dul·zar §04 tr. to sweeten; (suavizar) to soften, ease.

en·du·re·cer §17 tr. to harden; (robustecer) to toughen (up), make hardy —reflex. to harden; (robustecerse) to become tough or hardy; (encruelecerse) to become hardhearted or cruel.

e·ne·bro m. juniper.

e·ne·mi·go, a m.f. enemy, adversary —f. enmity.

e·ne·mis·tad f. animosity, enmity.

e·ne·mis·tar tr. to antagonize —reflex. to become enemies.

e·ner·gí·a f. energy; (vigor) vitality, vigor; (eficacia) efficacy, effectiveness; (ánimo) spirit.

e·nér·gi·co, a adj. energetic.

e·ne·ro m. January.

e·ner·va·ción f./**mien·to** m. enervation.

e·ner·var tr. to enervate, weaken.

e·né·si·mo, a adj. nth, umpteenth.

en·fa·da·di·zo, a adj. touchy, irritable.

en·fa·dar tr. to anger, annoy —reflex. to get angry or annoyed.

en·fa·do m. annoyance, anger.

en·fa·jar tr. to girdle.

en·fan·gar §47 tr. to cover with mud —reflex. (ensuciarse) to become muddy; COLL. to get involved in dirty business.

en·far·dar tr. to pack, bale.

én·fa·sis m. emphasis.

en·fá·ti·co, a adj. emphatic.

en·fer·mar intr. to get sick, become sick —tr. to make ill; (debilitar) to weaken.

en·fer·me·dad f. illness, sickness.

en·fer·me·rí·a f. infirmary.

en·fer·me·ro, a m.f. nurse.

en·fer·mi·zo, a adj. sickly, unhealthy.

en·fer·mo, a adj. & m.f. sick (person).

en·fer·vo·ri·zar §04 tr. to enliven, enthuse, (animar) to encourage.

en·fie·re·cer·se §17 reflex. to become furious.

en·fi·lar tr. to line up, put in line; (enhebrar) to thread, string; (apuntar) to direct, point; (seguir) to go down or along.

en·fi·se·ma m. emphysema.

en·fla·que·cer §17 tr. to make thin; (debilitar) to weaken, debilitate —intr. to grow thin, lose weight; (desanimarse) to weaken, lose heart.

en·fo·car §70 tr. to focus.

en·fo·que m. focus.

en·fren·tar tr. to bring or put face to face —intr. to face —reflex. to confront, face.

en·fren·te adv. facing, opposite; (delante) in front.

en·fria·mien·to m. cooling; MED. chill, cold.

en·friar §30 tr. to cool; COLL. to kill —intr. to cool, become cold —reflex. to be cold; (contraer un catarro) to catch a cold.

en·fun·dar tr. to put in a case, to sheathe.

en·fu·re·cer §17 tr. to madden, infuriate —reflex. to become furious, lose one's temper.

en·fu·re·ci·mien·to m. rage, fury.

en·ga·la·nar tr. to adorn, decorate; (vestir) to dress up, deck out —reflex. to adorn oneself, deck oneself out.

en·ga·llar·se reflex. to put on airs.

en·gan·char tr. to hook; (comprometer) to wheedle, persuade; MIL. to enlist, recruit

—reflex. to get caught or hooked up; MIL. to enlist.

en·gan·che m. *(acción)* hook (up); *(gancho)* hook; *(acoplamiento)* coupling; MIL. enlistment, recruitment.

en·ga·ña·bo·bos m.f.inv. COLL. cheat, swindler —m. fraud, swindle.

en·ga·ña·di·zo, a adj. gullible, credulous.

en·ga·ña·dor, ·ra I. adj. deceiving, deceptive **II.** m.f. deceiver, trickster.

en·ga·ñar tr. to deceive, trick; *(distraer)* to ward or stave off; *(pasar)* to kill, while away —intr. to be deceptive or misleading —reflex. to deceive oneself; *(equivocarse)* to be mistaken or wrong.

en·ga·ñi·f(l)a f. COLL. trick, swindle.

en·ga·ño m. *(equivocación)* error, mistake; *(trampa)* deception, trick; *(estafa)* swindle, fraud.

en·ga·ño·so, a adj. *(burlador)* deceiving, tricking; *(deshonesto)* dishonest, deceitful; *(mentiroso)* misleading, wrong.

en·gar·ce m. stringing, threading; *(encadenamiento)* linking, joining; JEWEL. setting.

en·gar·zar §04 tr. to string, thread; *(engastar)* to set, mount; *(rizar)* to curl; *(encadenar)* to link, join.

en·gas·ta·dor, ·ra I adj. setting **II.** m.f. setter, mounter.

en·gas·tar tr. JEWEL. to set, mount.

en·gas·te m. setting, mounting.

en·ga·tu·sa·dor, ·ra COLL. **I.** adj. coaxing, cajoling **II.** m.f. wheedler.

en·ga·tu·sar tr. COLL. to cajole, coax.

en·gen·drar tr. to engender.

en·gen·dro m. fetus; *(monstruo)* monster, freak.

en·glo·bar tr. to include, comprise.

en·go·la·do, a adj. presumptuous, arrogant.

en·go·lo·si·nar tr. to entice, tempt —reflex. to develop a taste (for), take a liking (to).

en·go·lle·ta·do, a adj. COLL. conceited, proud.

en·go·lle·tar·se reflex. to become conceited.

en·go·ma·do, a adj. gummy, gluey.

en·go·mar tr. to glue, gum.

en·go·mi·nar tr. to put on hair cream.

en·gor·dar tr. to fatten —intr. to get fat; *(hacerse rico)* to get rich.

en·gor·de m. fattening.

en·go·rro m. obstacle, impediment.

en·go·rro·so, a adj. annoying, troublesome.

en·goz·nar tr. to hinge.

en·gra·na·je m. MECH. gear; *(acción)* engaging, meshing; COLL. connection, link.

en·gra·nar intr. MECH. to mesh, engage; *(enlazar)* to connect, link.

en·gran·de·cer §17 tr. to augment, increase; *(alabar)* to laud, praise; *(elevar)* to enhance, heighten; *(exagerar)* to exaggerate —reflex. to become exalted; *(elevarse)* to rise, be promoted.

en·gra·pa·do·ra f. stapler.

en·gra·par tr. to clamp, cramp.

en·gra·sa·do m. lubrication, lubricant.

en·gra·sa·dor, ·ra I. adj. greasing, lubricating **II.** m. grease gun.

en·gra·sar tr. to grease; *(aceitar)* to oil; *(fertilizar)* to spread with manure.

en·gra·se/sa·mien·to m. lubrication, lubricant.

en·gre·í·do, a adj. conceited, arrogant; AMER.

spoiled.

en·grei·mien·to m. pride, haughtiness.

en·gre·ír §58 tr. to make vain or conceited; AMER. *(mimar)* to spoil, pamper —reflex. to become vain or conceited.

en·gri·llar tr. to put in irons, shackle; *(sujetar)* to bring under control, subdue.

en·gro·sar §19 tr. to make thick, thicken; *(aumentar)* to increase, swell —intr. to get fat, put on weight; *(crecer)* to grow.

en·gru·do m. paste.

en·guir·nal·dar tr. to decorate with garlands.

en·gu·llir §13 tr. to gulp down, gobble.

en·ha·ci·nar tr. to pile, heap.

en·ha·ri·nar tr. to flour, coat with flour.

en·he·bi·llar tr. to put a buckle on.

en·he·brar tr. to thread, string; FIG. to link, connect.

en·hes·tar §49 tr. to raise, lift; *(poner derecho)* to erect, set upright —reflex. to be raised or lifted; *(ponerse derecho)* to stand upright.

en·hies·to, a I. see enhestar **II.** adj. upright, erect.

en·hi·lar tr. to string, thread; *(ordenar)* to order, arrange; *(dirigir)* to direct, guide —intr. to set out for, make for.

en·ho·ra·bue·na I. f. congratulations **II.** adv. luckily, fortunately; *(con mucho gusto)* welcome, with pleasure.

en·hor·nar tr. to put in an oven.

e·nig·ma m. enigma, riddle.

e·nig·má·ti·co, a adj. enigmatic(al).

en·ja·bo·nar tr. to soap, wash with soap; *(adular)* to soft-soap, flatter; *(reprender)* to scold, reprimand.

en·ja·e·zar §04 tr. to harness, saddle.

en·jam·brar tr. to (collect into a) hive —intr. to swarm; FIG. to multiply, abound.

en·jam·bre m. swarm; FIG. crowd, throng.

en·jau·lar tr. to cage, put in a cage; *(encarcelar)* to jail.

en·jo·yar tr. to adorn or set with jewels; *(embellecer)* to embellish, beautify.

en·jua·ga·dien·tes m. COLL. mouthwash.

en·jua·gar §47 tr. & reflex. to rinse.

en·jua·gue/ga·to·rio m. rinse, rinsing water; *(recipiente)* washbowl, rinsing cup; *(estratagema)* scheme, plot.

en·ju·ga·ma·nos m.inv. AMER. towel.

en·ju·gar §47 tr. to dry; *(cancelar)* to wipe out, settle —reflex. to wipe dry; *(adelgazarse)* to grow thin or lean.

en·jui·cia·mien·to m. judgment, judging; *(proceso)* trial, prosecution; *(pleito)* lawsuit.

en·jui·ciar tr. *(juzgar)* to judge, examine; *(instruir una causa)* to institute legal proceedings against; *(sujetar a juicio)* to indict, prosecute.

en·jun·dia f. grease, fat; *(substancia)* essence, substance; *(vigor)* strength, vitality; *(carácter)* character, personality.

en·ju·to, a I. adj. dry; *(delgado)* skinny, lean **II.** m.pl. *(tascos)* brushwood, kindling; *(tapas)* snacks, tidbits.

en·la·ce m. connection, link; *(casamiento)* marriage, matrimony; *(parentesco)* tie, bond; *(intermediario)* intermediary, liaison; *(empalme de vías)* junction, crossing.

n·la·dri·lla·do m. brick pavement.

en·la·dri·llar tr. to pave with bricks.

en·la·na·do, a adj. covered with wool.

en·lar·dar tr. to lard, baste.

en·la·tar tr. to can, put in cans.

en·la·za·dor, ·ra I. adj. linking, connective II. m.f. binder, connector.

en·la·zar §04 tr. to lace, interlace; (trabar) to link, connect; (agarrar) to lasso, rope —intr. RAIL. to connect —reflex. to become connected; (casarse) to marry, get married; (contraer parentesco) to become related by marriage.

en·le·jiar §30 tr. to bleach, steep in lye.

en·lo·da·du·ra f./mien·to m. muddying.

en·lo·dar tr. to muddy; FIG. to besmirch, stain —reflex. to become muddy.

en·lo·que·ce·dor, ·ra adj. maddening.

en·lo·que·cer §17 tr. to drive mad or insane; (excitar) to excite, drive crazy —intr. & reflex. to go insane or crazy; (trastornarse) to get excited, go crazy.

en·lo·que·ci·mien·to m. madness, insanity.

en·lo·sa·do m. tiled floor.

en·lo·sa·dor m. tiler, tile layer.

en·lo·sar tr. to tile, pave with tiles.

en·lo·zar §04 tr. AMER. to coat with enamel.

en·lu·ci·do, a I. adj. plastered II. m. plaster, coat of plaster.

en·lu·ci·dor m. (de paredes) plasterer; (de metales) polisher.

en·lu·cir §44 tr. to plaster.

en·lu·ta·do, a adj. in mourning.

en·lu·tar tr. (cubrir de luto) to put in mourning, (poner de luto) to bereave, sadden; (obscurecer) to darken, make gloomy —reflex. to go into mourning; (obscurecerse) to get dark or gloomy.

en·llan·tar tr. to rim or shoe.

en·ma·de·ra·do/mien·to m. timbering.

en·ma·de·rar tr. to plank, timber.

en·ma·le·cer·se §17/zar·se §04 reflex. AMER. to become overgrown with weeds.

en·man·gar §47 tr. to put a handle or haft on.

en·man·tar tr. to cover with a blanket —reflex. to become melancholy or sad.

en·ma·ra·ña·mien·to m. tangle, confusion.

en·ma·ra·ñar tr. to entangle, snarl; (confundir) to muddle, confuse —reflex. to become tangled; (confundirse) to become muddled; METEOROL. to become cloudy or overcast.

en·ma·rar·se reflex. to sail the high seas.

en·mar·car §70 tr. to frame.

en·ma·ri·dar intr. & reflex. to marry, take a husband.

en·ma·ri·lle·cer·se §17 reflex. to turn yellow.

en·ma·ro·mar tr. to tie with a rope, rope.

en·mas·ca·ra·do, a m.f. masked person.

en·mas·ca·rar tr. to mask; (disfrazar) to conceal, disguise —reflex. to put on a mask.

en·ma·si·llar tr. to putty, caulk.

en·men·da·ble adj. amendable, rectifiable.

en·men·da·ción f. correction, amendment.

en·men·dar §49 tr. to correct, amend; (resarcir) to make amends for, compensate —reflex. to mend one's ways.

en·mien·da f. amendment; (reparo) reparation, compensation.

en·mien·de, do see enmendar.

en·mo·he·cer §17 tr. & reflex. to make moldy; (metales) to rust.

en·mo·he·ci·mien·to m. molding, mildewing; (de metales) rusting.

en·mor·da·zar §04 tr. to gag, muzzle.

en·mu·de·cer §17 tr. to silence, hush —intr. to be silent, keep quiet.

en·mu·gre·cer §17/grar tr. to soil, dirty —reflex. to become soiled or dirty.

en·ne·gre·cer §17 tr. to blacken; (obscurecer) to darken —reflex. to turn black; (obscurecerse) to darken.

en·ne·gre·ci·mien·to m. blackening, darkening.

en·no·ble·cer §17 tr. to ennoble.

e·no·ja·di·zo, a adj. quick-tempered, touchy.

e·no·jar tr. to anger, make angry —reflex. to become angry.

e·no·jo m. anger; (molestia) bother, annoyance.

e·no·jo·so, a adj. bothersome, annoying.

e·no·lo·gí·a f. oenology.

e·nó·lo·go, a I. adj. oenological II. m.f. oenologist.

en·or·gu·lle·cer §17 tr. to make proud, fill with pride —reflex. to be proud, pride oneself.

e·nor·me adj. enormous, huge.

e·nor·me·men·te adv. enormously, extremely.

e·nor·mi·dad f. enormity, hugeness.

en·quil·clar tr. to hang.

en·rai·zar §06 intr. to take root.

en·ra·le·cer §17 intr. to get thin.

en·ra·ma·da f. bower, arbor.

en·ra·mar tr. to embower, interweave; (adornar) to decorate with branches —intr. to put out branches.

en·ran·ciar tr. & reflex. to spoil.

en·ra·re·cer §17 tr. (el aire) to thin, rarefy; (hacer escaso) to make rare or scarce —intr. & reflex. to become rare or scarce.

en·ra·re·ci·mien·to m. thinning, rarefying; (escasez) scarcity.

en·ra·sar tr. CONSTR. to level, make flush; (allanar) to smooth, plane —intr. to be at the same level.

en·re·da·de·ra I. adj. climbing, trailing II. f. climbing plant, creeper.

en·re·da·dor, ·ra I. adj. gossipy II. m.f. gossip, busybody.

en·re·dar tr. (atrapar) to net; (tender) to lay, set; (enmarañar) to tangle up, snarl; (enemistar) to cause trouble between; (embrollar) to complicate, confuse; (comprometer) to involve, embroil —intr. to get into mischief, cause trouble —reflex. to get tangled up, become snarled; (complicarse) to become complicated or confused; (comprometerse) to become involved; COLL. (amancebarse) to get involved, have an affair.

en·re·do m. (maraña) tangle, snarl; (engaño) deceit; (llo) mess, muddle; (trama) plot ♦ pl. COLL. things, stuff.

en·re·ja·do m. railings; (celosía) latticework, trellis.

en·re·jar tr. to surround with railings; (una ventana) to put latticework on; (apilar tablas) to lay crosswise.

en·re·ve·sa·do, a adj. intricate, complicated; (travieso) mischievous, unruly.

en·rie·lar tr. METAL. to make into ingots or bars; (echar en la riclera) to cast into ingot molds; AMER. (poner rieles) to put rails on; (encarrilar) to put on rails.

en·ri·que·cer §17 tr. to enrich, make wealthy; (adornar) to adorn, embellish —intr. & reflex. to get rich, become wealthy.

en·ris·car §70 tr. to raise, lift.

en·ris·trar¹ tr. to thread.

en·ris·trar² tr. (ir derecho hacia) to go straight toward; (acertar una cosa difícil) to overcome.

en·ro·je·cer §17 tr. *(con fuego)* to make red-hot; *(dar color rojo)* to redden, make red —intr. to blush, turn red —reflex. *(por fuego)* to turn red-hot; *(ponerse rojo)* to redden, turn red; *(ruborizarse)* to blush, turn red.

en·ro·je·ci·mien·to m. reddening, blush.

en·ro·lar tr. to sign up, recruit.

en·ro·llar tr. to roll or wind up; *(enredar)* to entangle, involve —reflex. to be rolled or wound up; COLL. to get involved.

en·ron·que·cer §17 tr. make hoarse —reflex. to become hoarse.

en·ro·ñar tr. & reflex. to rust.

en·ros·ca·du·ra f. coil, twist.

en·ros·car §70 tr. to coil, twist; *(atornillar)* to screw in.

en·ru·lar tr. AMER. to curl.

en·sa·la·da f. CUL. salad; FIG. hodgepodge.

en·sa·la·de·ra f. salad bowl.

en·sal·mista m.f. quack, charlatan.

en·sa·lo·brar·se reflex. to become salty.

en·sal·za·mien·to m. praise, exaltation.

en·sal·zar §04 tr. to exalt, glorify.

en·sam·bla·dor m. joiner.

en·sam·bla·du·ra f./bla·je/ble m. CARP. joint, connection.

en·sam·blar tr. to join, connect.

en·san·cha·mien·to m. expansion, extension.

en·san·char tr. to widen, expand; *(extender)* to stretch, extend —intr. & reflex. *(envanecerse)* to get puffed up or conceited; *(engrandecerse)* to expand, broaden.

en·san·che m. extension, expansion; *(barrio nuevo)* suburban development.

en·san·gren·tar §49 tr. *(manchar)* to stain with blood; *(derramar)* to shed blood —reflex. *(mancharse)* to become blood-stained; *(encolerizarse)* to fly into a rage, become furious.

en·sa·ña·mien·to m. cruelty, brutality.

en·sa·ñar tr. to enrage, infuriate —reflex. to be cruel or merciless.

en·sar·tar tr. to string, thread; *(atravesar)* to run through, pierce; *(decir tonterías)* to rattle off —reflex. AMER. to get stuck with.

en·sa·ya·dor, ra m.f. assayer.

en·sa·yar tr. to test, try out; THEAT. to rehearse, practice; *(adiestrar)* to train, teach; *(intentar)* to try or attempt —reflex. to practice, rehearse.

en·sa·yis·ta m.f. essayist.

en·sa·yo m. test, trial; *(ejercicio)* exercise, practice; *(intento)* attempt; LIT. essay; METAL. assay, assaying; THEAT. rehearsal.

en·se·gui·da or en seguida adv. immediately, at once.

en·se·na·da f. cove, inlet.

en·se·ña f. badge, emblem.

en·se·ñan·za f. *(arte)* teaching; *(instrucción)* training; *(educación)* education; *(lección)* lesson; RELIG. doctrine, teaching.

en·se·ñar tr. to teach; *(indicar)* to indicate, point out; *(mostrar)* to show —reflex. to accustom oneself to, get used to.

en·se·ño·re·ar·se reflex. to take over, take possession.

en·se·res m.pl. equipment, accouterments ♦ e. domésticos household goods.

en·si·llar tr. to saddle, put a saddle on.

en·si·mis·ma·do, a adj. pensive, absorbed in thought; AMER. *(engreído)* conceited, vain.

en·si·mis·ma·mien·to m. pensiveness, absorption; AMER. *(engreimiento)* conceit, vanity.

en·si·mis·mar·se reflex. to be or become absorbed in thought; AMER. *(engreírse)* to become conceited or vain.

en·so·ber·be·cer §17 tr. to make proud or arrogant —reflex. to become proud or arrogant; MARIT. to become rough.

en·som·bre·cer §17 tr. to darken; *(eclipsar)* to overshadow, eclipse —reflex. to darken, get dark; *(entristecerse)* to become sad.

en·so·par tr. *(empapar)* to soak, drench; *(el pan)* to dip, dunk —reflex. to get soaked.

en·sor·de·ce·dor, ra adj. deafening.

en·sor·de·cer §17 tr. to make deaf, deafen; *(amortiguar)* to muffle —intr. to go or become deaf; *(enmudecer)* to pretend not to hear.

en·sor·de·ci·mien·to m. deafness.

en·sor·ti·jar tr. *(rizar)* to curl, put curls into; *(enrollar)* to coil —reflex. to become curly.

en·su·ciar tr. to dirty, soil; *(estropear)* to make a mess of, mess up; *(desacreditar)* to stain, besmirch —reflex. to become dirty or soiled; *(desacreditar)* to discredit oneself ♦ e. por dinero to accept or take bribes.

en·sue·ño m. dream; *(fantasía)* fantasy, illusion.

en·ta·bla·do m. floor, flooring.

en·ta·blar tr. to board (up); *(empezar)* to begin, start; MED. to splint, put in a splint; LAW to bring, file ♦ e. amistad to become friends —intr. AMER. to tie, draw —reflex. to begin, start.

en·ta·bli·llar tr. to splint, put in a splint.

en·ta·llar tr. to carve, sculpture; *(grabar)* to engrave; CARP. to notch, groove; SEW. to tailor, adjust —intr. to fit well.

en·ta·pi·zar §04 tr. *(paredes)* to tapestry, hang with tapestries; *(muebles)* to upholster; *(cubrir)* to grow over, cover.

en·ta·ri·ma·do m. parquet, parquetry.

en·ta·ri·mar tr. to parquet.

en·te m. entity, being; *(sujeto)* character; COM. firm, company ♦ e. de razón imaginary being • e. de ficción fictional character.

en·ten·de·de·ras f.pl. brains, intelligence.

en·ten·de·dor, ra I. adj. expert; *(listo)* clever, sharp II. m.f. one who understands; *(experto)* expert.

en·ten·der §50 I. tr. to understand, comprehend; *(creer)* to believe, think; *(querer)* to mean, intend —intr. ♦ e. en or de *(tener aptitud)* to be good at; *(ocuparse)* to deal with; *(tener autoridad)* to be in charge of • dar a e. to insinuate, hint at • e. mal to misunderstand —reflex. to be understood; *(interpretarse)* to be meant; *(comprenderse a sí mismo)* to understand oneself; *(tener motivo)* to have one's reasons; *(ponerse de acuerdo)* to come to an agreement; *(llevarse bien)* to get along; *(tener relaciones amorosas)* to have an affair II. m. opinion.

en·ten·di·do, a I. adj. expert, informed; *(inteligente)* intelligent, smart ♦ no darse por e. to pretend not to understand II. m.f. expert, connoisseur.

en·ten·di·mien·to m. understanding, comprehension; *(juicio)* judgment, sense; *(inteligencia)* intelligence, understanding.

en·te·ra·do, a adj. *(informado)* informed, aware; *(bien informado)* well-informed ♦ darse por e. de to be well aware of • estar e. to be informed, know.

en·te·rar tr. *(informar)* to inform, make aware;

AMER. to pay; S. AMER. to complete, make up —reflex. to find out, become aware.

en·te·re·za f. *(cualidad)* integrity, uprightness; *(fortaleza)* fortitude; *(severidad)* strictness.

en·te·ri·zo, a adj. entire, whole.

en·ter·ne·ce·dor, ra adj. touching, moving.

en·ter·ne·cer §17 tr. to soften, make tender; *(conmover)* to touch, move —reflex. *(conmoverse)* to be touched or moved; *(ceder)* to relent.

en·te·ro, a I. adj. entire, complete; *(robusto)* robust, healthy; *(justo)* just, fair; *(firme)* steadfast, resolute; MATH. whole, integral ♦ **por e.** entirely, completely **II.** m. integer, whole number; FIN. point; AMER. payment.

en·te·rrar §49 tr. to bury; *(clavar)* to sink or drive in; *(sobrevivir)* to outlive, survive —reflex. to withdraw, bury oneself.

en·ti·biar tr. to make lukewarm; *(templar)* to temper, moderate —reflex. to become lukewarm; *(moderar)* to relax, cool down.

en·ti·dad f. entity; *(organización)* organization; COM. company, concern.

en·tien·da do see entender.

en·tie·rre, rro see enterrar.

en·tie·rro m. burial, interment; *(funerales)* funeral; *(sepulcro)* tomb, grave.

en·tin·ta·do m. inking.

en·tin·tar tr. PRINT. to ink; *(teñir)* to dye, tint.

en·tol·dar tr. to put an awning over; *(tapizar)* to cover with a tapestry —reflex. to put on airs; METEOROL. to become overcast, cloud over.

en·to·mo·lo·gí·a f. entomology.

en·to·mó·lo·go m. f. entomologist.

en·to·na·ción f. intonation; *(arrogancia)* arrogance, conceit.

en·to·nar tr. *(cantar)* to sing in tune; *(dar cierto tono)* to modulate; *(empezar a cantar)* to intone —intr. *(cantar)* to sing in tune; *(empezar a cantar)* to intone; *(armonizar)* to harmonize; PAINT. to match (colors) —reflex. to be arrogant, put on airs.

en·ton·ces adv. *(en aquel momento)* then, at that time; *(en tal caso)* then, in that case ♦ **desde e.** since then, from then on • **en aquel e.** or **por e.** around that time, at that time • **hasta e.** till then.

en·tor·nar tr. to half-close, leave ajar.

en·tor·no m. environment.

en·tor·pe·cer §17 tr. to make torpid or slow; *(embrutecer)* to dull, deaden; *(obstaculizar)* to hamper, obstruct.

en·tra·da f. entry, entrance; *(vestíbulo)* vestibule, entrance hall; *(ingreso)* admission; *(privilegio)* admittance, entrée; *(billete)* admission ticket; *(taquilla)* gate, receipts; *(desembolso)* deposit, down payment; COM. entry; CUL. entrée; MECH. intake; COMPUT., ELEC., input; MIL. invasion, encroachment ♦ **de e.** right away, from the start • **tener e.** to be welcome ♦ pl. FIN. income, receipts.

en·tra·ma·do m. framework.

en·tra·mar tr. to build a frame for.

en·tram·par tr. to trap, snare; *(engañar)* to deceive, trick; *(enredar)* to entangle, make a mess of; *(gravar con deudas)* to burden with debts —reflex. COLL. to get into debt.

en·tran·te adj. *(próximo)* next, coming; *(nuevo)* new, incoming; ARCHIT. recessed.

en·tra·ña f. entrails, innards; *(esencia)* core, essence; *(centro)* center, middle; *(voluntad)*

will; *(genio)* disposition, nature ♦ pl. bowels, innermost part • **arrancar las e. a alguien** to break someone's heart • **dar hasta las e.** to give one's all • **sin e.** heartless, pitiless.

en·tra·ña·ble adj. intimate, close; *(querido)* beloved, dear.

en·tra·ñar tr. *(enterrar)* to bury deep; *(llevar en si)* to carry within; *(acarrear)* to entail —reflex. to become deeply attached.

en·trar intr. to enter, come in; *(ser admitido)* to be admitted; *(ingresar)* to join; *(encajar)* to go, fit; *(desaguar)* to flow; *(formar parte de)* to enter, be part; *(ser contado)* to be included or counted; *(emplearse)* to go, be used; *(empezar)* to begin, come in; *(atacar)* to attack, charge ♦ **e. a** to begin to • **e. en** to enter, go in; *(abrazar)* to take up, adopt • **no entrarle a uno** *(desagradar)* to dislike; *(no comprender)* to be unable to get —tr. *(meter)* to bring or put inside; *(introducir)* to introduce, bring in; *(invadir)* to invade, attack; *(influir)* to influence, get at —reflex. to get in, sneak in.

en·tre prep. between; *(en el número de)* among, amongst; *(en)* in <e. paréntesis in parentheses>; to <pensé e. mí I thought to myself> ♦ **de e.** out of, from among • **e. tanto** meanwhile • **por e.** through.

en·tre·a·bier·to, a I. see entreabrir **II.** adj. half-open, ajar.

en·tre·a·brir §80 tr. to open halfway, set ajar —reflex. to be open halfway, be ajar.

en·tre·ac·to m. intermission, entr'acte.

en·tre·ca·no, a adj. graying.

en·tre·ca·var tr. to dig shallowly.

en·tre·ce·jo m. ANAT. space between the eyebrows; *(ceño)* frown ♦ **arrugar** or **fruncir el e.** to frown.

en·tre·ce·rrar §49 tr. to half-close, leave ajar.

en·tre·co·mi·llar tr. to put in quotation marks.

en·tre·cor·tar tr. to cut into, cut partially; *(interrumpir)* to interrupt, cut off.

en·tre·cru·za·do, a adj. interwoven.

en·tre·cru·zar §04 tr. to intercross, interweave —reflex. to be intercrossed, be interwoven.

en·tre·di·cho, m. prohibition, interdiction; RELIG. interdict; *(en cuestión)* ♦ **estar en e.** to be in question.

en·tre·dós m. dresser, low cupboard; SEW. insert, panel.

en·tre·fi·no, a adj. of medium quality.

en·tre·ga f. delivery; *(rendición)* handing over.

en·tre·gar §47 tr. *(dar)* to deliver; *(poner en manos)* to hand over or in; *(traicionar)* to betray —reflex. *(rendirse)* to surrender, submit; *(abandonarse)* to abandon oneself *(a to)*.

en·tre·la·zar §04 tr. to interlace, interweave.

en·tre·me·dias adv. *(entre dos cosas)* in between, halfway; *(mientras tanto)* in the meantime, meanwhile ♦ **e. de** between, among.

en·tre·més¹ m. appetizer; hors d'oeuvre.

en·tre·més² m. THEAT. entr'acte, short play.

en·tre·me·ter tr. to insert, put or place in between —reflex. *(injerirse)* to meddle, interfere; *(una conversación)* to interrupt, butt in.

en·tre·me·ti·do, a I. adj. meddlesome, interfering **II.** m.f. meddler, busybody.

en·tre·mez·clar tr. to intermingle.

en·tre·na·dor, ra m.f. trainer, coach.

en·tre·na·mien·to m. training, coaching.

en·tre·nar tr. & reflex. to train.

en·tre·o·ír §45 tr. to half-hear, hear partially.

en·tre·pier·na(s) f.(pl.) crotch.

en·tre·pi·so m. mezzanine.

en·tre·sa·car §70 tr. to pick out, select.
en·tre·sue·lo m. mezzanine.
en·tre·ta·llar tr. to engrave, carve; *(detener)* to hinder, impede —reflex. to fit together.
en·tre·tan·to I. adv. meanwhile, in the meantime II. m. meantime, meanwhile.
en·tre·te·cho m. AMER. attic, loft.
en·tre·te·jer tr. to interweave, interlace.
en·tre·te·la f. SEW. interlining.
en·tre·te·lar tr. to interline.
en·tre·te·ner §69 tr. to entertain, amuse; *(ocupar)* to occupy, keep busy; *(detener)* to detain, delay —reflex. *(detenerse)* to dally, dawdle; *(divertirse)* to be entertained or amused.
en·tre·te·ni·do, a adj. amusing, entertaining.
en·tre·te·ni·mien·to m. amusement, entertainment; *(detenimiento)* detainment, delay.
en·tre·tiem·po m. between-season.
en·tre·tie·ne, tuviera, tuvo see **entretener**.
en·tre·ver §77 tr. to half-see, see partially; *(adivinar)* to guess, surmise.
en·tre·ve·rar tr. to intermingle, mix.
en·tre·ve·ro m. confusion, jumble.
en·tre·ví, vimos see **entrever**.
en·tre·vis·ta f. meeting, conference; JOURN. interview.
en·tre·vis·ta·dor, ·ra m.f. interviewer.
en·tre·vis·tar tr. to interview —reflex. to hold an interview or a meeting.
en·tri·pa·do, a I. adj. intestinal II. m. COLL. gnawing resentment.
en·tris·te·cer §17 tr. to sadden, grieve —reflex. to become sad or grieved.
en·tro·me·ter tr. & reflex. var. of **entremeter**.
en·trom·par·se reflex. COLL. to get drunk or intoxicated; AMER. to get angry.
en·tro·ni·zar §04 tr. to enthrone, put on the throne; *(ensalzar)* to revere, praise.
en·tu·ba·ción f./*bajar* m. tubing.
en·tu·bar tr. to tube, insert a tube in.
en·tuer·to m. wrong, injustice.
en·tu·me·cer §17 tr. to (make) numb —reflex. to go or become numb; *(hincharse)* to swell.
en·tu·me·ci·mien·to m. numbness, torpor; *(crecida)* swelling, rise.
en·tur·biar tr. to cloud *(ensuciar)* to become clouded or cloudy.
en·tu·sias·mar tr. to enthuse —reflex. to become enthusiastic.
en·tu·sias·mo m. enthusiasm.
en·tu·sias·ta I. adj. enthusiastic II. m.f. enthusiast.
e·nu·me·ra·ción f. enumeration.
e·nu·me·rar tr. to enumerate.
e·nun·cia·ción f. enunciation, declaration.
e·nun·cia·do m. enunciation, statement.
e·nun·ciar tr. to enunciate, express clearly.
en·vai·nar tr. to sheathe; *(envolver)* to enclose.
en·va·len·to·nar tr. to encourage, embolden —reflex. to become bold.
en·va·ne·cer §17 tr. make vain or conceited —reflex. to become vain or conceited.
en·va·sa·dor, ·ra m.f. packer; *(embotellador)* bottler —m. large funnel.
en·va·sar tr. to pack, package; *(embotellar)* to bottle; *(beber)* to drink to excess; *(apuñalar)* to stab.
en·va·se m. packing, packaging; *(paquete)* package; *(botella)* bottle.
en·ve·je·cer §17 tr. to age, make old —intr. & reflex. to grow old, age.
en·ve·je·ci·mien·to m. aging, age.

en·ve·ne·nar tr. to poison.
en·ver·ga·du·ra f. wingspan, wingspread; FIG. importance, significance.
en·ver·gar §47 tr. to fasten.
en·vés m. other side, back.
en·ve·sa·do, a adj. showing the opposite side.
en·via·do m. envoy.
en·viar §30 tr. to send, dispatch; *(transmitir)* to convey, transmit ♦ **e. a uno a pasear** or **a paseo** COLL. to send someone packing.
en·vi·ciar tr. to corrupt, pervert —reflex. *(aficionarse)* to become addicted (con, en to); *(corromperse)* to become corrupt or perverted.
en·vi·dia f. envy.
en·vi·diar tr. to envy, be envious of.
en·vi·dio·so, a adj. & m.f. envious (person).
en·vi·le·cer §17 tr. & reflex. to degrade (oneself).
en·vi·le·ci·mien·to m. degradation.
en·ví·o m. sending, dispatch; *(transmisión)* conveyance, transmission; *(paquete)* package, parcel; *(dinero)* remittance; *(mercancías)* shipment, consignment.
en·vión m. push, shove.
en·vi·te m. bet; *(empujón)* push, shove; *(ofrecimiento)* offering ♦ **al primer e.** right off (the bat), from the outset or start.
en·viu·dar intr. to be widowed.
en·vol·to·rio m. bundle; *(cubierta)* wrapper.
en·vol·tu·ra f. cover, covering.
en·vol·ven·te adj. enveloping.
en·vol·ver §78 tr. *(cubrir)* to envelop, cover; *(empaquetar)* to pack, bundle up; *(vestir)* to swaddle; *(arrollar)* to wind; MIL. to surround; FIG. to involve, mix up; *(ocultar)* to enshroud —reflex. *(cubrirse)* to be covered; *(complicarse)* to become involved or mixed up; *(amancebarse)* to have an affair; *(luchar)* to fight.
en·vuel·to, a I. see **envolver** II. f.pl. swaddling clothes.
en·vuel·ve, vo see **envolver**.
en·ye·sar tr. to plaster; MED. to set in plaster.
en·yu·gar §47/**yun·tar** tr. to yoke.
en·zar·zar §04 tr. to cover with brambles; *(malquistar)* to entangle, embroil —reflex. to get caught or entangled.
en·zi·ma f. enzyme.
e·ón m. eon.
¡e·pa! interj. AMER. *(¡hola!)* hey!, hello!; *(¡ea!)* come on!; *(¡cuidado!)* whoa!
e·pi·cen·tro m. epicenter.
é·pi·co, a adj. epic.
e·pi·cú·re·o, a adj. & m.f. epicurean.
e·pi·de·mia f. epidemic.
e·pi·dé·mi·co, a adj. epidemic.
e·pi·de·mio·lo·gí·a f. epidemiology.
e·pi·dér·mi·co, a adj. epidermal, epidermic.
e·pi·der·mis f.inv. epidermis, outer skin.
e·pi·glo·tis f.inv. epiglottis.
e·pí·gra·fe m. epigraph.
e·pi·lep·sia f. epilepsy.
e·pi·lép·ti·co, a adj. & m.f. epileptic.
e·pí·lo·go m. epilogue; *(resumen)* summary, compendium.
e·pis·co·pa·do m. episcopate.
e·pi·so·dio m. episode.
e·pis·te·mo·lo·gí·a f. epistemology.
e·pís·to·la f. epistle.
e·pi·ta·fio m. epitaph.
e·pi·te·lio m. epithelium.
e·pí·te·to m. epithet.
e·pí·to·me m. epitome, summary.

é·po·ca f. epoch, era; *(período)* time, period; GEOL. age **♦ en aquella é.** at that time **• formar o hacer é.** to make history.

e·pó·ni·mo, a I. adj. eponymous, eponymic II. m. eponym.

e·po·pe·ya f. epic poem, epic.

e·qui·dad f. equity.

e·qui·dis·tan·cia f. equidistance.

e·qui·dis·tan·te adj. equidistant.

e·qui·lá·te·ro, a adj. equilateral.

e·qui·li·bra·do, a adj. *(ecuánime)* stable, well-balanced; *(sensato)* sensible, reasonable.

e·qui·li·brar tr. & reflex. to balance.

e·qui·li·brio m. equilibrium.

e·qui·li·bris·mo m. acrobatics; *(del volatinero)* tightrope walking.

e·qui·li·bris·ta m.f. acrobat; *(volatinero)* tightrope walker, funambulist.

e·qui·no, a adj. equine, horse.

e·qui·noc·cio m. equinox.

e·qui·pa·je m. luggage, baggage; MARIT. crew.

e·qui·par tr. to equip, outfit.

e·qui·pa·ra·ble adj. comparable *(con* to, with).

e·qui·pa·ra·ción f. comparison, comparing.

e·qui·pa·rar tr. to compare.

e·qui·po m. *(acción)* equipping, outfitting; *(equipamiento)* equipment, gear; SPORT. team; *(de trabajadores)* shift, crew **♦ e. de primeros auxilios** first aid kit.

e·qui·ta·ción f. riding, equitation.

e·qui·ta·ti·vo, a adj. equitable, fair.

e·qui·va·len·cia f. equivalence, equivalency.

e·qui·va·len·te adj. & m. equivalent.

e·qui·va·ler §74 intr. to be equivalent, equal.

e·qui·vo·ca·ción f. error, mistake.

e·qui·vo·ca·da·men·te adv. mistakenly.

e·qui·vo·ca·do, a adj. wrong, mistaken.

e·qui·vo·car §70 tr. to mistake —intr. to equivocate, lie —reflex. to be mistaken.

e·quí·vo·co, a I. adj. equivocal II. m. ambiguity; *(malentendido)* misunderstanding.

e·ra¹ f. era, age; *(período)* period, time.

e·ra² see **ser²**.

e·ra·rio m. treasury.

er·bio m. erbium.

e·rec·ción f. erection.

e·rec·to, a adj. erect.

e·re·mi·ta m. hermit, eremite.

e·res see **ser²**.

er·go conj. ergo, therefore.

er·gui·mien·to m. erection, raising up.

er·guir §31 tr. to raise, lift up —reflex. to straighten up; *(envanecerse)* to become vain or conceited.

e·rial adj. & m. untilled, uncultivated (land).

e·ri·gir §32 tr. to erect, build; *(fundar)* to found, establish —reflex. to set, establish oneself.

e·ri·za·do, a adj. bristly, spiky.

e·ri·zar §04 tr. to make stand on end, set on end —reflex. to stand on end.

e·ri·zo m. ZOOL. hedgehog; BOT. burr.

er·mi·ta·ño, a m.f. hermit —m. hermit crab.

e·ro·ga·ción f. distribution; AMER. donation.

e·ró·ge·no, a adj. erogenous.

e·ro·sión f. erosion.

e·ró·ti·co, a adj. erotic.

e·ro·tis·mo m. eroticism, erotism.

e·rra·bun·do, a adj. wandering, roving.

e·rra·di·ca·ción f. eradication.

e·rra·di·car §70 tr. to eradicate, root out; *(descuajar)* to uproot, tear up by the roots.

e·rra·do, a adj. wrong, mistaken.

e·rran·te adj. errant, wandering.

e·rrar §33 tr. *(no acertar)* to miss; *(faltar)* to fail (someone) —intr. *(vagar)* to wander, roam; *(equivocarse)* to be mistaken, make a mistake —reflex. to be mistaken, make a mistake.

e·rra·ta f. erratum.

e·rró·ne·o, a adj. erroneous, mistaken.

e·rror m. error, mistake.

e·ruc·tar intr. to burp, belch.

e·ruc·to m. burp, belch.

e·ru·di·ción f. erudition, learning.

e·ru·di·to, a adj. & m.f. erudite.

e·rup·ción f. eruption.

es see **ser²**.

e·sa adj. see **ese, esa**.

é·sa pron. see **ése, ésa**.

es·bel·tez f. slenderness, svelteness.

es·bel·to, a adj. slender, svelte.

es·bo·zar §04 tr. to sketch, outline.

es·bo·zo m. sketch, outline.

es·ca·be·char tr. to pickle, marinate.

es·ca·be·che m. *(adobo)* marinade; *(pescado)* marinated fish salad; *(tinte)* hair dye.

es·ca·bel m. *(asiento)* stool, small seat; *(para los pies)* footstool.

es·ca·bro·so, a adj. *(desigual)* rough, rugged; *(aspero)* harsh, cruel; *(libreviano)* dirty, smutty.

es·ca·bu·llir·se §13 reflex. to escape.

es·ca·fan·dra f./bro m. diver's or diving suit.

es·ca·la f. scale; *(escalera de mano)* ladder, stepladder; *(gama)* range; MARIT. port of call; MIL. register, list; MUS. scale **♦ e. móvil** sliding scale **• hacer e.** MARIT. to put in, call.

es·ca·la·fón m. list.

es·ca·lar tr. to scale, climb; *(robar)* to break in or into, burgle —intr. to rise, climb (by dubious means); MIL., POL. to escalate.

es·cal·da·du·ra f. scald, scalding.

es·cal·dar tr. to scald, burn; *(abrasar)* to make red hot —reflex. to chafe, become chafed.

es·ca·le·ra f. stairs, staircase; *(escalerilla)* ladder; *(de naipes)* straight **♦ e. de caracol** winding staircase **• e. de mano** stepladder **• e. mecánica o automática** escalator.

es·ca·le·ri·lla f. stepladder; *(de naipes)* series of three cards; MARIT. gangway.

es·cal·far tr. to poach.

es·ca·li·na·ta f. flight of steps.

es·ca·lo·frí·o m. *(de miedo)* shiver, shudder; *(de fiebre)* chill, shiver.

es·ca·lón m. step, stair **♦ en escalones** unevenly.

es·ca·lo·nar tr. *(colocar)* to space out; *(horas)* to stagger; AGR. to terrace.

es·ca·lo·pe m. cutlet, scaloppini.

es·cal·par tr. to scalp.

es·cal·pe·lo m. scalpel.

es·ca·ma f. scale.

es·ca·ma·du·ra f. scaling.

es·ca·mar tr. to scale.

es·ca·mo·so, a adj. scaly.

es·ca·mo·te·a·dor, ·ra I. adj. conjuring II. m.f. conjurer, magician; COLL. *(ladrón)* thief.

es·ca·mo·te·ar tr. to make disappear or vanish (by sleight of hand); COLL. *(robar)* to filch, steal; *(evitar)* to avoid, evade.

es·cam·pa·da f. clear spell.

es·cam·pa·do, a adj. clear, open.

es·cam·par tr. & intr. to clear (up).

es·can·ciar tr. to serve, pour —intr. to drink wine.

es·can·da·li·zar §04 tr. to scandalize, shock —intr. to make a fuss —reflex. to be shocked.

es·can·da·lo m. scandal; (alboroto) uproar, ruckus ♦ armar un e. to make a scene.

es·can·da·lo·so, a adj. scandalous, shocking; (alborotoso) noisy, uproarious.

es·can·dio m. CHEM. scandium.

es·ca·pa·da f. (huida) escape, flight; (aventura) escapade.

es·ca·par intr. & reflex. to escape ♦ escaparse por un pelo COLL. to have a close call.

es·ca·pa·ra·te m. shop or display window; AMER. (ropero) wardrobe, closet.

es·ca·pa·to·ria f. escape, flight; COLL. (pretexto) excuse, pretext.

es·ca·pe m. escape, flight; (de un reloj) escapement; AUTO. exhaust (pipe).

es·ca·ra·ba·jo m. scarab, black beetle ♦ pl. COLL. scribbles, scrawls.

es·ca·ra·mu·za f. (combate) skirmish; (argumento) quarrel, dispute.

es·car·ba·dien·tes m.inv. toothpick.

es·car·bar tr. (rascar) to scrape, scratch; (los dientes) to pick; (atizar) to rake, poke; (averiguar) to poke around, investigate.

es·car·ce·os m.pl. wanderings, ramblings ♦ e. amorosos flirtation.

es·car·cha f. frost.

es·car·char intr. to become frosted —tr. to frost.

es·car·da f. weeding hoe.

es·car·dar tr. to weed (out).

es·ca·ri·fi·car §70 tr. to scarify.

es·car·la·ta adj. & f. scarlet.

es·car·la·ti·na f. scarlet fever.

es·car·me·nar tr. (peinar) to comb; (castigar) to punish, castigate; (estafar) to swindle little by little.

es·car·men·tar §49 tr. to chastise, teach a lesson to —intr. to learn one's lesson.

es·car·mien·to m. (aviso) warning, lesson; (castigo) punishment.

es·car·ne·cer §17 tr. to ridicule, mock.

es·car·nio m. ridicule, mocking.

es·ca·ro·la f. escarole.

es·car·pa·do, a adj. (pendiente) steep, sheer; (escabroso) craggy, rugged.

es·car·par tr. to rasp, scrape.

es·car·pe m. scarp, escarpment.

es·car·pia f. hook.

es·car·pín m. pump.

es·ca·sa·men·te adv. scarcely, just.

es·ca·se·ar tr. to skimp, give sparingly —intr. to become or be scarce.

es·ca·sez f. scarcity, lack; (mezquindad) stinginess; (pobreza) poverty, need.

es·ca·so, a adj. scarce, limited; (mezquino) miserly, stingy; (falto) scanty, insufficient.

es·ca·ti·mar tr. to skimp on, spare.

es·ca·to·lo·gí·a f. eschatology; (de excrementos) scatology.

es·ca·to·ló·gi·co, a adj. eschatological; (excrementicio) scatological.

es·ce·na f. scene; THEAT. stage; (arte dramático) theater, dramatic art ♦ poner en e. to stage, present.

es·ce·na·rio m. stage, scene.

es·ce·ni·fi·car §70 tr. to stage, dramatize.

es·ce·no·gra·fí·a f. scenery.

es·ce·nó·gra·fo, a m.f. set designer.

es·cép·ti·co, a I. adj. skeptical II. m.f. skeptic.

es·cin·dir tr. to divide, split —reflex. to split.

es·ci·sión f. division, split; MED. excision.

es·cla·re·cer §17 tr. to illuminate, light up; (elucidar) to clarify, elucidate; (ennoblecer) to ennoble —intr. to dawn.

es·cla·vis·ta adj. pro-slavery.

es·cla·vi·tud f. slavery.

es·cla·vi·zar §04 tr. to enslave.

es·cla·vo, a I. adj. enslaved II. m.f. slave —f. bracelet, bangle.

es·cle·ro·sis f.inv. sclerosis.

es·clu·sa f. lock, sluice; (compuerta) floodgate.

es·co·ba f. broom.

es·co·bar tr. to sweep.

es·co·bi·lla f. brush, small broom.

es·co·bi·llar tr. AMER. to brush.

es·co·bi·na f. sawdust; (de metal) filings.

es·co·cer §71 intr. to sting, smart —reflex. become chafed or irritated; (sentirse) to be hurt.

es·co·ger §34 tr. to choose, select.

es·co·gi·do, a adj. select, choice; (elegido) chosen, selected.

es·co·lar I. adj. scholastic, school II. m.f. pupil, student.

es·co·la·ri·dad f. education, schooling.

es·co·lás·ti·co, a adj. scholastic.

es·col·ta f. escort.

es·col·tar tr. to escort.

es·co·llar intr. to run aground.

es·co·lle·ra f. jetty, breakwater.

es·co·llo m. reef, shoal; FIG. stumbling block.

es·com·brar tr. to sweep, clear.

es·com·bro m. rubble, debris; MIN. slag.

es·con·der tr. & reflex. to hide, conceal.

es·con·di·da·men·te adv. secretly, covertly.

es·con·di·das f.pl. ♦ a e. secretly, covertly.

es·con·di·te m. hiding place; (juego) hide-and-seek.

es·con·dri·jo m. hiding place.

es·co·pe·ta f. shotgun, rifle.

es·co·pe·ta·zo m. gunshot (wound); (noticia) bad news, blow.

es·co·rar tr. MARIT. to list, heel; CONSTR. to shore or prop up —intr. & reflex. to list, heel.

es·cor·bu·to m. scurvy.

es·cor·char tr. to skin, flay.

es·co·ria f. scoria.

es·cor·pión m. scorpion.

es·co·tar tr. to cut, trim; (sacar agua) to drain water from; (partir un gasto) to go Dutch.

es·co·te m. neck, neckline ♦ ir or pagar a e. to go Dutch.

es·co·ti·lla f. hatch(way).

es·co·zor m. smarting; (pena) grief, sorrow.

es·cri·ba·ní·a f. notary public's position or office; (oficio de secretario) clerkship; (escritorio) writing desk; (recado de escribir) writing materials.

es·cri·ba·no m. notary public; (secretario) clerk, secretary.

es·cri·bien·te m.f. amanuensis, clerk.

es·cri·bir §80 tr. & intr. to write ♦ e. a máquina to type —reflex. to write to each other, correspond; (deletrearse) to be spelled; (inscribirse) to enroll, enlist.

es·cri·to, a I. see escribir II. adj. written ♦ e. a

mano handwritten • **e. a máquina** typed, typewritten **III.** m. document, writing ♦ **por e.** in writing.

es·cri·tor, ·ra m.f. writer.

es·cri·to·rio m. desk; *(despacho)* office, study.

es·cri·tu·ra f. writing; *(sistema de signos)* script; LAW document, instrument; *(contrato)* indenture, deed.

es·cri·tu·rar tr. to notarize, execute by deed; THEAT. to book, sign.

es·cro·to m. scrotum.

es·crú·pu·lo m. scruple.

es·cru·pu·lo·si·dad f. scrupulousness.

es·cru·pu·lo·so, a adj. & m.f. scrupulous (person).

es·cru·tar tr. to scrutinize, examine.

es·cru·ti·nio m. scrutiny, examination.

es·cru·ti·ña·dor, ·ra m.f. scrutinizer.

es·cua·dra f. triangle; CARP. carpenter's square; *(grapa)* angle iron; MIL. squad, squadron.

es·cua·dri·lla f. squadron.

es·cua·drón m. cavalry squadron.

es·cuá·li·do, a adj. squalid, filthy.

es·cu·cha f. listening; RELIG. chaperone ♦ **estar a la e.** or **en e.** to be listening —m. night scout.

es·cu·char tr. to listen to —reflex. to like to hear oneself talk.

es·cu·dar tr. & reflex. to shield, protect (oneself).

es·cu·de·rí·a f. *(servicio)* position of a page or squire; AUTO. fleet.

es·cu·de·ro m. squire, page; *(hidalgo)* nobleman.

es·cu·di·lla f. wide bowl.

es·cu·do m. shield; *(insignia)* escutcheon.

es·cu·dri·ña·mien·to m. scrutiny.

es·cu·dri·ñar tr. to scrutinize, examine.

es·cue·la f. school • **e. de artes y oficios** trade or technical school • **e. de párvulos** kindergarten • **tener buena e.** to be well-trained or schooled.

es·cuer·zo m. toad.

es·cue·to, a adj. concise, direct; *(libre)* free, unencumbered.

es·cue·za, zo see **escocer.**

es·cul·pir tr. to sculpt, carve; *(grabar)* to engrave.

es·cul·tor, ·ra m.f. sculptor —f. sculptress.

es·cul·tu·ra f. sculpture, carving.

es·cul·tu·ral adj. sculptural.

es·cu·pi·de·ra f. spittoon, cuspidor; AMER. *(orinal)* urinal.

es·cu·pir tr. to spit; COLL. *(pagar)* to cough up, fork over or out; *(confesar)* to spill, give —intr. to spit.

es·cu·rre·pla·tos m.inv. dish rack.

es·cu·rri·de·ro m. drainboard, draining rack; MIN. drainpipe.

es·cu·rri·di·zo, a adj. slippery.

es·cu·rri·dor m. colander.

es·cu·rrir tr. to drain; *(hacer que chorree)* to wring (out) —intr. to drip, trickle; *(deslizar)* to slip, slide —reflex. to drain, to drip; *(deslizar)* to slip, slide; *(escapar)* to slip out, escape; COLL. *(equivocarse)* to slip up.

e·se, e·sa adj. [pl. **esos, esas**] that ♦ pl. those.

é·se, é·sa pron. [pl. **ésos, ésas**] that one; *(el primero)* the former; *(allí)* there, your town ♦ pl. those.

e·sen·cia f. essence ♦ **quinta e.** quintessence.

e·sen·cial adj. essential.

es·fe·ra f. sphere; *(del reloj)* dial, face.

es·fé·ri·co, a I. adj. spherical **II.** m. ball.

es·fe·ro·grá·fi·ca f. ARG. ball-point pen.

es·fe·roi·de m. spheroid.

es·fin·ge f. sphinx.

es·fín·ter m. sphincter.

es·for·za·do, a adj. brave, courageous.

es·for·zar §37 tr. to strengthen; *(dar ánimo)* to encourage —reflex. to strive.

es·fuer·zo m. effort, exertion; *(valor)* courage, bravery; *(ánimo)* spirit, heart.

es·fu·mar tr. to stump; *(suavizar)* to tone down, soften —reflex. to disappear, vanish.

es·gri·ma f. fencing.

es·gri·mir tr. to wield, brandish; *(servirse de)* to use, make use of —intr. to fence.

es·gri·mis·ta m.f. fencer.

es·guin·ce m. *(regate)* dodge, swerve; *(gesto de desdén)* frown, grimace; MED. sprain, twist.

es·la·bón m. link; *(hierro)* steel.

es·la·bo·nar tr. to link —reflex. to be linked.

es·lo·ra f. length (of a ship).

es·mal·tar tr. to enamel; *(hermosear)* to embellish, adorn.

es·mal·te m. enamel; *(labor)* enameling, enamel work; *(color azul)* smalt, cobalt blue ♦ **e. de para uñas** nail polish.

es·me·ra·do, a adj. careful, meticulous.

es·me·ral·da f. emerald.

es·me·rar tr. to polish, brighten —reflex. to be painstaking, take great care.

es·me·ril m. emery.

es·me·ri·la·dor, ·ra m.f. polisher.

es·me·ri·lar tr. to polish with emery.

es·me·ro m. extreme care, meticulousness.

es·mi·rria·do, a adj. COLL. skinny, thin.

es·mo·quin m. dinner jacket, tuxedo.

es·nob m.f. snob.

e·so pron. that ♦ **a e. de** about, around • **e. es** that's it • **e. mismo** exactly, the same • **por e.** therefore, that's why.

e·só·fa·go m. esophagus.

e·sos see **ese.**

é·sos see **é·se.**

e·so·té·ri·co, a adj. esoteric.

es·pa·cia·dor m. space bar, spacer.

es·pa·cial adj. spatial; *(del espacio)* space.

es·pa·ciar tr. to space or spread out —reflex. *(dilatarse)* to expatiate, go on at length; *(solazarse)* to relax.

es·pa·cio m. space.

es·pa·cio·sa·men·te adv. slowly, deliberately.

es·pa·cio·so, a adj. spacious, roomy; *(lento)* slow, deliberate.

es·pa·da f. sword; *(espadachín)* swordsman; *(naipe)* spade ♦ **de capa y e.** cloak-and-dagger • **entre la e. y la pared** between a rock and a hard place.

es·pa·da·chín m. skilled swordsman; *(bravucón)* swashbuckler.

es·pa·dín m. dress or ceremonial sword.

es·pa·gue·ti m. spaghetti.

es·pal·da f. back ♦ **dar** or **volver la e.** to turn one's back • pl. back • **a e. de alguien** behind someone's back • **de e.** from behind • **tener buenas e.** to be very patient.

es·pal·dar m. back (of a chair); *(enrejado)* trellis, espalier.

es·pal·da·ra·zo m. blow or slap on the back; FIG. *(apoyo)* support, backing.

es·pan·ta·da f. *(huida)* flight, escape; *(miedo)*

sudden scare or fright.

es·pan·ta·di·zo, a adj. jumpy, skittish.

es·pan·ta·jo m. scarecrow; *(persona fea)* sight, fright.

es·pan·ta·pá·ja·ros m.inv. scarecrow.

es·pan·tar tr. to frighten, scare —reflex. to be frightened or scared.

es·pan·to m. fright, scare; *(fantasma)* ghost, phantom.

es·pan·to·so, a adj. frightening, terrifying.

es·pa·ra·dra·po m. adhesive tape.

es·par·ci·do, a adj. scattered, strewn; *(alegre)* merry, cheerful.

es·par·cir §35 tr. to scatter, spread —reflex. to scatter, be scattered; *(descansarse)* to relax, take it easy.

es·pá·rra·go m. asparagus.

es·par·te·ña f. espadrille.

es·par·to m. esparto.

es·pas·mo m. spasm.

es·pas·mó·di·co, a adj. spasmodic.

es·pá·tu·la f. CUL. spatula; ORNITH. spoonbill.

es·pe·cia f. spice.

es·pe·cial adj. special ♦ en e. especially.

es·pe·cia·li·dad f. specialty.

es·pe·cia·lis·ta adj. & m.f. specialist.

es·pe·cia·li·za·ción f. specialization.

es·pe·cia·li·za·do, a adj. specialized.

es·pe·cia·li·zar §04 tr., intr. & reflex. to specialize.

es·pe·cial·men·te adv. especially, specially.

es·pe·cie f. species; *(tipo)* type, kind; *(asunto)* matter, affair; *(noticia)* bit of news; *(pretexto)* pretext.

es·pe·ci·fi·ca·ción f. specification.

es·pe·ci·fi·car §70 tr. to specify.

es·pe·ci·fi·ci·dad f. specificity.

es·pe·cí·fi·co, a adj. & m. specific.

es·pé·ci·men m. [pl. **-címenes**] specimen.

es·pe·cio·so, a adj. specious; *(hermoso)* beautiful, perfect.

es·pec·ta·cu·lar adj. spectacular.

es·pec·tá·cu·lo, m. spectacle.

es·pec·ta·dor, ·ra m.f. spectator, onlooker ♦ pl. audience, public.

es·pec·tral adj. spectral; *(fantasmal)* ghostly.

es·pec·tro m. PHYS. spectrum; *(fantasma)* ghost, spook; *(horror)* specter, horror.

es·pe·cu·la·ción f. speculation.

es·pe·cu·la·dor, ·ra m.f. speculator.

es·pe·cu·lar tr. to examine, inspect; *(conjeturar)* to speculate —intr. to speculate in.

es·pe·cu·la·ti·vo, a adj. speculative.

es·pe·jis·mo/je·ro m. mirage.

es·pe·jo m. mirror; *(modelo)* model, example.

es·pe·luz·nan·te adj. COLL. hair-raising.

es·pe·luz·nar tr. to ruffle, muss; *(pelo)* to make stand on end —reflex. to become ruffled or mussed; *(pelo)* to stand on end.

es·pe·ra f. wait; LAW respite.

es·pe·ran·za f. hope.

es·pe·ran·zar §04 tr. to make hopeful.

es·pe·rar tr. *(tener esperanza)* to hope (for); *(aguardar)* to wait for, await; *(confiar en)* to expect ♦ e. en to trust, put one's faith in —intr. to wait.

es·per·ma f. sperm, semen.

es·per·ma·to·zoi·de m. spermatozoid.

es·per·pen·to m. COLL. *(espanto)* fright, sight; *(desatino)* absurdity, nonsense.

es·pe·sar tr. to thicken —reflex. to grow or become thicker.

es·pe·so, a adj. thick; *(sucio)* dirty, unkempt.

es·pe·sor m. thickness; *(densidad)* density.

es·pe·tar tr. CUL. to skewer, spit; *(atravesar)* to pierce, run through —reflex. *(ponerse tenso)* to become serious or solemn; COLL. *(asegurarse)* to establish oneself.

es·pí·a m.f. spy —f. MARIT. warping, warp.

es·piar §30 tr. to spy on —intr. to spy; MARIT. to warp.

es·pi·char tr. to prick —intr. COLL. to kick the bucket, die.

es·pi·ga f. BOT. spike, ear; CARP. tenon; *(clavija)* peg, pin.

es·pi·ga·do, a adj. spiky.

es·pi·gar §47 tr. to glean; CARP. to tenon, dovetail —reflex. to grow or shoot up.

es·pi·gón m. point; *(mazorca)* ear (of corn); MARIT. breakwater, jetty.

es·pi·na f. thorn; *(de pez)* fishbone; ANAT. spine, backbone; *(pesar)* grief, sorrow ♦ dar mala e. to cause suspicion ● estar en espinas to be on pins and needles.

es·pi·na·ca f. spinach.

es·pi·nar tr. to prick; FIG. to hurt, offend.

es·pi·na·zo m. ANAT. spine, backbone; ARCHIT. keystone.

es·pi·nel m. boulter, trotline.

es·pi·ni·lla f. shinbone; *(granillo)* blackhead.

es·pi·no m. hawthorn, thornbush.

es·pi·no·so, a adj. thorny, spiny; *(arduo)* difficult, sticky.

es·pio·na·je m. espionage, spying.

es·pi·ra·ción f. exhalation, expiration.

es·pi·ral I. adj. spiral, winding II. m. balance spring, hairspring; MED. coil —f. spiral.

es·pi·rar tr. to exhale, breathe out; *(exudar)* to give off, exude —intr. to exhale, breathe out.

es·pi·ri·tis·ta I. adj. spiritualistic, spiritistic II. m.f. spiritualist, spiritist.

es·pi·ri·to·so, a adj. spirited, lively; *(alcohólico)* spirituous, alcoholic.

es·pí·ri·tu m. spirit; *(alma)* soul; *(mente)* intelligence, wit ♦ exhalar el e. to die, give up the ghost ● e. de cuerpo esprit de corps.

es·pi·ri·tual adj. & m. spiritual.

es·pi·ri·tua·li·dad f. spirituality.

es·pi·ri·tua·lis·ta I. adj. spiritualistic II. m.f. spiritualist.

es·pi·ta f. tap, spigot; *(bebedor)* drunkard, boozer.

es·pi·tar tr. to tap, put a spigot on.

es·plen·den·te adj. shining, resplendent.

es·plén·di·do, a adj. splendid; *(generoso)* generous; *(resplandeciente)* resplendent.

es·plen·dor m. splendor.

es·plen·do·ro·so, a adj. resplendent.

es·plín m. melancholy, depression.

es·po·le·ar tr. EQUIT. to spur, prod with a spur; FIG. to incite, urge.

es·po·le·o m. spurring.

es·po·le·ta f. ARM. fuse; ORNITH. wishbone.

es·po·lón m. spur; ZOOL. fetlock; MARIT. cutwater; ARCHIT. buttress; MED chilblain.

es·pol·vo·re·ar tr. to dust (off).

es·pon·ja f. sponge ♦ beber como una e. COLL. to drink like a fish ● tirar or arrojar la e. to throw in the towel, give up.

es·pon·jar tr. to make spongy or fluffy —reflex. to become spongy; *(envanecerse)* to put on airs; COLL. *(rebozar)* to glow with health.

es·pon·je·ar intr. to snoop, pry.

es·pon·jo·so, a adj. spongy.

es·pon·sa·les m.pl. betrothal, engagement.

es·pon·ta·nei·dad f. spontaneity.

es·pon·tá·ne·o, a adj. spontaneous.

es·po·ra f. spore.

es·po·rá·di·co, a adj. sporadic.

es·po·sa f. wife, spouse ♦ pl. handcuffs.

es·po·sa·do, a adj. var. of **desposado**.

es·po·sar tr. to handcuff, put handcuffs on.

es·po·so m. husband, spouse.

es·pue·la f. spur.

es·pul·gar §47 tr. to delouse; (examinar) to scrutinize, examine closely.

es·pu·ma f. foam; (de un líquido) froth, spume; (de jabón) lather; (desechos) scum ♦ crecer como e. or la e. COLL. to shoot up, spread like wildfire • e. de caucho foam rubber.

es·pu·ma·de·ra f. skimmer.

es·pu·ma·je·ar intr. to foam at the mouth.

es·pu·man·te adj. foaming, frothing; (vino) sparkling.

es·pu·mar tr. to skim, remove foam from —intr. to foam, froth.

es·pu·ma·ra·jo m. foam, froth.

es·pu·mo·so, a adj. frothy, foamy.

es·pu·rio, a adj. spurious.

es·pu·tar tr. to spit, expectorate.

es·pu·to m. spit, spittle.

es·que·la f. note, short letter; (aviso) notice.

es·que·lé·ti·co, a adj. skeletal.

es·que·le·to m. skeleton.

es·que·ma m. scheme, outline.

es·que·má·ti·co, a adj. schematic.

es·que·ma·ti·zar §04 tr. to schematize.

es·quí m. [pl. **·s**] ski; (deporte) skiing.

es·quia·dor, **·ra** m.f. skier.

es·quiar §30 intr. to ski.

es·qui·la f. shearing, fleecing.

es·qui·lar tr. to shear, fleece.

es·quil·mar tr. to harvest, gather; (empobrecer) to impoverish; FIG. to exhaust.

es·qui·na f. corner ♦ a la vuel·ta de la e. just around the corner • doblar la e. (dar una vuelta) to turn the corner; AMER., FIG. to die, kick the bucket • hacer e. to be on the corner.

es·qui·na·do, a adj. cornered, angular.

es·qui·nar tr. (formar esquina) to form a corner with; (poner en esquina) to put in a corner; (poner a mal) to set against, estrange —intr. to form a corner (with) —reflex. ♦ e. con to quarrel with.

es·qui·na·zo m. COLL. corner; ARG., CHILE serenade ♦ dar e. a alguien COLL. to give someone the slip.

es·quir·la f. splinter.

es·qui·var tr. to avoid, evade; (rehusar) to shun, refuse —reflex. to withdraw, shy away.

es·qui·vez f. coldness, disdain.

es·qui·vo, a adj. cold, disdainful.

es·qui·zo·fre·nia f. schizophrenia.

es·qui·zo·fré·ni·co, a adj. & m.f. schizophrenic.

es·ta see **este**, a.

és·ta see **éste**, a.

es·ta·ba see **estar**.

es·ta·bi·li·dad f. stability.

es·ta·bi·li·zar §04 tr. to stabilize, make stable.

es·ta·ble adj. stable.

es·ta·ble·ce·dor, **·ra** I. adj. establishing, founding II. m.f. establisher, founder.

es·ta·ble·cer §17 tr. to establish, found; (decretar) to decree, ordain —reflex. to establish oneself.

es·ta·ble·ci·mien·to m. establishment.

es·ta·blo m. stable.

es·ta·ca f. stake, post; (garrote) club, cudgel; BOT. cutting; CARP. spike, nail.

es·ta·ca·da f. picket fence; MIL. stockade, palisade ♦ dejar a alguien en la e. COLL. to leave someone in the lurch • quedar en la e. COLL. to be defeated or beaten.

es·ta·car §70 tr. (atar) to tie to a stake or post; (señalar) to stake out; AMER. to fasten down with stakes —reflex. to freeze, stand stock-still.

es·ta·ción f. (estado) position; (tiempo) season; RAIL., TELEC. station.

es·ta·cio·na·mien·to m. stationing, positioning; AUTO. parking place or space.

es·ta·cio·nar tr. to station, place; AUTO. to park —reflex. to remain stationary; (colocarse) to station oneself.

es·ta·cio·na·rio, a adj. stationary.

es·ta·da/dí·a f. stay, stop.

es·ta·dio m. stadium; (fase) phase, stage.

es·ta·dis·ta m. statesman; (estadístico) statistician.

es·ta·dís·ti·co, a I. adj. statistical II. m. statistician —f. statistics; (dato) statistic.

es·ta·do m. state; (condición) condition (calidad) status; (jerarquía) rank, grade; estate <el cuarto e. the fourth estate>; (resumen) statement, report; MIL. post, garrison ♦ e. civil marital status • e. mayor general staff.

es·ta·fa f. swindle, hoax.

es·ta·fa·dor, **·ra** f. swindler, crook.

es·ta·far tr. to swindle, cheat.

es·ta·fe·ta f. mail, post; (casa de correo) post office; DIPL. diplomatic pouch.

es·ta·fi·lo·co·co m. staphylococcus.

es·ta·la f. port of call; (establo) stable.

es·ta·lac·ti·ta f. stalactite.

es·ta·lag·mi·ta f. stalagmite.

es·ta·llar intr. to burst, explode; (sobrevenir) to break out.

es·ta·lli·do/llo m. (explosión) explosion; ARM. report; FIG. outbreak, outburst.

es·tam·bre m. TEX. worsted yarn; BOT. stamen.

es·tam·pa f. (imagen) print; (huella) track, mark; (aspecto) aspect, appearance.

es·tam·pa·do, a I. adj. TEX. stamped II. m. printing, engraving.

es·tam·pa·dor m. printer, engraver.

es·tam·par tr. to print, stamp; (grabar) to emboss, engrave; (dejar huella) to leave a mark; COLL. (arrojar) to throw, hurl.

es·tam·pi·da f. explosion, bang; AMER. stampede.

es·tam·pi·do m. explosion, bang.

es·tam·pi·lla f. stamp, seal; AMER. postage stamp.

es·tam·pi·llar tr. to stamp, mark with a stamp.

es·tan·car §70 tr. to dam up, stem; COM. to monopolize —reflex. to stagnate, become stagnant; (detenerse) to come to a standstill.

es·tan·cia f. (mansión) country house, estate; (estadía) stay; AMER. ranch, farm.

es·tan·cie·ro m. AMER. rancher, farmer.

es·tan·dar·te m. standard, banner.

es·tan·que m. (charca) pond, pool; (depósito) tank, reservoir.

es·tan·te I adj. (existente) extant; (permanente) fixed II. m. shelving, shelves.

es·tan·te·rí·a f. shelving, shelves.
es·ta·ñar tr. to tin, plate with tin.
es·ta·ño m. tin.
es·ta·qui·lla f. wooden peg.
es·ta·qui·llar tr. to peg, fasten with pegs.
es·tar §36 intr. to be ♦ ¿a cuántos estamos? or ¿a qué estamos? what is the date? • ¿cómo estás? how are you? • está bien or bien está okay, all right • e. a to sell at, cost • e. al caer to be about to happen • e. bien (convenir) to be suitable or fitting; (gozar de buena salud) to be well or healthy • e. de más to be superfluous • e. en (entender) to understand; (consistir en) to depend on, lie in • e. en sí to know what one is doing • e. mal (no convenir) to be unsuitable or inappropriate; (padecer de mala salud) to be ill • e. para (gustar) to be in the mood for; to be about to <estamos para salir we are about to leave> • e. por (favorecer) to be for, be in favor of; to be about to <e. por terminarlo to be about to finish it>; (quedar) to remain to be; (tener ganas) to have a mind to, be inclined to.
es·tar·cir §35 tr. to stencil.
es·ta·tal adj. state, of the state.
es·tá·ti·co, a I. adj. static II. f. static; MECH. statics.
es·ta·tua f. statue; COLL. (persona) cold fish.
es·ta·tua·rio, a adj. & m.f.statuary.
es·ta·tuir §18 tr. to establish, enact; (demostrar) to demonstrate, prove.
es·ta·tu·ra f. stature.
es·ta·tu·to m. (ley) statute, law; (regla) rule.
es·te m. east.
es·te, a adj. [pl. estos, -tas] this ♦ pl. these.
és·te, a pron. [pl. éstos, -tas] this one; (el segundo) the latter; (aquí) here, this town ♦ pl. these.
es·té see estar.
es·te·la f. AVIA. trail; MARIT. wake.
es·te·lar adj. stellar.
es·te·no·gra·fí·a f. stenography, shorthand.
es·te·nó·gra·fo, a m.f. stenographer.
es·ten·tó·re·o, a adj. stentorian, loud.
es·te·pa f. steppe.
es·te·ra f. matting.
es·ter·co·lar¹ m. dung heap, manure pile.
es·ter·co·lar² tr. to manure, fertilize.
es·té·re·o adj. & f. stereo.
es·te·re·o·fo·ní·a f. stereophony, stereo.
es·te·re·o·fó·ni·co, a adj. stereophonic, stereo.
es·te·re·o·ti·par tr. to stereotype.
es·te·re·o·tí·pi·co, a adj. stereotypical.
es·te·re·o·ti·po m. stereotype.
es·té·ril adj. sterile, infertile; (árido) barren.
es·te·ri·li·dad f. sterility.
es·te·ri·li·za·ción f. sterilization.
es·te·ri·li·zar §04 tr. to sterilize.
es·ter·li·na adj. sterling.
es·ter·nón m. sternum, breastbone.
es·te·ro m. estuary; AMER. (pantano) marsh, swamp; AMER. (charca) puddle, pool.
es·ter·tor m. death rattle; MED. stertor.
es·te·ta m. aesthete.
es·té·ti·co, a I. adj. aesthetic II. m. aesthetic, aesthete —f. aesthetics.
es·te·tos·co·pio m. stethoscope.
es·te·va·do, a adj. & m.f. bowlegged (person).
es·ti·ba·dor m. stevedore.
es·ti·bar tr. to pack tightly, compress; MARIT. to stow.
es·tiér·col m. dung, manure.
es·tig·ma m. stigma ♦ pl. RELIG. stigmata.

es·tig·ma·ti·zar §04 tr. to stigmatize, brand; FIG. to censure, reproach.
es·ti·lar intr. & reflex. (usar) to be customary, be the custom; (estar de moda) to be in fashion —tr. to draw up.
es·ti·le·te m. stylus, style; (puñal) stiletto; MED. probe, stylet.
es·ti·lis·ta m.f. stylist.
es·ti·lís·ti·co, a I. adj. stylistic II. f. stylistics.
es·ti·li·zar §04 tr. to stylize.
es·ti·lo m. style ♦ por el e. like that.
es·ti·lo·grá·fi·co, a I. adj. stylographic II. f. fountain pen, stylograph.
es·ti·ma f. esteem, respect.
es·ti·ma·ble adj. estimable; (valioso) worthy of esteem, admirable.
es·ti·ma·ción f. esteem, respect; COM. appraisal, valuation.
es·ti·ma·dor, ·ra I. adj. appreciative II. m. COM. appraiser.
es·ti·mar tr. to esteem, hold in esteem; COM. to estimate, appraise; (juzgar) to consider, deem —reflex. to be esteemed.
es·ti·mu·lan·te I. adj. stimulating II. m. stimulant.
es·ti·mu·lar tr. to stimulate; (aguijonear) to prod, push; (incitar) to incite, urge on.
es·tí·mu·lo m. stimulus.
es·tí·o m. summer.
es·ti·pen·dio m. stipend, remuneration.
es·ti·pu·lar tr. to stipulate.
es·ti·ra·do, a adj. stretched; (vanidoso) pompous, haughty; (tacaño) stingy, tight.
es·ti·rar tr. to stretch; (extender) to extend ♦ e. la pata COLL. to die, kick the bucket —reflex. to stretch oneself.
es·ti·rón m. yank, tug ♦ dar un e. to shoot up.
es·tir·pe f. stock, lineage; LAW heirs.
es·ti·val adj. summer, estival.
es·to pron. this; (asunto) this business or matter ♦ por e. for this reason.
es·to·ca·da f. thrust, stab; (herida) stab wound.
es·to·fa f. TEX. brocade; FIG. class, quality.
es·to·fa·do, a I. adj. stewed; (acolchado) quilted II. m. stew; (acolchadura) quilting.
es·to·far tr. to stew.
es·toi·co, a adj. & m.f. stoic.
es·to·la f. stole.
es·tó·ma·go m. stomach.
es·to·pa f. (fibra) tow; (tela) burlap; MARIT. oakum ♦ e. de acero steel wool.
es·to·que·ar tr. to kill or wound with a sword.
es·tor·bar tr. to obstruct, block; (dificultar) to hinder, hamper.
es·tor·bo m. obstruction, obstacle; (dificultad) hindrance; (molestia) bother, annoyance.
es·tor·nu·dar intr. to sneeze.
es·tor·nu·do m. sneeze.
es·tos see este, a.
és·tos see éste, a.
es·toy see estar.
es·tra·do m. dais; (sala) drawing room.
es·tra·fa·la·rio, a COLL. I. adj. outlandish, bizarre; (desaliñado) slovenly II. m.f. eccentric.
es·tra·go m. destruction, devastation.
es·tra·gón m. tarragon.
es·tram·bó·ti·co, a adj. COLL. outlandish.
es·tran·gu·la·ción f. strangulation.
es·tran·gu·la·dor, ·ra I. adj. strangulating II. m.f. strangler —m. AUTO. choke.

es·tran·gu·lar tr. to strangle, strangulate; MECH. to choke.

ea·tra·ta·ge·ma f. stratagem.

es·tra·te·ga m.f. strategist.

es·tra·te·gia f. strategy.

es·tra·té·gi·co, a I. adj. strategic **II.** m.f. strategist.

es·tra·ti·fi·car §70 tr. & reflex. to stratify.

es·tra·to m. stratum; METEOROL. status.

es·tra·tos·fe·ra f. stratosphere.

es·tra·za f. rag ♦ **papel de e.** brown wrapping paper.

es·tre·cha·mien·to m. narrowing, tightening.

es·tre·char tr. *(reducir)* to narrow, *(apretar)* to tighten; *(sisar)* to take in; *(abrazar)* to hug; *(obligar)* to compel ♦ **e. la brecha** to close the gap • **e. la mano a** to shake hands with —reflex. to narrow; *(apretarse)* to tighten, become tight; *(ceñirse)* to squeeze together; *(reducir gastos)* to economize; *(amistarse)* to become close *or* intimate.

es·tre·chez f. narrowness; *(aprieto)* bind, jam; *(amistad)* closeness, intimacy; *(pobreza)* poverty, need; *(austeridad)* austerity.

es·tre·cho, a I. adj. narrow; *(apretado)* tight; *(tacaño)* stingy, mean; *(íntimo)* close, intimate; *(rígido)* rigid, severe; *(limitado)* narrow-minded **II.** m. strait, channel.

es·tre·lla f. star; *(asterisco)* asterisk ♦ **e. de mar** starfish.

es·tre·lla·do, a adj. star-shaped; *(con estrellas)* starry ♦ **huevos estrellados** fried eggs.

es·tre·llar tr. to cover with stars; COLL. *(romper)* to smash, shatter —reflex. to become starry; COLL. *(romperse)* to smash, crash.

es·tre·lla·to m. stardom.

es·tre·me·ce·dor, ra adj. frightening.

es·tre·me·cer §17 tr. to shake —reflex. to shake, tremble.

es·tre·me·ci·mien·to m. shake, shudder; *(de frío)* shiver, shivering.

es·tre·nar tr. to use *or* wear for the first time; *(representar)* to première, open —reflex. to première, debut.

es·tre·no m. opening, debut; *(representación)* première.

es·tre·nuo, a adj. strenuous.

ca·tre·ñi·do, a adj. constipated; FIG. stingy.

es·tre·ñi·mien·to m. constipation.

es·tre·ñir §59 tr. to constipate —reflex. to be *or* get constipated.

es·tré·pi·to m. uproar, din.

es·tre·pi·to·so, a adj. noisy, deafening.

es·trep·to·co·co m. streptococcus.

es·trep·to·mi·ci·na f. streptomycin.

es·tría f. ARCHIT. fluting, stria; *(ranura)* groove.

es·tria·do, a adj. striated, fluted.

es·triar §30 tr. ARCHIT. to striate, flute; *(hacer ranuras)* to groove —reflex. to be grooved.

es·tri·bar intr. to rest, lie on; *(fundarse)* to be based, rest.

es·tri·bi·llo m. POET. refrain; MUS. chorus.

es·tri·bo m. stirrup; *(de carruaje)* footboard; TECH. bracket, brace; GEOG. spur ♦ **perder los estribos** to lose one's head.

es·tri·bor m. starboard.

es·tric·ni·na f. strychnine.

es·tric·to, a adj. strict.

es·tri·den·cia f. stridence, shrillness.

es·tri·den·te adj. strident, shrill.

es·tri·ña, ño, ñera, ñó see **estreñir.**

es·tro·fa f. strophe, stanza.

es·tron·cio m. strontium.

es·tro·pa·jo m. dishcloth, rag.

es·tro·pe·ar tr. to damage, ruin; *(dañar)* to hurt, injure; *(maltratar)* to mistreat, mishandle.

es·tro·pi·cio m. COLL. uproar, clatter.

es·truc·tu·ra f. structure.

es·truc·tu·ra·ción f. construction.

es·truc·tu·ral adj. structural.

es·truc·tu·rar tr. to structure, construct.

es·truen·do m. clamor, uproar.

ce·truen·do·so, a adj. clamorous, noisy.

es·tru·jar tr. to squeeze, crush.

es·tru·jón m. squeezing, pressing.

es·tua·rio m. estuary.

es·tu·co m. stucco.

es·tu·che m. case, box; *(vaina)* sheath; *(conjunto)* set of instruments.

es·tu·dian·ta·do m. student body, pupils.

es·tu·dian·te m. student, pupil.

es·tu·dian·til adj. student.

es·tu·diar tr. & intr. to study.

es·tu·dio m. study; *(cuarto)* study, studio.

es·tu·dio·so, a adj. & m.f. studious (person).

es·tu·fa f. stove, heater; *(invernáculo)* hothouse, greenhouse; *(sauna)* steam room.

es·tu·pe·fac·ción f. stupefaction.

es·tu·pe·fa·cien·te I. adj. stupefying, astonishing; PHARM. narcotic, stupefacient **II.** m. narcotic, stupefacient.

es·tu·pe·fac·to, a adj. stupefied, astonished.

es·tu·pen·do, a adj. stupendous, tremendous.

es·tu·pi·dez f. stupidity, idiocy.

es·tú·pi·do, a I. adj. stupid, dumb **II.** m.f. idiot, dumbbell.

es·tu·por m. MED. stupor, torpor; FIG. stupefaction, astonishment.

es·tu·rión m. sturgeon.

es·tu·vie·ra, vo see **estar.**

es·vás·ti·ca f. swastika.

e·ta·pa f. phase, stage; MIL. field ration.

et·cé·te·ra adv. et cetera.

é·ter m. ether.

e·té·re·o, a adj. ethereal.

e·ter·ni·dad f. eternity.

e·ter·ni·zar §04 tr. to perpetuate; *(hacer durar)* to prolong indefinitely —reflex. to be everlasting *or* eternal; FIG. to drag on.

e·ter·no, a adj. eternal.

é·ti·co, a I. adj. ethical, moral **II.** m.f. moralist —f. ethics.

e·ti·lo m. ethyl.

e·ti·mo·lo·gía f. etymology.

e·ti·mo·ló·gi·co, a adj. etymological.

e·ti·mó·lo·go, a m.f. etymologist.

e·ti·que·ta f. etiquette, ceremony; *(rótulo)* tag, label ♦ **de e.** formal.

e·ti·que·tar tr. to label, pigeonhole.

ét·ni·co, a adj. ethnic.

et·no·ci·dio m. genocide.

et·nó·lo·go m.f. ethnologist.

eu·ca·lip·to m. eucalyptus.

eu·ca·ris·tía f. Eucharist.

eu·ca·rís·ti·co, a adj. Eucharistic.

eu·fe·mis·mo m. euphemism.

eu·fo·ria f. euphoria.

eu·fó·ri·co, a adj. euphoric, jubilant.

eu·nu·co m. eunuch.

eu·ro·pio m. europium.

eu·ta·na·sia f. euthanasia.

e·va·cua·ción f. evacuation.

e·va·cuar tr. to evacuate.

e·va·cua·ti·vo, a I. adj. evacuating; *(purgativo)* evacuant, purgative II. m. purgative.

e·va·cua·to·rio, a I. adj. evacuating; *(purgativo)* evacuant, purgative II. m. evacuation site; *(retrete)* public lavatory, rest room.

e·va·dir tr. to evade, avoid —reflex. to escape, sneak away.

e·va·luar §67 tr. to evaluate, assess.

e·va·nes·cen·te adj. evanescent, vanishing.

e·van·gé·li·co, a adj. evangelical.

e·van·ge·lio m. gospel.

e·van·ge·lis·ta m. evangelist.

e·van·ge·li·zar §04 tr. to evangelize.

e·va·po·ra·ción f. evaporation.

e·va·po·rar tr. & reflex. to evaporate.

e·va·po·ri·zar §04 tr. to vaporize, evaporate.

e·va·sión f. escape; *(evasiva)* evasion.

e·va·si·vo, a I. adj. evasive II. f. evasion.

e·va·sor, ·ra adj. evading, eluding.

e·ven·to m. chance event, contingency.

e·ven·tual adj. unexpected, incidental.

e·ven·tual·men·te adv. by chance, unexpectedly; *(posiblemente)* possibly, perhaps.

e·vic·ción f. eviction, dispossession.

e·vi·den·cia f. certainty, obviousness; AMER. proof, evidence.

e·vi·den·ciar tr. *(probar)* to prove, demonstrate; *(hacer patente)* to make evident or clear.

e·vi·den·te adj. evident, clear.

e·vi·tar tr. to avoid.

e·vo·ca·dor, ·ra adj. evocative.

e·vo·car §70 tr. to evoke; *(invocar)* to invoke.

e·vo·ca·ti·vo, a adj. evocative.

e·vo·lu·ción f. evolution.

e·vo·lu·cio·nar intr. to evolve.

e·vo·lu·ti·vo, a adj. evolutionary, evolutional.

ex·a·brup·to m. abrupt or sharp remark.

e·xa·cer·bar tr. to exacerbate, aggravate.

e·xac·ti·tud f. exactitude, exactness; *(puntualidad)* punctuality.

e·xac·to, a adj. exact, precise; *(puntual)* punctual.

e·xa·ge·ra·ción f. exaggeration.

e·xa·ge·ra·do, a adj. exaggerated.

e·xa·ge·rar tr. to exaggerate.

e·xá·go·no m. hexagon.

e·xal·ta·ción f. exaltation; *(aumento del espíritu)* exhilaration, over-excitement.

e·xal·ta·do, a I. adj. exalted; *(sobreexcitado)* over-excited, hotheaded II. m.f. hothead.

e·xal·tar tr. to exalt, glorify —reflex. to get worked up.

e·xa·men m. examination, test; *(interrogación)* interrogation.

e·xa·mi·na·dor, ·ra m.f. examiner.

e·xa·mi·nar tr. to examine —reflex. to take an exam.

e·xan·güe adj. exsanguine, bloodless; *(aniquilado)* weak, exhausted; *(muerto)* dead.

e·xá·ni·me adj. inanimate, lifeless; *(debilitado)* weak, faint.

e·xas·pe·ra·ción f. exasperation.

e·xas·pe·rar tr. to exasperate —reflex. to become exasperated.

ex·ca·va·ción f. excavation.

ex·ca·var tr. to excavate, dig.

ex·ce·den·te I. adj. excessive; *(sobrante)* excess, surplus II. m. excess, surplus.

ex·ce·der tr. to exceed, surpass —reflex. to exceed oneself; *(sobrepasarse)* to go too far.

ex·ce·len·cia f. excellence.

ex·ce·len·te adj. excellent.

ex·cel·so, a adj. sublime, lofty.

ex·cen·tri·ci·dad f. eccentricity.

ex·cén·tri·co, a adj. eccentric.

ex·cep·ción f. exception ♦ a or con e. de except for.

ex·cep·cio·nal adj. exceptional.

ex·cep·to prep. except, excepting.

ex·cep·tuar §67 tr. to exclude, exempt —reflex. to be excluded or exempted.

ex·ce·si·vo, a adj. excessive.

ex·ce·so m. excess; COM. surplus ♦ en e. to excess, too much.

ex·ci·sión f. excision.

ex·ci·ta·bi·li·dad f. excitability.

ex·ci·ta·ble adj. excitable.

ex·ci·ta·ción f. excitement; BIOL. excitation.

ex·ci·tan·te I. adj. stimulating II. m. stimulant.

ex·ci·tar tr. to excite —reflex. to become excited.

ex·cla·ma·ción f. exclamation; *(signo ortográfico)* exclamation point.

ex·cla·mar intr. to exclaim.

ex·cla·ma·ti·vo/to·rio, a adj. exclamatory.

ex·cluir §18 tr. to exclude; *(expulsar)* to throw out, expel.

ex·clu·sión f. exclusion.

ex·clu·si·ve adv. exclusively; *(no incluyendo)* exclusive of, not including.

ex·clu·si·vo, a I. adj. exclusive II. f. *(repulsa)* rejection; *(privilegio)* exclusive or sole right.

ex·clu·ya, yo, yera, yó see excluir.

ex·com·ba·tien·te adj. & m.f. veteran.

ex·co·mul·ga·do, a m.f. excommunicant.

ex·co·mul·gar tr. to excommunicate.

ex·co·mu·nión f. excommunication.

ex·co·riar tr. to excoriate, chafe.

ex·cre·ción f. excretion.

ex·cre·men·to m. excrement.

ex·cre·tar intr. to excrete.

ex·cul·par tr. to exculpate, exonerate.

ex·cur·sión f. excursion.

ex·cur·sio·nis·ta m.f. excursionist, sightseer.

ex·cu·sa f. excuse ♦ a e. secretly.

ex·cu·sa·do, a adj. exempt; *(reservado)* reserved, private; *(inútil)* unnecessary, superfluous II. m. toilet.

ex·cu·sar tr. to excuse; *(evitar)* to avoid, prevent; *(exentar)* to exempt —reflex. to excuse oneself ♦ e. de to refuse.

e·xe·cra·ción f. execration.

e·xe·crar tr. to execrate.

e·xé·ge·sis f. exegesis.

e·xe·ge·ta m.f. exegete.

e·xen·ción f. exemption.

e·xen·tar tr. to exempt, excuse —reflex. to exempt oneself.

e·xen·to, a I. see eximir and exentar II. adj. exempt, free; *(descubierto)* clear, unobstructed.

e·xe·quias f.pl. funeral rites, obsequies.

ex·ha·la·ción f. exhalation; *(vapor)* fumes, vapor; *(estrella)* shooting star; *(centella)* flash of lightning.

ex·ha·lar tr. to exhale; *(suspiros)* to breathe —reflex. *(respirar)* to breathe hard; *(correr)* to hurry, run.

ex·haus·ti·vo, a adj. exhaustive.

ex·haus·to, a adj. exhausted.

ex·hi·bi·ción f. exhibition, exhibit.

ex·hi·bi·cio·nis·ta m.f. exhibitionist.

ex·hi·bir tr. to exhibit, display —reflex. to show up, to show oneself.

ex·hor·ta·ción f. exhortation.
ex·hor·tar tr. to exhort.
ex·hu·mar tr. to exhume, disinter.
e·xi·gen·cia f. exigency, demand.
e·xi·gen·te adj. & m.f. demanding (person).
e·xi·gir §32 tr. to exact; *(requerir)* to demand, require.
e·xi·l(i)a·do, a I. adj. exiled, in exile II. m.f. exile.
e·xi·l(i)ar tr. to exile, banish —reflex. to be exiled *or* banished.
e·xi·lio m. exile, banishment.
e·xi·mio, a adj. *(distinguido)* distinguished, eminent; *(excelente)* select, choice.
e·xi·mir tr. to free, exempt —reflex. to excuse oneself.
e·xis·ten·cia f. existence ♦ pl. stock, goods.
e·xis·ten·cial adj. existential.
e·xis·ten·cia·lis·ta adj. & m.f. existentialist.
e·xis·ten·te adj. existent; COM. in stock.
e·xis·tir intr. to exist, be in existence.
é·xi·to m. success; *(resultado)* result, outcome ♦ **é. rotundo** huge success, hit • **tener é.** to be successful.
e·xi·to·so, a adj. AMER. successful.
é·xo·do m. exodus.
e·xo·ne·rar tr. to exonerate; *(despedir)* to dismiss ♦ **e. el vientre** to have a bowel movement.
e·xor·bi·tan·cia f. exorbitance, excess.
e·xor·bi·tan·te adj. exorbitant, excessive.
e·xor·cis·ta m. exorcist.
e·xor·ci·zar §04 tr. to exorcise.
e·xo·ti·ci·dad/quez f. exoticism.
e·xó·ti·co, a adj. exotic.
e·xo·tis·mo m. exoticism.
ex·pan·dir tr. & reflex. to expand, spread.
ex·pan·sión f. expansion; *(recreo)* relaxation, recreation; *(franqueza)* expansiveness.
ex·pan·sio·nis·ta adj. & m.f. expansionist.
ex·pan·si·vo, a adj. expandable, expansible; *(franco)* open, expansive.
ex·pa·tria·ción f. expatriation.
ex·pa·triar §30 tr. to expatriate, banish —reflex. to go into exile; *(emigrar)* to emigrate.
ex·pec·ta·ción f. expectation.
ex·pec·ta·ti·vo, a I. adj. expectant, hopeful II. f. expectation, anticipation.
ex·pec·to·ra·ción f. expectoration.
ex·pec·to·ran·te adj. & m. expectorant.
ex·pec·to·rar tr. & intr. to expectorate.
ex·pe·di·ción f. expedition; *(prontitud)* speed, dispatch; COM. shipping, shipment.
ex·pe·di·cio·na·rio, a I. adj. expeditionary II. m.f. member of an expedition; *(expedidor)* sender.
ex·pe·di·dor, ·ra m.f. sender, shipper —m. dispenser.
ex·pe·dien·te I. adj. expedient II. m. expedient; *(archivo)* file, dossier, record; LAW proceedings.
ex·pe·dir §48 tr. *(enviar)* to send, ship; *(despachar)* to expedite, dispatch; *(dictar)* to issue.
ex·pe·di·tar tr. S. AMER. to expedite, dispatch.
ex·pe·di·ti·vo, a adj. expeditious.
ex·pe·di·to, a adj. ready, free; *(una vía)* clear.
ex·pe·ler tr. to expel, eject.
ex·pen·de·dor, ·ra I. adj. spending II. m.f. dealer, retailer; THEAT. ticket agent.
ex·pen·der tr. to expend, spend; *(hacer circular)* to circulate; *(vender al por menor)* to retail, sell.
ex·pen·dio m. expense, outlay; AMER. *(tienda)*

store, shop; *(venta al por menor)* retailing.
ex·pen·sas f.pl. expenses, costs.
ex·pe·rien·cia f. experience; CHEM., PHYS. experiment.
ex·pe·ri·men·ta·ción f. experimentation.
ex·pe·ri·men·ta·do, a adj. experienced.
ex·pe·ri·men·tal adj. experimental.
ex·pe·ri·men·tar tr. to try out, test; *(sentir en sí)* to experience, undergo.
ex·pe·ri·men·to m. experiment, experimentation.
ex·per·to adj. & m. expert.
ex·pia·ción f. expiation, atonement.
ex·piar §30 tr. to atone for, expiate.
ex·pia·ti·vo, a adj. expiative, expiatory.
ex·pia·to·rio, a adj. expiatory.
ex·pi·ra·ción f. expiration.
ex·pi·rar intr. to expire.
ex·pla·na·da f. esplanade.
ex·pla·yar tr. to extend, spread out —reflex. *(dilatarse)* to expatiate, speak at length; *(divertirse)* to relax, unwind; *(confiarse)* to confide *(a, con* in).
ex·ple·ti·vo, a adj. expletive.
ex·pli·ca·ción f. explanation.
ex·pli·car §70 tr. to explain; *(exponer)* to expound; *(enseñar)* to teach —reflex. to explain oneself; *(comprender)* to understand.
ex·pli·ca·ti·vo, a adj. explanatory.
ex·plí·ci·to, a adj. explicit.
ex·plo·ra·ción f. exploration.
ex·plo·ra·dor, ·ra I. adj. exploring, exploratory II. m.f. explorer —m. boy scout.
ex·plo·rar tr. & intr. to explore.
ex·plo·sión f. explosion.
ex·plo·si·vo, a adj. & m.f. explosive.
ex·plo·ta·ción f. exploitation; *(operación)* running; *(cultivo)* cultivation.
ex·plo·tar tr. to exploit; *(operar)* to run, operate, *(una mina)* to work; *(cultivar)* to cultivate —intr. to go off, explode.
ex·po·nen·cial adj. & f. exponential.
ex·po·nen·te I. adj. explaining, expounding II. m.f. exponent —m. MATH. exponent; *(ejemplo)* example <un magnífico e. a magnificent example>; AMER. model, best <e. de calidad the best in quality>.
ex·po·ner §54 tr. to expose; *(explicar)* to propound, explain; *(exhibir)* to exhibit; *(abandonar)* to abandon —reflex. to expose oneself.
ex·por·ta·ción f. exportation, exporting; *(mercancías)* exports; *(artículo)* export (item).
ex·por·ta·dor, ·ra I. adj. exporting II. m.f. exporter.
ex·por·tar tr. & intr. to export.
ex·po·si·ción f. exhibition, show; *(explicación)* explanation; *(orientación)* exposure.
ex·pó·si·to, a I. adj. abandoned II. m.f. foundling.
ex·po·si·tor, ·ra I. adj. expository II. m.f. exponent; *(en una exposición)* exhibitor.
ex·pre·sa·do, a adj. above-mentioned.
ex·pre·sa·men·te adv. *(claramente)* clearly, explicitly; *(de propósito)* expressly, specifically.
ex·pre·sar tr. & reflex. to express (oneself).
ex·pre·sión f. expression.
ex·pre·si·vo, a adj. expressive.
ex·pre·so, a I. adj. express II. adj. express III. m. *(tren)* express train; *(correo)* express mail.
ex·pri·mi·dor m. squeezer, juicer.
ex·pri·mir tr. to squeeze.

ex·pro·piar tr. to expropriate.
ex·pues·to, a I. see **exponer** II. adj. dangerous, hazardous.
ex·pul·sar tr. to expel, drive out.
ex·pul·sión f. ejection, expulsion.
ex·pur·gar §47 tr. *(purificar)* to purge, purify; *(un libro)* to expurgate.
ex·pu·sie·ra, so see **exponer**.
ex·qui·si·tez f. exquisiteness.
ex·qui·si·to, a adj. exquisite.
ex·ta·siar·se §30 reflex. to become ecstatic.
éx·ta·sis f.inv. ecstasy, rapture.
ex·tá·ti·co, a adj. *(arrebatado)* ecstatic, enraptured; *(profundo)* deep, profound.
ex·tem·po·rá·nei·dad f. inopportuneness.
ex·tem·po·rá·ne·o, a adj. inopportune.
ex·ten·der §50 tr. to extend, enlarge; *(desdoblar)* to spread out, spread; *(despachar)* to draw up, issue —reflex. to stretch, extend; *(dilatarse)* to speak at length; *(propagarse)* to spread.
ex·ten·sa·men·te adv. extensively.
ex·ten·si·ble adj. extensible, extendible.
ex·ten·sión f. extension; *(amplitud)* expanse, stretch; *(dimensión)* extent, size.
ex·ten·si·vo, a adj. *(flexible)* extendible, extensible; *(grande)* extensive, wide; *(por extensión)* extended.
ex·ten·so, a I. see **extender** II. adj. extensive, ample, vast ♦ **por e.** at length, in (great) detail.
ex·te·nua·do, a adj. debilitated, weakened.
ex·te·nuar §67 tr. to debilitate, weaken.
ex·te·rior I. adj. exterior, outer; *(extranjero)* foreign II. m. exterior, outside; *(apariencia)* personal appearance.
ex·te·rio·ri·dad f. exteriority; *(apariencia)* outward appearance ♦ pl. pomp, show.
ex·te·rio·ri·zar §04 tr. to express, externalize.
ex·ter·mi·na·ción f. var. of **exterminio**.
ex·ter·mi·na·dor, ·ra m.f. exterminator.
ex·ter·mi·nar tr. to exterminate.
ex·ter·mi·nio m. extermination.
ex·ter·no, a I. adj. external, outward II. m.f. day school pupil.
ex·tien·da, de see **extender**.
ex·tin·ción f. extinction.
ex·tin·gui·ble adj. extinguishable.
ex·tin·guir §26 tr. to extinguish —reflex. *(apagarse)* to fade, go out; *(desaparecerse)* to become extinct, die out.
ex·tin·to, a I. see **extinguir** II. adj. extinguished; *(desaparecido)* extinct.
ex·tir·par tr. to extirpate.
ex·tor·sión f. extortion; *(molestia)* harm, trouble.
ex·tor·sio·na·dor, ·ra m.f. extortioner, extortionist.
ex·tor·sio·nar tr. to extort.
ex·tra I. adj. extra II. prep. ♦ **e. de** COLL. besides, in additon to III. m.f. CINEM., THEAT. extra —m. *(gaje)* extra, gratuity; *(gasto)* extra charge or expense; *(comida)* seconds.
ex·trac·ción f. extraction.
ex·trac·tar tr. to abstract, summarize.
ex·trac·to m. extract; *(compendio)* summary.
ex·trac·tor, ·ra m.f. extractor.
ex·tra·di·ción f. extradition.
ex·tra·er §72 tr. to extract.
ex·tra·li·mi·tar·se reflex. to overstep one's power or authority.
ex·tran·je·ro, a I. adj. alien, foreign II. m.f.

foreigner, alien —m. abroad.
ex·tra·ñar tr. *(desterrar)* to banish, exile; *(privar)* to estrange; *(sentir la novedad)* to find strange, not to be used to; AMER. to miss —reflex. to be surprised or astonished.
ex·tra·ño, a I. adj. *(extranjero)* foreign, alien; *(raro)* strange, odd; *(que no tiene que ver)* extraneous II. m.f. foreigner.
ex·tra·o·fi·cial adj. unofficial, nonofficial.
ex·tra·or·di·na·rio, a I. adj. extraordinary; *(extraño)* strange, odd II. m. *(correo urgente)* special delivery; *(periódico)* special edition; *(remuneración)* bonus.
ex·tra·po·lar tr. to extrapolate.
ex·tra·te·rre·no, a/rres·tre adj. & m.f. extraterrestrial.
ex·tra·va·gan·cia f. extravagance.
ex·tra·va·gan·te I. adj. extravagant II. m.f. eccentric.
ex·tra·ver·ti·do, a I. adj. extroverted, outgoing II. m.f. extrovert, outgoing person.
ex·tra·via·do, a adj. *(apartado)* out-of-the-way; *(perdido)* lost, missing.
ex·tra·viar §30 tr. *(desviar)* to lead astray, misguide; *(perder)* to misplace, lose —reflex. to get lost.
ex·tra·ví·o m. *(pérdida del camino)* going astray, losing one's way; *(pérdida)* misplacement, loss.
ex·tre·mar tr. to carry to an extreme —reflex. to take great pains, exert oneself to the utmost.
ex·tre·ma·un·ción f. extreme unction.
ex·tre·mi·dad f. *(punta)* end, tip; *(parte extrema)* extremity ♦ pl. extremities.
ex·tre·mis·ta adj. & m.f. extremist.
ex·tre·mo, a I. adj. *(último)* last, ultimate; *(intenso)* extreme, greatest, utmost; *(distante)* far, farthest II. m. extreme.
ex·tro·ver·sión f. extroversion, extraversion.
ex·tro·ver·ti·do, a I. adj. extroverted, extraverted II. m.f. extrovert, extravert.
e·xu·be·ran·cia f. exuberance, abundance.
e·xu·be·ran·te adj. exuberant, abundant.
e·xu·dar tr. & intr. to exude.
e·xul·tar intr. to exult, rejoice.
e·ya·cu·la·ción f. ejaculation.
e·ya·cu·lar tr. to ejaculate.

F

f, F f. seventh letter of the Spanish alphabet.
fá·bri·ca f. factory, works; *(fabricación)* manufacture; *(edificio)* building, construction; *(invención)* fabrication.
fa·bri·ca·ción f. manufacture; *(construcción)* construction ♦ **f. en serie** mass production.
fa·bri·can·te m.f. *(manufacturador)* manufacturer; *(dueño)* factory owner.
fa·bri·car §70 tr. to manufacture, make; *(construir)* to build, construct; *(inventar)* to fabricate, invent; *(labrar)* to work.
fa·bril adj. manufacturing.
fá·bu·la f. fable; *(invención)* lie, fiction; *(objeto de burla)* laughingstock; *(habladuría)* gossip, talk.
fa·bu·lo·sa·men·te adv. fabulously, extremely; *(fingidamente)* falsely.
fa·bu·lo·so, a adj. fabled, imaginary; *(extraordinario)* fabulous.
fac·ción f. faction, party; *(rasgo)* feature, facial feature; MIL. combat, battle ♦ **f. de guardia**

guard duty.
fa·ce·ta f. facet; FIG. facet, aspect.
fá·cil I. adj. easy; (*probable*) likely probable; (*dócil*) easygoing; (*liviana*) loose, of easy virtue II. adv. easily.
fa·ci·li·dad f. facility, ease; (*oportunidad*) opportunity, chance ♦ **tener f.** de to be apt to • **tener f. para** to have a gift *or* an aptitude for ♦ pl. terms.
fa·ci·li·tar tr. to facilitate, make easy; (*proporcionar*) to supply, furnish.
fa·ci·ne·ro·so, a adj. & m.f. criminal, delinquent; (*malévolo*) wicked (person).
fac·sí·mil/i·le m. facsimile.
fac·ti·ble adj. feasible, practicable.
fac·tor m. factor; COM. factor, agent.
fac·to·rí·a f. colonial trading post; AMER. plant, factory; ECUAD., PERU foundry, ironworks.
fac·tu·ra f. making; COM. invoice, bill.
fac·tu·ra·ción f. billing, invoicing.
fac·tu·rar tr. to invoice, bill.
fa·cul·tad f. faculty; (*virtud*) gift, advantage; (*derecho*) power, right; (*licencia*) license, permission; EDUC. school, college, faculty.
fa·cul·tar tr. to authorize, empower.
fa·cul·ta·ti·vo, a I. adj. facultative; (*profesional*) professional; MED. medical II. m. MED. physician, doctor.
fa·cha f. look, appearance ♦ **f. a f.** face to face • **estar hecho una f.** to look a mess *or* sight.
fa·cha·da f. (*dimensión*) frontage; (*portada*) title page ♦ **con f.** a facing • **hacer f. con** *or* **a** to be opposite, face.
fa·e·na f. manual labor; (*quehacer*) task, chore; (*trabajo mental*) mental task; COLL. (*trastada*) dirty trick ♦ **estar en plena f.** to be hard at work.
fai·sán m. pheasant.
fa·ja f. strip, belt; (*corsé*) girdle, corset; (*tira de papel*) wrapper; AMER. belt, waistband.
fa·ja·du·ra f. banding, belting; AMER. attack, beating.
fa·jar tr. to band, belt; (*vendar*) to bandage, swathe; (*envolver*) to wrap; AMER. to attack, assault —reflex. AMER. to set out to do something ♦ **f. con** *or* **a** to attack, fall on.
fa·ji·na f. AGR. shock, rick of sheaves; (*leña*) kindling; MIL. call to quarters, taps.
fa·jo m. bundle, sheaf; (*de billetes*) wad, roll; AMER. shot, swig.
fa·la·cia f. deception, deceitfulness; (*error*) fallacy.
fa·lan·ge f. phalanx; MIL. army, troops.
fa·lan·gis·ta adj. & m.f. Falangist.
fa·laz adj. deceitful, deceptive.
fal·da f. skirt; (*ala de sombrero*) brim, flap; (*de un monte*) foot; (*regazo*) lap ♦ pl. COLL. ladies, skirts • **aficionado a las f.** womanizer.
fal·de·ar tr. to skirt, go around.
fal·de·ro, a adj. skirt; lap <*perro f.* lap dog> ♦ **hombre f.** lady's man • **niño** *or* **niña f.** mama's boy *or* girl.
fal·dón m. tail; (*saya*) skirt; EQUIT. flap, skirt.
fa·li·ble adj. fallible.
fá·li·co, a adj. phallic.
fa·lo m. phallus, penis.
fal·se·ar tr. to falsify; (*contrahacer*) to fake, counterfeit; (*cerradura*) to pick; ARCHIT. to bevel —intr. (*flaquear*) to sag, become weak; (*torcerse*) to bend, warp.
fal·se·dad f. falseness; (*hipocresía*) hypocrisy;

(*mentira*) falsehood, lie.
fal·se·te m. (*corcho*) plug, bung; (*puerta*) small door; MUS. falsetto.
fal·si·fi·car §70 tr. to falsify; (*copiar*) to counterfeit, forge; CHEM. to adulterate.
fal·so, a I. adj. false; (*erróneo*) fallacious; (*engañoso*) deceitful, false; (*falsificado*) counterfeit, fake; (*inexacto*) inexact, inaccurate; (*fingido*) fake, phony II. m. reinforcement, patch ♦ **dar un paso en f.** to trip, stumble • **de** *or* **en f.** falsely.
fal·ta f. lack, shortage; (*ausencia*) absence; (*defecto*) defect, flaw; (*infracción*) misdemeanor; (*culpa*) fault; (*abuso*) breach; (*error*) error, mistake ♦ **a f. de** for lack of, for want of • **hacer f.** (*faltar*) to be lacking, need; (*ser necesario*) to be necessary; to miss <*me haces f.* I miss you> • **sin f.** without fail.
fal·tar intr. (*hacer falta*) to lack, need; (*carecer de*) to be lacking; (*estar ausente*) to be missing; (*no acudir a*) to be absent, miss; (*no responder*) to fail to function; (*morir*) to die; (*fallar*) to fail in; (*no cumplir*) to fail to keep, break; (*ofender*) to insult ♦ **f. mucho para** to be a long way off • **f. . . . para** to be • <*faltan diez minutos para las ocho* it is ten minutes to eight> • **f. poco** para not to be long before • **f. por** to remain to be.
fal·to, a adj. lacking, wanting; (*escaso*) short; (*mezquino*) poor, wretched.
fa·lla f. see **fallo.**
fa·llar tr. to fail, disappoint —intr. to fail; (*perder resistencia*) to give way ♦ **sin f.** without fail.
fa·lle·cer §17 intr. (*morir*) to die, expire; (*faltar*) to run out, end.
fa·lle·ci·mien·to m. death, demise.
fa·lli·do, a adj. unsuccessful; COM. bankrupt.
fa·llir intr. to run out, end.
fa·llo, a I. adj. void, lacking a suit (in cards) II. m. (*sentencia*) ruling, judgment; (*decisión*) decision; (*falta*) error, fault ♦ **tener fallos de memoria** to have lapses in one's memory —f. defect, fault; GEOG., MIN. fault; AMER. fault, failure.
fa·ma f. fame; (*reputación*) reputation ♦ **es f. que** it is rumored *or* reported that.
fa·mé·li·co, a adj. starving, famished.
fa·mi·lia f. family ♦ **venir de f.** to run in the family.
fa·mi·liar I. adj. (*relativo a la familia*) familial, family; (*llano*) casual; (*conocido*) familiar; (*corriente*) colloquial, familiar II. m. family *or* household member; (*amigo íntimo*) intimate friend.
fa·mi·lia·ri·zar §04 tr. & reflex. to familiarize (oneself).
fa·mo·so, a adj. famous; COLL. excellent.
fá·mu·la f. COLL. maid, servant.
fa·ná·ti·co, a I. adj. fanatic(al) II. m.f. fanatic; (*entusiasta*) fan.
fa·na·tis·mo m. fanaticism.
fa·na·ti·zar §04 tr. to fanaticize.
fan·dan·go m. fandango; COLL. row, uproar.
fan·fa·rre·ar intr. var. of **fanfarronear.**
fan·fa·rria f. COLL. bragging; MUS. fanfare.
fan·fa·rrón, o·na I. adj. COLL. bragging; (*presumido*) flashy, showy II. m.f. COLL. braggart.
fan·fa·rro·na·da f. bragging.
fan·fa·rro·ne·ar intr. to brag.
fan·fa·rro·ne·rí·a f. bragging.
fan·gal/gar m. quagmire, mudhole.

fan·go m. mud, mire.

fan·go·si·dad f. muddiness.

fan·go·so, a adj. muddy, miry.

fan·ta·se·ar intr. to daydream, dream.

fan·ta·sí·a f. fantasy ♦ **de f.** fancy.

fan·ta·sio·so, a adj. COLL. conceited, vain.

fan·tas·ma m. ghost, apparition; *(visión)* vision, illusion; *(persona seria)* stuffed shirt —f. scarecrow.

fan·tas·ma·gó·ri·co, a adj. phantasmagoric.

fan·tás·ti·co, a adj. fantastic.

fan·to·cha·da f. ridiculous action.

fan·to·che m. puppet, marionette; COLL. boastful nincompoop.

fa·rán·du·la f. theater, show business; *(compañía)* troupe.

fa·ran·du·le·ar intr. COLL. to boast, brag.

fa·ran·du·le·ro, a I. m.f. THEAT. wandering player; *(trapacero)* swindler II. adj. swindling.

fa·ra·ón m. Pharaoh, pharaoh.

far·do m. large bundle or parcel.

far·fu·llar COLL. tr. to jabber, gabble; FIG. *(chapucear)* to do hastily —intr. to jabber, gabble.

fa·ri·ná·ce·o, a adj. farinaceous.

fa·rin·ge f. pharynx.

fa·ri·se·o m. Pharisee, pharisee.

far·ma·céu·ti·co, a I. adj. pharmaceutical II. m.f. pharmacist, druggist.

far·ma·cia f. pharmacy.

far·ma·co·lo·gí·a f. pharmacology.

far·ma·co·pe·a f. pharmacopoeia.

fa·ro m. *(torre)* lighthouse; *(señal)* beacon; AUTO. headlight; FIG. guiding light.

fa·rol m. *(linterna)* lantern; *(luz pública)* street lamp; *(luz)* light; *(fachendoso)* show-off.

fa·ro·la f. *(farol)* streetlight, street lamp; *(faro)* beacon.

fa·ro·le·ar intr. COLL. to boast, brag.

fa·ro·le·rí·a f. COLL. boastfulness.

fa·ro·le·ro, a I. adj. boastful, bragging II. m.f. braggart; *(el que cuida de los faroles)* lamplighter.

fa·rra f. AMER. binge, spree.

fa·rre·ar intr. AMER. to go on a binge, carouse.

fa·rre·ro, a/rris·ta AMER. I. adj. carousing, reveling II. m.f. carouser, reveler.

far·sa f. farce; *(compañía)* company of actors; FIG. farce, sham.

far·san·te, a I. m.f. comic actor, farceur —m. fake, charlatan II. adj. COLL. fraud, fake.

far·se·ar intr. AMER. to fool around.

far·sis·ta m.f. writer of farces, farceur.

fas·cí·cu·lo m. fascicle.

fas·ci·na·ción f. fascination.

fas·ci·nan·te adj. fascinating.

fas·ci·nar tr. to fascinate; *(engañar)* to deceive.

fas·cis·ta adj. & m.f. fascist, Fascist.

fa·se f. phase; TECH. stage.

fas·ti·diar tr. *(molestar)* to annoy; *(cansar)* to tire, bore —reflex. to get annoyed.

fas·ti·dio m. *(molestia)* annoyance, bother; *(repugnancia)* repugnance; *(aburrimiento)* boredom.

fas·ti·dio·so, a adj. *(molesto)* annoying, bothersome; *(cargante)* tiresome, tedious.

fas·to, a I. adj. auspicious, happy II. m. pomp, splendor.

fas·tuo·si·dad f. pomp, splendor.

fas·t(u)o·so, a adj. lavish, splendid.

fa·tal adj. fatal; *(funesto)* mournful, unfortunate.

fa·ta·li·dad f. *(destino)* fate, destiny; *(desgracia)* misfortune, calamity.

fa·ta·lis·ta I. adj. fatalistic II. m.f. fatalist.

fa·tal·men·te adv. *(desdichadamente)* unfortunately, unhappily; *(inevitablemente)* fatefully, inevitably; *(muy mal)* wretchedly.

fa·tí·di·co, a adj. fatidic, prophetic.

fa·ti·ga f. fatigue; *(respiración)* shortness of breath ♦ **dar f.** to trouble, annoy • **f. visual** eyestrain ♦ pl. *(dificultades)* difficulties; *(penas)* sorrows.

fa·ti·gar §47 tr. to fatigue; *(molestar)* to annoy —reflex. to get tired.

fa·ti·go·so, a adj. fatigued, tired; *(que cansa)* fatiguing, tiring; COLL. *(cargante)* bothersome, annoying.

fa·tui·dad f. fatuity; *(tontería)* fatuous remark or act; *(presunción)* conceit, vanity.

fa·tuo, a I. adj. fatuous; *(presumido)* conceited, vain II. m.f. fool, fatuous person; *(presumido)* vain person.

fau·ces f.pl. fauces, gullet ♦ **las f. de la muerte** the jaws of death.

fau·na f. fauna, animal life.

faus·to, a I. adj. fortunate, lucky II. m. luxury, splendor.

fa·vor m. favor; *(amparo)* protection ♦ **a f. de** in favor of, in behalf of • **a f. de la noche** under cover of darkness ♦ **f.** complimentary, free • **en f. de** in favor of • **por f.** please.

fa·vo·ra·ble adj. favorable.

fa·vo·re·cer §17 tr. to favor, support; AMER. to protect —reflex. to help one another ♦ **f.** to avail oneself of.

fa·vo·ri·tis·mo m. favoritism, partiality.

fa·vo·ri·to, a adj. & m.f. favorite.

faz f. face; NUMIS. obverse ♦ **a la f. de** in front of.

fe f. faith; *(creencia)* credence; *(confianza)* trust, confidence; *(palabra de honor)* word of honor; *(documento)* certificate ♦ **a buena fe** undoubtedly, doubtless • **a** or **de fe** truly • **dar fe a** to confirm, certify • **fe de erratas** errata • **fe pública** legal authority • **hacer fe** to be sufficient proof.

fe·al·dad f. ugliness; *(torpeza)* turpitude, foulness.

fe·bre·ro m. February.

fe·cal adj. fecal.

fé·cu·la f. starch.

fe·cun·dar tr. to make fertile; *(engendrar)* to fertilize, fecundate.

fe·cun·di·dad f. fecundity; FIG. fruitfulness.

fe·cun·di·zar §04 tr. *(hacer fecundo)* to make fertile; *(engendrar)* to fertilize.

fe·cun·do, a adj. fecund; FIG. abundant, rich.

fe·cha f. date; *(día)* day; *(momento actual)* now, the present ♦ **con** or **de f. de** dated • **hasta la f.** so far, to date.

fe·cha·dor m. date stamp; AMER. *(matasellos)* postmark.

fe·char tr. to date.

fe·cho, a adj. done, executed (used in legal documents).

fe·cho·rí·a f. misdeed, misdemeanor.

fe·de·ral adj. & m.f. federal.

fe·de·ra·lis·ta adj. & m.f. federalist.

fe·de·rar tr. & reflex. to federate, confederate.

fe·ha·cien·te adj. authentic, reliable.

fe·li·ci·dad f. felicity, happiness; *(suerte feliz)*

good luck ♦ pl. *(enhorabuena)* congratulations; *(deseos amistosos)* best *or* warm wishes.

fe·li·ci·ta·ción f. congratulation(s).

fe·li·ci·tar tr. to congratulate; *(desear bien)* to wish well —reflex. to congratulate oneself; *(contentarse)* to be happy.

fe·li·grés, e·sa m.f. parishioner.

fe·li·gre·sí·a f. parish, parishioners.

fe·li·no, a adj. & m. feline.

fe·liz adj. happy; *(acertado)* felicitous, apt; *(oportuno)* lucky.

fe·lo·ní·a f. treachery, perfidy.

fel·pa f. TEX. plush; COLL. *(zurra)* beating, thrashing; *(represión)* telling off, scolding.

fel·pa·do, a adj. plush.

fel·par tr. to cover with plush.

fel·po m. mat, rug.

fel·po·so, a adj. plush, velvety.

fel·pu·do, a I. adj. plush, velvety II. m. mat, rug.

fe·me·ni·no, a adj. & m. feminine.

fe·mi·n(e)i·dad f. femininity.

fe·mi·nis·ta adj. & m.f. feminist.

fé·mur m. femur, thighbone.

fe·ne·cer §17 tr. to finish, settle —intr. *(morir)* to die, pass away; *(acabarse)* to come to an end, conclude.

té·ni·co, a adj. phenic, carbolic.

fé·nix f. *iny* phoenix.

fe·no·bar·bi·tal m. phenobarbital.

fe·nol m. phenol.

fe·no·me·nal adj. phenomenal.

fe·nó·me·no m. phenomenon; *(monstruo)* freak, monster.

fe·o, a I. adj. ugly ♦ **dejar f.** to slight, hurt — **más f. que Picio** as ugly as sin II. adv. AMER. nasty, awful III. m. COLL. *(desaire)* insult, slight; *(feúldud)* ugliness.

fé·re·tro m. *(ataúd)* coffin; *(andas)* bier.

fe·ria f. *(mercado)* market; *(exposición)* fair; *(día de fiesta)* holiday.

fe·ria·do, a adj. ♦ **día f.** holiday.

fe·rian·te I. adj. fair-going II. m.f. fairgoer; *(comerciante)* trader, exhibitor.

fe·ri·no, a adj. fierce, ferocious ♦ **tos f.** whooping cough.

fer·men·tar tr. & intr. to ferment.

fer·men·to m. ferment; BIOCHEM. enzyme; CUL. leaven(ing).

fer·mio m. fermium.

fe·ro·ci·dad f. ferocity.

fe·roz adj. *(cruel)* ferocious, fierce; COLL. *(tremendo)* tremendous, terrible.

fe·rrar §49 tr. to plate *or* trim with iron.

fé·rre·o, a adj. iron.

fe·rre·te·rí·a f. ironworks, foundry; *(comercio)* hardware store; *(quincalla)* hardware.

fe·rre·te·ro, a m.f. hardware dealer.

fe·rro·ca·rril m. railroad, railway.

fe·rro·via·rio, a adj. & m.f. railroad (employee).

fér·til adj. fertile ♦ **f. de** *or* **en** abundant *or* rich in.

fer·ti·li·dad f. fertility; *(abundancia)* abundance.

fer·ti·li·zan·te I. adj. fertilizing II. m. fertilizer.

fer·ti·li·zar §04 tr. to fertilize.

fer·vien·te adj. fervent, fervid.

fer·vor m. fervor.

fer·vo·ro·so, a adj. fervent, fervid.

fes·te·jar tr. to entertain; *(celebrar)* to celebrate; *(galantear)* to court, woo, MEX. to beat,

thrash.

fes·te·jo m. entertainment, feast; *(galanteo)* courting, wooing; AMER. celebration, party.

fes·tín m. banquet, feast.

fes·ti·val m. festival.

fes·ti·vi·dad f. festivity; *(día)* feast *or* holy day.

fes·ti·vo, a adj. festive; *(agudo)* witty, humorous.

fes·tón m. festoon.

fes·to·ne·ar/nar tr. to festoon.

fe·tal adj. fetal.

fe·ti·che m. fetish.

fe·ti·chis·ta adj. & m.f. fetishist(ic).

fe·ti·dez f. fetidness, stench.

fé·ti·do, a adj. fetid, foul-smelling.

fe·to m. fetus.

fe·ú·c(h)o, a adj. COLL. ugly, hideous.

feu·dal adj. feudal, feudalistic.

feu·do m. *(territorio)* feud, fee; *(tributo)* tribute, tithe; *(vasullaje)* vassalage, fealty.

fez m. fez.

fia·ble adj. reliable, dependable.

fia·do, a adj. trusting ♦ **al f.** on credit.

fia·dor, ·ra m.f. guarantor; LAW bailsman, bailer —m. *(presilla)* fastener; TECH. catch.

fiam·bre I. adj. CUL. *(servido)* cold; COLL. *(sin novedad)* old, stale ♦ **estar hecho f.** COLL. to kick the bucket, drop dead II. m. cold cut; AMER., COLL. boring party.

fiam·bre·rí·a f. S. AMER. delicatessen.

fian·za f. guaranty; *(depósito)* security, deposit; *(fiador)* guarantor.

fiar §30 tr. to guaranty; *(vender)* to sell on credit; *(confiar)* to entrust —intr. & reflex. to trust *(de, a* in).

fias·co m. fiasco, failure.

fi·bra f. fiber; *(de madera)* grain; *(vigor)* vigor, energy; MIN. vein; TEX. staple.

fi·bro·ce·men·to m. asbestos cement.

fi·bro·ma m. fibroma.

fi·bro·so, a adj. fibrous.

fic·ción f. fiction.

fic·ti·cio, a adj. fictitious.

fi·cha f. *(en los juegos)* counter, chip; *(dominó)* domino; *(disco de metal)* token; *(tarjeta)* index card —m. AMER. rogue, rascal.

fi·char tr. to keep on an index card; *(en bares, restaurantes)* to keep a tab; *(en fábricas)* to punch in *or* out; *(en dominó)* to play; COLL. *(cuidarse de)* to keep tabs on.

fi·che·ro m. file (cabinet).

fi·de·dig·no, a adj. trustworthy, reliable.

fi·dei·co·mi·sa·rio, a adj. & m.f. fiduciary.

fi·de·li·dad f. fidelity; *(exactitud)* exactness, accuracy.

fi·de·o m. noodle; COLL. *(persona delgada)* skinny person, rail.

fi·du·cia·rio, a adj. & m.f. fiduciary.

fie·bre f. fever ♦ **tener f.** to run a fever.

fiel I. adj. faithful, loyal; *(exacto)* exact, accurate; *(honrado)* honest, trustworthy; *(religioso)* faithful II. m. *(oficial)* public inspector; *(aguja)* needle, pointer; *(clavillo)* pin (of scissors).

fiel·tro m. felt; *(sombrero)* felt hat.

fie·re·za f. *(crueldad)* fierceness, ferocity; *(deformidad)* ugliness, deformity.

fie·ro, a I. adj. fierce, ferocious; *(grande)* enormous, huge II. m. bluff, threat ♦ **echar fie·ros** to bluster, make threats —f. *(bestia)* wild animal *or* beast; *(persona irritada)* hothead, ornery person; *(persona cruel)* beast, brute ♦ **ser una f. para** to be a fiend for.

fie·rra, rro see **ferrar.**

fie·rro AMER. m. brand, mark ♦ pl. tools.

fies·ta f. party, celebration; *(feriado)* holiday; RELIG. feast, holy day ♦ **aguar la f.** COLL. to spoil the fun ─ **hacer f.** to take a holiday ▪ **no estar para fiestas** to be in no mood for joking ▪ **se acabó la f.** COLL. the party's over.

fi·gu·ra f. figure; *(cara)* face, countenance; *(actor)* character; *(naipe)* face card; *(mudanza)* figure, step; MUS. note.

fi·gu·ra·ble adj. imaginable, conceivable.

fi·gu·ra·ción f. figuration; *(idea)* idea, invention.

fi·gu·ra·do, a adj. figurative.

fi·gu·ran·te, a m.f. THEAT. extra, walk-on; FIG. supernumerary.

fi·gu·rar tr. to represent, depict; *(fingir)* to feign, simulate ─intr. to figure, take part ─reflex. to imagine, figure ♦ **¡figúrate!** just imagine!

fi·gu·ra·ti·vo, a adj. figurative.

fi·gu·rín m. fashion plate ♦ pl. fashion magazines.

fi·ja f. see **fijo, a.**

fi·ja·ción f. fixing, fixation.

fi·ja·dor, ra I. adj. fixing, fixative II. m. CONST. pointer; *(para el pelo)* hair spray; PHOTOG. fixative.

fi·ja·men·te adv. firmly; *(atentamente)* fixedly, steadfastly.

fi·jar tr. to fix, fasten; *(establecer)* to establish ♦ **f. los ojos** *(mirar)* to stare; COLL. *(morir)* to die ─reflex. to settle, become fixed; *(atender)* to pay attention ♦ **¡fíjate!** just imagine!

fi·je·za f. firmness, steadfastness ♦ **mirar con f.** to stare at, look at fixedly.

fi·jo, a I. adj. fixed; *(permanente)* permanent; *(estable)* stable, steady; *(de colores)* fast, indelible ♦ **de f.** certainly, surely II. m. fixed salary ─f. *(bisagra)* large hinge; CONST. trowel; AMER. *(cosa segura)* sure thing.

fi·la f. *(hilera)* file; *(cola)* line, queue; *(línea)* row, tier; COLL. dislike, aversion; SL. *(rostro)* face; MIL. rank ♦ **alistarse en filas** to sign up, enlist ▪ **en filas** on active duty *or* service.

fi·la·men·to m. filament.

fi·lan·tro·pí·a f. philanthropy.

fi·lán·tro·po, a m.f. philanthropist.

fi·lar·mo·ní·a f. love of music.

fi·lar·mó·ni·co, a I. adj. & m.f. philharmonic.

fi·la·te·lis·ta m.f. philatelist, stamp collector.

fi·le·te m. CUL. fillet; TECH. thread.

fi·le·te·ar tr. CUL. to fillet; TECH. to thread.

fi·lia·ción f. filiation; *(señas personales)* description.

fi·lial I. adj. filial; COM. subsidiary, branch II. f. COM. branch (office); *(subdivisión)* subsidiary.

fi·li·bus·te·ro m. filibuster.

fi·li·gra·na f. filigree; PRINT. watermark.

fi·li·ll í m. [pl. **·lles.**] COLL. fineness, delicacy.

fi·lí·pi·ca f. philippic, invective.

fi·lis·te·o, a adj. & m.f. Philistine ─m. giant, big man.

film *or* **fil·me** m. film, movie.

fil·mar tr. to film, shoot.

fíl·mi·co, a adj. film, movie.

fi·lo m. (cutting) edge; C. AMER., MEX. hunger ♦ **al f. de la medianoche** at the stroke of midnight ▪ **dar f.** *or* **un f.** *(afilar)* to sharpen; *(inci-*

tar) to incite, excite ▪ **por f.** exactly.

fi·lo·lo·gí·a f. philology.

fi·ló·lo·go, a m.f. philologist, philologer.

fi·lón m. MIN. vein, lode; FIG. gold mine.

fi·lo·so, a adj. AMER. sharp, sharp-edged.

fi·lo·so·fal adj. ♦ **piedra f.** philosopher's stone.

fi·lo·so·far intr. to philosophize.

fi·lo·so·fí·a f. philosophy.

fi·ló·so·fo, a I. adj. philosophic(al) II. m.f. philosopher.

fil·tra·ción f. filtration.

fil·tran·te adj. filtering.

fil·trar tr. & intr. to filter ─reflex. *(pasarse)* to filter, pass through; *(disminuirse)* to disappear, dwindle.

fil·tro m. filter; *(bebedizo)* love potion, philter.

fin m. end; *(meta)* aim, end ♦ **a. f. de** in order to ▪ **a f. de cuentas** in the final analysis ▪ **a f. de que** so that ▪ **a fines de** at the end of ▪ **al f.** at last, finally ▪ **al f. y al cabo** after all, when all is said and done ▪ **dar f. a** to finish off ▪ **en f.** *(finalmente)* finally; *(en resumen)* in brief, in short ▪ **f. de semana** weekend ▪ **poner f. a** to finish, put an end to ▪ **por f.** finally, at last ▪ **sin f.** endless ▪ **un sin f.** no end.

fi·na·do, a m.f. deceased, dead person.

fi·nal I. adj. final, last II. m. *(fin)* end, ending; MUS. finale ─f. SPORT. final ♦ **al f.** in *or* at the end.

fi·na·li·dad f. purpose, objective.

fi·na·lis·ta m.f. finalist.

fi·na·li·za·ción f. conclusion, finish.

fi·na·li·zar §04 tr. to finish, conclude ─intr. to (come to an) end.

fi·nan·cia·ción f./**mien·to** m. financing.

fi·nan·ciar tr. to finance.

fi·nan·cie·ro, a I. adj. financial II. m.f. financier.

fi·nan·zas f.pl. finance(s).

fin·ca f. property, real estate; AMER. farm.

fin·car §70 tr. & intr. to acquire property *or* real estate; *(establecerse)* to settle, get established; AMER. to rest, lie ─reflex. to acquire property.

fi·ne·za f. fineness; *(cortesía)* courtesy, politeness; *(amabilidad)* kindness, affection; *(regalo)* gift, present.

fin·gi·do, a I. adj. false, feigned II. m.f. feigner, dissembler.

fin·gi·mien·to m. feigning, pretense.

fin·gir §32 tr. to pretend, feign.

fi·ni·qui·tar tr. to close, settle; *(concluir)* to conclude, finish; *(matar)* to bump off, rub out.

fi·ni·to, a adj. finite.

fi·no, a adj. fine; *(precioso)* precious; *(puro)* pure; *(cortés)* refined, elegant; *(delicado)* delicate; *(astuto)* astute, shrewd.

fi·nu·ra f. fineness; *(urbanidad)* refinement, politeness; *(sutileza)* subtlety, delicacy.

fiord *or* **fior·do** m. fjord, fiord.

fir·ma f. signature; *(acción)* signing; COM. firm, company ♦ **f. en blanco** carte blanche.

fir·ma·men·to m. firmament, heavens.

fir·man·te I. adj. signatory II. m.f. signer.

fir·mar tr. & reflex. to sign.

fir·me I. adj. firm; *(constante)* steadfast, staunch ♦ **de f.** hard ▪ **en f.** final, definitive ▪ **mantenerse** *or* **ponerse f.** to stand firm II. m. foundation, bed III. adv. firmly, steadily.

fir·me·za f. firmness.

fi·ru·le·tes m.pl. AMER. ornaments.

fis·cal I. adj. fiscal II. m. *(tesorero)* treasurer;

(abogado) district attorney, public prosecutor (G.B.); *(entremetido)* busybody, snooper.

fis·ca·li·zar §04 tr. *(controlar)* to supervise, oversee; *(investigar)* to investigate, inspect; *(curiosear)* to pry into, snoop.

fis·co m. public treasury, exchequer (G.B.).

fis·gar §47 tr. to spear, harpoon; *(husmear)* to pry into, snoop on —intr. & reflex. to make fun of.

fis·gón, o·na COLL. m.f. *(curioso)* snooper; *(burlador)* tease, mocker.

fis·go·ne·ar tr. COLL. to snoop, pry.

fí·si·co, a I. adj. physical II. m.f. *(persona)* physicist —m. physique, appearance —f. physics.

fi·sio·lo·gí·a f. physiology.

fi·sió·lo·go, a m.f. physiologist.

fi·sión f. fission.

fi·sio·te·ra·pia f. physiotherapy.

fi·s(i)o·no·mí·a f. physiognomy.

fís·tu·la f. fistula.

fi·su·ra f. fissure.

fla(c)·ci·dez f. flaccidity, flabbiness.

flá(c)·ci·do, a adj. flaccid, flabby.

fla·co, a I. adj. thin, lean; *(sin fuerza)* weak, feeble II. m. FIG. weak spot, weakness.

fla·ge·la·ción f. flagellation.

fla·ge·la·do, a adj. flagellate.

fla·ge·lar tr. to flagellate.

fla·ge·lo m. whip, scourge.

fla·gran·te adj. flagrant ♦ **en f. (delito)** in the act, red-handed.

fla·man·te adj. brilliant, bright; *(nuevo)* brand-new, like new.

fla·me·ar intr. *(llamear)* to blaze, flame; *(ondear)* to flap, flutter.

fla·men·co, a I. adj. flamenco; *(achulado)* cocky; C. AMER., MEX. skinny II. m. *(cuchillo)* dagger, sheath knife; ORNITH. flamingo.

flan m. flan, caramel custard.

flan·co m. side, flank; MIL. flank.

flan·que·ar tr. to flank.

fla·que·ar intr. to weaken.

fla·que·za f. thinness, leanness; *(debilidad)* weakness; *(fragilidad)* frailty.

fla·to m. flatus, gas; AMER. melancholy.

fla·tu·len·cia f. flatulence.

flau·ta f. flute ♦ **entre pitos y flautas** one thing or another ♦ **¡la gran f.!** AMER., COLL. my God! —m. flautist, flutist.

flau·tín m. piccolo.

flau·tis·ta m.f. flautist, flutist.

fle·bi·tis f. phlebitis.

fle·bo·to·mí·a f. phlebotomy, bloodletting.

fle·co m. *(adorno)* fringe; *(borde desgastado)* frayed edge; *(flequillo)* bangs.

fle·cha f. arrow.

fle·char tr. *(el arco)* to draw; *(asaetear)* to shoot or kill with an arrow; *(enamorar)* to infatuate, make a hit with.

fle·cha·zo m. *(disparo)* arrow shot or wound; COLL. *(amor)* love at first sight.

fle·je m. iron band or strip.

fle·ma f. phlegm.

fle·má·ti·co, a adj. phlegmatic(al).

fle·qui·llo m. bangs.

fle·tar tr. *(alquilar)* to charter; *(embarcar)* to load; AMER. to hire, rent.

fle·te m. *(alquiler)* charter fee; *(carga)* freight, cargo; AMER. freightage; *(precio de transporte)* freightage; AMER. *(caballo)* spirited horse.

fle·xi·bi·li·dad f. flexibility.

fle·xi·ble I. adj. flexible II. m. electric cord.

fle·xión f. flexion; GRAM. inflection.

fle·xor, ·ra adj. & m. flexor.

flir·te·ar intr. to flirt.

flir·te·o m. flirtation, flirting.

flo·je·ar intr. *(obrar con flojedad)* to slacken, idle; *(flaquear)* to weaken.

flo·je·dad f. *(flaqueza)* weakness, debility; *(pereza)* laziness, carelessness.

flo·je·ra f. laziness, carelessness.

flo·jo, a I. adj. *(suelto)* loose, slack; *(fláccido)* limp, flabby; *(débil)* weak; *(holgazán)* lazy, shiftless II. m.f. idler, loafer.

flor f. flower; blossom, bloom <en f. in bloom>; *(frescura)* bloom, prime; *(piropo)* compliment; *(de la piel)* grain ♦ **a f. de** on the surface of, level with • **f. de lis** jacobean lily; HER. fleur-de-lis • **f. y nata** the cream of the crop.

flo·ra f. flora.

flo·re·ar tr. to flower, decorate with flowers; *(cerner)* to sift —intr. to brandish a sword; COLL. *(echar flores)* to pay compliments; *(escoger lo mejor)* to pick the best.

flo·re·cer §17 intr. to flower, bloom; *(prosperar)* to thrive, flourish —reflex. to become moldy.

flo·re·ci·do, a adj. moldy.

flo·re·cien·te adj. flowering, blooming; *(próspero)* thriving, prosperous.

flo·re·ci·mien·to m. flowering.

flo·re·o m. chatter, small talk; *(dicho frívolo)* quip, jest; *(en esgrima)* flourish; MUS. arpeggio.

flo·re·rí·a f. flower or florist's shop.

flo·re·ro, a I. adj. joking, jesting II. m.f. florist —m. *(florero)* vase.

flo·res·cen·cia f. CHEM. efflorescence; BOT. florescence.

flo·res·ta f. *(bosque)* wood, forest; *(antología)* anthology.

flo·re·te I. adj. superfine II. m. foil.

flo·ri·cul·tor, ·ra m.f. floriculturist.

flo·ri·cul·tu·ra f. floriculture.

flo·ri·do, a adj. flowery; *(escogido)* choice, select.

flo·ris·ta m.f. florist.

flo·ta f. *(buques)* fleet; *(aviones)* squadron.

flo·ta·ción f. flotation, floating.

flo·ta·dor, ·ra I. adj. floating, buoyant II. m. float; MARIT. outrigger.

flo·tan·te adj. floating, buoyant.

flo·tar intr. to float.

flo·te m. ♦ **a f.** afloat.

flo·ti·lla f. flotilla.

fluc·tua·ción f. fluctuation.

fluc·tuan·te adj. fluctuating.

fluc·tuar §67 intr. to fluctuate; *(ondear)* to bob, undulate; *(estar en peligro)* to be in danger, be at risk; *(dudar)* to vacillate, waver.

fluen·cia f. *(acción)* stream, flow; *(fuente)* source, spring.

flui·dez f. fluidity.

flui·do, a I. adj. fluid; *(inseguro)* in flux II. m. fluid; ELEC. current.

fluir §18 intr. to flow; *(brotar)* to gush, stream.

flu·jo m. flow, flux; FIG. flood, stream ♦ **f. de risa** fit of laughter • **f. de sangre** hemorrhage • **f. de vientre** diarrhea • **f. y reflujo** ebb and flow.

flúor m. fluorine.

fluo·res·cen·te adj. fluorescent.

fluo·ri·za·ción f. fluoridation.

fluo·ros·co·pio m. fluoroscope.

fluo·ru·ro m. fluoride.

flu·vial adj. fluvial, river.

flux m.inv. flush ♦ **estar a f. de todo** AMER. to have nothing ● **hacer f.** AMER. to squander everything.

flu·ya, ye, yera, yó see **fluir.**

flu·yen·te adj. flowing.

fo·bia f. phobia.

fo·ca f. seal.

fo·cal adj. focal.

fo·co m. focus; *(fuente)* source; *(reflector)* spotlight.

fo·fo, a adj. soft, spongy.

fo·ga·ta f. bonfire.

fo·gón m. *(cocina)* stove, range; *(de caldera)* firebox; AMER. bonfire.

fo·go·na·zo m. powder flash.

fo·go·ne·ro m. stoker, fireman.

fo·go·si·dad f. fire, spirit.

fo·go·so, a adj. fiery, spirited.

fo·ja f. leaf, sheet (of paper).

fo·lia·ción f. foliation.

fo·liar I. tr. PRINT. to foliate, number II. adj. BOT. foliar.

fo·lí·cu·lo m. follicle.

fo·lio m. page, leaf; PRINT. running head *or* title ♦ **de a f.** COLL. very big, huge.

folk·lo·re m. folklore.

folk·ló·ri·co, a adj. folk(loric); *(pintoresco)* picturesque, quaint.

fo·lla·je m. foliage; *(adorno)* tasteless decoration; *(palabrería)* verbiage.

fo·lle·tín m. serial.

fo·lle·ti·nes·co, a adj. serial; *(melodramático)* melodramatic.

fo·lle·to m. pamphlet, brochure.

fo·men·tar tr. *(calentar)* to warm, incubate; *(instigar)* to foment, stir up; *(promover)* to promote, foster.

fo·men·to m. *(calor)* warmth; *(pábulo)* fuel; *(auxilio)* promotion, development.

fon·da f. *(posada)* inn; *(restaurante)* restaurant; AMER. tavern, bar; CHILE refreshment stand.

fon·da·ble adj. fit for anchoring.

fon·de·a·de·ro m. anchorage.

fon·de·a·do, a adj. AMER. rich, wealthy.

fon·de·ar tr. to sound, fathom; *(examinar)* investigate, probe —intr. to anchor, drop anchor —reflex. AMER. to get rich.

fon·di·llo m. rear (end), butt ♦ **pl.** seat of the pants.

fon·do m. *(base)* bottom; *(hondura)* depth, bed; *(parte más lejos)* rear, back; *(campo)* ground, background; *(colección)* collection; *(residuo)* residue; *(indole)* character, nature; *(lo principal)* essence, bottom; *(reserva)* store, reservoir ♦ **a f.** completely, thoroughly ● **bajos fondos** scum, dregs ● **dar f.** to drop anchor ● **de f.** main, leading ● **echar a f.** to sink ● **en f.** abreast ● **irse a f.** to sink, founder ● **sin f.** bottomless ♦ **pl.** funds, capital ● **estar con f.** to have money ● **f. disponibles** ready cash.

fo·ne·ma m. phoneme.

fo·né·ti·co, a I. adj. phonetic II. f. phonetics.

fo·ne·tis·ta m.f. phonetician, phoneticist.

fó·ni·co, a adj. phonic.

fo·no·grá·fi·co, a adj. phonographic.

fo·nó·gra·fo m. phonograph, record player.

fo·ra·ji·do, a adj. & m.f. fugitive, outlaw.

fo·rá·ne·o, a adj. foreign, alien.

fo·ras·te·ro, a I. adj. foreign, alien II. m.f. stranger, outsider.

for·ce·jar/je·ar intr. to struggle, resist.

for·ce·je·o/jo m. struggle, struggling.

fór·ceps m.inv. forceps.

fo·ren·se adj. forensic.

fo·res·ta·ción f. (re)forestation.

fo·res·tal adj. forest(al).

for·ja f. *(fragua)* forge; *(ferrería)* ironworks, foundry; *(argamasa)* mortar.

for·ja·du·ra f./**mien·to** m. forging.

for·jar tr. to forge, hammer; *(fabricar)* to make, form; *(inventar)* to invent, make up —reflex. to forge; AMER. to make a bundle.

for·ma f. form; *(dimensiones)* shape; *(silueta)* figure, outline; *(molde)* mold, pattern; *(formato)* format; *(documento)* form, questionnaire; *(manera)* way, method ♦ **de f.** so that, in such a way that ● **en debida f.** in due form, duly ● **formas sociales** manners, social conventions ● **guardar las formas** to keep up appearances ● **hacer f.** to line up.

for·ma·ción f. formation; *(educación)* upbringing, training.

for·ma·do, a adj. formed, shaped.

for·mal adj. formal.

for·mal·de·hí·do m. formaldehyde.

for·ma·li·dad f. formality.

for·ma·lis·mo m. formalism.

for·ma·li·zar §04 tr. to formalize —reflex. to take offense.

for·mar tr. to form; *(moldear)* to shape; *(criar)* to bring up, rear —intr. MIL. to fall in —reflex. to take form; *(desarrollarse)* to develop.

for·ma·ti·vo, a adj. formative.

for·ma·to m. format; *(tamaño)* size.

for·mi·da·ble adj. formidable.

for·món m. firmer chisel.

fór·mu·la f. formula; MED. prescription; CUL. recipe; *(expresión)* formality ♦ **por f.** as a matter of form.

for·mu·lar I. tr. to formulate II. adj. formulaic.

for·mu·la·rio I. m. formulary II. adj. formulistic.

for·ni·ca·ción f. fornication.

for·ni·car §70 intr. to fornicate.

for·ni·do, a adj. robust, strong.

fo·ro m. forum; LAW court, tribunal; *(profesión)* bar, legal profession.

fo·rra·je m. forage, fodder; *(fárrago)* hodgepodge, mess.

fo·rra·je·ar tr. & intr. to forage.

fo·rrar tr. *(coser)* to line; *(cubrir)* to cover —reflex. AMER., COLL. *(enriquecerse)* to get rich; *(atiborrarse)* to stuff oneself.

fo·rro m. lining; *(cubierta)* cover, covering; MARIT. sheathing; TECH. liner, lining.

for·ta·le·ce·dor, ·ra adj. fortifying.

for·ta·le·cer §17 tr. to fortify.

for·ta·le·ci·mien·to m. *(acción)* fortifying, strengthening; *(defensas)* fortifications, defenses.

for·ta·le·za f. *(vigor)* strength, vigor; *(virtud)* fortitude; *(fortín)* fortress, stronghold.

for·ti·fi·ca·ción f. fortification.

for·ti·fi·can·te I. adj. fortifying II. m. tonic.

for·ti·fi·car §70 tr. to fortify.

for·tín m. *(fuerte)* small, fort; *(refugio)* bunker.

for·tui·to, a adj. fortuitous, chance.

for·tu·na f. fortune; *(borrasca)* storm, tempest

♦ por f. fortunately **• probar f.** to try one's luck.

fo·rún·cu·lo m. boil, furuncle.

for·za·da·men·te adv. by force, forcibly.

for·za·do, a I. adj. forced **II.** m. convict.

for·zar §37 tr. to force; *(capturar)* to take by force; *(violar)* to rape; *(obligar)* to force, compel.

for·zo·sa·men·te adv. by force, forcibly; *(ineludiblemente)* unavoidably, inevitably.

for·zo·so, a adj. unavoidable, inevitable.

for·zu·do, a adj. strong, robust.

fo·sa f. *(sepultura)* grave, tomb; ANAT. fossa **♦ f. séptica** septic tank **• fosas nasales** nostrils.

fos·fa·to m. phosphate.

fos·fo·res·cen·cia f. phosphorescence.

fos·fo·res·cen·te adj. phosphorescent.

fós·fo·ro m. phosphorus; *(cerilla)* match.

fó·sil I. m. fossil **II.** adj. fossil, fossilized; COLL. *(antiguo)* old, outdated.

fo·si·li·za·ción f. fossilization.

fo·si·li·zar·se §04 reflex. to fossilize.

fo·so m. pit, ditch; THEAT. pit; MIL. moat, trench.

fo·to f. photo, picture **♦ sacar fotos** to take *or* snap pictures.

fo·to·com·po·si·ción f. photocomposition, phototypesetting.

fo·to·co·nia f. photocopy

fo·to·co·piar tr. to photocopy.

fo·to·gé·ni·co, a adj. photogenic.

fo·to·gra·ba·do m. photoengraving.

fo·to·gra·bar tr. to photoengrave.

fo·to·gra·fi·a f. photography; *(retrato)* photograph, picture; *(taller)* photography studio.

fo·to·gra·fiar §30 tr. to photograph.

fo·to·grá·fi·co, a adj. photographic.

fo·tó·gra·fo, a m.f. photographer.

fo·to·me·trí·a f. photometry.

fo·tó·me·tro m. photometer.

fo·tón m. photon.

fo·to·sen·si·ble adj. photosensitive.

fo·to·sín·te·sis f. photosynthesis.

fo·to·tro·pis·mo m. phototropism.

frac m. [pl. s *or* -ques] tails, formal coat.

fra·ca·sa·do, a I. adj. failed, unsuccessful **II.** m.f. failure, unsuccessful person.

fra·ca·sar intr. to fail.

fra·ca·so m. failure.

frac·ción f. fraction.

frac·cio·na·mien·to m. *(división)* division, breaking (into parts); MATH. fractionization; CHEM. fractionation.

frac·cio·nar tr. to divide, break (into parts); MATH. to fractionize; CHEM. to fractionate.

frac·tu·ra f. fracture, break.

frac·tu·rar tr. to fracture, break.

fra·gan·cia f. fragrance, perfume; *(fama)* good reputation.

fra·gan·te adj. fragrant, perfumed; *(flagrante)* flagrant.

fra·ga·ta f. MARIT. frigate; ORNITH. frigate bird.

frá·gil adj. fragile; *(fugaz)* perishable, fleeting.

frag·men·tar tr. to fragment.

frag·men·ta·rio, a adj. fragmentary.

frag·men·to m. fragment; *(trozo)* passage, excerpt.

fra·gor m. din, uproar.

fra·go·ro·so, a adj. roaring, thunderous.

fra·go·so, a adj. rough, rugged; *(ruidoso)* thunderous.

fra·gua f. forge, smithy.

fra·gua·do m. setting, hardening.

fra·guar §10 tr. *(hierro)* to forge; *(inventar)* to plan, plot —intr. to set, harden.

frai·le m. friar, monk.

fram·bue·sa f. raspberry.

fram·bue·so m. raspberry bush.

fran·ca·che·la f. COLL. *(comilona)* feast, spread; *(parranda)* spree, binge.

fran·cio m. francium.

fran·cis·ca·no/co, a adj. & m.f. Franciscan.

fran·co, a I. adj. *(sincero)* frank; *(liberal)* generous; *(desembarazado)* open, clear, *(exento)* exempt, free **♦ f. de porte** postpaid **II.** m. FIN. franc.

fra·ne·la f. TEX. flannel; AMER. undershirt.

fran·ja f. fringe, border; *(banda)* strip, band.

fran·je·ar tr. to fringe, trim.

fran·que·ar tr. *(eximir)* to exempt; *(conceder)* to grant; *(desembarazar)* to clear, open; *(pagar el porte)* to frank; *(liberar)* to free, enfranchise; *(atravesar)* to cross, pass through —reflex. *(acceder)* to yield, give in; *(confiar)* to confide.

fran·que·o m. *(de correo)* franking; *(sellos)* postage.

fran·que·za f. frankness, candor; *(exención)* freedom, exemption; *(generosidad)* generosity.

fran·qui·cia f. exemption **♦ f. postal** frank, franking privilege.

fra que ni n a t photocopy

fras·co m. small bottle; *(redoma)* flask, vial; ARM. powder flask.

fra·se f. sentence, phrase **♦ f. hecha** set expression.

fra·se·ar tr. to phrase.

fra·se·o m. phrasing.

fra·se·o·lo·gí·a f. phraseology; *(estilo)* phrasing, style.

fra·ter·nal adj. brotherly, fraternal.

fra·ter·nal·men·te adv. fraternally.

fra·ter·ni·dad f. brotherhood, fraternity.

fra·ter·ni·zar §04 intr. to fraternize.

fra·ter·no, a adj. fraternal.

fra·tri·ci·da I. adj. fratricidal **II.** m.f. fratricide.

fra·tri·ci·dio m. fratricide.

frau·de m. fraud.

frau·du·len·to, a adj. fraudulent.

fray m. Fra, Brother.

fra·za·da f. blanket.

fre·cuen·cia f. frequency.

fre·cuen·tar tr. to frequent.

fre·cuen·te adj. frequent; *(común)* habitual.

fre·ga·de·ro m. kitchen sink.

fre·ga·do, a I. m. scrubbing, scouring; COLL. *(enredo)* mess, tangle **II.** adj. AMER. stubborn, obstinate.

fre·ga·du·ra f./mien·to m. var. of **fregado.**

fre·gar §52 tr. to scour, scrub; *(lavar)* to wash; AMER., COLL. *(molestar)* to annoy, bother —reflex. AMER. to become annoyed.

fre·gón, o·na I. adj. AMER. bothersome, annoying **II.** m.f. AMER. pest, annoyance —f. scullery maid.

frei·du·ra f./mien·to m. frying.

fre·ír §58 tr. CUL. to fry; *(fastidiar)* to pester, annoy; AMER., COLL. *(matar a tiros)* to kill, shoot —reflex. COLL. to be excited **♦ f. de calor** to be boiling hot.

fre·nar tr. *(caballo)* to bridle; *(vehículo)* to brake, apply the brake to; *(hábito, vicio)* to curb, check.

fre·na·zo m. sudden braking.

fre·ne·sí m. [pl. **-íes**] *(delirio)* frenzy.
fre·né·ti·co, a adj. frenetic, frenzied; *(colérico)* mad, furious.
fre·ni·llo m. muzzle, bridle ♦ **no tener f. en la lengua** to speak one's mind.
fre·no m. EQUIT. bit; MECH. brake; *(obstáculo)* obstacle, check ♦ **tascar** *or* **morder el f.** COLL. to champ at the bit.
fren·te f. forehead, brow; *(rostro)* face, countenance; *(cabeza)* head ♦ **arrugar la f.** to knit one's brow • **f. a f.** face to face —m. front; *(fachada)* face, façade; *(anverso)* obverse; MIL., METEOROL. front ♦ **al** *or* **en f.** in front, opposite • **al f. de** at the head of, in charge of • **de f.** resolutely, without hesitation • **f. a** facing, opposite • **hacer f. a** to face, confront.
fre·sa adj. & f. strawberry.
fres·co, a I. adj. cool; *(nuevo)* fresh; *(descarado)* fresh, cheeky, impudent ♦ **estar** *or* **quedar f.** COLL. to fail, be disappointed • **¡que f.!** what a nerve! II. m. cool, coolness; *(aire)* fresh air; ARTS fresco; AMER. cool drink ♦ **al f.** in the open air, in the fresh air —f. fresh air; COLL. *(dicho desagradable)* biting *or* blunt remark.
fres·cor m. freshness, coolness.
fres·cu·ra f. freshness, coolness; *(chanza)* fresh remark; *(serenidad)* serenity, equanimity; *(descuido)* coolness.
freu·dia·no, a adj. & m.f. Freudian.
frial·dad f. coldness, frigidity; *(indiferencia)* indifference; *(falta de animación)* dullness; MED. frigidity, impotence; *(necedad)* nonsense, foolishness.
frí·a·men·te adv. coldly, coolly; *(sin gracia)* dully, colorlessly.
fri·ca·ti·vo, a adj. & f. fricative.
fric·ción f. friction; *(masaje)* massage, rubdown.
fric·cio·nar tr. to rub; *(dar masajes)* to massage.
frie·ga f. *(fricción)* massage, rubdown; AMER., COLL. *(fastidio)* bother, annoyance.
frie·go, gue see **fregar**.
frie·ra, frió see **freír**.
fri·gi·dai·re m. refrigerator.
fri·gi·dez f. frigidity.
frí·gi·do, a adj. frigid.
fri·go·rí·fi·co, a I. adj. refrigerator, refrigerating II. m. refrigerator; *(establecimiento industrial)* cold-storage plant; *(cámara)* locker, cold-storage room.
frí·jol *or* **fri·jol** m. bean.
frí·o, a I. adj. cold; *(sin gracia)* graceless, insipid II. m. cold, coldness; *(bebida)* cool drink ♦ **coger f.** to catch a cold • **hacer f.** to be cold *<hace mucho f. hoy* it is very cold today>* • **tener f.** to be cold *<tengo f.* I am cold>* ♦ pl. AMER. malaria; *(helados)* frozen treats.
frio·len·to, a adj. sensitive to the cold.
frio·le·ro, a I. adj. sensitive to the cold II. f. trifle, bauble; FIG. a mere, only.
fri·sa f. frieze.
fri·sar tr. to rub —intr. to be compatible, get along (with) ♦ **f. con** *or* **en** to be close to, border on.
fri·so m. frieze.
fri·ta·da f. fried dish, fry.
fri·to, a I. see **freír** II. adj. fried III. m. fried food.
fri·tu·ra f. fried food.
fri·vo·li·dad f. frivolity, frivolousness.

frí·vo·lo, a adj. frivolous.
fron·da f./de m. frond; *(hoja)* leaf, shoot ♦ pl. foliage, leaves.
fron·do·so, a adj. frondose, leafy.
fron·tal adj. frontal.
fron·te·ri·zo, a adj. *(contiguo)* border, frontier; *(de enfrente)* facing, opposite.
fron·te·ro, a I. adj. facing, opposite II. m. MIL. border commander —f. border, frontier; ARCHIT. façade.
fron·tis·pi·cio m. frontispiece.
fron·tón m. SPORT. *(pared)* front wall of a handball court; *(cancha)* handball court; ARCHIT. pediment, gable.
fro·ta·du·ra f./mien·to m. rubbing, rub.
fro·tar tr. to rub —reflex. to rub (together).
fro·te m. rub, rubbing.
fruc·tí·fe·ro, a adj. fructiferous.
fruc·ti·fi·car §70 intr. to bear *or* produce fruit; *(producir utilidad)* to be fruitful.
fruc·tuo·so, a adj. fruitful, productive.
fru·frú m. frou-frou.
fru·gal adj. frugal.
fru·ga·li·dad f. frugality, frugalness.
frui·ción f. fruition, enjoyment.
frun·ce·ci·do m. gather, shirr.
frun·cir §35 tr. SEW. to gather, shirr; *(los labios)* to purse; *(la frente)* to frown, knit one's brow; *(reducir)* to contract, reduce.
frus·le·rí·a f. trifle, trinket.
frus·tra·ción f. frustration.
frus·tra·do, a adj. frustrated, thwarted; *(malogrado)* failed.
frus·trar tr. to frustrate, thwart —reflex. *(fracasar)* to fail; *(privarse)* to be frustrated.
fru·ta f. fruit; COLL. *(resultado)* fruit, result.
fru·tal I. adj. fruit II. m. fruit tree.
fru·te·rí·a f. fruit store *or* stand.
fru·te·ro, a I. adj. fruit II. m.f. fruit seller *or* merchant —m. fruit bowl *or* plate.
fru·ti·lla f. rosary bead.
fru·to m. fruit.
fu·ci·lar intr. to sparkle, flash.
fue see **ser²** *or* **ir**.
fue·go m. fire; *(llama)* flame, heat; *(hogar)* hearth, home; *(fósforo)* light *<¿tienes f.?* do you have a light?>*; *(ardor)* heat, passion; *(faro)* beacon; MIL. fire, discharge; MED. rash ♦ **a f. lento** slowly, little by little; CUL. on a low flame • **entre dos fuegos** between a rock and a hard place • **¡f.!** fire!, shoot! • **f. fatuo** ignis fatuus, jack-o'-lantern • **fuegos artificiales** fireworks • **hacer f.** to fire, shoot • **pegar f.** to set on fire • **romper el f.** to open fire.
fue·lle m. *(implemento)* bellows; *(frunce)* pucker, gather; *(chismoso)* tattletale, gossip.
fuen·te f. *(manantial)* spring; *(aparato)* fountain, water fountain; *(pila)* font; *(plato)* platter, serving dish; *(cabecera)* source, headwater; *(origen)* source, origin ♦ **beber en buenas fuentes** to be well-informed.
fue·ra adv. outside, out ♦ **¡f.!** get out! • **f. de** outside of; *(además de)* besides, except for • **f. de que** aside from the fact that • **f. de sí** beside oneself • **por f.** on the outside.
fue·ra see **ser²** *or* **ir**.
fue·ro m. jurisdiction, power; *(cuerpo de leyes)* code; *(privilegio)* privilege, exemption ♦ pl. COLL. arrogance, pride.
fuer·te I. adj. strong; *(fortificado)* fortified; *(intenso)* powerful, forceful; loud *<un grito f.* a loud shout>* II. m. fort, fortress; *(talento)*

forte, strong point **III.** adv. hard; *(en voz alta)* loudly.

fuer·te·men·te adv. hard; *(en voz alta)* loudly.

fuer·za f. force, strength; *(violencia)* force, coercion; *(poder)* power ♦ **a f. de** by dint of • **a la f. or por f.** by force, forcibly; *(forzosamente)* perforce, necessarily • **a f. viva** by sheer force • **es f.** it is necessary to, one must • **f. mayor** act of God, force majeure.

fu·ga f. flight, escape; *(ardor)* ardor, impetuosity; *(escape)* leak, leakage; MUS. fugue ♦ **darse a la f. or ponerse en f.** to flee, take (to) flight.

fu·ga·ci·dad f. fugacity, brevity.

fu·gar·se §47 reflex. to flee, run away; *(salirse)* leak (out).

fu·gaz adj. fleeting, brief; ASTRON. shooting.

fu·gi·ti·vo, a adj. & m.f. fugitive.

fui, fuimos, fuiste see *ser* or *ir*.

fu·la·no, a m.f. so-and-so.

ful·gir §32 intr. to shine, sparkle.

ful·gor m. brilliance, radiance.

ful·gu·rar intr. to flash brilliantly.

ful·mi·nar tr. *(un rayo)* to strike (and kill) by lightning; *(hacer morir bruscamente)* to strike down *or* dead; *(arrojar)* to throw, hurl; FIG. to thunder.

fu·lle·rí·a f. *(en cartas)* cheating; *(astucia)* astuteness, guile.

fu·lle·ro, a I. adj. crooked, dishonest; *(astuto)* sharp, wily **II.** m.f. cardsharp, cheat; *(astuto)* sharpie.

fu·ma·da f. puff (of smoke).

fu·ma·dor, ·ra I. adj. smoking **II.** m.f. smoker.

fu·mar intr. & tr. to smoke —reflex. COLL. *(malgastar)* to squander; *(faltar)* to skip, cut <*f. la clase* to cut class>.

fu·mi·ga·dor, ·ra m.f. fumigator.

fu·mi·gar §47 tr. to fumigate.

fun·ción f. function, *(empleo)* position; THEAT. show, performance.

fun·cio·nal adj. functional, operative.

fun·cio·na·li·dad f. functionality.

fun·cio·na·mien·to m. functioning, operating.

fun·cio·nar intr. to work, run.

fun·cio·na·rio a m.f. civil servant, official.

fun·da f. cover, case.

fun·da·ción f. foundation.

fun·da·dor, ·ra I. adj. founding **II.** m f. founder.

fun·da·men·tal adj. fundamental.

fun·da·men·tar tr. to lay the foundations of; *(basar)* to base.

fun·da·men·to m. foundation; *(razón)* reason, ground.

fun·dar tr. to build, raise, *(instituir)* to found, establish; *(apoyar)* to base, rest —reflex. FIG. to be founded *or* based.

fun·di·ción f. melting, smelting; *(fábrica)* foundry, smeltery; *(hierro)* cast iron.

fun·dir tr. METAL. to melt, smelt; *(moldear)* to cast, mold; *(bombilla)* to burn out —reflex. to merge, fuse; AMER. to go bankrupt.

fú·ne·bre adj. funereal.

fu·ne·ral adj. & m. funeral.

fu·né·re·o, a adj. funeral.

fu·nes·to, a adj. unfortunate, regrettable; *(fatal)* ill-fated.

fun·gi·ci·da I. adj. fungicidal **II.** m. fungicide.

fu·ni·cu·lar I. adj. funicular **II.** m. cable car.

fu·ñi·que adj. & m.f. awkward, clumsy (person).

fur·gón f. *(carro)* van, wagon; RAIL. boxcar.

fur·go·ne·ta f. van, truck.

fu·ria f. fury.

fu·ri·bun·do, a adj. enraged, furious.

fu·rio·sa·men·te adv. furiously, frantically.

fu·rio·so, a adj. furious; *(grande)* tremendous.

fu·ror m. fury, rage.

fur·ti·vo, a adj. furtive, stealthy.

fu·rún·cu·lo m. boil, furuncle.

fu·se·la·je m. fuselage.

fu·si·ble I. adj. fusible **II.** m. fuse.

fu·sil m. rifle, gun.

fu·si·la·mien·to m. shooting, execution.

fu·si·lar tr. to shoot; COLL. *(plagiar)* to plagiarize.

fu·sión f. melting, fusion; COM. merger.

fu·sio·nar intr. to merge.

fus·te m. shaft; *(importancia)* importance, consequence.

fus·ti·ga·dor, ·ra I. adj. whipping; *(censurador)* censuring **II.** m.f. whipper; *(censurador)* censurer.

fus·ti·gar §47 tr. to whip, lash; *(criticar)* to censure, reprimand.

fút·bol or **fut·bol** m. soccer, football (G.B.) ♦ **f. americano** football.

fut·bo·lis·ta m.f. soccer player, footballer (G.B.).

fú·til adj. trivial, insignificant.

fu·ti·li·dad f. triviality, insignificance.

fu·tu·ris·ta adj. & m.f. futurist.

fu·tu·ro, a I. adj. future **II.** m future; COLL. *(novio)* fiancé, intended; COLL. *(novia)* fiancée, intended.

G

g, G f. eighth letter of the Spanish alphabet.

ga·ba·cho, a I. adj. DEROG. French **II.** m.f. DEROG. French person.

ga·bán m. overcoat, topcoat.

ga·bar·di·na f. gabardine; *(sobretodo)* raincoat.

ga·ba·zo m. bagasse.

ga·bi·ne·te m. *(cuarto)* study, office; *(de una mujer)* boudoir; *(laboratorio)* laboratory; POL. cabinet.

ga·ce·la f. gazelle.

ga·ce·ta f. gazette, journal; *(chismoso)* gossip, gossipmonger.

ga·ce·ti·lla f. *(noticia breve)* short news item; *(columna de chismes)* gossip column; *(chismoso)* gossipmonger.

ga·chí f. [pl. s] SL. girl, chick.

ga·cho, a I. adj. *(inclinado)* bowed, bent; *(flojo)* drooping, floppy ♦ **a gachas** on all fours **II.** m. AMER. slouch hat —f. mush, paste ♦ pl. porridge • **hacerse unas g.** COLL. to get mushy.

ga·do·li·nio m. gadolinium.

ga·fas f.pl.inv. (eye)glasses.

ga·fe m. COLL. jinx.

ga·fo, a I. adj. claw-handed **II.** f. *(gancho)* hook; *(grapa)* clamp.

ga·gá adj. doting, foolish.

gai·ta f. MUS. bagpipe; *(organillo)* hurdy-gurdy; COLL. *(pescuezo)* neck.

gai·te·ro, a I. adj. flamboyant, gaudy **II.** m.f. bagpiper.

ga·je m. salary ◆ pl. salary, wages • g. del oficio occupational hazard.

ga·jo m. (rama) branch; (racimo) bunch; (división) section; (punta) prong, tine; AMER. curl.

ga·la f. (vestido) full dress; (gracia) elegance; CUBA, MEX. tip ◆ hacer g. de or tener a g. to show off ◆ pl. (adornos) finery, trappings; (regalos) wedding gifts or presents.

ga·lác·ti·co, a adj. galactic.

ga·lán m. handsome man; (pretendiente) beau, suitor; THEAT. leading man.

ga·la·na·men·te adv. (con gala) smartly; (elegantemente) elegantly.

ga·lan·ce·te m. handsome young man.

ga·la·ní·a f. elegance.

ga·la·no, a adj. (bien vestido) spruce, smart; (elegante) elegant.

ga·lan·te adj. gallant; (amatorio) flirtatious.

ga·lan·te·a·dor, ·ra I. adj. flirtatious II. m. gallant, flirt.

ga·lan·te·ar tr. (cortejar) to woo, court; (coquetear) to flirt with.

ga·lan·te·o m. (cortejo) courting; (coqueteo) flirting.

ga·lan·te·rí·a f. gallantry; (gracia) grace, elegance; (liberalidad) generosity.

ga·la·nu·ra f. elegance.

ga·lá·pa·go m. ZOOL. sea turtle; METAL. ingot; EQUIT. English saddle.

ga·lar·dón m. reward.

ga·lar·do·nar tr. to reward.

ga·la·xia f. galaxy.

ga·le·na f. MIN. galena.

ga·le·no m. COLL. doctor.

ga·le·ón m. galleon.

ga·le·o·te m. galley slave.

ga·le·ra f. galley; (carro) covered wagon; (cárcel) women's prison; (sala) hospital ward.

ga·le·ra·da f. (carga) wagonload; PRINT. galley (proof).

ga·le·rí·a f. gallery.

gal·go, a m.f. greyhound.

gal·guer·ar intr. AMER. to be starved.

ga·li·llo m. uvula.

ga·li·ma·tí·as m.inv. gibberish, nonsense.

ga·lio m. gallium.

ga·lo·cha f. wooden or iron clog.

ga·lón m. (de líquidos) gallon; (cinta) braid, galloon; MIL. stripe.

ga·lo·ne·ar tr. SEW. to trim with braid.

ga·lo·pan·te adj. galloping.

ga·lo·par/pe·ar intr. to gallop.

ga·lo·pe m. gallop ◆ a g. tendido at full gallop • ir de g. to gallop, go at a gallop.

gal·pón m. AMER. large shed.

gal·vá·ni·co, a adj. galvanic.

gal·va·ni·za·ción f. galvanization.

gal·va·ni·za·do, a I. adj. galvanized II. m. galvanization.

gal·va·ni·zar §04 tr. to galvanize.

ga·llar·de·ar intr. to act with ease and grace.

ga·llar·de·te m. streamer, pennant.

ga·llar·dí·a f. (bizarría) elegance, grace; (valor) gallantry, bravery.

ga·llar·do, a adj. (airoso) elegant, graceful; (valiente) brave, valiant.

ga·lle·ar intr. (gritar) to shout; (sobresalir) to stand out, excel.

ga·lle·ta f. (bizcocho de mar) sea biscuit, hardtack; (bizcocho) biscuit, cracker; COLL. (bofetada) slap ◆ colgar or dar la g. a alguien AMER. to fire, dismiss someone.

ga·lli·na f. hen, chicken —m.f. FIG. chicken, coward ◆ como g. en corral ajeno COLL. like a fish out of water • g. ciega blindman's buff.

ga·lli·ná·ce·o, a adj. gallinaceous.

ga·lli·ne·rí·a f. (tienda) poultry shop; (bandada) flock of hens; (cobardía) cowardice.

ga·lli·ne·ro m. (jaula) chicken coop, henhouse; (sitio ruidoso) madhouse; THEAT. top balcony.

ga·lli·to m. (fanfarrón) braggart, showoff; (persona importante) somebody, celebrity.

ga·llo m. ORNITH. cock, rooster; (nota falsa) false note; (jefe) boss, chief; AMER. (valiente) cocky person; (carro) fire engine; (serenata) serenade; (objeto de segunda mano) secondhand object ◆ g. de pelea gamecock, fighting cock • tener mucho g. to be cocky.

ga·llón m. lawn, turf.

ga·ma f. gamut.

ga·ma·da adj. ◆ cruz g. swastika.

gam·ba f. prawn.

gam·ba·do, a adj. bowlegged.

gam·bar·se reflex. AMER. to become bowlegged.

gam·be·ta f. AMER. caper, prance.

gam·be·te·ar intr. to caper, prance.

ga·me·to m. gamete.

gam·ma f. gamma.

ga·mu·za f. chamois.

ga·na f. (deseo) desire, longing; (apetito) appetite ◆ darle ganas or darle la g. de to feel like • de buena, mala g. willingly, unwillingly • de g. energetically, eagerly ◆ pl. con g. heartily • tener g. de to want to, feel like • sin g. unwillingly.

ga·na·de·rí·a f. (ganado) cattle, livestock; (raza) breed, strain.

ga·na·de·ro, a I. adj. cattle II. m.f. cattle rancher, cattleman.

ga·na·do m. livestock, stock; AMER. cattle.

ga·na·dor, ·ra I. adj. winning, victorious II. m.f. (el que gana) winner; (asalariado) wage earner.

ga·nan·cia f. profit, gain.

ga·nan·cial adj. profit, pertaining to profit.

ga·nar tr. (lograr) to gain; (llevarse) to win, get; (recibir) to earn, make; (triunfar) to win; (vencer) to beat, defeat; (aventajar) to surpass; (captar) to win over; (merecer) to earn, merit; (alcanzar) to reach, arrive at —intr. to earn; (mejorar) to improve, advance —reflex. ◆ g. la vida to earn one's living.

gan·chi·llo m. (horquilla) hairpin; (aguja) crochet needle; (labor) crochet.

gan·cho m. (garfio) hook; (cayado) crook, staff; (puñetazo) hook; COLL. (timador) cajoler; (rufián) pimp; (atractivo) charm, allure; AMER. hairpin ◆ echar el g. to hook, snare.

gan·dul, ·la I. adj. COLL. lazy, shiftless II. m.f. COLL. loafer, good-for-nothing.

gan·du·le·ar intr. to loaf, idle.

gan·du·le·rí·a f. laziness.

gan·ga f. bargain, steal.

gan·glio m. ganglion.

gan·go·si·dad f. nasality (of voice).

gan·go·so, a adj. nasal, twangy.

gan·gre·na f. gangrene.

gan·gre·nar·se reflex. to become gangrenous.

gan·gue·ar intr. to speak nasally.

gan·gue·o m. nasal tone, twang.

ga·no·so, a adj. desirous, anxious.

gan·sa·da f. COLL. nonsense.

gan·se·ar intr. COLL. to do or say silly things.

gan·so, a m. gander —f. goose —m.f. *(torpe)* dummy; *(rústico)* bumpkin.

gan·zú·a f. *(instrumento)* picklock; *(ladrón)* picklock, thief.

ga·ño·te m. COLL. throat, gullet ♦ **de g.** COLL. free, gratis.

ga·ra·ba·te·ar intr. *(echar un garabato)* to hook; *(escribir)* to scribble; *(tergiversar)* to beat around the bush —tr. to scribble.

ga·ra·ba·to m. *(gancho)* hook, grapple; *(escarabajos)* scribble; COLL. *(gracia)* sex appeal, attractiveness.

ga·ra·je m. garage.

ga·ran·te I. adj. responsible II. m.f. guarantor.

ga·ran·tí·a f. guarantee; *(fianza)* security, deposit.

ga·ran·tir §38 tr. *(asegurar)* to guarantee; *(preservar)* to protect, defend.

ga·ran·ti·zar §04 tr. to guarantee.

ga·ra·pi·ña f. frozen state.

ga·ra·pi·ñar tr. *(helar)* to freeze; *(bañar)* to sugar-coat.

ga·ra·tu·sa f. compliment.

gar·ban·zo m. chickpea ♦ **g. negro** COLL. black sheep.

gar·be·ar intr. *(fanfarronear)* to swagger; *(robar)* to rob —tr. *(robar)* to steal —refl. COLL. *(arreglárselas)* to manage, get by; *(pasearse)* to go for a walk.

gar·bi·llar tr. AGR. to sieve.

gar·bi·llo m. sieve.

gar·bo m. *(gallardía)* elegance, grace; *(generosidad)* generosity.

gar·bo·so, a adj. *(airoso)* elegant, graceful; *(generoso)* generous.

gar·de·nia f. gardenia.

gar·du·ño, a m.f. COLL. thief, pickpocket.

ga·re·te m. ♦ **ir(se) al g.** to drift.

gar·fa f. claw.

gar·fe·ar intr. to hook, grab with a hook.

gar·fio m. grappling iron, grapple.

gar·ga·je·ar intr. to spit.

gar·ga·jo m. phlegm, spit.

gar·gan·ta f. throat; *(del pie)* instep; *(desfiladero)* gorge.

gar·gan·te·ar intr. to warble, trill.

gar·gan·ti·lla f. necklace, choker.

gár·ga·ra f. gargling ♦ pl. AMER. gargle.

gar·ga·ris·mo m. gargling; *(líquido)* gargle.

gar·ga·ri·zar §04 intr. to gargle.

gár·gol m. groove.

gár·go·la f. gargoyle.

gar·gue·ro/güe·ro m. windpipe, trachea.

ga·ri·ta f. *(de centinela)* sentry box; *(portería)* porter's office; *(retrete)* lavatory.

ga·ri·te·ro m. gambler.

ga·ri·to m. *(local)* gambling house; *(ganancia)* gambling profits.

gar·lar intr. COLL. to chatter, gab.

gar·li·to m. *(de pesca)* fish trap; COLL. *(trampa)* trap, snare.

gar·lo·pa f. jack plane.

gar·na·cha f. judge's robe or gown.

gar·nu·cho m. MEX. rap, fillip.

ga·rra f. claw, talon; MARIT. hook; AMER. *(fuerza)* bite, kick ♦ **caer en las garras de alguien** to fall into someone's clutches • **como una g.** AMER. very thin • **echar la g.** to lay one's hands on ♦ pl. AMER. tatters, rags.

ga·rra·fa f. carafe, decanter.

ga·rra·fal adj. COLL. huge, enormous.

ga·rra·fón m. demijohn.

ga·rra·pa·ta f. tick, mite; *(caballo)* nag.

ga·rra·pa·te·ar intr. to scribble, scrawl.

ga·rra·pa·to m. scribble, scrawl.

ga·rra·pi·ñar tr. to grab, snatch.

ga·rro·cha f. TAUR. lance, goad; SPORT. pole.

ga·rrón m. talon, claw.

ga·rro·ta·zo m. blow.

ga·rro·te m. *(palo)* club; *(tormento)* garrote; MEX. brake ♦ **dar g.** to garrote.

ga·rro·te·ar tr. AMER. to club.

ga·rro·ti·llo m. croup.

ga·rru·cha f. pulley.

ga·rru·lar intr. to chatter, prattle.

ga·rru·le·rí·a f. chatter, prattle.

gá·rru·lo, a adj. *(cantor)* noisy, chirping; *(hablador)* garrulous, talkative.

ga·rú·a/·ru·ja f. AMER. drizzle, fine rain.

ga·ruar §67 intr. AMER. to drizzle.

ga·ru·fa f. ARG., SL. spree, binge.

ga·ru·fe·ar intr. ARG., SL. to go on a spree.

gar·zo, a I. adj. blue II. f. heron.

gas m. gas.

ga·sa f. gauze; *(de luto)* crepe.

ga·se·ar tr. *(hacer gaseoso)* to carbonate; *(asfixiar)* to gas, asphyxiate.

ga·se·o·so, a I. adj. gaseous II. f. carbonated beverage.

ga·si·fi·ca·ción f. gasification.

ga·si·fi·ca·dor m. gasifier.

ga·si·fi·car §70 tr. to gasify.

ga·so·duc·to m. gas pipeline.

gas oil or **ga·soil/·só·le·o** m. gas or diesel oil.

ga·so·li·na f. gasoline, gas.

ga·so·li·ne·ra f. *(lancha)* motorboat; *(tienda)* gas station.

gas·ta·do, a adj. *(debilitado)* worn-out, exhausted; *(usado)* worn, threadbare; *(trillado)* hackneyed, worn-out.

gas·ta·dor, ·ra I. adj. spendthrift II. m.f. *(derrochador)* spendthrift; *(prisionero)* convict —m. MIL. sapper.

gas·tar tr. *(pagar)* to spend; *(consumir)* to consume, exhaust; *(echar a perder)* to wear out; *(malgastar)* to waste, squander; *(llevar)* to sport, wear • **gastarlas** COLL. to behave, act —intr. to spend —refl. *(consumirse)* to be used up, run out; *(deteriorarse)* to wear out; *(debilitarse)* to wear oneself out.

gas·to m. *(desembolso)* expenditure, expense; *(consumo)* use, consumption; *(deterioro)* wear and tear ♦ **hacer el g. de la conversación** COLL. to do all the talking.

gás·tri·co, a adj. gastric.

gas·tri·tis f. gastritis.

gas·tro·en·te·ri·tis f. gastroenteritis.

gas·tro·in·tes·ti·nal adj. gastrointestinal.

gas·tro·no·mí·a f. gastronomy.

gas·tro·nó·mi·co, a adj. gastronomic(al).

gas·tró·no·mo, a m.f. gastronome, gourmet.

ga·ta f. see **gato, a.**

ga·te·ar intr. to crawl, walk on all fours; *(trepar)* to climb (trees) —tr. *(arañar)* to scratch, claw; *(robar)* to swipe, steal.

ga·ti·llo m. ARM. *(percusor)* hammer, firing pin; *(disparador)* trigger; *(ratero)* petty thief.

ga·to, a m. cat, tomcat; *(gancho)* clamp, vice; *(cric)* jack; COLL. *(portamonedas)* moneybags; COLL. *(ladrón)* sneak thief; *(hombre astuto)* fox, slyboots ♦ **buscarle tres pies al g.** to complicate matters unnecessarily • **dar g. por liebre** COLL. to swindle, pull the wool over someone's eyes —f. cat, tabby; MEX. maid ♦ **a gatas** on all fours.

ga·tu·no, a adj. feline, catlike.

gau·cha·da f. AMER., COLL. clever trick.

gau·ches·co, a adj. gaucho.

gau·cho, a adj. & m. gaucho.

ga·ve·ta f. drawer.

ga·vi·lán m. sparrow hawk; *(escritura)* flourish (in penmanship); *(pluma)* nib.

ga·vi·lla f. *(cereales)* sheaf of grain; *(sarmientos)* bundle of vines; *(gente)* gang, band.

ga·vi·lle·ro m. stack *or* row of sheaves.

ga·vio·ta f. seagull, gull.

ga·za·pa f. COLL. lie, fib.

ga·za·pa·tón m. COLL. blunder.

ga·za·pe·ra f. *(madriguera)* rabbit warren; COLL. *(pandilla)* shady gang; *(riña)* brawl, scuffle.

ga·za·pi·na f. *(pandilla)* gang; *(riña)* fight, brawl.

ga·za·po m. young rabbit; COLL. *(hombre astuto)* sly fox; COLL. *(disparate)* slip of the tongue *or* pen.

ga·za·pón m. gambling house.

gaz·mo·ña·da/ñe·rí·a f. prudishness, priggishness.

gaz·mo·ñe·ro/ño, a I. adj. prudish, priggish II. m.f. prig, prude.

gaz·ná·pi·ro, a I. adj. simple-minded, dullwitted II. m.f. numbskull, dunce.

gaz·na·ta·da f. blow to the throat; AMER. slap.

gaz·na·te m. *(garguero)* throat, windpipe; *(fruta de sartén)* fritter.

gaz·pa·cho m. gazpacho.

géi·ser m. geyser.

ge·la·ti·na f. gelatin.

ge·la·ti·no·so, a adj. gelatinous.

gé·li·do, a adj. gelid, icy.

ge·ma f. gem; BOT. bud, gemma.

ge·me·bun·do, a adj. groaning loudly.

ge·me·lo, a I. adj. twin II. m.f. twin ♦ m.pl. *(anteojos)* binoculars, field glasses; *(de camisa)* cuff links ● **g. de teatro** opera glasses.

ge·mi·do m. moan, groan.

ge·mir §48 intr. *(quejarse)* to moan, groan; *(aullar)* to howl, wail.

gen *or* **ge·ne** m. [pl. **–es**] gene.

gen·dar·me m. gendarme, policeman.

gen·dar·me·rí·a f. gendarmerie.

ge·ne·a·lo·gí·a f. genealogy.

ge·ne·a·ló·gi·co, a adj. genealogical.

ge·ne·ra·ción f. generation.

ge·ne·ra·dor, ·ra I. adj. generating, engendering II. m.f. generator, engenderer —m. ELEC., MECH. generator —f. generatrix.

ge·ne·ral I. ♦ adj. general ♦ **en g.** *or* **por lo g.** generally, in general II. m. general ♦ **g. de brigada** brigadier general ● **g. de división** major general ● **g. en jefe** commander in chief.

ge·ne·ra·la·to m. generalship.

ge·ne·ra·li·dad f. generality; *(el mayor número)* majority.

ge·ne·ra·lí·si·mo m. generalissimo.

ge·ne·ra·li·za·ción f. generalization; *(extensión)* expansion.

ge·ne·ra·li·zar §04 tr. to generalize; *(ampliar)* to widen, expand.

ge·ne·rar tr. to generate, produce.

ge·ne·ra·ti·vo, a adj. generative.

ge·ne·ra·triz f. GEOM. generatrix; ELEC., MECH. generator.

ge·né·ri·ca·men·te adv. generically.

ge·né·ri·co, a adj. generic.

gé·ne·ro m. type, kind; *(manera)* manner, style; COM. commodity; TEX. fabric, material; BIOL. genus; GRAM. gender; ARTS, LIT. genre ♦ **g. humano** humankind.

ge·ne·ro·si·dad f. generosity.

ge·ne·ro·so, a adj. generous; *(ilustre)* highborn; *(excelente)* excellent, fine.

gé·ne·sis f.inv. origin, beginning.

ge·né·ti·co, a I. adj. genetic II. f. genetics.

ge·nial adj. brilliant, inspired; COLL. *(agradable)* genial, pleasant; *(característica)* typical.

ge·nia·li·dad f. *(rareza)* peculiarity, trait; *(obra)* brilliant *or* inspired work.

ge·nia·zo m. COLL. bad *or* violent temper.

ge·nio m. *(carácter)* temperament, disposition; *(talento)* genius; *(deidad pagana)* genius, spirit ♦ **de mal g.** bad-tempered.

ge·ni·tal adj. & m. genital ♦ pl. genitals, genitalia.

ge·ni·ti·vo, a m. genitive.

ge·ni·tor, ·ra I. adj. engendering, reproductive II. m. procreator, reproducer.

ge·no·ci·dio m. genocide.

ge·no·ti·po m. genotype.

gen·te f. people; *(nación)* nation, folk; COLL. *(facción)* clan, gang; *(familia)* family, folks; MIL. troops; AMER. decent folk ♦ **g. baja** common people ● **g. bien** upper class ● **g. de paz** friend ● **g. de trato** tradespeople ● **g. menuda** COLL. kids, small fry.

gen·til I. adj. RELIG. gentile; *(gracioso)* genteel, polite; *(notable)* remarkable, excellent II. m.f. RELIG. gentile.

gen·ti·le·za f. *(gracia)* genteelness; *(cortesía)* courtesy; *(amabilidad)* kindness; *(bizarría)* stylishness.

gen·til·hom·bre m. [pl. **-tileshombres**] handsome young man; HIST. gentleman-in-waiting.

gen·ti·li·cio, a I. adj. national; *(relativo al linaje)* hereditary II. m. GRAM. word indicating origin.

gen·ti·li·dad f./**lis·mo** m. RELIG. Gentile religion; *(personas)* (the) Gentiles.

gen·tí·o m. crowd, mob.

gen·tu·za f. riffraff, rabble.

ge·nu·fle·xión f. genuflection.

ge·nui·no, a adj. genuine.

ge·o·cén·tri·co, a adj. geocentric.

ge·o·da f. geode.

ge·o·fí·si·co, a I. adj. geophysical II. m.f. geophysicist —f. geophysics.

ge·o·gra·fí·a f. geography.

ge·o·grá·fi·co, a adj. geographic(al).

ge·ó·gra·fo, a m.f. geographer.

ge·o·lo·gí·a f. geology.

ge·o·ló·gi·co, a adj. geologic(al).

ge·ó·lo·go, a m.f. geologist.

ge·ó·me·tra m.f. geometrician, geometer.

ge·o·me·trí·a f. geometry.

ge·o·mé·tri·co, a adj. geometric(al); *(exacto)* exact, precise.

ge·o·po·lí·ti·co, a I. adj. geopolitical II. f. geopolitics.

ge·ra·nio m. geranium.

ge·ren·cia f. *(gestión)* management; *(cargo)* managership, directorship; *(oficina)* manager's *or* director's office.

ge·ren·te m. manager, director.

ge·ria·tra m.f. geriatrician, geriatrist.

ge·riá·tri·co, a adj. geriatric.

ger·ma·nes·co, a adj. slang.

ger·ma·ní·a f. slang of gypsies and thieves.
ger·ma·nio m. germanium.
ger·men m. germ.
ger·mi·ci·da I. adj. germicidal II. m. germicide, germ killer.
ger·mi·na·ción f. germination.
ger·mi·nar intr. to germinate.
ge·ron·to·lo·gí·a f. gerontology.
ge·ron·tó·lo·go, a m.f. gerontologist.
ge·run·dio m. GRAM. (del español) present participle; (del latín) gerund.
ges·ta f. exploits, heroic deeds.
ges·ta·ción f. gestation.
ges·tar tr. to gestate, carry —reflex. to develop, grow.
ges·te·ar intr. (hacer muecas) to grimace, make faces; (hacer ademanes) to gesture, gesticulate.
ges·ti·cu·la·ción f. (mueca) grimace, face; (ademán) gesture, gesticulation.
ges·ti·cu·lar tr. (que hace muecas) grimacing; (que hace ademanes) gesturing.
ges·ti·cu·lar intr. (hacer muecas) to grimace, make faces; (hacer ademanes) to gesture, gesticulate.
ges·tión f. (dirección) administration, management; (trámite) step, measure; (cuasicontrato) agreement.
ges·tio·nar tr. to take steps or measures to obtain.
ges·to m. (expresión) look, facial expression; (mueca) grimace, face; (ademán) gesture, gesticulation ♦ estar de buen, mal g. to be in a good, bad mood • hacer gestos (hacer muecas) to make faces, grimace; (hacer ademanes) to gesture, gesticulate.
ges·tor, ·ra I. adj. managing II. m.f. manager, administrator.
géy·ser m. geyser.
gi·ba f. (corcova) hump, hunch; (molestia) nuisance.
gi·bar tr. (corcovar) to bend, curve; COLL. (molestar) to annoy.
gi·bón m. gibbon.
gi·bo·so, a adj. & m.f. hunchback(ed).
gi·gan·ta f. giantess; BOT. sunflower.
gi·gan·te I. adj. giant, gigantic II. m. giant.
gi·gan·tes·co, a adj. gigantic, huge.
gi·gan·tez f. gigantic size.
gí·go·lo m. gigolo.
gi·ma, mo, miera, mió see **gemir**.
gim·na·sia f. gymnastics ♦ g. sueca calisthenics.
gim·na·sio m. gymnasium, gym; (escuela) high or secondary school.
gim·nas·ta m.f. gymnast.
gim·nás·ti·ca f. var. of **gimnasia**.
gi·mo·te·a·dor, ·ra I. adj. whining II. m.f. whiner.
gi·mo·te·ar intr. COLL. to whine.
gi·mo·te·o m. COLL. whine, whining.
gi·ne·bra f. (bebida) gin; (juego) gin (rummy); (ruido) din, uproar; (confusión) confusion, bedlam.
gi·ne·co·lo·gí·a f. gynecology.
gi·ne·có·lo·go, a m.f. gynecologist.
gin·gi·vi·tis f. gingivitis.
gi·ra f. trip, outing.
gi·ra·dis·cos m.inv. (tocadiscos) record player, phonograph; (plato) turntable.
gi·ra·do m. COM. drawee.
gi·ra·dor, ·ra m.f. drawer, one who draws money on an account.

gi·ral·da f. weather vane, weathercock.
gi·rar intr. (dar vueltas) to revolve, rotate; (moverse alrededor de un eje) to gyrate; (torcer) to turn, veer; (negociar) to do business; (enviar) to wire; COM. to draw ♦ g. en descubierto to overdraw —tr. (rodar) to rotate, turn; COM. to draw.
gi·ra·sol m. BOT. sunflower; FIG. social climber, sycophant.
gi·ra·to·rio, a adj. turning, rotating.
gi·ro m. (rotación) revolution, rotation; (vuelta) turn; (aspecto) turn, (fruse) turn of phrase, expression; COM. draft; (negocio) business, line of business ♦ andar de mal g. to be in a bad way • g. a la vista sight draft • g. en descubierto overdraft • g. postal money order.
gi·ro·a·vión m. gyroplane.
gi·ros·co·pio m. gyroscope, gyro.
gis m. (tiza) chalk; COL. slate pencil.
gi·ta·ne·ar intr. to wheedle, cajole.
gi·ta·ne·rí·a f. (reunión) band of gypsies; (adulación) wheedling, cajolery.
gi·ta·nes·co, a adj. gypsy, gypsy-like.
gi·ta·no, a I. adj. gypsy; (adulador) wheedling, cajoling; (socaliñero) sly, crafty II. m.f. gypsy.
gla·cia·ción f. glaciation.
gla·cial adj. glacial; (helado) icy, frozen; FIG. icy, cold.
gla·ciar I. m. glacier II. adj. glacial.
gla·dia·dor/tor m. gladiator.
gla·dí·o·lo/dio·lo m. gladiolus.
glan·de m. glans penis.
glán·du·la f. gland.
glan·du·lar adj. glandular.
gla·se·a·do, a adj. glazed, glossy.
gla·se·ar tr. to glaze.
glau·co·ma m. glaucoma.
gli·ce·ri·na f. glycerine, glycerol.
gli·ci·na f. BOT. wisteria; CHEM. glycine.
gli·col m. glycol.
glo·bal adj. global; COM. total.
glo·bal·men·te adv. as a whole.
glo·bo m. globe; (Tierra) Earth; (de goma) balloon ♦ en g. as a whole • g. ocular or del ojo eyeball • g. sonda sounding balloon.
glo·bu·lar adj. globular.
glo·bu·li·na m. globulin.
gló·bu·lo m. globule; ANAT. corpuscle.
glo·gló m. gurgle, gurgling.
glo·ria f. glory; (honor) fame, renown; (esplendor) splendor, greatness; (cielo) heaven ♦ a g. heavenly, divinely • estar en la g. or en su g. to be in seventh heaven • ganar la g. to go to heaven.
glo·riar §30 tr. to glorify —reflex. (preciarse) to boast; (complacerse mucho) to glory (in).
glo·rie·ta f. plaza, square; (cenador) bower, arbor.
glo·ri·fi·ca·ción f. glorification.
glo·ri·fi·ca·dor, ·ra I. adj. glorifying II. m.f. glorifier.
glo·ri·fi·car §70 tr. to glorify, praise —reflex. to glory.
glo·rio·so, a adj. glorious; (bendito) blessed; (vanidoso) boastful, conceited.
glo·sa f. gloss.
glo·sa·dor, ·ra I. adj. glossing II. m.f. commentator, glossarist.
glo·sar tr. to gloss; (comentar) to comment; (interpretar mal) to gloss, criticize.
glo·sa·rio m. glossary.
glo·se m. glossing, annotating.

glo·tis f. glottis.
glo·tón, o·na I. adj. gluttonous II. m.f. glutton.
glo·to·ne·ar intr. to eat gluttonously.
glo·to·ne·rí·a f. gluttony.
glu·ce·mia f. glycemia.
glu·co·sa f. glucose.
glu·glú m. (del agua) gurgle; (del pavo) gobble, gobbling.
glu·glu·te·ar intr. to gobble.
glu·ten m. gluten.
glu·ti·no·so, a adj. glutinous, sticky.
gno·mo m. gnome.
gnós·ti·co, a adj. & m.f. gnostic.
gnu m. gnu.
go·ber·na·ción f. government ♦ **Ministerio de la G.** Ministry of the Interior.
go·ber·na·dor I. adj. governing II. m. governor.
go·ber·nan·ta f. ARG. governess.
go·ber·nan·te I. adj. ruling, governing II. m.f. ruler, leader; COLL. (pez gordo) big shot.
go·ber·nar §49 tr. to govern; (dirigir) to control; (conducir) to steer —intr. MARIT. to steer.
go·bier·no m. government; (oficio y duración) governorship; (edificio) governor's house; MARIT. (timón) rudder; (manejo) steering, navigability ♦ **g. de la casa** housekeeping • **servir de g.** to serve as a guide.
go·ce m. enjoyment, pleasure.
go·fo, a adj. crude, ignorant.
gol m. [pl. (e)s] goal ♦ **marcar** or **meter un g.** to make or score a goal.
go·la f. (garganta) gullet, throat; (adorno) gorget, ruff.
go·le·a·da f. high score.
go·le·a·dor, ·ra m.f. goal scorer.
go·le·ar tr. to score many goals against —intr. to score.
go·le·ta f. schooner.
golf m. golf.
gol·fo, a m.f. urchin —m. gulf <el G. de México the Gulf of Mexico>; bay <el G. de Vizcaya the Bay of Biscay>.
go·li·lla f. collar, ruff; ORNITH. ruff; TECH. pipe collar or flange.
go·lon·dri·na f. swallow.
go·lon·dri·no m. ORNITH. male swallow; (vagabundo) vagrant, bum; MIL. deserter.
go·lo·sa·men·te adv. eagerly, with relish.
go·lo·si·na f. (manjar agradable) delicacy; (deseo) longing, craving; (gula) gluttony; (chuchería) trifle, frivolity.
go·lo·si·nar/ne·ar intr. to nibble on sweets.
go·lo·so, a I. m.f. sweet-toothed person II. adj. (glotón) sweet-toothed; (deseoso) gluttonous; (apetitoso) appetizing, tempting.
gol·pa·zo m./da f. heavy or hard blow.
gol·pe m. blow, hit <el policía le dio un g. the policeman dealt him a blow>; (sacudida) bump; (latido) heartbeat; (explosión) gust, blast; (multitud) crowd, throng; (desgracia) blow, shock; (pestillo) spring lock; (sorpresa) surprise; (gracia) wit, wittiness; SEW. pocket flap ♦ **a golpes** in fits and starts, sporadically • **al g.** AMER. instantly • **de g.** suddenly • **de g. y porrazo** hastily, hurriedly • **de un g.** at one fell swoop • **g. de estado** coup d'état • **g. de fortuna** or **de suerte** stroke of luck • **g. de gracia** coup de grâce, death blow • **g. de mano** coup de main, sudden attack • **g. de vista** glance, look • **g. en vano** miss • **no dar g.** not to do a lick of work.
gol·pe·a·du·ra f./pe·o m. beating.
gol·pe·ar tr. & intr. to beat, strike.
gol·pe·te·ar tr. to pound, pummel.
gol·pi·za f. ECUAD., MEX. beating, thrashing.
go·lle·te m. (cuello) throat, neck; (de una botella) bottleneck.
go·ma f. (savia) gum; (caucho) rubber; (pegamento) glue; (elástico) rubber band ♦ **g. arábiga** gum arabic • **g. de borrar** eraser • **g. de mascar** chewing gum • **g. laca** shellac.
go·mal m. AMER. rubber plantation.
go·me·ro, a I. adj. rubber, gum II. m. AMER. rubber tree; (productor) rubber planter; (obrero) rubber-plantation worker.
go·mi·na f. hair cream or dressing.
go·mo·si·dad f. gumminess, adhesiveness.
go·mo·so, a I. adj. gummy; C. AMER. hungover II. m. fop, dandy.
gó·na·da f. gonad.
gon·do·la f. gondola.
gon·do·le·ro m. gondolier.
gong or **gon·go** m. gong.
go·no·co·co m. gonococcus.
go·no·rre·a f. gonorrhea.
gor·di(n)·flón, o·na COLL. I. adj. chubby, tubby II. m.f. fatty, tub.
gor·do, a I. adj. (obeso) fat, plump; (abultado) big; (graso) fatty, greasy; (grueso) thick coarse; water <agua g. hard water>; (importante) important II. m.f. fat person —m. (sebo) fat, suet; (premio) first prize.
gor·du·ra f. (grasa) fat, grease; (corpulencia) obesity, fatness.
gor·go·jo m. (insecto) weevil; (persona) midget.
gor·go·ri·tos m.pl. COLL. trills.
gor·go·te·ar intr. to gurgle, burble.
gor·go·te·o m. gurgling, gurgle.
go·ri·la m. gorilla.
gor·jal m. priest's collar.
gor·je·a·dor, ·ra/je·an·te adj. warbling.
gor·je·ar intr. to warble, trill —reflex. COLL. to gurgle.
gor·je·o m. (quiebro) warble, trill; (habla de niños) gurgling.
go·rra f. (sombrero) cap; (de bebé) (baby) bonnet ♦ **pasar la g.** to pass the hat —m. sponger, freeloader ♦ **andar** or **vivir de g.** COLL. to sponge, freeload • **de g.** COLL. at another's expense.
go·rre·ar intr. AMER. to freeload.
go·rrín m. piglet, suckling pig.
go·rri·ne·ra f. pigpen, pigsty.
go·rri·ne·rí·a f. (porquería) filth, dirtiness; COLL. (acción grosera) dirty trick.
go·rri·no, a I. m.f. ZOOL. piglet, suckling pig; FIG. pig, slovenly person II. adj. filthy.
go·rrión m. ORNITH. sparrow; AMER. hummingbird.
go·rro m. (sombrero) cap; (de niños) bonnet.
go·rrón, o·na I. adj. sponging, freeloading; AMER. (egoísta) selfish, greedy II. m.f. sponger, freeloader.
go·rro·ne·ar intr. to sponge, freeload.
go·rro·ne·rí·a f. (acción) sponging, freeloading; AMER. (avaricia) selfishness, greediness.
go·ta f. drop; MED. gout; ARCHIT. gutta ♦ **g. a g.** bit by bit, little by little • **sudar la g. gorda** COLL. to sweat blood.
go·te·ar intr. to drip, trickle.

go·te·o m. dripping, trickling.
go·te·ra f. (*gotas de agua*) leak; (*señal de agua*) water mark; (*cenefa*) valance ♦ pl. aches and pains; AMER. outskirts, environs.
go·te·ro m. AMER. eyedropper.
go·te·rón m. large raindrops.
gó·ti·co, a adj. & m.f. Gothic.
go·zar §04 tr. (*poseer*) to have, enjoy —intr. (*disfrutar*) to enjoy, take pleasure in —reflex. to rejoice.
goz·ne m. hinge.
go·zo m. joy, pleasure.
go·zo·so, a adj. joyful.
gra·ba·ción f. recording ♦ g. en cinta tape recording.
gra·ba·do m. (*arte, obra*) engraving; (*ilustración*) print, illustration ♦ g. al agua fuerte etching • g. en madera woodcut.
gra·ba·dor, ·ra m.f. engraver —f. tape recorder.
gra·bar tr. ARTS to engrave; (*registrar sonidos*) to record, tape; (*fijar*) to engrave, imprint.
gra·ce·jo m. wit, humor.
gra·cia f. (*donaire*) charm, grace; (*beneficio*) favor, kindness; (*perdón*) pardon; (*buen trato*) good graces; RELIG. grace; (*agudeza*) witty remark, joke ♦ caer en g. de la g. to fall out of favor • caer en g. to please, find favor • de g. free, gratis • en g. a for the sake of or benefit of • hacer g. (*agradar*) to please; (*divertir*) to amuse, strike as funny • tener g. to be funny ♦ pl. thank you, thanks • dar g. to give thanks • g. a thanks to, owing to • g. a Dios thank God.
gra·cia·ble adj. (*afable*) affable, good-natured; (*fácil de conceder*) easily granted.
grá·cil adj. slender, thin.
gra·cio·sa·men·te adv. (*con gracia*) gracefully; (*de balde*) gratuitously, free.
gra·cio·so, a I. adj. (*encantador*) charming, graceful; (*divertido*) amusing, funny; (*gratuito*) free, gratis II. m.f. graciozo, clown; THEAT. fool.
gra·da f. (*peldaño*) step, stair; (*asientos*) tier ♦ pl. AMER. atrium.
gra·da·ción f. gradation.
gra·da·do, a adj. stepped, with steps.
gra·de·rí·a f./o m. (*gradas*) tiers, rows (of seats); (*escalera*) (flight of) steps.
gra·do m. (*calidad*) grade, quality; (*nivel*) degree; (*fase*) stage, step; (*peldaño*) step, stair; (*título académico*) degree, academic title; (*clase*) class, grade; MIL. rank ♦ de buen, mal g. willingly, unwillingly • de g. en g. by degrees, gradually • en alto g. to a high degree • en sumo g. to the highest degree.
gra·dua·ción f. graduation; (*proporción de alcohol*) alcoholic strength; MIL. rank, grade.
gra·dua·do, a I. adj. graduated II. m.f. graduate.
gra·dual adj. gradual.
gra·dual·men·te adv. gradually, by degrees.
gra·duar §67 tr. (*evaluar*) to gauge; (*dividir en grados*) to graduate; EDUC. to graduate, confer a degree on —reflex. to graduate.
grá·fi·co, a I. adj. graphic II. m.f. graph, chart.
gra·fi·to m. graphite.
gra·fo·lo·gí·a f. graphology.
gra·ge·a f. (*confite*) Jordan almond; (*píldora*) sugar-coated pill.
gra·jo m. rook, crow; AMER. body odor.

gra·ma·ti·cal adj. grammatical.
gra·má·ti·co, a I. adj. grammatical II. m.f. grammarian —f. grammar.
gra·mo m. gram, gramme (G.B.).
gra·mó·fo·no m. gramophone, phonograph.
gran adj. contr. of grande.
gra·na f. (*acción*) seeding; (*época*) seeding time; (*semilla*) seed; (*insecto*) cochineal; (*color*) scarlet ♦ dar g. to go to seed.
gra·na·da f. see granado, a.
gra·na·de·ro m. grenadier.
gra·na·di·lla f. (*planta y flor*) passionflower; (*fruto*) passion fruit.
gra·na·di·no, a m. pomegranate flower f. (*jarabe*) grenadine; TEX. grenadine.
gra·na·do, a I. adj. (*notable*) distinguished, notable; (*experto*) expert ♦ lo más g. de the cream or pick of II. m. pomegranate (tree) —f. BOT. pomegranate (fruit); MIL. grenade; ARTIL. shell ♦ g. de mano hand grenade • g. de mortero mortar shell.
gra·nar intr. to go to seed.
gra·na·te adj. & m. garnet.
gran·de I. adj. (*enorme*) large, big; (*considerable*) great; (*grandioso*) grand, impressive; (*eminente*) great, eminent ♦ en g. on a grand scale II. m. Spanish grandee.
gran·de·men·te adv. (*muy bien*) grandly, very well; (*en extremo*) extremely, greatly.
gran·de·za f. (*tamaño*) size; (*magnitud*) bigness, largeness; (*nobleza*) greatness, grandeur; (*dignidad*) grandeeship.
gran·di·lo·cuen·cia f. grandiloquence.
gran·di·lo·cuen·te, ·no adj. grandiloquent.
gran·dio·si·dad f. grandeur, magnificence.
gran·dio·so, a adj. grand, magnificent.
gran·dor m. size, magnitude.
gran·do·te, a adj. COLL. very big, huge.
gra·ne·a·do, a adj. (*granulado*) granulated, ground; (*punteado*) stippled; MIL. heavy, continuous <*fuego g.* heavy fire>.
gra·nel m. ♦ a g. (*sin envase*) in bulk, loose; (*abundantemente*) in abundance.
gra·ne·ro m. granary.
gra·ní·ti·co, a adj. granitic, granite.
gra·ni·to m. granite; MED. small pimple.
gra·ni·za·da f. (*copia de granizo*) hailstorm; (*multitud*) shower, torrent.
gra·ni·za·do m. iced drink.
gra·ni·zar §04 intr. to hail; FIG. to rain, shower.
gra·ni·zo m. hail; FIG. hail, torrent.
gran·ja f. (*hacienda*) farm, grange; (*quinta*) country house; (*lechería*) dairy.
gran·je·ar tr. (*conquistar*) to win over, capture —reflex. to gain, win.
gran·je·ro, a m.f. farmer.
gra·no m. (*semilla*) grain, seed; (*fruto*) grain, cereal; (*partícula*) grain, particle; MED. pimple; (*medida de peso*) grain; (*de la piel*) grain ♦ ir al g. COLL. to get down to brass tacks.
gra·no·so, a adj. granular, grainy.
gra·nu·ja f. loose grapes —m. COLL. ragamuffin, street urchin.
gra·nu·ja·da f. rascality, deviltry.
gra·nu·lar adj. granular, grainy; (*granujiento*) pimply.
grá·nu·lo m. (*grano*) small grain, granule; (*pildorilla*) small pill.
gra·pa f. (*para los papeles*) staple; (*para la madera*) clip, clamp.
gra·sien·to, a adj. greasy.

gra·so, a I. adj. fatty, greasy II. m. fattiness, greasiness —f. *(sebo)* fat, grease; *(suciedad)* grease, grime; *(grasilla)* pounce ♦ **g. de ballena** blubber ♦ pl. METAL. slag.

gra·so·so, a adj. greasy, oily.

gra·ta·men·te adv. *(de manera grata)* pleasingly; *(con agrado)* with pleasure; AMER. gratefully.

gra·ti·fi·ca·ción f. *(recompensa)* reward, recompense; *(propina)* tip, gratuity; S. AMER. gratification.

gra·ti·fi·car §70 tr. *(recompensar)* to reward; *(dar una propina)* to tip; *(satisfacer)* to gratify.

gra·tis adv. gratis, free.

gra·ti·tud f. gratitude.

gra·to, a adj. *(placentero)* pleasing; *(gratis)* free, gratis; AMER. grateful.

gra·tui·to, a adj. *(gratis)* free (of charge); *(arbitrario)* gratuitous.

gra·va f. gravel.

gra·va·men m. *(carga)* burden, obligation; *(impuesto)* tax; LAW encumbrance.

gra·var tr. *(cargar)* to burden, encumber; *(exigir un impuesto)* to levy, impose.

gra·ve adj. *(serio)* grave, serious; *(importante)* important; *(bajo)* deep, low; *(pesado)* weighty, heavy.

gra·ve·dad f. *(seriedad)* gravity, seriousness; *(importancia)* importance; PHYS. gravity; *(peso)* weight.

gra·ve·men·te adv. *(con formalidad)* seriously; *(de manera grave)* gravely.

grá·vi·do, a adj. pregnant.

gra·vi·ta·ción f. gravitation.

gra·vi·tar intr. to gravitate ♦ **g. sobre** to be a burden to, weigh on.

gra·vi·ta·to·rio, a/cio·nal adj. gravitational.

gra·vo·so, a adj. *(oneroso)* onerous, burdensome; *(costoso)* costly, expensive.

graz·nar intr. *(chillar)* to squawk; *(cacarear)* to quack; *(el cuervo)* to caw.

graz·ni·do m. *(chillido)* squawk; *(del cuervo)* caw; *(del pato)* quack; *(del ganso)* cackle.

gre·dal I. adj. clayey II. m. clay pit.

gre·ga·rio, a adj. gregarious; *(servil)* servile, slavish.

gre·mial I. adj. union, trade-union; HIST. guild II. m. union member; HIST. guildsman.

gre·mio m. *(sindicato)* union, trade union; *(asociación)* association, society; HIST. guild.

gre·ña f. *(cabellera)* shock or mop of hair; *(maraña)* entanglement ♦ **andar a la g.** COLL. to quarrel, squabble

gre·ñu·do, a adj. disheveled, unkempt.

gres·ca f. *(jaleo)* uproar, hubbub; *(riña)* quarrel, row.

grey f. *(rebaño)* flock, herd; *(raza)* people, nation; *(fieles)* congregation, flock.

grial m. Grail.

grie·ta f. crack, crevice; MED. chap.

grie·tar·se/te·ar·se reflex. *(agrietarse)* to crack; MED. to get chapped.

gri·fo, a I. adj. *(crespo)* curly, kinky; PRINT. italic; AMER. *(intoxicado por la marijuana)* stoned, high II. m. *(caño)* tap, spigot; MYTH. griffin, griffon —f. COLL. marijuana.

gri·fón m. *(grifo)* large faucet or spigot; *(perro)* griffon.

gri·lla f. female cricket; S. AMER. annoyance, bother.

gri·lle·te m. fetter, shackle.

gri·llo m. cricket; FIG. *(obstáculo)* obstacle,

hindrance ♦ pl. fetters, shackles.

gri·ma f. annoyance, disgust ♦ **dar g.** to grate on someone's nerves, annoy.

grin·go, a I. adj. *(extranjero)* foreign; *(norteamericano)* Yankee; S. AMER. blond, fair II. m.f. *(extranjero)* foreigner; *(norteamericano)* Yankee; S. AMER. blond, fair-haired person —m. COLL. gibberish.

gri·pe f. grippe, flu.

gris I. adj. *(color)* gray; *(triste)* dull, gloomy II. m. gray ♦ **hacer g.** COLL. to be brisk.

gri·sá·ce·o, a adj. grayish.

gri·se·o, a adj. gray.

gri·ta f. outcry, shouting ♦ **dar g. a** COLL. to boo at, hoot at.

gri·tar intr. *(dar gritos)* to shout, scream; *(abuchear)* to jeer, boo —tr. to jeer at, boo.

gri·te·rí·a f./o m. din, uproar.

gri·to m. *(alarido)* shout, scream; *(clamor)* outcry, clamor; ZOOL. cry, call ♦ **dar gritos** to shout, scream • **el último g.** the latest craze • **poner el g. en el cielo** COLL. to raise the roof.

gro·se·ra·men·te adv. COLL. noisy, loud-mouthed.

gro·se·lla f. currant ♦ **g. silvestre** gooseberry.

gro·se·ra·men·te adv. *(con descortesía)* rudely; *(con ignorancia)* crudely, stupidly; *(con indecencia)* coarsely, indelicately.

gro·se·rí·a f. *(tosquedad)* coarseness, roughness; *(rusticidad)* ignorance, stupidity; *(indecencia)* vulgarity; *(descortesía)* rudeness.

gro·se·ro, a I. adj. *(basto)* coarse, crude; *(descortés)* rude; *(rústico)* rustic, unpolished; *(craso)* gross II. m. boor.

gro·sor m. thickness.

gros·so mo·do adv. roughly, approximately.

gro·tes·co, a adj. grotesque.

grú·a f. *(máquina)* crane, derrick; *(camión de auxilio)* wrecker, tow truck.

grue·so, a I. adj. *(corpulento)* stout, fat; *(grande)* big, bulky; *(en grano)* coarse; *(de grosor)* thick II. m. *(espesor)* thickness; *(parte principal)* bulk ♦ **en g.** COM. in bulk, gross —f. gross (twelve dozen).

gru·lla f. ORNITH. crane.

gru·me·te m. cabin boy.

gru·mo m. *(de líquido)* lump; *(de sangre)* clot; *(de leche)* curd; *(de uvas)* bunch, cluster.

gru·mo·so, a adj. *(de líquido)* lumpy; *(de sangre)* clotty; *(de leche)* curdy; *(de uvas)* clustered.

gru·ñi·do m. *(de un cerdo)* grunt; *(de un perro)* growl; *(de una persona)* grumble, grunt.

gru·ñir §12 intr. *(un cerdo)* to grunt; *(un perro)* to growl; *(refunfuñar)* to grumble; *(chirriar)* to creak.

gru·ñón, o·na COLL. I. adj. grouchy, grumpy II. m.f. grouch, grump.

gru·pa f. rump (of a horse).

gru·po m. group.

gru·ta f. grotto, cavern.

gua·ba f. guava.

gua·ca f. AMER. *(sepultura)* Indian tomb; *(tesoro)* hidden treasure; *(hucha)* money box.

gua·ca·mol/mo·le m. C. AMER., MÉX. guacamole.

gua·co I. m. BOT. guaco; ORNITH. currasow II. adj. AMER. harelipped.

gua·cho, a I. adj. S. AMER. orphaned; CHILE, PERU *(desparejo)* unmatched, odd (sock) II. m. *(pollo)* chick, baby bird; S. AMER. orphan, foundling.

gua·da·ña f. scythe.

gua·da·ñar tr. to scythe, mow.

gua·gua f. *(cosa baladí)* trifle, triviality; S. AMER. *(nene)* baby, infant; CARIB. *(autobús)* bus ♦ **de g.** free, gratis.

gua·ji·ro, a I. adj. AMER. rustic, boorish II. m.f. peasant.

qual·dra·pa f. *(cobertura)* caparison, horse trappings; COLL. *(guiñapo)* tatter, rag.

gua·no m. guano, fertilizer; CUBA palm tree; AMER. money, cash.

guan·te m. glove ♦ **arrojar el g.** to throw down the gauntlet • **echar el g.** COLL. to grab, nab • **echar un g.** COLL. to pass the hat • **recoger el g.** to accept a challenge ♦ pl. tip.

guan·te·ar tr. AMER. to slap.

guan·te·le·te m. gauntlet.

guan·te·ro, a m.f. glover, glove maker —m. glove compartment.

gua·pe·ar intr. COLL. *(ser valiente)* to bluster; *(vestirse)* to show off; AMER. *(fanfarronear)* to brag, boast.

gua·pe·tón, o·na adj. COLL. *(lindo)* very attractive; *(animoso)* brave, bold; *(ostentoso)* flashy.

gua·pe·za f. COLL. *(bizarría)* boldness, daring; *(ostentación)* flashiness.

gua·po, a I. adj. COLL. *(lindo)* good-looking, attractive; *(ostentoso)* flashy; COLL. *(animoso)* brave, daring II. m. *(pendenciero)* bully; COLL. *(galán)* ladies' man.

gua·que·ro, a m.f. AMER. hunter of buried treasure.

gua·ra·cha f. CUBA, P. RICO *(diversión)* merrymaking, revelry; AMER. *(bulla)* noise, hubbub.

gua·ra·che m. MEX. huarache, sandal.

gua·ran·go, a adj. R.P. boorish, ill-mannered; S. AMER. dirty, filthy.

gua·ran·gue·ar intr. R.P. to behave boorishly.

gua·ra·ní m. PAR., FIN. guaraní.

gua·ra·pón m. AMER. broad-brimmed hat.

guar·da m.f. guard, custodian —f. *(tutela)* custody, guardianship; *(cumplimiento)* observance; *(de la llave)* ward; *(hoja de papel)* endpaper, flyleaf —m. ARG. bus driver.

guar·da·ba·rre·ra m.f. gatekeeper.

guar·da·ba·rros m.pl. fender, mudguard.

guar·da·bos·que m. forest ranger, forester.

guar·da·bri·sa m. windshield.

guar·da·ca·de·na m. bicycle chain guard.

guar·da·cos·tas m.inv. coast guard cutter.

guar·da·es·pal·das m.inv. bodyguard.

guar·da·fan·go m. AMER. var. of **guardabarros**.

guar·da·fre·nos m.inv. brakeman.

guar·da·gu·jas m.inv. switchman.

guar·da·me·ta m. goalkeeper, goalie.

guar·da·mon·te m. ARM. trigger guard; *(capote)* riding cape or cloak.

guar·da·pol·vo m. *(cubierta)* dust cover; *(vestido)* duster.

guar·da·pun·tas m.inv. pencil cap.

guar·dar tr. *(vigilar)* to guard, watch over; *(proteger)* to protect; *(animales)* to keep, tend; *(cumplir)* to keep; *(conservar)* to save, put away ♦ **g. cama** to be confined to bed • **g. silencio** to keep quiet —intr. ♦ **¡guarda!** COLL. watch out!, look out! —reflex. *(reservarse)* to keep; *(protegerse)* to be on one's guard ♦ **g. de** to guard against.

guar·da·rro·pa m. *(cuarto)* cloakroom, checkroom; *(ropas)* wardrobe —m.f. cloakroom attendant.

guar·de·rí·a f. *(empleo)* guardship; *(local)* daycare center, nursery.

guar·dia f. *(tropas)* guard; *(defensa)* defense, protection ♦ **en g.** on guard • **g. municipal** city police force —m. *(centinela)* guard, guardsman; *(policía)* policeman.

guar·dián, a·na m.f. guardian, custodian; *(vigilante)* watchman.

guar·di·lla f. attic, garret.

gua·re·cer §17 tr. to shelter, protect —reflex. to hide, take refuge.

gua·ri·da f. *(de animales)* lair, den; *(refugio)* shelter, refuge; *(querencia)* haunt, hangout; *(conuite)* hideout.

gua·ris·mo m. number, figure.

guar·ne·cer §17 tr. *(adornar)* to trim, border; *(proveer)* to supply, provide; JEWEL. to set; MIL. to garrison; MAS. to plaster; CUL. to garnish.

guar·ni·ción f. *(adorno)* trim, border; JEWEL. setting; MIL. garrison; CUL. garnish.

gua·sa·da f. ARG. vulgarism, coarse word.

guas·ca f. CHILE, PERU whip.

guas·ca·zo m. AMER. lash.

gua·se·ri·a f. ARG., CHILE coarseness.

gua·so, a I. m.f. AMER. farmer, peasant —f. COLL. *(pesadez)* slowness, dullness; *(burla)* joke, jest II. adj. AMER. crude, coarse.

guau m. bow wow.

gua·ya·ba f. BOT. guava; *(jalea)* guava jelly.

gua·ya·be·ro, a AMER. I. adj. lying II. m.f. liar —f. lightweight shirt.

gua·ya·bo m. guava.

gu·ber·na·men·tal adj. governmental.

gu·ber·na·ti·vo, a adj. governmental.

gue·rra f. *(combate)* war; *(ciencia)* warfare ♦ **dar g.** COLL. to give no peace to • **hacer la g.** to wage war • **Primera, Segunda Guerra Mundial** First, Second World War.

gue·rre·a·dor, ·ra I. adj. warring, fighting II. m.f. warrior, fighter.

gue·rre·ar intr. *(luchar)* to war, fight; *(resistir)* to oppose, resist.

gue·rre·ro, a I. adj. *(que guerrea)* warring, fighting; *(travieso)* mischievous II. m. warrior, fighter —f. MIL. tunic.

gue·rri·lla f. MIL. guerrilla warfare; *(partida)* band of guerrillas.

gue·rri·lle·ar intr. to wage guerrilla warfare.

gue·rri·lle·ro m. guerrilla.

gui·a m.f. guide; *(consejero)* adviser; *(director)* director, leader —f. *(faro)* guide; *(poste)* guidepost; *(libro)* guide, directory; *(manillas)* handlebars; BOT. leader, guide shoot; MECH. guide ♦ pl. reins.

gui·ar §30 tr. to guide, lead; *(conducir)* to drive.

gui·ja·rro m. pebble.

gui·llo·ti·na f. guillotine.

gui·llo·ti·nar tr. to guillotine.

guin·che *or* **güin·che** m. AMER. winch, hoist.

guin·da f. sour cherry.

guin·dar tr. *(colgar)* to hang high, hoist; *(obtener)* to get, land; *(ahorcar)* to hang.

guin·di·lla f. red pepper.

gui·ña·da f. wink.

gui·ñar tr. to wink.

gui·ño m. wink ♦ **hacer guiños** to wink.

guión m. *(bandera)* banner, standard; CINEM., THEAT. script; GRAM. hyphen.

guio·nis·ta m.f. scriptwriter.

guir·nal·da f. garland, wreath.

güi·ro m. AMER. gourd, calabash.

gui·sa f. manner, way ♦ **a g. de** as, like.
gui·sa·do m. stew.
gui·san·te m. pea.
gui·sar tr. (*cocinar*) to cook; (*estofar*) to stew; (*arreglar*) to arrange.
gui·so m. (*estofado*) stew; (*plato*) cooked dish.
gui·ta f. (*cuerda*) twine; SL. (*dinero*) bucks.
gui·ta·rra f. guitar.
gui·ta·rre·ar intr. to play the guitar.
gui·ta·rris·ta m.f. guitarist, guitar player.
gui·ta·rrón m. large guitar; (*pícaro*) sly rascal, scoundrel.
gu·la f. gluttony.
gul·den m. FIN. gulden, guilder.
gu·rí, i·sa m.f. ARG. Indian child.
gu·rru·mi·no, a I. adj. sickly, puny II. m. henpecked husband —f. COLL. uxoriousness.
gu·sa·ne·ar intr. to swarm, teem.
gu·sa·ni·llo m. ZOOL. small worm.
gu·sa·no m. worm; ENTOM. caterpillar.
gus·tar tr. (*probar*) to taste, sample; (*experimentar*) to test, try —intr. to like; (*agradar*) to please, be pleasing (to).
gus·ta·zo m. COLL. great pleasure or delight.
gus·ti·llo m. aftertaste.
gus·to m. taste; (*sabor*) flavor; (*placer*) pleasure; (*capricho*) whim, fancy ♦ **a g.** comfortable; (*a voluntad*) at will; CUL. to taste • **con mucho g.** with pleasure • **dar g. a** to please, gratify • **tener el g. de** to have the pleasure of • **tomar g. a** to take a liking to.
gus·to·sa·men·te adv. with pleasure
gus·to·so, a adj. (*sabroso*) tasty, savory; (*con placer*) pleased, glad; (*agradable*) pleasant, agreeable.

H

h, H f. ninth letter of the Spanish alphabet.
ha, has, han see haber[2].
ha·ba f. (*planta*) fava bean; (*fruto, semilla*) bean ♦ pl. **en todas partes se cuecen h.** COLL. it's the same all over the world.
ha·ber[1] m. COM. credit ♦ **tener uno en su h.** to have to one's credit ♦ pl. assets, property.
ha·ber[2] §39 aux. to have ♦ **h. de** to have to, must —impers. ♦ **hay ago** ago; **habidos y por h.** past, present and future • **hay** there is, there are • **hay que** it is necessary • **no hay de qué** don't mention it, you're welcome • **¿qué hay?** what's up?, what's happening? • **¿qué hay de nuevo?** what's new? • **todo lo habido y por h.** everything imaginable —tr. (*poseer*) to have; (*alcanzar*) to get one's hands on; (*capturar*) to catch —reflex. ♦ **habérselas con alguien** to have it out with someone.
há·bil adj. (*capaz*) capable; (*diestro*) skillful.
ha·bi·li·dad f. (*capacidad*) capability; (*ingeniosidad*) skill.
ha·bi·li·tar tr. (*permitir*) to enable; (*preparar*) to equip; COM. to finance.
ha·bi·ta·ble adj. inhabitable.
ha·bi·ta·ción f. (*cuarto*) room; (*domicilio*) dwelling; (*aposento*) room; BOT., ZOOL. habitat.
ha·bi·tan·te m.f. inhabitant.
ha·bi·tar tr. to inhabit, live in.
há·bi·to m. (*costumbre*) habit; RELIG. habit ♦ **colgar el h.** RELIG. to give up the cloth • **tomar el h.** RELIG. (*monjas*) to take the veil; (*sacerdotes*) to take holy orders ♦ pl. RELIG. vestments.

ha·bi·tual adj. habitual.
ha·bi·tuar §67 tr. to habituate —reflex. to become accustomed (to).
ha·bla f. (*facultad*) speech; (*idioma*) language ♦ **al h.** in contact • **perder el h.** or **quedarse sin h.** to be speechless • **quitar el h. a** to stop speaking to.
ha·bla·do, a I. adj. spoken II. f. MEX. gossip ♦ **bien h.** well-spoken • **cine h.** talking pictures • **mal h.** foul-mouthed.
ha·bla·dor, ·ra I. adj. (*que habla mucho*) talkative; (*chismoso*) gossipy II. m.f. (*charlatán*) chatterbox; (*chismoso*) gossip; MEX. boaster.
ha·bla·du·rí·a f. (*charla*) chatter; (*rumor*) rumor; (*chisme*) gossip.
ha·blan·chín, ina COLL. I. adj. (*parlanchín*) talkative; (*chismoso*) gossip II. m.f. (*charlatán*) chatterbox; (*chismoso*) gossip.
ha·blar intr. to speak, talk ♦ **h. alto** to speak loudly • **h. a tontas y a locas** to talk through one's hat • **h. bajo** to speak softly • **h. bien de** to speak well of • **h. claro** to speak frankly • **h. como un loro** to chatter • **h. de** to talk about • **h. en plata** to speak clearly • **h. entre dientes** to mumble • **h. mal de** to speak ill of • **h. por** to speak for • **h. por h.** to talk for talking's sake • **h. por los codos** to talk a blue streak • **¡eso es h.!** COLL. now you're talking! • **eso es puro h.** COLL. that's baloney! • **¡ni h.!** out of the question! —tr. to speak; (*decir*) to talk; (*dar a entender*) to speak of ♦ **hablarlo todo** to tell all —reflex. to speak to one another.
ha·brá, bría see haber[2].
ha·cer §40 tr. to make; (*efectuar*) to do; (*formar*) to form; (*componer*) to compose; (*causar*) to cause; (*obligar*) to force; (*representar*) to play the part of; (*igualar*) to equal; (*suponer*) to assume to be ♦ **h. agua** MARIT. to leak • **h. alarde** to boast • **h. cara** or **frente a** to face • **h. caso de** or **a** to pay attention to • **h. cola** to stand in line • **h. conocer** to make known • **h. daño** to hurt • **h. estimación** to estimate • **h. falta** (*faltar*) to be needed; (*echar de menos*) to be missed • **h. fe** to testify • **h. juego** to match • **h. la barba** to shave • **h. la guerra** to wage war • **h. mofa de** to mock • **h. pedazos** to smash • **h. presente** to notify • **h. recados** to run errands • **h. saber** to let know • **h. sombra** to cast a shadow • **h. un milagro** to work a miracle • **h. una apuesta** to place a bet • **h. una maleta** to pack a suitcase • **h. una pregunta** to ask a question • **h. una visita** to pay a visit • **h. una de las suyas** to be up to one's old tricks —intr. to matter, be relevant • **h. de** to serve as —impers. ♦ **desde hace** for • **hace frío** it is cold • **hace mucho** long ago • **hace poco** a little while ago • **hace tanto tiempo** so long ago —reflex. (*volverse*) to grow, become; (*convertirse*) to turn into; (*aumentarse*) to grow; (*proveerse*) to provide oneself; (*acostumbrarse*) to get used to • **h. atrás** to move back • **h. a un lado** to step aside • **h. con** to make off with • **h. la vida** to earn one's living • **hacérsele a uno** to strike, seem.
ha·cia prep. toward; (*alrededor de*) about, around ♦ **h. abajo** downward • **h. acá** here, this way • **h. adelante** forward • **h. arriba** upward • **h. atrás** backward.
ha·cien·da f. (*finca*) ranch; (*fortuna*) fortune; AMER. livestock.
ha·ci·na f. stack, pile.
ha·ci·nar tr. to stack, pile.

ha·cha f. *(herramienta)* ax, axe; *(del toro)* bull's horn ♦ **de h. y tiza** tough ♦ **h. de armas** battle-ax • **ser un h.** to be an ace.

ha·che f. ♦ **llámele h.** call it what you like (it's all the same).

ha·che·ro m. lumberjack.

ha·chís m. hashish.

ha·chón m. *(tea)* large torch; *(brasero)* cresset.

ha·da f. fairy ♦ **cuento de hadas** fairy tale.

ha·do m. destiny, fate.

ha·ga, go see **hacer**.

ha·la·gar §47 tr. *(lisonjear)* to flatter; *(mostrar afecto)* to show affection for; *(agradar)* to please; *(adular)* to cajole.

ha·la·go m. *(lisonja)* flattery; *(adulación)* cajolery.

ha·la·güe·ño, a adj. *(lisonjero)* flattering; *(alentador)* promising; *(agradable)* pleasing; *(atractivo)* attractive.

ha·lar tr. *(tirar)* to pull toward oneself; MARIT. to tow —intr. MARIT. to pull.

hal·cón m. falcon, hawk.

hal·co·ne·rí·a f. falconry, hawking.

hal·co·ne·ro m. falconer, hawker.

hal·da f. *(falda)* skirt; *(harpillera)* burlap.

há·li·to m. *(aliento)* breath; *(vapor)* vapor; POET. *(viento suave)* gentle breeze.

ha·llar tr. *(por casualidad)* to come across; *(encontrar)* to find; *(averiguar)* to find out; *(notar)* to note; *(descubrir)* to discover —reflex. *(encontrarse)* to be, find oneself; *(estar)* to be ♦ **h. uno en todo** to have one's hand in everything • **no h.** to feel out of place.

ha·llaz·go m. *(acción)* discovery; *(objeto)* good find.

ha·ma·ca f. *(cama)* hammock; *(vehículo)* palanquin; AMER. swing.

ham·bre f. hunger; *(de una nación)* famine; *(deseo)* longing ♦ **h. canina** ravenous hunger • **matar el h.** to stave off hunger • **morir** *or* **morirse de h.** to be starving • **tener h.** to be hungry.

ham·brien·to, a I. adj. *(famélico)* starved; *(con hambre)* hungry; *(deseoso)* longing II. m.f. starving *or* hungry person.

ham·bur·gue·sa f. hamburger.

ha·mo m. fishhook.

ham·pa f. underworld.

ham·pón I. adj. tough II. m. thug.

ha·rá, ría see **hacer**.

ha·ra·gán, a·na I. adj. lazy, idle II. m.f. loafer.

ha·ra·ga·ne·ar intr. to be idle, loaf.

ha·ra·pien·to, a adj. tattered.

ha·ra·po m. *(andrajo)* tatter; *(aguardiente)* weak *or* inferior alcohol, rotgut.

ha·ra·po·so, a adj. tattered.

ha·rén m. harem.

ha·ri·na f. *(trigo molido)* flour; *(cereal molido)* meal; *(polvo)* powder ♦ **h. de hueso** bone meal • **ser h. de otro costal** COLL. to be a horse of a different color.

ha·ri·ne·ro, a I. adj. flour II. m. *(persona)* flour dealer; *(receptáculo)* flour bin.

ha·ri·no·so, a adj. *(que tiene harina)* floury; *(farináceo)* farinaceous.

har·ne·ro m. sieve.

har·pi·lle·ra f. burlap.

har·tar tr. *(saciar el apetito)* to stuff; *(satisfacer)* to satisfy; *(fastidiar)* to annoy; *(aburrir)* to bore; *(cansar)* to tire.

har·taz·go m. fill ♦ **darse un h. de** *(comer mucho)* to eat one's fill of, FIG. to have had one's

fill of.

har·to, a I. adj. *(saciado)* satiated; *(cansado)* fed up II. adj. *(bastante)* enough; *(muy)* very.

har·tu·ra f. *(hartazgo)* bellyful, fill; POET. *(abundancia)* wealth; *(logro)* fulfillment.

has·ta I. prep. until; up to, as far as ♦ **h. la vista** *or* **h. luego** see you, so long • **h. mañana** see you tomorrow • **h. que** until II. adv. even.

has·tiar §30 tr. *(cansar)* to tire; *(asquear)* to sicken; *(fastidiar)* to annoy.

has·tí·o m. *(repugnancia)* repugnance; *(fastidio)* annoyance; *(tedio)* boredom.

ha·to[1] m. *(de ganado)* herd; *(cabaña)* pastor's hut; *(banda)* gang; *(montón)* bunch.

ha·to[2] m. everyday clothes, belongings ♦ **liar uno el h.** COLL. to pack one's things.

hay, haya see **haber[2]**.

haz[1] m. *(fardo)* bundle; *(de leña)* fagot; PHYS. pencil *(of light rays)* ♦ **pl. haces de rectas** MATH. pencil of lines.

haz[2] f. *(cara)* countenance; *(de tela)* right side.

haz[3] see **hacer**.

ha·za f. plot of arable land.

ha·za·ña f. feat, exploit.

ha·za·ño·so, a adj. *(heroico)* heroic; *(valiente)* gallant.

haz·me·rre·ír m. COLL. laughingstock.

he[1] adv. lo, behold ♦ **h. allí** there is *or* are • **h. aquí** here is *or* are • **helo aquí** here it is.

he[2] see **haber[2]**.

he·bi·lla f. buckle, clasp.

he·bra f. *(hilo)* thread; *(fibra)* fiber; *(filamento)* filament; *(veta)* grain; FIG. thread ♦ **de una h.** CHILE all at once, in one breath • **pegar la h.** to strike up a conversation.

he·chi·ce·rí·a f. *(brujería)* witchcraft; *(hechizo)* spell.

he·chi·ce·ro, a I. adj. bewitching II. m. *(brujo)* sorcerer; *(encantador)* charmer —f. *(bruja)* sorceress; *(encantadora)* charmer.

he·chi·zar §04 tr. *(encantar)* to bewitch; *(cautivar)* to charm.

he·chi·zo m. *(sortilegio)* spell; *(encanto)* charm; *(persona)* charmer.

he·cho, a I. see **hacer** II. adj. *(perfecto)* complete; *(terminado)* finished; *(acostumbrado)* used to; *(proporcionado)* proportioned; *(maduro)* mature; *(semejante a)* like; *(cocido)* done; *(ropa)* ready-made ♦ **h. y derecho** in every respect III. m. *(acto)* act, action, *(hazaña)* deed; *(suceso)* event; *(realidad)* fact; *(asunto)* point ♦ **a lo h., pecho** let's waste the rest of it now • **de h.** *(en realidad)* as a matter of fact; LAW de facto • **h. consumado** fait accompli.

he·chu·ra f. *(fabricación)* making; *(criatura)* creature; *(forma)* form; *(forma del cuerpo)* shape; *(confección)* workmanship.

he·der §50 intr. *(apestar)* to stink; *(enfadar)* to annoy.

he·dion·dez f. *(hedor)* stink; *(cosa hedionda)* foul-smelling thing.

he·dion·do, a adj. *(maloliente)* stinking, smelling; *(repugnante)* sickening; *(obsceno)* obscene; *(molesto)* annoying.

he·dor m. stench, stink.

he·ge·mo·ní·a f. hegemony.

he·la·de·rí·a f. ice-cream parlor.

he·la·de·ro, a m.f. ice-cream street vendor.

he·la·do, a I. adj. frozen; *(muy frío)* freezing, icy; *(atónito)* dumfounded; *(desdeñoso)* cold, frosty II. m. ice cream; *(sorbete)* sherbet —f. frost.

he·la·dor, ·ra I. adj. freezing II. f. ice cream machine.

he·lar §49 tr. *(congelar)* to freeze; *(dejar pasmado)* to dumfound; *(desanimar)* to discourage* —reflex. to freeze ♦ **se me heló la sangre** my blood curdled.

hé·li·ce f. helix; AVIA. propeller; ZOOL. snail.

he·li·cóp·te·ro m. helicopter.

he·lio m. helium.

he·li·puer·to m. heliport.

he·ma·to·lo·gí·a f. hematology.

hem·bra f. *(mujer)* woman; *(animal)* female; *(cola de caballo)* thin horse tail; BOT. female plant; SEW. *(corchete)* eye; MECH. female; ELEC. *(enchufe)* socket; *(tornillo)* nut; *(cerradura)* strike; *(molde)* hollow mold ♦ **h. de cerrojo** or **pestillo** strike plate • **h. del timón** gudgeon.

he·mi·ci·clo m. *(semicírculo)* semicircle; ARCHIT. hemicycle.

he·mis·fe·rio m. hemisphere ♦ **h. austral** southern hemisphere • **h. boreal** northern hemisphere • **h. cerebral** or **del cerebro** cerebral hemisphere • **h. occidental** western hemisphere.

he·mo·fi·lia f. hemophilia.

he·mo·fí·li·co, ·a I. adj. hemophilic II. m.f. hemophiliac.

he·mo·glo·bi·na f. hemoglobin.

he·mo·rra·gia f. hemorrhage ♦ **h. nasal** nosebleed.

he·mo·rroi·de f. hemorrhoid ♦ pl. hemorrhoids, piles.

he·mos see **haber²**.

he·nal m. hayloft.

hen·chi·mien·to m. *(henchidura)* filling; *(madera)* wood used to fill holes; *(suelo)* rough floor.

hen·chir §48 tr. to fill —reflex. to stuff oneself.

hen·der §50 tr. *(cortar)* to split; *(un fluido)* to cut through; *(abrirse paso)* to make one's way through.

hen·di·du·ra f. crack.

hen·di·mien·to m. cracking.

he·nil m. hayloft.

he·no m. hay ♦ **h. blanco** velvet grass.

he·ñir §59 tr. to knead.

he·pa·ti·tis f. hepatitis.

hep·tá·go·no, ·a I. adj. heptagonal II. m. heptagon.

he·rál·di·co, ·a I. adj. heraldic II. m.f. herald —f. heraldry.

her·bá·ce·o, ·a adj. herbaceous.

her·ba·rio, ·a I. adj. herbal II. m. *(experto)* herbalist; *(colección)* herbarium; *(libro)* herbal; ZOOL. rumen.

her·be·cer §17 intr. to begin to grow.

her·bí·vo·ro, ·a I. adj. herbivorous II. m. herbivore.

her·bo·la·rio, ·a I. adj. COLL. mad II. m. *(comerciante)* herbalist; *(tienda)* herbalist's shop —m.f. COLL. crazy person.

her·bo·so, ·a adj. herbaceous.

her·cú·le·o, ·a adj. Herculean; FIG. herculean.

he·re·dad f. country estate or property ♦ **h. residual** or **residuaria** residual estate.

he·re·dar tr. *(recibir)* to inherit; LAW *(dar)* to bequeath.

he·re·de·ro, ·a I. adj. inheriting ♦ **príncipe h.** crown prince II. m.f. inheritor —m. heir —f. heiress ♦ **h. forzoso** heir apparent • **h. legal** heir at law • **instituir h.** or **por h.** to appoint as one's heir.

he·re·di·ta·rio, ·a adj. hereditary; FIG. ancestral.

he·re·je m.f. heretic; FIG. rascal.

he·re·jí·a f. heresy; *(insulto)* insult.

he·ren·cia f. *(patrimonio)* inheritance; *(tradición)* heritage; BIOL. heredity ♦ **h. yacente** LAW unclaimed estate.

he·ré·ti·co, ·a adj. heretical.

he·ri·do, ·a I. adj. *(lesionado)* wounded; *(ofendido)* offended II. m.f. *(persona herida)* wounded or injured person —m. ♦ **los heridos** the wounded —f. *(lesión)* wound; *(ofensa)* offense; *(tormento)* torment ♦ **h. contusa** contusion • **renovar la h.** to reopen an old wound • **tocar en la h.** to touch a sore spot.

he·rir §65 tr. *(lesionar)* to wound; *(hacer doler)* to hurt; *(ofender)* to offend; *(el sol)* to shine on; *(tañer)* to pluck.

her·ma·fro·di·ta I. adj. hermaphroditic II. m.f. hermaphrodite.

her·ma·na f. see **hermano, a**.

her·ma·nar tr. *(juntar)* to join; *(fraternizar)* to treat as a brother —reflex. to be united.

her·ma·nas·tro, ·a m.f. stepbrother/sister.

her·man·dad f. *(fraternidad)* brotherhood; *(de hermanas)* sisterhood; *(semejanza)* likeness; *(amistad)* close friendship; *(liga)* league.

her·ma·no, ·a m. brother ♦ **h. carnal** blood brother • **h. de leche** foster brother • **h. gemelo** twin brother • **h. lego** lay brother • **h. mayor** older or oldest brother • **h. menor** younger or youngest brother • **h. político** brother-in-law • **hermanos siameses** Siamese twins • **medio h.** half brother • **primo h.** first cousin —f. sister ♦ **h. gemela** twin sister • **h. lega** lay sister • **h. mayor** older or oldest sister • **h. menor** younger or youngest sister • **h. política** sister-in-law • **prima h.** first cousin —m.f. twin, mate.

her·mé·ti·co, ·a adj. *(cerrado)* airtight; *(incomprensible)* impenetrable.

her·mo·se·ar tr. to beautify —intr. to show off one's beauty.

her·mo·so, ·a adj. *(bello)* beautiful; *(niño)* healthy; *(tiempo)* fine.

her·mo·su·ra f. *(belleza)* beauty; *(mujer)* beauty, beautiful woman.

her·nia f. hernia.

hé·ro·e m. hero; *(protagonista)* main character; *(semidiós)* demigod.

he·roi·co, ·a adj. heroic.

he·ro·í·na f. heroine; PHARM. heroin.

he·ro·ís·mo m. heroism; *(hazaña)* heroic deed.

her·pes m. or f.pl. herpes.

he·rra·dor m. blacksmith.

he·rra·du·ra f. *(hierro)* horseshoe; *(resguardo)* hoof guard; ZOOL. horseshoe bat ♦ **mostrar las herraduras** to take to one's heels.

he·rra·je m. hardware.

he·rra·mien·ta f. *(instrumento)* tool; *(conjunto de instrumentos)* tools, set of tools; *(dentadura)* grinders, choppers; *(arma)* weapon ♦ **h. cortante** or **de corte** cutting tool.

he·rrar §49 tr. *(caballos)* to fit with horseshoes; *(ganado)* to brand; *(guarnecer)* to trim with iron or metal.

he·rre·rí·a f. *(fábrica)* foundry; *(taller)* blacksmith's shop; *(oficio)* blacksmithing.

he·rre·ro m. blacksmith.

he·rrín m. rust.

he·rrum·brar tr. to rust.

he·rrum·bre f. (*orín*) rust; (*sabor*) iron taste; BOT. rust, mildew.

he·rrum·bro·so, a adj. rusty, rusted.

her·vi·de·ro m. boiling; (*manantial*) bubbling spring; (*muchedumbre*) swarm.

her·vi·dor m. (*utensilio*) kettle; TECH. heating tube *or* chamber.

her·vir §65 intr. to boil; MARIT. to become rough ♦ **h. a fuego lento** to simmer • **h. de** *or* **en** to seethe with; (*pasión*) to be consumed with.

her·vor m. boiling; (*fogosidad*) ardor ♦ **levantar el h.** to come to a boil • **h. de la sangre** skin rash.

her·vo·ro·so, a adj. (*hirviente*) boiling; (*fogoso*) ardent.

he·si·ta·ción f. hesitation.

he·si·tar intr. to hesitate.

he·te·ro·do·xia f. heterodoxy.

he·te·ro·gé·ne·o, a adj. heterogeneous; (*diferente*) dissimilar.

he·te·ro·se·xual adj. & m.f. heterosexual.

hé·ti·co, a I. adj. MED. consumptive; FIG. emaciated II. m.f. MED. consumptive.

he·xá·go·no, a I. adj. hexagonal II. m. hexagon.

hez f. (*de licor*) sediment; FIG. scum ♦ pl. feces.

hia·to m. hiatus.

hi·ber·na·ción f. hibernation.

hi·ber·nar intr. to hibernate.

hi·bis·co m. hibiscus.

hí·bri·do, a adj. & m.f. hybrid.

hi·cie·ra, ce see hacer.

hi·dal·go, a I. adj. (*noble*) noble; (*generoso*) magnanimous II. m.f. noble.

hi·dal·guez/guí·a f. (*nobleza*) nobility; (*generosidad*) generosity.

hi·dra f. (*pólipo*) hydra; (*culebra*) poisonous aquatic snake; (*peligro*) recurring danger.

hi·dra·ta·ción f. hydration.

hi·dra·tar tr. to hydrate.

hi·dra·to m. hydrate ♦ **h. amónico** ammonium hydroxide • **h. de calcio** calcium hydrate • **h. de carbono** carbohydrate.

hi·dráu·li·ca f. hydraulics.

hí·dri·co, a adj. hydric; MED. water.

hi·dro·a·vión m. hydroplane.

hi·dro·car·bu·ro m. hydrocarbon.

hi·dro·ce·fa·lia f. hydrocephaly.

hi·dro·e·léc·tri·co, a adj. hydroelectric.

hi·dro·fo·bia f. hydrophobia.

hi·dro·ge·nar tr. to hydrogenate.

hi·dró·ge·no m. hydrogen.

hi·dró·li·sis f. hydrolysis.

hi·dró·me·tro m. hydrometer.

hi·dro·pla·no m. MARIT. hydrofoil; AVIA. seaplane.

hi·dros·fe·ra f. hydrosphere.

hi·dro·tec·nia f. hydraulic engineering.

hi·dro·te·ra·pia f. hydrotherapy.

hi·dro·ter·mal adj. hydrothermal.

hi·dró·xi·do m. hydroxide.

hie·dra f. ivy.

hiel f. bile; FIG. bitterness ♦ **echar la h.** COLL. to sweat blood ♦ pl. sorrows.

hie·le, lo see helar.

hie·lo m. ice; (*frialdad*) coldness ♦ **estar hecho un h.** to be freezing cold • **ser más frío que el h.** *or* **ser como un pedazo de h.** to be cold as ice.

hie·ma·ción f. wintering; BOT. winter blooming.

hie·na f. hyena.

hie·ra, ro see herir.

hie·rá·ti·co, a adj. RELIG. hieratic; FIG. solemn.

hier·ba f. (*pasto*) grass; (*medicinal*) herb; COLL. (*droga*) grass ♦ **h. mate** *or* **del Paraguay** maté • **mala h.** weed; FIG. troublemaker ♦ pl. (*pastos*) pasture • **h. marinas** algae • **y otras h.** and so forth.

hier·ba·bue·na f. mint.

hie·rre, rro see herrar.

hie·rro m. iron; (*marca*) brand; (*punta*) iron tip; (*arma*) weapon ♦ **h. colado** *or* **fundido** cast iron • **h. dulce** soft iron • **h. forjado** wrought iron • **h. galvanizado** galvanized iron ♦ pl. shackles.

hier·va, vo see hervir.

hi·ga f. (*amuleto*) fist-shaped amulet; (*gesto*) nose-thumbing, (*desprecio*) mockery ♦ **dar una h. a alguien** to thumb one's nose at • **no dar dos higas** por not to give a damn about.

hí·ga·do m. liver ♦ pl. COLL. guts • **echar los h.** COLL. to break one's back • **hasta los h.** COLL. with heart and soul.

hi·gié·ni·co, a adj. hygienic.

hi·go m. fig ♦ **de higos a brevas** once in a blue moon • **h. de tuna** prickly pear • **no dársele a uno un h.** COLL. not to care a fig about.

hi·gue·ra f. fig tree ♦ **estar en la h.** COLL. to be in another world • **h. chumba** *or* **de Indias** *or* **de pala** prickly pear • **h. infernal** castor-oil plant.

hi·jas·tro, a m.f. stepchild, stepson/daughter.

hi·jo, a m. son; (*obra*) brain child; (*en nombres*) junior ♦ **cada h. de vecino** COLL. every mother's son • **h. de su padre** his father's son • **h. político** son-in-law —f. (*niña*) daughter ♦ **h. de su madre** her mother's daughter • **h. política** daughter-in-law; —m f. (*niño*) child; (*nativo*) native; (*descendiente*) descendant; (*querido*) dear • **h. adoptivo** adopted child • **h. bastardo** *or* **natural** illegitimate child • **h. de familia** minor • **h. de la cuna** foundling • **h. de leche** foster child ♦ pl. children; (*descendientes*) descendants.

hi·jue·la f. (*añadido*) widening strip *or* gore; (*colchón*) small mattress; (*acequia*) small irrigation ditch; (*camino*) branch; (*correo*) rural postal service; RELIG. pall; LAW schedule; (*bienes*) estate; BOT. palm seed.

hi·la f. (*fila*) line, row; (*acción*) spinning; (*tripa delgada*) thin gut ♦ **a la h.** single file • **h. de agua** irrigation ditch ♦ pl. lint (for dressing wounds).

hi·la·cha f./o m. raveled thread.

hi·la·cho·so, a adj. frayed.

hi·la·da f. (*hilera*) row; ARCHIT. course.

hi·la·do m. (*acción*) spinning; (*hilo*) thread.

hi·la·dor, ra m.f. spinner.

hi·lan·de·rí·a f. (*arte*) spinning; (*fábrica*) spinning mill.

hi·lar tr. to spin; FIG. to ponder ♦ **h. delgado** *or* **muy fino** COLL. to split hairs.

hi·la·ran·te adj. hilarious, uproarious.

hi·la·ri·dad f. hilarity.

hi·le·ra f. (*línea recta*) row, file; (*hilo*) thread; METAL. drawplate; ARCHIT. ridgepole ♦ pl. spinneret.

hi·le·ro m. eddy, current.

hi·lo m. (*hebra*) thread; (*filamento*) filament; (*alambre*) fine wire; (*tejido*) linen; (*filo*) edge; (*colgajo*) bunch; ZOOL. hilum; (*de sangre*) trickle; *(de conversación)* thread ♦ **a h.** uninterruptedly • **al h.** SEW. along the thread; *(nervioso)* on edge • **colgar de un h.** to hang by a thread • **cortar el h.** to interrupt • **de h.** straight, directly • **h. de bramante** twine • **h. de cajas** *or* **de monjas** fine thread • **h. de gallinero** chicken wire • **h. de la vida** course of life • **h. de perlas** string of pearls • **h. de tierra** ELEC. ground wire • **tener el alma en un h.** to have one's heart in one's throat.

hil·ván m. basting, tacking.

hil·va·nar tr. to baste, tack; COLL. *(hacer con prisa)* to throw together; *(enlazar)* to coordinate.

hi·men m. hymen.

him·na·rio m. hymnal, hymnbook.

him·no m. hymn ♦ **h. nacional** national anthem.

hin n. whinny, neigh.

hin·ca·du·ra f. sinking, driving.

hin·ca·pié m. planting one's feet ♦ **hacer h. en** COLL. to insist on, stress.

hin·car §70 tr. *(clavar)* to sink, drive (in); *(apoyar)* to brace, plant (against) ♦ **h. el pico** COLL. to kick the bucket —reflex. to sink into ♦ **h. de rodillas** to kneel down.

hin·co m. post, stake.

hin·cón m. mooring post; *(mojón)* marker.

hin·cha f. COLL. hatred, enmity ♦ **tener h. a alguien** to have *or* hold a grudge against someone —m. COLL. fan, supporter.

hin·cha, cho see henchir.

hin·cha·do, a I. adj. *(inflado)* inflated, blown up; *(lleno)* full, filled up; MED. swollen; *(vanidoso)* conceited; *(pomposo)* pompous II. f. ♦ **la h.** COLL. the fans.

hin·char tr. *(aumentar)* to swell; *(inflar)* to inflate, blow up; *(exagerar)* to exaggerate; MED. to swell —reflex. MED. to swell; *(comer)* to fill *or* stuff oneself; *(envanecerse)* to become conceited ♦ **h. las narices** COLL. to get one's dander up.

hin·cha·zón f. MED. swelling; *(vanidad)* conceit; *(pomposidad)* pomposity.

hi·no·jo¹ m. fennel.

hi·no·jo² m. knee ♦ **de hinojos** on one's knees, kneeling.

hi·ña, ño, ñera, ñó see heñir.

hi·par intr. *(tener hipo)* to have the hiccups; *(los perros)* to pant; *(fatigarse)* to wear *or* tire oneself out; *(gimotear)* to whimper ♦ **h. por** to long *or* yearn for.

hi·pér·bo·la f. GEOM. hyperbola.

hi·pér·bo·le f. RHET. hyperbole.

hi·per·bó·li·co, a adj. hyperbolic(al).

hi·per·crí·ti·co, a I. adj. hypercritical II. m.f. hypercritic, severe critic.

hi·per·gli·ce·mia/glu·ce·mia f. hyperglycemia.

hi·per·me·tro·pí·a f. hypermetropy, farsightedness.

hi·per·sen·si·ble adj. hypersensitive.

hi·per·ten·sión f. hypertension, high blood pressure.

hi·per·ten·so, a adj. hypertensive.

hi·per·ter·mia f. hyperthermia.

hi·per·ven·ti·la·ción f. hyperventilation.

hí·pi·co, a adj. horse, equine ♦ **concurso h.** horse show.

hi·pi·do m. whimper, whine.

hi·pis·mo m. horse racing.

hip·no·sis f. hypnosis.

hip·no·te·ra·pia f. hypnotherapy.

hip·nó·ti·co, a adj. & m. hypnotic.

hip·no·tis·mo m. hypnotism.

hip·no·ti·zar §04 tr. to hypnotize.

hi·po m. hiccup; *(ansia)* yearning, longing; *(odio)* grudge, aversion ♦ **quitar el h.** COLL. to astonish • **tener h.** to have (the) hiccups.

hi·po·cen·tro m. hypocenter.

hi·po·con·drí·a f. hypochondria.

hi·po·con·dria·co/drí·a·co, a adj. & m.f. hypochondriac.

hi·po·cre·sí·a f. hypocrisy.

hi·pó·cri·ta I. adj. hypocritical II. m.f. hypocrite.

hi·po·dér·mi·co, a adj. hypodermic.

hi·pó·dro·mo m. racetrack.

hi·po·gli·ce·mia/glu·ce·mia f. hypoglycemia.

hi·po·pó·ta·mo m. hippopotamus.

hi·po·tá·la·mo m. hypothalamus.

hi·po·te·ca f. mortgage.

hi·po·te·car §70 tr. to mortgage; *(comprometer)* to compromise.

hi·po·ten·sión f. hypotension, low blood pressure.

hi·po·te·nu·sa f. hypotenuse.

hi·po·ter·mia f. hypothermia.

hi·pó·te·sis f. hypothesis.

hi·po·té·ti·co, a adj. hypothetical.

hi·rien·te adj. *(arma)* cutting; *(mordaz)* offensive, cutting.

hi·rie·ra, rió see herir.

hir·su·to, a adj. *(peludo)* hirsute, hairy; *(erizado)* coarse, bristly; *(brusco)* gruff.

hir·vien·te adj. boiling.

hir·vie·ra, vió see hervir.

his·pa·no·ha·blan·te adj. & m.f. Spanish-speaking (person), Hispanophone.

his·te·rec·to·mí·a f. hysterectomy.

his·te·ria f. hysteria.

his·té·ri·co, a I. adj. *(uterino)* uterine; *(alterado)* hysteric(al) II. m. *(histerismo)* hysteria —m.f. hysteric, hysterical person.

his·to·ria f. history; *(cuento)* story, tale; *(chisme)* gossip ♦ **dejarse de historias** to get to the point • **h. antigua** ancient history — **pasar a la h.** COLL. to be past history.

his·to·ria·do, a adj. ornate; ARTS storied.

his·to·ria·dor, ra m.f. historian.

his·to·rial I. adj. historic, historical II. m. *(archivo)* file, dossier; *(reseña personal)* résumé, curriculum vitae.

his·to·riar tr. *(contar)* to tell the story of; *(escribir)* to chronicle.

his·tó·ri·co, a adj. historic(al).

his·to·rie·ta f. story, anecdote ♦ **pl. h. ilustradas** *or* **cómicas** comic strips.

his·trión m. *(actor)* actor; *(bufón)* clown; *(prestidigitador)* juggler.

his·trio·nis·mo m. *(oficio)* acting; *(mundo teatral)* theater world; *(teatralidad)* histrionics.

hi·to, a I. adj. *(inmediato)* adjoining; *(fijo)* fixed II. m. *(señal de límite)* boundary marker; *(señal de distancia)* milestone; *(juego)* quoits; *(blanco)* bull's-eye, target ♦ **a h.** firmly • **dar en el h.** to hit the nail on the head • **mirar de h. en h.** to stare at.

hi·zo see hacer.

ho·ci·car §70 tr. *(escarbar)* to nuzzle; COLL. *(besuquear)* to smooch —intr. *(golpearse)* to hit one's face (against); COLL. *(tropezar)* to run into (difficulties); COLL. *(darse por vencido)* to give up; MARIT. to pitch.

ho·ci·co m. ZOOL. muzzle, snout; COLL. *(boca)* mouth; *(labios)* kisser; *(gesto)* sour face ♦ **caer de hocicos** COLL. to fall flat on one's face • **dar de hocicos** COLL. to hit one's face (against something) • **estar de hocicos** SL. to be teed off • **meter el h. en todo** COLL. to stick one's nose into everything • **poner h.** COLL. to put on a sour face.

ho·ci·no m. *(angostura)* narrows; *(en una quebrada)* dale.

hoc·key m. hockey ♦ **h. sobre hielo** ice hockey.

ho·ga·ño adv. COLL. *(hoy en día)* these days, nowadays; *(en este año)* this year.

ho·gar m. *(de una chimenea)* hearth, fireplace; *(hoguera)* bonfire; *(casa)* home; *(vida familiar)* home or family life.

ho·ga·re·ño, a adj. home-loving, domestic.

ho·ga·za f. *(pan grande)* large loaf of bread; *(pan grueso)* coarse bread.

ho·gue·ra f. bonfire.

ho·ja f. leaf; *(pétalo)* petal; *(de papel)* sheet, leaf; *(lámina de metal)* sheet, foil; *(folio)* leaf, page; *(documento)* sheet, form; *(cuchilla)* blade; *(de una puerta)* leaf; *(de ventana)* pane, sheet (of glass); *(de tierra)* strip of fallow land; *(espada)* sword; *(periódico)* newspaper, sheet ♦ **h. de h. perenne** evergreen • **h. de aluminio** aluminum foil • **h. de estaño** tinfoil • **h. de lata** tin plate • **h. de parra** fig leaf • **h. de ruta** COM. waybill • **h. de servicios** service record • **h. suelta** leaflet • **volver la h.** *(hojear)* to turn the page; *(cambiar de tema)* to change the subject; *(empezar nueva vida)* to turn over a new leaf.

ho·ja·la·ta f. tin plate.

ho·ja·la·te·ro m. tinsmith.

ho·jal·dre m.f. puff pastry.

ho·ja·ras·ca f. *(hojas secas)* dead or fallen leaves; *(frondosidad)* excessive foliage; *(cosas inútiles)* rubbish.

ho·je·ar tr. *(trashojar)* to skim or leaf (through) —intr. METAL. to peel, flake; *(susurrar)* to rustle.

ho·jo·so adj. leafy.

ho·jue·la f. *(hoja pequeña)* small leaf; *(masa frita)* pancake; *(de aceituna)* pressed olive skin; *(de metal)* metal leaf or foil; BOT. leaflet, foliole.

¡ho·la! interj. hello!, hi!

hol·ga·do, a adj. *(ancho)* big, loose; *(que vive con bienestar)* comfortable, well-off.

hol·gan·za f. *(descanso)* rest, leisure; *(ociosidad)* idleness; *(placer)* pleasure.

hol·gar §16 intr. *(descansar)* to relax; *(estar ocioso)* to be idle; *(estar alegre)* to be happy or glad; *(ser inútil)* to be unnecessary; *(no ajustar)* to be too big ♦ **huelga decir que** needless to say • **¡huelgan los comentarios!** no comment! —reflex. *(divertirse)* to have a good time; *(alegrarse)* to be pleased.

hol·ga·zán, a·na I. adj. lazy II. m.f. loafer.

hol·ga·za·ne·ar intr. to loaf, be idle.

hol·ga·za·ne·rí·a f. laziness.

hol·go·rio m. COLL. boisterous merrymaking.

hol·gu·ra f. *(regocijo)* enjoyment; *(anchura)* fullness; *(bienestar)* comfort, affluence; MECH. play.

ho·lo·caus·to m. *(sacrificio)* holocaust, burnt offering; *(víctima)* sacrifice, victim.

ho·lo·gra·fí·a f. holography.

ho·ló·gra·fo, a I. m. holograph II. adj. holographic.

ho·lo·gra·ma m. hologram.

ho·lla·du·ra f. treading, trampling.

ho·llar §19 tr. *(pisar)* to tread or trample (on); *(humillar)* to trample on, humiliate.

ho·lle·jo m. skin, peel.

ho·llín m. soot.

ho·lli·nien·to, a adj. sooty.

hom·bra·da f. manly action.

hom·bre m. man; *(humanidad)* man, mankind; COLL. *(esposo)* husband, man ♦ **de h. a h. man-to-man** • **¡h.!** what a surprise!, my goodness! • **¡h. al agua!** man overboard! • **h. de honor** honorable man • **h. de estado** statesman • **h. de letras** scholar • **h. del momento** man of the hour • **h. de mar** seaman, sailor • **h. de mundo** man of experience • **h. de negocios** businessman • **h. de palabra** man of his word • **h. de paja** straw man, front • **h. de palabra** man of his word • **h. de pelo en pecho** COLL. real man • **h. de pro** or **de provecho** worthy man • **h. rana** frogman • **pobre h.** wretch, poor devil • **ser muy h.** to be a real man.

hom·bre·ar¹ intr. COLL. *(echárselas de hombre)* to act in a manly way; *(querer igualarse)* to strive to equal; MEX. to work in masculine occupations (said of women) —reflex. to strive to equal.

hom·bre·ar² intr. to push with the shoulders.

hom·bre·ra f. shoulder pad; ARM. shoulder plate; *(adorno)* epaulet, epaulette.

hom·brí·a f. manliness ♦ **h. de bien** integrity, honesty.

hom·bri·llo m. yoke.

hom·bro m. shoulder ♦ **a hombros** piggyback • **arrimar el h.** COLL. *(trabajar)* to put one's shoulder to the wheel; *(ayudar)* to lend a hand • **echar el h.** to shoulder, take on • **encogerse de hombros** to shrug • **mirar a uno por encima del h.** to look down on someone • **sobre los hombros** on one's shoulders.

hom·bru·no, a adj. COLL. manly, masculine.

ho·me·na·je m. homage.

ho·me·na·je·a·do, a m.f. person to whom homage is paid.

ho·me·na·je·ar tr. to pay homage to.

ho·mi·ci·da I. adj. homicidal, murderous II. m.f. homicide, murderer.

ho·mi·ci·dio m. homicide.

ho·mi·lí·a f. homily.

ho·mo·fi·lia f. homophilia.

ho·mó·ga·mo, a adj. homogamous.

ho·mo·ge·nei·dad f. homogeneity.

ho·mo·ge·nei·za·ción f. homogenization.

ho·mo·ge·nei·zar §04 tr. to homogenize.

ho·mo·gé·ne·o, a adj. homogeneous.

ho·mo·ni·mia f. homonymy.

ho·mó·ni·mo, a I. adj. homonymous II. m. homonym —m. or f. namesake.

ho·mo·se·xual adj. & m.f. homosexual.

ho·mo·se·xua·li·dad f. homosexuality.

hon·da·men·te adv. *(con hondura)* deeply; *(profundamente)* deeply, profoundly.

hon·da·zo m. shot from a sling.

hon·do, a I. adj. *(profundo)* deep; *(bajo)* low; *(intenso)* intense; *(recóndito)* innermost II. m. bottom ♦ **de h.** deep, in depth —f. sling, slingshot.

hon·dón m. *(fondo)* bottom; *(valle)* glen; *(ojo de aguja)* eye.

hon·do·na·da f. ravine, gorge.

hon·du·ra f. depth, profundity ♦ pl. **meterse en h.** to get in over one's depth.

ho·nes·ti·dad f. *(honradez)* honesty; *(decencia)* decency; *(pudor)* modesty.

ho·nes·to, a adj. *(honrado)* honest; *(decente)* decent; *(pudoroso)* modest; *(razonable)* reasonable.

hon·go m. BOT. mushroom; MED. fungus; *(sombrero)* derby, bowler (hat) ♦ **h. marino** sea anemone • **h. yesguero** tinder fungus.

ho·nor m. *(virtud)* honor; *(recato)* virtue; *(buena reputación)* good reputation, prestige; *(celebridad)* fame, glory ♦ **hacer h. a** to honor • **hacer los honores a** to do justice to.

ho·no·ra·ble adj. honorable.

ho·no·ra·rio, a I. adj. honorary II. m. honorarium ♦ pl. fees, emoluments.

ho·no·rí·fi·co, a adj. *(que da honor)* honorific; *(no oficial)* honorary, honorific.

hon·ra f. *(dignidad propia)* honor, self-respect; *(buena fama)* reputation; *(pudor)* virtue ♦ pl. last respects.

hon·ra·dez f. honesty, integrity.

hon·ra·do, a adj. honest, honorable.

hon·ra·dor, ·ra I. adj. honoring II. m.f. honorer.

hon·rar tr. to honor, respect.

hon·ro·so, a adj. *(que da honra)* honorable; *(decente)* decent.

ho·pe·ar intr. *(menear la cola)* to wag the tail; *(corretear)* to run or chase around.

ho·po I. m. *(cola)* bushy tail; *(copete)* tuft or shock of hair; *(tupé)* toupee II. interj. COLL. get out!, scram!

ho·ra I. f. hour; *(momento)* time ♦ **a buena h.** in good time, opportunely • **a la h.** on time, punctually • **a primera h.** first thing in the morning • **¿a qué h.?** at what time?, when? • **a todas horas** at all hours • **a última h.** at the last minute; *(por la noche)* last thing at night • **dar h.** to make an appointment • **de última h.** last-minute • **en h. buena** fortunately • **en h. mala** unfortunately • **h. de comer** mealtime • **h. legal** standard time • **h. punta** rush hour; ELEC. peak hour • **la última h.** death • **pedir h.** to request an appointment • **poner en h.** to set • **por h.** per hour, by the hour • **¿qué h. es?** what time is it? • h. RELIG. book of hours • **h. canónicas** canonical hours • **h. de oficina** office or business hours • **h. extraordinarias** overtime • **h. libres** free time • **por h.** by the hours • **tener las h. contadas** to be at death's door II. adv. now.

ho·ra·dar tr. to drill, bore.

ho·ra·do m. *(agujero)* bore or drill hole; *(caverna)* cavern, grotto.

ho·ra·rio, a I. adj. hourly II. m. *(mano del reloj)* hour hand; RAIL. schedule, timetable.

hor·ca f. *(aparato de suplicio)* gallows; AGR. pitchfork; *(ristra)* string.

hor·ca·ja·das adv. ♦ **a h.** astride, straddling.

hor·cón m. *(horca)* pitchfork; *(apoyo)* forked pole supporting tree branches; AMER. wooden column supporting ceiling beams.

ho·ri·zon·tal adj. & adv. horizontal.

ho·ri·zon·te m. horizon.

hor·ma f. *(forma)* form, mold; *(de zapatero)* (shoemaker's) last; *(para zapatos)* shoetree; *(de sombrero)* hat block; CONSTR. dry wall ♦ **hallar la h. de su zapato** to get what's coming to one.

hor·mi·ga f. ant ♦ **ser una h.** to be industrious or hard-working.

hor·mi·gón m. concrete ♦ **h. armado** reinforced concrete • **h. hidráulico** hydraulic lime

mortar • **h. precomprimido** or **pretensado** prestressed concrete.

hor·mi·go·ne·ra f. cement or concrete mixer.

hor·mi·gue·ar intr. *(sentir hormigueo)* to tingle; *(bullir)* to teem.

hor·mi·gue·o m. *(multitud)* swarm, throng; *(sensación)* tingling.

hor·mi·gue·ro m. ENTOM. anthill; ORNITH. wryneck; FIG. hub of activity.

hor·mi·gui·lla f. COLL. *(picazón)* tingling sensation; *(remordimiento)* remorse.

hor·mi·gui·llo m. VET. founder; *(de personas)* human chain; *(picazón)* tingling sensation ♦ **parecer tener h.** COLL. to have ants in one's pants.

hor·mi·gui·ta f. COLL. industrious or diligent person.

hor·mo·na f. hormone.

hor·na·chue·la f. hut, hovel.

hor·na·da f. CUL. batch (of baked goods); FIG. group (of people).

hor·na·gue·ro, a I. adj. *(amplio)* ample, wide; MIN. coal-bearing II. f. coal.

hor·ne·ar intr. & tr. to bake.

hor·ne·ro, a m.f. baker.

hor·ni·lla f. burner; ORNITH. pigeonhole.

hor·ni·llo m. *(cocina)* stove; MIN. blasthole; MIL. fougasse ♦ **h. de atanor** athanor.

hor·no m. oven; TECH. furnace; CERAM. kiln ♦ **h. reverbero** TECH. reverberatory furnace • **no está el h. para bollos** COLL. the time is not ripe.

ho·rós·co·po m. horoscope.

hor·que·ta f. AGR. pitchfork; *(del árbol)* fork; AMER. fork (in a road).

hor·qui·lla f. AGR. pitchfork; *(sostén)* forked stake; *(del cabello)* hairpin, hair clip; *(de una bicicleta)* fork.

ho·rren·do, a adj. horrendous.

ho·rri·ble adj. horrible.

ho·rri·dez f. horridness.

hó·rri·do, a adj. horrid.

ho·rri·fi·car §70 tr. to horrify.

ho·rrí·fi·co, a adj. horrific.

ho·rri·pi·lan·te adj. hair-raising, terrifying.

ho·rri·pi·lar tr. *(erizar)* to make one's hair stand on end, give one the creeps; *(horrorizar)* to terrify.

ho·rror m. horror; *(temor)* terror; *(repulsión)* revulsion; *(atrocidad)* atrocity; COLL. *(cantidad)* tons, loads.

ho·rro·ri·zar §04 tr. to horrify —reflex. to be horrified.

ho·rro·ro·so, a adj. *(horrible)* horrible; COLL. *(feo)* hideous; *(muy malo)* terrible.

ho·rru·ra f. filth, dirt ♦ pl. MIN. scoria, slag.

hor·ta·li·za f. vegetable.

hor·te·la·no, a I. adj. *(del jardín)* (of the) garden; *(del huerto)* (of the) orchard II. m. *(jardinero)* gardener; ORNITH. ortolan.

hor·ten·se adj. *(del jardín)* (of the) garden; *(del huerto)* (of the) orchard.

hor·ten·sia f. hydrangea.

hor·ti·co·la adj. horticultural.

hor·ti·cul·tor, ·ra m.f. horticulturist.

hor·ti·cul·tu·ra f. horticulture.

hos·co, a adj. *(obscuro)* gloomy; *(moreno)* dark-skinned; *(áspero)* gruff.

hos·pe·da·je m. lodging.

hos·pe·dar tr. to lodge, put up —reflex. to lodge or stay (at).

hos·pe·de·rí·a f. *(hotel)* inn, hostel; *(hospedaje)*

lodging; RELIG. hospice.

hos·pe·de·ro, a m.f. innkeeper.

hos·pi·cio m. (para pobres) poorhouse; (para huérfanos) orphanage; RELIG. hospice.

hos·pi·tal m. hospital ♦ **h. de sangre** MIL. field hospital.

hos·pi·ta·la·rio, a adj. (cordial) hospitable; (acogedor) inviting; RELIG. of the Hospitalers.

hos·pi·ta·li·cio, a adj. hospitable.

hos·pi·ta·li·dad f. (cordialidad) hospitality; (permanencia) hospital stay.

hos·pi·ta·li·za·ción f. hospitalization.

hos·pi·ta·li·zar §04 tr. to hospitalize.

hos·que·dad f. (obscuridad) gloominess; (de la piel) darkness; (aspereza) gruffness.

hos·te·le·rí·a f. (profesión) hotel management; (industria) hotel trade or business.

hos·te·le·ro, a m.f. innkeeper.

hos·te·rí·a f. inn, hostel.

hos·tia f. (sacrificio) sacrifice; RELIG. wafer; SL. (golpe) punch ♦ **darle una h. a alguien** COLL. to give someone a beating.

hos·ti·ga·mien·to m. (azotamiento) whipping; (acosamiento) harassment.

hos·ti·gar §47 tr. (azotar) to whip; (acosar) to harass; (incitar) to urge, press.

hos·til adj. hostile.

hos·ti·li·dad f. hostility ♦ pl. hostilities, fighting • **romper las h.** MIL. to begin or commence hostilities.

hos·ti·li·zar §04 tr. to antagonize; MIL. to harass.

ho·tel m. (hostería) hotel; (casa) house, villa.

ho·te·le·ro, a I. adj. hotel II. m.f. (dueño) hotelkeeper, hotel owner; (encargado) hotel manager.

hoy adv. (en este día) today; (en el tiempo presente) nowadays ♦ **de h. a mañana** at any moment • **de** or **desde h. en adelante** from now on, from this day forward • **h. (en) día** nowadays - **h. mismo** this very day • **h. por h.** at the present time • **por h.** for now, for the time being

ho·ya f. (hoyo) pit, hole; (sepultura) grave; (remolino) eddy; (valle) dale.

ho·yar tr. to dig holes.

ho·yo m. (cavidad) hole; (sepultura) grave; MED. pockmark; SPORT. hole.

ho·yue·lo m. (en las mejillas) dimple; (en la barbilla) cleft; (en la garganta) depression.

hoz f. sickle.

hu·bie·ra, bo SEE **haber** ♦.

hu·cha f. (alcancía) piggy bank; (arca) chest; (ahorros) savings.

hue·co, a I. adj. (vacío) hollow; (retumbante) deep; (mullido) spongy; (vacuo) vacuous; (vano) vain II. m. (cavidad) hollow; (agujero) hole; (espacio) space; COLL. (vacante) vacancy; (vacío) gap, void; ARCHIT. opening ♦ **h. de ascensor** elevator shaft.

hue·la, la SEE **oler**.

huel·ga f. (paro) strike; AGR. fallow ♦ **declararse en h.** to go on strike • **h. de brazos caídos** sit-down strike • **h. de hambre** hunger strike • **h. intermitente** slowdown • **h. patronal** lockout • **h. por solidaridad** sympathy strike.

huel·go, gue SEE **holgar**.

huel·go m. (aliento) breath; (anchura) room, space; MECH. play.

huel·guis·ta m.f. striker, striking worker.

hue·lla f. (del pie) footprint; (de un animal) track, print; (vestigio) trace, mark; (del escalón) tread; FIG. footstep ♦ **h. digital** or **dactilar** fingerprint.

hue·llo m. (camino) track; (pisada) tread, step; (del casco) sole.

huér·fa·no, a I. adj. (sin padres) orphan(ed); (sin amparo) defenseless; (sin hijos) childless ♦ **h. de** without, devoid of II. m.f. orphan.

huer·ta f. (sembrado) large vegetable garden; (de árboles) orchard; SP. (regadío) irrigated land.

huer·to m. (jardín) vegetable garden; (de árboles) orchard.

hue·sa f. grave.

hue·so m. ANAT. bone; BOT. pit, stone; (cosa difícil) drudgery; (lo inútil) piece of junk; (persona desagradable) pain in the neck; C. AMER., MEX. (empleo oficial) government job ♦ **dar** or **tropezar en un h.** to hit a snag • **de buen h.** lucky • **estar en los huesos** to be nothing but skin and bones • **h. colorado** MEX. northerly wind • **h. de la alegría** funny bone • **h. de la suerte** wishbone • **h. duro de roer** hard nut to crack • **h. palomo** coccyx • **la sin h.** COLL. tongue • **meterse a h. de puerco** MEX. to swagger, show off • **no dejar a uno h. salvo** to rake over the coals • **soltar la sin h.** COLL. to shoot off one's mouth • **tener los huesos molidos** COLL. to be dead tired.

hue·so·so, a adj. bony, osseous.

hués·ped, a m.f. (invitado) guest; BIOL. host —m. (invitante) host —f. (invitante) hostess.

hues·te f. (ejército) army, troop; (partidarios) followers.

hue·su·do, a adj. bony.

hue·va f. roe.

hue·vo m. egg ♦ **h. duro** hard-boiled egg • **h. escalfado** poached egg • **h. estrellado** or **frito** fried egg • **h. pasado por agua** soft-boiled egg • **huevos revueltos** scrambled eggs.

hui·do, a I. adj. (fugitiva) fugitive, fleeing; (reservado) withdrawn II. f. (fuga) escape; (pretexto) pretext; EQUIT. bolt.

hui·llón, o·na AMER. I. adj. cowardly II. m.f. coward.

huir §18 intr. (escapar) to escape, run away; (evitar) to avoid, flee from; (alejarse) to slip away —reflx. to escape, run away —tr. to avoid, shun.

hu·le m. (caucho) rubber; (tela) oilcloth.

hu·lla f. coal ♦ **h. blanca** water power, hydraulic power.

hu·ma·nar tr. to humanize —reflx. to become human; RELIG. to become man (God).

hu·ma·ni·dad f. humanity; (género) mankind; (bondad) humaneness; COLL. (corpulencia) corpulence ♦ pl. humanities.

hu·ma·nis·ta I. m.f. humanist II. adj. humanistic.

hu·ma·ni·ta·rio, a adj. humanitarian.

hu·ma·ni·zar §04 tr. to humanize —reflx. to become more human, soften.

hu·ma·no, a I. adj. human; (benévolo) humane II. m. human (being).

hu·ma·re·da f. /ma·zo m. dense smoke.

hu·me·an·te adj. (que humea) smoking, smoky; (que echa vapor) steaming.

hu·me·ar intr. (echar humo) to smoke; (echar vapor) to steam; (permanecer) to smolder; (presumir) to become conceited —tr. AMER. to fumigate.

hu·me·dad f. humidity; (calidad de húmedo) dampness, moisture.

hu·me·de·ce·dor m. humidifier.
hu·me·de·cer §17 tr. to humidify; *(mojar)* to dampen, moisten —reflex. to become damp or moist.
hú·me·do, a adj. humid; *(mojado)* damp, moist.
hu·me·ra f. COLL. drunkenness.
hu·me·ro m. chimney, smokestack.
hú·me·ro m. humerus.
hu·mil·dad f. *(virtud)* humility, humbleness; *(de cuna)* lowliness (of birth); *(acción)* humble act.
hu·mil·de adj. *(sumiso)* humble, meek; *(bajo)* humble, lowly; *(de poco monto)* modest.
hu·mi·lla·ción f. humiliation.
hu·mi·llan·te adj. humiliating.
hu·mi·llar tr. *(rebajar)* to humble; *(avergonzar)* humiliate; *(bajar la frente)* to bow (one's head) —reflex. to humble oneself.
hu·mi·llo m. pride.
hu·mo m. *(gas)* smoke; *(vapor)* steam ♦ **a h. de pajas** lightly, without thinking • **echar h.** to smoke • **hacerse h.** to vanish into thin air ♦ pl. airs • **bajarle los h.** a uno to put someone in his place • **tener muchos h.** to put on airs.
hu·mor m. humor; *(talante)* mood, humor; *(agudeza)* humor, wit.
hu·mo·ra·do, a adj. ♦ **bien, mal h.** good/bad-humored II. f. *(chiste)* joke; *(capricho)* whim, fancy.
hu·mo·ris·mo m. humor, wit.
hu·mo·ris·ta I. adj. humorous II. m.f. humorist.
hu·mo·rís·ti·co, a adj. humorous.
hu·mo·so, a adj. *(lleno de humo)* smoky; *(que echa humo)* smoking.
hun·di·do, a adj. *(sumido)* sunken; *(de ojos)* sunken, deep-set; *(mejillas)* hollow, sunken.
hun·di·mien·to m. *(naufragio)* sinking; *(derrumbe)* cave-in; *(ruina)* ruin, collapse.
hun·dir tr. *(sumergir)* to sink; *(confundir)* to confuse; *(arruinar)* to ruin; *(derrotar)* to defeat; *(clavar)* to plunge —reflex. *(sumergirse)* to sink; *(caer)* to fall down, collapse.
hu·ra·cán m. hurricane.
hu·ra·ño, a adj. unsociable.
hur·ga·dor, ·ra I. adj. poking II. m. poker.
hur·gar §47 tr. *(atizar)* to poke, stir; *(revolver)* to poke or rummage around in.
hur·gón m. poker.
hur·go·ne·ar tr. *(atizar)* to poke, stir; *(tirar estocadas)* to jab at.
hur·gui·llas m.f. busybody.
hu·rón, ·o·na m. ferret —m.f. COLL. *(curioso)* snoop; *(persona huraña)* unsociable person.
hu·ro·ne·ar intr. *(cazar)* to ferret, hunt with a ferret; COLL. *(curiosear)* to snoop, pry.
hu·ro·ne·ra f. ferret hole.
hu·rra·ca f. ORNITH. magpie; COLL. *(charlatán)* chatterbox.
hur·ta·di·llas adv. ♦ **a h.** secretly, furtively.
hur·tar tr. *(robar)* to steal, thieve; *(dar de menos)* to shortchange; *(plagiar)* to plagiarize.
hur·to m. *(robo)* theft, robbery; *(cosa hurtada)* stolen object.
hu·si·llo m. *(tornillo)* screw, worm; *(desaguadero)* drain, drainage canal.
hus·me·a·dor, ·ra I. adj. snooping, prying II. m.f. snoop.
hus·me·ar tr. *(olfatear)* to scent, smell out; *(indagar)* to snoop, pry —intr. *(oler mal)* to stink, smell; *(curiosear)* to snoop, pry.

hus·me·o m. *(olfateo)* smelling; *(fisgoneo)* snooping, prying.
hu·so m. SEW., TEX. spindle; MECH. drum; AER. fuselage ♦ **h. horario** time zone.
hu·ya, yo, yera, yó see huir.

I

i, I f. [pl. **íes**] tenth letter of the Spanish alphabet ♦ **poner los puntos sobre las íes** COLL. to dot the i's.
i·ba see ir.
i·bis f.inv. ibis.
i·co·no m. icon.
i·co·no·clas·ta adj. & m.f. iconoclast.
i·co·no·gra·fí·a f. iconography.
ic·te·ri·cia f. jaundice.
ic·tio·lo·gí·a f. ichthyology.
ic·tió·lo·go m. ichthyologist.
i·da f. see ido, a.
i·de·a f. idea; *(concepto)* concept; *(noción)* notion; *(imagen)* image, picture; *(ingenio)* imagination ♦ **cambiar de i.** to change one's mind • **darle a uno la i. de** to get it into one's head • **hacerse** or **metérsele a uno una i.** **en la cabeza** COLL. to get an idea into one's head • **¡ni i.!** COLL. search me! • **no puedes tener i.** you can't imagine • **tener i. de** to intend to.
i·de·al I. adj. ideal; *(perfecto)* perfect II. m. ideal ♦ **lo i.** the perfect thing.
i·de·a·lis·ta adj. & m.f. idealist.
i·de·a·li·zar §04 tr. to idealize.
i·de·ar tr. *(concebir)* to think up, plan; *(inventar)* to invent, design.
i·dén·ti·co, a adj. identical.
i·den·ti·dad f. identity.
i·den·ti·fi·ca·ble adj. identifiable.
i·den·ti·fi·car §70 tr. to identify —reflex. to identify (oneself) with, be identified with.
i·de·o·lo·gí·a f. ideology.
i·de·o·ló·gi·co, a adj. ideological.
i·dí·li·co, a adj. idyllic.
i·di·lio m. idyll.
i·dio·ma m. language, tongue.
i·dio·má·ti·co, a adj. idiomatic.
i·dio·sin·cra·sia f. idiosyncrasy.
i·dio·sin·crá·si·co, a adj. idiosyncratic.
i·dio·ta I. adj. foolish, idiotic II. m.f. idiot, imbecile.
i·dio·tez f. idiocy.
i·do, a I. see ir II. adj. COLL. *(chiflado)* nuts, crazy ♦ **estar i.** COLL. to be distracted III. f. *(acción)* going; *(viaje)* trip ♦ **i. y vuelta** round trip • **idas y venidas** comings and goings.
i·dó·la·tra I. adj. idolatrous, idolizing II. m.f. idolater, idolizer.
i·do·la·trar tr. to idolize.
i·do·la·trí·a f. idolatry.
í·do·lo m. idol.
i·do·nei·dad f. *(aptitud)* aptitude, capacity; *(conveniencia)* suitability, fitness.
i·dó·ne·o, a adj. *(apto)* capable, apt; *(conveniente)* suitable, fit.
i·gle·sia f. church ♦ **i. parroquial** parish church.
íg·ne·o, a adj. igneous.
ig·ni·ción f. ignition.
ig·no·mi·nia f. ignominy.
ig·no·mi·nio·so, a adj. ignominious.
ig·no·ran·cia f. ignorance.

ig·no·ran·te I. adj. *(sin educación)* ignorant, uneducated; *(que ignora)* uninformed, unaware **II.** m.f. ignoramus.

ig·no·rar tr. to be ignorant of, not to know.

ig·no·to, a adj. unknown, undiscovered.

i·gual I. adj. equal; *(semejante)* similar, alike; *(mismo)* like; *(parejo)* even, level ♦ **darle a uno i.** to be the same to one • **Ir iguales** to be even • **ser i. a** *(ser lo mismo)* to be the same as; *(igualar)* to equal • **todo me es i.** it's all the same to me **II.** m. MATH. equal sign —m.f. equal ♦ **al i. que** just like • **de i. a i.** as an equal • **i. que** the same as • **no tener i.** to have no equal, be unrivaled • **sin i.** unparalleled, unequaled.

i·gua·la·dor, ·ra I. adj. equalizing, leveling **II.** m.f. equalizer, leveler.

i·gua·la·mien·to m. equalization.

i·gua·lar tr. *(hacer igual)* to equalize, make equal; *(allanar)* to smooth; *(juzgar igual)* to consider equal, equate; *(comparar)* to compare; SPORT. to tie —intr. & reflex. *(ser iguales)* to be equal; SPORT. to be tied ♦ **i. a** or **con** to be equal to, be the equal of.

i·gual·dad f. equality; *(semejanza)* similarity, likeness; *(uniformidad)* evenness ♦ **en i. de condiciones** on an equal basis, on equal terms.

i·gua·li·ta·rio, a adj. & m.f. egalitarian.

i·gual·men·te adv. equally; *(también)* also, too; *(en la misma manera)* the same, in the same way.

i·gua·na m. iguana.

i·ja·da f. *(de un animal)* flank; *(del hombre)* side; *(dolor)* colic, pain in the side.

i·la·ción f. *(deducción)* inference; *(de ideas)* connectedness, cohesiveness.

i·le·gal adj. illegal.

i·le·ga·li·dad f. illegality.

i·le·gi·ble adj. illegible.

i·le·gi·ti·mi·dad f. illegitimacy.

i·le·gí·ti·mo, a adj. illegitimate.

i·le·so, a adj. unhurt, unscathed.

i·le·tra·do, a adj. & m.f. illiterate.

i·lí·ci·to, a adj. illicit.

i·ló·gi·co, a adj. illogical.

i·lu·mi·na·ción f. illumination; *(alumbrado)* lighting; *(espiritual)* enlightenment.

i·lu·mi·na·do, a I. adj. *(alumbrado)* lit (up), illuminated; *(realizado)* enlightened **II.** m.f. *(hereje)* illuminist; *(visionario)* visionary ♦ **los iluminados** the Illuminati.

i·lu·mi·na·dor, ·ra I. adj. illuminating, illuminative **II.** m.f. illuminator of a manuscript.

i·lu·mi·nar tr. to illuminate; *(alumbrar)* to light; *(espiritualmente)* to enlighten.

i·lu·sión f. illusion; *(esperanza)* hope ♦ **hacerse la i. de** to imagine that • **hacerse ilusiones de** to cherish hopes of • **tener i. por** to look forward to.

i·lu·sio·nar tr. *(forjar esperanzas)* to build up (someone's) hopes; *(engañar)* to deceive —reflex. to have hopes (of).

i·lu·sio·nis·ta m.f. illusionist, magician.

i·lu·so, a I. adj. deluded **II.** m.f. dreamer.

i·lu·so·rio, a adj. illusory, false.

i·lus·tra·ción f. illustration; *(grabado)* picture ♦ **la I.** the Enlightenment.

i·lus·tra·do, a I. adj. *(persona)* learned, erudite; *(libro)* illustrated **II.** m.f. erudite person.

i·lus·tra·dor, ·ra I. adj. illustrative **II.** m.f. illustrator.

i·lus·trar tr. to illustrate; *(aclarar)* to eluci-

date; *(instruir)* to instruct, enlighten.

i·lus·tra·ti·vo, a adj. illustrative.

i·lus·tre adj. illustrious, distinguished.

i·ma·gen f. image ♦ **i. fantasma** TELEV. double image, ghost • **ser la i. viva de** to be the living image of.

i·ma·gi·na·ble adj. imaginable.

i·ma·gi·na·ción f. imagination ♦ **dejarse llevar por la i.** to let the imagination run away with one • **pasar por la i.** to occur, cross one's mind.

i·ma·gi·nar tr. to imagine; *(inventar)* to invent; *(suponer)* to suppose, presume —reflex. to imagine.

i·ma·gi·na·rio, a adj. imaginary.

i·ma·gi·na·ti·vo, a adj. imaginative.

i·mán¹ m. RELIG. imam.

i·mán² m. magnet; FIG. magnetism.

i·ma·nar/man·tar tr. to magnetize.

im·bé·cil adj. & m.f. imbecile.

im·be·ci·li·dad f. imbecility.

im·bo·rra·ble adj. indelible.

im·buir §18 tr. to imbue.

i·mi·ta·ble adj. imitable.

i·mi·ta·ción f. imitation.

i·mi·ta·dor, ·ra m.f. imitator, mimic.

i·mi·tar tr. to imitate, mimic.

i·mi·ta·ti·vo, a adj. imitative.

im·pa·cien·cia f. impatience.

im·pa·cien·tar tr. to make (someone) lose patience —reflex. to lose one's patience.

im·pa·cien·te adj. impatient, restless.

im·pac·to m. impact; *(choque)* shock; *(repercusión)* repercussion.

im·pal·pa·ble adj. impalpable.

im·par adj. odd, uneven.

im·pa·ra·ble adj. unstoppable.

im·par·cial adj. impartial.

im·par·cia·li·dad f. impartiality.

im·par·tir tr. to grant, concede.

im·pa·si·bi·li·dad f. impassiveness.

im·pa·si·ble adj. impassive.

im·pa·vi·dez f. fearlessness, courage.

im·pá·vi·do, a adj. fearless, dauntless.

im·pe·ca·ble adj. impeccable.

im·pe·di·do, a adj. & m.f. disabled (person).

im·pe·di·men·to m. impediment.

im·pe·dir §48 tr. to prevent, obstruct.

im·pe·ler tr. to impel.

im·pe·ne·tra·ble adj. impenetrable.

im·pe·ni·ten·te I. adj. confirmed, inveterate **II.** m.f. stubborn *or* intractable person.

im·pen·sa·ble adj. unthinkable, unimaginable.

im·pen·sa·do, a adj. unexpected, fortuitous.

im·pe·ran·te adj. ruling, dominant.

im·pe·rar tr. to rule, reign.

im·pe·ra·ti·vo, a adj. & m. imperative ♦ **imperativos económicos** economic considerations.

im·per·cep·ti·ble adj. imperceptible.

im·per·di·ble m. safety pin.

im·per·do·na·ble adj. inexcusable.

im·pe·re·ce·de·ro, a adj. *(duradero)* indestructible; *(inmortal)* immortal.

im·per·fec·ción f. imperfection.

im·per·fec·to, a adj. imperfect.

im·pe·rial adj. imperial.

im·pe·ri·cia f. *(torpeza)* unskillfulness; *(incapacidad)* inexperience.

im·pe·rio m. empire; *(autoridad)* authority; *(duración)* reign.

im·pe·rio·si·dad f. imperiousness.

im·pe·rio·so, a adj. *(autoritario)* imperious, overbearing; *(imperativo)* imperative, urgent.

im·per·me·a·bi·li·dad f. impermeability.
im·per·me·a·bi·li·zar §04 tr. to (make) water-proof.
im·per·me·a·ble I. adj. impermeable, water-proof II. m. raincoat, mackintosh.
im·per·mu·ta·ble adj. unexchangeable.
im·per·so·nal adj. impersonal.
im·per·té·rri·to, a adj. intrepid, dauntless.
im·per·ti·nen·cia f. impertinence.
im·per·ti·nen·te I. adj. impertinent; *(insolente)* insolent; *(molesto)* meddlesome II. m. ♦ pl. lorgnette, opera glasses.
im·per·tur·ba·ble adj. imperturbable.
im·pé·ti·go m. impetigo.
im·pe·tra·ción f. impetration; *(súplica)* beseeching.
im·pe·trar tr. to impetrate; *(obtener)* to obtain by entreaty; *(suplicar)* to beseech.
ím·pe·tu m. impetus; *(violencia)* violence; *(energía)* energy; *(fogosidad)* impetuosity.
im·pe·tuo·si·dad f. *(ímpetu)* impetus; *(violencia)* violence; *(fogosidad)* impetuosity.
im·pe·tuo·so, a adj. *(violento)* violent; *(fogoso)* impetuous, impulsive.
im·pi·da, do, diera, dió see **impedir**.
im·pie·dad f. impiety.
im·pí·o, a I. adj. impious II. m.f. infidel.
im·pla·ca·ble adj. implacable.
im·plan·ta·ción f. implantation; *(introducción)* introduction.
im·plan·tar tr. to implant; *(introducir)* to introduce.
im·pli·ca·ción f. implication; *(complicidad)* complicity; *(consecuencia)* consequence.
im·pli·can·te adj. implicating.
im·pli·car §70 tr. to implicate; *(significar)* to imply, mean —reflex. to become involved.
im·plí·ci·to, a adj. implicit.
im·plo·rar tr. to implore.
im·pon·de·ra·ble adj. & m. imponderable.
im·po·nen·te adj. *(grandioso)* imposing; COLL. *(atractivo)* good-looking.
im·po·ner §54 tr. *(ordenar)* to impose; *(informar)* to inform; *(infundir)* to inspire, instill —reflex. *(ser impuesto)* to be imposed on or upon; *(ser necesario)* to be necessary; *(obligarse)* to take on ♦ i. a to dominate.
im·po·ni·ble adj. taxable, subject to tax.
im·po·pu·lar adj. unpopular.
im·por·ta·ción f. importation, importing; *(bienes importados)* imported goods.
im·por·ta·dor, ·ra I. adj. importing II. m.f. importer.
im·por·tan·cia f. importance; *(valor)* significance; *(autoridad)* authority; *(influencia)* influence ♦ darse i. to put on airs.
im·por·tan·te adj. important ♦ lo i. the most important thing.
im·por·tar intr. to be important, matter —tr. *(valer)* to cost, be worth; *(introducir en un país)* to import; *(llevar consigo)* to entail.
im·por·te m. amount, cost.
im·por·tu·nar tr. to importune.
im·por·tu·ni·dad f. importunity.
im·por·tu·no, a adj. inopportune.
im·po·si·bi·li·dad f. impossibility.
im·po·si·bi·li·ta·do, a adj. *(tullido)* disabled, crippled; *(impedido)* prevented.
im·po·si·bi·li·tar tr. *(prevenir)* to make impossible; *(impedir)* to prevent.
im·po·si·ble I. adj. impossible; *(inservible)* useless; *(intratable)* intractable, difficult; *(la-*

mentable) lamentable; AMER. dirty, filthy II. m. impossible ♦ hacer lo i. to do the impossible, do the utmost.
im·po·si·ción f. imposition.
im·pos·tor, ·ra I. adj. slanderous II. m. impostor, slanderer.
im·pos·tu·ra f. *(engaño)* imposture; *(calumnia)* slander.
im·po·ten·cia f. impotence.
im·po·ten·te adj. & m. impotent (man).
im·prac·ti·ca·ble adj. *(irrealizable)* impracticable, unfeasible; *(intransitable)* impassable.
im·pre·ca·ción f. imprecation, curse.
im·pre·car §70 tr. to imprecate, curse.
im·pre·ci·sión f. lack of precision, inexactness.
im·pre·ci·so, a adj. imprecise.
im·preg·na·ción f. impregnation.
im·preg·nar tr. to impregnate.
im·pre·me·di·ta·do, a adj. unpremeditated.
im·pren·ta f. *(arte)* printing; *(establecimiento)* printing house.
im·pres·cin·di·ble adj. indispensable.
im·pre·sión f. impression; *(edición)* printing; *(obra)* edition ♦ i. digital or dactilar fingerprint • tener la i. de or que to have the impression that.
im·pre·sio·na·ble adj. impressionable.
im·pre·sio·nan·te adj. impressive.
im·pre·sio·nar tr. to make an impression on, impress; *(conmover)* to move, touch —reflex. to be moved.
im·pre·sio·nis·ta adj. & m.f. impressionist.
im·pre·so, a I. see **imprimir** II. adj. printed III. m. leaflet.
im·pre·sor, ·ra m.f. owner of a printing house —m. printer.
im·pre·vi·si·ble adj. unpredictable.
im·pre·vi·sión f. lack of foresight.
im·pre·vis·to, a I. adj. unforeseen, unexpected II. m. ♦ pl. incidental expenses.
im·pri·mir §80 tr. *(reproducir)* to print; *(estampar)* to stamp, imprint; *(dejar una huella)* to imprint; *(transmitir)* to impart.
im·pro·ba·bi·li·dad f. improbability.
im·pro·ba·ble adj. improbable.
ím·pro·bo, a adj. *(sin probidad)* dishonest; *(muy duro)* arduous.
im·pro·ce·den·te adj. *(inadecuado)* inappropriate; LAW irrelevant.
im·pro·duc·ti·vo, a adj. unproductive.
im·pro·pie·dad f. impropriety.
im·pro·pio, a adj. *(inadecuado)* inappropriate; *(no exacto)* incorrect; MATH. improper.
im·pro·vi·sa·ción f. improvisation.
im·pro·vi·sa·do, a adj. *(de cosas)* makeshift, improvised; *(de un discurso)* impromptu, extemporaneous; MUS. improvised.
im·pro·vi·sar tr. to improvise; RHET. to extemporize.
im·pro·vi·so, a adj. unexpected♦ al or de i. unexpectedly, suddenly.
im·pru·den·cia f. imprudence.
im·pru·den·te adj. & m.f. imprudent (person).
im·pu·den·cia f. impudence.
im·pú·di·co, a adj. & m.f. shameless (person).
im·pu·dor m. *(desvergüenza)* shamelessness; *(falta de pudor)* impudicity.
im·pues·to, a I. see **imponer** II. m. tax, duty ♦ i. a las rentas income tax • i. a las ventas sales tax • i. de herencias inheritance tax • i. adicional ARG. surtax • i. de aduanas customs duty • i. inmobiliario real-estate tax • i.

sobre bienes property tax.
im·pug·na·ble adj. impugnable.
im·pug·na·ción f. refutation, contradiction.
im·pug·nar tr. to refute, impugn.
im·pul·sar tr. to impel, drive.
im·pul·sión f. impulsion, impulse.
im·pul·si·vi·dad f. impulsiveness.
im·pul·si·vo, a adj. & m.f. impulsive (person).
im·pul·so m. impulse.
im·pul·sor, ·ra I. adj. impelling, driving II. m.f. (fuerza) driving force; (instigador) instigator.
im·pu·ne adj. unpunished.
im·pu·ni·dad f. impunity.
im·pu·re·za f. impurity.
im·pu·ro, a adj. impure.
im·pu·sie·ra, so see imponer.
im·pu·ta·ble adj. imputable.
im·pu·ta·ción f. imputation, charge.
im·pu·tar tr. (atribuir) to impute, charge with; COM. (asignar) to assign.
i·na·bor·da·ble adj. unapproachable.
i·na·bro·ga·ble adj. irrevocable.
i·na·ca·ba·ble adj. interminable, endless.
i·na·ca·ba·do, a adj. unfinished.
i·nac·ce·si·ble adj. inaccessible.
i·nac·ción f. inaction.
i·na·cep·ta·ble adj. unacceptable.
i·nac·ces·tum bra do, a adj. unaccustomed.
i·nac·ti·vi·dad f. inactivity.
i·nac·ti·vo, a adj. inactive.
i·na·dap·ta·ble adj. unadaptable.
i·na·de·cua·do, a adj. unsuitable, inadequate.
i·nad·mi·si·ble adj. inadmissible.
i·nad·ver·ten·cia f. inadvertence, carelessness.
i·nad·ver·ti·do, a adj. (sin cuidado) careless; (no advertido) unnoticed.
i·na·go·ta·ble adj. inexhaustible, endless.
i·na·guan·ta·ble adj. unbearable, insufferable.
i·na·lám·bri·co, a adj. wireless.
i·nal·can·za·ble adj. unreachable.
i·nal·te·ra·ble adj. unalterable.
i·na·mo·vi·ble adj. immovable, unremovable.
i·na·ne adj. inane.
i·na·ni·dad f. inanity.
i·na·ni·ma·do, a adj. inanimate, lifeless.
i·na·pa·ga·ble adj. inextinguishable.
i·na·pla·za·ble adj. unpostponable.
i·na·pli·ca·ble adj. inapplicable.
i·na·pre·cia·ble adj. (inestimable) invaluable; (imperceptible) imperceptible.
i·na·pro·pia·do, a adj. inappropriate.
i·nar·ti·cu·la·do, a adj. inarticulate.
i·na·ta·ca·ble adj. impregnable, unassailable.
i·na·ten·ción f. inattention.
i·na·ten·to, a adj. unattentive.
i·nau·di·to, a adj. (no oído) unheard-of; (extraordinario) unprecedented; (monstruoso) outrageous.
i·nau·gu·ra·ción f. inauguration, opening.
i·nau·gu·rar tr. to inaugurate, open.
in·cal·cu·la·ble adj. incalculable.
in·ca·li·fi·ca·ble adj. indescribable.
in·can·des·cen·cia f. incandescence.
in·can·des·cen·te adj. incandescent.
in·can·sa·ble adj. untiring, indefatigable.
in·ca·pa·ci·dad f. incapacity.
in·ca·pa·ci·ta·do, a adj. incapacitated.
in·ca·pa·ci·tar tr. to incapacitate.
in·ca·paz adj. incapable, unable; (incompetente) incompetent; LAW incapacitated.
in·cau·ta·ción f. seizure, confiscation.

in·cau·tar·se reflex. to seize, confiscate.
in·cau·to, a adj. (imprudente) incautious, unwary; (inocente) gullible, naive.
in·cen·diar tr. to set on fire, set fire to —reflex. to catch fire.
in·cen·dia·rio, a adj. & m.f. incendiary.
in·cen·dio m. fire.
in·cen·sa·rio m. incense vessel.
in·cen·ti·vo m. incentive.
in·cer·ti·dum·bre f. uncertainty, doubt.
in·ce·sa·ble/san·te adj. incessant.
in·ces·to m. incest.
in·ces·tuo·so, a adj. incestuous.
in·ci·den·cia f. (incidente) incident, occurrence; PHYS. incidence.
in·ci·den·tal adj. (incidente) incidental; (en paréntesis) parenthetical.
in·ci·den·te adj. & m. incident.
in·cien·so m. incense.
in·cier·to, a adj. uncertain, doubtful.
in·ci·ne·ra·ción f. incineration, cremation.
in·ci·ne·rar tr. to incinerate, cremate.
in·ci·pien·te adj. incipient.
in·ci·sión f. incision.
in·ci·si·vo, a adj. cutting, incisive ♦ diente i. incisor.
in·ci·so m. article.
in·ci·tar tr. to incite, instigate.
in·ci·vil adj. uncivil, rude.
in·ci·vi·li·dad f. incivility, rudeness.
in·cle·men·cia f. inclemency.
in·cle·men·te adj. inclement.
in·cli·na·ción f. inclination; (del cuerpo) bowing; (pendiente) slope, slant; (tendencia) inclination.
in·cli·nar tr. (la cabeza) to bow, lower; (torcer) to slant, tilt; (persuadir) to persuade —intr. to resemble, take after —reflex. (doblarse) to bow; (desviar) to slant, slope; (parecerse) to resemble, take after; (estar dispuesto) to be or feel inclined.
in·cluir §18 tr. to include; (encerrar) to enclose; (contener) to contain; (comprender) to comprise.
in·clu·sión f. inclusion ♦ con i. de including.
in·clu·si·ve adv. inclusive, included.
in·clu·si·vo, a adj. inclusive, including.
in·clu·so, a I. see incluir II. adv. (inclusivamente) inclusively; (aun más) even <i. le avisé I even warned him>.
in·clu·ya, yo, yera, yó see incluir.
in·co·bra·ble adj. irrecoverable, uncollectable.
in·cóg·ni·to, a I. adj. unknown ♦ de i. incognito II. m. incognito —f. MATH. unknown quantity; (misterio) question.
in·co·he·ren·cia f. incoherence.
in·co·he·ren·te adj. incoherent.
in·co·lo·ro, a adj. (sin color) colorless; (sin brillo) dull.
in·có·lu·me adj. unharmed, unscathed.
in·com·bus·ti·ble adj. incombustible, fireproof.
in·co·mes·ti·ble adj. inedible.
in·co·mi·ble adj. COLL. inedible.
in·co·mo·dar tr. to inconvenience, bother —reflex. to become angry.
in·co·mo·do m./di·dad f. (falta de comodidad) discomfort; (molestia) inconvenience.
in·có·mo·do, a I. adj. uncomfortable, awkward II. m. discomfort, inconvenience.

in·com·pa·ra·ble adj. incomparable.
in·com·pa·ti·ble adj. incompatible.
in·com·pe·ten·te adj. incompetent.
in·com·ple·to, a adj. incomplete, unfinished.
in·com·pren·si·ble adj. incomprehensible.
in·co·mu·ni·ca·ble adj. incommunicable.
in·co·mu·ni·ca·do, a adj. *(aislado)* isolated, cut off; CRIMIN. incommunicado.
in·con·ce·bi·ble adj. inconceivable.
in·con·ci·lia·ble adj. irreconcilable.
in·con·clu·so, a adj. inconclusive.
in·con·di·cio·nal adj. unconditional.
in·co·ne·xo, a adj. disconnected, unconnected.
in·con·fe·sa·ble adj. unspeakable.
in·con·fun·di·ble adj. unmistakable.
in·con·gruen·cia f. incongruity.
in·con·gruen·te adj. incongruous.
in·con·men·su·ra·ble adj. *(inmensurable)* incommensurable; *(enorme)* enormous.
in·cons·cien·cia f. *(pérdida del conocimiento)* unconsciousness; *(irreflexión)* thoughtlessness.
in·cons·cien·te I. adj. *(sin conocimiento)* unconscious; *(sin consciencia)* unconscious, unaware; *(irreflexivo)* thoughtless II. m. unconscious.
in·con·se·cuen·te adj. inconsistent.
in·con·si·de·ra·do, a I. adj. *(no considerado)* inconsiderate; *(atolondrado)* rash II. m.f. inconsiderate person.
in·con·sis·ten·cia f. inconsistency.
in·con·sis·ten·te adj. inconsistent.
in·con·so·la·ble adj. inconsolable.
in·cons·tan·cia f. changeableness, fickleness.
in·cons·tan·te adj. & m.f. fickle (person).
in·cons·ti·tu·cio·nal adj. unconstitutional.
in·con·ta·ble adj. *(innumerable)* countless; *(que no puede narrarse)* unrepeatable.
in·con·te·ni·ble adj. irrepressible.
in·con·tes·ta·do, a adj. uncontested.
in·con·ti·nen·cia f. incontinence.
in·con·ti·nen·te adj. incontinent.
in·con·tro·la·ble adj. uncontrollable.
in·con·tro·ver·ti·ble adj. incontrovertible.
in·con·ven·ci·ble adj. steadfast, unshakable.
in·con·ve·nien·cia f. inconvenience; *(incomodidad)* discomfort; *(grosería)* crude remark.
in·con·ve·nien·te I. adj. inconvenient; *(inapropiado)* inappropriate; *(grosero)* crude II. m. *(obstáculo)* obstacle; *(objeción)* objection; *(desventaja)* drawback ♦ tener i. to mind, object.
in·con·ver·ti·ble adj. inconvertible.
in·cor·po·ra·ción f. incorporation.
in·cor·po·ral adj. incorporeal.
in·cor·po·rar tr. to incorporate —reflex. *(sentarse)* to sit up; *(formar parte)* to join ♦ i. a las filas to join the ranks.
in·cor·pó·re·o, a adj. incorporeal.
in·co·rrec·to, a adj. incorrect.
in·co·rre·gi·ble adj. incorrigible.
in·co·rrup·ti·ble adj. incorruptible.
in·co·rrup·to, a adj. incorrupt; *(virgen)* virginal.
in·cre·du·li·dad f. incredulity.
in·cré·du·lo, a I. adj. incredulous; RELIG. unbelieving II. m.f. RELIG. unbeliever.
in·cre·í·ble adj. incredible, unbelievable.
in·cre·men·tar tr. to increase, augment.
in·cre·men·to m. increment, increase.
in·cre·pa·ción f. severe rebuke or reproach.
in·cre·par tr. to rebuke, reprimand.
in·cri·mi·na·ción f. incrimination.
in·cri·mi·nar tr. to incriminate.

in·crus·ta·ción f. incrustation; ARTS inlaying.
in·crus·tar tr. GEOL. to encrust; ARTS to inlay —reflex. to become encrusted or embedded.
in·cu·ba·ción f. incubation.
in·cu·ba·dor, ·ra I. adj. incubating II. f. incubator.
in·cu·bar tr. & intr. to incubate.
in·cues·tio·na·ble adj. unquestionable.
in·cul·car §70 tr. to inculcate.
in·cul·to, a adj. uncultured, uneducated.
in·cum·ben·cia f. incumbency.
in·cum·bir §38 intr. to be of concern to.
in·cu·ra·ble I. adj. incurable II. m.f. incurably ill person.
in·cu·rrir intr. ♦ i. en to commit, incur.
in·cur·sión f. incursion, raid.
in·da·ga·ción f. investigation, inquiry.
in·da·gar §47 tr. to investigate, inquire into.
in·da·ga·to·rio, a adj. investigatory.
in·de·bi·do, a adj. *(ilegal)* illegal; *(desconsiderado)* improper.
in·de·cen·cia f. *(falta de decencia)* indecency; *(acto)* indecent action.
in·de·cen·te adj. indecent.
in·de·ci·ble adj. unspeakable.
in·de·ci·sión f. indecision.
in·de·ci·so, a adj. *(irresoluto)* undecided; *(incierto)* indecisive.
in·de·co·ro·so, a adj. indecorous.
in·de·fen·so, a adj. *(sin defensa)* defenseless; *(desamparado)* helpless.
in·de·fi·ni·do, a adj. *(no definido)* undefined; *(indeterminado)* indefinite; GRAM. indefinite.
in·de·le·ble adj. indelible.
in·dem·ne adj. uninjured, unhurt.
in·dem·ni·dad f. indemnity.
in·dem·ni·za·ción f. indemnity.
in·dem·ni·zar §04 tr. to indemnify.
in·de·pen·den·cia f. independence.
in·de·pen·dien·te I. adj & m.f. independent II. adv. independently.
in·de·pen·di·zar §04 tr. to free, liberate —reflex. to become independent.
in·des·ci·fra·ble adj. undecipherable; FIG. impenetrable.
in·des·crip·ti·ble adj. indescribable.
in·de·se·a·ble adj. & m.f. undesirable.
in·des·truc·ti·ble adj. indestructible.
in·de·ter·mi·na·ble adj. undeterminable.
in·de·ter·mi·na·do, a adj. indeterminate; GRAM. indefinite.
in·di·ca·ción f. indication; *(señal)* sign; *(sugerencia)* suggestion; *(señas)* directions; *(instrucción)* direction; *(observación)* remark.
in·di·ca·do, a adj. *(adecuado)* suitable; *(aconsejado)* recommended.
in·di·ca·dor, ·ra I. adj. indicating II. m. indicator ♦ i. de carretera road sign.
in·di·car §70 tr. to indicate; *(mostrar)* to show; *(sugerir)* to suggest.
in·di·ca·ti·vo, a I. adj. & m. indicative.
ín·di·ce I. m. *(general)* table of contents; *(alfabético)* index; *(de biblioteca)* catalogue; *(indicio)* indication; *(coeficiente)* rate; *(cifra)* index; *(dedo)* index finger II. adj. index.
in·di·cio m. indication, sign ♦ pl. clues.
in·di·fe·ren·cia f. indifference.
in·di·fe·ren·te adj. indifferent.
in·dí·ge·na adj. & m.f. native.
in·di·gen·cia f. indigence.
in·di·gen·te I. adj. indigent II. m. ♦ los indigentes the poor, the needy.

in·di·ges·tar tr. to cause indigestion —reflex. *(tener indigestión)* to have indigestion; COLL. *(no agradar)* to dislike.

in·di·ges·tión f. indigestion.

in·dig·na·ción f. indignation.

in·dig·nar tr. to anger, infuriate —reflex. to become indignant.

in·dig·ni·dad f. *(carácter)* unworthiness; *(afrenta)* indignity.

in·dig·no, a adj. *(sin mérito)* unworthy; *(vil)* despicable.

ín·di·go m. indigo.

in·di·rec·to, a I. adj. indirect **II.** f. hint ♦ lanzar *or* soltar *or* tirar una i. COLL. to hint at.

in·dis·ci·pli·na·do, a adj. undisciplined.

in·dis·cre·ción f. indiscretion.

in·dis·cre·to, a adj. & m.f. indiscreet (person).

in·dis·cu·ti·ble adj. indisputable.

in·dis·pen·sa·ble adj. indispensable.

in·dis·po·ner §54 tr. to set against —reflex. *(enfermarse)* to become indisposed; *(malquistarse)* to fall out.

in·dis·po·si·ción f. indisposition.

in·dis·pues·to, a adj. indisposed.

in·dis·pu·sie·ra, so see **indisponer.**

in·dis·pu·ta·ble adj. indisputable.

in·dis·tin·gui·ble adj. indistinguishable.

in·dis·tin·to, a adj. indistinct

in·di·vi·dual adj. individual; *(habitación)* single.

in·di·vi·dua·li·dad f. individuality.

in·di·vi·dua·lis·ta I. adj. individualistic **II.** m.f. individualist.

in·di·vi·dua·li·zar §04 tr. to individualize.

in·di·vi·duo, a I. adj. individual **II.** m. individual; *(de una sociedad)* member.

in·di·vi·si·bi·li·dad f. indivisibility.

in·di·vi·si·ble adj. indivisible.

in·dó·cil adj. indocile, unruly.

in·do·ci·li·dad f. indocility, unruliness.

in·do·cu·men·ta·do, a I. adj. undocumented **II.** m.f. person without identification papers.

ín·do·le f. *(naturaleza)* nature; *(tipo)* type.

in·do·len·cia f. indolence.

in·do·len·te I. adj. indolent **II.** m.f. idler.

in·do·lo·ro, a adj. indolent, painless.

in·do·ma·ble adj. *(animal)* untamable; *(caballo)* unbreakable; *(persona)* uncontrollable; *(pasión, valor)* indomitable.

in·dó·mi·to, a adj. *(no domado)* untamed; *(no domesticado)* untamable; *(persona)* unruly; *(carácter)* indomitable.

in·duc·ción f. induction.

in·du·cir §22 tr. *(llevar)* to induce, lead; *(deducir)* to induce, infer.

in·duc·ti·vo, a adj. inductive.

in·du·da·ble adj. indubitable, certain.

in·du·je·ra, jo see **inducir.**

in·dul·gen·cia f. indulgence.

in·dul·gen·te adj. indulgent.

in·dul·tar tr. *(perdonar)* to pardon; *(exonerar)* to exempt; LAW to grant amnesty.

in·dul·to m. *(perdón)* pardon; *(exoneración)* exemption.

in·du·men·ta·ria f. clothing, garments.

in·dus·tria f. industry.

in·dus·trial I. adj. industrial **II.** m. industrialist.

in·dus·tria·li·zar §04 tr. to industrialize —reflex. to become industrialized.

in·dus·trio·so, a adj. industrious.

i·né·di·to, a adj. unpublished.

i·ne·fa·ble adj. ineffable.

i·ne·fi·ca·cia f. inefficacy.

i·ne·fi·caz adj. ineffective, inefficacious.

i·ne·lu·di·ble adj. inescapable.

i·nep·ti·tud f. ineptitude.

i·nep·to, a adj. & m.f. inept (person).

i·ne·qui·vo·co, a adj. unequivocal.

i·ner·cia f. inertia.

i·ner·te adj. inert.

i·nes·cru·ta·ble adj. inscrutable.

i·nes·cu·dri·ña·ble adj. inscrutable.

i·nes·pe·ra·do, a adj. unexpected.

i·nes·ta·bi·li·dad f. instability.

i·nes·ta·ble adj. unstable.

i·nes·ti·ma·ble adj. inestimable.

i·ne·vi·ta·ble adj. inevitable.

i·ne·xac·to, a adj. inexact, inaccurate.

i·nex·cu·sa·ble adj. inexcusable.

i·ne·xis·ten·te adj. inexistent, nonexistent.

i·ne·xo·ra·ble adj. inexorable.

i·nex·per·to, a adj. & m.f. inexperienced (person).

i·nex·pli·ca·ble adj. inexplicable.

i·nex·plo·ra·do, a adj. unexplored.

i·nex·pug·na·ble adj. *(invencible)* impregnable; *(irreductible)* unshakable.

i·nex·tin·gui·ble adj. *(que no se apaga)* inextinguishable; *(que no se agota)* unquenchable; *(inagotable)* perpetual.

i·nex·tri·ca·ble adj. inextricable.

in·fa·li·bi·li·dad f. infallibility.

in·fa·li·ble adj. *(inequívoco)* infallible; *(inevitable)* inevitable.

in·fa·man·te adj. defamatory, slanderous.

in·fa·mar tr. to defame, slander.

in·fa·me I. adj. infamous; *(odioso)* thankless; *(vil)* vile **II.** m.f. infamous person.

in·fa·mia f. infamy.

in·fan·cia f. infancy.

in·fan·ta f. *(niña)* infant; *(del rey)* infanta.

in·fan·te m. *(niño)* infant; *(del rey)* infante; MIL. infantryman.

in·fan·te·ri·a f. infantry ♦ i. de marina marines.

in·fan·ti·ci·da I. adj. infanticidal **II.** m.f. infanticide.

in·fan·ti·ci·dio m. infanticide.

in·fan·til adj. infantile; FIG. childish.

in·far·to m. infarct, infarction.

in·fa·ti·ga·ble adj. indefatigable, untiring.

in·fa·tua·ción f. conceit.

in·fa·tuar §67 tr. to make conceited —reflex. to become conceited.

in·faus·to, a adj. unfortunate.

in·fec·ción f. infection.

in·fec·cio·so, a adj. infectious.

in·fec·tar tr. to infect —reflex. to become infected.

in·fe·cun·do, a adj. infecund, sterile.

in·fe·li·ci·dad f. unhappiness.

in·fe·liz I. adj. *(desgraciado)* unfortunate; *(miserable)* wretched; COLL. *(bondadoso)* good-hearted **II.** m.f. *(pobre diablo)* poor devil; COLL. *(persona bondadosa)* good-hearted person.

in·fe·ren·cia f. inference.

in·fe·rior I. adj *(de abajo)* lower; *(menor)* inferior; *(menos)* less **II.** m. inferior.

in·fe·rio·ri·dad f. inferiority.

in·fe·rir §65 tr. *(deducir)* to infer, deduce; *(ocasionar)* to cause, inflict.

in·fer·nal adj. infernal.

in·fes·ta·ción f. infestation.
in·fes·tar tr. to infest.
in·fi·de·li·dad f. infidelity.
in·fiel I. adj. *(falto de fidelidad)* unfaithful; *(desleal)* disloyal II. m.f. RELIG. infidel.
in·fie·ra, ró see **inferir.**
in·fier·no m. hell; FIG. madhouse ♦ **en el quinto i.** COLL. (out) in the boondocks.
in·fil·tra·ción f. infiltration.
in·fil·trar tr. & reflex. to infiltrate.
ín·fi·mo, a adj. *(muy bajo)* least, lowest; *(peor)* worst.
in·fi·ni·dad f. infinity; *(cantidad)* a lot ♦ **una i. de personas** countless people.
in·fi·ni·te·si·mal adj. infinitesimal.
in·fi·ni·ti·vo, a adj. & m. GRAM. infinitive.
in·fi·ni·to, a I. adj. infinite II. m. infinite; MATH., PHYS. infinity III. adv. ♦ **a lo i.** ad infinitum.
in·fla·ción f. inflation.
in·fla·cio·na·rio, a adj. inflationary.
in·fla·dor m. air pump, inflater.
in·fla·ma·ble adj. inflammable.
in·fla·ma·ción f. inflammation.
in·fla·mar tr. *(encender)* to set on fire; *(enardecer las pasiones)* to inflame —reflex. *(encenderse)* to catch fire; *(enardecerse)* to become aroused.
in·fla·ma·to·rio, a adj. inflammatory.
in·flar tr. to inflate —reflex. to become conceited *or* puffed up.
in·fle·xi·ble adj. inflexible, rigid.
in·fli·gir §32 tr. to inflict.
in·fluen·cia f. influence.
in·fluen·ciar tr. AMER. to influence.
in·fluen·za f. influenza, flu.
in·fluir §18 intr. to have influence.
in·flu·jo m. influence.
in·flu·yen·te adj. influential.
in·for·ma·ción f. information; *(datos)* data.
in·for·mal adj. informal; *(de poco fiar)* unreliable.
in·for·ma·li·dad f. informality; *(falta de seriedad)* irresponsibility.
in·for·mar tr. *(comunicar)* to inform; PHILOS. to form —reflex. to find out.
in·for·má·ti·ca f. data processing.
in·for·ma·ti·vo, a adj. informative.
in·for·me¹ adj. shapeless, formless.
in·for·me² m. report, piece of information.
in·for·tu·na·do, a adj. & m.f. unfortunate (person).
in·for·tu·nio m. misfortune, bad luck.
in·frac·ción f. infraction, transgression.
in·frac·tor, ·ra I. adj. transgressing II. m.f. transgressor.
in·fra·es·truc·tu·ra f. infrastructure.
in·fran·que·a·ble adj. insurmountable.
in·fra·rro·jo, a adj. infrared.
in·fre·cuen·te adj. infrequent.
in·frin·gir §32 tr. to infringe, violate.
in·fruc·tí·fe·ro, a adj. unfruitful, unprofitable.
in·fruc·tuo·so, a adj. fruitless, useless.
in·fun·da·do, a adj. unfounded, groundless.
in·fun·dio m. COLL. lie, false story.
in·fun·dio·so, a adj. lying, mendacious.
in·fun·dir tr. to instill, arouse.
in·fu·sión f. infusion.
in·ge·niar tr. to devise —reflex. to manage *(para)* to ♦ **ingeniárselas** to manage.
in·ge·nie·rí·a f. engineering.
in·ge·nie·ro m. engineer ♦ **i. agrónomo** agron-

omist.
in·ge·nio m. *(habilidad)* ingenuity; *(talento)* talent; *(agudeza)* wit; *(de azúcar)* sugar mill ♦ **afilar** *or* **aguzar el i.** to sharpen one's wits.
in·ge·nio·si·dad f. ingenuity.
in·ge·nio·so, a adj. ingenious.
in·ge·nuo, a adj. & m.f. naive (person).
in·ge·rir §65 tr. to ingest.
in·ges·tión f. ingestion.
in·gle f. groin.
in·gra·ti·tud f. ingratitude, ungratefulness.
in·gra·to, a adj. *(desagradecido)* ungrateful; *(que no satisface)* thankless, unrewarding.
in·gre·dien·te m. ingredient.
in·gre·sar intr. *(entrar)* to enter; *(hacerse miembro)* to become a member of —tr. to deposit.
in·gre·so m. *(acción)* entrance; *(entrada)* entryway; *(de dinero)* income ♦ pl. earnings.
in·há·bil adj. *(incapaz)* unskillful; *(inadecuado)* unfit.
in·ha·bi·li·dad f. *(falta de maña)* unskillfulness; *(ineptitud)* incompetence; *(impedimento)* handicap.
in·ha·bi·li·tar tr. to disqualify.
in·ha·bi·ta·ble adj. uninhabitable.
in·ha·bi·ta·do, a adj. uninhabited, deserted.
in·ha·lar tr. to inhale.
in·he·ren·te adj. inherent.
in·hi·bi·ción f. inhibition.
in·hi·bir tr. to inhibit —reflex. to withdraw.
in·hos·pi·ta·la·rio, a adj. inhospitable.
in·hu·ma·ni·dad f. inhumanity, cruelty.
in·hu·ma·no, a adj. inhuman, cruel.
i·ni·cia·ción f. initiation.
i·ni·cia·do, a I. adj. initiated II. m.f. initiate.
i·ni·cia·dor, ·ra I. adj. initiating II. m.f. initiator.
i·ni·cial adj. & f. initial.
i·ni·ciar tr. to initiate; *(admitir)* to introduce.
i·ni·cia·ti·va f. initiative.
i·ni·cio m. beginning.
i·ni·cuo, a adj. iniquitous, wicked.
i·ni·gua·la·do, a adj. unequaled.
i·ni·ma·gi·na·ble adj. unimaginable.
i·ni·mi·ta·ble adj. inimitable.
i·nin·te·li·gi·ble adj. unintelligible.
i·ni·qui·dad f. iniquity.
in·je·ren·cia f. interference.
in·je·rir §65 tr. to insert —reflex. to interfere.
in·jer·tar tr. to graft, implant.
in·jer·to m. graft, transplant.
in·ju·ria f. *(insulto)* insult; *(daño)* injury.
in·ju·riar tr. *(ofender)* to insult; *(dañar)* to injure.
in·ju·rio·so, a adj. injurious.
in·jus·ti·cia f. injustice.
in·jus·ti·fi·ca·ble adj. unjustifiable.
in·jus·to, a adj. unjust.
in·ma·cu·la·do, a adj. spotless, immaculate.
in·ma·du·rez f. immaturity.
in·ma·du·ro, a adj. *(fruta)* unripe, green; *(persona)* immature.
in·me·dia·ción f. immediacy ♦ pl. environs.
in·me·dia·to, a adj. next to, adjoining ♦ **de i.** immediately, at once.
in·me·mo·rial adj. immemorial.
in·men·si·dad f. immensity, vastness.
in·men·so, a adj. immense.
in·men·su·ra·ble adj. immeasurable.
in·me·re·ci·do, a adj. unmerited, undeserved.
in·mer·sión f. immersion.

in·mi·gra·ción f. immigration.
in·mi·gran·te adj. & m.f. immigrant.
in·mi·grar intr. to immigrate.
in·mi·gra·to·rio, a adj. immigrant.
in·mi·nen·cia f. imminence, imminency.
in·mi·nen·te adj. imminent.
in·mis·cuir §18 tr. to mix —reflex. to meddle, interfere.
in·mo·bi·lia·rio, a adj. real estate.
in·mo·de·ra·do, a adj. immoderate, excessive.
in·mo·des·to, a adj. immodest.
in·mo·la·ción f. immolation.
in·mo·lar tr. & reflex. to immolate (oneself).
in·mo·ral adj. immoral.
in·mo·ra·li·dad f. immorality.
in·mor·tal adj. immortal.
in·mor·ta·li·dad f. immortality.
in·mor·ta·li·zar §04 tr. to immortalize.
in·mo·vi·ble adj. immovable.
in·mó·vil adj. immobile.
in·mo·vi·li·dad f. immobility.
in·mo·vi·li·za·ción f. immobilization.
in·mo·vi·li·zar §04 tr. to immobilize; COM. to tie up capital.
in·mue·ble I. adj. ♦ bienes inmuebles real estate II. m. building.
in·mun·di·cia f. filth, dirt.
in·mun·do, a adj. dirty, filthy.
in·mu·ni·dad f. immunity.
in·mu·ni·za·ción f. immunization.
in·mu·ni·zar §04 tr. to immunize.
in·mu·no·lo·gí·a f. immunology.
in·mu·ta·bi·li·dad f. immutability.
in·mu·ta·ble adj. immutable.
in·mu·tar tr. to change —reflex. to lose one's composure.
in·na·to, a adj. innate.
in·ne·ce·sa·rio, a adj. unnecessary.
in·ne·ga·ble adj. undeniable.
in·no·ble adj. ignoble.
in·no·va·ción f. innovation.
in·no·va·dor, ·ra I. adj. innovative II. m.f. innovator.
in·no·var tr. to innovate.
in·nu·me·ra·ble adj. innumerable.
i·no·cen·cia f. innocence.
i·no·cen·te adj. & m.f. innocent ♦ día de los i. April Fools' Day.
i·no·cu·la·ción f. inoculation.
i·no·cu·lar tr. to inoculate.
i·no·cuo, a adj. innocuous.
i·no·do·ro, a I. adj. odorless II. m. toilet.
i·nol·vi·da·ble adj. unforgettable.
i·no·pe·ra·ble adj. inoperable.
i·no·por·tu·no, a adj. inopportune.
i·nor·gá·ni·co, a adj. inorganic.
i·no·xi·da·ble adj. rustproof ♦ acero i. stainless steel.
in·que·bran·ta·ble adj. unbreakable.
in·quie·tan·te adj. disquieting, disturbing.
in·quie·tar tr. (perturbar) to disturb; (alarmar) to alarm —reflex. to worry.
in·quie·to, a adj. (intranquilo) restless; (desasosegado) worried, anxious.
in·quie·tud f. (agitación) restlessness; (aprensión) uneasiness.
in·qui·li·na·to m. (alquiler) leasing; (derecho) tenancy.
in·qui·li·no, a m.f. tenant.
in·qui·na f. animosity, dislike ♦ tenerle i. a alguien to hold a grudge against.
in·qui·rir §02 tr. to investigate, probe.

in·qui·si·ción f. inquisition; HIST. Inquisition.
in·qui·si·dor, ·ra I. adj. inquisitive II. m.f. inquirer —m. HIST. Inquisitor.
in·qui·si·ti·vo, a adj. inquisitive.
in·sa·cia·ble adj. insatiable.
in·sa·lu·bre adj. insalubrious.
in·sa·no, a adj. (demente) insane; (insalubre) unhealthy.
in·sa·tis·fac·ción f. dissatisfaction.
in·sa·tis·fac·to·rio, a adj. unsatisfactory.
in·sa·tis·fe·cho, a adj. (no satisfecho) unsatisfied; (desilusionado) dissatisfied.
ins·cri·bir §80 tr. (grabar) to engrave; (matricular) to register; (anotar) to record —reflex. to register, enroll.
ins·crip·ción f. (acción) inscribing; (epígrafe) inscription; (anotación) record; (matriculación) enrollment.
in·sec·ti·ci·da I. adj. insecticidal II. m. insecticide.
in·sec·to m. insect.
in·se·gu·ri·dad f. insecurity.
in·se·gu·ro, a adj. insecure.
in·se·mi·na·ción f. insemination.
in·sen·sa·tez f. (estupidez) stupidity; (dicho) foolish remark.
in·sen·sa·to, a I. adj. foolish, senseless II. m.f. fool, dolt.
in·sen·si·ble adj. (que no siente) insensible; (sin compasión) unfeeling; (imperceptible) imperceptible; (inconsciente) unconscious.
in·se·pa·ra·ble adj. inseparable.
in·ser·ción f. insertion.
in·ser·tar tr. to insert.
in·si·dia f. malice.
in·si·dio·so, a adj. insidious.
in·sig·ne adj. famous, illustrious.
in·sig·nia f. badge, emblem.
in·sig·ni·fi·can·te adj. insignificant.
in·sin·ce·ri·dad f. insincerity.
in·sin·ce·ro, a adj. insincere.
in·si·nua·ción f. insinuation.
in·si·nuar §67 tr. to insinuate —reflex. to ingratiate oneself.
in·sí·pi·do, a adj. tasteless; FIG. dull.
in·sis·ten·cia f. insistence.
in·sis·ten·te adj. insistent.
in·sis·tir intr. to insist (en on).
in·so·bor·na·ble adj. incorruptible.
in·so·cia·ble adj. unsociable.
in·so·la·ción f. sunstroke, overexposure.
in·so·lar tr. to expose to the sun —reflex. to get sunstroke.
in·so·len·cia f. insolence.
in·so·len·te adj. insolent.
in·só·li·to, a adj. unusual, uncommon.
in·so·lu·ble adj. insoluble.
in·sol·ven·te adj. & m.f. insolvent.
in·som·nio m. insomnia, sleeplessness.
in·son·da·ble adj. unfathomable.
in·so·por·ta·ble adj. unbearable, intolerable.
in·sos·te·ni·ble adj. untenable.
ins·pec·ción f. inspection, examination.
ins·pec·cio·nar tr. to inspect, examine.
ins·pec·tor, ·ra m.f. inspector.
ins·pi·ra·ción f. inspiration; (de aire) inhalation.
ins·pi·rar tr. to inhale; (infundir sentimientos) to inspire —reflex. to be inspired (en by).
ins·ta·la·ción f. installation; (equipo) equipment ♦ i. sanitaria plumbing.
ins·ta·la·dor, ·ra m.f. installer, fitter.

ins·ta·lar tr. to install —reflex. to establish oneself.

ins·tan·cia f. instance ♦ **a i. de** at the request of • **en última i.** as a final resort.

ins·tan·tá·ne·o, a adj. instantaneous.

ins·tan·te m. instant, moment ♦ **a cada i.** constantly • **al i.** immediately.

ins·tar tr. to urge, press —intr. to be urgent.

ins·tau·ra·ción f. establishment.

ins·tau·rar tr. to establish.

ins·ti·ga·ción f. instigation.

ins·ti·gar §47 tr. to incite.

ins·ti·lar tr. to instill.

ins·tin·ti·vo, a adj. instinctive.

ins·tin·to m. instinct ♦ **por i.** by instinct.

ins·ti·tu·ción f. institution.

ins·ti·tu·cio·nal adj. institutional.

ins·ti·tu·cio·na·li·zar §04 tr. to institutionalize.

ins·ti·tuir §18 tr. to institute.

ins·ti·tu·to m. institute; *(escuela)* school.

ins·truc·ción f. instruction; *(enseñanza)* teaching; *(educación)* education; *(conocimiento)* learning; MIL. drill ♦ pl. directions.

ins·truc·ti·vo, a adj. instructive.

ins·truc·tor, ·ra m.f. instructor.

ins·truir §18 tr. to instruct, teach.

ins·tru·men·ta·ción f. arrangement.

ins·tru·men·tal I. adj. instrumental **II.** m. instruments.

ins·tru·men·tar tr. to orchestrate, arrange.

ins·tru·men·to m. instrument.

ins·tru·ya, yo, yera, yó see **instruir.**

in·su·bor·di·na·ción f. insubordination.

in·su·bor·di·na·do, a I. adj. insubordinate **II.** m.f. rebel.

in·su·bor·di·nar tr. to incite to rebellion —reflex. to rebel.

in·subs·tan·cial adj. *(sin substancia)* insubstantial; *(vacío)* shallow.

in·su·fi·cien·cia f. insufficiency; MED. failure.

in·su·fi·cien·te adj. insufficient.

in·su·li·na f. insulin.

in·sul·so, a adj. *(sin sabor)* tasteless; *(soso)* dull.

in·sul·tan·te adj. insulting.

in·sul·tar tr. to insult.

in·sul·to m. insult.

in·su·pe·ra·ble adj. insurmountable.

in·sur·gen·te adj. & m.f. insurgent.

in·su·rrec·ción f. insurrection.

in·su·rrec·to, a I. adj. insurgent **II.** m.f. rebel.

in·tac·to, a adj. intact.

in·ta·cha·ble adj. irreproachable, stainless.

in·tan·gi·ble adj. intangible.

in·te·gra·ción f. integration.

in·te·gra·dor, ·ra I. adj. integrating **II.** m.f. integrator.

in·te·gral adj. & f. integral.

in·te·grar tr. *(componer)* to make up, compose; *(hacer entrar)* to integrate; MATH. to integrate ♦ **estar integrado por** to be composed of.

in·te·gri·dad f. integrity.

ín·te·gro, a adj. *(entero)* whole, complete; *(honrado)* honest, upright.

in·te·lec·to m. intellect.

in·te·lec·tual adj. & m.f. intellectual.

in·te·lec·tua·li·zar §04 intr. to intellectualize.

in·te·li·gen·cia f. intelligence; *(comprensión)* understanding; *(habilidad)* ability.

in·te·li·gen·te adj. & m.f. intelligent (person).

in·te·li·gi·ble adj. intelligible.

in·tem·pe·ran·cia f. intemperance.

in·tem·pe·ran·te adj. intemperate.

in·tem·pe·rie f. bad weather ♦ **a la i.** outdoors.

in·tem·pes·ti·vo, a adj. inopportune, ill-timed.

in·ten·ción f. intention; *(voluntad)* wish ♦ **con i.** intentionally • **segunda i.** underhandedness • **tener malas intenciones** to be up to no good.

in·ten·cio·nal adj. intentional.

in·ten·si·dad f. intensity, strength.

in·ten·si·fi·ca·ción f. intensification.

in·ten·si·fi·car §70 tr. to intensify.

in·ten·si·vo, a adj. intensive.

in·ten·so, a adj. intense.

in·ten·tar tr. *(tener intención)* to intend, plan; *(ensayar)* to try, attempt.

in·ten·to m. *(propósito)* intent; *(tentativa)* attempt.

in·te·rac·ción f. interaction.

in·ter·ca·lar tr. to intercalate.

in·ter·cam·bia·ble adj. interchangeable.

in·ter·cam·biar tr. to interchange, exchange.

in·ter·cam·bio m. interchange, exchange.

in·ter·ce·der tr. to intercede.

in·ter·cep·tar tr. *(detener)* to intercept; *(obstruir)* to block; *(un teléfono)* to wiretap.

in·ter·ce·sión f. intercession.

in·ter·dic·ción f. prohibition, interdiction.

in·te·rés m. interest ♦ **devengar i.** to bear interest • **i. acumulado** accrued interest • **i. propio** self-interest • **sentir** or **tener i. en** to be interested in • **tipo de i.** rate of interest ♦ pl. possessions, interest • **i. creados** vested interests.

in·te·re·sa·do, a I. adj. *(que tiene interés)* interested; *(guiado por el interés)* selfish **II.** m.f. interested person or party.

in·te·re·san·te adj. interesting.

in·te·re·sar tr. *(inspirar interés)* to interest, arouse interest in; MED. to afflict —intr. to be of interest —reflex. to be or become interested *(en, por in).*

in·ter·fe·ren·cia f. interference.

in·ter·fe·rir §65 intr. to interfere.

ín·te·rin m. interim, meantime.

in·te·ri·no, a I. adj. *(provisorio)* interim; *(sustituto)* acting **II.** m.f. substitute.

in·te·rior I. adj. *(interno)* interior, inner; *(nacional)* domestic, internal; *(íntimo)* inner, innermost **II.** m. *(parte interna)* interior, inside; *(alma)* heart, soul; GEOG. interior.

in·ter·jec·ción f. interjection.

in·ter·lo·cu·tor, ·ra m.f. interlocutor.

in·ter·me·diar tr. to mediate.

in·ter·me·dia·rio, a I. adj. intermediate **II.** m. intermediary.

in·ter·me·dio, a I. adj. intermediate **II.** m. *(intervalo)* interval; THEAT. intermission.

in·ter·mi·na·ble adj. interminable.

in·ter·mi·ten·cia f. intermittence.

in·ter·mi·ten·te adj. intermittent.

in·ter·na·ción f. *(en hospital)* hospitalization; *(encerramiento)* confinement.

in·ter·na·cio·nal adj. international.

in·ter·na·cio·na·li·zar §04 tr. to internationalize.

in·ter·na·do, a I. adj. institutionalized **II.** m. boarding school.

in·ter·nar tr. *(hospitalizar)* to hospitalize; *(trasladar)* to send inland; *(encerrar)* to confine —reflex. to penetrate.

in·ter·no, a I. adj. *(de adentro)* internal; *(interior)* interior, inside; *(estudiante)* boarding

II. m.f. *(alumno)* boarding student; *(médico)* internist.

in·ter·pe·la·ción f. appeal, plea.

in·ter·pe·lar tr. *(a un oficial)* to question formally; *(rogar)* to plead.

in·ter·po·lar tr. to interpolate.

in·ter·po·ner §54 tr. to interpose; LAW to lodge *or* file —reflex. *(intervenir)* to intervene; *(estorbar)* to get in the way of.

in·ter·pre·ta·ción f. interpretation ♦ mala i. misinterpretation.

in·ter·pre·tar tr. to interpret; MUS. to perform; THEAT. to play.

in·ter·pre·ta·ti·vo, a adj. interpretative.

in·tér·pre·te m.f. *(traductor)* interpreter; *(actor)* actor; *(cantante)* singer.

in·ter·pu·sie·ra, so see interponer.

in·te·rro·ga·ción f. interrogation; *(pregunta)* question; GRAM. question mark.

in·te·rro·ga·dor, ·ra m.f. interrogator.

in·te·rro·gan·te I. adj. interrogating ♦ punto i. GRAM. question mark II. m.f. *(pregunta)* question; *(incógnita)* unanswered question.

in·te·rro·gar §47 tr. to interrogate, question.

in·te·rro·ga·ti·vo, a adj. & m. interrogative.

in·te·rro·ga·to·rio m. interrogation.

in·te·rrum·pir tr. to interrupt; *(obstruir)* to block, obstruct.

in·te·rrup·ción f. interruption.

in·te·rrup·tor m. switch; *(de circuito)* circuit breaker.

in·ter·sec·ción f. intersection.

in·ters·ti·cio m. interstice.

in·ter·va·lo m. interval ♦ a intervalos at intervals, intermittently.

in·ter·ven·ción f. *(mediación)* intervention, mediation; *(participación)* participation; *(de cuentas)* auditing, audit ♦ i. quirúrgica surgical procedure, operation.

in·ter·ve·nir §76 intr. *(participar)* to participate, take part; *(interceder)* to mediate; *(interponerse)* to intervene —tr. *(las cuentas)* to audit; *(la comunicación)* to wiretap; SURG. to operate on.

in·tes·ti·nal adj. intestinal.

in·tes·ti·no, a I. adj. internal II. m. intestine ♦ i. ciego caecum • i. delgado small intestine • i. grueso large intestine.

in·ti·ma·(ción) f. *(conminación)* ultimatum; *(indicio)* intimation; LAW notice.

in·ti·mar tr. *(hacer saber)* to make known; *(mandar)* to order —intr. to become friendly.

in·ti·mi·da·ción f. intimidation.

in·ti·mi·dad f. *(amistad)* close friendship; *(vida privada)* privacy; *(cercanía)* intimacy, closeness ♦ en la i. privately • en la i. de in the privacy of.

in·ti·mi·dar tr. to intimidate.

ín·ti·mo, a I. adj *(interior)* intimate, innermost; *(esencial)* essential; *(estrecho)* intimate, close; *(privado)* private II. m.f. intimate *or* close friend.

in·to·ca·ble adj. untouchable.

in·to·le·ra·ble adj. intolerable.

in·to·xi·ca·ción f. intoxication.

in·to·xi·car §70 tr. to intoxicate.

in·tran·qui·li·dad f. uneasiness.

in·tran·qui·lo, a adj. uneasy.

in·trans·cen·den·te adj. insignificant.

in·tran·si·gen·cia f. intransigence.

in·tran·si·gen·te adj. & m.f. intransigent.

in·tran·si·ta·ble adj. impassable.

in·tran·si·ti·vo, a adj. intransitive.

in·tra·ta·ble adj. *(incontrolable)* unmanageable; *(insociable)* unsociable; *(grosero)* rude.

in·tra·ve·no·so, a adj. intravenous.

in·tre·pi·dez f. intrepidness.

in·tré·pi·do, a adj. intrepid.

in·tri·ga f. intrigue.

in·tri·gar §47 intr. & tr. to intrigue.

in·trin·ca·do, a adj. *(complicado)* intricate; *(denso)* dense.

in·trín·se·co, a adj. intrinsic.

in·tro·duc·ción f. introduction; *(inserción)* insertion; *(prefacio)* preface; *(preámbulo)* preamble; MUS. overture.

in·tro·du·cir §22 tr. *(dar entrada)* to show (en into); *(meter)* to put in *or* into, stick in; *(insertar)* to insert; *(presentar)* to introduce —reflex. to enter, get in.

in·tro·duc·ti·vo, a adj. introductory.

in·tros·pec·ción f. introspection.

in·tros·pec·ti·vo, a adj. introspective.

in·tro·ver·ti·do, a I. adj. introverted II. m.f. introvert.

in·tru·sión f. intrusion.

in·tru·so, a I. adj. intrusive II. m.f. intruder.

in·tui·ción f. intuition.

in·tuir §18 tr. to intuit, sense.

in·tui·ti·vo, a adj. intuitive.

i·nun·da·ción f. flood.

i·nun·dar tr. to flood.

i·nu·si·ta·do, a adj. unusual, uncommon.

i·nu·sual adj. unusual, uncommon.

i·nú·til I. adj. *(inservible)* useless; *(vano)* vain, fruitless II. m.f. good-for-nothing.

i·nu·ti·li·zar §04 tr. *(arruinar)* to destroy; *(inhabilitar)* to make unusable.

in·va·dir tr. to invade.

in·va·li·da·ción f. invalidation.

in·va·li·dar tr. to invalidate.

in·va·li·dez f. invalidity.

in·vá·li·do, a I. adj. invalid, disabled; *(nulo)* invalid, null II. m.f. invalid, disabled person.

in·va·ria·ble adj. invariable.

in·va·sión f. invasion.

in·va·sor, ·ra I. adj. invading II. m.f. invader.

in·ven·ci·ble adj. invincible.

in·ven·ción f. invention.

in·ven·tar tr. to invent; *(forjar)* to fabricate, make up.

in·ven·ta·riar §30 tr. to inventory.

in·ven·ta·rio m. inventory.

in·ven·ti·vo, a I. adj. inventive II. f. inventiveness.

in·ven·to m. invention; *(creación)* creation; *(engaño)* fabrication; COLL. *(mentira)* lie.

in·ven·tor, ·ra I. adj. inventive II. m.f. inventor.

in·ver·na·de·ro m. *(invernáculo)* greenhouse; *(para el ganado)* winter pasture.

in·ver·nar §49 intr. *(pasar el invierno)* to winter; ZOOL. to hibernate.

in·ve·ro·sí·mil adj. *(improbable)* improbable, unlikely; *(increíble)* unbelievable.

in·ver·sión f. inversion; FIN. investment.

in·ver·sio·nis·ta m.f. investor.

in·ver·so, a adj. inverse, inverted ♦ a la i. the opposite way.

in·ver·te·bra·do, a adj. & m. invertebrate.

in·ver·tir §65 tr. to invert; COM., FIN. to invest; *(tiempo)* to spend time.

in·ves·ti·du·ra f. investiture.

in·ves·ti·ga·ción f. investigation; *(estudio)* research.

in·ves·ti·ga·dor, ·ra I. adj. investigative; *(que experimenta)* researching II. m.f. investigator; *(científico)* researcher.

in·ves·ti·gar §47 tr. to investigate; *(estudiar)* to research, study.

in·ves·tir §48 tr. to invest, confer (on).

in·ve·te·ra·do, a adj. inveterate.

in·vier·no m. winter.

in·vier·ta, to see invertir.

in·vio·la·ble adj. inviolable.

in·vir·tie·ra, tió see invertir.

in·vi·si·ble adj. invisible.

in·vi·ta·ción f. invitation.

in·vi·ta·do, a m.f. guest.

in·vi·tar tr. to invite.

in·vo·ca·ción f. invocation.

in·vo·car §70 tr. to invoke.

in·vo·lu·crar tr. to involve, implicate.

in·vo·lun·ta·rio, a adj. involuntary.

in·vul·ne·ra·ble adj. invulnerable.

in·yec·ción f. injection.

in·yec·tar tr. to inject.

ion m. ion.

ir §41 intr. to go; *(moverse)* to move; *(caminar)* to walk; *(viajar)* to travel; *(dirigirse)* to lead; *(extenderse)* to extend; *(proceder)* to proceed; *(quedar bien)* to suit, become; *(apostar)* to be at stake, ride • ¿cómo le va? how is it going? • ¿cómo va el asunto? how is the matter going? • i. a *(estar a punto de)* to be about to, to be going to <voy a comer en casa I am going to eat at home> • i. adelante to progress, go forward • i. de caza to go hunting • i. de compras to go shopping • i. de mal en peor to go from bad to worse • i. de paseo to go for a walk • i. de viaje to go on a trip • i. por to go for, fetch • ¡vaya! *(sorpresa)* you don't say!, is that so!; what a <¡vaya memoria! what a memory!> —reflex. *(partir)* to go away, leave; *(deslizarse)* to slip; *(morirse)* to die ♦ i. abajo to topple, collapse • i. a pique MARIT. to sink • vámonos let's go • vete a saber there's no telling.

i·ra f. *(cólera)* anger; *(furia)* fury ♦ llenarse de i. to become angry.

i·ra·cun·do, a adj. irate, angered.

i·ras·ci·ble adj. irascible.

ir·go, gue, guiera, guió see erguir.

i·ri·dis·cen·te adj. iridescent.

i·ris m. iris; MIN. noble opal ♦ arco i. rainbow.

i·ro·ní·a f. irony.

i·ró·ni·co, a adj. ironic(al).

i·rra·cio·nal adj. irrational.

i·rra·diar tr. to irradiate.

i·rra·zo·na·ble adj. absurd, ridiculous.

i·rre·al adj. unreal.

i·rre·a·li·dad f. unreality.

i·rre·ba·ti·ble adj. irrefutable, indisputable.

i·rre·con·ci·lia·ble adj. irreconcilable.

i·rre·fu·ta·ble adj. irrefutable.

i·rre·gu·lar adj. irregular.

i·rre·gu·la·ri·dad f. irregularity.

i·rre·le·van·te adj. irrelevant.

i·rre·pa·ra·ble adj. irreparable.

i·rre·pri·mi·ble adj. irrepressible.

i·rre·pro·cha·ble adj. irreproachable, faultless.

i·rre·sis·ti·ble adj. irresistible.

i·rre·so·lu·to, a adj. & m.f. irresolute (person).

i·rres·pe·tuo·so, a adj. & m.f. disrespectful (person).

i·rres·pon·sa·bi·li·dad f. irresponsibility.

i·rres·pon·sa·ble adj. & m.f. irresponsible.

i·rre·ve·ren·cia f. irreverence.

i·rre·ve·ren·te adj. & m.f. irreverent (person).

i·rre·ver·si·ble adj. irreversible.

i·rre·vo·ca·ble adj. irrevocable.

i·rri·ga·ción f. irrigation.

i·rri·gar §47 tr. to irrigate.

i·rri·so·rio, a adj. *(risible)* laughable; *(bajo)* ridiculously low.

i·rri·ta·ble adj. irritable.

i·rri·ta·ción f. irritation.

i·rri·tan·te adj. irritant.

i·rri·tar tr. to irritate.

i·rrum·pir intr. to burst (en into).

i·rrup·ción f. *(acometida)* bursting or rushing into; *(invasión)* invasion.

is·la f. island.

is·lá·mi·co, a adj. Islamic.

is·le·ta f. *(isla pequeña)* isle, islet; *(acera)* traffic island.

i·só·to·po m. isotope.

ist·mo m. isthmus.

i·tá·li·co, a adj. italic ♦ letra i. italics.

i·ti·ne·ra·rio, a adj. & m. itinerary.

iz·quier·dis·ta adj. & m.f. leftist.

iz·quier·do, a adj. left II. f. *(mano)* left hand; *(lado)* left ♦ a la i. *(dirección)* left, to the left; *(sitio)* on the left • de la i. on the left • a i. POL. the left or Left • por la i. on the left.

J

J, j f. eleventh letter of the Spanish alphabet.

ja·ba·lí m. [pl. -íes] wild boar.

ja·ba·li·na¹ f. ZOOL. wild sow.

ja·ba·li·na² f. javelin.

ja·bón m. soap ♦ dar un j. a R.P., COLL. to frighten; *(de afeitar)* shaving soap • j. de tocador or de olor toilet soap • j. en polvo soap powder • tener j. R.P., COLL. to be afraid.

ja·bo·na·do, a m. *(jabonadura)* soaping; *(ropa)* wash —f. AMER. soaping.

ja·bo·na·du·ra f. soaping.

ja·bo·nar tr. *(la ropa, el cuerpo)* to wash; *(la barba)* to lather.

ja·bon·ci·llo m. *(jabón)* bar of soap; BOT. soapberry.

ja·bo·ne·ro, a I. adj. soap II.m.f. soapmaker —f. soap dish.

ja·bo·no·so, a adj. soapy.

ja·ca f. pony, small horse.

ja·ca·ran·do·so, a adj. COLL. merry, lively.

ja·ca·re·ro, a/ris·ta adj. merry, lively.

já·ce·na f. girder, main beam.

ja·cin·to m. BOT. hyacinth; MIN. zircon ♦ j. occidental topaz • j. oriental ruby.

jaco m. *(jamelgo)* hack, nag; *(cota)* short-sleeved coat of mail.

jac·tan·cia f. *(alardeo)* boast; *(arrogancia)* arrogance.

jac·tan·cio·so, a adj. boastful, arrogant.

jac·tar·se reflex. to boast *(de* about).

ja·da f. hoe, spade.

ja·de m. jade.

ja·de·ar intr. to pant, gasp.

ja·diar tr. to hoe, dig with a spade.

ja·ez m. *(arreo)* harness; DEROG. *(carácter)* ilk, sort.

ja·guar m. jaguar.

ja·guay m. AMER. watering trough.

ja·güey m. AMER. pond.

ja·lar tr. COLL. *(tirar)* to pull; C. AMER. to make love to; COL., VEN. to do, perform —intr. AMER. to leave.

jal·be·gar §47 tr. to whitewash.

ja·le·a f. jelly ♦ **hacerse** *or* **volverse una j.** to go sweet (on).

ja·le·a·dor, ·ra I. adj. cheering II. m.f. cheerer.

ja·le·ar tr. *(animar)* to encourage; *(incitar)* to urge on; AMER. to pester.

ja·le·o m. *(animación)* clapping and cheering; *(incitación)* urging; *(baile)* popular Andalusian dance, COLL. *(tumulto)* fuss, uproar ♦ **armar un j.** to kick up a fuss • **estar de j.** to have a good time.

jal·ma f. packsaddle.

ja·lón¹ m. *(hito)* milestone; *(estaca)* stake.

ja·lón² m. AMER., COLL. *(tirón)* pull; *(trecho)* stretch, distance.

ja·lo·nar tr. *(con jalones)* to stake out; *(marcar)* to mark.

ja·más adv. *(nunca)* never; *(alguna vez)* ever ♦ **j. de los jamases** never ever • **nunca j.** never again • **para siempre j.** for ever and ever.

jam·ba f. jamb.

jam·ba·je m. *(de una puerta)* door frame; *(de una ventana)* window frame.

ja·mel·go m. nag, hack.

ja·món m. ham ♦ **j. ahumado** smoked ham • **j. serrano** cured ham.

ja·mo·na COLL. I. adj. plump II. f. buxom (middle-aged) woman ♦ **una mujer j.** a good-looking woman.

jan·ga·da f. *(armadía)* float; *(de árboles)* logjam.

ja·que¹ m. check ♦ **dar j.** to check • **dar j. y mate** to checkmate • **j.** mate checkmate • **tener en j.** *(amenazar)* to keep in check; *(hostigar)* to pester.

ja·que² m. COLL. braggart.

ja·que·ar tr. *(en ajedrez)* to check; *(hostigar)* to pester.

ja·que·ca f. *(migraña)* migraine headache; COLL. *(molestia)* pain in the neck.

ja·que·tón m. man-eating shark.

ja·ra f. BOT. rockrose; *(arma)* dart.

ja·ra·be m. syrup ♦ **dar j.** to butter up • **estar hecho un j.** to go sweet on • **j. de pico** COLL. lip service • **j. para la tos** cough syrup • **j. tapatío** hat dance.

ja·ra·na f. *(alboroto)* fuss, uproar; AMER. *(chanza)* joke ♦ **andar** *or* **ir de j.** to carouse • **estar de j.** to live it up.

ja·ra·ne·ar intr. *(divertirse)* to have a good time; AMER. *(chancear)* to joke.

ja·ra·ne·ro, ·a I. adj. fun-loving II. m.f. carouser.

jar·ca f. acacia.

jar·cia(s) f.(pl.) rigging, ropes.

jar·dín m. garden ♦ **j. de la infancia** kindergarten.

jar·di·ne·ra f. *(para flores)* flower stand or box; *(que cuida un jardín)* gardener.

jar·di·ne·rí·a f. gardening.

jar·di·ne·ro m. gardener.

ja·re·ta f. *(dobladillo)* hem; MARIT. cable.

ja·rra f. *(vasija)* jug, pitcher; *(de cerveza)* mug, beer mug ♦ **de** *or* **en jarra(s)** with arms akimbo.

ja·rre·tar tr. *(enervar)* to enervate; *(quitar las fuerzas)* to weaken.

ja·rre·te m. back of the knee; *(de un animal)* hock.

ja·rre·te·ra f. *(liga)* garter; *(orden militar)* Order of the Garter.

ja·rro m. pitcher, jug ♦ **echar un j. de agua fría a** COLL. to throw cold water on.

ja·rrón m. urn, vase.

jas·pe m. MIN. jasper; *(mármol)* veined marble.

jas·pe·ar tr. to marble, speckle.

ja·to, a m.f. calf.

jau·la f. cage; *(embalaje)* crate; *(para niños)* playpen; MIN. cage.

jau·rí·a f. pack (of animals).

jaz·mín m. jasmine ♦ **j. del Cabo** gardenia.

je·be m. alum; AMER., BOT. rubber plant.

je·fa f. boss, chief.

je·fa·tu·ra f. *(dirección)* management; *(oficina)* headquarters.

je·fe m. *(superior)* boss; *(gerente)* manager; *(líder)* leader; *(cabeza)* head ♦ **comandante en j.** commander-in-chief • **j. de escuadra** rear admiral • **j. de estación** stationmaster • **j. de estado mayor** chief of staff • **j. de redacción** editor-in-chief • **j. de taller** foreman.

je·me·que m. COLL. whine.

je·mi·que·ar intr. CHILE to whimper, whine.

en·gi·bre m. ginger.

e·rar·ca m. hierarch, high official.

e·rar·quí·a f. hierarchy, rank.

je·rár·qui·co, a adj. hierarchic(al).

jer·bo m. jerboa, mouse.

je·re·mi·a·da f. jeremiad, lamentation.

je·re·mí·as m.f. whiner, complainer.

je·rez m. sherry.

jer·ga¹ f. *(tela)* coarse woolen cloth; *(colchón)* straw mattress; AMER. saddle blanket.

jer·ga² f. *(jerigonza)* jargon; *(galimatías)* gibberish.

jer·gón m. straw mattress.

je·ri·be·que m. *(mueca)* grimace; *(guiño)* wink.

je·ri·gon·za f. *(jerga)* jargon, slang; *(galimatías)* gibberish.

je·rin·ga f. syringe; AMER., COLL. *(molestia)* nuisance ♦ **j. de engrase** grease gun.

je·rin·ga·dor, ·ra COLL. I. adj. irksome, annoying II. m.f. pest.

je·rin·gar §47 tr. *(inyectar)* to inject; COLL. *(fastidiar)* to pester.

je·rin·ga·zo m. injection.

je·rin·gón, o·na adj. AMER. annoying.

je·rin·gue·ar tr. AMER. to annoy, pester.

je·rin·gui·lla f. small syringe; BOT. mock orange.

je·ro·glí·fi·co, a I. adj. hieroglyphic II. m. hieroglyph.

je·ta f. *(hocico)* snout; *(labios)* thick lips; COLL. *(cara)* mug ♦ **poner j.** COLL. to make a face.

je·tu·do, a adj. thick-lipped.

ji·bia f. cuttlefish.

ji·fia f. swordfish.

jil·gue·ro m. goldfinch, linnet.

ji·li·po·lla·da/ez f. SL. *(acción)* stupid thing to do; *(dicho)* stupid thing to say ♦ **esos son jilipolleces** that's a lot of bull • **¡qué j.!** how stupid can you get!

ji·mio, a adj. & m.f. simian.

jin·da(·ma) f. COLL. fear, fright.

ji·ne·ta¹ f. ZOOL. genet.

ji·ne·ta² f. *(lanza corta)* short lance; *(hombrera)* epaulette; *(que cabalga)* horsewoman.

ji·ne·te m. *(cabalgador)* horseman; MIL. cavalryman; *(caballo)* thoroughbred horse.

ji·ne·te·ar intr. to ride on horseback —tr. AMER. to break in (horses).

jin·glar intr. to swing, rock.

jin·jol m. jujube.

ji·par intr. AMER., COLL. (*hipar*) to hiccup; (*jadear*) to pant.

ji·pi·do m. AMER., COLL. hiccup, hiccough.

ji·pi·ja·pa m. straw hat, Panama hat.

ji·qui·le·te m. indigo plant.

ji·ra f. (*tira*) strip; (*jirón*) shred; (*excursión*) excursion.

ji·ra·fa f. giraffe; (*del micrófono*) boom.

ji·rón m. (*pedazo*) shred, piece; (*ropa*) facing; (*estandarte*) pennant ♦ **hacer jirones** to tear to shreds.

ji·ro·na·do, a adj. torn, tattered.

jo·co·se·rio, a adj. tragicomic.

jo·co·si·dad f. (*gracia*) humor, wit; (*divertimiento*) fun; (*chiste*) joke.

jo·co·so, a adj. humorous, amusing.

jo·cun·di·dad f. jocundity, cheerfulness.

jo·cun·do, a adj. jocund, cheerful.

jo·fai·na f. washbasin, washbowl.

jol·go·rio m. merriment, fun ♦ **ir** *or* **estar de j.** COLL. to have a good time.

jo·pe·o m. stroll, walk.

jo·po m. tuft.

jor·na·da f. (*viaje*) journey, trip; (*día de trabajo*) workday; PRINT. day's print run ♦ **de media j.** part-time.

jor·nal m. (*sueldo*) day's wage; (*día de trabajo*) workday ♦ **a j.** by the day • **j. mínimo** minimum wage.

jor·na·le·ro, a m.f. day laborer.

jo·ro·ba f. (*giba*) hump; COLL. (*molestia*) nuisance.

jo·ro·ba·do, a I. adj. hunchbacked **II.** m.f. hunchback.

jo·ro·bar tr. COLL. to bother, pester.

jo·ro·be·ta f. COLL. hunchback.

jo·rrar tr. to tow, haul (a net).

jo·rro m. dragnet.

jo·ta¹ f. iota, bit ♦ **no decir ni j.** COLL. not to say a word • **no entender ni j.** COLL. not to understand at all • **sin faltar una j.** without missing a thing.

jo·ta² f. Spanish dance and its music.

jo·ta³ f. AMER. sandal.

jo·ven I. adj. young, youthful **II.** m.f. young person, youth.

jo·vial adj. jovial, cheerful.

jo·via·li·dad f. joviality.

jo·ya f. (*alhaja*) jewel; (*objeto de adorno*) piece of jewelry; FIG. gem ♦ pl. jewelry • **j. de fantasía** costume jewelry.

jo·yel m. small jewel.

jo·ye·ra f. jewelry box.

jo·ye·ría f. jewelry trade *or* business; (*tienda*) jewelry store.

jo·ye·ro, a m.f. jeweler, jeweller (G.B.) —m. (*caja*) jewelry box; AMER. goldsmith.

ju·bi·la·ción f. (*retiro*) retirement; (*rental*) pension.

ju·bi·la·do, a adj. & m.f. retired (person).

jubilar¹ adj. jubilee.

jubilar² tr. (*pensionar*) to retire; COLL. (*desechar*) to discard —reflex. to retire.

ju·bi·le·o m. (*aniversario*) jubilee; (*idas y venidas*) comings and goings ♦ **por j.** once in a lifetime.

jú·bi·lo m. jubilation, joy.

ju·bi·lo·so, a adj. jubilant, joyful.

ju·dai·co, a adj. Judaic, Jewish.

ju·das m. (*traidor*) traitor; (*muñeco de paja*) effigy of Judas burnt during Holy Week.

ju·dí·a f. see **judío, a.**

ju·di·ca·tu·ra f. (*cargo*) judicature; (*mandato*) judge's term of office; (*conjunto de jueces*) judiciary.

ju·di·cial adj. judicial, juridica!.

ju·di·cia·rio, a adj. judicial.

ju·dí·o, a I. adj. Jewish **II.** m.f. Jew —f. Jew, Jewess; BOT. bean ♦ **j. blanca** haricot bean • **j. escarlata** kidney bean.

jue·go m. (*recreo*) play, game; (*deporte*) sport; (*en tenis*) game; (*broma*) jest; (*vicio*) gambling; (*en naipes*) hand; MECH. play, slack; (*de loza, cristal*) set; (*de muebles*) set, suite; (*intención*) game, scheme ♦ **a j.** matching • **en j.** in play, at stake • **hacer doble j.** to be two-faced • **hacer j.** to match • **hacer j. de ojos** to flirt • **hacerle el j.** (*ceder la ventaja*) to play into someone's hands; (*cooperar*) to play along with someone • **¡hagan j.!** place your bets! • **j. de azar** *or* **de suerte** game of chance • **j. de billar** billiards • **j. de bolas** ball bearing • **j. de damas** checkers • **j. de ingenio** guessing game • **j. de manos** sleight of hand • **j. de niños** child's play • **j. de palabras** pun, play on words • **j. limpio, sucio** fair, foul play • **poner en j.** to put into play • **verle el j. a** to know someone's game *or* intentions ♦ pl. **j. malabares** juggling.

jue·go, gue see **jugar.**

juer·ga f. COLL. fun ♦ **ir de j.** to live it up.

juer·gue·ar·se reflex. COLL. to have a good time.

juer·guis·ta COLL. **I.** adj. carousing **II.** m.f. carouser.

jue·ves m.inv. Thursday ♦ **J. Santo** Holy Thursday.

juez m. judge; (*árbitro*) arbitrator; (*en los deportes*) referee ♦ **j. arbitrador** arbitrator • **j. de apelaciones** judge of the court of appeals • **j. de línea** SPORT. linesman • **j. de paz** justice of the peace.

ju·ga·da f. play, move ♦ **hacer una mala j.** to play a dirty trick.

ju·ga·dor, ·ra m.f. (*en los juegos*) player; (*en el azar*) gambler.

ju·gar §42 intr. (*divertirse*) to play, cavort; (*en el azar*) to gamble; (*hacer una jugada*) to make a play; (*en las damas, ajedrez*) to make a move ♦ **j. a** to play • **j. con dos barajas** to be two-faced • **j. sucio** to play dirty —tr. to play; (*apostar*) to wager; (*una carta*) to wield; (*hacer juego*) to match; (*tomar parte*) to take part, participate —reflex. to risk ♦ **j. el todo por el todo** to risk everything.

ju·ga·rre·ta f. COLL. dirty trick.

ju·glar I. adj. (*de trovadores*) of minstrels; (*chistoso*) comical **II.** m. (*trovador*) troubadour; (*bufón*) buffoon.

ju·go m. (*zumo*) juice; CUL. gravy; (*lo esencial*) essence; PHYSIOL. juice.

ju·go·si·dad f. juiciness.

ju·go·so, a adj. (*lleno de jugo*) juicy; FIG. substantial.

ju·gue·te m. (*de un niño*) toy; (*chanza*) joke, jest; THEAT. skit, short play; FIG. toy, plaything ♦ **de j.** toy.

ju·gue·te·ar intr. (*divertirse*) to play, cavort; (*jugar*) to toy.

ju·gue·te·rí·a f. toy store.

ju·gue·tón, o·na adj. playful, frisky.

jui·cio m. judgment; (discernimiento) discernment; (opinión) opinion; (razonamiento) reason; (sentido común) common sense; (cordura) good sense; LAW (pleito) trial; (sentencia) verdict ◆ **asentar el j.** to come to one's senses • **Día del J.** Judgment Day • **estar en su j.** to be of sound mind • **estar fuera de j.** to be out of one's mind • **j. final** Last Judgment • **perder el j.** to lose one's mind • **poner en tela de j.** to call into question.

jui·cio·so, a adj. judicious, wise.

ju·le·pe m. (poción) julep; (naipes) a card game; COLL. (reprimenda) tongue-lashing; AMER. scare, fright.

ju·lio¹ m. July.

ju·lio² m. PHYS. joule.

ju·mar·se reflx. AMER., COLL. to get drunk.

ju·men·to m. & f. ass, donkey; FIG. stupid person.

ju·me·ra f. AMER., COLL. drunk, drunken spree.

jun·cia f. sedge ◆ **vender j.** to brag, boast.

jun·co¹ m. BOT. rush; (bastón) cane ◆ **j. de Indias** rattan • **j. florido** flowering rush • **j. oloroso** camel grass.

jun·co² m. MARIT. Chinese junk.

ju·nio m. June.

ju·nior m. (el menor) junior; RELIG. novice priest.

ju·ní·pe·ro m. juniper; Col. idiot, fool.

jun·que·ra f. rush, bulrush.

jun·qui·llo m. (flor) jonquil; (junco de Indias) rattan; (moldura) rounded molding.

jun·ta f. see **junto, a.**

jun·tar tr. (unir) to join; (reunir) to assemble; (dinero) to amass; (entornar) to half-close —reflx. (reunirse) to gather; (asociarse) to get together; (copular) to mate, copulate; AMER. to live together.

jun·to, a I. adj. (unido) united, joined; (cercano) close II. adv. together, at the same time ◆ **j. a** close to, near • **j. con** along with, together with • **todo j.** at the same time, all together III. f. (de personas) board, junta; (reunión) meeting, session; (unión) union, junction; CONSTR. joint, scarf; TECH. gasket, washer; MARIT. seam; AMER. junction (of two rivers) • **j. administrativa** administrative council • **j. cardánica** or **universal** universal joint • **j. de educación, sanidad** board of education, health • **j. directiva** board of directors • **j. esférica** ball joint • **j. militar** military junta.

jun·tu·ra f. (punto de unión) juncture; ANAT., TECH. joint.

ju·ra f. (juramento) oath; (ceremonia) swearing in.

ju·ra·do, a I. adj. sworn, under oath II. m. (tribunal) jury; (miembro del tribunal) juror; (de una competición) panel of judges.

ju·ra·men·ta·do, a adj. sworn, under oath.

ju·ra·men·tar tr. to swear in, put under oath —reflx. to be sworn in, take an oath.

ju·ra·men·to m. (jura) oath; (ofensa) curse, swearword ◆ **bajo j.** under oath • **j. falso** perjury • **j. hipocrático** Hippocratic oath • **prestar j.** to take an oath • **soltar j.** to curse • **tomar j.** to swear in.

ju·rar tr. (prestar juramento) to swear, take an oath; (prometer) to swear, pledge (allegiance) —intr. (blasfemar) to swear, curse ◆ **j. en falso** to commit perjury —reflx. ◆ **jurársela a uno** to have it in for someone.

ju·rel m. saurel, jack mackerel.

ju·ri·di·ci·dad f. lawfulness.

ju·rí·di·co, a adj. juridical.

ju·ris·con·sul·to m. jurist, legal expert.

ju·ris·dic·ción f. jurisdiction ◆ **traslado de j.** change of venue.

ju·ris·dic·cio·nal adj. jurisdictional.

ju·ris·pe·ri·cia f. jurisprudence.

ju·ris·pe·ri·to, a m.f. legal expert, jurist.

ju·ris·pru·den·cia f. jurisprudence; (precedentes) case law, legislation.

ju·ris·ta m.f. (abogado) jurist, lawyer; (pensionado) pensioner; (dueño) one who has the right of ownership.

ju·ro m. (derecho) right of ownership; (renta) pension.

jus·ta f. see **justo, a.**

jus·ta·men·te adv. (con justicia) justly, fairly; (precisamente) exactly, precisely.

jus·ti·cia f. justice; (equidad) fairness; (castigo) retribution; (castigo de muerte) execution; (policía) law, police ◆ **de j.** justly, duly • **tomarse la j. por las manos** to take the law into one's own hands.

jus·ti·ciar tr. (ajusticiar) to execute; (condenar) to condemn.

jus·ti·cie·ro, a I. adj. (justo) just, fair; (riguroso) strict, severe II. m.f. just or righteous person.

jus·ti·fi·ca·ble adj. justifiable.

jus·ti·fi·ca·ción f. justification; (prueba) proof, evidence.

jus·ti·fi·ca·dor, ·ra I. adj. justifying II. m. justification bar.

jus·ti·fi·can·te I. adj. justifying II. m. voucher.

jus·ti·fi·car §70 tr. to justify; (defender) to defend —reflx. (explicarse) to justify or explain oneself; (probar la inocencia) to prove one's innocence.

jus·ti·fi·ca·ti·vo, a adj. justifying.

jus·ti·pre·ciar tr. to appraise, estimate.

jus·ti·pre·cio m. appraisal, estimate.

jus·to, a I. adj. just, fair; (legítimo) justified, legitimate; (honrado) righteous, upright; (exacto) exact, precise; (apretado) tight II. m.f. just person —f. (torneo) joust; FIG. (competencia) contest III. adv. (con justicia) justly; (exactamente) exactly; (frugalmente) sparingly.

ju·ve·nil adj. young, youthful.

ju·ven·tud f. (edad) youth; (vigor juvenil) youthfulness ◆ **la j.** (los jóvenes) the youth.

juz·ga·do m. (tribunal) court, tribunal; (judicatura) judicature.

juz·ga·dor, ·ra I. adj. judging II. m.f. judge.

juz·gar §47 tr. to judge; (arbitrar) to pass judgment on; (considerar) to consider; (estimar) to assess ◆ **a j. por** judging by or from • **j. mal** to misjudge.

K

k, K f. twelfth letter of the Spanish alphabet.

ka·ki adj. & m. khaki.

kan m. khan.

kan·gu·ro m. kangaroo.

ka·ra·te m. karate.

ke·ro·se·ne/sén m. AMER. kerosene.

ki·lo m. kilo, kilogram.

ki·lo·ci·clo m. kilocycle.

ki·lo·gra·mo m. kilogram.
ki·lo·li·tro m. kiloliter.
ki·ló·me·tro m. kilometer.
ki·lo·tón m. kiloton.
ki·lo·va·tio m. kilowatt.
ki·ne·si·te·ra·peu·ta m. masseur —f. masseuse.
ki·ne·si·te·ra·pia f. kinesitherapy, massage.
kirsch m. kirsch, cherry brandy.
ki·wi m. kiwi.
kla·xon m. horn.
ko·a·la m. koala.
ko·pek m. kopeck.
krip·tón m. krypton.

L

l, L f. thirteenth letter of the Spanish alphabet.
la¹ I. def. art. the ♦ **la** the one that, the one who II. pron. her <*la miré* I looked at her>; it <*buscó la cinta y finalmente la encontró* she looked for the ribbon and finally found it>; you <*no la vi a usted en la fiesta, Ana* I didn't see you at the party, Ann>.
la² MUS. la.
la·be·rin·to m. labyrinth.
la·bia f. COLL. eloquence ♦ **tener mucha l.** to have the gift of gab.
la·bio m. lip; (*borde*) lip, rim; (*órgano del habla*) lip, mouth ♦ **sellar los labios** to keep one's lips sealed • **l. leporino** harelip.
la·bor f. (*trabajo*) work; (*faena*) task, job; (*labranza*) farm work; (*bordado*) embroidery ♦ pl. **l. de aguja** needlework • **l. domésticas** household chores.
la·bo·ra·ble adj. work, working.
la·bo·ral adj. (*del trabajo*) labor; (*técnico*) technical.
la·bo·rar tr. (*trabajar*) to work; (*cultivar*) to cultivate; (*arar*) to plow —intr. to scheme.
la·bo·ra·to·rio m. laboratory.
la·bo·re·ar tr. to work —intr. MARIT. to reeve.
la·bo·rio·so, a adj. (*trabajador*) industrious; (*penoso*) arduous.
la·bra·do, a I. adj. (*forjado*) wrought; (*tallado*) carved; (*repujado*) tooled; (*cultivado*) cultivated; (*arado*) plowed; (*bordado*) embroidered II. m. (*campo*) cultivated or tilled land; (*de metales*) working; (*de madera, piedra*) carving; (*de cuero*) tooling; (*cultivo*) tilling; (*arada*) plowing; (*bordado*) embroidery.
la·bra·dor, ·ra I. adj. farm, farming II. m.f. (*agricultor*) farmer; (*arador*) plowman; (*campesino*) peasant.
la·bran·za f. (*cultivo*) farming; (*hacienda*) farm; (*tierra*) farmland.
la·brar tr. (*trabajar*) to work; (*metales*) to work; (*tallar*) to carve; (*cuero*) to tool; (*cultivar*) to cultivate; (*arar*) to plow; (*bordar*) to embroider; (*causar*) to bring about; (*edificar*) to build —intr. to work.
la·brie·go, a m.f. farm hand or worker.
la·ca f. (*resina*) lac; (*pintura*) lacquer, shellac; (*barniz*) lacquer; (*objeto*) lacquered object; (*pelo*) hair spray ♦ **l. de uñas** nail polish.
la·ca·yo m. (*criado*) lackey, valet; (*mozo de espuelas*) groom, attendant.
la·ce·ar tr. (*adornar*) to trim with bows; R.P. to whip with a lasso.
la·ce·ra·ción f. laceration.

la·ce·rar tr. to lacerate; (*dañar*) to injure.
la·ce·ria f. (*pobreza*) misery, want; (*trabajo penoso*) drudgery, toil.
la·cio, a adj. (*cabello*) straight; (*marchito*) wilted; (*flojo*) limp.
la·có·ni·co, a adj. laconic.
la·cra f. (*señal*) scar; (*defecto*) blemish.
la·crar tr. to seal with wax.
la·cre I. m. sealing wax II. adj. red.
la·cri·mó·ge·no, a adj. tear-producing ♦ **gas l.** tear gas.
la·cri·mo·so, a adj. (*que tiene lágrimas*) tearful; (*triste*) sorrowful.
lac·ta·ción f. nursing.
lac·tan·cia f. lactation.
lac·tan·te I. adj. nursing, suckling II. m.f. nursing infant.
lac·tar tr. & intr. to nurse, suckle.
lác·te·o, a adj. milky ♦ **Vía L.** Milky Way.
lác·ti·co, a adj. lactic.
lac·to·sa f. lactose.
la·de·ar tr. to bend, tilt —reflex. to lean, tilt.
la·de·o m. slope, inclination.
la·de·ra f. slope.
la·di·lla f. crab louse ♦ **pegarse a alguien como una l.** COLL. to stick to someone like a leech.
la·di·no, a adj. astute.
la·do m. side; (*sitio*) room; (*aspecto*) aspect; (*camino*) way; (*protección*) protection; MIL. flank; SPORT. end ♦ **al l.** near, close at hand • **al l. de** beside, next to • **a un l.** aside • **dar de l. a alguien** to give someone the cold shoulder • **dejar a un l.** to leave aside • **de l. a l.** from side to side • **echar a un l.** to cast aside • **hacerse a un l.** to get out of the way • **l. a l.** side by side • **l. débil** or **flaco** weak spot • **mirar de l.** to look sideways at • **poner a un l.** to put aside • **ponerse del l. de** to side with • **por el l. de** toward, in the direction of • **por otro l.** on the other hand • **por un l.** on the one hand.
la·drar intr. to bark; FIG. to growl, snarl.
la·dri·do m. bark.
la·dri·llo m. brick; (*azulejo*) tile ♦ **es un l.** it's or he's a bore • **l. crudo** adobe.
la·drón, o·na I. adj. thieving II. m.f. thief, robber ♦ **l. de corazones** COLL. lady-killer.
la·dro·ne·ra f. (*refugio*) den of thieves; (*de agua*) sluice gate; (*robo*) theft, robbery; (*alcancía*) money box.
la·dro·ne·rí·a f. larceny, theft.
la·dron·zue·lo, a m.f. petty thief.
la·ga·ña f. rheum.
la·gar·ta f. female lizard; ENTOM. gypsy moth; COLL. (*mujer*) crafty woman.
la·gar·ti·ja f. small lizard.
la·gar·ti·jo m. small lizard; MEX. sharp dresser.
la·gar·to m. lizard; COLL. (*hombre astuto*) sly devil; AMER. alligator.
la·gar·to·na f. COLL. crafty woman.
la·go m. lake.
lá·gri·ma f. tear; FIG. drop ♦ **llorar a l. viva** to cry one's heart out • pl. sorrows, troubles • **beberse las l.** to hold back one's tears • **deshacerse en l.** to burst into tears • **enjugarse las l.** to dry one's eyes or tears • **l. de cocodrilo** crocodile tears • **ser el paño de l. (de alguien)** to be someone's consolation.
la·gri·me·ar intr. (*ojos*) to water, tear; (*persona*) to cry, weep.
la·gri·mo·so, a adj. (*ojos*) watery, teary; (*lacrimoso*) tearful.

la·gu·na f. lagoon; *(texto)* hiatus; *(falta)* gap.
lai·ca·do m. laity.
lai·cal adj. lay, laical.
lai·co, a adj. lay, laical.
la·ja f. stone slab; MARIT. reef.
la·ma¹ f. *(cieno)* mud; BOT. algae; *(tela)* (silver *or* gold) lamé; AMER. slime.
la·ma² m.f. lama.
lam·ber tr. AMER. *(lamer)* to lick; *(adular)* to fawn on, suck up to.
la·me·du·ra f. lick, licking.
la·men·ta·ble adj. lamentable.
la·men·ta·ción f. lamentation.
la·men·tar tr. *(sentir)* to regret, be sorry for; *(llorar)* to bemoan —reflex. to grieve, lament.
la·men·to m. lament.
la·men·to·so, a adj. plaintive, mournful.
la·mer tr. *(con la lengua)* to lick; *(tocar suavemente)* to lap.
la·me·ta·da f. *or* **la·me·tón** m. AMER. licking, lick.
la·mi·do, a I. m.f. licking **II.** adj. *(flaco)* thin and pale; *(relamido)* polished, finely finished.
lá·mi·na f. *(plancha)* lamina, plate; PRINT. engraved plate; *(estampa)* print.
la·mi·na·ción f. lamination.
la·mi·na·do, a I. adj. laminated ♦ **hierro l.** sheet metal **II.** m. lamination.
la·mi·nar I. adj. laminar, laminal **II.** tr. to laminate.
lám·pa·ra f. lamp; RAD., TELEV. valve, tube ♦ **l. de alcohol** spirit lamp • **l. de arco** arc lamp • **l. de incandescencia** incandescent lamp • **l. de seguridad** safety lamp • **l. de soldar** blowtorch • **l. de techo** ceiling lamp • **l. fluorescente** fluorescent lamp • **l. neón** neon light.
lam·pa·ri·lla f. *(lámpara pequeña)* small lamp; *(que se enciende de noche)* night-light.
lam·pa·rón m. *(aceite)* grease spot *or* stain; MED. scrofula; VET. glanders.
lam·pi·ño, a adj. *(sin barba)* beardless; *(con poco vello)* hairless.
la·na f. wool; MEX., COLL. *(dinero)* dough, bread; AMER. *(mentira)* lie ♦ **cardarle a alguien la l.** COLL. to tell someone off • **de l.** wool, woolen • **ir por l. y salir trasquilado** to get more than one bargained for • **l. de acero** steel wool • **l. de vidrio** glass wool.
la·na·do, a adj. woolly, fleecy.
lan·ce m. *(acontecimiento)* event, occurrence; *(trance)* predicament; *(jugada)* move; *(riña)* quarrel, argument ♦ **l. apretado** COLL. tight spot, jam • **l. de honor** duel.
lan·ce·ar tr. to lance.
lan·ce·ro m. lancer ♦ pl. lancers (dance).
lan·ce·ta m. lancet.
lan·cha f. *(embarcación)* boat; *(piedra)* stone slab ♦ **l. motora** motorboat • **l. salvavidas** lifeboat • **l. torpedera** torpedo boat.
lan·char m. flagstone quarry.
lan·che·ro m. boatman, ferryman.
lan·chón m. barge.
lan·da f. moor, heath.
la·ne·ro, a I. adj. woolen **II.** m. *(negociante)* wool dealer; *(almacén)* wool warehouse.
lan·gos·ta f. ENTOM. locust; ZOOL. lobster.
lan·gos·ti·no/tín m. crayfish.
lan·gui·de·cer §17 intr. to languish.
lan·gui·dez f. *(flaqueza)* weakness, feebleness; *(falta de energía)* listlessness, lethargy.
lán·gui·do, a adj. languid.
lan·guor m. languor.
la·ni·lla f. *(pelillo)* nap; *(tejido)* flannel.

la·no·li·na f. lanolin.
la·no·so, a adj. woolly.
lan·za I. f. lance, spear; *(soldado)* lancer ♦ **correr lanzas** to joust • **estar con la l. en ristre** to be ready for action • **romper lanzas por** to defend, fight for **II.** adj. MEX. crafty, deceptive.
lan·za·bom·bas m.inv. *(de trinchera)* trench mortar; *(de aviones)* bomb release.
lan·za·co·he·tes m.inv. rocket launcher.
lan·za·da f. *(golpe)* lance thrust; *(herida)* lance wound.
lan·za·lla·mas m.inv. flame thrower.
lan·za·mien·to m. throw, throwing ♦ **l. de abastecimientos** airdrop • **l. del disco** discus throwing • **l. de un barco** launching of a ship.
lan·zar §04 tr. *(arrojar)* to throw, hurl; *(dardos, flechas)* to shoot, fire; *(un proyectil)* to launch; *(una bomba)* to drop; *(aves)* to release; COLL. *(vomitar)* to vomit, throw up; *(brotar)* to put forth; *(decir)* to let loose, let out; *(insultos)* to hurl; *(dar a conocer)* to launch; *(despojar)* to dispossess; *(desalojar)* to evict; SPORT. to throw —reflex. *(arrojarse)* to throw *or* hurl oneself; *(saltar)* to jump; *(asaltar)* to rush, attack ♦ **l. a** to launch into, embark upon.
lan·za·tor·pe·dos m.inv. MIL. torpedo tube.
la·pi·ce·ro m. *(instrumento mecánico)* pencil *(lápiz)* pencil; ARG., PERU penholder.
lá·pi·da f. tombstone.
la·pi·dar tr. *(matar)* to stone to death; AMER. to carve gems.
la·pi·da·rio, a I. adj. *(de las piedras preciosas)* lapidary; *(muy conciso)* concise, succinct ♦ **frase l.** memorable phrase **II.** m. lapidary.
lá·piz m. *(grafito)* graphite, lead; *(instrumento)* pencil ♦ **l. de color** colored pencil • **l. de labios** lipstick.
lap·so, a m. *(de tiempo)* lapse, interval; *(error)* lapse, slip.
lap·sus m. lapsus, slip ♦ **l. cálami** slip of the pen • **l. linguae** slip of the tongue.
la·que·ar tr. to lacquer, varnish.
lar·dar/de·ar tr. to baste, lard.
lar·do m. lard, animal fat.
lar·ga·men·te adv. *(con extensión)* at length; FIG. generously, liberally.
lar·gar §47 tr. *(aflojar)* to slacken; *(soltar)* to release, let go; *(despedir)* to fire, dismiss; *(tirar)* to throw, hurl; *(expulsar)* to throw out, expel; COLL. *(decir)* to let out, let fly ‹l. una palabrota to let fly an obscenity›; *(una bofetada)* to deal —reflex. COLL. *(marcharse)* to beat it, scram; *(comenzar)* to begin to.
lar·go, a I. adj. long; *(extenso)* lengthy; *(alto)* tall; *(abundante)* abundant; MARIT. loose, slack ♦ **a la l.** *(con el tiempo)* in the long run; *(poco a poco)* little by little • **a lo l.** lengthwise; *(por)* along; *(a través)* throughout • **de l.** in formal dress • **l. de manos** heavy-handed • **largos años** many years • **l. y tendido** COLL. at length **II.** m. length; MUS. largo ♦ **de l.** long ‹la piscina tiene quince pies de l. the pool is fifteen feet long› • **pasar de l.** *(no parar)* to pass by; *(no hacer caso de)* to ignore **III.** interj. get out! ♦ **¡l. de aquí!** get out of here!
lar·gor m. length.
lar·go·ru·to/gu·cho, a adj. lanky.
lar·gue·a·do, a adj. striped.
lar·gue·za f. *(liberalidad)* largesse; *(largura)* length.
lar·gui·ru·cho, a adj. lanky.

lar·gu·ra f. length.
la·rin·ge f. larynx.
la·rin·gi·tis f. laryngitis.
lar·va f. [pl. **-vae**] larva.
lar·val adj. larval.
las I. def. art. the II. pron. them.
las·ci·via f. lasciviousness.
las·ci·vo, a adj. & m.f. lascivious (person).
lá·ser m. laser ♦ **rayo l.** laser beam.
la·si·tud f. lassitude.
la·so, a adj. *(cansado)* tired, weary; *(flojo)* weak, languid; *(sin torcer)* limp.
lás·ti·ma f. *(sentimiento)* pity, compassion; *(cosa)* pity, shame ♦ **dar l.** to be pitiful • **es una l. que** it's a shame that • **¡qué l.!** what a shame! • **tener l.** to feel sorry for.
las·ti·ma·du·ra f. *(daño)* injury; *(herida)* wound.
las·ti·mar tr. *(dañar)* to injure, hurt; *(agraviar)* to. hurt, offend —reflex. to hurt or injure oneself.
las·ti·me·ro, a adj. sad, pitiful.
las·ti·mo·so, a adj. pitiful, deplorable.
las·tra f. flagstone, stone slab.
las·tre m. AER., MARIT. ballast; FIG. dead weight, burden.
la·ta f. *(hoja de lata)* tin plate; *(envase)* tin can, can; *(madero)* small log; *(para tejas)* roof lath; AMER., COLL. *(persona)* pest, nuisance ♦ **dar la l.** COLL. to annoy • **¡qué l.!** what a nuisance!
la·ta·zo m. COLL. bore.
la·te·ar tr. AMER., COLL. to bore, bend (someone's) ear.
la·ten·te adj. latent.
la·te·ral adj. lateral, side.
la·ti·do m. *(del corazón)* beat, beating; *(dolor)* throb, throbbing.
la·tien·te adj. *(pulso)* beating; *(herida)* throbbing.
la·ti·ga·zo m. *(golpe)* whiplash; *(chasquido)* whip-cracking ♦ **dar latigazos a** to whip, flog • **darse un l.** COLL. to have a snort.
lá·ti·go m. *(azote)* horsewhip; COL., ECUAD., PERU whiplash ♦ **l. de montar** riding crop.
la·ti·gue·ar intr. *(el látigo)* to crack the whip; AMER. to flog, whip.
la·tir intr. *(el corazón)* to beat; *(una herida)* to throb; MEX. to have an inkling or a hunch.
la·ti·tud f. *(ancho)* width, breadth; *(extensión)* extent, scope; GEOG. latitude; *(libertad)* freedom, latitude.
la·ti·tu·di·nal adj. latitudinal.
la·to, a adj. broad, wide.
la·tón m. brass ♦ **l. de aluminio** aluminum brass • **l. en hojas** or **planchas** sheet brass.
la·to·ne·rí·a f. brassworks.
la·to·ne·ro m. brassworker.
la·to·so, a adj. COLL. annoying, bothersome.
la·tro·ci·nio m. robbery, theft.
la·úd m. MUS. lute; MARIT. catboat; ZOOL. striped turtle.
lau·da·ble adj. laudable.
lau·dar tr. to rule, render a verdict on.
lau·da·to·rio, a I. adj. laudatory II. f. eulogy.
lau·de f. tombstone.
lau·do m. ruling, verdict.
lau·re·a·do, a adj. & m.f. laureate.
lau·re·ar tr. *(coronar)* to crown with laurel; *(premiar)* to honor, reward.
lau·re·dal m. laurel grove.
lau·rel m. laurel, bay ♦ pl. laurels, honors •

dormirse en los l. to rest on one's laurels.
láu·re·o, a adj. laurel.
lau·ré·o·la/re·o·la f. *(corona)* laurel wreath or crown; *(aureola)* halo, aureola.
la·va f. lava.
la·va·ble adj. washable.
la·va·bo m. *(lavamanos)* wash basin; *(cuarto)* bathroom.
la·va·ca·ras m.f.inv. COLL. toady, bootlicker.
la·va·co·ches m.inv. car washer.
la·va·da f. washing.
la·va·de·ro m. *(lavandería)* laundry; *(de un río)* washing place; MIN. placer.
la·va·do m. *(acción)* washing, wash; MED. lavage; PAINT. wash ♦ **l. de cabeza** COLL. reprimand • **l. de cerebro** brainwashing • **l. en seco** dry cleaning.
la·va·dor, ·ra I. adj. washing II. m.f. *(persona)* washer —m. PHOTOG. washer; ARM. ramrod —f. *(máquina)* washing machine, washer; *(mujer)* laundress ♦ **l. de platos** dishwasher.
la·va·du·ra f. *(acción)* washing, wash; *(lavazas)* dishwater, dirty water.
la·va·ma·nos m.inv. washbasin, washbowl.
la·van·da f. lavender.
la·van·de·ra f. washerwoman, laundrywoman.
la·van·de·rí·a f. laundry, laundromat.
la·van·de·ro m. laundryman, launderer.
la·va·o·jos m.inv. eyecup.
la·va·pla·tos m.inv. dishwasher.
la·var tr. *(limpiar)* to wash; *(purificar)* to wipe away, clean; PAINT. to paint in water colors; MAS. to whitewash; MIN. to wash ♦ **l. el cerebro** to brainwash —reflex. to wash (oneself) ♦ **l. las manos de** to wash one's hands of.
la·va·ti·va f. *(líquido)* enema; *(aparato)* enema bag; COLL. *(molestia)* nuisance.
la·xar tr. to loosen, slacken.
la·xan·te adj. & m. laxative.
la·xo, a adj. *(flojo)* loose, slack; *(relajado)* lax.
la·ya¹ f. AGR. spade.
la·ya² f. breed, kind ♦ **eso es de otra l.** that's a horse of a different color.
la·yar tr. to spade (up), dig with a spade.
la·za·da f. *(nudo)* bowknot; *(lazo)* lasso.
la·zar §04 tr. to lasso, rope.
la·za·ri·llo m. person who guides the blind.
la·za·ri·no, a I. adj. leprous II. m.f. leper.
lá·za·ro m. *(pobre)* ragged beggar; *(leproso)* leper.
la·za·ro·so, a I. adj. leprous II. f. m.f. leper.
la·zo m. *(nudo)* knot; *(para animales)* lasso; *(cordel)* lashing rope; *(trampa)* snare, trap; *(asechanza)* trap; *(vínculo)* bond, tie ♦ **l. corredizo** slipknot.
le pron. him <*la niña le siguió* the little girl followed him>; you <*no le vi a usted* I didn't see you>; to him, to her, to it, to you <*le dimos un regalo* we gave a present to him>; for him, for her, for it, for you <*le compré una cámara* I bought a camera for her>; from him, from her, from it, from you <*el gobierno le quitó la tierra* the government took his land from him>.
le·al adj. loyal, faithful ♦ **a mi l.** saber y entender to the best of my knowledge.
le·al·tad f. loyalty, fidelity.
lec·ción f. lesson; *(discurso)* lecture; *(capítulo)* lesson, chapter; *(lectura)* reading ♦ **dar a uno una l.** to teach someone a lesson.
lec·ti·vo, a adj. school ♦ **año l.** school year • **día l.** school day.

lec·tor, ·ra I. adj. reading **II.** m.f. reader.

lec·tu·ra f. *(acción)* reading; *(cosa leída)* reading matter; PRINT. pica ♦ **ser una persona de mucha l.** to be well-read.

le·cha·da f. *(de paredes)* whitewash; *(argamasa)* mortar, grout; *(papel)* pulp; *(emulsión)* emulsion ♦ **l. de cal** milk of lime.

le·char tr. AMER. to milk; C. AMER., MEX. to whitewash.

le·che f. milk; BOT. milky sap ♦ **dientes de l.** milk teeth • **l. desnatada** skim milk • **l. de vaca** cow's milk • **l. en polvo** powdered milk.

le·che·rí·a f. *(tienda)* dairy store; AMER. dairy farm.

le·che·ro, ·a I. adj. *(lechoso)* milky; *(que tiene leche)* milk, dairy **II.** f. *(vendedora)* milkmaid, dairymaid; *(recipiente)* milk can; *(jarra)* milk jug; AMER. *(vaca)* milk cow —m. milkman.

le·che·rón m. *(vasija)* milk pail; *(tela)* flannel wrap.

le·chi·ga·da f. *(nidada)* brood; *(cría)* litter.

le·cho m. bed; *(capa)* layer; ARCHIT. base; GEOL. bed, layer ♦ **abandonar el l.** to get out of bed • **l. de roca** bedrock.

le·chón m. *(cochinillo)* suckling pig; *(cerdo)* hog; *(persona)* pig, slob.

le·cho·so, ·a I. adj. milky **II.** m. papaya tree —f. papaya.

le·chu·ga f. lettuce; *(cuello)* ruff ♦ **como una l.** fresh as a daisy • **fresco como una l.** cool as a cucumber • **l. romana** romaine lettuce.

le·chu·za f. owl; COLL. *(mujer)* hag.

le·er §43 tr. to read ♦ **l. pruebas de imprenta** to proofread —intr. to read ♦ **l. a primera vista** MUS. to sight-read.

le·ga·ción f. legation.

le·ga·do m. legacy.

le·ga·jo m. file, dossier.

le·gal adj. legal.

le·ga·li·dad f. legality.

le·ga·lis·ta I. adj. legalistic **II.** m.f. legalist.

le·ga·li·za·ción f. legalization; *(validación)* authentication, validation.

le·ga·li·zar §04 tr. to legalize; *(certificar)* to authenticate, validate.

le·gar §47 tr. *(dejar)* to leave, bequeathe; *(enviar)* to delegate; *(transmitir)* to bequeathe, hand down.

le·ga·ta·rio, a m.f. legatee, heir ♦ **l. universal** general legatee.

le·gen·da·rio, a I. adj. legendary, fabled **II.** m. book of legends.

le·gi·ble adj. legible.

le·gión f. legion; *(multitud)* legion, multitude ♦ **la L. Extranjera** the Foreign Legion.

le·gio·na·rio, a I. adj. legionary **II.** m. legionary, legionnaire

le·gis·la·ción f. legislation.

le·gis·la·dor, ·ra I. adj. legislative **II.** m.f. legislator, lawmaker.

le·gis·lar intr. to legislate.

le·gis·la·ti·vo, a adj. legislative.

le·gis·la·tu·ra f. legislature.

le·gis·ta m. *(experto)* legist; *(profesor)* law professor; *(estudiante)* law student; *(abogado)* lawyer ♦ **médico l.** AMER. medical forensic expert.

le·gi·ti·mar tr. *(certificar)* to legitimize; *(un hijo)* to make legitimate.

le·gi·ti·mi·dad f. legitimacy; *(autenticidad)* authenticity.

le·gí·ti·mo, a adj. legitimate; *(cierto)* genuine;

(auténtico) real, authentic; *(válido)* valid.

le·go, a I. adj. *(seglar)* lay, secular; *(sin instrucción)* ignorant, uninformed; *(analfabeto)* illiterate ♦ **ser l. en** to know nothing about **II.** m. layman; RELIG. lay brother.

le·gua f. league ♦ **a la l.** far away, miles away • **se ve a la l.** you can see it a mile away.

le·gum·bre f. legume.

le·i·ble adj. legible, readable.

le·í·do, a I. see **leer II.** adj. well-read **III.** f. reading.

le·ja·ní·a f. *(distancia)* distance; *(paraje)* distant or remote place.

le·ja·no, a adj. distant, remote.

le·jí·a f. *(agua alcalina)* lye; *(detergente)* bleach; COLL. *(reprimenda)* scolding.

le·jos adv. far (away) ♦ **a lo l.** in the distance, far away • **de l.** from afar, from a distance • **desde l.** from afar, from a distance • **ir l.** to go too far, go a long way • **l. de** *(a gran distancia)* far from, a long way from; *(en lugar de)* far from • **más l.** farther, further.

le·lo, a I. adj. silly, foolish **II.** m.f. dolt, ninny ♦ **estar l. por** to be head over heels in love with • **quedarse l.** to be stunned.

le·ma m. motto; LIT. theme; LOG. lemma.

lem·pi·ra m. HOND., FIN. lempira.

len·ce·rí·a f. *(ropa blanca)* underwear; *(géneros)* linen goods; *(comercio)* linen trade.

len·gua f. tongue; *(idioma)* language; *(badajo)* bell clapper; CUL. tongue ♦ **buscarle a uno la l.** COLL. to pick a fight with someone • **estar con la l. fuera** to have one's tongue hanging out • **hablar en lenguas** RELIG. to speak in tongues • **írsele a uno la l.** COLL. to talk too much, run off at the mouth • **l. de víbora** COLL. backbiter, gossip • **l. de fuego** tongue of fire, flame • **l. de tierra** promontory, tongue of land • **l. franca** lingua franca • **l. materna** mother tongue, native language • **ligero de l.** indiscreet • **mala l.** backbiter, gossip • **morderse la l.** to bite one's tongue • **sacar la l.** to stick one's tongue out at • **tirar de la l.** to make someone talk • **trabársele a uno la l.** to become tongue-tied.

len·gua·do m. sole, flounder.

len·gua·je m. language, speech ♦ **l. cifrado** or **convenido** code language.

len·gua·raz adj. *(bilingüe)* bilingual; *(deslenguado)* foul-mouthed, vulgar; *(hablador)* talkative, garrulous.

len·guaz adj. garrulous.

len·güe·ta f. *(lengua pequeña)* small tongue; *(de zapato)* tongue; ANAT. epiglottis; *(de una balanza)* pointer, needle; MUS. reed; CARP. tongue ♦ **ensambladura de ranura y l.** tongue-and-groove joint.

le·ni·ti·vo, a I. adj. lenitive, soothing **II.** m. lenitive, palliative.

len·te m. or f. lens ♦ **l. de aumento** magnifying glass • **l. de contacto** contact lens • **l. electrónico** electron lens • **l. telegráfico** telephoto lens ♦ pl. eyeglasses, spectacles.

len·te·ja f. lentil.

len·te·jue·la f. sequin.

len·ti·lla f. contact lens.

len·ti·tud f. slowness.

len·to, a I. adj. *(tardo)* slow; MED. viscous **II.** adv. MUS. lento.

le·ña f. *(madera)* firewood; COLL. *(paliza)* beating ♦ **echar l. al fuego** to add fuel to the fire • **llevar l. al monte** to carry coals to Newcastle.

le·ña·dor, ·ra m.f. woodcutter.

le·ña·zo m. COLL. *(garrotazo)* clubbing, cudgeling; AMER. *(golpe)* blow, wallop.

le·ñe·ra f. woodshed.

le·ño m. *(trozo de árbol)* log; *(madera)* wood; POET. ship ♦ **dormir como un l.** COLL. to sleep like a log.

le·ño·so, a adj. woody.

le·ón m. lion; AMER. puma ♦ **ponerse como un l.** to get furious.

le·o·na f. lioness.

le·o·na·do, a adj. reddish-brown, tawny.

le·o·ne·ro, a I. adj. AMER. rowdy, disorderly **II.** m. MEX. place where brawls occur; COLL. *(tablajero)* gambler —m.f. lionkeeper —f. *(jaula)* lion cage; COLL. *(casa de juego)* gambling den; *(cuarto desarreglado)* messy room.

le·o·ni·no, a adj. leonine.

le·o·par·do m. leopard.

le·o·tar·do m. leotard.

le·po·ri·no, a adj. leporine ♦ **labio l.** harelip.

le·pra f. leprosy.

le·pro·so, a I. adj. leprous **II.** m.f. leper.

ler·do, a I. adj. sluggish **II.** m.f. dullwitted person.

les pron. to them, to you *<déles el libro* give the book to them>; for them, for you *<quiero comprarles unos zapatos* I want to buy shoes for you>; from them, from you *<les quitaron la oportunidad* they took the opportunity away from you>.

les·bia·na/bia adj. & f. lesbian.

le·sión f. lesion, injury.

le·sio·na·do, a I. adj. *(herido)* injured, wounded; *(dañado)* damaged, hurt **II.** m. ♦ **los lesionados** the wounded.

le·sio·nar tr. *(herir)* to wound, injure; *(dañar)* to damage —reflex. to get hurt, get injured.

les·na f. awl.

le·so, a adj. *(agraviado)* injured, wronged; *(perturbado)* perturbed; AMER. silly, stupid ♦ **l. majestad** lese majesty.

le·tal adj. lethal.

le·ta·ní·a f. litany.

le·tár·gi·co, a adj. lethargic.

le·tar·go m. lethargy.

le·tra f. letter; *(modo de escribir)* handwriting, writing; *(sentido)* letter, literal meaning; MUS. lyrics, words; COM. draft, bill of exchange ♦ **a la l.** to the letter, literally • **a l. vista** at sight, on sight • **l. a la vista** sight draft • **l. bastardilla** italics • **l. de cambio** bill of exchange • **l. de imprenta** type • **l. de mano** handwriting • **l. de molde** printed letter • **l. gótica** black letter • **l. magnética** laser printing • **l. mayúscula** capital letter • **l. minúscula** lower-case letter • **l. negrilla** boldface type • pl. letters, learning • **bellas l.** belles-lettres, literature • **l. humanas** humanities • **l. sagradas** Scriptures • **primeras l.** primary schooling.

le·tra·do, a I. adj. learned, educated **II.** m. attorney, lawyer.

le·tre·ro m. *(señal)* sign; *(etiqueta)* label.

le·tri·na f. latrine, privy.

leu·ce·mia f. leukemia.

leu·dar tr. to leaven, add yeast to.

le·va f. MARIT. weighing anchor, sailing; MIL. levy, conscription; MECH. *(palanca)* lever; *(álabe)* vane; *(rueda)* cam.

le·va·di·zo, a adj. which can be raised ♦ **puente l.** drawbridge.

le·va·du·ra f. *(fermento)* yeast; CARP. sawed-off plank; *(germen)* germ ♦ **l. de cerveza** brewer's

yeast • **l. en polvo** baking powder.

le·van·ta·dor, ·ra I. adj. raising, lifting **II.** m.f. lifter.

le·van·ta·mien·to m. *(acción)* raising, lifting; *(motín)* uprising ♦ **l. topográfico** (land) survey.

le·van·tar tr. *(alzar)* to raise, lift; *(elevar)* to lift up; *(enderezar)* to straighten up; *(quitar)* to remove; *(construir)* to raise, erect; *(establecer)* to found, set up; *(producir)* to raise; *(la caza)* to flush out; *(mudar)* to move; *(prohibición, embargo)* to raise, lift; *(los ánimos, la voz)* to raise; *(acusación)* to bring; *(el ancla)* to weigh; *(campamento)* to break ♦ **l. cabeza** to improve one's condition in life —reflex. *(elevarse)* to rise; *(ponerse de pie)* to stand up; *(de la cama)* to get out of bed; *(sobresalir)* to stand out; *(sublevarse)* to rebel; METEOROL. to rise ♦ **l. con** to make off with.

le·var tr. MARIT. to weigh.

le·ve adj. *(ligero)* light; *(de poca importancia)* slight, trivial.

le·vi·ta·ción f. levitation.

lé·xi·co, a I. adj. lexical **II.** m. *(diccionario)* dictionary, lexicon; *(de un escritor)* vocabulary, lexicon.

le·xi·co·gra·fí·a f. lexicography.

le·xi·có·gra·fo, a m.f. lexicographer.

le·xi·co·lo·gí·a f. lexicology.

ley f. *(estatuto)* law, statute; *(código)* law, body of laws; *(regla)* rule, regulation; *(acto)* act, bill; *(religión)* Law; *(norma)* standard; METAL. fineness ♦ **al margen de la l.** outside the law • **a toda l.** strictly • **de buena l.** sterling, excellent • **de mala l.** crooked, disreputable • **l. de prescripción** statute of limitations • **l. de quiebras** bankruptcy law • **l. humana** social law • **l. no escrita** unwritten law.

le·yen·da f. *(fábula)* legend, myth; *(de una moneda)* inscription; *(texto)* legend, caption.

le·ye·ra, yó see leer.

lez·na f. awl.

liar §30 tr. *(atar)* to tie, bind; *(envolver)* to wrap (up); *(un cigarrillo)* to roll; COLL. *(engañar)* to take in, fool; *(mezclar)* to mix up in ♦ **liarlas** COLL. *(huir)* to beat it, scram; *(morir)* to kick the bucket —reflex. *(amancebarse)* to live together; *(mezclarse)* to be mixed up in ♦ **l. a palos** to come to blows • **liárselas** COLL. *(huir)* to beat it, scram; *(morir)* to kick the bucket.

li·ba·ción f. libation.

li·bar tr. *(los insectos)* to suck; *(echar)* to pour; *(degustar)* to taste, sip.

li·be·lis·ta m. *(de escritos satíricos)* lampoonist; LAW libeler.

li·be·lo m. *(escrito satírico)* lampoon; *(infamatorio)* libel; LAW petition.

li·bé·lu·la f. dragonfly.

li·be·ra·ción f. liberation; *(del enemigo)* deliverance ♦ **l. condicional** parole.

li·be·ra·dor, ·ra I. adj. liberating **II.** m.f. liberator.

li·be·ral I. adj. liberal; *(generoso)* generous; *(progresista)* progressive **II.** m.f. liberal.

li·be·ra·li·dad f. liberality.

li·be·ra·li·zar §04 tr. to liberalize.

li·be·rar tr. *(librar)* to free, liberate; *(de una deuda)* to release, discharge —reflex. to be released or discharged.

li·ber·tad f. liberty, freedom; *(independencia)* independence; *(exención)* exemption; *(franqueza)* openness; *(derecho)* right, liberty ♦ **en l.**

freely • **l. condicional** probation • **l. de comercio** free trade • **l. de conciencia** freedom of worship • **l. de imprenta** or **de prensa** freedom of the press • **l. de palabra** freedom of speech • **l. provisional** parole • **poner en l.** to free, set free ♦ pl. *(inmunidades)* rights; *(maneras)* liberties • **tomarse l.** to take liberties.

li·ber·ta·dor, ·ra I. adj. liberating **II.** m.f. liberator.

li·ber·tar tr. to free, liberate; *(salvar)* to save, deliver; *(eximir)* to exempt, release.

li·ber·ta·rio, a adj. & m.f. libertarian.

li·ber·ti·na·je m. libertinism.

li·ber·ti·no, a adj. & m.f. libertine.

li·bi·di·no·so, a adj. libidinous.

li·bi·do m. libido.

li·bra f. pound ♦ **l. carnicera** kilogram • **l. esterlina** pound sterling.

li·brar tr. *(salvar)* to free, deliver; COM. to draw; *(eximir)* to exempt, release; *(batalla, duelo)* to wage ♦ **¡Dios me libre!** heaven forbid! —reflex. to avoid, escape.

li·bre adj. free; *(independiente)* independent; *(soltero)* single, unmarried; *(desembarazado)* clear, open; *(vacante)* free, unoccupied; *(sin trabas)* free, unrestrained; *(atrevido)* bold; *(exento)* free, exempt; *(en la natación)* freestyle ♦ **l. albedrío** free will • **l. cambio** free trade • **l. de derechos** duty-free.

li·bre·a f. livery, uniform.

li·bre·cam·bio m. free trade or exchange.

li·bre·pen·sa·dor, ·ra I. adj. freethinking **II.** m.f. freethinker.

li·bre·pen·sa·mien·to m. freethinking, free thought.

li·bre·rí·a f. *(tienda)* bookstore, bookshop; *(comercio)* book trade; *(oficio)* booksellers, book dealers; *(armario)* bookcase, bookshelf; *(biblioteca)* library.

li·bre·ro m. *(vendedor)* bookseller, book dealer; *(armario)* bookcase, bookshelf.

li·bre·ta f. *(cuaderno)* notebook; *(agenda)* calendar, appointment book ♦ **l. de ahorros** savings book, passbook • **l. de cheques** checkbook • **l. de direcciones** address book.

li·bre·tis·ta m.f. librettist.

li·bro m. book; *(registro)* register; MUS. libretto ♦ **examinar los libros** COM. to audit • **hacer l. nuevo** COLL. to turn over a new leaf • **l. borrador** blotter, daily record • **l. copiador** letter book • **l. de asiento** or **de cuentas** account book • **l. de caja** cashbook • **l. de horas** Book of Hours • **l. de texto** textbook • **l. diario** journal, daybook • **l. mayor** ledger • **l. en rústica** paperback • **libros sagrados** Scriptures.

li·cen·cia f. license; *(permiso)* permission; *(documento)* license, permit; EDUC. licentiate degree; MIL. discharge ♦ **l. absoluta** discharge • **l. por enfermedad** sick leave.

li·cen·cia·do, a I. adj. exempted **II.** m.f. *(graduado)* university graduate, bachelor; COLL. *(estudiante)* student; AMER. lawyer —m. discharged soldier.

li·cen·cia·mien·to m. MIL. discharge; EDUC. graduation.

li·cen·ciar tr. MIL. to discharge; *(dar permiso)* to license, permit; *(despedir)* to dismiss, discharge; EDUC. to graduate —reflex. to graduate.

li·cen·cia·tu·ra f. *(título)* bachelor's degree; *(acto)* graduation; *(estudios)* degree program.

li·cen·cio·so, a adj. licentious.

li·ce·o m. *(sociedad)* lyceum; AMER. *(escuela)* grammar or high school.

li·ci·ta·ción f. bid, tender.

li·ci·ta·dor m. bidder.

li·ci·tar tr. *(ofrecer precio)* to bid for or on; AMER. to auction.

lí·ci·to, a adj. licit.

li·cor m. liquor, spirits; *(cordial)* liqueur, cordial.

li·cua·do·ra f. mixer, blender.

li·cuar §67 tr. to liquefy; METAL. to liquate.

lid f. fight ♦ **en buena l.** in a fair fight.

lí·der m. leader, chief.

li·de·ra·to/raz·go m. leadership.

li·dia f. fight, battle ♦ **toro de l.** fighting bull.

li·dia·dor, ·ra m.f. *(luchador)* fighter, combatant —m. bullfighter.

li·diar tr. *(torear)* to fight —intr. *(luchar)* to fight, battle; *(oponerse a uno)* to oppose, face; *(contender)* to struggle, contend; *(soportar)* to put up with.

lie·bre f. hare; FIG. coward ♦ **levantar la l.** COLL. to spill the beans • **l. corrida** MEX. whore • **dar gato por l.** to swindle.

lien·zo m. *(tela)* linen, canvas; PAINT. canvas; ARCHIT. façade.

li·ga f. *(de medias)* garter; *(venda)* band; *(materia viscosa)* birdlime; *(aleación)* alloy; *(confederación)* alliance, league; SPORT. league; *(mezcla)* compound, mixture ♦ **hacer buena** or **mala l. con** to get along well or badly with.

li·ga·ción f. *(acción)* tying, binding; *(enlace)* bond, union; *(liga)* compound, mixture.

li·ga·du·ra f. *(acción)* tying, binding; *(atadura)* tie, bond; *(traba)* impediment; MED. *(torniquete)* tourniquet; *(de una vena)* ligature; MUS. tie, ligature.

li·ga·men·to m. tying, binding; ANAT. ligament.

li·gar §47 tr. *(atar)* to tie, bind; *(unir)* to join, link; *(obligar)* to bind, commit; METAL. to alloy; MUS. to slur —intr. AMER. *(entenderse)* to get along well; *(tener suerte)* to be lucky —reflex. to unite.

li·ga·zón f. bond, connection.

li·ge·re·za f. *(liviandad)* lightness; *(rapidez)* quickness, swiftness; *(agilidad)* agility, nimbleness; *(acción irreflexiva)* indiscretion.

li·ge·ro, a I. adj. *(leve)* light; *(rápido)* quick, swift; *(ágil)* agile, nimble; *(insignificante)* unimportant, insignificant; *(digerible)* light; *(tenue)* light; *(inconstante)* fickle ♦ **l. de cascos** COLL. featherbrained, empty-headed • **l. de dedos** or **de manos** light-fingered • **l. de pies** fleet-footed, quick **II.** adv. quickly, swiftly ♦ **a la l.** *(de prisa)* quickly; *(sin reflexión)* without much thought.

lig·ni·to m. lignite, brown coal.

lig·no·so, a adj. woody.

li·ja f. **I.** f. *(pez)* dogfish; *(papel)* sandpaper ♦ **darse l.** AMER. to put on airs **II.** adj. MEX., P. RICO shrewd, sharp.

li·ja·do·ra f. sander, sanding machine.

li·jar tr. to sand, sandpaper.

li·la f. & adj. lilac.

li·ma¹ f. *(fruto)* lime; *(limero)* lime tree.

li·ma² f. file ♦ **comer como una l.** to eat like a horse • **l. para las uñas** nail file.

li·ma·du·ra f. filing.

li·mar tr. *(desbastar)* to file down; *(pulir)* to polish, refine; *(cercenar)* to pare, trim ♦ **l. asperezas** to smooth over disputes.

li·ma·tón m. *(herramienta)* rasp; AMER. roof beam.

lim·bo m. THEOL. limbo; ASTRON., BOT. limb ♦ **estar en l.** to be in a daze.

li·mi·ta·ción f. limitation, limit.

li·mi·ta·do, a adj. limited; *(poco inteligente)* limited, slow-witted; *(pequeño)* small.

li·mi·tar tr. to limit; *(delimitar)* to delimit; *(restringir)* to restrict; *(acortar)* to reduce —intr. to be bounded —reflex. to limit oneself.

lí·mi·te m. limit; *(frontera)* boundary ♦ **fecha l.** deadline • **l. de elasticidad** ENGIN. elastic limit • **precio l.** final price.

li·mo m. mud, slime.

li·món m. *(fruto)* lemon; *(árbol)* lemon tree; AMER. *(de escalera)* string, shaft ♦ **refresco de l.** lemonade.

li·mo·na·do, a I. adj. lemon-colored II. f. lemonade ♦ **l. purgante** citrate of magnesia • **ni chicha ni l.** neither fish nor fowl.

li·mo·nar m. lemon grove.

li·mo·ne·ro, a m.f. lemon seller —m. lemon tree.

li·mo·si·dad f. *(cieno)* muddiness; DENT. tartar.

li·mo·si·na f. limousine.

li·mos·na f. charity, alms.

li·mos·ne·ar intr. to beg.

li·mos·ne·ro, a I. adj. charitable, generous II. m.f. *(recolector)* almoner; AMER. beggar —f. alms bag *or* box.

li·mo·so, a adj. muddy, slimy.

lim·pia f. *(limpieza)* cleaning; COLL. *(trago)* drink, shot; *(limpiabotas)* bootblack.

lim·pia·bo·tas m.inv. shoe shiner, bootblack.

lim·pia·chi·me·ne·as m.inv. chimney sweep.

lim·pia·dor, a adj. cleaning II. m.f. cleaner —f. cleaning woman *or* lady.

lim·pia·du·ra f. cleaning.

lim·pia·pa·ra·bri·sas m.inv. windshield wiper.

lim·piar tr. *(quitar lo sucio)* to clean, cleanse; *(purificar)* to clear, exonerate; *(desembarazar)* to clear, rid; COLL. *(robar)* to swipe; *(ganar)* to clean up; MEX. to beat, whip.

lím·pi·do, a adj. limpid.

lim·pie·za f. *(calidad)* cleanliness; *(acción)* cleaning, cleansing; *(precisión)* neatness, accuracy ♦ **l. de corazón** honesty, rectitude • **l. en seco** dry cleaning.

lim·pio, a I. adj. *(sin mancha)* clean, spotless; *(sin mezcla)* pure; *(cantidad)* net; *(exento)* free, clear; *(aseado)* neat, tidy; *(que ha perdido en el juego)* clean; COLL. *(sin dinero)* cleaned out, broke ♦ **en l.** free and clear, net • **quedar l.** COLL. to be broke, be cleaned out II. adv. fair ♦ **poner en l.** to make a clean copy • **quedar en l.** to become clear • **sacar algo en l.** to understand, get a clear idea of.

li·na·je m. *(familia)* lineage, ancestry; *(clase)* kind, genre.

li·na·za f. flaxseed, linseed ♦ **aceite de l.** linseed oil.

lin·ce I. m. lynx; FIG. shrewd person II. adj. sharp.

lin·char tr. to lynch.

lin·dan·te adj. bordering, adjacent.

lin·dar intr. to border (on), be adjacent (to).

lin·de m.f. boundary, limit.

lin·de·ro, a I. adj. bordering II. m. edge, border.

lin·do, a I. adj. pretty, lovely; *(perfecto)* perfect, exquisite II. m. COLL. *(hombre presumido)* showoff III. adv. R.P. prettily, nicely ♦

de lo l. much, a lot.

lí·ne·a f. line; *(ascendencia)* lineage; *(límite)* limit, boundary; *(silueta)* figure, outline ♦ **en toda la l.** all along the line, completely • **estar en l.** AMER. to be slim, in shape • **guardar la l.** to keep one's figure • **l. aérea** airline • **l. de agua** *or* **de flotación** water line • **l. de conducta** *or* **l. política** policy • **l. de fuego** firing line • **l. de montaje** assembly line • **l. de partido** party line • **l. de puntos** dotted line • **l. de tiro** line of fire • **l. equinoccial** equator • **l. térrea** railway • **l. telegráfica** telegraph line.

li·ne·al adj. linear.

li·ne·a·m(i)en·to m. lineament, contour.

li·ne·ar¹ adj. linear.

li·ne·ar² tr. *(tirar líneas)* to draw lines; *(bosquejar)* to outline, sketch.

lin·fa f. lymph.

lin·fá·ti·co, a I. adj. lymphatic II. m.f. person suffering from lymphatism.

lin·go·te m. ingot ♦ **lingotes de oro** gold bullion.

lin·güis·ta m.f. linguist.

lin·güís·ti·co, a I. adj. linguistic II. f. linguistics.

li·ni·men·to m. liniment.

li·no m. *(planta)* flax; *(tela)* linen; *(de vela)* canvas, sailcloth; ARG., P. RICO flaxseed, linseed.

li·nó·le·o/leum m. linoleum.

lin·tel m. lintel.

lin·ter·na f. *(luz)* lantern; *(de bolsillo)* flashlight; *(lámpara)* lamp, light; MECH. lantern wheel *or* pinion.

lí·o m. *(bulto)* bundle, package; COLL. *(embrollo)* jam, mess ♦ **armar un l.** COLL. to make a fuss *or* racket • **hacerse un l.** COLL. to get into a jam *or* fix.

lí·pi·do m. lipid.

li·po·so·lu·ble adj. fat-soluble.

li·que·fac·ción f. liquefaction.

li·quen m. lichen.

li·qui·da·ción f. *(un negocio)* liquidation; *(cuenta)* settlement; *(venta)* liquidation, clearance sale.

li·qui·dar tr. *(hacer líquido)* to liquefy; *(vender)* to sell off, liquidate; *(pagar)* to settle, clear; *(poner fin)* to resolve; AMER., COLL. *(matar)* to eliminate.

li·qui·dez f. liquidity.

lí·qui·do, a I. adj. liquid; *(sin gravamen)* net ♦ **dinero l.** ready cash II. m. liquid, fluid; COM. net amount ♦ **l. imponible** taxable income.

li·ra f. MUS. lyre; FIN. lira.

lí·ri·co, a adj. lyric(al).

li·rio m. iris ♦ **l. blanco** white *or* Madonna lily • **l. de agua** calla lily • **l. del valle** lily of the valley.

li·ris·mo m. lyricism.

li·rón m. dormouse ♦ **dormir como un l.** to sleep like a log.

li·siar tr. to cripple, disable.

li·so, a adj. *(parejo)* smooth; *(llano)* flat; *(sin labrar)* plain, unadorned ♦ **l. y llano** simple, straightforward.

li·son·ja f. flattery.

li·son·je·a·dor, ·ra I. adj. flattering II. m.f. flatterer.

li·son·je·ar tr. *(adular)* to flatter; *(deleitar)* to delight, please.

li·son·je·ro, a I. adj. *(que lisonjea)* flattering; *(agradable)* pleasing, gratifying II. m.f. flatterer.

lis·ta f. *(enumeración)* list; *(de personas)* roll; *(recuento)* roll call; *(tira)* strip; *(raya)* stripe ♦ **l. de comidas** menu • **l. de correos** general delivery • **l. negra** blacklist • **pasar l.** to call roll.

lis·ta·do, a adj. striped.

lis·te·za f. smartness, alertness.

lis·to, a adj. *(hábil)* skillful; *(inteligente)* smart, clever; *(preparado)* ready; *(sagaz)* shrewd ♦ **andar l.** to be careful or cautious • **¿estás l.?** are you ready? • **pasarse de l.** to be too clever for one's own good.

lis·tón m. *(cinta)* ribbon; ARCHIT. listel, fillet; CARP. lath, cleat.

li·su·ra f. *(igualdad)* smoothness, evenness; *(sinceridad)* sincerity, candor; AMER. *(atrevimiento)* boldness, impudence.

li·te·ra f. *(vehículo)* litter; *(en tren)* berth, bunk.

li·te·ral adj. literal.

li·te·ra·rio, a adj. literary.

li·te·ra·to, a I. adj. well-read, erudite **II.** m.f. man or woman of letters.

li·te·ra·tu·ra f. literature.

li·ti·ga·ción f. litigation.

li·ti·gan·te adj. & m.f. litigant.

li·ti·g(i)ar tr. to litigate —intr. to contend, dispute.

li·ti·gio m. lawsuit, litigation; *(contienda)* dispute.

li·tio m. lithium.

li·to·gra·fí·a f. *(arte)* lithography; *(imagen)* lithograph.

li·to·gra·fiar §30 tr. to lithograph.

li·tó·gra·fo m. lithographer.

li·to·ral adj. & m. littoral, coast.

li·tro m. liter.

li·tur·gia f. liturgy.

li·túr·gi·co, a adj. liturgical.

li·via·no, a adj. *(ligero)* light; *(inconstante)* fickle, faithless; *(de poca importancia)* slight, trivial.

li·vi·dez f. lividity, lividness.

lí·vi·do, a adj. livid.

lo I. def. art. the . . . thing, the . . . part <*lo mejor* the best part>; how <*no puedo creer lo rico que es* I cannot believe how rich he is> ♦ **lo de** the matter of, the business of <*¿y lo de vender la casa?* and the matter of selling the house?> • **lo que** what, which <*no revelarán lo que les dijiste* they will not reveal what you told them> • **lo que es** as to, as for **II.** pron. it <*no lo creo* I don't believe it>; him <*lo vi* I saw him>; [not translated] <*¿eres estudiante? no, no lo soy* are you a student? no, I am not>.

lo·a f. praise ♦ **cantar l.** or **hacer l. de** to sing the praises of.

lo·a·ble adj. laudable, praiseworthy.

lo·ar tr. to praise, laud.

lo·ba f. female wolf; *(vestido)* (ecclesiastical or academic) robe, gown.

lo·bo¹ m. wolf; ICHTH. loach; AMER., ZOOL. coyote ♦ **l. de mar** old salt, sea dog • **l. marino** seal.

lo·bo² m. BOT. lobe.

ló·bre·go, a adj. *(obscuro)* dark, somber; *(triste)* sad, gloomy.

lo·bre·guez f. darkness, obscurity.

ló·bu·lo m. lobe, lobule.

lo·ca·ción f. rental, leasing.

lo·cal I. adj. local **II.** m. *(edificio)* premises; *(lugar)* locale, site.

lo·ca·li·dad f. *(población)* district, locality; *(local)* locale, site; THEAT. *(asiento)* seat; *(billete)* ticket.

lo·ca·li·zar §04 tr. *(limitar a un punto)* to localize; *(encontrar)* to locate, find.

lo·ca·ta·rio, a m.f. tenant, lessee.

lo·ce·rí·a f. AMER. pottery shop, china shop.

lo·ción f. lotion.

lo·co, a I. adj. *(demente)* mad, crazy; *(imprudente)* crazy, reckless; *(extraordinario)* extraordinary, unbelievable ♦ **andar** or **volverse l.** to go mad, go crazy • **a tontas y a locas** COLL. without rhyme or reason • **como l.** like crazy, like mad • **estar l. de** or **por** to be crazy about • **estar l. de atar** or **de remate** COLL. to be stark raving mad • **estar l. de contento** COLL. to be wild with joy **II.** m.f. *(demente)* madman/woman, lunatic ♦ **cada l. con su tema** everyone has his own ax to grind • **hacerse el l.** COLL. to play dumb • **l. rematado** COLL. raving lunatic.

lo·co·mo·ción f. locomotion.

lo·co·mo·tor, triz adj. locomotor, locomotive.

lo·co·mo·to·ra f. locomotive.

lo·cua·ci·dad f. loquacity.

lo·cuaz adj. loquacious.

lo·cu·ción f. *(modo de hablar)* locution, expression; GRAM. phrase.

lo·cu·ra f. *(demencia)* madness, insanity; FIG. folly, lunacy ♦ **gastar una l.** to spend a fortune • **hacer locuras** to commit follies.

lo·cu·tor, ·ra m.f. radio announcer.

lo·do m. *(barro)* mud, sludge; MIN. sludge ♦ **arrastrar por el l.** to drag through the mud.

lo·ga·rit·mo m. logarithm.

lo·gia f. lodge.

lo·gi·cial m. COMPUT. software.

ló·gi·co, a I. adj. logical **II.** m.f. logician —f. logic.

lo·gís·ti·ca I. f. MIL. logistics; PHILOS. symbolic logic **II.** adj. logistic(al).

lo·grar tr. *(obtener)* to get, obtain; *(realizar)* to achieve ♦ **dar (algo) por logrado** to take (something) for granted —reflex. to succeed, be successful.

lo·gro m. *(éxito)* success, achievement; *(lucro)* profit, gain; *(usura)* usury.

lo·ma f. hillock, knoll.

lom·briz f. worm, earthworm ♦ **l. solitaria** tapeworm.

lo·mo m. ANAT., CUL. loin; ZOOL. back; *(de un libro)* spine; *(de un cuchillo)* back ♦ **pasar la mano por el l.** COLL. to pat on the back.

lon·che m. AMER. lunch.

lon·ga·ni·za f. pork sausage.

lon·ge·vi·dad f. longevity.

lon·ge·vo, a adj. long-lived.

lon·gi·tud f. *(dimensión)* length; GEOG. longitude ♦ **l. de onda** wavelength.

lon·gi·tu·di·nal adj. longitudinal.

lon·ja f. *(tira)* slice; COM. *(edificio)* marketplace, exchange; ARCHIT. porch, portico; R.P. leather strap.

lo·or m. praise.

lo·que·ar intr. to act like a crazy person; *(alborotar)* to frolic, romp.

lo·que·ra f. *(jaula)* padded cell; AMER. madness, insanity.

lo·que·rí·a f. AMER. insane asylum.

lo·que·ro m. asylum guard or attendant.

lo·ro m. parrot; COLL. hag.

los I. def. art. the **II.** pron. them.

lo·sa f. slab, stone ♦ **l. sepulcral** tombstone.

lo·sar tr. to tile.

lo·te m. *(parte)* lot, share; COM. *(grupo de objetos)* lot.

lo·te·ar tr. to divide into lots *or* shares.

lo·te·rí·a f. *(juego público)* lottery, raffle; *(juego casero)* bingo; *(cosa incierta)* gamble.

lo·za f. *(barro vidriado)* glazed pottery; *(platos)* china.

lo·za·ní·a f. *(de las plantas)* lushness; *(salud)* healthiness; *(orgullo)* pride, haughtiness.

lo·za·no, a adj. *(frondoso)* leafy, luxuriant; *(robusto)* robust, vigorous.

lu·bri·ca·ción f. lubrication.

lu·bri·can·te I. adj. lubricating **II.** m. lubricant.

lu·bri·(fi)·car §70 tr. to lubricate.

lu·ce·ro m. *(astro)* bright star; *(planeta)* Venus; *(de un animal)* white star ♦ **l. del alba** morning star • **l. de la tarde** evening star ♦ pl. POET. the eyes.

lu·ci·dez f. lucidity.

lú·ci·do, a adj. *(brillante)* bright, shining, *(inteligente)* brilliant, intelligent.

lu·cien·te adj. shining, brilliant.

lu·ciér·na·ga f. glowworm, firefly.

lu·ci·(l)(lo m. tomb, sarcophagus.

lu·ci·mien·to m. *(brillo)* brilliance, luster; *(éxito)* success, triumph.

lu·cir §44 intr. *(brillar)* to shine; *(distinguirse)* to shine, excel; *(tener apariencia)* to show —tr. *(alardear)* to show off, display; *(iluminar)* to illuminate, light up —reflex. *(vestir bien)* to dress up; *(salir bien)* to come out with flying colors; *(distinguirse)* to shine, distinguish oneself.

lu·crar tr. to win, profit.

lu·cra·ti·vo, a adj. lucrative.

lu·cro m. profit, gain.

lu·cu·bra·ción f. lucubration.

lu·cha f. *(conflicto)* struggle, conflict; SPORT. wrestling ♦ **l. de clases** class struggle.

lu·cha·dor, ·ra m.f. fighter; SPORT. wrestler.

lu·char intr. *(pelear)* to fight, struggle; *(disputar)* to argue, quarrel; SPORT. to wrestle.

lue·go I. adv. *(después)* then, afterward; *(más tarde)* later, later on; *(pronto)* soon ♦ **desde l.** of course, naturally • **hasta l.** so long, until later • **l. de** after • **l. que** as soon as • **tan l. como** as soon as **II.** conj. therefore.

lu·gar m. *(sitio)* place; *(espacio)* room, space; *(pueblo)* town, village; *(puesto)* position ♦ **en l. de** instead of • **en primer l.** in the first place, first • **no ha l.** LAW petition denied • **tener l.** to take place, happen.

lu·ga·re·ño, a I. adj. of a village **II.** m.f. villager.

lu·gar·te·nen·cia f. lieutenancy.

lu·gar·te·nien·te m. lieutenant.

lú·gu·bre adj. lugubrious.

lu·jo m. luxury ♦ **artículos de l.** luxury goods • **de l. de luxe** • **vivir en l. asiático** to live like a king.

lu·jo·so, a adj. luxurious.

lu·ju·ria f. *(lascivia)* lust, lechery; *(exceso)* excess.

lu·ju·rian·te adj. lush, luxurious.

lu·ju·rio·so, a adj. lustful, lascivious.

lum·ba·go m. lumbago.

lum·bar adj. lumbar.

lum·bre f. *(luz)* light; *(fuego)* fire; *(fósforo, encendedor)* light ♦ **dar l.** to give (someone) a light.

lum·bre·ra f. *(cuerpo luminoso)* light, luminary; *(en un techo)* skylight; MECH. port, vent; CARP. mouth (of a plane); MARIT. porthole; *(persona)* luminary; MEX. box (in a bullring).

lu·mi·na·ria f. RELIG. altar lamp ♦ pl. *(decorative)* lights.

lu·mi·nis·cen·cia/nes·cen·cia f. luminescence.

lu·mi·nis·cen·te/nes·cen·te adj. luminescent.

lu·mi·no·si·dad f. luminosity.

lu·mi·no·so, a adj. *(que despide luz)* luminous; *(excelente)* bright, brilliant.

lu·na f. moon; *(vidrio)* plate glass; *(espejo)* mirror; *(lente)* lens; *(capricho)* notion, wild idea ♦ **estar de buena, mala l.** to be in a good, bad mood • **estar en la l.** to be daydreaming • **l. creciente** crescent moon • **l. de miel** honeymoon • **l. llena** full moon • **l. menguante** waning moon • **l. nueva** new moon • **media l.** half moon; AMER. *(pastry)* croissant.

lu·nar¹ m. *(de la piel)* mole, beauty mark; *(defecto)* flaw ♦ **vestido de lunares** polka-dot dress.

lu·nar² adj. lunar.

lu·ná·ti·co, a adj. & m.f. lunatic.

lu·nes m. Monday.

lu·ne·ta f. *(de anteojos)* lens; THEAT. orchestra seat; ARCHIT. *(bocateja)* front tile (of roof); *(bovedilla)* lunette.

lú·nu·la f. half-moon of fingernails; GEOM. arc.

lu·pa f. magnifying glass, loupe.

lu·pa·nar m. brothel.

lu·pi·no, a I. adj. lupine, wolf-like **II.** m. BOT. lupine.

lú·pu·lo m. hops.

lus·tra·bo·tas m.inv. AMER. shoe shiner.

lus·trar tr. *(limpiar)* to polish, shine; *(purificar)* to lustrate, purify.

lus·tre m. *(brillo)* luster, shine; *(esplendor)* splendor, glory; *(betún)* shoe polish.

lus·tro·so, a adj. lustrous, shiny.

lu·to m. mourning ♦ **ponerse de l.** to go into mourning.

luz f. *(claridad)* light; *(lámpara)* light, lamp; *(día)* day, daylight; *(guía)* guiding light; ARCHIT. window; AUTO. light; PAINT. lighting ♦ **a primera l.** at daybreak • **a todas luces** clearly, from every angle • **dar a l.** PHYSIOL. to give birth; *(publicar)* to publish, print • **l. de Bengala** Bengal light, sparkler • **l. de tráfico** traffic light • **sacar a l.** *(revelar)* to bring to light; *(publicar)* to bring out, publish • **salir a l.** *(publicarse)* to come out, publish; *(descubrirse)* to come to light ♦ pl. enlightenment, learning • **corto de l.** COLL. not very bright.

LL

ll, Ll f. fourteenth letter of the Spanish alphabet.

lla·ga f. *(herida)* wound, sore; *(úlcera)* ulcer, sore; *(daño)* wound, injury ♦ **poner el dedo en la ll.** to touch on a sore spot.

lla·gar §47 tr. to wound, injure.

lla·ma¹ f. flame; FIG. flame, passion ♦ **en llamas** in flames, aflame.

lla·ma² f. ZOOL. llama.

lla·ma·da f. call, calling; *(de timbre)* ring; *(de puerta)* knock; *(telefónica)* telephone call; *(seña)* reference mark; *(ademán)* gesture, signal; *(atracción)* call, lure; MEX. cowardice ♦ II. **al orden** call to order • II. **de socorro** distress signal.

lla·ma·dor, ·ra m.f. caller —m. *(aldaba)* door knocker; *(timbre)* doorbell.

lla·ma·mien·to m. calling; *(convocación)* call, summons; RELIG. calling, vocation.

lla·mar tr. *(dar voces)* to call, *(convocar)* to call, summon; *(telefonear)* to call, telephone; *(apellidar)* to call; *(nombrar)* to call; *(atraer)* to call, attract; *(suplicar)* to call upon, appeal to ♦ II. **al orden** to call to order • II. **a voces** to shout • II. **por teléfono** to telephone, phone —intr. *(hacer sonar un timbre)* to ring a doorbell; *(tocar a la puerta)* to knock at the door; *(por teléfono)* to call, telephone ♦ **¿quién llama?** who is it? —reflex. to be called *or* named.

lla·ma·ra·da f. *(fuego)* flare; *(bochorno)* flush; *(arrebato)* outburst.

lla·ma·ti·vo, a adj. showy, flashy.

lla·me·an·te adj. flaming, blazing.

lla·me·ar intr. to flame, blaze.

lla·ne·za f. simplicity.

lla·no, a I. adj. *(liso)* flat, even; *(sencillo)* natural, simple; *(claro)* clear, evident; *(corriente)* clear, open; *(simple)* simple, plain ♦ **de II.** plainly, clearly II. m. GEOG. plain —f. MAS. trowel, float; *(de papel)* side; *(llanura)* plain.

llan·ta f. *(de una rueda)* rim; AMER. tire.

llan·to m. crying, weeping.

lla·nu·ra f. *(lisura)* evenness; *(planicie)* plain.

lla·ve f. key; *(grifo)* tap, faucet; ELEC. switch; MECH. wrench; *(corchete)* bracket; MUS. clef; *(en lucha libre)* lock ♦ **ama de llaves** housekeeper • **bajo II.** under lock and key • **echar II.** to lock • **la II. del éxito** the key to success • II. **de bola** *or* **de flotador** ball cock • II. **de paso** water valve • II. **inglesa** monkey wrench.

lla·ve·ro m. key ring.

lle·ga·da f. arrival; SPORT. finish.

lle·gar §47 intr. *(venir)* to arrive, come; *(durar)* to reach, last; *(alcanzar)* to reach, extend *<la falda le llega hasta las rodillas* the skirt reaches her knees>; *(ascender)* to amount, come *<la cuenta llegó a quinientos pesos* the bill came to five hundred pesos>; *(suceder)* to arrive, come *<llegó el momento de la verdad* the moment of truth arrived> ♦ II. **a** *(destino)* to arrive at, reach; *(acuerdo)* to reach; *(lograr)* to manage to *<llegó a controlar la situación* he managed to control the situation> • II. **a las manos** COLL. to come to blows • II. **a saber** to find out • II. **a ser** to become —reflex. *(acercarse)* to move closer, come near; *(ir)* to stop by.

lle·nar tr. to fill (up) *<llene el vaso de vino* fill the glass with wine>; *(ocupar)* to fill, occupy *<él llena el puesto de la persona que se fue* he is filling the position of the person who left>; *(cumplir)* to fulfill, meet *<ll. las condiciones del contrato* to meet the conditions of the contract>; *(formulario)* to fill out; *(satisfacer)* to satisfy *<su explicación no me llena* his explanation does not satisfy me>; *(colmar)* to heap *<ll. de insultos a* to heap insults on> —intr. ASTRON. to be full —reflex. to fill up, be filled *<la sala se llenaba de gente* the room was filling up with people>; COLL. *(hartarse)* to stuff oneself, gorge; COLL. *(irritarse)* to be fed up.

lle·no, a I. adj. *(ocupado)* full, filled; *(redondo)* full ♦ **de II.** fully, completely • II. **de** full of, filled with II. m. THEAT. full house.

lle·var tr. *(transportar)* to carry, take *<le llevó flores al hospital* he took flowers to her in the hospital>; *(vestir)* to wear *<lleva medias negras* he is wearing black socks>; *(traer)* to carry, have *<no llevo dinero conmigo* I have no money with me>; *(conducir)* to take, lead *<este camino te llevará a Barcelona* this road will take you to Barcelona>; *(vivir)* to lead *<ll. una vida de perros* to lead a dog's life>; *(encargarse de)* to manage, run *<ella lleva las cuentas de la casa* she manages the household accounts>; *(tolerar)* to endure, put up with; *(cobrar)* to charge; *(arrancar)* to tear off, sever *<la metralla le llevó la pierna* the shrapnel severed his leg>; *(pasar)* to have spent, have been *<llevo cinco noches sin dormir* I have spent five nights without sleep>; *(ser mayor)* to be older *<mi hermana me lleva tres años* my sister is three years older than I>; MATH. to carry ♦ II. **a cabo** to carry out • II. **adelante** to go ahead *or* forward with • **llevarla hecha** COLL. to have it all figured out • II. **la peor parte** to get the worst of it • II. **las de perder** COLL. to be on the losing end —intr. to lead *<la carretera lleva a la ciudad* the highway leads to the city> —reflex. *(llevar)* to take away, carry off *<se llevó el premio gordo* she carried off the first prize>; *(robar)* to take *<se llevó el dinero del banco* he took the money from the bank>; *(conseguir)* to get *<se llevó lo que quería* he got what he wanted> ♦ II. **bien, mal** to get along well, badly.

llo·rar intr. *(derramar lágrimas)* to cry, weep; *(los ojos)* to water, run ♦ II. **a lágrima viva** to cry one's heart out —tr. *(lamentar)* to mourn; *(sentir mucho)* to regret, bemoan.

llo·ri·que·ar intr. to whine, whimper.

llo·ri·que·o m. whining, whimpering.

llo·ro m. crying, weeping.

llo·rón, o·na I. adj. crying, weeping ♦ **sauce II.** weeping willow II. m.f. *(llorador)* weeper; *(lloraduelos)* crybaby.

llo·ro·so, a adj. *(que ha llorado)* tearful; *(triste)* sad, sorrowful.

llo·ver §78 intr. to rain; FIG. to rain, shower ♦ **como llovido del cielo** unexpectedly • II. **a cántaros** *or* **a mares** to rain cats and dogs, rain buckets • **llueva o no** rain or shine.

llo·viz·na f. drizzle.

llo·viz·nar intr. to drizzle.

llue·va, ve see **llover**.

llu·via f. *(acción)* rain, raining; *(agua)* rain; *(cantidad)* rainfall; *(abundancia)* shower ♦ II. **atómica** fallout.

llu·vio·so, a adj. rainy, wet.

M

m, M f. fifteenth letter of the Spanish alphabet.

ma·ca·bro, a adj. macabre, funereal.

ma·ca·dam m. [pl. **s**] macadam.

ma·ca·rrón m. macaroon ♦ pl. macaroni.

ma·ce·ra·ción f./**mien·to** m. maceration; FIG. mortification.

ma·ce·rar tr. to macerate.

ma·ce·ta[1] f. *(mango)* handle; *(martillo)* stonemason's hammer; AMER. mallet.

ma·ce·ta[2] f. flowerpot.

ma·ce·te·ro m. flowerpot stand.

ma·ci·len·to, a adj. emaciated, lean.

ma·ci·zo, a I. adj. *(fuerte)* strong, solid; *(sin*

hueco) solid; (fundado) well-founded, solid II. m. (masa) mass; ARCHIT. section of a wall (between two bays); GEOG., GEOL. massif; (de edificios) block; (de plantas) flowerbed.

ma·co·na f. large basket.

ma·cro·bió·ti·co, a I. adj. macrobiotic II. f. macrobiotics.

ma·cro·cos·mo m. macrocosm.

ma·cro·e·co·no·mí·a f. macroeconomics.

ma·cro·mo·lé·cu·la f. macromolecule.

má·cu·la f. (mancha) stain, spot; COLL. (engaño) deception, trick; ASTRON. macula.

ma·cu·to m. alms basket.

ma·cha·ca f. (instrumento) crusher, pounder —m.f. (persona pesada) bore, boring person.

ma·cha·ca·dor, ·ra I. adj. crushing, pounding II. m.f. (que machaca) crusher, pounder —f. (máquina) crusher, crushing machine.

ma·cha·car §70 tr. to crush, pound —intr. (importunar) to bother, pester; (insistir) to insist, go on about ♦ m. en hierro frío to bang one's head against a wall.

ma·cha·cón, o·na I. adj. insistent, tiresome II. m.f. bore, pest.

ma·cha·da f. (hato) flock of billy goats; COLL. (necedad) stupidity, foolish remark; (hombrada) manly action.

ma·cha·do m. hatchet.

ma·cha·que·o m. (trituración) crushing, pounding; (insistencia) insistence.

ma·che·ta·zo m. blow with a machete.

ma·che·te m. machete.

ma·che·te·ar tr. (herir) to wound with a machete; (talar) to cut down with a machete.

ma·che·te·ro m. (desmontador) cutter, clearer (of a path); (de caña) cane-cutter.

ma·chi·hem·bra·do m. tongue and groove.

ma·chi·na f. (grúa grande) crane, derrick; (martinete) pile driver.

ma·cho[1] I. adj. male; (fuerte) strong, tough; (viril) manly, virile II. m. (animal) male; (mulo) mule; MECH. pin, plug; ELEC. plug; COLL. (necio) he-man ♦ m. cabrío billy goat.

ma·cho[2] m. (mazo) sledgehammer; (banco de yunque) anvil block; (yunque) square anvil.

ma·chón, o·na I. m. abutment, pilaster II. adj. AMER. mannish woman.

ma·cho·te m. COLL. virile man, he-man ♦ dárselas de m. to act like a he-man.

ma·chu·ca·du·ra f. (golpe) pounding, beating; (magullamiento) bruising, bruise.

ma·chu·car §70 tr. (golpear) to pound, beat; (magullar) to bruise.

ma·de·ja f. skein; (de pelo) mop of (hair) ♦ enredar or enredarse la m. to get complicated.

ma·de·ra f. wood; (de construcción) timber, lumber; ZOOL. horny part of a hoof ♦ de m. wooden, of wood ♦ m. flotante driftwood ♦ m. fósil lignite ♦ m. laminada or contrachapada plywood ♦ tocar m. to knock on wood.

ma·de·ra·da f. raft, float.

ma·de·ra·je f. /men m. wooden framework.

ma·de·re·rí·a f. lumberyard.

ma·de·re·ro, a I. adj. lumber, timber II. m. (comerciante) lumber or timber dealer; (carpintero) carpenter.

ma·de·ro m. log, length of timber.

ma·dras·tra f. stepmother.

ma·dre f. mother; (matrona) matron; (cauce) riverbed; (acequia) main irrigation ditch; (causa) cause ♦ ¡m. mía! my goodness! ♦ m. patria mother country, old country ♦ m. polí-

tica mother-in-law ♦ m. soltera unwed mother ♦ salirse de m. to overflow.

ma·dre·per·la f. pearl oyster; (nácar) mother-of-pearl.

ma·dre·sel·va f. honeysuckle.

ma·dri·gue·ra f. (cuevecilla) burrow, hole; (cubil) den; (escondrijo) hideout, lair.

ma·dri·na f. (de bautismo) godmother; (de boda) bridesmaid; (protectora) protectress, patroness; (yegua) lead mare.

ma·dru·ga·da f. (amanecer) dawn; (levantada) early rising ♦ a las dos de la m. at two o'clock in the morning ♦ de m. at daybreak, very early.

ma·dru·ga·dor, ·ra I. adj. early-rising II. m.f. early riser.

ma·dru·gar §47 intr. (levantarse temprano) to get up early; (ganar tiempo) to anticipate, be ahead ♦ a quien madruga, Dios le ayuda the early bird catches the worm —tr. ARG., MEX., SL. to get the better of (someone).

ma·dru·gón, o·na I. adj. early-rising II. m. ♦ darse un m. to get up very early.

ma·du·ra·ción f. maturation, ripening.

ma·du·ra·dor, ·ra adj. maturing, ripening.

ma·du·rar tr. AGR. to ripen, mature; (problema) to think out, work out; MED. to induce suppuration; (persona) to mature —intr. AGR. to ripen, mature; (persona) to mature; MED. to maturate, suppurate.

ma·du·rez f. AGR. ripeness; (sabiduría) sound judgment; (edad adulta) maturity.

ma·du·ro, a adj. AGR. ripe; (juicioso) wise; (entrado en años) mature; MED. ripe.

ma·es·tra f. see maestro, a.

ma·es·tran·za f. MIL. (almacén) armory; (talleres) arsenal; (operarios) arsenal workers.

ma·es·tre m. master.

ma·es·trí·a f. (habilidad) mastery, skill; (título avanzado) Master's degree; (título de maestro) teaching degree.

ma·es·tro, a I. adj. (perfecto) master; (principal) main, principal II. m. (profesor) teacher; (perito) expert, master; (artesano) master; EDUC. master; MUS. maestro ♦ m. de capilla choirmaster ♦ m. de cocina chef ♦ m. de escuela schoolmaster ♦ m. de obras master builder —f. (profesora) teacher, schoolmistress; (listón) guide line.

ma·gan·ce·rí·a f. deception, trickery.

ma·ga·ña f. trick, cunning stratagem.

ma·gia f. magic ♦ como por arte de m. as if by magic.

má·gi·co, a I. adj. (de la magia) magic(al); (maravilloso) marvellous, amazing II. f. magic.

ma·gín m. COLL. imagination, mind.

ma·gis·te·rio m. (profesión) teaching profession; (conjunto) teaching staff.

ma·gis·tra·do m. magistrate.

ma·gis·tral adj. (del maestro) magisterial, imposing; (excelente) skillful, masterful.

ma·gis·tra·tu·ra f. magistracy, magistrature.

mag·na·ni·mi·dad f. magnanimity.

mag·ná·ni·mo, a adj. magnanimous.

mag·na·te m. magnate.

mag·ne·sia f. magnesia.

mag·ne·sio m. magnesium.

mag·né·ti·co, a adj. magnetic.

mag·ne·tis·mo m. magnetism.

mag·ne·ti·zar §04 tr. to magnetize; (hipnotizar) to hypnotize, mesmerize.

mag·ne·to·fó·ni·co, a adj. magnetic ♦ cinta m. magnetic tape.

mag·ne·tó·fo·no/to·fón m. tape recorder.
mag·ni·fi·ca·dor, ·ra adj. magnifying.
mag·ni·fi·car §70 tr. *(engrandecer)* to magnify, exaggerate; *(ensalzar)* to exalt, glorify; OPT. to magnify, enlarge.
mag·ni·fi·cen·cia f. *(opulencia)* magnificence; *(generosidad)* generosity.
mag·ni·fi·cen·te adj. magnificent.
mag·ni·fi·co, a adj. *(hermoso)* magnificent, beautiful; *(excelente)* excellent; *(generoso)* generous.
mag·ni·tud f. *(tamaño)* magnitude, size; *(importancia)* importance, order; ASTRON. magnitude; MATH. quantity.
mag·no, a adj. great, grand.
mag·no·lia f. magnolia.
ma·go, a I. adj. magic, magical ♦ **los Reyes Magos** the Magi II. m. *(hechicero)* magician, wizard; *(sacerdote)* magus, sage.
ma·gro, a I. adj. lean, thin II. m. lean pork.
ma·gu·lla·du·ra f./**mien·to** m. bruise, contusion.
ma·gu·llar tr. to bruise, batter.
ma·gu·llón m. AMER. bruise.
mai·ce·na f. cornstarch.
mai·ti·nes m.pl. matins ♦ **llamar** or **tocar a m.** to call or ring to matins.
ma·íz m. [pl. **-íces**] corn, maize (G.B.) ♦ **rosetas de m.** popcorn.
mai·zal m. cornfield.
ma·ja f. see **majo, a.**
ma·ja·da f. *(redil)* sheepfold; *(estiércol)* manure, dung; ARG., CHILE flock of sheep.
ma·ja·de·rí·a f. nonsense, stupid act or remark.
ma·ja·de·ro, a I. adj. silly, foolish II. m.f. silly person, fool.
ma·ja·do m. mash, pulp.
ma·ja·du·ra f. mashing, pounding.
ma·jal m. shoal, school (of fish).
ma·jar tr. to mash, pound; COLL. *(molestar)* to annoy, bother; *(azotar)* to beat, flog.
ma·jes·tad f. *(poder)* majesty, sovereignty; *(grandeza)* grandeur, stateliness ♦ **Su M.** Your Majesty.
ma·jes·tuo·si·dad f. majesty, grandeur.
ma·jes·tuo·so, a adj. majestic, grand.
ma·jo, a SP. I. adj. *(vistoso)* flashy, showy; *(bonito)* pretty, attractive; *(simpático)* nice, sweet; *(elegante)* smart, well-dressed II. m. gay blade, cocky youth —f. *(majadero)* pestle; SP. flashy young woman.
mal¹ I. adj. see **malo, a** II. m. *(vicio)* evil; *(daño)* damage, harm; *(desgracia)* misfortune; *(enfermedad)* illness, disease ♦ **echar a m.** to scorn, despise • **hacer m.** to harm, hurt • **m. de mar** seasickness • **m. de montaña** altitude sickness • **m. de ojo** evil eye • **¡m. haya!** damn! • **tomar a m.** to be offended, take offense.
mal² adv. *(pobremente)* badly, poorly; *(desacertadamente)* wrongly, incorrectly; *(difícilmente)* hardly <*m. puedo ayudarte* I can hardly help you> ♦ **de m. en peor** from bad to worse • **menos m.** just as well • **si m. no recuerdo** if I remember correctly.
ma·la·bar m. ♦ **hacer juegos malabares** to juggle.
ma·la·ba·ris·ta m. juggler.
ma·la·ca·te m. *(cabrestante)* winch; AMER. spindle.
ma·la·con·se·ja·do, a adj. ill-advised.
ma·la·cos·tum·bra·do, a adj. having had habits; *(mal criado)* ill-bred, ill-mannered; *(mi-*

mado) spoiled.
ma·la·cos·tum·brar·se reflex. to get into bad habits.
ma·la·crian·za f. AMER. bad manners.
ma·la·gra·de·ci·do, a adj. AMER. ungrateful, unappreciative.
ma·lan·dan·za f. misfortune, calamity.
ma·lan·drín, ·i·na I. adj. wicked, evil II. m.f. rascal, scoundrel.
ma·la·pa·ta f. COLL. bad luck —m.f. unlucky person.
ma·lar I. adj. malar, cheek II. m. malar.
ma·la·ria f. malaria.
ma·la·san·gre adj. mean or evil-minded.
ma·la·ve·ni·do, a adj. incompatible.
ma·la·ven·tu·ra f. misfortune, adversity.
ma·la·ven·tu·ra·do, a I. adj. ill-fated, unfortunate II. m.f. unfortunate person, poor soul.
ma·la·ven·tu·ran·za f. misfortune, ill fortune.
mal·ba·ra·ta·dor, ·ra I. adj. *(que malvende)* underselling; *(malgastador)* squandering II. m.f. *(que malvende)* underseller; *(malgastador)* squanderer, spendthrift.
mal·ba·ra·tar tr. *(malvender)* to undersell; *(malgastar)* to squander.
mal·ca·sa·do, a adj. *(infiel)* unfaithful, adulterous; *(casado con persona de condición inferior)* married to someone below one's station.
mal·ca·sar tr. *(ser incompatibles)* to mismatch; *(casar con persona de condición inferior)* to marry below one's station —reflex. to be mismarried or mismatched.
mal·co·mer intr. to eat poorly.
mal·co·mi·do, a adj. malnourished, underfed.
mal·con·si·de·ra·do, a adj. inconsiderate.
mal·con·ten·to, a I. adj. *(disgustado)* discontented, unhappy; *(rebelde)* malcontent, rebellious II. m.f. malcontent.
mal·cria·dez/de·za f. AMER. bad manners, lack of breeding.
mal·cria·do, a adj. spoiled, ill-bred.
mal·criar §30 tr. to spoil, pamper.
mal·dad f. *(carácter de malo)* wickedness, evil; *(acto)* evil act ♦ **cometer maldades** to do evil or wrong.
mal·de·ci·do, a adj. & m.f. evil, wicked (person).
mal·de·cir §11 tr. *(echar una maldición)* to curse, damn; *(calumniar)* to slander; *(renegar de)* to curse —intr. to curse.
mal·di·cien·te I. adj. slandering, defaming II. m.f. *(calumniador)* slanderer; *(detractor)* detractor; *(persona que maldice)* curser.
mal·di·ción I. f. curse, damnation II. interj. damn!, damnation!
mal·di·ga, o, jera, jo see **maldecir.**
mal·dis·pues·to, a adj. *(de mala gana)* reluctant; *(enfermo)* indisposed.
mal·di·to, a adj. *(desagradable)* damned, lousy <*esta m. lluvia* this damned rain>; *(de mal carácter)* bad, wicked; THEOL. damned, condemned ♦ **¡m. lo que me importa!** damned if I care!
ma·le·a·bi·li·dad f. malleability.
ma·le·a·ble adj. malleable.
ma·le·an·te I. adj. *(que pervierte)* vicious, corrupting; *(perverso)* perverse; *(maligno)* malicious, wicked II. m.f. crook, evildoer.
ma·le·ar tr. *(estropear)* to spoil, ruin; *(pervertir)* to pervert, corrupt —reflex. *(estropearse)* to be ruined; *(pervertirse)* to be perverted or corrupted.
ma·le·cón m. sea wall, dike.

ma·le·di·cen·cia f. slander.

ma·le·du·ca·do, a adj. bad-mannered.

ma·le·fi·cen·cia f. maleficence, evil.

ma·le·fi·cen·te adj. maleficent.

ma·le·fi·cio m. spell, curse.

ma·lé·fi·co, a adj. *(dañino)* maleficent, evil; *(que hace maleficios)* spell-casting, bewitching.

ma·len·ten·di·do m. misunderstanding.

ma·les·tar m. *(del cuerpo)* malaise, indisposition; *(inquietud)* malaise, uneasiness.

ma·le·ta f. suitcase, valise ◆ **hacer la m.** to pack one's bag —m. COLL. bungler, incompetent.

ma·le·te·ro m. station porter; AUTO. trunk.

ma·le·tín m. small suitcase.

ma·le·tón m. AMER. hunchback, humpback.

ma·le·tu·do, a adj. AMER. hunchbacked.

ma·le·vo·len·cia f. malevolence.

ma·lé·vo·lo, a adj. & m.f. malevolent (person).

ma·le·za f. *(hierbas)* weeds; *(zarzales)* underbrush.

mal·for·ma·ción f. malformation.

mal·gas·ta·dor, ra adj. & m.f. spendthrift.

mal·gas·tar tr. to waste, misspend.

mal·ha·bla·do, a adj. foul-mouthed, vulgar.

mal·ha·da·do, a adj. wretched, unfortunate.

mal·ha·ya adj. AMER., COLL. damned, cursed ◆ ¡**m. seal** damn it!

mal·he·chor, ra I. adj. evil, doing evil II. m.f. wrongdoer, evildoer.

mal·he·rir §65 tr. to wound or injure badly.

mal·hu·mor m. bad temper.

mal·hu·mo·ra·do, a adj. bad-tempered.

mal·hu·mo·rar tr. to annoy, irritate.

ma·li·cia f. *(perversidad)* malice, wickedness; *(disimulo)* slyness, cunning; *(travesura)* mischievousness, naughtiness; COLL. *(sospecha)* suspicion.

ma·li·ciar·se reflex. to be suspicious ◆ **algo me malicio en ese lío** there's something fishy about this business.

ma·li·cio·so, a I. adj. malicious; *(astuto)* sly, cunning II. m.f. malicious person.

ma·lig·ni·dad f. malignancy.

ma·lig·no, a adj. malignant.

ma·lin·ten·cio·na·do, a adj. & m.f. ill-intentioned (person).

mal·man·da·do, a adj. disobedient.

mal·mi·ra·do, a adj. disliked, disfavored.

ma·lo, a I. adj. bad; *(pobre)* poor; *(perverso)* evil; *(dañino)* harmful; *(desagradable)* unpleasant, nasty <pasamos un mal rato we had an unpleasant time>; *(enfermo)* sick, ill; *(travieso)* naughty; *(nocivo)* noxious <un mal olor a noxious odor>; COLL. *(malicioso)* mean, malicious ◆ **a la m.** AMER. by force • **a (las) malas** on bad terms • **de m. gana** reluctantly • **de malas** *(con desgracia)* unlucky, out of luck <estar de malas to be out of luck>; *(con mala intención)* with bad intentions; COLL. *(molesto)* upset, out of sorts <hoy estoy de malas I am out of sorts today> • **lo m. es que** the trouble is... • **ponerse m.** to become sick • **por las malas** by force II. m. ◆ **el m.** the bad guy, the villain.

ma·lo·gra·do, a adj. frustrated, abortive.

ma·lo·grar tr. to waste, lose; *(estropear)* to spoil, ruin —reflex. *(fracasar)* to fail, come to nothing; *(morir prematuramente)* to come to an untimely end.

ma·lo·gro m. *(fracaso)* failure; *(fin)* untimely end.

ma·lo·lien·te adj. smelly, foul-smelling.

ma·lón m. AMER. surprise Indian attack.

mal·pa·rar tr. *(maltratar)* to hurt, harm; *(dañar)* to damage.

mal·pa·rir intr. to miscarry, have a miscarriage.

mal·par·to m. miscarriage.

mal·pen·sa·do, a adj. & m.f. evil-minded or malicious (person).

mal·que·rer §55 tr. to bear ill will toward, dislike.

mal·quis·tar tr. to alienate, estrange.

mal·quis·to, a adj. disliked, unpopular.

mal·sa·no, a adj. unhealthy.

mal·so·nan·te adj. *(que suena mal)* ill-sounding, harsh; *(indecente)* nasty, offensive.

mal·su·fri·do, a adj. impatient.

mal·ta f. malt; *(grano tostado)* toasted grain; R.P. black beer.

mal·te·ar tr. to malt.

mal·tra·ta·mien·to m. mistreatment.

mal·tra·tar tr. to maltreat, mistreat.

mal·tra·to m. var. of **maltratamiento**.

mal·tre·cho, a adj. damaged, battered.

mal·va I. f. mallow; MEX., COLL. marijuana, weed —m. *(color)* mauve, light violet ◆ **m. arbórea** or **loca** or **rósea** rose mallow, hollyhock II. adj. mauve, light violet.

mal·va·do, a I. adj. evil, wicked II. m.f. evildoer, wicked person.

mal·ven·der tr. to sell at a loss, sell off cheap.

mal·ver·sa·ción f. embezzlement.

mal·ver·sa·dor, ra I. adj. embezzling II. m.f. embezzler.

mal·ver·sar tr. to embezzle.

mal·vi·vir intr. to live badly.

ma·lla f. *(de red)* mesh, netting; *(de armadura)* mail, chain mail; AMER. *(traje de baño)* swimsuit, bathing trunks.

ma·llo m. *(mazo)* mallet, maul; *(juego y terreno)* mall, pall mall.

ma·má f. mamma, mammary gland; COLL. *(madre)* mommy.

ma·má f. COLL. mama, mommy.

ma·ma·ca·llos m.inv. COLL. fool, sucker.

ma·ma·de·ra f. AMER. *(biberón)* baby bottle; *(tetina de biberón)* rubber nipple.

ma·ma·do, a I. adj. COLL. drunk, sloshed II. f. COLL. *(acción)* nursing, sucking; *(cantidad de leche tomada)* amount of milk that a child takes in sucking or nursing ◆ **agarrarse una m.** ARG., COLL. to get drunk.

ma·man·tón, o·na adj. suckling.

ma·mar tr. *(chupar)* to suckle, nurse; FIG. *(aprender)* to learn (from childhood) —intr. to suck, nurse —reflex. AMER., COLL. to get drunk or smashed ◆ **m. el dedo** COLL. to let oneself be sucked in, be fooled.

ma·ma·rio, a adj. mammary.

ma·ma·rra·cha·da f./**cho** m. COLL. *(cuadro malo)* junk, bad painting; *(basura)* junk, rubbish; *(idiota)* fool, idiot; *(sandez)* stupidity, idiocy.

ma·me·lón m. nipple.

ma·mí·fe·ro I. adj. mammalian II. m. mammal, mammalian.

ma·mi·la f. *(de la hembra)* woman's breast around the nipple; *(del hombre)* nipple.

ma·món, o·na I. adj. unweaned, still nursing II. m.f. *(bebé que mama todavía)* unweaned baby, baby who still nurses —m. BOT. shoot, sucker.

ma·mo·tre·to m. *(libro de apuntes)* notebook, memo book; COLL. *(legajo grueso)* thick bundle of papers; *(libraco)* large, bulky book; AMER. *(armatoste)* monstrosity.

mam·pa·ra f. *(cancel)* movable room divider *or* partition; *(biombo)* screen.

mam·po·rro m. COLL. bump (on the head).

ma·mu·jar tr. to nurse intermittently.

ma·mu·llar tr. *(comer o masticar)* to suck in; COLL. *(mascullar)* to mumble, mutter.

ma·ná m. manna.

ma·na·da f. *(hato)* flock, herd; *(de lobos)* pack; COLL. *(bunda)* gang, bunch ♦ **a manadas** COLL. in droves or crowds.

ma·na·de·ro, a I. adj. flowing, running **II.** m. *(manantial)* spring, source; *(pastor)* shepherd.

ma·nan·te adj. flowing, running.

ma·nan·tial I. adj. spring, running **II.** m. *(fontanal)* spring, source; *(origen)* source, origin.

ma·nan·tí·o, a adj. flowing, running.

ma·nar tr. & intr. to run *or* flow *(de from)*.

ma·na·tí [pl. **-íes**] m. manatee, sea cow; *(piel)* manatee hide.

ma·na·za f. large *or* hefty hand.

ma·na·zas I. adj. clumsy, all thumbs **II.** m.f. inv. clumsy person.

man·ca·mien·to m. disabling.

man·car §70 tr. to maim, disable.

man·ca·rrón, o·na I. adj. worn-out **II.** m. AMER. nag, worn-out horse.

man·ce·ba f. mistress, concubine.

man·ce·bí·a f. brothel, whorehouse.

man·ce·bo m. *(joven)* young man, youth; *(soltero)* bachelor, single man.

man·ce·ra f. plow handle.

man·ci·lla f. stain, blemish.

man·ci·llar tr. to stain, blemish.

man·ci·par tr. to enslave.

man·co, a I. adj. *(de una mano)* one-handed; *(de un brazo)* one-armed; *(sin el uso de un miembro)* maimed, disabled; POET. halting ♦ **no ser manco** COLL. to be important, count **II.** m.f. *(persona con una mano)* one-handed person; *(persona con un brazo)* one-armed person, *(persona sin el uso de un miembro)* person with a disabled extremity.

man·co·mu·nar tr. *(unir)* to unite, join; *(combinar)* to combine, pool; LAW to make jointly liable —reflex. to unite, join together.

man·co·mu·ni·dad f. *(asociación)* association, union; *(comunidad)* community.

man·cor·nar §19 tr. *(derribar los cuernos)* to hold down by the horns; *(atar los cuernos)* to tie together by the horns.

man·cuer·na f. ♦ pl. MEX. cufflinks.

man·cha f. stain, spot; *(borrón)* blot, smudge; FIG. stain, blot ♦ **m. solar** sunspot • **sin m.** unblemished.

man·char tr. *(hacer manchas)* to stain, spot; *(ensuciar)* to soil, dirty; FIG. to soil, stain; PAINT. to daub —reflex. *(hacerse manchas)* to become stained *or* spotted; *(ensuciarse)* to get dirty, become soiled.

man·chón m. *(mancha grande)* large spot *or* stain; AGR. patch of thick vegetation.

man·da f. legacy, bequest.

man·da·de·ro, a m.f. messenger, errand boy *or* girl.

man·da·do m. *(orden)* order; *(encargo)* task, assignment; *(recado)* errand.

man·da·más m.inv. COLL. honcho, big shot.

man·da·mien·to m. *(orden)* order, command; BIBL. commandment; LAW writ ♦ **m. de arresto** *or* **de detención** arrest warrant • **m. de em-**

bargo writ of attachment.

man·dar tr. *(ordenar)* to order, command; *(enviar)* to send; *(legar)* to leave, bequeath ♦ **m. a volar** MEX., COLL. to kiss off, get rid of • **m. al otro barrio** COLL. to kill, knock off • **m. a paseo** COLL. to send packing —intr. to be in command, be in charge ♦ **¿mande?** MEX. pardon me?, come again?

man·da·ri·na f. mandarin orange, tangerine.

man·da·ta·rio m. agent, mandatary ♦ **el primer m.** the president.

man·da·to m. *(orden)* order, command; *(encargo)* charge, trust; DIPL., POL. mandate; *(contrato)* power of attorney ♦ **m. jurídico** court order, injunction.

man·dí·bu·la f. jaw, mandible ♦ **reír a m. batiente** to laugh one's head off.

man·dil m. *(delantal)* apron, pinafore; *(bayeta)* cloth for grooming horses; *(red)* fine-meshed fishing net; AMER. *(manta de caballo)* horse blanket.

man·di·lón m. COLL. coward, weakling.

man·dio·ca f. cassava, manioc; *(tapioca)* tapioca.

man·do m. *(autoridad)* authority, power; *(dirección)* command, leadership; POL. term of office; MECH. control ♦ **entregar el m.** to hand over command • **estar al m.** to be in command • **m. doble** MECH. dual control; AUTO. dual drive • **tablero de mandos** instrument panel.

man·do·lín m./**li·na** f. mandolin.

man·dón, o·na adj. & m.f. bossy (person).

man·dra·cho m. gambling house.

man·dria I. adj. *(cobarde)* cowardly, timid; *(inútil)* useless, worthless **II.** m.f. *(cobarde)* coward; *(necio)* fool, useless person.

man·dril m. mandrill.

man·du·car §70 tr. & intr. COLL. to eat, chow down.

ma·ne·a f. hobble, shackle.

ma·ne·ar tr. to hobble.

ma·ne·ci·lla f. *(del reloj)* hand; *(broche)* clasp; PRINT. index (mark); *(palanquilla)* small lever.

ma·ne·ja·ble adj. manageable.

ma·ne·jar tr. *(situación)* to handle; *(empresa)* to run, manage; *(caballo)* to handle; *(automóvil)* to drive —reflex. *(moverse)* to get or move around; *(comportarse)* to behave —intr. AMER. to drive.

ma·ne·jo m. *(uso)* handling; *(funcionamiento)* running, operation; *(dirección)* handling, management; *(maquinación)* machination, trick; EQUIT. horsemanship; *(de auto)* driving ♦ **instrucciones de m.** directions.

ma·ne·ra f. manner; *(modo)* manner, way; *(tipo)* type; *(estilo)* style ♦ **a (la) m. de** like, in the manner of • **de alguna m.** somehow, in some way • **de cualquier m.** anyhow, any old way • **de la misma m.** similarly, in the same way • **de mala m.** badly, rudely • **de m.** que so, so that • **de ninguna m.** by no means, in no way • **de otra m.** otherwise • **de tal m.** in such a way • **de todas maneras** at any rate, anyway • **en gran m.** in large measure, greatly • **m. de ser** personality, the way one is • **m. de ver** outlook, point of view • **¡qué m. de. . .!** what a way to . . .! • **sobre m.** exceedingly.

man·ga f. sleeve; *(manguera)* hose; *(red)* tubular fishing net; *(tromba de agua)* waterspout; *(colador)* strainer; MARIT. beam, breadth ♦ **en mangas de camisa** in shirt sleeves • **sin mangas** sleeveless.

man·ga·ne·so m. manganese.

man·ga·ni·lla f. trick, ruse.

man·gar §47 tr. COLL. *(robar)* to steal, swipe; AMER. *(pedir)* to mooch, sponge.

man·go¹ m. handle, haft.

man·go² m. mango (tree and fruit).

man·gón m. second-hand dealer; AMER. corral; COL. pastureland.

man·go·ne·ar intr. *(entremeterse)* to meddle, pry; COLL. *(mandar)* to boss people about, take charge; AMER. to profit by illicit means; MEX. to steal.

man·go·ne·ro, a adj. COLL. meddlesome.

man·gos·ta f. mongoose.

man·gue·ar tr. AMER. *(caza)* to flush, startle; *(ganado)* to drive into a gangway.

man·gue·ra f. *(de riego)* hose, garden hose; MARIT. pump hose.

man·gue·ro m. *(bombero)* fireman; *(tabla)* board for ironing sleeves; MEX. mango.

man·gue·ta f. *(enema)* enema; ARCHIT. beam, tie; *(palanca)* lever; *(de retrete)* U-tube.

man·gui·ta f. case, cover.

man·gui·te·ro m. furrier.

man·gui·to m. *(de piel)* muff; *(mangote)* oversleeve; *(manopla)* glove; TECH. sleeve, bushing.

ma·ní m. [pl. **-níes**] peanut.

ma·ní·a f. *(locura)* mania; *(capricho)* craze, fad; *(costumbre)* habit; COLL. *(tirria)* dislike, aversion ♦ **m. persecutoria** persecution mania or complex • **tenerle m. a alguien** COLL. to dislike someone.

ma·nia·bier·to, a adj. & m.f. generous (person).

ma·ní·a·co, a adj. & m.f. maniac.

ma·nia·tar tr. to manacle, handcuff.

ma·nia·tí·co, a I. adj. maniacal **II.** m.f. maniac.

ma·ni·co·mio m. insane asylum.

ma·ni·cor·to, a COLL. **I.** adj. stingy, tightfisted **II.** m.f. skinflint, miser.

ma·ni·cu·ro, a m.f. *(persona)* manicurist —f. *(cuidado)* manicure.

ma·ni·do, a adj. trite, hackneyed.

ma·ni·fes·ta·ción f. manifestation.

ma·ni·fes·tan·te m.f. demonstrator.

ma·ni·fes·tar §49 tr. *(expresar)* to manifest, express; *(anunciar)* to show, reveal —intr. to demonstrate —reflex. to reveal oneself.

ma·ni·fies·to, a I. adj. manifest, obvious **II.** m. manifest.

ma·ni·gue·ta f. handle, haft.

ma·ni·ja f. *(mango)* handle; *(abrazadera)* clamp.

ma·ni·lar·go, a adj. *(de manos largas)* longhanded; COLL. *(generoso)* generous, openhanded; AMER. *(ladrón)* light-fingered.

ma·ni·lla f. *(pulsera)* bracelet; *(manija)* handle; *(grillete)* handcuff, manacle.

ma·ni·llar m. handlebars (of a bicycle).

ma·nio·bra f. *(acto)* handling, operation; *(artificio)* maneuver, stratagem; MIL. maneuver; MARIT. *(arte)* seamanship; *(aparejos)* rigging, gear ♦ pl. MARIT., MIL. maneuvers; RAIL. shunting ♦ **estar de m.** to be on maneuvers.

ma·nio·brar intr. & tr. to maneuver.

ma·ni·pu·la·ción f. manipulation; COM. handling.

ma·ni·pu·la·dor, ·ra I. adj. manipulating **II.** m.f. manipulator —m. TELEC. telegraph key.

ma·ni·pu·lar tr. to manipulate; *(manejar)* to

handle; COM. to manage; *(mercancías)* to handle.

ma·ni·pu·le·o m. COLL. manipulation.

ma·ni·quí m. [pl. **-íes**] mannequin.

ma·nir tr. *(ablandar)* to age; *(sobar)* to knead —reflex. to become gamy.

ma·ni·rro·to, a adj. & m.f. spendthrift.

ma·ni·tas m. inv. handyman.

ma·ni·va·cí·o, a COLL. empty-handed.

ma·ni·ve·la f. crank.

man·jar m. *(alimento)* food; *(plato)* dish.

ma·no¹ f. hand; *(pata)* forefoot, front paw; *(trompa del elefante)* elephant's trunk; CUL. foot, trotter; *(del reloj)* hand; *(almirez)* pestle, pounder; *(capa)* coat; *(lado)* side <*el río está a m. izquierda* the river is on the left side>; *(lance)* hand, round <*echar una m. de dominó* to play a round of dominoes>; *(el primero a jugar)* lead <*yo soy m.* I am the first>; *(ayuda)* hand, help ♦ **a m.** on hand, at hand • **alzar la m. a** to raise one's hand to, threaten • **a m.** by hand <*escrito a m.* written by hand>; *(cerca)* at hand, on hand • **a m. armada** armed, by force • **a manos llenas** generously, openly • **bajo m.** underhandedly, secretly • **buena m.** skill, dexterity • **cargar la m.** to be heavyhanded • **coger a alguien con las manos en la masa** COLL. to catch someone red-handed, catch in the act • **con el corazón en la m.** straight from the heart • **con las manos vacías** empty-handed • **dar la m. a** to shake hands with • **dar la última m. a** to put the finishing touches on • **darse las manos** *(unirse)* to join hands, unite; *(saludarse)* to shake hands • **dar una m. a** to lend a hand to • **dejar de la m.** to abandon • **de m.** hand <*equipaje de m.* hand luggage> • **de m. a m.** from hand to hand • **de primera m.** firsthand • **de segunda m.** secondhand • **echar m. de** to make use of • **estrechar la m. a** to shake hands with • **hacer lo que está en sus manos** to do everything within one's power • **hecho a m.** handmade • **imponer las manos** RELIG. to lay on hands • **m. a m.** *(juntos)* hand in hand, jointly; *(sin ventaja)* even • **m. de obra** labor • **m. derecha** or **diestra** right-hand man • **¡manos a la obra!** let's get to work! • **¡manos arriba!** hands up! • **meter m. en** COLL. to interfere, butt in • **pedir la m. a** to ask for someone's hand • **tener algo entre manos** to be working on something • **traer algo entre manos** to be involved or mixed up in something • **untar la m. a alguien** to grease someone's palm • **venir a m.** to be convenient • **venir** or **llegar a las manos** to come to blows.

ma·no² m. AMER., MEX., COLL. friend, pal.

ma·no·jo m. *(haz)* bundle, bunch; *(puñado)* handful ♦ **a manojos** abundantly.

ma·no·se·ar tr. to handle, touch.

man·se·dum·bre f. *(suavidad)* gentleness, mildness; *(de un animal)* tameness.

man·sión f. residence.

man·so, a I. adj. *(suave)* gentle, mild; *(domesticado)* tame **II.** m. bellwether (of a flock).

man·ta f. *(frazada)* blanket; *(para caballos)* horse blanket; *(mantón)* shawl; COLL. *(paliza)* beating, drubbing; AMER. *(poncho)* poncho; COL., MEX. *(algodón)* coarse cotton cloth; AMER., ICHTH. manta ray.

man·te·ca f. *(grasa)* grease, fat; *(de cerdo)* lard; *(de vaca)* butter ♦ **como m.** soft, smooth.

man·te·cón m. COLL. milksop, mollycoddle.

man·te·co·so, a adj. buttery.

man·tel m. *(de la mesa)* tablecloth; *(del altar)* altar cloth.

man·te·le·rí·a f. table linen.

man·te·ne·dor m. president (of a tournament) ♦ m. de familia breadwinner.

man·te·nen·cia f *(acto)* maintenance; *(sostenimiento)* support; *(sustento)* sustenance, food.

man·te·ner §69 tr. *(alimentar)* to feed; *(sustentar)* to maintain, support; *(sostener)* to support, hold up; *(conservar)* to maintain, keep; *(continuar)* to maintain, keep up; *(afirmar)* to affirm ♦ m. a distancia *or* a raya to keep at a distance • m. en buen uso to keep in good condition —reflex. *(alimentarse)* to feed oneself; *(sustentarse)* to maintain *or* support oneself; *(perseverar)* to remain *or* stand firm; *(permanecer)* to remain, keep oneself ♦ m. a distancia to keep one's distance • m. en sus trece COLL. to stick to one's guns • m. firme to hold one's ground.

man·te·ni·mien·to m. *(mantenencia)* maintenance; *(sostenimiento)* support; *(sustento)* sustenance, food.

man·te·que·rí·a f. creamery, dairy.

man·te·que·ro, a I. m. *(persona)* dairyman; *(vasija)* butter dish —f. *(persona)* dairymaid, dairy vendor; *(máquina)* butter churn; *(vasija)* butter dish II. adj. butter, of butter.

man·te·qui·lla f. *(de vaca)* butter; *(con azúcar)* butter cream.

man·te·qui·lle·ra f. AMER. butter dish.

man·tie·ne see **mantener**.

man·ti·lla f. mantilla; *(de un niño)* swaddling clothes; *(del caballo)* saddlecloth; PRINT. blanket.

man·to m. *(capa)* cloak, mantle; *(mantilla)* long mantilla; *(vestidura)* robe; *(de la chimenea)* mantel; FIG. cloak, cover; ZOOL. mantle; MIN. layer, stratum; MEX., BOT. bellflower.

man·tón m. shawl.

man·tu·vie·ra, vo see **mantener**.

ma·nual adj. & m. manual.

ma·nu·brio m. TECH. crank; *(manija)* handle; *(de bicicleta)* handlebars.

ma·nu·fac·tu·ra f. *(fábrica)* factory; *(artículo)* manufactured article; *(fabricación)* manufacture.

ma·nu·fac·tu·rar tr. to manufacture.

ma·nu·fac·tu·re·ro, a adj. manufacturing.

ma·nu·mi·sión f. manumission, emancipation.

ma·nus·cri·to, a I. adj. handwritten II. m. manuscript.

ma·nu·ten·ción f. *(acción)* maintenance; *(conservación)* conservation.

man·za·na f. apple; *(cuadra)* block; *(de espada)* pommel.

man·za·nal m. *(huerto)* apple orchard; *(árbol)* apple tree.

man·za·nar m. apple orchard.

man·za·ni·lla f. chamomile; *(infusión)* chamomile tea; *(aceituna)* olive; *(jerez)* manzanilla.

man·za·no m. apple tree.

ma·ña f. *(habilidad)* skill, dexterity; *(astucia)* craftiness, guile; *(hábito)* bad habit ♦ darse m. para to manage *or* • más vale m. que fuerza brain is better than brawn • tener m. para to have a knack for.

ma·ña·na I. f. morning ♦ a la m. siguiente the next morning • ayer por la m. yesterday morning • de *or* en *or* por la m. in the morning • de la noche a la m. overnight • (muy) de m. very early (in the morning) —m. tomorrow, future

II. adv. *(el próximo día)* tomorrow; *(en el futuro)* in the future ♦ a partir de m. starting tomorrow, as of tomorrow • hasta m. see you tomorrow • m. por la m. tomorrow morning • pasado m. the day after tomorrow.

ma·ñe·ar tr. to manage *or* handle cleverly —intr. to be artful *or* crafty.

ma·ñe·ro, a adj. *(astuto)* clever, shrewd; R.P. *(mañoso)* hard to manage.

ma·ño·so, a adj. *(hábil)* skillful; *(astuto)* cunning; *(con malas mañas)* hard to manage.

ma·pa m. map, chart ♦ desaparecer del m. to vanish from the face of the earth • m. mudo blank *or* skeleton map • no estar en el m. COLL. to be out of this world.

ma·pa·che/chín m. raccoon.

ma·pa·mun·di m. map of the world.

ma·que·ar tr. *(poner laca)* to lacquer; MEX. to varnish —reflex. COLL. to dress up.

ma·qui·lla·je m. *(acción)* making up (of one's face); *(cosmético)* makeup, cosmetics.

ma·qui·llar tr. to make up (one's face), apply cosmetics to.

má·qui·na f. *(aparato)* machine; *(motor)* engine; *(locomotora)* locomotive, engine; LIT., THEAT. machine, deus ex machina ♦ a toda m. at full speed • hecho a m. machine-made • m. de escribir typewriter • m. de lavar washing machine • m. herramienta machine tool • m. neumática air pump • m. registradora S. AMER. cash register.

ma·qui·na·ción f. machination, plotting.

ma·qui·na·dor, ·ra I. adj. plotting, scheming II. m.f. plotter, schemer.

ma·qui·nal adj. mechanical.

ma·qui·nar tr. to plot, scheme.

ma·qui·na·ria f. *(conjunto)* machinery; *(mecanismo)* mechanism.

ma·qui·ni·lla f. small machine *or* device ♦ m. de afeitar *or* de seguridad safety razor • m. para cortar el pelo hair clippers.

ma·qui·nis·mo m. mechanization; PHILOS. mechanism.

ma·qui·nis·ta m. machinist; RAIL. engineer, engine driver; THEAT. stagehand.

mar m. *or* f. sea; *(marejada)* tide, swell; FIG. sea, flood ♦ alta m. high seas • correr a mares to stream, flow • hablar de la m. to speak of the impossible • hacerse a la m. to put out to sea • la m. de *(muchos)* loads of, lots of <la m. de trabajo loads of work>; *(muy)* very <él es la m. de tonto he is very foolish> • llover a mares to rain cats and dogs • m. agitado *or* picado choppy sea • m. bravo rough seas • m. de fondo ground swell.

ma·ra·ña f. *(maleza)* thicket; BOT. kermes oak; *(enredo)* tangle, mess.

ma·ras·mo m. MED. marasmus; *(apatía)* apathy; *(estancación)* stagnation, paralysis.

ma·ra·tón m. marathon.

ma·ra·vi·lla f. *(fenómeno)* wonder, marvel; *(asombro)* wonder, astonishment; *(caléndula)* marigold ♦ a las mil maravillas wonderfully, excellently • a m. marvellously • hacer maravillas to work wonders • venirle a uno de m. to be just what the doctor ordered.

ma·ra·vi·llar tr. to amaze, astonish —reflex. to marvel, be amazed *(con, de* at, by).

ma·ra·vi·llo·so, a adj. marvelous, wonderful.

mar·be·te m. *(etiqueta)* label, tag; *(orilla)* border, edge.

mar·ca f. *(señal)* mark; *(de ganadería)* brand;

(tipo) make, brand <*¿de qué m. es su auto?* what make is your car?>; *(estampa)* stamp; COM. trademark; *(medidor)* measuring stick, rule; *(medida)* standard (size); *(cicatriz)* scar; SPORT. mark, record; MARIT. seamark; GEOG. march, frontier ♦ **de m.** excellent, outstanding • **de m. mayor** high quality, first-class • **m. de agua** watermark • **m. de fábrica** trademark • **m. registrada** (registered) trademark.

mar·ca·do I. adj. marked, notable **II.** m. marking.

mar·ca·dor, ·ra I. adj. marking **II.** m.f. *(que marca)* marker; *(lápiz)* marker, marking pen —m. *(de bordado)* embroidery sampler; *(de herrero)* blacksmith's hammer; PRINT. feeder operator; SPORT. scoreboard.

mar·ca·pa·so(s) m. pacemaker.

mar·car §70 tr. *(poner marca)* to mark; *(herrar)* to brand; *(estampillar)* to stamp; *(la ropa)* to label; *(anotar)* to observe, note; *(indicar)* to say, indicate <*la balanza marca tres kilos* the scale indicates three kilos>; *(aplicar)* to assign, destine; *(subrayar)* to mark, underline; *(poner el precio)* to mark, price; *(el pelo)* to set; *(un número de teléfono)* to dial; PRINT. to feed; SPORT. to score ♦ **m. el compás** MUS. to keep time • **m. el paso** MIL. to mark time.

mar·cial adj. martial; *(militar)* military <*porte m.* military bearing>.

mar·co m. *(cerco)* frame; FIN. mark (monetary unit); *(peso)* mark (unit of weight); *(patrón)* standard; *(estructura)* framework <*dentro del m. del pensamiento hegeliano* within the framework of Hegelian thought>.

mar·cha f. *(movimiento)* march, movement; *(velocidad)* speed, velocity; *(salida)* departure; *(progresión)* march <*la m. del tiempo* the march of time>; *(curso)* course, progress; *(funcionamiento)* operation, running ♦ **a toda m.** at full speed • **dar m. atrás** to go into reverse • **estar en m.** *(comenzar)* to be underway; *(funcionar)* to be running or working • **m. atrás** AUTO. reverse • **m. forzada** MIL. forced march • **m. fúnebre** funeral march • **poner en m.** to start • **ponerse en m.** to start off • **sobre la m.** on the double.

mar·chan·te, a m.f. *(vendedor)* merchant, dealer; *(cliente)* customer, patron.

mar·char intr. *(ir)* to go; *(andar)* to walk; *(moverse)* to move, go; *(funcionar)* to run, work; *(progresar)* to go, proceed <*todo marcha bien* everything is going well>; MIL. to march —reflex. to go (away), leave.

mar·chi·tar tr. *(secar)* to wilt; *(debilitar)* to debilitate, weaken —reflex. *(secarse)* to wilt; *(debilitarse)* to become weak, languish.

mar·chi·to, a adj. wilted.

mar·cho·so, a adj. COLL. cheerful, merry.

ma·re·a f. tide; *(viento)* sea breeze; FIG. flood ♦ **contra viento y m.** against all odds • **m. alta** high tide • **m. baja** low tide • **m. creciente** rising tide • **m. menguante** low tide.

ma·re·a·do, a adj. *(malo)* sick; *(en el mar)* seasick; *(bebido)* drunk; *(aturdido)* dizzy.

ma·re·a·mien·to m. seasickness.

ma·re·ar tr. to navigate, sail; *(fastidiar)* to annoy, bother —reflex. *(tener náuseas)* to become nauseated; *(en barcos)* to become seasick; *(malograrse)* to become damaged.

ma·re·ja·da f. *(del mar)* swell, turbulence; *(agitación)* agitation, ferment.

ma·re·o m. *(náusea)* sickness, nausea; *(en bar-*

cos) seasickness; *(en vehículos)* motion sickness.

mar·fil m. ivory ♦ **m. vegetal** ivory nut.

mar·ga·ri·na f. margarine.

mar·ga·ri·ta f. BOT. daisy; *(perla)* margarite, pearl; ZOOL. periwinkle ♦ **echar margaritas a los cerdos** to throw pearls before swine.

mar·gen m. *(borde)* margin, border; *(nota)* marginal note; *(amplitud)* leeway, margin <*me dejaron m. en mis trabajos* they gave me leeway in my work>; COM. margin ♦ **al m.** *(de papel)* in the margin; *(afuera)* on the fringe <*vive al m. de la sociedad* he lives on the fringe of society> • **dar m. para** to give occasion for, give an opportunity for • **m. de ganancias** COM. profit margin —f. bank.

mar·gi·nal adj. marginal.

mar·gi·nar tr. *(dejar márgenes)* to marginate, leave a margin on; *(poner notas)* to make marginal notes on; *(apartar)* to leave out.

ma·ri·ca m. COLL., DEROG. gay man, sissy.

ma·ri·cas·ta·ña f. ♦ **en tiempos de M.** in days of yore, in the olden days.

ma·ri·cón m. SL., DEROG. *(homosexual)* gay man; *(pesado)* jerk.

ma·ri·dar intr. *(casar)* to marry, wed; *(vivir juntos)* to live together —tr. to join, unite.

ma·ri·do m. husband, spouse.

ma·ri·gua·na/hua·na/jua·na f. marijuana.

ma·ri·ma·cho m. COLL. mannish woman.

ma·rim·ba f. *(tambor)* drum; AMER. *(tímpano)* kettledrum; *(xilófono)* marimba, xylophone.

ma·ri·na f. see **marino, a.**

ma·ri·nar tr. to marinate; MARIT. to man.

ma·ri·ne·rí·a f. *(profesión)* seafaring, sailoring; *(tripulación)* ship's crew, seamen.

ma·ri·ne·ro, a I. adj. *(gobernable)* seaworthy; *(marino)* marine, sea; *(marinesco)* sailor, of sailors **II.** m. sailor, mariner ♦ **m. de agua dulce** landlubber —f. *(blusa)* middy blouse, sailor top; CHILE, ECUAD., PERU marinera (folk dance).

ma·ri·no, a I. adj. marine, sea ♦ **azul m.** navy blue **II.** m. sailor, mariner —f. *(costa)* coast; *(náutica)* navigation, seamanship; MIL. navy ♦ **Infantería de M.** Marine Corps • **m. de guerra** navy • **m. mercante** merchant marine.

ma·rio·ne·ta f. marionette, puppet.

ma·ri·po·sa I. f. butterfly; TECH. *(llave)* butterfly valve; *(tuerca)* butterfly or wing nut; *(lamparilla)* night light —m. DEROG. fairy, queer **II.** adj. SPORT. butterfly.

ma·ri·po·se·ar intr. *(ser inconstante)* to be fickle or capricious; *(dar vueltas)* to hover or flit about.

ma·ri·qui·ta f. ENTOM. *(coleóptero)* ladybug; *(hemíptero)* firebug; ORNITH. parakeet —m. COLL., DEROG. sissy, pansy.

ma·ris·cal m. marshal ♦ **m. de campo** field marshal.

ma·ris·co m. shellfish, crustacean.

ma·ris·ma f. salt marsh.

ma·ri·tal adj. marital.

ma·rí·ti·mo, a adj. maritime, sea ♦ **por vía m.** by sea.

mar·mi·ta f. pot, saucepan.

mar·mi·tón m. kitchen helper.

már·mol m. marble ♦ **de m.** hardhearted, cold.

mar·mo·le·rí·a f. *(conjunto)* marblework; *(obra)* marble; *(taller)* workshop, studio.

mar·mó·re·o, a adj. marble, marmoreal.

mar·mo·ta f. marmot; FIG. sleepyhead ♦ **dor-**

mir **como una** m. to sleep like a log.

ma·ro·me·ro, a m.f. AMER. tightrope walker.

mar·qués m. marquis.

mar·que·sa f. *(persona)* marquise, marchioness; AMER. *(sillón)* armchair, easy chair.

mar·que·si·na f. marquee, canopy.

mar·que·te·rí·a f. *(taracea)* marquetry, inlaid work; *(ebanistería)* cabinet work.

ma·rra·na·da/ne·rí·a f. COLL. *(mala pasada)* dirty or rotten trick; *(suciedad)* filth, filthiness.

ma·rra·no, a I. adj. dirty, filthy II. m. ZOOL. pig, hog; COLL. *(sucio)* pig, slob; *(canalla)* swine —f. ZOOL. sow; DEROG. *(mujer)* slut; TECH. axle (of a water wheel).

ma·rrar intr. *(errar)* to miss (a shot); *(fallar)* to fail; *(desviarse)* to go astray or wrong.

ma·rro m. *(juego de niños)* tag; *(con bolos)* ninepins; *(ladeo)* dodge, swerve; *(falta)* slip, error; MEX. mallet.

ma·rrón I. adj. brown II. m. *(color)* brown; *(castaña)* candied chestnut.

ma·rru·lla/lle·rí·a f. coaxing, wheedling.

ma·rru·lle·ro, a I. adj. conniving II. m.f. conniver, flatterer.

mar·so·p(l)a f. porpoise.

mar·su·pial adj. & m. marsupial.

mar·ta f. pine marten ♦ m. cebellina ZOOL. sable.

mar·tes m. Tuesday. ♦ m. de carnaval or carnestolendas RELIG. Shrove Tuesday.

mar·ti·lla·da f. hammer blow.

mar·ti·llar tr. to hammer.

mar·ti·lla·zo m. hard blow of a hammer.

mar·ti·lle·ro m. AMER. auctioneer.

mar·ti·llo m. hammer; *(mallo)* gavel <m. de subastador auctioneer's gavel>; ICHTH. hammerhead (shark); *(establecimiento)* auction house; ANAT. malleus, hammer; MUS. tuning hammer; ♦ m. de fragua or m. pilón MECH. drop hammer • m. neumático pneumatic drill.

mar·tín pes·ca·dor m. kingfisher.

mar·ti·ne·te¹ m. heron.

mar·ti·ne·te² m. *(de piano)* hammer; *(mazo)* drop hammer; *(de estacas)* pile driver ♦ m. a vapor steam hammer • m. de fragua trip hammer.

már·tir m.f. martyr.

mar·ti·rio m. martyrdom.

mar·ti·ri·zar §04 tr. *(hacer sufrir martirio)* to martyr, martyrize; *(atormentar)* to torment.

mar·zo m. March.

mas conj. but <no lo vi, m. lo escuché I didn't see it, but I heard it>.

más I. adv. more <m. importante more important>; most <la alumna m. inteligente the most intelligent student>; longer <durar m. to last longer>; rather <m. quiero morir I would rather die> ♦ a lo m. at most, at the most • a m. besides, in addition • a m. de besides, in addition to • a m. no poder as much as possible or as can be • a m. y mejor a lot, really <llovía a m. y mejor it was really raining> • como el que m. as much as anyone • de m. too much, extra • en lo m. mínimo in the slightest • en m. more • estar de m. to be superfluous or unnecessary • m. allá further • m. bien rather • m. de more than • m. que more than <yo sé m. que él I know more than he>; *(sino)* but, except <nadie puede hacerlo m. que Carlos no one can do it except Charles> • ni m. ni menos no more, no less • no m. only, no more • no m. que only • por m. que no matter how much •

¿qué m. da? what difference does it make? • sin m. ni m. without further ado II. m. plus sign ♦ el m. y el menos the pros and the cons • tener sus m. y sus menos COLL. to have good points and bad points III. prep. plus <cinco m. ocho son trece five plus eight is thirteen>.

ma·sa f. mass; *(volumen)* volume, bulk; *(cuerpo compacto)* lump <una m. de arcilla a lump of clay>; *(el pueblo)* people, masses; *(pasta)* dough; ELEC. ground; MAS. mortar ♦ con las manos en la m. in the act, redhanded • en m. *(todos juntos)* all together, en masse; *(en gran escala)* mass <protesta en m. mass protest> • m. atómica atomic mass • m. de aire air mass • producción en m. mass production.

ma·sa·crar tr. to massacre.

ma·sa·cre f. massacre.

ma·sa·je m. massage.

ma·sa·jis·ta m. masseur —f. masseuse.

mas·car §70 tr *(masticar)* to chew; COLL. *(mascullar)* to mumble.

más·ca·ra f. *(careta)* mask; *(traje)* disguise, costume; *(pretexto)* mask, pretense —m.f. *(persona)* masker, masquerader ♦ baile de máscaras masquerade, masked ball • m. antigás gas mask • m. de oxígeno oxygen mask • quitarse la m. to drop one's pretenses.

mas·ca·ra·da f. *(fiesta)* masquerade, masked ball; *(desfile)* masked parade; *(cosa falsa)* masquerade, charade.

mas·ca·rón m. sculpted head or face ♦ m. de proa MARIT. figurehead.

mas·co·ta f. mascot.

mas·cu·li·ni·dad f. masculinity.

mas·cu·li·no, a I. adj. male; *(propio de los hombres)* masculine, manly; GRAM. masculine II. m. GRAM. masculine (gender).

mas·cu·llar tr. COLL. to mumble, mutter.

ma·si·lla f. putty.

ma·si·vo, a adj. *(grande)* massive; mass <comunicación m. mass communication>.

ma·so·quis·ta adj. & m.f. masochist.

mas·ti·car §70 tr. *(triturar)* to chew, masticate; *(rumiar)* to ponder over, ruminate.

más·til m. mast; *(palo)* pole; *(de una pluma)* quill ♦ m. totémico totem pole.

mas·tín m. mastiff ♦ m. danés Great Dane.

más·ti·que m. mastic.

mas·toi·des adj. & f.inv. mastoid.

mas·tur·ba·ción f. masturbation.

mas·tur·bar tr. & reflex. to masturbate.

ma·ta f. *(arbusto)* bush, shrub; *(pie de una planta)* sprig, tuft; *(campo de árboles)* orchard, grove • m. de pelo head of hair.

ma·ta·can·de·las m.inv. candle snuffer.

ma·ta·de·ro m. *(de ganado)* slaughterhouse; COLL. *(trabajo)* drudgery, chore.

ma·ta·dor, a I. adj. *(que mata)* killing; COLL. *(penoso)* killing, deadly II. m.f. *(asesino)* killer, murderer —m. *(en naipes)* trump card; TAUR. bullfighter, matador.

ma·ta·fue·go m. fire extinguisher.

má·ta·las·ca·llan·do m.f. COLL. sly dog, wolf in sheep's clothing.

ma·ta·mos·cas m.inv. fly swatter.

ma·tan·za f. *(acción)* killing, slaughtering; *(de personas)* massacre; *(de animales)* slaughtering, butchering.

ma·tar tr. to kill; *(animales)* to butcher, slaughter; *(apagar)* to put out, extinguish <m. el fuego to put out the fire>; *(cal)* to slake; *(en naipes)* to beat, top; *(arruinar)* to ruin, break

<*m. un proyecto* to ruin a project> **estar a m. con** to be at loggerheads with • **matarlas callando** (*quitarse la vida*) to kill oneself; to be killed <*su hijo se mató en un accidente* his son was killed in an accident>; FIG. to kill oneself —intr. to kill.

ma·ta·ri·fe m. butcher, slaughterer.

ma·ta·rra·tas m.inv. (*raticida*) rat poison; COLL. (*aguardiente malo*) rotgut, firewater.

ma·ta·sa·nos m. COLL. quack (doctor).

ma·ta·se·llar tr. to cancel, postmark.

ma·ta·se·llos m.inv. (*instrumento*) canceller; (*marca*) postmark, cancellation.

ma·te¹ m. (*sin brillo*) matte; (*apagado*) dull.

ma·te² m. checkmate, mate **dar jaque m.** to checkmate.

ma·te³ m. AMER., BOT. (*arbusto*) maté tree; (*calabaza*) maté gourd; (*bebida*) maté; COLL. (*cabeza*) noodle • **yerba m.** maté (tea).

ma·te·má·ti·co, a I. adj. mathematical II. m.f. mathematician —f. mathematics **pl.** mathematics.

ma·te·ria f. matter; (*material*) material, substance; EDUC. subject • **en m. de** as regards, in the matter of • **entrar en m.** to come to the point, get down to business • **índice de materias** table of contents • **m. colorante** dyestuff • **m. de estado** POL. affair of state • **m. gris** gray matter • **m. prima** raw material.

ma·te·rial I. adj. material; (*corpóreo*) physical; (*materialista*) materialistic II. m. (*aparato*) materials, equipment; (*substancia*) material, substance <*hecho de buen m.* made of good material>; (*ingrediente*) ingredient.

ma·te·ria·li·dad f. materiality; (*apariencia*) outward appearance.

ma·te·ria·lis·ta I. adj. materialistic II. m.f. materialist.

ma·ter·nal adj. maternal.

ma·ter·ni·dad f. (*estado*) maternity; (*establecimiento*) maternity hospital.

ma·ter·no, a adj. (*maternal*) maternal, motherly; maternal <*abuelo m.* maternal grandfather>; (*nativo*) mother, native <*lengua m.* native language>.

ma·ti·nal adj. morning, matinal.

ma·tiz m. (*de color*) shade, tint; (*aspecto*) shade, nuance.

ma·ti·zar §04 tr. (*combinar*) to match, harmonize; (*teñir*) to tint, shade; (*variar*) to vary <*m. la voz* to vary one's tone of voice>.

ma·tón m. COLL. bully.

ma·to·rral m. (*maleza*) brushwood, scrub; (*soto*) thicket.

ma·tra·ca·la·da f. crowd, mob.

ma·tre·ro, a I. adj. cunning, shrewd II. m. AMER. bandit.

ma·triar·ca·do m. matriarchy.

ma·triar·cal adj. matriarchal.

ma·tri·ci·dio m. matricide.

ma·trí·cu·la f. (*lista*) register, list; (*inscripción*) registration, matriculation; (*gente matriculada*) roll; AUTO. registration.

ma·tri·cu·la·ción f. registration.

ma·tri·cu·lar tr. & reflex. to register, matriculate.

ma·tri·mo·nial adj. matrimonial.

ma·tri·mo·niar intr. to marry, get married.

ma·tri·mo·nio m. (*casamiento*) marriage, matrimony; COLL. (*marido y mujer*) married couple **contraer m.** to marry • **fuera del m.** out of wedlock • **m. civil** civil marriage • **m. por poderes** marriage by proxy • **partida de m.** marriage certificate.

ma·triz I. f. womb, uterus; (*molde*) mold, die; (*tuerca*) nut; MATH., MIN. matrix II. adj. original **casa m.** headquarters, main office.

ma·tro·na f. (*madre de familia*) matron; (*partera*) midwife; (*encargada*) matron.

ma·tro·nal adj. matronly.

ma·tu·te m. (*acción*) smuggling; (*contrabando*) contraband, smuggled goods.

ma·tu·te·ar intr. to smuggle.

mau·la m.f. swindler, cheat.

mau·llar intr. to meow, mew.

mau·lli·do/·ú·llo m. (*voz*) meow, mew; (*acción*) meowing, mewing.

mau·so·le·o m. mausoleum.

má·xi·ma·men·te adv. principally, chiefly.

má·xi·me adv. principally, all the more.

má·xi·mo, a I. adj. maximum, greatest <*m. común divisor* greatest common denominator>; highest <*el punto m.* the highest point>; greatest <*el pensador m. de su tiempo* the greatest thinker of his time> II. m. maximum **al m.** to the maximum • **como m.** at the most • **hacer el m.** to do one's utmost —f. (*aforismo*) maxim; (*temperatura*) maximum temperature.

ma·yo m. May.

ma·yó·li·ca f. majolica ware.

ma·yo·ne·sa f. mayonnaise.

ma·yor I. adj. (*más grande*) bigger, larger <*m. parte* the larger part>; (*el más grande*) biggest, largest; (*importante*) greater; (*el más importante*) greatest <*el problema m.* the greatest problem>; (*de más edad*) older, elder <*mi hermano m.* my older brother>; elderly <*un señor m.* an elderly gentleman>; (*el más viejo*) oldest, eldest; (*adulto*) adult; (*principal*) main <*calle m.* main street>; RELIG. high <*misa m.* high mass>; MUS. major **al por m.** COM. wholesale • **caza m.** big game hunting • **estado m.** MIL. staff • **m. de edad** of age II. m. MIL. major; (*jefe*) chief **pl.** elders, ancestors.

ma·yo·raz·go m. (*derecho*) right of primogeniture; (*herencia*) estate inherited by primogeniture; (*heredero*) inheritor of an entailed estate; (*hijo primogénito*) first-born son; COLL. (*primogenitura*) seniority.

ma·yor·do·mí·a f. (*cargo*) stewardship; (*oficina*) majordomo's office.

ma·yor·do·mo m. majordomo.

ma·yo·rí·a f. majority **en la m. de los casos** in most cases • **en su m.** in the main • **m. absoluta** absolute majority • **m. de edad** legal age.

ma·yo·ri·dad f. majority, adult age.

ma·yo·ris·ta I. adj. wholesale II. m. wholesaler.

ma·yús·cu·lo, a I. adj. (*letra*) capital; (*importante*) important, prominent; COLL. (*grande*) enormous, tremendous II. f. capital letter.

ma·za f. (*arma*) mace; (*utensilio para machacar*) mallet; (*martinete*) drop hammer, pile driver.

ma·za·co·te m. COLL. (*plato*) lumpy mess <*el flan se ha hecho un m.* the pudding is a lumpy mess>; (*obra artística fea*) monstrosity.

ma·za·mo·rra f. cornmeal mush.

ma·za·pán m. marzipan.

maz·mo·rra f. dungeon.

ma·zo m. (*martillo*) mallet; (*manojo*) bunch.

ma·zor·ca f. ear, cob (of corn).

me pron. me <*me vieron en el jardín* they saw me in the garden>; me, to me <*dame la llave* give me the key>; me, for me <*ella me compró* *un regalo* she bought a present for me>; from me <*me quitó el pañuelo* he took the handkerchief from me>; myself <*me miré en el espejo* I looked at myself in the mirror>.

me·cá·ni·co, a I. adj. *(de la mecánica)* mechanical, machine-operated; *(automático)* automatic, machine-like II. m. *(maquinista)* mechanic; *(chófer)* driver —f. *(ciencia)* mechanics; *(mecanismo)* mechanism.

me·ca·nis·mo m. *(aparato)* mechanism, working parts; *(estructura)* structure, workings.

me·ca·ni·zar §04 tr. to mechanize.

me·ca·no·gra·fí·a f. typing, typewriting.

me·ca·no·gra·fiar §30 tr. to type.

me·ca·nó·gra·fo, a m.f. typist.

me·ce·de·ro m. stirrer, swizzle stick.

me·ce·do·ra f. rocking chair, rocker.

me·ce·nas m.inv. patron (of the arts).

me·cer §75 tr. *(acunar)* to rock; *(columpiar)* to swing; *(balancear)* to move to and fro, sway; *(agitar)* to shake —reflex. to rock < *m. en una mecedora* to rock in a rocking chair>; *(columpiarse)* to swing; *(balancearse)* to move to and fro.

me·cha f. *(de lámpara)* wick; *(espoleta)* fuse; *(para encender)* match; *(mechón)* lock; MED., SURG. tent; AMER. *(del taladro)* drill bit ♦ **a toda m.** at full speed ♦ **aguantar la m.** to grin and bear it.

me·char tr. to stuff.

me·che·ra f. shoplifter.

me·che·ro m. *(boquilla)* burner, jet <*m. de gas* gas burner>; *(encendedor)* lighter, cigarette lighter; *(canutillo)* wick, holder; *(del candelero)* candle socket.

me·chón m. *(de pelo)* lock, tuft; *(de lana)* tuft.

me·da·lla f. medal; *(joya)* medallion ♦ **el reverso de la m.** the other side of the coin.

me·da·llis·ta m.f. medalist.

me·da·llón m. *(medalla grande)* medallion; *(joya)* locket.

mé·da·no *or* **me·da·no** m. *(duna)* dune, sand dune; *(banco de arena)* sandbank.

me·dia f. *(de mujer)* stocking; *(de hombre)* sock; *(tiempo)* half past <*las dos y media* half past two>.

me·dia·ción f. mediation, arbitration.

me·dia·do, a adj. half full ♦ **a mediados de** halfway through, in the middle of.

me·dia·dor, ·ra I. adj. mediating II. m.f. mediator.

me·dia·ne·ro, a I. adj. *(que está en medio)* dividing; *(mediador)* mediating II. m.f. *(intercesor)* mediator —f. adjoining wall.

me·dia·no, a I. adj. *(regular)* average, medium; COLL. *(mediocre)* mediocre, poor II. f. GEOM. median.

me·dia·no·che f. midnight.

me·dian·te I. adj. interceding II. adv. through, by means of ♦ **Dios m.** God willing.

me·diar intr. *(llegar a la mitad)* to get halfway; *(estar en medio)* to be in the middle; *(interponerse)* to intercede, come between; *(transcurrir)* to elapse, go by.

me·di·ca·ción f. *(tratamiento)* medication, medical treatment; *(medicamentos)* medication, medicines.

me·di·ca·men·to m. medicine, medicament.

me·di·car §70 tr. to medicate.

me·di·cas·tro m. quack, medicaster.

me·di·ci·na f. *(ciencia)* medicine, art of healing; *(medicamento)* medicine, medication ♦

doctor en m. doctor of medicine.

me·di·ci·nal adj. medicinal.

me·di·ci·nar tr. to treat (with medicine), give medicine to.

me·di·ción f. measurement, measuring.

mé·di·co, a I. adj. medical II. m.f. doctor, physician ♦ **m. de cabecera** family doctor ♦ **m. de consulta** consulting physician ♦ **m. general** general practitioner.

me·di·da f. measure, measurement <*m. para líquidos* liquid measure>; *(medición)* measuring, measurement; *(recipiente)* measure, measuring device; *(norma)* standard, gauge <*todo depende de la m. en que se juzgue* it all depends on the standard by which one judges>; *(proporción)* proportion, degree <*me pagan a m. de mi trabajo* they pay me in porportion to my work>; *(prevención)* measure, step <*tomó medidas para evitar más problemas* he took steps to avoid further problems>; *(prudencia)* measure, moderation; POET. measure, meter ♦ **a m. que** as, while ♦ **en la m. en que** insofar as ♦ **en menor m.** to a lesser extent ♦ **hecho a la m.** made-to-order ♦ **pasarse de la m.** to carry things too far ♦ **sin m.** immoderately, in excess.

me·di·dor, ·ra I. adj. measuring II. m.f. *(persona)* measurer —m. AMER. *(contador)* meter.

me·die·val adj. medieval.

me·dio, a I. adj. half <*tres horas y m.* three and a half hours>; *(mediano)* middle, medium <*una persona de talla m.* a person of medium height>; *(central)* middle, midway <*el punto m.* the midway point>; *(regular)* average <*el español m.* the average Spaniard>; MATH. average, mean ♦ **m. hermana** half sister ♦ **m. hermano** half brother ♦ **m. luna** half-moon ♦ **m. pasaje** half fare II. m. *(centro)* middle, center; *(ambiente)* environment, medium; *(medida)* measure, step <*procedió adoptando los medios necesarios* he proceeded, taking the necessary measures>; *(medium)* medium, spiritualist; *(moderación)* middle ground; MATH. half; BIOL. medium; LOG. middle term; SPORT. halfback ♦ **de m. a m.** *(en el centro)* in the middle; *(completamente)* completely, entirely ♦ **de por m.** in between ♦ **en m. de** *(en la mitad)* in the middle; *(sin embargo)* notwithstanding; *(entre tanto)* in the midst of <*en m. de todo eso logró salir bien* in the midst of all that, he managed to come out all right> ♦ **estar de por m.** *(mediar)* to intervene, mediate; *(involucrarse)* to be in the middle, be involved ♦ **m. ambiente** environment ♦ **meterse de por m.** *or* **en m.** to intervene ♦ **por m. de** by means of ♦ **por todos los medios** by all means, at all costs ♦ **quitar de en m.** to get rid of, do away with ♦ **quitarse de en m.** to get out of the way III. adv. half, partially <*m. terminado* half finished> ♦ **a m.** half <*a m. vestir* half-dressed> ♦ **a medias** halfway <*no lo reparó sino a medias* he just repaired it halfway>; *(no del todo)* half <*dormido a medias* half asleep>.

me·dio·cre adj. mediocre.

me·dio·cri·dad f. mediocrity.

me·dio·dí·a m. midday, noon.

me·dir §48 tr. to measure; *(comparar)* to compare; *(moderar)* to weigh <*mide sus palabras cuidadosamente* he weighs his words carefully> —reflex. to be moderate, act with restraint.

me·di·ta·bun·do, a adj. meditative, thoughtful.

me·di·ta·ción f. meditation.

me·di·tar tr. & intr. to meditate.
me·di·ta·ti·vo, a adj. meditative.
mé·dium m.inv. medium.
me·drar intr. *(crecer)* to grow, thrive; *(mejorar)* to improve; *(prosperar)* to prosper.
me·dro·so, a I. adj. fearful, timorous II. m.f. coward.
me·du·la or **mé·du·la** f. medulla, marrow; BOT. medulla, pith; *(esencia)* essence ♦ **hasta la m.** to the core • **m. espinal** spinal cord • **m. ósea** bone marrow.
me·du·sa f. medusa, jellyfish.
me·gá·fo·no m. megaphone.
me·ga·lo·ma·ní·a f. megalomania.
me·ga·ló·ma·no, a I. adj. megalomaniacal II. m.f. megalomaniac.
me·ga·tón m. megaton.
me·ji·lla f. cheek.
me·ji·llón m. mussel.
me·jor I. adj. *(superior)* better <*este coche es m. que el otro* this car is better than the other>; best <*el m. estudiante de la clase* the best student in the class> ♦ **lo m. posible** as well as possible II. adv. *(más bien)* better <*ella escribe m. que él* she writes better than he does>; *(antes)* rather <*m. morirme que perder la honra* I would rather die than lose my honor> ♦ **a lo m.** maybe, perhaps • **en el m. de los casos** at best • **m. dicho** rather, more specifically • **m. que m.** all the better, so much the better • **tanto m.** better still, so much the better.
me·jo·ra f. *(adelanto)* improvement, betterment; *(aumento)* increase.
me·jo·ra·mien·to m. improvement.
me·jo·rar tr. *(poner mejor)* to improve, make better; *(aumentar)* to raise ♦ **mejorando lo presente** present company excepted —intr. & reflex. *(ponerse mejor)* to improve, get better; *(el tiempo)* to clear up.
me·jo·rí·a f. *(mejora)* improvement, betterment; *(convalecencia)* improvement.
me·lan·co·lí·a f. *(tristeza)* melancholy, sadness; MED. melancholia.
me·lan·có·li·co, a adj. & m.f. melancholy (person).
me·la·za f. molasses.
mel·co·cha f. taffy.
me·le·na f. *(cabello)* long hair, mop (of hair); *(de león)* mane.
me·le·ro I. m. honey vendor II. adj. honey.
me·li·fluo, a adj. mellifluous.
me·lin·dre·rí·a f. affectation, fussiness.
me·lin·dro·so/dre·ro, a adj. & m.f. affected or fussy (person).
me·lo·co·tón m. *(fruto)* peach; *(árbol)* peach tree.
me·lo·co·to·ne·ro m. peach tree.
me·lo·dí·a f. *(canto)* melody, tune; *(calidad)* melody, melodiousness.
me·ló·di·co, a adj. melodic, tuneful.
me·lo·dio·so, a adj. melodious, tuneful.
me·lo·dra·ma m. melodrama.
me·lo·dra·má·ti·co, a adj. melodramatic(al).
me·lón m. melon; FIG. idiot, fool.
me·lo·so, a adj. *(dulce)* sweet, honeyed; *(suave)* smooth; FIG. sweet, gentle.
me·lo·te m. molasses; SP. honey preserves.
me·lla f. *(abolladura)* dent; *(en un filo)* nick, notch; *(en la porcelana)* chip; *(hueco)* gap, hole ♦ **hacer m. a** to have an effect upon, impress • **hacer m. en** to harm.
me·llar tr. *(metal)* to dent; *(un filo)* to nick,

notch; *(porcelana)* to chip; *(menoscabar)* to harm —intr. *(superficie)* to become dented or chipped; *(dañarse)* to be harmed or injured.
me·lli·zo, a m.f. & adj. twin.
mem·bra·na f. membrane.
mem·bre·te m. *(del remitente)* letterhead; *(del destinatario)* addressee's name and address.
mem·bri·llo m. *(árbol)* quince tree; *(fruta)* quince; *(dulce)* quince jam or jelly.
mem·bru·do, a adj. robust, muscular.
me·mo·ra·ble adj. memorable.
me·mo·rán·dum m. [pl. **pl. inv.** or **-da**] *(nota)* memorandum, memo; *(libreta)* memo book.
me·mo·rar tr. to remember, recall.
me·mo·ria f. memory; *(recuerdo)* memory, remembrance; COM. *(informe)* financial report or statement ♦ **borrar de la m.** to forget completely • **conservar la m. de** to remember • **de m.** by heart • **digno de m.** memorable • **en m. de** in memory of • **falta de m.** forgetfulness • **hacer m. de** to remember • **irse de la m.** to slip one's mind • **traer a la m. de uno** to remind one • **venir a la m.** to come to mind • pl. *(libro)* memoirs.
me·mo·rial m. *(libreta)* memo book, notebook; *(petición)* memorial, petition; *(publicación)* publication, bulletin.
me·mo·ri·za·ción f. memorization, memorizing.
me·mo·ri·zar §04 tr. to memorize, learn by heart.
men·ción f. mention ♦ **hacer m. de** to make mention of, mention • **m. honorífica** honorable mention.
men·cio·nar tr. to mention ♦ **sin m.** not to mention.
men·da·ci·dad f. *(hábito)* mendacity; *(mentira)* lie.
men·daz I. adj. mendacious, lying II. m.f. liar.
men·di·can·te adj. & m.f. mendicant.
men·di·gar §47 tr. to beg (for) —intr. to beg.
men·di·go, a m.f. beggar, mendicant.
men·dru·go m. crust, crumb.
me·ne·ar tr. & reflex. *(mover)* to move; *(agitar)* to shake, wag; *(oscilar)* to sway, swing.
me·ne·o m. *(movimiento)* movement; *(agitación)* shake; *(oscilación)* sway, swing.
me·nes·ter m. *(falta)* need, want; *(ocupación)* occupation ♦ **haber** or **tener m. de** to need or want • **ser m. que** to be necessary that.
men·gua f. *(disminución)* diminution, decrease; *(falta)* lack; *(pobreza)* poverty; *(descrédito)* discredit, disgrace.
men·gua·do, a I. adj. *(disminuido)* diminished, decreased; *(cobarde)* cowardly, timid II. m. drop stitch.
men·guan·te I. adj. *(que disminuye)* diminishing, decreasing; ASTRON. waning; MARIT. ebb II. m. *(disminución)* diminution, decrease; ASTRON. waning; MARIT. ebb; *(decadencia)* decline, decadence ♦ **cuarto m.** last quarter (of the moon).
men·guar §10 intr. *(disminuir)* to diminish, decrease; ASTRON. to wane; MARIT. to ebb; *(en tejido)* to decrease; *(declinar)* to decline, go downhill —tr. *(disminuir)* to diminish, decrease; *(velocidad)* to reduce; *(peso, responsabilidad)* to lessen, diminish; *(menoscabar)* to detract from <*esto no mengua en nada su fama* this in no way detracts from his reputation>.
me·nin·gi·tis f. meningitis.
me·no·pau·sia f. menopause.

me·nor I. adj. less, lesser <*de m. importancia* of lesser importance>; least <*no tengo la m. idea* I don't have the least idea>; (*más joven*) younger <*mi hermano m.* my younger brother>; (*el más joven*) youngest; COLL. (*más pequeño*) smaller; (*el más pequeño*) smallest; MUS., RELIG. minor ♦ **al por m.** COM. retail • **m. de edad** minor, under age **II. m.** minor, juvenile ♦ **tribunal de menores** juvenile court.

me·no·rí·a f. (*subordinación*) subordination; (*edad*) minority (of age).

mo·no·ris·ta m. AMER. retailer, retail dealer.

me·nos I. adv. less <*ella tiene m. dinero que él* she has less money than he>; least <*Paco es el m. listo de la clase* Frank is the least clever boy in the class>; fewer <*había m. de cincuenta personas en la reunión* there were fewer than fifty people at the meeting> ♦ **al m.** at least • **a m. que** unless • **cada vez m.** less and less • **cuanto m. . . . m.** the less . . . the less • **de m.** short <*dos kilos de m.* two kilograms short> • **echar a alguien de m.** to miss someone • **más o m.** more or less • **lo m.** the least • **m. de** less than <*m. de cien dólares* less than one hundred dollars> • **m. que** less than • **ni más ni m.** exactly • **no ser para m.** to be no wonder, little wonder that • **por lo m.** at least • **ser lo de m.** to be the least important thing • **tener a m.** to consider it beneath oneself • **venir a m.** to decline, come down in the world **II. m.** minus sign **III.** conj. but, except <*todo m. eso* all but that> **IV.** prep. minus <*quince m. siete son ocho* fifteen minus seven is eight>.

me·nos·ca·bar tr. to damage, impair.

me·nos·ca·bo m. (*mengua*) diminishing, lessening; (*daño*) damage; (*descrédito*) damage ♦ **con m. de** to the detriment of.

me·nos·pre·cia·ble adj. despicable, contemptible.

me·nos·pre·ciar tr. (*despreciar*) to despise, scorn; (*subestimar*) to underestimate, underrate.

me·nos·pre·cia·ti·vo, a adj. disdainful, contemptuous.

me·nos·pre·cio m. (*desprecio*) contempt, scorn; (*subestimación*) underestimation, underrating; (*falta de respeto*) disrespect ♦ **hacer m. de** to make light of, scoff at.

men·sa·je m. message ♦ **m. en clave** coded message.

men·sa·je·ro, a adj. & m.f. messenger.

mens·trua·ción f. menstruation.

mens·trual adj. menstrual.

mens·tru·ar §67 intr. to menstruate.

men·sual adj. monthly.

men·sua·li·dad f. (*salario*) monthly wage; (*pago*) monthly installment.

men·su·ra f. measure, measurement.

men·su·ra·ble adj. mensurable, measurable.

men·su·ra·dor, ·ra I. adj. measuring **II.** measurer, meter.

men·su·rar tr. to measure.

men·ta f. mint.

men·ta·do, a adj. famous, renowned.

men·tal adj. mental.

men·ta·li·dad f. mentality, mind ♦ **m. abierta** open mind.

men·tar §49 tr. to name, mention.

men·te f. (*potencia intelectual*) mind, intellect; (*inteligencia*) intelligence; (*pensamiento*) mind <*tener en la m.* to have in mind>; (*propósito*) mind, intention <*tener en m.* to have in mind (to do)>.

men·te·ca·to, a I. adj. silly, foolish **II.** m.f. fool, simpleton.

men·tir §65 intr. to lie, tell lies.

men·ti·ra f. (*falsedad*) lie, falsehood; (*manchita blanca*) white spot (on a fingernail) ♦ **¡m.!** that's a lie! • **m. inocente** or **piadosa** white lie • **parece m.** it seems unbelievable.

men·ti·rón m. whopping lie, whopper.

men·ti·ro·so, a I. adj. lying **II.** m.f. liar.

men·tol m. menthol.

men·to·la·do, a adj. mentholated.

men·tor m. mentor.

me·nú m. menu, bill of fare.

me·nu·de·o m. (*repetición*) frequent repetition; (*venta al por menor*) retail ♦ **vender al m.** to sell retail.

me·nu·do, a I. adj. (*pequeño*) small, little; (*sin importancia*) small, insignificant <*problemas menudos* small problems>; (*fino*) fine <*lluvia m.* fine rain>; (*irónico*) fine <*¡en m. llo estamos!* a fine mess we're in!> ♦ **a m.** often, frequently • **por m.** in detail, minutely **II.** m. (*moneda*) loose change • pl. innards; (*de las reses*) offal; (*de las aves*) giblets.

me·ñi·que I. adj. (*del dedo*) little, baby; (*pequeño*) tiny **II.** m. little finger, pinkie.

me·o·llo m. (*médula*) marrow; (*seso*) brain, gray matter; (*inteligencia*) brains.

me·que·tre·fe m. COLL. jackanapes.

mer·ca·chi·fle m. (*buhonero*) peddler, hawker; (*comerciante*) small-time merchant; DEROG. (*avaro*) shark, money grubber.

mer·ca·de·o m. marketing.

mer·ca·de·rí·a f. var. of **mercancía**.

mer·ca·do m. (*feria*) market; (*sitio*) marketplace ♦ **acaparar el m. de** to corner the market in • **m. de cambios** foreign exchange market • **m. de valores** stock market • **m. exterior** foreign market • **m. interior** or **nacional** domestic market.

mer·ca·do·tec·nia f. marketing (research).

mer·can·cí·a f. (*artículo*) piece of merchandise, article; (*existencias*) merchandise, goods.

mer·can·te adj. & m. merchant.

mer·can·til adj. mercantile, commercial ♦ **derecho m.** commercial law • **sociedad m.** trading company.

mer·car §70 tr. to purchase, buy.

mer·ced f. (*beneficio*) gift, favor; RELIG. mercy; ARCH. (*título*) grace, worship ♦ **a la m. de** at the mercy of • **m. a** thanks to • **tenga la m. de** please be so kind as.

mer·ce·na·rio, a adj. & m. mercenary.

mer·ce·rí·a f. notions shop.

mer·cu·rial adj. mercurial.

mer·cu·rio m. mercury.

mer·cu·ro·cro·mo m. mercurochrome.

me·re·ce·dor, a adj. worthy, deserving ♦ **m. de confianza** trustworthy.

me·re·cer §17 tr. (*ser digno de*) to deserve, be worthy of; (*lograr*) to earn, get ♦ **m. la pena** to be worthwhile, be worth the trouble —reflex. to be deserving or worthy.

me·re·ci·do m. just deserts, due <*llevar su m.* to get one's just deserts>.

me·re·ci·mien·to m. merit, worth.

me·ren·dar §49 tr. to snack on —intr. to have a snack.

me·ren·gue m. meringue; R.P. COLL. mess.

me·re·triz f. prostitute, whore.

me·ri·dia·no, a adj. & m. meridian.

me·rien·da f. snack.
me·rien·de, do see **merendar.**
mé·ri·to m. *(virtud)* merit; *(valor)* worth, value ♦ **de m.** of merit, notable • **hacer méritos para** to strive to be deserving of.
me·ri·to·rio, a I. adj. meritorious **II.** m. unpaid trainee.
mer·lu·za f. hake.
mer·mar tr. & intr. to decrease, diminish.
mer·me·la·da f. marmalade.
me·ro m. ICHTH. grouper.
me·ro, a adj. *(puro)* mere, pure; MEX. *(verdadero)* real ♦ **ser el m. malo** to be wickedness itself.
me·ro·de·a·dor, ra I. adj. marauding **II.** m.f. marauder.
me·ro·de·ar intr. to maraud, plunder.
mes m. *(período del año)* month; *(sueldo)* monthly salary *<cobrar el m.* to draw one's monthly salary>; COLL. *(menstruo)* menstruation ♦ **al** or **por m.** by the month.
me·sa f. *(mueble)* table; *(junta)* board, council *<m. electoral* electoral board>; GEOG. meseta, plateau; JEWEL. facet, face; *(comida)* fare, food ♦ **de m. table** *<vino de mesa* table wine> • **levantar** or **alzar la m.** to clear the table • **m. de noche** night table, nightstand • **m. de operaciones** operating table • **m. de tijera** or **de doblar** card table, folding table • **poner la m.** to set the table.
me·se·ro, a MEX. m. *(camarero)* waiter —f. *(camarera)* waitress.
me·se·ta f. *(de escalera)* landing; GEOG. plateau.
me·siá·ni·co, a adj. messianic.
me·són m. inn, tavern.
me·so·ne·ro, a m.f. innkeeper.
mes·ti·zo, a I. adj. of mixed parentage **II.** m.f. mestizo (of white and Indian parentage).
me·su·ra f. moderation, restraint.
me·su·ra·do, a adj. moderate, circumspect.
me·ta f. *(fin)* goal, objective; *(de carrera)* finish; *(guardameta)* goalkeeper.
me·ta·bó·li·co, a adj. metabolic.
me·ta·bo·lis·mo m. metabolism.
me·ta·fí·si·co, a I. adj. metaphysical **II.** m. metaphysician —f. metaphysics.
me·tá·fo·ra f. metaphor.
me·ta·fó·ri·co, a adj. metaphoric(al).
me·tal m. metal; *(latón)* brass; *(calidad)* nature, quality; *(timbre)* tone, ring ♦ **m. blanco** nickel • **m. de imprenta** type metal • **m. en láminas** sheet metal.
me·tá·li·co, a I. adj. metallic **II.** m. cash, currency.
me·ta·li·zar §04 tr. to metalize —reflex. to become metalized.
me·ta·lur·gia f. metallurgy.
me·ta·lúr·gi·co, a I. adj. metallurgical **II.** m. metallurgist, metalworker.
me·ta·lur·gis·ta m. metallurgist, metalworker.
me·ta·mór·fi·co, a adj. GEOL. metamorphic.
me·ta·mor·fo·sis/mór·fo·sis f. inv. BIOL. metamorphosis; *(transformación)* transformation.
me·ta·no m. methane.
me·te·ó·ri·co, a adj. meteoric.
me·te·o·ri·to m. meteorite.
me·te·o·ro/té·o·ro m. meteor.
me·te·o·ro·lo·gí·a f. meteorology.
me·te·o·ro·lo·gis·ta/ró·lo·go, a m.f. meteorologist.

me·ter tr. *(introducir)* to put in, insert *<ella metió el dinero en el bolsillo* she put the money in her pocket>; *(promover)* to start, cause *<m. enredos* to start trouble>; *(causar)* to make *<m. ruido* to make noise>; *(implicar)* to involve, get into *<metió a su hermano en el negocio* he got his brother into the business>; *(apretar)* to squeeze into, squash together; *(apostar)* to stake, wager; COLL. *(golpe)* to give, deal; SEW. to take in ♦ **m. de contrabando** to smuggle in • **m. en vereda** COLL. to bring into line —reflex. *(entrar)* to get into, enter *<se metieron en el coche* they got into the car>; *(entremeterse)* to intervene, butt in; *(enredarse)* to get mixed up in ♦ **m. a** *(empezar)* to start; *(hacerse)* to set oneself up as • **m. con** to provoke, annoy • **m. de** AMER. to become • **m. en sí mismo** to withdraw into one's shell • **m. en todo** to meddle.
me·ti·cu·lo·so, a adj. meticulous.
me·ti·do, a I. see **meter II.** adj. *(abundante)* full; *(interesado)* involved; AMER. meddlesome ♦ **m. en sí** withdrawn **III.** m.f. AMER. meddler.
me·ti·lo m. methyl.
me·tó·di·co, a adj. methodical.
mé·to·do m. method, technique ♦ **con m.** methodically.
me·to·do·lo·gí·a f. methodology.
me·tra·je m. footage, length (of a film) ♦ **corto m.** short (film) • **largo m.** full-length or feature film.
me·tra·lle·ta f. submachine gun, tommy gun.
mé·tri·co, a I. adj. metric; POET. metrical ♦ **cinta m.** tape measure **II.** f. metrics.
me·tro¹ m. *(medida)* meter, metre (G.B.); *(regla)* ruler ♦ **m. cuadrado** square meter • **m. cúbico** cubic meter.
me·tro² m. abbr. of **metropolitano.**
me·tró·po·li f. *(capital)* capital; *(nación)* metropolis.
me·tro·po·li·ta·no, a I. adj. metropolitan **II.** m. subway, underground (G.B.).
mez·ca·li·na f. mescaline.
mez·cla f. *(acción)* mixing; *(combinación)* mixture, combination; *(de personas)* mixture, assortment; *(tejido)* tweed; CONST. mortar.
mez·cla·dor, ra I. adj. mixing, blending **II.** m.f. *(persona)* mixer —f. *(máquina)* mixing machine; CONST. cement mixer.
mez·cla·du·ra f./**mien·to** m. mixture, blend.
mez·clar tr. *(unir)* to mix, blend; *(reunir)* to mix, mingle; *(desordenar)* to mix up; *(en naipes)* to shuffle —reflex. *(unirse)* to mix, blend; *(reunirse)* to mix, mingle; *(meterse)* to become involved or mixed up.
mez·co·lan·za f. COLL. hodgepodge, jumble.
mez·quin·dad f. *(avaricia)* stinginess, miserliness; *(acción tacaña)* ill turn, act of meanness.
mez·qui·no, a I. adj. *(pobre)* poor, wretched; *(avaro)* stingy, miserly; *(miserable)* petty, small; *(pequeño)* small, tiny **II.** m. MEX. wart.
mez·qui·ta f. mosque.
mí pron. [pl. **used after prepositions**] me *<lo compró para mí* he bought it for me> ♦ **me toca a mí** it's my turn • **¿(y) a mí qué?** so what?
mi, mis adj. my *<mis hermanas* my sisters>.
miau m. meow.
mi·co m. mico, long-tailed monkey.
mi·cro·bio m. microbe.
mi·cro·bio·lo·gí·a f. microbiology.
mi·cro·bús m. microbus, minibus.

mi·cro·cir·cui·to m. microcircuit.

mi·cro·ci·ru·gí·a f. microsurgery.

mi·cro·cós·mi·co, a adj. microcosmic.

mi·cro·cos·mo(s) m. microcosm.

mi·cro·e·co·no·mí·a f. microeconomics.

mi·cro·fi·cha f. microfiche.

mi·cro·fil·me) m. microfilm.

mi·cró·fo·no m. microphone.

mi·cro·on·das f.pl. microwaves.

mi·cro·or·de·na·dor m. microcomputer.

mi·cro·pla·que·ta f. microchip.

mi·cros·có·pi·co, a adj. microscopic.

mi·cros·co·pio m. microscope ♦ **m. electrónico** electron microscope.

mi·da, do, diera, dió see **medir**.

mie·do m. *(temor)* fear, dread, *(aprensión)* apprehension ♦ **dar m. a** to frighten • **meterle m. a** to frighten • **morirse de m.** to be scared to death • **que da** *or* **mete m.** frightening, fearsome • **tener m.** to be afraid • **tener m. a** *or* **de** to be afraid of, fear • **tener m. (de) que** to be afraid that.

mie·do·so, a I. adj. fearful, cowardly II. m. coward.

miel f. honey; *(jarabe)* molasses; *(dulzura)* honey, sweetness ♦ **no hay m. sin hiel** every rose has a thorn • **m. de caña** molasses • **panal de m.** honeycomb.

miel·ga f. alfalfa.

miem·bro m. member; ANAT. *(extremidad)* member, limb; *(pene)* penis ♦ **m. viril** penis • **m. vitalicio** life member.

mien·ta, to see **mentir**.

mien·tras I. adv. ♦ **m. más** the more <*m. más consigue más quiere* the more he gets, the more he wants> • **m. tanto** meanwhile, in the meantime II. conj. *(pero)* while, whereas <*mi casa es pequeña m. la tuya es grande* my house is small whereas yours is large>; *(durante)* while, as long as <*m. la huelga duraba* while the strike lasted> ♦ **m. que** while.

miér·co·les m. inv. Wednesday ♦ **m. de ceniza** RELIG. Ash Wednesday ♦ ¡m.! AMER., COLL. shoot!, darn it!

mies f. *(cereal)* grain; *(tiempo de la siega)* harvest time ♦ pl. grain fields.

mi·ga f. *(pedacito)* bit, scrap; *(del pan)* crumb; *(substancia)* substance, pith ♦ **hacer buenas, malas migas con** to get along well, badly with.

mi·ga·ja f. *(del pan)* crumb; *(pedacito)* scrap, bit ♦ **m. de pan** bread crumb ♦ pl. scraps.

mi·gra·ción f. migration.

mi·gra·ña f. migraine (headache).

mi·gra·to·rio, a adj. migratory.

mil I. adj. thousand; *(milésimo)* thousandth; *(muchos)* thousand, countless <*m. veces* a thousand times> ♦ **a las m. y quinientas** at the last minute • **m. millones** billion, milliard (G.B.) II. m. a thousand, one thousand.

mi·la·gro m. miracle ♦ **hacer milagros** to work wonders • **vivir de m.** COLL. to be *or* stay alive by a miracle.

mi·la·gro·so, a adj. miraculous.

mi·le·nio m. millennium.

mi·lé·si·mo, a adj. & m. thousandth.

mi·li f. COLL. military service.

mi·li·cia f. *(arte militar)* art of war; *(tropa)* military, soldiery; *(de ciudadanos)* militia; *(servicio militar)* military service ♦ **m. nacional** national guard.

mi·li·cia·no, a I. adj. military II. m. mili-

---

tiaman.

mi·li·gra·mo m. milligram.

mi·li·li·tro m. milliliter.

mi·lí·me·tro m. millimeter.

mi·li·tan·te I. adj. militant II. m.f. militant, activist.

mi·li·tar¹ I. adj. military II. m. soldier ♦ **los militares** the military.

mi·li·tar² intr. *(como soldado)* to serve; *(en un partido)* to be active ♦ **m. en favor de** to lend support to.

mi·li·ta·ri·zar §04 tr. to militarize.

mil·piés m.inv. millipede.

mi·lla f. *(medida inglesa)* mile; MARIT. mile, nautical mile ♦ **m. náutica** nautical mile.

mi·llar m. *(conjunto de mil)* thousand <*un m. de hombres* a thousand men> ♦ pl. thousands, scores • **a m.** by the thousands.

mi·llón m. million ♦ **tener millones** COLL. to be a millionaire.

mi·llo·na·rio, a adj. & m.f. millionaire.

mi·mar tr. *(acariciar)* to caress, fondle; *(consentir)* to pamper, spoil.

mim·bre m. *(arbusto)* osier; *(tallo)* wicker.

mi·me·o·gra·fí·a f. *(acción)* mimeographing; *(copia)* mimcograph.

mi·me·o·gra·fiar §30 tr. to mimeograph.

mimeógrafo m. mimeograph (machine).

mí·mi·co, a I. adj. mimic, imitative II. f. THEAT. mime; *(imitación)* imitation, mimicry.

mi·mo m. THEAT. mime; *(caricia)* caressing, fondling ♦ **hacerle mimos a alguien** to pamper *or* indulge someone.

mi·mo·so, a adj. pampered, spoiled.

mi·na f. mine; *(galería)* underground passage; FIG. mine, storehouse; *(de lápiz)* pencil lead; AMER. mistress.

mi·na·dor, ra I. adj. mining II. m. *(ingeniero)* mining engineer; *(obrero)* miner; MIL. miner, sapper; MARIT. minelayer.

mi·nar tr. to mine; *(debilitar)* to undermine, destroy <*m. la salud* to undermine one's health>.

mi·na·re·te m. minaret.

mi·ne·ral adj. & m. mineral.

mi·ne·ra·lo·gí·a f. mineralogy.

mi·ne·ra·ló·gi·co, a adj. mineralogical.

mi·ne·ra·lo·gis·ta m. mineralogist.

mi·ne·rí·a f. *(trabajo)* mining; *(minas)* mines; *(mineros)* miners.

mi·ne·ro, a I. adj. mining II. m. *(trabajador)* miner; *(propietario)* mine owner.

min·gi·to·rio m. urinal.

min·go m. object ball (in billiards).

mi·nia·tu·ra f. miniature.

mi·nia·tu·ris·ta m.f. miniaturist.

mi·ni·fal·da f. miniskirt.

mi·ni·fun·dio m. small farm.

mi·ni·mi·zar §04 tr. to minimize.

mí·ni·mo, a I. adj. *(pequeño)* minimum, least; *(minucioso)* minute, minimal II. m. *(límite inferior)* minimum; METEOROL. low pressure zone ♦ **al m.** *or* **a lo más m.** to a minimum • **como m.** at least, at the very least • **en lo más m.** in the slightest • **m. común múltiplo** lowest common multiple • **m. vital** subsistence income —f. MUS. half note, minim; METEOROL. minimum temperature.

mi·nis·te·rial adj. ministerial.

mi·nis·te·rio m. ministry; *(cuerpo de ministros)* cabinet ♦ **M. de Agricultura** Department of Agriculture • **M. de Comercio** Department of Commerce • **M. de Hacienda** Treasury Department • **M. de Guerra** Defense Department • **M. de Trabajo** Department of Labor • **M. de Marina** Department of the Navy • **M. de Relaciones Exteriores** State Department.

mi·nis·trar tr. to hold office.

mi·nis·tro m.f. minister ♦ **M. de Agricultura** Secretary of Agriculture • **M. de Comercio** Secretary of Commerce • **M. de Hacienda** Secretary of the Treasury • **M. de Guerra** Defense Secretary • **M. de Marina** Secretary of the Navy • **M. de Relaciones Exteriores** Secretary of State • **primer m.** POL. prime minister.

mi·no·ra·ción f. diminution, reduction.

mi·no·rar tr. to diminish, reduce.

mi·no·rí·a/ri·dad f. minority.

mi·no·ris·ta I. adj. retail II. m.f. retailer.

mi·no·ri·ta·rio, a I. adj. minority II. m.f. member of a minority.

min·tie·ra, tió see **mentir.**

mi·nu·cia f. small thing, trifle.

mi·nu·cio·so, a adj. thorough, minute.

mi·nús·cu·lo, a I. adj. *(muy pequeño)* minuscule, tiny; *(insignificante)* insignificant ♦ **letra m.** small or lowercase letter II. f. small or lowercase letter.

mi·nu·ta f. *(borrador)* rough draft; *(acta)* minutes, record; *(nota)* note, memorandum; *(cuenta)* lawyer's bill; *(de una comida)* menu, bill of fare.

mi·nu·te·ro m. minute hand.

mi·nu·to m. minute ♦ **al m.** at once.

mí·o, a I. adj. mine *<estos libros son míos* these books are mine>; of mine *<un amigo m.* a friend of mine>; my *<¡Dios m.!* my God!>; *(querido)* my dear *<madre m.* my dear mother>> II. pron. mine *<¿dónde está el m.?* where is mine?> ♦ **ésta es la m.** COLL. this is my big chance • **lo m.** my affair, my business • **los míos** my people, my folks.

mio·pe I. adj. myopic, nearsighted II. m.f. myope, myopic person.

mio·pí·a f. myopia, nearsightedness.

mi·ra f. ARM., TECH. sight; *(intención)* aim, intention ♦ **con miras a** with an eye to, with a view to • **estar a la m. de** COLL. to be on the lookout for • **poner la m. en** to aim to, aspire to.

mi·ra·do, a I. adj. *(circunspecto)* cautious, circumspect; regarded *<mal m.* ill-regarded> II. f. *(acción)* look, glance; *(apariencia)* look, expression ♦ **echar una m. a** to cast a glance at • **m. fija** stare • **m. perdida** distant look.

mi·ra·dor, ·ra I. adj. looking, watching II. m.f. *(observador)* observer, spectator —m. *(balcón)* balcony, terrace.

mi·rar tr. *(ver)* to look at; *(observar)* to watch, observe; *(contemplar)* to gaze at; *(reflexionar)* to think about, consider ♦ **m. bien** or **con buenos ojos** to look with favor on, approve of • **m. de arriba abajo** to look up and down • **m. de hito en hito** to stare at • **m. de reojo** to look askance at • **m. de soslayo** to look sideways at • **m. mal** or **con malos ojos** to disapprove of • **m. por** to look out for, look after *<sólo miran por sus intereses>* they only look out for their own interests>; to look out (of) *<miraban por la ventana>* they were looking out the window> • **m. por encima** to glance at, look over • **m. por encima del hombro** to look down on —intr. *(ver)* to look; *(observar)* to watch; *(dar a)* to look out on, overlook *<el balcón mira a la plaza* the balcony overlooks the plaza> ♦ **¡mira!** *(como*

advertencia) watch out!, be careful!; *(como amenaza)* look here! • **mire** well, let me say this —reflex. to look at oneself *<me miré en el espejo* I looked at myself in the mirror>; to look at one another *<se miraban con amor* they looked at one another lovingly> ♦ **m. unos a otros** FIG. to look at each other helplessly.

mi·ra·sol m. sunflower.

mi·rí·a·da f. myriad.

mi·ri·lla f. *(para observar)* peephole; SURV. target, sight.

mir·lo m. blackbird.

mi·rón, ·o·na adj. & m.f. nosy or inquisitive (person).

mi·sa f. Mass ♦ **decir m.** to say or celebrate Mass • **m. de difuntos** or **de requiem** Requiem Mass • **m. de gallo** Midnight Mass • **m. mayor** High Mass • **m. rezada** Low Mass.

mi·sán·tro·po m. misanthrope.

mis·ce·lá·ne·o, a I. adj. miscellaneous II. f. miscellany.

mi·se·ra·ble I. adj. *(pobre)* poor, wretched; *(tacaño)* stingy, miserly; *(lastimoso)* miserable, pitiful; *(despreciable)* despicable, vile ♦ **¡m. de mí!** woe is me! II. m.f. *(pobre)* wretch, unfortunate person; *(tacaño)* miser, skinflint; *(canalla)* cad, scoundrel.

mi·se·ria f. *(infortunio)* misery, suffering; *(pobreza)* poverty; *(avaricia)* stinginess, miserliness; COLL. *(cosa pequeña)* pittance ♦ **estar en la m.** to be down and out.

mi·se·ri·cor·dia f. mercy, compassion.

mi·se·ri·cor·dio·so, a adj. & m.f. compassionate or merciful (person).

mí·se·ro, a adj. wretched, unfortunate.

mi·sil m. missile.

mi·sión f. mission.

mi·sio·nal adj. missionary.

mi·sio·ne·ro, a adj. & m.f. missionary.

mi·si·va f. missive, letter.

mis·mo, a I. adj. *(idéntico)* same *<leí el m. libro* I read the same book>; *(exacto)* very *<en ese m. momento* at that very moment> ♦ **ahora m.** right now • **así m.** *(de esta manera)* in the same way, likewise; *(también)* also • **lo m.** the same thing • **por lo m.** for that reason, for that very reason • **yo m.** I myself.

mi·so·gi·nia f. misogyny.

mis·te·rio m. mystery.

mis·te·rio·so, a adj. mysterious.

mis·ti·cis·mo m. mysticism.

mís·ti·co, a I. adj. mystic(al) II. m.f. mystic —f. mystical theology.

mis·ti·fi·car §70 tr. to mystify, trick.

mis·tu·ra f. mixture.

mi·tad f. *(una de dos partes)* half *<la m. de la población* half of the population>; *(medio)* middle *<durante la m. de la película* during the middle of the movie> ♦ **a** or **en la m. de** in the middle of • **mi cara m.** COLL. my better half • **por la m.** in half, in two.

mí·ti·co, a adj. mythic(al).

mi·ti·ga·ción f. mitigation.

mi·ti·ga·dor, ·ra/gan·te I. adj. mitigating II. m.f. mitigator.

mi·ti·gar §47 tr. to mitigate.

mi·tin m. [pl. **mí·ti·nes**] meeting, rally.

mi·to m. *(relato)* myth; *(leyenda)* myth, legend.

mi·to·lo·gí·a f. mythology.

mi·to·lo·gis·ta/tó·lo·go m. mythologist.

mi·tón m. mitt.

mi·tra f. *(toca de obispo)* miter; *(obispado)* bishopric; *(arzobispado)* archbishopric.

mix·to, a I. adj. *(mezclado)* mixed; *(mestizo)* of mixed race II. m. explosive compound.

mix·tu·ra f. *(mezcla)* mixture; PHARM. compound, mixture.

mix·tu·rar tr. to mix.

mne·mo·tec·nia/téc·ni·ca f. mnemonics.

mne·mo·téc·ni·co, a adj. mnemonic.

mo·bi·lia·rio, a I. adj. movable II. m. furniture, furnishings.

mo·bla·je m. furniture, furnishings.

mo·blar §19 tr. to furnish.

mo·ca·sín m. moccasin.

mo·ce·dad f. youth.

mo·co m. mucus; COLL. snot ♦ **limpiarse los mocos** COLL. to blow one's nose • **llorar a m. tendido** COLL. to cry like a baby.

mo·co·so, a I. adj. snotty, bratty II. m.f. snotty kid, brat.

mo char tr. to hack or lop off.

mo·cha·zo m. blow with a rifle butt.

mo·chi·la f. *(de caminante)* pack, knapsack; *(de cazador)* game bag; MIL. ration.

mo·cho, a I. adj. *(sin punta)* blunt; *(sin cuernos)* hornless; COLL. *(pelado)* shorn, cropped II. m. *(mango)* handle; *(culata)* stock, butt.

mo·da f. style, fashion ♦ **a la m.** or **de m.** fashionable, in fashion • **estar** or **ser de m.** to be in fashion • **fuera de m.** out of fashion • **pasado de m.** old-fashioned • **pasarse de m.** to go out of fashion • **ponerse de m.** to come into fashion • **ser la última m.** to be the latest fashion.

mo·dal I. adj. modal II. m.pl. manners, behavior.

mo·da·li·dad f. modality, nature.

mo·de·lar tr. to model —reflex. to model oneself after someone, emulate.

mo·de·lo I. m. model —m.f. fashion model ♦ **desfile de modelos** fashion show • **m. a escala** scale model II. adj. model, exemplary.

mo·de·ra·ción f. moderation.

mo·de·ra·do, a adj. & m.f. moderate.

mo·de·ra·dor, ·ra I. adj. moderating II. m.f. moderator —m. PHYS. moderator.

mo·de·rar tr. *(templar)* to moderate, regulate; *(contener)* contain, restrain —reflex. to contain or restrain oneself.

mo·der·nis·ta I. adj. modernist, modernistic II. m.f. modernist.

mo·der·ni·za·ción f. modernization.

mo·der·ni·zar §04 tr. to modernize.

mo·der·no, a I. adj. modern II. m.f. modern ♦ **a la moderna** or **a lo moderno** in the modern manner or fashion.

mo·des·tia f. modesty.

mo·des·to, a adj. & m.f. modest (person).

mó·di·co, a adj. moderate, reasonable.

mo·di·fi·ca·ción f. modification.

mo·di·fi·ca·dor, ·ra I. adj. modifying II. m.f. modifier.

mo·di·fi·car §70 tr. to modify —reflex. to change, become modified.

mo·dis·mo m. idiom, idiomatic expression.

mo·dis·ta m.f. dressmaker, modiste.

mo·dis·te·rí·a f. dress shop.

mo·do m. *(manera)* manner, way; GRAM. mood; MUS. mode ♦ **a** or **al m. de** like, in the manner of • **a mi m.** in my own way • **del mismo m.** in the same way • **de m. que** so that • **de ningún m.** by no means • **de todos modos** at any rate, in any case • **en cierto m.** to a

certain extent • **m. de ser** character, way of being ♦ pl. manners.

mo·do·rra f. drowsiness, heaviness.

mo·do·so, a adj. well-behaved, well-mannered.

mo·du·la·ción f. modulation ♦ **m. de amplitud** RAD. amplitude modulation, AM • **m. de frecuencia** RAD. frequency modulation, FM.

mo·du·la·dor, ·ra I. adj. modulating II. m.f. modulator.

mo·du·lar tr. & intr. to modulate.

mó·du·lo m. ARCHIT. module; PHYS. modulus; MUS. modulation ♦ **m. lunar** lunar module.

mo·fa f. mockery, ridicule ♦ **hacer m. de** to mock, ridicule.

mo·far intr. & reflex. to mock, ridicule ♦ **mofarse de** to mock, ridicule.

mo·he·cer §17 tr. *(hacer mohoso)* to make moldy; *(aherrumbrar)* to make rusty —reflex. *(hacerse mohoso)* to mildew; *(aherrumbrarse)* to rust.

mo·hín m. grimace, face ♦ **hacer mohines** to grimace, make faces.

mo·hí·no, a adj. *(triste)* sad, melancholy; *(enfadado)* ill-humored, sulky II. —m. ORNITH. blue magpie —f. *(enojo)* anger, displeasure; *(melancolía)* sadness, melancholy.

mo·ho m. *(hongo)* mold, mildew; *(herrumbre)* rust, corrosion; *(desidia)* laziness, indolence ♦ **criar m.** to get moldy.

mo·ho·so, a adj. *(lleno de hongos)* moldy, mildewed; *(herrumbroso)* rusty, corroded.

mo·ja·dor, ·ra I. adj. wetting II. m.f. wetter —m. PRINT. moistening tank; *(esponja)* sponge.

mo·jar tr. *(humedecer)* to wet, make wet; *(empapar)* to drench, soak; to dip <mojar el pan en aceite to dip the bread in oil> —reflex. to get wet.

mo·ja·se·llos m.inv. moistener, sponge (for stamps).

mo·je m. gravy, juice.

mo·ji·gan·ga f. *(fiesta de máscaras)* masquerade, costume party; THEAT. farce, comedy; *(burla)* mockery, joke.

mo·ji·ga·te·rí·a f. *(hipocresía)* hypocrisy, dissimulation; *(santurronería)* sanctimoniousness.

mo·ji·ga·to, a I. adj. *(hipócrita)* hypocritical; *(santurrón)* sanctimonious II. m.f. *(hipócrita)* hypocrite; *(santurrón)* sanctimonious person.

mo·jón m. *(de término)* boundary marker; *(de gula)* road marker.

mo·jo·nar tr. to set up boundary markers around.

mo·lo·ne·ro m. appraiser, assessor.

mo·lar adj. & m. molar.

mol·de m. mold; *(forma)* pattern, model; *(persona ejemplar)* role model; PRINT. form ready for printing ♦ **de m.** fitting, opportune • **letra de m.** print • **venir de m.** or **venir como de m.** to be just what one needs.

mol·de·a·do m. molding, casting.

mol·de·ar tr. *(sacar el molde)* to mold, shape; *(vaciar)* to cast.

mo·lé·cu·la f. molecule.

mo·le·cu·lar adj. molecular.

mo·le·dor, ·ra I. adj. grinding II. m. grinder.

mo·ler §78 tr. *(trigo)* to grind, mill; *(caña)* to press; *(cansar)* to exhaust, drain; *(destruir)* to beat up, cream ♦ **m. a golpes** or **palos** to beat to a pulp.

mo·les·tar tr. *(fastidiar)* to bother, annoy; *(interrumpir)* to disturb, disrupt; *(causar dolor)* to bother, trouble —reflex. to bother, take the trouble ♦ **no se moleste** don't bother.

mo·les·tia f. *(fastidio)* bother, annoyance; *(incomodidad)* inconvenience, trouble; *(malestar)* discomfort ♦ **si no es m.** if it isn't too much trouble.

mo·les·to, a adj. *(fastidioso)* bothersome, annoying; *(enojado)* bothered, annoyed; *(incómodo)* uncomfortable, awkward; *(inconveniente)* inconvenient, troublesome.

mo·li·do, a adj. *(aplastado)* ground, milled; *(derrengado)* beat, worn-out.

mo·lien·da f. *(acción)* grinding, milling; *(molino)* mill; *(temporada)* milling season.

mo·li·fi·car §70 tr. to mollify, soften.

mo·li·mien·to m. grinding, milling.

mo·li·ne·ro, a I. adj. milling II. m. miller, grinder.

mo·li·ne·te m. *(ventilador)* ventilating fan; *(juguete de papel)* pinwheel.

mo·li·ni·llo m. *(para moler)* mill, grinder; *(para batir)* whisk, beater.

mo·li·no m. mill ♦ **m. de viento** windmill • **molinos de viento** imaginary enemies.

mo·lus·co m. mollusk.

mo·llar adj. soft, tender.

mo·lle·ra f. *(cráneo)* crown (of the head); *(fontanela)* fontanelle; *(seso)* brains, ability ♦ **cerrado de m.** COLL. stupid.

mo·men·tá·ne·o, a adj. momentary.

mo·men·to m. moment; *(ocasión)* occasion, time ♦ **a cada m.** continually, at every instant • **a partir de este m.** from this moment (on) • **al m.** immediately, at once • **de m.** at present, for the moment • **de un m. a otro** any moment, from one minute to the next • **dentro de un m.** in a moment • **desde este m.** from this moment (on) • **¡m.!** just a minute! • **momentos después** moments later.

mo·mi·fi·car §70 tr. to mummify —reflex. to become mummified.

mo·mio, a I. adj. lean, thin II. m. cushy job —f. mummy ♦ **estar hecho una m.** to be all skin and bones.

mo·mo m. funny face.

mo·na f. *(hembra)* female monkey; COLL. *(mimo)* ape, mimic; *(borrachera)* drunkenness; MEX. coward ♦ **coger** or **pillar una m.** COLL. to get loaded or plastered • **dormir la m.** COLL. to sleep it off.

mo·na·cal adj. monastic.

mo·na·da f. *(gesto)* monkey or funny face; *(cosa o persona graciosa)* pretty or lovely thing.

mo·na·gui·llo m. acolyte, altar boy.

mo·nar·ca m. monarch, sovereign.

mo·nar·quí·a f. monarchy.

mo·nár·qui·co, a I. adj. monarchic(al) II. m.f. monarchist.

mo·nas·te·rio m. monastery.

mo·nás·ti·co, a adj. monastic(al).

mon·da f. *(limpieza)* cleaning; *(poda)* pruning, trimming; *(peladura)* peeling, skinning; *(parte podada)* trimmings; *(parte pelada)* peelings, peels.

mon·da·dien·tes m.inv. toothpick.

mon·da·dor, ·ra I. adj. *(podador)* pruning, trimming; *(que pela)* peeling II. m.f. *(podador)* pruner, trimmer; *(pelador)* peeler.

mon·da·du·ra f. *(poda)* pruning, trimming; *(peladura)* peeling; *(parte pelada)* trimmings; *(parte pelada)* peelings.

mon·dar tr. *(fruta)* to peel, skin; *(nueces)* to

shell; *(podar)* to prune, trim.

mo·ne·da f. coin; FIN. mint; COLL. *(caudal)* wealth, money ♦ **acuñar m.** to mint money • **m. corriente** currency • **pagar con la misma m.** to give someone a taste of his own medicine.

mo·ne·de·ro m. change purse.

mo·ne·rí·a f. *(monada)* cute or amusing thing; *(gesto)* funny or monkey face; *(tontería)* silliness, foolishness.

mo·ne·ta·rio, a I. adj. monetary II. m. coin collection.

mo·ne·ti·zar §04 tr. *(amonedar)* to mint, coin; *(dar curso legal)* to monetize.

mon·gó·li·co, a adj. & m.f. MED. mongoloid.

mon·go·lis·mo m. mongolism, Down's syndrome.

mo·nín, ·i·na adj. COLL. cute, pretty.

mo·ni·tor m. *(admonitor)* monitor, adviser; *(entrenador)* trainer; COMPUT. monitor.

mon·ja f. nun; MEX. round sweet bread.

mon·je m. *(fraile)* monk; *(solitario)* recluse.

mo·no, a I. adj. COLL. cute, darling II. m. monkey, ape; *(imitador)* mimic, ape; *(traje)* coveralls.

mo·nó·cu·lo, a m. *(lente)* monocle; *(vendaje)* eye patch.

mo·no·ga·mia f. monogamy.

mo·nó·ga·mo, a adj. monogamous.

mo·no·gra·fí·a f. monograph.

mo·no·gra·ma m. monogram.

mo·no·lin·güe adj. monolingual.

mo·no·li·to m. monolith.

mo·no·lo·gar §47 intr. to soliloquize.

mo·no·lo·go m. monologue, soliloquy.

mo·no·pla·no m. monoplane.

mo·no·po·lio m. monopoly.

mo·no·po·li·zar §04 tr. to monopolize.

mo·no·to·ní·a f. monotony.

mo·nó·to·no, a adj. monotonous.

mons·truo m. monster.

mons·truo·si·dad f. monstrosity.

mons·truo·so, a adj. monstrous.

mon·ta f. *(acción)* mounting; *(suma)* sum, total ♦ **de poca m.** of no account, insignificant.

mon·ta·car·gas m.inv. freight elevator.

mon·ta·do, a I. adj. *(que va a caballo)* mounted; *(caballo)* saddled; *(máquina)* assembled; THEAT. staged II. m. assembly.

mon·ta·je m. assembly, installation; CINEM. montage ♦ **cadena de m.** assembly line.

mon·tan·te m. *(de una armazón)* upright, strut; *(ventana)* transom; *(listón)* mullion.

mon·ta·ña f. mountain; FIG. mountain, heap ♦ **hacer de todo una m.** to make a mountain out of a molehill • **m. rusa** rollercoaster ♦ pl. highlands.

mon·ta·ñe·ro, a m.f. mountaineer, mountain climber.

mon·ta·ñés, ·e·sa I. adj. mountain, highland II. m.f. mountain dweller, highlander.

mon·ta·ño·so, a adj. mountainous.

mon·ta·pla·tos m.inv. dumbwaiter.

mon·tar intr. *(subir)* to mount, get on; *(subir a caballo)* to mount a horse; *(cabalgar)* to ride (horseback); *(alcanzar)* to reach ♦ **m. a caballo** to ride horseback • **m. en** to ride <**m. en bicicleta** to ride a bicycle> • **m. en cólera** to get angry —tr. *(subir)* to mount <**m. un caballo** to mount a horse>; *(valer)* to mount or amount to <**sus cuentas montaron mil dólares** his bills mounted to one thousand dollars>; *(armar)* to assemble, set up; *(establecer)* to set up <**m. un**

negocio to set up a business>; CINEM. to edit; THEAT. to produce; JEWEL. to set; *(acoplar)* to mount.

mon·te m. *(montaña)* mount, mountain; *(bosque)* forest, woodland; COLL. *(establecimiento)* pawnshop; *(juego de naipes)* monte ♦ **m. alto** forest, woodland (with tall trees) • **m. bajo** brush, brushwood.

mon·te pí·o m. pawnshop.

mon·tés adj. wild, undomesticated.

mon·tí·cu·lo m. knoll, hillock.

mon·to m. amount, total.

mon·tón m. *(acopio)* pile, heap; COLL. *(mucho)* heaps, lots ♦ **a montones** by the truckload • **del m.** COLL. ordinary, average • **ser del m.** COLL. to be one of the herd.

mon·tu·ra f. *(cabalgadura)* mount; *(silla)* saddle, mount; *(de una máquina)* assembly, installation; JEWEL. setting.

mo·nu·men·tal adj. monumental, huge.

mo·nu·men·to m. monument.

mon·zón m.f. monsoon.

mo·ño m. *(de la mujer)* bun, chignon; *(lazo)* bow, knot; ORNITH. crest.

mo·que·ar intr. to snivel, have a runny nose.

mo·ra·do, a I. adj. purple, violet **II.** m. purple —f. *(casa)* house, dwelling; *(estancia)* stay, sojourn.

mo·ra·dor, ·ra I. adj. living, residing **II.** m.f. tenant, resident.

mo·ral I. adj. moral **II.** f. *(ética)* morals, ethics; *(ánimo)* morale, spirits.

mo·ra·le·ja f. moral.

mo·ra·li·dad f. morality; *(moraleja)* moral.

mo·ra·li·zar §04 tr. & intr. to moralize.

mo·rar intr. to live, reside.

mo·ra·to·ria f. moratorium.

mor·bi·dez f. softness, delicateness.

mór·bi·do, a adj. soft, delicate; MED. morbid.

mor·bi·li·dad/di·dad f. morbidity.

mor·bo·sl·dad f. morbidity, disease.

mor·bo·so, a adj. *(no sano)* morbid; *(enfermo)* sick, diseased.

mor·ci·lla f. CUL. blood pudding or sausage; THEAT., COLL. ad lib, improvisation ♦ **¡que te den m.!** COLL. take a walk!, get lost!

mor·da·ci·dad f. mordacity.

mor·daz adj. *(corrosivo)* corrosive, mordant; *(picante)* burning, pungent; *(punzante)* biting, mordant.

mor·da·za f. *(silencio)* gag; TECH. clamp.

mor·de·du·ra f. bite.

mor·der §78 tr. to bite; *(mordiscar)* to nibble (at); *(asir)* to bite, grip; ARTS, PRINT. to etch —intr. to bite.

mor·dien·te I. adj. mordant, biting **II.** m. *(agua fuerte)* caustic acid; *(de tintorero)* color fixative.

mor·dis·car §70/**que·ar** tr. to nibble (at).

mor·dis·co m. nibble, bite ♦ **dar or pegar un m.** to take a bite (of).

mo·re·no, a I. adj. *(pardo)* brown; *(tostado)* brown-skinned, dark-skinned; *(pelo)* brown, brunet; AMER., COLL. *(mulato)* mulatto **II.** m.f. *(negro)* Black, Negro; *(de pelo castaño)* brunet, brunette; AMER. *(mulato)* mulatto.

mor·fi·na f. morphine.

mor·fo·lo·gí·a f. morphology.

mor·gue f. morgue.

mo·ri·bun·do, a I. adj. moribund, dying **II.** m.f. dying person.

mo·rir §27 intr. to die; *(extinguirse)* to die, go

out; *(desaparecer)* to die, die out ♦ **m. ahogado** to drown • **m. ahorcado** to be hanged • **m. de frío** to freeze to death • **m. de risa** to die laughing • **m. fusilado** to be shot —reflex. *(fallecer)* to die; *(extinguirse)* to die, go out ♦ **m. de aburrimiento** to be bored to death • **m. de ganas** to be dying to • **m. por** *(estar loco por)* to be crazy about; *(querer)* to be dying to <*me muero por ir a Francia* I am dying to go to France>.

mo·ro·si·dad f. *(lentitud)* slowness; *(demora)* delay, lateness; *(falta de actividad)* inactivity.

mo·ro·so, a adj. *(lento)* slow; *(perezoso)* lazy; *(tardío)* tardy; *(en el pago)* in arrears, delinquent.

mo·rro m. snout, nose.

mo·rru·do, a adj. *(que tiene hocico)* snouted; *(que tiene labios gruesos)* thick-lipped; R.P. brawny.

mor·sa f. walrus.

mor·se m. Morse code.

mor·ta·ja f. shroud.

mor·tal I. adj. mortal; FIG. dreadful, awful **II.** m. man, mortal.

mor·ta·li·dad f. mortality.

mor·tan·dad f. death toll, mortality.

mor·te·ci·no, a adj. dying, fading.

mor·te·ro m. mortar.

mor·tí·fe·ro, a adj. fatal, lethal.

mor·ti·fi·ca·ción f. mortification; FIG. annoyance.

mor·ti·fi·ca·dor, ·ra adj. mortifying.

mor·ti·fi·can·te adj. mortifying.

mor·ti·fi·car §70 tr. to mortify, FIG. to annoy.

mor·tuo·rio, a I. adj. mortuary, funereal **II.** m. funeral.

mos·ca f. fly; *(cebo)* fly (for fishing); COLL. *(dinero)* dough, bread; COLL. *(persona)* pest, pain in the neck ♦ **aflojar or soltar la m.** COLL. to fork it out or over, cough it up • **cazar moscas** COLL. to waste time • **m. muerta** COLL. hypocrite • **no matar una m.** not to hurt a fly • **papar moscas** to daydream • **peso m.** lightweight • **por si las moscas** just in case –m. MEX. stowaway, tramp.

mos·ca·tel adj. muscatel.

mos·que·ar tr. *(ahuyentar moscas)* to swat; *(responder)* to answer back (with a fresh remark) —intr. MEX. to travel as a tramp, slow away.

mos·que·ro m. *(trampa)* flytrap; AMER. swarm of flies.

mos·que·te m. musket.

mos·qui·te·ro m. mosquito net.

mos·qui·to m. mosquito; *(mosca pequeña)* gnat, midge.

mos·ta·za f. mustard; *(mostacilla)* bird shot.

mos·to m. *(zumo)* must; COLL. *(vino)* wine.

mos·tra·dor, ·ra I. adj. demonstrative **II.** m.f. demonstrator —m. counter, table top.

mos·trar §19 tr. *(enseñar)* to show; *(explicar)* to demonstrate, show; *(indicar)* to point out; *(expresar)* to show, express —reflex. *(darse a conocer)* to show oneself or prove to be <*se muestra buen profesor* he shows himself to be a good professor>; *(aparecer)* to show oneself, appear.

mos·tren·co, a I. adj. ownerless <*bienes mostrencos* ownerless property> **II.** m.f. COLL. *(persona ruda)* dolt; *(persona torpe)* dim-witted person

mo·te[1] m. *(enigma)* riddle; *(divisa)* motto;

(apodo) nickname ♦ **poner m. a alguien** to nickname someone.

mo·te² m. AMER. stewed corn.

mo·tel m. motel.

mo·tín m. insurrection, riot.

mo·ti·va·ción f. motivation.

mo·ti·var tr. *(causar)* to motivate, cause; *(explicar)* to explain; *(justificar)* justify.

mo·ti·vo m. *(causa)* motive, cause; MUS. theme; ART. motif ♦ **bajo ningún m.** under no circumstances • **con mayor m.** even more so • **dar m.** to give cause • **no ser m. para** to be no reason to *or* for • **sin m.** without reason.

mo·to f. COLL. cycle, motorcycle.

mo·to·ci·cle·ta f. motorcycle.

mo·to·ci·clis·ta I. adj. motorcycle II. m.f. motorcyclist.

mo·to·náu·ti·ca I. adj. motorboat II. f. motorboating.

mo·to·na·ve f. motorboat, motor ship.

mo·tor, ·ra I. adj. motor II. m. motor engine ♦ **m. auxiliar** booster (engine) • **m. de arranque** starter • **m. de cilindro en V** V-engine • **m. de cohete** rocket engine • **m. de combustión interna** *or* **de explosión** internal combustion engine • **m. de reacción** *or* **de chorro** jet engine • **m. de vapor** steam engine • **m. diesel** diesel (engine) • **m. fuera de borda** outboard motor.

mo·to·ris·ta m.f. *(motociclista)* motorcyclist; *(de automóvil)* motorist.

mo·to·ri·zar §04 tr. to motorize.

mo·ve·di·zo, a adj. *(que se mueve)* moving, shifting; *(inconstante)* fickle, changeable ♦ **arenas movedizas** quicksand.

mo·ver §78 tr. to move about, stir; *(la cabeza)* to shake; MECH. to drive, power; *(inducir)* to induce, move; *(incitar)* to incite, provoke; *(conmover)* to excite, stir ♦ **m. a** to move to <**m. a compasión** to move to pity> —intr. ARCHIT. to spring; AGR. to sprout, bud —reflex. to move.

mo·vi·ble adj. movable.

mo·vi·do, a adj. *(persona)* active, lively; *(mar)* choppy, rough; *(fotografía)* fuzzy, blurry.

mó·vil I. adj. *(que puede moverse)* mobile, movable; *(inestable)* unstable, variable II. m. *(motivo)* motive, reason; PHYS. moving body; ARTS mobile.

mo·vi·li·dad f. mobility.

mo·vi·li·za·ción f. mobilization.

mo·vi·li·zar §04 tr. to mobilize.

mo·vi·mien·to m. *(acción)* movement, motion; *(efecto)* move, movement; *(actividad)* activity, movement; *(sentimiento)* feeling; MECH. motion; MIL., MUS. movement; COM. activity ♦ **m. perpetuo** perpetual motion • **m. sísmico** earth tremor • **poner en m.** to put in motion.

mo·zo, a I. adj. young II. m. *(camarero)* waiter; *(tentemozo)* prop, shore ♦ **buen m.** AMER. handsome • **m. de caballos** stable boy, groom • **m. de cordel** *or* **de cuerda** porter —f. girl • **buena m.** AMER. good-looking.

mo·zue·lo, a m.f. *(muchacho)* lad; *(muchacha)* girl.

mu·ci·la·go/ci·la·go m. mucilage.

mu·co·si·dad f. mucosity.

mu·co·so, a adj. & f. mucous (membrane).

mu·cus m. mucus.

mu·cha·cha·da f. AMER. group of youngsters.

mu·cha·cho, a m.f. *(niño)* child, youngster; COLL. *(adolescente)* youth, kid —m. *(chico)* boy; *(mozo)* houseboy, servant —f. *(chica)*

girl; *(moza)* maid, servant.

mu·che·dum·bre f. multitude, crowd.

mu·cho, a I. adj. *(abundante)* much, a lot of <**m. agua** a lot of water>; very <**hace m. frío** it is very cold> ♦ pl. many, a lot of <**muchos problemas** many problems> II. pron. a lot <**¿tienes dinero?** no, pero mi amiga tiene m. do you have any money? no, but my friend has a lot> ♦ pl. many <**muchos vinieron tarde** many came late> III. adv. a lot, much <**ellos trabajan m.** they work a lot>; much <**m. después** much later>; *(largo tiempo)* for a long time <**hace m. que viven en Portugal** they have lived in Portugal for a long time> ♦ **ni m. menos** not by a long shot, far from it • **por m. que** however much, no matter how much • **tener en m.** to hold in high regard, think a lot of.

mu·da f. *(de ropa)* change of clothing; *(de plumas)* molting, molt; *(tiempo)* molting season.

mu·da·ble adj. *(cambiable)* changeable; *(inconstante)* inconstant, fickle.

mu·dan·za f. *(cambio)* change; *(traslado)* move, moving; *(figura de baile)* figure; *(inconstancia)* inconstancy, fickleness ♦ **estar de m.** to be moving.

mu·dar tr. *(cambiar)* to change; *(trasladar)* to move; ORNITH., ZOOL. to molt, shed ♦ **m. de idea** *or* **de opinión** to change one's mind —reflex. *(cambiarse)* to change; *(trasladarse)* to move.

mu·dez f. dumbness, muteness.

mu·do, a I. adj. *(que no puede hablar)* mute, dumb; *(silencioso)* silent, mute; GRAM. silent II. m.f. dumb *or* mute person.

mue·bla·je m. furniture.

mue·ble I. adj. movable II. m. piece of furniture ♦ pl. furniture.

mue·ble, blo see **moblar**.

mue·ble·rí·a f. furniture store.

mue·ca f. face, grimace ♦ **hacer muecas** to make faces.

mue·la f. *(de molino)* millstone; *(de afilar)* grindstone, whetstone; ANAT. molar ♦ **m. de juicio** wisdom tooth.

mue·la, lo see **moler**.

mue·lle¹ I. adj. *(blando)* soft, tender; *(elástico)* elastic, springy II. m. spring.

mue·lle² m. pier, dock; RAIL. loading platform.

mue·ra, re see **morir**.

muer·da, do see **morder**.

muér·da·go m. mistletoe.

muer·te f. death; *(homicidio)* murder, homicide ♦ **a m.** to the death <**un duelo a m.** a duel to the death>; *(implacablemente)* to the death, relentlessly <**odiar a m.** to hate relentlessly> • **de mala m.** COLL. crummy, lousy • **de m.** seriously, fatally <**enfermo de m.** fatally ill> • **hasta la m.** until death.

muer·to, a I. see **morir** II. adj. dead; *(apagado)* lifeless; *(marchito)* faded; *(cansado)* exhausted ♦ **más m. que vivo** half-dead • **m. de** dying of <**estoy m. de sed** I am dying of thirst> • **no tener dónde caerse m.** COLL. to be penniless III. m.f. *(difunto)* dead person; *(cadáver)* corpse ♦ **cargar con el m.** COLL. to be left holding the bag • **echarle el m. a** COLL. to put the blame on • **hacerse el m.** COLL. to play possum, play dead • **los muertos** the dead.

mues·tra¹ f. *(ejemplo)* sample, specimen; *(señal)* sign, indication <**una m. de buena fe** an indication of good faith>; *(modelo)* model,

guide ♦ **dar muestras de** to show signs of.
mues·tra² f. show, exhibition.
mues·tre, tro see **mostrar**.
mue·va, ve see **mover**.
mu·gir §32 intr. *(las vacas)* to moo; *(los toros)* to bellow; *(bramar)* to roar, howl.
mu·gre f. filth, grime.
mu·grien·to, a adj. filthy, grimy.
mu·gue·ta m. lily of the valley.
mu·jer f. *(hembra)* woman; *(esposa)* wife ♦ **m. de la limpieza** cleaning woman • **m. de su casa** housewife, homemaker • **m. de la vida** or **de mal vivir** prostitute.
mu·je·rie·go, a adj. womanizing, philandering ♦ **ser un m.** to be a womanizer or ladies' man.
mu·la f. female mule ♦ **ser una m.** to be stubborn as a mule.
mu·la·to, a I. adj. *(de raza mixta)* mulatto; *(de color moreno)* dark, dark-skinned **II.** m.f. *(persona)* mulatto —m. AMER., MIN. dark silver ore.
mu·le·ro m. muleteer.
mu·le·ta f. *(para andar)* crutch; *(sostén)* crutch, support.
mu·lo m. mule; FIG. brute, beast.
mul·ta f. fine; AUTO. parking ticket.
mul·tar tr. to fine.
mul·ti·co·lor adj. multicolor.
mul·ti·co·pis·ta f. duplicating machine, copier.
mul·ti·mi·llo·na·rio, a adj. & m.f. multimillionaire.
mul·ti·na·cio·nal adj. multinational.
múl·ti·ple adj. multiple.
mul·ti·pli·ca·ción f. multiplication.
mul·ti·pli·car §70 tr. & reflex. to multiply.
mul·ti·pli·ci·dad f. muliplicity.
mul·ti·pro·ce·sa·dor adj. & m. COMPUT. multiprocessor.
mul·ti·tud f. multitude.
mul·ti·tu·di·na·rio, a adj. multitudinous.
mu·lli·do, a I. adj. fluffy, soft **II.** m. stuffing, filling.
mu·llir §13 tr. *(esponjar)* to fluff (up); *(la tierra)* to loosen.
mun·da·nal adj. worldly, mundane.
mun·da·no, a adj. *(del mundo)* worldly, mundane; *(que mundanea)* worldly-minded.
mun·dial I. adj. *(del mundo)* world <*guerra m.* world war>; *(universal)* worldwide, universal **II.** m. world championship <*m. de fútbol* world soccer championship>.
mun·do m. *(universo)* world; *(tierra)* earth; *(género humano)* world, society; *(agrupación)* world <*el m. de las artes* the art world> ♦ **correr el m.** to travel far and wide • **desde que el m. es m.** since time began • **echar al m.** to bring into the world, bring forth • **echarse al m.** to enter the life of prostitution • **irse al otro m.** to pass away • **medio m.** COLL. crowd of people, multitude • **no ser del otro m.** COLL. to be no big deal • **tener m.** to know one's way around • **todo el m.** everyone, everybody • **venir al m.** to come into the world, be born • **ver m.** to travel, see the world.
mu·ni·ción f. *(pertrechos)* ammunition, munitions; *(bastimentos)* provisions, rations.
mu·ni·cio·nar tr. *(con armas)* to munition, supply with munitions; *(con bastimentos)* to provision, provide with food or rations.
mu·ni·ci·pal adj. municipal.
mu·ni·ci·pa·li·dad f. municipality.
mu·ni·ci·pio m. *(ayuntamiento)* town council,

municipality; *(pueblo)* township, district.
mu·ni·fi·cen·cia f. munificence, generosity.
mu·ni·fi·cen·te adj. munificent, generous.
mu·ñe·ca f. wrist; *(juguete)* doll; *(maniquí)* mannequin; COLL. *(presumida)* conceited girl; *(muchacha bonita)* doll, pretty girl ♦ **m. de trapo** rag doll.
mu·ñe·co m. *(juguete)* doll; *(marioneta)* puppet.
mu·ñón m. stump.
mu·ral I. adj. & m. mural.
mu·ra·lis·ta I. adj. mural **II.** m.f. muralist.
mu·ra·lla f. wall, rampart.
mur·cie·la·go m. bat.
mu·rie·ra, rió see **morir**.
mur·mu·llo m. *(ruido sordo)* murmur, murmuring; *(de la gente)* murmur; *(del agua)* babbling, gurgle; *(del viento)* sighing, sigh; *(de las hojas)* rustling, rustle; *(queja)* grumble, complaint.
mur·mu·ra·ción f. gossip.
mur·mu·ra·dor, ra I. adj. *(murmurante)* murmuring; *(chismoso)* gossiping **II.** m.f. gossip.
mur·mu·rar intr. to murmur; *(hablar quedo)* to whisper; *(agua)* to babble, gurgle; *(viento)* to sigh; *(hojas)* to rustle; *(quejar)* to grumble; COLL. *(chismear)* to gossip.
mu·ro m. *(pared)* wall; *(muralla)* rampart.
mu·sa f. muse ♦ **las musas** the liberal arts.
mus·cu·lar adj. muscular.
mus·cu·la·tu·ra f. musculature.
mús·cu·lo m. muscle.
mus·cu·lo·so, a adj. muscular.
mu·se·o m. museum ♦ **m. de cera** wax museum.
mus·go m. moss.
mu·si·cal adj. & m. musical.
mú·si·co, a I. adj. musical **II.** m.f. *(instrumentista)* musician —f. *(arte)* music; *(papel)* sheet music; *(obra musical)* musical composition ♦ **irse con la m. a otra parte** COLL. to take one's troubles elsewhere • **m. de cámara** chamber music • **m. de fondo** background music • **m. y letra** words and music • **poner m. a** to set music to, set to music.
mu·si·co·lo·gí·a f. musicology.
mu·si·có·lo·go, a m.f. musicologist.
mu·si·tar tr. *(susurrar)* to whisper; *(murmurar)* to mumble, mutter.
mus·lo m. thigh; *(de pollo)* drumstick, leg.
mus·tiar·se reflex. to wither, become withered.
mus·tio, a adj. *(triste)* sad, gloomy; *(marchito)* withered, wilted; MEX. hypocritical.
mu·ta·bi·li·dad f. mutability.
mu·ta·ble adj. mutable.
mu·ta·ción f. mutation.
mu·ti·la·ción f. mutilation.
mu·ti·la·do, a I. adj. mutilated; *(inválido)* disabled **II.** m.f. disabled person, cripple ♦ **m. de guerra** disabled veteran.
mu·ti·lar tr. to mutilate; *(destruir)* to deface; *(acortar)* to cut up.
mu·tual I. adj. mutual **II.** f. mutual benefit society.
mu·tua·li·dad f. *(calidad)* mutuality; *(corporación)* mutual benefit society.
mu·tuo, a I. adj. mutual **II.** m. FIN., LAW loan, mutuum.
muy adv. very <*m. alto* very tall>; greatly, quite <*estoy m. satisfecho* I am quite satisfied>; *(demasiado)* too <*ella es m. joven para ocupar ese puesto* she is too young to occupy that post>; quite a, very much a <*él es m.*

hombre he is quite a man> ♦ **m. de noche** late at night • **m. señor mío** Dear Sir • **ser m. de** to be just like, be very much like <*eso es m. de ella* that is just like her> • **ser m. de su casa** COLL. to be a homebody.

N

n, N f. sixteenth letter of the Spanish alphabet.

na·bo m. *(planta)* turnip; ARCHIT. *(bolo)* newel, newel post; *(eje)* central pillar; MARIT. mast.

ná·car m. nacre, mother-of-pearl.

na·ca·ri·no/cá·re·o, a adj. nacreous.

na·cer §17 intr. *(venir al mundo)* to be born; *(salir del huevo)* to be hatched; *(germinar)* to sprout, begin to grow; *(florecer)* to bud, blossom; *(los astros)* to rise; *(brotar)* to start, start to flow; *(provenir)* to stem or originate from <*el vicio nace de la ociosidad* vice stems from idleness>; *(originar)* to originate, be conceived ♦ **al n.** at birth • **n. de pie** COLL. to be born lucky • **n. para** to be born to <*nació para cantar* he was born to sing> • **volver a n.** COLL. to have a narrow escape.

na·ci·do, a I. adj. born ♦ **bien n.** well-born, well-bred • **mal n.** ill-bred, mean • **recién n.** newborn II. m. human being ♦ **ningún n.** nobody • **todos los nacidos** everybody.

na·cien·te I. adj. *(que nace)* nascent; *(inicial)* incipient, initial; *(reciente)* recent, growing <*la n. curiosidad* the growing curiosity>; rising <*el sol n.* the rising sun> II. m. Orient, East.

na·ci·mien·to m. birth; *(de pájaros)* hatching; *(de ríos)* source; *(manantial)* spring; *(linaje)* descent, origin; *(natividad)* crèche, Nativity scene ♦ **dar n. a** to give rise to • **de n.** from birth • **por n.** by birth.

na·ción f. nation; *(pueblo)* country, people.

na·cio·nal adj. national, domestic.

na·cio·na·li·dad f. nationality, citizenship ♦ **doble n.** dual citizenship.

na·cio·na·lis·ta adj. & m.f. nationalist.

na·cio·na·li·za·ción f. *(expropiación)* nationalization, expropriation; *(naturalización)* naturalization.

na·cio·na·li·zar §04 tr. *(convertir en nacional)* to nationalize; *(naturalizar)* to naturalize —reflex. to become naturalized.

na·da I. pron. nothing, not anything <*no he visto n.* I have not seen anything> ♦ **antes de n.** first, before anything else • **de n.** you're welcome • **n. de no,** none <*n. de quejas* no complaints> • **n. de eso** none of that, not at all • **n. menos** no less, nothing less • **ni n.** COLL. or anything <*no iré ni n.* I will not go or anything> • **no es n.** it's nothing • **no hay n. como** there is nothing like • **por n. del mundo** not for all the world II. adv. in no way, not at all <*no es n. extraño* it's not at all strange> III. f. *(inexistencia)* nothingness, nothing; *(cosa mínima)* the slightest thing <*una n. le hace llorar* the slightest thing makes him cry>.

na·da·dor, ·ra I. adj. swimming II. m.f. swimmer.

na·dar intr. to swim ♦ **n. de espalda** or **de pecho** to do the backstroke or breaststroke • **n. en** to have an abundance of • **n. entre dos aguas** to sit on the fence, be undecided.

na·de·rí·a f. insignificant thing, trifle.

na·die I. pron. nobody, no one II. m. a no-

body ♦ **no ser n.** to be a nobody • **un don n.** a nobody, an unimportant person.

naf·ta f. naphtha; AMER. gasoline.

naf·ta·li·na f. naphthalene; COLL. *(contra la polilla)* mothballs.

nai·pe m. card, playing card ♦ **barajar los naipes** to shuffle the cards • **castillo de n.** house of cards ♦ pl. deck (of cards).

nal·ga f. buttock ♦ pl. bottom, behind.

na·na f. COLL. *(abuela)* granny; *(arrullo)* lullaby; AMER. *(niñera)* nanny.

na·ran·ja I. f. orange —m. orange (color) ♦ **media n.** COLL. better half • **n. de ombligo** navel orange • **n. tangerina, mandarina** tangerine, mandarin orange II. adj. orange.

na·ran·ja·da f. orangeade.

na·ran·jal m. orange grove.

na·ran·je·ro, a I. adj. orange II. m.f. *(vendedor)* orange seller; *(cultivador)* orange grower.

na·ran·jo m. orange tree.

nar·ci·sis·ta I. adj. narcissistic II. m.f. narcissist.

nar·có·ti·co, a adj. & m. narcotic.

nar·co·ti·zan·te adj. & m.f. narcotic.

nar·co·ti·zar §04 tr. to narcotize, drug.

nar·co·tra·fi·can·te m. drug dealer.

nar·do m. nard, spikenard.

na·ri·gu·do, a adj. large-nosed.

na·riz f. nose; *(cada orificio)* nostril; *(olfato)* sense of smell; MECH. socket (of a bolt) ♦ **estar hasta las narices** to have had it up to here, be fed up • **meter las narices en** COLL. to interfere, stick one's nose into • **n. aguileña** aquiline nose • **n. chata** pug nose • **n. respingada** or **respingona** snub nose • **no ver más allá de las narices** COLL. not to see past one's nose • **sonarse la n.** to blow one's nose • **tener de las narices** COLL. to lead around by the nose.

na·rra·ción f. *(narrativa)* narrative, account; *(acción)* narration.

na·rra·dor, ·ra I. adj. narrative II. m.f. narrator.

na·rrar tr. to narrate, relate.

na·rra·ti·vo, a I. adj. narrative II. f. *(narración)* narrative, account; *(habilidad)* narrative skill.

nar·val m. narwhal.

na·sal adj. & f. nasal.

na·ta f. *(crema)* cream; *(capa)* skim; *(lo mejor)* (the) cream, (the) best; AMER. *(de metal)* scum.

na·ta·ción f. swimming.

na·tal adj. *(relativo al nacimiento)* natal, pertaining to birth; *(nativo)* native <*ciudad n.* native city>.

na·ta·li·cio adj. & m. birthday.

na·ta·li·dad f. natality, birthrate.

na·ta·to·rio, a I. adj. swimming, bathing II. m. swimming pool.

na·ti·llas f.pl. custard.

Na·ti·vi·dad f. *(Navidad)* Christmas; *(retablo)* Nativity scene, crèche.

na·ti·vo, a I. adj. *(indígena)* native, indigenous; *(natural)* innate, inborn; MIN. native, pure II. m.f. native.

na·to, a adj. born, natural <*él es un criminal n.* he is a born criminal>.

na·tu·ra f. nature ♦ **contra n.** unnatural.

na·tu·ral I. adj. natural; *(nativo)* native, indigenous; *(innato)* innate, native; *(ilegítimo)* illegitimate <*hijo n.* illegitimate son>; MUS.

natural ♦ **al n.** naturally, without adornment II. m.f. native.

na·tu·ra·le·za f. nature ♦ **contra la n.** against nature, unnatural • **n. muerta** still life • **por n.** by nature, naturally.

na·tu·ra·li·dad f. naturalness.

na·tu·ra·li·za·ción f. naturalization.

na·tu·ra·li·zar §04 tr. (nacionalizar) to naturalize, nationalize; (aclimatar) to acclimate, adapt —reflex. to be naturalized or nationalized.

nau·fra·gar §47 intr. MARIT. to be shipwrecked, FIG. to fail, flounder.

nau·fra·gio m. MARIT. shipwreck; FIG. failure.

náu·fra·go, a adj. & m.f. shipwrecked (person).

náu·se·a f. nausea; (repugnancia) disgust ♦ **dar náuseas** to disgust, nauseate • **sentir náuseas** to feel sick.

nau·se·a·bun·do, a/se·ante adj. nauseating, sickening.

nau·se·ar intr. to feel sick, feel nauseous.

náu·ti·co, a I. adj. nautical, maritime ♦ **club n.** yacht club • **deportes náuticos** water sports II. f. navigation.

na·va·ja f. (cortaplumas) jackknife, penknife; ZOOL. razor clam ♦ **n. de afeitar** razor • **n. de resorte** switchblade.

na·val adj. naval, maritime.

na·ve f. ship, vessel; ARCHIT. nave ♦ **n. aérea** airship • **n. de guerra** battleship • **n. espacial** spaceship • **quemar las naves** to burn one's bridges.

na·ve·ga·ble adj. navigable.

na·ve·ga·ción f. navigation, sailing ♦ **n. aérea** aerial navigation • **n. costera** coastal navigation • **n. fluvial** river navigation.

na·ve·gar §47 intr. (viajar) to travel by boat, sail; MEX. to tolerate, bear —tr. to navigate, steer.

Na·vi·dad f. Christmas, Nativity ♦ **¡Feliz N.!** Merry Christmas!

na·vie·ro, a I. adj. shipping <compañía n. shipping company> II. m.f. ship owner.

na·ví·o m. ship, vessel.

ne·bli·na f. mist, fog.

ne·bli·no·so, a adj. misty, foggy.

ne·bu·lo·si·dad f. (bruma) cloudiness, haziness; FIG. vagueness.

ne·bu·lo·so, a adj. (sombrío) cloudy, nebulous; (difícil de entender) hazy, vague; ASTRON. nebular.

ne·ce·dad f. foolishness, nonsense.

ne·ce·sa·rio, a adj. necessary; (esencial) essential.

ne·ce·ser m. (de tocador) toilet case, dressing case; (estuche) kit.

ne·ce·si·dad f. necessity, need; (pobreza) need, poverty; (menester) jam, tight spot ♦ **de n.** necessarily, by necessity • **en caso de n.** if necessary • **n. extrema** extreme need, dire straits • **por n.** out of necessity.

ne·ce·si·ta·do, a I. adj. (pobre) needy, poor; (falto) in need, lacking II. m.f. needy person.

ne·ce·si·tar tr. (hacer falta) to need, want; (requerir) to require, necessitate; (deber) to have to, need to <necesitamos escribirlo we have to write it> —intr. ♦ **n. de** to need, be in need of.

ne·cio, a I. adj. (tonto) ignorant, foolish; (terco) stubborn, obstinate; ARG., P. RICO touchy II. m.f. fool ♦ **a necias** foolishly.

ne·cro·fi·lia f. necrophilia.

ne·cro·lo·gí·a f. necrology, obituary.

ne·cro·man·cia f. necromancy, black magic.

néc·tar m. nectar.

nec·ta·ri·na f. nectarine.

ne·fas·to, a adj. ominous, unlucky.

ne·frí·ti·co, a adj. nephritic, renal.

ne·fri·tis f. nephritis.

ne·ga·ble adj. deniable, refutable.

ne·ga·ción f. (negativa) negation, denial; (denegación) refusal; GRAM. negative (particle).

ne·gar §52 tr. to deny; (contradecir) to deny, refute; (rehusar) to refuse; (prohibir) to prohibit, forbid; (repudiar) to disclaim, disavow —reflex. (rehusar) to refuse; (privarse) to deny oneself.

ne·ga·ti·vi·dad f. negativity, negativeness.

ne·ga·ti·vo, a I. adj. negative II. m. PHOTOG. negative —f. (negación) negation, denial; (rechazo) refusal, denial.

ne·gli·gé m. negligee.

ne·gli·gen·cia f. (irresponsabilidad) negligence, carelessness; (descuido) neglect, disregard.

ne·gli·gen·te adj. & m.f. negligent (person).

ne·go·cia·ble adj. negotiable.

ne·go·cia·ción f. (acción) negotiation; (negocio) business deal, transaction.

ne·go·cia·do m. (departamento) department, office; (negocio) business deal, transaction; (negocio ilícito) shady deal.

ne·go·cia·dor, ra I. adj. negotiating II. m.f. negotiator.

ne·go·cian·te m.f. (comerciante) merchant, dealer; (de negocios) businessman/woman.

ne·go·ciar intr. (tratar) to negotiate, discuss; (comerciar) to deal, do business (con, en, in) —tr. to negotiate.

ne·go·cio m. (comercio) business, business concern; (trabajo) job, occupation; (transacción) transaction, deal; (utilidad) profit, return; (asunto) affair, concern; R.P. shop, store ♦ **de negocios** business <hombre de negocios businessman> • **encargado de negocios** chargé d'affaires • **n. redondo** profitable deal • **n. sucio** shady deal.

ne·gri·lla f. PRINT. boldface (type).

ne·gro, a I. adj. black; (oscuro) dark, black ♦ **n. como boca de lobo** pitch-black • **pasarlas negras** COLL. to have a hard time • **poner a alguien n.** to anger someone • **ponerse n.** (enojarse) to get angry; (broncearse) to get a tan • **ver todo n.** to be pessimistic II. m.f. (persona) Black, Negro; AMER. (querido) dear, darling —m. (color) black ♦ **en blanco y n.** in black and white • **n. de humo** lampblack —f. MUS. quarter note.

ne·gru·ra f. blackness, darkness.

ne·gruz·co, a adj. blackish, dark.

né·me·sis f. nemesis.

ne·ne, a m.f. COLL. (bebé) baby, infant; (querido) dear, darling.

ne·nú·far m. water lily.

ne·o·clá·si·co, a I. adj. neoclassic(al) II. m.f. neoclassicist.

ne·ó·fi·to, a m.f. neophyte, novice.

ne·o·lí·ti·co, a I. adj. neolithic II. m.f. neolith.

ne·o·lo·gis·mo m. neologism.

ne·ón m. neon.

ne·o·na·to m. newborn baby.

ne·po·tis·mo m. nepotism.

ner·vio m. nerve; (tendón) tendon, sinew; BOT. rib, vein ♦ pl. **crisparle los n. a alguien** to get on someone's nerves • **tener los n. de punta** to be on edge.

ner·vio·si·dad f. nervousness, agitation.

ner·vio·so, a adj. nervous; nerve <*célula n.* nerve cell> ♦ **ponerse n.** to get nervous.

ner·vo·si·dad f. nervousness.

ne·to, a adj. *(claro)* pure, simple; net <*precio n.* net price>.

neu·má·ti·co, a I. adj. pneumatic **II.** m. tire ♦ **n. de repuesto** spare tire.

neu·mo·ní·a f. pneumonia.

neu·ral·gia f. neuralgia.

neu·ro·ci·ru·ja·no, a m.f. neurosurgeon.

neu·ro·ci·ru·gí·a f. neurosurgery.

neu·ro·lo·gí·a f. neurology.

neu·ro·ló·gi·co, a adj. neurological.

neu·ró·lo·go, a m.f. neurologist.

neu·ro·na f. neuron(e).

neu·ro·sis f.inv. neurosis.

neu·ró·ti·co, a adj. & m.f. neurotic.

neu·to·nio m. newton.

neu·tral adj. & m.f. neutral.

neu·tra·li·dad f. neutrality.

neu·tra·li·za·ción f. neutralization.

neu·tra·li·zan·te I. adj. neutralizing **II.** m.f. neutralizer.

neu·tra·li·zar §04 tr. to neutralize —reflex. to be neutralized.

neu·tro, a I. adj. *(indiferente)* neutral; BIOL. neuter, sexless; GRAM. *(género)* neuter; *(verbos)* intransitive; CHEM., ELEC. neutral **II.** m. GRAM. neuter.

neu·trón m. neutron.

ne·va·do, a I. adj. snowy, snow-covered; FIG. snow-white **II.** f. snowfall.

ne·var §49 intr. to snow —tr. to whiten, make white.

ne·ve·ra f. refrigerator, icebox.

ne·vis·ca f. light snowfall, snow flurry.

ne·vis·car §70 tr. to snow lightly.

ne·xo m. nexus, link ♦ **sin n.** unrelated.

ni conj. neither, nor <*no tomo ni fumo* I neither drink nor smoke>; not even <*ni (siquiera)me hablaron* they did not even speak to me> ♦ **ni que** not even if.

ni·co·ti·na f. nicotine.

ni·cho m. *(en la pared)* niche, recess; *(tumba)* tomb, vault.

ni·da·da f. *(de huevos)* nestful (of eggs); *(de pájaros)* brood.

ni·dal m. *(nido)* nest; *(huevo)* nest egg; *(lugar frecuentado)* hangout, haunt.

ni·do m. nest; *(morada)* abode, home; *(guarida)* den, lair; *(centro)* center, hotbed <*n. de discordia*s a hotbed of controversy> ♦ **caerse del n.** COLL. to be extremely gullible • **patearle el n.** a R.P. to pull the rug out from under.

nie·bla f. *(bruma)* fog, mist; *(nube)* cloud.

nie·go, gue see **negar.**

nie·to, a m.f. grandchild, grandson/daughter ♦ pl. grandchildren.

nie·va see **nevar.**

nie·ve f. snow; *(blancura)* whiteness ♦ **a punto de n.** stiff.

ni·gro·man·cia f. necromancy, black magic.

ni·gro·man·te m.f. necromancer.

ni·hi·lis·ta I. adj. nihilistic **II.** m.f. nihilist.

ni·lón m. nylon.

nim·bo m. *(aureola)* halo; METEOROL. nimbus.

ni·mie·dad f. trifle, trivial detail.

ni·mio, a adj. trivial, insignificant.

nin·fa f. nymph; ZOOL. nymph, pupa.

nin·fe·a f. water lily.

nin·fo m. COLL. fop, dandy.

nin·fó·ma·na f. nymphomaniac.

nin·fo·ma·ní·a f. nymphomania.

nin·gún adj. contr. of **ninguno.**

nin·gu·no, a I. adj. none, no, not any <*no tengo n. opinión* I have no opinion> ♦ **de n. manera** or **de ningún modo** in no way, by no means • **en n. parte** nowhere **II.** pron. none, not any <*no quiero n. de ellos* I do not want any of them>; *(nadie)* no one, nobody.

ni·ña f. see **niño.**

ni·ñe·rí·a f. childish act; FIG. trifle.

ni·ñe·ro, a I. adj. fond of children **II.** f. nursemaid, babysitter.

ni·ñez f. *(infancia)* childhood; *(principio)* infancy, beginning.

ni·ño, a I. adj. *(joven)* young, childlike; *(impulsivo)* immature, childish; *(inexperto)* inexperienced **II.** m.f. *(muchacho)* child; S. AMER. master (used by servants); CHILE scoundrel —m. boy ♦ **de n.** as a child • **desde n.** from childhood • **n. explorador** Boy Scout • **n. prodigio** child prodigy ♦ pl. children —f. *(muchacha)* girl; *(del ojo)* pupil (of the eye).

ní·quel m. nickel; AMER. coin.

ni·que·lar tr. to nickel, nickel-plate.

ni·ti·dez f. *(claridad)* clarity; *(de fotos)* sharpness.

ní·ti·do, a adj. *(claro)* clear; *(de fotos)* sharp.

ni·tra·to m. nitrate ♦ **n. de potasio** potassium nitrate • **n. de sodio** sodium nitrate.

ní·tri·co, a adj. nitric.

ni·tri·to m. nitrite.

ni·tró·ge·no m. nitrogen.

ni·tro·gli·ce·ri·na f. nitroglycerin.

ni·vel m. *(altura)* level, height; *(grado)* level, standard <*n. cultural* cultural level> ♦ **a n.** level • **de alto n.** high-level • **n. de agua** water level • **n. de vida** standard of living • **n. del mar** sea level • **paso a n.** railroad crossing.

ni·ve·lar tr. *(igualar)* to make level; SURV. to survey, grade; *(equilibrar)* to balance.

no I. adv. no <*¿puedes verlo?* no can you see it? no>; not <*n. vengo* I'm not coming>; non <*no intervención* nonintervention> ♦ **¿a qué no?** COLL. do you want to bet? • **¿cómo no?** of course, why not? • **no bien** no sooner • **no más** no more, only; AMER., COLL. feel free to <*continúe no más* feel free to continue> • **no obstante** nevertheless, notwithstanding • **no sea que** in case, lest **II.** m. no <*un no definitivo* a definite no>.

no·ble I. adj. *(aristocrático)* noble, aristocratic; *(elevado)* noble, honorable **II.** m.f. nobleman/woman.

no·ble·za f. *(aristocracia)* nobility, aristocracy; *(honradez)* nobleness, gentility.

no·ción f. notion, idea.

no·ci·vi·dad f. noxiousness, harmfulness.

no·ci·vo, a adj. noxious, harmful.

noc·tám·bu·lo, a I. adj. night-wandering **II.** m.f. night owl.

noc·tur·nal adj. nocturnal.

noc·tur·no, a I. adj. nocturnal, nightly; *(triste)* sad, melancholy **II.** m. RELIG. nocturn; MUS. nocturne.

no·che f. *(anochecer)* night, evening; *(oscuridad)* darkness ♦ **a primera n.** at nightfall, just after dark • **buenas noches** good evening, good night • **cerrar la n.** to become completely dark • **de la n. a la mañana** suddenly, overnight • **de n.** *(por la noche)* at night; evening, night <*traje de n.* evening gown> • hacer n. to spend the night • esta n. tonight • hacerse de n. to grow dark • n. cerrada dark night • por la n. at night.

no·dri·za f. wet nurse.

nó·du·lo m. nodule.

no·gal m. walnut.

nó·ma·da/de l. adj. nomadic II. m.f. nomad.

nom·bra·do, a adj. (*célebre*) renowned, famous; (*sobredicho*) aforementioned.

nom·bra·mien·to m. (*acción*) naming; (*nominación*) nomination, appointment.

nom·brar tr. (*llamar*) to name, mention by name; (*nominar*) to nominate, appoint.

nom·bre m. name; GRAM. noun; (*renombre*) name, reputation ♦ de n. by name; in name only <*presidente de n.* president in name only> • en n. de in the name of, by the authority of • no tener n. to be unspeakable <*su conducta no tiene n.* his conduct is unspeakable> • n. artístico stage name; LIT. pen name • n. común or apelativo common noun • n. y apellido full name • poner n. a to name • sin n. nameless.

no·men·cla·tu·ra f. nomenclature.

no·me·ol·vi·des f.inv. forget-me-not.

nó·mi·na f. (*lista*) list, roll; COM. payroll.

no·mi·na·ción f. nomination, appointment.

no·mi·na·dor, ra l. adj. nominating II. m.f. nominator.

no·mi·nal adj. nominal, titular; COM. face <*valor n.* face value>; GRAM. nominal, substantival.

no·mi·nar tr. to nominate, appoint.

no·mi·na·ti·vo, a l. adj. personal GRAM. nominative II. m. nominative case.

non l. adj. odd, uneven II. m. MATH. odd number ♦ pl. repeated denial.

no·na·da f. trifle, nothing much.

no·na·ge·na·rio/gé·si·mo, a adj. & m.f. nonagenarian.

no·na·gé·si·mo, a adj. & m. ninetieth.

no·no, a l. adj. ninth II. m. (*noveno*) ninth; R.P., COLL. grandpa —f. grandma.

no·que·ar tr. SPORT. to knock out.

nor·des·te or no·res·te m. northeast.

no·ria f. water wheel.

nor·ma f. (*modelo*) norm; (*regla*) rule.

nor·mal l. adj. normal, standard ♦ escuela n. teachers training school II. f. GEOM. perpendicular.

nor·ma·li·dad f. normality, normalcy.

nor·ma·lis·ta m.f. student teacher.

nor·ma·li·za·ción f. normalization; INDUS. standardization.

nor·ma·li·zar §04 tr. to normalize; INDUS. to standardize.

nor·ma·ti·vo, a adj. normative.

no·ro·es·te m. northwest.

nor·te m. north; (*guía*) guide, lodestar.

nor·te·ño, a l. adj. northern II. m.f. northerner.

nór·ti·co, a adj. northern, northerly.

nos pron. us <*ellos os vieron* they saw us>; us, to us, for us, from us <*él n. vendió la casa* he sold the house to us>; one another, each other <*n. queremos* we love each other>; ourselves <*n. estamos mirando en el espejo* we are looking at ourselves in the mirror>.

no·so·tros, as pron. we <*n. lo hicimos* we did it>; us, ourselves <*no es para n.* it is not for us>.

nos·tal·gia f. nostalgia, homesickness.

nos·tál·gi·co, a adj. nostalgic, homesick.

no·ta f. (*comentario*) note, observation; (*apostilla*) note, notation; (*reparo*) notice, heed; (*calificación*) grade, mark; MUS. note ♦ dar la n. to stand out • de mala n. with a bad reputation • de n. of note, famous • forzar la n. to go too far • n. falsa wrong note.

no·ta·ble adj. (*apreciable*) notable, noteworthy; (*superior*) outstanding, striking.

no·ta·ción f. (*anotación*) note, annotation; ARTS, MATH. notation.

no·tar tr. (*indicar*) to note, point out; (*observar*) to notice, observe —reflex. to see, notice <*se nota la diferencia* one can see the difference>.

no·ta·rio, a m. notary, notary public.

no·ti·cia f. news item, piece of news ♦ pl. news • n. de última hora the latest news.

no·ti·cia·rio m. RAD. newscast; CINEM. newsreel.

no·ti·cie·ro, a l. adj. news II. m. news report.

no·ti·cio·so, a l. adj. informed, well-informed II. m. AMER. news report.

no·ti·fi·ca·ción f. notification, notice.

no·ti·fi·car §70 tr. to notify, inform.

no·to·rie·dad f. (*reputación*) notoriety; (*fama*) fame, renown.

no·to·rio, a adj. notorious, well known.

no·va·to, a COLL. l. adj. beginning II. m.f. beginner, novice.

no·ve·cien·tos, as adj. & m. nine hundred.

no·ve·dad f. (*calidad de nuevo*) newness; (*innovación*) novelty, innovation; (*cambio*) change; (*noticia*) recent event ♦ no hay n. nothing is new • sin n. (*nada nuevo*) as usual, no change; (*bien*) safely, well.

no·ve·do·so, a adj. novel, new.

no·vel adj. new, inexperienced.

no·ve·la f. novel ♦ n. policíaca detective story.

no·ve·les·co, a adj. novelesque.

no·ve·lis·ta m.f. novelist.

no·ve·no, a adj. & m. ninth —f. RELIG. novena.

no·ven·ta l. adj. ninety; (*nonagésimo*) ninetieth II. m. ninety.

no·ven·ta·vo, a adj. & m. ninetieth.

no·ven·tón, o·na adj. & m.f. nonagenarian.

no·via l. see novio, a.

no·viaz·go m. (*relaciones amorosas*) courtship; (*compromiso*) engagement, betrothal.

no·vi·cia·do m. novitiate.

no·vi·cio, a l. adj. beginning, new II. m.f. novice; (*aprendiz*) beginner, apprentice.

no·viem·bre m. November.

no·vi·llo m. young bull —f. heifer, young cow.

no·vio, a m. (*amigo*) boyfriend; (*prometido*) fiancé; (*recién casado*) groom ♦ pl. (*casados*) newlyweds; (*prometidos*) engaged couple —f. (*amiga*) girlfriend; (*prometida*) fiancée; (*recién casada*) bride.

nu·ba·rrón m. large black cloud.

nu·be f. cloud; (*sombra*) shadow; (*multitud*) swarm, multitude; (*en los ojos*) cloud, film; JEWEL. flaw ♦ estar en las nubes to have one's head in the clouds • n. de lluvia rain cloud • por las nubes sky-high.

nú·bil adj. nubile, marriageable.

nu·bi·li·dad f. nubility.

nu·bla·do, a adj. cloudy, overcast.

nu·blar tr. to cloud, darken —reflex. to become cloudy or overcast.

nu·bo·si·dad f. cloudiness.
nu·bo·so, a adj. cloudy, overcast.
nu·ca f. nape (of the neck).
nu·cle·ar adj. nuclear.
nu·clei·co, a adj. nucleic.
nú·cle·o m. nucleus; ELEC. core; BOT. kernel, pit; (esencial) core, essence.
nu·cle·ón m. nucleon.
nu·di·llo m. knuckle.
nu·dis·ta m.f. nudist.
nu·do m. (lazo) knot; ANAT. node, lump; BOT., MARIT. KNOT; (lazo) bond, tie; (enredo) crux, core <el n. de la trama the crux of the plot> ♦ **n. corredizo** slipknot, noose • **n. gordiano** Gordian knot • **tener un n. en la garganta** to have a lump in one's throat.
nu·do·so, a adj. knotty, knotted.
nue·ra f. daughter-in-law.
nues·tro, a I. adj. our, of ours <n. coche our car> II. pron. ours, of ours <el n. es rojo ours is red> ♦ **los nuestros** our people, our side.
nue·ve I. adj. nine; (noveno) ninth ♦ **las n.** nine o'clock II. m. nine.
nue·vo, a I. adj. new; (otro) new, another <compró un n. libro she bought a new book> ♦ **de n.** again • **N. Mundo** New World • **N. Testamento** New Testament • **¿qué hay de n.?** what's new? II. f. news, tidings.
nuez f. nut; (del nogal) walnut; ANAT. Adam's apple; MUS. nut ♦ **n. moscada** or **de especie** nutmeg.
nu·li·dad f. nullity; (incapacidad) inability, incompetence; (inutilidad) worthlessness; COLL. (persona) useless person.
nu·lo, a adj. null, void; (sin mérito) useless, worthless ♦ **n. y sin valor** null and void.
nu·me·ra·ción f. numeration, numbering; (números) numbers, numerals ♦ **n. arábiga, romana** Arabic, Roman numerals.
nu·me·ra·dor m. numerator.
nu·me·ral adj. numeral.
nu·me·rar tr. (foliar) to number; (contar) to count, enumerate.
nu·me·ra·rio, a I. adj. numerary II. m. cash, currency.
nu·mé·ri·co, a adj. numerical.
nú·me·ro m. number; (signo) numeral; (ejemplar) issue, copy; (medida) size; THEAT. number, act ♦ **n. arábigo** Arabic numeral • **n. atrasado** back issue • **n. cardinal** cardinal number • **n. complejo** compound number • **n. dígito** digit • **n. entero** whole number • **n. extraordinario** special edition or issue • **n. fraccionario** or **quebrado** fraction • **n. impar** odd number • **n. ordinal** ordinal number • **n. par** even number • **n. primo** prime number • **n. redondo** round number • **n. romano** Roman numeral • **n. uno** the best, the first • **sin n.** countless, numberless.
nu·me·ro·so, a adj. numerous.
nu·mis·má·ti·co, a I. adj. numismatic II. m.f. numismatist —f. numismatics.
nun·ca adv. never, not ever ♦ **más que n.** more than ever • **n. jamás** or **n. más** never again.
nup·cial adj. nuptial.
nup·cias f.pl. nuptials, wedding.
nu·tria f. otter.
nu·tri·cio, a adj. nutritious.
nu·tri·ción f. nutrition.
nu·tri·do, a adj. (alimentado) nourished, fed <bien n. well-fed>; (abundante) large, abundant <una concurrencia muy n. a large crowd>.
nu·tri·mien·to m. nourishment.
nu·trir tr. (alimentar) to nourish, feed; (fortalecer) to nurture, strengthen.
nu·tri·ti·vo, a adj. nutritious, nutritive.

Ñ

ñ, Ñ f. seventeenth letter of the Spanish alphabet.
ña·me m. yam.
ñan·dú m. American ostrich.
ña·pa f. AMER. bonus, extra ♦ **de ñ.** AMER. to boot, into the bargain.
ña·que m. odds and ends.
ña·to, a adj. AMER. snub-nosed.
ñe·que I. m. AMER. strength, vigor; C. AMER., MEX. slap, blow II. adj. AMER. strong, vigorous ♦ **hombre de ñ.** COLL. he-man.
ño·ñe·rí·a or **ño·ñez** f. foolishness, simplemindedness.
ño·ño, a adj. & m.f. COLL. (apocado) bashful (person); (soso) dull (person).
ño·que/qui m. AMER. gnocchi.
ñor·bo m. ARG., ECUAD., PERU passionflower.
ñu·do m. ARCH. knot ♦ **al ñ.** R.P. in vain.

O

o, O f. eighteenth letter of the Spanish alphabet.
o conj. or <blanco o negro black or white>; either <lo harás o de buen grado o por la fuerza you will do it, either willingly or unwillingly> ♦ **o sea** that is to say.
o·a·sis m.inv. oasis.
ob·ce·ca·da·men·te adv. blindly.
ob·ce·car §70 tr. to obfuscate, blind.
o·be·de·cer §17 tr. to obey —intr. to obey ♦ **o. a** (responder a) to respond to <esta enfermedad obedece al tratamiento this illness responds to treatment>; (deberse a) to be due to, arise from <su ausencia obedece a varias circunstancias his absence is due to a number of circumstances>.
o·be·dien·cia f. obedience.
o·be·dien·te adj. obedient.
o·be·lis·co m. obelisk.
o·ber·tu·ra f. overture.
o·be·si·dad f. obesity.
o·be·so, a adj. obese.
ó·bi·ce m. obstacle, impediment.
o·bis·po m. bishop.
ob·je·ción f. objection ♦ **hacer** or **levantar una o.** to object, raise an objection.
ob·je·ta·ble adj. objectionable.
ob·je·tar tr. to object to, raise objections to ♦ **no tener nada que o.** to have no objection or objections.
ob·je·ti·var tr. to objectify.
ob·je·ti·vi·dad f. objectivity.
ob·je·ti·vis·mo m. objectivism.
ob·je·ti·vo, a adj. & m. objective.
ob·je·to m. object; (tema) subject, theme; (fin) aim; GRAM. object ♦ **carecer de o.** to be useless • **con o. de** in order to • **¿con qué o.?** to what end? • **ser o. de** to be the object of • **tener por o.** to be one's aim.

o·ble·a f. wafer; PHARM. capsule.

o·bli·cuo, a adj. *(inclinado)* oblique, slanting; ANAT., GEOM. oblique.

o·bli·ga·ción f. obligation; *(responsabilidad)* responsibility; *(deber)* duty; FIN. bond ♦ **o. colectiva** joint obligation • **o. implícita** implied obligation ♦ pl. family obligations • **faltar a sus o.** to fail in one's duties.

o·bli·gar §47 tr. *(imponer)* to oblige, obligate; *(compeler)* to force, compel; *(favorecer)* to oblige, favor <*nos obligó con su presencia he favored us with his presence*> —reflex. to obligate oneself.

o·bli·ga·to·rie·dad f. compulsoriness.

o·bli·ga·to·rio, a adj. obligatory, compulsory.

o·blon·go, a adj. oblong.

o·bo·e m. MUS. oboe; *(músico)* oboist.

o·bra f. work; *(acto)* act <*una o. de misericordia* an act of mercy>; *(labor)* workmanship; *(construcción)* construction site ♦ **de o.** in deed • **¡manos a la o.!** let's get to work! • **o. de caridad** charitable deed • **o. maestra** masterpiece • **obras públicas** public works • **por o. de** thanks to.

o·brar tr. to work —intr. to act, proceed ♦ **o. en** to be in <*la carta obra en manos de Juan* the letter is in John's hands>.

o·bre·ro, a I. adj. working *<clase o.* working class> ♦ **sindicato o.** labor union II. m.f. *(trabajador)* worker; *(jornalero)* laborer ♦ **o. portuario** dockworker.

obs·ce·ni·dad f. obscenity.

obs·ce·no, a adj. obscene.

obs·cu·ro, a adj. var. of **oscuro, a.**

obs·cu·ri·dad f. var. of **oscuridad.**

ob·se·quiar tr. *(regalos)* to give as a gift; *(agasajar)* to entertain.

ob·se·quio m. *(regalo)* gift, present; *(agasajo)* attention, kindness ♦ **deshacerse en obsequios (con alguien)** to lavish attention (on someone) • **en o. de** in honor of, for the sake of.

ob·se·quio·so, a adj. *(cortés)* obliging, attentive; *(servil)* obsequious, deferential; MEX. fond of giving gifts.

ob·ser·va·ción f. observation; *(nota aclaratoria)* observation, explanatory note or remark; *(objeción)* objection ♦ **en** or **bajo o.** under observation • **hacer una o.** to make a remark.

ob·ser·va·dor, ·ra I. adj. observant, observing II. m.f. observer ♦ **o. de pájaros** birdwatcher.

ob·ser·van·cia f. observance.

ob·ser·var tr. to observe; *(cumplir)* to obey; *(espiar)* to watch; *(notar)* to notice; *(comentar)* to remark.

ob·ser·va·to·rio m. observatory.

ob·se·sión f. obsession.

ob·se·sio·nan·te adj. obsessive.

ob·se·sio·nar tr. to obsess.

ob·se·si·vo, a adj. obsessive.

ob·se·so, a adj. & m.f. obsessive.

ob·so·le·to, a adj. obsolete.

obs·ta·cu·li·zar §04 tr. to obstruct, hinder.

obs·tá·cu·lo m. obstacle ♦ **carrera de obstáculos** steeplechase, obstacle course • **poner obstáculos** *(impedir)* to obstruct, hinder; *(objetar)* to object.

obs·tan·te adj. obstructing ♦ **no o.** nevertheless, however.

obs·tar intr. *(impedir)* to obstruct, hinder; *(oponerse una cosa a otra)* to stand in the way of.

obs·té·tri·co, a adj. obstetric(al).

obs·ti·na·ción f. obstinacy.

obs·ti·na·do, a adj. obstinate.

obs·ti·nar·se reflex. to be or become obstinate.

obs·truc·ción f. obstruction.

obs·truc·cio·nis·ta I. m.f. obstructionist II. adj. obstructionist(ic).

obs·truir §18 tr. to obstruct.

ob·ten·ción f. obtaining.

ob·te·ner §69 tr. *(conseguir)* to obtain, get; *(conservar)* to have, keep.

ob·tu·ra·dor, a I. adj. obturating, plugging II. m. *(tapón)* plug, stopper; PHOTOG. shutter ♦ **o. de plano focal** focal plane shutter.

ob·tu·rar tr. to obturate, stop up.

ob·tu·so, a adj. obtuse.

ob·tu·vie·ra, vo see **obtener.**

ob·viar tr. to obviate, prevent —intr. to stand in the way.

ob·vio, a adj. obvious.

o·ca·sión f. occasion; *(oportunidad)* opportunity; *(motivo)* reason, cause; *(tiempo)* time <*en aquella o.* at that time>; *(circunstancia)* circumstance; AMER. bargain ♦ **aprovechar una o.** to take advantage of an opportunity • **con o. de** on the occasion of • **de o.** *(de segunda mano)* secondhand; *(de precio reducido)* bargain • **dar o. a** to give rise to • **en cierta o.** once, on a certain occasion • **en la primera o.** at the first opportunity • **en ocasiones** sometimes.

o·ca·sio·nal adj. occasional; *(fortuito)* chance.

o·ca·sio·nar tr. *(causar)* to occasion, cause; *(provocar)* to stir up, provoke.

o·ca·so m. *(del sol)* sunset, sundown; *(de un astro)* setting; *(occidente)* occident, west; *(decadencia)* decline.

oc·ci·den·tal I. adj. western, occidental II. m.f. westerner, occidental.

oc·ci·den·te m. west, occident.

oc·ci·pi·tal adj. & m. occipital (bone).

o·cé·a·no m. ocean; FIG. ocean, sea.

o·ce·a·no·gra·fí·a f. oceanography.

o·ce·a·no·grá·fi·co, a adj. oceanographic.

o·cio m. *(inactividad)* idleness, inactivity; *(tiempo libre)* leisure, free time.

o·cio·si·dad f. idleness ♦ **la o. es la madre de todos los vicios** idleness is the root of all evil.

o·cio·so, a I. adj. idle II. m.f. idler, loafer.

o·cre m. ocher, ochre.

oc·ta·vo, a adj. & m. eighth —f. MUS. octave.

oc·te·to m. octet.

oc·to·ge·na·rio, a adj. & m.f. octogenarian.

oc·to·gé·si·mo, a adj. & m. eightieth.

oc·to·go·nal adj. octagonal.

oc·tó·go·no, a I. adj. octagonal II. m. octagon.

oc·tu·bre m. October.

o·cu·lar I. adj. ocular, pertaining to the eye II. m. eyepiece, ocular.

o·cu·lis·ta m.f. oculist.

o·cul·ta·men·te adv. stealthily, secretly.

o·cul·tar tr. *(esconder)* to hide, conceal *(de from)*; *(callar)* to hush, silence; *(disfrazar)* to disguise.

o·cul·tis·mo m. occultism.

o·cul·to, a adj. *(escondido)* hidden, concealed; *(sobrenatural)* occult ♦ **en o.** secretly.

o·cu·pa·ción f. occupation; *(empleo)* profession, trade; *(trabajo)* daily activities or routine.

o·cu·pa·do, a adj. *(teléfono, línea)* engaged, busy; *(ciudad, territorio)* occupied; *(seat)* taken <*¿está o. este asiento?* is this seat taken?>.

o·cu·pan·te I. adj. occupying II. m.f. occupant.

o·cu·par tr. (*apoderarse*) to occupy, take possession of; (*llenar*) to occupy, fill; (*habitar*) to occupy, live in; to hold, fill <ocupó el puesto de ministro he held the post of minister>; (*emplear*) to employ, give work to; (*encargar*) to occupy, keep busy —reflex. (*emplearse*) to occupy oneself; (*interesarse*) to concern oneself; (*atender a*) to attend, pay attention (*de* to).

o·cu·rren·cia f. (*ocasión*) occurrence, event; (*chiste*) witticism ♦ ¡qué o.! what a thought! • tener ocurrencias to be witty.

o·cu·rren·te adj. witty, funny.

o·cu·rrir intr. (*suceder*) to occur, happen; (*acudir*) to go to, show up for ♦ ¿qué ocurre? what's the matter? —reflex. to occur to, strike <se me ocurrió que estaba en peligro it occured to me that I was in danger>.

o·chen·ta adj. & m. eighty.

o·chen·ta·vo o adj. & m. eightieth.

o·chen·tón, o·na adj. & m.f. COLL. octogenarian.

o·cho I. adj. eight; (*octavo*) eighth ♦ las o. eight o'clock • o. días a week II. m. eight.

o·cho·cien·tos, as adj. & m. eight hundred.

o·da f. ode.

o·da·lis·ca f. odalisque.

o·diar tr. to hate, loathe.

o·dio m. hatred, loathing.

o·dio·so, a adj. odious.

o·di·se·a f. odyssey.

o·don·to·lo·gí·a f. odontology, dentistry.

o·don·tó·lo·go, a m.f. odontologist, dentist.

o·dre m. wineskin.

o·es·te m. west.

o·fen·der tr. (*injuriar*) to offend, insult; (*dañar*) to hurt, injure —intr. to be offensive —reflex. to take offense.

o·fen·sa f. offense.

o·fen·si·vo, a adj. & f. offensive.

o·fen·sor, ·ra I. adj. offending II. m.f. offender.

o·fer·ta f. (*propuesta*) offer, proposal; COM. bid, tender ♦ o. en firme firm offer • o. y demanda supply and demand.

o·fer·tar tr. to tender; AMER. to offer.

o·fi·cial I. adj. official II. m. (*funcionario*) official, officer; (*obrero*) skilled worker; MIL. officer ♦ o. de guardia officer of the watch • o. del día officer of the day • o. mayor chief clerk • primer o. MARIT. first mate.

o·fi·cia·li·dad f. officer corps, officers; (*carácter oficial*) official character.

o·fi·cia·li·zar §04 tr. to make official.

o·fi·cian·te m. officiant.

o·fi·ciar tr. RELIG. to celebrate; (*comunicar*) to communicate officially —intr. RELIG. to officiate ♦ o. de to act as.

o·fi·ci·na f. office; (*de farmacia*) laboratory ♦ horas de o. business hours • o. de colocación employment agency.

o·fi·ci·nis·ta m.f. clerk, office worker.

o·fi·cio m. (*ocupación*) labor, work; (*empleo*) office, post; (*artesanía*) trade, craft; (*función*) function, role; (*comunicación*) communiqué, official notice; RELIG. office, service ♦ artes y oficios arts and crafts • buenos oficios good offices • de o. (*oficialmente*) ex officio, officially; (*de profesión*) by trade • gajes del o. occupational hazards • Santo O. Holy Office, Inquisition.

o·fi·cio·sa·men·te adv. (*con diligencia*) dili-

gently; (*con complacencia*) obligingly; (*con entremetimiento*) officiously.

o·fi·cio·so, a adj. (*laborioso*) hard-working, diligent; (*solícito*) solicitous, obliging; (*importuno*) officious, meddlesome.

o·fre·cer §17 tr. to offer; COM. to offer, bid; RELIG. to offer up, dedicate —reflex. to offer oneself, volunteer.

o·fre·ci·mien·to m. offer, offering.

o·fren·da f. offering, gift.

o·fren·dar tr. to make an offering.

of·tal·mo·lo·gí·a f. ophthalmology.

of·tal·mó·lo·go m. ophthalmologist.

o·fus·ca·ción f./**mien·to** m. (*acción*) blinding, dazzling; (*confusión*) confusion, bewilderment.

o·fus·car §70 tr. (*cegar*) to blind, dazzle; (*confundir*) to confuse, bewilder.

o·gro m. ogre.

¡oh! interj. oh!

oh·mio or **ohm** m. ohm.

o·í·do I. see oír II. m. (*sentido*) hearing, sense of hearing; ANAT. ear <o. interno inner ear>; MUS. ear <ella tiene buen o. she has a good ear> ♦ abrir los oídos to listen attentively • aguzar el o. to prick up one's ears • al o. confidentially • caer en oídos sordos to fall on deaf ears • cerrar los oídos a to turn a deaf ear to • dar oídos a (*escuchar*) to listen to; (*dar crédito a*) to believe, credit • de o. by ear • duro de o. hard of hearing • prestar oídos a to lend an ear to • ser todo oídos to be all ears.

o·ír §45 tr. (*escuchar*) to hear; (*atender*) to listen to, pay attention to; (*entender*) to understand; (*asistir*) to attend ♦ o. bien to listen well • o. hablar de to hear about • ¡oye! or ¡oiga! (*para llamar la atención*) listen!; (*para reprender*) look here!

o·jal m. (*en la ropa*) buttonhole; (*agujero*) hole.

¡o·ja·lá! interj. would to God!, I hope that.

o·je·a·da f. glance, glimpse.

o·je·ar tr. (*mirar*) to eye, look at; (*aojar*) to cast the evil eye on.

o·je·ra f. dark circle or ring (under the eyes).

o·je·ri·za f. animosity, grudge.

o·je·ro·so/ru·do, a adj. having dark circles under the eyes, haggard.

o·je·te m. SEW. eyelet, drawstring hole.

o·jo m. eye; (*ojo de la cerradura* keyhole>; (*de un puente*) span, arch; (*malla*) mesh; (*atención*) attention <pon o. en lo que haces pay attention to what you are doing>; (*aptitud*) eye <él tiene buen o. he has a good eye> ♦ abrir los ojos to be on the alert, keep one's eyes open • a o. or a o. de buen cubero roughly, by a rough estimate • a ojos cerrados blindly, with one's eyes closed • a ojos vistas visibly, openly • cerrar los ojos COLL. (*dormir*) to sleep; (*morir*) to die • clavar los ojos en to stare at • comerse con los ojos COLL. to devour with one's eyes • con mucho o. very carefully • costar un o. de la cara COLL. to cost an arm and a leg • cuatro ojos DEROG. four-eyes • dichosos los ojos que te ven COLL. you're a sight for sore eyes • echar un o. a to have one's eye on • en un abrir y cerrar de ojos COLL. in the twinkling of an eye • írsele los ojos por or tras not to be able to keep one's eyes off of • mirar con buenos, malos ojos to look favorably, unfavorably on • ¡mucho o.! be careful! • no pegar o. not to sleep a wink • no quitar los ojos de not to take one's eyes off of • ¡ojo! look out!, watch out! • o. avizor eagle eye • o.

de buey *(ventana)* bull's eye; MARIT. porthole • **o. de la tempestad** eye of the storm • **o. de vidrio** glass eye • **o. morado** black eye • **o. por o.** an eye for an eye • **ojos rasgados** slanted eyes • **ojos reventones** *or* **saltones** popeyes, bulging eyes • **tener entre ojos** to have a grudge against.

o·jo·ta f. AMER. sandal.

o·la f. wave ✦ **o. de frío** cold spell.

o·le·a·da f. *(embate de ola)* beating of waves; *(movimiento)* wave, surge <*una o. de gente* a surge of people>; *(cantidad)* wave, large number <*una o. de protestas* a wave of protests>.

o·le·a·gi·no·so, a adj. oily, oleaginous.

o·le·a·je m. *(olas)* surf, waves; *(marejada)* swell.

ó·le·o m. oil ✦ **pintura al ó.** oil painting.

o·le·o·duc·to m. oil pipeline.

o·le·o·mar·ga·ri·na f. oleomargarine.

o·ler §46 tr. *(olfatear)* to smell; *(averiguar)* to smell out, uncover; *(inquirir)* to nose or pry into —intr. *(tener olor)* to smell; *(parecer)* to smell of or like ✦ **no o. bien** to smell fishy.

ol·fa·te·ar tr. *(oler)* to sniff; COLL. *(descubrir)* to get wind of; *(curiosear)* to pry into.

ol·fa·to m. *(sentido)* sense of smell; *(intuición)* intuition; *(instinto)* instinct ✦ **tener o. para los negocios** to have a good nose for business.

ol·fa·to·rio, a adj. olfactory.

o·li·gar·ca m. oligarch.

o·li·gar·quí·a f. oligarchy.

o·li·gár·qui·co, a adj. oligarchic.

o·lim·pia·da/pí·a·da f. Olympic games.

o·lím·pi·co, a adj. Olympian, Olympic ✦ **juegos olímpicos** Olympic games.

o·li·va adj. & f. olive.

o·li·var m. olive grove.

o·li·va·re·ro, a adj. olive-growing <*región o.* olive-growing region>; olive <*industria o.* olive industry>.

o·li·vo m. olive tree; *(color)* olive.

ol·mo m. elm (tree) ✦ **pedir peras al o.** to ask for the moon.

o·ló·gra·fo, a I. adj. holographic II. m. holograph.

o·lor m. *(sensación)* smell; *(perfume)* smell, odor ✦ **tener o.** a to smell of.

o·lo·ro·so, a adj. perfumed, fragrant.

ol·vi·da·di·zo, a adj. *(desmemoriado)* forgetful, absent-minded; *(ingrato)* ungrateful ✦ **hacerse el o.** to pretend to forget.

ol·vi·da·do, a adj. *(desconocido)* forgotten; *(olvidadizo)* forgetful, absent-minded; *(ingrato)* ungrateful.

ol·vi·dar tr. & reflex. *(no recordar)* to forget; *(dejar)* to leave (behind) <*me olvidé los libros* I left the books behind>; *(omitir)* to leave out or off <*olvidaron incluir su nombre en el registro* they left his name off the register>; *(descuidar)* to neglect ✦ **olvidarse de** to forget to.

ol·vi·do m. *(desmemoria)* forgetfulness; *(estado)* oblivion <*los planes cayeron en el o.* the plans fell into oblivion> ✦ **echar al** or **en o.** to forget • **enterrar en el o.** to cast into oblivion.

o·lla f. *(vasija)* pot, kettle; *(cocido)* stew ✦ **o. de presión** pressure cooker.

om·bli·go m. navel.

om·bli·gue·ro m. bellyband (for infants).

o·mi·sión f. omission.

o·mi·so, a adj. neglectful, careless.

o·mi·tir tr. to omit.

óm·ni·bus m. omnibus, bus.

om·ni·po·ten·cia f. omnipotence.

om·ni·po·ten·te adj. omnipotent.

om·ni·sa·pien·te adj. omniscient.

o·mó·pla·to m. shoulder blade.

o·na·nis·mo m. onanism.

on·ce I. adj. eleven; *(undécimo)* eleventh ✦ **las o.** eleven o'clock II. m. eleven.

on·ce·no, a adj. eleventh.

on·co·lo·gí·a f. oncology.

on·da f. wave ✦ **estar en la o.** COLL. to be with it.

on·de·a·do, a adj. wavy.

on·de·ar intr. *(agua)* to ripple; *(ondular)* to wave, flutter.

on·du·la·ción f. *(movimiento)* undulation; *(sinuosidad)* winding; *(del cabello)* wave.

on·du·la·do, a adj. wavy.

on·du·lar tr. to wave —intr. to undulate.

o·ne·ro·so, a adj. onerous.

ó·nix f. onyx.

o·no·más·ti·co, a adj. onomastic ✦ **fiesta** or **día o.** saint's day.

o·no·ma·to·pe·ya f. onomatopoeia.

o·no·ma·to·pé·yi·co, a adj. onomatopoeic.

on·za f. ounce.

on·za·vo adj. & m. eleventh.

o·pa AMER. I. adj. stupid, foolish II. m.f. COLL. fool, dolt.

o·pa·ci·dad f. opacity, opaqueness.

o·pa·co, a adj. opaque.

ó·pa·lo m. opal.

op·ción f. option, choice.

op·cio·nal adj. optional.

ó·pe·ra f. opera ✦ **o. bufa** comic opera.

o·pe·ra·ción f. operation; FIN. transaction ✦ **o. cesárea** Caesarean section.

o·pe·ra·dor, ·ra I. adj. operating II. m.f. MECH. operator m. CINEM. cameraman.

o·pe·ran·te adj. operating, working <*capital o.* working capital>.

o·pe·rar intr. to operate; COM. to deal, do business —tr. to operate on.

o·pe·ra·rio, a m.f. operator, worker.

o·pe·ra·ti·vo, a adj. operative.

o·pi·nar intr. *(formar opinión)* to think, have an opinion; *(expresar la opinión)* to express an opinion ✦ **o. en** or **sobre** to give an opinion on.

o·pi·nión f. opinion.

o·pio m. opium.

o·pió·ma·no m. opium addict.

o·pí·pa·ro, a adj. sumptuous, magnificent.

o·po·ner §54 tr. *(contraponer)* to set up or put against; *(poner enfrente)* to oppose, put opposite —reflex. *(objetar)* to oppose, object to; *(ser contrario)* to be in opposition to, be contrary <*sus ideas nunca se oponen a las mías* his ideas are never contrary to mine>.

o·por·to m. port (wine).

o·por·tu·na·men·te adv. opportunely, conveniently.

o·por·tu·ni·dad f. *(ocasión)* opportunity, chance; *(de una medida)* appropriateness.

o·por·tu·nis·ta adj. & m.f. opportunist.

o·por·tu·no, a adj. *(conveniente)* opportune, timely; *(apropiado)* suitable, fitting; *(ocurrente)* witty II. m.f. witty person.

o·po·si·ción f. opposition.

o·po·si·tor, ·ra m.f. opponent.

o·pre·sión f. oppression ✦ **o. del pecho** tightness in the chest.

o·pre·si·vo, a adj. oppressive.

o·pre·so, a I. see **oprimir** II. adj. oppressed.

o·pre·sor, ·ra I. adj. oppressive, tyrannical II. m.f. oppressor, tyrant.

o·pri·mi·do, a adj. oppressed ♦ **tener el cora-zón o.** to be sick at heart.

o·pri·mir tr. *(tiranizar)* to oppress, tyrannize; *(apretar)* to press, squeeze.

o·pro·biar tr. to vilify, defame.

o·pro·bio m. shame, disgrace.

o·pro·bio·so, a adj. shameful, disgraceful.

op·tar tr. to choose, select.

op·ta·ti·vo, a I. adj. *(facultativo)* optional; GRAM. optative II. m. GRAM. optative.

óp·ti·co, a I. adj. optical II. m. optician —f. PHYS. optics.

op·ti·mis·ta I. adj. optimistic II. m.f. optimist.

óp·ti·mo, a adj. optimal, best.

op·tó·me·tra m.f. optometrist.

op·to·me·trí·a f. optometry.

o·pues·to, a I. see **oponer** II. adj. *(enfrente)* opposite; *(contrario)* opposing, contrary.

o·pu·len·cia f. opulence.

o·pu·len·to, a adj. opulent.

o·pu·sie·ra, so see **oponer.**

o·ra conj. *(ahora)* now <o. de este lado, o. del otro lado now this way, now the other way>; *(o bien)* either <o. de día, o. de noche either by day or by night>.

o·ra·ción f. *(discurso)* speech, oration; RELIG. prayer; GRAM. *(frase)* sentence; *(cláusula)* clause ♦ **o. adjetiva** adjectival clause • **o. adverbial** adverbial clause • **o. compuesta** or **coordinada** compound or complex sentence • **o. sustantiva** noun clause.

o·rá·cu·lo m. oracle.

o·ra·dor, ·ra m.f. orator.

o·ral adj. oral.

o·ran·gu·tán m. orangutan.

o·rar intr. *(hablar)* to speak, make a speech; *(rezar)* to pray.

o·ra·to·rio, a I. adj. oratory, oratorical II. m. *(capilla)* oratory, chapel; MUS. oratorio —f. oratory, rhetoric.

or·be m. *(esfera)* orb, sphere; *(mundo)* world.

ór·bi·ta f. orbit; *(esfera)* sphere, field.

or·den m. *(disposición)* order <o. cronológico chronological order>; *(sistema)* method, system; *(paz)* order, peace <el o. público public order>; *(categoría)* nature, character <asuntos de o. filosófico matters of a philosophical nature>; ARCHIT., BIOL. order ♦ **de primer o.** of the first order, first-rate • **en o.** in order • **llamar al o.** to call to order • **o. de antigüedad** seniority • **o. del día** agenda • **poner en o.** to put in order • **por o.** in its turn —f. order ♦ **a la o. de** at the order of • **a sus órdenes** at your service • **o. de arresto** arrest warrant • **o. del día** MIL. order of the day • **o. de registro** search warrant • **o. judicial** court order.

or·de·na·ción f. *(orden)* arrangement; *(acción)* ordering, arranging; RELIG. ordination.

or·de·na·da f. ordinate.

or·de·na·do, a adj. orderly, methodical.

or·de·na·dor, ·ra I. adj. ordering, arranging II. m. or f. computer.

or·de·nan·za f. regulation, ordinance —m. MIL. orderly; *(empleado)* messenger.

or·de·nar tr. *(organizar)* to order, put in order; *(arreglar)* to arrange; *(mandar)* to order, command; *(dirigir)* to direct; RELIG. to ordain —reflex. RELIG. to be ordained.

or·de·ña·dor, ·ra I. adj. milking II. m.f. milker —f. milking machine.

or·de·ñar tr. to milk.

or·di·nal adj. ordinal.

or·di·na·riez f. COLL. vulgarity, commonness.

or·di·na·rio, a adj. *(común)* ordinary, common; *(inculto)* coarse, uncouth; *(mediocre)* ordinary, mediocre; *(diario)* daily.

o·re·ar tr. to air, ventilate —reflex. to get some air, take a walk.

o·re·ja f. ear; *(parte lateral)* flap; *(asa)* handle; MECH. lug, flange ♦ **aguzar las orejas** to prick up one's ears • **con las orejas caídas** or **gachas** crestfallen • **mojarle la o. a alguien** —tr. COLL. to pick a fight with someone.

o·re·je·ra f. *(de gorra)* earflap; *(de arado)* moldboard.

o·re·jón, ·na m. *(fruta)* dried peach half; HIST. Inca nobleman.

or·fa·na·to m. orphanage.

or·fan·dad f. *(estado de huérfano)* orphanhood; *(privación)* abandonment.

or·fe·bre m. goldsmith or silversmith.

or·fe·bre·rí·a f. *(arte)* gold or silver work; *(taller)* gold or silver workshop.

or·fe·li·na·to m. orphanage.

or·gá·ni·co, a adj. organic.

ór·ga·ni·llo m. barrel organ, hurdy-gurdy.

or·ga·nis·mo m. organism; *(organización)* organization, institution.

or·ga·nis·ta m.f. organist.

or·ga·ni·za·ción f. organization.

or·ga·ni·za·dor, ·ra I. adj. organizing II. m.f. organizer.

or·ga·ni·zar §04 tr. to organize —reflex. to be organized.

ór·ga·no m. organ; *(medio)* medium, agency; *(periódico)* journal.

or·gas·mo m. orgasm.

or·gí·a f. orgy.

or·gia·co/giás·ti·co, a adj. orgiastic.

or·gu·llo m. *(arrogancia)* arrogance, conceit; *(sentimiento legítimo)* pride ♦ **no caber en sí de o.** to be bursting with pride.

or·gu·llo·so, a I. adj. *(que tiene orgullo)* proud; *(engreído)* conceited, arrogant II. m.f. proud person.

o·rien·ta·ción f. orientation; *(colocación)* positioning; *(consejo)* guidance, direction.

o·rien·tal I. adj. oriental, eastern II. m.f. oriental.

o·rien·tar tr. *(colocar)* to position <o. un cañón to position a cannon>; *(un edificio)* to orient, orientate; *(encaminar)* to guide.

o·rien·te m. east, orient.

o·ri·fi·cio m. orifice, opening.

o·ri·gen m. origin; *(principio)* source; *(linaje)* birth <de o. noble of noble birth>; *(causa)* cause ♦ **dar o. a** to give rise to • **en su o.** originally.

o·ri·gi·nal I. adj. original; *(primero)* first; *(nuevo)* new, novel <un concepto o. a novel concept>; *(inventivo)* inventive; *(raro)* odd, singular; *(auténtico)* authentic II. m. original; *(manuscrito)* manuscript.

o·ri·gi·na·li·dad f. *(novedad)* originality, novelty; *(carácter excéntrico)* eccentricity.

o·ri·gi·nar tr. & reflex. to originate.

o·ri·gi·na·ria·men·te adv. originally.

o·ri·gi·na·rio, a adj. coming or arising *(de* from).

o·ri·lla f. *(borde)* border, edge; *(del mar)* shore; *(de un río)* bank ♦ **a la o.** or **a orillas de** by, beside <*a orillas del mar* by the seashore>.

o·ri·llar tr. *(poner orilla)* to border, edge; *(guarnecer)* to trim, decorate.

o·rín¹ m. rust.

o·rín² m. urine.

o·ri·na f./nes m.inv. urine.

o·ri·nal m. urinal.

o·ri·nar intr. to urinate —reflex. to wet oneself, wet one's pants.

o·riun·do, a adj. native ♦ **ser o. de** to come from, be native to.

or·la f. border; COST. fringe, trimming; HER. orle.

or·lar tr. to border, edge.

or·na·men·tal adj. ornamental.

or·na·men·tar tr. to ornament, adorn.

or·na·men·to m. *(adorno)* ornament, adornment; ARCHIT. ornamentation, molding.

or·nar tr. to bedeck, embellish.

or·ni·to·lo·gí·a f. ornithology.

or·ni·tó·lo·go m.f. ornithologist.

o·ro m. gold; *(moneda)* gold coin; *(riqueza)* wealth, riches ♦ **comprar a peso de o.** to buy dearly, pay a fortune for • **chapado de o.** gold-plated • **de o.** gold, golden • **o. batido** gold leaf • **o. en barras** gold bars, bullion • **o. en polvo** gold dust • **o. negro** black gold, oil ♦ pl. suit in Spanish deck of cards.

o·ron·do, a adj. COLL. *(hinchado)* puffed up, self-satisfied; *(una vasija)* pot-bellied.

o·ro·pel m. tinsel.

or·ques·ta f. orchestra.

or·ques·ta·ción f. orchestration.

or·ques·tal adj. orchestral.

or·ques·tar tr. to orchestrate.

or·quí·de·a f. orchid.

or·ti·ga f. nettle.

or·to·don·cia f. orthodontia.

or·to·don·tis·ta I. adj. orthodontic II. m.f. orthodontist.

or·to·do·xo, a adj. orthodox.

or·to·gra·fí·a f. orthography.

or·to·grá·fi·co, a adj. orthographic.

or·to·pé·di·co, a I. adj. orthopedic II. m.f. orthopedist.

or·to·pe·dis·ta m.f. orthopedist.

o·ru·ga f. ENTOM. caterpillar; AUTO. caterpillar tread.

o·ru·jo m. marc, residue (of pressed grapes).

or·zue·lo m. sty.

os pron. you <*os vi en el museo* I saw you in the museum>; you, to you <*os dieron la oportunidad de discutirlo* they gave you the opportunity to discuss it>; you, for you <*os buscaba un asiento* he was looking for a seat for you>; from you <*os robaron un coche* they stole a car from you>; yourselves <*vosotros os laváis* you wash yourselves>; each other <*vosotros os amáis* you love each other>.

o·sa·dí·a f. boldness, audacity.

o·sa·do, a adj. bold, daring.

o·sa·men·ta f. *(conjunto de huesos)* bones; *(esqueleto)* skeleton.

o·sar intr. to dare.

os·ci·la·ción f. oscillation; *(balanceo)* swing, swinging movement; *(vacilación)* vacillation, wavering.

os·ci·la·dor m. oscillator.

os·ci·lar intr. to oscillate; *(balancearse)* to swing, move back and forth; *(fluctuar)* to fluctuate, vary; *(vacilar)* to vacillate, waver.

os·ci·la·to·rio, a adj. oscillatory.

ós·cu·lo m. kiss.

os·cu·re·cer §17 tr. *(volver oscuro)* to obscure, darken; *(volver poco inteligible)* to obscure, conceal; *(eclipsar)* to overshadow, eclipse; *(debilitar el brillo)* to tarnish, dim; PAINT. to shade, shadow —intr. to be getting dark —reflex. *(ponerse oscuro)* to darken, grow dark; *(nublarse)* to become cloudy or overcast.

os·cu·re·ci·mien·to m. darkening.

os·cu·ri·dad f. *(sombra)* darkness; *(imprecisión)* obscurity, haziness; *(incertidumbre)* uncertainty.

os·cu·ro, a adj. *(sin luz)* dark; *(desconocido)* obscure <*un poeta o.* an obscure poet>; *(negro)* dark; *(sombrío)* gloomy; *(confuso)* hazy, unclear; *(incierto)* uncertain; *(nebuloso)* cloudy, overcast ♦ **a oscuras** in the dark • **hacer o.** to become dark • **o. como boca de lobo** pitch-black, pitch-dark • **quedarse a oscuras** to be left in the dark.

ó·se·o, a adj. osseous, bony.

o·si·fi·car·se §70 reflex. to ossify.

os·mio m. osmium.

ós·mo·sis or os·mo·sis f. osmosis.

o·so m. bear ♦ **o. gris** grizzly bear.

os·ten·si·ble adj. ostensible.

os·ten·si·vo, a adj. ostensive.

os·ten·ta·ción f. ostentation.

os·ten·tar tr. *(mostrar)* to show; *(hacer gala)* to flaunt, make a show of.

os·ten·to·so, a adj. showy, grandiose.

os·te·ó·lo·go, a m.f. osteologist.

os·te·o·pa·tí·a f. osteopathy.

os·tra f. oyster.

os·tra·cis·mo m. ostracism.

o·te·ar tr. *(desde lugar alto)* to scan, survey; *(escudriñar)* to watch, observe.

o·ti·tis f. otitis, inflammation of the ear.

o·to·ñal adj. autumnal.

o·to·ño m. autumn, fall.

o·tor·ga·dor, ·ra I. adj. granting II. m.f. grantor.

o·tor·gar §47 tr. *(consentir)* to grant, give; LAW to execute, draw up.

o·to·rri·no·la·rin·go·lo·gí·a f. otorhinolaryngology.

o·tro, a I. adj. *(distinto)* other, another <*¿quieres o. taza de café?* do you want another cup of coffee?>; *(igual)* another <*ella es o. María Callas* she is another Maria Callas> ♦ **o. cosa** something else • **o. vez** again • **por o. parte** on the other hand II. pron. another one <*no tengo o.* I do not have another one> ♦ **¡o.!** THEAT. encore! • **unos a otros** each other, one another ♦ pl. others.

o·va·ción f. ovation.

o·va·cio·nar tr. to give an ovation to.

o·val or o·va·la·do, a adj. oval.

ó·va·lo m. oval.

o·vá·ri·co adj. ovarian.

o·va·rio m. ovary.

o·ve·ja f. ewe, female sheep ♦ **o. descarriada** lost sheep.

o·ve·je·ro, a I. m. shepherd —f. shepherdess II. adj. ♦ **perro o.** sheepdog.

o·ver·tu·ra f. overture.

o·vi·llar tr. to roll or wind —reflex. to roll or curl up.

o·vi·llo m. *(de hilo)* ball; *(cosa enredada)* tangle, snarl ♦ **hacerse un o.** COLL. *(acurrucarse)* to curl up; *(embrollarse)* to get tangled up.

o·vi·no, a adj. ovine, of sheep.

o·ví·pa·ro, a I. adj. oviparous II. m.f. oviparous animal.

ov·ni m. UFO, unidentified flying object.

o·vu·la·ción f. ovulation.

o·vu·lar I. adj. ovular II. intr. to ovulate.

ó·vu·lo m. ovule.

o·xi·da·ción f. oxidation.

o·xi·dar tr. & reflex. to oxidize, rust.

ó·xi·do m. oxide.

o·xi·ge·na·do, a adj. oxygenated ♦ **agua o.** hydrogen peroxide.

o·xi·ge·nar tr. to oxygenate —reflex. to breathe fresh air.

o·xí·ge·no m. oxygen.

o·yen·te I. adj. hearing, listening II. m.f. *(persona que oye)* hearer, listener; EDUC. auditor ♦ **los oyentes** the audience.

o·ye·ra, yó see **oír.**

o·zo·no m. ozone.

P

p, P f. nineteenth letter of the Spanish alphabet.

pa·be·llón m. *(bandera)* flag, banner; *(tienda de campaña)* bell tent; *(dosel)* bed canopy; *(edificio)* pavilion; MARIT. registration; ANAT. outer ear ♦ **arriar el p.** to lower the flag • **p. de caza** shooting box.

pa·bi·lo m. candle wick.

pá·bu·lo m. *(alimento)* food, pabulum; *(sustento)* support, encouragement ♦ **dar p. a** to encourage.

pa·cer §17 intr. to graze.

pa·cien·cia f. patience ♦ **acabársele** or **agotársele a uno la p.** to lose one's patience • **armarse de p.** to arm oneself with patience • **perder la p.** to lose one's temper.

pa·cien·te adj. & m.f. patient.

pa·ci·fi·ca·ción f. pacification.

pa·ci·fi·ca·dor, ra I. adj. pacifying II. m.f. pacifier, peacemaker.

pa·ci·fi·car §70 tr. to pacify —reflex. to calm down.

pa·cí·fi·co, a adj. peaceful, pacific.

pa·ci·fis·ta adj. & m.f. pacifist.

pa·co·ti·lla f. ♦ **de p.** shoddy, junky.

pac·tar tr. to agree to or upon —intr. to come to an agreement, make a pact ♦ **p. con el diablo** to sell one's soul to the devil.

pac·to m. pact, agreement.

pa·chón m. COLL. dull fellow.

pa·cho·rra f. AMER., COLL. slowness, sluggishness.

pa·de·cer §17 tr. *(sufrir)* to suffer *(de from)*; *(soportar)* to endure, bear; *(ser víctima)* to be the victim of <*padece una equivocación* he is the victim of an error> —intr. *(sufrir)* to suffer; *(recibir daño)* to be damaged ♦ **p. del corazón** to have heart trouble.

pa·de·ci·mien·to m. *(sufrimiento)* suffering; *(enfermedad)* ailment, illness.

pa·dras·tro m. stepfather; *(pellejo)* hangnail.

pa·dre I. m. father; FIG. father, creator; RELIG. father, priest ♦ **p. espiritual** confessor • **P. Eterno** Heavenly Father • **P. Nuestro** Lord's Prayer • **p. político** father-in-law • **Santo P.** RELIG. Holy Father ♦ pl. parents II. adj. COLL. terrific, tremendous.

pa·dre·nues·tro m. Lord's Prayer, Our Father ♦ **en un p.** COLL. in the wink of an eye.

pa·dri·llo m. AMER. sire, stallion.

pa·dri·no m. *(de niño)* godfather; *(de boda)* best man; *(de desafío)* second; *(patrocinador)* sponsor ♦ pl. godparents.

pa·drón m. *(censo)* census, register; *(columna)* memorial column or pillar; AMER. sire, stallion. ¡**paf!** interj. bang!, thud!

pa·ga f. *(acción)* payment; *(sueldo)* wages ♦ **buena p.** good pay.

pa·ga·de·ro, a adj. payable, due ♦ **p. a la vista, entrega** payable on sight, delivery.

pa·ga·do, a adj. ♦ **p. de sí mismo** self-satisfied.

pa·ga·no, a adj. & m.f. pagan.

pa·gar §47 tr. to pay; *(recompensar)* to repay <*p. un favor>* to repay a favor> ♦ **p. a crédito** or **a plazos** to pay in installments • **p. con la misma moneda** to give (someone) a taste of their own medicine • **pagarla(s)** to pay for it • **p. por adelantado** to pay in advance —intr. to pay.

pa·ga·ré m. promissory note, IOU.

pá·gi·na f. page.

pa·gi·nar tr. to paginate, number the pages of.

pa·go¹ adj. COLL. paid ♦ **estar p.** to be even.

pa·go² m. *(entrega)* payment; *(recompensa)* repayment, recompense.

pa·ís m. *(territorio)* country, nation; *(región)* region, territory.

pai·sa·je m. landscape.

pai·sa·jis·ta I. adj. landscape II. m.f. landscape painter.

pai·sa·no, a I. adj. of the same country or region II. m.f. *(campesino)* peasant; *(compatriota)* fellow countryman/woman.

pa·ja f. straw; *(lo desechable)* deadwood, chaff; *(cosa sin substancia)* rubbish; *(para beber)* (drinking) straw.

pa·jar m. straw loft, barn.

pa·ja·re·ar intr. *(cazar)* to hunt birds; *(holgazanear)* to loaf about.

pa·ja·re·ra f. bird cage.

pa·ja·re·rí·a f. bird shop.

pa·ja·re·ro, a I. adj. bird II. m. *(vendedor)* bird seller; *(cazador)* bird catcher.

pá·ja·ro m. bird ♦ **matar dos pájaros de un tiro** COLL. to kill two birds with one stone • **p. carpintero** woodpecker • **tener la cabeza llena de pájaros** COLL. to be a featherbrain.

pa·ja·rra·co m. *(pájaro)* large ugly bird; COLL. *(pillo)* clever bastard.

pa·je m. HIST. page.

pa·la f. *(herramienta)* shovel, spade; *(contenido)* shovelful; *(parte plana)* blade; *(del remo)* blade; *(del curtidor)* fleshing knife; *(de bisagra)* leaf; *(de la hélice)* (propeller) blade ♦ **p. mecánica** power shovel.

pa·la·bra f. word; *(facultad)* speech; *(elocuencia)* eloquence; *(promesa)* word, promise ♦ **bajo p.** on one's word of honor • **coger la p.** **a alguien** to take someone at his word • **conceder** or **dar la p. a** to give the floor to • **correr la p.** to pass the word • **cruzar p.** to talk, converse • **cumplir** or **mantener su p. uno** to keep one's word • **decir** or **tener la última p.** to have the last word • **dejar a alguien con la p. en la boca** to turn one's back on someone who is speaking • **de p.** orally • **dirigir la p. a** to address, speak to • **empeñar la p.** to pledge one's word • **en dos** or **en pocas palabras** in brief • **en una p.** in a word, in short • **faltar a su p.** to go back on one's word • **medir uno sus palabras** to weigh one's words • **no decir**

p. not to say a word • **no tener p.** to be unreliable • **¡p.!** on my word of honor! • **p. de honor** word of honor • **p. de matrimonio** promise of marriage • **p. por p.** word for word, verbatim • **palabras mayores** strong language • **pedir la p.** to ask for the floor • **quedarse sin palabras** to be left speechless • **quitarle a alguien la p. de la boca** to take the words right out of someone's mouth • **tomar la p.** to take the floor.

pa·la·bre·o m. chatter.

pa·la·bre·rí·a f./o m. COLL. idle chatter.

pa·la·bro·ta f. COLL. swearword, dirty word ♦ **decir palabrotas** to swear.

pa·la·ce·te m. elegant house.

pa·la·cie·go, a adj. (*magnífico*) palatial, magnificent; (*del palacio*) court, palace.

pa·la·cio m. palace ♦ **p. de justicia** courthouse.

pa·la·da f. shovelful.

pa·la·dar m. (*de la boca*) palate, roof of the mouth; (*gusto*) taste.

pa·la·de·ar tr. to savor, relish.

pa·la·dín m. paladin; FIG. champion.

pa·la·dio m. palladium.

pa·la·frén m. palfrey.

pa·la·fre·ne·ro m. groom, equerry.

pa·lan·ca f. lever; (*utensilio*) crowbar; (*palo*) shaft, pole; COLL. (*influencia*) pull, influence ♦ **p. de cambio** gearshift • **p. del timón** rudder bar.

pa·lan·ga·na f. washbasin.

pa·lan·quín m. palanquin.

pa·la·tal adj. & f. palatal.

pal·co m. THEAT. box.

pa·le·ar tr. to shovel.

pa·len·que m. hitching post.

pa·le·o·lí·ti·co, a adj. & m. Paleolithic.

pa·le·on·to·lo·gí·a f. paleontology.

pa·le·on·tó·lo·go, a m.f. paleontologist.

pa·le·o·zoi·co, a adj. & m. Paleozoic.

pa·les·tra f. (*lugar de lucha*) palestra, gymnasium; (*campo*) arena ♦ **salir a la p.** to enter the fray or the arena.

pa·le·ta f. (*pala pequeña*) small shovel or spade; (*del pintor*) palette; (*del albañil*) trowel; ANAT. shoulder blade; MECH. (*álabe*) paddle (of water wheel); (*de la hélice*) blade; (*diente*) front tooth.

pa·le·ti·lla f. shoulder blade.

pa·le·tó m. coat, greatcoat.

pa·lia·ti·vo, a adj. & m. palliative.

pa·li·de·cer §17 intr. (*ponerse pálido*) to turn pale, grow pale; (*descolorarse*) to fade.

pa·li·dez f. paleness, pallor.

pá·li·do, a adj. (*descolorido*) pale, pallid; FIG. pallid, lackluster.

pa·li·du·cho, a adj. COLL. pale.

pa·li·llo m. (*palito*) small stick; (*para agujas*) knitting-needle holder; (*mondadientes*) toothpick; (*de tambor*) drumstick.

pa·li·to m. small stick ♦ **pisar el p.** AMER., COLL. to fall into the trap.

pa·li·za f. beating, thrashing.

pal·ma f. (*de la mano*) palm; (*palmera*) palm (tree); (*hoja*) palm leaf; (*victoria*) victory, triumph; VET. palm (of a hoof) ♦ **llevarse la p.** to carry the day ♦ pl. applause • **andar en p.** to be applauded ♦ **batir p.** to applaud.

pal·ma·do, a adj. (*de forma de palma*) palmate, palm-shaped; (*ligado*) webbed II. f. (*golpe*) slap, pat; (*ruido*) hand clap ♦ **dar palmadas** to clap one's hands.

pal·mar I. adj. ANAT. palmar II. m. palm grove.

pal·mar² intr. COLL. to die, kick the bucket.

pal·me·a·do, a adj. (*de forma de palma*) palmate, palm-shaped; (*ligado*) webbed.

pal·me·ar intr. (*batir palmas*) to clap, applaud —tr. R.P. to pat, slap.

pal·me·ra f. palm tree.

pal·mí·pe·do, a adj. & m. webfooted (animal).

pal·mi·to m. palm heart.

pal·mo m. span, palm ♦ **crecer a palmos** to shoot up • **dejar a alguien con un p. de narices** to let someone down • **p. a p.** little by little, inch by inch.

pal·mo·te·ar intr. to applaud.

pa·lo m. (*vara*) stick, pole; (*mango*) stick, handle <p. de escoba broomstick>; MARIT. mast, spar; (*golpe*) hit, whack ♦ **dar de palos** to whack • **de tal p., tal astilla** like father, like son • **de p.** wooden • **p. ensebado** AMER. greased pole • **p. mayor** mainmast • **p. santo** lignum vitae • **palos de golf** golf clubs.

pa·lo·ma f. dove, pigeon ♦ **p. buchona** pouter pigeon • **p. mensajera** homing pigeon.

pa·lo·mar m. dovecote, pigeon loft.

pa·lo·me·ta f. (*pez*) saurel, yellow jack; (*tuerca*) wing or butterfly nut.

pa·lo·mi·lla f. (*de graneros*) grain moth; (*de caballerías*) back, fore-rump; (*tuerca*) wing or butterfly nut; (*sostén*) wall bracket.

pa·lo·mi·ta f. popcorn.

pa·lo·mo m. (*macho*) cock pigeon; (*paloma torcaz*) ring-necked dove.

pa·lo·te m. MUS. drumstick; (*trazo*) pothook.

pal·pa·ble adj. palpable.

pal·par tr. (*tocar*) to touch, feel; (*experimentar*) to appreciate —reflex. to be felt, be perceptible.

pal·pi·ta·ción f. palpitation.

pal·pi·tan·te adj. palpitating; FIG. burning.

pal·pi·tar intr. (*temblar*) to palpitate, throb; (*latir*) to beat; (*emocionarse*) to quiver, be aflutter (with emotion); (*manifestar*) to throb <en su verso palpita la emoción his poetry throbs with emotion>.

pál·pi·to m. COLL. hunch, presentiment.

pal·ta f. AMER. avocado.

pa·lu·dis·mo m. malaria.

pa·lur·do, a I. adj. boorish II. m.f. boor.

pa·llar¹ intr. to sing improvised songs —tr. MIN. to sort.

pa·llar² m. (*alubia*) lima or butter bean; (*judía*) haricot bean.

pam·pa f. pampa, plain.

pám·pa·no m. (*pimpollo*) tendril, vine shoot; (*hoja*) vine leaf; ICHTH. salp.

pam·pe·ro, a I. adj. of or from the pampas II. m.f. AMER. pampero (inhabitant).

pam·pli·na f. COLL. (*tontería*) nonsense; (*insignificancia*) trifle.

pam·pli·na·da f. COLL. nonsense.

pan m. bread; (*pieza*) loaf of bread <un p. grande a big loaf of bread>; (*masa*) dough; cake <un p. de jabón a cake of soap>; (*sustento*) bread, food; METAL. leaf, foil ♦ **a p. y agua** on bread and water • **contigo p. y cebolla** COLL. for better or for worse • **ganarse el p.** to earn a living • **p. de maíz** cornbread • **p. fermentado** leavened bread • **p. integral** whole-wheat bread • **ser más bueno que el p.** to be kindness itself • **ser p. comido** COLL. to be a cinch.

pa·na f. corduroy.

pa·na·ce·a f. panacea.
pa·na·de·rí·a f. bakery.
pa·na·de·ro, a m.f. baker.
pa·nal m. honeycomb.
pa·na·má m. Panama hat.
pa·na·me·ri·ca·no, a adj. Pan-American.
pa·na·te·la f. long thin sponge cake.
pán·cre·as m.inv. pancreas.
pan·cre·á·ti·co, a adj. pancreatic.
pan·cro·má·ti·co, a adj. panchromatic.
pan·cho, a COLL. I. adj. calm, unruffled ♦ **quedarse tan p.** to keep one's cool II. m. R.P. hot dog.
pan·da m. panda.
pan·de·ar intr. & reflex. *(la madera)* to warp; *(la pared)* to bulge.
pan·de·mo·nio/mó·nium m. pandemonium.
pan·de·re·ta f. tambourine.
pan·de·ro m. tambourine.
pan·de·re·te·ar intr. to play the tambourine.
pan·di·lla f. gang, band.
pan·di·lle·ro/llis·ta m. member of a gang.
pa·ne·ci·llo m. roll, bun.
pa·ne·gí·ri·co, a I. adj. panegyrical II. m. panegyric.
pa·nel m. panel ♦ pl. paneling.
pa·ne·ra f. breadbasket.
pán·fi·lo, a adj. *(cachazudo)* slow; *(bobo)* foolish.
pan·fle·to m. pamphlet.
pa·nia·gua·do m. favorite, protégé.
pá·ni·co, a adj. & m. panic.
pa·ni·zo m. *(mijo)* millet; *(maíz)* corn, maize.
pa·no·plia f. panoply.
pa·no·ra·ma m. panorama.
pa·no·rá·mi·co, a adj. panoramic.
pan·que·que m. AMER. pancake.
pan·ta·lón m./lo·nes m.pl. *(de hombre)* trousers, pants; *(de mujer)* slacks ♦ **llevar los pantalones** COLL. to wear the pants in the family • **p. corto** shorts • **p. vaquero** jeans.
pan·ta·lo·ne·ra f. trouser maker.
pan·ta·lla f. *(de lámpara)* lamp shade; *(de hogar)* fire screen; *(telón)* movie screen; *(de radar)* screen; *(de cine)* film <*las estrellas de la p.* film stars>; *(protección)* shield.
pan·ta·nal m. marsh, bog.
pan·ta·no m. marsh; FIG. difficulty.
pan·ta·no·so, a adj. boggy, marshy.
pan·te·ís·ta I. adj. pantheistic II. m.f. pantheist.
pan·te·ón m. pantheon.
pan·te·ra f. panther.
pan·tó·gra·fo m. pantograph.
pan·to·mi·ma f. pantomime.
pan·to·rri·lla f. calf.
pan·tu·fla f. slipper.
pan·za f. COLL. *(barriga)* belly, paunch; ZOOL. rumen; *(de vasija)* belly.
pan·za·da f. push given with the belly ♦ **darse una p. de** to gorge oneself on.
pan·za·zo m. ♦ **darse un p.** to do a bellyflop.
pan·zón, o·na/zu·do, a adj. paunchy.
pa·ñal m. diaper ♦ **dejar en pañales a alguien** COLL. to leave someone standing • **estar en pañales** *(ser niño)* to be in diapers; *(ser novato)* to be wet behind the ears.
pa·ño m. *(tela)* cloth; *(de lana)* woolen cloth; *(tapiz)* drapery; *(ancho)* panel; *(trapo)* rag ♦ **p. de lágrimas** shoulder to cry on • **paños menores** underwear.
pa·ño·le·ta f. scarf, fichu.

pa·ño·lón m. shawl.
pa·ñue·lo m. handkerchief; *(pañoleta)* scarf ♦ **p. de bolsillo** pocket handkerchief.
pa·pa¹ m. Pope ♦ **ser más papista que el p.** to be more Catholic than the Pope.
pa·pa² f. AMER. potato ♦ **p. dulce** sweet potato • **no saber ni p. de** COLL. not to know a thing about ♦ pl. COLL. *(comida)* food, grub; *(puches)* pap, mush.
pa·pá m. papa, daddy ♦ **P. Noel** Father Christmas.
pa·pa·da f. double chin.
pa·pa·ga·yo m. parrot.
pa·pal I. adj. papal II. m. AMER. potato field.
pa·pa·lo·te/pe·lo·te m. C. AMER., MEX. kite.
pa·pa·mos·cas m.inv. COLL. simpleton, fool.
pa·pa·na·tas m.inv. COLL. fool.
pa·par tr. ♦ **p. moscas** to gape.
pa·pa·ya f. papaya.
pa·pel m. paper; *(hoja)* piece of paper; *(documento)* document; *(función)* role; THEAT. role ♦ **hacer buen p.** to do well • **hacer el p. de** to act as • **hacer mal p.** to do poorly • **p. cuadriculado** graph paper • **p. de arroz** rice paper • **p. de calcar** tracing paper • **p. de cartas** stationery • **p. de estraza** brown wrapping paper • **p. de lija** sandpaper • **p. de seda** tissue paper • **p. encerado** wax paper • **p. higiénico** toilet paper • **p. moneda** paper money • **p. para escribir** writing paper • **p. rayado** lined paper • **p. secante** blotting paper ♦ pl. *(documentos)* papers, documents; *(identificación)* identification papers.
pa·pe·le·o m. FIG. red tape, paper work.
pa·pe·le·ro, a I. adj. paper II.m.f. *(fabricante)* paper manufacturer; *(vendedor)* stationer.
pa·pe·le·ta f. *(cédula)* card; *(cucurucho)* paper cone or bag; *(de voto)* ballot paper ♦ **p. de empeño** pawn ticket.
pa·pe·lón m. ♦ **hacer un p.** to make a fool of oneself.
pa·pe·ra f. goiter ♦ pl. mumps.
pa·pi m. COLL. daddy, pop.
pa·pi·la f. papilla.
pa·pi·lla f. pap, soft food ♦ **estar hecho p.** COLL. to be exhausted *or* beat • **hacer p. a** COLL. to make mincemeat of.
pa·pi·ro m. papyrus.
pa·pis·ta adj. & m.f. papist.
pa·que·bo·te m. packet boat, packet.
pa·que·te I. m. *(bulto)* package; *(caja)* pack, packet <*un p. de cigarrillos* a pack of cigarettes>; *(paquebote)* packet boat, packet; COLL. *(mentira)* lie II. adj. AMER. smart, elegant.
pa·que·te·rí·a f. elegance, chic.
pa·qui·der·mo m. pachyderm.
par I. adj. *(igual)* equal; MATH. even; ZOOL. paired II. m. *(dos)* couple <*un p. de huevos* a couple of eggs>; pair <*un p. de pantalones* a pair of pants>; *(yunta)* pair, team; *(dignidad)* peer; MATH. even number; ARCHIT. rafter ♦ **a la p.** *(igualmente)* on a par, equally; *(a un tiempo)* at the same time; COM. at par • **al p. de** on the same level as • **a pares** *or* **en pares** in pairs, by twos • **de p. en p.** wide <*abierto de p. en p.* wide open> • **sin p.** without peer *or* equal.
pa·ra prep. *(movimiento)* towards, for; *(destino, fin)* for, to, in order to; *(duración, tiempo)* for, by, about to, on the point of, to, for; *(comparación)* for, to, considering; *(en provecho de)* for; *(no se traduce)* <*crema p. afeitar* shaving cream> ♦ **p.**

con toward • **p. concluir** in conclusion • **p. que** so that, in order that • ¿**p. qué?** why <*p. qué has venido?* why have you come?>; for what <*¿p. qué sirve esa manija?* what is this handle for?> • **p. siempre** forever.

pa·ra·bién m. congratulations.

pa·rá·bo·la f. *(cuento)* parable; GEOM. parabola.

pa·ra·bri·sas m.inv. windshield, windscreen (G.B.)

pa·ra·caí·das f.inv. parachute.

pa·ra·cai·dis·ta m.f. *(aficionado)* parachutist; MIL. paratrooper.

pa·ra·cho·ques m.inv. bumper, fender.

pa·ra·da f. see parado, a.

pa·ra·de·ro m. *(sitio)* whereabouts; *(destino)* destination • **averiguar el p. de** to locate • **ignorar el p. de algo, alguien** not to know where something, someone is.

pa·ra·dig·ma m. paradigm.

pa·ra·di·sía·co/·sí·a·co, a adj. heavenly.

pa·ra·do, a I. adj. *(inmóvil)* stationary; *(detenido)* stopped; *(inactivo)* idle; *(sin empleo)* unemployed; AMER. standing • **salir bien, mal p.** to come off well, badly II. f. *(acto)* stop; *(suspensión)* halt; *(sitio)* stop <*p. de autobús* bus stop>; MIL. parade • **p. de taxis** taxi or cab stand • **p. en firme** or **en seco** dead stop.

pa·ra·do·ja f. paradox.

pa·ra·dó·ji·co, a adj. paradoxical.

pa·ra·dor m. inn, roadhouse.

pa·ra·fi·na f. paraffin.

pa·ra·fi·nar tr. to paraffin, treat with paraffin.

pa·ra·fra·se·ar tr. to paraphrase.

pa·rá·fra·sis f.inv. paraphrase.

pa·ra·guas m.inv. umbrella.

pa·ra·güe·rí·a f. umbrella shop.

pa·ra·güe·ro, a m.f. umbrella maker or seller —m. umbrella stand.

pa·ra·í·so m. paradise; THEAT. top balcony.

pa·ra·je m. *(lugar)* spot; *(región)* area.

pa·ra·le·lo, a I. adj. parallel II. m. GEOG. parallel; *(comparación)* parallel, comparison • **correr p.** to run parallel to • **establecer un p.** to draw a parallel between, compare —f. *(línea)* parallel line • pl. SPORT. parallel bars.

pa·ra·le·lo·gra·mo m. parallelogram.

pa·rá·li·sis f.inv. paralysis • **p. cerebral** cerebral palsy • **p. infantil** poliomyelitis.

pa·ra·lí·ti·co, a adj. & m.f. paralytic.

pa·ra·li·za·ción f. immobilization, paralyzation; COM. *(estancamiento)* stagnation.

pa·ra·li·zar §04 tr. *(causar parálisis)* to paralyze; FIG. *(estorbar)* to impede, stop —reflex. to become paralyzed.

pa·ra·mé·di·co, a adj. paramedical.

pa·rá·me·tro m. parameter.

pá·ra·mo m. high barren plain.

pa·ran·gón m. comparison, parallel • **sin p.** matchless.

pa·ra·no·ia f. paranoia.

pa·ra·noi·co, a adj. & m.f. paranoid.

pa·ra·pe·tar·se reflex. MIL. to defend oneself with parapets; FIG. to protect oneself.

pa·ra·pe·to m. parapet.

pa·ra·plé·ji·co, a adj. & m.f. paraplegic.

pa·ra·psi·co·lo·gí·a f. parapsychology.

pa·rar intr. *(cesar)* to stop, halt; COLL. *(terminar)* to end up <*¿adónde vas a p. con esos preparativos?* where are you going to end up with all those preparations?>; *(alojarse)* to lodge, stay; *(caer)* to end up, land <*la carta paró en manos*

de su hija the letter ended up in the hands of his daughter> • **ir a p.** to end up • **p. en** to end up, result in • **p. en seco** to stop dead • **sin p.** ceaselessly, nonstop —tr. *(detener)* to stop, halt; *(impedir)* to check; *(prevenir)* to forestall • **p. la oreja** AMER. to prick up one's ears —reflex. *(detenerse)* to stop; COLL. *(beneficiarse)* to prosper; AMER. to stand up • **p. a** to stop, pause <*p. a pensar* to stop to think>.

pa·ra·rra·yos m. lightning rod.

pa·ra·sí·ti·co, a adj. parasitic.

pa·rá·si·to, a I. adj. parasitic II. m. parasite.

pa·ra·sol m. parasol.

par·ce·la f. parcel, plot.

par·ce·lar tr. to divide into plots, parcel.

par·cial I. adj. partial II. m. *(partidario)* partisan, follower; *(examen)* periodic exam.

par·cia·li·dad f. partiality; *(prejuicio)* bias.

par·co, a adj. *(corto)* sparing <*p. en el hablar* sparing in words>; *(frugal)* frugal, economical; *(moderado)* moderate.

par·che m. *(emplasto)* plaster; *(remiendo)* patch; *(de tambor)* drumhead.

¡par·diez! interj. COLL. good God!, by Jove!

par·do, a I. adj. *(moreno)* brown; *(oscuro)* dark II. m.f. AMER. mulatto.

par·dus·co, a adj. brownish.

pa·re·ar tr. to match, pair.

pa·re·cer¹ m. *(opinión)* opinion, view; *(aspecto)* appearance • **al p.** apparently • **cambiar de p.** to change one's mind • **ser del p. que** to be of the opinion that.

pa·re·cer² §17 intr. *(dar la impresión)* to seem; *(querer)* to like <*si te parece, saldremos inmediatamente* if you like, we will leave immediately>; *(semejarse)* to resemble, seem like; *(tener cierto aspecto)* to look, appear • **al p.** apparently • **así parece** so it seems • **p. mentira** to be hard to believe —reflex. to look alike • **p. a** to resemble, look like.

pa·re·ci·do, a I. adj. similar • **bien p.** good-looking • **ser p. a** to resemble, be like II. m. similarity.

pa·red f. wall • **darse contra la p.** to knock one's head against the wall • **p. por medio** next door.

pa·re·dón m. large thick wall.

pa·re·jo, a I. adj. *(igual)* alike, equal; *(liso)* even, smooth; *(llano)* flat, level • **ir parejos** *(cosas, personas)* to be equal; *(caballos)* to go neck and neck II. f. *(par)* pair; *(hombre y mujer)* couple; *(dos compañeros)* pair, couple; *(de baile)* dancing partner; *(de juego)* partner in card games • **por parejas** two by two, in pairs.

pa·ren·te·la f. relations, relatives.

pa·ren·tes·co m. *(vínculo)* kinship; *(lazo)* tie.

pa·rén·te·sis m.inv. parenthesis; *(frase)* parenthetical statement; *(interrupción)* break, interruption • **entre p.** in parentheses • **sea dicho entre p.** incidentally.

pa·ria m.f. pariah.

pa·ri·dad f. parity.

pa·rien·te, a m.f. relative, relation • **p. consanguíneo** blood relation.

pa·rie·tal adj. & m. parietal (bone).

pa·ri·hue·las f.pl. stretcher.

pa·rir intr. & tr. to give birth (to).

pa·ri·ta·rio, a adj. joint.

par·la·men·ta·rio, a/·ris·ta I. adj. parliamentary II. m.f. member of parliament.

par·la·men·to m. *(asamblea)* parliament; *(discurso)* address; THEAT. long speech.

par·lan·chín, i·na I. adj. talkative, chattering II. m.f. chatterbox.

par·lan·te adj. speaking, talking.

par·lar intr. to chatter.

par·lo·te·ar intr. COLL. to chatter.

par·lo·te·o m. COLL. chatter.

pa·ro m. (suspensión) stoppage, standstill; (desempleo) unemployment ♦ **p. forzoso** layoff • **p. laboral** strike.

pa·ro·dia f. parody.

pa·ro·diar tr. to parody.

pa·ro·dis·ta m.f. parodist.

pa·ró·ni·mo, a I. adj. paronymous II. m. paronym.

pa·ro·xis·mo m. paroxysm.

par·pa·de·ar intr. (párpados) to blink; (luz) to flicker; (estrellas) to twinkle.

par·pa·de·o m. (ojos) blink; (luz) flicker; (stars) twinkle.

pár·pa·do m. eyelid.

par·que m. park; (estacionamiento) parking lot ♦ **p. de atracciones** amusement park.

par·qué m. parquet.

par·que·ar tr. AMER. to park.

par·que·o m. AMER. (acción) parking; (lugar) parking lot.

par·que·dad f. (prudencia) economy; (templanza) moderation.

par·quí·me·tro m. parking meter.

pa·rra f. grapevine ♦ **hoja de p.** fig leaf (on statue).

pá·rra·fo m. paragraph ♦ **echar un p.** COLL. to have a chat • **hacer p. aparte** COLL. to change the subject.

pa·rral m. (lugar) vineyard; (parra con armazón) vine arbor.

pa·rran·da f. COLL. party, spree ♦ **andar** or **estar de p.** to be out for a good time.

pa·rran·de·ar intr. COLL. to go out partying.

pa·rran·dis·ta m.f. COLL. reveler.

pa·rri·ci·da m.f. parricide.

pa·rri·ci·dio m. parricide.

pa·rri·lla f. grill; (rejilla) grating; (restaurant) steak house.

pa·rri·lla·da f. dish of grilled fish or seafood; R.P. dish of grilled meats.

pá·rro·co I. m. parish priest II. adj. parish.

pa·rro·quia f. (territorio) parish; (habitantes) parishioners; (iglesia) parish church.

pa·rro·quial adj. parochial, parish.

pa·rro·quia·no, a I. adj. parochial, parish II. m.f. (feligrés) parishioner; (cliente) customer.

par·si·mo·nia f. (templanza) moderation; (calma) calm.

par·si·mo·nio·so, a adj. (sobrio) parsimonious; (tranquilo) unhurried.

par·te f. part; (porción) portion; (cantidad asignada) share; (sitio) place, spot; (lado) side; (facción) side; COM., LAW party; THEAT. role ♦ **a esta p.** ago, past <de un mes a esta p. a month ago> • **de p. de** (a nombre de) in the name of, on behalf of; (en favor de) on the side of; (por orden de) at the command of • **¿de p. de quién?** who's calling? • **en alguna p.** somewhere • **en cualquier p.** anywhere • **en gran p.** for the most part • **en ninguna p.** nowhere • **en p.** partly • **en** or **por todas partes** everywhere • **hacer su p.** to do one's share • **la mayor p.** the majority • **llevar la mejor p.** to have the upper hand • **no ser p. de** to have nothing to do with • **p. actora** LAW plaintiff • **p. de la**

oración GRAM. part of speech • **p. por p.** bit by bit • **poner de su p.** to do what one can • **ponerse de p. de** to side with • **por la mayor p.** for the most part • **por mí p.** as far as I am concerned • **por otra p.** on the other hand • **por partes** step by step • **tener** or **tomar p. en** to take part in, participate in —m. (escrito) note; (despacho) dispatch, message; (informe) report ♦ **dar p.** to report • **dar p. a** to notify, inform.

par·te·no·gé·ne·sis f. parthenogenesis.

par·te·ra f. midwife.

par·te·ro m. male midwife.

par·ti·ción f. division, partition.

par·ti·ci·pa·ción f. participation; (contribución) contribution; (de lotería) share in a lottery ticket; COM. (acción) share, interest ♦ **p. de boda** wedding invitation • **p. en las utilidades** profit sharing.

par·ti·ci·pan·te I. adj. participating, sharing II. m.f. (que toma parte) participant; SPORT. competitor.

par·ti·ci·par tr. to inform —intr. (tomar parte) to participate, take part; (compartir) to share.

par·tí·ci·pe I. adj. participating II. m.f. (colaborador) participant; (interesado) interested party ♦ **hacer a alguien p. de** to inform someone of.

par·ti·ci·pio m. participle.

par·tí·cu·la f. particle.

par·ti·cu·lar I. adj. (privado) private; (individual) individual, personal; (especial) particular, special <un talento p. a special talent> II. m.f. (individuo) individual, private person; (asunto) matter, point ♦ **nada de p.** nothing special.

par·ti·cu·la·ri·dad f. peculiarity.

par·ti·cu·la·ri·zar §04 tr. (especificar) to specify; (detallar) to detail —reflex. to stand out.

par·ti·cu·lar·men·te adv. particularly.

par·ti·da·rio, a adj. & m.f. partisan.

par·ti·dis·ta I. adj. party II. m.f. partisan.

par·ti·do, a II. adj. divided II. m. (bando) (political) party; (provecho) profit, advantage; (distrito) district; SPORT. game ♦ **sacar p. de** to benefit from • **tomar p.** (decidir) to decide; (ponerse de parte) to take sides —f. (salida) departure; (expedición) party; (mano de juego) hand, round; COM. (artículo) entry, item; (porción) lot, batch ♦ **p. de defunción** death certificate • **p. de matrimonio** marriage certificate • **p. simple** COM. single entry.

par·tir tr. (dividir) to divide, split; to crack <p. nueces to crack nuts>; (romper) to break, split open; (repartir) to share —intr. to leave ♦ **a p. de** as of, starting from.

par·ti·ti·vo, a adj. partitive.

par·ti·tu·ra f. score.

par·to m. childbirth, delivery.

par·tu·rien·ta f. woman in labor.

par·va f. unthreshed grain; FIG. heap, pile.

pár·vu·lo, a m.f. small child, tot.

pa·sa f. see **paso, a.**

pa·sa·di·zo m. (pasillo) passage; (callejón) alley.

pa·sa·do, a I. adj. past, gone by <en años pasados in past years>; (anterior) last <el mes p. last month>; GRAM. past, preterit; CUL. (podrido) spoiled; (poco fresco) stale; (muy cocido) overdone ♦ **p. de moda** old-fashioned • **p. la una** after one (o'clock) • **p. mañana** day after tomorrow II. m. past ♦ **lo p.,** p. let bygones be bygones —f. (acto) passage, passing; SEW. stitch ♦ **de p.** (de paso) on the way; (ligera-

mente) cursorily • **mala p.** dirty trick.

pa·sa·dor, ·ra I. adj. passing II. m. (*barra*) bolt; (*chaveta*) cotter (pin); (*de pelo*) hairpin.

pa·sa·je m. passage; (*billete*) ticket; (*pasajeros*) passengers; (*paso público*) passageway.

pa·sa·je·ro, a I. adj. passing, fleeting II. m.f. passenger, traveler.

pa·sa·ma·no m. handrail.

pa·sa·mon·ta·ñas m.pl. balaclava (hat).

pa·sa·por·te m. passport.

pa·sar tr. (*alcanzar*) to pass, hand; (*atravesar*) to cross; (*ir más allá*) to go beyond <*p. los límites* to go beyond the limits>; COLL. (*contrabandear*) to smuggle; (*poner en circulación*) to circulate; (*transferir*) to transfer; (*introducir*) to insert; (*colar*) to filter; (*disfrutar*) to spend, pass <*pasamos el verano en la playa* we spent the summer at the beach>; (*sufrir*) to suffer, undergo <*hemos pasado muchas desgracias* we have undergone many misfortunes>; (*desecar*) to dry in the sun; (*aprobar*) to pass <*p. un examen* to pass a test> • **p. en limpio** to make a clear copy • **p. la noche en blanco** to spend a sleepless night • **p. las de Caín** to go through hell • **p. lista** to call roll • **pasarla bien, mal** to have a good, bad time • **p. por las armas** to execute • **p. por alto** to omit —intr. (*transcurrir*) to go by; (*entrar*) to come in; (*ocurrir*) to happen, occur <*¿qué pasó?* what happened?>; (*durar*) to last; (*cesar*) to pass, be over; (*conceder*) to yield, pass; (*transferirse*) to be handed down • **hacerse p.** por to pass oneself off as • **ir pasándola** to get along • **p. a** to proceed to • **p. a mejor vida** to go on to the great beyond • **p. a ser** to become • **p. de** (*exceder*) to exceed, surpass; (*edad*) to be over • **p. de moda** to go out of fashion • **p. por** (*simular ser*) to pretend to be; (*detenerse*) to stop by; (*padecer*) to go through, undergo • **p. por encima** to go over someone's head • **p. sin** to do or go without —reflex. (*cumbiar de partido*) to pass over; (*olvidarse*) to forget; (*deslizar*) to run <*se pasó la mano por la frente* she ran her hand across her brow>; (*excederse*) to go too far; (*echarse a perder*) to go bad; (*estar muy cocido*) to be overcooked • **p. sin** to do without • **p. de la raya** to go too far • **p. la gran vida** to live it up.

pa·sa·re·la f. (*puentecillo*) footbridge; MARIT. gangway; THEAT. catwalk.

pa·sa·tiem·po m. pastime.

Pas·cua f. (*de resurrección*) Easter; (*Navidad*) Christmas; (*Epifanía*) Epiphany; (*Pentecostés*) Pentecost; (*fiesta judía*) Passover • **dar las pascuas** to wish (someone) a Merry Christmas • **estar como unas pascuas** COLL. to be happy as a lark • **P. florida** RELIG. Easter • **santas pascuas** COLL. that's all there is to it • pl. Christmastide.

pa·se m. pass.

pa·se·ar intr. (*andar*) to go for a walk; (*a caballo*) to ride (on a horse); (*en coche*) to go for a ride; (*en bicicleta*) to go for a bicycle ride —tr. to take for a walk.

pa·se·o m. (*caminata*) stroll; (*a caballo, coche*) ride; (*excursión*) outing, (*avenida*) avenue; TAUR. parade (of toreadors before the bullfight) • **dar un p.** (*andar*) to go for a walk; (*en coche*) to go for a ride • **echar** or **mandar a p.** to send (someone) packing • **ir de p.** (*andar*) to walk; (*viajar*) to go on a trip • **¡vete a p.!** take a walk!

pa·si·llo m. corridor.

pa·sión f. passion.

pa·sio·nal adj. passionate, emotional • **crimen p.** crime of passion.

pa·si·vo, a I. adj. passive II. m. COM. liabilities.

pas·ma·do, a adj. COLL. (*atónito*) astounded, astonished; (*helado*) frozen.

pas·mar tr. (*enfriar*) to freeze, chill; (*dejar atónito*) to stun; (*asombrar*) to astound —reflex. (*enfriarse*) to freeze; (*atontarse*) to be stunned; (*asombrarse*) to be astounded.

pas·mo m. (*enfriamiento*) chill; (*asombro*) astonishment.

pas·mo·so, a adj. astonishing, amazing.

pa·so, a I. adj. dried (fruit) • **ciruela pasa** prune • **uvas pasas** raisins II. f. raisin • **estar** or **quedarse hecho una p.** COLL. to become all dried and wrinkled • **p. de Corinto** currant.

pa·so m. step; (*marcha*) walk; EQUIT. gait; (*distancia*) pace; (*acción*) passing, passage; (*camino*) passage; GEOG. pass; MARIT. strait; (*pisada*) footstep; (*en el baile*) step • **abrir p. a** to make way for • **a buen p.** quickly • **a cada p.** at every turn • **a dos pasos** at a short distance • **a ese p.** at that rate • **aflojar el p.** to slow down • **a grandes pasos** by leaps and bounds • **apretar el p.** to go faster • **al p. que** (*al mismo tiempo*) while; at the rate that <*al p. que vas, nunca vas a terminar* at the rate that you are going, you will never finish> • **a p. de tortuga** at a snail's pace • **a p. lento** slowly • **a pocos pasos** at a short distance • **ceder el p.** to step aside • **cerrar el p.** to block the way • **cortar el p.** to cut off • **de p.** in passing • **marcar el p.** to keep time • **p. a nivel** grade crossing • **p. a p.** little by little • **p. por p.** step by step • **salir del p.** to get out of a jam • **salirle al p.** (*salir al encuentro*) to intercept; (*confrontar*) to confront • **seguirle los pasos a alguien** to tail someone • **volver sobre sus pasos** to retrace one's steps.

pas·quín m. rag, scandal sheet.

pas·ta f. (*masa*) paste; PAINT. impasto • **p. de dientes** toothpaste • **tener p. de** to have the makings of • pl. noodles, pasta.

pas·tar tr. to take to pasture —intr. to graze.

pas·tel m. CUL. (*dulce*) cake; (*de carne, queso*) pie; PAINT. pastel; COLL. (*ardid*) scheme, game • pl. pastry.

pas·te·le·rí·a f. (*sitio*) pastry shop; (*oficio*) pastry-making.

pas·te·le·ro, a m, f. pastry cook.

pas·te(u)·ri·zar §04 tr. to pasteurize.

pas·te(u)·ri·za·ción f. pasteurization.

pas·ti·lla f. (*de jabón*) bar, cake; (*medicinal*) lozenge, drop; (*de menta*) mint.

pas·ti·zal m. pasture, grazing land.

pas·to m. (*hierba*) grass; (*sitio*) pasture; (*comida*) feed, fodder; FIG. food, fuel.

pas·tor, ·ra m. (*ovejero*) shepherd; (*prelado*) pastor —f. shepherdess.

pas·to·ral I. adj. pastoral II. f. MUS. pastorale.

pas·to·re·ar tr. to take to pasture.

pas·to·so, a adj. (*blando*) doughy; (*voz*) mellow; (*lengua*) coated.

pa·ta f. ZOOL. (*pie*) paw, foot; (*pierna*) leg; COLL. (*pierna humana*) leg; (*base*) leg <*las patas de la mesa* the legs of the table>; ORNITH. female duck • **a cuatro patas** on all fours • **a p.** COLL. on foot • **estirar la p.** COLL. to kick the bucket • **meter la p.** COLL. to put one's foot in it • **p. de gallo** crowfoot; (*arruga*) crow's-foot

• **p. de palo** wooden leg • **patas arriba** COLL. *(boca arriba)* upside-down; *(en desorden)* topsy-turvy • **salir** *or* **ser p.** *or* **patas** to end in a draw *or* a tie • **tener mala p.** COLL. to be unlucky.

pa·ta·da f. kick ♦ **a patadas** COLL. in abundance • **dar la p. a alguien** COLL. to give someone the boot • **darle a alguien una p.** to kick someone • **echar a alguien a patadas** to kick someone out.

pa·ta·le·ar intr. *(dar patadas)* to kick; *(pisar)* to stamp.

pa·ta·le·ta f. COLL. tantrum, fit.

pa·tán m. COLL. lout, boor.

pa·ta·ta f. potato • **patatas fritas** French fries.

pa·ta·tín pa·ta·tán interj. ♦ **que p.** COLL. this and that.

pa·ta·tús m. COLL. fainting spell.

pa·te·ar tr. COLL. to kick —intr. COLL. *(dar patadas)* to stamp one's feet <**p. de rabia** to stamp with rage>; AMER., COLL. *(andar mucho)* to chase all over the place; *(cocear)* to kick.

pa·ten·tar tr. to patent, register.

pa·ten·te I. adj. patent, obvious ♦ **hacer p.** to make evident II. f. *(permiso)* warrant; *(licencia)* licence; *(de invención)* patent ♦ **p. de navegación** certificate of registration.

pa·ter·nal adj. paternal.

pa·ter·ni·dad f. paternity; FIG. authorship.

pa·ter·no, a adj. paternal.

pa·té·ti·co, a adj. pathetic.

pa·tí·bu·lo m. scaffold, gallows.

pa·ti·llas f.pl. sideburns.

pa·ti·llu·do, a adj. having long and heavy sideburns.

pa·tín m. skate; AVIA. skid ♦ **p. de hielo** ice skate • **p. de ruedas** roller skate.

pá·ti·na f. patina.

pa·ti·na·dor, ·ra I. adj. skating II. m.f. skater.

pa·ti·na·je m. skating ♦ **p. artístico** figure skating • **p. sobre hielo** ice skating • **p. sobre ruedas** roller skating.

pa·ti·nar intr. *(con patines)* to skate; *(un vehículo)* to skid; *(resbalar voluntariamente)* to slide; *(resbalar sin querer)* to slip; *(meter la pata)* to slip up —tr. to give a patina to.

pa·ti·na·zo m. skid.

pa·tio m. patio, courtyard ♦ **p. de escuela** schoolyard.

pa·ti·tie·so, a adj. *(paralizado)* stiff-legged; *(aturdido)* paralyzed ♦ **dejar p.** to dumbfound.

pa·ti·zam·bo, a adj. & m.f. knock-kneed (person).

pa·to m. *(ave)* duck; *(pato macho)* drake; AMER. *(bacineta)* bedpan; COLL. *(pelmazo)* bore, drip ♦ **estar hecho un p.** to be soaked to the skin • **pagar el p.** COLL. to take the rap • **p. flojel** eider duck • **p. real** *or* **silvestre** mallard, wild duck.

pa·tó·ge·no, a I. adj. pathogenic II. m. pathogen.

pa·to·lo·gí·a f. pathology.

pa·tó·lo·go, a m.f. pathologist.

pa·tón, o·na adj. COLL. big-footed.

pa·to·ta f. R.P. street gang.

pa·to·te·ro m. R.P. COLL. member of a street gang.

pa·tra·ña f. COLL. hoax.

pa·triar·ca m. patriarch.

pa·triar·cal adj. patriarchal.

pa·tri·cio, a adj. & m.f. patrician.

pa·tri·mo·nio m. patrimony, heritage.

pa·trio, a I. adj. *(de la patria)* native; *(del padre)* paternal II. f. homeland, native land ♦ **madre p.** motherland.

pa·trio·ta m.f. patriot.

pa·trio·te·rí·a f. exaggerated patriotism.

pa·trio·te·ro, a I. adj. COLL. excessively patriotic II. m.f. jingoist.

pa·trió·ti·co, a adj. patriotic.

pa·tro·ci·na·dor, ·ra I. adj. sponsoring II. m.f. sponsor, patron.

pa·tro·ci·nar tr. to sponsor, patronize.

pa·trón, o·na m.f. RELIG. patron saint —m. *(amo)* master, boss; MARIT. skipper, captain; *(modelo)* pattern; *(unidad)* standard ♦ **cortado por el mismo p.** cut of the same cloth.

pa·tro·nal adj. employers', management.

pa·tro·na·to m. *(protección)* patronage, sponsorship; *(organización)* board, council ♦ **p. de las artes** arts council.

pa·tro·no, a m.f. *(jefe)* boss; *(empresario)* employer; *(santo)* patron saint —m. *(dueño)* landlord; *(señor)* lord —f. *(casera)* landlady; *(señora)* lady.

pa·tru·lla f. squad, patrol.

pa·tru·llar intr. & tr. to patrol.

pa·tru·lle·ro, a I. adj. patrol II. m. *(coche)* patrol car; *(buque)* patrol boat; *(avión)* patrol plane.

pa·tu·do, a adj. COLL. big-footed.

pau·la·ti·na·men·te adv. gradually.

pau·la·ti·no, a adj. gradual.

pau·pé·rri·mo, a adj. very poor.

pau·sa f. *(interrupción)* pause, break; *(lentitud)* slowness, calm; MUS. rest ♦ **con p.** slowly.

pau·sa·do, a I. adj. slow II. adv. slowly.

pau·ta f. *(regla)* rule, guide; *(rayas)* guidelines ♦ **dar la p.** to set the example.

pa·va¹ f. turkey-hen.

pa·va² f. *(fuelle)* furnace bellows; R.P. teapot.

pa·va·da f stupidity, foolishness.

pa·vi·men·ta·ción f. paving.

pa·vi·men·tar tr. *(piso)* to floor; *(calle)* to pave.

pa·vi·men·to m. pavement.

pa·vo, a I. adj. foolish II. m. turkey; *(hombre soso)* fool ♦ **edad del p.** awkward age • **p. real** peacock.

pa·vo·na·do, a I. adj. dark blue II. m. METAL. bluing, browning.

pa·vo·ne·ar intr. & reflex. to show off.

pa·vor m. fright, terror.

pa·vo·ro·so, a adj. frightening, terrifying.

pa·vu·ra f. fright, terror.

pa·ya·da f. R.P. improvisation by singing gauchos.

pa·ya·dor m. R.P. singing gaucho.

pa·yar intr. R.P. *(cantar)* to improvise songs; *(contar cuentos)* to tell stories.

pa·ya·sa·da f. buffoonery ♦ **hacer payasadas** to fool around.

pa·ya·se·ar intr. AMER. to clown around.

pa·ya·so m. clown, buffoon.

paz f. peace; *(tratado)* peace treaty; *(tranquilidad)* peacefulness, tranquility ♦ **dejar en p.** to leave alone • **estar en p.** to be at peace; FIG. to be even • **hacer las paces** to make peace • **poner p. entre** to make peace between.

paz·gua·te·rí·a f. foolishness.

paz·gua·to, a I. adj. foolish II. m.f. fool.

pe·a·je m. toll.

pe·al m. *(pie)* foot (of a stocking); *(pial)* lasso.

pe·a·tón m. pedestrian.

pe·a·to·nal adj. pedestrian.
pe·be·te, a m.f. R.P. kid, child.
pe·be·te·ro m. incense burner.
pe·ca f. freckle.
pe·ca·do m. sin ♦ **siete pecados capitales** seven deadly sins.
pe·ca·dor, ·ra I. adj. sinful, II. m.f. sinner.
pe·ca·mi·no·so, a adj. sinful.
pe·car §47 intr. to sin; *(faltar)* to transgress.
pe·ca·rí *or* **pé·ca·ri** m. peccary.
pe·ce·ra f. fishbowl, aquarium.
pe·cí·o·lo/cio·lo m. petiole.
pé·co·ra f. head of sheep.
pe·co·so, a adj. freckled.
pec·ti·na f. pectin.
pec·to·ral I. adj. pectoral II. m. pectoral; *(cruz)* pectoral cross.
pe·cu·liar adj. peculiar.
pe·cu·lia·ri·dad f. peculiarity.
pe·cu·lio m. LAW peculium; FIG. one's own *or* personal money.
pe·cu·nia f. COLL. money.
pe·cu·nia·rio, a adj. pecuniary, financial.
pe·cha·zo m. R.P. touch for a loan.
pe·cha·dor m. AMER., COLL. sponger.
pe·char tr. *(pagar tributo)* to pay; *(asumir)* to shoulder; AMER., COLL. *(dinero)* to hit for a loan; *(empujar)* to shove (with the chest)
pe·che·ro, a m. bib —f. shirt front.
pe·cho m. chest; *(busto)* breast; *(seno)* bosom, breast; ORNITH. breast ♦ **abrir el p.** to unbosom oneself • **dar el p.** to suckle, nurse • **de p.** nursing • **hombre de pelo en p.** he-man • **poner el p. a** to face • **tomar a p.** to take to heart.
pe·chu·ga f. *(del ave)* breast; *(de persona)* chest, breast.
pe·da·go·gí·a f. pedagogy.
pe·da·go·go m. pedagogue.
pe·dal m. *(de pie)* (foot) pedal, treadle; MUS. pedal; *(nota)* sustained note ♦ **p. de embrague** clutch pedal • **p. de freno** brake pedal.
pe·da·le·ar intr. to pedal.
pe·da·le·o m. pedaling.
pe·dan·te I. adj. pedantic II. m.f. pedant.
pe·dan·te·rí·a f./**tis·mo** m. pedantry.
pe·da·zo m. piece ♦ **a pedazos** in pieces *or* bits • **caerse a pedazos** COLL. *(deshacerse)* to fall to pieces; *(estar cansadísimo)* to be dead tired • **hacer pedazos** *(romper)* to smash into pieces; *(desgarrar)* to tear into pieces • **p. de bruto** COLL. blockhead • **ser un p. de pan** COLL. to be an angel.
pe·de·ras·ta m. pederast.
pe·de·ras·tia f. pederasty.
pe·der·nal m. flint.
pe·des·tal m. pedestal; FIG. foundation.
pe·des·tre adj. pedestrian.
pe·dí·a·tra/dia·tra m.f. pediatrician.
pe·dia·trí·a f. pediatrics.
pe·dí·cu·lo m. peduncle.
pe·di·cu·ro, a m.f. podiatrist.
pe·di·do m. *(encargo)* order; *(petición)* request ♦ **a p. de** at the request of • **a p. del público** by public demand • **hacer un p.** to place an order • **p. en firme** firm order.
pe·di·gre·e/grí m. pedigree.
pe·di·güe·ño, a I. adj. persistent, pestering II. m.f. pest, nuisance.
pe·dir §48 tr. *(rogar)* to ask, request; to ask for <*le pedí diez dólares* I asked him for ten dollars>; *(demandar)* to demand; *(mendigar)* to

beg; to order <*pidió una taza de café* he ordered a cup of coffee>; COM. to ask ♦ **a p. de boca** to one's heart's content • **p. disculpas** to apologize • **p. prestado** to borrow.
pe·dra·da f. blow with a stone ♦ **matar a pedradas** to stone to death • **pegar una p. a alguien** to throw a stone at someone.
pe·dre·gal m. rocky terrain.
pe·dre·go·so, a adj. rocky.
pe·dre·rí·a f. precious stones, gems.
pe·dre·ro m. stonecutter.
pe·dris·ca f. *(granizo)* hail; *(granizada)* hailstorm.
pe·drus·co m. COLL. rough *or* uncut stone.
pe·dún·cu·lo m. peduncle.
pe·ga f. *(acción)* sticking; *(dificultad)* snag.
pe·ga·da f. COLL. stroke of luck.
pe·ga·di·zo, a adj. *(que se pega)* adhesive; *(que se contagia)* catching; *(que capta la atención)* catchy.
pe·ga·du·ra f. *(acción)* sticking; *(unión)* adhesion.
pe·ga·jo·si·dad f. stickiness.
pe·ga·jo·so, a adj. *(pegadizo)* adhesive; *(contagioso)* catching; COLL. *(meloso)* cloying; *(excesivamente meloso)* gooey.
pe·ga·mien·to m. sticking, gluing.
pegapega f. Amer. bindline.
pe·gar §47 tr. *(engomar)* to glue; *(arrimar)* to move closer <*p. el sofá a la pared* to move the sofa closer to the wall>; *(unir)* to fasten; *(botón)* to sew on; *(golpear)* to hit; to give <*p. un grito* to give a yell> ♦ **no p. un ojo** not to sleep a wink • **p. fuego** to set fire to • **p. un salto** to jump • **p. un susto** to frighten • **p. un tiro** to shoot —intr. *(adherir)* to adhere; *(golpear)* to hit; *(armonizar)* to go together; MED. to be catching —reflex. *(unirse)* to adhere, CUL. *(quemarse)* to stick to the pan; to pick up <*el vicio de fumar se le pegó de mí* she picked up the vice of smoking from me> • **p. un tiro** to shoot oneself.
pe·go·te m. *(cosa pegajosa)* gooey mess; *(guisado)* thick stew.
pei·na·da f. COLL. combing ♦ **darse una p.** to comb one's hair.
pei·na·do m. hair style, coiffure.
pei·na·dor, ·ra m.f. hairdresser —f. woolcombing machine.
pei·nar tr. *(el cabello)* to comb; *(lana)* to card ♦ **p. canas** COLL. to be old —reflex. to comb one's hair.
pei·ne m. *(para el pelo)* comb; *(para la lana)* card ♦ **pasarse el p.** to comb one's hair.
pei·ne·ta f. ornamental comb.
pe·la·do, a I. adj. *(calvo)* bald; *(con el pelo cortado)* shorn; *(frutos)* peeled; *(desplumado)* plucked; *(sin carne)* bare; *(desnudo)* barren; *(pobre)* broke II. m. *(corte de pelo)* haircut; *(esquileo)* shearing; *(pobre)* pauper —f. *(cabeza)* bald head; *(corte de pelo)* crew cut.
pe·la·du·ra f. peeling.
pe·la·ga·tos m.inv. COLL. poor devil.
pe·la·gra f. pellagra.
pe·lam·bre m. *(pieles)* hides; *(pelo)* matted hair.
pe·lar tr. *(cortar el pelo)* to cut; *(mondar)* to peel; *(desplumar)* to pluck; *(quitar la piel)* to strip; COLL. *(despojar)* to clean out; *(desplumar)* to tear down ♦ **duro de p.** hard nut to crack • **p. la pava** COLL. to court.
pel·da·ño m. rung.

pe·le·a f. (fight ♦ p. de gallos cockfight.
pe·le·a·dor, ·ra adj. (que pela) fighting; (propenso a pelear) quarrelsome.
pe·le·ar intr. to fight; (disputar) to quarrel; (batallar) to battle.
pe·le·le m. (muñeco) rag doll; COLL. (tonto) nincompoop; (traje) child's pajamas.
pe·le·te·rí·a f. (oficio) fur trade; (tienda) fur shop; (pieles finas) furs.
pe·le·te·ro m. (fabricante) fur maker; (vendedor) furrier.
pe·lia·gu·do, a adj. COLL. difficult, tricky.
pe·li·ca·no m. pelican.
pe·lí·cu·la f. (piel) skin; ,zilla) film; PHOTOG. film; CINEM. motion picture ♦ de p. COLL. extraordinary • p. del oeste western • p. en colores film in color; PHOTOG. color film • p. hablada talking picture • p. muda silent movie.
pe·li·grar intr. to be in danger.
pe·li·gro m. danger ♦ correr el p. de to run the risk of • correr p. or estar en p. to be in danger • poner en p. to endanger.
pe·li·gro·so, a adj. dangerous.
pe·li·llo m. (pelo corto) short hair; COLL. (nadería) trifle.
pe·li·rro·jo, a I. adj. red-haired, redheaded II. m.f. redhead.
pel·ma·zo m. (cosa aplastada) flattened mass; (en el estómago) lump; COLL. (persona) bore.
pe·lo m. (cabello) hair; (de la barba) whisker; (de cepillo) bristle; ZOOL. (piel) fur, coat; BOT., ORNITH. down; (filamento) strand; TECH. hairspring; (del tejido) nap; JEWEL. flaw ♦ agarrarse a un p. to grasp at straws • al p. COLL. perfectly • a p. with the grain • contra p. against the grain • estar hasta los pelos COLL. to be fed up • hombre de p. en pecho he-man • no tener pelos en la lengua COLL. not to mince words • p. de camello camel hair • ponérsele a uno los pelos de punta COLL. to make one's hair stand on end • por los pelos or por un p. by the skin of one's teeth • tomar a alguien el p. to pull someone's leg • traído por los pelos farfetched • venir al p. COLL. (ser perfecto) to be just right; (ser oportuno) to come in handy.
pe·lo·ta f. ball; (juego) ball game ♦ p. vasca jai alai.
pe·lo·ta·ri m.f. pelota or jai alai player.
pe·lo·te·ar intr. (jugar) to kick a ball around; (lanzar) to toss back and forth; (reñir) to quarrel, argue.
pe·lo·te·ra f. COLL. brawl, scuffle.
pe·lo·tón m. squad.
pel·tre m. pewter.
pe·lu·ca f. wig.
pe·lu·che f. plush.
pe·lu·do, a I. adj. hairy, shaggy II. m. (felpudo) thick mat; ARG., ZOOL. armadillo.
pe·lu·que·rí·a f. (para hombres) barber shop; (para mujeres) beauty shop or parlor.
pe·lu·que·ro, a m.f. (para hombres) barber; (para hombres y mujeres) hairdresser.
pe·lu·quín m. (peluca) small wig; (bisoñé) toupee.
pe·lu·sa f. (de plantas) down; (de telas) fuzz.
pel·vis f.inv. pelvis.
pe·lla f. (masa redonda) round mass; BOT. head (of cauliflower); (de cerdo) raw lard.
pe·lle·jo m. (de animal) hide; (de fruta) peel; (piel) skin; (odre) wineskin ♦ estar en el p. de

otro FIG. to be in another's shoes • jugarse el p. to risk one's neck • no tener más que el p. to be as thin as a rail • quitarle el p. a alguien COLL. to criticize • salvar el p. to save one's skin.
pe·lliz·car §70 tr. (apretar) to pinch; (comer un poco) to nibble.
pe·lliz·co m. (acción) pinch; (pizca) small portion.
pe·llón m. sheepskin.
pe·na f. (castigo) punishment; (aflicción) sorrow; (dolor) pain ♦ a duras penas with great difficulty • a penas hardly, scarcely • bajo or so p. de under penalty of • dar p. to grieve • p. de muerte death penalty • ¡qué p.! what a shame! • valer la p. to be worthwhile.
pe·na·cho m. (copete) crest; (adorno) plume.
pe·na·do, a I. adj. grieved II. m.f. convict.
pe·nal I. adj. penal II. m. prison.
pe·na·li·dad f. (pena) hardship; LAW penalty.
pe·na·li·zar §04 tr. to penalize.
pe·nar tr. to punish —intr. to suffer.
pen·co m. COLL. hack, nag.
pen·de·ja·da f. SL. (tontería) stupidity; (cobardía) cowardliness.
pen·de·jo, a SL. I. adj. (cobarde) cowardly; (tonto) stupid II. m.f. (cobarde) coward; AMER. (tonto) jerk —m. (pelo) pubic hair.
pen·den·ciar tr. to quarrel.
pen·den·cie·ro, a I. adj. quarrelsome II. m.f. troublemaker.
pen·der intr. (colgar) to hang; (cernerse) to hover; (estar pendiente) to be pending.
pen·dien·te I. adj. (colgante) hanging; (sin solucionar) pending II. m. (arete) earring; (colgante) pendant —f. (cuesta) slope; (del tejado) pitch.
pen·dón m. (bandera) banner; (estandarte) standard.
pén·du·lo, a I. adj. hanging II. m. pendulum.
pe·ne m. penis.
pe·ne·tra·ble adj. penetrable.
pe·ne·tra·ción f. penetration; (sagacidad) insight.
pe·ne·tran·te adj. (que penetra) penetrating; (inteligencia) acute; (voz, mirada) piercing; (frío) biting.
pe·ne·trar tr. to penetrate; (empapar) to permeate; (afectar) to pierce —intr. to penetrate, enter —reflex. (comprender) to fathom; (empaparse) to steep oneself (de in).
pe·ni·ci·li·na f. penicillin.
pe·nín·su·la f. peninsula.
pe·nin·su·lar I. adj. peninsular II. m.f. inhabitant of a peninsula.
pe·ni·que m. penny.
pe·ni·ten·cia f. (sentimiento) penitence; (castigo) penance ♦ hacer p. to do penance.
pe·ni·ten·cia·rio, a adj. & m. penitentiary.
pe·ni·ten·te adj. & m.f. penitent.
pe·no·so, a adj. (difícil) arduous; (triste) sad.
pen·sa·do, a adj. ♦ bien p. (bien reflexionado) well thought-out; (con pensamientos favorables) well-intentioned • el día menos p. when least expected • mal p. (mal reflexionado) poorly thought-out; (con pensamientos malos) evilminded • tener p. to have in mind
pen·sa·dor, ·ra I. adj. thinking II. m. thinker ♦ libre p. freethinker.
pen·sa·mien·to¹ m. thought; (idea) idea; (sentencia) maxim ♦ no pasarle por el p. not to

cross one's mind.
pen·sa·mien·to² m. BOT. pansy.
pen·san·te adj. thinking.
pen·sar §49 tr. *(considerar)* to think about, consider; *(creer)* to think, believe; *(planear)* to intend ♦ **pensándolo mejor** or **bien** on second thought —intr. to think ♦ **p. en** or **sobre** to think about ♦ **p. entre sí** or **para sí** to think to oneself **¿qué piensas de . . . ?** what is your opinion about . . . ? ♦ **sin p.** without thinking.
pen·sa·ti·vo, a adj. pensive.
pen·sión f. *(en un hotel)* room and board; *(de retiro)* pension, annuity; *(de estudios)* grant; *(casa)* boarding house.
pen·sio·na·do, a I. adj. pensioned II. m.f. pensioner —m. boarding school.
pen·sio·nar tr. to pension.
pen·sio·nis·ta m.f. *(retirado)* pensioner; *(en hotel)* boarder.
pen·tá·go·no, a I. adj. pentagonal II. m. pentagon.
pen·ta·gra·ma m. MUS. stave, staff.
pen·to·tal m. pentothal.
pe·núl·ti·mo, a adj. & m.f. penultimate.
pe·num·bra f. shadow; PHYS. penumbra.
pe·nu·ria f. penury, want.
pe·ña f. *(roca)* boulder; *(círculo)* circle.
pe·ñas·co m. large rock, crag.
pe·ñas·co·so, a adj. rocky.
pe·ñón m. craggy rock ♦ **p. de Gibraltar** Rock of Gibraltar.
pe·ón m. AMER. farmhand, peon; *(jornalero)* unskilled laborer; *(en ajedrez)* pawn; *(en damas)* man; MIL. infantryman.
pe·o·na·da f./**pe** m. gang of laborers.
pe·or I. adj. worse <*éste es p. que el otro* this one is worse than the other>; worst <*soy el p. jugador* I am the worst player> ♦ **cada vez p.** worse and worse ♦ **y lo que es p.** and what's worse II. adv. worse ♦ **p. que p.** or **tanto p.** worse still III. m.f. worse <*soy el p. de los dos* I am the worse of the two>; worst <*ella es la p. de las bailarinas* she is the worst of the dancers> ♦ **en el p. de los casos** if worst comes to worst • **lo p.** the worst thing.
pe·pa f. AMER. pip, seed.
pe·pi·no m. cucumber ♦ **no importar un p.** COLL. not to matter a whit.
pe·pi·ta f. pip, seed; VET. pip; MIN. nugget.
pép·ti·co, a adj. peptic.
pe·que·ñez f. *(calidad)* smallness, littleness; *(menudencia)* trifle ♦ **p. de miras** narrow-mindedness.
pe·que·ñín, i·na I. adj. teeny, tiny II. m.f. child, tot.
pe·que·ño, a I. adj. small; *(corto)* short; *(joven)* young II. m.f. child ♦ **de p.** as a child.
pe·que·ñue·lo, a I. adj. tiny, teeny II. m.f. little one, tot ♦ **los pequeñuelos** the little ones.
pe·ra f. *(fruta)* pear; *(barba)* goatee ♦ **pedir peras al olmo** COLL. to ask for the moon.
pe·ral m. pear tree.
per·cal m. percale.
per·can·ce m. mishap.
per·ca·tar intr. to notice —reflex. to become aware.
per·cep·ción f. *(de dinero)* receiving; *(sensación)* perception.
per·cep·ti·vo, a adj. perceptive.
per·ci·bir tr. *(distinguir)* to perceive, sense; *(cobrar)* to collect, receive.
per·cu·dir tr. to tarnish, dull —reflex. to be-

come stained.
per·cu·sión f. percussion.
per·cu·tir intr. to percuss, strike.
per·cu·tor m. firing pin.
per·cha f. *(madero)* pole, prop; *(perchero)* clothes rack, *(de colgar)* hanger, coat hanger.
per·che·ro m. clothes rack.
per·de·dor, ra I. adj. losing II. m.f. loser.
per·der §50 tr. to lose; *(desperdiciar)* to miss; *(arruinar)* to spoil ♦ **echar a p.** to spoil ♦ **de vista** to lose sight of • **p. el juicio** to lose one's mind • **p. la vista** to lose one's eyesight —intr. to lose; *(desteñirse)* to fade —reflex. to lose, mislay; *(desorientarse)* to get lost; *(dejar de ser útil)* to go to waste; *(arruinarse)* to go astray ♦ **p. de vista** to disappear.
per·di·ción f. *(ruina)* ruin; RELIG. damnation.
pér·di·da f. *(privación)* loss, waste; *(daño)* damage, harm ♦ **pérdidas y ganancias** profit and loss.
per·di·da·men·te adv. madly.
per·di·do, a I. adj. *(extraviado)* lost, lost; *(bala)* stray; *(rematado)* confirmed <*un borracho p.* a confirmed drunkard>; *(incorregible)* dissolute ♦ **estar p. por** to be madly in love with II. m. libertine.
per·di·gón m. partridge; ARM. small shot.
per·di·gue·ro m. pointer.
per·diz f. partridge.
per·dón m. pardon, forgiveness ♦ **¡p.!** sorry!
per·do·nar tr. *(disculpar)* to pardon, forgive; *(la vida)* to spare; *(renunciar)* to forego.
per·du·ra·ble adj. *(eterno)* eternal, everlasting; *(duradero)* durable, lasting.
per·du·rar intr. to last.
pe·re·ce·de·ro, a adj. perishable.
pe·re·cer §17 intr. to perish, die.
pe·re·ci·mien·to m. demise.
pe·re·gri·na·ción f./**pe** m. pilgrimage.
pe·re·gri·nar intr. *(andar)* to journey; *(a un santuario)* to make a pilgrimage.
pe·re·gri·no, a I. adj. *(que viaja)* traveling; *(en una peregrinación)* on a pilgrimage; ORNITH. migratory II. m.f. pilgrim.
pe·re·jil m. parsley.
pe·ren·ga·no, a m.f. so-and-so.
pe·ren·ne adj. perennial.
pe·ren·to·ria·men·te adv. peremptorily.
pe·ren·to·rie·dad f. peremptoriness.
pe·ren·to·rio, a adj. *(terminante)* peremptory; *(apremiante)* urgent.
pe·re·za f. *(holgazanería)* laziness; *(lentitud)* slowness.
pe·re·zo·so, a I. adj. *(holgazán)* lazy; *(pesado)* slow II. m. ZOOL. sloth.
per·fec·ción f. perfection ♦ **a la p.** to perfection.
per·fec·cio·na·mien·to m. *(perfección)* perfection; *(mejora)* improvement.
per·fec·cio·nar tr. *(hacer perfecto)* to make perfect; *(mejorar)* to improve.
per·fec·cio·nis·ta adj. & m.f. perfectionist.
per·fec·ta·men·te adv. perfectly ♦ **¡p.!** right!
per·fec·to, a adj. perfect.
per·fi·dia f. perfidy.
pér·fi·do, a I. adj. unfaithful II. m.f. traitor.
per·fil m. profile; *(contorno)* outline; *(sección)* cross section ♦ **de p.** in profile • **de medio p.** three-quarter.
per·fi·la·do, a adj. *(rostro)* long and thin; *(nariz)* perfect.
per·fi·lar tr. PAINT. to profile; *(pulir)* to polish

—reflex. *(colocarse de perfil)* to show one's profile; *(tomar forma)* to take shape.

per·fo·ra·ción f. perforation; MIN. drilling.

per·fo·ra·do, ·a adj. perforation.

per·fo·ra·dor, ·ra I. adj. perforating; MIN. drilling II. f. *(para papeles)* punch; MIN. drill.

per·fo·rar tr. to perforate; MIN. to drill.

per·fu·mar tr. to perfume.

per·fu·me m. perfume; *(aroma)* fragrance.

per·fu·me·rí·a f. perfumery.

per·fu·me·ro, ·a/mis·ta m.f. perfumer.

per·ga·mi·no m. *(papel)* parchment; *(diploma)* diploma; *(documento)* manuscript.

pér·go·la f. pergola.

pe·ri·car·dio m. pericardium.

pe·ri·car·pio m. pericarp.

pe·ri·cia f. skill, expertise.

pe·ri·co m. parakeet.

pe·ri·fe·ria f. periphery.

pe·ri·fo·llo m. BOT. chervil; COLL. ornaments.

pe·ri·lla f. *(adorno)* pear-shaped ornament; *(barbilla)* goatee; *(tirador)* knob, handle ♦ **venir de perillas** COLL. to come in handy.

pe·rí·me·tro m. perimeter.

pe·rió·di·ca·men·te adv. periodically.

pe·rió·di·co, ·a I. adj. periodic(al) II. m. newspaper.

pe·rio·dis·mo m. journalism.

pe·rio·dis·ta m.f. journalist.

pe·rí·o·do/rí·o·do m. period; GEOL. age.

pe·ri·pa·té·ti·co, ·a adj. Aristotelian; COLL. *(ridículo)* ridiculous.

pe·ri·pe·cia f. vicissitude.

pe·rís·to·le f. peristalsis.

pe·ri·que·te m. ♦ **en un p.** COLL. in a jiffy.

pe·ri·qui·to m. parakeet.

pe·ris·co·pio m. periscope.

pe·ris·ti·lo m. peristyle.

pe·ri·to, ·a adj. & m.f. expert.

pe·ri·to·ne·o m. peritoneum.

per·ju·di·car §70 tr. *(dañar)* to damage; *(estropear)* to harm.

per·ju·di·cial adj. harmful, detrimental.

per·jui·cio m. *(material)* damage; *(moral)* injury; FIN. loss.

per·ju·rar intr. to commit perjury.

per·ju·rio m. perjury.

per·ju·ro, ·a I. adj. perjured II. m.f. perjurer.

per·la f. pearl; FIG. treasure ♦ **de perlas** perfectly ♦ **p. de cultivo** cultured pearl ♦ **venir de perlas** to come at the right moment.

per·la·do, ·a adj. pearl-colored, pearly.

per·ma·ne·cer §17 intr. to stay, remain.

per·ma·nen·cia f. *(duración)* permanence; *(estancia)* stay.

per·ma·nen·te I. adj. permanent II. f. permanent wave.

per·mi·si·ble adj. permissible.

per·mi·si·vo, ·a adj. permissive.

per·mi·so m. *(autorización)* permission; *(documento)* permit; MIL. leave ♦ **con (su) p.** *(perdóneme)* excuse me; *(con su autorización)* with your permission ♦ **p. de conducir** driver's license.

per·mi·ti·do, ·a adj. permitted, allowed.

per·mi·tir tr. *(autorizar)* to permit, let; *(tolerar)* to allow, tolerate ♦ **permítame** allow me • **si lo permite el tiempo** weather permitting —reflex. to be permitted *or* allowed ♦ **no se permite fumar** no smoking.

per·mu·ta/ción f. exchange; MATH. permutation.

per·mu·tar tr. to exchange; MATH. to permute.

per·ne·ra f. pant leg.

per·ni·cio·so, ·a adj. pernicious.

per·nil m. *(de animal)* haunch and thigh; *(de cerdo)* ham.

per·no m. bolt, pin.

per·noc·tar intr. to spend the night.

pe·ro I. conj. but <*es bonita p. antipática* she is pretty but disagreeable>; yet <*gana mucho dinero p. nunca tiene un centavo* he earns a lot of money yet he is always broke> II. m. ♦ **no hay p. que valga** COLL. there are no buts about it ♦ **poner peros** COLL. to raise objections.

pe·ro·gru·lla·da f. COLL. trite remark.

pe·ro·né m. fibula.

pe·ro·rar intr. to perorate, make a speech.

pe·ro·ra·ta f. long-winded speech.

pe·ró·xi·do m. peroxide.

per·pen·di·cu·lar adj. & f. perpendicular.

per·pe·tra·ción f. perpetration.

per·pe·tra·dor, ·ra I. adj. perpetrating II. m.f. perpetrator.

per·pe·trar tr. to perpetrate.

per·pe·tua·ción f. perpetuation.

per·pe·tua·men·te adv. perpetually.

per·pe·tuar §67 tr. to perpetuate —reflex. to be perpetuated.

per·pe·tui·dad f. perpetuity.

per·pe·tuo, ·a adj. perpetual ♦ **cadena p.** life imprisonment.

per·ple·ji·dad f. perplexity.

per·ple·jo, ·a adj. perplexed.

pe·rre·ra f. *(lugar)* dog kennel; *(carro)* dog-catcher's wagon.

pe·rre·rí·a f. *(jauría)* pack of dogs; *(mala acción)* dirty trick.

pe·rro, ·a I. m.f. dog; FIG. dirty dog ♦ **¡a otro p. con ese hueso!** COLL. tell it to the Marines! • **p. cobrador** retriever • **p. de aguas** *or* **de lanas** poodle • **p. dogo** *or* **de presa** bulldog • **p. faldero** lap dog • **p. galgo** greyhound • **p. lebrel** whippet • **p. lobo** wolfhound • **p. mastín** mastiff • **p. ovejero** sheep dog • **p. sabueso** bloodhound • **una vida de perros** a lousy life —f. bitch; COLL. *(moneda)* five- or ten-cent piece II. adj. lousy, rotten.

pe·rru·no, ·a adj. canine, of dogs.

per·se·cu·ción f. *(tormento)* persecution; *(seguimiento)* pursuit, chase.

per·se·gui·dor, ·ra I. adj. *(que atormenta)* persecuting; *(que sigue)* chasing II. m.f. *(que atormenta)* persecutor; *(que sigue)* pursuer.

per·se·guir §64 tr. *(seguir)* to pursue, chase; *(acosar)* to persecute; *(atormentar)* to torment; *(molestar)* to pester.

per·se·ve·ran·cia f. perseverance.

per·se·ve·ran·te adj. persevering.

per·se·ve·rar intr. to persevere.

per·sia·na f. blind.

per·si·ga, go see **perseguir.**

per·sig·nar tr. to cross.

per·si·guie·ra, guió see **perseguir.**

per·sis·ten·cia f. persistence.

per·sis·ten·te adj. persistent.

per·sis·tir intr. to persist.

per·so·na f. person ♦ **p. jurídica** LAW legal entity ♦ **por p.** per person, each • **tercera p.** GRAM. third person; *(mediador)* third party ♦ **pl.** people.

per·so·na·je m. celebrity; LIT. character.

per·so·nal I. adj. personal II. m. personnel ♦ **p. de tierra** ground crew.

per·so·na·li·dad f. personality; *(personaje)* public figure.

per·so·na·li·zar §04 tr. to personalize; GRAM. to make personal.

per·so·ni·fi·ca·ción f. personification.

per·so·ni·fi·car §70 u. to personify.

pers·pec·ti·va f. perspective; *(vista)* view; *(contingencia)* outlook; *(apariencia)* appearance.

pers·pi·ca·cia/ci·dad f. perspicacity.

pers·pi·caz adj. *(agudo)* sharp, keen; *(sagaz)* shrewd, perspicacious.

per·sua·dir tr. *(a hacer)* to persuade; *(a creer)* to convince —reflex. to be persuaded *or* convinced.

per·sua·sión f. persuasion.

per·sua·si·vo, a adj. persuasive.

per·te·ne·cer §17 intr. *(ser de)* to belong, be; *(ser parte)* to belong <*el anillo pertenece a la colección real* the ring belongs to the royal collection>; *(concernir)* to pertain (a to).

per·te·ne·cien·te adj. pertaining (a to).

per·te·nen·cia f. *(derecho)* ownership; *(posesión)* belonging.

pér·ti·ga f. pole ♦ **salto de p.** pole vault.

pér·ti·go m. shaft.

per·ti·naz adj. obstinate, tenacious.

per·ti·nen·cia f. pertinence, relevance

per·ti·nen·te adj. pertinent, relevant.

per·tre·char tr. MIL. to supply, equip; *(disponer)* to prepare —reflex. ♦ **p. de o con** to supply oneself with.

per·tre·chos m.pl. *(víveres)* supplies, *(instrumentos)* equipment.

per·tur·ba·ción f. disturbance.

per·tur·ba·dor, ·ra I. adj. disturbing II. m.f. disturber.

per·tur·bar tr. *(trastornar)* to disturb; *(desasosegar)* to perturb.

pe·rú m. ♦ valer un p. to be worth a fortune.

per·ver·si·dad f. perversity.

per·ver·sión f. perversion.

per·ver·so, a adj. & m. wicked (person).

per·ver·ti·do, a I. adj. perverted II. m.f. pervert.

per·ver·tir §65 tr. to pervert —reflex. to become perverted.

pe·sa f. weight ♦ pl. dumbbells, weights.

pe·sa·car·tas m.inv. letter scale.

pe·sa·da f. quantity weighed at one time.

pe·sa·dez f. *(calidad)* heaviness; *(molestia)* nuisance.

pe·sa·di·lla f. nightmare.

pe·sa·do, a adj. *(que pesa)* heavy; *(sueño)* deep; *(corazón)* heavy; *(tiempo)* oppressive; *(aburrido)* boring; *(molesto)* annoying; *(fatigante)* tedious; *(difícil)* tough; *(ofensivo)* offensive; *(obeso)* obese.

pe·sa·dum·bre f. *(pesadez)* heaviness, *(pesar)* grief.

pé·sa·me m. condolence ♦ **dar el p.** to express condolences.

pe·sar[1] m. *(pena)* sorrow; *(arrepentimiento)* regret ♦ **p. de** in spite of, despite • **a p. de uno** against one's will • **a p. de todo** in spite of everything.

pe·sar[2] tr. *(determinar el peso)* to weigh; to weigh down <*me pesa el fardo* the bundle is weighing me down>; *(examinar)* to weigh, consider; *(agobiar)* to sadden —intr. *(tener peso)* to weigh; *(ser pesado)* to weigh a lot; *(ser importante)* to carry weight ♦ **pese a quien le**

pese say what they will.

pe·sa·ro·so, a adj. *(arrepentido)* sorry; *(triste)* sad.

pes·ca f. *(acción)* fishing; *(lo pescado)* catch ♦ **p. de alta mar** deep-sea fishing.

pes·ca·de·rí·a f. fish market.

pes·ca·de·ro, a m.f. fishmonger.

pes·ca·di·lla f. whiting.

pes·ca·do m. fish (out of water).

pes·ca·dor m. fisherman.

pes·can·te m. *(de las cocheras)* coachman's seat; CONSTR. jib; MARIT. davit.

pes·car §70 tr. *(coger peces)* to fish (for); *(lograr)* to land <*p. un marido* to land a husband>; *(sorprender)* to catch.

pes·cue·zo m. *(de animal)* neck; *(de persona)* scruff of the neck.

pe·se·bre f. manger.

pe·se·ta f. FIN. peseta.

pe·si·mis·ta I. adj. pessimistic II. m.f. pessimist.

pé·si·mo, a adj. very bad, terrible.

pe·so m. weight; FIN. peso; *(pesa)* counterweight; *(carga)* burden; SPORT. shot <*lanzamiento del p.* shot-put> ♦ **caerse de su propio p.** COLL. to be self-evident • **levantamiento de pesos** weightlifting • **levantar en p.** to lift up • **p. bruto** gross weight • **p. específico** density • **p. gallo** bantamweight • **p. liviano** lightweight • **p. medio** middleweight • **p. mosca** flyweight • **p. pesado** heavyweight • **p. semimedio** welterweight • **quitarle a alguien un p. de encima** to take a load off someone's mind.

pes·pun·tar/te·ar tr. to backstitch.

pes·pun·te m. backstitch.

pes·que·ro, a adj. fishing.

pes·qui·sa f. *(averiguación)* investigation —m. ARG., ECUAD. secret police.

pes·ta·ña f. eyelash; *(de una rueda)* rim; *(borde)* edge; SEW. fringe ♦ **no pegar p.** not to sleep a wink • **quemarse las pestañas** COLL. to burn the midnight oil.

pes·ta·ñe·ar intr. to blink, wink.

pes·ta·ñe·o m. blinking, winking.

pes·te f. plague; *(olor)* stench; *(molestia)* nuisance ♦ **huir de alguien como de la p.** to avoid someone like the plague ♦ pl. offensive words • **echar p.** to complain bitterly.

pes·ti·len·cia f. *(peste)* pestilence, plague; *(olor)* stench, stink.

pes·ti·llo m. bolt (of a lock).

pes·to·so, a adj. foul.

pe·ta·ca f. *(bolsa)* tobacco pouch; *(estuche)* cigarette case; *(baúl)* leather trunk.

pé·ta·lo m. petal.

pe·tar·do m. MIL. petard; *(cohete)* firecracker.

pe·ta·te m. *(estera)* sleeping mat; *(de ropa)* bundle.

pe·ti·ción f. petition; LAW claim ♦ **a p. de** at the request of.

pe·ti·cio·nar tr. to petition.

pe·ti·cio·na·rio, a/na I. adj. petitioning II. m.f. petitioner.

pe·ti·me·tre m. fop.

pe·ti·so, a AMER. I. adj. short II. m. small horse.

pe·ti·to·rio, a I. adj. petitionary II. m. petition.

pé·tre·o, a adj. rocky.

pe·tri·fi·car §70 tr. to petrify —reflex. to become petrified.

pe·tro·dó·la·res m.pl. petrodollars.

pe·tró·le·o m. petroleum, oil ♦ **p. bruto** or **crudo** crude oil • **p. combustible** fuel oil.

pe·tro·le·ro, a I. adj. oil, petroleum II. m. oil tanker.

pe·tro·lí·fe·ro, a adj. oil-bearing.

pe·tro·quí·mi·ca f. petrochemistry.

pe·tro·quí·mi·co, a adj. petrochemical.

pe·tu·lan·cia f. arrogance.

pe·tu·lan·te adj. arrogant.

pe·tu·nia f. petunia.

pe·yo·ra·ti·vo, a adj. pejorative.

pe·yo·te m. peyote.

pez[1] m. fish ♦ **estar como el p. en el agua** COLL. to feel completely at home • **p. espada** swordfish • **p. gordo** COLL. big shot.

pez[2] f. pitch, tar.

pe·zón m. (de la teta) nipple; (extremo) point.

pe·zo·ne·ra f. (de eje) linchpin; (de mujeres) nipple shield.

pe·zu·ña f. (cloven) hoof.

¡pf! interj. hah!

pia·do·so, a adj. (que compadece) compassionate; (devoto) pious.

pia·nis·ta m.f. pianist.

pia·no I. m. piano ♦ **p. de cola** grand piano • **p. de media cola** baby grand • **p. vertical** upright piano II. adv. MUS. softly.

pia·no·for·te m. pianoforte, piano.

piar §30 intr. to cheep, chirp.

pi·be, a m.f. R.P. COLL. kid.

pi·ca·de·ro m. (para caballos) ring; MARIT. boat skid or block.

pi·ca·di·llo m. chopped meat ♦ **hacer p.** to make mincemeat of.

pi·ca·do, a I. adj. (perforado) perforated; COLL. (ofendido) ticked off II. m. (acción) perforating; MUS. staccato; AVIA. nose dive.

pi·ca·dor m. (de caballos) horsebreaker; TAUR. picador.

pi·ca·du·ra f. bite.

pi·ca·flor m. hummingbird; AMER. flirt.

pi·ca·ma·de·ros m.inv. woodpecker.

pi·ca·na f. R.P. goad.

pi·ca·ne·ar tr. R.P. to goad.

pi·can·te adj. spicy; (arriesgado) risqué.

pi·ca·plei·tos m.inv. COLL. shyster.

pi·ca·por·te m. (barrita) latch; (llave) latchkey; (aldaba) doorknocker.

pi·car §70 tr. (punzar) to prick; (agujerear) to perforate; to punch <p. los billetes to punch tickets>; TAUR. to goad; (espolear) to spur; (morder) to bite; ICHTH. to bite; ORNITH. to peck (at); (comer) to nibble; (quemar) to burn, sting; (cortar) to mince; (estimular) to arouse, pique; (enojar) to pique, vex; PAINT. to stipple —intr. (escocer) to itch; (morder) to sting; (calentar) to be hot; AVIA., ORNITH. to dive; ICHTH. to bite —reflex. (agujerearse) to become moth-eaten; (echarse a perder) to rot; (avinagrarse) to turn sour; MARIT. to become choppy; (irritarse) to get annoyed.

pi·car·dí·a f. (acción baja) dirty trick; (travesura) mischief.

pi·ca·res·co, a adj. mischievous; LIT. picaresque.

pí·ca·ro, a I. adj. (astuto) sly; (malicioso) wicked; (en sentido cariñoso) impish II. m.f. (bribón) scoundrel; (astuto) sly person; (en sentido cariñoso) rascal —m. LIT. rogue.

pi·ca·rón, o·na I. adj. COLL. mischievous II. m.f. COLL. rascal.

pi·ca·zón f. itch, itching.

pi·co m. (de aves) beak; (punta) tip; (de vasija) spout; (herramienta) pick; (cima) peak ♦ **callar** or **cerrar el p.** COLL. to shut one's trap • **tener mucho p.** COLL. to gab a lot • **y p.** odd <veinte dólares y p. twenty-odd dollars>; a little after <son las ocho y p. it is a little after eight>.

pi·cor m. itching.

pi·co·ta·da f./zo m. peck.

pi·co·te·ar tr. (con el pico) to peck; (comer) to nibble, pick (at).

pic·tó·ri·co, a adj. pictorial.

pi·chón m. (paloma) young pigeon; COLL. (nombre cariñoso) honey; AMER. novice.

pi·da, do, diera, dió see pedir.

pie m. foot; (base) base, stand; (sedimento) sediment; (tronco) trunk; (tallo) stalk ♦ **al p. de la letra** to the letter • **a p.** on foot • **a p. firme** steadfastly • **a p. juntillas** steadfastly • **caer de p.** to land on one's feet • **con pies de plomo** (lentamente) slowly; (con prudencia) cautiously • **dar a p.** to give rise to • **de p.** upright • **de pies a cabeza** from head to foot • **en p. de guerra** ready for war • **entrar con buen p.** to get off to a good start • **estar con el p. en el estribo** to be about to leave • **estar con un p. en la sepultura** to have one foot in the grave • **hacer p.** (hallar fondo) to touch bottom; (estar seguro) to be on a firm footing • **levantarse con el p. izquierdo** COLL. to get up on the wrong side of the bed • **nacer de p.** COLL. to be born lucky • **no dar p. con bola** COLL. to do nothing right • **no tener pies ni cabeza** to make no sense whatsoever • **perder p.** to slip • **p. de atleta** athlete's foot • **pies planos** flatfeet • **poner pies en polvorosa** COLL. to run away • **ponerse de p.** to stand up.

pie·dad f. (devoción) piety; (lástima) pity.

pie·dra f. (peña) stone, rock; (granizo) hailstone ♦ **p. de afilar** grindstone • **p. de amolar** whetstone • **p. angular** cornerstone • **p. caliza** limestone • **p. de chispa** flint • **p. de molino** millstone • **p. filosofal** philosophers' stone • **p. fundamental** keystone • **p. pómez** pumice stone • **p. preciosa** precious stone.

piel f. skin; ZOOL. (sin pelo) skin, hide; (con pelo) fur, pelt; (cuero) leather; BOT. peel ♦ **de p.** (de cuero) leather <valija de p. leather suitcase>; fur <abrigo de p. fur coat> • **p. de cabra** goat-skin • **p. de cerdo** pigskin • **p. de gallina** goose pimples • **ser de la p. del diablo** COLL. to be a little devil.

pien·se, so see pensar[1].

pien·so m. fodder.

pier·da, do see perder.

pier·na f. leg; R.P. player (in a card game) ♦ **dormir a p. suelta** COLL. to sleep like a log.

pie·za f. piece; (de maquinaria) part; (moneda) coin; (de tela) bolt; (habitación) room; (animal) head; (ficha) man ♦ **de una p.** (sólido) solid; (honesto) honest • **dejar de una p.** COLL. to leave speechless • **p. de repuesto** spare part • **quedarse de una p.** COLL. to be left speechless.

pi·fia f. (en billar) miscue; COLL. (error) slip.

pi·fiar intr. & tr. (en billar) to miscue ♦ COLL. (chapucear) to bungle; AMER. to mock.

pig·men·ta·ción f. pigmentation.

pig·men·tar tr. to pigment.

pig·men·to m. pigment.

pig·me·o adj. & m.f. pygmy.

pi·ja·ma m. pajamas.

pi·la f. (recipiente) basin; (de cocina) sink;

(fuente) fountain; *(montón)* pile; *(de bautismo)* baptismal font; *(de agua bendita)* holy water font; ELEC. battery, cell ♦ **nombre de p.** Christian name • **p. atómica** atomic reactor.

pi·lar m. *(columna)* pillar, column; *(de puente)* pier.

pil·cha f. R.P. piece of clothing.

píl·do·ra f. pill ♦ **dorar la p.** COLL. to sugarcoat the pill.

pi·le·ta f. *(pila)* sink; AMER. *(piscina)* swimming pool.

pi·lón¹ m. *(pila)* basin, trough; *(mortero)* pounding mortar; *(pan de azúcar)* sugarloaf; *(pesa móvil)* movable weight.

pi·lón² m. ARCHIT. pylon.

pi·lo·tar/te·ar tr. to pilot; *(conducir)* to drive.

pi·lo·te m. stake.

pi·lo·to I. m. pilot; *(navegante)* navigator; *(segundo de un buque)* first mate; *(guía)* guide; *(llama)* pilot light ♦ **p. automático** automatic pilot • **p. de pruebas** test pilot • **p. de puerto** harbor pilot • **p. práctico** coastal pilot II. adj. pilot, model.

pil·tra·fa f. *(carne)* gristly meat; *(persona)* wretch.

pi·llar tr. *(robar)* to plunder; *(coger)* to catch.

pi·lle·rí·a f. prank, trick.

pi·lle·te/llín m. COLL. rascal.

pi·llo, a COLL. I. adj. mischievous II. m.f. scoundrel.

pi·llue·lo, a I. adj. mischievous II. m.f. rascal.

pi·men·tón m. paprika.

pi·mien·ta f. pepper.

pi·mien·to m. BOT. pepper; *(pimentón)* paprika ♦ **p. chile** chili pepper • **p. morrón** sweet pepper.

pim·pan·te adj. *(bien vestido)* elegant, spruce; *(garboso)* graceful, poised.

pim·po·llo m. *(capullo)* rosebud; *(vástago)* shoot —m.f. COLL. attractive youth.

pi·na·co·te·ca f. art gallery.

pi·ná·cu·lo m. pinnacle.

pi·nar m. pine grove.

pin·cel m. brush.

pin·ce·la·da f./zo m. brush stroke ♦ **dar la última p.** a to put the last touches on.

pin·cha·du·ra f. puncture.

pin·char tr. to puncture; FIG. to annoy ♦ **ni pincha ni corta** COLL. he has little say.

pin·cha·zo m. puncture.

pin·che I. m. *(de cocina)* kitchen boy; AMER. *(de oficina)* clerk II. adj. MEX., COLL. miserable, lousy.

pin·cho m. *(aguijón)* prickle, thorn; *(de aduanero)* sampling stick; *(de sombrero)* hatpin.

pin·ga·jo m. COLL. tatter, rag.

pin·go m. COLL. *(pingajo)* tatter; *(pendón)* bum, good-for-nothing; R.P. fast horse.

pin·güe adj. *(graso)* greasy; *(grande)* huge.

pin·güi·no m. penguin.

pi·ni·to m. first step.

pi·no m. pine (tree) ♦ **p. albar** Scotch pine.

pin·ta f. see **pinto, a.**

pin·ta·do, a I. adj. spotted, mottled ♦ **como p.** just right • **no poder ver (a alguien) ni p.** COLL. not to be able to stand (someone) • **venir como p.** to suit to a tee.

pin·tar tr. to paint; *(describir)* to depict —intr. to paint —reflex. to put on make-up.

pin·ta·rra·jar/je·ar COLL. tr. to paint amateurishly —reflex. to put on heavy make-up.

pin·to, a I. adj. speckled II. f. *(mancha)* spot; COLL. *(aspecto)* look; *(medida)* pint ♦ **tener p. de** COLL. to look like.

pin·tón, o·na adj. *(de frutas)* ripening; *(de ladrillos)* half-baked; R.P., COLL. *(elegante)* sharp.

pin·tor, ·ra m.f. painter ♦ **p. de brocha gorda** house painter; FIG. bad painter.

pin·to·res·co, a adj. picturesque.

pin·tu·ra f. *(arte)* painting; *(cuadro)* painting, picture; *(color)* paint; *(descripción)* portrayal ♦ **p. a la acuarela** water color • **p. al fresco** fresco painting • **p. al óleo** oil painting • **p. al pastel** pastel (drawing).

pin·za f. *(de langosta)* claw; SEW. dart ♦ pl. *(tenacillas)* tweezers; *(tenazas)* tongs.

pi·ña f. *(del pino)* pine cone; *(ananás)* pineapple; COLL. *(puñetazo)* blow ♦ **darse piñas** AMER., COLL. to come to blows.

pi·ñón¹ m. *(simiente)* pine nut; *(arbusto)* nut pine.

pi·ñón² m. MECH. pinion (wheel).

pí·o, a I. adj. *(devoto)* pious; *(compasivo)* compassionate II. m. chirping ♦ **no decir ni p.** COLL. not to say a word.

pio·jo m. louse ♦ **p. resucitado** COLL. upstart.

pio·jo·so, a adj. *(lleno de piojos)* lousy; *(sucio)* dirty; *(miserable)* stingy.

pio·la f. string, cord.

pio·ne·ro, a m.f. & adj. pioneer.

pio·rre·a f. pyorrhea.

pi·pa¹ f. *(tonel)* barrel; *(para fumar)* pipe.

pi·pa² f. pip, seed.

pi·per·min m. peppermint.

pi·pe·ta f. pipette.

pi·pí m. COLL. wee-wee ♦ **hacer p.** COLL. to make wee-wee.

pi·piar §30 intr. to chirp.

pi·pón, o·na adj. AMER. *(lleno)* full; *(barrigón)* paunchy.

pi·que¹ m. resentment.

pi·que² m. ♦ **echar a p.** to sink; FIG. to ruin • **irse a p.** to sink; FIG. to be ruined.

pi·qué m. piqué.

pi·que·ta f. pick.

pi·que·te m. picket, squad.

pi·ra·gua f. pirogue.

pi·ra·mi·dal adj. pyramidal.

pi·rá·mi·de f. pyramid.

pi·ra·ña f. AMER. piranha.

pi·rar·se reflex. COLL. to take off, leave.

pi·ra·ta m. & adj. pirate ♦ **p. aéreo** hijacker.

pi·ra·te·rí·a f. *(de barcos)* piracy; *(robo)* theft ♦ **p. aérea** hijacking.

pi·ri·ta f. pyrites.

pi·ró·ma·no, a I. adj. pyromaniacal II. m.f. pyromaniac.

pi·ro·pe·ar tr. COLL. to pay flirtatious compliments to.

pi·ro·po m. *(requiebro)* flattering remark; *(granate)* garnet ♦ **decir piropos** to pay flirtatious compliments (a to).

pi·ro·tec·nia f. pyrotechnics, pyrotechny.

pi·ro·téc·ni·co, a I. adj. pyrotechnic(al) II. m. pyrotechnist.

pí·rri·co, a adj. Pyrrhic.

pi·rue·ta f. pirouette.

pi·ru·lí m. [pl. **-ís**] lollipop.

pis m. COLL. wee-wee ♦ **hacer p.** to pee.

pi·sa·da f. *(acción)* step; *(huella)* footprint.

pi·sa·pa·pe·les m.inv. paperweight.

pi·sar tr. *(andar)* to step or walk on; *(frutas)* to

press; *(tierra)* to pack down; ORNITH. to copulate with; *(cubrir)* to cover.

pi·sa·ú·vas m.inv. grape treader.

pis·ci·cul·tu·ra f. pisciculture.

pis·ci·na f. *(para nadar)* swimming pool; *(para peces)* fishpond.

pis·co·la·bis m.inv. COLL. snack.

pi·so m. *(suelo)* ground; *(de una habitación)* floor; *(pavimento)* pavement; *(planta)* floor, story; *(apartamento)* apartment, flat (G.B.) ♦ **p. bajo** ground floor • **primer p.** second floor, first floor (G.B.).

pi·són m. rammer, tamper.

pi·so·ne·ar tr. to ram down, tamp.

pi·so·te·ar tr. *(pisar)* to trample; *(maltratar)* to abuse.

pi·so·tón m. ♦ **dar un p.** to step on someone's foot.

pis·ta f. *(huella)* trail; *(de carrera)* racetrack; *(de bailar)* dance floor; *(del circo)* ring; *(de aterrizaje)* runway; *(indicio)* clue; *(camino)* trail ♦ **estar sobre la p.** to be on the trail *or* track.

pis·ta·cho m. pistachio (nut).

pis·ti·lo m. pistil.

pis·to·la f. *(arma)* pistol; *(para pintar)* paint sprayer ♦ **p. ametralladora** submachine gun • **p. de engrase** grease gun.

pis·to·le·ro m. COLL. gunman.

pis·to·le·ta·zo m. pistol shot.

pis·tón m. piston; AMER. cornet.

pi·ta f. BOT. agave; TEX. pita.

pi·ta·da f. whistle; AMER. puff, drag.

pi·tan·za f. *(reparto)* ration; *(alimento)* daily bread.

pi·tar intr. *(tocar el pito)* to blow a whistle; S. AMER. *(fumar)* to smoke ♦ **salir pitando** to go off like a shot —tr. *(silbar)* to hiss at; S. AMER. *(fumar)* to smoke.

pi·te·cán·tro·po m. pithecanthropus.

pi·ti·do m. whistling.

pi·ti·lle·ra f. cigarette case.

pi·ti·llo m. cigarette.

pi·to m. whistle ♦ **no darle** *or* **importarle a uno un p.** COLL. not to give a damn • **no tocar p. en** to have nothing to do with • **no valer un p.** to be worthless.

pi·tón[1] m. ZOOL. python.

pi·tón[2] m. *(cuerno)* horn; *(pitorro)* spout; *(del árbol)* shoot; AMER. nozzle.

pi·to·ni·sa f. pythoness.

pi·tui·ta·rio, a adj. pituitary.

pi·vo·te m. pivot.

pi·ya·ma m. var. of **pijama**.

pi·za·rra f. *(troca)* slate; *(pizarrón)* blackboard.

pi·za·rrín m. slate pencil.

pi·za·rrón m. AMER. blackboard.

piz·ca[1] f. pinch ♦ **ni p.** COLL. not (at all).

piz·pe·re·ta/piz·pi·re·ta adj. COLL. lively.

pla·ca f. plaque; *(chapa)* plate; *(insignia)* badge; *(disco)* record; ELEC., PHOTOG. plate; COMPUT. chip ♦ **p. de matrícula** license plate.

pla·ce·bo m. placebo.

plá·ce·me m. congratulations.

pla·cen·ta f. placenta.

pla·cen·te·ro, a adj. pleasant.

pla·cer[1] m. *(deleite)* pleasure; *(diversión)* delight; *(voluntad)* desire.

pla·cer[2] §51 tr. to please *<me place hacerlo it pleases me to do it>*.

pla·ci·dez f. placidness, placidity.

plá·ci·do, a adj. *(quieto)* placid; *(grato)* pleasant.

pla·ga f. plague; BOT. blight.

pla·gar §47 tr. to plague —reflex. to become infested with.

pla·giar tr. to plagiarize.

pla·gia·rio, a I. adj. plagiarizing **II.** m.f. plagiarist.

pla·gio m. plagiarism.

plan m. plan; *(esquema)* scheme; *(proyecto)* project; *(programa)* program ♦ **p. de estudios** curriculum, course of study.

pla·na f. *(página)* page, side; PRINT. page; MAS. trowel ♦ **de primera p.** front page.

plan·cha f. *(lámina)* sheet; *(utensilio)* iron *<p. a vapor steam iron>*; COLL. *(error)* blooper; PRINT. plate ♦ **a la p.** grilled • **hacer la p.** to float on one's back.

plan·cha·do, a m. *(acción)* ironing; *(ropa)* ironing, clothes to be ironed —f. *(puentecillo)* gangplank; AMER., COLL. *(metedura de pata)* blunder.

plan·cha·dor, ·ra m.f. presser.

plan·char tr. to iron.

plan·cha·zo m. COLL. blunder.

pla·ne·a·ción f./**mien·to** m. planning.

pla·ne·a·dor m. glider.

pla·ne·ar tr. to plan —intr. AER. to glide.

pla·ne·ta m. planet.

pla·ne·ta·rio, a I. adj. planetary **II.** m. planetarium.

pla·ne·toi·de m. planetoid.

pla·ni·fi·ca·ción f. planning.

pla·ni·fi·ca·dor, ·ra I. adj. planning **II.** m.f. planner.

pla·ni·fi·car §70 tr. to plan.

pla·ni·lla f. AMER. *(lista)* list; *(cuadro)* table; *(formulario)* form.

pla·no, a I. adj. *(llano)* level, even; *(liso)* smooth; *(chato)* flat **II.** m. plane; *(superficie)* surface; *(diagrama)* diagram; *(mapa)* map, chart; *(de una espada)* flat ♦ **caer de p.** to fall flat • **de p.** plainly • **levantar un p.** TOP. to make a survey • **primer p.** CINEM. *(foto)* close-up; *(área)* foreground.

plan·ta f. plant; *(del pie)* sole; *(diseño)* floor plan; *(piso)* floor; *(proyecto)* plan, project ♦ **p. baja** ground floor, first floor • **primera p.** second floor, first floor (G.B.).

plan·ta·ción f. *(acción)* planting; *(explotación)* plantation.

plan·ta·do, a adj. planted ♦ **bien p.** COLL. good-looking • **dejar (a alguien) p.** to stand (someone) up.

plan·tar tr. to plant, sow; *(colocar)* to put; COLL. *(un golpe)* to land; *(abandonar)* to leave —reflex. *(resistir)* to stand firm; COLL. *(pararse)* to balk *<el caballo se plantó frente al arroyo the horse balked at the stream>*; *(en naipes)* to stand.

plan·te·a·mien·to m. *(exposición)* exposition; *(propuesta)* proposal; *(establecimiento)* establishment; *(enfoque)* focus.

plan·te·ar tr. *(exponer)* to expound; *(empezar)* to start; *(planear)* to outline; *(establecer)* to establish; *(proponer)* to propose.

plan·tel m. *(conjunto)* group; *(criadero)* nursery, seedbed.

plan·te·o m. var. of **planteamiento**.

plan·ti·lla f. *(suela)* insole; TECH. *(patrón)* template; *(de una lámina)* form.

plan·tón m. *(pimpollo)* seedling; *(estaca)* cutting ♦ **estar de p.** COLL. to be standing around a long time • **dar un p.** to keep (someone) waiting.

pla·ñi·de·ro, a adj. plaintive.

pla·ñi·do m. moan, lament.

pla·ñir §12 intr. to lament.

pla·que·ta f. blood platelet.

plas·ma m. plasma.

plas·mar tr. to shape, mold.

plás·ti·co, a adj. & m. plastic —f. plastic arts.

plas·ti·fi·ca·ción f./do m. shellacking.

plas·ti·fi·car §70 tr. to shellac.

pla·ta f. silver; *(moneda)* silver (coin); AMER. money.

pla·ta·for·ma f. platform; FIG. *(trampolín)* stepping stone; *(vagón)* open wagon ♦ **p. continental** continental shelf • **p. de lanzamiento** launching pad.

pla·tal m. AMER., COLL. fortune.

plá·ta·no m. *(de banano)* banana; *(de sombra)* plane tree; BOT., CUL. plantain.

pla·te·a f. orchestra seat or section.

pla·te·a·do, a I. adj. *(bañado)* silver-plated; *(de color)* silvery; MFX. wealthy II. m. silver plating.

pla·te·ar tr. to silver-plate.

pla·te·rí·a f. *(arte)* silversmithing; *(tienda)* silversmith's shop.

pla·te·ro m. silversmith.

plá·ti·ca f. chat, talk.

pla·ti·car §70 intr. to chat, talk *(sobre over, about)*.

pla·ti·llo m. *(plato pequeño)* saucer; *(balanza)* tray; MUS. cymbal ♦ **p. volador** flying saucer.

pla·ti·na f. PRINT. *(mesa)* imposing table; *(de prensa)* platen; TECH. plate (of air pump); *(microscopio)* slide.

pla·ti·nar tr. to platinize; *(hair)* to bleach.

pla·ti·no m. platinum.

pla·to m. plate, dish; *(contenido)* plateful, dish; *(comida)* dish; course <p. **fuerte** main course>; *(de la balanza)* pan; MECH. plate ♦ **pagar los platos rotos** COLL. to pay the consequences.

pla·tó·ni·co, a adj. platonic.

pla·tu·do, a adj. AMER., COLL. rich, wealthy.

plau·si·ble adj. plausible.

pla·ya f. beach ♦ **p. de estacionamiento** AMER. parking lot.

pla·ye·ro, a adj. beach <sombrero **p.** beach hat>.

pla·za f. *(lugar público)* plaza, square; *(mercado)* marketplace; *(sitio)* place; *(empleo)* position ♦ **p. de toros** bullring.

pla·zo m. *(término)* term, period; *(pago)* installment ♦ **a corto p.** short-term • **a largo p.** long-term • **comprar a plazos** to buy on credit • **en breve p.** within a short time • **vender a plazos** to sell on credit.

pla·zo·le·ta f. small square.

ple·a·mar f. high tide or water.

ple·be f. *(multitud)* masses; DEROG. riffraff.

ple·be·yo, a adj. & m.f. plebeian.

ple·bis·ci·to m. plebiscite.

ple·ga·ble adj. folding, collapsible.

ple·ga·de·ra f. paperknife; PRINT. folder.

ple·ga·di·zo, a adj. *(que se dobla)* folding; *(fácil de doblar)* foldable, easy to fold.

ple·ga·do m.f. *(acción)* folding; *(pliegue)* fold.

ple·ga·mien·to m. fold.

ple·gar §52 tr. *(hacer pliegues)* to pleat; *(doblar)* to fold —reflex. *(doblarse)* to bend, fold; *(someterse)* to yield; *(adherirse)* to join.

ple·ga·ria f. prayer.

plei·te·ar intr. to litigate.

plei·te·sí·a f. homage, tribute ♦ **rendir p.** to pay homage.

plei·to m. LAW lawsuit; *(disputa)* quarrel ♦ **entablar p.** to bring suit • **ganar el p.** to obtain a favorable judgment • **poner p.** to sue.

ple·na·mar f. var. of **pleamar.**

ple·na·rio, a adj. plenary.

ple·ni·lu·nio m. full moon.

ple·ni·po·ten·cia f. unlimited powers.

ple·ni·po·ten·cia·rio, a adj. & m.f. plenipotentiary.

ple·ni·tud f. fullness; FIG. prime.

ple·no, a I. adj. full ♦ **en p.** right in the middle of <en **p. calle** right in the middle of the street> • **en p. día** in broad daylight II. m. joint session.

plé·to·ra f. plethora.

pleu·re·sí·a f. pleurisy.

ple·xo m. plexus ♦ **p. solar** solar plexus.

plie·go m. *(papel doblado)* folded sheet of paper; *(hoja de papel)* sheet of paper; *(documento cerrado)* sealed document; PRINT. signature ♦ **p. de condiciones** specifications.

plie·go, gue see **plegar.**

plie·gue m. fold; SEW. pleat.

pli·sa·do m. *(acción)* pleating; *(efecto)* pleat.

pli·sar tr. to pleat.

plo·ma·da f. plumb (line); MARIT. plumb or sounding line; *(perdigonada)* shot with pellets.

plo·me·rí·a f. *(techo)* lead roofing; AMER. *(oficio)* plumbing.

plo·me·ro m. AMER. plumber.

plo·mi·zo, a adj. leaden.

plo·mo, a I. adj. leaden II. m. lead; COLL. *(bala)* bullet; *(persona)* bore ♦ **a p.** plumb.

plu·ma f. feather; *(conjunto de plumas)* feather, down <una **almohada de plumas** a down pillow>; *(para escribir)* quill; *(estilográfica)* pen; *(adorno)* plume ♦ AMER. **p. fuente** or **estilográfica** fountain pen.

plu·ma·da f. pen stroke.

plu·ma·fuen·te f. AMER. fountain pen.

plu·ma·je m. *(plumas)* plumage; *(adorno)* plume.

plu·ma·zo m. pen stroke ♦ **de un p.** with one stroke of the pen.

plu·me·ro m. *(para polvo)* feather duster; *(penacho)* plume.

plu·mi·lla f. nib.

plu·món m. *(pluma)* down; *(colchón)* feather mattress.

plu·ral adj. & m. plural.

plu·ra·li·dad f. plurality.

plu·ra·li·zar §04 tr. to pluralize.

plus·cuam·per·fec·to m. pluperfect.

plus·va·lí·a f. appreciation.

plu·to·cra·cia f. plutocracy.

plu·tó·cra·ta m.f. plutocrat.

plu·to·nio m. plutonium.

plu·vial adj. pluvial, rain.

po·bla·ción f. population; *(lugar)* locality; *(ciudad)* city; *(pueblo)* town.

po·bla·do m. *(habitantes)* population; *(ciudad)* city; *(pueblo)* town.

po·bla·dor, ·ra m.f. resident, inhabitant.

po·blar §19 tr. to populate; AGR. to plant —reflex. to become populated; *(llenarse)* to become crowded *(de with)*.

po·bre I. adj. poor; *(necesitado)* needy; *(desprovisto)* lacking *(de, en in)*; *(humilde)* humble;

FIG. unfortunate ♦ **más p. que una rata** COLL. as poor as a church mouse II. m. beggar, pauper ♦ **los pobres** the poor.

po·bre·men·te adv. *(con pobreza)* poorly, indigently; *(con escasez)* poorly, inadequately.

po·bre·tón, o·na I. adj. wretched II. m.f. wretch.

po·bre·za f. poverty; *(indigencia)* indigence; *(escasez)* lack.

po·ce·ro m. well digger.

po·cil·ga f. pigsty.

po·ci·llo m. cup.

pó·ci·ma f. *(cocimiento medicinal)* potion; *(bebida)* concoction.

po·ción f. potion.

po·co, a I. adj. little ♦ **p. tiempo** short while *or* time ♦ **ser p. cosa** to be unimportant ♦ pl. few, not many ♦ **pocas veces** not very often, rarely II. m. little ♦ **dentro de p.** in a short while, soon ♦ **otro p.** a little more ♦ **tener en p.** to have a low opinion *(a of)* ♦ **un p. de** a little, some <*tiene un p. de dinero* he has a little money> ♦ pl. <*p. saben la respuesta* few know the answer> III. adv. *(con escasez)* little, not much <*habló p. durante la clase* he spoke little during the class>; *(en corta duración)* not long, a short while <*tardó p. en terminar* he did not take long to finish>; *(no muy)* not very ♦ **a p. de** shortly after <*a p. de comer fuimos al cine* shortly after eating, we went to the movies> ♦ **falta p. para** it will not be long before <*falta p. para comer* it will not be long before we eat> ♦ **hace p.** a short time ago ♦ **p. a p.** little by little ♦ **p. después** a little after ♦ **p. más o menos** more or less ♦ **por p.** almost.

po·da f. *(acción)* pruning; *(tiempo)* pruning season.

po·da·de·ra f. AGR. pruning shears.

po·da·dor, ra I. adj. pruning II. m.f. pruner.

po·dar tr. to prune.

po·den·co, a adj. & m.f. spaniel (dog).

po·der¹ m. power; *(autoridad)* authority; *(vigor)* might; *(fuerza física)* strength; *(capacidad)* capacity; *(posesión)* hands <*tengo en mi p. su carta del once de mayo* I have in my hands your letter of the eleventh of May>; MIL. strength; POL. government; LAW power of attorney ♦ **dar p. a** to empower ♦ **p. adquisitivo** purchasing power ♦ **p. ejecutivo** the executive ♦ **p. judicial** the judiciary ♦ **p. legislativo** the legislative branch ♦ **por poderes** by proxy.

po·der² §53 tr. *(lograr)* to be able to <*podremos salir a las ocho* we will be able to leave at eight o'clock>; can <*¿puedes acompañarme?* can you come with me?> —intr. to be able, can <*me gustaría ayudarte pero no puedo* I would like to help you but I am not able to>; to be possible, may <*puede que llueva mañana* it may rain tomorrow> ♦ **a más no p.** to the utmost ♦ **no p. con** *(no lograr)* not to be able to handle; *(no soportar)* not to be able to stand ♦ **no p. más** *(estar fatigado)* to be exhausted; *(estar harto)* to be fed up ♦ **no p. menos que** not to be able to help but ♦ **no p. valerse por sí mismo** to be helpless ♦ **no puede ser** that is not possible ♦ **puede ser** maybe ♦ **¿se puede?** may I?

po·de·rí·o m. power.

po·de·ro·so, a adj. *(fuerte)* powerful; *(rico)* wealthy; *(eficaz)* effective.

po·dí·a·tra/dia·tra m. AMER. podiatrist.

po·drá, drías see **poder²**.

po·dre·dum·bre f. putrefaction.

po·dri·do, a adj. rotten ♦ **estar p. en plata** AMER., COLL. to be rolling in money.

po·drir tr. & reflex. to rot, putrefy.

po·e·ma m. poem.

po·e·sí·a f. poetry; *(poema)* poem.

po·e·ta m. poet.

po·é·ti·co, a I. adj. poetic II. f. poetics.

po·e·ti·sa f. poetess.

pó·ker m. poker.

po·lai·na f. legging.

po·lar adj. polar; ELEC. pole.

po·la·ri·za·ción f. polarization.

po·la·ri·zar §04 tr. to polarize —intr. to become polarized.

po·le·a f. pulley.

po·lé·mi·co, a I. adj. polemic(al) II. f. *(arte)* polemics; *(controversia)* polemic.

po·le·mi·zar §04 intr. to argue *(sobre* about).

po·len m. pollen.

po·li m. SL. cop —f. cops <*¡la p.!* the cops!>.

po·li·cí·a f. police —m. policeman.

po·li·cia·co/cí·a·co, a adj. *(de policía)* police; detective <*novela p.* detective novel>.

po·li·cial I. adj. *(de policía)* police; *(de detective)* detective II. m. AMER. policeman.

po·li·clí·ni·ca f. polyclinic.

po·li·cro·mí·a f. polychromy.

po·lie·dro m. polyhedron.

po·li·fo·ní·a f. polyphony.

po·li·ga·mia f. polygamy.

po·lí·glo·to/lí·glo·to, a adj. & m.f. polyglot.

po·lí·go·no m. polygon.

po·li·lla f. moth.

po·lí·me·ro m. polymer.

po·li·ni·za·ción f. pollination.

po·li·no·mio m. polynomial.

po·lio(·mie·li·tis) f. polio, poliomyelitis.

pó·li·po m. polyp.

po·li·téc·ni·co, a adj. polytechnic.

po·li·ti·cas·tro m. DEROG. politician.

po·lí·ti·co, a I. adj. political; *(de parentesco)* -in-law <*hermana p.* sister-in-law> II. m.f. politician —f. politics; *(modo de obrar)* policy <*p. monetaria* monetary policy>.

po·li·ti·que·ar intr. COLL. to talk politics.

po·li·ti·que·ro, a m.f. political maneuverer.

po·li·ti·zar §04 tr. to politicize.

po·liu·re·ta·no m. polyurethane.

po·li·va·len·te adj. polyvalent.

pó·li·za f. *(de seguros)* insurance policy; *(contrato)* contract; *(sello)* stamp.

po·li·zón m. stowaway.

po·lo¹ m. pole ♦ **p. antártico** *or* **austral** South Pole ♦ **p. ártico** *or* **boreal** North Pole ♦ **ser el p. opuesto de** to be the opposite of.

po·lo² m. polo ♦ **p. acuático** water polo.

pol·trón, o·na I. adj. lazy II. f. easy chair.

po·lu·ción f. pollution.

pol·va·re·da f. *(nube)* cloud of dust; *(alboroto)* rumpus.

pol·ve·ra f. compact.

pol·vo m. *(tierra)* dust; *(substancia pulverizada)* powder; *(porción)* pinch ♦ **en. p.** powdered ♦ **estar hecho p.** COLL. *(exhausto)* to be exhausted; *(desmoralizado)* to be overwhelmed ♦ **hacer morder el p.** to beat up a alguien to defeat ♦ **hacer p.** COLL. *(romper)* to smash; *(aniquilar)* to annihilate ♦ pl. cosmetic powder.

pól·vo·ra f. powder ♦ **ser una p.** to be a whip.

pol·vo·rien·to, a adj. dusty.

pol·vo·rín m. *(explosivo)* fine gunpowder; *(lugar)* powder magazine.

po·lla f. young hen.

po·lle·ra f. henouse; AMER. skirt.

po·lle·rí·a f. poultry shop.

po·lle·ro m. poulterer.

po·llo m. (cria) chick; CUL. chicken; SL. (gargajo) spit.

po·ma·da f. pomade.

po·me·lo m. (fruta) grapefruit; (árbol) grapefruit tree.

pó·mez adj. ♦ **piedra p.** pumice stone.

po·mo m. pome; (para licores) flagon; (para perfumes) perfume bottle.

pom·pa f. pomp; (ostentación) display; (procesión) procession; (burbuja) bubble ♦ **pompas fúnebres** funeral.

pom·po·si·dad f. (esplendor) pomp; (arrogancia) pomposity.

pom·po·so, a adj. (espléndido) magnificent; (arrogante) pompous.

pó·mu·lo m. (hueso) cheekbone; (mejilla) cheek.

pon see poner.

pon·cha·da f. AMER., COLL. large quantity.

pon·che m. punch.

pon·che·ra f. punch bowl.

pon·cho m. poncho.

pon·de·ra·ble adj. ponderable; (digno de ponderación) worthy of consideration.

pon·de·ra·ción f. (examinación) consideration; (peso) weighing; (equilibrio) balance.

pon·de·ra·do, a adj. prudent, careful.

pon·de·rar tr. (alabar) to praise; (examinar) to ponder; (pesar) to weigh.

pon·drá, dría see poner.

po·ne·dor, ·ra adj. egg-laying.

po·ner §54 tr. (colocar) to put, place <¿dónde pusiste la tijera? where did you put the scissors?>; (disponer) to set <María puso la mesa Mary set the table>; (escribir) to write; (instalar) to set up <p. casa to set up house>; (suponer) to suppose <pongamos que esto es así let's suppose that this is so>; (tardar) to take; (dejar) to leave <lo pongo en tus manos I leave it in your hands>; (asignar) to assign <le pusimos a hacer las decoraciones we assigned him to do the decorations>; (nombrar) to give <le pusieron el apodo de Paco they gave him the nickname of Frank>; ORNITH. to lay; THEAT. to put on; (apostar) to put, stake; (contribuir) to contribute; (imponer) to levy; (exponer) to put <sin darme cuenta puse a Tomás en una situación peligrosa without realizing it I put Thomas in a dangerous situation>; (insultar) to insult <¡cómo lo pusieron! how they insulted him!>; (causar) to put <eso lo pondrá de mal humor that will put him in a bad mood>; (enviar) to send <me puso un telegrama she sent me a telegram> ♦ **p. al corriente** or **al día** to bring up to date ♦ **p. aparte** or **a un lado** to put aside ♦ **p. de la parte de uno** to do what one can ♦ **p. en claro** to make clear ♦ **p. en duda** to call into question ♦ **p. en movimiento** to set in motion ♦ **p. en práctica** to put into practice ♦ **p. en ridículo** to ridicule ♦ **p. en venta** to put up for sale ♦ **p. fin a** to put a stop to ♦ **p. manos a la obra** to get to work ♦ **p. miedo** to frighten ♦ **p. por encima** to prefer ♦ **p. por escrito** to put in writing ♦ **p. por las nubes** to praise to the skies —intr. ORNITH. to lay —reflex. (colocarse) to put or place oneself; (vestirse) to put on <se puso el sombrero he put on his hat>; (arriesgarse) to put oneself <p. en peligro to put oneself in danger>; ASTRON. to set; (hacerse) to become <se pusieron furiosos they became furious>; (dedicarse) to apply oneself ♦ **p. a** to begin to ♦ **p. al corriente** to bring oneself up to date ♦ **p. bien** to get well ♦ **p. colorado** to blush ♦ **p. de acuerdo** to reach an agreement ♦ **p. de pie** to stand up ♦ **p. en camino** to set out.

po·nien·te m. (occidente) west; (viento) west wind.

pon·ti·fi·cal adj. pontifical.

pon·ti·fi·car §70 intr. to pontificate.

pon·ti·fi·ce m. RELIG. pontiff ♦ **Sumo P.** Sovereign Pontiff.

pon·tón m. (barco chato) pontoon; (puente) pontoon bridge.

pon·zo·ña f. venom.

pon·zo·ño·so, a adj. poisonous.

po·pa f. stern ♦ **a p.** MARIT. astern, abaft ♦ **viento en p.** FIG. smoothly, well.

po·pu·la·cho m. populace.

po·pu·lar adj. (del pueblo) of the people, people's; (grato al pueblo) popular, well-liked; (coloquial) colloquial; (música) folk.

po·pu·la·ri·dad f. popularity.

po·pu·la·ri·zar §04 tr. to popularize —reflex. to become popular.

po·pu·rrí m. potpourri.

po·que·dad f. (escasez) scantiness, paucity; (timidez) timidity.

pó·quer m. poker.

por prep. (sitio) by, on, along, through, around, over, towards, throughout; (tiempo) for, around, about, in, at not yet, still to be; (agente) by, via; (causa, motivo) because of, out of, on account of, on behalf of, for, for the sake of, in order to; (modo) by, by means of, in, after, as, for; (distributiva) for, in exchange for, per, a, by, times; (concesión) however, no matter how ♦ **p. acá** or **aquí** around here ♦ **p. ahí** or **allí** around there ♦ **p. ahora** for the time being ♦ **p. casualidad** perchance ♦ **p. causa de** because of ♦ **p. ciento** per cent ♦ **p. cierto** indeed ♦ **p. completo** completely ♦ **p. consiguiente** therefore ♦ **p. correo** by mail ♦ **p. cuenta de uno** (sin ayuda) by oneself; (sin requerimiento) of one's own accord ♦ **p. desgracia** unfortunately ♦ **¡p. Dios!** for Heaven's sake! ♦ **p. entre** between, among ♦ **p. eso** therefore ♦ **p. lo bajo** softly ♦ **p. lo menos** at least ♦ **p. lo tanto** therefore ♦ **p. medio de** through ♦ **p. otra parte** or **p. lo demás** on the other hand ♦ **¿p. qué?** why? ♦ **p. regla general** as a general rule ♦ **p. si acaso** in case ♦ **p. sí mismo** by oneself ♦ **p. sobre dove** ♦ **p. supuesto** of course ♦ **p. todos lados** everywhere ♦ **p. valor de** in the amount of.

por·ce·la·na f. porcelain; (vajilla) china; (esmalte) porcelain enamel; (color) porcelain blue.

por·cen·ta·je m. percentage.

por·cen·tual adj. percentage.

por·ci·no, a I. adj. (del puerco) porcine, pig II. m. small pig.

por·ción f. portion; (parte) part; (cuota) share.

por·che m. porch.

por·dio·se·ar intr. to beg.

por·dio·se·ro, a m.f. beggar.

por·fí·a f. stubbornness.

por·fia·do, a adj. & m.f. stubborn (person).

por·fiar §30 intr. (disputar) to argue stubbornly; (insistir) to persist.

por·me·nor m. detail, particular.
por·no·gra·fí·a f. pornography.
por·no·grá·fi·co, a adj. pornographic.
po·ro m. interstice; BIOL. pore.
po·ro·si·dad f. porosity.
po·ro·so, a adj. porous.
po·ro·to m. AMER. bean.
por·que conj. *(por causa de que)* because *<tra­bajo p. quiero comer* I work because I want to eat>; *(para que)* in order that, so that ♦ **p. sí** just because.
por·qué m. reason *(de* for), cause.
por·que·rí·a f. *(suciedad)* filth; *(basura)* garbage; *(grosería)* vulgarity; *(jugarreta)* dirty trick; *(cosa de poco valor)* junk.
por·que·ri·za f. pigsty.
po·rra f. *(clava)* club; *(de herrero)* sledgehammer; COLL. *(cabellera)* long hair.
po·rra·zo m. *(golpe)* blow; *(choque)* bump ♦ **pegarse un p. contra algo** to bump into something.
po·rro m. leek.
por·ta·a·vio·nes m.inv. aircraft carrier.
por·ta·ban·de·ra f. flag holder.
por·ta·bom·bas m.inv. bomb carrier.
por·ta·da f. ARCHIT. facade; PRINT. *(frontispicio)* title page; *(tapa)* cover.
por·ta·dor, ra I. adj. bearing II. m.f. carrier.
por·ta·e·qui·pa·jes m.inv. *(baúl)* trunk (of a car); *(rejilla)* luggage rack.
por·ta·es·tan·dar·te m. standard-bearer.
por·ta·fo·lio m. briefcase.
por·tal m. *(zaguán)* entrance hall; *(porche)* porch.
por·ta·lám·pa·ras m.inv. socket.
por·ta·li·bros m.inv. book straps.
por·ta·plu·mas m.inv. penholder.
por·tar tr. to carry, bear —reflex. to behave.
por·ta·rre·tra·tos m.inv. picture frame.
por·tá·til adj. portable.
por·ta·voz m.f. spokesman/woman.
por·ta·zo m. slam ♦ **dar un p. a alguien** to slam the door in someone's face.
por·te m. *(acción)* transporting; *(costo)* transport charge; *(presencia)* demeanor.
por·ten·to m. marvel.
por·ten·to·so, a adj. marvelous.
por·te·ño, a I. adj. of Buenos Aires II. m.f. native of Buenos Aires.
por·te·rí·a f. *(oficina)* concierge's office; SPORT. goal.
por·te·ro, a m.f. *(conserje)* concierge; *(de vivienda)* janitor; SPORT. goalkeeper.
pór·ti·co m. portico.
por·ti·lla f. *(paso)* gate; MARIT. porthole.
por·ti·llo m. *(de muro)* opening; *(puerta)* gate; *(paso angosto)* pass.
por·tón m. *(puerta grande)* large door; *(del zaguán)* vestibule door.
por·tua·rio, a adj. port, harbor.
por·ve·nir m. future.
pos adv. ♦ **en p. de** in pursuit of.
po·sa·da f. *(mesón)* inn; *(hogar)* home; *(hospedaje)* shelter.
po·sa·de·ras f.pl. buttocks.
po·sa·de·ro, a m.f. innkeeper.
po·sar intr. *(hospedarse)* to lodge; *(descansar)* to rest; *(las aves)* to perch; PAINT., PHOTOG. to pose —reflex. *(las aves)* to perch; AVIA. to land —tr. to put.
pos·da·ta f. postscript.
po·se f. pose.

po·se·e·dor, ra I. adj. who possesses II. m.f. *(dueño)* owner; holder *<el p. de una marca mun­dial* the holder of a world record> ♦ **p. de acciones** stockholder.
po·se·er §43 tr. to possess; *(tener)* to have *<ella posee una buena biblioteca* she has a good library>; to hold *<posee el record mundial* he holds the world record>.
po·se·í·do, a I. adj. possessed *(de* by) II. m.f. possessed person.
po·se·sión f. possession; *(propiedad)* property; AMER. property, estate ♦ pl. possessions, personal property.
po·se·sio·nar tr. to give possession of —reflex. to take possession of, take over.
po·se·si·vo, a adj. & m. possessive.
po·se·so, a adj. & m.f. possessed (person).
po·se·sor, ra adj. & m.f. var. of poseedor, ra.
po·se·ye·ra, yó see poseer.
pos·fe·cha f. postdate.
pos·gue·rra f. postwar period.
po·si·bi·li·dad f. possibility ♦ pl. chances.
po·si·bi·li·tar tr. to make possible.
po·si·ble adj. possible ♦ **de ser p.** if possible • **dentro de** *or* **en lo p.** as far as possible • **hacer p.** to make possible • **hacer (todo) lo p.** to do everything possible • **lo antes p.** as soon as possible.
po·si·ción f. position; *(postura)* posture; *(condición social)* status.
po·si·ti·vis·ta adj. & m.f. positivist.
po·si·ti·vo, a I. adj. positive II. m. PHOTOG. print; GRAM. positive.
po·so m. *(sedimento)* sediment; *(de café)* coffee grounds.
po·so·lo·gí·a f. dosage.
pos·po·ner §54 *(poner detrás)* to put behind; *(diferir)* to postpone.
pos·ta f. *(de caballos)* relay; *(lugar)* staging post; *(tajada)* slice.
pos·tal I. adj. postal ♦ **giro p.** money order II. f. postcard.
post·da·ta f. var. of posdata.
pos·te m. post ♦ **p. indicador** signpost.
pos·ter·ga·ción f. postponement.
pos·ter·gar §47 tr. *(aplazar)* to postpone; *(en un empleo)* to pass over.
pos·te·ri·dad f. posterity.
pos·te·rior adj. *(ulterior)* subsequent *(a* to), later; *(trasero)* rear, back.
pos·te·rio·ri·dad f. posteriority ♦ **con p.** later *(a* than), subsequently *(a* to).
pos·te·rior·men·te adv. later (on).
post·gue·rra f. var. of posguerra.
pos·ti·go m. *(puerta falsa)* hidden door; *(contraventana)* shutter; *(de ciudad)* side gate.
pos·ti·zo, a I. adj. false *<dentadura p.* false teeth>; artificial *<brazo p.* artificial arm>; *(de quitapón)* detachable II. m. hair piece.
pos·to·pe·ra·to·rio, a adj. postoperative.
pos·tor m. bidder ♦ **mejor p.** highest bidder.
pos·trar tr. *(humillar)* to humiliate; *(debilitar)* to debilitate —reflex. *(arrodillarse)* to kneel down; *(debilitarse)* to become debilitated.
pos·tre m. dessert ♦ **a la p.** in the end.
pos·tre·mo, a adj. last, final.
pos·trer adj. contr. of postrero.
pos·tre·ro, a adj. last, final.
pos·tri·me·rí·a f. last years, final stages.
pos·tu·la·do m. postulate.
pos·tu·lan·te, a m.f. applicant.
pos·tu·lar tr. to ask for, seek.

pós·tu·mo, a adj. posthumous.

pos·tu·ra f. posture; (posición) position; (actitud) attitude; (opinión) stand; (de huevos) laying of eggs.

po·ta·ble adj. potable.

po·ta·je m. (guiso) stew; (bebida) brew.

po·ta·sio m. potassium.

po·te m. pot, jar.

po·ten·cia f. (poder) power; (fuerza) potency, strength; (nación) power <una p. mundial a world power>; ARM. range; PHILOS. potential ♦ **segunda p.** square • **tercera p.** cube.

po·ten·ta·do m. (soberano) potentate; (rico) tycoon.

po·ten·te adj. (poderoso) powerful; (que engendra) potent, virile; (grande) big, mighty.

po·les·tad f. power, authority ♦ **patria p.** parental authority.

po·to m. S. AMER., COLL. buttocks.

po·tra f. young mare.

po·tran·ca f. young mare.

po·tre·ar tr. to romp, frolic.

po·tre·ro m. (dehesa) pasture; R.P. playground (in a vacant lot).

po·tri·llo m. colt.

po·tro m. colt; SPORT. horse; (de tormento) rack.

po·zo m. (de agua) well; (en un río) deep pool; (hoyo) pit MARIT. bilge; FIG. mine, source ♦ **p. de petróleo** oil well • **p. negro** cesspool.

prac·ti·can·te a I. adj. practicing II. m.f. (que ejerce) practitioner; (aprendiz) medical intern.

prac·ti·car §70 tr. to practice; (hacer) to perform, carry out.

prác·ti·co, a I. adj. practical; (conveniente) useful; (diestro) experienced II. m. MARIT. pilot —f. practice; (experiencia) experience ♦ **en la p.** in practice • **poner en p.** to put into practice.

pra·de·ra f. meadow.

pra·do m. (campo) meadow; (paseo) promenade.

prag·má·ti·co, a adj. pragmatic.

pre·ám·bu·lo m. (prólogo) preamble; (rodeo) digression.

pre·ca·rio, a adj. precarious.

pre·cau·ción f. precaution; (prudencia) caution ♦ **por p.** as a precaution.

pre·ca·ver tr. to take precautions against —reflex. to take precautions ♦ **p. contra** to guard against.

pre·ca·vi·do, a adj. cautious.

pre·ce·den·te I. adj. preceding II. m. precedent ♦ **sentar un p.** to set a precedent.

pre·ce·der tr. to precede.

pre·cep·to m. precept.

pre·cep·tor, ·ra m.f. preceptor, tutor; (profesor) teacher —f. governess.

pre·ces f.pl. RELIG. prayers.

pre·cia·do, a adj. (de valor) precious; (estimado) prized.

pre·ciar·se reflex. to brag, boast ♦ **p. de** to consider or think oneself.

pre·cin·ta f. (en un paquete) strap; (en las aduanas) official stamp or seal.

pre·cin·ta·do, a I. adj. sealed II. m. sealing.

pre·cin·tar tr. (un paquete) to bind, strap; (sellar) to seal, stamp.

pre·cin·to m. (de un paquete) strapping; (acción) sealing; (ligadura) strap.

pre·cio m. (valor pecuniario) price, cost; (valor) value, worth <es una obra de gran p. it is a work

of great worth>; (sacrificio) price, cost ♦ **al p. de** at the cost of • **no tener p.** to be priceless • **p. al contado** cash price • **p. de cierre** closing price • **p. de compra** purchase price • **p. de factura** invoice price • **p. de lista** list price • **p. de venta** selling price.

pre·cio·si·dad f. (objeto) beauty; (persona) jewel.

pre·cio·so, a adj. (de valor) precious, valuable; (lindo) lovely.

pre·cio·su·ra f. AMER., COLL. beauty.

pre·ci·pi·cio m. precipice, cliff.

pre·ci·pi·ta·ción f. precipitation ♦ **con p.** hastily • **p. radioactiva** (radioactive) fallout.

pre·ci·pi·ta·do, a adj. & m. precipitate.

pre·ci·pi·tar tr. (lanzar) to hurl; (apresurar) to hasten; CHEM. to precipitate —reflex. (darse prisa) to hurry; (lanzarse) to rush headlong.

pre·ci·sa·men·te adv. (justamente) precisely; (especialmente) specially.

pre·ci·sar tr. (explicar) to explain; (fijar) to set; (necesitar) to need —reflex. to be necessary or needed.

pre·ci·sión f. precision.

pre·ci·so, a adj. (necesario) necessary; (fijo) precise; (exacto) exact; (claro) distinct ♦ **cuando sea p.** when necessary • **tener tiempo p. para** to have just enough time for.

pre·ci·ta·do, a adj. abovementioned.

pre·cla·ro, a adj. illustrious.

pre·co·ci·dad f. precocity.

pre·cog·ni·ción f. precognition.

pre·co·lom·bi(a)·no, a adj. pre-Columbian.

pre·con·ce·bi·do, a adj. preconceived.

pre·con·ce·bir §48 tr. to preconceive.

pre·co·ni·zar §04 tr. to recommend.

pre·coz adj. precocious.

pre·cur·sor, ·ra I. adj. precursory II. m.f. precursor.

pre·de·ce·sor, ·ra m.f. predecessor.

pre·de·cir §11 tr. to predict.

pre·des·ti·na·ción f. predestination.

pre·des·ti·nar tr. to predestine.

pre·de·ter·mi·nar tr. to predetermine.

pré·di·ca f. sermon.

pre·di·ca·ción f. (acción) preaching; (sermón) sermon.

pre·di·ca·do m. GRAM., LOG. predicate.

pre·di·ca·dor, ·ra I. adj. preaching II. m. preacher.

pre·di·car §70 tr. to preach —intr. to preach ♦ **p. con el ejemplo** to set an example.

pre·dic·ción f. prediction.

pre·di·cho, a adj. aforesaid.

pre·di·lec·ción f. predilection.

pre·di·lec·to, a adj. favorite.

pre·dio m. property.

pre·dis·po·ner §54 tr. to predispose ♦ **p. contra** to prejudice against.

pre·dis·po·si·ción f. predisposition.

pre·do·mi·nan·te adj. predominant.

pre·do·mi·nar intr. to prevail.

pre·do·mi·nio m. predominance.

pre·e·mi·nen·te adj. pre-eminent.

pre·es·co·lar adj. preschool.

pre·es·ta·ble·ci·do, a adj. pre-established.

pre·fa·bri·ca·do, a adj. prefabricated.

pre·fa·bri·car §70 tr. to prefabricate.

pre·fa·cio m. preface.

pre·fec·to m. prefect.

pre·fec·tu·ra f. prefecture.

pre·fe·ren·cia f. preference.

pre·fe·ren·te adj. (*principal*) preferential; (*preferible*) preferable.

pre·fe·ren·te·men·te adv. preferably.

pre·fe·ri·ble adj. preferable.

pre·fe·ri·do, a adj. preferred.

pre·fe·rir §65 tr. to prefer.

pre·fi·jar tr. to prearrange.

pre·fi·jo m. prefix; TELEC. area code.

pre·fi·rie·ra, rió see **preferir**.

pre·gón m. street vendor's shout.

pre·go·nar tr. (*publicar*) to proclaim; (*un vendedor*) to hawk; (*revelar*) to divulge.

pre·go·ne·ro, a m.f. (*anunciador*) announcer; (*vendedor*) hawker, peddler —m. (*oficial*) town crier.

pre·gun·ta f. question ♦ **hacer una p.** to ask a question.

pre·gun·tar tr. (*una pregunta*) to ask; (*interrogar*) to question ♦ **p. por** (*noticias*) to inquire about; (*persona*) to ask for —reflex. to wonder.

pre·gun·tón, o·na adj. & m.f. COLL. nosy *or* inquisitive (person).

pre·his·to·ria f. prehistory.

pre·his·tó·ri·co, a adj. prehistoric.

pre·jui·cio m. prejudice.

pre·juz·gar §47 tr. to prejudge.

pre·la·do m. prelate.

pre·li·mi·nar adj. & m. preliminary.

pre·lu·dio m. prelude.

pre·ma·tu·ro, a adj. premature.

pre·me·di·ta·ción f. premeditation.

pre·me·di·ta·da·men·te adv. deliberately.

pre·me·di·ta·do, a adj. premeditated.

pre·me·di·tar tr. to premeditate.

pre·miar tr. (*recompensar*) to reward; (*en certamen*) to award a prize to.

pre·mio m. (*recompensa*) reward; (*en certamen*) prize; FIN. premium ♦ **p. en efectivo** cash prize • **p. gordo** COLL. jackpot.

pre·mi·sa f. premise.

pre·mo·ni·ción f. premonition.

pre·mo·ni·to·rio, a adj. premonitory.

pre·mu·ra f. urgency.

pre·na·tal adj. prenatal.

pren·da f. (*garantía*) guaranty; (*de vestir*) article of clothing; (*señal*) token ♦ **en p.** as security • **en p. de** as token of • **no soltar p.** to be very discreet • **p. interior** undergarment.

pren·dar tr. to pawn —reflex. to become fond.

pren·de·dor m. (*broche*) clasp; JEWEL. pin.

pren·der tr. (*asir*) to grasp; (*aprehender*) to apprehend; (*encarcelar*) to put in prison; (*clavar*) to fasten; AMER. (*con fuego*) to light; (*un aparato*) to turn *or* switch on ♦ **p. con alfileres** to pin • **p. fuego a** to set fire to —intr. (*planta*) to take root; (*fuego*) to catch fire; (*vacuna*) to take (effect).

pren·sa f. press; (*imprenta*) printing press.

pren·sar tr. to press.

pren·sil adj. prehensile.

pre·nup·cial adj. prenuptial.

pre·ña·da, o adj. pregnant.

pre·ñar tr. to impregnate.

pre·ñez f. pregnancy.

pre·o·cu·pa·ción f. preoccupation; (*inquietud*) anxiety.

pre·o·cu·pa·do, a adj. preoccupied; (*inquieto*) worried.

pre·o·cu·par tr. to preoccupy; (*inquietar*) to worry —reflex. (*inquietarse*) to worry (*con, de,*

por about); (*cuidarse*) to take care.

pre·pa·ra·ción f. preparation.

pre·pa·ra·dor, ·ra m.f. SPORT. trainer, coach.

pre·pa·rar tr. & reflex. to prepare (oneself).

pre·pon·de·ran·cia f. preponderance.

pre·pon·de·ran·te adj. preponderant.

pre·po·si·ción f. preposition.

pre·po·si·cio·nal adj. prepositional.

pre·po·ten·cia f. prepotency.

pre·po·ten·te adj. prepotent.

pre·pu·cio m. prepuce.

pre·rro·ga·ti·va f. prerogative.

pre·sa f. (*acción*) capture; (*cosa apresada*) catch; (*en la caza*) prey; (*víctima*) victim; (*conducto*) ditch; (*porción*) morsel; ZOOL. fang ♦ **hacer p.** to capture.

pre·sa·giar tr. to presage.

pre·sa·gio m. (*señal*) omen; (*adivinación*) premonition.

pres·bí·te·ro m. presbyter, priest.

pres·cin·den·cia f. AMER. omission ♦ **con p. de** without.

pres·cin·di·ble adj. nonessential.

pres·cin·dir intr. (*ignorar*) to ignore; (*privarse*) to do without ♦ **prescindiendo de** regardless of.

pres·cri·bir §80 tr. & intr. to prescribe.

pres·crip·ción f. prescription.

pre·se·lec·ción f. preselection.

pre·sen·cia f. presence; (*figura*) appearance ♦ **hacer acto de p.** to put in an appearance • **p. de ánimo** presence of mind.

pre·sen·cial adj. ♦ **testigo p.** eyewitness.

pre·sen·ciar tr. to witness.

pre·sen·ta·ción f. presentation; (*exhibición*) exhibition.

pre·sen·tar tr. to present; (*mostrar*) to show; (*exhibir*) to display; (*dar*) to give; (*proponer*) to nominate; (*introducir*) to introduce; LAW to bring —reflex. (*mostrarse*) to present oneself; (*venir*) to show up <*el alumno se presentó al terminar la clase* the student showed up as the class ended>; (*aparecer*) to present itself, appear; (*dar el nombre*) to introduce oneself.

pre·sen·te I. adj. present; (*actual*) current ♦ **hacer p.** (*declarar*) to state; (*notificar*) to notify • **tener p.** to keep in mind II. m. (*regalo*) present, gift; GRAM. present (tense) ♦ **al p.** at present • **hasta el p.** up to the present • **la p.** this letter • **los presentes** those present III. interj. present, here.

pre·sen·ti·mien·to m. premonition.

pre·sen·tir §65 tr. to have a premonition of.

pre·ser·va·ción f. preservation.

pre·ser·var tr. to preserve.

pre·ser·va·ti·vo, a I. adj. preservative II. m. (*remedio*) preservative; (*anticonceptivo*) prophylactic, condom.

pre·si·den·cia f. (*de nación*) presidency; (*de reunión*) chairmanship; (*silla*) chair; (*oficina*) president's office.

pre·si·den·cial adj. presidential.

pre·si·den·ta f. (woman) president; (*de reunión*) chairwoman.

pre·si·den·te m. president; (*de reunión*) chairman; (*del parlamento*) speaker; (*de tribunal*) presiding judge.

pre·si·dia·rio m. convict.

pre·si·dio m. prison.

pre·si·dir tr. (*dirigir*) to preside over; (*predominar*) to dominate.

pre·si·lla f. (*lazo*) loop; (*para papeles*) paper

clip.

pre·sión f. pressure ♦ **olla a p.** pressure cooker • **p. arterial** blood pressure.

pre·sio·nar tr. *(apretar)* to press; *(hacer presión)* to put pressure on.

pre·so, a I. see **prender II.** adj. under arrest **III.** m.f. prisoner.

pres·ta·ción f. services ♦ **p. de juramento** swearing-in.

pres·ta·do adj. *(dado)* lent; *(tomado)* borrowed ♦ **dar p.** to lend • **de p.** as a loan • **pedir** *or* **tomar p.** to borrow.

pres·ta·dor, ·ra I. adj. lending **II.** m.f. lender.

pres·ta·men·te adv. quickly.

pres·ta·mis·ta m.f. moneylender.

prés·ta·mo m. *(acción de dar)* lending; *(acción de recibir)* borrowing; *(empréstito)* loan ♦ **a plazo fijo** COM. time loan.

pres·tar tr. to lend ♦ **p. atención** to pay attention • **p. auxilio** *or* **ayuda** to help, assist • **p. juramento** to take the oath • **p. oídos** to lend an ear —reflex. *(consentir)* to consent; *(ser apto para)* to lend itself *(a, para* to); *(ofrecerse)* to offer.

pres·te·za f. promptness.

pres·ti·di·gi·ta·ción f. prestidigitation.

pres·ti·di·gi·ta·dor, ·ra m.f. prestidigitator.

pres·ti·giar tr. to lend prestige to.

pres·ti·gio m. prestige.

pres·ti·gio·so, a adj. prestigious.

pres·to, a I. adj. prompt; MUS. presto **II.** adv. promptly.

pre·su·mi·ble adj. presumable.

pre·su·mi·do, a adj. & m.f. presumptuous *or* conceited (person).

pre·su·mir tr. to presume —intr. ♦ **p. de** to think oneself.

pre·sun·ción f. *(vanidad)* presumptuousness; *(suposición)* presumption; LAW presumption.

pre·sun·ta·men·te adv. presumably.

pre·sun·to, a I. see **presumir II.** adj. presumed.

pre·sun·tuo·so, a adj. & m.f. presumptuous *or* conceited (person).

pre·su·po·ner §54 tr. to presuppose.

pre·su·po·si·ción f. presupposition.

pre·su·pues·tar tr. to budget.

pre·su·pues·ta·rio, a adj. budgetary.

pre·su·pues·to, a I. see **presuponer II.** m. budget estimate ♦ **equilibrar el p.** to balance the budget.

pre·su·ri·zar §04 tr. to pressurize.

pre·su·ro·so, a adj. *(rápido)* quick; *(con prisa)* in a hurry.

pre·ten·cio·so, a adj. pretentious.

pre·ten·der tr. *(buscar)* to seek; *(intentar)* to try, attempt; *(a una mujer)* to court; *(afirmar)* to claim.

pre·ten·dien·te, a I. adj. *(que reclama)* seeking; *(al trono)* pretending to; *(a una mujer)* courting **II.** m.f. *(reclamante)* claimant; *(a un puesto)* candidate; *(al trono)* claimant —m. suitor.

pre·ten·sión f. *(aspiración)* desire; *(derecho)* claim; AMER. *(vanidad)* pretentiousness ♦ **sin pretensiones** unpretentious • **tener la p. de** to think one is going to.

pre·ten·sio·so, a adj. pretentious.

pre·té·ri·to, a adj. & m. past.

pre·tex·tar tr. to allege.

pre·tex·to m. pretext.

pre·va·le·cer §17 intr. *(sobresalir)* to prevail;

BOT. to take root.

pre·va·le·cien·te adj. prevailing.

pre·va·ler §74 intr. to prevail.

pre·ven·ción f. prevention; *(apresto)* preparedness; *(precaución)* precautionary measure; *(providencia)* foresight.

pre·ve·ni·do, a adj. *(preparado)* prepared; *(advertido)* forewarned; *(precavido)* prudent.

pre·ve·nir §76 tr. *(preparar)* to prepare; *(prever)* to foresee; *(impedir)* to prevent; *(avisar)* to forewarn ♦ **p. de** to provide with —reflex. *(disponerse)* to prepare oneself; *(tomar precauciones)* to take precautions.

pre·ven·ti·vo, a adj. preventive.

pre·ver §77 tr. to foresee.

pre·via·men·te adv. previously.

pre·vio, a adj. *(anterior)* previous, former; *(preparatorio)* preliminary, prior <**p. aviso** prior notice>; *(a condición de)* subject to <**p. acuerdo de las partes interesadas** subject to the agreement of the interested parties>; *(después)* after, upon <**p. pago** after or upon payment>.

pre·vi·si·ble adj. foreseeable.

pre·vi·sión f. *(clarividencia)* foresight; *(prudencia)* precaution ♦ **p. social** social security.

pre·vi·sor, ·ra adj. & m.f. cautious *or* prudent (person).

pre·vis·to, a I. see **prever II.** adj. *(anticipado)* foreseen; *(estipulado)* provided <**p. por la ley** provided by law>.

prez m. honor, glory.

prie·to, a adj. dark.

pri·ma¹ f. *(indemnización)* insurance premium; *(recompensa)* premium; MUS. treble.

pri·ma² f. see **primo, a.**

pri·ma·cí·a f. superiority.

pri·ma·do m. RELIG. primate.

pri·ma·rio, a adj. primary; *(primero)* first.

pri·ma·te m. primate.

pri·ma·ve·ra f. *(estación)* spring; *(época)* springtime; *(de la vida)* prime.

pri·ma·ve·ral adj. spring(like).

pri·mer adj. contr. of **primero.**

pri·me·ra·men·te adv. first, in the first place.

pri·me·ro, a I. adj. first; front <**la p. página** the front page>; *(mejor)* best <**ella es la p. alumna de la clase** she is the best student in the class>; *(fundamental)* basic <**las primeras necesidades** the basic needs>; *(anterior)* former ♦ **a p. vista** at first sight • **de buenas a primeras** all at once • **de primera** first-class • **en primer lugar** first of all • **primer actor** leading man • **p. actriz** leading lady **II.** m.f. first <**Pedro fue el p. en llegar** Peter was the first to arrive>; *(el mejor)* best —f. AUTO. first gear **III.** adv. first; *(más bien)* first, sooner <**p. morir que pedir ayuda** sooner dead than ask for help>.

pri·mi·cia f. exclusive news.

pri·mi·ti·vo, a adj. & m.f. primitive.

pri·mo, a I. adj. first; MATH. prime **II.** m.f. cousin • **p. hermano** *or* **carnal** first cousin.

pri·mo·gé·ni·to, a adj. & m.f. first-born.

pri·mor m. *(finura)* delicacy; *(cosa exquisita)* exquisite thing.

pri·mor·dial adj. primordial.

pri·mo·ro·so, a adj. beautiful, exquisite.

prin·ce·sa f. princess.

prin·ci·pa·do m. *(título)* princedom; *(territorio)* principality.

prin·ci·pal I. adj. principal; *(más importante)* main; *(esencial)* essential; GRAM. main (clause) ♦ **lo p.** the main thing **II.** m. FIN. principal.

prín·ci·pe I. adj. first **II.** m. prince ♦ **p. consorte** prince consort • **p. heredero** crown prince.

prin·ci·pes·co, a adj. princely.

prin·ci·pian·te, a I. adj. beginning **II.** m.f. beginner, novice.

prin·ci·piar tr. to begin.

prin·ci·pio m. *(comienzo)* beginning; *(fundamento)* principle; *(causa primitiva)* source ♦ **a p.** or **principios de** at the beginning of • **al p.** at first, in or at the beginning • **dar p. a** to start off • **del p. al fin** or **desde el p. hasta el fin** from beginning to end • **en un p.** at the beginning • **por p.** on principle • **sin principios** unprincipled • **tener por p.** to make a point of.

prin·gar §47 tr. *(ensuciar)* to get grease on; *(empapar)* to dip in fat.

prin·go·so, a adj. greasy.

prin·gue m.f. grease; FIG. filth.

prio·ri·dad f. priority.

pri·sa f. *(apuro)* haste; *(velocidad)* speed; *(urgencia)* urgency ♦ **a** or **de p.** quickly • **a toda p.** as quickly as possible • **andar** or **estar de p.** to be in a hurry • **dar** or **meter p. a alguien** to rush someone • **darse p.** to hasten, hurry (up) • **tener p.** to be in a hurry *(por, en* to).

pri·sión f. prison; *(de afecto)* bond, tie ♦ **p. preventiva** LAW preventive custody.

pri·sio·ne·ro, a m.f. prisoner.

pris·ma m. prism.

pris·má·ti·co, a I. adj. prismatic **II.** m.pl. binoculars.

prís·ti·no, a adj. pristine.

pri·va·ción f. *(acción)* deprivation; *(falta)* lack.

pri·va·do, a I. adj. private ♦ **p. de** without, bereft of • **vida p.** privacy **II.** m. protégé.

pri·var tr. *(despojar)* to deprive; *(prohibir)* to forbid —reflex. to abstain *(de* from).

pri·va·ti·za·ción f. privatization.

pri·va·ti·zar §04 tr. to privatize.

pri·vi·le·giar tr. to favor.

pri·vi·le·gio m. privilege.

pro m.f. profit, benefit ♦ **en p. de** pro, in favor of • **el p. y el contra** pro and con.

pro·a f. prow, bow.

pro·ba·bi·li·dad f. probability ♦ **probabilidades de vida** life expectancy.

pro·ba·ble adj. probable; *(demostrable)* provable.

pro·ba·dor, ·ra I. adj. proving **II.** m. fitting room.

pro·bar §19 tr. *(ensayar)* to test; *(confirmar)* to prove; *(ropa)* to try on; *(comida)* to taste ♦ **p. ventura** to try one's luck —intr. to try ♦ **p. de todo** to take a taste of everything —reflex. to try on.

pro·be·ta f. test tube.

pro·bi·dad f. probity, integrity.

pro·ble·ma m. problem.

pro·ble·má·ti·co, a I. adj. problematic(al). **II.** f. issues.

pro·bo, a adj. upright.

pro·ca·ci·dad f. indecency.

pro·caz adj. *(insolente)* insolent; *(indecente)* indecent.

pro·ce·den·cia f. *(origen)* origin; *(punto de salida)* point of departure; *(de conducta)* properness.

pro·ce·den·te adj. *(que procede)* (coming) from; LAW admissible.

pro·ce·der[1] m. conduct.

pro·ce·der[2] intr. *(originarse)* to originate in;

(ejecutar) to go on (to); *(ir con orden)* to proceed; *(portarse)* to behave; *(continuar)* to go on or ahead with; *(ser apropiado)* to be fitting or appropriate.

pro·ce·di·mien·to m. *(método)* procedure; *(proceso)* process; LAW proceedings.

pró·cer adj. & m. eminent or illustrious (person).

pro·ce·sa·do, a m.f defendant.

pro·ce·sa·mien·to m. LAW prosecution; COMPUT. processing ♦ **p. de datos** data processing.

pro·ce·sar tr. LAW to prosecute; COMPUT. to process.

pro·ce·sión f. procession ♦ **la p. va por dentro** COLL. still waters run deep.

pro·ce·so m. process; *(transcurso)* course; LAW *(causa)* trial; *(autos)* proceedings.

pro·cla·ma·ción f. proclamation.

pro·cla·mar tr. & reflex. to proclaim (oneself).

pro·cli·ve adj. inclined *(a* to).

pro·cre·a·ción f. procreation.

pro·cre·ar tr. to procreate.

pro·cu·ra·dor, ·ra I. adj. procuring **II.** m.f. *(apoderado)* proxy; *(abogado)* attorney.

pro·cu·rar tr. *(intentar)* to endeavor; *(obtener)* to obtain —reflex. to obtain.

pro·di·gar §47 tr. to lavish —reflex. to go out of one's way.

pro·di·gio m. *(persona)* prodigy; *(fenómeno)* wonder.

pro·di·gio·so, a adj. marvelous.

pró·di·go, a adj. *(malgastador)* prodigal, wasteful; *(muy generoso)* generous.

pro·duc·ción f. production; *(producto)* product ♦ **p. en serie** mass production.

pro·du·cir §22 tr. to produce; *(engendrar)* to bear; *(elaborar)* to manufacture; *(ocasionar)* to cause; FIN. to yield ♦ **p. en serie** to mass-produce —reflex. to take place.

pro·duc·ti·vi·dad f. productivity.

pro·duc·ti·vo, a adj. productive; *(lucrativo)* lucrative.

pro·duc·to, a m. product; COM. *(beneficio)* profit; *(ingresos)* proceeds ♦ **p. derivado** byproduct • **productos de consumo** consumer goods.

pro·duc·tor, ·ra I. adj. productive, producing **II.** m.f. producer.

pro·du·je·ra, jo see **producir.**

pro·e·za f. feat.

pro·fa·na·ción f. desecration.

pro·fa·nar tr. *(maltratar)* to desecrate; *(deshonrar)* to disgrace.

pro·fa·no, a adj. profane; *(irreverente)* irreverent; *(no iniciado)* uninitiated **II.** m.f. layman/woman.

pro·fe·cí·a f. prophecy.

pro·fe·rir §65 tr. to utter.

pro·fe·sar tr. *(ejercer)* to practice; *(enseñar)* to teach; *(creer)* to believe in; *(declarar)* to profess; *(afecto)* to feel —intr. to take vows.

pro·fe·sión f. profession ♦ **de p.** by trade.

pro·fe·sio·nal adj. & m.f. professional.

pro·fe·sor, ·ra m.f. *(de escuela)* teacher; *(de universidad)* professor ♦ **p. auxiliar** assistant professor • **p. suplente** substitute teacher.

pro·fe·so·ra·do m. *(cargo)* teaching position; *(cuerpo docente)* faculty.

pro·fe·ta m. prophet.

pro·fe·ti·sa f. prophetess.

pro·fe·ti·zar §04 tr. to prophesy.

pro·fie·ra, ro see **proferir.**

pro·fi·lác·ti·co, a I. adj. prophylactic II. m. condom —f. prophylaxis.

pro·fi·la·xis f. prophylaxis.

pro·fi·rie·ra, rió see **proferir**.

pró·fu·go, a adj. & m.f. fugitive.

pro·fun·di·dad f. profundity, depth ♦ **de p.** deep, in depth.

pro·fun·di·zar §04 tr. (cavar) to make deeper; (estudiar) to delve into —intr. to go deeply into a subject.

pro·fun·do, a I. adj. (hondo) deep; (intenso) profound; (difícil) difficult; (penetrante) deep; (sincero) heartfelt II. m. depth.

pro·fu·sión f. profusion.

pro·fu·so, a adj. profuse.

pro·ge·nie f. progeny.

pro·ge·ni·tor m. progenitor ♦ pl. (antepasados) ancestors; (padres) parents.

pro·gra·ma m. program ♦ **p. de estudios** curriculum — **p. doble** CINEM. double feature.

pro·gra·ma·ción f. programming.

pro·gra·ma·dor, ·ra I. adj. programming II. m.f. programmer.

pro·gra·mar tr. (planificar) to plan; COMPUT. to program.

pro·gre·sar intr. to progress.

pro·gre·sión f. progression.

pro·gre·sis·ta adj. & m.f. progressive.

pro·gre·si·vo, a adj. progressive.

pro·gre·so m. progress.

pro·hi·bi·ción f. prohibition.

pro·hi·bi·do, a adj. prohibited, forbidden ♦ **p. estacionar** no parking ▪ **p. la entrada** no admittance.

pro·hi·bir tr. to prohibit, forbid ♦ **p. a alguien hacer algo** to prohibit someone from doing something, forbid someone to do something ▪ **se prohibe fumar** no smoking.

pro·hi·bi·ti·vo/to·rio, a adj. prohibitive.

pró·ji·mo m. (otra persona) fellow man, (humanidad) mankind; COLL. (sujeto) fellow.

pro·le f. progeny.

pro·le·ta·ria·do m. proletariat.

pro·le·ta·rio, a adj. & m.f. proletarian.

pro·li·fe·ra·ción f. proliferation.

pro·li·fe·rar intr. to proliferate.

pro·lí·fi·co, a adj. prolific.

pro·li·jo, a adj. (pesado) long-winded; (meticuloso) meticulous.

pró·lo·go m. prologue.

pro·lon·ga·ción f. prolongation; (parte) continuation.

pro·lon·ga·da·men·te adv. at great length.

pro·lon·ga·do, a adj. prolonged.

pro·lon·ga·mien·to m. var. of **prolongación**.

pro·lon·gar §47 tr. (continuar) to prolong; (alargar) to lengthen —reflex. (extenderse) to extend; (durar más tiempo) to last longer.

pro·me·diar tr. (sacar el promedio) to average; (dividir en dos) to divide in half —intr. to be halfway through ♦ **al p. el mes** halfway through the month.

pro·me·dio m. average; (mitad) middle ♦ **por p.** on average.

pro·me·sa f. promise; RELIG. vow ♦ **cumplir (con) una p.** to keep a promise ▪ **faltar a una p.** to break a promise.

pro·me·te·dor, ·ra adj. promising.

pro·me·ter tr. to promise ♦ **p. el oro y el moro** to promise the moon and stars —intr. to be promising —reflex. (esperar) to expect; (apalabrar) to become engaged.

pro·me·ti·do, a m. fiancé —f. fiancée.

pro·mi·nen·cia f. prominence.

pro·mi·nen·te adj. prominent.

pro·mis·cui·dad f. promiscuity.

pro·mis·cuo, a adj. promiscuous.

pro·mi·so·rio, a adj. promising.

pro·mo·ción f. promotion; EDUC. graduating class.

pro·mo·cio·nar tr. to promote.

pro·mon·to·rio m. promontory; (pila) heap.

pro·mo·tor, ·ra I. adj. (que promociona) promoting; (instigador) instigating II. m.f. (que promociona) promoter; (instigador) instigator.

pro·mo·ve·dor, ·ra I. adj. (que promociona) promoting; (instigador) instigating II. m.f. (que promociona) promoter; (instigador) instigator.

pro·mo·ver §78 tr. to promote; (fomentar) to foster; (provocar) to cause.

pro·mul·ga·ción f. promulgation.

pro·mul·gar §47 tr. to promulgate; (proclamar) to proclaim.

pro·no, a adj. prone.

pro·nom·bre m. pronoun.

pro·no·mi·nal adj. pronominal.

pro·nos·ti·car §70 tr. (predicción) prediction; (señal) omen ♦ **p. del tiempo** weather forecast.

pron·ti·tud f. (velocidad) speed; (diligencia) promptness; (ingenio) sharpness (of mind).

pron·to, a I. adj. (veloz) quick; (diligente) prompt; (preparado) ready ♦ **p. a** quick to <p. a enfadarse quick to anger> II. adv. (velozmente) quickly; (diligentemente) promptly; (en seguida) at once; (dentro de poco) soon; (temprano) early ♦ **de p.** suddenly ▪ **lo más p. posible** as soon as possible ▪ **por lo p.** for the moment ▪ **tan p. como** as soon as.

pron·tua·rio m. dossier; AMER., CRIMIN. record, file.

pro·nun·cia·ción f. pronunciation.

pro·nun·cia·mien·to m. (golpe de estado) military coup; LAW pronouncement.

pro·nun·ciar tr. to pronounce; (decir) to utter; (discurso) to deliver —reflex. (sublevarse) to rebel; (sentencia) to pass; (declararse) to declare oneself.

pro·pa·ga·ción f. propagation.

pro·pa·gan·da f. propaganda; (publicidad) advertising ♦ **hacer p.** to advertise.

pro·pa·gan·dís·ti·co, a adj. propagandistic.

pro·pa·gar §47 tr. & reflex. to propagate; FIG. to spread.

pro·pa·lar tr. to divulge.

pro·pa·sar tr. to go beyond —reflex. to go too far.

pro·pen·der intr. to tend (a to, toward).

pro·pen·sión f. propensity; MED. predisposition.

pro·pen·so, a adj. prone (a to).

pro·pia·men·te adv. (con propiedad) properly; (realmente) exactly ♦ **p. dicho** strictly speaking.

pro·pi·ciar tr. AMER. to sponsor.

pro·pi·cio, a adj. propitious.

pro·pie·dad f. property; (posesión) ownership; (heredad) estate <es dueño de una gran p. he's the owner of a great estate>; (exactitud) accuracy; (conveniencia) appropriateness <la p. de una palabra the appropriateness of a word> ♦ **hablar con p.** to speak correctly ▪ **p. horizontal** cooperative property ▪ **p. inmobiliaria** real es-

tate • **p. intelectual** copyright.
pro·pie·ta·rio, a I. adj. proprietary II. m. owner, proprietor —f. owner, proprietress.
pro·pi·na f. tip, gratuity.
pro·pi·nar tr. COLL. to give <*p. una paliza* to give a beating>.
pro·pio, a adj. own <*mató a su p. padre* he killed his own father>; *(original)* own, very <*ésas son sus propias palabras* those are her very words>; *(natural)* own, natural <*su p. pelo* his own hair>; *(mismo)* -self <*el p. interesado debe asistir a la reunión* the interested party himself must attend the meeting>; *(conveniente)* proper, suitable <*no·es p. para este caso* it is not suitable for this case>; *(característico)* typical, characteristic <*eso es p. de ella* that is typical of her>; GRAM., MATH. proper.
pro·po·ne·dor, ·ra/nen·te I. adj. proposing II. m.f. proponent.
pro·po·ner §54 tr. *(sugerir)* to propose; *(exponer)* to propound; *(plantear)* to pose; *(presentar)* to propose, nominate <*lo propuse para la vacante* I proposed him for the vacant post>; *(opinar)* to move <*propongo que se aplace la sesión* I move that the meeting be postponed> —reflex. to intend to do.
pro·por·ción f. proportion; *(tamaño)* size ♦ **en p. a** in proportion to • **guardar p. con** to be in proportion with ♦ pl. proportions, dimensions.
pro·por·cio·na·do, a adj. *(con proporción)* proportionate; *(adecuado)* commensurate.
pro·por·cio·nal adj. proportional.
pro·por·cio·nar tr. *(distribuir)* to apportion; *(suministrar)* to provide —reflex. to get, obtain.
pro·po·si·ción f. proposition; *(propuesta)* proposal; *(moción)* motion; GRAM. clause.
pro·pó·si·to m. *(intención)* intention; *(objetivo)* purpose ♦ **a p.** *(por cierto)* by the way; *(adrede)* deliberately • **a p. de** apropos of • **con el p. de** in order to • **con este p.** to this end.
pro·pues·ta f. *(proposición)* proposition; *(oferta)* proposal; COM. bid.
pro·pug·nar tr. to advocate.
pro·pul·sar tr. to propel.
pro·pul·sión f. propulsion ♦ **p. a chorro** jet propulsion • **p. delantera** front wheel drive.
pro·pul·sor, ·ra I. adj. propellant II. m. propeller.
pro·pu·sie·ra, yo see **proponer**.
pro·rra·ta f. share.
pro·rra·te·ar tr. to prorate.
pró·rro·ga f. extension.
pro·rro·gar §47 tr. to extend.
pro·rrum·pir intr. to burst *(en* into).
pro·sa f. prose.
pro·sai·co, a adj. prosaic.
pro·sa·pia f. lineage.
pros·ce·nio m. proscenium.
pros·cri·bir §80 tr. *(desterrar)* to exile; *(prohibir)* to proscribe.
pros·crip·ción f. *(destierro)* exile; *(prohibición)* proscription.
pro·se·cu·ción f. continuation.
pro·se·guir §64 tr. & intr. *(seguir)* to pursue; *(continuar)* to carry on with.
pro·se·li·tis·ta adj. proselytizing.
pros·pec·to m. prospectus, brochure.
pros·pe·rar intr. to prosper.
pros·pe·ri·dad f. prosperity.
prós·pe·ro, a adj. prosperous.
prós·ta·ta f. prostate (gland).

pros·ter·nar·se reflex. to prostrate oneself.
pros·tí·bu·lo m. brothel.
pros·ti·tu·ción f. prostitution.
pros·ti·tuir §18 tr. & reflex. to prostitute (oneself).
pros·ti·tu·ta f. prostitute.
pro·ta·go·nis·ta m.f. protagonist —m. hero —f. heroine.
pro·ta·go·ni·zar §04 tr. to star in.
pro·tec·ción f. protection.
pro·tec·cio·nis·ta adj. & m.f. protectionist.
pro·tec·tor, ·ra I. adj. *(defensor)* protective; *(patrocinador)* supporting II. m.f. *(defensor)* protector; *(patrocinador)* patron. —f. patroness.
pro·tec·to·ra·do m. protectorate.
pro·te·ger §34 tr. to protect.
pro·te·gi·do, a m. protégé —f. protégée.
pro·teí·na f. protein.
pró·te·sis f. MED. prosthesis; GRAM. prothesis.
pro·tes·ta f. protest; LAW protestation.
pro·tes·tan·te adj. & m.f. RELIG. Protestant.
pro·tes·tar tr. *(asegurar)* to affirm; *(la fe)* to profess; COM. to protest —intr. to protest.
pro·tes·to m. COM. protest.
pro·to·co·lo m. *(registro)* record book; *(de un congreso)* minutes; DIPL. protocol.
pro·tón m. proton.
pro·to·plas·ma m. protoplasm.
pro·to·ti·po m. prototype.
pro·to·zo·a·rio/zo·o m. protozoan.
pro·tu·be·ran·cia f. protuberance.
pro·ve·cho m. *(beneficio)* benefit; *(ganancia)* profit; *(adelantamiento)* advancement ♦ **¡buen p.!** COLL. enjoy your meal! • **en p. de** to the benefit of • **en propio** to one's own advantage • **sacar p. de** *(beneficiarse)* to benefit from; *(aprovecharse)* to take advantage of.
pro·ve·cho·so, a adj. *(beneficioso)* profitable; *(bueno)* good; *(ventajoso)* advantageous.
pro·ve·e·dor, ·ra m.f. supplier.
pro·ve·er §43 tr. *(suministrar)* to provide *(de* with); *(conferir)* to grant.
pro·ve·nien·te adj. proceeding *(de* from).
pro·ve·nir §76 intr. *(proceder)* to proceed *(de* from); *(originarse)* to come *(en* from).
pro·ver·bial adj. proverbial.
pro·ver·bio m. proverb.
pro·vi·ye·ra, yo see **proveer**.
pro·vi·den·cia f. *(disposición)* provision; LAW ruling ♦ **P.** RELIG. Providence • **tomar providencias** to take measures.
pro·vi·den·cial adj. providential.
pro·vin·cia f. province.
pro·vin·cia·no, a adj. & m.f. provincial.
pro·vi·sión f. provision; *(surtido)* supply; *(medida)* measure; FIN. funds, cover ♦ **p. de fondos** FIN. funds ♦ pl. supplies.
pro·vi·sio·nal adj. temporary.
pro·vi·so·rio, a adj. AMER. temporary.
pro·vo·ca·ción f. provocation; *(insulto)* insult; *(desafío)* challenge.
pro·vo·ca·dor, ·ra I. adj. *(irritante)* provoking; *(sensual)* provocative II. m.f. provoker.
pro·vo·car §70 tr. *(incitar)* to provoke; *(irritar)* to annoy; *(motivar)* to move; *(despertar)* to rouse; *(causar)* to cause.
pro·vo·ca·ti·vo, a adj. inviting, tempting.
pro·xe·ne·ta m. procurer, pimp —f. procuress.
pró·xi·ma·men·te adv. soon, before long.

pro·xi·mi·dad f. proximity.

pró·xi·mo, a adj. (cercano) near; (siguiente) next <el año p. next year> ♦ **p. a** (al lado de) near to; (a punto de) about to.

pro·yec·ción f. projection; CINEM. screening.

pro·yec·tar tr. (lanzar) to hurl; (planear) to plan; (sombra) to cast; ARCHIT., TECH. to design; CINEM., GEOM. to project.

pro·yec·til m. projectile, missile ♦ **p. antiaéreo** antiaircraft missile • **p. balístico intercontinental** intercontinental ballistic missile • **p. de avión** a tierra air-to-surface missile • **p. dirigido** or **teledirigido** guided missile.

pro·yec·to m. (plan) plan; (boceto) design; (bosquejo) draft ♦ **en p.** in the planning stages • **p. experimental** pilot project • **p. de ley** bill.

pro·yec·tor m. (reflector) searchlight; CINEM. projector; OPT. condenser; THEAT. spotlight ♦ **p. cinematográfico** movie projector.

pru·den·cia f. prudence.

pru·den·te adj. prudent.

prue·ba f. (razón) proof, evidence; (indicio) sign; (ensayo) sample; (examen) test; (dificultad) ordeal; MATH., PRINT. proof; CHEM., TECH. test; PHOTOG. proof, print; SEW. fitting; COM. trial <a p. on trial> ♦ **a p. de agua** waterproof • **a p. de aire** airtight ♦ **a p. de balas** bulletproof • poner a p. to put to the test.

prue·be, bo see **probar.**

pseu·do adj. pseudo.

psi·co·a·ná·li·sis m. or f. psychoanalysis.

psi·co·a·na·lis·ta m.f. psychoanalyst.

psi·co·a·na·li·zar §04 tr. to psychoanalyze.

psi·co·dé·li·co, a adj. psychedelic.

psi·co·lo·gí·a f. psychology.

psi·có·lo·go, a m.f. psychologist.

psi·có·pa·ta m.f. psychopath.

psi·co·pa·tí·a f. psychopathy.

psi·co·sis f.inv. psychosis.

psi·co·te·ra·peu·ta m.f. psychotherapist.

psi·co·te·ra·pia f. psychotherapy.

psi·que/quis f. psyche.

psi·quí·a·tra/quia·tra m.f. psychiatrist.

psi·quia·trí·a f. psychiatry.

psí·qui·co, a adj. psychic.

pso·ria·sis f. psoriasis.

pú·a f. (punta) sharp point; BOT. thorn; AGR. graft; ZOOL. quill; (de fonógrafo) needle; (espolón) spur; COLL. (persona) cunning person.

pu·ber·tad f. puberty.

pu·bis m.inv. (vientre) pubic region; (hueso) pubis (bone).

pu·bli·ca·ción f. publication.

pu·bli·car §70 tr. (proclamar) to proclaim; (editar) to publish.

pu·bli·ci·dad f. publicity; (anuncio) advertisement ♦ **agencia de p.** advertising agency.

pú·bli·co, a I. adj. public; (patente) known <es p. que it is known that>; (del pueblo) common <el bien p. the common good> II. m. public; (auditorio) audience; (espectadores) spectators; (lectores) readers; TELEV. viewers.

pu·che·ro m. CUL. stew; COLL. (alimento diario) daily bread; COLL. (gesto) pout ♦ **ganarse el p.** COLL. to earn one's daily bread • **hacer pucheros** COLL. to pout.

pu·cho m. COLL. (colilla) cigarette stub; (poco) trifle, bit; (sobrante) leftover.

pú·di·co, a adj. modest.

pu·dien·te adj. & m.f. rich or wealthy (person).

pu·die·ra, do see **poder²**.

pu·dor m. (recato) shyness; (vergüenza) shame ♦ **sin p.** shameless(ly).

pu·do·ro·so, a adj. shy.

pu·dri·ción f. putrefaction, rot.

pu·drir tr. (descomponer) to rot; COLL. (molestar) to annoy —reflex. (descomponerse) to rot; COLL. (molestarse) to be annoyed ♦ **¡ahí te pudras!** COLL. to hell with you! —intr. to rot.

pue·ble, blo see **poblar.**

pue·blo m. (población) town; (habitantes) population; (nación) people, nation; (gente común) (the) common or working people.

pue·da, do see **poder².**

puen·te m. bridge ♦ **p. aéreo** airlift • **p. colgante** suspension bridge • **p. levadizo** drawbridge.

puer·co, a I. adj. (sucio) filthy; (bajo) contemptible; (asqueroso) disgusting II. m. ZOOL. pig, hog; COLL. (hombre) pig, swine ♦ **echar margaritas a los puercos** COLL. to throw pearls before swine —f. ZOOL. sow.

pue·ril adj. childish.

pue·ri·li·dad f. (calidad) childishness; (bagatela) trifle.

pue·rro m. leek.

puer·ta f. door; (armazón) gate; (entrada) doorway; (camino) gateway <la virtud es p. de la felicidad virtue is the gateway to happiness> ♦ **a p. cerrada** behind closed doors • **dar a alguien con la p. en las narices** to slam the door in someone's face • **de p. en p.** from door to door • **echar las puertas abajo** to knock the door down • **p. corrediza** sliding door • **p. giratoria** revolving door • **p. trasera** back door • **p. de vidrio** glass door.

puer·to m. port, harbor; (ciudad) port, seaport ♦ **p. de escala** port of call.

pues I. conj. since, as <cómpralo, p. a ti te gusta buy it, since you like it> II. adv. (en tal caso) well, all right <¿no quieres escucharme? ¡p. te arrepentirás! you don't want to listen to me? well, you'll regret it!>; (partícula continuativa) then <repito, p., que hace bien I repeat, then, that he's doing the right thing> ♦ **p. bien** well then • **¡p. claro!** of course! • **¿p. qué?** so what? • **sí p.** yes, of course.

¡puf! interj. ugh!, ycch!

pú·gil m. (gladiador) pugilist; SPORT. boxer.

pu·gi·lis·ta m. boxer.

pug·na f. (lucha) battle; (oposición) conflict ♦ **estar en p. con** to clash with.

pug·nar intr. to struggle (por to).

pug·naz adj. pugnacious, aggressive.

pu·ja f. (esfuerzo) struggle; (acción de licitar) bidding.

pu·jan·te adj. strong.

pu·jan·za f. strength.

pu·jar tr. to raise (a bid) —intr. to struggle (por, para to).

pul·cri·tud f. (esmero) neatness; (cuidado) care.

pul·cro, a adj. neat.

pul·ga f. flea ♦ **tener malas pulgas** COLL. to be touchy.

pul·ga·da f. inch.

pul·gar adj. & m. thumb.
pu·li·do, a adj. *(metal)* polished; *(pulcro)* neat; *(refinado)* refined.
pu·li·dor, ·ra I. adj. polishing II. m. polisher.
pu·lir tr. *(bruñir)* to polish; *(alisar)* to smooth; FIG. to put the finishing touches on; *(perfeccionar)* to polish; *(civilizar)* to refine.
pul·món m. lung.
pul·mo·nar adj. pulmonary.
pul·mo·ní·a f. pneumonia.
pul·pa f. pulp.
púl·pi·to m. pulpit.
pul·po m. octopus.
pul·po·so, a adj. fleshy.
pul·sa·dor, ·ra I. adj. pulsating II. m. buzzer.
pul·sar tr. *(tocar)* to play; *(apretar)* to push; *(sondear)* to sound out —intr. to beat.
pul·se·ar intr. to arm-wrestle.
pul·se·ra f. bracelet; *(de reloj)* watch band.
pul·so m. *(latido)* pulse; *(muñeca)* wrist; *(seguridad)* steady hand; *(cuidado)* caution.
pu·lu·lar intr. to swarm.
pul·ve·ri·za·dor m. pulverizer; *(para pintar)* paint sprayer; *(de perfume)* atomizer.
pul·ve·ri·zar §04 tr. *(reducir a polvo)* to pulverize; *(perfume)* to spray; FIG. to smash.
pu·lla f. *(palabra grosera)* obscenity; *(chanza)* gibe; *(crítica mordaz)* cutting remark.
¡pum! interj. bang!, boom!
pu·ma m. puma, American panther.
pun·do·nor m. honor.
pu·ni·ti·vo, a adj. punitive.
pun·ta f. point; *(extremidad)* tip; *(cima)* top; *(colilla)* stub; *(clavo)* small nail; ZOOL. *(asta)* horn ♦ **de p. a cabo** from one end to the other • **de p. en blanco** COLL. to the nines • **estar hasta la p. de los pelos** COLL. to be fed up • **hacer p.** to go first • **poner los nervios de p.** to put someone's nerves on edge • **p. de lanza** spearhead • **sacar p. a** to sharpen.
pun·ta·da f. SEW. stitch; *(dolor)* sharp pain.
pun·tal m. *(madero)* brace; *(elemento principal)* foundation.
pun·ta·pié m. kick *<dar un p. to kick>* ♦ **echar a puntapiés** to kick out.
pun·te·rí·a f. aim ♦ **afinar la p.** to aim carefully • **dirigir la p. en** or **hacia** to aim at • **tener buena p.** to be a good shot.
pun·te·ro, a I. adj. leading II. m. *(vara)* pointer; *(punzón)* metal punch —f. *(de media)* toe patch; *(de calzado)* toecap.
pun·tia·gu·do, a adj. sharp, pointed.
pun·ti·lla f. *(tachuela)* tack; *(encaje)* lace trim; *(puñal)* dagger; CARP. tracing point.
pun·ti·llo·so, a adj. punctilious.
pun·to m. point; *(señal pequeña)* dot; *(sitio)* spot; *(momento)* moment; *(asunto)* matter; *(cuestión)* question; GRAM.; *(sobre letra)* dot; *(de oración)* period, full stop (G.B.); SEW. *(puntada)* stitch *<p. por encima overcast stitch>*; *(malla)* mesh; SURG. stitch ♦ **al p.** at once • **a p.** just in time • **a p. de** about to • **de p.** knitted • **dos puntos** colon • **en p.** on the dot, sharp *<llegaron a las dos en p. they arrived at two on the dot>* • **estar a p. de** to be on the verge of • **hasta cierto p.** up to a point • **poner p. final a** to put a stop to • **p. atrás** SEW. backstitch • **p. culminante** climax • **p. de apoyo** fulcrum • **p. de arranque** starting point • **p. de congelación** freezing point • **p. de vista** point of view, viewpoint • **p. final** period • **p. muerto**

dead center; AUTO. neutral; FIG. stalemate • **p. por p.** in detail • **puntos suspensivos** suspension points • **p. y aparte** new paragraph • **p. y coma** semicolon • **subir de p.** COLL. to heat up *<la conversación estaba subiendo de p. the conversation was heating up>* • **¡y p.!** COLL. and that's all!
pun·tua·ción f. punctuation; *(calificación)* grade.
pun·tual adj. prompt.
pun·tua·li·zar §04 tr. *(concretar)* to finalize; *(referir detalladamente)* to describe in detail.
pun·tual·men·te adv. promptly
pun·za·da f. *(dolor agudo)* stabbing pain; *(herida)* stab; *(de conciencia)* pang.
pun·zan·te adj. sharp.
pun·zar §04 tr. to prick; FIG. to torment.
pun·zón m. *(instrumento)* punch; *(para estampar)* stamp.
pu·ña·do m. handful.
pu·ñal m. dagger.
pu·ña·la·da f. stab; FIG. stab of pain ♦ **coser a puñaladas** COLL. to cut someone to pieces.
pu·ñe·ta·zo m. punch ♦ **pl. a p.** with one's fists • **dar a alguien de p.** to punch someone.
pu·ño m. fist; SEW. cuff ♦ **apretar los puños** to clench one's fists • **de propio p.** or **de p. y letra de uno** by one's own hand.
pu·pa f. *(en los labios)* cold sore; *(daño)* booboo.
pu·pi·lo, a m.f. student (at a boarding school) ♦ **medio p.** student who eats lunch at school —f. ANAT. pupil.
pu·pi·tre m. writing desk.
pu·ra·men·te adv. purely.
pu·ré m. CUL. purée.
pu·re·za f. purity.
pur·ga f. *(medicina)* purgative; *(eliminación)* purge.
pur·ga·ción f. *(acción)* purging; *(purificación)* purification; *(expiación)* atonement.
pur·gan·te adj. & m. laxative.
pur·gar §47 tr. *(eliminar)* to purge; *(limpiar)* to cleanse; *(purificar)* to purify; *(a un enfermo)* to purge; *(expiar)* to atone; MECH. to drain or vent; POL. to purge —reflex. to take a purgative.
pur·ga·to·rio m. Purgatory; FIG. purgatory.
pu·ri·fi·ca·ción f. purification.
pu·ri·fi·car §70 tr. *(volver puro)* to purify; *(limpiar)* to cleanse —intr. to become purified.
pu·ris·ta adj. & m.f. purist.
pu·ri·ta·no, a I. adj. Puritan; *(estricto)* puritan(ical) II. m.f. Puritan; *(estricto)* puritan.
pu·ro, a I. adj. pure; *(no aguado)* unadulterated *<vino p.* unadulterated wine>; *(casto)* chaste; *(incorrupto)* disinterested; *(mero)* mere *<por p. casualidad* by mere chance>; *(simple)* absolute *<la p. verdad* the absolute truth>; *(sin agua, soda)* straight ♦ **de p.** out of sheer *<de p. cansado* out of sheer tiredness>* II. m. cigar.
púr·pu·ra f. *(color)* purple; *(colorante)* purple dye; MED. purpura.
pur·pú·re·o, a adj. purple.
pus m. pus.
pu·sie·ra, so see **poner.**
pu·si·lá·ni·me adj. pusillanimous.
pús·tu·la f. pustule.
pu·ta·ti·vo, a adj. putative.
pu·tre·fac·ción f. rotting.
pu·tre·fac·to, a adj. rotten.

Q

q, Q f. twentieth letter of the Spanish alphabet.

quan·tum m. [pl. **-ta**] quantum.

que I. rel. pron. that, which <*el coche q. compraron es azul* the car that they bought is blue>; who <*los niños, que jugaban afuera, no vieron nada* the children, who were playing outside, saw nothing>; whom <*los amigos con q. cuento* the friends on whom I am relying> • **el q.** he who, the one who or that • **la q.** she who, the one who or that • **las q.** or **los q.** those who, the ones who or that • **lo q.** which <*murió joven, lo q. no le permitió alcanzar fama* he died young, which did not allow him to achieve fame>; what <*no entiendo lo q. dices* I don't understand what you're saying> II. conj. that <*me escribieron q. venían* they wrote to me that they were coming>; than <*yo sé más q. tú* I know more than you>; (*porque*) because, since; that <*habla tan rápido q. no lo comprendemos* he speaks so fast that we do not understand him>; (*si*) whether <*q. quiera, q. no quiera, lo tiene que hacer* whether he wants to or not, he has to do it>; that <*te pido q. salgas* I ask that you leave>; and <*uno habla q. habla pero ella nunca escucha* one talks and talks but she never listens>; [not translated] <*hay mucha q. hacer* there is a lot to do> • **a q.** I bet that • **yo q. tú** if I were you.

qué I. adj. which <*¿q. libros necesitan ustedes?* which books do you need?>; what <*¡q. tiempo hace!* what nice weather we're having!> II. pron. what <*¿q. quieres?* what do you want?>; how <*¡q. precioso!* how lovely!> • **¡a mí q.!** so what! • **no hay de q.** you're welcome, don't mention it • **¿para q.?** what for? • **¿por q.?** why? • **q. de** how many <*¡q. de desgracias sufrieron!* how many misfortunes they suffered!>; **¿q. hay?** or **¿q. tal?** how goes it? • **¿q. pasa?** what's the matter? • **¡q. va!** nonsense!, come on! • **un no sé q.** a certain something • **¿y q.?** so what?

que·bra·cho m. quebracho.

que·bra·da f. (*desfiladero*) ravine; (*hendedura*) crack, gap; AMER. stream.

que·bra·di·zo, a adj. brittle, fragile.

que·bra·do, a I. adj. (*roto*) broken; (*en quiebra*) bankrupt; GEOG. rough; MED. herniated II. m.f. (*en quiebra*) bankrupt person; MED. person with a hernia • m. MATH. fraction.

que·bra·du·ra f. (*grieta*) crack; (*rotura*) fracture; MED. (*hernia*) rupture; (*fractura*) fracture.

que·bra·jar tr. to crack.

que·bran·ta·dor, ·ra I. adj. (*rompedor*) breaking; (*machacador*) crushing, smashing II. m. crushing machine.

que·bran·ta·mien·to m. (*rompimiento*) breaking; (*hendimiento*) cracking; (*acción*) crushing; (*debilitación*) weakening, deterioration; (*violación*) violation.

que·bran·tar tr. (*romper*) to break; (*hender*) to crack; (*machacar*) to crush; (*forzar*) to force, break <*q. la voluntad de alguien* to break someone's will>; (*debilitar*) to weaken; (*la ley*) to break • **q. la salud** to ruin one's health —reflex. (*romperse*) to break; (*henderse*) to crack.

que·bran·to m. (*debilitación*) weakening; (*pérdida*) loss; (*aflicción*) sorrow.

que·brar §49 tr. (*romper*) to break <*q. un vaso*

to break a glass>; (*torcer*) to twist; (*interrumpir*) to interrupt —intr. to break off or up <*q. con el novio* to break up with one's boyfriend>; COM. to go bankrupt —reflex. (*romperse*) to be broken; (*hacerse una hernia*) to get a hernia.

que·da f. curfew • **toque de q.** curfew bell or signal.

que·da·men·te adv. calmly, softly.

que·dar intr. (*permanecer*) to remain, stay <*el hombre quedó atrás* the man stayed behind>; (*estar*) to be <*el teatro queda muy lejos* the theater is very far away>; (*restar*) to be left <*me quedan cinco dólares* I have five dollars left>; (*acabar*) to be, end up <*quedamos conformes* we are in agreement>; MATH. to leave • **¿en qué quedamos?** what have we decided? • **q. bien** (*salir bien*) to come out well; FIG. to look good <*ese vestido te queda bien* that dress looks good on you> • **q. en** to agree • **q. mal** to come out badly • **q. por** to remain to be <*el contrato queda por firmar* the contract remains to be signed> —reflex. (*permanecer*) to stay; (*estar*) to be <*se quedó perplejo* he was perplexed>; to become <*q. sordo* to become deaf> • **q. con** to keep • **q. sin** to run out of • **q. para vestir santos** COLL. to be an old maid.

que·do, a I. adj. still, calm II. adv. low, softly.

que·ha·ce·res m.pl. chores.

que·ja f. (*lamento*) moan, groan; (*resentimiento*) grudge; LAW complaint.

que·jar·se reflex. (*gemir*) to moan; (*lamentarse*) to whine, complain (*de* about).

que·ji·do m. moan, groan • **dar quejidos** to groan.

que·jón, o·na adj. whining.

que·jo·so, a adj. annoyed, complaining.

que·jum·bro·so, a adj. grumbling, complaining.

que·ma f. (*acción*) burning; (*incendio*) fire.

que·ma·de·ro m. incinerator.

que·ma·do, a adj. burned, burnt; (*resentido*) resentful; (*agotado*) burned out • **q. por el sol** sunburned.

que·ma·dor, ·ra I. adj. burning; (*incendiario*) incendiary II. m.f. (*incendiario*) arsonist, incendiary —m. burner <*q. de gas* gas burner>.

que·ma·du·ra f. burn.

que·mar tr. (*arder*) to burn; (*incendiar*) to set on fire; (*consumir con fuego*) to burn (up); (*destruir con fuego*) to burn (down); (*chamuscar*) to scorch; (*escaldar*) to scald; (*calentar mucho*) to heat up; (*plantas*) to blight; (*picar*) to sting; (*malbaratar*) to sell cheaply; (*fusible*) to blow • **q. balas** to fire shots • **q. las naves** to burn one's bridges behind one —intr. (*arder*) to burn; (*estar muy caliente*) to be burning hot —reflex. (*arderse*) to burn, be or get burned; to burn oneself <*se quemó con la plancha* she burned herself on the iron>; (*consumir con fuego*) to burn (up); (*destruirse*) to burn (down); (*sentir calor*) to feel hot; (*plantas*) to be blighted; (*broncearse*) to get a tan; (*fusible*) to blow; COLL. (*estar cerca de encontrar*) to be warm or hot (in a game) • **q. con** or **por algo** to get annoyed over or by something • **q. las pestañas** COLL. to burn the midnight oil.

que·ma·rro·pa adv. • **a q.** at pointblank range.

que·ma·zón f. (*quema*) burning; (*calor*) intense heat; COLL. (*comezón*) itching.

que·na f. AMER. Peruvian reed flute.

que·re·lla f. (*queja*) complaint, lament; (*dis-*

puta) dispute, quarrel; LAW complaint.

que·re·llan·te I. adj. complaining II. m.f. plaintiff.

que·ren·cia f. COLL. home, nest.

que·ren·cio·so, a adj. homing.

que·ren·dón, o·na I. adj. AMER. loving, affectionate II. m.f. COLL. darling, sweetheart.

que·rer¹ m. love, affection.

que·rer² §55 tr. *(desear)* to want *<¿quieres otra taza de té?* do you want another cup of tea?>; *(amar)* to love; *(resolver)* to want *<quiero subir a la cima* I want to climb to the top>; *(requerir)* to require ♦ **como quien no quiere la cosa** offhandedly, casually • **como quiera que sea** in whatever way • **cuando quiera** at any time • **no q.** to refuse • **¿qué más quieres?** COLL. what more do you want? • **q. decir** to mean • **q. es poder** where there's a will, there's a way • **q. más** to prefer • **quiera que no** like it or not • **sin q.** *(sin intención)* unintentionally; *(por acaso)* by chance —intr. to. look as if it is going to snow *<quiere nevar* it looks as if it is going to snow>.

que·ri·do, a I. adj. dear, beloved II. f. *(amante)* lover —m.f. COLL. darling, dear.

que·rrá, rría see querer².

que·ru·bín m. cherubim.

que·sa·di·lla f. CUL. *(pastel)* cheesecake; AMER. cornmeal pie filled with cheese.

que·se·rí·a f. cheese store.

que·so m. cheese ♦ **q. de nata** cream cheese.

quet·zal m. ORNITH. quetzal; GUAT., FIN. quetzal.

qui·cio m. pivot hole ♦ **estar fuera de q.** COLL. to be beside oneself • **sacar de q.** COLL. to exasperate.

quid m. gist, crux.

quie·bra f. *(rotura)* break; *(en la tierra)* crack; *(pérdida)* loss; COM. bankruptcy.

quie·bre, bro see quebrar.

quien pron. [pl. **es**] who *<los jefes, quienes estaban ausentes, tenían la información necesaria* the managers, who were absent, had the necessary information>; whom *<la chica de q. hablo se llama Isabel* the girl of whom I am speaking is named Elizabeth>; whoever, he or she who *<q. mal anda mal acaba* whoever lies down with dogs gets up with fleas>.

quién pron. [pl. **es**] who *<¿q. es ese chico?* who is that boy?>; whom *<no sé de q. hablas* I do not know of whom you are speaking> ♦ **de q. or de quiénes** whose *<¿de q. es ese libro?* whose book is that?>.

quien·quie·ra pron. [pl. **quienesquiera**] whoever, whomever *<q. que sea* whoever it is>.

quie·ra, ro see querer².

quie·to, a adj. *(inmóvil)* still; *(sosegado)* quiet.

quie·tud f. *(inmovilidad)* motionlessness; *(sosiego)* calm, tranquillity.

qui·ja·da f. jawbone, jaw.

qui·jo·ta·da f. quixotism, quixotic action.

qui·jo·tes·co, a adj. quixotic.

qui·la·te m. carat; FIG. value.

qui·lo m. kilo, kilogram.

qui·lom·bo m. R.P., SL. brothel.

qui·lla f. keel; ORNITH. breastbone, keel ♦ **dar de q.** MARIT. to keel (over).

qui·me·ra f. chimera; *(ilusión)* illusion.

qui·mé·ri·co, a adj. chimerical.

quí·mi·ca f. chemistry • **q. analítica** analytic chemistry • **q. atómica** atomic chemistry • **q. biológica** biochemistry.

quí·mi·co, a I. adj. chemical ♦ **producto** *or* **sustancia q.** chemical (substance) II. m.f. chemist.

qui·mio·te·ra·pia f. chemotherapy.

qui·mo·no m. kimono.

qui·na f. BOT. cinchona bark; MED. quinine ♦ **más malo que la q.** COLL. terrible, horrible • **tragar q.** SL. to put up with a lot.

quin·ca·lla f. hardware.

quin·ca·lle·rí·a f. hardware store.

quin·ce I. adj. fifteen; *(decimoquinto)* fifteenth ♦ **q. días** fortnight II. m. fifteen ♦ **dar q. y raya a** to get the better of, be superior to.

quin·ce·na f. *(quince días)* fortnight, fifteen days; *(paga)* fortnightly pay.

quin·ce·nal adj. biweekly, semimonthly.

quin·ce·nal·men·te adv. every two weeks.

quin·cua·ge·na·rio, a I. adj. *(de cincuenta unidades)* having fifty parts; *(de cincuenta años)* fifty years old II. m.f. quinquagenarian.

quin·cua·gé·si·mo, a adj. & m. fiftieth.

qui·nie·las f.pl. betting against the bank (on football and other games), quinella.

qui·nien·tos, as adj. & m. five hundred.

qui·ni·na f. quinine.

quin·que·nal adj. five-year.

quin·que·nio m. five-year period.

quin·ta f. see quinto, a.

quin·ta·e·sen·cia f. quintessence.

quin·tal m. quintal, hundredweight ♦ **q. métrico** 100 kilograms.

quin·tar tr. *(sacar uno de cada cinco)* to take one out of every five; MIL. to draft.

quin·te·to m. quintet.

quin·ti·lli·zos, as m.f.pl. quintuplets.

quin·to, a I. adj. fifth II. m. fifth —f. *(casa)* country house; MIL. draft II. MUS. fifth.

quín·tu·plo, a I. adj. quintuple, fivefold II. m. quintuple.

quin·za·vo, a adj. & m. fifteenth.

quios·co m. kiosk ♦ **q. de música** bandstand • **q. de refrescos** refreshment stand • **q. de periódicos** newsstand.

qui·qui·ri·quí m. cock-a-doodle-do.

qui·ró·fa·no m. operating room.

qui·ro·man·cia f. palmistry.

qui·ro·man·te m. AMER., ZOOL. armadillo.

qui·rúr·gi·co, a adj. surgical.

qui·sie·ra, so see querer².

quis·qui·llo·so, a adj. & m.f. *(melindroso)* finicky (person); *(susceptible)* touchy (person).

quis·te m. cyst.

qui·ta f. acquittance, release (from a debt) ♦ **de q. y pon** detachable.

qui·ta·es·mal·te m. nail polish remover.

qui·ta·man·chas m. *or* f.inv. stain remover.

qui·ta·nie·ves m.inv. snowplow.

qui·tar tr. *(apartar)* to take away; *(hurtar)* to rob of; *(restar)* to subtract; *(abrogar)* to repeal; *(prohibir)* to forbid; *(impedir)* to hinder; *(librar)* to free from; *(privar)* to deprive of ♦ **q. la mesa** to clear the table • **quitarle a uno las palabras de la boca** to take the words out of one's mouth • **sin q. ni poner** verbatim —reflex. to take off *<se quitó la chaqueta* he took off his jacket>; *(mancha)* to come out ♦ **q. de encima** to get rid of • **q. de en medio** to get out of the way • **q. el sombrero** to take one's hat off.

qui·ta·sol m. parasol.

qui·zá(s) adv. maybe, perhaps.

quó·rum m. quorum.

R

r, R f. twenty-first letter of the Spanish alphabet.

ra·ba·di·lla f. tailbone; COLL. rump.

¡a·ba·no m. radish ♦ **me importa un r.** COLL. I couldn't care less.

ra·bí m. [pl. **-íes**] rabbi.

ra·bia f. rabies; FIG. fury ♦ **cogerle r. a alguien** to get furious with someone • **dar r.** to infuriate.

ra·biar intr. to have rabies; FIG. to be furious ♦ **a r.** rabid <*un aficionado de béisbol a r.* a rabid baseball fan> • **que rabia** COLL. like mad or crazy • **r. de hambre** to be dying of hunger • **r. por algo** to be dying for something.

ra·bi·cor·to, a adj. short-tailed.

ra·bie·ta f. COLL. tantrum.

ra·bi·llo m. (*cola*) small tail; (*para pantalones*) strap; (*de una hoja*) leaf stalk; (*de una fruta*) stem.

ra·bi·no m. rabbi.

ra·bio·so, a adj. rabid; FIG. furious; COLL. (*un color*) garish.

ra·bo m. tail; (*ángulo*) corner <*mirar con el r. del ojo* to look out of the corner of one's eye>; BOT. stem ♦ **salir con el r. entre las piernas** COLL. to leave one's tail between the legs.

ra·bón, o·na I. adj. (*rabicorto*) short-tailed; (*sin rabo*) tailless **II.** f. ♦ **hacer la r.** COLL. to play hooky.

ra·bo·ne·ar intr. COLL. to play hooky.

ra·cial adj. racial.

ra·ci·mar AGR. tr. to pick the remaining grapes from —reflex. to form clusters.

ra·ci·mo m. raceme; FIG. cluster.

ra·cio·ci·nio m. (*razón*) reason; (*razonamiento*) reasoning.

ra·ción f. ration; RELIG prebend ♦ **poner a media r.** to put on short rations.

ra·cio·nal I. adj. rational **II.** m. breastplate.

ra·cio·na·lis·ta adj. & m.f. rationalist.

ra·cio·na·li·zar §04 tr. to rationalize.

ra·cio·na·mien·to m. rationing.

ra·cio·nar tr. to ration.

ra·cis·ta adj. & m.f. racist.

ra·cha f. (*viento*) gust; (*suerte*) run (of luck) ♦ **a rachas** by fits and starts.

ra·da f. bay.

ra·dar m. radar ♦ **r. acústico** sound radar.

ra·dia·ción f. radiation.

ra·diac·ti·vi·dad f. radioactivity.

ra·diac·ti·vo, a adj. radioactive.

ra·dia·dor m. radiator.

ra·dial adj. radial; R.P. radio <*locutor r.* radio announcer>.

ra·dian·te adj. radiant.

ra·diar intr. to radiate; RAD. to broadcast.

ra·di·ca·ción f. taking root.

ra·di·cal adj. & m.f. radical.

ra·di·car §70 intr. (*arraigar*) to take root; (*estar*) to be located; (*habitar*) to reside —reflex. (*arraigarse*) to take root; (*domiciliarse*) to establish oneself.

ra·dio¹ m. radius; (*rayo*) spoke.

ra·dio² m. radium.

ra·dio³ m. or f. radio.

ra·dio·ac·ti·vi·dad f. var. of **radiactividad.**

ra·dio·ac·ti·vo, a adj. var. of **radiactivo, a.**

ra·dio·a·fi·cio·na·do, a m.f. ham radio operator.

ra·dio·di·fun·dir tr. & intr. to broadcast.

ra·dio·di·fu·sión/e·mi·sión f. broadcasting.

ra·dio·di·fu·so·ra/e·mi·so·ra f. (broadcasting) station.

ra·dio·es·cu·cha m.f. radio listener.

ra·dio·gra·fí·a f. (*técnica*) radiography; (*imagen*) x-ray.

ra·dio·gra·fiar §30 tr. to x-ray.

ra·dio·gra·ma m. radiogram.

ra·dio·lo·gí·a f. radiology.

ra·dió·lo·go, a m.f. radiologist.

ra·dio·na·ve·ga·olón f. radio navigation.

ra·dio·rre·cep·tor m. receiver.

ra·dios·oo·pia f. radioscopy.

ra·dio·te·le·fo·ní·a f. radiotelephony.

ra·dio·te·lé·gra·fo m. radiotelegraph.

ra·dio·te·ra·pia f. radiotherapy.

ra·dio·trans·mi·sor m. radio transmitter.

ra·dio·yen·te m.f. radio listener.

ra·e·du·ra f. scrapings.

ra·er §56 tr. (*raspar*) to scrape; COLL. (*la ropa*) to wear out.

rá·fa·ga f. (*de viento*) gust (of wind); (*de ametralladora*) burst.

raid m. raid.

ra·í·do, a adj. worn.

rai·ga, go see raer.

rai·gam·bre f. roots; FIG. stability; (*tradición*) tradition.

ra·íz f. root; FIG. root, origin ♦ **a r. de** as a result of • **bienes raíces** real estate • **de r.** completely • **echar raíces** to take root; (*instalarse*) to settle (down) • **r. cuadrada** square root.

ra·ja f. (*hendidura*) crack; (*de madera*) splinter; (*de fruta*) slice.

ra·já m. [pl. **-aes**] rajah.

ra·ja·do, a adj. cracked.

ra·ja·du·ra f. crack.

ra·jar tr. (*dividir*) to slice, (*hender*) to crack; R.P. COLL. to fire —reflex. (*henderse*) to crack; COLL. (*acobardarse*) to chicken out; C. AMER. to spend lavishly; R.P., CARIB. to rush off.

ra·le·ar intr. (*una tela*) to become worn; AGR. to yield thin bunches of grapes; (*una persona*) to reveal one's true nature.

ra·lo, a adj. thin.

ra·lla·dor m. grater.

ra·llar tr. to grate; COLL. (*molestar*) to grate on.

ra·ma f. branch; PRINT. chase ♦ **andarse por las ramas** COLL. to digress • **en r.** raw.

ra·ma·da f. grove.

ra·ma·je m. branches.

ra·mal m. (*cabo*) strand; (*ronzal*) halter; (*de escalera*) flight; (*ramificación*) branch.

ra·ma·la·zo m. (*de viento*) gust; (*señal*) welt ♦ **un r. de enojo** a burst of anger.

ram·bla f. boulevard; AMER. promenade.

ra·me·ra f. prostitute.

ra·mi·fi·ca·ción f. ramification.

ra·mi·fi·car·se §70 reflex. to branch off or out.

ra·mi·lle·te m. (*conjunto*) cluster; (*de flores*) bouquet.

ra·mo m. (*ramillete*) bouquet; (*rama pequeña*) small branch; (*rama cortada*) cut branch; (*subdivisión*) branch ♦ **Domingo de Ramos** Palm Sunday.

ra·mo·ne·ar tr. (*los árboles*) to prune; (*los animales*) to graze.

ram·pa f. ramp ♦ **r. de lanzamiento** ASTRONAUT. launching pad.

ra·na f. frog ♦ **no ser r.** COLL. to be nobody's fool ♦ **r. de zarzal** tree frog • **r. mugidora** bullfrog.

ran·ciar tr. to make rancid —reflex. to turn rancid.

ran·ci·dez/cie·dad f. rancidity.

ran·cio, a adj. *(comida)* rancid; *(anticuado)* old-fashioned.

ran·che·rí·a f. settlement.

ran·che·ro m. *(cocinero)* camp cook; *(dueño)* rancher.

ran·cho m. AMER. *(choza)* hut; *(granja)* farm; *(comida)* mess; *(campamento)* camp; R.P. straw hat ♦ **alborotar el r.** COLL. to cause trouble • **hacer r.** COLL. to make room • **hacer r. aparte** to go one's own way.

ran·go m. rank; AMER. pomp.

ra·nu·ra f. groove.

ra·pa·ce·rí·a f. childish prank.

ra·pa·ci·dad f. rapacity.

ra·pa·du·ra f./**mien·to** m. *(afeitada)* shave; *(de pelo)* haircut.

ra·pa·piés m.inv. firecracker.

ra·pa·pol·vo m. COLL. scolding.

ra·par tr. *(la barba)* to shave; *(el pelo)* to crop; COLL. *(hurtar)* to snatch.

ra·paz, a I. m.f. youngster II. adj. rapacious.

ra·pe m. *(afeitada)* quick shave; COLL. *(reprensión)* scolding ♦ **al r.** close-cropped.

ra·pé adj. & m. powdered (tobacco).

ra·pi·dez f. speed.

rá·pi·do, a I. adj. quick II. m. *(tren)* express train; *(en un río)* rapids III. adv. quickly.

ra·pi·ña f. robbery ♦ **ave de r.** bird of prey.

ra·po·sa f. vixen.

rap·so·dia f. rhapsody.

rap·tar tr. to abduct.

rap·to m. *(arrebato)* burst; *(delito)* kidnaping; *(éxtasis)* rapture; MED. faint.

rap·tor, ra I. adj. kidnaping II. m.f. kidnaper.

ra·que·ta f. racket; *(para nieve)* snowshoe; *(en casinos)* croupier's rake.

ra·quí·de·o, a adj. rachidian.

ra·quí·ti·co, a adj. & m.f. rachitic (person).

ra·qui·tis·mo m./**tis** f. rickets.

ra·ra·men·te adv. rarely.

ra·re·za f. rarity; *(cosa rara)* rare thing.

ra·ro, a adj. rare; *(extraño)* odd; *(insigne)* notable ♦ **rara vez** rarely.

ras m. ♦ **a r. de** level with.

ra·san·te I. adj. *(just)* touching ♦ **tiro r.** low-angle fire • **vuelo r.** low-level flight II. f. slope.

ra·sar tr. to brush.

ras·ca·cie·los m.inv. skyscraper.

ras·ca·du·ra f. *(acción)* scratching; *(rasguño)* scratch.

ras·ca·mo·ño m. hairpin.

ras·car §70 tr. *(con la uña)* to scratch; *(raspar)* to scrape —reflex. to scratch oneself.

ras·ca·zón f. itch.

ra·se·ro m. leveler.

ras·ga·do, a I. adj. *(desgarrado)* torn; *(ojos)* almond-shaped II. m. tear.

ras·ga·du·ra f. tear.

ras·gar §47 tr. to tear.

ras·go m. *(trazo)* stroke; *(carácter)* trait, feature ♦ **a grandes rasgos** in broad strokes ♦ pl. features.

ras·gón m. tear.

ras·gue·ar tr. to strum.

ras·gue·o m. strumming.

ras·gu·ñar tr. to scratch.

ras·gu·ño m. scratch.

ra·so, a I. adj. *(llano)* flat; *(el cielo)* clear; *(hasta el borde)* level; MIL. private <soldado r. private soldier> ♦ **al r.** in the open air • **cielo r.** ceiling II. m. satin.

ras·pa f. *(de pescado)* spine; AGR. bear; AMER., COLL. reprimand.

ras·pa·dor m. scraper.

ras·pa·du·ra f. scraping; COLL. *(rapadura)* shave.

ras·pan·te adj. *(vino)* sharp; *(abrasivo)* abrasive.

ras·par tr. *(raer)* to scrape (off); *(rasar)* to graze.

ras·pón m. AMER. *(reprimenda)* scolding; *(desolladura)* scratch ♦ **de r.** in passing.

ras·qui·ña f. AMER. itch.

ras·tra f. *(señal)* trail; *(ristra)* string of dried fruit; AGR. hoe; MARIT. dredge ♦ **a rastras** dragging.

ras·tre·a·dor, ra I. adj. tracking II. m. tracker ♦ **r. de minas** MIL. mine sweeper.

ras·tre·ar tr. *(seguir el rastro)* to trail; *(pescar)* to trawl; *(indagar)* to inquire into; MARIT. to dredge.

ras·tre·o m. *(seguimiento)* tracking; *(pesca)* trawling; MARIT. dragging; AGR. raking.

ras·tre·ro, a adj. *(arrastrándose)* trailing; *(bajo)* vile ♦ **perro r.** tracker.

ras·tri·llar tr. TEX. to comb; AGR. to rake.

ras·tri·llo m. rake; TEX. comb.

ras·tro m. *(pista)* trail; *(señal)* trace.

ras·tro·jar tr. to clear of stubble.

ras·tro·jo m. *(residuo)* stubble; *(campo segado)* stubble field.

ra·su·rar tr. *(afeitar)* to shave; *(raer)* to scrape.

ra·ta f. rat ♦ **más pobre que una r.** COLL. as poor as a church mouse.

ra·te·ar tr. to pilfer —intr. to creep.

ra·te·rí·a f. pilfering.

ra·te·ro, a I. adj. *(ladrón)* thieving; *(bajo)* base II. m.f. thief.

ra·ti·fi·ca·ción f. ratification.

ra·ti·fi·car §70 tr. to ratify.

ra·ti·fi·ca·to·rio, a adj. ratifying.

ra·to m. while ♦ **a cada r.** all the time • **al poco r.** shortly after • **de r. en r.** from time to time • **un buen r.** quite some time.

ra·tón m. mouse ♦ **r. de biblioteca** bookworm.

ra·to·ne·ro, a I. adj. mouselike • **perro r.** ratter (dog) II. f. *(trampa)* mousetrap; *(agujero)* mousehole.

rau·dal m. torrent; FIG. abundance.

rau·do, a adj. swift.

ra·vio·les m.pl. ravioli.

ra·ya¹ f. *(lista)* stripe; *(línea)* line; *(veta)* streak; *(arañazo)* scratch; *(en el peb)* part; *(pliegue)* crease; *(límite)* limit; *(punto)* point; GRAM., TELEC. dash; PHYS. line; SPORT. line, mark; AMER. hopscotch; MEX. pay ♦ **a rayas** striped • **hacerse la r.** to part one's hair • **mantener a r. (a alguien)** COLL. to keep (someone) in his place • **pasarse de la r.** COLL. to go too far • **tener a r.** to keep at bay.

ra·ya² f. ICHTH. ray.

ra·ya·no, a adj. adjacent ♦ **r. en** bordering on.

ra·yar tr. to draw lines on —intr. *(lindar)* to be next to; *(amanecer)* to dawn; *(aparecer)* to appear; *(arañar)* to scratch; *(aproximar)* to be approaching; *(sobresalir)* to stand out ♦ **al r. el alba** at the crack of dawn • **r. a gran altura** to excel —reflex. to get scratched.

ra·yo m. ray; *(de rueda)* spoke; *(descarga)* thunderbolt; *(infortunio)* blow; *(dolor)* flash of pain; *(persona)* fast worker; *(relámpago)* flash of lightning ♦ **echar rayos y centellas** to be furious • **r. del radio** radio beam.

ra·yón m. rayon.

ra·yue·la f. pitch and toss; AMER. hopscotch.

ra·za f. race; *(de animales)* breed ♦ **de pura r.** *(caballos)* thoroughbred; *(perros)* pedigreed.

ra·zón f. reason; *(recado)* message; *(cómputo)* rate; MATH. ratio, proportion ♦ **asistirle a uno la r.** to be in the right • **con mayor r.** with all the more reason • **con r.** with good reason • **dar la r. a alguien** to side with someone • **entrar en r.** to come to one's senses • **meter a alguien en r.** to talk sense into someone • **perder la r.** to go out of one's mind • **r. social** business name • **tener r.** to be right.

ra·zo·na·ble adj. reasonable.

ra·zo·na·da·men·te adv. rationally.

ra·zo·na·do, a adj. reasoned.

ra·zo·nar intr. *(pensar)* to reason; *(hablar)* to speak —tr. to give reasons for.

re m. re, D.

re·ac·ción f. reaction ♦ **avión de r.** jet plane • **r. en cadena** chain reaction.

re·ac·cio·nar intr. to react.

re ac cio na rio, a adj. & m.f. reactionary.

re·a·cio, a adj. stubborn.

re·ac·ti·va·ción f. reactivation; ECON. recovery.

re·ac·ti·var tr. to reactivate.

re·ac·tor m. jet engine; PHYS. reactor.

re·a·dap·ta·ción f. readaptation.

re·a·dap·tar tr. to readapt.

re·a·fir·mar tr. to reaffirm.

re·a·jus·tar tr. to readjust.

re·a·jus·te m. readjustment.

re al adj. real.

re·al I. adj. royal; FIG. fine II. m. *(moneda)* real; MIL. army camp ♦ **no tener un r.** COLL. not to have a penny.

re·al·ce m. *(lustre)* luster; PAINT. highlight, *(adorno)* embossment ♦ **poner de r.** to highlight.

re·a·le·za f. royalty.

re·a·li·dad f. reality ♦ **en r.** actually.

re·a·lis·ta adj. & m.f. *(realidad)* realist; *(monárquico)* royalist.

re·a·li·za·ble adj. attainable.

re·a·li·za·ción f. *(ejecución)* execution; *(cumplimiento)* fulfillment; CINEM. production.

re·a·li·za·dor, ra I. adj. fulfilling II. m.f. CINEM. producer.

re·a·li·zar §04 tr. *(cumplir)* to realize; *(ejecutar)* to accomplish; COM. to sell —reflex. to come true.

re·al·zar §04 tr. to enhance.

re·a·ni·mar tr. to revive —reflex. to recover.

re·a·nu·da·ción f. resumption.

re·a·nu·dar tr. to resume —reflex. to begin again.

re·a·pa·re·cer §17 intr. to reappear.

re·a·pa·ri·ción f. reappearance.

re·a·su·mir tr. to resume.

re·a·vi·var tr. to revive.

re·ba·ja f. *(acción)* reduction; *(descuento)* discount.

re·ba·jar tr. *(reducir)* to reduce; *(bajar)* to lower; *(humillar)* to humiliate —reflex. to degrade oneself ♦ **r. a** to stoop to.

re·bal·sa f. puddle.

re·bal·sar tr. & intr. *(estancarse)* to form a pool; *(rebosar)* to overflow.

re·bal·se m. *(piscina)* pool; *(presa)* dam.

re·ba·na·da f. slice.

re·ba·nar tr. to slice.

re·ba·ño m. herd.

re·ba·sar tr. to surpass —intr. to overflow.

re·ba·tir tr. *(argumento)* refute; *(ataque)* to ward off; *(tentación)* to resist.

re·be·lar·se reflex. to rebel.

re·bel·de I. adj. rebellious; MED. resistant; LAW in default II. m.f. rebel; LAW defaulter.

re·bel·dí·a f. rebelliousness; LAW default.

re·be·lión f. rebellion.

re·ben·ca·zo m. lash (of a whip).

re·ben·que m. AMER. whip.

re·bién adv. COLL. extremely well.

re·bor·de m. border.

re·bo·san·te adj. ♦ **r. de** bursting with.

re·bo·sar intr. & reflex. to overflow *(de* with).

re·bo·tar intr. *(pelota)* to bounce; *(bala)* to ricochet.

re·bo·te m. rebound ♦ **de r.** on the rebound.

re·bo·zo m. shawl.

re·bue·no, a adj. COLL. excellent.

re·bu·jar tr. to tuck in.

re·bus·ca f. *(acción)* hunt; *(fruto)* gleanings.

re·bus·ca·do, a adj. pedantic.

re·buz·nar intr. to bray.

re·buz·no m. braying.

re·ca·bar tr. to request.

re·ca·do m. *(mensaje)* message; *(mandado)* errand; AMER., EQUIT. riding gear ♦ **mandar r.** to send word.

re·ca·er §15 intr. to relapse ♦ **r. en** to fall to.

re·ca·í·da f. relapse.

re·ca·lar tr. to saturate —intr. MARIT. to sight land; S. AMER. to arrive.

re·cal·car §70 tr. *(apretar)* to squeeze (in); *(insistir)* to stress —reflex. to sprain.

re·cal·ci·tran·te adj. recalcitrant.

re·ca·len·ta·mien·to m. reheating.

re·ca·len·tar §49 tr. *(volver a calentar)* to reheat; *(calentar demasiado)* to overheat.

re·ca·ma·do m. relief embroidery.

re·ca·mar tr. to do relief embroidery on.

re·cá·ma·ra f. dressing room; ARTIL. gun breech; MEX. bedroom.

re·cam·bio m. *(acción)* changing again; *(pieza)* spare part.

re·ca·pa·ci·tar tr. to reconsider.

re·ca·pi·tu·la·ción m. recapitulation.

re·ca·pi·tu·lar tr. to recapitulate.

re·car·ga·do, a adj. overloaded; FIG. overdone.

re·car·gar §47 tr. to reload; *(aumentar)* to increase; *(sobrecargar)* to overload; *(abrumar)* to overburden; *(adornar)* to overdecorate; *(cobrar más)* to charge extra; *(cobrar demasiado)* to overcharge; TECH. to recharge.

re·car·go m. surcharge.

re·ca·ta·do, a adj. *(cauteloso)* reserved; *(tímido)* shy; *(pudoroso)* modest.

re·ca·tar tr. to cover up —reflex. *(mostrar recelo)* to behave prudently.

re·ca·to m. *(cautela)* caution; *(modestia)* modesty.

re·cau·chu·tar tr. AMER. to retread.

re·cau·da·ción f. *(cobranza)* collection; *(cantidad)* receipts.

re·cau·da·dor m. tax collector.

re·cau·dar tr. to collect.

re·cau·do m. caution ♦ poner a buen r. to place in safekeeping.

re·ca·ye·ra, yó see recaer.

re·ce·lar tr. to suspect.

re·ce·lo m. suspicion.

re·ce·lo·so, a adj. suspicious.

re·cep·ción f. reception; (admisión) admission; (reunión) party; (en un hotel) front desk.

re·cep·cio·nis·ta m.f. receptionist.

re·cep·tá·cu·lo m. receptacle.

re·cep·ti·vi·dad f. receptivity.

re·cep·ti·vo, a adj. receptive.

re·cep·tor, ·ra I. adj. receiving II. m. receiver.

re·ce·sión f. recession.

re·ce·so m. (separación) withdrawal; AMER. adjournment.

re·ce·ta f. MED. prescription; CUL. recipe; FIG. formula.

re·ce·tar tr. to prescribe.

re·ce·ta·rio m. prescription book.

re·ci·bi·dor, ·ra I. adj. receiving II. m.f. receiver —m. (entrance) hall.

re·ci·bi·mien·to m. reception; (vestíbulo) (entrance) hall.

re·ci·bir tr. & intr. to receive —reflex. ♦ r. de to graduate as.

re·ci·bo m. receipt; (sala) reception room ♦ acusar r. de to acknowledge receipt of.

re·ci·cla·je m. (persona) retraining; (cosa) recycling.

re·ci·clar tr. to recycle —reflex. to be retrained.

re·cién adv. recently ♦ r. nacido newborn.

re·cien·te adj. recent; (moderno) modern.

re·cien·te·men·te adv. recently.

re·cin·to m. place.

re·cio, a adj. (vigoroso) strong; (abultado) bulky; (tiempo) severe; (lluvia) heavy; (veloz) swift ♦ en lo más r. de in the thick of.

re·ci·pien·te I. adj. receiving II. m. container.

re·ci·pro·ca·men·te adv. reciprocally.

re·ci·pro·car §70 tr. to reciprocate.

re·ci·pro·ci·dad f. reciprocity.

re·cí·pro·co, a adj. reciprocal.

re·ci·ta·do m. recitative.

re·ci·ta·dor, ·ra I. adj. reciting II. m.f. reciter.

re·ci·tal m. MUS. recital; LIT. reading.

re·ci·tar tr. to recite.

re·cla·ma·ción f. (petición) claim; (protesta) complaint.

re·cla·ma·dor, ·ra I. adj. claiming <parte r. claiming party> II. m.f. claimant.

re·cla·mar tr. (pedir) to claim; (exigir) to demand; LAW to summon —intr. to protest.

re·cla·mo m. (llamada) birdcall; (instrumento) decoy whistle; (reclamación) claim; COM. advertisement; PRINT. catchword.

re·cli·nar tr. to lean or rest on —reflex. to recline.

re·cli·na·to·rio m. kneeling-stool.

re·cluir §18 tr. (encerrar) to seclude; (encarcelar) to imprison —reflex. to shut oneself in.

re·clu·sión f. (encierro) seclusion; (prisión) imprisonment.

re·clu·so, a I. see recluir II. adj. (encerrado) secluded; (preso) imprisoned III. m.f. prisoner.

re·clu·ta f. recruitment —m. recruit.

re·clu·ta·mien·to m. recruitment.

re·clu·tar tr. to recruit.

re·clu·ya, yo, yera, yó see recluir.

re·co·brar tr. & reflex. to recover.

re·co·bro m. recovery.

re·co·dar intr. & reflex. to lean one's elbows (on).

re·co·do m. bend.

re·co·ge·dor, ·ra I. adj. collecting II. m.f. collector —m. AGR. gleaner.

re·co·ger §34 tr. (volver a coger) to pick up; (juntar) to gather; (coleccionar) to save; (dar asilo) to shelter; (encerrar) to lock up; AGR. to harvest; MARIT., SEW. to take in —reflex. to withdraw ♦ r. las mangas to roll up one's sleeves.

re·co·gi·do, a I. adj. (apartado) withdrawn; (pequeño) small; (tranquilo) quiet, tranquil II. f. gathering.

re·co·gi·mien·to m. (acción) collecting; (retiro) retirement; (ensimismamiento) withdrawal.

re·co·lec·ción f. (acción) collection; (resumen) summary; AGR. harvest; RELIG. spiritual absorption.

re·co·lec·tar tr. to gather.

re·co·lec·tor, ·ra m.f. (de cosechas) harvester; (recaudador) collector.

re·co·men·da·ble adj. recommendable.

re·co·men·da·ción f. recommendation.

re·co·men·da·do, a m. protégé —f. protégée.

re·co·men·dar §49 tr. to recommend.

re·com·pen·sa f. reward.

re·com·pen·sar tr. (premiar) to recompense; (compensar) to compensate.

re·con·ci·lia·ble adj. reconcilable.

re·con·ci·lia·ción f. reconciliation.

re·con·ci·liar tr. & reflex. to reconcile.

re·cón·di·to, a adj. recondite, hidden.

re·con·for·tar tr. to comfort; MED. to fortify.

re·co·no·cer §17 tr. to recognize; (identificar) to identify; (agradecer) to appreciate; (examinar) to examine; MIL. to reconnoiter; SURV. to survey ♦ r. la evidencia to bow to the evidence —reflex. to be clear or apparent; (confesar) to confess <r. culpable to admit one's guilt>.

re·co·no·ci·da·men·te adv. (con gratitud) gratefully; (evidentemente) clearly.

re·co·no·ci·do, a adj. (agradecido) grateful; (aceptado) recognized; (confesado) acknowledged.

re·co·no·ci·mien·to m. (identificación) recognition; (confesión) acknowledgement; (gratitud) gratitude; (examinación) examination; MIL. reconnaissance ♦ en r. de in gratitude for.

re·con·quis·tar tr. to recover.

re·con·si·de·rar tr. to reconsider.

re·cons·ti·tuir §18 tr. to reconstitute.

re·cons·ti·tu·yen·te I. adj. reconstituent II. m. tonic.

re·cons·truc·ción f. reconstruction; CONSTR. rebuilding.

re·cons·truir §18 tr. to reconstruct; CONSTR. to rebuild.

re·con·tar §19 tr. to recount.

re·co·pi·la·ción f. compilation.

re·co·pi·la·dor m. compiler.

re·co·pi·lar tr. to compile.

ré·cord m. & adj. inv. record <una cosecha r. a record crop>.

re·cor·da·ción f. memory.

re·cor·dar §19 tr. to remember; (avisar) to remind; (evocar) to remind of —intr. to remember; (contar recuerdos) to reminisce; (despertar) to wake up —reflex. to be remembered ♦ r. que to remind oneself that.

re·co·rrer tr. (viajar) to travel; (mirar) to look over ♦ **r. el mundo** to see the world.

re·co·rri·do m. (viaje) journey; (trayecto) path; (de cartero, recadero) route.

re·cor·tar tr. (cortar) to trim; (reducir) to reduce; ARTS to cut out —reflex. to stand out.

re·cor·te m. (acción) trimming; (de periódico) newspaper clipping; (de pelo) trim.

re·cos·tar §19 tr. to lean (on) —reflex. (reclinarse) to recline; (acostarse) to lie down ♦ **r. en or sobre** to lean on.

re·co·va f. poultry market; AMER. market.

re·co·ve·co m. nook ♦ pl. recesses • **sin r.** frank, open.

re·cre·a·ción f. recreation.

re·cre·ar tr. (divertir) to entertain; (crear de nuevo) to re-create —reflex. to enjoy.

re·cre·a·ti·vo, a adj. (divertido) entertaining; recreational <terapia r. recreational therapy>.

re·cre·o m. (acción) recreation; (en escuela) recess ♦ **de r.** pleasure <barco de r. pleasure boat>.

re·cri·mi·na·ción f. recrimination.

re·cri·mi·nar intr. & reflex. to recriminate (each other).

re·cru·de·cer §17 intr. & reflex. to worsen.

re·cru·de·ci·mien·to m. worsening.

rec·ta f. see recto, a.

rec·tán·gu·lo I. adj. rectangular II. m. rectangle.

rec·ti·fi·ca·ción f. rectification.

rec·ti·fi·car §70 tr. (enderezar) to straighten; (corregir) to rectify; CHEM., ELEC., MATH. to rectify; MECH. to resurface.

rec·ti·tud f. straightness; FIG. honesty.

rec·to, a I. adj. (derecho) straight; (honrado) honest; FIG. sound; GEOM. right II. m. ANAT. rectum; PRINT. recto —f. GEOM. straight line ♦ **r. final** home stretch III. adv. straight.

rec·tor, ·ra I. adj. ruling II. m.f. (de colegio) principal —m (cura) parish priest; (de universidad) president.

re·cua·dro m. ARCHIT. panel; PRINT. box.

re·cuen·te to see recontar.

re·cuen·to m. (segunda enumeración) recount; (enumeración) count.

re·cuer·de, do see recordar.

re·cuer·do m. (memoria) memory; (regalo) souvenir ♦ pl. regards.

re·cues·te to see recostar.

re·cu·la·da f. backward movement; (de vehículo) backing (up); ARM. recoil, COLL. (acción de ceder) backing down.

re·cu·lar intr. to back up; ARM. to recoil; COLL. (ceder) to retreat.

re·cu·pe·ra·ble adj. recoverable.

re·cu·pe·ra·ción f. recovery.

re·cu·pe·rar tr. (recobrar) to recover; (fuerzas, sentido) to regain consciousness; (reconquistar) to win back; (por pérdida) to recoup; (el tiempo) to make up for; TECH. to reclaim —reflex. to recover.

re·cu·rren·te I. adj. recurrent II. m.f. LAW appellant

re·cu·rrir intr. (acudir) to turn or appeal (to); (volver) to return or revert (to).

re·cur·so m. (acción) recourse; (medio) means; resource <recursos naturales natural resources>.

re·cu·sa·ción f. rejection; LAW challenge.

re·cu·sar tr. to reject, refuse; LAW to challenge.

re·cha·za·mien·to m. rejection; (negativa) refusal; (del enemigo) repelling.

re·cha·zar §04 tr. to reject; (declinar) to refuse; (repeler) to repel; (tentación) to resist; (negar) to deny.

re·cha·zo m. rejection.

re·chi·fla f. (abucheo) hissing; (burla) derision.

re·chi·flar tr. to hiss.

re·chi·nar intr. (hacer ruido) to grate; (los dientes) to grind.

re·chon·cho, a adj. COLL. chubby.

re·chu·pe·te COLL. ♦ **de r.** (fantástico) terrific; (delicioso) scrumptious.

red f. net; (malla) mesh; (redecilla) hairnet; (de tiendas) chain; (conspiración) network; RAIL., TELEC. network ♦ **caer en la r.** to fall into a trap • **tender las redes** to cast one's net.

re·dac·ción f. (escritura) writing; (oficina) editorial office; (personal) editorial staff.

re·dac·tar tr. to draft.

re·dac·tor, ·ra I. adj. writing II. m.f. (escritor) writer; (revisor) editor ♦ **r. jefe** editor in chief.

re·da·da f. (de pescados) catch, (de la policía) roundup, dragnet.

re·de·ci·lla f. (tejido) mesh; (para el pelo) hairnet; (bolsa) string bag.

re·de·dor m. surroundings ♦ **al r.** around.

re·den·ción f. redemption.

re·den·tor, ·ra I. adj. redeeming II. m.f. redeemer.

re·dil m. fold.

re·di·mir tr. to redeem; (de obligación) to exempt.

ré·di·to m. interest.

re·di·tua·ble adj. interest-yielding.

re·di·tuar §67 tr. to yield.

re·do·bla·do, a adj. stocky; MECH. reinforced ♦ **paso r.** MIL. double time.

re·do·blar tr. (intensificar) to intensify; (doblar) to fold —intr. to roll.

re·do·ble m. (redoblamiento) redoubling; (de tambor) roll.

re·don·da f. see redondo, a.

re·don·de·a·do, a adj. round.

re·don·de·ar tr. to make round; MATH. to round off —reflex. to become round.

re·don·del m. COLL. circle; TAUR. arena.

re·don·dez f. roundness.

re·don·do, a I. adj. round ♦ **caer (en) r.** to collapse • **en r.** around ♦ **girar en r.** COLL. to turn around • **salir r. (a alguien)** to go well (for someone) II. f. region; MUS. whole note ♦ **a la r.** around.

re·duc·ción f. reduction; (sumisión) subjecting.

re·du·ci·do, a adj. reduced; (estrecho) narrow; (pequeño) small, limited.

re·du·ci·mien·to m. var. of reducción.

re·du·cir §22 tr. to reduce; (sujetar) to subjugate —reflex. to be reduced; (venir a ser) to boil down (a to).

re·duc·tor, ·ra I. adj. reducing II. m. CHEM., ELEC. reducer.

re·du·je·ra, jo see reducir.

re·dun·dan·cia f. redundancy.

re·dun·dan·te adj. redundant.

re·dun·dar intr. (rebosar) to overflow; (resultar) to redound (en to).

re·e·le·gir §54 tr. to re-elect.

re·em·bol·sa·ble adj. reimbursable.

re·em·bol·sar tr. to reimburse.

re·em·bol·so m. reimbursement ♦ **enviar con-**

tra r. to send C.O.D.

re·em·pla·zan·te I. adj. replacing II. m.f. replacement.

re·em·pla·zar §04 tr. to replace.

re·em·pla·zo m. replacement.

re·en·car·na·ción f. reincarnation.

re·en·car·nar intr. to reincarnate —reflex. to be reincarnated.

re·en·cuen·tro m. ♦ tener un r. to meet again.

re·en·gan·char tr. & reflex. to re-enlist.

re·es·truc·tu·ra·ción f. restructuring.

re·es·truc·tu·rar tr. to restructure.

re·fac·ción f. (colación) snack; (reparación) renovation.

re·fac·cio·nar tr. AMER. to renovate.

re·fa·jo m. underskirt.

re·fec·to·rio m. refectory.

re·fe·ren·cia f. reference.

re·fe·ren·te adj. referring (a to).

re·fe·rir §65 tr. to refer; (contar) to relate, tell —reflex. to refer (a to).

re·fi·lón adv. ♦ de r. obliquely; (de pasada) in passing.

re·fi·na·do, a adj. refined.

re·fi·na·mien·to m. refinement.

re·fi·nar tr. to refine —reflex. to become refined.

re·fi·ne·rí·a f. refinery.

re·fi·rie·ra, rió see referir.

re·flec·tor, ·ra I. adj. reflecting II. m. OPT. reflector; (proyector) spotlight; MIL. searchlight.

re·fle·jar tr. to reflect —reflex. to be reflected.

re·fle·jo, a I. adj. PHYS. reflected; PHYSIOL. reflex II. m. reflection; PHYSIOL. reflex; (brillo) gleam.

re·fle·xión f. reflection.

re·fle·xio·nar intr. & tr. to reflect (en, sobre on).

re·fle·xi·vo, a adj. reflective; GRAM. reflexive.

re·flo·re·cer §17 intr. to bloom again.

re·flu·jo m. ebb.

re·fo·res·ta·ción f. AMER. reforestation.

re·for·ma f. reform; (modificación) alteration.

re·for·ma·do, a adj. reformed; (modificado) altered.

re·for·mar tr. to reform; (mejorar) to improve; (restaurar) to renovate; (modificar) to alter —reflex. to reform.

re·for·ma·to·rio, a adj. & m. reformatory.

re·for·mis·ta adj. & m.f. reformist.

re·for·za·do, a adj. reinforced.

re·for·zar §37 tr. to reinforce; FIG. to encourage.

re·frac·ción f. refraction.

re·frac·tar tr. to refract.

re·frán m. saying ♦ como dice or según reza el r. as the saying goes.

re·fre·gar §52 tr. (frotar) to scrub; COLL. (reprochar) to throw back at.

re·fre·nar tr. to restrain.

re·fren·dar tr. (firmar) to endorse; (pasaporte) to stamp.

re·fren·da·rio m. countersigner.

re·fres·can·te adj. refreshing.

re·fres·car §70 tr. to refresh —intr. & reflex. to become cool; (tomar fuerzas) to refresh (oneself).

re·fres·co m. (alimento) refreshment; (bebida) soft drink.

re·frie·ga f. skirmish, scuffle.

re·frie·go, gue see refregar.

re·fri·ge·ra·ción f. refrigeration; (de aire) air

conditioning ♦ r. por agua water-cooling.

re·fri·ge·ra·dor, ·ra I. adj. refrigerating II. m. or f. refrigerator.

re·fri·ge·ran·te I. adj. refrigerating II. m. cooling bath.

re·fri·ge·rar tr. to refrigerate.

re·fri·ge·rio m. snack.

re·fri·to, a I. adj. refried II. m. COLL. rehash.

re·fuer·zo m. reinforcement; (sostén) support.

re·fu·gia·do, a adj. & m.f. refugee.

re·fu·giar tr. to give refuge —reflex. to take refuge.

re·fu·gio m. refuge ♦ r. antiaéreo air-raid shelter.

re·ful·gen·te adj. refulgent.

re·ful·gir §32 intr. to shine brightly.

re·fun·fu·ña·dor, ·ra I. adj. grumbling, whining II. m.f. grumbler.

re·fun·fu·ñar intr. to grumble.

re·fun·fu·ño m. grumble.

re·fun·fu·ñón, ·o·na I. adj. grumbling II. m.f. grumbler.

re·fu·ta·ción f. rebuttal.

re·fu·tar tr. to rebut.

re·ga·de·ra f. watering can.

re·ga·dí·o, a I. adj. irrigable II. m. irrigated land.

re·ga·la·do, a adj. (delicado) dainty; (con comodidades) easy; (barato) dirt-cheap.

re·ga·lar tr. (dar) to give (as a present); (donar) to give away; (halagar) to flatter —reflex. to indulge oneself.

re·ga·li·a f. (derecho real) royal privilege; (excepción) privilege; (sueldo) bonus; (de autor) royalties.

re·ga·liz m./li·za f. licorice.

re·ga·lo m. (obsequio) present, gift; (placer) joy, pleasure; (comodidad) comfort, ease.

re·ga·lón, ·o·na adj. COLL. spoiled.

re·ga·ña·dien·tes ♦ a r. COLL. grudgingly.

re·ga·ñar intr. (reñir) to quarrel, argue; (refunfuñar) to grumble —tr. COLL. to scold.

re·ga·ño m. scolding.

re·ga·ñón, ·o·na I. adj. grumbling II. m.f. grumbler.

re·gar §52 tr. to water; (esparcir) to strew; (con lágrimas) to bathe; (con bebida) to wash down.

re·ga·ta f. regatta.

re·ga·te·a·dor, ·ra AMER. I. adj. haggling II. m.f. haggler.

re·ga·te·ar tr. (negociar) to bargain for; (vender) to retail —intr. (negociar) to bargain; (poner dificultades) to be difficult.

re·ga·te·o m. haggling.

re·ga·zo m. lap.

re·ge·ne·ra·ción f. regeneration.

re·ge·ne·ra·dor, ·ra I. adj. regenerating, regenerative II. m.f. regenerator.

re·ge·ne·rar tr. to regenerate.

re·gen·tar/te·ar tr. to direct.

re·gen·te m.f. regent —m. RELIG. director of studies; (gerente) manager.

ré·gi·men m. regime; (sistema) system; (reglas) regulations; MED. diet.

re·gi·men·tar §49 tr. to regiment.

re·gi·mien·to m. government; MIL. regiment.

re·gio, a adj. regal; FIG. magnificent.

re·gión f. region.

re·gio·nal adj. regional.

re·gio·na·lis·mo m. regionalism.

re·gir §57 tr. (gobernar) to govern; (manejar)

to run; LAW to govern; GRAM. to take —intr. to apply —reflex. ♦ **r. por** to be guided by.

re·gis·tra·dor, ·ra I. adj. *(que inspecciona)* examining; *(que registra)* registering ♦ **caja r.** cash register II. m.f. *(que inspecciona)* examiner; *(que registra)* register —f. cash register.

re·gis·trar tr. *(inspeccionar)* to examine; *(en un registro)* to register; *(rebuscar)* to search; *(anotar)* to note —intr. to search —reflex. to register; *(ocurrir)* to happen.

re·gis·tro m. *(acción)* registration; *(inspección)* examination; *(búsqueda)* search, *(libro)* register; *(oficina)* registry; *(asiento)* entry; *(padrón)* census list; *(género de voces)* register ♦ **tocar todos los registros** COLL. to use all possible means • **r. de la propiedad** real estate registry.

re·gla f. *(para trazar)* ruler; *(norma)* rule; *(modelo)* model; *(instrucciones)* instructions; *(menstruación)* period ♦ **en r.** by the book • **poner algo en r.** to put *or* set something straight • **r. de cálculo** slide rule.

re·gla·men·ta·ción f. *(acción)* regulation; *(regla)* rule.

re·gla·men·tar tr. to regulate.

re·gla·men·ta·rio, ·a adj. prescribed.

re·gla·men·to m. *(reglas)* rules.

re·glar tr. *(rayar)* to rule; *(regular)* to regulate —reflex. to be guided *(por* by).

re·go·ci·jar tr. to delight —reflex. to be delighted.

re·go·ci·jo m. joy.

re·go·de·ar·se reflex. COLL. *(deleitarse)* to take pleasure in; *(bromear)* to joke.

re·go·de·o m. pleasure.

re·gor·de·te, ·a adj. COLL. plump.

re·gre·sar tr., intr. & reflex. AMER. to return.

re·gre·sión f. regression.

re·gre·si·vo, ·a adj. regressive.

re·gre·so m. return ♦ **estar de r.** to be back.

re·gue·ro m. *(chorro)* stream; AGR. irrigation ditch; *(señal)* trail: *(de sangre)* trickle.

re·gu·la·ción f. regulation; *(control)* control.

re·gu·la·do, ·a adj. *(según una regla)* according to rule; *(ajustado)* regulated; *(controlado)* controlled.

re·gu·la·dor, ·ra I. adj. regulating II. m. regulator; RAD. control knob.

re·gu·lar[1] I. adj. regular; *(aceptable)* fairly good; *(mediano)* average; GRAM. regular ♦ **por lo r.** as a rule II. adv. ♦ **estar r.** COLL. to be so-so.

re·gu·lar[2] tr. *(ajustar)* to regulate; *(controlar)* to control; *(ordenar)* to put in order.

re·gu·la·ri·dad f. regularity ♦ **con r.** regularly.

re·gu·la·ri·zar §04 tr. to regularize.

re·gu·lar·men·te adv. regularly; *(medianamente)* fairly well.

re·gur·gi·ta·ción f. regurgitation.

re·gur·gi·tar intr. to regurgitate.

re·ha·bi·li·ta·ción f. rehabilitation; *(reinstalación)* reinstatement.

re·ha·bi·li·tar tr. to rehabilitate; *(en un puesto)* to reinstate.

re·ha·cer §40 tr. *(hacer)* to redo; *(elaborar)* to remake.

re·hén m. hostage.

re·hi·lar tr. to twist too hard —intr. to whiz.

re·hi·le·te m. *(flechilla)* dart; TAUR. banderilla.

re·ho·gar §47 tr. to brown.

re·huir §18 tr. to avoid —reflex. to flee *or* shrink from.

re·hu·sar tr. to refuse.

re·hu·ya, yo, yera, yó see **rehuir.**

re·im·pri·mir §80 tr. to reprint.

rei·na f. queen.

rei·na·do m. reign.

rei·nan·te adj. ruling; FIG. prevailing.

rei·nar tr. to reign.

re·in·ci·den·cia f. relapse; CRIMIN. recidivism.

re·in·ci·den·te I. adj. *(que recae)* relapsing; CRIMIN. recidivous II. m.f. recidivist.

re·in·ci·dir intr. to relapse.

re·in·cor·po·ra·ción f. reincorporation.

re·in·cor·po·rar tr. to reincorporate.

re·in·gre·sar intr. to re-enter.

rei·no m. kingdom

re·ins·ta·la·ción f. reinstallation; *(en un puesto)* reinstatement.

re·ins·ta·lar tr. to reinstall; *(en un puesto)* to reinstate.

re·in·te·gra·ción f. reintegration; *(reembolso)* refund.

re·in·te·grar tr. *(restablecer)* to reintegrate; *(reembolsar)* to refund —reflex. *(recibir reembolso)* to be reimbursed; *(volver)* to rejoin.

re·in·te·gro m. *(restablecimiento)* reintegration; *(reembolso)* reimbursement; *(pólizas)* fiscal stamps.

re·ír §58 intr. to laugh; *(los ojos)* to sparkle ♦ **r. a carcajadas** to laugh out loud • **r. de** to laugh at —tr. to laugh at —reflex. to laugh; *(burlarse de)* to laugh at.

rei·te·ra·ción f. reiteration.

rei·te·rar tr. to reiterate.

rei·te·ra·ti·vo, ·a adj. reiterative.

rei·vin·di·ca·ción f. LAW recovery; *(vindicación)* vindication.

rei·vin·di·car §70 tr. LAW to recover; *(vindicar)* to vindicate.

re·ja f. *(del arado)* plowshare; *(de ventana)* grating ♦ **estar entre rejas** to be behind bars.

re·ji·lla f. grille; *(de una silla)* wickerwork; *(de un horno)* fire grate; RAIL. luggage rack.

re·jun·tar tr. to gather.

re·ju·ve·ne·cer §17 tr., intr. & reflex. to rejuvenate.

re·ju·ve·ne·ci·mien·to m. rejuvenation.

re·la·ción f. relation; *(conexión)* connection; *(relato)* account; *(informe)* report; *(lista)* list; MATH. ratio ♦ **con** *or* **en r. a** in relation to • **guardar r. con** to bear relation with ♦ pl. *(cortejo)* courtship; *(conocidos)* acquaintances • **estar en buenas r. con** to be on good terms with • **mantener r. con** to be in touch with • **tener buenas r.** to be well-connected.

re·la·cio·na·do, ·a adj. related *(con* to, with).

re·la·cio·nar tr. to relate —reflex. to be related; *(hacer amistades)* to make friends.

re·la·ja·ción f. relaxation; *(aflojamiento)* loosening; *(moral)* laxity.

re·la·ja·do, ·a adj. relaxed; *(aflojado)* loose; AMER. *(depravado)* depraved.

re·la·ja·mien·to m. var. of **relajación.**

re·la·jar tr. *(mente, cuerpo)* to relax; *(aflojar)* to loosen; *(la tensión)* to ease; *(divertir)* to amuse —reflex. to relax; *(viciarse)* to let oneself go.

re·la·jo m. AMER. COLL. *(desorden)* commotion; *(depravación)* debauchery.

re·la·mer tr. to lick —reflex. to lick one's lips.

re·la·mi·do, ·a adj. affected.

re·lám·pa·go m. lightning; FIG. flash.

re·lam·pa·gue·ar intr. to flash with lightning; FIG. to sparkle.

re·lam·pa·gue·o m. lightning.

re·lap·so, a I. adj. relapsed II. m.f. backslider.

re·la·ta·dor, ·ra m.f. narrator.

re·la·tar tr. to narrate.

re·la·ti·vi·dad f. relativity.

re·la·ti·vo, a adj. & m. GRAM. relative ♦ **en lo r.** a with regard to.

re·la·to m. narration; *(informe)* account; *(cuento)* story.

re·la·tor, ·ra I. adj. narrating II. m.f. *(de cuentos)* narrator; *(de expedientes)* court reporter.

re·le·er §43 tr. to reread.

re·le·gar §47 tr. to relegate ♦ **r. al olvido una cosa** to cast something into oblivion.

re·le·van·te adj. outstanding.

re·le·var tr. *(exonerar)* to relieve *(de of, from)*; *(absolver)* to pardon; *(exaltar)* to praise; *(reemplazar)* to relieve *(de from)*; PAINT. to paint in relief —reflex. to take turns.

re·le·vo m. *(acto)* change of the guard; *(soldado)* relief; SPORT. relay.

re·li·ca·rio m. reliquary; *(medallón)* locket.

re·lie·ve m. ART., GEOG. relief; *(estampado)* embossing; *(renombre)* prominence ♦ **poner en r.** to emphasize.

re·li·gión f. religion.

re·li·gio·si·dad f. religiosity.

re·li·gio·so, a I. adj. religious II. m. monk —f. nun.

re·lin·char intr. to neigh.

re·lin·cho m. neigh; FIG. whoop.

re·li·quia f. relic ♦ **r. de familia** family heirloom.

re·loj m. *(de pared)* clock; *(de pulsera)* watch ♦ **como un r.** like clockwork • **r. de caja** grandfather's clock • **r. de sol** sundial • **r. despertador** alarm clock.

re·lo·je·rí·a f. *(arte)* watchmaking, clockmaking; *(taller)* watch *or* clock factory; *(tienda)* jewelry store.

re·lo·je·ro, a m.f. watchmaker.

re·lu·cien·te adj. shining.

re·lu·cir §44 intr. to shine ♦ **sacar a r.** *(mencionar)* to bring up; *(poner en relieve)* to bring out • **salir a r.** to come to light.

re·lum·bran·te adj. dazzling.

re·lum·brar intr. to dazzle.

re·lla·nar tr. to level again —reflex. to stretch out in one's chair.

re·lla·no m. landing.

re·lle·nar tr. *(llenar)* to refill; *(llenar completamente)* to fill up; CUL. to stuff; SEW. to pad.

re·lle·no, a I. adj. stuffed II. m. stuffing; SEW. padding.

re·ma·char tr. *(roblonar)* to rivet; *(machacar)* to clinch; FIG. to drive home.

re·ma·che m. *(de clavo)* clinching; *(roblón)* rivet.

re·ma·llar tr. to mend.

re·ma·nen·te m. remnant; COM. surplus.

re·man·gar §47 tr. to roll *or* tuck up.

re·man·so m. backwater.

re·mar intr. to row.

re·ma·ta·do, a adj. utter; LAW convicted.

re·ma·ta·dor, ·ra m. goal scorer —m.f. R.P. auctioneer.

re·ma·tar tr. *(acabar)* to finish (off); *(agotar)* to use up; *(matar)* to kill off; *(subastar)* to auction (off); ARCHIT. to top; SPORT. to shoot, kick (a goal) —intr. to end.

re·ma·te m. *(fin)* conclusion; *(toque final)* finishing touch; *(subasta)* auction; SPORT. shot ♦ **como r.** to top it all (off) • **de r.** utter.

re·me·dar tr. *(imitar)* to imitate; *(burlarse)* to mimic.

re·me·dia·ble adj. remediable ♦ **fácilmente r.** easy to remedy.

re·me·diar tr. to remedy; *(ayudar)* to assist; *(librar)* to save; *(evitar)* to prevent.

re·me·dio m. remedy; *(ayuda)* relief ♦ **como último r.** as a last resort • **no haber (más) r.** to be unavoidable • **no tener más r.** to have no alternative *(que but)* • **no tener r.** to be hopeless.

re·me·do m. imitation; *(parodia)* travesty.

re·mem·bran·za f. remembrance.

re·me·mo·ra·ción f. remembrance.

re·me·mo·rar tr. to remember.

re·men·dar §49 tr. *(reparar)* to mend; SEW. to darn; *(corregir)* to correct.

re·men·dón, o·na m.f. mender; *(zapatero)* cobbler.

re·me·ro, a m.f. rower.

re·me·sa f. *(de dinero)* remittance; *(de mercancías)* consignment.

re·me·sar tr. *(dinero)* to remit; *(mercancías)* to consign.

re·mien·de, do see **remendar.**

re·mien·do m. *(acción)* mending; *(enmienda)* correction; SEW. patch.

re·mil·ga·do, a adj. affected.

re·mil·gar·se §47 reflex. to behave affectedly.

re·mil·go m. affectedness.

re·mi·nis·cen·cia f. reminiscence.

re·mi·sión f. *(envío)* remittance; *(entrega)* delivery; *(perdón)* pardon; MED. remission.

re·mi·so, a adj. remiss.

re·mi·ten·te I. remitting II. m.f. sender.

re·mi·tir tr. *(enviar)* to send; *(dinero)* to remit; *(perdonar)* to forgive; *(demorar)* to put off; *(ceder)* to diminish; *(al juicio de otro)* to leave to *(someone's)* judgment; *(referir)* to refer; COM. to ship —intr. to diminish —reflex. to refer *(a to).*

re·mo m. *(grande)* oar; *(pequeño)* paddle; SPORT. rowing.

re·mo·jo m. soaking ♦ **poner en r.** to soak.

re·mo·la·cha f. beet.

re·mol·ca·dor, ·ra I. adj. towing II. m. AUTO. tow truck; MARIT. tugboat.

re·mol·car §70 tr. to tow.

re·mo·li·ne·ar tr. & intr. to whirl.

re·mo·li·no m. *(de agua)* whirlpool; *(de aire)* whirlwind; *(de pelo)* cowlick.

re·mo·lón, o·na I. adj. lazy II. m.f. loafer.

re·mo·lo·ne·ar intr. COLL. to loaf.

re·mol·que m. *(acción)* towing; *(vehículo que remolca)* tow truck; *(vehículo remolcado)* towed vehicle ♦ **a r.** in tow.

re·mon·tar tr. *(calzado)* to repair; *(un río)* to go up; *(superar)* to surmount; *(elevar)* to raise; *(encumbrar)* to honor —reflex. *(volar)* to soar; *(hasta el origen)* to go back *(a to).*

ré·mo·ra f. remora.

re·mor·der §78 tr. to bite, gnaw; FIG. to trouble ♦ **r. la conciencia** to weigh on one's conscience —reflex. to show remorse.

re·mor·di·mien·to m. remorse.

re·mo·to, a adj. remote.

re·mo·ver §78 tr. *(mover)* to move; *(quitar)* to remove; *(destituir)* to dismiss; *(mezclar)* to stir; *(recuerdos)* to revive —reflex. to shake.

re·mo·zar §04 tr. to rejuvenate; FIG. to bring up to date —reflex. to be rejuvenated.

rem·pu·jón m. COLL. var. of **empujón.**

re·muer·da, do see **remorder.**

re·mue·va, vo see **remover.**

re·mu·ne·ra·ción f. remuneration.

re·mu·ne·rar tr. to remunerate.

re·mu·ne·ra·ti·vo, a adj. remunerative.

re·na·cen·tis·ta I. adj. Renaissance II. m.f. expert on the Renaissance.

re·na·cer §17 intr. *(nacer de nuevo)* to be reborn; *(recobrar fuerzas)* to recover; *(reaparecer)* to reappear.

re·na·ci·mien·to m. revival ♦ **R.** Renaissance.

re·na·cua·jo m. tadpole; FIG. shrimp.

re·nal adj. renal.

ren·ci·lla f. quarrel.

ren·cor m. rancor ♦ **guardar r. a alguien** to hold a grudge against someone.

ren·co·ro·so, a adj. resentful.

ren·di·ción f. *(entrega)* surrender; *(utilidad)* yield.

ren·di·do, a adj. *(obsequioso)* obsequious; *(sumiso)* submissive; *(cansado)* exhausted.

ren·di·ja f. crack.

ren·di·mien·to m. *(cansancio)* exhaustion; *(sumisión)* submissiveness; *(obsequiosidad)* obsequiousness; *(producto)* yield; *(funcionamiento)* performance.

ren·dir §48 tr. *(vencer)* to defeat; *(sujetar)* to dominate; *(entregar)* to surrender; *(restituir)* to give back; *(producir)* to yield; *(dar fruto)* to bear; *(cansar)* to tire out; *(las armas)* to lay down ♦ **r. cuentas de** to give an account of • **r. culto a** *(venerar)* to worship; *(homenajear)* to pay tribute to • **r. examen** to take an examination • **r. homenaje a** to pay homage to —intr. *(dar utilidad)* to yield; AMER. *(durar mucho)* to last longer than usual —reflex. *(someterse)* to surrender; *(entregarse)* to yield <**r. a la fuerza** to yield to force>; *(cansarse)* to exhaust oneself.

re·ne·ga·do, a adj. & m.f. *(apóstata)* apostate; COLL. *(de mal carácter)* gruff (person).

re·ne·gar §52 tr. to deny strongly —intr. RELIG. to apostatize; *(blasfemar)* to swear; COLL. *(quejarse)* to grumble ♦ **r. de** to renounce.

re·ne·gri·do, a adj. black.

ren·glón m. *(línea)* line (of words); *(partida)* item ♦ **a r. seguido** COLL. right after.

ren·go, a adj. & m.f. lame (person).

ren·gue·ar intr. AMER. to limp.

re·nie·gue, go see **renegar.**

re·no m. reindeer.

re·nom·bra·do, a adj. renowned.

re·nom·bre m. renown.

re·no·va·ción f. *(extensión)* renewal; *(restauración)* renovation.

re·no·var §19 tr. *(extender)* to renew; *(reemplazar)* to replace; *(restaurar)* to renovate.

ren·ta f. *(ingresos)* income; *(ganancia)* profit; *(interés)* interest; *(alquiler)* rent; *(anual)* annuity; *(deuda pública)* national debt ♦ **r. bruta** gross income.

ren·ta·ble adj. profitable.

ren·tar tr. *(producir renta)* to yield; AMER. *(alquilar)* to rent.

ren·tis·ta m.f. *(accionista)* bondholder; *(rico)* wealthy person.

re·nuen·cia f. reluctance.

re·nuen·te adj. reluctant.

re·nue·ve, vo see **renovar.**

re·nun·cia f. *(abandono)* renunciation; *(a un puesto)* resignation.

re·nun·cia·ción f./**mien·to** m. renunciation.

re·nun·ciar tr. *(abandonar)* to renounce; *(a un*

puesto) to resign; *(no aceptar)* to reject.

re·nun·cio m. COLL. lie.

re·ñi·de·ro m. pit ♦ **r. de gallos** cockpit.

re·ñi·do, a adj. *(enemistado)* at odds; *(difícil)* hard-fought ♦ **r. con** contrary to.

re·ñi·dor, ·ra adj. quarrelsome.

re·ñir §59 intr. to quarrel ♦ **r. en buena lid** to have a fair fight • **r. por** to fight for or over —tr. *(regañar)* to scold; *(llevar a cabo)* to wage.

re·o, a m.f. defendant.

re·o·jo adv. ♦ **mirar de r.** to look out of the corner of one's eye.

re·or·ga·ni·za·ción f. reorganization

re·or·ga·ni·zar §04 tr. to reorganize.

re·pan·chi·gar·se/ti·gar·se §47 reflex. COLL. to stretch or sprawl out.

re·pa·ra·ción f. *(compostura)* repair.

re·pa·ra·dor, ·ra I. adj. restorative II. m.f. *(que compone)* repairer; *(reparón)* faultfinder — m. repairman.

re·pa·rar tr. *(componer)* to repair; *(notar)* to notice; *(desagraviar)* to make amends for; *(remediar)* to redress; *(restablecer)* to restore —intr. to stop ♦ **no r. en nada** to stop at nothing.

re·pa·ro m. *(objeción)* objection; *(duda)* misgiving; *(defensa)* protection ♦ **no andar con reparos** not to hesitate.

re·par·ti·ción f. sharing.

re·par·ti·dor, ·ra I. adj. distributing II. m.f. *(que reparte)* distributor; *(entregador)* deliverer ♦ **r. de periódicos** newspaper boy.

re·par·ti·ja f. AMER., COLL. var. of **reparto.**

re·par·tir tr. *(dividir)* to divide; *(distribuir)* to distribute; *(entregar)* to deliver; *(esparcir)* to spread out.

re·par·to m. *(distribución)* distribution; *(entrega)* delivery; CINEM., THEAT. cast.

re·pa·sar tr. *(pasar)* to pass (by) again; *(examinar)* to review; *(hojear)* to glance over; *(explicar, hacer)* to go over again —intr. to pass (by) again.

re·pa·so m. review ♦ **dar un r.** to look over or through.

re·pa·tria·ción f. repatriation.

re·pa·tria·do, a I. adj. repatriated II. m.f. repatriate.

re·pa·triar §30 tr. & reflex. to repatriate (oneself).

re·pe·cho m. short steep incline ♦ **a r.** uphill.

re·pe·len·te adj. repellent.

re·pe·ler tr. to repel; *(rechazar)* to reject.

re·pen·te m. start ♦ **de r.** suddenly.

re·pen·ti·no, a adj. sudden.

re·per·cu·sión f. repercussion.

re·per·cu·tir intr. *(rebotar)* to rebound; *(resonar)* to reverberate ♦ **r. en** to have repercussions on.

re·per·to·rio m. repertory, repertoire.

re·pe·ti·ción f. repetition; *(mecanismo)* repeater.

re·pe·tir §48 tr. to repeat; *(comer más)* to have a second helping of; *(recitar)* to recite —intr. to repeat —reflex. to repeat itself or oneself.

re·pe·ti·ti·vo, a adj. repetitive.

re·pi·car §70 intr. to ring out.

re·pi·que·te·ar intr. *(las campanas)* to ring; *(tambor)* to beat; *(golpear)* to drum.

re·pi·que·te·o m. *(de campanas)* lively ringing; *(de lluvia)* pitter-patter; *(con los dedos)* tapping.

re·pi·sa f. shelf.

re·pi·ta, to, tiera, tió see **repetir**.

re·plan·tar tr. to replant.

re·plan·te·ar tr. *(exponer)* to restate; ARCHIT. to lay out a ground plan of.

re·ple·gar §52 tr. to fold over; AER. to retract —reflex. MIL. to retreat.

re·ple·to, a adj. full ♦ **r. de** packed with.

ré·pli·ca f. *(contestación)* retort; *(copia)* replica; LAW replication.

re·pli·car §70 intr. to retort.

re·plie·go, gue see **replegar**.

re·po·bla·ción f. repopulation.

re·po·blar §19 tr. to repopulate.

re·po·llo m. cabbage.

re·po·ner §54 tr. *(poner)* to put back; *(reemplazar)* to replace; *(replicar)* to reply; THEAT. to revive —reflex. *(recuperarse)* to recover; *(serenarse)* to calm down.

re·por·ta·je m. *(artículo)* report; *(de noticias)* news coverage; *(entrevista)* interview.

re·por·tar tr. to bring —reflex. to control oneself.

re·por·te m. *(chisme)* gossip; *(noticia)* news.

re·por·te·ro, a I. adj. reporting II. m.f. reporter.

re·po·sa·piés m.inv. footrest.

re·po·sar intr. *(descansar)* to rest; *(yacer)* to lie.

re·po·si·ción f. *(acción)* replenishment; THEAT. revival.

re·po·so m. repose.

re·pos·te·rí·a f. *(tienda)* pastry shop; *(oficio)* confectionery.

re·pos·te·ro m.f. confectioner.

re·pren·der tr. to reprimand.

re·pren·sión f. reprimand.

re·pre·sa f. dam.

re·pre·sa·lia f. reprisal.

re·pre·sar tr. to dam.

re·pre·sen·ta·ción f. representation; THEAT. performance.

re·pre·sen·tan·te I. adj. representing II. m.f. representative.

re·pre·sen·tar tr. to represent; *(volver a presentar)* to present again; *(aparentar)* to appear to be; THEAT. to perform —intr. to picture.

re·pre·sen·ta·ti·vo, a adj. representative.

re·pre·sión f. repression.

re·pre·si·vo, a adj. repressive.

re·pre·sor, ra I. adj. repressing II. m.f. repressor.

re·pri·men·da f. reprimand.

re·pri·mir tr. & reflex. to repress (oneself).

re·pro·bar §19 tr. *(desaprobar)* to disapprove; *(en exámenes)* to fail.

ré·pro·bo, a adj. & m.f. reprobate.

re·pro·char tr. to reproach.

re·pro·che m. reproach.

re·pro·duc·ción f. reproduction.

re·pro·du·cir §22 tr. & reflex. to reproduce.

re·pro·duc·tor, ra I. adj. *(que copia)* reproducing; BIOL. reproductive; ZOOL. breeding II. m.f. BIOL. reproducer; ZOOL. breeder.

re·prue·be, bo see **reprobar**.

rep·tar intr. to crawl.

rep·til I. adj. reptilian II. m. reptile.

re·pú·bli·ca f. republic.

re·pu·bli·ca·no, a adj. & m.f. republican.

re·pu·dia·ción f. repudiation.

re·pu·diar tr. to repudiate; LAW to renounce.

re·pu·dio m. repudiation.

re·pu·drir tr. & reflex. to rot away; FIG. to eat one's heart out.

re·pues·to, a I. see **reponer** II. adj. MED. recovered III. m. *(reserva)* supply; *(pieza)* spare (part) ♦ **de r.** spare.

re·pug·nan·cia f. repugnance.

re·pug·nan·te adj. repugnant.

re·pug·nar intr. to detest <*las arañas me repugnan* I detest spiders>.

re·pu·jar tr. to do repoussé on.

re·pul·gar §47 tr. to hem.

re·pul·sar tr. to reject.

re·pul·sión f. repulsion.

re·pul·si·vo, a adj. repulsive.

re·pun·tar intr. to turn.

re·pun·te m. turning.

re·pu·ta·ción f. reputation.

re·pu·tar tr. to deem.

re·que·brar §49 tr. *(volver a quebrar)* to break again; *(lisonjear)* to flatter.

re·que·mar tr. to burn.

re·que·ri·mien·to m. requirement; LAW summons; *(demanda)* request.

re·que·rir §65 tr. *(necesitar)* to require; *(intimar)* to order; *(solicitar)* to request ♦ **r. (de amores)** to woo.

re·que·són m. *(queso)* cottage or pot cheese; *(cuajada)* curd.

re·que·te·bién adv. COLL. wonderfully.

re·quie·bro m. flattery.

ré·quiem m. requiem.

re·quie·ra, ro, quiriera, quirió see **requerir**.

re·qui·sa f. *(revista)* inspection; MIL. requisition; AMER. search.

re·qui·sar tr. to requisition; AMER. to search.

re·qui·si·ción f. requisition.

re·qui·si·to m. requirement.

res f. animal ♦ **r. vacuna** head of cattle.

re·sa·bi·do, a adj. well-known.

re·sa·bio m. *(sabor)* unpleasant aftertaste; *(vicio)* bad habit.

re·sa·ca f. MARIT. undertow; COM. redraft.

re·sa·la·do, a adj. COLL. charming.

re·sa·lir §63 intr. to jut out.

re·sal·tar intr. to jut out; FIG. to stand out ♦ **hacer r.** to stress.

re·sar·ci·ble adj. indemnifiable.

re·sar·cir §35 tr. to indemnify —reflex. to make up (de for).

res·ba·la·di·zo, a adj. slippery.

res·ba·lar intr. to slip; AUTO to skid.

res·ba·lón m. slip; AUTO. skid.

res·ba·lo·so, a adj. slippery.

res·ca·ta·dor, ra I. adj. rescuing II. m.f. rescuer.

res·ca·tar tr. *(recobrar)* to recover; *(cautivos)* to ransom; *(salvar)* to rescue.

res·ca·te m. *(acción)* rescue; *(recobro)* recovery; *(dinero)* ransom money.

res·cin·dir tr. to rescind.

res·ci·sión f. rescission.

res·col·do m. embers.

re·se·car §70 tr. & reflex. to dry out.

re·sen·ti·do, a adj. resentful.

re·sen·ti·mien·to m. resentment.

re·sen·tir·se §65 reflex. *(sentir los efectos)* to feel the effects; *(debilitarse)* to be impaired; FIG. to feel hurt ♦ **r. por** to take offense at.

re·se·ña f. MIL. inspection; *(descripción)* outline; *(relación)* account; *(análisis)* review.

re·se·ñar tr. MIL. to inspect; *(describir)* to de-

scribe; *(analizar)* to review.
re·se·ro m. AMER. herdsman.
re·ser·va f. reserve; *(provisión)* stock; *(reservación, excepción)* reservation; *(discreción)* discretion; COM., MIL. reserve ♦ **a r. de** except for • **a r. de que** unless • **sin r.** openly.
re·ser·va·ción f. reservation.
re·ser·va·do, a I. adj. reserved; *(discreto)* discreet; *(confidencial)* confidential **II.** m. reserved room *or* area.
re·ser·var tr. to reserve; *(guardar)* to save; *(encubrir)* to conceal; *(no comunicar)* to withhold; *(dilatar)* to put off; *(dispensar)* to exempt —reflex. to save one's strength *or* oneself.
re·ser·vis·ta I. adj. reserve **II.** m. reservist.
res·fria·do m. cold.
res·friar §30 tr. *(enfriar)* to cool; *(moderar)* to temper —intr. to cool —reflex. to catch a cold.
res·guar·dar tr. & reflex. to protect (oneself).
res·guar·do m. *(protección)* protection; *(documento)* safeguard.
re·si·den·cia f. residence.
re·si·den·cial adj. residential.
re·si·den·te adj. & m.f. resident.
re·si·dir intr. to reside.
re·si·duo m. residue ♦ pl. waste.
re·sien·ta, to see **resentirse.**
re·sig·na·ción f. resignation.
re·sig·nar tr. & reflex. to resign (oneself).
re·si·na f. resin.
re·sin·tie·ra, tió see **resentirse.**
re·sis·ten·cia f. resistance; *(aguante)* endurance ♦ **oponer r.** to resist • **r. de tensión** tensile strength.
re·sis·ten·te adj. resistant; BOT. hardy.
re·sis·tir intr. to resist; *(durar)* to endure —tr. to resist; *(aguantar)* to bear —reflex. to resist; *(luchar)* to fight; *(negarse)* to refuse (a to).
res·ma f. ream.
re·so·lu·ción f. resolution, *(decisión)* decision; *(solución)* solution.
re·so·lu·to, a adj. resolute.
re·sol·ver §78 tr. to resolve; *(solucionar)* to solve; *(resumir)* to sum up; CHEM. to dissolve —reflex. to resolve; *(ser solucionado)* to resolve itself ♦ **r. por** to decide in favor of —intr. to decide.
re·so·llar §19 intr. to breathe heavily; FIG. to show signs of life ♦ **sin r.** COLL. without a word.
re·so·nan·cia f. resonance; FIG. repercussion ♦ **tener r.** to cause a stir.
re·so·nan·te adj. resounding.
re·so·nar §19 intr. to resound; FIG. to have repercussions.
re·so·plar intr. to puff.
re·so·pli·do/plo m. puffing.
re·sor·te m. spring ♦ pl. **tocar los r.** to pull the strings.
res·pal·dar[1] m. back of a chair.
res·pal·dar[2] tr. *(apuntar)* to endorse; *(garantizar)* to back —reflex. to lean back; *(basarse)* to base oneself (en on).
res·pal·do m. *(de silla)* back; *(garantía)* backing.
res·pec·ti·vo, a adj. respective.
res·pec·to m. respect ♦ **al r.** about the matter • **r. a** *or* **de** with respect to.
res·pe·tar tr. to respect.
res·pe·to m. respect ♦ **faltar al r.** to be disrespectful.

res·pe·tuo·so, a adj. respectful.
res·pin·gar §47 intr. to balk.
res·pin·go m. start; COLL. *(movimiento)* gesture of impatience.
res·pi·ra·ción f. respiration.
res·pi·ra·de·ro m. *(abertura)* vent; *(cañería)* ventilation shaft; *(descanso)* rest.
res·pi·ra·dor m. *(máquina)* respirator; ANAT. respiratory muscle.
res·pi·rar intr. to breathe; FIG. to breathe a sigh of relief ♦ **no dejar r. a alguien** not to give someone a moment's peace • **no r.** COLL. not to breathe a word —tr. to breathe (in); FIG. to exude <*r. honradez* to exude honesty>.
res·pi·ro m. *(respiración)* respiration; *(descanso)* rest, respite; FIG. break.
res·plan·de·cer §17 intr. to shine.
res·plan·de·cien·te adj. resplendent.
res·plan·dor/de·ci·mien·to m. brightness; *(de llamas)* glow; *(brillo)* shine; *(esplendor)* splendor.
res·pon·der tr. to answer —intr. *(contestar)* to answer; *(corresponder)* to return; *(replicar)* to answer back; *(resultar)* to perform <*la máquina nueva responde bien* the new machine performs well>; *(reaccionar)* to respond ♦ **r. a una descripción** to fit a description • **r. a una necesidad** to meet a need • **r. a una obligación** to honor an obligation • **r. por** to be responsible for.
res·pon·sa·bi·li·dad f. responsibility ♦ **r. limitada** limited liability.
res·pon·sa·bi·li·zar §04 tr. to make responsible —reflex. to take the responsibility.
res·pon·sa·ble adj. responsible; LAW liable ♦ **hacerse r. de** to assume responsibility for.
res·pon·so m. RELIG. prayer for the dead.
res·pues·ta f. answer.
res·que·bra·(ja·)du·ra f./ja·mien·to crack.
res·que·bra·jar tr. & reflex. to crack.
res·que·brar §49 intr. to crack.
res·que·mor m. *(resentimiento)* resentment; *(remordimiento)* remorse.
res·qui·cio m. crack; FIG. glimmer <*un r. de esperanza* a glimmer of hope>.
res·ta f. subtraction.
res·ta·ble·cer §17 tr. to reestablish —reflex. to recover.
res·ta·ble·ci·mien·to m. reestablishment, restoration; MED. recovery.
res·ta·llar intr. to crack.
res·tan·te I. adj. remaining **II.** m. remainder.
res·tar tr. MATH. to subtract; *(quitar)* to take away —intr. to remain; MATH. to subtract.
res·tau·ra·ción f. restoration.
res·tau·ra·dor, ·ra I. adj. restoring **I.** m.f. restorer.
res·tau·ran·te m. restaurant.
res·tau·rar tr. to restore.
res·ti·tu·ción f. restitution.
res·ti·tuir §18 tr. to restore —reflex. to come back.
res·to m. remainder; COM. balance ♦ pl. leftovers • **r. mortales** mortal remains.
res·to·rán m. restaurant.
res·tre·gar §52 tr. to rub.
res·tric·ción f. restriction.
res·tric·ti·vo, a adj. restrictive.
res·trin·gir §32 tr. to restrict; MED. to contract —reflex. to cut down on.
res·tri·ñir §12 tr. *(astringir)* to constrict; *(estreñir)* to constipate.

re·su·ci·tar tr. to resuscitate; FIG. to revive —intr. to be resuscitated.

re·suel·to, a I. see **resolver** II. adj. determined.

re·suel·va, vo see **resolver**.

re·sue·lle, llo see **resollar**.

re·sue·llo m. breathing ♦ **perder el r.** to be out of breath.

re·sue·ne see **resonar**.

re·sul·ta f. result, consequence ♦ **de resultas** as a result of.

re·sul·ta·do m. result; (*consecuencia*) outcome; MATH. answer ♦ **dar r.** to produce results.

re·sul·tar intr. to turn out to be <*si resulta posible, te acompañaremos* if it turns out to be possible, we'll go with you>; (*salir*) to turn out <*la investigación no resultó como pronosticaban* the investigation didn't turn out as they predicted>; (*funcionar*) to work (out); (*encontrar*) to find <*ella me resulta muy simpática* I find her very nice> ♦ **estar resultando** to be beginning <*este tema me está resultando aburrido ya* this topic is beginning to bore me> • **r. de** to result or stem from • **r. que** to turn out that.

re·su·men m. summary ♦ **en r.** in short.

re·su·mi·da·men·te adv. briefly.

re·su·mi·de·ro m. AMER. sewer.

re·su·mir tr. to summarize; (*acortar*) to shorten —reflex. to be summed up ♦ **r. en** to boil down to.

re·sur·gi·mien·to m. resurgence.

re·sur·gir §32 intr. to reappear.

re·su·rrec·ción f. resurrection.

re·ta·dor, ·ra I. adj. challenging II. m.f. challenger.

re·ta·guar·dia f. rear.

re·ta·hí·la f. string.

re·tar tr. (*desafiar*) to challenge; (*censurar*) to scold.

re·tar·dar tr. to delay.

re·tar·do m. delay.

re·ta·zo m. (*de tela*) remnant; (*de discurso*) fragment.

re·te·ner §69 tr. to retain; (*deducir*) to withhold.

re·te·ni·mien·to m. retention.

re·ten·ti·vo, a I. adj. retentive II. f. memory.

re·ti·cen·cia f. reticence.

re·ti·cen·te adj. reticent.

re·ti·cu·lar adj. reticular.

re·tí·cu·lo m. BIOL. reticulum; OPT. reticle.

re·ti·na f. retina.

re·ti·ni·tis f. retinitis.

re·tin·to, a adj. dark brown.

re·ti·ra·da f. retreat ♦ **emprender una r.** to beat a retreat.

re·ti·ra·do, a adj. (*apartado*) secluded; (*jubilado*) retired II. m.f. retired person.

re·ti·rar tr. (*remover*) to remove; (*separar*) to move away; (*de circulación*) to withdraw; (*quitar*) to take away; (*retractar*) to retract; (*jubilar*) to retire; DIPL. to recall; FIN. to withdraw —reflex. (*apartarse*) to withdraw; (*irse para atrás*) to move back; (*jubilarse*) to retire; MIL. to retreat ♦ **a dormir** to go to bed.

re·ti·ro m. (*retirada*) withdrawal; (*lugar*) retreat; (*jubilación*) retirement; (*pensión*) pension; RELIG. retreat.

re·to m. challenge.

re·to·ba·do, a adj. AMER. stubborn.

re·to·bar AMER. tr. to wrap in leather —reflex. to become irritated.

re·to·car §70 tr. PHOTOG. to touch up; SEW. to alter; FIG. to put the finishing touch on.

re·to·mar tr. to take back.

re·to·ñar intr. to sprout; FIG. to reappear.

re·to·ño m. sprout.

re·to·que m. PHOTOG. retouching; SEW. alteration.

re·tor·cer §71 tr. to twist; (*los bigotes*) to twirl; (*interpretar mal*) to misinterpret, twist —reflex. to twist; (*de dolor*) to writhe.

re·tor·ci·do, a adj. twisted.

re·tor·ci·jón m. var. of **retortijón.**

re·tor·ci·mien·to m. (*torsión*) twisting; (*contorsión*) writhing.

re·tó·ri·co, a I. adj. rhetorical II. m. rhetorician —f. rhetoric.

re·tor·nar tr. to return, give back —intr. to return, go back.

re·tor·no m. return; (*trueque*) exchange.

re·tor·ti·jón m. twisting ♦ **r. de tripas** stomach cramps.

re·to·zar §04 intr. to frolic.

re·to·zo m. frolic.

re·to·zón, o·na adj. frolicsome.

re·trac·tar tr. & reflex. to retract.

re·trác·til adj. retractable.

re·tra·er §72 tr. to dissuade; LAW to redeem —reflex. (*refugiarse*) to take refuge; (*retirarse*) to retreat.

re·traí·do, a adj. (*solitario*) reclusive; (*poco comunicativo*) withdrawn.

re·trai·mien·to m. seclusion.

re·tran·ca f. breeching.

re·trans·mi·tir tr. to retransmit; (*difundir*) to rebroadcast; TELEC. to relay.

re·tra·sa·do, a adj. (*tardío*) late; (*persona*) retarded; (*país*) backward.

re·tra·sar tr. (*demorar*) to delay; (*aplazar*) to postpone; (*un reloj*) to set back —intr. to lag, fall behind; (*un reloj*) to be slow —reflex. to be late *or* delayed.

re·tra·so m. delay; (*subdesarrollo*) backwardness ♦ **con r.** late.

re·tra·tar tr. PAINT. to paint a portrait of; (*describir*) to depict; PHOTOG. to photograph —reflex. PAINT. to have one's portrait painted; PHOTOG. to have one's photograph taken; (*reflejarse*) to be reflected.

re·tra·tis·ta m.f. PAINT. portrait painter; PHOTOG. photographer.

re·tra·to m. PAINT. portrait; (*descripción*) trait, description; AMER. photograph.

re·tre·ta f. MIL. retreat; AMER. (*retahíla*) series, string; MUS. open-air band concert.

re·tre·te m. toilet.

re·tri·bu·ción f. retribution.

re·tri·buir §18 tr. (*pagar*) to pay; (*recompensar*) to reward; AMER. to reciprocate.

re·tro·ac·ti·vi·dad f. retroactivity.

re·tro·ac·ti·vo, a adj. retroactive.

re·tro·ce·der intr. (*volver atrás*) to go back; (*un paso*) to step back; (*nivel*) to recede; MIL. to withdraw.

re·tro·ce·so m. (*regresión*) retrocession; ARM. recoil; MIL. withdrawal; MECH. return.

re·tró·gra·do, a I. adj. retrogressive; ASTRON. retrograde; POL. reactionary II. m.f. reactionary.

re·tro·pro·pul·sión f. jet propulsion.

re·tros·pec·ción f. retrospection.

re·tros·pec·ti·vo, a adj. & f. retrospective.

re·tro·tra·er §72 tr. to antedate.

re·tro·vi·sor m. rearview mirror.

re·tru·car §70 intr. R.P., COLL. to retort.

re·trué·ca·no m. play on words.

re·tum·bar intr. to resound.

re·ú·ma or reu·ma m. var. of reumatismo.

reu·má·ti·co, a adj. & m.f. rheumatic.

reu·ma·tis·mo m. rheumatism.

reu·nión f. (de negocios) meeting; (de ex-alumnos) reunion; (fiesta) party.

reu·nir §60 tr. (juntar) to unite; (agrupar) to gather; (requisitos) to fulfill; (fondos) to collect; MIL. to assemble —reflex. (juntarse) to unite; (en una reunión) to meet.

re·vá·li·da f. revalidation; (examen) final examination; (certificado) certificate.

re·va·li·da·ción f. revalidation; (renovación) renewal.

re·va·li·dar tr. to revalidate; (renovar) to renew.

re·va·lo·ri·za·ción f. revaluation.

re·va·lo·ri·zar §04 tr. to revalue.

re·van·cha f. revenge.

re·ve·la·ción f. revelation.

re·ve·la·do m. PHOTOG. developing.

re·ve·la·dor, ·ra I. adj. revealing II. m. PHOTOG. developer.

re·ve·lar tr. to reveal; PHOTOG. to develop.

re·ven·de·dor, ·ra I. adj. reselling II. m.f. (que revende) reseller; (detallista) retailer ♦ r. de entradas ticket scalper.

re·ven·der tr. to resell; COM. to retail.

re·ven·ta f. resale.

re·ven·tar §49 intr. (globo) to burst; (neumático) to blow; (olas) to break; COLL. (morir) to kick the bucket ♦ r. de cansancio to be exhausted ♦ r. de envidia to be bursting with envy —tr. to burst; (aplastar) to smash; (cansar) to exhaust; (causar daño) to wreck; COLL. (molestar) to annoy —reflex. to burst; (cansarse) to exhaust oneself.

re·ven·tón m. burst; (de neumático) flat tire.

re·ver §65 intr. to review; LAW to retry.

re·ver·be·ra·ción f. reverberation.

re·ver·be·ran·te adj. reverberating.

re·ver·be·rar intr. to reverberate.

re·ve·ren·cia f. reverence; (saludo) bow ♦ hacer una r. to bow.

re·ve·ren·ciar tr. to revere.

re·ve·ren·dí·si·mo, a adj. Most Reverend.

re·ve·ren·do, a adj. reverend; COLL. huge.

re·ve·ren·te adj. respectful.

re·ver·so, a adj. & m. reverse.

re·ver·tir §65 intr. to revert.

re·vés m. (envés) back; (desgracia) setback ♦ al r. (al contrario) backwards; (con lo de dentro fuera) inside out ♦ al r. de contrary to.

re·ve·sa·do, a adj. intricate.

re·ves·ti·mien·to m. covering.

re·ves·tir §48 tr. to cover; FIG. to take on.

re·vien·te, to see reventar.

re·vier·ta, to, virtiera, virtió see revertir.

re·vi·sar tr. to check.

re·vi·sión f. revision.

re·vi·sio·nis·ta adj. & m.f. revisionist.

re·vi·sor, ·ra I. adj. revising, checking II. m. inspector ♦ r. de cuentas auditor.

re·vis·ta f. (periódico) magazine; (revisión) review; THEAT. revue ♦ pasar r. to review ♦ r. literaria literary review.

re·vis·ta, to see revestir.

re·vis·te·ro, a m.f. (persona) reviewer; (mueble) magazine rack.

re·vis·tie·ra, tió see revestir.

re·vi·ta·li·zar §04 tr. to revitalize.

re·vi·vi·fi·car §70 tr. to revive.

re·vi·vir intr. to revive.

re·vo·ca·ción f. revocation; DIPL. recall.

re·vo·ca·dor m. plasterer.

re·vo·car §70 tr. (anular) to repeal; (destituir) to dismiss; CONSTR. to plaster.

re·vol·car §73 tr. to knock down —reflex. (en el suelo) to roll; (en el fango) to wallow.

re·vol·cón m. COLL. fall.

re·vo·lo·te·ar intr. to flutter.

re·vo·lo·te·o m. fluttering.

re·vol·ti·jo/llo m. jumble ♦ r. de huevos scrambled eggs.

re·vol·to·so, a I. adj. troublemaking II. m.f. troublemaker; (rebelde) rebel.

re·vo·lu·ción f. revolution.

re·vo·lu·cio·nar tr. to revolutionize.

re·vo·lu·cio·na·rio, a adj. & m.f. revolutionary.

re·vol·ver §78 tr. (mezclar) to mix; (líquidos) to stir; (agitar) to shake; (desordenar) to mix up; (producir náuseas) to turn —reflex. (dar vueltas) to turn around; (revolcarse) to roll; (retorcerse) to writhe ♦ r. contra alguien to turn against someone.

re·vól·ver m. revolver.

re·vo·que m. plaster.

re·vuel·co m. (en el suelo) roll; (en el fango) wallowing.

re·vue·lo m. (revoloteo) fluttering; (turbación) commotion ♦ de r. in passing.

re·vuel·ta f. revolt; (riña) quarrel.

re·vuel·to, a I. see revolver II. adj. (en desorden) jumbled; (inquieto) turbulent; (travieso) mischievous; (enrevesado) complicated ♦ huevos revueltos scrambled eggs.

rey m. king ♦ a cuerpo de r. like a king ♦ día de Reyes Epiphany.

re·yer·ta f. quarrel.

re·za·gar §47 tr. (dejar atrás) to leave behind; (aplazar) to put off —reflex. to lag behind.

re·zar §04 tr. to say —intr. to pray. ♦ según reza el refrán as the saying goes.

re·zo m. prayer.

re·zon·ga·dor, ·ra I. adj. grumbling II. m.f. grumbler.

re·zon·gar §47 intr. to grumble.

re·zu·mar tr., intr. & reflex. to ooze.

ri·a, río see reír.

ria·cho/chue·lo m. stream.

ri·be·ra f. shore.

ri·be·re·ño/ra·no, a I. adj. the shore, riparian II. shore dweller.

ri·be·te m. (borde) trimming; (a un cuento) embellishment.

ri·be·te·a·do I. adj. trimmed II. m. trimming.

ri·be·te·ar tr. to trim.

ri·ca·cho, a/chón, o·na m.f. COLL. moneybags.

ri·ca·men·te adv. richly.

ri·ci·no m. castor-oil plant ♦ aceite de r. castor oil.

ri·co, a I. adj. rich; (acaudalado) wealthy, (fértil) fertile; (abundante) abundant; (magnífico) luxurious; (sabroso) delicious; COLL. (simpático) adorable ♦ hacerse r. to get rich II. m.f. rich person ♦ los ricos the rich.

ric·tus m. rictus ♦ r. de dolor wince of pain.

ri·cu·ra f. tastiness; FIG. cutie.

ri·dí·cu·lez f. absurdity; (insignificancia) trifle.

ri·di·cu·li·zar §04 tr. to ridicule.

ri·dí·cu·lo, a I. adj. ridiculous II. m. ridiculous situation ♦ **hacer el r.** to make a fool of oneself • **poner en r.** to make a fool of.

rie·go m. irrigation ♦ **boca de r.** hydrant.

rie·go, gue see **regar**.

riel m. rail ♦ **andar sobre rieles** to go like clockwork.

rien·da f. rein; (*sujeción*) restraint ♦ **a r. suelta** (*con velocidad*) at full speed; (*sin sujeción*) without restraint.

rie·ra, rió see **reír**.

ries·go m. risk.

ri·fa f. raffle.

ri·far tr. to raffle.

ri·fle m. rifle.

ri·gi·dez f. rigidity.

rí·gi·do, a adj. stiff.

ri·gie·ra, gió see **regir**.

ri·gor m. rigor ♦ **de r.** de rigueur.

ri·gu·ro·so, a adj. rigorous.

ri·ja, o see **regir**.

ri·ma f. rhyme ♦ pl. poems.

ri·mar intr. & tr. to rhyme.

rim·bom·ban·cia f. bombast.

rim·bom·ban·te adj. resounding, echoing; (*pomposo*) bombastic; (*ostentoso*) showy.

rí·mel m. mascara.

rin·cón m. corner.

rin·co·ne·ra f. corner furniture.

rin·da, dio, diera, dió see **rendir**.

ri·no·ce·ron·te m. rhinoceros.

ri·ña f. quarrel.

ri·ña, ñe, ñera, ñó see **reñir**.

ri·ñón m. kidney ♦ **costar un r.** COLL. to cost a fortune ♦ pl. lower back.

rí·o m. river; FIG. flood ♦ **r. abajo** downstream.

ri·que·za f. (*abundancia*) wealth; (*opulencia*) opulence; (*fecundidad*) richness ♦ pl. riches • **r. naturales** natural resources.

ri·sa f. laugh <*una r. ahogada* a stifled laugh>; laughter <*no hizo caso de la r. de los estudiantes* he took no notice of the students' laughter>; laugh, joke <*la explicación que dio fue una r.* the explanation he gave was a laugh>; (*hazmerreír*) laughingstock ♦ **desternillarse** or **reventar de r.** to burst with laughter • **contener la r.** to keep a straight face • **dar r. a alguien** to make someone laugh • **¡qué r.!** how funny! • **tener un ataque de r.** to have a fit of laughter • **tomar a r.** to take as a joke.

ris·co m. cliff.

ri·si·ble adj. laughable.

ri·so·ta·da f. guffaw.

ris·tra f. string <*r. de ajos* string of garlic>.

ri·sue·ño, a adj. smiling; (*agradable*) pleasant; (*favorable*) bright.

rít·mi·co, a adj. rhythmic.

rit·mo m. rhythm.

ri·to m. rite, ceremony.

ri·tual adj. & m. ritual.

ri·val adj & m.f. rival.

ri·va·li·dad f. rivalry.

ri·va·li·zar §04 intr. to rival.

ri·za·do m. curling.

ri·zar §04 tr. (*pelo*) to curl; (*olas*) to ripple —reflex. (*pelo*) to curl (up); (*mar*) to become choppy.

ri·zo m. (*mechón*) ringlet; TEX. ribbed velvet.

ró·ba·lo or **ro·ba·lo** m. ICHTH. bass.

ro·bar tr. to rob; (*saquear*) to burgle; (*la voluntad*) to steal (away).

ro·ble m. oak; FIG. pillar of strength.

ro·blón m. (*clavo*) rivet; (*teja*) ridge of tiles.

ro·bo m. robbery; (*en naipes*) draw.

ro·bus·te·cer §17 tr. to strengthen.

ro·bus·to, a adj. robust.

ro·ca f. rock.

ro·ce m. (*acción*) rubbing; (*toque*) touch; (*trato frecuente*) close contact; (*fricción*) animosity.

ro·cia·dor m. sprayer.

ro·cia·du·ra f./**mien·to** m. sprinkling.

ro·ciar §30 intr. to fall (dew) —tr. (*mojar*) to sprinkle; (*arrojar*) to scatter.

ro·cín m. (*asno*) donkey; (*caballo bajo*) workhorse.

ro·cí·o m. dew; (*llovizna*) sprinkle.

ro·co·so, a adj. rocky.

ro·da·ba·llo m. turbot, flounder.

ro·da·do m. R.P. vehicle.

ro·da·ja f. (*de metal*) disc; (*de fruta*) slice.

ro·da·je m. (*conjunto de ruedas*) wheels; (*impuesto*) vehicle tax; CINEM. filming.

ro·da·mien·to m. bearing.

ro·dar §19 intr. (*girar*) to roll; (*funcionar*) to run; (*moverse con ruedas*) to run (on wheels); (*caer dando vueltas*) to tumble (down); (*vagar*) to roam; CINEM. to shoot —tr. (*hacer rodar*) to roll; CINEM. to shoot.

ro·de·ar intr. to go around; (*ir por el camino más largo*) to go by a roundabout way; (*hablar con rodeos*) to beat around the bush —tr. to surround; (*dar la vuelta*) to go around; AMER. to round up —reflex. ♦ **r. de** to surround oneself with.

ro·de·o m. (*acción*) surrounding; (*camino indirecto*) roundabout way; (*fiesta*) rodeo; (*de ganado*) roundup; (*circunloquio*) circumlocution; (*subterfugio*) subterfuge ♦ **andar con rodeos** to beat around the bush.

ro·de·te m. bun.

ro·di·lla f. knee ♦ **de rodillas** on one's knees.

ro·di·lla·da f./**zo** m. blow with the knee.

ro·di·lle·ra f. knee guard.

ro·di·llo m. roller; CUL. rolling pin.

ro·e·dor, ra I. adj. gnawing II. m. rodent.

ro·ent·gen/ge·nio m. roentgen.

ro·er §61 tr. to gnaw; (*molestar*) to worry; (*gastar*) to erode.

ro·gar §16 tr. to beg —intr. to pray ♦ **hacerse de r.** to play hard to get.

ro·ji·zo, a adj. reddish.

ro·jo, a I. adj. (*colorado*) red; (*mejillas*) ruddy ♦ **mal r.** VET. swine fever • **ponerse r.** to blush • **ponerse r. de ira** to become furious II. m.f. red, revolutionary —m. (*color*) red ♦ **al r. rojo-hot** • **estar al r. vivo** to be heated or tense.

rol·da·na f. pulley wheel.

ro·lli·zo, a I. adj. (*redondo*) round; (*grueso*) chubby, plump II. m. round log.

ro·llo m. roll <*un r. de cinta adhesiva* a roll of adhesive tape>; (*de escritura*) scroll; (*de cuerda*) coil; MECH., TECH. roller; CUL. rolling pin ♦ **en r.** rolled (up) • **soltar el r.** COLL. to go on and on.

ro·ma·na f. steelyard.

ro·man·ce I. adj. Romance (language) II. m. (*lengua moderna*) Romance language; (*castellano*) Spanish (language); LIT. ballad; POET. romance ♦ **en buen r.** in clear language.

ro·man·ce·ro, a m.f. writer of romances —m. collection of romances.

ro·ma·no, a adj. Roman ♦ **número r.** Roman numeral.

ro·mán·ti·co, a adj. & m.f. romantic.

rom·bo m. rhombus.

ro·me·rí·a f. *(peregrinación)* pilgrimage; *(fiesta)* festival.

ro·me·ro m. rosemary.

ro·mo, a adj. GEOM. obtuse; ANAT. snub-nosed.

rom·pe·ca·be·zas m.inv. jigsaw puzzle; FIG. riddle.

rom·pe·de·ro, a adj. fragile.

rom·pe·hie·los m.inv. icebreaker.

rom·pe·nue·ces m.inv. nutcracker.

rom·pe·o·las m.inv. breakwater.

rom·per §80 tr. to break; *(en pedazos)* to tear or rip (up); *(surcar)* to plow; *(iniciar)* to begin; *(cancelar)* to break off; AGR. to plow; MIL. to break through ◆ **r. el paso** to break step • **r. filas** to fall out • **r. la cara** *or* **las narices a alguien** to smash someone's face in • **r. la marcha** to lead the way —intr. to break ◆ **r. a** to begin suddenly to *<rompió a cantar* she began suddenly to sing> • **r. con** to break up with • **r. en** to burst into —reflex. *(quebrarse)* to break; *(descomponerse)* to break (down); *(separarse en pedazos)* to tear; *(partirse)* to snap; MED. to fracture ◆ **r. el alma** to break one's neck • **r. la cabeza** to rack one's brains.

rom·pi·mien·to m. break; *(de noviazgo)* breakup.

ron m. rum.

ron·ca·dor, ·ra I. adj. snoring II. m.f. *(persona)* snorer.

ron·car §70 intr. to snore.

ron·co, a adj. *(afónico)* hoarse; *(áspero)* harsh.

ron·cha f. *(herida)* welt; *(cardenal)* bruise.

ron·da f. *(de músicos)* street serenaders; AMER. *(de gente)* circle.

ron·da·na f. gasket; AMER. pulley wheel.

ron·dar intr. *(vigilar)* to patrol; *(dar una serenata)* to serenade; *(vagar)* to prowl around —tr. *(dar vueltas)* to hover around; *(galantear)* to court; *(asediar)* to pursue.

ron·que·ar intr. to speak hoarsely.

ron·que·ra/quez f. hoarseness.

ron·qui·do m. snore; FIG. roar.

ron·ro·ne·ar intr. to purr.

ro·ña f. *(sarna)* rash; *(mugre)* filth; COLL. *(tacañería)* stinginess.

ro·ño·so, a adj. *(sarnoso)* scabby; *(sucio)* filthy; *(tacaño)* stingy.

ro·pa f. clothes, clothing ◆ **a quema r.** *(de cerca)* pointblank; *(de improviso)* suddenly • **r. de cama** bed linen • **r. interior** underwear • **r. sucia** laundry.

ro·pa·je m. vestments.

ro·pe·ro m. closet.

ro·sa I. f. rose; *(color)* pink; ARCHIT. rose window; JEWEL. rose-cut diamond ◆ **verlo todo de color de r.** to see everything through rose-colored glasses II. adj. pink.

ro·sá·ce·o, a adj. rosy.

ro·sa·do, a I. adj. *(color)* pink; *(vino)* rosé II. m. rosé.

ro·sal m. rosebush; AMER. rose garden.

ro·sa·le·da/ra f. rose garden.

ro·sa·rio m. rosary; FIG. string.

ros·bif m. roast beef.

ros·ca f. *(círculo)* ring, circle; *(espiral)* thread; CUL. ring; R.P. *(discusión)* argument ◆ **hacer la r. a alguien** COLL. to flatter someone.

ros·car §70 tr. to thread.

ros·tro m. face.

ro·ta·ción f. rotation.

ro·ta·ti·vo, a I. adj. revolving II. f. MECH. rotary press —m. newspaper.

ro·ta·to·rio, a adj. rotating.

ro·to, a I. see **romper** II. adj. *(dañado)* broken; *(quebrado)* smashed; torn, ripped *<una página r.* a torn page>.

ro·ton·da f. rotunda.

ro·tor m. rotor.

ro·to·so, a adj. AMER. tattered.

ró·tu·la f. kneecap; MECH. rounded joint.

ro·tu·la·do·m label.

ro·tu·la·dor, ·ra I. adj. labeling II. m.f. labeling device.

ro·tu·lar tr. to label.

ró·tu·lo m. label ◆ pl. CINEM. subtitles.

ro·tun·do, a adj. *(sonoro)* resounding; *(definitivo)* categorical.

ro·tu·ra f. break; *(en papel, tela)* tear.

ro·tu·ra·dor, ·ra I. adj. plowing II. m.f. plower —f. plow.

ro·tu·rar tr. to plow.

ro·za·gan·te adj. splendid.

ro·za·mien·to m. rubbing; FIG. friction.

ro·zar §04 tr. *(frotar)* to rub; *(raer)* to scrape; *(tocar)* to brush against; *(volar a ras de)* to skim; *(rayar en)* to border on; MED. to chafe —intr. to touch lightly —reflex. to rub *(con* against).

roz nai hir. to bray.

roz·ni·do m. braying noise.

ru·bé·o·la f. rubella.

ru·bí m. [pl. **-íes**] ruby.

ru·bi·cun·do, a adj. ruddy.

ru·bio, a I. adj. blond(e) II. m. blond —f. blonde.

ru·blo m. ruble.

ru·bor m. blush; *(vergüenza)* embarrassment ◆ **sentir r.** to be embarrassed.

ru·bo·ri·zar·se §04 reflex. to blush.

ru·bo·ro·so, a adj. red in the face.

rú·bri·ca f. rubric; *(firma)* signature flourish.

ru·bri·car §70 tr. *(firmar y sellar)* to sign and seal; *(con iniciales)* to initial.

ru·bro m. title; ACC. item.

ru·da f. rue.

ru·de·za f. *(tosquedad)* roughness; *(falta de pulimento)* rudeness.

ru·di·men·ta·rio, a adj. rudimentary.

ru·di·men·to m. rudiment.

ru·do, a adj. *(tosco)* rough; *(sin pulimento)* rude; *(arte)* crude; *(tiempo)* severe.

rue·ca f. distaff.

rue·da f. wheel; *(de un mueble)* roller; *(rodaja)* slice; *(corro)* ring (of people); *(suplicio)* rack ◆ **hacer r.** to make a circle • **ir sobre ruedas** to go smoothly • **r. de presos** lineup • **r. dentada** cogwheel.

rue·de, do see **rodar**.

rue·do m. *(borde)* edge; *(circunferencia)* circumference; *(dobladillo)* hem; TAUR. bullring ◆ **dar la vuelta al r.** TAUR. to go around the bullring receiving applause • **echarse al r.** to enter the fray.

rue·ga, go see **rogar**.

rue·go m. request.

ru·fián m. *(chulo)* pimp; *(granuja)* ruffian.

ru·gi·do m. roar.

ru·gi·dor, a/gien·te adj. roaring.

ru·gir §32 intr. to roar; FIG. to howl.

ru·go·so, a adj. wrinkled.

rui·do m. noise; *(alboroto)* din; FIG. stir ◆ **hacer r.** to create a stir • **mucho r. y pocas**

nueces much ado about nothing • sin r. silently.
rui·do·so, a adj. noisy, loud; FIG. smashing.
ruin adj. (despreciable) despicable; (avaro) stingy; (animales) mean; (miserable) poor; (raquítico) puny.
rui·na f. (destrucción) ruin; (hundimiento) downfall ♦ estar hecho una r. to be a wreck.
rui·no·so, a adj. dilapidated.
rui·se·ñor m. nightingale.
ru·le·ta f. roulette.
ru·lo m. (cilindro) roller; R.P. (de pelo) ringlet.
rum·ba f. rumba.
rum·be·ar intr. AMER. to head (para, hacia for).
rum·bo m. direction; AER., MARIT. course ♦ con r. a bound for • ir con r. a to be heading for • perder el r. to lose one's bearings • tomar buen r. to take a turn for the better.
ru·mian·te adj. & m. ruminant.
ru·miar tr. to ruminate; FIG. to grumble.
ru·mor m. murmur; (de árboles) rustle; (chismes) rumor.
ru·mo·re·ar·se/rar·se reflex. to be rumored.
rup·tu·ra f. (acción) breaking; MED. fracture; (de relaciones) breakup.
ru·ral I. adj. rural II. m.f. AMER. peasant.
rús·ti·co, a I. adj. rustic; (grosero) rough II. m.f. peasant.
ru·ta f. route.
ru·ti·lan·te adj. brilliant.
ru·ti·lar intr. to shine.
ru·ti·na f. routine.
ru·ti·na·rio, a adj. routine.

S

s, S f. twenty-second letter of the Spanish alphabet.
sá·ba·do m. Saturday; RELIG. Sabbath ♦ S. de Gloria or Santo Easter Saturday.
sa·ba·na f. AMER. savannah.
sá·ba·na f. bed sheet ♦ pegársele a uno las sábanas COLL. to oversleep.
sa·ban·di·ja f. bug; FIG. louse.
sa·ba·ñón m. chilblain.
sa·be·lo·to·do m.f. COLL. know-it-all.
sa·ber[1] m. learning, knowledge ♦ según mi leal s. y entender to the best of my knowledge.
sa·ber[2] §62 tr. to know <ella sabe lo que ocurrió she knows what happened>; (tener habilidad) to know how <¿sabes cocinar? do you know how to cook?>; to learn <supe la noticia demasiado tarde I learned the news too late> ♦ hacer s. to inform • no s. dónde meterse COLL. not to know where to hide • ¿qué sé yo? how should I know? • que yo sepa as far as I know • s. de buena tinta to have on good authority • s. de memoria to know by heart • sin saberlo yo without my knowledge • un no sé qué a certain something • véte a s. your guess is as good as mine —intr. to know; (acostumbrar) to be in the habit of <él sabe llegar temprano he is in the habit of arriving early> ♦ a s. namely • no se sabe nobody knows • ¿quién sabe? who knows? • s. a to taste like; FIG. to smack of • s. de (conocer) to know about, to be familiar with; to hear from <hace mucho tiempo que no sabemos de José we have not heard from Joe in a long time> —reflex. to be known ♦ sabérselo todo to know it all.

sa·bi·do, a adj. (conocido) known; COLL. (docto) learned.
sa·bi·du·rí·a f. (prudencia) wisdom; (conocimiento) knowledge ♦ s. popular folk wisdom.
sa·bien·das adv. ♦ a s. knowingly.
sa·bi·hon·do, a COLL. adj. & m.f. know-it-all.
sa·bio, a I. adj. (prudente) wise; (instruido) learned II. m.f. (persona prudente) wise person; (instruido) learned person.
sa·bla·zo m. (golpe) saber blow; (herida) saber wound; COLL. sponging ♦ dar un s. a alguien COLL. to sponge money off someone.
sa·ble m. saber.
sa·ble·ar intr. COLL. to sponge.
sa·bor m. (gusto) taste, flavor; (carácter) flavor, color ♦ con s. a limón lemon-flavored • sin s. tasteless • tener s. a to taste of.
sa·bo·re·ar tr. (notar el sabor) to taste; (apreciar) to relish.
sa·bo·ta·je m. sabotage.
sa·bo·te·a·dor, ·ra I. adj. sabotaging II. m.f. saboteur.
sa·bo·te·ar tr. to sabotage.
sa·brá, bría see saber[2].
sa·bro·su·ra f. AMER. delicious or tasty thing.
sa·bro·so, a adj. (delicioso) tasty; (agradable) delightful; (picante) racy.
sa·bue·so m. bloodhound.
sa·ca·bo·ca·dos m.inv. punch.
sa·ca·cla·vos m.inv. nail puller or claw.
sa·ca·cor·chos m.inv. corkscrew.
sa·ca·man·chas m. or f.inv. stain remover.
sa·ca·pun·tas m.inv. pencil sharpener.
sa·car §70 tr. to take out <sacó su cartera del bolsillo he took his wallet out of his pocket>; (quitar) to remove <s. una mancha to remove a stain>; (arrancar) to pull out; (un arma) to draw; (de un apuro) to bail out; (información) to get out; (deducir) to take it <de tu expresión saco que estás preocupado from your expression I take it that you are worried>; (resolver) to figure out; (conseguir) to get; (ganar) to win; (elegir) to elect; (moda, estilo) to come out with; (publicar) to publish; (restar) to subtract; (fotografiar) to take <quiero s. una foto del grupo I want to take a picture of the group>; (apuntar) to take <s. apuntes to take notes>; (citar) to quote (de from); SPORT. to serve; CHEM. to extract ♦ s. a bailar to ask to dance • s. adelante (lograr) to carry out; (criar) to bring up • s. a luz (revelar) to bring to light; (publicar) to publish • s. a relucir to bring up • s. de quicio or de sí to infuriate • s. el jugo COLL. to bleed dry • s. en claro to figure out • s. la cara por COLL. to stand for • s. en claro or en limpio to understand • s. provecho de to benefit from • s. sangre to bleed • s. una copia to make a copy • s. ventaja to take advantage —reflex. to take off.
sa·ca·ri·na f. saccharin.
sa·cer·do·cio m. priesthood.
sa·cer·do·te m. priest ♦ sumo s. high priest.
sa·cer·do·ti·sa f. priestess.
sa·ciar tr. to satiate ♦ s. la sed to quench one's thirst —reflex. to be satiated.
sa·co m. (bolsa) bag; AMER. (chaqueta) jacket; ANAT. sac ♦ no echar en s. roto COLL. to keep in mind, not to forget • s. de dormir sleeping bag • s. de huesos COLL. bag of bones.
sa·cra·men·to m. sacrament ♦ recibir los sacramentos to receive the last rites.

sa·cri·fi·car §70 tr. to sacrifice; *(animales)* to slaughter —reflex. to sacrifice oneself.

sa·cri·fi·cio m. sacrifice; *(de animales)* slaughter.

sa·cri·le·gio m. sacrilege.

sa·cri·le·go, a adj. & m.f. sacrilegious (person).

sa·cris·tán m. sacristan.

sa·cro, a I. adj. *(sagrado)* sacred; ANAT. sacral II. m. ANAT. sacrum.

sa·cro·san·to, a adj. sacrosanct.

sa·cu·di·da f. *(acción)* shake; *(tirón)* tug; *(sismo)* tremor; *(de explosión)* blast; *(emoción)* jolt ♦ **s. eléctrica** electric shock.

sa·cu·dir tr. *(agitar)* to shake; *(quitar el polvo)* to dust; *(tirar)* to tug; *(golpear)* to beat; *(un ala)* to flap; *(alterar)* to jolt —reflex. *(agitarse)* to shake; *(la ropa)* to shake or brush off.

sa·cu·dón m. AMER. var. of **sacudida.**

sá·di·co, a I. adj. sadistic II. m.f. sadist.

sa·do·ma·so·quis·ta I. adj. sadomasochistic II. m.f. sadomasochist.

sa·e·ta f. *(flecha)* dart; *(del reloj)* hand; *(copla)* short song sung in religious ceremonies.

sa·ga f. saga.

sa·ga·ci·dad f. sagacity.

sa·gaz adj. sagacious, astute.

sa·gra·do, a adj. sacred.

sa·hu·ma·dor m. incense burner.

sa·hu·mar tr. to perfume with incense.

sa·hu·me·rio m. *(humo)* aromatic smoke; *(materia)* incense.

sai·ne·te m. one-act farce.

sa·í·no m. peccary.

sa·ke m. sake.

sal[1] f. salt; *(gracia)* charm; *(agudeza)* wit ♦ **echar s. a** to salt • **la s. de la vida** the spice of life • **s. de mesa** table salt • **sales aromáticas** smelling salts • **sales de baño** bath salts.

sal[2] see **salir.**

sa·la f. *(sala grande)* living room; *(cuarto grande)* large room; *(teatro)* house; MED. hospital ward ♦ **s. de clase** classroom • **s. de conferencias** lecture hall • **s. de espectáculos** theater, hall • **s. de espera** waiting room • **s. de estar** living room • **s. de máquinas** engine room • **s. de partos** delivery room.

sa·la·do, a adj. salt, salty ‹*agua s.* salt water›; salty, salted ‹*un plato muy s.* a highly salted dish›; *(gracioso)* witty, amusing; R.P. *(caro)* expensive.

sa·la·man·dra f. salamander.

sa·la·me m. AMER. salami.

sa·lar tr. to salt; *(curar)* to cure.

sa·la·rial adj. wage ‹*aumento s.* wage increase›.

sa·la·rio m. wage ♦ **s. vital** living wage • **s. a destajo** piece rate • **s. por hora** hourly wage.

sa·laz adj. salacious.

sal·chi·cha f. pork sausage.

sal·chi·che·rí·a f. sausage shop.

sal·chi·chón m. sausage.

sal·dar tr. COM. *(liquidar)* to pay off; *(vender)* to remainder.

sal·do m. COM. *(liquidación)* payment; *(cifra)* balance; *(mercancías)* remnants ♦ **s. acreedor o a favor** credit balance • **s. deudor** debit balance • **s. disponible** available balance.

sal·drá, drías see **salir.**

sa·le·ro m. *(de mesa)* saltshaker; *(gracia)* wit.

sa·le·ro·so, a adj. COLL. witty.

sal·ga, go see **salir.**

sa·li·da f. *(acción)* departure; *(abertura)* exit;

(escapatoria) way out; *(solución)* solution; *(ocurrencia)* witty remark; COM. *(venta)* sale; *(posibilidad de venta)* market; ACC. entry; ELEC., MECH. outlet ♦ **dar s. a** to vent • **s. del sol** sunrise • **tener s.** COM. to sell well.

sa·lien·te I. adj. *(que sobresale)* projecting; *(prominente)* salient; *(el sol)* rising II. f. projection.

sa·li·ne·ra f. salt mine or pit.

sa·li·no, a I. adj. saline II. f. salt mine or pit.

sa·lir §63 intr. to leave ‹*salimos de la casa a las tres* we left the house at three o'clock›; to go out ‹*no es prudente s. por la noche solo* it is not wise to go out alone at night›; *(partir)* to leave *(para for)*; *(librarse)* to get out; *(aparecer)* to come out; *(el sol)* to rise; *(flor, fruto)* to come up *(de from)*; *(idea, concepto)* to emerge; *(mancha)* to come out; *(libro)* to come out; *(oportunidad)* to come or turn up ‹*cuando salga la oportunidad* when the opportunity comes up›; *(costar)* to cost; *(cálculo)* to work out; *(en el juego)* to lead; *(ir a parar)* to lead ‹*esta calle sale a la plaza* this street leads to the plaza›; *(parecerse)* to take after; *(ser elegido)* to be elected ♦ **salga lo que salga** COLL. come what may • **s. adelante** to get ahead • **s. bien, mal** to turn out well, badly • **s. con** to come out with ‹*él salió con una observación importante* he came out with an important observation›; to go out with, date ‹*Juan sale con Anita ahora* John is dating Anita now› • **s. del paso** to get out of a jam • **s. pitando** COLL. *(correr)* to run out quickly; *(enfadarse)* to blow up —reflex. *(derramarse)* to leak; *(rebosar)* to boil over ♦ **s. con la suya** to get one's own way • **s. de la regla** to break the rule • **s. de madre** to overflow • **s. del tema** to digress.

sa·li·tral m. saltpeter bed or deposit.

sa·li·tre m. saltpeter.

sa·li·tro·so, a adj. saltpetrous.

sa·li·va f. saliva, spit ♦ **gastar s. en balde** COLL. to waste one's breath.

sa·li·va·de·ra f. AMER. spittoon.

sa·li·val/var adj. salivary.

sa·li·var intr. to salivate; *(escupir)* to spit.

sa·li·va·zo m. COLL. spit, spittle.

sa·li·ver·ses f.pl. knobs on a horse's bit.

sal·mo m. psalm.

sal·món m. salmon.

sal·mue·ra f. brine.

sa·lo·bre adj. briny.

sa·lón m. *(sala grande)* hall ‹*s. de conferencias* lecture hall›; *(para visitas)* drawing room; *(exposición)* exhibition; *(tertulia)* salon ♦ **s. de actos o sesiones** assembly hall • **s. de baile** ballroom • **s. de belleza** beauty parlor • **s. de té** tearoom • **s. de ventas** salesroom.

sal·pi·ca·du·ra f. *(acción)* splashing; *(salpicón)* splash.

sal·pi·car §70 tr. *(con un líquido)* to splash; *(rociar)* to sprinkle; *(motear)* to fleck.

sal·pi·cón m. *(carne picada)* cold hash; COLL. *(cosa picada)* shredded or minced item; *(salpicadura)* splash.

sal·pi·men·tar §49 tr. to season; FIG. to spice.

sal·pu·lli·do m. var. of **sarpullido.**

sal·sa f. sauce, gravy ♦ **en su propia s.** in one's element • **s. rusa** Russian dressing.

sal·se·ra f. gravy boat.

sal·se·ro m. CHILE salt vendor.

sal·si·fí m. [pl. **-íes**] BOT. goat's beard.

sal·ta·dor, ·ra I. adj. jumping II. m.f. jumper

♦ **s. de pértiga** or **con garrocha** pole vaulter.
sal·ta·mon·tes m.inv. grasshopper.
sal·tar intr. (*brincar*) to jump (*de* with); (*levantarse*) to jump up; (*dar saltitos*) to hop; (*lanzarse*) to jump (*a* into); (*rebotar*) to bounce; (*desprenderse*) to come off; (*salir con ímpetu*) to bound; (*enfadarse*) to blow up ♦ **s. a la vista** or **a los ojos** to be self-evident • **s. sobre** to pounce on —tr. (*atravesar*) to jump over; (*omitir*) to skip over.
sal·ta·rre·gla f. bevel square.
sal·te·a·do, a adj. sautéed.
sal·te·ar tr. (*robar*) to hold up; (*hacer algo con interrupciones*) to skip; (*sofreír*) to sauté.
sal·tim·ban·qui m. COLL. (*charlatán*) charlatan; (*acróbata*) acrobat; (*malabarista*) juggler.
sal·to m. (*brinco*) jump; (*obstáculo*) hurdle; (*despeñadero*) ravine; (*juego*) leapfrog; (*ascenso*) promotion, jump; SPORT. jump <s. de altura high jump> ♦ **s. de mata** COLL. from hand to mouth • **a saltos** by leaps and bounds • **en un s.** in a jiffy • **s. de cama** negligée • **s. de la carpa** jackknife dive • **s. de pértiga** or **con garrocha** pole vault.
sa·lu·bre adj. healthful.
sa·lud I. f. health; (*bienestar*) welfare, wellbeing ♦ **beber a la s. de** to drink to the health of • **estar bien, mal de s.** to be in good, bad health II. interj. COLL. (*al estornudar*) (God) bless you!; (*brindis*) cheers!
sa·lu·da·ble adj. (*sano*) healthy; (*provechoso*) beneficial.
sa·lu·dar tr. (*mostrar cortesía*) to greet; (*honrar*) to salute; MARIT. to dip the flag to ♦ **Le saluda atentamente** Yours faithfully or truly.
sa·lu·do m. (*cortesía*) greeting; (*inclinación*) bow; MIL. salute ♦ pl. regards.
sa·lu·ta·ción f. greeting.
sal·va f. see **salvo, a**.
sal·va·ción f. salvation.
sal·va·da f. AMER., COLL. good fortune or luck.
sal·va·guar·dar tr. to safeguard.
sal·va·guar·dia f. (*salvoconducto*) safe-conduct; (*protección*) safeguard.
sal·va·ja·da f. savagery.
sal·va·je I. adj. (*silvestre*) wild; (*no domesticado*) wild, untamed; (*feroz*) savage; (*rudo*) rude; (*primitivo*) uncivilized II. m.f. (*bárbaro*) savage; COLL. (*bruto*) boor.
sal·va·men·to m. rescue; RELIG. salvation.
sal·var tr. (*librar*) to save; (*resolver*) to overcome; (*evitar*) to avoid; (*recorrer*) to cover; RELIG. to save ♦ **salvando a los presentes** present company excluded • **s. las apariencias** to save face —reflex. to escape ♦ **¡sálvese quien pueda!** every man for himself! • **s. por los pelos** COLL. to escape by the skin of one's teeth.
sal·va·vi·das I. m.inv. (*artefacto*) life preserver; (*bote*) lifeboat —m.f. (*bañero*) lifeguard II. adj. lifesaving.
sal·ve·dad f. (*condición*) proviso; (*excepción*) exception; (*reserva*) reservation.
sal·via f. sage.
sal·vo, a I. adj. safe ♦ **a s.** safe (and sound) • **a s. de** safe from • **poner a s.** to rescue • **ponerse a s.** to reach safety II. adv. except (for), save • **s. que** unless III. f. MIL. salvo ♦ **s. de aplausos** round of applause.
sal·vo·con·duc·to m. safe-conduct.
san adj. contr. of **santo**.
sa·na·lo·to·do m. cure-all.
sa·na·men·te adv. (*con sanidad*) wholesomely;

(*sinceramente*) sincerely.
sa·nar tr. to heal —intr. (*enfermedad*) to recover (from illness); (*herida*) to heal.
sa·na·to·rio m. sanatorium; (*hospital*) hospital.
san·ción f. (*ratificación*) ratification; (*pena*) punishment; (*aprobación*) sanction.
san·cio·nar tr. (*ratificar*) to sanction; (*autorizar*) to sanction; (*castigar*) to punish.
san·co·char tr. to parboil.
san·co·cho m. AMER. stew containing parboiled meat, yucca and bananas; FIG. mishmash.
san·da·lia f. sandal.
sán·da·lo m. sandalwood.
san·dez f. nonsense.
san·dí·a f. watermelon.
san·dun·gue·ro, a adj. COLL. witty, charming.
sa·ne·a·mien·to m. (*mejora*) improvement; (*limpieza*) sanitation; (*corrección*) righting.
sa·ne·ar tr. (*mejorar*) to improve; (*limpiar*) to sanitize; (*corregir*) to right; LAW to indemnify.
san·fa·són m. ♦ **a la s.** AMER., COLL. carelessly.
san·grar tr. to bleed; (*un terreno*) to drain; (*un árbol*) to tap; PRINT. to indent —intr. to bleed.
san·gre f. blood; (*linaje*) lineage ♦ **a s. fría** in cold blood • **chupar la s. a alguien** COLL. to be a bloodsucker • **de s. caliente** warm-blooded • **de s. fría** cold-blooded • **echar a. s.** to bleed • **llevar en la s.** to have in one's blood • **no llegar la s. al río** COLL. not to be a serious matter • **pura s.** thoroughbred.
san·grí·a f. (*extracción*) bloodletting; (*de líquidos*) draining; (*bebida*) sangria; PRINT. indentation; (*gasto*) bleeding.
san·grien·ta·men·te adv. cruelly.
san·grien·to, a adj. (*que echa sangre*) bloody; (*manchado de sangre*) blood-stained; (*sanguinario*) bloodthirsty; (*cruel*) cruel.
san·gui·jue·la f. leech.
san·gui·na·rio, a adj. bloodthirsty, cruel.
san·guí·ne·o, a adj. blood <grupo s. blood group>.
san·gui·no·len·to, a adj. (*manchado*) blood-stained; (*inflamado*) bloodshot.
sa·ni·dad f. health, healthiness ♦ **s. pública** board of health.
sa·ni·ta·rio, a adj. sanitary.
sa·no, a adj. (*de salud*) healthy; (*saludable*) healthful; (*provechoso*) wholesome; (*en condición*) sound; (*sin daño*) unharmed; (*sin vicio*) wholesome; (*entero*) whole ♦ **cortar por lo s.** to take drastic measures • **s. y salvo** safe and sound.
san·se·a·ca·bó adv. COLL. that's the end of it <no voy y s. I'm not going and that's the end of it>.
san·tia·mén m. COLL. jiffy.
san·ti·dad f. sanctity ♦ **Su S.** His Holiness.
san·ti·fi·car §70 tr. (*hacer santo*) to sanctify; (*consagrar*) to consecrate; (*venerar*) to revere.
san·ti·guar §10 tr. to make the sign of the cross on —reflex. to cross oneself.
san·tí·si·mo, a I. adj. most holy II. m. Holy Sacrament.
san·to, a I. adj. holy; (*bendito*) blessed; COLL. blessed <esperamos todo el s. día we waited the whole blessed day> ♦ **S. Padre** Holy Father II. m.f. saint —m. (*imagen*) image of a saint; (*festividad*) saint's day ♦ **¿a s. de qué?** what on earth for? • **dar el s. y seña** to give the

password • **desnudar a un s. para vestir a otro** to rob Peter to pay Paul • **no ser s. de su devoción** to not be keen on.

san·tua·rio m. sanctuary; *(intimidad)* privacy.

san·tu·rrón/lón, o·na adj. & m.f. sanctimonious *or* hypocritical (person).

sa·ña f. fury.

sa·pien·cia f. wisdom.

sa·pien·te adj. wise.

sa·po m. toad • **echar sapos y culebras** COLL. to swear.

sa·que m. *(tenis)* serve; *(fútbol)* kickoff; *(raya)* service line.

sa·que·ar tr. to plunder.

sa·que·o m. plundering.

sa·ram·pión m. measles.

sa·ra·o m. soirée, evening party.

sar·cas·mo m. sarcasm.

sar·cás·ti·co, a adj. sarcastic.

sar·có·fa·go m. sarcophagus.

sar·di·na f. sardine • **como s. en lata** COLL. packed like sardines.

sar·dó·ni·co, a adj. sardonic.

sar·ga f. TEX. serge; PAINT. painted wall fabric.

sar·ga·zo m. sargasso.

sar·gen·te·ar tr. to command as a sergeant; FIG. to boss —intr. to be bossy.

sar·gen·to m. sergeant.

sa·ri·lla f. marjoram.

sar·na f. scabies; VET. mange • **más viejo que la s.** COLL. as old as the hills.

sar·no·so, a I. adj. scabby; VET. mangy II. m.f. person suffering from scabies.

sar·pu·lli·do m. rash.

sa·rro m. crust; DENT. tartar.

sar·ta f. string.

sar·tén f. frying pan; *(sartenada)* panful • **tener la s. por el mango** COLL. to have the upper hand.

sa·sa·frás m. sassafras.

sas·tre m. tailor; THEAT. costumer • **traje s.** woman's tailored suit.

sas·tre·rí·a f. tailor's (shop).

sa·tá·ni·co, a adj. BIBL. Satanic; FIG. satanic.

sa·té·li·te adj. & m. satellite.

sa·tén/tín m. satin.

sa·ti·na·do, a I. adj. satiny • **papel s.** glossy *or* coated paper II. m. *(acción)* calendering; *(brillo)* gloss.

sa·ti·nar tr. PRINT., TEX. to calender.

sá·ti·ra f. satire.

sa·tí·ri·co, a I. adj. satiric(al) II. m.f. satirist.

sa·ti·ri·zar §04 tr. & intr. to satirize.

sá·ti·ro m. satyr.

sa·tis·fac·ción f. satisfaction • **a s.** satisfactorily • **a s. de** to the satisfaction of • **pedir s.** to demand satisfaction.

sa·tis·fa·cer §40 tr. to satisfy; *(pagar)* to pay; *(cumplir)* to meet <**s.** *los requisitos* to meet the requirements> —reflex. to satisfy oneself.

sa·tis·fac·to·rio, a I. see **satisfacer** II. adj. satisfactory.

sa·tis·fe·cho, a I. see **satisfacer** II. adj. satisfied • **darse por s. con** to be satisfied *or* content with • **estar** *or* **quedar s.** to be full *or* sated.

sa·tis·fi·cie·ra, ce, zo see **satisfacer**.

sa·tu·ra·ción f. saturation.

sa·tu·ra·do, a adj. saturated.

sa·tu·rar tr. to saturate.

sau·ce m. willow • **s. llorón** weeping willow.

sau·da·de f. nostalgia.

sau·zal m. willow grove.

sa·via f. sap.

sa·xó·fo·no/tón m. saxophone.

sa·ya f. *(falda)* skirt; *(enaguas)* petticoat.

sa·yo m. *(casaca)* cassock; *(túnica)* tunic.

sa·zón f. season <*fruta en s.* fruit in season>; *(condimento)* seasoning • **a la s.** at that time.

sa·zo·na·do, a adj. seasoned, flavorful.

sa·zo·nar tr. *(dar sabor)* to season; *(madurar)* to ripen —intr. & reflex. to ripen.

se reflex. pron. oneself, himself, herself, yourself, itself, themselves, yourselves <*las chicas se están mirando en el espejo* the girls are looking at themselves in the mirror>; to oneself, to himself, to herself, to yourself, to itself, to themselves, to yourselves <*ese viejo se habla a sí mismo* that old man talks to himself>; [to indicate the owner of the direct object of a verb] <*Juan se puso el sombrero* John put on his hat>; [to provide reflex. form to verbs not reflex. in meaning] <*mi tío se murió* my uncle died>; *(uno a otro)* each other, one another <*mis padres se aman* my parents love each other>; to each other, to one another <*ellos se mandaron regalos* they sent presents to one another> —indef. pron. one, they, people <*se dice que la economía mejorará* they say that the economy will improve> —aux. pron. [to give passive meaning to active verbs] <*se venden libros aquí* books are sold here> —pers. pron. [used instead of **le** *or* **les** before **lo, la, los** *or* **las**] to him, to her, to you, to it, to them <*Ana se lo dijo a él* Ann said it to him>; for him, for her, for you, for it, for them <*se la voy a comprar a usted* I am going to buy it for you>; from him, from her, from you, from it, from them <*él se lo robó a ellos* he stole it from them>.

sé see **saber²** *or* **ser⁶**.

se·bá·ce·o, a adj. sebaceous.

se·bo m. *(para velas)* tallow; *(grasa)* grease; *(gordura)* fat.

se·bo·rre·a f. seborrhea.

se·ca f. see **seco, a**.

se·ca·de·ro m. drying room.

se·ca·do m. drying.

se·ca·dor m. hair dryer.

se·ca·do·ra f. clothes dryer.

se·ca·men·te adv. dryly.

se·can·te I. adj. *(que seca)* drying; GEOM. secant; *(fastidioso)* annoying II. f. GEOM. secant —m. blotting paper.

se·car §70 tr. to dry; *(fastidiar)* to annoy, bother —reflex. to dry (out) <*la ropa se secó en unas horas* the clothes dried in a few hours>; to dry oneself, dry off; *(ríos y fuentes)* to dry up, run dry; BOT. to wither.

sec·ción f. section; *(división)* department <*s. de niños* children's department> • **s. transversal** cross section.

sec·cio·nar tr. to section.

se·ce·sión f. secession.

se·ce·sio·nis·ta adj. & m.f. secessionist.

se·co, a I. adj. dry; *(desecado)* dried; *(corto y brusco)* sharp <*un golpe s.* a sharp blow>; *(poco cariñoso)* undemonstrative; *(ronco)* harsh; *(desabrido)* laconic • **a secas** curtly • **dejar a alguien s.** COLL. to kill instantly <*lo atropelló el tren y lo dejó s.* the train hit him and killed him instantly>; *(dejar atónito)* to stun • **en s.** COLL. *(bruscamente)* suddenly; *(sin causa)* without cause *or* reason; *(sin medios)* without resources • **limpiar en s.** to dry-clean

II. f. drought.

se·co·ya f. sequoia.

se·cre·ción f. secretion.

se·cre·ta·men·te adv. secretly.

se·cre·ta·ría f. secretary.

se·cre·ta·rí·a f. *(cargo)* secretaryship; *(oficina)* secretary's office; *(oficina administrativa)* secretariat ♦ **S. de Estado** State Department.

se·cre·ta·ria·do m. *(oficina)* secretariat; *(cargo)* secretaryship.

se·cre·ta·rio m. secretary ♦ **s. municipal** *or* **de ayuntamiento** town clerk.

se·cre·te·ar intr. COLL. to whisper.

se·cre·te·o m. whispering.

se·cre·ter m. writing desk.

se·cre·to, a I. m. secret; *(reserva)* secrecy <**s. profesional** professional secrecy; MUS. sounding-board ♦ **en s.** secretly • **guardar un s.** to keep a secret • **s. a voces** COLL. open secret • **s. de Estado** state secret • **s. de confesión** RELIG. seal of confession **II.** adj. secret; *(invisible)* hidden; *(confidencial)* confidential; *(reservado)* secretive.

sec·ta f. sect.

sec·ta·rio, a adj. & m.f. sectarian.

sec·tor m. sector.

sec·to·rial adj. sectorial.

se·cuaz m.f. *(subalterno)* henchman; *(partidario)* partisan.

se·cue·la f. consequence.

se·cuen·cia f. sequence.

se·cues·tra·dor, ·ra I. adj. *(de personas)* kidnapping; *(de vehículos)* hijacking **II.** m.f. *(de personas)* kidnapper; *(de vehículos)* hijacker.

se·cues·trar tr. *(personas)* to kidnap; *(vehículos)* to hijack.

se·cues·tro m. *(de personas)* kidnapping; *(de vehículos)* hijacking.

se·cu·lar adj. secular.

se·cu·la·ris·mo m. secularism.

se·cu·la·ri·zar §04 tr. to secularize.

se·cun·dar tr. to second.

se·cun·da·rio, a adj. & m. secondary.

sed f. thirst.

se·da f. silk ♦ **como una s.** *(suave)* as smooth as silk; *(dócil)* as gentle as a lamb.

se·dal m. fishing line; SURG. seton.

se·dan·te adj. & m. sedative.

se·dar tr. to soothe; MED. to sedate.

se·da·ti·vo, a adj. & m. sedative.

se·de f. *(del gobierno)* seat; *(de organización)* headquarters ♦ **Santa S.** Holy See.

se·den·ta·rio, a adj. sedentary.

se·de·rí·a f. *(negocios)* silk trade; *(tienda)* silk shop.

se·di·ción f. sedition.

se·dien·to, a adj. *(con sed)* thirsty; *(árido)* dry; *(deseoso)* desirous.

se·di·men·to m. sediment.

se·do·so, a adj. silky.

se·duc·ción f. seduction; *(atractivo)* allure.

se·du·cir §22 tr. to seduce; *(cautivar)* to captivate.

se·duc·ti·vo, a/tor, ·ra I. adj. *(que seduce)* seductive; *(fascinante)* captivating **II.** m.f. *(que seduce)* seducer; *(que encanta)* charmer.

se·ga·dor, ·ra I. adj. mowing **II.** m.f. harvester —f. *(máquina)* harvester, combine.

se·gar §52 tr. *(la mies)* to harvest; *(la hierba)* to mow; FIG. to cut off.

se·glar I. adj. secular **II.** m.f. layman/woman.

seg·men·ta·ción f. segmentation.

seg·men·to m. segment.

se·gre·ga·ción f. segregation.

se·gre·ga·cio·nis·ta adj. & m.f. segregationist.

se·gre·gar §47 tr. to segregate; MED. to secrete.

se·gui·da·men·te adv. *(sin interrupción)* continuously; *(después)* next.

se·gui·do, a I. adj. *(continuo)* continuous; *(consecutivo)* consecutive **II.** adv. AMER. often ♦ **en seguida** immediately, at once

se·gui·dor, ·ra I. adj. following **II.** m.f. follower.

se·guir §64 tr. to follow; *(venir después)* to come after <**el reinado de Juan Carlos siguió a la dictadura de Franco** the reign of Juan Carlos came after Franco's dictatorship>; *(continuar)* to keep or go on; *(ir en pos)* to pursue; *(perseguir)* to chase; *(espiar)* to watch closely; *(observar)* to watch <**s. los acontecimientos mundiales** to watch world events>; *(prestar atención)* to pay attention (to); *(emular)* to emulate; *(estudiar)* to study <**sigo medicina I** study medicine> —intr. *(continuar)* to continue; *(estar de salud)* to feel <**¿cómo sigue el enfermo hoy?** how is the patient feeling today?>.

se·gún I. prep. according to <**s. este informe** according to this report> **II.** adv. *(como)* depending on <**s. como te comportes te llevaré al cine** depending on how you behave I'll take you to the movies>; according to <**el Evangelio s. San Mateo** the Gospel according to Saint Matthew> ♦ **s. y conforme** *(de igual manera)* exactly as; *(de acuerdo a las circunstancias)* de pending on the circumstances.

se·gun·de·ro m. second hand.

se·gun·do, a I. adj. second <**febrero es el s. mes del año** February is the second month of the year>; *(otro)* another <**él es un s. Mozart** he is another Mozart> ♦ **de s. clase** second-class • **de s. mano** secondhand • **s. enseñanza** secondary education • **s. intención** double meaning **II.** m. second; *(subjefe)* second-in-command; *(asistente)* assistant —f. AUTO. second gear.

se·gur *(hacha)* ax; *(hoz)* sickle.

se·gu·ra·men·te adv. *(ciertamente)* certainly; *(probablemente)* probably.

se·gu·ri·dad f. security, safety ♦ **con toda s.** with absolute certainty • **de s.** safety <**cinturón de s.** safety belt> • **tener la s. de que** to be certain that.

se·gu·ro, a I. adj. *(protegido)* safe; *(cierto)* certain; *(confiado)* sure; *(confiable)* trustworthy; *(firme)* stable **II.** m. *(aseguración)* insurance; *(dispositivo)* safety catch ♦ **s. contra accidentes** accident insurance • **s. de vida** life insurance **III.** adv. certainly, for sure.

seis I. adj. six; *(sexto)* sixth ♦ **las s.** six o'clock **II.** m. six.

seis·cien·tos, tas adj. & m. six hundred.

se·lec·ción f. selection.

se·lec·cio·nar tr. to select.

se·lec·ti·vo, a adj. selective.

se·lec·to, a adj. select.

sel·va f. *(bosque)* woods; *(jungla)* jungle.

sel·vá·ti·co, a adj. forest.

se·llar tr. *(imprimir)* to stamp; *(cerrar)* to seal, close; FIG. to conclude.

se·llo m. stamp; *(de documento)* seal; PHARM. cachet • **s. de correo** *or* **s. postal** postage stamp • **s. fiscal** LAW revenue stamp.

se·má·fo·ro m. semaphore.

se·ma·na f. week; *(salario)* weekly pay ♦ **entre s.** during the week • **s. laboral** working week.
se·ma·nal adj. weekly.
se·ma·nal·men·te adv. weekly.
se·ma·na·rio, a I. adj. weekly II. m. weekly publication.
se·mán·ti·co, a I. adj. semantic II. f. semantics.
sem·blan·te m. *(rostro)* face; *(apariencia)* appearance ♦ **estar de mal s.** to look ill.
sem·blan·za f. biographical sketch *or* profile.
sem·bra·dí·o/do m. sown field *or* land.
sem·bra·dor, ·ra I. adj. sowing II. m.f. *(persona)* sower f. *(máquina)* seed drill.
sem·brar §49 tr. to sow; *(esparcir)* to scatter.
se·me·jan·te I. adj. *(similar)* similar; *(tal)* such, like that <*nunca he visto hombre s.* I have never seen such a man> II. m.f. fellow man.
se·me·jan·za f. similarity; RHET. simile ♦ **a s. de** as.
se·me·jar intr. & reflex. to resemble (one another) ♦ **s. a** to look like.
se·men m. semen, sperm; BOT. seed.
se·men·tar §49 tr. to seed.
se·men·te·ra f. *(tierra)* sown field; *(temporada)* seedtime, sowing time.
se·mes·tral adj. semiannual, biannual.
se·mes·tre m. six months, semester; COM. half-yearly payment.
se·mia·ca·ba·do, a adj. half-finished.
se·miau·to·má·ti·co, a adj. semiautomatic.
se·mi·cir·cu·lar adj. semicircular.
se·mi·cír·cu·lo m. semicircle.
se·mi·cor·che·a f. sixteenth note, semiquaver (G.B.).
se·mi·des·nu·do adj. half-naked.
se·mi·diós m. demigod.
se·mi·fi·na·lis·ta adj. & m.f. semifinalist.
se·mi·lla f. seed.
se·mi·lle·ro m. *(plantación)* seed bed, *(vivero)* nursery; FIG. breeding ground.
se·mi·nal adj. seminal.
se·mi·na·rio m. seminary.
se·mi·na·ris·ta m. seminarian.
se·mi·pe·sa·do adj. & m. light heavyweight.
se·mi·pre·cio·so, a adj. semiprecious.
se·mí·ti·co, a adj. Semitic.
se·mi·to·no m. half tone.
sé·mo·la f. semolina.
sem·pi·ter·no, a adj. everlasting.
se·na·do m. senate.
se·na·dor m. senator.
sen·ci·lla·men·te adv. simply, plainly.
sen·ci·llez f. *(simplicidad)* simplicity; *(ingenuidad)* innocence.
sen·ci·llo, a I. adj. *(fácil)* easy; *(sin adorno)* plain; CHEM., PHYS. simple; *(ingenuo)* innocent II. m. AMER. change.
sen·da f./**de·ro** m. path; FIG. road.
sen·dos, as adj. each <*los niños recibieron s. regalos* the children each received a present>.
se·nec·tud f. old age.
se·nil adj. senile.
se·no m. *(hueco)* hollow; *(regazo)* bosom; *(pecho)* breast; *(cavidad)* cavity <*senos nasales si­nus cavities*>; *(matriz)* womb; FIG. bosom; MATH. sine; ARCHIT. spandrel; MARIT. inlet.
sen·sa·ción f. sensation; *(impresión)* feeling.
sen·sa·cio·nal adj. sensational.
sen·sa·cio·na·lis·ta adj. sensational(istic).
sen·sa·tez f. good sense.
sen·sa·to, a adj. sensible.

sen·si·bi·li·dad f. *(facultad)* sensibility; *(emotividad)* sensitivity, sensitiveness; *(susceptibilidad)* sensitivity.
sen·si·bi·li·zar §04 tr. to sensitize.
sen·si·ble adj. *(que percibe)* sentient; *(sentimental)* sentimental; *(impresionable)* sensitive; *(susceptible)* sensitive.
sen·si·ble·rí·a f. sentimentality.
sen·si·ble·ro, a adj. overly sentimental.
sen·si·ti·vo, a adj. *(sensible)* sensitive; *(capaz de sentir)* sentient; *(sensorial)* sense <*órgano s.* sense organ>.
sen·so·rio, a/rial adj. sensorial.
sen·sual adj. *(sensitivo)* sensuous; *(lujurioso)* sensual.
sen·sua·li·dad f. sensuality.
sen·ta·do, a I. adj. *(establecido)* settled; *(juicioso)* judicious ♦ **dar por s.** to take for granted II. f. sitting.
sen·tar §49 tr. to sit; *(establecer)* to set <*s. precedente* to set a precedent> —intr. *(la comida)* to agree with; *(la ropa)* to fit; *(favorecer)* to become <*esos aires no te sientan bien* those airs do not become you> —reflex. to sit (down).
sen·ten·cia f. *(juicio)* sentence; *(decisión)* ruling; *(refrán)* maxim ♦ **pronunciar la s.** to pass sentence • **cumplir la s.** to serve one's sentence • **s. de muerte** death sentence.
sen·ten·ciar tr. *(juzgar)* to pass judgment; *(condenar)* to sentence.
sen·ten·cio·so, a adj. *(conceptuoso)* sententious; *(grave)* grave.
sen·ti·do, a I. adj. *(sincero)* heartfelt <*un s. pésame* heartfelt condolences>; *(quisquilloso)* touchy II. m. sense; *(interpretación)* interpretation; *(conciencia)* consciousness <*recobrar el s.* to regain consciousness>; *(dirección)* direction ♦ **aguzar el s.** COLL. to prick up one's ears • **con todos los cinco sentidos** heart and soul • **doble s.** double meaning • **en el s. de que** to the effect that • **no tener s.** not to make sense • **poner los cinco sentidos en** to give one's all to • **sin s.** *(insensato)* meaningless; *(inconsciente)* unconscious • **tener s.** to make sense.
sen·ti·men·tal adj. sentimental.
sen·ti·mien·to m. *(emoción)* sentiment; *(pesar)* sorrow.
sen·tir¹ m. *(sentimiento)* feeling; *(opinión)* opinion.
sen·tir² §65 tr. to feel <*siento el calor del sol en la cara* I feel the heat of the sun on my face>; *(experimentar)* to experience; *(oír)* to hear; *(lamentar)* to regret; *(opinar)* to think <*siempre dice lo que siente* he always says what he thinks>; *(presentir)* to sense; *(apreciar)* to appreciate ♦ **lo siento** I'm sorry —intr. to feel —reflex. to feel; AMER. *(ofenderse)* to take offense ♦ **s. a sus anchas** to feel at ease • **s. como en (su) casa** to feel at home.
se·ña f. *(indicio)* sign; *(señal)* signal <*los dos niños tenían una s. secreta* the two children had a secret signal>; *(marca)* mark; MIL. password ♦ **dar señas de** to show signs of • **hablar por señas** to communicate by gestures • **hacer señas** to signal • **s. personales** description.
se·ñal f. *(marca)* sign; *(mojón)* landmark; *(seña)* reminder; *(para libros)* bookmark; *(vestigio)* trace; *(prodigio)* mark of distinction; *(aviso)* signal <*s. de peligro* danger signal>; *(síntoma)* symptom; COM. deposit ♦ **dar señales de vida** to show signs of life • **en s. de** as a sign of • **ni s.** not a trace.

se·ña·la·do, a adj. (notable) outstanding; (fijado) appointed.

se·ña·lar tr. (poner señal) to put a mark or sign on; (indicar) to point (at); (determinar) to determine, set <pronto señalaremos el día para la fiesta soon we will set the day for the party>; (hacer señal) to signal; (nombrar) to appoint; AMER. (ganado) to brand.

se·ña·li·za·ción f. (colocación) posting of signs; (señales) road or railway signs.

se·ña·li·zar §04 tr. to place signposts.

se·ñe·ro, a adj. (solitario) solitary; (único) extraordinary.

se·ñor, a I. adj. COLL. hell of a <me dio una s. bofetada he dealt me a hell of a blow> II. m. Mister, Mr. <vi al s. Márquez en el mercado I saw Mr. Márquez in the market>; sir <siéntese, s. sit down, sir>; (dueño) master <el s. de la casa the master of the house>; (noble) lord; (caballero) gentleman ♦ la S. RELIG. the Lord • muy s. mío Dear Sir • ¡S.! COLL. Good Lord! —f. Mistress, Mrs. <aquí viene la s. Martínez here comes Mrs. Martínez>; madam <buenas tardes, s. good afternoon, madam>; (dueña, noble) lady; (esposa) wife ♦ muy s. mía Dear Madam • Nuestra S. RELIG. Our Lady.

se·ño·rial adj. (propio de señor) of a lord; (majestuoso) majestic.

se·ño·río m. (dominio) dominion; (territorio) domain; (título) lordship; (propiedad) estate; (dignidad) solemnity.

se·ño·ri·ta f. (joven) young lady; (antes del apellido) Miss.

se·ño·ri·to m. (joven) young man; COLL. (amo) master; DEROG. (ocioso) rich kid.

se·ño·rón, o·na I. adj. lordly II. m. great gentleman —f. great lady.

se·ñue·lo m. (para aves) decoy; (cebo) bait; (trampa) trap.

se·pa see saber².

sé·pa·lo m. sepal.

se·pa·ra·ción f. separation.

se·pa·ra·da·men·te adv. separately.

se·pa·ra·do, a I. adj. separate, separated ♦ por s. (separadamente) separately; (correos) under separate cover II. m.f. separated man/woman.

se·pa·rar tr. to separate; (partir) to divide; (boxeadores) to break; (despedir) to dismiss —reflex. to separate.

se·pa·ra·tis·ta adj. & m.f. separatist.

se·pe·lio m. burial.

se·pia f. sepia.

sep·ten·trio·nal adj. northern(ly).

sep·te·to m. septet.

sép·ti·co, a adj. septic.

sep·tiem·bre m. September.

sép·ti·mo, a adj. & m. seventh —f. MUS. seventh.

sep·tin·gen·té·si·mo, a adj. & m. seven-hundredth.

sep·tua·ge·na·rio, a adj. & m.f. septuagenarian.

sep·tua·gé·si·mo, a adj. & m. seventieth.

se·pul·cral adj. sepulchral; (lúgubre) gloomy.

se·pul·cro m. sepulcher.

se·pul·tar tr. to bury.

se·pul·to, a adj. buried.

se·pul·tu·ra f. (entierro) burial; (tumba) grave ♦ dar s. a to bury • estar con un pie en la s. to have one foot in the grave.

se·pul·tu·re·ro m. gravedigger.

se·que·dad f. dryness.

se·quí·a f. drought.

sé·qui·to m. entourage.

ser¹ m. (ente) being; (esencia) essence ♦ s. humano human being • s. vivo living creature.

ser² §66 aux. to be <el Nuevo Mundo fue descubierto por Colón en 1492 the New World was discovered by Columbus in 1492> —intr. to be ♦ a or de no s. por if it were not for • a no s. que unless • así sea so be it • ¡cómo es eso! what do you mean by that! • de no s. así otherwise • érase que se era once upon a time • es de it is to be <es de esperar it is to be hoped>; (valer) to be worth <es de verse it is worth seeing> • no es para menos COLL. rightly so • no sea que lest • o sea or esto es that is to say • o sea que in other words • sea como sea one way or the other • sea lo que sea be that as it may • s. de (pertenecer) to belong to <este libro es de Marta this book belongs to Martha>; to be made of <la cadena es de oro the chain is made of gold>; (tener origen) to be or come from <mi madre era de Inglaterra my mother was from England>; (formar parte) to be or come from <el profesor es de la Universidad de Madrid the professor is from the University of Madrid>; (suceder) to become of <¿que será de nosotros? what will become of us?>; (corresponder) to be suitable for <su conducta no es la de un profesional his conduct is not suitable for a professional> • s. de lo que no hay COLL. to be unique • siendo que since • ya sea ... ya sea either ... or.

se·ra·fín m. angel.

se·re·nar tr. (calmar) to calm; (apaciguar) to soothe —reflex. to grow calm.

se·re·na·ta f. serenade ♦ dar la s. COLL. to pester.

se·re·ni·dad f. serenity.

se·re·no, a I. adj. calm II. m. (rocío) evening dew; (guarda) night watchman ♦ al s. in the night air.

se·rial adj. & m. serial.

se·ria·men·te adv. seriously.

se·rie f. series ♦ fabricar or producir en s. to mass-produce • fuera de s. COLL. out of sight.

se·rie·dad f. seriousness; (comportamiento) dependability.

se·ri·gra·fí·a f. silk-screening.

se·rio, a adj. serious; (grave) grave; (concienzudo) earnest; (sombrío) solemn; (severo) stern; (confiable) reliable ♦ en s. (gravemente) seriously; (sinceramente) truly • hablar en s. to be serious • tomar en s. to take seriously.

ser·món m. sermon.

ser·mo·ne·ar tr. to lecture.

ser·pien·te f. snake ♦ s. de cascabel rattlesnake.

se·rra·do, a adj. (cortado) sawed; (con dientes) serrated.

se·rra·ní·a f. mountains.

se·rra·no, a I. adj. (que habita) mountain-dwelling; (de las sierras) mountain II. m.f. highlander.

se·rrar §49 tr. to saw.

se·rre·rí·a f. sawmill.

se·rru·cho m. saw.

ser·vi·ble adj. useful.

ser·vi·cial adj. obliging.

ser·vi·cio m. service; (criados) help; (utilidad) usefulness; (orinal) urinal; (retrete) bathroom ♦ al s. de in the service of • prestar un s. to perform a service.

ser·vi·dor, ·ra m.f. servant ♦ **s. de usted** at your service • **su seguro s.** yours truly.

ser·vi·dum·bre f. *(esclavitud)* slavery; *(conjunto)* staff of servants.

ser·vil adj. servile.

ser·vi·lle·ta f. napkin.

ser·vi·lle·te·ro m. napkin ring.

ser·vir §47 intr. to serve ♦ **no s. para nada** to be useless • **s. de** *(hacer el papel de)* to act or serve as *<s. de guía* to act as a guide*>*; *(valer)* to be of use • **s. para** to be of use — tr. to serve; *(a un cliente)* to wait on — reflex. *(valerse)* to make use of ♦ **sírvase** please.

ser·vo·fre·no m. power brake.

ser·vo·mo·tor m. servomotor.

sé·sa·mo m. sesame.

se·se·ar intr. to lisp.

se·sen·ta I. adj. sixty; *(sexagésimo)* sixtieth II. m. sixty.

se·sen·ta·vo, a adj. & m. sixtieth.

se·sen·tón, o·na adj. & m.f. COLL. sexagenarian.

se·se·o m. lisp.

ses·gar §47 tr. *(inclinar)* to slant; SEW. *(cortar)* to cut on the bias.

ses·go m. slant; SEW. bias ♦ **al s.** obliquely; SEW. on the bias • **tomar un mal s.** COLL. to take a turn for the worse.

se·sión f. session, meeting ♦ **levantar la s.** to adjourn the meeting • **s. espiritista** seance.

se·sio·nar intr. to hold a meeting.

se·so m. brain; FIG. sense ♦ **perder el s.** to lose one's mind, go crazy ♦ pl. brains • **devanarse los s.** to rack one's brains.

se·su·do, a adj. wise.

se·te·cien·tos, as adj. & m. seven hundred.

se·ten·ta I. adj. seventy; *(septuagésimo)* seventieth II. m. seventy.

se·ten·ta·vo, a adj. & m. seventieth.

se·ten·tón, o·na COLL. adj. & m.f. septuagenarian.

se·tiem·bre m. September.

se·to m. fence ♦ **s. vivo** hedge.

seu·dó·ni·mo, a LIT. I. adj. pseudonymous II. m. pseudonym.

se·ve·ra·men·te adv. severely; *(con rigor)* rigorously; *(inexorablemente)* relentlessly; *(rigidamente)* strictly; *(gravemente)* gravely; *(duramente)* harshly.

se·ve·ri·dad f. severity; *(rigor)* rigor; *(inexorabilidad)* relentlessness; *(rigidez)* strictness; *(gravedad)* graveness; *(dureza)* harshness.

se·ve·ro, a adj. severe; *(riguroso)* rigorous, *(inexorable)* unyielding; *(rígido)* strict; *(grave)* grave; *(duro)* harsh.

se·xa·ge·na·rio, a adj. & m.f. sexagenarian.

se·xa·gé·si·mo, a adj. & m. sixtieth.

se·xis·ta adj. & m.f. sexist.

se·xo m. sex; *(órganos)* genitals ♦ **el bello s.** the fair sex.

sex·tan·te m. sextant.

sex·te·to m. sextet.

sex·to, a adj. & m. sixth.

se·xua·do, a adj. sexed.

se·xual adj. sexual.

se·xua·li·dad f. sexuality.

si¹ m. MUS. ti.

si² conj. if; whether *<no sabemos si está casado o no* we do not know whether he is married or not*>* ♦ **como si as if** *<por si acaso* just in case • **si bien** although • **si no** if not, otherwise.

sí¹ pron. oneself, himself, herself, yourself, it-

self, themselves, yourselves ♦ **dar de sí** to give of oneself • **de por sí** or **en sí** in itself • **de sí** in itself • **fuera de sí** beside oneself • **para sí** oneself • **sí mismo** oneself *<Mateo piensa sólo en sí mismo* Matthew thinks only of himself*>*.

sí² adv. yes; *(en votación)* aye; *(ciertamente)* certainly *<ellos sí vendrán* they will certainly come*>*; so *<creo que sí* I think so*>* II. m. yes *<un sí categórico* a categorical yes*>*; *(consentimiento)* consent, permission *<conseguimos el sí del maestro* we got the teacher's permission*>* ♦ **dar el sí** to say yes.

si·ba·ri·ta I. adj. sybaritic II. m.f. sybarite.

si·ba·rí·ti·co, a adj. sybaritic.

si·bi·la f. sibyl.

si·bi·lan·te adj. & m.f. sibilant.

si·co·a·ná·li·sis m. var. of **psicoanálisis.**

si·co·lo·gí·a f. var. of **psicología.**

si·có·lo·go, a adj. & m.f. var. of **psicólogo, a.**

si·co·mo·ro m. sycamore.

si·co·sis f. var. of **psicosis.**

si·co·te·ra·pia f. var. of **psicoterapia.**

SIDA m. AIDS.

si·de·ral/dé·re·o adj. astral.

si·de·rur·gia f. iron and steel industry.

si·de·rúr·gi·co, a adj. iron and steel *<industria s.* iron and steel industry*>*.

si·dra f. alcoholic cider.

sie·ga f. *(acción)* harvesting; *(temporada, cosecha)* harvest.

siem·bra f. *(acción)* sowing; *(temporada)* sowing season; *(sembrado)* sown land.

siem·pre adv. always ♦ **como s.** as always • **de s.** usual • **para** or **por s.** forever • **s. jamás** forever and ever • **s. lo mismo** always the same • **s. que** *(cada vez)* every time *<s. que entro en la casa, me quito los zapatos* every time I enter the house, I take off my shoes*>*; *(a condición de)* provided that • **s. y cuando** provided that.

sien f. temple.

sien·ta, te, to see **sentir²** or **sentar.**

sie·rra f. *(instrumento)* saw; ICHTH. sawfish; GEOL. mountain range ♦ **s. de cinta** band saw • **s. de mano** handsaw.

sier·vo, a m.f. *(esclavo)* slave; *(esclavo feudal)* serf; *(servidor)* servant.

sies·ta f. afternoon nap ♦ **dormir** or **echar la s.** to take a nap after lunch.

sie·te I. adj. seven; *(séptimo)* seventh ♦ **las s.** seven o'clock II. m. seven.

sí·fi·lis f. syphilis.

si·fi·lí·ti·co, a adj. & m.f. syphilitic.

si·fón m. *(tubería)* U-bend; *(para líquidos)* siphon; COLL. *(agua gaseosa)* soda water.

si·ga, go see **seguir.**

si·gi·lo m. secrecy; *(discreción)* discretion.

si·gi·lo·so, a adj. *(secreto)* secretive; *(prudente)* discreet.

si·gla f. acronym.

si·glo m. century; *(época)* age *<el s. del átomo* the atomic age*>*; FIG. ages ♦ **en** or **por los siglos de los siglos** forever and ever • **S. de las Luces** the Enlightenment • **S. de Oro** Golden Age.

sig·ni·fi·ca·ción f. *(significado)* meaning; *(importancia)* significance.

sig·ni·fi·ca·do, a I. adj. significant II. m. meaning.

sig·ni·fi·can·te adj. significant.

sig·ni·fi·car §70 tr. *(querer decir)* to mean; *(hacer saber)* to indicate; *(representar)* to signify

—reflex. to distinguish oneself (*como as*).

sig·ni·fi·ca·ti·vo, a adj. significant.

sig·no m. sign; (*de puntuación*) mark; (*destino*) fate ♦ **s. de admiración** exclamation point • **s. de interrogación** question mark • **s. diacrítico** diacritical mark • **s. de igual** equal sign • **s. de más** plus sign • **s. de menos** minus sign.

si·guien·te adj. following, next.

si·guie·ra, guió see **seguir**.

sí·la·ba f. syllable.

si·la·be·ar intr. to syllable.

si·la·be·o m. syllabication.

sil·ba f. booing.

sil·bar intr. to whistle; (*una bala*) to whizz; (*chiflar*) to boo.

sil·ba·ti·na f. AMER. booing.

sil·ba·to m. whistle.

sil·bi·do m. (*silbo*) whistle; (*de culebra*) hissing; (*de bala*) whizzing; MED. wheeze ♦ **s. de oídos** ringing in the ears • **dar un s.** to whistle.

si·len·cia·dor m. silencer; AUTO. muffler, silencer (G.B.).

si·len·ciar tr. (*guardar en silencio*) to keep silent about; (*ahogar*) to muffle; (*ocultar*) to hush up; (*hacer callar*) to silence.

si·len·cio m. silence; MUS. rest ♦ **guardar s.** to keep silent.

si·len·cio·so, a adj. quiet, silent.

si·li·co·na f. silicone.

si·lo m. silo.

si·lo·gis·mo m. syllogism.

si·lo·gís·ti·co, a adj. syllogistic.

si·lue·ta f. outline.

sil·ves·tre adj. wild.

sil·vi·cul·tor m. forester.

si·lla f. (*asiento*) chair; (*para montar*) saddle ♦ **s. de ruedas** wheelchair.

si·lle·rí·a f. (*conjunto*) set of chairs; RELIG. choir stalls; (*taller*) chair shop; (*tienda*) chair store.

si·llín m. (*de bicicleta*) seat; (*silla ligera*) light riding cycle.

si·llón m. armchair ♦ **s. giratorio** swivel chair.

si·ma f. chasm.

sim·bio·sis f. symbiosis.

sim·bió·ti·co, a adj. symbiotic.

sim·bó·li·co, a adj. symbolic(al).

sim·bo·li·zar §04 tr. to symbolize.

sím·bo·lo m. symbol ♦ **s. de prestigio** status symbol.

si·me·trí·a f. symmetry.

si·mé·tri·co, a adj. symmetric(al).

si·mien·te f. seed.

si·mil adj. similar.

si·mi·lar adj. similar.

si·mi·li·tud f. similarity.

si·mio, a m.f. simian.

sim·pa·tí·a f. (*afecto*) affection; (*afinidad*) affinity; (*amabilidad*) congeniality ♦ **ganarse la s. de** to win the affection of • **tener s. a** or **por** to like • **tomarle s. a** to take a liking to.

sim·pá·ti·co, a I. adj. pleasant **II.** m. ♦ **gran s.** sympathetic nervous system.

sim·pa·ti·zan·te I. adj. sympathizing **II.** m.f. sympathizer.

sim·pa·ti·zar §04 intr. to get along (together) <*no simpatizan para nada* they don't get along at all>.

sim·ple I. adj. simple; (*fácil*) easy; (*sin adornos*) plain; (*modesto*) modest; (*tonto*) simpleminded **II.** m.f. simpleton; MED. simple.

sim·ple·za f. (*necedad*) simpleness; (*ingenuidad*) simplicity ♦ pl. foolish remarks.

sim·pli·ci·dad f. simplicity.

sim·pli·fi·ca·ción f. simplification.

sim·pli·fi·car §70 tr. to simplify.

sim·plón, o·na/plo·te COLL. **I.** adj. simple **II.** m.f. simpleton.

sim·po·sio/sium m. symposium.

si·mu·la·ción f. pretense.

si·mu·la·cro m. pretense; MIL. war games.

si·mu·la·dor, ·ra I. adj. simulating **II.** m.f. simulator.

si·mu·lar tr. to feign.

si·mul·tá·ne·o, a adj. simultaneous.

sin prep. without <*salió s. abrigo* he went out without a coat>; (*fuera de*) not including <*nos cobraron cien dólares s. los gastos de envío* they charged us one hundred dollars, not including the postage>; without <*salieron s. advertirnos* they went out without telling us>; un- <*dejaron mucho s. hacer* they left much undone>; -less <*me quedé s. un centavo* I was left penniless> ♦ **s. embargo** however, nevertheless • **s. que** without <*robaron el banco s. que la policía los capturara* they robbed the bank without being caught by the police>.

si·na·go·ga f. synagogue.

sin·ce·ri·dad f. sincerity ♦ **con toda s.** in all sincerity.

sin·ce·ro, a adj. sincere.

sín·co·pa f. GRAM. syncope; MUS. syncopation.

sin·co·pa·do, a adj. syncopated.

sín·co·pe m. GRAM., MED. syncope ♦ **s. car·díaco** heart attack.

sin·cro·ní·a f. synchrony.

sin·cro·ni·za·ción f. synchronization.

sin·cro·ni·zar §04 tr. to synchronize —intr. RAD. to tune in.

sin·di·cal adj. trade-union <*movimiento s.* trade-union movement>.

sin·di·ca·lis·ta I. adj. trade-union **II.** m.f. trade unionist.

sin·di·ca·li·za·ción f. unionization.

sin·di·ca·li·zar §04 tr. to unionize —reflex. (*formar*) to form a labor union; (*unirse*) to join a labor union.

sin·di·car §70 tr. (*un sindicato*) to unionize; (*acusar*) to accuse.

sin·di·ca·to m. labor or trade union.

sín·di·co m. LAW trustee; (*de una quiebra*) receiver.

sín·dro·me m. syndrome ♦ **s. de inmunodeficiencia adquirida** acquired immune deficiency syndrome.

si·ne·cu·ra f. sinecure.

si·ner·gí·a f. synergy.

sin·fín m. endless number or quantity <*hizo un s. de sugerencias* she made an endless number of suggestions>.

sin·fo·ní·a f. symphony.

sin·fó·ni·co, a adj. symphonic, symphony <*orquesta s.* symphony orchestra>.

sin·gu·lar I. adj. singular; (*excepcional*) unique; (*peculiar*) peculiar **II.** m. GRAM. singular ♦ **en s.** in particular.

sin·gu·la·ri·dad f. singularity; (*carácter excepcional*) uniqueness; (*peculiaridad*) peculiarity.

sin·gu·la·ri·zar §04 tr. (*distinguir*) to distinguish; GRAM. to make singular —reflex. to distinguish oneself (*por by*).

sin·hue·so f. COLL. tongue ♦ **soltar la s.** COLL. to shoot off one's mouth.

si·nies·tro, a I. adj. (*izquierdo*) left, left-hand; (*perverso*) wicked; (*funesto*) fateful **II.** m. disaster.

sin·nú·me·ro m. countless or endless number <*un s. de invitados* a countless number of guests>.

si·no¹ m. fate.

si·no² conj. but <*no llegué el martes s. el jueves* I did not arrive on Tuesday but on Thursday>; *(excepto)* except <*nadie lo sabía s. Pedro* no one knew it except Peter> ♦ **no sólo...s.** not only...but also <*no sólo es rico s. generoso* he is not only rich but also generous>.

si·no·ni·mia f. synonymy.

si·nó·ni·mo, a I. adj. synonymous II. m. synonym.

si·nop·sis f.inv. synopsis.

si·nóp·ti·co, a adj. synoptic(al).

sin·ra·zón f. injustice.

sin·sa·bor m. *(disgusto)* discontent; *(pena)* grief.

sin·tác·ti·co, a adj. syntactic.

sin·ta·xis m.inv. syntax.

sín·te·sis f.inv. synthesis.

sin·té·ti·co, a adj. synthetic.

sin·te·ti·za·dor m. synthesizer.

sin·te·ti·zar §04 tr. to synthesize.

sin·tie·ra, tió see *sentir².*

sín·to·ma m. symptom.

sin·to·má·ti·co, a adj. symptomatic.

sin·to·ní·a f. tuning (in).

sin·to·ni·za·dor m. tuner.

sin·to·ni·zar §04 tr. to tune (in) ♦ **s. con** to be tuned to.

si·nuo·si·dad f. sinuosity.

si·nuo·so, a adj. sinuous; FIG. devious.

sin·ver·güen·za adj. & m.f. COLL. shameless or brazen (person).

sin·ver·güen·za·da f. AMER. COLL. dirty trick.

si·quí·a·tra/quia·tra m.f. psychiatrist.

si·quia·trí·a f. psychiatry.

si·quí·co, a adj. psychic.

si·quie·ra I. conj. even though, if only II. adv. at least <*espéreme diez minutos s.* wait for me for ten minutes at least> ♦ **ni s.** not even.

si·re·na f. siren; MYTH. mermaid ♦ **s. de niebla** foghorn.

sir·va, vo see *servir.*

sir·vien·ta f. maid.

sir·vien·te m. servant.

sir·vie·ra, vió see *servir.*

si·sa f. armhole.

si·se·ar tr. & intr. to boo.

sís·mi·co, a adj. seismic.

sis·mo m. earthquake.

sis·mó·gra·fo m. seismograph.

sis·te·ma m. system ♦ **con s.** systematically • **s. métrico (decimal)** metric system • **s. nervioso** nervous system.

sis·te·má·ti·co, a I. adj. systematic II. f. systematics.

sis·te·ma·ti·za·ción f. systematization.

sis·te·ma·ti·zar §04 tr. to systematize.

sís·to·le f. systole.

si·tial m. seat of honor.

si·tiar tr. MIL. to lay siege; *(rodear)* to surround.

si·tio m. *(localidad)* site; *(lugar)* place <*el libro no está en su s.* the book is not in its place>; MIL. siege.

si·to, a adj. situated.

si·tua·ción f. situation; *(estado)* position.

si·tuar §67 tr. to place.

smo·king m. tuxedo.

snob I. adj. snobbish II. m.f. snob.

so¹ m. COLL. you ♦ **¡s. tonto!** you idiot!

so² prep. under ♦ **s. pena de muerte** under penalty of death.

so·a·sar tr. to roast lightly, brown.

so·ba·co m. armpit.

so·ba·que·ra f. *(refuerzo)* armhole reinforcement; *(resguardo)* underarm shield.

so·ba·qui·na f. underarm odor.

so·bar tr. *(la masa)* to knead; *(las pieles)* to full; *(zurrar)* to thrash; *(toquetear)* to fondle; AMER. *(adular)* to flatter.

so·be·o m. strap.

so·be·ra·ní·a f. sovereignty.

so·be·ra·no, a adj. & m.f. sovereign.

so·ber·bio, a I. adj. *(orgulloso)* arrogant; *(magnífico)* superb II. f. arrogance.

so·bón, o·na adj. & m.f. COLL. mushy or overly fond (person).

so·bor·nar tr. to bribe.

so·bor·no m. bribery.

so·bra f. excess ♦ **de s.** superfluous • **estar de s.** to be one too many ♦ pl. leftovers.

so·bra·da·men·te adv. only too well.

so·bra·do, a adj. plenty of.

so·bran·te I. adj. *(que sobra)* remaining; *(excesivo)* surplus II. m. surplus.

so·brar tr. to surpass —intr. *(estar de más)* to be more than enough; *(quedar)* to remain; *(ser inútil)* to be superfluous.

so·bre¹ m. envelope.

so·bre² prep. *(encima)* above, over <*los pájaros volaban s. los verdes campos* birds flew over the green fields>; *(en)* on, on top of <*ella puso el mantel s. la mesa* she put the tablecloth on the table>; *(superior a)* above, over <*el rango de capitán está s. el de teniente* the rank of captain is above that of lieutenant>; *(acerca de)* about, on <*escribí s. los problemas* I wrote about the problems>; *(más o menos)* about <*vendremos s. las dos* we will come at about two o'clock>; *(además de)* on top of, over <*me dieron cincuenta dólares s. lo acordado* they gave me fifty dollars over what was agreed upon>; *(tras)* on top of, upon <*insulto s. insulto* one insult on top of another>; *(en prenda de)* on, against <*un préstamo s. la finca* a loan on the farm>; on <*un impuesto s. la mercancía importada* a tax on imported goods>; *(de)* in, out of <*seis s. cien* six out of one hundred> ♦ **dar s.** to face • **s. manera** exceedingly • **s. todo** especially.

so·bre·a·bun·dan·cia f. superabundance.

so·bre·a·bun·dan·te adj. superabundant.

so·bre·a·bun·dar intr. to be overabundant ♦ **s. en** to superabound in.

so·bre·a·li·men·tar tr. to overfeed.

so·bre·car·ga f. overload.

so·bre·car·gar §47 tr. to overload; FIG. to overburden.

so·bre·ce·jo/ño m. frown.

so·bre·co·ger §34 tr. to scare —reflex. to be scared.

so·bre·co·si·do m./**cos·tu·ra** f. whipstitch.

so·bre·cu·bier·ta f. cover; *(de un libro)* dust jacket.

so·bre·cue·llo m. overcollar.

so·bre·di·cho, a adj. above-mentioned.

so·bre·dien·te m. snaggletooth.

so·bre·en·ten·der §50 tr. & reflex. var. of **sobrentender.**

so·bre·en·ten·di·do, a adj. understood.

so·bre·ex·ci·ta·ción f. overexcitement.

so·bre·ex·ci·tar tr. to overexcite.
so·bre·fal·da f. overskirt.
so·bre·hue·so m. bony tumor.
so·bre·hu·ma·no, a adj. superhuman.
so·bre·lle·nar tr. to overfill.
so·bre·lle·var tr. to bear.
so·bre·ma·ne·ra adv. exceedingly.
so·bre·me·sa f. after-dinner conversation ♦ **de s.** after-dinner.
so·bre·na·tu·ral adj. supernatural.
so·bre·nom·bre m. nickname.
so·bren·ten·der §50 tr. to understand —reflex. to be understood.
so·bre·pa·sar intr. to surpass.
so·bre·pe·so m. overload.
so·bre·po·ner §54 tr. to superimpose —reflex. (controlarse) to control oneself; (vencer) to triumph.
so·bre·pre·cio m. surcharge.
so·bre·pues·to, a I. see **sobreponer** II. adj. (puesto encima) superimposed; SEW. appliqué III. m. SEW. appliqué.
so·bre·sa·lien·te I. adj. outstanding II. m. highest mark.
so·bre·sa·lir §63 intr. (resaltar) to project; (sobrepujar) to be outstanding.
so·bre·sal·tar tr. to startle —reflex. to be startled (con, por by, at).
so·bre·sal·to m. fright.
so·bres·cri·to m. address.
so·bres·drú·ju·lo, a I. adj. accented on the syllable preceding the antepenult II. f. word accented on the syllable preceding the antepenult.
so·bre·sei·mien·to m. LAW stay (of proceedings) ♦ **s. definitivo** dismissal.
so·bres·ti·mar tr. to overestimate.
so·bre·suel·do m. bonus.
so·bre·to·do m. overcoat.
so·bre·ve·nir §76 intr. to occur unexpectedly.
so·bre·vi·vien·te I. adj. surviving II. m.f. survivor.
so·bre·vi·vir intr. to survive.
so·brie·dad f. moderation.
so·bri·no, a m. nephew —f. niece.
so·brio, a adj. (sin beber) sober; (conservador) moderate.
so·ca·rrar tr. to scorch.
so·ca·rrón, o·na adj. & m.f. sarcastic (person).
so·ca·rro·ne·rí·a f. sarcasm.
so·ca·var tr. to excavate; FIG. to undermine.
so·ca·vón m. (mina) tunnel; (hundimiento) cave-in.
so·cia·bi·li·dad f. friendliness.
so·cia·ble adj. sociable.
so·cial adj. social.
so·cia·lis·ta adj. & m.f. socialist.
so·cia·li·za·ción f. socialization.
so·cia·li·zar §04 tr. to socialize.
so·cie·dad f. society; COM. corporation ♦ **formar s.** to associate • **s. anónima** corporation • **s. en comandita** limited partnership • **s. cooperativa** cooperative partnership • **s. de control** holding company • **s. de crédito** credit union • **s. de responsabilidad limitada** limited-liability company • **s. gremial** trade union • **s. mercantil** trading company • **s. regular colectiva** general partnership, copartnership.
so·cio, a m.f. (asociado) member; (accionista) business associate; COLL. (amigo) pal ♦ **s. capitalista** financial partner • **s. comanditario** silent partner • **s. honorario** honorary member.

so·cio·e·co·nó·mi·co, a adj. socioeconomic.
so·cio·lo·gí·a f. sociology.
so·cio·ló·gi·co, a adj. sociological.
so·ció·lo·go, a m.f. sociologist.
so·co·rrer tr. to aid.
so·co·rro I. m. (apoyo) aid; MIL. (tropas) relief; (provisiones) supplies ♦ **puesto de s.** first-aid station • **señal de s.** distress signal II. interj. help!
so·dio m. sodium.
so·do·mí·a f. sodomy.
so·do·mi·ta I. adj. sodomitical II. m.f. sodomite.
so·ez adj. vulgar.
so·fá f. sofa.
so·fis·ma m. sophism.
so·fis·ta I. adj. sophistic II. m.f. sophist.
so·fis·ti·ca·ción f. sophistication.
so·fis·ti·ca·do, a adj. sophisticated.
so·fo·ca·ción f. suffocation; FIG. embarrassment.
so·fo·ca·dor, ·ra/·can·te adj. suffocating.
so·fo·car §70 tr. (asfixiar) to suffocate; (un fuego) to put out; (una rebelión) to suppress; (avergonzar) to embarrass —reflex. to suffocate; FIG. to get embarrassed.
so·fo·co m. suffocation; (ahogo) choking sensation ♦ **pasar un s.** to suffer an embarrassment.
so·fo·cón m. COLL. annoyance ♦ **darle un s. (a uno)** COLL. to have a fit.
so·fre·ír §58 tr. to fry lightly.
so·fri·to I. see **sofreír** II. m. lightly-fried dish.
so·ga f. rope ♦ **dar s. a alguien** COLL. to excite someone • **con la s. al cuello** COLL. with the knife at one's throat.
so·ja f. soya, soybean.
so·juz·gar §47 tr. to subjugate.
sol¹ m. sun; (luz) sun, sunlight; PERU., FIN. sol ♦ **al ponerse el s.** at sunset • **al salir el s.** at sunrise • **arrimarse al s. que más calienta** COLL. to know on which side one's bread is buttered • **de s. a s.** from sunrise to sunset • **hacer s.** to be sunny • **no dejar ni a s. ni a sombra** to give someone no peace • **tomar el s.** to sunbathe.
sol² m. MUS. sol.
so·la·men·te adv. only.
so·la·no m. east wind.
so·la·pa f. (de sobre) flap; (de chaqueta) lapel.
so·la·pa·do, a adj. underhanded.
so·la·par tr. SEW. to put lapels on; (traslapar) to overlap; FIG. to conceal —intr. to overlap.
so·lar¹ adj. solar.
so·lar² m. (terreno) lot; (bajo construcción) building site; (casa) ancestral home.
so·la·rie·go, a adj. (del patrimonio) ancestral; (noble) noble.
so·la·rium/rio m. solarium.
so·laz m. (descanso) relaxation; (consuelo) solace.
so·la·zar §04 tr. & reflex. to amuse (oneself).
so·la·zo m. COLL. scorching sunshine.
sol·da·do m. soldier • **s. raso** private • **s. de caballería** cavalryman • **s. de infantería** infantryman • **s. de marina** marine.
sol·da·dor m. (obrero) solderer; (soplete) blow torch.
sol·da·du·ra f. (acción) soldering; (material) solder; (compostura) repair ♦ **s. autógena** welding • **s. por arco** arc welding.
sol·dar §19 tr. to solder —reflex. (pegarse) to

join together; *(huesos)* to knit.

so·le·a·do adj. sunny.

so·le·ar tr. to expose to the sun —reflex. to sun oneself.

so·le·cis·mo m. solecism.

so·le·dad f. *(aislamiento)* solitude; *(sentirse solo)* loneliness; *(lugar)* solitary place.

so·lem·ne adj. solemn.

so·lem·ni·dad f. solemnity.

so·ler §78 intr. *(acostumbrar)* to be in the habit of <*Miguel suele levantarse temprano* Michael is in the habit of getting up early>; *(ser frecuente)* to tend to <*suele llover mucho en Londres* it tends to rain a lot in London>; *(equivalentes adverbiales)* usually, often <*yo suelo levantarme tarde* I usually get up late>; <*suele nevar mucho aquí* it often snows a lot here>.

so·le·ra f. *(soporte)* crossbeam; *(piedra)* plinth; *(del molino)* lower millstone; *(del horno)* floor.

so·le·van·tar tr. to lift; FIG. to stir up.

sol·fa f. MUS. musical notation ♦ **poner en s.** COLL. to ridicule.

sol·fe·ar tr. to sing sol-fa.

sol·fe·o m. solfeggio.

so·li·ci·ta·ción f. request.

so·li·ci·tan·te I. adj. petitioning II. m.f. petitioner.

so·li·ci·tar tr. *(pedir)* to request; *(gestionar)* to apply for; *(atraer)* to attract.

so·li·ci·to, a adj. solicitous.

so·li·ci·tud f. *(cuidado)* solicitude; *(petición)* request; *(instancia)* petition; *(gestión)* application ♦ **a s.** on request ♦ **a s. de** at the request of ♦ **presentar una s.** to submit an application.

so·li·da·ri·dad f. solidarity ♦ **por s. con** in solidarity with.

so·li·da·rio, a adj. *(en común)* joint; *(obligatorio)* mutually binding; TECH. integral.

so·li·da·ri·zar·se §04 reflex. to join together.

so·li·dez f. solidity; *(fuerza)* strength.

so·li·di·fi·ca·ción f. solidification.

so·li·di·fi·car §70 tr. & reflex. to solidify.

só·li·do, a I. adj. solid; *(fuerte)* strong II. m. solid.

so·li·lo·quio m. soliloquy.

so·lis·ta m.f. soloist.

so·li·ta·rio, a I. adj. *(solo)* lone; *(desierto)* solitary II. m.f. *(ermitaño)* recluse —m. *(diamante, juego)* solitaire; ZOOL. hermit crab —f. ZOOL. tapeworm.

so·li·vian·tar tr. *(excitar)* to stir up; *(irritar)* to irritate; *(preocupar)* to worry.

so·li·viar tr. to lift.

so·lo, a I. adj. *(sin compañía)* alone; *(único)* sole; *(aislado)* lonely ♦ **a solas** alone II. m. MUS. solo.

só·lo adv. only.

so·lo·mi·llo m. sirloin.

sols·ti·cio m. solstice.

sol·tar §19 tr. *(aflojar)* to loosen; *(desasir)* to let go of <*suelta mi brazo* let go of my arm>; *(liberar)* to free; *(irrumpir)* to let out <*el prisionero soltaba gritos de terror* the prisoner let out cries of terror>; *(decir)* to blurt out; *(en tejidos)* to drop —reflex. *(adquirir soltura)* to become proficient; *(volverse desenvuelto)* to loosen up; COLL. *(empezar)* to begin.

sol·te·rí·a f. bachelorhood.

sol·te·ro, a I. adj. single II. m. bachelor —f. unmarried woman.

sol·te·rón, o·na I. adj. old and unmarried II. m. confirmed bachelor —f. spinster; COLL.

old maid.

sol·tu·ra f. *(aflojamiento)* looseness; *(seguridad)* confidence; *(agilidad)* agility; *(al hablar)* fluency; *(descaro)* brazenness ♦ **con s.** confidently.

so·lu·ble adj. CHEM. soluble; *(que se puede resolver)* solvable.

so·lu·ción f. solution; *(desenlace)* ending.

so·lu·cio·nar tr. to solve.

sol·ven·cia f. solvency; FIN. settlement; *(fiabilidad)* reliability ♦ **s. moral** character.

sol·ven·tar tr. *(pagar)* to settle; *(costear)* to finance; *(resolver)* to resolve.

sol·ven·te I. adj. *(libre de deudas)* solvent; *(responsable)* reliable II. m. solvent.

so·llo·zar §04 intr. to sob.

so·llo·zo m. sob ♦ **estallar** *or* **prorrumpir en sollozos** to burst into sobs.

so·má·ti·co, a adj. somatic.

so·ma·ti·za·ción f. somatization.

so·ma·ti·zar §04 intr. to somatize.

som·bra f. *(obscuridad)* darkness; *(área)* shade; *(imagen)* shadow <*la s. del molino* the shadow of the windmill>; *(penumbra)* shade <*a la s. del manzano* in the shade of the apple tree>; *(espectro)* ghost; *(confusión)* confusion ♦ **dar s.** to cast a shadow ♦ **poner a la s.** COLL. to put in jail.

som·brar tr. to shade.

som·bre·a·dor m. eye shadow.

som·bre·ar tr. *(poner sombra)* to shade; *(dar sombra)* to throw shadow on.

som·bre·re·ra f. *(para señoras)* milliner; *(para hombres)* hat maker; *(caja)* hatbox.

som·bre·re·rí·a f. *(señoras)* milliner's (shop); *(hombres)* hatter's (shop).

som·bre·re·ro m. *(para señoras)* milliner; *(para hombres)* hat maker.

som·bre·ro m. hat; BOT., MECH. cap ♦ **s. de copa** top hat ♦ **s. hongo** derby, bowler (G.B.).

som·bri·lla f. parasol.

som·brí·o, a adj. *(lugar)* gloomy; *(persona)* sullen.

so·me·ra·men·te adv. superficially.

so·me·ro, a adj. *(sin profundidad)* shallow; *(superficial)* superficial; *(breve)* brief.

so·me·ter tr. *(subyugar)* to subjugate; *(subordinar)* to subordinate; *(entregar)* to submit; to subject *or* put to <*lo sometieron a una prueba científica* they subjected it to a scientific test> ♦ **s. a prueba** to test ♦ **s. a tratamiento** to put under treatment ♦ **s. algo a una autoridad** to refer something to an authority —reflex. *(rendirse)* to surrender; to undergo <*s. a una operación* to undergo an operation>.

so·me·ti·mien·to m. submission.

som·ní·fe·ro, a I. adj. sleep-inducing II. m. sleeping pill.

som·no·len·cia f. somnolence.

so·mos see **ser²**.

son¹ m. COLL. tune ♦ **¿a s. de qué?** for what reason? ♦ **en s. de** as <*en s. de broma* as a joke> ♦ **sin ton ni s.** COLL. without rhyme or reason.

son² see **ser²**.

so·na·do, a adj. *(muy divulgado)* talked-about; SL. *(chiflado)* crazy.

so·na·je·ro m. rattle.

so·nám·bu·lo, a I. adj. sleep II. m.f. sleepwalker.

so·nar¹ m. TECH. sonar.

so·nar² §19 intr. *(producir sonido)* to sound;

(tintinear) to ring; *(parecer)* to sound like <*esto me suena a tontería* this sounds like foolishness to me>; *(el reloj)* to strike; *(recordar)* to ring a bell <*ese nombre no me suena* that name does not ring a bell with me>; PHONET. to be pronounced ♦ **como suena** literally —tr. *(hacer que suene)* to sound; *(tocar)* to play; *(repicar)* to ring; *(la nariz)* to blow —reflex. to blow.

son·da f. *(sondeo)* sounding; *(instrumento)* sounding line *or* lead; ASTRONAUT. probe <*s. espacial* space probe>; MED. probe; TECH. drill ♦ **s. acústica** sonic depth finder.

son·de·ar/dar tr. to sound; MED. to probe; TECH. to drill; *(explorar)* to explore, inquire into; *(averiguar)* to sound out.

son·de·o m. sounding; MED. probing; TECH. drilling; *(encuesta)* poll.

so·ne·to m. sonnet.

so·ni·do m. sound; MED. murmur.

so·no·ri·dad f. sonority.

so·no·ro, a adj. *(sonido)* sound; *(resonante)* sonorous.

son·re·ír §58 intr. to smile; FIG. to smile on <*la fortuna le sonríe* luck smiles on him> —reflex. to smile.

son·ri·en·te adj. smiling.

son·ri·sa f. smile.

son·ro·jar·se reflex. to blush.

son·ro·jo m. blush.

son·ro·sar tr. to turn pink.

son·sa·car §70 tr. to wheedle.

son·se·ar intr. AMER. to fool around.

son·so, a AMER., COLL. I. adj. silly II. m.f. fool.

son·so·ne·te m. singsong.

so·ña·do, a adj. dream, of one's dreams.

so·ña·dor, ·ra I. adj. dreamy II. m.f. dreamer.

so·ñar §19 tr. & intr. to dream ♦ ¡**ni soñarlo!** not on your life! • **s. con** to dream of *or* about • **s. con los angelitos** COLL. to have sweet dreams • **s. despierto** to daydream.

so·ño·len·cia f. somnolence.

so·ño·lien·to, a adj. sleepy.

so·pa f. soup; *(pan mojado)* sop ♦ **estar** *or* **quedar hecho una s.** COLL. to be soaking wet.

so·pa·pe·ar tr. to slap.

so·pa·po m. slap.

so·pe·ro, a I. adj. soup <*plato s.* soup plate *or* bowl> II. m. soup plate *or* bowl —f. soup tureen.

so·pe·sar tr. to weigh.

so·pe·tón m. slap ♦ **de s.** suddenly.

so·pla·do, a m. glassblowing.

so·pla·dor, ·ra I. adj. blowing II. m. glass blower.

so·plar intr. to blow —tr. *(mover el viento)* to blow (away) <*el viento sopla la hojarasca en el otoño* the wind blows the dead leaves during the fall>; *(velas)* to blow out; *(globos)* to blow up; COLL. *(apuntar)* to prompt; *(hurtar)* to swipe.

so·ple·te m. blowtorch ♦ **s. de arena** sandblast • **s. oxiacetilénico** oxyacetylene torch.

so·plo m. blow; FIG. instant.

so·plón, o·na I. adj. COLL. squealing II. m.f. COLL. stool pigeon.

so·pon·cio m. COLL. faint.

so·por m. MED. sopor; FIG. sleepiness.

so·po·rí·fe·ro/fi·co, a I. adj. sleep-inducing, FIG. boring II. m. sleeping pill.

so·por·ta·ble adj. bearable.

so·por·tar tr. *(sostener)* to support; *(sufrir)* to bear.

so·por·te m. *(sostén)* support; *(base)* stand.

so·pra·no m.f. soprano.

sor f. RELIG. sister.

sor·ber tr. *(beber)* to sip; *(absorber)* to absorb.

sor·be·te m. sherbet.

sor·bo m. sip <*un s. de vino* a sip of wine>; *(trago)* swallow, gulp.

sor·de·ra f. deafness.

sor·di·dez f. *(suciedad)* squalor; *(vileza)* sordidness.

sór·di·do, a adj. *(sucio)* squalid; *(vil)* sordid.

sor·di·na f. MUS. damper.

sor·do, a I. adj. deaf; *(silencioso)* silent; *(apagado)* muffled; FIG. indifferent; GRAM. voiceless ♦ **a sordas** silently • **quedarse s.** to go deaf • **s. como una tapia** stone deaf II. m.f. *(persona)* deaf person; GRAM. surd ♦ **hacerse el s.** to pretend not to hear.

sor·do·mu·do, a adj. & m.f. deaf-mute.

sor·go m. sorghum.

sor·na f. sarcasm.

so·ro·char·se reflex. AMER., MED. to get mountain sickness.

so·ro·che m. AMER. mountain sickness.

sor·pren·den·te adj. *(admirable)* surprising; *(raro)* unusual.

sor·pren·der tr. *(coger desprevenido)* to take by surprise; *(asombrar)* to surprise; *(descubrir)* to discover —reflex. to be surprised *or* amazed.

sor·pre·sa f. surprise; *(asombro)* amazement ♦ **coger de s.** to take by surprise.

sor·pre·si·vo, a adj. unexpected.

sor·te·ar tr. *(echar a suertes)* to draw lots for; *(rifar)* to raffle; *(evitar)* to avoid.

sor·te·o m. *(acción)* drawing; *(rifa)* raffle ♦ **por s.** by lot.

sor·ti·ja f. *(anillo)* ring; *(de pelo)* ringlet.

sor·ti·le·gio m. *(hechicería)* witchcraft; *(hechizo)* spell ♦ **echar un s.** to cast a spell on.

so·sa f. BOT. saltwort; CHEM. soda ♦ **s. cáustica** caustic soda.

so·se·ga·do, a adj. quiet, peaceful.

so·se·gar §52 tr. & intr. to calm (down) —reflex. to calm down.

so·sie·go m. tranquility, quiet.

sos·la·yar tr. *(poner al soslayo)* to put on a slant; *(evitar)* to sidestep.

sos·la·yo, a I. adj. slanted II. adv. ♦ **al** *or* **de s.** *(oblicuamente)* on a slant; *(de lado)* sideways; *(de pasada)* in passing • **mirar de s.** to look out of the corner of one's eye (at); *(desaprobar)* to look askance (at).

so·so, a adj. *(de poco sabor)* tasteless; *(sin sal)* unsalted; *(zonzo)* dull.

sos·pe·cha f. suspicion.

sos·pe·char tr. to suspect —intr. to be suspicious.

sos·pe·cho·so, a adj. & m.f. suspicious (person).

sos·tén¹ see **sostener.**

sos·tén² m. *(acción)* sustenance; *(apoyo)* support; *(prenda)* bra ♦ **s. de familia** breadwinner.

sos·ten·drá, dría see **sostener.**

sos·te·ne·dor, ·ra I. adj. supporting II. m.f. supporter.

sos·te·ner §69 tr. *(sustentar)* to support; *(sujetar)* to hold (up); *(mantener)* to keep up; *(defender)* to uphold; *(apoyar)* to back —reflex. *(mantenerse parado)* to hold oneself up; *(mantenerse)* to support oneself; *(continuar)* to continue.

sos·te·ni·do, a I. adj. *(continuo)* sustained; MUS. sharp II. m. MUS. sharp.

sos·te·ni·mien·to m. *(apoyo)* support; *(mantenimiento)* maintenance; *(sustento)* sustenance.

sos·tie·ne, tuviera, tuvo see **sostener**.

so·ta·na f. soutane.

só·ta·no m. basement.

so·ta·ven·to m. MARIT. leeward ♦ **a s.** to leeward.

so·to m. *(arboleda)* grove; *(matorral)* thicket.

soy see **ser**.

Sr. m. [abbr. of **Señor**] Mr.

Sra. f. [abbr. of **Señora**] Mrs.

stan·dard adj. & m. standard ♦ **s. de vida** standard of living.

su, sus adj. one's, his, her, your, its, their.

sua·ve adj. soft; *(liso)* smooth; *(dulce)* sweet; *(tranquilo)* gentle.

sua·vi·dad f. softness; *(lisura)* smoothness; *(dulzura)* sweetness; *(tranquilidad)* gentleness.

sua·vi·za·dor, ·ra I. adj. softening II. m. razor strop.

sua·vi·zar §04 tr. to soften; *(hacer plano)* to smooth; *(moderar)* to temper —reflex. to soften; *(volver plano)* to become smooth; *(moderarse)* to be tempered.

su·ba f. R.P. rise.

su·ba·cuá·ti·co, a adj. underwater.

su·bal·ter·no, a adj. & m.f. subordinate.

su·ba·rren·da·mien·to n. sublease.

su·ba·rren·dar §49 tr. to sublet.

su·ba·rrien·do m. *(contrato)* sublease; *(precio)* sublease rent.

su·bas·ta f. auction ♦ **en s.** for auction • **sacar a s.** to put up for auction • **vender en s.** to auction off.

su·bas·tar tr. to auction.

sub·co·mi·sión f. subcommittee.

sub·cons·cien·cia f. subconscious mind.

sub·cons·cien·te I. adj. subconscious II. m. subconscious mind.

sub·cu·tá·ne·o, a adj. subcutaneous.

sub·de·sa·rro·lla·do, a adj. underdeveloped.

sub·di·rec·tor, ·ra m.f. assistant manager.

súb·di·to, a I. adj. subject II. m.f. *(de un monarca)* subject; *(ciudadano)* citizen.

sub·di·vi·dir tr. & reflex. to subdivide.

sub·di·vi·sión f. subdivision.

su·bes·ti·mar tr. to underestimate.

sub·go·ber·na·dor, ·ra m.f. lieutenant governor.

su·bi·ba·ja m. seesaw.

su·bi·do, a I. adj. *(fuerte)* deep <*rojo s.* deep red>; *(elevado)* high II. f. *(ascensión)* climb; *(aumento)* increase; *(cuesta)* hill.

su·bir tr. *(escalar)* to climb, go up <*subí la cuesta* I climbed the hill>; *(llevar arriba)* to take *or* carry up; *(levantar, extender)* to raise; *(aumentar)* to raise —intr. *(elevarse)* to rise <*el humo subía* the smoke was rising>; *(ascender)* to go up; *(montar)* to get on *or* into <*sube al coche* get into the car>; *(cabalgar)* to mount; *(crecer)* to rise; *(alcanzar)* to come *or* amount to <*la cuenta sube a cincuenta dólares* the bill comes to fifty dollars>; *(aumentar)* to rise <*los precios han subido* prices have risen>; *(en un empleo)* to be promoted; *(agravarse)* to get worse <*le subió la fiebre* his fever got worse>; MUS. to raise the pitch ♦ **s. al trono** to ascend to the throne • **s. de punto** to increase • **s. de tono** *(sonido)* to get louder; *(conversación)*

to become heated —reflex. *(ascender)* to go up; *(montar)* to get on *or* into <*el niño se subió al tren* the little boy got on the train> ♦ **subírsele a uno a la cabeza** to go to one's head.

sú·bi·ta·men·te adv. suddenly.

sú·bi·to, a I. adj. *(imprevisto)* sudden; *(precipitado)* hasty ♦ **de s.** suddenly, all of a sudden II. adv. suddenly.

sub·je·fe m. assistant manager.

sub·je·ti·vi·dad f. subjectivity.

sub·je·ti·vo, a adj. & m. subjective.

sub·jun·ti·vo, a adj. & m. subjunctive.

su·ble·va·ción f./**mien·to** m. uprising.

su·ble·var tr. *(agitar)* to incite to rebellion; *(enojar)* to annoy —reflex. to revolt.

su·bli·ma·ción f. sublimation.

su·bli·mar tr. to sublimate —reflex. to be sublimated.

su·bli·me adj. sublime.

sub·ma·ri·no, a adj. & m. submarine.

su·bo·fi·cial adj. MIL. non-commissioned *or* warrant officer; MARIT. petty officer.

su·bor·di·na·ción f. subordination.

su·bor·di·na·do, a adj. & m.f. subordinate.

su·bor·di·nar tr. to subordinate —intr. to become subordinate.

sub·pro·duc·to m. by-product.

su·bra·ya·do m. underlining.

su·bra·yar tr. *(señalar)* to underline, *(poner énfasis)* to emphasize.

su·brep·ti·cio, a adj. surreptitious.

su·bro·gar §47 tr. LAW to subrogate.

sub·sa·nar tr. to correct.

subs·cri·bir §80 tr. *(documento)* to sign; *(idea, moción)* to subscribe to; COM. to underwrite —reflex. to subscribe *(a to).*

subs·crip·ción f. subscription.

subs·crip·tor, ·ra m.f. subscriber.

sub·se·cre·ta·rí·a f. *(oficio)* undersecretaryship, *(oficina)* undersecretary's office.

sub·se·cre·ta·rio, a m.f. *(en una oficina)* assistant secretary; *(de un ministro)* undersecretary.

sub·se·cuen·te adj. subsequent.

sub·si·diar tr. to subsidize.

sub·si·dia·rio, a adj. subsidiary; LAW ancillary.

sub·si·dio m. *(subvención)* subsidy; *(ayuda)* aid.

sub·si·guien·te adj. subsequent.

sub·sis·ten·cia f. *(vida)* subsistence; *(provisión)* sustenance.

sub·sis·ten·te adj. subsistent.

sub·sis·tir intr. *(vivir)* to subsist; *(permanecer)* to remain.

subs·tan·cia f. substance; *(materia)* matter; *(esencia)* essence; *(jugo)* extract; *(juicio)* sense.

subs·tan·cia·ción f. substantiation.

subs·tan·cial adj. substantial.

subs·tan·cial·men·te adv. *(en substancia)* substantially; *(esencialmente)* essentially.

subs·tan·ciar tr. to substantiate.

subs·tan·cio·so, a adj. substantial.

subs·tan·ti·va·ción f. substantivation.

subs·tan·ti·var tr. to substantivate.

subs·tan·ti·vo, a I. adj. substantive II. m. noun.

subs·ti·tu·ción f. substitution.

subs·ti·tuir §18 tr. to substitute.

subs·ti·tu·ti·vo, a adj. & m. substitute.

subs·ti·tu·to, a m.f. replacement; THEAT. understudy.

subs·trac·ción f. *(acción)* taking away; *(deduc-*

ción) deduction; *(robo)* theft; MATH. subtraction.

subs·tra·en·do m. subtrahend.

subs·tra·er §72 tr. *(quitar)* to take away; *(deducir)* to deduce; *(robar)* to steal; MATH. to subtract —reflex. to avoid.

subs·tra·to m. substratum; PHILOS. essence.

sub·sue·lo m. basement; GEOL. subsoil.

sub·te m. R.P., COLL. subway.

sub·te·nien·te m. second lieutenant.

sub·ter·fu·gio m. subterfuge.

sub·te·rrá·ne·o, a I. adj. underground II. m. *(lugar)* underground place; AMER. *(tren)* subway.

sub·tí·tu·lo m. subtitle.

su·bur·ba·no, a I. adj. suburban II. m.f. suburbanite.

su·bur·bio m. *(arrabal)* suburb; *(barrio pobre)* slum.

sub·ven·ción f. subsidy.

sub·ven·cio·nar tr. to subsidize.

sub·ver·sión f. *(acción)* subversion; *(revolución)* revolution.

sub·ver·si·vo, a adj. subversive.

sub·ya·cen·te adj. underlying.

sub·yu·ga·dor, ·ra I. adj. subjugating; FIG. captivating II. m.f. subjugator; FIG. captivator.

sub·yu·gar §47 tr. to subjugate; FIG. to captivate.

suc·ción f. suction.

su·ce·dá·ne·o, a adj. & m. substitute.

su·ce·der intr. *(reemplazar)* to succeed; *(ocurrir)* to occur —reflex. to follow one another.

su·ce·di·do m. COLL. event.

su·ce·sión f. succession; *(herederos)* heirs; *(herencia)* inheritance.

su·ce·si·va·men·te adv. successively ♦ **y así s.** and so on.

su·ce·si·vo, a adj. consecutive ♦ **en lo s.** in the future.

su·ce·so m. event; *(transcurso)* course; *(resultado)* outcome.

su·ce·sor, ·ra I. adj. succeeding II. m.f. successor; *(heredero)* heir.

su·cie·dad f. *(mugre)* dirt; *(inmundicia)* filth.

su·cin·to, a adj. succinct.

su·cio, a adj. *(no limpio)* dirty; *(asqueroso)* filthy; *(vil)* vile; *(deshonesto)* indecent.

su·cre m. ECUAD., FIN. sucre.

su·cu·len·cia f. succulence.

su·cu·len·to, a adj. succulent.

su·cum·bir intr. to succumb.

su·cur·sal I. adj. branch II. f. *(oficina)* branch (office); *(de empresa)* subsidiary.

sud m. south.

su·dar intr. to sweat; FIG. to work hard; *(empapar en sudor)* to sweat; FIG. to work hard for; BOT. to ooze ♦ **s. la gota gorda** COLL. to be dripping with sweat; FIG. to work hard.

su·da·rio m. shroud.

su·des·ta·da f. R.P. rainy southeast wind.

su·des·te m. southeast.

su·do·es·te m. southwest.

su·dor m. sweat ♦ **con el s. de la frente** by the sweat of one's brow.

su·do·rí·fe·ro/fi·co, a I. adj. sudoriferous II. m. sudorific.

su·do·ro·so, a adj. sweaty.

sue·gra f. mother-in-law.

sue·gro m. father-in-law ♦ pl. in-laws.

sue·la f. sole; *(cuero)* tanned leather; TECH. washer ♦ **media s.** half sole ♦ **un pícaro de**

siete suelas COLL. an out-and-out rascal.

sue·la, lo see **soler.**

suel·de, do see **soldar.**

suel·do m. salary ♦ **a s.** on a salary.

sue·lo m. *(tierra)* ground; *(terreno)* soil; *(territorio)* land; *(piso)* floor; *(pavimento)* pavement; *(tierra)* earth, world ♦ **estar por los suelos** COLL. to be dirt cheap ♦ **s. natal** homeland ♦ **venir** or **venirse al s.** to fall down, collapse; FIG. to fail.

suel·te, to see **soltar.**

suel·to, a I. adj. loose; *(desatado)* untied; *(que no hace juego)* odd; *(ágil)* nimble; *(atrevido)* daring ♦ **s. de lengua** *(charlatán)* loose-tongued; *(insolente)* sharp-tongued ♦ **venderse s.** *(por peso)* to be sold in bulk; *(por separado)* to be sold singly II. m. *(artículo)* insert; *(dinero)* loose change.

sue·ne, no see **sonar².**

sue·ñe, ño see **soñar.**

sue·ño m. *(acto)* sleep; *(representación)* dream; *(adormecimiento)* drowsiness; *(ilusión)* dream; *(encanto)* dream <este bebé es un s. this baby is a dream> ♦ **caerse de s.** to be falling asleep on one's feet ♦ **dar s.** to make sleepy ♦ **echar un s.** to take a nap ♦ **entre sueños** while half asleep ♦ **ni en** or **por sueños** not even in one's dreams ♦ **no poder conciliar el s.** not to be able to sleep ♦ **perder el s. por algo** to lose sleep over something ♦ **quitar el s.** to keep awake ♦ **s. dorado** life's dream ♦ **s. hecho realidad** dream come true ♦ **s. pesado** heavy sleep ♦ **tener el s. liviano** to be a light sleeper ♦ **tener s.** to be sleepy.

sue·ro m. serum; *(de la leche)* whey.

suer·te f. *(destino)* fate; *(fortuna)* luck; *(condición)* lot <mejorar la s. del pueblo to improve the lot of the people>; *(género)* kind ♦ **buena s.** good luck ♦ **caerle** or **tocarle a uno en s.** to fall to one's lot ♦ **dar** or **traer s.** to bring luck ♦ **de otra s.** otherwise ♦ **de s. que** in a way that ♦ **echar suertes** to draw lots ♦ **estar de mala s.** to be out of luck ♦ **estar de s.** to be in luck ♦ **la s. está echada** the die is cast ♦ **por s.** *(por casualidad)* by chance; *(por fortuna)* luckily ♦ **s. negra** very bad luck ♦ **tener s.** to be lucky.

sué·ter m. sweater.

su·fi·cien·cia f. *(aptitud)* competence; COLL. *(presunción)* smugness.

su·fi·cien·te adj. *(bastante)* sufficient; *(presumido)* pedantic.

su·fi·jo m. suffix.

su·fra·gar §47 tr. to pay (for) —intr. AMER. to vote.

su·fra·gio m. *(derecho)* suffrage; *(voto)* vote.

su·fra·gis·ta POL. m.f. suffragist —f. suffragette.

su·fri·do, a adj. patient.

su·fri·mien·to m. suffering.

su·frir tr. *(padecer)* to suffer; *(experimentar)* to undergo; *(soportar)* to endure —intr. *(padecer)* to suffer; *(preocuparse)* to worry ♦ **s. de** to suffer from.

su·ge·ren·cia f. suggestion.

su·ge·rir §65 tr. to suggest.

su·ges·tión f. suggestion.

su·ges·tio·nar tr. *(influenciar)* to influence; *(hipnotizar)* to hypnotize.

su·ges·ti·vo, a adj. *(sugerente)* suggestive; *(interesante)* appealing.

su·gie·ra, ro, riera, rió see **sugerir.**

sui·ci·da I. adj. suicidal II. m.f. suicide.

sui·ci·diar·se reflex. to commit suicide.

sui·ci·dio m. suicide.

su·je·ción f. (dominación) subjection; (ligadura) fastening ♦ **con s.** a subject to.

su·je·ta·dor, ·ra I. adj. fastening II. m.f. (objeto que sujeta) fastener; (horquilla) clip —m. (sostén) bra.

su·je·ta·li·bros m.inv. bookend.

su·je·ta·pa·pe·les m.inv. paper clip or clamp.

su·je·tar tr. (fijar) to fasten; (agarrar) to grasp; (dominar) to subject ♦ **s. con clavos** to nail down • **s. con grapas** to staple —reflex. (someterse) to subject oneself; (agarrarse) to hang or hold on; (ajustarse) to conform.

su·je·to, a I. see **sujetar** II. adj. (susceptible) subject (a to); (fijado) fastened III. m. subject; COLL. (tipo) individual.

sul·fa·to m. sulfate, sulphate.

sul·fu·ro m. sulfide.

sul·tán, a·na m. sultan —f. sultana.

su·ma f. sum; MATH. (adición) addition; (cantidad) amount of money; FIG. summary ♦ **en s.** in short.

su·ma·men·te adv. extremely.

su·man·do m. addend.

su·mar tr. (resumir) to add (up); (totalizar) to add up to —reflex. to join (in) ♦ **s. a** (añadirse a) to be added to; (agregarse a) to join; (adherirse a) to adhere to.

su·ma·ria·men·te adv. summarily.

su·ma·rio, a I. adj. brief; LAW summary II. m. summary; LAW indictment.

su·mer·gi·ble adj & m. submersible.

su·mer·gir §32 tr. to submerge; FIG. plunge —reflex. to dive, submerge ♦ **s. en** to become immersed or absorbed in.

su·mi·de·ro m. drain.

su·mi·nis·tra·dor, ·ra m.f. supplier.

su·mi·nis·trar tr. to supply.

su·mi·nis·tro m. supply ♦ **s. a domicilio** home delivery.

su·mir tr. to sink, submerge —reflex. (hundirse) to sink; (en duda, depresión) to become immersed.

su·mi·sión f. (acción) submission; (carácter) submissiveness; (obediencia) obedience.

su·mi·so, a adj. (sometido) submissive; (obediente) obedient.

su·mo, a adj. greatest; FIG. enormous ♦ **a lo sumo** at (the) most ♦ **de sumo** completely.

sun·tua·rio, a adj. luxury.

sun·tuo·si·dad f. sumptuousness.

sun·tuo·so, a adj. sumptuous.

su·pe·di·tar tr. to subordinate ♦ **estar supeditado a** to depend on.

su·pe·ra·bun·dan·te adj. superabundant.

su·pe·ra·bun·dar intr. to superabound.

su·pe·ra·ción f. (de dificultad) overcoming; (de uno mismo) self-improvement.

su·pe·rar tr. (sobrepujar) to surpass; (dificultades) to overcome; (adversario) to beat ♦ **estar superado** to be over or finished —reflex. to improve oneself.

su·pe·rá·vit m. [pl. inv. or **s**] surplus.

su·per·che·rí·a f. deceit.

su·per·do·ta·do, a adj. & m.f. exceptionally gifted (child).

su·per·es·truc·tu·ra f. superstructure.

su·per·fi·cial adj. superficial; FIG. shallow.

su·per·fi·cie f. surface; GEOM. area ♦ **salir a la s.** to (come to the) surface.

su·per·fi·no, a adj. extra-fine.

su·per·fluo, a adj. superfluous.

su·per·hom·bre m. superman.

su·pe·rin·ten·den·te m.f. superintendent.

su·pe·rior I. m. superior II. adj. (de más altura) upper <pisos superiores upper floors>; (más alto) higher <enseñanza s. higher education>; (mejor) better; (excelente) superior.

su·pe·rio·ra f. mother superior.

su·pe·rio·ri·dad f. (calidad) superiority; (autoridad) higher authority.

su·per·la·ti·vo, a adj. & m. superlative.

su·per·mer·ca·do m. supermarket.

su·per·nu·me·ra·rio, a adj. & m.f. supernumerary.

su·per·po·bla·ción f. overpopulation.

su·per·po·bla·do, a adj. overpopulated.

su·per·po·ner §54 tr. (poner encima de) to superimpose; (anteponer) to place above or before.

su·per·po·ten·cia f. superpower.

su·per·pro·duc·ción f. overproduction.

su·per·só·ni·co, a adj. supersonic.

su·pers·ti·ción f. superstition.

su·pers·ti·cio·so, a adj. superstitious.

su·per·vi·sar tr. to supervise.

su·per·vi·sión f. supervision.

su·per·vi·sor, ·ra I. adj. supervisory II. m.f. supervisor.

su·per·vi·ven·cia f. survival.

sú·pie·ra, po see saber².

su·pi·no, a I. adj. supine ♦ **ignorancia s.** crass ignorance II. m. supine.

su·plan·tar tr. to supplant.

su·ple·men·tal/ta·rio, a adj. supplemental, supplementary.

su·ple·men·to m. supplement; RAIL., THEAT. supplementary or extra charge.

su·plen·cia f. replacement.

su·plen·te I. adj. (que suple) substitute; SPORT. reserve II. m.f. replacement; SPORT. reserve player; THEAT. understudy.

sú·pli·ca f. (ruego) plea; (petición) request.

su·pli·can·te I. adj. (que ruega) pleading; (que pide) petitioning II. m.f. supplicant.

su·pli·car §70 tr. to implore.

su·pli·cio m. (tortura) torture; (castigo corporal) corporal punishment; (dolor) suffering.

su·plir tr. (compensar) to make up for; (reemplazar) to replace.

su·pón, pondrá, dría see suponer².

su·po·ner¹ m. COLL. supposition.

su·po·ner² §54 tr. (presumir) to suppose; (imaginar) to imagine; (traer consigo) to entail <el proyecto supone grandes gastos the project entails a considerable outlay> ♦ **ser de s.** to be possible or likely.

su·pon·ga, go see suponer².

su·po·si·ción f. supposition; (conjetura) assumption.

su·po·si·to·rio m. suppository.

su·pra·rre·nal adj. suprarenal.

su·pre·ma·cí·a f. supremacy.

su·pre·mo, a adj. supreme; (definitivo) final.

su·pre·sión f. elimination.

su·pri·mir tr. to eliminate.

su·pues·to, a I. see **suponer²** II. adj. (fingido) assumed <nombre s. assumed name>; (que se supone) supposed; (imaginario) imaginary; (hipotético) hypothetical ♦ **dar por s.** to take for granted • **por s.** of course III. m. supposition ♦ **en el s. de que** supposing that.

su·pu·rar intr. to suppurate.

su·pu·sie·ra, so see **suponer²**.
sur m. south.
sur·car §70 tr. AGR. to plow; MARIT. to cut or plow through.
sur·co m. *(en la tierra)* trench; *(en el rostro)* wrinkle.
sur·gir §32 intr. *(surtir)* to shoot up; *(aparecer)* to arise.
sur·me·na·je m. mental strain or fatigue.
su·rrea·lis·ta I. adj. surrealistic II. m.f. surrealist.
sur·ti·do, a I. adj. assorted II. m. selection.
sur·ti·dor, ·ra I. adj. supplying II. m. *(proveedor)* supplier; *(chorro)* spout; *(fuente)* fountain ♦ **s. de gasolina** filling station.
sur·tir tr. to supply ♦ **s. efecto** to have the desired effect —intr. to gush.
sus·cep·ti·bi·li·dad f. susceptibility, sensitivity.
sus·cep·ti·ble/ti·vo, a adj. susceptible; *(quisquilloso)* sensitive.
sus·ci·tar tr. to stir up.
sus·cri·bir §80 tr. & reflex. var. of **subscribir**.
sus·crip·ción f. var. of **subscripción**.
sus·crip·tor, ·ra m.f. var. of **subscriptor, a**.
su·so·di·cho, a adj. abovementioned.
sus·pen·der tr. to suspend; *(colgar)* to hang; *(interrumpir)* to interrupt; *(reprobar)* to fail; LAW to adjourn.
sus·pen·sión f. suspension; LAW adjournment ♦ **s. de hostilidades** cease-fire ♦ **s. de garantías** suspension of constitutional rights.
sus·pen·si·vo, a adj. suspensive ♦ **puntos suspensivos** ellipsis.
sus·pen·so, a I. see **suspender** II. m. EDUC. failing mark ♦ **de s.** suspense <*una película de s.* a suspense movie> ♦ **en s.** pending • **mantener en s.** to keep guessing.
sus·pen·so·res m.pl. AMER. suspenders.
sus·pen·so·rio, a I. adj. suspensory II. m. MED. truss; SPORT. athletic supporter.
sus·pi·ca·cia f. distrust.
sus·pi·caz adj. distrustful.
sus·pi·rar intr. to sigh ♦ **s. por** to long for.
sus·pi·ro m. sigh ♦ **dar** or **exhalar el último s.** to breathe one's last.
sus·tan·cia f. var. of **substancia**.
sus·tan·ti·vo, a adj. & m. var. of **substantivo**.
sus·ten·ta·mien·to m./**ción** f. *(alimento)* sustenance; *(base)* support; AER. lift.
sus·ten·tar tr. *(alimentar)* to sustain; *(apoyar)* to support; *(afirmar)* to uphold —reflex. *(alimentarse)* to nourish oneself; *(mantenerse)* to support oneself ♦ **s. con** or **de** to feed on.
sus·ten·to m. *(alimento)* sustenance; *(apoyo)* support; *(medios)* livelihood ♦ **ganarse el s.** to earn one's living.
sus·ti·tu·ción f. var. of **substitución**.
sus·ti·tuir §18 tr. var. of **substituir**.
sus·ti·tu·to, a adj. & m.f. var. of **substituto, a**.
sus·to m. *(miedo)* scare; *(preocupación)* dread ♦ **caerse del s.** COLL. to be frightened to death • **darse** or **pegarse un s.** COLL. to get a scare • **dar un s. a alguien** to frighten someone.
sus·trac·ción f. var. of **substracción**.
sus·tra·er §72 tr. var. of **substraer**.
su·su·rran·te adj. *(que susurra)* whispering; *(follaje)* rustling.
su·su·rrar intr. *(murmurar)* to whisper; *(el agua)* to murmur; *(hojas)* to rustle —reflex. to be rumored.
su·su·rro m. *(murmullo)* whisper; *(de hojas)*

rustling.
su·til adj. subtle; *(perspicaz)* sharp.
su·ti·le·za/li·dad f. subtlety; *(agudeza)* sharpness.
su·tu·ra f. suture.
su·tu·rar tr. to suture.
su·yo, a I. adj. his, her, your, their <*la casa s. es elegantísima; la nuestra es bastante fea* their house is very elegant; ours is rather ugly>; of his, of hers, of yours, of theirs <*ese amigo s.* that friend of yours> II. pron. his, hers, yours, theirs <*estos libros son suyos* these books are yours> ♦ **hacer de las suyas** COLL. to be up to one's old tricks • **ir a lo s.** to look after one's own interest • **lo s.** one's share • **los suyos** one's friends or family • **salirse con la s.** COLL. to get one's way.
svás·ti·ca f. swastika.

T

t, T f. twenty-third letter of the Spanish alphabet.
ta·ba f. ANAT. anklebone ♦ pl. knucklebones.
ta·ba·cal m. tobacco field.
ta·ba·ca·le·ro, a I. adj. tobacco II. m.f. *(cultivador)* tobacco grower or dealer.
ta·ba·co m. tobacco.
tá·ba·no m. gadfly.
ta·ba·que·rí·a f. tobacco store.
ta·ba·que·ro, a I. adj. tobacco II. m.f. tobacco processor or dealer —f. tobacco box or pouch.
ta·ber·na f. tavern.
ta·ber·ná·cu·lo m. tabernacle.
ta·ber·ne·ro, a m.f. bartender.
ta·bi·que m. partition ♦ **t. nasal** nasal bone.
ta·bla f. *(de madera)* board; *(de mármol)* slab; *(índice)* index; *(lista)* table; *(faja de tierra)* strip of land; PAINT., SEW. panel ♦ **hacer t. rasa de** to disregard • **t. de lavar** washboard • **t. de planchar** ironing board • **t. de salvación** last resort • **t. rasa** tabula rasa ♦ pl. *(empate)* tie; THEAT. boards.
ta·bla·do m. *(tablas)* floorboards; *(plataforma)* wooden platform; THEAT. stage; CRIMIN. execution scaffold.
ta·blao m. SP. stage of flamenco nightclub.
ta·ble·a·do, a I. adj. pleated II. m. pleats.
ta·ble·ar tr. CARP. to divide wood into planks; SEW. to divide into pleats.
ta·ble·ro m. *(tabla)* board; *(en el juego)* board <*t. de ajedrez* chessboard>; *(pizarra)* blackboard; ELEC. switchboard ♦ **poner** or **traer al t.** to risk, stake • **t. contador** abacus • **t. de dibujo** drawing board • **t. de instrumentos** instrument panel; AUTO. dashboard.
ta·ble·ta f. tablet.
ta·ble·te·o m. machine-gun fire.
ta·bli·lla f. *(para anuncios)* bulletin board; *(en billar)* cushion between side pockets; MED. splint.
ta·blón m. thick plank.
ta·bú adj. & m. [pl. -úes] taboo.
ta·bu·la·dor m.f. tabulator.
ta·bu·re·te m. stool.
ta·ca·ñe·ar intr. COLL. to be stingy.
ta·ca·ñe·rí·a f. stinginess.
ta·ca·ño, a I. adj. stingy II. m.f. miser.
ta·ca·zo m. blow (with a billiard cue).
tá·ci·to, a adj. tacit.

ta·ci·tur·no, a adj. taciturn.

ta·co m. (cuña) wedge; (en billar) billiard cue; (canuto) blowpipe; (de papel) pad; (de billetes) book of tickets; ARM. wad; (baqueta) ramrod; (atasco) obstruction; MEX. taco.

ta·cón m. heel.

ta·co·na·zo m. blow with the heel.

ta·co·ne·ar intr. to tap one's heels.

tác·ti·co, a I. adj. tactical II. m.f. tactician —f. tactics.

tác·til adj. tactile.

tac·to m. (sentido) (sense of) touch; (acción) touching; (delicadeza) tact ♦ **al t.** to the touch.

ta·cua·ra f. ARG., BOT. kind of bamboo.

ta·cha f. flaw ♦ **sin t.** upright.

ta·cha² f. large tack.

ta·cha·du·ra f. erasure.

ta·char tr. to cross out ♦ **t. de** to accuse of.

ta·cho m. AMER. can ♦ **irse al t.** R.P., COLL. to fail ♦ **t. de basura** AMER. garbage can.

ta·cho·nar tr. to stud.

ta·chue·la f. tack.

ta·fe·tán m. taffeta.

ta·fi·le·te m. morocco leather.

ta·húr, u·ra m.f. cardsharp.

tai·ma·do, a adj. & m.f. cunning or crafty (person).

ta·ja·da f. slice ♦ **sacar t.** to benefit or profit (de from).

ta·jan·te adj. sharp; FIG. categorical.

ta·jar tr. to slice.

ta·jo m. (corte) cut; (con la espada) slash.

tal I. adj. such (a) <nunca he visto t. cosa I have never seen such a thing>; (cierto) certain <un t. José Gómez te llamó a certain Joseph Gómez called you> ♦ **como si t. cosa** as if there were nothing to it ♦ **t. cual** such as <te lo venderé t. cual es I will sell it to you such as it is> ♦ **t. vez** perhaps, maybe II. pron. such a thing <yo no haría t. I would not do such a thing>; (alguno) some, someone ♦ **fulano de t.** so and so ♦ **t. para cual** COLL. two of a kind III. adv. thus, so ♦ **con t. que** provided that ♦ **¿qué t.?** COLL. how goes it?

ta·la f. (de árboles) felling; (destrucción) destruction, ruin.

ta·la·bar·te·rí·a f. saddlery.

ta·la·bar·te·ro m. saddler.

ta·la·dor, ·ra I. adj. cutting II. m.f. cutter.

ta·la·dra·dor, ·ra I. adj. drilling II. m.f. (persona) driller —f. (máquina) drill.

ta·la·drar tr. to drill ♦ **t. los oídos** to pierce the ears.

ta·la·dro m. (taladradora) drill; (barrena) gimlet; (agujero) drill hole; ENTOM. shipworm.

tá·la·mo m. nuptial bed; ANAT., BOT. thalamus.

ta·lán m. ding dong.

ta·lan·te m. (humor) mood; (voluntad) will ♦ **hacer algo de buen t.** to do something willingly ♦ **hacer algo de mal t.** to do something unwillingly.

ta·lar tr. (un árbol) to fell, cut down; (destruir) to destroy.

tal·co m. talc; PHARM. talcum powder.

ta·le·ga f. (saco) sack; (dinero) wealth.

ta·len·to m. talent.

ta·len·to·so/tu·do, a adj. talented.

ta·lión m. talion ♦ **ley del t.** principle of an eye for an eye.

ta·lis·mán m. talisman.

tal·mud m. Talmud.

tal·mú·di·co, a adj. Talmudic.

ta·lón m. heel; (moldura) talon; (de cubierta) rim; (comprobante) receipt; (de cheque) stub ♦ **pisarle a alguien los talones** FIG. to be at someone's heels.

ta·lo·na·rio m. (de recibos) receipt book; (de cheques) checkbook.

ta·lo·ne·ra f. heel piece.

ta·lla f. (estatura) height; (medida) size; (escultura) wood carving ♦ **tener t. para** to be cut out for.

ta·lla·do, a I. adj. (madera) carved; (metal) engraved; JEWEL. cut ♦ **bien t.** well-built II. m. (en madera) carving; (en metal) engraving; JEWEL. cutting.

ta·lla·dor m. engraver.

ta·llar tr. (madera) to carve; (en metal) to engrave; JEWEL. to cut; ARTS to sculpt.

ta·lla·rín m. noodle.

ta·lle m. (de mujer) figure; (de hombre) physique; (cintura) waist; SEW. bodice.

ta·ller m. (de obreros) shop; (de artistas) studio ♦ **t. de reparaciones** AUTO. body shop.

ta·llo m. stem.

ta·mal m. AMER., CUL. tamale.

ta·man·go m. R.P., COLL. shoe.

ta·ma·ño, a I. adj. (tan grande) so large or big, such a large or big <nunca podremos reembolsar t. deuda we can never repay such a large debt>; (muy grande) very big or wide <abrir tamaños ojos to open one's eyes wide>; (igual) such a II. m. (dimensión) size; (volumen) volume ♦ **del t. de** as large as ♦ **t. natural** life-size.

ta·ma·rin·do m. tamarind.

tam·ba·le·an·te adj. staggering.

tam·ba·le·ar intr. to stagger.

tam·bién adv. (además) also, too; (asimismo) likewise.

tam·bo m. R.P. dairy farm.

tam·bor m. drum; (persona) drummer; ANAT. eardrum; TECH. cylinder; SEW. embroidery frame; (del revólver) cylinder ♦ **a t. batiente** FIG. triumphantly.

tam·bo·ra f. drum.

tam·bo·re·te m. MARIT. cap.

tam·bo·ril m. small drum.

tam·bo·ri·le·ar intr. (el tamboril) to beat; (con los dedos) to tap.

tam·bo·ri·le·o m. beating (of a drum).

tam·bo·ri·le·ro, a m.f. drummer.

ta·miz m. sieve.

ta·mi·zar §04 tr. (con tamiz) to sift; (luz) to filter; FIG. to screen.

tam·po·co adv. neither, nor.

tam·pón m. ink pad; PHARM. tampon.

tam·tam m. tom-tom.

tan adv. so, as <no soy t. alto como Enrique I am not as tall as Henry> ♦ **t. pronto como** as soon as ♦ **t. siquiera** at least ♦ **t. sólo** only.

tan·da f. (turno) turn; (de trabajadores) shift; (capa) layer <una t. de ladrillos a layer of bricks>; COLL. (gran cantidad) bunch.

tan·gen·te adj. & f. tangent ♦ **irse** or **salir por la t.** to go off on a tangent.

tan·gi·ble adj. tangible.

tan·go m. tango.

tan·gue·ar intr. to tango.

ta·ni·no m. tannin.

tan·que m. tank; (barco) tanker.

tan·te·ar tr. (calcular) to do a rough calculation of; (medir) to gauge; (considerar) to consider carefully; (explorar) to test; (sondear) to sound out; (bosquejar) to sketch —intr. to feel one's way.

tan·te·o m. rough calculation ♦ **al t.** roughly.

tan·to, a I. adj. so much, so many <*jamás he visto t. dinero* I have never seen so much money> **II.** pron. that <*a t. arrastra la codicia* that is what greed leads to> ♦ **las tantas** wee hours • **por (lo) t.** therefore • **t. como** or **cuanto** as much as **III.** m. *(cantidad)* certain amount; *(en deportes)* point ♦ **a tantos de** on a certain date in <*a tantos de junio* on a certain date in June> • **en** or **entre t.** in the meantime • **no ser para t.** not to be so bad • **otro t.** the same thing • **t. por ciento** per cent • **y tantos** and some, odd <*mil y tantos* a thousand odd> **IV.** adv. *(de tal modo)* so much <*comí t.* I ate so much>; so long <*tardaron t.* it took them so long>; *(hasta tal grado)* to such an extent ♦ **t. como** as much as • **t. más** all the more • **t. mejor** all the better • **t. que** so much that.

ta·ñer §68 tr. *(instrumento)* to play; *(campana)* to toll.

ta·ñi·do m. tolling.

ta·pa f. *(de olla)* lid; *(de libro)* cover; *(bocado)* hors d'oeuvre ♦ **levantarse la t. de los sesos** COLL. to blow someone's brains out.

ta·pa·do m. coat.

ta·par tr. *(cubrir)* to cover (up); *(cerrar)* to plug up; *(ocultar)* to block; FIG. to conceal —reflex. to cover oneself up.

ta·pa·rra·bo m. loincloth.

ta·pe·te m. *(alfombra)* small rug or carpet; *(de mesa)* table runner ♦ **estar sobre el t.** to be under discussion • **poner sobre el t.** to bring up for discussion.

ta·pia f. *(pared de tierra)* mud or adobe wall; *(cerca)* (adjoining) wall ♦ **más sordo que una t.** COLL. deaf as a post.

ta·pial m. (adjoining) wall.

ta·piar tr. to wall in.

ta·pi·ce·rí·a f. *(de tapices)* tapestry-making; *(de muebles)* upholstery; *(tienda)* upholsterer's shop.

ta·pi·ce·ro, a m.f. *(de tapices)* tapestry maker; *(de muebles)* upholsterer.

ta·pio·ca f. tapioca.

ta·pir m. tapir.

ta·piz m. tapestry.

ta·pi·zar §04 tr. *(adornar)* to hang with tapestries; *(muebles)* to upholster; *(el suelo)* to carpet.

ta·pón m. *(de botellas)* cork; *(de tonel)* plug; SURG. tampon ♦ **t. de desagüe** drain plug.

ta·po·nar tr. *(un agujero)* to plug; SURG. to tampon.

ta·po·na·zo m. pop (of a cork).

ta·pu·jo m. ♦ **andar con tapujos** COLL. to be full of secrecy.

ta·que·ra f. rack for billiard cues.

ta·qui·gra·fí·a f. stenography.

ta·qui·gra·fiar §30 tr. to write in shorthand.

ta·quí·gra·fo, a m.f. stenographer.

ta·qui·lla f. THEAT. *(ventanilla)* box office; *(cantidad)* receipts ♦ **hacer t.** to be a box-office hit.

ta·qui·lle·ro, a I. m.f. ticket agent **II.** adj. ♦ **éxito t.** box-office hit.

ta·ra¹ f. *(peso)* tare; *(defecto)* defect ♦ **tener una t.** COLL. to be an idiot.

ta·ra² f. tally stick.

ta·ra·do, a adj. & m.f. AMER., COLL. idiot.

ta·ram·ba·na f. scatterbrain.

ta·rán·tu·la f. tarantula.

ta·ra·re·ar tr. to hum.

ta·ra·re·o m. humming.

ta·ras·ca·da f. bite.

ta·ras·car §70 tr. to bite.

tar·dan·za f. delay.

tar·dar intr. *(demorarse)* to delay <*no tardes en avisarnos* don't delay in informing us>; *(durar)* to take <*el tren tardó tres horas en llegar* the train took three hours to arrive>; *(tomar tiempo)* to take a long time <*él tardó en contestar* he took a long time to answer>; *(llegar tarde)* to be late ♦ **a más t.** at the latest.

tar·de I. f. afternoon, (early) evening ♦ **buenas tardes** good afternoon **II.** adv. *(a hora avanzada)* late <*nos acostamos t.* we went to bed late>; *(fuera de tiempo)* too late <*el médico llegó t.* the doctor arrived too late> ♦ **a la caída de la t.** at dusk • **hacerse t.** to get late • **lo más t.** at the latest • **más vale t. que nunca** better late than never • **por** or **en la t.** in the afternoon • **t. o temprano** sooner or later.

tar·dí·o, a adj. late; *(lento)* slow.

ta·re·a f. task ♦ **t. escolar** homework.

ta·ri·fa f. *(tasa)* tariff; *(precio)* fare; *(tabla)* price list.

ta·ri·far tr. to apply a tariff or rate to.

ta·ri·ma f. movable platform.

tar·je·ta f. card <*t. de identidad* identity card> ♦ **t. de crédito** credit card • **t. de visita** calling card • **t. perforada** punch card • **t. postal** post card.

tar·je·te·ro m. card case.

tar·quín m. mud.

tar·ra·ja f. MECH. diestock.

ta·rro m. *(vasija)* jar; *(de lata)* tin can ♦ **tener t.** SL. to be lucky.

tar·so m. tarsus.

tar·ta f. pie.

tar·ta·mu·de·ar intr. to stammer.

tar·ta·mu·de·o m./**dez** f. stammering.

tar·ta·mu·do, a I. adj. stammering **II.** m.f. stammerer.

tar·tán m. tartan.

tár·ta·ro, a adj. & m. tartar.

tar·te·ra f. baking pan.

ta·ru·go m. *(clavija)* wooden peg; *(taco)* wooden block; FIG. blockhead.

ta·sa f. rate ♦ **t. aduanera** customs duty.

ta·sa·ción f. appraisal.

ta·sa·dor, ·ra I. adj. appraising **II.** m.f. appraiser.

ta·sa·je·ar tr. AMER., CUL. to jerk.

ta·sa·jo m. jerky.

ta·sar tr. *(poner precio)* to set the price of; *(valorar)* to appraise.

tas·ca f. SL. dive, joint.

tas·car §70 tr. to chomp ♦ **t. el freno** FIG. to chomp at the bit.

ta·ta m. AMER., COLL. daddy.

ta·ta·ra·bue·lo, a m. great-great-grandfather —f. great-great-grandmother ♦ pl. great-great-grandparents.

ta·ta·ra·nie·to, a m. great-great-grandson —f. great-great-granddaughter ♦ pl. great-great-grandchildren.

ta·tua·je m. tattoo.

ta·tuar §67 tr. to tattoo.

tau·ri·no, a adj. taurine.

tau·ro·ma·quia f. bullfighting.

tau·to·lo·gí·a f. tautology.

ta·xi m. taxi.

ta·xi·der·mia f. taxidermy.

ta·xí·me·tro m. *(reloj)* meter; *(vehículo)* taxi.

ta·xis·ta m.f. taxi driver.

ta·xo·no·mí·a f. taxonomy.

ta·za f. cup; *(contenido)* cupful; *(de fuente)* basin; *(de retrete)* bowl.

ta·zón m. large cup.

te pron. you *<te quiero I love you>;* you, to you *<te mandaron una carta they sent a letter to you>;* you, for you *<te compré un regalo I bought a present for you>;* from you *<no le dejes quitarte la pelota don't let him take the ball from you>;* yourself *<cálmate calm yourself>.*

té m. tea ♦ **t. del Paraguay** maté.

te·a f. torch.

te·a·tral adj. theatrical.

te·a·tra·li·dad f. theatricality.

te·a·tro m. theater.

te·cla f. key ♦ **dar en la t.** COLL. to hit the nail on the head.

te·cla·do m. keyboard.

te·cle·a·do m. fingering.

te·cle·ar intr. *(las teclas)* to finger a keyboard; COLL. *(los dedos)* to drum with the fingers; *(el piano)* to play the piano; FIG. to be doing poorly.

te·cle·o m. drumming with the fingers.

téc·ni·co, a I. adj. technical II. m.f. *(especialista)* technician; *(ingeniero)* engineer ♦ **t. agrícola** agronomist • **t. electricista** electrical engineer —f. *(método, habilidad)* technique; *(tecnología)* technology; *(ingeniería)* engineering ♦ **t. electrónica** electronics.

tec·no·cra·cia f. technocracy.

tec·no·lo·gí·a f. technology.

tec·no·ló·gi·co, a adj. technological.

te·cha·do m. *(techo)* roof; *(cobertizo)* shed ♦ **bajo t.** indoors.

te·cha·dor m. roofer.

te·char tr. to roof.

te·cho m. *(tejado)* roof; *(parte interior)* ceiling; AVIA. ceiling ♦ **no tener t.** not to have a roof over one's head.

te·dio m. tedium.

te·dio·so, a adj. tedious.

te·gu·men·to m. tegument.

te·ja f. *(mosaico)* tile; *(de techo)* slate.

te·ja·do m. roof ♦ **empezar la casa por el t.** to put the cart before the horse.

te·jar¹ m. brick or tile factory.

te·jar² tr. to tile.

te·je·dor, ·ra I. adj. weaving II. m.f. weaver —m. weaverbird —f. AMER. weaving machine.

te·je·ma·ne·je m. COLL. intrigue.

te·jer intr. *(con telar)* to weave; *(hacer punto)* to knit.

te·ji·do m. *(tela)* fabric; *(textura)* weave; ANAT., BIOL. tissue ♦ **t. de alambre** wire mesh • **t. de punto** jersey.

te·jo m. *(para jugar)* chip; *(juego)* quoits; *(de metal)* metal disk; MEX., TECH. step bearing; BOT. yew tree.

te·jón¹ m. ZOOL. badger.

te·jón² m. gold ingot or disk.

te·la f. *(paño)* fabric; *(membrana)* membrane; *(nata)* film; *(de araña)* web; ANAT. film; BOT. skin; ARTS *(lienzo)* canvas; *(pintura)* painting ♦ **poner en t. de juicio** to call into question • **t. adhesiva** adhesive tape • **t. aislante** electrical tape • **t. metálica** wire netting.

te·lar m. TEX. loom; *(de puerta)* frame; BKB. sewing press ♦ **en el t.** in the making.

te·la·ra·ña f. spider web ♦ pl. **tener t. en los ojos** COLL. to have blinders on.

te·le·co·mu·ni·ca·ción f. telecommunication.

te·le·di·fun·dir tr. to telecast.

te·le·di·fu·sión f. telecast.

te·le·di·ri·gi·do, a adj. remote-controlled.

te·le·di·ri·gir §32 tr. to guide by remote control.

te·le·fo·na·zo m. COLL. phone call.

te·le·fo·ne·ar tr. to phone.

te·le·fo·ní·a f. telephony.

te·le·tó·ni·ca·men·te adv. by phone.

te·le·fó·ni·co, a adj. phone ♦ **cabina t.** phone booth • **guía t.** telephone directory.

te·le·fo·nis·ta m.f. telephone operator.

te·lé·fo·no m. telephone.

te·le·fo·to m. telephoto.

te·le·fo·to·gra·fí·a f. telephotography.

te·le·gra·fí·a f. telegraphy.

te·le·gra·fiar §30 tr. to telegraph.

te·le·grá·fi·co, a adj. telegraphic.

te·le·gra·fis·ta m.f. telegrapher.

te·lé·gra·fo m. telegraph.

te·le·gra·ma m. telegram.

te·le·guia·do, a adj. remote-controlled.

te·le·im·pre·sor m. teleprinter.

te·le·man·do m. remote control.

te·le·me·trí·a f. telemetry.

te·le·ob·je·ti·vo m. telephoto lens.

te·le·pa·tí·a f. telepathy.

te·le·pá·ti·co, a adj. telepathic.

te·les·có·pi·co, a adj. telescopic.

te·les·co·pio m. telescope.

te·les·pec·ta·dor, ·ra m.f. television viewer.

te·le·ti·po m. teletype.

te·le·vi·den·te m.f. television viewer.

te·le·vi·sar tr. to televise.

te·le·vi·sión f. television.

te·le·vi·sor m. television (set).

té·lex m. télex.

te·lón m. THEAT. curtain; MEX. riddle ♦ **t. de boca** drop curtain • **t. de fondo** backdrop.

te·lú·ri·co, a adj. telluric.

te·lu·rio m. tellurium.

te·ma m. *(asunto)* subject; *(escrito)* composition; *(idea fija)* obsession; MUS. theme.

te·ma·rio m. agenda.

te·má·ti·co, a I. adj. *(del tema)* thematic; *(terco)* obstinate II. f. subject.

tem·bla·de·ra f. *(acción)* trembling fit; *(vasija)* thin two-handled cup.

tem·blar §49 intr. *(temblequear)* to tremble; *(tener miedo)* to be afraid ♦ **t. de frío** to shiver with cold • **t. de miedo** to quiver with fear.

tem·ble·que m. *(persona)* trembler; *(terremoto)* earthquake.

tem·ble·que·ar intr. to tremble.

tem·blor m. tremor; AMER. earthquake ♦ **t. de tierra** earthquake.

tem·blo·(ro·)so, a adj. shaking.

te·mer tr. & intr. to fear ♦ **t. a** to be afraid of • **t. por** to fear for.

te·me·ra·rio, a adj. reckless.

te·me·ri·dad f. temerity.

te·me·ro·so, a adj. *(temible)* frightening; *(tímido)* timid.

te·mi·ble adj. frightful.

te·mor m. *(miedo)* fear; *(presunción)* foreboding.

tém·pa·no m. *(de hielo)* iceberg; *(tapa de tonel)* barrel head.

tem·pe·ra·men·tal adj. temperamental.

tem·pe·ra·men·to m. *(naturaleza)* temperament; *(temperie)* weather.

tem·pe·ran·cia f. temperance.

tem·pe·rar tr. *(calmar)* to calm; *(moderar)* to temper.

tem·pe·ra·tu·ra f. temperature.

tem·pes·tad f. storm ♦ **t. en un vaso de agua** tempest in a teapot.

tem·pes·tuo·so, a adj. stormy.

tem·pla·do, a adj. *(moderado)* moderate; *(tibio)* lukewarm; *(el clima)* mild.

tem·plan·za f. *(sobriedad)* temperance; *(moderación)* moderation; *(del clima)* mildness.

tem·plar tr. *(moderar)* to temper; *(la temperatura)* to make lukewarm; METAL. to temper; MUS. to tune; *(mitigar)* to mitigate; *(apaciguar)* to appease —intr. to warm up.

tem·ple m. *(de metales)* temper; *(indole)* nature; *(disposición)* mood <**estar de buen t.** to be in a good mood>; *(valentía)* courage.

tem·plo m. temple.

tem·po·ra·da f. *(del año)* season; *(período)* period ♦ **de fuera de t.** off-season • **por temporadas** off and on • **t. baja** off season.

tem·po·ral I. adj. *(pasajero)* temporary; *(secular)* temporal II. m. *(tempestad)* storm; *(lluvia persistente)* rainy spell.

tem·po·rá·ne·o/ra·rio, a adj. temporary.

tem·pra·ne·ro, a adj. early ♦ **ser t.** to be an early riser.

tem·pra·no, a adj. & adv. early.

ten see **tener**.

te·na·ci·dad f. tenacity.

te·naz adj. tenacious.

te·na·za(s) f.(pl.) *(herramienta)* pliers; ZOOL. pincers; *(del fuego)* tongs; MED. forceps ♦ **t. de rizar** curling iron.

ten·de·de·ro m. clothesline.

ten·den·cia f. *(propensión)* tendency; *(de moda, mercado)* trend.

ten·den·cio·so, a adj. tendentious.

ten·der §50 tr. *(extender)* to spread (out); *(alargar)* to stretch out <**me tendió la mano** he stretched out his hand to me>; *(ropa)* to hang out; *(cable)* to lay; *(puente)* to build —intr. to tend *(a* to) —reflex. to lie down.

ten·de·ro, a m.f. shopkeeper.

ten·di·do, a I. adj. *(extendido)* stretched *or* spread out; EQUIT. full II. m. *(acción)* spreading; *(ropa)* load of wash.

ten·dien·te adj. AMER. tending.

ten·dón m. tendon.

ten·drá, dría see **tener**.

te·ne·bro·so, a adj. *(sombrío)* dark; *(secreto)* shady; *(oscuro)* obscure.

te·ne·dor, ·ra m.f. *(poseedor)* owner; COM. bearer —m. fork ♦ **t. de acciones** stockholder • **t. de libros** bookkeeper.

te·ne·du·rí·a f. bookkeeping.

te·nen·cia f. possession.

te·ner §69 tr. to have; *(poseer)* to possess; *(asir)* to take hold of <**ten el cable** take hold of the rope>; *(contener)* to contain; *(mantener)* to maintain; *(considerar)* to consider <**tuvo a menos trabajar en tal cosa** he considered it beneath her to work on anything like that>; to be <**tiene sesenta años de edad** he is sixty years of age>; *(cumplir)* to keep, fulfill ♦ **no t. sobre qué caerse muerto** not to have a cent to one's name • **t. a bien** to see fit to • **t. calor, frío** to be hot, cold • **t. celos** to be jealous • **t. cuidado** to be careful • **t. en cuenta** to take into account • **t. en mucho** to esteem • **t. en poco** to think little of • **t. éxito** to succeed • **t. ganas de** to feel like • **t. hambre, sed** to be hungry, thirsty • **t. la bondad de** to be kind enough to • **t. la culpa** to be to blame • **t. lugar** to take place • **t. miedo** to be afraid • **t. mucho de** to resemble • **t. por** to think <**lo tengo por sabio** I consider him wise> • **t. presente** to bear in mind • **t. prisa** to be in a hurry • **t. que** to have to <**tenemos que hacerlo** we have to do it> • **t. que ver con** to have to do with • **t. razón** to be right • **t. sueño** to be sleepy • **t. suerte** to be lucky —intr. to be well-off —reflex. to steady oneself ♦ **t. de pie** to stand up • **t. por** to consider oneself.

te·nia f. tapeworm.

te·nien·te m. lieutenant; *(sustituto)* substitute, deputy.

te·nis m. tennis ♦ **t. de mesa** Ping-Pong.

te·nis·ta m.f. tennis player.

te·nor¹ m. tenor; tone ♦ **a t. de** in accordance with.

te·nor² m. MUS. tenor.

te·no·rio m. Don Juan.

ten·sar tr. to stretch.

ten·sión f. tension; *(emocional)* stress ♦ **t. arterial** blood pressure.

ten·so, a adj. *(tirante)* tense; *(nervios, situación)* strained; *(emocionalmente)* stressed.

ten·sor, ·ra I. adj. tensile II. m. *(aparato)* tightener; TECH. turnbuckle.

ten·ta·ción f. temptation.

ten·tá·cu·lo m. tentacle.

ten·ta·dor, ·ra I. adj. tempting II. m. tempter.

ten·tar §49 tr. *(palpar)* to grope; *(seducir)* to tempt; *(intentar)* to try.

ten·ta·ti·vo, a I. adj. tentative II. f. attempt ♦ **t. de delito** LAW attempted crime.

te·nue adj. *(delgado)* thin; *(luz)* soft.

te·ñir §59 tr. to dye; PAINT. to darken; FIG. to imbue.

te·o·cra·cia f. theocracy.

te·o·lo·gí·a f. theology.

te·ó·lo·go, a m.f. theologian.

te·o·re·ma m. theorem.

te·o·ré·ti·co, a adj. theoretical.

te·o·rí·a f. theory.

te·ó·ri·co, a I. adj. theoretical II. m.f. theoretician.

te·o·ri·zar §04 tr. to theorize.

te·o·so·fí·a f. theosophy.

te·ó·so·fo, a m.f. theosophist.

te·qui·la f. tequila.

te·ra·peu·ta m.f. therapist.

te·ra·péu·ti·co, a I. adj. therapeutic II. f. therapy.

te·ra·pia f. therapy.

ter·cer adj. contr. of **tercero**.

ter·cer·mun·dis·ta adj. third-worldist.

ter·ce·ro, a I. adj. third <**ella vive en la t. casa a la derecha** she lives in the third house on the right> II. m. *(mediador)* mediator; LAW third party —f. MUS. third; AUTO. third gear.

ter·ce·to m. POET. tercet; MUS. trio.

ter·cia·do, a adj. *(azúcar)* brown; *(atravesado)* crosswise.

ter·ciar tr. to place diagonally across —intr. *(interponerse)* to mediate; *(participar)* to take part <**t. en una conversación** to take part in a conversation>; *(completar)* to fill in.

ter·cio, a adj. & num. third.

ter·cio·pe·lo m. velvet.

ter·co, a adj. stubborn.

ter·gi·ver·sa·ción f. distortion.

ter·gi·ver·sar tr. to distort.

ter·mal adj. thermal.

ter·mas f.pl. hot baths *or* springs.

ter·mi·na·ción f. ending.

ter·mi·nal I. adj. terminal **II.** m. ELEC. terminal —f. *(estación)* terminal.

ter·mi·nan·te adj. definite.

ter·mi·nar tr. *(poner término)* to end; *(acabar)* to complete —intr. *(tener término)* to come to an end ◆ **t. de** *(acabar de)* to have just; *(concluir)* to finish <*terminamos de comer* we finished eating> • **t. en** to end up in • **t. por** to end up <*terminó por marcharse enfadado* he ended up going away angry> —reflex. to come to an end.

tér·mi·no m. *(conclusión)* end; *(palabra, tiempo)* term; *(límite)* boundary; LOG., MATH. term ◆ **dar t. a** to finish off • **en buenos términos con** on good terms with • **en último t.** in the last analysis • **llevar a t.** to carry out • **poner t. a** to put an end to • **por t. medio** on the average • **t. medio** MATH. average; *(compromiso)* middle ground.

ter·mi·no·lo·gí·a f. terminology.

ter·mi·ta f. termite.

ter·mo m. thermos (bottle).

ter·mo·di·ná·mi·ca f. thermodynamics.

ter·mo·e·léc·tri·co, a adj. thermoelectric.

ter·mó·me·tro m. thermometer.

ter·mo·nu·cle·ar adj. thermonuclear.

ter·mo·rre·gu·la·dor m. thermostat.

ter·mos·ta·to m. thermostat.

ter·na f. *(lista)* list of three candidates; *(en dados)* pair of three.

ter·ne·ra f. *(animal)* female calf; *(carne)* veal.

ter·ne·ro m. male calf.

ter·no m. *(tres)* set of three; *(vestido)* three-piece suit; *(en lotería)* set of three numbers.

ter·nu·ra f. tenderness.

ter·que·dad f. stubbornness.

te·rra·co·ta f. terra cotta.

te·rra·mi·ci·na f. terramycin.

te·rra·plén m. embankment.

te·rra·ple·nar tr. *(llenar)* to fill up with earth; *(hacer terraplén)* to embank.

te·rrá·que·o, a adj. terrestrial ◆ **globo t.** the earth.

te·rra·te·nien·te m. landowner.

te·rra·za f. *(balcón)* terrace; *(azotea)* roof terrace; *(de un café)* veranda.

te·rre·mo·to m. earthquake.

te·rre·nal adj. earthly.

te·rre·no, a I. adj. *(terrestre)* earthly; *(terrenal)* worldly **II.** m. *(tierra)* land; *(campo)* piece of land; *(suelo)* ground; GEOL. terrain; SPORT. field ◆ **preparar el t.** to pave the way • **reconocer el t.** to get the lay of the land • **t. conocido** familiar territory.

te·rres·tre adj. terrestrial.

te·rri·ble adj. terrible.

te·rrí·co·la m.f. earthling.

te·rri·to·rial adj. territorial.

te·rri·to·rio m. territory; *(comarca)* zone.

te·rrón m. *(de tierra)* clod; *(de azúcar)* lump.

te·rror m. terror.

te·rro·rí·fi·co, a adj. terrifying.

te·rro·ris·ta adj. & m.f. terrorist.

te·rru·ño m. *(tierra)* land; *(país)* native land.

ter·so, a adj. *(limpio)* clear; *(estilo)* smooth.

ter·tu·lia f. *(reunión)* social gathering; THEAT.

upper gallery ◆ **t. literaria** literary circle.

te·sis f.inv. thesis; *(opinión)* theory.

te·si·tu·ra f. tessitura; *(actitud)* frame of mind.

te·són m. tenacity.

te·so·ne·ro, a adj. tenacious.

te·so·re·rí·a f. treasury.

te·so·re·ro, a m.f. COM. treasurer —m. RELIG. custodian.

te·so·ro m. *(dinero)* treasure; *(fondos públicos)* treasury; FIG. gem.

tes·ta f. head.

tes·ta·dor, ·ra m.f. testator.

tes·ta·fe·rro m. figurehead.

tes·ta·men·ta·rio, a I. adj. testamentary **II.** m. executor —f. executrix.

tes·ta·men·to m. will ◆ **Antiguo T.** Old Testament • **Nuevo T.** New Testament.

tes·tar intr. to make a will.

tes·ta·ru·do, a adj. & m.f. stubborn (person).

tes·te m. testicle.

tes·tí·cu·lo m. testicle.

tes·ti·fi·car §70 tr. to testify (to).

tes·ti·go m.f. witness ◆ **t. de cargo** witness for the prosecution • **t. de descargo** witness for the defense • **t. ocular** eyewitness —m. FIG. proof.

tes·ti·mo·niar tr. to testify (to).

tes·ti·mo·nio m. testimony; *(atestación)* affidavit; FIG. token ◆ **falso t.** perjury.

tes·tuz m. *(frente)* forehead; *(nuca)* nape.

te·ta f. *(pecho)* breast; *(de vaca)* udder; *(pezón)* nipple ◆ **dar la t. a** to nurse • **niño de t.** nursing infant • **quitar la t. a** to wean.

té·ta·no(s) m. tetanus.

te·te·ra f. teapot.

te·ti·lla f. *(de mamíferos)* teat; *(de biberón)* nipple.

te·tra·e·dro m. tetrahedron.

té·tri·co, a adj. gloomy.

tex·til adj. & m. textile.

tex·to m. *(contenido)* text; *(libro)* textbook.

tex·tual adj. textual.

tex·tu·ra f. texture.

tez f. complexion.

ti pron. you <*lo compré para ti* I bought it for you>; yourself <*hazlo para ti* do it for yourself>

tí·a f. aunt; COLL. *(mujer cualquiera)* dame ◆ **cuéntaselo a tu t.** COLL. tell it to the marines • **no hay tu tí.** COLL. no use • **t. abuela** great-aunt.

tia·ra f. tiara.

ti·bia f. tibia.

ti·bio, a adj. lukewarm.

ti·bu·rón m. shark.

tic m. tic.

tic·tac *or* **tic tac** m. ticking.

tiem·ble, blo see **temblar.**

tiem·po m. time; *(época)* times <*en t. de Napoleón* in the times of Napoleon>; *(ocasión)* moment; *(estación)* season; METEOROL. weather ◆ **al mismo t.** at the same time • **al t. que** just as • **andando el t.** in the course of time • **a su t.** in due time • **a t.** in *or* on time • **cargarse el t.** to become overcast • **con t.** *(por adelantado)* in advance; *(en el momento oportuno)* in good time • **dar t. al t.** to bide one's time • **de algún t. a esta parte** for some time now • **de t.** from time to time • **en los buenos tiempos** in the good old days • **en t. de Maricastaña** COLL. in olden times • **fuera de t.** at the wrong time • **ganar t.** to save time • **perder el t.** to

waste time • **t. atrás** some time ago.
tien·da f. dress shop ♦ **ir de tiendas** to go shopping • **t. de campaña** tent • **t. de modas** boutique.
tien·da, do see tender.
tie·ne see tener.
tien·ta f. ♦ **a tientas** gropingly • **andar a tientas** to feel one's way.
tien·te, to see tentar.
tien·to m. *(tacto)* touch; *(palo de ciego)* blindman's cane; *(balancín)* balancing pole; *(pulso)* steady hand; *(prudencia)* caution; *(correa)* leather strip ♦ **con t.** cautiously.
tier·no, a adj. *(afectuoso)* loving; *(blando)* soft; tender <*carne t.* tender meat>.
tie·rra f. *(superficie)* land <*viajar por t.* to travel by land>; *(suelo)* ground; *(patria)* country; *(comarca)* region; *(campo)* land <*t. de cultivo* arable land>; ELEC. ground ♦ **caer a t.** to fall down • **dar en t. con** to knock down • **poner t. de por medio** to make oneself scarce • **T.** Earth • **t. adentro** inland • **t. de nadie** FIG., no man's land • **venir(se) a t.** to collapse.
tie·so, a adj. *(rígido)* stiff; *(estirado)* arrogant.
ties·to m. *(pedazo)* piece of earthenware; *(maceta)* flowerpot; *(vasija)* bowl.
ti·foi·de·o, a I. adj. typhoid II. f. typhoid fever.
ti·fón m. typhoon.
ti·fus m. typhus.
ti·gre m. tiger ♦ **t. americano** jaguar.
ti·gre·sa f. tigress.
ti·gri·llo m. AMER. wildcat.
ti·je·ra(s) f.(pl.) *(instrumento)* scissors; *(zanja)* drainage ditch ♦ **cortado por la misma t.** cut from the same cloth.
ti·je·re·ta f. BOT. tendril; ENTOM. earwig; ORNITH. scissortail.
ti·je·re·ta·da f./**zo** m. snip.
ti·je·re·te·ar tr. to snip —intr. COLL. to butt in.
ti·je·re·te·o m. *(acción)* snipping; *(ruido)* snip-snip.
til·dar tr. *(poner acento)* to put a tilde on; *(llamar)* to call <*t. a alguien de necio* to call someone a fool>.
til·de m.f. *(sobre la ñ)* tilde; *(acento)* accent; *(tacha)* flaw —f. iota.
ti·lin·go, a adj. & m.f. COLL. silly (person).
ti·lo m. linden.
ti·ma·dor, ·ra m.f. cheat.
ti·mar tr. to cheat.
tim·ba f. COLL. *(partida)* hand of cards; *(garito)* gambling den.
tim·bal m. kettledrum; CUL. meat pie.
tim·ba·le·ro, a m.f. kettledrummer.
tim·bra·do, a adj. stamped.
tim·brar tr. to stamp.
tim·bra·zo m. loud ringing.
tim·bre m. *(sello)* stamp; *(sello oficial)* tax stamp; *(aparato)* buzzer; *(sonido)* ring; *(sonoridad)* timbre.
ti·mi·dez f. timidity.
tí·mi·do, a adj. timid.
ti·mo¹ m. thymus.
ti·mo² m. swindle.
ti·món m. MARIT. rudder; AVIA. control stick; AGR. plow beam; *(pértigo)* whippletree; FIG. helm ♦ **manejar el t.** to be at the helm.
ti·mo·ne·ar tr. & intr. to steer.
ti·mo·nel m. helmsman.
ti·mo·ra·to, a adj. shy.

tím·pa·no m. MUS. kettledrum; ANAT. eardrum.
ti·na *or* **ti·na·ja** f. *(vasija)* large earthen vat; *(cubo)* vat; *(baño)* bathtub.
tin·gla·do m. *(cobertizo)* shed; *(tablado)* platform; *(enredo)* ruse.
ti·nie·blas f.pl. darkness; FIG. ignorance.
ti·no m. *(puntería)* good aim; *(juicio)* good judgment ♦ **sacar de t.** to drive crazy • **sin t.** recklessly.
tin·ta f. ink; *(color)* dye ♦ **media t.** ARTS halftone • **saber de buena t.** COLL. to have it on good authority • **sudar t.** COLL. to sweat blood • **t. china** India ink • **t. simpática** invisible ink ♦ pl. colors • **a medias t.** vaguely • **cargar** *or* **recargar las t.** to exaggerate.
tin·te m. *(acción)* dyeing; *(colorante)* dye; *(color)* tint; FIG. tinge.
tin·te·ro m. inkwell; PRINT. ink fountain ♦ **quedársele a uno en el t. una cosa** COLL. to slip one's mind.
tin·tín/ti·(lí·)ne·o m. *(de vasos)* clinking; *(de campanilla)* jingling.
tin·ti·nar/ne·ar intr. *(vasos)* to clink; *(campanilla)* to jingle.
tin·to, a I. see teñir II. adj. dark-red III. m. red wine.
tin·to·re·rí·a f. dry cleaner's shop.
tin·to·re·ro, a m.f. *(que tiñe)* dyer; *(que limpia)* dry cleaner.
tin·tu·ra f. dye; PHARM. tincture.
ti·ña f. MED. ringworm; COLL. *(miseria)* squalor, poverty; *(mezquindad)* stinginess.
ti·ña, ño, ñera, ñó see teñir.
ti·ño·so, a I. adj. scabby; FIG. stingy II. m.f. MED. person suffering from ringworm; FIG. miser.
tí·o m. *(pariente)* uncle; COLL. *(persona cualquiera)* guy ♦ **t. abuelo** great-uncle ♦ pl. aunt and uncle.
tio·vi·vo m. merry-go-round.
ti·pa f. AMER., DEROG. trollop.
tí·pi·co, a adj. typical.
ti·pi·fi·car §70 tr. to typify.
ti·ple m. MUS. *(voz)* soprano; *(instrumento)* treble guitar; MARIT. single-piece mast —m.f. MUS. soprano.
ti·po m. *(clase)* kind; *(modelo)* type; *(figura)* figure; DEROG. character; *(persona)* guy <*¿quién es ese t.?* who is that guy?>; PRINT. type; COM. rate <*t. de interés* interest rate>.
ti·po·gra·fí·a f. typography.
ti·pó·gra·fo, a m.f. typesetter.
ti·ra f. strip.
ti·ra·bo·tas m.inv. bootjack.
ti·ra·bu·zón m. *(sacacorchos)* corkscrew; *(bucle)* ringlet.
ti·ra·da f. *(lanzamiento)* throw; *(distancia)* distance; *(serie)* series; *(edición)* edition ♦ **de una t.** at one stretch.
ti·ra·do, a adj. dirt-cheap.
ti·ra·dor, ·ra m. *(de pistola)* shot; *(de cajón)* knob; *(de campanilla)* bellpull, catapult ♦ pl. suspenders —f. shot.
ti·ra·lí·ne·as m.inv. ruling pen.
ti·ra·ní·a f. tyranny.
ti·ra·ni·zar §04 tr. to tyrannize.
ti·ra·no, a I. adj. tyrannical II. m.f. tyrant.
ti·ran·te I. adj. *(tenso)* tight; *(relaciones)* strained II. m. *(correa)* strap; ARCHIT. tie beam; TECH. brace ♦ pl. suspenders.
ti·ran·tez f. tightness; FIG. strain.
ti·rar tr. *(arrojar)* to throw; *(desechar)* to throw

away; *(derribar)* to knock down; *(estirar)* to stretch; *(disparar)* to fire; *(trazar)* to draw <*t. paralelas* to draw parallel lines>; *(dar)* to give <*le tiré una patada* I gave him a kick>; *(imprimir)* to print; *(malgastar)* to waste ♦ **t. a alguien de la lengua** to draw someone out • **tirarla de** to boast of being wise <*tirarla de sabio* to boast of being wise> —intr. *(atraer)* to attract <*el imán tira del metal* the magnet attracts metal>; *(traer hacia sí)* to pull; *(producir corriente)* to draw <*esta chimenea no tira bien* this chimney does not draw well>; *(torcer)* to turn, go <*t. hacia la izquierda* to turn towards the left>; *(durar)* to last <*los zapatos no tirarán otro año* his shoes will not last another year>; *(aspirar)* to aspire; *(atraer el ánimo)* to have an appeal; *(asemejarse)* to take after <*ella tira a su madre* she takes after her mother>; *(parecerse)* to have a touch of <*este color tira a rojo* this color has a touch of red>; COLL. *(funcionar)* to run <*el coche tira bien* the car runs well> ♦ **ir tirando** COLL. to manage • **t. de** to pull • **tira y afloja** give-and-take —reflex. *(arrojarse)* to throw or hurl oneself; *(tenderse)* to lie down.

ti·ri·lla f. neckband.

ti·ri·tar intr. to shiver.

ti·ro m. *(lanzada)* throw; *(disparo)* shot; *(campo)* shooting range or gallery; *(de tela)* length; *(caballos)* team (of horses); *(de chimenea)* draft; *(de escalera)* flight ♦ **a t. de** within reach or range of • **a t. limpio** or **a tiros** with gunfire • **darse** or **pegarse un t.** to shoot oneself • **ni a tiros** COLL. not by a long shot • **salirle a uno el t. por la culata** to backfire • **t. al blanco** target practice.

ti·roi·des adj. & m. thyroid.

ti·rón m. *(acción)* pull; *(estirón)* yank; COLL. *(distancia)* distance ♦ **de un t.** in one stretch.

ti·ro·te·ar tr. to snipe or fire at —reflex. to exchange fire.

ti·ro·te·o m. shooting.

ti·rria f. COLL. dislike.

ti·sa·na f. infusion.

tí·si·co, a adj. & m.f. consumptive.

ti·sis f. tuberculosis.

ti·sú m. gold or silver lamé.

tí·te·re m. puppet ♦ **no dejar t. con cabeza** COLL. to leave nothing standing ♦ pl. puppet show.

ti·ti·lar intr. *(temblar)* to quiver; *(una estrella)* to twinkle.

ti·ti·le·o m. *(temblor)* quivering; *(de estrella)* twinkling.

ti·ti·ri·tar intr. to tremble.

ti·ti·ri·te·ro, a m.f. puppeteer.

ti·tu·be·ar intr. *(oscilar)* to stagger; *(vacilar)* to hesitate.

ti·tu·be·o m. *(al andar)* staggering; *(vacilación)* hesitation.

ti·tu·la·do, a adj. *(libro)* entitled; *(persona)* titled.

ti·tu·lar¹ I. adj. *(que tiene título)* titular; regular <*el profesor t.* the regular professor> II. m. PRINT. headline —m.f. holder (of a passport, office).

ti·tu·lar² tr. to entitle —intr. to receive a title —reflex. EDUC. to receive one's degree.

tí·tu·lo m. title; *(encabezado)* heading; *(diploma)* degree ♦ **a t. de** by way of.

ti·za f. chalk.

tiz·nar tr. to smudge; FIG. to stain.

tiz·ne m. or f. soot.

ti·zo·ne·ar intr. to poke.

to·a·lla f. towel.

to·a·lle·ro m. towel rack.

to·bi·lle·ra f. ankle support.

to·bi·llo m. ankle.

to·bo·gán m. *(para niños)* slide; *(para mercancías)* chute; *(para la nieve)* sled.

to·ca f. *(sombrero)* hat, *(de religiosa)* wimple.

to·ca·dis·cos m.inv. record player.

to·ca·do, a I. adj. COLL. touched II. m. *(peinado)* hairdo; *(sombrero)* hat.

to·ca·dor m. *(mueble)* dressing table; *(cuarto)* dressing room ♦ **artículos de t.** toiletries.

to·can·te adj. ♦ **t. a** concerning.

to·car §70 tr. to touch; *(palpar)* to feel <*lo toqué con el dedo* I felt it with my finger>; *(manosear)* to handle; *(hacer sonar)* to sound; *(tañer)* to ring; MUS. to play; *(aludir)* to touch on ♦ **t. fondo** to hit bottom • **t. la diana** MIL. to play reveille —intr. *(corresponder)* to be up to, fall to <*me toca a mí darle la noticia* it is up to me to give him the news>; to be one's turn <*¿a quién le toca?* whose turn is it?>; *(recibir)* to get <*le toca la mitad* he gets half>; *(caer en suerte)* to win <*le tocó el premio gordo* he won the grand prize>; to knock <*t. a la puerta* to knock at the door>; *(llegar el momento)* to be time <*ahora toca pagar* now it is time to pay> ♦ **t. a rebato** to sound the alarm • **t. a su fin** to come to an end • **t. de cerca** to hit home.

to·ca·yo, a m.f. namesake.

to·ci·no m. salt pork.

to·da·ví·a adv. still <*t. están durmiendo* they are still sleeping>; *(sin embargo)* nevertheless; *(aún)* even <*él es t. más inteligente que ella* he is even more intelligent than she> ♦ **t. no** not yet.

to·do, a I. adj. all <*se comió t. el pan* he ate all the bread>; *(cada)* each, every <*t. delito merece castigo* every crime deserves punishment>; all <*este jardín es t. hierbas* this garden is all weeds>; whole, entire <*t. el universo* the whole universe> • **t. el mundo** everybody II. m. whole <*el t. es mayor que sus partes* the whole is greater than its parts>; all, everything <*t. está listo* everything is ready> ♦ **ante t.** first of all • **así y t.** for all that • **con t.** still • **del t.** entirely • **sobre t.** above all ♦ pl. everybody, everyone III. adv. all.

to·do·po·de·ro·so, a adj. almighty ♦ **El T.** the Almighty.

to·ga f. *(de los romanos)* toga; *(de los magistrados)* robe.

tol·do m. awning.

to·le m. COLL. uproar.

to·le·ran·cia f. tolerance.

to·le·ran·te adj. tolerant.

to·le·rar tr. to tolerate; *(condescender)* to be tolerant of; *(permitir)* to allow.

to·lon·drón, o·na I. adj. scatterbrained II. m.f. *(persona)* scatterbrain; *(chichón)* bump ♦ **a tolondrones** COLL. by fits and starts.

to·ma f. *(acción)* taking; *(captura)* capture; *(dosis)* dose; *(entrada)* intake; CINEM. take ♦ **t. de conciencia** awareness • **t. de corriente** ELEC. plug • **t. de posesión** *(investidura)* inauguration; MIL. occupation • **t. y daca** give-and-take.

to·ma·dor, ·ra I. adj. AMER. drinking II. m.f. AMER. *(bebedor)* drinker; COM. drawee.

to·ma·du·ra f. *(toma)* taking; MIL. capture ♦ **t. de pelo** practical joke.

to·mar tr. to take; *(capturar)* to capture;

(comer) to have <*tomé el desayuno a las siete* I had breakfast at seven o'clock>; *(beber)* to have <*¿quieres t. una cerveza conmigo?* do you want to have a beer with me?>; *(agarrar)* to take up <*t. la pluma* to take up one's pen>; *(cobrar)* to gather <*t. fuerzas* to gather strength>; *(robar)* to steal; *(escoger)* to pick <*tome uno de estos naipes* pick one of these cards>; *(considerar)* to mistake <*lo tomé por el jefe* I mistook him for the boss>; *(adquirir)* to acquire <*t. malas costumbres* to acquire bad habits>; *(imitar)* to adopt <*tomó los modales de su hermana mayor* she adopted the manners of her older sister>; *(alquilar)* to rent; *(contratar)* to hire; *(padecer)* to catch <*t. frío* to catch cold> ♦ **t. a bien, mal** to take well, badly • **t. a pecho** to take to heart • **t. asiento** to take a seat • **t. conciencia** to become aware • **t. el fresco** to take the air • **t. el pelo a alguien** to pull someone's leg • **t. en broma** to take as a joke • **t. en cuenta** to take into account • **t. las de Villadiego** COLL. to beat it • **t. parte** to participate • **t. partido** to take sides • **t. prestado** to borrow —intr. to go <*tomamos por la izquierda* we went to the left> ♦ **¡toma!** really!

to·ma·te m. tomato ♦ **ponerse como un t.** to become red as a beet.

tóm·bo·la f. charity raffle.

to·mi·llo m. thyme.

to·mo m. tome.

ton m. ♦ **sin t. ni son** without rhyme or reason.

to·na·da f. *(canción)* tune; AMER. regional accent.

to·na·li·dad f. tonality.

to·nel m. barrel.

to·ne·la·da f. ton.

to·ne·la·je m. tonnage.

tó·ni·co, a adj. & m.f. tonic ♦ **dar la t.** to set the tone.

to·ni·fi·ca·dor, ·ra/can·te adj. strengthening.

to·ni·fi·car §70 tr. to tone.

to·ni·na f. ICHTH. tuna; ZOOL. dolphin.

to·no m. tone ♦ **a t.** in tune • **bajar el t.** to tone down • **dar el t.** to set the tone • **darse t.** to put on airs • **fuera de t.** out of place • **subir el t.** *(acalorarse)* to become heated; *(gritar)* to get louder.

ton·su·rar tr. *(un clérigo)* to tonsure; *(el pelo)* to cut; *(la lana)* to shear.

ton·te·ar intr. to act foolishly.

ton·te·rí·a/dad/ra f. *(cualidad)* foolishness; *(acción)* foolish action; *(dicho)* stupid remark; *(nadería)* trifle ♦ **decir tonterías** to talk nonsense.

ton·to, a I. adj. foolish ♦ **a tontas y a locas** COLL. any which way II. m.f. *(necio)* fool; *(payaso)* clown ♦ **hacerse el t.** to play the fool • **t. de capirote** COLL. total fool.

to·pa·cio m. topaz.

to·par tr. *(chocar)* to bump (into); *(encontrar)* to run into —intr. to butt ♦ **t. con** or **contra** to bump into.

to·pe I. m. *(extremo)* butt; *(para sostener)* catch ♦ **estar hasta los topes** *(estar lleno)* to be filled to the brim; *(estar harto)* to be fed up II. adj. top <*precio t.* top price>.

to·pe·tar/te·ar tr. *(animales)* to butt; COLL. *(chocar)* to bump (into).

to·pe·ta·zo m. bump (with the head).

tó·pi·co m. topic; MED. local application.

to·po m. ZOOL. mole; COLL. *(persona)* clumsy person.

to·po·gra·fí·a f. topography.

to·pó·gra·fo, a m.f. topographer.

to·que m. touch; *(de campana)* chime; *(de sirena)* blast; *(de tambor)* beat; *(golpe)* tap ♦ **dar el último t.** a to give the finishing touch to • **t. de diana** MIL. reveille • **t. de queda** curfew.

to·que·te·ar tr. to handle.

to·que·te·o m. handling.

to·rá·ci·co, a adj. thoracic.

tó·rax m. thorax.

tor·be·lli·no m. *(viento)* whirlwind; *(agua)* vortex; FIG. lively.

tor·ce·du·ra f. *(acción)* twisting; *(efecto)* twist; MED. sprain.

tor·cer §71 tr. to twist; *(doblar)* to bend; *(la cara)* to contort; MED. to sprain —intr. to turn ♦ **no dar el brazo a t.** to stand firm —reflex. *(estar torcido)* to be twisted; *(doblarse)* to be bent.

tor·ci·do, a adj. *(no recto)* crooked; *(doblado)* bent.

tor·ci·jón m. stomach cramp.

tor·do I. m. *(caballo)* dapple-gray horse; ORNITH. thrush II. adj. dapple-gray.

to·re·a·dor m. toreador.

to·re·ar tr. to fight —intr. to fight bulls.

to·re·o m. bullfighting.

to·re·ro, a I. adj. of bullfighting II. m. bullfighter.

tor·men·ta f. storm; FIG. turmoil.

tor·men·to m. torment.

tor·men·to·so, a adj. stormy.

tor·na·do m. tornado.

tor·nar tr. *(devolver)* to return; *(mudar)* to turn <*la sangre tornó el agua roja* the blood turned the water red> —intr. to return —reflex. to become.

tor·na·sol m. BOT. sunflower; CHEM. litmus.

tor·na·so·la·do, a adj. iridescent.

tor·ne·ar tr. to turn.

tor·ne·o m. tournament.

tor·ne·ro, a m.f. lathe operator.

tor·ni·llo m. screw ♦ **apretar a alguien los tornillos** to put the screws on someone • **faltarle un t.** to have a loose screw.

tor·ni·que·te m. tourniquet.

tor·no m. lathe; *(elevador)* winch; *(giratorio)* revolving dumbwaiter ♦ **en t. a** around • **t. de alfarero** potter's wheel.

to·ro m. bull ♦ **echar a alguien un t.** COLL. to give someone a piece of one's mind • **t. de lidia** fighting bull ♦ pl. bullfight.

to·ron·ja f. grapefruit.

tor·pe adj. *(desmañado)* clumsy; *(necio)* stupid.

tor·pe·de·ar tr. to torpedo.

tor·pe·do m. torpedo fish; MIL. torpedo ♦ **t. de fondo** ground torpedo • **t. flotante** submarine mine.

tor·pe·za f. *(cualidad)* clumsiness; *(necedad)* stupidity ♦ **cometer una t.** to make a blunder.

tor·por m. torpor.

to·rrar tr. to roast.

to·rre f. tower; *(de ajedrez)* castle; *(de petróleo)* oil derrick; MARIT. turret ♦ **t. de vigía** observation tower; MARIT. crow's nest.

to·rre·ja f. French toast.

to·rren·cial adj. torrential.

to·rren·te m. *(de agua)* torrent; *(de sangre)* bloodstream; FIG. avalanche.

to·rre·ón m. large fortified tower.

tó·rri·do, a adj. torrid.

tor·sión f. torsion ♦ **momento de t.** torque.

tor·so m. torso.

tor·ta f. cake; COLL. *(bofetada)* slap; PRINT. font; MEX. sandwich ♦ **ni t.** COLL. not a thing.

tor·ta·zo m. COLL. blow.

tor·te·ra f. baking pan.

tor·ti·co·li(s) m. stiff neck.

tor·ti·lla f. CUL. omelet; AMER. tortilla ♦ **hacer t. a** COLL. to flatten • **volverse la t.** COLL. to turn the tables.'

tór·to·la f. turtledove.

tor·tu·ga f. turtle.

tor·tuo·so, a adj. tortuous; FIG. devious.

tor·tu·ra f. torture.

tor·tu·rar tr. to torture.

tor·vo, a adj. grim.

tos f. cough, coughing ♦ **acceso de t.** coughing fit • **t. convulsiva** whooping cough.

tos·co, a adj. *(basto)* crude; *(una persona)* coarse.

to·ser intr. to cough.

tos·que·dad f. coarseness.

tos·ta·do, a I. adj. *(pan)* toasted; *(café)* roasted; FIG. tanned II. m. *(de pan)* toasting; *(de café)* roasting —f. toast.

tos·ta·dor, ·ra m.f. toaster.

tos·tar §19 tr. *(pan)* to toast; *(café)* roast; *(calentar mucho)* to scorch; *(la piel)* to tan —reflex. to become tanned.

tos·tón m. *(crostin)* *(cosa demasiado asada)* burned or scorched thing; *(cochinillo)* roast suckling pig; MEX. silver coin ♦ pl. CARIB., CUL. fried plantain chips.

to·tal I. adj. & m. total II. adv. so *<t. que se fue* so, he left>.

to·ta·li·dad f. totality.

to·ta·li·ta·rio, a adj. & m.f. totalitarian.

to·ta·li·zar §04 tr. to total.

tó·tem m. [pl. **es** or **totems**] totem.

to·to·ra f. AMER. cattail.

to·xe·mia f. toxemia.

to·xi·ci·dad f. toxicity.

tó·xi·co, a I. adj. toxic II. m. poison.

to·xi·có·lo·go, a m.f. toxicologist.

to·xi·có·ma·no, a I. m.f. drug addict II. adj. addicted to drugs.

to·xi·na f. toxin.

to·zu·do, a adj. stubborn.

tra·ba f. *(liga)* tie; *(para caballos)* hobble; *(para puertas)* bolt; *(estorbo)* obstacle ♦ **poner trabas a** to put obstacles in the way of.

tra·ba·ja·do, a adj. *(cansado)* worn-out; *(elaborado)* elaborate.

tra·ba·ja·dor, ·ra I. adj. hard-working II. m.f. worker.

tra·ba·jar intr. to work ♦ **hacer t. el dinero** to make one's money work • **poner a t.** to put to work • **ponerse a t.** to get to work • **t. de** to work as —tr. to work; AGR. to till.

tra·ba·jo m. work; *(labor)* labor *<t. manual* manual labor>; *(tarea)* job; *(esfuerzo)* trouble *<tomarse el t. de* to take the trouble to> ♦ **costar t.** to be hard • **t. a destajo** piecework • **trabajos forzados** hard labor.

tra·ba·jo·so, a adj. demanding.

tra·ba·len·guas m.inv. tongue twister.

tra·bar tr. *(unir)* to join; *(atar)* to fasten; *(asegurar)* to bolt; *(echar trabas a)* to hobble; *(una sierra)* to set; *(empezar)* to start up *<t. una conversación* to start up a conversation> ♦ **t. amistad** to strike up a friendship —tr. *(espesar)* to thicken; *(agarrar)* to take hold —reflex. *(atascarse)* to jam; *(enredarse)* to get

tangled up ♦ **t. a golpes** to come to blows • **trabársele a uno la lengua** to get tongue-tied.

tra·bi·lla f. *(del pantalón)* foot strap; *(de cintura)* half belt; *(punto)* dropped stitch.

tra·bu·car §70 tr. to mix up.

tra·bu·co m. blunderbuss.

trac·ción f. traction ♦ **t. delantera** front-wheel drive.

trac·to m. *(de tiempo)* interval; MED., RELIG. tract.

trac·tor m. tractor ♦ **t. oruga** caterpillar tractor.

tra·di·ción f. tradition.

tra·di·cio·nal adj. traditional.

tra·duc·ción f. translation.

tra·du·cir §22 tr. *(una lengua)* to translate; *(expresar)* to express.

tra·duc·tor, ·ra I. adj. translating II. m.f. translator.

tra·er §72 tr. to bring *<traiga los libros a la clase* bring your books to class>; *(llevar)* to wear *<traía un sombrero nuevo* he was wearing a new hat>; *(atraer)* to attract; *(causar)* to bring about *<esto trae muchos problemas* this brings about many problems>; *(alegar)* to adduce *<t. ejemplos* to adduce examples>; *(publicar)* to carry *<este periódico traía un artículo sobre el escándalo* this newspaper carried an article about the scandal> ♦ **t. a mal** *(maltratar)* to abuse; *(molestar)* to pester • **t. al mundo** to bring into the world • **t. cola** *(tener consecuencias)* to have serious consequences; *(venir acompañado)* to bring a friend along • **t. consigo** to entail • **t. entre manos** to be up to.

tra·ge·dia f. tragedy.

trá·gi·co, a I. adj. tragic II. m.f. tragedian.

tra·gi·co·me·dia f. tragicomedy.

tra·gi·có·mi·co, a adj. tragicomic.

tra·go m. *(bebida)* drink; *(porción)* gulp ♦ **de un t.** in one shot • **pasar un t. amargo** to have a bad time of it.

trai·ción f. treason.

trai·cio·nar tr. to betray.

trai·cio·ne·ro, a I. adj. traitorous II. m.f. traitor.

trai·dor, ·ra I. adj. traitorous II. m.f. traitor.

trai·ga, go see traer.

trai·lla f. leash.

tra·je m. *(vestido)* dress; *(conjunto)* suit; THEAT. costume ♦ **t. de baño** bathing suit • **t. de luces** bullfighter's costume.

tra·je·a·do, a adj. dressed.

tra·je·ar tr. to dress.

tra·je·ra, jo see traer.

tra·jín m. *(trabajo)* work; COLL. *(ajetreo)* hustle

tra·ga·dor, ·ra I. adj. *(que traga)* swallowing; *(glotón)* gluttonous II. m.f. *(persona que traga)* swallower; *(glotón)* glutton.

tra·ga·de·ras m.f.inv. COLL. glutton.

tra·ga·le·guas m.f.inv. person who walks a lot.

tra·ga·luz m. skylight.

tra·ga·pe·rras adj. COLL. coin-operated.

tra·gar §47 intr. to swallow —tr. *(ingerir)* to swallow; *(comer)* to devour; *(hundirse)* to swallow up *<el mar se tragó el barco* the sea swallowed up the boat>; *(aceptar)* to fall for; *(soportar)* to stomach *<no trago a ese chico* I cannot stomach that boy>; *(consumir)* to eat up.

tra·fi·can·te I. adj. dealing II. m.f. dealer.

tra·fi·car §70 intr. to deal *(en, con* in).

trá·fi·co m. traffic.

and bustle.

tra·ji·nar tr. to carry —intr. COLL. to bustle about.

tra·ma f. *(de un tejido)* weft; *(intriga)* scheme; *(de novela)* plot; *(en fotograbado)* line screen.

tra·ma·dor, ·ra I. adj. weaving II. m.f. weaver.

tra·mar tr. *(un tejido)* to weave; COLL. *(maquinar)* to scheme.

tra·mi·ta·ción f. *(de un asunto)* transaction; *(trámites)* procedures.

tra·mi·tar tr. *(un asunto)* to negotiate; *(tomar medidas)* to take the necessary steps.

trá·mi·te m. procedure ♦ pl. formalities.

tra·mo m. *(de terreno)* stretch; *(de una escalera)* flight.

tra·mo·ya f. THEAT. stage machinery; *(enredo)* plot.

tra·mo·yis·ta m.f. THEAT. stagehand; COLL. *(tramposo)* swindler.

tram·pa f. *(cepo)* trap; *(puerta)* trap door; *(ardid)* trick ♦ **caer en la t.** to fall into a trap • **hacer trampas** to cheat.

tram·pe·ar intr. COLL. *(con dinero)* to cheat; *(vivir de su ingenio)* to live by one's wits —tr. COLL. to trick, deceive.

tram·po·lín m. *(del gimnasta)* trampoline; *(del nadador)* diving board; FIG. springboard.

tram·po·so, a adj. I. cheating II. m.f. *(engañador)* swindler; *(en naipes)* cardsharp.

tran·ca f. *(garrote)* cudgel; *(de puerta)* crossbar; AMER. gate ♦ **agarrarse una t.** COLL. to get loaded.

tran·ca·da f. stride ♦ **en dos trancadas** COLL. in a jiffy.

tran·car §70 tr. to bar.

tran·ca·zo m. *(garrotazo)* blow with a stick; COLL. *(gripe)* flu.

tran·ce m. *(crisis)* crisis; *(apuro)* tight spot; *(del médium)* trance ♦ **a todo t.** at all costs • **en t. de muerte** on the point of death.

tran·co m. *(paso largo)* stride; *(umbral)* threshold; AMER. gallop ♦ **en dos trancos** COLL. in a jiffy.

tran·que·ra f. *(estacada)* stockade; AMER. gate.

tran·qui·li·dad f. tranquility.

tran·qui·li·zan·te I. adj. tranquilizing II. m. tranquilizer.

tran·qui·li·zar §04 tr. to quiet —reflex. to be quieted.

tran·qui·lo, a adj. tranquil ♦ **¡déjame t.!** leave me alone!

tran·sac·ción f. COM. transaction; *(acuerdo)* settlement.

tran·sar intr. AMER. to compromise.

tran·sat·lán·ti·co, a I. adj. transatlantic II. m. ocean liner.

trans·bor·da·dor m. ferry ♦ **t. espacial** space shuttle.

trans·bor·dar tr. to transfer, transship.

trans·bor·do m. transfer, transshipment.

trans·cen·den·cia f. transcendence.

trans·cen·den·tal adj. transcendental.

trans·cen·den·te adj. transcendent(al).

trans·cen·der §50 tr. to transcend.

trans·con·ti·nen·tal adj. transcontinental.

trans·cri·bir §80 tr. to transcribe.

trans·crip·ción f. transcription.

trans·cu·rrir intr. to elapse.

trans·cur·so m. course *<en el t. de un mes* in the course of a month>.

tran·se·ún·te I. adj. passing, transient II. m.f. *(que pasa)* passerby; *(que reside transitoria-*

mente) transient.

tran·se·xual adj. & m.f. transsexual.

trans·fe·ren·cia f. transfer(ence).

trans·fe·rir §65 tr. *(trasladar)* to transfer; *(aplazar)* to postpone.

trans·fi·gu·ra·ción f. transfiguration.

trans·for·ma·ción f. transformation.

trans·for·ma·dor, ·ra I. adj. transforming II. m.f. transformer —m. ELEC. transformer.

trans·for·mar tr. *(cambiar)* to transform; *(mejorar)* to improve; SPORT. to convert —reflex. to undergo a transformation.

tráns·fu·ga m.f./**go** m. *(fugitivo)* fugitive; *(desertor)* deserter.

trans·fun·dir tr. to transfuse.

trans·fu·sión f. transfusion.

trans·gre·dir §38 tr. to transgress.

trans·gre·sión f. transgression.

trans·gre·sor, ·ra I. adj. transgressing II. m.f. transgressor.

tran·si·ción f. transition.

tran·si·do, a adj. overcome.

tran·si·gen·te adj. accommodating.

tran·si·gir §32 intr. to compromise.

tran·sis·tor m. transistor.

tran·si·ta·ble adj. passable.

tran·si·tar intr. *(pasar)* to go; *(viajar)* to travel.

tran·si·ti·vo, a adj. transitive.

trán·si·to m. *(paso)* transit; *(tráfico)* traffic; *(lugar de parada)* stop ♦ **de mucho t.** busy *<una calle de mucho t.* a busy street> • **de t.** in transit.

tran·si·to·rio, a adj. temporary.

trans·la·ción f. translation.

trans·li·te·ra·ción f. transliteration.

trans·lú·ci·do, a adj. translucent.

trans·lu·cir·se §44 reflex. *(ser translúcido)* to be translucid; *(ser evidente)* to be evident.

trans·mi·gra·ción f. transmigration.

trans·mi·grar intr. to transmigrate.

trans·mi·sión f. *(acción)* transmission; RAD., TELEV. broadcast ♦ **t. delantera** AUTO. front-wheel drive • **t. del pensamiento** telepathy.

trans·mi·sor, ·ra I. adj. transmitting II. m. ELEC. transmitter.

trans·mi·tir tr. *(comunicar)* to transmit; RAD., TELEV. to broadcast.

trans·mu·ta·ción f. transmutation.

trans·mu·tar tr. to transmute —reflex. to be transmuted.

trans·o·ce·á·ni·co, a adj. transoceanic.

trans·pa·ren·cia f. *(cualidad)* transparence; PHOTOG. slide.

trans·pa·ren·tar·se reflex. *(verse)* to show through; *(ser transparente)* to be transparent; *(ser evidente)* to be obvious.

trans·pa·ren·te I. adj. *(un objeto)* transparent; *(evidente)* obvious II. m. shade.

trans·pi·ra·ción f. perspiration.

trans·pi·rar intr. *(sudar)* to perspire; *(rezumarse)* to leak out.

trans·plan·tar tr. to transplant.

trans·po·ner §54 tr. *(mudar de sitio)* to move; *(trasplantar)* to transplant; *(intercambiar)* to transpose; *(desaparecer)* to disappear around *<los agresores transpusieron la esquina* the assailants disappeared around the corner>.

trans·por·ta·ción f. transportation, transport.

trans·por·ta·dor, ·ra I. adj. transporting II. m.f. transporter —m. MATH. protractor; MECH. conveyor.

trans·por·tar tr. *(llevar)* to transport; MUS. to

transpose —reflex. FIG. to get carried away.

trans·por·te m. transportation; COM. transport; *(embarcación)* transport ship.

trans·por·tis·ta m.f. carrier.

trans·po·si·ción f. transposition.

trans·pu·sie·ra, so see **transponer.**

trans·va·sar tr. to decant.

trans·ver·sal I. adj. *(que atraviesa)* transverse; *(pariente)* collateral II. m.f. collateral relative —f. side street.

trans·ver·so, a adj. & m. transverse (muscle).

tran·ví·a m. streetcar.

tran·via·rio, a I. adj. streetcar <*red t.* streetcar system> II. m. *(empleado)* streetcar worker; *(conductor)* streetcar driver.

tra·pe·ar tr. AMER. to mop.

tra·pe·cio m. GEOM. trapezoid; *(de gimnasia)* trapeze; ANAT. *(músculo)* trapezius; *(hueso)* trapezium.

tra·pe·cis·ta m.f. trapeze artist.

tra·pe·rí·a f. *(trapos)* rags; *(tienda)* old clothing store.

tra·pe·ro, a m.f. ragpicker.

tra·pe·zoi·de m. trapezoid; ANAT. trapezium.

tra·pi·che m. *(de aceituna)* olive press; *(de azúcar)* sugar mill; AMER. *(ingenio)* sugar plantation; *(de mineral)* grinding machine.

tra·pien·to, a adj. ragged.

tra·pi·son·da f. COLL. *(jaleo)* racket; *(enredo)* scheme.

tra·po m. rag; MARIT. sails; TAUR. muleta ♦ **a todo t.** under full sail • **poner a alguien como un t.** COLL. to rake someone over the coals • **sacar los trapos a relucir** COLL. to wash one's dirty linen in public ♦ pl. clothing.

trá·que·a or **tra·que·ar·te·ria** f. trachea.

tra·que·(te·)ar intr. *(un cohete)* to go off; *(hacer ruido)* to clatter, rattle; *(agitarse)* to shake, jolt —tr. *(agitar)* to shake; COLL. *(manosear)* to handle.

tra·que·te·o m. AMER. *(ruido)* bang; *(movimiento)* shaking.

tras prep. *(después de)* after <*día t. día* day after day>; *(detrás de)* behind <*caminaban t. un carretón* they walked behind a wagon>; *(además)* in addition <*t. de ser rico, es guapo* in addition to being rich, he is good-looking>; *(en busca de)* in search of.

tra·sat·lán·ti·co, a adj. transatlantic.

tras·cen·den·cia f. PHILOS. transcendence; *(importancia)* significance.

tras·cen·den·tal adj. PHILOS. transcendental; *(que se extiende)* far-reaching; *(importante)* very significant.

tras·cen·den·te adj. transcendent.

tras·cen·der §50 intr. *(divulgarse)* to become known; *(extenderse)* to extend; *(oler)* to smell.

tras·co·rral m. backyard.

tra·se·char tr. to lie in wait for.

tra·se·gar §52 tr. *(trastornar)* to mix up; *(un líquido)* to decant; COLL. *(beber mucho)* to guzzle.

tra·se·ro, a I. adj. back II. m. ANAT. behind; ZOOL. rump —f. back.

tras·fon·do m. background.

tras·ho·jar tr. to leaf through.

tra·sie·go m. decanting.

tra·sie·go, gue see **trasegar.**

tras·la·ción f. *(transporte)* moving; *(traducción)* translation; RHET. metaphor; MECH., PHYS. translation.

tras·la·dar tr. *(mover)* to move; *(a un empleado)* to transfer; *(aplazar)* to postpone; *(traducir)* to translate; *(copiar)* to transcribe —reflex. to change residence.

tras·la·do m. *(copia)* copy <*fiel t.* true copy>; *(de un empleado)* transfer; *(de residencia)* change of residence; LAW notification ♦ **dar t.** to send a copy.

tras·luz m. *(luz)* light seen through a transparent body; *(luz reflejada)* reflected light ♦ **al t.** against the light.

tras·ma·no m. ♦ **a t.** *(del alcance)* out of reach; *(lugar)* out of the way.

tras·mun·do m. the other world.

tras·no·cha·do, a adj. *(macilento)* haggard; *(trillado)* trite.

tras·no·cha·dor, ·ra I. adj. staying up late II. m.f. night owl.

tras·no·char intr. to stay up all night.

tras·pa·pe·lar tr. to misplace —reflex. to get lost.

tras·pa·pe·la·do, a adj. misplaced.

tras·pa·sar tr. *(perforar)* to pierce; *(atravesar)* to cross <*t. el río* to cross the river>; *(transferir)* to transfer; *(violar)* to break; FIG. to pierce <*t. el corazón de dolor* to pierce someone's heart with pain> —reflex. to go too far.

tras·pa·so m. *(cesión)* transfer; *(venta)* sale; *(lo traspasado)* transferred property; *(precio)* transfer fee.

tras·pié m. stumble ♦ **dar traspiés** to stumble.

tras·plan·tar tr. to transplant —reflex. to uproot oneself.

tras·plan·te m. *(acción)* transplanting; *(injerto)* transplant.

tras·pun·te m. prompter.

tras·qui·la·dor, ·ra m.f. shearer.

tras·qui·lar tr. *(el pelo)* to clip; *(el ganado)* to shear.

tras·ta·bi·llar intr. to stagger.

tras·ta·bi·llón m. slip.

tras·ta·da f. COLL. dirty trick.

tras·ta·zo m. COLL. whack.

tras·te m. MUS. fret; *(chisme)* thingamajig, whatnot; SP. wine-taster's glass; AMER., COLL. behind ♦ **dar al t. con** COLL. to spoil • **ir al t.** COLL. to fall through.

tras·te·ar intr. to move furniture —tr. TAUR. to tease (a bull) with a red cape; MUS. to strum.

tras·tien·da f. stock room.

tras·to m. *(mueble)* old piece of furniture; *(utensilio)* utensil <*trastos de cocina* kitchen utensils>; *(cosa inútil)* piece of junk; THEAT. flat, piece of scenery ♦ **tirarse los trastos a la cabeza** COLL. to have a terrible fight ♦ pl. gear.

tras·to·car §70 tr. to twist —reflex. to go mad.

tras·tor·nar tr. *(derribar)* to turn upside down; *(perturbar)* to disrupt; *(inquietar)* to worry; *(enloquecer)* to drive mad ♦ **trastornarle la mente a alguien** to drive someone mad —reflex. to go mad.

tras·tor·no m. upset.

tras·tra·bi·llar intr. to stagger.

tras·tro·car §73 tr. to twist.

tra·sun·tar tr. *(copiar)* to copy; *(compendiar)* to summarize.

tra·ta f. slave trade ♦ **t. de blancas** white slavery.

tra·ta·ble adj. sociable.

tra·ta·do m. *(obra)* treatise; *(entre gobiernos)*

treaty; *(entre compañías)* agreement.

tra·ta·mien·to m. treatment; *(título)* form of address; TECH. process ♦ **dar t. de** to address as • **t. de la información** COMPUT. data processing.

tra·tan·te m.f. dealer.

tra·tar tr. to treat *<no me trates mal* do not treat me badly>; *(manejar)* to handle *<hay que t. este asunto con cuidado* it is necessary to handle this matter carefully>; *(dar el tratamiento de)* to address as *<le traté de doña* I addressed her as Madame>; *(comerciar)* to manage *<t. la venta del negocio* to manage the sale of the business>; CHEM. to process; MED. to treat —intr. ♦ **t. con** to have dealings with • **t. de** *(discutir)* to be about *<este artículo trata de la economía* this article is about the economy>; *(procurar)* to try *<traté de salir temprano* I tried to leave early> —reflex. to treat each other ♦ **t. de** to be a question of *<se trata de encontrar una solución* it is a question of finding a solution>.

tra·to m. treatment *<t. especial* preferential treatment>; *(título)* form of address; *(relaciones)* dealings; *(negocio)* trade; *(convenio)* agreement ♦ **¡t. hecho!** COLL. it's a deal!

trau·ma m. trauma.

trau·má·ti·co, a adj. traumatic.

trau·ma·ti·zar §04 tr. to traumatize.

tra·vés m. *(inclinación)* slant; *(torcimiento)* bend; SEW. bias ♦ **a** or **al t.** through • **de t.** crosswise.

tra·ve·sa·ño m. *(barra)* crossbeam; *(almohada)* bolster.

tra·ve·sí·a f. *(camino)* crossroad; *(de una carretera)* part of a highway that goes through a town; *(distancia)* distance across; *(viaje)* crossing; *(viento)* crosswind.

tra·ves·tí/ti·do m. transvestite.

tra·ve·su·ra f. mischief.

tra·vie·so, a adj. mischievous ♦ **a campo traviesa** cross-country.

tra·yec·to m. *(distancia)* distance; *(recorrido)* way.

tra·yec·to·ria f. trajectory.

tra·za f. *(diseño)* design; *(plan)* plan; *(aspecto)* appearance; GEOM. trace ♦ **darse trazas para** to find a way to.

tra·za·do, a I. adj. ♦ **bien t.** good-looking • **mal t.** unattractive II. m. *(diseño)* design; *(plan)* plan; *(bosquejo)* sketch.

tra·zar §04 tr. *(diseñar)* to design; *(bosquejar)* to outline; *(discurrir)* to draw up; *(describir)* to depict.

tra·zo m. *(línea)* line *<t. rectilíneo* straight line>; *(diseño)* design; *(de una letra)* stroke ♦ **al t.** drawn in outline.

tra·zu·mar·se reflex. to seep.

tré·bol m. BOT. clover; ARCHIT. trefoil ♦ pl. clubs.

tre·ce I. adj. thirteen; *(decimotercero)* thirteenth II. m. thirteen ♦ **mantenerse** or **seguir en sus treces** COLL. to stick to one's guns.

tre·cho m. *(distancia)* stretch; *(de tiempo)* spell ♦ **a trechos** *(en ciertas partes)* in places, in parts; *(con interrupción)* in stages • **de t.** *(distancia)* at intervals; *(tiempo)* every now and then.

tre·fi·lar tr. to make into wire.

tre·gua f. truce; *(descanso)* rest; *(pausa)* lull ♦ **no dar t.** never to let up.

trein·ta I. adj. thirty; *(trigésimo)* thirtieth

II. m. thirty.

trein·ta·vo, a adj. & m. thirtieth.

trein·te·na f. *(treinta unidades)* thirty; *(treintava parte)* thirtieth part.

tre·me·bun·do, a adj. dreadful.

tre·men·do, a adj. *(horrendo)* horrible; *(digno de respeto)* tremendous; COLL. *(grandísimo)* tremendous, terrible *<un disparate t.* a terrible blunder> ♦ **tomarlo a la t.** COLL. to make a big fuss.

tre·men·ti·na f. turpentine ♦ **esencia de t.** oil of turpentine.

tre·mo·lar tr. *(enarbolar)* to hoist; *(agitar)* to wave.

tre·mo·li·na f. rustling; FIG. racket ♦ **armar la t.** COLL. to kick up a rumpus.

tré·mo·lo m. tremolo.

tre·mor m. tremor.

tré·mu·lo, a adj. *(tembloroso)* trembling; *(voz)* quivering; *(luz)* flickering.

tren m. *(ferrocarril)* train; *(instrumentos)* gear, equipment *<t. de dragado* dredging gear>; MIL. convoy; MEX., URUG. streetcar ♦ **t. de aterrizaje** landing gear • **t. de vida** way of life • **t. directo** or **expreso** express train • **vivir a todo t.** COLL. to live in style.

tren·ci·lla f. braid.

tren·ci·llar tr. to trim with braid.

tren·ci·llo m. gold or silver hatband.

tren·za f. braid.

tren·za·do m. braid.

tren·zar §04 tr. to braid.

tre·pa·na·ción f. trephination.

tre·pa·nar tr. to trephine.

tré·pa·no m. SURG. trephine; *(perforadora)* drill.

tre·par[1] intr. to climb.

tre·par[2] tr. *(taladrar)* to drill; SEW. to trim, edge —reflex. to lean backwards.

tre·pi·da·ción f. trepidation.

tre·pi·dar intr. to vibrate.

tres I. adj. three; *(tercero)* third ♦ **las t.** three o'clock II. m. three.

tres·cien·tos, as adj. & m. three hundred.

tres cuar·tos m. three-quarter-length coat.

tre·si·llo m. *(naipes)* ombre; *(muebles)* three-piece suite; *(sortija)* ring with three stones; MUS. triplet.

tres·piés m.inv. *(trébede)* trivet; *(trípode)* tripod.

tre·ta f. *(ardid)* trick; SPORT. feint.

tre·za·vo, a adj. & m. thirteenth.

trí·a·da f. triad.

trian·gu·lar adj. triangular.

trián·gu·lo I. adj. triangular II. m. triangle ♦ **t. rectángulo** right triangle.

tri·bal adj. tribal.

tri·bu f. tribe.

tri·bu·la·ción f. tribulation.

tri·bu·na f. *(de un orador)* rostrum; SPORT. bleachers.

tri·bu·nal m. *(lugar)* court; *(magistrados)* bench; *(jueces de exámenes)* board of examiners ♦ **t. de menores** juvenile court.

tri·bu·no m. HIST. tribune; *(orador)* orator.

tri·bu·ta·ble adj. taxable.

tri·bu·tar tr. to pay.

tri·bu·ta·rio, a I. adj. *(de los impuestos)* tax *<régimen t.* tax system>; *(un río)* tributary II. m.f. *(que paga impuestos)* taxpayer; *(que paga tributo)* tributary.

tri·bu·to m. *(impuesto)* tax; *(respeto)* tribute.

tri·cen·te·na·rio m. tricentennial.
tri·cen·té·si·mo, a adj. & m. three-hundredth.
trí·ceps adj. & m.inv. triceps.
tri·ci·clo m. tricycle.
tri·co·lor adj. tricolor.
tri·cor·nio I. adj. three-cornered. II. m. three-cornered hat.
tri·cot m. tricot.
tri·cús·pi·de adj. & f. tricuspid.
tri·den·te I. adj. tridentate II. m. trident.
tri·di·men·sion·al adj. three-dimensional.
trie·dro, a I. adj. trihedral II. m. trihedron.
trie·nal adj. triennial.
trie·nio m. triennium.
tri·ful·ca f. COLL. rumpus <*armar una t.* to kick up a rumpus>.
tri·fur·car·se §70 reflex. to divide into three.
tri·gal m. wheat field.
tri·ga·za adj. wheat <*paja t.* wheat chaff>.
tri·gé·si·mo, a adj. & m. thirtieth.
tri·go m. wheat ♦ **no ser t. limpio** COLL. to be dishonest • **t. candeal** white wheat • **t. sarraceno** buckwheat.
tri·go·no·me·trí·a f. trigonometry.
tri·gue·ño, a adj. *(tez)* olive-skinned; *(pelo)* dark blond.
tri·gue·ro, a I. adj. wheat <*campo t.* wheat field> II. m. wheat sieve.
tri·la·te·ral adj. trilateral.
tri·lá·te·ro, a adj. trilateral.
tri·lin·güe adj. trilingual.
tri·lo·gí·a f. trilogy.
tri·lla f. *(trillo)* thresher; *(acción)* threshing; ICHTH. gurnard.
tri·lla·de·ra f. thresher.
tri·lla·do, a adj. *(muy común)* trite; *(camino)* beaten.
tri·lla·dor, ·ra I. adj. threshing II. f. threshing machine ♦ **t. segadora** combine.
tri·llar tr. to thresh; COLL. *(emplear mucho)* to use frequently; *(maltratar)* to beat.
tri·lli·zo, a I. adj. triple II. m.f. triplet.
tri·llo m. thresher; AMER. route, path, lane.
tri·llón m. one million billion (U.S.), trillion (G.B.).
tri·mes·tral adj. quarterly.
tri·mes·tral·men·te adv. quarterly.
tri·mes·tre I. adj. trimestral II. m. *(tres meses)* quarter; *(pago)* quarterly payment; *(revista)* quarterly.
tri·nar intr. MUS. to trill; ORNITH. to warble; COLL. *(enojarse)* to fume.
trin·ca f. triad, MARIT. cable.
trin·car §70 tr. to smash.
trin·cha·dor, ·ra I. adj. carving II. carver, slicer —m. *(cuchillo)* carving knife; MEX. carving board.
trin·chan·te I. adj. carving II. m. *(persona)* carver; *(tenedor)* carving fork.
trin·char tr. to carve.
trin·che·ra f. MIL. trench; RAIL. cutting; *(abrigo)* trench coat; MEX. sharp instrument ♦ **guerra de trincheras** trench warfare.
trin·che·te m. shoemaker's knife.
tri·ne·o m. sleigh.
tri·ni·ta·ria f. wild pansy.
tri·no, a m. trill.
tri·no·mio m. trinomial.
trin·que·te m. MARIT. *(palo)* foremast; *(vela)* foresail; SPORT. covered pelota court; MECH. pawl.
trí·o m. trio.

tri·pa f. intestine; *(de una vasija)* belly; *(de cigarro)* tobacco filling ♦ **echar las tripas** COLL. to retch, vomit • **hacer de tripas corazón** COLL. to pluck up one's courage • **tener malas tripas** to be hardhearted ♦ pl. *(panza)* guts; BOT. core; FIG. innards.
tri·par·ti·to, a adj. tripartite.
tri·pi·ca·llos m.pl. tripe (stew).
tri·ple adj. & m. triple.
tri·pli·ca·ción f. triplication.
tri·pli·ca·do m. triplicate ♦ **por t.** in triplicate.
tri·pli·car §70 tr. to triplicate.
tri·plo, a adj. & m. triple.
trí·po·de I. m.f. tripod II. adj. three-legged.
tri·pón, o·na COLL. adj. & m.f. pot-bellied (person).
tríp·ti·co m. triptych.
trip·ton·go m. triphthong.
tri·pu·do, a adj. & m.f. pot-bellied (person).
tri·pu·la·ción f. AVIA., MARIT. crew ♦ **t. de tierra** AVIA. ground crew.
tri·pu·lan·te m.f. crew member.
tri·pu·lar tr. AVIA., MARIT. to man.
tri·qui·no·sis f. trichinosis.
tri·qui·ñue·la f. COLL. trick, ruse ♦ **andar con triquiñuelas** to have tricks up one's sleeve.
tri·qui·tra·que m. *(de un tren)* clickety-clack; *(cohete)* firecracker ♦ **a cada t.** at every step.
tris m. *(ruido)* crack; *(instante)* jiffy ♦ **estar en un t. de** COLL. to be within an inch of.
tris·ca f. *(ruido)* crack; *(jaleo)* racket.
tris·car §70 intr. *(patear)* to stamp; *(retozar)* to frolic.
tris·te adj. sad; *(melancólico)* melancholy; *(deplorable)* miserable <*una vida t.* a miserable life>; *(insuficiente)* measly.
tris·te·za f. sadness; *(dolor)* sorrow.
tris·tón, o·na adj. melancholy.
tri·tón m. newt.
tri·tu·ra·ción f. crushing.
tri·tu·rar tr. TECH. to triturate; *(moler)* to crush; *(mascar)* to chew; *(una persona)* to beat up; *(un argumento)* to demolish.
triun·fa·dor, ·ra I. adj. triumphant II. m.f. winner.
triun·fal adj. triumphal; *(brillante)* triumphant <*una acogida t.* a triumphant reception>.
triun·fan·te adj. triumphant.
triun·far intr. to win; FIG. to succeed.
triun·fo m. triumph; FIG. success.
triun·vi·ra·to m. triumvirate.
tri·va·len·te adj. trivalent.
tri·vial adj. trivial.
tri·via·li·dad f. triviality.
tri·za f. piece ♦ **hacer trizas** to tear to pieces.
tro·car §73 tr. *(cambiar)* to barter; *(confundir)* to mix up —reflex. to change.
tro·ce·ar tr. to divide into pieces.
tro·ce·o m. cutting up.
tro·cla or **tró·co·la** f. pulley.
tro·cha f. *(atajo)* shortcut; *(camino)* path; AMER., RAIL. gauge.
tro·che·mo·che adv. ♦ **a t.** or **a troche y moche** COLL. helter-skelter.
tro·fe·o m. *(objeto)* trophy; *(despojos)* spoils (of war); *(victoria)* triumph.
tro·glo·di·ta I. adj. *(de cavernas)* troglodytic; *(bárbaro)* barbarous; *(comilón)* gluttonous II. m.f. *(habitante de cavernas)* troglodyte; *(bruto)* brute; *(comilón)* glutton.
troi·ca f. troika.
tro·le m. trolley.

tro·le·bús m. trolley bus.
tro·le·ro, a COLL. I. adj. lying II. m.f. liar.
trom·ba f. waterspout ♦ **como una t.** FIG. violently.
trom·bón m. *(instrumento)* trombone; *(músico)* trombonist ♦ **t. de pistones** valve trombone • **t. de varas** slide trombone.
trom·bo·sis f. thrombosis.
trom·pa f. MUS. horn; ZOOL. trunk; ENTOM. proboscis ♦ **t. de caza** hunting horn • **t. de Falopio** Fallopian tube —m. MUS. horn player.
trom·pa·da f. COLL. *(golpe)* punch; *(encontrón)* bump.
trom·paz·o m. punch ♦ **darse un t. con la pared** to bump into the wall.
trom·pe·ar tr. AMER. to punch.
trom·pe·ta f. trumpet —m.f. *(persona)* trumpeter; COLL. *(persona despreciable)* rascal.
trom·pe·ta·zo m. trumpet blast.
trom·pe·te·ro m. *(tocador)* trumpeter; *(fabricante)* trumpet maker; ICHTH. trumpet fish.
trom·pe·ti·lla f. *(para oír)* ear trumpet; *(cigarro)* cheroot.
trom·pe·tis·ta m.f. trumpeter.
trom·pi·car §70 intr. to trip.
trom·pi·cón m. *(tropezón)* trip; AMER. COLL. *(mojicón)* punch in the nose ♦ **a trompicones** by fits and starts.
trom·pis m.inv. COLL. punch.
trom·po m. top.
trom·pón m. *(juguete)* large spinning top; *(golpe)* blow.
trom·pu·do, a adj. AMER. thick-lipped.
tro·na·da f. thunderstorm.
tro·na·dor, ·ra I. adj. *(que truena)* thundering; *(un cohete)* detonating II. f. MEX. begonia.
tro·nan·te adj. thundering.
tro·nar §19 intr. to thunder; COLL. *(arruinarse)* to go broke ♦ **estar que truena** COLL. to be in a rage • **por lo que pueda t.** COLL. just in case.
tron·cal adj. trunk.
tron·car §70 tr. to truncate.
tron·co m. trunk; GEOM. frustum; *(caballos)* team (of horses); COLL. *(torpe)* dimwit, blockhead ♦ **dormir como un t.** COLL. to sleep like a log • **t. de cono** truncated cone.
tron·cha f. AMER. *(tajada)* chunk, slice; COLL. *(ganga)* cushy job.
tron·char tr. *(un árbol)* to fell; *(romper)* to split ♦ **troncharse de risa** COLL. to split one's sides laughing.
tro·ne·ra f. MIL. loophole; MARIT. porthole; *(en billar)* pocket.
tro·ní·do m. *(de trueno)* thunderclap; *(de cañón)* roar.
tro·no m. throne; RELIG. tabernacle.
tron·zar §04 tr. to cut up.
tro·pa f. *(muchedumbre)* crowd; MIL. *(ejército)* army; AMER. *(ganado)* herd ♦ pl. troops • **t. de asalto** storm troops.
tro·pel m. confusion ♦ **en t.** in a mad rush.
tro·pe·lí·a f. *(prisa)* rush; *(ultraje)* abuse; *(violencia)* violence.
tro·pe·zar §29 intr. *(dar un traspié)* to stumble; *(encontrar un estorbo)* to trip; *(cometer un error)* to slip up ♦ **t. con** COLL. to bump into.
tro·pe·zón m. *(traspiés)* stumble; *(obstáculo)* stumbling block; *(desliz)* slip ♦ **a tropezones** COLL. by fits and starts.
tro·pi·cal adj. tropical.
tró·pi·co, a m. tropic ♦ **t. de Cáncer,** Capricor-

nio Tropic of Cancer, Capricorn.
tro·pie·zo m. *(obstáculo)* stumbling block; *(traspiés)* stumble; *(desliz)* slip.
tro·pis·mo m. tropism.
tro·po m. trope.
tro·pos·fe·ra f. troposphere.
tro·quel m. (stamping) die.
tro·que·lar tr. to mint.
tro·ta·ca·lles m.f.inv. COLL. gadabout.
tro·ta·da f. trot.
tro·ta·dor, ·ra adj. trotting.
tro·ta·mun·dos m.f.inv. globetrotter.
tro·tar intr. to trot; FIG. to run around.
tro·te m. *(andar)* trot; COLL. *(actividad)* bustle; *(apuro)* chore ♦ **al t.** *(trotando)* trotting; *(de prisa)* quickly • **de** or **para todo t.** COLL. for everyday use.
tro·tón, ·o·na I. adj. trotting II. m. trotter.
tro·va f. ballad.
tro·va·dor, ·ra I. adj. versifying II. m. *(poeta)* poet; HIST. troubadour —f. poetess.
tro·va·do·res·co, a adj. troubadour <*canción t.* troubadour song>.
tro·var intr. to write verses or poetry.
tro·za f. *(de madera)* log; MARIT. parrel truck.
tro·zar §04 tr. *(hacer pedazos)* to cut into pieces; *(un árbol)* to cut into logs.
tro·zo m. *(pedazo)* piece; *(de madera, queso)* chunk; *(de una obra)* excerpt.
tru·co m. trick; *(juego de naipes)* card game ♦ **cogerle el t. a algo** COLL. to get the hang of something.
tru·cu·len·cia f. truculence.
tru·cu·len·to, a adj. *(cruel)* ferocious; *(atroz)* atrocious.
tru·cha f. ICHTH. trout; MECH. derrick.
true·co, que see trocar.
true·ne, no see tronar.
true·no m. thunder; *(de un arma)* shot.
true·que m. barter.
tru·fa¹ f. truffle.
tru·far¹ intr. to lie.
tru·far² tr. to stuff with truffles.
tru·hán, ·a·na I. adj. crooked II. m.f. scoundrel.
tru·ha·ne·ar intr. to cheat.
trun·ca·do, a adj. truncated.
trun·ca·mien·to m. truncation.
trun·car §70 tr. *(cortar)* to truncate; *(dejar incompleto)* to leave unfinished.
trun·co, a adj. *(truncado)* truncated; AMER. incomplete.
tse·tsé f. tsetse fly.
tú pron. you, thou ♦ **¡más eres tú!** COLL. look who's talking! • **tratar de tú** to address as *tú*.
tu, tus adj. your <*tu amigo* your friend>.
tu·ba f. tuba.
tu·ber·cu·li·na f. tuberculin.
tu·bér·cu·lo m. BOT. tuber; MED. tubercle.
tu·ber·cu·lo·sis f. tuberculosis.
tu·ber·cu·lo·so, a I. adj. BOT. tuberous; MED. tubercular II. m.f. MED. tuberculosis sufferer.
tu·be·rí·a f. *(serie)* pipes; *(tubo)* pipe; *(instalación)* plumbing; *(fábrica)* pipe factory.
tu·be·ro·so, a adj. tuberous.
tu·bo m. tube; ANAT., ZOOL. canal <*t. digestivo* alimentary canal> ♦ **t. de desagüe** drainpipe • **t. de escape** exhaust pipe • **t. lanzallamas** flame thrower • **t. lanzatorpedos** torpedo tube.
tu·bu·la·do, a adj. tubular.
tu·bu·lar adj. tubular.

tu·cán m. toucan.

tu·co m. R.P. (*salsa*) tomato sauce; ORNITH. owl.

tuer·ca f. MECH. nut ♦ **t. de alas** *or* **de mariposa** wing nut.

tuer·ce see **torcer.**

tue·ro m. (*leño grueso*) thick log; (*leña*) firewood.

tuer·to, a I. adj. (*torcido*) crooked; (*que no ve*) one-eyed II. m.f. one-eyed person —m. wrong.

tuer·za, zo see **torcer.**

tues·te m. toasting.

tues·te, to see **tostar.**

tué·ta·no m. marrow ♦ pl. **estar enamorado hasta los t.** COLL. to be head over heels in love • **hasta los t.** through and through.

tu·fo m. fume; FIG. stench.

tu·gu·rio m. (*habitación*) hole, dump; (*casucha*) shack; (*bar*) dive, joint.

tul m. tulle.

tu·li·pa f. (*pantalla*) tulip-shaped lampshade; BOT. small tulip.

tu·li·pán m. tulip.

tu·lli·do, a adj. crippled.

tu·llir §13 tr. to cripple —reflex. to become crippled.

tum·ba f. (*sepulcro*) tomb; (*voltereta*) somersault; (*caída*) fall.

tum·bar tr. (*derribar*) to knock down; COLL. (*atontar*) to knock out <*tanto alcohol nos tumbó* so much alcohol knocked us out> —intr. (*caer*) to fall down; MARIT. to keel over, capsize —reflex. to lie down.

tum·bo m. (*caída*) fall; (*sacudida*) jolt ♦ **dar tumbos** to jolt.

tum·bón, o·na I. adj. COLL. lazy II. m.f. COLL. lazy person —f. deck chair.

tu·me·fac·to, a adj. swollen.

tu·mes·cen·cia f. tumescence.

tu·mes·cen·te adj. tumescent.

tu·mor m. tumor <*t. cerebral* brain tumor>.

tú·mu·lo m. (*sepulcro*) burial mound; (*catafalco*) catafalque; (*sepultura*) tomb.

tu·mul·to m. tumult.

tu·mul·tuo·so, a adj. tumultuous.

tu·na f. prickly pear.

tu·nal m. (*niguera*) prickly pear; (*sitio*) prickly pear grove.

tu·nan·ta COLL. I. adj. cunning II. f. hussy.

tu·nan·te I. adj. crooked II. m.f. rascal.

tu·nan·te·ar intr. to be a crook *or* rascal.

tu·nan·te·rí·a f. (*acción*) dirty trick; (*cualidad*) crookedness.

tun·da f. (*del paño*) shearing; COLL. (*azotaina*) beating.

tun·de·ar tr. to beat.

tun·di·dor, ·ra I. adj. shearing II. m.f. shearer —f. shearing machine.

tun·di·du·ra f. shearing.

tun·dir tr. (*el paño*) to shear; COLL. (*golpear*) to beat.

tun·dra f. tundra.

tú·nel m. tunnel <*t. aerodinámico* wind tunnel>.

tu·ne·rí·a f. roguishness.

tungs·te·no m. tungsten.

tú·ni·ca f. tunic.

tu·pé m. (*pelo*) toupee; COLL. (*descaro*) gall.

tu·pi·do, a adj. (*espeso*) thick, dense; (*paño*) tightly-woven; COLL. (*torpe*) thickheaded.

tu·pir tr. (*apretar*) to pack tightly; (*una tela*) to

weave closely.

tur·ba[1] f. mob.

tur·ba[2] f. peat.

tur·ba·ción f. (*emoción*) upset; (*desorden*) confusion.

tur·ba·dor, ·ra I. adj. disturbing II. m.f. disturber.

tur·ba·mul·ta f. COLL. mob.

tur·ban·te m. turban.

tur·bar tr. (*perturbar*) to upset; (*desconcertar*) to embarrass —reflex. to be upset.

túr·bi·do, a adj. muddy.

tur·bie·dad f. (*de líquidos*) muddiness; (*oscuridad*) opaqueness.

tur·bi·na f. turbine.

tur·bio, a I. adj. (*un líquido*) muddy; (*un negocio*) shady; (*agitado*) turbulent <*un periodo t.* a turbulent period>; (*vista*) blurred; (*oscuro*) confused II. m.pl. sediment.

tur·bión m. shower; FIG. torrent.

tur·bo·hé·li·ce/pro·pul·sor m. turboprop.

tur·bo·rre·ac·tor m. turbojet.

tur·bu·len·cia f. turbulence.

tur·bu·len·to, a adj. turbulent.

túr·gi·do, a *or* **tur·gen·te** adj. turgid.

tu·ris·ta m.f. tourist.

tu·rís·ti·co, a adj. tourist.

tur·nar intr. & reflex. to take turns.

tur·nio, a adj. & m.f. cross-eyed (person).

tur·no m. (*vez*) turn; (*de obreros*) shift ♦ **de t.** on duty • **por t.** in turn • **por turnos** by turns • **trabajar por turnos** to work shifts • **t. de día** *or* **de noche** day *or* night shift.

tur·que·sa f. turquoise.

tur·quí [pl. **-íes**]/**qui·no, a** adj. indigo.

tu·rrón m. nougat.

tu·ru·la·to, a adj. COLL. stunned.

tu·rum·bón m. COLL. bump on the head.

tu·sa f. AMER. (*del maíz*) cornhusk; (*cigarro*) cigar rolled in a cornhusk; (*del caballo*) mane.

tu·sar tr. AMER., COLL. to trim.

tu·te·ar tr. to address as **tú**.

tu·te·la f. (*de personas*) guardianship; (*de territorios*) trusteeship; (*protección*) protection; (*dirección*) guidance ♦ **territorio bajo t.** trust territory.

tu·te·lar adj. protective.

tu·te·o m. addressing as **tú**.

tu·tor, ·ra m.f. guardian.

tu·to·rí·a f. guardianship.

tu·vie·ra, vo see **tener.**

tu·yo, a I. adj. yours <*¿es t. el coche?* is the car yours?>; of yours <*un pariente t.* a relative of yours> II. pron. yours <*¿quién tiene el t.?* who has yours?> ♦ **lo t.** your affair • **los tuyos** your people.

U

u, U f. twenty-fourth letter of the Spanish alphabet.

u conj. var. of **o** used before (*h*)*o*.

u·bé·rri·mo, a adj. (*tierra*) very fertile; (*vegetación*) luxuriant.

u·bi·ca·ción f. (*sitio*) location; (*acción*) placing.

u·bi·car §70 tr. AMER. to locate —reflex. to be located; (*encontrar trabajo*) to get hired.

u·bi·cuo, a adj. ubiquitous.

u·bre f. udder.

Ud., Uds. pron. abbrev. of **usted, ustedes.**

¡uf! interj. *(cansancio)* whew!; *(repugnancia)* ugh!

u·fa·nar·se reflex. to boast.

u·fa·no, a adj. *(orgulloso)* proud; *(satisfecho)* pleased.

u·jier m. doorkeeper.

úl·ce·ra f. ulcer.

ul·ce·ra·ción f. ulceration.

ul·ce·rar tr. & reflex. to ulcerate.

ul·ce·ro·so, a adj. ulcerous.

ul·te·rior adj. *(más allá)* ulterior; *(que ocurre después)* subsequent.

ul·te·rior·men·te adv. subsequently.

úl·ti·ma·men·te adv. *(por último)* ultimately; *(recientemente)* lately.

ul·ti·mar tr. *(acabar)* to conclude; AMER., COLL. to finish off.

ul·ti·má·tum m. ultimatum.

úl·ti·mo, a adj. *(final)* last <*la ú. partida de la temporada* the last game of the season>; *(de dos)* latter; *(más reciente)* latest, most recent; *(remoto)* farthest; *(mejor)* finest; *(de abajo)* bottom; *(de arriba)* top; *(de atrás)* back; FIG. *(definitivo)* last <*como ú. remedio* as a last resort>; COM. lowest ♦ **a últimos de** at or towards the end of (a month) ♦ **la ú. grito (de la moda)** the latest craze ♦ **estar a lo ú. de** to be nearly at the end of ♦ **estar en las últimas** COLL. *(estar moribundo)* to be on one's last legs; *(estar en la miseria)* to be down and out ♦ **llegar el ú.** to arrive last ♦ **por ú.** lastly.

ul·tra I. adv. besides II. m.f. extremist.

ul·tra·de·re·cha f. far right.

ul·tra·de·re·chis·ta adj. & m.f. far rightist.

ul·tra·jan·te adj. offensive, outrageous.

ul·tra·jar intr. to insult, outrage.

ul·tra·je m. insult, outrage.

ul·tra·mar m. overseas country.

ul·tra·ma·ri·no, a I. adj. overseas II. m.pl. *(comestibles)* imported foods; *(tienda)* grocery store.

ul·tra·mo·der·no, a adj. ultramodern.

ul·tran·za adj. ♦ **a u.** *(a muerte)* to the death; *(resueltamente)* determinedly.

ul·tra·rro·jo, a adj. ultrared.

ul·tra·só·ni·co, a adj. ultrasonic.

ul·tra·so·ni·do m. ultrasound.

ul·tra·tum·ba f. otherworld.

ul·tra·vio·le·ta adj. ultraviolet.

u·lu·lar intr. to howl.

um·bi·li·cal adj. umbilical.

um·bral m. threshold.

um·brí·o, a I. adj. shady II. f. shade.

um·bro·so, a adj. shady.

un contr. of **uno.**

u·ná·ni·me adj. unanimous.

u·na·ni·mi·dad f. unanimity ♦ **por u.** unanimously.

un·ción f. unction; RELIG. extreme unction.

un·cir §35 tr. to yoke.

un·dé·ci·mo, a adj. & m. eleventh.

un·du·lan·te adj. undulating.

un·du·lar intr. to undulate.

un·gir §32 tr. to anoint.

un·güen·to m. ointment.

u·ni·ce·lu·lar adj. unicellular.

u·ni·ci·dad f. uniqueness.

ú·ni·co, a I. adj. *(solo)* only; *(extraordinario)* unique II. m.f. only one <*es el ú. que me queda* it's the only one I have left> ♦ **lo ú.** only thing <*¡lo ú. que faltaba!* that's the only thing that was missing!>.

u·ni·cor·nio m. unicorn.

u·ni·dad f. *(acuerdo)* unity; *(armonía)* harmony; *(cada uno)* each (one) <*valen veinte pesos la u.* they cost twenty pesos each>; MATH., MIL., TECH. unit ♦ **u. monetaria** monetary unit.

u·ni·do, a adj. *(juntos)* united; *(que se quieren)* close.

u·ni·fi·car §70 tr. to unify.

u·ni·for·mar tr. to make uniform.

u·ni·for·me I. adj. *(igual)* uniform; *(terreno)* level; *(ritmo)* steady; *(sin variedad)* plain <*estilo u.* plain style> II. m. uniform.

u·ni·for·mi·dad f. uniformity.

u·ni·gé·ni·to, a I. adj. only <*hijo u.* only child> II. m. RELIG. Son of God.

u·ni·la·te·ral adj. unilateral.

u·nión f. union; *(armonía)* unity; *(conexión)* joint.

u·nir tr. *(juntar)* to unite; *(combinar)* to join (together); *(casar)* to unite (by marriage); *(mezclarse)* to mix; *(aliar)* to combine <*u. la teoría con la experiencia práctica* to combine theory with practical experience>; COM. to merge; MECH., TECH. to join —reflex. *(juntarse)* to join; *(casarse)* to marry; *(mezclarse)* to mix; COM. to merge ♦ **u. a** or **u. con** to join ♦ **u. en matrimonio** to be united in marriage.

u·ni·se·xo adj. unisex.

u·ní·so·no, a I. adj. in unison II. m. unison ♦ **al u.** in unison.

u·ni·ta·rio, a I. adj. unified; RELIG. Unitarian II. m.f. RELIG. Unitarian.

u·ni·ver·sal adj. universal; *(del mundo)* world <*historia u.* world history>.

u·ni·ver·sa·li·dad f. universality.

u·ni·ver·sa·li·zar §04 tr. to universalize.

u·ni·ver·si·dad f. university.

u·ni·ver·si·ta·rio, a I. adj. university II. m.f. university student.

u·ni·ver·so m. universe.

u·no, a I. m. one II. adj. one ♦ **la u.** one o'clock ♦ **u. que otro** a few ♦ pl. some, a few <*unos estudiantes* some students>; about; approximately <*unos veinte kilómetros de aquí* about twenty kilometers from here> III. indef. pron. one <*u. de mis amigos* one of my friends>; one, you <*u. no puede escaparse de aquí* you cannot escape from here>; *(alguien)* somebody <*u. lo hizo* somebody did it> ♦ **cada u.** each one, every one ♦ **de u. en u.** one by one ♦ **u. a otro** or **con otro** each other, one another <*se miraron u. a otro* they looked at each other> ♦ **u. a or por u.** one at a time ♦ **u. y otro** both ♦ **u. tras otro** one after another ♦ pl. **u. a otros** one another ♦ **u. cuantos** a few, some IV. indef. art. **a, an** <*necesito u. pluma* I need a pen>.

un·tar tr. *(engrasar)* to grease; *(manchar)* to smear; to spread <*u. el pan con mermelada* to spread bread with jam>; MED. to rub ♦ **u. la mano a alguien** COLL. to grease someone's palm.

un·to m. *(materia grasa)* grease; *(del animal)* fat ♦ **u. de México** COLL. bribe.

un·tuo·si·dad f. greasiness.

un·tuo·so, a adj. greasy.

un·tu·ra f. *(acción)* greasing; *(sustancia)* ointment.

u·ña f. *(de la mano)* fingernail; *(del pie)* toenail; *(garra)* claw; *(pezuña)* hoof; *(garfio)* claw; *(gancho)* hook ♦ **comerse las uñas** to

bite one's nails • **sacar las uñas** COLL. to show
one's claws • **ser u. y carne** to be inseparable.
ju·pa! interj. upsy-daisy! ♦ **a u.** in arms.
u·ra·nio m. uranium.
ur·ba·ni·dad f. urbanity.
ur·ba·nis·ta m.f. city planner.
ur·ba·nís·tl·co, a adj. (de la ciudad) urban; (del
urbanismo) city-planning.
ur·ba·ni·za·ción f. (urbanismo) urbanization,
city planning; (desarrollo) development.
ur·ba·ni·zar §04 tr. (civilizar) to civilize; (un
terreno) to develop ♦ **zona sin u.** undeveloped
area.
ur·ba·no, a adj. (de la ciudad) urban; (cortés)
urbane.
ur·be f. large city.
ur·di·dor, ·ra TEX. I. adj. warping II. m.f.
warper.
ur·dim·bre f. TEX. warping; FIG. scheming.
ur·dir tr. TEX. to warp; FIG. to scheme.
u·re·a f. urea.
u·ré·ter m. ureter.
u·re·tra f. urethra.
ur·gen·cia f. urgency ♦ **con u.** urgently • **cura
de u.** first aid.
ur·gen·te adj. urgent.
ur·gir §32 intr. to be urgent.
u·ri·na·rio, a I. adj. urinary II. m. urinal.
ur·na f. (caja) urn, (urta) ballot box, (cuja de
cristales) glass case ♦ **acudir** or **ir a las urnas**
to go to the polls.
u·ró·lo·go, a m.f. urologist.
u·rra·ca f. magpie.
ur·ti·ca·ria f. hives.
u·sa·do, a adj. (deteriorado) worn-out; (de segunda mano) secondhand.
u·san·za f. custom.
u·sar tr. (emplear) to use; (llevar ropa) to wear
♦ **sin u.** unused —intr. (soler) to be accustomed (to) <uso nadar todos los días I'm accustomed to swimming every day>; (emplear) to
use, make use of <u. de artimaña to use trick-
ery> ♦ **u. mal de** to misuse —reflex. (estar de
moda) to be the custom or the fashion; (estar
en uso) to be used.
u·so m. (empleo) use <el u. de fibras sintéticas
the use of synthetic fibers>; (goce) exercise <el
u. del privilegio hereditario the exercise of hereditary privilege>; (moda) fashion; (costumbre) custom; (desgaste) wear and tear ♦ **al u.**
de in the style of • **deteriorado con el u.** well-
used • **estar fuera de u.** to be obsolete • **hacer
mal u. de** to misuse • **hacer u. de** to use •
hacer u. de la palabra to speak • **para todo u.**
all-purpose • **ser de u.** (emplearse) to be used;
(llevarse) to be worn • **u. de razón** power of
reason.
us·ted pron. you ♦ **de u.** yours • **hablar** or
tratar de u. to use the polite form of address ♦
pl. you, all of you.
u·sual adj. usual.
u·sua·rio, a I. adj. usufructuary <derechos
usuarios usufructuary rights> II. m.f. user.
u·su·fruc·to m. usufruct.
u·su·ra f. usury.
u·su·re·ro, a I. adj. usurious II. m.f. usurer.
u·sur·pa·ción f. usurpation.
u·sur·pa·dor, ·ra I. adj. usurping II. m.f.
usurper.
u·sur·par tr. to usurp.
u·ten·si·lio m. utensil.
u·te·ri·no, a adj. uterine.

ú·te·ro m. uterus.
ú·til I. adj. (que sirve) useful; (apto) fit II. m.
tool, utensil ♦ pl. implements • **ú. de pesca**
fishing tackle.
u·ti·li·dad f. (cualidad) usefulness; (provecho)
profit ♦ **u. bruta** gross profit ♦ pl. profits • **u.
de capital** capital gains • **u. impositivas** taxable profits • **u. líquidas** net profits.
u·ti·li·zar §04 tr. to utilize.
u·to·pí·a f. utopia.
u·tó·pi·co, a adj. & m.f. utopian.
u·va f. grape ♦ **estar hecho una u.** COLL. to be
drunk as a skunk • **u. pasa** raisin.
ú·vu·la f. uvula.
u·xo·ri·ci·da I. adj. uxoricidal II. m. uxoricide.
¡uy! interj. (sorpresa) oh!; (dolor) ouch!

V

v, V f. twenty-fifth letter of the Spanish alphabet ♦ **v. doble** double-u, w.
va·ca f. cow; CUL. beef; (cuero) cowhide,
leather; (dinero) gambling pool ♦ **v. de San An-
tón** ladybug • **v. lechera** milk cow • **v. marina**
manatee, sea cow • **vacas gordas** years of
plenty.
va·ca·ción f. vacation ♦ **estar de vacaciones**
to be on vacation.
va·can·te I. adj. vacant II. f. vacancy.
va·cia·de·ro m. dump.
va·cia·do m. (de metales) casting; (figura) cast.
va·ciar §30 tr. (dejar vacío) to empty <v. una
caja to empty a box>; (verter) to drain <v. una
botella to drain a bottle>; (fundir) to cast; (sacar filo) to sharpen; (ahuecar) to hollow out
—intr. to empty —reflex. to empty.
va·ci·la·ción f. hesitation ♦ **sin v.** unhesitatingly.
va·ci·lan·te adj. (persona) hesitating; (luz)
flickering.
va·ci·lar intr. (moverse) to sway; (la luz) to
flicker; (dudar) to hesitate; MEX. to go on a
spree ♦ **sin v.** unhesitatingly.
va·cí·o, a I. adj. empty; (desocupado) vacant;
(hueco) hollow; (falto) devoid <una cabeza v.
de ideas a mind devoid of ideas> II. m. (cavidad) emptiness; (hueco) hollow; (espacio)
empty space; (falta) void <su muerte ha dejado
un gran v. his death has left a great void>;
PHYS. vacuum ♦ **envasado al v.** vacuum-
packed • **hacer el v. a alguien** COLL. to give
someone the cold shoulder.
va·cui·dad f. vacuity.
va·cu·na·ción f. vaccination.
va·cu·nar tr. to vaccinate.
va·cu·no, a adj. bovine ♦ **ganado v.** cattle.
va·cuo, a adj. vacuous.
va·de·ar tr. (un río) to ford; (a pie) to wade
across; (una dificultad) to overcome.
va·do m. (de un río) ford; (recurso) remedy.
va·ga·bun·de·ar intr. to wander.
va·ga·bun·do, a adj. & m.f. vagabond.
va·ga·men·te adv. vaguely.
va·gan·cia f. (delito) vagrancy; (ociosidad)
idleness.
va·gar §47 intr. (errar) to wander; (andar
ocioso) to be idle.
va·gi·do m. cry.
va·gi·na f. vagina.
va·go, a I. adj. (indeterminado) vague; (holga-

zán) lazy; *(vagabundo)* vagrant **II.** m. *(holgazán)* loafer; *(vagabundo)* vagrant; ANAT. vagus nerve.

va·gón m. RAIL. use, coach; *(para mercancías)* truck, van ♦ **v. cama** sleeping car • **v. de carga** freight car • **v. de equipajes** baggage car • **v. de pasajeros** passenger car • **v. de primera** first-class car • **v. restaurante** dining car.

va·go·ne·ta f. small wagon *or* cart.

va·gue·ar intr. to wander.

va·gue·dad f. *(cualidad)* vagueness; *(expresión vaga)* vague remark.

va·hí·do m. dizzy spell.

va·ho m. steam.

vai·na I. f. *(envoltura)* sheath; BOT. pod; MARIT. casing; AMER., COLL. *(molestia)* nuisance **II.** adj. AMER., COLL. annoying.

vai·ni·lla f. vanilla; SEW. hemstitch.

vai·vén m. *(oscilación)* oscillation; *(balanceo)* swaying; *(fluctuación)* fluctuation.

va·ji·lla f. tableware ♦ **lavar la v.** to wash the dishes • **v. de plata** silverware • **v. de porcelana** china.

val·drá, dría see **valer.**

va·le m. *(pagaré)* voucher; *(recibo)* receipt.

va·le·de·ro, a adj. valid.

va·len·cia f. valence.

va·len·tí·a f. *(valor)* bravery; *(ánimo)* boldness.

va·len·tón, o·na I. adj. boastful **II.** m.f. braggart.

va·len·to·na·da f. boast.

va·ler §74 I. intr. *(tener valor)* to be worth; *(tener mérito)* to be of value; *(ser válido)* to be valid *<esta moneda no vale* this coin is not valid>; *(tener autoridad)* to have authority *<el supervisor no vale para esto* the supervisor does not have authority in this matter>; *(servir)* to be useful, be of use *<no le valdrán todas sus palancas* all of his connections will be of no use to him> ♦ **más vale** it is better —tr. *(tener un valor de)* to be worth *<el reloj vale cien dólares* the watch is worth a hundred dollars>; *(costar)* to be *<¿cuánto vale?* how much is it?>; *(representar)* to be worth *<una blanca vale dos negras* a half note is worth two quarter notes>; *(producir)* to yield *<esa inversión le valió cien mil pesos* that investment yielded him a hundred thousand pesos>; *(causar)* to cause *<nuestra conducta nos valió muchos disgustos* our conduct caused us a lot of trouble> ♦ **hacer v. sus derechos** to assert one's rights • **v. la pena** to be worthwhile • **v. lo que pesa en oro** to be worth its weight in gold —reflex. to manage for oneself ♦ **v. de** to make use of **II.** m. worth.

va·le·ro·so, a adj. courageous.

va·le·tu·di·na·rio, a adj. & m.f. sickly (person).

val·ga, go see **valer.**

va·lí·a f. worth.

va·li·da·ción f. validation.

va·li·dar tr. to validate.

va·li·dez f. validity.

vá·li·do, a adj. valid.

va·lien·te I. adj. *(inútil)* brave; *(osado)* bold; COLL. a fine *<¡v. amigo eres tú!* a fine friend you are!> *<¡v. frío!* it's freezing! **II.** m. *(valeroso)* brave man; *(valentón)* braggart.

va·li·ja f. *(maleta)* suitcase; *(saco de correo)* mailbag ♦ **v. diplomática** diplomatic pouch.

va·lio·so, a adj. valuable.

va·lor m. *(cualidad)* worth; *(precio)* price *<el v. de la propiedad* the price of the property>; *(importancia)* importance; *(osadía)* nerve *<tener el*

v. de negarlo to have the nerve to deny it>; *(coraje)* valor; MATH., MUS. value ♦ **dar v. a** to attach importance to • **de v.** valuable • **sin v.** worthless • **v. adquisitivo** purchasing power • **v. comercial** market value • **v. nominal** COM. face value ♦ pl. COM. securities • **v. inmuebles** real estate.

va·lo·ra·ción f. appraisal.

va·lo·rar tr. *(dar mérito)* to appreciate; *(valuar)* to appraise; *(aumentar el valor)* to increase the value of.

va·lo·ri·za·ción f. appraisal.

va·lo·ri·zar §04 tr. *(evaluar)* to appraise; *(aumentar el valor)* to raise the value of.

vals m. waltz.

va·lua·ción f. appraisal.

va·luar §67 tr. to appraise, value.

vál·vu·la f. valve; MECH. RAD. tube.

va·lla f. *(cerca)* fence; *(obstáculo)* obstacle; SPORT. hurdle.

va·llar tr. to fence in.

va·lle m. *(entre montañas)* valley; *(de un río)* river basin ♦ **v. de lágrimas** vale of tears.

va·mos, van see **ir.**

vam·pi·re·sa f. vamp.

vam·pi·ro m. vampire.

va·na·glo·ria f. pride.

va·na·glo·riar·se reflex. to boast.

va·na·glo·rio·so, a adj. & m.f. boastful (person).

va·na·men·te adv. *(inútilmente)* vainly; *(con vanidad)* presumptuously; *(tontamente)* foolishly.

van·da·lis·mo m. vandalism.

van·guar·dia f. MIL. vanguard; ARTS, LIT. avant-garde ♦ **ir a la v.** to be in the forefront.

van·guar·dis·ta adj. & m.f. avant-garde (artist).

va·ni·dad f. *(cualidad)* vanity; *(ostentación)* ostentation; *(orgullo)* conceit.

va·ni·do·so, a adj. & m.f. vain *or* conceited (person).

va·no, a I. adj. *(inútil)* vain; *(frívolo)* frivolous; *(vanidoso)* conceited ♦ **en v.** in vain, vainly **II.** m. ARCHIT. window.

va·por m. *(gas)* steam; *(vaho)* vapor; *(buque)* steamship ♦ **al v.** CUL. steamed • **v. de ruedas** paddle steamer.

va·po·ri·za·dor m. vaporizer.

va·po·ri·zar §04 tr. to vaporize.

va·po·ro·so, a adj. *(que despide vapores)* vaporous; *(tejido)* sheer.

va·pu·le·ar tr. to thrash.

va·que·ro, a I. adj. pertaining to cowhands ♦ **pantalón v.** jeans **II.** m. cowboy.

va·que·ta f. cowhide.

va·ra f. *(palo)* stick; *(rama)* rod; *(bastón)* staff; BOT. stalk; *(medida)* linear measurement (.84 meters); *(de trombón)* slide; TAUR. *(pica)* pike; *(garrochazo)* thrust with a pike.

va·ra·de·ro m. dry dock.

va·ra·du·ra f. running aground.

va·rar MARIT. tr. to beach —intr. to run aground.

va·ra·zo m. *(golpe)* blow with a stick; TAUR. thrust with a lance.

va·re·a·dor, ·ra m.f. *(de árboles)* beater; *(del ganado)* cowhand.

va·re·ar tr. *(derribar)* to knock down; *(dar golpes)* to cudgel; TAUR. to jab with the lance.

va·ria·ble adj. & f. MATH. variable.

va·ria·ción f. variation.

va·ria·do, a adj. varied.

va·rian·te I. adj. varying II. f. variant.

va·riar §30 tr. & intr. to vary.

va·ri·ce f. varicose vein.

va·ri·ce·la f. chicken pox.

va·rie·dad f. variety ♦ pl. (cosas diversas) miscellany; THEAT. variety show.

va·ri·lla f. (vara) rod; (de un paraguas) rib; (de corsé) stay; MEX. peddler's wares ♦ v. de pistón piston rod • v. mágica magic wand.

va·rio, a I. adj. (que varía) varied; (cambiadizo) varying, changeable ♦ pl. several II. m.f. ♦ pl. several <varios piensan que sí several think so>.

va·rón m. (hombre) male; (niño) boy <tienen dos hijas y un v. they have two girls and one boy> ♦ santo v. COLL. plain simple man.

va·ro·nil adj. (masculino) virile; (dicho de mujer) mannish.

va·sa·lla·je m. servitude.

va·sa·llo, a I. adj. subordinate II. m.f. HIST. vassal; (súbdito) subject.

vas·cu·lar adj. vascular.

va·sec·to·mí·a f. vasectomy.

va·se·li·na f. Vaseline (trademark).

va·si·ja f. container.

va·so m. glass; (jarrón) vasc; ZOOL. hoof; ANAT., BOT. vessel.

vás·ta·go m. BOT. shoot; (hijo) offspring; MECH. rod ♦ v. de válvula or de distribución valve rod or stem.

vas·to, a adj. vast.

va·ti·ci·na·dor, ·ra I. adj. prophesying II. m.f. prophet.

va·ti·ci·nar tr. to predict.

va·ti·ci·nio m. prediction.

va·tio m. watt.

va·tio·ho·ra m. watt-hour.

va·ya see ir.

ve see ir or ver².

ve·a, veo see ver².

ve·ci·nal adj. local.

ve·cin·dad f. (cualidad) nearness; (vecindario) neighbors; (cercanías) vicinity ♦ casa de v. apartment building.

ve·cin·da·rio m. neighborhood.

ve·ci·no, a I. adj. (próximo) next ♦ v. a or de near II. m.f. neighbor ♦ cualquier hijo de v. COLL. anybody.

ve·da f. (prohibición) prohibition; HUNT. closed season.

ve·da·do, a I. adj. prohibited II. m. game preserve.

ve·dar tr. (prohibir) to prohibit; (impedir) to prevent.

ve·e·dor, ·ra I. adj. prying II. m.f. busybody —m. supervisor.

ve·ge·ta·ción f. vegetation.

ve·ge·tal I. adj. vegetable ♦ reino v. plant kingdom II. m. vegetable; (planta) plant.

ve·ge·tar intr. to vegetate.

ve·ge·ta·ria·no, a adj. & m.f. vegetarian.

ve·ge·ta·ti·vo, a adj. vegetative.

ve·he·men·cia f. vehemence.

ve·he·men·te adj. vehement.

ve·hí·cu·lo m. vehicle; MED. carrier.

ve·í·a see ver².

vein·ta·vo, a adj. & m. twentieth.

vein·te I. adj. twenty; (vigésimo) twentieth II. m. twenty.

vein·te·na f. score.

vein·ti·dós adj. & m. twenty-two.

vein·ti·tan·tos, as adj. (cantidad) twenty or so;

(del mes) around the twentieth.

vein·ti·ún adj. contr. of veintiuno.

vein·tiu·no, a I. adj. twenty-one; (vigésimo primero) twenty-first II. m. twenty-one.

ve·ja·ción f. vexation.

ve·ja·men m. (molestia) vexation; (insulto) affront; (represión satírica) derision.

ve·jar tr. to vex.

ve·jes·to·rio m. DEROG. (persona) old fool; (cosa) old wreck.

ve·je·te COLL. I. adj. old II. m. old man.

ve·jez f. old age.

ve·ji·ga f. ANAT. bladder; (en la piel) blister ♦ v. de la bilis gall bladder • v. natatoria swim bladder.

ve·la¹ f. (vigilia) vigil; (trabajo) night shift; (luz) candle <v. de cera wax candle>; MEX. reprimand ♦ en v. awake • estar a dos velas FIG. to be broke • no darle a alguien v. en un entierro FIG. not to give someone a say in the matter.

ve·la² f. MARIT. sail ♦ a toda v. under full sail • barco de v. sailboat • buque de v. sailing ship • hacerse a la v. to set sail • v. de cuchillo staysail • v. mayor mainsail.

ve·la·da f. evening ♦ quedarse de v. to spend the evening.

ve·la·do, a adj. (oculto) veiled; (voz) muffled; (imagen) blurred.

ve·la·dor, ·ra I. adj. watching II. m.f. (persona que vela) vigil-keeper —m. (mesita) night table; R.P. bedside lamp; MEX. glass lampshade.

ve·la·me(n) m. sails.

ve·lar tr. (vigilar) to keep watch over; (cuidar) to sit up with <v. a un niño enfermo to sit up with a sick child>; (cubrir) to cover with a veil; (esconder) to hide —intr. (no dormir) to stay awake; (trabajar) to work late; RELIG. to keep vigil ♦ v. por to care for, look after —reflex. PHOTOG. to blur.

ve·la·to·rio m. wake.

ve·lei·dad f. (deseo vano) whim; (inconstancia) fickleness.

ve·lei·do·so, a adj. fickle.

ve·le·ro, a I. adj. swift-sailing II. m.f. (de velas para buques) sailmaker; (de velas de cera) candlemaker —m. sailboat.

ve·le·ta f. weather vane —m.f. COLL. weathercock.

ve·lo m. veil; (humeral) humeral veil ♦ correr or echar un v. sobre algo to hush something up • tomar el v. to take the veil • v. del paladar soft palate.

ve·lo·ci·dad f. velocity; AUTO. gear ♦ exceso de v. speeding • v. de ascensión AER. climbing speed • v. límite speed limit • v. máxima top speed.

ve·lo·cí·me·tro m. speedometer.

ve·ló·dro·mo m. velodrome.

ve·lo·rio m. wake; R.P. dull party.

ve·loz adj. swift.

ve·lu·do m. plush.

ve·llo m. (pelo) hair; (pelusilla) fuzz.

ve·llón m. (lana) fleece; (piel) sheepskin; (mechón) tuft of wool.

ve·llo·ci·no m. fleece.

ve·llu·do, a I. adj. hairy II. m. TEX. velveteen.

ven see venir.

ve·na f. vein; (inspiración) inspiration ♦ darle a uno la v. to feel like doing something crazy • estar en v. to be in the mood.

ve·na·blo m. javelin.

ve·na·do m. stag; CUL. venison ♦ **pintar el v.** MEX. to play hooky.

ven·ce·de·ro, a adj. COM. payable.

ven·ce·dor, ·ra I. adj. (conquistador) conquering; (victorioso) winning II. m.f. (conquistador) conqueror; (ganador) winner.

ven·cer §75 tr. (conquistar) to conquer; (derrotar) to defeat; (aventajar) to surpass; (superar) to overcome; to be overcome <le venció el sueño he was overcome by sleep>; to control, master <v. las pasiones to control one's emotions> —intr. (ganar) to win; COM. (cumplir un plazo) to expire; (una deuda) to fall due —reflex. (combarse) to bend; (romperse) to collapse.

ven·ci·do, a I. adj. (derrotado) defeated; COM. (una deuda) due; (cumplido) expired II. m.f. loser —fr. ♦ **a la tercera va la v.** (exhortando) the third time is the charm; (amenazando) three strikes and you're out.

ven·ci·mien·to m. (victoria) victory; (derrota) defeat; (torcimiento) bending; (al romperse) collapse; COM. (término) expiration; (de una deuda) maturity.

ven·da f. bandage; (de cabeza) headband ♦ **tener una v. en los ojos** to be blindfolded.

ven·da·je m. bandage.

ven·dar tr. to bandage ♦ **v. los ojos** to blindfold.

ven·da·val m. gale.

ven·de·dor, ·ra I. adj. selling II. m.f. (persona que vende) seller; (de tienda) salesperson ♦ **v. ambulante** peddler.

ven·der tr. to sell; (hacer comercio) to market; (sacrificar) to sell (out); (traicionar) to betray ♦ **v. al contado** to sell for cash • **v. al por mayor** to sell wholesale • **v. al por menor** to sell retail • **v. a plazos** to sell on installment • **v. caro** to be expensive —reflex. to sell, be sold <las manzanas se venden por docena apples are sold by the dozen>; (dejarse sobornar) to sell oneself ♦ **se vende** for sale.

ven·di·mia f. (cosecha) grape harvest; (año) vintage.

ven·di·mia·dor, ·ra m.f. grape picker.

ven·drá, dría see venir.

ve·ne·no m. (toxina) poison; FIG. venom.

ve·ne·no·so, a adj. poisonous.

ve·ne·ra·ble adj. venerable.

ve·ne·ra·ción f. veneration.

ve·ne·rar tr. to venerate.

ve·né·re·o, a adj. & m. venereal (disease).

ven·ga, go see venir.

ven·ga·dor, ·ra I. adj. avenging II. m.f. avenger.

ven·gan·za f. vengeance.

ven·gar §47 tr. & reflex. to avenge (oneself) ♦ **v. de alguien** to take revenge on someone.

ven·ga·ti·vo, a adj. vindictive.

ve·nia f. (perdón) forgiveness; (permiso) permission; AMER., MIL. salute.

ve·ni·da f. (llegada) arrival; (regreso) return.

ve·ni·de·ro, a adj. coming, upcoming.

ve·nir §76 intr. to come; (llegar) to arrive; (ropa) to fit <esta chaqueta ya no me viene this jacket no longer fits me>; (tener) to get <me vino un dolor de cabeza I got a headache>; (inferirse) to follow <esta conclusión viene de tal postura this conclusion follows from such a posture>; (presentarse) to occur <la idea me vino inesperadamente the idea occurred to me unexpectedly>; (producirse) to grow <el trigo

viene bien en esta región wheat grows well in this region>; (suceder) to end up <vino a morir he ended up dying>; (resultar) to end up <viene a ser lo mismo it ends up being all the same>; (repetir) to keep <vengo diciéndolo desde hace cinco meses I have been saying so for five months> ♦ **que viene** next <el año que viene next year> • **v. a la memoria** to come to mind • **v. al caso** to be relevant • **v. al mundo** to come into the world • **v. al pelo** COLL. to come in the nick of time • **venga lo que venga** come what may • **venirle ancho a uno** to be too big for one • **ver v.** to see it coming —reflex. ♦ **v. abajo** or **por tierra** or **al suelo** to collapse, fall down.

ven·ta f. sale ♦ **servicio de v.** sales department • **v. al contado** cash sale • **v. a crédito** credit sale • **v. al por mayor** wholesale • **v. al por menor** retail.

ven·ta·ja f. (superioridad) advantage; (en una carrera) lead; (provecho) benefit ♦ **llevar v.** to have the lead over • **sacar v. a** to be ahead of • **sacar v. de** to profit from.

ven·ta·jo·so, a adj. advantageous.

ven·ta·na f. window; ANAT. nostril ♦ **echar** or **tirar por la v.** to squander.

ven·ta·nal m. large window.

ven·ta·ni·lla f. (de vehículo) window; (portilla) porthole; (taquilla) box office.

ven·ta·rrón m. COLL. gale.

ven·ti·la·ción f. ventilation.

ven·ti·la·dor m. fan.

ven·ti·lar tr. (un lugar) to air out; (discutir) to air; (hacer público) to make public —reflex. COLL. to get some fresh air.

ven·tis·ca f. blizzard.

ven·tis·car §70 intr. to snow heavily.

ven·tis·que·ro m. (ventisca) blizzard; (de un monte) snowcap.

ven·to·le·ra f. gust of wind ♦ **darle a uno la v. de hacer algo** COLL. to take it into one's head to do something.

ven·to·se·ar intr. to break wind.

ven·to·si·dad f. gas.

ven·to·so, a I. adj. windy II. f. MED. cupping glass; ZOOL. sucker; (abertura) air hole.

ven·tre·ra f. (faja) bellyband; (armadura) stomach plate (of armor); (del caballo) cinch.

ven·tri·cu·lar adj. ventricular.

ven·trí·cu·lo m. ventricle.

ven·trí·lo·cuo, a m.f. ventriloquist.

ven·tri·lo·quia f. ventriloquism.

ven·tro·so/tru·do, a adj. paunchy.

ven·tu·ra f. (felicidad) happiness; (suerte) luck ♦ **a la (buena) v.** with no set plan • **decir la buena v. a alguien** to tell someone's fortune • **por v.** as luck would have it • **probar v.** to try one's luck.

ven·tu·ro·so, a adj. fortunate.

ver¹ m. (apariencia) appearance; (opinión) opinion <a mi v. in my opinion>.

ver² §77 tr. to see; (mirar) to look at; (televisión, películas) to watch; (visitar) to visit; (averiguar) to look and see <vea usted si está Pedro look and see if Peter is here>; (examinar) to examine <veamos este párrafo let's examine this paragraph>; (observar) to observe ♦ **a** or **hasta más** v. so long • **a v.** let's see • **estar** or **quedar en veremos** AMER. to be a long way off • **tener que v. con** to have to do with • **veremos** we'll see • **v. venir** to see it coming —reflex. (ser visto) to be seen; (ser obvio) to be obvious or clear; (*mirarse*) to see oneself <*v. en el espejo* to see oneself in the mirror>; (*hallarse*) to find oneself <*me veo pobre y sin amigos* I find myself poor and without friends>; (*visitarse*) to see one another; (*encontrarse*) to meet <*v. con los amigos* to meet with friends> ♦ **estar por v.** to remain to be seen • **véase** see (in references) • **vérselas con** COLL. to have to deal with • **vérselas negras** COLL. to be in a jam.

ve·ra f. edge ♦ **a la v. de** next to.

ve·ra·ci·dad f. veracity.

ve·ra·ne·an·te m.f. summer resident.

ve·ra·ne·ar intr. to spend the summer.

ve·ra·ne·o m. vacationing ♦ **ir de v.** to go on vacation • **lugar de v.** summer resort.

ve·ra·nie·go, a adj. (*del verano*) summer; (*ligero*) light.

ve·ra·no m. summer.

ve·ras f.pl. (*verdad*) truth; (*seriedad*) earnestness ♦ **de v.** really.

ve·raz adj. truthful.

ver·ba f. loquaciousness.

ver·bal adj. verbal.

ver·be·na f. verbena, vervain; (*fiesta*) festival held on the eve of a saint's day.

ver·bi·gra·cia or **ver·bi gra·tia** adv. for example, for instance.

ver·bo m. GRAM. verb; RELIG. Word.

ver·bo·rre·a f. COLL. verbosity.

ver·bo·si·dad f. verbosity.

ver·bo·so, a adj. verbose.

ver·dad f. truth <*decir la v.* to tell the truth>; (*veracidad*) truthfulness ♦ **a decir v. or a la v.** to be honest • **de v.** (*de veras*) truly; (*verdadero*) real <*él es un héroe de v.* he is a real hero> • **¿de v.?** really? • **decirle a alguien cuatro verdades** FIG. to tell it like it is • **en v.** truly • **faltar a la v.** to lie • **la pura v.** the plain truth • **¿no es v.?** isn't that so? • **¿v.?** is that so?

ver·da·de·ro, a adj. (*real*) true; (*auténtico*) genuine; (*veraz*) truthful.

ver·de I. adj. green; unseasoned <*leña v.* unseasoned wood>; (*inmaduro*) unripe; (*obsceno*) dirty; COLL. (*libertino*) dirty <*un viejo v.* a dirty old man> ♦ **poner v. a uno** to tell someone off • **v. de envidia** green with envy II. m. (*color*) green; (*verdor*) verdure; (*hierba*) grass; (*follaje*) foliage; (*alcacer*) fresh fodder; R.P. maté ♦ **v. esmeralda** emerald green • **v. mar** sea green • **v. oliva** olive green.

ver·de·mar I. adj. sea-green II. m. sea green.

ver·dín m. (*de las plantas*) fresh green; (*musgo*) moss.

ver·dor m. verdancy.

ver·do·so, a adj. greenish.

ver·du·go m. BOT. twig; (*de justicia*) executioner; (*de ladrillos*) layer of bricks.

ver·du·gón m. (*roncha*) welt; BOT. shoot.

ver·du·le·rí·a f. grocery store.

ver·du·le·ro, a m.f. greengrocer.

ver·du·ra f. (*verdor*) greenness; (*legumbre*) vegetable; (*follaje*) greenery.

ver·dus·co, a adj. dark greenish.

ve·re·da f. (*senda*) trail; AMER. sidewalk ♦ **entrar en v.** to fall in line.

ve·re·dic·to m. verdict.

ver·ga f. ANAT. penis; (*de ballesta*) steel bow; MARIT. yard.

ver·ga·jo m. pizzle.

ver·gel m. orchard.

ver·gon·zan·te adj. shamefaced.

ver·gon·zo·so, a I. adj. (*ignominioso*) shame-

---

ful; (*tímido*) shy II. m.f. shy person.

ver·güen·za f. (*bochorno*) shame; (*desconcierto*) embarrassment; (*timidez*) shyness; (*oprobio*) disgrace <*él es la v. de su familia* he is the disgrace of his family> ♦ **darle a uno to be ashamed** <*me da v. decírtelo* I am ashamed to tell you> • **no tener v.** to be shameless • **perder la v.** to lose all sense of shame • **¡que v.!** what a disgrace! • **sin v.** shameless(ly) • **tener v.** to be ashamed.

ve·ri·cue·to m. rugged path.

ve·rí·di·co, a adj. true.

ve·ri·fi·ca·ción f. verification.

ve·ri·fi·ca·dor, ·ra I. adj. checking II. m.f. checker.

ve·ri·fi·car §70 tr. (*la verdad*) to verify; (*una máquina*) to check; (*realizar*) to carry out —reflex. (*tener lugar*) to take place; (*una predicción*) to come true.

ve·ris·mo m. verism.

ver·ja f. (*de cerca*) railings; (*de ventana*) grating.

ver·me m. intestinal worm.

ver·mi·ci·da I. adj. vermicidal II. m. vermicide.

ver·mí·fu·go, a I. adj. vermifugal II. m. vermifuge.

ver·mut/mú m. (*aperitivo*) vermouth —f. AMER., CINEM., THEAT. matinée.

ver·ná·cu·lo, a adj. vernacular.

ver·nal adj. vernal.

ve·ró·ni·ca f. BOT. veronica, speedwell; TAUR. pass with the cape.

ve·ro·sí·mil adj. probable.

ve·ro·si·mi·li·tud f. probability.

ve·rru·ga f. wart.

ver·sa·do, a adj. versed.

ver·sar intr. ♦ **v. sobre** to deal with.

ver·sá·til adj. versatile; FIG. changeable.

ver·sa·ti·li·dad f. fickleness.

ver·sí·cu·lo m. versicle.

ver·si·fi·car §70 intr. & tr. to versify.

ver·sión f. version.

ver·so[1] m. verse; (*versículo*) versicle ♦ **echar versos** MEX. to gab.

ver·so[2] m. PRINT. verso.

vér·te·bra f. vertebra.

ver·te·bra·do, a adj. & m. vertebrate.

ver·te·bral adj. vertebral.

ver·te·de·ro m. (*desaguadero*) drain; (*de basura*) garbage dump.

ver·te·dor, ·ra I. adj. emptying II. m. (*canal*) drain; MARIT. bailer.

ver·ter §50 tr. (*derramar*) to spill; (*lágrimas, sangre*) to shed; (*vaciar*) to empty out; (*volcar*) to turn upside down; (*traducir*) to translate —intr. to flow.

ver·ti·cal adj. & f. vertical.

ver·ti·ca·li·dad f. verticality.

vér·ti·ce m. apex.

ver·tien·te I. adj. flowing II. f. (*declive*) slope; (*manantial*) spring.

ver·ti·gi·no·si·dad f. vertiginousness.

ver·ti·gi·no·so, a adj. vertiginous.

vér·ti·go m. vertigo; (*arrebato*) frenzy ♦ **tener v.** to feel dizzy.

ve·sí·cu·la f. vesicle ♦ **v. biliar** gall bladder.

ve·si·cu·lar adj. vesicular.

ves·per·ti·no, a adj. evening.

ves·tal adj. & f. vestal.

ves·tí·bu·lo m. (*antesala*) vestibule; (*en un hotel, teatro*) lobby.

ves·ti·do m. *(de mujer)* dress; *(de hombre)* suit ♦ **v. de noche** evening gown.

ves·ti·du·ra f. *(prenda de vestir)* garment; *(ropa)* clothes ♦ pl. RELIG. vestments.

ves·ti·gio m. vestige.

ves·ti·men·ta f. clothes.

ves·tir §48 tr. to dress <*vistieron a la novia* they dressed the bride>; *(llevar)* to wear <*vestía un traje rosado* she was wearing a pink suit>; *(cubrir)* to cover <*v. una puerta de acero* to cover a door with steel>; *(proveer con ropa)* to clothe <*v. a los pobres* to clothe the poor>; *(hacer ropa)* to dress <*este sastre viste a mis hermanos* this tailor dresses my brothers>; FIG. to dress up ♦ **quedarse para v. santos** COLL. to be an old maid —intr. *(ir vestido)* to dress <*ellos visten bien* they dress well>; *(lucir)* to look good <*la seda viste mucho* silk looks very good> ♦ **v. de** to wear <*él viste de uniforme* he wears a uniform> —reflex. *(ataviarse)* to get dressed; *(ir vestido)* to dress <*v. a la moda* to dress fashionably>; *(cubrirse)* to be covered <*el campo se viste de flores* the field is covered with flowers>.

ves·tua·rio m. wardrobe; *(cuarto)* dressing room; SPORT. locker room.

ve·ta f. *(de madera)* grain; MIN. vein.

ve·tar tr. to veto.

ve·te·a·do, a adj. streaked.

ve·te·ar tr. to streak.

ve·te·ra·ní·a f. *(larga experiencia)* long experience; *(antigüedad)* seniority.

ve·te·ra·no, a adj. & m.f. veteran.

ve·te·ri·na·rio, a I. adj. veterinary II. m.f. veterinarian —f. veterinary medicine.

ve·to m. veto ♦ **poner el v. a** to veto.

ve·tus·to, a adj. decrepit.

vez f. time <*te lo dije cuatro veces* I told you four times>; *(ocasión)* time <*hay veces que conviene no hablar* there are times when it is best not to talk>; *(turno)* turn <*la v. que me tocó no estuve aquí* when it was my turn, I was not here> ♦ **a la v.** at the same time • **a la v. que** while • **alguna que otra v.** once in a while • **algunas veces** sometimes • **a su v.** in turn • **a veces** at times • **cada v.** every time • **cada v. más** more and more • **cada v. menos** less and less • **cada v. que** whenever • **de una v.** all at once • **de una v. por todas** once and for all • **de v. en cuando** from time to time • **dos veces** twice • **en v. de** instead of • **érase una v.** once upon a time • **hacer las veces de** to stand in for • **muchas veces** often • **otra v.** again • **pocas o raras veces** rarely • **por enésima v.** COLL. for the umpteenth time • **repetidas veces** repeatedly • **tal v.** perhaps • **una que otra v.** once in a while • **una v.** once • **una v. que** as soon as.

vi, vimos see **ver²**.

ví·a¹ prep. via <*vamos v. Quito* we are going via Quito>.

ví·a² f. *(camino)* road; *(ruta)* route <*v. terrestre* land route>; RAIL. *(carril)* track; ANAT. tract; CHEM. process; LAW proceedings ♦ **en vías de** in the process of • **por v. oral** orally • **v. aérea** airway; *(correo)* airmail • **V. Crucis** Way of the Cross; FIG. ordeal • **v. de comunicación** channel of communication • **v. férrea** railroad • **v. fluvial** waterway • **V. Láctea** Milky Way • **v. marítima** seaway.

via·ble adj. viable.

via·duc·to m. viaduct.

via·jan·te adj. & m. traveling (salesman).

via·jar intr. to travel.

via·je m. trip ♦ **¡buen v.!** bon voyage! • **de un v.** AMER. all at once • **ir de v.** to go on a trip • **v. de ida y vuelta** round trip ♦ pl. travel.

via·je·ro, a I. adj. traveling II. m.f. traveler.

vial adj. road, traffic.

via·li·dad f. highway administration.

vian·da f. food.

viá·ti·co m. *(dietas)* per diem; RELIG. viaticum.

ví·bo·ra f. viper.

vi·bra·ción f. vibration.

vi·brar —intr. *(sacudirse)* to vibrate; *(sentirse conmovido)* to be moved.

vi·ca·rí·a f. *(oficio o territorio)* vicariate; *(residencia)* vicarage.

vi·ca·rio, a I. adj. deputy II. m. vicar.

vi·ce·al·mi·ran·te m. vice admiral.

vi·ce·can·ci·ller m. vice chancellor.

vi·ce·cón·sul m. vice consul.

vi·ce·ge·ren·te m. assistant manager.

vi·ce·go·ber·na·dor, ·ra m.f. lieutenant governor.

vi·ce·pre·si·den·cia f. *(en un país)* vicepresidency; *(en reunión)* vice-chairmanship.

vi·ce·pre·si·den·te m.f. *(en un país)* vice president; *(en reunión)* vice chairman.

vi·ce·ver·sa adv. vice versa.

vi·ciar tr. *(contaminar)* to pollute; *(pervertir)* to corrupt; *(adulterar)* to adulterate; *(falsificar)* to falsify; *(anular)* to invalidate —reflex. *(contaminarse)* to become polluted; *(entregarse al vicio)* to become corrupt.

vi·cio m. *(perversión)* vice; *(mala costumbre)* bad habit ♦ **v.** without reason.

vi·cio·so, a I. adj. *(incorrecto)* incorrect; *(depravado)* depraved II. m.f. *(persona depravada)* depraved person; *(toxicómano)* drug addict.

vi·ci·si·tud f. vicissitude.

víc·ti·ma f. victim.

vic·to·re·ar tr. to cheer.

vic·to·ria f. victory; *(éxito)* success; *(coche)* victoria.

vic·to·ria·no, a adj. & m.f. HIST. Victorian.

vic·to·rio·so, a I. adj. victorious II. m.f. victor.

vi·cu·ña f. vicuña.

vid f. grapevine.

vi·da f. life; *(duración)* lifetime; *(sustento)* living <*ganarse la v.* to earn one's living>; *(modo de vivir)* way of life; *(biografía)* life story; *(viveza)* liveliness ♦ **así es la v.** such is life • **buscarse la v.** COLL. to hustle • **dar mala v. a** to mistreat • **darse buena v.** to lead the good life • **echarse a la v.** to become a prostitute • **en la v.** never • **entre la v. y la muerte** at death's door • **escapar con v.** to come out alive • **la otra v.** the hereafter • **pasar a mejor v.** to pass away • **quitarse la v.** to take one's life • **v. mía** COLL. my dear • **v. y milagros** COLL. life history • **vivir la v.** to lead the good life.

vi·den·te m.f. clairvoyant.

ví·de·o m. or f. video.

ví·de·o·ca·se·te m. or f. videocassette.

ví·de·o·cin·ta f. videotape.

ví·de·o·dis·co m. videodisc/disk.

vi·do·rra f. COLL. life of ease.

vi·dria·do, a I. adj. glazed II. m. *(barniz)* glaze; *(loza)* glazed earthenware.

vi·driar tr. to apply a glaze to —intr. to become glazed.

vi·drie·ra f. window.

vi·drie·ro, a m.f. glazier.

vi·drio m. glass; R.P. window-pane ♦ **v. tallado** cut glass.

vi·drio·so, a adj. *(quebradizo)* fragile; *(suelo)* slippery; *(delicado)* tricky; *(ojos)* glassy.

vie·jo, a I. adj. old II. m. old man ♦ pl. old folks —f. old woman.

vie·ne see **venir**.

vien·to m. wind; *(cuerda)* guide rope; MUS. wind <*instrumentos de v.* wind instruments> ♦ **a los cuatro vientos** to the four winds • **contra v. y marea** against all odds • **hacer v.** to be windy • **ir v. en popa** to go smoothly *or* well.

vien·tre m. *(abdomen)* belly; *(matriz)* womb; *(intestino)* bowels <*evacuar el v.* to move one's bowels>; FIG. belly ♦ **bajo v.** lower abdomen.

vier·nes m.inv. Friday ♦ **V. Santo** Good Friday.

vier·ta, to see **verter**.

vi·ga f. *(madero)* beam; *(de metal)* girder ♦ **v. transversal** crossbeam.

vi·gen·cia f. force <*en v.* in force>.

vi·gen·te adj. in force.

vi·gé·si·mo, a adj. & m. twentieth.

vi·gí·a m. MARIT. lookout —f. watchtower; MARIT. reef.

vi·gi·lan·cia f. vigilance.

vi·gi·lan·te I. adj. vigilant II. m. *(guarda)* watchman; AMER. policeman.

vi·gi·lar tr. to watch over; intr. to watch.

vi·gi·lia f. *(vela)* vigil; *(falta de sueño)* sleeplessness; *(víspera)* eve ♦ **día de v.** day of abstinence.

vi·gor m. vigor; *(de una ley)* force, effect <*entrar en v.* to go into force>.

vi·go·ri·zar §04 tr. to invigorate.

vi·go·ro·so, a adj. vigorous.

vi·hue·la f. guitar.

vil adj. & m.f. base, despicable (person).

vi·le·za f. *(cualidad)* vileness; *(acción)* contemptible action.

vi·li·pen·diar tr. to vilify.

vi·li·pen·dio m. vilification.

vi·lo adv. ♦ **en v.** up in the air.

vi·lla f. *(pueblo)* village; *(casa)* villa.

vi·llan·ci·co m. Christmas carol.

vi·lla·ní·a f. despicable act.

vi·lla·no, a I. adj. *(que no es noble)* common; *(paisano)* peasant; *(grosero)* coarse, rude; *(vil)* base II. m.f. *(paisano)* commoner; *(persona mala)* villain.

vi·na·gre m. vinegar ♦ **cara de v.** COLL. sourpuss.

vi·na·gre·ra f. vinegar bottle ♦ pl. cruet.

vi·na·gre·ta f. vinaigrette.

vi·na·te·rí·a f. wine shop.

vi·na·te·ro, a adj. & m.f. wine *(merchant)*.

vin·cu·la·ción f. link.

vin·cu·lar tr. *(enlazar)* to link; LAW to entail.

vín·cu·lo m. link; LAW entailment.

vin·cha f. headband.

vin·di·ca·ción f. *(venganza)* revenge; *(defensa)* vindication.

vin·di·car §70 tr. *(vengar)* to avenge; *(defender)* to vindicate; LAW to claim, recover.

vin·dic·ta f. revenge.

vi·ní·co·la I. adj. wine-making II. m. winemaker.

vi·ni·cul·tor, ra m.f. grape grower.

vi·ni·cul·tu·ra f. viniculture.

vi·nie·ra, no see **venir**.

vi·ní·li·co, a adj. of vinyl.

vi·ni·lo m. vinyl.

vi·no m. wine ♦ **bautizar el v.** COLL. to water the wine • **v. añejo** vintage wine • **v. de Jerez** sherry • **v. de mesa** table wine • **v. de Oporto** port wine • **v. tinto** red wine.

vi·ña f. vineyard.

vi·ña·te·ro, a AMER. I. adj. grape-growing II. m.f. grape grower.

vi·ñe·do m. vineyard.

vi·ñe·ta f. vignette.

vio·la f. viola —m.f. violist.

vio·lá·ce·o, a adj. violet.

vio·la·ción f. violation; *(de mujer)* rape; *(profanación)* desecration.

vio·la·dor, ra m.f. violator —m. rapist.

vio·lar tr. *(las leyes)* to violate; *(a una mujer)* to rape; *(cosas sagradas)* to desecrate.

vio·len·cia f. *(fuerza)* violence; *(violación)* rape; *(turbación)* embarrassment.

vio·len·tar tr. *(forzar)* to force; *(entrar por fuerza)* to break into; *(torcer)* to distort; *(atropellar)* to infuriate.

vio·len·to, a adj. violent; *(intenso)* intense <*una discusión v.* an intense discussion>; *(molesto)* embarrassing <*es v. que me traten así* it is embarrassing to be treated like this>.

vio·le·ta f. & adj. violet.

vio·lín m. violin —m.f. violinist.

vio·li·nis·ta m.f. violinist.

vio·lón m. *(instrumento)* double bass, bass viol, *(persona)* double bass player.

vio·lon·c(h)e·lo m. cello.

vi·pe·ri·no, a adj. venomous.

vi·ra·da f. turn; MARIT. tack.

vi·ra·je m. *(acción)* veering; *(giro)* turn; MARIT. tack; *(cambio)* turning point; PHOTOG. toning.

vi·rar tr. MARIT. *(de rumbo)* to turn; *(el cabrestante)* to wind; PHOTOG. to tone —intr. to swerve.

vir·gen adj. & f. virgin.

vir·gi·nal/ne·o, a adj. virginal.

vir·gi·ni·dad f. virginity.

vir·go m. *(virginidad)* virginity; ANAT. hymen.

vír·gu·la f. *(vara)* small rod; PRINT. virgule; BACT. cholera bacillus.

vi·ril adj. virile.

vi·ri·li·dad f. virility.

vir·tual adj. virtual.

vir·tud f. *(cualidad)* virtue; *(eficacia)* ability ♦ **en v. de** by virtue of.

vir·tuo·si·dad f./sis·mo m. virtuosity.

vir·tuo·so, a I. adj. virtuous II. m.f. virtuoso.

vi·rue·la f. *(enfermedad)* smallpox; *(cicatriz)* pockmark.

vi·ru·len·to, a adj. virulent.

vi·rus m.inv. virus.

vi·ru·ta f. shavings.

vi·sa f. AMER. visa.

vi·sar tr. *(pasaporte)* to visa; *(documento)* to endorse; ARTIL., SURV. to sight.

vís·ce·ra f. organ ♦ pl. viscera.

vis·co·si·dad f. viscosity.

vis·co·so, a adj. viscous.

vi·se·ra f. visor.

vi·si·bi·li·dad f. visibility.

vi·si·ble adj. visible; COLL. *(decente)* decent.

vi·si·llo m. window curtain.

vi·sión f. vision; *(vista)* eyesight ♦ **quedarse como quien ve visiones** COLL. to look as though one has seen a ghost • **ver visiones** COLL. to see things.

vi·sio·na·rio, a adj. & m.f. visionary.

vi·sir m. vizir.

vi·si·ta f. *(acción)* visit; *(persona)* visitor ♦ **hacer una v.** *or* **ir de v.** to pay a visit • **v. de cortesía** *or* **de cumplido** courtesy call • **v. de médico** COLL. brief visit.

vi·si·tar tr. & reflex. to visit (one another).

vis·lum·brar tr. to glimpse.

vis·lum·bre f. glimmer.

vi·so m. *(reflejo)* sheen; *(destello)* gleam; *(forro)* colored undergarment; *(apariencia)* appearance <*tener v. de verdad* to have the appearance of truth>; FIG. veneer.

vi·són m. mink.

vi·sor m. PHOTOG. viewfinder; ARTIL. sight.

vís·pe·ra f. eve ♦ **en v. de** on the eve of ♦ pl. RELIG. vespers.

vis·ta, to, tiera, tió see **vestir**.

vis·ta·zo m. glance ♦ **dar un v. a** to take a glance at.

vis·to, a I. see **ver²** II. adj. ♦ **bien v.** proper • **es** *or* **está v.** it is commonly accepted • **mal v.** improper • **nunca v.** unheard-of • **por lo v.** apparently • **v.** LAW whereas • **v. bueno** O.K. • **v. que** since III. f. *(visión)* sight; eyesight <*él tiene buena v.* he has good eyesight>; *(panorama)* view; *(cuadro)* scene; *(mirada)* eyes <*dirigió la v. a la pantalla* he turned his eyes toward the screen>; *(vistazo)* look, glance; LAW hearing ♦ **aguzar la v.** to keep one's eyes open • **a la v.** COM. at sight • **a la v. de todos** publicly • **alzar la v.** to look up • **apartar la v. de** to look away; FIG. to turn a blind eye to • **a primera** *or* **a simple v.** at first sight • **a simple v.** *(de paso)* at a glance; *(con los ojos)* with the naked eye • **bajar la v.** to look down • **clavar** *or* **fijar la v. en** to stare at • **comerse** *or* **tragarse con la v.** COLL. to devour with one's eyes • **con vistas a** with a view to • **conocer de v.** to know by sight • **corto de v.** nearsighted • **en v. de** considering • **estar a la v.** *(poder verse)* to be visible; *(ser evidente)* to be obvious; *(estar al acecho)* to keep an eye on • **hacer la v. gorda** COLL. to turn a blind eye • **hasta la v.** so long • **medir con la v.** to size up • **no perder de v. a** not to lose sight of • **perder de v.** to lose sight of • **perderse de v.** to disappear • **saltar a la v.** to hit the eye • **v. cansada** tired eyes • **v. de águila** *or* **de lince** hawk eye • **v. doble** MED. double vision • **volver la v. atrás** to look back —m. customs inspector.

vis·to·so, a adj. colorful.

vi·sual I. adj. visual II. f. line of vision.

vi·sua·li·za·ción f. AMER. visualization.

vi·sua·li·zar §04 tr. AMER. to visualize.

vi·tal adj. vital.

vi·ta·li·cio, a adj. life <*miembro v.* life member>.

vi·ta·li·dad f. vitality.

vi·ta·li·zar §04 tr. to vitalize.

vi·ta·mi·na f. vitamin.

vi·te·la f. vellum.

vi·ti·vi·ní·co·la I. adj. vine-growing II. m.f. vine grower.

vi·to·re·ar tr. to cheer.

vi·tral m. stained-glass window.

ví·tre·o, a adj. vitreous.

vi·tri·fi·car tr. & reflex. to vitrify.

vi·tri·na f. *(caja)* display case; *(de tienda)* window.

vi·trió·li·co, a adj. vitriolic.

vi·tua·llar tr. to provision.

vi·tua·llas f.pl. provisions.

vi·tu·pe·ra·dor, ·ra I. vituperative II. m.f. vi-

tuperator, scold.

vi·tu·pe·rar tr. to vituperate.

vi·tu·pe·rio m. *(insulto)* insult; *(censura)* vituperation.

viu·dez f. *(de viudo)* widowerhood; *(de viuda)* widowhood.

viu·do, a I. adj. widowed II. m. widower —f. *(mujer)* widow; BOT. mourning bride.

vi·vac m. [pl. -ques] MIL. bivouac.

vi·va·ci·dad f. *(en las acciones)* vivacity; *(del espíritu)* sharpness; *(de color)* vividness.

vi·va·men·te adv. *(rápidamente)* rapidly; *(profundamente)* deeply.

vi·va·ra·cho, a adj. COLL. lively.

vi·vaz adj. quick-witted; BOT. perennial.

vi·ven·cia f. *(personal)* experience.

ví·ve·res m.pl. provisions.

vi·ve·ro m. BOT. nursery; *(de peces)* fish hatchery; *(de moluscos)* farm.

vi·ve·za f. *(vivacidad)* liveliness; *(prontitud)* quickness; *(agudeza)* sharpness; *(brillo)* vividness.

ví·vi·do, a adj. vivid.

vi·vi·dor, ·ra m.f. COLL. sponger.

vi·vien·da f. *(lugar)* housing <*escasez de v.* housing shortage>; *(morada)* dwelling; *(casa)* house.

vi·vien·te adj. living.

vi·vi·fi·ca·dor, ·ra/can·te adj. vivifying.

vi·vi·fi·car §70 tr. to vivify.

vi·vir¹ m. life ♦ **de mal v.** disreputable.

vi·vir² intr. to live ♦ **¿quién vive?** MIL. who goes there? • **saber v.** to know how to live • **¡viva!** hurrah! • **v. al día** to live from hand to mouth • **v. a lo grande** to live it up • **v. de** to live on *or* off <*ella vive de sus rentas* she lives off her investments> • **v. del aire** to live on next to nothing —tr. to live; *(experimentar)* to go through.

vi·vi·sec·ción f. vivisection.

vi·vo, a I. adj. *(con vida)* alive; *(intenso)* deep; *(brillante)* vivid; *(listo)* sharp; *(astuto)* sly; MED. raw <*carne v. raw skin*> ♦ **al rojo v.** red-hot • **en v.** TELEC. live II. m. *(borde)* edge; SEW. piping; VET. mange; COLL. *(hombre listo)* wise guy ♦ **los vivos** the living.

viz·ca·cha f. viscacha.

viz·con·de m. viscount.

viz·con·de·sa f. viscountess.

vo·ca·blo m. term.

vo·ca·bu·la·rio m. vocabulary.

vo·ca·bu·lis·ta m.f. lexicographer.

vo·ca·ción f. vocation.

vo·ca·cio·nal adj. vocational.

vo·cal I. adj. vocal II. m.f. *(en una junta)* board or committee member —f. vowel.

vo·ca·lis·ta m.f. vocalist.

vo·ca·li·za·ción f. vocalization.

vo·ca·li·zar §04 intr. to vocalize.

vo·ce·a·dor, ·ra m.f. *(vocinglero)* loud *or* vociferous person —m. *(pregonero)* town crier; MEX. street hawker.

vo·ce·ar intr. & tr. to shout.

vo·ce·o m. shouting.

vo·ce·rí·a f./o m. *(gritería)* shouting; *(clamor)* uproar.

vo·ce·ro, a mf. spokesman/woman.

vo·ci·fe·ra·dor, ·ra I. adj. vociferous II. m.f. vociferator.

vo·ci·fe·rar tr. & intr. to shout.

vo·la·da f. short flight.

vo·lan·do adv. COLL. in a flash.

vo·lan·te I. adj. flying II. m. MECH. flywheel; AUTO. steering wheel; *(del reloj)* balance wheel; *(papel)* flier; *(juego)* badminton.

vo·lan·tín, i·na I. adj. flying II. m. *(para pescar)* fishing line with several hooks; S. AMER. *(cometa)* small kite.

vo·lar §19 intr. to fly; *(irse volando)* to fly away; *(desaparecer)* to disappear; *(divulgarse)* to spread quickly —tr. to blow up.

vo·lá·til adj. *(que vuela)* flying; CHEM. volatile.

vo·la·tín m. acrobatic stunt.

vo·la·ti·ne·ro, a m.f. tightrope walker.

vol·cán m. volcano.

vol·cá·ni·co, a adj. volcanic.

vol·car §73 tr. *(verter)* to dump; *(persuadir)* to make (someone) change his mind —intr. to overturn —reflex. *(derribarse)* to tip over; *(entregarse)* to do one's utmost.

vo·le·ar tr. SPORT. to volley; AGR. to scatter.

vo·le·o m. SPORT. volley ♦ **del primer** *or* **de un v.** COLL. quickly • **sembrar a v.** AGR. to scatter (seed).

vo·li·ción f. volition.

vol·tai·co, a adj. voltaic <arco v. voltaic arc>.

vol·ta·je m. voltage.

vol·tá·me·tro m. voltammeter.

vol·te·ar tr. *(volcar)* to turn over; *(dar la vuelta a)* to turn around; *(poner al revés)* to turn upside down; *(derribar)* to knock down or over —intr. to tumble.

vol·te·re·ta f. somersault.

vol·tí·me·tro m. voltmeter.

vol·tio m. volt.

vo·lu·ble adj. voluble; FIG. fickle.

vo·lu·men m. volume; *(cuerpo)* bulk ♦ **a todo v.** loud.

vo·lu·mi·no·so, a adj. voluminous.

vo·lun·tad f. *(facultad)* will; *(firmeza)* will power <faltarle la v. de hacerlo to lack the will power to do it>; *(intención)* intention; *(deseo)* wish ♦ **a v.** at will • **buena, mala v.** good, ill will • **fuerza de v.** will power • **ganar la v. de alguien** to win someone over • **última v.** last will and testament.

vo·lun·ta·rio, a I. adj. voluntary II. m.f. volunteer.

vo·lun·ta·rio·so, a adj. *(caprichoso)* willful; *(deseoso)* willing.

vo·lup·tuo·si·dad f. voluptuousness.

vo·lup·tuo·so, a adj. voluptuous.

vol·ver §78 tr. to turn <v. la hoja to turn the page>; *(dar vuelta)* to turn around; to turn over <v. el colchón to turn over the mattress>; to turn inside out <v. los calcetines to turn socks inside out>; *(dirigir)* to turn <volvió los ojos hacia la puerta she turned her eyes toward the door>; to return <¿volviste el libro al estante? did you return the book to the shelf?>; *(corresponder)* to repay; *(restablecer)* to restore; *(dar)* to give back ♦ **v. la cara** to turn around • **v. la espalda a alguien** to turn one's back on someone • **v. loco a alguien** COLL. to drive someone crazy —intr. *(regresar)* to return <volvimos a casa muy tarde we returned home very late>; *(reanudar)* to get back ♦ **v. a** to . . . again <volví a empezar I began again> • **v. en sí** to come to —reflex. *(darse vuelta)* to turn around; *(hacerse)* to become <v. religioso to become religious> ♦ **v. atrás** *(desdecirse)* to back down; *(no cumplir)* to back out • **v. contra** to turn against *or* on • **v. loco** to go crazy.

vo·mi·tar tr. to vomit; *(decir)* to spew; *(un se-*

creto) to spill —intr. to vomit.

vo·mi·ti·vo, a adj. & m. vomitive.

vó·mi·to m. *(acción)* vomiting; *(resultado)* vomit.

vo·ra·ci·dad f. voracity.

vo·rá·gi·ne f. whirlpool.

vo·ra·gi·no·so, a adj. turbulent.

vo·raz adj. voracious.

vór·ti·ce m. *(torbellino)* vortex; *(de ciclón)* center of a cyclone.

vos pron. you, thou, ye; S. AMER. you.

vo·se·ar tr. to address as *vos*.

vo·se·o m. use of *vos* in addressing someone.

vo·so·tros, as pron. you, yourselves <entre v. among yourselves>.

vo·ta·ción f. *(acción)* voting; *(voto)* vote.

vo·tan·te I. adj. voting II. m.f. voter.

vo·tar intr. *(en elección)* to vote; RELIG. to make a vow —tr. to vote.

vo·ti·vo, a adj. votive.

vo·to m. vote <depositar un v. to cast a vote>; vow <v. de castidad vow of chastity>; *(deseo)* wish ♦ **hacer votos por** to sincerely hope for.

voz f. voice; *(vocablo)* term; *(rumor)* rumor <se corrió la v. the rumor got around>; *(opinión)* opinion <v. pública public opinion> ♦ **alzar** *or* **levantar la v.** to raise one's voice • **a media v.** in a low voice • **a una v.** unanimously • **a vozes** shouting • **a v. en cuello** at the top of one's voice • **dar voces** to shout • **en v. alta** in a loud voice • **llevar la v. cantante** to call the shots • **pedir a voces** to cry out for • **tener v.** to have a say • **tener v. ronca** to be hoarse.

vo·za·rrón m. booming voice.

vuel·co m. overturning ♦ **darle un v. el corazón** COLL. to skip a beat • **dar un v.** *(un coche)* to overturn; *(un barco)* to capsize.

vuel·co, que see volcar.

vue·le, lo see volar.

vue·lo m. *(acción)* flight; *(plumas)* flight feathers; SEW. *(de falda)* flare; *(adorno)* ruffle ♦ **al v.** COLL. immediately • **de alto v.** big-time • **levantar el v.** *(echar a volar)* to take flight; *(imaginarse)* to let one's imagination go; *(engreírse)* to become arrogant • **v. espacial** space flight.

vuel·to, a I. see volver II. f. *(giro)* turn; *(revolución)* revolution; *(curvatura)* curve <v. cerrada sharp curve>; *(regreso)* return <te veré a la v. I will see you upon my return>; *(revés)* reverse; *(repetición)* recurrence; SPORT. lap; SEW. facing; *(bóveda)* vault; MUS. ritornello ♦ **ayudarle a alguien** *or* **algo la v.** COLL. to find out what makes someone *or* something tick • **a la v.** *(al volver)* on the way back; *(al revés)* on the other side; *(cerca)* around the corner • **a la v. de la esquina** around the corner • **a v. de correo** by return mail • **darle vueltas a** to turn over in one's mind • **darle vueltas** to go around in circles • **dar** *or* **darse una v.** *(pasear)* to take a walk; *(en auto)* to go for a ride • **dar vueltas** *(girar)* to go around; *(torcer)* to twist and turn <la carretera da muchas vueltas the highway twists and turns a great deal> • **de ida y v.** round-trip • **déjate de vueltas** COLL. stop beating around the bush • **estar de v.** *(volver)* to be back; COLL. *(saber)* to have been there and back • **media v.** MIL. about-face • **no tener v. de hoja** COLL. to be undeniable • **poner a alguien de v. y media** COLL. to let someone have it —m. AMER. change <quédese con el v. keep the change>.

vuel·va, ve see volver.
vues·tro, a poss. adj. *(su)* your; *(suyo)* (of) yours <*uno de vuestros parientes* a relative of yours> ♦ **los vuestros** *or* **las vuestras** yours.
vul·ca·ni·zar §04 tr. to vulcanize.
vul·gar adj. *(común)* common; *(grosero)* vulgar.
vul·ga·ri·dad f. vulgarity.
vul·ga·ris·mo m. vulgarism.
vul·ga·ri·zar §04 tr. *(hacer vulgar)* to vulgarize; *(hacer asequible)* to popularize.
vul·gar·men·te adv. *(groseramente)* coarsely; *(comúnmente)* commonly.
vul·go m. masses.
vul·ne·ra·bi·li·dad f. vulnerability.
vul·ne·ra·ble adj. vulnerable.
vul·ne·rar tr. *(herir)* to wound; *(la ley)* to violate.
vul·va f. vulva.

W

w, W f. letter which, although not a part of the Spanish alphabet, is used in the spelling of words of foreign origin.
wat m. watt.
wel·ter m. welterweight.
whis·ky m. whiskey.

X

x, X f. twenty-sixth letter of the Spanish alphabet.
xe·no·fo·bia f. xenophobia.
xe·nó·fo·bo, a I. adj. xenophobic II. m.f. xenophobe.
xe·ro·gra·fí·a f. xerography.
xe·ro·gra·fiar §30 tr. to Xerox.
xe·ro·grá·fi·co, a adj. xerographic.
xi·ló·fo·no m. xylophone.
xi·lo·gra·fí·a f. *(arte)* xylography; *(impresión)* xylograph.

Y

y, Y f. twenty-seventh letter of the Spanish alphabet.
y conj. and ♦ **¿y bien?** and then? • **y eso que** even though • **¿y qué?** so what?
ya I. adv. *(finalmente)* already <*ya hemos terminado* we have already finished>; *(ahora)* now <*ya es famoso* now he is famous>; *(pronto)* soon; *(en seguida)* right away; *(por último)* now <*ya es hora de tomar una decisión* now it is time to make a decision> ♦ **ya lo creo** of course • **ya no** no longer • **ya que** since II. conj. now, at times <*demuestra su talento ya en las artes, ya en las ciencias* she demonstrates her talent at times in the arts, at times in the sciences> III. interj. I see!
yac m. yak.
ya·ca·ré m. AMER. alligator.
ya·cen·te I. adj. lying II. m. MIN. floor of a vein.
ya·cer §79 intr. *(estar tendido)* to lie; *(estar)* to be.

ya·cien·te adj. & m. var. of yacente.
ya·ci·mien·to m. GEOL. deposit ♦ **y. petrolífero** oil field.
ya·guar m. jaguar.
yám·bi·co, a adj. iambic.
yam·bo m. POET. iamb.
yan·qui adj. & m.f. Yankee.
ya·pa f. AMER. *(adehala)* bonus; MEX. gratuity.
yar·da f. yard.
ya·te m. yacht.
ye·gua f. mare.
ye·gua·da f. herd of horses; C. AMER. blunder.
ye·gua·ri·zo, a I. adj. equine II. m. R.P. stud.
ye·güe·rí·a f. herd of horses.
ye·ís·mo m. pronunciation of Spanish *ll* as *y*.
yel·mo m. helmet.
ye·ma f. *(del huevo)* yolk; BOT. bud ♦ **y. del dedo** finger tip.
yen m. FIN. yen.
yer·ba f. grass; S. AMER. maté.
yer·bal m. R.P. field of maté.
yer·ba·te·ro, a I. adj. AMER. of maté II. m.f. *(curandero)* quack; *(vendedor)* maté seller.
yer·go, gue see erguir.
yer·mar tr. to strip.
yer·mo, a I. adj. barren II. m. desert.
yer·no m. son-in-law.
ye·rra f. AMER. cattle branding.
ye·rre, rro see errar.
ye·rro I.n. *(falta)* fault; *(pecado)* sin; *(error)* error.
yer·to, a adj. ♦ **y. de frío** frozen stiff.
ye·se·ro, a I. adj. plaster II. m. plasterer.
ye·so m. GEOL. gypsum; ARTS, CONSTR. plaster; *(vaciado)* plaster cast.
yo I. pron. I <*yo lo hice* I did it> ♦ **soy yo** it's I or me • **yo mismo** I myself II. m. ego.
yo·da·do, a adj. iodized.
yo·da·to m. iodate.
yo·do m. iodine.
yo·du·ro m. iodide.
yo·ga m. yoga.
yo·g(h)i m. yogi.
yo·gur(t) m. yogurt.
yo·yo m. yo-yo.
yu·ca f. *(mandioca)* manioc; *(izote)* yucca.
yu·cal m. yucca field.
yu·do m. judo.
yu·ga·da f. *(tierra)* day's plowing; *(de bueyes)* yoke (of oxen).
yu·go m. *(arreo)* yoke; *(opresión)* oppression; *(carga pesada)* burden; MARIT. transom.
yu·gu·lar adj. & f. jugular.
yun·que m. anvil; ANAT. incus.
yun·ta f. yoke (of oxen).
yu·te m. jute.
yux·ta·po·ner §54 tr. to juxtapose.
yux·ta·po·si·ción f. juxtaposition.
yu·yal m. AMER. weed patch.
yu·yo m. AMER. weed.
yu·yu·ba f. jujube.

Z

z, Z f. twenty-eighth letter of the Spanish alphabet.
za·fa·do, a adj. & m.f. R.P. brazen (person).
za·far tr. MARIT. *(un nudo)* to untie; *(una vela)* to unbend —reflex. *(de peligro)* to escape *(de from)*; *(de compromiso)* to get out of; *(de persona)*

to get rid of; *(una correa)* to come off; AMER, ANAT. to become dislocated.

za·fa·rran·cho m. MARIT. clearing the decks; COLL. *(trastorno)* havoc ♦ **z. de combate** clearing for action.

za·flo, a adj. crude.

za·fí·ro m. sapphire.

za·fra¹ f. jar.

za·fra² f. *(cosecha)* sugar cane harvest; *(fabricación)* sugar-making; *(temporada)* sugar cane harvest season.

za·ga f. *(parte)* rear; SPORT. defense ♦ **a la z.** behind • **no irle uno en z. a otro** to be just as good as another —m. *(en el juego)* last player.

za·guán m. front hall, vestibule.

za·gue·ro, a I. adj. *(trasero)* rear; *(que va en zaga)* lagging behind **II.** m. *(en fútbol)* defense; *(en pelota)* backstop.

za·he·rir §65 tr. *(criticar)* to criticize; *(ridiculizar)* to mock.

za·hon·dar tr. to dig —intr. to sink.

zai·no, a adj. *(caballo)* pure chestnut; *(ganado)* pure black.

za·la·me·rí·a f. flattery.

za·la·me·ro, a I. adj. flattering **II.** m.f. flatterer.

za·ma·rra f. *(chaqueta)* sheepskin jacket; *(piel)* sheepskin.

za·ma·rre·ar tr. *(sacudir)* to shake, *(maltratar)* to push around.

za·ma·rre·o m. *(sacudimiento)* shaking; *(trato malo)* rough treatment.

za·ma·rro m. *(chaqueta)* sheepskin jacket; *(piel)* sheepskin; FIG., COLL. *(hombre tosco)* boor.

zam·bar·do m. luck.

zam·bo, a adj. & m.f. bowlegged *(person)*.

zam·bom·ba f. zambomba (drum-like folk instrument) ♦ **¡z.!** wow!

zam·bom·bo m. COLL. boor.

zam·bra f. *(fiesta morisca)* Moorish festival; *(baile gitano)* Andalusian gypsy dance.

zam·bu·lli·da f. *(en agua)* plunge; *(en esgrima)* thrust ♦ **darse una z.** to take a dip.

zam·bu·llir §13 tr. to plunge —reflex. *(en el agua)* to dive; *(esconderse)* to hide, duck out of sight.

zam·bu·llo m. AMER. waste barrel.

zam·pa·li·mos·nas m.f.inv. COLL. bum.

zam·par tr. *(esconder)* to hide quickly; *(comer)* to gobble.

zam·pa·tor·tas m.f.inv. COLL. *(persona glotona)* pig; *(torpe)* blockhead.

zam·po·ña f. reed flute.

zam·pu·zar §04 tr. to hide quickly.

za·na·ho·ria f. carrot; R.P., FIG. nitwit.

zan·ca f. bird's leg; COLL. *(pierna)* long thin leg; *(de escalera)* stringboard.

zan·ca·da f. stride ♦ **en dos zancadas** COLL. in a jiffy.

zan·ca·di·lla f. *(caída)* tripping; COLL. *(engaño)* trick; *(trampa)* trap ♦ **hacerle una z. a alguien** to trip someone.

zan·ca·je·ar intr. to rush or dash around.

zan·ca·jo m. *(hueso)* heel bone; *(talón)* heel.

zan·ca·jo·so, a adj. bowlegged.

zan·co m. stilt.

zan·cón, o·na adj. COLL. long-legged.

zan·cu·do, a I. adj. long-legged; ORNITH. wading **II.** f.pl. wading birds —m. AMER. mosquito.

zan·ga·na·da f. COLL. stupid remark.

zan·gan·don·go/dun·go m. COLL. *(holgazán)*

lazybones; *(desmañado)* clumsy ox.

zan·ga·ne·ar intr. COLL. to loaf *(around)*.

zan·ga·ne·rí·a f. loafing *(around)*.

zán·ga·no f. ENTOM. drone; COLL. *(holgazán)* parasite.

zan·go·lo·te·ar COLL. tr. to jiggle —intr. to fidget —reflex. to rattle.

zan·go·lo·te·o m. COLL. rattling.

zan·guan·go, a COLL. **I.** adj. lazy, idle **II.** m.f. loafer, bum —f. malingering, faking illness.

zan·ja f. ditch, trench ♦ **z. de desagüe** drainage ditch.

zan·jar tr. to dig a ditch around, trench.

zan·jón m. large ditch.

zan·que·ar intr. to walk a lot.

za·pa f. spade.

za·pa·dor m. sapper.

za·pa·llo m. AMER. pumpkin.

za·pa·pi·co m. pickax.

za·pa·rras·tro·so, a I. adj. COLL. ragged, shabby **II.** m.f. bum, tramp.

za·pa·ta f. *(calzado)* half boot; MECH. shoe; *(arandela)* washer.

za·pa·ta·zo m. *(golpe)* blow with a shoe; MARIT. sail-flapping ♦ **pl. dar z.** to stamp one's feet.

za·pa·te·a·do m. heel-tapping dance.

za·pa·te·a·dor, ·ra I. adj. tap dancing **II.** m.f. tap dancer.

za·pa·te·ar intr. *(golpear)* to hit with the shoe; *(bailar)* to tap-dance —intr. *(bailar)* to tap one's feet.

za·pa·te·o m. *(acción)* tapping; *(baile)* tap dancing.

za·pa·te·rí·a f. *(taller)* shoemaker's shop; *(tienda)* shoe store.

za·pa·te·ro, a I. adj. underdone, undercooked *(vegetables)* **II.** m.f. *(fabricación)* shoemaker; *(venta)* shoe seller; *(remendón)* cobbler ♦ **z., a tus zapatos** mind your own business.

za·pa·ti·lla f. *(pantufla)* slipper; *(de baile)* dancing shoe.

za·pa·to m. shoe ♦ **saber uno dónde le aprieta el z.** to know what is best for oneself.

za·pa·tu·do, a adj. *(zapatos)* wearing clodhoppers; *(pezuña)* thick-hoofed.

za·po·tal m. sapodilla grove.

za·po·te m. sapodilla tree or fruit.

za·po·te·ro m. sapodilla tree.

za·qui·za·mí m. [pl. **-íes**] *(desván)* attic; *(cuarto)* hole.

zar m. czar.

za·ra·ban·da f. sarabande.

za·ra·ga·ta f. COLL. ruckus.

za·ran·da f. sieve.

za·ran·da·ja f. COLL. trifles.

za·ran·dar/de·ar tr. *(cribar)* to sift; *(sacudir)* to shake —reflex. to be on the go.

za·ran·de·o m. *(criba)* sifting; *(colador)* straining; *(sacudida)* shaking; *(prisa)* bustle.

za·ra·za f. chintz.

zar·ci·llo m. *(pendiente)* earring; BOT. tendril.

zar·co, a adj. light blue.

za·ri·güe·ya f. opossum.

za·ri·na f. czarina.

za·ris·ta m.f. czarist.

zar·pa f. claw.

zar·pa·da f. clawing.

zar·par tr. to weigh —intr. to set sail.

zar·pa·zo m. lash of a paw.

za·rra·pas·tro·so, a I. adj. ragged, shabby **II.** m.f. bum, tramp.

zar·za f. bramble.

zar·zal m. bramble patch.

zar·za·mo·ra f. blackberry.

zar·za·pa·rri·lla f. sarsaparilla.

zar·zo·so, a adj. prickly, thorny.

zar·zue·la f. MUS., THEAT. Spanish comedy *or* operetta; SP., CUL. rice and seafood dish.

¡zas! interj. bang!

ze·nit m. zenith.

zi·go·to m. zygote.

zig·zag m. zigzag.

zig·za·gue·ar intr. to zigzag.

zig·za·gue·o m. zigzagging.

zinc m. zinc.

zín·ga·ro, a adj. & m.f. gypsy.

zó·ca·lo m. *(de edificio)* socle; *(pedestal)* plinth; *(de pared)* skirting board; GEOL. shelf; MEX. public square.

zo·dia·cal adj. zodiacal.

zo·dia·co/di·a·co m. zodiac.

zo·na f. zone; *(distrito)* district.

zo·nal adj. zonal.

zon·ce·ra f. nonsense.

zo·ni·fi·ca·ción f. zoning.

zo·ni·fi·car §70 tr. to zone.

zon·zo, a COLL. **I.** adj. foolish **II.** m.f. fool.

zo·o m. zoo.

zo·o·gra·fi·a f. zoography.

zo·o·lo·gi·a f. zoology.

zo·o·ló·gi·co, a adj. zoological ♦ **jardín z.** zoo.

zo·ó·lo·go, a m.f. zoologist.

zoom m. zoom lens.

zo·pen·co, a COLL. **I.** adj. dumb, dopey **II.** m.f. dummy, dope.

zo·pi·lo·te m. buzzard.

zo·pi·sa f. tar, pitch.

zo·po, a adj. & m.f. deformed (person).

zo·que·te m. *(de madera)* chunk of wood; *(de pan)* hunk of bread; *(tonto)* dummy.

zo·rra f. fox; *(hembra)* vixen; *(astuta)* sly fox;

COLL. *(prostituta)* whore; *(carro)* dray; MEX., COLL. *(borrachera)* drunkenness.

zo·rre·rí·a f. COLL. cunning.

zo·rri·llo/no m. AMER. skunk.

zo·rro m. fox; COLL. *(astuto)* sly fox ♦ **hacerse el z.** to play dumb.

zo·rru·no, a adj. foxlike.

zor·zal m. thrush.

zo·zo·bra f. *(hundimiento)* capsizing, sinking; METEOROL. dangerous weather; *(inquietud)* anxiety.

zo·zo·brar intr. to capsize, sink; FIG. to fail.

zue·co m. clog.

zu·ma·que m. sumac.

zum·ba f. bullroarer.

zum·bar intr. *(un insecto)* to buzz; *(los oídos)* to ring.

zum·bi·do m. *(de insecto)* buzzing; *(de los oídos)* ringing.

zum·bón, o·na **I.** adj. teasing **II.** m.f. joker.

zu·mo m. juice.

zu·mo·so, a adj. juicy.

zun·char tr. to fasten with a metal strap.

zun·cho m. metal strap.

zur·ci·do m. darn.

zur·cir §35 tr. to darn ♦ **¡anda y que te zurzan!** COLL. go jump in the lake!

zur·do, a **I.** adj. left-handed **II.** m.f. left-handed person ♦ **no ser z.** to be agile and clever.

zu·rra f. tanning; FIG. thrashing.

zu·rra·pa f. dregs.

zu·rrar tr. to tan; FIG. to give a beating.

zu·rri·do m. *(golpe)* whack; *(ruido)* harsh noise.

zu·rrón m. *(bolsa)* leather bag; BOT. husk; MED. amniotic sac.

zu·rro·na f. COLL. loose woman.

zu·ru·llo m. round lump of soft material.

zu·ta·no, a COLL. m. what's-his-name —f. what's-her-name —m.f. so-and-so.

Inglés/Español

A

a, A (ā) s. primera letra del alfabeto inglés; MÚS. la *m* ♦ **from A to Z** de cabo a rabo.
a (ə, ā), an (ən, ăn) art. indef. un <*a book* un libro>; *(per)* a, por, cada, el <*twice an hour* dos veces por hora>.
a·back (ə-băk') adv. ♦ **to be taken a.** quedar desconcertado ♦ **to take a.** desconcertar.
a·ban·don (ə-băn'dən) I. tr. abandonar; *(to desert)* desertar, dejar ♦ **to a. oneself to** entregarse a II. s. abandono, desenfreno.
a·ban·doned (:dənd) adj. abandonado, desierto.
a·base (ə-bās') tr. rebajar, humillar.
a·bash (ə-băsh') tr. avergonzar.
a·bate (ə-bāt') tr. intr. menguar, amainar.
ab·bess (ăb'ĭs) s. abadesa.
ab·bey (ăb'ē) s. abadía, convento.
ab·bot (ăb'ət) s. abad *m.*
ab·bre·vi·ate (ə-brē'vē-āt') tr. abreviar, resumir.
ab·bre·vi·a·tion (-'-ā'shən) s. *(shortening)* abreviación *f; (shortened form)* abreviatura.
ab·di·cate (ăb'dĭ-kāt') tr. & intr. abdicar.
ab·do·men (ăb'də-mən) s. abdomen *m,* vientre *m.*
ab·duct (ăb-dŭkt') tr. secuestrar, raptar.
ab·duc·tion (ăb-dŭk'shən) s. rapto, secuestro.
ab·duc·tor (:tər) s. *(kidnapper)* raptor *m,* secuestrador *m;* ANAT. abductor *m.*
a·bed (ə-bĕd') adv. en cama, acostado.
ab·er·rant (ă-bĕr'ənt) adj. aberrante.
ab·er·ra·tion (ăb'ə-rā'shən) s. aberración *f.*
a·bet (əbĕt') tr. -tt- incitar, instigar (a cometer un delito) ♦ **to aid and a.** ser cómplice de.
a·bet·tor/ter (:ər) s. instigador *m.*
a·bey·ance (ə-bā'əns) s. ♦ **in a.** en suspenso.
ab·hor (ăb-hôr') tr. -rr- aborrecer, detestar.
ab·hor·rence (:əns) s. aborrecimiento, odio.
a·bide (ə-bīd') tr. -d o **abode** tolerar, soportar —intr. permanecer, continuar ♦ **to a. by** cumplir con, acatar.
a·bid·ing (ə-bī'dĭng) adj. constante, duradero.
a·bil·i·ty (ə-bĭl'ĭ-tē) s. *(skill)* capacidad *f,* habilidad *f; (talent)* aptitud *f; (power)* facultad *f.*
ab·ject (ăb'jĕkt') adj. abyecto, vil.
ab·jure (ăb-jŏŏr') tr. abjurar.
a·blaze (ə-blāz') adj. ardiente, encendido.
a·ble (ā'bəl) adj. **-er, -est** capaz, hábil ♦ **to be a.** to poder, ser capaz (de).
a·ble-bod·ied (:bŏd'ēd) adj. sano, fuerte.
ab·lu·tion (ə-blŭ'shən) s. ablución *f* ♦ pl. FAM. lavabo.
a·bly (ā'blē) adv. hábilmente, diestramente.
ab·nor·mal (ăb-nôr'məl) adj. anormal.
ab·nor·mal·i·ty ('-măl'ĭ-tē) s. anormalidad *f.*
a·board (ə-bôrd') adv. & prep. a bordo (de) ♦ **all a.!** ¡pasajeros al tren!
a·bode (ə-bōd') I. cf. **abide** II. s. morada.

a·bol·ish (ə-bŏl'ĭsh) tr. abolir, eliminar.
ab·o·li·tion (ăb'ə-lĭsh'ən) s. abolición *f.*
A-bomb (ā'bŏm') s. bomba atómica.
a·bom·i·nate (ə-bŏm'ə-nāt') tr. abominar, detestar.
ab·o·rig·i·ne (ăb'ə-rĭj'ə-nē) s. aborigen *mf,* indígena *mf.*
a·bort (ə-bôrt') tr. & intr. abortar.
a·bor·tion (ə-bôr'shən) s. aborto.
a·bor·tion·ist (:shə-nĭst) s. abortista *mf.*
a·bor·tive (:tĭv) adj. MED. abortivo; FIG. fracasado, frustrado.
a·bound (ə-bound') intr. abundar.
a·bout (ə-bout') I. prep. *(concerning)* acerca de, sobre; *(with regard to)* con respecto a; *(approximately)* a eso de, alrededor de <*a. ten o'clock* alrededor de las diez>; *(all around)* acá y allá, a la redonda ♦ **how a. that!** ¡qué te parece! ♦ **how a. you?** ¿y tú? ♦ **to be a.** to estar a punto de II. adv. aproximadamente, casi; *(all around)* aquí y allá, por todas partes ♦ **all a.** por todas partes ♦ **to be up and a.** estar levantado (de la cama).
a·bout-face (:fās') s. media vuelta.
a·bove (ə-bŭv') I. adv. en lo alto, encima; *(in a text)* más arriba ♦ **a. all** sobre todo • **from a.** desde lo alto II. prep. *(over)* sobre, por encima de; *(greater than)* superior a ♦ **a. and beyond** mucho más allá de III. adj. precitado, antedicho IV. s. ♦ **the a.** lo dicho, lo anterior.
a·bove·board (:bôrd') adj. franco, abierto.
a·bove-men·tioned (:mĕn'shənd) adj. anteriormente citado, de referencia.
a·bra·sion (ə-brā'zhən) s. abrasión *f.*
a·bra·sive (:sĭv) adj. & s. abrasivo.
a·breast (ə-brĕst') adv. en una línea ♦ **to keep a. of** mantenerse al corriente de • **two a.** de dos en fondo.
a·bridge (ə-brĭj') tr. abreviar, condensar.
a·bridg(e)·ment (:mənt) s. abreviación *f,* condensación *f; (synopsis)* compendio, resumen *m.*
a·broad (ə-brôd') adv. en el extranjero; *(out and about)* fuera de casa ♦ **to go a.** ir al extranjero.
ab·ro·gate (ăb'rə-gāt') tr. abrogar, revocar.
a·brupt (ə brŭpt') adj. *(curt)* abrupto, brusco; *(sudden)* inesperado, repentino; *(steep)* escarpado.
ab·scess (ăb'sĕs') s. absceso.
ab·scond (ăb-skŏnd') intr. largarse.
ab·sence (ăb'səns) s. ausencia, falta.
ab·sent I. adj. (ăb'sənt) ausente; *(lacking)* que falta; *(distracted)* abstraído II. tr. (ăb-sĕnt') ♦ **to a. oneself from** ausentarse de.
ab·sen·tee (ăb'sən-tē') s. ausente *mf.*
ab·sen·tee·ism (:ĭz'əm) s. absentismo.
ab·sent-mind·ed (ăb'sənt-mīn'dĭd) adj. distraído.
ab·sinthe (ăb'sĭnth') s. licor *m* de ajenjo.
ab·so·lute (ăb'sə-lŏŏt') adj. absoluto; *(unconditional)* total; *(monarchy)* autocrático.

ab·so·lut·ist (:lŏo'tĭst) s. & adj. absolutista *mf*.
ab·solve (əb-zŏlv') tr. absolver; *(of obligation)* eximir; *(of guilt)* exculpar.
ab·sorb (əb-sôrb') tr. absorber; *(to muffle)* amortiguar; FIG. ocupar (tiempo).
ab·sorbed (əb-sôrbd') adj. absorto, abstraído.
ab·sorb·ent (əb-sôr'bənt) adj. & s. absorbente *m*.
ab·sorp·tion (əb-sôrp'shən) s. absorción *f*; FIG. concentración *f*, ensimismamiento.
ab·stain (ăb-stān') intr. abstenerse *(from de)*.
ab·sti·nence (ăb'stə-nəns) s. abstinencia *f*.
ab·sti·nent (:nənt) adj. abstemio.
ab·stract (ăb-străkt') I. adj. abstracto II. s. ('') sumario, resumen *m* ♦ **in the a.** en abstracto III. tr. extraer, quitar.
ab·stract·ed (ăb-străk'tĭd) adj. ensimismado.
ab·strac·tion (:shən) s. abstracción *f*; *(idea)* idea abstracta; *(distraction)* distracción *f*.
ab·struse (ăb-strōos') adj. abstruso.
ab·surd (əb-sûrd') adj. absurdo, ridículo.
ab·surd·i·ty (əb-sûr'dĭ-tē) s. ridiculez *f*.
a·bun·dance (ə-bŭn'dəns) s. abundancia *f*.
a·bun·dant (:dənt) adj. abundante.
a·buse I. tr. (ə-byōoz') abusar de; *(to hurt)* maltratar; *(to berate)* insultar II. s. (ə-byōos') abuso; *(injury)* maltrato; *(sexually)* violación *f*; *(insult)* insulto.
a·bu·sive (ə-byōo'sĭv) adj. *(abusing)* abusivo; *(insulting)* injurioso, insultante.
a·but (ə-bŭt') tr. -tt- lindar con.
a·bys·mal (ə-bĭz'məl) adj. malísimo, pésimo.
a·byss (ə-bĭs') s. abismo; FIG. infierno.
ac·a·de·mi·a (ăk'ə-dē'mē-ə) s. el mundo académico.
ac·a·dem·ic (:dĕm'ĭk) I. adj. académico, universitario; *(speculative)* teórico II. s. catedrático.
ac·a·de·mi·cian (:də-mĭsh'ən) s. académico.
a·cad·e·my (ə-kăd'ə-mē) s. academia *f*.
ac·cede (ăk-sēd') intr. ♦ **to a.** to consentir en, acceder a; *(the throne, office)* subir a, ascender a.
ac·cel·er·ate (ăk-sĕl'ə-rāt') tr. acelerar, apresurar —intr. apresurarse, darse prisa.
ac·cel·er·a·tor (:rā'tər) s. acelerador *m*.
ac·cent (ăk'sĕnt') I. s. ♦ **written a.** acento ortográfico II. tr. acentuar.
ac·cen·tu·ate (ăk-sĕn'chōo-āt') tr. acentuar.
ac·cept (ăk-sĕpt') tr. aceptar; *(to admit)* admitir, dar acogida a.
ac·cept·a·ble (ăk-sĕp'tə-bəl) adj. aceptable, admisible.
ac·cep·tance (:təns) s. aceptación *f*; *(reception)* (buena) acogida; *(approval)* aprobación *f*.
ac·cept·ed (:tĭd) adj. aceptado; *(widely used)* corriente, normal.
ac·cess (ăk'sĕs') s. acceso, entrada.
ac·ces·si·ble (-'ə-bəl) adj. accesible.
ac·ces·sion (ăk-sĕsh'ən) s. accesión *f*, ascenso; *(addition)* ampliación *f*, expansión *f*; *(outburst)* arrebato.
ac·ces·so·ry (ăk-sĕs'ə-rē) I. s. accesorio *f*; DER. cómplice *mf* II. adj. accesorio, adjunto.
ac·ci·dent (ăk'sĭ-dənt) s. *(mishap)* accidente *m*; *(chance)* casualidad *f* ♦ **by a.** por casualidad.
ac·ci·den·tal·ly ('-dĕn'tl-ē) adv. *(by chance)* por casualidad; *(unintentionally)* sin querer.
ac·claim (ə-klām') I. tr. aclamar, ovacionar II. s. aclamación *f*, ovación *f*.
ac·cla·ma·tion (ăk'klə-mā'shən) s. aclamación *f*, aprobación *f* unánime.

ac·cli·mate (ăk'lə-māt') tr. & intr. aclimatar(se).
ac·cli·ma·tion ('-mā'shən) s. aclimatación *f*.
ac·cli·ma·tize (ə-klī'mə-tīz') tr. aclimatar.
ac·co·lade (ăk'ə-lād') s. aprobación *f*, elogio.
ac·com·mo·date (ə-kŏm'ə-dāt') tr. *(to oblige)* hacer un favor a, complacer; *(to hold)* dar cabida a —intr. adaptarse.
ac·com·mo·dat·ing (:dā'tĭng) adj. *(obliging)* solícito, servicial; *(adaptable)* acomodadizo.
ac·com·mo·da·tion (-'-dā'shən) s. acomodación *f*; *(convenience)* favor *m*, servicio ♦ pl. alojamiento.
ac·com·pa·ni·ment (ə-kŭm'pə-nē-mənt) s. acompañamiento.
ac·com·pa·ny (ə-kŭm'pə-nē) tr. & intr. acompañar(se).
ac·com·plice (ə-kŏm'plĭs) s. cómplice *mf*.
ac·com·plish (ə-kŏm'plĭsh) tr. lograr, realizar.
ac·com·plished (:plĭsht) adj. *(completed)* consumado, realizado; *(skilled)* competente.
ac·com·plish·ment (:plĭsh-mənt) s. *(completion)* realización *f*, logro; *(skill)* pericia, consumación *f*.
ac·cord (ə-kôrd') I. tr. conceder, otorgar —intr. avenirse, concordar II. s. acuerdo, convenio ♦ **in a. with** de acuerdo con ♦ **of one's own a.** de propia voluntad.
ac·cor·dance (ə-kôr'dns) s. acuerdo *f*, conformidad *f* ♦ **in a. with** de conformidad con.
ac·cord·ing·ly (:dĭng-lē) adv. *(in keeping with)* en conformidad; *(consequently)* por consiguiente.
according to prep. conforme a, según.
ac·cor·di·on (ə-kôr'dē-ən) s. acordeón *m*.
ac·cost (ə-kôst') tr. abordar, dirigirse a.
ac·count (ə-kount') I. s. *(report)* relato, informe *m*; *(explanation)* explicación *f*, motivo; COM. cuenta ♦ **by all accounts** según el decir *o* la opinión general ♦ **charge a.** cuenta corriente ♦ **joint a.** cuenta indistinta ♦ **of no a.** de poca monta ♦ **on a. of** a causa de, por ♦ **on no a.** de ninguna manera ♦ **to give an a. of (oneself)** dar buena cuenta de (sí) ♦ **to take into a.** tomar en cuenta ♦ pl. COM. estado de cuenta II. intr. ♦ **to a. for** dar razón de.
ac·count·a·ble (ə-koun'tə-bəl) adj. responsable *(for* por); *(explicable)* justificable.
ac·count·ant (:tənt) s. contador *m*, contable *mf*.
ac·count·ing (:tĭng) s. contabilidad *f*.
ac·cou·ter·ment (ə-kōo'tər-mənt) s. equipaje *m*, atavío ♦ pl. adornos, atavío.
ac·cred·it (ə-krĕd'ĭt) tr. acreditar, reconocer.
ac·cred·i·ta·tion (-'ĭ-tā'shən) s. EDUC. autorización *f*; DIPL. acreditación *f*.
ac·cred·it·ed (-'-tĭd) adj. autorizado, reconocido.
ac·crue (ə-krōo') intr. acumularse ♦ **to a. from** resultar de.
ac·cul·tur·ate (ə-kŭl'chə-rāt') intr. adaptarse por asimilación cultural.
ac·cu·mu·late (ə-kyōom'yə-lāt') tr. & intr. acumular(se), amontonar(se).
ac·cu·mu·la·tion (-'-lā'shən) s. acumulación *f*.
ac·cu·ra·cy (ăk'yər-ə-sē) s. exactitud *f*, precisión *f*.
ac·cu·rate (ăk'yər-ĭt) adj. exacto, preciso.
ac·curs·ed (ə-kûr'sĭd) adj. odioso, infausto.
ac·cu·sa·tion (ăk'yə-zā'shən) s. acusación *f*.
ac·cuse (ə-kyōoz') tr. acusar.
ac·cused (ə-kyōozd') adj. acusado ♦ **the a.** el

acusado, el inculpado.

ac·cus·er (ə-kyōō′zər) s. acusador *m*.

ac·cus·tom (ə-kŭs′təm) tr. acostumbrar.

ac·cus·tomed (:təmd) adj. acostumbrado, habitual ♦ **a. to** acostumbrado a.

ace (ās) s. as *m* ♦ **a. in the hole** FAM. as de reserva.

a·cer·bi·ty (ə-sûr′bĭ-tē) s. acerbidad *f*, acritud *f*; FIG. aspereza.

ac·e·tate (ăs′ĭ-tāt′) s. acetato.

a·ce·tic (ə-sē′tĭk) adj. acético.

a·cet·y·lene (ə-sĕt′l-ēn′) s. acetileno ♦ **a. torch** soplete oxiacetilénico.

ache (āk) I. intr. doler ♦ **to a. for** anhelar, ansiar II. s. dolor *m*.

a·chieve (ə-chēv′) tr. llevar a cabo, lograr.

a·chieve·ment (:mənt) s. (act) ejecución *f*, realización *f*; (accomplishment) logro, hazaña.

a·chiev·er (ə-chē′vər) s. ganador *m*.

ac·id (ăs′ĭd) I. s. ácido; JER. LSD *m*, prueba decisiva II. adj. ácido; (sour) agrio; FIG. mordaz, punzante.

ac·id-fast (:făst′) adj. a prueba de ácidos.

a·cid·ic (ə-sĭd′ĭk) adj. ácido.

a·cid·i·fy (ə-sĭd′ə-fī′) tr. & intr. acidificar(se).

a·cid·i·ty (:ĭ-tē) s. acidez *f*.

ac·id·u·lous (ə-sĭj′ə-ləs) adj. acídulo, cáustico.

ac·knowl·edge (ăk-nŏl′ĭj) tr. (to admit) admitir, reconocer; (to recognize) reconocer; (to thank) agradecer ♦ **to a. receipt of** acusar recibo de.

ac·knowl·edged (:ĭjd) adj. reconocido.

ac·knowl·edg(e)·ment (:ĭj-mənt) s. (confession) admisión *f*; (recognition) reconocimiento; (receipt) acuse *m* de recibo.

ac·me (ăk′mē) s. cumbre *f*, cima.

ac·ne (ăk′nē) s. acné *m*.

ac·o·lyte (ăk′ə-līt′) s. acólito, monaguillo.

a·corn (ā′kôrn′) s. bellota.

a·cous·tic/ti·cal (ə-kōō′stĭk) adj. acústico ♦ **a. nerve** nervio auditivo ♦ **acoustics** s.sg. acústica

ac·quaint (ə-kwānt′) tr. familiarizar, poner al corriente ♦ **to be acquainted** conocerse • **to be acquainted with** conocer, estar al corriente de.

ac·quain·tance (ə-kwān′təns) s. (knowledge) conocimiento; (person) conocido.

ac·qui·esce (ăk′wē-ĕs′) intr. consentir, asentir.

ac·qui·es·cence (:əns) s. aquiescencia.

ac·quire (ə-kwīr′) tr. adquirir, obtener ♦ **acquired immune deficiency syndrome** síndrome de inmunodeficiencia adquirida.

ac·qui·si·tion (ăk′wĭ-zĭsh′ən) s. adquisición *f*.

ac·quis·i·tive (ə-kwĭz′ĭ-tĭv) adj. codicioso.

ac·quit (ə-kwĭt′) tr. **-tt-** absolver, exculpar ♦ **to a. oneself** portarse, conducirse.

ac·quit·tal (:l) s. absolución *f*, descargo.

a·cre (ā′kər) s. acre *m*.

ac·rid (ăk′rĭd) adj. acre, cáustico.

ac·ri·mo·ny (ăk′rə-mō′nē) s. acrimonia.

ac·ro·bat (ăk′rə-băt′) s. acróbata *mf*.

ac·ro·bat·ic (′-′ĭk) adj. acrobático ♦ **acrobatics** s. acrobacia.

ac·ro·nym (ăk′rə-nĭm′) s. siglas (f).

a·cross (ə-krôs′) I. prep. (through) por, a través de; (on the other side of) al *o* en el otro lado de II. adv. (on the other side) a través, del otro lado; (crosswise) transversalmente, en cruz ♦ **to be ten feet a.** tener diez pies de ancho • **to come** *o* **run a.** encontrarse con • **to go a.** atravesar, cruzar.

a·cross-the-board (′-thə-bôrd′) adj. general, para todos.

a·cros·tic (ə-krô′stĭk) s. acróstico.

a·cryl·ic (ə-krĭl′ĭk) adj. acrílico.

act (ăkt) I. intr. actuar, hacer algo; (to behave) conducirse, comportarse; (to perform) hacer un papel, actuar ♦ **to a. like** *o* hacer como que • **to a. on** *o* **upon** influir en, obrar sobre • **to a. up** portarse mal —tr. representar, hacer el papel de II. s. (action) acto, hecho; (deed) acción *f*; (performance) número; TEAT. acto; (pretense) simulación *f*, fingimiento; (a law) ley *f*, decreto ♦ **to catch in the a.** coger con las manos en la masa • **to put on an a.** simular, fingir.

act·ing (ăk′tĭng) I. adj. interino, suplente II. s. TEAT. actuación *f*.

ac·tion (ăk′shən) s. acción *f*; (act) acto, hecho; (motion) operación *f*, movimiento; (activity) actividad *f*; (effect) influencia, efecto; MIL. batalla, acción *f* de guerra ♦ **to put out of a.** destrozar, inutilizar • **to take a.** tomar medidas ♦ pl. conducta.

ac·ti·vate (ăk′tə-vāt′) tr. activar, agitar.

ac·tive (ăk′tĭv) adj. activo, en movimiento; (energetic) enérgico, vigoroso ♦ **a. duty** MIL. servicio activo • **to take an a. interest in** interesarse vivamente por.

ac·tiv·ist (ăk′tə-vĭst) adj. & s. activista *mf*.

ac·tiv·i·ty (ăk-tĭv′ĭ-tē) s. actividad *f*.

ac·tor (ăk′tər) s. actor *m*.

ac·tress (ăk′trĭs) s. actriz *f*.

ac·tu·al (ăk′chōō-əl) adj. real, verdadero.

ac·tu·al·i·ty (′-ăl′ĭ-tē) s. realidad *f*.

ac·tu·al·ly (′-ə-lē) adv. en realidad.

ac·tu·ar·y (ăk′chōō-ĕr′ē) s. actuario de seguros.

ac·tu·ate (ăk′chōō-āt′) tr. activar, impulsar.

a·cu·men (ə-kyōō′mən) s. perspicacia, ingenio.

ac·u·punc·ture (ăk′yə-pŭngk′chər) s. acupuntura.

a·cute (ə-kyōōt′) adj. agudo; (sensitive) sagaz, perspicaz; (critical) grave.

ad (ăd) s. FAM. anuncio, publicidad *f*.

ad·age (ăd′ĭj) s. adagio, proverbio.

ad·a·mant (ăd′ə-mənt) adj. inexorable, inflexible.

ad·a·man·tine (′-măn′tēn) adj. inflexible.

Ad·am's apple (ăd′əmz) s. nuez *f* de la garganta.

a·dapt (ə-dăpt′) tr. & intr. adaptar(se), acomodar(se).

a·dapt·a·ble (ə-dăp′tə-bəl) adj. adaptable, acomodable.

ad·ap·ta·tion (ăd′ăp-tā′shən) s. adaptación *f*.

a·dapt·er/or (ə-dăp′tər) s. adaptador *m*.

add (ăd) tr. añadir, agregar; MAT. sumar ♦ **adding machine** sumadora ♦ **to a. up** sumar • **to a. up to** FAM. venir a ser, equivaler a —intr. aumentar, acrecentar; MAT. sumar ♦ **to a. up** FAM. tener sentido.

ad·dend (ăd′ĕnd′) s. sumando.

ad·den·dum (ə-dĕn′dəm) s. [pl. **-da**] addenda *m*, apéndice *m*.

ad·der (ăd′ər) s. víbora, culebra.

ad·dict I. tr. (ə-dĭkt′) ♦ **addicted to** (drugs) adicto a; FAM. dedicado a, entregado a II. s. (ăd′ĭkt) adicto; FAM. fanático.

ad·dic·tion (ə-dĭk′shən) s. vicio; FAM. afición *f*.

ad·dic·tive (:tĭv) adj. que forma hábito.

ad·di·tion (ə-dĭsh′ən) s. adición *f*; MAT. suma ♦ **in a.** además, también.

ad·di·tion·al (ə-nəl) adj. adicional.

ad·di·tive (ăd′ĭ-tĭv) adj. & s. aditivo.

ad·dle (ăd′l) tr. enturbiar, confundir.

ad·dress I. s. (ə-drĕs′, ăd′rĕs′) (postal) direc-

ción *f*, señas; *(lecture)* discurso, alocución *f* ♦
home a. (dirección de) domicilio II. tr. (ə-
drēs') *(a person)* dirigirse a, dirigir la palabra a;
(a group) dar un discurso a; *(letter)* dirigir, poner las señas a ♦ **to a. oneself to** aplicarse a ◆ **to
a. someone as** dar a alguien el tratamiento de.
ad·dress·ee (ăd'rĕ-sē') s. destinatario.
a·dept (ə-dĕpt') adj. perito.
ad·e·qua·cy (ăd'ĭ-kwə-sē) s. suficiencia.
ad·e·quate (ăd'ĭ-kwĭt) adj. adecuado.
ad·here (ăd-hîr') intr. *(to stick)* pegarse; *(to be
loyal)* adherirse; *(to follow)* ceñirse.
ad·her·ence (:əns) s. adherencia; *(devotion)*
adhesión *f*.
ad·he·sion (ăd-hē'zhən) s. adhesión *f*.
ad·he·sive (:sĭv) I. adj. adhesivo, pegajoso ♦ **a.
tape** cinta adhesiva II. s. adhesivo.
ad·ja·cent (ə-jā'sənt) adj. adyacente, contiguo.
ad·jec·tive (ăj'ĭk-tĭv) s. adjetivo.
ad·join (ə-join') tr. estar contiguo a, lindar con.
ad·join·ing (ə-joi'nĭng) adj. contiguo.
ad·journ (ə-jûrn') tr. suspender, levantar (una
sesión) —intr. *(a meeting)* aplazarse; *(to move)*
cambiarse, trasladarse (to a).
ad·journ·ment (:mənt) s. *(closing)* suspensión
f, clausura; *(transfer)* traslación *f*.
ad·judge (ə-jŭj') tr. DER. considerar.
ad·ju·di·cate (ə-jōō'dĭ-kāt') tr. juzgar, fallar.
ad·junct (ăj'ŭngkt') adj. & s. adjunto.
ad·just (ə-jŭst') tr. *(to fit)* ajustar; *(to fix)* arreglar; *(to adapt)* adaptar; COM. liquidar, ajustar
(reclamo) —intr. ajustarse.
ad·just·a·ble (ə-jŭs'tə-bəl) adj. ajustable.
ad·just·er/·tor (:tər) s. MEC. regulador m; COM.
ajustador m, liquidador m (de reclamos).
ad·just·ment (ə-jŭst'mənt) s. ajuste m; *(fixing)*
arreglo; COM. liquidación *f* (de una cuenta).
ad·ju·tant (ăj'ə-tnt) s. ayudante m.
ad lib (lĭb') adv. de manera improvisada.
ad·min·is·ter (ăd-mĭn'ĭ-stər) tr. administrar;
(to manage) dirigir, manejar ♦ **to a. an oath to**
tomar juramento a ♦ **to a. to** ayudar, cuidar (de
una persona).
ad·min·is·trate (:strāt') tr. administrar.
ad·min·is·tra·tion (-'-strā'shən) s. administración *f*, manejo; POL. dirección *f*, gobierno ♦ **the
A.** el gobierno.
ad·min·is·tra·tor (-'-strā'tər) s. administrador
m.
ad·mi·ra·ble (ăd'mər-ə-bəl) adj. admirable.
ad·mi·ral (ăd'mər-əl) s. almirante m.
ad·mi·ra·tion (ăd'mə-rā'shən) s. admiración *f*.
ad·mire (ăd-mîr') tr. admirar.
ad·mir·er (:ər) s. admirador m; *(suitor)* enamorado.
ad·mis·si·ble (ăd-mĭs'ə-bəl) adj. admisible,
aceptable.
ad·mis·sion (ăd-mĭsh'ən) s. admisión *f*; *(fee)*
entrada; *(acceptance)* ingreso (al foro, universidad); *(confession)* admisión, concesión *f*.
ad·mit (ăd-mĭt') tr. **-tt-** *(to let in)* admitir, dar
entrada a; *(to confess)* confesar, reconocer; *(to
concede)* conceder —intr. dar entrada ♦ **to a.
of** permitir, dejar lugar a.
ad·mit·tance (:ns) s. *(admission)* admisión *f*;
(permission to enter) acceso, entrada.
ad·mix·ture (ăd-mĭks'chər) s. mixtura, mezcla.
ad·mon·ish (ăd-mŏn'ĭsh) tr. *(to reprove)* amonestar; *(to caution)* advertir.
ad·mo·ni·tion (ăd'mə-nĭsh'ən) s. *(reproof)* admonición *f*; *(warning)* advertencia.
a·do (ə-dōō') s. bulla, alboroto.

ad·o·les·cence (ăd'l-ĕs'əns) s. adolescencia.
ad·o·les·cent (:ənt) s. & adj. adolescente *mf*.
a·dopt (ə-dŏpt') tr. adoptar.
a·dopt·ed (ə-dŏp'tĭd) adj. *(a child)* adoptivo;
(assumed) adoptado.
a·dop·tion (:shən) s. adopción *f*.
a·dop·tive (:tĭv) adj. adoptivo.
a·dor·a·ble (ə-dôr'ə-bəl) adj. adorable.
ad·o·ra·tion (ăd'ə-rā'shən) s. adoración *f*.
a·dore (ə-dôr') tr. adorar.
a·dorn (ə-dôrn') tr. adornar, decorar.
a·dorn·ment (:mənt) s. adorno, decoración *f*.
ad·re·nal (ə-drē'nəl) adj. adrenal, suprarrenal.
a·dren·a·line (ə-drĕn'ə-lĭn) s. adrenalina.
a·drift (ə-drĭft') adv. & adj. a la deriva.
a·droit (ə-droit') adj. diestro, hábil.
ad·u·la·tion (ăj'ə-lā'shən) s. adulación *f*.
a·dult (ə-dŭlt', ăd'ŭlt') s. adulto ♦ pl. mayores.
a·dul·ter·ate (ə-dŭl'tə-rāt') tr. adulterar.
a·dul·ter·er (:tər-ər) s. adúltero.
a·dul·ter·ess (:ĭs) s. adúltera.
a·dul·ter·ous (:əs) adj. adúltero.
a·dul·ter·y (ə-dŭl'tə-rē) s. adulterio.
ad·vance (ăd-văns') I. tr. avanzar, adelantar;
(to propose) proponer, presentar; *(to further)*
fomentar, promover; *(to hasten)* adelantar; *(to
lend)* anticipar —intr. avanzar; *(to improve)*
hacer progresos; *(to rise)* elevarse, subir (valor,
posición) II. s. avance m, adelanto; *(progress)*
progreso; *(rise)* alza, aumento (de valor); *(loan)*
anticipo ♦ pl. propuesta amorosa III. adj. adelantado, anticipado ♦ **a. guard** avanzada, vanguardia ♦ **in a.** por anticipado, de antemano.
ad·vanced (ăd-vănst') adj. *(in level, degree)*
avanzado, superior; *(in time, ability)* adelantado.
ad·vance·ment (ăd-văns'mənt) s. avance m;
(improvement) adelanto; *(development)* progreso; *(promotion)* ascenso.
ad·van·tage (ăd-văn'tĭj) s. ventaja; *(gain)* provecho, partido ♦ **to one's a.** para ventaja propia ♦ **to take a. of** *(to make use of)* aprovechar,
valerse de; *(to exploit)* abusarse de.
ad·van·ta·geous ('-tā'jəs) adj. ventajoso.
ad·vent (ăd'vĕnt') s. advenimiento, llegada.
ad·ven·ture (ăd-vĕn'chər) I. s. aventura ♦ **a.
story** historia de aventuras II. tr. & intr. aven-
turar(se), arriesgar(se).
ad·ven·tur·er (:ər) s. aventurero.
ad·ven·tur·ous (:əs) adj. aventurero, emprendedor.
ad·verb (ăd'vûrb') s. adverbio.
ad·ver·sar·y (ăd'vər-sĕr'ē) s. adversario.
ad·verse (ăd-vûrs', '') adj. adverso, desfavorable.
ad·ver·si·ty (ăd-vûr'sĭ-tē) s. adversidad *f*.
ad·ver·tise (ăd'vər-tīz') tr. anunciar ♦ **to a. for**
buscar por medio de avisos —intr. poner un
anuncio, hacer publicidad.
ad·ver·tise·ment (:mənt, ăd-vûr'tĭs-) s. anuncio, publicidad *f*.
ad·ver·tis·er (ăd'vər-tī'zər) s. anunciante *mf*.
ad·ver·tis·ing (:zĭng) s. publicidad *f*, propaganda.
ad·vice (ăd-vīs') s. consejo ♦ **to take a.** seguir
el consejo.
ad·vis·a·ble (ăd-vī'zə-bəl) adj. prudente.
ad·vise (ăd-vīz') tr. *(to counsel)* dar consejo a,
aconsejar; *(to suggest)* recomendar, sugerir; *(to
notify)* notificar.
ad·vise·ment (:mənt) s. deliberación *f* ♦ **to**

take under a. someter a consideración.

ad·vis·er/·sor (ăd-vī'zər) s. consejero, asesor *m*.

ad·vi·so·ry (:zə-rē) **I.** adj. consultivo, asesor **II.** s. aviso de precaución.

ad·vo·ca·cy (ăd'və kə-sē) s. apoyo, promoción *f* (de una causa o idea).

ad·vo·cate (ăd'və-kāt') **I.** tr. abogar por (causa, idea) **II.** s. (*o* :kĭt) defensor *m*, partidario; G.B. abogado.

adz(e) (ădz) s. azuela.

ae·gis (ē'jĭs) s. ♦ **under the a.** of bajo el patrocinio de.

aer·ate (âr'āt') tr. gasear (un líquido); oxigenar (la sangre); *(to air)* airear.

aer·i·al (âr'ē-əl) **I.** adj. aéreo, de aire **II.** s. antena.

aer·ie (âr'ē, ĭr'ē) s. aguilera.

aer·o·bic (â-rō'bĭk) adj. aeróbico.

aer·o·dy·nam·ic (âr'ō-dī-năm'ĭk) adj. aerodinámico ♦ **aerodynamics** s.sg. aerodinámica.

aer·o·naut (âr'ə-nôt') s. aeronauta *mf*.

aer·o·nau·tic/ti·cal (:nô'tĭk) adj. aeronáutico ♦ **aeronautics** s.sg. aeronáutica.

aer·o·sol (âr'ə-sôl') s. aerosol *m* ♦ **a. bomb** bomba de aerosol, vaporizador.

aer·o·space (âr'ō-spās') adj. aeroespacial.

aes·thete (ĕs'thēt') s. esteta *mf*.

aes·thet·ic (ĕs-thĕt'ĭk) adj. estético ♦ **aesthetics** s.sg. estética.

a·far (ə-fär') adv. ♦ **from a.** de lejos.

af·fa·ble (ăf'ə-bəl) adj. afable, amable.

af·fair (ə-fâr') s. *(business)* asunto; *(event)* incidente *m*; *(liaison)* amorío; *(gathering)* acontecimiento social ♦ pl. **world affairs** situación mundial ♦ pl. asuntos mundiales.

af·fect[1] (ə-fĕkt') tr. *(to influence)* afectar, influir en; *(to move)* afectar, conmover.

af·fect[2] tr. *(to feign)* fingir, simular.

af·fec·ta·tion (ăf'ĕk-tā'shən) s. afectación *f*.

af·fect·ed (ə-fĕk'tĭd) adj. *(influenced)* afectado; *(moved)* conmovido, impresionado.

af·fect·ed adj. *(mannered)* afectado, amanerado.

af·fect·ing (:tĭng) adj. sensible, conmovedor.

af·fec·tion (:shən) s. afecto, cariño.

af·fec·tion·ate (·shə-nĭt) adj. afectuoso, cariñoso.

af·fi·da·vit (ăf'ĭ-dā'vĭt) s. afidávit *m*.

af·fil·i·ate (ə-fĭl'ē-āt') **I.** tr. & intr. afiliar(se), asociar(se) *(with a)* **II.** s. (:ĭt) socio, asociado.

af·fil·i·a·tion (·'-ā'shən) s. afiliación *f*.

af·firm (ə-fûrm') tr. afirmar, aseverar.

af·firm·a·tive (ə-fûr'mə-tĭv) **I.** adj. afirmativo **II.** s. afirmativa.

af·fix (ə-fĭks') tr. *(to attach)* pegar, adherir; *(to append)* agregar, añadir; *(a signature)* poner.

af·flict (ə-flĭkt') tr. afligir, acongojar ♦ **to be afflicted with** padecer de, sufrir de.

af·flic·tion (ə-flĭk'shən) s. aflicción *f*.

af·flu·ence (ăf'lōō-əns) s. riqueza, opulencia.

af·flu·ent (:ənt) adj. rico, opulento.

af·ford (ə-fôrd') tr. *(monetarily)* tener con qué comprar; *(to spare)* poder disponer de; *(to risk)* afrontar; *(to provide)* proporcionar, dar.

af·ford·a·ble (ə-fôr'də-bəl) adj. que se puede comprar o dar.

af·front (ə-frŭnt') **I.** tr. afrentar, insultar **II.** s. afrenta, insulto.

a·field (ə-fēld') adv. ♦ **far a.** muy lejos.

a·fire (ə-fīr') adj. & adv. ardiendo, en llamas.

a·flame (ə-flām') adj. & adv. en llamas.

a·float (ə-flōt') adj. & adv. *(floating)* a flote, flotando; *(at sea)* a bordo; COM. en circulación, corriente.

a·foot (ə-fŏōt') adj. & adv. a pie; FIG. en marcha.

a·fore·said (ə-fôr'sĕd') adj. antedicho.

a·fore·thought ('thôr') adj. ♦ **with malice a.** con premeditación.

a·foul (ə foul') adv. ♦ **to run a. of** enredarse con, meterse en líos con.

a·fraid (ə-frād') adj. asustado, atemorizado ♦ **to be a. (of)** tener miedo (de *o* a) • **to be a. that** temer que.

a·fresh (ə-frĕsh') adv. de nuevo, otra vez.

aft (ăft) adj. & adv. a, en, *o* hacia popa.

af·ter (ăf'tər) **I.** prep. *(in place, order)* después de, detrás de; *(in time)* después de; *(following)* tras <*day a. day* día tras día>; *(in pursuit of)* en pos, tras; *(at the end of)* al cabo de ♦ **a. all** al fin y al cabo • **to be a. someone** perseguir a alguien **II.** conj. después (de) que **III.** adv. *(afterward)* después; *(behind)* atrás.

af·ter·birth (:bûrth') s. secundinas, placenta.

af·ter·bur·ner (:bûr'nər) s. quemador *m* auxiliar.

af·ter·ef·fect (:ĭ-fĕkt') s. consecuencia.

af·ter·im·age (:ĭm'ĭj) s. imagen consecutiva *o* accidental.

af·ter·life (:līf') s. vida venidera.

af·ter·math (:măth') s. consecuencias, resultados.

af·ter·noon (:nōōn') s. tarde *f* ♦ **good a.!** ¡buenas tardes!

af·ter·taste (:tāst') s. *(taste)* dejo, resabio; FIG. sabor *m*, impresión *f*.

af·ter·ward(s) (:ward[z]) adv. después, luego.

af·ter·world (:wûrld') s. el otro mundo.

a·gain (ə-gĕn') adv. otra vez, de nuevo ♦ **a. and a.** una y otra vez • **and then a.** por otra parte • **as much a.** otro tanto más • **never a.** nunca más • **now and a.** de vez en cuando.

a·gainst (ə-gĕnst') prep. *(touching)* contra; *(in opposition to)* en contra de, contra; *(in contrast to)* en contraste con, sobre; *(as a defense from)* como protección contra.

a·gape (ə-gāp') adv. & adj. boquiabierto.

ag·ate (ăg'ĭt) s. ágata.

age (āj) **I.** s. edad *f*; *(era)* época, era ♦ **a. of consent** edad núbil • **middle a.** edad mediana • **of a.** mayor de edad • **old a.** vejez, senectud • **to come of a.** llegar a la mayoría de edad • **under a.** menor de edad **II.** tr. & intr. envejecer(se), madurar(se); *(wine)* añejar.

ag·ed adj. (ā'jĭd) *(old)* envejecido, anciano; (ājd) *(of the age of)* de la edad de, de.

age·less (āj'lĭs) adj. eternamente joven.

age·long (āj'lông') adj. eterno, de siempre.

a·gen·cy (ā'jən-sē) s. *(a means)* medio, acción *f*; *(business)* agencia; POL. ministerio, dependencia gubernamental.

a·gen·da (ə-jĕn'də) s. agenda, temario.

a·gent (ā'jənt) s. *(person)* agente *mf*, representante *mf*; *(means)* instrumento, medio; CHEM. agente *m*, factor *m*.

age-old (āj'ōld') adj. antiquísimo.

ag·glu·ti·na·tion (ə-glōōt'n-ā'shən) s. aglutinación *f*.

ag·gran·dize (ə-grăn'dīz') tr. agrandar, engrandecer.

ag·gra·vate (ăg'rə-vāt') tr. *(to worsen)* agravar, empeorar; *(to annoy)* irritar, exasperar ♦ **aggra-**

vated **assault** asalto con intención de crimen.
ag·gra·va·tion ('-vā'shən) s. *(worsening)* agravación *f; (annoyance)* irritación *f.*
ag·gre·gate (ăg'rĭ-gĭt) I. adj. & s. agregado ♦ **in the a.** en total II. tr. (-gāt') agregar, unir.
ag·gress (ə-grĕs') intr. agredir.
ag·gres·sion (ə-grĕsh'ən) s. agresión *f.*
ag·gres·sive (ə-grĕs'ĭv) adj. *(hostile)* agresivo, ofensivo; *(assertive)* emprendedor, dinámico.
ag·gres·sor (:ər) s. agresor *m.*
ag·grieve (ə-grēv') tr. apenar, afligir.
a·ghast (ə-găst') adj. espantado, horrorizado.
ag·ile (ăj'əl, ăj'īl') adj. ágil, ligero.
a·gil·i·ty (ə-jĭl'ĭ-tē) s. agilidad *f*, ligereza.
ag·ing (ā'jĭng) s. añejamiento.
ag·i·tate (ăj'ĭ-tāt') tr. *(physically)* agitar; *(to upset)* inquietar —intr. agitar.
ag·i·tat·ed (:tā'tĭd) adj. agitado, inquieto.
ag·i·ta·tion ('-shən) s. agitación *f*, perturbación *f.*
ag·i·ta·tor ('-'tər) s. agitador *m.*
a·glow (ə-glō') adj. resplandeciente ♦ **a. with** radiante de.
ag·nos·tic (ăg-nŏs'tĭk) s. & adj. agnóstico.
a·go (ə-gō') adj. & adv. hace <*two years a.* hace dos años> ♦ **how long a.?** ¿cuánto tiempo hace?
a·gog (ə-gŏg') adj. ansioso, anhelante.
ag·o·nize (ăg'ə-nīz') intr. hacer grandes esfuerzos ♦ **to a. over** atormentarse por (una duda, decisión).
ag·o·ny (:nē) s. *(pain)* dolor *m*, tortura; *(anguish)* angustia, tormento.
a·grar·i·an (ə-grâr'ē-ən) adj. agrario.
a·gree (ə-grē') intr. *(to consent)* consentir, acceder a; *(to concur)* estar de acuerdo, coincidir; *(to match)* corresponder a, concordar; GRAM. concordar ♦ **don't you a.?** ¿no le parece? • **to a. on** avenirse a, ponerse de acuerdo con • **to a. that** quedar en • **to a. with one** sentarle bien.
a·gree·a·ble (:ə-bəl) adj. *(pleasant)* agradable; *(willing to agree)* complaciente.
a·greed (ə-grēd') adj. convenido, entendido.
a·gree·ment (ə-grē'mənt) s. *(accord)* concordancia, conformidad *f; (contract)* acuerdo, pacto ♦ **in a. with** de acuerdo con • **to enter into an a.** firmar un contrato.
ag·ri·cul·tur·al (ăg'rĭ-kŭl'chər-əl) adj. agrícola.
ag·ri·cul·ture (ăg'rĭ-kŭl'chər) s. agricultura.
ag·ri·cul·tur·ist ('-'-ĭst) s. agrónomo.
a·gron·o·mist (ə-grŏn'ə-mĭst) s. agrónomo.
a·gron·o·my (:mē) s. agronomía.
a·ground (ə-ground') adv. & adj. varado, encallado ♦ **to run a.** encallar.
a·head (ə-hĕd') adv. *(at or to the front)* delante, al frente, adelante; *(in advance)* por adelantado ♦ **a. of** antes que • **go a.!** ¡adelante! • **to be a. of** llevar ventaja a • **to get a.** progresar, adelantar.
a·hoy (ə-hoi') interj. ♦ **ship a.!** ¡barco a la vista!
aid (ād) I. tr. & intr. ayudar, auxiliar II. s. ayuda, auxilio ♦ **first a.** primeros auxilios.
aide (ād) s. asistente *mf*, ayudante *mf.*
aide-de-camp (ād'dĭ-kămp') s. [pl. **aides-**] ayudante *m* de campo, edecán *m.*
AIDS (ādz) s. SIDA.
ail (āl) intr. estar enfermo —tr. afligir, doler.
ail·ing (ā'lĭng) adj. enfermizo, achacoso.
ail·ment (āl'mənt) s. dolencia, enfermedad *f.*
aim (ām) I. tr. apuntar —intr. *(a weapon)* apuntar; *(to aspire)* aspirar, proponerse II. s. *(of a weapon)* puntería, apunte *m; (goal)* obje-

tivo, meta ♦ **to take a. at** apuntar a.
aim·less (:lĭs) adj. sin objeto, a la deriva.
ain't (ānt) FAM. contr. de **am not, is not, are not, has not, y have not.**
air (âr) I. s. aire *m; (aura)* apariencia, aspecto ♦ **a. brake** freno neumático • **a. conditioner** acondicionador de aire • **a. conditioning** aire acondicionado • **a. force** fuerza aérea • **a. freight** carga aérea, flete por avión • **a. letter** carta aérea • **a. mattress** colchón de aire • **to be on the a.** RAD., TELEV. estar emitiéndose (un programa) • **to clear the a.** aclarar las cosas • **up in the a.** incierto, no resuelto ♦ pl. aires, afectación • **to put on a.** darse aires II. tr. *(to expose to air)* orear, ventilar; FIG. hacer público, divulgar.
air·borne (âr'bôrn') adj. *(by aircraft)* aerotransportado; *(flying)* volando, en el aire; *(pollen, seeds)* llevado por el aire.
air·brush ♦ **air brush** (âr'brŭsh') s. aerógrafo.
air·con·di·tion (âr'kən-dĭsh'ən) tr. acondicionar el aire, climatizar.
air·cool (âr'kōol') tr. enfriar por aire.
air·craft (âr'krăft') s.inv. nave aérea ♦ **a. carrier** portaaviones.
air·drome (âr'drōm') s. aeródromo.
air·fare (âr'fâr') s. tarifa aérea.
air·field (âr'fēld') s. campo de aviación.
air·i·ly (âr'ə-lē) adv. ligeramente, alegremente.
air·ing (âr'ĭng) s. *(exposure to air)* ventilación *f*, oreo; FIG. ventilación (de ideas, opiniones).
air·less (âr'lĭs) adj. sin aire, sofocante.
air·lift (âr'lĭft') I. s. puente aéreo II. tr. transportar por vía aérea.
air·line (âr'līn') s. aerolínea.
air·lin·er (âr'lī'nər) s. avión *m* de pasajeros.
air·mail (âr'māl') s. ♦ **by a.** por vía aérea.
air·man (âr'mən) s. [pl. **-men**] MIL. soldado de la fuerza aérea; *(aviator)* aviador *m.*
air·plane (âr'plān') s. avión *m*, aeroplano.
air·port (âr'pôrt') s. aeropuerto, aeródromo.
air·sick (âr'sĭk') adj. mareado (en avión).
air·space (âr'spās') s. espacio aéreo.
air·strip (âr'strĭp') s. pista de aterrizaje.
air·tight (âr'tīt') adj. hermético.
air·wor·thy (âr'wûr'thē) adj. en condiciones de vuelo.
air·y (âr'ē) adj. -i- *(breezy)* bien ventilado; *(delicate)* diáfano, ligero; *(light-hearted)* alegre; *(casual)* despreocupado.
aisle (īl) s. pasillo; *(of church)* nave *f.*
a·jar (ə-jär') adv. & adj. entreabierto.
a·kim·bo (ə-kĭm'bō) adj. & adv. en jarras.
a·kin (ə-kĭn') adj. ♦ **a. to** parecido a.
al·a·bas·ter (ăl'ə-băs'tər) s. alabastro.
a·lac·ri·ty (ə-lăk'rĭ-tē) s. presteza, prontitud *f.*
a·larm (ə-lärm') I. s. *(fear)* alarma, temor *m; (device)* señal *f* de alarma; MIL. rebato ♦ **a. clock** (reloj) despertador II. tr. *(to frighten)* alarmar; *(to warn)* dar la alarma.
a·larm·ing (ə-lär'mĭng) adj. alarmante.
a·larm·ist (:mĭst) s. alarmista *mf.*
a·las (ə-lăs') interj. ¡ay!, ¡ay de mí!
al·ba·tross (ăl'bə-trôs') s. [pl. inv. o **es**] albatros *m;* FIG. pena, sufrimiento.
al·be·it (ôl-bē'ĭt) conj. aunque, si bien.
al·bi·no (ăl-bī'nō) s. albino.
al·bum (ăl'bəm) s. álbum *m; (record)* elepé *m.*
al·che·mist (ăl'kə-mĭst) s. alquimista *mf.*
al·che·my (mē) s. alquimia.
al·co·hol (ăl'kə-hôl') s. alcohol *m.*
al·co·hol·ic ('-hŏl'ĭk) I. adj. alcohólico II. s.

bebedor alcoholizado.
al·co·hol·ism ('-'lĭz'əm) s. alcoholismo.
al·cove (ăl'kōv) s. trasalcoba.
al·de·hyde (ăl'də-hīd') s. aldehído.
al·der (ôl'dər) s. aliso.
al·der·man (ôl'dər-mən) s. [pl. **-men**] concejal m.
ale (āl) s. ale f.
a·lem·bic (ə-lĕm'bĭk) s. alambique m.
a·lert (ə-lûrt') **I.** adj. alerta **II.** s. alarma **♦ to be on the a.** estar sobre aviso **III.** tr. (to warn) alertar; (to inform) poner sobre aviso.
al·fal·fa (ăl-făl'fə) s. alfalfa, mielga.
al·gae (ăl'jē) s.pl. algas.
al·ge·bra (ăl'jə-brə) s. álgebra.
al·ge·bra·ic ('-brā'ĭk) adj. algebraico.
al·go·rithm (ăl'gə-rĭth'əm) s. algoritmia, algoritmo.
a·li·as (ā'lē-əs) **I.** s. alias m, seudónimo **II.** adv. alias, conocido por.
al·i·bi (ăl'ə-bī') **I.** s. DER. coartada, alibi m; FAM. excusa **II.** intr. FAM. excusarse.
a·li·en (ā'lē-ən) **I.** adj. (foreign) extranjero; (unfamiliar) ajeno, extraño **♦ a. to** contrario a **II.** s. (foreigner) extranjero; CIENC. FIC. ser m de otro planeta.
a·lien·ate (āl'yə-nāt') tr. alienar, enajenar; DER. enajenar, traspasar.
a·lien·a·tion (-nā'shən) s. alienación f.
a·light¹ (ə-līt') intr. **-ed** o **alit** (to perch) posarse; (to dismount) bajar, apearse.
a·light² adj. iluminado.
a·lign (ə-līn') tr. & intr. alinear(se) **♦ to a. oneself with** ponerse del lado de.
a·lign·ment (:mənt) s. (in a line) alineación f; POL. alineamiento.
a·like (ə-līk') **I.** adj. semejante, parecido **II.** adv. igualmente, de la misma manera.
al·i·men·ta·ry (ăl'ə-mĕn'tə-rē) adj. alimental, alimentario **♦ a. canal** tubo digestivo.
al·i·mo·ny (ăl'ə-mō'nē) s. pensión f (por divorcio o separación).
a·line (ə-līn') tr. alinear, poner en línea.
a·lit (ə-lĭt') cf. **alight¹**.
a·live (ə-līv') adj. vivo **♦ a. to** sensible a **♦ a. with** rebosante de **♦ to be a. and kicking** estar vivito y coleando **♦ to come a.** FIG. cobrar vida.
al·ka·li (ăl'kə-lī') s. [pl. **(e)s**] álcali m.
al·ka·line (:līn, :lĭn') adj. alcalino.
al·ka·loid (:loid') s. alcaloide m.
al·kyl (ăl'kəl) s. alcohilo, alquilo.
all (ôl) **I.** adj. todo **♦ and a. that** y otras cosas por el estilo **♦ of a. things!** ¡imagínate! **II.** pron. todo(s), todo el mundo **♦ above a.** sobre todo **♦ after a.** al fin y al cabo **♦ a. in a.** en resumen **♦ not at a.** nada, en absoluto; (you're welcome) no hay de qué **III.** s. todo **♦ that's a.** eso es todo, nada más **IV.** adv. (completely) completamente; (exclusively) solamente; (apiece) por (cada) bando <a score of five a. cinco puntos por bando> **♦ a. along** siempre, desde el principio **♦ a. around** por todas partes **♦ a. at once** de repente, de golpe **♦ a. but** casi **♦ a. of a sudden** de repente **♦ a. over** (finished) terminado; (everywhere) por todas partes **♦ a. right** (satisfactory) satisfactorio, bueno; (uninjured) ileso, sin daño; (very well) muy bien; (yes) sí **♦ a. the better, worse** tanto mejor, peor **♦ a. too** demasiado, muy.
all-a·round (ôl'ə-round') adj. (comprehensive) completo; (versatile) versátil.
al·lay (ə-lā') tr. calmar, aquietar.

al·le·ga·tion (ăl'ĭ-gā'shən) s. alegación f; DER. alegato.
al·lege (ə-lĕj') tr. (to declare) alegar; (to assert) sostener, pretender.
al·leged (ə-lĕjd') adj. alegado, supuesto.
al·le·giance (ə-lē'jəns) s. lealtad f.
al·le·gor·ic/i·cal (ăl'i-gôr'ĭk) adj. alegórico.
al·le·go·ry (ăl'ĭ-gôr'ē) s. alegoría.
al·ler·gen (ăl'ər-jən) s. alérgeno.
al·ler·gic (ə-lûr'jĭk) adj. alérgico.
al·ler·gist (ăl'ər-jĭst) s. alergista mf.
al·ler·gy (:jē) s. alergia.
al·le·vi·ate (ə-lē'vē-āt') tr. aliviar.
al·le·vi·a·tion (-'-ā'shən) s. alivio.
al·ley (ăl'ē) s. (street) callejón m, callejuela; (in bowling) pista **♦ blind a.** callejón sin salida **♦ bowling a.** bolera **♦ up one's a.** lo de uno.
al·li·ance (ə-lī'əns) s. alianza, unión f.
al·lied (ə-līd', ăl'īd') adj. aliado.
al·li·ga·tor (ăl'ĭ-gā'tər) s. caimán m.
al·lit·er·a·tion (ə-lĭt'ə-rā'shən) s. aliteración f.
al·lo·cate (ăl'ə-kāt') tr. destinar, asignar.
al·lo·ca·tion ('-kā'shən) s. asignación f, reparto.
al·lot (ə-lŏt') tr. **-tt-** (to apportion) asignar, distribuir; (to allocate) destinar.
al·lot·ment (:mənt) s. (act) distribución f; (object, quantity) lote m, porción f.
all-out (ôl'out') adj. extremo, máximo.
al·low (ə-lou') tr. (to permit) dejar, permitir; (to give) conceder, dar; (to set aside) dar, poner aparte; (to admit) confesar, admitir; (to discount) deducir, descontar **♦ a. me** permítame **♦ to a. for** tener en cuenta, tomar en consideración **♦ to a. oneself** darse el gusto de.
al·low·a·ble (:ə-bəl) adj. permisible.
al·low·ance (:əns) s. (permission) permiso; (rebate) rebaja; (money) dinero de bolsillo (que se da a los niños) **♦ to make a. for** tener en cuenta, tomar en consideración.
al·loy s. (ăl'oi') aleación f **II.** tr. (ə-loi') alear.
all-pur·pose (ôl'pûr'pəs) adj. de uso múltiple.
all-right (ôl'rīt') adj. JER. bueno, excelente.
all·spice (ôl'spīs') s. pimienta de Jamaica.
all-star (ôl'stär') adj. de primeras figuras.
all-time (ôl'tīm') adj. nunca visto o alcanzado.
al·lude (ə-lōōd') intr. aludir, referirse.
al·lure (ə-lōōr') **I.** tr. atraer, fascinar **II.** s. atracción f, fascinación f.
al·lu·sion (ə-lōō'zhən) s. alusión f.
al·lu·vi·al (ə-lōō'vē-əl) adj. aluvial, de aluvión.
al·ly I. tr. & intr. (ə-lī') unir(se), aliar(se) **II.** s. (ăl'ī') aliado.
al·ma ma·ter (ăl'mə mä'tər) s. la universidad donde uno se ha recibido.
al·ma·nac (ôl'mə-năk') s. almanaque m.
al·might·y (ôl-mī'tē) adj. todopoderoso.
al·mond (ä'mənd) s. (tree) almendro; (nut) almendra.
al·most (ôl'mōst', -') adv. casi, por poco.
alms (ämz) s.pl. limosna, caridad f.
al·oe (ăl'ō) s. áloe m, alcíbar m.
a·loft (ə-lôft') adv. (in the air) en el aire; (in flight) en vuelo; MARÍT. en la arboladura.
a·lone (ə-lōn') **I.** adj. solo; (with nothing added) solamente, en sí mismo **♦ let a.** sin mencionar, mucho menos **♦ to leave** o **let a.** no molestar, dejar en paz **♦ to stand a.** ser único **II.** adv. (only) sólo, solamente; (by oneself) solo.
a·long (ə-lông') **I.** adv. (in line with) a lo largo de; (forward) adelante; (with one) consigo **♦ all**

a. desde el principio • **a. about** FAM. a eso de • **a. with** junto con • **to get a. with someone** llevarse bien con alguien • **to go a. with** JER. aceptar, estar conforme con (idea, plan) **II.** prep. a lo largo de, por.

a·long·side (:sīd′) adv. & prep. a lo largo (de), junto (a); MARÍT. al costado (de).

a·loof (ə-lōōf′) **I.** adj. distante, reservado **II.** adv. a distancia (de los otros), aparte ♦ **to keep a. from** mantenerse apartado de.

a·loud (ə-loud′) adv. en voz alta.

al·pha (ăl′fə) s. alfa ♦ **a. ray** rayo alfa.

al·pha·bet (ăl′fə-bĕt′) s. alfabeto, abecedario.

al·pha·bet·ic/i·cal ('-′ĭk) adj. alfabético.

al·pha·bet·ize (ăl′fə-bĭ-tīz′) tr. alfabetizar.

al·pha·nu·mer·ic ('-nŌŌ-mĕr′ĭk) adj. alfanumérico.

al·pine (ăl′pīn′) adj. alpino.

al·read·y (ôl-rĕd′ē) adv. ya.

al·so (ôl′sō) adv. también, además.

al·tar (ôl′tər) s. altar ♦ **a. boy** monaguillo.

al·tar·piece (:pēs′) s. retablo.

al·ter (ôl′tər) tr. alterar, cambiar; COST. arreglar —intr. cambiarse, transformarse.

al·ter·a·tion (ôl′tə-rā′shən) s. alteración f; COST. arreglo.

al·ter·cate (ôl′tər-kāt′) intr. altercar, disputar.

al·ter·ca·tion ('-kā′shən) s. altercado, disputa.

al·ter·nate (ôl′tər-nāt′) **I.** tr. & intr. alternar **II.** adj. (:nĭt) *(substitute)* sustituto, alterno; *(every other)* alterno **III.** s. (:nĭt) sustituto, suplente mf.

al·ter·nate·ly (:nĭt-lē) adv. alternativamente, por turnos.

al·ter·na·tive (ôl-tûr′nə-tĭv) **I.** s. alternativa **II.** adj. alternativo.

al·ter·na·tor (ôl′tər-nā′tər) s. alternador m.

al·though (ôl-thō′) conj. aunque, si bien.

al·tim·e·ter (ăl-tĭm′ĭ-tər) s. altímetro.

al·ti·tude (ăl′tĭ-tōōd′) s. altitud f, altura ♦ **a. sickness** mal de altura, puna.

al·to (ăl′tō) adj. & s. contralto.

al·to·geth·er (ôl′tə-gĕth′ər) adv. *(entirely)* enteramente, del todo; *(all told)* en total ♦ **in the a.** FAM. en cueros.

al·tru·is·tic (ăl′trōō-ĭs′tĭk) adj. altruista.

al·um (ăl′əm) s. alumbre m.

a·lu·mi·num (ə-lōō′mə-nəm) s. aluminio.

a·lum·na (ə-lŭm′nə) s. [pl. **-nae**] graduada.

a·lum·nus (:nəs) s. [pl. **-ni**] graduado.

al·ways (ôl′wāz) adv. siempre; *(forever)* para siempre.

am (ăm, əm) primera persona sing. de **be**.

a·mal·gam (ə-măl′gəm) s. QUÍM. amalgama, aleación f; *(mixture)* mezcla.

a·mal·ga·mate (:gā-māt′) tr. & intr. QUÍM. amalgamar(se); COM. unir(se).

am·a·ryl·lis (ăm′ə-rĭl′ĭs) s. amarilis f.

a·mass (ə-măs′) tr. acumular, amontonar.

am·a·teur (ăm′ə-tûr′, -ə-chŌŌr′) **I.** s. *(nonprofessional)* amateur mf; *(unskillful person)* chapucero **II.** adj. amateur.

am·a·to·ry (ăm′ə-tôr′ē) adj. amoroso, amatorio.

a·maze (ə-māz′) tr. asombrar, sorprender.

a·mazed (ə-māzd′) adj. asombrado.

a·maze·ment (ə-māz′mənt) s. asombro.

a·maz·ing (ə-mā′zĭng) adj. *(astonishing)* asombroso; *(surprising)* sorprendente; *(marvelous)* maravilloso.

am·bas·sa·dor (ăm-băs′ə-dər) s. embajador m ♦ **a. at large** embajador viajero.

am·ber (ăm′bər) **I.** s. ámbar m **II.** adj. amba-

rino.

am·bi·ance (ăm′bē-əns) s. ambiente m.

am·bi·dex·trous (ăm′bĭ-dĕk′strəs) adj. ambidextro.

am·bi·ent (ăm′bē-ənt) adj. ambiente.

am·bi·gu·i·ty (ăm′bĭ-gyŌŌ′ĭ-tē) s. ambigüedad f.

am·big·u·ous (ăm-bĭg′yŌŌ-əs) adj. ambiguo.

am·bi·tion (ăm-bĭsh′ən) s. ambición f, afán m.

am·bi·tious (:əs) adj. ambicioso; *(grand)* grandioso.

am·biv·a·lence (ăm-bĭv′ə-ləns) s. ambivalencia.

am·biv·a·lent (:lənt) adj. ambivalente.

am·ble (ăm′bəl) intr. deambular.

am·bu·lance (ăm′byə-ləns) s. ambulancia.

am·bu·la·to·ry (:lə-tôr′ē) adj. ambulatorio.

am·bush (ăm′bŏŏsh′) **I.** s. emboscada, celada **II.** tr. emboscar, tender una celada a.

a·me·lio·rate (ə-mēl′yə-rāt′) tr. & intr. mejorar(se), aliviar(se).

a·me·lio·ra·tion (-′-rā′shən) s. mejora, alivio.

a·men (ă-mĕn′, ä-mĕn′) interj. amén.

a·me·na·ble (ə-mē′nə-bəl) adj. receptivo ♦ **to be a. to** estar dispuesto a.

a·mend (ə-mĕnd′) tr. *(to correct)* corregir, rectificar; *(to revise)* enmendar.

a·mend·ment (:mənt) s. *(correction)* corrección f; *(alteration)* enmienda.

a·mends (ə-mĕndz′) s.pl. ♦ **to make a. for** dar satisfacción por.

a·men·i·ty (ə-mĕn′ĭ-tē) s. amenidad f, afabilidad f ♦ pl. *(civilities)* modales, cortesías; *(comforts)* comodidades.

A·mer·i·can (ə-mĕr′ĭ-kən) adj. americano; *(of U.S.A.)* norteamericano.

A·mer·i·can·ism (:kə-nĭz′əm) s. americanismo.

A·mer·i·can·ize (:nīz′) tr. americanizar.

am·e·thyst (ăm′ə-thĭst) s. amatista.

a·mi·a·ble (ā′mē-ə-bəl) adj. amable, afable.

am·i·ca·ble (ăm′ĭ-kə-bəl) adj. amigable.

a·mid(st) (ə-mĭd[st]′) prep. en medio de, entre.

a·mi·no acid (ə-mē′nō) s. aminoácido.

a·miss (ə-mĭs′) **I.** adj. fuera de orden **II.** adv. ♦ **to go a. salir mal** • **to take a.** tomar a mal.

am·i·ty (ăm′ĭ-tē) s. amistad f, concordia.

am·me·ter (ăm′mē′tər) s. amperímetro.

am·mo (ăm′ō) s. munición f.

am·mo·ni·a (ə-mōn′yə) s. *(gas)* amoníaco; *(cleanser)* agua amoniacal.

am·mo·ni·um (ə-mō′nē-əm) s. amonio.

am·mu·ni·tion (ăm′yə-nĭsh′ən) s. municiones f.

am·ne·sia (ăm-nē′zhə) s. amnesia.

am·ne·si·ac (:zē-ăk′) s. & adj. amnésico.

am·nes·ty (ăm′nĭ-stē) **I.** s. amnistía, indulto **II.** tr. indultar.

a·moe·ba (ə-mē′bə) s. [pl. **s** o **-bae**] ameba.

a·moe·bic (:bĭk) adj. ♦ **a. dysentery** amebiasis.

a·mong(st) (ə-mŭng[st]′) prep. entre, en medio de.

a·mor·al (ă-môr′əl) adj. amoral.

am·o·rous (ăm′ər-əs) adj. amativo.

a·mor·phous (ə-môr′fəs) adj. amorfo, informe.

am·or·tize (ăm′ər-tīz′) tr. amortizar.

a·mount (ə-mount′) **I.** s. cantidad f, monto **II.** intr. ♦ **to a. to** *(to come to)* subir a, ascender a; *(to be equivalent to)* ser igual a, (venir a) ser lo mismo que.

am·per·age (ăm′pər-ĭj) s. amperaje m.

am·pere (ăm′pĭr′) s. amperio.

am·phet·a·mine (ăm-fĕt′ə-mēn′) s. anfetamina.

am·phib·i·an (ăm-fĭb'ē-ən) adj. & s. anfibio.
am·phib·i·ous (:ē-əs) adj. anfibio.
am·phi·the·a·ter (ăm'fə-thē'ə-tər) s. anfiteatro.
am·ple (ăm'pəl) adj. **-er, -est** (large) extenso, amplio; (generous) generoso; (adequate) suficiente.
am·pli·fi·er (ăm'plə-fī'ər) s. amplificador m.
am·pli·fy (ăm'plə-fī') tr. ELECTRÓN. amplificar; (an idea) desarrollar.
am·pli·tude (ăm'plĭ-tūd') s. amplitud f ♦ a. modulation modulación de amplitud.
am·ply (ăm'plē) adv. ampliamente.
am·pu·tate (ăm'pyə-tāt') tr. amputar.
am·pu·ta·tion ('-tā'shən) s. amputación f.
am·pu·tee (:tē') s. amputado.
a·muck (ə·mŭk') adv. ♦ **to run a.** abandonarse a la furia, volverse loco.
am·u·let (ăm'yə-lĭt) s. amuleto, talismán m.
a·muse (ə·myōōz') tr. entretener, divertir ♦ **to a. oneself** divertirse, entretenerse.
a·muse·ment (:mənt) s. (pastime) entretenimiento; (laughter) risa.
a·mus·ing (ə·myōō'zĭng) adj. entretenido, divertido.
am·yl (ăm'əl) s. amilo.
an (ən, ăn) cf. a.
a·nach·ro·nism (ə·năk'rə·nĭz'əm) s. anacronismo.
a·nach·ro·nis·tic ('-'nĭs'tĭk) adj. anacrónico.
an·a·gram (ăn'ə·grăm') s. anagrama m.
a·nal (ā'nəl) adj. anal.
an·al·ge·sic (ăn'əl·jē'zĭk) s. & adj. analgésico.
an·a·log computer (ăn'ə·lôg') s. computadora analógica.
a·nal·o·gous (ə·năl'ə·gəs) adj. análogo.
a·nal·o·gy (ə·năl'ə·jē) s. (correspondence) analogía, semejanza; (correlation) correlación f.
a·nal·y·sis (ə·năl'ĭ·sĭs) s. [pl. **-ses**] análisis m; PSIC. psicoanálisis m.
an·a·lyst (ăn'ə·lĭst) s. analista mf.
an·a·lyt·ic/i·cal ('-lĭt'ĭk) adj. analítico.
an·a·lyze (ăn'ə·līz') tr. analizar; PSIC. psicoanalizar.
an·ar·chic/chi·cal (ăn·är'kĭk) adj. anárquico.
an·ar·chist (ăn'ər·kĭst) s. anarquista mf.
an·ar·chy (:kē) s. anarquía.
a·nath·e·ma (ə·năth'ə·mə) s. anatema m.
a·nath·e·ma·tize (:tīz') tr. anatematizar.
an·a·tomic/ical (ăn'ə·tŏm'ĭk) adj. anatómico.
a·nat·o·mist (ə·năt'ə·mĭst) s. anatomista mf.
a·nat·o·mize (:mīz') tr. anatomizar.
a·nat·o·my (:mē) s. anatomía; FIG. análisis m (de obra, crimen); (body) cuerpo humano.
an·ces·tor (ăn'sĕs'tər) s. antepasado.
an·ces·tral (-'trəl) adj. ancestral.
an·ces·try (''trē) s. linaje m, abolengo.
an·chor (ăng'kər) I. s. ancla, áncora; FIG. soporte m; TELEV. locutor m, anunciador m ♦ at **a.** anclado ♦ **to cast a.** echar anclas ♦ **to weigh a.** levar anclas, zarpar II. intr. anclar, fondear —tr. sujetar, asegurar.
an·chor·age (:ĭj) s. ancladero, fondeadero.
an·chor·man (:măn') s. [pl. **-men**] locutor m, anunciador m.
an·cho·vy (ăn'chō'vē) s. [pl. inv. o **-vies**] anchoa.
an·cient (ăn'shənt) I. adj. antiguo, vetusto II. s. anciano ♦ pl. (los) antiguos.
an·cil·lar·y (ăn'sə·lĕr'ē) adj. auxiliar.
and (ənd, ănd) conj. y, e ♦ **try a. come** trata de venir ♦ **go a. see** anda a ver.

and·i·ron (ănd'ī'ərn) s. morillo.
an·droid (ăn'droid') s. androide m, robot m.
an·ec·do·tal (ăn'ĭk·dōt'l) adj. anecdótico.
an·ec·dote (ăn'ĭk·dōt') s. anécdota.
a·ne·mi·a (ə·nē'mē·ə) s. anemia.
a·ne·mic (:mĭk) adj. anémico.
an·e·mom·e·ter (ăn'ə·mŏm'ĭ·tər) s. anemómetro.
a·nem·o·ne (ə·nĕm'ə·nē) s. anémona.
an·es·the·sia (ăn'ĭs·thē'zhə) s. anestesia.
an·es·the·si·ol·o·gy (:thē·zē·ŏl'ə·jē) s. anestesiología.
an·es·thet·ic (:thĕt'ĭk) s. & adj. anestésico.
a·nes·the·tist (ə·nĕs'thĭ·tĭst) s. anestesista mf.
a·nes·the·tize (:tīz') tr. anestesiar.
an·eu·rysm (ăn'yə·rĭz'əm) s. aneurisma m.
a·new (ə·nōō') adv. nuevamente, de nuevo.
an·gel (ăn'jəl) s. ángel m.
an·gel·ic/i·cal (ăn·jĕl'ĭk) adj. angélico, angelical.
an·ger (ăng'gər) I. s. ira, enojo II. tr. & intr. airar(se), enojar(se).
an·gle¹ (ăng'gəl) intr. pescar con caña ♦ **to a. for** FIG. ir a la pesca de.
an·gle² (ăng'gəl) I. s. ángulo; (corner) esquina, codo; (point of view) ángulo, punto de vista; (scheme) ardid m ♦ **at an a.** en diagonal ♦ **at right angles** en ángulo recto II. tr. & intr. mover(se) en ángulo.
an·gler (:glər) s. pescador m (de caña).
an·gle·worm (:gəl·wûrm') s. lombriz f.
An·gli·can (ăng'glĭ·kən) adj. & s. anglicano.
An·gli·cize (:sīz') tr. anglicanizar.
an·gling (:glĭng) s. pesca con caña.
An·glo-Sax·on (ăng'glō·săk'sən) adj. & s. anglosajón m.
an·gri·ly (ăng'grə·lē) adv. con enojo, con ira.
an·gry (ăng'grē) adj. **-i-** enojado, enfadado; (sky) amenazador; MED. inflamado ♦ **to be a. at** o **about** (something) estar enojado por (algo) ♦ **to make** (someone) **a.** enojar (a alguien).
angst (ängkst) s. angustia, ansiedad f.
an·guish (ăng'gwĭsh) I. s. angustia, congoja II. tr. & intr. angustiar(se), acongojar(se).
an·guished (:gwĭsht) adj. angustiado, acongojado.
an·hy·drous (ăn·hī'drəs) adj. anhidro.
an·i·line (ăn'ə·lĭn) s. anilina ♦ **a. dye** color de anilina.
an·i·ma (ăn'ə·mə) s. alma, espíritu m.
an·i·mal (ăn'ə·məl) adj. & s. animal m.
an·i·mal·cule ('-măl'kyōōl) s. animáculo.
an·i·mal·is·tic (:mə·lĭs'tĭk) adj. como o de animal.
an·i·mate (ăn'ə·māt') I. tr. animar II. adj. (:mĭt) animado, viviente.
an·i·mat·ed (:mā'tĭd) adj. animado, vivaz ♦ **a. cartoon** dibujos animados.
an·i·ma·tion ('-'shən) s. animación f, vivacidad f ♦ **suspended a.** muerte aparente.
an·i·mism (ăn'ə·mĭz'əm) s. animismo.
an·i·mos·i·ty (ăn'ə·mŏs'ĭ·tē) s. animosidad f.
an·i·mus ('-məs) s. animosidad f.
an·i·on (ăn'ī'ən) s. anión m, ion negativo.
an·ise (ăn'ĭs) s. anís m.
an·i·sette (ăn'ĭ·sĕt') s. anisete m.
an·kle (ăng'kəl) s. tobillo.
an·kle·bone (:bōn') s. hueso del tobillo, taba.
an·klet (ăng'klĭt) s. (ornament) ajorca para el tobillo; (socks) media tobillera.
an·nals (ăn'əlz) s.pl. anales m.
an·neal (ə·nēl') tr. recocer (cristal, metales).

an·ne·lid (ăn′ə-lĭd) adj. & s. anélido.

an·nex I. tr. (ə-něks′) anexar, anexionar II. s. (ăn′ĕks′) anexo.

an·nex·a·tion (ăn′ĭk-sā′shən) s. anexión f.

an·ni·hi·late (ə-nī′ə-lāt′) tr. aniquilar.

an·ni·hi·la·tion (-′-lā′shən) s. aniquilación f.

an·ni·ver·sa·ry (ăn′ə-vûr′sə-rē) s. aniversario.

an·no·tate (ăn′ə-tāt′) tr. anotar.

an·no·ta·tion (-′-tā′shən) s. anotación f, nota.

an·nounce (ə-nouns′) tr. anunciar, declarar.

an·nounce·ment (:mənt) s. anuncio, declaración f.

an·nounc·er (ə-noun′sər) s. anunciador m, locutor m.

an·noy (ə-noi′) tr. molestar, fastidiar.

an·noy·ance (:əns) s. molestia, fastidio.

an·noy·ing (:ĭng) adj. molesto, irritante.

an·nu·al (ăn′yōo-əl) I. adj. anual II. s. (year-book) anuario; BOT. planta anual.

an·nu·al·ly (:ə-lē) adj. anualmente, cada año.

an·nu·i·ty (ə-nōō′ĭ-tē) s. (payment) anualidad f, (income for life) renta vitalicia.

an·nul (ə-nŭl′) tr. -ll- (to nullify) anular, invalidar; (to cancel) cancelar.

an·nul·ment (:mənt) s. (invalidation) anulación f, invalidación f; (cancellation) cancelación f.

an·ode (ăn′ōd′) s. ánodo.

an·o·dyne (ăn′ə-dīn′) adj. & s. anodino.

a·noint (ə-noint′) tr. untar; RELIG. ungir.

a·nom·a·lous (ə-nŏm′ə-ləs) adj. anómalo.

a·nom·a·ly (:lē) s. anomalía.

an·o·nym·i·ty (ăn′ə-nĭm′ĭ-tē) s. anonimato.

a·non·y·mous (ə-nŏn′ə-məs) adj. anónimo.

a·noph·e·les (ə-nŏf′ə-lēz′) s. anofeles m.

an·oth·er (ə-nŭth′ər) I. adj. otro; (different) (otro) distinto; (additional) más ♦ **a. one** otro más • **a. time** otro día • **without a. word** sin más palabras II. pron. otro ♦ **one a.** uno(s) a otro(s).

an·swer (ăn′sər) I. s. respuesta, contestación f; (solution) solución f, resultado; (reason) explicación f, razón f ♦ **to know all the answers** saberlo todo II. intr. dar contestación, responder; (to suffice) servir; (to match) corresponder (to a) ♦ **answering machine** contestador automático (de teléfono) • **to a. back** replicar con insolencia —tr. responder a, contestar a; (correctly) resolver, solucionar (problema, enigma) ♦ **to a. for** ser responsable por • **to a. the telephone** contestar el teléfono.

an·swer·a·ble (ə-bəl) adj. responsable (for por).

ant (ănt) s. hormiga.

ant·ac·id (ănt-ăs′ĭd) adj. & s. antiácido.

an·tag·o·nism (ăn-tăg′ə-nĭz′əm) s. antagonismo, rivalidad f.

an·tag·o·nis·tic (-′-nĭs′tĭk) adj. antagónico.

an·tag·o·nize (-′-nīz′) tr. provocar la hostilidad de.

an·te (ăn′tē) s. apuesta inicial (en póker).

ant·eat·er (ănt′ē′tər) s. oso hormiguero.

an·te·cede (ăn′tĭ-sēd′) tr. & intr. anteceder.

an·te·ce·dent (:nt) adj. & s. antecedente m.

an·te·date (ăn′tĭ-dāt′) tr. preceder (en tiempo); (a document) antedatar.

an·te·di·lu·vi·an (′-də-lōō′vē-ən) adj. antediluviano; FIG. anticuado.

an·te·lope (ăn′tl-ōp′) s. [pl. inv. o **s**] antílope m.

an·ten·na (ăn-těn′ə) s. ZOOL. [pl. -nae] antena; RAD. [pl. -nas] antena.

an·te·room (ăn′tē-rōōm′) s. antesala.

an·them (ăn′thəm) s. (hymn) himno <national a. himno nacional>; RELIG. antífona.

an·ther (ăn′thər) s. antera, borlilla.

ant·hill (ănt′hĭl′) s. hormiguero.

an·thol·o·gize (ăn-thŏl′ə-jīz′) tr. compilar.

an·thol·o·gy (:jē) s. antología.

an·thra·cite (ăn′thrə-sīt′) s. antracita.

an·thrax (ăn′thrăks′) s. ántrax m.

an·thro·po·cen·tric (ăn′thrə-pə-sĕn′trĭk) adj. antropocéntrico.

an·thro·pol·o·gist (:pŏl′ə-jĭst) s. antropólogo.

an·thro·pol·o·gy (:pŏl′ə-jē) s. antropología.

an·ti·a·bor·tion (ăn′tē-ə-bôr′shən) adj. que se opone al aborto.

an·ti·air·craft (:âr′krăft′) adj. antiaéreo.

an·ti·bal·lis·tic (:bə-lĭs′tĭk) adj. antibalístico.

an·ti·bi·ot·ic (:bī-ŏt′ĭk) s. & adj. antibiótico.

an·ti·bod·y (ăn′tĭ-bŏd′ē) s. anticuerpo.

an·tics (ăn′tĭks) s.pl. travesuras.

an·ti·christ (ăn′tĭ-krīst′) s. anticristo.

an·tic·i·pate (ăn-tĭs′ə-pāt′) tr. (to foresee) anticipar, prever; (to expect) esperar, contar con; (with pleasure) gozar de antemano; (to forestall) adelantarse, anticiparse a.

an·tic·i·pa·tion (-′-pā′shən) s. (act) anticipación f; (expectation) expectación f, esperanza; (eagerness) ilusión f.

an·ti·cli·mac·tic (ăn′tē-klī-măk′tĭk) adj. decepcionante.

an·ti·cli·max (:klī′măks′) s. anticlímax m, decepción f.

an·ti·com·mu·nist (:kŏm′yə-nĭst) s. & adj. anticomunista mf.

an·ti·dote (ăn′tĭ-dōt′) s. antídoto.

an·ti·freeze (:frēz′) s. anticongelante m.

an·ti·gen (:jən) s. antígeno.

an·ti·he·ro (:hîr′ō) s. [pl. **es**] protagonista m que es todo lo contrario del héroe clásico.

an·ti·his·ta·mine (ăn′tē-hĭs′tə-mēn′) s. antihistamínico.

an·ti·ma·lar·i·al (:mə-lâr′ē-əl) I. adj. antipalúdico II. s. droga antipalúdica.

an·ti·mat·ter (ăn′tĭ-măt′ər) s. antimateria.

an·ti·mo·ny (ăn′tə-mō′nē) s. antimonio.

an·tip·a·thy (ăn-tĭp′ə-thē) s. antipatía.

an·ti·per·spi·rant (ăn′tē-pûr′spər-ənt) adj. & s. antisudoral m, desodorante m.

an·tip·o·des (ăn-tĭp′ə-dēz′) s.pl. antípodas f.

an·ti·quar·i·an (ăn′tĭ-kwâr′ē-ən) s. anticuario.

an·ti·quat·ed (′-kwā′tĭd) adj. anticuado.

an·tique (ăn-tēk′) I. adj. (ancient) antiguo; (old) viejo, anticuado; (furniture) de época II. s. antigüedad f, antigualla.

an·tiq·ui·ty (ăn-tĭk′wĭ-tē) s. antigüedad f.

an·ti·rust (ăn′tē-rŭst′) adj. & s. antioxidante m.

an·ti·Sem·ite (:sĕm′īt′) s. antisemita mf.

an·ti·Se·mit·ic (:sə-mĭt′ĭk) adj. antisemítico.

an·ti·sep·tic (ăn′tĭ-sĕp′tĭk) adj. & s. antiséptico.

an·ti·se·rum (′-sîr′əm) s. [pl. **s** o -ra] antisuero.

an·ti·slav·er·y (ăn′tē-slā′və-rē) adj. en contra de la esclavitud, antiesclavista.

an·ti·so·cial (:sō′shəl) adj. antisocial.

an·ti·tank (:tăngk′) adj. antitanque.

an·ti·ter·ror·ism (:tĕr′ə-rĭz′əm) s. antiterrorismo.

an·ti·theft device (:thĕft′) s. dispositivo antirrobo.

an·tith·e·sis (ăn-tĭth′ĭ-sĭs) s. [pl. -ses] antítesis f, contraste m.

an·ti·thet·i·cal (ăn′tĭ-thĕt′ĭ-kəl) adj. antitético.

an·ti·tox·in (ăn′tē-tŏk′sĭn) s. antitoxina.

an·ti·trust (:trŭst′) adj. antimonopolio.
an·ti·ven·in (:vĕn′ən) s. contraveneno.
ant·ler (ănt′lər) s. asta, mogote *m*.
an·to·nym (ăn′tə-nĭm′) s. antónimo.
a·nus (ā′nəs) s. ano.
an·vil (ăn′vĭl) s. yunque *m*.
anx·i·e·ty (ăng-zī′ĭ-tē) s. ansiedad *f*, ansia; PSIC. angustia.
anx·ious (ăngk′shəs) adj. *(worried)* ansioso, inquieto; *(eager)* deseoso, anhelante.
an·y (ĕn′ē) I. adj. *(no matter which)* cualquier <*a. book* cualquier libro>; *(some)* algún <*do you have a. doubt?* ¿tienes alguna duda?>; *(negative)* algún, ningún <*there isn't a. reason* no hay ninguna razón>; *(every)* cualquiera, todo <*we must avoid a. contact* debemos evitar todo contacto> ✦ **a. minute** pronto • **at a. cost** a toda costa • **at a. rate** *o* **in a. case** de todos modos II. pron. alguno, cualquiera; *(negative)* ninguno ✦ **if a.** si los hay III. adv. algo, de algún modo <*do you feel a. better?* ¿te sientes algo mejor?>; *(negative)* nada, para nada <*I don't feel a. better* no me siento nada mejor> ✦ **a. longer** más tiempo, todavía.
an·y·bod·y (:bŏd′ē) pron. cualquiera, quienquiera, cualquier persona <*a. could do it* cualquiera podría hacerlo>; *(interrogative)* alguien, alguno <*did you see a?* ¿viste a alguien?>; *(negative)* ninguno, nadie <*I didn't see a.* no vi a nadie>.
an·y·how (:hou′) adv. *(even so)* de todas maneras, de todos modos; *(carelessly)* de cualquier manera.
an·y·more (′-môr′) adv. *(negative)* nunca más, ya más, ya no <*I don't run a.* ya no corro más>; *(interrogative)* aún, todavía <*do you run a.?* ¿corres todavía?>.
an·y·one (′-wŭn′) cf. **anybody**.
an·y·place (:plās′) cf. **anywhere**.
an·y·thing (:thĭng′) pron. *(interrogative)* algo, alguna cosa <*are you doing a. now?* ¿estás haciendo algo ahora?>; *(negative)* nada, ninguna cosa <*I can't see a.* no veo nada>; *(affirmative)* cualquier cosa, todo lo que <*take a. you like* toma todo lo que quieras> ✦ **a. else?** ¿algo más?, ¿alguna otra cosa? • **like a.** FAM. a más no poder.
an·y·time (:tīm′) adv. a cualquier hora, en cualquier momento.
an·y·way (:wā′) adv. *(in any case)* de cualquier manera, de cualquier modo; *(even so)* lo mismo, de todos modos.
an·y·where (:hwâr′) adv. *(affirmative)* dondequiera, a *o* en cualquier sitio *o* parte; *(negative)* en, a, *o* por ninguna parte *o* ningún lado; *(interrogative)* en algún lugar, en alguna parte ✦ **a. from** FAM. entre <*you can save a. from five to ten dollars* puedes ahorrar entre cinco y diez dólares>.
A-OK *o* **A-o·kay** (ā′ō-kā′) adj. & adv. perfecto, excelente.
a·pace (ə-pās′) adv. rápidamente, velozmente.
a·part (ə-pärt′) adv. aparte, a distancia ✦ **a. from** aparte de, con la excepción de • **to come a.** desprenderse, desunirse • **to fall a.** descomponerse; FIG. venirse abajo • **to keep a.** apartar, separar • **to take a.** desarmar, desmontar • **to tear a.** despedazar, destrozar • **to tell a.** distinguir, diferenciar • **to stand a.** mantenerse apartado; FIG. distinguirse • **to set a.** reservar, poner a un lado.
a·part·ment (ə-pärt′mənt) s. *(residence)* departamento, apartamento; *(room)* cuarto ✦ **a. house** casa *o* edificio de departamentos.
ap·a·thet·ic (ăp′ə-thĕt′ĭk) adj. apático.
ap·a·thy (′-thē) s. apatía.
ape (āp) I. s. mono; FIG. imitamonos *mf* II. tr. imitar, remedar.
a·per·i·tif (ä′pə-lĭ-tēf′) s. aperitivo.
ap·er·ture (ăp′ər-chər) s. abertura.
a·pex (ā′pĕks′) s. [pl. **es** *o* **-pices**] ápice *m*; FIG. cima, cumbre *m*.
a·pha·sia (ə-fā′zhə) s. afasia.
a·phid (ā′fĭd) s. pulgón *m*.
aph·o·rism (ăf′ə-rĭz′əm) s. aforismo, refrán *m*.
aph·ro·dis·i·ac (ăf′rə-dĭz′ē-ăk′) adj. & s. afrodisíaco.
a·pi·ar·y (ā′pē-ĕr′ē) s. abejar *m*, colmenar *m*.
a·piece (ə-pēs′) adv. por cabeza, cada uno.
a·plomb (ə-plŏm′) s. aplomo.
a·poc·a·lypse (ə-pŏk′ə-lĭps′) s. revelación *f*.
a·poc·a·lyp·tic (-′-lĭp′tĭk) adj. apocalíptico.
a·poc·ry·phal (ə-pŏk′rə-fəl) adj. apócrifo.
ap·o·gee (ăp′ə-jē) s. apogeo.
a·po·lit·i·cal (ā′pə-lĭt′ĭ-kəl) adj. apolítico.
a·pol·o·get·ic (ə-pŏl′ə-jĕt′ĭk) adj. lleno de disculpas.
a·pol·o·get·i·cal·ly (:ĭ-kə-lē) adv. disculpándose.
a·pol·o·gize (:jīz′) intr. disculparse *(for por, de)* *(to* con).
a·pol·o·gy (:jē) s. *(for an offense)* disculpa; *(formal defense)* apología ✦ **to make an a.** disculparse.
ap·o·plec·tic (ăp′ə-plĕk′tĭk) adj. apoplético.
ap·os·tate (ə-pŏs′tāt′) s. apóstata *mf*.
a·pos·tle (ə-pŏs′əl) s. apóstol *mf*.
ap·os·tol·ic (ăp′ə-stŏl′ĭk) adj. apostólico.
a·pos·tro·phe (ə-pŏs′trə-fē) s. GRAM. apóstrofo; RET. apóstrofe *m*.
a·poth·e·car·y (ə-pŏth′ĭ-kĕr′ē) s. boticario.
a·poth·e·o·sis (ə-pŏth′ē-ō′sĭs) s. [pl. **ses**] apoteosis *f*.
ap·pall (ə-pôl′) tr. pasmar, horrorizar.
ap·pall·ing (ə-pô′lĭng) adj. pasmoso, horrendo.
ap·pa·ra·tus (ăp′ə-rā′təs, -răt′əs) s. [pl. inv. *o* **es**] aparato; *(mechanism)* mecanismo.
ap·par·el (ə-păr′əl) s. ropa, indumentaria.
ap·par·ent (ə-păr′ənt) adj. *(seeming)* aparente; *(perceptible)* evidente, claro.
ap·par·ent·ly (:lē) adv. *(seemingly)* aparentemente, por lo visto; *(obviously)* evidentemente.
ap·pa·ri·tion (ăp′ə-rĭsh′ən) s. aparición *f*.
ap·peal (ə-pēl′) I. s. *(plea)* súplica; *(a call for)* llamada; *(petition)* petición *f*, instancia; *(charm)* atracción *f*, encanto; DER. apelación *f*, recurso ✦ **without a.** DER. sin recurso, inapelable II. intr. ✦ **a. to** suplicar a; DER. recurrir a, apelar a; *(to be attractive)* tener atractivo para —tr. llevar a un tribunal superior.
ap·peal·ing (ə-pē′lĭng) adj. atrayente.
ap·pear (ə-pîr′) intr. *(to come into view)* aparecer, asomarse; *(to seem)* parecer; *(to present oneself)* presentarse; *(on the stage)* actuar; *(in court)* comparecer; *(in print)* publicarse.
ap·pear·ance (′-əns) s. *(act)* aparición *f*; *(looks)* aspecto, apariencia; *(pretense)* pretensión *f*, simulación *f* ✦ **to make an a.** hacer acto de presencia ✦ pl. apariencias, exterioridad.
ap·pease (ə-pēz′) tr. apaciguar, aplacar.
ap·pease·ment (:mənt) s. apaciguamiento.
ap·pel·lant (ə-pĕl′ənt) I. adj. de apelación II. s. apelante *mf*.

ap·pel·late (:īt) adj. de apelación.
ap·pel·la·tion (ăp'ə-lā'shən) s. nombre m.
ap·pend (ə-pĕnd') tr. anexar, adjuntar.
ap·pend·age (ə-pĕn'dĭj) s. apéndice m.
ap·pen·dec·to·my (ăp'ən-dĕk'tə-mē) s. apendectomía.
ap·pen·di·ci·tis (ə-pĕn'dĭ-sī'tĭs) s. apendicitis f.
ap·pen·dix (ə-pĕn'dĭks) s. [pl. **es** o **-dices**] apéndice m.
ap·pe·tite (ăp'ĭ-tīt') s. apetito, apetencia.
ap·pe·tiz·er (:tī'zər) s. aperitivo.
ap·pe·tiz·ing (:zĭng) adj. apetitoso, gustoso.
ap·plaud (ə-plôd') tr. & intr. aplaudir.
ap·plause (ə-plôz') s. aplauso.
ap·ple (ăp'əl) s. manzana ♦ **a. tree** manzano.
ap·ple·sauce (:sôs') s. compota de manzana.
ap·pli·ance (ə-plī'əns) s. artefacto, aparato ♦ **household a.** aparato electrodoméstico.
ap·pli·cant (ăp'lĭ-kənt) s. aspirante mf.
ap·pli·ca·tion ('-kā'shən) s. (act) aplicación f; (relevance) correspondencia, pertinencia; (diligence) esmero; (request) solicitación f; (form) solicitud f, aplicación.
ap·pli·ca·tor ('-kā'tər) s. aplicador m.
ap·pli·qué (ăp'lĭ-kā') s. aplicado, aplicación f.
ap·ply (ə-plī') tr. (to put on) aplicar; (to use) emplear, usar (to para) ♦ **to a. oneself** to aplicarse a —intr. ser pertinente o aplicable ♦ **to a. for** solicitar (empleo, admisión).
ap·point (ə-point') tr. (to designate) nombrar, designar; (a date) fijar, determinar.
ap·point·ed (ə-poin'tĭd) adj. nombrado, designado.
ap·point·ee (-'tē') s. persona designada.
ap·point·ment (ə-point'mənt) s. (act) nombramiento, designación f; (post) puesto, cargo; (date) cita, compromiso.
ap·por·tion (ə-pôr'shən) tr. prorratear.
ap·prais·al (ə-prā'zəl) s. tasación f.
ap·praise (ə-prāz') tr. evaluar, tasar.
ap·pre·cia·ble (ə-prē'shə-bəl) adj. perceptible, sensible.
ap·pre·cia·bly (:blē) adv. sensiblemente.
ap·pre·ci·ate (ə-prē'shē-āt') tr. (to recognize) darse cuenta de, reconocer; (to value) apreciar, estimar; (to be grateful for) agradecer —intr. valorizarse, subir de precio o valor.
ap·pre·ci·a·tion (-'-ā'shən) s. (recognition) apreciación f, reconocimiento; (gratitude) gratitud f; COM. valorización f.
ap·pre·cia·tive (ə-prē'shə-tĭv) adj. apreciador, agradecido.
ap·pre·hend (ăp'rĭ-hĕnd') tr. (to arrest) aprehender, arrestar; (to understand) comprender.
ap·pre·hen·sion (:hĕn'shən) s. (dread) aprensión f; (arrest) aprehensión f; (understanding) comprensión f.
ap·pre·hen·sive (:sĭv) adj. aprensivo.
ap·pren·tice (ə-prĕn'tĭs) I. s. aprendiz m II. tr. poner de aprendiz.
ap·pren·tice·ship (:shĭp') s. aprendizaje m.
ap·prise (ə-prīz') tr. informar, notificar.
ap·proach (ə-prōch') I. intr. aproximarse, acercarse —tr. aproximarse a, acercarse a; (to make overtures to) abordar; (to take up) abordar, emprender (tarea, asunto) II. s. (act) acercamiento; (access) acceso, vía de entrada; (overture) proposición f, propuesta; (method) método, enfoque m (de un asunto, situación).
ap·proach·ing (ə-prōch'ĭng) adj. (upcoming) venidero, próximo; (nearing) que se acerca.
ap·pro·ba·tion (ăp'rə-bā'shən) s. aprobación f.

ap·pro·pri·ate (ə-prō'prē-ĭt) I. adj. apropiado, adecuado II. tr. (:āt') (to set apart) destinar, consignar; (to seize) apropiarse de.
ap·pro·pri·a·tion (-'-ā'shən) s. (act) apropiación f; (allocation) asignación f.
ap·prov·al (ə-prō'vəl) s. aprobación f, sanción f ♦ **on a.** a prueba.
ap·prove (ə-prōōv') tr. (to endorse) aprobar, consentir; (to ratify) sancionar, ratificar —intr. dar su aprobación, aprobar.
ap·prox·i·mate (ə-prŏk'sə-mĭt) I. adj. aproximado II. tr. & intr. (:māt') aproximar(se), acercar(se).
ap·prox·i·ma·tion (-'-mā'shən) s. aproximación f.
ap·pur·te·nance (ə-pûr'tn-əns) s. accesorio.
a·pri·cot (ăp'rĭ-kŏt', ā'prĭ-) s. albaricoque m.
A·pril (ā'prəl) s. abril m.
a·pron (ā'prən) s. delantal m; AVIA. pista (delante de los hangares) ♦ **to be tied to (a mother's) a. strings** estar cosido a las faldas de (la madre).
ap·ro·pos (ăp'rə-pō') I. adj. adecuado, oportuno II. adv. & prep. a propósito (de).
apse (ăps) s. ábside m.
apt (ăpt) adj. (suitable) apropiado, acertado; (inclined) propenso; (bright) apto, listo.
ap·ti·tude (ăp'tĭ-tōōd') s. aptitud f, capacidad f.
aq·ua·ma·rine (ăk'wə-mə-rēn') s. (color) aguamarina.
aq·ua·plane (ăk'wə-plān') s. acuaplano.
a·quar·i·um (ə-kwâr'ē-əm) s. [pl. **s** o **-ia**] acuario.
a·quat·ic (ə-kwŏt'ĭk) adj. acuático, acuátil.
aq·ua·tint (ăk'wə-tĭnt') s. (process) acuatinta; (etching) grabado al acuatinta.
aq·ue·duct (ăk'wĭ-dŭkt') s. acueducto.
a·que·ous (ā'kwē-əs) adj. acuoso, ácueo.
aq·ui·fer (ăk'wə-fər) s. roca acuífera.
aq·ui·line (ăk'wə-līn') adj. aguileño, aquilino.
ar·a·besque (ăr'ə-bĕsk') s. arabesco.
Ar·a·bic numeral (ăr'ə-bĭk) s. número arábigo.
ar·a·ble (ăr'ə-bəl) adj. arable, cultivable.
a·rach·nid (ə-răk'nĭd) s. arácnido.
ar·bi·ter (är'bĭ-tər) s. árbitro.
ar·bi·trar·y (:trĕr'ē) adj. arbitrario.
ar·bi·trate (:trāt') tr. & intr. arbitrar.
ar·bi·tra·tion ('-trā'shən) s. arbitraje m.
ar·bi·tra·tor ('-tər) s. arbitrador m, árbitro.
ar·bor (är'bər) s. enramada, pérgola.
ar·bo·re·al (är-bôr'ē-əl) adj. arbóreo.
ar·bor·vi·tae (är'bər-vī'tē) s. árbol m de la vida.
arc (ärk) I. s. arco ♦ **a. lamp** lámpara de arco • **electric a.** arco voltaico II. intr. **-c(k)-** formar arco.
ar·cade (är-kād') s. arcada; (roofed passageway) galería.
ar·cane (är-kān') adj. arcano.
arch¹ (ärch) I. s. arco II. tr. (to bend) enarcar, arquear; (to span) atravesar —intr. arquearse.
arch² adj. (principal) principal; (mischievous) astuto, socarrón.
ar·chae·o·log·i·cal (är'kē-ə-lŏj'ĭ-kəl) adj. arqueológico.
ar·chae·ol·o·gist (:ŏl'ə-jĭst) s. arqueólogo.
ar·chae·ol·o·gy (:jē) s. arqueología.
ar·cha·ic (är-kā'ĭk) adj. arcaico.
arch·an·gel (ärk'ān'jəl) s. arcángel m.
arch·bish·op (ärch'bĭsh'əp) s. arzobispo.
arched (ärcht) adj. arqueado, enarcado.
arch·en·e·my (ärch-ĕn'ə-mē) s. enemigo acé-

rrimo, el mayor enemigo.
arch·er (är'chər) s. arquero (de arco y flecha).
arch·er·y (är'chə-rē) s. tiro de arco y flecha.
ar·che·type (är'kĭ-tīp') s. arquetipo, prototipo.
ar·chi·pel·a·go (är'kə-pĕl'ə-gō') s. [pl. **(e)s**] archipiélago.
ar·chi·tect (är'kĭ-tĕkt') s. arquitecto.
ar·chi·tec·tur·al ('-tĕk'chər-əl) adj. arquitectónico.
ar·chi·tec·ture (är'kĭ-tĕk'chər) s. arquitectura.
ar·chive (är'kīv') s. archivo.
ar·chi·vist (är'kə-vĭst) s. archivista *mf.*
arch·priest (ärch-prēst') s. arcipreste *m.*
arch·way (ärch'wā') s. arcada, arco.
arc·tic (ärk'tĭk, är'tĭk) adj. frígido, glacial.
ar·dent (är'dnt) adj. ardiente, vehemente.
ar·du·ous (är'jōō-əs) adj. arduo, penoso.
are (är) segunda persona sing. y pl. de **be.**
ar·e·a (âr'ē-ə) s. área; *(region)* zona, región *f* ♦ **a. code** prefijo telefónico.
a·re·na (ə-rē'nə) s. *(circus ring)* arena, pista; *(auditorium)* estadio; FIG. área, campo.
aren't (ärnt, är'ənt) contr. de **are not.**
ar·gon (är'gŏn') argón *m*, argo.
ar·got (är'gō, :gət) s. argot *m.*
ar·gu·a·ble (är'gyōō-ə-bəl) adj. discutible, disputable
ar·gue (är'gyōō) tr. *(to debate)* argüir, presentar; *(to maintain)* razonar, argumentar; *(to persuade)* persuadir, convencer —intr. *(to debate)* argumentar, argüir (in favor o en contra de algo); *(to quarrel)* disputar, discutir.
ar·gu·ment (är'gyə-mənt) s. *(debate)* discusión *f*, debate *m*; *(quarrel)* pelea, disputa; *(contention)* razonamiento, argumento.
ar·gu·men·ta·tion (:mĕn-tā'shən) s. *(act)* argumentación *f*; *(debate)* debate *m.*
ar·gu·men·ta·tive ('-tā-tĭv) adj. discutidor.
a·ri·a (ä'rē-ə) s. aria.
ar·id (är'ĭd) adj. árido, seco.
a·rid·i·ty (ə-rĭd'ĭ-tē) s. aridez *f*, sequedad *f.*
a·right (ə-rīt') adv. correctamente, rectamente.
a·rise (ə-rīz') intr. **arose**, **-n** *(to get up)* levantarse, ponerse en pie; *(to ascend)* ascender, elevarse; *(to originate)* surgir, originarse.
ar·is·toc·ra·cy (är'ĭ-stŏk'rə-sē) s. aristocracia.
a·ris·to·crat (ə-rĭs'tə-krăt') s. aristócrata *mf.*
a·ris·to·crat·ic ('-'ĭk) adj. aristocrático.
Ar·is·to·te·lian (ə-rĭs'tə-tē'lē-ən) adj. aristotélico.
a·rith·me·tic (ə-rĭth'mĭ-tĭk) s. aritmética.
ar·ith·met·ic·al (är'ĭth-mĕt'ĭk) adj. aritmético.
ark (ärk) s. arca, barcaza.
arm¹ (ärm) s. ANAT. brazo ♦ **a. in a.** tomados del brazo ♦ **to keep at a.'s length** mantener a distancia prudencial.
arm² I. s. MIL. arma ♦ **arms race** carrera de armamentos ♦ **to be up in arms** alzarse en armas; FIG. poner el grito en el cielo ♦ **to bear arms** llevar las armas ♦ **to lay down one's arms** rendir las armas II. tr. armar.
ar·ma·ment (är'mə-mənt) s. armamento ♦ pl. armas, armamento.
ar·ma·ture (är'mə-chŏr') s. armadura.
arm·band (ärm'bănd') s. brazalete *m*, brazal *m.*
arm·chair (:châr') s. sillón *m*, butaca ♦ **a. politician** político de café.
armed (ärmd) adj. armado ♦ **a. forces** fuerzas armadas.
arm·ful (ärm'fŏŏl') s. brazada.

ar·mi·stice (är'mĭ-stĭs) s. armisticio, tregua.
ar·moire (ärm-wär') s. armario, ropero.
ar·mor (är'mər) I. s. armadura; *(metal plating)* blindaje *m* ♦ **a. plate** plancha de blindaje, coraza II. tr. blindar, acorazar.
ar·mor·clad (:klăd') adj. acorazado, blindado.
ar·mored (är'mərd) adj. acorazado, blindado.
ar·mor·y (är'mə-rē) s. *(arsenal)* armería, arsenal *m*; *(factory)* fábrica de armas.
arm·pit (ärm'pĭt') s. axila.
ar·my (är'mē) s. ejército; FIG. multitud *f.*
a·ro·ma (ə-rō'mə) s. aroma *m*, fragancia.
ar·o·mat·ic (är'ə-măt'ĭk) adj. aromático.
a·rose (ə-rōz') cf. **arise.**
a·round (ə-round') I. adv. *(in all directions)* por todos lados, en derredor; *(here and there)* por aquí, por allá; *(in circumference)* de circunferencia ♦ **all a.** por todos lados ♦ **the other way a.** al contrario, al revés ♦ **to get a.** *(person)* viajar, ir a lugares; *(news)* divulgarse, propalarse ♦ **to have been a.** tener experiencia, haber corrido mundo II. prep. *(about)* cerca de, alrededor de; *(encircling)* alrededor de; *(here and there)* por todos lados, en torno de ♦ **a. the corner** a la vuelta de la esquina.
a·round-the-clock ('-thə-klŏk') adj. continuamente.
a·rous·al (ə-rou'zəl) s. despertar *m.*
a·rouse (ə-rouz') tr. *(to awaken)* despertar; *(to stir up)* estimular, incitar.
ar·peg·gi·o (är-pĕj'ē-ō) s. arpegio.
ar·raign (ə-rān') tr. *(before a court)* citar, hacer comparecer; *(to charge)* denunciar, acusar.
ar·raign·ment (:mənt) s. DER. citación *f.*
ar·range (ə-rānj') tr. *(to order)* arreglar, ordenar; *(to settle upon)* fijar, señalar (fechas, convenios); *(to plan)* preparar; MÚS. arreglar —intr. acordar, convenir en.
ar·range·ment (:mənt) s. arreglo; *(order)* disposición *f*, *(agreement)* convenio ♦ pl. planes, medidas.
ar·rant (är'ənt) adj. notorio, consumado.
ar·ray (ə-rā') I. tr. *(to arrange)* arreglar, disponer; *(to adorn)* adornar (con lujo); MIL. formar II. s. *(impressive display)* conjunto impresionante; *(attire)* vestimenta lujosa; MIL. orden *m* de batalla.
ar·rears (ə-rîrz') s.pl. ♦ **to be in a.** estar atrasado en pagos de deuda.
ar·rest (ə-rĕst') I. tr. *(to halt)* detener, parar; *(to seize)* arrestar, detener; *(to engage)* cautivar II. s. arresto, detención *f* ♦ **under a.** detenido.
ar·rest·ing (ə-rĕs'tĭng) adj. llamativo, impresionante.
ar·ri·val (ə-rī'vəl) s. llegada, arribo.
ar·rive (ə-rīv') intr. llegar; *(by boat)* arribar; FAM. tener éxito, llegar ♦ **to a. at** llegar a (conclusión, objetivo).
ar·ro·gance (är'ə-gəns) s. arrogancia, altivez *f.*
ar·ro·gant (:gənt) adj. arrogante, altivo.
ar·row (är'ō) s. flecha.
ar·row·head (:hĕd') s. punta de flecha.
ar·row·root (:rōōt') s. arrurruz *m.*
ar·se·nal (är'sə-nəl) s. arsenal *m.*
ar·se·nic (är'sə-nĭk) s. & adj. arsénico.
ar·son (är'sən) s. incendio premeditado.
ar·son·ist (är'sə-nĭst) s. incendiario.
art (ärt) s. arte *m*; *(skill)* destreza, técnica ♦ **fine arts** bellas artes.
ar·ter·y (är'tə-rē) s. arteria.
art·ful (ärt'fəl) adj. *(skillful)* ingenioso, diestro;

(clever) artificioso; *(deceitful)* mañoso.

ar·thrit·ic (är-thrĭt´ĭk) adj. & s. artrítico.

ar·thri·tis (är-thrī´tĭs) s. artritis f.

ar·ti·choke (är´tĭ-chōk´) s. alcachofa.

ar·ti·cle (är´tĭ-kəl) s. artículo; *(of a document)* cláusula ♦ **a. of clothing** prenda de vestir • **articles and conditions** COM. pliego de condiciones • **articles of incorporation** COM. estatutos de una sociedad anónima.

ar·tic·u·late (är-tĭk´yə-lĭt) **I.** adj. *(speaking)* que habla; *(distinct)* articulado; *(well-expressed)* inteligible, claro; BIOL. articulado **II.** tr. (:lāt´) *(to enunciate)* articular, enunciar; *(to form a joint)* articular.

ar·ti·fact (är´tə-fākt´) s. artefacto.

ar·ti·fice (är´tə-fĭs) s. artificio; *(trickery)* engaño.

ar·ti·fi·cial (´-fĭsh´əl) adj. artificial.

ar·til·ler·y (är-tĭl´ə-rē) s. artillería.

ar·ti·san (är´tĭ-zən) s. artesano, artífice mf.

art·ist (är´tĭst) s. artista mf.

ar·tis·tic (är-tĭs´tĭk) adj. artístico.

art·ist·ry (är´tĭ-strē) s. arte mf, talento artístico.

art·less (ärt´lĭs) adj. *(naive)* sencillo, ingenuo; *(natural)* natural; *(crude)* desmañado, torpe.

Ar·y·an (âr´ē-ən) adj. & s. ario.

as (ăz, əz) **I.** adv. *(equally)* así de, tan; *(for example)* (tal) como • **as a ... as** tan ... como <*as strong as an ox* tan fuerte como un buey> • **as far as I'm concerned** en cuanto a mí respecta • **as far as I know** hasta que yo sepa **II.** conj. *(to the same degree)* igual que, como <*sweet as sugar* dulce como el azúcar>; *(while)* mientras; *(because)* ya que, porque • **as from** a partir de • **as if** como si • **as it to** como para • **as it were** por así decirlo • **as long as** *(since)* ya que; *(on the condition that)* siempre y cuando; *(while)* mientras • **as to** en cuanto a • **as yet** hasta ahora **III.** prep. como • **as a rule** por regla general • **as for** en cuanto a **IV.** pron. *(which)* que <*do the same things as I do* haz las mismas cosas que yo hago>; *(a fact that)* como <*she is very careful, as her work shows* ella es muy cuidadosa, como lo demuestra su trabajo>.

as·bes·tos (ăs-bĕs´təs) s. asbesto, amianto **♦ a. cement** fibrocemento.

as·cend (ə-sĕnd´) intr. *(to rise)* elevarse, remontarse; *(to slope upward)* ascender, subir —tr. *(to climb)* subir (escalera, montaña); *(the throne)* subir a, ascender a.

as·cen·dance/ence (ə-sĕn´dəns) s. ascendiente m, predominio.

as·cen·dant/ent (:dənt) adj. ascendiente.

as·cend·ing (:dĭng) adj. ascendente.

as·cen·sion (:shən) s. ascensión f.

as·cent (ə-sĕnt´) s. *(act)* subida, ascensión f; *(in rank)* ascenso; *(upward slope)* cuesta.

as·cer·tain (ăs´ər-tān´) tr. determinar.

as·cet·ic (ə-sĕt´ĭk) **I.** s. asceta mf **II.** adj. ascético.

as·cot (ăs´kət) s. corbata (a la inglesa).

as·cribe (ə-skrīb´) tr. atribuir, imputar.

a·sep·tic (ə-sĕp´tĭk) adj. aséptico.

ash[1] (ăsh) s. *(from fire)* ceniza.

ash[2] s. BOT. fresno.

a·shamed (ə-shāmd´) adj. avergonzado **♦ to be a.** tener vergüenza.

ash·en (ăsh´ən) adj. pálido, ceniciento.

a·shore (ə-shôr´) adv. a o en tierra **♦ to go a.** bajar a tierra, desembarcar.

ash·tray (ăsh´trā´) s. cenicero.

a·side (ə-sīd´) **I.** adv. *(to one side)* al lado, a un

lado <*step a.* hágase a un lado>; *(apart)* de lado, aparte <*joking a.* bromas aparte> **♦ a. from** a no ser por **II.** s. TEAT. aparte m; *(digression)* digresión f.

as·i·nine (ăs´ə-nīn´) adj. estúpido, necio.

ask (ăsk) tr. preguntar <*he asked me my age* me preguntó mi edad>; *(to request)* solicitar, pedir; *(to demand)* exigir; *(to invite)* invitar **♦ to a. a favor** pedir un favor • **to a. a question** hacer una pregunta —intr. preguntar *(about, after por)* **♦ to a. for** pedir • **to a. for it** FAM. buscársela • **to be had for the asking** basta pedirlo para conseguirlo.

a·skance (ə-skăns´) adv. *(sidewise)* de reojo, de soslayo; *(with suspicion)* con recelo.

a·skew (ə-skyōō´) **I.** adj. ladeado, torcido **II.** adv. oblicuamente, sesgadamente.

a·sleep (ə-slēp´) adj. dormido; *(inactive)* inactivo; *(numb)* adormecido **♦ to fall a.** dormirse, quedarse dormido.

asp (ăsp) s. áspid m, áspide m.

as·par·a·gus (ə-spăr´ə-gəs) s. espárrago.

as·pect (ăs´pĕkt´) s. aspecto.

as·pen (ăs´pən) s. álamo temblón.

as·per·i·ty (ă-spĕr´ĭ-tē) s. aspereza.

as·per·sion (ə-spûrs´zhən) s. calumnia.

as·phalt (ăs´fôlt´) s. asfalto **II.** tr. asfaltar.

as·phyx·i·ate (ăs-fĭk´sē-āt) tr. & intr. asfixiar(se), sofocar(se).

as·phyx·i·a·tion (´-´-´shən) s. asfixia.

as·pic (ăs´pĭk) s. gelatina (de carne o tomate).

as·pi·rant (ăs´pər-ənt) s. aspirante mf.

as·pi·rate (ăs´pə-rāt´) **I.** tr. aspirar **II.** s. (:pər-ĭt) aspiración f.

as·pi·ra·tion (ăs´pə-rā´shən) s. aspiración f.

as·pire (ə-spīr´) intr. aspirar, ambicionar.

as·pi·rin (ăs´pər-ĭn) s. aspirina.

ass (ăs) s. asno, burro; *(fool)* tonto, imbécil mf.

as·sail (ə-sāl´) tr. asaltar, atacar.

as·sail·ant (ə-sāl´ənt) s. asaltante mf.

as·sas·sin (ə-săs´ĭn) s. asesino.

as·sas·si·nate (:ə-nāt´) tr. asesinar.

as·sas·si·na·tion (´-´-nā´shən) s. asesinato.

as·sault (ə-sôlt´) **I.** s. asalto, ataque m **♦ a. and battery** asalto y agresión **II.** tr. & intr. asaltar, atacar.

as·say (ăs´ā´) **I.** s. ensaye m **II.** tr. (ă-sā´) ensayar (metales o aleación).

as·sem·ble (ə-sĕm´bəl) tr. *(to gather)* congregar, reunir; MEC. armar, montar —intr. congregarse, reunirse.

as·sem·bly (:blē) s. *(meeting)* asamblea, congreso; MEC. montaje m; MIL. asamblea **♦ a. language** lenguaje ensamblador • **a. line** línea de montaje.

as·sent (ə-sĕnt´) **I.** intr. asentir, convenir **II.** s. asentimiento, aprobación f.

as·sert (ə-sûrt´) tr. *(to declare)* asertar, afirmar; *(one's right)* mantener, hacer valer **♦ to a. oneself** imponerse, hacer valer uno sus derechos.

as·ser·tion (ə-sûr´shən) s. aserción f.

as·ser·tive (:tĭv) adj. agresivo.

as·sess (ə-sĕs´) tr. *(to appraise)* evaluar, tasar *(at en)*; *(to levy)* gravar, multar; *(to evaluate)* evaluar, juzgar.

as·sess·ment (:mənt) s. *(appraisal)* evaluación f, tasación f; *(amount assessed)* tasa.

as·ses·sor (:ər) s. tasador m (de impuestos).

as·set (ăs´ĕt´) s. *(item)* posesión f, bien m; *(advantage)* ventaja **♦ pl.** bienes, activo.

as·sid·u·ous (ə-sĭj´ōō-əs) adj. asiduo.

as·sign (ə-sīn´) tr. asignar; *(a task)* señalar; *(to*

ascribe) indicar; DER. transferir, traspasar.

as·sig·na·tion (ās′ĭg-nā′shən) s. asignación *f*; *(date)* cita *(amorosa).*

as·sign·ment (ə-sīn′mənt) s. *(act)* asignación *f*; *(task)* tarea, deber *m*; *(position)* puesto.

as·sim·i·late (ə-sĭm′ə-lāt′) tr. & intr. asimilar(se).

as·sim·i·la·tion (-′-lā′shən) s. asimilación *f.*

as·sist (ə-sĭst′) I. tr. & intr. asistir, auxiliar II. s. ayuda, auxilio.

as·sis·tance (ə-sĭs′təns) s. asistencia, ayuda ♦ **to be of a. to** ayudar a.

as·sis·tant (:tənt) s. & adj. ayudante *mf*, auxiliar *m.*

as·so·ci·ate (ə-sō′shē-āt′, -sē-) I. tr. & intr. asociar(se) ♦ **to a. with someone** juntarse *o* tratarse con alguien II. s. (:ĭt) *(partner)* socio, consocio; *(companion)* compañero III. adj. (:ĭt) asociado, adjunto.

as·so·ci·a·tion (-′-ā′shən) s. asociación *f.*

as·so·nance (ās′ə-nəns) s. asonancia.

as·sort (ə-sôrt′) tr. clasificar, ordenar.

as·sort·ed (ə-sôr′tĭd) adj. surtido, variado.

as·sort·ment (ə-sôrt′mənt) s. surtido, colección variada.

as·suage (ə-swāj′) tr. *(to ease)* aliviar, mitigar; *(to satisfy)* satisfacer, saciar.

as·sum·able (ə-sōō′mə-bəl) adj. asumible.

as·sume (ə-sōōm′) tr. asumir; *(to arrogate)* arrogarse (un derecho); *(to feign)* fingir, simular; *(to presume)* presumir, suponer.

as·sumed (ə-sōōmd′) adj. *(feigned)* simulado, fingido; *(taken for granted)* supuesto, presunto.

as·sum·ing (ə-sōō′mĭng) adj. pretensioso.

as·sump·tion (ə-sŭmp′shən) s. *(act)* asunción *f*; *(supposition)* suposición *f.*

as·sur·ance (ə-shŏŏr′əns) s. *(guarantee)* garantía, promesa; *(certainty)* certeza, seguridad *f*; *(self-confidence)* aplomo.

as·sure (ə-shŏŏr′) tr. asegurar; *(to reassure)* tranquilizar; *(to ensure)* garantizar.

as·sured (ə-shŏŏrd′) adj. *(sure)* seguro, cierto; *(self-confident)* seguro (de sí mismo).

as·ter·isk (ās′tə-rĭsk′) s. asterisco.

a·stern (ə-stûrn′) adv. a *o* de popa.

as·ter·oid (ās′tə-roid′) s. asteroide *m.*

asth·ma (āz′mə) s. asma.

asth·mat·ic (āz-māt′ĭk) adj. & s. asmático.

as·tig·mat·ic (ās′tĭg-māt′ĭk) adj. astigmático.

a·stir (ə-stûr′) adj. *(moving about)* activo, en movimiento; *(out of bed)* levantado.

as·ton·ish (ə-stŏn′ĭsh) tr. asombrar.

as·ton·ish·ing (:ĭ-shĭng) adj. asombroso.

as·ton·ish·ment (:ĭsh-mənt) s. asombro.

a·stound (ə-stound′) tr. maravillar, asombrar.

a·stray (ə-strā′) adv. por mal camino ♦ **to go a.** extraviarse *o* **to lead a.** descarriar.

a·stride (ə-strīd′) adv. & prep. a horcajadas (sobre).

as·trin·gent (ə-strĭn′jənt) I. adj. MED. astringente; *(harsh)* áspero II. s. astringente *m.*

as·trol·o·ger (ə-strŏl′ə-jər) s. astrólogo.

as·tro·log·i·cal (ās′trə-lŏj′ĭk) adj. astrológico.

as·trol·o·gy (ə-strŏl′ə-jē) s. astrología.

as·tro·naut (ās′trə-nôt′) s. astronauta *mf.*

as·tron·o·mer (ə-strŏn′ə-mər) s. astrónomo.

as·tro·nom·ic/i·cal (ās′trə-nŏm′ĭk) adj. astronómico.

as·tron·o·my (ə-strŏn′ə-mē) s. astronomía.

as·tro·phys·ics (ās′trō-fĭz′ĭks) s.sg. astrofísica.

as·tute (ə-stōōt′) adj. astuto, sagaz.

a·sun·der (ə-sŭn′dər) adv. en pedazos, en dos.

a·sy·lum (ə-sī′ləm) s. asilo.

a·sym·me·try (ā-sĭm′ĭ-trē) s. asimetría.

at (āt, ət) prep. en <*at right angles* en ángulo recto>; a <*at noon* al mediodía>; por <*to be angry at something* estar enfadado por algo>; de <*don't laugh at me!* ¡no te rías de mí!>; en casa de <*I'll be at Roberto's* estaré en casa de Roberto>.

at·a·vism (āt′ə-vĭz′əm) s. atavismo.

at·a·vis·tic (′-vĭs′tĭk) adj. atávico.

ate (āt) cf. **eat.**

a·the·ism (ā′thē-ĭz′əm) s. ateísmo.

a·the·ist (:ĭst) s. ateo.

ath·lete (āth′lēt′) s. atleta *mf* ♦ **a.'s foot** pie de atleta.

ath·let·ic (āth-lĕt′ĭk) adj. atlético ♦ **athletics** s. atletismo.

a·thwart (ə-thwôrt′) I. adv. de través II. prep. a través de.

at·las (āt′ləs) s. atlas *m.*

at·mos·phere (āt′mə-sfîr′) s. atmósfera.

at·mos·pher·ic (′-sfîr′ĭk) adj. atmosférico.

a·toll (āt′ôl′, ā′tôl′) s. atolón *m.*

at·om (āt′əm) s. átomo ♦ **a. bomb** bomba atómica.

a·tom·ic (ə-tŏm′ĭk) adj. atómico.

at·om·ize (āt′ə-mīz′) tr. atomizar.

at·om·iz·er (:mī′zər) s. atomizador *m.*

a·to·nal (ā-tō′nəl) adj. atonal.

a·tone (ə-tōn′) intr. dar reparación *(for por),* expiar.

a·tone·ment (:mənt) s. expiación *f*, reparación *f.*

a·top (ə-tŏp′) adv. & prep. encima (de).

a·tri·um (ā′trē-əm) s. [pl. **s** *o* **-ia**] atrio.

a·tro·cious (ə-trō′shəs) adj. atroz, abominable.

a·troc·i·ty (ə-trŏs′ĭ-tē) s. atrocidad *f.*

at·ro·phy (āt′rə-fē) I. s. atrofia II. tr. & intr. atrofiar(se).

at·tach (ə-tāch′) tr. *(to fasten)* ligar, sujetar; *(to bond)* unir, pegar; *(to ascribe)* dar, atribuir (importancia, significado); DER. incautarse de.

at·ta·ché (āt′ə-shā′) s. agregado ♦ **a. case** portafolio, maletín.

at·tached (ə-tācht′) adj. *(fastened)* adherido, adjunto ♦ **a. to** *(fond of)* encariñado con, apegado a.

at·tach·ment (ə-tāch′mənt) s. *(act)* unión *f*; *(extra part)* accesorio; *(affection)* afición *f*; MEC. acoplamiento; DER. incautación *f.*

at·tack (ə-tāk′) I. tr. atacar, agredir; FIG. acometer (tarea, problema) —intr. ir al ataque II. s. ataque *m*, agresión *f.*

at·tack·er (:ər) s. agresor *m*, asaltante *mf.*

at·tain (ə-tān′) tr. *(to accomplish)* lograr, conseguir; *(to arrive at)* llegar a, alcanzar.

at·tain·a·ble (ə-tā′nə-bəl) adj. lograble, alcanzable.

at·tain·der (ə-tān′dər) s. proscripción *f*, muerte civil *f.*

at·tain·ment (:mənt) s. logro, realización *f.*

at·tempt (ə-tĕmpt′) I. tr. intentar, tratar de II. s. *(try)* intento, prueba; *(attack)* atentado.

at·tend (ə-tĕnd′) tr. *(to go to)* atender, asistir a; *(to accompany)* acompañar; *(to wait upon)* asistir, servir; *(to take care of)* atender, cuidar ♦ **to a. to** prestar atención a.

at·ten·dance (ə-tĕn′dəns) s. asistencia, concurrencia.

at·ten·dant (:dənt) I. s. asistente *m*, mozo II. adj. concomitante, concurrente.

at·ten·tion (ə-těn′shən) s. atención *f*; *(attentiveness)* cuidado ♦ **a.!** MIL. ¡firmes! • **to pay a. (to)** prestar atención (a) ♦ **pl.** cortesías, atenciones.

at·ten·tive (:tĭv) adj. atento.

at·ten·u·ate (ə-těn′yŏŏ-āt′) tr. & intr. atenuar(se), disminuir(se).

at·test (ə-těst′) tr. atestiguar —intr. ♦ **to a. to** dar fe de.

at·tes·ta·tion (ăt′ĕ-stā′shən) s. atestación *f*.

at·tic (ăt′ĭk) s. desván *m*, guardilla.

at·tire (ə-tīr′) I. tr. ataviar, vestir II. s. atavío, vestido.

at·ti·tude (ăt′ĭ-tōōd′) s. actitud *f*.

at·tor·ney (ə-tûr′nē) s. abogado, apoderado ♦ **a. general** fiscal *o* procurador general.

at·tract (ə-trăkt′) tr. & intr. atraer.

at·trac·tion (ə-trăk′shən) s. atracción *f*; *(allure)* atractivo.

at·trac·tive (:tĭv) adj. atractivo, atrayente.

at·trib·ute (ə-trĭb′yŏŏt) I. tr. atribuir II. s. (ăt′rə-byōōt′) atributo.

at·tri·tion (ə-trĭsh′ən) s. reducción *f* (en el número del personal por retiro, renuncia, etc.).

at·tune (ə-tōōn′) tr. adaptar, armonizar.

a·typ·i·cal (ā-tĭp′ĭ-kəl) adj. anormal, irregular.

au·burn (ô′bərn) adj. castaño.

auc·tion (ôk′shən) I. s. subasta, remate *m* II. tr. subastar, rematar.

auc·tion·eer (ôk′shə-nîr′) s. subastador *m*.

au·da·cious (ô-dā′shəs) adj. *(bold)* audaz; *(insolent)* atrevido, descarado.

au·dac·i·ty (ô-dăs′ĭ-tē) s. *(boldness)* audacia; *(insolence)* atrevimiento, descaro.

au·di·ble (ô′də-bəl) adj. audible, oíble.

au·di·ence (ô′dē-əns) s. *(public)* auditorio, público; *(formal hearing)* audiencia.

au·di·o (ô′dē-ō′) I. adj. de frecuencia audible ♦ **a. frequency** audiofrecuencia.

au·di·o·vi·su·al (:vĭzh′ōō-əl) adj. audiovisual ♦ **a. aids** material audiovisual.

au·dit (ô′dĭt) I. s. intervención *f* (de cuentas) II. tr. intervenir.

au·di·tion (ô—dĭsh′ən) I. s. audición *f* II. tr. dar audición a —intr. actuar en una audición.

au·di·tive (ô′dĭ-tĭv) adj. auditivo.

au·di·tor (:tər) s. COM. auditor *m*, interventor *m*; EDUC. alumno libre.

au·di·to·ri·um (ô′dĭ-tôr′ē-əm) s. auditorio.

au·di·to·ry (ô′dĭ-tôr′ē) adj. auditorio, auditivo.

au·ger (ô′gər) s. barrena.

aught (ôt) s. cero.

aug·ment (ôg-měnt′) tr. & intr. aumentar(se).

aug·men·ta·tion (ôg′měn-tā′shən) s. aumento.

au·gur (ô′gər) I. s. adivino II. tr. & intr. augurar ♦ **to a. ill, well** ser de mal, bien agüero.

au·gu·ry (ô′gyə-rē) s. augurio.

au·gust (ô-gŭst′) adj. augusto.

Au·gust (ô′gəst) s. agosto.

aunt (ănt, änt) s. tía.

au·ra (ôr′ə) s. aura.

au·ral (ôr′əl) adj. auricular.

au·ri·cle (ôr′ĭ-kəl) s. aurícula.

au·ro·ra (ə-rôr′ə) s. aurora.

aus·pice (ô′spĭs) s. auspicio ♦ **under the auspices of** bajo los auspicios de.

aus·pi·cious (ô-spĭsh′əs) adj. propicio, favorable.

aus·tere (ô-stîr′) adj. austero.

aus·ter·i·ty (ô-stěr′ĭ-tē) s. austeridad *f*.

au·then·tic (ô-thěn′tĭk) adj. auténtico.

au·then·ti·cate (:tĭ-kāt′) tr. autenticar.

au·then·tic·i·ty (′-tĭs′ĭ-tē) s. autenticidad *f*.

au·thor (ô′thər) I. s. autor *m* II. tr. escribir.

au·thor·i·tar·i·an (ə-thôr′ĭ-târ′ē-ən) adj. & s. autoritario.

au·thor·i·tar·i·an·ism (:ə-nĭz′əm) s. autoritarismo.

au·thor·i·ta·tive (ə-thôr′ĭ-tā′tĭv) adj. *(official)* autorizado; *(imperious)* autoritario.

au·thor·i·ty (:ĭ-tē) s. autoridad *f* ♦ **on good a.** de buena tinta.

au·thor·i·za·tion (ô′thər-ĭ-zā′shən) s. autorización *f*, permiso.

au·thor·ize (ô′thə-rīz′) tr. autorizar.

au·thor·ized (:rīzd) adj. autorizado.

au·thor·ship (ô′thər-shĭp′) s. paternidad literaria.

au·tism (ô′tĭz′əm) s. autismo.

au·to (ô′tō) s. FAM. automóvil *m*, auto.

au·to·bi·o·graph·ic/i·cal (ô′tō-bī′ə-grăf′ĭk) adj. autobiográfico.

au·to·bi·og·ra·phy (′-ŏg′rə-fē) s. autobiografía.

au·toc·ra·cy (ô-tŏk′rə-sē) s. autocracia.

au·to·crat (ô′tə-krăt′) s. autócrata *mf*.

au·to·crat·ic (′-′ĭk) adj. autocrático.

au·to·di·dact (ô′tō-dī′dăkt) s. autodidacta.

au·to·graph (ô′tə-grăf′) I. s. autógrafo II. tr. autografiar.

au·to·im·mune (ô′tō-ĭ-myōōn′) adj. autoinmune.

au·to·load·ing (:lō′dĭng) adj. semiautomático.

au·to·mate (ô′tə-māt′) tr. automatizar.

au·to·mat·ic (′-măt′ĭk) I. adj. automático ♦ **a. rifle** fusil ametrallador II. s. arma automática.

au·to·ma·tion (′-mā′shən) s. automación *f*, automatización *f*.

au·tom·a·tize (ô-tŏm′ə-tīz′) tr. automatizar.

au·tom·a·ton (:tən) s. [pl. **s** o **-ta**] autómata *mf*.

au·to·mo·bile (ô′tə-mō-bēl′) s. automóvil *m*.

au·to·mo·tive (′-′tĭv) adj. automotor, automotriz; *(industry)* automovilístico.

au·ton·o·mous (ô-tŏn′ə-məs) adj. autónomo.

au·ton·o·my (:mē) s. autonomía.

au·top·sy (ô′tŏp′sē) s. autopsia.

au·tumn (ô′təm) s. otoño.

au·tum·nal (ô-tŭm′nəl) adj. otoñal, de otoño.

aux·il·ia·ry (ôg-zĭl′yə-rē) I. adj. auxiliar II. s. *(assistant)* auxiliar *mf*, asistente *mf*; *(group)* grupo auxiliar.

a·vail (ə-vāl′) I. tr. beneficiar ♦ **to a. oneself of** aprovecharse de, valerse de II. s. ♦ **of** *o* **to no a.** en vano.

a·vail·a·bil·i·ty (ə-vā′lə-bĭl′ĭ-tē) s. disponibilidad *f*.

a·vail·a·ble (-′-bəl) adj. *(obtainable)* obtenible; *(at hand)* disponible ♦ **to make a. to** poner a la disposición de.

av·a·lanche (ăv′ə-lănch′) s. avalancha.

a·vant-garde (ä′vänt-gärd′) adj. & s. (de) vanguardia.

av·a·rice (ăv′ər-ĭs) s. avaricia, codicia.

av·a·ri·cious (ăv′ə-rĭsh′əs) adj. avaricioso.

a·venge (ə-věnj′) tr. & intr. vengar(se).

a·veng·er (ə-věn′jər) s. vengador *m*.

av·e·nue (ăv′ə-nōō′) s. avenida; FIG. medios, camino.

a·ver (ə-vûr′) tr. **-rr-** afirmar, declarar.

av·er·age (ăv′ər-ĭj) I. s. promedio, término medio ♦ **on the a.** por término medio, como promedio II. adj. *(de término)* medio *<a. cost* costo medio*>*; *(ordinary)* regular III. tr. *(to compute)* calcular el promedio de; *(to obtain)* alcanzar un promedio de; *(to prorate)* prorratear.

a·verse (ə-vûrs') adj. opuesto, contrario ◆ **to be a. to** oponerse a.

a·ver·sion (ə-vûr'zhən) s. aversión f.

a·vert (ə-vûrt') tr. *(to turn away)* desviar, apartar (mirada); *(to prevent)* prevenir (peligro).

a·vi·ar·y (ā'vē-ĕr'ē) s. pajarera.

a·vi·a·tion (ā'vē-ā'shən) s. aviación f.

a·vi·a·tor ('-' tər) s. aviador m.

av·id (ăv'ĭd) adj. ávido; *(ardent)* entusiasta.

a·vid·i·ty (ə-vĭd'ĭ-tē) s. avidez f.

av·o·ca·do (ăv'ə-kä'dō) s. aguacate m, palta.

av·o·ca·tion (ăv'ō-kā'shən) s. pasatiempo.

a·void (ə-void') tr. evitar.

a·void·a·ble (ə-voi'də-bəl) adj. evitable.

a·void·ance (ə-void'ns) s. evitación f.

a·vow (ə-vou') tr. reconocer, confesar.

a·vowed (ə-voud') adj. reconocido, declarado.

a·vun·cu·lar (ə-vŭng'kyə-lər) adj. avuncular.

a·wait (ə-wāt') tr. & intr. esperar, aguardar.

a·wake (ə-wāk') I. tr. & intr. awoke, -d despertar(se) II. adj. despierto.

a·wak·en (ə-wā'kən) tr. & intr. despertar(se).

a·wak·en·ing (:kə-nĭng) s. despertar m.

a·ward (ə-wôrd') I. tr. *(to bestow)* premiar; *(legally)* adjudicar II. s. *(prize)* premio, recompensa; *(decision)* decisión f, fallo.

a·ware (ə-wâr') adj. consciente, percatado ◆ **to be a. of** o **that** tener conciencia de o que ◆ **to become a. of** enterarse de.

a·ware·ness (:nĭs) s. conciencia, conocimiento.

a·wash (ə-wŏsh') adj. & adv. inundado.

a·way (ə-wā') I. adv. lejos de, a *<a house two miles a. from here* una casa a dos millas de aquí>; *(continuously)* sin parar *<to fire a. disparar sin parar>*; *(aside)* en el sentido opuesto ◆ **far a.** lejos ◆ **right a.** inmediatamente II. adj. *(absent)* ausente, fuera *<she's a from home* está fuera de la casa>; *(at a distance)* distante, lejano.

awe (ô) I. s. temor m o admiración f reverente ◆ **to stand in a. of** temer a, admirar a II. tr. infundir temor o admiración reverente.

a·weigh (ə-wā') adj. pendiente (ancla) ◆ **anchors a.!** ¡levanten anclas!

awe·some (ô'səm) adj. pasmoso, asombroso.

awe·struck/strick·en (ô'strŭk'/strĭk'ən) adj. pasmado, asombrado.

aw·ful (ô'fəl) adj. *(terrible)* pavoroso; *(atrocious)* atroz, horrible; *(great)* enorme, tremendo.

aw·ful·ly (ô'fə-lē) adv. *(atrociously)* horriblemente, muy mal; *(very)* muchísimo, muy.

a·while (ə-hwīl') adv. un rato, algún tiempo.

awk·ward (ôk'wərd) adj. *(clumsy)* torpe, desmañado; *(embarrassing)* embarazoso; *(situation)* delicado, difícil; *(shape)* inconveniente, difícil de manejar.

awk·ward·ness (:nĭs) s. *(clumsiness)* torpeza; *(embarrassment)* desconcierto.

awl (ôl) s. lezna, punzón m.

awn·ing (ô'nĭng) s. toldo.

a·woke (ə-wōk') cf. **awake.**

a·wry (ə-rī') adv. de soslayo ◆ **to go a.** salir mal.

ax(e) (ăks) I. s. hacha ◆ **to get the a.** JER. ser despedido ◆ **to have an a. to grind** FAM. tener intereses personales II. tr. cortar (con hacha).

ax·i·om (ăk'sē-əm) s. axioma.

ax·i·o·mat·ic/i·cal ('-ə-măt'ĭk) adj. axiomático.

ax·is (ăk'sĭs) s. [pl. **axes**] eje m.

ax·le (ăk'səl) s. eje m, árbol m.

a·ya·tol·lah (ī'ə-tō'lə) s. RELIG. líder religioso islámico de la secta chiita.

ay(e) (ī) I. s. [pl. **es**] voto a favor ◆ **the ayes** los que votan a favor II. adv. sí.

az·ure (ăzh'ər) adj. & s. azul m celeste.

B

b, B (bē) s. segunda letra del alfabeto inglés; MÚS. si m.

baa (bă, bä) I. intr. balar II. s. balido.

bab·ble (băb'əl) I. intr. *(to prattle)* barbotar; *(to chatter)* parlotear; *(a brook)* murmurar, susurrar II. s. *(prattle)* barboteo; *(chatter)* parloteo; *(murmur)* murmullo.

babe (bāb) s. bebé m; JER. *(girl)* bebé, monada.

ba·boon (bă-bōōn') s. babuino.

ba·by (bā'bē) I. s. *(infant)* bebé m, nene m; *(childish person)* niño; JER. *(girl)* bebé, monada ◆ **b. brother, sister** hermanito, hermanita ◆ **b. carriage** cochecito de niños ◆ **b. talk** balbuceo II. tr. mimar, consentir.

ba·by·hood (:hŏod') s. *(primera)* infancia, niñez f.

ba·by·ish (:ĭsh) adj. infantil, de niño.

ba·by·sit (:sĭt') intr. -**sat**, -**tting** cuidar niños.

bac·cha·nal (băk'ə-năl') s. bacanal f.

bach·e·lor (băch'ə-lər) s. soltero; EDUC. *(degree)* bachillerato; *(graduate)* bachiller m.

bach·e·lor·hood (:hŏod') s. soltería.

bach·e·lor's-but·ton (băch'ə-lərz-bŭt'n) s. aciano.

ba·cil·lus (bə-sĭl'əs) s. [pl. -**li**] bacilo.

back (băk) I. s. *(person)* espalda; *(animal)* lomo, espinazo; *(reverse side)* envés m, revés m; *(coin, check)* dorso, reverso; *(chair)* respaldo; *(room, house)* fondo; DEP. defensa, zaga ◆ **b. to b.** uno detrás del otro ◆ **behind someone's b.** a espaldas de alguien ◆ **on one's b.** postrado, en cama ◆ **with one's b. to the wall** entre la espada y la pared II. adv. atrás, hacia atrás ◆ **as far b. as** ya en ◆ **b. and forth** de acá para allá ◆ **in b. of** detrás de, tras de ◆ **to be b.** estar de vuelta ◆ **to go** o **come b.** volver, regresar ◆ **to go b. on one's word** desdecirse, faltar a una promesa ◆ **years b.** años atrás, hace años III. adj. *(in the rear)* de atrás, posterior; *(remote)* lejano; *(overdue)* atrasado ◆ **b. door, stairs** puerta, escalera de servicio ◆ **b. talk** impertinencia(s) ◆ **b. yard** traspatio ◆ **to take a b. seat** pasar al segundo plano IV. tr. mover hacia atrás; *(vehicle)* dar marcha atrás a; *(to support)* respaldar, apoyar ◆ **to b. up** *(vehicle)* dar marcha atrás; *(drain)* atascar(se); *(to support)* respaldar; *(to justify)* justificar con pruebas; *(to guarantee)* respaldar (fondos) —intr. moverse hacia atrás, retroceder ◆ **to b. away** alejarse retrocediendo ◆ **to b. down** ceder, echarse atrás ◆ **to b. out** retractarse, volverse atrás ◆ **to b. up** o **off** retroceder.

back·ache (băk'āk') s. dolor m de espalda.

back·bit·ing (:bī'tĭng) s. calumnia, murmuración f.

back·bone (:bōn') s. *(spine)* espinazo, columna vertebral; FIG. carácter m, firmeza.

back·break·ing (:brā'kĭng) adj. agobiador.

back·date (:dāt') tr. antedatar.

back·drop (:drŏp') s. telón m de fondo.

back·er (:ər) s. patrocinador *m*, promotor *m*.
back·fire (:fīr′) I. s. petardeo II. intr. AUTO. petardear; *(scheme)* salir al revés.
back·gam·mon (:găm′ən) s. chaquete *m*.
back·ground (:ground′) s. fondo, trasfondo; *(of events)* antecedentes *m*; *(experience)* experiencia.
back·hand (:hănd′) adv. & s. (de) revés *m*.
back·hand·ed (:hăn′dĭd) adj. ambiguo.
back·ing (:ĭng) s. respaldo (moral, económico).
back·lash (:lăsh′) s. *(motion)* contragolpe *m*, sacudida; *(reaction)* reacción *f*.
back·log (:lôg′) s. acumulación *f* (de trabajo, pedidos).
back·pack (:păk′) s. mochila.
back·rest (:rĕst′) s. respaldo (de un asiento).
back·side (:sīd′) s. FAM. trasero, nalgas.
back·slide (:slīd′) intr. **-slid, slid(den)** reincidir (en el pecado, delito).
back·space (:spās′) intr. hacer retroceder (el carro de una máquina de escribir).
back·stage (:lăsh′) adv. entre bastidores.
back·stair(s) (:stăr[z]′) adj. furtivo.
back·stitch (:stĭch′) I. s. pespunte *m* II. tr. pespuntear.
back·stop (:stŏp′) s. red o valla para retener la pelota.
back·stretch (:strĕch′) s. pista opuesta a la recta final.
back·stroke (:strōk′) s. *(backhand)* revés *m*; *(in swimming)* brazada de espalda.
back·track (:trăk′) intr. desandar.
back·up (:ŭp′) I. s. *(reserve)* reserva; *(substitute)* suplente *mf*; *(support)* respaldo; *(clog)* atascamiento; MÚS. acompañamiento II. adj. suplente, de reserva.
back·ward (:wərd) I. adv. *o* **-wards** hacia *o* para atrás <to look b. mirar para atrás>; de espaldas <to fall b. caerse de espaldas>; al revés, al contrario <they do everything b. lo hacen todo al revés> ♦ **to know backwards and forwards** saberse al dedillo II. adj. hacia atrás <a b. look una mirada hacia atrás>; *(motion)* de retroceso; *(reverse)* al revés, inverso; *(unprogressive)* atrasado (país, época).
back·ward·ness (:wərd-nĭs) s. atraso, retraso.
back·wa·ter (:wô′tər) s. *(water)* agua estancada; *(place)* lugar atrasado.
back·woods (:wo͝odz′) s.pl. monte *m*, selva.
ba·con (bā′kən) s. tocino ♦ **to bring home the b.** FAM. ganar el pan.
bac·te·ri·a (băk-tîr′ē-ə) cf. **bacterium**.
bac·te·rial (:ē-əl) adj. bacteriano.
bac·te·ri·cide (:ĭ-sīd′) s. bactericida *m*.
bac·te·ri·um (:ē-əm) s. [pl. **-ria**] bacteria.
bad (băd) **worse, worst** I. adj. malo; *(shoddy)* inferior; *(defective)* defectuoso; *(check)* sin fondos; *(naughty)* desobediente; *(harmful)* perjudicial; *(severe)* fuerte <a b. cold un catarro fuerte>; *(rotten)* podrido ♦ **from b. to worse** de mal en peor • **not b.** FAM. no está mal • **to feel b.** *(ill)* sentirse mal; *(sad)* estar triste • **to feel b. about** sentir, lamentar • **to go b.** echarse a perder • **too b.!** ¡qué lástima!, ¡mala suerte! II. s. lo malo III. adv. FAM. mucho <it hurts b. me duele mucho> ♦ **to be b. off** FAM. estar mal.
bade (băd, bād) cf. **bid.**
badge (băj) s. distintivo, insignia.
badg·er (băj′ər) I. s. tejón *m* II. tr. importunar, molestar.
bad·lands (băd′lăndz′) s.pl. pedregal *m*.
bad·ly (:lē) adv. mal; *(very much)* mucho, con

urgencia; *(seriously)* gravemente, de gravedad ♦ **to take something b.** tomar a mal algo.
bad·min·ton (băd′mĭn′tən) s. volante *m*.
bad-mouth (băd′mouth′) tr. JER. hablar pestes de, poner por los suelos.
bad-tem·pered (:tĕm′pərd) adj. *(character)* de mal genio; *(mood)* malhumorado.
baf·fle (băf′əl) I. tr. *(to bewilder)* confundir, desconcertar; *(to foil)* eludir II. s. deflector *m*.
baf·fle·ment (:mənt) s. confusión *f*.
baf·fling (băf′lĭng) adj. desconcertante.
bag (băg) I. s. bolsa, saco; *(purse)* bolso, cartera; *(suitcase)* valija, maletín *m*; DEP. caza *f* ♦ **b. and baggage** totalmente • **in the b.** JER. en el bolsillo, seguro ♦ pl. equipaje II. tr. **-gg-** meter en una bolsa; *(to hunt)* cazar; FAM. *(to capture)* coger, pescar —intr. formar bolsas, abultarse
bag·gage (:ĭj) s. equipaje *m*, maletas; MIL. bagaje *m*.
bag·gy (:ē) adj. **-i-** bombacho.
bag·man (:mən) s. [pl. **-men**] JER. recaudador *m* (de dinero mal habido).
bag·pipe (:pīp′) s. gaita.
bail¹ (bāl) I. s. fianza, caución *f* ♦ **out on b.** en libertad bajo fianza • **to go b. for** dar fianza por II. tr. dar fianza *o* caución por ♦ **to b. out** sacar de apuros.
bail² tr. & intr. MARÍT. achicar (agua) ♦ **to b. out** saltar (en paracaídas).
bail·ee (bā-lē′) s. DER. depositario.
bail·iff (bā′lĭf) s. alguacil *m*.
bail·i·wick (bā′lə-wĭk′) s. alguacilazgo.
bail·or (bā′lər) s. fiador *m*, fianza.
bail·out (bāl′out′) s. rescate financiero.
bails·man (bālz′mən) s. [pl. **-men**] fiador *m*, fianza.
bait (bāt) I. s. cebo, carnada ♦ **to take the b.** tragarse el anzuelo II. tr. poner el cebo en (anzuelo, trampa); *(to torment)* atormentar.
baize (bāz) s. bayeta.
bake (bāk) I. tr. cocer al horno —intr. cocerse II. s. cocción *f* (al horno).
bak·er (bā′kər) s. panadero.
bak·er·y (bā′kə-rē) s. panadería.
bak·ing (bā′kĭng) s. cocción *f* ♦ **b. powder** levadura en polvo • **b. soda** bicarbonato de sodio.
bal·ance (băl′əns) I. s. *(scale)* balanza; *(equilibrium)* equilibrio; TEN. *(equality)* balance *m*; *(difference)* saldo; FAM. *(remainder)* resto; *(sanity)* juicio ♦ **b. due** saldo deudor • **b. sheet** balance • **b. wheel** volante compensador • **off b.** *(unstable)* en desequilibrio; *(off guard)* desprevenido • **to be in the b.** estar en la balanza • **to strike a b.** encontrar el término medio • **to throw off b.** desconcertar II. tr. *(to bring into equilibrium)* balancear, equilibrar; *(to counterbalance)* compensar, contrarrestar; TEN. equilibrar ♦ **to b. the books** pasar balance —intr. equilibrarse; *(to sway)* balancearse; TEN. cuadrar.
bal·anced (:ənst) adj. balanceado, equilibrado.
bal·co·ny (băl′kə-nē) s. balcón *m*; TEAT. galería, paraíso.
bald (bôld) adj. calvo; *(blunt)* categórico, sin rodeos ♦ **to go b.** quedarse calvo.
bald-faced (:fāst′) adj. descarado.
bald·ness (:nĭs) s. calvicie *f*.
bale (bāl) I. s. bala, fardo II. tr. embalar, enfardar.
ba·leen (bə-lēn′) s. barba de ballena.

bale·ful (bāl'fəl) adj. maléfico, funesto.

balk (bôk) I. intr. *(to stop)* plantarse; *(to refuse)* oponerse *(at* a) —tr. impedir, frustar II. s. obstáculo, impedimento.

balk·y (bô'kē) adj. -i- reacio.

ball¹ (bôl) I. s. bola; DEP. pelota, balón m; *(cannonball)* bala de cañón ♦ **b. bearing** cojinete de bolas • **to be on the b.** JER. estar atento • **to play b.** FAM. cooperar II. tr. ♦ **to b. (something) up** enredar, embrollar (algo).

ball² s. baile m de etiqueta ♦ **to have a b.** JER. divertirse mucho, pasarla muy bien.

bal·lad (bāl'əd) s. balada.

ball-and-sock·et joint (bôl'ən-sŏk'ĭt) s. articulación f de rótula.

bal·last (bāl'əst) s. *(weight)* lastre m; *(gravel)* balasto.

bal·le·ri·na (bāl'ə-rē'nə) s. bailarina (de ballet).

bal·let (bă-lā') s. ballet m.

bal·lis·tic (bə-lĭs'tĭk) adj. balístico ♦ **ballistics** s.sg. balística.

bal·loon (bə-lōōn') I. s. globo II. intr. *(to swell)* hincharse, inflarse; *(to increase)* aumentar rápidamente.

bal·lot (bāl'ət) I. s. *(paper)* papeleta (electoral); *(voting)* votación f; *(electoral ticket)* candidaturas ♦ **b. box** urna electoral II. intr. votar.

ball·park o **ball park** (bôl'pärk') s. estadio ♦ **in the b. FAM.** aproximado.

ball-point pen (:point') s. bolígrafo.

ball·room (:rōōm') s. salón m de baile.

bal·ly·hoo (bāl'ē-hōō') s. FAM. bombo, propaganda exagerada.

balm (bäm) s. bálsamo.

balm·y (bä'mē) adj. -i- *(weather)* agradable, suave; JER. *(silly)* chiflado, tocado.

ba·lo·ney (bə-lō'nē) s. FAM. *(bologna)* salchicha de Bolonia; *(nonsense)* disparates m.

bal·sa (bôl'sə) s. balsa.

bal·sam (bôl'səm) s. *(ointment)* bálsamo; *(tree)* abeto balsámico.

bal·us·ter (bāl'ə-stər) s. balaustre m.

bal·us·trade (:strād') s. balaustrada.

bam·boo (băm-bōō') s. *(tree)* bambú m; *(stem)* caña (de bambú).

bam·boo·zle (băm-bōō'zəl) tr. FAM. embaucar.

ban (băn) I. tr. **-nn-** prohibir, proscribir II. s. prohibición f, proscripción f.

ba·nal (bə-nāl' băn'əl) adj. banal, trivial.

ba·nan·a (bə-nān'ə) s. plátano, banana ♦ **b. tree** plátano, banano ♦ pl. JER. chiflado.

band¹ (bănd) I. s. banda, faja; *(of paper)* tira; *(stripe)* franja, lista; JOY. anillo *(de boda)*; *(on hat, dress)* cinta II. tr. fajar, atar.

band² s. banda; *(gang)* cuadrilla; MÚS. *(military)* banda; *(jazz)* orquesta; *(rock)* conjunto II. tr. & intr. ♦ **to b. together** agrupar(se), juntar(se).

band·age (băn'dĭj) I. s. venda II. tr. vendar.

ban·dan·(n)a (băn-dăn'ə) s. pañuelo grande.

ban·dit (băn'dĭt) s. bandido, bandolero.

ban·do·leer/lier (băn'də-lîr') s. bandolera.

band·stand (bănd'stănd') s. quiosco de orquesta.

band·wag·on (:wăg'ən) s. ♦ **to get o jump on the b.** FAM. arrimarse al que lleva la batuta.

ban·dy (băn'dē) tr. *(to toss)* pasarse, tirar (de un lado a otro); *(words)* intercambiar.

ban·dy-leg·ged (:lĕg'ĭd) adj. patizambo.

bane (bān) s. ♦ **to be the b. of someone's existence** hacerle la vida imposible a alguien.

bane·ful (:fəl) adj. pernicioso, nocivo.

bang (băng) I. s. *(explosion)* estallido; *(loud slam)* golpe m, golpetazo; JER. *(thrill)* emoción f, excitación f II. tr. *(to bump, pound)* golpear; *(to slam)* cerrar de un golpetazo ♦ **to b. up** estropear —intr. *(to explode)* detonar; *(to make a loud noise)* dar un golpetazo; *(to crash)* chocar *(into* con) III. adv. exactamente IV. interj. *(shot)* ¡pum!; *(blow)* ¡zas!

bangs (băngz) s.pl. cerquillo, flequillo.

ban·gle (băng'gəl) s. esclava, ajorca.

bang-up (băng'ŭp') adj. JER. excelente.

ban·ish (băn'ĭsh) tr. *(to exile)* exiliar, desterrar; *(to cast out)* echar fuera, ahuyentar.

ban·ish·ment (:mənt) s. *(exile)* exilio, destierro; *(ban)* proscripción f.

ban·is·ter (băn'ĭ-stər) s. barandilla, baranda.

ban·jo (băn'jō) s. [pl. **(e)s**] banjo.

bank¹ (băngk) I. s. *(of a river)* ribera, orilla; *(hillside)* loma; *(of snow)* montón m; AVIA. inclinación f lateral ♦ pl. MARÍT. bajío, banco (de arena) II. tr. *(a fire)* cubrir; *(to bank, a road)* peraltar; AVIA. inclinar —intr. AVIA. inclinarse.

bank² s. COM. banco; *(in gambling)* banca ♦ **b. account** cuenta bancaria • **b. note** billete de banco II. tr. depositar en un banco —intr. COM. tener cuenta ♦ **to b. on** contar con, confiar en.

bank³ s. *(row)* hilera, fila.

bank·book (:bŏŏk') s. libreta de banco.

bank·er (băng'kər) s. banquero.

bank·ing (:kĭng) s. *(occupation)* banca; *(bank business)* operaciones bancarias.

bank·roll (băngk'rōl') FAM. I. s. dinero en el banco, fondos II. tr. costear, financiar.

bank·rupt (:rəpt) I. adj. COM. insolvente; *(ruined)* arruinado; *(lacking)* falto, carente ♦ **to go b.** declararse en quiebra, quebrar II. tr. hacer quebrar, arruinar.

bank·rupt·cy (:sē) s. quiebra, bancarrota.

ban·ner (băn'ər) I. s. bandera, estandarte m; PERIOD. titular m a toda plana II. adj. sobresaliente.

banns (bănz) s.pl. amonestaciones f.

ban·quet (băng'kwĭt) I. s. banquete m II. tr. & intr. banquetear.

ban·ter (băn'tər) I. s. broma, burla II. intr. burlar, bromear.

bap·tism (băp'tĭz'əm) s. bautismo.

bap·tist (:tĭst) s. bautista m/f.

bap·tis·ter·y/try (:tĭ-strē) s. baptisterio.

bap·tize (tīz') tr. bautizar.

bar (bär) I. s. barra; *(of gold)* lingote m; *(lever)* palanca; *(of a prison)* barrote m; *(of soap)* pastilla; *(of chocolate)* tableta; *(obstacle)* obstáculo; *(tavern)* bar m; *(counter)* mostrador m; MARÍT. banco (de arena, grava); DER. *(tribunal)* tribunal m; *(legal profession)* abogacía; MÚS. compás m ♦ **behind bars** entre rejas II. tr. **-rr-** *(to fasten)* cerrar con barras; *(to obstruct)* obstruir; *(to exclude)* excluir; *(to prohibit)* prohibir III. prep. ♦ **b. none** sin excepción.

barb (bärb) s. púa; *(cutting remark)* observación f mordaz.

bar·bar·i·an (bär-bâr'ē-ən) s. & adj. bárbaro.

bar·bar·ic (:băr'ĭk) adj. bárbaro.

bar·ba·rism (:bə-rĭz'əm) s. barbarie f.

bar·bar·i·ty ('băr'ĭ-tē) s. barbaridad f.

bar·ba·rous (:bər-əs) adj. bárbaro.

bar·be·cue (bär'bĭ-kyōō') I. s. barbacoa, parrillada II. tr. asar a la parrilla.

barbed (bärbd) adj. con púas; *(cutting)* mordaz ♦ **b. wire** alambre de púas.

bar·bell (bär'běl') s. barra con pesas, haltera.

bar·ber (bär'bər) I. s. barbero, peluquero II. tr. *(to shave)* afeitar; *(to cut hair)* cortar el pelo.

bar·ber·shop (:shŏp') s. barbería, peluquería.

bar·bi·tu·rate (bär-bĭch'ər-ĭt) s. barbitúrico.

bard (bärd) s. poeta *m*, bardo.

bare (bâr) I. adj. desnudo; *(head)* descubierto; *(feet)* descalzo; *(undisguised)* descubierto, a la vista; *(empty)* desprovisto, vacío; *(plain)* puro, sencillo; *(mere)* mínimo ♦ **to lay b.** revelar, poner al descubierto II. tr. desnudar; *(to reveal)* revelar, descubrir.

bare·back ('băk') adv. & adj. a *o* en pelo.

bare·faced (:fāst') adj. descarado.

bare·foot·ed (:fŏot'ĭd) adv. & adj. descalzo.

bare·hand·ed (:hăn'dĭd) adj. & adv. sin guantes; *(without tools)* sólo con las manos; *(unarmed)* desarmado.

bare·head·ed (:hĕd'ĭd) adj. & adv. con la cabeza descubierta.

bare·ly (bâr'lē) adv. apenas.

bar·gain (bär'gən) I. s. *(deal)* pacto, convenio; *(good buy)* ganga ♦ **into the b.** por añadidura ♦ **to strike a b.** llegar a un acuerdo II. intr. *(to negotiate)* negociar, pactar; *(to haggle)* regatear ♦ **to b. for** *o* **on** esperar —tr. trocar, cambiar.

bar·gain·ing (:gə-nĭng) s. *(haggling)* regateo; *(negotiation)* negociación *f*.

barge (bärj) I. s. barcaza, gabarra II. intr. ♦ **to b. in** entremeterse ♦ **to b. into** irrumpir en.

bar·i·tone (băr'ĭ-tōn') s. barítono.

bar·i·um (bâr'ē-əm) s. bario.

bark¹ (bärk) I. s. ladrido ♦ **his b. is worse than his bite** perro que ladra no muerde II. tr. & intr. ladrar ♦ **to b. up the wrong tree** equivocarse.

bark² s. BOT. corteza.

bar·keep·(er) (bär'kēp'[ər]) s. barman *m*.

bar·ley (bär'lē) s. cebada.

bar·maid (bär'mād') s. camarera, cantinera.

barn (bärn) s. *(for grain)* granero; *(for livestock)* establo.

bar·na·cle (bär'nə-kəl) s. percebe *m*.

barn·yard (bärn'yärd') adj. & s. (de) corral *m*.

ba·rom·e·ter (bə-rŏm'ĭ-tər) s. barómetro.

bar·o·met·ric/ri·cal (băr'ə-mĕt'rĭk) adj. barométrico.

bar·on (băr'ən) s. barón *m*.

bar·on·ess (:ə-nĭs) s. baronesa.

ba·roque (bə-rōk') adj. & s. barroco.

bar·racks (băr'əks) s.pl. cuartel *m*, barraca.

bar·rage (bə-räzh') s. MIL. bombardeo, cortina de fuego; FIG. *(burst)* avalancha.

bar·rel (băr'əl) I. s. barril *m*, tonel *m*; *(of a gun)* cañón *m*; MAQ. cubilo, tambor *m* ♦ **to be a b. of fun** ser divertidísimo ♦ **to be over a b.** estar con el agua al cuello II. tr. entonelar, embarrilar —intr. JER. ir a gran velocidad.

bar·ren (băr'ən) I. adj. *(sterile)* estéril, infecundo; *(land)* yermo; *(unproductive)* infructuoso, vano II. s. ♦ **pl.** tierra yerma, páramo.

bar·rette (bə-rĕt') s. pasador *m*.

bar·ri·cade (băr'ĭ-kād') I. s. barricada, barrera II. tr. levantar barricadas.

bar·ri·er (băr'ē-ər) s. barrera, valla.

bar·ring (bär'ĭng) prep. salvo, excepto.

bar·ris·ter (băr'ĭ-stər) s. G.B. abogado.

bar·room (bär'rōom') s. bar *m*.

bar·row (băr'ō) s. carretilla.

bar·tend·er (bär'těn'dər) s. camarero, barman *m*.

bar·ter (bär'tər) I. intr. & tr. trocar, cambiar II. s. trueque *m*, cambio.

bas·al (bā'səl) adj. fundamental, básico.

ba·salt (bə-sôlt') s. basalto.

base¹ (bās) I. s. base *f*; ARQ. basa ♦ **to be off b.** estar equivocado II. adj. de la base III. tr. ♦ **to b. (up)on** basar en *o* sobre.

base² adj. *(vile)* ruin; *(lowly)* bajo; *(metal)* inferior, de baja ley.

base·ball ('bôl') s. béisbol *m*; *(ball)* pelota.

base·board (:bôrd') s. zócalo.

base·born (:bôrn') adj. *(of birth)* de humilde cuna; *(contemptible)* bajo, despreciable.

base·less (:lĭs) adj. infundado.

base·ment (:mənt) s. sótano.

bas·es (bā'sēz') cf. **basis.**

bash (băsh) FAM. I. tr. golpear II. s. *(blow)* golpazo, porrazo; *(party)* fiesta, parranda.

bash·ful (băsh'fəl) adj. tímido, encogido.

ba·sic (bā'sĭk) I. adj. básico II. s. base *f*.

ba·sic·i·ty (bā-sĭs'ĭ-tē) s. basicidad *f*.

bas·il (băz'əl, bā'zəl) s. albahaca.

ba·sil·i·ca (bə-sĭl'ĭ-kə) s. basílica.

ba·sin (bā'sĭn) s. palangana, jofaina; *(washbowl)* pila, pileta; GEOG. cuenca.

ba·sis (bā'sĭs) s. [pl. **-ses**] base *f*, fundamento ♦ **on the b. of** en base a.

bask (băsk) intr. gozar, complacerse.

bas·ket (băs'kĭt) s. cesta, canasta.

bas·ket·ball (:bôl') s. baloncesto; *(ball)* pelota.

bas·ket·ry (băs'kĭ-trē) s. cestería.

bas·ket·weave (:kĭt-wēv') s. tejido esterilla.

bas·re·lief (bā'rĭ-lēf') s. bajo relieve.

bass¹ (băs) s. [pl. inv. *o* **es**] ICT. róbalo.

bass² (bās) s. *(voice)* bajo; *(instrument)* contrabajo ♦ **b. clef** clave de fa ♦ **b. drum** bombo.

bas·si·net (băs'ə-nĕt') s. cuna.

bas·soon (bə-sōōn') s. fagot *m*, bajón *m*.

bas·tard (băs'tərd) I. s. bastardo; JER. *(scoundrel)* canalla II. adj. ilegítimo; *(spurious)* espurio.

baste (bāst) tr. *(to sew)* hilvanar; CUL. lardear.

bas·tion (băs'chən) s. baluarte *m*.

bat (băt) I. s. DEP. bate *m*; ZOOL. murciélago ♦ **right off the b.** FAM. inmediatamente ♦ **to go to b. for** FAM. sacar la cara por II. tr. -tt- golpear; DEP. batear ♦ **not to b. an eye** no pestañear ♦ **to b. around** FAM. discutir mucho.

batch (băch) s. CUL. hornada; *(lot)* partida, lote *m*; *(group)* grupo, tanda.

bate (bāt) tr. moderar, disminuir.

bat·ed (bā'tĭd) adj. ♦ **with b. breath** con aliento entrecortado *o* pasmado.

bath (băth) s. baño; *(bathroom)* cuarto de baño ♦ **pl. casa de baños.**

bathe (bāth) intr. bañarse —tr. *(to wet)* bañar; *(to wash)* lavar; *(to flood)* inundar.

bath·ing suit (bā'thĭng) s. traje *m* de baño.

bath·robe (băth'rōb') s. bata, albornoz *m*.

bath·room (:rōōm') s. cuarto de baño.

bath·tub (:tŭb') s. bañera.

ba·tiste (bə-tēst') s. batista.

ba·ton (bə-tŏn') s. batuta.

bat·tal·ion (bə-tăl'yən) s. batallón *m*.

bat·ter¹ (băt'ər) tr. *(to beat)* golpear, apalear; *(to damage)* deteriorar, estropear.

bat·ter² s. CUL. pasta; DEP. bateador *m*.

bat·ter·ing-ram (:ĭng-răm') s. ariete *m*.

bat·ter·y (băt'ə-rē) s. ELEC., MIL. batería; *(dry cell)* pila; *(storage)* acumulador *m*; DER. asalto.

bat·tle (băt'l) **I.** s. MIL. batalla, combate *m*; FIG. lucha **II.** intr. & tr. combatir, luchar.
bat·tle-ax(e) (:ăks') s. hacha (de combate).
bat·tle·field (:fēld') s. campo de batalla.
bat·tle·ground (:ground') s. campo de batalla.
bat·tle·ship (:shĭp') s. acorazado.
bat·ty (băt'ē) adj. -i- JER. chiflado.
bau·ble (hô'bǝl) s. chuchería, baratija.
baud (bôd) s. baudio.
baux·ite (bôk'sīt') s. bauxita.
bawd (bôd) s. ramera.
bawd·y (bô'dē) adj. -i- obsceno.
bawd·y·house (:hous') s. burdel *m*.
bawl (bôl) intr. *(to cry)* llorar; *(to shout)* gritar —tr. gritar, vociferar ♦ **to b. out** regañar.
bay¹ (bā) s. GEOG. bahía.
bay² s. ARQ. compartmiento ♦ **b. window** ventana saledíza.
bay³ adj. & s. *(horse, color)* hayo.
bay⁴ **I.** s. aullido ♦ **to keep at b.** mantener a raya **II.** intr. & tr. ladrar (a), aullar (a).
bay⁵ s. BOT. laurel *m*.
bay·o·net (bā'ǝ-nĕt') s. bayoneta.
ba·za(a)r (bǝ-zär') s. bazar *m*.
ba·zoo·ka (bǝ-zōō'kǝ) s. bazuca *m*.
be (bē) intr. **I.** *(inherent quality, time, possession, passive voice)* ser *<ice is cold* el hielo es frío> *<what time is it?* ¿qué hora es?> *<is it yours?* ¿es tuyo?> *<it was done yesterday* fue hecho ayer> *<it is possible* es posible> **II.** *(location, impermanence)* estar *<where are you?* ¿dónde estás?> *<my coffee is cold* mi café está frío> **III.** *(age, physical sensation)* tener; *(weather)* hacer, hacer; *(reaction)* quedarse *<she was speechless* se quedó sin palabras> ♦ **as it were** por así decirlo ♦ **be that as it may** sea como fuere ♦ **so be it** así sea ♦ **there is** *o* **are** hay ♦ **to be to** tener que, deber *<you are to leave tonight* tienes que *o* debes partir esta noche>.
beach (bēch) **I.** s. playa **II.** tr. varar.
beach·head (:hed') s. cabeza de playa.
bea·con (bē'kǝn) s. *(lighthouse)* faro; *(signal fire)* almenara; AVIA. *(light)* baliza; *(radio)* radiofaro; *(signal)* faro, guía *m*.
bead (bēd) **I.** s. *(ornament)* cuenta, abalorio; *(drop)* gota ♦ **to draw a b. on** apuntar a ♦ pl. JOY. collar; RELIG. rosario **II.** intr. formarse en gotas.
bead·y (bē'dē) adj. -i- ♦ **b. eyes** ojos pequeños y brillantes.
beak (bēk) s. pico.
beak·er (bē'kǝr) s. vaso de precipitación.
beam (bēm) **I.** s. *(of light)* haz *m*, rayo; ARQ. viga; MARÍT. manga; RAD. onda dirigida ♦ **to be on the b.** FAM. estar sobre la pista **II.** tr. emitir, dirigir —intr. *(to shine)* destellar, irradiar; *(to smile)* sonreír radiantemente.
bean (bēn) s. habichuela, judía, frijol *m*; *(seed)* haba; *(of coffee)* grano; JER. *(head)* coco ♦ **to spill the beans** FAM. descubrir el pastel **II.** tr. JER. pegar en el coco.
bean·bag ('băg') s. bolsita con frijoles secos usado por los niños para jugar.
bean·pole (:pōl') s. JER. persona larguirucha.
bean·stalk (:stôk') s. tallo de la planta de frijoles.
bear¹ (bâr) tr. **bore, born(e)** *(to support)* sostener; *(to carry, display)* llevar; *(a grudge)* guardar; *(oneself)* conducirse; *(to take on)* hacerse cargo de; *(to endure)* aguantar; *(to give birth to)* dar a luz; *(to yield)* producir, dar ♦ **to b. in mind** tener en cuenta ♦ **to b. mention** merecer

mencionarse ♦ **to b. off** llevarse ♦ **to b. out** corroborar ♦ **to b. with** tener paciencia con —intr. *(to produce)* producir, rendir; *(to pressure)* pesar; *(to go)* mantenerse sobre *<b. right* manténgase sobre la derecha> ♦ **to b. on** *o* **upon** relacionarse con ♦ **to b. up** resistir ♦ **to bring to b.** aplicar, utilizar.
bear² s. oso; FIN. bajista *mf*.
bear·a·ble ('ǝ-bǝl) adj. soportable.
beard (bîrd) s. barba.
beard·ed (bîr'dĭd) adj. barbudo.
bear·er (bâr'ǝr) s. *(carrier)* portador *m*; *(of message, check)* portador *m*.
bear·ing (:ĭng) s. *(poise)* porte *m*; MEC. cojinete *m*; AER., MARÍT. rumbo ♦ **to have a b. on** tener relación con ♦ pl. orientación ♦ **to get one's b.** orientarse.
beast (bēst) s. bestia, bruto ♦ **b. of burden** bestia de carga.
beast·ly (:lē) **I.** adj. -i- bestial, brutal **II.** adv. G.B. sumamente.
beat (bēt) **I.** tr. **beat, beat(en)** *(to hit)* golpear; *(to flog)* pegar, aporrear; *(to pound, flap, stir)* batir; *(to defeat)* vencer, derrotar; *(to surpass)* superar a; JER. *(to perplex)* confundir, dejar perplejo; MÚS. *(a drum)* tocar; *(rhythm)* marcar, llevar ♦ **b. it!** ¡lárgate! ♦ **off the beaten path** fuera de lo común ♦ **to b. back** *o* **off** repeler ♦ **to b. down** derribar —intr. *(to hit)* golpear, caer con violencia; *(to throb)* latir, pulsar; *(drums)* redoblar ♦ **to b. around the bush** andarse con rodeos ♦ **to b. down on** azotar (el sol) **II.** s. *(throb)* latido, pulsación *f*; *(tempo)* compás *m*, ritmo; *(route)* ronda **III.** adj. FAM. rendido, deslomado.
beat·er (bē'tǝr) s. batidor *m*.
be·a·tif·ic (bē'ǝ-tĭf'ĭk) adj. beatífico.
be·at·i·fy (bē-ăt'ǝ-fī') tr. beatificar.
beat·ing (bē'tĭng) s. *(thrashing)* paliza; *(defeat)* derrota; *(of the heart)* latido.
be·at·i·tude (bē-ăt'ĭ-tōōd') s. beatitud *f*.
beau (bō) s. [pl. **s** *o* **-x**] *(suitor)* pretendiente *m*; *(dandy)* galán *m*.
beau·ti·cian (byōō-tĭsh'ǝn) s. cosmetólogo.
beau·ti·ful (byōō'tǝ-fǝl) adj. bello, hermoso.
beau·ti·ful·ly (:fǝ-lē) adv. *(attractively)* bellamente; *(very well)* espléndidamente.
beau·ti·fy (:fī') tr. embellecer.
beau·ty (byōō'tē) s. belleza, hermosura; *(person, thing)* belleza ♦ **b. parlor** *o* **salon** salón de belleza ♦ **that was a (real) b.!** ¡qué golpe más bueno!
bea·ver (bē'vǝr) s. castor *m*.
be·cause (bĭ-kôz', -kŭz') conj. porque ♦ **b. of** a causa de, por.
beck (bĕk) s. ♦ **at someone's b. and call** al servicio de alguien.
beck·on (bĕk'ǝn) tr. & intr. *(to summon)* hacer señas; *(to entice)* atraer, llamar.
be·come (bĭ-kŭm') intr. **-came, -come** *(to turn into)* llegar a ser, convertirse en; *(angry, etc.)* hacerse, ponerse, volverse ♦ **b. of** ser, hacerse *<what was of George?* ¿qué se ha hecho de Jorge?> —tr. quedar *o* sentar bien.
be·com·ing (:ĭng) adj. *(suitable)* apropiado, conveniente; *(attractive)* que sienta bien.
bed (bĕd) **I.** s. cama, lecho; *(lodging)* alojamiento; *(of flowers)* macizo ♦ **b. and board** pensión completa ♦ **to go to b.** acostarse **II.** intr. **-dd-** ♦ **to b. down** acostarse.
be·daz·zle (bĭ-dăz'ǝl) tr. deslumbrar.
bed·bug (bĕd'bŭg') s. chinche *f*.

bed·cham·ber (:chām′bər) s. alcoba.
bed·clothes (:klō*th*z′) s.pl. ropa de cama.
bed·ding (:ĭng) s. ropa de cama.
be·dev·il (bĭ-dĕv′əl) tr. fastidiar, dificultar.
bed·fel·low (bĕd′fĕl′ō) s. *(bedmate)* compañero de cama; *(associate)* socio.
bed·lam (bĕd′ləm) s. algarabía, alboroto.
bed·pan (bĕd′păn′) s. orinal *m*, chata.
bed·post (:pōst′) s. pilar *m* de la cama.
bed·rid·den (:rĭd′n) adj. postrado en cama.
bed·roll (:rōl′) s. lecho portátil que se enrolla.
bed·room (:rōōm′) s. dormitorio, alcoba.
bed·side (:sīd′) adj. & s. (de) cabecera.
bed·sore (:sôr′) s. úlcera por decúbito.
bed·spread (:sprĕd′) s. cubrecama *m*, colcha.
bed·spring (:sprĭng′) s. colchon *m* de muelles.
bed·stead (:stĕd′) s. armadura de la cama.
bed·time (:tīm′) s. hora de acostarse.
bed·wet·ting (:wĕt′ĭng) s. enuresis nocturna.
bee (bē) s. abeja; FAM. *(contest)* concurso.
beech (bēch) s. haya.
beef (bēf) I. s. [pl. **-ves**] carne *f* de res; JER. *(complaint)* [pl. **s**] queja ♦ **to have a b.** quejarse II. intr. JER. quejarse —tr. ♦ **to b. up** JER. reforzar.
beef·steak (′stāk′) s. bistec *m*, biftec *m*.
beef·y (bē′fē) adj. **-i-** fornido, musculoso.
bee·hive (bē′hīv′) s. colmena.
bee·keep·ing (bē′kē′pĭng) s. apicultura.
bee·line (bē′līn′) s. línea recta.
been (bĭn) part. p. de **be**.
beep (bēp) I. s. sonido agudo II. intr. & tr. sonar con sonido agudo.
beep·er (bē′pər) s. dispositivo de llamada.
beer (bĭr) s. cerveza ♦ **dark, light b.** cerveza negra, dorada.
bees·wax (bēz′wăks′) s. cera.
beet (bēt) s. remolacha.
bee·tle (bēt′l) s. escarabajo.
be·fall (bĭ-fôl′) tr. **-fell, -en** acontecer a.
be·fit·ting (bĭ-fĭt′ĭng) adj. propio, conveniente.
be·fore (bĭ-fôr′) I. adv. *(earlier)* antes; *(in the past)* anteriormente, ya una vez ♦ **to go b.** ir delante (de) II. prep. *(in time)* antes de o que; *(in space)* delante de; *(in front of)* ante III. conj. *(in advance)* antes de que; *(rather than)* antes que.
be·fore·hand (:hănd′) adv. *(earlier)* antes; *(in anticipation)* de antemano.
be·friend (bĭ-frĕnd′) tr. entablar amistad con.
be·fud·dle (bĭ-fŭd′l) tr. confundir.
beg (bĕg) tr. & intr. **-gg-** *(for charity)* mendigar, pedir (limosna); *(to entreat)* suplicar, rogar ♦ **b. for mercy** implorar clemencia • **to b. pardon** pedir perdón • **to b. off** disculparse.
be·gan (bē-găn′) cf. **begin**.
be·get (bē-gĕt′) tr. **-got, -got(ten)** engendrar.
beg·gar (bĕg′ər) s. mendigo, pobre *mf*.
beg·gar·ly (:lē) adj. mísero, pobre.
beg·gar·y (bĕg′ə-rē) s. miseria, penuria.
be·gin (bĭ-gĭn′) tr. & intr. **-gan, -gun, -nn-** empezar, comenzar ♦ **to b. by** empezar por • **to b. with** para empezar.
be·gin·ner (:ər) s. principiante *mf*, novato.
be·gin·ning (:ĭng) s. comienzo, principio; *(source)* origen *m* ♦ **b. with** a partir de.
be·gone (bĭ-gôn′) interj. ¡fuera!
be·grudge (bĭ-grŭj′) tr. *(to envy)* envidiar; *(to give reluctantly)* dar de mala gana.
be·guile (bĭ-gīl′) tr. encantar, seducir.
be·gun (bē-gŭn′) cf. **begin**.
be·half (bĭ-hăf′) s. ♦ **in b. of** para, a favor de •

on b. of en nombre de.
be·have (bĭ-hāv′) tr. & intr. portarse, comportarse; *(properly)* portarse bien; *(machine)* funcionar.
be·hav·ior (:yər) s. comportamiento, conducta.
be·head (bĭ-hĕd′) tr. decapitar, descabezar.
be·hind (bĭ-hīnd′) I. adv. *(in back)* atrás, detrás; *(late)* atrasado; *(slow)* con retraso II. prep. *(in back of)* detrás de; *(in a prior place)* atrás; *(underlying)* detrás de; *(in support of)* detrás ♦ **b. schedule** atrasado III. s. FAM. trasero, nalgas.
be·hold (bĭ-hōld′) tr. **-held** mirar, contemplar —interj. ¡mirad!, he aquí.
be·hold·en (bĭ-hōl′dən) adj. obligado *(to* con).
be·hoove (bĭ-hōōv′) tr. convenir.
beige (bāzh) s. & adj. beige *m*.
be·ing (bē′ĭng) s. existencia; *(entity, essence)* ser *m* ♦ **human b.** ser humano • **to bring into b.** realizar, crear.
be·la·bor (bĭ-lā′bər) tr. *(to scold)* regañar; *(to harp on)* machacar.
be·lat·ed (bĭ-lā′tĭd) adj. atrasado, tardío.
belch (bĕlch) I. intr. & tr. eructar; FIG. arrojar, vomitar II. s. eructo.
be·lea·guer (bĭ-lē′gər) tr. asediar, acosar.
bel·fry (bĕl′frē) s. campanario.
be·lie (bĭ-lī′) tr. **-lying** desmentir, contradecir.
be·lief (bĭ-lēf′) s. creencia, fe *f*; *(conviction)* convicción *f*, opinión *f*; *(confidence)* confianza.
be·liev·a·ble (bĭ-lē′və-bəl) adj. creíble.
be·lieve (bĭ-lēv′) tr. & intr. creer; *(to trust)* confiar; *(to support)* ser partidario (de *in*) ♦ **to make b.** fingir.
be·liev·er (bĭ-lē′vər) s. creyente *mf*.
be·lit·tle (bĭ-lĭt′l) tr. menospreciar.
bell (bĕl) I. s. campana; *(of a door)* timbre *m*; *(of animals)* cencerro; *(of collar)* cascabel *m* ♦ **b. jar** campana de cristal • **b. tower** campanario • **to ring a b.** FIG. sonarle a uno II. tr. ♦ **to b. the cat** poner el cascabel al gato.
bell-bot·tom (′bŏt′əm) adj. acampanado.
bell·boy (:boi′) s. botones *m*, paje *m*.
belle (bĕl) s. belleza, mujer bella.
bell·flow·er (bĕl′flou′ər) s. campanilla.
bell·hop (:hŏp′) s. botones *m*, paje *m*.
bel·li·cose (bĕl′ĭ-kōs′) adj. belicoso, agresivo.
bel·lig·er·en·cy (bə-lĭj′ər-əns) s. beligerancia, hostilidad *f*.
bel·lig·er·ent (:ənt) adj. & s. beligerante *mf*.
bel·low (bĕl′ō) I. intr. bramar, rugir —tr. vociferar II. s. bramido, rugido.
bel·lows (bĕl′ōz) s. fuelle *m*, barquín *m*.
bel·ly (bĕl′ē) I. s. vientre *m*; *(stomach)* estómago; FAM. *(paunch)* panza, barriga ♦ **b. flop** panzazo • **b. laugh** carcajada II. intr. & tr. inflar(se), hinchar(se).
bel·ly·ache (:āk′) I. s. *(pain)* dolor *m* de barriga; JER. *(gripe)* queja II. intr. JER. quejarse.
bel·ly·but·ton (:bŭt′n) s. FAM. ombligo.
bel·ly·ful (:fŏōl′) s. FAM. panzada, hartazgo.
be·long (bĭ-lông′) intr. *(to have a place)* deber estar, corresponder; *(to fit into a group)* estar en su ambiente ♦ **b. to** *(as property)* pertenecer a, ser de; *(as a member)* ser miembro de; *(as part of)* corresponder a.
be·long·ings (:ĭngz) s.pl. efectos personales.
be·lov·ed (bĭ-lŭv′ĭd) adj. & s. querido.
be·low (bĭ-lō′) I. adv. abajo; *(in a text)* más abajo II. prep. (por) debajo de; *(on a scale)* bajo <*b. zero* bajo cero>.
belt (bĕlt) I. s. cinturón *m*, cinto; *(region)*

zona, faja; JER. *(punch)* golpe *m*; *(of whiskey)* trago; TEC. *(band)* correa ♦ **seat** *or* **safety b.** cinturón de seguridad • **to hit below the b.** golpear bajo II. tr. *(clothing)* ceñir; JER. *(to punch)* golpear, asestar un golpe ♦ **to b. out** cantar (con voz chillona).

be·moan (bǐ-mōn´) tr. lamentar.

be·muse (bǐ-myōōz´) tr. dejar perplejo.

bench (běnch) s. *(seat, workbench)* banco; DER. *(office of the judge)* judicatura; *(court)* tribunal *m*; G.B. *(in Parliament)* escaño ♦ **b. warrant** DER. auto de detención.

bend (běnd) I. tr. **bent** *(the head)* inclinar; *(the knee)* doblar; *(one's back)* encorvar; *(to curve)* doblar, plegar; *(to subdue)* doblegar —intr. *(to curve)* doblarse, curvarse; *(to swerve)* desviarse, torcer ♦ **to b. back** doblarse hacia atrás • **to b. down** *o* **over** encorvarse • **to b. over backwards** hacer el mayor esfuerzo posible II. s. *(curve)* curva; *(turn)* vuelta, recodo ♦ pl. parálisis que afecta a los buceadores.

bend·er (běn´dər) s. FAM. borrachera, juerga.

be·neath (bǐ-nēth´) I. prep. *(below)* (por) debajo de; *(under)* bajo; *(unworthy)* indigno de II. adv. *(below)* abajo; *(underneath)* abajo.

ben·e·dic·tion (běn´ǐ-dǐk´shən) s. bendición *f.*

ben·e·fac·tor (běn´ə-fǎk´tər) s. benefactor.

ben·e·fac·tress (:trǐs) s. benefactora.

ben·e·fice (běn´ə-fǐs) s. beneficio.

be·nef·i·cent (bə-něf´ǐ-sənt) adj. benéfico.

ben·e·fi·cial (běn´ə-fǐsh´əl) adj. provechoso.

ben·e·fi·ci·ar·y (:ē-ĕr´ē) s. beneficiario.

ben·e·fit (běn´ə-fǐt) I. s. *(profit)* beneficio, provecho, *(advantage)* ventaja; *(fund-raiser)* beneficio ♦ **for the b. of** en beneficio de • **to give someone the b. of** dar el beneficio de la duda a alguien por anticipado ♦ pl. asistencia II. tr. beneficiar —intr. ♦ **to b. by** *o* **from** sacar provecho de.

be·nev·o·lence (bə-něv´ə-ləns) s. benevolencia; *(kindly act)* acto de caridad.

be·nev·o·lent (:lənt) adj. benévolo; *(philanthropic)* benéfico.

be·night·ed (bǐ-nī´tǐd) adj. ignorante.

be·nign (bǐ-nīn´) adj. benigno.

bent (běnt) I. cf. **bend** II. adj. *(crooked)* doblado, torcido; *(determined)* empeñado III. s. inclinación *f*, tendencia.

be·numb (bǐ-nǔm´) tr. entumecer; *(to stupefy)* entorpecer.

ben·zene (běn´zēn´) s. benceno.

be·queath (bǐ-kwēth´, -kwēth´) tr. legar.

be·quest (bǐ-kwěst´) s. legado.

be·rate (bǐ-rāt´) tr. reprender, regañar.

be·reaved (bǐ-rēvd´) adj. afligido (por la muerte) ♦ **the b.** los deudos del difunto.

be·reave·ment (bǐ-rēv´mənt) s. *(grief)* luto, duelo; *(loss)* pérdida (de un ser querido).

be·reft (bǐ-rěft´) adj. privado (*of* de).

be·ret (bə-rā´) s. boina.

ber·ry (běr´ē) s. baya.

ber·serk (bər-sûrk´) adj. frenético, loco ♦ **to go b.** volverse loco.

berth (bûrth) s. *(on a train)* litera; MARÍT. *(cabin)* camarote *m*; *(at a wharf)* atracadero; *(employment)* puesto ♦ **to give a wide b. to** evitar.

be·ryl·li·um (bə-rǐl´ē-əm) s. berilio.

be·seech (bǐ-sēch´) tr. -ed *o* **-sought** suplicar, implorar.

be·set (bǐ-sět´) tr. -set, -tting *(to harass)* asediar, acosar; *(to surround)* rodear.

be·side (bǐ-sīd´) prep. junto a, al lado de ♦ **to be b. oneself** estar fuera de sí • **to be b. the point** no venir al caso.

be·sides (bǐ-sīdz´) I. adv. *(in addition)* además, también; *(moreover)* además; *(otherwise)* por otro lado, aparte de eso II. prep. *(in addition to)* además de; *(except)* aparte de, fuera de.

be·siege (bǐ-sēj´) tr. MIL. sitiar; *(to hem in)* rodear; *(to harass)* asediar, abrumar ♦ **to be besieged with** *(calls, requests)* haber recibido un torrente de (llamadas, peticiones).

be·smirch (bǐ-smûrch´) tr. ensuciar, manchar.

be·speak (bǐ-spēk´) tr. **-spoke, -spoke(n)** indicar, revelar.

best (běst) [superl. de **good**] I. adj. mejor; *(favorite)* favorito <*my b. friend* mi amigo favorito> ♦ **b. man** padrino (de una boda) • **b. seller** libro de gran éxito • **to know what is b. for one** saber lo que más le conviene a uno II. adv. mejor; *(most)* más <*which do you like b.?* ¿cuál te gusta más?> III. s. el mejor, lo mejor ♦ **at b.** a lo más • **to do one's b.** hacer lo mejor que uno puede • **to make the b. of it** salir de un mal negocio lo mejor posible • **to the b. of my recollection** que yo recuerde IV. tr. vencer, ganar.

bes·tial (běs´chəl) adj. bestial.

bes·ti·al·i·ty (´chē-ǎl´ǐ-tē) s. bestialidad *f.*

be·stir (bǐ-stûr´) tr. ♦ **to b. oneself** rebullirse.

be·stow (bǐ-stō´) tr. otorgar, conceder.

be·stow·al (:əl) s. otorgamiento.

be·strewn (bǐ-strōōn´) adj. salpicado (*with* de).

bet (bět) I. s. apuesta ♦ **to be a sure b.** ser cosa segura II. tr. **bet(ted), -tting** apostar ♦ **I b.. . .** FAM. a que. . . , seguro que. . . —intr. *(to wager)* apostar; *(to gamble)* jugar ♦ **I b.!** FAM. ¡ya lo creo! • **you b.!** FAM. ¡claro!

be·to·ken (bǐ-tō´kən) tr. indicar, presagiar.

be·tray (bǐ-trā´) tr. traicionar; *(to inform on)* delatar; *(a secret)* revelar.

be·tray·al (:əl) s. traición *f*, delación *f*; *(of a secret)* revelación *f.*

be·troth (bǐ-trōth´) tr. ♦ **to become betrothed** desposarse.

be·troth·al (bǐ-trō´thəl) s. compromiso matrimonial.

be·trothed (bǐ-trōthd´) s. prometido, novio.

bet·ter (bět´ər) [comp. de **good**] I. adj. mejor; *(preferable)* más apropiado, preferible ♦ **the b. part of** la mayor parte de • **to be b.** to valer más, ser mejor II. adv. mejor ♦ **all the b.** *o* **so much the b.** tanto mejor • **b. and b.** cada vez mejor • **b. late than never** más vale tarde que nunca • **b. off** en mejores condiciones • **had b.** más vale que <*we had b. go* más vale que nos vayamos> • **to get b.** mejorar III. tr. & intr. mejorar(se) IV. s. el mejor ♦ **for b. or worse** en la fortuna como en la desventura • **to get the b. of** superar, vencer ♦ pl. superiores.

bet·ter·ment (:mənt) s. mejora, mejoramiento.

bet·tor (bět´ər) s. apostador *m*, apostante *mf.*

be·tween (bǐ-twēn´) I. prep. entre ♦ **b. now and then** de aquí a entonces • **b. you and me** entre nosotros II. adv. en medio, de por medio ♦ **far b.** a grandes intervalos • **in b.** mientras tanto.

be·twixt (bǐ-twǐkst´) adv. ♦ **b. and between** entre una cosa y otra.

bev·el (běv´əl) I. s. bisel *m* II. tr. biselar.

bev·eled (:əld) adj. biselado.

bev·er·age (běv´ər-ǐj) s. bebida.

bev·y (běv´ē) s. *(of birds)* bandada; *(of people)* grupo.

be·wail (bǐ-wāl′) tr. lamentar.
be·ware (bǐ-wâr′) I. tr. & intr. tener cuidado (con) ♦ **b. of** cuidado con II. interj. ¡cuidado!
be·wil·der (bǐ-wǐl′dər) tr. aturdir, dejar perplejo.
be·wil·der·ment (:mənt) s. aturdimiento.
be·witch (bǐ-wǐch′) tr. hechizar.
be·witch·ment (:mənt) s. hechizo.
be·yond (bǐ-yǒnd′) I. prep. *(greater than)* más allá, fuera de; *(after)* después de ♦ **b. belief** increíble • **b. dispute** incontestable • **b. (a) doubt** fuera de duda • **b. help** sin remedio • **it's b. me** no alcanzo a comprender II. adv. más lejos, más allá.
bi·an·nu·al (bī-ăn′yōō-əl) adj. semestral.
bi·as (bī′əs) I. s. *(tendency)* inclinación *f*; *(prejudice)* prejuicio; *(partiality)* preferencia; COST. bies *m* II. tr. predisponer, influenciar ♦ **to be biased** ser parcial.
bib (bĭb) s. babero; *(of an apron)* peto.
Bi·ble (bī′bəl) s. Biblia ♦ **b.** biblia.
Bib·li·cal *o* **bib·li·cal** (bĭb′lǐ-kəl) adj. bíblico.
bib·li·og·ra·pher (bĭb′lē-ǒg′rə-fər) s. bibliógrafo.
bib·li·og·ra·phy (:fē) s. bibliografía.
bib·li·o·phile (bĭb′lē-ə-fīl′) s. bibliófilo.
bi·car·bon·ate (bī-kär′bə-nāt′) s. bicarbonato ♦ **b. of soda** bicarbonato de sosa.
bi·cen·ten·ni·al (bī′sĕn-tĕn′ē-əl) adj. & s. bicentario.
bi·ceps (bī′sĕps′) s. [pl. inv. *o* **es**] bíceps *m*.
bick·er (bĭk′ər) intr. reñir, disputar.
bi·cy·cle (bī′sĭk′əl) I. s. bicicleta II. intr. montar *o* ir en bicicleta.
bi·cy·clist (:lĭst) s. ciclista *mf*.
bid (bĭd) I. tr. **bid** *o* **bade, bid(den), -dd-** *(to order)* ordenar, mandar; *(to offer)* licitar; *(in cards)* declarar ♦ **to b. farewell** *o* **good-bye** to decir adiós a —intr. hacer una oferta II. s. *(offer)* licitación *f*, oferta; *(in cards)* declaración *f*; *(effort)* tentativa.
bid·der (:ər) s. postor *m*.
bid·ding (:ĭng) s. *(command)* orden *f*; *(at an auction)* oferta; *(in cards)* declaración *f*.
bid·dy (bĭd′ē) s. gallina; JER. vieja chacharera.
bide (bīd) tr. **-d** *o* **bode, -d** ♦ **to b. one's time** aguardar el momento propicio.
bi·en·ni·al (bī-ĕn′ē-əl) adj. bienal.
bier (bîr) s. féretro.
bi·fo·cal (bī-fō′kəl) I. adj. bifocal II. s. ♦ pl. anteojos bifocales.
bi·fur·cate (bī′fər-kāt′) intr. bifurcarse.
bi·fur·ca·tion (′-kā′shən) s. bifurcación *f*.
big (bĭg) **-gg-** I. adj. gran, grande; *(great in intensity)* fuerte; *(older)* mayor <*my* **b.** *brother* mi hermano mayor>; *(important)* importante, de gran significado ♦ **b. shot** *o* **wheel** pez gordo II. adv. ♦ **to be b. on** FAM. ser entusiasta de • **to make it b.** tener gran éxito • **to talk b.** jactarse.
big·a·mist (bĭg′ə-mĭst) s. bígamo.
big·a·my (:mē) s. bigamia.
big-heart·ed (bĭg′här′tĭd) adj. generoso.
big·ness (:nĭs) s. grandor *m*, grandeza.
big·ot (bĭg′ət) s. intolerante *mf*.
big·ot·ed (:ə-tĭd) adj. intolerante.
big·ot·ry (:trē) s. intolerancia.
big-time (bĭg′tīm′) adj. JER. de los grandes.
big·wig (:wĭg′) s. FAM. pez gordo.
bike (bīk) s. *(bicycle)* bici *f*; *(motorcycle)* moto *f* II. intr. montar en bici, manejar una moto.

bik·er (bī′kər) s. motociclista *mf*.
bi·lat·er·al (bī-lăt′ər-əl) adj. bilateral.
bile (bīl) s. *(fluid)* bilis *f*; *(ill temper)* mal genio.
bilge (bĭlj) s. MARÍT. sentina; JER. *(nonsense)* disparates *m* ♦ **b. water** agua de sentina.
bi·lin·gual (bī-lĭng′gwəl) adj. bilingüe.
bil·ious (bĭl′yəs) adj. bilioso.
bilk (bĭlk) tr. estafar, defraudar.
bill¹ (bĭl) I. s. *(invoice)* cuenta, factura; *(poster)* cartel *m*; *(bank note)* billete *m*; POL. proyecto de ley ♦ **b. of exchange** letra de cambio • **b. of fare** carta, menú • **b. of lading** conocimiento de embarque • **b. of rights** declaración de derechos • **b. of sale** boleto de compra y venta • **to fill the b.** FAM. satisfacer todos los requisitos • **to foot the b.** FAM. correr con los gastos II. tr. *(a customer)* pasar la cuenta a; *(expenses, goods)* facturar; *(to promote)* anunciar, promocionar.
bill² s. *(beak)* pico; *(visor)* visera.
bill·board (′bôrd′) s. cartelera.
bil·let (bĭl′ĭt) MIL. I. s. alojamiento II. tr. alojar.
bill·fold (bĭl′fōld′) s. billetera, cartera.
bil·liards (bĭl′yərdz) s.sg. billar *m*.
bill·ing (bĭl′ĭng) s. publicidad *f* ♦ pl. facturación.
bil·lion (bĭl′yən) s. E.U. mil millones *m*; G.B. billón *m*.
bil·lion·aire (:yə-nâr′) s. & adj. billonario.
bil·low (bĭl′ō) I. s. oleada, ola II. intr. *(sea)* ondular; *(sails)* hincharse.
bil·low·y (:ē) adj. ondulante.
bil·ly (bĭl′ē) ♦ **b. club** porra, bastón (de policía) • **b. goat** macho cabrío.
bi·month·ly (bī-mŭnth′lē) adj. & adv. bimestral(mente).
bin (bĭn) s. *(box)* cajón *m*; *(container)* recipiente *m*, compartimiento.
bi·na·ry (bī′nə-rē) adj. binario.
bind (bīnd) I. tr. **bound** *(to tie)* amarrar, atar; *(to restrain)* ceñir; *(a wound)* vendar; *(morally, legally)* obligar, comprometer a; *(by sentiment)* ligar, vincular; *(a contract)* ratificar; *(a book)* encuadernar, empastar; *(sheaves)* agavillar; *(to constipate)* estreñir ♦ **to be bound up with** estar ligado *o* relacionado con • **to b. over** poner bajo fianza —intr. *(to be tight)* apretar; *(a mix)* aglutinarse; *(a contract)* tener fuerza obligatoria II. s. ♦ **to be in a b.** estar en un aprieto, en un apuro.
bind·er (bīn′dər) s. IMPR. encuadernador *m*; *(fastener)* atadura; *(notebook cover)* carpeta; *(payment)* garantía; *(contract)* contrato provisional.
bind·er·y (:də-rē) s. taller *m* de encuadernación.
bind·ing (:ĭng) I. s. IMPR. encuadernación *f*; COST. ribete *m* II. adj. *(tight)* apretado; DER. obligatorio; *(promise)* que compromete a uno.
binge (bĭnj) s. JER. parranda ♦ **to go on a (shopping, eating) b.** darse un banquete (comprando, comiendo).
bin·oc·u·lar (bə-nŏk′yə-lər) I. adj. binocular II. s. ♦ pl. gemelos, prismáticos.
bi·no·mi·al (bī-nō′mē-əl) adj. & s. binomio.
bi·o·chem·i·cal (bī′ō-kĕm′ĭ-kəl) adj. bioquímico.
bi·o·chem·ist (:ĭst) adj. bioquímico.
bi·o·chem·is·try (:ĭ-strē) s. bioquímica.
bi·o·feed·back (bī′ō-fēd′băk′) s. biorreacción *f*.

bi·og·ra·pher (bī-ŏg'rə-fər) s. biógrafo.
bi·o·graph·ic/i·cal (bī'ə-grăf'ĭk) adj. biográfico.
bi·og·ra·phy (bī-ŏg'rə-fē) s. biografía.
bi·o·log·ic/i·cal (bī'ə-lŏj'ĭk) adj. biológico.
bi·ol·o·gist (bī-ŏl'ə-jĭst) s. biólogo.
bi·ol·o·gy (:jē) s. biología.
bi·on·ics (bī-ŏn'ĭks) s.sg. biónica.
bi·o·phys·ics (bī'ō-fĭz'ĭks) s.sg. biofísica.
bi·op·sy (bī'ŏp'sē) s. biopsia.
bi·o·rhythm (bī'ō-rĭth'əm) s. ritmo biológico.
bi·o·sci·ence ('sī'əns) s. ciencia natural.
bi·par·ti·san (bī-pär'tĭ-zən) adj. bipartidista.
bi·par·tite (:tīt') adj. bipartito.
bi·ped (bī'pĕd') s. & adj. bípedo.
bi·plane (bī'plān') s. biplano.
bi·ra·cial (bī-rā'shəl) adj. de dos razas.
birch (bûrch) s. abedul m.
bird (bûrd) I. s. pájaro; (large) ave f; (game) caza de pluma • **birds of a feather** lobos de la misma camada • **for the birds** cosa de bobos • **odd b.** bicho raro II. intr. observar pájaros.
bird·cage ('kāj') s. jaula.
bird·call (:kôl') s. canto; (device) reclamo.
bird·house (:hous') s. pajarera, aviario.
bird·lime (:īm') s. liga.
bird·seed (:sēd') s. alpiste m.
bird's-eye (bûrdz'ī') adj. • **b. view** vista panorámica.
birth (bûrth) s. nacimiento; (ancestry) linaje m; MED. parto ♦ **b. control** control de la natalidad • **by b.** de nacimiento • **to give b. to** dar a luz a.
birth·day ('dā') s. cumpleaños • **on one's (15th, 25th) b.** al cumplir los (15, 25) años.
birth·mark (:märk') s. lunar m.
birth·place (:plās') s. lugar m de nacimiento.
birth·rate (:rāt') s. índice m de natalidad.
birth·right (:rīt') s. derechos de nacimiento.
bis·cuit (bĭs'kĭt) s. bizcocho; G.B. galletita.
bi·sect (bī'sĕkt') tr. bisecar.
bi·sec·tion (bī-sĕk'shən) s. bisección f.
bi·sex·u·al (bī-sĕk'shōō-əl) adj. & s. bisexual mf.
bish·op (bĭsh'əp) s. obispo; (in chess) alfil m.
bis·muth (bĭz'məth) s. bismuto.
bi·son (bī'sən) s. bisonte m.
bit¹ (bĭt) s. (piece) pedacito, trocito; (amount) poco <a b. larger un poco más grande> (moment) ratito ♦ **a good b.** bastante • **a little b.** un poquito • **b. by b.** poco a poco • **b. part** papel secundario • **bits and pieces** cosas sueltas • **not a b.** en absoluto • **the whole b.** FAM. todo • **to blow to bits** hacer pedazos o añicos • **to do one's b.** poner de la parte de uno.
bit² s. (drill) broca, barrena; (of a bridle) freno, bocado.
bit³ s. COMPUT. bit m, bitio.
bitch (bĭch) I. s. (dog) perra; JER. (shrew) zorra, arpía; (complaint) queja II. intr. JER. quejarse.
bitch·y ('ē) adj. -i- rencoroso.
bite (bīt) I. tr. & intr. **bit, bit(ten)** morder; (insects, snakes, fish) picar; (to cut into) cortar ♦ **to b. off** arrancar de un mordisco • **to b. the bullet** apretar los dientes y aguantar • **to b. the dust** morder el polvo II. s. mordisco, dentellada; (wound) mordedura; (sting) picada; (in fishing) picada; (mouthful) mordisco, bocado • **to have a b. to eat** FAM. tomar un piscolabis • **to have b.** ser incisivo o penetrante.
bit·ing (bī'tĭng) adj. (wind) cortante; (incisive)

penetrante; (sarcastic) mordaz.
bit·ter (bĭt'ər) I. adj. **-er, -est** amargo; (wind, cold) cortante, penetrante; (hard to accept) duro; (fierce) encarnizado, implacable; (resentful) resentido, amargado ♦ **to the b. end** hasta vencer o morir II. s. ♦ pl. biter m.
bit·ter·ness (:nĭs) s. amargura; (fierceness) encarnizamiento; (resentment) rencor m.
bit·ter·sweet (:swēt') adj. agridulce.
bi·tu·men (bī-tōō'mən) s. betún m.
bi·tu·mi·nous (:mə-nəs) adj. bituminoso.
bi·va·lent (bī-vā'lənt) adj. bivalente.
bi·valve (bī'vălv') s. & adj. bivalvo.
bi·week·ly (bī-wēk'lē) adj. quincenal.
bi·zarre (bĭ-zär') adj. extravagante, extraño.
blab (blăb) I. tr. **-bb-** soltar, descubrir (secreto) —intr. (to tell secrets) descubrir el pastel; (to chatter) cotorrear II. s. charloteo, cotorreo.
blab·ber (:ər) I. intr. cotorrear II. s. cotorreo.
blab·ber·mouth (:mouth') s. JER. cotorra.
black (blăk) I. s. negro ♦ **B.** o **b.** (person) negro • **in b. and white** por escrito • **in the b.** estar haciendo ganancias • **to wear b.** estar de luto II. adj. negro; (gloomy) sombrío; (wicked) malvado; (sullen) hosco ♦ **B.** o **b.** (Negroid) negro • **b. box** AVIA. registrador de vuelo • **b. eye** ojo a la funerala • **b. market** mercado negro, estraperlo III. tr. ♦ **to b. out** MIL. apagar las luces; MED. perder el conocimiento.
black-and-blue ('ən-blōō') adj. FAM. amoratado.
black·ball ('bôl') I. s. bola negra II. tr. dar o echar bola negra.
black·ber·ry (:bĕr'ē) s. zarzamora.
black·bird (:bûrd') s. mirlo.
black·board (:bôrd') s. pizarra, pizarrón m.
black·en (:ən) tr. ennegrecer; (to defame) mancillar, difamar —intr. ennegrecerse.
black·head (:hĕd') s. espinilla, grano.
black·jack (:jăk') s. (bludgeon) cachiporra; (game) veintiuna.
black·list (:lĭst') I. s. lista negra II. tr. poner en la lista negra.
black·mail (:māl') I. s. chantaje m II. tr. chantajear.
black·mail·er (:mā'lər) s. chantajista mf.
black·out (:out') s. (of a city) apagón m; MED. desmayo, pérdida de la memoria; (of news) supresión f.
black·smith (:smĭth') s. herrero.
black·top (:tŏp') s. asfalto.
blad·der (blăd'ər) s. vejiga.
blade (blād) s. hoja; (of a razor, skate) cuchilla; (of an oar) pala; (of a propeller, fan) aleta; (of grass) brizna; (young man) galán m.
blahs (bläz) s.pl. JER. ♦ **to get the b.** desanimarse.
blame (blām) I. tr. ♦ **to be to b. for** tener la culpa de • **to b. on** echar la culpa a II. s. culpa ♦ **to put the b. on** echar la culpa a.
blame·less (:lĭs) adj. libre de culpa.
blame·wor·thy (:wûr'thē) adj. -i- censurable, culpable.
bland (blănd) adj. (mild) suave; (dull) insulso.
blan·dish·ment (blăn'dĭsh-mənt) s. lisonja.
blank (blăngk) I. adj. (paper, tape) en blanco; (wall) liso; (look) vago; (mind) vacío ♦ **b. check** cheque en blanco; FIG. carta blanca • **to go b.** quedarse en blanco II. s. (space) blanco, vacío; (form) formulario (en blanco); (car-

tridge) cartucho de fogueo ♦ **to draw a b.** no saber qué decir o contestar **III.** tr. ♦ **to b. out** borrar.

blan·ket (blăng'kĭt) **I.** s. manta, frazada; FIG. manto, capa ♦ **wet b.** aguafiestas **II.** adj. general, comprensivo **III.** tr. tapar, cubrir.

blare (blâr) **I.** intr. resonar —tr. proclamar, pregonar **II.** s. estruendo.

blar·ney (blär'nē) s. FAM. labia.

bla·sé (blä-zā') adj. hastiado, indiferente.

blas·pheme (blăs-fēm') tr. & intr. blasfemar (contra).

blas·phe·mous ('fə-məs) adj. blasfemo.

blas·phe·my (:mē) s. blasfemia.

blast (blăst) **I.** s. *(gust)* ráfaga; *(explosion)* explosión *f*; *(explosive)* carga explosiva; *(shock)* onda de choque; MÚS. toque *m*, soplido ♦ **b. furnace** alto horno • **(at) full b.** a todo vapor • **to have a b.** JER. pasarla muy bien **II.** tr. *(to blow up)* volar; *(hopes)* acabar con; *(a hole)* abrir, perforar (con barrenos); FAM. *(to criticize)* criticar ♦ **to b. away** disparar repetidamente • **to b. off** despegar.

blast·ed (blăs'tĭd) adj. FAM. condenado, maldito.

blast·off o **blast-off** (blăst'ôf') s. lanzamiento.

bla·tant (blāt'nt) adj. patente, evidente.

blath·er (blăth'ər) **I.** intr. decir disparates **II.** s. disparates *m*.

blaze¹ (blāz) **I.** s. llamarada; *(glare)* resplandor *m*; *(fire)* fuego, hoguera; *(outburst)* arranque *m* **II.** intr. arder ♦ **blazing with (lights, colors)** resplandeciente de (luces, colores) • **to b. away** disparar continuamente.

blaze² **I.** s. *(white spot)* lucero; *(trail mark)* marca **II.** tr. ♦ **to b. a trail** abrir un camino.

blaz·er (blā'zər) s. chaqueta deportiva.

bla·zon·ry (blā'zən-rē) s. blasón *m*.

bleach (blēch) **I.** tr. blanquear; *(clothes)* colar; *(hair)* des(s)colorar —intr. des(s)colorarse **II.** s. des(s)colorante *m*; *(for clothes)* lejía.

bleach·ers (blē'chərz) s.pl. gradas.

bleak (blēk) adj. desolado, frío; *(dreary)* sombrío; *(prospect)* poco prometedor.

blear (blîr) tr. nublar.

blear·y ('ē) adj. **-i-** *(eyes)* nublado; *(exhausted)* agotado, exhausto.

bleat (blēt) **I.** s. balido **II.** intr. balar.

bleed (blēd) intr. **bled** sangrar, perder sangre; BOT. exudar, perder savia; *(colors)* correrse ♦ **to b. to death** morir desangrado —tr. desangrar a, sacar sangre a; *(liquids)* sangrar; JER. *(to extort)* desplumar a ♦ **to b. white** o **dry** FAM. chuparle la sangre a.

bleep (blēp) tr. & s. (hacer un) sonido electrónico agudo.

blem·ish (blĕm'ĭsh) **I.** tr. manchar, mancillar **II.** s. mancha; *(flaw)* tacha.

blend (blĕnd) **I.** tr. **-ed** o **blent** *(to mix)* mezclar; *(to harmonize)* armonizar —intr. *(to mix)* mezclarse, entremezclarse; *(to harmonize)* armonizar, hacer juego **II.** s. mezcla.

blend·er (blĕn'dər) s. licuadora, batidora.

bless (blĕs) tr. **-ed** o **blest** bendecir ♦ **b. my soul!** o **b. me!** ¡válgame Dios! • **to b. with** dotar de.

bless·ed ('ĭd) adj. bendito, santo ♦ **b. event** feliz acontecimiento • **not a b. thing** FAM. nada en absoluto.

bless·ing (:ĭng) s. bendición *f*; *(benefit)* ventaja; *(approval)* aprobación *f*.

blew (blōō) cf. **blow¹**.

blight (blīt) **I.** s. BOT. añublo; *(decay)* ruina, decadencia **II.** tr. arruinar, destruir.

blimp (blĭmp) s. dirigible no rígido.

blind (blīnd) **I.** adj. ciego; *(hidden)* escondido; *(street)* sin salida ♦ **b. as a bat** ciego como un topo • **b. in one eye** tuerto • **b. date, navigation** cita, navegación a ciegas • **b. spot** ángulo muerto; FIG. punto flaco • **b. with** ciego de • **to turn a b. eye** hacer la vista gorda **II.** s. persiana **III.** adv. a ciegas ♦ **b. drunk** borracho como una cuba **IV.** tr. cegar; *(to dazzle)* deslumbrar.

blind·ers (blīn'dərz) s.pl. anteojeras.

blind·fold (blīnd'fōld') **I.** tr. vendar los ojos a **II.** s. venda.

blind·ing (:ĭng) adj. cegador, deslumbrante.

blind·ly (:ē) adv. ciegamente, a ciegas.

blind·ness (:nĭs) s. ceguera.

blink (blĭngk) **I.** intr. parpadear, pestañear; *(signal)* brillar intermitentemente; *(to back down)* ceder, echarse atrás —tr. abrir y cerrar ♦ **to b. an eye** hacer la vista gorda • **without blinking an eye** sin pestañear **II.** s. parpadeo, pestañeo ♦ **on the b.** JER. descompuesto.

blink·er (blĭng'kər) s. intermitente *m* ♦ pl. anteojeras.

blink·ing (:kĭng) adj. parpadeante; *(intermittent)* intermitente; G.B., JER. maldito.

blip (blĭp) s. ELECTRÓN. cresta de eco.

bliss (blĭs) s. dicha, felicidad *f*.

bliss·ful ('fəl) adj. dichoso, feliz.

blis·ter (blĭs'tər) **I.** s. ampolla; BOT. verruga **II.** tr. & intr. ampollar(se).

blis·ter·ing (:ĭng) adj. *(hot)* abrasador; *(harsh)* feroz (palabras); *(fast-paced)* forzado.

blithe (blīth) adj. alegre, despreocupado.

blitz (blĭts) s. MIL. ataque relámpago.

bliz·zard (blĭz'ərd) s. ventisca; FIG. torrente *m*.

bloat (blōt) tr. & intr. hinchar(se), inflar(se).

blob (blŏb) s. masa informe; *(of color)* mancha.

bloc (blŏk) s. bloque *m*.

block (blŏk) **I.** s. bloque *m*; *(chunk)* trozo; *(for chopping)* tajo; *(hat mold)* horma; *(chock)* calza; *(toy)* tarugo; *(pulley)* polea; *(of a city)* cuadra, manzana; *(street)* calle *f*, cuadra; *(obstacle)* obstrucción *f*, obstáculo; JER. *(head)* coco, cabeza; DEP., MED., PSICOL. bloqueo, obstrucción ♦ **b. and tackle** aparejo de poleas **II.** tr. *(to obstruct)* bloquear, obstruir (tráfico, avance); *(a wheel)* calzar; MED., PSICOL. obstruir, interrumpir.

block·ade (blŏ-kād') **I.** s. bloqueo **II.** tr. bloquear.

block·age (blŏk'ĭj) s. obstrucción *f*.

block·bust·er (:bŭs'tər) s. FAM. éxito rotundo.

block·head (:hĕd') s. FAM. zoquete *m*.

bloke (blōk) s. G.B., FAM. tipo, fulano.

blond (blŏnd) s. & adj. rubio.

blonde (blŏnd) s. & adj. rubia.

blood (blŭd) **I.** s. sangre *f*; *(bloodshed)* derrame *m* de sangre; *(lineage)* linaje *m*; *(kinship)* parentesco *m* ♦ **b. bath** matanza • **b. count** recuento globular • **b. relation** consanguíneo • **b. test** análisis de sangre • **b. type** tipo sanguíneo.

blood·cur·dling ('kûrd'lĭng) adj. espeluznante.

blood·hound (:hound') s. sabueso.

blood·less (:lĭs) adj. exangüe; *(coup)* sin derramamiento de sangre.

blood·shed (:shĕd') s. derramamiento de

sangre.

blood·shot (:shŏt') adj. inyectado de sangre.

blood·stain I. s. mancha de sangre
II. tr. ensangrentar.

blood·stream (:strēm') s. corriente sanguínea.

blood·thirst·y (:thûr'stē) adj. sanguinario.

blood·y (:ē) I. adj. -i- sangriento; G.B., JER.
maldito, infame II. adv. G.B., JER. muy III.
tr. ensangrentar.

bloom (blūm) I. s. flor *f*; *(flowering)* florecimiento; *(vigor)* lozanía ♦ **in b.** en flor II. intr.
florecer.

bloom·ers (blō'mərz) s.pl. calzón bombacho.

bloop·er (blō'pər) s. FAM. mancha de pata.

blos·som (blŏs'əm) I. s. flor *f*, *(flowering)*
florecimiento ♦ **in b.** en flor II. intr. florecer.

blot (blŏt) I. s. mancha, borrón *m* II. tr. -tt-
manchar; *(ink)* secar ♦ **blotting paper** papel
secante • **to b. out** borrar.

blotch (blŏch) I. s. mancha, manchón *m*
II. tr. & intr. cubrir(se) de manchas.

blot·ter (blŏt'ər) s. *(paper)* secante *m*; *(register)*
registro.

blouse (blous) s. blusa; *(smock)* blusón *m*;
MIL. guerrera.

blow¹ (blō) I. intr. **blew, -n** soplar; *(a horn)*
sonar; *(a whale)* respolar; *(a fuse)* quemarse;
(to pant) resollar; *(to burst)* explotar ♦ **to b. in**
FAM. llegar inesperadamente • **to b. out** *(tire)*
estallar, reventarse; *(fuse)* fundirse, quemarse •
to b. over *(storm)* pasar; *(scandal)* olvidarse •
to b. up *(to explode)* explotar; *(with anger)* encolerizarse —tr. soplar; *(instrument)* tocar;
(smoke) echar; *(the nose)* sonarse; *(a fuse)*
fundir; *(to waste)* malgastar; FAM. *(to leave
town)* irse, largarse de ♦ **to b. away** llevarse • **to
b. down** derribar • **to b. off steam** desahogarse
emocionalmente • **to b. out** soplar, apagar • **to
b. over** derribar • FIG. sorprender • **to b. up** *(to
destroy)* volar, hacer saltar; *(to inflate)* inflar;
FOTOG. ampliar II. s. soplido, soplo; *(storm)*
tormenta.

blow² s. golpe *m*; *(setback)* revés *m* ♦ **to come
to blows** agarrarse a puñetazos.

blow-by-blow (′bī') adj. detallado.

blow-dry·er (:drī'ər) s. secador *m* de cabello.

blow·gun (:gŭn') s. cerbatana.

blow·hard (:härd') s. JER. fanfarrón *m*.

blow·hole (:hōl') s. respiradero.

blown (blōn) cf. **blow¹**.

blow·out (:out') s. AUTO. reventón *m*, pinchazo; JER. *(bash)* gran festín *m*, comilona.

blow·torch (:tôrch') s. soplete *m*.

blow-up (:ŭp') s. explosión *f*; *(of temper)* estallido; FOTOG. ampliación *f*.

blub·ber (blŭb'ər) I. intr. lloriquear, gimotear
—tr. decir llorando II. s. grasa de ballena;
(body fat) grasa, gordura.

bludg·eon (blŭj'ən) I. s. cachiporra, maza
II. tr. aporrear.

blue (blōō) I. s. azul *m* ♦ **out of the b.** de
repente ♦ pl. melancolía; MÚS. jazz melancólico
II. adj. azul; *(gloomy)* tristón, melancólico ♦
b. chip acción selecta • **b. jay** arrendajo • **b.
jeans** pantalones vaqueros.

blue·bell (′bĕl') s. campanilla.

blue·bot·tle (:bŏt'l) s. moscarda, mosca azul.

blue-col·lar (:kŏl'ər) adj. de obreros.

blue-pen·cil (:pĕn'səl) tr. corregir, revisar.

blue·print (:prĭnt') s. cianotipo, anteproyecto;
FIG. proyecto detallado.

blue·stock·ing (:stŏk'ĭng) s. marisabidilla.

bluff¹ (blŭf) I. tr. *(to fool)* engañar —intr.
farolear, aparentar II. s. engaño, farol *m* ♦ **to
call someone's b.** desenmascarar.

bluff² s. *(cliff)* acantilado; *(river bank)* ribera
escarpada.

bluff·er (′ər) s. fanfarrón *m*, farolero.

blu·ing (blōō'ĭng) s. añil *m*, azulete *m*.

blun·der (blŭn'dər) I. s. error craso, metida
de pata II. intr. *(to move)* andar a tropezones;
(to err) cometer un error craso.

blunt (blŭnt) I. adj. desafilado; *(frank)* franco,
brusco II. tr. desafilar, embotar.

blur (blûr) I. tr. -rr- empañar, nublar —intr.
oscurecerse, ponerse borroso II. s. borrón *m*,
manchón *m*.

blurb (blûrb) s. propaganda.

blur·ry (blûr'ē) adj. -i- confuso, borroso.

blurt (blûrt) tr. ♦ **to b. out** dejar escapar, decir
impulsivamente.

blush (blŭsh) I. intr. ruborizarse, sonrojarse ♦
to b. at avergonzarse de II. s. rubor *m*, sonrojo.

blus·ter (blŭs'tər) I. intr. *(wind)* bramar; *(to
boast)* echar bravatas II. s. fanfarronada.

boar (bôr) s. *(hog)* verraco; *(wild pig)* jabalí *m*.

board (bôrd) I. s. madero, tabla; *(for games)*
tablero; *(table)* mesa; *(meals)* pensión *f*; *(council)* junta, consejo ♦ **above b.** honesto, sin reservas • **b. of directors** directorio • **b. of trade**
junta de comercio • **on b.** a bordo ♦ **b.** TEAT.
tablas, escenario II. tr. embarcar(se) en ♦ **to b.
up** tapar con tablas —intr. hospedarse con
comida.

board·er (bôr'dər) s. pensionista *mf*.

board·ing·house (:dĭng-hous') s. pensión *f*.

board·walk (bôrd'wôk') s. paseo entablado.

boast (bōst) I. intr. jactarse, alardear ♦ **to b. of** *o*
about jactarse de, hacer alarde de • **to be
nothing to b. about** no ser cosa para jactarse
—tr. ostentar II. s. jactancia, alarde *m*.

boast·ful (′fəl) adj. jactancioso.

boast·ing (bō'stĭng) s. jactancia, vanagloria.

boat (bōt) s. *(small craft)* bote *m*, barca; *(ship)*
barco, buque *m* ♦ **to be in the same b.** estar en
la misma situación.

boat·ing (bō'tĭng) s. paseo en bote.

boat·man (bōt'mən) s. [pl. -men] lanchero.

boat·swain (bō'sən) s. contramaestre *m*.

bob¹ (bŏb) I. s. *(dip)* sacudida; CARP. plomo,
peso II. intr. -bb- balancearse (esp. en el
agua).

bob² s.inv. G.B., JER. chelín *m*.

bob·ber (′ər) s. flotador *m* (de pescador).

bob·bin (bŏb'ĭn) s. bobina, carrete *m*.

bob·ble (bŏb'əl) tr. dejar caer (una pelota).

bob·by (bŏb'ē) s. G.B., FAM. policía *mf* ♦ **b. pin**
horquilla • **b. socks** *o* **sox** tobilleras.

bob·cat (bŏb'kăt') s. gato montés, lince *m*.

bob·tail (′tāl') s. cola cortada.

bode¹ (bōd) tr. presagiar ♦ **to b. well, ill** ser de
buen, mal agüero.

bode² cf. **bide**.

bod·ice (bŏd'ĭs) s. cuerpo, corpiño.

bod·i·ly (bŏd'l-ē) I. adj. corporal II. adv.
(physically) corporalmente; *(as a whole)* en
pleno.

bod·ing (bō'dĭng) adj. presagioso, ominoso.

bod·y (bŏd'ē) I. s. *(trunk)* torso; *(corpse)* cadáver *m*; *(organization)* organismo;
(group) grupo, conjunto; *(of matter)* masa;
AVIA. fuselaje *m*; AUTO. carrocería ♦ **b. and
soul** completamente, con toda el alma II. tr. ♦

to b. forth representar, simbolizar (idea, concepto).

bod·y·guard (:gärd') s. guardaespaldas m.

bog (bŏg) I. s. pantano, ciénaga II. tr. & intr. -gg- ♦ to b. down empantanar(se), atascar(se).

bog·ey·man (bŏg'ē-mǎn') s. [pl. -men] FAM. cuco, coco.

bog·gle (bŏg'əl) tr. & intr. sobresaltar(se) ♦ it boggles the mind es de volverse loco.

bo·gus (bō'gəs) adj. falso, fraudulento.

boil[1] (boil) I. intr. hervir; *(to cook)* cocer; FIG. bullir ♦ to b. down reducirse (a) • to b. over *(pot)* rebosar (al hervir); *(person)* enfurecerse —tr. hacer hervir; *(to cook)* cocer, herventar; *(an egg)* pasar por agua II. s. hervor m ♦ to bring to a b. calentar hasta que hierva • to come to a b. comenzar a hervir.

boil[2] s. MED. furúnculo, divieso.

boil·er (boi'lər) s. caldera.

boil·ing (:ĭng) I. adj. hirviente II. s. ebullición f ♦ b. point FÍS. punto de ebullición; FAM. límite de la paciencia.

bois·ter·ous (boi'stər-əs) adj. bullicioso, alborotador.

bold (bōld) adj. *(fearless)* intrépido; *(daring)* audaz; *(impudent)* descarado ♦ in b. face en letra negrilla.

boll (bōl) s. vaina, cápsula.

bo·lo·gna (bə-lō'nē) s. salchicha de Bolonia.

bol·ster (bōl'stər) I. s. cabezal m II. tr. *(to strengthen)* reforzar, apoyar; *(to hearten)* animar.

bolt (bōlt) I. s. MEC. tornillo, perno; *(lock)* cerrojo, pestillo; *(of cloth)* rollo; *(dash)* salto brusco o rápido; *(thunderbolt)* rayo ♦ a b. from the blue suceso inesperado • b. and nut perno y tuerca • to make a b. for precipitarse hacia II. tr. *(to lock)* echar el cerrojo a, cerrar con pestillo; *(to fasten)* sujetar con tornillos o pernos; *(to gulp)* engullir —intr. *(to dash off)* fugarse; *(a horse)* desbocarse ♦ to b. off fugarse, huir • to b. out salir de repente.

bomb (bŏm) I. s. bomba; JER. *(failure)* fracaso, fiasco ♦ b. shelter refugio contra bombardeos II. tr. bombardear —intr. arrojar bombas; JER. *(to fail)* fracasar.

bom·bard (-bärd') tr. *(to bomb)* bombardear; *(to harass)* abrumar, acosar.

bom·bar·dier ('bər-dîr') s. bombardero.

bom·bard·ment (-bärd'mənt) s. bombardeo.

bom·bast ('bǎst') s. discurso grandilocuente.

bomb·er (:ər) s. bombardero.

bomb·ing (:ĭng) s. bombardeo.

bomb·proof (:prōf') adj. a prueba de bombas.

bomb·shell (:shĕl') s. MIL., FIG. bomba.

bomb·sight (:sīt') s. visor m de bombardeo.

bo·na fide (bō'nə fīd') adj. auténtico.

bo·nan·za (bə-nǎn'zə) s. bonanza, mina.

bond (bŏnd) I. s. lazo, atadura; DER. fianza, garantía; FIN. bono, obligación f; QUÍM. enlace m ♦ in b. en depósito, afianzado ♦ pl. cadenas II. tr. unir; DER. afianzar, dar fianza a; —intr. unirse, pegarse.

bond·age (bŏn'dĭj) s. esclavitud f.

bond·ed (bŏn'dĭd) adj. depositado bajo fianza.

bond·hold·er (bŏnd'hōl'dər) s. obligacionista mf.

bond·ser·vant (:sûr'vənt) s. esclavo, siervo.

bonds·man (bŏndz'mən) s. [pl. -men] DER. fiador m; *(bondservant)* esclavo.

bone (bōn) I. s. hueso; *(of fish)* espina ♦ b. of contention manzana de la discordia • to make no bones of o about no andarse con rodeos • to the b. FIG. al máximo, completamente II. tr. deshuesar; *(fish)* quitar las espinas a —intr. ♦ to b. up on JER. estudiar duro.

bone-dry ('drī') adj. completamente seco.

bon·er (bō'nər) s. FAM. metedura de pata.

bon·fire (bŏn'fîr') s. fogata, hoguera.

bon·net (bŏn'ĭt) s. *(hat)* gorra, cofia; MEC. sombrerete m; G.B., AUTO. capó.

bo·nus (bō'nəs) s. plus m, sobresueldo.

bon·y (bō'nē) adj. -i- óseo; *(thin)* esquelético, flaco; *(fish)* espinoso.

boo (bōō) I. s. abucheo, rechifla II. interj. ¡bú! III. intr. & tr. abuchear (a), rechiflar (a).

boob (bōōb) s. FAM. *(fool)* bobalicón m; JER. *(breast)* teta.

boo-boo (bōō'bōō) s. JER. *(blunder)* metida de pata; *(injury)* nana, pupa.

boo·by (:bē) s. FAM. bobalicón m; JER. teta ♦ b. prize premio al peor • b. trap engañabobos.

book (bŏŏk) I. s. libro; *(notebook)* libreta; *(register)* registro ♦ to go by the b. proceder según las reglas • to throw the b. at someone JER. castigar severamente II. tr. *(a suspect)* asentar, registrar; *(to reserve)* reservar, hacer reservación de; *(to hire)* contratar (artistas) ♦ to be booked up *(hotel, restaurant)* estar completo; *(person)* tener otro compromiso.

book·bind·ing ('bīn'dĭng) s. encuadernación f.

book·case (:kās') s. estantería para libros.

book·end (:ĕnd') s. sujetalibros m.

book·ie (:ē) s. FAM. corredor m (de apuestas).

book·ing (:ĭng) s. *(engagement)* contratación f; *(reservation)* reservación f, reserva.

book·ish (:ĭsh) adj. libresco.

book·keep·er (:kē'pər) s. tenedor m de libros.

book·keep·ing (:kē'pĭng) s. teneduría de libros, contabilidad f.

book·let (:lĭt) s. folleto.

book·plate (:plāt') s. ex libris m.

book·sell·er (:sĕl'ər) s. librero.

book·shelf (:shĕlf') s. [pl. -ves] estante m para libros.

book·store (:stôr') s. librería.

book·worm (:wûrm') s. *(larva)* polilla (que roe los libros); FIG. ratón m de biblioteca.

boom[1] (bōōm) I. s. *(sound)* estampido, trueno; COM. auge m II. intr. *(to thunder)* tronar, retumbar; COM. estar en auge.

boom[2] s. MARÍT. botalón m; MEC. pescante m (de grúa); CINEM. jirafa (de micrófono).

boo·mer·ang (bōō'mə-rǎng') I. s. bumerang m II. intr. ser contraproducente.

boon (bōōn) s. bendición f, dicha.

boon·docks (bōōn'dŏks') s.pl. JER. los quintos infiernos.

boon·dog·gle (bōōn'dŏ'gəl) s. FAM. trabajo pagado innecesario.

boor (bŏŏr) s. patán m.

boor·ish (ʹĭsh) adj. tosco, rudo.

boost (bōōst) I. tr. *(to lift)* alzar, levantar; *(to increase)* aumentar II. s. *(push)* impulso; *(increase)* aumento.

boost·er (bōō'stər) s. promotor m ♦ b. rocket cohete acelerador • b. shot inyección de refuerzo.

boot (bōōt) I. s. bota; G.B. *(trunk)* portaequipajes m ♦ to b. FAM. además • to get the b. FAM. ser despedido del empleo II. tr. *(to kick)* patear; JER. *(to fire)* despedir.

booth (bōōth) s. *(compartment)* cabina; *(stand)*

puesto, quiosco.

boot·leg (bŏŏt′lĕg′) I. tr. & intr. **-gg-** contrabandear II. adj. & s. (de) contrabando.

boot·leg·ger (′lĕg′ər) s. contrabandista *mf.*

boot·lick·er (′lĭk′ər) s. adulón *m.*

boot·strap (′străp′) s. tirante *m* ♦ **by one's bootstraps** por sí mismo.

boo·ty (bōō′tē) s. botín *m.*

booze (bōōz) FAM. I. s. bebida alcohólica II. intr. beber.

bop (bŏp) FAM. I. tr. **-pp-** golpear II. s. golpe *m.*

bor·der (bôr′dər) I. s. *(boundary)* frontera; *(edge)* borde *m*, orilla II. tr. *(to edge)* bordear; *(to adjoin)* lindar con —intr. ♦ **to b. on** lindar con; FIG. aproximarse a.

bor·der·line (:līn′) I. s. frontera II. adj. dudoso.

bore¹ (bôr) I. tr. & intr. *(to drill)* taladrar, barrenar II. s. *(hole)* agujero; *(diameter)* diámetro interior; *(caliber)* calibre *m.*

bore² I. tr. *(to weary)* aburrir, cansar II. s. *(person)* pesado, pelmazo; *(thing)* pesadez *f.*

bore³ cf. **bear¹.**

bore·dom (′dəm) s. aburrimiento.

bo·ric (bôr′ĭk) adj. bórico.

bor·ing (bôr′ĭng) adj. aburrido, pesado.

born (bôrn) I. cf. **bear¹** ♦ **to be b.** nacer; *(to originate)* originarse II. adj. nato ♦ **a b. fool** un tonto de nacimiento • **a b. liar** un mentiroso innato.

born·a·gain (′ə-gĕn′) adj. renacido.

borne (bôrn) cf. **bear¹.**

bo·ron (bôr′ŏn′) s. boro *m.*

bor·ough (bûr′ō) s. municipio.

bor·row (bŏr′ō) tr. *(a loan)* tomar prestado; *(to use)* apropiarse (de) —intr. tomar un préstamo.

bor·row·er (:ər) s. prestatario.

bo's'n o **bos'n** (bō′sən) var. de **boatswain.**

bos·om (bŏŏz′əm) s. pecho, FIG. seno ♦ **b. buddy** FAM. amigo del alma.

boss (bôs) I. s. *(supervisor)* supervisor *m*, capataz *m*; *(leader)* jefe *m*, cacique *m* II. tr. dirigir, mandar.

boss·y (bô′sē) adj. **-i-** mandón.

bo·tan·ic/i·cal (bə-tăn′ĭk) adj. botánico.

bot·a·nist (bŏt′n-ĭst) s. botánico.

bot·a·ny (:ē) s. botánica.

botch (bŏch) I. tr. chapucear II. s. chapucería.

both (bōth) I. pron. & adj. ambos, los dos ♦ **b. of us, you** nosotros dos, vosotros dos • **to have it both ways** sacar ventaja de una manera u otra II. conj. ... y ... además *<he is b. strong and healthy* es fuerte y sano además*>.*

both·er (bŏth′ər) I. tr. & intr. molestar(se) *(about, with, por)* II. s. molestia, fastidio.

both·er·some (:səm) adj. molesto, fastidioso.

bot·tle (bŏt′l) I. s. botella; *(baby's)* biberón *m* ♦ **to hit the b.** JER. beber II. tr. embotellar, envasar ♦ **to b. up** reprimir.

bot·tle·neck (:nĕk′) s. cuello; FIG. embotellamiento.

bot·tom (bŏt′əm) s. fondo; *(of a list)* final *m*; *(foot)* pie *m*; *(of sea, river)* lecho; *(essence)* meollo, base *f*; FAM. *(buttocks)* trasero ♦ **b. dollar** precio más bajo • **b. line** FIN. balance; FIG. quid.

bot·tom·less (:lĭs) adj. sin fondo.

bot·u·lism (bŏch′ə-lĭz′əm) s. botulismo.

bough (bou) s. rama.

bought (bôt) cf. **buy.**

bouil·lon (bŏŏl′yŏn′) s. caldo.

boul·der (bōl′dər) s. canto rodado.

boul·e·vard (bŏŏl′ə-värd′) s. bulevar *m.*

bounce (bouns) I. intr. rebotar; *(to jump)* saltar, dar brincos; FAM. *(a check)* ser rechazado ♦ **to b. back** recuperarse —tr. hacer rebotar; JER. *(to expel)* echar; *(to fire)* despedir II. s. *(leap)* salto, brinco; *(rebound)* rebote *m*; *(springiness)* elasticidad *f.*

bounc·er (bouns′ər) s. JER. persona encargada de echar a los alborotadores.

bounc·ing (:ĭng) adj. robusto, fuerte.

bounc·y (:sē) adj. **-i-** vivo, exuberante.

bound¹ (bound) I. intr. saltar, dar brincos II. s. *(leap)* salto, brinco; *(bounce)* rebote *m.*

bound² I. cf. **bind** II. adj. *(tied)* atado, amarrado; *(certain)* seguro; *(obliged)* obligado; IMPR. encuadernado ♦ **b. up in** entregado a • **b. up with** estrechamente relacionado con • **it is b. to happen** tiene forzosamente que ocurrir.

bound³ adj. ♦ **b. for** con destino a.

bound·a·ry (boun′də-rē) s. límite *m*, frontera.

bound·less (bound′lĭs) adj. ilimitado, infinito.

bounds (boundz) s.pl. límite *m* ♦ **out of b.** DEP. fuera de la cancha; *(behavior)* fuera de los límites; *(prohibited)* prohibido.

boun·ti·ful (boun′tə-fəl) adj. generoso.

boun·ty (boun′tē) s. *(generosity)* generosidad *f*; *(gift)* regalo, *(reward)* recompensa.

bou·quet (bō-kā′, bōō-) s. *(of flowers)* ramillete *m*; *(of wine)* buqué *m.*

bour·geois (bŏŏr-zhwä′) s. & adj. burgués *m.*

bour·geoi·sie (′ zē′) s. burguesía.

bout (bout) s. *(contest)* combate *m*; *(spell)* ataque *m* (de una enfermedad).

bou·tique (bōō-tēk′) s. tienda pequeña de artículos de moda.

bo·vine (bō′vīn′) adj. & s. bovino.

bow¹ (bou) s. MARÍT. proa.

bow² (bou) I. intr. *(to stoop)* inclinarse, doblegarse; *(to nod)* saludar; *(in obeisance)* inclinarse, hacer una reverencia; *(to submit)* someterse ♦ **to b. out** retirarse, renunciar —tr. *(the head, body)* inclinar; *(the knee)* doblar II. s. *(obeisance)* reverencia; *(greeting)* saludo.

bow³ (bō) s. ARM., MÚS. *(weapon)* arco; *(knot)* lazo; *(curve)* arco, curva ♦ **b. tie** corbata de lazo.

bow·el (bou′əl) s. intestino ♦ **b. pl.** entrañas.

bowl¹ (bōl) s. *(dish)* fuente *f*, cuenco; *(cup)* tazón *m*; *(washbasin)* jofaina; *(toilet)* taza; DEP. estadio.

bowl² intr. DEP. jugar a los bolos —tr. lanzar, tirar (la bola) ♦ **to b. over** derribar; FIG. pasmar.

bow·leg·ged (bō′lĕg′ĭd) adj. estevado.

bowl·er¹ (bō′lər) s. jugador *m* de bolos.

bowl·er² (:lər) s. *(hat)* sombrero hongo, bombín *m.*

bowl·ing (bō′lĭng) s. bolos ♦ **b. alley** bolera.

box¹ (bŏks) I. s. caja; *(large)* cajón *m*; *(small)* estuche *m*; *(pigeonhole)* casilla; *(printed)* casilla, cuadro; TEAT. palco; *(in newspaper)* recuadro ♦ **b. office** taquilla, boletería • **b. spring** colchón de resortes II. tr. ♦ **to b. in** encerrar • **to b. up** encajonar, empaquetar.

box² I. s. *(blow)* bofetada, cachete *m* II. tr. abofetear; DEP. boxear —intr. boxear.

box·car (′kär′) s. F.C. furgón *m.*

box·er (bŏk′sər) s. boxeador *m*, púgil *m.*

box·ing (:sĭng) s. boxeo ♦ **b. glove** guante de boxeo.

box·wood (bŏks′wŏŏd′) s. boj *m.*

boy (boi) I. s. niño; *(youth, servant)* muchacho

II. interj. ¡chico!, ¡hombre!

boy·cott (boi′kŏt′) I. tr. boicotear II. s. boicoteo, boicot *m*.

boy·friend (boi′frĕnd′) s. FAM. novio.

boy·hood (:hŏŏd′) s. niñez *f*, infancia.

bra (brä) s. sostén *m*, corpiño.

brace (brās) I. s. *(support)* refuerzo, puntal *m*; TEC. tirante *m*; MED. braguero *m*; IMPR. corchete *m* ✦ pl. ODONT. aparato de ortodoncia II. tr. *(to support)* apuntalar, reforzar; *(to hold steady)* asegurar; *(to invigorate)* vigorizar ✦ **to b. one-self** for prepararse para (golpe, noticia) ✦ **to b. up** cobrar ánimo.

brace·let (brās′lĭt) s. brazalete *m*, pulsera.

brac·ing (brā′sĭng) adj. fortificante, vigorizante.

brack·et (brăk′ĭt) I. s. *(support)* soporte *m*, escuadra; *(shelf)* repisa; *(category)* categoría, grupo; IMPR. corchete *m* II. tr. agrupar, clasificar.

brack·ish (brăk′ĭsh) adj. salino, salobre.

bract (brăkt) s. bráctea.

brad (brăd) s. puntilla, clavito.

brag (brăg) I. tr. & intr. **-gg-** jactarse (de) II. s. jactancia, alarde *m*.

brag·gart (′ərt) s. & adj. fanfarrón *m*.

braid (brād) I. tr. *(to plait)* trenzar; COST. galonear II. s. *(plait)* trenza; *(trim)* galón *m*.

brain (brān) I. s. cerebro ✦ **b. child** FAM. invento, creación ✦ pl. CUL. sesos; *(intelligence)* cabeza ✦ **to rack one's b.** devanarse los sesos II. tr. JER. romper la crisma a.

brain·storm (′stôrm′) s. idea genial.

brain·wash (:wŏsh′) tr. lavar el cerebro.

brain·y (brā′nē) adj. **-i-** FAM. inteligente, listo.

braise (brāz) tr. dorar a fuego lento en cazuela tapada.

brake (brāk) I. s. freno ✦ **b. drum** tambor de freno II. tr. frenar —intr. aplicar el freno.

bram·ble (brăm′bəl) s. zarzamora.

bran (brăn) s. salvado, afrecho.

branch (brănch) I. s. rama; *(division)* ramo, rama; *(of a river)* brazo; F.C. ramal *m* ✦ **b. office** sucursal II. intr. *(trees)* echar ramas; *(to spread out)* ramificarse; *(to split)* bifurcarse ✦ **to b. out** extender las actividades.

brand (brănd) I. s. COM. marca (de fábrica); *(style)* modo, manera; *(type)* clase *f*; *(on cattle)* marca (de hierro); *(firebrand)* tizón *m* II. tr. *(cattle)* marcar, herrar; *(to stigmatize)* calificar de, tildar de.

brand·ing (brăn′dĭng) s. herradero, hierra ✦ **b. iron** hierro de marcar.

bran·dish (brăn′dĭsh) tr. blandir, esgrimir.

brand-new (brănd′nŏŏ′) adj. flamante.

bran·dy (brăn′dē) s. coñac *m*, aguardiente *m*.

brash (brăsh) adj. *(rash)* impetuoso; *(impudent)* descarado, insolente.

brass (brăs) s. latón *m*; FAM. *(gall)* descaro ✦ **b. hat** MIL., JER. oficial de estado mayor ✦ **b. knuckles** manopla ✦ pl. MÚS. cobres.

bras·siere (brə-zîr′) s. sostén *m*, corpiño.

brass·y (brăs′ē) adj. **-i-** *(sound)* metálico; FAM. *(impudent)* descarado.

brat (brăt) s. niño malcriado, mocoso.

bra·va·do (brə-vä′dō) s. [pl. **(e)s**] bravata.

brave (brāv) I. adj. valiente, bravo II. s. guerrero indio III. tr. *(to face)* afrontar; *(to defy)* desafiar.

brav·er·y (brā′və-rē) s. valentía, valor *m*.

brawl (brôl) I. s. pelea II. intr. pelear.

brawn (brôn) s. fuerza muscular.

brawn·y (brô′nē) adj. **-i-** musculoso.

bray (brā) I. s. rebuzno II. intr. rebuznar.

bra·zen (brā′zən) adj. descarado.

bra·zier (brā′zhər) s. brasero.

breach (brēch) I. s. *(of law)* violación *f*; *(of promise)* incumplimiento; *(of relations)* ruptura; MIL. brecha II. tr. MIL. abrir brecha en; DER. violar.

bread (brĕd) I. s. pan *m*; JER. *(money)* plata, pasta ✦ **b. and butter** FAM. pan de cada día II. tr. CUL. empanar.

bread·bas·ket (′băs′kĭt) s. panera; *(region)* granero.

bread·board (:′bôrd′) s. tabla para cortar pan.

breadth (brĕdth) s. *(width)* anchura; *(scope)* extensión *f*; *(openness)* liberalidad *f*.

bread·win·ner (brĕd′wĭn′ər) s. sostén *m* de la familia.

break (brāk) I. tr. broke, broken romper; *(to crack)* quebrar, fracturar; *(to damage)* estropear, descomponer; *(a law)* infringir, violar; *(spirit, will)* quebrantar; *(a horse)* domar; *(a blow, fall)* amortiguar, parar; *(a bill)* cambiar; *(a record)* saldar; *(a code)* descifrar; ELEC. interrumpir, cortar ✦ **to b. down** *(to analyze)* detallar, analizar; *(to destroy)* derrumbar • **to b. in** *(shoes)* amoldar; *(machine)* ajustar • **to b. off** *(to detach)* romper, separar; *(relations)* romper; *(talks)* suspender • **to b. one's back** romperse el alma • **to b. oneself of a habit** quitarse una costumbre • **to b. open** abrir forzando, forzar • **to b. someone's heart** partirle el corazón a alguien • **to b. up** *(to crumble)* desmenuzar; *(to put an end to)* acabar, terminar; *(to upset)* quebrantar, apesadumbrar; *(with laughter)* hacer morir de risa • **to b. (up) with** romper con (una relación) —intr. *(to shatter)* romperse; *(to come apart)* partirse; *(to become unusable)* estropearse, descomponerse; *(fever)* bajar; *(day)* apuntar, rayar; *(the heart)* partirse, romperse; *(the voice)* fallar; *(news)* revelarse; DEP. separarse (los púgiles) • **to b. away** *(to withdraw)* separarse; *(to escape)* escaparse; *(to start suddenly)* arrancar • **to b. down** *(to malfunction)* averiarse, descomponerse; *(physically)* debilitarse; *(emotionally)* abatirse, sufrir un colapso • **to b. even** salir sin ganar o perder • **to b. in** *(to enter)* entrar forzadamente (con intención de robar); *(to interrupt)* interrumpir • **to b. into** *(to enter)* entrar forzadamente en; *(tears, laughter)* echarse a • **to b. loose** *(to come off)* soltarse, desprenderse; *(to escape)* escaparse • **to b. off** *(to come off)* soltarse, desprenderse; *(to stop)* detenerse • **to b. out** *(to escape)* escaparse; *(to erupt)* estallar; MED. salirle a uno (sarpullido, manchas) • **to b. through** atravesar, abrirse paso • **to b. up** *(to end)* acabarse, terminarse *(partido, reunión)*; *(to split up)* separarse (una relación); *(to scatter)* dispersarse, levantarse II. s. *(act)* ruptura, rompimiento; *(fracture)* fractura; *(crack)* grieta, raja; *(gap)* abertura; *(change)* cambio, interrupción *f*; *(pause)* intervalo, pausa; *(sudden dash)* salida, arrancada; *(escape)* fuga, evasión *f*; ELEC. interrupción, corte *m* ✦ **at the b. of day** al amanecer • **lucky b.** coyuntura feliz • **to give someone a b.** dar una oportunidad a alguien • **to take a b.** descansar • **without a b.** sin parar.

break·a·ble (brā′kə-bəl) I. adj. rompible, frágil II. s. ✦ pl. objetos frágiles.

break·age (:kĭj) s. rotura; *(loss)* daños de rotura.

break·down (brāk′doun′) s. MEC. avería; *(fail-*

ure) fracaso; MED. colapso, depresión *f; (of costs)* desglose *m;* QUÍM. descomposición *f.*

break·er (brā'kər) s. ELEC. interruptor automático; *(wave)* cachón *m.*

break·fast (brĕk'fəst) I. s. desayuno II. intr. desayunar, tomar el desayuno.

break-in (brāk'ĭn') s. *(illegal entry)* entrada forzada; *(testing)* período de prueba.

break·neck (:nĕk') adj. ♦ **at b. speed** a mata caballo.

break·through (:thrō') s. MIL. ruptura; *(achievement)* adelanto, progreso.

break·up (:ŭp') s. *(separation)* separación *f; (of marriage, firm)* disolución *f,* desintegración *f.*

break·wa·ter (:wô'tər) s. rompeolas *m.*

breast (brĕst) s. pecho; *(of a woman)* pecho, seno; *(of a fowl)* pechuga ♦ **b. stroke** brazada de pecho.

breast·bone ('bōn') s. esternón *m.*

breast-feed (:fēd') tr. **-fed** amamantar.

breath (brĕth) s. respiración *f,* aliento; *(of an animal)* hálito; *(of air)* soplo ♦ **in one b.** de un tirón • **in the same b.** al mismo tiempo • **out of b.** sin aliento • **short of b.** corto de resuello • **to catch one's b.** recobrar el aliento • **under one's b.** en voz baja • **to waste one's b.** gastar saliva en balde.

breathe (brēth) intr. respirar; *(to blow)* soplar suavemente —tr. respirar; *(to impart)* infundir; *(to whisper)* susurrar, decir ♦ **to b. in** inhalar, aspirar • **to b. one's last** exhalar el último suspiro • **to b. out** exhalar.

breath·er (brē'thər) s. FAM. respiro, pausa.

breath·ing (:thĭng) s. respiración *f* ♦ **b. space** respiro, pausa.

breath·less (brĕth'lĭs) adj. sin aliento; *(panting)* jadeante; *(amazed)* sin resuello, pasmado.

breath·tak·ing (:tā'kĭng) adj. impresionante.

breath·y (:ē) adj. **-i-** velado (voz).

breech (brēch) s. ANAT. trasero; ARM. recámara ♦ pl. (brĭch'ĭz) calzones; FAM. pantalones.

breech·cloth (:klôth') s. taparrabo.

breed (brēd) I. tr. **bred** *(to engender)* engendrar; *(to raise, bring up)* criar —intr. procrear, reproducirse II. s. *(strain)* raza; *(type)* casta, especie *f.*

breed·er (brē'dər) s. criador *m.*

breed·ing (:dĭng) s. crianza, educación *f.*

breeze (brēz) I. s. brisa, FAM. *(easy task)* paseo, papa II. intr. ♦ **to b. in** entrar alegremente • **to b. through** pasar como si tal cosa.

breez·y (brē'zē) adj. **-i-** *(windy)* ventoso; *(casual)* despreocupado.

brev·i·ty (brĕv'ĭ-tē) s. brevedad *f.*

brew (brōō) I. tr. *(beer)* fabricar; *(tea)* preparar, hacer —intr. *(to loom)* amenazar II. s. *(beverage)* infusión *f;* FAM. *(beer)* cerveza; *(concoction)* brebaje *m,* mezcla.

brew·er ('ər) s. cervecero.

brew·er·y (:ə-rē) s. cervecería.

bri·ar (brī'ər) s. brezo, zarza.

bribe (brīb) I. s. soborno ♦ **to take bribes** dejarse sobornar II. tr. sobornar.

brib·er·y (brī'bə-rē) s. soborno.

bric-a-brac (brĭk'ə-brăk') s. baratijas.

brick (brĭk) I. s. ladrillo II. tr. ♦ **to b. up** tapiar con ladrillos.

brick·bat ('băt') s. crítica cortante, pulla.

brick·lay·er (:lā'ər) s. albañil *m.*

bri·dal (brīd'l) I. s. boda, casamiento II. adj. nupcial ♦ **b. gown** traje de boda.

bride (brīd) s. novia, desposada.

bride·groom ('grōōm') s. novio, desposado.

brides·maid (brīdz'mād') s. dama de honor.

bridge (brĭj) I. s. puente *m; (of the nose)* caballete *m* ♦ **to burn one's bridges** quemar las naves II. tr. *(to build)* tender un puente sobre; *(to span)* extenderse a través de.

bri·dle (brīd'l) I. s. brida ♦ **b. path** camino de herradura II. tr. *(a horse)* embridar; *(passions)* refrenar, dominar —intr. picarse *(at por).*

brief (brēf) I. adj. *(in time)* breve; *(in length)* corto; *(succinct)* conciso II. s. *(summary)* sumario, resumen *m;* DER. escrito ♦ **in b.** en resumen ♦ pl. calzoncillos III. tr. informar; *(to give instructions)* dar instrucciones.

brief·case ('kās') s. portafolio, cartera.

brief·ing (brē'fĭng) s. reunión *f* de información.

brig (brĭg) s. MIL., FAM. calabozo.

bri·gade (brĭ-gād') s. brigada.

brig·a·dier (brĭg'ə-dîr') s. general *m* de brigada.

brig·and (brĭg'ənd) s. bandido, bandolero.

brig·an·tine (brĭg'ən-tēn') s. bergantín *m.*

bright (brīt) I. adj. *(shining)* brillante, resplandeciente; *(color)* subido; *(smart)* inteligente, despierto; *(happy)* alegre II. s. ♦ pl. AUTO. luces altas *o* de carretera.

bright·en ('n) tr. & intr. *(with light)* aclarar(se), iluminar(se); *(with joy)* alegrar(se), animar(se).

bright·ness (:nĭs) s. *(quality)* claridad *f,* brillantez *f; (degree)* minosidad *f.*

bril·liance/·cy (brĭl'yəns) s. brillo.

bril·liant (brĭl'yənt) adj. *(shining)* brillante; *(inventive)* genial; *(splendid)* magnífico.

brim (brĭm) I. s. *(of a cup)* borde *m; (of a hat)* ala II. intr. **-mm-** estar lleno hasta el tope ♦ **to b. over** desbordarse.

brim·ful ('fŏōl') adj. lleno hasta el tope.

brine (brīn) s. CUL. salmuera; *(sea)* mar *mf.*

bring (brĭng) tr. **brought** traer; *(to carry)* llevar; *(to persuade)* convencer; *(a price)* rendir; *(charges)* formular ♦ **to b. about** *(to effect)* efectuar, realizar; *(to cause)* causar, provocar • **to b. around** *(to revive)* volver; *(to persuade)* convencer • **to b. back** *(to return)* devolver; *(a memory)* hacer recordar, traer (a la mente); *(to cause to return)* traer de vuelta • **to b. before** encomendar a, someter a • **to b. down** *(to lower)* bajar; *(to overthrow)* derribar • **to b. forth** *(to bear)* producir (frutos); *(to reveal)* poner de manifiesto • **to b. in** *(to harvest)* recoger; *(money)* rendir, producir; DER. *(a verdict)* pronunciar • **to b. off** conseguir, lograr hacer • **to b. on** ocasionar, causar • **to b. oneself** resignarse a • **to b. out** *(a product)* presentar; *(to highlight)* hacer resaltar; *(to reveal)* revelar, mostrar • **to b. up** *(children)* criar, educar; *(a topic)* plantear, traer a colación • **to b. upon oneself** buscarse, acarrearse.

brink (brĭngk) s. borde *m,* margen *f* ♦ **on the b. of** a punto de.

brink·man·ship ('mən-shĭp') s. política arriesgada.

bri·quet(te) (brĭ-kĕt') s. briqueta.

brisk (brĭsk) adj. *(energetic)* enérgico, vigoroso; *(invigorating)* estimulante.

bris·ket (brĭs'kĭt) s. falda (de una res).

bris·tle (brĭs'əl) I. s. cerda II. intr. ♦ **to b. with** estar lleno *o* erizado de.

britch·es (brĭch'ĭz) s.pl. FAM. pantalones *m* ♦ **too big for one's b.** FAM. arrogante, engreído.

brit·tle (brĭt'l) I. adj. **-er, -est** quebradizo, frá-

gil II. s. caramelo de nueces.
broach (brōch) I. s. broche *m* II. tr. *(a subject)* abordar, sacar a colación; *(a cask)* espitar.
broad (brōd) I. adj. *(wide)* ancho; *(spacious)* extenso, amplio; *(general)* general; *(obvious)* evidente, claro; *(tolerant)* liberal, de miras amplias; *(accent)* marcado ♦ **b. jump** salto de longitud • **in b. daylight** en pleno día II. s. JER. *(woman)* mina, fulana III. adv. plenamente, completamente.
broad·cast (brōd'kăst') I. tr. **-cast(ed)** RAD. emitir, radiar; TELEV. transmitir, televisar; *(to make known)* difundir, divulgar; AGR. sembrar a voleo —intr. RAD. emitir, radiar un programa; TELEV. transmitir, televisar un programa II. s. *(act)* transmisión *f*, emisión *f*; *(program)* programa *m*.
broad·cast·er (:kăs'tər) s. locutor *m*.
broad·cast·ing (:tĭng) s. radiodifusión *f*; TELEV. transmisión *f*, difusión *f*.
broad·cloth (:klŏth') s. paño fino.
broad·en (:n) tr. & intr. ensanchar(se).
broad·mind·ed (:mīn'dĭd) adj. tolerante, comprensivo.
broad·side (:sīd') I. s. MARÍT. costado; MIL., FIG. andanada; IMPR. pliego suelto II. adv. de costado.
bro·cade (brō-kād') s. brocado.
broc·co·li (brŏk'ə-lē) s. brécol *m*, bróculi *m*.
bro·chure (brō-shŏŏr') s. folleto.
brogue (brōg) s. *(shoe)* zapato grueso; *(accent)* acento irlandés.
broil (broil) tr. asar a la parrilla —intr. asarse, achicharrarse.
broil·er (broi'lər) s. parrilla; *(chicken)* pollo para asar.
broke (brōk) I. cf. **break** II. adj. JER. pelado.
bro·ken (brō'kən) I. cf. **break** II. adj. roto, quebrado; *(out of order)* descompuesto; *(language)* chapurreado; *(health, law)* quebrantado; *(line)* quebrado; *(ground)* accidentado; *(spirit)* sumiso; *(heart)* destrozado.
bro·ken-down (:doun') adj. decrépito.
bro·ken-heart·ed (:här'tĭd) adj. con el corazón destrozado.
bro·ker (brō'kər) s. agente *mf*, corredor *m* de bolsa.
bro·ker·age (:ĭj) s. corretaje *m*.
bro·mide (brō'mīd') s. QUÍM. bromuro; *(platitude)* trivialidad *f*.
bro·mine (brō'mēn') s. bromo.
bron·chi·al (brŏng'kē-əl) adj. bronquial ♦ **b. tube** bronquio.
bron·chi·tis (-kī'tĭs) s. bronquitis *f*.
bron·co (brŏng'kō) s. mustango, potro cerril.
bronze (brŏnz) I. s. bronce *m* II. adj. de bronce; *(color)* bronceado III. tr. broncear.
brooch (brōch, brōōch) s. broche *m*.
brood (brōōd) I. s. ORNIT. nidada; *(children)* progenie *f*, prole *f* II. tr. empollar —intr. empollar; *(to ponder)* cavilar III. adj. de cría.
brook¹ (brŏŏk) s. arroyo.
brook² tr. tolerar, aguantar.
broom (brōōm) s. escoba; BOT. retama.
broom·stick ('stĭk') s. palo de escoba.
broth (brŏth) s. caldo.
broth·el (brŏth'əl) s. burdel *m*, lupanar *m*.
broth·er (brŭth'ər) s. hermano; *(fellow member)* compañero; RELIG. hermano.
broth·er·hood (:hŏŏd') s. hermandad *f*, fraternidad *f*; *(guild)* gremio.

broth·er-in-law (:ĭn-lŏ') s. [pl. **brothers-**] cuñado, hermano político.
broth·er·ly (:lē) adj. fraternal, fraterno.
brought (brŏt) cf. **bring**.
brow (brou) *(eyebrow)* ceja; *(forehead)* frente *f*.
brow·beat ('bēt') tr. **-beat, -en** intimidar.
brown (broun) I. s. marrón *m*, castaño II. adj. marrón; *(hair)* castaño; *(skin, sugar)* moreno III. tr. & intr. CUL. dorar(se).
brown·ie (brou'nē) s. bizcocho de chocolate.
brown·out (broun'out') s. apagón *m* parcial.
browse (brouz) intr. *(shop)* curiosear; *(book)* hojear un libro; *(to graze)* pacer.
bruise (brōōz) I. s. *(skin)* magulladura, contusión *f*; *(fruit)* daño II. tr. magullar, contusionar; *(fruit)* dañar; *(feelings)* herir —intr. magullarse, dañarse.
brunch (brŭnch) s. combinación de desayuno y almuerzo.
bru·net (brōō-nĕt') adj. & s. moreno ♦ **brunette** morena.
brunt (brŭnt) s. fuerza, impacto (de ataque, crítica) ♦ **to bear the b. of** llevar el peso de.
brush¹ (brŭsh) I. s. cepillo; *(paintbrush)* brocha; *(of an artist)* pincel *m*; *(brushing)* cepillado; *(encounter)* encuentro II. tr. cepillar; *(to sweep)* quitar, barrer *(off* de); *(to graze)* rozar al pasar ♦ **to b. off** o **aside** hacer caso omiso de • **to b. up** repasar, retocar • **to b. up on** refrescar los conocimientos de —intr. pasar rozando.
brush² s. maleza.
brush-off ('ŏf') s. FAM. despedida brusca.
brush·wood (:wŏŏd') s. maleza.
brusque o **brusk** (brŭsk) adj. brusco.
bru·tal (brōōt'l) adj. brutal, bestial.
bru·tal·i·ty (-tăl'ĭ-tē) s. brutalidad *f*.
bru·tal·ize (brōōt'l-īz') tr. brutalizar.
brute (brōōt) I. s. *(animal)* bestia; *(person)* bestia *mf*, bruto II. adj. *(instinctive)* bruto; *(cruel)* brutal.
bub·ble (bŭb'əl) I. s. burbuja; *(of soap)* pompa ♦ **b. gum** chicle de globo • **to blow bubbles** hacer pompas de jabón • **to burst someone's b.** desengañar a alguien II. intr. burbujear ♦ **to b. over** with rebosar de.
bub·bly (:lē) adj. **-i-** efervescente.
bu·bon·ic plague (bōō-bŏn'ĭk) s. peste bubónica.
buc·ca·neer (bŭk'ə-nîr') s. bucanero.
buck¹ (bŭk) I. s. ZOOL. macho; *(deer)* ciervo; FAM. *(youth)* joven despierto II. intr. *(horse)* botar, corcovear; *(to balk)* resistirse ♦ **to b. up** FAM. animarse —tr. *(to unseat)* derribar; *(to oppose)* oponerse.
buck² s. JER. dólar *m*.
buck·a·roo/er·oo (bŭk'ə-rōō') s. vaquero.
buck·et (bŭk'ĭt) s. cubo, balde *m* ♦ **to kick the b.** FAM. estirar la pata.
buck·le¹ (bŭk'əl) I. s. *(fastener)* hebilla II. tr. & intr. abrochar(se) ♦ **to b. down** to dedicarse con empeño a.
buck·le² I. tr. & intr. *(to bend)* combar(se) II. s. comba.
buck·shot (bŭk'shŏt') s. perdigón *m*, posta.
buck·skin (:skĭn') s. ante *m*.
buck·tooth (:tōōth') s. [pl. **-teeth**] diente *m* saliente.
buck·wheat (:hwēt') s. trigo sarraceno.
bud (bŭd) I. s. *(shoot)* brote *m*, yema; *(flower)* capullo ♦ **in the b.** en cierne(s) • **to nip in the b.** cortar de raíz II. intr. **-dd-** *(plant)* echar brotes o

capullos; *(flower)* brotar; *(to show promise)* estar en cierne.

bud·dy (bŭd'ē) s. FAM. amigo, compadre *m*.

budge (bŭj) tr. & intr. *(object)* mover(se) un poco; *(person)* (hacer) ceder.

budg·et (bŭj'ĭt) I. s. presupuesto II. tr. presupuestar.

budg·et·ar·y (:ĭ-tĕr'ē) adj. presupuestario.

buff[1] (bŭf) I. s. *(leather)* cuero, ante *m* ♦ **in the b.** en cueros II. adj. de color del ante III. tr. pulir.

buff[2] s. FAM. entusiasta *mf*, aficionado.

buf·fa·lo (bŭf'ə-lō') I. s. [pl. inv. *o* **es**] búfalo, bisonte *m* II. tr. JER. intimidar, confundir.

buff·er (bŭf'ər) s. *(shock absorber)* amortiguador *m*; *(intercessor)* intercesor *m*; *(for polishing)* pulidor *m* ♦ **b. state** estado tapón.

buf·fet[1] (bə-fā') s. *(sideboard)* aparador *m*; *(restaurant)* cantina, buffet *m*.

buf·fet[2] (bŭf'ĭt) I. s. bofetada II. tr. abofetear.

buf·foon (bə-fōōn') s. bufón *m*, payaso.

buf·foon·er·y (bə-fōō'nə-rē) s. bufonada, payasada.

bug (bŭg) I. s. insecto, bicho; FAM. *(germ)* microbio; *(defect)* defecto, falla (en un sistema); JER. *(enthusiast)* entusiasta *mf*; *(microphone)* micrófono oculto II. tr. **-gg-** JER. *(to pester)* fastidiar, importunar; *(a room, phone)* Instalar un micrófono oculto en.

bug·gy (bŭg'ē) s. *(horse-drawn)* calesa; *(baby carriage)* coche *m* de niño.

bug·house (bŭg'hous') s. JER. manicomio.

bu·gle (byōō'gəl) s. clarín *m*, corneta.

build (bĭld) I. tr. **built** construir, edificar; *(monuments)* erigir; *(fire)* preparar; *(to make)* hacer; *(to assemble)* armar ♦ **to b. up** *(theory)* elaborar; *(collection)* hacer, reunir; *(reputation)* crear, *(sales)* aumentar; *(health)* fortalecer —intr. ♦ **to b. up** *(to increase)* aumentar; *(to intensify)* intensificarse, ir en aumento II. s. talle *m*, figura.

build·er (bĭl'dər) s. constructor *m*, contratista *mf*.

build·ing (:dĭng) s. edificio, casa.

build·up (bĭld'ŭp') s. aumento; MIL. *(of troops)* concentración *f*; FAM. *(publicity)* publicidad *f* ♦ **arms b.** incremento bélico.

built-in (bĭlt'ĭn') adj. *(closet)* empotrado; *(as integral part)* que es parte integral.

built-up (:ŭp') adj. urbanizado.

bulb (bŭlb) s. BOT. bulbo; *(lamp)* bombilla.

bul·bous (bŭl'bəs) adj. protuberante.

bulge (bŭlj) I. s. protuberancia, bulto; *(in wall)* pandeo II. intr. & tr. hinchar(se), abultar.

bulg·ing (bŭl'jĭng) adj. *(swollen)* hinchado; *(protuberant)* saltón.

bulk (bŭlk) I. s. volumen *m*, tamaño; *(largest part)* grueso ♦ **in b.** *(loose)* a granel, suelto; *(in large amounts)* en grandes cantidades II. intr. ♦ **to b. large** ser importante.

bulk·head (:hĕd') s. MARIT. mamparo.

bulk·y (bŭl'kē) adj. **-i-** *(massive)* voluminoso; *(unwieldy)* pesado.

bull[1] (bōōl) I. s. toro; *(elephant, seal)* macho; FIN. alcista *mf*; JER. *(nonsense)* tontería ♦ **b. session** FAM. tertulia ♦ **to shoot the b.** JER. charlar, parlotear II. tr. ♦ **to b. one's way** abrirse paso III. adj. macho ♦ **b. market** mercado en alza ♦ **b. neck** cuello de toro.

bull[2] s. RELIG. bula.

bull·dog (bōōl'dôg') s. buldog *m*, dogo.

bull·doze (:dōz') tr. nivelar *o* excavar con una excavadora.

bull·doz·er (:dō'zər) s. excavadora.

bul·let (bōōl'ĭt) s. bala.

bul·le·tin (bōōl'ĭ-tn) s. *(periodical)* boletín *m*; *(report)* comunicado ♦ **b. board** tablero de anuncios.

bul·let-proof (bōōl'ĭt-prōōf') adj. a prueba de balas.

bull·fight (bōōl'fīt') s. corrida de toros.

bull·fight·er (:fī'tər) s. torero.

bull·frog (:frôg') s. rana toro.

bull·head·ed (:hĕd'ĭd) adj. testarudo, terco.

bull·horn (:hôrn') s. megáfono eléctrico.

bul·lion (bōōl'yən) s. oro *o* plata en lingotes.

bull·ish (bōōl'ĭsh) adj. FIN. en alza.

bul·lock (:ək) s. buey *m*.

bull·ring (:rĭng') s. plaza de toros.

bull's-eye (bōōlz'ī') s. *(target)* blanco; *(shot)* acierto ♦ **to hit the b.** dar en el blanco.

bull·whip (bōōl'hwĭp') s. látigo (de cuero).

bul·ly (bōōl'ē) I. s. matón *m*, abusador *m* II. tr. intimidar, amedrentar —intr. abusar.

bul·rush (bōōl'rŭsh') s. espadaña.

bul·wark (bōōl'wərk) s. baluarte *m*.

bum (bŭm) I. s. *(hobo)* vagabundo; *(loafer)* vago, holgazán *m*; G.B., FAM. *(buttocks)* trasero II. tr. & intr. **-mm-** *(to cadge)* gorronear, sablear II. s. JER. *(sore)* dolorido.

bum·ble (bŭm'bəl) intr. obrar con torpeza.

bum·ble·bee (bŭm'bəl-bē') s. abejorro.

bump (bŭmp) I. tr. *(to collide with)* topar, chocar contra; *(to knock against)* golpear contra; *(to displace)* desplazar; FAM. *(to oust)* quitar el puesto ♦ **to b. into** tropezarse con ♦ **to b. off** JER. matar, despachar —intr. chocar contra; *(to jolt)* moverse a sacudidas II. s. *(collision)* choque *m*, topetón *m*; *(swelling)* hinchazón *f*, chichón *m*; *(in a road)* bache *m*.

bump·er (bŭm'pər) s. parachoques *m*.

bump·kin (bŭmp'kĭn) s. patán *m*, palurdo.

bump·y (bŭm'pē) adj. **-i-** *(uneven)* desigual, accidentado; *(jolty)* agitado, sacudido.

bun (bŭn) s. CUL. bollo, panecillo; *(hair)* moño.

bunch (bŭnch) I. s. *(of grapes)* racimo; *(of flowers)* ramillete *m*; *(handful)* montón *m*, puñado; FAM. *(of people)* grupo II. tr. & intr. agrupar(se), juntar(se).

bun·dle (bŭn'dl) I. s. bulto, fardo; *(papers)* fajo, *(tied)* atado; JER. *(money)* montón *m* de dinero II. tr. *(to tie)* atar; *(to wrap)* envolver; *(to dress warmly)* arropar bien —intr. ♦ **to b. up** arroparse, abrigarse.

bun·gle (bŭng'gəl) I. tr. & intr. chapucear II. s. chapucería.

bun·ion (bŭn'yən) s. juanete *m*.

bunk[1] (bŭngk) I. s. *(bed)* litera II. intr. dormir en una litera.

bunk[2] s. JER. *(nonsense)* tontería, sandez *f*.

bun·ker (bŭng'kər) s. MARIT. pañol *m* del carbón; MIL. refugio subterráneo.

bun·ny (bŭn'ē) s. FAM. conejo, conejito.

bunt·ing (bŭn'tĭng) s. tela para banderas.

buoy (bōō'ē, boi) I. s. boya ♦ **life b.** salvavidas II. tr. MARIT. aboyar; *(to keep afloat)* mantener a flote; FIG. *(to hearten)* animar, alentar.

buoy·an·cy (boi'ən-sē) s. *(capacity)* flotabilidad *f*; *(cheerfulness)* optimismo.

buoy·ant (:ənt) adj. boyante; *(animated)* animado; *(cheerful)* optimista.

bur (bûr) s. erizo, parte espinosa.

bur·den (bûr′dn) I. s. carga ♦ **the b. of proof** la carga de la prueba II. tr. *(to load)* cargar; *(to oppress)* agobiar.

bu·reau (byŏŏr′ō) s. [pl. **s** *o* **-x**] *(dresser)* tocador *m*; POL. departamento; *(business)* agencia; G.B. *(desk)* escritorio.

bu·reauc·ra·cy (byŏŏ-rŏk′rə-sē) s. burocracia.

bu·reau·crat (byŏŏr′ə-krăt′) s. burócrata *mf*.

bur·geon (bûr′jən) intr. crecer, florecer.

burg·er (bûr′gər) s. FAM. hamburguesa.

burgh·er (bûr′gər) s. burgués *m*.

bur·glar (bûr′glər) s. ladrón *m* ♦ **b. alarm** alarma antirrobo.

bur·glar·ize (:glə-rīz′) tr. robar (casa, tienda).

bur·gla·ry (:rē) s. robo con allanamiento de morada.

bur·i·al (bĕr′ē-əl) s. entierro ♦ **b. ground** cementerio, camposanto.

bur·lap (bûr′lăp′) s. arpillera.

bur·lesque (bər-lĕsk′) I. s. *(parody)* parodia; *(vaudeville)* espectáculo de variedades II. tr. parodiar III. adj. burlesco.

bur·ly (bûr′lē) adj. -i- fuerte, robusto.

burn (bûrn) I. tr. -ed *o* -t quemar; *(a building)* incendiar; *(to expend)* gastar (dinero, energías) ♦ **to b. down** incendiar • **to b. into** grabar en • **to b. oneself out** JER. agotarse, gastarse (uno) • **to b. the candle at both ends** vivir una vida agitada • **to b. to a crisp** achicharrar • **to b. to the ground** reducir a cenizas • **to b. up** *(to consume)* consumir; FAM. *(to enrage)* enfurecer, indignar • **to get burned** FAM. estar embaucado —intr. quemarse, arder; *(building)* consumirse; *(light bulb)* estar encendido; *(with fever)* arder; *(with passion)* consumirse; *(food)* quemarse ♦ **to b. down** quemarse por completo • **to b. out** *(fire)* apagarse; *(fuse, bulb)* quemarse, fundirse • **to b. up** *(in flames)* quemarse *o* consumirse completamente; *(with anger)* enfurecerse, indignarse • **to b. up with** arder de II. s. *(injury)* quemadura; *(sunburn)* quemadura de sol.

burn·er (bûr′nor) s. quemador *m*, mechero.

burn·ing (:nǐng) adj. *(hot)* ardiente, abrasador; *(passionate)* ardiente; *(urgent)* urgente.

bur·nish (bûr′nǐsh) I. tr. pulir, bruñir II. s. brillo, lustre *m*.

bur·noose (bər-nōōs′) s. albornoz *m*.

burn·out (bûrn′out′) s. *(failure)* extinción *f*; *(exhaustion)* agotamiento.

burp (bûrp) I. s. eructo II. intr. eructar —tr. hacer eructar (a un niño).

burr (bûr) s. *(tool)* taladro; *(roughness)* rebaba; BOT. erizo, parte espinosa.

bur·row (bûr′ō) I. s. madriguera II. intr. *(to dig)* hacer una madriguera; *(to hide)* amadrigarse —tr. cavar, excavar.

bur·sar (bûr′sər) s. tesorero.

burst (bûrst) I. intr. -t *(to break open)* estallar, reventarse; *(to explode)* explotar; *(to be full)* rebosar (**with** de) ♦ **to b. in** *(to interrupt)* interrumpir • **to b. into** irrumpir en • **to b. into bloom** brotar • **to b. into flame(s)** estallar en llamas • **to b. open** abrirse violentamente • **to b. out** *(to exclaim)* exclamar; *(to emerge)* surgir; *(to burst forth)* brotar; *(crying, laughing)* echarse a —tr. *(to shatter)* reventar; *(to force open)* romper ♦ **to b. into** *(a room)* irrumpir en; *(tears, laughter)* desatarse en • **to b. with** rebosar de II. s. reventón *m*, explosión *f*; *(of laugh-*

ter) estallido; *(of gunfire)* ráfaga; *(of energy)* explosión; *(of anger)* arranque *m*; *(of applause)* salva.

bur·y (bĕr′ē) tr. enterrar; *(to inter, conceal)* sepultar ♦ **to b. oneself** sumergirse, sepultarse.

bus (bŭs) I. s. [pl. **es** *o* **-ses**] autobús *m*, ómnibus *m* II. tr. **-s-** *o* **-ss-** transportar en autobús.

bus·boy (bŭs′boi′) s. ayudante *m* de camarero.

bush (bŏŏsh) s. *(shrub)* arbusto; *(thicket)* maleza; *(land)* matorral *m*.

bushed (bŏŏsht) adj. FAM. agotado, hecho polvo.

bush·el (bŏŏsh′əl) s. medida de áridos (35,24 litros); FAM. *(great deal)* montón *m*.

bush·whack (bŏŏsh′hwăk′) intr. abrirse paso en la maleza —tr. tender una emboscada.

bush·y (:ē) adj. -i- *(land)* breñoso, lleno de arbustos; *(hair)* tupido, espeso.

bus·i·ly (bǐz′ə-lē) adv. diligentemente.

busi·ness (bǐz′nǐs) s. *(establishment)* comercio, negocio; *(firm)* firma, empresa; *(commerce)* negocios; *(matter, concern)* asunto ♦ **b. school** escuela de comercio • **that's none of your b.** eso no es cosa tuya • **to mean b.** no andar con juegos.

busi·ness·like (:līk′) adj. metódico, serio.

busi·ness·man (:măn′) s. [pl. **-women**] hombre *m* de negocios, comerciante *m*.

busi·ness·wom·an (:wŏŏm′ən) s. [pl. **-women**] mujer *f* de negocios, comerciante *f*.

bust¹ (bŭst) s. ARTE., ANAT. busto.

bust² (bŭst) FAM. I. tr. *(to break)* romper; *(to damage)* descomponer; *(to punch)* pegar; *(to arrest)* arrestar —intr. romperse, descomponerse II. s. *(flop)* chasco, fracaso; COM. quiebra; ECON. época de depresión económica; *(punch)* puñetazo; *(arrest)* arresto; *(raid)* redada, batida.

bus·tle (bŭs′əl) I. intr. apresurarse II. s. bullicio, animación *f*.

bus·y (bǐz′ē) I. adj. -i- *(person)* atareado, ocupado; *(place)* animado, concurrido; *(telephone)* ocupado ♦ **b. signal** señal de ocupado II. tr. & intr. mantener(se) ocupado.

bus·y·bod·y (:bŏd′ē) s. entremetido.

but (bŭt, bət) I. conj. *(on the other hand)* pero, mas; *(rather)* sino; *(nevertheless)* no obstante, sin embargo; *(except)* excepto ♦ **b. then** pero por otra parte • **cannot (help) b.** no poder menos que • **none b.** solamente II. adv. nada más que, solamente ♦ **all b.** casi • **to do nothing b.** no hacer más que III. prep. menos, excepto ♦ **b. for** a no ser por IV. s. pero.

bu·tane (byōō′tān′) s. butano.

butch·er (bŏŏch′ər) I. s. carnicero ♦ **b. shop** carnicería II. tr. *(animals)* matar; *(to murder)* asesinar; FAM. *(to botch)* chapucear.

butch·er·y (:ə-rē) s. *(carnage)* matanza; *(botch)* chapucería.

but·ler (bŭt′lər) s. mayordomo.

butt¹ (bŭt) I. tr. & intr. topar, dar un topetazo ♦ **to b. in(to)** FAM. entremeterse en II. s. topetazo.

butt² tr. *(to attach)* empalmar; *(to abut)* colindar —intr. estar empalmado.

butt³ s. *(object of ridicule)* hazmerreír *m*.

butt⁴ s. *(of a rifle)* culata; *(cigarette end)* colilla; JER. *(cigarette)* rubio, pitillo; FAM. *(buttocks)* trasero.

but·ter (bŭt′ər) I. s. mantequilla II. tr. untar con mantequilla ♦ **to b. up** adular, lisonjear.

but·ter·cup (:kŭp′) s. botón *m* de oro.

but·ter·fat (:făt') s. grasa o nata de la leche.
but·ter·fin·gers (:fĭng'gərz) s. FAM. persona torpe.
but·ter·fly (:flī') s. mariposa ✦ **to have butterflies in one's stomach** tener cosquillas en el estómago.
but·ter·milk (:mĭlk') s. suero de la leche.
but·ter·scotch (:skŏch') s. caramelo.
but·tock (bŭt'ək) s. nalga ✦ pl. trasero.
but·ton (bŭt'n) I. s. botón m; (switch) botón, pulsador m; (badge) insignia, distintivo ✦ **on the b.** FAM. correcto, exacto II. tr. & intr. abotonar(se), abrochar(se).
but·ton·hole (:hōl') I. s. ojal m II. tr. retener (a alguien y obligarlo a escuchar).
but·tress (bŭt'rĭs) I. s. ARQ. contrafuerte m; (support) apoyo, sostén m II. tr. reforzar, apoyar.
bux·om (bŭk'səm) adj. rollizo, frescachón.
buy (bī) I. tr. **bought** comprar, adquirir; FAM. (to bribe) sobornar; FAM. (to believe) creer, aceptar ✦ **to b. into** comprar cantidades importantes de acciones de (una empresa) • **to b. off** sobornar • **to b. out** COM. comprar la parte de • **to b. up** acaparar —intr. hacer compras II. s. (purchase) compra; FAM. (bargain) ganga ✦ **a good b.** ganga.
buy·er (bī'ər) s. comprador m.
buzz (bŭz) I. intr. (insect, motor) zumbar; (room) llenarse de charla; (buzzer) sonar; (to ring) tocar el timbre ✦ **to b. around** o **about** jetrearse • **b. off!** FAM. ¡lárgate! —tr. hacer zumbar; FAM. (to fly) volar muy cerca de; (with a buzzer) llamar con un timbre; FAM. (to telephone) telefonear, dar un telefonazo II. s. (drone) zumbido; (murmur) murmullo; FAM. (telephone call) telefonazo ✦ **b. saw** sierra circular.
buz·zard (bŭz'ərd) s. buitre m.
buzz·er (bŭz'ər) s. timbre m.
by (bī) I. prep. (agent, measure, route) por <made by hecho por> <by the dozen por docena> <by mail por correo>; (origin, time) de <by birth de nacimiento> <by night de noche>; (next to) junto a, cerca de <by the bed junto a la cama>; (according to) según, de acuerdo con <by the rules de acuerdo con las reglas>; (not later than) para <by noon para el mediodía>; (after) a <day by day día a día ✦ **by the by** de paso, a propósito • **by the way** de paso, entre paréntesis • **by this time** (hour) a esta hora; (point) a estas alturas II. adv. (nearby) cerca, al lado de; (aside) a un lado, aparte ✦ **by and by** (soon) pronto; (after a while) más tarde • **by and large** en términos generales • **by then** para entonces.
by-and-by (bī'ən-bī') s. ✦ **in the b.** en el futuro.
bye (bī) s. ✦ **by the b.** incidentalmente.
bye(-bye) (bī[-bī]) interj. FAM. ¡adiós!; ¡chau!
by·gone (bī'gôn') I. adj. pasado II. s. ✦ **to let bygones be bygones** olvidar lo pasado.
by·law (bī'lô') s. (of an organization) reglamento; (of a city) ordenanza municipal.
by-line (bī'līn') s. PERIOD. renglón m con el nombre del autor.
by-pass o **by·pass** (bī'păs') I. s. (road) carretera de circunvalación; ELEC. derivación f ✦ **coronary b.** desviación coronaria II. tr. evitar, pasar por alto.
by-prod·uct (bī'prŏd'əkt) s. INDUS. subproducto, derivado; (side effect) efecto secundario.
by·road (bī'rōd') s. carretera secundaria.

by·stand·er (bī'stăn'dər) s. espectador m, circunstante mf.
byte (bīt) s. byte m, octeto.
by·way (bī'wā') s. carretera secundaria.
by·word (bī'wûrd') s. (proverb) refrán m; (synonym) sinónimo.

C

c, C (sē) s. tercera letra del alfabeto inglés; MÚS. do.
cab (kăb) s. taxi m, (of vehicle) cabina.
ca·bal (kə-băl') s. (plot) cábala, intriga; (conspirators) camarilla.
cab·a·la (kăb'ə-lə, kə-bä'-) s. cábala.
cab·a·ret (kăb'ə-rā') s. cabaret m.
cab·bage (kăb'ĭj) s. col f, berza.
cab·by/bie (kăb'ē) s. FAM. taxista mf.
cab·driv·er (:drī'vər) s. taxista m.
cab·in (kăb'ĭn) s. (house) barraca, choza; (of ship) camarote m; (of plane) cabina ✦ **c. cruiser** yate de recreo.
cab·i·net (kăb'ə-nĭt) s. armario; POL. consejo o gabinete m de ministros.
cab·i·net·mak·er (:mā'kər) s. ebanista mf.
cab·i·net·work (:wûrk') s. ebanistería.
ca·ble (kā'bəl) I. s. cable m; (telegram) cablegrama m; TELEV. televisión f por cable ✦ **c. car** funicular II. tr. & intr. cablegrafiar.
ca·ble·gram (:grăm') s. cablegrama m.
ca·ble·vi·sion (:vĭzh'ən) s. televisión f por cable.
ca·boo·dle (kə-bōōd'l) s. FAM. ✦ **the whole c.** el montón entero.
ca·boose (kə-bōōs') s. furgón m de cola.
cab·stand (kăb'stănd') s. parada de taxis.
ca·ca·o (kə-kā'ō) s. cacao.
cache (kăsh) I. s. (place) escondrijo, (goods) reserva escondida II. tr. guardar en un escondrijo.
ca·chet (kă-shā') s. sello.
cack·le (kăk'əl) I. intr. (hen) cacarear; (to laugh) reírse estridentemente II. s. (of hens) cacareo; (laughter) risa estridente.
ca·coph·o·ny (kə-kŏf'ə-nē) s. cacofonía.
cac·tus (kăk'təs) s. [pl. es o -ti] cactus m, cacto.
cad (kăd) s. desvergonzado, sinvergüenza m.
ca·dav·er (kə-dăv'ər) s. cadáver m.
ca·dav·er·ous (:əs) adj. cadavérico.
cad·die (kăd'ē) I. s. caddy m II. intr. **-dying** (servir de) caddy.
cad·dy (kăd'ē) s. cajita para el té.
ca·dence/·cy (kād'ns) s. cadencia.
ca·det (kə-dět') s. cadete m.
cadge (kăj) tr. & intr. FAM. gorronear.
cad·mi·um (kăd'mē-əm) s. cadmio.
cad·re (kăd'rē) s. cuadro.
ca·du·ce·us (kə-dōō'sē-əs) s. [pl. -cei] caduceo.
Cae·sar·e·an section (sĭ-zâr'ē-ən) s. operación cesárea.
ca·fé/·fe (kă-fā') s. café m.
caf·e·te·ri·a (kăf'ĭ-tîr'ē-ə) s. cafetería.
caf·fein(e) (kăf'tăn') s. cafeína.
caf·tan (kăf'tăn') s. túnica.
cage (kāj) I. s. jaula II. tr. enjaular.
cag·(e)y (kā'jē) adj. **-i-** astuto.
ca·hoots (kə-hōōts') s.pl. FAM. ✦ **to be in c. with** estar en connivencia con.
cai·man (kā'mən) s. caimán m.

cairn (kârn) s. montón *m* de piedras.

cais·son (kā'sŏn') s. CONSTR. cajón hidráulico; MARIT. camello; MIL. cajón de municiones.

ca·jole (kə-jōl') tr. engatusar.

cake (kāk) **I.** s. pastel *m*; *(sponge)* bizcocho; *(pancake)* torta; *(of soap)* pastilla ♦ **to take the c.** FAM. ser el colmo **II.** tr. & intr. endurecer(se).

cal·a·bash (kāl'ə-bāsh') s. *(vine)* calabaza; *(tree)* güira; *(bowl)* totumo.

cal·a·boose (kāl'ə-bōōs') s. JER. calabozo.

cal·a·mine (kāl'ə-mīn') s. calamina.

ca·lam·i·ty (kə-lăm'ĭ-tē) s. calamidad *f.*

cal·ci·fy (kāl'sə-fī') tr. & intr. calcificar(se).

cal·ci·mine (kāl'sə-mīn') s. encalado.

cal·ci·um (kāl'sē-əm) s. calcio.

cal·cu·late (kāl'kyə-lāt') tr. calcular —intr. hacer cálculos; *(to guess)* suponer ♦ **to c. on** FAM. contar con.

cal·cu·lat·ed (:lā'tĭd) adj. deliberado, intencional.

cal·cu·lat·ing (:tĭng) adj. calculador.

cal·cu·la·tion ('-'shən) s. cálculo.

cal·cu·la·tor ('-'tər) s. calculadora.

cal·cu·lus (kāl'kyə-ləs) s. [pl. **es** o **-li**] cálculo.

cal·dron (kŏl'drən) s. caldera.

cal·en·dar (kāl'ən-dər) s. calendario; *(schedule)* agenda.

calf¹ (kāf) s. [pl. **-ves**] *(of cow)* becerro, ternero; *(of whale, elephant)* cría.

calf² s. [pl. **-ves**] ANAT. pantorrilla.

calf·skin ('skĭn') s. piel *f* de becerro.

cal·i·ber (kāl'ə-bər) s. calibre *m.*

cal·i·brate (:brāt') tr. calibrar.

cal·i·co (kāl'ĭ-kō') s. [pl. **(e)s**] calicó.

cal·i·per(s) (kāl'ə-pər[z]) s. calibrador *m* ♦ **vernier c.** calibrador micrométrico.

ca·liph (kā'lĭf) s. califa *m.*

ca·liph·ate (kā'lĭ-fāt') s. califato.

cal·is·then·ics (kāl'ĭs-thĕn'ĭks) s. calistenia.

ca·lix (kā'lĭks) s. [pl. **-ces**] cáliz *m.*

call (kŏl) **I.** tr. llamar; *(a meeting)* convocar; *(to telephone)* telefonear, llamar a; *(birds)* reclamar a; *(to consider)* considerar, juzgar <*I c. that fair* lo considero razonable>; *(to label)* calificar (de); *(a strike)* declarar; *(to predict)* predecir ♦ **to c. back** hacer volver; TEL. volver a llamar ▪ **to c. down** FAM. *(to scold)* regañar, reñir; *(to invoke)* invocar ▪ **to c. forth** hacer surgir ▪ **to c. in** *(to summon)* hacer venir, llamar; COM. *(a debt, loan)* pedir el reembolso de ▪ **to c. into play** hacer entrar en juego ▪ **to c. off** *(to cancel)* cancelar; *(to halt)* parar, suspender ▪ **to c. oneself** llamarse ▪ **to c. out** *(to mobilize)* convocar a la acción; *(to shout)* llamar ▪ **to c. together** convocar, reunir ▪ **to c. to account** pedir cuentas ▪ **to c. to mind** evocar, traer a la memoria ▪ **to c. to order** llamar al orden ▪ **to c. (one's) attention to** hacer notar o reparar en ▪ **to c. up** llamar a, telefonear; MIL. llamar a las armas —intr. *(to telephone)* hacer una llamada (telefónica), llamar; *(to visit)* hacer una visita; *(to yell)* llamar, gritar; ORNIT., ZOOL. reclamarse ♦ **to c. again** volver otra vez ▪ **to c. at** MARÍT. hacer escala en ▪ **to c. back** volver a llamar por teléfono ▪ **to c. for** requerir, necesitar ▪ **to c. on** o **upon** *(to visit)* visitar a, ir a ver a; *(to appeal)* recurrir a; *(God)* invocar ▪ **to c. out** exclamar, gritar **II.** s. llamada; ORNIT., ZOOL. reclamo, canto; *(of bugle)* toque *m*; *(short visit)* visita; *(summons, appeal)* llamamiento; COM. *(demand)* demanda, pedido *f* ♦

button botón de llamada ▪ **c. girl** FAM. prostituta ▪ **on c. de guardia** ▪ **port of c.** puerto de escala ▪ **to pay a c. on** hacer visita a ▪ **within c.** al alcance de la voz.

call·er (kŏ'lər) s. visita, visitante *mf.*

cal·lig·ra·pher (kə-lĭg'rə-fər) s. calígrafo.

cal·lig·ra·phy (:fē) s. caligrafía.

call·ing (kŏ'lĭng) s. vocación *f* ♦ **c. card** tarjeta de visita.

cal·li·o·pe (kə-lī'ə-pē) s. órgano de vapor.

cal·lous (kāl'əs) **I.** adj. insensible, duro de corazón **II.** intr. *(skin)* encallecerse; hacerse insensible.

cal·low (kāl'ō) adj. **-er, -est** *(person)* inmaturo.

call-up (kŏl'ŭp') s. MIL. llamada a filas.

cal·lus (kāl'əs) **I.** s. [pl. **es**] callo **II.** intr. encallecerse.

calm (käm) **I.** adj. sereno, tranquilo **II.** s. calma **III.** tr. & intr. aplacar(se), calmar(se).

calm·ness ('nĭs) s. tranquilidad *f.*

ca·lor·ic (kə-lôr'ĭk) adj. & s. calórico.

cal·o·rie (kāl'ə-rē) s. caloría.

ca·lum·ni·ate (kə-lŭm'nē-āt') tr. calumniar.

cal·um·ny (kāl'əm-nē) s. calumnia.

cal·va·ry (kāl'və-rē) s. calvario.

calve (kāv) intr. parir (la vaca).

calves (kāvz) cf. **calf¹,²**.

ca·lyx (kā'lĭks) s. [pl. **es** o **-ces**] cáliz *m.*

cam (kām) s. leva.

ca·ma·ra·der·ie (kä'mə-rä'də-rē) s. compañerismo, camaradería.

cam·ber (kām'bər) s. *(of road)* peralte *m*; AUTO. inclinación *f.*

cam·bi·um (kām'bē-əm) s. cambium *m.*

came (kām) cf. **come**.

cam·el (kām'əl) s. camello.

ca·mel·lia (kə-mēl'yə) s. camelia.

cam·e·o (kām'ē-ō') s. camafeo.

cam·er·a (kām'ər-ə) s. FOTOG. cámara, máquina; CINEM. cámara ♦ **in c.** DER. en sesión secreta.

cam·er·a·man (:măn') s. [pl. **-men**] cameraman *m.*

cam·i·sole (kām'ĭ-sōl') s. cubrecorsé *m.*

cam·ou·flage (kām'ə-fläzh') **I.** s. camuflaje *m* **II.** tr. & intr. camuflar.

camp (kāmp) **I.** s. campo; *(encampment)* campamento **II.** intr. & tr. acampar.

cam·paign (kām-pān') intr. & s. (hacer una) campaña.

cam·pa·ni·le (kām'pə-nē'lē) s. [pl. **s** o **-li**] campanil *m*, campanario.

camp·er (kām'pər) s. AUTO. campista *mf*; caravana.

camp·fire (kāmp'fīr') s. hoguera de campamento.

camp·ground (:ground') s. camping *m.*

cam·phor (kām'fər) s. alcanfor *m.*

camp·ing (kām'pĭng) s. camping *m.*

camp·site (:sīt') s. camping *m.*

cam·pus (kām'pəs) s. [pl. **es**] ciudad universitaria.

cam·shaft (kām'shăft') s. árbol *m* de levas.

can¹ (kăn, kən) aux. [pret. **could**] *(to be able to)* poder; *(to know how to)* saber <*he c. cook* él sabe cocinar>.

can² (kăn) **I.** s. *(tin)* lata; *(for trash)* tacho, cubo; JER. *(jail)* chirona; *(toilet)* retrete *m*; *(buttocks)* nalgas ♦ **c. opener** abrelatas **II.** tr. **-nn-** *(food)* enlatar; JER. *(to fire)* despedir ♦ **c. it!** JER. ¡a callar!, ¡basta!

ca·nal (kə-năl') s. canal *m.*

ca·nard (kə-närd′) s. bulo, patraña.
ca·nar·y (kə-nâr′ē) s. canario.
can·cel (kăn′səl) I. tr. anular, cancelar; *(to cross out)* tachar; *(a stamp)* matar; *(to offset)* contrarrestar II. s. cancelación f, anulación f.
can·cel·la·tion ('sə-lā′shən) s. cancelación f; *(of stamp)* matasellos m.
can·cer (kăn′sər) s. cáncer m.
can·cer·ous (:əs) adj. canceroso.
can·de·la·brum (kăn′dl-ä′brəm) s. [pl. **s** o **-ra**] candelabro.
can·des·cent (kăn-dĕs′ənt) adj. candente.
can·did (kăn′dĭd) adj. *(frank)* franco; *(not posed)* espontáneo.
can·di·da·cy (kăn′dĭ-də-sē) s. candidatura.
can·di·date (kăn′dĭ-dāt′) s. candidato.
can·died (kăn′dēd) adj. escarchado.
can·dle (kăn′dl) s. vela, bujía; *(in church)* cirio
    ♦ **not to hold a c.** to no llegar ni a la suela del zapato de.
can·dle·hold·er (:hōl′dər) s. candelero.
can·dle·light (:līt′) s. luz f de una vela.
can·dle·pow·er (:pou′ər) s. candela.
can·dle·stick (:stĭk′) s. candelero.
can·dor (kăn′dər) s. franqueza.
can·dy (kăn′dē) I. s. caramelo ♦ **c. store** confitería II. tr. & intr. escarchar(se).
cane (kān) I. s. *(stick)* bastón m; *(switch)* vara; *(plant)* caña, *(wicker)* mimbre m; *(sugar cane)* caña de azúcar II. tr. golpear con una vara.
cane·brake ('brāk′.) s. cañaveral m.
ca·nine (kā′nīn′) I. adj. canino II. s. *(animal)* animal canino; *(tooth)* diente canino.
can·is·ter (kăn′ĭ-stər) s. lata.
can·ker (sore) (kăng′kər) s. úlcera en la boca.
can·ker·ous (:əs) adj. ulceroso.
can·na·bis (kăn′ə-bĭs) s. cáñamo índico.
canned (kănd) adj. enlatado; FAM. *(taped)* grabado.
can·ner·y (kăn′ə-rē) s. fábrica de conservas.
can·ni·bal (kăn′ə-bəl) s. caníbal m, antropófago.
can·ni·bal·ism (:bə-lĭz′əm) s. canibalismo.
can·ni·bal·is·tic (:bə′lĭs′tĭk) adj. caníbal.
can·ni·bal·ize ('-lĭz′) tr. recuperar las piezas servibles de (avión, tanque).
can·ning (kăn′ĭng) s. conservería.
can·non (kăn′ən) [pl. inv. o **s**] cañón m.
can·non·ade ('ə-nād′) I. tr. & intr. cañonear II. s. cañoneo.
can·non·ball ('ən-bôl′) s. bala de cañón.
can·non·eer ('ə-nîr′) s. artillero.
can·not (kăn′ŏt′, kə-nŏt′) negación de **can't**.
can·ny (kăn′ē) adj. **-i-** astuto.
ca·noe (kə-nōō′) intr. **-oeing** & s. (ir en) canoa.
can·on (kăn′ən) s. *(church law)* canon m; *(priest)* canónigo.
ca·non·ic/i·cal (kə-nŏn′ĭk) adj. RELIG. canónico; FIG. ortodoxo.
can·on·ize (kăn′ə-nīz′) tr. canonizar.
can·o·py (kăn′ə-pē) s. dosel m; *(of leaves, stars)* bóveda.
cant[1] (kănt) I. s. inclinación f II. tr. inclinar.
cant[2] s. *(whine)* quejido, *(insincere talk)* hipocresía; *(jargon)* jerga.
can't (kănt) contr. de **cannot**.
can·ta·loup(e) (kăn′tl-ōp′) s. cantalupo.
can·tan·ker·ous (kăn-tăng′kər-əs) adj. FAM. malhumorado, pendenciero.
can·teen (kăn-tēn′) s. *(store, cafeteria)* cantina; *(flask)* cantimplora.

can·ter (kăn′tər) intr. & s. (ir a) medio galope.
can·ti·cle (kăn′tĭ-kəl) s. cántico.
can·ti·le·ver (kăn′tl-ē′vər) tr. & s. (construir con una) ménsula.
can·ton (kăn′tən) s. cantón m.
can·tor (kăn′tər) s. solista m (de una sinagoga).
can·vas (kăn′vəs) s. lona; *(painting)* lienzo; *(sails)* velamen m.
can·vass (kăn′vəs) I. tr. & intr. *(to solicit)* solicitar (votos); *(to poll)* hacer una encuesta (de); *(to examine)* examinar II. s. *(of votes)* solicitación f; *(survey)* encuesta, *(examination)* examen m.
can·yon (kăn′yən) s. cañón m.
cap (kăp) I. s. *(hat)* gorro, gorra; *(academic)* birrete m; *(cover)* tapa; *(limit)* tope m; ARM. cápsula, pistón m ♦ **c. gun** pistola de fulminante II. tr. **-pp-** *(to cover)* cubrir, poner una gorra; *(to complete)* terminar ♦ **to c. off** culminar.
ca·pa·bil·i·ty (kā′pə-bĭl′ĭ-tē) s. capacidad f.
ca·pa·ble (kā′pə-bəl) adj. capaz.
ca·pa·cious (kə-pā′shəs) adj. espacioso.
ca·pac·i·tor (kə-păs′ĭ-tər) s. condensador m.
ca·pac·i·ty (kə-păs′ĭ-tē) s. capacidad f; *(production)* rendimiento máximo ♦ **in the c.** of en calidad de ♦ **to fill to c.** llenar completamente.
ca·par·i·son (kə-păr′ĭ-sən) s. caparazón m.
cape[1] (kāp) s. GEOG. cabo.
cape[2] s. *(garment)* capa.
ca·per[1] (kā′pər) I. s. *(leap)* cabriola; *(prank)* travesura; JER. *(plot)* conspiración criminal f ♦ **to cut a c.** hacer cabriolas II. intr. brincar.
ca·per[2] s. CUL. alcaparra.
cap·il·lar·y (kăp′ə-lĕr′ē) s. & adj. (vaso) capilar.
cap·i·tal[1] (kăp′ĭ-tl) I. s. *(city)* capital f; *(assets, wealth)* capital m; IMPR. *(letter)* mayúscula f ♦ **c. assets** activo fijo ♦ **c. gain** ganancias sobre el capital ♦ **c. punishment** pena capital o de muerte II. adj. *(foremost)* capital; *(excellent)* excelente, *(involving death)* capital; IMPR. mayúscula.
cap·i·tal[2] s. ARQ. capitel m.
cap·i·tal·ism (:tĭz′əm) s. capitalismo.
cap·i·tal·ist (:tĭst) s. capitalista mf.
cap·i·tal·is·tic ('-ĭs′tĭk) adj. capitalista.
cap·i·tal·i·za·tion (:ĭ-zā′shən) s. ECON. capitalización f; IMPR. uso de letras mayúsculas.
cap·i·tal·ize ('-līz′) tr. FIN. capitalizar; IMPR. escribir con mayúscula —intr. ♦ **to c. on** aprovechar, sacar provecho de.
cap·i·tal·ly (:ē) adv. admirablemente.
cap·i·tol (kăp′ĭ-tl) s. capitolio.
ca·pit·u·late (kə-pĭch′ə-lāt′) intr. capitular.
ca·pon (kā′pŏn′) s. capón m.
ca·price (kə-prēs′) s. capricho, antojo.
ca·pri·cious (kə-prĭsh′əs) adj. caprichoso.
cap·size (kăp′sīz′) tr. & intr. (hacer) volcar.
cap·stan (kăp′stən) s. *(hoist)* cabrestante m; *(of tape recorder)* espiga.
cap·sule (kăp′səl, -sōōl) s. cápsula; *(summary)* resumen m breve.
cap·tain (kăp′tən) I. s. capitán m II. tr. capitanear.
cap·tion (kăp′shən) I. s. *(of picture)* pie m, leyenda; CINEM. subtítulo; *(heading)* encabezamiento II. tr. *(to title)* encabezar; *(a picture)* poner una leyenda.
cap·tious (kăp′shəs) adj. *(carping)* criticón; *(deceptive)* capcioso.
cap·ti·vate (kăp′tĭ-vāt′) tr. cautivar, fascinar.
cap·ti·va·tion ('-vā′shən) s. encanto.

cap·tive (kăp'tĭv) I. s. cautivo II. adj. *(confined)* cautivo; *(charmed)* cautivado.

cap·tiv·i·ty (-'ĭ-tē) s. cautividad *f*, cautiverio.

cap·tor (kăp'tər) s. capturador *m*.

cap·ture (:chər) I. tr. capturar; *(a prize)* ganar II. s. captura.

car (kär) s. AUTO. coche *m*, carro; F.C. coche *m*, vagón *m*; *(tramcar)* tranvía *m*.

ca·rafe (kə-răf') s. garrafa.

car·a·mel (kăr'ə-məl) s. *(candy)* caramelo; *(burnt sugar)* azúcar quemado.

car·a·pace (kăr'ə-pās') s. caparazón *m*.

car·at (kăr'ət) s. quilate *m*.

car·a·van (kăr'ə-văn') s. caravana.

car·a·vel (kăr'ə-věl') s. carabela.

car·a·way seed (kăr'ə-wā') s. carvi *m*.

car·bide (kär'bīd') s. carburo.

car·bine (kär'bīn') s. carabina.

car·bi·neer ('bə-nîr') s. carabinero.

car·bo·hy·drate (kär'bō-hī'drāt') s. carbohidrato.

car·bon (kär'bən) s. QUÍM. carbono; *(paper)* papel *m* carbón; *(copy)* copia ♦ **c. copy** copia al carbón • **c. dioxide** bióxido de carbono • **c. paper** papel carbón.

car·bon·ate (:bə-nāt') tr. carbonatar ♦ **carbonated water** gaseosa.

car·bon·if·er·ous (:nĭf'ər-əs) adj. carbonífero.

car·bun·cle (kär'bŭng'kəl) s. carbunco.

car·bu·re·tion (kär'bə-rā'shən) s. carburación *f*.

car·bu·re·tor ('-'tər) s. carburador *m*.

car·bu·ret·tor (kär'bə-rĕt'ər) G.B. var. de **carburetor**.

car·cass (kär'kəs) s. res muerta, cadáver *m*; FAM. *(body)* cuerpo.

car·cin·o·gen (kär-sĭn'ə-jən) s. agente cancerígeno.

car·cin·o·gen·ic (kär'sə-nə-jĕn'ĭk) adj. cancerígeno.

card¹ (kärd) I. s. *(playing)* naipe *m*, carta; *(greeting)* tarjeta; *(post)* (tarjeta) postal *f*; *(index)* ficha; *(ID)* carnet *m*; FAM. *(jokester)* bromista *mf* ♦ **c. catalog** fichero ♦ pl. naipes • **house of c.** castillo de naipes • **it's in the c.** está escrito • **to hold all the c.** tener todos los triunfos en la mano • **to play one's c.** maniobrar bien II. tr. FAM. comprobar la edad de.

card² TEJ. I. s. carda II. tr. cardar.

card·board ('bôrd') s. cartón *m*.

car·di·ac (kär'dē-ăk') adj. cardiaco, cardíaco.

car·di·gan (kär'dĭ-gən) s. chaqueta de punto.

car·di·nal (kär'dn-əl) I. adj. cardinal; *(red)* purpúreo II. s. ORNIT., RELIG. cardenal *m*; *(red)* púrpura.

car·di·o·gram (kär'dē-ə-grăm') s. cardiograma *m*.

car·di·ol·o·gy ('-ŏl'ə-jē) s. cardiología.

card·sharp (kärd'shärp') s. fullero, tahúr *m*.

care (kâr) I. s. *(worry)* inquietud *f*, preocupación *f*; *(grief)* pena; *(charge)* cargo <*in my c.* a mi cargo>; *(caution)* cuidado <*with c.* con cuidado>; *(custody)* custodia; *(close attention)* esmero ♦ **(in) c. of** para entregar a • **to take c. (not to)** tener cuidado (de que no) • **to take c. of** *(person)* cuidar de; *(thing)* (pre)ocuparse de; *(expenses)* correr con • **to take c. of itself** resolverse por sí mismo • **under (someone's) c.** a cargo de (alguien) II. intr. *(to be concerned)* preocuparse; *(to mind)* importar <*I don't c.* no me importa> ♦ **I couldn't c. less** FAM. me importa un pito • **to c. for** *(to look after)* cuidar;

(to love, want) querer • **to c. to** tener ganas de, querer.

ca·reen (kə-rēn') intr. dar bandazos —tr. inclinar (un bote).

ca·reer (kə-rîr') I. s. carrera, profesión *f*; *(course)* curso (de la vida) II. intr. precipitarse.

care·free (kâr'frē') adj. despreocupado.

care·ful (:fəl) adj. *(cautious)* cauteloso, prudente; *(thorough)* cuidadoso ♦ **to be c.** tener cuidado.

care·less (:lĭs) adj. *(negligent)* descuidado; *(unconcerned)* indiferente; *(offhand)* espontáneo.

ca·ress (kə-rĕs') I. s. caricia II. tr. acariciar.

care·tak·er (kâr'tā'kər) s. guardián *m*; *(of a residence)* portero.

care·worn (:wôrn') adj. agobiado.

car·fare (kär'fâr') s. precio de trayecto.

car·go (kär'gō) s. [pl. **(e)s**] carga, cargamento.

car·i·ca·ture (kär'ĭ-kə-chŏor') I. s. caricatura II. tr. caricaturizar.

car·il·lon (kăr'ə-lŏn') s. carillón *m*.

car·mine (kär'mĭn) s. & adj. carmín *m*.

car·nage (kär'nĭj) s. carnicería, matanza.

car·nal (kär'nəl) adj. carnal.

car·na·tion (kär-nā'shən) s. clavel *m*.

car·ni·val (kär'nə-vəl) s. *(season)* carnaval *m*; *(fair)* feria, parque *m* de atracciones.

car·ni·vore (kär'nə-vôr') s. carnívoro.

car·niv·o·rous (-nĭv'ər-əs) adj. carnívoro.

car·ob bean (kär'əb) s. algarroba.

car·ol (kär'əl) I. s. villancico II. tr. & intr. cantar (villancicos).

car·om (kär'əm) s. & intr. (hacer) carambola.

ca·rous·al (kə-rou'zəl) s. jarana, juerga.

ca·rouse (kə-rouz') intr. andar de jarana.

ca·rou·sel (kär'ə-sĕl') s. carrusel *m*, tiovivo.

carp¹ (kärp) intr. quejarse ♦ **to c. at** criticar.

carp² s. ICT. carpa.

car·pen·ter (kär'pən-tər) s. carpintero.

car·pen·try (:trē) s. carpintería.

car·pet (kär'pĭt) I. s. alfombra ♦ **to be on the c.** estar recibiendo una regañina II. tr. alfombrar.

car·pet·bag (:băg') s. maleta hecha de alfombra.

carp·ing (kär'pĭng) adj. criticón.

car·port (kär'pôrt') s. cobertizo para automóviles.

car·rel (kär'əl) s. cubículo de estudio.

car·riage (kär'ĭj) s. carruaje *m*, coche *m*; *(posture)* porte *m*; MEC. carro; COM. transporte *m*; G.B., F.C. vagón *m* ♦ **baby c.** cochecito de niños.

car·ri·er (kär'ē-ər) s. portador *m*, transportador *m*; COM. transportista *mf* ♦ **c. pigeon** paloma mensajera.

car·ri·on (kär'ē-ən) s. carroña.

car·rot (kär'ət) s. zanahoria.

car·ry (kär'ē) I. tr. llevar; *(a disease)* transmitir; *(merchandise)* tener surtido de; *(a penalty)* llevar aparejado, acarrear; *(an election)* ganar; *(a motion)* aprobar; *(to extend)* prolongar, extender; *(to impel)* mover, impulsar; *(to contain)* contener; *(to print)* publicar; *(to broadcast)* transmitir; MAT. llevarse ♦ **to be carried away (by)** estar entusiasmado (con) • **to c. along** arrastrar • **to c. forward** TEN. llevar, transportar a (columna, cuenta) • **to c. off** *(prize)* llevarse; *(plan)* realizar, llevar a cabo • **to c. on** *(conversation)* mantener, sostener; *(business)* dirigir, asumir el manejo • **to c. out** realizar, llevar a cabo • **to c. over** TEN. pasar a otra columna *o* página • **to c. something too far** llevar algo al exceso • **to c. through** *(to complete)* completar, llevar a cabo; *(to sustain)* sostener • **to c. weight** ser de peso *o* influencia —intr. *(motion, proposal)* ganar, aprobarse; *(to extend)* llegar, extenderse; *(sound)* oírse; *(voice)* proyectarse ♦ **c. on!** ¡siga!, ¡continúe! • **to c. on** *(to continue)* seguir, continuar; *(to misbehave)* portarse mal • **to c. over** conservarse (del pasado) **II.** s. *(portage)* transporte *m*; *(range)* alcance *m*.

car·ry·all (:ôl′) s. maletín *m*.

car·ry·o·ver (:ō′vər) s. remanente *m*.

car·sick (kär′sĭk′) adj. mareado.

cart (kärt) **I.** s. carro; *(handcart)* carretilla **II.** tr. acarrear; *(to lug)* arrastrar ♦ **to c. away** *o* **off** llevar.

cart·age (kär′tĭj) s. acarreo, porte *m*.

carte blanche (kärt blänch′) s. carta blanca.

car·tel (kär-těl′) s. cártel *m*.

car·ti·lage (kär′tl-ĭj) s. cartílago.

cart·load (kärt′lōd′) s. carretada.

car·tog·ra·pher (kär-tŏg′rə-fər) s. cartógrafo.

car·tog·ra·phy (:fē) s. cartografía.

car·ton (kär′tn) s. caja de cartón.

car·toon (kär-tōōn′) s. *(political)* caricatura; *(comic)* tira, historieta; *(film)* dibujos animados.

car·toon·ist (·tōō′nĭst) s. caricaturista *mf*.

car·tridge (kär′trĭj) s. cartucho; *(phonograph pickup)* fonocaptor *m*; *(cassette)* casete *m*; *(ink refill)* repuesto ♦ **c. belt** cartuchera.

cart·wheel (kärt′hwēl′) s. voltereta lateral.

cart·wright (:rīt′) s. carretero.

carve (kärv) tr. CUL. trinchar; ARTE. *(to sculpt)* tallar, cincelar; *(to engrave)* grabar ♦ **to c. out** labrar —intr. trinchar carne.

carv·ing (kär′vĭng) s. talla, escultura.

cas·cade (kă-skād′) **I.** s. cascada; FIG. chorro, torrente *m* **II.** intr. caer en forma de cascada.

case[1] (kās) **I.** s. *(instance)* caso; *(example)* ejemplo, *(matter)* cuestión *f*; *(a c. of honor)* una cuestión de honor>; *(argument)* argumento; MED., GRAM. GEOL. DER. causa, pleito ♦ **a c. in point** un caso pertinente • **c. history** hoja *o* historia clínica • **in any c.** en todo caso • **in no c.** de ningún modo • **in that c.** en tal caso • **it is not a c. of** no se trata de • **that being the c.** si ése es el caso • **to bring a c. against** poner un pleito a • **to make one's c.** probar la tesis de uno • **to put o state one's c.** presentar unos los argumentos • **to rest one's c.** terminar uno el alegato **II.** tr. JER. espiar, planificar.

case[2] **I.** s. *(box)* caja; *(outer covering)* estuche *m*; *(slipcover)* funda; ARQ. *(frame)* bastidor *m*, marco **II.** tr. empacar, embalar.

case·ment (′mənt) s. *(frame)* marco de ventana; *(window)* ventana batiente.

case·work (:wûrk′) s. estudio de los antecedentes personales *o* familiares.

cash (kăsh) **I.** s. efectivo ♦ **c. register** caja registradora • **to pay (in)** cash pagar al contado **II.** tr. hacer efectivo, cobrar ♦ **to c. in** convertir en efectivo • **to c. in on** sacar partido de.

cash·book (′bŏŏk′) s. libro de caja.

cash·box (:bŏks′) s. caja.

cash·ew (kăsh′ōō) s. anacardo.

cash·ier (kă-shîr′) s. cajero ♦ **c.'s check** cheque de caja.

cash·mere (kăzh′mîr′) s. cachemira.

cas·ing (kā′sĭng) s. cubierta, envoltura.

ca·si·no (kə-sē′nō) s. casino.

cask (kăsk) s. barril *m*, tonel *m*.

cas·ket (kăs′kĭt) s. ataúd *m*; *(box)* estuche *m*.

cas·sa·va (kə-sä′və) s. mandioca; *(flour, bread)* cazabe *m*.

cas·se·role (kăs′ə-rōl′) s. cazuela, cacerola.

cas·sette (kə-sět′) s. *(film)* cartucho; *(tape)* casete *mf*.

cas·sock (kăs′ək) s. sotana.

cast (kăst) **I.** tr. **cast** *(to hurl)* tirar, arrojar; *(anchor)* echar; *(vote)* echar, depositar; *(glance)* volver, dirigir; *(light, shadow)* proyectar; *(dice)* tirar; CINEM. *(roles)* repartir; *(actor)* asignar una parte a; METAL. *(to mold)* moldear ♦ **to c. aside** *o* **away** desechar, descartar • **to c. doubt (up)on** poner en duda • **to c. down** *(eyes)* bajar; *(spirits)* desanimar • **to c. light on** esclarecer • **to c. off** desechar • **to c. out** echar fuera, arrojar —intr. ♦ **to c. about (for)** buscar • **to c. off** MARÍT. desamarrar; COST. terminar una vuelta **II.** s. tirada, lanzamiento; *(of dice)* tirada; *(of color)* tinte *m*; *(appearance)* apariencia; *(tendency)* tendencia; METAL. molde *f*, forma; MED. enyesadura; CINEM., TEAT. reparto ♦ **c. iron** hierro fundido.

cas·ta·nets (kăs′tə-nĕts′) s.pl. castañuelas.

cast·a·way (kăst′ə-wā′) adj. & s. náufrago.

caste (kăst) s. casta.

cast·er (kăs′tər) s. *(wheel)* ruedecilla; *(stand)* convoy, vinagrera.

cas·ti·gate (kăs′tĭ-gāt′) tr. castigar, reprobar.

cast·ing (kăs′tĭng) s. METAL. pieza fundida; TEAT. reparto.

cast-i·ron (kăst′ī′ərn) adj. de hierro fundido; *(tough)* férreo.

cas·tle (kăs′əl) **I.** s. castillo; *(in chess)* torre *f*, roque *m* **II.** tr. & intr. enrocar (al rey).

cast-off (kăst′ôf′) adj. desechado.

cas·tor oil (kăs′tər) s. aceite *m* de ricino.

cas·trate (kăs′trāt′) tr. castrar, capar.

cas·tra·tion (kă-strā′shən) s. castración *f*.

ca·su·al (kăzh′ōō-əl) adj. *(accidental)* casual; *(occasional)* que ocurre de vez en cuando; *(indifferent)* despreocupado; *(informal)* informal; *(superficial)* superficial.

ca·su·al·ly (:ē) adv. *(by chance)* casualmente; *(by the by)* de paso; *(informally)* informalmente.

ca·su·al·ty (:tē) s. *(accident)* accidente *m*; *(victim)* víctima; MIL. baja.

ca·su·ist·ry (kăzh′ōō-ĭ-strē) s. casuística.

cat (kăt) s. gato; JER. *(guy)* tipo ♦ **to let the c. out of the bag** revelar un secreto.

ca·tab·o·lism (kə-tăb′ə-lĭz′əm) s. catabolismo.

cat·a·combs (kăt′ə-kōmz′) s.pl. catacumbas.

cat·a·log(ue) (kăt′l-ôg′) **I.** s. catálogo **II.** tr. catalogar —intr. hacer un catálogo.

cat·a·lyst (kăt′l-ĭst) s. catalizador *m*.

cat·a·lyt·ic (′-ĭt′ĭk) adj. catalítico.

cat·a·lyze (′-īz′) tr. catalizar.

cat·a·pult (kăt′ə-pŭlt′) **I.** s. catapulta **II.** tr. catapultar.

cat·a·ract (kăt′ə-răkt′) s. catarata.

ca·tarrh (kə-tär′) s. catarro.

ca·tas·tro·phe (kə-tăs′trə-fē) s. catástrofe *f*.

cat·a·stroph·ic (kăt′ə-strŏf′ĭk) adj. catastrófico.

cat·a·ton·ic (kăt′ə-tŏn′ĭk) adj. catatónico.

cat·call (kăt′kôl′) s. silbido, silbatina.

catch (kăch, kĕch) **I.** tr. **caught** *(with the hands)* coger, agarrar; *(to capture)* prender, capturar; *(animals)* atrapar, cazar; *(fish)* pescar; *(bus, train)* alcanzar, tomar; *(to snag, hook)* engan-

charse *(on en)*; *(to pinch)* agarrarse *(in con)*; *(an illness)* coger, contraer; *(to surprise)* coger desprevenido, sorprender; *(to understand)* entender, captar; FAM. *(to take in)* (ir a) ver (película, espectáculo) ♦ **to c. hold of** agarrarse a, asirse a • **c. it** FAM. ganarse una paliza *o* reprimenda • **to c. oneself** *(to check oneself)* contenerse; *(to realize)* darse cuenta • **to c. up on** ponerse al corriente en cuanto a • **to c. up with** alcanzar —intr. *(to become fastened, hooked)* engancharse; *(to snag)* enredarse; *(to hold)* agarrar, engancharse; *(to catch fire)* prender fuego, encenderse ♦ **to c. on** *(to understand)* comprender; *(to become aware)* caer en la cuenta; *(a fad)* hacerse *o* volverse muy popular • **to c. up** ponerse al día *o* al corriente II. s. *(act)* cogida; *(lock)* cerradura; *(in hunting)* presa; *(in fishing)* pesca; *(capture)* captura; FAM. *(hitch)* truco, trampa; *(good match)* buen partido.
catch·er (kăch'ər) s. DEP. receptor *m.*
catch·ing (:ĭng) adj. contagioso.
catch·word (:wûrd') s. lema *m*, slogan *m.*
catch·y (:ē) adj. -i- *(easy to remember)* pegadizo; *(tricky)* capcioso.
cat·e·chism (kăt'ĭ-kĭz'əm) s. catecismo.
cat·e·chist (:kĭst) s. catequista *mf.*
cat·e·chize (:kīz') tr. catequizar.
cat·e·gor·ic/i·cal (kăt'ĭ-gôr'ĭk) adj. categórico.
cat·e·go·rize (:gə-rīz') tr. clasificar.
cat·e·go·ry (:gôr'ē) s. categoría.
ca·ter (kā'tər) intr. abastecer de comida *o* servicios ♦ **to c. to** intentar satisfacer los deseos de.
cat·er-cor·ner(ed) (kăt'ər-kôr'nər[d]) adj. & adv. *(en)* diagonal.
ca·ter·er (kā'tər-ər) s. encargado de banquetes.
ca·ter·ing (:ĭng) s. servicio de banquetes.
cat·er·pil·lar (kăt'ər-pĭl'ər) s. oruga.
cat·er·waul (kăt'ər-wôl') intr. *(to meow)* maullar; *(to screech)* chillar.
cat·fish (kăt'fĭsh') s. [pl. inv. *o* es] siluro, bagre *m.*
cat·gut (:gŭt') s. cuerda de tripa.
ca·thar·sis (kə-thär'sĭs) s. [pl. **-ses**] catarsis *f.*
ca·'ne·dral (kə-thē'drəl) s. catedral *f.*
cath·e·ter (kăth'ĭ-tər) s. catéter *m.*
cath·ode (kăth'ōd') s. cátodo ♦ **c. ray** rayo catódico.
cath·o·lic (kăth'ə-lĭk) I. adj. general, universal ♦ **C.** católico II. s. ♦ **C.** católico.
cat·kin (kăt'kĭn') s. amento.
cat·nap (kăt'năp') s. & intr. **-pp-** (echar una) siesta corta.
cat·nip (:nĭp') s. nébeda.
cat-o'-nine-tails (' ə-nīn'tālz) s. látigo de nueve colas.
cat·sup (kăt'səp, kăch'əp) var. de **ketchup.**
cat·tail (kăt'tāl') s. anea, espadaña.
cat·tle (kăt'l) s. ganado vacuno.
cat·tle·man (:măn') s. [pl. **-men**] ganadero.
cat·ty (kăt'ē) adj. -i- malicioso.
cat·walk (:wôk') s. pasadizo, pasarela.
cau·cus (kô'kəs) I. s. [pl. **es** *o* **-ses**] reunión *f* electoral II. intr. celebrar reunión electoral.
caught (kôt) cf. **catch.**
cau·li·flow·er (kô'lĭ-flou'ər) s. coliflor *f.*
caulk (kôk) tr. calafatear.
cau·sa·tion (kô-zā'shən) s. causalidad *f.*
caus·a·tive (kô'zə-tĭv) adj. causativo.
cause (kôz) I. s. causa; *(reason)* motivo, razón *f* II. tr. causar, provocar.
cause·way (:wā') s. carretera elevada.
caus·tic (kô'stĭk) adj. & s. cáustico.

cau·ter·ize (kô'tə-rīz') tr. cauterizar.
cau·tion (kô'shən) I. s. cautela, precaución *f*; *(warning)* advertencia II. tr. advertir, amonestar.
cau·tion·ar·y (kô'shə-nĕr'ē) adj. *(preventive)* preventivo; *(exemplary)* aleccionador.
cau·tious (kô'shəs) adj. cauteloso, precavido.
cav·al·cade (kăv'əl-kād') s. cabalgata.
cav·a·lier (kăv'ə-lîr') I. s. caballero II. adj. arrogante.
cav·al·ry (kăv'əl-rē) s. caballería.
cav·al·ry·man (:mən) s. [pl. **-men**] soldado de caballería.
cave (kāv) I. s. cueva ♦ **c. dweller** *o* **man** cavernícola, troglodita II. intr. ♦ **to c. in** *(to collapse)* derrumbarse; *(to yield)* ceder.
cave-in ('ĭn') s. hundimiento, socavón *m.*
cav·ern (kăv'ərn) s. caverna.
cav·ern·ous (:ər-nəs) adj. cavernoso.
cav·i·ty (kăv'ĭ-tē) s. cavidad *f*; ODONT. caries *f.*
ca·vort (kə-vôrt') intr. cabriolar, juguetear.
caw (kô) I. s. graznido II. intr. graznar.
cay (kē, kā) s. cayo.
cay·enne pepper (kī-ĕn') s. pimienta del ají.
cease (sēs) I. tr. *(to stop)* dejar de; *(to discontinue)* suspender ♦ **c. fire!** MIL. ¡alto el fuego! —intr. cesar II. s. cese *m* ♦ **without c.** incesantemente.
cease-fire ('fīr') s. suspensión *f* de fuego.
cease·less (:lĭs) adj. incesante, continuo.
ce·dar (sē'dər) s. cedro.
cede (sēd) tr. ceder.
ceil·ing (sē'lĭng) s. cielo raso, techo; AER. techo; *(limit)* tope *m.*
cel·e·brant (sĕl'ə-brənt) s. celebrante *mf.*
cel·e·brate (:brāt') I. tr. celebrar; *(an occasion)* festejar, conmemorar —intr. festejarse.
cel·e·brat·ed (:brā'tĭd) adj. célebre, famoso.
cel·e·bra·tion ('-'shən) s. celebración *f.*
ce·leb·ri·ty (sə-lĕb'rĭ-tē) s. celebridad *f.*
cel·er·y (sĕl'ə-rē) s. apio.
ce·les·tial (sə-lĕs'chəl) adj. *(of the sky)* celeste; *(divine)* celestial.
cel·i·ba·cy (sĕl'ə-bə-sē) s. celibato.
cel·i·bate (:bĭt) adj. & s. célibe *mf.*
cell (sĕl) s. *(room)* celda; BIOL., ELEC., POL. célula.
cel·lar (sĕl'ər) s. sótano; *(of wines)* bodega.
cel·lo (chĕl'ō) s. violoncelo.
cel·lo·phane (sĕl'ə-fān') s. celofán *m.*
cel·lu·lar (sĕl'yə-lər) adj. celular.
cel·lu·loid (:loid') s. celuloide *m.*
cel·lu·lose (:lōs') s. celulosa.
ce·ment (sĭ-mĕnt') I. s. cemento; *(glue)* pegamento ♦ **c. mixer** hormigonera II. tr. unir con cemento; *(to glue)* pegar; FIG. *(to strengthen)* cimentar.
cem·e·ter·y (sĕm'ĭ-tĕr'ē) s. cementerio.
cen·ser (sĕn'sər) s. incensario.
cen·sor (sĕn'sər) I. s. censor *m* II. tr. censurar.
cen·so·ri·ous (sĕn-sôr'ē-əs) adj. censurador.
cen·sor·ship (sĕn'sər-shĭp') s. censura.
cen·sure (sĕn'shər) I. s. censura II. tr. censurar.
cen·sus (sĕn'səs) s. censo.
cent (sĕnt) s. centavo, céntimo.
cen·taur (sĕn'tôr') s. centauro.
cen·ten·ni·al (sĕn-tĕn'ē-əl) adj. & s. centenario.
cen·ter (sĕn'tər) I. s. centro II. tr. centrar; *(to concentrate)* concentrar —intr. concentrarse ♦ **to c. on** centrarse en.

cen·ter·piece (:pēs') s. centro de mesa; FIG. foco principal.

cen·ti·grade (sĕn'tĭ-grād') adj. centígrado.

cen·ti·gram ('grăm') s. centigramo.

cen·ti·li·ter (:lē'tər) s. centilitro.

cen·ti·me·ter (:mē'tər) s. centímetro.

cen·ti·pede (:pēd') s. ciempiés m.

cen·tral (sĕn'trəl) adj. central.

cen·tral·ize (:trə-līz') tr. & intr. centralizar(se).

cen·tre (sĕn'tər) G.B. var. de **center**.

cen·tric (:trĭk) adj. céntrico, central.

cen·trif·u·gal (:trĭf'yə-gəl) adj. centrífugo.

cen·tri·fuge ('trə-fyōoj') s. centrifugadora.

cen·trip·e·tal (:trĭp'ĭ-tl) adj. centrípeto.

cen·trist ('trĭst) s. centrista mf.

cen·tu·ry (sĕn'chə-rē) s. siglo ♦ **c. plant** maguey.

ce·phal·ic (sə-făl'ĭk) adj. cefálico.

ce·ram·ic (sə-răm'ĭk) s. (clay) arcilla, barro; (porcelain) porcelana ♦ **ceramics** sg. cerámica.

ce·re·al (sĭr'ē-əl) s. cereal m.

cer·e·bral (sĕr'ə-brəl, sə-rē'-) adj. cerebral.

cer·e·brum (:brəm) s. [pl. **s** o **-ra**] cerebro.

cer·e·mo·ni·al (sĕr'ə-mō'nē-əl) adj. & s. ceremonial m.

cer·e·mo·ni·ous (:əs) adj. ceremonioso.

cer·e·mo·ny (sĕr'ə-mō'nē) s. ceremonia.

cer·tain (sûr'tn) adj. (definite) cierto; (sure) seguro; (some) algunos, ciertos ♦ **for a.** por cierto • **to make c.** asegurarse.

cer·tain·ly (:lē) adv. (surely) cierto; (of course) por supuesto; (without fail) seguro.

cer·tain·ty (:tē) s. certeza; (fact) cosa segura.

cer·ti·fi·a·ble (sûr'tə-fī'ə-bəl) adj. certificable.

cer·tif·i·cate (sər-tĭf'ĭ-kĭt) s. certificado, partida.

cer·ti·fi·ca·tion (sûr'tə-fĭ-kā'shən) s. certificación f; (document) certificado.

cer·ti·fied ('-fīd') adj. certificado ♦ **c. public accountant** contador público titulado.

cer·ti·fy (sûr'tə-fī') tr. & intr. certificar.

cer·ti·tude (:tōod') s. certidumbre f, certeza.

cer·vix (sûr'vĭks) s. [pl. **es** o **-ces**] (neck) cerviz f; (of the uterus) cuello del útero.

ce·si·um (sē'zē-əm) s. cesio.

ces·sa·tion (sĕ-sā'shən) s. cesación f, cese m.

ces·sion (sĕsh'ən) s. cesión f.

cess·pool (sĕs'pōol') s. pozo negro; FIG. cloaca, sentina.

ce·ta·ce·an (sĭ-tā'shən) adj. & s. cetáceo.

chafe (chāf) tr. (to rub) rozar; (to annoy) irritar; (to warm) frotar —intr. rozarse ♦ **to c.** at enfadarse por.

chaff (chăf) I. s. AGR. ahechaduras; (trifle) paja; (banter) chanza II. tr. zumbar, chasquear.

cha·grin (shə-grĭn') I. s. desilusión f, desazón f II. tr. desilusionar.

chain (chān) I. s. cadena ♦ **c. gang** cadena de presidiarios • **c. mail** cota de mallas • **c. reaction** reacción en cadena • **c. saw** sierra de cadena • **c. store** sucursal de una cadena de tiendas II. tr. encadenar.

chain-smoke ('smōk') intr. & tr. fumar un cigarrillo tras otro.

chair (châr) I. s. silla; (chairman) presidente m; EDUC. cátedra ♦ **c. lift** telesilla II. tr. presidir.

chair·man ('mən) s. [pl. **-men**] presidente m.

chair·man·ship (:mən-shĭp') s. presidencia.

chair·per·son (:pûr'sən) s. presidente m, presidenta.

chair·wom·an (:wŏm'ən) s. [pl. **-women**] presidénta.

chal·ced·o·ny (kăl-sĕd'n-ē) s. calcedonia.

cha·let (shă-lā') s. chalet m.

chal·ice (chăl'ĭs) s. cáliz m.

chalk (chôk) I. s. MIN. creta; (marker) tiza II. tr. marcar, escribir (con tiza) ♦ **to c. up** apuntarse (tanto, victoria).

chalk·board ('bôrd') s. pizarrón m, pizarra.

chal·lenge (chăl'ənj) I. s. desafío, reto; MIL. quién vive m; DER. recusación f II. tr. desafiar, retar; (to contest) disputar, MIL. dar el quién vive; DER. recusar.

chal·leng·er ('ən-jər) s. desafiador m, retador m.

chal·leng·ing (:jĭng) adj. arduo, difícil.

cham·ber (chām'bər) s. cámara ♦ **c. pot** orinal ♦ pl. despacho (de un juez).

cham·ber·lain (:lən) s. chambelán m.

cham·ber·maid (:mād') s. camarera, criada.

cha·me·le·on (kə-mēl'yən) s. camaleón m.

cham·ois (shăm'ē) s.inv. gamuza.

cham·o·mile (kăm'ə-mīl') s. manzanilla.

champ (chămp) s. FAM. campeón m.

cham·pagne (shăm-pān') s. champaña m.

cham·pi·on (chăm'pē-ən) I. s. campeón m II. tr. abogar por.

cham·pi·on·ship (:shĭp') s. campeonato.

chance (chăns) I. s. casualidad f; (luck) suerte f; (opportunity) oportunidad f <give me a c. to go déme la oportunidad de ir>; (possibility) posibilidad f; (risk) riesgo <to take a c. correr un riesgo> ♦ **by any c.** por casualidad • **to stand a c.** tener una posibilidad II. intr. suceder, acaecer —tr. arriesgar ♦ **to c. on** o **upon** encontrarse con III. adj. casual, fortuito.

chan·cel (chăn'səl) s. antealtar m.

chan·cel·ler·y (:sə-lə-rē) s. cancillería.

chan·cel·lor (:lər) s. POL. canciller m; EDUC. rector m.

chanc·y (chăn'sē) adj. s. arriesgado.

chan·de·lier (shăn'də-lîr') s. araña.

change (chānj) I. tr. & intr. cambiar (de); (clothes, color) mudar (de); (to transform) convertir(se) ♦ **to c. off** turnarse • **to c. over** cambiar II. s. (act) cambio; (substitution) sustitución f, relevo; (of clothing) muda; (money) cambio, vuelto, (coins) suelto ♦ **c. for the better** un cambio beneficioso • **c. of heart** arrepentimiento • **for a c.** para variar • **keep the c.** quédese con el vuelto.

change·a·ble (chān'jə-bəl) adj. cambiable; (inconstant) variable.

change·ling (chānj'lĭng) s. niño cambiado por otro.

change·o·ver (:ō'vər) s. cambio.

chang·er (chān'jər) s. (device) cambiador m; FIN. cambiante mf, cambista mf.

chan·nel (chăn'əl) I. s. canal m; (riverbed) cauce m; (groove) ranura II. tr. canalizar.

chant (chănt) I. s. canto; (psalm) cántico, salmodia II. tr. & intr. cantar, salmodiar.

chan·ti·cleer (chăn'tĭ-klîr') s. gallo.

cha·os (kā'ŏs') s. caos m.

cha·ot·ic (kā-ŏt'ĭk) adj. caótico.

chap[1] (chăp) tr. & intr. **-pp-** paspar(se).

chap[2] s. FAM. (fellow) tipo, muchacho.

chap·el (chăp'əl) s. capilla.

chap·er·on(e) (shăp'ə-rōn') I. s. carabina II. tr. hacer de carabina con.

chap·lain (chăp'lĭn) s. capellán m.

chaps (chăps, shăps) s.pl. zahones m.

chap·ter (chăp'tər) s. capítulo; *(of a club)* sección *f.*

char (chär) tr. & intr. **-rr-** *(to scorch)* chamuscar(se); *(to reduce to coal)* carbonizar(se).

char·ac·ter (kăr'ək-tər) s. carácter *m.*; LIT. *(role)* personaje *m.*, papel *m.*; FAM. *(guy)* tipo ♦ **in c.** característico.

char·ac·ter·is·tic ('-tə-rĭs'tĭk) **I.** adj. característico **II.** s. característica *f.*

char·ac·ter·ize ('-rīz') tr. caracterizar.

cha·rade (shə-rād') s. charada.

char·coal (chär'kōl') s. carbón *m* vegetal o de leña; DIB. carboncillo.

chard (chärd) s. acelga.

charge (chärj) **I.** tr. *(to entrust)* encargar, encomendar; DER. *(to instruct)* instruir; *(to accuse)* acusar; COM. *(a price)* pedir, cobrar; *(on credit)* cargar; *(to saturate)* impregnar; MIL. *(to attack)* atacar, acometer; ELEC. cargar —intr. atacar, ir a la carga; COM. cobrar **II.** s. *(management)* cargo, dirección *f*; *(accusation)* acusación *f*; *(burden)* carga, peso; *(cost)* costo, precio; *(tax)* impuesto; *(attack)* carga; ARM., ELEC. carga ♦ **in c.** encargado de ● **to appear on a c. of** DER. comparecer acusado de ● **to be in c.** ser el encargado ● **to bring charges against** DER. hacer acusaciones contra ● **to reverse the charges** TEL. llamar a cobro revertido ● **to take c.** asumir el mando ● **to take c. of** encargarse de, hacerse cargo de.

char·gé d'af·faires (shär-zhā' də-fâr') s. [pl. **chargés**] encargado de negocios.

charg·er (chär'jər) s. caballo de batalla.

char·i·ot (chär'ē-ət) s. carro de batalla.

cha·ris·ma (kə-rĭz'mə) s. carisma *m.*

char·i·ta·ble (chär'ĭ-tə-bəl) adj. caritativo.

char·i·ty (chär'ĭ-tē) s. caridad *f*, beneficencia; *(institution)* beneficencia.

char·la·tan (shär'lə-tn) s. charlatán *m.*

charm (chärm) **I.** s. encanto; *(amulet)* amuleto ♦ **like a c.** como por encanto **II.** tr. encantar; *(to beguile)* seducir; *(to bewitch)* embrujar.

charm·er (chär'mər) s. encantador *m.*

charm·ing (chär'mĭng) adj. encantador.

chart (chärt) **I.** s. MARÍT. carta de navegación **II.** tr. trazar.

char·ter (chär'tər) **I.** s. POL. carta; *(of organization)* estatutos; *(lease)* fletamento ♦ **c. flight** vuelo fletado ● **c. member** socio fundador **II.** tr. establecer los estatutos de; *(to rent)* fletar.

char·ter·house (:hous') s. cartuja.

char·wom·an (chär'wŏm'ən) s. [pl. **-women**] G.B. criada, empleada de limpieza.

char·y (chär'ē) adj. **-i-** parco.

chase¹ (chās) **I.** tr. perseguir *(after* a) ♦ **to c. away** o **off** ahuyentar ● **to c. out** echar fuera —intr. ir corriendo **II.** s. persecución *f* ♦ **the c.** *(sport)* la cacería; *(quarry)* caza, presa.

chase² **I.** s. *(groove)* ranura, estría **II.** tr. acanalar.

chasm (kăz'əm) s. abismo.

chas·sis (shăs'ē, chăs'ē) s.inv. chasis *m.*

chaste (chāst) adj. casto.

chas·ten (chā'sən) tr. castigar, disciplinar.

chas·tise (chăs-tīz') tr. castigar.

chas·ti·ty (chăs'tĭ-tē) s. castidad *f.*

chat (chăt) **I.** intr. **-tt-** charlar, platicar **II.** s. charla, plática.

chat·tel (chăt'l) s. bien *m* mueble.

chat·ter (chăt'ər) **I.** intr. parlotear, chacharear; *(teeth)* castañetear **II.** s. parloteo, cháchara.

chat·ter·box (:bŏks') s. parlanchín *m.*

chat·ty (chăt'ē) adj. **-i-** parlanchín.

chauf·feur (shō'fər, shō-fûr') **I.** s. chofer o chófer *m* **II.** tr. conducir.

chau·vin·ist (shō'və-nĭst) s. chauvinista *mf.*

chau·vin·is·tic ('-nĭs'tĭk) adj. chauvinista.

cheap (chēp) **I.** adj. barato; *(inferior)* de mala calidad; *(tawdry)* charro; *(stingy)* tacaño ♦ **dirt c.** baratísimo ● **to feel c.** sentirse rebajado **II.** adv. barato.

cheap·en (chē'pən) tr. & intr. rebajar(se), degradar(se).

cheap·ly (chēp'lē) adv. barato, a bajo precio ♦ **c. made** de baja calidad.

cheap·ness (:nĭs) s. bajo precio; *(quality)* mala calidad; *(stinginess)* tacañería.

cheap·skate (:skāt') s. JER. tacaño.

cheat (chēt) **I.** tr. *(to swindle)* defraudar, estafar; *(to deceive)* engañar —intr. hacer trampa; *(on exam)* copiar **II.** s. *(swindler)* tramposo; *(trick)* trampa; *(swindle)* estafa.

cheat·er (chē'tər) s. tramposo.

cheat·ing (:tĭng) **I.** adj. tramposo, fraudulento **II.** s. trampa.

check (chĕk) **I.** s. *(halt)* parada, detención *f*; *(restraint)* freno, impedimento; *(verification)* comprobación *f*, chequeo; *(mark)* marca, señal *f*; *(ticket)* talón *m*; *(bill)* cuenta de restaurante); *(bank draft)* cheque *m*; *(pattern)* cuadros; *(square)* cuadro; *(in chess)* jaque *m* ♦ **c. list** lista de control ● **to keep** o **to hold in c.** tener a raya, tener controlado **II.** interj. ¡jaque! **III.** tr. *(to halt)* detener; *(to restrain)* refrenar, contener; *(an emotion)* reprimir; *(to test)* examinar, controlar; *(to verify)* verificar; *(hat, coat)* depositar; *(luggage)* facturar; *(in chess)* dar jaque ♦ **c. it out!** JER. ¡mire esto! ● **to c. against** chequear, cotejar ● **to c. off** marcar (uno por uno), chequear ● **to c. out** FAM. comprobar ● **to c. up on** comprobar, verificar ● **to c. with** consultar con —intr. *(to halt)* detenerse; *(to agree)* concordar (listas, cifras) ♦ **to c. in (to)** registrarse (en un hotel) ● **to c. out (of)** pagar la cuenta y marcharse (de un hotel).

check·book (:bŏŏk') s. chequera, talonario.

check·er (:ər) s. *(examiner)* verificador *m*; *(cashier)* cajero; *(in the game)* pieza del juego de damas ♦ **pl.** damas.

check·er·board (:bôrd') s. tablero de damas.

check·ered (chĕk'ərd) adj. *(design)* cuadriculado, a cuadros; FIG. *(uneven)* con altibajos.

check·mate (:māt') **I.** tr. dar jaque y mate **II.** s. jaque y mate *m.*

check·out (:out') s. *(exit)* salida (de hotel, supermercado); *(inspection)* inspección *f.*

check·point (:point') s. lugar *m* de inspección.

check·room (:rōōm') s. guardarropa *m*; *(for luggage)* consigna.

check·up (:ŭp') s. chequeo, reconocimiento médico general.

cheek (chēk) s. mejilla; *(impudence)* descaro ♦ **c. by jowl** codo con codo.

cheek·bone (:bōn') s. pómulo.

cheek·y (chē'kē) adj. **-i-** descarado, caradura.

cheep (chēp) **I.** s. piada **II.** tr. & intr. piar.

cheer (chîr) **I.** tr. *(to gladden)* animar, alegrar; *(to encourage)* alentar; *(to shout)* vitorear, ovacionar ♦ **to c. on** animar, alentar ● **to c. up** alegrar, animar —intr. aplaudir ♦ **c. up!** ¡ánimo! ● **to c. up** alegrarse **II.** s. alegría, ánimo; *(shout)* viva, hurra ♦ **pl. c.!** ¡salud!

cheer·ful ('fəl) adj. alegre.

cheer·i·ly (:ə-lē) adv. alegremente.
cheer·lead·er (:lē'dər) s. persona que dirige los vivas en una encuesta deportiva.
cheer·less (:lĭs) adj. triste.
cheer·y (:ē) adj. -i- alegre.
cheese (chēz) s. queso.
cheese·cake ('kāk') s. quesadilla.
cheese·cloth (:klôth') s. estopilla.
chees·y (chē'zē) adj. -i- caseoso; *(cheap)* vulgar, de pacotilla.
chef (shĕf) s. cocinero, jefe m de cocina.
chem·i·cal (kĕm'ĭ-kəl) I. adj. químico II. s. sustancia química.
che·mise (shə-mēz') s. camisa (de mujer).
chem·ist (kĕm'ĭst) s. químico; G.B. *(pharmacist)* farmacéutico.
chem·is·try (kĕm'ĭ-strē) s. química.
che·mo·ther·a·py (kē'mō-thĕr'ə-pē) s. quimioterapia.
cheque (chĕk) s. G.B. cheque m.
cher·ish (chĕr'ĭsh) tr. *(to hold dear)* querer, estimar; *(thoughts, ideas)* abrigar.
cher·ry (chĕr'ē) I. s. cereza ♦ c. tree cerezo II. adj. de color rojo cereza.
cher·ub (chĕr'əb) s. [pl. -im] querubín m.
che·ru·bic (chə-rōō'bĭk) adj. querúbico.
chess (chĕs) s. ajedrez m ♦ c. player ajedrecista.
chess·board ('bôrd') s. tablero de ajedrez.
chess·man (:măn') s. [pl. -men] trebejo.
chest (chĕst) s. pecho; *(box)* cofre m, arca m; *(dresser)* cómoda.
chest·nut (chĕs'nət) I. s. *(nut)* castaña; *(horse)* zaino; *(color)* castaño ♦ c. tree castaño II. adj. castaño, marrón.
chew (chōō) I. tr. & intr. masticar, mascar ♦ to c. out regañar, reprender ♦ to c. over rumiar, meditar ♦ to c. the fat charlar, parlotear II. s. mascada (esp. de tabaco).
chew·ing ('ĭng) s. masticación f ♦ c. gum chicle, goma de mascar.
chew·y (ē) adj. -i- *(meat)* fibroso, duro; *(sweets)* que se pega a los dientes.
chic (shēk) s. & adj. chic m.
chi·can·er·y (shĭ-kā'nə-rē) s. trapacería.
chick (chĭk) s. polluelo; JER. *(girl)* chavala.
chick·en (chĭk'ən) I. s. gallina, pollo ♦ c. pox varicela II. adj. FAM. miedoso, cobarde III. intr. ♦ to c. out acobardarse.
chick·en-heart·ed (:här'tĭd) adj. cobarde.
chick·pea (chĭk'pē') s. garbanzo.
chic·o·ry (chĭk'ə-rē) s. achicoria.
chide (chīd) tr. -d o chid regañar, reprender.
chief (chēf) I. s. jefe m ♦ c. executive primer mandatario ♦ c. justice presidente del tribunal ♦ c. of staff jefe del estado mayor II. adj. principal.
chief·ly ('lē) adv. principalmente.
chief·tain (:tən) s. cacique m, caudillo.
chif·fon (shĭ-fŏn') s. chifón m, gasa.
chig·ger (chĭg'ər) s. pique m, nigua.
child (chīld) s. [pl. -ren] niño; *(offspring)* hijo; FIG. *(product)* fruto, embarazada ♦ c.'s play juego de niños ♦ with c. embarazada.
child·bear·ing ('bâr'ĭng) s. maternidad f.
child·birth (:bûrth') s. parto, alumbramiento.
child·hood (:hŏŏd') s. niñez f, infancia.
child·ish (chīl'dĭsh) adj. infantil, pueril.
child·less (chīld'lĭs) adj. sin hijos.
child·like (:līk') adj. infantil.
chil·dren (chĭl'drən) cf. **child**.
chil·i (chĭl'ē) s. chile m, ají m.

chill (chĭl) I. s. *(coolness)* frío; *(shiver)* escalofrío; *(damper)* enfriamiento ♦ to catch a c. resfriarse ♦ to take the c. off calentar II. adj. frío III. tr. *(to cool)* enfriar; *(food)* refrigerar.
chill·er ('ər) s. historia escalofriante.
chill·ing (:ĭng) adj. *(cold)* frío; *(frightening)* escalofriante; *(discouraging)* frío.
chill·y (:ē) adj. -i- frío.
chime (chīm) I. s. carillón m; *(sound)* repique m ♦ pl. carillón II. intr. repicar, sonar ♦ to c. in intervenir (en una conversación) —tr. dar (la hora).
chi·me·ra (kĭ-mîr'ə) s. quimera.
chim·ney (chĭm'nē) s. chimenea; *(of a lamp)* tubo de vidrio ♦ c. sweep deshollinador.
chim·ney·piece (:pēs') s. repisa de una chimenea.
chimp (chĭmp) s. FAM. chimpancé m.
chim·pan·zee (chĭm'păn-zē') s. chimpancé m.
chin (chĭn) I. s. barbilla, mentón m ♦ c. up! ¡ánimo! ♦ to keep one's c. up no desanimarse II. tr. -nn- ♦ to c. oneself hacer flexiones en la barra tocándola con la barbilla.
chi·na (chī'nə) s. china, porcelana; *(crockery)* loza.
chink¹ (chĭngk) s. *(crack)* grieta, rajadura.
chink² (chĭngk) s. *(metallic sound)* tintín m II. tr. & intr. tintinear.
chintz (chĭnts) s. zaraza.
chintz·y (chĭnt'sē) adj. -i- FAM. de oropel.
chip (chĭp) I. s. pedacito, trozo; *(splinter)* astilla; *(of stone)* lasca; *(in china)* desportilladura; *(in gambling)* ficha; ELECTRÓN. placa ♦ a c. off the old block de tal palo, tal astilla ♦ in the chips JER. forrado de dinero ♦ the chips are down JER. la suerte está echada ♦ to have a c. on one's shoulder estar resentido ♦ pl. patatas fritas II. tr. -pp- *(to splinter)* hacer astillas; *(to chop)* picar; *(to chisel)* cincelar ♦ to c. off desportillar —intr. *(china)* desportillarse; *(wood)* astillarse ♦ to c. in contribuir.
chip·munk (chĭp'mŭngk') s. ardilla listada.
chip·per (chĭp'ər) adj. FAM. animado, jovial.
chi·ro·prac·tor (kī'rə-prăk'tər) s. quiropráctico.
chirp (chûrp) I. s. *(bird)* gorjeo; *(cricket)* chirrido II. intr. *(bird)* gorjear; *(cricket)* chirriar.
chis·el (chĭz'əl) I. s. cincel m II. tr. cincelar; FAM. *(to cheat)* estafar.
chis·el·er (:ə-lər) s. cincelador m; FAM. *(swindler)* estafador m.
chit (chĭt) s. vale m, cuenta.
chit·chat (chĭt'chăt') s. charla, cháchara.
chiv·al·rous (shĭv'əl-rəs) adj. caballeresco.
chiv·al·ry (:rē) s. caballerosidad f.
chive (chīv) s. cebollino.
chlo·ride (klôr'īd') s. cloruro.
chlo·ri·nate (:ə-nāt') tr. tratar con cloro.
chlo·rine (klôr'ēn') s. cloro.
chlo·ro·form (:ə-fôrm') I. s. cloroformo II. tr. cloroformizar.
chlo·ro·phyl(l) (:fĭl') s. clorofila.
chock (chŏk) I. s. calza, cuña II. tr. calzar.
chock-full (:fŏŏl') adj. repleto, colmado.
choc·o·late (chôk'lĭt) adj. & s. (de) chocolate m.
choice (chois) I. s. elección f, selección f; *(option)* opción f; *(assortment)* surtido; *(alternative)* alternativa ♦ by c. por gusto ♦ to have no c. no tener alternativa ♦ to make a c. escoger, elegir II. adj. escogido, superior.
choir (kwīr) s. coro.

choir·boy ('boi') s. niño de coro.
choke (chōk) I. tr. *(to strangle)* estrangular, ahogar; *(to suffocate)* sofocar; *(food)* atragantar; *(to clog)* atorar, atascar; AUTO. estrangular ♦ **to c. back** contener, ahogar • **to c. down** tragar con asco • **to c. off** cortar *o* terminar abruptamente • **to c. up** obstruir, atascar —intr. sofocarse, ahogarse; *(on food)* atragantarse; *(to clog)* atorarse ♦ **to c. up** FAM. emocionarse II. s. sofocación *f*, ahogo; AUTO. estrangulador *m*.
chok·er (chō'kər) s. gargantilla.
chol·er (kŏl'ər) s. ira, cólera.
chol·er·a (kŏl'ər-ə) s. MED. cólera *m*.
chol·er·ic (kŏl'ə-rĭk) adj. colérico.
cho·les·ter·ol (kə-lĕs'tə-rōl') s. colesterol *m*.
chomp (chŏmp) tr. & intr. ronzar.
choose (chōz) tr. **chose, chosen** elegir, escoger; *(to prefer)* preferir —intr. ♦ **to do as one chooses** hacer lo que quiere.
choos·ing (chō'zĭng) s. elección *f*, selección *f*.
choos·y (:zē) adj. **-i-** FAM. quisquilloso.
chop (chŏp) I. tr. **-pp-** cortar; *(to mince)* picar ♦ **to c. down** talar • **to c. up** cortar en trozos II. s. corte *m*, tajo; CUL. chuleta.
chop·per (:ər) s. FAM. helicóptero ♦ pl. JER. dientes *(postizos)*.
chop·ping block (:ĭng) s. tajo.
chop·py (:ē) adj. **-i-** picado, agitado.
chops (chŏps) s.pl. quijada ♦ **to lick one's c.** relamerse.
chop·sticks (chŏp'stĭks') s.pl. palillos chinos.
cho·ral (kôr'əl) adj. & s. coral *f*.
chord (kôrd) s. MÚS. acorde *m*; GEOM. cuerda.
chore (chôr) s. quehacer *m*, faena.
cho·re·o·graph (kôr'ē-ə-grăf') tr. hacer la coreografía de.
cho·re·og·ra·pher ('-ŏg'rə-fər) s. coreógrafo.
cho·re·og·ra·phy (:fē) s. coreografía.
cho·ris·ter (kôr'ĭ-stər) s. corista *mf*.
chor·tle (chôr'tl) I. intr. reír entre dientes II. s. risa ahogada.
cho·rus (kôr'əs) s. [pl. **es**] coro; *(refrain)* estribillo ♦ **c. girl** corista • **in c.** al unísono.
chose (chōz) cf. **choose**.
cho·sen (chō'zən) I. cf. **choose** II. adj. & s. elegido, escogido.
chow (chou) I. s. FAM. comida II. intr. ♦ **to c. down** comer.
chow·der (chou'dər) s. sopa de pescado.
chris·ten (krĭs'ən) tr. bautizar.
Chris·ten·dom (:dəm) s. cristiandad *f*.
chris·ten·ing (:ĭng) s. bautismo, bautizo.
Chris·tian (krĭs'chən) adj. & s. cristiano ♦ **C. name** nombre de pila.
Chris·ti·an·i·ty ('chē-ăn'ĭ-tē) s. cristianismo; *(Christendom)* cristiandad *f*.
Chris·tian·ize ('chə-nīz') tr. cristianizar.
Christ·mas (krĭs'məs) s. Navidad *f*.
chro·mat·ic (krō-măt'ĭk) adj. cromático.
chrome (krōm) s. cromo.
chro·mi·um (krō'mē-əm) s. cromo.
chro·mo·some (krō'mə-sōm') s. cromosoma *m*.
chron·ic (krŏn'ĭk) adj. crónico.
chron·i·cle (krŏn'ĭ-kəl) I. s. crónica II. tr. hacer la crónica de.
chron·o·log·i·cal (krŏn'ə-lŏj'ĭk) adj. cronológico.
chro·nol·o·gy (krə-nŏl'ə-jē) s. cronología.
chro·nom·e·ter (krə-nŏm'ĭ-tər) s. cronómetro.
chrys·a·lis (krĭs'ə-lĭs) s. crisálida.

chry·san·the·mum (krĭ-săn'thə-məm) s. crisantemo.
chub·by (chŭb'ē) adj. **-i-** rechoncho.
chuck¹ (chŭk) I. tr. *(to pat)* hacer la mamola ♦ **to c. out** FAM. tirar, botar II. s. *(pat)* mamola; MEC. mandril *m*.
chuck² s. CUL. paletilla.
chuck·hole (chŭk'hōl') s. FAM. bache *m*.
chuck·le (chŭk'əl) I. intr. reírse entre dientes II. s. risita, risa ahogada.
chug (chŭg) I. s. traqueteo II. intr. **-gg-** traquetear.
chum (chŭm) s. compañero, compinche *m*.
chum·my (:ē) adj. **-i-** amistoso.
chunk (chŭngk) s. pedazo, trozo; *(amount)* cantidad *f* grande.
chunk·y (chŭng'kē) adj. **-i-** corto y grueso; *(in chunks)* en pedazos.
church (chûrch) s. iglesia.
church·go·er (:gō'ər) s. devoto (que va a misa regularmente).
church·man (:mən) s. [pl. **-men**] clérigo.
church·yard (:yärd') s. camposanto.
churl (chûrl) s. patán *m*.
churl·ish (chûr'lĭsh) adj. maleducado.
churn (chûrn) I. s. mantequera II. tr. CUL. hacer (mantequilla); *(to shake)* agitar, revolver ♦ **to c. out** producir en profusión —intr. agitarse, revolverse.
chute (shōt) s. *(ramp)* rampa, tobogán *m*; *(conduit)* conducto; FAM. paracaídas *m*.
ci·ca·da (sĭ-kā'də) s. [pl. **s** *o* **-ae**] cigarra.
ci·der (sī'dər) s. sidra.
ci·gar (sĭ-gär') s. cigarro, puro.
cig·a·ret(te) (sĭg'ə-rĕt') s. cigarrillo.
cil·i·um (sĭl'ē-əm) s. [pl. **-ia**] cilio.
cinch (sĭnch) I. s. EQUIT. cincha; FAM. *(snap)* cosa fácil II. tr. EQUIT. cinchar; FAM. *(to make certain)* asegurar.
cin·der (sĭn'dər) s. carbonilla ♦ pl. cenizas.
cin·e·ma (sĭn'ə-mə) s. cine *m*.
cin·e·mat·ic ('-măt'ĭk) adj. fílmico.
cin·e·ma·tog·ra·phy (:mə-tŏg'rə-fē) s. cinematografía.
cin·na·mon (sĭn'ə-mən) s. canela.
ci·pher (sī'fər) I. s. *(code)* cifra; *(zero)* cero II. intr. hacer un cálculo —tr. cifrar.
cir·cle (sûr'kəl) I. s. círculo; *(orbit)* órbita; *(turn)* vuelta ♦ **to come full c.** volver al punto de partida • **to go around in circles** estar en un círculo vicioso II. tr. *(to enclose)* cercar, rodear; *(to draw)* hacer un círculo alrededor de; *(to revolve around)* girar alrededor de —intr. dar vueltas.
cir·cuit (sûr'kĭt) I. s. circuito ♦ **c. breaker** cortacircuitos • **c. court** tribunal de distrito II. intr. & tr. dar la vuelta (a).
cir·cu·i·tous (sər-kyōō'ĭ-təs) adj. indirecto.
cir·cuit·ry (sûr'kĭ-trē) s. sistema *m* de circuitos.
cir·cu·lar (sûr'kyə-lər) adj. & s. circular *f*.
cir·cu·late (:lāt') intr. & tr. circular.
cir·cu·lat·ing (:lā'tĭng) adj. circulante.
cir·cu·la·tion ('-lā'shən) s. circulación *f*.
cir·cum·cise (sûr'kəm-sīz') tr. circuncidar.
cir·cum·cised (:sīzd') adj. circunciso.
cir·cum·fer·ence (sər-kŭm'fər-əns) s. circunferencia.
cir·cum·flex (sûr'kəm-flĕks') s. acento circunflejo.
cir·cum·lo·cu·tion (sûr'kəm-lō-kyōō'shən) s. circunlocución *f*, circunloquio.
cir·cum·nav·i·gate (:năv'ĭ-gāt') tr. circunnave-

gar.
cir·cum·scribe ('-skrīb') tr. circunscribir.
cir·cum·spect (:spĕkt') adj. circunspecto.
cir·cum·stance (sûr'kəm-stāns') s. circunstancia; *(ceremony)* ceremonia ♦ **to c.** situación, posición • **under no c.** de ninguna manera.
cir·cum·stan·tial ('-stăr'shəl) adj. circunstancial ♦ **c. evidence** pruebas indirectas.
cir·cum·vent (:vĕnt') tr. evitar.
cir·cus (sûr'kəs) s. circo.
cir·rho·sis (sī-rō'sĭs) s. cirrosis *f.*
cir·rus (sĭr'əs) s. [pl. **-ri**] cirro.
cis·tern (sĭs'tərn) s. cisterna, aljibe *m.*
cit·a·del (sĭt'ə-dəl) s. ciudadela.
ci·ta·tion (sī-tā'shən) s. *(quote)* cita; DER. citación *f*; MIL. mención *f.*
cite (sīt) tr. *(to quote)* citar; DER. citar; MIL. mencionar.
cit·i·fied (sĭt'ĭ-fīd') adj. urbanizado.
cit·i·zen (sĭt'ĭ-zən) s. ciudadano.
cit·i·zen·ry (:rē) s. ciudadanos.
cit·i·zen·ship (:shĭp') s. ciudadanía.
cit·ric (sĭt'rĭk) adj. cítrico.
cit·ron (:rən) s. cidra.
cit·rus (:rəs) adj. cítrico ♦ **c. fruits** agrios.
cit·y (sĭt'ē) s. ciudad *f* ♦ **c. hall** ayuntamiento.
civ·et (sĭv'ĭt) s. civeta.
civ·ic (sĭv'ĭk) adj. cívico ♦ **civics** s.sg. estudio del gobierno civil.
civ·il (sĭv'əl) adj. civil ♦ **c. liberty** libertad ciudadana • **c. servant** empleado público • **c. service** administración pública.
ci·vil·ian (sĭ-vĭl'yən) adj. & s. civil *m,* (de) paisano.
ci·vil·i·ty (:ĭ-tē) s. urbanidad *f*, civilidad *f.*
civ·i·li·za·tion (sĭv'ə-lĭ-zā'shən) s. civilización *f.*
civ·i·lize (sĭv'ə-līz') tr. civilizar.
clack (klăk) I. intr. castañetear II. s. castañeteo.
clad (klăd) of. **clothe.**
claim (klām) I. tr. *(to demand)* reclamar; *(to state)* afirmar; *(to deserve)* merecer II. s. *(demand)* reclamación *f*; *(assertion)* afirmación *f*; *(right)* derecho, título; MIN. concesión *f*; DER. demanda.
claim·ant (klā'mənt) s. DER. demandante *mf*; *(to a position)* pretendiente *mf.*
clair·voy·ance (klâr-voi'əns) s. clarividencia.
clair·voy·ant (:ənt) adj. & s. clarividente *mf.*
clam (klăm) I. s. almeja II. intr. **-mm-** pescar almejas ♦ **to c. up** callarse como un muerto.
clam·ber (klăm'bər) intr. subir gateando.
clam·my (klăm'ē) adj. **-i-** frío y húmedo.
clam·or (klăm'ər) I. s. clamor *m* II. tr. & intr. clamar.
clam·or·ous (:əs) adj. clamoroso.
clamp (klămp) I. s. TEC. grapa, abrazadera; CARP. cárcel *f* II. tr. sujetar con abrazadera; FIG. agarrar firmemente ♦ **to c. down on** FAM. *(person)* apretar las clavijas a; *(expression)* reprimir.
clan (klăn) s. clan *m.*
clan·des·tine (klăn-dĕs'tĭn) adj. clandestino.
clang (klăng) intr. & s. (sonar con) sonido metálico.
clan·gor (:ər) s. estruendo.
clank (klăngk) I. s. ruido metálico II. intr. hacer un ruido metálico.
clan·nish (klăn'ĭsh) adj. exclusivo.
clans·man (klănz'mən) s. [pl. **-men**] miembro de un clan.
clap (klăp) I. intr. **-pp-** dar palmadas; *(objects)*

golpearse ♦ **to c. shut** cerrarse de golpe —tr. aplaudir; *(to tap)* dar una palmada a ♦ **to c. together** FAM. improvisar II. s. aplauso; *(tap)* palmada; *(bang)* estampido.
clap·per (:ər) s. badajo.
clap·ping ('ing) s. aplausos; *(in time)* palmadas.
clap·trap (:trăp') s. charlatanería, palabrería.
claque (klăk) s. claque *f.*
clar·et (klăr'ĭt) s. clarete *m.*
clar·i·fi·ca·tion (klăr'ə-fĭ-kā'shən) s. aclaración *f.*
clar·i·fy (klăr'ə-fī') tr. & intr. aclarar(se).
clar·i·net (klăr'ə-nĕt') s. clarinete *m.*
clar·i·on (klăr'ē·ən) adj. estentóreo, sonoro.
clar·i·ty (klăr'ĭ-tē) s. claridad *f.*
clash (klăsh) I. intr. *(to collide)* chocar, entrechocarse; *(to conflict)* chocar, estar en conflicto II. s. *(noise)* estruendo; *(collision)* choque *m*; *(conflict)* desacuerdo.
clasp (klăsp) I. s. *(device)* cierre *m*, broche *m*; *(hug)* abrazo; *(of the hands)* apretón *m* ♦ **c. knife** navaja de muelle II. tr. *(to hook)* abrochar, enganchar; *(to hug)* abrazar; *(to clutch)* agarrar; *(the hand)* apretar.
class (klăs) I. s. clase *f* ♦ **c. of 1988** promoción de 1988 II. tr. clasificar.
class-con·scious ('kŏn'shəs) adj. con conciencia de clase social.
clas·sic (klăs'ĭk) adj. & s. clásico.
clas·si·cal (:ĭ-kəl) adj. clásico.
clas·si·cism (:sĭz'əm) s. clasicismo.
clas·si·cist (:sĭst) s. clasicista *mf.*
clas·si·fi·ca·tion ('-fĭ-kā'shən) s. clasificación *f.*
clas·si·fied (klăs'ə-fīd') adj. clasificado; *(secret)* secreto.
clas·si·fy (klăs'ə-fī') tr. clasificar; *(to restrict)* restringir.
class·mate (klăs'māt') s. compañero de clase.
class·room (:rōōm') s. aula, sala de clase.
class·y (klăs'ē) adj. **-i-** JER. elegante.
clat·ter (klăt'ər) I. intr. traquetear II. s. traqueteo; *(din)* estruendo.
clause (klôz) s. cláusula *f*; GRAM. oración *f.*
claus·tro·pho·bi·a (klô' strə-fō'bē-ə) s. claustrofobia.
clav·i·chord (klăv'ĭ-kôrd') s. clavicordio.
clav·i·cle (klăv'ĭ-kəl) s. clavícula.
claw (klô) I. s. garra; *(of cat)* uña; *(of crab)* tenaza, pinza ♦ **c. hammer** martillo sacaclavos II. tr. & intr. arañar.
clay (klā) s. arcilla.
clean (klēn) I. adj. limpio; *(pure)* puro; *(total)* completo, radical; JER. *(innocent)* inocente (de sospechas) ♦ **c. as a whistle** limpio como una patena • **to make a c. breast of it** confesar de plano II. adv. limpiamente; FAM. *(entirely)* completamente ♦ **to come c.** confesarlo todo III. tr. limpiar; CUL. *(meat)* quitar la grasa a; *(vegetables)* pelar; *(fish)* escamar y abrir ♦ **to c. out** *(to empty out)* vaciar; *(to use up)* agotar; FAM. *(to leave penniless)* sacarle hasta el último centavo a • **to c. up** acabar con *(un asunto)* —intr. limpiar(se) ♦ **to c. up** FIG. poner las cosas en orden • **to c. up** FAM. ganarse una fortuna.
clean-cut ('kŭt') adj. *(sharp)* nítido, definido; *(wholesome)* sano.
clean·er (klē'nər) s. limpiador *m*, quitamanchas *m* ♦ **c.'s** tintorería.
clean·ing (:ning) s. limpieza.

clean·li·ness (klĕn′lē-nĭs) s. limpieza, aseo.
cleanse (klĕnz) tr. limpiar, purificar.
cleans·er (klĕn′zər) s. limpiador *m.*
clean-shav·en (klēn′shā′vən) adj. bien afeitado.
clean-up (:ŭp′) s. limpieza general *o* a fondo.
clear (klîr) I. adj. claro; *(sky, view)* despejado; *(air, water)* transparente; *(evident)* evidente; *(conscience)* limpio, tranquilo; *(net)* neto, en limpio ♦ **as c. as day** más claro que el agua ♦ **as c. as mud** nada claro ♦ **c. of** libre de ♦ **c. profit** beneficio neto ♦ **to make oneself c.** explicar claramente II. adv. claro, con claridad ♦ **to stand c.** mantenerse aparte III. tr. *(to make clear)* aclarar; *(to unobstruct)* despejar; *(a path, way)* abrir; *(the table)* levantar; *(to remove)* quitar; *(to pass over)* salvar; *(to pass by)* pasar sin rozar; *(the throat)* aclararse; *(conscience)* descargar, aliviar; *(to exonerate)* limpiar; *(to acquit)* absolver; *(to approve)* aprobar; *(a profit)* ganar; *(a check)* compensar; *(debt)* liquidar; *(customs)* sacar de la aduana ♦ **to c. away** quitar ♦ **to c. off** despejar ♦ **to c. out** *(empty)* vaciar; *(to clean)* limpiar ♦ **to c. up** *(doubt)* disipar; *(mystery)* aclarar —intr. *(to become clear)* aclararse; *(sky)* despejarse; *(crowd)* dispersarse; *(impurities)* limpiarse ♦ **to c. out** irse, largarse ♦ **to c. through** pasar por, ser aprobado por ♦ **to c. up** despejarse IV. s. ♦ **in the c.** fuera de sospecha.
clear·ance (′əns) s. *(removal)* despejo; *(sale)* liquidación *f.,* saldo; *(leeway)* espacio, margen *m.; (permission)* permiso; *(by customs)* despacho; *(of a check)* compensación *f.*
clear-cut (:kŭt′) adj. claro.
clear·ing (:ĭng) s. claro.
clear·ing-house (:hous′) s. oficina de compensación.
clear·ly (klîr′lē) adv. claramente; *(evidently)* evidentemente; *(of course)* por supuesto.
clear-sight·ed (:sī′tĭd) adj. perspicaz.
cleat (klēt) s. MARÍT. cornamusa; *(on shoes)* clavo, tapón *m.*
cleav·age (klē′vĭj) s. hendidura, división *f.*
cleave (klēv) tr. & intr. **-d** *o* **cleft** partir(se), hender(se).
cleav·er (klē′vər) s. cuchillo de carnicero).
clef (klĕf) s. clave *f.*
cleft (klĕft) I. cf. **cleave** II. adj. hendido, partido ♦ **c. palate** fisura palatina III. s. fisura.
clem·en·cy (klĕm′ən-sē) s. clemencia.
clench (klĕnch) I. tr. apretar II. s. apretón *m.*
cler·gy (klûr′jē) s. clero.
cler·gy·man (:mən) s. [pl. **-men**] clérigo *m.*
cler·ic (klĕr′ĭk) s. clérigo.
cler·i·cal (′ĭ-kəl) adj. de oficina; RELIG. clerical.
clerk (klûrk) s. *(in office)* oficinista *mf; (in store)* dependiente *mf;* DER. escribano, amanuense *mf.*
clev·er (klĕv′ər) adj. **-er, -est** *(bright)* listo, inteligente; *(witty)* ingenioso; *(skillful)* hábil.
clev·er·ness (:nĭs) s. *(skill)* habilidad *f.; (intelligence)* inteligencia.
cli·ché (klē-shā′) s. cliché *m,* clisé *m.*
click (klĭk) I. s. chasquido, ruido seco II. intr. chasquear; JER. *(to succeed)* salir bien —tr. *(tongue)* chasquear; *(heels)* taconear.
cli·ent (klī′ənt) s. cliente *mf.*
cli·en·tele (klī′ən-tĕl′) s. clientela.
cliff (klĭf) s. acantilado, precipicio.
cli·mac·tic (klī-mǎk′tĭk) adj. culminante.
cli·mate (klī′mĭt) s. clima *m.*

cli·mat·ic (-mǎt′ĭk) s. climático.
cli·max (klī′mǎks′) I. s. culminación *f;* LIT., RET. clímax *m* II. intr. culminar.
climb (klīm) I. tr. & intr. subir; *(to scale)* escalar, trepar ♦ **to c. down** descender, bajar II. s. subida, ascenso.
climb·er (klī′mər) s. alpinista *mf.*
climb·ing (:mĭng) I. adj. trepador II. s. alpinismo.
clinch (klĭnch) I. tr. *(a nail)* remachar; *(to secure)* afianzar; *(a deal)* decidir, concluir; *(a title)* ganar —intr. luchar cuerpo a cuerpo (en boxeo) II. s. lucha cuerpo a cuerpo (en boxeo).
cling (klĭng) intr. **clung** *(to hold fast)* asirse, agarrarse; *(to stick)* pegarse; *(to persist in)* aferrarse.
clin·ic (klĭn′ĭk) s. clínica.
clin·i·cal (:ĭ-kəl) adj. clínico.
cli·ni·cian (klĭ-nĭsh′ən) s. clínico.
clink (klĭngk) I. tr. & intr. tintinear II. s. tintín *m,* tintineo.
clink·er (klĭng′kər) s. *(residue)* escoria; *(mistake)* error *m.*
clip¹ (klĭp) I. tr. **-pp-** cortar, recortar; *(to trim)* podar; *(to shear)* esquilar (ovejas); FAM. *(to hit)* pegar; *(to overcharge)* estafar ♦ **to c. along** ir a buen paso II. s. FAM. *(blow)* golpe *m; (pace)* paso rápido.
clip² I. s. *(fastener)* sujetador *m; (for paper)* sujetapapeles *m; (for hair)* horquilla; *(of rifle)* cargador *m* II. tr. **-pp-** sujetar.
clip·board (′bôrd′) s. tablilla con sujetapapeles.
clip·per (:ər) s. *(shears)* tijeras; *(for sheep)* esquiladora; MARÍT. clíper *m* ♦ pl. tijeras • **nail c.** cortaúñas.
clip·ping (:ĭng) s. recorte *m.*
clique (klēk, klĭk) s. pandilla, camarilla.
cloak (klōk) I. s. capa, manto II. tr. encubrir.
cloak-and-dag·ger (′ən-dǎg′ər) adj. de capa y espada.
cloak·room (′rōōm′) s. guardarropa *m.*
clob·ber (klŏb′ər) tr. JER. *(to hit)* golpear; *(to defeat)* dar una paliza.
clock (klŏk) I. s. reloj *m* (de pie, de mesa); *(chronometer)* cronómetro II. tr. cronometrar.
clock·wise (:wīz′) adv. & adj. en el sentido de las agujas del reloj.
clock·work (:wûrk′) s. mecanismo de relojería ♦ **like c.** como un reloj.
clod (klŏd) s. *(of dirt)* terrón *m; (dolt)* bobo.
clog (klŏg) I. s. *(blockage)* obstrucción *f,* atasco; *(shoe)* zueco II. tr. & intr. **-gg-** obstruir(se), atascar(se).
clois·ter (kloi′stər) I. s. claustro; *(monastery)* monasterio, convento II. tr. enclaustrar.
clomp (klŏmp) intr. andar pesada y ruidosamente.
clone (klōn) I. s. clon *m* II. tr. & intr. reproducir(se) asexualmente.
close I. adj. *(near)* cercano; *(relationship)* íntimo; *(similar)* parecido; *(contest)* reñido; *(resemblance)* casi igual; *(copy)* fiel, exacto; *(rigorous)* minucioso; *(attention)* total; *(enclosed)* encerrado; *(tight-fitting)* apretado; *(stuffy)* mal ventilado; *(confining)* estrecho; *(strict)* estricto ♦ **a c. resemblance** un gran parecido ♦ **at c. range** a quemarropa, de cerca • **c. call** FAM. escape difícil • **c. combat** MIL. combate cuerpo a cuerpo • **c. quarters** lugar estrecho II. tr. (klōz) cerrar; *(letter)* concluir; *(session)* levantar; *(gap, distance)* acortar ♦ **to**

c. down cerrar definitivamente • **to c. in** rodear, cercar • **to c. out** *(account)* cerrar; *(product)* liquidar • **to c. up** *(shop)* cerrar; *(opening)* tapar • **to c. up shop** cesar toda actividad —intr. cerrarse; *(shop)* cerrar; *(story, show)* terminarse, concluirse; *(to agree)* ponerse de acuerdo ♦ **to c. down** clausurarse, cerrarse definitivamente • **to c. in** *(to surround)* rodear; *(to draw near)* acercarse • **to c. up** *(shop)* cerrar; *(wound)* cerrarse, cicatrizarse III. s. *(klōz)* final *m*, conclusión *f* ♦ **at the c. of the day** a la caída de la tarde ♦ **to bring to a c.** terminar IV. adv. *(klōs)* cerca ♦ **c. at hand** a mano • **c. by** muy cerca • **c. to** muy cerca de, junto a • **c. together** muy juntos • **to come c.** acercarse.

closed (klōzd) adj. cerrado; *(finished)* concluido; *(season)* vedado; *(restricted)* reservado; *(mind)* estrecho.

closed-cir·cuit television (:sûr′kĭt) s. televisión *f* en circuito cerrado.

close·down (klōz′doun′) s. cierre *m*.

close·ly (klōs′lē) adv. (de) cerca; *(intimately)* estrechamente; *(exactly)* con fidelidad; *(attentively)* atentamente.

close·ness (:nĭs) s. cercanía, proximidad *f*; *(intimacy)* intimidad *f*.

close-out (klōz′out′) s. liquidación *f*.

clos·et (klŏz′ĭt) s. armario, ropero.

close-up (klōs′ŭp′) s. primer plano.

clos·ing (klō′zĭng) s. cierre *m* ♦ **c. remarks** observaciones finales • **in c.** para concluir.

clot (klŏt) I. s. coágulo II. intr. -tt- coagularse, cuajarse.

cloth (klôth) s. [pl. **s**] tela, paño; *(strip)* trapo ♦ **the c.** el clero.

clothe (klōth) tr. -d o **clad** vestir, arropar.

clothes (klōthz) s.pl. ropa, vestimenta.

clothes·line (:līn′) s. cuerda para tender ropa.

clothes·pin (:pĭn′) s. pinza para tender ropa.

cloth·ing (klō′thĭng) s. ropa, indumentaria.

cloud (kloud) I. s. nube *f*; *(shadow)* sombra ♦ **on c. nine** FAM. contentísimo • **under a c.** bajo sospecha II. tr. & intr. nublar(se), anublar(se) ♦ **to c. over** o **up** nublarse.

cloud·burst (′bûrst′) s. aguacero.

cloud·y (klou′dē) adj. -i- *(overcast)* nublado; *(vague)* nebuloso; *(liquid)* turbio.

clout (klout) I. s. *(blow)* bofetada; FAM. *(influence)* poder *m* II. tr. abofetear.

clove (klōv) s. *(spice)* clavo de especia; *(of garlic)* diente *m*.

clo·ven hoof (klō′vən) s. pezuña hendida.

clo·ver (klō′vər) s. trébol *m* ♦ **to be in c.** vivir como un rey.

clo·ver·leaf (:lēf′) s. cruce *m* en trébol.

clown (kloun) I. s. payaso II. intr. payasear.

cloy·ing (kloi′ĭng) adj. empalagoso.

club (klŭb) I. s. *(cudgel)* porra; *(golf)* palo; *(in cards)* trébol *m*, basto; *(association)* club *m* ♦ **c. car** F.C. coche salón II. tr. -bb- aporrear.

club·foot (′fŏot′) s. pie *m* deforme.

club·house (:hous′) s. club *m*.

cluck (klŭk) I. s. *(sound)* cloqueo; FAM. *(dolt)* estúpido, tonto II. intr. cloquear.

clue (klōō) I. s. pista, indicio; *(in puzzle)* indicación *f* ♦ **I haven't a c.** no tengo ni idea II. tr. -(e)ing ♦ **to c. in** poner al tanto de la situación.

clump (klŭmp) I. s. *(lump)* masa; *(trees)* grupo II. intr. andar con pisadas fuertes —tr. agrupar.

clum·sy (klŭm′zē) adj. -i- *(awkward)* torpe; *(unwieldy)* incómodo; *(unrefined)* crudo.

clung (klŭng) cf. **cling.**

clunk (klŭngk) s. sonido sordo.

clus·ter (klŭs′tər) I. s. grupo; *(bunch)* racimo, ramo II. tr. & intr. agrupar(se), arracimar(se).

clutch (klŭch) I. tr. agarrar, asir —intr. ♦ **to c. at** agarrarse a II. s. *(grasp)* apretón *m*; MEC. embrague *m* ♦ **in the c.** en situación crítica ♦ pl. FIG. garras.

clut·ter (klŭt′ər) I. s. desorden *m* II. tr. esparcir desordenadamente.

coach (kōch) I. s. *(carriage)* coche *m*, carruaje *m*; *(bus)* ómnibus *m*; F.C. vagón *m* de pasajeros; AVIA. clase económica; *(trainer)* entrenador *m*; *(tutor)* maestro particular II. tr. & intr. *(to tutor)* dar lecciones suplementarias; *(to train)* entrenar.

coach·man (′mən) s. [pl. **-men**] cochero.

co·ag·u·late (kō-ăg′yə-lāt′) tr. & intr. coagular(se).

coal (kōl) s. carbón *m*, hulla; *(ember)* ascua ♦ **c. tar** alquitrán de hulla • **hard c.** antracita, hulla seca • **soft c.** carbón bituminoso.

co·a·lesce (kō′ə-lĕs′) intr. unirse.

coal·field (kōl′fēld′) s. cuenca carbonífera.

co·a·li·tion (kō′ə-lĭsh′ən) s. coalición *f*.

coarse (kōrs) adj. *(inferior)* basto; *(uncouth)* vulgar; *(rough)* áspero, tosco; *(grainy)* granular.

coars·en (kōr′sən) intr. volverse tosco o vulgar —tr. vulgarizar.

coarse·ness (kōrs′nĭs) s. *(of manners)* grosería; *(texture)* aspereza.

coast (kōst) I. s. costa ♦ **c. guard** guardacostas • **the c. is clear** no hay moros en la costa II. intr. *(to slide)* deslizarse; *(bicycle, car)* rodar sin impulso.

coast·al (kō′stəl) adj. costero.

coast·er (kō′stər) s. *(sled)* trineo; *(mat)* posavasos.

coast·line (kōst′līn′) s. costa, litoral *m*.

coat (kōt) I. s. *(overcoat)* abrigo; *(jacket)* saco, chaqueta; *(of animal)* piel *f*, pelo; *(paint)* mano *f*, capa; *(coating)* baño ♦ **c. of arms** escudo de armas • **c. of mail** cota de malla II. tr. *(to cover)* revestir; *(to paint)* dar una mano o capa; *(to plate)* bañar.

coat·ed (kō′tĭd) adj. cubierto, bañado.

coat·ing (kō′tĭng) s. *(layer)* capa, mano *f*; *(gold, silver)* baño, revestimiento.

coat·tail (kōt′tāl′) s. faldón *m* ♦ **on someone's coattails** a base del éxito de otra persona.

coax (kōks) tr. engatusar.

coax·ing (kōk′sĭng) I. s. engatusamiento II. adj. engatusador.

cob (kŏb) s. elote *m*, mazorca.

co·balt (kō′bôlt′) s. cobalto.

cob·bler (kŏb′lər) s. zapatero; *(pie)* tarta de fruta.

cob·ble·stone (kŏb′əl-stōn′) s. piedra redonda ♦ **c. pavement** empedrado.

co·bra (kō′brə) s. cobra.

cob·web (kŏb′wĕb′) s. telaraña.

co·ca (kō′kə) s. coca.

co·caine (kō-kān′) s. cocaína.

coc·cyx (kŏk′sĭks) s. [pl. **-yges**] cóccix *m*.

cock (kŏk) I. s. *(rooster)* gallo; *(male bird)* macho; *(faucet)* grifo, llave *f*; ARM. *(hammer)* martillo II. tr. ARM. amartillar; *(a hat)* inclinar (hacia arriba); *(fist, ears)* alzar, levantar.

cock·ade (kō-kād′) s. escarapela.

cock·a·ma·mie (kŏk′ə-mā′mē) adj. JER. absurdo.

cock-and-bull story (kŏk′ən-bŏŏl′) s. FAM. patraña, cuento increíble.

cock·a·too (kŏk′ə-tōō′) s. cacatúa.

cock·er·el (kŏk′ər-əl) s. gallo joven.

cock·eyed (kŏk′īd′) adj. OFTAL. bizco; JER. *(crooked)* oblicuo, torcido; *(foolish)* absurdo.

cock·fight (kŏk′fīt′) s. pelea de gallos.

cock·i·ness (kŏk′ē-nĭs) s. presunción *f.*

cock·le (kŏk′əl) s. berberecho ♦ **the cockles of one's heart** las entretelas del corazón.

cock·ney (kŏk′nē) s. lenguaje *m* o habitante *mf* de los barrios bajos de Londres.

cock·pit (kŏk′pĭt′) s. *(arena)* cancha; AVIA. cabina.

cock·roach (kŏk′rōch′) s. cucaracha.

cocks·comb (kŏks′kōm′) s. ZOOL. cresta de gallo; *(fop)* petimetre *m,* fatuo.

cock·sure (kŏk′shŏŏr′) adj. demasiado seguro.

cock·tail (kŏk′tāl′) s. cóctel *m.*

cock·y (kŏk′ē) adj. -i- FAM. presumido, engreído.

co·coa (kō′kō) s. cacao.

co·co(a)·nut (kō′kə-nət) s. coco ♦ **c. palm** cocotero.

co·coon (kə-kōōn′) s. capullo.

cod (kŏd) s. [pl. inv. *o* **s**] bacalao.

cod·dle (kŏd′l) tr. *(to cook)* cocer a fuego lento; *(to pamper)* mimar, consentir.

code (kōd) I. s. código; *(cipher)* clave *f,* cifra ♦ **Morse c.** alfabeto Morse II. tr. codificar; *(a message)* cifrar.

co·de·fend·ant (kō′dĭ-fĕn′dənt) s. coacusado.

co·deine (kō′dēn′) s. codeína.

cod·fish (kŏd′fĭsh′) s. [pl. inv. *o* **es**] bacalao.

codg·er (kŏj′ər) s. FAM. vejete *m.*

cod·i·fy (kŏd′ə-fī′, kō′də-) tr. codificar.

co·di·rec·tion (kō′dĭ-rĕk′shən) s. codirección *f.*

cod-liv·er oil (kŏd′lĭv′ər) aceite *m* de hígado de bacalao.

co·ed (kō′ĕd′) s. FAM. I. s. alumna de una universidad mixta II. adj. coeducacional.

co·ed·u·ca·tion (kō-ĕj′ə-kā′shən) s. coeducación *f,* enseñanza mixta.

co·ed·u·ca·tion·al (:shə-nəl) adj. coeducacional.

co·ef·fi·cient (kō′ə-fĭsh′ənt) s. coeficiente *m.*

co·erce (kō-ûrs′) tr. coaccionar, obligar.

co·er·cion (kō-ûr′zhən) s. coacción *f;* DER. *(restraint)* coerción *f.*

co·e·val (kō-ē′vəl) adj. & s. coetáneo.

co·ex·ist (kō′ĭg-zĭst′) intr. coexistir.

co·ex·is·tence (:zĭs′təns) s. coexistencia.

co·ex·ten·sive (kō′ĭk-stĕn′sĭv) adj. coextenso.

cof·fee (kŏ′fē) s. café *m* ♦ **c. shop** café, cafetería ♦ **c. table** mesa de café o de centro.

cof·fee·pot (:pŏt′) s. cafetera.

cof·fer (kŏ′fər) s. cofre *m* ♦ pl. fondos.

cof·fin (kŏ′fĭn) s. ataúd *m.*

cog (kŏg) s. MEC. diente *m.*

co·gent (kō′jənt) adj. profundamente pensado.

cog·i·tate (kŏj′ĭ-tāt′) intr. & tr. reflexionar.

co·gnac (kōn′yăk′) s. coñac *m.*

cog·nate (kŏg′nāt′) adj. & s. (palabra) afín.

cog·ni·tion (kŏg-nĭsh′ən) s. *(faculty)* cognición *f; (knowledge)* percepción *f.*

cog·ni·zance (kŏg′nĭ-zəns) s. conocimiento ♦ **to take c. of** tener en cuenta.

cog·ni·zant (:zənt) adj. enterado, informado ♦ **to be c. of** saber.

cog·wheel (kŏg′hwēl′) s. rueda dentada.

co·hab·it (kō-hăb′ĭt) intr. cohabitar.

co·here (kō-hîr′) intr. *(objects)* adherirse;

(thoughts) tener coherencia, ser coherente.

co·her·ence/·cy (:əns) s. coherencia.

co·her·ent (:ənt) adj. coherente.

co·he·sion (kō-hē′zhən) s. cohesión *f.*

co·he·sive (:sĭv) adj. cohesivo.

co·hort (kō′hôrt′) s. FAM. socio, compañero.

coif·fure (kwä-fyŏŏr′) s. tocado, peinado.

coil (koil) I. s. rollo; *(single)* anillo, vuelta; *(of pipe)* serpentín *m;* ELEC. bobina II. tr. & intr. enrollar(se), enroscar(se).

coin (koin) I. s. moneda II. tr. *(to mint)* acuñar; *(phrase, word)* inventar.

co·in·cide (kō′ĭn-sīd′) intr. coincidir.

co·in·ci·dence (kō-ĭn′sĭ-dəns) s. *(identicalness)* coincidencia; *(chance)* casualidad *f.*

co·in·ci·den·tal (-′-dĕn′təl) adj. *(identical)* coincidente; *(accidental)* casual, fortuito.

co·i·tus (kō′ĭ-təs) s. coito.

coke¹ (kōk) s. MIN. coque *m.*

coke² s. JER. cocaína.

co·la (kō′lə) s. cola (nuez, bebida).

col·an·der (kŭl′ən-dər) s. colador *m.*

cold (kōld) I. adj. frío; *(impassive)* impasible; *(fact, truth)* mero, sencillo; FAM. *(unconscious)* sin conocimiento; *(unprepared)* sin preparación ♦ **c. comfort** poco consuelo ♦ **c. cream** crema para el cutis ♦ **c. cuts** fiambres ♦ **c. feet** JER. miedo ♦ **c. shoulder** FAM. indiferencia, frialdad ♦ **c. snap** *o* **spell** ola de frío ♦ **c. sore** afta (labial) ♦ **in c. blood** a sangre fría ♦ **to be c.** *(object)* estar frío; *(person)* tener frío; *(weather)* hacer frío II. adv. *(totally)* completamente, *(unprepared)* sin preparación, en seco ♦ **to know c.** saber al dedillo III. s. frío; MED. catarro, resfriado ♦ **out in the c.** en la estacada • **to catch (a) c.** resfriarse.

cold-blood·ed (′blŭd′ĭd) adj. impasible; *(murder)* a sangre fría; ZOOL. de sangre fría.

cold-heart·ed (:här′tĭd) adj. insensible.

cold·ness (:nĭs) s. frío, frialdad *f.*

cole (kōl) s. colza, col *f.*

cole·slaw (′slō′) s. ensalada de col.

col·ic (kŏl′ĭk) s. cólico.

col·i·se·um (kŏl′ĭ-sē′əm) s. coliseo.

co·li·tis (kō-lī′tĭs) s. colitis *f.*

col·lab·o·rate (kə-lăb′ə-rāt′) intr. colaborar.

col·lab·o·ra·tion (-′-rā′shən) s. colaboración *f; (treason)* colaboracionismo.

col·lab·o·ra·tion·ist (:shə-nĭst) s. colaboracionista *mf.*

col·lab·o·ra·tive (-′-′ tĭv) adj. cooperativo.

col·lab·o·ra·tor (:tər) s. colaborador *m; (traitor)* colaboracionista *mf.*

col·lage (kə-läzh′) s. collage *m,* montaje *m.*

col·lapse (kə-lăps′) I. intr. caerse, derrumbarse; *(person)* desplomarse; *(business)* fracasar; *(to fold)* plegarse —tr. plegar II. s. caída, derrumbe *f; (business)* fracaso; MED. colapso.

col·laps·i·ble/a·ble (kə-lăp′sə-bəl) adj. plegable.

col·lar (kŏl′ər) I. s. cuello; JOY., MEC. collar *m; (harness)* collera II. tr. *(an animal)* poner un collar a; FAM. *(to nab)* agarrar, detener.

col·lar·bone (:bōn′) s. clavícula.

col·late (kə-lāt′, kŏl′āt′) tr. *(texts)* colacionar; *(pages)* ordenar.

col·lat·er·al (kə-lăt′ər-əl) I. adj. colateral; *(evidence)* corroborante; FIN. con garantía de pago II. s. prenda, hipoteca.

col·league (kŏl′ēg′) s. colega *mf.*

col·lect (kə-lĕkt′) I. tr. *(to gather)* juntar, reunir; *(as hobby)* coleccionar; *(payments)* recaudar ♦ **to c. oneself** controlarse —intr. juntarse, acumularse **II.** adj. & adv. *(telephone call)* de cobro revertido.

col·lect·ed (kə-lĕk′tĭd) adj. recogido, sosegado ♦ **c. works** obras completas.

col·lec·tion (:shən) s. colección *f*; *(heap)* acumulación *f*; *(of money)* cobro; *(donation)* colecta.

col·lec·tive (:tĭv) **I.** adj. colectivo ♦ **c. farm** granja cooperativa **II.** s. cooperativa.

col·lec·tiv·ize (:tə-vīst) s. colectivista *mf*.

col·lec·tiv·ize (:tə-vīz′) tr. colectivizar.

col·lec·tor (:tər) s. colector *m*; *(of taxes)* recaudador *m*; *(of bills)* cobrador *m*; *(as hobby)* coleccionista *mf*.

col·lege (kŏl′ĭj) s. universidad *f*; *(department)* facultad *f*; RELIG. colegio.

col·le·gian (kə-lē′jən) s. estudiante *mf* universitario.

col·le·giate (:jĭt) adj. universitario.

col·lide (kə-līd′) intr. chocar.

col·lie (kŏl′ē) s. perro pastor escocés.

col·lier (kŏl′yər) s. G.B. minero de carbón.

col·li·sion (kə-lĭzh′ən) s. choque *m*.

col·loid (kŏl′oid′) s. & adj. coloide *m*.

col·lo·qui·al (kə-lō′kwē-əl) adj. familiar.

col·lo·qui·al·ism (:ə-lĭz′əm) s. estilo *o* expresión *f* familiar.

col·lo·qui·um (:əm) s. [pl. *s o* -**ia**] coloquio.

col·lo·quy (kŏl′ə-kwē) s. coloquio.

col·lude (kə-lōōd′) intr. confabularse.

col·lu·sion (kə-lōō′zhən) s. confabulación *f*.

co·logne (kə-lōn′) s. colonia *(perfume)*.

co·lon[1] (kō′lən) s. GRAM. dos puntos.

co·lon[2] s. [pl. *s o* -**la**] ANAT. colon *m*.

colo·nel (kûr′nəl) s. coronel *m*.

co·lo·ni·al (kə-lō′nē-əl) **I.** adj. *(of a colony)* colonial; *(colonizing)* colonizador **II.** s. colono.

co·lo·ni·al·ist (:ə-lĭst) s. & adj. colonialista *mf*.

col·o·nist (kŏl′ə-nĭst) s. *(colonizer)* colonizador *m*; *(inhabitant)* colono.

col·o·nize (:nīz′) tr. colonizar.

col·o·niz·er (:nī′zər) s. colonizador *m*.

col·on·nade (kŏl′ə-nād′) s. columnata.

col·o·ny (kŏl′ə-nē) s. colonia.

col·or (kŭl′ər) **I.** s. color *m*; ARTE., MÚS. colorido ♦ **c. guard** escolta de bandera • **c. line** FIG. barrera racial • **c. photography** cromofotografía • **c. television** televisión en color • **in c.** en colores • **in full c.** a todo color • **of c.** verde • **to change c.** mudar de color • **to lose c.** palidecer ♦ pl. *(flag)* bandera, estandarte; *(of school)* insignia; *(character)* carácter *m* • **with flying c.** con mucho éxito **II.** tr. colorear; *(to paint)* pintar; *(to dye)* teñir; *(to distort)* alterar, embellecer; *(to influence)* influir en —intr. sonrojarse, ruborizarse.

col·or·a·tion (′ə-rā′shən) s. coloración *f*.

col·or·blind (′ər-blīnd′) adj. MED. daltoniano; FIG. insensible a distinciones raciales.

col·ored (:ərd) **I.** adj. coloreado, de color; *(person)* de color **II.** s. persona de color.

col·or·fast (:ər-făst′) adj. de color fijo.

col·or·ful (:fəl) adj. *(vivid)* de gran colorido; *(picturesque)* pintoresco.

col·or·ing (:ĭng) s. *(coloration)* coloración *f*; *(dye)* colorante *m*.

col·or·less (:lĭs) adj. incoloro.

co·los·sal (kə-lŏs′əl) adj. colosal.

co·los·sus (:əs) s. [pl. **es** *o* -**si**] coloso.

co·los·to·my (kə-lŏs′tə-mē) s. colostomía.

col·our (kŭl′ər) G.B. var. de **color.**

colt (kōlt) s. potro.

col·umn (kŏl′əm) s. columna.

col·um·nist (:nĭst) s. columnista *mf*.

co·ma (kō′mə) s. coma *m*.

co·ma·tose (:tōs′) adj. comatoso.

comb (kōm) **I.** s. peine *m*; ORNIT. *(crest)* cresta; *(honeycomb)* panal *m* **II.** tr. peinar; *(to search)* registrar (detalladamente) ♦ **to c. one's hair** peinarse.

com·bat **I.** tr. (kəm-băt′, kŏm′băt′) pelear contra, dar batalla; FIG. combatir, resistir **II.** s. (kŏm′băt′) combate *m*.

com·bat·ant (kəm-băt′nt) s. combatiente *m*.

com·bat·ive (:ĭv) adj. combativo.

com·bi·na·tion (kŏm′bə-nā′shən) s. combinación *f*; *(mix)* mezcla.

com·bine **I.** tr. & intr. (kəm-bīn′) combinar(se); *(to mix)* mezclar **II.** s. (kŏm′bīn′) AGR. segadora; *(association)* asociación *f*.

com·bo (kŏm′bō) s. conjunto.

com·bus·ti·ble (kəm-bŭs′tə-bəl) adj. & s. combustible *m*.

com·bus·tion (:chən) s. combustión *f*.

come (kŭm) **I.** intr. came, come venir; *(to arrive at, extend to)* llegar; *(to amount to)* ascender a ♦ **c. what may** pase lo que pase • **to c. about** suceder, ocurrir; MARÍT. virar • **to c. across** *(to find)* encontrarse con; *(to be understood)* ser comprendido • **to c. after** *(to follow)* seguir; *(to pursue)* venir en busca de • **to c. along** *(to accompany)* acompañar; *(to progress)* progresar • **to c. around** *(to visit)* hacer una visita; *(to revive)* volver en sí • **to c. at** atacar • **to c. away** irse, retirarse • **to c. back** volver • **to c. before** preceder; DER. comparecer ante (juez, tribunal) • **to c. between** interponerse entre • **to c. by** *(to visit)* hacer una visita; *(to obtain)* obtener, lograr • **to c. down** bajar; *(to collapse)* derrumbarse; *(to fall)* caer(se) • **to c. down with** FAM. caer enfermo con • **to c. in** *(to enter)* entrar; *(in a race)* llegar; *(to figure into)* figurar, entrar • **to c. in for** FAM. recibir • **to c. into** heredar • **to c. of** resultar de, suceder por • **to c. off** *(to detach)* soltarse, separarse; *(to acquit oneself)* salir (bien, mal); *(to happen)* tener lugar • **to c. on** TEAT. salir a escena; *(to present oneself)* presentarse *(as como)* • **to c. out** FAM. tirarse a • **to c. out** salir; *(to detach)* desprenderse; *(to appear)* asomar; *(book)* publicarse; *(to result)* resultar (bien, mal); *(for o against)* declararse; *(stain)* quitarse; *(truth)* salir a la luz, revelarse; *(to bloom)* florecer • **to c. out with** *(to announce)* revelar, publicar; *(a product)* salir con, ofrecer; FAM. *(to say)* saltar con, soltar (comentario, maldición) • **to c. over** *(to happen to)* sobrevenir, invadir; FAM. *(to visit)* venir • **to c. through** *(to do what is wanted)* cumplir; *(to be apparent)* manifestarse; *(to endure)* pasar por, salir de • **to c. through** with JER. cumplir con • **to c. to** *(to revive)* recobrar los sentidos, volver en sí; *(to amount to)* reducirse a • **to c. to one** ocurrírsele • **to c. under** *(a category)* figurar entre; *(to be subject to)* caer bajo, estar sometido a (poder, influencia) • **to c. up** subir; *(to arise)* presentarse, surgir; *(to be mentioned)* ser mencionado • **to c. up against** tropezar *o* dar con • **to c. up to** *(in quality)* estar a la altura de; *(in height)* llegar hasta; *(to approach)* acercarse a • **to c. up with** *(to produce)* producir; *(to propose)* sugerir, proponer • **to c.**

within entrar *o* estar dentro de • **when it comes to** cuando se trata de **II.** interj. ¡venga!, ¡ven! ♦ **c. again?** ¿cómo? • **c. in!** ¡adelante!, ¡pase! • **c. off it!** FAM. ¡no me vengas con eso! • **c. now!** ¡vamos!, ¡no es para tanto! • **c. on!** FAM. *(hurry up!)* ¡date prisa!, ¡apúrate!; *(you're kidding!)* ¡no me digas!

come·back ('băk') s. réplica, respuesta ingeniosa ♦ **to make a c.** restablecerse, reaparecer.

co·me·di·an (kə-mē'dē-ən) s. *(entertainer)* cómico; *(actor)* comediante m.

co·me·di·enne (-'-ĕn') s. *(entertainer)* cómica; *(actress)* comedianta.

come·down (kŭm'doun') s. *(in status)* bajón m, pérdida de rango; *(disappointment)* revés m.

com·e·dy (kŏm'ĭ-dē) s. comedia.

come·ly (kŭm'lē) adj. **-i-** atractivo.

come-on (:ŏn') s. aliciente m, incentivo.

com·er (:ər) s. *(arrival)* persona que llega; FAM. *(rising star)* persona prometedora.

com·et (kŏm'ĭt) s. cometa m.

come·up·pance (kŭm-ŭp'əns) s. FAM. castigo merecido.

com·fort (kŭm'fərt) **I.** tr. confortar, consolar; *(to relieve)* aliviar **II.** s. *(well-being)* confort m; *(relief)* alivio; *(consolation)* consuelo; *(ease)* comodidad f ♦ **c. station** excusado público • **to be a c.** ser un consuelo.

com·fort·a·ble (:fər-tə-bəl) adj. *(easy)* confortable, cómodo; FAM. *(sufficient)* adecuado.

com·fort·er (:tər) s. *(person)* consolador m; *(quilt)* edredón m.

com·fy (kŭm'fē) adj. **-i-** FAM. cómodo.

com·ic (kŏm'ĭk) adj. & s. cómico ♦ **c. book** revista de historietas ilustradas • **c. strip** tira cómica.

com·i·cal (:ĭ-kəl) adj. cómico.

com·ing (kŭm'ĭng) **I.** adj. venidero **II.** s. venida, llegada ♦ **comings and goings** idas y venidas.

com·ma (kŏm'ə) s. GRAM. coma.

com·mand (kə-mănd') **I.** tr. mandar; *(to give orders)* ordenar; *(to rule)* regir; *(to have available)* disponer de, poseer; *(to deserve)* infundir; *(to overlook)* dominar —intr. mandar, dar órdenes **II.** s. mando; *(order)* orden f; *(authority)* mandato, mando; *(mastery)* dominio; MIL. *(jurisdiction)* comando ♦ **at one's c.** a la disposición de uno • **c. headquarters** centro de comando • **c. post** puesto de mando ♦ **to be in c. of** estar al mando de • **under the c. of** al mando de.

com·man·dant (kŏm'ən-dănt') s. comandante m.

com·man·deer (:dîr') tr. *(to confiscate)* confiscar; FAM. *(to seize)* apoderarse de.

com·mand·er (kə-măn'dər) s. jefe m; MARÍT. capitán m de fragata; MIL. comandante m.

com·mand·ing (:dĭng) adj. que está al mando; *(impressive)* imponente; *(position)* dominante.

com·mand·ment (kə-mănd'mənt) s. orden f; RELIG. mandamiento.

com·man·do (kə-măn'dō) s. [pl. **(e)s**] comando.

com·mem·o·rate (kə-mĕm'ə-rāt') tr. conmemorar.

com·mence (kə-mĕns') tr. & intr. comenzar.

com·mence·ment (:mənt) s. comienzo, principio; EDUC. ceremonia de entrega de diplomas.

com·mend (kə-mĕnd') tr. *(to praise)* elogiar, alabar; *(to recommend)* recomendar; *(to entrust)* encomendar.

com·mend·a·ble (kə-mĕn'də-bəl) adj. loable.

com·men·da·tion (kŏm'ən-dā'shən) s. *(praise)* elogio; *(recommendation)* recomendación f; *(citation)* mención f.

com·men·su·rate (kə-mĕn'sər-ĭt) adj. proporcionado.

com·ment (kŏm'ĕnt') **I.** s. comentario; *(remark)* observación f **II.** intr. comentar, observar.

com·men·tar·y (:ən-tĕr'ē) s. comentario.

com·men·tate (:tāt') tr. & intr. comentar.

com·men·ta·tor (:tā'tər) s. locutor m.

com·merce (kŏm'ərs) s. comercio.

com·mer·cial (kə-mûr'shəl) **I.** adj. comercial **II.** s. anuncio.

com·mer·cial·ism (:shə-lĭz'əm) s. comercialismo.

com·mer·cial·ize (:līz') tr. comercializar.

com·mie (kŏm'ē) s. FAM. rojo, comunista mf.

com·min·gle (kə-mĭng'gəl) intr. mezclarse.

com·mis·er·ate (kə-mĭz'ə-rāt') intr. compadecerse *(with* de).

com·mis·sar (kŏm'ĭ-sär') s. comisario.

com·mis·sar·i·at ('-sär'ē-ĭt) s. intendencia militar.

com·mis·sar·y ('-sĕr'ē) s. economato.

com·mis·sion (kə-mĭsh'ən) **I.** s. comisión f; MIL. nombramiento ♦ **out of c.** fuera de servicio; *(broken)* descompuesto • **to put out of c.** *(to ruin)* inutilizar; FAM. *(to sideline)* poner fuera de combate, acabar con • **to work on c.** trabajar a comisión **II.** tr. MIL. nombrar; *(to order)* encargar, mandar a hacer; *(ship)* poner en servicio.

com·mis·sion·er (:ə-nər) s. miembro de una comisión; *(official)* comisario.

com·mit (kə-mĭt') tr. **-tt-** cometer; *(to entrust)* encomendar; *(to jail)* encarcelar; *(to institutionalize)* internar; *(to dispose of)* entregar ♦ **to c. oneself** comprometerse • **to c. to paper** *o* **writing** consignar por escrito.

com·mit·ment (:mənt) s. *(pledge)* compromiso; *(institutionalization)* internamiento, reclusión f; *(obligation)* obligación f.

com·mit·tal (:l) s. *(confinement)* confinamiento, reclusión f; *(pledging)* obligación f.

com·mit·tee (kə-mĭt'ē) s. comité m, comisión f.

com·mode (kə-mōd') s. *(bureau)* cómoda; *(washbowl)* palangenero; *(toilet)* retrete m.

com·mo·di·ous (kə-mō'dē-əs) adj. espacioso, amplio.

com·mod·i·ty (kə-mŏd'ĭ-tē) s. mercancía.

com·mo·dore (kŏm'ə-dôr') s. comodoro.

com·mon (kŏm'ən) adj. **-er, -est** común; *(public)* público • *(widespread)* general; *(frequent)* usual, frecuente; *(quality)* mediocre, inferior ♦ **c. cold** resfriado, catarro • **c. fraction** fracción ordinaria • **c. ground** tema de interés mutuo • **c. law** derecho consuetudinario • **c. sense** sentido común • **c. stock** acciones ordinarias **II.** s. ejido, campo comunal ♦ **Commons** G.B. Cámara de los Comunes.

com·mon·er (:ə-nər) s. plebeyo.

com·mon-law marriage (:ən-lô') s. matrimonio consensual.

com·mon·place (:plās') **I.** adj. común, ordinario **II.** s. lugar m común.

com·mon·wealth (:wĕlth') s. *(people)* comunidad f; *(state)* república.

com·mo·tion (kə-mō'shən) s. tumulto, alboroto.

com·mu·nal (kə-myōo'nəl) adj. comunal.

com·mune¹ (kə-myōōn') intr. comunicarse, comulgar.

com·mune² (kŏm'yōōn) s. POL. comuna; *(community)* vivienda colectiva.

com·mu·ni·ca·ble (kə-myōō'nĭ-kə-bəl) adj. comunicable; *(contagious)* contagioso.

com·mu·ni·cant (:kənt) S. RELIG. comulgante *m*; *(communicator)* comunicante *m.*

com·mu·ni·cate (:kāt') tr. & intr. comunicar(se).

com·mu·ni·ca·tion (-'-kā'shən) s. comunicación *f.*

com·mu·ni·ca·tive (-'-'tĭv) adj. comunicativo.

com·mu·ni·ca·tor (:kā'tər) s. comunicante *mf.*

com·mun·ion (kə-myōōn'yən) s. comunión *f.*

com·mu·ni·qué (kə-myōō'nĭ-kā') s. comunicado oficial.

com·mu·nism (kŏm'yə-nĭz'əm) s. comunismo.

com·mu·nist (:nĭst) s. & adj. comunista *mf.*

com·mu·nis·tic ('-nĭs'tĭk) adj. comunista.

com·mu·ni·ty (kə-myōō'nĭ-tē) s. comunidad *f*; *(local inhabitants)* vecindario.

com·mu·nize (kŏm'yə-nīz') tr. convertir en propiedad comunal.

com·mu·ta·tion (kŏm'yə-tā'shən) s. conmutación *f* ♦ **c. ticket** billete de abono.

com·mu·ta·tive ('-'tə-tĭv) adj. conmutativo.

com·mute (kə myōōt') I. tr. conmutar — intr. viajar diariamente al lugar en que se trabaja II. s. viaje diario.

com·mut·er (kə-myōō'tər) s. persona que viaja diariamente (esp. al trabajo).

com·pact¹ I. adj. (kəm-pākt', kŏm'pākt') compacto; *(concise)* conciso II. tr. (kəm-pākt') comprimir III. s. (kŏm'pākt') polvera; AUTO. automóvil compacto.

com·pact² (kŏm'pākt') s. pacto, convenio.

com·pan·ion (kəm-păn'yən) s. compañero.

com·pan·ion·a·ble (:yə nə bəl) adj. sociable.

com·pan·ion·ship (:yən-shĭp') s. compañerismo.

com·pan·ion·way (:wā') s. escalera de cámara.

com·pa·ny (kŭm'pə-nē) s. compañía; *(group)* grupo; *(guests)* invitado(s) ♦ **to keep c.** with asociarse con • **to keep someone c.** hacerle compañía a alguien • **to part c.** separarse.

com·pa·ra·ble (kŏm'pər-ə-bəl, kəm-pār'-) adj. comparable

com·par·a·tive (kəm-pār'ə-tĭv) I. adj. comparativo; *(relative)* relativo ♦ **c. literature** literatura comparada II. s. comparativo.

com·pare (kəm pâr') I. tr. & intr. (poderse) comparar • **as compared with** comparado con II. s. ♦ **beyond c.** incomparable.

com·par·i·son (:ī-sən) s. comparación *f* ♦ **by c.** en comparación.

com·part·ment (kəm-pärt'mənt) s. compartimiento.

com·pass (kŭm'pəs) I. s. *(magnetic)* brújula, compás *m*; *(perimeter)* perímetro; *(scope)* alcance *m* ♦ **c.** *o* pl. GEOM. compás II. tr. circundar, rodear.

com·pas·sion (kəm-păsh'ən) s. compasión *f.*

com·pas·sion·ate (:ə-nĭt) adj. compasivo.

com·pat·i·ble (kəm-păt'ə-bəl) adj. compatible.

com·pa·tri·ot (kəm-pā'trē-ət) s. compatriota *mf.*

com·pel (kəm-pĕl') tr. **-ll-** compeler, obligar; *(respect, belief)* imponer.

com·pel·ling (:ĭng) adj. obligatorio; *(evidence)* incontestable; *(need)* apremiante.

com·pen·di·um (kəm-pĕn'dē-əm) [pl. **s** *o* **-ia**] s. compendio.

com·pen·sate (kŏm'pən-sāt') tr. compensar; COM. indemnizar — intr. ♦ **to c. for** compensar.

com·pen·sa·tion ('-sā'shən) s. compensación *f*; COM. indemnización *f.*

com·pete (kəm-pēt') intr. competir ♦ **to c. in** concursar *o* tomar parte en.

com·pe·tence (kŏm'pĭ-tns) s. competencia.

com·pe·tent (:tnt) adj. competente.

com·pe·ti·tion ('-tĭsh'ən) s. competencia ♦ **the c.** nuestros competidores.

com·pet·i·tive (kəm-pĕt'ĭ-tĭv) adj. competitivo; *(person)* competidor; *(spirit)* de competencia.

com·pet·i·tor (:tər) s. competidor *m.*

com·pi·la·tion (kŏm'pə-lā'shən) s. compilación *f*, recopilación *f.*

com·pile (kəm-pīl') tr. compilar, recopilar.

com·pla·cen·cy/·cence (kəm-plā'sən-sē/-səns) s. *(gratification)* complacencia; *(smugness)* satisfacción *f* de sí mismo.

com·pla·cent (:sənt) adj. pagado de sí mismo.

com·plain (kəm-plān') intr. quejarse *(about de).*

com·plain·ant (:plā'nənt) s. demandante *mf.*

com·plaint (:plānt') s. queja; *(protest)* reclamación *f*; DER. querella, demanda.

com·plai·sant (kəm-plā'sənt) adj. complaciente.

com·ple·ment (kŏm'plə-mənt) I. s. complemento II. tr. complementar.

com·ple·men·ta·ry (-'-mĕn'tə-rē) adj. complementario.

com·plete (kəm-plēt') I. adj. completo; *(thorough)* total; *(utter)* verdadero II. tr. completar, llevar a cabo; *(a form)* llenar; *(to conclude)* terminar.

com·ple·tion (-plē'shən) s. terminación *f* ♦ **to be near c.** estar al terminarse.

com·plex I. adj. (kəm-plĕks', kŏm'plĕks') *(composite)* compuesto; *(intricate)* intrincado, complejo II. s. (kŏm'plĕks') complejo.

com·plex·ion (kəm-plĕk'shən) s. *(skin)* tez *f*; *(character)* aspecto, carácter *m.*

com·pli·ance (kəm-plī'əns) s. *(with an order)* acatamiento; *(acquiescence)* conformidad *f* ♦ **in c. with** conforme a.

com·pli·ant (:ənt) adj. obediente, dócil.

com·pli·cate (kŏm'plĭ-kāt') tr. complicar.

com·pli·cat·ed (:kā'tĭd) adj. complicado.

com·pli·ca·tion ('-shən) s. complicación *f.*

com·plic·i·ty (kəm-plĭs'ĭ-tē) s. complicidad *f.*

com·pli·ment (kŏm'plə-mənt) I. s. *(praise)* elogio; *(honor)* honor *m*; *(flattery)* piropo ♦ **to pay a c.** to elogiar • **to take it as a c. that** ser un honor para uno que ♦ pl. saludos • **with the c. of** obsequio de II. tr. elogiar, felicitar.

com·pli·men·ta·ry ('-mĕn'tə-rē) adj. elogioso, halagador; *(free)* de favor.

com·ply (kəm-plī') intr. *(with an order)* acatar, obedecer; *(with a request)* acceder.

com·po·nent (kəm-pō'nənt) I. s. componente *m*, elemento II. adj. componente; *(system)* de elementos.

com·port·ment (kəm-pòrt'mənt) s. comportamiento, conducta.

com·pose (kəm-pōz') tr. & intr. componer ♦ **to be composed of** estar integrado por • **to c. oneself** tranquilizarse.

com·posed (:pōzd') adj. sosegado, tranquilo.

com·pos·er (:pō'zər) s. compositor *m.*

com·pos·ite (:pŏz'ĭt) adj. & s. compuesto.

com·po·si·tion (kŏm′pə-zĭsh′ən) s. composición f.

com·po·sure (kəm-pō′zhər) s. serenidad f.

com·pound¹ (kŏm′pound′) I. adj. compuesto ♦ **c. fracture** MED. fractura complicada II. s. compuesto; GRAM. palabra compuesta III. tr. (kəm-pound′) (to combine) mezclar, combinar; (interest) calcular cumulativamente; (to add to) agravar.

com·pound² s. (buildings) conglomerado encerrado de residencias.

com·pre·hend (kŏm′prĭ-hěnd′) tr. comprender.

com·pre·hen·si·ble (:hěn′sə-bəl) adj. comprensible.

com·pre·hen·sion (:shən) s. comprensión f.

com·pre·hen·sive (:sĭv) adj. (broad) amplio, general; (overall) de conjunto; (knowledge) comprensivo; (charge) total; (insurance) a todo riesgo.

com·press I. tr. (kəm-prěs′) comprimir; (to shorten) condensar II. s. (kŏm′prěs′) compresa.

com·pressed (kəm-prěst′) adj. comprimido.

com·pres·sion (:prěsh′ən) s. compresión f.

com·prise (kəm-prīz′) tr. (to include) comprender, incluir; (to consist of) constar de.

com·pro·mise (kŏm′prə-mīz′) I. s. compromiso, acuerdo; (concession) concesión f II. tr. (to settle) componer; (to endanger) comprometer —intr. hacer concesiones.

com·pro·mis·ing (:mī′zĭng) adj. (accommodating) transigente; (detrimental) comprometedor.

com·pul·sion (kəm-pŭl′shən) s. compulsión f; (impulse) impulso ♦ **to feel a c.** to sentirse obligado o impelido ♦ **under c.** a la fuerza.

com·pul·sive (:sĭv) adj. (desire) incontrolable; (person) obsesivo.

com·pul·so·ry (:sə-rē) adj. (coercive) compulsorio; (required) obligatorio.

com·punc·tion (kəm-pŭngk′shən) s. compunción f ♦ **without c.** sin escrúpulo.

com·pu·ta·tion (kŏm′pyōō-tā′shən) s. cálculo.

com·pute (kəm-pyōōt′) tr. computar, calcular.

com·put·er (:pyōō′tər) s. computadora, ordenador m ♦ **c. language** lenguaje de máquina.

com·put·er·ize (:tə-rīz′) tr. (data) computarizar; (office) instalar computadoras en ♦ **to be computerized** hacerse computarizar.

com·rade (kŏm′răd′) s. camarada mf.

con¹ (kŏn) adv. & s. contra m.

con² JER. I. tr. **-nn-** estafar, engañar II. s. estafa ♦ **c. game** estafa ♦ **c. man** estafador.

con·cat·e·nate (kən-kăt′n-āt′) tr. concatenar.

con·cave (kŏn-kāv′) adj. cóncavo.

con·ceal (kən-sēl′) tr. ocultar; (a crime) encubrir.

con·ceal·ment (:mənt) s. ocultación f; (of a crime) encubrimiento.

con·cede (kən-sēd′) tr. conceder —intr. hacer una concesión.

con·ceit (kən-sēt′) s. vanidad f, presunción f; (metaphor) concepto.

con·ceit·ed (:sē′tĭd) adj. vanidoso, engreído.

con·ceiv·a·ble (kən-sē′və-bəl) adj. concebible.

con·ceive (kən-sēv′) tr. & intr. concebir.

con·cen·trate (kŏn′sən-trāt′) I. tr. & intr. concentrar(se) II. s. concentrado.

con·cen·tra·tion (′-trā′shən) s. concentración f ♦ **c. camp** campo de concentración.

con·cen·tric (kən-sěn′trĭk) adj. concéntrico.

con·cept (kŏn′sěpt′) s. concepto.

con·cep·tion (kən-sěp′shən) s. concepción f; (plan) proyecto; (idea) concepto, idea.

con·cep·tu·al (:chōō-əl) adj. conceptual.

con·cern (kən-sûrn′) I. tr. (to be about) tratar de; (to affect) concernir a; (to trouble) preocupar ♦ **as concerns** en lo que concierne a ♦ **to c. oneself with** ocuparse de, interesarse por ♦ **those concerned** los interesados ♦ **to whom it may c.** a quien corresponda II. s. (affair) asunto; (interest) interés m; (worry) preocupación f ♦ **to be of no c.** carecer de importancia.

con·cerned (:sûrnd′) adj. (interested) interesado; (worried) preocupado.

con·cern·ing (:sûr′nĭng) prep. referente a.

con·cert I. s. (kŏn′sûrt′) concierto ♦ **in c. with** de concierto con II. tr. & intr. (kən-sûrt′) concertar(se).

con·cert·ed (kən-sûr′tĭd) adj. conjunto.

con·cer·to (kən-chěr′tō) s. [pl. **s** o **-ti**] concierto.

con·ces·sion (kən-sěsh′ən) s. concesión f.

con·ces·sion·aire (-′-ə-nâr′) s. concesionario.

conch (kŏngk, kŏnch) s. [pl. **(e)s**] caracol marino; (shell) caracola.

con·cil·i·ate (kən-sĭl′ē-āt′) tr. conciliar.

con·cil·i·a·tor (:ā′tər) s. mediador m.

con·cise (kən-sīs′) adj. conciso, sucinto.

con·clude (kən-klōōd′) tr. & intr. concluir.

con·clu·sion (:klōō′zhən) s. conclusión f ♦ **to bring to a c.** concluir.

con·clu·sive (:sĭv) adj. concluyente, decisivo.

con·coct (kən-kŏkt′) tr. (food) confeccionar, preparar; (to invent) fabricar.

con·coc·tion (:kŏk′shən) s. confección f; (brew) brebaje m; (lie) fabricación f.

con·cord (kŏn′kôrd′) s. concordia; (treaty) tratado.

con·course (kŏn′kôrs′) s. (throng) multitud f; (for passengers) salón m, vestíbulo.

con·crete (kŏn-krēt′) I. adj. concreto; CONSTR. (′′) de concreto o hormigón II. s. (′′) concreto, hormigón m.

con·cu·bine (kŏng′kyə-bīn′) s. concubina.

con·cu·pis·cent (kŏn-kyōō′pĭ-sənt) adj. concupiscente.

con·cur (kən-kûr′) intr. **-rr-** (to agree) convenir; (to coincide) concurrir, coincidir.

con·cur·rence (:əns) s. (agreement) acuerdo; (coincidence) concurrencia, coincidencia.

con·cur·rent (:ənt) adj. concurrente.

con·cus·sion (kən-kŭsh′ən) s. (shock) concusión f; (injury) conmoción f cerebral.

con·demn (kən-děm′) tr. condenar; (a building) declarar inhabitable.

con·dem·na·ble (:nə-bəl) adj. condenable.

con·den·sa·tion (kŏn′děn-sā′shən) s. condensación f; LIT. versión condensada.

con·dense (kən-děns′) tr. & intr. condensar(se).

con·dens·er (:děn′sər) s. condensador m.

con·de·scend (kŏn′dĭ-sěnd′) intr. dignarse.

con·de·scend·ing (:sěn′dĭng) adj. condescendiente.

con·de·scen·sion (:shən) s. condescendencia.

con·di·ment (kŏn′də-mənt) s. condimento.

con·di·tion (kən-dĭsh′ən) I. s. condición f; (health) estado de salud ♦ **on c. that** a condición que ♦ **on one c.** con una condición ♦ **to be in no c. to** no estar en condiciones de ♦ **to keep in c.** mantenerse en forma II. tr. (to qualify, train) condicionar; (to make fit) poner en condiciones; *(by exercising)* poner en forma; *(to adapt)* acostumbrar.

con·di·tion·al (·ʼə-nəl) adj. condicional ♦ **to be c. on** depender de.

con·di·tion·er (·nər) s. acondicionador *m.*

con·di·tion·ing (:nǐng) s. acondicionamiento.

con·do·lence (kən-dō´ləns) s. condolencia ♦ **to offer condolences to** dar el pésame a.

con·dom (kŏn´dəm) s. preservativo.

con·do·min·i·um (kŏn´də-mǐn´ē-əm) s. condominio.

con·done (kən-dōn´) tr. condonar.

con·dor (kŏn´dôr´) s. cóndor *m.*

con·du·cive (kən-dōō´sǐv) adj. ♦ **c. to** conducente a.

con·duct I. tr. (kən-dŭkt´) *(to direct)* dirigir (negocio, orquesta); *(to carry out)* llevar a cabo, hacer; *(a tour)* servir de guía a; FÍS. conducir ♦ **to c. oneself** conducirse II. s. (kŏn´dŭkt´) *(behavior)* conducta, comportamiento; *(management)* dirección *f.*

con·duc·tor (kən-dŭk´tər) s. *(train, bus)* conductor *m,* cobrador *m;* MÚS. director *m;* FÍS. conductor.

con·duit (kŏn´dǐt, :dōō-ǐt) s. conducto.

cone (kōn) s. cono; CUL. barquillo, cucurucho.

con·fect (kən-fĕkt´) tr. confeccionar.

con·fec·tion (:fĕk´shən) s. confección *f; (sweet)* confitura.

con·fec·tion·er (:shə-nər) s. confitero.

con·fed·er·a·cy (kən-fĕd´ər-ə-sē) s. confederación *f; (conspiracy)* complot *m.*

con·fed·er·ate I. adj. & s. (:ər-ǐt) confederado II. tr. & intr. (:ə-rāt´) confederar(se).

con·fer (kən-fûr´) tr. & intr. **-rr-** conferir.

con·fer·ence (kŏn´fər-əns) s. *(assembly)* conferencia, congreso; *(meeting)* reunión *f.*

con·fer·ral (kən-fûr´əl) s. concesión *f.*

con·fess (kən-fĕs´) tr. confesar —intr. confesar; RELIG. confesarse.

con·fessed (:fĕst´) adj. declarado.

con·fes·sion (:fĕsh´ən) s. confesión *f.*

con·fes·sion·al (:ə-nəl) I. adj. confesional II. s. confesionario.

con·fes·sor (kən-fĕs´ər) s. *(priest)* confesor *m; (sinner)* penitente *mf.*

con·fet·ti (kən-fĕt´ē) s.pl. confeti *m.*

con·fi·dant (kŏn´fǐ-dänt´) s. confidente *mf.*

con·fide (kən-fīd´) tr. & intr. confiar.

con·fi·dence (kŏn´fǐ-dəns) s. confianza; *(secret)* confidencia ♦ **c. man** estafador • **to place one's c. in** confiar en • **to take someone into one's c.** confiarse a alguien.

con·fi·dent (:dənt) adj. *(certain)* seguro; *(self-assured)* confiado; *(manner)* de confianza.

con·fi·den·tial (´-dĕn´shəl) adj. confidencial, privado.

con·fi·den·ti·al·i·ty (´-´shē-ăl´ǐ-tē) s. carácter confidencial o privado.

con·fid·ing (kən-fī´dǐng) adj. confiado.

con·fig·u·ra·tion (kən-fǐg´yə-rā´shən) s. configuración *f.*

con·fine (kən-fīn´) I. tr. *(person)* confinar, recluir; *(answer)* limitar ♦ **to be confined to bed** tener que guardar cama II. s. (kŏn´fīn´) ♦ pl. confines.

con·fine·ment (:mənt) s. *(seclusion)* confinamiento, reclusión *f; (restriction)* limitación *f; (lying-in)* parto ♦ **in solitary c.** incomunicado.

con·firm (kən-fûrm´) tr. confirmar; POL. ratificar.

con·firmed (:fûrmd´) adj. confirmado; POL. ra-

tificado; *(inveterate)* habitual.

con·fis·cate (kŏn´fǐ-skāt´) tr. confiscar.

con·fla·gra·tion (kŏn´flə-grā´shən) s. conflagración *f.*

con·flict I. s. (kŏn´flǐkt´) conflicto ♦ **to be in c. with** estar en pugna con • **to come into c.** chocar II. intr. (kən-flǐkt´) contradecirse.

con·flict·ing (kən-flǐk´tǐng) adj. contradictorio.

con·flu·ence (kŏn´flōō-əns) s. confluencia.

con·form (kən-fôrm´) intr. conformarse, concordar; *(to standards, rules)* ajustarse —tr. ajustar.

con·form·ist (:fôr´mǐst) s. conformista *mf.*

con·for·mi·ty (:mǐ-tē) s. conformidad *f* ♦ **in c. with** conforme a.

con·found (kən-found´) tr. confundir ♦ **c. it!** ¡maldito sea!

con·front (kən-frŭnt´) tr. *(to face)* enfrentar, hacer frente a; *(to encounter)* encontrar; *(dangers)* arrostrar.

con·fuse (kən-fyōōz´) tr. confundir.

con·fused (:fyōōzd´) adj. *(bewildered)* confundido, desconcertado; *(disordered)* confuso.

con·fus·ing (:fyōō´zǐng) adj. confuso.

con·fu·sion (:zhən) s. confusión *f* ♦ **to be in c.** *(person)* estar confundido; *(things)* estar en desorden.

con·fute (kən-fyōōt´) tr. confutar, refutar.

con·geal (kən-jēl´) tr. & intr. *(to freeze)* congelar(se); *(to coagulate)* coagular(se).

con·gen·ial (kən-jēn´yəl) adj. *(kindred)* afín; *(sociable)* simpático; *(suitable)* agradable.

con·gen·i·tal (kən-jĕn´ǐ-tl) adj. congénito.

con·ger eel (kŏng´gər) s. congrio.

con·gest (kən-jĕst´) tr. & intr. congestionar(se).

con·gest·ed (:jĕs´tǐd) adj. *(by traffic)* congestionado; *(area)* superpoblado; *(chest, nose)* constipado.

con·ges·tion (:chən) s. congestión *f.*

con·glom·er·ate I. s. (kən-glŏm´ə-rǐt) I. tr. & intr. conglomerar(se) II. s. & adj. (:ər-ǐt) conglomerado.

con·glom·er·a·tion (´-´-rā´shən) s. conglomeración *f.*

con·grat·u·late (kən-grăch´ə-lāt´) tr. felicitar ♦ **to c. oneself** congratularse.

con·grat·u·la·tion (´-´shən) s. felicitación *f,* congratulación *f* ♦ **congratulations!** ¡felicidades!, ¡enhorabuena!

con·grat·u·la·to·ry (´-lə-tôr´ē) adj. de felicitación.

con·gre·gate (kŏng´grǐ-gāt´) intr. & tr. congregar(se).

con·gre·ga·tion (´-gā´shən) s. congregación *f,* reunión *f;* RELIG. *(worshipers)* feligreses *m; (order)* congregación.

con·gress (kŏng´grǐs) s. congreso.

con·gres·sion·al (kŏng´grǐsh´ə-nəl) adj. del congreso.

con·gress·man (kŏng´grǐs-mən) s. [pl. **-men**] E.U. diputado de la Cámara de Representantes.

con·gress·wom·an (:wŏm´ən) s. [pl. **-women**] E.U. diputada de la Cámara de Representantes.

con·gru·ous (kŏng´grōō-əs) adj. congruente.

con·ic/·i·cal (kŏn´ǐk) adj. cónico.

con·i·fer (kŏn´ə-fər) s. conífera.

co·nif·er·ous (kə-nǐf´ər-əs) adj. conífero.

con·jec·tur·al (kən-jĕk´chər-əl) adj. conjetural.

con·jec·ture (:chər) I. s. conjetura II. tr. conjeturar —intr. hacer conjeturas.

con·ju·gal (kŏn´jə-gəl) adj. conyugal.

con·ju·gate (kŏn'jə-gāt') I. tr. & intr. conjugar(se) II. adj. (:gĭt) conjugado.
con·ju·ga·tion ('-gā'shən) s. conjugación f.
con·junc·tion (kən-jŭngk'shən) s. conjunción f ♦ **in c. with** conjuntamente con.
con·junc·ti·vi·tis (-'tə-vī'tĭs) s. conjuntivitis f.
con·junc·ture (-'chər) s. coyuntura.
con·jure (kŏn'jər) tr. ♦ **to c. up** (a spirit) invocar; (by magic) hacer aparecer por arte de magia; (to evoke) evocar —intr. hacer juegos de manos.
con·jur·er/·or (:ər) s. mago.
conk (kŏngk) tr. FAM. golpear en el coco —intr. ♦ **to c. out** (machine) romperse; (person) caerse redondo.
con·nect (kə-nĕkt') tr. (to join) conectar, unir; (to associate) vincular, relacionar; TEL. poner en comunicación; ELEC. conectar —intr. unirse; (rooms) comunicarse; (buses, trains) hacer combinación.
con·nect·ed (kə-nĕk'tĭd) adj. conectado; (socially) relacionado, enchufado.
con·nec·tion (:shən) s. conexión f; (association) vínculo, relación f; (social) enchufe m, relación; (buses, trains) combinación f ♦ **in c. with** en relación con.
con·nec·tive (:tĭv) adj. conectivo.
con·nec·tor/·er (:tər) s. MEC. conectador m; ELEC. hilo de conexión.
con·ning tower (kŏn'ĭng) s. torre f (de mando).
con·nive (kə-nīv') intr. intrigar, conspirar.
con·niv·ing (kə-nī'vĭng) adj. confabulador.
con·nois·seur (kŏn'ə-sûr') s. conocedor m.
con·no·ta·tion (:tā'shən) s. connotación f.
con·note (kə-nōt') tr. connotar.
con·quer (kŏng'kər) tr. conquistar; (enemy, disease) vencer —intr. vencer, triunfar.
con·quer·or (:ər) s. conquistador m, vencedor m.
con·quest (kŏng'kwĕst') s. conquista.
con·science (kŏn'shəns) s. conciencia ♦ **in all c.** en conciencia • **to have something on one's c.** tener un cargo de conciencia.
conscience-strick·en (:strĭk'ən) adj. arrepentido, con remordimientos de conciencia.
con·sci·en·tious (kŏn'shē-ĕn'shəs) adj. concienzudo ♦ **c. objector** objetor de conciencia.
con·scious (kŏn'shəs) adj. consciente; (intentional) deliberado ♦ **to become c.** volver en sí • **to become c. of** darse cuenta de.
con·scious·ness (:nĭs) s. (awareness) conciencia; FISIOL. conocimiento.
con·script MIL. I. tr. (kən-skrĭpt') reclutar, alistar II. s. (kŏn'skrĭpt') recluta m, conscripto.
con·scrip·tion (kən-skrĭp'shən) s. conscripción f, reclutamiento.
con·se·crate (kŏn'sĭ-krāt') tr. consagrar.
con·sec·u·tive (kən-sĕk'yə-tĭv) adj. consecutivo.
con·sen·sus (kən-sĕn'səs) s. consenso ♦ **c. of opinion** opinión o consenso general.
con·sent (kən-sĕnt') I. intr. consentir II. s. consentimiento.
con·se·quence (kŏn'sĭ-kwĕns) s. consecuencia; (importance) importancia ♦ **in c.** por consiguiente.
con·se·quent (:kwĕnt') adj. consiguiente.
con·se·quen·tial ('-kwĕn'shəl) adj. consiguiente; (significant) de consecuencia.
con·se·quent·ly ('-kwĕnt'lē) adv. por consiguiente.
con·ser·va·tion (kŏn'sər-vā'shən) s. conservación f.
con·ser·va·tism (kən-sûr'və-tĭz'əm) s. conservadurismo.
con·ser·va·tive (:tĭv) I. adj. (traditional) conservador; (moderate) moderado; (cautious) prudente II. s. conservador m.
con·ser·va·tor (:tər) s. DER. tutor m.
con·ser·va·to·ry (:tôr'ē) s. (for plants) invernadero; (school) conservatorio.
con·serve (kən-sûrv') tr. conservar.
con·sid·er (kən-sĭd'ər) tr. & intr. considerar ♦ **all things considered** considerando todos los puntos • **to c. oneself** considerarse.
con·sid·er·a·ble (:ə-bəl) adj. considerable.
con·sid·er·ate (:ĭt) adj. considerado, atento.
con·sid·er·a·tion (kən-sĭd'ə-rā'shən) s. consideración f; (payment) retribución f ♦ **after due c.** después de un detenido examen • **in c. of** en reconocimiento de • **out of c. for** por respeto a • **under c.** en consideración.
con·sid·er·ing (-'ər-ĭng) I. prep. considerando II. adv. FAM. después de todo.
con·sign (kən-sīn') tr. consignar.
con·sign·ee (:sī'nē') s. consignatario.
con·sign·ment (:sīn'mənt) s. consignación f.
con·sig·nor (:sī'nôr') s. consignador m.
con·sist (kən-sĭst') intr. consistir (of, in en).
con·sis·ten·cy (:sĭs'tən-sē) s. (agreement) coherencia, acuerdo; (texture) consistencia.
con·sis·tent (:tənt) adj. (in agreement) coherente, de acuerdo; (uniform) consistente.
con·so·la·tion (kŏn'sə-lā'shən) s. consolación f, consuelo.
con·sole¹ (kən-sōl') tr. consolar.
con·sole² (kŏn'sōl') s. (cabinet) gabinete m (de radio o televisor); TEC. tablero de mando.
con·sol·i·date (kən-sŏl'ĭ-dāt') tr. & intr. consolidar(se); (to merge) fusionar(se).
con·so·nant (kŏn'sə-nənt) adj. & s. consonante f.
con·sort I. s. (kŏn'sôrt') consorte mf II. tr. & intr. (kən-sôrt') asociar(se), juntar(se).
con·sor·ti·um (kən-sôr'shē-əm) s. [pl. -ia] consorcio.
con·spic·u·ous (kən-spĭk'yōō-əs) adj. (noticeable) destacado, evidente; (remarkable) conspicuo ♦ **to be c.** destacar(se) • **to be c. by one's absence** brillar uno por su ausencia.
con·spir·a·cy (kən-spĭr'ə-sē) s. conspiración f.
con·spir·a·tor (:tər) s. conspirador m.
con·spire (kən-spīr') intr. conspirar.
con·sta·ble (kŏn'stə-bəl) s. (peace officer) alguacil m; G.B. policía m.
con·stab·u·lar·y (kən-stăb'yə-lĕr'ē) s. policía f.
con·stan·cy (kŏn'stən-sē) s. constancia; (faithfulness) lealtad f.
con·stant (kŏn'stənt) I. adj. constante; (faithful) leal; (changeless) invariable II. s. constante f.
con·stel·la·tion (kŏn'stə-lā'shən) s. constelación f.
con·ster·na·tion (kŏn'stər-nā'shən) s. consternación f.
con·sti·pate (kŏn'stə-pāt') tr. estreñir.
con·sti·pa·tion ('-pā'shən) s. estreñimiento.
con·stit·u·en·cy (kən-stĭch'ōō-ən-sē) s. (voters) electorado; (district) distrito electoral.
con·stit·u·ent (:ənt) I. adj. constituyente; (electoral) electoral II. s. componente m; (voter) elector m.

con·sti·tute (kŏn'stĭ-tōōt') tr. constituir.

con·sti·tu·tion ('-tōō'shən) s. constitución f.

con·sti·tu·tion·al (:shə-nəl) adj. constitucional.

con·strain (kən-strān') tr. (to oblige) constreñir, compeler; (to restrict) restringir.

con·straint (:strānt') s. (coercion) constreñimiento; (restriction) limitación f; (embarrassment) molestia.

con·strict (kən-strĭkt') tr. & intr. estrechar(se), encoger(se); (to compress) comprimir(se).

con·struct (kən-strŭkt') tr. construir.

con·struc·tion (:strŭk'shən) s. construcción f; (structure) estructura; (interpretation) interpretación f ♦ under c. en construcción.

con·struc·tive (:tĭv) adj. constructivo.

con·strue (kən-strōō') tr. interpretar.

con·sul (kŏn'səl) s. cónsul m.

con·su·late (:sə-lĭt) s. consulado.

con·sult (kən-sŭlt') tr. & intr. consultar.

con·sult·ant (:sŭl'tənt) s. consultor m.

con·sum·a·ble (kən-sōō'mə-bəl) I. adj. consumible ♦ c. resources recursos de consumo II. s. artículo de consumo.

con·sume (kən-sōōm') tr. consumir; (food) tragar; (time, effort) tomar ♦ to be consumed with consumirse de.

con·sum·er (:sōō'mər) s. consumidor m ♦ c. goods bienes de consumo.

con·sum·er·ism (:mə·rĭz'əm) s. movimiento de protección al consumidor.

con·sum·mate I. tr. (kŏn'sə-māt') consumar II. adj. (:mət, kən-sŭm'ĭt) consumado.

con·sum·ma·tion (kŏn'sə-mā'shən) s. consumación f; (of a goal) culminación f.

con·sump·tion (kən-sŭmp'shən) s. consumo; MED. consunción f.

con·sump·tive (:tĭv) I. adj. consuntivo; MED. tísico II. s. tísico.

con·tact (kŏn'tăkt') s. contacto; (connection) relación f ♦ c. lens lente de contacto • to come, get in c. with entrar, ponerse en contacto con II. tr. ponerse en contacto con III. adj. de contacto.

con·ta·gion (kən-tā'jən) s. contagio.

con·ta·gious (:jəs) adj. contagioso.

con·tain (kən-tān') tr. contener ♦ to c. oneself contenerse.

con·tain·er (:tā'nər) s. recipiente m, envase m; COM. contenedor m ♦ c. ship buque de carga (en contenedores).

con·tain·er·ize (:nə-rīz') tr. embalar en contenedor.

con·tain·ment (kən-tān'mənt) s. contención f.

con·tam·i·nant (kən-tăm'ə-nənt) s. contaminador m, contaminante m.

con·tam·i·nate (:nāt') tr. contaminar.

con·tem·plate (kŏn'təm-plāt') tr. contemplar; (to intend) pensar, proyectar.

con·tem·pla·tion ('-plā'shən) s. contemplación f; (intention) intención f, perspectiva.

con·tem·po·ra·ne·ous (kən-těm'pə-rā'nē-əs) adj. contemporáneo.

con·tem·po·rar·y (-'-rĕr'ē) adj. & s. contemporáneo, coetáneo.

con·tempt (kən-tĕmpt') s. desprecio, desdén m; DER. desacato ♦ beneath c. despreciable • to hold in c. despreciar.

con·tempt·i·ble (:tĕmp'tə-bəl) adj. despreciable.

con·temp·tu·ous (:chōō-əs) adj. despreciativo.

con·tend (kən-tĕnd') intr. contender — tr. mantener, sostener.

con·tend·er (:tĕn'dər) s. contendiente mf.

con·tent¹ (kŏn'tĕnt') s. contenido; (meaning) significado ♦ pl. contenido, materia.

con·tent² (kən-tĕnt') I. adj. contento, satisfecho ♦ to be c. with conformarse con II. tr. contentar, satisfacer III. s. satisfacción f.

con·tent·ed (:tĕn'tĭd) adj. contento, satisfecho.

con·ten·tion (kən-tĕn'shən) s. (conflict) disputa; (rivalry) competencia; (assertion) argumento.

con·tent·ment (kən-tĕnt'mənt) s. satisfacción f.

con·test I. s. (kŏn'tĕst') (struggle) contienda; (competition) competencia, concurso II. tr. (kən-tĕst') cuestionar, impugnar —intr. contender.

con·tes·tant (kən-tĕs'tənt) s. (rival) contendiente mf; (participant) concursante mf.

con·text (kŏn'tĕkst') s. contexto.

con·tig·u·ous (kən-tĭg'yōō-əs) adj. contiguo.

con·ti·nence (kŏn'tə-nəns) s. continencia.

con·ti·nent (:nənt) adj. & s. continente m.

con·ti·nen·tal (kŏn'tə-nĕn'tl) adj. continental ♦ C. europeo ♦ c. breakfast desayuno completo.

con·tin·gen·cy (kən-tĭn'jən-sē) s. contingencia.

con·tin·gent (:jənt) I. adj. contingente, eventual ♦ to be c. on depender de II. s. contingente m.

con·tin·u·al (kən-tĭn'yōō-əl) adj. continuo.

con·tin·u·a·tion (-'-ā'shən) s. continuación f.

con·tin·ue (kən-tĭn'yōō) intr. continuar, seguir; (to last) prolongarse, durar ♦ to be continued continuará —tr. continuar; (to prolong) prolongar; DER. (to postpone) aplazar.

con·ti·nu·i·ty (kŏn'tə-nōō'ĭ-tē) s. continuidad f.

con·tin·u·ous (kən-tĭn'yōō-əs) adj. continuo.

con·tin·u·um (:əm) s. [pl. s o -ua] continuo.

con·tort (kən-tôrt') tr. torcer, retorcer —intr. desfigurarse (el rostro).

con·tor·tion (:tôr'shən) s. contorsión f.

con·tour (kŏn'tōōr') s. contorno; TOP. curva de nivel.

con·tra·band (kŏn'trə-bănd') adj. & s. (de) contrabando.

con·tra·bass (:bās') s. contrabajo.

con·tra·cep·tion ('-sĕp'shən) s. contracepción f.

con·tra·cep·tive (:tĭv) adj. & s. anticonceptivo.

con·tract I. s. (kŏn'trăkt') contrato II. tr. (kən-trăkt') (to agree to) contratar; (to acquire) contraer; (to shrink) contraer, encoger —intr. contraerse, encogerse.

con·trac·tion (kən-trăk'shən) s. contracción f.

con·trac·tor (kŏn'trăk'tər) s. contratista mf.

con·tra·dict (kŏn'trə-dĭkt') tr. contradecir ♦ to c. oneself contradecirse.

con·tra·dic·tion (:dĭk'shən) s. contradicción f.

con·trail (kŏn'trāl') s. estela de condensación.

con·trap·tion (kən-trăp'shən) s. artefacto.

con·tra·pun·tal (kŏn'trə-pŭn'tl) adj. de contrapunto.

con·tra·ri·e·ty (:rī'ə-tē) s. contrariedad f.

con·trar·y (kŏn'trĕr'ē) I. adj. contrario; (ornery) terco II. s. lo contrario, lo opuesto ♦ on o to the c. al o por el contrario • quite the c.! ¡todo lo contrario! III. adv. ♦ c. to en contra de.

con·trast I. tr. & intr. (kən-trăst') (hacer) contrastar II. s. (kŏn'trăst') contraste m ♦ in c. por contraste • in c. to a diferencia de.

con·tra·vene (kŏn'trə-vēn') tr. contravenir.

con·trib·ute (kən-trĭb′yōōt) tr. contribuir; *(an article)* escribir *(to para)*; *(information)* aportar —intr. contribuir; PERIOD. colaborar.

con·tri·bu·tion (kŏn′trĭ-byōō′shən) s. contribución f.

con·trib·u·tor (kən-trĭb′yə-tər) s. contribuidor m, colaborador m.

con·trite (kən-trīt′, kŏn′trīt′) adj. contrito.

con·tri·tion (kən-trĭsh′ən) s. contrición f.

con·tri·vance (kən-trī′vəns) s. invento.

con·trive (kən-trīv′) tr. inventar, idear ♦ **to c. to** conseguir (hacer algo).

con·trived (:trīvd′) adj. artificial.

con·trol (kən-trōl′) I. tr. **-ll-** controlar, dirigir; *(to regulate)* regular; *(passions)* dominar ♦ **to c. oneself** dominarse II. s. control m; *(restraint)* dominio ♦ **out of** o **beyond c.** fuera de control • **to be in c.** tener el mando • **to get out of c.** desmandarse ♦ pl. mandos, controles.

con·trol·la·ble (:trō′lə-bəl) adj. controlable.

con·trol·ler (:lər) s. MEC. regulador m, control m; AVIA. controlador m; POL. interventor m.

con·trol·ling (:lĭng) adj. predominante, determinante ♦ **c. interest** mayoría de acciones.

con·tro·ver·sial (kŏn′trə-vûr′shəl) adj. polémico, discutible.

con·tro·ver·sy (′-′sē) s. controversia, polémica.

con·tu·sion (kən-tōō′zhən) s. contusión f.

co·nun·drum (kə-nŭn′drəm) s. enigma m.

con·va·lesce (kŏn′və-lĕs′) intr. convalecer.

con·va·les·cence (′:əns) s. convalecencia.

con·vec·tion (kən-vĕk′shən) s. convección f.

con·vene (kən-vēn′) intr. reunirse —tr. convocar.

con·ven·ience (kən-vēn′yəns) s. *(suitability)* conveniencia; *(comfort)* comodidad f; *(device)* dispositivo útil; G.B. *(toilet)* baño ♦ **at your c.** cuando guste • **at your earliest c.** tan pronto como le sea posible.

con·ven·ient (:yənt) adj. *(suitable)* conveniente; *(handy)* útil; *(comfortable)* cómodo.

con·vent (kŏn′vənt) s. convento.

con·ven·tion (kən-vĕn′shən) s. convención f; *(custom)* costumbre f, regla convencional.

con·ven·tion·al (:shə-nəl) adj. convencional; *(accepted)* corriente; *(war, weapons)* clásico.

con·ven·tion·al·i·ty (′-′nǎl′ĭ-tē) s. convencionalismo.

con·ven·tion·eer (:nîr′) s. convencionista mf.

con·verge (kən-vûrj′) intr. converger.

con·ver·sant (kən-vûr′sənt) adj. ♦ **c. with** versado en.

con·ver·sa·tion (kŏn′vər-sā′shən) s. conversación f ♦ **to make c.** dar conversación, platicar.

con·ver·sa·tion·al (:shə-nəl) adj. *(tone)* familiar; *(method)* de conversación.

con·verse¹ (kən-vûrs′) intr. conversar.

con·verse² (kŏn′vûrs′) adj. & s. (lo) opuesto, (lo) contrario.

con·verse·ly (kən-vûrs′lē) adv. a la inversa.

con·ver·sion (kən-vûr′zhən) s. conversión f.

con·vert I. tr. & intr. (kən-vûrt′) convertir(se) II. s. (kŏn′vûrt′) converso.

con·vert·er/·tor (kən-vûr′tər) s. convertidor m.

con·vert·i·ble (:tə-bəl) I. adj. convertible II. s. AUTO. descapotable m.

con·vex (kŏn′vĕks′, kən-vĕks′) adj. convexo.

con·vey (kən-vā′) tr. *(to carry)* transportar, llevar; *(to transmit)* transmitir; *(a meaning)* comunicar, dar a entender.

con·vey·ance (:əns) s. transporte m; *(vehicle)* vehículo; DER. *(transfer)* cesión f, traspaso.

con·vey·er/·or (:ər) s. transportador m; *(belt)* cinta transportadora.

con·vict I. tr. (kən-vĭkt′) declarar culpable, condenar II. s. (kŏn′vĭkt′) convicto.

con·vic·tion (kən-vĭk′shən) s. convicción f; DER. condena ♦ **to carry c.** ser convincente.

con·vince (kən-vĭns′) tr. convencer.

con·viv·i·al (kən-vĭv′ē-əl) adj. *(sociable)* sociable; *(festive)* jovial, festivo.

con·vo·ca·tion (kŏn′və-kā′shən) s. convocación f; *(assembly)* asamblea.

con·voke (kən-vōk′) tr. convocar.

con·vo·lut·ed (kŏn′və-lōō′tĭd) adj. *(coiled)* enrollado; *(intricate)* intrincado, complicado.

con·vo·lu·tion (:shən) s. enrollamiento.

con·voy (kŏn′voi′) I. tr. convoyar II. s. convoy m.

con·vulse (kən-vŭls′) tr. convulsionar ♦ **to be convulsed with laughter** estar muerto de risa —intr. padecer convulsiones.

con·vul·sion (:vŭl′shən) s. convulsión f; *(laughter)* ataque m de risa.

coo (kōō) I. s. arrullo II. intr. arrullar.

cook (kŏŏk) I. tr. cocinar, guisar; TEC. cocer ♦ **to c. up** FAM. inventar —intr. *(food)* cocinarse; *(chef)* cocinar ♦ **what's cooking?** FAM. ¿qué pasa? II. s. cocinero.

cook·book (′bŏŏk′) s. libro de cocina.

cook·ie (:ē) var. de **cooky**.

cook·ing (:ĭng) adj. & s. (de) cocina.

cook·out (:out′) s. comida cocinada al aire libre.

cook·y (:ē) s. galletita, bizcochito.

cool (kōōl) I. adj. fresco; *(calm)* tranquilo; *(unenthusiastic)* frío; JER. *(excellent)* fenomenal ♦ **a c. (million)** la friolera de (un millón de dólares) • **as c. as a cucumber** más fresco que una lechuga • **to keep c.** no perder la calma • **to play it c.** tomarlo con calma II. tr. & intr. refrescar(se), enfriar(se); *(passions)* entibiar(se) ♦ **c. it!** JER. ¡cálmate! • **to c. off** o **down** *(to get colder)* refrescarse; *(to calm down)* calmarse III. s. fresco, frescor m ♦ **to keep, lose one's c.** conservar, perder la serenidad.

cool·ant (kōō′lənt) s. líquido refrigerante.

cool·er (:lər) s. enfriador m.

coo·lie (kōō′lē) s. culi m.

cool·ing (kōō′lĭng) adj. refrescante.

cool·ly (kōōl′lē) adv. *(coldly)* friamente, con frialdad; *(calmly)* tranquilamente.

cool·ness (:nĭs) s. frescor m, fresco; *(calmness)* calma; *(lack of enthusiasm)* frialdad f.

coon (kōōn) s. FAM. mapache m.

coop (kōōp) I. s. gallinero ♦ **to fly the c.** fugarse, escaparse II. tr. ♦ **to c. up** enjaular.

co-op (kō′ŏp′) s. FAM. cooperativa f.

coo·per (kōō′pər) s. barrilero, cubero.

co·op·er·ate (kō-ŏp′ə-rāt′) intr. cooperar.

co·op·er·a·tive (:ər-ə-tĭv′) I. adj. *(joint)* cooperativo; *(helpful)* servicial II. s. cooperativa.

co·or·di·nate (kō-ôr′dn-ĭt′) I. s. coordenada II. adj. coordinado; *(equal)* igual, semejante III. tr. & intr. (:āt′) coordinar(se).

co·or·di·na·tor (:ā′tər) s. coordinador m.

cop (kŏp) I. s. FAM. policía m II. tr. **-pp-** JER. robar ♦ **to c. out** echarse atrás.

co·part·ner (kō-pärt′nər) s. consocio.

cope (kōp) intr. FAM. *(to strive)* arreglárselas *(with para)*; *(to face up)* hacer frente a *(with a)*.

cop·i·er (kŏp′ē-ər) s. copiadora.

co·pi·lot (kō′pī′lət) s. copiloto.

cop·ing (kō′pĭng) s. albardilla.

co·pi·ous (kō'pē-əs) adj. copioso, abundante.
co·plain·tiff (kō-plān'tĭf) s. codemandante mf.
cop-out (kŏp'out') s. JER. rendición f, resignación f.
cop·per¹ (kŏp'ər) I. s. cobre m II. adj. (de) cobre; (color) cobrizo.
cop·per² s. JER. policía m.
cop·per·y (-ē) adj. cobrizo.
copse (kŏps) s. bosquecillo, soto.
cop·ter (kŏp'tər) s. FAM. helicóptero.
cop·u·late (kŏp'yə-lāt') intr. copularse.
cop·u·la·tion (:lā'shən) s. cópula.
cop·y (kŏp'ē) I. s. copia; (book, magazine) ejemplar m; IMPR. original m, material m • c. editor redactor • to make a c. of copiar, sacar una copia de II. tr. copiar, sacar en limpio; (to imitate) imitar —intr. hacer una copia; (to cheat) copiar (en un examen).
cop·y·cat (:kăt') s. FAM. imitador m.
cop·y·ed·it (:ĕd'ĭt) tr. corregir (manuscrito).
cop·y·right (·rīt') I. s. propiedad literaria II. tr. registrar como propiedad literaria.
cop·y·writ·er (:rī'tər) s. redactor m de textos publicitarios.
co·quette (kō-kĕt') s. coqueta.
cor·al (kôr'əl) adj. & s. (de) coral m.
cord (kôrd) s. cuerda; ELEC. cordón m; TEJ. pana ♦ pl. FAM. pantalones de pana.
cor·dial (kôr'jəl) I. adj. amable II. s. cordial m.
cor·dial·i·ty (kôr-jăl'ĭ-tē) s. amabilidad f.
cord·less (kôrd'lĭs) adj. a baterías, a pilas.
cor·don (kôr'dn) I. s. cordón m II. tr. ♦ to c. off acordonar.
cor·do·van (kôr'də-vən) s. cordobán m.
cor·du·roy (kôr'də-roi') s. pana ♦ pl. pantalones de pana.
core (kôr) I. s. (essence) corazón m, médula; (center) núcleo, foco; (of fruit) corazón; (of reactor) núcleo; COMPUT. núcleo magnético ♦ to the c, hasta la médula II. tr quitar el corazón de.
co·re·spon·dent (kō'rĭ-spŏn'dənt) s. cómplice m del demandado en un divorcio.
co·ri·an·der (kôr'ē-ăn'dər) s. cilantro.
cork (kôrk) I. s. corcho ♦ to blow one's c. FAM. explotar, enojarse II. tr. encorchar.
cork·er (kôr'kər) s. FAM. mentira grande.
cork·screw (kôrk'skrōō') s. tirabuzón m, sacacorchos m.
cor·mo·rant (kôr'mər-ənt) s. cuervo marino.
corn¹ (kôrn) s. maíz m; JER. (sentimentality) sensiblería; G.B. (wheat) trigo ♦ c. flakes copos de maíz • c. on the cob maíz en la mazorca.
corn² s. MED. callo, callosidad f.
corn·ball ('bôl') adj. JER. demasiado obvio.
corn·cob (:kŏb') s. mazorca.
corn·crib (:krĭb') s. granero.
cor·ne·a (kôr'nē-ə) s. córnea.
corned beef (kôrnd) s. carne f en conserva.
cor·ner (kôr'nər) I. s. esquina; (inside) rincón m; (of eye) rabillo; (of mouth) comisura; (predicament) aprieto, apuro; (spot, region) rincón; COM. monopolio ♦ out of the c. of one's eye con el rabillo del ojo • the four corners of the earth las cinco partes del mundo • to cut corners hacer economías • to drive someone into a c. acorralar a alguien • to turn the c. doblar la esquina; (to improve) pasar el punto crítico II. tr. (to trap) arrinconar, acorralar; COM. monopolizar, acaparar.

cor·nered (:nərd) adj. arrinconado.
cor·ner·stone (:nər-stōn') s. piedra angular.
cor·net s. (kôr-nĕt') cornetín m.
cor·nice (kôr'nĭs) s. cornisa.
corn·meal (kôrn'mēl') s. harina de maíz.
corn·stalk (:stôk') s. tallo del maíz.
corn·starch (:stärch') s. maicena.
corn·y (kôr'nē) adj. -i- (mawkish) sensiblero; (joke) demasiado obvio.
co·rol·la (kə-rŏl'ə, -rō'lə) s. corola.
cor·ol·lar·y (kôr'ə-lĕr'ē) I. s. corolario II. adj. consecuente.
cor·o·nar·y (kôr'ə-nĕr'ē) adj. & s. coronario.
cor·o·na·tion (kôr'ə-nā'shən) s. coronación f.
cor·o·ner (kôr'ə-nər) s. pesquisidor m (que investiga la causa de un fallecimiento).
cor·o·net (kôr'ə-nĕt') s. corona, diadema.
cor·po·ral¹ (kôr'pər-əl) adj. corporal ♦ c. punishment castigo corporal.
cor·po·ral² s. MIL. cabo.
cor·po·rate (kôr'pər-ĭt) adj. corporativo; (joint) colectivo.
cor·po·ra·tion ('pə-rā'shən) s. corporación f, sociedad anónima.
cor·po·re·al (kôr-pôr'ē-əl) adj. corpóreo.
corps (kôr) s.inv. cuerpo.
corpse (kôrps) s. cadáver m.
cor·pu·lence (kôr'pyə-ləns) s. corpulencia.
cor·pu·lent (:lənt) adj. corpulento.
cor·pus (kôr'pəs) s. [pl. -pora] cuerpo.
cor·pus·cle (kôr'pə-səl) s. corpúsculo.
cor·ral (kə-răl') I. s. corral m II. tr. -ll- acorralar; FAM. (to seize) capturar.
cor·rect (kə-rĕkt') I. tr. corregir; (to remedy) remediar; (to adjust) ajustar —intr. hacer correcciones o ajustes ♦ to stand corrected confesar que uno se equivocó II. adj. correcto ♦ to be c. tener razón.
cor·rec·tion (kə-rĕk'shən) s. corrección f; (punishment) castigo; (adjustment) ajuste m.
cor·rec·tive (:tĭv) adj. correctivo.
cor·rect·ness (kə-rĕkt'nĭs) s. (propriety) corrección f; (accuracy) exactitud f.
cor·re·late (kôr'ə-lāt') I. tr. correlacionar —intr. estar en correlación II. adj. & s. correlativo.
cor·rel·a·tive (kə-rĕl'ə-tĭv) adj. & s. correlativo.
cor·re·spond (kôr'ĭ-spŏnd') intr. corresponder; (to write) escribirse.
cor·re·spon·dence (:spŏn'dəns) s. correspondencia ♦ c. course curso por correspondencia.
cor·re·spon·dent (·dənt) I. s. correspondiente mf; PERIOD. corresponsal mf II. adj. correspondiente.
cor·re·spond·ing (:dĭng) adj. correspondiente.
cor·ri·dor (kôr'ĭ-dər) s. pasillo, corredor m.
cor·rob·o·rate (kə-rŏb'ə-rāt') tr. corroborar.
cor·rode (kə-rōd') tr. & intr. corroer(se).
cor·ro·sion (kə-rō'zhən) s. corrosión f.
cor·ro·sive (:sĭv') I. adj. corrosivo II. s. sustancia corrosiva.
cor·ru·gate (kôr'ə-gāt') tr. & intr. estriar(se).
cor·ru·gat·ed (:gā'tĭd) adj. (cardboard) estriado; (metal) acanalado.
cor·rupt (kə-rŭpt') I. adj. corrompido, (dishonest) corrupto II. tr. & intr. corromper(se).
cor·rupt·ing (kə-rŭp'tĭng) adj. corruptor.
cor·rup·tion (:shən) s. corrupción f.
cor·sage (kôr-säzh') s. ramillete m.
cor·sair (kôr'sâr') s. corsario.
cor·set (kôr'sĭt) s. corsé m.
cor·tege (kôr-tĕzh') s. cortejo, séquito.

cor·tex (kôr'těks') s. [pl. **es** o **-ices**] corteza.

cor·ti·sone (kôr'tĭ-sōn') s. cortisona.

co·run·dum (kə-rŭn'dəm) s. corindón m.

cor·vette (kôr-vět') s. corbeta.

co·sign (kō-sīn') tr. firmar junto con otro; FIN. *(to endorse)* avalar.

co·sig·na·to·ry (kō-sĭg'nə-tôr'ē) s. cosignatario.

co·sign·er (kō-sī'nər) s. cosignatario.

cos·met·ic (kŏz-mět'ĭk) s. & adj. cosmético.

cos·mic (kŏz'mĭk) adj. cósmico.

cos·mol·o·gy (kŏz-mŏl'ə-jē) s. cosmología.

cos·mo·naut (kŏz'mə-nôt') s. cosmonauta mf.

cos·mo·pol·i·tan (kŏz'mə-pŏl'ĭ-tn) adj. & s. cosmopolita mf.

cos·mo·po·lite (-môp'ə-līt') s. cosmopolita mf.

cos·mos (kŏz'məs) s. cosmos m.

cost (kôst) I. s. costo, coste m; *(in time, effort)* costa ♦ **at all costs** o **at any c.** cueste lo que cueste ♦ **at c.** a precio de costo ♦ **at the c. of** a costa de ♦ pl. gastos; *(risks)* riesgos II. intr. cost costar.

co·star o **co-star** (kō'stär') I. s. actor m de uno de los papeles estelares II. intr. **-rr-** ♦ **co·starring** con.

cost·ly (kôst'lē) adj. **-i-** caro; *(entailing loss)* costoso.

cost-plus (:plŭs') s. costo de producción más una utilidad fija.

cos·tume (kŏs'tōōm') I. s. *(dress)* traje m; *(disguise)* máscara, disfraz m ♦ **c. ball** baile de disfraces ♦ pl. TEAT. vestuario II. tr. vestir, disfrazar.

cos·tum·er (:tōō'mər) sastre m de teatro.

co·sy (kō'zē) var. de **cozy.**

cot (kŏt) s. catre m.

cote (kōt) s. redil m.

co·te·nant (kō-těn'ənt) s. coinquilino.

co·te·rie (kō'tə-rē) s. tertulia, camarilla.

co·ter·mi·nous (kō-tûr'mə-nəs) adj. limítrofe.

co·til·lion (kō-tĭl'yən) s. cotillón m.

cot·tage (kŏt'ĭj) s. casa de campo, chalet m ♦ **c. cheese** requesón, cuajada.

cot·ter pin (kŏt'ər) s. pasador m de chaveta.

cot·ton (kŏt'n) I. s. algodón m ♦ **c. gin** desmotadora ♦ **c. wool** G.B. algodón absorbente II. intr. ♦ **to c. to** FAM. sentirse atraído por.

cot·ton·seed (:sēd') s. [pl. inv. o **s**] semilla de algodón.

cot·ton·tail (:tāl') s. liebre f de cola blanca.

cot·ton·wood (:wŏd') s. álamo de Virginia.

couch (kouch) I. s. sofá m II. tr. expresar, formular.

cou·gar (kōō'gər) s. puma m.

cough (kôf) I. intr. toser —tr. ♦ **to c. up** escupir; JER. *(money)* soltar II. s. tos f ♦ **c. drop** pastilla para la tos.

could (kŏod) cf. **can¹.**

coun·cil (koun'səl) s. consejo, junta; RELIG. concilio ♦ **city c.** concejo municipal.

coun·cil·man (:mən) s. [pl. **-men**] concejal m.

coun·cil·(l)or (koun'sə-lər) s. consejero.

coun·sel (koun'səl) I. s. *(advice)* consejo; *(consultation)* consulta; *(attorney)* abogado ♦ **c. for the defense** abogado defensor ♦ **to keep one's own c.** guardar secreto ♦ **to take c.** consultar II. tr. aconsejar —intr. consultar.

coun·sel·(l)or (:sə-lər) s. *(adviser)* consejero; *(lawyer)* abogado.

count¹ (kount) I. tr. contar; *(to deem)* considerar ♦ **to c. against** pesar contra ♦ **to c. for** valer por ♦ **to c. in** incluir ♦ **to c. on** contar con ♦ **to c. out** excluir ♦ **to c. up** contar —intr. contar; *(to matter)* tener importancia, valer ♦ **to c. down** contar hacia atrás II. s. *(act)* cuenta; *(number)* cómputo, cálculo ♦ **to keep, lose c. of** llevar, perder la cuenta de.

count² s. *(nobleman)* conde m.

count·down ('doun') s. cuenta atrás.

coun·te·nance (koun'tə-nəns) I. s. semblante m, cara ♦ **to be out of c.** estar desconcertado ♦ **to give c. to** sancionar II. tr. sancionar, aprobar.

coun·ter¹ (koun'tər) I. adj. & s. (lo) contrario, (lo) opuesto II. tr. *(a blow)* contrarrestar; *(to oppose)* oponerse a; *(to respond)* contestar III. adv. de modo contrario ♦ **to go** o **run c. to** ir en contra de.

count·er² s. mostrador m; *(of a kitchen)* tablero; *(chip, token)* ficha ♦ **over the c.** FIN. mediante un corredor de bolsa; *(drugs)* sin receta ♦ **under the c.** por debajo del tapete.

coun·ter·act ('-äkt') tr. contrarrestar.

coun·ter·at·tack I. s. ('-ə-tăk') contraataque m II. intr. & tr. ('-ə-tăk') contraatacar.

coun·ter·bal·ance I. s. ('-băl'əns) contrapeso m II. tr. ('-'-') contrapesar.

coun·ter·claim ('-klām') s. contrademanda.

coun·ter·clock·wise ('-klŏk'wīz') adv. & adj. en sentido contrario de las agujas del reloj.

coun·ter·cul·ture ('-kŭl'chər) s. contracultura.

coun·ter·es·pi·o·nage ('-ěs'pē-ə-näzh') s. contraespionaje m.

coun·ter·feit (koun'tər-fĭt') I. tr. falsificar, contrahacer; *(to feign)* fingir II. adj. contrahecho, falso; *(feigned)* fingido III. s. falsificación f, imitación f; *(money)* moneda falsa.

coun·ter·feit·er (:ər). s. falsificador m.

coun·ter·in·tel·li·gence (koun'tər-ĭn-těl'ə-jəns) s. contraespionaje m.

coun·ter·mand (:mănd') tr. contramandar.

coun·ter·mea·sure ('-mězh'ər) s. contramedida.

coun·ter·of·fen·sive (:ə-fěn'sĭv) s. contraofensiva.

coun·ter·pane (:pān') s. colcha.

coun·ter·part (:pärt') s. complemento.

coun·ter·plot (:plŏt') s. contracomplot m.

coun·ter·point (:point') s. contrapunto.

coun·ter·poise (:poiz') I. s. contrapeso; *(equilibrium)* equilibrio II. tr. contrapesar.

coun·ter·pro·duc·tive ('-prə-dŭk'tĭv) adj. contraproducente.

coun·ter·ref·or·ma·tion (:rěf'ər-mā'shən) s. contrarreforma.

coun·ter·rev·o·lu·tion (:rěv'ə-lōō'shən) s. contrarrevolución f.

coun·ter·sign (:sīn') I. tr. refrendar II. s. refrendata; *(password)* contraseña.

coun·ter·sig·na·ture ('-sĭg'nə-chər) s. refrendata, aval m.

coun·ter·spy ('-spī') s. contraespía mf.

coun·ter·weight (:wāt') s. contrapeso.

count·ess (koun'tĭs) s. condesa.

count·ing (koun'tĭng) s. cuenta, contaje m.

count·ing·house (:hous') s. oficina de contabilidad.

count·less (kount'lĭs) adj. incontable.

coun·try (kŭn'trē) s. país m; *(rural area)* campo; *(homeland)* patria ♦ **c. house** casa de campo, quinta.

coun·try·man (:mən) s. [pl. **-men**] compatriota mf.

coun·try·side (:sīd') s. campo, paisaje m.

coun·try·wom·an (:wŏŏm ən) s. [pl. **-women**] compatriota.

coun·ty (koun'tē) s. condado, distrito ♦ **c. seat** cabeza de distrito.

coup (kōō) s. golpe maestro; *(coup d'état)* golpe (de estado) ♦ **c. de grâce** golpe de gracia.

coup d'é·tat (kōō' dā-tä') s. golpe *m* de estado.

coupe/·pé (kōōp/kōō-pā') s. cupé *m*.

cou·ple (kŭp'əl) I. s. par *m*; *(of people)* pareja; *(several)* unos cuantos II. tr. juntar; TEC. acoplar —intr. juntarse; *(to mate)* acoplarse.

cou·pler (:lər) s. acoplador *m*; F.C. empalme *m*.

cou·plet (kŭp'lĭt) s. pareado.

cou·pon (kōō'pŏn') s. cupón *m* ♦ **to take c.** animarse.

cou·ra·geous (kə-rā'jəs) adj. valiente.

cou·ri·er (kŏŏr'ē-ər) s. correo, cosario.

course (kôrs) I. s. *(flow, path)* curso; *(duration)* transcurso; *(route)* rumbo; *(policy)* línea de conducta; *(of a meal)* plato; *(of studies)* programa *m*; *(subject)* curso; *(racetrack)* pista; *(in golf)* campo; *(of bricks)* hilada ♦ **c. of action** línea de acción • **in due c.** a su debido tiempo • **of c.** por supuesto, claro • **of c. not** por supuesto que no, claro que no • **to change c.** cambiar de rumbo • **to take** o **run its c.** seguir a su curso II. intr. correr.

court (kôrt) I. s. corte *f*; *(tribunal)* tribunal *m*; *(session)* audiencia; DEP. cancha ♦ **c. jester** bufón de la corte • **c. order** orden judicial • **to pay c. to** cortejar • **to settle out of c.** llegar a un arreglo • **to take to c.** llevar a los tribunales II. tr. *(to curry favor)* cortejar; *(to woo)* enamorar; *(to seek)* buscar; *(to invite)* ir en busca de —intr. hacer la corte.

cour·te·ous (kûr'tē-əs) adj. cortés, atento.

cour·te·san (kôr'tĭ-zən) s. cortesana.

cour·te·sy (kôr'tĭ-sē) s. cortesía ♦ **c. of** de parte de • **out of c.** por cortesía • **to do someone the c. of** tener la amabilidad de.

court·house (kôrt'hous') s. palacio de justicia.

court·i·er (kôr'tē-ər) s. cortesano.

court·ly (kôrt'lē) adj. -i- cortés.

court·mar·tial (:mär'shəl) s. [pl. **courts-**] consejo de guerra.

court·room (:rōōm') s. sala de justicia.

court·ship (:shĭp') s. corte *f*; *(period)* noviazgo.

court·yard (:yärd') s. patio.

cous·in (kŭz'in) s. primo ♦ **first, second c.** primo hermano, segundo.

cove (kōv) s. abra, cala.

cov·en (kŭv'ən) s. reunión *f* de brujas.

cov·e·nant (kŭv'ə-nənt) s. convenio, pacto.

cov·er (kŭv'ər) I. tr. cubrir; *(to coat)* revestir; *(with a lid)* tapar; *(a book, chair)* forrar; *(a subject)* tratar; *(to clothe)* tapar; *(to encompass)* abarcar; *(to conceal)* ocultar; *(to insure)* asegurar ♦ **covered wagon** carromato • **to c. over** cubrir por completo • **to c. up** disimular, encubrir —intr. cubrir • **to c. for** *(to substitute)* cubrir el puesto; *(to shield)* encubrir, servir de pantalla • **to c. up** cubrirse, abrigarse II. s. cubierta; *(lid)* tapa; *(slipcover, case)* funda, forro; *(jacket)* forro; *(of a magazine)* portada; *(bedspread)* sobrecama; *(pretense)* pretexto; *(shelter)* refugio; *(protection)* amparo; *(hiding place)* escondite *m*; *(table setting)* cubierto ♦ **c. charge** precio del cubierto • **c. girl** modelo fotográfica • **c. letter** carta adjunta o explicato-

ria • **to break c.** salir del escondite • **to take c.** refugiarse, ponerse a cubierto • **under c.** cubiertamente, clandestinamente • **under separate c.** por separado, aparte ♦ pl. ropa de cama.

cov·er·age (:ĭj) s. *(of a topic)* tratamiento; *(news)* reportaje *m*; *(insurance)* riesgos incluidos, protección *f*.

cov·er·alls (:ôlz') s.pl. mono.

cov·er·ing (:ĭng) s. cubierta; *(wrapping)* envoltura; *(clothing)* ropa; *(layer)* capa.

cov·ert (kŭv'ərt, kō-vûrt') adj. secreto, clandestino.

cov·er-up o **cov·er·up** (kŭv'ər-ŭp') s. encubrimiento, ocultamiento.

cov·et (kŭv'ĭt) tr. codiciar.

cov·et·ous (:ĭ-təs) adj. codicioso.

cov·ey (kŭv'ē) s. nidada.

cow¹ (kou) s. vaca; *(whale, elephant)* hembra.

cow² tr. intimidar, atemorizar.

cow·ard (kou'ərd) s. cobarde *mf*.

cow·ard·ice (:ər-dĭs) s. cobardía.

cow·ard·ly (:ərd-lē) I. adj. cobarde II. adv. cobardemente.

cow·bell (kou'běl') s. cencerro.

cow·boy (:boi') s. vaquero.

cow·er (kou'ər) intr. encogerse de miedo.

cow·girl (kou'gûrl') s. vaquera.

cow·herd (:hûrd') s. vaquero.

cow·hide (:hīd') s. cuero (de vaca).

cowl (koul) s. capucha; AVIA. capota.

cow·lick (kou'lĭk') s. mechón *m* (de pelo).

cow·man (:mən) s. [pl. **-men**] ganadero.

co·work·er (kō'wûr'kər) s. compañero de trabajo.

cow·poke (kou'pōk') s. FAM. vaquero.

cow·pox (:pŏks') s. VET. vacuna.

cow·punch·er (:pŭn'chər) s. FAM. vaquero.

cow·ry/rie (kou'rē) s. cauri *m*.

cox·comb (kŏks'kōm') s. petimetre *m*.

coy (koi) adj. remilgado, evasivo.

coy·o·te (kī-ō'tē, kī'ōt') s. coyote *m*.

co·zi·ness (kō'zē-nĭs) s. *(comfort)* comodidad *f*; *(privacy)* intimidad *f*.

co·zy (kō'zē) I. adj. -i- cómodo, calentito • **to play it c.** JER. actuar con cautela II. intr. ♦ **to c. up to** FAM. arrimarse a.

crab¹ (krăb) I. s. cangrejo; *(louse)* ladilla ♦ **c. apple** manzana silvestre II. intr. **-bb-** pescar cangrejos; *(to move)* moverse oblicuamente.

crab² I. s. refunfuñón *m*, cascarrabias *mf* II. intr. **-bb-** FAM. refunfuñar.

crab·by (:ē) adj. -i- de malas pulgas.

crab·grass (:grăs') s. garranchuelo.

crack (krăk) I. intr. *(to break)* romperse; *(whip)* restallar; *(to snap)* chasquear; *(bones, knuckles)* crujir; *(to split)* rajarse, agrietarse; *(to splinter)* astillarse; *(the voice)* cascarse; FAM. *(to give in)* ceder, quebrarse; *(to go mad)* chiflarse ♦ **to c. down** tomar medidas represivas • **to c. up** *(to wreck)* estrellarse; *(mentally)* chiflarse; *(to laugh)* morirse de risa • **to get cracking** FAM. poner manos a la obra —tr. *(to break)* romper; *(a whip)* chasquear; *(to pop)* hacer crujir; *(to split)* rajar, agrietar; *(to splinter)* astillar; *(to break open)* partir; *(a safe)* forzar; *(eggs, nuts)* cascar; *(to solve)* solucionar; *(a code)* descifrar; FAM. *(a joke)* contar ♦ **to c. open** abrir un poquito (ventana, puerto) • **to c. up** *(to wreck)* estrellar; *(with laughter)* hacer morir de risa II. s. *(snap)* chasquido; *(of a whip)* restallido; *(of the knuckles)* crujido; *(of a* *gun)* estallido; *(split)* rajadura, grieta; *(slit)* rendija; *(blow)* golpe *m,* porrazo; *(chance)* oportunidad *f; (joke)* salida, chiste *m; (gibe)* pulla ♦ **at the c. of dawn** al romper el alba • **to fail through the cracks** ser pasado por alto • **to take a c. at** probar, intentar III. adj. experto; *(marksman)* certero.

crack·down (:doun') s. medidas represivas.

cracked (krăkt) adj. FAM. chiflado, loco.

crack·er (krăk'ər) s. galleta.

crack·er·jack (:jăk') adj. JER. maravilloso.

crack·le (krăk'əl) I. intr. crepitar, crujir —tr. hacer crujir II. s. crepitación *f,* chisporroteo; *(rustle)* crujido.

crack·pot (krăk'pŏt') s. chiflado, excéntrico.

crack·up (:ŭp') s. *(plane)* choque *m; (plane)* caída; *(mental)* colapso.

cra·dle (krād'l) I. s. cuna; *(of a phone)* horquilla, gancho ♦ **to rob the c.** FAM. salir *o* casarse con una persona muy joven II. tr. mecer en los brazos; *(to support)* sostener.

craft (krăft) s. habilidad *f,* arte *m; (guile)* astucia; *(trade)* oficio; *(boat)* embarcación *f; (airplane)* avión *m.*

crafts·man (krăfts'mən) s. [pl. **-men**] artesano.

crafts·man·ship (:shĭp') s. artesanía; *(skill)* arte *m,* destreza.

craft·y (krăf'tē) adj. **-i-** hábil, astuto.

crag (krăg) s. risco, peñasco.

crag·gy (:ē) adj. **-i-** peñascoso.

cram (krăm) tr. **-mm-** *(to force)* meter a la fuerza; *(to stuff)* abarrotar, rellenar; *(with food)* atiborrarse de —intr. FAM. estudiar a última hora.

cramp¹ (krămp) MED. I. s. calambre *m* ♦ pl. retortijones II. intr. ♦ **to c. up** acalambrarse.

cramp² I. s. TEC. grapa, cárcel *f; (limitation)* restricción *f* II. tr. engrapar; *(to restrict)* restringir ♦ **to c. one's style** JER. cortar los vuelos a uno.

cramped (krămpt) adj. apretado, apiñado; *(financially)* incómodo; *(illegible)* ilegible.

cran·ber·ry (krăn'bĕr'ē) s. arándano.

crane (krān) I. s. ORNIT. grulla; TEC. grúa II. tr. estirar (el cuello).

cra·ni·um (krā'nē-əm) s. [pl. s *o* **-ia**] cráneo.

crank (krăngk) I. s. manivela; FAM. *(grouch)* cascarrabias *mf; (eccentric)* chiflado II. tr. arrancar (un motor) dando vueltas a la manivela ♦ **to c. out** producir como si fuera una máquina • **to c. up** echar a andar.

crank·case ('kās') s. cárter *m* del cigüeñal *m.*

crank·shaft (:shăft') s. cigüeñal *m.*

crank·y (:kē) adj. **-i-** *(irritable)* quisquilloso; *(odd)* estrafalario.

cran·ny (krăn'ē) s. grieta.

crape (krāp) s. crespón *m,* crepé *m.*

craps (krăps) s.pl. dados ♦ **to shoot c.** jugar a los dados.

crash (krăsh) I. intr. estrellarse, chocar; *(to break)* hacerse pedazos; *(to resound)* retumbar; *(to fail)* quebrar, fracasar; JER. *(to sleep)* irse a dormir ♦ **to c. through** irrumpir en —tr. estrellar, hacer pedazos; FAM. *(a party)* zamparse en II. s. *(noise)* estrépito; *(collision)* choque *m,* colisión *f;* AVIA. caída; COM. *(failure)* ruina, quiebra ♦ **c. helmet** casco protector III. adj. *(course, diet)* intensivo; AVIA. de emergencia.

crash-land ('lănd') intr. hacer un aterrizaje forzoso.

crass (krăs) adj. craso, burdo.

crate (krāt) I. s. cajón *m* II. tr. encajonar.

cra·ter (krā'tər) s. cráter *m.*

cra·vat (krə-văt') s. corbata.

crave (krāv) tr. ansiar, morirse por.

cra·ven (krā'vən) adj. & s. cobarde *mf.*

crav·ing (krā'vĭng) s. anhelo, antojo.

craw (krô) s. buche *m.*

crawl (krôl) I. intr. arrastrarse, reptar; *(baby)* gatear; *(traffic)* avanzar a paso de tortuga; *(skin)* erizarse; DEP. nadar estilo crol II. ♦ **to be crawling with** hervir de • **to c. up** trepar II. s. gateado; DEP. crol *m* ♦ **at a c.** a paso de tortuga.

cray·fish (krā'fĭsh') s. [pl. inv. *o* **es**] astaco.

cray·on (krā'ŏn') s. & tr. (dibujar al) pastel *m.*

craze (krāz) I. tr. enloquecer, volver loco II. s. moda.

crazed (krāzd) adj. loco, enloquecido.

cra·zy (krā'zē) adj. **-i-** loco; *(foolish)* de locos, disparatado ♦ **to be c. about** *(person)* estar loco por; *(fad)* estar loco con • **to go c.** volverse loco.

creak (krēk) I. intr. crujir, chirriar II. s. crujido, chirrido.

creak·y (krē'kē) adj. **-i-** que cruje, chirriante; *(dilapidated)* desvencijado.

cream (krēm) I. s. crema ♦ **c. cheese** queso crema • **c. of tartar** cremor tártaro • **c. puff** pastelito de crema • **c. sauce** salsa bechamel • **the c. of the crop** la flor y nata • **whipped c.** *(crema)* chantilli II. tr. batir; JER. *(to defeat)* hacer polvo, aplastar.

cream·y (krē'mē) adj. **-i-** cremoso.

crease (krēs) I. s. pliegue *m; (of trousers)* filo, raya; *(wrinkle)* arruga II. tr. plegar; *(to press)* hacer el filo a —intr. arrugarse.

cre·ate (krē-āt') tr. crear; *(to cause)* producir.

cre·a·tion (:ā'shən) s. creación *f.*

cre·a·tive (:tĭv) adj. creador, imaginativo ♦ **c. writing** composición literaria.

cre·a·tiv·i·ty ('-tĭv'ĭ-tē) s. originalidad *f.*

cre·a·tor (krē-ā'tər) s. creador *m.*

crea·ture (krē'chər) s. criatura; *(being)* ente *m,* ser *m; (animal)* bestia, bicho.

crèche (krěsh) s. nacimiento; G.B. *(nursery)* guardería.

cre·dence (krēd'ns) s. crédito, fe *f.*

cre·den·tial (krĭ-děn'shəl) s. credencial *f.*

cred·i·ble (krěd'ə-bəl) adj. creíble.

cred·it (krěd'ĭt) I. s. crédito; *(merit)* mérito; *(recognition)* reconocimiento; *(praise)* encomio; TEN. haber *m* ♦ **c. card, line** tarjeta, límite de crédito • **on c.** a crédito • **to give c.** COM. dar crédito; *(to praise, name)* reconocer (el mérito, a autor) • **to take c. for** atribuirse el mérito de ♦ pl. títulos de crédito II. tr. dar crédito a, creer; *(to recognize)* otorgar reconocimiento; *(to attribute)* atribuir; COM. abonar en cuenta.

cred·it·a·ble (:ə-bəl) adj. encomiable, loable.

cred·i·tor (:tər) s. acreedor *m.*

cred·u·lous (krěj'ə-ləs) adj. crédulo.

creed (krēd) s. credo.

creek (krēk) s. riachuelo, arroyo ♦ **up the c.** FAM. en apuros.

creel (krēl) s. nasa.

creep (krēp) I. intr. **crept** arrastrarse, deslizarse; *(to crawl)* gatear; *(cautiously)* avanzar con cautela; *(traffic)* ir a paso de tortuga; BOT. trepar ♦ **to c. by** pasar lentamente • **to c. up on someone** acercarse a alguien sigilosamente • **to make one's flesh c.** hacer ponérsele la piel de gallina II. s. *(crawl)* gateado; *(pace)* paso lento; JER. *(jerk)* desgraciado, cretino ♦ pl. FAM. escalofrío, pavor.

creep·er (krē'pər) s. enredadera.

creep·y (:pē) adj. -i- FAM. horripilante, espeluznante.

cre·mate (krē'māt') tr. incinerar.

cre·ma·tion (krī mā'shən) s. cremación *f.*

cre·ma·to·ri·um (krē'mə-tôr'ē-əm) s. [pl. **s** o **-ia**] crematorio.

cre·o·sote (krē'ə-sōt') s. creosota.

crepe o **crêpe** (krāp) s. *(fabric)* crespón *m,* crepé *m; (rubber)* crepé; CUL. panqueque *m* ♦ **c. paper** papel crepé.

crept (krĕpt) cf. **creep.**

cres·cent (krĕs'ənt) I. s. medialuna; *(semicircle)* semicírculo II. adj. creciente.

crest (krĕst) I. s. cresta, *(on a helmet)* penacho, cimera; HER. timbre *m* II. tr. llegar hasta la cumbre de.

crest·fall·en (:fô'lən) adj. alicaído, abatido.

cre·tin (krēt'n) s. cretino.

cre·vasse (krĭ-văs') s. fisura (esp. de glaciar).

crev·ice (krĕv'ĭs) s. grieta, rajadura.

crew (krōō) s. AVIA., MARÍT. tripulación *f;* MIL. dotación *f; (of workers)* equipo; *(staff)* personal *m* ♦ **c. cut** pelado al cepillo.

crib (krĭb) I. s. cuna; *(corncrib)* granero; FAM. *(plagiarism)* plagio ♦ **c. sheet** FAM. chuleta II. tr. **-bb-** FAM. plagiar —intr. usar una chuleta.

crick (krĭk) s. ♦ **c. in the neck** torticolis *f.*

crick·et¹ (krĭk'ĭt) s. ENTOM. grillo.

crick·et² s. DEP. críquet *m* ♦ **it's not c.** FAM. no es jugar limpio.

cri·er (krī'ər) s. pregonero.

crime (krīm) s. crimen *m* ♦ **c. rate** criminalidad.

crim·i·nal (krĭm'ə-nəl) adj. & s. criminal *mf* ♦ **c. record** antecedentes penales.

crim·i·nol·o·gist ('-nŏl'ə-jĭst) s. criminalista *mf.*

crimp (krĭmp) I. tr. *(cloth)* plisar; *(hair)* rizar, encrespar II. s. pliegue *m,* rizo ♦ **to put a c. in** poner trabas a.

crim·son (krĭm'zən) I. adj. & s. carmesí *m* II. tr. teñir de carmesí —intr. sonrojarse.

cringe (krĭnj) intr. encogerse, acobardarse.

crin·kle (krĭng'kəl) I. tr. & intr. arrugar(se) II. s. arruga.

crin·o·line (krĭn'ə-lĭn) s. crinolina.

crip·ple (krĭp'əl) I. s. lisiado, cojo II. tr. lisiar, tullir; FIG. inutilizar, estropear.

cri·sis (krī'sĭs) s. [pl. **-ses**] crisis *f.*

crisp (krĭsp) I. adj. *(crunchy)* tostado, crujiente; *(fresh)* fresco; *(bracing)* vivificante; *(precise)* preciso, claro II. s. ♦ **to burn** o **fry to a c.** achicharrar(se) ♦ pl. G.B. papas fritas.

crisp·y (krĭs'pē) adj. -i- tostado, crujiente.

criss·cross (krĭs'krôs') I. tr. & intr. entrecruzar(se) II. s. entrecruzamiento III. adj. entrecruzado IV. adv. en cruz.

cri·te·ri·on (krī-tîr'ē-ən) s. [pl. **s** o **-ia**] criterio.

crit·ic (krĭt'ĭk) s. crítico.

crit·i·cal ('ĭ-kəl) adj. crítico; *(carping)* criticón ♦ **in c. condition** grave ♦ **to be c. of** criticar.

crit·i·cal·ly (:kə-lē) adv. gravemente.

crit·i·cism (:sĭz'əm) s. crítica.

crit·i·cize (:sīz') tr. & intr. criticar.

cri·tique (krĭ-tēk') s. crítica.

crit·ter (krĭt'ər) s. FAM. bicho, animal *m.*

croak (krōk) I. s. *(of frog)* croar *m; (of crow)* graznido II. intr. *(frog)* croar, cantar; *(crow)*

graznar; JER. *(to die)* estirar la pata.

cro·chet (krō-shā') tr. & s. (tejer a) ganchillo.

crock (krŏk) s. vasija de barro.

crocked (krŏkt) adj. JER. hecho una uva.

crock·er·y (krŏk'ə-rē) s. vajilla de barro, loza.

croc·o·dile (krŏk'ə-dīl') s. cocodrilo.

cro·cus (krō'kəs) s. [pl. **es** o **-ci**] azafrán *m.*

croft (krôft) s. G.B. finca en arrendamiento.

crone (krōn) s. arpía.

cro·ny (krō'nē) s. compinche *mf,* amigote *m.*

crook (krŏŏk) I. s. *(staff)* báculo; *(curve)* ángulo; *(of river, path)* recodo; FAM. *(thief)* tramposo, ladrón *m* II. tr. & intr. doblar(se).

crook·ed (:ĭd) adj. *(road, thief)* torcido; *(nose)* corvo; *(back)* encorvado.

croon (krōōn) I. intr. canturrear; *(pop singer)* cantar de modo sentimental II. s. canturreo.

croon·er (krōō'nər) s. cantante *mf* sentimental.

crop (krŏp) I. s. cosecha; *(variety)* cultivo; *(haircut)* pelado corto; *(whip)* fusta; ORNIT. buche *m* II. tr. **-pp-** *(to trim)* cortar, recortar; *(hair)* cortar muy corto; *(ears)* desmochar ♦ **to c. up** surgir.

cross (krôs) I. s. cruz *f; (mixture)* mezcla; *(crossbreed)* híbrido II. tr. cruzar; *(one's arms)* cruzarse de; FAM. *(to oppose)* contrariar ♦ **to c. off** o **out** tachar ♦ **to c. oneself** santiguarse ♦ **to c. over** atravesar —intr. *(to intersect, breed)* cruzarse; *(to go across)* cruzar, atravesar III. adj. *(intersecting)* transversal; *(angry)* de mal humor; *(reciprocal)* recíproco ♦ **c. hair** retículo ♦ **c. section** sección transversal; FIG. muestra representativa ♦ **c. street** (calle) transversal ♦ **to get c.** enfadarse.

cross·bar ('bär') s. travesaño; *(of door)* tranca.

cross·beam (:bēm') s. traviesa.

cross·bow (:bō') s. ballesta.

cross·breed (:brēd') I. tr. & intr. **-bred** cruzar(se) II. s. híbrido.

cross-coun·try (:kŭn'trē) adj. a campo traviesa; *(flight, drive)* a través del país.

cross·cur·rent (:kûr'ənt) s. contracorriente *f.*

cross-ex·am·i·na·tion ('ĭg-zăm'ə-nā'shən) s. repregunta, interrogatorio.

cross-ex·am·ine ('-'īn) tr. repreguntar, interrogar.

cross-eyed (krôs'īd') adj. bizco.

cross-fer·til·i·za·tion ('fûr'tl-ĭ-zā'shən) s. fecundación cruzada.

cross·fire ('fīr') s. fuego cruzado.

cross·ing (krô'sĭng) s. cruce *m; (ford)* vado; F.C. paso a nivel.

cross·piece (krôs'pēs') s. travesaño.

cross-pol·li·na·tion ('pŏl'ə-nā'shən) s. polinización cruzada.

cross-pur·pose ('pûr'pəs) s. ♦ **to be at cross-purposes** no entenderse.

cross-ques·tion (:kwĕs'chən) I. tr. repreguntar, interrogar II. s. repregunta, interrogación *f.*

cross-ref·er·ence (:rĕf'ər-əns) s. remisión *f.*

cross·road (:rōd') s. vía transversal *f* ♦ pl. encrucijada.

cross-stitch (:stĭch') s. punto cruzado.

cross·talk (:tôk') s. interferencias.

cross·tie (:tī') s. traviesa.

cross·walk (:wôk') s. paso de peatones.

cross·wind (:wĭnd') s. viento de costado.

cross·wise/ways (:wīz'/wāz') adv. al través.

cross·word puzzle (:wûrd') s. crucigrama *m.*

crotch (krŏch) s. *(of tree)* horquilla; ANAT. entrepiernas.

crotch·et·y (krŏch'ĭ-tē) adj. caprichoso.

crouch (krouch) intr. agacharse, acuclillarse.

croup¹ (krōōp) s. MED. crup *m*, garrotillo.

croup² s. grupa (del caballo).

crow¹ (krō) s. cuervo ♦ **as the c. flies** en línea recta • **to eat c.** FAM. besar la correa.

crow² I. intr. -ed *o* crew cantar, cacarear ♦ **to c. over** jactarse de II. s. canto, cacareo.

crow·bar (*bär'*) s. pata de cabra, palanca.

crowd (kroud) I. s. multitud *f*, muchedumbre *f*; (mob) gentío; (spectators) público; (clique) gente *f* ♦ **to follow the c.** hacer lo que todos • **to rise above the c.** destacarse II. intr. agolparse, amontonarse ♦ **to c. into** atestar, apiñarse dentro —tr. apiñar, amontonar; (to fill) atestar, llenar ♦ **to c. out** empujar.

crowd·ed (krou'dĭd) adj. lleno, concurrido; (cramped) apretado.

crown (kroun) I. s. corona; (of a hat, tree) copa; (summit, honor) cima; (achievement) coronación *f* ♦ **c. prince** príncipe heredero II. tr. coronar; (to top off) rematar; FAM. (to hit) dar un cocotazo a ♦ **to c. it all** para rematar.

crown·ing (krou'nĭng) s. coronación *f*.

crow's-feet (krōz'fēt') s.pl. patas de gallo.

crow's-nest (*·nĕst'*) s. cofa de vigía.

cru·cial (krōō'shəl) adj. crucial, decisivo.

cru·ci·ble (krōō'sə-bəl) s. crisol *m*.

cru·ci·fix (krōō'sə-fĭks') s. crucifijo.

cru·ci·fix·ion (*·fĭk'shən*) s. crucifixión *f*.

cru·ci·fy (*·fī'*) tr. crucificar.

crude (krōōd) I. adj. (vulgar) ordinario, grosero; (rough) tosco, basto; (raw) crudo, bruto II. s. (petróleo) crudo.

crude·ness (*·nĭs*) *o* **cru·di·ty** (krōō'dĭ-tē) s. (vulgarity) grosería; (roughness) tosquedad *f*, baste-dad *f*.

cru·el (krōō'əl) adj. -er, -est cruel, despiadado.

cru·el·ty (*·tē*) s. crueldad *f*.

cru·et (krōō'ĭt) s. vinagrera, aceitera.

cruise (krōōz) I. intr. (to sail) navegar; (as a tourist) hacer un crucero; (car) circular; (to patrol) patrullar ♦ **to c. for** FAM. circular en busca de —tr. (ship) cruzar; (car) circular o patrullar por II. s. crucero.

cruis·er (krōō'zər) s. (warship) crucero; (motorboat) yate *m* con camarotes; (police car) patrullero.

crumb (krŭm) s. miga, migaja.

crum·ble (krŭm'bəl) tr. & intr. desmigajar(se); FIG. desmoronar(se).

crum·my *o* **crumb·y** (krŭm'ē) adj. -i- (miserable) malísimo; (cheap) de mala muerte.

crum·pet (krŭm'pĭt) s. G.B. panecillo blando.

crum·ple (krŭm'pəl) tr. & intr. (to crush) arrugar(se), estrujar(se); (to collapse) derribar(se).

crunch (krŭnch) I. tr. triturar —intr. crujir II. s. crujido; FAM. (crisis) aprieto, crisis *f*; (shortage) escasez *f*.

crunch·y (krŭn'chē) adj. crujiente.

cru·sade (krōō-sād') s. & intr. (hacer una) cruzada.

cru·sad·er (*·sā'dər*) s. cruzado.

crush (krŭsh) I. tr. (to squash) aplastar; (to squeeze) exprimir; (to crumple) estrujar; (to hug forcefully) apretar; (to grind) triturar, moler; (enemy, revolt) aplastar; (to overwhelm) agobiar II. s. aplastamiento; (crowd) multitud *f*; (infatuation) enamoramiento ♦ **to have a c. on someone** FAM. perder la chaveta por alguien.

crust (krŭst) I. s. (bread, pie) corteza; (coating, scab) costra; (layer) capa II. tr. & intr. encostrar(se).

crus·ta·cean (krŭ-stā'shən) s. & adj. crustáceo.

crust·y (krŭs'tē) adj. -i- de corteza dura; (surface) costroso; (surly) áspero, brusco.

crutch (krŭch) s. muleta; FIG. sostén *m*.

crux (krŭks) s. [pl. es *o* -ces] punto crítico; (of an argument) quid *m*.

cry (krī) I. intr. llorar; (to shout) gritar; (animals) aullar ♦ **to c. for** clamar por • **to c. for joy** llorar de alegría • **to c. out** exclamar, gritar • **to c. over** lamentarse por —tr. gritar, decir a gritos; (in public) pregonar ♦ **to c. down** menospreciar • **to c. forgiveness** implorar perdón II. s. grito; (weeping) llanto; (entreaty) petición *f*; (peddler's call) pregón *m* ♦ **a far c. from** muy distante de • **in full c.** en plena persecución • **to have a good c.** llorar a lágrima viva.

cry·ba·by (brī'bē) s. llorón *m*.

crypt (krĭpt) s. cripta.

cryp·tic (krĭp'tĭk) adj. enigmático, misterioso.

cryp·to·gram ('tə-grăm') s. criptograma *m*.

cryp·tog·ra·phy (*·tŏg'rə-fē*) s. criptografía.

crys·tal (krĭs'təl) I. s. cristal *m* ♦ **c. ball** bola de cristal • **c. clear** claro como el agua II. adj. de cristal; (transparent) cristalino.

crys·tal·line ('*tə-lĭn*) adj. cristalino.

crys·tal·lize (*:līz'*) tr. & intr. cristalizar(se).

crys·tal·log·ra·phy ('*-lŏg'rə-fē*) s. cristalografía.

cub (kŭb) s. cachorro; (novice) novato.

cub·by·hole (kŭb'ē-hōl') s. (room) cuchitril *m*; (cupboard) armario pequeño.

cube (kyōōb) I. s. cubo ♦ **c. root** raíz cúbica • **sugar c.** terrón de azúcar II. tr. MAT. cubicar; (to cut) picar en cubos.

cu·bic (kyōō'bĭk) adj. cúbico.

cu·bi·cle (*·bĭ-kəl*) s. compartimiento.

cub·ist (*·bĭst*) s. cubista *mf*.

cuck·old (kŭk'əld) I. s. cornudo II. tr. poner los cuernos a.

cuck·oo (kōō'kōō) I. s. (bird) cuco, cuclillo; (call) cucú *m* II. adj. loco, chiflado.

cu·cum·ber (kyōō'kŭm'bər) s. pepino.

cud (kŭd) s. bolo alimenticio ♦ **to chew the c.** rumiar.

cud·dle (kŭd'l) I. tr. & intr. abrazar(se), acurrucar(se) II. s. abrazo.

cud·dly (:lē) adj. -i- mimoso.

cudg·el (kŭj'əl) s. garrote *m*, bastón *m* ♦ **to take up the cudgels for** salir en defensa de.

cue¹ (kyōō) s. (billiard stick) taco ♦ **c. ball** mingo, bola blanca.

cue² I. s. TEAT. pie *m*, señal *f* ♦ **to take one's c. from** guiarse por II. tr. dar el pie *o* la señal a.

cuff¹ (kŭf) s. (shirt) puño; (pant) bajos, vuelta *f* ♦ **c. links** gemelos, yugos • **off the c.** FAM. de improviso ♦ pl. esposas.

cuff² I. tr. abofetear II. s. bofetada.

cui·rass (kwĭ-răs') s. coraza.

cui·sine (kwĭ-zēn') s. cocina, arte culinario.

cu·li·nar·y (kyōō'lə-něr'ē, kŭl'ə-) adj. culinario.

cull (kŭl) tr. entresacar, seleccionar ♦ **to c. out** sacar, separar.

cul·mi·nate (kŭl'mə-nāt') intr. culminar.

cul·pa·ble (kŭl'pə-bəl) adj. culpable.

cul·prit (kŭl'prĭt) s. culpable *mf*.

cult (kŭlt) s. culto; (sect) secta.

cult·ist (kŭl'tĭst) s. fanático, devoto.

cul·ti·vate (kŭl'tə-vāt') tr. cultivar.

cul·ti·va·tion ('-vā'shən) s. cultivo; *(refinement)* cultura, refinamiento.

cul·ti·va·tor ('-' tər) s. cultivador *m.*

cul·tur·al (kŭl'chər-əl) adj. cultural.

cul·ture (kŭl'chər) s. cultura; AGR., BIOL. cultivo

cul·tured (:chərd) adj. *(person)* culto; *(pearl)* de cultivo.

cul·vert (kŭl'vərt) s. alcantarilla.

cum·ber (kŭm'bər) tr. agobiar, embarazar.

cum·ber·some (:səm) adj. embarazoso, incómodo.

cum·in (kŭm'ĭn) s. comino.

cum·mer·bund (kŭm'ər-bŭnd') s. faja.

cu·mu·late (kyoom'yə-lāt') tr. & intr. cumular(se), acumular(se).

cu·mu·la·tive (:lā'tĭv, -lə-tĭv) adj. acumulativo.

cu·mu·lus (ləs) s. [pl. -li] cúmulo.

cun·ning (kŭn'ĭng) I. adj. *(crafty)* astuto, taimado; *(masterful)* hábil, ingenioso; *(cute)* mono, precioso II. s. astucia, habilidad *f.*

cup (kŭp) I. s. taza; *(trophy)* copa; *(chalice)* cáliz *m; (hollow)* hoyo ♦ **that's not my c. of tea** eso no es de mi gusto • **in one's cups** FAM. borracho, bebido II. tr. **-pp-** ahuecar.

cup·board (kŭb'ərd) s. *(cabinet)* aparador *m; (closet)* alacena.

cup·cake (kŭp'kāk') s. bizcochito redondo.

cup·ful (:fŏol') s. taza.

cu·pid·i·ty (kyōō-pĭd'ĭ-tē) s. codicia, avaricia.

cu·po·la (kyōō'pə-lə) s. cúpula.

cu·pric (kŏo'prĭk) adj. cúprico.

cur (kûr) s. perro cruzado; *(person)* canalla *m.*

cur·a·ble (kyŏor'ə-bəl) adj. curable.

cu·ras·sow (kŏor'ə-sō') s. guaco.

cu·rate (kyŏor'ĭt) s. cura *m.*

cu·ra·tor (kyōō-rā'tər) s. conservador *m.*

curb (kûrb) I. s. *(of a street)* bordillo; *(restraint)* freno; *(of bridle)* barbada II. tr. refrenar.

curb·stone ('stōn') s. bordillo.

curd (kûrd) s. cuajada, requesón *m.*

cur·dle (kûr'dl) tr. & intr. cuajar(se) ♦ **to c. one's blood** helarle la sangre a uno.

cure (kyŏor) I. s. cura; *(remedy)* remedio II. tr. & intr. curar(se).

cure·all (:ôl') s. curalotodo, panacea.

cu·ret·tage (kyŏor'ĭ-täzh') s. raspado.

cur·few (kûr'fyōō) s. *(toque m de)* queda.

cu·ri·o (kyŏor'ē-ō') s. curiosidad *f*, baratija.

cu·ri·os·i·ty (kyŏor'ē-ŏs'ĭ-tē) s. curiosidad.

cu·ri·ous (kyŏor'ē-əs) adj. curioso ♦ **to be c. to** tener deseos de.

curl (kûrl) I. tr. & intr. *(to twist)* rizar(se), ensortijar(se); *(to coil)* enrollar(se); *(the lips)* fruncir(se); *(smoke)* formar volutas ♦ **to c. up** hacerse un ovillo, acurrucarse II. s. riza, crespo; *(of smoke)* voluta.

curl·er (kûr'lər) s. bigudí *m.*

curl·i·cue (:li-kyōō') s. rasgo, plumada.

curl·y (:lē) adj. -i- rizado, crespo.

cur·mudg·eon (kər-mŭj'ən) s. cascarrabias *mf.*

cur·rant (kûr'ənt) s. grosella; *(raisin)* pasa de Corinto.

cur·ren·cy (kûr'ən-sē) s. *(money)* moneda, dinero (corriente); *(use)* vigencia, boga ♦ **foreign c.** divisas, moneda extranjera.

cur·rent (kûr'ənt) I. adj. *(present-day)* actual; *(in progress)* corriente, en curso; *(edition)* último; *(accepted)* corriente, en boga ♦ **c. events** actualidades • **c. liabilities** pasivo exigible II. s. corriente *f* ♦ **alternating, direct c.**

corriente alterna, continua.

cur·rent·ly (:lē) adv. *(now)* actualmente; *(commonly)* corrientemente.

cur·ric·u·lum (kə-rĭk'yə-ləm) s. [pl. **s** *o* **-la**] programa *m* de estudios ♦ **c. vitae** historial profesional.

cur·ry¹ (kûr'ē) tr. *(a horse)* almohazar; *(hides)* zurrar ♦ **to c. favor with** congraciarse con.

cur·ry² s. CUL. (salsa de) cari *m.*

curse (kûrs) I. s. maldición *f; (scourge)* desgracia, calamidad *f; (obscenity)* mala palabra, grosería II. tr. **-d** *o* **curst** maldecir; *(to afflict)* desgraciar, afligir; *(to swear at)* insultar a ♦ **to be cursed with** tener la desgracia de —intr. decir malas palabras ♦ **to c. at** insultar a.

curs·ed (kûr'sĭd, kûrst) adj. maldito.

cur·sive (kûr'sĭv) adj. cursiva.

cur·sor (kûr'sər) s. cursor *m.*

cur·so·ry (kûr'sə-rē) adj. superficial, rápido.

curt (kûrt) adj. brusco, seco.

cur·tail (kər-tāl') tr. cortar, reducir.

cur·tain (kûr'tn) I. s. cortina; TEAT. telón *m* ♦ **c. call** llamada a escena • **c. time** hora de subir el telón • **to draw the c.** over o on correr un velo sobre • **to raise the c. on** poner al descubierto ♦ pl. JER. fin II. tr. velar, encubrir ♦ **to c. off** separar con cortinas.

curt·sy (kûrt'sē) s. & intr. (hacer una) reverencia.

cur·va·ceous (kûr-vā'shəs) adj. voluptuoso.

cur·va·ture (kûr'və-chŏor') s. curvatura; *(of the spine)* encorvamiento.

curve (kûrv) I. s. curva II. intr. curvear; *(surface)* doblarse —tr. encorvar; *(to bend)* doblar.

curved (kûrvd) adj. curvo, curvado; *(bent)* doblado.

cush·ion (kŏosh'ən) I. s. cojín *m*, almohadilla; FIG. amortiguador *m*, resguardo II. tr. *(to pad)* acolchar; *(a blow)* amortiguar.

cush·y (kŏosh'ē) adj. -i- JER. fácil, cómodo.

cusp (kŭsp) s. cúspide *f; (of moon)* cuerno.

cus·pid (kŭs'pĭd) s. diente canino, colmillo.

cus·pi·dor (kŭs'pĭ-dôr') s. escupidera.

cuss (kŭs) FAM. I. intr. decir palabrotas —tr. maldecir ♦ **to c. out** insultar a II. s. palabrota; *(person)* majadero.

cus·tard (kŭs'tərd) s. natilla ♦ **caramel c.** flan.

cus·to·di·an (kŭ-stō'dē-ən) s. custodio, guardián *m; (janitor)* conserje *m.*

cus·to·dy (kŭs'tə-dē) s. custodia; *(detention)* detención *f* ♦ **to be in c.** estar detenido • **to take into c.** detener, arrestar.

cus·tom (kŭs'təm) I. s. costumbre *f; (patronage)* clientela ♦ pl. aduana • **to go through c.** pasar la aduana II. adj. hecho a la medida.

cus·tom·ar·i·ly ('tə-mâr'ə-lē) adv. acostumbradamente; *(ordinarily)* normalmente.

cus·tom·ar·y (-'-mēr'ē) adj. acostumbrado, de costumbre ♦ **to be c.** ser costumbre.

cus·tom·er (:mər) s. cliente *mf.*

cus·tom·house (kŭs'təm-hous') s. aduana.

cus·tom·ize (kŭs'tə-mīz') tr. preparar a gusto del comprador.

cus·tom-made (kŭs'təm-mād') adj. hecho a gusto del comprador.

cut (kŭt) I. tr. **cut** cortar; *(to divide)* dividir, repartir; *(to omit)* omitir, excluir; *(to harvest)* segar; *(to fell)* talar; *(to carve)* tallar; *(hole)* practicar, abrir; *(teeth)* echar; *(the size of)* reducir, acortar; *(time)* abreviar; *(prices)* rebajar; *(grease)* disolver; *(to hurt feelings)* lastimar, herir; *(to shut off)* parar; *(a record)* grabar; *(to quit)* dejarse de, acabar con; FAM. *(classes)* fumarse, faltar a ♦ **c. it out!** ¡basta ya! • **to c. back** *(to trim)* recortar; *(to reduce)* reducir, disminuir • **to c. down** *(a tree)* talar; JER. *(to kill)* matar • **to c. off** *(to sever)* cortar; *(to shut off)* parar; *(to block)* aislar, bloquear; *(a view)* tapar; *(to disinherit)* desheredar • **to c. out** *(to remove)* cortar; *(designs)* recortar; *(to delete)* suprimir; *(to quit)* dejar de • **to c. to the bone** reducir al mínimo • **to c. up** cortar en pedazos, partir —intr. cortar; *(a substance)* cortarse; *(to turn sharply)* virar, doblar ♦ **to be c. out for** estar hecho para • **to c. across** cortar por; *(categories)* derribar • **to c. back (on)** hacer reducciones (en) • **to c. both ways** tener doble filo • **to c. down on** reducir(se), aminorar • **to c. in** *(a line of people)* colarse; *(to interrupt)* interrumpir • **to c. loose** JER. hablar *o* actuar sin cuidarse • **to c. up** hacer diabluras II. s. corte *m*; *(notch)* muesca; *(reduction)* reducción *f*; *(discount)* rebaja; FAM. *(share)* tajada, parte *f*; JOY. talla; IMPR. grabada; CINEM. corte, interrupción *f* ♦ **a c. above** un poco mejor que.

cut-and-dried (kŭt'ən-drīd') adj. rutinario.

cu-ta-ne-ous (kyōō-tā'nē-əs) adj. cutáneo.

cut-back (kŭt'băk') s. reducción *f*.

cute (kyōōt) adj. *(pretty)* mono; *(contrived)* afectado ♦ **to get c. with** hacerse el listo con.

cu-ti-cle (kyōō'tĭ-kəl) s. cutícula.

cut-ie (kyōō'tē) s. JER. monada.

cut-lass (kŭt'ləs) s. sable *m*.

cut-ler (:lər) s. cuchillero.

cut-ler-y (:lə-rē) s. cubiertos.

cut-let (kŭt'lĭt) s. chuleta.

cut-off (kŭt'ôf') s. *(limit)* límite *m*; *(short cut)* atajo; *(device)* cierre *m*, obturador *m*.

cut-rate (:rāt') adj. rebajado, de descuento.

cut-ter ('ər) s. cortador *m*; MARÍT. cúter *m* ♦ **coast guard c.** guardacostas.

cut-throat (:thrōt') I. s. degollador *m*, asesino II. adj. *(cruel)* cruel, sanguinario; *(competition)* implacable.

cut-ting (:ĭng) I. s. *(clipping)* recorte *m*; AGR. rampollo II. adj. cortante; *(remark)* mordaz.

cut-tle-fish (kŭt'l-fĭsh') s. [pl. inv. *o* **es**] jibia.

cy-a-nide (sī'ə-nīd') cianuro.

cy-ber-net-ics (sī'bər-nĕt'ĭks) s.sg. cibernética.

cy-cla-mate (sī'klə-māt') s. ciclamato.

cy-cle (sī'kəl) I. s. ciclo; *(bike)* bici *f*, moto *f* II. intr. ocurrir cíclicamente; *(to go)* ir en bicicleta *o* motocicleta.

cy-clic/cli-cal (sĭk'lĭk) adj. cíclico.

cy-clist (sī'klĭst) s. *(bicycle)* ciclista *mf*; *(motorcycle)* motociclista *mf*.

cy-clone (sī'klōn') s. ciclón *m*.

cy-clo-tron (sī'klə-trŏn') s. ciclotrón *m*.

cyg-net (sĭg'nĭt) s. pichón *m* de cisne.

cyl-in-der (sĭl'ən-dər) s. cilindro.

cy-lin-dri-cal (sə-lĭn'drĭ-kəl) adj. cilíndrico.

cym-bal (sĭm'bəl) s. címbalo, platillo.

cyn-ic (sĭn'ĭk) s. & adj. cínico.

cyn-i-cal (:ĭ-kəl) adj. cínico.

cyn-i-cism (sī'sĭz'əm) s. cinismo.

cy-no-sure (sī'nə-shōōr') s. centro de atracción.

cy-press (sī'prəs) s. ciprés *m*.

cyst (sĭst) s. quiste *m*.

cys-tic (sĭs'tĭk) adj. enquistado.

cys-ti-tis (sĭ-stī'tĭs) s. cistitis *f*.

cy-to-plasm (sī'tə-plăz'əm) s. citoplasma *m*.

czar (zär) s. zar *m*.

czar-e-vitch ('ə-vĭch') s. zarevitz *m*.

cza-ri-na (zä-rē'nə) s. zarina.

D

d, D (dē) s. cuarta letra del alfabeto inglés; MÚS. re *m*.

dab (dăb) I. tr. **-bb-** dar toques a, retocar suavemente II. s. *(bit)* pizca; *(pat, tap)* golpe ligero.

dab-ble (dăb'əl) tr. salpicar —intr. *(to splash)* chapotear; *(as amateur)* interesarse superficialmente *(in, at* por).

dab-bler (:lər) s. diletante *mf*.

dachs-hund (däks'hŏŏnt') s. perro salchicha.

dad (dăd) s. FAM. papá *m*.

dad-dy ('ē) s. FAM. papacito, papito.

daf-fo-dil (dăf'ə-dīl') s. narciso.

daf-fy (dăf'ē) adj. **-i-** FAM. chalado, chiflado.

dag-ger (dăg'ər) s. daga, puñal *m*; IMPR. obelisco ♦ **to look daggers at** apuñalar con la mirada.

da-guerre-o-type (də-gâr'ə-tīp') s. daguerrotipo.

dahl-ia (dăl'yə) s. dalia.

dai-ly (dā'lē) I. adj. & s. diario II. adv. diariamente, cada día.

dain-ty (dān'tē) adj. **-i-** exquisito, delicado; *(affected)* remilgado.

dair-y (dâr'ē) s. lechería ♦ **d. cattle** vacas lecheras • **d. farm** granja lechera.

dair-y-man (:mən) s. [pl. **-men**] lechero.

da-is (dā'ĭs) s. tarima, estrado.

dai-sy (dā'zē) s. margarita.

dale (dāl) s. valle *m*.

dal-li-ance (dăl'ē-əns) s. *(dawdling)* gandulería; *(flirtation)* coqueteo.

dal-ly (dăl'ē) tr. *(to flirt)* coquetear; *(to waste time)* gandulear.

dam[1] (dăm) I. s. *(barrier)* presa; *(reservoir)* embalse *m* II. tr. **-mm-** embalsar, represar.

dam[2] s. madre *f* (de cuadrúpedos).

dam-age (dăm'ĭj) I. s. daño; *(mechanical)* avería; FIG. perjuicio ♦ pl. daños *o* perjuicios II. tr. & intr. dañar(se), estropear(se).

dam-ask (dăm'əsk) s. damasco.

dame (dām) s. dama; JER. hembra.

damn (dăm) I. tr. condenar; *(to swear at)* maldecir II. interj. ♦ **d. (it)!** ¡maldito sea!, ¡maldición! III. s. ♦ **I don't give a d.** no me importa un comino • **it's not worth a d.** no vale un comino IV. adj. maldito V. adv. muy.

dam-na-tion (-nă'shən) I. s. condenación *f* II. interj. ¡maldición!

damned (dămd) I. adj. **-er, -est** condenado, maldito; FAM. *(huge)* tremendo II. adv. FAM. muy, sumamente III. s. ♦ **the d.** los condenados.

damp (dămp) I. adj. húmedo II. s. humedad *f*; *(gas)* mofeta III. tr. humedecer; *(a fire)* apagar; *(to discourage)* desanimar.

damp-en (dăm'pən) tr. humedecer; *(spirit, zeal)* deprimir, disminuir —intr. humedecerse.

damp-er (dăm'pər) s. TEC. compuerta de tiro; FÍS. amortiguador *m*; MÚS. sordina ♦ **to put a d. on** desanimar, apagar (entusiasmo *o* ánimo).

damp-ness (dămp'nĭs) s. humedad *f*.

dam·sel (dăm′zəl) s. damisela.
dance (dăns) I. tr. & intr. bailar II. s. baile m.
danc·er (dăn′sər) s. bailador m; (ballet) bailarín m.
danc·ing (:sĭng) adj. & s. (de) baile m.
dan·de·li·on (dăn′dl-ī′ən) s. diente m de león.
dan·der (dăn′dər) s. FAM. cólera ♦ **to get someone's d. up** hacer que alguien rabie.
dan·dle (dăn′dl) tr. mecer.
dan·druff (dăn′drəf) s. caspa.
dan·dy (dăn′dē) I. s. dandi m, petimetre m II. adj. -i- FAM. excelente.
dan·ger (dān′jər) s. peligro.
dan·ger·ous (:əs) adj. peligroso.
dan·gle (dăng′gəl) tr. & intr. colgar(se), balancear(se) en el aire.
dank (dăngk) adj. malsano y húmedo.
dap·per (dăp′ər) adj. atildado, apuesto.
dap·ple (dăp′əl) I. tr. motear II. adj. moteado.
dare (dâr) I. intr. osar, atreverse —tr. (to face) arrostrar; (to challenge) retar, desafiar ♦ **I d. say** me parece probable II. s. desafío, reto.
dare·dev·il (′dĕv′əl) adj. & s. atrevido.
dar·ing (:ĭng) I. adj. temerario, audaz II. s. audacia, atrevimiento.
dark (därk) I. adj. oscuro; (skin) moreno, moreno; (sky) amenazador; (dismal) triste; (evil) siniestro; (unknown) misterioso; (ignorant) ignorante ♦ **Dark Ages** Alta Edad Media • **d. horse** candidato con un apoyo inesperado II. s. oscuridad f; (nightfall) anochecer m, noche f ♦ **to be in the d.** no estar informado.
dark·en (där′kən) tr. & intr. oscurecer(se); (to sadden) entristecer(se).
dark·ness (därk′nĭs) s. oscuridad f.
dark·room (:rōōm′) s. cuarto oscuro.
dar·ling (där′lĭng) I. s. querido, amado; (favorite) predilecto II. adj. querido, amado, FAM. (charming) adorable.
darn[1] (därn) COST. I. tr. zurcir —intr. hacer zurcidos II. s. zurcido.
darn[2] I. interj. ¡maldición! II. adj. maldito III. adv. FAM. muy.
darned (därnd) I. adj. maldito II. adv. muy.
darn·ing (där′nĭng) s. COST. zurcido.
dart (därt) I. intr. correr, lanzarse —tr. lanzar, arrojar II. s. dardo; (movement) movimiento rápido; COST. (tuck) pinza.
dash (dăsh) I. tr. (to smash) estrellar, romper; (to hurl) tirar; (to splash) salpicar; (to spoil) arruinar, frustrar ♦ **to d. off** hacer rápidamente —intr. correr, lanzarse ♦ **to d. in**, **out** entrar, salir corriendo II. s. (bit) pizca; (rush) prisa; (race) carrera corta; (verve) brío; IMPR. raya; AUTO. salpicadero ♦ **at a d.** de un golpe • **to make a d. at**, **for** precipitarse sobre, hacia • **to make a d. for it** echarse a correr, huir.
dash·board (′bōrd′) s. tablero de instrumentos, salpicadero.
dash·ing (:ĭng) adj. gallardo.
das·tard·ly (dăs′tərd-lē) adj. vil, ruin.
da·ta (dā′tə, dăt′ə) s.pl. o sg. información f, datos ♦ **d. bank** base o banco de datos • **d. processing** procesamiento de datos • **d. processor** ordenador.
da·ta·base (:bās′) s. base f de datos.
date[1] (dāt) I. s. fecha; (epoch) época; (appointment) cita, compromiso; (companion) acompañante mf ♦ **d. line** meridiano de cambio de fecha • **to d.** hasta la fecha II. tr. & intr. fechar; (socially) salir (con) ♦ **to d. back to** remontar(se) a • **to d. from** datar de.

date[2] s. (fruit) dátil m ♦ **d. palm** datilero.
dat·ed (dā′tĭd) adj. fechado; (out-of-date) pasado de moda, anticuado.
date·line (dāt′līn′) s. fecha y lugar m de origen.
da·tum (dā′təm, dăt′əm) s. [pl. -ta] dato.
dauh (dôh) I. tr. revestir, embadurnar —intr. pintarrajear II. s. revestimiento, capa.
daugh·ter (dô′tər) s. hija.
daugh·ter-in-law (:ĭn-lô′) s. [pl. daughters-] nuera, hija política.
daunt (dônt) tr. intimidar; (to dishearten) desanimar.
daunt·less (′lĭs) adj. intrépido.
dau·phin (dô′fĭn) s. delfín m.
dav·en·port (dăv′ən pôrt′) s. sofá m grande.
daw·dle (dôd′l) intr. andar despacio, demorarse —tr. ♦ **to d. away** perder, malgastar.
dawn (dôn) I. s. amanecer m, alba; FIG. albor m II. intr. amanecer ♦ **it dawned on me** caí en la cuenta.
day (dā) s. día m, (workday) jornada; (epoch) época ♦ **d. bed** sofá cama • **d. care** cuidado de niños durante el día • **day-care center** guardería • **d. in, d. out** día tras día • **d. laborer** jornalero, peón • **d. off** día franco • **d. school** externado • **from d. to d.** de un día para otro • **the d. after al día siguiente • the d. before . . .**, la víspera de . . . • **these days** hoy en día • **to call it a d.** dar por acabado, retirarse • **to carry the d.** triunfar, llevarse la palma • **to have had one's d.** haber pasado de moda.
day·book (dā′bŏŏk′) s. diario.
day·break (dā′brāk′) s. amanecer m, alba.
day·dream (dā′drēm′) I. s. ensueño II. intr. ed o -t soñar despierto.
day·light (dā′līt′) s. luz f del día; (dawn) amanecer m; (daytime) día m ♦ **to scare the daylights out of** FAM. asustar mucho • **to see d.** llegar a comprender.
day·light-sav·ing (′-sā′vĭng) hora de verano.
day·long (′-lông′) adj. & adv. (que dura) todo el día.
day·time (dā′tīm′) s. día m.
day-to-day (dā′tə-dā′) adj. (daily) cotidiano; (a day at a time) al día.
daze (dāz) I. tr. (to stun) aturdir; (to dazzle) deslumbrar II. s. aturdimiento.
daz·zle (dăz′əl) I. tr. deslumbrar II. s. deslumbramiento.
daz·zling (:ĭng) adj. deslumbrante.
dea·con (dē′kən) s. diácono.
dea·con·ess (dē′kə-nĭs) s. diaconisa.
de·ac·ti·vate (dē-ăk′tə-vāt′) tr. desactivar.
dead (dĕd) I. adj. muerto; (numb) insensible; (motionless) estancado; (dull) triste, aburrido; (sounds) sordo; (a ball) sin rebote; (utter) completo, absoluto; (exact) exacto, certero; DEP. fuera de juego; ELEC. sin corriente; (battery) descargado ♦ **d. center, weight** punto, peso muerto • **d. end** callejón sin salida • **d. letter** carta no reclamada • **d. reckoning** estima II. s. muerto ♦ **the d.** los muertos • **the d. of night, winter** plena noche, pleno invierno III. adv. (absolutely) completamente, absolutamente, (exactly) exactamente, justo.
dead·beat (′bēt′) s. JER. gorrón m, holgazán m.
dead·en (:n) tr. amortiguar.
dead-end (:ĕnd′) adj. sin salida; FIG. sin porvenir.
dead·line (:līn′) s. fecha tope, plazo.
dead·lock (:lŏk′) I. s. estancamiento II. tr. & intr. estancar(se).

dead·ly (:lē) I. adj. -i- *(lethal)* mortífero; *(implacable)* mortal; *(destructive)* devastador; *(aim)* certero; *(sin)* capital; FAM. *(dull)* pesado II. adv. extremadamente.

dead·pan (:păn′) JER. I. s. cara impasible II. adj. & adv. (de forma) impasible.

dead·wood (:wŏŏd′) s. rama muerta; FIG. persona o cosa inútil.

deaf (dĕf) adj. sordo.

deaf-and-dumb (′ən-dŭm′) s. & adj. sordomudo.

deaf·en (′ən) tr. ensordecer.

deaf·en·ing (:ə-nĭng) adj. ensordecedor.

deaf-mute (:myŏŏt′) s. & adj. sordomudo.

deaf·ness (:nĭs) s. sordera.

deal (dēl) I. tr. **dealt** *(to apportion)* repartir, distribuir; *(a blow)* asestar; *(cards)* dar, repartir —intr. comerciar *(in en)* ♦ **to d. with** COM. tratar con; *(a situation)* enfrentarse con; *(to manage)* dirigir; *(to treat)* tratar de o sobre; *(to handle)* ocuparse de, encargarse de; *(to punish)* castigar II. s. *(agreement)* arreglo, convenio; *(in cards)* reparto; FAM. *(dealings)* trato ♦ **a good** o **great d.** mucho • **big d.!** ¡gran cosa! • **it's a d.!** ¡trato hecho! • **to make a big d. out of nothing** FAM. hacer un escándalo por nada.

deal·er (:ər) s. negociante mf, traficante mf; *(in cards)* banquero.

deal·er·ship (:shĭp′) s. negocio.

deal·ings (:lĭngz) s.pl. *(business)* negocios; *(relations)* trato.

dean (dēn) s. EDUC. decano; RELIG. deán m.

dear (dîr) I. adj. querido; *(esteemed)* estimado; *(precious)* valioso; *(costly)* caro ♦ **D. Sir** Muy o Estimado señor mío II. adv. caro III. s. querido.

dear·ly (:lē) adv. *(costly)* caro; *(fondly)* con cariño; *(very much)* mucho.

dearth (dûrth) s. escasez f.

dear·y (dîr′ē) s. FAM. querido.

death (dĕth) s. muerte f ♦ **d. certificate** partida de defunción • **d. mask** mascarilla • **d. penalty** pena de muerte • **d. rate** índice de mortalidad • **d. warrant** orden de ejecución • **to be bored to d.** repetir hasta el aburrimiento • **to put to d.** ejecutar.

death·bed (′bĕd′) s. lecho de muerte.

death·less (:lĭs) adj. inmortal.

death·ly (:lē) I. adj. cadavérico, sepulcral II. adv. mortalmente, muy.

death's-head (dĕths′hĕd′) s. calavera.

death·trap (dĕth′trăp′) s. construcción f o situación peligrosa.

death·watch (:wŏch′) s. velatorio.

de·ba·cle (dĭ-bä′kəl) s. desastre m, fracaso.

de·bar (dē-bär′) tr. -rr- excluir, prohibir.

de·bark (dĭ-bärk′) tr. & intr. desembarcar.

de·bar·ka·tion (dē′bär-kā′shən) s. *(of people)* desembarco; *(of cargo)* desembarque m.

de·base (dĭ-bās′) tr. *(to devalue)* desvalorizar; *(to degrade)* degradar, rebajar.

de·bat·a·ble (dĭ-bā′tə-bəl) adj. discutible.

de·bate (dĭ-bāt′) I. tr. & intr. discutir, debatir II. s. discusión f, debate m.

de·bat·er (dĭ-bā′tər) s. polemista mf.

de·bauch (dĭ-bôch′) tr. corromper, pervertir.

de·bauch·er·y (dĭ-bô′chə-rē) s. libertinaje m.

de·bil·i·tate (dĭ-bĭl′ĭ-tāt′) tr. debilitar.

deb·it (dĕb′ĭt) I. s. débito, debe m ♦ **d. balance** saldo deudor II. tr. cargar en cuenta.

deb·o·nair (dĕb′ə-nâr′) adj. alegre, garboso.

de·brief (dē-brēf′) tr. someter a un interrogato-

rio *(después de cumplida una misión)*.

de·bris o **dé·bris** (də-brē′, dā-) s. escombros m, desechos m; GEOL. detrito.

debt (dĕt) s. deuda ♦ **to be in someone's d.** estar en deuda con alguien • **to get** o **run into d.** contraer deudas.

debt·or (:ər) s. deudor m.

de·bug (dē-bŭg′) tr. -gg- anular un dispositivo electrónico secreto; COMPUT. suprimir errores.

de·but o **dé·but** (dā-byŏŏ′) I. s. estreno, debut m II. intr. FAM. debutar.

de·bu·tante o **dé·bu·tante** (dĕb′yŏŏ-tänt′) s. debutante f.

dec·ade (dĕk′ād′) s. decenio, década.

dec·a·dence (dĕk′ə-dns) s. decadencia.

de·ca·dent (:dnt) adj. & s. decadente mf.

de·cal (dē′kăl′, dĭ-kăl′) s. calcomanía.

dec·a·me·ter (dĕk′ə-mē′tər) s. decámetro.

de·camp (dĭ-kămp′) intr. FAM. largarse; MIL. decampar.

de·cant (dĭ-kănt′) tr. decantar.

de·cant·er (dĭ-kăn′tər) s. garrafa, jarra.

de·cap·i·tate (dĭ-kăp′ĭ-tāt′) tr. decapitar.

de·cath·lon (dĭ-kăth′lŏn) s. decatlón m.

de·cay (dĭ-kā′) I. intr. pudrirse, descomponerse; *(a tooth)* cariarse; FIS. desintegrarse; *(to get worse)* decaer II. s. descomposición f; *(of a tooth)* caries f; FIS. desintegración f; *(of morals)* decadencia.

de·cease (dĭ-sēs′) I. intr. morir, fallecer II. s. muerte f, fallecimiento.

de·ceased (dĭ-sēst′) adj. & s. difunto.

de·ce·dent (dĭ-sēd′nt) s. difunto.

de·ceit (:sēt′) s. engaño, fraude m.

de·ceit·ful (:fəl) adj. engañoso.

de·ceive (dĭ-sēv′) tr. & intr. engañar.

de·ceiv·er (dĭ-sē′vər) s. embustero.

de·cel·er·ate (dē-sĕl′ə-rāt′) tr. disminuir la velocidad de —intr. decelerar.

De·cem·ber (dĭ-sĕm′bər) s. diciembre m.

de·cen·cy (dē′sən-sē) s. decencia, decoro.

de·cent (dē′sənt) adj. decente; *(kind)* bueno; FAM. *(dressed)* vestido.

de·cen·tral·ize (dē-sĕn′trə-līz′) tr. descentralizar.

de·cep·tion (dĭ-sĕp′shən) s. engaño, fraude m.

de·cep·tive (:tĭv) adj. engañoso.

dec·i·bel (dĕs′ə-bĕl′) s. decibel m, decibelio.

de·cide (dĭ-sīd′) tr. & intr. decidir ♦ **to d. (up) on** optar por.

de·cid·ed (dĭ-sī′dĭd) adj. *(resolute)* decidido; *(definite)* claro, indudable.

de·cid·u·ous (dĭ-sĭj′ŏŏ-əs) adj. caduco.

dec·i·mal (dĕs′ə-məl) s. & adj. decimal m ♦ **d. point** coma.

dec·i·mate (:māt′) tr. diezmar.

dec·i·me·ter (:mē′tər) s. decímetro.

de·ci·pher (dĭ-sī′fər) tr. descifrar.

de·ci·sion (dĭ-sĭzh′ən) s. decisión f.

de·ci·sive (dĭ-sī′sĭv) adj. decisivo.

de·ci·sive·ness (:nĭs) s. firmeza, decisión f.

deck¹ (dĕk) I. s. cubierta; *(of cards)* baraja ♦ **d. hand** marinero de cubierta • **to clear the d.** FAM. preparar para la acción II. tr. JER. tumbar.

deck² (dĕk) tr. adornar, engalanar ♦ **to d. oneself out** emperifollarse.

de·claim (dĭ-klām′) tr. & intr. declamar.

dec·la·ra·tion (dĕk′lə-rā′shən) s. declaración f.

de·clar·a·tive (dĭ-klăr′ə-tĭv) adj. declaratorio.

de·clare (dĭ-klâr′) tr. declarar —intr. hacer una declaración ♦ **to d. against, for** pronunciarse en contra, a favor de.

de·clas·si·fy (dē-klǎs'ə-fī') tr. anular la clasificación confidencial de.

de·clen·sion (dǐ-klěn'shən) s. declinación f.

de·cline (dǐ-klīn') I. intr. *(to refuse)* rehusar, negarse; *(to slope)* inclinarse; *(to deteriorate)* deteriorarse; *(health)* decaer; *(prices)* bajar —tr. rehusar, rechazar; GRAM. declinar II. s. *(decrease)* disminución f; *(deterioration)* deterioro, declive m; *(of prices)* descenso.

de·clin·ing (dǐ-klī'nǐng) adj. declinante.

de·cliv·i·ty (dǐ-klǐv'ǐ-tē) s. declive m.

de·code (dē-kōd') tr. descifrar, descodificar.

dé·col·le·tage (dā'kŏl-täzh') s. escote m.

de·col·o·nize (dē-kŏl'ə-nīz') tr. descolonizar.

de·com·pose (dē'kəm-pōz') tr. & intr. *(into parts)* descomponer(se); *(to rot)* pudrir(se).

de·com·po·si·tion (dē-kŏm'pə-zǐsh'ən) s. descomposición f, putrefacción f.

de·com·press (dē'kəm-prĕs') tr. descomprimir.

de·com·pres·sor (:ər) s. descompresor m.

de·con·ges·tant (dē'kən-jĕs'tənt) s. descongestionante m.

de·con·tam·i·nate (dē'kən-tăm'ə-nāt') tr. descontaminar.

de·con·trol (dē'kən-trōl') I. tr. -ll- librar de control (gubernamental) II. s. anulación f del control.

dé·cor o **de·cor** (dā'kôr') s. decoración f.

dec·o·rate (dĕk'ə-rāt') tr. decorar; *(with medals)* condecorar.

dec·o·ra·tion ('-rā'shən) s. decoración f; *(medal)* condecoración f.

dec·o·ra·tive (dĕk'ər-ə-tǐv) adj. decorativo.

dec·o·ra·tor (:rā'tər) s. decorador m.

dec·o·rous (:ər-əs) adj. decoroso.

de·co·rum (dǐ-kôr'əm) s. decoro.

de·coy I. s. (dē'koi') señuelo II. tr. (dǐ-koi') atraer con señuelo.

de·crease I. intr. & tr. (dǐ-krēs') disminuir, reducir II. s. (dē'krēs') disminución f.

de·creas·ing (dǐ-krē'sǐng) adj. decreciente.

de·cree (dǐ-krē') I. s. decreto II. tr. decretar.

de·crep·it (dǐ-krĕp'ǐt) adj. decrépito.

de·crim·i·nal·ize (dē-krǐm'ə-nə-līz') tr. legalizar.

de·cry (dǐ-krī') tr. despreciar, criticar.

ded·i·cate (dĕd'ǐ-kāt') tr. dedicar.

ded·i·ca·tion ('-kā'shən) s. dedicación f; *(inscription)* dedicatoria f.

de·duce (dǐ-dōōs') tr. deducir, inferir.

de·duct (dǐ-dŭkt') tr. restar, substraer.

de·duct·i·ble (dǐ-dŭk'tə-bəl) adj. deducible.

de·duc·tion (:shən) s. deducción f.

de·duc·tive (:tǐv) adj. deductivo.

deed (dēd) I. s. *(act)* acto; *(action)* hecho; *(feat)* proeza; DER. *(title)* escritura (de propiedad) II. tr. traspasar por escritura.

deem (dēm) tr. considerar, juzgar.

deep (dēp) I. adj. profundo; *(measuring)* de profundidad; *(thick)* de espesor; *(distant)* distante; *(shrewd)* astuto; *(in thought)* absorto; *(colors)* subido; MÚS. bajo, grave ♦ **d. down** en el fondo ♦ **d. in debt** cargado de deudas ♦ **to go off the d. end** ponerse histérico II. adv. profundamente, en lo más hondo ♦ **d. into the night** hasta muy entrada la noche III. s. profundidad f; *(of night, winter)* lo más profundo; POÉT. el mar.

deep·en (dē'pən) tr. & intr. ahondar(se).

deep-fry (dēp'frī') tr. freír (por inmersión en aceite).

deep-sea (:sē') adj. de mar profundo.

deep-seat·ed (:sē'tǐd) adj. profundamente arraigado.

deep-set (:sĕt') adj. hundidos (los ojos).

deer (dîr) s.inv. ciervo, venado.

deer·skin ('skǐn) s. gamuza.

de·es·ca·late (dē-ĕs'kə-lāt') tr. disminuir.

de·face (dǐ-fās') tr. desfigurar, mutilar.

de·fam·a·to·ry (dǐ-făm'ə-tôr'ē) adj. difamatorio.

de·fame (dǐ-fām') tr. difamar, calumniar.

de·fault (dǐ-fôlt') I. s. incumplimiento; DER. contumacia ♦ **to win by d.** ganar por abandono II. intr. dejar de cumplir, faltar a un compromiso; DER. estar en rebeldía; DEP. dejar de presentarse.

de·feat (dǐ-fēt') I. tr. *(to beat)* derrotar, vencer; *(to thwart)* frustrar II. s. *(loss)* derrota; *(failure)* fracaso; *(frustration)* frustración f.

de·feat·ist (dǐ-fē'tǐst) s. derrotista m/f.

def·e·cate (dĕf'ǐ-kāt') intr. defecar.

de·fect I. s. (dē'fĕkt') defecto, desperfecto II. intr. (dǐ-fĕkt') desertar.

de·fec·tion (dǐ-fĕk'shən) s. defección f.

de·fec·tive (:tǐv) adj. *(faulty)* defectuoso; *(subnormal)* deficiente; GRAM. defectivo.

de·fec·tor (:tər) s. desertor m.

de·fend (dǐ-fĕnd') tr. defender; *(to justify)* justificar; *(a theory)* sostener —intr. hacer una defensa.

de·fen·dant (dǐ-fĕn'dənt) s. acusado, demandado.

de·fend·er (:dər) s. defensor m.

de·fend·ing (:dǐng) adj. defensor.

de·fense (dǐ-fĕns') s. defensa.

de·fense·less (:lǐs) adj. indefenso.

de·fen·sive (dǐ-fĕn'sǐv) adj. defensivo.

de·fer (dǐ-fûr') tr. -rr- aplazar, postergar; MIL. otorgar una prórroga a —intr. deferir.

def·er·ence (dĕf'ər-əns) s. deferencia.

def·er·en·tial (-ə-rĕn'shəl) adj. deferente.

de·fer·ment (dǐ-fûr'mənt) s. aplazamiento; MIL. prórroga.

de·fer·ra·ble (:ə-bəl) adj. diferible, aplazable.

de·fer·ral (:əl) var. de **deferment**.

de·fi·ance (dǐ-fī'əns) s. desafío, reto.

de·fi·ant (:ənt) adj. provocador, desafiante.

de·fi·cient (dǐ-fǐsh'ənt) adj. deficiente, carente ♦ **to be d. in** carecer de.

def·i·cit (dĕf'ǐ-sǐt) s. déficit f ♦ **d. spending** gasto deficitario.

de·file (dǐ-fīl') tr. *(to dirty)* ensuciar, contaminar; *(to desecrate)* profanar; *(to rape)* violar.

de·fine (dǐ-fīn') tr. definir.

def·i·nite (dĕf'ə-nǐt) adj. definido; *(certain)* definitivo; *(explicit)* claro, explícito.

def·i·nite·ly (:lē) I. adv. definitivamente II. interj. ¡por supuesto!, ¡desde luego!

def·i·ni·tion (dĕf'ə-nǐsh'ən) s. definición f; *(of power, authority)* limitación f.

de·fin·i·tive (dǐ-fǐn'ǐ-tǐv) adj. definitivo.

de·flate (dǐ-flāt') tr. desinflar; *(pride)* rebajar; *(currency)* desvalorizar —intr. desinflarse.

de·fla·tion (dǐ-flā'shən) s. desinflamiento; *(of currency)* deflación f.

de·flect (dǐ-flĕkt') tr. & intr. desviar(se).

de·flow·er (dē-flou'ər) tr. desflorar.

de·fo·li·ant (dē-fō'lē-ənt) s. defoliante m.

de·fo·li·ate (:āt') tr. & intr. deshojar(se).

de·for·est (dē-fôr'ǐst) tr. desmontar.

de·form (dĭ-fôrm′) tr. & intr. deformar(se).
de·formed (dĭ-fôrmd′) adj. deforme, desfigurado.
de·for·mi·ty (dĭ-fôr′mĭ-tē) s. deformidad *f.*
de·fraud (dĭ-frôd′) tr. defraudar.
de·fray (dĭ-frā′) tr. sufragar, costear.
de·fray·al (:əl) s. subvención de gastos *f.*
de·frock (dē-frŏk′) tr. expulsar de una orden religiosa.
de·frost (dē-frôst′) tr. & intr. descongelar(se).
de·frost·er (dē-frô′stər) s. descongelador *m.*
deft (dĕft) adj. hábil, diestro.
deft·ness (:nĭs) s. habilidad *f*, destreza.
de·funct (dĭ-fŭngkt′) adj. difunto.
de·fuse (dē-fyo͞oz′) tr. quitar la espoleta a; *(hostility)* templar, minorar.
de·fy (dĭ-fī′) tr. desafiar; *(to resist)* resistir.
de·gen·er·a·cy (dĭ-jĕn′ər-ə-sē) s. degeneración *f.*
de·gen·er·ate (:ĭt) I. adj. & s. degenerado II. intr. (:ə-rāt′) degenerar.
de·gen·er·a·tive (:ər-ə-tĭv) adj. degenerativo.
de·grade (dĭ-grād′) tr. degradar.
de·grad·ing (dĭ-grā′dĭng) adj. degradante.
de·gree (dĭ-grē′) s. grado; EDUC. título ♦ **by degrees** gradualmente, poco a poco ♦ **doctor's d.** doctorado ♦ **to a certain d.** hasta cierto punto ♦ **to take a d.** in licenciarse en.
de·hu·man·ize (dē-hyo͞o′mə-nīz′) tr. deshumanizar.
de·hu·mid·i·fy (dē′hyo͞o-mĭd′ə-fī′) tr. deshumedecer.
de·hy·drate (dē-hī′drāt′) tr. deshidratar.
de·ice (dē-īs′) tr. deshelar.
de·i·cide (dē′ĭ-sīd′) s. deicidio; *(killer)* deicida *mf.*
de·i·fy (dē′ə-fī′) tr. deificar.
deign (dān) tr. & intr. dignarse (a).
de·ism (dē′ĭz′əm) s. deísmo.
de·i·ty (dē′ĭ-tē) s. deidad *f* ♦ **D.** Dios.
de·ject (dĭ-jĕkt′) tr. desanimar.
de·ject·ed (dĭ-jĕk′tĭd) adj. desanimado.
de·jec·tion (:shən) s. depresión *f.*
de·lay (dĭ-lā′) I. tr. *(to postpone)* postergar; *(to make late)* retrasar, demorar; *(to stall)* entretener —intr. demorarse, tardar II. s. demora, retraso; *(postponement)* postergación *f* ♦ **a five minute d.** cinco minutos de atraso.
de·lec·ta·ble (dĭ-lĕk′tə-bəl) adj. delicioso.
del·e·gate I. s. (dĕl′ĭ-gĭt) delegado, diputado II. tr. (:gāt′) delegar.
de·lete (dĭ-lēt′) tr. tachar, suprimir.
del·e·te·ri·ous (dĕl′ĭ-tîr′ē-əs) adj. deletéreo.
de·le·tion (dĭ-lē′shən) s. tachadura, supresión *f.*
de·lib·er·ate I. adj. (dĭ-lĭb′ər-ĭt) deliberado, a propósito; *(slow)* pausado II. intr. & tr. (:ə-rāt′) deliberar.
de·lib·er·a·tion (dĭ-lĭb′ə-rā′shən) s. deliberación *f*; *(slowness)* lentitud *f.*
del·i·ca·cy (dĕl′ĭ-kə-sē) s. delicadeza; *(fine food)* manjar *m*, gollería.
del·i·cate (dĕl′ĭ-kĭt) adj. delicado.
del·i·ca·tes·sen (dĕl′ĭ-kə-tĕs′ən) s. fiambrería.
de·li·cious (dĭ-lĭsh′əs) adj. delicioso.
de·light (dĭ-līt′) I. s. deleite *m*; *(person, thing)* encanto II. tr. deleitar, encantar —intr. ♦ **to d. in** deleitarse con o en.
de·light·ed (dĭ-lī′tĭd) adj. encantado.
de·light·ful (dĭ-līt′fəl) adj. delicioso, encantador.
de·lin·e·ate (dĭ-lĭn′ē-āt′) tr. delinear; *(to depict)* describir, pintar.

de·lin·quen·cy (dĭ-lĭng′kwən-sē) s. delincuencia.
de·lin·quent (:kwənt) I. adj. delincuente; *(in payment)* moroso II. s. delincuente *mf.*
del·i·quesce (dĕl′ĭ-kwĕs′) intr. licuarse.
de·lir·i·ous (dĭ-lĭr′ē-əs) adj. delirante.
de·lir·i·um (:əm) s. delirio, desvarío.
de·liv·er (dĭ-lĭv′ər) tr. *(to free)* liberar; *(to hand over)* entregar; *(mail)* repartir; *(a blow, speech)* dar; *(missile)* lanzar; *(baby)* asistir al parto de ♦ **to d. oneself of an opinion** opinar —intr. cumplir *(on* con); *(to give birth)* alumbrar ♦ **we d.** entregamos a domicilio.
de·liv·er·ance (:əns) s. liberación *f.*
de·liv·er·er (:ər) s. liberador *m.*
de·liv·er·y (dĭ-lĭv′ə-rē) s. entrega; *(release)* liberación *f*; *(birth)* parto; *(style)* elocución *f.*
de·liv·er·y·man (:măn′) s. [pl. -men] repartidor *m.*
dell (dĕl) s. valle pequeño.
de·louse (dē-lous′) tr. despiojar, espulgar.
del·phin·i·um (dĕl-fĭn′ē-əm) s. delfinio.
de·lude (dĭ-lo͞od′) tr. engañar, despistar.
del·uge (dĕl′yo͞oj) I. tr. inundar II. s. inundación *f*, diluvio.
de·lu·sion (dĭ-lo͞o′zhən) s. engaño, ilusión *f*; MED. delirio.
de·lu·sive (:sĭv) adj. ilusorio, falso.
de luxe *o* **de·luxe** (dĭ-lŭks′) adj. de lujo, lujoso.
delve (dĕlv) intr. indagar, hurgar.
dem·a·gog·ic (dĕm′ə-gŏj′ĭk) adj. demagógico.
dem·a·gogue (dĕm′ə-gŏg′) s. demagogo.
dem·a·gogu·er·y (:gô′gə-rē) s. demagogia.
de·mand (dĭ-mănd′) I. tr. *(to ask for)* demandar; *(to claim, require)* reclamar, exigir II. s. *(request)* solicitud *f*; *(claim)* reclamación *f*; *(requirement)* necesidad *f*; COM. demanda ♦ **d. deposit** depósito a la vista ♦ **on d.** COM. a la vista; *(by request)* a petición ♦ **to be in d.** ser popular.
de·mand·ing (dĭ-măn′dĭng) adj. exigente.
de·mar·cate (dĭ-mär′kāt′) tr. demarcar.
de·mean (dĭ-mēn′) tr. rebajar ♦ **to d. oneself** rebajarse.
de·mean·or (dĭ-mē′nər) s. comportamiento.
de·ment·ed (dĭ-mĕn′tĭd) adj. demente, loco.
de·mer·it (dĭ-mĕr′ĭt) s. desmerecimiento.
dem·i·god (dĕm′ē-gŏd′) s. semidiós *m.*
dem·i·john (:jŏn′) s. damajuana, garrafón *m.*
de·mil·i·ta·rize (dē-mĭl′ĭ-tə-rīz′) tr. desmilitarizar.
de·mise (dĭ-mīz′) s. fallecimiento, defunción *f*; DER. traspaso (de bienes).
dem·i·tasse (dĕm′ē-tăs′) s. tacita de café.
de·mo·bil·ize (dē-mō′bə-līz′) tr. desmovilizar.
de·moc·ra·cy (dĭ-mŏk′rə-sē) s. democracia.
dem·o·crat (dĕm′ə-krăt′) s. demócrata *mf.*
dem·o·crat·ic (′-ĭk) adj. democrático.
de·moc·ra·tize (dĭ-mŏk′rə-tīz′) tr. democratizar.
dem·o·graph·ic (dĕm′ə-grăf′ĭk) adj. demográfico ♦ **demographics** s.pl. datos demográficos.
de·mog·ra·phy (dĭ-mŏg′rə-fē) s. demografía.
de·mol·ish (dĭ-mŏl′ĭsh) tr. demoler, derribar.
dem·o·li·tion (dĕm′ə-lĭsh′ən) s. demolición *f.*
de·mon (dē′mən) s. demonio.
de·mon·ic (dĭ-mŏn′ĭk) adj. demoniaco.
dem·on·strate (dĕm′ən-strāt′) tr. demostrar —intr. protestar, manifestarse.
dem·on·stra·tion (′-strā′shən) s. demostración *f*; *(rally)* manifestación *f.*
de·mon·stra·tive (dĭ-mŏn′strə-tĭv) adj. demos-

ing

trativo; *(expressive)* expresivo, efusivo.

dem·on·stra·tor (děm'ən-strā'tər) s. *(sample)* modelo de muestra; *(person)* manifestante *mf.*

de·mor·al·ize (dĭ-môr'ə-līz') tr. desmoralizar.

de·mote (dĭ-mōt') tr. degradar.

de·mo·tion (dĭ-mō'shən) s. degradación *f.*

de·mur (dĭ-mûr') intr. intr. hacer objeciones.

de·mure (dĭ-myŏŏr') adj. **-er, -est** recatado.

den (děn) s. *(lair)* cubil *m; (study)* estudio.

de·na·ture (dē-nā'chər) tr. desnaturalizar.

de·ni·al (dĭ-nī'əl) s. negativa; *(disavowal)* repudio; DER. denegación *f.*

den·i·grate (děn'ĭ-grāt') tr. denigrar.

den·im (děn'ĭm) s. dril *m* de algodón ♦ pl. vaqueros.

den·i·zen (děn'ĭ-zən) s. habitante *mf.*

de·nom·i·na·tion (dĭ-nŏm'ə-nā'shən) s. denominación *f; (sect)* secta, creencia.

de·nom·i·na·tion·al (:shə-nəl) adj. sectario.

de·nom·i·na·tor (-'-'-tər) s. denominador *m.*

de·note (dĭ-nōt') tr. denotar.

dé·noue·ment (dā'nōō-mä') s. desenlace *m.*

de·nounce (dĭ-nouns') tr. denunciar.

dense (děns) adj. denso; FAM. estúpido.

den·si·ty (děn'sĭ-tē) s. densidad *f;* FAM. estupidez *f.*

dent (děnt) I. s. abolladura, mella II. tr. & intr. abollar(se), mellar(se).

den·tal (děn'tl) adj. dental ♦ **d. plate** dentadura postiza.

den·ti·frice (:tə-frĭs) s. dentífrico.

den·tist (děn'tĭst) s. dentista *mf.*

den·tist·ry (:tĭ-strē) s. odontología.

den·ture (:chər) s. dentadura postiza.

de·nude (dĭ-nōōd') tr. denudar, despojar.

de·nun·ci·a·tion (dĭ-nŭn'sē-ā'shən) s. denuncia; *(criticism)* censura, crítica.

de·ny (dĭ-nī') tr. negar; *(to withhold)* rehusar; *(to repudiate)* repudiar ♦ **to d. oneself** privarse de.

de·o·dor·ant (dē-ō'dər-ənt) s. desodorante *m.*

de·o·dor·ize (:ə-rīz') tr. desodorizar.

de·part (dĭ-pärt') intr. marcharse, irse; *(train, bus)* salir ♦ **to d. from** apartarse de —tr. partir de.

de·part·ed (dĭ-pär'tĭd) adj. & s. difunto.

de·part·ment (dĭ-pärt'mənt) s. departamento; POL. ministerio ♦ **d. store** gran almacén

de·par·ture (dĭ-pär'chər) s. partida, salida; *(deviation)* desviación *f.*

de·pend (dĭ-pěnd') intr. ♦ **to d. (up)on** *(as a dependent, consequence)* depender de; *(to trust)* confiar en, fiar; *(to count on)* contar con ♦ **you can d. on it!** ¡puedes estar seguro!

de·pend·a·bil·i·ty (dĭ-pěn'də-bĭl'ĭ-tē) s. *(person)* seriedad *f; (machine)* seguridad *f* de funcionamiento.

de·pend·a·ble (-'-bəl) adj. *(trustworthy)* (digno) de confianza; *(reliable)* seguro.

de·pend·ence/ance (dĭ-pěn'dəns) s. dependencia *(on, upon de); (trust)* confianza *(on, upon en).*

de·pend·ent/ant (:dənt) I. adj. ♦ **d. (up)on** dependiente de II. s. persona a cargo.

de·per·son·al·ize (dē-pûr'sə-nə-līz') tr. despersonalizar.

de·pict (dĭ-pĭkt') tr. representar, pintar.

de·pil·a·to·ry (dĭ-pĭl'ə-tôr'ē) I. adj. depilatorio II. s. crema depilatoria.

de·plane (dē-plān') intr. bajar del avión.

de·plete (dĭ-plēt') tr. agotar, reducir.

de·ple·tion (dĭ-plē'shən) tr. agotamiento.

de·plor·a·ble (dĭ-plôr'ə-bəl) adj. deplorable.

de·plore (dĭ-plôr') tr. deplorar, desaprobar.

de·ploy (dĭ-ploi') tr. & intr. desplegar(se).

de·ploy·ment (:mənt) s. despliegue *m.*

de·po·nent (dĭ-pō'nənt) s. declarante *mf.*

de·pop·u·late (dē-pŏp'yə-lāt') tr. despoblar.

de·port (dĭ-pôrt') tr. deportar, expulsar.

de·port·ee (dē'pôr-tē') s. deportado.

de·port·ment (dĭ-pôrt'mənt) s. conducta

de·pose (dĭ-pōz') tr. deponer.

de·pos·it (dĭ-pŏz'ĭt) I. tr. depositar; COM. *(down payment)* dar de señal *o* de entrada II. s. depósito; *(down payment)* señal *f,* entrada.

de·po·si·tion (děp'ə-zĭsh'ən) s. POL. deposición *f;* DER. declaración *f.*

de·pos·i·tor (dĭ-pŏz'ĭ-tər) s. cuentacorrentista *mf.*

de·pos·i·to·ry (:tôr'ē) s. depositaría, almacén *m.*

de·pot (dē'pō) s. *(bus, train)* estación *f; (warehouse)* almacén *m,* depósito.

de·prave (dĭ-prāv') tr. depravar, pervertir.

de·prav·i·ty (dĭ-prăv'ĭ-tē) s. depravación *f.*

dep·re·cate (děp'rĭ-kāt') tr. desaprobar.

de·pre·ci·ate (dĭ-prē'shē-āt') tr. *(to devalue)* depreciar, desvalorar; *(to belittle)* despreciar —intr. depreciarse.

de·pre·ci·a·tion (-'-ā'shən) s. depreciación *f,* desvalorización *f.*

dep·re·da·tion (děp'rĭ-dā'ənən) s. depredación *f,* pillaje *m.*

de·press (dĭ-prěs') tr. *(to dispirit)* deprimir, desanimar; *(to press down)* presionar; *(prices)* bajar.

de·pres·sant (:ənt) s. sedante *m.*

de·pressed (dĭ-prěst') adj. deprimido; ECON. *(period)* de depresión; *(economy)* deprimido.

de·press·ing (dĭ-prěs'ĭng) adj. deprimente.

de·pres·sion (dĭ-prěsh'ən) s. *(a hollow)* cavidad *f,* hueco; ECON., MED. depresión *f.*

de·pres·sur·ize (dē-prěsh'ə-rīz') tr. descomprimir.

dep·ri·va·tion (děp'rə-vā'shən) s. privación *f.*

de·prive (dĭ-prīv') tr. privar.

de·prived (dĭ-prīvd') adj. pobre, necesitado.

depth (děpth) s. profundidad *f; (most intense part)* lo más profundo; *(color)* intensidad *f* ♦ **charge** carga de profundidad • **in d.** a fondo ♦ pl. lo más hondo; FIG. lo más recóndito.

dep·u·tize (děp'yə-tīz') tr. diputar, delegar

dep·u·ty (:tē) s. *(delegate)* delegado; *(assistant)* asistente *m; (legislator)* diputado.

de·rail (dē-rāl') tr. & intr. (hacer) descarrilar.

de·range (dĭ-rānj') tr. *(to disturb)* perturbar, desordenar; *(to make insane)* enloquecer.

de·ranged (dĭ-rānjd') adj. loco, trastornado.

de·range·ment (dĭ-rānj'mənt) s. desorden *m,* desarreglo; MED. trastorno (mental).

der·by (dûr'bē) s. *(race)* carrera; *(hat)* sombrero hongo.

de·reg·u·late (dē-rěg'yə-lāt') tr. quitar las reglamentaciones de.

der·e·lict (děr'ə-lĭkt') I. s. *(person)* vago; *(ship)* derrelicto II. adj. *(remiss)* remiso; *(property)* abandonado.

de·ride (dĭ-rīd') tr. burlarse de, mofarse de.

de·ri·sion (dĭ-rĭzh'ən) s. burla, mofa.

de·ri·sive/so·ry (dĭ-rī'sĭv/sə-rē) adj. *(mocking)* burlón, mofador; *(ridiculous)* irrisorio

de·rive (dĭ-rīv') tr. & intr. derivar *(from de).*

der·ma·tol·o·gy (dûr'mə-tŏl'ə-jē) s. dermatología

der·o·ga·tion (děr'ə-gā'shən) s. *(disparagement)* menosprecio; DER. derogación *f.*

de·rog·a·to·ry/tive (dǐ-rǒg'ə-tôr'ē/tǐv) adj. *(disparaging)* despectivo; DER. derogatorio.

der·rick (děr'ǐk) s. *(crane)* grúa; *(of oil well)* torre *f* de perforación.

der·ring-do (děr'ǐng-dōō') s. intrepidez *f.*

der·vish (dûr'vǐsh) s. derviche *m.*

de·sal·i·nate (dē-sǎl'ə-nāt') tr. desalar.

de·scend (dǐ-sěnd') intr. descender; *(inheritance)* transmitirse por herencia ♦ **to d. on** *o* **upon** caer encima de —tr. descender, bajar.

de·scen·dant (dǐ-sěn'dənt) s. descendiente *mf.*

de·scent (dǐ-sěnt') s. descenso; *(slope)* declive *m*; *(lineage)* descendencia; MIL. embestida.

de·scribe (dǐ-skrīb') tr. describir.

de·scrip·tion (dǐ-skrǐp'shən) s. descripción *f* ♦ **of every d.** de toda clase.

de·scrip·tive (:tǐv) adj. descriptivo.

de·scry (dǐ-skrī') tr. divisar, descubrir.

des·e·crate (děs'ǐ-krāt') tr. profanar.

de·seg·re·gate (dē-sěg'rǐ-gāt') intr. & tr. eliminar la segregación racial (en).

de·sen·si·tize (dē-sěn'sǐ-tīz') tr. desensibilizar.

des·ert¹ (děz'ərt) s. desierto ♦ **d. heat** calor desértico.

de·sert² (dǐ-zûrt') s. ♦ pl. *(one's due)* merecido.

de·sert³ (dǐ-zûrt') tr. abandonar; MIL. desertar de —intr. desertar.

de·sert·er (dǐ-zûr'tər) s. desertor *m.*

de·ser·tion (:shən) s. deserción *f.*

de·serve (dǐ-zûrv') tr. & intr. merecer(se).

de·serv·ing (dǐ-zûr'vǐng) adj. digno, meritorio.

des·ic·cate (děs'ǐ-kāt') tr. & intr. desecar(se).

de·sign (dǐ-zīn') I. tr. *(to invent)* idear; *(a plan)* diseñar; *(pattern)* dibujar; *(to intend)* proyectar —intr. hacer diseños II. s. diseño; ARTE. dibujo; ARQ. plano; *(intention)* propósito ♦ **by d.** intencionalmente ● **to have designs on** poner las miras en.

des·ig·nate (děz'ǐg-nāt') I. tr. designar; *(to characterize)* describir II (:nǐt) adj. designado.

de·sign·er (dǐ-zī'nər) s. diseñador *m.*

de·sir·a·ble (dǐ-zīr'ə-bəl) adj. deseable.

de·sire (dǐ-zīr') I. tr. desear II. s. deseo.

de·sir·ous (:əs) adj. deseoso.

de·sist (dǐ-zǐst') intr. dejar de hacer algo.

desk (děsk) s. escritorio; *(at school)* pupitre *m*; *(in hotel)* recepción *f*; *(counter, booth)* mesa.

des·o·late (děs'ə-lǐt) (děs'ə-lǐt) adj. desolado II. tr. (:lāt') *(to distress)* desconsolar.

de·spair (dǐ-spâr') I. s. desesperación *f* II. intr. desesperar(se).

des·per·a·do (děs'pə-rä'dō) s. [pl. **(e)s**] forajido, bandolero.

des·per·ate (děs'pər-ǐt) adj. desesperado; *(grave)* crítico; *(urgent)* apremiante.

des·per·a·tion ('pə-rā'shən) s. desesperación *f.*

des·pi·ca·ble (děs'pǐk'ə-bəl) adj. odioso, vil.

de·spise (dǐ-spīz') tr. despreciar.

de·spite (dǐ-spīt') prep. a pesar de, no obstante.

de·spoil (dǐ-spoil') tr. expoliar, saquear.

de·spon·dence/cy (dǐ-spǒn'dəns) s. desánimo.

de·spon·dent (:dənt) adj. desanimado.

des·pot (děs'pət) s. déspota *mf.*

des·pot·ic (dǐ-spǒt'ǐk) adj. despótico.

des·pot·ism (děs'pə-tǐz'əm) s. despotismo.

des·sert (dǐ-zûrt') s. CUL. postre *m.*

de·sta·bi·lize (dē-stā'bə-līz') tr. desestabilizar.

des·ti·na·tion (děs'tə-nā'shən) s. destino.

des·tine (děs'tǐn) tr. destinar ♦ **destined for** con destino a.

des·ti·ny (děs'tə-nē) s. destino, sino.

des·ti·tute (děs'tǐ-tōōt') adj. indigente.

des·ti·tu·tion ('-tōō'shən) s. miseria.

de·stroy (dǐ-stroi') tr. destruir.

de·stroy·er (:ər) s. destructor *m.*

de·struct (dǐ-strǔkt') s. destrucción deliberada de un vehículo espacial.

de·struc·tion (dǐ-strǔk'shən) s. destrucción *f.*

de·struc·tive (:tǐv) adj. destructivo, destructor ♦ **d. of** *o* **to** perjudicial para.

de·sul·to·ry (děs'əl-tôr'ē) adj. sin entusiasmo.

de·tach (dǐ-tǎch') tr. separar, desprender.

de·tach·a·ble (:ə-bəl) adj. desmontable.

de·tached (dǐ-tǎcht') adj. separado; *(aloof)* indiferente, despreocupado.

de·tach·ment (dǐ-tǎch'mənt) s. separación *f*; *(impartiality)* objetividad *f*; *(aloofness)* indiferencia; MIL. destacamento.

de·tail (dǐ-tāl', dē'tāl') I. s. detalle *m*, pormenor *m*; MIL. destacamento II. tr. detallar.

de·tailed (dǐ-tāld', dē'tāld') adj. detallado, minucioso.

de·tain (dǐ-tān') tr. *(to delay)* retardar, demorar; *(in custody)* detener.

de·tect (dǐ-těkt') tr. percibir, detectar.

de·tec·tion (dǐ-těk'shən) s. descubrimiento.

de·tec·tive (dǐ-těk'tǐv) s. detective *mf* ♦ **d. story** novela policial.

de·tec·tor (:tər) s. detector *m.*

dé·tente (dā-tänt') s. distensión *f.*

de·ten·tion (dǐ-těn'shən) s. detención *f.*

de·ter (dǐ-tûr') tr. **-rr-** impedir.

de·ter·gent (dǐ-tûr'jənt) s. detergente *m.*

de·te·ri·o·rate (dǐ-tîr'ē-ə-rāt') intr. empeorar, degenerar.

de·ter·mi·nant (dǐ-tûr'mə-nənt) adj. & s. determinante *m.*

de·ter·mi·nate (:nǐt) adj. definitivo.

de·ter·mi·na·tion (-'-nā'shən) s. determinación *f*; *(resolve)* resolución *f*; DER. *(ruling)* decisión *f.*

de·ter·mine (dǐ-tûr'mǐn) tr. determinar —intr. decidir.

de·ter·mined (:mǐnd) adj. determinado.

de·ter·min·ing (:mǐ-nǐng) adj. decisivo.

de·ter·rence (:əns) s. disuasión *f.*

de·ter·rent (:ənt) I. s. agente disuasivo; MIL. fuerza de disuasión II. adj. impeditivo; MIL. de disuasión.

de·test (dǐ-těst') tr. detestar, aborrecer.

de·throne (dē-thrōn') tr. destronar.

det·o·nate (dět'n-āt') tr. & intr. (hacer) detonar.

det·o·na·tor (:ā'tər) s. detonador *m.*

de·tour (dē'tōōr') I. s. desvío II. tr. & intr. desviar(se).

de·tox·i·fi·ca·tion (dē-tŏk'sə-fǐ-kā'shən) s. desintoxicación *f.*

de·tract (dǐ-trǎkt') intr. ♦ **to d. from** disminuir.

de·trac·tion (dǐ-trǎk'shən) s. disminución *f.*

de·train (dē-trān') intr. bajar de un tren.

det·ri·ment (dět'rə-mənt) s. detrimento.

det·ri·men·tal (-'-měn'tl) adj. perjudicial.

deuce (dōōs) s. dos *m.*

deu·te·ri·um (dōō-tîr'ē-əm) s. deuterio.

de·val·u·ate/val·ue (dē-vǎl'yōō-āt'/vǎl'yōō) tr. devaluar, desvalorizar.

dev·as·tate (děv'ə-stāt') tr. devastar, asolar; *(to overwhelm)* abrumar.

dev·as·tat·ing (:stā'tǐng) adj. devastador.

dev·as·ta·tion ('-'shən) s. devastación f.
de·vel·op (dĭ-vĕl'əp) tr. desarrollar; *(the body)* fortalecer; *(an ability)* formar; *(land)* urbanizar; *(taste)* adquirir; *(habit, disease)* contraer; FOTOG. revelar —intr. desarrollarse; *(to advance)* progresar; *(to be disclosed)* descubrirse, revelarse.
de·vel·op·er (.ə-pər) s. urbanizador m; FOTOG. revelador m.
de·vel·op·ing (:pĭng) adj. en (vías de) desarrollo.
de·vel·op·ment (dĭ-vĕl'əp-mənt) s. desarrollo; *(event)* suceso; FOTOG. revelado.
de·vi·ance (dē'vē-əns) s. desviación f.
de·vi·ant (:ənt) adj. & s. pervertido.
de·vi·ate (dē'vē-āt') intr. desviarse.
de·vi·a·tion ('-ā'shən) s. desviación f; *(from the truth)* alejamiento.
de·vice (dĭ-vīs') s. *(scheme)* ardid m; *(mechanism)* dispositivo, aparato; LIT. recurso.
dev·il (dĕv'əl) s. diablo ♦ a d. of *(something)* (algo) del diablo • d.'s advocate abogado de diablo • to give the d. his due dar a cada uno lo suyo.
dev·il·ish (:ə-lĭsh) I. adj. diabólico, malvado; *(mischievous)* travieso.
dev·il·try/ry (:əl-trē/rē) s. diablura.
de·vi·ous (dē'vē-əs) adj. tortuoso.
de·vise (dĭ-vīz') tr. *(to conceive)* idear, concebir; *(to contrive)* trazar, tramar.
de·vi·tal·ize (dē-vīt'l-īz') tr. debilitar.
de·void (dĭ-void') adj. desprovisto, carente.
de·volve (dĭ-vŏlv') tr. transferir, delegar.
de·vote (dĭ-vōt') tr. dedicar, consagrar.
de·vot·ed (dĭ-vō'tĭd) adj. *(loving)* afectuoso; *(dedicated)* devoto; *(ardent)* fervoroso.
dev·o·tee (dĕv'ə-tē') s. devoto.
de·vo·tion (dĭ-vō'shən) s. devoción f ♦ pl. oraciones, rezos.
de·vo·tion·al (:shə-nəl) I. adj. devoto II. s. oficio religioso breve.
de·vour (dĭ-vour') tr. devorar, engullir.
de·vour·ing (dĭ-vou'rĭng) adj. devorador.
de·vout (dĭ-vout') adj. -er, -est *(pious)* devoto; *(earnest)* fervoroso.
de·vout·ness (:nĭs) s. devoción f, piedad f.
dew (dōō) s. rocío ♦ d. point punto de condensación.
dew·drop (:drŏp') s. gota de rocío.
dew·y (:ē) adj. rociado; FIG. puro, fresco.
dex·ter·i·ty (dĕk-stĕr'ĭ-tē) s. destreza.
dex·ter·ous (dĕk'stər əs) adj. diestro, hábil.
dex·trose (dĕk'strōs') s. dextrosa.
di·a·be·tes (dī'ə-bē'tĭs) s. diabetes f.
di·a·bet·ic (:bĕt'ĭk) adj. & s. diabético.
di·a·bol·ic/i·cal (dī'ə-bŏl'ĭk) adj. diabólico.
di·a·crit·ic (dī'ə-krĭt'ĭk) s. signo diacrítico.
di·a·dem (dī'ə dĕm') s. diadema f.
di·ag·nose (dī'əg-nōs') tr. diagnosticar.
di·ag·no·sis (:nō'sĭs) s. [pl. -ses] diagnóstico.
di·ag·nos·tic (:nōs'tĭk) adj. diagnóstico.
di·ag·o·nal (dī-ăg'ə-nəl) adj. & s. diagonal f.
di·a·gram (dī'ə-grăm') I. s. diagrama m II. tr. -mm- representar con un diagrama.
di·al (dī'əl) I. s. *(scale, clock)* esfera, cuadrante m; RAD., TELEV. dial m, botón m selector; TEL. disco ♦ d. tone TEL. tono para marcar II. tr. RAD., TELEV. sintonizar; TEL. marcar (un número).
di·a·lect (dī'ə-lĕkt') s. dialecto.
di·a·lec·tic (dī'ə-lĕk'tĭk) I. s. dialéctica II. adj. /ti·cal dialéctico.

di·a·lec·tics (:tĭks) s.sg. dialéctica.
di·a·log(ue) (dī'ə-lôg') s. diálogo.
di·al·y·sis (dī-ăl'ĭ-sĭs) s. diálisis f.
di·am·e·ter (dī-ăm'ĭ-tər) s. diámetro.
di·a·met·ric/ri·cal (dī'ə-mĕt'rĭk) adj. diametral, del diámetro; *(contrary)* opuesto.
di·a·mond (dī'ə-mənd) s. diamante m; *(shape)* rombo ♦ d. ring sortija de diamantes.
di·a·per (dī'pər) I. s. pañal m II. tr. poner el pañal a.
di·aph·a·nous (dī-ăf'ə-nəs) adj. diáfano.
di·a·phragm (dī'ə-frăm') s. diafragma m.
di·a·rist (dī'ə-rĭst) s. diarista mf.
di·ar·rh(o)e·a (dī'ə-rē'ə) s. diarrea f.
di·a·ry (dī'ə-rē) s. diario.
di·as·to·le (dī-ăs'tə-lē) s. diástole f.
di·a·tribe (dī'ə-trīb') s. diatriba f.
dice (dīs) I. s.pl. [sg. **die**] dados II. tr. picar en cubitos.
di·chot·o·my (dī-kŏt'ə-mē) s. dicotomía f.
dick (dĭk) s. JER. sabueso, detective m.
dick·ens (dĭk'ənz) s. diablo, demonio.
dick·er (dĭk'ər) intr. ♦ to d. over ragatear.
dic·tate I. tr. (dĭk'tāt', -') *(letter)* dictar; *(policy)* imponer —intr. mandar II. s. ('') mandato ♦ pl. dictados.
dic·ta·tion (dĭk-tā'shən) s. dictado.
dic·ta·tor (dĭk'tā'tər) s. dictador m.
dic·ta·tor·ship ('-shĭp) s. dictadura f.
dic·tion (dĭk'shən) s. dicción f.
dic·tion·ar·y (dĭk'shə-nĕr'ē) s. diccionario.
dic·tum (dĭk'təm) s. [pl. s o -ta] dictamen m.
did (dĭd) cf. **do.**
di·dac·tic/ti·cal (dī-dăk'tĭk) adj. didáctico.
did·n't (dĭd'nt) contr. de **did not.**
die[1] (dī) intr. **dy·ing** *(to lose force)* apagarse, disminuir; *(to become extinct)* extinguirse, desaparecer.
die[2] s. [pl. **s**] MAQ. cuño, troquel m; [pl. **dice**] *(for gambling)* dado ♦ **the d. is cast** la suerte está echada.
die-hard (dī'härd') s. testarudo.
die·sel engine (dē'zəl) s. motor diesel.
di·et[1] (dī'ĭt) s. & intr. *(estar a)* dieta.
di·et[2] s. POL. dieta.
di·e·tar·y (dī'ĭ-tĕr'ē) adj. dietético.
di·et·er (:tər) s. persona que hace dieta.
di·e·tet·ic (dī'ĭ-tĕt'ĭk) adj. dietético.
di·e·ti·tian/cian (dī'ĭ-tĭsh'ən) s. dietista mf.
dif·fer (dĭf'ər) intr. disentir, no estar de acuerdo ♦ to d. from diferir con, ser diferente de.
dif·fer·ence (:əns) s. diferencia ♦ it makes no d da lo mismo • what d. does it make? ¿qué más da? • what's the d.? ¿qué importa?
dif·fer·ent (:ənt) adj. diferente, distinto.
dif·fer·en·ti·ate (dĭf'ə-rĕn'shē-āt') tr. & intr. diferenciar(se), distinguir(se).
dif·fi·cult (dĭf'ĭ-kəlt) adj. difícil.
dif·fi·cul·ty (:kəl-tē) s. dificultad f ♦ pl. apuros.
dif·fi·dent (dĭf'ĭ-dnt) adj. tímido.
dif·frac·tion (dĭ-frăk'shən) s. difracción f.
dif·fuse I. tr. & intr. (dĭ-fyōōz') difundir(se) II. adj. (dĭ-fyōōs') difuso.
dig (dĭg) I. tr. **dug**, **-gging** cavar, excavar; *(well, tunnel)* hacer, abrir; MIN. excavar; JER. *(to understand)* comprender; *(to like)* gustar ♦ to d. in(to) hincar, hundir en • to d. out *(hole)* excavar; *(object)* extraer; *(facts)* sacar • to d. up *(object)* extraer, desenterrar; *(facts)* descubrir —intr. cavar ♦ to d. for buscar • to d. in *(to entrench oneself)* atrincherarse; FAM. *(to eat)* atacar II. s. *(prod)* golpe m; *(with the*

elbow) codazo; *(gibe)* pulla, indirecta; ARQUEOL. excavación *f* ♦ pl. G.B., FAM. *(lodgings)* alojamiento.

di·gest I. tr. & intr. (dǐ-jěst', dī-) digerir(se) II. s. (dī'jěst') compendio, sinopsis *f.*

di·gest·i·ble (dĭ-jěs'tə-bəl, dī-) adj. digestible.

di·ges·tion (:chən) s. digestión *f.*

di·ges·tive (:tĭv) adj. & s. digestivo.

dig·ger (dĭg'ər) s. *(person)* cavador *m*; *(tool)* azadón *m*; *(machine)* excavadora *f.*

dig·ging (:ĭng) s. excavación *f.*

digit (dĭj'ĭt) s. ANAT. dedo; MAT. dígito.

dig·i·tal (:ĭ-tl) adj. digital ♦ **d. clock** reloj numérico.

dig·i·tal·is (dĭj'ĭ-tăl'ĭs) s. digitalina.

dig·ni·fied (dĭg'nə-fīd') adj. digno, decoroso.

dig·ni·fy (:fī') tr. dignificar.

dig·ni·tar·y (dĭg'nĭ-těr'ē) s. dignatario.

dig·ni·ty (dĭg'nĭ-tē) s. dignidad *f.*

di·gress (dī-grěs', dī-) intr. divagar.

di·gres·sive (:ĭv) adj. digresivo, inconexo.

dike (dīk) s. dique *m*, represa.

di·lap·i·dat·ed (dĭ-lăp'ĭ-dā'tĭd) adj. desvencijado.

di·late (dī-lāt') tr. & intr. dilatar(se).

di·la·tion (dī-lā'shən) s. dilatación *f.*

dil·a·to·ry (dĭl'ə-tôr'ē) adj. dilatorio.

di·lem·ma (dĭ-lěm'ə, dī-) s. dilema *m.*

dil·et·tante (dĭl'ĭ-tänt') s. diletante *mf.*

dil·i·gence (dĭl'ə-jəns) s. diligencia.

dil·i·gent (dĭl'ə-jənt) adj. diligente.

dill (dĭl) s. eneldo.

dil·ly (dĭl'ē) s. FAM. joya, perla.

dil·ly-dal·ly (:dăl'ē) intr. perder el tiempo.

di·lute (dĭ-lōōt', dī-) I. tr. diluir, desleir II. adj. diluido.

dim (dĭm) **-mm-** I. adj. *(dark)* oscuro; *(lights)* bajo, débil; *(outline)* borroso; *(vision)* turbio; *(memory)* vago; *(person)* de pocas luces ♦ **to take a d. view of** ver de modo poco favorable II. tr. *(room)* oscurecer; *(lights)* bajar —intr. oscurecerse; *(lights)* perder intensidad; *(outline, memory)* borrarse.

dime (dīm) s. E.U. moneda de diez centavos ♦ **d. store** tienda de baratijas.

di·men·sion (dĭ-měn'shən, dī-) s. dimensión *f.*

di·min·ish (dĭ-mĭn'ĭsh) tr. & intr. disminuir.

dim·i·nu·tion (dĭm'ə-nōō'shən) s. disminución *f.*

di·min·u·tive (dĭ-mĭn'yə-tĭv) I. adj. *(tiny)* diminuto; GRAM. diminutivo II. s. diminutivo.

dim·ple (dĭm'pəl) s. hoyuelo.

dim·wit (dĭm'wĭt') s. JER. mentecato.

din (dĭn) s. estrépito; *(of a crowd)* clamoreo.

dine (dīn) intr. comer; *(in the evening)* cenar.

din·er (dī'nər) s. comensal *mf*; F.C. vagón *m* restaurante; *(restaurant)* restaurante *m* popular.

di·nette (dī-nět') s. comedor pequeño.

ding-dong (dĭng'dông') s. talán talán *m.*

din·ghy (dĭng'ē) s. bote *m* (de remo).

din·gy (dĭn'jē) adj. **-i-** sórdido, sucio.

dining (dī'nĭng) adj. ♦ **d. car** vagón restaurante • **d. hall** refectorio • **d. room** comedor.

din·ky (dĭng'kē) adj. **-i-** FAM. diminuto.

din·ner (dĭn'ər) s. cena; *(at noon)* comida (principal); *(formal)* banquete *m* ♦ **d. jacket** smoking.

di·no·saur (dī'nə-sôr') s. dinosaurio.

dint (dĭnt) s. ♦ **by d. of** a fuerza de.

di·o·cese (dī'ə-sĭs) s. diócesis *f.*

di·ode (dī'ōd') s. diodo.

di·ox·ide (dī-ŏk'sīd') s. dióxido.

dip (dĭp) I. tr. **-pp-** *(to dunk)* bañar, mojar; *(to immerse)* sumergir, meter; *(to scoop)* sacar; *(to lower)* inclinar, bajar —intr. *(to plunge)* sumergirse; *(prices, road)* bajar; *(out of sight)* hundirse; AVIA. bajar en picado ♦ **to d. into** *(a subject)* meterse en; *(a book)* hojear; *(savings)* echar mano a II. s. *(immersion)* inmersión *f*; *(swim)* chapuzón *m*; *(liquid)* baño; *(slope, drop)* bajada; *(of magnetic needle)* inclinación *f*; *(hollow)* depresión *f*; *(in a road)* badén *m*; CUL. salsa; AVIA. bajón *m* ♦ **to take a d.** darse un chapuzón.

diph·the·ri·a (dĭf-thîr'ē-ə, dĭp-) s. difteria.

diph·thong (dĭf'thông', dĭp'-) s. diptongo.

di·plo·ma (dĭ-plō'mə) s. diploma *m.*

di·plo·ma·cy (dĭ-plō'mə-sē) s. diplomacia.

dip·lo·mat (dĭp'lə-măt') s. diplomático.

dip·lo·mat·ic ('-'ĭk) adj. diplomático.

di·pole (dī'pōl') s. dipolo.

dip·per (dĭp'ər) s. cazo, cucharón *m.*

dip·stick (:stĭk') s. indicador *m* de nivel.

dire (dīr) adj. terrible, espantoso; *(extreme)* extremo ♦ **to be in d. need of** necesitar urgentemente.

di·rect (dĭ-rěkt', dī-) I. tr. dirigir; *(to order)* ordenar ♦ **to d. one's attention to** fijarse en II. adj. directo; *(candid)* franco ♦ **the d. opposite** exactamente lo contrario III. adv. directamente.

di·rec·tion (dĭ-rěk'shən, dī-) s. dirección *f*; *(order)* orden *f* ♦ pl. instrucciones.

di·rec·tive (:tĭv) s. directiva.

di·rect·ly (dĭ-rěkt'lē, dī-) adv. directamente; *(immediately)* inmediatamente.

di·rec·tor (dĭ-rěk'tər, dī-) s. director *m.*

di·rec·tor·ship (:shĭp') s. dirección *f.*

di·rec·tor·ate (:ĭt) s. directorio.

di·rec·to·ry (dĭ-rěk'tə-rē) s. guía telefónica ♦ **d. assistance** información telefónica.

dirge (dûrj) s. endecha, canto fúnebre.

dirt (dûrt) s. tierra; *(grime)* mugre *f*; *(filth)* suciedad; *(gossip)* chisme *m*; *(smut)* porquería ♦ **to treat like d.** tratar como un trapo.

dirt-cheap ('chēp') adj. & adv. FAM. baratísimo, tirado.

dirt·y (dûr'tē) I. adj. **-i-** sucio; *(joke)* verde; *(language)* grosero; *(weather)* malo ♦ **d. language** groserías • **d. trick** mala jugada • **d. word** taco • **d. work** trabajo pesado o desagradable • **to give a d. look** mirar con mala cara II. tr. & intr. ensuciar(se), manchar(se).

dis·a·bil·i·ty (dĭs'ə-bĭl'ĭ-tē) s. incapacidad *f*; *(handicap)* invalidez *f*, inhabilidad *f.*

dis·a·ble (dĭs-ā'bəl) tr. incapacitar; *(to cripple)* lisiar.

dis·a·bled (:bəld) adj. incapacitado; *(crippled)* lisiado, inválido; *(vehicle)* averiado.

dis·a·buse (dĭs'ə-byōōz') tr. desengañar.

dis·ad·van·tage (dĭs'əd-văn'tĭj) s. desventaja, inconveniente *m* ♦ **to be, put at a d.** estar, poner en situación desventajosa • **to the d. of** en detrimento de.

dis·ad·van·taged (:tĭjd) adj. desvalido.

dis·ad·van·ta·geous (dĭs-ăd'vən-tā'jəs) adj. desventajoso, desfavorable.

dis·af·fect (dĭs'ə-fěkt') tr. indisponer.

dis·af·fect·ed (:fěk'tĭd) adj. desafecto.

dis·af·fec·tion (:shən) s. desafección *f.*

dis·a·gree (dĭs'ə-grē') intr. no estar de acuerdo, estar en desacuerdo; *(food)* sentar mal; *(to quarrel)* reñir.

dis·a·gree·a·ble (:ə-bəl) adj. desagradable.

dis·a·gree·ment (:mənt) s. desacuerdo; *(quarrel)* riña.

dis·al·low (dĭs'ə-lou') tr. prohibir; DEP. anular.

dis·ap·pear (dĭs'ə-pîr') intr. desaparecer.

dis·ap·pear·ance (:əns) s. desaparición f.

dis·ap·point (dĭs'ə-point') tr. decepcionar, desilusionar; *(to fail to please)* defraudar.

dis·ap·point·ed (:point'tĭd) adj. decepcionado; *(a lover)* desengañado.

dis·ap·point·ing (:tĭng) adj. decepcionante.

dis·ap·point·ment (dĭs'ə-point'mənt) s. desilusión f, decepción f; *(in love)* desengaño.

dis·ap·prov·al (dĭs'ə-prōō'vəl) s. desaprobación f.

dis·ap·prove (dĭs'ə-prōōv') tr. desaprobar —intr. ♦ to d. of no gustarle a uno.

dis·arm (dĭs-ärm') I. tr. & intr. desarmar(se).

dis·arm·a·ment (:är'mə-mənt) s. desarme m.

dis·arm·ing (dĭs-är'mĭng) adj. cautivante.

dis·ar·range (dĭs'ə-rānj') tr. desarreglar.

dis·ar·ray (dĭs'ə-rā') I. s. desarreglo, desorden m; *(clothing)* desaliño II. tr. desarreglar.

dis·as·sem·ble (dĭs'ə-sĕm'bəl) tr. desmontar.

dis·as·so·ci·ate (dĭs'ə-sō'shē-āt') tr. disociar.

dis·as·ter (dĭ-zăs'tər) s. desastre m.

dis·as·trous (:trəs) adj. desastroso.

dis·a·vow (dĭs'ə-vou') tr. desconocer.

dis·a·vow·al (:əl) s. negación f, repudio.

dis·band (dĭs-bănd') tr. & intr. dispersar(se).

dis·bar (dĭsk) s. disco ♦ d. jockey animador.

dis·bar·ment (:mənt) s. exclusión f del foro.

dis·be·lief (dĭs'bĭ-lēf') s. incredulidad f.

dis·be·lieve (:lēv') tr. no creer —intr. ser incrédulo.

dis·burse (dĭs-bûrs') tr. desembolsar.

dis·burse·ment (:mənt) s. desembolso.

disc (dĭsk) s. disco ♦ d. jockey animador.

dis·card I. tr. (dĭs-kärd') descartar; *(clothing, books)* desechar —intr. descartarse II. s. ('') descarte m.

dis·cern (dĭ-sûrn') tr. discernir; *(to perceive)* percibir —intr. hacer distinciones.

dis·cern·ing (dĭ-sûr'nĭng) adj. perspicaz.

dis·cern·ment (dĭ-sûrn'mənt) s. discernimiento.

dis·charge I. tr. (dĭs-chärj') descargar; *(soldiers)* licenciar; *(patients)* dar de alta; *(employees)* despedir; *(pus)* arrojar; *(duty)* desempeñar, ejecutar; *(promise)* cumplir (con); *(debt)* saldar; *(prisoner)* librar —intr. *(river, pipe)* descargar; ELEC. descargarse II. s. ('') descarga; *(emission)* escape m; *(secretion)* secreción f; *(flow)* flujo; *(of duty)* desempeño; *(from hospital)* alta; *(of soldiers)* licenciamiento.

dis·ci·ple (dĭ-sī'pəl) s. discípulo.

dis·ci·pli·nar·y (dĭs'ə-plə-nĕr'ē) adj. disciplinario.

dis·ci·pline (dĭs'ə-plĭn) I. s. disciplina; *(punishment)* castigo II. tr. disciplinar; *(to punish)* castigar.

dis·claim (dĭs-klām') tr. desconocer, denegar.

dis·claim·er (dĭs-klā'mər) s. denegación f, repudio.

dis·close (dĭ-sklōz') tr. divulgar, revelar.

dis·clo·sure (dĭ-sklō'zhər) s. divulgación f.

dis·co (dĭs'kō') s. *(baile m de)* discoteca.

dis·col·or (dĭs-kŭl'ər) tr. descolorar, desteñir.

dis·com·bob·u·late (dĭs'kəm-bŏb'yə-lāt') tr. FAM. confundir, trastornar.

dis·com·fit (dĭs-kŭm'fĭt) tr. *(to thwart)* frustrar;

(to disconcert) desconcertar.

dis·com·fi·ture (:fĭ-chŏŏr') s. frustración f.

dis·com·fort (dĭs-kŭm'fərt) I. s. molestia, malestar m II. tr. molestar.

dis·com·pose (dĭs'kəm-pōz') tr. perturbar.

dis·com·po·sure (:pō'zhər) s. agitación f.

dis·con·cert (dĭs'kən-sûrt') tr. desconcertar.

dis·con·nect (dĭs'kə-nĕkt') tr. separar; ELEC., TEL. desconectar.

dis·con·nect·ed (:nĕk'tĭd) adj. desconectado; *(unrelated)* sin relación; *(illogical)* inconexo.

dis·con·so·late (dĭs-kŏn'sə-lĭt) adj. desconsolado.

dis·con·tent (dĭs'kən-tĕnt') adj. & s. descontento.

dis·con·tent·ed (:tĕn'tĭd) adj. descontento.

dis·con·tin·ue (dĭs'kən-tĭn'yōō) tr. discontinuar, suspender.

dis·con·tin·u·ous (:əs) adj. discontinuo.

dis·cord (dĭs'kôrd') s. discordia; MÚS. disonancia.

dis·cor·dant (dĭs-kôr'dnt) adj. discorde.

dis·co·theque/thèque (dĭs'kə-tĕk') s. discoteca.

dis·count (dĭs'kount') I. tr. descontar II. s. descuento, rebaja ♦ d. rate tasa de descuento • d. store tienda de rebajas.

dis·cour·age (dĭ-skûr'ĭj) tr. desanimar, desalentar; *(to hinder)* no fomentar, impedir ♦ to d. from disuadir o reconvenir que no.

dis·cour·age·ment (:ĭj-mənt) s. desaliento, desánimo.

dis·cour·ag·ing (:ə-jĭng) adj. desalentador.

dis·course I. s. (dĭs'kôrs') discurso; *(conversation)* plática II. intr. (dĭ-skôrs') conversar ♦ to d. on disertar sobre.

dis·cour·te·ous (dĭs-kûr'tē-əs) adj. descortés.

dis·cov·er (dĭ-skŭv'ər) tr. descubrir; *(to realize)* darse cuenta de.

dis·cov·er·er (:ər) s. descubridor m.

dis·cov·er·y (dĭ-skŭv'ə-rē) s. descubrimiento.

dis·cred·it (dĭs-krĕd'ĭt) I. tr. *(to disbelieve)* no dar crédito a; *(to disparage)* desprestigiar, desacreditar II. s. deprestigio, descrédito ♦ to be a d. to deshonrar a • to be to the d. of ir en descrédito de.

dis·creet (dĭ-skrēt') adj. discreto.

dis·crep·an·cy (dĭ-skrĕp'ən-sē) s. discrepancia.

dis·crete (dĭ-skrēt') adj. separado, inconexo.

dis·cre·tion (dĭ-skrĕsh'ən) s. discreción f ♦ at the d. of a juicio de, según el deseo de.

dis·cre·tion·ar·y (:ə-nĕr'ē) adj. discrecional.

dis·crim·i·nate (dĭ-skrĭm'ə-nāt') intr. & tr. discriminar *(against en contra de; from de)*.

dis·crim·i·nat·ing (:nā'tĭng) adj. discerniente.

dis·crim·i·na·tion (-'-nā'shən) s. *(prejudice)* discriminación f; *(perception)* discernimiento; *(distinction)* distinción f.

dis·crim·i·na·to·ry (-'-nə-tôr'ē) adj. *(biased)* discriminatorio; *(selective)* exigente.

dis·cur·sive (dĭ-skûr'sĭv) adj. digresivo.

dis·cus (dĭs'kəs) s. disco.

dis·cuss (dĭ-skŭs') tr. *(to talk over)* hablar de o sobre; *(formally)* discutir, tratar.

dis·cus·sion (dĭ-skŭsh'ən) s. *(conversation)* discusión f; *(discourse)* disertación f ♦ to be under d. estar en discusión.

dis·dain (dĭs-dān') I. tr. desdeñar, menospreciar ♦ to d. to no dignarse a II. s. desdén m, menosprecio.

dis·dain·ful (:fəl) adj. desdeñoso.

dis·ease (dĭ-zēz') s. enfermedad f.

dis·eased (dĭ-zēzd′) adj. enfermo.

dis·em·bark (dĭs′ĕm-bärk′) tr. & intr. desembarcar.

dis·em·bod·ied (dĭs′ĕm-bŏd′ēd) adj. incorpóreo.

dis·em·bod·y (:ē) tr. separar del cuerpo.

dis·em·bow·el (dĭs′ĕm-bou′əl) tr. desentrañar.

dis·en·chant (dĭs′ĕn-chănt′) tr. desencantar.

dis·en·chant·ment (:mənt) s. desencanto.

dis·en·cum·ber (dĭs′ĕn-kŭm′bər) tr. librar.

dis·en·fran·chise (dĭs′ĕn-frăn′chīz′) tr. privar de derechos civiles.

dis·en·gage (dĭs′ĕn-gāj′) tr. & intr. *(to uncouple)* desenganchar(se); *(gears)* desengranar(se); MIL. retirar(se); AUTO. desembragar(se).

dis·en·gaged (:gājd′) adj. *(free)* desembarazado, libre; AUTO. desembragado.

dis·en·tan·gle (dĭs′ĕn-tăng′gəl) tr. & intr. desenredar(se), desenmarañar(se).

dis·e·qui·lib·ri·um (dĭs-ē′kwə-lĭb′rē-əm) s. desequilibrio.

dis·fa·vor (dĭs-fā′vər) I. s. desaprobación f ♦ to fall into d. caer en desgracia II. tr. desfavorecer, desaprobar.

dis·fig·ure (dĭs-fĭg′yər) tr. desfigurar, afear.

dis·fran·chise (dĭs-frăn′chīz′) tr. privar de derechos civiles.

dis·gorge (dĭs-gôrj′) tr. vomitar.

dis·grace (dĭs-grās′) I. s. deshonra; *(ignominy)* ignominia II. tr. deshonrar.

dis·grace·ful (:fəl) adj. vergonzoso.

dis·grun·tled (dĭs-grŭn′tld) adj. disgustado.

dis·guise (dĭs-gīz′) I. s. disfraz m II. tr. disfrazar.

dis·gust (dĭs-gŭst′) tr. repugnar, asquear II. s. repugnancia.

dis·gust·ed (:gŭs′tĭd) adj. asqueado, repugnado.

dis·gust·ing (:tĭng) adj. repugnante, asqueroso.

dish (dĭsh) I. s. plato; RAD., TELEV. disco (de antena) II. tr. ♦ to d. out *(food)* servir; *(advice, abuse)* repartir, dar.

dis·har·mo·ny (dĭs-här′mə-nē) s. discordia.

dis·heart·en (dĭs-här′tn) tr. desanimar, desalentar.

di·shev·el(l)ed (dĭ-shĕv′əld) adj. desaliñado.

dis·hon·est (dĭs-ŏn′ĭst) adj. deshonesto, deshonrado; *(dealings)* fraudulento.

dis·hon·es·ty (:ĭ-stē) s. falta de honradez; *(fraud)* fraude m.

dis·hon·or (:ər) I. s. deshonra; *(shame)* vergüenza II. tr. deshonrar; COM. rechazar.

dis·hon·or·a·ble (:ə-bəl) adj. deshonroso.

dish·rag (dĭsh′răg′) s. trapo de fregar.

dish·wash·er (:wŏsh′ər) s. lavaplatos m.

dis·il·lu·sion (dĭs′ĭ-lo͞o′zhən) I. s. desilusionar II. s. desilusión f.

dis·il·lu·sion·ment (:mənt) s. desilusión f.

dis·in·cen·tive (dĭs′ĭn-sĕn′tĭv) s. falta de incentivo.

dis·in·clined (dĭs′ĭn-klīnd′) adj. maldispuesto.

dis·in·fect (dĭs′ĭn-fĕkt′) tr. desinfectar.

dis·in·fec·tant (:fĕk′tənt) s. & adj. desinfectante m.

dis·in·for·ma·tion (dĭs-ĭn′fər-mā′shən) s. información incorrecta (para despistar).

dis·in·gen·u·ous (dĭs′ĭn-jĕn′yo͞o-əs) adj. insincero, falso.

dis·in·her·it (dĭs′ĭn-hĕr′ĭt) tr. desheredar.

dis·in·te·grate (dĭs-ĭn′tĭ-grāt′) tr. & intr. desintegrar(se).

dis·in·ter (dĭs′ĭn-tûr′) tr. -**rr**- desenterrar.

dis·in·ter·est (dĭs-ĭn′tər-ĭst) s. desinterés m.

dis·in·ter·est·ed (:trĭ-stĭd) adj. *(impartial)* desinteresado; *(indifferent)* indiferente.

dis·in·vest·ment (dĭs′ĭn-vĕst′mənt) s. disminución f del capital invertido.

dis·join (dĭs-join′) tr. desunir, separar.

dis·joint·ed (dĭs-join′tĭd) adj. desarticulado; *(incoherent)* incoherente, inconexo.

dis·junc·tion (dĭs-jŭngk′shən) s. disyunción f.

disk (dĭsk) s. disco ♦ **d. jockey** animador.

disk·ette (dĭ-skĕt′) s. disco.

dis·lik(e)·a·ble (dĭs-lī′kə-bəl) adj. antipático.

dis·like (dĭs-līk′) I. tr. tener aversión a, no gustarle a uno II. s. antipatía, aversión f.

dis·lo·cate (dĭs′lō-kāt′) tr. dislocar; FIG. trastornar, desarreglar.

dis·lo·ca·tion (′-kā′shən) s. dislocación f.

dis·lodge (dĭs-lŏj′) tr. desalojar, echar fuera.

dis·loy·al (dĭs-loi′əl) adj. desleal.

dis·loy·al·ty (:tē) s. deslealtad f.

dis·mal (dĭz′məl) adj. triste, deprimente.

dis·man·tle (dĭs-măn′tl) tr. *(to tear down)* desmantelar; *(to disassemble)* desarmar.

dis·may (dĭs-mā′) I. tr. *(to upset)* consternar; *(to dishearten)* desalentar II. s. consternación f, desaliento.

dis·mem·ber (dĭs-mĕm′bər) tr. desmembrar.

dis·miss (dĭs-mĭs′) tr. dar permiso para salir; *(employee)* despedir; *(officials)* destituir; *(doubt)* alejar; *(claim)* desestimar.

dis·miss·al (:əl) s. *(employee)* despido; *(official)* destitución f; *(idea)* abandono; DER. desestimación f.

dis·mount (dĭs-mount′) tr. & intr. desmontar(se).

dis·o·be·di·ent (dĭs′ə-bē′dē-ənt) adj. desobediente.

dis·o·bey (dĭs′ə-bā′) tr. & intr. desobedecer.

dis·or·der (dĭs-ôr′dər) I. s. desorden m; MED. trastorno II. tr. desordenar; MED. trastornar.

dis·or·der·ly (:lē) adj. desordenado; *(unruly)* alborotador ♦ **d. conduct** conducta escandalosa.

dis·or·gan·ize (dĭs-ôr′gə-nīz′) tr. desorganizar.

dis·o·ri·ent (dĭs-ôr′ē-ĕnt′) tr. desorientar.

dis·own (dĭs-ōn′) tr. repudiar.

dis·par·age (dĭ-spăr′ĭj) tr. menospreciar.

dis·par·ag·ing (:ĭ-jĭng) adj. menospreciativo.

dis·pa·rate (dĭs′pər-ĭt) adj. dispar, desigual.

dis·par·i·ty (dĭ-spăr′ĭ-tē) s. disparidad f.

dis·pas·sion·ate (dĭs-păsh′ə-nĭt) adj. desapasionado; *(unbiased)* imparcial.

dis·patch (dĭ-spăch′) I. tr. despachar II. s. despacho; *(speed)* diligencia.

dis·pel (dĭ-spĕl′) tr. -**ll**- disipar.

dis·pen·sa·ble (dĭ-spĕn′sə-bəl) adj. prescindible.

dis·pen·sa·ry (dĭ-spĕn′sə-rē) s. dispensario.

dis·pen·sa·tion (dĭs′pən-sā′shən) s. reparto, distribución f; *(exemption)* dispensa.

dis·pense (dĭ-spĕns′) tr. dispensar.

dis·per·sal (dĭ-spûr′səl) s. dispersión f.

dis·perse (dĭ-spûrs′) tr. & intr. dispersar(se).

dis·pir·it·ed (dĭ-spĭr′ĭ-tĭd) adj. desalentado.

dis·place (dĭs-plās′) tr. desplazar; *(to supplant)* substituir, suplantar ♦ **displaced person** persona expatriada.

dis·place·ment (:mənt) s. desplazamiento; *(substitution)* reemplazo, sustitución f.

dis·play (dĭ-splā′) I. tr. exhibir, mostrar; *(to show off)* ostentar; *(to unfurl)* desplegar II. s.

exhibición *f; (show)* despliegue *m; (ostentation)* ostentación *f;* COMPUT. representación *f* visual.

dis·please (dĭs-plēz') tr. & intr. desagradar.

dis·pleas·ing (:plē'zĭng) adj. desagradable.

dis·pleas·ure (:plĕzh'ər) s. desagrado.

dis·pos·a·ble (dĭ-spō'zə-bəl) adj. *(available)* disponible; *(discardable)* desechable.

dis·pos·al (:zəl) s. disposición *f; (of waste)* eliminación *f; (sale)* venta ♦ **at your d.** a su disposición.

dis·pose (dĭ-spōz') tr. disponer; *(to incline)* volver propenso a ♦ **to d. of** *(property, business)* despachar; *(waste)* eliminar, desechar.

dis·posed (dĭ-spōzd') adj. dispuesto.

dis·po·si·tion (dĭs'pə-zĭsh'ən) s. disposición *f; (tendency)* predisposición *f.*

dis·pos·sess (dĭs'pə-zĕs') tr. desposeer.

dis·proof (dĭs-prōōf') s. refutación *f.*

dis·pro·por·tion·ate (dĭs'prə-pôr'shə-nĭt) adj. desproporcionado.

dis·prove (dĭs-prōōv') tr. refutar.

dis·pu·tant (dĭs'pyə-tənt) s. disputador *m.*

dis·pute (dĭ-spyōōt') I. tr. disputar; *(to doubt)* cuestionar; *(in court)* litigar, contender —intr. disputar, discutir; *(to quarrel)* pelear II. s. *(debate)* disputa; *(conflict)* conflicto;- *(quarrel)* pelea.

dis·qual·i·fi·ca·tion (dĭs-kwŏl'ə-fĭ-kā'shən) s. descalificación *f; (unfitness)* incapacidad *f.*

dis·qual·i·fy (dĭs-kwŏl'ə-fī') tr. descalificar; *(to render unfit)* incapacitar.

dis·qui·et (dĭs-kwī'ĭt) I. tr. inquietar II. s. inquietud *f.*

dis·re·gard (dĭs'rĭ-gärd') I. tr. no hacer caso de, desatender II. s. desatención *f,* negligencia.

dis·re·pair (dĭs'rĭ-pâr') s. mal estado, falta de arreglo ♦ **to fall into d.** *(machinery)* descomponerse; *(a house)* caer en ruina.

dis·rep·u·ta·ble (dĭs-rĕp'yə-tə-bəl) adj. de mala fama, desacreditado.

dis·re·pute (dĭs'rĭ-pyōōt') s. mala fama, descrédito ♦ **to bring (fall) into d.** desprestigiar(se).

dis·re·spect (dĭs'rĭ-spĕkt') I. s. falta de respeto, descortesía II. tr. faltar al respeto.

dis·re·spect·ful (:fəl) adj. irrespetuoso.

dis·robe (dĭs-rōb') tr. & intr. desvestir(se).

dis·rupt (dĭs-rŭpt') tr. *(to upset)* perturbar; *(to interrupt)* interrumpir; *(to rupture)* romper.

dis·rup·tion (dĭs-rŭp'shən) s. *(upset)* perturbación *f; (interruption)* interrupción *f; (rupture)* rompimiento.

dis·rup·tive (:tĭv) adj. *(upsetting)* perturbador; *(interfering)* interruptor, obstructor.

dis·sat·is·fac·tion (dĭs-săt'ĭs-făk'shən) s. insatisfacción *f,* descontento.

dis·sat·is·fy (dĭs-săt'ĭs-fī') tr. no contentar.

dis·sect (dĭ-sĕkt', dī-) tr. disecar.

dis·sec·tion (dĭ-sĕk'shən, dī-) s. disección *f.*

dis·sem·ble (dĭ-sĕm'bəl) tr. & intr. disimular.

dis·sem·i·nate (dĭ-sĕm'ə-nāt') tr. & intr. diseminar(se).

dis·sen·sion (dĭ-sĕn'shən) s. disensión *f.*

dis·sent (dĭ-sĕnt') I. intr. disentir II. s. disención *f;* RELIG. disidencia.

dis·sent·er (dĭ-sĕn'tər) s. disidente *mf.*

dis·ser·ta·tion (dĭs'ər-tā'shən) s. *(discourse)* disertación *f; (thesis)* tesis *f.*

dis·ser·vice (dĭs-sûr'vĭs) s. perjuicio, daño.

dis·si·dent (dĭs'ĭ-dnt) adj. & s. disidente *mf.*

dis·sim·i·lar (dĭ-sĭm'ə-lər) adj. disímil.

dis·sim·u·late (:yə-lāt') tr. & intr. disimular.

dis·si·pate (dĭs'ə-pāt') tr. & intr. disipar(se).

dis·si·pat·ed (:pā'tĭd) adj. disipado.

dis·so·ci·ate (dĭ-sō'shē-āt') tr. disociar ♦ **to d. oneself from** disociarse de.

dis·so·lute (dĭs'ə-lōōt') adj. disoluto, disipado.

dis·so·lu·tion ('-lōō'shən) s. disolución *f.*

dis·solve (dĭ-zŏlv') tr. & intr. disolver(se) ♦ **to d. in tears** deshacerse en lágrimas.

dis·so·nant (dĭs'ə-nənt) adj. disonante.

dis·suade (dĭ-swād') tr. disuadir.

dis·taff (dĭs'tăf') s. *(staff)* rueca; *(women)* las mujeres ♦ **d. side** línea femenina.

dis·tance (dĭs'təns) I. s. distancia; *(range)* alcance *m; (stretch)* trecho, tirada; *(coolness)* frialdad *f,* reserva ♦ **a good d. away** bastante lejos • **at** o **from a d.** a (la) distancia • **in the d.** a lo lejos • **to keep one's d.** guardar las distancias • **within walking d.** suficientemente cerca como para ir andando II. tr. alejar, distanciar.

dis·tant (dĭs'tənt) adj. distante, alejado; *(in relationship)* lejano; *(aloof)* reservado, frío.

dis·taste (dĭs-tāst') s. aversión *f.*

dis·taste·ful (:fəl) adj. desagradable.

dis·tem·per (dĭs-tĕm'pər) s. moquillo.

dis·tend (dĭ-stĕnd') tr. & intr. *(to expand)* distender(se); *(to swell)* hinchar(se).

dis·ten·tion/sion (dĭ-stĕn'shən) s. *(expansion)* distensión *f; (swelling)* hinchazón *f.*

dis·till (dĭ-stĭl') tr. & intr. destilar.

dis·til·late (dĭs'tə-lāt') s. destilado.

dis·till·er·y (dĭ-stĭl'ə-rē) s. destilería.

dis·tinct (dĭ-stĭngkt') adj. distinto; *(clear)* claro; *(unquestionable)* marcado, indudable.

dis·tinc·tion (dĭ-stĭngk'shən) s. distinción *f* ♦ **to gain d.** distinguirse • **with d.** con mérito.

dis·tinc·tive (:tĭv) adj. distintivo.

dis·tin·guish (dĭ-stĭng'gwĭsh) tr. & intr. distinguir ♦ **to d. oneself** distinguirse, descollar.

dis·tin·guish·a·ble (:gwĭ-shə-bəl) adj. distinguible.

dis·tin·guished (:gwĭsht) adj. distinguido.

dis·tort (dĭ-stôrt') tr. *(to contort)* distorsionar; *(to misrepresent)* tergiversar, alterar.

dis·tor·tion (dĭ-stôr'shən) s. distorsión *f; (misrepresentation)* tergiversación *f,* alteración *f.*

dis·tract (dĭ-străkt') tr. distraer; *(to bewilder)* aturdir, turbar.

dis·trac·tion (dĭ-străk'shən) s. distracción *f; (frenzy)* frenesí *m.*

dis·traught (dĭ-strôt') adj. *(worried)* aturdido, turbado; *(crazed)* desequilibrado.

dis·tress (dĭ-strĕs') I. s. *(suffering)* aflicción *f,* pena; *(anxiety)* ansiedad *f; (need)* apuro; *(danger)* peligro II. tr. afligir.

dis·tressed (dĭ-strĕst') adj. afligido, angustiado; *(in danger)* en peligro; *(poor)* en apuros.

dis·trib·ute (dĭ-strĭb'yōōt) tr. distribuir.

dis·tri·bu·tion (dĭs'trə-byōō'shən) s. distribución *f,* reparto.

dis·trib·u·tor (dĭ-strĭb'yə-tər) s. distribuidor *m.*

dis·trict (dĭs'trĭkt) s. región *f,* comarca; *(of a city)* zona, barrio; POL. distrito, partido ♦ **d. attorney** fiscal • **d. court** tribunal federal.

dis·trust (dĭs-trŭst') I. s. desconfianza, recelo II. tr. desconfiar de, sospechar.

dis·trust·ful (:fəl) adj. desconfiado.

dis·turb (dĭ-stûrb') tr. *(to alter)* perturbar; *(to upset)* turbar, trastornar; *(to interrupt)* interrumpir; *(to bother)* molestar; *(to disarrange)* desordenar; PSIC. desequilibrar ♦ **do not d.** no molestar.

dis·tur·bance (dĭ-stûr'bəns) s. perturbación *f; (worry)* trastorno; *(interruption)* interrupción *f; (bother)* molestia; *(disorder)* desorden *m; (riot)* disturbio; PSIC. desequilibrio.

dis·u·ni·ty (dĭs-yōō′nĭ-tē) s. desunión *f.*

dis·use (dĭs-yōōs′) s. desuso.

ditch (dĭch) **I.** s. *(trench)* zanja; *(irrigation)* acequia; *(drainage)* canal *m; (of a road)* cuneta **II.** tr. cavar zanjas en; FAM. *(to discard)* abandonar.

dith·er (dĭth′ər) s. nerviosismo, agitación *f.*

dit·to (dĭt′ō) **I.** s. idem *m; (copy)* copia, duplicado **II.** adv. idem **III.** tr. sacar un duplicado de.

dit·ty (dĭt′ē) s. cancioncita.

di·van (dĭ-văn′) s. diván *m.*

dive (dīv) **I.** intr. **-d** *o* **dove, -d** *(headfirst)* zambullirse *(de cabeza)*; DEP. saltar; *(submarine)* sumergirse; *(scuba)* bucear; *(airplane)* bajar en picado; *(to plummet)* caer a plomo; FIG. lanzarse, meterse de lleno **II.** s. *(headfirst)* zambullida; DEP. salto; *(plane)* picado; *(submarine)* sumersión *f; (drop)* caída, baja; JER. *(bar)* garito.

dive-bomb (′bŏm′) tr. bombardear en picada.

div·er (dī′vər) s. DEP. saltador *m* (de trampolín); *(underwater)* buzo, buceador *m.*

di·verge (dĭ-vûrj′, dī-) intr. divergir.

di·ver·gent (dĭ-vûr′jənt, dī-) adj. divergente.

di·vers (dī′vərz) adj. diversos, varios.

di·verse (dĭ-vûrs′, dī-) adj. diverso; *(varied)* variado.

di·ver·si·fy (dĭ-vûr′sə-fī′, dī-) tr. & intr. diversificar(se).

di·ver·sion (dĭ-vûr′zhən, dī-) s. diversión *f; (detour)* desviación *f.*

di·ver·si·ty (:sĭ-tē) s. diversidad *f,* variedad *f.*

di·vert (dĭ-vûrt′, dī-) tr. divertir; *(to turn aside)* desviar.

di·vest (dĭ-vĕst′, dī-) tr. despojar, desposeer.

di·ves·ti·ture (dĭ-vĕs′tĭ-chər) s. despojo, desposeimiento.

di·vide (dĭ-vīd′) **I.** tr. & intr. dividir(se) ♦ **to d. up** *(to apportion)* repartir; *(to separate)* dividir(se) **II.** s. divisoria.

di·vid·ed (dĭ-vī′dĭd) adj. dividido; BOT. seccionado ♦ **d. highway** carretera con barrera divisoria.

div·i·dend (dĭv′ĭ-dĕnd′) s. dividendo.

di·vid·er (dĭ-vī′dər) s. divisor *m; (partition)* separación *f* ♦ pl. compás de punta seca.

div·i·na·tion (dĭv′ə-nā′shən) s. adivinación *f.*

di·vine¹ (dĭ-vīn′) **I.** adj. **-er, -est** divino **II.** s. clérigo.

di·vine² tr. & intr. adivinar.

div·ing (dī′vĭng) s. DEP. salto; *(scuba)* buceo ♦ **d. board** trampolín • **d. suit** escafandra.

di·vin·i·ty (dĭ-vĭn′ĭ-tē) s. divinidad *f; (theology)* teología ♦ **D.** Dios.

di·vi·sion (dĭ-vĭzh′ən) s. división *f; (section)* sección *f,* departamento.

di·vi·sive (dĭ-vī′sĭv) adj. divisivo.

di·vi·sor (dĭ-vī′zər) s. divisor *m.*

di·vorce (dĭ-vôrs′) **I.** s. divorcio **II.** tr. *(things, couple)* divorciar; *(a spouse)* divorciarse de.

di·vor·cé (dĭ-vor·sā′, :sā′) s. divorciado ♦ **divorcée** divorciada.

di·vulge (dĭ-vŭlj′) tr. divulgar.

diz·zi·ness (dĭz′ē-nĭs) s. vertigo, mareo.

diz·zy (dĭz′ē) **I.** adj. **-i-** *(giddy)* mareado; *(bewildered)* aturdido; *(speed, height)* vertiginoso; FAM. *(foolish)* bobo **II.** tr. marear, dar vértigo.

do (dōō) **I.** tr. **did, done** hacer; *(one's duty)* cumplir con; *(to wash)* limpiar; *(dishes)* fregar;

(one's hair, nails) arreglarse; *(justice, homage)* rendir, tributar; *(to work as)* dedicarse a; *(to prepare)* preparar; *(to cook)* cocinar; *(to work on)* trabajar en; *(to tour)* recorrer; *(to decorate)* decorar; JER. *(drugs)* tomar, usar ♦ **to do again** volver a hacer, hacer de nuevo • **to do away with** *(to eliminate)* eliminar; *(to abolish)* abolir; FAM. *(to kill)* matar • **to do for** servir de, hacer el papel de • **to do in** JER. *(to kill)* liquidar; *(to ruin)* arruinar; *(to exhaust)* agotar, cansar • **to do over** *(to do again)* volver a hacer; FAM. *(to redecorate)* redecorar • **to do up** *(laces)* atarse; *(buttons)* abrocharse; FAM. *(to do with style)* hacer con estilo • **to do with** *(to get along on)* conformarse con; *(to find desirable)* venirle a uno (muy) bien • **what can I do for you?** ¿en qué puedo servirle? —intr. *(to behave)* conducirse, comportarse; *(to perform)* obrar, actuar; *(to get along)* andar, irle a uno; *(to feel)* encontrarse, sentirse; *(to serve the purpose)* servir ♦ **how do you do?** ¿cómo está usted? • **nothing doing!** JER. ¡nada de eso!, ¡ni hablar! • **that will do!** ¡basta ya! • **that will never do** *o* **that won't do** *(it is improper)* eso no se hace; *(it is unsuitable)* eso no conviene • **to be doing badly** irle mal • **to do or die** vencer o morir —aux. *(interrogative)* <*do you think it's funny?* ¿crees que eso es gracioso?>; *(negative)* <*I don't know no* sé>; *(emphatic)* <*do behave* pórtate bien>; *(substitute)* <*do you understand me? Yes, I do* ¿me entiendes? sí> **II.** s. [pl. **s** *o* **-s**] *(party)* fiesta; *(hairdo)* peinado ♦ **the do's and don'ts** lo que se debe y lo que no se debe hacer.

doc·ile (dŏs′əl, :īl′) adj. dócil.

dock¹ (dŏk) **I.** s. *(wharf)* muelle *m,* embarcadero; *(for trucks, trains)* andén *m* **II.** tr. & intr. *(ship)* (hacer) atracar al muelle; *(spacecraft)* acoplar(se).

dock² tr. VET. cercenar (la cola); *(to deduct)* descontar (de un salario).

dock³ s. *(in court)* banquillo del acusado.

dock·et (dŏk′ĭt) s. *(agenda)* agenda *f;* DER. sumario de causas.

dock·hand (dŏk′hănd′) s. estibador *m.*

dock·work·er (:wûr′kər) s. estibador *m.*

dock·yard (:yärd′) s. astillero.

doc·tor (dŏk′tər) **I.** s. médico, doctor *m;* EDUC. doctor **II.** tr. *(to treat)* tratar, atender; *(to repair)* remendar; *(to falsify)* adulterar.

doc·tor·ate (:ĭt) s. doctorado.

doc·tri·naire (dŏk′trə-nâr′) s. & adj. doctrinario.

doc·trine (dŏk′trĭn) s. doctrina.

doc·u·ment (dŏk′yə-mənt) **I.** s. documento **II.** tr. documentar, probar con documentos.

doc·u·men·ta·ry (′-mĕn′tə-rē) adj. & s. documental *m.*

dod·der·ing (dŏd′ər-ĭng) adj. senil.

dodge (dŏj) **I.** tr. esquivar; *(by cunning)* evadir, eludir —intr. echarse a un lado **II.** s. regate *m.*

doe (dō) s. [pl. inv. *o* **s**] gama.

does (dŭz) tercera persona sg. de **do.**

doe·skin (dō′skĭn′) s. piel *f* de gamo, ante *m.*

doff (dŏf) tr. quitarse.

dog (dôg) **I.** s. perro; *(scoundrel)* canalla *mf;* FAM. *(fellow)* tipo; *(fiasco)* bomba, desastre *m* ♦ **d. days** canícula ♦ pl. JER. pies *m,* patas **II.** tr. **-gg-** perseguir, seguir.

dog·catch·er (′kăch′ər) s. lacero.

doge (dōj) s. dux *m.*

dog-eat-dog (dôg′ĕt-dôg′) adj. atrozmente

competitivo.

dog·fight ('fīt') s. combate aéreo reñido.

dog·ged (dò'gĭd) adj. terco, obstinado.

dog·ger·el (dò'gər-əl) s. coplas de ciego.

dog·gone (dòg'gôn') s. FAM. maldito.

dog·gy/ie (dò'gē) s. FAM. perrito.

dog·house (dòg'hous') s. caseta de perro ♦ **in the d.** JER. en desgracia.

do·gie (dò'gē) s. becerro sin madre.

dog·ma (dòg'mə) s. dogma m.

dog·mat·ic (-măt'ĭk) adj. dogmático.

dog·ma·tist ('mə-tĭst) s. dogmatizador m.

do-good·er (dōō'gŏŏd'ər) s. FAM. bienhechor m.

dog·trot (dòg'trŏt') s. trote m suave, trote lento.

dog·wood ('wŏŏd') s. cornejo, sanguiñuelo.

doi·ly (doi'lē) s. tapete m.

do·ing (dōō'ĭng) s. (act) hecho, obra; (effort) esfuerzo m ♦ pl. fiestas, actividades.

do-it-your·self (dōō'ĭt-yər-sĕlf') adj. FAM. diseñado para ser hecho por uno mismo.

dol·drums (dōl'drəmz') s.pl. (inactivity) estancamiento; (listlessness) decaimiento; MARÍT. calmas ecuatoriales.

dole (dōl) I. s. limosna; G.B. (welfare) subsidio de paro ♦ **to be on the d.** estar acogido al paro II. tr. dar limosna ♦ **to d. out** repartir, distribuir.

dole·ful (dōl'fəl) adj. triste.

doll (dŏl) I. s. muñeca II. intr. & tr. ♦ **to d.** (oneself) **up** JER. emperifollar(se).

dol·lar (dŏl'ər) s. dólar m ♦ **to bet one's bottom d.** JER. apostarse la cabeza.

dol·ly (dŏl'ē) I. s. (toy) muñeca; (platform) carretilla; CINEM. travelín m, plataforma rodante II. intr. ♦ **to d. in** acercarse la cámara.

dol·phin (dŏl'fĭn) s. ZOOL. delfín m; ICT. dorado.

dolt (dōlt) s. tonto, idiota mf.

do·main (dō-mān') s. dominio; FIG. campo.

dome (dōm) s. cúpula, domo.

do·mes·tic (də-mĕs'tĭk) I. adj. doméstico; (home-loving) casero; ECON. (not foreign) nacional, del país ♦ **d. science** economía doméstica II. s. doméstico.

do·mes·ti·cate (-tĭ-kāt') tr. (animal) domesticar, amansar; (person) volver casero.

do·mes·tic·i·ty (dō'mĕ-stĭs'ĭ-tē) s. (of animals) domesticidad; (home life) vida casera.

dom·i·cile (dŏm'ĭ-sīl', dom'ĭ-) I. s. domicilio II. tr. domiciliar —intr. residir.

dom·i·nance (dŏm'ə-nəns) s. dominación f.

dom·i·nant (:nənt) adj. & s. dominante f.

dom·i·nate (:nāt') tr. & intr. dominar.

dom·i·neer ('-nîr') tr. & intr. tiranizar.

do·min·ion (də-mĭn'yən) s. dominio.

dom·i·no (dŏm'ə-nō') s. [pl. (e)s] (mask) dominó; (game piece) ficha ♦ pl. (game) dominó.

don¹ (dŏn) s. (Spanish gentleman) hidalgo; G.B. (head) catedrático ♦ **D.** don, señor.

don² tr. (clothes) ponerse; (an air) asumir.

do·nate (dō'nāt') tr. donar.

do·na·tion (dō-nā'shən) s. donación f; (gift) donativo.

done (dŭn) I. cf. **DO** II. adj. terminado, hecho; CUL. cocido, hecho ♦ **d. I** ¡trato hecho! ♦ **d. for** FAM. vencido ♦ **well d.!** ¡muy bien!

don·key (dŏng'kē) s. burro, asno.

do·nor (dō'nər) s. donador o, donante mf.

do-no·thing (dōō'nŭth'ĭng) I. adj. que no hace nada II. s. perezoso, persona sin iniciativa.

don't (dōnt) contr. de **do not**.

doo·dle (dōōd'l) FAM. I. intr. hacer garabatos (distraídamente) II. s. garabato.

doom (dōōm) I. s. (sentence) condena; (ruin) ruina, perdición f; (death) muerte f II. tr. condenar.

doom·say·er ('sā'ər) s. pesimista mf.

dooms·day (dōōmz'dā') s. día m del juicio final.

door (dôr) s. puerta; AUTO. portezuela; (doorway) entrada ♦ **to knock the d. down** echar la puerta abajo ♦ **to lay at the d. of** echar la culpa a ♦ **to lie at one's d.** recaer sobre uno.

door·bell ('bĕl') s. timbre m.

door·keep·er (:kē'pər) s. portero.

door·knob (:nŏb') s. perilla.

door·man (:măn') s. [pl. -men] portero.

door·mat (:măt') s. felpudo, estera.

door·nail (:nāl') s. clavo de puerta ♦ **dead as a d.** completamente muerto.

door·step (:stĕp') s. escalón m de la puerta ♦ **at one's d.** cerca de uno.

door-to-door (dôr'tə-dôr') adj. de puerta en puerta; (salesman) que vende a domicilio.

door·way (dôr'wā') s. puerta, entrada.

dope (dōp) I. s. (varnish) barniz m; FAM. (narcotic) narcótico, droga; JER. (dolt) tonto; (information) datos II. tr. FAM. drogar ♦ **to d. out** calcular, deducir.

dop·(e)y (dō'pē) adj. ♦ JER. (drugged) drogado; (lethargic) atontado, aletargado; (stupid) tonto.

dorm (dôrm) s. FAM. (room) dormitorio; (building) residencia para estudiantes.

dor·mant (dôr'mənt) adj. durmiente, ZOOL. en estado letárgico; BOT. en estado latente.

dor·mer (dôr'mər) s. buharda, buhardilla.

dor·mi·to·ry (dôr'mĭ-tôr'ē) s. (room) dormitorio; (building) residencia.

dor·mouse (dôr'mous') s. lirón m.

do·ry (dôr'ē) s. esquife f de fondo plano.

dos·age (dō'sĭj) s. dosificación f; (amount) dosis f.

dose (dōs) I. s. dosis f II. tr. medicinar.

dos·si·er (dŏs'ē-ā') s. expediente m.

dot (dŏt) I. s. punto ♦ **on the d.** FAM. (on time) a la hora; (exactly) exactamente; (o'clock) en punto II. tr. -tt- poner el punto a; (to scatter) salpicar ♦ **dotted line** línea de puntos.

dot·age (dō'tĭj) s. chochez f.

dote (dōt) intr. chochear ♦ **to d. on** adorar.

dot·ty (dŏt'ē) adj. ♦ chiflado.

dou·ble (dŭb'əl) I. adj. doble; (folded) doblado ♦ **d. agent** espía doble ♦ **d. base** contrabajo ♦ **d. chin** papada ♦ **d. entry** partida doble ♦ **d. take** reacción tardía ♦ **d. talk** lenguaje ambiguo ♦ **d. time** (wage) paga doble; MIL. paso ligero; MÚS. compás binario II. s. doble m; MAT. duplo ♦ **on the d.** FAM. con toda rapidez; MIL. a paso ligero III. tr. doblar; (to repeat) redoblar —intr. doblarse, duplicarse ♦ **to d. as** servir como ♦ **to d. back** volver uno sobre sus pasos ♦ **to d. for** sustituir a ♦ **to d. up** (from pain) doblarse en dos; (to share) compartir la misma habitación o cama ♦ **to d. up with laughter** desternillarse de risa IV. adv. doble, doblemente; (two together) dos juntos ♦ **d. or nothing** doble o nada.

dou·ble-bar·reled ('-băr'əld) adj. ARM. de dos cañones; FIG. de doble efecto.

dou·ble-breast·ed (:brĕs'tĭd) adj. cruzado.

dou·ble-check (:chĕk') tr. & intr. verificar por

segunda vez.

dou·ble-cross (:krŏs') JER. I. tr. traicionar (a un cómplice) II. s. traición *f*.

dou·ble-deal·er (:dē'lər) s. embustero.

dou·ble-deck·er (:dĕk'ər) s. *(bus)* ómnibus *m* de dos pisos; *(sandwich)* emparedado doble.

dou·ble-dig·it (:dĭj'ĭt) adj. de dos dígitos.

dou·ble-edged (:ĕjd') adj. de doble filo.

dou·ble-joint·ed (:join'tĭd) adj. de articulaciones dobles.

dou·ble-park (:pärk') tr. & intr. estacionar en doble fila.

dou·ble-quick (:kwĭk') adj. rapidísimo.

dou·ble-space (:spās') intr. & tr. escribir a máquina con doble espacio.

doub·let (dŭb'lĭt) s. *(pair)* pareja; *(jacket)* jubón *m*; GRAM. *(word)* doblete *m*.

dou·bloon (dŭb-blōōn') s. doblón *m*.

dou·bly (dŭb'lē) adv. doblemente.

doubt (dout) I. tr. dudar; *(to distrust)* desconfiar de —intr. dudar II. s. duda ♦ **beyond d.** fuera de duda ♦ **in d.** dudoso ♦ **no d.** sin duda.

doubt·er (dou'tər) s. escéptico.

doubt·ful (dout'fəl) adj. dudoso.

doubt·less (:lĭs) I. adj. seguro II. adv. *(certainly)* sin duda; *(probably)* probablemente.

douche (dōōsh) I. s. ducha II. tr. & intr. duchar(se).

dough (dō) s. masa, pasta; JER. *(money)* plata.

dough·nut (dō'nət) s. buñuelo.

dour (dŏŏr, dour) adj. *(stern)* severo; *(sullen)* hosco.

douse (dous) tr. *(to immerse)* sumergir; *(to drench)* empapar; *(to extinguish)* extinguir.

dove¹ (dŭv) s. paloma; FIG. pacifista *mf*.

dove² (dōv) cf. **dive.**

dove·tail (dŭv'tāl') s. cola de milano.

dow·a·ger (dou'ə-jər) s. *(widow)* viuda con viudedad; *(elderly woman)* señora mayor.

dow·dy (dou'dē) adj. -**i**- desaliñado.

dow·el (dou'əl) s. clavija.

dow·er (dou'ər) s. viudedad *f*.

down¹ (doun) I. adv. *(downward)* (hacia) abajo; *(on the ground)* en tierra; *(in writing)* por escrito; COM. *(in advance)* como adelanto ♦ **d. and out** sin un real, pobrísimo ♦ **d. below** abajo ♦ **d. with ... !** ¡abajo ... ! II. adj. *(descending)* que va hacia abajo; *(depressed)* deprimido; COM. inicial, a cuenta ♦ **to be d. on** tenerle inquina a ♦ **to be d. with** estar enfermo con III. prep. abajo ♦ **d. the centuries** a través de los siglos ♦ **d. the road** más abajo IV. s. descenso, caída V. tr. *(food)* tragar, engullir; *(liquids)* vaciar de un trago; *(an airplane)* derribar.

down² s. *(feathers)* plumón *m*; *(hair, fibers)* pelusa, vello.

down·cast ('kăst') adj. *(depressed)* abatido, desalentado; *(eyes)* hacia abajo.

down·er (dou'nər) s. JER. *(pill)* tranquilizante *m*; *(experience)* experiencia que deprime.

down·fall (doun'fôl') s. ruina, caída.

down·grade (:grād') I. s. bajada, pendiente *f* II. tr. disminuir (de categoría, importancia).

down·heart·ed (:här'tĭd) adj. abatido.

down·hill (:hĭl') adv. cuesta abajo ♦ **to go d.** deteriorarse; *(health)* debilitarse, decaer.

down·play (:plā') tr. minimizar.

down·pour (:pôr') s. chaparrón *m*, aguacero.

down·right (:rīt') I. adj. *(complete)* absoluto, completo; *(forthright)* categórico II. adv. completamente, categóricamente.

down·stage (:stāj') adv. & s. (hacia el) proscenio.

down·stairs (:stârz') I. adv. & adj. *(lower floor)* en *o* del piso de abajo; *(main floor)* en *o* de la planta baja ♦ **to go d.** bajar (de un piso a otro) II. s.pl. planta baja.

down·stream (:strēm') adv. agua *o* río abajo.

down-to-earth ('tə-ûrth') adj. práctico.

down·town (:toun') I. adv. & s. (hacia *o* en el) centro de una ciudad II. adj. del centro.

down·trod·den (:trŏd'n) adj. pisoteado.

down·turn (:tûrn') s. baja, bajón *m*.

down·ward (:wərd) I. adv. *o* -**wards** hacia abajo II. adj. descendente.

down·wind (:wĭnd') adv. & adj. de *o* a sotavento, a favor del viento.

dow·ry (dou'rē) s. dote *f*.

doze (dōz) I. intr. dormitar ♦ **to d. off** dormirse, echar una cabezada II. s. sueño ligero.

doz·en (dŭz'ən) I. s.inv. docena ♦ **dozens of** miles de II. adj. docena de.

drab (drăb) adj. -**bb**- *(brownish)* pardusco; *(dull)* ordinario, monótono.

draft (drăft) I. s. corriente *f* de aire; *(of a chimney)* tiro; *(sketch)* bosquejo; *(written)* borrador *m*, versión *f*; *(gulp)* trago; MIL. conscripción *f*, quinta; MARÍT. calada; COM. giro ♦ **d. board** junta de reclutamiento ♦ **on d.** de barril II. tr. *(a bill)* hacer un anteproyecto de; *(a writing)* hacer un borrador de; *(a speech, plan)* redactar; MIL. quintar, reclutar III. adj. *(horse)* de tiro; *(beer)* de barril.

draft·ee (drăf-tē') s. recluta *m*, conscripto.

drafts·man (drăfts'mən) s. [pl. -**men**] dibujante *m*, diseñador *m*.

drag (drăg) I. tr. & intr. -**gg**- arrastrar; *(river, lake)* dragar; *(to bring forcibly)* llevar de los pelos ♦ **to d. along** arrastrar ♦ **to d. out** *(to extract)* sacar; *(to prolong)* alargar interminablemente —intr. *(to trail)* arrastrar(se); *(to pass slowly)* hacerse interminable; JER. *(on a cigarette)* dar una pitada ♦ **to d. on** hacerse interminable II. s. *(act)* arrastre *m*; *(hindrance)* estorbo; AER. resistencia al avance; JER. *(bore)* pesado; *(puff)* chupada, pitada ♦ **in d.** JER. vestido de mujer (un hombre, o viceversa) ♦ **main d.** JER. calle principal.

drag·net (drăg'nĕt') s. *(net)* red barredera; *(roundup)* pesquisa.

drag·on (drăg'ən) s. dragón *m*.

drag·on·fly (:flī') s. libélula.

dra·goon (drə-gōōn') I. s. dragón *m* II. tr. coaccionar.

drain (drān) I. tr. drenar, desaguar; *(to drink)* beber; *(to empty)* vaciar; *(to exhaust)* agotar —intr. desaguarse, vaciarse II. s. desagüe *m*, desaguadero; FIG. desgaste *m* ♦ **down the d.** por la ventana.

drain·age (drā'nĭj) s. drenaje *m*.

drain·pipe (drān'pīp') s. caño de desagüe.

drake (drāk) s. pato (macho).

dram (drăm) s. *(weight)* dracma *f*; *(small drink)* traguito, copita; *(a bit)* pizca.

dra·ma (drä'mə) s. drama *m*.

dra·mat·ic (drə-măt'ĭk) adj. dramático ♦ **dra·matics** s.pl. histrionismo; s.sg. TEAT. arte dramático.

dram·a·tist (dră'mə-tĭst, drăf'-) s. dramaturgo.

dram·a·tize (:tīz') tr. TEAT. escenificar; *(an issue, presentation)* dramatizar.

drank (drăngk) cf. **drink.**

drape (drāp) I. tr. *(to adorn)* adornar con col-

gaduras; *(to cover)* cubrir; *(to arrange in folds)* **drapear;** *(to hang)* colgar; *(arms, legs)* echar —intr. caer **II.** s. caída ♦ pl. cortinas.

drap·er (drā′pər) s. G.B. pañero.

drap·er·y (:pə-rē) s. *(cloth)* paños; G.B. *(business)* pañería ♦ pl. cortinas.

dras·tic (drās′tïk) adj. drástico.

draught (drăft, drăft) G.B. var. de **draft.**

draughts (drăfts) s. G.B. juego de damas.

draw (drô) **I.** tr. **drew, -n** *(to pull)* tirar de, halar; *(to lead)* conducir, llevar; *(to attract)* atraer; *(liquid, gun, conclusion)* sacar; *(breath)* tomar; *(curtain)* correr; *(lots, straws)* echar *(suertes)*; *(fire, criticism)* provocar; *(salary)* cobrar; *(cards)* robar; *(game, contest)* empatar; *(to stretch taut)* tensar; *(a line)* trazar; ARTE. dibujar; MARIT. calar; COM. *(interest)* ganar, devengar; *(savings)* sacar, retirar ♦ **to d. a blank** no recordar nada • **to d. attention** llamar la atención • **to d. in** *(to retract)* retraer; *(to sketch)* esbozar • **to d. out** *(information)* sonsacar; *(to prolong)* prolongar • **to d. together** unir, juntar • **to d. the line** trazar un límite ♦ **to d. up** redactar, preparar —intr. *(to take in air)* tirar; DEP. *(to tie)* empatar; ARTE. dibujar ♦ **to d. away** apartarse • **to d. back** echarse para atrás • **to d. in** encogerse • **to d. near** acercarse • **to d. on** *(a supply)* servirse de, recurrir a; *(an account)* girar contra • **to d. up** pararse **II.** s. *(attraction)* atracción *f*; *(air intake)* tiro, *(lottery)* sorteo • **to d.** empate *m*.

draw·back (′băk′) s. desventaja.

draw·bridge (:brïj′) s. puente levadizo.

draw·er (drôr) s. cajón *m*, gaveta ♦ pl. *(women's)* bombachas; *(men's)* calzoncillos.

draw·ing (drô′ïng) s. dibujo; *(lottery)* lotería, sorteo ♦ **d. card** atractivo, atracción • **d. room** salón.

drawl (drôl) intr. & s. (hablar con) voz lenta y cansina.

drawn (drôn) cf. **draw.**

draw·string (drô′strïng′) s. cordón *m*.

dread (drĕd) **I.** s. pavor *m*, terror *m*; *(anticipation)* aprensión **II.** tr. temer; *(to anticipate)* anticipar (con temor) **III.** adj. espantoso, terrible.

dread·ful (′fəl) adj. espantoso, terrible.

dread·nought (:nôt′) s. acorazado.

dream (drēm) **I.** s. sueño; *(daydream)* ensueño **II.** tr. & intr. **-ed** *o* **-t** soñar *(of, about* con); *(to daydream)* soñar despierto ♦ **to d. up** inventar.

dream·er (drē′mər) s. soñador *m*.

dream·y (:mē) adj. **-i-** como un sueño, de ensueño; FAM. *(wonderful)* maravilloso, precioso.

drea·ry (drîr′ē) adj. **-i-** *(bleak)* deprimente, sombrío; *(dull)* monótono, aburrido.

dredge (drĕj) **I.** s. draga, rastra **II.** tr. & intr. dragar, rastrear ♦ **to d. up** desenterrar.

dregs (drĕgz) s.pl. poso, heces *f*; FIG. escoria.

drench (drĕnch) tr. empapar.

dress (drĕs) **I.** s. *(garment)* vestido, traje *m*; *(apparel)* vestimenta, ropa ♦ **d. ball** baile de etiqueta • **d. code** reglamento de la vestimenta • **d. rehearsal** ensayo general **II.** tr. vestir; *(to decorate)* decorar; *(hair)* peinar, arreglar; *(wounds)* curar; *(food)* aderezar ♦ **dressed to kill** vestido muy elegantemente • **dressed to the nines** de punta en blanco —intr. vestirse ♦ **to d. down** regañar • **to d. up** vestirse de etiqueta **III.** adj. *(clothing)* de vestir; *(occasion)*

de etiqueta.

dress·er (′ər) s. cómoda, tocador *m*.

dress·ing (:ïng) s. MED. vendaje *m*; *(sauce)* aliño, salsa; *(stuffing)* relleno ♦ **d. gown** bata • **d. room** camerino • **d. table** tocador, coqueta.

dress·mak·er (:mā′kər) s. costurera.

dress·mak·ing (:kïng) s. costura.

dress·y (drĕs′ē) adj. **-i-** elegante.

drew (drōō) cf. **draw.**

drib·ble (drïb′əl) **I.** intr. *(to trickle)* gotear; *(to drool)* babear; DEP. *(soccer)* gambetear; *(basketball)* driblear —tr. *(to trickle)* echar a gotas; DEP. gambetear, driblear **II.** s. *(trickle)* goteo, hilo; *(bit)* gota, pizca; DEP. gambeta, dribling *m*.

dri·er (drī′ər) var. de **dryer.**

drift (drïft) **I.** intr. *(off course)* ir a la deriva; *(on a current)* ser arrastrado por la corriente; *(to roam)* vagar, vagabundear; *(snow, sand)* amontonarse —tr. llevar, arrastrar **II.** s. AVIA., MARIT. deriva; *(of sand, snow)* pila, montón *m*; *(general idea)* dirección *f*, rumbo ♦ **to get the d.** FAM. caer en la cuenta.

drift·er (drïf′tər) s. vagabundo.

drift·wood (:wŏŏd′) s. madera flotante.

drill (drïl) **I.** s. *(tool)* torno, taladro; *(oil rig)* perforadora; *(machine)* taladradora; *(exercises)* ejercicios repetitivos; *(cloth)* dril *m* ♦ **d. press** prensa taladradora **II.** intr. & tr. taladrar, perforar; *(to exercise)* ejercitar; *(to teach)* enseñar por medio de repetición.

drink (drïngk) **I.** tr. & intr. **drank, drunk** beber, tomar ♦ **to d. in** devorar • **to d. to** brindar por, beber a la salud de • **to d. up** FAM. bebérselo todo **II.** s. bebida; *(swallow)* trago, buche *m* ♦ **to take to d.** darse a la bebida • **to give someone a d.** dar de beber a alguien.

drink·a·ble (drïng′kə-bəl) adj. potable, bebible.

drink·er (:kər) s. bebedor *m*.

drink·ing (:kïng) s. beber *m*; *(habit)* bebida.

drip (drïp) **I.** tr. *pp* echar *(a gotas)* —intr. gotear **II.** s. gota; *(sound)* goteo, goteadero *m*; JER. *(bore)* pelma *m*, pesado.

drip-dry (′drī′) adj. que seca rápidamente sin arrugas al estar colgado.

drive (drīv) **I.** tr. **drove, -n** *(a vehicle)* conducir, guiar; *(passengers)* llevar; *(distance)* recorrer; *(to push)* empujar; *(to compel)* forzar, obligar; *(a nail)* clavar; *(a machine)* hacer funcionar, accionar; *(a stake)* hincar ♦ **to d. away** *o* **off** alejar, apartar • **to d. back** hacer retroceder • **to d. in** clavar, hincar • **to d. out** *(to expel)* echar; *(into the open)* hacer salir —intr. *(a vehicle)* conducir, guiar; *(to travel by car)* ir en coche; *(rain, snow)* azotar ♦ **to d. at** insinuar, querer decir • **to d. by** *o* **through** pasar (por) • **to d. on** seguir el camino **II.** s. *(ride)* vuelta en coche; *(journey)* viaje *m*; *(road)* carretera, camino; *(campaign)* campaña; *(vigor)* vigor *m*, energía; *(push)* empuje *m*, agresividad; MEC. transmisión *f*; AUTO. tracción *f*; PSIC. impulso; MIL. ofensiva ♦ **d. belt** correa de transmisión • **to go for a d.** dar una vuelta en coche.

drive-in (′ïn′) s. lugar que atiende a los clientes sin que se bajen del automóvil.

driv·el (drïv′əl) s. *(saliva)* baba; *(nonsense)* boberías.

driv·en (drïv′ən) cf. **drive.**

driv·er (drī′vər) s. chofer *mf*, conductor *m*.

drive·way (drīv′wā′) s. camino de entrada.

driv·ing (drī′vïng) **I.** adj. *(impelling)* impulsor,

motriz; *(rain)* torrencial; AUTO. de conducción II. s. acción *f* de conducir; *(motoring)* automovilismo.

driz·zle (drĭz'əl) I. intr. lloviznar, garuar —tr. salpicar II. s. llovizna, garúa.

droll (drōl) adj. cómico, gracioso.

drone[1] (drōn) s. *(bee)* zángano; *(aircraft)* aeroplano de control remoto.

drone[2] I. intr. *(to buzz)* zumbar; *(to speak)* hablar monótonamente —tr. decir en forma monótona II. s. zumbido; *(bagpipe)* roncón *m*.

drool (drōl) I. intr. babosear, babear; FAM. *(to show desire)* caérsele la baba II. s. baba, saliva.

droop (drōp) I. intr. *(to hang)* inclinarse, doblarse; *(trees, eyelids)* caerse; *(head)* inclinarse; *(shoulders)* encorvarse; *(spirits)* desanimarse II. s. caída; *(shoulders)* encorvadura; *(head)* inclinación *f*.

drop (drŏp) I. s. gota; *(trace)* poco, pizca; *(lozenge)* pastilla; *(fall)* bajada, caída; *(height of fall)* altura; *(in prices)* baja; *(in value, quality)* disminución *f*; *(abyss)* precipicio; *(by parachute)* lanzamiento; *(for messages)* buzón *m* ♦ **a d. in the bucket** una gota de agua en el mar II. intr. **-pp-** *(to drip)* gotear; *(to fall)* caer a tierra, desplomarse; *(wind)* amainar; *(temperature, prices)* bajar; *(value, quality)* disminuir; *(conversation)* terminarse; *(to die)* morir de repente ♦ **to d. behind** quedarse atrás • **to d. in** o **by** pasar (por casa de alguien) • **to d. off** *(leaves)* caer; *(part)* caerse, desprenderse; *(to diminish)* disminuir • **to d. out** *(to omit)* omitir; *(to quit)* dejar de participar —tr. *(to let fall)* dejar caer, soltar; *(to let go of)* soltar; *(a letter)* echar; *(conversation)* interrumpir; *(plan)* abandonar; *(to omit)* omitir, suprimir; *(habit)* dejar de; *(hint)* soltar; *(voice, prices)* bajar; *(bombs)* lanzar ♦ **to d. off** dejar • **to d. someone a line** poner unas líneas a alguien.

drop·let ('lĭt) s. gotita.

drop-off (:ôf') s. *(slope)* bajada escarpada; *(decrease)* disminución significativa.

drop·out (:out') s. *(student)* estudiante *mf* que abandona sus estudios; *(from society)* persona que rechaza a la sociedad.

drop·per (:ər) s. gotero, cuentagotas *m*.

drop·pings (:ĭngz) s.pl. excremento de animales.

dross (drôs) s. TEC. escoria; FIG. desperdicio.

drought (drout) s. sequía, seca; FIG. escasez *f*.

drove[1] (drōv) s. *(herd)* manada; FIG. multitud *f* ♦ **in droves** a manadas.

drove[2] cf. **drive**.

drov·er (drō'vər) s. *(of cattle, mules)* arriero, vaquero; *(of sheep)* pastor *m*.

drown (droun) intr. ahogarse —tr. ahogar; *(to flood)* anegar.

drowse (drouz) intr. adormecerse, estar medio dormido.

drows·y (drou'zē) adj. **-i-** soñoliento, amodorrado.

drub (drŭb) tr. **-bb-** *(to thrash)* apalear; *(to defeat)* derrotar por completo.

drub·bing (:ĭng) s. paliza, zurra; *(defeat)* derrota severa.

drudge (drŭj) s. esclavo del trabajo.

drudg·er·y ('ə-rē) s. faena pesada y aburrida.

drug (drŭg) I. s. droga; MED. medicamento; *(narcotic)* narcótico ♦ **d. addict** narcómano, drogadicto II. tr. **-gg-** MED. dar medicamento; *(with a narcotic)* drogar, narcotizar; *(food,*

drink) poner una droga en.

drug·gist ('ĭst) s. farmacéutico, boticario.

drug-store (:stôr') s. farmacia, botica.

drum (drŭm) I. s. cilindro, tambor *m*; *(barrel)* tonel *m*; MÚS. tambor ♦ pl. batería II. intr. & tr. **-mm-** tocar (el tambor); *(fingers)* tamborilear (con) ♦ **to d. into someone's head** meterle a alguien en la cabeza • **to d. out** echar, expulsar • **to d. up** conseguir.

drum·beat ('bēt') s. toque *m* del tambor.

drum·mer (:ər) s. baterista *mf*, tambor *mf*.

drum·stick (:stĭk') s. MÚS. baqueta, palillo; CUL. muslo.

drunk (drŭngk) I. cf. **drink** II. adj. ebrio, borracho ♦ **to get d.** emborracharse III. s. *(drunkard)* borracho; *(bout)* juerga.

drunk·ard (drŭng'kərd) s. borracho.

drunk·en ('kən) adj. borracho, bebido; *(song, brawl)* de borrachos; *(state)* de embriaguez.

dry (drī) I. adj. **-i-** o **-y-** seco; *(arid)* árido; *(thirsty)* sediento; *(toast)* sin mantequilla; *(boring)* pesado; *(wit, style)* agudo, satírico; *(county, state)* prohibicionista ♦ **d. cleaner's** tintorería, tinte • **d. cleaning** limpieza en seco • **d. dock** carenero • **d. goods** mercería, lencería • **d. land** tierra firme • **d. measure** sistema de medidas para áridos • **d. run** práctica, simulacro • **to run d.** secarse, agotarse II. tr. & intr. secar(se), desecar(se) ♦ **d. up!** ¡cállate la boca! • **to d. out** secar(se); *(drunkard)* dejar de beber • **to d. up** desecar(se); *(supply)* esfumarse, desaparecer.

dry-clean (:klēn') tr. limpiar en seco.

dry·er (:ər) s. *(appliance)* secador *m*; *(machine)* secadora.

dry·ness (:nĭs) s. sequedad *f*.

du·al (dōō'əl) adj. dual, doble.

du·al·i·ty (dōō-ăl'ĭ-tē) s. dualidad *f*.

du·al-pur·pose (dōō'əl-pûr'pəs) adj. de doble propósito, de doble función.

dub[1] (dŭb) tr. **-bb-** *(to knight)* armar, hacer caballero; *(to nickname)* apodar.

dub[2] tr. **-bb-** MÚS. mezclar; CINEM. doblar.

du·bi·ous (dōō'bē-əs) adj. *(doubtful)* dudoso, incierto; *(questionable)* sospechoso.

duch·ess (dŭch'ĭs) s. duquesa.

duch·y (:ē) s. ducado.

duck[1] (dŭk) s. pato; *(female)* pata.

duck[2] tr. *(head)* agachar; *(to dodge)* eludir, evadir; *(to plunge)* zambullir —intr. agacharse, zambullirse ♦ **to d. out** desaparecer • **to d. out on** eludir.

duck·ling ('lĭng) s. patito, anadón *m*.

duct (dŭkt) s. conducto, tubo; ANAT. canal *m*.

dud (dŭd) s. FAM. *(bomb)* bomba que no estalla; *(failure)* fracaso ♦ pl. FAM. *(clothes)* trapos; *(belongings)* posesiones.

dude (dōōd) s. FAM. hombre *m* de ciudad; *(dandy)* petimetre *m*; JER. *(guy)* tipo, tío.

due (dōō) I. adj. *(payable)* pagadero; *(amount)* sin pagar; *(just)* debido, merecido; *(sufficient)* suficiente ♦ **d. date** vencimiento • **d. process** proceso legal correspondiente • **to be d.** deber o, a causa de • **to become** o **fall d.** vencer II. s. *(comeuppance)* merecido; *(reward)* recompensa ♦ pl. cuota II. adv. derecho hacia.

du·el (dōō'əl) intr. batirse en duelo.

du·el·er·ist (:ə-lər/ĭst) s. duelista *m*.

du·et (dōō-ĕt') s. dueto, dúo.

duf·fel bag (dŭf'əl) s. bolsa de lona.

dug (dŭg) cf. **dig**.

dug·out (dŭg'out') s. *(boat)* piragua; *(shelter)*

trinchera.

duke (dōōk) s. duque m.

dukes (dōōks) s.pl. JER. puños ♦ **put** o **stick up your d.!** ¡ponte en guardia!

dul·cet (dŭl′sĭt) adj. suave, dulce.

dull (dŭl) I. adj. (stupid) tonto, torpe; (insensitive) lento, embotado; (blunt) desafilado, romo; (sound, pain) sordo; (boring) aburrido; (sluggish) flojo; (color, sound) apagado; (cloudy) nublado, gris II. tr. & intr. (to blunt) desafilar(se), enromar(se); (pain) aliviar(se); (feelings) embotar(se); (to muffle) amortiguar(se), apagar(se).

dull·ard (′ərd) s. estúpido, idiota mf.

dul(l)·ness (:nĭs) s. (blade, senses) embotamiento; (stupidity) torpeza; (flatness) monotonía, insipidez f.

du·ly (dōō′lē) adv. correctamente, debidamente; (punctually) al debido tiempo.

dumb (dŭm) adj. (mute) mudo; FAM. (stupid) tonto, estúpido ♦ **d. show** pantomima • **to strike d.** dejar sin habla.

dumb·bell (′běl′) s. (weight) pesas; JER. (dolt) estúpido, tonto.

dumb·wait·er (:wā′tər) s. montaplatos m.

dum(b)·found (:found′) tr. pasmar, asombrar.

dum·my (:ē) I s. (puppet) muñeco, títere m; (mannequin) maniquí m; (front) testaferro; FAM. (dolt) tonto, bobo II. adj. falso, ficticio.

dump (dŭmp) I. tr. tirar, deshacerse de; (to empty) vaciar, descargar; COM. inundar el mercado con; COMPUT. imprimir (información) —intr. caerse, desplomarse ♦ **to d. out** vaciar(se) II. s. vertedero, muladar m; (depot) depósito; JER. (unkept place) pocilga ♦ **d. truck** volquete ♦ pl. FAM. abatimiento.

dump·ling (:lĭng) s. bola de masa cocida.

dun¹ (dŭn) tr. -nn- apremiar (a un deudor).

dun² s. (color) pardo.

dunce (dŭns) s. FAM. zopenco, burro ♦ **d. cap** orejas de burro.

dune (dōōn) s. duna ♦ **d. buggy** automóvil para andar sobre dunas.

dung (dŭng) s. estiércol m.

dun·ga·rees (dŭng′gə-rē′z′) s.pl. pantalones vaqueros.

dun·geon (dŭn′jən) s. mazmorra.

dunk (dŭngk) tr. sumergir, hundir; (food) ensopar, remojar.

du·o (dōō′ō) s. FAM. (pair) pareja; MÚS. dúo.

du·o·dec·i·mal (dōō′ə-dĕs′ə-məl) I. adj. duodecimal II. s. duodécimo.

du·o·de·num (:dē′nəm) s. [pl. s o -na] duodeno.

dupe (dōōp) I. FAM. primo II. tr. embaucar, engañar.

du·plex (dōō′plĕks) I. adj. doble II. s. (apartment) apartamento de dos pisos; (house) casa de dos viviendas.

du·pli·cate (:plĭ-kĭt) I. s. duplicado, copia ♦ **in d.** por duplicado II. tr. (:kāt′) copiar, duplicar; (on a machine) multicopiar III. adj. duplicado.

du·plic·i·ty (dōō-plĭs′ĭ-tē) s. engaño.

du·ra·ble (dŏŏr′ə-bəl) adj. duradero ♦ **d. goods** productos no perecederos.

du·ra·tion (dŏŏ-rā′shən) s. duración f.

du·ress (dŏŏ-rĕs′) s. coerción f ♦ **under d.** por coacción.

dur·ing (dŏŏr′ĭng) prep. durante.

dusk (dŭsk) s. crepúsculo ♦ **at d.** al atardecer.

dusk·y (dŭs′kē) adj. -i- oscuro, fusco; (color)

negruzco, moreno.

dust (dŭst) I. s. polvo ♦ **d. cloud** polvareda • **d. jacket** sobrecubierta • **to bite the d.** morirse • **to let the d. settle** dejar que se calme la situación II. tr. limpiar el polvo de; (to cover) empolvar; (to sprinkle) espolvorear —intr. limpiar el polvo.

dust·bin (′bĭn′) s. G.B. basurero.

dust·er (dŭs′tər) s. (cloth) trapo (para limpiar); (with feathers) plumero; (smock) guardapolvo.

dust·ing (:tĭng) s. limpieza de polvo; (covering) capa de polvo; G.B., FAM. (thrashing) paliza.

dust·man (dŭst′mən) s. [pl. -men] G.B. basurero.

dust·pan (:păn′) s. recogedor m.

dust·y (dŭs′tē) adj. -i- polvoriento.

du·ti·ful (dōō′tĭ-fəl) adj. obediente, cumplidor.

du·ty (dōō′tē) s. deber m, obligación f; (task) función f; (tax) impuesto, arancel ♦ **in the line of d.** en cumplimiento del deber • **to be on (off) d.** (no) estar de servicio • **to do one's d.** cumplir con su deber.

du·ty-free (:frē′) adj. & adv. exento de derechos de aduana.

du·ty-paid (:pād′) adj. con los derechos de aduana pagados.

dwarf (dwôrf) I. adj. & s. [pl. s o -ves] enano II. tr. achicar, empequeñecer.

dwell (dwĕl) tr. -ed o dwelt morar, residir; FIG. persistir, existir ♦ **to d. on (in, upon)** detenerse en, insistir en; (to expatiate) dilatarse sobre.

dwell·er (′ər) s. morador m, habitante mf.

dwell·ing (:ĭng) s. residencia, morada.

dwin·dle (dwĭn′dl) tr. & intr. disminuir, menguar.

dye (dī) I. s. tintura, tinte m II. tr. dyeing teñir, colorar.

dy·er (dī′ər) s. tintorero.

dye·stuff (dī′stŭf′) s. tinte m, colorante m.

dy·ing (dī′ĭng) I. cf. die¹ II. adj. moribundo; (final) último.

dy·nam·ic (dī-năm′ĭk) adj. dinámico ♦ **dynamics** s. dinámica.

dy·na·mite (dī′nə-mīt′) I. s. dinamita II. interj. JER. estupendo, maravilloso.

dy·na·mo (:mō′) s. dinamo f.

dy·nas·ty (dī′nə-stē) s. dinastía.

dys·en·ter·y (dĭs′ən-tĕr′ē) s. disentería.

dys·func·tion (dĭs-fŭngk′shən) s. disfunción f.

dys·pep·sia (dĭs-pĕp′shə) s. dispepsia.

dys·tro·phy (dĭs′trə-fē) s. distrofia.

E

e, E (ē) s. quinta letra del alfabeto inglés; MÚS. mi m.

each (ēch) I. adj. cada • **e. and every one** todos sin excepción II. pron. cada uno • **e. for himself** cada cual por su cuenta • **e. other** uno a otro, mutuamente • **e. his own** cada uno con su gusto III. adv. por persona, cada uno.

ea·ger (ē′gər) adj. -er, -est (avid) ansioso, ávido; (desirous) deseoso, ardiente ♦ **e. beaver** FAM. persona de exagerado entusiasmo • **to be e. for** ansiar, anhelar.

ea·ger·ness (:nĭs) s. ansia, anhelo.

ea·gle (ē′gəl) s. águila.

ear¹ (îr) s. oreja; (organ of hearing) oído ♦ **e. lobe** lóbulo de la oreja • **to fall on deaf ears**

caer en saco roto • **to give an e. to** prestar atención a • **to have a good e. (for)** tener un buen oído (para) • **to have someone's e.** tener la atención de alguien • **to keep** *o* **have one's e. to the ground** mantenerse alerta *o* al corriente • **to listen with half an e.** escuchar a medias • **to play by e.** tocar de oído • **to play it by e.** improvisar sobre la marcha • **to turn a deaf e.** hacerse el sordo.

ear² s. BOT. espiga, mazorca.

ear·ache (ĭr'āk') s. dolor *m* de oído.

ear·drum (ĭr'drŭm') s. tímpano.

ear·flap (ĭr'flăp') s. orejera.

earl (ûrl) s. conde *m*.

earl·dom ('dəm) s. condado.

ear·ly (ûr'lē) -i- I. adj. temprano; *(near the beginning)* primero; *(quick)* rápido, pronto; *(premature)* prematuro; *(primitive)* primitivo ♦ **at an e. date** en fecha cercana • **at the earliest** lo más pronto • **at your earliest convenience** con la mayor brevedad • **e. bird** FAM. *(riser)* madrugador; *(arrival)* persona que llega temprano • **e. show** primera función II. adv. *(soon)* temprano, pronto; *(before)* antes; *(in advance)* con tiempo, con anticipación; *(prematurely)* prematuramente ♦ **as e. as** ya en • **as e. as possible** lo más pronto posible • **bright and e.** muy temprano • **e. in** a principios de • **e. in the morning** de madrugada • en serio.

ear·mark (ĭr'märk') I. s. marca característica, señal *f* II. tr. marcar ♦ **to be earmarked for** estar reservado para.

ear·muff (ĭr'mŭf') s. orejera.

earn (ûrn) tr. *(to make)* ganar; *(to deserve)* ganarse, merecer; *(to acquire)* obtener; *(interest)* devengar.

ear·nest¹ (ûr'nĭst) adj. sincero, serio; *(important)* grave ♦ **in e.** en serio.

ear·nest² s. *(deposit)* arras *f*; *(token)* prenda.

earn·ings (ûr'nĭngz) s.pl. *(salary)* sueldo; COM. *(income)* ingresos; *(profits)* utilidades *f*.

ear·phone (ĭr'fōn') s. audífono.

ear·ring (ĭr'rĭng) s. pendiente *m*, arete *m*.

ear·shot (ĭr'shŏt') s. ♦ **within e.** al alcance del oído.

ear·split·ting (ĭr'splĭt'ĭng) adj. ensordecedor.

earth (ûrth) s. tierra; *(world)* mundo ♦ **down to e.** sensato, realista • **E.** Tierra • **to come back to e.** volver a la realidad • **who, what on e.** quién, qué diablo.

earth·en (ûr'thən) adj. de tierra.

earth·en·ware (:wâr') I. s. loza II. adj. de barro.

earth·ling (ûrth'lĭng) s. terrícola *mf*.

earth·ly (:lē) adj. mundanal, terreno; FAM. *(conceivable)* concebible, posible ♦ **to be of no e. use** no servir para nada.

earth·quake (:kwāk') s. terremoto, temblor *m*.

earth·shak·ing (:shā'kĭng) adj. importantísimo, de enormes consecuencias.

earth·work (:wûrk') s. terraplén *m*.

earth·worm (:wûrm') s. lombriz *f*.

earth·y (ûr'thē) adj. -i- vulgar, tosco.

ear·wax (ĭr'wăks') s. cerumen *m*.

ease (ēz) I. s. *(comfort)* comodidad *f*; *(relief)* alivio, desahogo; *(naturalness)* desenvoltura; *(facility)* facilidad *f*, soltura; *(affluence)* afluencia ♦ **at e.** cómodo; MIL. en posición de descanso • **at e.!** ¡descanso! • **to put at e.** poner cómodo • **with e.** fácilmente, sin esfuerzo II. tr. & intr. *(pain)* aliviar(se), mitigar(se); *(pressure)* descargar(se); *(tension)* relajar(se);

(to loosen) aflojar(se) ♦ **to e. in(to)** (hacer) entrar con cuidado • **to e. up** bajar, disminuir • **to e. up on** tratar con menos rigor.

ea·sel (ē'zəl) s. caballete *m*.

ease·ment (ēz'mənt) s. servidumbre *f*.

eas·i·ly (ē'zə-lē) adv. fácilmente; *(possibly)* muy probablemente.

eas·i·ness (ē'zē-nĭs) s. facilidad *f*; *(comfort)* comodidad *f*.

east (ēst) I. s. este *m*, oriente *m* II. adj. del este, oriental III. adv. al este, hacia el este.

east·bound ('bound') adj. con rumbo al este.

Eas·ter (ē'stər) s. Pascua de Resurrección; *(period)* Semana Santa ♦ **E. Sunday** domingo de Pascua.

east·ern (ē'stərn) adj. oriental, del este.

east·ward (ēst'wərd) I. adv. hacia el este II. adj. oriental, que va al este.

eas·y (ē'zē) -i- I. adj. fácil; *(free from worry)* tranquilo; *(comfortable)* cómodo; *(easygoing)* desenvuelto, natural; *(simple)* sencillo; *(not strict)* suave, leve; *(wanton)* desordenado; *(unhurried)* lento, pausado ♦ **e. chair** sillón • **e. to get along with** acomodadizo • **to be easy on the street** vivir acomodado II. adv. fácilmente ♦ **e. does it** con calma • **to come e.** costar poco esfuerzo, resultar fácil • **to go e. on** FAM. *(to use moderately)* usar con moderación; *(to be lenient to)* no tratar con mucha severidad • **to take it e.** FAM. *(to relax)* descansar; *(to stay calm)* no agitarse; *(to go slow)* no apurarse.

eas·y·go·ing ('-gō'ĭng) adj. despreocupado, descuidado; *(tolerant)* tolerante.

eat (ēt) tr. ate, eaten comer; *(lunch, dinner)* tomar (el almuerzo, la cena); *(to corrode)* corroer; JER. *(to annoy)* molestar, fastidiar ♦ **to e. away** corroer, carcomer • **to e. up** *(to devour)* comérselo todo; *(to use up)* consumir, gastar; *(to be credulous)* creer sin crítica; *(to enjoy)* deleitarse en • **what's eating you?** ¿qué mosca te ha picado? —intr. comer, alimentarse ♦ **to e. (away) at** roer, corroer • **to e. into** *(to corrode)* corroer; *(to use up)* (des)gastar • **to e. out** comer fuera (de casa) • **to e. through** corroer.

eats (ēts) s.pl. JER. comida, alimento.

eaves (ēvz) s.pl. alero.

eaves·drop ('drŏp') intr. -pp- escuchar disimulada *o* secretamente.

ebb (ĕb) I. s. menguante *f* ♦ **e. and flow** flujo y reflujo; FIG. altibajos • **to be at a low e.** tener poca energía II. intr. menguar.

eb·on·y (ĕb'ə-nē) I. s. abano II. adj. negro.

e·bul·lient (ĭ-bŭl'yənt) adj. *(lively)* entusiasta; *(bubbly)* burbujeante.

ec·cen·tric (ĭk-sĕn'trĭk) I. adj. excéntrico II. s. *(person)* excéntrico; MEC. excéntrica.

ec·cen·tric·i·ty (ĕk'sĕn-trĭs'ĭ-tē) s. excentricidad *f*.

ec·cle·si·as·tic (ĭ-klē'zē-ăs'tĭk) adj. & s. eclesiástico.

ech·e·lon (ĕsh'ə-lŏn') s. escalón *m*.

ech·o (ĕk'ō) I. s. [pl. es] eco ♦ **e. chamber** cámara de resonancia II. tr. *(to repeat)* repetir; *(to imitate)* imitar —intr. producir eco, resonar.

e·clec·tic (ĭ-klĕk'tĭk) adj. & s. ecléctico.

e·clipse (ĭ-klĭps') I. s. eclipse *m* II. tr. eclipsar.

e·clip·tic (ĭ-klĭp'tĭk) s. eclíptica.

ec·o·log·i·cal (ĕk'ə-lŏj'ĭ-kəl) adj. ecológico.

ec·ol·o·gy (ĭ-kŏl'ə-jē) s. ecología.

ec·o·nom·ic (ĕk'ə-nŏm'ĭk, ē'kə-) adj. económico ♦ **economics** s.sg. economía.

ec·o·nom·i·cal (:ĭ-kəl) adj. económico.

e·con·o·mist (ĭ-kŏn′ə-mĭst) s. economista mf.

e·con·o·mize (:mīz′) intr. economizar (on en).

e·con·o·my (:mē) s. economía f ♦ e. car automóvil económico.

ec·o·sys·tem (ĕk′ə-sĭs′təm) s. ecosistema m.

ce·sta·sy (ĕk′stə sē) s. éxtasis m.

ec·stat·ic (ĕk-stăt′ĭk) adj. extático.

ec·u·men·i·cal (ĕk′yə-mĕn′ĭ-kəl) adj. ecuménico.

ec·ze·ma (ĕk′sə-mə) s. eczema m.

ed·dy (ĕd′ē) I. s. remolino II. intr. arremolinarse, remolinar.

edge (ĕj) I. s. (cutting side) filo, corte m; (border, rim) borde m; (shore, hem) orilla; (boundary) límite m; (angle) arista; (of table, coin) canto; (farthest part) extremidad f; FIG. (sharpness) filo, mordacidad f; FAM. (advantage) ventaja ♦ e. of town afueras • on e. de canto • to be on e. tener los nervios de punta • to be on the e. of estar al borde o al punto de • to set one's teeth o nerves on e. dar dentera, ponerle a uno los pelos de punta • to take the e. off (to blunt) embotar; (the appetite) acallar II. tr. (to sharpen) afilar; (to border) bordear; (to trim) ribetear ♦ to e. out vencer por un margen pequeño —intr. andar o moverse cautelosamente ♦ to e. away, toward retirarse, adelantarse poco a poco.

edge·wise/ways (ĕj′wīz′/wāz′) adv. (on end) de filo o de canto; (sideways) sesgadamente ♦ I couldn't get a word in e. no podía meter baza.

edg·y (ĕj′ē) adj. -i- nervioso, tenso.

ed·i·ble (ĕd′ə-bəl) adj. & s. comestible m.

e·dict (ē′dĭkt′) s. edicto.

ed·i·fi·ca·tion (ĕd′ə-fĭ-kā′shən) s. edificación f.

ed·i·fice (ĕd′ə-fĭs) s. edificio.

ed·i·fy (:fī′) tr. edificar.

ed·it (ĕd′ĭt) tr. (to draft) redactar; (to correct) corregir, editar; (edition, text) preparar; (a publication) dirigir; CINEM. montar ♦ to e. out quitar, suprimir.

ed·it·ing (ĕd′ĭ-tĭng) s. (of text) redacción f; (correction) corrección f, revisión f; (of a publication) dirección f; (of film) montaje m.

e·di·tion (ĭ-dĭsh′ən) s. edición f; (number of copies) tiraje m, tirada; FIG. versión f.

ed·i·tor (ĕd′ĭ-tər) s. editor m; (supervisor) redactor jefe m; CINEM. montador m ♦ e. in chief jefe de redacción, redactor en jefe.

ed·i·to·ri·al (:tôr′ē-əl) adj. & s. editorial m ♦ e. staff redacción.

ed·i·tor·ship (′tər-shĭp′) s. dirección f, redacción f.

ed·u·cate (ĕj′ə-kāt′) tr. educar.

ed·u·cat·ed (:kā′tĭd) adj. (cultured) culto; (schooled) educado.

ed·u·ca·tion (′-′shən) s. educación f.

ed·u·ca·tion·al (:shə-nəl) adj. (institution, staff) docente; (instructive) educativo.

ed·u·ca·tor (ĕj′ə-kā′tər) s. educador m.

eel (ēl) s. [pl. inv. o s] anguila.

ee·rie/ry (îr′ē) adj. -i- (creepy) espeluznante; (mysterious) sobrenatural, misterioso.

ef·face (ĭ-fās′) tr. borrar ♦ to e. oneself comportarse sin llamar la atención.

ef·fect (ĭ-fĕkt′) I. s. efecto; (result) resultado ♦ for e. para impresionar • in e. (in fact) efectivamente; (virtually) casi, prácticamente; (in operation) en vigor, vigente • to be in e. estar vigente • to go into e. entrar en vigor • to have no e. no dar resultado • to no e. inútilmente,

sin resultado • to take e. (medication) surtir efecto; (laws, schedule) entrar en vigor ♦ pl. bienes, pertenencias II. tr. efectuar, realizar.

ef·fec·tive (ĭ-fĕk′tĭv) adj. efectivo; (striking) impresionante; (operative) vigente.

ef·fec·tive·ness (:nĭs) s. eficacia.

ef·fec·tu·al (ĭ-fĕk′chŏŏ-əl) adj. eficaz.

ef·fem·i·na·cy (ĭ-fĕm′ə-nə-sē) s. afeminación f.

ef·fem·i·nate (:nĭt) adj. afeminado.

ef·fer·ves·cent (ĕf′ər-vĕs′ənt) adj. efervescente.

ef·fete (ĭ-fēt′) adj. (worn out) gastado; (decadent) decadente.

ef·fi·ca·cy (ĕf′ĭ-kə-sē) s. eficacia.

ef·fi·cien·cy (ĭ-fĭsh′ən-sē) s. eficiencia; FAM. (apartment) apartamento de un cuarto con cocina y baño; MEC. rendimiento.

ef·fi·cient (ĭ-fĭsh′ənt) adj. eficaz, eficiente; MEC. de buen o gran rendimiento.

ef·fi·gy (ĕf′ə-jē) s. efigie f.

ef·flu·ent (ĕf′lōō-ənt) I. adj. efluente II. s. chorro.

ef·fort (ĕf′ərt) s. esfuerzo; (achievement) obra ♦ to spare no e. hacer todo lo posible.

ef·fort·less (:lĭs) adj. fácil, sin esfuerzo.

ef·fron·ter·y (ĭ-frŭn′tə-rē) s. descaro.

ef·fu·sion (ĭ-fyōō′zhən) s. efusión f.

ef·fu·sive (:sĭv) adj. efusivo.

e·gal·i·tar·i·an (ĭ-găl′ĭ-târ′ē-ən) adj. & s. igualitario.

egg (ĕg) I. s. huevo; BIOL. óvulo; JER. (fellow) tío, tipo ♦ bad e. JER. calavera • good e. JER. buen tipo • to put all one's eggs in one basket jugárselo todo en una carta • to walk o tread on eggs andar con extremo cuidado • with e. on one's face pasando vergüenza II. tr. ♦ to e. on incitar.

egg·beat·er (ĕg′bē′tər) s. batidor m de huevos.

egg·head (ĕg′hĕd′) s. JER. intelectual mf.

egg·nog (ĕg′nŏg′) s. ronpopo.

egg·plant (ĕg′plănt′) s. berenjena.

egg·shell (ĕg′shĕl′) s. cascarón m.

e·go (ē′gō) s. yo, ego, (egoism) egoísmo.

e·go·ist (:ĭst) s. egoísta mf.

e·go·is·tic/ti·cal (′-ĭs′tĭk) adj. egoísta.

e·go·ma·ni·a (:mā′nē-ə) s. preocupación obsesiva con el ego.

e·go·tist (ē′gə-tĭst) s. egotista mf.

e·go·tis·tic/ti·cal (′-tĭs′tĭk) adj. egotista.

e·gre·gious (ĭ-grē′jəs) adj. atroz, flagrante.

e·gress (ē′grĕs′) s. salida.

e·gret (ē′grĭt) s. airón m.

ei·der·down (ī′dər-doun′) s. edredón m.

eight (āt) s. & adj. ocho ♦ e. hundred ochocientos • e. o'clock las ocho.

eight·een (ā-tēn′) s. & adj. dieciocho.

eight·eenth (ā-tēnth′) I. s. dieciocho; (part) dieciochava parte II. adj. (place) décimoctavo; (part) dieciochavo.

eighth (ātth) s. & adj. octavo.

eight·i·eth (ā′tē-ĭth) I. s. ochenta; (part) octogésima parte II. adj. octogésimo.

eight·y (ā′tē) s. & adj. ochenta m.

ei·ther (ē′thər, ī′-) I. pron. & adj. uno u otro, cualquiera de los dos; (negative) ni uno ni otro, ninguno de los dos II. conj. o...o ♦ <e. we go now, or we stay o nos vamos ahora o nos quedamos> III. adv. tampoco.

e·jac·u·late (ĭ-jăk′yə-lāt′) tr. & intr. FISIOL. eyacular; (to exclaim) exclamar.

e·jac·u·la·tion (′-lā′shən) s. eyaculación f; (exclamation) exclamación f; (prayer) jaculatoria.

e·ject (ĭ-jĕkt′) tr. expeler, expulsar —intr.

AVIA. eyectar.

e·jec·tion (ĭ-jĕk'shən) s. expulsión *f*; AER. eyección *f* ♦ **e. seat** asiento eyectable *o* lanzable.

eke (ēk) tr. ♦ **to e. out** suplir para que sea apenas suficiente • **to e. out a living** ganarse la vida a duras penas.

e·lab·o·rate (ĭ-lăb'ər-ĭt) I. adj. *(detailed)* esmerado; *(intricate)* complicado II. tr. (:ə-rāt') elaborar, desarrollar —intr. explicarse ♦ **to e. on** explayarse.

e·lab·o·ra·tion (:ə-rā'shən) s. elaboración *f*; *(explanation)* explicación *f*.

e·lapse (ĭ-lăps') intr. transcurrir, pasar.

e·las·tic (ĭ-lăs'tĭk) adj. elástico.

e·las·tic·i·ty (ĭ-lă-stĭs'ĭ-tē) s. elasticidad *f*.

e·late (ĭ-lāt') tr. regocijar, alborozar.

e·lat·ed (ĭ-lā'tĭd) adj. contento, alborozado.

e·la·tion (:shən) s. regocijo, alegría.

el·bow (ĕl'bō') I. s. codo ♦ **e. grease** FAM. energía física II. tr. dar un codazo ♦ **to e. one's way** abrirse paso a codazos.

el·bow·room (:rōōm') s. espacio suficiente.

eld·er (ĕl'dər) I. adj. mayor ♦ **to be (two) years (his) e.** ser (dos) años mayor que (él) II. s. *(old person)* mayor *m*; *(leader)* anciano.

eld·er·ly (:lē) adj. mayor (de edad).

eld·est (ĕl'dĭst) adj. mayor.

e·lect (ĭ-lĕkt') I. tr. & intr. elegir II. adj. electo ♦ **the e.** los elegidos.

e·lec·tion (ĭ-lĕk'shən) s. *(choice)* elección *f*; POL. elecciones *f*.

e·lec·tion·eer (-'shə-nîr') intr. hacer campaña electoral.

e·lec·tive (-'tĭv) I. adj. electivo II. s. curso electivo.

e·lec·tor·al (ĭ-lĕk'tər-əl) adj. electoral.

e·lec·tor·ate (:ĭt) s. electorado.

e·lec·tric/tri·cal (ĭ-lĕk'trĭk) adj. eléctrico; *(thrilling)* emocionante.

e·lec·tri·cian (--trĭsh'ən) s. electricista *mf*.

e·lec·tric·i·ty (:trĭs'ĭ-tē) s. electricidad *f*.

e·lec·tri·fy (ĭ-lĕk'trə-fī') tr. electrizar; *(a building, town)* electrificar.

e·lec·tro·car·di·o·gram (-'trō-kär'dē-ə-grăm') s. electrocardiograma *m*.

e·lec·tro·cute (-'trə-kyōōt') tr. electrocutar.

e·lec·trode (ĭ-lĕk'trōd') s. electrodo.

e·lec·tro·dy·nam·ics (-'trō-dī-năm'ĭks) s.sg. electrodinámica.

e·lec·trol·y·sis (--trŏl'ĭ-sĭs) s. electrólisis *f*.

e·lec·tro·lyte (-'trə-līt') s. electrólito.

e·lec·tro·mag·net (-'trō-măg'nĭt) s. electroimán *m*.

e·lec·tro·mag·net·ic (:măg-nĕt'ĭk) adj. electromagnético.

e·lec·tro·mo·tive (:mō'tĭv) s. electromotriz.

e·lec·tron (ĭ-lĕk'trŏn') s. electrón *m*.

e·lec·tron·ic (--trŏn'ĭk) adj. electrónico ♦ **electronics** s.sg. electrónica.

e·lec·tro·plate (-'trə-plāt') tr. galvanizar.

e·lec·tro·shock (-'trə-shŏk') s. electrochoque *m*.

e·lec·tro·stat·ic (:stăt'ĭk) adj. electrostático.

e·lec·tro·type (ĭ-lĕk'trə-tīp') s. electrotipo.

el·e·gance (ĕl'ĭ-gəns) s. elegancia.

el·e·gant (:gənt) adj. elegante.

el·e·gi·ac (ĕl'ə-jī'ək) adj. elegíaco.

el·e·gy (ĕl'ə-jē) s. elegía.

el·e·ment (ĕl'ə-mənt) s. elemento ♦ **an e. of** algo de ♦ pl. *(weather)* los elementos; RELIG. especies eucarísticas.

el·e·men·tal ('-mĕn'tl) adj. elemental.

el·e·men·ta·ry (:tə-rē) adj. elemental ♦ **e. school** escuela primaria.

el·e·phant (ĕl'ə-fənt) s. elefante *m*.

el·e·phan·tine ('-făn'tēn') adj. enorme; *(clumsy)* torpe.

el·e·vate (ĕl'ə-vāt') tr. elevar; *(to promote)* ascender (to a).

el·e·vat·ed (:vā'tĭd) I. adj. elevado II. s. FAM. ferrocarril elevado.

el·e·va·tion ('-shən) s. elevación *f*; GEOG. altitud *f*.

el·e·va·tor ('-'tər) s. ascensor *m*; AGR. elevador *m*; AVIA. timón *m* de profundidad.

el·ev·en (ĭ-lĕv'ən) s. & adj. once *m* ♦ **e. o'clock** las once.

el·ev·enth (:ənth) s. & adj. undécimo; *(part)* onzavo.

elf (ĕlf) s. [pl. **-ves**] duende *m*.

e·lic·it (ĭ-lĭs'ĭt) tr. sonsacar, sacar.

el·i·gi·ble (ĕl'ĭ-jə-bəl) adj. elegible.

e·lim·i·nate (ĭ-lĭm'ə-nāt') tr. eliminar.

e·lim·i·na·tion (-'nā'shən) s. eliminación *f*.

e·lite *o* **é·lite** (ĭ-lēt', ā-lēt') s. élite *f*.

e·lit·ist (ĭ-lē'tĭst, ā-lē'-) adj. elitista.

elk (ĕlk) s. [pl. inv. *o* **s**] alce *m*.

e·lipse (ĭ-lĭps') s. elipse *f*.

el·lip·sis (ĭ-lĭp'sĭs) s. [pl. **-ses**] elipsis *f*.

el·lip·tic/ti·cal (:tĭk) adj. elíptico.

elm (ĕlm) s. olmo.

el·o·cu·tion (ĕl'ə-kyōō'shən) s. elocución *f*.

e·lon·ga·tion (ĭ-lông'gā'shən) s. extensión *f*, alargamiento.

e·lope (ĭ-lōp') intr. fugarse (con un amante).

e·lope·ment (:mənt) s. fuga.

el·o·quence (ĕl'ə-kwəns) s. elocuencia.

el·o·quent (:kwənt) adj. elocuente.

else (ĕls) adj. & adv. ♦ **all** *o* **everything e.** todo lo demás • **anybody** *o* **anyone e.** cualquier otro, cualquier otra persona; *(negative)* ningún otro, nadie más • **anything e.** cualquier otra cosa, algo más; *(negative)* ninguna otra cosa, nada más • **anywhere e.** *(place)* en cualquier otra parte; *(direction)* a cualquier otra parte; *(negative) (place)* a ningún otro lugar; *(in existence)* en ningún otro lugar • **everyone e.** todos los demás • **everywhere e.** en *o* a todas partes • **how e.?** ¿de qué otro modo? • **much e.** mucho, muchas cosas • **nobody** *o* **no one e.** nadie más, ningún otro • **nothing e.** nada más • **nowhere e.** en *o* a ninguna otra parte • **or e.** si no • **somebody** *o* **someone e.** otro, otra persona • **something e.** otra cosa; *(something additional)* algo más • **somewhere e.** en *o* a otra parte • **what e.** ¿qué más? • **where e.?** ¿en *o* a qué otro sitio? • **who e?** ¿quién más?

else·where ('hwâr') adv. a *o* en otra parte.

e·lu·ci·date (ĭ-lōō'sĭ-dāt') tr. elucidar.

e·lude (ĭ-lōōd') tr. eludir, esquivar; *(to escape understanding)* escapársele a uno.

e·lu·sive (ĭ-lōō'sĭv) adj. evasivo; *(hard to describe)* difícil de describir.

e·ma·ci·at·ed (ĭ-mā'shē-ā'tĭd) adj. demacrado.

em·a·nate (ĕm'ə-nāt') intr. proceder, emanar *(from de)*.

e·man·ci·pate (ĭ-măn'sə-pāt') tr. emancipar ♦ **to become emancipated** emanciparse.

e·man·ci·pa·tor (:pā'tər) s. emancipador *m*.

e·mas·cu·late (ĭ-măs'kyə-lāt') tr. emascular; FIG. debilitar, disminuir.

em·balm (ĕm-bäm') tr. *(a corpse)* embalsamar.

em·bank·ment (ĕm-băngk'mənt) s. terraplén *m*.

em·bar·go (ĕm·bär′gō) **I.** s. [pl. **es**] embargo **II.** tr. embargar.

em·bark (ĕm·bärk′) tr. & intr. embarcar(se) ♦ **to e. on** lanzarse a.

em·bar·ka·tion (ĕm′bär·kā′shən) s. *(of people)* embarco; *(of goods)* embarque *m.*

em·bar·rass (ĕm·băr′əs) tr. *(to disconcert)* desconcertar, turbar; *(to shame)* avergonzar; *(to cause trouble for)* poner en aprieto ♦ **to be o feel embarrassed** sentirse confuso o avergonzado.

em·bar·rass·ing (:ĭng) adj. *(disconcerting)* desconcertante; *(situation)* violento.

em·bar·rass·ment (:mənt) s. *(shame)* vergüenza, turbación *f; (trouble)* embarazo; *(confusion)* desconcierto.

em·bas·sy (ĕm′bə·sē) s. embajada.

em·bat·tled (ĕm·băt′ld) adj. asediado.

em·bed (ĕm·bĕd′) tr. & intr. **-dd-** implantar(se), incrustar(se); FIG. fijar(se).

em·bel·lish (ĕm·bĕl′ĭsh) tr. embellecer; *(a story)* añadir detalles a.

em·ber (ĕm′bər) s. ascua, brasa.

em·bez·zle (ĕm·bĕz′əl) tr. malversar, desfalcar.

em·bez·zle·ment (:mənt) s. malversación *f,* desfalco *f.*

em·bez·zler (ĕm·bĕz′lər) s. malversador *m,* desfalcador *m.*

em·bit·ter (ĕm·bĭt′ər) tr. amargar, agriar.

em·blem (ĕm′bləm) s. emblema *m.*

em·blem·at·ic (ĕm′blə·măt′ĭk) adj. simbólico.

em·bod·i·ment (ĕm·bŏd′ē·mənt) s. personificación *f.*

em·bod·y (ĕm·bŏd′ē) tr. encarnar, personificar; *(to include)* incorporar.

em·bold·en (ĕm·bōl′dən) tr. alentar.

em·bo·lism (ĕm′bə·lĭz′əm) s. embolia.

em·boss (ĕm·bôs′) tr. grabar en relieve; *(leather, silver)* repujar.

em·brace (ĕm·brās′) **I.** tr. abrazar; *(to accept eagerly)* aprovecharse de —intr. abrazarse **II.** s. abrazo; *(acceptance)* adopción *f.*

em·broi·der (ĕm·broi′dər) tr. bordar; *(a story)* exagerar —intr. hacer bordado.

em·broi·der·y (:də·rē) s. bordado.

em·broil (ĕm·broil′) tr. embrollar, enredar.

em·bry·o (ĕm′brē·ō′) s. embrión *m.*

em·bry·ol·o·gy (′·ŏl′ə·jē) s. embriología.

em·bry·on·ic (:ŏn′ĭk) adj. embrionario.

em·cee (ĕm′sē′) s. & intr. FAM. (actuar de) maestro de ceremonias.

e·mend (ĭ·mĕnd′) tr. enmendar, corregir.

e·men·da·tion (ē′mĕn·dā′shən) s. enmienda.

em·er·ald (ĕm′ər·əld) s. esmeralda.

e·merge (ĭ·mûrj′) intr. emerger, surgir; *(to become known)* darse a entender.

e·mer·gen·cy (ĭ·mûr′jən·sē) s. emergencia; MED. caso de urgencia; *(need)* necesidad *f* urgente ♦ **e. landing** aterrizaje forzoso.

e·mer·gent (:jənt) adj. emergente.

em·er·y (ĕm′ə·rē) s. esmeril *m* ♦ **e. board** lima de uñas.

e·met·ic (ĭ·mĕt′ĭk) adj. & s. emético, vomitivo.

em·i·grant (ĕm′ĭ·grənt) s. & adj. emigrante *m.*

em·i·grate (:grāt′) intr. emigrar.

em·i·nence (ĕm′ə·nəns) s. eminencia.

em·i·nent (:nənt) adj. eminente.

em·is·sar·y (ĕm′ĭ·sĕr′ē) s. emisario.

e·mis·sion (ĭ·mĭsh′ən) s. emisión *f.*

e·mit (ĭ·mĭt′) tr. **-tt-** emitir.

e·mol·lient (ĭ·mŏl′yənt) adj. & s. emoliente *f.*

e·mo·tion (ĭ·mō′shən) s. emoción *f.*

e·mo·tion·al (:shə·nəl) adj. emocional; *(scene, person)* emotivo.

em·pa·thize (ĕm′pə·thīz′) intr. identificarse.

em·pa·thy (:thē) s. identificación *f.*

em·per·or (ĕm′pər·ər) s. emperador *m.*

em·pha·sis (ĕm′fə·sĭs) s. [pl. **-ses**] énfasis *m;* GRAM. *(stress)* acento.

em·pha·size (:sīz′) tr. enfatizar, hacer hincapié en; GRAM. acentuar.

em·phat·ic (ĕm·făt′ĭk) adj. enfático; *(vigorous)* enérgico; GRAM. acentuado.

em·phy·se·ma (ĕm′fĭ·sē′mə) s. enfisema *m.*

em·pire (ĕm′pīr′) s. imperio.

em·pir·ic·i·cal (ĕm·pĭr′ĭk) adj. empírico.

em·pir·i·cism (:ĭ·sĭz′əm) s. empirismo.

em·ploy (ĕm·ploi′) **I.** tr. emplear ♦ **to be employed** tener empleo **II.** s. empleo ♦ **in the e.** of empleado por.

em·ploy·ee (:ē′) s. empleado.

em·ploy·er (:ər) s. empleador *m.*

em·ploy·ment (:mənt) s. empleo.

em·po·ri·um (ĕm·pôr′ē·əm) s. [pl. **s** o **-ria**] emporio.

em·pow·er (ĕm·pou′ər) tr. autorizar.

em·press (ĕm′prĭs) s. emperatriz *f.*

emp·ti·ness (ĕmp′tē·nĭs) s. vacío; *(of a person, words)* vacuidad *f.*

emp·ty (ĕmp′tē) **I.** adj. **-i-** vacío; *(unpopulated)* desierto; *(vain)* vano, hueco; *(idle)* ocioso; *(devoid)* falto **II.** tr. vaciar; *(to vacate)* dejar vacío, desalojar; *(to unload)* descargar —intr. vaciarse ♦ **to e. into** desembocar en **III.** s. envase vacío.

emp·ty-hand·ed (′-hăn′dĭd) adj. manivacío.

emp·ty-head·ed (:hĕd′ĭd) adj. frívolo.

em·py·re·an (ĕm′pī·rē′ən) s. & adj. empíreo.

em·u·late (ĕm′yə·lāt′) tr. emular.

em·u·la·tor (:lā′tər) s. emulador *m.*

e·mul·si·fy (ĭ·mŭl′sə·fī′) tr. emulsionar.

e·mul·sion (:shən) s. emulsión *f.*

en·a·ble (ĕn·ā′bəl) tr. *(to make able)* capacitar; *(to make possible)* posibilitar; DER. autorizar.

en·act (ĕn·ăkt′) tr. promulgar; TEAT. representar.

en·act·ment (:mənt) s. promulgación *f;* TEAT. representación *f.*

e·nam·el (ĭ·năm′əl) **I.** s. esmalte *m* **II.** tr. esmaltar.

e·nam·el·ware (:wâr′) s. utensilios de hierro esmaltado.

en·am·or (ĭ·năm′ər) tr. enamorar ♦ **to become enamored of** enamorarse de.

en·camp·ment (ĕn·kămp′mənt) s. campamento.

en·cap·su·late (ĕn·kăp′sə·lāt′) tr. encerrar en una cápsula.

en·case (ĕn·kās′) tr. encerrar, encajonar.

en·ceph·a·li·tis (ĕn·sĕf′ə·lī′tĭs) s. encefalitis *f.*

en·chant (ĕn·chănt′) tr. encantar.

en·chant·ing (ĕn·chănt′tĭng) adj. encantador.

en·chant·ment (:mənt) s. *(bewitchment)* encantamiento; *(charm)* encanto.

en·cir·cle (ĕn·sûr′kəl) tr. rodear, circundar.

en·close (ĕn·klōz′) tr. encerrar; *(a document)* adjuntar; *(to fence in)* cercar ♦ **enclosed herewith** encontrará adjunto.

en·clo·sure (ĕn·klō′zhər) s. encierro; *(land)* cercado; *(document)* adjunto, documento; *(fence)* cerco, valla.

en·code (ĕn·kōd′) tr. codificar.

en·com·pass (ĕn·kŭm′pəs) tr. *(to surround)* rodear; *(to include)* abarcar.

en·core (ŏn´kôr´) I. s. repetición f, bis m II. interj. ¡otra!, ¡bis!

en·coun·ter (ĕn-koun´tər) I. s. encuentro; *(clash)* choque m II. tr. encontrar; MIL. enfrentarse con.

en·cour·age (ĕn-kûr´ĭj) tr. animar, alentar; *(to embolden)* fortalecer; *(to foster)* fomentar.

en·cour·age·ment (:mənt) s. ánimo, aliento; *(incentive)* incentivo.

en·cour·ag·ing (ĕn-kûr´ə-jĭng) adj. alentador.

en·croach (ĕn-krōch´) intr. ♦ **to e. on** meterse en, invadir.

en·crust (ĕn-krŭst´) tr. incrustar.

en·crypt (ĕn-krĭpt´) tr. codificar.

en·cum·ber (ĕn-kŭm´bər) tr. *(to overburden)* sobrecargar; *(to impede)* impedir.

en·cum·brance (:brəns) s. obstáculo, impedimento; DER. gravamen m.

en·cy·clo·p(a)e·di·a (ĕn-sī´klə-pē´dē-ə) s. enciclopedia.

end (ĕnd) I. s. *(tip)* extremo, punta; *(boundary)* límite m; *(conclusion)* fin m, final m; *(outcome)* desenlace m; *(death)* fin, muerte f; *(goal)* propósito; *(destruction)* destrucción f ♦ **at the e. of** al cabo de ♦ **e. to e.** punta con punta • **for days on end** día tras día • **from e. to e.** de un extremo al otro • **in the e.** al fin, al final • **odds and ends** restos, sobrante • **on e.** *(upright)* de pie, derecho; *(nonstop)* sin parar; *(hair)* de punta • **to bring (come) to an e.** terminar(se), acabar(se) • **to make ends meet** cubrir las necesidades con el dinero que se tiene • **to meet one's e.** encontrar la muerte • **to no e.** en vano, inútilmente • **to put an e. to** poner fin a • **to what end?** ¿con qué finalidad? II. tr. acabar, concluir; *(to destroy)* destruir ♦ **to e. it all** acabar con la vida —intr. terminar(se), acabar(se) ♦ **to e. up** terminar, ir a parar.

en·dan·ger (ĕn-dān´jər) tr. poner en peligro.

en·dear·ing (ĕn-dîr´ĭng) adj. atractivo.

en·dear·ment (:mənt) s. cariño, afecto.

en·deav·or (ĕn-dĕv´ər) I. s. *(effort)* esfuerzo; *(attempt)* intento II. intr. intentar.

en·dem·ic (ĕn-dĕm´ĭk) adj. endémico.

end·ing (ĕn´dĭng) s. conclusión f, fin m; *(of a story)* desenlace m, final m.

en·dive (ĕn´dīv´) s. escarola, endibia.

end·less (ĕnd´lĭs) adj. interminable; *(infinite)* infinito; *(continuous)* continuo.

en·do·crine (ĕn´də-krĭn) adj. endocrino.

en·dorse (ĕn-dôrs´) tr. endosar; *(to support)* apoyar; *(to approve)* sancionar.

en·dors·ee (´-sē´) s. endosatorio, endosado.

en·dorse·ment (ĕn-dôrs´mənt) s. endoso; *(approval)* aprobación f; *(support)* apoyo.

en·dors·er (ĕn-dôr´sər) s. endosante mf.

en·dow (ĕn-dou´) tr. dotar.

en·dow·ment (:mənt) s. dotación f; *(natural gift)* dote m, don m.

en·dur·ance (ĕn-dŏŏr´əns) s. resistencia, aguante m.

en·dure (ĕn-dŏŏr´) tr. resistir, aguantar; *(to tolerate)* tolerar —intr. aguantarse, resistir; *(to last)* durar.

en·dur·ing (:ĭng) adj. perdurable, duradero; *(long-suffering)* sufrido.

end·wise (ĕnd´wīz´/wāz´) adv. *(upright)* de punta, de pie; *(end foremost)* con la punta al frente; *(lengthwise)* longitudinalmente; *(end to end)* extremo con extremo.

en·e·ma (ĕn´ə-mə) s. enema m.

en·e·my (ĕn´ə-mē) s. & adj. enemigo.

en·er·get·ic (ĕn´ər-jĕt´ĭk) adj. enérgico.

en·er·gize (ĕn´ər-jīz´) tr. dar energía a, vigorizar; ELEC. *(to charge)* excitar.

en·er·gy (ĕn´ər-jē) s. energía.

en·er·vate (ĕn´ər-vāt´) tr. enervar.

en·fee·ble (ĕn-fē´bəl) tr. debilitar.

en·fold (ĕn-fōld´) tr. *(to envelop)* envolver; *(to surround)* rodear; *(to embrace)* abrazar.

en·force (ĕn-fôrs´) tr. *(a law)* hacer cumplir o respetar; *(to impose)* imponer.

en·force·a·ble (ĕn-fôr´sə-bəl) adj. *(law)* aplicable; *(contract)* ejecutorio.

en·force·ment (ĕn-fôrs´mənt) s. aplicación f, ejecución f.

en·fran·chise (ĕn-frăn´chīz´) tr. otorgar el derecho al voto; *(to free)* libertar, manumitir.

en·gage (ĕn-gāj´) tr. *(to hire)* emplear; *(to reserve)* contratar, reservar; *(to engross)* cautivar; *(to promise)* comprometer, empeñar; MIL. trabar combate con; MEC. *(gears)* engranar; *(clutch)* embragar —intr. comprometerse, obligarse (a pagar, ayudar); MIL. trabarse en combate ♦ **to e. in** ocuparse o tomar parte en.

en·gaged (ĕn-gājd´) adj. *(employed)* empleado; *(busy)* ocupado; *(reserved)* contratado; *(betrothed)* comprometido; MIL. combatiente; MEC. engranado ♦ **to be e.** *(busy)* estar ocupado; *(betrothed)* estar comprometido • **to get e.** prometerse.

en·gage·ment (ĕn-gāj´mənt) s. compromiso; *(appointment)* cita; MIL. batalla, combate m; MEC. engranaje m.

en·gag·ing (ĕn-gā´jĭng) adj. atractivo.

en·gen·der (ĕn-jĕn´dər) tr. engendrar.

en·gine (ĕn´jĭn) s. máquina, motor m; F.C. locomotora ♦ **e. block** bloque de cilindros.

en·gi·neer (ĕn´jə-nîr´) I. s. ingeniero; F.C. maquinista m; FIG. artífice mf II. tr. maniobrar, maquinar.

en·gi·neer·ing (:ĭng) s. ingeniería.

Eng·lish-speak·ing (ĭng´glĭsh-spē´kĭng) adj. de habla inglesa.

en·gorge (ĕn-gôrj´) tr. devorar, engullir; MED. congestionar.

en·grave (ĕn-grāv´) tr. grabar; *(on stone)* tallar.

en·grav·er (ĕn-grā´vər) s. grabador m.

en·grav·ing (:vĭng) s. grabado.

en·gross (ĕn-grōs´) tr. absorber, cautivar.

en·gross·ing (ĕn-grō´sĭng) adj. absorbente.

en·gulf (ĕn-gŭlf´) tr. *(to surround)* encerrar, rodear; *(to swallow up)* tragarse.

en·hance (ĕn-hăns´) tr. *(to increase)* aumentar; *(to intensify)* dar realce a, realzar.

en·hance·ment (:mənt) s. *(increase)* aumento; *(of flavor, beauty)* realce m.

e·nig·ma (ĭ-nĭg´mə) s. enigma m.

en·ig·mat·ic (ĕn´ĭg-măt´ĭk) adj. enigmático.

en·join (ĕn-join´) tr. *(to command)* mandar; *(to prohibit)* prohibir.

en·join·der (:dər) s. mandato.

en·joy (ĕn-joi´) tr. gozar (de), disfrutar; *(to like)* gustar a ♦ **to e. oneself** divertirse, pasarlo bien.

en·joy·a·ble (:ə-bəl) adj. agradable, encantador; *(fun)* divertido.

en·joy·ment (:mənt) s. placer m, goce m; disfrute m.

en·large (ĕn-lärj´) tr. agrandar, aumentar; *(to magnify)* magnificar; FOTOG. ampliar —intr. agrandarse ♦ **to e. on** explayarse sobre.

en·larg·er (ĕn-lär´jər) s. ampliadora.

en·light·en (ĕn-līt´n) tr. iluminar, ilustrar; *(to*

inform) aclarar.

en·light·ened (:nd) adj. culto, ilustrado; *(spiritually)* iluminado.

en·light·en·ment (:n-mənt) s. iluminación *f,* ilustración *f* ♦ **the E.** la Ilustración.

en·list (ĕn-lĭst') tr. MIL. alistar, *(to engage)* ganar el apoyo de —intr. alistarse ♦ **enlisted man** soldado de tropa.

en·list·ment (:mənt) s. alistamiento.

en·liv·en (ĕn-lī'vən) tr. alegrar, animar.

en·mesh (ĕn-mĕsh') tr. enredar, enmarañar.

en·mi·ty (ĕn'mĭ-tē) s. enemistad *f.*

en·no·ble (ĕn-nō'bəl) tr. ennoblecer.

en·nui (ŏn-wē') s. lasitud *f,* aburrimiento.

e·nor·mi·ty (ĭ-nôr'mĭ-tē) s. enormidad *f.*

e·nor·mous (:məs) adj. enorme.

e·nough (ĭ-nŭf') I. adj. bastante, suficiente ♦ **to be e.** ser suficiente, bastar II. adv. bastante, suficientemente ♦ **curiously** o **oddly e.** por raro que parezca • **sure e.** en efecto • **well e.** bastante bien III. s. lo bastante, lo suficiente ♦ **e. is e.** basta y sobra • **it is e. to drive you mad** es para volverse loco • **to have had e.** *(to be satisfied)* estar satisfecho; *(to be tired of)* estar harto IV. interj. ¡basta! ♦ **e. of this!** ¡basta ya!

en·rage (ĕn-rāj') tr. enfurecer, encolerizar.

en·rap·ture (ĕn-răp'chər) tr. embelesar.

en·rich (ĕn-rĭch') tr. enriquecer; *(to fertilize)* abonar.

en·rol(l) (ĕn-rōl') tr. & intr. -ll- registrar(se), inscribir(se); *(a student)* matricular(se).

en·rol(l)·ment (:mənt) s. inscripción *f;* *(in school)* matriculación *f;* *(record)* registro.

en·sconce (ĕn-skŏns') tr. ♦ **to e. oneself** establecerse cómodamente.

en·sem·ble (ŏn-sŏm'bəl) s. conjunto; TEAT. compañía.

en·shrine (ĕn-shrīn') tr. guardar en un relicario; FIG. conservar religiosamente.

en·sign (ĕn'sən) s. *(flag)* pabellón *m;* *(officer)* alférez *m.*

en·slave (ĕn-slāv') tr. esclavizar.

en·snare (ĕn-snâr') tr. entrampar.

en·sue (ĕn-sōō') intr. seguir(se), resultar.

en·su·ing (:ĭng) adj. resultante.

en·sure (ĕn-shŏŏr') tr. asegurar, garantizar.

en·tail (ĕn-tāl') tr. implicar, comportar; DER. vincular.

en·tan·gle (ĕn-tăng'gəl) tr. enmarañar, enredar.

en·tente (ŏn-tŏnt') s. *(agreement)* acuerdo, convenio; *(signatories)* aliados.

en·ter (ĕn'tər) tr. entrar en; *(to penetrate)* penetrar en, perforar; *(to insert)* introducir, insertar; *(to participate in)* participar en; *(to embark upon)* emprender, empezar; *(to join)* afiliarse a; *(to obtain admission to)* ingresar, entrar a; *(a profession)* iniciar, abrazar; *(in a register)* asentar, anotar; DER. entablar, presentar ♦ **to e. one's head** o **mind** ocurrírsele a uno —intr. entrar; *(to gain entry)* ingresar; *(to register)* inscribirse, matricularse; TEAT. salir ♦ **not to e. into** it no figurar para nada • **to e. into** *(a contract)* celebrar, concertar; *(to begin)* iniciar.

en·ter·prise (ĕn'tər-prīz') s. empresa; *(initiative)* iniciativa.

en·ter·pris·ing (:prī'zĭng) adj. emprendedor *m.*

en·ter·tain (ĕn'tər-tān') tr. divertir, entretener; *(to host)* agasajar; *(an idea)* considerar ♦ **to e. oneself** divertirse —intr. recibir invitados.

en·ter·tain·er (:tā'nər) s. artista *mf.*

en·ter·tain·ing (:nĭng) adj. entretenido, diver-

tido.

en·ter·tain·ment (ĕn'tər-tān'mənt) s. entretenimiento, diversion *f;* *(show)* espectáculo.

en·thrall (ĕn-thrôl') tr. cautivar; *(to enslave)* esclavizar.

en·throne (ĕn-thrōn') tr. entronizar.

en·thuse (ĕn-thōōz') tr. & intr. FAM. entusiasmar(se).

en·thu·si·asm (ĕn-thōō'zē-ăz'əm) s. entusiasmo.

en·thu·si·ast (:ăst') s. entusiasta *mf.*

en·thu·si·as·tic (-'-ăs'tĭk) adj. entusiástico.

en·tice (ĕn-tīs') tr. atraer, tentar.

en·tire (ĕn-tīr') adj. entero, total; *(in one piece)* intacto.

en·tire·ly (:lē) s. totalidad *f.*

en·ti·tle (ĕn-tīt'l) tr. titular; *(to give a right)* dar derecho a ♦ **to be entitled to** tener derecho a.

en·ti·tle·ment (:mənt) s. derecho.

en·ti·ty (ĕn'tĭ-tē) s. ser *m;* *(thing)* ente *m.*

en·tomb (ĕn-tōōm') tr. sepultar, enterrar.

en·to·mol·o·gy (ĕn'tə-mŏl'ə-jē) s. entomología.

en·tou·rage (ŏn'tŏŏ-räzh') s. séquito.

en·trails (ĕn'trālz') s.pl. entrañas, vísceras.

en·train (ĕn-trān') intr. subir al tren.

en·trance¹ (ĕn'trəns) s. entrada; TEAT. salida (a escena).

en·trance² (ĕn-trăns') tr. encantar.

en·trant (ĕn'trənt) s. concursante *mf.*

en·trap (ĕn-trăp') tr. -pp- entrampar.

en·treat (ĕn-trēt') tr. implorar, suplicar.

en·treat·y (ĕn-trē'tē) s. pedido, súplica.

en·trée/tree (ŏn'trā') s. *(admittance)* entrada; *(main dish)* plato principal.

en·trench (ĕn-trĕnch') tr. atrincherar ♦ **to e. oneself** atrincherarse.

en·tre·pre·neur (ŏn'trə-prə-nûr') s. empresario.

en·trust (ĕn-trŭst') tr. confiar ♦ **to e. with** encargar, encomendar.

en·try (ĕn'trē) s. entrada; *(in a register)* registro, DEF. *(entrant)* competidor *m;* TEN. ariento.

en·twine (ĕn-twīn') tr. & intr. entrelazar(se).

e·nu·mer·ate (ĭ-nōō'mə-rāt') tr. enumerar.

e·nun·ci·ate (ĭ-nŭn'sē-āt') tr. enunciar; *(to proclaim)* proclamar.

en·vel·op (ĕn-vĕl'əp) tr. envolver.

en·ve·lope (ĕn'və-lōp', ŏn'-) s. sobre *m;* *(wrapping)* envoltura; *(cover)* cobertura.

en·vi·a·ble (ĕn'vē-ə-bəl) adj. envidiable.

en·vi·ous (ĕn'vē-əs) adj. envidioso.

en·vi·ron·ment (ĕn-vī'rən-mənt) s. medio ambiente; *(atmosphere)* ambiente *m.*

en·vi·rons (:rənz) s.pl. alrededores *m.*

en·vis·age (ĕn-vĭz'ĭj) tr. concebir; *(to imagine)* imaginarse, concebir.

en·voy (ĕn'voi', ŏn'-) s. mensajero; POL. representante diplomático.

en·vy (ĕn'vē) I. s. envidia; *(object)* cosa o persona envidiada II. tr. envidiar, tener envidia de —intr. sentir envidia.

en·zyme (ĕn'zīm') s. enzima.

e·on (ē'ŏn') s. eón *m.*

ep·au·let(te) (ĕp'ə-lĕt') s. charretera.

e·phem·er·al (ĭ-fĕm'ər-əl) adj. efímero.

ep·ic (ĕp'ĭk) I. s. epopeya II. adj. épico.

ep·i·cen·ter (ĕp'ĭ-sĕn'tər) s. epicentro.

ep·i·cure (ĕp'ĭ-kyŏŏr') s. gastrónomo.

ep·i·dem·ic (ĕp'ĭ-dĕm'ĭk) I. adj. epidémico II. s. MED. epidemia; FIG. ola.

ep·i·der·mis (ĕp'ĭ-dûr'mĭs) s. epidermis *f.*

ep·i·gram (ĕp'ĭ-grăm') s. epigrama *m.*

ep·i·graph (ĕp′ĭ-grăf′) s. epígrafe *m*.

ep·i·lep·sy (ĕp′ə-lĕp′sē) s. epilepsia.

ep·i·log(ue) (ĕp′ə-lôg′) s. epílogo.

e·piph·a·ny (ĭ-pĭf′ə-nē) s. revelación *f*.

e·pis·co·pal (ĭ-pĭs′kə-pəl) adj. episcopal.

ep·i·sode (ĕp′ĭ-sōd′) s. episodio.

e·pis·te·mol·o·gy (ĭ-pĭs′tə-mŏl′ə-jē) s. epistemología.

e·pis·tle (ĭ-pĭs′əl) s. epístola.

e·pis·to·lar·y (ĭ-pĭs′tə-lĕr′ē) adj. epistolar.

ep·i·taph (ĕp′ĭ-tăf′) s. epitafio.

ep·i·thet (ĕp′ə-thĕt′) s. epíteto; *(insult)* insulto.

e·pit·o·me (ĭ-pĭt′ə-mē) s. epítome *m*; *(embodiment)* personificación *f*.

e·pit·o·mize (:mīz′) tr. *(to sum up)* resumir; *(to embody)* personificar.

ep·och (ĕp′ək) s. época; *(milestone)* hito.

ep·ox·y (ĭ-pŏk′sē) s. resina epoxídica.

eq·ua·ble (ĕk′wə-bəl) adj. *(unvarying)* invariable; *(even-tempered)* calmo, tranquilo.

e·qual (ē′kwəl) **I.** adj. igual; *(evenhanded)* equitativo ♦ **all things being e.** si todo sigue igual • **on e. terms** en un plano de igualdad • **to be e. to** *(same as)* ser igual que; *(capable)* ser apto para **II.** s. igual *mf* ♦ **between equals** de igual a igual • **e. sign** signo de igualdad • **without e.** sin par **III.** tr. igualar a; *(to match)* igualar.

e·qual·i·ty (ĭ-kwŏl′ĭ-tē) s. igualdad *f*.

e·qual·ize (ē′kwə-līz′) tr. & intr. igualar.

e·qual·ly (:lē) adv. igualmente, por igual.

e·qua·nim·i·ty (ē′kwə-nĭm′ĭ-tē, ĕk′wə-) s. ecuanimidad *f*.

e·quate (ĭ-kwāt′) tr. igualar; MAT. poner en ecuación —intr. ser iguales.

e·qua·tion (ĭ-kwā′zhən) s. ecuación *f*.

e·qua·tor (ĭ-kwā′tər) s. ecuador *m*.

e·ques·tri·an (ĭ-kwĕs′trē-ən) **I.** adj. ecuestre **II.** s. jinete *mf*.

e·qui·lat·er·al (ē′kwə-lăt′ər-əl) adj. equilátero.

e·qui·lib·ri·um (:lĭb′rē-əm) s. [pl. **s** *o* **-ia**] equilibrio.

e·qui·nox (:nŏks′) s. equinoccio.

e·quip (ĭ-kwĭp′) tr. **-pp-** equipar; FIG. preparar.

e·quip·ment (:mənt) s. equipo; *(tools)* avíos; FIG. aptitud *f*; AUTO. accesorios.

eq·ui·ta·ble (ĕk′wĭ-tə-bəl) adj. equitativo.

eq·ui·ty (ĕk′wĭ-tē) s. equidad *f*, imparcialidad *f*; FIN. valor líquido.

e·quiv·a·lence/len·cy (ĭ-kwĭv′ə-ləns) s. equivalencia.

e·quiv·a·lent (:lənt) adj. & s. equivalente *m*.

e·quiv·o·cal (ĭ-kwĭv′ə-kəl) adj. equívoco.

e·quiv·o·cate (:kāt′) intr. usar intencionalmente lenguaje equívoco *o* ambiguo.

e·ra (ĭr′ə, ĕr′ə) s. era.

e·rad·i·cate (ĭ-răd′ĭ-kāt′) tr. erradicar.

e·rase (ĭ-rās′) tr. borrar.

e·ras·er (ĭ-rā′sər) s. goma de borrar, borrador *m*.

e·ra·sure (:shər) s. borradura.

e·rect (ĭ-rĕkt′) **I.** adj. erecto, erguido; *(hair)* erizado **II.** tr. *(to construct)* erigir, construir; *(to raise, establish)* levantar.

e·rec·tion (ĭ-rĕk′shən) s. erección *f*; *(of a building)* construcción *f*.

erg (ûrg) s. ergio.

er·go (ûr′gō, ĕr′gō) conj. & adv. por (lo) tanto.

er·go·nom·ics (ûr′gə-nŏm′ĭks) s.sg. ergonomía.

er·mine (ûr′mĭn) s. armiño.

e·rode (ĭ-rōd′) tr. & intr. erosionar(se), desgas-

tar(se); *(to corrode)* corroer(se).

e·rog·e·nous (ĭ-rŏj′ə-nəs) adj. erógeno.

e·ro·sion (ĭ-rō′zhən) s. erosión *f*.

e·rot·ic (ĭ-rŏt′ĭk) adj. erótico.

e·rot·i·cism (:ĭ-sĭz′əm) s. erotismo.

err (ûr, ĕr) intr. errar, equivocarse; *(to sin)* pecar.

er·rand (ĕr′ənd) s. mandado, recado.

er·rant (ĕr′ənt) adj. errante, errabundo.

er·rat·ic (ĭ-răt′ĭk) adj. irregular; *(eccentric)* excéntrico, extravagante.

er·ra·tum (ĭ-rä′təm) s. [pl. **-ta**] errata, error *m*.

er·ro·ne·ous (ĭ-rō′nē-əs) adj. erróneo.

er·ror (ĕr′ər) s. error *m*.

er·satz (ĕr′zäts′) adj. artificial.

er·u·dite (ĕr′yə-dīt′) adj. erudito.

e·rupt (ĭ-rŭpt′) intr. *(to spew)* brotar violentamente; *(emotions, riot)* estallar, explotar; GEOL., MED. hacer erupción; ODONT. salir.

e·rup·tion (ĭ-rŭp′shən) s. erupción *f*; *(outburst)* estallido.

es·ca·late (ĕs′kə-lāt′) tr. & intr. *(war)* extender(se), intensificar(se); *(prices)* subir.

es·ca·la·tion (′-lā′shən) s. *(of war)* intensificación *f*; *(of prices)* subida.

es·ca·la·tor (ĕs′kə-lā′tər) s. escalera mecánica.

es·ca·pade (ĕs′kə-pād′) s. aventura.

es·cape (ĭ-skāp′) **I.** intr. escaparse —tr. escapar de, librarse de; *(name, meaning)* eludir, escapársele a uno **II.** s. escapatoria; *(evasion)* evasión *f*; *(leakage)* escape *m*, salida.

es·cap·ee (ĭ-skā′pē′) s. prófugo, fugitivo.

es·cap·ist (ĭ-skā′pĭst) **I.** adj. escapista **II.** s. persona que se evade de la realidad.

es·carp·ment (ĭ-skärp′mənt) s. escarpa.

es·cha·tol·o·gy (ĕs′kə-tŏl′ə-jē) s. escatología.

es·chew (ĭs-chŏō′) tr. evitar.

es·cort **I.** s. (ĕs′kôrt′) escolta; *(companion)* acompañante *m* **II.** tr. (ĭ-skôrt′) acompañar, escoltar.

es·crow (ĕs′krō′) s. plica ♦ **e. account** cuenta en plica • **in e.** en depósito.

e·soph·a·gus (ĭ-sŏf′ə-gəs) s. [pl. **-gi**] esófago.

e·so·ter·ic (ĕs′ə-tĕr′ĭk) adj. esotérico.

es·pe·cial (ĭ-spĕsh′əl) adj. especial.

es·pe·cial·ly (:ə-lē) adv. especialmente.

es·pi·o·nage (ĕs′pē-ə-näzh′) s. espionaje *m*.

es·pla·nade (ĕs′plə-näd′) s. explanada.

es·pous·al (ĭ-spou′zəl) s. adhesión *f*, apoyo.

es·pouse (ĭ-spouz′) tr. casarse con; *(a cause)* adoptar.

es·quire (ĕs′kwīr′) s. G.B. terrateniente *m* ♦ **E.** [abr. **Esq.**] Don, Señor <*John Smith, Esq.* Sr. John Smith>.

es·say **I.** tr. (ĕ-sā′) ensayar **II.** s. (ĕs′ā′) ensayo.

es·say·ist (ĕs′ā′ĭst) s. ensayista *mf*.

es·sence (ĕs′əns) s. esencia ♦ **in e.** esencialmente.

es·sen·tial (ĭ-sĕn′shəl) adj. & s. *(element)* esencial ♦ **to get down to the essentials** ir al grano.

es·tab·lish (ĭ-stăb′lĭsh) tr. establecer; *(to prove)* demostrar; *(facts)* verificar ♦ **to e. oneself** establecerse.

es·tab·lished (:lĭsht) adj. establecido; *(custom)* arraigado; *(fact)* conocido; *(business)* de buena fama *o* reputación; *(staff)* de plantilla; *(religion)* oficial.

es·tab·lish·ment (:lĭsh-mənt) s. establecimiento ♦ **E.** RELIG. iglesia oficial; POL. clase dirigente.

es·tate (ĭ-stāt′) s. *(land)* hacienda, finca; *(property)* propiedad *f*; *(inheritance)* herencia; DER. testamentaría ♦ **real e.** bienes raíces • **the fourth e.** la prensa.

es·teem (ĭ-stēm′) I. tr. estimar II. s. estimación *f*, aprecio ♦ **to hold someone in high e.** tenerle gran estima a alguien.

es·thet·ic (ĕs-thĕt′ĭk) var. de **aesthetic**.

es·ti·mate (ĕs′tə-māt′) I. tr. estimar II. s. (:mĭt) estimación *f*; *(of costs)* presupuesto; *(opinion)* opinión *f* ♦ **rough e.** cálculo aproximado.

es·ti·ma·tion (′-mā′shən) s. estimación *f*, valoración *f*; *(opinion)* opinión *f*.

es·trange·ment (ĭ-strānj′mənt) s. enajenación *f*, alejamiento.

es·tro·gen (ĕs′trə-jən) s. estrógeno.

es·trus (ĕs′trəs) s. estro.

es·tu·ar·y (ĕs′chōō-ĕr′ē) s. estuario.

et cet·er·a (ĕt-sĕt′ər-ə) etcétera.

etch (ĕch) tr. & intr. grabar al agua fuerte.

etch·ing (ĭng) s. aguafuerte *m*, grabado.

e·ter·nal (ĭ-tûr′nəl) adj. & s. eterno.

e·ter·ni·ty (:nĭ-tē) s. eternidad *f*.

e·ther (ē′thər) s. éter *m*.

e·the·re·al (ĭ-thîr′ē-əl) adj. etéreo.

eth·ic (ĕth′ĭk) s. ética ♦ **ethics** sg. ética.

eth·i·cal (:ĭ-kəl) adj. ético, moral.

eth·nic (ĕth′nĭk) adj. étnico.

eth·nol·o·gy (ĕth-nŏl′ə-jē) s. etnología.

e·thos (ē′thŏs′) s. genio.

eth·yl (ĕth′əl) s. etilo ♦ **e. alcohol** alcohol etílico.

et·i·quette (ĕt′ĭ-kĕt′) s. etiqueta, protocolo.

et·y·mol·o·gy (ĕt′ə-mŏl′ə-jē) s. etimología.

eu·ca·lyp·tus (yōō′kə-lĭp′təs) s. [pl. **es** *o* **-ti**] eucalipto.

eu·lo·gize (yōō′lə-jīz′) tr. elogiar, encomiar.

eu·lo·gy (:jē) s. panegírico.

eu·nuch (yōō′nək) s. eunuco.

eu·phe·mism (yōō′fə-mĭz′əm) s. eufemismo.

eu·pho·ny (yōō′fə-nē) s. eufonía.

eu·pho·ri·a (yōō-fôr′ē-ə) s. euforia.

eu·phor·ic (:ĭk) adj. eufórico.

eu·tha·na·sia (yōō′thə-nā′zhə) s. eutanasia.

e·vac·u·ate (ĭ-văk′yōō-āt′) tr. evacuar — intr. retirarse.

e·vac·u·a·tion (′-ā′shən) s. evacuación *f*.

e·vac·u·ee (:ē′) s. evacuado.

e·vade (ĭ-vād′) tr. evitar, evadir.

e·val·u·ate (ĭ-văl′yōō-āt′) tr. evaluar; *(to appraise)* tasar, valuar.

e·val·u·a·tion (′-ā′shən) s. evaluación *f*, valoración *f*; *(judgment)* opinión *f*.

ev·a·nes·cent (ĕv′ə-nĕs′ənt) adj. evanescente.

e·van·gel·ic/i·cal (ē′văn-jĕl′ĭk/ĭ-kəl) adj. evangélico.

e·van·gel·ist (ĭ-văn′jə-lĭst) s. evangelizador *m*.

e·vap·o·rate (ĭ-văp′ə-rāt′) tr. & intr. evaporar(se).

e·vap·o·ra·tion (′-rā′shən) s. evaporación *f*.

e·va·sion (ĭ-vā′zhən) s. evasión *f*.

e·va·sive (:sĭv) adj. evasivo.

eve (ēv) s. víspera ♦ *(before a feast)* vigilia ♦ **on the e. of** en vísperas de.

e·ven (ē′vən) I. adj. *(flat)* plano, llano; *(smooth)* liso; *(level)* a nivel; *(uniform)* regular; *(equally matched)* parejo; *(score)* empatado; *(exact)* justo; *(equal)* igual; *(temper)* sereno; *(fair)* equitativo; MAT. par ♦ **to be e.** estar mano a mano ♦ **to get e.** desquitarse • **to make e.** allanar • **to stay e.** cubrir los gastos II. adv. todavía, aun <*e.* worse aun peor>; siquiera <*he didn't e.* cry ni siquiera lloró> ♦ **e. as** precisamente, justo cuando ♦ **e. if** *o* **though** aunque, aun cuando • **e. so** aun así • **e. now** ahora mismo III. tr. *(to level, smooth)* emparejar, nivelar; *(to make equal)* igualar ♦ **to e. up the score** DEP. igualar; FAM. *(to get revenge)* ajustar cuentas.

e·ven·hand·ed (′-hăn′dĭd) adj. equitativo.

eve·ning (ēv′nĭng) s. tarde *f*; *(dusk)* anochecer *m*, noche *f*; *(entertainment)* velada ♦ **e. class** clase nocturna • **e. dress** *(for men)* traje de etiqueta; *(for women)* traje de noche • **e. performance** función de noche • **good e.!** ¡buenas tardes!; *(after sunset)* ¡buenas noches! • **in the e.** por la tarde.

e·ven·ness (ē′vən-nĭs) s. igualdad *f*; *(of temper, judgment)* ecuanimidad *f*.

e·ven·song (ē′vən-sông′) s. vísperas.

e·vent (ĭ-vĕnt′) s. suceso, acontecimiento; *(outcome)* resultado; DEP. evento ♦ **in any e.** en todo caso • **in the e. of** en caso de (que).

e·vent·ful (:fəl) adj. lleno de acontecimientos; *(momentous)* extraordinario, memorable.

e·ven·tu·al (ĭ-vĕn′chōō-əl) adj. final.

e·ven·tu·al·ly (:ē) adv. con el tiempo, a la larga.

ev·er (ĕv′ər) adv. *(always)* siempre; *(at any time)* alguna vez <have you e. been to Paris? ¿estuviste alguna vez en París?>; *(at all)* nunca, jamás <nobody has e. treated me this way nunca nadie me trató así> ♦ **as e.** como siempre • **better than e.** mejor que nunca • **e. since** *(from the time)* desde que; *(since then)* desde entonces • **e. so** *(happy)* tan (feliz) • **e. so little** muy poco • **e. so much** mucho, muchísimo • **for e. and e.** por siempre jamás, para siempre • **hardly e.** casi nunca • **not e.** nunca.

ev·er·chang·ing (′-chān′jĭng) adj. cambiadizo.

ev·er·green (′-grēn′) adj. & s. (planta, árbol *m*) de hoja perenne.

ev·er·last·ing (′-lăs′tĭng) adj. eterno, *(long lasting)* perdurable; *(tedious)* interminable.

eve·ry (ĕv′rē) adj. cada <e. two hours cada dos horas>; todo(s) <e. man todo hombre> ♦ **e. day** todos los días • **e. one** cada uno, cada cual • **e. one of them** todos (sin excepción) • **e. other day** cada dos días • **e. time** cada vez, cada cual • **e. which way** por todas partes; *(in no order)* en total desorden.

eve·ry·bod·y (:bŏd′ē, :bŭd′ē) pron. cada uno, cada cual; *(all)* todos, todo el mundo.

eve·ry·day (:dā′) adj. diario, cotidiano; *(usual)* común; *(clothes)* de todos los días.

eve·ry·one (:wŭn′) pron. cada uno, cada cual; *(all)* todos, todo el mundo ♦ **e. for himself** cada uno por su cuenta.

eve·ry·thing (:thĭng′) pron. todo.

eve·ry·where (:hwâr′) adv. en, a *o* por todas partes; *(wherever)* dondequiera que.

e·vict (ĭ-vĭkt′) tr. expulsar; DER. desahuciar.

e·vic·tion (ĭ-vĭk′shən) s. desahucio.

ev·i·dence (ĕv′ĭ-dəns) s. prueba; *(data)* hechos, datos; *(testimony)* declaración *f* ♦ **to be in e.** estar a la vista • **to give e.** declarar como testigo • **to show e. of** presentar señales de • **to turn state's e.** dar testimonio en contra de los cómplices II. tr. evidenciar, probar.

ev·i·dent (:dənt) adj. evidente.

e·vil (ē′vəl) I. adj. malo, malvado; *(harmful)* nocivo, perjudicial; *(influence)* pernicioso; *(look)* nefasto ♦ **e. eye** mal de ojo II. s. mal, maldad *f*; *(harm)* perjuicio; *(immorality)* perversidad *f.*

e·vil·do·er (:dōō'ər) s. malhechor *m,* malvado.

e·vil-mind·ed ('-mīn'dĭd) adj. malicioso, malintencionado.

e·vis·cer·ate (ĭ-vĭs'ə-rāt') tr. destripar.

e·voc·a·tive (ĭ-vŏk'ə-tĭv) adj. evocador.

e·voke (ĭ-vōk') tr. evocar.

ev·o·lu·tion (ĕv'ə-lōō'shən) s. evolución *f.*

ev·o·lu·tion·ar·y ('-'shə-nĕr'ē) adj. evolutivo.

ev·o·lu·tion·ist (:nĭst) s. evolucionista *mf.*

e·volve (ĭ-vŏlv') tr. & intr. desarrollar(se), BIOL. (hacer) evolucionar.

ewe (yōō) s. oveja hembra.

ew·er (yōō'ər) s. aguamanil *m.*

ex·ac·er·bate (ĭg-zăs'ər-bāt') tr. exacerbar.

ex·act (ĭg-zăkt') I. adj. exacto II. tr. quitar con la fuerza ♦ **to e. from** *o* **of** exigir a.

ex·act·ing (ĭg-zăk'tĭng) adj. *(demanding)* exigente; *(severe)* severo; *(rigorous)* riguroso.

ex·act·ly (ĭg-zăkt'lē) adv. exactamente; *(wholly)* precisamente; *(time)* en punto; *(quite true)* es verdad, así es.

ex·ag·ger·ate (ĭg-zăj'ə-rāt') tr. & intr. exagerar.

ex·ag·ger·a·tion ('-'rā'shən) s. exageración *f.*

ex·alt (ĭg-zôlt') tr. exaltar.

ex·am (ĭg-zăm') s. FAM. examen *m.*

ex·am·i·na·tion (ĭg-zăm'ə-nā'shən) s. examen *m;* DER. interrogatorio; *(inquiry)* investigación *f* ♦ **to take an e.** sufrir un examen.

ex·am·ine (ĭg-zăm'ĭn) tr. examinar; *(to scrutinize)* escudriñar; DER. interrogar.

ex·am·in·er (:ə-nər) s. examinador *m.*

ex·am·ple (ĭg-zăm'pəl) s. ejemplo ♦ **to set an e.** dar ejemplo.

ex·as·per·ate (ĭg-zăs'pə-rāt') tr. exasperar.

ex·ca·vate (ĕk'skə-vāt') tr. *(to dig)* excavar; *(ruins)* desenterrar.

ex·ceed (ĭk-sēd') tr. exceder; *(limits, authority)* propasarse en, excederse en.

ex·ceed·ing·ly (ĭk-sē'dĭng-lē) adv. extremadamente.

ex·cel (ĭk-sĕl') tr. -**ll**- superar, aventajar —intr. distinguirse.

ex·cel·lence (ĕk'sə-ləns) s. excelencia.

Ex·cel·len·cy (:lən-sē) s. Excelencia.

ex·cel·lent (ĕk'sə-lənt) adj. excelente.

ex·cept (ĭk-sĕpt') I. prep. excepto, menos ♦ **e. for** *(were it not for)* si no fuera por, a no ser por; *(apart from)* aparte de II. conj. *(only)* sólo que; *(otherwise than)* sino ♦ **e. that** salvo *o* excepto que III. tr. exceptuar, excluir.

ex·cept·ing (ĭk-sĕp'tĭng) prep. salvo, con excepción de.

ex·cep·tion (:shən) s. excepción *f* ♦ **to take e. to** estar en desacuerdo con, oponerse a ♦ **with the e. of** a excepción de, excepto.

ex·cep·tion·al (:shə-nəl) adj. excepcional.

ex·cerpt (:s. ĕk'sûrpt') extracto II. tr. (ĭk-sûrpt') extractar ♦ **to e. from** citar de.

ex·cess (ĭk-sĕs', ĕk'sĕs') I. s. exceso ♦ **in e.** *o* más que ♦ **to e.** en *o* con exceso II. adj. excesivo.

ex·ces·sive (ĭk-sĕs'ĭv) adj. excesivo.

ex·change (ĭks-chānj') I. tr. cambiar, intercambiar; *(glances, words)* cruzar; *(prisoners, goods)* canjear ♦ **to e. for** cambiar por II. s. cambio, intercambio; *(of prisoners, goods)* canje *m;* COM. bolsa; TEL. central telefónica ♦ **e.** rate tipo de cambio ♦ **in e. for** a cambio de.

ex·change·a·ble (:chān'jə-bəl) adj. canjeable.

ex·cheq·uer (ĭks-chĕk'ər) s. tesoro público ♦ E.

G.B. Ministerio de Hacienda.

ex·cise tax (ĕk'sīz') s. impuesto indirecto.

ex·ci·sion (ĭk-sĭzh'ən) s. excisión *f.*

ex·cite (ĭk-sīt') tr. excitar; *(to thrill)* entusiasmar, emocionar.

ex·cit·ed (ĭk-sī'tĭd) adj. excitado; *(emotions)* agitado; *(thrilled)* entusiasmado ♦ **to get e.** excitarse, agitarse; *(with glee)* entusiasmarse.

ex·cite·ment (ĭk-sīt'mənt) s. emoción *f,* agitación *f; (enthusiasm)* entusiasmo.

ex·cit·ing (ĭk-sī'tĭng) adj. emocionante.

ex·claim (ĭk-sklām') intr. exclamar —tr. gritar, proclamar.

ex·cla·ma·tion (ĕk'sklə-mā'shən) s. exclamación *f* ♦ **e.** point signo de admiración.

ex·clude (ĭk-sklōōd') tr. excluir.

ex·clud·ing (ĭk-sklōō'dĭng) prep. excepto, exceptuando a.

ex·clu·sive (:sĭv) I. adj. exclusivo; *(select)* selecto, elegante ♦ **e. rights** exclusividad ♦ **mutually e.** que se excluyen II. s. noticia de exclusividad.

ex·com·mu·ni·cate (ĕks'kə-myōō'nĭ-kāt') I. tr. excomulgar II. s. & adj. (:kĭt) excomulgado.

ex·com·mu·ni·ca·tion ('-'kā'shən) s. excomunión *f.*

ex·co·ri·ate (ĭk-skôr'ē-āt') tr. *(to abrade)* excoriar; *(to upbraid)* reprochar, recriminar.

ex·cre·ment (ĕk'skrə-mənt) s. excremento.

ex·crete (ĭk-skrēt') tr. excretar.

ex·cre·to·ry (ĕk'skrī-tôr'ē) adj. excretor(io).

ex·cru·ci·at·ing (ĭk-skrōō'shē-ā'tĭng) adj. insoportable, dolorosísimo.

ex·cul·pate (ĕk'skəl-pāt') tr. exculpar.

ex·cur·sion (ĭk-skûr'zhən) s. excursión *f,* paseo; *(digression)* digresión *f.*

ex·cur·sive (:sĭv) adj. digresivo.

ex·cuse (ĭk-skyōōz') I. tr. excusar, disculpar; *(to exempt)* dispensar *(from* de) ♦ **e. me** *(I'm sorry!)* ¡discúlpeme!; *(pardon me)* con permiso ♦ **to be excused from** estar dispensado de ♦ **to e. oneself** for disculparse de II. s. (:skyōōs') excusa ♦ **to make excuses (for)** dar excusas (por).

ex·e·cute (ĕk'sī-kyōōt') tr. ejecutar; *(to do)* hacer; *(to validate)* formalizar.

ex·e·cu·tion ('-kyōō'shən) s. ejecución *f; (validation)* legalización *f.*

ex·e·cu·tion·er (:shə-nər) s. verdugo.

ex·ec·u·tive (ĭg-zĕk'yə-tĭv) I. s. ejecutivo; POL. *(officer)* presidente *m,* jefe *m* de estado; *(branch)* poder ejecutivo II. adj. ejecutivo.

ex·ec·u·tor (:tər) s. (ejecutor) testamentario.

ex·ec·u·trix (:trĭks') s. [pl. es *o* -**ices**] (ejecutora) testamentaria.

ex·em·plar (ĭg-zĕm'plər) s. ejemplar *m.*

ex·em·pla·ry (:plə-rē) adj. ejemplar.

ex·em·pli·fy (:plə-fī') tr. ejemplificar.

ex·empt (ĭg-zĕmpt') I. tr. eximir *(from* de) II. adj. exento.

ex·emp·tion (ĭg-zĕmp'shən) s. exención *f.*

ex·er·cise (ĕk'sər-sīz') I. s. ejercicio ♦ pl. *(ceremony)* ceremonia II. tr. *(to use)* usar de, proceder con; *(to drill)* ejercitar, entrenar; *(rights)* ejercer —intr. ejercitarse.

ex·ert (ĭg-zûrt') tr. *(strength)* emplear; *(influence)* ejercer ♦ **to e. oneself** esforzarse.

ex·er·tion (ĭg-zûr'shən) s. *(of strength)* empleo; *(of influence)* ejercicio; *(effort)* esfuerzo.

ex·ha·la·tion (ĕks'hə-lā'shən) s. exhalación *f.*

ex·hale (ĕks-hāl') intr. & tr. exhalar.

ex·haust (ĭg-zôst') I. tr. *(to use up)* agotar; *(to*

tire) cansar; *(soil)* empobrecer; *(gases)* vaciar, extraer II. s. AUTO. escape *m*, descarga; *(fumes)* gases *m* de escape ♦ **e. pipe** tubo de escape.

ex·haust·i·ble (ĭg-zôs′stə-bəl) adj. agotable.

ex·haus·tion (ĭg-zôs′chən) s. agotamiento.

ex·haus·tive (ĭg-zô′stĭv) adj. exhaustivo.

ex·hib·it (ĭg-zĭb′ĭt) I. tr. exhibir; *(at a show)* exponer; *(emotion, trait)* manifestar —intr. exponer II. s. *(display)* exhibición *f*; *(object)* objeto exhibido; DER. prueba instrumental.

ex·hi·bi·tion (ĕk′sə-bĭsh′ən) s. exhibición *f*, exposición *f*, G.B. *(scholarship)* beca.

ex·hi·bi·tion·ist (:ə-nĭst) s. exhibicionista *mf*.

ex·hib·i·tor (ĭg-zĭb′ĭ-tər) s. expositor *m*.

ex·hil·a·rant (ĭg-zĭl′ər-ənt) s. estimulante *m*.

ex·hil·a·rate (:ə-rāt′) tr. *(to elate)* alborozar; *(to invigorate)* animar; *(to stimulate)* estimular.

ex·hil·a·rat·ing (:ə-rā′tĭng) adj. *(invigorating)* vigorizante; *(stimulating)* estimulante.

ex·hil·a·ra·tion (-′-′shən) s. entusiasmo, exaltación *f*.

ex·hort (ĭg-zôrt′) tr. exhortar.

ex·hume (ĭg-zyōōm′, ĭk-syōōm′) tr. exhumar.

ex·i·gen·cy (ĕk′sə-jən-sē) s. exigencia; *(emergency)* caso de urgencia.

ex·ile (ĕg′zīl′, ĕk′sīl′) I. s. exilio, destierro; *(person)* desterrado II. tr. exiliar, desterrar.

ex·ist (ĭg-zĭst′) intr. existir, ser; *(to live)* vivir; *(to subsist)* subsistir.

ex·is·tence (:təns) s. existencia; *(life)* vida ♦ **to come into e.** empezar a existir.

ex·is·tent (:tənt) adj. viviente; *(current)* existente, actual.

ex·is·ten·tial (ĕg′zĭ-stĕn′shəl, ĕk′sĭ-) adj. existencial.

ex·is·ten·tial·ist (:shə-lĭst) s. & adj. existencialista *mf*.

ex·ist·ing (ĭg-zĭs′tĭng) adj. existente.

ex·it (ĕg′zĭt, ĕk′sĭt) I. s. salida ♦ **to make one's e.** salir, marcharse II. intr. salir.

ex·o·dus (ĕk′sə-dəs) s. éxodo.

ex·on·er·ate (ĭg-zŏn′ə-rāt′) tr. *(from responsibility)* exonerar; *(from blame)* disculpar.

ex·or·bi·tant (ĭg-zôr′bĭ-tənt) adj. exorbitante.

ex·or·cise (ĕk′sôr-sīz′) tr. exorcizar.

ex·or·cist (:sĭst) s. exorcista *mf*.

ex·ot·ic (ĭg-zŏt′ĭk) adj. exótico.

ex·pand (ĭk-spănd′) tr. & intr. extender(se); *(to enlarge)* expandir(se); *(to develop)* desarrollar(se); FÍS. dilatar(se).

ex·panse (ĭk-spăns′) s. extensión *f*.

ex·pan·sion (ĭk-spăn′shən) s. expansión *f*; FÍS. dilatación *f*; *(of a town)* ensanche *m*; *(of an idea)* ampliación *f*, *(of trade)* expansión.

ex·pan·sive (:sĭv) adj. expansivo.

ex·pa·tri·ate (ĕks-pā′trē-āt′) I. tr. expatriar II. s. (:ĭt, :āt′) exiliado.

ex·pect (ĭk-spĕkt′) tr. *(to await)* esperar; *(to require)* contar con; *(to suppose)* suponer.

ex·pec·tan·cy (ĭk-spĕk′tən-sē) s. expectación *f*, expectativa.

ex·pec·tant (:tənt) adj. expectante; *(pregnant)* embarazada.

ex·pec·ta·tion (ĕk′spĕk-tā′shən) s. expectación *f*, expectativa; *(prospect)* esperanza ♦ **beyond e.** más de lo esperado • **contrary to e.** contrariamente a lo esperado.

ex·pec·to·rate (ĭk-spĕk′tə-rāt′) tr. & intr. expectorar.

ex·pe·di·ence/en·cy (ĭk-spē′dē-əns) s. conveniencia.

ex·pe·di·ent (:ənt) I. adj. conveniente II. s. expediente *m*, recurso.

ex·pe·dite (ĕk′spĭ-dīt′) tr. apresurar; *(to facilitate)* facilitar; *(to dispatch)* expedir.

ex·pe·di·tion (′-dĭsh′ən) s. expedición *f*.

ex·pel (ĭk-spĕl′) tr. -ll- expeler; *(to dismiss)* echar, expulsar.

ex·pend (ĭk-spĕnd′) tr. *(to spend)* gastar; *(to consume)* consumir.

ex·pend·a·ble (ĭk-spĕn′də-bəl) adj. prescindible.

ex·pen·di·ture (:dĭ-chər) s. desembolso, gasto.

ex·pense (ĭk-spĕns′) s. gasto ♦ **at the e. of** a expensas de ♦ pl. expenses • **legal e.** costas ♦ **to meet e.** hacer frente a los gastos.

ex·pen·sive (ĭk-spĕn′sĭv) adj. costoso, caro.

ex·pe·ri·ence (ĭk-spîr′ē-əns) I. s. experiencia II. tr. *(to undergo)* experimentar; *(to feel)* sentir; *(difficulties)* tener.

ex·pe·ri·enced (:ənst) adj. experimentado.

ex·per·i·ment (ĭk-spĕr′ə-mənt) I. s. experimento II. intr. experimentar *(on en)*.

ex·per·i·men·tal (-′-mĕn′tl) adj. experimental.

ex·pert (ĕk′spûrt′) s. & adj. experto, perito.

ex·per·tise (ĕk′spər-tēz′) s. pericia.

ex·pi·ate (ĕk′spē-āt′) tr. & intr. expiar.

ex·pi·ra·tion (ĕk′spə-rā′shən) s. *(end, death)* expiración *f*; *(lapse)* caducidad *f*; *(breath)* espiración *f*, espiramiento.

ex·pire (ĭk-spīr′) intr. *(to end, die)* expirar; *(to lapse)* vencer, caducar; *(to exhale)* espirar.

ex·plain (ĭk-splān′) tr. explicar —intr. dar explicaciones ♦ **to e. oneself** explicarse.

ex·pla·na·tion (ĕk′splə-nā′shən) s. explicación *f*.

ex·plan·a·to·ry (ĭk-splăn′ə-tôr′ē) adj. explicativo.

ex·ple·tive (ĕk′splĭ-tĭv) s. obscenidad *f*.

ex·pli·cate (ĕk′splĭ-kāt′) tr. explicar.

ex·plic·it (ĭk-splĭs′ĭt) adj. explícito.

ex·plode (ĭk-splōd′) intr. explotar estallar; FIG. prorrumpir —tr. hacer explotar; *(to detonate)* detonar; *(to disprove)* desbaratar ♦ **exploded view** vista esquemática.

ex·ploit I. s. (ĕk′sploit′) hazaña, proeza II. tr. (ĭk-sploit′) explotar.

ex·ploit·er (ĭk-sploi′tər) s. explotador *m*.

ex·plo·ra·tion (ĕk′splə-rā′shən) s. exploración *f*.

ex·plore (ĭk-splôr′) tr. explorar; FIG. investigar.

ex·plor·er (:ər) s. explorador *m*.

ex·plo·sion (ĭk-splō′zhən) s. explosión *f*.

ex·plo·sive (:sĭv) adj. & s. explosivo.

ex·po·nent (ĭk-spō′nənt) s. representante *mf*, exponente *m*; MAT. exponente *m*.

ex·po·nen·tial (ĕk′spə-nĕn′shəl) adj. exponencial.

ex·port I. tr. (ĭk-spôrt′) exportar II. s. (ĕk′spôrt′) exportación *f*.

ex·por·ta·tion (ĕk′spôr-tā′shən) s. exportación *f*.

ex·port·er (ĭk-spôr′tər) s. exportador *m*.

ex·pose (ĭk-spōz′) tr. exponer; *(to reveal)* revelar; *(to unmask)* desenmascarar ♦ **to be exposed to** estar expuesto a.

ex·po·sé (ĕk′spō-zā′) s. revelación *f*.

ex·po·si·tion (ĕk′spə-zĭsh′ən) s. exposición *f*.

ex·pos·tu·late (ĭk-spŏs′chə-lāt′) intr. objetar ♦ **to e. with** reconvenir a.

ex·po·sure (ĭk-spō′zhər) s. exposición *f*; *(revelation)* revelación *f*, descubrimiento ♦ **e. meter**

exposímetro • **to make an e.** sacar una fotografía.

ex·pound (ĭk-spound') tr. exponer, explicar —intr. hacer una exposición detallada (*on* de).

ex·press (ĭk-sprĕs') **I.** tr. expresar; *(to show)* manifestar; *(to squeeze)* exprimir; COM. enviar por expreso **II.** adj. expreso; *(explicit)* explícito; *(mail)* de entrega inmediata **III.** adv. por expreso **IV.** s. transporte rápido; *(train)* expreso, rápido.

ex·pres·sion (ĭk-sprĕsh'ən) s. expresión *f*; *(sign)* señal *f*; *(gesture)* gesto.

ex·pres·sion·ist (:ə-nĭst) s. & adj. expresionista *mf*.

ex·pres·sion·less (:ən-lĭs) adj. inexpresivo.

ex·pres·sive (ĭk-sprĕs'ĭv) adj. expresivo ♦ **e. of** que expresa.

ex·press·ly (:lē) adv. expresamente.

ex·press·way (:wā') s. autopista.

ex·pro·pri·ate (ĕks-prō'prē-āt') tr. expropiar.

ex·pro·pri·a·tion (-'ā'shən) s. expropiación *f*.

ex·pul·sion (ĭk-spŭl'shən) s. expulsión *f*.

ex·punge (ĭk-spŭnj') tr. borrar, tachar.

ex·pur·gate (ĕk'spər-gāt') tr. expurgar.

ex·qui·site (ĕk'skwĭ-zĭt, ĭk-swĭz'ĭt) adj. exquisito; *(acute)* agudo, vivo.

ex·tant (ĕk'stənt, ĕk-stănt') adj. existente.

ex·tem·po·ra·ne·ous (ĭk-stĕm'pə-rā'nē-əs) adj. improvisado.

ex·tem·po·rize (-'-rīz') tr. & intr. improvisar.

ex·tend (ĭk-stĕnd') tr. extender; *(road, visit)* prolongar; *(hand, arm)* alargar; *(to enlarge)* agrandar, ampliar; *(to offer)* ofrecer; FIN. *(payment)* prorrogar ♦ **to e. an invitation** invitar ♦ **to e. oneself** esforzarse —intr. extenderse; *(to reach)* alcanzar.

ex·ten·sion (ĭk-stĕn'shən) s. extensión *f*; *(expansion)* ampliación *f*; *(annex)* anexo; *(continuation)* prolongación *f*; FIN. prórroga ♦ **e. ladder** escalera extensible.

ex·ten·sive (:sĭv) adj. extenso.

ex·tent (ĭk-stĕnt') s. extensión *f*; *(degree)* grado ♦ **to a certain e.** hasta cierto punto • **to a large e.** en gran parte • **to what e.?** ¿hasta qué punto?

ex·ten·u·ate (ĭk-stĕn'yŏŏ-āt') tr. atenuar.

ex·ten·u·at·ing (:ā'tĭng) adj. atenuante.

ex·te·ri·or (ĭk-stîr'ē-ər) **I.** adj. exterior; *(external)* externo **II.** s. exterior *m*.

ex·ter·mi·nate (ĭk-stûr'mə-nāt') tr. exterminar.

ex·ter·mi·na·tor (:nā'tər) s. exterminador *m*.

ex·ter·nal (ĭk-stûr'nəl) **I.** adj. externo; *(exterior, foreign)* exterior ♦ **e. ear** oreja **II.** s. ♦ pl. apariencia, aspecto exterior.

ex·ter·nal·ize (:nə-līz') tr. exteriorizar.

ex·tinct (ĭk-stĭngkt') adj. extinto, desaparecido; *(inactive)* inactivo.

ex·tin·guish (ĭk-stĭng'gwĭsh) tr. extinguir, apagar.

ex·tin·guish·er (:gwĭ-shər) s. extintor *m*.

ex·tir·pate (ĕk'stər-pāt') tr. extirpar.

ex·tol(l) (ĭk-stōl') tr. **-ll-** alabar.

ex·tort (ĭk-stôrt') tr. *(money)* extorsionar; *(confession)* arrancar, sacar por la fuerza.

ex·tor·tion (ĭk-stôr'shən) s. extorsión *f*; *(graft)* concusión *f*.

ex·tra (ĕk'strə) **I.** adj. extra; *(additional)* adicional **II.** s. extra *m*; PERIOD. extraordinario; *(worker)* supernumerario; CINEM., TEAT. extra *mf* **III.** adv. excepcionalmente.

ex·tract **I.** tr. (ĭk-străkt') extraer; *(to excerpt)*

extractar **II.** s. (ĕk'străkt') extracto.

ex·trac·tion (ĭk-străk'shən) s. extracción *f*; *(origin)* origen *m*.

ex·tra·cur·ric·u·lar (ĕk'strə-kə-rĭk'yə-lər) adj. extracurricular.

ex·tra·dite ('-dīt') tr. entregar por extradición.

ex·tra·di·tion ('-dĭsh'ən) s. extradición *f*.

ex·tra·mar·i·tal (:măr'ĭ-tl) adj. adúltero.

ex·tra·mu·ral (:myŏŏr'əl) adj. de o situado extramuros.

ex·tra·ne·ous (ĭk-strā'nē-əs) adj. ajeno.

ex·traor·di·nar·y (ĭk-strôr'dn-ĕr'ē, ĕk'strə-ôr'-) adj. extraordinario.

ex·trap·o·late (ĭk-străp'ə-lāt') tr. extrapolar.

ex·tra·sen·so·ry perception (ĕk'strə-sĕn'sə-rē) adj. percepción *f* por medios extrasensibles.

ex·tra·ter·res·tri·al (:tə-rĕs'trē-əl) adj. extraterrestre *mf*.

ex·trav·a·gance (ĭk-străv'ə-gəns) s. extravagancia; *(of spending)* despilfarro.

ex·trav·a·gant (:gənt) adj; *(lavish)* pródigo, *(wasteful)* derrochador; *(exorbitant)* costoso.

ex·trav·a·gan·za (-'-găn'zə) s. entretenimiento espectacular.

ex·treme (ĭk-strēm') **I.** adj. extremo; *(extraordinary)* excepcional; *(drastic)* drástico ♦ **e. unction** extremaunción **II.** s. extremo ♦ **in the e.** en extremo • **to go to extremes** tomar medidas extremas.

ex·treme·ly (:lē) adv. extremadamente.

ex·trem·ist (ĭk-strē'mĭst) adj. & s. extremista *mf*.

ex·trem·i·ty (ĭk-strĕm'ĭ-tē) s. extremidad *f*; *(utmost degree)* extremo; *(danger)* grave peligro; *(distress)* adversidad *f*.

ex·tri·cate (ĕk'strĭ-kāt') tr. *(from a difficulty)* librar, sacar; *(to disengage)* desprender.

ex·trin·sic (ĭk-strĭn'sĭk) adj. extrínseco.

ex·tro·vert (ĕk'strə-vûrt') s. extrovertido.

ex·trude (ĭk-strŏŏd') tr. empujar hacia afuera; TEC. extruir —intr. sobresalir.

ex·u·ber·ant (ĭg-zŏŏ'bər-ənt) adj. exuberante; *(mood, spirits)* efusivo.

ex·ude (ĭg-zŏŏd') intr. & tr. exudar, rezumar.

ex·ult (ĭg-zŭlt') intr. exultar, regocijarse.

ex·ul·tant (ĭg-zŭl'tənt) adj. exultante, jubiloso.

eye (ī) **I.** s. ojo ♦ **e. opener** revelación, sorpresa • **e. shadow** sombreador • **in the twinkling of an e.** en un abrir y cerrar de ojos • **my e.!** ¡de ningún modo! • **to catch someone's e.** llamar la atención de alguien • **to give someone the e.** FAM. lanzar una mirada incitante a alguien • **to keep an e. on** vigilar • **to keep one's eyes open** mantenerse alerta • **to make eyes at** echar miradas a • **to roll one's eyes** poner los ojos en blanco • **to see e. to e.** estar de acuerdo • **to set eyes on** alcanzar a ver • **with an e. to** con miras a • **without batting an e.** sin pestañear **II.** tr. eyeing o eying ojear, mirar.

eye·ball (ī'bôl') s. globo ocular.

eye·brow (ī'brou') s. ceja.

eye·drop·per (ī'drŏp'ər) s. cuentagotas *m*.

eye·ful (ī'fŏŏl') s. vistazo, ojeada.

eye·glass (ī'glăs') s. monóculo ♦ pl. lentes.

eye·lash (ī'lăsh') s. pestaña.

eye·let (ī'lĭt) s. ojete *m*.

eye·lid (ī'lĭd') s. párpado.

eye·piece (ī'pēs') s. ocular *m*.

eye·sight (ī'sīt') s. vista ♦ **within e.** al alcance de la vista.

eye·sore (ī'sôr') s. cosa que ofende la vista.

eye·strain (ī'strān') s. vista fatigada.
eye·tooth (ī'tōoth') s. [pl. **-teeth**] colmillo.
eye·wash (ī'wŏsh') s. colirio; FAM. *(nonsense)* tontería.
eye·wit·ness (ī'wĭt'nəs) s. testigo ocular.
ey·rie (âr'ē, îr'ē) s. aguilera.

F

f, F (ĕf) s. sexta letra del alfabeto inglés, MÚS. fa *m.*
fa·ble (fā'bəl) s. fábula; *(lie)* mentira.
fa·bled (fā'bəld) adj. legendario.
fab·ric (făb'rĭk) s. tela; FIG. estructura.
fab·ri·cate (făb'rĭ-kāt') tr. fabricar.
fab·ri·ca·tion ('-kā'shən) s. fabricación *f*; *(falsehood)* mentira.
fab·u·list (făb'yə-lĭst) s. fabulista *m/f.*
fab·u·lous (făb'yə-ləs) adj. fabuloso.
fa·çade (fə-säd') s. fachada.
face (fās) **I.** s. cara; *(grimace)* mueca, gesto; FIG. apariencia; *(countenance)* rostro; *(façade)* frente *m*; *(of a clock)* esfera ♦ **f. card** figura (naipe) • **f. cloth** paño • **f. down, up** boca abajo, arriba • **f. of the earth** faz de la tierra • **f. value** FIN. valor nominal; FIG. valor aparente • **in the f. of** frente a • **on the f. of it** a primera vista • **to lose f.** desprestigiarse • **to one's f.** en la cara de uno • **to save f.** salvar las apariencias • **to show one's f.** hacer acto de presencia **II.** tr. *(to turn toward)* ponerse de cara a, mirar hacia; *(to look out on)* estar frente a, dar a; *(to confront)* hacer frente a, arrostrar; TEC. revestir; COST. guarnecer (un borde) ♦ **let's f. it** reconozcámoslo • **to be faced with** enfrentarse con • **to f. down** resistir firmemente —intr. *(to be situated)* estar orientado hacia, mirar hacia; *(to turn)* volverse, voltear la cara ♦ **to f. up to** encararse con, enfrentarse a.
face·less ('lĭs) adj. sin cara; FIG. anónimo.
face-lift (:lĭft') o **face·lift·ing** (:lĭf'tĭng) s. cirugía estética; FIG. modernización *f*, embellecimiento.
face-off (:ôf') s. confrontación *f.*
face-sav·ing (:sā'vĭng) adj. que salva la dignidad.
fac·et (făs'ĭt) s. faceta.
fa·ce·tious (fə-sē'shəs) adj. jocosamente irónico, humorístico.
fa·cial (fā'shəl) adj. & s. *(treatment)* facial.
fac·ile (făs'əl) adj. fácil; *(superficial)* superficial.
fa·cil·i·tate (fə-sĭl'ĭ-tāt') tr. facilitar.
fa·cil·i·ty (:tē) s. facilidad *f* ♦ pl. COM. facilidades; *(buildings)* instalaciones; *(public toilet)* servicio, baño.
fac·sim·i·le (făk-sĭm'ə-lē) s. & adj. facsímil *m.*
fact (făkt) s. hecho ♦ **in fact** en realidad • **the f. of the matter is** la verdad es • **the f. remains that** a pesar de todo • **to know for a f.** saber a ciencia cierta ♦ pl. datos, información.
fact-find·ing ('f ĭn'dĭng) adj. investigador.
fac·tion (făk'shən) s. facción *f.*
fac·tion·al (:sha-nəl) adj. faccioso.
fac·tor (făk'tər) s. factor *m.*
fac·to·ry (făk'tə-rē) s. fábrica.
fac·tu·al (făk'chōō-əl) adj. verdadero.
fac·ul·ty (făk'əl-tē) s. facultad *f*; EDUC. cuerpo docente, profesorado.
fad (făd) s. manía, novedad *f.*

fad·dish (:ĭsh) adj. que sigue la moda.
fade (fād) intr. *(light)* palidecer, apagarse; *(sound, hope)* desvanecerse; *(flower)* marchitarse; *(strength)* debilitarse; *(color)* desteñirse ♦ **to f. away** *(to waste away)* consumirse; *(to leave gradually)* desvanecerse • **to f. in, out** CINEM. aparecer, desaparecer gradualmente —tr. desvanecer.
fade-in ('ĭn') s. fundido, aparición *f* gradual.
fade-out (:out') s. desvanecimiento gradual.
fag¹ (făg) **I.** s. trabajo, faena **II.** intr. **-gg-** trabajar duro ♦ **to be fagged out** estar rendido —tr. ♦ **to f. out** fatigar.
fag² s. JER. cigarrillo.
fag·(g)ot (făg'ət) s. haz *m* de leña.
fail (fāl) **I.** intr. fracasar; *(motor, health, support)* fallar; *(to be inadequate)* faltar; *(to weaken)* decaer, debilitarse; *(in school)* no aprobar, aplazarse; COM. quebrar ♦ **to f. to** *(to be unsuccessful in)* no lograr, no alcanzar a; *(to neglect to)* dejar de —tr. fallar, frustrar; *(course, exam)* salir mal en; *(student)* no aprobar a **II.** s. ♦ **without f.** sin falta.
fail·ing (fā'lĭng) s. falla, defecto.
fail-safe (fāl'sāf') adj. que no falla.
fail·ure (fāl'yər) s. fracaso; *(person)* fracasado; *(weakening)* decaimiento; *(nonfulfillment)* incumplimiento; *(of crops)* pérdida; ELEC. corte *m*; suspenso; COM. quiebra ♦ **heart f.** ataque al corazón.
faint (fānt) **I.** adj. *(indistinct)* borroso; *(slight)* vago, ligero; *(pale)* pálido; *(dizzy)* mareado; *(timid)* tímido; *(weak)* débil **II.** s. desmayo **III.** intr. desmayarse.
faint-heart·ed (:här'tĭd) adj. tímido.
fair¹ (fâr) **I.** adj. *(beautiful)* bello; *(blond)* rubio; *(skin)* blanco; *(impartial)* imparcial; *(just)* justo, equitativo; *(reasonable)* razonable; *(mediocre)* regular; *(weather)* bueno; *(sky)* despejado ♦ **f. and square** honrado a carta cabal • **f. enough!** ¡vale!, ¡bien! • **f. game** FIG. presa fácil • **f. play** juego limpio • **f. shake** JER. oportunidad • **f. to middling** regular, bastante bueno • **no f.!** ¡no hay derecho! • **one's f. share** lo que le corresponde a uno • **to give someone f. warning** prevenir a alguien **II.** adv. honradamente ♦ **to play f.** jugar limpio.
fair² s. *(market)* mercado; *(exhibition)* exposición *f*, feria; *(church bazaar)* tómbola.
fair·ground ('ground') s. campo para ferias.
fair·ly (:lē) adv. *(justly)* justamente, equitativamente; *(moderately)* bastante.
fair-mind·ed (:mīn'dĭd) adj. imparcial.
fair·ness (:nĭs) s. *(beauty)* belleza; *(justness)* imparcialidad *f* ♦ **in all f.** para ser justo.
fair·y (fâr'ē) s. hada ♦ **f. tale** cuento de hadas.
fair·y·land (:lănd') s. país *m* de las hadas.
fait ac·com·pli (fa'tä-kòm-plē') s. [pl. **faits ac·complis**] hecho consumado.
faith (fāth) s. *(confidence)* confianza; *(belief)* fe *f*; *(set of beliefs)* doctrina ♦ **in good, bad f.** de buena, mala fe • **of every f.** de todas las religiones • **to break f. with** faltar a la palabra dada a • **to have f. in** fiarse de • **to keep f. with** cumplir la palabra dada a.
faith·ful ('fəl) **I.** adj. fiel; *(reliable)* digno de confianza **II.** s.pl. ♦ **the f.** los fieles.
faith·less ('lĭs) adj. infiel, desleal.
fake (fāk) **I.** adj. falso, fraudulento **II.** s. impostor *m*; *(fraud)* engaño; *(forgery)* falsificación *f* **III.** tr. falsificar; *(to feign)* fingir ♦ **to f. out** engañar —intr. engañarse, fingirse

fak·er (fā'kər) s. falsificador *m*, impostor *m*.
fa·kir (fə-kîr') s. faquir *m*.
Fa·lan·gist (fə-lăn'jĭst) s. & adj. falangista *mf*.
fal·con (făl'kən, fôl'-) s. halcón *m*.
fal·con·ry (:rē) s. halconería.
fall (fôl) I. intr. **fell, fallen** caer(se); *(light)* dar *(on, across* sobre*); (prices, temperature)* bajar; *(wind, voice)* disminuir; *(to become)* quedarse, volverse *<to f. silent* quedarse mudo*>* ◆ **falling star** estrella fugaz • **to f. away** *(to slope)* descender; *(to come loose)* desprenderse; *(to decline)* declinar • **to f. back** caerse de espaldas; *(to retreat)* replegarse; *(to lag)* quedarse atrás • **to f. behind** quedarse atrás, rezagarse; *(to be late)* atrasarse; *(in payments)* retrasarse; *(in class)* quedar a la zaga • **to f. down** caer(se); *(building)* venirse abajo, derrumbarse • **to f. due** vencer, ser pagadero • **to f. flat** fracasar • **to f. flat on one's face** caer de bruces; *(to fail)* fracasar • **to f. for** FAM. *(person)* volverse loco por; *(trick)* tragarse • **to f. from grace** caer en desgracia • **to f. in** *(roof)* hundirse, venirse abajo; *(soldiers)* formar filas • **to f. into** estar comprendido en • **to f. off** *(to come loose)* desprenderse; *(to decrease)* disminuir, decaer; *(quality)* empeorar • **to f. (up)on** *(head, knees)* caer de; *(duty)* tocar a; *(to attack)* caer sobre • **to f. out** *(of bed)* caerse; *(of a car)* salirse; *(to quarrel)* reñir, pelear • **to f. over** *(to fall)* caerse, volcarse; *(to trip over)* tropezar con • **to f. through** venirse abajo, fracasar • **to f. to** *(to begin to)* empezar a; *(to befall)* tocar a, corresponder a • **to f. within** estar dentro de, estar incluido en II. s. caída; *(autumn)* otoño; *(reduction)* bajada, descenso; *(decline)* decadencia, ruina ◆ **to ride for a f.** ir al fracaso ◆ **to take a bad f.** darse una mala caída, caerse duro ◆ pl. catarata, cascada.
fal·la·cious (fə-lā'shəs) adj. falaz, engañoso.
fal·la·cy (făl'ə-sē) s. idea falsa; LÓG. falacia.
fal·li·ble (făl'ə-bəl) adj. falible.
fall·ing-out (fô'lĭng-out') s. desacuerdo, pelea.
fall·out (fôl'out') s. lluvia radioactiva; *(side effects)* consecuencias.
fal·low (făl'ō) I. adj. durmiente, inactivo; AGR. barbechada II. tr. barbechar.
false (fôls) I. adj. falso; *(hope)* infundado; *(teeth)* postizo; MÚS. desafinado ◆ **f. arrest** a-rresto ilegal • **f. pretense** intención fraudulenta • **f. start** salida mala *o* nula • **f. step** paso en falso, desliz II. adv. falsamente, con falsedad; *(wrong)* mal.
false-heart·ed ('här'tĭd) adj. pérfido.
false·hood (:hŏŏd') s. mentira.
false·ness (:nĭs) s. falsedad *f*.
fal·set·to (fôl-sĕt'ō) adv. & s. (en) falsete *m*.
fal·si·fy (fôl'sə-fī') tr. falsificar, falsear.
fal·ter (fôl'tər) I. intr. titubear; *(to fail)* fallar II. s. vacilación *f*, titubeo.
fame (fām) s. fama, renombre *m*.
famed (fāmd) adj. famoso.
fa·mil·ial (fə-mĭl'yəl) adj. familiar, de familia.
fa·mil·iar (fə-mĭl'yər) I. adj. familiar; *(well-known)* conocido; *(common)* corriente; *(intimate)* de confianza; *(forward)* confianzudo ◆ **that does not sound f.** eso no me suena • **to be f. with** conocer • **to be on f. terms with** tener confianza con II. s. *(friend)* amigo íntimo; *(spirit)* espíritu *m* protector.
fa·mil·iar·i·ty (-'yăr'ĭ-tē) s. familiaridad *f*; *(impropriety)* atrevimiento ◆ pl. libertades.
fa·mil·iar·ize (-'yə-rīz') tr. familiarizar.

fam·i·ly (făm'ə-lē) s. familia ◆ **f. doctor** médico de cabecera • **f. name** apellido • **f. planning** planeamiento del tamaño de la familia • **f. skeleton** secreto de familia • **f. tree** árbol genealógico.
fam·ine (făm'ĭn) s. hambre *f*.
fam·ished (:ĭsht) adj. muerto de hambre.
fa·mous (fā'məs) adj. famoso.
fa·mous·ly (:lē) adv. FAM. muy bien.
fan¹ (făn) I. s. *(paper)* abanico; *(electric)* ventilador *m* ◆ **f. belt** correa del ventilador II. tr. **-nn-** abanicar; FIG. avivar, excitar ◆ **f. out** abrirse en abanico.
fan² s. FAM. *(enthusiast)* aficionado ◆ **f. mail** cartas de admiradores.
fa·nat·ic (fə-năt'ĭk) s. & adj. fanático.
fa·nat·i·cal (:ĭ-kəl) adj. fanático.
fa·nat·i·cism (:sĭz'əm) s. fanatismo.
fan·ci·er (făn'sē-ər) s. conocedor, aficionado.
fan·ci·ful (făn'sĭ-fəl) adj. imaginativo.
fan·cy (făn'sē) I. s. imaginación *f*, fantasía; *(whim)* capricho ◆ **to strike one's f.** antojárselo a uno ◆ **to take a f. to** tomar cariño *o* gusto a II. adj. **-i-** *(elaborate)* muy adornado; *(superior)* fino, selecto; *(luxurious)* lujoso ◆ **f. dress** disfraz III. tr. imaginar; *(to like)* cobrar afecto por, gustarle a uno; *(to suppose)* suponer ◆ **f. that!** ¡imagínese! • **to f. oneself** imaginarse.
fan·cy-free (:frē') adj. despreocupado.
fan·cy·work (:wûrk') s. bordado.
fan·fare (făn'fâr') s. fanfarria.
fang (făng) s. colmillo; *(of snake)* diente *m*.
fan·ny (făn'ē) s. JER. trasero.
fan·ta·size (făn'tə-sīz') tr. & intr. fantasear.
fan·tas·tic (făn-tăs'tĭk) adj. fantástico.
fan·ta·sy (făn'tə-sē) s. fantasía.
far (fär) **-ther** *o* **further, -thest** *o* **furthest** I. adv. lejos; *(much)* mucho *<f. more* mucho más*>*; *(very)* muy *<f. different* muy diferente*>* ◆ **as f. as** *(up to)* hasta; *(to the extent that)* por lo que • **as f. as I am concerned** por mi parte • **as f. as possible** en lo posible • **by f.** con mucho • **f. and away** con mucho • **f. and wide** por todas partes • **f. away** *o* **f. off** (a lo) lejos • **f. be it from me** no me propongo • **f. from** lejos de • **f. from it** al contrario • **f. into** *(very late)* hasta muy avanzado; *(very deep)* hasta muy adentro de • **how f.?** *(distance)* ¿a qué distancia?; *(place)* ¿hasta dónde?; *(degree)* ¿hasta qué punto? • **so f.** *(place)* hasta aquí; *(up to now)* hasta ahora; *(extent)* hasta cierto punto • **so f. so good** hasta ahora todo va bien • **thus f.** hasta ahora • **to go f.** llegar lejos, realizar mucho; *(money)* rendir • **to go so f. as to** llegar inclusive a • **to go too f.** pasarse de la raya II. adj. lejano; *(side, corner)* otro, opuesto; *(journey)* largo; POL. extremo ◆ **a f. cry** una gran diferencia.
far·a·way ('ə-wā') adj. lejano, remoto; *(dreamy)* distraído, soñador.
farce (färs) s. farsa.
far·ci·cal (fär'sĭ-kəl) adj. ridículo, absurdo.
fare (fâr) I. intr. ir *<to f. badly* ir mal*>* II. s. pasaje *m*; *(passenger)* pasajero; *(food)* comida.
fare·well (fâr-wĕl') s. & interj. adiós *m*.
far·fetched (fär'fĕcht') adj. traído de los pelos.
far-flung (:flŭng') adj. vasto, extenso; *(remote)* remoto, distante.
farm (färm) I. s. granja, finca ◆ **f. hand** peón • **f. machinery** maquinaria agrícola II. tr. cultivar ◆ **to f. out** ceder por contrato —intr. labrar la tierra, ser agricultor.
farm·er (fär'mər) s. granjero, agricultor *m* ◆

small f. labrador.
farm·house (färm'hous') s. granja, cortijo.
farm·land (:länd') s. tierra de labrantía.
farm·yard (:yärd') s. corral m.
far-off (fär'ôf') adj. remoto.
far-reach·ing (:rē'chĭng) adj. de mucho alcance.
far·row (făr'ō) s. lechigada de cerdos.
far-sight·ed (fär'sī'tĭd) adj. prudente, previsor; OFTAL. présbite.
far·ther (fär'thər) [comp. de **far**] I. adv. (in space) más lejos; (in time) más adelante; (degree) más ♦ **f. on** más adelante II. adj. más lejano.
far·thest (:thĭst) [superl. de **far**] I. adj. más remoto II. adv. más lejos.
fas·ci·nate (făs'ə-nāt') tr. fascinar, encantar.
fas·ci·nat·ing (:nā'tĭng) adj. fascinante.
fas·ci·na·tion ('-'shən) s. fascinación f, encanto.
fas·cist (făsh'ĭst) s. fascista mf.
fash·ion (făsh'ən) I. s. manera, modo; (style) moda ♦ **after a f.** en cierto modo • **f. plate** figurín • **in f.** de moda • **in one's own f.** al estilo personal • **latest f.** la última moda • **to be in f.** estar de moda • **to go out of f.** pasar de moda II. tr. formar, moldear; (to adapt) amoldar ♦ **to f. out of** o **from** hacer con.
fash·ion·a·ble ('ə-nə-bəl) adj. de moda; (elegant) elegante, de buen tono.
fast¹ (făst) I. adj. (quick) rápido; (swift) veloz; (clock) adelantado; (dissipated) disipado; (color) inalterable; (secure) firme (en su lugar); (stuck) atascado; (loyal) leal ♦ **f. friend** amigo leal • **to pull a f. one** hacer una maldad (a alguien) II. adv. rápidamente, velozmente; (securely) firmemente; (clock) adelantadamente ♦ **f. and furious** a todo meter • **f. and loose** irresponsablemente • **to make f.** atar, sujetar • **to stand f.** mantenerse firme.
fast² I. intr. ayunar II. s. ayuno.
fas·ten (făs'ən) tr. fijar, sujetar; (to tie) atar; (to close) cerrar; blame echar ♦ **f. the door** echar el cerrojo —intr. fijarse, afirmarse.
fas·ten·er (:ə-nər) s. sujetador m.
fas·tid·i·ous (fă-stĭd'ē-əs) adj. meticuloso.
fat (făt) I. s. grasa; CUL. manteca ♦ **f. of the land** el meollo de la tierra II. adj. -tt- gordo; (lucrative) lucrativo; (thick) grueso; (large) grande ♦ **f. cat** JER. persona rica • **f. chance** JER. ninguna posibilidad • **to get f.** ponerse gordo, engordar.
fa·tal (fāt'l) adj. fatal, mortal.
fa·tal·ist (:ĭst) s. fatalista mf.
fa·tal·is·tic ('-lĭs'tĭk) adj. fatalista.
fa·tal·i·ty (fā-tăl'ĭ-tē) s. fatalidad f; (victim) muerto, víctima.
fate (fāt) s. destino, sino; (doom) fatalidad f.
fat·ed (fā'tĭd) adj. predestinado.
fate·ful (fāt'fəl) adj. fatídico, fatal.
fat·head (făt'hĕd') s. JER. imbécil mf, estúpido.
fa·ther (fä'thər) I. s. padre m ♦ **like f. like son** de tal palo tal astilla II. tr. engendrar.
fa·ther·hood (:hŏŏd') s. paternidad f.
fa·ther-in-law (:ĭn-lô') s. [pl. **fathers-**] suegro.
fa·ther·land (:länd') s. patria.
fa·ther·ly (:lē) adj. paternal, paterno.
fath·om (făth'əm) I. s. braza II. tr. comprender a fondo; MARÍT. (to sound) sondear.
fa·tigue (fə-tēg') I. s. fatiga; MIL. faena ♦ pl. traje de faena II. tr. fatigar, cansar.
fat·ness (făt'nĭs) s. gordura.

fat·so (:sō) s. [pl. **es**] JER. gordo.
fat·ten (:n) tr. engordar, cebar; FIG. aumentar —intr. engordar.
fat·ten·ing (:ĭng) adj. que engorda.
fat·ty (făt'ē) adj. graso, adiposo.
fat·u·ous (făch'ŏŏ-əs) adj. fatuo.
fau·cet (fô'sĭt) s. grifo, canilla.
fault (fôlt) I. s. culpa; (shortcoming) defecto; ELEC., GEOL. falla ♦ **at f.** culpable • **to be at f.** tener la culpa • **to find f.** criticar II. tr. encontrar defectos en.
fault·find·ing (:fīn'dĭng) adj. criticón.
fault·less (:lĭs) adj. perfecto, impecable.
fault·y (fôl'tē) adj. -i- defectuoso, imperfecto.
faun (fôn) s. fauno.
fa·vor (fā'vər) I. s. favor m; (esteem) estimación f, aprecio; (approval) aprobación f, apoyo ♦ **in f. of** a favor de; (made out to) a nombre de • **to be in (out of) f.** (dejar de) ser popular • **to be in f. of** estar a favor de, ser partidario de II. tr. favorecer; (to be partial to) preferir; (to resemble) parecerse a.
fa·vor·a·ble (:ə-bəl) adj. favorable.
fa·vored (fā'vərd) adj. favorecido; (favorite) preferido; (blessed) dotado.
fa·vor·ite (fā'vər-ĭt) I. s. favorito; (protégé) privado II. adj. favorito, preferido.
fa·vour (fā'vər) G.B. var. de **favor**.
fawn¹ (fôn) intr. hacer fiestas ♦ **to f. on** adular.
fawn² I. s. cervato, (color) color m de gamuza.
fawn·ing (:ĭng) adj. adulador, servil.
faze (fāz) tr. perturbar, desconcertar.
fe·al·ty (fē'əl-tē) s. lealtad f.
fear (fĭr) I. s. miedo, temor m; (dread) aprensión f ♦ **for f. that** por miedo de que • **to be in f. of** tener miedo de II. tr. & intr. tener miedo (de), temer ♦ **never f.** ¡no hay cuidado!
fear·ful (:fəl) adj. espantoso; (frightened) temeroso; (anxious) aprehensivo; FAM. (dreadful) tremendo ♦ **to be f.** of temer.
fear·less (:lĭs) adj. intrépido, audaz.
fear·some (:səm) adj. (frightening) temible, terrible.
fea·si·ble (fē'zə-bəl) adj. factible, viable.
feast (fēst) I. s. banquete m, comilona; (treat) gozo; RELIG. fiesta ♦ **f. day** día festivo II. tr. & intr. banquetear ♦ **to f. (one's eyes) on** regalarse (la vista) con.
feat (fēt) s. proeza, hazaña.
feath·er (fĕth'ər) I. s. pluma ♦ **a f. in one's cap** un triunfo de uno • **f. bed** colchón de plumas • **in fine f.** de muy buen humor ♦ pl. plumas, plumaje II. tr. emplumar ♦ **to f. one's nest** hacer su agosto.
feath·er·brain (:brān') s. FAM. pelele m.
feath·er·weight (:wāt') s. peso pluma.
feath·er·y (fĕth'ə-rē) adj. plumoso.
fea·ture (fē'chər) I. s. característica, rasgo; CINEM. película principal; PERIOD. artículo de primera plana ♦ pl. facciones, rasgos II. tr. (to showcase) presentar; (to be a characteristic of) tener, incorporar; (to draw) representar ♦ **f. that!** ¡imagínate eso!
fea·tured (fē'chərd) adj. (film) principal; (role) estelar; (article) de primera plana.
feb·rile (fĕb'rəl, fē'brəl) adj. febril.
Feb·ru·ar·y (fĕb'rŏŏ-ĕr'ē, fĕb'yŏŏ-) s. febrero.
fe·ces (fē'sēz) s.pl. excrementos, heces f.
feck·less (fĕk'lĭs) adj. irresponsable.
fe·cund (fē'kənd) adj. fecundo.
fe·cun·date (fē'kən-dāt') tr. fecundar.
fed (fĕd) I. cf. **feed** II. adj. ♦ **f. up with** harto

de.
fed·er·al (fĕd'ər-əl) adj. federal.
fed·er·al·ist (:ə-lĭst) adj. & s. federalista *mf*.
fed·er·ate (fĕd'ə-rāt') I. tr. & intr. federar(se), confederar(se) II. adj. (:ər-ĭt) federado.
fed·er·a·tion ('-rā'shən) s. federación *f*.
fee (fē) s. honorarios, emolumentos ♦ **admission, membership f.** cuota de admisión, socio • **registration f.** derechos de matrícula.
tee·ble (fē'bəl) adj. **-er, -est** débil.
tee·ble-mind·ed (:mīn'dĭd) adj. imbécil.
feed (fēd) I. tr. **fed** dar de comer a; *(to nourish, supply)* alimentar; *(anger, suspicion)* avivar; *(to breast-feed)* amamantar; *(to bottle-feed)* dar el biberón a ♦ **to f. on** alimentarse con; FIG. derivar satisfacción de —intr. comer ♦ **to f. one-self** alimentarse II. s. *(fodder)* pienso, forraje *m*; FAM. *(meal)* comida; MEC. alimentación *f*.
feed·back (:'băk') s. información *f*; ELECTRÓN. realimentación *f*, retroacción *f*.
feed·bag (:băg') s. morral *m*.
feed·ing (fē'dĭng) s. alimentación *f*.
feel (fēl) I. tr. **felt** sentir; *(to touch)* tocar; *(to examine)* palpar; *(to sense)* percibir ♦ **it feels cold, hot** hace frío, calor ♦ **to f. in one's bones that** FAM. tener el presentimiento que • **to f. out** averiguar, sondear —intr. sentir (por tacto); *(physically)* ser ... al tacto *<the sheets f. smooth* las sábanas son suaves al tacto*>*; *(emotionally)* sentirse, estar; *(to seem)* parecer; *(to grope)* andar a tientas; *(to believe)* creer, pensar ♦ **to f. cold, hot** tener o sentir frío, calor • to **f. for** *(to sympathize)* compadecer; *(to grope for)* buscar a tientas • **to f. hungry, sleepy** tener hambre, sueño • **to f. like** FAM. *(to want to)* tener ganas de; *(to the touch)* parecer (como) • **to f. up to** FAM. sentirse con ánimos para II. s. *(touch)* tacto; *(perception)* sensación *f*; *(atmosphere)* atmósfera ♦ **to get the f. of** coger el truco de • **to have a f. for** tener sentido para.
feel·er (fē'lər) s. *(probe)* sondeo; ZOOL. antena, tentáculo ♦ **to put out feelers** sondear.
feel·ing (fē'lĭng) I. s. *(touch)* tacto; *(sensation)* sensación *f*; *(emotion)* emoción *f*; *(impression)* impresión *f*; *(premonition)* presentimiento; *(passion)* pasión *f*; *(opinion)* opinión *f*; *(aptitude)* sentido ♦ pl. sensibilidades • **hard f.** resentimiento • **ill f.** malos sentimientos II. adj. sensible.
feet (fēt) cf. **foot.**
feign (fān) tr. & intr. aparentar, fingir.
feint (fānt) s. finta; MIL. maniobra fingida.
feist·y (fī'stē) adj. **-i-** intrépido, arrojado.
feld·spar (fĕld'spär') s. feldespato.
fe·lic·i·tous (fĭ-lĭs'ĭ-təs) adj. oportuno, apto.
fe·lic·i·ty (:tē) s. felicidad *f*; *(phrase)* dicho feliz.
fe·line (fē'līn') adj. felino.
fell[1] I. tr. cortar, talar; *(to kill)* acogotar.
fell[2] adj. cruel, feroz ♦ **in one f. swoop** de un solo golpe.
fell[3] cf. **fall.**
fel·low (fĕl'ō) I. s. *(boy)* muchacho; *(man)* hombre *m*; *(friend)* compañero; *(guy)* tipo; *(of a society)* socio ♦ **poor f.!** ¡pobre! II. adj. ♦ **f. citizens** (con)ciudadanos • **f. man** prójimo • **f. member** (con)socio • **f. worker** compañero de trabajo.
fel·low·ship (:shĭp') s. comunidad *f* (de intereses, ideas); *(fraternity)* fraternidad *f*; *(friendship)* compañerismo; EDUC. beca ♦ **good f.** espíritu de paz y concordia.

fel·on (fĕl'ən) s. criminal *m*, felón *m*.
fel·o·ny (:ə-nē) s. felonía, delito mayor.
felt[1] (fĕlt) adj. & s. (de) fieltro.
felt[2] cf. **feel.**
fe·male (fē'māl') I. adj. femenino; *(clothes, manners)* de mujer; *(group)* de mujeres; BIOL., MEC. hembra II. s. mujer; BIOL., BOT. hembra.
fem·i·nine (fĕm'ə-nĭn) adj. & s. femenino.
fem·i·nin·i·ty ('-'ĭ-tē) s. feminidad *f*.
fem·i·nist (fĕm'ə-nĭst) s. feminista *mf*.
fem·i·nize (:nīz') tr. & intr. afeminar(se).
fen (fĕn) s. ciénaga, pantano.
fence (fĕns) I. s. cerca, empalizada; JER. traficante *mf* de artículos robados ♦ **to sit on the f.** nadar entre dos aguas II. tr. cercar, vallar; *(to close off)* encerrar ♦ **to f. in** *(property)* cercar; *(animals)* encerrar • **to f. off** cercar • **to f. out** excluir —intr. DEP. practicar la esgrima; JER. traficar con artículos robados.
fenc·er (fĕn'sər) s. esgrimista *mf*.
fence-sit·ting (fĕns'sĭt'ĭng) s. irresolución *f*.
fend (fĕnd) tr. ♦ **to f. off** *(blow)* parar; *(attack)* repeler —intr. ♦ **to f. for oneself** valerse por sí mismo.
fend·er (fĕn'dər) s. AUTO. guardafango; F.C. quitapiedras *m*; *(fireplace screen)* pantalla.
fen·es·tra·tion (fĕn'ĭ-strā'shən) s. ventanaje *m*.
fen·nel (fĕn'əl) s. hinojo.
fer·ment I. s. *(ferment)* fermento; *(unrest)* agitación *f* II. tr. & intr. (fər-mĕnt') fermentar.
fern (fûrn) s. helecho.
fe·ro·cious (fə-rō'shəs) adj. feroz.
fe·roc·i·ty (fə-rŏs'ĭ-tē) s. ferocidad *f*.
fer·ret (fĕr'ĭt) I. s. hurón *m* II. tr. ♦ **to f. out** descubrir.
fer·ric (fĕr'ĭk) adj. férrico.
Fer·ris wheel (fĕr'ĭs) s. noria, vuelta al mundo.
fer·rite (fĕr'īt') s. QUÍM. ferrito; MIN. ferrita.
fer·ro·con·crete (fĕr'ō-kŏn'krēt') s. hormigón armado.
fer·ro·mag·net·ic (:măg-nĕt'ĭk) adj. ferromagnético.
fer·rous (fĕr'əs) adj. ferroso.
fer·rule (fĕr'əl) s. virola, contera.
fer·ry (fĕr'ē) I. tr. transportar en barco *o* avión II. s. transbordador *m*; *(pier)* embarcadero.
fer·ry·boat (:bōt') s. transbordador *m*, ferry *m*.
fer·ry·man (:mən) s. [pl. **-men**] barquero.
fer·tile (fûr'tl) adj. fértil; BIOL. fecundo.
fer·til·i·ty (fər-tĭl'ĭ-tē) s. fertilidad *f*, fecundidad *f*.
fer·til·ize (fûr'tl-īz') tr. abonar; BIOL. fecundar.
fer·til·iz·er (:ī'zər) s. fertilizante *m*, abono.
fer·vent (fûr'vənt) adj. ferviente, fervoroso.
fer·vid (fûr'vĭd) adj. fervoroso.
fer·vor (fûr'vər) s. fervor *m*.
fes·ter (fĕs'tər) intr. *(to rankle)* enconarse; *(to suppurate)* supurar.
fes·ti·val (fĕs'tə-vəl) I. s. fiesta; *(art, film)* festival *m* II. adj. festivo, de fiesta.
fes·tive (fĕs'tĭv) adj. festivo, de fiesta.
fes·tiv·i·ty (fĕ-stĭv'ĭ-tē) s. festividad *f*, fiesta; *(merriment)* regocijo ♦ pl. diversiones.
fes·toon (fĕ-stōon') I. s. festón *m* II. tr. festonear.
fetch (fĕch) tr. traer, ir a buscar; *(a sigh)* dar; *(blood, tears)* hacer brotar; *(a price)* venderse por —intr. cobrar la presa ♦ **fetch!** ¡tráelo! (a un perro).
fetch·ing (fĕch'ĭng) adj. atractivo, encantador.
fete (fāt, fĕt) I. s. fiesta, festín *m* II. tr. festejar.
fet·id (fĕt'ĭd) adj. fétido, hediondo.

fet·ish (fĕt´ĭsh) s. fetiche *m* ♦ **to make a f. of** venerar.

fet·ish·ist (:ĭ-shĭst´) s. fetichista *mf*.

fet·ter (fĕt´ər) I. s. *(shackle)* grillete *m*; *(restraint)* traba II. tr. poner grilletes *o* trabas a.

fet·tle (fĕt´l) s. ♦ **in fine f.** *(condition)* en forma; *(spirits)* de buen humor.

fe·tus (fē´təs) s. [pl. **es**] feto.

feud (fyōōd) I. s. enemistad prolongada II. intr. pelear, contender.

feu·dal (´l) adj. feudal.

fe·ver (fē´vər) s. fiebre *f*.

fe·ver·ish (:ĭsh) adj. febril.

few (fyōō) I. adj. poco ♦ **a f.** unos • **a f. times** varias veces • **every f. (miles)** cada dos o tres (millas) • **the last f. (days)** estos últimos (días) II. s. & pron. pocos ♦ **a f.** unos cuantos • **a f.** of algunos de • **quite a f.** muchos.

few·er (´ər) adj. & pron. menos *(than de)* ♦ **the f. the better** cuantos menos mejor.

few·est (:ĭst) I. adj. menos II. pron. el menor número.

fi·an·cé (fē´än-sā´) s. novio, prometido ♦ **fian·cée** novia, prometida.

fi·as·co (fē-ăs´kō) s. [pl. **(e)s**] fiasco.

fi·at (fē´ăt´, fē´ät´) s. fiat *m*.

fib (fĭb) I. s. mentirilla II. intr. **-bb-** decir mentirillas.

fib·ber (´ər) s. mentirosillo.

fi·ber (fī´bər) s. fibra; FIG. carácter *m*, nervio ♦ **f. glass** fibra de vidrio.

fi·ber·board (:bôrd´) s. madera de bagazo.

fi·brous (fī´brəs) adj. fibroso.

fick·le (fĭk´əl) adj. inconstante, variable.

fic·tion (fĭk´shən) s. ficción *f*; *(lie)* mentira.

fic·tion·al (:shə-nəl) adj. ficticio; LIT. novelístico, de ficción.

fic·tion·al·ize (:nə-līz´) tr. novelar, novelizar.

fic·ti·tious (fĭk-tĭsh´əs) adj. ficticio.

fid·dle (fĭd´l) FAM. I. s. violín *m* ♦ **fit as a f.** sano como una manzana • **to play second f.** desempeñar un papel secundario II. intr. tocar el violín ♦ **to f. around** perder el tiempo • **to f. with** juguetear con —tr. tocar ♦ **to f. away** perder.

fid·dler (:lər) s. FAM. violinista *mf*.

fid·dle·sticks (:l-stĭks´) interj. ¡tonterías!

fi·del·i·ty (fĭ-dĕl´ĭ-tē) s. fidelidad *f*.

fidg·et (fĭj´ĭt) intr. moverse, no estarse quieto.

fidg·et·y (:ĭ-tē) adj. nervioso, inquieto.

fi·du·cial (fĭ-dōō´shəl) adj. fiduciario.

fi·du·ci·ar·y (:shē-ĕr´ē) adj. & s. fiduciario.

fief (fēf) s. feudo.

field (fēld) I. s. campo; *(profession)* profesión *f*; *(contestants)* competidores *m* ♦ **f. glasses** gemelos • **f. goal** gol de patada • **f. gun** cañón de campaña • **f. hand** peón • **f. marshal** mariscal de campo • **f. of view** campo visual • **f. trip** excursión • **to take the f.** DEP. salir a jugar; MIL. entrar en campaña II. tr. *(team)* poner en el campo; *(question)* manejar.

field·work (´wûrk´) s. trabajo en el terreno.

fiend (fēnd) s. demonio; FAM. *(addict)* vicioso.

fiend·ish (fēn´dĭsh) adj. diabólico.

fierce (fîrs) adj. feroz; *(violent)* violento; *(hard-fought)* reñido; *(ardent)* furioso.

fier·y (fîr´ē) adj. **-i-** *(blazing)* llameante; *(hot)* abrasador; *(color)* encendido; *(temper)* fogoso; *(words)* enardecido.

fife (fīf) s. pífano, flautín *m*.

fif·teen (fĭf-tēn´) s. & adj. quince *m*.

fif·teenth (:tēnth´) s. & adj. *(place)* decimoquinto; *(part)* quinzavo.

fifth (fĭfth) adj. & s. quinto.

fif·ti·eth (fĭf´tē-ĭth) I. s. *(place)* cincuenta; *(part)* quincuagésimo II. adj. *(place)* quincuagésimo; *(part)* cincuentavo.

fif·ty (fĭf´tē) adj. & s. cincuenta *m*.

fif·ty-fif·ty (´ ´) adj. FAM. mitad y mitad ♦ **to go f.** ir a medias.

fig (fĭg) s. higo ♦ **f. leaf** hoja de parra • **not to care a f.** importarle a uno un bledo.

fight (fīt) I. intr. *fought* luchar, pelear; *(to box)* boxear; *(to argue)* reñir ♦ **to f. back** defenderse —tr. luchar con *o* contra; *(to resist, combat)* combatir; *(a battle)* dar, librar; DER. litigar, contender ♦ **to f. it out** decidirlo luchando • **to f. off** rechazar, repeler II. s. lucha; *(combat)* combate *m*; *(quarrel)* riña, disputa; *(brawl, boxing)* pelea; *(bellicosity)* combatividad *f* ♦ **fair f.** buena lid • **to have a f.** pelearse.

fight·er (fī´tər) s. luchador *m*, combatiente *mf*; *(boxer)* boxeador *m* ♦ **f. plane** avión de caza.

fig·ment (fĭg´mənt) s. invención *f* ♦ **f. of one's imagination** producto de la imaginación.

fig·u·ra·tive (fĭg´yər-ə-tĭv) adj. figurativo.

fig·ure (fĭg´yər) I. s. figura; *(number)* cifra; *(price)* precio; *(illustration)* diseño, dibujo; *(silhouette)* silueta ♦ **f. of speech** figura, tropo • **f. skating** patinaje artístico • **to cut a fine f.** causar una buena impresión • **to keep one's f.** guardar la línea • pl. cálculos, operaciones • **in round f.** en números redondos • **to be good at f.** ser fuerte en aritmética II. tr. computar, calcular; *(to depict)* figurar, representar; FAM. *(to reckon)* imaginar(se), figurar(se) • **to f. out** *(to solve)* resolver; *(to understand)* comprender —intr. hacer cálculos; *(to appear)* figurar, encontrarse ♦ **to f. as** pasar por • **to f. on** FAM. contar con.

fig·ure·head (:hĕd´) s. *(leader)* testaferro; MARIT. mascarón de proa.

fig·u·rine (fĭg´yə-rēn´) s. estatuilla.

fil·a·ment (fĭl´ə-mənt) s. filamento.

fil·bert (fĭl´bərt) s. avellana.

filch (fĭlch) tr. hurtar, robar.

file¹ (fīl) s. archivo; *(for cards)* fichero; *(dossier)* expediente *m*; *(folder)* carpeta; MIL. fila, columna ♦ **f. card** ficha • **f. clerk** archivista • **to be on f.** estar archivado II. tr. archivar; *(to put in order)* clasificar, ordenar; *(claim, suit)* entablar; *(complaint)* sentar; *(petition, appeal)* presentar —intr. marchar en fila ♦ **to f. by** *(to parade)* desfilar; *(single file)* pasar uno por uno • **to f. in, out** entrar, salir en fila.

file² I. s. *(tool)* lima II. tr. limar.

fi·let (fĭ-lā´) s. filete *m*.

fil·i·bus·ter (fĭl´ə-bŭs´tər) I. s. maniobra obstruccionista II. tr. obstruir *(moción, propuesta).*

fil·i·gree (fĭl´ĭ-grē´) s. filigrana.

fil·ing (fī´lĭng) s. colocación *f* en un archivo.

fil·ings (fī´lĭngz) s.pl. limaduras.

fill (fĭl) I. tr. llenar; *(to plug up)* tapar; *(a tooth)* empastar; *(to fulfill)* cumplir con; FARM. preparar *(receta)*; *(to occupy)* ocupar; CONSTR., CUL. rellenar; COM. *(order)* despachar; MARIT. hinchar *(velas)* ♦ **to f. in** *(a form)* llenar; *(to complete)* completar con *(información, detalles)* • **to f. out** *(to enlarge)* ensanchar; *(a form)* completar; COM. *(order)* despachar • **to f. someone in on** poner a alguien al corriente de • **to f. up** llenar *(hasta el tope)* —intr. llenarse ♦ **to f. in for** reemplazar a • **to f. out** ensancharse • **to f.**

up llenarse **II.** s. *(enough)* hartura, hartazgo; CONSTR. terraplén *m*, relleno ♦ **to have had one's f.** of estar harto de.

fill·er ('ər) s. relleno.

fil·let (fĭ-lā', fĭl'ĭt) **I.** s. filete *m* **II.** tr. cortar en filetes.

fill·ing (fĭl'ĭng) s. relleno; ODONT. empaste *m* ♦ **f. station** gasolinera.

fil·ly (fĭl'ē) s. potranca, potra.

film (fĭlm) **I.** s. película; *(coating)* capa; *(in eyes)* tela; *(cinema)* cinema *m* ♦ **f. studio** estudio cinematográfico **II.** tr. *(an event)* filmar; *(a scene)* rodar; *(a play)* hacer una versión fílmica de —intr. rodar.

film·mak·er ('mā'kər) s. cineasta *mf.*

film·strip (:strĭp') s. tira de película.

film·y (fĭl'mē) adj. -i- tenue, diáfano.

fil·ter (fĭl'tər) **I.** s. filtro **II.** tr. & intr. filtrar(se) ♦ **f. in** entrar poco a poco.

filth (fĭlth) s. mugre *f*, suciedad *f.*

filth·y (fĭl'thē) adj. -i- sucio, mugriento.

fil·trate (fĭl'trāt') **I.** tr. filtrar **II.** s. filtrado.

fin (fĭn) s. aleta; AER. plano de deriva.

fi·na·gle (fə-nā'gəl) JER. tr. agenciarse.

fi·nal (fī'nəl) **I.** adj. último; *(concluding)* final; *(unalterable)* definitivo **II.** s. DEP. final *f*; EDUC. examen final.

fi·nal·e (fə-năl'ē) s. final *m*; TEAT. último acto.

fi·nal·ist (fī'nə-lĭst) s. finalista *mf.*

fi·nal·ize (:līz') tr. finalizar, concluir.

fi·nal·ly (:lē) adv. finalmente, por último.

fi·nance (fə-năns', fī'năns') **I.** s. finanzas *f* ♦ **company** sociedad financiera ♦ pl. finanzas, fondos **II.** tr. financiar.

fin·an·cier (fĭn'ən-sîr') s. financiero.

fi·nanc·ing (fə-năn'sĭng, fī'-năn'-) s. financiamiento, financiación *f.*

finch (fĭnch) s. pinzón *m.*

find (fīnd) **I.** tr. **found** encontrar; *(to notice)* hallar; *(to discover)* descubrir; *(a target)* dar en; *(to regain)* recuperar; DER. declarar ♦ **to f. oneself** verse, encontrarse ♦ **to f. out** averiguar, descubrir —intr. ♦ **to f. for** fallar a favor de ♦ **to f. out about** informarse sobre **II.** s. descubrimiento, hallazgo.

find·ings (fīn'dĭngz) s.pl. *(of research)* resultados; *(of a report)* conclusiones; DER. fallo.

fine¹ (fīn) **I.** adj. fino; *(skillful)* excelente; *(weather)* lindo; *(sharp)* afilado; *(healthy)* bien; *(subtle)* sutil ♦ **f. arts** bellas artes • **f. print** letra menuda • **(it's) f. with me** FAM. estoy de acuerdo • **one f. day** un buen día • **that's f.!** ¡está bien! **II.** adv. estupendamente; *(minutely)* finamente; FAM. muy bien.

fine² (fīn) **I.** s. multa **II.** tr. multar.

fine·ness (nĭs) s. fineza, delicadeza; *(excellence)* perfección *f*; *(thinness)* finura.

fin·er·y (fī'nə-rē) s. adornos, galas.

fi·nesse (fə-nĕs') s. *(skill)* finura, delicadeza; *(subtlety)* delicadeza, tacto.

fine-tune (fīn'tōōn') tr. afinar.

fin·ger (fĭng'gər) **I.** s. dedo ♦ **index f.** (dedo) índice • **little f.** (dedo) meñique • **not to lift a f.** no mover un dedo • **ring f.** (dedo) anular • **to get one's fingers burned** cogerse los dedos • **to keep one's fingers crossed** esperar que todo salga bien • **to put one's f. on** acertar **II.** tr. *(to handle, play)* tocar; JER. *(to inform on)* denunciar; *(a victim)* marcar.

fin·ger·board (:bôrd') s. diapasón *m.*

fin·ger·ing (:ĭng) s. digitación *f.*

fin·ger·nail (:nāl') s. uña.

fin·ger·print (:prĭnt') **I.** s. huella digital **II.** tr. tomar las huellas digitales.

fin·ger·tip (:tĭp') s. punta o yema del dedo.

fin·ick·y (fĭn'ĭ-kē) adj. -i- quisquilloso.

fin·ish (fĭn'ĭsh) **I.** tr. acabar (con); *(to terminate)* terminar; *(a journey)* llegar al final de; *(to perfect)* rematar ♦ **to f. off** acabar con; *(to perfect)* rematar • **to f. up** acabar, terminar —intr. acabar, terminar ♦ **to f. (first)** llegar o quedar (en primer lugar) • **to f. with someone** romper (relaciones) con alguien **II.** s. final *m*, fin *m*; *(substance)* pulimento; *(perfection)* perfección *f*; TEC. acabado ♦ **f. line** línea de llegada.

fin·ished (:ĭsht) adj. acabado, FIG. consumado, excelente; *(ruined)* arruinado.

fin·ish·ing (:ĭsh-ĭng) adj. último ♦ **f. school** colegio para señoritas • **f. touch** último toque.

fi·nite (fī'nīt') adj. finito.

fink (fĭngk) s. JER. persona odiosa.

fir (fûr) s. abeto.

fire (fīr) **I.** s. fuego; *(destructive)* incendio ♦ **f. bomb** bomba incendiaria • **f. department** o **brigade** cuerpo de bomberos • **f. drill** ejercicios contra incendios • **f. engine** camión de bomberos • **f. escape** salida de urgencia • **f. wall** muro refractario • **to be on f.** estar en llamas o ardiendo • **to be** o **to come under f.** FIG. ser blanco de ataques • **to catch f.** encenderse, coger fuego • **to set on f.** o **to f.** prenderle o pegarle fuego a **II.** tr. *(to ignite)* encender; *(to arouse)* enardecer; *(gun, bullet)* disparar; *(a shot)* tirar; *(a rocket)* lanzar; FAM. *(to hurl)* tirar, arrojar; *(from a job)* despedir, echar; CERÁM. cocer ♦ **to f. questions at** bombardear a preguntas —intr. disparar *(on contra)* ♦ **to f. away** disparar sin cesar • **to get fired up** apasionarse.

fire·arm ('ärm') s. arma de fuego.

fire·ball (:bôl') s. bola incandescente.

fire·base (:bās') s. base *f* de fuego.

fire·boat (:bōt') s. barco bomba.

fire·brand (:brănd') s. *(torch)* tizón *m*, tea; FIG. agitador *m*, cizañero.

fire·break (:brāk') s. cortafuego.

fire·crack·er (:krăk'ər) s. cohete *m*, petardo.

fire·fight·er (:fī'tər) s. bombero.

fire·fly (:flī') s. luciérnaga.

fire·house (:hous') s. estación *f* de bomberos.

fire·light (:līt') s. luz *f* del hogar, lumbre *f.*

fire·man (:mən) s. [pl. **-men**] bombero.

fire·place (:plās') s. hogar, chimenea *m.*

fire·plug (:plŭg') s. boca de incendios.

fire·pow·er (:pou'ər) s. potencia de fuego.

fire·proof (:prōōf') adj. a prueba de fuego; *(incombustible)* incombustible.

fire·side (:sīd') s. hogar *m.*

fire·wa·ter (:wô'tər) s. JER. aguardiente *m.*

fire·wood (:wŏōd') s. leña.

fire·works (:wûrks') s.pl. fuegos artificiales.

fir·ing (:ĭng) s. *(of guns)* disparo, descarga; *(shots)* disparos; FAM. *(from a job)* despido ♦ **f. pin** percusor • **f. squad** pelotón de fusilamiento.

firm¹ (fûrm) adj. & adv. firme ♦ **to stand f.** mantenerse firme.

firm² s. COM. firma, casa.

fir·ma·ment (fûr'mə-mənt) s. firmamento.

firm·ness (fûrm'nĭs) s. firmeza.

first (fûrst) **I.** adj. primero; *(elementary)* primario; *(outstanding)* sobresaliente; *(principal)*

principal ♦ f. **aid** primeros auxilios • **(at)** f. **hand** de primera mano ♦ f. **mate** segundo oficial • f. **name** nombre de pila • f. **papers** E.U. solicitud de nacionalización • **in the** f. **place** en primer lugar • **not to know the** f. **thing about** no saber absolutamente nada de II. adv. primero; *(before anything else)* antes; *(firstly)* en primer lugar; *(for the first time)* por primera vez. ♦ **at** f. en un principio • f. **and foremost** antes que nada • f. **of all** ante todo • **to come** f. ser lo más importante • **to go** f. ser el primero III. s. primero; *(beginning)* principio; AUTO. primera.

first-born ('bŏrn') adj. & s. primogénito.

first-class (:klăs') I. adj. de primera clase; *(first-rate)* de primera categoría II. adv. en primera.

first·hand (:hănd') adv. & adj. de primera mano.

first·ly (:lē) adv. en primer lugar.

first-rate (:rāt') I. adj. de primera categoría o clase II. adv. FAM. muy bien.

firth (fûrth) s. estuario.

fis·cal (fĭs′kəl) s. & adj. fiscal m.

fish (fĭsh) I. s. [pl. **-es** o **-**] pez m; *(food)* pescado ♦ **a cold** f. FAM. persona sin sentimientos • **neither** f. **nor fowl** ni chicha ni limonada • **to have other** f. **to fry** FAM. tener otras cosas en que ocuparse II. intr. pescar ♦ **to** f. **for** andar a la pesca de • **to go fishing** ir de pesca —tr. pescar; *(from pocket)* buscar, sacar ♦ **to** f. **out** agotar los peces en.

fish·bone (:bōn') s. espina.

fish·bowl (:bōl') s. pecera; FIG. vidriera.

fish·er (:ər) s. pescador m.

fish·er·man (:ər-mən) s. [pl. **-men**] pescador m.

fish·er·y (:ə-rē) s. pesca; *(place)* pesquería.

fish·eye (:ī′) adj. de ángulo plano, de 180°

fish·hook (:hŏŏk′) s. anzuelo.

fish·ing (:ĭng) s. pesca ♦ f. **ground** zona de pesca • f. **rod** caña de pescar.

fish·mar·ket (:mär′kĭt) s. pescadería.

fish·mon·ger (:mŭng′gər) s. G.B. pescadero.

fish·net (:nĕt′) s. red f.

fish·tail (:tāl′) intr. colear.

fish·wife (:wīf′) s. [pl. **-ves**] FAM. verdulera.

fish·y (:ē) adj. -i- a pescado; FAM. sospechoso.

fis·sile (fĭs′əl, fĭs′īl′) adj. fisionable, fisil.

fis·sion (fĭsh′ən) s. fisión f.

fis·sure (fĭsh′ər) s. fisura.

fist (fĭst) s. puño.

fist·fight (′fĭt′) s. pelea a puñetazos.

fist·ful (:fŏŏl′) s. puñado.

fist·i·cuffs (fĭs′tĭ-kŭfs′) s.pl. pelea a puñetazos.

fit¹ (fĭt) I. tr. **fit(ted)**, **-tting** *(to go on, in)* entrar en; *(to put on, in)* colocar, meter; *(to alter, adjust, match)* ajustar; *(to suit)* sentar bien ♦ **to** f. **in** tener tiempo para • **to** f. **out** proveer; *(a ship)* armar —intr. caber; *(part, piece)* ajustar, encajar; *(to agree)* concordar; *(clothes)* sentar bien • **to** f. **in(to)** encajar o caber en • **to** f. **in with** *(people)* congeniar con; *(things)* cuadrar II. adj. -tt- oportuno, conveniente; *(healthy)* sano; *(competent)* idóneo; *(suitable)* apropiado, digno ♦ f. **to be tied** FAM. fuera de sí • **to keep** f. mantenerse en buen estado físico • **to see** f. juzgar conveniente III. s. ajuste m, encaje m; *(clothes)* corte m, entalladura.

fit² s. ataque m; *(convulsion)* convulsión f ♦ **by fits and starts** a tropezones.

fit·ful (′fəl) adj. intermitente, irregular.

fit·ness (:nĭs′) s. propiedad f, conveniencia;

(healthiness) salud f, estado físico.

fit·ted (:ĭd) adj. apto, capacitado; *(clothes)* entallado; *(suit)* hecho a la medida.

fit·ting (:ĭng) I. adj. apropiado, oportuno; *(proper)* propio, justo II. s. *(of clothes)* prueba; MEC. parte suelta.

five (fīv) s. & adj. cinco ♦ f. **hundred** quinientos • f. **o'clock** las cinco.

five-and-ten ('ən-tĕn′) o **five-and-dime** (:dīm′) s. tienda que vende artículos baratos.

fix (fĭks) I. tr. fijar; *(to repair)* reparar, componer; *(hair)* arreglar; *(meal)* preparar; FAM. *(to get even with)* ajustarle las cuentas a; *(race, election)* arreglar; *(to solve)* solucionar ♦ **to** f. **up** FAM. *(to repair)* componer; *(to arrange)* organizar; *(to tidy)* arreglar —intr. fijarse ♦ **to** f. **on** decidir II. s. apuro, aprieto; RAD. posición f; *(bribery)* soborno; JER. dosis f de narcótico.

fix·a·tion (fĭk-sā′shən) s. fijación f.

fix·a·tive (fĭk′sə-tĭv) s. fijador m.

fixed (fĭkst) adj. fijo; *(stationary)* estacionario; FAM. *(contest)* arreglado; QUÍM. estable.

fix·er (fĭk′sər) s. fijador m.

fix·ture (fĭks′chər) s. instalación fija; *(appliance)* accesorio, artefacto.

fizz (fĭz) I. s. sonido de efervescencia II. intr. hacer sonido de efervescencia.

fiz·zle ('əl) I. s. FAM. fracaso II. intr. chisporrotear ♦ **to** f. **out** FAM. quedarse sin energía.

fjord (fyôrd) s. fiordo.

flab (flăb) s. FAM. carne o piel fláccida.

flab·ber·gast (flăb′ər-găst′) tr. FAM. asombrar.

flab·by (flăb′ē) adj. -i- fláccido.

flac·cid (flăk′sĭd, flăs′ĭd) adj. fláccido.

flag¹ (flăg) I. s. bandera II. tr. **-gg-** marcar *(con una señal)*; *(taxi, bus)* hacer parar con señales a.

flag² intr. **-gg-** *(to weaken)* debilitarse; *(to falter)* disminuir.

flag·el·lant (flăj′ə-lənt) s. flagelante mf.

flag·el·late (:lāt′) tr. flagelar.

flag·on (flăg′ən) s. jarra grande, pichel m.

flag·pole (flăg′pōl′) s. mástil m, asta m.

fla·gran·cy (flā′grən-sē) s. escándalo.

fla·grant (flā′grənt) adj. *(glaring)* descarado; *(shocking)* escandaloso.

flag·ship (flăg′shĭp′) s. buque m insignia.

flag·stone (flăg′stōn′) s. lastra, losa.

flag·wav·ing (flăg′wā′vĭng) s. patriotería.

flail (flāl) I. s. mayal m II. tr. *(to thresh)* desgranar; *(to thrash)* golpear —intr. agitarse.

flair (flâr) s. *(knack)* don m; *(style)* elegancia.

flak (flăk) s. MIL. artillería antiaérea; FAM. *(criticism)* crítica excesiva.

flake (flāk) I. s. escama, hojuela; *(snowflake)* copo; JER. persona rara II. intr. *(skin)* descamarse; *(paint)* desprenderse en escamillas.

flak·y (flā′kē) adj. -i- escamoso; JER. raro, loco.

flam·boy·ant (flăm-boi′ənt) I. adj. rimbombante, llamativo II. s. framboyán m.

flame (flām) I. s. llama; FAM. *(sweetheart)* novio, -a II. intr. arder, llamear ♦ **to** f. **up** *(person)* inflamarse; *(situation)* estallar.

flame·proof ('prŏŏf′) adj. incombustible.

flame·throw·er (:thrō′ər) s. lanzallamas m.

flam·ing (flā′mĭng) adj. ardiente, llameante.

fla·min·go (flə-mĭng′gō) s. [pl. **(e)s**] flamenco.

flam·ma·ble (flăm′ə-bəl) adj. inflamable.

flank (flăngk) s. ijada II. tr. flanquear.

flan·nel (flăn′əl) s. franela ♦ f. pl. pantalones o ropa interior de franela.

flap (flăp) I. s. *(of wings)* aleteo; *(of flags)* ondulación *f*; *(of envelopes)* solapa; *(of pockets)* cartera; *(of garments)* faldón *m*; *(of hats)* ala; AVIA. alerón *m*; JER. *(uproar)* jaleo II. tr. & intr. **-pp-** *(wings)* aletear, batir; *(arms)* agitar; *(sails)* gualdrapear; *(to sway)* sacudir(se).

flare (flâr) I. intr. llamear; *(to glow)* brillar; *(to widen)* acampanarse ♦ **t. up** llamear; *(in anger)* encolerizarse; *(conflict)* estallar II. s. llamarada; *(signal)* señal luminosa; *(outburst)* arrebato; COST. vuelo; ASTRON. erupción *f*.

flare-up ('ŭp') s. llamarada repentina; *(outburst)* estallido.

flash (flăsh) I. tr. *(to emit)* lanzar, despedir (luz); *(to reflect)* reflejar; *(to aim)* dirigir; FAM. *(to flaunt, show)* enseñar; *(a smile)* echar —intr. *(to sparkle)* brillar, destellar; *(to flare up)* llamear; *(thought, idea)* pasar o cruzar como un relámpago; *(eyes)* relampaguear *(with de)* ♦ **t. by** pasar como un rayo II. s. destello, resplandor *m*; FOTOG. flash *m*; *(of understanding)* rayo de luz; *(news)* noticia de último momento; *(of lightning)* relámpago; FAM. ostentación *f* ♦ **a t. in the pan** mucho ruido y pocas nueces • **t. bulb** lámpara de flash • **t. flood** riada • **t. point** punto de inflamación • **in a t.** en un instante • **like a t.** como un rayo.

flash-back ('băk') s. escena retrospectiva intercalada en la acción presente.

flash-er (:ər) s. destellador *m*.

flash-ing (:ĭng) adj. centelleante, intermitente.

flash-light (:līt') s. linterna eléctrica.

flash-y (ē) adj. **-i-** llamativo, chillón.

flask (flăsk) s. frasco; QUÍM. matraz *m*.

flat¹ (flăt) **-tt-** I. adj. *(level)* plano, llano; *(smooth)* liso, raso; *(prone)* tendido; *(definite)* categórico; *(fixed)* fijo, *(dull)* monótono; *(tasteless)* soso; *(tire)* desinflado; *(color)* sin brillo; MÚS. *(key)* bemol; *(pitch)* desafinado II. adv. horizontalmente, de plano; *(completely)* sin más ni más ♦ **t. broke** FAM. pelado • **t. out** a toda velocidad III. s. plano, superficie *f*; *(tire)* pinchazo; MÚS. bemol *m* ♦ **the t. of the hand** la palma de la mano ♦ pl. llanura, llano.

flat² s. *(apartment)* apartamento.

flat-boat ('bōt') s. barca chata, chalana.

flat-car (:kär') s. vagón *m* de plataforma.

flat-footed (:fŏŏt'ĭd) adj. de pies planos.

flat-land (:lănd') s. llano, llanura.

flat-ten (:n) tr. allanar, achatar; *(to knock down)* derribar —intr. achatarse.

flat-ter (flăt'ər) tr. adular, halagar; *(to suit)* favorecer —intr. emplear lisonjas.

flat-ter-er (:ər) s. adulador *m*, lisonjero.

flat-ter-y (flăt'ə-rē) s. lisonja, halago.

flat-u-lent (flăch'ə-lənt) adj. flatulento.

flaunt (flônt) tr. hacer ostentación de.

fla-vor (flā'vər) I. s. gusto, sabor *m* <mint *f* sabor a menta>; *(flavoring)* condimento II. tr. condimentar, aderezar.

fla-vor-ful (:fəl) adj. sabroso, gustoso.

fla-vor-ing (:ĭng) s. condimento, aderezo.

fla-vour (flā'vər) G.B. var. de **flavor.**

flaw (flô) s. imperfección *f*, defecto.

flawed (flôd) adj. defectuoso, estropeado.

flaw-less (flô'lĭs) adj. perfecto, sin defecto.

flax (flăks) s. lino; *(fiber)* fibra de lino.

flax-en (flăk'sən) adj. de lino; *(blond)* rubio.

flay (flā) tr. desollar, despellejar.

flea (flē) s. pulga ♦ **t. market** mercado de artículos usados.

fleck (flĕk) I. s. pinta, mota II. tr. motear.

fledg(e)-ling (flĕj'lĭng) s. pajarito; *(novice)* novato.

flee (flē) intr. **fled** huir, escaparse; *(to vanish)* desvanecerse —tr. huir de.

fleece (flēs) I. s. lana; *(sheared)* vellón *m*; *(lining)* muletón *m* II. tr. *(to shear)* esquilar; *(to rob)* desplumar, pelar.

fleec-y (flē'sē) adj. **-i-** lanudo.

fleet¹ (flēt) s. *(of ships)* flota; *(of cars)* escuadra; MIL. armada, fuerza naval.

fleet² adj. *(fast)* rápido, ligero.

fleet-ing (flē'tĭng) adj. fugaz, efímero.

flesh (flĕsh) I. s. carne *f*; *(fat)* gordura; *(of fruits)* pulpa ♦ **t. wound** herida superficial • **in the f.** en persona II. tr. ♦ **to t. out** extender, completar.

flesh-y (ē) adj. **-i-** carnoso; *(fat)* corpulento.

flew (flōō) cf. **fly¹.**

flex (flĕks) I. tr. & intr. doblar(se), encorvar(se) II. s. G.B. flexible m.

flex-i-ble (flĕk'sə-bəl) adj. flexible.

flick¹ (flĭk) I. s. golpecito; *(of tail)* coleada; *(of fingers)* capirotazo II. tr. golpear rápida y ligeramente; *(to snap)* dar un golpecito a —intr. colear ♦ **to t. through** hojear.

flick² FAM. *(film)* película, filme *m*.

flick-er (:ər) I. intr. oscilar, temblar; *(light)* parpadear, vacilar II. s. luz *f* vacilante.

fli-er (flī'ər) s. aviador *m*; *(circular)* volante *m*.

flight¹ (flīt) s. vuelo; *(flock)* bandada; *(swift movement)* paso fugaz; *(floor)* piso; *(of stairs)* tramo ♦ **t. attendant** aeromozo, -a • **t. deck** cubierta de aterrizaje ♦ **to take t.** alzar el vuelo.

flight² s. *(act of fleeing)* huida, fuga.

flight-less (:lĭs) adj. incapaz de volar.

flight-y (flī'tē) adj. **-i-** frívolo, casquivano.

flim-sy (flĭm'zē) adj. **-i-** insubstancial, endeble; *(excuse)* flojo.

flinch (flĭnch) I. intr. *(to wince)* sobresaltarse; *(to retreat)* recular II. s. reculada.

fling (flĭng) I. tr. **flung** arrojar, tirar ♦ **to t. about** agitar (brazos) • **to t. aside** abandonar, desechar • **to t. down** echar al suelo • **to t. one-self** precipitarse, lanzarse II. s. lanzamiento; FAM. *(spree)* juerga; *(attempt)* tentativa (breve) ♦ **to have a f.** echar una cana al aire.

flint (flĭnt) s. pedernal *m*.

flint-lock ('lŏk') s. llave *f* o trabuco de chispa.

flip (flĭp) I. tr. **-pp-** lanzar, tirar; *(coin)* echar (a cara o cruz) ♦ **to t. over** dar la vuelta o —intr. agitarse, dar vueltas ♦ **to t. out** enloquecerse *(over por)* • **to t. over** voltearse, volcarse • **to t. through** hojear II. s. golpe *m*; *(shake)* sacudida; *(somersault)* salto mortal ♦ **t. side** reverso (de un disco) III. adj. FAM. descarado.

flip-flop ('flŏp') s. FAM. cambio brusco.

flip-pant (flĭp'ənt) adj. frívolo, impertinente.

flip-per (flĭp'ər) s. aleta.

flirt (flûrt) I. intr. flirtear, coquetear; *(with danger)* jugar II. s. *(man)* galanteador *m*; *(woman)* coqueta.

flir-ta-tion (flûr-tā'shən) s. flirteo, coqueteo.

flit (flĭt) intr. **-tt-** revolotear.

float (flōt) I. tr. hacer flotar, poner a flote; FIN. *(a loan)* negociar; *(currency)* dejar fluctuar —intr. flotar; FIN. *(currency)* fluctuar; *(to wander)* vagar, errar II. s. flotador *m*; *(buoy)* boya; *(platform)* balsa, plataforma flotante.

float-ing (flō'tĭng) adj. flotante, boyante.

flock (flŏk) I. s. *(of birds)* bandada; ZOOL., RELIG. rebaño II. intr. congregarse ♦ **to t. to** lle-

gar en tropel a.
floe (flō) s. témpano o masa de hielo flotante.
flog (flŏg) tr. **-gg-** azotar, flagelar.
flog·ging ('ĭng) s. paliza, flagelación f.
flood (flŭd) **I.** s. inundación f; (torrent) torrente m; (floodlight) luz f de proyector ♦ **f. plain** terreno aluvial ♦ **f. tide** pleamar ♦ **the F.** el Diluvio **II.** tr. & intr. inundar(se).
flood·gate ('gāt') s. compuerta de exclusa.
flood·light (:līt') s. luz f de proyector.
floor (flôr) **I.** s. piso; (of a dance hall) pista; (bottom) fondo; (assembly members) congresistas mf ♦ **f. lamp** lámpara de pie ♦ **f. show** espectáculos ♦ **to ask for** o **take the f.** pedir o tener la palabra ♦ **top f.** piso alto **II.** tr. (to knock down) derribar; FAM. (the accelerator) pisar a fondo; (to stun) apabullar.
floor·board ('bôrd') s. tabla de piso.
floor·walk·er (:wô'kər) s. superintendente m de departamento (en un almacén).
flop (flŏp) **I.** s. sonido sordo; FAM. (failure) fracaso **II.** tr. **-pp-** dejar caer (pesadamente) —intr. dejarse caer; (to move about) agitarse; FAM. (to fail) fracasar.
flop·house ('hous') s. JER. pensión f de mala muerte.
flop·py (:ē) adj. **-i-** FAM. flojo, blando ♦ **f. disk** COMPUT. disco flexible (de memoria auxiliar).
flo·rid (flôr'ĭd) adj. (face) rojo; (style) florido.
flo·rist (flôr'ĭst) s. florista mf.
floss (flôs) s. (waste) borra; COST. seda; (dental) seda vegetal.
flo·ta·tion (flō-tā'shən) s. flotación f.
flot·sam (flŏt'səm) s. pecios.
flounce¹ (flouns) s. COST. volante m, cairel m.
flounce² **I.** intr. sacudirse ♦ **to f. out** salir enfadado **II.** s. sacudida.
floun·der¹ (floun'dər) intr. luchar o esforzarse inútilmente.
floun·der² s. ICT. platija, lenguado.
flour (flour) **I.** s. harina **II.** tr. enharinar.
flour·ish (flûr'ĭsh) **I.** intr. florecer, prosperar —tr. blandir **II.** s. floreo; (signature) rúbrica.
flout (flout) tr. & intr. burlarse (de).
flow (flō) **I.** intr. fluir; ELEC., FIG. correr; (to circulate) circular; (to gush) manar; (tide) subir; (blood, tears) derramar ♦ **to f. from** FIG. provenir de ♦ **to f. into** desaguar ♦ **to f. together** confluir **II.** s. flujo; (of blood, traffic) circulación f; (stream) corriente f; (volume) caudal m; (course) curso ♦ **f. chart** diagrama de fabricación.
flow·er (flou'ər) **I.** s. flor f; FIG. flor y nata ♦ **f. shop** florería **II.** intr. florecer, dar flor.
flow·er·pot (:pŏt') s. maceta.
flow·er·y (flou'ə-rē) adj. florido.
flown (flōn) cf. **fly¹.**
flu (flōō) s. FAM. gripe f.
fluc·tu·ate (flŭk'chōō-āt') intr. fluctuar.
flue (flōō) s. cañón humero.
flu·en·cy (flōō'ən-sē) s. (in a language) dominio; (effortlessness) fluidez f, soltura.
flu·ent (flōō'ənt) adj. perfecto; (fluid) fluyente ♦ **f. in** hablar perfectamente, dominar.
flu·ent·ly (:lē) adv. con soltura.
fluff (flŭf) **I.** s. (down) pelusa; (trifle) nadería **II.** tr. mullir; FAM. (to botch) chapucear.
fluff·y ('ē) adj. **-i-** lanoso; (soft) mullido.
flu·id (flōō'ĭd) s. & adj. fluido, líquido ♦ **f. ounce** onza líquida.
fluke¹ (flōōk) s. (of anchor) uña; (of whale) aleta (de la cola).

fluke² s. (luck) chiripa, tiro de suerte.
flung (flŭng) cf. **fling.**
flunk (flŭngk) intr. FAM. sacar suspenso ♦ **to f. out** ser expulsado (por malas notas) —tr. (a course) sacar suspenso en, fracasar en; (a student) colgar, suspender.
flun·ky (flŭng'kē) s. lacayo.
flu·o·res·cence (flŏŏ-rĕs'əns) s. fluorescencia.
flu·o·res·cent (:ənt) adj. fluorescente.
fluor·i·da·tion (flôr'ĭ-dā'shən, flōr'-) s. fluorización f.
fluor·ide ('īd') s. fluoruro.
fluor·ine (:ēn') s. flúor m.
flur·ry (flûr'ē) s. (gust) ráfaga; (snowfall) nevisca; (bustle) fiebre f, frenesí m; FIG. lluvia.
flush (flŭsh) **I.** intr. fluir abundantemente; (to blush) ruborizarse —tr. (to redden) enrojecer; (to excite) exaltar; (to clean) limpiar con agua ♦ **to f. the toilet** apretar el botón del inodoro, tirar la cadena **II.** s. (gush) chorro; (blush) rubor m; (glow) resplandor m; (exhilaration) animación f **III.** adj. copioso, abundante ♦ **f. against** contra, pegado a ♦ **f. with** a nivel con **IV.** adv. al mismo nivel.
flush² tr. hacer salir del escondite a.
flus·ter (flŭs'tər) tr. poner nervioso.
flute (flōōt) s. MÚS. flauta; ARQ. estría.
flut·ing (flōō'tĭng) s. estriado, acanaladura.
flut·ist (flōō'tĭst) s. flautista mf.
flut·ter (flŭt'ər) **I.** intr. revolotear, aletear; (in the wind) ondear, ondular; (to tremble) temblar; (heart) palpitar —tr. agitar, mover **II.** s. revoloteo, aleteo; (waving) ondulación f; (agitation) agitación f; MED. palpitación f ♦ **to be in a f.** estar nervioso.
flux (flŭks) s. flujo; (fluctuation) cambio.
fly¹ (flī) **I.** intr. **flew, flown** volar; (hair, flag) flotar; (to flee) huir, escapar; (to hurry) darse prisa; (to rush by) pasar o irse volando; (sparks, chips) saltar ♦ **to f. at** FAM. lanzarse sobre ♦ **to f. in the face of** ir contra, hacer frente a ♦ **to f. into a rage** encolerizarse ♦ **to f. open** abrirse repentinamente —tr. hacer volar; (to pilot) pilotear; (to transport) transportar en avión; (to cross) atravesar o cruzar en avión; (a flag) desplegar; (kite) remontar **II.** s. (of trousers) bragueta; (tent flap) toldo; G.B. (carriage) coche m de punto ♦ pl TRAT. telares.
fly² s. ENTOM. mosca f ♦ **f. swatter** matamoscas.
fly·ing ('ĭng) adj. volador; (swift) veloz, ligero ♦ **f. buttress** contrafuerte ♦ **f. saucer** platillo volador ♦ **f. time** duración del vuelo ♦ **to get off to a f. start** empezar muy bien.
fly·leaf (:lēf') s. [pl. **-ves**] guarda.
fly·o·ver (:ō'vər) s. G.B. cruce elevado.
fly·pa·per (:pā'pər) s. papel m matamoscas.
foal (fōl) **I.** s. potro **II.** intr. parir un potro.
foam (fōm) **I.** s. espuma ♦ **f. rubber** espuma de caucho **II.** intr. hacer espuma ♦ **f. at the mouth** espumajear, rabiar.
foam·y (fō'mē) adj. **-i-** espumoso.
fob¹ (fŏb) s. (chain) leontina, leopoldina.
fob² tr. **-bb-** ♦ **to f. something off on someone** encajarle algo a alguien.
fo·cal (fō'kəl) adj. focal ♦ **f. point** foco.
fo·cus (fō'kəs) **I.** s. [pl. **es** o **-ci**] foco ♦ **in f.** enfocado ♦ **out of f.** desenfocado ♦ **to bring into f.** enfocar **II.** tr. enfocar; (a lens) ajustar; FIG. concentrar —intr. enfocarse ♦ **to f. on** enfocar.
fod·der (fŏd'ər) s. forraje m, pienso ♦ **cannon f.** carne de cañón.

foe (fō) s. enemigo; *(opponent)* adversario.

foe·tus (fē'təs) var. de **fetus.**

fog (fôg) I. s. neblina, niebla; *(at sea)* bruma; FOTOG. velo ♦ **f. bank** nube de bruma • **in a f.** confundido II. tr. **-gg-** *(glass)* empañar; *(sky, mind)* nublar —intr. ♦ **to f. up** *(glass)* empañarse; *(sky)* nublarse; FOTOG. velarse.

fog·gy (fô'gē) adj. **-i-** neblinoso; *(glass)* empañado; *(bewildered)* ofuscado ♦ **not to have the foggiest idea** no tener ni la más mínima idea.

fog·horn (fôg'hôrn') s. sirena de niebla.

fo·gy (fô'gē) s. persona chapada a la antigua.

foi·ble (foi'bəl) s. punto flaco, debilidad *f.*

foil[1] (foil) tr. frustrar, hacer fracasar.

foil[2] s. *(sheet)* lámina fina de metal; *(contrast)* contraste *m* ♦ **to act as a f. to** servir de contraste a.

foil[3] s. DEP. florete *m.*

foist (foist) tr. ♦ **to f. off on** encajar a.

fold[1] (fōld) I. tr. doblar, plegar; *(arms)* cruzar; *(hands)* enlazar; *(wings)* plegar, recoger ♦ **to f. back** doblar • **to f. down** *o* **out** bajar (asiento de silla, mesa plegadiza) • **to f. in** CUL. incorporar • **to f. up** *(to wrap up)* envolver; *(to collapse)* plegar (sillas) —intr. doblarse, plegarse; *(to fail)* fracasar; FAM. *(to give in)* doblegarse ♦ **to f. up** doblarse, plegarse II. s. pliegue *m; (crease)* doblez *m,* arruga.

fold[2] s. *(corral)* redil *m; (flock)* rebaño.

fold·er (fōl'dər) s. carpeta.

fold·ing (fōl'dĭng) adj. plegable, plegadizo ♦ **f. screen** biombo • **f. seat** traspuntín.

fold·out (fōld'out') s. lámina desplegable.

fo·li·age (fō'lē-ĭj) s. follaje *m.*

fo·li·o (fō'lē-ō') s. folio; *(book)* infolio.

folk (fōk) I. s. [pl. inv. *o* **s**] pueblo, nación *f* ♦ **country f.** campesinos • **f. dance** baile folklórico • **f. medicine** medicina popular • pl. **folks** gente; FAM. *(relatives)* familia • **the old f.** los viejos II. adj. popular.

folk·lore (fōk'lôr') s. folklore *m.*

folk·sy (fōk'sē) adj. **-i-** campechano, afable.

folk·tale (fōk'tāl') s. cuento tradicional.

fol·li·cle (fōl'ĭ-kəl) s. folículo.

fol·lies (fōl'ēz) s.pl. revista teatral.

fol·low (fōl'ō) tr. seguir; *(to chase)* perseguir; *(a road, course)* proseguir, continuar por; *(rules)* observar; *(a profession)* dedicarse a; *(speech, book)* prestar atención a; *(to understand)* comprender ♦ **to f. through** *o* **up** llevar a cabo —intr. seguir ♦ **as follows** *(to do)* de la siguiente manera; *(to reply)* lo siguiente • **it follows that** se deduce que.

fol·low·er (:ər) s. *(disciple)* discípulo; *(supporter)* partidario; *(admirer)* admirador *m.*

fol·low·ing (:ĭng) I. adj. siguiente II. s. adherentes *mf; (admirers)* admiradores *m.*

fol·low-up (:ŭp') I. adj. complementario II. s. complemento (de un proceso); *(continuation)* resultado, consecuencia.

fol·ly (fōl'ē) s. tontería; *(silly idea or action)* disparate *m.*

fo·ment (fō-mĕnt') tr. fomentar.

fond (fōnd) adj. cariñoso; *(doting)* indulgente; *(cherished)* caro ♦ **to be f. of** *(person)* tener cariño a; *(thing)* ser aficionado a.

fon·dle (fōn'dl) tr. & intr. acariciar.

fond·ness (fōnd'nĭs) s. cariño, afecto; *(inclination)* inclinación *f; (taste)* afición *f.*

font (fônt) s. fuente *f;* RELIG. pila bautismal.

food (fōōd) s. comida; *(nourishment)* alimento ♦ **f. poisoning** intoxicación alimenticia • **f. pro-**

cessor procesador de alimentos.

food·stuff ('stŭf') s. comestible.

fool (fōōl) I. s. tonto, necio; *(jester)* bufón *m; (dupe)* simplón *m* ♦ **f.'s errand** empresa inútil • **to make a f. of** *(to deceive)* poner en ridículo a; *(to tease)* tomar el pelo a II. tr. *(to trick)* engañar; *(to surprise)* sorprender —intr. jugar ♦ **to f. around** jugar (sin propósito).

fool·har·dy ('här'dē) adj. **-i-** temerario.

fool·ing (fōō'lĭng) s. broma, chacota ♦ **no f.** hablando en serio • **no f.!** ¡no me digas! • **to be just f.** estar sólo bromeando.

fool·ish (:lĭsh) adj. *(silly)* tonto, absurdo; *(embarrassed)* ridículo.

fool·ish·ness (:nĭs) s. tontería.

fool·proof (fōōl'prōōf') adj. infalible; *(impossible to misuse)* a prueba contra mal uso.

fools·cap (fōōlz'kăp') s. hoja de papel.

foot (fōōt) I. s. [pl. **feet**] pie *m;* ZOOL. pata; *(base)* base *f* ♦ **by** *o* **on f. a pie • f. brake** freno de pedal • **f. soldier** soldado de infantería • **my f.!** JER. ¡tonterías! • **to drag one's feet** FIG. roncear • **to get cold feet** FAM. coger miedo • **to get one's f. in the door** abrir una brecha • **to land on one's feet** caer de pie • **to put one's f. down** ponerse firme • **to put one's f. in one's mouth** meter la pata • **to stand on one's own two feet** valerse por sí mismo II. intr. ♦ **to f. it** andar a pie —tr. ♦ **to f. the bill** pagar la cuenta.

foot·age ('ĭj') s. medida de superficie *o* longitud (expresada en pies); CINEM. metraje *m.*

foot-and-mouth disease ('n-mouth') s. glosopeda, fiebre aftosa.

foot·ball ('bôl') s. fútbol *m; (ball)* pelota.

foot·bridge (:brĭj') s. puente *m* para peatones.

foot·hill (:hĭl') s. estribación *f* (de montaña).

foot·hold (:hōld') s. *(support)* lugar *m* de apoyo (para el pie); *(starting point)* posición *f.*

foot·ing (:ĭng) s. pie *m,* equilibrio; *(basis)* base *f* ♦ **on equal f.** en pie de igualdad • **to lose one's f.** perder el pie.

foot·lights (:'lĭts') s.pl. candilejas.

foot·loose (:lōōs') adj. sin obligaciones ♦ **f. and fancy free** libre, ligero y contento.

foot·man (:mən) s. [pl. **-men**] lacayo.

foot·note (:nōt') I. s. anotación *f* II. tr. anotar.

foot·path (:păth') s. sendero.

foot·print (:prĭnt') s. huella.

foot·race (:rās') s. carrera pedestre.

foot·sore (:sôr') adj. con los pies cansados.

foot·step (:stĕp') s. pisada.

foot·stool (:stōōl') s. taburete *m.*

foot·wear (:wâr') s. calzado.

foot·work (:wûrk') s. juego de piernas.

fop (fŏp) s. petimetre *m.*

fop·per·y (:ə-rē) s. afectación *f.*

fop·pish (:ĭsh) adj. afectado.

for (fôr, fər) I. prep. para, por; *(destination)* para, hacia; *(beneficiary)* para; *(exchange)* por; *(duration)* por, desde hace; *(on account of)* de, por; *(in spite of)* a pesar de, con; *(considering)* para ♦ **as f.** en cuanto a • **f. all that** con todo • **to be f. it** FAM. estar completamente a favor de • **to be f.** estar de parte de • **to be f. someone** tocarle a alguien II. conj. ya que, pues, porque.

for·age (fôr'ĭj) I. s. forraje *m* II. intr. hurgar ♦ **to f. for** buscar hurgando.

for·ay (fôr'ā') s. incursión *f.*

for·bear (fôr-bâr') tr. **-bore, -borne** abstener *o*

desistir de —intr. *(to refrain)* abstenerse; *(to be tolerant)* ser tolerante.

for·bear·ance (:əns) s. tolerancia, paciencia.

for·bid (far-bĭd') tr. **-bad(e), -bid(den), -dding** prohibir.

for·bid·ding (:ĭng) adj. amenazante.

force (fôrs) I. fuerza; *(efficacy)* eficacia, peso; *(corps)* cuerpo; DER *(effect)* vigencia, validez *f* ♦ **by f.** por la fuerza • **by f. of** a fuerza de • **in f.** DER. vigente, en vigor; *(in numbers)* en masa • **to put in f.** poner en vigor II. tr. compeler, obligar; *(to obtain)* obtener por la fuerza; *(to coerce, break open)* forzar; *(to impose)* imponer; AGR. hacer crecer temprano ♦ **to f. back** *(to repel)* rechazar; *(tears)* contener, reprimir • **to f. down** obligar a bajar • **to f. from** echar *o* sacar fuera • **to f. one's way** abrirse paso • **to f. open** forzar • **to f. out** obtener por la fuerza • **to f. up(on)** obligar a tomar *o* aceptar.

forced (fôrst) adj. forzado; *(landing)* forzoso; *(unnatural)* fingido.

force·ful (fôrs'fəl) adj. fuerte, enérgico.

for·ceps (fôr'səps) s.inv. pinzas, fórceps *m*.

forc·i·ble (fôr'sə-bəl) adj. forzado.

forc·i·bly (:blē) adv. a la fuerza.

ford (fôrd) I. s. vado II. tr. vadear.

fore (fôr) I. adj. delantero II. s. frente *m*, delantera ♦ **to come to the f.** comenzar a destacarse III. adv. hacia el frente.

fore·arm¹ (-ärm') tr. prepararse de antemano.

fore·arm² (ärm') s. antebrazo.

fore·bear (:bâr') s. antepasado.

fore·bod·ing (-bō'dĭng) s. presentimiento.

fore·cast ('kăst') I. tr. & intr. **-cast(ed)** pronosticar II. s. pronóstico.

fore·cast·er (:kăs'tər) s. pronosticador *m*.

fore·cas·tle (fōk'səl, fôr'kăs'əl) s. castillo de proa.

fore·close (fôr-klōz') intr. privar del derecho de redimir una hipoteca.

fore·clo·sure (:klō'zhər) s. pérdida del derecho a redimir una hipoteca.

fore·fa·ther ('fä'thər) s. antepasado.

fore·fin·ger (:f'ĭng'gər) s. dedo índice.

fore·foot (:fŏŏt') s. [pl. **-feet**] pata delantera.

fore·front (:frŭnt') s. vanguardia.

fore·go (-gō') tr. **-went, -gone** preceder.

fore·gone ('gôn') adj. previo, pasado.

fore·ground (:ground') s. primer plano.

fore·hand (:hănd') adj. & s. (golpe) derecho.

fore·head (:hĕd') s. frente *f*.

for·eign (fôr'ĭn) adj. extranjero; *(trade)* exterior; *(uncharacteristic)* ajeno ♦ **f. exchange** *(currency)* divisas; COM. cambio exterior • **f. office** G.B. Ministerio de Asuntos Exteriores • **f. service** servicio diplomático y consular

for·eign·er (:ə-nər) s. extranjero, forastero.

fore·knowl·edge (fôr-nŏl'ĭj) s. presciencia.

fore·leg ('lĕg') s. pata delantera, brazo.

fore·lock (:lŏk') s. mechón *m*.

fore·man (:mən) s. [pl. **-men**] capataz *m*; DER. presidente *m* de un jurado.

fore·men·tioned (:mĕn'shənd) adj. antedicho.

fore·most (:mōst') adj. primero, delantero; *(paramount)* máximo, supremo.

fo·ren·sic (fə-rĕn'sĭk) adj. forense.

fore·run·ner (fôr'rŭn'ər) s. precursor *m*, predecesor *m*; *(harbinger)* anunciador *m*.

fore·said (:sĕd') adj. antedicho, susodicho.

fore·see (-sē') tr. **-saw, -seen** prever, anticipar.

fore·see·a·ble (:ə-bəl) adj. previsible.

fore·shad·ow (fôr-shăd'ō) tr. presagiar.

fore·short·en·ing (:shôr'tn-ĭng) s. escorzo.

fore·sight ('sīt') s. previsión *f*.

fore·sight·ed (:sī'tĭd) adj. prudente.

fore·skin (:skĭn') s. prepucio.

for·est (fôr'ĭst) I. s. bosque *m*, selva ♦ **f. ranger** guardabosque II. tr. poblar de árboles III. adj. forestal, selvático.

fore·stall (fôr-stôl') tr. impedir, prevenir.

fore·stland (fôr'ĭst-lănd') s. área boscosa.

for·est·ry (:ĭ-strē) s. silvicultura.

fore·taste (fôr'tāst') s. goce anticipado.

fore·tell (-tĕl') tr. **-told** predecir.

fore·thought ('thôt') s. deliberación *f*, premeditación *f*.

for·ev·er (fôr-ĕv'ər, fər-) adv. por *o* para siempre, eternamente, *(always)* siempre

for·ev·er·more (-'-môr') adv. para siempre jamás.

fore·warn (fôr-wôrn') tr. prevenir, avisar.

fore·word ('wərd) s. prólogo, prefacio.

for·feit (fôr'fĭt) I. s. *(penalty)* penalidad *f*; *(loss)* pérdida legal de un derecho; *(forfeiture)* prenda perdida II. tr. perder como castigo.

for·fei·ture (:fĭ-chŏor') s. pérdida (de título, derecho); *(security)* prenda perdida.

for·gave (fər-gāv') cf. **forgive.**

forge¹ (fôrj) I. s. *(smithy)* forja, fragua II. tr. fraguar, forjar; *(to counterfeit)* falsificar.

forge² intr. avanzar ♦ **to f. ahead** adelantar con esfuerzo.

forg·er (fôr'jər) s. falsificador *m*.

for·ger·y (jə-rē) s. falsificación *f*.

for·get (fər-gĕt') tr. & intr. **-got, got(ten), -tting** olvidar, olvidarse de ♦ **to f. oneself** propasarse, extralimitarse • **to f. to** olvidarse de.

for·get·ful (:fəl) adj. olvidadizo, desmemoriado; *(negligent)* descuidado.

for·get-me-not (:mē-nŏt') s. nomeolvides *f*.

for·give (fər-gĭv') tr. & intr. **-gave, -given** perdonar.

for·give·ness (:nĭs) s. perdón *m*.

for·giv·ing (:ĭng) adj. clemente, indulgente.

for·go (fôr-gō') tr. **-went, -gone** renunciar, prescindir de

for·got(·ten) (fər-gŏt[n]') cf. **forget.**

fork (fôrk) I. s. tenedor *m*; AGR. horca; *(of a road)* bifurcación *f*; *(of a tree)* horqueta; *(in a river)* horcajo ♦ **f. lift** montacargas II. tr. levantar con la horca ♦ **to f. over** FAM. aflojar, desembolsar —intr. bifurcarse.

forked (fôrkt) adj. *(fork-shaped)* ahorquillado; *(tail)* hendido.

for·lorn (fər-lôrn', fôr-) adj. *(sad)* acongojado; *(deserted)* abandonado, desolado; *(hopeless)* sin esperanzas

form (fôrm) I. s. forma; *(figure)* figura; *(type)* clase *f*, tipo; *(convention)* convencionalismo; *(manners)* conducta, modales *m*; *(formality)* formalidad *f*; *(document)* formulario, EDUC. *(grade)* año, grado ♦ **bad f.** algo que no se hace • **for f.'s sake** por pura fórmula • **f. letter** circular II. tr. formar; *(to model)* moldear, modelar; *(to develop)* desarrollar; *(to conceive)* idear, concebir; *(a habit)* contraer, adquirir —intr. formarse, tomar forma.

for·mal (fôr'məl) I. adj. formal; *(according to conventions)* convencional; *(official)* oficial; *(done in proper form)* en debida forma; *(correct)* muy correcto; *(ceremonious)* ceremonioso; *(dinner, dress)* de etiqueta; *(for the sake of form)* de cumplido, formulario II. s. ceremonia de etiqueta; *(attire)* traje *m* de etiqueta.

for·mal·de·hyde (fôr-măl′də-hīd′) s. formaldehído.

for·mal·i·ty (fôr-măl′ĭ-tē) s. ceremonia; *(requirement)* formalidad *f,* trámite *m; (custom)* fórmula ♦ **as a mere f.** para *o* por cumplir ♦ pl. ceremonias, cumplidos.

for·mal·ize (fôr′mə-līz′) tr. formalizar.

for·mal·ly (:lē) adv. formalmente; *(officially)* oficialmente; *(ceremoniously)* protocolariamente, ceremoniosamente.

for·mat (fôr′măt′) s. *(plan)* concepción *f,* plan *m; (layout)* formato.

for·ma·tion (fôr-mā′shən) s. formación *f.*

for·mer (fôr′mər) adj. *(earlier)* antiguo, pasado; *(of two)* primero, anterior; *(no longer)* antiguo, ex ♦ **the f.** el primero, aquél.

for·mer·ly (:lē) adv. anteriormente, antes.

form·fit·ting (fôrm′fĭt′ĭng) adj. ajustado.

for·mi·da·ble (fôr′mĭ-də-bəl) adj. formidable; *(awesome)* tremendo, imponente.

form·less (fôrm′lĭs) adj. informe, sin forma.

for·mu·la (fôr′myə-lə) s. [pl. **s** *o* **-lae**] fórmula; *(baby food)* mezcla nutritiva preparada.

for·mu·late (:lāt′) tr. formular.

for·ni·cate (fôr′nĭ-kāt′) intr. fornicar.

for·sake (fər-sāk′) tr. **-sook, -saken** *(to give up)* dejar, renunciar a; *(to abandon)* abandonar.

for·swear (fôr-swâr′) tr. **-swore, -sworn** abjurar de ♦ **to f. oneself** perjurar, jurar en falso.

fort (fôrt) s. fuerte *m; (base)* base *f* militar ♦ **to hold down the f.** FAM. permanecer en el puesto.

forte (fôrt, fôr′tā′) s. *(punto)* fuerte *m.*

forth (fôrth) adv. en adelante ♦ **and so f.** y cosas así ♦ **to come f.** aparecer, adelantarse ♦ **to go f.** ir(se) ♦ **to put f.** *(leaves)* echar; *(argument)* adelantar.

forth·com·ing (-kŭm′ĭng) adj. *(upcoming)* próximo, venidero; *(available)* disponible.

forth·right (′rīt′) adj. directo, franco.

for·ti·eth (fôr′tē-ĭth) I. s. *(place)* cuarenta *m,* *(part)* cuadragésimo II. adj. *(place)* cuadragésimo; *(part)* cuarentavo

for·ti·fy (fôr′tə-fī′) tr. fortificar; *(to invigorate)* fortalecer; *(food)* enriquecer; *(wine)* encabezar.

for·ti·fy·ing (:īng) adj. fortificante.

for·ti·tude (fôr′tĭ-tōōd′) s. fortaleza.

fort·night (fôrt′nīt′) s. quincena, quince días *m.*

fort·night·ly (:lē) I. adj. & s. *(publicación f)* quincenal II. adv. quincenalmente.

for·tress (fôr′trĭs) s. fortaleza.

for·tu·i·tous (fôr-tōō′ĭ-təs) adj. fortuito.

for·tu·nate (fôr′chə-nĭt) adj. afortunado ♦ **to be f.** *(person)* tener suerte; *(event)* ser una suerte.

for·tu·nate·ly (:lē) adv. afortunadamente.

for·tune (fôr′chən) s. fortuna; *(good luck)* suerte *f* ♦ **to make a f.** hacerse rico.

for·tune·tell·er (:tĕl′ər) s. adivino.

for·tune·tell·ing (:ĭng) s. adivinación *f.*

for·ty (fôr′tē) adj. & s. cuarenta *m.*

fo·rum (fôr′əm) s. [pl. **s** *o* **-ra**] foro.

for·ward (fôr′wərd) I. adj. *(frontal)* delantero; *(bold)* descarado; *(progressive)* avanzado; *(precocious)* adelantado II. adv. hacia adelante ♦ **looking f. to seeing you** a la espera de volverle a ver ♦ **to bring f.** *(topic)* presentar, ofrecer; TEN. llevar *(saldo)* ♦ **to come f.** presentarse, ofrecerse ♦ **to look f. to** anticipar III. s. DEP. delantero IV. tr. *(mail)* enviar, reexpedir; *(to help advance)* promover, fomentar.

for·ward·er (:wər-dər) s. agente *m* expedidor.

for·ward·ing (:dĭng) s. envío, expedición *f.*

for·wards (fôr′wərdz) adv. *(hacia)* adelante.

fos·sil (fŏs′əl) s. & adj. fósil *m.*

fos·ter (fô′stər) I. tr. *(to bring up)* criar; *(to promote)* fomentar, promover; *(hope)* abrigar II. adj. adoptivo.

fought (fôt) cf. **fight.**

foul (foul) I. adj. *(revolting)* asqueroso; *(rotten)* podrido; *(dirty)* sucio; *(polluted)* contaminado, viciado; *(obscene)* obsceno, grosero; FAM. *(horrible)* atroz ♦ **f. play** maniobra *o* juego sucio ♦ **to fall f. of** ponerse a malas con II. s. DEP. falta III. adv. sucio, contra las reglas IV. tr. ensuciar; *(to obstruct)* obstruir, atascar; *(to entangle)* enredarse en *o* con; DEP. cometer una falta contra ♦ **to f. up** FAM. chapucear —intr. DEP. cometer una falta; *(to tangle)* enredarse ♦ **to f. up** FAM. hacer una chapuceada.

foul-mouthed (′mouthd′) adj. malhablado.

foul-up (:up′) s. FAM. maraña, confusión *f;* MEC. falla mecánica.

found[1] (found) tr. *(to establish)* fundar; *(building, theory)* fundamentar.

found[2] tr. METAL. fundir.

found[3] cf. **find.**

foun·da·tion (foun-dā′shən) s. fundación *f; (basis)* fundamento; *(for cosmetics)* base *f;* CONSTR. cimientos ♦ **f. stone** primera piedra ♦ **to lay the foundations** sentar las bases.

found·er[1] (foun′dər) intr. *(to break down)* fracasar, venirse abajo; VET. despearse; *(to sink)* hundir.

found·er[2] s. fundador *m.*

found·ling (found′lĭng) s. expósito.

foun·dry (foun′drē) s. fundición *f.*

fount (fount) s. fuente *f.*

foun·tain (foun′tən) s. fuente *f; (for drinking)* surtidor *m* ♦ **f. pen** estilográfica.

foun·tain·head (:hĕd′) s. fuente *f.*

four (fôr) s. & adj. cuatro ♦ **f. hundred** cuatrocientos ♦ **f. o'clock** las cuatro.

four-foot·ed (:fŏŏt′ĭd) adj. *(:fŏŏt′ĭd)* cuadrúpedo.

four-let·ter word (lĕt′ər) s. palabrota.

four·square (:skwâr′) adj. *(firm)* inequívoco; *(forthright)* franco, sincero.

four·teen (fôr-tēn′) s. & adj. catorce *m.*

four·teenth (:tēnth′) s. & adj. *(place)* decimocuarto; *(part)* catorzavo.

fourth (fôrth) adj. & s. cuarto.

fourth-class (′klăs′) adj. & adv. *(por correo)* abierto.

fowl (foul) I. s. [pl. inv. *o* **s**] aves *f* *(en general); (domesticated)* ave de corral; *(meat)* carne *f* de ave II. intr. cazar aves.

fox (fŏks) I. s. zorro II. tr. engañar.

fox·hole (′hōl′) s. pozo de tirador.

fox·hound (:hound′) s. perro raposero.

fox·y (fŏk′sē) adj. **-i-** taimado, astuto.

foy·er (foi′ər, foi′ā′) s. salón *m* de entrada.

fra·cas (frā′kəs) s. riña, reyerta.

frac·tion (frăk′shən) s. MAT. fracción *f,* quebrado; *(bit)* porción minúscula, pizca.

frac·tion·al (:shə-nəl) adj. fraccionario, fraccionado; *(tiny)* minúsculo.

frac·tious (frăk′shəs) adj. indócil, rebelde.

frac·ture (frăk′chər) I. s. fractura II. tr. & intr. fracturar(se).

frag·ile (frăj′əl, :īl′) adj. frágil.

fra·gil·i·ty (frə-jĭl′ĭ-tē) s. fragilidad *f.*

frag·ment (frăg′mənt) I. s. fragmento II. tr. & intr. (′mĕnt′) fragmentar.

frag·men·tar·y (′mən-tĕr′ē) adj. fragmentario.

fra·grance (frā′grəns) s. fragancia, perfume *m.*

fra·grant (:grənt) adj. fragante.

frail (frāl) adj. *(fragile)* frágil; *(weak)* débil.

frail·ty (:tē) s. fragilidad *f*; *(moral)* flaqueza.

frame (frām) I. s. *(structure)* armadura, armazón *f*; *(border)* cerco, marco; *(body)* estructura corporal; CINEM. fotograma *m*; JER. *(frame-up)* conspiración *f*; AUTO. chasis *m*; *(bicycle)* cuadro; *(glasses)* montura ♦ **t. of mind** estado de ánimo, disposición *f* II. tr. construir, armar; *(to formulate)* formular; *(picture)* enmarcar, encuadrar; JER. *(to incriminate)* acriminar falsamente III. adj. de tablas, de madera.

frame-up ('up') s. JER. estratagema *m*, maquinación *f* para incriminar a alguien.

frame·work (:wûrk') s. estructura; *(system)* sistema *m*, CONSTR. armazón *f*, esqueleto.

franc (frăngk) s. FIN. franco.

fran·chise (frăn'chīz') s. derecho de voto; COM. concesión *f*, licencia.

frank[1] (frăngk) I. adj. franco, sincero II. tr. franquear III. s. franquicia postal.

frank[2] s. FAM. *(hot dog)* perro caliente.

frank·furt·er ('fər·tər) s. salchicha, perro caliente.

frank·in·cense (frăng'kĭn-sĕns') s. incienso.

frank·ness (frăngk'nĭs) s. franqueza.

fran·tic (frăn'tĭk) adj. desesperado; *(pace)* frenético.

fra·ter·nal (frə-tûr'nəl) adj. fraternal, fraterno ♦ **f. twins** mellizos.

fra·ter·ni·ty (:nĭ-tē) s. (con)fraternidad *f*; *(organization)* asociación estudiantil masculina.

frat·er·nize (frăt'ər-nīz') intr. fraternizar.

fraud (frôd) s. fraude *m*; *(person)* impostor *m*.

fraud·u·lence (frô'jə-ləns) s. fraudulencia.

fraught (frôt) adj. cargado, lleno.

fray[1] (frā) s. *(brawl)* riña, pelea.

fray[2] tr. & intr. desgastar(se), deshilachar(se).

fraz·zle (frăz'əl) I. tr. desgastar, agotar II. s. ♦ **worn to a f.** completamente agotado.

freak (frēk) I. s. cosa extraña o imprevista; *(monstrosity)* fenómeno; *(whim)* capricho; JER. *(drug user)* narcómano; *(fan)* fanático II. intr. & tr. ♦ **to f. out** JER. alucinar; *(emotionally)* agitar(se), excitar(se).

freak·ish (frē'kĭsh) adj. extraño, raro; *(abnormal)* anormal; *(capricious)* caprichoso.

freak·y (frē'kē) adj. -i- raro, extraño.

freck·le (trĕk'əl) I. s. peca II. tr. motear, salpicar —intr. cubrirse de pecas.

freck·led (:əld) adj. pecoso.

free (frē) I. adj. libre; *(independent)* independiente; *(gratis)* gratis, gratuito; *(not occupied)* desocupado; *(frank)* franco; *(liberal)* generoso; *(untied)* suelto ♦ **for f.** gratis ♦ **and clear** libre de trabas o gravámenes ♦ **f. enterprise** libre empresa ♦ **f. from** o **of sin f. of charge** gratis ♦ **f. on board** franco a bordo ♦ **f. trade** librecambio ♦ **f. will** libre albedrío ♦ **to be f.** to tener la libertad para, poder ♦ **to break f.** soltarse, librarse ♦ **to feel f.** to sentirse con la libertad de ♦ **to give, have a f. hand** dar, tener carta blanca ♦ **to set f.** poner en libertad; *(slave)* emancipar; *(animal)* soltar II. adv. libremente; *(gratis)* gratis III. tr. libertar, poner en libertad; *(to emancipate)* emancipar; *(to let loose)* soltar; *(to rid)* liberar, librar; *(to untangle)* desembarazar; *(to exempt)* eximir.

free-base ('bās') intr. inhalar cocaína que ha sido purificada con éter.

free·bie/bee (:bē) s. JER. dádiva.

free·boot·er (:bōō'tər) s. pirata *m*.

free-born (:bôrn') adj. nacido libre.

freed·man (frĕd'mən) s. [pl. **-men**] manumiso.

free·dom (frē'dəm) s. libertad *f*; *(exemption)* exención *f*; *(immunity)* inmunidad *f*; *(privilege)* privilegio; *(ease)* soltura.

free-for-all (:fər-ôl') s. refriega, pelea.

free·hand (:hănd') adj. a pulso.

free-lance ('lăns') I. intr. trabajar independientemente II. adj. independiente.

free·lanc·er (:lăn'sər) o **free lance** s. persona que trabaja independientemente.

free·load (:lōd') intr. JER. vivir de arriba.

free·load·er (:lō'dər) s. JER. parásito.

free·ly (:lē) adv. libremente; *(generously)* liberalmente.

free·man (:mən) s. [pl. **-men**] ciudadano.

Free·ma·son (:mā'sən) s. francmasón *m*.

free-spo·ken (:spō'kən) adj. franco.

free·style (:stīl') s. estilo libre (de natación).

free·think·er (:thĭng'kər) s. librepensador *m*.

free·way (:wā') s. autopista.

freeze (frēz) I. intr. **troze, frozen** helarse, congelarse; *(person)* tener frío, helarse; *(from fear)* quedarse paralizado ♦ **to f. over** helarse, congelarse ♦ **to f. to death** morirse de frío ♦ **to f. he·lar**; *(food, assets)* congelar; *(to chill)* enfriar, refrigerar ♦ **to f. out** excluir II. s. congelación *f*; *(cold snap)* ola de frío.

freeze-dry ('drī') tr. secar por congelación.

freez·er (frē'zər) s. congelador *m*.

freez·ing (:zĭng) I. adj. glacial ♦ **it's f. cold** hace un frío tremendo II. s. congelación *f*

freight (frāt) I. s. carga, flete *m* ♦ **f. car, train** vagón, tren de carga II. tr. *(to transport)* transportar, fletar; *(to load)* cargar.

freight·er (frā'tər) s. carguero, buque *m* de carga *m*.

French (frĕnch) ♦ **F. door** puertaventana • **F. fries** patatas fritas • **F. horn** corno francés • **F. window** puertaventana.

fre·net·ic (frə-nĕt'ĭk) adj. frenético.

fren·zied (frĕn'zēd) adj. frenético.

fren·zy (frĕn'zē) s. frenesí *m*; *(delirium)* desvarío; *(craze)* furor *m*

fre·quen·cy (frē'kwən-sē) s. frecuencia.

fre·quent (frē'kwənt) I. adj. frecuente II. tr. (-kwĕnt') frecuentar.

fres·co (frĕs'kō) s. [pl. **(e)s**] fresco.

fresh (frĕsh) I. adj. fresco; *(new, additional)* nuevo; *(water)* dulce; *(air)* puro; *(recent)* reciente ♦ **f. from** recién llegado de ♦ **to be f. out of** FAM. acabarse de quedar sin II. adv. recientemente, acabado de.

fresh·en ('ən) intr. *(wind)* refrescar ♦ **to f. up** refrescarse, asearse —tr refrescar.

fresh·en·er (:ə-nər) s. purificador *m*.

fresh·man (:mən) s. [pl. **-men**] estudiante *mf* de primer año; *(novice)* novato.

fresh·ness (:nĭs) s. frescura; *(novelty)* novedad *f*; *(purity)* pureza.

fresh·wa·ter (:wô'tər) adj. de agua dulce.

fret[1] (frĕt) intr. -tt- *(to worry)* preocuparse; *(to fuss)* quejarse; *(to wear away)* desgastarse.

fret[2] s. MÚS. traste *m*.

fret·ful (:fəl) adj. irritable, molesto.

fret·work (:wûrk') s. calado.

Freu·di·an (froi'dē·ən) adj. & s. freudiano.

fri·ar (frī'ər) s. fraile *m*.

fric·tion (frĭk'shən) s. fricción *f* ♦ **f. match** fósforo, cerilla • **f. tape** cinta aisladora.

Fri·day (frī'dē) s. viernes *m*.

fridge (frĭj) s. FAM. refrigerador *m*, nevera.
fried (frīd) pret. y part. p. de **fry¹**.
friend (frĕnd) s. amigo ♦ **a f. of mine** un amigo mío • **f. of the family** un amigo de la casa • **to be (best) friends with** ser (muy) amigo de • **to have friends in high places** tener influencia • **to make friends** ganarse amigos • **to make friends with** trabar amistad con • **to part friends** separarse en buenos términos.
friend·less ('lĭs) adj. sin amigos.
friend·li·ness (:lē-nĭs) s. amigabilidad *f.*
friend·ly (frĕnd'lē) adj. -i- amable, simpático; *(warm)* amistoso; *(not hostile)* amigo; *(allied)* aliado; *(favorable)* favorable ♦ **f. advice** consejo de amigo • **f. to** favorable a • **to be f. with** ser amigo de • **to become f. (with)** hacerse amigo (de).
friend·ship (:shĭp') s. amistad *f.*
frieze (frēz) s. *(band)* cenefa; ARQ. friso.
frig·ate (frĭg'ĭt) s. fragata.
fright (frīt) s. miedo, susto; FAM. *(mess)* esperpento.
fright·en ('n) tr. & intr. asustar(se), alarmar(se).
fright·en·ing (:ĭng) adj. espantoso.
fright·ful (frīt'fəl) adj. espantoso, horrible; *(terrifying)* aterrador; FAM. *(awful)* tremendo.
frig·id (frĭj'ĭd) adj. muy frío, helado; *(indifferent)* frío; MED. frígido ♦ **f. zone** zona glacial.
fri·gid·i·ty (frĭ-jĭd'ĭ-tē) s. frialdad *f.*
frill (frĭl) s. faralá *m* ♦ **pl.** FAM. adornos.
frill·y ('ē) adj. -i- con volantes o faralás; *(frivolous)* con muchos adornos.
fringe (frĭnj) s. *(trim)* franja; *(flounce)* fleco, orla; *(border)* ribete *m*; POL. grupo marginal o extremista ♦ **f. benefits** beneficios suplementarios • **on the f.** o **fringes** al margen de.
frisk (frĭsk) I. intr. retozar, juguetear —tr. FAM. cachear, palpar (de armas) II. s. cacheo, registro (de armas).
frisk·y (frĭs'kē) adj. -i- *(playful)* retozón, juguetón; *(horse)* fogoso.
frit·ter¹ (frĭt'ər) tr. ♦ **to f. away** malgastar.
frit·ter² s. CUL. fritura, fritada.
friv·o·lous (frĭv'ə-ləs) adj. frívolo.
frizz (frĭz) I. tr. & intr. rizar(se), encrespar(se) II. s. rizos, bucles *m*.
friz·zle (frĭz'əl) intr. freírse chirriando.
friz·zy (frĭz'ē) adj. -i- muy rizado, encrespado.
fro (frō) adv. *(hacia)* atrás ♦ **to and f.** de aquí para allá.
frock (frŏk) s. vestido; *(smock)* guardapolvo; RELIG. vestido talar ♦ **f. coat** levita.
frog (frŏg) s. rana; FAM. *(in throat)* ronquera.
frog·man ('măn') s. [pl. -men] *(diver)* buceador *m*, buzo; MIL. hombre *m* rana.
frol·ic (frŏl'ĭk) I. s. jugueteo, diversión *f* II. intr. -ck- juguetear, retozar.
from (frŭm, frŏm) prep. *(distance, place)* de, desde; *(time)* de, desde, a partir de; *(origin, reason)* de, *(de)* parte de, a causa de, por; *(removal)* de, a; *(according to)* por, según; *(against)* de; *(among)* entre.
frond (frŏnd) s. fronda.
front (frŭnt) I. s. frente *m*; *(forefront)* parte delantera; *(first part)* principio, comienzo; *(demeanor)* postura, posición *f*; *(appearance)* apariencia; FAM. *(cover)* pantalla, fachada ♦ **from the f.** por delante, de frente • **in f.** o **in f. of** delante de, frente a, en frente de • **out f.** afuera • **to put on a bold f.** hacer de tripas corazón II. adj. delantero, frontal ♦ **f. door** puerta de entrada •

f. man testaferro • **f. money** depósito o pago inicial • **f. page** primera plana • **f. row** primera fila III. tr. *(to face)* dar frente a, dar a; *(to confront)* hacer frente a, afrontar —intr. ♦ **to f. on(to)** mirar hacia, dar frente a • **to f. for** servir de fachada a.
front·age (frŭn'tĭj) s. anchura de un solar o terreno; *(adjacent land)* terreno frontero ♦ **with f. on** con fachada a.
fron·tal (:tl) adj. frontal.
fron·tier (frŭn-tîr') I. s. frontera, límite *m*; FIG. campo II. adj. fronterizo.
fron·tiers·man (:tîrz'mən) s. [pl. -men] habitante *m* de la frontera.
fron·tis·piece (frŭn'tĭ-spēs') s. frontispicio.
front-line (frŭnt'līn') adj. de la vanguardia.
front-page (:pāj') adj. de primera plana.
front-run·ner (:rŭn'ər) s. el que está en ventaja en una competencia *(esp. política)*.
front·ward (:wərd) adj. & adv. [o **-wards**] al frente, hacia el frente.
frost (frôst) I. s. escarcha; *(freezing weather)* helada II. tr. *(window)* empañar; CUL. escarchar; TEC. deslustrar; AGR. quemar —intr. ♦ **to f. over** o **up** cubrir con escarcha, empañar.
frost·bite ('bīt') I. s. congelación *f* II. tr. -bit, -bitten congelar.
frost·ed (frô'stĭd) adj. *(ground, cake)* escarchado; *(window)* empañado; *(glassware)* deslustrado; *(foods)* helado, congelado.
frost·ing (:stĭng) s. alcorza, escarchado.
frost·y (:stē) adj. -i- muy frío, de helada; *(welcome)* frío, glacial; *(hair)* canoso, cano.
froth (frôth) I. s. espuma; *(saliva)* espumarajo; FIG. trivialidades *f* II. intr. hacer espuma; *(at the mouth)* espumajear.
froth·y (frô'thē) adj. -i- espumoso, de espuma; *(frivolous)* frívolo, insubstancial.
frown (froun) I. s. ceño, entrecejo II. intr. fruncir el entrecejo ♦ **to f. at** mirar con ceño • **to f. (up)on** desaprobar.
frow·zy/sy (frou'zē) adj. -i- desaseado, desaliñado.
froze (frōz) cf. **freeze**.
fro·zen (frō'zən) I. cf. **freeze** II. adj. helado; *(food, assets)* congelado; *(very cold)* frígido; *(numb)* entumecido; *(with fear)* paralizado.
fruc·tose (frŭk'tōs') s. fructosa.
fru·gal (frō'gəl) adj. frugal, parco.
fruit (frōt) I. s. [pl. inv. o **s**] fruta; BOT. fruto ♦ **to bear f.** dar fruto; FIG. dar resultado ♦ **pl.** resultados II. intr. dar fruto.
fruit·cake ('kāk') s. torta de frutas; JER. *(crazy person)* loco.
fruit·ful (:fəl) adj. fructuoso, fructífero.
fru·i·tion (frō-ĭsh'ən) s. fruición *f* ♦ **to bring (come) to f.** realizar(se).
fruit·less (frōt'lĭs) adj. infructuoso.
fruit·y (frō'tē) adj. -i- de olor o sabor de fruta; *(sentimental)* sentimental.
frump·y (frŭm'pē) adj. -i- *(dowdy)* desaliñado; *(old-fashioned)* anticuado.
frus·trate (frŭs'trāt') tr. frustrar.
fry¹ (frī) I. tr. & intr. freír(se) ♦ **frying pan** sartén II. s. fritada ♦ **pl.** patatas o papas fritas.
fry² s.inv. *(young fish)* pececillos.
fry·er ('ər) s. *(pan)* sartén *f*; *(chicken)* pollo para freír.
fuch·sia (fyōō'shə) s. fucsia.
fud·dle (fŭd'l) I. tr. atontar, confundir II. s. confusión *f* ♦ **to be in a f.** estar atontado.
fud·dy-dud·dy (fŭd'ē-dŭd'ē) s. carcamal *m*.

fudge (fŭj) I. s. *(candy)* dulce *m* de chocolate; *(nonsense)* tontería II. tr. falsificar —intr. engañar ♦ to f. on dejar de cumplir con.

fu·el (fyōō'əl) I. s. combustible *m* ♦ f. cell celda electroquímica • f. oil aceite fuel *o* combustible • to add f. to the fire echar leña al fuego • to be f. for dar pábulo a II. tr. *(furnace)* alimentar; *(auto)* echar gasolina a; *(ship, plane)* abastecer de combustible a; FIG. dar pábulo a.

fu·gi·tive (fyōō'jĭ-tĭv) adj. & s. fugitivo.

fugue (fyōōg) s. fuga.

ful·fill(l) (fŏŏl-fĭl') tr. -ll- *(requirements)* llenar; *(duty)* desempeñar; *(contract, promise)* cumplir (con); *(need)* satisfacer; *(ambition)* realizar.

full (fŏŏl) I. adj. lleno; *(complete)* completo; *(detailed)* detallado; *(maximum)* máximo; *(crowded)* atestado; *(hotel, theater)* completo; *(entire)* entero; *(total)* total; *(figure)* amplio ♦ f. house sala repleta • f. powers plenos poderes • f. sail vela llena • f. stop GRAM. punto • f. swing en plena actividad • f. tilt a todo dar • in f. view of a plena vista de • to be f. *(person)* estar satisfecho; *(hotel)* no tener lugar • to the fullest extent al máximo II. adv. *(very)* extremadamente, muy; *(directly)* directamente, de lleno ♦ in f. swing en plena operación III. s. ♦ f. completamente, detalladamente • to pay in f. pagar íntegramente.

full-blood·ed ('blŭd'ĭd) adj. *(purebred)* de raza *o* casta; *(vigorous)* robusto.

full-blown (:blōn') adj. BOT. abierto; FIG. desarrollado, maduro.

full-fledged (:flĕjd') adj. *(having full status)* cabal; ORNIT. de plumaje completo.

full-grown (:grōn') adj. crecido, maduro.

full-length (:lĕngkth') adj. *(portrait)* de cuerpo entero; *(of standard length)* de tamaño normal; *(film)* de largo metraje.

full·ness (:nĭs) s. abundancia, plenitud *f*; *(satiety)* saciedad *f*, hartura.

full-scale (:skāl') adj. *(model)* de tamaño natural; *(all-out)* en gran escala, a todo dar.

full-size(d) (:sīz[d]') adj. de tamaño natural.

full-time (:tīm') adj. de jornada completa.

ful·ly (:ē) adv. *(totally)* completamente, enteramente; *(at least)* por lo menos.

ful·mi·nate (fŏŏl'mə-nāt') I. intr. *(to denounce)* tronar; *(to explode)* fulminar II. s. fulminato.

fum·ble (fŭm'bəl) intr. *(to handle)* enredarse; *(to grope)* buscar torpemente • f. for words buscar las palabras —tr. *(to handle)* manejar torpemente; *(to bungle)* estropear; DEP. *(to drop)* dejar caer ♦ to f. one's way a tientas.

fum·bling (:blĭng) adj. torpe.

fume (fyōōm) I. s. humo, tufo ♦ pl. gases, humo II. intr. echar humo, enfurecerse.

fu·mi·gate (fyōō'mĭ-gāt') tr. & intr. fumigar.

fun (fŭn) s. diversión *f*, alegría ♦ for f. *(as a joke)* en broma, bromeando; *(to have fun)* para divertirse • for the f. of it para divertirse • in f. en broma, bromeando • to be f. ser divertido • to have f. divertirse, pasarlo bien • to make f. of reírse *o* burlarse de • to spoil the f. aguar la fiesta • what f.! ¡qué divertido!

func·tion (fŭngk'shən) I. s. función *f*; *(ceremony)* acto, ceremonia ♦ in one's f. as en calidad de • to be a f. of estar en relación con II. intr. funcionar ♦ to f. as servir en la capacidad de.

func·tion·al (:shə-nəl) adj. funcional.

func·tion·ar·y (:nĕr'ē) s. funcionario.

fund (fŭnd) I. s. fondo ♦ pl. fondos, dinero disponible • the f. G.B. deuda pública II. tr. COM. suministrar fondos para; *(to finance)* costear; *(a debt)* consolidar.

fun·da·men·tal (fŭn'də-mĕn'tl) I. adj. fundamental II. s. fundamento.

fun·da·men·tal·ist (:ĭst) s. fundamentalista *mf*.

fund·ing (fŭn'dĭng) s. financiamiento.

fund-rais·ing (fŭnd'rā'zĭng) adj. para recaudar fondos, de recaudación de fondos.

fu·ner·al (fyōō'nər-əl) s. funeral(es) *m*; *(procesion)* cortejo fúnebre ♦ f. home funeraria • f. march marcha fúnebre • f. service misa de cuerpo presente.

fu·ner·ar·y (:nə-rĕr'ē) adj. funerario.

fu·ne·re·al (fyōō-nîr'ē-əl) adj. fúnebre.

fun·gi·cide (fŭn'jĭ-sīd', fŭng'gĭ-) s. fungicida *m*.

fun·gous (fŭng'gəs) adj. fungoso.

fun·gus (fŭng'gəs) s. [pl. es *o* -gi] BOT. hongo; MED. fungo.

funk (fŭngk) s. FAM. depresión *f* ♦ to be in a f. estar desanimado.

fun·nel (fŭn'əl) I. s. *(utensil)* embudo; *(stack)* chimenea II. intr. tomar forma de embudo, encañonarse ♦ to f. through encauzarse, pasar por —tr. encauzar, dirigir.

fun·ny (fŭn'ē) I. adj. -i- *(amusing)* divertido, cómico, gracioso; *(odd)* raro, extraño; *(fishy)* sospechoso ♦ f. bone hueso de la alegría; FAM. sentido del humor • f. papers tiras cómicas, muñequitos • that's not f. eso no es ninguna gracia • to try to be f. hacerse el gracioso II. s. ♦ pl. tiras cómicas.

fur (fûr) I. s. pelo, pelaje *m*; *(pelt)* piel *f* ♦ f. coat abrigo de piel(es) II. tr. -rr- cubrir *o* forrar con pieles.

fu·ri·ous (fyŏŏr'ē-əs) adj. furioso; *(speed)* vertiginoso ♦ at a f. pace a toda velocidad.

furl (fûrl) tr. & intr. enrollar(se), plegar(se).

fur·long (fûr'lông') s. estadio.

fur·lough (fûr'lō) I. s. permiso ♦ to be on f. estar de permiso II. tr. dar permiso a.

fur·nace (fûr'nĭs) s. horno.

fur·nish (fûr'nĭsh) tr. *(room, house)* amueblar; *(supplies)* suministrar; *(opportunity)* dar; *(proof)* aducir ♦ to f. with proveer de.

fur·nish·ings (:nĭ-shĭngz) s.pl. mobiliario, moblaje *m*.

fur·ni·ture (:chər) s. muebles *m*, mobiliario ♦ a piece of f. un mueble • f. store mueblería.

fu·ror (fyōŏr'ôr) s. furor *m*; *(commotion)* conmoción *f*.

fur·ri·er (fûr'ē-ər) s. peletero.

fur·row (fûr'ō) I. s. surco II. tr. surcar; *(the brow)* arrugar.

fur·ry (fûr'ē) adj. -i- peludo; *(tongue)* sarroso.

fur·ther (fûr'thər) I. adj. [comp. de far] *(more distant)* más lejano *o* alejado; *(additional)* otro, más; *(renewed)* nuevo II. adv. [comp. de far] *(extent, degree)* más; *(distance)* más lejos, más allá ♦ f. back *(space)* más atrás; *(time)* antes • f. on más adelante III. tr. promover, fomentar.

fur·ther·more (:môr') adv. además.

fur·thest (fûr'thĭst) [superl. de far] I. adj. *(more distant)* más lejano; *(remotest)* más remoto II. adv. *(extent, degree)* al extremo; *(distance)* más lejos.

fur·tive (fûr'tĭv) adj. furtivo.

fu·ry (fyŏŏr'ē) s. furia ♦ to be in a f. estar furioso.

fuse¹ (fyōōz) s. *(wick)* mecha; ARM. espoleta.

fuse² (fyōōz) I. tr. & intr. fundir(se) II. s. ELEC. fusible *m*, plomo ♦ **f. box** caja de fusibles *o* plomos • **to blow a f.** ELEC. fundir(se) un plomo; FIG. enfurecerse.

fu·se·lage (fyo͞o′sə-läzh′) s. fuselaje *m*.

fu·sil·lade (fyo͞o′sə-läd′) s. fusilería.

fu·sion (fyo͞o′zhən) s. fusión *f*.

fuss (fŭs) I. s. *(commotion)* alboroto, bulla; *(concern)* aspavientos; *(formalities)* cumplidos; *(quarrel)* lío • **it's not worth the f.** no vale la pena • **to kick up** *o* **to make a f.** armar un lío • **to make a f. over** *(to worry)* preocuparse por; *(to pamper)* mimar II. intr. inquietarse *(over por)*; *(to whimper)* lloriquear; *(to object)* quejarse ♦ **to f. about** *o* **around** andar de acá para allá • **to f.** with jugar con, toquetear.

fuss-budg·et (′bŭj′ĭt) s. quisquilloso.

fuss·i·ness (:ē-nĭs) s. carácter quisquilloso *o* melindroso; *(meticulousness)* escrupulosidad *f*.

fuss·y (fŭs′ē) adj. **-i-** *(touchy)* susceptible, irritable; *(baby)* lloricón; *(fastidious)* quisquilloso, melindroso; *(meticulous)* concienzudo.

fu·tile (fyo͞ot′l, fyo͞o′tīl′) adj. inútil, vano.

fu·til·i·ty (fyo͞o-tĭl′ĭ-tē) s. inutilidad *f*.

fu·ture (fyo͞o′chər) I. s. futuro, porvenir *m* ♦ **in the f.** en lo sucesivo • **in the near f.** dentro de poco ♦ pl. COM. futuros, bienes de entrega futura II. adj. futuro, venidero.

fu·tur·is·tic (′chə-rĭs′tĭk) adj. futurista.

fuzz¹ (fŭz) s. pelusa.

fuzz² s. JER. policía, poli *f*.

fuzz·y (′ē) adj. **-i-** velloso, velludo; *(indistinct)* borroso; *(confused)* confuso.

G

g, G (jē) s. séptima letra del alfabeto inglés; MÚS. sol *m*; FÍS. signo de la gravedad.

gab (găb) FAM. I. intr. **-bb-** parlotear, picotear II. s. parloteo, palique *m* ♦ **to have the gift of g.** tener mucha labia.

gab·ar·dine (găb′ər-dēn′) s. gabardina.

gab·ble (găb′əl) I. intr. *(to babble)* cotorrear; *(geese)* graznar II. s. *(geese)* cotorreo; graznido.

gab·by (găb′ē) adj. **-i-** FAM. locuaz, hablador.

ga·ble (gā′bəl) s. aguilón *m*.

gad·fly (găd′flī′) s. moscardón *m*.

gadg·et (găj′ĭt) s. FAM. artilugio, dispositivo.

gadg·et·ry (:ĭ-trē) s. artilugios, dispositivos.

gaff (găf) I. s. *(hook)* garfio, gancho; *(spar)* cangrejo II. tr. enganchar.

gaffe (găf) s. metida de pata.

gag (găg) I. s. mordaza; FAM. *(joke)* chiste *m* II. tr. **-gg-** amordazar; *(to choke)* atorar, ahogar; *(to nauseate)* dar náuseas a —intr. atorarse, ahogarse.

ga·ga (gä′gä) adj. JER. chocho, chiflado.

gage¹ (gāj) s. *(pledge)* prenda; *(challenge)* reto.

gage² s. BOT. ciruela verdal.

gag·gle (găg′əl) s. manada (de gansos).

gai·e·ty (gā′ĭ-tē) s. regocijo, alegría.

gain (gān) I. tr. ganar; *(to acquire)* adquirir; *(respect, confidence)* granjearse; *(strenth, momentum)* cobrar; *(clock)* adelantarse; *(to advance)* avanzar —intr. *(to become greater)* aumentar; *(to become better)* mejorar; *(in value)* subir (valor) ♦ **to g. on** ganar terreno, acercarse a II. s. *(profit)* ganancia, beneficio; *(increase)* aumento ♦ pl. *(profits)* ganancias; *(acquisitions)* adquisiciones.

gain·ful (′fəl) adj. ventajoso, lucrativo.

gain·say (gān-sā′) tr. **-said** negar.

gait (gāt) s. paso.

gal (găl) s. FAM. muchacha, chica.

ga·la (gā′lə, găl′ə) adj. & s. (de) gala, (de) fiesta.

ga·lac·tic (gə-lăk′tĭk) adj. galáctico.

gal·ax·y (găl′ək-sē) s. galaxia; FIG. *(assemblage)* constelación *f*.

gale (gāl) s. *(wind)* vendaval *m*, ventarrón *m*; *(of laughter)* explosión *f*.

gall¹ (gôl) s. FISIOL. hiel *f*; FIG. *(bitterness)* rencor *m*; *(impudence)* descaro.

gall² I. s. *(sore)* matadura, rozadura II. tr. *(to chafe)* rozar; *(to exasperate)* molestar, irritar.

gal·lant (găl′ənt) I. adj. *(courageous)* gallardo, bizarro; *(dashing)* galano; *(chivalrous)* galante; *(flirtatious)* galanteador II. s. galán *m*.

gal·lant·ry (′ən-trē) s. galantería.

gall·blad·der (gôl′blăd′ər) s. vesícula biliar.

gal·ler·y (găl′ə-rē) s. galería ♦ **to play to the g.** actuar para la galería, complacer al vulgo.

gal·ley (găl′ē) s. *(ship)* galera; *(kitchen)* cocina; IMPR. *(proof)* galerada.

gall·ing (gô′lĭng) adj. irritante, exasperante.

gal·li·vant (găl′ə-vănt′) intr. callejear.

gal·lon (găl′ən) s. galón *m*.

gal·lop (găl′əp) I. s. galope *m* ♦ **at a g.** al galope • **at full g.** a galope tendido II. tr. hacer galopar ♦ **to g. through** hacer de prisa —intr. galopar.

gal·lows (găl′ōz) s. [pl. inv. *o* **es**] horca ♦ **g. humor** humor negro.

gall·stone (gôl′stōn′) s. cálculo biliar.

ga·lore (gə-lôr′) adj. FAM. en cantidad, a granel.

ga·losh (gə-lŏsh′) s. chanclo.

gal·van·ic (găl-văn′ĭk) adj. galvánico.

gal·va·nize (′və-nīz′) tr. galvanizar.

gam·bit (găm′bĭt) s. *(chess move)* gambito; *(strategy)* estratagema, maniobra.

gam·ble (găm′bəl) I. intr. *(to bet)* jugar; *(to risk)* arriesgarse ♦ **to g. on** contar con que —tr. *(to bet)* jugar, apostar; *(to risk)* arriesgar ♦ **to g. away** perder en el juego II. s. *(bet)* jugada; *(risk)* riesgo, empresa arriesgada.

gam·bler (:blər) s. jugador *m*.

gam·bling (:blĭng) s. juego.

gam·bol (găm′bəl) I. intr. brincar, cabriolar II. s. brinco, cabriola.

game¹ (gām) I. s. juego; *(of checkers, etc.)* partida; *(of baseball, etc.)* partido; *(wild animals)* caza; *(quarry)* presa ♦ **big g.** caza mayor • **board g.** juego de mesa • **g. show** concurso televisivo • **the g. is up!** ¡se acabó la jugada! • **to be on to someone's g.** conocer el juego a alguien • **to play games** FIG. jugar, andar con trucos II. adj. *(plucky)* valeroso; FAM. *(willing)* listo.

game² adj. cojo, lisiado.

game·cock (′kŏk′) s. gallo de pelea.

game·keep·er (:kē′pər) s. guardabosque *mf*.

games·man·ship (gāmz′mən-shĭp′) s. maestría en juegos.

gam·ut (găm′ət) s. gama ♦ **to run the g.** abarcarlo todo.

gam·y (gā′mē) adj. **-i-** salvajino.

gan·der (găn′dər) s. ganso ♦ **to take a g. at** JER. echar una ojeada a.

gang (găng) s. pandilla; *(laborers)* cuadrilla; *(tools)* juego II. intr. ♦ **to g. up** formar una pandilla • **g. up on** atacar en grupo.

gang·bust·er ('bŭs'tər) s. JER. funcionario que combate el crimen organizado ♦ **like gangbusters** FAM. a todo trapo.
gan·gling (găng'glĭng) adj. larguirucho.
gan·gly (:glē) adj. **-i-** larguirucho.
gang·plank (găng'plăngk') s. plancha.
gan·grene (găng'grēn') s. gangrena.
gan·gre·nous (:grə-nəs) adj. gangrenoso.
gang·ster (găng'stər) s. gángster m, bandido.
gang·way (găng'wā') s. (passageway) pasillo; (gangplank) plancha ♦ **g.!** ¡paso!
gaol (jāl) G.B. var. de **jail**.
gap (găp) I. s. boquete m, hueco; (crack) hendedura; GEOG. (pass) desfiladero; (blank) espacio; (of time) intervalo; (disparity) diferencia, discrepancia; (void) vacío; ELEC. separación f ♦ **to bridge the g.** salvar las diferencias ♦ **to fill a g.** compensar una deficiencia II. intr. **-pp-** abrirse, estar abierto.
gape (găp) I. intr. (to yawn) bostezar; (to stare) quedarse boquiabierto; (chasm, hole) abrirse ♦ **to g. at** mirar boquiabierto II. s. (yawn) bostezo; (stare) mirada atónita; (hole) boquete m, brecha.
gap·ing (gā'pĭng) adj. muy abierto.
ga·rage (gə-räzh', -räj') s. garaje m.
garb (gärb) I. s. vestidura II. tr. vestir.
gar·bage (gär'bĭj) s. basura, desperdicio; FIG. porquería ♦ **g. disposal** aparato triturador para la eliminación de basura.
gar·ble (gär'bəl) tr. (message) desvirtuar; (words) mezclar.
gar·den (gär'dn) I. s. jardín m; (for vegetables) huerto, huerta II. intr. trabajar en el jardín, cultivar el huerto III. adj. de jardín, del huerto ♦ **g. apartments** edificios de apartamentos con jardines.
gar·den·er (gärd'nər) s. jardinero; (of vegetables) hortelano.
gar·de·nia (gär-dēn'yə) s. gardenia.
gar·den·ing (gärd'nĭng) s. jardinería; (of vegetables) horticultura.
gar·gan·tu·an (gär-găn'chōo-ən) adj. enorme.
gar·gle (gär'gəl) I. intr. gargarizar, hacer gárgaras II. s. gárgara; (medication) gargarismo.
gar·goyle (gär'goil') s. gárgola.
gar·ish (gâr'ĭsh) adj. chillón, charro.
gar·land (gär'lənd) I. s. guirnalda II. tr. enguirnaldar.
gar·lic (gär'lĭk) s. ajo.
gar·ment (gär'mənt) s. vestido, prenda de vestir.
gar·ner (gär'nər) tr. (to store) almacenar, acopiar; (to accumulate) acumular.
gar·net (gär'nĭt) s. granate m.
gar·nish (gär'nĭsh) I. tr. (to embellish) adornar; CUL. guarnecer, aderezar; DER. embargar II. s. ornamento; CUL. guarnición f.
gar·nish·ment (:mənt) s. DER. embargo.
gar·ret (găr'ĭt) s. buhardilla, desván m.
gar·ri·son (găr'ĭ-sən) s. guarnición f II. tr. (troops) poner en guarnición; (post) guarnecer.
gar·rot(t)e (gə-rŏt') I. s. garrote m II. tr. agarrotar.
gar·ru·lous (găr'ə-ləs) adj. gárrulo, locuaz.
gar·ter (gär'tər) s. liga ♦ **Order of the G.** Orden de la Jarretera.
gas (găs) I. s. [pl. **-(s)es**] gas m; (gasoline) gasolina; (asphyxiant) gas asfixiante; (anesthetic) gas anestésico; JER. (idle talk) cháchara ♦ **g. mask** máscara antigás • **g. station** gasolinera • **to be a g.** JER. ser divertidísimo • **to step**

on the g. pisar el acelerador II. tr. **-ss-** asfixiar con gas —intr. JER. chacharear ♦ **to g. up** FAM. llenar el tanque (con gasolina).
gas·e·ous (găs'ē-əs, găsh'əs) adj. gaseoso.
gash (găsh) I. tr. acuchillar II. s. cuchillada.
gas·ket (găs'kĭt) s. junta, arandella.
gas·light (găs'līt') s. luz f o lámpara de gas.
gas·o·line/ene (găs'ə-lēn') s. gasolina, nafta.
gasp (găsp) I. intr. (in surprise) quedar boquiabierto; (to pant) jadear ♦ **to g. for air** hacer esfuerzos para respirar II. s. jadeo.
gas·sy (găs'ē) adj. **-i-** gaseoso.
gas·tric (găs'trĭk) adj. gástrico.
gas·tro·nom·ic ('trə-nŏm'ĭk) adj. gastronómico.
gas·tron·o·my (gă-strŏn'ə-mē) s. gastronomía.
gas·works (găs'wûrks') s.pl. fábrica de gas.
gate (gāt) s. puerta; (of iron) verja; FIG. (pathway) camino; MEC. válvula; TEAT. (attendance) taquilla ♦ **to get the g.** JER. ser puesto de patitas en la calle.
gate·crash·er ('krăsh'ər) s. JER. calado, persona que entra sin pagar.
gate·keep·er (:kē'pər) s. portero.
gate·way (:wā') s. (opening) pórtico; (access) puerta, entrada; FIG. (pathway) camino.
gath·er (găth'ər) I. tr. reunir, juntar; (to congregate) congregar; (to infer) deducir; (flowers) coger; (crops, thoughts) recoger; (to amass) acumular; (speed) ganar; (strength) cobrar; COST. fruncir ♦ **to g. from** concluir • **to g. together** reunir, juntar • **to g. up** recoger —intr. reunirse, congregarse; (to accumulate) acumularse, amontonarse; (to build up) aumentar ♦ **g. round!** ¡acérquense! • **to g. together** reunirse, juntarse II. s. frunce m, pliegue m.
gath·er·ing (:ĭng) s. (collection) recolección f; (assembly) asamblea, reunión f.
gauche (gōsh) adj. torpe, sin tacto.
gaud·y (gô'dē) adj. **-i-** llamativo, chillón.
gauge (gāj) I. s. (measurement) medida; (size) tamaño, extensión f; TEC. calibrador m; FIG. muestra de carácter, habilidad); F.C. entrevía; ARM. calibre m II. tr. (to measure) medir; (to evaluate) estimar, evaluar; (to determine) determinar.
gaunt (gônt) adj. macilento, demacrado.
gaunt·let¹ (gônt'lĭt) s. (glove) guante m de manópla ♦ **to throw down, take up the g.** arrojar, recoger el guante.
gaunt·let² s. (punishment) baqueta ♦ **to run the g.** sufrir una desaprobación general.
gauze (gôz) s. gasa.
gave (gāv) cf. **give**.
gav·el (găv'əl) s. martillo.
gawk (gôk) intr. FAM. papar moscas.
gawk·y (gô'kē) adj. **-i-** torpe, desgarbado.
gay (gā) adj. alegre; (bright) vistoso; JER. homosexual II. s. JER. homosexual mf.
gaze (gāz) I. intr. mirar con fijeza, contemplar II. s. mirada fija.
ga·ze·bo (gə-zē'bō) s. [pl. **(e)s**] pérgola.
ga·zelle (gə-zěl') s. gacela.
ga·zette (gə-zět') s. gaceta.
gaz·et·teer (găz'ĭ-tîr') s. diccionario geográfico.
gear (gîr) I. s. MEC. rueda dentada, engranaje m; AUTO. velocidad f, marcha; (assembly) tren m; (equipment) equipo, aparejos; FAM. (belongings) cosas ♦ **in g.** engranado • **to change o shift gears** AUTO. cambiar de velocidad; FIG. cambiar de objetivo • **to put into g.** engranar II. tr. MEC. engranar ♦ **to g. to** ajustar o adaptar

a • **to g. (oneself) up** prepararse.
gear·box ('bŏks') s. caja de cambios.
gear·ing (:ing) s. engranaje *m*.
gear·shift (:shĭft') s. palanca de cambios.
gear·wheel (:hwēl') s. rueda dentada.
gee (jē) interj. FAM. ¡caramba!
geese (gēs) cf. **goose.**
gee·zer (gē'zər) s. JER. viejo excéntrico, tío.
Gei·ger counter (gī'gər) s. contador *m* Geiger.
gel (jĕl) s. gel *m*.
gel·a·tin(e) (jĕl'ə-tn) s. gelatina.
gel·at·i·nous (jə-lăt'n-əs) adj. gelatinoso.
geld (gĕld) tr. castrar, capar.
geld·ing (gĕl'dĭng) s. caballo castrado.
gem (jĕm) s. piedra preciosa, gema; FIG. tesoro, joya.
gem·stone ('stōn') s. piedra preciosa.
gen·der (jĕn'dər) s. GRAM. género; (*sex*) sexo.
gene (jēn) s. gene *m*.
ge·ne·al·o·gy (jē'nē-ŏl'ə-jē) s. genealogía.
gen·er·al (jĕn'ər-əl) I. adj. general ♦ **g. delivery** lista de correos • **g. practitioner** médico general • **g. store** almacén • **in g.** por lo general II. s. general *m*.
gen·er·al·i·ty (jĕn'ə-răl'ĭ-tē) s. generalidad *f*.
gen·er·al·i·za·tion (jĕn'ər-ə-lĭ-zā'shən) s. generalización *f*.
gen·er·al·ize ('--līz') tr. generalizar —intr. hacer generalizaciones.
gen·er·al-pur·pose (jĕn'ə-rəl-pûr'pəs) adj. de uso general.
gen·er·ate (jĕn'ə-rāt') tr. generar; FIG. (*to produce*) producir, engendrar.
gen·er·a·tion ('-rā'shən) s. generación *f* ♦ **the younger g.** los jóvenes.
gen·er·a·tor ('-'tər) s. generador *m*.
ge·ner·ic (jə-nĕr'ĭk) adj. genérico.
gen·er·os·i·ty (jĕn'ə-rŏs'ĭ-tē) s. generosidad *f*.
gen·er·ous ('ər-əs) adj. generoso.
gen·e·sis (jĕn'ĭ-sĭs) s. [pl. **-ses**] génesis *f*.
ge·net·ic (jə-nĕt'ĭk) adj. genético ♦ **genetics** s.sg. genética.
gen·ial (jēn'yəl) adj. (*friendly*) afable, simpático; (*benign*) benigno, suave.
ge·ni·al·i·ty (jē'nē-ăl'ĭ-tē) s. afabilidad *f*, simpatía; (*pleasantness*) templanza.
ge·nie (jē'nē) s. genio.
gen·i·tal (jĕn'ĭ-tl) I. adj. genital II. s. ♦ pl. órganos genitales.
gen·i·ta·li·a (-tă'lē-ə) s.pl. órganos genitales.
gen·ius (jēn'yəs) s. [pl. **es**] genio.
gen·o·cide (jĕn'ə-sīd') s. genocidio.
gen·re (zhän'rə) s. género, clase *f*.
gent (jĕnt) s. FAM. señor *m*, individuo.
gen·teel (jĕn-tēl') adj. (*refined*) fino, cortés; (*stylish*) gallardo, elegante.
gen·tile (jĕn'tīl') s. gentil *m*, pagano ♦ **G.** persona no judía.
gen·til·i·ty (jĕn-tĭl'ĭ-tē) s. (*gentry*) nobleza; (*politeness*) gentileza, cortesía.
gen·tle (jĕn'tl) adj. **-er, -est** (*kind*) bondadoso, amable; (*tender*) dulce; (*mild*) suave; (*tame*) manso, dócil ♦ **of g. birth** bien nacido.
gen·tle·man (:mən) s. [pl. **-men**] caballero, señor *m* ♦ **g.'s agreement** pacto de honor ♦ pl. (*in letters*) muy señores míos o nuestros; (*form of address*) caballeros, señores.
gen·tle·ness (:nĭs) s. bondad *f*; (*mildness*) suavidad *f*; (*tameness*) mansedumbre *f*.
gen·tle·wom·an (:wŏŏm'ən) s. [pl. **-women**] dama, señora; (*attendant*) dama de compañía.

gen·try (jĕn'trē) s. personas bien nacidas; G.B. (*upper classes*) alta burguesía.
gen·u·flect (jĕn'yə-flĕkt') intr. hacer una genuflexión.
gen·u·flec·tion ('-flĕk'shən) s. genuflexión *f*.
gen·u·ine (jĕn'yŏŏ-ĭn) adj. (*real*) verdadero; (*authentic*) genuino; (*sincere*) sincero.
ge·nus (jē'nəs) s. [pl. **-nera**] género.
ge·o·graph·ic/i·cal (jē'ə-grăf'ĭk) adj. geográfico.
ge·og·ra·phy (jē-ŏg'rə-fē) s. geografía.
ge·o·log·ic/i·cal (jē'ə-lŏj'ĭk) adj. geológico.
ge·ol·o·gist (jē-ŏl'ə-jĭst) s. geólogo.
ge·ol·o·gy (:jē) s. geología.
ge·o·met·ric/i·cal (jē'ə-mĕt'rĭk) adj. geométrico.
ge·om·e·try (jē-ŏm'ĭ-trē) s. geometría.
ge·o·phys·i·cist (jē'ō-fĭz'ĭ-sĭst) s. geofísico.
ge·o·phys·ics (:fĭz'ĭks) s.sg. geofísica.
ge·o·po·lit·i·cal (:pə-lĭt'ĭ-kəl) adj. geopolítico.
ge·o·pol·i·tics (:pŏl'ĭ-tĭks) s.sg. geopolítica.
ge·o·ther·mal (:thûr'məl) adj. geotérmico.
ge·ra·ni·um (jə-rā'nē-əm) s. geranio.
ger·i·at·ric (jĕr'ē-ăt'rĭk) adj. & s. (*paciente mf*) geriátrico ♦ **geriatrics** s.sg. geriatría.
germ (jûrm) s. BIOL., FIG. germen *m*; MED. (*microbe*) microbio; (*bacillus*) bacilo.
ger·mane (jər-mān') adj. pertinente.
German (jûr'mən) ♦ **G. measles** rubéola • **G. shepherd** pastor alemán.
ger·mi·cide (jûr'mĭ-sīd') s. germicida *m*.
ger·mi·nal (:mə-nəl) adj. germinal.
ger·mi·nate (:nāt') tr. & intr. (hacer) germinar.
ger·mi·na·tion ('-nā'shən) s. germinación *f*.
ger·on·tol·o·gy (jĕr'ən-tŏl'ə-jē) s. gerontología.
ger·ry·man·der (jĕr'ē-măn'dər) tr. dividir (una entidad política) injustamente.
ger·und (jĕr'ənd) s. gerundio.
ges·tate (jĕs'tāt') tr. gestar.
ges·ta·tion (jĕ-stā'shən) s. gestación *f*.
ges·tic·u·late (jĕ-stĭk'yə-lāt') intr. gesticular.
ges·tic·u·la·tion (-'-lā'shən) s. gesticulación *f*, gesto.
ges·ture (jĕs'chər) I. s. gesto, ademán *m*; (*token*) detalle *m*, muestra II. intr. hacer ademanes —tr. expresar con ademán.
get (gĕt) tr. **got, got(ten), -tt-** (*to obtain*) obtener, conseguir; (*to buy*) comprar; (*to receive*) recibir; (*to win*) sacar; (*to attract*) atraer; (*to seize*) agarrar, capturar; (*flu, cold*) coger, contraer; (*to cause to become*) hacer que <*that got me angry* eso hizo que me enfadara>; (*a meal*) hacer, preparar; (*to bring*) traer, alcanzar <*g. my slippers, please* tráeme las pantuflas, por favor>; (*to persuade*) lograr, hacer que <*we got her to come with us* logramos que ella viniera con nosotros>; FAM. (*to possess*) poseer, tener <*what have you got in your hand?* ¿qué tienes en la mano?>; (*must*) tener que <*we have got to win* tenemos que ganar>; (*to annoy*) molestar, irritar; (*to punish*) castigar; (*to understand*) comprender; (*to hear*) oír bien; (*to puzzle*) desconcertar, confundir; (*to capture*) coger, captar <*to get the feel of* coger el truco de> ♦ **to g. across** hacer comprender • **to g. away (from)** quitar (a) • **to g. back** recuperar, recobrar • **to g. down** poner por escrito • **to g. off** (*to send*) mandar, enviar; (*defendant*) lograr la absolución para; (*day*) tener libre • **to g. out** (*to remove*) sacar; (*news*) difundir; (*stain*) quitar • **to g. out of** (*information*) sonsacar de; (*pleasure, benefit*) sacar o obtener de • **to g. over**

(with) acabar con • **to g. up** (petition) organizar; (courage) armarse —intr. (to become) ponerse <he got well se puso bien>; (to turn) ponerse, hacer <it's getting cold empieza a hacer frío> ♦ **I can't g. over it** no lo puedo creer • **to g. across** cruzar • **to g. along** (in years) ponerse viejo; (to manage) arreglárselas (on con); (to be friendly) llevarse bien (with con) • **to g. along without** pasar sin, prescindir de • **to g. around** (to travel) viajar; (socially) salir mucho; (news) difundirse; (an obstacle) lograr pasar; (a person) engatusar • **to g. around to** encontrar tiempo para • **to g. at** (the truth) averiguar, descubrir; (to mean) querer decir • **to g. away** (to escape) escaparse (from de); (to leave) (conseguir) irse; (on vacation) ir de vacaciones • **to g. back** regresar, volver • **to g. back at** vengarse de • **to g. back to** (to return) volver a; (to call back) volver a llamar • **to g. by** arreglárselas • **to g. down to** (business) ponerse a; (details) pasar a considerar • **to g. in** (to arrive) llegar; (to gain entry) entrar; (to return home) regresar a casa • **to g. in with** trabar amistad con • **to g. into** (car) subir a; (bed, trouble) meterse en; (a habit) adquirir; FAM. (to enjoy) apasionarse por • **to g. off** (train, horse) apearse; (work) salir (del trabajo); (to escape punishment) librarse • **to g. on** (train, horse) montar en; (to be friendly) llevarse bien (with con) • **to g. on with** seguir con • **to g. out** (to be over) terminar; (to manage to leave) lograr salir • **to g. out of** (bed, chair) levantarse de; (town) alejarse de; (obligation) librarse de; (trouble) sacarse de; (the way) quitarse (de en medio); (car) apearse de • **to g. over** (to finish) terminar; (illness) reponerse de; (shyness, disappointment) superar; (person) olvidar; (difficulty) vencer; (loss) sobreponerse a • **to g. through** (exam) aprobar; (the day, crowd) pasar; (to finish) terminar; (to manage to arrive) llegar a su destino (provisiones, mensaje) • **to g. through to** (by phone) conseguir comunicación con; (to be understood) hacer comprender • **to g. to** (to manage to) lograr; (to arrive) llegar a; FAM. (to begin) abordar, comenzar a; (to upset) molestar a (alguien); (to affect) impresionar, conmover • **to g. up** (to stand up) levantarse, ponerse de pie; (out of bed) levantarse (de la cama) ♦ **what's gotten into him?** ¿qué le pasa?
get·a·way (gĕt'ə-wā') s. fuga, escape m.
get-to·geth·er (:tə-gĕth'ər) s. FAM. fiestecita.
get-up (gĕt'ŭp') s. atavío, vestimenta.
get-up-and-go (gĕt'ŭp ən-gō') s. ambición f, arrojo.
gey·ser (gī'zər) s. géiser m.
ghast·ly (găst'lē) adj. -i- horrible, horroroso; (ghostly) cadavérico; (awful) atroz.
gher·kin (gûr'kĭn) s. pepinillo.
ghet·to (gĕt'ō) s. [pl. (e)s] ghetto.
ghost (gōst) s. fantasma m, espectro; (haunting image) visión f; (trace) sombra, asomo ♦ **g. town** pueblo desierto • **not to have a g. of a chance** no tener la más remota posibilidad • **the Holy G.** BIBL. el Espíritu Santo • **to give up the g.** entregar el alma.
ghost·ly (:lē) adj. -i- espectral, fantasmal.
ghost-writ·er (:rī'tər) s. escritor m que escribe para otro, negro.
ghoul (gōōl) s. demonio necrófago.
ghoul·ish (gōō'lĭsh) adj. diabólico, malvado.
GI (jē'ī') s. [pl. s o 's] soldado (de los E.U.).
gi·ant (jī'ənt) adj. & s. gigante m.

gib·ber (jĭb'ər) intr. farfullar.
gib·ber·ish (:ĭsh) s. galimatías m, jerga.
gib·bet (jĭb'ĭt) I. s. horca II. tr. ahorcar.
gib·bon (jĭb'ən) s. gibón m.
gibe (jīb) I. intr. & tr. burlarse, mofarse (de) II. s. burla, mofa.
gib·lets (jĭb'lĭts) s.pl. menudos (de ave).
gid·dy (gĭd'ē) adj. -i- (dizzy) mareado; (causing dizziness) vertiginoso; (frivolous) frívolo.
gift (gĭft) s. regalo, obsequio; (donation) donación f; (talent) talento, aptitud f.
gift·ed (gĭf'tĭd) adj. (person) dotado, de muchas dotes; (performance) excepcional.
gig[1] (gĭg) s. (carriage) calesa.
gig[2] s. (spear) arpón m de pesca.
gig[3] s. JER., MÚS. actuación f, presentación f.
gi·gan·tic (jī-găn'tĭk) adj. gigantesco.
gig·gle (gĭg'əl) I. intr. reírse tontamente II. s. risita entrecortada y tonta ♦ **to get o have the giggles** estar tentado de risa.
gig·gly (:lē) adj. de risa fácil.
gild (gĭld) tr. -ed o gilt dorar.
gill[1] (gĭl) s. ICT. agalla, branquia ♦ **to look green about the gills** tener mala cara.
gill[2] (jĭl) s. E.U. cuatro onzas (líquidas); G.B. cinco onzas (líquidas).
gilt (gĭlt) I. cf. gild II. adj. dorado III. s. lámina o chapa de oro.
gilt-edge(d) ('ĕj[d]') adj. de bordes dorados ♦ **g. securities** valores de primer orden.
gim·let (gĭm'lĭt) s. barrena de mano.
gim·mick (gĭm'ĭk) s. truco <sales g. truco publicitario>; (gadget) artefacto.
gim·mick·ry (:ĭ-krē) s. (tricks) trucos; (gadgetry) artefactos innecesarios.
gimp (gĭmp) s. JER. (limp) renguera, cojera; (person) rengo, paticojo.
gimp·y (gĭm'pē) adj. JER. rengo, cojo.
gin[1] (jĭn) s. (liquor) ginebra.
gin[2] I. s. (cotton gin) desmotadora II. tr. -nn- desmotar (algodón).
gin·ger (jĭn'jər) s. jengibre m; FAM. (liveliness) garra, chispa.
gin·ger·bread (:brĕd') s. CUL. pan m de jengibre; (decoration) ornamentación excesiva.
gin·ger·ly (:lē) I. adv. cuidadosamente, cautelosamente II. adj. cuidadoso, cauteloso.
gin·ger·snap (:snăp') s. galletita con sabor a jengibre.
ging·ham (gĭng'əm) s. guinga.
gin·gi·vi·tis (jĭn'jə-vī'tĭs) s. gingivitis f.
gin·seng (jĭn'sĕng') s. ginsén m, ginseng m.
gi·raffe (jə-răf') s. [pl. inv. o s] jirafa.
gird (gûrd) tr. -ed o girt (to strap) ceñir, atar; (to surround) rodear ♦ **to g. oneself** prepararse.
gird·er (gûr'dər) s. viga.
gir·dle (gûr'dl) I. s. (sash) faja; (belt) cinturón m; (undergarment) faja II. tr. (to encircle) rodear; (to belt) ceñir, atar.
girl (gûrl) s. muchacha, chica; (child) niña; (unmarried young woman) joven f, señorita; (daughter) hija; (sweetheart) novia.
girl·friend o **girl friend** ('frĕnd') s. amiga; (sweetheart) novia.
girl·hood (:hŏŏd') s. niñez f, juventud f.
girl·ish (gûr'lĭsh) adj. de niña.
girth (gûrth) s. circunferencia; (bulk) tamaño, dimensiones f; (cinch) cincha.
gis·mo (gĭz'mō) s. JER. cosa, artefacto.
gist (jĭst) s. esencia, quid m.
give (gĭv) I. tr. gave, given dar; (a gift) regalar; (to pay) pagar; (to bestow) conferir, otor-

gar; *(to donate)* donar; *(to cause)* ocasionar, causar; *(a speech)* pronunciar; *(an illness)* transmitir, contagiar; *(to supply, provide)* proporcionar, proveer de; *(to dispense)* administrar (medicina, sacramentos); *(to yield)* ceder; *(to host)* dar (baile, fiesta); *(to devote)* dedicar, consagrar ♦ **to g. away** *(bride)* entregar (la novia) al novio; *(awards)* entregar; *(to divulge)* contar, revelar (secreto, trama); *(to sell cheaply)* regalar • **to g. back** devolver • **to g. chase** perseguir • **to g. it to someone** FAM. castigar o reprender a alguien • **to g. notice** *(to resign)* renunciar a (empleo); *(to fire)* despedir (de un empleo) • **to g. off** emitir, despedir (olor, vapor) • **to g. oneself up** entregarse (a las autoridades) • **to g. oneself up to** *(vice, despair)* abandonarse a; *(study, work)* dedicarse a • **to g. out** distribuir, repartir • **to g. over** entregar (autoridad, presos) • **to g. someone his due** reconocer a alguien sus méritos • **to g. up** *(to abandon)* abandonar, renunciar a (intento, tarea); *(to hand over)* entregar; *(business, activity)* retirarse de; *(to stop)* dejar de; *(to consider as lost)* dar por perdido • **to g. warning** prevenir, advertir —intr. hacer regalos, dar; *(to fail)* fallar; *(to yield)* ceder; *(to collapse)* caerse ♦ **to g. as good as one gets** pagar con la misma moneda • **to g. in** *(to collapse)* ceder, caerse; *(to accede)* acceder; *(to admit defeat)* darse por vencido • **to g. on(to)** dar a • **to g. out** *(from exhaustiom)* perder las fuerzas; *(to fail)* fallar, pararse; *(funds, luck)* agotarse • **to g. up** *(to resign oneself)* resignarse; *(to concede defeat)* darse por vencido; *(to lose hope)* perder las esperanzas • **to g. way** *(to yield)* ceder; *(to collapse)* caerse II. s. elasticidad *f*, flexibilidad *f*.

give-and-take ('ən-tāk') s. *(compromise)* toma y daca; *(of ideas)* intercambio.

give·a·way ('ə-wā') s. FAM. *(gift)* regalo; *(accidental exposure)* revelación involuntaria.

giv·en (:ən) I. cf. give II. adj. dado ♦ **g. name** nombre de pila • **g. that** dado que.

giv·ing (:ǐng) adj. generoso, liberal.

giz·zard (gǐz'ərd) s. molleja.

gla·cial (glā'shəl) adj. glacial.

gla·cier (:shər) s. glaciar *m*, ventisquero.

glad (glăd) adj. **-dd-** *(happy)* alegre, contento; *(cheerful)* bueno ♦ **to g. meet you** mucho gusto en conocerle • **to be g. to** alegrarse de.

glad·den ('n) tr. alegrar.

glade (glād) s. claro.

glad·i·a·tor (glăd'ē-ā'tər) s. gladiador *m*.

glad·i·o·lus (glăd'ē-ō'ləs) s. [pl. **es** o **-li**] gladiolo, gladíolo.

glam·o(u)r (glăm'ər) s. encanto, hechizo.

glam·o(u)r·ize (:ə-rīz') tr. *(to idealize)* idealizar, glorificar.

glam·o(u)r·ous (:ər-əs) adj. elegante, hechicero.

glance (glăns) I. intr. echar un vistazo o una mirada ♦ **to g. off** rozar, rebotar contra • **to g. through** o **at** echar un vistazo a, hojear II. s. *(glimpse)* vistazo, mirada; *(deflection)* rebote *m* ♦ **at a g.** de un vistazo • **at first g.** a primera vista • **to cast a g. at** echar una mirada a.

gland (glănd) s. glándula.

glan·du·lar (glăn'jə-lər) adj. glandular.

glare (glâr) I. intr. *(to stare angrily)* mirar con rabia; *(to dazzle)* relumbrar; *(to stand out)* saltar a la vista —tr. expresar con una mirada furibunda II. s. mirada furibunda; *(blinding light)* deslumbramiento, resplandor *m*.

glar·ing ('ǐng) adj. *(irate)* airado; *(light)* deslumbrador; *(error)* patente, manifiesto.

glass (glăs) s. vidrio, cristal *m*; *(glassware)* cristalería; *(drinking vessel)* vaso; *(mirror)* espejo ♦ pl. *(eyeglasses)* lentes, anteojos; *(binoculars)* gemelos • **dark g.** espejuelos de sol.

glass·ful ('fōl') s. vaso.

glass·mak·ing (:mā'kǐng) s. vidriería.

glass·ware (:wâr') s. cristalería.

glass·works (:wûrks') s.sg. fábrica de vidrio.

glau·co·ma (glou-kō'mə) s. glaucoma *m*.

glaze (glāz) I. s. *(ice)* capa de hielo; CERÁM. vidriado, barniz *m*; CUL. capa de almíbar, garapiña II. tr. *(a window)* poner vidrios a; CERÁM. barnizar; CUL. garapiñar —intr. ponerse vidrioso, nublarse.

gla·zier (glā'zhər) s. vidriero.

gleam (glēm) I. s. destello; *(of intelligence)* chispa, pizca II. intr. destellar.

glean (glēn) tr. espigar.

glean·ings (glē'nǐngz) s.pl. cosecha, acopio.

glee (glē) s. regocijo, alegría ♦ **g. club** orfeón.

glee·ful ('fəl) adj. regocijado, alegre.

glen (glēn) s. valle estrecho, cañada.

glib (glǐb) adj. **-bb-** *(self-assured)* desenvuelto; *(insincerely eloquent)* locuaz, de mucha labia.

glide (glīd) I. intr. deslizarse; *(furtively)* escurrirse; AVIA. planear —tr. hacer planear II. s. deslizamiento; AVIA. planeo; MÚS. ligadura.

glid·er (glī'dər) s. planeador *m*.

glim·mer (glǐm'ər) I. s. luz trémula; *(trace)* indicio ♦ **a g. of hope** un rayo de esperanza II. intr. brillar con luz trémula, lucir débilmente.

glimpse (glǐmps) I. s. vistazo, ojeada ♦ **to catch a g. of** vislumbrar II. tr. vislumbrar.

glint (glǐnt) I. s. destello, fulgor *m* II. intr. destellar.

glis·ten (glǐs'ən) intr. resplandecer, brillar.

glitch (glǐch) s. JER. malfuncionamiento.

glit·ter (glǐt'ər) I. s. centelleo, destello; COST. lentejuelas II. intr. relucir, centellear.

gloat (glōt) I. intr. regodearse II. s. regodeo.

glob (glŏb) s. gotita; *(lump)* pelota, masa.

glob·al (glō'bəl) adj. *(spherical)* esférico; *(worldwide)* mundial; *(total)* global.

globe (glōb) s. globo (terrestre).

globe·trot·ter ('trŏt'ər) s. trotamundos *mf.*

glob·u·lar (glŏb'yə-lər) adj. globular.

glob·ule (:yōl) s. glóbulo.

glob·u·lin (:yə-lǐn) s. globulina.

gloom (glōm) s. *(partial)* penumbra; *(total)* tinieblas *f*; *(melancholy)* melancolía, tristeza.

gloom·y (glō'mē) adj. **-i-** *(dark)* oscuro; *(dreary)* lúgubre; *(melancholy)* triste; *(pessimistic)* pesimista.

glop (glŏp) JER. I. s. amasijo, plasta II. tr. **-pp-** llenar de plasta.

glo·ri·fy (glôr'ə-fī') tr. glorificar; *(to exalt inordinately)* idealizar, poner por las nubes.

glo·ri·ous (:ē-əs) adj. glorioso; *(magnificent)* esplendoroso; FAM. *(wonderful)* magnífico.

glo·ry (glôr'ē) I. s. gloria ♦ **to be in one's g.** estar en la gloria II. intr. ♦ **to g. in** gloriarse de.

gloss¹ (glŏs) I. s. *(luster)* lustre *m*, brillo; *(deceptive appeal)* falso brillo, oropel *m* II. tr. ♦ **to g. over** prestar poca atención a.

gloss² I. s. *(explanation)* glosa; *(glossary)* glosario II. tr. glosar.

gloss·a·ry (glŏ'sə-ĭ) s. glosario.
gloss·y (glŏ'sē) I. adj. -i- lustroso, brillante; *(paper)* glaseado; *(showy)* vistoso II. s. fotografía impresa en papel glaseado.
glove (glŭv) s. guante *m* ♦ **g. compartment** guantera • **hand in g.** inseparables • **to fit like a g.** quedar como anillo al dedo.
glow (glō) I. intr. resplandecer, brillar; *(coals, sky)* arder; *(from passion)* encenderse II. s. resplandor *m*, brillo; *(heat)* calor *m*; *(of sunset)* arrebol *m*; *(blush)* rubor *m*; *(physical warmth)* sensación *f* de bienestar; *(ardor)* ardor *m*, enardecimiento.
glow·er (glou'ər) I. intr. echar chispas por los ojos II. s. mirada furiosa.
glow·ing (glō'ĭng) adj. ardiente, incandescente; *(shining)* resplandeciente; *(face)* radiante; *(enthusiastic)* fervoroso.
glow-worm (:wûrm') s. gusano de luz.
glu·cose (glo̅o̅'kōs') s. glucosa.
glue (glo̅o̅) I. s. goma de pegar, pegamento; *(for wood)* cola II. tr. pegar.
glu·ey (:ē) adj. pegajoso, viscoso.
glum (glŭm) adj. -mm- *(dejected)* abatido, triste; *(gloomy)* taciturno; *(dismal)* sombrío.
glut (glŭt) I. tr. -tt- hartar, atracar ♦ **to g. the market** inundar el mercado II. s. exceso.
glu·ten (glo̅o̅t'n) s. gluten *m*.
glu·ti·nous (:əs) adj. glutinoso, pegajoso.
glut·ton (glŭt'n) s. glotón *m*.
glut·ton·ous (:əs) adj. glotón.
glut·ton·y (:ē) s. glotonería, gula.
glyc·er·ide (glĭs'ə-rīd') s. glicérido.
glyc·er·in(e) (:ər-ĭn) s. glicerina.
glyc·er·ol (:ə-rôl') s. glicerol *m*.
gly·col (glī'kôl') s. glicol *m*.
G-man (jē'măn') s. [pl. **-men**] agente *m* del F.B.I.
gnarled (närld) adj. *(wood)* nudoso; *(hands)* rugoso.
gnash (năsh) tr. rechinar (los dientes).
gnat (năt) s. jején *m*.
gnaw (nô) tr. & intr. roer.
gnome (nōm) s. gnomo.
gnos·tic (nŏs'tĭk) adj. & s. gnóstico.
gnu (no̅o̅) s. ñu *m*.
go (gō) I. intr. **went, gone** ir; *(to proceed)* seguir adelante; *(to leave)* irse, marcharse; *(to take its course)* andar, marchar <how is everything going? ¿cómo anda todo?>; *(to turn out)* salir, resultar <to go well salir bien>; *(to extend)* llegar; *(to function)* funcionar, andar; *(to be acceptable)* aceptarse <anything goes nowadays todo se acepta hoy en día>; *(to be sold)* venderse; *(to become)* tornarse, volverse <he went mad se volvió loco>; *(to say)* decir; *(to be abolished)* ser suprimido; *(to pass away)* desaparecer <the pain has gone el dolor desapareció>; *(to be used up)* gastarse; *(to fail, give out)* fallar; *(to have validity)* valer, ser ley <whatever he says goes lo que él dice es ley>; *(inheritance)* pasar; FAM. *(to wait)* esperar <we still have another hour to go tenemos que esperar otra hora todavía>; *(to be left)* faltar <there are ten miles to go before we arrive faltan diez millas para llegar> ♦ **to go about** hacer, emprender • **to go about one's business** ocuparse en sus asuntos propios • **to go after** *(to follow)* seguir a; *(to attack)* caerle a, atacar • **to go around** circular • **to go away** *(to leave)* irse, marcharse; *(to pass)* pasar (dolor, molestia) • **to go before** preceder, ir antes • **to go by** *(to pass by)* pasar por; *(time*

pasar, *(to follow)* ajustarse a (las reglas), *(to be guided by)* juzgar por; *(the name of)* ser conocido por • **to go down** *(to descend)* bajar; *(the sun)* ponerse; *(a ship)* hundirse; *(airplane)* caerse; *(in history)* dejar huella • **to go for** *(to fetch)* ir por, ir a traer; FAM. *(to delight in)* gustar mucho; *(to attack)* atacar; *(to be alloted)* destinarse a • **to go forward** adelantar(se) • **to go in** *(to enter)* entrar en; *(to fit)* caber, encajar • **to go in for** FAM. dedicarse a • **to go into** *(to enter)* entrar en; *(to fit)* caber o encajar en; *(a profession)* dedicarse a; *(to examine)* examinar, investigar • **to go off** *(gun)* dispararse; *(bomb)* hacer explosión; *(to sound)* sonar; *(to turn out)* resultar, salir <everything went off well todo salió bien> • **to go on** *(to continue)* continuar, seguir; *(to take place)* suceder, ocurrir; *(to fit)* caber en • **to go out** *(to exit, socially)* salir; *(light)* apagarse; *(fire, matches)* extinguirse • **to go over** *(to examine)* examinar; *(to rehearse)* ensayar; *(to review)* repasar; *(to succeed)* salir bien • **to go through** *(to get approval)* aprobarse; *(to experience)* pasar por, sufrir • **to go to** *(to toward)* dirigirse o acercarse a • **to go under** *(to drown)* ahogarse; *(to become bankrupt)* quebrar; *(to fail)* fracasar • **to go up** *(to ascend)* subir; *(building)* levantarse • **to go up to** acercarse a • **to go with** *(to accompany)* acompañar; *(to match)* hacer juego con; *(to date)* salir con — ti. *(to wager)* apostar; *(to tolerate)* tolerar, soportar; *(to follow)* seguir <to go the same way seguir el mismo camino> ♦ **to go it alone** obrar solo y sin ayuda II. s. [pl. **es**] *(try)* intento; *(turn)* turno; *(energy)* energía ♦ **on the go** en actividad, ocupado • **to have a go at something** intentar algo • **to make a go of something** tener éxito en sacar adelante.
goad (gōd) I. s. aguijada; FIG. *(incentive)* aguijón *m* II. tr. aguijonear.
go-a·head (gō'ə-hĕd') s. FAM. autorización *f*.
goal (gōl) s. meta; DEP. *(structure)* portería; *(score)* gol *m*, tanto ♦ **g. post** poste.
goal·keep·er ('kē'pər) s. portero, guardameta *m*.
goat (gōt) s. cabra, macho cabrío; *(scapegoat)* cabeza de turco ♦ **to get someone's g.** FAM. molestar o enojar a alguien.
goat·ee (gō-tē') s. perilla, barbas de chivo.
goat·skin (gōt'skĭn') s. piel *f* de cabra; *(container)* bota.
gob (gŏb) s. pedazo ♦ **g.** FAM. gran cantidad.
gob·ble¹ (gŏb'əl) tr. devorar, engullir ♦ **to g. up** FAM. agotar rápidamente, acabar con.
gob·ble² I. s. gluglú *m*, graznido *(del pavo)* II. intr. gluglutear.
gob·ble·dy·gook (:dē-go̅o̅k') s. FAM. blablablá.
go-be·tween (gō'bĭ-twēn') s. intermediario.
gob·let (gŏb'lĭt) s. copa.
gob·lin (gŏb'lĭn) s. duende *m*, trasgo.
god (gŏd) s. dios; *(idol)* ídolo ♦ **G.** Dios.
god·child ('chīld') s. [pl. **-dren**] ahijado, -a.
god·daugh·ter (:dô'tər) s. ahijada.
god·dess (:ĭs) s. diosa.
god·fa·ther (:fä'thər) s. padrino.
god·for·sak·en (:fər-sā'kən) adj. remoto; *(desolate)* desolado, abandonado.
god·head (:hĕd') s. divinidad *f* ♦ **G.** Dios.
god·less (:lĭs) adj. descreído, ateo.
god·like (:līk') adj. como dios; *(divine)* divino.
god·li·ness (:lē-nĭs) s. piedad *f*; *(divinity)* divinidad *f*.
god·ly (:lē) adj. -i- piadoso, pío; *(divine)* di-

vino.

god·moth·er (:mŭth'ər) s. madrina.

god·par·ent (:pâr'ənt) s. padrino, madrina.

god·send (:sĕnd') s. cosa llovida del cielo.

god·son (:sŭn') s. ahijado.

go·get·ter (gō'gĕt'ər) s. FAM. buscavidas *mf*.

gog·gle (gŏg'əl) **I.** intr. mirar con los ojos de-sorbitados **II.** s. ♦ pl. gafas, anteojos.

gog·gle-eyed (:īd') adj. de ojos saltones.

go·ing (gō'ĭng) **I.** s. *(departure)* ida, partida; *(condition underfoot)* piso; FAM. *(progress)* progreso, marcha ♦ **good g.!** ¡muy bien! **II.** adj. *(working)* que funciona; *(flourishing)* que marcha; *(prevailing)* actual, corriente.

go·ing-o·ver (:ō'vər) s. FAM. inspección *f*; *(beating)* paliza; *(reprimand)* castigo.

go·ings-on (gō'ĭngz-ŏn') s.pl. actividades *f*.

goi·ter (goi'tər) s. bocio.

gold (gōld) **I.** s. oro **II.** adj. *(made of gold)* de oro; *(golden)* dorado.

gold·en (gōl'dən) adj. dorado; *(voice, epoch)* de oro; *(hair)* rubio; *(opportunity)* excelente ♦ **g. mean** justo medio.

gold-filled (gōld'fĭld') adj. chapado de oro.

gold·finch (:fĭnch') s. jilguero, cardelina.

gold·fish (:fĭsh') s. [pl. inv. *o* es] pececillo de color.

gold·smith (:smĭth') s. orfebre *m*, orífice *m*.

golf (gŏlf) **I.** s. golf *m* **II.** intr. jugar al golf.

golf·er (gŏl'fər) s. golfista *mf*.

gol·ly (gŏl'ē) interj. FAM. ¡Dios mío!, ¡caramba!

go·nad (gō'năd') s. gónada.

gon·do·la (gŏn'dl-ə) s. góndola; F.C. batea.

gon·do·lier ('-lîr') s. gondolero.

gone (gŏn) **I.** cf. **go II.** adj. *(past)* pasado, ido; *(dead)* muerto; *(ruined)* arruinado; *(lost)* per-dido; *(exhausted)* agotado ♦ **to be g.** *(departed)* haberse ido; *(disappeared)* haber desaparecido, faltar; *(used up)* haberse acabado; *(away)* estar afuera, irse ♦ **to be g. on** FAM. estar loco por.

gon·er (gŏ'nər) s. FAM. persona condenada *o* arruinada.

gong (gŏng) s. gong *m*, batintín *m*.

gon·or·rhe·a (gŏn'ə-rē'ə) s. gonorrea.

goo (gōō) s. FAM. substancia pegajosa; *(drivel)* sentimentalismo.

goo·ber (gōō'bər) s. cacahuete *m*, maní *m*.

good (gŏŏd) **I.** adj. **better, best** bueno; *(benefi-cial)* beneficioso; *(thorough)* completo; *(valid)* válido; *(genuine)* auténtico; *(ample)* abun-dante; *(full)* más de <I waited a g. hour esperé más de una hora>; *(pleasant)* agradable; *(favor-able)* favorable; *(reliable)* digno de confianza ♦ **a g.** turn un favor, una bondad • **as g. as** prác-ticamente, casi • **g. for nothing** inútil • **how g. of you** muy amable de su parte • **g.** looks buen parecer • **in g. standing** de buena reputa-ción • **that's a g. one!** ¡un buen chiste! • **to be g. at** tener capacidad *o* talento para • **to be g. for** *(to last)* durar; *(to have credit)* tener cré-dito hasta; *(to be beneficial)* hacer bien • **to be g. to someone** ser bueno para con alguien • **to be no g.** ser inútil, no servir para nada • **to be g. enough to** tener la bondad de • **to have a g. time** divertirse, pasarlo bien • **to hold g.** valer, tener validez • **to make g.** *(to prosper)* prospe-rar; *(a debt)* cubrir; *(a promise)* cumplir **II.** s. bien *m*; *(goodness)* bondad *f* ♦ **for g.** para siempre • **the g.** lo bueno • **to come to no g.** terminar mal ♦ pl. *(wares, belongings)* bienes; *(merchandise)* mercancías, géneros; *(fabric)* tela • **g. and chattels** muebles y enseres • **to**

deliver the g. cumplir lo prometido • **to have the g. on someone** tener pruebas de culpabili-dad contra alguien **III.** adv. FAM. bien ♦ **g. and proper** por las buenas • **to do one g.** sentarle bien • **to feel g.** *(satisfied)* estar satisfecho; *(well)* sentirse bien; *(pleasurable)* ser agrada-ble, dar gusto **IV.** interj. ¡bueno!, ¡muy bien!

good-by(e) (-bī') **I.** interj. ¡adiós!, ¡hasta luego! **II.** s. [pl. **(e)s**] adiós, despedida.

good-for-noth·ing ('fər-nŭth'ĭng) **I.** s. haragán *m*, inútil *m* **II.** adj. inútil, sin valor.

good-heart·ed (:här'tĭd) adj. bondadoso.

good-hu·mored (:hyōō'mərd) adj. jovial, ale-gre.

good-look·ing (:lŏŏk'ĭng) adj. bien parecido.

good·ly (:lē) adj. -i- *(attractive)* atractivo, agra-dable; *(large)* grande, considerable.

good-na·tured (:nā'chərd) adj. afable, amable.

good·ness (:nĭs) **I.** s. bondad *f* **II.** interj. ¡Dios mío!, ¡Ave María!

good-sized (:sīzd') adj. bastante grande.

good-tem·pered (:tĕm'pərd) adj. afable.

good·y (:ē) FAM. **I.** s. golosina, dulce *m* **II.** in-terj. ¡qué bien!

good·y-good·y (:ē:ē) adj. & s. santurrón *m*.

goo·ey (gōō'ē) adj. pegajoso, viscoso.

goof (gōōf) JER. **I.** s. *(fool)* bobo, simplón *m*; *(mistake)* disparate *m*, pifia **II.** intr. meter la pata ♦ **to g. off** *o* **around** holgazanear.

goof-off ('ôf') s. JER. haragán *m*, holgazán *m*.

goof·y (gōō'fē) adj. -i- JER. tonto, ridículo.

gook (gŏŏk) s. JER. mugre *f*, suciedad *f*.

goon (gōōn) s. FAM. *(thug)* terrorista pagado; JER. *(stupid person)* estúpido, tonto.

goose (gōōs) s. [pl. **geese**] ganso ♦ **g. bumps** *o* **flesh** carne de gallina • **to cook one's g.** FAM. malograrle los planes a uno.

goose-step ('stĕp') intr. **-pp-** ir a paso de ganso.

go·pher (gō'fər) s. ardilla terrestre.

Gor·di·an knot (gôr'dē-ən) s. nudo gordiano.

gore[1] (gôr) tr. cornear.

gore[2] s. *(cloth)* sesga, nesga.

gore[3] s. *(blood)* sangre coagulada.

gorge (gôrj) JER. **I.** s. *(ravine)* desfiladero; *(throat)* garganta **II.** tr. hartar, atiborrar —intr. ♦ **to g. oneself** hartarse y atiborrarse.

gor·geous (gôr'jəs) adj. *(beautiful)* hermosísi-mo; *(magnificent)* magnífico, espléndido.

go·ril·la (gə-rĭl'ə) s. gorila *m*.

go·ry (gôr'ē) adj. -i- *(bloody)* ensangrentado; *(fight)* sangriento.

gosh (gŏsh) interj. ¡cielos!, ¡Dios!

gos·ling (gŏz'lĭng) s. ansarino.

gos·pel (gŏs'pəl) s. evangelio ♦ **g. meeting** reunión evangélica.

gos·sa·mer (gŏs'ə-mər) **I.** s. telaraña fina; *(fabric)* gasa **II.** adj. muy delgado, muy fino.

gos·sip (gŏs'ĭp) **I.** s. chismes *m*; *(gossiper)* chismoso ♦ **g. column** noticias sociales **II.** intr. chismear, chismorrear.

gos·sip·mon·ger (:mŭng'gər) s. chismoso.

gos·sip·y (gŏs'ĭ-pē) adj. chismoso.

got, got·ten (gŏt, gŏt'n) cf. **get.**

Goth·ic (gŏth'ĭk) adj. gótico.

gouge (gouj) **I.** s. *(tool)* gubia; *(cut)* muesca **II.** tr. escoplear (con una gubia); JER. *(to over-charge)* estafar ♦ **to g. out** excavar.

gourd (gôrd) s. calabaza.

gour·mand (gŏŏr-mänd') s. goloso, glotón *m*.

gour·met (gŏŏr-mā') s. gastrónomo.

gout (gout) s. gota.

gov·ern (gŭv'ərn) tr. gobernar; *(to determine)* determinar —intr. gobernar.

gov·ern·a·ble (:ər-nə-bəl) adj. gobernable.

gov·er·nance (:nəns) s. gobierno.

gov·ern·ess (:nĭs) s. institutriz f.

gov·ern·ment (gŭv'ərn-mənt) s. & adj. (del) gobierno.

gov·ern·ment·al ('-měn'tl) adj. gubernamental, gubernativo.

gov·er·nor (gŭv'ər-nər) s. gobernador m; MEC. *(regulator)* regulador automático.

gov·er·nor·ship (:shĭp') s. gobernación.

gown (goun) s. vestido (de etiqueta); *(nightgown)* camisón m; *(ceremonial robe)* toga.

grab (grăb) I. tr. **-bb-** *(to seize)* agarrar, coger; *(to snatch)* arrebatar; JER. *(to attract)* cautivar ♦ **to g. a bite to eat** comer algo a la carrera —intr. ♦ **to g. at** tratar de arrebatar II. s. ♦ **to make a g. at** tratar de agarrar • **up for grabs** disponible.

grab·by (ē) adj. **-i-** codicioso.

grace (grās) I. s. gracia; *(reprieve)* plazo; *(at table)* bendición f de la mesa ♦ **by the g. of** gracias a • **g. period** plazo de respiro • **to be in the good graces of** gozar del favor de • **to fall from g.** caer en desgracia • **to say g.** bendecir la mesa II. tr. adornar, embellecer ♦ **to g. with** honrar con.

grace·ful (:fəl) adj. agraciado, elegante.

grace·less (:lĭs) adj. sin gracia; *(clumsy)* torpe.

gra·cious (grā'shəs) adj. *(courteous)* amable, cortés; *(kind)* compasivo; *(elegant)* elegante ♦ **goodness g.! o g. me!** ¡válgame Dios!

grad (grăd) s. FAM. graduado.

gra·date (grā'dāt') tr. & intr. graduar(se).

gra·da·tion (grā-dā'shən) s. gradación f, graduación f; *(of colors)* degradación f.

grade (grād) I. s. *(degree, rank)* grado; *(quality)* calidad f; EDUC. *(class)* año, curso; *(mark)* nota; *(slope)* pendiente f ♦ **g. A** de primera • **g. crossing** paso a nivel • **g. school** escuela primaria • **to make the g.** FAM. tener éxito II. tr. *(to classify)* clasificar; *(an exam)* calificar; *(a student)* dar nota a; *(to level)* nivelar.

gra·di·ent (grā'dē-ənt) s. inclinación f.

grad·u·al (grăj'ōō-əl) adj. gradual, paulatino.

grad·u·ate (grăj'ōō-āt') I. tr. & intr. graduar(se) ♦ **to g. as** recibirse de II. adj. & s. graduado, diplomado ♦ **g. school** escuela para graduados.

grad·u·a·tion ('-'shən) s. graduación f; *(commencement)* entrega de diplomas.

graf·fi·ti (grə-fē'tē) s.pl. inscripciones f en las paredes.

graft[1] (grăft) AGR., MED. I. tr. & int. injertar(se) II. s. injerto.

graft[2] I. s. *(crime)* concusión f, extorsión f II. tr. & intr. extorsionar.

gra·ham (grā'əm) s. harina de trigo entero.

grain (grān) s. grano; *(cereals)* cereales m; *(bit)* pizca, asomo; *(in wood)* fibra; *(in leather)* flor f; *(texture)* textura ♦ **to go against one's g.** ir contra el carácter de uno • **with a g. of salt** con reservas.

grain·y (grā'nē) adj. **-i-** *(granular)* granoso, granular; *(veined)* veteado.

gram (grăm) s. gramo.

gram·mar (grăm'ər) s. gramática ♦ **g. school** escuela primaria; G.B. escuela secundaria.

gram·mar·ian (grə-mâr'ē-ən) s. gramático.

gram·mat·i·cal (:măt'ĭ-kəl) adj. gramatical.

gramme (grăm) G.B. var. de **gram**.

gram·o·phone (grăm'ə-fōn') s. gramófono.

gran·a·ry (grăn'ə-rē) s. granero.

grand (grănd) I. adj. grandioso, magnífico; *(principal)* principal; *(sumptuous)* suntuoso; *(dignified)* ilustre, distinguido; *(style)* elevado; *(wonderful)* fenomenal ♦ **g. jury** jurado de acusación • **g. larceny** robo de mayor cuantía • **g. piano** piano de cola • **the g. total** la suma total • **to have a g. time** pasarlo fenomenalmente II. s. piano de cola; JER. mil dólares.

grand·aunt ('ănt', 'änt') s. tía abuela.

grand·child (:chīld') s. [pl. **-dren**] nieto, -a.

grand·dad(·dy) (grăn'dăd'[ē]) s. abuelo, abuelito; *(archetype)* arquetipo.

grand·daugh·ter (:dô'tər) s. nieta.

gran·deur (grăn'jər) s. grandeza.

grand·fa·ther (grănd'fä'thər) s. abuelo ♦ **g. clock** reloj de pie o de caja.

gran·dil·o·quence (grăn-dĭl'ə-kwəns) s. grandilocuencia.

gran·dil·o·quent (:kwənt) adj. grandilocuente.

gran·di·ose (grăn'dē-ōs') adj. grandioso; *(style)* pomposo; *(scheme)* ambicioso.

grand·ma (grănd'mä') s. FAM. abuelita.

grand·moth·er (grănd'mŭth'ər) s. abuela.

grand·pa (grănd'pä') s. FAM. abuelo, abuelito.

grand·par·ent (grănd'pâr'ənt) s. abuelo, -a.

grand·son (:sŭn') s. nieto.

grand·stand (:stănd') I. s. tribuna II. intr. actuar de manera ostentosa.

grange (grānj) s. G.B. granja, finca.

gran·ite (grăn'ĭt) s. granito.

gran·ny/nie (grăn'ē) s. abuelita; *(fussy person)* persona minuciosa.

grant (grănt) I. tr. *(to concede)* conceder; *(to bestow)* otorgar; *(to admit)* admitir ♦ **granted o granting that** suponiendo que • **to take it for granted** dar por sentado • **to take someone for granted** no apreciar suficientemente a alguien II. s. concesión f; *(donation)* donación f; *(scholarship)* beca; DER. *(transfer)* cesión f.

gran·u·lar (grăn'yə-lər) adj. granular.

gran·u·late (:lāt') tr. & intr. granular(se).

gran·ule (grăn'yōōl) s. gránulo.

grape (grāp) s. uva.

grape·fruit (frōōt') s. toronja, pomelo.

grape·shot (:shŏt') s. metralla.

grape·vine (:vīn') s. vid f, parra ♦ **through the g.** por medio de chismes.

graph (grăf) I. s. gráfico, diagrama m ♦ **g. paper** papel cuadriculado II. tr. representar mediante un gráfico o diagrama.

graph·ic ('ĭk) I. adj. gráfico II. s. ilustración gráfica ♦ **graphics** sg. o pl. *(drawing)* dibujo lineal; ARTE. artes gráficas.

graph·ite (grăf'īt') s. grafito.

grap·ple (grăp'əl) I. s. garfio II. tr. MARÍT. aferrar (con un garfio); *(to grip)* agarrar —intr. luchar cuerpo a cuerpo ♦ **to g. with** afrontar.

grasp (grăsp) I. tr. *(to seize)* agarrar, asir; *(to clasp)* apretar; *(to comprehend)* captar —intr. ♦ **to g. at** tratar de agarrar II. s. *(grip)* apretón m; *(embrace)* abrazo; FIG. comprensión f ♦ **beyond, within one's g.** fuera del, al alcance de uno • **to have a good g. of** dominar.

grasp·ing (grăs'pĭng) adj. avaricioso.

grass (grăs) s. hierba; *(lawn)* césped m; *(pasture)* pasto; JER. *(marijuana)* yerba.

grass·hop·per ('hŏp'ər) s. saltamontes m.

grass·land (:lănd') s. pradera, prado.

grass·roots (:rōōts′) s.pl. nivel *m* local (de la organización política).

grass·y (:ē) adj. -i- con mucha hierba.

grate¹ (grāt) I. tr. CUL. rallar; *(teeth)* hacer rechinar; FIG. irritar —intr. rechinar ♦ **to g. on** irritar II. s. *(of metal)* chirrido; *(of teeth)* rechinamiento.

grate² s. *(grill)* reja, verja; *(for coals)* parrilla.

grate·ful (grāt′fəl) adj. agradecido.

grat·er (grā′tər) s. rallador *m*.

grat·i·fi·ca·tion (grăt′ə-fĭ-kā′shən) s. gratificación *f*.

grat·i·fy (grăt′ə-fī′) tr. complacer, satisfacer.

grat·ing (grā′tĭng) adj. *(rasping)* discordante, malsonante; *(irritating)* molesto.

grat·is (grăt′ĭs) adj. & adv. gratis.

grat·i·tude (grăt′ĭ-tōōd′) s. gratitud *f*.

gra·tu·i·tous (grə-tōō′ĭ-təs) adj. gratuito.

gra·tu·i·ty (:tē) s. propina.

grave¹ (grāv) s. tumba, sepultura; *(pit)* fosa.

grave² adj. grave, serio; *(dignified)* solemne.

grave·dig·ger (′dĭg′ər) s. sepulturero.

grav·el (grăv′əl) s. ripio, grava.

grave·stone (grāv′stōn′) s. lápida.

grave·yard (:yärd′) s. cementerio, camposanto.

grav·i·tate (grăv′ĭ-tāt′) intr. gravitar ♦ **to g. toward** tender hacia, ser atraído por.

grav·i·ta·tion (′-tā′shən) s. gravitación *f*.

grav·i·ty (grăv′ĭ-tē) s. gravedad *f*; *(solemnity)* solemnidad *f*.

gra·vy (grā′vē) s. *(juices)* jugo; *(sauce)* salsa; JER. *(easy gain)* breva ♦ **g. boat** salsera.

gray (grā) I. s. gris II. adj. gris; *(hair)* cano ♦ **g. area** zona no definida ♦ **to go** o **turn g.** encanecer.

gray·ish (′ĭsh) adj. grisáceo.

graze¹ (grāz) intr. *(to feed)* pacer, pastar —tr. apacentar.

graze² I. tr. & intr. *(to brush against)* rozar II. s. rozadura.

grease (grēs) I. s. grasa ♦ **g. monkey** JER. mecánico • **g. paint** maquillaje II. tr. engrasar, untar.

greas·y (grē′sē, grē′zē) adj. -i- *(grease-coated)* engrasado; *(fatty)* grasoso; *(dirty)* grasiento.

great (grāt) I. adj. grande; *(age)* avanzado; FAM. *(very good)* magnífico, bárbaro ♦ **a g. while** mucho tiempo • **to be g. at** FAM. ser un hacha en • **to be g.** friends FAM. ser muy amigos • **to have a g. time** pasarlo en grande II. s. grande *m* III. adv. FAM. muy bien.

great·coat (:kōt′) s. sobretodo, abrigo.

great-grand·child (-grănd′chĭld′) s. [pl. **-dren**] bisnieto, -a.

great-grand·daugh·ter (:dô′tər) s. bisnieta.

great-grand·fa·ther (:fä′thər) s. bisabuelo.

great-grand·moth·er (:mŭth′ər) s. bisabuela.

great-grand·par·ent (:pâr′ənt) s. bisabuelo, -a.

great-grand·son (:sŭn′) s. bisnieto.

great·ly (grāt′lē) adv. muy, mucho.

greed (grēd) s. *(for wealth)* codicia, avaricia; *(for food)* gula, glotonería.

greed·y (grē′dē) adj. -i- *(avaricious)* codicioso; *(gluttonous)* glotón *m*; *(eager)* ávido.

green (grēn) s. verde *m*; *(verdure)* verdor *m*; *(lawn)* césped *m* ♦ **g. bean** habichuela o judía verde • **g. thumb** FAM. habilidad para la jardinería ♦ pl. verduras II. adj. verde; *(sickly)* pálido; *(raw)* inexperto, novato ♦ **he is g. with envy** se le come la envidia.

green·back (′băk′) s. FAM. billete *m*.

green·er·y (grē′nə-rē) s. follaje *m*, verdor *m*.

green·gro·cer (grēn′grō′sər) s. G.B. verdulero.

green·horn (:hôrn′) s. novato, bisoño.

green·house (:hous′) s. invernadero.

green·ish (grē′nĭsh) adj. verdoso.

greet (grēt) tr. dar la bienvenida, saludar; *(news, fact)* recibir; *(one's eyes, ears)* presentarse a.

greet·ing (grē′tĭng) s. saludo ♦ **g. card** tarjeta.

gre·gar·i·ous (grĭ-gâr′ē-əs) adj. *(group-forming)* gregario; *(sociable)* sociable.

grem·lin (grĕm′lĭn) s. duende *mf*.

gre·nade (grə-nād′) s. granada.

grew (grōō) cf. **grow**.

grey (grā) var. de **gray**.

grey·hound (′hound′) s. galgo.

grid (grĭd) s. *(grating)* rejilla; *(on a map)* cuadrícula; ELEC. *(network)* red *f*.

grid·dle (grĭd′l) s. plancha.

grid·i·ron (grĭd′ī′ərn) s. CUL. parrilla; *(football field)* campo de rugby americano.

grid·lock (grĭd′lŏk′) s. embotellamiento de tráfico.

grief (grēf) s. *(sorrow)* pena, congoja; *(trouble)* desgracia ♦ **to come to g.** fracasar, sufrir un desastre.

griev·ance (grē′vəns) s. *(cause)* motivo de queja; *(complaint)* queja.

grieve (grēv) tr. dar pena, afligir —intr. apenarse, afligirse; *(to mourn)* lamentarse.

griev·ous (grē′vəs) adj. *(causing grief)* penoso; *(serious)* serio, grave.

grill (grĭl) I. tr. *(to broil)* asar a la parrilla; FAM. *(to cross-examine)* asar II. s. *(rack)* parrilla; *(food)* asado; *(restaurant)* restaurante *m*.

grill(e) (grĭl) s. *(grate)* reja; *(at window)* verja.

grim (grĭm) adj. -mm- *(unrelenting)* implacable; *(forbidding)* imponente, terrible; *(ghastly)* macabro; *(gloomy)* lúgubre ♦ **the g. truth** la escueta verdad.

grim·ace (grĭm′ĭs) I. s. mueca II. intr. hacer muecas.

grime (grīm) s. mugre *f*.

grim·y (grī′mē) adj. -i- mugriento.

grin (grĭn) I. intr. -nn- sonreír ♦ **to g. and bear it** soportar estoicamente II. s. sonrisa abierta.

grind (grīnd) I. tr. **ground** *(to crush)* triturar, pulverizar; *(to sharpen)* amolar; *(a lens)* pulir; *(glass)* esmerilar; *(teeth)* hacer rechinar; *(coffee, wheat)* moler; *(meat)* picar ♦ **to g. down** *(to wear away)* desgastar; *(to oppress)* agobiar, oprimir • **to g. out** producir rutinariamente • **to g. up** triturar —intr. *(to mill)* molerse; *(brake, gears)* chirriar, ir dando chirridos; FAM. *(to study hard)* quemarse las pestañas estudiando; *(to work hard)* trabajar mucho II. s. FAM. *(student)* empollón *m*; *(task)* trabajo pesado ♦ **to get back to the g.** volver a los libros o al trabajo.

grind·stone (′stōn′) s. muela.

grip (grĭp) I. s. *(firm grasp)* asimiento; *(of hands)* apretón *m*; *(control)* control *m*; *(handle)* asidero; *(suitcase)* maleta ♦ **to come to grips with** afrontar, habérselas con • **to get a good g. on** agarrar bien • **to get a g. on oneself** controlarse, calmarse • **to have a good g. on** tener un buen dominio de II. tr. -pp- *(to seize)* asir, agarrar; *(to clasp)* apretar; FAM. *(to enthrall)* cautivar —intr. agarrarse.

gripe (grīp) FAM. I. tr. fastidiar —intr. quejarse *(about* de) II. s. queja.

grippe (grĭp) s. gripe *f*, influenza.

gris·ly (grĭz′lē) adj. espantoso, horroroso.

grist (grĭst) s. molienda ♦ **to be g. for the mill** ser provechoso.

gris·tle (grĭs′əl) s. cartílago.

grit (grĭt) **I.** s. *(granules)* granitos de arena; FAM. *(pluck)* agallas, valor m **II.** tr. **-tt-** ♦ **to g. one's teeth** FAM. apretar las dientes.

grits (grĭts) s.pl. maíz m a medio moler.

grit·ty (grĭt′ē) adj. **-i-** arenoso.

griz·zly (grĭz′lē) **I.** adj. **-i-** grisáceo **II.** s. oso gris.

groan (grōn) **I.** intr. *(to moan)* gemir; *(to creak)* crujir *(bajo mucho peso)* —tr. decir o indicar con gemidos **II.** s. gemido.

gro·cer (grō′sər) s. tendero, almacenero.

gro·cer·y (;sə-rē) s. tienda de comestibles, almacén m ♦ **g. store** almacén ♦ pl. comestibles.

grog (grŏg) s. grog m (esp. ron con agua).

grog·gy (grŏg′ē) adj. **-i-** *(dazed)* atontado; *(shaky)* tambaleante.

groin (groin) s. ANAT. ingle f; ARQ. arista.

groom (grōōm) **I.** s. mozo de caballos; *(bridegroom)* novio **II.** tr. *(horses)* cuidar; *(person)* preparar *(for para)* ♦ **grooming** acicaladura • **to g. oneself** arreglarse, acicalarse.

groove (grōōv) **I.** s. ranura; *(of a record)* surco; *(routine)* rutina ♦ in the g. JER. en plena forma • **to get into the g. of things** acostumbrarse **II.** tr. acanalar —intr. ♦ **to g. on** JER. disfrutar de.

grope (grōp) intr. andar a tientas ♦ **to g. for** buscar a tientas —tr. tentar.

gross (grōs) **I.** adj. *(income, weight)* bruto; *(error, ignorance)* craso; *(vulgar)* grosero; *(disgusting)* repugnante; *(unrefined)* ordinario, tosco ♦ **g. amount** suma total • **g. injustice** injusticia notoria • **g. national product** producto nacional bruto **II.** s. total m; *(twelve dozen)* gruesa ♦ **by the g.** en gruesas **III.** tr. recaudar dinero en bruto ♦ **to g. out** JER. dar asco a.

gro·tesque (grō-tĕsk′) adj. grotesco.

grot·to (grŏt′ō) s. [pl. **-es** o **-s**] gruta.

grouch (grouch) **I.** intr. gruñir, refunfuñar **II.** s. gruñón m.

grouch·y (grou′chē) adj. **-i-** malhumorado.

ground (ground) **I.** s. tierra, suelo; *(area)* terreno, campo; ELEC. toma de tierra ♦ **from the g. up** completamente • **g. crew** personal de tierra • **g. floor** planta baja • **g. hog** marmota • **g. rule** regla de procedimiento o comportamiento • **g. swell** mar de fondo • **g. water** agua subterránea • **g. zero** sitio de una explosión nuclear • **to break g.** empezar (esp. a construir) • **to break new g.** marcar nuevos rumbos • **to cover the g.** *(distance)* recorrer el trecho; FIG. tratar extensamente un tópico • **to get off the g.** tomar vuelo • **to give, gain g.** ceder, ganar terreno • **to hold o stand one's g.** mantenerse firme, no ceder • **to run into the g.** agotar *(un tema)* ♦ pl. *(piece of land)* terreno; *(basis)* base; *(cause)* causa, motivo ♦ **g. for divorce** motivo de divorcio>; *(sediment)* poso **II.** tr. *(theory)* basar, fundar; AVIA. impedir volar; FAM. *(to punish)* prohibir salir; ELEC. conectar con tierra; MARÍT. hacer varar o encallar ♦ **to be well-grounded** in ser versado en.

ground² cf. **grind.**

ground·less (′lĭs) adj. infundado, sin base.

ground·work (:wûrk′) s. fundamento, base f.

group (grōōp) **I.** s. grupo; *(organization)* agrupación f; MÚS. conjunto **II.** tr. & intr. agrupar(se).

group·ing (grōō′pĭng) s. agrupación f.

grouse¹ (grous) s.inv. ORNIT. urogallo.

grouse² FAM. **I.** intr. quejarse, refunfuñar **II.** s. queja, refunfuño.

grout (grout) s. lechada.

grove (grōv) s. bosquecillo, soto.

grov·el (grŭv′əl) intr. *(to cringe)* rebajarse; *(to debase oneself)* envilecerse.

grow (grō) tr. **grew, grown** cultivar <to g. flowers cultivar flores> *(beard, hair)* dejar(se) crecer —intr. *(business, industry)* expandirse, agrandarse; *(to increase)* aumentar; *(to mature)* madurar (persona) ♦ **to g. accustomed to** acostumbrarse a • **to g. dark** oscurecerse • **to g. into** llegar a ser • **to g. old** envejecer • **to g. on trees** encontrarse dondequiera • **to g. on one** llegar a gustarle a uno • **to g. out of** *(a habit)* perder; *(to result from)* deberse a • **to g. up** *(physically)* crecer; *(mentally)* madurar, hacerse adulto; *(to be raised)* criarse.

growl (groul) **I.** s. gruñido **II.** intr. gruñir —tr. expresar con gruñidos.

grown (grōn) **I.** cf. **grow II.** adj. *(mature)* mayor, adulto.

grown-up (′ŭp′) adj. & s. adulto.

growth (grōth) s. crecimiento; *(development)* desarrollo; *(increase)* aumento; *(of beard)* barba; *(of grass)* brote m; MED. tumor m.

grub (grŭb) **I.** tr. **-bb-** *(to dig up)* desarraigar; JER. *(to sponge)* gorronear —intr. *(to dig)* cavar; *(to rummage)* hurgar **II.** s. ZOOL. larva, gusano; JER. *(food)* comida.

grub·by (′ē) adj. **-i-** sucio.

grudge (grŭj) **I.** tr. escatimar, dar a regañadientes **II.** s. rencor m ♦ **to hold a g. against** guardar rencor a.

grudg·ing·ly (′ĭng-lē) adv. de mala gana.

gru·el (grōō′əl) s. gachas f, avenate m.

gru·el·(l)ing (′ə-lĭng) adj. *(demanding)* abrumador; *(exhausting)* agotador, penoso.

grue·some (grōō′səm) adj. horrible, horrendo.

gruff (grŭf) adj. brusco, *(hoarse)* ronco.

grum·ble (grŭm′bəl) **I.** intr. quejarse, gruñir **II.** s. queja, gruñido.

grum·bler (:blər) s. gruñidor m, gruñón m.

grum·bling (:blĭng) adj. gruñón, refunfuñón.

grump (grŭmp) **I.** s. gruñón m ♦ pl. mal humor **II.** intr. quejarse, refunfuñar.

grump·y (grŭm′pē) adj. **-i-** malhumorado.

grunt (grŭnt) **I.** intr. gruñir **II.** s. gruñido.

guar·an·tee (găr′ən-tē′) **I.** s. garantía; *(promise)* palabra, promesa; *(guarantor)* garante mf ♦ **to be a g. of** asegurar, garantizar **II.** tr. garantizar; *(to promise)* prometer; *(someone's actions)* responder de.

guar·an·tor (:tôr′) s. garante mf.

guar·an·ty (′-tē) s. garantía.

guard (gärd) **I.** tr. guardar; *(to protect)* proteger; *(to watch over)* custodiar —intr. ♦ **to g. against** guardarse de **II.** s. *(sentinel)* guardia m, guardián m; *(body of troops)* guardia f; *(escort)* escolta; DEP. *(players)* defensa m; *(defensive posture)* guardia; *(act of guarding)* custodia, guardia; *(of a prisoner)* vigilancia; *(safeguard)* protección f ♦ **off (one's) g.** desprevenido • **on (one's) g.** prevenido, en guardia • **to be on g.** MIL. estar de guardia • **under g.** a buen recaudo.

guard·ed (gär′dĭd) adj. *(cautious)* cauto; *(restrained)* mesurado; *(protected)* protegido.

guard·house (gärd′hous′) s. cuerpo de guardia; *(jail)* cárcel f militar.

guard·i·an (gär'dē-ən) s. guardián *m*, guarda *m*; (of an orphan) tutor *m*, curador *m*.

gua·va (gwä'və) s. guayaba.

gu·ber·na·to·ri·al (gōō'bər-nə-tôr'ē-əl) adj. del gobernador.

guck (gŭk) s. JER. mugre *f*.

gue(r)·ril·la (gə-rĭl'ə) s. guerrillero ♦ **g. warfare** guerrilla.

guess (gĕs) I. tr. & intr. conjeturar; (to suppose) suponer; (to estimate correctly) adivinar ♦ **I g. so** me imagino que sí • **g. who!** ¡adivina! • **to g. right** adivinar, acertar • **to keep someone guessing** mantener a alguien con en suspenso II. s. conjetura, suposición *f* ♦ **rough g.** cálculo aproximado • **to take a g.** tratar de adivinar.

guess·work ('wûrk') s. conjetura.

guest (gĕst) s. (at home) invitado; (at hotel) huésped *m* ♦ **be my g.** FAM. hazlo si quieres • **g. room** cuarto de huéspedes.

guff (gŭf) s. JER. disparate *m*, tontería.

guf·faw (gə-fô') I. s. carcajada, risotada II. intr. reírse a carcajadas.

guid·ance (gīd'ns) s. (direction) dirección *f*; (leadership) gobierno; (counseling) consejo ♦ **under the g.** of guiado por.

guide (gīd) I. s. (leader) guía *mf*; (book, device) guía *f* II. tr. guiar; (to steer, govern) dirigir; (to advise) aconsejar ♦ **guided missile** proyectil teledirigido —intr. servir de guía.

guide·book ('bŏŏk') s. guía.

guide·line (:līn') s. pauta.

guide·post (:pōst') s. poste *m* indicador.

guild (gĭld) s. gremio, asociación *f*.

guile (gīl) s. engaño.

guile·less ('lĭs) adj. inocente, cándido.

guil·lo·tine (gĭl'ə-tēn') I. s. guillotina II. tr. guillotinar.

guilt (gĭlt) s. culpabilidad *f*; (blame, remorse) culpa.

guilt·less ('lĭs) adj. inocente.

guilt·y (gĭl'tē) adj. -i- culpable ♦ **not g.** inocente • **to find g.** declarar culpable • **to have a g. conscience** remorderle a uno la conciencia.

guinea pig s. conejillo de Indias.

guise (gīz) s. (aspect) apariencia; (pretext) pretexto; (dress) traje *m*.

gui·tar (gĭ-tär') s. guitarra.

gulf (gŭlf) s. golfo; (abyss) abismo.

gul·let (gŭl'ĭt) s. esófago; (throat) garganta.

gul·li·ble (gŭl'ə-bəl) adj. bobo, crédulo.

gul·ly (gŭl'ē) s. badén *m*, barranco.

gulp (gŭlp) I. tr. tragar, engullir ♦ **to g. down** tragarse —intr. tragar en seco; (in fear) quedar boquiabierto II. s. trago.

gum¹ (gŭm) I. s. (sap, glue) goma; (for chewing) chicle *m* II. tr. -mm- engomar ♦ **to g. up** (to clog) atascar; (to ruin) estropear.

gum² s. ODONT. encía.

gum·bo (gŭm'bō) s. (sopa de) quingombó.

gump·tion (gŭmp'shən) s. FAM. espíritu *m*.

gun (gŭn) I. s. arma de fuego; (cannon) cañón *m*; (handgun) pistola; (rifle) fusil *m*; (shotgun) escopeta; (killer) pistolero II. tr. -nn- disparar; AUTO. acelerar a fondo ♦ **to g. down** matar (a tiros).

gun·boat ('bōt') s. cañonero.

gun·fight (:fīt') s. pelea a tiros.

gun·fire (:fīr') s. disparos, tiros; (from artillery) cañonazos; (shooting) tiroteo.

gunk (gŭnk) s. FAM. mugre *f*, porquería.

gun·man (gŭn'mən) s. [pl. -men] pistolero.

gun·ner (:ər) s. MIL. artillero.

gun·ner·y (:ə-rē) s. artillería.

gun·ny·sack (gŭn'ē-săk') s. saco de arpillera.

gun·pow·der (gŭn'pou'dər) s. pólvora.

gun·run·ner (:rŭn'ər) s. traficante *mf* de armas.

gun·shot (:shŏt') s. tiro; (artillery) cañonazo; (range) alcance *m* ♦ **within g.** a tiro de fusil.

gun·shy (:shī') adj. asustadizo, receloso.

gun·sling·er (:slĭng'ər) s. pistolero.

gun·smith (:smĭth') s. armero.

gun·wale (gŭn'əl) s. regala, borda.

gur·gle (gûr'gəl) I. intr. (water) gorgotear; (baby) gorjear II. s. gorgoteo, gorjeo.

gu·ru (gŏŏr'ōō) s. maestro.

gush (gŭsh) I. intr. brotar, chorrear; (person) hablar con efusión excesiva II. s. chorro; (display) efusión excesiva.

gush·er (:ər) s. pozo brotante de petróleo.

gust (gŭst) I. s. ventolera, ráfaga; (of anger) acceso II. intr. soplar (el viento).

gus·to (gŭs'tō) s. deleite *m*, entusiasmo.

gust·y (gŭs'tē) adj. -i- ventoso, borrascoso.

gut (gŭt) I. s. intestino, tripa ♦ pl. (entrails) tripas; JER. (courage) agallas II. tr. -tt- destripar; FIG. acabar con el interior de III. adj. JER. (feeling) hondo; (reaction) instintivo; (issue) fundamental.

gut·less ('lĭs) adj. JER. sin agallas, cobarde.

guts·y (:sē) adj. -i- JER. con agallas, atrevido.

gut·ter (gŭt'ər) I. s. (street) cuneta; (roof) canalón *m*, canal *m* ♦ **g. language** lenguaje obsceno • **to come from the g.** venir de lo más bajo II. intr. parpadear (una vela).

guy¹ (gī) I. s. (tether) tirante *m* II. tr. atirantar.

guy² s. FAM. (fellow) tipo, tío ♦ pl. muchachos.

guz·zle (gŭz'əl) tr. soplarse, beber mucho.

guz·zler (:lər) s. bebedor *m*, borracho.

gym (jĭm) s. FAM. gimnasio.

gym·na·si·um (jĭm-nā'zē-əm) s. gimnasio.

gym·nast ('năst') s. gimnasta *mf*.

gym·nas·tic (:năs'tĭk) adj. gimnástico ♦ **gymnastics** s.sg. gimnasia.

gy·ne·col·o·gist (gī'nĭ-kŏl'ə-jĭst) s. ginecólogo.

gy·ne·col·o·gy (:jē) s. ginecología.

gyp (jĭp) FAM. I. tr. -pp- estafar II. s. (swindle) estafa; (swindler) estafador *m*.

gyp·sum (jĭp'səm) s. yeso.

gyp·sy (jĭp'sē) s. gitano ♦ **G. gitano.**

gy·rate (jī'rāt') intr. girar, rotar.

gy·ra·tion (jī-rā'shən) s. giro, rotación *f*.

gyre (jīr) s. espiral *m*.

gy·ro (jī'rō) s. giroscopio.

gy·ro·scope (jī'rə-skōp') s. giroscopio.

H

h, H (āch) s. octava letra del alfabeto inglés.

ha (hä) interj. ¡ah!, ¡ja!

ha·be·as cor·pus (hā'bē-əs kôr'pəs) s. hábeas corpus *m*.

hab·er·dash·er (hăb'ər-dăsh'ər) s. vendedor *m* de artículos para caballeros.

hab·er·dash·er·y (:ə-rē) s. (tienda de) artículos para caballeros.

hab·it (hăb'ĭt) s. costumbre *f*; (addiction) dependencia; (dress) hábito ♦ **out of h.** por costumbre • **to be in the h. of** acostumbrarse de • **to kick the h.** FAM. dejar el vicio.

hab·it·a·ble (hăb'ĭ-tə-bəl) adj. habitable.

hab·i·tat (:tăt') s. hábitat *m*.

hab·i·ta·tion ('-tā'shən) s. habitación f.
hab·it-form·ing (hăb'ĭt-fôr'mĭng) adj. que crea hábito.
ha·bit·u·al (hə-bĭch'ōō-əl) adj. inveterado, empedernido, (usual) acostumbrado.
ha·bit·u·ate (:āt') tr. & intr. habituar(se).
hack[1] (hăk) I. tr. (to chop) cortar, tajar; FAM. (to cope) aguantar —intr. toser II. s. tajo, hachazo; (cough) tos seca.
hack[2] I. s. (nag) jamelgo, penco; (hireling) asalariado; (carriage) coche m de alquiler; FAM. taxista mf II. intr. FAM. trabajar de taxista III. adj. comercializado; (hackneyed) trillado.
hack·le (hăk'əl) s. pluma del cuello ♦ pl. pelos del cuello • to get one's h. up sacar las garras.
hack·ney (hăk'nē) I. s. (horse) trotón m, caballo de silla; (carriage) coche m de alquiler.
hack·neyed (:nēd) adj. gastado, trillado.
hack·saw (hăk'sô') s. sierra para metales.
had (hăd) cf. **have**.
had·dock (hăd'ək) s. [pl. inv. o s] abadejo.
hag (hăg) s. vieja bruja, arpía.
hag·gard (hăg'ərd) adj. demacrado.
hag·gle (hăg'əl) intr. regatear.
hag·gler (:lər) s. regateador m.
hag·gling (:lĭng) s. regateo.
hag·rid·den (hăg'rĭd'n) adj. atormentado.
ha-ha (hä'hä') interj. ja, ja, ja!
hail[1] (hāl) I. s. (ice) granizo; (barrage) lluvia, andanada II. intr. granizar.
hail[2] I. tr. saludar; (to acclaim) aclamar; (cab) llamar —intr. ♦ to h. from ser de II. s. saludo III. interj. ¡salve! ♦ h. to viva.
hail·stone (hāl'stōn') s. granizo.
hail·storm (:stôrm') s. granizada.
hair (hâr) s. pelo, cabello ♦ gray h. canas • h. piece tupé, peluquín • h. spray gomina, laca • h. style peinado • to comb one's h. peinarse • to get in someone's h. tener a alguien hasta la coronilla • to let one's h. down echar una cana al aire • to make one's h. stand on end ponerle a uno los pelos de punta • to tear one's h. out tirarse de los pelos • to split hairs hilar demasiado fino.
hair·brush ('brŭsh') s. cepillo (para el pelo).
hair·cut (:kŭt') s. corte m de pelo ♦ to get a h. cortarse el pelo.
hair·do (:dōō') s. peinado.
hair·dress·er (:drĕs'ər) s. peluquero.
hair·dress·ing (:ĭng) s. (occupation) peluquería; (act) peinado.
hair·less (hâr'lĭs) adj. sin pelo; (face) lampiño.
hair·line (:līn') s. nacimiento del pelo; (line) rayita ♦ receding h. entradas.
hair·net (:nĕt') s. redecilla para el cabello.
hair·pin (:pĭn') s. (pin) horquilla; (curve) curva cerrada (de una carretera).
hair·rais·ing (:rā'zĭng) adj. espeluznante.
hairs·breadth (hârz'brĕdth') s. pelo, tris m.
hair·split·ting (hâr'splĭt'ĭng) s. argucias.
hair·trig·ger (hâr'trĭg'ər) adj. impulsivo.
hair·y (hâr'ē) adj. -i- peludo; JER. (hazardous) espinoso.
hake (hāk) s. [pl. inv. o s] merluza.
hal·cy·on (hăl'sē-on) adj. venturoso.
hale[1] (hāl) adj. robusto, fuerte.
hale[2] tr. llevar a la fuerza, arrastrar.
half (hăf) I. s. [pl. -ves] mitad f; (part) parte f; DEP. tiempo • and a h. y medio • better h. FAM. cara mitad, costilla • by h. a la mitad • by halves a medias • h. brother, sister hermanas-

tro, -a • h. note MÚS. blanca • h. past (two) (dos) y media II. adj. & adv. medio, a medias ♦ h. price a mitad de precio • not h. bad FAM. no tan malo.
half-alive ('ə-līv') adj. medio muerto.
half-and-half ('ən-hăf') I. adj. mitad y mitad II. adv. a medias III. s. leche f con crema.
half·back (:băk') s. DEP. medio.
half-baked (:băkt') adj. a medio cocer; FAM. (ill-conceived) disparatado, precipitado.
half-breed (:brēd') s. & adj. JER. mestizo.
half-caste (:kăst') s. & adj. mestizo.
half-cocked (:kŏkt') adj. FAM. descabellado.
half-heart·ed (:här'tĭd) adj. sin entusiasmo.
half hour (:our') s. media hora.
half-life (:līf') s. período de desintegración radioactiva.
half-mast (:măst') s. ♦ at h. a media asta.
half-moon (:mōōn') s. media luna.
half-o·pen (:ō'pən) adj. entreabierto.
half-slip (:slĭp') s. enagua corta.
half-truth (:trōōth') s. verdad f a medias.
half·way (:wā') I. adj. medio, intermedio; (measures) parcial II. adv. a la mitad; (partially) a medias ♦ to meet h. partir la diferencia, hacer concesiones.
half-wit (:wĭt') s. retrasado mental.
half-wit·ted (:ĭd) adj. necio, tonto.
hal·i·but (hăl'ə-bət) s. halibut m.
hall (hôl) s. corredor m, (lobby) vestíbulo; (auditorium) sala; EDUC. (building) facultad f ♦ h. of fame museo conmemorativo.
hal·le·lu·jah (hăl'ə-lōō'yə) interj. aleluya.
hall·mark (hôl'märk') s. sello.
hal·low (hăl'ō) tr. santificar; (to revere) venerar.
hal·lu·ci·nate (hə-lōō'sə-nāt') tr. & intr. alucinar(se).
hal·lu·ci·na·tion (-'-nā'shən) s. alucinación f.
hal·lu·ci·na·to·ry (-'-nə-tôr'ē) adj. alucinante.
hal·lu·ci·no·gen (:nə-jən) s. alucinógeno.
hal·lu·ci·no·gen·ic ('-jĕn'ĭk) adj. alucinógeno.
hall·way (hôl'wā') s. pasillo, corredor m.
ha·lo (hā'lō) s. [pl. (e)s] halo; (aura) aura.
halt[1] (hôlt) I. s. (stop) alto, parada; (pause) interrupción f ♦ to call a h. to poner fin a II. tr. & intr. parar(se), detener(se); (briefly) interrumpir(se) ♦ halt ¡alto!
halt[2] intr. (to hobble) cojear; (to waver) titubear.
hal·ter (hôl'tər) I. s. dogal m; (bodice) corpiño sin espalda II. tr. encabestrar; (to restrain) restringir.
halt·ing (hôl'tĭng) adj. cojo; (wavering) titubeante.
halve (hăv) tr. partir o reducir a la mitad; (a number) dividir por dos.
halves (hăvz) cf. **half**.
ham (hăm) I. s. jamón m, pernil m; ANAT. corva; FAM. (performer) comicastro; RAD. radioaficionado II. tr. -mm- exagerar.
ham·burg·er (hăm'bûr'gər) s. hamburguesa.
ham·let (hăm'lĭt) s. aldea, caserío.
ham·mer (hăm'ər) I. s. martillo; (of gun) percusor m; (of piano) martinete m II. tr. martillar ♦ to h. away at FAM. (an opponent) castigar a; (a task) trabajar con ahínco en • to h. home FIG. machacar incansablemente • to h. out (dent) sacar a martillazos; (contract) elaborar, llegar a.
ham·mered (:ərd) adj. repujado.

ham·mer·head (:ər-hĕd') s. cabeza de martillo; ICT. pez martillo.

ham·mock (hăm'ək) s. hamaca.

ham·per¹ (hăm'pər) tr. poner trabas a.

ham·per² s. *(basket)* cesto.

ham·ster (hăm'stər) s. hámster *m*.

ham·string (hăm'strĭng') I. s. tendón *m* de la corva II. tr. **-strung** cortar el tendón de la corva a; *(to hinder)* incapacitar.

hand (hănd) I. s. mano *f*; *(of clock, gauge)* aguja, manecilla; *(side)* lado; *(script)* letra; *(applause)* aplauso; *(laborer)* obrero, jornalero; *(on ship)* tripulante *m*; *(expert)* perito; *(cards)* mano; EQUIT. palmo menor; *(bananas)* racimo ♦ **at the hands of** en manos de • **by h.** a mano • **by the h.** de la mano • **(close) at h.** muy cerca, a mano • **h. in h.** tomados de la mano • **h. over fist** FAM. a manos llenas • **hands down** fácilmente • **hands off!** ¡no tocar! • **on h.** disponible • **on one's hands and knees** a gatas • **on the one (other) h.** por una (otra) parte • **out of h.** fuera de control • **out of my hands** fuera de mi alcance • **the matter at h.** el asunto que se está estudiando • **to be an old h.** at tener mucha experiencia en • **to be someone's right h.** ser el brazo derecho de alguien • **to bite the h. that feeds you** ser mal agradecido • **to change hands** cambiar de dueño • **to clap one's hands** batir palmas • **to get o lay one's hands on** encontrar, localizar • **to give o lend a h.** (with) echar una mano (a) • **to have a h.** in tener parte en • **to have one's hands full** tener mucho que hacer • **to keep one's h.** in no perder la práctica de • **to know like the back of one's h.** conocer como la palma de la mano • **to live from h. to mouth** vivir al día • **to play into someone's hands** hacerle el juego a alguien • **to shake hands** darse la mano • **to take one's life in(to) one's hands** jugarse uno la vida • **to take something off someone's hands** quitarle a alguien algo • **to throw up one's hands** echarse o llevarse las manos a la cabeza • **to wait on someone h.** and foot desvivirse por alguien II. tr. entregar, dar ♦ **to h. down** transmitir; *(verdict)* dictar • **to h. in** presentar, entregar • **to h. out** *(to administer)* dar, aplicar; *(to distribute)* repartir • **to h. over (to)** ceder (a) • **to have to h. it to** JER. tener que felicitar a o reconocer los méritos de.

hand·bag ('băg') s. cartera, bolso.

hand·ball (:bôl') s. pelota (vasca).

hand·bill (:bĭl') s. volante *m*, octavilla.

hand·book (:bŏŏk') s. manual *m*.

hand·car (:kär') s. zorrilla.

hand·cart (:kärt') s. carretilla.

hand·cuff (:kŭf') I. s. esposas II. tr. esposar; FIG. maniatar.

hand·ful (:fŏŏl') s. puñado ♦ **a real h.** una verdadera lata.

hand·gun (:gŭn') s. pistola.

hand·i·cap (hăn'dē-kăp') I. s. hándicap *m*; *(hindrance)* obstáculo; *(physical)* defecto; *(mental)* retraso II. tr. **-pp-** asignar un hándicap a; *(to impede)* poner en desventaja.

hand·i·capped (:kăpt') adj. impedido.

hand·i·craft (hăn'dē-krăft') s. destreza manual; *(occupation, product)* (artículo de) artesanía.

hand·i·work (:wûrk') s. trabajo manual; *(doing)* obra.

hand·ker·chief (hăng'kər-chĭf') s. pañuelo.

han·dle (hăn'dl) I. tr. tocar, andar con; *(conveyance)* manejar, dirigir; *(to deal with)* encar-

garse de; *(to represent)* ser el agente de; *(to cope with)* poder con; *(to trade in)* comerciar en ♦ **h. with care** frágil • **to h. oneself** comportarse —intr. manejarse II. s. mango; *(of door)* manija; *(grip)* asa, asidero; JER. nombre *m* ♦ **to fly off the h.** perder los estribos.

han·dle·bars (:bärz') s.pl. manillar *m*.

han·dler (hănd'lər) s. COM. tratante *m*; DEP. entrenador *m*.

han·dling (:lĭng) s. manejo; *(treatment)* forma de tratar ♦ **shipping and h.** gastos de flete; FIG. liberal, generoso.

hand·made (hănd'mād') adj. hecho a mano.

hand-me-down (:mē-doun') s. & adj. (prenda de vestir) de segunda mano.

hand·out (:out') s. limosna; *(leaflet)* folleto.

hand·pick (:pĭk') tr. escoger, seleccionar.

hand·rail (:rāl') s. pasamano, barandilla.

hand·saw (:sô') s. serrucho.

hand·shake (:shāk') s. apretón *m* de manos.

hands-off (hăndz'ôf') adj. de no intervención.

hand·some (hăn'səm) adj. **-er, est** guapo, bien parecido; FIG. liberal, generoso.

hands-on (hăndz'ŏn') adj. práctico.

hand·spring (hănd'sprĭng') s. DEP. voltereta.

hand·stand (:stănd') s. parada de cabeza.

hand-to-hand (:tə-hănd') adj. cuerpo a cuerpo.

hand-to-mouth (:tə-mouth') adj. precario.

hand·writ·ing (:rī'tĭng) s. escritura; *(style)* letra.

hand·writ·ten (:rĭt'ən) adj. escrito a mano.

hand·y (hăn'dē) adj. **-i-** mañoso; *(accessible)* a mano; *(useful)* conveniente ♦ **to be h. with** saber manejar • **to come in h.** venir bien.

hand·y·man (:măn') s. [pl. **-men**] hombre *m* que hace bricolajes.

hang (hăng) I. tr. **hung** suspender, colgar; *(to execute)* ahorcar; *(pictures)* fijar; *(one's head)* bajar, inclinar ♦ **h. up** *(to delay)* demorar; *(telephone)* colgar —intr. colgar; *(to be executed)* ser ahorcado; *(in air)* flotar; *(to droop)* inclinarse; *(fabric)* caer; *(paintings)* inclinar ♦ **h. in there!** FAM. ¡ánimo! • **to h. around** o **out** FAM. haraganear • **to h. back** quedarse atrás • **to h. loose** JER. estar tranquilo • **to h. on** *(to wait)* esperar; *(to grasp)* asirse de; *(to persevere)* persistir; *(to depend on)* depender de • **to h. onto** guardar, quedarse con II. s. caída (de tela, prenda) ♦ **not to give a h.** FAM. importarle a uno un comino • **to get the h. of something** FAM. cogerle el truco a algo.

han·gar (hăng'ər) s. hangar *m*.

hang·er (hăng'ər) s. colgadero, percha.

hang·er-on (hăng'ər-ŏn') s. [pl. **hangers-**] parásito, gorrón *m*.

hang·ing (hăng'ĭng) I. s. ejecución *f* en la horca II. adj. colgante, pendiente.

hang·out (:out') s. guarida, punto de reunión.

hang·o·ver (:ō'vər) s. resaca; FIG. vestigio.

hang-up (:ŭp') s. FAM. complejo, problema *m*; *(obstacle)* traba.

hank (hăngk) s. madeja.

han·ker (hăng'kər) intr. anhelar.

han·ker·ing (:ĭng) s. deseo, ganas; *(nostalgia)* añoranza.

han·kie/ky (hăng'kē) s. FAM. pañuelo.

han·ky-pan·ky (hăng'kē-păng'kē) s. JER. truquitos, jueguitos; *(foolishness)* boberías ♦ **there's some h. going on** hay algo que no huele bien.

hap·haz·ard (hăp-hăz'ərd) adj. fortuito.

hap·less (hăp'lĭs) adj. desventurado.

hap·pen (hăp'ən) intr. *(to come to pass)* pasar, suceder; *(to take place)* producirse, ocurrir ♦ **how does it h. that . . .?** ¿cómo es posible que . . . ? • **it you h. to talk to him** si por casualidad hablaras con él • **it (so) happens that o as it happens** da la casualidad que • **to h. to be** dar la casualidad de ser o estar.

hap·pen·stance (:stăns') s. casualidad f.

hap·pi·ness (hăp'ē-nĭs) s. felicidad f, dicha; *(merriment)* alegría.

hap·py (hăp'ē) adj. **-i-** feliz, dichoso; *(fortunate)* dichoso; *(fulfilled)* contento; *(merry)* alegre; *(fitting)* acertado; *(overly fond of)* obsesionado ♦ **h. birthday!** ¡feliz cumpleaños!, ¡felicidades! • **to be h. for,** to alegrarse por, de.

hap·py-go-luck·y ('-gō-lŭk'ē) adj. despreocupado.

ha·rangue (hə-răng') I. s. arenga II. tr. & intr. arengar.

ha·rass (hə-răs', hăr'əs) tr. acosar; *(to annoy)* molestar; *(to wear out)* agobiar; MIL. hostilizar.

ha·rass·ment (:mənt) s. acoso, hostigamiento.

har·bin·ger (här'bĭn-jər) s. heraldo; *(omen)* presagio; *(forerunner)* precursor m.

har·bor (här'bər) I. s. puerto, bahía; *(refuge)* refugio II. tr. proteger; *(hopes)* abrigar; *(resentment)* guardar.

hard (härd) I. adj. duro, sólido; *(firm)* firme; *(resistant)* resistente; *(difficult)* difícil, arduo; *(robust)* fuerte; *(strong-minded)* decidido, resuelto; *(diligent)* diligente; *(inclement)* duro; *(stern)* severo; *(trying)* difícil; *(callous)* cruel, de piedra; *(damaging)* dañino; *(facts)* incontestable; *(liquor)* fuerte ♦ **h. and fast** riguroso, invariable • **h. cash** metálico • **h. core** núcleo, médula • **h. drugs** drogas adictivas • **h. labor** trabajos forzados • **h. line** postura firme • **h. luck** mala suerte II. adv. *(intensely)* mucho; *(vigorously)* con fuerza; *(badly)* gravemente; *(firmly)* fuertemente ♦ **h. on** the heels of pisándole los talones a • **to be h. at it** trabajar con ahínco • **to be h. hit** estar severamente afectado • **to be h. up** encontrarse sin dinero.

hard·back (:băk') adj. & s. (libro) encuadernado.

hard·boiled (:boild') adj. *(egg)* duro; FAM. *(callous)* duro; *(unsentimental)* práctico.

hard·bound (:bound') var. de hardback.

hard·core o **hard-core** (:kôr') adj. empedernido; *(pornography)* explícito.

hard·cov·er (:kŭv'ər) var. de hardback.

hard·en (här'dn) tr. & intr. endurecer(se); *(to inure)* acostumbrar(se).

hard·en·ing (:ĭng) s. endurecimiento.

hard·head·ed (härd'hĕd'ĭd) adj. *(stubborn)* testarudo; *(realistic)* práctico.

hard·heart·ed (:här'tĭd) adj. duro de corazón.

har·di·hood (här'dē-hŏod') s. temeridad f; *(impudence)* atrevimiento.

hard-line o **hard·line** (härd'līn') adj. firme; *(uncompromising)* intransigente.

hard-lin·er (:lī'nər) s. intransigente mf.

hard·ly (:lē) adv. *(just)* apenas <I had h. closed my eyes apenas había cerrado los ojos>; *(scarcely)* escasamente, casi no.

hard-nosed (:nōzd') adj. cabezón, obstinado.

hard·ship (:shĭp') s. sufrimiento; *(privation)* penuria.

hard·ware (:wâr') s. (artículos de) ferretería, COMPUT. equipo, maquinaria; FAM. *(weapons)* hierros ♦ **h. store** ferretería.

hard-won (:wŭn') adj. ganado con dificultad.

hard·wood (:wŏod') s. & adj. *(arbol m)* de madera dura.

har·dy (här'dē) adj. robusto, resistente; *(intrepid)* temerario.

hare (hâr) s. liebre f.

hare-brained ('brānd') adj. atolondrado.

hare-lip (:lĭp') s. labio leporino.

har·em (hâr'əm) s. harén m.

hark (härk) intr. escuchar, prestar atención ♦ **to h. back to** remontarse a.

har·lot (här'lət) s. ramera.

harm (härm) I. s. daño, perjuicio; *(evil)* mal m ♦ **out of h.'s way** a salvo II. tr. hacer daño.

harm·ful ('fəl) adj. perjudicial; *(damaging)* dañino.

harm·less (:lĭs) adj. inocuo.

har·mon·ic (här-mŏn'ĭk) adj. & s. armónico.

har·mon·i·ca (:ĭ-kə) s. armónica.

har·mo·ni·ous (här-mō'nē-əs) adj. armonioso.

har·mo·nize ('mə-nīz') tr. & intr. armonizar.

har·mo·ny (:nē) s. armonía.

har·ness (här'nĭs) I. s. arreos II. tr. *(horse)* enjaezar; *(energy)* aprovechar, utilizar.

harp (härp) I. s. arpa II. intr. tocar la arpa ♦ **to h. on** machacar, insistir en.

har·poon (här-pōōn') I. s. arpón m II. tr. arponear.

harp·si·chord (härp'sĭ-kôrd') s. clavicémbalo.

har·py (här'pē) s. arpía.

har·row·ing (hăr'ō-ĭng) adj. espantoso.

har·ry (hăr'ē) tr. merodear; *(to harass)* atormentar.

harsh (härsh) adj. áspero; *(stern)* cruel, severo.

har·vest (här'vĭst) I. s. cosecha; *(of sugar cane)* zafra; *(of grapes)* vendimia; *(result)* fruto II. tr. & intr. cosechar, hacer la cosecha.

har·vest·er (:vĭ-stər) s. *(of fruit)* recolector m; *(of sugar cane)* cortador m; *(machine)* segadora.

has (hăz) tercera persona sing. de **have**.

has-been (hăz'bĭn') s. FAM. persona acabada.

hash¹ (hăsh) I. s. CUL. picadillo; *(jumble)* revoltillo II. tr. picar; FAM. *(to mangle)* mutilar ♦ **to h. out** o over discutir a fondo.

hash² s. JER. *(hashish)* hachís m.

hash·ish ('ĕsh') s. hachís m.

has·sle (hăs'əl) FAM. I. s. reyerta, jaleo II. tr. fastidiar, molestar.

has·sock (hăs'ək) s. cojín m, almohadón m.

haste (hāst) s. prisa; *(rashness)* precipitación f ♦ **in h.** de prisa, precipitadamente • **to make h.** darse prisa.

has·ten (hā'sən) intr. darse prisa, apresurarse —tr. apresurar.

hast·y (hā'stē) adj. **-i-** apresurado; *(rash)* precipitado ♦ **to be h.** precipitarse.

hat (hăt) s. sombrero ♦ **at the drop of a h.** al menor pretexto • **h. in hand** humildemente • **my h.!** ¡naranjas! • **to keep under one's h.** no decir nada de • **to take one's h. off to** reconocer el mérito de • **to throw one's h. into the ring** postularse como candidato.

hatch¹ (hăch) s. trampa; MARIT. escotilla.

hatch² intr. salir del cascarón —tr. *(to produce young)* sacar pollos; *(an egg)* empollar; *(plot)* tramar.

hatch·er·y ('ə-rē) s. criadero (de peces, aves).

hatch·et (hăch'ĭt) s. hachuela ♦ **h. man** JER. matón; *(henchman)* esbirro • **to bury the h.** envainar la espada.

hatch·way (hăch'wā') s. MARIT. escotilla.

hate (hāt) I. tr. odiar —intr. sentir odio II. s.

odio.

hate·ful ('fəl) adj. odioso; *(full of hatred)* rencoroso.

ha·tred (hā'trĭd) s. odio, aborrecimiento.

hat·ter (hăt'ər) s. sombrerero.

haugh·ty (hô'tē) adj. -i- altivo.

haul (hôl) I. intr. & tr. halar, tirar (de); *(to transport)* transportar ♦ **to h. off** coger impulso II. s. tirada; *(distance)* tramo; *(load)* carga; *(of fish)* redada ♦ **over the long h.** a la larga.

haunch (hônch) s. cuarto trasero; *(hip)* cadera.

haunt (hônt) I. tr. *(ghosts)* aparecer a o en; *(to frequent)* rondar; *(to obsess)* perseguir ♦ **to be haunted** estar embrujado o encantado II. s. lugar predilecto.

haunt·ing (hôn'tĭng) adj. inolvidable.

have I. tr. had tener; *(to possess)* poseer; *(in mind)* retener; *(to acquire)* obtener; *(letter)* recibir; *(disease)* sufrir de; *(good time)* pasar; *(words)* encontrar; *(to cause to be done)* hacer, mandar; *(to permit)* tolerar; *(baby)* dar a luz, alumbrar; *(to be obligated to)* deber <I h. to get there on time debo llegar a tiempo> ♦ **to be had** ser engañado • **to h. had it** estar hasta la coronilla • **to h. it in for** FAM. tenérsela jurada a • **to h. it out with** habérselas con • **to h. on** llevar puesto • **to h. to do with** tener que ver con —aux. haber <he had lost his temper se había enojado>; hacer <it has been snowing for a week hace una semana que está nevando> ♦ **had better** más vale que <I had better leave más vale que me vaya> II. s. ♦ **the haves and the have-nots** los ricos y los pobres.

ha·ven (hā'vən) s. puerto; *(shelter)* refugio.

have-not (hăv'nŏt') s. pobre *mf*.

hav·er·sack (hăv'ər-săk') s. mochila.

hav·oc (hăv'ək) s. estragos; *(chaos)* caos *m*.

hawk¹ (hôk) s. halcón *m*; FIG. tiburón *m*; FAM. *(warmonger)* militarista *mf*.

hawk² intr. & tr. *(to peddle)* pregonar.

hawk·er (hô'kər) s. pregonero.

hawk·ish (hô'kĭsh) adj. militarista.

haw·ser (hô'zər) s. guindaleza.

haw·thorn (hô'thôrn') s. espino.

hay (hā) I. s. heno ♦ **h. fever** fiebre del heno • **to hit the h.** FAM. acostarse, irse a roncar II. intr. secar heno.

hay·loft (hā'lôft') s. henil *m*.

hay·seed (hā'sēd') s. JER. patán *m*.

hay·stack (hā'stăk') s. almiar *m*.

hay·wire (hā'wīr') adj. FAM. descontrolado.

haz·ard (hăz'ərd) I. s. riesgo; *(chance)* azar *m*; *(in golf)* obstáculo II. tr. arriesgar; *(a guess)* aventurar.

haz·ard·ous (:ər-dəs) adj. peligroso; *(chancy)* azaroso; *(harmful)* perjudicial.

haze¹ (hāz) s. niebla ligera; *(mental)* ofuscación.

haze² tr. someter a ritos de iniciación.

ha·zel (hā'zəl) adj. & s. (de) avellano.

ha·zel·nut (:nŭt') s. avellana.

haz·y (hā'zē) adj. -i- nebuloso; *(unclear)* confuso.

H-bomb (āch'bŏm') s. bomba H.

he (hē) I. pron. él II. s. varón *m*.

head (hĕd) I. s. cabeza; *(sense)* inteligencia; *(ability)* habilidad *f*; *(composure)* aplomo; *(person)* persona; *(chief)* jefe *m*; *(top)* tope *m*; *(of table, bed)* cabecera; *(of steam)* presión *f*; *(on beer)* espuma; *(point)* punta; *(of drum)* parche *m*; *(of page)* principio; *(headline)* titular *m*;

GEOG. cabo; BOT. repollo; MARIT. letrina; AUTO. culata (de cilindro) ♦ **from h. to foot** de arriba abajo • **h. of hair** cabellera • **h. over heels** patas arriba; FIG. locamente • **h. start** ventaja • **h. wind** viento en contra • **off the top of one's h.** sin pensar mucho en ello • **to be over one's h.** estar (algo) fuera de la capacidad de uno • **to be soft in the h.** FAM. estar tocado de la cabeza • **to bring to a h.** forzar el desenlace • **to come to a h.** madurar, definirse • **to get it into one's h. (to)** FAM. metérsele a uno la idea (de) • **to get it through one's h.** comprender algo • **to go to one's h.** subírsele a la cabeza • **to keep one's h. above water** mantenerse a flote • **to stand on one's h. (to)** hacer lo imposible (para) • **to talk one's h. off** FAM. hablar hasta por los codos ♦ pl. cara (de moneda) • **h. or tails** cara o cruz • **not to make h. or tails of** FAM. no encontrar ni pies ni cabeza a II. tr. encabezar; *(to be first)* ir a la cabeza de; *(to turn)* apuntar; DEP. cabecear ♦ **to h. off** prevenir —intr. dirigirse • **to h. back** regresar • **to h. for** ir con rumbo a III. adj. principal, central; *(at the head)* delantero.

head·ache ('āk') s. dolor *m* de cabeza; FAM. *(annoyance)* quebradero de cabeza.

head·band (:bănd') s. cinta.

head·board (:bôrd') s. cabecera (de cama).

head·er (:ər) s. FAM. salto o caída de cabeza.

head·first (:fûrst') adv. de cabeza; *(impetuously)* precipitadamente.

head·gear (:gîr') s. *(headdress)* tocado; *(helmet)* casco.

head·hunt·er (:hŭn'tər) s. cazador *m* de cabezas; JER. *(recruiter)* reclutador *m*.

head·ing (:ĭng) s. encabezamiento; *(section)* apartado; *(course)* derrotero.

head·lamp (:lămp') s. faro, luz delantera.

head·land (:lənd) s. promontorio.

head·light (:līt') s. faro, luz delantera.

head·line (:līn') I. s. titular *m* ♦ pl. sumario de noticias • **to make the h.** aparecer en primera plana II. tr. poner titular a.

head·long (:lòng') I. adv. precipitadamente II. adj. precipitado.

head·mas·ter (:măs'tər) s. director *m* (de un colegio).

head·mis·tress (:mĭs'trĭs) s. directora (de un colegio).

head-on (:ŏn') adj. & adv. de frente.

head·phone (:fōn') s. audífono, auricular *m*.

head·quar·ter (:kwôr'tər) tr. acuartelar.

head·quar·ters (:tərz) s.pl. cuartel *m* general; *(police)* jefatura; COM. oficina central.

head·rest (hĕd'rĕst') s. cabecera; AUTO. apoyo para la cabeza.

head·set (:sĕt') s. auriculares *m*, audífonos.

head·stone (:stōn') s. lápida sepulcral.

head·strong (:strŏng') adj. voluntarioso.

head·wait·er (:wā'tər) s. jefe *m* de comedor.

head·wa·ter (:wô'tər) s. cabecera.

head·way (:wā') s. avance *m*, progreso; *(clearance)* altura libre, espacio sobrante ♦ **to make h.** avanzar, progresar.

head·y (:ē) adj. -i- embriagador.

heal (hēl) tr. curar; *(to remedy)* remediar —intr. sanar.

heal·er (hē'lər) s. curandero.

heal·ing (:lĭng) I. adj. curativo II. s. curación *f*.

health (hĕlth) s. salud *f*; *(of community)* sanidad *f* ♦ **h. food** alimentos naturales • **h. insur-**

ance seguro médico • **h. spa** centro de ejercicios • **to be in bad, good h.** estar mal, bien de salud • **to your h.!** ¡salud!

health·ful ('fəl) adj. sano, saludable.

health·y (:thē) adj. -i- sano; *(air, place)* saludable, salubre; *(appetite)* bueno; *(sizable)* generoso, considerable • **to feel h.** sentirse bien de salud.

heap (hēp) I. s. montón; JER. *(jalopy)* cacharro II. tr. amontonar, apilar.

hear (hîr) tr. **heard** (hûrd; *(to listen to)* escuchar; *(Mass, lecture)* asistir a, oír; *(a faint sound)* sentir; *(to know)* enterarse de; *(legal case)* ver ♦ **to have never heard of** no conocer • **to h. about** oír hablar de • **to h. out** escuchar hasta el final —intr. oír ♦ **I won't h. of it!** ¡ni hablar! • **to h. from** tener noticias de.

hear·ing ('ĭng) s. oído; *(earshot)* alcance m del oído; DER. audiencia ♦ **hard of** h. duro de oído • **h. aid** audífono • **to give a fair h.** escuchar sin prejuicios.

hear·ken (härkən) intr. escuchar, atender.

hear·say (hîr'sā') s. rumores m.

hearse (hûrs) s. carroza fúnebre.

heart (härt) s. corazón m; JER. *(cards)* copa; *(of lettuce)* cogollo ♦ **at h.** en el fondo • **by h.** de memoria • **h. and soul** en cuerpo y alma • h. **attack** ataque cardíaco • **h. failure** colapso (cardíaco) • **in the h. of winter** en pleno invierno • **not to have one's h. in something** hacer algo sin entusiasmo • **the h. of the matter** el quid, el meollo • **to be near** o **dear to one's h.** tocarle a uno en el alma • **to have h. trouble** no andar bien del corazón • **to have one's h. set on** encapricharse con • **to have the h. to** tener valor para • **to lose h.** descorazonarse • **to one's h.'s content** hasta saciarse • **to take h.** cobrar ánimo • **to take h. to** tomar a pecho • **to wear one's h. on one's sleeve** mostrar fácilmente los sentimientos • **with all** o **from one's h.** de todo corazón.

heart·ache ('āk') s. tristeza, pena.

heart·beat (:bēt') s. latido.

heart·break (:brāk') s. angustia, pena; *(disappointment)* decepción f.

heart·bro·ken (:brō'kən) adj. angustiado, apenado; *(disappointed)* decepcionado ♦ **to be h.** tener partido el corazón.

heart·burn (:bûrn') s. acedía.

heart·en (härtn) tr. alentar.

heart·felt (härt'fĕlt') adj. sincero; *(grief, sympathy)* más sentido.

hearth (härth) s. hogar m.

heart·land (härt'lănd') s. región f central.

heart·less (:lĭs) adj. despiadado, cruel.

heart·rend·ing (:rĕn'dĭng) adj. desgarrador.

heart·throb (:thrŏb') s. *(heartbeat)* latido del corazón; *(sweetheart)* enamorado.

heart-to-heart (:tə-härt') adj. cándido.

heart·y (här'tē) adj. cordial, sincero; *(robust)* robusto; *(appetite)* bueno; *(meal)* abundante ♦ **to be a h. eater** ser de buen comer.

heat (hēt) I. s. calor m; *(for building)* calefacción f; *(estrus)* estro, celo; DEP. carrera; JER. *(police)* jara, poli ♦ **h. rash** miliaria • **h. stroke** insolación • **the h. of the day** lo más caluroso del día II. tr. & intr. calentar(se); *(to excite)* acalorar(se) ♦ **h. up** recalentar.

heat·ed (hē'tĭd) adj. caliente; *(debate)* acalorado.

heat·er (hē'tər) s. radiador calorífero; *(stove)* estufa, calentador m; JER. revólver m.

heath (hēth) s. brezo; *(land)* brezal m.

hea·then (hē'thən) s. [pl. inv. o s] & adj. pagano; *(savage)* salvaje m.

heath·er (hĕth'ər) s. brezo.

heat·ing (hē'tĭng) I. adj. calentador; FIS. calorífico II. s. calentamiento; *(system)* calefacción f.

heave (hēv) I. tr. alzar (con esfuerzo), *(to hurl)* arrojar; *(sigh)* exhalar —intr. levantarse; FAM. *(to retch)* nausear II. s. tiro; GEOL. desplazamiento, levantamiento ♦ pl. arcadas.

heav·en (hĕv'ən) s. cielo; *(paradise)* paraíso ♦ **for h.'s sake!** ¡por (amor de) Dios! • **h. forbid** that Dios nos libre de • **h. knows** Dios es testigo • **thank h.!** ¡gracias a Dios! ♦ pl. cielo, firmamento • **good h.!** ¡Dios mío!, ¡cielos!

heav·en·ly (:lē) adj. celestial; *(delightful)* divino, sublime.

heav·y (hĕv'ē) I. adj. -i- pesado; *(thick)* espeso; *(rain)* fuerte; *(sea)* borrascoso; *(clumsy)* torpe; *(excessive)* fuerte; *(grave)* serio; *(arduous)* dificultoso; *(large-scale)* en gran escala; *(onerous)* gravoso; *(coarse)* grueso; *(heart)* oprimido; *(foul)* cargado; *(eyelids)* amodorrado II. adv. pesadamente; *(slowly)* lentamente III. s. TEAT. villano.

heav·y-du·ty ('-dōō'tē) adj. de servicio pesado.

heav·y-hand·ed (:hăn'dĭd) adj. torpe; *(oppressive)* de mano dura.

heav·y-heart·ed (:här'tĭd) adj. afligido.

heav·y-set (:sĕt') adj. corpulento.

heav·y·weight ('-wāt') s. peso pesado; FAM. persona importante.

heck (hĕk) I. interj. ¡diablos! II. s. infierno.

heck·le (hĕk'əl) tr. interrumpir (a un orador).

heck·ler (:lər) s. persona que interrumpe a un orador.

hec·tic (hĕk'tĭk) adj. ajetreado.

hedge (hĕj) I. s. seto (vivo); FIN. inversión defensiva; *(excuse)* evasiva II. tr. encerrar (con un seto); *(to limit)* restringir —intr. FIN. hacer operaciones compensatorias; *(to skirt)* andarse con rodeos.

hedge·hog (hĕj'hŏg') s. erizo.

hedge·row (hĕj'rō') s. seto (vivo).

he·don·ist (hēd'n-ĭst) s. hedonista mf.

hee·bie-jee·bies (hē'bē-jē'bēz) s.pl. JER. desasosiego, nervios.

heed (hēd) I. intr. & tr. hacer caso n, (a, de) II. s. atención ♦ **to pay h.** to prestar atención a.

heed·ful ('fəl) adj. atento, cuidadoso.

heed·less (:lĭs) adj. descuidado, incauto ♦ **to be h.** of no hacer caso a.

hee-haw (hē'hô') s. rebuzno; *(guffaw)* risotada.

heel¹ (hēl) I. s. talón m; *(of shoe)* tacón m; *(of bread)* punta; JER. *(cad)* canalla ♦ **to be on someone's heels** andar pisándole los talones a alguien • **to cool one's heels** hacer antesala larga • **to take to one's heels** poner pies en polvorosa • **to turn on one's h.** dar media vuelta II. tr. poner el tacón a —intr. seguir de cerca.

heel² (hēl) tr. & intr. MARÍT. escorar, inclinar(se).

heft (hĕft) I. s. peso II. tr. *(to test the weight of)* sopesar; *(to lift)* alzar.

heft·y (hĕf'tē) adj. -i- pesado; *(strong)* robusto; *(amount)* cuantioso.

he·gem·o·ny (hĭ-jĕm'ə-nē) s. hegemonía.

heif·er (hĕf'ər) s. novilla.

height (hīt) s. altura, alto; *(summit)* cumbre f; *(of stupidity)* colmo; *(of person)* estatura; *(hill)* colina.

height·en ('n) tr. & intr. *(to increase)* aumentar(se); *(to make higher)* elevar(se).

hei·nous (hā'nəs) adj. atroz, nefando.

heir (âr) s. heredero ♦ **h. apparent** heredero forzoso.

heir·ess (âr'ĭs) s. heredera (de una fortuna).

heir·loom (âr'lŏŏm') s. reliquia de familia.

heist (hīst) JER. I. tr. robar II. s. robo.

held (hĕld) cf. **hold**[1].

hel·i·cop·ter (hĕl'ĭ-kŏp'tər) s. helicóptero.

he·li·o·cen·tric (hē'lē-ō-sĕn'trĭk) adj. heliocéntrico.

he·li·o·graph ('ə-grăf') s. heliógrafo.

he·li·o·trope (hĕl'yə-trōp') s. heliotropo.

hel·i·port (hĕl'ə-pôrt') s. helipuerto.

he·li·um (hē'lē-əm) s. helio.

he·lix (hē'lĭks) s. [pl. **es** *o* **-ces**] hélice *f*.

hell (hĕl) s. infierno ♦ FAM. **a h. of a** *(bad)* más malo que el diablo; *(good)* buenísimo ♦ **a h. of a lot** muchísimo • **come h. or high water** contra viento y marea • **for the h. of it** por puro gusto • **like h.** muchísimo • **to give someone h.** encenderle los pelos a alguien • **to go to h.** echarse a perder • **to h. with it!** ¡al diablo! • **to raise h.** armar una de todos los diablos • **what, who the h. ...** qué, quién diablos ...

hell-bent ('bĕnt') adj. empeñado.

hell·cat (:kăt') s. *(shrew)* arpía; *(fiend)* demonio.

hell·fire (:fīr') s. fuego del infierno.

hell·hole (:hōl') s. lugar m de mala muerte.

hell·ion (:yən) s. FAM. bribón *m*, diablo.

hell·ish (:ĭsh) adj. infernal.

hel·lo (hĕ-lō', hə-) I. interj. ¡hola! II. s. ♦ **to say h.** saludar.

helm (hĕlm) s. timón *m*.

hel·met (hĕl'mĭt) s. casco.

help (hĕlp) I. tr. ayudar; *(to relieve)* aliviar; *(to save)* auxiliar; *(to prevent)* evitar; *(to serve)* servir ♦ **to h. oneself** *(food)* servirse; *(to mooch)* tomar, mangar —intr. *(to serve)* ser útil; *(to assist)* prestar asistencia ♦ **to h. out** dar una mano II. s. ayuda; *(succor)* auxilio; *(relief)* alivio; *(remedy)* remedio; *(employees)* empleados; *(servants)* sirvientes.

help·er (hĕl'pər) s. ayudante *mf*.

help·ful (hĕlp'fəl) adj. útil; *(beneficial)* provechoso; *(kind)* amable.

help·ing (hĕl'pĭng) s. ración *f* ♦ **to have another h.** servirse más, repetir.

help·less (hĕlp'lĭs) adj. indefenso; *(powerless)* incapaz; *(disabled)* inválido.

help·mate (:māt') s. compañero; *(spouse)* esposo.

hel·ter-skel·ter (hĕl'tər-skĕl'tər) I. adj. atropellado; *(haphazard)* desordenado II. s. desorden m III. adv. FAM. a troche y moche.

hem[1] (hĕm) I. s. dobladillo II. tr. **-mm-** dobladillar; *(to enclose)* encerrar.

hem[2] I. interj. ¡ejem! II. intr. **-mm-** decir ¡ejem! ♦ **to h. and haw** vacilar al hablar.

he-man (hē'măn') s. [pl. **-men**] FAM. macho.

hem·i·sphere (hĕm'ĭ-sfîr') s. hemisferio.

hem·i·spher·ic/·i·cal ('-sfîr'ĭk) adj. hemisférico.

hem·line (hĕm'līn') s. COST. bastilla, ruedo.

hem·lock (hĕm'lŏk') s. abeto, pinabete m; *(poisonous plant)* cicuta.

he·mo·glo·bin (hē'mə-glō'bĭn) s. hemoglobina.

he·mo·phil·i·a ('-fĭl'ē-ə) s. hemofilia.

he·mo·phil·i·ac (:ăk') s. hemofílico.

hem·or·rhage (hĕm'ər-ĭj) s. & intr. (sufrir una) hemorragia.

hem·or·rhoid (:ə-roid') s. almorrana.

hemp (hĕmp) s. cáñamo.

hem·stitch (hĕm'stĭch') s. vainica.

hen (hĕn) s. gallina; *(female bird)* hembra.

hence (hĕns) adv. por lo tanto; *(from now)* de aquí a *<a year h.* de aquí a un año*>*.

hence·forth ('fôrth') adv. de ahora en adelante.

hench·man (hĕnch'mən) s. [pl. **-men**] hombre *m* de confianza; *(supporter)* secuaz *m*.

hen·house (hĕn'hous') s. gallinero.

hen·na (hĕn'ə) s. alcana, alheña.

hen·peck (hĕn'pĕk') tr. FAM. dominar (al marido).

he·pat·ic (hĭ-păt'ĭk) adj. hepático.

hep·a·ti·tis (hĕp'ə-tī'tĭs) s. hepatitis *f*.

hep·ta·gon (hĕp'tə-gŏn') s. heptágono.

her (hər, hûr) I. pron. pers. la *<I saw h.* la vi*>*; le *<I told h.* le dije*>*; ella *<for h.* para ella*>* II. adj. pos. su, de ella.

her·ald (hĕr'əld) I. s. heraldo, anunciador *m*; *(harbinger)* precursor *m* II. tr. proclamar.

her·ald·ry (:əl-drē) s. blasón *m*; *(pageantry)* pompa heráldica.

herb (ûrb, hûrb) s. hierba ♦ pl. finas hierbas.

her·ba·ceous (hûr-bā'shəs, ûr-) adj. herbáceo.

herb·al (hûr'bəl, ûr'-) adj. herbario.

her·bal·ist (:bə-lĭst) s. herbolario.

her·bi·cide (:bĭ-sīd') s. herbicida.

her·biv·o·rous (hûr-bĭv'ər-əs, ûr-) adj. herbívoro.

her·cu·le·an (hûr'kyə-lē'ən) adj. hercúleo.

herd (hûrd) I. s. manada; *(crowd)* muchedumbre *f* II. tr. & intr. reunir(se) en manada.

herd·er (hûr'dər) s. *(of cattle)* vaquero; *(of sheep)* pastor *m*; *(livestock owner)* ganadero.

here (hîr) I. adv. aquí; *(to this place)* acá; *(now)* ahora; *(on this point)* en este punto ♦ **h. we are** ya llegamos • **that's neither h. nor there** eso no viene al caso II. adj. este *<my friend h.* este amigo mío*>*.

here·a·bout(s) ('ə-bout[s]') adv. por aquí.

here·af·ter (:ăf'tər) I. adv. en lo sucesivo; *(at a future time)* en un futuro II. s. el más allá.

here·by (:bī') adv. por este medio.

he·red·i·tar·y (hə-rĕd'ĭ-tĕr'ē) adj. hereditario.

he·red·i·ty (:tē) s. herencia.

here·in (hîr-ĭn') adv. en esto.

here·of (:ŭv') adv. (acerca) de esto.

here·on (:ŏn') adv. sobre esto.

her·e·sy (hĕr'ĭ-sē) s. herejía.

her·e·tic (:tĭk) s. hereje *mf*.

he·ret·i·cal (hə-rĕt'ĭ-kəl) adj. herético.

here·to·fore (hîr'tə-fôr') adv. hasta ahora.

here·up·on (:ə-pŏn') adv. a continuación.

here·with (hîr-wĭth') adv. adjunto.

her·i·ta·ble (hĕr'ĭ-tə-bəl) adj. hereditario.

her·i·tage (:tĭj) s. herencia; *(legacy)* patrimonio.

her·maph·ro·dite (hər-măf'rə-dīt') s. hermafrodita *mf*.

her·mit (hûr'mĭt) s. ermitaño.

her·mit·age (:mĭ-tĭj) s. RELIG. ermita.

her·ni·a (hûr'nē-ə) s. [pl. **s** *o* **-ae**] hernia.

he·ro (hîr'ō) s. [pl. **es**] héroe *m*; LIT. protagonista *mf*; JER. *(sandwich)* emparedado grande.

he·ro·ic (hĭ-rō'ĭk) adj. heroico ♦ **heroics** s.pl. rimbombancia.

her·o·in (hĕr'ō-ĭn) s. heroína (narcótico).

her·o·ine (hĕr'ō-ĭn) s. heroína; LIT. protago-

nista.
her·o·ism (:ĭz′əm) s. heroísmo.
her·on (hĕr′ən) s. garza.
her·pes (hûr′pēz) s. herpes *m*.
her·ring (hĕr′ĭng) s. [pl. inv. *o* **s**] arenque *m*.
her·ring·bone (·hōn′) s. *(pattern)* espinapez *f*; *(in cloth)* punto de espina.
hers (hûrz) pron. pos. (el) suyo, el de ella.
her·self (hûr-sĕlf′) pron. pers. *(reflexive)* se <she hurt h. se lastimó>; *(emphatic)* ella misma <she h. ella misma>; *(after preposition)* (sí) misma ♦ **by h.** sola.
hes·i·tan·cy (hĕz′ĭ-tn-sē) s. indecisión *f*.
hes·i·tant (:tnt) adj. vacilante.
hes·i·tate (:tāt′) intr. vacilar, *(not to dare)* no atreverse.
hes·i·ta·tion (′-tā′shən) s. indecisión *f*; *(vacillation)* titubeo.
het·er·o·dox (hĕt′ər-ə-dŏks′) adj. heterodoxo; *(heretic)* herético.
het·er·o·dox·y (:dŏk′sē) s. heterodoxia.
het·er·o·ge·ne·ous (′--jē′nē-əs) adj. heterogéneo.
het·er·o·sex·u·al (hĕt′ə-rō-sĕk′shōō-əl) adj. & s. heterosexual.
het·er·o·sex·u·al·i·ty (:sĕk′shōō-ăl′ĭ-tē) s. heterosexualidad *f*.
hew (hyōō) tr. **-ed, -ed** *o* **-n** *(to shape)* tallar; *(to cut down)* talar —intr. conformarse.
hex (hĕks) I. s. embrujo; *(jinx)* aojo II. tr. embrujar.
hex·a·gon (hĕk′sə-gŏn′) s. hexágono.
hex·ag·o·nal (hĕk-săg′ə-nəl) adj. hexagonal.
hey (hā) interj. ¡eh!, ¡oiga!
hey·day (hā′dā′) s. auge *m*.
hi (hī) interj. ¡oye!, ¡hola!
hi·a·tus (hī-ā′təs) s. [pl. inv. *o* **es**] grieta; *(gap)* laguna; ANAT., FONÉT. hiato.
hi·ber·na·tion (′-nā′shən) s. hibernación *f*.
hi·bis·cus (hī-bĭs′kəs) s. hibisco.
hic·cup/cough (hĭk′əp) I. s. hipo II. intr. **-pp-** tener hipo, hipar.
hick (hĭk) s. FAM. aldeano.
hick·o·ry (hĭk′ə-rē) s. nogal americano.
hide[1] (hīd) tr. **hid, hid(den)** ocultar, esconder; *(to conceal)* disimular; *(to cover up)* tapar —intr. esconderse; *(to seek refuge)* refugiarse.
hide[2] s. cuero ♦ **not to see h. nor hair of** no ver el pelo de.
hide-and-seek (hīd′n-sēk′) s. escondidas.
hide·a·way (′ə-wā′) s. escondite *m*; *(retreat)* retiro.
hide·ous (hīd′ē-əs) adj. espantoso; *(atrocious)* atroz.
hide-out (hīd′out′) s. escondite *m*.
hid·ing (hī′dĭng) s. ♦ **h. place** escondite ♦ **in h.** escondido ♦ **to come out of h.** salir de su escondite ♦ **to go into h.** esconderse.
hi·er·ar·chy (hī′ə-rär′kē) s. jerarquía.
hi·er·o·glyph·ic (hī′ər-ə-glĭf′ĭk) adj. & s. jeroglífico.
hi-fi (hī′fī′) s. (aparato de) alta fidelidad.
high (hī) I. adj. alto; *(tall)* de altura; *(peaking)* culminante; *(lofty)* grande; *(wind, fever)* fuerte; *(Mass)* mayor; *(voice)* agudo; *(advanced)* avanzado; *(crime)* grave; FAM. *(drunk)* borracho; *(drugged)* drogado ♦ **h. and dry** de desamparado ♦ **h. and mighty** FAM. arrogante ♦ **h. jump** salto de altura ♦ **h. noon** pleno mediodía ♦ **h. priority** primera importancia ♦ **h. seas** alta mar ♦ **h. school** escuela secundaria ♦ **h. tide**

pleamar ♦ **to be h. in** tener un alto contenido de ♦ **to be h. time** ya ser hora ♦ **to be in h. spirits** estar de excelente humor II. adv. en lo alto, alto ♦ **h. above** muy por encima de ♦ **h. priced** caro, de lujo ♦ **to look h. and low** buscar por todas partes ♦ **to run h.** estar exaltado ♦ **to sing h.** cantar en un tono alto *o* agudo III. s. altura; *(gear)* directa; METEOR. zona de alta presión ♦ **on h.** en las alturas ♦ **to be on a h.** JER. estar de excelente humor.
high·ball (hī′bôl′) s. whisky *m* con gaseosa.
high·born (hī′bôrn′) adj. de noble cuna.
high·boy (hī′boi′) s. cómoda alta.
high·brow (hī′brou′) FAM. I. s. intelectual *mf*; *(pedant)* pedante *mf* II. adj. culto.
high·chair (hī′châr′) s. silla alta para niños.
high-class (hī′klăs′) adj. de primera clase.
high·er (hī′ər) adj. más alto; *(greater)* mayor; *(advanced)* superior.
high·er-up (hī′ər-ŭp′) s. FAM. superior *m*.
high-fa·lu·tin (hī′fə-lōōt′n) adj. FAM. pretencioso.
high-grade (hī′grād′) adj. de calidad superior.
high-hand·ed (hī′hăn′dĭd) adj. arrogante; *(dictatorial)* despótico.
high-hat (hī′hăt′) adj. desdeñoso, engreído.
high·land (hī′lənd) s. terreno montañoso.
high-lev·el (hī′lĕv′əl) adj. de alto nivel.
high·light (hī′līt′) I. s. toque *m* de luz; *(event)* suceso *o* atracción *f* principal II. tr. iluminar; *(to emphasize)* destacar.
high·ly (hī′lē) adv. altamente; *(extremely)* extremadamente; *(well)* muy bien.
high-mind·ed (hī′mīn′dĭd) adj. noble.
high·ness (hī′nĭs) s. altura ♦ **H.** Alteza.
high-per·for·mance (hī′pər-fôr′məns) adj. de alto rendimiento.
high-pitched (hī′pĭcht′) adj. agudo; *(voice)* chillón; *(activity)* frenético.
high-pow·er(ed) (hī′pou′ər[d]) adj. de alta potencia, de gran fuerza *o* energía.
high-pres·sure (hī′prĕsh′ər) adj. de alta presión; FAM. *(tenacious)* insistente.
high-rise (hī′rīz′) s. edificio de muchos pisos.
high-spir·it·ed (hī′spĭr′ĭ-tĭd) adj. animoso; *(energetic)* vivo.
high-strung (hī′strŭng′) adj. muy nervioso.
high·tail (hī′tāl′) intr. JER. salir corriendo.
high-tech (hī′tĕk′) adj. de tecnología avanzada.
high-test (hī′tĕst′) adj. de alta octanaje.
high·way (hī′wā′) s. carretera, autopista.
hi·jack (hī′jăk′) tr. FAM. *(vehicle)* secuestrar; *(goods)* robarse.
hi·jack·er (:ər) s. secuestrador *m*; *(of plane)* pirata aéreo.
hi·jack·ing (:ĭng) s. secuestro; *(of plane)* piratería aérea.
hike (hīk) I. intr. caminar ♦ **to h. up** subirse —tr. aumentar (precios) II. s. *(walk)* caminata; *(rise)* aumento ♦ **take a h.!** JER. ¡váyase a paseo! ♦ **to go on a h.** ir de excursión.
hik·er (hī′kər) s. excursionista *mf*.
hi·lar·i·ous (hĭ-lâr′ē-əs) adj. para morirse de risa.
hi·lar·i·ty (:ĭ-tē) s. hilaridad *f*.
hill (hĭl) s. colina; *(heap)* montón *m* ♦ **to be over the h.** FAM. ir cuesta abajo.
hill·bil·ly (′bĭl′ē) s. FAM. patán *m*.
hill·side (:sīd′) s. ladera (de un cerro).
hill·top (:tŏp′) s. cima (de un cerro).
hill·y (:ē) adj. **-i-** montuoso.
hilt (hĭlt) s. mango ♦ **to the h.** totalmente.

him (hǐm) pron. pers. le, lo <*they accepted h.* lo aceptaron>; le <*they sent h. a letter* le mandaron una carta>; él <*to h. a* él>.

him·self (:sĕlf´) pron. pers. *(reflexive)* se <*he hit h. se* golpeó>; *(emphatic)* él mismo <*he h.* él mismo>; *(after preposition)* (sí) mismo ♦ **by h.** solo.

hind¹ (hīnd) adj. trasero, posterior.

hind² s. *(deer)* cierva.

hin·der (hǐn´dər) tr. impedir, obstaculizar.

hind·most (hīnd´mōst´) adj. postrero, último.

hin·drance (hǐn´drəns) s. impedimento.

hind·sight (hīnd´sīt´) s. retrospección *f.*

hinge (hǐnj) **I.** s. bisagra **II.** tr. poner bisagras a —intr. ♦ **to h. on** depender de.

hint (hǐnt) **I.** s. insinuación *f*; *(tip)* sugerencia; *(clue)* idea ♦ **not a h. of** ni rastro de • **to drop a h.** tirar una indirecta • **to take a h.** darse por aludido **II.** tr. insinuar, dar a entender —intr. ♦ **to h. at** insinuar; *(to allude to)* aludir a.

hin·ter·land (hǐn´tər-lănd´) s. interior *m* (de un país).

hip¹ (hǐp) s. ANAT. cadera.

hip² adj. **-pp-** JER. al tanto, informado.

hip³ interj. ♦ **h., h., hurrah!** ¡hurra!, ¡viva!, ¡olé!

hip·bone (:bōn´) s. cía, hueso de la cadera.

hip·pie (hǐp´ē) s. hippie *mf.*

hip·po (hǐp´ō) s. FAM. hipopótamo.

Hip·po·crat·ic oath (hǐp´ə-krăt´ĭk) s. juramento hipocrático.

hip·po·drome (hǐp´ə-drōm´) s. hipódromo.

hip·po·pot·a·mus (hǐp´ə-pŏt´ə-məs) s. [pl. **es** o **-mi**] hipopótamo.

hire (hīr) **I.** tr. emplear; *(to rent)* alquilar ♦ **now hiring** se necesitan empleados —intr. ♦ **to h. out** se aceptar trabajo de **II.** s. *(wages)* sueldo; *(rent)* alquiler *m* ♦ **for h.** se alquila.

hire·ling (´lĭng) s. asalariado, mercenario.

hir·ing (:ĭng) s. contratación *f*; *(renting)* alquiler *m.*

hir·sute (hûr´sōōt´) adj. hirsuto.

his (hĭz) **I.** adj. pos. su, de él **II.** pron. pos. (el) suyo, el de él.

His·pan·o·phone (hĭ-spăn´ə-fōn´) s. hispanohablante *mf.*

hiss (hĭs) **I.** s. siseo; *(whistling)* silbido **II.** tr. & intr. silbar.

his·to·ri·an (hĭ-stôr´ē-ən) s. historiador *m.*

his·tor·ic/·cal (:ĭk) adj. histórico.

his·to·ry (hĭs´tə-rē) s. historia; *(background)* historial *m* ♦ **to go down in h.** pasar a la historia • **to make h.** dejar huella en la historia.

his·tri·on·ic (hĭs´trē-ŏn´ĭk) adj. histriónico ♦ **histrionics** s.pl. histrionismo.

hit (hĭt) **I.** tr. **hit** golpear; *(to collide with)* chocar contra o con; *(target)* dar en; *(to reach)* alcanzar; FAM. *(idea)* ocurrir ♦ **to h. home** tocar un punto vulnerable • **to h. it off (with)** FAM. hacer buenas migas con • **to h. on** FAM. encontrar, dar con —intr. ocurrir ♦ **to h. below the belt** dar un golpe bajo **II.** s. golpe *m; (collision)* choque *m; (shot)* tiro; *(success)* éxito ♦ **h. or miss** al azar • **to be a h. with** caerle simpático a.

hit-and-run (´n-rŭn´) adj. que atropella y huye *(conductor de un vehículo).*

hitch (hĭch) **I.** tr. enganchar ♦ **to h. a ride** FAM. hacerse llevar en automóvil • **to h. up** uncir —intr. FAM. *(to hitchhike)* viajar a dedo; *(to fasten)* engancharse ♦ **to get hitched** FAM. casarse **II.** s. FAM. tropiezo; MIL. período de servicio; *(knot)* vuelta de cabo; *(tug)* tirón *m;*

(device) enganche *m* ♦ **without a h.** sin dificultad.

hitch·hike (´hīk´) intr. hacer autostop.

hitch·hik·er (:hī´kər) s. autostopista *mf.*

hith·er (hĭth´ər) **I.** adv. (hacia) acá **II.** adj. citerior, más cercano.

hith·er·to (:tōō´) adv. hasta ahora.

hive (hīv) s. colmena; *(colony)* enjambre *m.*

hives (hīvz) s.pl. urticaria.

ho (hō) interj. ¡eh!, ¡oiga!.

hoa·gie (hō´gē) s. FAM. sandwich *m* grande.

hoar (hôr) s. escarcha.

hoard (hôrd) **I.** s. provisión acumulada **II.** tr. & intr. acaparar, atesorar.

hoar·frost (hôr´frôst´) s. escarcha.

hoarse (hôrs) adj. ronco.

hoar·y (hôr´ē) adj. **-i-** cano; *(old)* vetusto.

hoax (hōks) s. engaño, trampa.

hob·ble (hŏb´əl) **I.** intr. cojear —tr. *(an animal)* trabar, manear; *(to hamper)* impedir **II.** s. *(walk)* cojera; *(device)* maniota.

hob·by (hŏb´ē) s. pasatiempo, afición *f.*

hob·by·horse (:hôrs´) s. caballito de madera; *(topic)* tema favorito.

hob·gob·lin (hŏb´gŏb´lĭn) s. duende *m; (bugbear)* espantajo.

hob·nob (hŏb´nŏb´) intr. **-bb-** codearse.

ho·bo (hō´bō) [pl. **(e)s**] vago, vagabundo.

hock¹ s. ZOOL. jarrete *m.*

hock² FAM. **I.** tr. empeñar **II.** s. empeño.

hock·ey (hŏk´ē) s. hockey *m* ♦ **ice h.** hockey sobre hielo.

hock·shop (hŏk´shŏp´) s. FAM. casa de empeños.

ho·cus-po·cus (hō´kəs-pō´kəs) **I.** s. pasapasa *m; (trickery)* engaño **II.** interj. abracadabra.

hodge·podge (hŏj´pŏj´) s. mezcolanza.

hoe (hō) **I.** s. azada **II.** tr. & intr. azadonar.

hog (hôg, hŏg) **I.** s. cerdo, puerco; FAM. cochino ♦ **to live high on the h.** FAM. vivir en la abundancia **II.** tr. **-gg-** acaparar.

hog-tie o **hog·tie** (´tī´) tr. **-tying/-tieing** atar juntas las patas de; *(to impede)* poner trabas.

hog·wash (:wŏsh´) s. *(swill)* bazofia; *(nonsense)* tonterías.

ho-hum (hō´hŭm´) interj. expresa aburrimiento.

hoist (hoist) **I.** tr. izar **II.** s. grúa, cabria.

hok·ey (hō´kē) adj. **-i-** JER. *(trite)* banal; *(phony)* falso.

hold¹ (hōld) **I.** tr. **held** asir, agarrar; *(to take)* tener; *(to support)* sostener; *(to secure)* sujetar; *(to own)* ser dueño de; *(for questioning)* tener bajo custodia; *(to keep)* retener; *(to accommodate)* tener capacidad para; *(to control)* contener; *(to occupy)* ocupar; *(fort)* defender; *(course)* mantener; *(to reserve)* reservar; *(to consider)* creer; *(meeting)* celebrar; *(elections)* convocar; *(title)* poseer; MÚS. sostener; *(room)* reservar; *(one's liquor)* aguantar ♦ **h. everything!** ¡paren! • **h. it!** ¡no se muevan! • **h. the phone!** ¡un momento! • **h. your horses!** FAM. ¡espérate un momento! • **to be left holding the bag** FAM. cargar con el muerto • **to h. a gun on** apuntar con una pistola a • **to h. back** *(to repress)* reprimir, contener; *(to impede)* impedir • **to h. captive** mantener cautivo • **to h. dear** estimar • **to h. down** *(to oppress)* oprimir; *(to pin down)* mantener sujeto; *(prices)* moderar • **to h. down a job** tener un trabajo • **to h. hands** ir cogidos de la mano • **to h. it in** JER. aguantarse • **to h. it in** JER. aguantarse • **to h. off** alejar • **to h. one's own** defenderse •

to h. on tight agarrar fuertemente • **to h. on to** *(to grip)* agarrarse a; *(to keep)* seguir con • **to h. over** *(to threaten)* amenazar con; *(to extend)* continuar • **to h. to** hacer cumplir • **to h. up** FAM. *(to delay)* atrasar; *(to rob)* atracar; *(to lift)* levantar; *(to stop)* detener —intr. asirse, agarrar-se; *(to be firm)* sostenerse; *(to be valid)* seguir en vigor ♦ **to h. back** contenerse • **to h. forth** on hablar de • **to h. off** demorarse • **to h. on** *(to grip)* agarrarse bien; *(to continue)* proseguir; *(to wait)* aguardar, esperar • **to h. out** *(to last)* durar; *(to resist)* aguantar • **to h. out on** FAM. tener secretos con • **to h. over** aplazar • **to h. to** seguir firme en II. s. *(grip)* asidero; *(influence)* influencia; *(cell)* celda (de prisión); MÚS. calderón *m* ♦ **to get h. of** *(to grasp)* coger; *(to obtain)* conseguir; *(to find)* encontrar • **to get h. of oneself** controlarse, dominarse.

hold² s. MARIT. bodega; AFR. cabina de carga.
hold·ing (hōl'dĭng) s. inquilinato ♦ pl. propiedades.
hold·out (hōld'out') s. persona que obstaculiza un acuerdo.
hold·o·ver (:ō'vər) s. remanente *m*, resto.
hold·up (:ŭp') s. *(delay)* demora; *(robbery)* asalto, atraco (a mano armada).
hole (hōl) I. s. hueco; *(in ground)* hoyo; *(in road)* bache *m*; *(small)* agujero; *(large)* boquete *m*; *(burrow)* madriguera; *(dwelling)* ratonera; *(flaw)* falla; *(predicament)* aprieto; *(in golf)* hoyo ♦ in the h. FAM. endeudado II. tr. agujerear —intr. ♦ **to h. up** esconderse.
hol·i·day (hŏl'ĭ-dā') s. día feriado; RELIG. día de fiesta ♦ pl. G.B. vacaciones.
ho·li·er-than-thou (hō'lē-ər-thən-thou') adj. santurrón.
hol·ler (hŏl'ər) I. intr. & tr. gritar II. s. grito.
hol·low (hŏl'ō) I. adj. hueco; *(concave)* cóncavo; *(reverberating)* retumbante; *(empty)* vacío II. s. hueco; *(depression)* depresión *f*; *(emptiness)* vacío III. tr. ♦ **to h. out** ahuecar.
hol·ly (hŏl'ē) s. acebo.
hol·ly·hock (hŏl'ē-hŏk') s. malva loca.
ho·lo·caust (hŏl'ə-kôst', hō'lə-) s. destrucción completa (por el fuego).
ho·lo·gram (hŏl'ə-grăm', hō'lə-) s. holograma *m*.
ho·lo·graph (:grăf') s. ológrafo.
hol·ster (hōl'stər) s. pistolera.
ho·ly (hō'lē) adj. -i- sacro; *(revered)* venerable; *(saintly)* santo, pío ♦ **h. day** fiesta de guardar.
hom·age (hŏm'ĭj, ŏm'-) s. homenaje *m*.
home (hōm) I. casa; *(residence)* domicilio; *(household)* hogar *m*; *(headquarters)* sede *f*; *(institution)* asilo ♦ **a h. away from h.** lugar donde uno está como en su propia casa • **at h. and abroad** dentro y fuera del país • **to be away from h.** estar de viaje • **to feel at h.** sentirse a gusto • **to make oneself at h.** ponerse cómodo • **to make one's h.** establecerse II. adj. casero; *(native)* natal; *(team)* de casa; *(game)* en casa ♦ **h. economics** economía doméstica • **h. front** frente civil • **h. port** puerto de origen • **h. run** DEP. jonrón III. adv. ♦ **at h.** en casa • **to be h.** estar (en casa); *(after a trip)* estar de vuelta • **to come, go h.** regresar, irse a casa • **to see h.** acompañar hasta casa • **to hit h.** dar en el blanco IV. intr. volver a casa; *(missile)* autodirigirse ♦ **homing pigeon** paloma mensajera.
home·bod·y (ʹbŏd'ē) s. persona hogareña.
home·com·ing (:kŭm'ĭng) s. regreso al hogar.

home·grown (:grōn') s. adj. de cosecha propia.
home·land (:lănd') s. patria.
home·less (:lĭs) adj. sin hogar.
home·ly (:lē) adj. -i- sin atractivo; *(domestic)* casero; *(plain)* sencillo, rústico.
home·made (:mād') adj. hecho en casa.
home·mak·er (:mā'kər) s. ama de casa.
hom·er (hō'mər) s. jonrón *m*.
home·sick (:sĭk') adj. nostálgico.
home·spun (:spŭn') adj. tejido en casa, *(simple)* sencillo.
home·stead (:stĕd') I. s. *(farm)* granja; FAM. casa II. intr. & tr. tomar posesión legalmente (de tierras).
home·stretch (:strĕch') s. etapa final.
home·town (:toun') s. ciudad *f* de origen o de residencia.
home·ward (:wərd) I. adj. de vuelta, de regreso II. adv. [o -wards] hacia casa.
home·work (:wûrk') s. deberes *m*, tareas escolares; FIG. trabajo preliminar.
hom·ey (hō'mē) adj. -i- FAM. hogareño; *(intimate)* íntimo.
hom·i·cid·al (hŏm'ĭ-sīd'l, hō'mĭ-) adj. homicida.
hom·i·cide (ʹ-sīd') s. homicidio; *(murderer)* homicida *mf*.
hom·i·ly (hŏm'ə-lē) s. homilía, sermón *m*.
ho·mo·ge·ne·ous (hō'mə-jē'nē-əs) adj. homogéneo.
ho·mog·e·nize (hō-mŏj'ə-nīz') tr. homogeneizar.
hom·o·graph (hŏm'ə-grăf') s. homógrafo.
hom·o·nym (:nĭm') s. homónimo.
hom·o·phone (:fōn') s. homófono.
ho·mo·sex·u·al (hō'mō-sĕk'shōō-əl) adj. & s. homosexual *mf*.
ho·mo·sex·u·al·i·ty (:sĕk'shōō-ăl'ĭ-tē) s. homosexualidad *f*.
hon·cho (hŏn'chō) JER. s. jefe *m*.
hone (hōn) I. s. piedra de afilar II. tr. afilar; *(to perfect)* pulir.
hon·est (ŏn'ĭst) I. adj. honesto; *(honorable)* recto; *(truthful)* veraz; *(sincere)* franco; *(genuine)* legítimo II. interj. te lo juro.
hon·es·ty (:ĭ-stē) s. honestidad *f*; *(integrity)* honradez *f*; *(truthfulness)* veracidad *f*; *(sincerity)* franqueza.
hon·ey (hŭn'ē) s. miel *f*; *(sweetness)* dulzura; *(darling)* tesoro, encanto ♦ **a h. of** una maravilla de.
hon·ey·bee (:bē') s. abeja (melera).
hon·ey·comb (:kōm') I. s. panal *m* II. tr. acribillar.
hon·ey·dew (:dōō') s. secreción dulce de algunos insectos; *(melon)* variedad de melón dulce.
hon·eyed (hŭn'ēd) adj. con miel; *(sweet)* meloso.
hon·ey·moon (:ē-mōōn') s. & intr. (pasar la) luna de miel.
hon·ey·suck·le (:sŭk'əl) s. madreselva.
honk (hŏngk) I. s. *(goose)* graznido; *(horn)* bocinazo II. tr. & intr. tocar la bocina.
hon·or (ŏn'ər) I. s. honor *m*, honra; *(decoration)* condecoración *f*; *(probity)* probidad *f* ♦ **on my h.!** ¡palabra de honor! • **to be on one's h.** estar obligado por el honor • **to consider it an h. to** tener la honra de • **to do the honors** rendir honores • **your H.** Su Señoría II. tr. honrar; *(check)* aceptar; *(contract)* cumplir.
hon·or·a·ble (ʹ-ə-bəl) adj. honorable; *(praiseworthy)* honroso; *(honest)* honrado; *(illustri-*

ous) excelentísimo; *(honorific)* honorífico ♦ **h. mention** accésit.
hon·or·a·bly (:blē) adv. honorablemente.
hon·o·rar·i·um (ŏn'ə-râr'ē-əm) s. [pl. **s** o **-ia**] honorarios.
hon·or·ar·y ('-rĕr'ē) adj. honorario.
hon·or·if·ic (:rĭf'ĭk) adj. honorífico.
hood (hŏŏd) s. capucha, caperuza; *(of car)* capó.
hood·ed ('ĭd) adj. encapuchado; *(hood-shaped)* con forma de capucha.
hood·lum (hŏŏd'ləm, hŏŏd'-) s. *(gangster)* maleante m; *(ruffian)* rufián m.
hood·wink (hŏŏd'wĭngk') tr. engañar; *(to trick)* embaucar.
hoo·ey (hŏō'ē) s. JER. tonterías.
hoof (hŏŏf) I. s. [pl. **s** o **-ves**] pezuña II. tr. ♦ **to h. it** FAM. ir andando —intr. JER. bailar.
hoofed (hŏŏft) adj. ungulado.
hook (hŏŏk) I. s. *(for fishing)* anzuelo; *(for clothes)* percha ♦ **by h. or by crook** por las buenas o por las malas • **h., line, and sinker** JER. del todo • **off the h.** *(telephone)* descolgado; *(absolved)* eximido II. tr. enganchar; FAM. *(to snare)* pescar; JER. *(to steal)* robar; *(to bend)* encorvar ♦ **to get hooked on** JER. enviciarse con • **to h. up** enganchar; ELEC. conectar; *(to assemble)* armar —intr. doblar, torcer; *(to be fastened)* engancharse.
hooked (hŏŏkt) adj. ganchudo; *(addicted)* adicto; *(trapped)* enviciado ♦ **h. rug** alfombra de nudo.
hook·er (:ər) s. FAM. prostituta.
hook·nosed (:nōzd') adj. de nariz aguileña.
hook·up (:ŭp') s. sistema m de conexión.
hook·worm (:wûrm') s. anquilostoma m.
hook·y (hŏŏk'ē) s. ♦ **to play h.** hacer novillos.
hoo·li·gan (hŏō'lĭ-gən) s. FAM. rufián m.
hoop (hŏŏp) s. aro; *(band)* zuncho.
hoop·la (hŏŏp'lä') s. alboroto; *(misleading talk)* galimatías.
hoot (hŏŏt) I. intr. ulular; *(to boo)* abuchear II. s. ululato; *(shout)* risotada ♦ **not to give a h.** no importarle a uno un comino.
hooves (hŏŏvz) cf. **hoof.**
hop[1] (hŏp) I. intr. **-pp-** brincar; *(to skip)* saltar con un pie ♦ **to h. to it** echar manos a la obra II. brinco; *(rebound)* rebote m; FAM. *(dance)* baile m; *(short trip)* vuelo corto ♦ **h., skip, and a jump** distancia corta.
hop[2] s. lúpulo ♦ pl. frutos desecados del lúpulo.
hope (hŏp) I. intr. esperar ♦ **I should h. so!** ¡eso espero! • **to h. for** tener esperanzas de II. s. esperanza ♦ **to build up one's hopes** hacerse ilusiones.
hope·ful ('fəl) I. adj. esperanzado; *(promising)* prometedor II. s. aspirante m.
hope·ful·ly (:fə-lē) adv. esperanzadamente; *(one hopes)* se espera que.
hope·less (:lĭs) adj. desesperado; *(impossible)* imposible ♦ **h. case** caso perdido.
hop·scotch (hŏp'skŏch') s. rayuela.
horde (hôrd) s. horda, multitud f.
ho·ri·zon (hə-rī'zən) s. horizonte m.
hor·i·zon·tal (hôr'ĭ-zŏn'tl) adj. & s. horizontal f.
hor·mo·nal (hôr-mō'nəl) adj. hormonal.
hor·mone ('mōn') s. hormona.
horn (hôrn) I. s. cuerno; TEC. bocina; MÚS. trompa; FAM. saxófono, trompeta ♦ **h. of plenty** cornucopia • **to blow one's own h.** echarse flo-

res II. intr. ♦ **to h. in** JER. entremeterse.
horn·bill ('bĭl') s. cálao.
horned (hôrnd) adj. cornudo.
hor·net (hôr'nĭt) s. avispón m.
horn·y (hôr'nē) adj. **-i-** córneo; *(calloused)* calloso.
ho·ro·scope (hôr'ə-skōp') s. horóscopo.
hor·ren·dous (hô-rĕn'dəs) adj. horrendo.
hor·ri·ble (hôr'ə-bəl) adj. horrible; *(disagreeable)* desagradable.
hor·rid (hôr'ĭd) adj. hórrido; *(offensive)* repulsivo.
hor·rif·ic (hô-rĭf'ĭk) adj. horrendo.
hor·ri·fy (hôr'ə-f ī') tr. horrorizar; *(to shock)* escandalizar.
hor·ror (:ər) s. *(fear)* horror m; *(abhorrence)* aversión f; FAM. *(ugly thing)* espanto ♦ **h. film** película de miedo.
hors d'oeuvre (ôr dûrv') s. [pl. inv. o **s**] entremés m.
horse (hôrs) I. s. caballo; *(frame)* caballete m; DEP. potro ♦ **a h. of another color** otro cantar • **from the h.'s mouth** de buena tinta • **h. sense** FAM. sentido común II. intr. ♦ **to h. around** jugar alborotosamente III. adj. hípico.
horse·back ('băk') adv. a caballo.
horse·drawn (:drôn') adj. tirado por caballos.
horse·flesh (:flĕsh') s. caballos (en general).
horse·fly (:flī') s. tábano.
horse·hair (:hâr') s. pelo de caballo; *(cloth)* tela de crín.
horse·man (:mən) s. [pl. **-men**] caballista m; *(breeder)* criador m (de caballos).
horse·play (:plā') s. FAM. juego rudo.
horse·pow·er (:pou'ər) s. caballo de fuerza.
horse·rad·ish (:răd'ĭsh) s. rábano picante.
horse·shoe (:shŏō') s. herradura ♦ pl. juego en que se tira a un hito con herraduras.
horse·wom·an ('wŏom'ən) s. [pl. **-women**] caballista; *(breeder)* criadora (de caballos).
hors·(e)y (hôr'sē) adj. **-i-** caballuno, caballar.
hor·ti·cul·ture (hôr'tĭ-kŭl'chər) s. horticultura.
hose (hōz) I. s. [pl. inv.] medias; *(socks)* calcetines m; *(tube)* [pl. **s**] manguera II. tr. regar o lavar (con manguera).
ho·sier·y (hō'zhə-rē) s. medias.
hos·pice (hŏs'pĭs) s. hospicio.
hos·pi·ta·ble (hŏs'pĭ-tə-bəl, hŏ-spĭt'ə-) adj. hospitalario; *(receptive)* receptivo.
hos·pi·tal (hŏs'pĭt'l) s. hospital m.
hos·pi·tal·i·ty (hŏs'pĭ-tăl'ĭ-tē) s. hospitalidad f.
hos·pi·tal·ize (hŏs'pĭt'l-īz') tr. hospitalizar.
host[1] (hŏst) I. s. *(at a meal, party)* anfitrión m; *(of inn)* mesonero; TELEV. presentador m II. tr. FAM. ser el anfitrión de.
host[2] s. multitud f; *(army)* hueste f.
hos·tage (hŏs'tĭj) s. rehén mf.
hos·tel (hŏs'təl) s. albergue m (para jóvenes); *(inn)* hostería.
hos·tel·ry (:rē) s. hostería.
host·ess (hō'stĭs) s. *(host)* anfitriona; *(waitress)* camarera; *(stewardess)* azafata.
hos·tile (hŏs'təl, -tĭl') adj. hostil; *(antagonistic)* antagónico.
hos·til·i·ty (hŏ-stĭl'ĭ-tē) s. hostilidad f; *(act)* acto hostil ♦ pl. hostilidades, actos de guerra.
hot (hŏt) adj. **-tt-** caliente; *(climate)* cálido; *(sun)* abrasador; *(spicy)* picante; *(temper)* vivo; *(controversial)* muy discutido; *(heated)* acalorado; *(stolen)* robado; *(excellent)* excelente; *(lucky)* con mucha suerte; MÚS. rítmico ♦ **h. air** JER. palabrería • **h. dog** salchicha • **h. line** línea de emergencia • **h. off the press**

de última hora • **h. on the trail** sobre la pista • **in h. pursuit** tras los talones • **h. pepper** ají • **h. plate** infiernillo • **h. rod** automóvil modificado • **h. seat** FAM. situación crítica • **in h. water** FAM. en un lío • **to be h.** *(person)* tener calor; *(weather)* hacer calor.

hot·bed ('bĕd') s. almajara; FIG. semillero.

hot·blood·ed (:blŭd'ĭd) adj. fogoso.

ho·tel (hō-tĕl') s. hotel *m.*

hot·foot (hŏt'fŏŏt') intr. ♦ **to h. it** ir de prisa.

hot·head (:hĕd') s. persona arrebatada.

hot·head·ed (''ĭd) adj. arrebatado.

hot·house (hŏt'hous') s. invernadero.

hot·shot (:shŏt') s. JER. as *mf* (persona brillante)

hot·wa·ter bottle (-wô'tər) s. bolsa de agua caliente.

hound (hound) I. s. podenco; *(enthusiast)* aficionado II. tr. *(to harass)* acosar; *(to nag)* importunar.

hour (our) s. hora.

hour·glass ('glăs') s. reloj *m* de arena.

hour·ly (:lē) I. adj. horario; *(by the hour)* por hora II. adv. a cada hora; *(by the hour)* por horas.

house (hous) I. s. casa; *(home)* hogar *m;* *(auditorium)* teatro; *(audience)* público *m;* *(of parliament)* cámara ♦ **h. arrest** arresto domiciliario II. tr. (houz) alojar; *(to shelter)* proteger; *(to contain)* contener.

house·boat ('bōt') s. casa flotante.

house·bro·ken (:brō'kən) adj. enseñado en limpieza (un animal casero).

house·clean·ing (:klē'nĭng) s. limpieza de la casa.

house·coat (:kōt') s. bata (de casa).

house·fly (:flī') s. mosca común.

house·hold (:hōld') s. casa *(establecimiento doméstico).*

house·keep·er (:kē'pər) s. ama de llaves.

house·keep·ing (:kē'pĭng) s. manejo de una casa.

house·warm·ing ('wôr'mĭng) s. fiesta para el estreno de una casa.

house·wife (:wīf') s. [pl. **-ves**] ama de casa.

house·work (:wûrk') s. quehaceres domésticos.

hous·ing (hou'zĭng) s. casas *f;* *(place to live)* vivienda; MEC. cárter *m* ♦ **h. development** unidad vecinal.

hov·el (hŭv'əl, hŏv'-) s. cuchitril *m.*

hov·er (hŭv'ər, hŏv'-) intr. *(soar)* cernerse; *(flutter)* revolotear ♦ **to h. around** rondar • **to h. between** vacilar.

how (hou) I. adv. cómo; *(in what condition)* qué tal; *(to what extent)* cuánto, qué ♦ **and h.!** ¡y cómo! • **h. about . . . ?** ¿qué te parece . . . ? • **h. about me?** ¿y yo, qué? • **h. are you?** ¿cómo está usted? • **h. big is it?** ¿cómo es de grande? • **h. come?** FAM. ¿cómo es posible? • *(is possible)* que? • **h. could you!** ¡no te da vergüenza? • **h. do you do?** ¿cómo está usted? • **h. far?** *(away)* ¿a qué distancia?; *(to what point?)* ¿hasta dónde? • **h. fast?** *(speed)* ¿a qué velocidad?; *(how quickly)* ¿con qué rapidez? • **h. is it** *(that)* ¿cómo es que? • **h. is that again?** ¿cómo? • **h. long?** *(length)* ¿cómo . . . de largo? *(time)* ¿cuánto tiempo? • **h. many?** ¿cuántos? • **h. much?** ¿cuánto? • **h. old are you?** ¿cuántos años tienes?, ¿qué edad tienes? • **h. so?** ¿cómo? II. conj. cómo; *(that)* que III. s. ♦ **the h.** el cómo.

how·dy (hou'dē) interj. REG. ¡hola!

how·e·ver (hou-ĕv'ər) I. adv. de cualquier modo, como quiera que; *(by what means)* cómo; *(to whatever degree)* por . . . que ‹*h. tired she was* por cansada que estuviera› ♦ **h. it may be** sea lo que sea • **h. much** por más o por mucho que II. conj. no obstante.

howl (houl) I. intr. aullar; *(with pain)* dar alaridos —tr. gritar II. s. aullido; *(of pain)* alarido.

how·so·ev·er (hou'sō-ĕv'ər) adv. de cualquier modo; *(to whatever degree)* por muy.

hub (hŭb) s. cubo, FIG. centro, foco.

hub·bub (hŭb'ŭb') s. bullicio.

huck·le·ber·ry (hŭk'əl-bĕr'ē) s. BOT. arándano.

huck·ster (hŭk'stər) s. buhonero; JER. *(ad writer)* agente *mf* de publicidad.

hud·dle (hŭd'l) I. s. *(crowd)* group, turba; *(conference)* reunión *f* (pequeña o privada) II. tr. & intr. apiñar(se) ♦ **to h. up** acurrucarse.

hue (hyōō) s. color *m,* tinte *m;* *(shade)* matiz *m* ♦ **h. and cry** protesta pública.

huff (hŭf) I. s. arranque *m* de furia II. intr. resoplar.

huff·y ('ē) adj. -i- *(touchy)* quisquilloso; *(indignant)* indignado; *(arrogant)* altivo.

hug (hŭg) I. tr. -gg- abrazar; *(to cling to)* ceñirse a —intr. abrazarse II. s. abrazo.

huge (hyōōj) adj. enorme.

huh (hŭ) interj. expresa interrogación, sorpresa o indiferencia.

hulk (hŭlk) I. s. carraca; *(hull)* casco; *(large thing)* armatoste *m* II. intr. *(to loom)* surgir amenazadoramente.

hulk·ing (hŭl'kĭng) adj. pesado.

hull (hŭl) I. s. *(pod)* vaina; *(shell)* cáscara; MARÍT. casco II. tr. descascarillar.

hul·la·ba·loo (hŭl'ə-bə-lōō') s. FAM. alboroto.

hum (hŭm) I. intr. -mm- tararear; *(bees)* zumbar; FAM. *(to be active)* estar muy activo —tr. tararear II. s. zumbido.

hu·man (hyōō'mən) adj. & s. (ser) humano ♦ **h. being** ser humano.

hu·mane (-mān') adj. compasivo; *(humanistic)* humanístico.

hu·man·ist (:nĭst) s. humanista *mf.*

hu·man·i·tar·i·an (-mān'ĭ-târ'ē-ən) I. adj. humanitario II. s. filántropo, persona humanitaria

hu·man·i·ty (-'ĭ-tē) s. humanidad *f;* *(humanness)* naturaleza humana.

hu·man·ize ('mə-nīz') tr. humanizar.

hu·man kind (:mən kīnd') s. raza humana.

hu·man·oid (:mə-noid') adj. & s. humanoide.

hum·ble (hŭm'bəl) I. adj. -er, -est humilde; *(submissive)* sumiso; *(unpretentious)* sin pretensiones ♦ **to eat h. pie** rectractarse, disculparse de manera humillante II. tr. humillar.

hum·ble·ness (:nĭs) s. humildad *f.*

hum·bug (hŭm'bŭg') I. s. patraña; *(trickster)* embaucador *m;* *(nonsense)* tontería II. tr. & intr. -gg- embaucar.

hum·ding·er (hŭm'dĭng'ər) s. JER. maravilla.

hum·drum (hŭm'drŭm') adj. monótono.

hu·mer·us (hyōō'mər-əs) s. húmero.

hu·mid (hyōō'mĭd) adj. húmedo.

hu·mid·i·fi·er (-'ə-fī'ər) s. humedecedor *m.*

hu·mid·i·fy (:ə-fī') tr. humedecer.

hu·mid·i·ty (:ĭ-tē) s. humedad *f.*

hu·mi·dor (hyōō'mĭ-dôr') s. bote *m* que mantiene húmedo el tabaco.

hu·mil·i·ate (hyōō-mĭl′ē-āt′) tr. humillar.
hu·mil·i·a·tion (-′-ā′shən) s. humillación f.
hu·mil·i·ty (hyōō-mĭl′ĭ-tē) s. humildad f.
hum·ming·bird (hŭm′ĭng-bûrd′) s. colibrí m.
hu·mor (hyōō′mər) s. humor m.
hu·mor·ist (:ĭst) s. humorista mf.
hu·mor·less (:lĭs) adj. sin humor, solemne.
hu·mor·ous (:əs) adj. cómico; (employing humor) humorista.
hump (hŭmp) s. joroba; (in the ground) montecillo ♦ to be over the h. haber vencido la mayor dificultad.
hump·back (′băk′) s. jorobado; MED. cifosis f.
hump·backed (:băkt′) adj. jorobado.
humph (hŭmf) interj. ¡puf!, ¡uh!
hunch (hŭnch) I. s. (feeling) corazonada; (hump) giba II. tr. doblar (la espalda) —intr. agacharse; (to thrust forward) adelantarse ♦ to h. up estar con el cuerpo encorvado.
hunch·back (′băk′) s. jorobado.
hun·dred (hŭn′drĭd) s. [pl. inv. o s] & adj. cien, ciento; MAT. centena ♦ pl. centenares.
hun·dred·fold (:fōld′) adj. & s. céntuplo, centavo.
hun·dredth (hŭn′drĭdth) adj. & s. centésimo, centavo.
hung (hŭng) I. cf. hang II. adj. ♦ h. jury jurado que no llega a un fallo unánime ♦ h. over que sufre una resaca ♦ h. up FAM. preocupado ♦ to be h. up on estar obsesionado con ▪ to get h. up demorarse.
hun·ger (hŭng′gər) I. s. hambre f; (desire) sed f II. intr. tener hambre o sed.
hun·gry (:grē) adj. -i- hambriento; (avid) ávido; (look) de hambre.
hunk (hŭngk) s. FAM. trozo (grande).
hun·ker (hŭng′kər) intr. agacharse.
hun·ky-do·ry (hŭng′kē-dôr′ē) adj. JER. muy bien, estupendo.
hunt (hŭnt) I. tr. cazar; (to pursue) perseguir; (to search for) buscar ♦ to h. down capturar —intr. ♦ to go hunting ir de caza II. s. caza; (pursuit) persecución f; (search) búsqueda.
hunt·er (hŭn′tər) s. cazador m; (searcher) buscador m.
hunt·ing (:tĭng) I. s. cacería II. adj. de caza.
hur·dle (hûr′dl) I. s. valla; FIG. barrera II. tr. saltar; (to overcome) vencer.
hurl (hûrl) I. tr. lanzar II. s. lanzamiento.
hur·rah (hŏŏ-rä′) interj. ¡hurra!, ¡ole!
hur·ri·cane (hûr′ĭ-kān′) s. huracán m.
hur·ried (hûr′ēd) adj. apresurado.
hur·ry (:ē) I. intr. darse prisa, apurarse ♦ to h. away, back marcharse, volver de prisa ▪ to h. up apresurarse —tr. apurar; (to rush) dar prisa a II. s. prisa; (urgency) apuro ♦ in a h. de prisa ▪ to be in a h. (to) tener prisa (por).
hurt (hûrt) I. tr. hacer daño; (to distress) angustiar; (to damage) perjudicar ♦ to h. someone's feelings ofender a alguien —intr. doler <my head hurts me duele la cabeza> ♦ to get h. o to h. oneself lastimarse II. s. (harm) daño; (pain) dolor m; (injury) herida; (anguish) angustia.
hurt·ful (′fəl) adj. dañoso; (wounding) hiriente; (detrimental) perjudicial.
hur·tle (hûr′tl) intr. abalanzarse —tr. arrojar.
hus·band (hŭz′bənd) I. s. marido II. tr. economizar.
hus·band·ry (:bən-drē) s. agricultura; (livestock) cría de ganado; (economy) economía.
hush (hŭsh) I. tr. & intr. callar(se); (to calm) calmar(se) ♦ to h. up silenciar(se) II. s. silen-

cio; (stillness) quietud f III. interj. ¡silencio! ♦ h. up! ¡cállate!
hush-hush (′hŭsh′) adj. FAM. secreto.
husk (hŭsk) I. s. vaina; (shell) cáscara II. tr. desvainar.
husk·y¹ (hŭs′kē) adj. -i- (hoarse) ronco.
husk·y² (hŭs′kē) adj. -i- FAM. (burly) fornido.
hus·ky³ s. perro esquimal.
hus·sy (hŭz′ē, hŭs′ē) s. (saucy) pícara; (immoral) mujer libertina.
hus·tle (hŭs′əl) I. tr. empujar; FAM. (to hurry) apurar; (to swindle) estafar —intr. FAM. (to hurry) ajetrearse; (prostitute) trabajar de prostituta II. s. FAM. ajetreo; (swindle) estafa.
hus·tler (:lər) s. persona enérgica; (swindler) estafador m; (prostitute) prostituta.
hut (hŭt) s. choza.
hutch (hŭch) s. jaula (para conejos); (cupboard) alacena; (hut) choza.
hy·a·cinth (hī′ə-sĭnth) s. jacinto.
hy·brid (hī′brĭd) s. híbrido.
hy·drant (hī′drənt) s. boca de agua.
hy·drate (hī′drāt′) I. s. hidrato II. tr. & intr. hidratar(se).
hy·drau·lic (hī-drô′lĭk) adj. hidráulico, de la hidráulica ♦ hydraulics s.sg. hidráulica.
hy·dro·car·bon (hī′drə-kär′bən) s. hidrocarburo.
hy·dro·ceph·a·lous (hī′drō-sěf′ə-ləs) adj. hidrocéfalo, hidrocefálico.
hy·dro·chlo·ride (hī′drə-klôr′īd′) s. clorhidrato.
hy·dro·e·lec·tric (hī′drō-ĭ-lěk′trĭk) adj. hidroeléctrico.
hy·dro·gen (hī′drə-jən) s. hidrógeno.
hy·dro·gen·ate (:jə-nāt′, hī-drŏj′ə-) tr. hidrogenar.
hy·drol·o·gy (hī-drŏl′ə-jē) s. hidrología.
hy·drol·y·sis (:ĭ-sĭs) s. hidrólisis f.
hy·dro·lyze (hī′drə-līz′) tr. hidrolizar.
hy·dro·pho·bi·a (′-fō′bē-ə) s. hidrofobia.
hy·dro·plane (:plān′) I. s. hidroavión m; (boat) hidroplano II. intr. deslizarse sobre agua.
hy·dro·ther·a·py (′-thěr′ə-pē) s. hidroterapia.
hy·drous (hī′drəs) adj. hidratado.
hy·drox·ide (hī-drŏk′sīd′) s. hidróxido.
hy·e·na (hī-ē′nə) s. hiena.
hy·giene (hī′jēn′) s. higiene f.
hy·gien·ic (hī′jē-ěn′ĭk, hī-jēn′-) adj. higiénico, de la higiene; (sanitary) sanitario.
hy·gien·ist (hī-jēn′ĭst) s. higienista mf.
hy·men (hī′mən) s. himen m.
hymn (hĭm) s. himno.
hym·nal (′nəl) s. himnario.
hype (hīp) I. s. JER. superchería; (promotion) publicidad exagerada II. tr. promocionar (con exageraciones).
hyped-up (hīpt′ŭp′) adj. JER. entusiasmado.
hy·per·ac·tive (hī′pər-ăk′tĭv) adj. hiperactivo.
hy·per·bo·la (hī′pûr′bə-lə) s. [pl. s o -ae] hipérbola.
hy·per·bo·le (:lē) s. hipérbole f.
hy·per·crit·i·cal (hī′pər-krĭt′ĭ-kəl) adj. hipercrítico.
hy·per·sen·si·tive (:sěn′sĭ-tĭv) adj. hipersensible.
hy·per·ten·sion (:těn′shən) s. hipertensión f.
hy·per·ten·sive (:těn′sĭv) adj. & s. hipertenso.
hy·per·mi·a (:thûr′mē-ə) s. hipertermia.
hy·phen (hī′fən) s. guión m.
hy·phen·ate (:fə-nāt′) tr. unir o separar con

guión.

hyp·no·sis (hǐp-nō'sǐs) s. [pl. **-ses**] hipnosis f.
hyp·not·ic (:nǒt'ǐk) adj. & s. hipnótico.
hyp·no·tism ('nə-tǐz'əm) s. hipnotismo.
hyp·no·tist (:tǐst) s. hipnotizador m.
hyp·no·tize (:tīz') tr. hipnotizar; FIG. magnetizar.
hy·po·chon·dri·a (hī'pə-kŏn'drē-ə) s. hipocondria.
hy·po·chon·dri·ac (:ǎk') s. & adj. hipocondríaco.
hy·poc·ri·sy (hǐ-pŏk'rǐ sē) s. hipocresia.
hyp·o·crite (hǐp'ə-krǐt') s. hipócrita mf.
hyp·o·crit·i·cal ('-kəl) adj. hipócrita.
hy·po·der·mic (hī' pə-dûr'mǐk) I. adj. hipodérmico II. s. inyección f o jeringa hipodérmica.
hy·po·gly·ce·mi·a (hī'pō-glī-sē'mē-ə) s. hipoglicemia.
hy·po·ten·sion (:tĕn'shən) s. hipotensión f.
hy·pot·e·nuse (hī-pŏt'n-ōōs') s. hipotenusa.
hy·po·thal·a·mus (hī'pō-thǎl'ə mos) s. hipotálamo.
hy·po·ther·mi·a (:thûr'mē-ə) s. hipotermia.
hy·poth·e·sis (hī-pŏth'ǐ-sǐs) s. [pl. **-ses**] hipótesis f, suposición f.
hy·poth·e·size (:sīz') intr. formar una hipótesis.
hy·po·thet·i·cal (hī'pə-thĕt'ǐ-kəl) adj. hipotético; (contingent) dependiente.
hys·ter·ec·to·my (hǐs'tə-rĕk'tə-mē) s. histerectomía.
hys·ter·i·a (hǐ-stĕr'ē-ə, -stǐr'-) s. MED. histerismo; FAM. (fit) emoción f incontrolable.
hys·ter·ic (stĕr'ǐk) s. histérico ♦ **hysterics** s.pl. (fit) paroxismo; (hysteria) ataque m de histeria.
hys·ter·i·cal (:ǐ-kəl) adj. histérico; (emotional) emocional (persona).

I

i, I (ī) s. novena letra del alfabeto inglés.
I (ī) I. pron. yo II. s. [pl. **I's**] yo, ego.
i·bis (ī'bǐs) s. ibis m.
ice (īs) I. s. hielo; (dessert) helado escarchado ♦ **i. age** período glaciar ♦ **i. cap** casquete polar ♦ **i. cream** helado ♦ **i. cube** cubito de hielo ♦ **i. skate** patín de hielo ♦ **to break the i.** (to relax) romper el hielo; (to begin) dar el primer paso ♦ **to cut no i.** FAM. no convencer, no surtir efecto ♦ **to keep on i.** FAM. tener en reserva ♦ **to tread on thin i.** pisar terreno peligroso II. tr. (cake) escarchar; (to freeze) helar; (to chill) congelar —intr. ♦ **to i. over** helarse.
ice·berg (īs'bûrg') s. iceberg m.
ice·box (īs'bŏks') s. nevera, refrigerador m.
ice-cold (īs'kōld') adj. helado.
ice-cream cone (īs'krēm') s. helado en barquillo o cucurucho.
iced (īst) adj. congelado, helado; (cooled) refrigerado; (cake) escarchado, garapiñado.
ice-skate (īs'skāt') intr. patinar sobre hielo.
ich·thy·ol·o·gy (ĭk'thē-ŏl'ə-jē) s. ictiología.
i·ci·cle (ī'sǐ-kəl) s. carámbano.
i·ci·ly (ī'sə-lē) adv. fríamente, con frialdad.
ic·ing (ī'sǐng) s. alcorza, escarchado.
i·con (ī'kŏn') s. icono.
i·con·o·clast (ī'kŏn'ə-klǎst') s. iconoclasta mf.
ic·y (ī'sē) adj. -i- ♦ helado; (person, look) glacial.
ID card (ī'dē') s. carnet m de identificación.
i·de·a (ī-dē'ə) s. idea; (plan) proyecto ♦ **bright**

i. idea genial ♦ **that's the i.!** ¡eso es! ♦ **to get an i. of** hacerse una idea de ♦ **to get an i.** into one's head metérsele a uno una idea en la cabeza ♦ **to get ideas** hacerse ilusiones ♦ **to get the i.** darse cuenta ♦ **what's the big i.?** FAM. ¿a qué viene eso?
i·de·al (ī-dē'əl) adj. & s. ideal m.
i·de·al·ist (:ə-lǐst) s. idealista mf.
i·de·al·is·tic ('-lǐs'tǐk) adj. idealista.
i·de·al·ize ('-līz') tr. idealizar.
i·den·ti·cal (ī-dĕn'tǐ-kəl) adj. idéntico.
i·den·ti·fi·a·ble (:fī'ə-bəl) adj. identificable ♦ **easily i.** de fácil identificación.
i·den·ti·fi·ca·tion ('-fǐ-kā'shən) s. identificación f ♦ **i. card, papers** carnet m, documentos de identidad.
i·den·ti·fy (ī-dĕn'tə-fī') tr. & intr. identificar(se).
i·den·ti·ty (ī-dĕn'tǐ-tē) s. identidad f ♦ **i. card, papers** tarjeta, documentos de identidad.
i·de·o·log·i·cal (ī'dē-ə-lŏj'ǐ-kəl, īd'ē-) adj. ideológico.
i·de·o·logue (:lŏg') s. ideólogo.
i·de·ol·o·gy (ī'dē-ŏl'ə-jē, īd'ē-) s. ideología.
id·i·o·cy (ĭd'ē-ə-sē) s. idiotez f; (foolish deed) necedad f.
id·i·om (ĭd'ē-əm) s. (expression) modismo, locución f; (jargon) jerga, idioma m.
id·i·o·mat·ic ('-ə-mǎt'ǐk) adj. idiomático ♦ **i. expression** modismo.
id·i·o·syn·cra·sy (ĭd'ē-ō-sǐng'krə-sē) s. idiosincrasia.
id·i·o·syn·crat·ic (:sǐn-krǎt'ǐk) adj. idiosincrásico.
id·i·ot (ĭd'ē-ət) s. idiota mf; (fool) tonto.
id·i·ot·ic ('-ŏt'ǐk) adj. idiota, tonto.
i·dle (īd'l) I. adj. -er, -est ocioso; (unemployed) parado; (threat) vano ♦ **i. gossip** cuentos de viejas ♦ **i. talk** palabras vacías II. intr. (to loaf) haraganear; (machinery) funcionar en vacío —tr. (a worker) dejar parado; (a motor) hacer funcionar en vacío.
i·dol (īd'l) s. ídolo.
i·dol·a·trous (ī-dŏl'ə-trəs) adj. idólatra.
i·dol·a·try (ī-dŏl'ə-trē) s. idolatría.
i·dol·ize (īd'l-īz') tr. idolatrar.
i·dyll (īd'l) s. idilio.
i·dyl·lic (ī-dĭl'ǐk) adj. idílico.
if (ĭf) I. conj. si; (granting that) en caso que; (even though) si bien, aunque ♦ **if and when** siempre y cuando ♦ **if at all** si es que ♦ **if I were you** yo que tú II. s. ♦ **no ifs, ands, or buts** no hay pero que valga.
ig·loo (ĭg'lōō) s. iglú m.
ig·ne·ous (ĭg'nē'əs) adj. ígneo.
ig·nite (ĭg-nīt') tr. & intr. encender(se).
ig·ni·tion (ĭg-nǐsh'ən) s. ignición f; AUTO. encendido.
ig·no·ble (ĭg-nō'bəl) adj. innoble, bajo.
ig·no·min·i·ous (ĭg'nə-mǐn'ē-əs) adj. ignominioso.
ig·no·min·y (ĭg'nə-mǐn'ē) s. ignominia.
ig·no·ra·mus (ĭg'nə-rā'məs) s. ignorante mf.
ig·no·rance (ĭg'nər-əns) s. ignorancia.
ig·no·rant (:ənt) adj. ignorante.
ig·nore (ĭg-nôr') tr. (to disregard) no hacer caso de; (to leave out) pasar por alto.
i·gua·na (ĭ-gwä'nə) s. iguana.
ilk (ĭlk) s. clase f, índole f.
ill (ĭl) adj. worse, worst I. adj. enfermo, malo; (hostile) malo ♦ **i. effects** consecuencias ♦ **i. will** enemistad ♦ **to be in i. health** estar mal de sa-

lud • **to feel i.** sentirse mal II. adv. *(not well)* mal *<i. paid* mal remunerado>; *(scarcely)* mal, poco *<i. prepared* poco preparado> ♦ **i. at ease** incómodo III. s. mal *m.*

ill·ad·vised (ĭl'əd-vīzd') adj. imprudente.

ill-bred (ĭl'brĕd') adj. mal educado.

ill-con·sid·ered (ĭl'kən-sĭd'ərd) adj. imprudente.

il·le·gal (ĭ-lē'gəl) I. adj. ilegal, ilícito II. s. inmigrante *mf* ilegal.

il·le·gal·i·ty ('-găl'ĭ-tē) s. ilegalidad *f*; *(unlawful act)* acto ilegal.

il·leg·i·bil·i·ty (ĭ-lĕj'ə-bĭl'ĭ-tē) s. ilegibilidad *f.*

il·leg·i·ble (-'-bəl) adj. ilegible.

il·le·git·i·ma·cy (ĭl'ə-jĭt'ə-mə-sē) s. ilegitimidad *f.*

il·le·git·i·mate (ĭl'ə-jĭt'ə-mĭt) adj. *(illegal)* ilegal; *(bastard)* ilegítimo, bastardo.

ill-fat·ed (ĭl'fā'tĭd) adj. malaventurado.

ill-got·ten (ĭl'gŏt'n) adj. mal habido.

ill-hu·mored (ĭl'hyŏo'mərd) adj. malhumorado.

il·lic·it (ĭ-lĭs'ĭt) adj. ilícito.

il·lit·er·a·cy (ĭ-lĭt'ər-ə-sē) s. analfabetismo.

il·lit·er·ate (:ĭt) s. & adj. analfabeto; *(ignorant)* ignorante *mf.*

ill-man·nered (ĭl'măn'ərd) adj. mal educado.

ill·ness (ĭl'nĭs) s. enfermedad *f.*

il·log·i·cal (ĭ-lŏj'ĭ-kəl) adj. ilógico.

ill-pre·pared (ĭl'prĭ-pârd') adj. mal preparado.

ill-suit·ed (ĭl'sŏo'tĭd) adj. impropio.

ill-tem·pered (ĭl'tĕm'pərd) adj. de mal genio.

ill-treat (ĭl'trēt') tr. maltratar.

il·lu·mi·nate (ĭ-lŏo'mə-nāt') tr. iluminar.

il·lu·mi·nat·ing (:nā'tĭng) adj. *(book)* instructivo; *(solution, remark)* revelador.

il·lu·mi·na·tion (-'-nā'shən) s. iluminación *f.*

il·lu·sion (ĭ-lŏo'zhən) s. ilusión *f*; *(magic trick)* truco ♦ **to be under an i.** engañarse.

il·lu·sive (ĭ-lŏo'sĭv) adj. ilusivo, ilusorio.

il·lu·so·ry (:sə-rē) adj. ilusivo, ilusorio.

il·lus·trate (ĭl'ə-strāt') tr. & intr. ilustrar.

il·lus·tra·tion (-'-strā'shən) s. ilustración *f.*

il·lus·tra·tive (ĭ-lŭs'trə-tĭv, ĭl'ə-strā'tĭv) adj. ilustrativo ♦ **to be i.** of ilustrar, ejemplificar.

il·lus·tra·tor (ĭl'ə-strā'tər) s. ilustrador *m.*

il·lus·tri·ous (ĭ-lŭs'trē-əs) adj. ilustre.

im·age (ĭm'ĭj) I. s. imagen *f*; *(reputation)* reputación *f* ♦ **in one's own i.** a imagen de uno • **mirror i.** espejo II. tr. representar, retratar.

im·age·ry (:rē) s. imágenes *f*; ARTE. imaginería.

i·mag·i·na·ble (ĭ-măj'ə-nə-bəl) adj. imaginable.

i·mag·i·nar·y (:nĕr'ē) adj. imaginario.

i·mag·i·na·tion (ĭ-măj'ə-nā'shən) s. imaginación ♦ **to have no i.** ser una persona sin imaginación.

i·mag·i·na·tive (-'-nə-tĭv) adj. imaginativo.

i·mag·ine (ĭ-măj'ĭn) tr. imaginar; *(to suppose)* imaginarse, suponer ♦ **just i.!** ¡imagínate!

im·bal·ance (ĭm-băl'əns) s. desequilibrio.

im·be·cile (ĭm'bə-sĭl) adj. & s. imbécil *mf.*

im·be·cil·i·ty ('-'ĭ-tē) s. imbecilidad *f.*

im·bibe (ĭm-bīb') tr. beber; FIG. absorber.

im·bue (ĭm-byŏo') tr. imbuir.

im·i·tate (ĭm'ĭ-tāt') tr. imitar.

im·i·ta·tion ('-tā'shən) s. imitación *f* ♦ **i. leather** cuero artificial • **in i. of** a imitación de.

im·mac·u·late (ĭ-măk'yə-lĭt) adj. inmaculado.

im·ma·nent (ĭm'ə-nənt) adj. inmanente.

im·ma·te·ri·al (ĭm'ə-tîr'ē-əl) adj. inmaterial; *(unimportant)* sin importancia ♦ **to be i.** no ve-

nir al caso.

im·ma·ture (ĭm'ə-chŏŏr') adj. inmaduro.

im·ma·tur·i·ty (:ĭ-tē) s. falta de madurez.

im·meas·ur·a·ble (ĭ-mĕzh'ər-ə-bəl) adj. inmensurable; *(vast)* inconmensurable, ilimitado.

im·me·di·a·cy (ĭ-mē'dē-ə-sē) s. *(proximity)* inmediación *f*; *(of a problem)* urgencia.

im·me·di·ate (ĭ-mē'dē-ĭt) adj. inmediato; *(near, soon)* próximo; *(danger)* inminente; *(problem)* urgente ♦ **i. vicinity** inmediaciones.

im·me·mo·ri·al (ĭm'ə-môr'ē-əl) adj. inmemorial.

im·mense (ĭ-mĕns') adj. inmenso, enorme.

im·men·si·ty (ĭ-mĕn'sĭ-tē) s. inmensidad *f.*

im·merse (ĭ-mûrs') tr. sumergir; *(to baptize)* bautizar por inmersión; FIG. absorber.

im·mer·sion (ĭ-mûr'zhən) s. inmersión *f.*

im·mi·grant (ĭm'ĭ-grənt) s. inmigrante *mf.*

im·mi·grate (:grāt') intr. inmigrar.

im·mi·gra·tion (-'-grā'shən) s. inmigración *f.*

im·mi·nence (ĭm'ə-nəns) s. inminencia.

im·mi·nent (:nənt) adj. inminente.

im·mo·bile (ĭ-mō'bəl, -bĭl') adj. *(not moving)* inmóvil; *(not movable)* inmovible; *(fixed)* fijo.

im·mo·bi·lize (:bə-līz') tr. inmovilizar.

im·mod·er·ate (ĭ-mŏd'ər-ĭt) adj. inmoderado.

im·mod·est (ĭ-mŏd'ĭst) adj. inmodesto; *(boastful)* jactancioso.

im·mo·late (ĭm'ə-lāt') tr. inmolar.

im·mor·al (ĭ-môr'əl) adj. inmoral.

im·mo·ral·i·ty (ĭm'ô-răl'ĭ-tē) s. inmoralidad *f.*

im·mor·tal (ĭ-môr'tl) adj. & s. inmortal *mf.*

im·mor·tal·i·ty (ĭm'ôr-tăl'ĭ-tē) s. inmortalidad *f.*

im·mor·tal·ize (ĭ-môr'tl-īz') tr. inmortalizar.

im·mov·a·ble (ĭ-mŏo'və-bəl) adj. *(not movable)* inamovible; *(unyielding)* inflexible.

im·mune (ĭ-myŏŏn') adj. inmune *(from* de).

im·mu·ni·ty (ĭ-myŏŏ'nĭ-tē) s. inmunidad *f.*

im·mu·ni·za·tion (ĭm'yə-nĭ-zā'shən) s. inmunización *f.*

im·mu·nize (-'nīz') tr. inmunizar.

im·mu·nol·o·gy (-'-nŏl'ə-jē) s. inmunología.

im·mure (ĭ-myŏŏr') tr. emparedar.

im·mu·ta·ble (ĭ-myŏŏ'tə-bəl) adj. inmutable.

imp (ĭmp) s. diablillo; *(child)* niño travieso.

im·pact I. s. (ĭm'păkt') impacto, choque *m*; *(influence)* efecto, consecuencias II. tr. (-') chocar contra; FAM. *(to affect)* afectar.

im·pair (ĭm-pâr') tr. deteriorar, dañar.

im·pair·ment (:mənt) s. deterioro, daño.

im·pale (ĭm-pāl') tr. empalar.

im·pal·pa·ble (ĭm-păl'pə-bəl) adj. impalpable; *(imperceptible)* imperceptible.

im·pan·el (ĭm-păn'əl) tr. elegir (un jurado).

im·part (ĭm-pärt') tr. *(to bestow)* impartir; *(to disclose)* dar a conocer.

im·par·tial (ĭm-pär'shəl) adj. imparcial.

im·par·ti·al·i·ty (-'shē-ăl'ĭ-tē) s. imparcialidad *f.*

im·pass·a·ble (ĭm-păs'ə-bəl) adj. *(road)* intransitable; *(obstacle)* infranqueable.

im·passe (ĭm'păs) s. *(street)* callejón *m* sin salida; FIG. atolladero, estancamiento.

im·pas·sion (ĭm-păsh'ən) tr. apasionar.

im·pas·sioned (:ənd) adj. apasionado.

im·pas·sive (ĭm-păs'ĭv) adj. impasible.

im·pa·tience (ĭm-pā'shəns) s. impaciencia.

im·pa·tient (:shənt) adj. impaciente ♦ **to be i. with** no tener paciencia con • **to get i.** perder la paciencia • **to make i.** impacientar.

im·peach (ĭm-pēch') tr. *(to charge)* acusar, denunciar; *(to prosecute)* enjuiciar.

im·peach·ment (:mənt) s. *(charging)* acusa-

ción *f.; (prosecution)* enjuiciamiento.
im·pec·ca·ble (ĭm-pĕk′ə-bəl) adj. impecable.
im·pede (ĭm-pēd′) tr. impedir; *(to delay)* retardar.
im·ped·i·ment (ĭm-pĕd′ə-mənt) s. impedimento; *(defect)* defecto.
im·pel (ĭm-pĕl′) tr. -ll- impeler, impulsar.
im·pend (ĭm-pĕnd′) intr. ser inminente.
im·pen·e·tra·ble (ĭm-pĕn′ĭ-trə-bəl) adj. impenetrable.
im·per·a·tive (ĭm-pĕr′ə-tĭv) adj. *(tone)* imperioso; *(urgent)* urgente; GRAM. imperativo.
im·per·cep·ti·ble (ĭm′pər-sĕp′tə-bəl) adj. imperceptible.
im·per·fect (ĭm-pûr′fĭkt) adj. imperfecto.
im·per·fec·tion (ĭm′pər-fĕk′shən) s. imperfección *f.*
im·pe·ri·al (ĭm-pîr′ē-əl) adj. imperial; *(majestic)* augusto, señorial.
im·pe·ri·al·ist (:ə-lĭst) s. imperialista *mf.*
im·pe·ri·al·is·tic (:lĭs′tĭk) adj. imperialista.
im·per·il (ĭm-pĕr′əl) tr. poner en peligro.
im·pe·ri·ous (ĭm-pîr′ē-əs) adj. imperioso.
im·per·ish·a·ble (ĭm-pĕr′ĭ-shə-bəl) adj. imperecedero.
im·per·ma·nent (ĭm-pûr′mə-nənt) adj. no permanente, temporal.
im·per·me·a·ble (ĭm-pûr′mē-ə-bəl) adj. impermeable.
im·per·mis·si·ble (ĭm′pər-mĭs′ə-bəl) adj. no permisible, inadmisible.
im·per·son·al (ĭm-pûr′sə-nəl) adj. impersonal.
im·per·son·ate (ĭm-pûr′sə-nāt′) tr. hacerse pasar por.
im·per·son·a·tion (-′-nā′shən) s. imitación *f.*
im·per·son·a·tor (-′-′tər) s. imitador *m.*
im·per·ti·nence (ĭm-pûr′tn-əns) s. impertinencia.
im·per·ti·nent (:ənt) adj. impertinente.
im·per·turb·a·ble (ĭm′pər-tûr′bə-bəl) adj. imperturbable.
im·per·vi·ous (ĭm-pûr′vē-əs) adj. insensible.
im·pet·u·ous (ĭm-pĕch′ōō-əs) adj. *(rash)* impetuoso.
im·pe·tus (ĭm′pĭ-təs) s. ímpetu *m*, impulso.
im·pinge (ĭm-pĭnj′) intr. ♦ **to i. on** *(to invade)* invadir, violar; *(to affect)* impresionar.
im·pi·ous (ĭm′pē-əs, ĭm-pī′əs) adj. impío.
imp·ish (ĭm′pĭsh) adj. pícaro.
im·plac·a·ble (ĭm-plăk′ə-bəl) adj. implacable.
im·plant I. tr. (ĭm-plănt′) implantar II. s. (′′) MED. injerto.
im·plan·ta·tion (ĭm′plăn-tā′shən) s. implantación *f.*
im·plau·si·ble (ĭm-plô′zə-bəl) adj. *(unbelievable)* inverosímil; *(improbable)* improbable.
im·ple·ment I. s. (ĭm′plə-mənt) utensilio, instrumento II. tr. (:mĕnt′) poner en práctica; *(a law)* aplicar.
im·ple·men·ta·tion (′-mən-tā′shən) s. *(of plan)* puesta en práctica; *(of law)* aplicación *f.*
im·pli·cate (ĭm′plĭ-kāt′) tr. implicar.
im·pli·ca·tion (-′-kā′shən) s. implicación *f; (inference)* inferencia.
im·plic·it (ĭm-plĭs′ĭt) adj. implícito; *(unquestioning)* absoluto.
im·plied (ĭm-plīd′) adj. implícito.
im·plore (ĭm-plôr′) tr. implorar.
im·ply (ĭm-plī′) tr. *(to entail)* implicar, significar; *(to hint)* dar a entender, insinuar.
im·po·lite (ĭm′pə-līt′) adj. descortés.
im·pol·i·tic (ĭm-pŏl′ĭ-tĭk) adj. imprudente.

im·port I. tr. (ĭm-pôrt′) *(goods)* importar; *(to signify)* significar —intr. tener importancia II. s. (′′) *(item)* artículo importado; *(business)* importación *f; (significance)* importancia.
im·por·tance (ĭm-pôr′tns) s. importancia ♦ **to be of i.** ser importante, tener importancia.
im·por·tant (:tnt) adj. importante ♦ **it's not i.** no importa.
im·por·ta·tion (ĭm′pôr-tā′shən) s. importación *f.*
im·port·er (-′tər) s. importador *m.*
im·por·tu·nate (ĭm-pôr′chə-nĭt) adj. importuno, fastidioso.
im·por·tune (ĭm′pôr-tōōn′, ĭm-pôr′chən) tr. importunar, fastidiar.
im·por·tu·ni·ty (′-tōō′nĭ-tē) s. importunidad *f.*
im·pose (ĭm-pōz′) tr. imponer ♦ **to i. oneself** imponerse —intr. ♦ **to i. (up)on** abusar de.
im·pos·ing (ĭm-pō′zĭng) adj. imponente.
im·po·si·tion (ĭm′pə-zĭsh′ən) s. *(act)* imposición *f; (unfair demand)* abuso.
im·pos·si·bil·i·ty (ĭm-pŏs′ə-bĭl′ĭ-tē) s. imposibilidad *f.*
im·pos·si·ble (ĭm-pŏs′ə-bəl) adj. imposible.
im·pos·tor (ĭm-pŏs′tər) s. impostor *m.*
im·po·tence/ten·cy (ĭm′pə-tns) s. impotencia.
im·po·tent (:tnt) adj. impotente.
im·pound (ĭm-pound′) tr. *(to confine)* encerrar; DER. *(to seize)* embargar, confiscar.
im·pov·er·ish (ĭm-pŏv′ər-ĭsh) tr. *(people)* empobrecer; *(resources)* agotar.
im·prac·ti·ca·ble (ĭm-prăk′tĭ-kə-bəl) adj. impracticable.
im·prac·ti·cal (:kəl) adj. poco práctico.
im·prac·ti·cal·i·ty (-′-kăl′ĭ-tē) s. impracticabilidad *f.*
im·pre·cise (ĭm′prĭ-sīs′) adj. impreciso.
im·pre·ci·sion (:sĭzh′ən) s. imprecisión *f.*
im·preg·na·ble (ĭm-prĕg′nə-bəl) adj. *(fortress)* inexpugnable; FIG. invulnerable.
im·preg·nate (ĭm-prĕg′nāt′) tr. dejar preñada; *(ovum)* fecundar; *(to permeate)* impregnar.
im·pre·sa·ri·o (ĭm′prĭ-sär′ē-ō′) s. empresario.
im·press¹ (ĭm-prĕs′) I. tr. *(to imprint)* imprimir; *(to affect)* impresionar, causar impresión ♦ **I was not impressed** no me pareció gran cosa II. s. (′′) *(mark)* marca, señal *f; (seal)* sello.
im·press² tr. MIL. reclutar a la fuerza.
im·pres·sion (ĭm-prĕsh′ən) s. impresión *f; (memory)* idea; IMPR. tirada ♦ **to be under the i.** **that** tener la impresión de que.
im·pres·sion·a·ble (:ə-nə-bəl) adj. impresionable.
im·pres·sion·is·tic (-′-nĭs′tĭk) adj. ARTE. impresionista; *(subjective)* subjetivo.
im·pres·sive (ĭm-prĕs′ĭv) adj. impresionante.
im·pri·ma·tur (ĭm′prə-mä′tŏŏr′) s. imprimátur *m.*
im·print (ĭm-prĭnt′) I. tr. imprimir II. s. (′′) impresión *f; (influence)* impronta; IMPR. pie *m* de imprenta.
im·pris·on (ĭm-prĭz′ən) tr. aprisionar.
im·pris·on·ment (:mənt) s. aprisionamiento.
im·prob·a·bil·i·ty (ĭm-prŏb′ə-bĭl′ĭ-tē) s. improbabilidad *f.*
im·prob·a·ble (ĭm-prŏb′ə-bəl) adj. improbable.
im·promp·tu (ĭm-prŏmp′tōō) I. adj. improvisado II. adv. improvisadamente.
im·prop·er (ĭm-prŏp′ər) adj. impropio; *(indecorous)* incorrecto, indebido.
im·pro·pri·e·ty (ĭm′prə-prī′ĭ-tē) s. impropiedad *f; (improper act)* falta de corrección.

im·prove (ĭm-prōōv′) tr. mejorar; *(to upgrade)* hacer mejoras en; *(productivity)* aumentar, incrementar; *(skill, product)* perfeccionar; *(one's mind)* desarrollar ♦ **to i. one's appearance** hacerse más presentable —intr. mejorar; *(patient)* mejorar(se) ♦ **to i. (up)on** mejorar.

im·prove·ment (:mənt) s. mejora, mejoramiento; *(in productivity, quality)* aumento; *(of a skill)* perfeccionamiento; *(in attitude)* reforma; *(mental)* desarrollo; *(in school)* adelanto, progreso; *(in health)* mejoría; *(in a building)* reforma; *(in a facility)* ampliación f ♦ **to make improvements in** perfeccionar.

im·prov·i·dent (ĭm-prŏv′ĭ-dənt) adj. imprevisor.

im·pro·vi·sa·tion (ĭm-prŏv′ĭ-zā′shən) s. improvisación f.

im·pro·vise (ĭm′prə-vīz′) tr. & intr. improvisar.

im·pru·dent (ĭm-prōōd′nt) adj. imprudente.

im·pu·dence (ĭm′pyə-dns) s. impudencia.

im·pu·dent (:dnt) adj. impudente, descarado.

im·pugn (ĭm-pyōōn′) tr. impugnar.

im·pulse (ĭm′pŭls′) s. impulso ♦ **on i.** sin reflexionar.

im·pul·sive (ĭm-pŭl′sĭv) adj. impetuoso.

im·pu·ni·ty (ĭm-pyōō′nĭ-tē) s. impunidad f.

im·pure (ĭm-pyōōr′) adj. impuro; *(adulterated)* mezclado; *(air)* contaminado.

im·pu·ri·ty (:tē) s. impureza; *(contamination)* contaminación f; *(substance)* contaminante m.

im·pute (ĭm-pyōōt′) tr. imputar.

in (ĭn) I. prep. en, dentro de, por; *(time)* a, por, durante, de; *(arrival)* a; *(method)* a, en, por; *(with verbs)* al, mientras <in running after the bus mientras corría para tomar el autobús> II. adv. *(inside)* (a)dentro; *(in power)* en el poder; *(in fashion)* de moda ♦ **to be in** estar <is the doctor in? ¿está el doctor?>; *(in power)* estar en el poder • **to be in for it** FAM. ir a recibir un castigo (por algo hecho) • **to be in on** *(to participate)* tomar parte en; *(to know)* estar enterado de • **to be in with someone** FAM. gozar del favor de alguien • **to have it in for someone** FAM. tenerle antipatía a alguien III. adj. *(fashionable)* de moda; *(entering)* de entrada ♦ **the in party** FAM. el partido en el poder IV. s. influencia ♦ **the ins and outs** los pormenores, los detalles ♦ **to have an in somewhere** tener influencia en algún sitio.

in·a·bil·i·ty (ĭn′ə-bĭl′ĭ-tē) s. incapacidad f.

in·ac·ces·si·ble (ĭn′ăk-sĕs′ə-bəl) adj. inaccesible.

in·ac·cu·ra·cy (ĭn-ăk′yər-ə-sē) s. inexactitud f; *(error)* error m.

in·ac·cu·rate (:ĭt) adj. inexacto.

in·ac·tive (ĭn-ăk′tĭv) adj. inactivo; MIL. en o de reserva.

in·ac·tiv·i·ty (′-′ĭ-tē) s. inactividad f.

in·ad·e·qua·cy (ĭn-ăd′ĭ-kwə-sē) s. inadecuación f; *(insufficiency)* insuficiencia.

in·ad·e·quate (:kwĭt) adj. inadecuado; *(insufficient)* insuficiente.

in·ad·mis·si·ble (ĭn′əd-mĭs′ə-bəl) adj. inadmisible.

in·ad·ver·tent (ĭn′əd-vûr′tnt) adj. *(inattentive)* descuidado; *(unintentional)* accidental.

in·ad·vis·a·ble (ĭn′əd-vī′zə-bəl) adj. imprudente, no aconsejable.

in·al·ien·a·ble (ĭn-āl′yə-nə-bəl) adj. inalienable.

in·al·ter·a·ble (ĭn-ôl′tər-ə-bəl) adj. inalterable.

in·ane (ĭn-ān′) adj. tonto, necio.

in·an·i·mate (ĭn-ăn′ə-mĭt) adj. *(not living)* inanimado; *(dull)* desanimado, apagado.

in·an·i·ty (:ĭ-tē) s. necedad f, insensatez f.

in·ap·pli·ca·ble (ĭn-ăp′lĭ-kə-bəl, ĭn′ə-plĭk′ə-) adj. que no viene al caso.

in·ap·pre·cia·ble (ĭn′ə-prē′shə-bəl) adj. inapreciable, insignificante.

in·ap·pro·pri·ate (ĭn′ə-prō′prē-ĭt) adj. impropio, inadecuado.

in·ar·tic·u·late (ĭn′är-tĭk′yə-lĭt) adj. *(sound)* inarticulado; *(person)* incapaz de expresarse.

in·as·much as (ĭn′əz-mŭch′əz) conj. ya que.

in·at·ten·tion (ĭn′ə-tĕn′shən) s. desatención f.

in·at·ten·tive (:tĭv) adj. desatento, distraído.

in·au·di·ble (ĭn-ô′də-bəl) adj. inaudible.

in·au·gu·ral (ĭn-ô′gyər-əl) adj. inaugural.

in·au·gu·rate (:gyə-rāt′) tr. *(to begin)* inaugurar; POL. investir del cargo a.

in·au·gu·ra·tion (-′-rā′shən) s. inauguración f; POL. investidura, toma de posesión.

in·aus·pi·cious (ĭn′ô-spĭsh′əs) adj. desfavorable, poco propicio.

in·born (ĭn′bôrn′) adj. congénito, innato.

in·bound (ĭn′bound′) adj. que viene, de venida.

in·bred (ĭn′brĕd′) adj. consanguíneo; *(innate)* innato.

in·breed·ing (ĭn′brē′dĭng) s. procreación f en consanguinidad; *(people)* endogamia.

in·cal·cu·la·ble (ĭn-kăl′kyə-lə-bəl) adj. incalculable.

in·can·des·cent (ĭn′kən-dĕs′ənt) adj. incandescente.

in·can·ta·tion (ĭn′kăn-tā′shən) s. invocación f; *(spell)* sortilegio, conjuro.

in·ca·pa·ble (ĭn-kā′pə-bəl) adj. incapaz; *(incompetent)* incompetente.

in·ca·pac·i·tate (ĭn′kə-păs′ĭ-tāt′) tr. incapacitar.

in·ca·pac·i·ty (:tē) s. incapacidad f.

in·car·cer·ate (ĭn-kär′sə-rāt′) tr. encarcelar.

in·car·cer·a·tion (-′-rā′shən) s. encarcelamiento.

in·car·nate (ĭn-kär′nĭt) I. adj. encarnado II. tr. (:nāt′) encarnar.

in·car·na·tion (′-nā′shən) s. encarnación f.

in·cen·di·ar·y (ĭn-sĕn′dē-ĕr′ē) adj. incendiario.

in·cense[1] (ĭn-sĕns′) tr. encolerizar, enfurecer.

in·cense[2] (″) s. *(sticks, smoke)* incienso.

in·cen·tive (ĭn-sĕn′tĭv) s. incentivo.

in·cep·tion (ĭn-sĕp′shən) s. principio.

in·ces·sant (ĭn-sĕs′ənt) adj. incesante.

in·cest (ĭn′sĕst′) s. incesto.

in·ces·tu·ous (ĭn-sĕs′chōō-əs) adj. incestuoso.

inch (ĭnch) I. s. pulgada ♦ **every i. of the way** todo el camino • **i. by i.** poco a poco • **to know every i. of** conocer como la palma de la mano • **within an i. of** a punto de II. intr. avanzar poco a poco —tr. mover poco a poco.

in·ci·dence (ĭn′sĭ-dəns) s. incidencia; *(rate)* frecuencia, índice m.

in·ci·dent (:dənt) adj. & s. incidente m ♦ **without i.** sin novedad.

in·ci·den·tal (′-dĕn′tl) I. adj. *(related)* incidente; *(minor)* secundario; *(expense)* accesorio ♦ **i. to** propio de II. s.pl. imprevistos.

in·cin·er·ate (ĭn-sĭn′ə-rāt′) tr. incinerar.

in·cin·er·a·tor (′-rā′tər) s. incinerador m.

in·cip·i·ent (ĭn-sĭp′ē-ənt) adj. incipiente.

in·cise (ĭn-sīz′) tr. cortar; *(to engrave)* tallar.

in·ci·sion (ĭn-sĭzh′ən) s. incisión f.

in·ci·sive (ĭn-sī′sĭv) adj. *(mentally)* penetrante,

águdo; *(biting)* incisivo, mordaz.

in·ci·sor (:zər) s. (diente) incisivo.

in·cite (ĭn-sīt') tr. incitar.

in·cite·ment (:mənt) s. incitación f.

in·clem·ent (ĭn-klĕm'ənt) adj. inclemente.

in·cli·na·tion (ĭn'klə-nā'shən) s. inclinación f; *(tendency)* tendencia; *(preference)* gusto.

in·cline (ĭn-klīn') I. tr. & intr. inclinar(se) ♦ **if you feel so inclined** si usted desea ♦ **to be inclined to** estar dispuesto a ♦ **to i. to** tender a II. s. ('') inclinación f, pendiente f.

in·clined (ĭn-klīnd') adj. inclinado ♦ **i. to** dispuesto a ♦ **musically i.** que le atrae la música

in·clude (ĭn-klōōd') tr. incluir, abarcar.

in·clud·ed (ĭn-klōō'dĭd) adj. incluido, incluso.

in·clu·sion (:zhən) s. inclusión f.

in·clu·sive (:sĭv) adj. *(including)* inclusive; *(comprehensive)* inclusivo.

in·cog·ni·to (ĭn-kŏg'nĭ-tō', '-nē'tō) I. adj. & s. incógnito II. adv. de incógnito.

in·co·her·ence (ĭn'kō-hîr'əns) s. incoherencia f.

in·co·her·ent (:ənt) adj. incoherente.

in·com·bus·ti·ble (ĭn'kəm-bŭs'tə-bəl) adj. & s. (substancia) incombustible.

in·come (ĭn'kŭm') s. ingresos m, entrada f; *(on investments)* renta; *(profit)* utilidades f ♦ **gross, net i.** entrada bruta, neta ♦ **i. tax** impuesto sobre los ingresos o utilidades.

in·com·ing (ĭn'kŭm'ĭng) adj. entrante, que entra; *(new)* nuevo.

in·com·mu·ni·ca·do (ĭn'kə-myōō'nĭ-kä'dō) adj. incomunicado.

in·com·pa·ra·ble (ĭn-kŏm'pər-ə-bəl) adj. incomparable.

in·com·pat·i·bil·i·ty (ĭn'kəm-păt'ə-bĭl'ĭ-tē) s. incompatibilidad f.

in·com·pat·i·ble ('-'-bəl) adj. incompatible.

in·com·pe·tence/ten·cy (ĭn-kŏm'pĭ-tns) s. incompetencia, incapacidad f.

in·com·pe·tent (:tnt) I. adj. incompetente, incapaz II. s. persona incompetente.

in·com·plete (ĭn'kəm-plēt') adj. incompleto.

in·com·pre·hen·si·ble (ĭn-kŏm'prĭ-hĕn'sə-bəl) adj. incomprensible.

in·con·ceiv·a·ble (ĭn'kən-sē'və-bəl) adj. inconcebible; *(incredible)* increíble.

in·con·clu·sive (ĭn'kən-klōō'sĭv) adj. no concluyente, inconcluyente.

in·con·gru·ent (ĭn-kŏn grōō'ənt) adj. incongruente.

in·con·gru·i·ty (:i-tē) s. incongruencia f.

in·con·gru·ous (ĭn-kŏng'grōō-əs) adj. incongruo, incongruente.

in·con·se·quen·tial (ĭn kŏn'sĭ kwĕn'shəl) adj. insignificante, sin trascendencia f.

in·con·sid·er·ate (ĭn'kən-sĭd'ər-ĭt) adj. desconsiderado

in·con·sis·ten·cy (ĭn'kən-sĭs'tən-sē) s. inconsecuencia; *(irregularity)* irregularidad f.

in·con·sis·tent (:tənt) adj. inconsecuente; *(irregular)* irregular; *(contradictory)* contradictorio ♦ **i. with** en contradicción con.

in·con·sol·a·ble (ĭn'kən-sō'lə-bəl) adj. inconsolable, desconsolado.

in·con·spic·u·ous (ĭn'kən-spĭk'yōō-əs) adj. no conspicuo, discreto.

in·con·test·a·ble (ĭn'kən-tĕs'tə-bəl) adj. incontestable.

in·con·ti·nent (ĭn-kŏn'tə-nənt) adj. incontinente.

in·con·tro·vert·i·ble (ĭn-kŏn'trə-vûr'tə-bəl) adj. incontrovertible, indiscutible.

in·con·ven·ience (ĭn'kən-vēn'yəns) I. s. inconveniencia; *(bother)* molestia II. tr. incomodar, molestar.

in·con·ven·ient (:yənt) adj. inconveniente; *(bothersome)* molesto.

in·cor·po·rate (ĭn-kôr'pə-rāt') tr. *(to include)* incorporar, incluir; COM. constituir en sociedad —intr. constituirse en sociedad.

in·cor·po·rat·ed (:rā'tĭd) adj. incorporado; COM. constituido en sociedad.

in·cor·rect (ĭn'kə-rĕkt') adj. incorrecto.

in·cor·ri·gi·ble (ĭn-kôr'i-jə-bəl) adj. incorregible.

in·crease (ĭn-krēs') I. tr. & intr. aumentar; *(prices)* subir; *(production)* incrementar, tomar incremento II. s. ('') aumento; *(in prices)* subida, alza; *(in production)* incremento ♦ **to be on the i.** ir en aumento.

in·creas·ing (ĭn-krē'sĭng) adj. creciente.

in·creas·ing·ly (:lē) adv. cada vez más.

in·cred·i·ble (ĭn-krĕd'ə-bəl) adj. increíble.

in·cre·du·li·ty (ĭn'krĭ-dōō'lĭ-tē) s. incredulidad f.

in·cred·u·lous (ĭn krĕj'ə-ləs) adj. incrédulo.

in·cre·ment (ĭng'krə-mənt) s. incremento ♦ **un·earned i.** plusvalía.

in·crim·i·nate (ĭn-krĭm'ə-nāt') tr. incriminar.

in·crim·i·na·tion ('-'-nā'shən) s. incriminación f.

in·cu·bate (ĭng'kyə-bāt') tr. & intr. incubar.

in·cu·ba·tion ('-'bā'shən) s. incubación f.

in·cu·ba·tor ('-'-tər) s. incubadora f.

in·cul·cate (ĭn-kŭl'kāt') tr. inculcar.

in·cum·bent (ĭn-kŭm'bənt) I. adj. *(resting)* apoyado; POL. actual ♦ **to be i. on** corresponderle a alguien II. s. POL. titular m.

in·cur (ĭn-kûr') tr. incurrir.

in·cur·a·ble (ĭn-kyōōr'ə-bəl) adj. incurable.

in·cur·sion (ĭn-kûr'zhən) s. incursión f.

in·debt·ed (ĭn-dĕt'ĭd) adj. endeudado; *(owing gratitude)* agradecido.

in·de·cen·cy (ĭn'dē'sən-sē) s. indecencia f.

in·de·cent (:sənt) adj. indecente ♦ **i. exposure** exhibicionismo.

in·de·ci·pher·a·ble (ĭn'dĭ-sī'fər-ə-bəl) adj. indescifrable.

in·de·ci·sion (ĭn'dĭ-sĭzh'ən) s. indecisión f.

in·de·ci·sive (:sī'sĭv) adj. *(inconclusive)* dudoso, *(irresolute)* indeciso, irresoluto.

in·deed (ĭn-dēd') I. adv. *(truly)* verdad, verdaderamente; *(in fact)* en efecto; *(of course)* claro ♦ **i.?** ¿de verdad? • **that is i. a luxury** eso sí que es lujo • **yes i.!** ¡claro que sí! II. interj. de veras, verdad.

in·de·fen·si·ble (ĭn'dĭ-fĕn'sə-bəl) adj. indefensible; *(inexcusable)* imperdonable.

in·de·fin·a·ble (ĭn'dĭ-fī'nə-bəl) adj. indefinible.

in·def·i·nite (ĭn-dĕf'ə-nĭt) adj. indefinido; *(uncertain)* incierto, impreciso; *(vague)* vago.

in·del·i·ble (ĭn-dĕl'ə-bəl) adj. indeleble.

in·del·i·ca·cy (ĭn-dĕl'ĭ-kə-sē) s. indelicadeza f.

in·del·i·cate (:kĭt) adj. indelicado.

in·dem·ni·fy (ĭn-dĕm'nə-fī'), tr. *(to insure)* asegurar; *(to compensate)* indemnizar.

in·dem·ni·ty (:tē) s. *(security, exemption)* indemnidad f; *(compensation)* indemnización f.

in·dent (ĭn-dĕnt') I. tr. IMPR. sangrar; *(to serrate)* dentar; *(to notch)* hacer muescas en II. s. ('') IMPR. sangría; *(notch)* muesca.

in·den·ta·tion (ĭn'dĕn-tā'shən) s. *(notch)* muesca; *(recess)* hueco; IMPR. sangría.

in·den·ture (ĭn-dĕn'chər) tr. ligar por contrato.

in·de·pend·ence (ĭn'dĭ-pĕn'dəns) s. independencia.

in·de·pend·ent (:dənt) adj. & s. independiente *mf* ♦ **of i. means** con recursos propios, adinerado ♦ **to be i.** of no depender de.

in·depth (ĭn'dĕpth') adj. profundo.

in·de·scrib·a·ble (ĭn'dĭ-skrī'bə-bəl) adj. indescriptible.

in·de·struc·ti·ble (ĭn'dĭ-strŭk'tə-bəl) adj. indestructible.

in·de·ter·mi·nate (ĭn'dĭ-tûr'mə-nĭt) adj. indeterminado, incierto.

in·dex (ĭn'dĕks') I. s. [pl. **es** o **-dices**] índice *m*; *(sign)* indicio; IMPR. *(fist)* manecilla; TEC. *(pointer)* indicador *m* ♦ **i. card** ficha, tarjeta II. tr. poner un índice a; *(to indicate)* indicar, señalar; *(to regulate)* regular (precios).

In·di·a (ĭn'dē-ə) ♦ **I. ink** tinta china ♦ **I. rubber** caucho.

in·di·cate (ĭn'dĭ-kāt') tr. indicar.

in·di·ca·tion ('-kā'shən) s. indicación *f*; *(sign)* indicio, seña; *(symptom)* síntoma *m*.

in·dic·a·tive (ĭn-dĭk'ə-tĭv) adj. & s. indicativo ♦ **to be i.** of indicar, ser un indicio de.

in·di·ca·tor (ĭn'dĭ-kā'tər) s. indicador *m*.

in·di·ces (ĭn'dĭ-sēz') cf. **index**.

in·dict (ĭn-dīt') tr. acusar.

in·dict·a·ble (ĭn-dī'tə-bəl) adj. que merece acusación legal.

in·dict·ment (ĭn-dīt'mənt) s. acusación *f*.

in·dif·fer·ence (ĭn-dĭf'ər-əns) s. indiferencia.

in·dif·fer·ent (:ənt) adj. indiferente; *(impartial)* desinteresado; *(mediocre)* regular.

in·di·gence (ĭn'dĭ-jəns) s. indigencia.

in·dig·e·nous (ĭn-dĭj'ə-nəs) adj. indígena.

in·di·gent (ĭn'dĭ-jənt) adj. & s. indigente *mf*.

in·di·gest·i·ble (ĭn'dĭ-jĕs'tə-bəl, ĭn'dī-) adj. indigestible.

in·di·ges·tion (:chən) s. indigestión *f*.

in·dig·nant (ĭn-dĭg'nənt) adj. indignado.

in·dig·na·tion ('-nā'shən) s. indignación *f*.

in·dig·ni·ty (ĭn-dĭg'nĭ-tē) s. indignidad *f*; *(humiliation)* humillación *f*.

in·di·go (ĭn'dĭ-gō') s. [pl. **(e)s**] índigo, añil *m*.

in·di·rect (ĭn'dĭ-rĕkt', ĭn'dī-) adj. indirecto.

in·dis·cern·i·ble (ĭn'dĭ-sûr'nə-bəl) adj. indiscernible, imperceptible.

in·dis·creet (ĭn'dĭ-skrēt') adj. indiscreto.

in·dis·cre·tion (:skrĕsh'ən) s. indiscreción *f*.

in·dis·crim·i·nate (ĭn'dĭ-skrĭm'ə-nĭt) adj. *(undiscriminating)* sin criterio; *(random)* al azar; *(admiration, praise)* ciego.

in·dis·pens·a·ble (ĭn'dĭ-spĕn'sə-bəl) adj. indispensable, imprescindible.

in·dis·posed (ĭn'dĭ-spōzd') adj. *(slightly ill)* indispuesto; *(averse)* adverso, maldispuesto.

in·dis·po·si·tion (ĭn-dĭs'pə-zĭsh'ən) s. *(aversion)* aversión *f*; *(ailment)* indisposición *f*.

in·dis·put·a·ble (ĭn'dĭ-spyoo'tə-bəl) adj. indisputable.

in·dis·tinct (ĭn'dĭ-stĭngkt') adj. indistinto.

in·dis·tin·guish·a·ble (:stĭng'gwĭ-shə-bəl) adj. indistinguible.

in·di·vid·u·al (ĭn'də-vĭj'ōō-əl) I. adj. individual; *(style, manner)* particular, propio II. s. individuo.

in·di·vid·u·al·ist (:ə-lĭst) s. individualista *mf*.

in·di·vid·u·al·is·tic ('-'-ə-lĭs'tĭk) adj. individualista.

in·di·vid·u·al·i·ty (:ăl'ĭ-tē) s. individualidad *f*, particularidad *f*.

in·di·vid·u·al·ize ('-'-ə-līz') tr. individualizar.

in·di·vis·i·ble (ĭn'də-vĭz'ə-bəl) adj. indivisible.

in·doc·tri·nate (ĭn-dŏk'trə-nāt') tr. adoctrinar.

in·doc·tri·na·tion (-'-nā'shən) s. adoctrinamiento.

in·do·lence (ĭn'də-ləns) s. indolencia.

in·do·lent (:lənt) adj. indolente.

in·dom·i·ta·ble (ĭn-dŏm'ĭ-tə-bəl) adj. indomable, indómito.

in·door (ĭn'dôr') adj. *(interior)* interior, interno; *(event)* de puertas adentro.

in·doors (ĭn-dôrz') adv. adentro, bajo techo.

in·duce (ĭn-dōōs') tr. *(to cause)* ocasionar; *(childbirth)* provocar; *(to infer)* inducir ♦ **to i.** to lograr convencer de que.

in·duce·ment (:mənt) s. *(incentive)* incentivo, aliciente *m*; *(lure)* atractivo.

in·duct (ĭn-dŭkt') tr. POL. instalar; MIL. reclutar; *(new member)* admitir.

in·duc·tion (ĭn-dŭk'shən) s. inducción *f*; POL. instalación *f*; *(into a society)* admisión *f*; MIL. incorporación *f* a filas.

in·duc·tive (:tĭv) adj. inductivo.

in·dulge (ĭn-dŭlj') tr. *(to pamper)* consentir, mimar; *(to gratify)* satisfacer ♦ **to i. oneself** darse gusto —intr. ♦ **to i. in** permitirse el lujo de.

in·dul·gence (ĭn-dŭl'jəns) s. *(humoring)* complacencia; *(pampering)* consentimiento; *(in pleasures)* gratificación *f*; *(treat)* gusto, capricho; *(favor)* favor *m*; RELIG. indulgencia.

in·dul·gent (:jənt) adj. indulgente.

in·dus·tri·al (ĭn-dŭs'trē-əl) adj. industrial ♦ **i. park** zona industrial ♦ **i. relations** relaciones laborales II. s. ♦ pl. valores industriales.

in·dus·tri·al·ist (:ə-lĭst) s. industrial *m*.

in·dus·tri·al·ize (:ə-līz') tr. & intr. industrializar(se).

in·dus·tri·ous (:əs) adj. industrioso.

in·dus·try (ĭn'də-strē) s. industria; *(management)* empresariado; *(diligence)* diligencia.

in·e·bri·ate (ĭn-ē'brē-āt') I. tr. embriagar, emborrachar II. adj. & s. (:ĭt) ebrio.

in·e·bri·at·ed (:ā'tĭd) adj. embriagado.

in·e·bri·a·tion (-'-'shən) s. embriaguez *f*.

in·ed·i·ble (ĭn-ĕd'ə-bəl) adj. incomestible.

in·ef·fec·tive (ĭn'ĭ-fĕk'tĭv) adj. ineficaz.

in·ef·fec·tu·al (:chōō-əl) adj. vano, inútil.

in·ef·fi·cien·cy (ĭn'ĭ-fĭsh'ən-sē) s. ineficacia.

in·ef·fi·cient (:ənt) adj. ineficiente, ineficaz.

in·el·i·gi·ble (ĭn-ĕl'ĭ-jə-bəl) adj. inelegible.

in·ept (ĭn-ĕpt') adj. inepto, incapaz.

in·ep·ti·tude (ĭn-ĕp'tĭ-tōōd') s. ineptitud *f*.

in·e·qual·i·ty (ĭn'ĭ-kwŏl'ĭ-tē) s. desigualdad *f*; *(injustice)* injusticia.

in·eq·ui·ty (ĭn-ĕk'wĭ-tē) s. injusticia.

in·ert (ĭn-ûrt') adj. inerte.

in·er·tia (ĭn-ûr'shə) s. inercia.

in·es·cap·a·ble (ĭn'ĭ-skā'pə-bəl) adj. ineludible, inevitable.

in·ev·i·ta·ble (ĭn-ĕv'ĭ-tə-bəl) adj. inevitable.

in·ex·act (ĭn'ĭg-zăkt') adj. inexacto.

in·ex·cus·a·ble (ĭn'ĭk-skyōō'zə-bəl) adj. inexcusable, imperdonable.

in·ex·haust·i·ble (ĭn'ĭg-zô'stə-bəl) adj. inagotable.

in·ex·o·ra·ble (ĭn-ĕk'sər-ə-bəl) adj. inexorable.

in·ex·pen·sive (ĭn'ĭk-spĕn'sĭv) adj. barato.

in·ex·pe·ri·ence (ĭn'ĭk-spîr'ē-əns) s. inexperiencia.

in·ex·pe·ri·enced (:ənst) adj. inexperto.

in·ex·pli·ca·ble (ĭn'ĭk-splĭk'ə-bəl) adj. inexplicable.

in·ex·tin·guish·a·ble (ĭn'ĭk-stĭng'gwĭ-shə-bəl)

adj. inextinguible.

in·fal·li·ble (ĭn-făl′ə-bəl) adj. infalible.

in·fa·mous (ĭn′fə-məs) adj. infame.

in·fa·my (:mē) s. infamia.

in·fan·cy (ĭn′fən-sē) s. infancia.

in·fant (ĭn′fənt) s. infante mf, niño.

in·fan·tile (ĭn′fən-tīl′) adj. infantil.

in·fan·try (ĭn′fən-trē) s. infantería.

in·farct (ĭn′färkt′) s. infarto.

in·fat·u·at·ed (ĭn-făch′ōō-ā′tĭd) adj. locamente enamorado; (foolish) encaprichado.

in·fat·u·a·tion (-′shən) s. encaprichamiento.

in·fect (ĭn-fĕkt′) tr. infectar; (to contaminate) contaminar; (another person) contagiar.

in·fec·tion (ĭn-fĕk′shən) s. infección f.

in·fec·tious (:shəs) adj. infeccioso.

in·fer (ĭn-fûr′) tr. -rr- inferir, deducir.

in·fer·ence (ĭn′fər-əns) s. inferencia.

in·fer·en·tial (ĭn′fə-rĕn′shəl) adj. que se infiere.

in·fe·ri·or (ĭn-fîr′ē-ər) adj. & s. inferior m.

in·fe·ri·or·i·ty (-′ôr′ĭ-tē) s. inferioridad f.

in·fer·nal (ĭn-fûr′nəl) adj. infernal.

in·fer·no (ĭn-fûr′nō) s. infierno.

in·fer·tile (ĭn-fûr′tl) adj. infértil, estéril.

in·fer·til·i·ty (ĭn′fər-tĭl′ĭ-tē) s. infertilidad f.

in·fest (ĭn-fĕst′) tr. infestar, plagar.

in·fes·ta·tion (:fĕ-stā′shən) s. infestación f.

in·fi·del (ĭn′fĭ-dəl) s. infiel mf.

in·fi·del·i·ty (′-fĭ-dĕl′ĭ-tē) s. infidelidad.

in·fight·ing (ĭn′fī′tĭng) s. lucha interna.

in·fil·trate (ĭn-fĭl′trāt′) tr. infiltrar; (an organization) infiltrarse en.

in·fil·tra·tion (-′trā′shən) s. infiltración f.

in·fi·nite (ĭn′fə-nĭt) adj. & s. infinito.

in·fin·i·tes·i·mal (ĭn-fĭn′ĭ-tĕs′ə-məl) adj. infinitesimal.

in·fin·i·tive (ĭn-fĭn′ĭ-tĭv) s. infinitivo.

in·fin·i·ty (:tē) s. infinidad f; MAT. infinito.

in·firm (ĭn-fûrm′) adj. débil, enfermizo.

in·fir·ma·ry (ĭn-fûr′mə-rē) s. enfermería.

in·fir·mi·ty (:mĭ-tē) s. (weakness) debilidad f; (illness) enfermedad f, achaque m.

in·flame (ĭn-flām′) tr. inflamar.

in·flam·ma·ble (ĭn-flăm′ə-bəl) adj inflamable

in·flam·ma·tion (ĭn′flə-mā′shən) s. inflamación f.

in·flam·ma·to·ry (ĭn-flăm′ə-tôr′ē) adj. (arousing) incendiario; MED. inflamatorio.

in·flate (ĭn-flāt′) tr. inflar; FIG. hinchar; ECON., FIN. causar la inflación de — intr. inflarse, hincharse.

in·flat·ed (ĭn-flā′tĭd) adj. inflado, hinchado; (bombastic) pomposo; (wages, prices) excesivo.

in·fla·tion (ĭn-flā′shən) s. inflación f.

in·fla·tion·ar·y (:shə-nĕr′ē) adj. inflacionario.

in·flect (ĭn-flĕkt′) tr. (voice) modular; GRAM. (verb) conjugar; (noun) declinar.

in·flec·tion (ĭn-flĕk′shən) s. inflexión f.

in·flex·i·ble (ĭn-flĕk′sə-bəl) adj. inflexible.

in·flict (ĭn-flĭkt′) tr. infligir, causar ♦ to i. (up)on imponer a.

in·flic·tion (ĭn-flĭk′shən) s. imposición f.

in·flow (ĭn′flō′) s. afluencia, flujo.

in·flu·ence (ĭn′flōō-əns) I. s. influencia, influjo ♦ to be an i. on tener influencia sobre • to have i. ser influyente • under the i. embriagado II. tr. influir en, ejercer influencia sobre.

in·flu·en·tial (-′ĕn′shəl) adj. influyente.

in·flu·en·za (ĭn′flōō-ĕn′zə) s. influenza.

in·flux (ĭn′flŭks′) s. afluencia, entrada.

in·form (ĭn-fôrm′) tr. informar, avisar ♦ to i. someone that comunicarle a alguien que

— intr. ♦ to i. on delatar, denunciar.

in·for·mal (ĭn-fôr′məl) adj. (casual) familiar, llano; (unofficial) extraoficial; (agreement) no legalizado; (unceremonious) sin ceremonia; (dress) de diario, de calle.

in·for·mal·i·ty (-′măl′ĭ-tē) s. familiaridad f, llaneza; (of occasion) ausencia de ceremonia.

in·form·ant (ĭn-fôr′mənt) s. informador m.

in·for·ma·tion (ĭn′fər-mā′shən) s. información f; (data) datos; (knowledge) conocimientos ♦ for your i. para su conocimiento.

in·form·a·tive (ĭn-fôr′mə-tĭv) adj. informativo.

in·formed (ĭn-fôrmd′) adj. informado, enterado ♦ to keep someone i. tener a alguien al corriente.

in·form·er (ĭn-fôr′mər) s. delator m, soplón m.

in·frac·tion (ĭn-frăk′shən) s. infracción f.

in·fra·red (ĭn′frə-rĕd′) adj. infrarrojo.

in·fra·struc·ture (ĭn′frə-strŭk′chər) s. infraestructura.

in·fre·quent (ĭn-frē′kwənt) adj. infrecuente.

in·fringe (ĭn-frĭnj′) tr. infringir —intr. ♦ to i. (up)on usurpar, abusar de.

in·fringe·ment (:mənt) s. (of law) infracción f; (of rights) usurpación f.

in·fu·ri·ate (ĭn-fyŏŏr′ē-āt′) tr. enfurecer.

in·fuse (ĭn-fyōōz′) tr. infundir.

in·fu·sion (ĭn-fyōō′zhən) s. infusión f.

in·gen·ious (ĭn-jēn′yəs) adj. ingenioso.

in·gé·nue (ăn′zhə-nōō′) s. joven ingenua.

in·ge·nu·i·ty (ĭn′jə-nōō′ĭ-tē) s. ingenio.

in·gen·u·ous (ĭn-jĕn′yōō-əs) adj. ingenuo.

in·gest (ĭn-jĕst′) tr. ingerir.

in·ges·tion (ĭn-jĕs′chən) s. ingestión f.

in·got (ĭng′gət) s. lingote m, barra.

in·grained (ĭn-grānd′) adj. arraigado.

in·gra·ti·ate (ĭn-grā′shē-āt′) tr. congraciarse.

in·grat·i·tude (ĭn-grăt′ĭ-tōōd′) s. ingratitud f.

in·gre·di·ent (ĭn-grē′dē-ənt) s. ingrediente m.

in·hab·it (ĭn-hăb′ĭt) tr. habitar, vivir en.

in·hab·it·a·ble (ĭn-hăb′ĭ-tə-bəl) adj. habitable.

in·hab·i·tant (:tənt) s. habitante mf.

in·ha·la·tion (ĭn′hə-lā′shən) s. inhalación f.

in·hale (ĭn-hāl′) tr. aspirar; (smoke) tragar; MED. inhalar —intr. aspirar aire.

in·her·ent (ĭn-hĕr′ənt) adj. inherente.

in·her·it (ĭn-hĕr′ĭt) tr. heredar.

in·her·i·tance (:ĭ-tns) s. (act) sucesión f; (thing) herencia; (heritage) patrimonio.

in·hib·it (ĭn-hĭb′ĭt) tr. inhibir; (to prevent) impedir; (to prohibit) prohibir.

in·hi·bi·tion (ĭn′hĭ-bĭsh′ən) s. inhibición f.

in·hos·pi·ta·ble (ĭn hŏs′pĭ tə bəl, ĭn′hŏspĭt′ə-) adj. inhospitalario; (barren) inhóspito.

in·house (ĭn′hous′) adj. interno, de la casa.

in·hu·man (ĭn-hyōō′mən) adj. inhumano, cruel; (monstrous) no humano.

in·hu·mane (′-mān′) adj. inhumano.

in·im·i·cal (ĭn-ĭm′ĭ-kəl) adj. adverso, hostil.

in·im·i·ta·ble (ĭn-ĭm′ĭ-tə-bəl) adj. inimitable.

in·iq·ui·ty (ĭ-nĭk′wĭ-tē) s. iniquidad f.

in·i·tial (ĭ-nĭsh′əl) I. adj. & s. inicial f ♦ s.pl. (person) iniciales; (organization) siglas II. tr. firmar con las iniciales.

in·i·ti·ate (ĭ-nĭsh′ē-āt′) I. tr. iniciar; (proceedings) entablar II. adj. & s. (:ĭt) iniciado.

in·i·ti·a·tion (-′-ā′shən) s. iniciación f.

in·i·ti·a·tive (ĭ-nĭsh′ə-tĭv) s. iniciativa f.

in·ject (ĭn-jĕkt′) tr. inyectar; (a patient) poner una inyección a; FIG. introducir.

in·jec·tion (ĭn-jĕk′shən) s. inyección f.

in·junc·tion (ĭn-jŭngk′shən) s. (command) or-

den *f; (prohibition)* entredicho.
in·jure (ĭn'jər) tr. lastimar, herir; *(to impair)* dañar, averiar; *(to wrong)* injuriar.
in·ju·ri·ous (ĭn-jŏŏr'ē-əs) adj. *(harmful)* dañino, perjudicial; *(offensive)* injurioso.
in·ju·ry (ĭn'jə-rē) s. *(damage, wrong)* daño, perjuicio; *(wound)* herida.
in·jus·tice (ĭn-jŭs'tĭs) s. injusticia.
ink (ĭngk) I. s. tinta II. tr. entintar.
in·kling (ĭng'klĭng) s. *(hint)* indicio; *(suspicion)* sospecha.
ink·well (ĭngk'wĕl') s. tintero.
in·laid (ĭn'lād') adj. incrustado.
in·land (ĭn'lənd') I. adj. (del) interior II. adv. tierra adentro, hacia el interior.
in·law (ĭn'lô') s. pariente político.
in·lay I. tr. (ĭn-lā') -laid incrustar II. s. ('') incrustación *f*.
in·let (ĭn'lĕt') s. *(bay)* cala; *(estuary)* estuario.
in·mate (ĭn'māt') s. *(of asylum)* asilado; *(prisoner)* presidiario, preso.
inn (ĭn) s. posada, hostería; *(tavern)* taverna.
in·nards (ĭn'ərdz) s.pl. FAM. entrañas.
in·nate (ĭ-nāt') adj. innato.
in·ner (ĭn'ər) adj. interior, interno; *(profound)* profundo, recóndito; *(intimate)* íntimo ♦ i. cir·cle esfera de mayor influencia • i. tube cámara del centro de una ciudad • i. tube cámara.
in·ner·most (:mōst') adj. más interno, más adentro; FIG. más profundo, más íntimo.
in·no·cence (ĭn'ə-səns) s. inocencia.
in·no·cent (:sənt) adj. & s. inocente *mf*.
in·noc·u·ous (ĭ-nŏk'yōŏ-əs) adj. inocuo.
in·no·vate (ĭn'ə-vāt') tr. & intr. innovar.
in·no·va·tion ('-vā'shən) s. innovación *f*.
in·no·va·tive ('-tĭv) adj. innovador.
in·no·va·tor (:tər) s. innovador *m*.
in·nu·en·do (ĭn'yōō-ĕn'dō) s. [pl. es] insinuación *f*, indirecta.
in·nu·mer·a·ble (ĭ-nōō'mər-ə-bəl) adj. innumerable.
in·ob·ser·vant (ĭn'əb-zûr'vənt) adj. desatento.
in·ob·tru·sive (ĭn'əb-trōō'sĭv) adj. discreto.
in·oc·u·late (ĭ-nŏk'yə-lāt') tr. inocular.
in·oc·u·la·tion ('-lā'shən) s. inoculación *f*.
in·of·fen·sive (ĭn'ə-fĕn'sĭv) adj. inofensivo.
in·op·er·a·ble (ĭn-ŏp'ər-ə-bəl) adj. *(not functioning)* que no funciona; CIR. inoperable.
in·op·er·a·tive (:tĭv) adj. *(not in effect)* inoperante; *(not functioning)* que no funciona.
in·op·por·tune (ĭn-ŏp'ər-tōōn') adj. inoportuno.
in·or·di·nate (ĭn-ôr'dn-ĭt) adj. inmoderado.
in·or·gan·ic (ĭn'ôr-găn'ĭk) adj. inorgánico.
in·pa·tient (ĭn'pā'shənt) s. paciente *mf* internado en un hospital.
in·put (ĭn'pōōt') s. COMPUT., ELEC. entrada; MEC. energia consumida; FIG. intervención *f*.
in·quest (ĭn'kwĕst') s. indagatoria, encuesta.
in·quire (ĭn-kwīr') intr. preguntar, hacer una pregunta ♦ to i. about *(a person)* preguntar por; *(a matter)* pedir informes sobre • to i. into investigar (sobre) —tr. preguntar por, averiguar.
in·quir·y (ĭng'kwə-rē) s. pregunta; *(investigation)* investigación *f*, inquisición *f*.
in·qui·si·tion (ĭn'kwĭ-zĭsh'ən) s. inquisición *f*.
in·quis·i·tive (ĭn-kwĭz'ĭ-tĭv) adj. *(prying)* preguntón, inquisitivo; *(curious)* curioso.
in·quis·i·tor (:tər) s. inquisidor *m*.
in·road (ĭn'rōd') s. invasión *f*, incursión *f*.
in·sane (ĭn-sān') adj. loco, demente; *(absurd)* disparatado ♦ i. asylum manicomio.

in·san·i·ty (ĭn-săn'ĭ-tē) s. locura, demencia; *(folly)* insensatez *f*, locura.
in·sa·tia·ble (ĭn-sā'shə-bəl) adj. insaciable.
in·scribe (ĭn-skrīb') tr. inscribir; *(to dedicate)* dedicar, firmar.
in·scrip·tion (ĭn-skrĭp'shən) s. inscripción *f*; *(dedication)* dedicatoria.
in·scru·ta·ble (ĭn-skrōō'tə-bəl) adj. inescrutable.
in·sect (ĭn'sĕkt') s. insecto.
in·sec·ti·cide (ĭn-sĕk'tĭ-sīd') s. insecticida *m*.
in·se·cure (ĭn'sĭ-kyŏŏr') adj. inseguro.
in·se·cu·ri·ty (:ĭ-tē) s. inseguridad *f*.
in·sem·i·nate (ĭn-sĕm'ə-nāt') tr. inseminar.
in·sem·i·na·tion (-'nā'shən) s. inseminación *f*.
in·sen·sate (ĭn-sĕn'sāt') adj. insensible.
in·sen·si·ble (:sə-bəl) adj. insensible.
in·sen·si·tive (:sĭ-tĭv) adj. insensible.
in·sep·a·ra·ble (ĭn-sĕp'ər-ə-bəl) adj. inseparable.
in·sert (ĭn-sûrt') I. tr. *(into)* insertar, introducir; *(between)* intercalar II. s. ('') inserción *f*; *(page)* encarte *m*; COST. entredos *m*.
in·ser·tion (ĭn-sûr'shən) s. inserción *f*.
in·side (ĭn-sīd', '') I. s. interior *m*, parte *f* de adentro ♦ to be on the i. tener acceso a información confidencial • to know i. out conocer a fondo • to turn i. out volver al revés ♦ pl. FAM. entrañas, tripas II. adj. *(inner)* interior, interno; *(confidential)* confidencial, secreto ♦ i. job delito cometido por un empleado de la casa • i. track DEP. pista interior; FIG. ventaja III. adv. *(within)* dentro, adentro; *(on the inner side)* por dentro IV. prep. dentro de ♦ i. of FAM. dentro de.
in·sid·er (ĭn-sī'dər) s. miembro de un grupo; *(well-informed person)* persona enterada.
in·sid·i·ous (ĭn-sĭd'ē-əs) adj. insidioso.
in·sight (ĭn'sīt') s. perspicacia; *(revelation)* revelación *f*, idea.
in·sight·ful adj. perspicaz.
in·sig·ni·a (ĭn-sĭg'nē-ə) s. [pl. inv. o s] insignia.
in·sig·nif·i·cant (ĭn'sĭg-nĭf'ĭ-kənt) adj. insignificante.
in·sin·cere (ĭn'sĭn-sîr') adj. insincero.
in·sin·cer·i·ty (:sĕr'ĭ-tē) s. insinceridad *f*.
in·sin·u·ate (ĭn-sĭn'yōō-āt') tr. insinuar.
in·sip·id (ĭn-sĭp'ĭd) adj. insípido.
in·sist (ĭn-sĭst') intr. insistir ♦ to i. (up)on insistir en • to i. that insistir en que.
in·sis·tence (ĭn-sĭs'təns) s. insistencia.
in·sis·tent (:tənt) adj. insistente.
in·so·far as (ĭn'sō-fär' ăz) conj. en cuanto a, en la medida en que.
in·sole (ĭn'sōl') s. plantilla (del zapato).
in·so·lence (ĭn'sə-ləns) s. insolencia, descaro.
in·so·lent (:lənt) adj. insolente, descarado.
in·sol·u·ble (ĭn-sŏl'yə-bəl) adj. insoluble.
in·sol·vent (:vənt) adj. & s. insolvente *mf*.
in·som·ni·a (ĭn-sŏm'nē-ə) s. insomnio.
in·som·ni·ac (:ăk') adj. & s. *(persona)* insomne.
in·so·much as (ĭn'sō-mŭch' ăz) conj. ya que.
in·sou·ci·ant (ĭn-sōō'sē-ənt) adj. despreocupado.
in·spect (ĭn-spĕkt') tr. inspeccionar; MIL. pasar revista.
in·spec·tion (ĭn-spĕk'shən) s. inspección *f*; MIL. revista.
in·spec·tor (:tər) s. inspector *m*.
in·spi·ra·tion (ĭn'spə-rā'shən) s. inspiración *f* ♦ to be an i. to servir de ejemplo a.

in·spi·ra·tion·al (:shə-nəl) adj. inspirador.
in·spire (ĭn-spīr′) tr. inspirar, motivar; *(emotion)* suscitar, infundir ♦ **to i. with** infundir, llenar de.
in·spired (ĭn-spīrd′) adj. inspirado, de inspiración.
in·spir·ing (ĭn-spīr′ĭng) adj. inspirador.
in·sta·bil·i·ty (ĭn′stə-bĭl′ĭ-tē) s. inestabilidad *f.*
in·stall (ĭn-stôl′) tr. instalar.
in·stal·la·tion (ĭn′stə-lā′shən) s. instalación *f*; MIL. base *f.*
in·stall·ment (:mənt) s. *(payment)* plazo, pago; *(of a publication)* entrega ♦ **i. plan** pago a plazos • **monthly i.** mensualidad.
in·stance (ĭn′stəns) s. *(example)* ejemplo, muestra; *(case)* caso ♦ **for i.** por ejemplo • **in many instances** en muchos casos.
in·stant (ĭn′stənt) I. s. instante *m*, momento ♦ **the i. (that)** en cuanto • **this i.** al instante, en seguida II. adj. inmediato; *(urgent)* apremiante; *(food, success)* instantáneo ♦ **i. replay** repetición inmediata por videocinta.
in·stan·ta·ne·ous (ĭn′stən-tā′nē-əs) adj. instantáneo.
in·stant·ly (ĭn′stənt-lē) adv. instantáneamente, inmediatamente.
in·stead (ĭn-stĕd′) adv. en su lugar; *(rather than)* en cambio ♦ **i. of** en lugar de, en vez de.
in·step (ĭn′stĕp′) s. empeine *m.*
in·sti·gate (ĭn′stĭ-gāt′) tr. fomentar.
in·sti·ga·tion (′-gā′shən) s. instigación *f.*
in·sti·ga·tor (′-′tər) s. instigador *m.*
in·still (ĭn-stĭl′) tr. instilar.
in·stinct (ĭn′stĭngkt′) s. instinto.
in·stinc·tive (ĭn-stĭngk′tĭv) adj. instintivo.
in·sti·tute (ĭn′stĭ-tōōt′) I. tr. instituir, establecer; *(to initiate)* iniciar II. s. instituto.
in·sti·tu·tion (′-tōō′shən) s. institución *f*; *(asylum)* asilo; *(for the insane)* manicomio.
in·sti·tu·tion·al (:shə-nəl) adj. institucional ♦ **i. care** atención médica con asilo, manicomio).
in·sti·tu·tion·al·ize (:nə-līz′) tr. institucionalizar; *(a person)* meter en un asilo o manicomio.
in·struct (ĭn-strŭkt′) tr. instruir; *(to order)* dar instrucciones, mandar.
in·struc·tion (ĭn-strŭk′shən) s. instrucción *f.*
in·struc·tor (:tər) s. instructor *m.*
in·stru·ment (ĭn′strə-mənt) s. instrumento.
in·stru·men·tal (′-mĕn′tl) adj. instrumental ♦ **to be i.** in *o* to ayudar a, contribuir a.
in·sub·or·di·nate (ĭn′sə-bôr′dn-ĭt) adj. insubordinado.
in·sub·stan·tial (ĭn′səb-stăn′shəl) adj. insubstancial; *(flimsy)* flojo.
in·suf·fer·a·ble (ĭn-sŭf′ər-ə-bəl) adj. intolerable.
in·suf·fi·cient (ĭn′sə-f ĭsh′ənt) adj. insuficiente.
in·su·lar (ĭn′sə-lər) adj. insular; *(narrowminded)* estrecho de miras.
in·su·late (ĭn′sə-lāt′) tr. aislar.
in·su·la·tion (′-lā′shən) s. aislamiento; *(material)* aislador *m*, material *m* aislante.
in·su·lin (ĭn′sə-lĭn) s. insulina.
in·sult (ĭn-sŭlt′) I. tr. insultar II. s. (′′) insulto.
in·sult·ing (ĭn-sŭl′tĭng) adj. insultante.
in·sup·port·a·ble (ĭn′sə-pôr′tə-bəl) adj. insoportable; *(claim)* injustificable.
in·sur·a·ble (ĭn-shōōr′ə-bəl) adj. asegurable.
in·sur·ance (:əns) s. seguro; FIG. seguridad *f* ♦ **to take out i.** sacar(se) un seguro.
in·sure (ĭn-shōōr′) tr. asegurar.

in·sured (ĭn-shōōrd′) s. asegurado.
in·sur·er (ĭn-shōōr′ər) s. asegurador *m.*
in·sur·gence/·cy (ĭn-sûr′jəns) s. insurrección *f.*
in·sur·gent (:jənt) adj. & s. insurgente *mf.*
in·sur·mount·a·ble (ĭn′sər-moun′tə-bəl) adj. insuperable.
in·sur·rec·tion (ĭn′sə-rĕk′shən) s. insurrección *f.*
in·tact (ĭn-tăkt′) adj. intacto.
in·take (ĭn′tāk′) s. entrada, toma; *(valve)* admisión *f.*
in·tan·gi·ble (ĭn-tăn′jə-bəl) adj. & s. *(cosa)* intangible.
in·te·ger (ĭn′tĭ-jər) s. (número) entero.
in·te·gral (ĭn′tĭ-grəl) I. adj. integral; *(part)* integrante II. s. integral *f.*
in·te·grate (:grāt′) tr. & intr. integrar(se).
in·te·grat·ed (:grā′tĭd) adj. integrado.
in·te·gra·tion (′-′shən) s. integración *f.*
in·teg·ri·ty (ĭn-tĕg′rĭ-tē) s. integridad *f.*
in·tel·lect (ĭn′tl-ĕkt′) s. intelecto.
in·tel·lec·tu·al (′-ĕk′chōō-əl) adj. & s. intelectual *mf.*
in·tel·lec·tu·al·ize (:ə-līz′) tr. intelectualizar.
in·tel·li·gence (ĭn-tĕl′ĭ-jəns) s. inteligencia; *(information)* información secreta.
in·tel·li·gent (:jənt) adj. inteligente.
in·tel·li·gent·si·a (-′-jĕnt′sē-ə) s. intelectualidad *f.*
in·tel·li·gi·ble (-′jə-bəl) adj. inteligible.
in·tem·per·ate (ĭn-tĕm′pər-ĭt) adj. intemperante; *(climate)* inclemente.
in·tend (ĭn-tĕnd′) tr. *(to plan)* proponerse, tener la intención (de); *(to contemplate)* pensar; *(to mean)* querer decir.
in·tend·ed (ĭn-tĕn′dĭd) I. adj. *(planned)* proyectado; *(intentional)* deliberado; *(future)* futuro ♦ **i. for** destinado a, para; *(remark)* dirigido a II. s. FAM. prometido, -a.
in·tense (ĭn-tĕns′) adj. intenso.
in·ten·si·fy (ĭn-tĕn′sə-f ī′) tr. & intr. intensificar(se), aumentar(se).
in·ten·si·ty (:sĭ-tē) s. intensidad *f.*
in·ten·sive (:sĭv) adj. intensivo.
in·tent (ĭn-tĕnt′) I. s. *(purpose)* intención *f*, propósito; *(meaning)* sentido ♦ **for all intents and purposes** en efecto II. adj. fijo ♦ **i. (up)on** resuelto a.
in·ten·tion (ĭn-tĕn′shən) s. intención *f*, propósito ♦ **to be one's i.** proponerse.
in·ten·tion·al (:shə-nəl) adj. intencional.
in·ter (ĭn-tûr′) tr. -rr- enterrar.
in·ter·act (ĭn′tər-ăkt′) intr. actuar recíprocamente, influenciar uno a otro.
in·ter·ac·tion (:ăk′shən) s. interacción *f.*
in·ter·breed (:brēd′) tr. & intr. -bred cruzar(se) animales de especie diferente.
in·ter·cede (:sēd′) intr. interceder.
in·ter·cept (ĭn′tər-sĕpt′) tr. interceptar.
in·ter·cep·tion (:sĕp′shən) s. interceptación *f.*
in·ter·ces·sion (:sĕsh′ən) s. intercesión *f.*
in·ter·change (:chānj′) I. tr. intercambiar; *(places)* alternar II. s. (′-′) intercambio; *(highway junction)* empalme *m.*
in·ter·change·a·ble (:chān′jə-bəl) adj. intercambiable.
in·ter·col·le·giate (:kə-lē′jĭt) adj. interuniversitario.
in·ter·com (′-kŏm′) s. sistema *m* de intercomunicación.
in·ter·con·nect (′-kə-nĕkt′) intr. & tr. conectar.
in·ter·con·nec·tion (:kə-nĕk′shən) s. inter-

conexión f.

in·ter·course ('-kôrs') s. relaciones f sociales; *(trade)* comercio, tráfico; *(coitus)* coito.

in·ter·de·pend·ent ('-dĭ-pĕn'dənt) adj. interdependiente.

in·ter·dict (:dĭkt') interdecir, prohibir.

in·ter·est (ĭn'trĭst, ĭn'tər-ĭst) I. s. interés m; *(benefit)* beneficio; COM. *(share)* acción f; *(on money)* interés ♦ **in one's own i.** en beneficio propio • **to be in one's best i.** to ser mejor para uno que • **to be of i.** ser interesante • **to take an i. in** interesarse por II. tr. interesar ♦ **to i. someone in** hacer que alguien se interese en o por.

in·ter·est·ed (ĭn'trĭ-stĭd, ĭn'tər-ĭ-) adj. interesado ♦ **to be i.** in interesarle a uno.

in·ter·est·ing (:stĭng) adj. interesante.

in·ter·fere (ĭn'tər-fîr') intr. interferir; *(to meddle)* entrometerse ♦ **to i. with** obstruir, impedir.

in·ter·fer·ence (:əns) s. interferencia.

in·ter·im (ĭn'tər-ĭm) I. s. interín m II. adj. interino, provisional.

in·te·ri·or (ĭn-tîr'ē-ər) adj. & s. interior m.

in·ter·ject (ĭn'tər-jĕkt') tr. interponer.

in·ter·jec·tion (:jĕk'shən) s. interposición f; GRAM. interjección f.

in·ter·lock (:lŏk') intr. trabarse.

in·ter·loc·u·tor (:lŏk'yə-tər) s. interlocutor m.

in·ter·lop·er (ĭn'tər-lō'pər) s. entrometido.

in·ter·lude (:lŏōd') s. intermedio; TEAT. entremés m.

in·ter·mar·ry ('-măr'ē) intr. *(races, religions)* casarse personas de distintos grupos; *(family)* casarse entre parientes.

in·ter·me·di·ar·y (:mē'dē-ĕr'ē) s. intermediario.

in·ter·me·di·ate (:ĭt) I. adj. intermedio II. s. intermediario.

in·ter·ment (ĭn-tûr'mənt) s. entierro.

in·ter·mi·na·ble (ĭn-tûr'mə-nə-bəl) adj. interminable.

in·ter·mis·sion (ĭn'tər-mĭsh'ən) s. intermisión f; TEAT. intermedio, entreacto.

in·ter·mit·tent (:mĭt'nt) adj. intermitente.

in·tern (ĭn'tûrn') I. s. interno, médico residente II. intr. (-') trabajar como interno —tr. internar, recluir (esp. en tiempo de guerra).

in·ter·nal (ĭn-tûr'nəl) adj. interno; *(domestic)* interior, nacional ♦ **i. revenue** rentas públicas.

in·ter·nal-com·bus·tion engine (:kəm-bŭs'-chən) s. motor m de explosión.

in·ter·nal·ize (:nə-līz') tr. hacer interno.

in·ter·na·tion·al (ĭn'tər-năsh'ə-nəl) adj. internacional.

in·ter·na·tion·al·ize (:nə-līz') tr. internacionalizar.

in·ter·nist (ĭn-tûr'nĭst) s. internista mf.

in·tern·ment (ĭn-tûrn'mənt) s. internamiento.

in·ter·of·fice (ĭn'tər-ô'fĭs) adj. interno.

in·ter·per·son·al (:pûr'sə-nəl) adj. personal.

in·ter·play ('-plā') s. interacción f.

in·ter·po·late (ĭn-tûr'pə-lāt') tr. interpolar.

in·ter·pose (ĭn'tər-pōz') tr. & intr. interponer(se).

in·ter·pret (ĭn-tûr'prĭt) tr. interpretar —intr. servir de intérprete.

in·ter·pre·ta·tion ('-prĭ-tā'shən) s. interpretación f ♦ **to bear a different i.** poder entenderse de otro modo.

in·ter·pret·er (:tər) s. intérprete mf.

in·ter·pre·tive (:tĭv) adj. interpretativo.

in·ter·ra·cial (ĭn'tər-rā'shəl) adj. entre las razas.

in·ter·re·lat·ed (ĭn'tər-rĭ-lā'tĭd) adj. correlativo, mutuamente relacionado.

in·ter·ro·gate (ĭn-tĕr'ə-gāt') tr. interrogar.

in·ter·ro·ga·tion (-'gā'shən) s. interrogación f; *(close questioning)* interrogatorio.

in·ter·rog·a·tive (ĭn'tə-rŏg'ə-tĭv) adj. & s. interrogativo.

in·ter·ro·ga·tor (ĭn-tĕr'ə-gā'tər) s. interrogador m.

in·ter·rupt (ĭn'tə-rŭpt') tr. interrumpir.

in·ter·rup·tion (:rŭp'shən) s. interrupción f.

in·ter·sect (ĭn'tər-sĕkt') tr. *(to cut)* cruzar; *(to cross)* cruzarse con —intr. cruzarse.

in·ter·sec·tion (:sĕk'shən) s. intersección f; *(of streets)* bocacalle f; *(of roads)* cruce m.

in·ter·sperse (:spûrs') tr. *(to distribute)* entreverar, entremezclar; *(to scatter)* salpicar.

in·ter·state (:stāt') adj. entre estados o provincias ♦ **i. highway** carretera nacional.

in·ter·twine (:twīn') tr. & intr. entrelazar(se), entretejer(se).

in·ter·val (ĭn'tər-vəl) s. intervalo ♦ **at intervals** a ratos • **at regular intervals** con regularidad.

in·ter·vene (ĭn'tər-vēn') intr. intervenir.

in·ter·ven·tion (:vĕn'shən) s. intervención f.

in·ter·view (ĭn'tər-vyōō') I. s. entrevista II. tr. & intr. entrevistar(se).

in·ter·view·er (:ər) s. entrevistador m.

in·ter·weave (ĭn'tər-wēv') tr. & intr. **-wove, -woven** entretejer(se).

in·tes·ta·cy (ĭn-tĕs'tə-sē) s. falta de testamento.

in·tes·tate (:tāt') adj. & s. intestado.

in·tes·ti·nal (ĭn-tĕs'tə-nəl) adj. intestinal.

in·tes·tine (:tĭn) s. intestino ♦ **large, small i.** intestino grueso, delgado.

in·ti·ma·cy (ĭn'tə-mə-sē) s. intimidad f.

in·ti·mate¹ (ĭn'tə-mĭt) adj. & s. íntimo ♦ **to become i.** intimar.

in·ti·mate² (:māt') tr. dar a entender, insinuar.

in·tim·i·date (ĭn-tĭm'ĭ-dāt') tr. intimidar.

in·tim·i·da·tion (-'dā'shən) s. intimidación f.

in·ti·ma·tion (ĭn'tə-mā'shən) s. insinuación f.

in·to (ĭn'tōō) prep. en, a, dentro de, contra ♦ **well i.** bien entrado o avanzado.

in·tol·er·a·ble (ĭn-tŏl'ər-ə-bəl) adj. intolerable.

in·tol·er·ant (:ənt) adj. intolerante ♦ **to be i. of** no poder tolerar.

in·to·na·tion (ĭn'tə-nā'shən) s. entonación f.

in·tone (ĭn-tōn') tr. recitar melódicamente.

in·tox·i·cate (ĭn-tŏk'sĭ-kāt') tr. embriagar.

in·tox·i·ca·tion (-'kā'shən) s. embriaguez f.

in·trac·ta·ble (ĭn-trăk'tə-bəl) adj. intratable, obstinado; MED. rebelde.

in·tran·si·gent (ĭn-trăn'sə-jənt) adj. intransigente.

in·tran·si·tive (ĭn-trăn'sĭ-tĭv) adj. & s. (verbo) intransitivo.

in·tra·ve·nous (ĭn'trə-vē'nəs) adj. intravenoso.

in·trep·id (ĭn-trĕp'ĭd) adj. intrépido.

in·tri·ca·cy (ĭn'trĭ-kə-sē) s. complejidad f.

in·tri·cate (:kĭt) adj. complejo, intrincado.

in·trigue (ĭn'trēg') I. s. intriga; *(love affair)* amorío secreto II. intr. & tr. (-') intrigar.

in·trigu·er (ĭn-trē'gər) s. intrigante mf.

in·trin·sic (ĭn-trĭn'sĭk) adj. intrínseco.

in·tro·duce (ĭn'trə-dōōs') tr. presentar; *(to insert, bring into use)* introducir; *(a product)* lanzar al mercado; *(a topic)* sacar a colación; *(to initiate)* familiarizar (to con); *(into a new surrounding)* traer; *(to preface)* prologar.

in·tro·duc·tion (:dŭk'shən) s. introducción f; *(of people)* presentación f; *(of a product)* lanza-

invento.

in·tro·duc·to·ry (:tə-rē) adj. preliminar.

in·tro·mis·sion (ĭn'trə-mĭsh'ən) s. inserción f.

in·tro·spec·tion (:spĕk'shən) s. introspección f.

in·tro·spec·tive (:tĭv) adj. introspectivo.

in·tro·vert (ĭn'trə-vûrt') s. introvertido.

in·tro·vert·ed (·vûr'tĭd) adj. introvertido.

in·trude (ĭn-trōōd') tr. meter por fuerza (en) —intr. *(to meddle)* inmiscuirse, entrometerse; *(to interrupt)* molestar, interrumpir.

in·trud·er (ĭn-trōō'dər) s. intruso.

in·tru·sion (:zhən) s. intrusión f; *(invasion)* invasión f; *(imposition)* molestia.

in·tru·sive (:sĭv) adj. intruso.

in·tu·it (ĭn-tōō'ĭt) tr. intuir.

in·tu·i·tion ('-ĭsh'ən) s. intuición f.

in·tu·i·tive (-'ĭ-tĭv) adj. intuitivo.

in·un·date (ĭn'ŭn-dāt') tr. inundar.

in·un·da·tion (:dā'shən) s. inundación f.

in·ure (ĭn-yŏŏr') tr. curtir, endurecer.

in·vade (ĭn-vād') tr. invadir; *(privacy)* no respetar; *(rights)* violar —intr. hacer una invasión.

in·vad·er (ĭn-vā'dər) s. invasor m.

in·va·lid¹ (ĭn'və-lĭd) adj. & s. inválido.

in·val·id² (ĭn-văl'ĭd) adj. nulo, inválido; *(faulty)* defectuoso, imperfecto.

in·val·i·date (:ĭ-dāt') tr. invalidar.

in·val·i·da·tion (-'-dā'shən) s. invalidación f.

in·va·lid·i·ty (ĭn-və-lĭd'ĭ-tē) s. nulidad f.

in·val·u·a·ble (ĭn-văl'yŏō-ə-bəl) adj. inestimable.

in·var·i·a·ble (ĭn-vâr'ē-ə-bəl) adj. invariable.

in·va·sion (ĭn-vā'zhən) s. invasión f; *(of privacy)* entrometimiento; *(of rights)* transgresión f.

in·vec·tive (ĭn-vĕk'tĭv) s. invectiva, vituperio.

in·veigh (ĭn-vā') intr. ♦ **to i. against** vituperar.

in·vei·gle (ĭn-vā') tr. sonsacar.

in·vent (ĭn vĕnt') tr. inventar.

in·ven·tion (ĭn vĕn'shən) s. invención f; *(new device)* invento; *(skill)* inventiva.

in·ven·tive (:tĭv) adj. inventivo.

in·ven·tor (:tər) s. inventor m.

in·ven·to·ry (ĭn'vən-tôr'ē) I. s. inventario; *(stock)* existencias II. tr. inventariar.

in·verse (ĭn'vûrs') adj. & s. (lo) inverso.

in·ver·sion (ĭn-vûr'zhən) s. inversión f.

in·vert (ĭn-vûrt') tr. invertir.

in·ver·te·brate (ĭn-vûr'tə-brĭt) adj. & s. invertebrado.

in·vest (ĭn-vĕst') tr. *(money)* invertir; *(effort)* dedicar; *(to endow)* conferir; *(to install in office)* investir —intr. hacer una inversión.

in·ves·ti·gate (ĭn-vĕs'tĭ-gāt') tr. investigar.

in·ves·ti·ga·tion ('-gā'shən) s. investigación f.

in·ves·ti·ga·tive (-'-tĭv) adj. de investigación.

in·ves·ti·ga·tor (:tər) s. investigador m.

in·ves·ti·ture (ĭn-vĕs'tĭ-chŏŏr') s. investidura f.

in·vest·ment (ĭn-vĕst'mənt) s. inversión f.

in·ves·tor (ĭn-vĕs'tər) s. inversionista mf.

in·vet·er·ate (ĭn-vĕt'ər-ĭt) adj. *(deep-rooted)* inveterado; *(confirmed)* incorregible.

in·vid·i·ous (ĭn-vĭd'ē-əs) adj. provocador.

in·vig·o·rate (ĭn-vĭg'ə-rāt') tr. dar vigor a.

in·vin·ci·ble (ĭn-vĭn'sə-bəl) adj. invencible.

in·vi·o·la·ble (ĭn-vī'ə-lə-bəl) adj. inviolable.

in·vi·o·late (:lĭt) adj. inviolado.

in·vis·i·ble (ĭn-vĭz'ə-bəl) adj. invisible ♦ **i. ink** tinta simpática.

in·vi·ta·tion (ĭn'vĭ-tā'shən) s. invitación f.

in·vite I. tr. (ĭn-vīt') invitar; *(for food, drink)* convidar; *(a response)* solicitar; *(trouble)* provocar, buscar II. s. (") FAM. invitación f.

in·vit·ing (ĭn-vī'tĭng) adj. atrayente, tentador.

in·vo·ca·tion (ĭn'və-kā'shən) s. invocación f.

in·voice (ĭn'vois') I. factura II. tr. facturar.

in·voke (ĭn-vōk') tr. invocar.

in·vol·un·tar·y (ĭn-vŏl'ən-tĕr'ē) adj. involuntario.

in·vo·lu·tion (ĭn'və-lōō'shən) s. complicación f.

in·volve (ĭn-vŏlv') tr. *(to include)* comprender, incluir; *(to entail)* implicar, entrañar; *(in a matter)* comprometer, involucrar; *(to engross)* absorber; *(to complicate)* enredar.

in·volved (ĭn-vŏlvd') adj. complicado, enredado ♦ **to be i. in** estar involucrado en • **to get i. in** meterse o involucrarse en.

in·volve·ment (ĭn-vŏlv'mənt) s. *(entanglement)* envolvimiento, comprometimiento; *(in a matter)* participación f; *(engrossment)* abstraimiento; *(intricateness)* intrincación f.

in·vul·ner·a·ble (ĭn-vŭl'nər-ə-bəl) adj. invulnerable.

in·ward (ĭn'wərd) I. adj. interior, interno II. adv. o **-wards** hacia adentro.

i·o·dine (ī'ə-dīn', :dĭn) s. yodo.

i·o·dize (ī'ə-dīz') tr. yodar.

i·on (ī'ən, ī'ŏn') s. ion m.

i·on·ic (ī-ŏn'ĭk) FÍS iónico, de los iones.

Ionic order s. ARQ. orden jónico.

i·on·ize (ī'ə-nīz') tr. & intr. ionizar(se).

i·o·ta (ī-ō'tə) s. iota; *(bit)* ápice m, pizca.

IOU (ī'ō-yōō') s. [pl. **s** o **'s**] pagaré m, vale m.

IQ o **I.Q.** (ī'kyōō') s. cociente m intelectual.

i·ras·ci·ble (ĭ-rǎs'ə-bəl) adj. irascible, iracundo.

i·rate (ī-rāt') adj. colérico, airado.

ire (īr) s. ira.

i·ri·des·cence (ĭr'ĭ-dĕs'əns) s. irisación f.

i·ri·des·cent (:ənt) adj. iridiscente, irisado.

i·ris (ī'rĭs) s. [pl. **es** o **irides**] *(of the eye)* iris m; BOT. lirio.

irk (ûrk) tr. irritar, sacar de quicio.

irk·some ('sŏm) adj. irritante.

i·ron (ī'ərn) I. s. hierro; *(for clothes)* plancha ♦ **I. Curtain** cortina de hierro • **i. horse** FAM. locomotora, ferrocarril • **i. lung** pulmón de acero • **i. ore** mineral de hierro ♦ pl. grilletes • **in i.** encadenado II. tr. & intr. planchar ♦ **to i. out** allanar, resolver.

i·ron·clad (:klǎd') I. adj. *(sheathed)* acorazado, blindado; *(strict)* riguroso II. s. acorazado.

i·ron·ic/i·cal (ī-rŏn'ĭk) adj. irónico.

i·ron·ing (ī'ər-nĭng) s. planchado ♦ **i. board** tabla de planchar.

i·ro·ny (ī'rə-nē) s. ironía.

ir·ra·di·ate (ĭ-rā'dē-āt') tr. irradiar.

ir·ra·di·a·tion (-'-ā'shən) s. irradiación f.

ir·ra·tion·al (ĭ-rǎsh'ə-nəl) adj. irracional.

ir·rec·on·cil·a·ble (ĭ-rĕk'ən-sī'lə-bəl) adj. *(differences)* insuperable; *(ideas)* inconciliable.

ir·re·cov·er·a·ble (ĭr'ĭ-kŭv'ər-ə-bəl) adj. irrecuperable; *(irreparable)* irreparable.

ir·re·deem·a·ble (ĭr'ĭ-dē'mə-bəl) adj. *(loan)* irredimible; *(situation)* irremediable.

ir·re·duc·i·ble (ĭr'ĭ-dōō'sə-bəl) adj. irreducible.

ir·ref·u·ta·ble (ĭ-rĕf'yə-tə-bəl) adj. irrefutable.

ir·reg·u·lar (ĭ-rĕg'yə-lər) I. adj. irregular; *(uneven)* desigual; *(merchandise)* imperfecto II. s. soldado irregular.

ir·reg·u·lar·i·ty (-'-lǎr'ĭ-tē) s. irregularidad f; *(of a surface)* desigualdad f; MED. estreñimiento.

ir·rel·e·vance/cy (ĭ-rĕl'ə-vəns) s. improcedencia, falta de pertinencia.

ir·rel·e·vant (:vənt) adj. inaplicable, improcedente ♦ **to be i.** no venir al caso ♦ **to be i. to** no tener nada que ver con.

ir·re·lig·ious (ĭr'ĭ-lĭj'əs) adj. irreligioso.

ir·re·me·di·a·ble (ĭr'ĭ-mē'dē-ə-bəl) adj. irremediable.

ir·rep·a·ra·ble (ĭ-rĕp'ər-ə-bəl) adj. irreparable.

ir·re·place·a·ble (ĭr'ĭ-plā'sə-bəl) adj. irreemplazable.

ir·re·pres·si·ble (ĭr'ĭ-prĕs'ə-bəl) adj. incontenible.

ir·re·proach·a·ble (ĭr'ĭ-prō'chə-bəl) adj. irreprochable, intachable.

ir·re·sist·i·ble (ĭr'ĭ-zĭs'tə-bəl) adj. irresistible.

ir·res·o·lute (ĭ-rĕz'ə-lōōt') adj. irresoluto.

ir·re·spec·tive (ĭr'ĭ-spĕk'tĭv) adj. ♦ **i. of** sin tener en cuenta, no obstante.

ir·re·spon·si·bil·i·ty (ĭr'ĭ-spŏn'sə-bĭl'ĭ-tē) s. irresponsabilidad f.

ir·re·spon·si·ble ('-'-bəl) adj. irresponsable.

ir·re·triev·a·ble (ĭr'ĭ-trē'və-bəl) adj. (not recoverable) irrecuperable; (mistake) irreparable.

ir·rev·er·ence (ĭ-rĕv'ər-əns) s. irreverencia.

ir·rev·er·ent (:ənt) adj. irreverente.

ir·re·vers·i·ble (ĭr'ĭ-vûr'sə-bəl) adj. irreversible; (damage) irreparable; (decision) irrevocable.

ir·rev·o·ca·ble (ĭ-rĕv'ə-kə-bəl) adj. irrevocable.

ir·ri·gate (ĭr'ĭ-gāt') tr. irrigar.

ir·ri·ga·tion ('-gā'shən) s. irrigación f.

ir·ri·ta·ble (ĭr'ĭ-tə-bəl) adj. irritable.

ir·ri·tant (:tnt) adj. & s. (substancia) irritante.

ir·ri·tate (:tāt') tr. irritar.

ir·ri·tat·ing (:tā'tĭng) adj. irritante, molesto.

ir·ri·ta·tion ('-tā'shən) s. irritación f.

ir·rupt (ĭ-rŭpt') tr. irrumpir.

ir·rup·tion (ĭ-rŭp'shən) s. irrupción f.

is (ĭz) tercera persona sg. de **be.**

Is·lam·ic (ĭs-läm'ĭk, ĭz-) s.) islámico.

is·land (ī'lənd) s. isla; (in a street) isleta.

isle (īl) s. isla; (islet) isleta.

is·let (ī'lĭt) s. isleta, islote m.

i·so·late (ī'sə-lāt') tr. aislar; (a prisoner) incomunicar.

i·so·la·tion (:lā'shən) s. aislamiento; (in prison) incomunicación f; (quarantine) cuarentena

i·so·la·tion·ist (:shə-nĭst) s. aislacionista mf.

i·so·mer (ī'sə-mər) s. isómero.

i·sos·ce·les (ī-sŏs'ə-lēz') adj. isósceles.

i·so·tope (ī'sə-tōp') s. isótopo.

is·su·ance (ĭsh'ōō-əns) s. emisión f.

is·sue (ĭsh'ōō) I. s. (money, stamps) emisión f; (edition) tirada; (copy) número; (result) consecuencia; (offspring) progenie f; (point under discussion) punto, cuestión f; (problem) problema m; (outlet) salida ♦ **at i.** en discusión • **to force the i.** forzar una decisión • **to raise the i.** de plantear el problema de • **to take i. with** estar en desacuerdo con II. intr. salir; (to emanate) surgir de; (to result) resultar (from de, in en) —tr. (to distribute) repartir; (to publish) publicar; (orders) dar; (decree) promulgar; (stamps, money) emitir.

isth·mus (ĭs'məs) s. istmo.

it (ĭt) pron. lo, la <do you know this song? yes, I know it ¿conoces esta canción? sí, la conozco>; le <give it a push dale un empujón>; ello, eso <we thought about it pensábamos en eso>; (not translated) él, ella, ello <has the mail come? yes, it just arrived ¿ha llegado el correo? sí, acaba de llegar> ♦ **it is cold** hace frío • **it is good es**

bueno • **it is snowing** está nevando.

i·tal·ic (ĭ-tăl'ĭk, ī-tăl'-) s. & adj. cursiva.

i·tal·i·cize (:ī-sīz') tr. imprimir en cursiva.

itch (ĭch) I. s. picazón f; (rash) sarna; (desire) comezón f ♦ **to have an i.** to tener el prurito de II. intr. picar <my ear itches me pica el oído> ♦ **to be itching** to estar desesperado por —tr. dar picazón; (to scratch) rascarse.

itch·y (:ē) adj. **-i-** que da picazón; (restless) impaciente.

i·tem (ī'təm) s. artículo; (on an agenda) punto; (of a document) ítem m; (of a form) casilla; TEN. (entry) partida; (of information) detalle m.

i·tem·ize (ī'tə-mīz') tr. enumerar, detallar.

it·er·ate (ĭt'ə-rāt') tr. iterar, repetir.

i·tin·er·ant (ī-tĭn'ər-ənt) adj. & s. (persona) ambulante.

i·tin·er·ar·y (:ə-rĕr'ē) s. itinerario.

its (ĭts) adj. pos. su.

it·self (ĭt-sĕlf') pron. se <it turns i. off automatically se apaga automáticamente>; sí mismo <the cat saw i. in the mirror el gato se vio a sí mismo en el espejo>; sólo <the yarn i. cost $20 la lana sóla cuesta 20 dólares>; mismo <the trouble is in the motor i. el problema es el motor mismo> ♦ **(all) by i.** solo • **of** o **in i.** de sí.

i·vo·ry (ī'və-rē) s. marfil m ♦ **i. tower** torre de marfil ♦ pl. FAM. (piano keys) teclas; (teeth) colmillos.

i·vy (ī'vē) s. hiedra, yedra.

J

J, j (jā) s. décima letra del alfabeto inglés.

jab (jăb) I. tr. **-bb-** (to poke) hurgonear; (to stab) clavar; (to punch) golpear; (with the elbow) dar un codazo a —intr. ♦ **to j.** at asestar un golpe rápido a II. s. (prick) pinchazo; (with the elbow) codazo; (punch) golpe corto.

jab·ber (jăb'ər) I. intr. parlotear, farfullar II. s. parloteo, farfulla.

jack (jăk) I. s. (in cards) sota; (jackass) burro; (flag) pabellón m; FAM. (fellow) tipo, tío; ELEC. toma de corriente; MEC. gato, cric m ♦ **j. rabbit** liebre norteamericana ♦ pl. tabas II. tr. ♦ **to j. up** alzar con el gato; FAM. (prices) aumentar.

jack·al (jăk'əl) s. chacal m.

jack·ass (jăk'ăs') s. asno, burro.

jack·et (jăk'ĭt) s. saco, chaqueta; (covering) cubierta; (of a book) sobrecubierta; (of a record) envoltura.

jack·ham·mer (jăk'hăm'ər) s. perforadora neumática.

jack-in-the-box ('ĭn-thə-bŏks') s. caja de sorpresa (con muñeco de resorte).

jack·knife (:nīf') I. s. [pl. **-ves**] navaja, cortaplumas m; (dive) salto de carpa II. intr. doblarse como una navaja.

jack-of-all-trades (' əv-ôl'trădz') s. [pl. **jacks-**] persona de muchos oficios.

jack-o'-lantern ('ə-lăn'tərn) s. lámpara hecha con una calabaza o zapallo.

jack·pot (:pŏt') s. premio gordo ♦ **to hit the j.** sacarse el premio gordo; FIG. tener gran suerte.

jade¹ (jād) s. MIN. jade m.

jade² I. s. (horse) jamelgo II. tr. agotar.

jad·ed (jā'dĭd) adj. (wearied) agotado; (sated) harto; (cynical) cínico.

jag¹ (jăg) s. (sharp point) punta saliente

jag² s. FAM. juerga ♦ **to go on a j.** ir de juerga.

jag·ged (jăg'ĭd) adj. *(notched)* dentado, mellado; *(uneven)* cortado irregularmente.

jag·uar (jăg'wär') s. jaguar m.

jai a·lai (hī' lī', hī' ə-lī') s. jai alai m.

jail (jāl) I. s. cárcel f II. tr. encarcelar.

jai·ler/or (jā'lər) s. carcelero.

ja·lop·y (jə-lŏp'ē) s. FAM. cacharro.

ja·lou·sie (jăl'ə-sē) s. celosía.

jam¹ (jăm) I. tr. **-mm-** *(to lock)* trabar, atascar; *(to fill, crowd)* atestar; *(to clog)* atorar; *(one's finger)* pillarse; RAD. causar interferencias en **• jammed with** atestado *o* atiborrado de **• to j.** in apretar, forzar **• to j. on the brakes** frenar en seco intr. atascarse, trabarse; *(firearm)* encasquillarse; *(brakes)* agarrotarse; MÚS. improvisar II. s. *(blockage)* atasco; *(congestion)* aprieto **• j. session** sesión de jazz improvisado **• to be in a j.** FAM. estar en un apuro *o* aprieto.

jam² s. CUL. mermelada.

jamb (jăm) s. jamba.

jan·gle (jăng'gəl) I. tr. & intr. (hacer) sonar de modo discordante **• to j. one's nerves** irritar a uno II. s. sonido metálico discordante.

jan·i·tor (jăn'ĭ-tər) s. empleado de limpieza.

Jan·u·ar·y (jăn'yōō-ĕr'ē) s. enero.

jar¹ (jär) s. *(jug)* jarra; *(pot)* tarro, pote m.

jar² I. tr. **-rr-** *(to squeal, grate)* chirriar; *(to shake)* sacudirse **• to j.** on one's nerves ponerle a uno los nervios de punta **• to j.** with no concordar con —tr. sacudir; *(to startle)* estremecer **• to j. one's nerves** irritar II. s. *(jolt, shock)* choque m; *(harsh sound)* chirrido.

jar·gon (jär'gən) s. jerga.

jas·mine (jăz'mĭn) s. jazmín m.

jaun·dice (jôn'dĭs) s. ictericia.

jaunt (jônt) I. s. paseo, excursión f II. intr. ir de paseo *o* de excursión.

jaunt·y (jôn'tē) adj. **-i-** *(sprightly)* vivaz; *(self confident)* desenvuelto; *(stylish)* apuesto.

jave·lin (jăv'lən) s. jabalina.

jaw (jô) I. s. mandíbula, quijada; JER. *(back talk)* réplica insolente **•** pl. boca **• the j. of death** las garras de la muerte II. intr. JER. chacharear.

jay (jā) s. arrendajo.

jay·walk (jā'wôk') intr. cruzar la calle sin prudencia.

jay·walk·er (-ər) s. peatón m imprudente.

jazz (jăz) I. s. jazz m; JER. palabrería, cuentos **• all that j.** FAM. la mar de cosas II. tr. **• to j. up** FAM. avivar, animar.

jaz·zy (-ē) adj. **-i-** de jazz, sincopado; JER. *(showy)* llamativo.

jea·lous (jĕl'əs) adj. celoso; *(suspicious)* receloso; *(envious)* envidioso **• to be j.** of tener celos de.

jeal·ous·y (-ə-sē) s. celos m, envidia.

jeans (jēns) s. pantalones vaqueros.

jeer (jîr) I. intr. *(to mock)* mofarse, burlarse *(at de)*; *(to boo)* abuchear —tr. insultar II. s. *(mockery)* mofa, burla; *(boo)* abucheo.

jell (jĕl) tr. & intr. coagular(se), cuajar(se); FAM. *(idea, plan)* formar(se).

jel·ly (jĕl'ē) I. s. jalea II. tr. & intr. convertir(se) en jalea.

jel·ly·bean (:bēn') s. confite m de goma.

jel·ly·fish (:fĭsh') s. [pl. inv. *o* **es**] medusa.

jeop·ard·ize (jĕp'ər-dīz') tr. poner en peligro.

jeop·ard·y (:dē) s. riesgo, peligro.

jerk¹ (jûrk) I. tr. dar un tirón a, tironear de —intr. *(to jolt)* moverse a sacudidas; *(to twitch)* moverse espasmódicamente II. s. *(yank)* tirón

m, sacudida; *(twitch)* espasmo; FAM. *(fool)* idiota mf, estúpido.

jerk² tr. CUL. tasajear, charquear.

jerk·y¹ (jûr'kē) adj. **-i-** espasmódico; *(uneven)* desigual; *(ride)* zarandeado.

jerk·y² s. CUL. tasajo, charqui m.

jer·ry-build (jĕr'ē-bĭld') tr. **-built** construir rápidamente y con mala calidad.

jer·sey (jûr'zē) s. *(fabric)* tejido de jersey; *(garment)* jersey m.

jest (jĕst) I. s. chiste m, broma **• in j.** en broma II. intr. bromear, chancear.

jes·ter (jĕs'tər) s. bufón m, bromista mf.

jet¹ (jĕt) s. MIN. azabache m **• j. black** azabachado.

jet² I. s. *(spurt)* chorro; *(nozzle)* boquilla; *(airplane)* jet m, avión m a reacción; *(engine)* reactor m **• j. lag** cansancio causado por viajar larga distancia en avión II. intr. **-tt-** volar en jet; *(to spurt)* salir a chorro.

jet·lin·er s. ('lī'nər) avión m de pasajeros a reacción.

jet-pro·pelled (':prə-pĕld') adj. propulsado por motor a chorro.

jet·ti·son (jĕt'ĭ-sən) tr. *(cargo)* echar al mar; FIG. *(to discard)* desechar.

jet·ty (jĕt'ē) s. desembarcadero, muelle m.

Jew (jōō) s. judío.

jew·el (jōō'əl) I. s. joya, alhaja; *(gem)* gema; *(in watches)* rubí m. II. tr. enjoyar, alhajar.

jew·el·(l)er (:ə-lər) s. joyero **• j.'s** joyería.

jew·el·ry (:əl-rē) s. joyas, alhajas.

Jew·ess (jōō'ĭs) s. judía.

Jew·ish (:ĭsh) adj. judío.

jib¹ (jĭb) s. MARÍT. foque m; MEC. aguilón m.

jib² intr. **-bb-** resistirse.

jibe¹ (jīb) intr. FAM. concordar.

jibe² var. de **gibe**.

jif·fy (jĭf'ē) *o* **jiff** (jĭf) s. FAM. **• in a j.** en un santiamén.

jig (jĭg) I. s. *(dance)* giga; MEC. patrón m, guía **• the j. is up** JER. se acabó la fiesta II. intr. **-gg-** bailar la giga; *(to bob)* andar a saltitos.

jig·ger¹ (jĭg'ər) s. medida para licores; *(gadget)* chuchería, chisme m.

jig·ger² s. ENTOM. nigua.

jig·gle (jĭg'əl) I. tr. & intr. zangolotear(se), menear(se) II. s. zangoloteo, meneo.

jig·saw (jĭg'sô') s. sierra de vaivén **• j. puzzle** rompecabezas.

jilt (jĭlt) tr. dejar plantado, dar calabazas.

jim·my (jĭm'ē) I. s. palanca II. tr. forzar con una palanca.

jin·gle (jĭng'gəl) I. tr. & intr. (hacer) cascabelear *o* tintinear II. s. cascabeleo, tintineo; *(ad)* anuncio rimado y cantado.

jinx (jĭngks) FAM. I. s. *(person, object)* gafe m, cenizo; *(condition)* mala suerte II. tr. traer mala suerte a.

jit·ter (jĭt'ər) I. intr. estar inquieto II. s. **•** pl. nerviosismo **• to give someone the j.** poner nervioso a alguien **• to have the j.** estar nervioso.

jit·ter·y (:ə-rē) adj. **-i-** FAM. nervioso.

jive (jīv) s. JER., MÚS. jazz m; *(jargon)* jerga de los músicos de jazz; *(empty talk)* cháchara.

job (jŏb) s. *(task)* tarea; *(work)* obra, trabajo; *(employment)* empleo <*to look for a j.* buscar un empleo>; *(responsibility)* deber m, responsabilidad f; JER. *(robbery)* golpe m **• by the j.** a destajo **• j. action** huelga **• on the j.**

FAM. en su puesto, vigilante • **to be out of a j.** estar sin trabajo • **to do a j. on** FAM. dañar, arruinar II. intr. **-bb-** *(to do piecework)* trabajar a destajo; *(as a jobber)* trabajar como intermediario —tr. ♦ **to j. out** dar a destajo.

job·ber ('ər) s. intermediario.

job·hold·er (:hōl'dər) s. empleado.

job·less (:lĭs) adj. sin trabajo.

jock (jŏk) s. JER. atleta *m*.

jock·ey (jŏk'ē) I. s. jockey *mf* II. tr. montar (como jockey); FIG. maniobrar, manipular.

jock·strap (:străp) s. suspensorio *m*.

jo·cose (jō-kōs') adj. jocoso, divertido.

joc·u·lar (jŏk'yə-lər) adj. jocoso, humorístico.

jodh·purs (jŏd'pərz) s.pl. pantalones *m* de montar.

jog (jŏg) I. tr. **-gg-** *(to push)* empujar levemente; *(to nudge)* dar un codazo a; *(the memory)* refrescar —intr. *(to trot)* cabalgar a trote corto; *(to run)* correr despacio II. s. *(push)* empujoncito, codazo; *(slow pace)* paso lento.

jog·ger ('ər) s. persona que corre despacio para hacer ejercicio.

jog·gle (:əl) I. tr. sacudir ligeramente, traquetear II. s. sacudida, traqueteo.

john (jŏn) s. JER. *(toilet)* retrete *m*; *(customer)* cliente *m* (de una prostituta).

join (join) tr. juntar, unir; *(forces)* aunar; *(land)* lindar con; *(a cause)* abrazar; *(political party)* afiliarse a; *(church, club)* hacerse socio de; *(business firm)* entrar en; *(road, river)* dar o empalmar con; *(people)* encontrarse o reunirse con; MIL. alistarse en • **to j. forces with** aliarse con • **to j. hands** FIG. darse la manos • **to j. in marriage** unir en matrimonio • **to j. together** juntar —intr. juntarse, unirse; *(in marriage)* unirse; *(roads, lines)* empalmar; *(rivers)* confluir ♦ **to j. in** participar en ♦ **to j. up** MIL. alistarse • **to j. up with** reunirse con.

join·er (joi'nər) s. persona que se une a grupos o causas; G.B. *(carpenter)* ebanista *m*.

joint (joint) I. s. junta, unión *f*; ANAT. coyuntura; BOT. nudo; CUL. corte *m* para asar; JER. *(marijuana)* cigarrillo de marihuana; *(bar)* tugurio ♦ **out of j.** *(bone)* dislocado; *(disordered)* en desorden; *(grouchy)* de mal humor II. adj. (en) común; *(collective)* mutuo ♦ **j. ownership** propiedad en común III. tr. juntar, ensamblar.

joist (joist) s. viga.

joke (jōk) I. s. chiste *m*; *(amusing remark)* gracia <*not to get the j.* no verle la gracia>; *(prank)* broma <*he can't take a j.* él no sabe tomar una broma> ♦ **as a j.** en broma • **to crack a j.** decir un chiste • **to make a j. of** tomar en broma • **to play a j. on** hacerle una broma a II. intr. contar chistes, bromear ♦ **joking apart** bromas aparte • **to j. around** bromear • **you must be joking** tú estás bromeando.

jok·er (jō'kər) s. bromista *mf*; *(cards)* comodín *m*; FAM. *(clause)* cláusula engañadora; *(wise guy)* tío, sujeto.

jol·ly (jŏl'ē) I. adj. **-i-** *(person)* alegre, jovial; *(occasion)* agradable; G.B. *(very)* muy II. tr. complacer, consentir.

jolt (jōlt) I. tr. *(to bump)* dar un tumbo o sacudida; *(to shake)* sacudir; *(to shock)* sobresaltar —intr. sacudirse, traquetear II. s. *(jerk)* sacudida, tumbo; *(shock)* choque *m*.

josh (jŏsh) tr. & intr. bromear.

jos·tle (jŏs'əl) I. s. tr. empujar, dar empellones II. s. empujón *m*, empellón *m*.

jot (jŏt) I. s. pizca, ápice *m* II. tr. **-tt-** ♦ **to j.**

down anotar, apuntar.

jounce (jouns) I. intr. dar tumbos —tr. sacudir, traquetear II. s. tumbo.

jour·nal (jûr'nəl) s. diario; TEN. (libro) diario; *(periodical)* revista, boletín *m*.

jour·nal·ism (:nə-lĭz'əm) s. periodismo.

jour·nal·ist (:nə-lĭst) s. periodista *mf*.

jour·nal·is·tic ('-lĭs'tĭk) adj. periodístico.

jour·ney (jûr'nē) I. s. viaje *m*; *(distance)* jornada II. intr. viajar —tr. recorrer.

jour·ney·man (:mən) s. [pl. **-men**] oficial *m*.

joust (joust) I. s. justa II. intr. justar, tornear.

jo·vi·al (jō'vē-əl) adj. jovial, alegre.

jowl (joul) s. *(jaw)* quijada; *(flesh)* carrillo.

joy (joi) s. alegría, júbilo; *(person, thing)* regocijo, motivo de alegría.

joy·ful ('fəl) adj. alegre, jubiloso.

joy·less (:lĭs) adj. sin alegría.

joy·ous (:əs) adj. alegre, gozoso.

joy·ride (:rīd') s. FAM. paseo alocado en coche.

ju·bi·lant (jōō'bə-lənt) adj. jubiloso.

ju·bi·la·tion ('-lā'shən) s. júbilo, exultación *f*.

ju·bi·lee ('-lē') s. *(anniversary)* aniversario (esp. el quincuagésimo); *(celebration)* celebración *f*.

Ju·da·ic (jōō-dā'ĭk) adj. judaico.

Ju·da·ism ('dē-ĭsm) s. judaísmo.

judge (jŭj) I. tr. juzgar; *(to determine)* determinar, evaluar; *(innocent, guilty)* declarar —intr. juzgar ♦ **judging from** o **by** juzgar por II. s. juez *mf*; *(in a contest)* árbitro; *(expert)* conocedor *m*.

judge·ship ('shĭp') s. magistratura, juzgado.

judg(e)·ment (:mənt) s. *(good sense, opinion)* juicio; *(ruling)* opinión *f*, dictamen *m*; *(estimate)* cálculo aproximado; DER. decisión *f*, fallo • **Last J.** juicio final • **to pass j. on** *(person)* juzgar a; *(issue)* juzgar sobre.

ju·di·ca·ture ('dĭ-kə-chŏŏr') s. judicatura.

ju·di·cial (jōō-dĭsh'əl) adj. judicial.

ju·di·ci·ar·y (:ē-ĕr'ē) s. *(branch)* el poder judicial *m*; *(judicature)* judicatura, los jueces.

ju·di·cious (:əs) adj. sensato, juicioso.

ju·do (jōō'dō) s. judo.

jug (jŭg) s. *(jar)* jarra, cántaro; JER. cárcel *f*, chirona.

jug·ger·naut (jŭg'ər-nôt') s. fuerza irresistible.

jug·gle (jŭg'əl) I. tr. hacer malabares con; *(figures)* hacer trampas con —intr. hacer juego de manos.

jug·gler (:lər) s. malabarista *mf*.

jug·u·lar (jŭg'yə-lər) adj. & s. yugular *f*.

juice (jōōs) I. s. jugo; *(of fruits, vegetables)* zumo, jugo; JER. *(electricity)* electricidad *f*; *(fuel)* gasolina II. tr. exprimir ♦ **to j. up** FAM. animar, vigorizar.

juic·y (jōō'sē) adj. **-i-** zumoso, jugoso; *(gossip)* picante, sabroso; *(lucrative)* lucrativo.

juke box (jōōk) s. tocadiscos *m* automático de moneda.

Ju·ly (jōō-lī') s. julio.

jum·ble (jŭm'bəl) I. tr. mezclar; *(to muddle)* embarullar, confundir II. s. *(mess)* revoltijo, embrollo; *(state)* mezcolanza, confusión *f*.

jum·bo (jŭm'bō) I. s. coloso II. adj. muy grande, enorme.

jump (jŭmp) I. intr. saltar; *(to be startled)* sobresaltarse; *(to respond quickly)* moverse; *(prices, temperature)* dar un salto; *(to skip)* pasar por alto, saltear; FAM. *(club, party)* animarse ♦ **to j. at** *(a chance)* aprovechar; *(offer, invitation)* apresurarse a aceptar • **to j. down** bajar de un salto • **to j. in(to)** *(a car, water)*

saltar a; *(new project)* emprender • **to j. off** saltar de; *(a vehicle)* salir de • **to j. on** subir de un salto a • **to j. on someone (for)** echarse encima de alguien (por) • **to j. out of** saltar de • **to j. over** saltar • **to j. to conclusions** sacar conclusiones precipitadamente • **to j. up** levantarse de un salto —tr. saltar (por encima de); *(to attack)* agredir, atacar; *(prices, stakes)* elevar; *(in checkers)* comer ♦ **to j. bail** fugarse estando bajo fianza • **to j. ship** FIG. irse, abandonar • **to j. the gun** adelantarse • **to j. the tracks** descarrilarse II s. salto; *(leap)* brinco; *(sudden movement)* sobresalto; *(checkers)* captura ♦ **j. suit** uniforme de paracaidistas • **to get o have a j. on** llevar o tener una ventaja sobre.
jump·er¹ (jŭm'pər) s. saltador *m*; ELEC. cable *m* de empalme.
jump·er² s. *(dress)* vestido sin mangas.
jump-start (jŭmp'stärt') tr. hacer arrancar a (un motor) usando un cable de empalme
jump·y (jŭm'pē) adj. **-i-** nervioso.
junc·tion (jŭngk'shən) s. juntura, conexión *f*; *(of rivers)* confluencia; F.C., ELEC. empalme *m*.
junc·ture (:chər) s. juntura, unión *f* ♦ **at this j.** a estas alturas.
June (jōōn) s. junio.
jun·gle (jŭng'gəl) s. selva, jungla; *(tangle)* maraña.
jun·ior (jōōn'yər) I. adj. *(younger)* más joven; *(for children)* juvenil, para gente joven; *(in rank)* subalterno; *(in school)* de penúltimo año II. s. joven *mf*; menor *mf*; *(rank)* subordinado; *(student)* estudiante *mf* de penúltimo año.
ju·ni·per (jōō'nə-pər) s. enebro, junípero.
junk¹ (jŭngk) I. s. *(scrap)* chatarra; FAM. *(useless objects)* trastos viejos, cachivaches *m*; JER. heroína ♦ **j. food** alimentos preparados de poco valor nutritivo • **j. mail** FAM. propaganda no solicitada II. tr. *(to discard)* echar a la basura, desechar; *(to scrap)* reducir a chatarra.
junk² s. MARIT. junco.
junk·et (jŭng'kĭt) s. CUL. crema de leche y cuajo; *(trip)* viaje *m* (pagado con fondos públicos).
junk·ie (jŭng'kē) s. JER. drogadicto; *(devotee)* adicto.
junk·man (jŭngk'măn') s. [pl. **-men**] trapero, chatarrero.
junk·yard (:yärd') s. depósito de chatarra.
jun·ta (hŏōn'tə) s. junta militar.
ju·rid·ic/i·cal (jŏō-rĭd'ĭk) jurídico.
ju·ris·dic·tion (jŏōr-ĭs-dĭk'shən) s. jurisdicción *f*.
ju·ris·pru·dence ('-prŏŏd'ns) s. jurisprudencia.
ju·rist (jŏōr'ĭst) s. jurista *mf*.
ju·ror (:ər) s. jurado *mf* (persona).
ju·ry (:ē) s. jurado, tribunal *m* ♦ **j. duty** deber cívico de formar parte de un jurado.
just (jŭst) I. adj. *(fair, right)* justo; *(equitable)* imparcial; *(legitimate)* justificado; *(accurate)* exacto II. adv. *(exactly)* justo, justamente <*j. the right amount* justamente la cantidad correcta>; *(recently)* recién <*j. published* recién publicado>; *(nearby)* no más que, apenas; *(barely)* por muy poco <*you j. missed the bus* perdiste el ómnibus por muy poco>; *(merely)* simplemente, sólo <*j. because* sólo porque>; *(really)* verdaderamente <*it is j. beautiful* es verdaderamente hermoso>; *(possibly)* posiblemente, quizás ♦ **j. about** *(not quite)* casi; *(posi-*

tively) ya <*I'm j. about fed up* ya estoy harto>; *(soon)* pronto <*it's j. about dinnertime* pronto será la hora de cenar> • **j. about** to a punto de • **j. as** *(precisely)* lo mismo que; *(in every way)* tal como <*j. as I thought!* ¡tal como pensaba!>; *(when)* justo cuando <*he came j. as I was leaving* llegó justo cuando me iba> • **j. as if** lo mismo que si • **j. in case** por si acaso • **j. in time** to o for justo a tiempo para • **j. like** *(same as)* como, igual que; *(typical of)* muy de <*that's j. like him!* ¡eso es muy de él!> • **j. my luck!** ¡qué suerte la mía! • **j. now** en este momento • **j. so** a su gusto, ni más ni menos • **j. the same** sin embargo • **not j. yet** todavía no • **to have j.** acabar de <*I've j. gotten here* acabo de llegar>.
jus·tice (jŭs'tĭs) s. justicia, *(righteousness)* rectitud *f*; *(judge)* juez *mf* ♦ **to do j.** to *(to enjoy)* apreciar debidamente; *(to show)* tratar debidamente • **to bring to j.** aprehender y enjuiciar • **j. of the peace** juez de paz.
jus·ti·fi·a·ble (jŭs'tə-fī'ə-bəl) adj. justificable.
jus·ti·fi·ca·tion ('-fĭ-kā'shən) s. justificación *f*.
jus·ti·fy ('-fī') tr. justificar.
just·ness (jŭst'nĭs) s. justicia, *(righteousness)* rectitud *f*; *(fairness)* imparcialidad *f*.
jut (jŭt) intr. **-tt-** ♦ **to j. out** resaltar, sobresalir.
ju·ve·nile (jōō'və-nəl, :nīl') I. adj. joven, juvenil; *(immature)* infantil; *(of minors)* de menores II. s. joven *mf* ♦ **j. court** tribunal de menores • **j. delinquent** delincuente juvenil.
jux·ta·pose (jŭk'stə-pōz') tr. yuxtaponer.
jux·ta·po·si·tion ('-pə-zĭsh'ən) s. yuxtaposición *f*.

K

k, K (kā) s. undécima letra del alfabeto inglés; FAM. *(thousand)* mil *m*; COMPUT. mil bitios.
kale (kāl) s. col rizada.
ka·lei·do·scope (kə-lī'də-skōp') s. calidoscopio.
ka·lei·do·scop·ic ('-'-skŏp'ĭk) s. calidoscópico.
kan·ga·roo (kăng'gə-rōō') s. canguro ♦ **k. court** tribunal desautorizado.
ka·put (kä-pŏŏt') adj. FAM. acabado.
kar·at (kăr'ət) s. quilate *m*.
ka·ra·te (kə-rä'tē) s. karate *m*.
kar·ma (kär'mə) s. karma *m*; FAM. *(atmosphere)* ambiente *m*, aura.
ka·ty·did (kā'tē-dĭd') s. saltamontes *m*.
kay·ak (kī'ăk') s. kayac *m*.
kay·o (kā-ō') JER. I. s. knock-out *m* II. tr. poner fuera de combate.
ka·zoo (kə-zōō') s. chicharra (instrumento).
ke·bab (kə-bŏb') s. carne asada en espetones.
keel (kēl) I. s. quilla ♦ **on an even k.** tranquilo II. intr. irse a pique ♦ **to k. over** desplomarse.
keel·boat ('-bōt') s. chalana fluvial (con quilla).
keen¹ (kēn) adj. agudo; *(blade)* afilado; *(interest)* vivo; *(appetite)* bueno; *(competition)* reñido, fuerte; *(enthusiastic)* entusiasta; JER. *(great)* fantástico ♦ **to be k. on** *(to like)* gustarle a uno; *(to wish to)* tener muchas ganas de.
keen² intr. lamentarse.
keen·ness ('nĭs) s. agudeza; *(of a blade)* filo; *(of emotions)* intensidad *f*; *(enthusiasm)* entusiasmo.
keep (kēp) I. tr. **kept** *(in one's possession)* quedarse con; *(to put aside)* guardar <*k. some for later* guarda algo para más tarde>; *(a family)*

sostener, mantener; *(in a place)* guardar <*where do you k. your saw?* ¿en dónde guardas la sierra?>; *(boarders)* dar hospedaje a, alojar; *(garden)* cultivar; *(animals)* criar; *(to manage)* dirigir, llevar; *(to preserve)* conservar <*to k. food fresh* conservar la comida fresca>; *(order, tradition)* mantener; *(diary, accounts)* llevar; *(to detain)* detener <*what is keeping you?* ¿qué es lo que te detiene?>; *(to fulfill)* cumplir, guardar <*to k. one's word* cumplir la palabra de uno>; *(an appointment)* acudir a; *(holiday)* celebrar, observar ♦ **to k. away** mantener alejado • **to k. back** *(tears)* contener; *(information)* ocultar; *(to withhold)* quedarse con • **to k. down** *(to oppress)* oprimir, sojuzgar; *(costs, temperature)* mantener bajo; *(to restrict)* limitar • **to k. from** *(to prevent)* impedir <*they kept me from speaking out* me impidieron expresar mi opinión>; *(to conceal)* ocultar • **to k. house** manejar una casa • **to k. in** no dejar salir, mantener dentro • **to k. on** *(clothing)* no quitarse; *(an employee)* no despedir, retener • **to k. one's head** no perder la cabeza • **to k. out** no dejar entrar • **to k. out of** FIG. no meterse <*k. out of my affairs* no te metas en mis asuntos> • **to k. (someone) quiet** hacer callar (a alguien) • **to k. (someone) waiting** hacer esperar (a alguien) • **to k. up** *(to continue)* continuar, proseguir <*k. up the good work* continúe haciendo tan buen trabajo>; *(to prevent from sleeping)* tener en vela; *(to maintain)* mantener <*to k. up a property* mantener una propiedad> • **to k. up appearances** guardar las apariencias • **to k. up with** *(work)* tener al día; *(the neighbors)* achantar a (los vecinos) • **to k. up with the times** ser muy de su época —intr. ♦ *(to stay)* permanecer, quedarse; *(food)* conservarse; *(to continue)* seguir; *(to not stop)* no dejar de <*he kept shouting* no dejó de gritar> ♦ **it can k.** puede esperar • **k. off** prohibido pisar • **k. out** prohibida la entrada • **k. at it** FAM. perseverar, persistir • **to k. away** mantenerse a distancia • **to k. going** *(to proceed)* seguir; *(to manage)* ir tirando • **to k. on** seguir, continuar <*k. on talking* continúa hablando> • **to k. quiet** quedarse callado • **to k. to** *(promise, word)* cumplir con; *(the right, left)* mantenerse a • **to k. up** ir al paso, alcanzar **II.** s. *(care)* custodia, protección *f*; *(of a castle)* torreón *m* ♦ **for keeps** para siempre • **to earn one's k.** ganarse la vida.

keep·er (kē'pər) s. guarda *m*, guardián *m*.

keep·ing (kē'pĭng) s. *(guarding)* guardia, custodia; *(custody)* cuidado, cargo <*in his k.* a cargo suyo> ♦ **in safe k.** a buen recaudo • **to be in (out of) k. with** (no) estar de acuerdo con.

keep·sake (kēp'sāk') s. recuerdo.

keg (kĕg) s. barril *m*.

kelp (kĕlp) s. kelp *m*, varec *m*.

ken (kĕn) s. ♦ **beyond one's k.** fuera de comprensión o alcance.

ken·nel (kĕn'əl) tr. & s. (meter en la) perrera.

kept (kĕpt) cf. **keep.**

ker·chief (kûr'chĭf) s. pañuelo.

ker·nel (kûr'nəl) s. grano; *(of a nut)* masa; FIG. meollo ♦ **k. of truth** un fondo de verdad.

ker·o·sene/sine (kĕr'ə-sēn') s. queroseno.

ketch (kĕch) s. queche *m*.

ketch·up (kĕch'əp, kăch'-) s. salsa de tomate.

ket·tle (kĕt'l) s. *(pot)* marmita, caldera; *(teakettle)* tetera ♦ **a fine k. of fish** un berenjenal.

ket·tle·drum (:drŭm') s. timbal *m*.

key¹ (kē) **I.** s. llave *f*; *(code, solution)* clave *f*;

(of a piano, typewriter) tecla; MÚS. tonalidad *f*, tono; TELEG. manipulador *m*; *(pitch)* tono <*she spoke in a high k.* habló en un tono alto> ♦ **in k.** afinado • **master k.** llave maestra • **off k.** desafinado **II.** adj. clave, importante **III.** tr. *(to encode)* codificar; MÚS. afinar ♦ **to be keyed to** *(to be appropriate for)* ser apropiado para; *(information)* explicarse por medio de una clave • **to be keyed up about** estar entusiasmado o nervioso a causa de.

key² s. GEOG. cayo.

key·board (kē'bôrd') **I.** s. teclado **II.** tr. IMPR. componer (mediante teclado).

key·hole (kē'hōl') s. bocallave *f*.

key·note (kē'nōt') **I.** s. MÚS. (nota) tónica; FIG. idea fundamental ♦ **k. address** discurso inaugural.

key·punch (kē'pŭnch') **I.** s. perforadora de tarjetas **II.** tr. procesar en una perforadora de teclado.

key·punch·er (kē'pŭn'chər) s. perforador *m* de tarjetas.

key·stone (kē'stōn') s. clave *f*.

key·stroke (kē'strōk') s. golpe *m* de la tecla.

kha·ki (kăk'ē) **I.** s. caqui *m* ♦ pl. uniforme de color caqui **II.** adj. de color caqui.

kib·itz (kĭb'ĭts) intr. FAM. dar consejos no solicitados.

ki·bosh (kī'bŏsh') s. ♦ **to put the k. on something** FAM. ponerle fin o término a algo.

kick (kĭk) **I.** intr. patear, dar puntapiés; *(animals)* cocear, dar coces; *(firearm)* dar un culatazo; FAM. *(to complain)* quejarse ♦ **to k. around** FAM. andar rodando • **to k. off** DEP. dar el puntapié inicial; FIG. *(to die)* estirar la pata • **to k. oneself** reprocharse —tr. patear, dar un puntapié a; *(animals)* dar coces a; *(firearm)* dar un culatazo en; DEP. patear; *(a goal)* marcar, meter ♦ **to k. around** FAM. *(to abuse)* maltratar; *(idea)* considerar, hablar de • **to k. in** *(one's share)* aportar (dinero); *(a door)* derribar a patadas • **to k. off** poner en marcha • **to k. out** echar a patadas **II.** s. patada; *(person)* puntapié *m*; *(animal)* coz *f*; *(firearm)* culatazo; JER. *(complaint)* queja; *(of a drink, motor)* fuerza ♦ **to be on a k.** estar obsesionado con • **to get a k. out of** FAM. encontrar placer en ♦ pl. sensación, emoción • **for k.** FAM. por gusto, por diversión.

kick·back ('băk') s. JER. tajada, coima.

kick·er (:ər) s. FAM. sorpresa.

kick·off (:ôf') s. DEP. saque *m* inicial; FIG. comienzo.

kick·stand (:stănd') s. soporte *m* (de bicicleta).

kick·y (:ē) adj. **-i-** JER. excitante.

kid (kĭd) **I.** s. *(goat)* cabrito; *(other animals)* cría; *(leather)* cabritilla; FAM. *(child)* niño; JER. *(pal)* muchachón *m* ♦ **k. brother** hermano menor • **k. stuff** juego de niños • **to handle with k. gloves** tratar con guante blanco **II.** tr. & intr. FAM. bromear o jugar (con) ♦ **are you kidding?** *(really?)* ¿de verdad?; *(of course not)* ¡ni en broma! • **no kidding!** ¡mentira!, ¡no me digas! • **to k. oneself** engañarse.

kid·der (:ər) s. bromista *mf*.

kid·dy/die (:ē) s. FAM. niñito, crío.

kid·nap (kĭd'năp') tr. secuestrar, raptar.

kid·nap·(p)er (:ər) s. secuestrador *m*, raptor *m*.

kid·nap·(p)ing (:ĭng) s. secuestro, rapto.

kid·ney (kĭd'nē) s. riñón *m* ♦ **k. bean** frijol colorado • **k. stone** cálculo renal.

kid·skin (kĭd'skĭn') s. cabritilla.

kill (kĭl) **I.** tr. matar; *(to destroy)* destruir; *(to overpower)* arruinar <*garlic killed the taste of the meat* el ajo arruinó el sabor de la carne>; FAM. *(motor, light)* apagar; *(bottle)* agotar; *(to veto)* vetar; *(to delete)* suprimir; *(to make laugh)* hacer morir de risa ♦ to k. off exterminar • to k. time *(to wait)* hacer tiempo; *(to idle)* matar el tiempo —intr. matar; *(to murder)* asesinar **II.** s. *(slaughter)* matanza; *(animal)* cacería; *(final blow)* golpe *m* final, acabamiento.

kill·er (:ər) s. asesino ♦ k. whale orca • to be a k. ser mortal (una enfermedad).

kill·ing (:ĭng) **I.** s. *(murder)* asesinato; *(slaughter)* matanza ♦ to make a k. FAM. ganar gran cantidad de dinero **II.** adj. que mata, mortal; *(exhausting)* agotador; *(funny)* graciosísimo.

kill·joy (:joi´) s. aguafiestas *mf.*

kiln (kĭln, kĭl) s. horno.

ki·lo (kē´lō) s. kilo.

kil·o·cy·cle (kĭl´ə-sī´kəl) s. kilociclo.

kil·o·gram (:grăm´) s. kilogramo.

kil·o·li·ter (:lē´tər) s. kilolitro.

kil·o·me·ter (:mē´tər, kĭ-lŏm´ĭ-tər) s. kilómetro.

kil·o·met·ric (kĭl´ə-mĕt´rĭk) adj. kilométrico.

kil·o·ton (´ə-tŭn´) s. kilotón *m*.

kil·o·watt (´ə-wŏt´) s. kilovatio.

kilt (kĭlt) s. falda escocesa, kilt *m*.

kil·ter (kĭl´tər) s. FAM. buena condición ♦ to be out of k. no funcionar bien.

ki·mo·no (kĭ-mō´nō) s. kimono, quimono.

kin (kĭn) s. parientes *m* ♦ kith and k. parientes y amigos • next of k. pariente más cercano.

kind¹ (kīnd) adj. bueno, afable; *(generous)* generoso, bondadoso; *(courteous)* cortés, amable <*it is very k. of you* es muy amable de su parte> ♦ would you be so k. as to? ¿tendrá usted la bondad de?

kind² s. *(class)* género, especie *f; (type)* tipo, clase *f* <*what k. of airplane is that?* ¿qué tipo de avión es ése?> ♦ a k. of un cierto • all kinds of FAM. *(plenty of)* de sobra, *(many different)* de todas clases, toda clase • in k. del mismo modo • k. of FAM. un poco <*it's k. of cold today* hace un poco de frío hoy> • nothing of the k. nada por el estilo • to repay in k. pagar con la misma moneda • two of a k. un par.

kin·der·gar·ten (kĭn´dər-gär´tn) s. jardín *m* de infantes.

kind-heart·ed (kīnd´här´tĭd) adj. bondadoso.

kin·dle (kĭn´dl) tr. & intr. encender(se).

kin·dling (kĭnd´lĭng) s. leña, astillas.

kind·ly (kīnd´lē) **I.** adj. -i- *(benevolent)* benigno, bondadoso; *(friendly)* amable, agradable **II.** adv. bondadosamente ♦ k. take a seat tenga la bondad de sentarse • to take k. to aceptar de buena gana.

kind·ness (:nĭs) s. bondad *f, (favor)* favor *m* ♦ have the k. to tenga la bondad de.

kin·dred (kĭn´drĭd) **I.** s. parientes *m* **II.** adj. afín, similar ♦ k. spirits almas gemelas.

kin·e·scope (kĭn´ĭ-skōp´) s. cinescopio.

kin·es·the·sia (kĭn´ĭs-thē´zhə) s. quinestesia.

ki·net·ic (kĭ-nĕt´ĭk) adj. cinético ♦ kinetics s.sg. cinética.

kin·folk(s) (kĭn´fōk[s]´) s.pl. parientes *m*.

king (kĭng) s. rey *m; (in checkers)* dama ♦ to live like a k. vivir a cuerpo de rey.

king·bird (:bûrd´) s. tirano.

king·dom (:dəm) s. reino ♦ to blow someone to k. come mandar a alguien de cabeza al otro mundo.

king·fish·er (:fĭsh´ər) s. martín *m* pescador.

king·ly (:lē) adj. -i- real, majestuoso.

king·pin (:pĭn´) s. FAM. persona clave, líder *m*.

king·ship (:shĭp´) s. trono; *(reign)* reinado.

king-size(d) (:sīz[d]´) adj. grande.

kink (kĭngk) **I.** s. *(in a wire)* rosca; *(tight curl)* rizo; *(muscle spasm)* calambre *m; (flaw)* falla; *(mental quirk)* extravagancia **II.** tr. & intr. *(a wire)* enroscar(se); *(hair)* rizar(se).

kink·y (kĭng´kē) adj. -i- *(wire)* enroscado; *(hair)* rizado; FAM. *(perverted)* pervertido.

kin·ship (kĭn´shĭp´) s. parentesco.

kins·man (kĭnz´mən) s. [pl. -men] *(relative)* pariente *m; (compatriot)* compatriota *m*.

kins·wom·an (:wŏm´ən) s. [pl. -women] *(relative)* parienta, *(compatriot)* compatriota.

ki·osk (kē´ŏsk´) s. quiosco.

kip·per (kĭp´ər) s. arenque ahumado.

kis·met (kĭz´mĕt´) s. destino.

kiss (kĭs) **I.** tr. besar, dar un beso a; *(to brush against)* rozar ♦ to k. away borrar con besos • to k. off FAM. despachar, despedir • to k. something goodbye FAM. decir adiós a algo —intr. besarse **II.** s. beso; *(slight touch)* roce *m* ♦ to blow a k. tirar un beso.

kiss·er (:ər) s. JER. hocico, trompa.

kiss-off (:ôf´) s. FAM. despido.

kit (kĭt) s. *(set of tools)* equipo, conjunto; *(collection of items)* juego; *(container)* estuche *m* ♦ first-aid k. botiquín • model k. juego de armar • the whole k. and caboodle FAM. la colección entera.

kitch·en (kĭch´ən) s. cocina ♦ k. sink fregadero.

kitch·en·ette (´ə-nĕt´) s. cocina pequeña.

kitch·en·ware (:ən-wâr´) s. batería de cocina.

kite (kīt) s. *(toy)* cometa; ORNIT. milano ♦ go fly a k.! FAM. ¡piérdete!

kit·ten (kĭt´n) s. gatito.

kit·ty¹ (kĭt´ē) s. *(in cards)* puesta del ganador; *(pool of money)* banca.

kit·ty² s. FAM. *(cat)* gato; *(kitten)* gatito.

kit·ty-cor·nered (:kôr´nərd) adj. diagonal.

klep·to·ma·ni·a (klĕp´tə-mā´nē-ə) s. cleptomanía.

klep·to·ma·ni·ac (:ăk´) s. cleptómano.

klutz (klŭts) s. JER. chambón *m*.

knack (năk) s. *(skill)* facilidad *f (for* para*); (natural talent)* don *m (for* de*)*.

knap·sack (năp´săk´) s. mochila.

knave (nāv) s. bribón *m*, bellaco.

knav·er·y (nā´və-rē) s. bribonada, bellaquería.

knav·ish (nā´vĭsh) adj. bribón, bellaco.

knead (nēd) tr. amasar, heñir.

knee (nē) **I.** s. rodilla; ZOOL. codillo; *(of garment)* rodillera ♦ to bring someone to his knees poner a alguien de rodillas • to go down on one's knees caer de hinojos **II.** tr. dar con la rodilla.

knee·cap (nē´kăp´) s. rótula.

knee-deep (nē´dēp´) adj. *(knee-high)* que llega hasta las rodillas; *(submerged)* metido hasta las rodillas.

knee-high (nē´hī´) adj. que llega hasta las rodillas.

kneel (nēl) intr. -ed o knelt arrodillarse.

knee·pad (nē´păd´) s. rodillera.

knell (nĕl) **I.** intr. sonar lúgubremente **II.** s. toque *m*, tañido ♦ death k. toque a muerto • to sound the death k. of presagiar el fin de.

knelt (nĕlt) cf. kneel.

knew (nōō) cf. know.

knick·ers (nĭk′ərz) s.pl. *(bloomers)* bragas *f*; *(knee breeches)* calzones *m*, bombachos.
knick-knack (nĭk′năk′) s. chuchería.
knife (nīf) I. s. [pl. **-ves**] cuchillo; *(blade, pocketknife)* cuchilla II. tr. *(to cut)* cortar; *(to stab)* apuñalar; FAM. *(to betray)* apuñalar por la espalda, traicionar.
knife-edge (′ĕj′) s. filo.
knight (nīt) I. s. caballero; *(in chess)* caballo II. tr. armar caballero; G.B. conceder el título de *Sir* a.
knight·hood (′hŏŏd′) s. rango *o* título de caballero; *(chivalry)* caballerosidad *f*.
knit (nĭt) I. tr. & intr. **knit(ted), -tting** tejer, hacer punto; *(to unite)* unir(se); *(brows)* fruncir(se); *(bone)* soldarse II. s. *(garment)* prenda de punto; *(cloth)* género de punto.
knit·ting (′ĭng) s. tejido, labor *f* de punto ♦ k. **needle** aguja de tejer *o* de hacer punto.
knit·wear (:wâr′) s. artículos de punto.
knives (nīvz) cf. **knife**.
knob (nŏb) s. *(of a door)* perilla, tirador *m*; *(dial)* botón *m*; *(bulge)* protuberancia.
knock (nŏk) I. tr. *(to hit)* golpear, pegar; *(to break through)* hacer <to k. a hole in the wall hacer un agujero en la pared>; JER. *(to criticize)* criticar, menospreciar ♦ k. **it off!** ¡no lo digas ya! • to **k. around** FAM. *(idea)* considerar; *(to abuse)* maltratar • to **k. down** derribar, tumbar; FAM. *(price)* rebajar • to **k. off** hacer caer, tirar <to k. the lamp off the table hacer caer la lámpara de la mesa>; FAM. *(to stop)* parar, suspender *(tarea, trabajo); (to do quickly)* terminar con; *(to deduct)* rebajar en; JER. *(to kill)* liquidar • to **k. out** *(a person)* dejar sin sentido; *(in boxing)* poner fuera de combate; *(to render inoperative)* estropear, inutilizar; *(power)* cortar; FAM. *(to impress)* impresionar • to **k. over** tirar (vasa, lámpara) —intr. *(at the door)* golpear, llamar; AUTO. pistonear *o* detonar (un motor) ♦ to **k. around** FAM. vagar, merodear • to **k. against** chocar contra • to **k. off** FAM. salir del trabajo • to **k. oneself out** FAM. matarse II. s. *(blow)* golpe *m*; *(rap)* toque *m*, llamada; AUTO. pistoneo; FAM. *(criticism)* crítica.
knock·down (′doun′) I. adj. demoledor, que derriba II. s. caída.
knock·er (:ər) s. aldaba, picaporte.
knock·ing (′ĭng) s. aldabonazo, llamada (a la puerta); *(sound)* golpeteo.
knock-kneed (:nēd′) adj. patizambo.
knock·out (:out′) s. knock-out *m*; JER. *(person)* maravilla; *(success)* exitazo ♦ k. **punch** golpe demoledor.
knoll (nŏl) s. loma, montículo.
knot (nŏt) I. s. nudo; *(group)* grupo, corrillo; *(difficulty)* problema *m* ♦ to **get tied up in knots** FAM. enredarse • to **tie the k.** FAM. casarse II. tr. & intr. **-tt-** anudar(se); *(to entangle)* enredar(se).
knot·hole (:hōl′) s. agujero (que deja un nudo).
knot·ted (:ĭd) adj. anudado; *(intricate)* enredado, enmarañado; *(gnarled)* nudoso.
knot·ty (:ē) adj. **-i-** *(rope)* lleno de nudos; *(wood)* nudoso; *(problem)* enredado.
know (nō) I. tr. **knew, known** saber <I know arithmetic sé aritmética>; *(a person, place)* conocer; *(to perceive)* comprender <I k. how you feel comprendo cómo te sientes>; *(to recognize)* reconocer; *(to distinguish)* distinguir <to k. right from wrong distinguir el bien del mal> ♦ to **get to k. someone** llegar a conocer a al-

guien • to **let someone k.** hacer saber a alguien • to **make known** hacer saber • to **k. about** saber de • to **k. how** to saber —intr. saber ♦ as **far as I k.** que yo sepa • how **should I k.!** ¡yo qué sé! • I **ought to k.!** ¡lo sabré yo! • to **k. best** saber mejor que nadie • to **k. better** saber lo que debe hacerse • to **k. better than to** saber que no se debe • to **k. each other** conocerse II. s. ♦ to **be in the k.** FAM. estar al tanto.
know·a·ble (nō′ə-bəl) adj. conocible.
know-how (nō′hou′) s. *(ability)* habilidad *f*; *(experience)* experiencia.
know·ing (nō′ĭng) adj. *(shrewd)* astuto, hábil; *(look, smile)* de complicidad.
know·ing·ly (:ĭng-lē) adv. *(shrewdly)* astutamente; *(deliberately)* a sabiendas ♦ to **glance k.** at dirigir una mirada de complicidad a.
know-it-all (nō′ĭt-ôl′) s. FAM. sabelotodo *mf*.
knowl·edge (nŏl′ĭj) s. *(understanding)* conocimiento; *(information)* conocimientos, saber *m* <k. about genetics conocimientos sobre la genética>; *(erudition)* erudición *f* ♦ it is common k. that todo el mundo sabe que • it has come to my k. that me enteré de que • to have a working k. of tener conocimientos prácticos de • to have a thorough k. of conocer a fondo • to have no k. of no saber nada de • (not) to my k. (no) que yo sepa • to the best of my k. según mi entender • without my k. sin saberlo yo.
knowl·edge·a·ble (:ĭ-jə-bəl) adj. instruido, informado ♦ to **be k. about** conocer bien.
known (nōn) I. cf. **know** II. adj. conocido.
know-noth·ing (nō′nŭth′ĭng) s. ignorante *mf*.
knuck·le (nŭk′əl) I. s. nudillo ♦ to **rap someone's knuckles** dar en los nudillos II. intr. ♦ to **k. down** aplicarse duro • to **k. under** ceder.
knuck·le·head (:hĕd′) s. alcornoque *m*.
KO DEP., JER. I. tr. *(kā′ō′)* **'d, 'ing** noquear II. s. *(kā-ō′)* [pl. **'s**] knock-out *m*.
ko·a·la (kō-ä′lə) s. koala *m*.
kook (kŏŏk) s. JER. alocado, excéntrico.
kook·y (kŏō′kē) adj. **-i-** JER. alocado, excéntrico.
ko·sher (kō′shər) adj. conforme al régimen alimenticio judío; JER. *(proper)* conforme a las reglas; *(genuine)* legítimo.
kow·tow (kou-tou′) intr. hacer una reverencia china; *(to fawn)* humillarse, postrarse.
ku·dos (kyōō′dōz′) s. prestigio, fama.
kum·quat (kŭm′kwŏt′) s. naranjita china.

L

l, L (ĕl) s. duodécima letra del alfabeto inglés.
lab (lăb) s. laboratorio.
la·bel (lā′bəl) I. s. rótulo, etiqueta; *(brand name)* marca de fábrica, FIG. *(epithet)* etiqueta II. tr. rotular, marcar; *(to describe)* describir.
la·bi·al (lā′bē-əl) adj. labial.
la·bor (lā′bər) I. s. trabajo, labor *f*; *(task)* tarea, faena; *(effort)* esfuerzo; *(workers)* mano *f* de obra, obreros; *(union)* sindicato; *(childbirth)* parto ♦ **hard l.** trabajos forzosos • **l. union** sindicato II. intr. trabajar; *(to strive)* esforzarse; *(to plod)* moverse con dificultad; MED. estar de parto • **l. over** tomarse trabajo en —tr. insistir en III. adj. laboral ♦ **l. camp** campo de trabajo • **l. pains** dolores de parto.
lab·o·ra·to·ry (lăb′rə-tôr′ē) s. laboratorio.
la·bored (lā′bərd) adj. trabajoso, dificultoso;

(strained) forzado.

la·bor·er (lā′bər-ər) s. trabajador *m*, obrero; *(unskilled)* peón *m*, jornalero.

la·bo·ri·ous (lə-bôr′ē-əs) adj. laborioso.

la·bor·sav·ing (lā′bər-sā′vīng) adj. que conserva mano de obra.

la·bour (lā′bər) G.B. var. de **labor**.

lab·y·rinth (lăb′ə-rĭnth′) s. laberinto.

lac (lăk) s. laca.

lace (lās) I. s. encaje *m*; *(trim)* puntilla; *(shoelace)* cordón *m* de zapato II. tr. encordonar; *(a drink)* echar licor a ♦ **to l. into** reprochar.

lac·er·ate (lăs′ə-rāt′) tr. lacerar.

lac·er·a·tion (′-rā′shən) s. laceración *f*; *(wound)* rasgón *m*.

lach·ry·mal (lăk′rə-məl) adj. lagrimal.

lack (lăk) I. s. *(deficiency)* falta, carencia; *(need)* escasez *f* ♦ **for l. of** por falta de II. tr. *(to be without)* carecer de, faltar; *(to need)* necesitar; *(to require)* hacer falta, requerir(se); *(to have no)* no tener —intr. hacer falta.

lack·a·dai·si·cal (lăk′ə-dā′zĭ-kəl) adj. indiferente, apático.

lack·ey (lăk′ē) s. lacayo; *(toady)* adulador *m*.

lack·ing (lăk′ĭng) I. adj. deficiente, falto de ♦ **to be l.** faltar II. prep. sin.

lack·lus·ter (lŭs′tər) adj. deslucido.

la·con·ic (lə-kŏn′ĭk) adj. lacónico.

lac·quer (lăk′ər) I. s. laca II. tr. laquear.

lac·tase (lăk′tās′) s. lactasa.

lac·tate (tāt′) I. intr. lactar II. s. lactato.

lac·ta·tion (-tā′shən) s. lactancia.

lac·tic (′tĭk) adj. láctico.

lac·tose (′tōs′) s. lactosa.

la·cu·na (lə-kyōō′nə) s. [pl. **s** o **-ae**] laguna.

lac·y (lā′sē) adj. -i- de encaje; FIG. diáfano.

lad (lăd) s. joven *m*, muchacho.

lad·der (lăd′ər) s. escalera, escala; *(status)* jerarquía; G.B. *(in a stocking)* carrera.

lad·die (lăd′ē) s. joven *m*, chico.

lade (lād) tr. **d, d** o **n** cargar; FIG. agobiar.

lad·en (lād′n) I. cf. **lade** II. adj. cargado; FIG. agobiado, abrumado.

lad·ing (lā′dĭng) s. carga, flete *m*.

la·dle (lād′l) I. s. cucharón *m* II. tr. servir con cucharón.

la·dy (lā′dē) s. dama; *(married woman)* señora ♦ **l. in waiting** dama de honor ♦ **l. of the evening** prostituta ♦ **l. of the house** ama de la casa ♦ **l.'s man** hombre galanteador ♦ **young l.** señorita.

la·dy·bird (·bûrd′) s. mariquita.

la·dy·bug (·bŭg′) s. mariquita.

la·dy·kill·er (·kĭl′ər) s. JER. tenorio.

la·dy·like (·līk′) adj. bien educada.

la·dy·ship (·shĭp′) s. excelencia, señoría.

lag (lăg) I. intr. **-gg-** *(to straggle)* rezagarse, retrasarse; *(to flag)* aflojar(se) ♦ **to l. behind** retrasarse II. s. dilación *f*, retraso.

la·ger (lä′gər) s. cerveza de Alemania.

lag·gard (lăg′ərd) adj. & s. rezagado.

la·goon (lə-gōōn′) s. laguna.

la·ic/i·cal (lā′ĭk) adj. laico, secular.

laid (lād) cf. **lay**[1].

laid-back (lād′băk′) adj. FAM. despreocupado.

lain (lān) cf. **lie**[1].

lair (lâr) s. guarida, madriguera.

lais·sez faire (lĕs′ā fâr′) s. doctrina de no intervención.

la·i·ty (lā′ĭ-tē) s. laicos; *(non-professionals)* profanos.

lake (lāk) s. lago.

lam (lăm) JER. I. intr. **-mm-** fugarse, huir II. s. fuga, escape *m* ♦ **to take it on the l.** largarse.

lamb (lăm) s. cordero; *(dear)* cielo, amor *m*; *(dupe)* inocente *mf*.

lam·baste (lăm-bāst′) tr. *(to thrash)* dar una paliza; *(to scold)* regañar duramente.

lame (lām) I. adj. cojo, renco; FIG. débil II. tr. lisiar, baldar.

la·mé (lă-mā′) s. lamé *m*.

lame·brain (lām′brān′) s. tonto.

la·ment (lə-mĕnt′) I. tr. lamentar, llorar; *(to regret)* deplorar —intr. lamentarse II. s. lamento; *(elegy)* elegía.

la·men·ta·ble (lə-mĕn′tə-bəl) adj. lamentable.

la·ment·ed (:tĭd) adj. lamentado.

lam·i·na (lăm′ə-nə) s. [pl. **s** o **-ae**] lámina.

lam·i·nate (·nāt′) I. tr. laminar II. adj. & s. laminado.

lam·i·nat·ed (:nā′tĭd) adj. laminado.

lam·i·na·tion (′-nā′shən) s. laminación *f*; *(lamina)* lámina.

lamp (lămp) s. lámpara.

lamp·black (′blăk′) s. negro de humo.

lamp·light (:līt′) s. luz *f* de la lámpara.

lam·poon (lăm-pōōn′) I. s. pasquín *m*, sátira II. tr. pasquinar, satirizar.

lamp·post (lămp′pōst′) s. poste *m* de farol.

lam·prey (lăm′prē) s. lamprea.

lance (lăns) I. s. lanza; CIR. lanceta II. tr. lancear, CIR. abrir con una lanceta.

lan·cet (lăn′sĭt) s. lanceta.

land (lănd) I. s. tierra; *(soil)* suelo; *(tract)* campo, terreno; *(country)* tierra, país *m*; *(people)* pueblo; *(real estate)* bienes *m* raíces ♦ **l. bank** banco hipotecario ♦ **l. mine** mina terrestre ♦ **l. of milk and honey** tierra de Jauja ♦ **no man's l.** tierra de nadie ♦ **to get the lay of the l.** tantear el terreno ♦ pl. tierras, posesiones II. tr. *(to unload)* desembarcar; *(to bring to earth)* aterrizar; FAM. *(fish)* coger, atrapar; *(to win)* lograr, conseguir; *(a blow)* dar, asestar ♦ **to l.** *(someone)* **in** llevar *(a alguien)* a —intr. *(to arrive)* arribar; *(to disembark)* desembarcar; *(to alight)* posarse; *(to come to rest)* caer; *(plane)* aterrizar ♦ **to l. up** ir a parar.

land·ed (lăn′dĭd) adj. hacendado ♦ **l. gentry** terratenientes.

land·fall (lănd′fôl′) s. recalada.

land·fill (:fĭl′) s. tierra rehabilitada.

land·hold·er (:hōl′dər) s. terrateniente *mf*.

land·hold·ing (:dĭng) s. tenencia de tierras.

land·ing (lăn′dĭng) s. *(on land)* aterrizaje *m*; *(on the sea)* amaraje *m*; *(on the moon)* alunizaje *m*; *(of passengers)* desembarco; *(of cargo)* desembarque *m*; *(site)* desembarcadero; *(of a staircase)* descanso.

land·la·dy (lănd′lā′dē) s. propietaria, dueña.

land·locked (:lŏkt′) adj. sin salida al mar.

land·lord (:lôrd′) s. propietario, arrendador *m*.

land·lub·ber (:lŭb′ər) s. FAM. marinero de agua dulce.

land·mark (:märk′) s. mojón *m*; *(event)* acontecimiento histórico; *(site)* monumento histórico.

land·mass (:măs′) s. área de terreno grande.

land·own·er (:ō′nər) s. terrateniente *mf*.

land·scape (:skāp′) I. s. paisaje *m*, panorama *m* II. tr. ornamentar (un terreno).

land·scap·ing (:skā′pĭng) s. jardinería ornamental.

land·slide (:slīd′) s. derrumbe *m* (de tierra), corrimiento; POL. triunfo electoral aplastante.

land·ward (:wərd) I. adj. más cerca de la tierra II. adv. hacia la tierra.

lane (lān) s. *(path)* senda, vereda; *(road)* camino; *(for ships, aircraft)* ruta; *(of a highway)* vía, carril *m*; DEP. calle *f*; *(in bowling)* pista.

lan·guage (lăng′gwĭj) s. lenguaje *m*; *(dialect)* lengua, idioma *m*; *(of a document)* términos ♦ **strong l.** palabras mayores *o* fuertes • **to use bad l.** ser mal hablado.

lan·guid (lăng′gwĭd) adj. lánguido.

lan·guish (:gwĭsh) intr. languidecer; *(to dwindle)* decaer; *(to stagnate)* estancarse; *(to waste away)* pudrirse.

lan·guish·ing (′′ĭng) adj. lánguido.

lan·guor (lăng′gər) s. languidez *f*.

lan·guor·ous (:əs) adj. lánguido.

lank (lăngk) adj. *(gaunt)* delgado; *(limp)* lacio.

lank·y (lăng′kē) adj. -**i**- larguirucho.

lan·o·lin (lăn′ə-lĭn) s. lanolina.

lan·tern (lăn′tərn) s. linterna; *(in a lighthouse)* fanal *m*.

lan·yard (lăn′yərd) s. MARÍT. acollador *m*, cuerda; MIL. cuerda y gancho de disparo.

lap¹ (lăp) s. falda, regazo; *(of a garment)* falda ♦ **in the l. of luxury** rodeado de lujo • **l. dog** perro faldero • **to fall into one's l.** caerle a uno del cielo.

lap² I. tr. -**pp**- *(to fold)* doblar, plegar; *(to overlap)* cubrir parcialmente, traslapar ♦ **to l.** *(to overlap)* imbricarse, traslaparse; *(to extend out)* sobresalir II. s. *(overlap)* traslapo, solapa; *(of a race)* vuelta a la pista; *(of a swimming pool)* largo; *(segment)* etapa.

lap³ I. tr. -**pp**- *(to drink)* beber a lengüetadas; *(to wash)* bañar, besar ♦ **to l. up** *(to drink)* lamer, beber a lengüetadas; *(to accept)* aceptar con entusiasmo —intr. *(to drink)* lengüetear, sorber; *(waves)* chapotear II. s. chapoteo.

la·pel (lə-pĕl′) s. solapa (de una vestimenta).

lap·i·dar·y (lăp′ĭ-dĕr′ē) s. & adj. lapidario.

lapse (lăps) I. intr. *(to drift)* caer, deslizarse; *(to fail)* faltar; *(to subside)* decaer, desvanecerse; *(to elapse)* pasar, transcurrir; *(to expire)* caducar II. s. *(slip)* desliz *m*, fallo; *(error, interval)* lapso; *(expiration)* caducidad *f*.

lapsed (lăpst) adj. *(elapsed)* transcurrido; *(expired)* caduco.

lar·ce·nist (lär′sə-nĭst) s. ladrón *m*, ratero.

lar·ce·nous (:nəs) adj. culpable de robo.

lar·ce·ny (:nē) s. hurto, robo.

larch (lärch) s. alerce *m*, lárice *m*.

lard (lärd) I. s. lardo II. tr. lardar, mechar; FIG. adornar.

lar·der (lär′dər) s. despensa.

large (lärj) I. adj. grande; *(comprehensive)* extenso, amplio ♦ **l. as life** de tamaño natural II. adv. grande ♦ **at l.** *(at liberty)* libre, en libertad; *(at length)* extensamente • **by and l.** por lo general • **l. order** FAM. tarea peliaguda.

large-heart·ed (′′här′tĭd) adj. magnánimo.

large·ly (:lē) adv. en gran parte.

large-scale (:skāl′) adj. en *o* a gran escala.

lar·gess(e) (lär-zhĕs′) s. largueza, generosidad *f*; *(gift)* dádiva, donativo.

lar·i·at (lăr′ē-ət) s. lazo.

lark¹ (lärk) s. ORNIT. alondra.

lark² (:) s. *(spree)* calaverada; *(prank)* broma ♦ **to do something for a l.** hacer algo para divertirse.

lar·va (lär′və) s. [pl. -**ae**] larva.

lar·val (:vəl) adj. larval.

lar·yn·gi·tis (lăr′ən-jī′tĭs) s. laringitis *f*.

lar·ynx (lăr′ĭngks) s. [pl. **es** *o* -**ges**] laringe *f*.

lar·civ·i·ous (lə-sĭv′ē-əs) adj. lascivo.

lase (lāz) intr. funcionar como láser.

la·ser (lā′zər) s. láser *m*.

lash¹ (lăsh) I. s. *(blow)* azote *m*, latigazo; *(whip)* azote, látigo; *(eyelash)* pestaña II. tr. azotar, dar latigazos a; *(tail)* agitar con fuerza; *(to criticize)* fustigar ♦ **to l. out** al fulminar contra, fustigar —intr. dar latigazos, restallar ♦ **to l. out** estallar de ira.

lash² tr. *(to tie)* atar.

lash·ing (′ĭng) s. *(whipping)* azotaina; *(criticism)* fustigación *f*; *(for binding)* atadura.

lass (lăs) s. muchacha, joven *f*.

las·sie (′ē) s. muchacha, joven *f*.

las·si·tude (lăs′ĭ-tōd′) s. lasitud *f*.

las·so (lăs′ō, lă-sō′) I. s. [pl. **(e)s**] lazo II. tr. coger con un lazo.

last¹ (lăst) I. adj. *(final)* último; *(past)* pasado; *(newest)* último; *(authoritative)* definitivo, final; *(least likely)* último ♦ **l. but not least** el último en orden pero no en importancia • **l. name** apellido • **l. night** anoche II. adv. el último, en último lugar; *(most recently)* la última vez; *(finally)* por último, finalmente III. s. el último; *(the end)* final *m* ♦ **at (long) l.** ¡por fin!, ¡al fin! • **to the l.** hasta el fin.

last² intr. durar; *(to survive)* sobrevivir; *(to endure)* perdurar; *(to be enough)* bastar, alcanzar —tr. bastar; *(to survive)* resistir, aguantar.

last³ s. horma (de zapato).

last-ditch (′dĭch′) adj. desesperado, último.

last·ing (lăs′tĭng) adj. duradero, perdurable.

last·ly (lăst′lē) adv. por último, finalmente.

last-min·ute (:mĭn′ĭt) adj. de última hora.

latch (lăch) I. s. pestillo, aldabilla II. tr. cerrar con pestillo *o* aldabilla.

latch·key (′kē′) s. llave *f* (de picaporte).

late (lāt) I. adj. *(behind schedule)* retrasado, atrasado; *(at an advanced hour)* a una hora avanzada; *(at the end)* a fines de; *(recent)* reciente, último; *(former)* antiguo, anterior; *(dead)* fallecido, difunto ♦ **to get l.** hacerse tarde • **to make someone l.** retrasar a alguien II. adv. tarde; *(at the end)* tardíamente, recientemente; *(recently)* hasta ♦ **l. in life** a una edad avanzada • **of l.** recientemente, últimamente.

late·com·er (′kŭm′ər) s. retrasado; *(newcomer)* recién llegado.

late·ly (:lē) adv. recientemente, últimamente.

la·ten·cy (lāt′n-sē) s. latencia.

late·ness (lāt′nĭs) s. tardanza; *(delay)* demora, retraso.

la·tent (lāt′nt) adj. latente.

lat·er (lā′tər) I. adj. posterior; *(more recent)* más reciente II. adv. más tarde, después ♦ **l. on** luego, después • **(I'll) see you l.** hasta luego.

lat·er·al (lăt′ər-əl) adj. lateral.

lat·est (lā′tĭst) I. adj. último; *(newest)* más reciente II. adv. el último III. s. lo último, lo más reciente ♦ **at the l.** a más tardar • **the very l.** el último grito.

la·tex (lā′tĕks′) s. látex *m*.

lath (lăth) s. *(wood)* listón *m*; *(metal)* lata; *(lathing)* listonería, enlistonado.

lathe (lāth) s. torno II. tr. tornear.

lath·er (lăth′ər) I. s. *(of soap)* espuma; *(of the mouth)* espumarajo; *(agitation)* agitación *f* II. tr. enjabonar —intr. espumar.

lat·i·tude (lăt′ĭ-tōd′) I. s. amplitud *f*; *(freedom)* libertad *f*; ASTRON., GEOG. latitud *f*.

la·trine (lə-trēn′) s. letrina, retrete *m*.

lat·ter (lăt'ər) adj. *(second)* éste, *(neuter the end)* último; *(later)* más reciente, último.

lat·ter-day (:dā') adj. reciente.

lat·tice (lăt'ĭs) I. s. enrejado, celosía; *(window)* ventana con celosía II. tr. enrejar.

lat·tice·work (:wûrk') s. enrejado, celosía.

laud (lôd) tr. *(to glorify)* loar, alabar; *(to give praise to)* elogiar, encomiar.

laud·a·ble (lô'də-bəl) adj. loable, laudable.

laud·a·to·ry (:tôr'ē) adj. laudatorio.

laugh (lăf) I. intr. reír(se) ♦ **to be nothing to l. about** no ser cosa de risa • **to burst out laughing** echarse a reír a carcajadas • **to l. at** *(to show amusement)* reírse con; *(to ridicule)* reírse de, burlarse de • **to l. it up** divertirse • **t l. off** *o* **away** tomar a risa • **to l. one's head off** reírse a más no poder • **to l. out loud** reírse a carcajadas • **to l. up one's sleeve** reírse para los adentros II. s. risa; *(joke)* chiste *m*, cosa de risa ♦ **for laughs** para hacer reír • **good for a l.** divertido • **to have a good l.** reírse mucho • **to have the last l.** ser el último que ríe.

laugh·a·ble ('ə-bəl) adj. cómico; *(ludicrous)* ridículo, absurdo.

laugh·ing (:ĭng) adj. risueño ♦ **it's no l. matter** no es cosa de risa • **l. gas** gas hilarante.

laugh·ing·stock (:stôk') s. hazmerreír *m*.

laugh·ter (lăf'tər) s. risa(s); *(loud)* carcajadas.

launch¹ (lônch) I. tr. lanzar; *(into the water)* botar; *(to initiate)* iniciar, emprender —intr. lanzarse ♦ **to l. forth** *o* **out** emprender II. s. lanzamiento; *(into the sea)* botadura ♦ **l. pad** plataforma de lanzamiento.

launch² s. MARÍT. lancha.

launch·er (lôn'chər) s. lanzador *m*.

launch·ing (:chĭng) s. lanzamiento; *(of a ship)* botadura ♦ **l. pad** plataforma de lanzamiento.

laun·der (lôn'dər) tr. & intr. lavar(se).

laun·dered (:dərd) adj. lavado; *(money)* que ha pasado por otras manos.

laun·der·er (:dər-ər) s. lavandero.

laun·dress (:drĭs) s. lavandera.

laun·dry (:drē) s. *(soiled)* ropa sucia; *(clean)* ropa limpia; *(place)* lavandería.

lau·re·ate (lôr'ē-ĭt) adj. & s. laureado.

lau·rel (lôr'əl) s. laurel *m* ♦ **to rest on one's laurels** dormirse en los laureles.

la·va (lä'və, lăv'ə) s. lava.

lav·a·to·ry (lăv'ə-tôr'ē) s. servicios; *(washbasin)* lavamanos *m*, lavabo.

lav·en·der (lăv'ən-dər) I. s. lavanda, alhucema II. adj. de color lavanda.

lav·ish (lăv'ĭsh) I. adj. generoso; *(extravagant)* lujoso, espléndido II. tr. prodigar, derrochar ♦ **to l. (something) on someone** colmar a alguien de (algo).

law (lô) s. ley *f*; *(code)* fuero, código; *(study)* derecho; *(principle)* ley, principio; FAM. *(police)* policía; LÓG., MAT. regla ♦ **case l.** jurisprudencia • **l. and order** orden público • **l. school** facultad de derecho • **to lay down the l.** dictar la ley • **to practice l.** ejercer la abogacía • **to take the l. into one's hands** tomarse la ley por la propia mano.

law·a·bid·ing (lô'ə-bī'dĭng) adj. respetuoso de la ley.

law·break·er (lô'brā'kər) s. infractor *m* de la ley.

law·ful (lô'fəl) adj. *(allowed by law)* legal, lícito; *(recognized)* legítimo.

law·less (lô'lĭs) adj. *(conduct)* desordenado; *(region)* sin leyes, ingobernable.

law·mak·er (lô'mā'kər) s. legislador *m*.

lawn (lôn) s. césped *m* ♦ **l. mower** cortacéspedes.

law·suit (lô'sōōt') s. pleito, juicio.

law·yer (lô'yər) s. abogado, jurista *mf*.

lax (lăks) adj. *(morals)* laxo; *(negligent)* descuidado; *(discipline)* flojo.

lax·a·tive (lăk'sə-tĭv) s. & adj. laxante *m*.

lax·i·ty (lăk'sĭ-tē) *o* **lax·ness** (lăks'nĭs) s. laxitud *f*; *(slackness)* flojedad *f*, *(negligence)* negligencia, descuido.

lay¹ (lā) tr. **laid** poner; *(to cause to lie)* acostar; *(blame)* achacar, atribuir; *(plans)* trazar, hacer; *(to submit)* presentar, someter; *(to wager)* apostar; *(to impose)* imponer; *(eggs)* poner ♦ **to be laid up** guardar cama • **to l. an egg** JER. *(to fail)* fracasar • **to l. aside** *(to give up)* abandonar; *(to put aside)* guardar, dejar a un lado • **to l. away, by,** *o* **in** guardar para el futuro • **to l. claim to** reclamar los derechos a • **to l. down** dictar, establecer • **to l. down one's life for** sacrificar la vida por • **to l. hands on** FAM. *(to catch)* coger, atrapar; *(to hit)* poner la mano encima • **to l. into** JER. *(to beat)* apalear; *(to scold)* regañar, reñir • **to l. it on (thick)** JER. exagerar • **to l. off** *(to dismiss)* despedir (esp. temporalmente); *(a habit)* dejar, abandonar • **to l. out** *(to plan)* planear, proyectar; *(to spread out)* preparar; *(to prepare for burial)* amortajar; *(to spend)* gastar • **to l. to rest** *(to bury)* enterrar; *(to refute)* refutar —intr. *(to produce eggs)* poner huevos, aovar; *(to bet)* apostar; MARÍT. situarse, colocarse • **to l. over** pararse, detenerse • **to l. to** MARÍT. pairar el barco.

lay² adj. secular, laico; *(not professional)* lego.

lay³ s. *(song)* cantar *m*.

lay⁴ cf. **lie¹**.

lay·er (lā'ər) I. s. capa; GEOL. estrato II. tr. separar en capas.

lay·ette (lā-ĕt') s. ajuar *m* de niño.

lay·man (lā'mən) s. [pl. **-men**] laico, seglar *m*; *(nonprofessional)* lego.

lay·off (lā'ôf') s. *(suspension)* suspensión *f* temporaria de empleados; *(dismissal)* despido.

lay·out (lā'out') s. disposición *f*, distribución *f*; *(sketch)* trazado.

lay·o·ver (lā'ō'vər) s. escala, parada.

laze (lāz) intr. holgazanear, gandulear —tr. ♦ **to l. away** perder, desperdiciar.

la·zi·ness (lā'zē-nĭs) s. pereza.

la·zy (lā'zē) adj. **-i-** perezoso ♦ **l. Susan** bandeja giratoria.

la·zy·bones (:bōnz') s.pl. JER. remolón *m*.

leach (lēch) tr. & intr. lixiviar(se).

lead¹ (lēd) tr. **led** *(to guide)* guiar, conducir; *(to command)* dirigir, mandar; *(to induce)* inducir; *(to head)* ser el primero en, encabezar; *(to be ahead of)* llevar una ventaja de; *(to live)* llevar; *(in cards)* salir con ♦ **to l. astray** descarriar • **to l. on** *(to entice)* seducir, tentar; *(to deceive)* engañar —intr. ser primero, estar a la cabeza; *(to go first)* enseñar el camino; *(in command)* mandar; *(to go)* llevar, conducir; *(in cards)* ser mano ♦ **to l. off** empezar, dar comienzo II. s. *(position)* primer lugar *m*, delantera; *(margin)* ventaja; *(clue)* indicación *f*, pista; CINEM., TEAT. *(role)* papel *m* principal; *(actor)* protagonista *mf*; PERIOD. párrafo introductor; *(news story)* artículo principal; *(in cards)* mano; *(leash)* traílla, correa ♦ **in the l.** a la cabeza, primero • **to follow the l. of** seguir el ejemplo de • **to take the l.** tomar la delantera, adelan-

tarse III. adj. principal.
lead² (lĕd) I. s. plomo; *(pencil)* mina ♦ l. **poi·soning** saturnismo II. tr. cubrir *o* forrar con plomo; *(window)* emplomar.
lead·en (lĕd'n) adj. plúmbeo, de plomo; *(gray)* plomizo; *(heavy)* pesado; *(sluggish)* lento; *(depressed)* deprimido.
lead·er (lē'dər) s. jefe *m*, líder *m*; *(guide)* guía *mf*; *(politician)* caudillo; *(first)* primero; *(pipe)* canalón *m*, conducto.
lead·er·ship (:shĭp') s. dirección *f*, mando; *(capacity)* dotes *f* de mando.
lead·in (lēd'ĭn') I. s. introducción *f* II. adj. de entrada.
lead·ing¹ (lē'dĭng) adj. *(foremost)* primero, que va a la cabeza; *(main)* principal; TEAT. primero ♦ l. **edge** puesto de avanzada • l. **question** pregunta capciosa.
lead·ing² (lĕd'ĭng) s. emplomado.
lead·off (lēd'ôf') s. *(move)* comienzo, principio; *(person)* iniciador *m*.
lead-time (:tīm') s. tiempo requerido para completar un proyecto.
leaf (lēf) I. s. [pl. **-ves**] hoja; *(foliage)* follaje *m*, hojas; *(page)* página; *(metal)* lámina ♦ **gold l.** pan de oro • **to shake like a l.** temblar como una hoja *o* un azogado • **to turn over a new l.** empezar una nueva vida II. intr. BOT. echar hojas ♦ **to l.** through hojear.
leaf·let ('lĭt) s. folleto, panfleto; *(flier)* volante *m*.
leaf·y (lē'fē) adj. **-i-** frondoso, hojoso.
league¹ (lēg) s. liga; *(organization)* asociación *f*; DEP. liga ♦ **to be in l. with** estar aliado con • **out of one's l.** en competencia desigual.
league² s. *(distance)* legua.
leak (lēk) I. intr. *(container)* salirse; *(pipe)* tener pérdidas; *(roof, faucet)* gotear; *(boat)* hacer agua ♦ **to l. in** filtrarse, colarse • **to l. out** salirse, escaparse; *(to become known)* divulgarse —tr. divulgar II. s. *(container)* agujero; *(pipe)* pérdida; *(faucet, roof)* gotera; *(boat)* vía de agua; *(escape)* salida, escape; *(disclosure)* divulgación *f*.
leak·y (lē'kē) adj. **-i-** que se sale, que gotea; *(boat)* que hace agua.
lean¹ (lēn) intr. **-ed** *o* **-t** inclinarse; *(to rest on)* apoyarse, reclinarse; *(to rely)* depender de, contar con; *(to tend)* inclinarse; *(to exert pressure)* hacer presión ♦ **to l. back** *(against the wall)* recostarse; *(in a chair)* reclinarse • **to l. forward** inclinarse • **to l. over backwards to** FAM. hacer todo lo posible para —tr. *(to rest)* apoyar, recostar; *(to cause to incline)* inclinar, ladear.
lean² I. adj. *(thin)* delgado, flaco; *(meat)* magro, sin grasa ♦ **l. years** años de escasez II. s. CUL. carne *f* sin grasa.
lean·ing (lē'nĭng) s. proclividad *f*, inclinación *f*.
lean-to (lēn'tōō') s. cobertizo.
leap (lēp) I. intr. **-ed** *o* **-t** saltar ♦ **to l. at the chance** no dejar escapar la oportunidad —tr. saltar por encima de; *(a horse)* hacer saltar II. s. salto, brinco; FIG. paso ♦ **by leaps and bounds** a grandes pasos • **l. year** año bisiesto.
leap·frog ('frôg') I. s. pídola II. tr. **-gg-** saltar por encima de.
learn (lûrn) tr. **-ed** *o* **-t** aprender; *(to find out)* saber, enterarse de ♦ **to l. by heart** aprender de memoria —intr. aprender; *(from mistakes)* escarmentar ♦ **to l. how to** aprender a.
learn·ed (lûr'nĭd) adj. erudito.
learn·er ('nər) s. principiante *mf* ♦ **to be a fast**

l. aprender rápidamente.
learn·ing ('nĭng) s. aprendizaje *m*; *(knowledge)* saber *m*, erudición *f* ♦ **l. disability** dificultad de aprendizaje.
lease (lēs) I. s. contrato de arrendamiento; *(duration)* alquiler *m* ♦ **to get a new l. on life** empezar una nueva vida II. tr. arrendar, dar en arriendo; *(to rent)* alquilar.
lease·hold ('hōld') s. inquilinato, arrendamiento; *(property)* propiedad arrendada.
lease·hold·er (:hōl'dər) s. inquilino, arrendatario.
leash (lēsh) I. s. correa, trailla II. tr. atraillar; *(to control)* controlar, dominar.
leas·ing (lē'sĭng) s. alquiler *m*, arrendamiento.
least (lēst) I. cf. **little** II. adj. menor; *(smallest)* mínimo, más pequeño ♦ **that's the l. of my worries** eso es lo de menos III. adv. menos IV. s. lo menos ♦ **at l.** *(not less than)* por lo menos; *(in any event)* al menos • **at the very l.** como mínimo • **not in the l.** en absoluto, de ningún modo • **to say the l.** sin exagerar; IRÓN. por no decir otra cosa.
least·wise ('wīz') adv. FAM. *(anyway)* de todas maneras; *(at least)* por lo menos.
leath·er (lĕth'ər) s. cuero, piel *f*.
leath·er·y ('ə-rē) adj. parecido al cuero; *(weathered)* curtido; *(meat)* correoso, duro.
leave¹ (lēv) tr. **left** salir de; *(to forget)* olvidar, dejar; *(to let stay, result in)* dejar; *(to bequeath)* dejar, legar; *(to entrust)* encomendar; *(to abandon)* dejar, abandonar ♦ **to l. alone** dejar en paz • **to l. behind** dejar atrás; *(to depart without)* irse *o* partir sin • **to l. in the dark** dejar a oscuras • **to l. out** omitir, excluir —intr. irse, marcharse; *(to depart)* salir, partir ♦ **to be left over** • **to be left over** quedar, sobrar • **to l. off** dejar, parar.
leave² s. permiso ♦ **to take (one's) l. of** someone despedirse de alguien.
leav·en (lĕv'ən) I. s. levadura; FIG. estímulo, fermento II. tr. leudar; *(to ferment)* fermentar.
leav·en·ing (:ə-nĭng) s. levadura.
leaves (lēvz) cf. **leaf**.
leave-tak·ing (lēv'tā'kĭng) s. despedida.
leav·ing (lē'vĭng) s. partida, salida.
lech·er (lĕch'ər) s. libertino, lujurioso.
lech·er·ous (:əs) adj. libertino, lujurioso.
lech·er·y (lĕch'ə-rē) s. libertinaje *m*, lujuria.
lec·tern (lĕk'tərn) s. atril *m*, facistol *m*.
lec·tor (:tər) s. lector *m*.
lec·ture (:chər) I. s. conferencia; *(class)* curso, clase *f*; *(reprimand)* reprimenda, sermón *m* II. intr. dictar conferencia —tr. dar una conferencia a; *(to scold)* sermonear.
lec·tur·er (:ər) s. conferenciante *mf*, conferencista *mf*.
led (lĕd) cf. **lead¹**.
ledge (lĕj) s. *(of a wall)* repisa, anaquel *m*; *(on a cliff)* reborde *m*, saliente *m*; *(in the ocean)* banco de arrecifes.
ledg·er (lĕj'ər) s. libro mayor.
lee (lē) s. MARÍT. sotavento; FIG. abrigo.
leech (lēch) I. s. sanguijuela; FIG. parásito, vividor *m* II. tr. ♦ **to l. off someone** pegarse a alguien como parásito.
leek (lēk) s. puerro.
leer (lîr) I. intr. mirar de reojo II. s. mirada de reojo.
leer·y (:ē) adj. **-i-** suspicaz, cauteloso.
lees (lēz) s.pl. sedimento de un líquido.

lee·ward (lē'wərd) adj. & s. (de) sotavento.

lee·way (lē'wā') s. *(drift)* deriva; FIG. *(margin)* margen *m*; *(latitude)* campo, libertad *f*.

left¹ (lĕft) **I.** adj. izquierdo **II.** s. izquierda **III.** adv. a *o* hacia la izquierda.

left² cf. **leave¹**.

left-hand ('hănd') adj. *(on the left)* a *o* de la izquierda; *(left-handed)* para zurdos.

left-hand·ed ('hăn'dĭd) **I.** adj. *(person)* zurdo; *(utensil)* para zurdos; *(compliment)* de doble filo **II.** adv. con la mano izquierda.

left·ist (lĕf'tĭst) s. & adj. POL. izquierdista *mf*.

left·o·ver (lĕft'ō'vər) **I.** adj. sobrante, restante **II.** s. ◆ pl. sobras, restos; CUL. plato hecho de restos de comida.

left-wing (lĕft'wĭng') adj. izquierdista.

left-wing·er (lĕft'wĭng'ər) s. izquierdista *mf*.

left·y (lĕf'tē) s. s. JER. zurdo.

leg (lĕg) s. pierna; *(of an animal)* pata; *(of furniture)* pata, pie *m*; *(of pants)* pierna, pernera; *(in a journey)* etapa; *(in races)* tramo, trecho ◆ **not to have a l. to stand on** FAM. carecer de una razón válida • **on its last legs** FAM. sin recursos, en las últimas • **to pull someone's l.** FAM. tomarle el pelo a alguien • **to shake a l.** FAM. apresurarse, darse prisa • **to stretch one's legs** *(to stretch)* estirar las piernas; *(to take a walk)* dar un paseo.

leg·a·cy (lĕg'ə-sē) s. herencia.

le·gal (lē'gəl) adj. legal; *(relating to the law)* jurídico; *(statutory)* legítimo ◆ **l. tender** moneda de curso legal • **of l. age** mayor de edad.

le·gal·ese (lē'gə-lēz') s. vocabulario legal.

le·gal·ist ('-lĭst) s. legalista *mf*.

le·gal·is·tic ('-lĭs'tĭk) adj. legalista.

le·gal·i·ty (lē-găl'ĭ-tē) s. legalidad *f* ◆ pl. trámites jurídicos.

le·gal·ize (lē'gə-līz') tr. legalizar, legitimar.

leg·ate (lĕg'ĭt) s. legado (enviado papal).

le·ga·tion (lĭ-gā'shən) s. legación *f*.

leg·end (lĕj'ənd) s. leyenda; *(person)* mito; *(caption)* pie *m*.

leg·en·dar·y (:ən-dĕr'ē) adj. legendario.

leg·ged (lĕg'ĭd, lĕgd) adj. *(people)* de piernas, *(animals, furniture)* de patas.

leg·gings (lĕg'ĭngz) s.pl. polainas.

leg·gy (:ē) adj. -i- de piernas largas.

leg·i·bil·i·ty (lĕj'ə-bĭl'ĭ-tē) s. legibilidad *f*.

leg·i·ble (lĕj'ə-bəl) adj. legible.

le·gion (lē'jən) s. legión *f*.

le·gion·ar·y (lē'jə-nĕr'ē) adj. & s. legionario.

le·gion·naire ('-nâr') s. legionario.

leg·is·late (lĕj'ĭ-slāt') intr. legislar. tr. disponer o establecer por ley.

leg·is·la·tion ('-slā'shən) s. legislación *f*.

leg·is·la·tive ('-'tĭv) adj. legislativo.

leg·is·la·tor (:tər) s. legislador *m*.

leg·is·la·ture (:chər) s. legislatura.

le·git (lə-jĭt') adj. JER. legítimo.

le·git·i·ma·cy (:ə-mə-sē) s. legitimidad *f*.

le·git·i·mate (:mĭt) adj. *(lawful)* lícito; *(reasonable)* válido; *(authentic)* legítimo, auténtico; *(child)* legítimo.

le·git·i·mize (:mīz') tr. legitimar.

leg·ume (lĕg'yŏom') s. legumbre *f*.

leg·work (lĕg'wûrk') s. FAM. trabajo que requiere caminar mucho.

lei·sure (lē'zhər, lĕzh'ər) s. ocio ◆ **at one's l.** cuando uno tenga tiempo ◆ **l. time** tiempo libre.

lei·sure·ly (:lē) adj. & adv. sin prisa.

lem·ming (lĕm'ĭng) s. lemming *m*.

lem·on (lĕm'ən) **I.** s. limón *m*; FAM. *(car)* ca-

charro ◆ **l. tree** limonero **II.** adj. limonado.

lem·on·ade ('-ə-nād') s. limonada.

lend (lĕnd) tr. **lent** prestar; *(to impart)* dar, impartir ◆ **to l. itself to** prestarse a • **to l. a hand** ayudar —intr. hacer préstamos.

lend·er (lĕn'dər) s. prestador *m*; COM. prestamista *mf*.

length (lĕngkth) s. largo, longitud *f*; *(quality)* largura, extensión *f*; *(piece)* pedazo, tramo; *(in a race)* cuerpo; *(duration)* duración *f* ◆ **at l.** *(eventually)* al cabo, por fin; *(fully)* por extenso, detenidamente • **to go to great lengths** hacer todo lo posible • **to keep somebody at arm's l.** mantener a alguien a distancia.

length·en (lĕngk'thən) tr. & intr. alargar(se), estirar(se); *(time)* prolongar(se).

length·wise (lĕngkth'wīz') adj. & adv. longitudinal(mente).

length·y (lĕngk'thē) adj. -i- prolongado; *(long)* largo.

le·ni·ence/·cy (lē'nyəns) s. indulgencia.

le·ni·ent (:yənt) adj. indulgente.

lens (lĕnz) s. lente *mf*.

lent (lĕnt) cf. **lend**.

len·til (lĕn'təl) s. lenteja.

le·o·nine (lē'ə-nīn') adj. leonino.

leop·ard (lĕp'ərd) s. leopardo.

le·o·tard (lē'ə-tärd') s. malla de bailarines.

lep·er (lĕp'ər) s. leproso.

lep·re·chaun (lĕp'rĭ-kŏn') s. duende *m*.

lep·ro·sy (lĕp'rə-sē) s. lepra.

lep·rous (:rəs) adj. leproso.

les·bi·an (lĕz'bē-ən) s. lesbiana.

le·sion (lē'zhən) s. lesión *f*.

less (lĕs) **I.** cf. **little II.** adj. menos; *(not as great)* menor ◆ **in l. than no time** en un abrir y cerrar de ojos • **l. than** menos de (lo que) • **no l. than** *(as much as)* nada menos que; *(at least)* por lo menos • **nothing l. than** nada menos que **III.** prep. menos **IV.** adv. menos ◆ **l. and l.** cada vez menos • **l. than** *(not at all)* nada <*you are being l. than honest* no estás siendo nada honesto>; *(far from)* ni mucho menos • **much l.** mucho menos **IV.** s. menos *m*.

les·see (lĕ-sē') s. locatario, arrendatario.

less·en (lĕs'ən) tr. & intr. disminuir.

less·er (:ər) adj. menor; *(smaller)* más pequeño.

les·son (lĕs'ən) s. lección *f* ◆ **to learn one's l.** escarmentar • **to take lessons** tomar clases.

les·sor (lĕs'ôr') s. locador *m*, arrendador *m*.

lest (lĕst) conj. para (que) no.

let¹ (lĕt) **I.** tr. **let, -tting** permitir; *(to allow)* dejar <*l. the water run* deja correr el agua>; *(to rent)* alquilar; *(to lease)* arrendar ◆ **to l. by** *o* **through** dejar pasar • **to l. down** bajar; *(to lengthen)* alargar; *(hair)* dejar caer; *(to disappoint)* fallar • **to l. go** *(to free)* despedir; *(to set free)* dejar en libertad; *(to release)* soltar • **to l. in** dejar entrar • **to l. it go at that** dejarlo así • **to l. know** avisar, dar a conocer • **to l. off** *(steam)* dejar salir; *(to exempt)* eximir, dispensar de; *(to forgive)* perdonar • **to l. oneself go** *(to enjoy)* soltarse, desatarse; *(to neglect)* descuidarse • **to l. out** dejar salir; *(to set free)* poner en libertad; *(garments)* ensanchar, extender; *(to divulge)* divulgar; *(scream)* dejar, despedir; *(to rent)* alquilar —intr. *(to be rented)* alquilarse; *(to be leased)* arrendarse • **to l. on** *(to divulge)* admitir, revelar el secreto; *(to pretend)* fingir • **to l. up** FAM. *(to cease)* cesar; *(to slacken)* aflojarse, disminuirse

—aux. <*l. us pray* oremos> <*let's see* veamos> <*l. x equal y* supongamos que x es igual a y> II. conj. ♦ **l. alone** y mucho menos, ni siquiera.
let² s. obstáculo; *(in tennis)* let m.
let·down ('doun') s. disminución f; *(disappointment)* decepción f, desilusión f.
le·thal (lē'thəl) adj. letal, mortífero.
le·thar·gic (lə-thär'jĭk) adj. letárgico.
leth·ar·gy (lĕth'ər-jē) s. letargo.
let·ter (lĕt'ər) I. s. *(of alphabet)* letra; *(note)* carta ♦ **capital l.** mayúscula • **l. bomb** carta explosiva • **l. opener** abrecartas • **small l.** minúscula • **to the l.** al pie de la letra ♦ pl. letras, erudición II. tr. inscribir letras en.
let·ter·box (:bŏks') s. apartado, buzón m.
let·tered (lĕt'ərd) adj. literato, letrado; *(erudite)* erudito; *(with letters)* rotulado.
let·ter·head (lĕt'ər-hĕd') s. *(heading)* membrete m; *(stationery)* papel membreteado.
let·ter·ing (:ĭng) s. rotulado, rótulo.
let·ter·per·fect ('-pûr'fĭkt) adj. preciso.
let·tuce (lĕt'əs) s. lechuga.
let·up (lĕt'ŭp') s. disminución f; *(pause)* pausa, interrupción f.
leu·ke·mi·a (lōō-kē'mē-ə) s. leucemia.
lev·ee (lĕv'ē) s. *(on a river)* ribero, dique m; *(pier)* muelle m fluvial.
lev·el (lĕv'əl) I. s. nivel m; *(height)* altura; *(flat land)* llano, llanura; *(rank)* posición f, categoría ♦ **at ground l.** a ras de tierra • **on the l.** FIG. honesto, limpio II. adj. plano, llano; *(horizontal)* horizontal, a nivel; *(even)* parejo, igual; *(steady)* uniforme; *(rational)* equilibrado; CUL. *(not heaping)* al ras, raso ♦ **to do one's l. best** FAM. hacer todo lo posible III. tr. nivelar; *(to make flat)* allanar, aplanar; *(to make uniform)* emparejar, igualar; *(to raze)* arrasar, echar por tierra; *(gun)* apuntar; *(accusation)* dirigir ♦ **to l. off** nivelar —intr. nivelarse, igualarse ♦ **to l. off** estabilizarse.
lev·el·head·ed (:hĕd'ĭd) adj. equilibrado.
lev·er (lĕv'ər, lē'vər) I. s. palanca II. tr. apalancar.
lev·er·age (:ĭj) s. apalancamiento; *(power)* fuerza de una palanca; FIG. poder m, influencia.
le·vi·a·than (lə-vī'ə-thən) s. gigante m.
lev·i·tate (lĕv'ĭ-tāt') tr. & intr. mantener(se) en el aire por levitación.
lev·i·ta·tion ('-tā'shən) s. levitación f.
lev·i·ty (lĕv'ĭ-tē) s. ligereza, frivolidad f.
lev·y (lĕv'ē) I. tr. *(to impose)* exigir, imponer; *(to collect)* recaudar; *(to draft)* levar, reclutar; *(a war)* hacer II. s. *(imposition)* exacción f, imposición f; *(collection)* recaudación f; *(draft)* leva, reclutamiento f; *(tax)* impuesto; *(surcharge)* sobretasa.
lewd (lōōd) adj. *(lustful)* lujurioso, lascivo; *(obscene)* obsceno, indecente.
lewd·ness ('nĭs) s. lujuria, lascivia.
lex·i·cal (lĕk'sĭ-kəl) adj. léxico.
lex·i·cog·ra·pher ('-kŏg'rə-fər) s. lexicógrafo.
lex·i·cog·ra·phy (:fē) s. lexicografía.
lex·i·con (lĕk'sĭ-kŏn') s. lexicón m, diccionario; *(vocabulary)* léxico, vocabulario.
li·a·bil·i·ty (lī'ə-bĭl'ĭ-tē) s. responsabilidad f, obligación f; *(to prosecution)* sujeción f; *(debt)* deuda; *(hindrance)* desventaja, inconveniente m; *(tendency)* susceptibilidad f ♦ **l. insurance** seguro de responsabilidad civil ♦ pl. COM. el pasivo.
li·a·ble (lī'ə-bəl) adj. responsable; *(obligated)*

obligado; *(subject)* sujeto; *(tending to)* susceptible; *(likely)* probable.
li·ai·son (lē'ā-zŏn', lē-ā'-) s. enlace m; *(love affair)* romance m.
li·ar (lī'ər) s. mentiroso.
li·ba·tion (lī-bā'shən) s. libación f; *(beverage)* bebida.
li·bel (lī'bəl) I. s. libelo, difamación f II. tr. difamar.
li·bel·er (lī'bə-lər) s. libelista mf, difamador m.
li·bel·ous (:ləs) adj. difamatorio.
lib·er·al (lĭb'ər-əl) I. adj. liberal; *(tolerant)* tolerante; *(generous)* generoso; *(abundant)* abundante, amplio; *(not liberal)* libre ♦ **l. arts** artes liberales, humanidades II. s. liberal mf.
lib·er·al·i·ty (lĭb'ə-răl'ĭ-tē) s. liberalidad f.
lib·er·al·ize ('ər-ə-līz') tr. & intr. liberalizar(se).
lib·er·ate (:ə-rāt') tr. liberar, libertar.
lib·er·a·tion ('-rā'shən) s. liberación f.
lib·er·a·tor ('-'tər) s. liberador m.
lib·er·tar·i·an (lĭb'ər-târ'ē-ən) s. libertario.
lib·er·tine (lĭb'ər-tēn') s. & adj. libertino.
lib·er·ty (lĭb'ər-tē) s. libertad f; MARIT. permiso, licencia ♦ **at l.** libre, en libertad.
li·bid·i·nous (lĭ-bĭd'n-əs) adj. libidinoso.
li·brar·i·an (lī-brâr'ē-ən) s. bibliotecario.
li·brar·y (lī'brĕr'ē) s. biblioteca.
li·bret·to (lĭ-brĕt'ō) s. [pl. **s** o **-ti**] libreto.
lice (līs) cf. **louse.**
li·cense (lī'səns) I. s. licencia, permiso; *(card)* carnet m; *(latitude, freedom)* libertad f ♦ **l. plate** patente, placa (de matrícula) II. tr. licenciar, autorizar; *(to accredit)* acreditar.
li·cens·er (lī'sən-sər) s. expedidor m de una licencia.
li·cen·ti·ate (lī-sĕn'shē-ĭt) s. licenciado.
li·cen·tious (:shəs) adj. licencioso.
li·chen (lī'kən) s. liquen m.
lic·it (lĭs'ĭt) adj. lícito.
lick (lĭk) I. tr. lamer; *(to beat)* cascar, zurrar; *(to defeat)* vencer; *(to overcome)* superar ♦ **to l. someone's boots** adular servilmente a alguien —intr. lamer II. s. lametazo; *(little bit)* pizca, ápice m; *(salt)* salegar m; *(blow)* golpe m.
lick·e·ty·split (lĭk'ĭ-tē-splĭt') adv. FAM. rapidísimamente, a gran velocidad.
lick·ing (lĭk'ĭng) s. JER. *(beating)* paliza; *(defeat)* derrota.
lic·o·rice (lĭk'ər-ĭs, :ĭsh) s. regaliz m.
lid (lĭd) s. tapa; *(eyelid)* pestaña ♦ **to blow the l. off** FAM. descubrir, revelar • **to flip one's l.** JER. pegar el grito en el cielo • **to put the l. on** FAM. poner frenos a.
lie¹ (lī) I. intr. **lay, lain, lying** *(to recline)* tenderse, acostarse; *(to be stretched out)* estar tendido, yacer; *(to remain)* quedarse; *(to be situated)* estar situado; *(to be buried)* estar enterrado; *(to be admissible)* ser admisible; FIG. *(to consist)* radicar, residir (in en) ♦ **to l. back** inclinarse hacia atrás • **to l. low** FAM. esconderse, ocultarse • **to l. lying down** FAM. aceptar (algo) sin protestar II. s. posición f.
lie² I. s. mentira, embuste m ♦ **l. detector** aparato detector de mentiras • **to give the l. to** desmentir II. intr. **lying** mentir.
liege (lēj) I. s. *(lord)* señor m feudal; *(vassal)* vasallo II. adj. leal, fiel.
lien (lēn, lē'ən) s. derecho de retención.
lieu (lōō) s. ♦ **in l. of** en lugar de, en vez de.
lieu·ten·ant (lōō-tĕn'ənt) s. MIL. teniente m; MARIT. alférez m de navío; *(deputy)* lugarteniente m ♦ **l. commander** capitán de corbeta •

l. governor vice gobernador.

life (līf) s. [pl. **-ves**] vida; *(usefulness)* duración *f*; *(activity)* animación *f*; *(imprisonment)* cadena perpetua ♦ **for dear l.** *o* for one's l. como para salvar la propia vida ♦ **in later l.** en los últimos años ♦ **l. jacket** chaleco salvavidas ♦ **l. of the party** alma de la fiesta ♦ **l. preserver** salvavidas ♦ **not on your l.!** ¡de ninguna manera! ♦ **that's l.!** ¡así es la vida! ♦ **to bring back to l.** reanimar, resucitar ♦ **to have the time of one's l.** divertirse mucho ♦ **to take one's own l.** suicidarse ♦ **true to l.** verosímil.

life·blood ('blŭd') s. sangre *f*; FIG. alma, parte *f* vital.

life·boat ('bōt') s. bote *m* salvavidas.

life·guard ('gärd') s. bañero, salvavidas *mf*.

life·less (līs) adj. inanimado; *(dead)* muerto; *(dull)* sin vida.

life·like ('līk') adj. que parece vivo; *(natural)* natural.

life·long ('lông') adj. de toda la vida.

lif·er (lī'fər) s. JER. presidiario condenado a prisión perpetua.

life·sav·er (līf'sā'vər) s. *(life preserver)* salvavidas *m*; FIG salvación *f*.

life·sav·ing (:sā'vĭng) I. s. salvamento, socorrismo II. adj. de salvamento.

life-size(d) (:sīz[d]') adj. de tamaño natural.

life·style (:stīl') s. estilo de vida.

life-sup·port system (:sə-pôrt') s. sistema *m* de mantenimiento de vida.

life·time (:tīm') s. vida.

life·work (:wûrk') s. obra principal de la vida.

lift (lĭft) I. tr. alzar, levantar; *(to hoist)* elevar, izar; *(to revoke)* revocar; *(to steal)* escamotear, birlar; *(to plagiarize)* plagiar —intr. levantarse, ascender; *(fog)* disiparse ♦ **to l. off** AER. despegar II. s. alzamiento, levantamiento; *(load)* carga; *(elevation)* elevación *f*; *(elation)* exaltación *f*; AFR. fuerza ascensional; MEC. gato; G.B. ascensor *m* ♦ **to give someone a l.** llevar a alguien en un vehículo; *(to cheer up)* levantarle a alguien el ánimo.

lift-off ('ôf') s. despegue *m*.

lig·a·ment (lĭg'ə-mənt) s. ligamento.

li·gate (lī'gāt') tr. ligar.

li·ga·tion (lī-gā'shən) s. ligadura.

lig·a·ture (lĭg'ə-chŏr') s. ligadura.

light[1] (līt) I. s. luz *f*; *(flame)* fuego; *(viewpoint)* aspecto, punto de vista; *(luminary)* lumbrera, eminencia; *(gleam)* brillo ♦ **in l. of** en vista de, considerando ♦ **l. bulb** bombilla ♦ **l. meter** fotómetro ♦ **to bring to l.** sacar a luz, revelar ♦ **to shed** *o* throw l. on aclarar ♦ **to come to l.** salir a la luz ♦ **to give the green l.** aprobar ♦ **to see the l.** comprender, darse cuenta ♦ pl. FIG. *(opinions)* luces, conocimientos II. tr. **-ed** *o* lit encender; *(to illuminate)* alumbrar, iluminar ♦ **to l. up** iluminar; *(cigarette)* encender —intr. encenderse ♦ **to l. up** iluminarse III. adj. *(colors)* claro; *(complexion)* blanco; *(hair)* rubio; *(bright)* bien iluminado.

light[2] I. adj. *(not heavy)* ligero, liviano; *(not forceful)* suave, leve; *(rain)* fino; *(food)* ligero; *(faint)* débil; *(frivolous)* superficial; *(happy)* alegre ♦ **l. in the head** mareado ♦ **to make l. of** no tomar en serio II. adv. ligeramente ♦ **to travel l.** viajar con poco equipaje III. intr. **-ed** *o* lit *(to dismount)* apearse, desmontar; *(to alight)* posarse ♦ **to l. into** atacar ♦ **to l. (up)on** *(to land on)* posarse; *(to come across)* tropezar con ♦ **to l. out** FAM. largarse.

light·en[1] (līt'n) tr. & intr. iluminar(se), aclarar(se).

light·en[2] tr. & intr. *(less heavy)* aligerar(se); *(to relieve)* aliviar(se); *(to gladden)* alegrar(se).

light·er[1] (līt'ər) s. encendedor *m*.

light·er[2] s. MARIT. barcaza, gabarra.

light-fin·gered (līt'f ĭng'gərd) adj. listo de manos, ligero de dedos.

light-foot·ed (:fŏŏt'ĭd) adj. ligero de pies.

light·head·ed ('hĕd'ĭd) adj. *(dizzy)* mareado; *(frivolous)* frívolo, ligero de cascos.

light·heart·ed ('här'tĭd) adj. despreocupado.

light·house (:hous') s. faro.

light·ing (lī'tĭng) s. iluminación *f*, alumbrado.

light·ly (līt'lē) adv. ligeramente; *(superficially)* levemente; *(nimbly)* ágilmente; *(blithely)* despreocupadamente; *(indifferently)* a la ligera ♦ **to let off l.** dar un castigo leve a ♦ **to take l.** no dar importancia a.

light·ness[1] (līt'nĭs) s. luminosidad *f*, claridad *f*.

light·ness[2] s. ligereza; *(agility)* agilidad *f*, gracia; *(blitheness)* despreocupación *f*.

light·ning (līt'nĭng) I. s. rayo, relámpago II. intr. descargar un rayo *o* relámpago III. adj. *(quick)* relámpago ♦ **l. bug** luciérnaga ♦ **l. rod** pararrayos.

light·weight (:wāt') s. persona de poco peso; *(boxer)* peso ligero; FAM. pelele *m*.

light-year *o* **light year** (:yïr') s. año luz.

lik·a·ble (lī'kə-bəl) adj. agradable, grato.

like[1] (līk) I. tr. gustar <*I l. the movies* me gusta el cine>; *(to want)* desear, querer —intr. querer ♦ **as you l.** como usted quiera II. s. gusto.

like[2] I. prep. como; *(typical of)* típico, propio (de); *(such as)* (tal) como ♦ **l. this** *o* that así ♦ **something l.** algo así como ♦ **that's more l. it!** ¡eso es mucho mejor! II. adj. similar, parecido III. s. semejante *mf*, igual *mf* ♦ **and the l.** FAM. y cosas por el estilo ♦ **the likes of** personas como IV. conj. como.

like·li·hood ('lē-hŏŏd') s. probabilidad *f*.

like·ly (:lē) I. adj. -i- probable; *(plausible)* verosímil, *(promising)* prometedor ♦ **that's a l. story!** ¡vaya cuento! II. adv. probablemente.

like-mind·ed (:mīn'dĭd) adj. del mismo parecer.

lik·en (lī'kən) tr. comparar.

like·ness (līk'nĭs) s. semejanza; *(appearance)* apariencia; *(representation)* retrato, imagen *f*.

like·wise (:wīz') adv. del mismo modo, lo mismo; *(also)* además.

lik·ing (lī'kĭng) s. afición *f*; *(taste)* gusto ♦ **to take a l. to** *(something)* aficionarse a; *(someone)* coger *o* tener simpatía a.

li·lac (lī'lək, lī'lăk') s. & adj. (de color) lila.

lilt (lĭlt) I. s. canción *f* alegre; *(cadence)* ritmo; *(accent)* deje *m* II. tr. cantar alegremente.

lil·y (lĭl'ē) s. lirio ♦ **l. of the valley** muguete ♦ **l. pad** hoja de nenúfar.

lil·y-liv·ered (-lĭv'ərd) adj. cobarde, tímido.

lil·y-white ('-hwīt') adj. blanco como la nieve; *(irreproachable)* intachable.

li·ma bean (lī'mə) s. frijol *m*, haba.

limb (lĭm) s. BOT. rama; ANAT. miembro, extremidad *f* ♦ **out on a l.** FAM. en una situación precaria ♦ **to tear l. from l.** despedazar.

lim·ber (lĭm'bər) I. adj. flexible; *(agile)* ágil II. intr. ♦ **to l. up** prepararse haciendo ejercicios.

lim·bo (lĭm'bō) s. nada ♦ L. TEOL. limbo.

lime[1] (līm) s. *(tree, fruit)* lima.

lime² I. s. cal *f*; *(birdlime)* liga II. tr. *(wall, surface)* encalar; *(soil)* abonar con cal.
lime·light ('līt') s. luz *f* de calcio; FIG. centro de atención.
lim·er·ick (lǐm'ər-ĭk) s. poema humorístico.
lime·stone (līm'stōn') s. (piedra) caliza.
lim·it (lǐm'ĭt) I. s. límite *m*; *(maximum)* máximo ♦ **the sky's the l.** FAM. todo es posible ♦ pl. límites, confines • **within l.** hasta cierto punto II. tr. limitar.
lim·i·ta·tion ('ĭ-tā'shən) s. limitación *f*, restricción *f* ♦ pl. restricciones; *(shortcomings)* deficiencias.
lim·it·ed ('-tĭd) I. adj. limitado, reducido; *(qualified)* módico ♦ **for a l. time only** por corto plazo solamente • **l. company** COM. sociedad anónima • **of l. means** corto de recursos II. s. (tren) expreso.
lim·it·ing (:tĭng) adj. limitativo.
lim·it·less (lǐm'ĭt-lĭs) adj. ilimitado, sin límites.
lim·o (lǐm'ō) s. limosina.
lim·ou·sine (lǐm'ə-zēn') s. limosina.
limp (lǐmp) I. intr. cojear II. s. cojera III. adj. fláccido; *(hanging)* caído; *(hair)* lacio; *(weak)* débil.
lim·pid (lǐm'pǐd) adj. límpido, claro.
lin·age (lǐ'nǐj) s. número de líneas.
linch·pin (lǐnch'pǐn') s. *(pin)* pezonera; *(essential)* parte *f* esencial.
lin·den (lǐn'dən) s. tilo.
line¹ (līn) I. s. línea; *(mark)* raya; *(wrinkle)* arruga; *(boundary)* frontera, límite *m*; *(wire)* cable *m*; *(rope)* cabo; *(cord)* cordón *m*, cordel *m*; *(fishing)* sedal *m*; *(transportation)* línea; *(company)* compañía; *(trajectory)* trayectoria; *(method)* línea, curso; *(occupation)* ocupación *f*; *(specialty)* especialidad *f*, rama; *(merchandise)* surtido; *(row)* hilera, fila; *(queue)* cola; *(verse)* verso; *(brief letter)* letras, líneas ♦ along the lines of algo como • in l. with de acuerdo con • down the l. en el futuro • l. of work ocupación • on the l. en el teléfono; *(in jeopardy)* en peligro • the end of the l. FIG. el final, el fin • to be in l. for ser candidato para • to be out of l. comportarse incorrectamente • to draw the l. fijar límites • to drop someone a l. ponerle a alguien unas letras • to feed, give o hand someone a l. embaucar a alguien • to hold the l. no restringir • to lay it on the l. hablar con franqueza • to step out of l. salirse de lo que está establecido • to toe the l. conformarse II. tr. rayar, trazar líneas en • to l. up poner en fila —intr. • to l. up hacer cola.
line² tr. *(to put lining in)* forrar; *(to cover)* cubrir; TEC. revestir; *(brakes)* guarnecer ♦ **to l. one's pockets** enriquecerse.
lin·e·age (lǐn'ē-ǐj) s. linaje *m*, estirpe *m*.
lin·e·al (:əl) adj. en línea directa; *(linear)* lineal.
lin·e·ar (:ər) adj. linear, lineal ♦ **l. measure** medida de longitud.
lined (līnd) adj. *(ruled)* rayado; *(with a lining)* forrado.
lin·en (lǐn'ən) I. s. lino, hilo; *(goods)* lencería ♦ pl. ropa de cama II. adj. de lino *o* hilo.
lin·er¹ (lǐ'nər) s. trasatlántico, barco de travesía; AVIA. avión *m* de línea *o* travesía.
lin·er² s. *(lining)* forro, revestimiento.
lines·man (līnz'mən) s. [pl. **-men**] ELEC. guardalínea *m*; DEP. juez *m* de línea.
line·up *o* **line-up** (līn'ŭp') s. CRIMIN. fila (de personas); DEP. alineación *f*.

lin·ger (lǐng'gər) intr. quedarse; *(to lag behind)* quedarse atrás; *(before dying)* durar; *(to persist)* persistir, subsistir.
lin·ge·rie (län'zhə-rē', :rā') s. lencería, ropa interior (de mujer).
lin·ger·ing (lǐng'gər-ǐng) adj. persistente.
lin·go (lǐng'gō) s. [pl. **es**] FAM. jerigonza.
lin·gual (lǐng'gwəl) adj. lingual.
lin·guist (:gwǐst) s. políglota; *(specialist)* lingüista *mf*.
lin·guis·tic (-gwǐs'tǐk) adj. lingüístico ♦ **linguistics** s.sg. lingüística.
lin·i·ment (lǐn'ə-mənt) s. linimento, untura.
lin·ing (lǐ'nǐng) s. forro.
link (lǐngk) I. s. eslabón *m*; *(element)* enlace *m*; *(connection)* unión *f*, conexión *f*; *(bond)* vínculo, lazo ♦ **weak l.** punto débil II. tr. & intr. *(to unite)* unir(se), enlazar(se); *(to connect)* eslabonar(se), conectar(se).
link·age (lǐng'kǐj) s. eslabonamiento, *(bond)* unión *f*, enlace *m*.
linked (lǐngkt) adj. conectado, enlazado; *(united)* vinculado, *(combined)* ligado.
links (lǐngks) s.pl. campo de golf.
li·no·le·um (lǐ-nō'lē-əm) s. linóleo.
lint (lǐnt) s. pelusa, tamo; MED. hilas.
lin·tel (lǐn'tl) s. dintel *m*, lintel *m*.
li·on (lī'ən) s. león *m*; *(celebrity)* celebridad *f* ♦ **the l.'s share** la mejor parte.
li·on·ess (lī'ə-nǐs) s. leona.
li·on·heart·ed (lī'ən-här'tǐd) adj. muy valiente.
li·on·ize (lī'ə-nīz') tr. agasajar.
lip (lǐp) s. labio; *(edge)* reborde *m*; *(rim)* pico; JER. insolencia, impertinencia ♦ **to keep a stiff upper l.** poner a mal tiempo buena cara • **to lick one's lips** FIG. relamerse • **to pay l. service** to fingir estar de acuerdo con • **to smack one's lips** hacer un chasquido con los labios.
lip-read (lǐp'rēd') intr. **-read** leer los labios.
lip·stick (:stǐk') s. lápiz *m* labial.
liq·ue·fac·tion (lǐk'wə-fǎk'shən) s. licuefacción *f*.
liq·ue·fy ('-fī') tr. & intr. licuar(se).
li·queur (lǐ-kûr') s. licor *m*.
liq·uid (lǐk'wǐd) I. s. líquido II. adj. líquido; *(clear)* claro, transparente; *(flowing)* límpido ♦ **l. assets** activo líquido.
liq·ui·date (:wǐ-dāt') tr. liquidar; *(assets)* convertir en efectivo; FAM. *(to murder)* asesinar.
liq·ui·da·tion ('-dā'shən) s. liquidación *f*.
liq·uid·i·ty (lǐ-kwǐd'ǐ-tē) s. liquidez *f*, fluidez *f*.
liq·ui·fy (lǐk'wə-fī') var. de **liquefy**.
liq·uor (lǐk'ər) s. licor *m*.
lisp (lǐsp) I. s. ceceo II. intr. cecear.
lis·some (lǐs'əm) adj. flexible; *(willowy)* elástico; *(nimble)* ágil.
list¹ (lǐst) I. s. lista II. tr. hacer una lista de, enumerar; *(to register)* poner en una lista.
list² MARÍT. I. s. escora II. intr. escorar.
lis·ten (lǐs'ən) intr. escuchar; *(to heed advice)* prestar atención ♦ **to l. up** escuchar bien.
lis·ten·er (:ə-nər) s. oyente *mf*.
list·ing (lǐs'tǐng) s. alistamiento; *(list entry)* listado; *(list)* lista.
list·less (lǐst'lǐs) adj. apático.
lit (lǐt) adj. cf. **light¹**, **light²**.
lit·a·ny (lǐt'n-ē) s. letanía.
li·ter (lē'tər) s. litro.
lit·er·a·cy (lǐt'ər-ə-sē) s. alfabetismo.
lit·er·al (lǐt'ər-əl) adj. literal; *(true)* escueto, llano; *(by letters)* alfabético.
lit·er·ar·y (lǐt'ə-rěr'ē) adj. literario.

lit·er·ate (:ər-ĭt) adj. que sabe leer y escribir; *(educated)* letrado, instruido; *(literary)* literato.

lit·er·a·ture (:ə-chŏŏr') s. literatura; *(printed material)* folletos, impresos.

lithe (lῑth) adj. flexible, elástico.

lith·i·um (lῑth'ē-əm) s. litio.

lith·o·graph (lῑth'ə-grăf') s. litografía.

li·thog·ra·pher (lĭ-thŏg'rə-fər) s. litógrafo.

li·thog·ra·phy (:fē) s. litografía.

lit·i·gant (lῑt'ĭ-gənt) s. & adj. litigante *mf.*

lit·i·gate (:gāt') tr. & intr. litigar, pleitear.

lit·i·ga·tion ('-gā'shən) s. litigio, pleito.

li·ti·gious (lĭ-tĭj'əs) adj. litigioso.

lit·mus (lῑt'məs) s. tornasol *m* ♦ **l. test** prueba de ácidez, FIG. prueba determinante.

li·tre (lē'tər) G.B. var. de **liter.**

lit·ter (lῑt'ər) I. s. *(conveyance)* litera, *(stretcher)* camilla; *(animal bedding)* lecho de paja; *(animal's young)* camada, cría; *(trash)* basura II. tr. *(with trash)* tirar basura en; *(to cover)* estar esparcido por; *(to scatter)* esparcir, regar —intr. tirar basura.

lit·ter·bug (:bŭg') s. FAM. persona que arroja basura en lugares públicos.

lit·tle (lῑt'l) I. adj. **-er** o **less, -est** o **least** *(small)* pequeño; *(short)* bajo; *(brief)* breve; *(not much)* poco; *(petty)* estrecho ♦ **l. ones** niños, gente menuda II. adv. **less, least** *(not much)* poco; *(not at all) l. did I know that* no me imaginé que>; *(somewhat)* un poco, algo <she's a l. better está algo mejor> ♦ **l. by l.** poco a poco III. s. poco; *(short time)* momento.

li·tur·gi·cal (lĭ-tûr'jĭ-kəl) adj. litúrgico.

lit·ur·gy (lῑt'ər-jē) s. liturgia.

live¹ (lῑv) intr. vivir ♦ **to l. and learn** vivir para ver • **to l. in** vivir donde se trabaja • **to l. on** vivir, perdurar —tr. vivir, llevar ♦ **to l. down** lograr borrar de la memoria • **to l. it up** FAM. correr las grandes juergas, vivir la vida • **to l. off** *(someone)* vivir a expensas de; *(the land)* vivir de • **to l. through** sobrevivir • **to l. up to** *(to conform with)* actuar en conformidad con; *(to fulfill)* cumplir • **to l. with** tolerar, aceptar.

live² (lῑv) I. adj. vivo; *(of interest)* actual; *(burning)* encendido; ARM. sin estallar; RAD., TELEV. en directo ♦ **l. wire** ELEC. cable con corriente; FIG. persona vivaz y activa II. adv. en directo.

live-in (lῑv'ĭn') adj. residente, con cama.

live·li·hood (lῑv'lē-hŏŏd') s. medios de ganarse la vida.

live·li·ness (:nĭs) s. vida, animación *f.*

live·long (lῑv'lông') adj. entero, completo ♦ **all the l. day** todo el santo día.

live·ly (lῑv'lē) adj. **-i-** lleno de vida, vivaz; *(spirited)* alegre; *(animated)* animado; *(keen)* vivo, grande; *(vivid)* vivo.

liv·en (lῑv'ən) tr. & intr. animar(se).

liv·er¹ (lῑv'ər) s. ANAT., CUL. hígado.

liv·er² s. ♦ **fast l.** juerguista *mf.*

liv·er·wurst (:wûrst') s. salchicha de hígado.

liv·er·y (lῑv'ə-rē) s. *(uniform)* librea; *(stable)* caballeriza de alquiler.

lives (lῑvz) cf. **life.**

live·stock (lῑv'stŏk') s. ganado.

liv·id (lῑv'ĭd) adj. lívido; *(pale)* pálido; *(furious)* furioso.

liv·ing (lῑv'ĭng) I. adj. vivo; *(extant)* viviente, contemporáneo; *(vivid)* lleno de vida, vívido ♦ **l. expenses** gastos de manutención ♦ **l. quar-**

ters vivienda, alojamiento ♦ **l. room** sala de estar • **l. wage** salario vital II. s. vida ♦ **to earn** o **to make a l.** ganarse la vida.

liz·ard (lῑz'ərd) s. lagarto.

lla·ma (lä'mə) s. llama.

load (lōd) I. s. *(weight)* peso; *(cargo)* carga, cargamento; *(burden)* peso, presión *f* ♦ **get a l. of this!** JER. ¡fíjate!, ¡mira ésto! • **to take a l. off one's mind** sacarse un peso de encima ♦ pl. FAM. montón, muchísimo II. tr. *(to fill)* cargar, llenar; *(to burden)* agobiar, abrumar; *(to adulterate)* adulterar —intr. cargar(se).

load·ed (lō'dĭd) adj. *(full)* cargado; *(tricky)* intencionado; *(drunk)* borracho, embriagado; *(rich)* rico, forrado de dinero.

loaf¹ (lōf) s. [pl. **-ves**] pan *m*; *(shaped mass)* hogaza, barra; *(of sugar)* pilón *m.*

loaf² intr. haraganear, holgazanear.

loaf·er (lō'fər) s. holgazán *m*; *(shoe)* mocasín *m.*

loam (lōm) s. mantillo, tierra labrantía.

loan (lōn) I. s. préstamo ♦ **l. shark** FAM. usurero • **on l.** prestado II. tr. prestar.

loath (lōth) adj. poco dispuesto, renuente.

loathe (lōth) tr. aborrecer.

loath·ing (lō'thĭng) s. aborrecimiento.

loath·some (lōth'səm) adj. repugnante.

loaves (lōvz) cf. **loaf¹.**

lob (lŏb) I. tr. **-bb-** volear II. s. volea *uns.*

lob·by (lŏb'ē) I. s. *(foyer)* vestíbulo; *(waiting room)* sala de espera; POL. grupo de presión II. intr. POL. ejercer presiones.

lobe (lōb) s. lóbulo.

lo·bot·o·my (lō-bŏt'ə-mē) s. lobotomía.

lob·ster (lŏb'stər) s. langosta, bogavante.

lo·cal (lō'kəl) I. adj. local ♦ **l. call** TEL. llamada urbana • **l. government** gobierno municipal • **l. news** noticias de la ciudad II. s. tren o ómnibus local; *(chapter)* sección *f* local.

lo·cale (lō-kăl') s. sitio, lugar *m.*

lo·cal·i·ty (:ĭ-tē) s. localidad *f.*

lo·cal·ize (lō'kə-līz') tr. & intr. localizar(se).

lo·cate (lō'kāt') tr. localizar; *(to place)* ubicar, colocar —intr. establecerse, asentarse.

lo·ca·tion (lō-kā'shən) s. lugar *m*, sitio; CINEM. exteriores <to film on l. rodar los exteriores>.

lock¹ (lŏk) I. s. *(device)* cerradura; *(of a canal)* esclusa; *(gunlock)* llave *f* ♦ **l., stock, and barrel** FAM. por completo, completamente • **under l. and key** bajo llave II. tr. cerrar con llave; *(to interlock)* trabar ♦ **l. arms** tomarse del brazo • **to l. horns with** reñir con • **to l. out of (the house)** cerrar la puerta a; *(employees)* dejar sin trabajo • **to l. up** *(to confine)* encerrar; *(to fasten)* cerrar con llave; *(in jail)* encarcelar —intr. cerrarse; *(to interlock)* trabarse; *(to jam)* agarrotarse; *(a firearm)* encasquillarse ♦ **to be locked out** estar fuera sin llave • **to l. up** echar la llave.

lock² s. *(of hair)* mecha ♦ pl. cabello.

lock·er ('ər) s. ropero, armario; *(trunk)* baúl *m*; *(refrigerator)* cámara frigorífica ♦ **l. room** vestuario (de un gimnasio, club).

lock·et (:ĭt) s. guardapelo, relicario.

lock·jaw (:jô') s. trismo.

lock·smith (:smĭth') s. cerrajero.

lock·up (:ŭp') s. FAM. calabozo.

lo·co (lō'kō) adj. FAM. loco, chiflado.

lo·co·mo·tion (lō'kə-mō'shən) s. locomoción *f.*

lo·co·mo·tive (:tĭv) I. s. locomotora II. adj. locomotor, locomotivo.

lo·cus (lō'kəs) s. [pl. **-ci**] lugar *m*, localidad *f*;

GEOM. lugar geométrico.

lo·cust (lō′kəst) s. ENTOM. langosta, saltamontes *m*; *(cicada)* cigarra; BOT. acacia blanca.

lo·cu·tion (lō-kyōō′shən) s. locución *f*.

lode (lōd) s. veta, filón *m*.

lode·star (:stär′) s. estrella polar; FIG. guía *m*.

lode·stone (:stōn′) s. piedra imán.

lodge (lŏj) I. s. *(cabin)* casa de campo; *(inn)* posada; *(meeting hall)* logia II. tr. *(to house)* alojar, hospedar; *(to deposit)* depositar; *(to place)* colocar; *(to embed)* alojar, incrustar; *(complaint)* presentar, sentar; *(authority)* conferir —intr. alojarse.

lodg·er (′ər) s. inquilino.

lodg·ing (:ĭng) s. alojamiento.

loft (lôft) I. s. *(upper floor)* piso sin dividir; *(attic)* desván *m*; *(gallery)* galería; *(hayloft)* pajar *m* II. tr. lanzar (en alto).

loft·y (lôf′tē) adj. -i- alto, elevado; *(noble)* noble; *(arrogant)* arrogante, altanero.

log[1] (lôg) I. s. leño, tronco; MARÍT. diario de navegación; AVIA. diario de vuelo ♦ **l. cabin** cabaña de troncos • **to sleep like a l.** dormir como un tronco II. tr. -gg- *(trees)* aserrar; AVIA., MARÍT. consignar en un diario de navegación *o* de vuelo • **to l. miles** recorrer una distancia de millas —intr. cortar y transportar árboles.

log[2] s. MAT. logaritmo.

log·a·rithm (lô′gə-rĭth′əm) s. logaritmo.

log·book (lôg′bŏŏk′) s. AVIA., MARÍT. diario de navegación *o* de vuelo.

loge (lōzh) s. TEAT. *(box)* palco; *(mezzanine)* primer balcón *m* de butacas.

log·ger·head (lô′gər-hĕd′) s. tortuga de mar ♦ **to be at loggerheads** estar en desacuerdo.

log·ic (lŏj′ĭk) s. lógica.

log·i·cal (′ĭ-kəl) adj. lógico.

lo·gi·cian (lō-jĭsh′ən) s. lógico, dialéctico.

lo·gis·tic/ti·cal (lō-jĭs′tĭk) adj. logístico ♦ **logistics** s.sg. *o* pl. logística.

log·jam (lôg′jăm′) s. atasco de troncos flotantes; FIG. *(deadlock)* atolladero.

loin (loin) s. ANAT. lomo; *(flank)* ijada, ijar *m*; CUL. *(of beef)* solomillo; *(of pork)* lomo ♦ pl. ANAT. ingle *f*; *(genitals)* órganos genitales.

loi·ter (loi′tər) intr. holgazanear; *(to delay)* retrasarse; *(to dawdle)* perder el tiempo.

loll (lŏl) intr. *(to slouch)* repantigarse; *(to droop)* pender.

lol·li·pop/ly·pop (lŏl′ē-pŏp′) s. pirulí *m*.

lone (lōn) adj. solo, solitario; *(sole)* único.

lone·li·ness (:lē-nĭs) s. soledad *f*.

lone·ly (:lē) adj. -i- *(alone)* solo; *(isolated)* solitario.

lon·er (lō′nər) s. FAM. solitario.

lone·some (lōn′səm) adj. solo, solitario.

long[1] (lông) I. adj. largo; *(in distance)* de largo, de longitud ♦ **in the l. run** a la larga • **l. johns** FAM. calzón interior largo • **l. jump** salto de longitud • **l. shot** *(entry)* competidor con poca probabilidad de ganar; *(bet)* apuesta arriesgada • **l. suit** punto fuerte • **not by a l. shot** ni mucho menos • **to be l. on** tener mucho • **to take a l. time** tardar mucho II. adv. mucho tiempo ♦ **as l. as** *(while)* mientras; *(if)* si, siempre y cuando • **how l.?** *(time)* ¿cuánto tiempo?; *(length)* ¿qué largo? • **l. live the king!** ¡viva el rey! • **no longer** ya no, no más • **so l.!** FAM. ¡hasta luego!, ¡adiós! • **so l. as** con tal que, siempre que III. s. mucho tiempo ♦ **before l.** dentro de poco • **for l.** mucho

tiempo • **the l. and the short of** la esencia de.

long[2] intr. ♦ **to l. for** añorar, desear con ansia • **to l. to** anhelar, desear ardientemente.

long·bow (′bō′) s. arco.

long-dis·tance (:dĭs′təns) adj. & adv. de larga distancia.

lon·gev·i·ty (lŏn-jĕv′ĭ-tē) s. longevidad *f*.

long·hair (lông′hâr′) s. FAM. bohemio.

long-haired (:hârd′) adj. pelilargo.

long·hand (:hănd′) s. letra cursiva.

long·ing (:ĭng) s. anhelo, deseo.

lon·gi·tude (lŏn′jĭ-tōōd′) s. longitud *f*.

long-lived (lông′līvd′, :līvd′) adj. de larga vida.

long-play·ing (:plā′ĭng) adj. de larga duración.

long-range (:rănj′) adj. de largo alcance.

long·shore·man (′shôr′mən) s. [pl. -men] estibador *m*.

long-stand·ing (:stăn′dĭng) adj. duradero.

long-suf·fer·ing (:sŭf′ər-ĭng) adj. resignado.

long-term (:tûrm′) adj. a largo plazo.

long-time (:tīm′) adj. antiguo, viejo.

long-wind·ed (:wĭn′dĭd) adj. verboso.

long·wise (:wīz′) adv. a lo largo, longitudinalmente.

look (lŏŏk) I. intr. mirar; *(to search)* buscar; *(to seem)* parecer; *(to face)* estar orientado hacia, dar a ♦ **l. alive!** ¡apresúrate! • **l. out!** ¡cuidado! • **to l. alike** parecerse • **to l. away** apartar la mirada • **to l. back** mirar hacia atrás; *(to remember)* recordar el pasado • **to l. down** bajar la mirada, bajar los ojos • **to l.** levantar la mirada, FIG. ir mejorando, ponerse mejor —tr. mirar ♦ **to l. after** *(someone)* cuidar a, ocuparse de; *(something)* ocuparse de, encargarse de • **to l. around** for estar en busca de, buscar • **to l. back on** recordar • **to l. down** despreciar • **to l. down one's nose at** FAM. menospreciar • **to l. for** buscar; *(to expect)* esperar • **to l. forward to** anticipar • **to l. in on** pasar por casa de • **to l. into** investigar • **to l. like** parecer(se) • **to l. (up)on** estimar, considerar • **to l. out for** *(to watch for)* estar al acecho de; *(to expect)* esperar; *(to take care of)* cuidar a • **to l. out on** dar a • **to l. over** examinar, repasar • **to l. (someone) up** ir a ver *o* visitar (a alguien) • **to l. (something) up** buscar • **to l. up to** respetar, tener en estima II. s. *(quick glance)* ojeada, vistazo; *(gaze)* mirada; *(aspect)* aspecto, apariencia; *(in fashion)* moda, estilo ♦ **by the l. of things** según parece • **to take** *o* **have a l. at** mirar, echar un vistazo a • **to take a good l. at** mirar bien ♦ pl. *(appearance)* aspecto; *(beauty)* belleza.

look-a·like (′ə-līk′) s. doble *mf*.

look·ing glass (:ĭng) s. espejo.

look·out (:out′) s. *(watch)* vigilancia; *(watchtower)* atalaya; *(vantage point)* mirador *m*; *(outlook)* perspectiva, panorama *m* ♦ **to be on the l. for** estar al acecho de.

loom[1] (lōōm) intr. *(to appear)* aparecer, surgir; *(to impend)* amenazar.

loom[2] s. telar *m*.

loon[1] (lōōn) s. ORNIT. somorgujo.

loon[2] s. *(simpleton)* bobo.

loon·y (lōō′nē) FAM. I. adj. -i- bobo ♦ **l. bin** manicomio II. s. loco, lunático.

loop (lōōp) I. s. lazo; *(coil)* vuelta; AVIA. rizo ♦ **to knock** *o* **throw for a l.** desconcertar II. tr. hacer un lazo en; *(to coil)* dar una vuelta a; *(to tie)* enlazar —intr. *(length of line)* hacer un lazo; *(to coil)* tener vueltas.

loop·hole (′hōl′) s. MIL. tronera, aspillera; FIG.

escapatoria, pretexto.

loose (lōōs) I. adj. *(unfastened)* suelto; *(slack)* flojo; *(not tight)* holgado; *(not compact)* poco compacto; *(vague)* vago, indefinido; *(idle)* irresponsable; *(promiscuous)* ligero, liviano; *(not literal)* libre; *(not packaged)* a granel ♦ **l. end** *(rope)* cabo suelto; FIG. asunto pendiente • **to be at l. ends** FIG. no saber qué hacer • **to tie up l. ends** FIG. atar cabos II. adv. ♦ **to come l.** aflojarse, desatarse • **to hang l.** JER. quedarse calmo • **to turn l.** soltar, libertar III. tr. soltar, poner en libertad; *(a volley)* disparar —intr. soltarse IV. s. ♦ **on the l.** FAM. suelto, en libertad.

loose-leaf ('lēf') adj. de hojas sueltas.

loose·ly (:ē) adv. sueltamente; *(vaguely)* vagamente; *(freely)* libremente.

loos·en (lōōʹsən) tr. aflojar; *(to untie)* desatar ♦ **to l. someone's tongue** hacer soltar la lengua a alguien • **to l. up on someone** ser menos riguroso con alguien —intr. aflojarse.

loot (lōōt) I. s. botín *m*, presa; JER. *(money)* dinero II. tr. *(to pillage)* pillar, saquear; *(to take as booty)* llevar como botín —intr. entregarse al saqueo.

loot·er (lōōʹtər) s. saqueador *m*.

loot·ing (:tĭng) s. saqueo.

lop (lŏp) tr. **-pp-** *(to trim)* podar; *(to eliminate)* eliminar.

lope (lōp) I. intr. correr a paso largo II. s. paso largo.

lop·sid·ed (lŏpʹsīʹdĭd) adj. desproporcionado; *(leaning)* inclinado, ladeado.

lo·qua·cious (lō-kwāʹshəs) adj. locuaz.

lo·quac·i·ty (lō-kwăsʹĭ-tē) s. locuacidad *f*.

lord (lôrd) I. s. señor *m* ♦ **l. and master** dueño y señor • **L. of the manor** señor feudal II. intr. ♦ **to l. it over** dominar.

lord·ship ('shĭp') s. *(title)* señoría; *(authority)* señorío.

lore (lôr) s. *(tradition)* tradición *f*; *(belief)* creencia popular; *(knowledge)* ciencia, saber *m*.

lor·gnette (lôrn-yĕtʹ) s. impertinentes *m*.

lor·ry (lôrʹē) s. G.B. camión *m*.

lose (lōōz) tr. **lost** perder; *(to cost)* costar, hacer perder <*his arrogance lost him his job* su arrogancia le costó el empleo>; *(clock)* atrasar ♦ **to l. oneself in** perderse en —intr. perder ♦ **to l. out** perder, salir perdiendo.

los·er (lōōʹzər) s. perdedor *m*, *(one that fails)* fracasado; *(lost cause)* causa perdida ♦ **to be a good l.** saber perder.

loss (lôs) s. pérdida; *(defeat)* derrota; *(game)* juego perdido; *(destruction)* estrago, daño ♦ **to be at a l.** *(to be puzzled)* no saber qué hacer; *(for words)* no encontrar palabras con qué expresarse ♦ **pl.** MIL. bajas; COM. pérdidas • **to cut one's l.** cortar por lo sano.

lost (lôst) I. cf. **lose** II. adj. perdido; *(engrossed)* absorto ♦ **get l.!** JER. ¡vete al demonio! • **l. and found** oficina de objetos perdidos • **to get l.** perderse.

lot (lŏt) s. *(drawing)* sorteo; *(share)* parte *f*, porción *f*; *(fate)* suerte *f*, sino; *(people)* grupo de personas; *(articles for sale)* lote *m*, partida; *(large amount)* gran cantidad, mucho; *(land)* solar *m*, lote; CINEM. estudio ♦ **by l.** por sorteo • **lots of** cantidades de, mucho • **to draw lots** echar suertes • **to improve one's l.** mejorar la suerte • **to throw in one's l. with** compartir la suerte de.

lo·tion (lōʹshən) s. loción *f*

lot·ter·y (lŏtʹə-rē) s. lotería.

lo·tus (lōʹtəs) s. loto.

loud (loud) I. adj. alto, fuerte; *(noisy)* ruidoso, bullicioso; *(gaudy)* chillón, llamativo; *(loud-mouthed)* gritón ♦ **in a l. voice** en voz alta, a gritos II. adv. *(to sound, yell, sing)* fuerte ♦ **out l.** en voz alta

loud·mouth ('mouth') FAM. s. gritón *m*.

loud·ness (:nĭs) s. volumen *m*, fuerza.

loud·speak·er (:spēʹkər) s. altavoz *m*, altoparlante *m*.

lounge (lounj) I. intr. repantigarse II. s. *(waiting room)* sala de espera; *(bar)* cantina, *(couch)* sofá *m* ♦ **l. chair** tumbona.

lour (louʹər) var. de **lower¹**.

louse (lous) I. s. ENTOM. [pl. **lice**] piojo; JER. [pl. **es**] canalla *mf*, sinvergüenza *mf* II. tr. ♦ **to l. up on** *(on)* estropear, echar a perder —intr. ♦ **to l. up** hacer una pifia.

lous·y (louʹzē) adj. **-i-** piojoso, lleno de piojos; *(unpleasant)* vil, malísimo; *(worthless)* pésimo.

lout (lout) s. patán *m*, bruto.

lou·ver/vre (lōōʹvər) s. *(blind)* persiana; *(slat)* tablilla.

lov·a·ble (lŭvʹə-bəl) adj. adorable; *(endearing)* cautivador.

love (lŭv) I. s. amor *m*, cariño; *(lover)* amor; DEP. cero (en tenis) ♦ **l. with l.** *(affectionately)* un cariñoso saludo; *(cordially)* un cordial saludo (al terminar una carta) • **l. affair** *(romance)* amorío; *(enthusiasm)* gran entusiasmo • **l. potion** filtro amoroso • **l. seat** confidente • **in l.** enamorado • **to fall in l.** enamorarse • **to make l.** hacer el amor II. tr. amar, querer; *(to enjoy)* gustarle a uno, encantar • **I'd l. to!** ¡con mucho gusto! —intr. amar, querer.

love·bird ('bûrd') s. periquito.

love·less (:lĭs) adj. sin amor.

love·li·ness (:lē-nĭs) s. belleza, hermosura.

love·lorn (:lôrn') adj. herido de amor.

love·ly (:lē) adj. **-i-** hermoso, bello; *(nice)* encantador.

love·mak·ing (:māʹkĭng) s. *(sexual)* relaciones *f* sexuales; *(courtship)* galanteo.

lov·er (:ər) s. amante *mf*, querido; *(devotee)* aficionado.

love·sick (:sĭk') adj. enfermo de amor.

lov·ing (:ĭng) adj. amoroso, cariñoso ♦ **l. cup** *(wine vessel)* copa de la amistad; *(prize)* trofeo, copa.

low¹ (lō) I. adj. bajo; *(in quality)* inferior; *(humble)* plebeyo, humilde; *(mean)* vil, malo; *(unfavorable)* desfavorable, malo; *(coarse)* vulgar, grosero ♦ **in l. spirits** abatido, deprimido • **l. relief** bajo relieve • **l. tide** bajamar • **to be l. on** estar escaso de • **to keep a l. profile** comportarse reservadamente • **to lie l.** FAM. esconderse temporalmente II. adv. bajo III. s. punto más bajo; METEOR. depresión *f*; AUTO. primera.

low² I. s. mugido II. intr. mugir.

low·brow (lōʹbrou') s. ignorante *mf*, persona inculta.

low-cost (lōʹkôstʹ) adj. barato, de bajo costo.

low-cut (lōʹkŭtʹ) adj. muy escotado (vestido).

low·down (lōʹdounʹ) s. JER. la pura verdad.

low·er¹ (lōʹər) intr. *(to scowl)* fruncir el ceño, *(to cloud over)* nublarse, encapotarse.

low·er² (lōʹər) adj. más bajo, inferior ♦ **l. case** IMPR. minúsculas II. tr. & intr. bajar; *(to diminish)* disminuir, reducir.

low·er·case ('-kās') adj. minúscula.

low-grade (lōʹgrādʹ) adj. de calidad inferior.

low·ing (lō′ĭng) s. mugido.
low-key(ed) (lō′kē[d]′) adj. de baja intensidad.
low·land (lō′lənd) s. tierra baja.
low-lev·el (lō′lĕv′əl) adj. de bajo nivel; *(rank)* de grado inferior, subalterno.
low·life (lō′līf′) s. plebeyo; *(despicable person)* persona ruin, perverso.
low·ly (lō′lē) adj. **-i-** bajo, inferior; *(humble)* humilde; *(prosaic)* prosaico, ordinario.
low·ness (lō′nĭs) s. *(shortness)* falta de altura; *(meanness)* bajeza, vileza.
low-pitched (lō′pĭcht′) adj. *(voice)* grave, bajo; *(roof)* poco inclinado; *(room)* de techo bajo.
low-pres·sure (lō′prĕsh′ər) adj. de baja presión; *(person)* relajado.
low-priced (lō′prīst′) adj. de bajo precio.
low-ten·sion (lō′tĕn′shən) adj. de baja tensión.
lox¹ (lŏks) s. CUL. salmón ahumado.
lox² (lŏks) s. FÍS. oxígeno líquido.
loy·al (loi′əl) adj. leal.
loy·al·ist (:ə-lĭst) s. gubernamental *mf.*
loy·al·ty (:əl-tē) s. lealtad *f.*
loz·enge (lŏz′ənj) s. GEOM. rombo; *(cough drop)* pastilla, tableta.
lu·bri·cant (lōō′brĭ-kənt) s. lubricante *m.*
lu·bri·cate (:kāt′) tr. lubricar.
lu·bri·cious (lōō-brĭsh′əs) adj. lúbrico.
lu·cent (lōō′sənt) adj. luminoso.
lu·cid (lōō′sĭd) adj. lúcido, claro; *(sane)* cuerdo; *(translucent)* translúcido.
lu·cid·i·ty (-′ĭ-tē) s. *(clarity)* lucidez *f*, claridad *f*; *(brilliance)* brillantez *f*, transparencia.
luck (lŭk) I. s. fortuna, suerte *f* **♦ for l.** para que traiga buena suerte **• good l.** ¡buena suerte! **• no such l.!** ¡ojalá! **• to be in l.** estar de suerte **• to be out of l.** no tener suerte **• to push one's l.** FAM. arriesgarse innecesariamente **• to try one's l.** probar suerte II. intr. **♦ to l. out** FAM. tener suerte.
luck·less (′lĭs) adj. desafortunado.
luck·y (:ē) adj. **-i-** afortunado; *(fortuitous)* fortuito, oportuno; *(bringing good luck)* que trae suerte **♦ l. break** coyuntura favorable **• thank your l. stars!** ¡bendice tu buena estrella!
lu·cra·tive (lōō′krə-tĭv) adj. lucrativo.
lu·cre (:kər) s. lucro, ganancia.
lu·di·crous (lōō′dĭ-krəs) adj. absurdo, ridículo.
luff (lŭf) I. s. orza II. intr. orzar.
lug¹ (lŭg) s. MEC. *(handle)* agarradera, asa; *(nut)* orejera; *(blockhead)* mentecato.
lug² tr. & intr. **-gg-** arrastrar, halar.
lug·gage (lŭg′ĭj) s. equipaje *m.*
lu·gu·bri·ous (lōō-gōō′brē-əs) adj. lúgubre.
luke·warm (lōōk′wôrm′) adj. tibio.
lull (lŭl) I. tr. *(to soothe)* calmar, sosegar; *(to deceive)* embaucar II. s. momento de calma, cese *m* temporal; *(pause)* pausa.
lull·a·by (′ə-bī′) s. canción *f* de cuna, nana.
lum·bar (lŭm′bər) adj. & s. *(parte f)* lumbar.
lum·ber¹ (lŭm′bər) s. maderos; *(plank)* tabla; G.B. *(junk)* trastos viejos II. tr. *(to fell timber)* talar; *(to cut wood)* cortar madera.
lum·ber² intr. avanzar pesadamente.
lum·ber·ing (:ĭng) I. adj. *(movement)* pesado, torpe; *(person)* que anda pesadamente *o* ruidosamente II. s., industria maderera.
lum·ber·jack (:jăk′) s. leñador *m.*
lum·ber·yard (:yärd′) s. almacén *m o* depósito de madera.
lu·mi·nance (lōō′mə-nəns) s. luminancia.
lu·mi·nar·y (:nĕr′ē) s. luminar *m.*
lu·mi·nes·cence (′-nĕs′əns) s. luminiscencia.

lu·mi·nes·cent (:nĕs′ənt) adj. luminiscente.
lu·mi·nos·i·ty (:nŏs′ĭ-tē) s. luminosidad *f.*
lu·mi·nous (′-nəs) adj. luminoso; *(illuminated)* iluminado; *(lucid)* lúcido, claro.
lum·mox (lŭm′əks) s. FAM. porro, necio.
lump¹ (lŭmp) I. s. montón *m*, masa; *(of soil, sugar)* terrón *m*; *(glob)* grumo; *(piece)* pedazo, trozo; *(totality)* conjunto; *(dolt)* alcornoque *m*; MED. bulto; *(on the head)* chichón *m* **♦ to have a l. in one's throat** tener un nudo en la garganta **• to take one's lumps** aguantar II. tr. *(to amass)* amontonar; *(to make into a mass)* apelotonar **♦ to l. together** juntar.
lump² tr. FAM. soportar, tolerar.
lump·y (lŭm′pē) adj. **-i-** aterronado; *(liquid)* grumoso.
lu·na·cy (lōō′nə-sē) s. locura *f*; *(act)* desatino.
lu·nar (:nər) adj. lunar, de la luna.
lu·na·tic (:nə-tĭk) I. adj. loco; *(for the insane)* de *o* para locos; *(foolish)* disparatado, descabellado II. s. lunático.
lunch (lŭnch) I. s. almuerzo II. intr. almorzar **♦ out to l.** FAM. chiflado **• to have** *o* **to eat l.** almorzar, comer.
lunch·eon (lŭn′chən) s. almuerzo.
lunch·eon·ette (′chə-nĕt′) s. restaurante pequeño, cafetería.
lunch·room (lŭnch′rōōm′) s. restaurante pequeño.
lunch·time (:tīm′) s. hora de comer.
lung (lŭng) s. pulmón *m.*
lunge (lŭnj) I. s. arremetida, embestida; *(in fencing)* estocada II. intr. lanzarse, arrojarse; *(in fencing)* dar una estocada **♦ to l. at** arremeter contra.
lu·pine (lōō′pīn) s. lupino.
lurch¹ (lûrch) I. intr. tambalearse, hacer eses; *(of a ship)* guiñar, dar guiñadas II. s. tambaleo, bamboleo; *(of a ship)* guiñada, bandazo.
lurch² s. **♦ to leave someone in the l.** dejar a alguien plantado *o* en la estacada.
lure (lŏŏr) I. s. tentación *f*; *(appeal)* atracción *f*; *(bait)* cebo, carnada II. tr. tentar, seducir.
lu·rid (lŏŏr′ĭd) adj. *(gruesome)* horrible, espeluznante; *(sensational)* sensacional, chocante; *(glowing)* resplandeciente.
lurk (lûrk) intr. estar al acecho; *(to sneak)* andar a hurtadillas, moverse furtivamente.
lus·cious (lŭsh′əs) adj. suculento, exquisito.
lush¹ (lŭsh) adj. *(thick)* lujuriante, exuberante; *(plentiful)* abundante; *(luxurious)* suntuoso.
lush² s. JER. borrachín *m*, borracho.
lust (lŭst) I. s. lujuria, lascivia; *(overwhelming desire)* ansia, anhelo II. intr. **♦ to l. after** *(something)* codiciar; *(someone)* desear.
lus·ter (lŭs′tər) s. lustre *m.*
lus·ter·less (:lĭs) adj. deslustrado.
lust·ful (lŭst′fəl) adj. lujurioso, lascivo.
lus·trous (lŭs′trəs) adj. lustroso, brillante.
lust·y (lŭs′tē) adj. **-i-** fuerte.
lute¹ (lōōt) s. MÚS. laúd *m.*
lute² s. TEC. zulaque *m*, luten *m.*
lux·u·ri·ant (lŭg-zhŏŏr′ē-ənt) adj. lujuriante.
lux·u·ri·ate (:āt′) intr. crecer con exuberancia **♦ to l.** in deleitarse con.
lux·u·ri·ous (:əs) adj. lujoso; *(lush)* suntuoso.
lux·u·ry (lŭg′zhə-rē, lŭk′shə-) s. lujo; *(frill)* cosa superflua **♦ to live in l.** vivir espléndidamente.
ly·ce·um (lī-sē′əm) s. *(hall)* auditorio, sala de conferencias; *(organization)* ateneo.
lye (lī) s. lejía.

ly·ing¹ (līʹĭng) I. cf. **lie¹** II. adj. *(reclining)* tendido, acostado; *(located)* situado.
ly·ing² (līʹĭng) I. cf. **lie²** II. adj. mentiroso III. s. mentira; *(lies)* mentiras.
ly·ing-in (līʹĭng-ĭnʹ) s. parto.
lymph (lĭmf) s. linfa.
lym·phat·ic (lĭm-fătʹĭk) adj. linfático.
lym·pho·cyte (ʹfə-sītʹ) s. linfocito.
lym·pho·ma (-lōʹmə) s. [pl. **s** o **-mata**] linfoma *m.*
lynch (lĭnch) tr. linchar.
lynx (lĭngks) s. lince *m.*
lyre (līr) s. lira.
lyr·ic (lĭrʹĭk) I. adj. lírico II. s. *(poem)* poema lírico; *(genre)* lírica; *(poet)* lírico ♦ pl. MÚS. letra (de una canción).
lyr·i·cal (ʹĭ-kəl) adj. lírico.
lyr·i·cist (ʹsĭst) s. autor *m* de la letra de una canción.

M

m, M (ĕm) s. decimotercera letra del alfabeto inglés.
ma (mä) s. FAM. mamá.
ma·ca·bre (mə-käʹbrə) adj. macabro.
mac·a·ro·ni (măkʹə-rōʹnē) s.pl. macarrones *m.*
mac·a·roon (măkʹə-rōōnʹ) s. mostachón *m.*
ma·caw (mə-kôʹ) s. guacamayo.
mace¹ (mās) s. maza; *(staff)* maza ceremonial.
mace² s. *(spice)* macia, macis *f.*
mac·er·ate (măsʹə-rātʹ) tr. & intr. macerar(se).
ma·chet·e (mə-shĕtʹē) s. machete *m.*
mach·i·nate (măkʹə-nātʹ, măshʹ-) tr. & intr. maquinar.
mach·i·na·tion (ʹ-nāʹshən) s. maquinación *f.*
ma·chine (mə-shēnʹ) I. s. máquina; *(device)* mecanismo; *(person)* autómata *mf*; *(political)* maquinaria ♦ **m. gun** ametralladora ♦ **m. shop** taller de maquinaria ♦ **slot m.** tragaperras ♦ **washing m.** lavadora II. tr. labrar a máquina.
ma·chine-gun (ʹgŭnʹ) tr. **-nn-** ametrallar.
ma·chin·er·y (mə-shēʹnə-rē) s. maquinaria; *(working parts)* mecanismo.
ma·chin·ist (ʹnĭst) s. maquinista *mf.*
mack·er·el (măkʹər-əl) s [pl. inv. o **s**] caballa.
mack·i·naw (măkʹə-nôʹ) s. chamarra de lana.
mac(k)·in·tosh (măkʹĭn-tŏshʹ) s. G.B. impermeable *m.*
mac·ra·mé (măkʹrə-māʹ) s. macramé *m.*
mac·ro·bi·ot·ics (măkʹrō-bī-ŏtʹĭks) s.sg. macrobiótica.
mac·ro·code (măkʹrə-kōdʹ) s. macrocódigo.
mac·ro·cosm (ʹkŏzʹəm) s. macrocosmo.
mac·ro·scop·ic (ʹ-skŏpʹĭk) adj. macroscópico.
mad (măd) adj. **-dd-** loco; FAM. enojado, *(senseless)* insensato; *(frantic)* frenético; *(dog)* rabioso ♦ **like m.** como un loco ♦ **m. as a hatter** o **March hare** más loco que una cabra ♦ **raving m.** loco de atar ♦ **to be mad about** estar loco por; *(angry)* estar enfadado por ♦ **to be m. at** estar enojado con ♦ **to drive someone m.** volver loco a alguien ♦ **to get m.** enfadarse ♦ **to make someone m.** hacer que alguien se enoje.
Mad·am (mădʹəm) s. [pl. **Mesdames**] señora ♦ **m.** [g.] señora; *(of brothel)* patrona.
mad·cap (mădʹkăpʹ) I. s tarambana *mf* II. adj. alocado, atolondrado.
mad·den (mădʹn) tr. enloquecer; *(to make angry)* enfurecer —intr. enfurecerse.

mad·den·ing (ʹĭng) adj. enloquecedor; *(irritating)* exasperante.
made (mād) I. cf. **make** II. adj. hecho ♦ **to have it m.** tener éxito.
made-to-or·der (ʹtōō-ôrʹdər) adj. hecho a la medida.
made-up (ʹŭpʹ) adj. inventado; *(with make-up)* maquillado.
mad·house (mădʹhousʹ) s. manicomio; FIG. casa de locos.
mad·man (ʹmănʹ) s. [pl. **-men**] demente *m.*
mad·ness (nĭs) s. locura; *(fury)* rabia.
Ma·don·na (mə-dŏnʹə) s. Madona.
mad·wom·an (mădʹwōōmʹən) s. [pl. **-women**] demente *f.*
mael·strom (mālʹstrəm) s. remolino; FIG. torbellino.
mag·a·zine (măgʹə-zēnʹ) s. revista; *(for ammunition)* polvorín *m*; *(of gun)* peine *m* (de balas); FOTOG. depósito (de la película).
ma·gen·ta (mə-jĕnʹtə) s. rojo purpúreo.
mag·got (măgʹət) s. gusano.
ma·gi (māʹjīʹ) cf. **magus.**
mag·ic (măjʹĭk) I. s. magia; FIG. encanto II. adj. mágico.
mag·i·cal (ʹĭ-kəl) adj. mágico.
ma·gi·cian (mə-jĭshʹən) s. mago.
mag·is·te·ri·al (măjʹĭ-stîrʹē-əl) adj. magistral; *(authoritarian)* autoritario; *(of a magistrate)* de magistrado.
mag·is·tra·cy (ʹstrə-sē) s. magistratura; *(district)* jurisdicción *f* de magistrado.
mag·is·trate (ʹstrātʹ) s. magistrado.
mag·nan·i·mous (măg-nănʹə-məs) adj. magnánimo.
mag·nate (măgʹnātʹ, nĭt) s. magnate *m.*
mag·ne·si·um (măg-nēʹzē-əm) s. magnesio.
mag·net (măgʹnĭt) s FIS. imán *m*; *(something attractive)* persona o cosa atractiva.
mag·net·ic (ʹnĕtʹĭk) adj. magnético.
mag·net·ism (ʹnĭ-tĭzʹəm) s. magnetismo.
mag·net·ize (ʹnĭ-tīzʹ) tr. magnetizar, imantar.
mag·ni·fi·ca·tion (măgʹnə-fĭ-kāʹshən) s. ampliación *f*; ÓPT. aumento.
mag·nif·i·cence (măg-nĭfʹĭ-səns) s. magnificencia.
mag·nif·i·cent (ʹsənt) adj. magnífico.
mag·ni·fi·er (măgʹnə-fīʹər) s. lupa; ÓPT. sistema *m* amplificador.
mag·ni·fy (ʹfīʹ) tr. aumentar; *(to exaggerate)* exagerar; *(to praise)* glorificar ♦ **magnifying glass** lente de aumento.
mag·ni·tude (măgʹnĭ-tōōdʹ) s. magnitud *f.*
mag·num (măgʹnəm) s. mágnum *m* ♦ **m. opus** obra maestra.
mag·pie (măgʹpīʹ) s. urraca.
ma·gus (māʹgəs) s. [pl. **-gi**] mago ♦ **the Magi** los Reyes Magos.
ma·hog·a·ny (mə-hŏgʹə-nē) s. caoba.
maid (mād) s. criada; *(unwed girl)* soltera; *(virgin)* doncella ♦ **m. of honor** dama de honor.
maid·en (ʹn) s. doncella II. adj. virginal; *(unmarried)* soltera; *(virgin)* virgen; *(first)* primero ♦ **m. name** apellido de soltera.
maid·en·head (ʹhĕdʹ) s. virginidad *f*; ANAT. himen *m.*
maid·en·hood (ʹhōōdʹ) s. doncellez *f.*
maid·ser·vant (mādʹsûrʹvənt) s. sirvienta.
mail¹ (māl) I. s. correo ♦ **air m.** vía aérea ♦ **by return m.** a vuelta de correo II. tr. enviar por correo; *(to post)* echar al correo III. adj. postal.

mail² s. (cota de) malla.
mail·box (māl'bŏks') s. buzón m.
mail·ing (mā'lǐng) s. envío.
mail·man (māl'măn') s. [pl. -men] cartero.
maim (mām) tr. lisiar; FIG. estropear.
main (mān) I. adj. principal; *(office)* central; *(valve)* maestro; MARÍT. mayor ◆ **the m. thing** lo principal o esencial II. s. tubería o cable m principal; *(might)* fuerzas ◆ **in the m.** principalmente.
main·frame ('frām') s. computador m central.
main·land (:lănd') s. tierra firme.
main·sail (:sǒl) s. vela mayor.
main·spring (:sprǐng') s. MEC. muelle m real; FIG. causa principal, fuerza motriz.
main·stay (:stā') s. MARÍT. estay m mayor; FIG. soporte m principal.
main·stream (:strēm') s. corriente f principal.
main·tain (mān-tān') tr. mantener; *(silence)* guardar; *(to preserve)* conservar; *(to repair)* cuidar ◆ **to m. one's composure** mantenerse sereno ◆ **to m. one's ground** mantenerse firme.
main·te·nance ('tə-nəns) s. mantenimiento; *(upkeep)* cuidado, conservación f ◆ **m. staff** personal de servicio.
maize (māz) s. maíz m.
ma·jes·tic (mə-jĕs'tĭk) adj. majestuoso.
maj·es·ty (măj'ĭ-stē) s. majestad f; *(splendor)* majestuosidad f.
ma·jor (mā'jər) I. adj. mayor; *(chief)* principal; *(extensive)* amplio; *(serious)* grave II. s. MIL. comandante m; EDUC. especialidad f III. intr. ◆ **to m.** EDUC. especializarse en.
ma·jor-do·mo ('-dō'mō) s. mayordomo.
ma·jor·i·ty (mə-jôr'ĭ-tē) s. mayoría, mayor parte f ◆ **to be in a m.** constituir la mayoría.
ma·jor-league (mā'jər-lēg') adj. FAM. importante, principal.
make (māk) I. tr. made hacer; *(to build)* construir; *(to manufacture)* fabricar; *(decision)* tomar; *(payment)* efectuar; *(a speech)* pronunciar; *(agreement)* concertar; *(excuses)* presentar; DEP. *(goal)* marcar; FAM. *(train)* alcanzar; *(to appoint)* nombrar; *(problems)* causar; *(food)* preparar; *(to establish)* establecer como; *(to attain)* llegar a; *(team)* entrar en; *(to earn)* ganar; *(money)* producir; *(to compel)* obligar a; *(to be good for)* servir para hacer; *(to become)* ser; *(to think of)* pensar; *(to add up to)* equivaler a; *(to count as)* ser; JER. seducir ◆ **to m. a mistake** cometer un error ◆ **to m. a move** *(to move)* moverse; *(to act)* obrar ◆ **to m. an appointment** citar ◆ **to m. a point** hacer una observación ◆ **to m. clear** poner en claro ◆ **to m. easy** facilitar ◆ **to m. for** ir hacia; *(problems)* crear ◆ **to m. into** convertir en ◆ **to m. it** tener éxito ◆ **to m. out** *(check)* hacer; *(to comprehend)* entender; *(to perceive)* divisar ◆ **to m. ready** preparar ◆ **to m. up** preparar; *(to assemble)* confeccionar; *(story)* inventar; *(to compensate)* recobrar; *(to constitute)* integrar; TEAT. maquillar(se) ◆ **to m. worse** empeorar —intr. ◆ **to m. for** continuar a ◆ **to m. off** huir ◆ **to m. out** salir (bien, mal); *(to embrace)* abrazar(se) ◆ **to m. up** hacer las paces II. s. fabricación f; *(in clothes)* confección f; *(style)* corte m; *(brand)* marca ◆ **to be on the m.** buscar su propio provecho; JER. *(seduction)* tener intención de seducir.
make-be·lieve ('bǐ-lēv') I. s. fingimiento, simulación f II. adj. fingido, simulado.
mak·er (mā'kər) s. fabricante m ◆ **M.** Hacedor.

make-shift (māk'shĭft') I. s. reemplazo provisional II. adj. improvisado, temporal.
make-up o **make·up** (:ŭp') s. construcción f, composición f; *(temperament)* carácter m; *(cosmetics)* maquillaje m.
mak·ing (mā'kǐng) s. creación f; *(manufacture)* fabricación f; *(of a meal)* preparación f; *(of a will)* redacción f ◆ **in the m.** *(plans)* en preparación; *(country)* en desarrollo; *(history)* en marcha ◆ **to be of one's own m.** ser obra propia ◆ **to have the makings of** tener los elementos necesarios para llegar a ser.
mal·ad·just·ed (măl'ə-jŭs'tĭd) adj. inadaptado.
mal·a·droit (măl'ə-droit') adj. desmañado.
mal·a·dy (măl'ə-dē) s. dolencia.
mal·aise (mă-lāz') s. malestar m.
mal·a·prop·ism (măl'ə-prŏp'ĭz'əm) s. uso cómicamente incorrecto de una palabra.
ma·lar·i·a (mə-lâr'ē-ə) s. malaria, paludismo.
ma·lar·k(e)y (mə-lär'kē) s. JER. charlatanería.
mal·con·tent (măl'kən-tĕnt') I. adj. malcontento II. s. (-') malcontento.
male (māl) I. adj. varón m; *(masculine)* masculino; *(manly)* varonil; *(for men)* de hombres; *(school)* de varones; BIOL., MEC. macho II. s. varón m; BIOL. macho.
mal·e·dic·tion (măl'ĭ-dĭk'shən) s. maldición f.
mal·e·fac·tor (măl'ə-făk'tər) s. malhechor m.
ma·lef·ic (mə-lĕf'ĭk) adj. maléfico.
ma·lev·o·lence (mə-lĕv'ə-ləns) s. malevolencia.
ma·lev·o·lent (:lənt) adj. malévolo.
mal·fea·sance (măl-fē'zəns) s. DER. mala conducta (esp. de un empleado público).
mal·formed (măl-fôrmd') adj. mal formado.
mal·func·tion (:fŭngk'shən) I. intr. funcionar mal II. s. funcionamiento defectuoso.
mal·ice (măl'ĭs) s. malicia; DER. intención maliciosa.
ma·li·cious (mə-lĭsh'əs) adj. malicioso; DER. premeditado, delictuoso.
ma·lign (mə-līn') I. tr. difamar II. adj. maligno.
ma·lig·nan·cy (mə-lĭg'nən-sē) s. malignidad f.
ma·lig·nant (:nənt) adj. maligno; *(harmful)* pernicioso.
ma·lin·ger (mə-lĭng'gər) intr. fingirse enfermo.
mall (môl) s. alameda; *(for shopping)* galería.
mal·lard (măl'ərd) s. [pl. inv. o s] pato silvestre.
mal·le·a·ble (măl'ē-ə-bəl) adj. maleable.
mal·let (măl'ĭt) s. mazo; DEP. mallo.
mal·nour·ished (măl-nûr'ĭsht) adj. desnutrido.
mal·nu·tri·tion ('nŏŏ-trĭsh'ən) s. desnutrición f.
mal·prac·tice (-prăk'tĭs) s. MED. tratamiento erróneo; *(misconduct)* conducta inmoral.
malt (môlt) s. malta; *(beer)* cerveza de malta.
mal·treat (măl-trēt') tr. maltratar.
mal·treat·ment (:mənt) s. maltratamiento.
ma(m)·ma (mä'mə) s. mamá, mama.
mam·mal (măm'əl) s. mamífero.
mam·ma·li·an (mə-mā'lē-ən) adj. mamífero.
mam·ma·ry (măm'ə-rē) adj. mamario.
mam·moth (măm'əth) I. s. mamut m II. adj. enorme, gigantesco.
man (măn) I. s. [pl. **men**] hombre m; *(male)* varón m; *(mankind)* el hombre; *(servant)* sirviente m; *(in chess)* pieza ◆ **m. about town** hombre de mundo ◆ **m. and wife** marido y mujer ◆ **m. of his word** hombre de palabra ◆ **men's room** servicio o baño para caballeros ◆ **no man's land** tierra de nadie ◆ **the M.** JER. la policía ◆ **to a m.** hasta el último ◆ **to be one's**

own m. ser un hombre independiente ♦ pl.
(workers) obreros; *(servicemen)* soldados **II.** tr.
-nn- *(vessel)* tripular; *(station)* manejar
III. interj. ¡hombre!

man·a·cle (măn'ə-kəl) **I.** s. manilla ♦ pl. esposas; FIG. restricción **II.** tr. esposar; FIG. restringir.

man·age (măn'ĭj) tr. controlar; *(business)* dirigir; *(property)* administrar; *(to handle)* poder con —intr. arreglárselas.

man·age·a·ble (:ĭ-jə-bəl) adj. manejable; *(tame)* dócil; *(task)* realizable ♦ **of m. size** manuable.

man·age·ment (:ĭj-mənt) s. gerencia; *(directors)* gerentes mf; *(skill)* habilidad directiva.

man·ag·er (:ĭ·jər) s. gerente mf; *(agent)* apoderado.

man·a·ge·ri·al (:'ə-jîr'ē-əl) adj. directivo, ejecutivo.

man-at-arms (măn'ət-ärmz') s. [pl. **men-**] soldado *(esp. de caballería)*.

man·da·rin (măn'də-rĭn) **I.** s. mandarín *m*
II. adj. ♦ **m. orange** mandarina.

man·date (măn'dāt') **I.** s. mandato; *(territory)* territorio bajo mandato **II.** tr. ordenar.

man·da·to·ry (:də-tôr'ē) adj. obligatorio; *(holding a mandate)* mandante.

man·do·lin (măn'dl-ĭn') s. mandolina.

mane (mān) s. *(of horse)* crin f; *(of lion)* melena.

man·eat·er (măn'ē'tər) s. animal *m* que come carne humana; *(cannibal)* caníbal mf.

ma·neu·ver (mə-nōō'vər) **I.** s. maniobra
II. intr. maniobrar; *(to manipulate)* manipular.

ma·neu·ver·a·ble (:ə-bəl) s. maniobrable.

man·ful (măn'fəl) adj. varonil, masculino.

man·ga·nese (măng'gə-nēz') s. manganeso.

mange (mānj) s. sarna.

man·ger (măn'jər) s. pesebre *m*.

man·gle¹ (măng'gəl) tr. s. & adj. mutilar.

man·gle² s. planchadora a rodillo.

man·go (măng'gō) s. [pl. **(e)s**] mango.

man·grove (măng'grōv') s. mangle *m*.

mang·y (măn'jē) adj. **-i-** sarnoso; FAM. *(shabby)* sucio.

man·han·dle (măn'hăn'dl) tr. tratar duramente.

man·hole (măn'hōl') s. boca de acceso.

man·hood (:hŏŏd') s. madurez f, *(manliness)* hombría; *(men)* hombres *m* ♦ **to grow to m.** hacerse hombre.

man·hunt (:hŭnt') s. búsqueda de un criminal.

ma·ni·a (mā'nē-ə) s. manía.

ma·ni·ac (mā'nē-ăk') s. & adj. maníaco.

ma·ni·a·cal (mə-nī'ə-kəl) adj. maníaco, maniaco; FIG. loco.

man·ic (măn'ĭk) adj. maníaco, maniaco.

man·ic-de·pres·sive (:'-dĭ-prĕs'ĭv) s. maníaco-depresivo, maniacodepresivo.

man·i·cure (măn'ĭ-kyŏŏr') **I.** s. manicura **II.** tr. hacer la manicura a; *(to trim)* recortar.

man·i·cur·ist (:ĭst) s. manicuro.

man·i·fest (măn'ə-fĕst') **I.** adj. manifiesto
II. tr. manifestar **III.** s. *(cargo)* manifiesto; *(passengers)* relación f de pasajeros.

man·i·fes·ta·tion (:'-fĕ-stā'shən) s. manifestación f.

man·i·fes·to (:fĕs'tō) s. [pl. **(e)s**] manifiesto.

man·i·fold (măn'ə-fōld') **I.** adj. diverso; *(of many parts)* variado **II.** s. AUTO. colector *m* de escape **III.** tr. multiplicar, diversificar.

ma·ni·kin (măn'ĭ-kĭn) s. enano; *(model)*

maniquí *m*.

ma·nip·u·late (mə-nĭp'yə-lāt') tr. manipular.

ma·nip·u·la·tion (:'-lā'shən) s. manipulación f; *(deceit)* manipuleo.

ma·nip·u·la·tive (:'-'tĭv) adj. de manipuleo.

ma·nip·u·la·tor (:tər) s. manipulador *m*.

man·kind (măn'kīnd') s. género humano; *(men)* los hombres.

man·like (:līk') adj. parecido al hombre.

man·li·ness (:lē-nĭs) s. hombría; *(masculinity)* masculinidad f.

man·ly (:lē) **I.** adj. **-i-** varonil; *(masculine)* masculino **II.** adv. como un hombre.

man·made (:mād') adj. artificial.

man·na (măn'ə) s. maná *m*.

manned (mănd) adj. tripulado.

man·ne·quin (măn'ĭ-kĭn) s. maniquí *m*.

man·ner (măn'ər) s. manera, modo; *(bearing)* comportamiento ♦ **all m. of** todo tipo de • **in a m. of speaking** por así decirlo ♦ pl. modales; *(politeness)* educación ♦ **pl.** modales.

man·nered (:ərd) adj. amanerado ♦ **ill-m.** de malos modales.

man·ner·ism (:ə rĭz'əm) s. amaneramiento; *(peculiarity)* peculiaridad f.

man·ner·ly (:ər-lē) adj. de buenos modales.

man·ni·kin (măn'ĭ-kĭn) var. de **manikin**.

man·nish (măn'ĭsh) adj. hombruno.

man-of-war (măn'ə-wôr') s. [pl. **men-**] buque *m* de guerra.

man·or (măn'ər) s. *(estate)* finca; *(mansion)* casa solariega; *(fief)* señorío, feudo.

man·pow·er (măn'pou'ər) s. fuerza humana; *(labor)* mano de obra disponible.

manse (măns) s. rectoría.

man·ser·vant (măn'sûr'vənt) s. [pl. **menservants**] sirviente *m*.

man·sion (măn'shən) s. casa grande.

man-size(d) (măn'sīz[d]') adj. FAM. de gran tamaño, muy grande.

man·slaugh·ter (:slô'tər) s. homicidio impremeditado o involuntario.

man·ta (măn'tə) s. chal *m*. ♦ **m. ray** ICT. manta.

man·tel (măn'tl) s. *(facing)* manto (de la chimenea); *(shelf)* repisa de la chimenea.

man·tel·piece (:pēs') s. repisa de la chimenea.

man·tle (măn'tl) s. manto **II.** tr. tapar.

man-to-man (măn'tə-măn') adj. de hombre a hombre.

man·u·al (măn'yōō-əl) **I.** adj. manual **II.** s. manual *m*; MÚS. teclado; MIL. ejercicio de armas.

man·u·fac·ture (măn'yə-făk'chər) **I.** tr. manufacturar; *(clothing)* confeccionar; *(to produce)* fabricar **II.** s. manufactura, fabricación f; *(product)* producto manufacturado.

man·u·fac·tured (:chərd) adj. manufacturado.

man·u·fac·tur·er (:chər-ər) s. fabricante mf.

man·u·fac·tur·ing (:ĭng) **I.** adj. manufacturero **II.** s. manufactura.

man·u·mit (măn'yə-mĭt') tr. **-tt-** manumitir.

ma·nure (mə-nŏŏr') **I.** s. estiércol *m* **II.** tr. estercolar.

man·u·script (măn'yə-skrĭpt') s. & adj. manuscrito.

man·y (mĕn'ē) **I.** adj. **more, most** muchos ♦ **how m.?** ¿cuántos? • **m. a man** muchos hombres • **m. people** mucha gente • **too m.** demasiado • **twice as m.** dos veces más **II.** s. & pron. muchos ♦ **a great m.** muchísimos • **as m. as** *(the same number)* tantos como; *(up to)* hasta • **the m.** las masas.

map (măp) **I.** s. mapa *m* ♦ **to put on the m.** dar fama a **II.** tr. **-pp-** trazar un mapa de; *(to plan)* planear.

ma·ple (mā′pəl) s. arce *m* ♦ **m. syrup** jarabe de arce.

map·mak·er (măp′mā′kər) s. cartógrafo.

map·mak·ing (:kĭng) s. cartografía.

map·ping (măp′ĭng) s. cartografía.

mar (mär) tr. **-rr-** *(to damage)* dañar, estropear; *(to disfigure)* desfigurar.

mar·a·thon (măr′ə-thŏn′) s. maratón *m*; *(contest)* competencia de resistencia.

ma·raud (mə-rôd′) intr. merodear —tr. pillar.

ma·raud·er (:rô′dər) s. merodeador *m*.

mar·ble (mär′bəl) **I.** s. mármol *m*; *(glass ball)* canica, bolita ♦ **to lose one's marbles** JER. aflojársele a uno un tornillo **II.** tr. jaspear **III.** adj. marmóreo, de mármol.

mar·bled (:bəld) adj. jaspeado.

mar·bling (:blĭng) s. marmoración *f*.

march[1] (märch) **I.** intr. MIL. marchar; *(to walk)* ir a pie; *(to advance)* avanzar ♦ **forward m.!** ¡de frente! ♦ **marching orders** órdenes de movilización ♦ **to m. on** seguir la marcha ♦ **to m. up to** acercarse a —tr. MIL. hacer marchar **II.** s. marcha; *(pace)* paso; *(of time)* transcurso; *(distance)* caminata ♦ **on the m.** en marcha.

march[2] s. *(frontier)* marca.

March (märch) s. marzo.

march·er (mär′chər) s. manifestante *mf*.

mare (mâr) s. yegua.

mar·ga·rine (mär′jər-ĭn) s. margarina.

mar·gin (mär′jĭn) s. margen *mf*; FIN. *(collateral)* garantía.

mar·gin·al (:jə-nəl) adj. marginal; *(barely acceptable)* mínimo.

mar·i·gold (măr′ĭ-gōld′) s. maravilla.

mar·i·jua·na/hua·na (măr′ə-wä′nə) s. mariguana; *(hemp)* cáñamo índico.

ma·ri·na (mə-rē′nə) s. marina.

mar·i·nade (măr′ə-nād′) s. escabeche *m*.

mar·i·nate (:nāt′) tr. escabechar, marinar.

ma·rine (mə-rēn′) **I.** adj. marítimo; *(life)* marino ♦ **m. engineer** ingeniero naval **II.** s. *(fleet)* marina; *(soldier)* soldado de marina ♦ **merchant m.** marina mercante ♦ pl. infantería de marina.

mar·i·ner (măr′ə-nər) s. marinero, marino.

mar·i·o·nette (măr′ē-ə-nĕt′) s. marioneta.

mar·i·tal (măr′ĭ-tl) adj. matrimonial, marital.

mar·i·time (măr′ĭ-tīm′) adj. marítimo.

mar·jo·ram (mär′jər-əm) s. mejorana.

mark[1] (märk) **I.** s. marca; *(punctuation)* signo de puntuación; *(grade)* nota; *(indication)* signo; *(standard)* altura; *(attention)* atención *f*; *(target)* blanco; *(goal)* objetivo; *(reference point)* señal *f*; *(impression)* sello; DEP. *(starting line)* línea de salida; *(record)* récord *m* ♦ **to be off the m.** no alcanzar el fin deseado; *(inaccurate)* estar incorrecto ♦ **to hit the m.** *(to succeed)* tener éxito; *(to fit rightly)* dar en el clavo ♦ **to make one's m.** distinguirse ♦ pl. *(appraisal)* evaluación; *(rating)* calificación **II.** tr. marcar; *(to draw)* dibujar; *(a spot)* señalar; *(to characterize)* caracterizar; *(to grade)* calificar; *(to heed)* prestar atención ♦ **m. down** *(to write down)* anotar; *(prices)* rebajar ♦ **to m. off** *(to demarcate)* demarcar; *(to note)* apuntar ♦ **to m. time** marcar el paso ♦ **to m. up** *(to deface)* estropear; *(prices)* aumentar.

mark[2] s. FIN. marco.

mark·down (märk′doun′) s. rebaja.

marked (märkt) adj. marcado; *(noticeable)* notable ♦ **a m. man** un hombre señalado.

mark·er (mär′kər) s. marcador *m*; JER. *(promissory note)* pagaré *m*.

mar·ket (mär′kĭt) **I.** s. mercado; *(demand)* salida; *(stock market)* bolsa ♦ **buyer's, seller's m.** mercado que favorece al comprador, vendedor ♦ **foreign exchange m.** mercado de cambios ♦ **m. price** precio corriente *o* de mercado ♦ **m. research** análisis de mercados ♦ **m. value** valor comercial ♦ **to be in the m. for** querer comprar ♦ **to be on the m.** estar en venta ♦ **to find a ready m.** tener fácil salida ♦ **to play the m.** jugar a la bolsa ♦ **to put on the m.** poner en venta **II.** tr. vender —intr. hacer las compras.

mar·ket·a·ble (:kĭ-tə-bəl) adj. vendible.

mar·ket·er (:tər) s. vendedor *m*; *(of new products)* mercantilizador *m*.

mar·ket·ing (:tĭng) s. comercio; *(of new products)* mercadeo.

mar·ket·place (mär′kĭt-plās′) s. (plaza del) mercado; *(business world)* mundo mercantil.

mark·ing (mär′kĭng) s. marca; *(act)* marcación *f*; ZOOL. pinta.

marks·man (märks′mən) s. [pl. **-men**] tirador *m* (al blanco).

marks·man·ship (:shĭp′) s. (buena) puntería.

mark·up (märk′ŭp′) s. *(of prices)* aumento; *(profit margin)* margen *m* de ganancia bruta.

mar·ma·lade (mär′mə-lād′) s. mermelada.

ma·roon[1] (mə-rōōn′) tr. abandonar; *(to isolate)* aislar.

ma·roon[2] s. & adj. *(color)* marrón *m*, castaño.

mar·quee (mär-kē′) s. *(tent)* tienda de campaña (grande); *(of theater, hotel)* marquesina.

mar·quis (mär′kwĭs, mär-kē′) s. marqués *m*.

mar·quise (mär-kēz′) s. marquesa.

mar·riage (mär′ĭj) s. matrimonio; *(wedding)* boda, casamiento; *(close union)* unión *f* ♦ **m. articles** contrato matrimonial ♦ **m. certificate** partida de matrimonio ♦ **to be related by m.** tener parentesco político ♦ **to take in m.** contraer matrimonio con.

mar·riage·a·ble (:ĭ-jə-bəl) adj. casadero.

mar·ried (:ēd) adj. casado; *(conjugal)* conyugal ♦ **m. couple** matrimonio ♦ **m. name** apellido de casada ♦ **to get m.** casarse.

mar·row (măr′ō) s. médula.

mar·ry (măr′ē) tr. *(to join in marriage)* casar; *(to take in marriage)* casarse con; *(to give in marriage)* dar en casamiento; *(to unite)* unir —intr. casarse; *(to unite)* unirse ♦ **to m. beneath oneself** casarse con alguien de clase inferior ♦ **to m. into** emparentar con.

marsh (märsh) s. pantano; *(salt)* marisma.

mar·shal (mär′shəl) **I.** s. MIL. mariscal *m*; *(chief)* jefe **II.** tr. poner en orden; *(to usher)* acompañar ceremoniosamente ♦ **to m. (forces) against** movilizar (fuerzas) en contra de.

marsh·land (märsh′lănd′) s. terreno pantanoso.

marsh·mal·low (märsh′mĕl′ō, :mäl′ō) s. bombón *m* de merengue blando.

marsh·y (mär′shē) adj. **-i-** pantanoso.

mar·su·pi·al (mär-sōō′pē-əl) adj. & s. marsupial *m*.

mart (märt) s. mercado.

mar·tial (mär′shəl) adj. marcial; *(military)* militar.

mar·ti·net (mär′tn-ĕt′) s. ordenancista *mf*.

mar·tyr (mär′tər) **I.** s. mártir *mf* **II.** tr. martirizar.

mar·tyr·dom (:dəm) s. martirio.

mar·vel (mär'vəl) I. s. maravilla; *(astonishment)* asombro II. intr. maravillarse.

mar·vel·lous (:və-ləs) adj. maravilloso; *(superb)* excelente.

mas·car·a (mă-skăr'ə) s. rimel m.

mas·cot (măs'kŏt) s. mascota.

mas·cu·line (măs'kyə-lĭn) adj. & s. masculino.

mas·cu·lin·i·ty ('-ĭn'ĭ-tē) s. masculinidad f.

mash (măsh) I. s. malta remojada; *(for animals)* mezcla de granos molidos; *(mixture)* mezcolanza II. tr. *(to crush)* majar; *(to grind)* moler.

mash·er ('ər) s. majador m.

mask (măsk) I. s. máscara; *(face covering)* antifaz m, careta; *(funeral)* mascarilla; FOTOG. ocultador m II. tr. *(to cover)* enmascarar; *(to disguise)* disimular; *(to conceal)* ocultar.

masked (măskt) adj. enmascarado; *(disguised)* disfrazado ✦ **m. ball** baile de máscaras.

masking tape s. cinta adhesiva opaca.

mas·o·chist (măs'ə-kĭst) s. masoquista mf.

mas·o·chis·tic ('-kĭs'tĭk) adj. masoquista.

ma·son (mā'sən) s. *(bricklayer)* albañil m; *(stonecutter)* cantero ✦ **M.** masón.

ma·son·ry (:rē) s. *(trade)* albañilería; *(brickwork)* obra de albañilería; *(rubblework)* mampostería; *(stonework)* cantería ✦ **M.** masonería.

masque (măsk) s. espectáculo alegórico; *(masked ball)* baile m de disfraces.

mas·quer·ade (măs'kə-rād') I. s. mascarada; *(costume)* disfraz m; *(pretense)* farsa II. intr. ✦ **to m. as** disfrazarse de; FIG. *(to pose as)* hacerse pasar por.

mass (măs) I. s. masa; *(large amount)* montón m; *(majority)* mayor parte f; *(physical bulk)* volumen m II. tr. amontonar —intr. congregarse en masa III. adj. de las masas ✦ **m. hysteria** histeria colectiva • **m. media** medios de comunicación de masa.

Mass o **mass** (măs) s. RELIG. misa ✦ **High, Low M.** misa mayor, rezada.

mas·sa·cre (măs'ə-kər) I. s. masacre f II. tr. masacrar.

mas·sage (mə-säzh', mə-säj') I. s. masaje m II. tr. dar masajes a, masajear.

mas·seur (mă-sûr') s. masajista m.

mas·seuse (mă-sœz') s. masajista f.

mas·sive (măs'ĭv) adj. masivo; *(huge)* monumental.

mass-pro·duce (măs'prə-dōōs') tr. fabricar en gran escala.

mast (măst) s. mástil m, *(pole)* palo.

mas·tec·to·my (mă-stĕk'tə-mē) s. mastectomía.

mas·ter (măs'tər) I. s. maestro; *(expert)* perito; *(degree)* maestría (título académico entre la licenciatura y el doctorado); *(owner)* amo; *(of household)* señor m; MARIT. capitán m de barco mercante ✦ **M.** señorito II. adj. maestro; *(main)* principal; *(copy)* original III. tr. ✦ **to** lograr dominar; *(to overcome)* superar.

mas·ter·ful (:fəl) adj. *(imperious)* dominante; *(skillful)* hábil.

mas·ter·ly (:lē) I. adj. magistral, genial II. adv. magistralmente, genialmente.

mas·ter·mind (:mīnd') I. s. genio creador y director II. tr. ser el cerebro de, dirigir.

mas·ter·piece (:pēs') s. obra maestra.

mas·ter·y (măs'tə-rē) s. *(skill)* maestría, *(rule)* gobierno.

mast·head (măst'hĕd') s. *(of mast)* tope m;

IMPR. cabecera.

mas·tic (măs'tĭk) s. mástique m.

mas·ti·cate (măs'tĭ-kāt') tr. masticar.

mas·tiff (măs'tĭf) s. mastín m.

mas·toid (măs'toid') I. s. mastoides f II. adj. mastoideo, mastoidal.

mas·tur·bate (măs'tər-bāt') tr. & intr. masturbar(se).

mas·tur·ba·tion ('-bā'shən) s. masturbación f.

mat¹ (măt) I. s. estera; *(doormat)* esterilla f, DEP. *(floor pad)* colchoneta; *(tangled mass)* maraña II. tr. & intr. -tt- enmarañar(se).

mat² I. s. *(border)* marco de cartón; *(finish)* acabado mate II. tr. -tt- *(a picture)* poner un marco de cartón a; *(glass, metal)* dar un acabado mate a III. adj. mate.

match¹ (măch) I. s. par m; *(pair)* juego; *(marriage)* matrimonio; DEP. partido ✦ **to be a good m.** *(mate)* ser un buen partido; *(to harmonize)* hacer juego • **to be a m.** for poder competir con • **to meet one's m.** hallar un rival digno de uno II. tr. corresponder a; *(to go with)* hacer juego con; *(to pit)* oponer; *(to equal)* igualar —intr. hacer juego.

match² s. *(stick)* fósforo.

match·book ('bŏk') s. sobre m de fósforos.

match·box (:bŏks') s. caja de fósforos, fosforera.

match·less (măch'lĭs) adj. sin igual, sin par.

match·mak·er (:mā'kər) s. casamentero.

mate¹ (māt) I. s. compañero; *(male)* macho; *(female)* hembra; *(buddy)* socio; MARIT. piloto; *(assistant)* ayudante m II. tr. & intr. *(to join)* hermanar(se); *(to marry)* casar(se); ZOOL. aparear(se).

mate² I. s. *(chess)* mate m (en ajedrez) II. intr. & tr. dar mate (a).

ma·te·ri·al (mə-tîr'ē-əl) I. s. material m; *(cloth)* tela II. adj. material; *(noticeable)* notable; *(relevant)* pertinente.

ma·te·ri·al·ist (-ə-lĭst) s. materialista mf.

ma·te·ri·al·is·tic (-'-ə-lĭs'tĭk) adj. materialista.

ma·te·ri·al·i·ty (:ăl'ĭ-tē) s. materialidad f; DER. pertinencia.

ma·te·ri·al·ize (-'-ə-līz') tr. materializar —intr. concretizarse; *(to appear)* materializarse.

ma·te·ri·el/té·ri·el ('-'-ĕl') s. material m, suministros y pertrechos.

ma·ter·nal (mə-tûr'nəl) adj. maternal; *(of one's mother)* materno.

ma·ter·ni·ty (:nĭ-tē) s. maternidad f; *(motherliness)* cariño maternal.

math (măth) s. matemática(s).

math·o·mat·i·cal ('ə-măt'ĭ-kəl) adj. matemático.

math·e·ma·ti·cian (:mə-tĭsh'ən) s. matemático.

math·e·mat·ics (:măt'-ĭks) s.sg. matemática(s).

mat·i·nee/née (măt'n-ā') s. matinée f.

mat·ing (mā'tĭng) s. *(of persons)* unión f; *(of animals)* apareamiento.

ma·tri·arch (mā'trē-ärk') s. matriarca.

ma·tri·ar·chal ('-är'kəl) adj. matriarcal.

ma·tri·ar·chy ('-'-kē) s. matriarcado.

mat·ri·cide (măt'rĭ-sīd') s. matricidio; *(person)* matricida mf.

ma·tric·u·late (mə-trĭk'yə-lāt') tr. & intr. matricular(se).

ma·tric·u·la·tion (-'-lā'shən) s. matriculación f, matrícula.

mat·ri·mo·ni·al (măt'rə-mō'nē-əl) adj. matrimonial.

mat·ri·mo·ny ('-'nē) s. matrimonio.

ma·trix (mā'trĭks) s. [pl. **es** o **-ces**] matriz f.

ma·tron (mā'trən) s. matrona; *(head nurse)* enfermera jefe; *(prison guard)* celadora.

ma·tron·ly (:lē) adj. matronal, de matrona.

matte (măt) s. acabado mate.

mat·ted (măt'ĭd) adj. *(with mats)* esterado; *(tangled)* enmarañado.

mat·ter (măt'ər) **I.** s. materia; *(concern)* cuestión f; *(approximate quantity)* cosa ♦ **as a m. of course** normalmente, por costumbre • **as a m. of fact** de hecho • **as matters stand** tal y como están las cosas • **for that m.** en cuanto a eso • **in the m. of** en lo tocante a • **no m.** no importa • **no m. how** sea como sea • **no m. what happens** pase lo que pase • **nothing's the m.** no pasa nada • **printed m.** impresos • **small m.** asunto sin importancia • **to be another m.** ser cosa aparte • **to be no laughing m.** no ser cosa de risa • **to make matters worse** para colmo de males • **what's the m.?** ¿qué sucede? **II.** intr. importar.

mat·ter-of-fact ('əv-făkt') adj. práctico; *(factual)* realista; *(prosaic)* prosaico.

mat·ting (măt'ĭng) s. estera.

mat·tress (măt'rĭs) s. colchón m.

mat·u·ra·tion (măch'ə-rā'shən) s. maduración f.

ma·ture (mə-chŏŏr', mə-tŏŏr') **I.** adj. **-er, -est** maduro; *(considered)* meditado; FIN. *(due)* pagadero **II.** tr. & intr. madurar.

ma·tur·i·ty (:ĭ-tē) s. madurez f; FIN. vencimiento ♦ **to reach m.** llegar a la madurez; FIN. ser pagadero, vencer.

maud·lin (môd'lĭn) adj. sensiblero.

maul (môl) **I.** s. almádena **II.** tr. *(to handle roughly)* maltratar; *(to injure)* lacerar.

mau·so·le·um (mô'sə-lē'əm) s. [pl. **s** o **-lea**] mausoleo.

mauve (mōv) s. & adj. malva m.

mav·er·ick (măv'ər-ĭk) s. res f sin marcar; *(dissenter)* disidente mf.

maw (mô) s. *(of a lion)* fauces f; *(opening)* abertura profunda.

mawk·ish (mô'kĭsh) s. sensiblero.

max·im (măk'sĭm) s. máxima.

max·i·mal (măk'sə-məl) adj. máximo.

max·i·mize (:mīz') tr. llevar al máximo.

max·i·mum (măk'sə-məm) adj. & s. máximo.

may (mā) aux. [pret. **might**] *(permission)* poder <*m. I go?* yes, you *m.* ¿puedo irme? sí, puedes>; *(possibility)* ser posible (que); *(wish)* ojalá que ♦ **be that as it m.** sea como fuere • **come what m.** pase lo que pase • **if I m.** si me lo permite • **long m. he live!** ¡que viva muchos años! • **m. as well** más vale que, mejor que • **m. I . . .?** ¿me permite . . .?

May (mā) s. mayo.

may·be (mā'bē) adj. *(perhaps)* quizá(s); *(possibly)* tal vez.

may·day (mā'dā') s. señal f de socorro.

may·flow·er (mā'flou'ər) s. espino.

may·hem (mā'hĕm') s. DER. mutilación f criminal; *(havoc)* estrago.

may·on·naise (mā'ə-nāz') s. mayonesa.

may·or (mā'ər) s. alcalde m.

may·or·al·ty (:əl-tē) s. alcaldía.

maze (māz) s. laberinto.

me (mē) pron. me; *(after preposition)* mi ♦ **it's me** FAM. soy yo • **with me** conmigo.

mead (mēd) s. aguamiel f, hidromel m.

mead·ow (mĕd'ō) s. pradera.

mea·ger (mē'gər) adj. *(lean)* magro; *(scanty)* exiguo; *(feeble)* pobre.

meal¹ (mēl) s. *(ground grain)* harina.

meal² s. comida ♦ **m. ticket** JER. sustento.

meal·time (mēl'tīm') s. hora de comer.

meal·y (mē'lē) adj. **-i-** *(granular)* harinoso; *(made of meal)* de harina; *(sprinkled with meal)* enharinado; *(pale)* pálido.

meal·y-mouthed (:mouthd') adj. meloso, camandulero.

mean¹ (mēn) tr. **meant** *(to signify)* querer decir; *(to intend)* tener la intención de; *(to allude to)* referirse a; *(to entail)* implicar ♦ **not to m. to do something** hacer algo sin querer • **to m. it** hablar en serio —intr. importar ♦ **to m. well** tener buenas intenciones.

mean² adj. inferior; *(base)* ruin; *(stingy)* tacaño; *(malicious)* mal intencionado; FAM. *(illtempered)* de malas pulgas; JER. *(difficult)* malo ♦ **to be m.** to tratar mal a • **to play a m. game of** JER. ser un bárbaro en.

mean³ **I.** s. *(middle)* punto medio; MAT. *(average)* promedio; *(arithmetic)* media ♦ pl. medios; *(method)* forma ♦ **by all m.** *(certainly)* sin duda; *(of course)* por supuesto • **by any m.** del modo que sea, como sea • **by m. of** por medio de, mediante • **by no m.** *(in no way)* de ningún modo; *(in no sense)* nada • **to live beyond one's m.** gastar más de lo que uno tiene **II.** adj. medio.

me·an·der (mē-ăn'dər) **I.** intr. serpentear; *(to wander)* vagar **II.** s. meandro.

mean·ing (mē'nĭng) s. sentido; *(intent)* significado ♦ **full of m.** cargado de sentido • **what's the m. of?** *(a word)* ¿qué significa?, ¿qué quiere decir?; *(a look)* ¿a qué viene?

mean·ing·ful (:fəl) adj. significativo.

mean·ing·less (:lĭs) adj. insignificante; *(senseless)* sin sentido.

meant (mĕnt) cf. **mean¹**.

mean·time (mēn'tīm') **I.** s. ínterin m **II.** adv. entretanto, mientras tanto.

mean·while (:hwīl') **I.** s. ínterin m **II.** adv. entretanto, mientras tanto.

mea·sles (mē'zəlz) s. sarampión m; *(German measles)* rubéola.

mea·sly (mēz'lē) adj. **-i-** JER. exiguo, ínfimo.

meas·ure (mĕzh'ər) **I.** s. medida; *(unit)* unidad f de medida; *(system)* sistema m (de medidas); *(limited amount)* cierto <*a m. of recognition* cierto reconocimiento>; *(bounds)* límite m; *(bill)* proyecto de ley; MÚS. compás m ♦ **beyond m.** sin límite • **for good m.** por añadidura • **in great m.** en gran parte • **to take the m. of** poner a prueba **II.** tr. medir; *(to estimate)* estimar ♦ **to m. off** medir • **to m. out** repartir (midiendo) —intr. ♦ **to m. up to** estar a la altura de.

meas·ured (:ərd) adj. acompasado; *(restrained)* mesurado.

meas·ure·ment (:ər-mənt) s. medición f; *(unit)* medida; *(system)* sistema m (de medidas).

meat (mēt) s. carne f; *(fleshy part)* parte f interior de algo comestible; *(essence)* meollo.

meat·ball ('bôl') s. albóndiga.

meat·less (:lĭs) adj. sin carne.

meat·y (mē'tē) adj. **-i-** carnoso, carnudo; FIG. substancioso.

mec·ca (mĕk'ə) s. meca.

me·chan·ic (mĭ-kăn'ĭk) s. mecánico ♦ **mechanics** sg. o pl. FÍS. mecánica; TEC. mecanismo;

FIG. técnica (de un arte, ciencia, sistema).

me·chan·i·cal (·ĭ-kəl) adj. MEC. mecánico, de máquinas; FIG. *(machine-like)* maquinal.

mech·a·nism (mĕk′ə-nĭz′əm) s. mecanismo.

mech·a·nis·tic (′-nĭs′tĭk) adj. mecanicista; *(mechanical)* mecánico.

mech·a·nize (′-nīz′) tr. mecanizar

med·al (mĕd′l) s. medalla.

med·al·ist (:ĭst) s. DEP. ganador *m.*

me·dal·lion (mĭ-dăl′yən) s. medallón *m.*

med·dle (mĕd′l) intr. entremeterse ♦ **to m. with** manosear.

med·dler (:lər) s. entremetido.

med·dle·some (:l-səm) adj. entremetido.

me·di·a (mē′dē-ə) [pl. de **medium**] s.pl. medios publicitarios (prensa, radio, televisión) ♦ **advertising m.** medios de publicidad • **broadcast m.** medios de (radio)difusión.

me·di·an (mē′dē-ən) I. adj. mediano; *(value)* medio II. s. punto medio; *(middle value)* valor medio.

me·di·ate (mē′dē-āt′) tr. ser mediador en; *(to negotiate)* negociar como mediador —intr. mediar.

me·di·a·tion (′-ā′shən) s. intervención *f;* DER. *(arbitration)* mediación *f.*

me·di·a·tor (′-′tər) s. mediador *m*

med·ic (mĕd′ĭk) s. médico; *(surgeon)* cirujano; *(student)* estudiante *mf* de medicina; MIL. auxiliar médico.

med·i·cal (:ĭ-kəl) adj. médico ♦ **m. examiner** DER. médico forense.

me·dic·a·ment (mĭ-dĭk′ə-mənt, mĕd′ĭ-kə-) s. medicamento.

med·i·cate (mĕd′ĭ-kāt′) tr. medicinar; *(to permeate)* impregnar (de sustancia medicinal).

med·i·ca·tion (′-kā′shən) s. medicamento; *(treatment)* tratamiento médico.

med·i·cine (mĕd′ĭ sĭn) s. medicina ♦ **m. man** hechicero ♦ **to give someone a taste of his own m.** pagarle a uno con la misma moneda ♦ **to take one's m.** atenerse a las consecuencias.

me·di·e·val (mē′dē-ē′vəl, mĕ-dē′vəl) adj. medieval.

me·di·o·cre (mē′dē-ō′kər) adj. mediocre.

me·di·oc·ri·ty (:ŏk′rĭ-tē) s. mediocridad *f.*

med·i·tate (mĕd′ĭ-tāt′) tr. & intr. meditar; *(to contemplate)* contemplar

med·i·ta·tion (′-tā′shən) s. meditación *f.*

med·i·ta·tive (′-tā′tĭv) adj. meditabundo.

me·di·um (mē′dē-əm) I. s. [pl. **s** o **-ia**] medio; *(spiritualist)* médium *mf* II. adj. mediano.

med·ley (mĕd′lē) s. mezcolanza; MÚS. popurrí *m.*

meek (mēk) adj. *(humble)* humilde; *(submissive)* manso.

meet (mēt) I. tr. met encontrar(se) con; *(to be present at arrival)* recibir; *(to be introduced)* conocer; *(to confer with)* entrevistarse con; *(to join)* unirse con; *(to confront)* hacer frente a; *(a challenge)* salir adelante; *(requirements)* satisfacer; *(debts)* pagar —intr. encontrarse, verse; *(to join)* unirse; *(to contend)* enfrentarse; *(to make acquaintance)* conocerse; *(to assemble)* reunirse II. s. DEP. encuentro.

meet·ing (mē′tĭng) s. reunión *f;* *(rally)* mitin *m.*

meet·ing·house (:hous′) s. templo.

meg·a·lo·ma·ni·a (mĕg′ə-lō-mā′nē-ə) s. megalomanía.

meg·a·lop·o·lis (′-lŏp′ə-lĭs) s. megalópolis *f.*

meg·a·phone (mĕg′ə-fōn′) s. megáfono.

meg·a·ton (:tŭn′) s. megatón *m.*

meg·a·watt (:wŏt′) s. megavatio.

mel·an·chol·ic (mĕl′ən-kŏl′ĭk) adj. melancólico.

mel·an·chol·y (′-ē) I. s. melancolía II. adj. melancólico; *(depressing)* triste.

meld (mĕld) tr. & intr. fusionar(se).

me·lee *o* **mê·lée** (mā′lā′) s. refriega; *(tumult)* tumulto.

mel·io·rate (mĕl′yə-rāt′) tr. & intr. mejorar(se)

mel·io·ra·tion (′-rā′shən) s. mejoramiento.

mel·lif·lu·ous (mə-lĭf′lŏo-əs) adj. melifluo.

mel·low (mĕl′ō) I. adj. **-er, -est** maduro; *(wine)* añejo; *(tone)* dulce; *(relaxed)* reposado II. tr. & intr. madurar; *(wine)* añejar(se); FIG. suavizar(se).

me·lod·ic (mə-lŏd′ĭk) adj. melódico.

me·lo·di·ous (mə-lō′dē-əs) adj. melodioso.

mel·o·dra·ma (mĕl′ə-drä′mə) s. melodrama *m.*

mel·o·dra·mat·ic (′-drə-măt′ĭk) adj. melodramático ♦ **melodramatics** s.pl. teatralidad.

mel·o·dy (mĕl′ə-dē) s. melodía.

mel·on (mĕl′ən) s. melón *m.*

melt (mĕlt) intr. derretirse; *(to dissolve)* disolverse; *(to vanish)* desvanecerse; *(to merge)* fusionarse; *(to soften)* ablandarse —tr. licuar, derretir; *(to dissolve)* disolver; *(to soften)* ablandar.

melt·down (′doun′) s. fusión *f* del núcleo del reactor nuclear.

mem·ber (mĕm′bər) s. miembro.

mem·ber·ship (:shĭp′) s. *(in group)* calidad *f* de miembro; *(number)* número total de socios o miembros

mem·brane (mĕm′brān′) s. membrana.

me·men·to (mə-mĕn′tō) s. [pl. **(e)s**] recuerdo.

mem·o (mĕm′ō) s. memorándum *m.*

mem·oir (mĕm′wär′) s. *(auto)*biografía ♦ pl. memorias.

mem·o·ra·bil·i·a (mĕm′ər-ə-bĭl′ē-ə) s.pl. eventos memorables; *(mementos)* recuerdos.

mem·o·ra·ble (′-bəl) adj. memorable.

mem·o·ran·dum (mĕm′ə-răn′dəm) s. [pl. **s** o **-da**] nota; *(communiqué)* memorándum *m.*

me·mo·ri·al (mə-môr′ē-əl) I. s. monumento conmemorativo; *(petition)* memorial *m* II. adj. conmemorativo.

me·mo·ri·al·ize (:ə-līz′) tr. conmemorar.

mem·o·rize (mĕm′ə-rīz′) tr. memorizar.

mem·o·ry (:rē) s. memoria; *(recollection)* recuerdo ♦ **from m.** de memoria • **if my m. serves me** si no me falla la memoria • **to commit to m.** aprender de memoria.

men (mĕn) cf. **man**

men·ace (mĕn′ĭs) I. s. amenaza; *(annoying person)* pesado II. tr. & intr. amenazar.

me·nag·er·ie (mə-năj′ə-rē) s. colección *f* de animales salvajes.

mend (mĕnd) I. tr. remendar; *(to reform)* reformar ♦ **to m. one's ways** enmendarse —intr. sanar II. s. remiendo ♦ **to be on the m.** ir mejorando.

men·da·cious (mĕn-dā′shəs) adj. mendaz.

men·dac·i·ty (:dăs′ĭ-tē) s. mendacidad *f.*

men·di·cant (mĕn′dĭ-kənt) I. adj. mendicante II. s. *(beggar)* mendigo; RELIG. mendicante *mf.*

men·folk(s) (mĕn′fōk[s]′) s.pl. hombres *m.*

me·ni·al (mē′nē-əl) I. adj. doméstico; *(servile)* servil II. s. criado.

men·in·gi·tis (mĕn′ĭn-jī′tĭs) s. meningitis *f.*

men·o·pause (mĕn′ə-pôz′) s. menopausia.

men·stru·al (mĕn′strōo-əl) adj. menstrual.

men·stru·ate (:āt') intr. menstruar.
men·stru·a·tion ('-ā'shən) s. menstruación f.
men·su·ra·ble (měn'sə-rə-bəl) adj. mensurable.
men·su·ra·tion ('-rā'shən) s. mensura.
mens·wear (měnz'wâr') s. ropa para hombres.
men·tal (měn'tl) adj. mental; (hospital) psiquiátrico ♦ m. derangement alienación mental.
men·tal·i·ty (měn-tǎl'ī-tē) s. mentalidad f; (attitude) modo de pensar.
men·thol (měn'thôl') s. mentol m.
men·tho·lat·ed (:thə-lā'tĭd) adj. mentolado.
men·tion (měn'shən) I. tr. mencionar II. s. mención f.
men·u (měn'yōō, mā'nyōō) s. menú m, carta.
me·ow (mē-ou') I. s. maullido II. intr. maullar.
mer·can·tile (mûr'kən-tēl', :tīl') adj. mercantil.
mer·ce·nar·y (mûr'sə-něr'ē) adj. & s. mercenario.
mer·chan·dise (mûr'chən-dīs') I. s. mercancía, mercadería II. tr. (:dīz') comerciar.
mer·chant (mûr'chənt) I. s. mercader m, comerciante mf; (shopkeeper) tendero II. adj. mercante.
mer·chant·man (:mən) s. [pl. -men] buque m mercante.
mer·ci·ful (mûr'sĭ-fəl) adj. misericordioso.
mer·ci·less (:lĭs) adj. despiadado.
mer·cu·ri·al (mər-kyŏŏr'ē-əl) adj. volátil; QUÍM. mercurial.
mer·cu·ro·chrome (:ə-krōm') s. mercurocromo.
mer·cu·ry (mûr'kyə-rē) s. mercurio.
mer·cy (mûr'sē) s. clemencia; (compassion) misericordia; (relief) alivio ♦ m. killing eutanasia • to be at the m. of estar a (la) merced de • to have m. on tener piedad de.
mere (mîr) adj. (simple) puro; (no more than) no más que <he is a m. employee no es más que un empleado>.
mere·ly (lē) adv. simplemente; (no more than) no más que <she's m. an assistant no es más que una ayudanta>.
mer·e·tri·cious (měr'ĭ-trĭsh'əs) adj. (gaudy) llamativo; (insincere) engañoso.
merge (mûrj) tr. & intr. unir(se); COM. fusionar(se).
merg·er (mûr'jər) s. unión f; COM. fusión f.
me·rid·i·an (mə-rĭd'ē-ən) I. s. meridiano; (apex) cenit m II. adj. meridiano.
me·ringue (mə-rǎng') s. merengue m.
mer·it (měr'ĭt) I. s. mérito; (advantage) ventaja ♦ m. raise aumento (de sueldo) por excelencia • on one's merits según las cualidades de uno ♦ pl. DER. fondo II. tr. & intr. merecer.
mer·i·to·ri·ous (měr'ĭ-tôr'ē-əs) adj. meritorio.
mer·maid (mûr'mād') s. sirena.
mer·ri·ment (měr'ĭ-mənt) s. alegría; (amusement) diversión f.
mer·ry (měr'ē) adj. -i- alegre; (entertaining) divertido; (brisk) ligero ♦ M. Christmas Feliz Navidad • to make m. divertirse.
mer·ry-go-round (:gō-round') s. tiovivo; (whirl) remolino.
mer·ry·mak·ing (:mā'kĭng) s. juerga.
mes·cal (mĕ-skǎl') s. mezcal m; (liquor) aguardiente m de mezcal.
mes·ca·line (měs'kə-lēn') s. mescalina.
mesh (měsh) I. s. malla; (of gears) engranaje m ♦ pl. malla; (snares) redes II. tr. enredar ♦ to m. together enlazar —intr. (to become entangled) enredarse; MEC. engranar; (to harmo-

nize) encajar.
mes·mer·ize (měz'mə-rīz') tr. hipnotizar; (to enthrall) cautivar.
mes·o·morph (měz'ə-môrf') s. mesomorfo.
mes·quite (mě-skēt') s. mezquite m.
mess (měs) I. s. desorden m; (dirty condition) asquerosidad f; (difficulty) lío; (serving) ración f; (meal) rancho ♦ m. hall comedor II. tr. ♦ to m. up o make a m. of (to soil) ensuciar; (to disarrange) desordenar, desarreglar; (to spoil) echar a perder —intr. ♦ to m. around FAM. entretenerse • to m. with FAM. molestar.
mes·sage (měs'ĭj) s. mensaje m.
mes·sen·ger (měs'ən-jər) s. mensajero.
mess·y (měs'ē) adj. -i- desordenado; (filthy) asqueroso; (slovenly) desaseado; (complicated) complicado.
met (mět) cf. meet.
met·a·bol·ic (mět'ə-bŏl'ĭk) adj. metabólico.
me·tab·o·lism (mĭ-tǎb'ə-lĭz'əm) s. metabolismo.
me·tab·o·lize (:līz') tr. & intr. metabolizar(se).
met·al (mět'l) s. metal m; (mettle) temple m.
me·tal·lic (mə-tǎl'ĭk) adj. metálico.
met·al·lur·gy (mět'l-ûr'jē) s. metalurgia.
met·al·work (:wûrk') s. (craft) metalistería; (things) objetos de metal.
met·a·mor·phic (mět'ə-môr'fĭk) adj. metamórfico.
met·a·mor·phose (mět'ə-môr'fōz', :fōs') tr. & intr. metamorfosear(se).
met·a·mor·pho·sis (:fə-sĭs) s. [pl. -ses] metamorfosis f.
met·a·phor (mět'ə-fôr') s. metáfora.
met·a·phor·i·cal ('-'ĭ-kəl) adj. metafórico.
met·a·phys·i·cal (mět'ə-fĭz'ĭ-kəl) adj. metafísico.
met·a·phys·ics (:ĭks) s.sg. metafísica.
me·tas·ta·sis (mə-tǎs'tə-sĭs) s. [pl. -ses] metástasis f.
mete (mēt) tr. ♦ to m. out repartir.
me·te·or (mē'tē-ər) s. meteoro.
me·te·or·ic ('-ôr'ĭk) adj. meteórico.
me·te·or·ite ('-ə-rīt') s. meteorito.
me·te·or·o·log·i·cal (mē'tē-ə-rə-lŏj'ĭ-kəl) adj. meteorológico.
me·te·or·ol·o·gist (:rŏl'ə-jĭst) s. meteorólogo, meteorologista mf.
me·te·or·ol·o·gy (:jē) s. meteorología.
me·ter¹ (mē'tər) s. (measurement, verse) metro; (device) contador m; MÚS. compás m.
meth·ane (měth'ān') s. metano.
meth·od (měth'əd) s. método; (order) orden m.
me·thod·ic/i·cal (mə-thŏd'ĭk) adj. metódico.
meth·od·ol·o·gy (měth'ə-dŏl'ə-jē) s. metodología.
meth·yl (měth'əl) s. metilo.
me·tic·u·lous (mə-tĭk'yə-ləs) adj. meticuloso; (overscrupulous) minucioso.
mé·tier (mā-tyā') s. especialidad f.
me·tre (mē'tər) G.B. var. de meter.
met·ric (mět'rĭk) adj. métrico.
met·ri·cal (:ĭ-kəl) adj. GRAM. métrico, de la métrica; (of measurement) métrico, del metro.
met·ro·nome (mět'rə-nōm') s. metrónomo.
me·trop·o·lis (mə-trŏp'ə-lĭs) s. metrópoli f.
met·ro·pol·i·tan (mět'rə-pŏl'ĭ-tn) adj. metropolitano.
met·tle (mět'l) s. (character) entereza; (courage) temple m ♦ on one's m. puesto a prueba.
met·tle·some (:səm) adj. animoso.
mew¹ (myōō) s. (small street) callejuela.

mew² I. intr. maullar II. s. maullido.

mewl (myōōl) intr. lloriquear.

mez·za·nine (mĕz′ə-nēn′) s. entresuelo.

mi·as·ma (mī-ăz′mə) s. miasma *m.*

mice (mīs) cf. **mouse**.

mi·cro (mī′krō) s. FAM. microcomputadora.

mi·crobe (mī′krōb′) s. microbio.

mi·cro·bi·ol·o·gy (mī′krō-bī-ŏl′ə-jē) s. microbiología.

mi·cro·bus (′-bŭs′) s. microbús *m.*

mi·cro·chip (′-chĭp′) s. microplaqueta.

mi·cro·cir·cuit (:sûr′kĭt) s. microcircuito.

mi·cro·com·put·er (:kəm-pyōō′tər) s. microordenador *m.*

mi·cro·cosm (mī′krə-kŏz′əm) s. microcosmo.

mi·cro·ec·o·nom·ics (mī′krō-ĕk′ə-nŏm′ĭks) s.sg. microeconomía.

mi·cro·fiche (′-fēsh′) s. [pl. inv. o ·es] microficha.

mi·cro·film (mī′krə-fĭlm′) I. s. microfilm *m* II. tr. reproducir en microfilm.

mi·cron (mī′krŏn′) s. [pl. s o -cra] micrón *m.*

mi·cro·or·gan·ism (mī′krō-ôr′gə-nĭz′əm) s. microorganismo.

mi·cro·phone (mī′krə-fōn′) s. micrófono.

mi·cro·proc·es·sor (mī′krō-prŏs′ĕs-ər) s. microprocesador *m.*

mi·cro·scope (mī′krə-skōp′) s. microscopio.

mi·cro·scop·ic/i·cal (′-skŏp′ĭk) adj. microscópico.

mi·cro·sur·ger·y (mī′krō-sûr′jə-rē) s. microcirugía.

mi·cro·wave (mī′krə-wāv′) s. microonda.

mid¹ (mĭd) adj. medio ♦ **in mid-April** a mediados de abril ♦ **in m. course** a media carrera.

mid² prep. POÉT. en medio de.

mid·air (:âr′) s. punto en medio del aire ♦ **m. collision** AVIA. choque en pleno vuelo.

mid·day (:dā′) s. mediodía *m.*

mid·dle (mĭd′l) I. adj. medio; (intermediate) intermedio ♦ **M. Ages** Edad Media ♦ **m. ground** punto de vista intermedio II. s. medio; (waist) cintura ♦ **in the m. of** en medio de.

mid·dle-aged (′-ājd′) adj. de edad madura.

mid·dle-class (:klăs′) adj. de la clase media.

mid·dle·man (′-măn′) s. [pl. -men] intermediario.

mid·dle-of-the-road (′-əv-thə-rōd′) adj. moderado.

mid·dle·weight (′-wāt′) s. DEP. peso medio.

mid·dling (mĭd′lĭng) adj. (medium) mediano; (mediocre) ordinario.

midg·et (mĭj′ĭt) s. (person) enano; (object) objeto pequeño.

mid·land (mĭd′lənd) s. región *f* central.

mid·night (:nīt′) s. medianoche *f* ♦ **to burn the m. oil** quemarse las cejas o pestañas.

mid·point (:point′) s. punto céntrico.

mid·riff (:rĭf′) s. abdomen *m* superior.

mid·sec·tion (:sĕk′shən) s. sección media.

mid·ship (:shĭp′) adj. del medio del barco.

mid·ship·man (:shĭp′mən) s. [pl. -men] guardiamarina *m.*

mid·ships (:shĭps′) adv. en medio del barco.

midst (mĭdst) I. s. medio ♦ **in our m.** entre nosotros ♦ **in the m. of** en medio de II. prep. entre, en medio de.

mid·stream (mĭd′strēm′) s. pleno río.

mid·sum·mer (:sŭm′ər) s. pleno verano; (summer solstice) solsticio de verano.

mid·term (:tûrm′) s. mitad *f* del semestre; (exam) examen *m* parcial.

mid·town (:toun′) s. centro de una ciudad.

mid·way (:wā′) I. s. avenida central (de una feria o exposición) II. adv. & adj. a mitad o medio del camino.

mid·week (:wēk′) s. medio de la semana.

mid·wife (:wīf′) [pl. -ves] I. s. comadrona, partera II. tr. -f- o -v- partear.

mid·wife·ry (:wīf′rē, :wīf′-) s. partería.

mid·win·ter (:wĭn′tər) s. pleno invierno, (winter solstice) solsticio de invierno.

mid·year (:yîr′) s. mitad *f* del año; (exam) examen *m* parcial de mitad del año.

mien (mēn) s. (hearing) porte *m*; (aspect) aspecto.

miff (mĭf) tr. disgustar.

might¹ (mīt) s. fuerzas.

might² aux. [prét. de **may**] poder <she m. help if she knew the truth ella podría ayudar si supiera la verdad>; ser posible que <it m. rain es posible que llueva>.

might·y (mī′tē) I. adj. -i- poderoso; (imposing) imponente II. adv. FAM. extremadamente.

mi·graine (mī′grān′) s. jaqueca, migraña.

mi·grant (mī′grənt) I. s. emigrante *mf*; (worker) trabajador *m* ambulante II. adj. migratorio.

mi·grate (mī′grāt′) intr. emigrar.

mi·gra·tion (mī-grā′shən) s. migración *f.*

mi·gra·to·ry (mī′grə-tôr′ē) adj. migratorio.

mike (mīk) s. FAM. micrófono.

mild (mīld) adj. suave; (in character) apacible; (climate) templado; (lenient) poco severo; (cold, cough) leve.

mil·dew (mĭl′dōō′) I. s. moho II. tr. & intr. enmohecer(se).

mile (mīl) s. milla ♦ **to be off by a m.** estar lejos de la cuenta.

mile·age (mī′lĭj) s. distancia en millas; (miles traveled) recorrido en millas; (allowance) gastos de viaje (pagados por millas); FAM. (usefulness) rendimiento, utilidad *f.*

mile·stone (mīl′stōn′) s. piedra miliaria; (event) hito.

mi·lieu (mēl-yōō′) s. ambiente *m.*

mil·i·tan·cy (mĭl′ĭ-tn-sē) s. belicosidad *f.*

mil·i·tant (:tnt) adj. & s. militante *mf.*

mil·i·ta·rist (:tər-ĭst) s. militarista *mf.*

mil·i·ta·ris·tic (′-tə-rĭs′tĭk) adj. militarista.

mil·i·ta·rize (′-tə-rīz′) tr. militarizar.

mil·i·tar·y (:tĕr′ē) I. adj. militar II. s. los militares, las fuerzas armadas.

mil·i·tate (:tāt′) intr. militar.

mi·li·tia (mə-lĭsh′ə) s. milicia.

mi·li·tia·man (:mən) s. [pl. -men] miliciano.

milk (mĭlk) I. s. leche *f* ♦ **chocolate m.** leche con chocolate ♦ **m. products** productos lácteos ♦ **m. shake** batido de leche ♦ **not to cry over spilled m.** a lo hecho, pecho ♦ **powdered m.** leche en polvo ♦ **skim m.** leche desnatada ♦ **whole m.** leche sin desnatar II. tr. ordeñar; (to draw out) sacar ♦ **to m. dry** exprimir como una naranja.

milk·weed (:wēd′) s. algodoncillo.

milk·y (mĭl′kē) adj. -i- lechoso ♦ **M. Way** Vía Láctea.

mill (mĭl) I. s. molino; (for spices, coffee) molinillo; (factory) fábrica ♦ **run of the m.** corriente y moliente ♦ **to go through the m.** aprender a golpes II. tr. moler; (to process) tratar —intr. arremolinarse.

mil·len·ni·um (mə-lĕn′ē-əm) s. [pl. s o -ia] milenio; RELIG. reinado de los mil años; (golden age) época de paz y prosperidad.

mill·er (mĭl′ər) s. molinero.

mil·li·gram (mĭl′ə-grăm′) s. miligramo.

mil·li·li·ter (:lē′tər) s. mililitro.

mil·li·me·ter (:mē′tər) s. milimetro.

mil·li·ner (mĭl′ə-nər) s. sombrerero.

mil·li·ner·y (:nĕr′ē) s. sombrería de señoras.

mil·lion (mĭl′yən) s. [pl. inv. *o* **s**] millón *m.*

mil·lion·aire (mĭl′yə-nâr′) s. millonario.

mil·li·pede (mĭl′ə-pēd′) s. milpiés *m.*

mill·stone (mĭl′stōn′) s. piedra de molino.

milque·toast (mĭlk′tōst′) s. persona de carácter tímido y reservado.

mime (mīm) I. s. pantomima; *(performer)* pantomimo II. tr. *(to mimic)* remedar; *(to pantomime)* hacer una pantomima de —intr. actuar en pantomima.

mim·e·o·graph (mĭm′ē-ə-grăf′) I. s. mimeógrafo II. tr. & intr. mimeografiar.

mim·ic (mĭm′ĭk) I. tr. **-ck-** remedar; *(resemble)* simular II. s. pantomimo; *(impersonator)* imitador *m*; *(copy)* imitación *f.*

mim·ic·ry (:ĭ-krē) s. mímica; BIOL. mimetismo.

mi·mo·sa (mĭ-mō′sə) s. mimosa.

mince (mĭns) tr. *(meat)* picar; *(words)* abstenerse de usar.

mince·meat (′mēt′) s. mezcla de fruta picada y especias ♦ **to make m.** of JER. hacer pedazos de.

minc·ing (mĭn′sĭng) adj. remilgado.

mind (mīnd) I. s. mente *f*; *(intelligence)* inteligencia; *(intellect)* cerebro; *(memory)* memoria; *(psychology)* psicología; *(opinion)* opinión *f*; *(attention)* atención ♦ **to be in one's right m.** estar uno en sus cabales • **to be out of one's m.** haber perdido el juicio • **to bring to m.** recordar • **to change one's m.** cambiar de opinión *o* parecer • **to come to m.** venir a la memoria • **to cross one's m.** ocurrírsele a uno • **to have a (good) m.** to estar dispuesto a • **to have in m.** planear • **to know one's (own) m.** saber lo que uno quiere • **to lose one's m.** perder la razón • **to make up one's m.** decidirse • **to my m.** a mi parecer • **to set one's m. on** estar resuelto a • **to speak one's m.** hablar con franqueza II. tr. *(to heed)* prestar atención a; *(to obey)* obedecer; *(to watch out for)* tener cuidado con; *(to dislike)* molestar <they do not m. the cold no les molesta el frío>; *(to look after)* cuidar ♦ **m. your own business!** ¡no te entrometas! • **not to m.** no tener inconveniente —intr. *(to give heed)* prestar atención; *(to obey)* obedecer ♦ **never m.** no importa, da igual.

mind·ed (mīn′dĭd) adj. de mentalidad <commercially m. de mentalidad mercantil>; *(disposed toward)* dispuesto.

mind·ful (mīnd′fəl) adj. atento.

mind·less (:lĭs) adj. estúpido; *(senseless)* sin sentido; *(careless)* descuidado.

mind·set (:sĕt′) s. predisposición *f* mental.

mine[1] (mīn) I. s. mina ♦ **land m.** mina terrestre II. tr. extraer; *(to dig a mine)* minar, poner minas en ♦ **to m. for** cavar en busca de.

mine[2] pron. (el) mío.

mine·field (mīn′fēld′) s. campo de minas.

min·er (mī′nər) s. minero.

min·er·al (mĭn′ər-əl) s. & adj. mineral *m.*

min·er·al·ize (:ə-līz′) tr. & intr. mineralizar(se).

min·er·al·o·gy (mĭn′ə-rŏl′ə-jē) s. mineralogía.

min·gle (mĭng′gəl) tr. & intr. mezclar(se).

min·i (mĭn′ē) s. algo más pequeño de lo normal.

min·i·a·ture (:ə-chŏŏr′, :ə-chər) I. s. miniatura II. adj. en miniatura.

min·i·a·tur·ize (:ə-chə-rīz′) tr. miniaturizar.

min·i·bike (:bīk′) s. pequeña motocicleta.

min·i·bus (:bŭs′) s. microbús *m.*

min·i·com·put·er (′-kəm-pyŏŏ′tər) s. computadora pequeña.

min·i·mal (mĭn′ə-məl) adj. & s. mínimo.

min·i·mize (:mīz′) tr. minimizar.

min·i·mum (:məm) s. & adj. [pl. **s** *o* **-ma**] mínimo ♦ **m. wage** salario vital.

min·ing (mī′nĭng) s. (la) minería; MIL. minado, siembra de minas.

min·ion (mĭn′yən) s. favorito; *(sycophant)* paniaguado; *(subordinate)* funcionario subordinado.

min·is·ter (mĭn′ĭ-stər) I. s. ministro ♦ **Prime M.** primer ministro II. intr. cuidar.

min·is·te·ri·al (′-stîr′ē-əl) adj. POL. ministerial; RELIG. pastoral.

min·is·try (′-strē) s. POL. ministerio; RELIG. sacerdocio ♦ **to enter the m.** hacerse clérigo.

mink (mĭngk) s. [pl. inv. *o* **s**] visón *m.*

min·now (mĭn′ō) s. [pl. inv. *o* **s**] pez pequeño.

mi·nor (mī′nər) I. adj. menor; *(not serious)* pequeño; *(secondary)* de poca importancia; *(in age)* menor de edad II. s. menor *mf* de edad; EDUC. especialización secundaria III. intr. ♦ **to m. in** EDUC. estudiar como especialización secundaria.

mi·nor·i·ty (mə-nôr′ĭ-tē, mī-) s. minoría.

mi·nor-league (mī′nər-lēg′) adj. FAM. de importancia secundaria.

min·ster (mĭn′stər) s. G.B. iglesia de un monasterio; *(cathedral)* catedral *f.*

min·strel (mĭn′strəl) s. trovador *m*; *(performer)* cantor y actor cómico.

mint[1] (mĭnt) I. s. casa de moneda; *(fortune)* cantidad *f* grande II. tr. acuñar; *(to invent)* idear III. adj. sin usar ♦ **in m. condition** como nuevo.

mint[2] s. BOT. menta, hierbabuena; *(candy)* (pastilla de) menta.

min·u·end (mĭn′yŏŏ-ĕnd′) s. minuendo.

min·u·et (mĭn′yŏŏ-ĕt′) s. minué *m.*

mi·nus (mī′nəs) I. prep. MAT. menos; FAM. *(without)* sin II. adj. MAT. negativo III. s. MAT. *(signo)* menos *m.*

min·us·cule (mĭn′ə-skyŏŏl′) I. s. minúscula II. adj. minúsculo.

min·ute[1] (mĭn′ĭt) s. minuto; *(moment)* momento ♦ **any m.** de un momento a otro • **at the last m.** a última hora • **just a m.!** ¡un momento! • **m. hand** minutero • **the m. something happens** en cuanto algo suceda • **this (very) m.** ahora mismo • **to take a m.** detenerse un momento a ♦ pl. acta.

mi·nute[2] (mĭ-nŏŏt′, mī-) adj. diminuto; *(insignificant)* insignificante; *(thorough)* minucioso.

min·ute·man (mĭn′ĭt-măn′) s. [pl. **-men**] miliciano (en la guerra de independencia de E.U.).

mi·nu·ti·a (mĭ-nŏŏ′shē-ə) s. [pl. **-iae**] minucias.

minx (mĭngks) s. joven coqueta *o* descarada.

mir·a·cle (mĭr′ə-kəl) s. milagro; FIG. maravilla.

mi·rac·u·lous (mĭ-răk′yə-ləs) adj. milagroso.

mi·rage (mĭ-räzh′) s. espejismo.

mire (mīr) I. s. lodazal *m*; *(mud)* fango II. tr. & intr. atascar(se).

mir·ror (mĭr′ər) I. s. espejo II. tr. reflejar.

mirth (mûrth) s. alegría; *(laughter)* hilaridad *f.*

mirth·ful (′fəl) adj. alegre.

mirth·less (:lĭs) adj. sin alegría.

mis·ad·ven·ture (mĭs′əd-vĕn′chər) s. desventura.

mis·ad·vise (:əd-vīz′) tr. aconsejar mal.

mis·a·ligned (:ə-līnd') adj. mal alineado.

mis·a·lign·ment (:līn'mənt) s. desalineación f.

mis·al·li·ance (:lī'əns) s. mala unión; *(marriage)* matrimonio con persona de clase inferior.

mis·an·thrope (mĭs'ən-thrōp') s. misántropo.

mis·an·throp·ic ('-thrŏp'ĭk) adj. misantrópico.

mis·an·thro·pist (mĭs-ăn'thrə-pĭst) s. misántropo.

mis·an·thro·py (:pē) s. misantropía.

mis·ap·pli·ca·tion (mĭs-ăp'lĭ-kā'shən) s. mala aplicación; *(misuse)* uso indebido.

mis·ap·ply ('ə-plī') tr. aplicar mal.

mis·ap·pre·hend (mĭs-ăp'rĭ-hĕnd') tr. comprender mal.

mis·ap·pre·hen·sion (:hĕn'shən) s. malentendido.

mis·ap·pro·pri·ate (mĭs'ə-prō'prē-āt') tr. apropiar erróneamente; *(to embezzle)* malversar.

mis·ap·pro·pri·a·tion ('-'-ā'shən) s. malversación f.

mis·be·got·ten (mĭs'bĭ-gŏt'n) adj. ilegítimo; *(ill-conceived)* mal concebido.

mis·be·have (:hāv') intr. portarse mal.

mis·be·hav·ior (:yər) s. mala conducta.

mis·cal·cu·late (mĭs-kăl'kyə-lāt') tr. & intr. calcular mal.

mis·cal·cu·la·tion ('-lā'shən) s. cálculo erróneo, *(mistake)* error m.

mis·call (mĭs-kôl') tr. llamar erróneamente.

mis·car·riage (mĭs-kăr'ĭj) s. *(failure)* fracaso; MED. aborto.

mis·car·ry (:ē) intr. *(to fail)* malograrse; MED. abortar.

mis·ceg·e·na·tion (mĭ-sĕj'ə-nā'shən, mĭs'ĭ-jə-) s. cruce m de razas.

mis·cel·la·ne·ous (mĭs'ə-lā'nē-əs) adj. misceláneo ♦ **m. assortment** surtido variado.

mis·cel·la·ny ('-'nē) s. miscelánea.

mis·chance (mĭs-chăns') s. infortunio; *(bad luck)* mala suerte.

mis·chief (mĭs'chĭf) s. *(damage)* daño; *(prank)* travesura; *(perverseness)* malicia.

mis·chie·vous (:chə-vəs) adj. malicioso; *(playful)* travieso; *(troublesome)* molesto.

mis·clas·si·fy (mĭs-klăs'ə-fī') tr. clasificar incorrectamente.

mis·con·ceive ('kən-sēv') tr. interpretar incorrectamente.

mis·con·cep·tion (:sĕp'shən) s. concepto erróneo.

mis·con·duct (mĭs-kŏn'dŭkt) s. mala conducta; *(mismanagement)* mala administración.

mis·con·strue ('kən-strōō') tr. interpretar mal.

mis·count (:t) tr. & intr. (mĭs-kount') contar mal II. s. ('kount') recuento erróneo.

mis·cre·ant (mĭs'krē-ənt) I. s. malhechor m II. adj. bellaco.

mis·cue (mĭs-kyōō') I. s. pifia II. intr. pifiar.

mis·deal I. tr. & intr. (mĭs-dēl') **-dealt** repartir mal (los naipes) II. s. ('dēl') reparto erróneo.

mis·deed (mĭs-dēd') s. fechoría.

mis·de·mean·or (mĭs'dĭ-mē'nər) s. *(misdeed)* fechoría; DER. delito menor.

mis·di·ag·nose (mĭs-dī'əg-nōs') tr. diagnosticar incorrectamente.

mis·di·ag·no·sis ('-'ō'sĭs) s. [pl. **-ses**] diagnóstico incorrecto.

mis·di·rect (mĭs'dĭ-rĕkt') tr. dirigir erradamente.

mis·di·rec·tion (:rĕk'shən) s. mala dirección.

mi·ser (mī'zər) s. avaro.

mis·er·a·ble (mĭz'ər-ə-bəl) adj. *(unhappy)* desdichado; *(disagreeable)* desagradable; *(mean)* abyecto; *(inadequate)* miserable; *(inferior)* de mala calidad.

mi·ser·ly (mī'zər-lē) adj. avariento.

mis·er·y (mĭz'ə-rē) s. miseria; *(unhappiness)* desdicha.

mis·es·ti·mate (mĭs-ĕs'tə-māt') tr. estimar erróneamente.

mis·fea·sance (:fē'zəns) s. DER. ejecución f ilegal de un procedimiento lícito.

mis·file (·fīl') tr. archivar mal.

mis·fire (:fīr') I. intr. fallar II. s. ('fīr') fallo de encendido; FIG. fracaso.

mis·fit ('fĭt') s. cosa o prenda que encaja o cae mal; *(person)* persona inadaptada.

mis·for·tune (mĭs-fôr'chən) s. mala suerte; *(mischance)* infortunio.

mis·giv·ing (:gĭv'ĭng) s. duda.

mis·gov·ern (:gŭv'ərn) tr. gobernar mal.

mis·guide (:gīd') tr. dirigir mal.

mis·guid·ed (:gī'dĭd) adj. descaminado.

mis·han·dle (:hăn'dl) tr. *(to botch)* manejar mal; *(to maltreat)* maltratar.

mis·hap (:hăp') s. desgracia.

mish·mash (mĭsh'măsh') s. revoltijo.

mis·i·den·ti·fy (mĭs'ī-dĕn'tə-fī') tr. identificar mal o erróneamente.

mis·in·form (:ĭn-fôrm') tr. dar informes erróneos.

mis·in·for·ma·tion ('-fər-mā'shən) s. información errónea.

mis·in·ter·pret ('-tûr'prĭt) tr. interpretar mal.

mis·in·ter·pre·ta·tion ('-'-prĭ-tā'shən) s. mala interpretación.

mis·judge (:jŭj') tr. & intr. juzgar mal.

mis·judg·ment (:mənt) s. juicio equivocado.

mis·la·bel (mĭs-lā'bəl) tr. clasificar mal.

mis·lay (:lā') tr. **-laid** perder.

mis·lead (:lēd') tr. **-led** descaminar; *(to deceive)* engañar.

mis·lead·ing (:lē'dĭng) adj. engañoso.

mis·led (:lĕd') c/f. **mislead**.

mis·man·age (:măn'ĭj) tr. administrar mal.

mis·man·age·ment (:mənt) s. mala administración.

mis·mar·riage (mĭs-măr'ĭj) s. matrimonio desacertado.

mis·match (:măch') I. tr. emparejar mal II. s. ('măch') emparejamiento mal hecho.

mis·name (mĭs-nām') tr. dar nombre que no corresponde a la realidad.

mis·no·mer (:nō'mər) s. nombre poco apto.

mi·sog·a·my (mĭ-sŏg'ə-mē) s. misogamia.

mi·sog·y·ny (mĭ-sŏj'ə-nē) s. misoginia.

mis·per·ceive (mĭs'pər-sēv') tr. percibir mal.

mis·place (mĭs-plās') tr. *(to mislay)* colocar fuera de su lugar; *(to lose)* extraviar; *(to bestow mistakenly)* otorgar indebidamente.

mis·print (mĭs'prĭnt') s. error m de imprenta.

mis·pro·nounce ('prə-nouns') tr. & intr. pronunciar mal o incorrectamente.

mis·quote (:kwōt') tr. citar incorrectamente.

mis·read (:rēd') tr. **-read** leer mal; *(to misinterpret)* interpretar mal.

mis·rep·re·sent ('rĕp'rĭ-zĕnt') tr. tergiversar.

mis·rep·re·sen·ta·tion (:zĕn-tā'shən) s. *(distortion)* tergiversación f; *(fraud)* representación fraudulenta.

mis·rule (mĭs-rōōl') I. tr. desgobernar II. s. desgobierno.

miss¹ (mĭs) I. tr. perder; *(a shot)* errar; *(not to*

meet) no encontrar; *(not to see)* no ver; *(not to perceive)* no darse cuenta de; *(not to achieve)* no conseguir; *(to regret the absence of)* echar de menos, extrañar ♦ **to m. one's turn** perder el turno • **to m. out on** perderse • **to m. the boat** FAM. írsele a uno el tren • **to m. the mark** equivocarse • **to m. the point** no comprender • **you can't miss it** lo encontrarás fácilmente —intr. fallar ♦ **to be missing** faltar • **you can't m.** FAM. no hay forma de perder II. s. fallo; *(failure)* fracaso.

miss² s. señorita ♦ **M. Brown** la señorita Brown.

mis·shap·en (mĭs-shā′pən) adj. deformado.

mis·sile (mĭs′əl, :īl′) s. proyectil m; *(guided)* misil teledirigido; *(ballistic)* proyectil balístico.

mis·sile·ry (:əl-rē) s. (ciencia de) cohetes teledirigidos.

miss·ing (mĭs′ĭng) adj. *(lost)* perdido; *(disappeared)* desaparecido; *(absent)* ausente; *(lacking)* que falta ♦ **m. link** eslabón perdido.

mis·sion (mĭsh′ən) s. misión f; DIPL. embajada; *(welfare organization)* beneficencia.

mis·sion·ar·y (:ə-nĕr′ē) s. & adj. misionero.

mis·sis (mĭs′ĭz) s. FAM. esposa, doña.

mis·sive (mĭs′ĭv) s. misiva.

mis·spell (mĭs-spĕl′) tr. **-ed** *o* **-spelt** ortografiar *o* deletrear mal.

mis·spend (:spĕnd′) tr. **-spent** malgastar.

mis·state (:stāt′) tr. exponer *o* relatar mal.

mis·step (:stĕp′) s. tropezón m; *(blunder)* desacierto.

mist (mĭst) I. s. *(fog)* neblina; *(at sea)* bruma; *(haze)* calina; FIG. oscuridad f II. intr. *(to fog up)* cubrirse de niebla; *(to blur)* empañarse.

mis·take (mĭ-stāk′) I. s. error m II. tr. **-took, -taken** interpretar mal ♦ **to m. . . . for** confundir . . . con —intr. ♦ **to be mistaken** equivocarse.

mis·tak·en (mĭ-stāk′kən) adj. *(wrong)* equivocado, errado; *(inexact)* erróneo.

Mis·ter (mĭs′tər) s. señor m.

mis·tle·toe (mĭs′əl-tō′) s. muérdago.

mis·took (mĭ-stŏok′) cf. **mistake.**

mis·treat (mĭs-trēt′) tr. maltratar.

mis·treat·ment (:mənt) s. maltrato.

mis·tress (mĭs′trĭs) s. *(head of household)* señora; *(lover)* amante f; *(controller)* dueña.

mis·tri·al (mĭs-trī′əl) s. juicio nulo (por error de procedimiento *o* desacuerdo del jurado).

mis·trust (:trŭst′) I. s. desconfianza II. tr. & intr. desconfiar (de).

mist·y (mĭs′tē) adj. **-i-** nebuloso; *(obscured)* empañado; *(vague)* vago.

mis·un·der·stand (mĭs-ŭn′dər-stănd′) tr. **-stood** entender *o* interpretar mal.

mis·un·der·stand·ing (:stăn′dĭng) s. malentendido; *(disagreement)* desacuerdo.

mis·use I. s. (mĭs-yōos′) mal empleo; *(mistreatment)* maltrato II. tr. (:yōoz′) emplear mal; *(to mistreat)* maltratar.

mite¹ (mīt) s. ENTOM. arador m, ácaro.

mite² s. *(money)* suma ínfima; *(object)* pizca.

mi·ter (mī′tər) I. s. RELIG. mitra; CARP. inglete m II. tr. unir a inglete.

mit·i·gate (mĭt′ĭ-gāt′) tr. mitigar.

mit·i·ga·tion (′-gā′shən) s. mitigación f.

mitt (mĭt) s. *(woman's)* mitón m; *(for baseball)* guante m de béisbol; JER. *(hand)* mano.

mit·ten (mĭt′n) s. manopla.

mix (mĭks) I. tr. mezclar; *(a drink)* preparar; *(to crossbreed)* cruzar ♦ **to get mixed up in** me-

terse en • **to m. in** agregar • **to m. it up** JER. llegar a las manos • **to m. up** *(to confuse)* confundir; *(to jumble)* mezclar —intr. mezclarse; *(to go together)* pegar II. s. mezcla; *(for a cake)* masa.

mixed (mĭkst) adj. mezclado; *(conflicting)* contradictorio; *(composite)* mixto ♦ **m. drink** trago combinado.

mixed-up (′ŭp′) adj. FAM. confundido, que no sabe lo que quiere.

mix·er (mĭk′sər) s. *(person)* persona sociable; *(machine)* mezcladora; *(appliance)* batidora; *(beverage)* bebida (para mezclar); *(gathering)* fiesta informal para que la gente se conozca.

mix·ture (mĭks′chər) s. mezcla; *(compound)* mixtura.

mix-up (mĭks′ŭp′) s. confusión f, lío.

mne·mon·ic (nĭ-mŏn′ĭk) I. adj. mnemotécnico, nemónico II. s. fórmula *o* rima mnemotécnica ♦ **mnemonics** sg. mnemotécnica, nemónica.

moan (mōn) I. s. gemido II. intr. gemir.

moat (mōt) s. foso (de un castillo).

mob (mŏb) I. s. turba; *(masses)* populacho; FAM. *(gang)* pandilla II. tr. **-bb-** *(to crowd in)* atestar; *(to throng around)* rodear.

mo·bile (mō′bəl, mō′bīl′) I. adj. móvil; *(character)* cambiadizo; *(society)* sin divisiones rígidas (de clase) II. s. (mō′bēl′) ARTE. móvil m.

mo·bil·i·ty (mō-bĭl′ĭ-tē) s. movilidad f.

mo·bi·lize (mō′bə-līz′) tr. & intr. movilizar(se).

mob·ster (mŏb′stər) s. JER. pandillero.

moc·ca·sin (mŏk′ə-sĭn) s. mocasín m.

mo·cha (mō′kə) s. moca.

mock (mŏk) I. tr. mofarse de; *(to imitate)* imitar II. adj. simulado.

mock·er·y (′ə-rē) s. mofa; *(object of ridicule)* objeto de burla; *(imitation)* imitación f; *(parody)* parodia ♦ **to make a m. of** parodiar a.

mock·ing·bird (:ĭng-bûrd′) s. sinsonte m.

mock-up *o* **mock-up** (′ŭp′) s. maqueta.

mod (mŏd′) s. moda II. adj. de moda.

mo·dal (mōd′l) adj. modal.

mo·dal·i·ty (mō-dăl′ĭ-tē) s. modalidad f.

mode (mōd) s. modo; *(fashion)* moda.

mod·el (mŏd′l) I. s. & adj. modelo II. tr. modelar; *(fashions)* presentar ♦ **to m. after** *o* **on** *(thing)* construir según; *(oneself)* tomar como modelo a —intr. modelar; *(to pose)* posar.

mod·el·ing (:ĭng) s. profesión f de modelo; *(production of designs)* creación f de modelos; *(representation)* modelado.

mod·er·ate (mŏd′ər-ĭt) I. adj. moderado; *(price)* módico; *(medium)* mediano II. s. moderado III. tr. (:ə-rāt′) moderar; *(to preside over)* presidir —intr. moderarse; *(to preside)* servir de moderador.

mod·er·a·tion (′ə-rā′shən) s. moderación f.

mod·er·a·tor (′-′ tər) s. moderador m.

mod·ern (mŏd′ərn) adj. & s. moderno.

mod·ern·ize (:ər-nīz′) tr. & intr. modernizar(se).

mod·est (mŏd′ĭst) adj. modesto; *(reserved)* recatado; *(in dress)* pudoroso; *(in price)* módico.

mod·es·ty (:ĭ-stē) s. modestia; *(decency)* pudor; *(in price)* modicidad f.

mod·i·cum (mŏd′ĭ-kəm) s. [pl. **s** *o* **-ca**] pizca.

mod·i·fi·ca·tion (mŏd′ə-fĭ-kā′shən) s. modificación f.

mod·i·fi·er (′-fī′ər) s. modificador m; GRAM. modificativo.

mod·i·fy (:fī′) tr. modificar; *(to moderate)*

moderar.
mod·ish (mō′dĭsh) adj. de moda.
mod·u·lar (mŏj′ə-lər) adj. modular, del módulo; *(furniture)* de módulos.
mod·u·late (mŏj′ə-lāt′) tr. & intr. modular.
mod·u·la·tion (′-lā′shən) s. modulación f.
mod·u·la·tor (′-lər) s. modulador m.
mod·ule (mŏj′ōol) s. módulo; ELECTRÓN. componente m.
mod·u·lus (mŏj′ə-ləs) s. [pl. -li] módulo.
mo·hair (mō′hâr′) s. mohair m.
moist (moist) adj. *(wet)* mojado; *(damp)* húmedo.
mois·ten (moi′sən) tr. & intr. humedecer(se).
moist·ness (moist′nĭs) s. humedad f.
mois·ture (mois′chər) s. humedad f.
mois·tur·ize (:chə-rīz′) tr. humedecer.
mois·tur·iz·er (:rī′zər) s. cosa que humedece; *(lotion)* loción f humectante.
mo·lar (mō′lər) s. & adj. molar m.
mo·las·ses (mə-lăs′ĭz) s. melaza.
mold¹ (mōld) I. s. *(hollow form)* molde m; *(model)* patrón m; *(molded item)* vaciado; *(shape)* forma; *(character)* temple m ♦ **to be cast in the m. of** estar cortado por el patrón de II. tr. moldear ♦ **to m. oneself on** tomar como modelo a.
mold² BIOL. I. s. moho II. intr. enmohecerse.
mold' *(wall)* martillo
mold·er (mōl′dər) tr. & intr. desmoronar(se).
mold·ing (mōl′dĭng) s. pieza moldeada; ARQ. moldura.
mold·y (mōl′dē) adj. -i- mohoso; *(musty)* enmohecido.
mole¹ (mōl) s. ANAT. lunar m.
mole² s. ZOOL. topo.
mo·lec·u·lar (mə-lĕk′yə-lər) adj. molecular.
mol·e·cule (mōl′ĭ-kyōol′) s. molécula.
mole·hill (mōl′hĭl′) s. topera
mo·lest (mə-lĕst′) tr. molestar; *(sexually)* abusar sexualmente.
mo·lest·er (mə-lĕs′tər) s. *(sexually)* persona que comete abusos sexuales.
moll (mōl) s. JER. querida de un gángster
mol·li·fy (mōl′ə-fī′) tr. *(to placate)* apaciguar; *(to soften)* mollificar.
mol·lusk/lusc (mōl′əsk) s. molusco.
mol·ly·cod·dle (mŏl′ē-kŏd′l) tr. FAM. mimar.
molt (mōlt) I. tr. & intr. mudar *(las plumas o la piel)* II. s. muda (de las plumas o la piel).
mol·ten (mōl′tən) adj. *(melted)* derretido; *(made by melting)* fundido.
mom (mŏm) s. FAM. mamá.
mo·ment (mō′mənt) s. momento ♦ **any m.** de un momento a otro • **at the last m.** a última hora • **at the m.** en este momento • **just a m.!** ¡un momento! • **m. of truth** hora de la verdad • **not for a m.!** ¡ni muerto! • **the m. something happens** en cuanto algo suceda • **this very m.** ahora mismo.
mo·men·tar·i·ly (mō′mən-târ′ə-lē) adv. *(for a moment)* momentáneamente; *(at any moment)* de un momento a otro; *(soon)* en un momento.
mo·men·tar·y (′-těr′ē) adj. momentáneo.
mo·men·tous (mō-měn′təs) adj. de gran importancia.
mo·men·tum (:təm) s. [pl. s o -ta] momento; *(impulse)* ímpetu m.
mon·arch (mŏn′ərk) s. monarca m; ENTOM. mariposa de color anaranjado y negro.
mo·nar·chic/chi·cal (mə-när′kĭk) adj. monárquico.

mon·ar·chist (mŏn′ər-kĭst) s. & adj. monárquico.
mon·ar·chy (:kē) s. monarquía.
mon·as·ter·y (mŏn′ə-stěr′ē) s. monasterio.
mo·nas·tic (mə-năs′tĭk) adj. monástico.
Mon·day (mŭn′dē) s. lunes m.
mon·e·tar·y (mŏn′ĭ-těr′ē) adj. monetario.
mon·ey (mŭn′ē) s. [pl. s o -ies] dinero; *(currency)* moneda ♦ **m. order** giro postal • **m. talks** el dinero todo lo puede • **not for all the m. in the world** ni por todo el oro del mundo • **ready m.** dinero disponible • **to be in the m.** estar entre los ganadores • **to be made of m.** ser millonario • **to make m.** ganar dinero • **to put m. on** apostar a • **your m. or your life!** ¡la bolsa o la vida! ♦ pl. fondos.
mon·ey·bag (:băg′) s. monedero ♦ pl. FAM. ricachón.
mon·ey·chang·er (:chān′jər) s. cambista mf; *(machine)* máquina que cambia monedas.
mon·eyed (mŭn′ēd) adj. adinerado.
mon·ey·lend·er (:ě lěn′dər) s. prestamista mf.
mon·ey·mak·er (:mā′kər) s. amasador m de dinero; *(thing)* fuente f de dinero.
mon·ey·mak·ing (:kĭng) I. s. enriquecimiento II. adj. lucrativo.
mon·gol·ism (mŏng′gə-lĭz′əm) s. MED. mongolismo.
mon·gol·oid (:loid′) adj. & s. MED. mongólico.
mon·goose (mŏng′gōos′) s. mangosta
mon·grel (mŭng′grəl, mŏng′-) s. & adj. híbrido *(esp. perro cruzado)*.
mon·i·ker (mŏn′ĭ-kər) s. JER. nombre m.
mo·ni·tion (mə-nĭsh′ən) s. admonición f.
mon·i·tor (mŏn′ĭ-tər) I. s. monitor m II. tr. *(signal, quality)* comprobar; *(for radiation)* determinar la contaminación radioactiva de; *(to keep track of)* vigilar (electrónicamente); *(for content)* escuchar —intr. servir de monitor.
mon·i·to·ry (mŏn′ĭ-tôr′ē) adj. admonitorio
monk (mŭngk) s. monje m.
mon·key (mŭng′kē) I. s. mono II. intr. ♦ **to m. around** hacer payasadas • **to m. (around) with** manosear o jugar con algo.
mon·key·shines (:shīnz′) s.pl. JER. payasadas.
monk·hood (mŭngk′hŏōd′) s. monacato.
monk·ish (mŭng′kĭsh) adj. monacal; *(of friars)* frailesco.
mon·o¹ (mŏn′ō) s. MED. mononucleosis f
mon·o² adj. monoaural.
mon·o·chro·mat·ic (mŏn′ə-krō-măt′ĭk) adj. monocromático.
mon·o·cle (mŏn′ə-kəl) s. monóculo.
mo·noc·u·lar (mə nŏk′yə-lər) adj. monocular.
mo·nog·a·mist (mə-nŏg′ə-mĭst) s. monógamo.
mo·nog·a·mous (:məs) adj. monógamo.
mo·nog·a·my (:mē) s. monogamia.
mon·o·gram (mŏn′ə-grăm′) I. s. monograma f II. tr. marcar con un monograma.
mon·o·graph (:grăf′) s. monografía.
mon·o·lin·gual (′-lĭng′gwəl) adj. monolingüe.
mon·o·lith (′-lĭth′) s. monolito.
mon·o·lith·ic (′-lĭth′ĭk) adj. monolítico.
mon·o·log(ue) (mŏn′ə-lôg′) s. monólogo.
mo·no·ma·ni·a (′-mā′nē-ə) s. monomanía.
mon·o·mor·phic (mŏn′ō-môr′fĭk) adj. monomórfico.
mon·o·nu·cle·o·sis (:-nōō′klē-ō′sĭs) s. mononucleosis f
mon·o·plane (mŏn′ə-plān′) s. monoplano.
mo·nop·o·list (mə-nŏp′ə-list) s. monopolizador m.

mo·nop·o·lis·tic (-'-lĭs'tĭk) adj. monopoliza-dor.

mo·nop·o·lize (-'-līz') tr. monopolizar.

mo·nop·o·ly (:lē) s. monopolio.

mon·o·rail (mŏn'ə-rāl') s. monocarril m.

mon·o·syl·lab·ic ('-sĭ-lăb'ĭk) adj. *(word)* mo-nosílabo; *(language)* monosilábico.

mon·o·tone (mŏn'ə-tōn') s. monotonía.

mo·not·o·nous (mə-nŏt'n-əs) adj. monótono.

mo·not·o·ny (:ē) s. monotonía.

mon·ox·ide (mŏn-ŏk'sīd') s. monóxido.

mon·soon (mŏn-sŏn') s. monzón m.

mon·ster (mŏn'stər) s. monstruo.

mon·strance (mŏn'strəns) s. custodia.

mon·stros·i·ty (mŏn-strŏs'ĭ-tē) s. monstruosi-dad f.

mon·strous ('strəs) adj. monstruoso.

mon·tage (mŏn-täzh') s. montaje m.

month (mŭnth) s. [pl. **s**] mes m. ♦ **in a m. of Sundays** nunca.

month·ly ('lē) I. adj. mensual ♦ **m. installment, payment** mensualidad II. adv. mensualmente III. s. publicación f mensual.

mon·u·ment (mŏn'ə-mənt) s. monumento.

mon·u·men·tal ('-mĕn'tl) adj. monumental.

moo (mŏ) I. intr. mugir II. s. mugido.

mooch (mŏch) JER. tr. conseguir gratis —intr. gorronear.

mooch·er (mŏ'chər) s. JER. gorrón m.

mood (mŏd) s. humor m; *(disposition)* disposición f ♦ **to be in a bad, good m.** estar de mal, buen humor • **to be in the m. for** tener ganas de.

mood·y (mŏ'dē) adj. -i- malhumorado; *(whimsical)* caprichoso.

moon (mŏn) I. s. luna; *(moonlight)* claro de luna ♦ **crescent m.** media luna • **once in a blue m.** de Pascuas a Ramos II. intr. FAM. estar en la luna.

moon·beam ('bēm') s. rayo de luna.

moon·light (:līt') I. s. luz f de la luna II. intr. FAM. tener otro empleo además del principal.

moon·shine (:shīn') s. claro de luna; FAM. *(foolishness)* pamplinas f; JER. *(whiskey)* alcohol destilado ilegalmente.

moon·stone (:stōn') s. piedra de la luna.

moon·struck (:strŭk') adj. chiflado, atontado.

moon·walk (:wŏk') s. caminata exploratoria sobre la superficie lunar.

moon·y (mŏ'nē) adj. -i- soñador.

moor¹ (mŏr) tr. MARÍT. amarrar.

moor² s. GEOG. terreno pantanoso.

moor·age (mŏr'ĭj) s. *(place)* amarradero; *(act)* amarradura.

moor·ing (:ĭng) s. *(cable)* amarra; *(act)* amarradura; *(place)* amarradero.

moose (mŏs) s.inv. anta.

moot (mŏt) adj. ♦ **m. point** punto debatible.

mop (mŏp) I. s. estropajo; *(of hair)* greña II. tr. -pp- fregar —intr. ♦ **to m. up** FAM. dar cabo a una tarea.

mope (mōp) intr. estar abatido.

mo·ped (mō'pĕd') s. ciclomotor m.

mop·pet (mŏp'ĭt) s. niño.

mor·al (mŏr'əl) I. adj. moral; *(person)* recto II. s. moraleja ♦ pl. principios morales • **loose m.** costumbres relajadas.

mo·rale (mə-răl') s. moral f, estado de ánimo.

mor·al·ist (mŏr'ə-lĭst) s. moralista mf; *(moralizer)* moralizador m.

mor·al·is·tic ('-lĭs'tĭk) adj. moralizador.

mo·ral·i·ty (mə-răl'ĭ-tē) s. moralidad f; *(morals)*

moral f.

mor·al·ize (mŏr'ə-līz') intr. moralizar.

mo·rass (mə-răs') s. ciénaga; FIG. embrollo.

mor·a·to·ri·um (mŏr'ə-tôr'ē-əm) s. [pl. **s** o **-ia**] moratoria.

mo·ray (mŏr'ā) s. morena.

mor·bid (mŏr'bĭd) adj. morboso.

mor·bid·i·ty (-'-tē) s. FAM. imbecil m.

mor·dant (mŏr'dnt) adj. mordaz.

more (mŏr) I. adj. más; *(greater in quantity)* superior II. s. más ♦ **the m. . . . the m. . . .** cuanto más . . . más . . . • **the m. the merrier** cuanto más, mejor III. adv. más IV. adv. más ♦ **m. and m.** cada vez más • **m. or less** más o menos • **m. than** *(with adjectives)* más que; *(with numbers)* más de • **to be no m.** ya no existir.

more·o·ver (:ō'vər) adv. además.

mo·res (mŏr'āz') s.pl. costumbres f, usos.

morgue (mŏrg) s. depósito de cadáveres.

mor·i·bund (mŏr'ə-bənd) adj. moribundo.

morn (mŏrn) s. POÉT. mañana.

morn·ing (mŏr'nĭng) s. mañana ♦ **good m.!** ¡buenos días! • **in the m.** por la mañana.

morn·ing-glo·ry (:glôr'ē) s. dondiego de día.

mo·ron (mŏr'ŏn') s. FAM. imbécil m.

mo·ron·ic (mə-rŏn'ĭk) adj. FAM. imbécil.

mo·rose (mə-rōs') adj. malhumorado.

mor·pheme (mŏr'fēm') s. morfema m.

mor·phine (mŏr'fēn') s. morfina.

mor·phol·o·gy (mŏr-fŏl'ə-jē) s. morfología.

mor·row (mŏr'ō) s. día m siguiente.

Morse code (mŏrs) s. morse m.

mor·sel (mŏr'səl) s. *(bite)* bocado, pedacito; *(delicacy)* manjar m.

mor·tal (mŏr'tl) I. adj. mortal; *(human)* humano; *(terrible)* terrible II. s. mortal m.

mor·tal·i·ty (mŏr-tăl'ĭ-tē) s. mortalidad f.

mor·tar (mŏr'tər) s. mortero.

mor·tar·board (:bôrd') s. *(tool)* esparavel m; *(hat)* birrete m.

mort·gage (mŏr'gĭj) I. s. hipoteca; *(contract)* contrato de hipoteca II. tr. hipotecar.

mort·ga·gee ('gĭ-jē') s. acreedor hipotecario.

mort·ga·gor ('-jər) s. deudor hipotecario.

mor·ti·cian (mŏr-tĭsh'ən) s. agente funerario.

mor·ti·fi·ca·tion (mŏr'tə-fĭ-kā'shən) s. mortificación f; *(torment)* tormento; MED. necrosis f.

mor·ti·fy ('-fī') tr. & intr. mortificar(se).

mor·ti·fy·ing (:ĭng) adj. mortificador.

mor·tise (mŏr'tĭs) s. mortaja.

mor·tu·ar·y (mŏr'chŏ-ĕr'ē) s. mortuorio.

mo·sa·ic (mō-zā'ĭk) s. mosaico.

mo·sey (mō'zē) intr. FAM. deambular.

mosque (mŏsk) s. mezquita.

mos·qui·to (mə-skē'tō) s. [pl. **(e)s**] mosquito ♦ **m. net** mosquitero.

moss (mŏs) s. musgo.

moss·y (mŏ'sē) adj. -i- musgoso; *(resembling moss)* parecido al musgo.

most (mōst) I. adj. *(in quantity)* más . . . que todos los demás; *(in measure)* mayor; *(almost all)* la mayoría de ♦ **for the m. part** en su mayoría II. s. la mayor parte; *(the majority)* la mayoría ♦ **at (the) m.** a lo sumo • **the m.** lo más • **to make the m. of** aprovechar al máximo III. pron. la mayoría, la mayor parte IV. adv. más . . . que todos los demás; *(superlative)* más; *(very)* muy ♦ **m. certainly** con toda seguridad • **m. likely** muy probablemente • **m. of all** sobre todo.

most·ly ('lē) adv. en su mayor parte.

mote (mōt) s. *(dust)* partícula; *(speck)* mota.

mo·tel (mō-tĕl′) s. motel *m*.

moth (môth) s. [pl. **s**] mariposa nocturna; *(clothes moth)* polilla.

moth·ball ('bôl') I. s. bola de naftalina ♦ **in mothballs** en condición de almacenamiento prolongado II. tr. almacenar.

moth-eat·en (:ēt′n) adj. apolillado; *(old)* viejo.

moth·er (mŭth′ər) I. s. madre *f*; *(superior)* superiora II. adj. materno; *(country)* madre III. tr. *(to give birth to)* dar a luz a; *(to protect)* cuidar como una madre.

moth·er·hood (:hŏod′) s. maternidad *f*.

moth·er-in-law (:ĭn-lô′) s. [pl. **mothers-**] suegra.

moth·er·land (:lănd′) s. patria; *(of ancestors)* madre patria.

moth·er·ly (:lē) adj. materno, maternal.

moth·er-of-pearl ('-əv-pûrl′) s. madreperla.

moth·proof (môth′prōōf′) I. adj. a prueba de polillas II. tr. proteger contra las polillas.

moth·y (mō′thē) adj. -i- apolillado.

mo·tif (mō-tēf′) s. motivo.

mo·tion (mō′shən) I. s. movimiento; *(gesture)* ademán *m*, *(proposal)* moción *f* ♦ **m. picture** película cinematográfica ♦ **m. sickness** mareo ♦ **to set in m.** poner en marcha II. intr. hacer señas *o* una señal.

mo·tion·less (:lĭs) adj. inmóvil.

mo·ti·vate (mō′tə-vāt′) tr. motivar.

mo·ti·va·tion ('-vā′shən) s. motivación *f*.

mo·tive (mō′tĭv) I. s. motivo; *(criminal)* móvil *m* II. adj. motriz; *(impelling)* impulsor.

mot·ley (mŏt′lē) adj. abigarrado.

mo·tor (mō′tər) I. s. motor *m* II. adj. motor; *(driven by a motor)* de motor ♦ **m. home** casa a remolque con motor • **m. inn** *o* **lodge** motel, hotel con estacionamiento • **m. vehicle** vehículo automotor III. intr. ir en automóvil.

mo·tor·bike (:bīk′) s. motocicleta liviana.

mo·tor·boat (:bōt′) s. bote *m* a motor.

mo·tor·cade (:kād′) s. caravana de automóviles.

mo·tor·car (:kär′) s. automóvil *m*, coche *m*.

mo·tor·cy·cle (:sī′kəl) s. motocicleta, moto *f*.

mo·tor·cy·clist (:sī′klĭst) s. motociclista *mf*.

mo·tor·ist (:ĭst) s. automovilista *mf*.

mo·tor·ize (:tə-rīz′) tr. motorizar.

mo·tor·man (mō′tər-mən) s. [pl. -men] maquinista *mf* (de tranvía o tren eléctrico).

mot·tle (mŏt′l) tr. motear, jaspear.

mot·tled (:ld) adj. moteado, jaspeado.

mot·to (mŏt′ō) s. [pl. (e)s] lema *m*

mould (mōld) G.B. var. de **mold.**

mound (mound) s. *(hill)* montículo.

mount¹ (mount) I. s. *(to climb)* subir (a); *(a horse)* montar; *(to fix in place)* fijar; MEC. montar; *(an attack)* lanzar —intr. *(to move upward)* subir; *(to ride)* montar II. s. montura; *(base)* soporte *m*.

mount² s. *(hill)* monte *m*.

moun·tain (moun′tən) s. montaña ♦ **m. laurel** calmia • **m. lion** león americano • **m. range** cordillera.

moun·tain·eer ('tə-nîr′) s. *(inhabitant)* montañés *m*; *(climber)* alpinista *mf*, montañero.

moun·tain·ous ('tə-nəs) adj. montañoso; *(immense)* inmenso.

moun·tain·side (:tən-sīd′) s. ladera *o* falda de una montaña.

moun·tain·top (:tŏp′) s. cima de una montaña.

moun·te·bank (moun′tə băngk′) s. saltabanco.

mount·ed (moun′tĭd) adj. montado.

mount·ing (:tĭng) s. montura; *(of jewel)* engaste *m*.

mourn (môrn) intr. & tr. llorar; *(a death)* lamentar(se).

mourn·er (môr′nər) s. persona que está de luto; *(at a funeral)* doliente *mf*.

mourn·ful (môrn′fəl) adj. dolorido, triste; *(arousing grief)* penoso

mourn·ing (môr′nĭng) s. duelo; *(period)* luto ♦ **m. dove** paloma torcaza • **to be in m.** estar de luto.

mouse (mous) s. [pl. **mice**] ratón *m*.

mouse·trap (′trăp′) s. ratonera.

mousse (mōōs) s. postre frío.

mous·tache (mŭs′tăsh′, mə-stăsh′) var. de **mustache.**

mous·y (mou′sē) adj. -i- FAM. *(dull gray)* pardusco; *(timid)* tímido.

mouth (mouth) I. s. [pl. **s**] boca ♦ **not to open one's m.** no decir esta boca es mía • **to be down in the m.** estar deprimido • **to have a big m.** ser un bocazas • **to keep one's m. shut** callar(se) • **to make one's m. water** hacérsele a uno la boca agua • **water one's m.!** FAM. ¡ten cuidado con lo que dices! II. tr. *(mouth)* pronunciar; *(to utter)* decir (de forma afectada); *(soundlessly)* articular en silencio; *(to take into the mouth)* meter en la boca —intr. ♦ **to m. off** hablar con descaro.

mouth·ful (′fŏol′) s. bocado; *(of smoke)* bocanada ♦ **you said a m.!** FAM. ¡muy bien dicho!

mouth·piece (:pēs′) s. boquilla; FAM. *(spokesman)* vocero.

mouth-to-mouth (:tə-mouth′) adj. de boca a boca.

mouth·wash (:wŏsh′) s. enjuague *m* bucal.

mouth·y (mou′thē, :thē) adj. -i- bombástico.

mov(e)·a·bil·i·ty (mōō′və-bĭl′ĭ-tē) s. movilidad *f*.

mov(e)·a·ble ('-bəl) adj. movible, móvil.

move (mōōv) I. tr. *intr.* mover(se); *(to change position)* cambiar de postura; *(to relocate)* mudarse; *(to act)* entrar en acción; *(to make a motion)* proponer; *(in a game)* jugar ♦ **to m. about** *o* **around** cambiar de sitio • **to m. along** *o* **forward** seguir adelante • **to m. away** alejarse • **to m. in** instalarse • **to m. in on** intentar apoderarse de • **to m. up** ascender —tr. mover; *(to change the place of)* trasladar; *(to prompt)* impulsar; MEC. *(to set in motion)* poner en marcha; *(to stir)* conmover ♦ **to m. up** subir; *(to advance)* adelantar (una fecha); *(to promote)* ascender II. s. movimiento; *(change of residence)* mudanza; *(of a piece)* jugada; *(player's turn)* turno; *(step)* paso ♦ **on the m.** andando de acá para allá; *(active)* activo • **to get a m. on** FAM. empezar a moverse.

move·ment ('mənt) s. movimiento; *(gesture)* gesto; *(trend)* tendencia; *(of bowels)* evacuación (del vientre) *f*; *(watch)* mecanismo.

mov·er (mōō′vər) s. persona que hace mudanzas ♦ **pl.** agencia de mudanzas.

mov·ie (:vē) s. película ♦ **m. star** estrella de cine • **m. theater** cine ♦ **pl.** cine.

mov·ie·go·er (:gō′ər) s. aficionado al cine.

mov·ie·mak·er (:mā′kər) s. cineasta *mf*.

mov·ing (mōō′vĭng) adj. móvil; *(changing residence)* de mudanza; *(in motion)* en marcha; *(touching)* conmovedor.

mow (mō) tr. -ed, -ed *o* -n segar.

mow·er (mō′ər) s. segador *m*; *(machine)* segadora; *(for lawn)* cortacéspedes *m.*

mow·ing (mō'ĭng) s. AGR. siega; *(lawn)* corte *m* ♦ m. machine segadora.

mown (mōn) cf. **mow.**

mox·ie (mŏk'sē) s. *(pluck)* coraje *m; (pep)* brío.

Mr. (mĭs'tər) s. [abr. de Mister] Sr.

Mrs. (mĭs'ĭz) s. [abr. de Mistress] Sra.

much (mŭch) I. adj. **more, most** mucho ♦ as m. . . . as tanto . . . como • how m.? ¿cuánto? • three times as m. tres veces más • too m. demasiado II. s. mucho; *(large part)* gran parte *f* ♦ as m. as tanto como • as m. as to say como si dijera • I thought as m. ya me lo figuraba • it's as m. as anybody can do es todo lo que se puede hacer • not so m. as ni siquiera • not to be m. no ser gran cosa • not to be m. of no ser gran cosa como • not to think m. of no tener un gran concepto de • so m. tanto • so m. for that borrón y cuenta nueva • so m. so that tanto que • so m. the better tanto mejor • there's not m. to it no es muy complicado • this, that m. un tanto así • to make m. of dar mucha importancia a • to say this m. for decir esto en defensa de • twice as m. el doble III. adv. mucho ♦ however m. por mucho que • how m.? ¿cuánto? • to my amazement con gran sorpresa mía • very m. muchísimo.

mu·ci·lage (myōō'sə-lĭj) s. mucílago; *(adhesive)* goma de pegar (esp. de origen vegetal).

muck (mŭk) I. s. lodo; *(filth)* suciedad *f; (manure)* estiércol *m; (fertile soil)* mantillo II. tr. ♦ to m. up ensuciar; *(to bungle)* chapucear.

muck·a·muck (mŭk'ə-mŭk') s. JER. persona importante.

muck·rake (mŭk'rāk') intr. descubrir *o* revelar escándalos.

muck·rak·er (:rā'kər) s. revelador *m* de escándalos públicos.

muck·y (:ē) adj. -i- fangoso.

mu·cous (myōō'kəs) adj. mucoso.

mu·cus (:kəs) s. mucosidad *f,* mucus *m.*

mud (mŭd) s. barro, lodo; *(slander)* difamación *f* ♦ to sling m. at calumniar a.

mud·dle (mŭd'l) tr. *(to muddy)* enturbiar; *(to jumble)* embrollar; *(to befuddle)* atontar; *(to bungle)* chapucear ♦ to m. through salir bien a pesar de torpezas.

mud·dy (mŭd'ē) I. adj. -i- fangoso; *(cloudy)* turbio II. tr. enfangar; *(a river)* llenar de fango; *(to make cloudy)* enturbiar ♦ to m. the waters complicar una situación.

mud·sling·er (:slĭng'ər) s. difamador *m.*

muff¹ (mŭf) I. tr. hacer mal II. s. chapucería.

muff² s. *(hand covering)* manguito.

muf·fin (mŭf'ĭn) s. mollete *m.*

muf·fle (mŭf'əl) tr. embozar; *(sound)* amortiguar; *(to make vague)* confundir.

muf·fler (mŭf'lər) s. *(scarf)* bufanda; AUTO. silenciador *m.*

mug¹ (mŭg) s. *(cup)* jarra.

mug² I. s. JER. *(face)* jeta; FAM. *(hoodlum)* rufián *m* II. tr. **-gg-** *(to take a mugshot)* fotografiar; *(to assault)* asaltar —intr. JER. exagerar los gestos faciales.

mug·ger (:ər) s. asaltante *mf.*

mug·ging (:ĭng) s. asalto (con intento de robo).

mug·gy (mŭg'ē) adj. -i- bochornoso.

mu·lat·to (mə-lä'tō) s. [pl. (e)s] mulato.

mul·ber·ry (mŭl'bĕr'ē) s. mora.

mulch (mŭlch) I. s. pajote *m.* II. tr. cubrir con pajote.

mule¹ (myōōl) s. mulo; FAM. *(person)* testarudo.

mule² s. *(slipper)* chinela, pantufla.

mule·skin·ner (myōōl'skĭn'ər) s. FAM. arriero.

mu·le·teer (myōō'lə-tîr') m. mulero.

mul·ish ('lĭsh) adj. terco.

mull¹ (mŭl) tr. CUL. calentar (vino).

mull² tr. & intr. ponderar (sobre).

mul·let (mŭl'ĭt) s. [pl. inv. *o* s] mújol *m,* lisa.

mul·ti·col·ored (mŭl'tĭ-kŭl'ərd) adj. multicolor.

mul·ti·di·men·sion·al ('tē-dĭ-mĕn'shə-nəl) adj. multidimensional.

mul·ti·far·i·ous (:tə-fâr'ē-əs) adj. variado.

mul·ti·fold ('-fōld') adj. doblado varias veces; *(multiple)* múltiple.

mul·ti·form ('-fôrm') adj. multiforme.

mul·ti·lat·er·al (mŭl'tē-lăt'ər-əl) adj. multilátero; POL. multilateral.

mul·ti·lev·el(ed) (:lĕv'əl[d]) adj. de varios niveles.

mul·ti·lin·gual (:lĭng'gwəl) adj. políglota.

mul·ti·me·di·a (:mē'dē-ə) adj. que incluye el uso de varios medios de comunicación.

mul·ti·mil·lion·aire ('mĭl'yə-nâr') s. multimillonario.

mul·ti·na·tion·al (:năsh'ə-nəl) adj. & s. multinacional *f.*

mul·ti·ple (mŭl'tə-pəl) I. adj. múltiple; MAT. múltiplo II. s. múltiplo.

mul·ti·plex (:plĕks') adj. múltiple; ELECTRÓN. múltiplex.

mul·ti·pli·cand ('-plĭ-kănd') s. multiplicando.

mul·ti·pli·ca·tion (:plĭ-kā'shən) s. multiplicación *f* ♦ m. table tabla de multiplicar.

mul·ti·plic·i·ty (:plĭs'ĭ-tē) s. multiplicidad *f.*

mul·ti·pli·er ('-plī'ər) s. multiplicador *m.*

mul·ti·ply (:plī') tr. & intr. multiplicar(se).

mul·ti·pur·pose (mŭl'tē-pûr'pəs) adj. multiuso.

mul·ti·tude ('tī-tōōd') s. multitud *f.*

mul·ti·tu·di·nous ('-'-n-əs) adj. multitudinario.

mul·ti·va·lent (mŭl'tə-vā'lənt) adj. polivalente.

mum¹ (mŭm) adj. silencioso ♦ to keep m. guardar silencio.

mum² s. G.B., FAM. mamá.

mum³ s. BOT., FAM. crisantemo.

mum·ble (mŭm'bəl) I. tr. mascullar —intr. balbucir II. s. refunfuño.

mum·bo jum·bo (mŭm'bō jŭm'bō) s. FAM. galimatías *m.*

mum·mer (mŭm'ər) s. mimo; *(masked person)* máscara *mf.*

mum·mer·y (:ə-rē) s. *(pantomime)* pantomima; *(mascarade)* mascarada.

mum·mi·fy (mŭm'ə-fī') tr. & intr. momificar(se).

mum·my¹ (:ē) s. *(corpse)* momia.

mum·my² s. FAM. mamá.

mumps (mŭmps) s.pl. paperas *f.*

munch (mŭnch) tr. ronzar.

mun·dane (mŭn'dān') adj. mundano.

mu·nic·i·pal (myōō-nĭs'ə-pəl) adj. municipal.

mu·nic·i·pal·i·ty ('-'-păl'ĭ-tē) s. municipalidad *f.*

mu·nif·i·cence (myōō-nĭf'ĭ-səns) s. munificencia.

mu·nif·i·cent (:sənt) adj. munífico.

mu·ni·tion (myōō-nĭsh'ən) s. municiones *f.*

mu·ral (myŏŏr'əl) s. pintura mural.

mur·der (mûr'dər) I. s. asesinato; *(massacre)* matanza; JER. *(trouble)* cosa espantosa ♦ first-, second-degree m. homicidio premeditado, impremeditado • **to get away with** m. FAM. salirse con la suya II. tr. asesinar; *(to destroy)* destrozar; *(to defeat)* aplastar.

mur·der·er (:ər) s. asesino.

mur·der·ess (:ĭs) s. asesina.

mur·der·ous (:əs) adj. asesino; FAM. terrible.

murk (mûrk) s. lobreguez *f.*

murk·y (mûr'kē) adj. -i- lóbrego.

mur·mur (mûr'mər) I. s. murmullo; MED. soplo cardíaco II. tr. & intr. murmurar.

mus·ca·tel (mŭs'kə-tĕl') s. vino moscatel.

mus·cle (mŭs'əl) I. s. ANAT. músculo; *(power)* fuerza II. intr. abrirse paso a la fuerza.

mus·cle-bound (:bound') adj. con los músculos abarrotados *o* endurecidos.

mus·cu·lar (mŭs'kyə lər) adj. muscular; *(strong)* musculoso.

mus·cu·la·ture (:lə-chŏŏr') s. musculatura.

muse (myōz) intr. meditar.

mu·se·um (myōō-zē'əm) s. museo.

mush (mŭsh) s. CUL. gachas de harina de maíz; *(soft thing)* masa muy blanda; FAM. *(sentimentality)* sentimentalismo.

mush·room (mŭsh'rōōm') I. s. BOT. hongo; CUL. champiñón *m* II. intr. crecer rápidamente.

mush·y (mŭsh'ē) adj. -i- blando; FAM. *(sentimental)* sensiblero; *(amorous)* enamoradizo.

mu·sic (myōō'zĭk) s. música ♦ **m. hall** sala de conciertos • **to be m. to one's ears** ser lo que uno quiere escuchar • **to face the m.** FAM. afrontar las consecuencias • **to set to m.** poner música a.

mu·si·cal (:zĭ-kəl) I. adj. de música; *(like music)* musical; *(fond of music)* aficionado a la música ♦ **m. chairs** juego de las sillas vacías II. s. comedia musical.

mu·si·cal·i·ty (:-kăl'ĭ-tē) s. musicalidad *f.*

mu·si·cian (:-zĭsh'ən) s. músico.

mu·si·col·o·gy ('zĭ-kŏl'ə-jē) s. musicología.

mus·ing (myōō'zĭng) I. adj. contemplativo II. s. contemplación *f.*

musk (mŭsk) s. almizcle *m.*

mus·ket (mŭs'kĭt) s. mosquete *m.*

mus·ket·eer ('kĭ-tîr') s. mosquetero.

mus·ket·ry ('-trē) s. mosquetes *m; (firing)* mosquetazos; *(technique)* mosquetería.

musk·mel·on (mŭsk'mĕl'ən) s. melón *m.*

musk·rat (mŭsk'răt') s. [pl. inv. o **s**] rata almizclera *o* almizclada.

musk·y (mŭsk'ē) adj. -i- almizcleño.

mus·lin (mŭz'lĭn) s. muselina.

muss (mŭs) I. tr. desordenar; *(to rumple)* arrugar II. s. desorden *m; (squabble)* riña.

mus·sel (mŭs'əl) s. mejillón *m.*

mus·sy (mŭs'ē) adj. -i- FAM. desordenado.

must[1] (mŭst) I. aux. deber, tener que; *(indicating probability)* deber de ♦ **it m. not be** eso no debe permitirse II. s. FAM. cosa indispensable ♦ **to be a m.** ser para no perdérselo.

must[2] s. *(juice)* mosto; *(mold)* moho.

mus·tache (mŭs'tăsh', mə-stăsh') s. bigote(s) *m.*

mus·tang (mŭs'tăng') s. mustang *m.*

mus·tard (mŭs'tərd) s. mostaza ♦ **to cut the m.** FAM. hacer lo que se espera de uno.

mus·ter (mŭs'tər) I. tr. & intr. reunir(se) ♦ **to m. up** armarse de II. s. MIL. revista; *(meeting)* asamblea ♦ **to pass m.** ser aceptable.

must·y (mŭs'tē) adj. -i- *(moldy)* mohoso; *(smelly)* que huele a cerrado.

mu·ta·ble (myōō'tə-bəl) adj. *(variable)* mudable, *(inconstant)* inconstante.

mu·tant (myōōt'nt) s. mutante *m.*

mu·tate (myōō'tāt') tr. & intr. mudar(se); BIOL. transformar(se).

mu·ta·tion (-tā'shən) s. alteración *f;* BIOL. mutación *f*

mute (myōōt) I. adj. mudo; *(silent)* callado II. s. mudo; MÚS. sordina III. tr. amortiguar; MÚS. poner sordina a.

mut·ed (myōō'tĭd) adj. sordo.

mu·ti·late (myōōt'l-āt') tr. mutilar.

mu·ti·la·tion ('-ā'shən) s. mutilación *f.*

mu·ti·neer (myōōt'n-îr') s. amotinador *m.*

mu·ti·nous ('-əs) adj. amotinador.

mu·ti·ny (:ē) I. s. motín *m* II. intr. amotinarse.

mutt (mŭt) s. JER. perro cruzado.

mut·ter (mŭt'ər) I. intr. & tr. murmurar; *(to grumble)* refunfuñar II. s. murmullo; *(grumbling)* refunfuño.

mut·ton (mŭt'n) s. carne *f* de carnero.

mu·tu·al (myōō'chōō-əl) adj. mutuo ♦ **by m. agreement** de común acuerdo • **m. fund** fondo mutualista (de inversión).

muz·zle (mŭz'əl) I. s. *(snout)* hocico; *(restraint)* mordaza; *(gun)* boca (de un arma de fuego) II. tr. poner bozal a; *(to restrain)* amordazar.

my (mī) I. adj. pos. mi ♦ **my dear sir** muy señor mío II. interj. ¡caramba!

my·o·pi·a (mī-ō'pē-ə) s. miopía.

my·op·ic (mī-ŏp'ĭk, mī-ō'pĭk) adj. miope.

myr·i·ad (mĭr'ē-əd) I. adj. innumerable II. s. miríada.

myrrh (mûr) s. mirra.

myr·tle (mûr'tl) s. mirto.

my·self (mī-sĕlf') pron. yo mismo; *(reflexive)* me; *(after preposition)* mí (mismo) ♦ **(all) by m.** completamente solo.

mys·te·ri·ous (mĭ-stîr'ē-əs) adj. misterioso.

mys·ter·y (mĭs'tə-rē) s. misterio; CINEM. película policíaca; LIT. novela policíaca.

mys·tic (:tĭk) adj. & s. místico.

mys·ti·cal (:tĭ-kəl) adj. místico.

mys·ti·fy (:tə-fī') tr. mistificar.

mys·tique (mĭ-stēk') s. misterio secreto.

myth (mĭth) s. mito.

myth·i·cal ('ĭ-kəl) adj. mítico.

myth·o·log·i·cal ('ə-lŏj'ĭ-kəl) adj. mitológico.

my·thol·o·gist (mĭ-thŏl'ə-jĭst) s. mitologista *m.*

my·thol·o·gize (:jīz') tr. convertir en mito —intr. crear un mito.

my·thol·o·gy (:jē) s. mitología.

N

n, N (ĕn) s. decimocuarta letra del alfabeto inglés.

nab (năb) tr. **-bb-** JER. *(to arrest)* arrestar; *(to grab)* coger, agarrar.

na·dir (nā'dər) s. nadir *m;* FIG. punto más bajo.

nag[1] (năg) I. tr. **-gg-** *(to scold)* regañar; *(to pester)* importunar —intr. *(to find fault)* criticar; *(to complain)* quejarse II. s. regañón *m.*

nag[2] s. *(old horse)* jamelgo

nail (nāl) I. s. clavo; *(finger, toe)* uña ♦ **n. polish** esmalte de uñas • **to be as hard as nails** tener corazón de piedra • **to bite one's nails** comerse las uñas • **to hit the n. on the head** dar en el clavo II. tr. clavar, asegurar con clavos; FAM. *(to catch)* coger, atrapar; *(to knock down)* derribar; *(to hit)* pegar ♦ **to n. down** *(to fasten)* clavar; *(to get)* obtener; *(to establish)* establecer firmemente.

na·ive/ive (nä-ēv′) adj. cándido, ingenuo.

na·ive·té/ive·té (′-tā′) s. ingenuidad f.

naked (nā′kĭd) adj. desnudo ♦ **the n. truth** la pura verdad ♦ **to the n. eye** a simple vista.

name (nām) I. s. nombre m; *(surname)* apellido; *(reputation)* fama, reputación f; FAM. *(celebrity)* celebridad f ♦ **full n.** nombre y apellido • **my n. is** me llamo • **n. brand** FAM. marca conocida • **to call someone names** insultar a alguien • **to go by the n. of** ser conocido por el nombre de • **to make a n. for oneself** hacerse un nombre • **what's your n.?** ¿cómo se llama Ud.? II. tr. llamar; *(a baby)* poner nombre a; *(to identify)* dar el nombre de; *(to mention)* nombrar, mencionar; *(to specify)* dar, fijar (hora, precio); *(to appoint)* nombrar ♦ **to be named** llamarse.

name·less (′lĭs) adj. sin nombre, anónimo.

name·ly (:lē) adv. es decir, a saber.

name·plate (:plāt′) s. placa o letrero con el nombre.

name·sake (:sāk′) s. tocayo.

nan·ny (nǎn′ē) s. niñera.

nap[1] (nǎp) I. s. siesta ♦ **to take a n.** dormir la siesta II. intr. **-pp-** echar o dormir la siesta ♦ **to be napping** FIG. estar desprevenido.

nap[2] s. *(of cloth)* lanilla, peluza.

na·palm (nā′päm′) s. napalm m.

nape (nāp, nǎp) s. nuca.

nap·kin (nǎp′kĭn) s. servilleta.

narc (närk) s. JER. agente m de policía que se ocupa de detener a los traficantes de drogas.

nar·cis·sism (när′sĭ-sĭz′əm) s. narcisismo.

nar·cis·sus (när-sĭs′əs) s. [pl. **es** o **-si**] narciso.

nar·cot·ic (när-kŏt′ĭk) s. & adj. narcótico.

nar·rate (när′āt′) tr. narrar.

nar·ra·tion (nǎ-rā′shən) s. narración f.

nar·ra·tive (nǎr′ə-tĭv) I. s. *(mode)* narrativa; *(account)* relato II. adj. narrativo.

nar·ra·tor (:āt′ər) s. narrador m.

nar·row (nǎr′ō) I. adj. **-er, -est** angosto, estrecho; *(mind)* estrecho, rígido; *(interests, interpretation)* limitado; *(barely sufficient)* escaso; *(strict)* estricto; *(intolerant)* intolerante, de miras estrechas ♦ **to have a n. escape** escaparse por un pelo II. tr. estrechar; *(to limit)* limitar, reducir ♦ **to n. down** limitar, reducir • **to n. it down to** reducirse a —intr. estrecharse III. s. ♦ pl. estrecho.

nar·row·ing (:ĭng) s. estrechamiento; FIG. *(limitation)* limitación f.

nar·row-mind·ed (:mīn′dĭd) adj. de miras estrechas.

na·sal (nā′zəl) adj. nasal.

na·sal·i·ty (nā-zǎl′ĭ-tē) s. nasalidad f.

nas·ty (nǎs′tē) adj. **-i-** *(filthy)* sucio; *(unpleasant)* asqueroso; *(cruel)* antipático; *(malicious)* malicioso; *(morally offensive)* obsceno, repugnante; *(cough, cold)* molesto; *(accident, fall)* grave; *(problem, affair)* difícil ♦ **to be n. to** tratar mal a • **to have a n. mind** ser un mal pensado.

na·tal (nāt′l) adj. natal.

na·tal·i·ty (nā-tǎl′ĭ-tē) s. natalidad f.

na·tion (nā′shən) s. nación f; *(people)* pueblo.

na·tion·al (nǎsh′ə-nəl) adj. & s. nacional.

na·tion·al·ist (:nə-lĭst) s. nacionalista mf.

na·tion·al·is·tic (′-nə-lĭs′tĭk) adj. nacionalista.

na·tion·al·i·ty (:nǎl′ĭ-tē) s. nacionalidad f, ciudadanía.

na·tion·al·ize (′-nə-līz′) tr. nacionalizar.

na·tion·hood (nā′shən-hŏŏd′) s. la condición de ser una nación, independencia.

na·tion·wide (′-wīd′) adj. por toda la nación.

na·tive (nā′tĭv) I. adj. *(inborn)* natural, innato; *(inhabitant)* nativo; *(country, town)* natal; *(language)* materno; *(customs)* originario; *(product)* del país ♦ **to be n.** to ser originario de II. s. nativo, indígena mf ♦ **to be a n. of** ser nativo de.

na·tiv·i·ty (nə-tĭv′ĭ-tē) s. nacimiento ♦ **N.** natividad (de Cristo).

nat·ty (nǎt′ē) adj. **-i-** FAM. elegante.

nat·u·ral (nǎch′ər-əl) I. adj. natural; *(inherent)* nato; *(fitting)* lógico; *(one's own)* propio ♦ **n. resource** recurso natural II. s. MÚS. *(note)* nota natural; *(sign)* becuadro ♦ **to be a n.** tener talento.

nat·u·ral·ist (:ə-lĭst) s. naturalista mf.

nat·u·ral·is·tic (′-lĭs′tĭk) adj. naturalista.

nat·u·ral·ize (′-līz′) tr. & intr. *(an alien)* naturalizar(se); *(to adapt)* adaptar(se).

nat·u·ral·ly (:lē) adv. naturalmente; *(by nature)* por naturaleza; *(of course)* por supuesto, claro.

na·ture (nā′chər) s. (la) naturaleza, natura; *(character)* índole f <*of a confidential n.* de índole confidencial>; *(essence)* naturaleza; *(temperament)* natural m ♦ **by n.** por naturaleza • **something in the n. of** algo así como • **to be in someone's n.** ser propio de alguien.

naught (nôt) s. nada; MAT. cero.

naugh·ty (nô′tē) adj. **-i-** *(mischievous)* travieso; *(disobedient)* desobediente; *(joke)* verde.

nau·sea (nô′zhə) s. náusea; *(disgust)* asco.

nau·se·ate (nô′zē-āt′) tr. dar náusea a; *(to disgust)* dar asco a.

nau·se·at·ing (:ā′tĭng) adj. nauseabundo, asqueroso.

nau·seous (nô′shəs) adj. nauseabundo ♦ **to feel n.** tener náuseas.

nau·ti·cal (nô′tĭ-kəl) adj. náutico ♦ **n. mile** milla marina.

na·val (nā′vəl) adj. naval.

nave (nāv) s. nave f.

na·vel (nā′vəl) s. ombligo.

nav·i·ga·ble (nǎv′ĭ-gə-bəl) adj. navegable.

nav·i·gate (nǎv′ĭ-gāt′) intr. & tr. navegar.

nav·i·ga·tion (′-gā′shən) s. navegación f.

nav·i·ga·tor (′-tər) s. navegante m.

na·vy (nā′vē) s. marina de guerra, flota; *(color)* azul marino ♦ **n. bean** judía blanca • **the N.** la marina, la armada.

nay (nā) I. adv. no; *(and moreover)* más bien II. s. voto en contra; *(refusal)* negativa.

neap tide (nēp) s. marea muerta.

near (nîr) I. adv. cerca, próximo; *(almost)* casi; *(closely related)* íntimo, cercano ♦ **n. and far** por todas partes • **to come** o **draw n.** acercarse • **to come** o **draw n.** acercarse II. adj. inmediato, próximo; *(relation)* cercano, allegado; *(direct)* directo, corto ♦ **n. and dear** íntimo • **to be a n. miss** fallar por poco III. prep. *(close to)* cerca de; *(almost)* casi IV. tr. & intr. acercarse (a), aproximarse (a).

near·by (′bī′) I. adj. cercano, próximo II. adv. cerca.

near·ly (:lē) adv. casi.

near·sight·ed (:sī′tĭd) adj. miope.

neat (nēt) adj. *(tidy)* limpio, pulcro; *(orderly)* ordenado; *(work)* esmerado, bien hecho; *(writing)* claro; *(clever)* ingenioso; *(liquor)* solo; JER. *(terrific)* fantástico.

neb·u·la (nĕb'yə-lə) s. [pl. **s** o **-ae**] nebulosa.
neb·u·lar (:lər) adj. nebuloso.
neb·u·lous (:ləs) adj. nebuloso.
nec·es·sar·y (nĕs'ĭ-sĕr'ē) I. adj. necesario; *(inevitable)* inevitable II. s. cosa necesaria.
ne·ces·si·tate (nə-sĕs'ĭ-tāt') tr. necesitar.
ne·ces·si·ty (:tē) s. necesidad *f* ♦ **out of n** por necesidad.
neck (nĕk) I. s. cuello; *(of animals)* pescuezo, cogote *m; (of bottles)* gollete *m;* MÚS. mástil *m; (of land)* istmo ♦ **by a n.** DEP. por una cabeza • **n. and n.** parejos • **n. of the woods** parajes • **to break one's n.** desnucarse; FIG. deslomarse • **to risk** o **stick out one's n.** arriesgarse • **to save someone's n.** salvarle el pellejo a alguien • **up to one's n.** metido hasta el cuello II. intr. JER. besuquearse.
neck·er·chief ('ər-chĭf) s. pañuelo para el cuello.
neck·lace (:lĭs) s. collar *m.*
neck·line (:līn') s. escote *m.*
neck·tie (:tī') s. corbata.
nec·rol·o·gy (nə-krŏl'ə-jē) s. necrologia.
nec·ro·man·cy (nĕk'rə-măn'sē) s. necromancia, nigromancia.
ne·crop·o·lis (nə-krŏp'ə-lĭs) s. [pl. **es** o **-leis**] necrópolis *f.*
ne·cro·sis (nə-krō'sĭs) s. necrosis *f.*
nec·tar (nĕk'tər) s. néctar *m.*
nec·tar·ine (nĕk'tə-rēn') s. griñón *m,* pelón *m.*
need (nēd) I. s. necesidad *f; (trouble)* apuro ♦ **if n. be** si fuera necesario • **there's no n.** to no hace falta • **to be in n.** estar necesitado • **to be in n. of** necesitar II. tr. necesitar —intr. estar necesitado ♦ **n. to** *(to have to)* deber, tener que; *(to be necessary)* ser necesario <*she needs to be told* es necesario decírselo>.
need·ful ('fəl) adj. necesario, requerido.
nee·dle (nēd'l) I. s. aguja II. tr. FAM. hacer rabiar, pinchar
nee·dle·point (:point') s. encaje *m* de aguja.
need·less (nēd'lĭs) adj. innecesario, superfluo ♦ **n. to say** huelga decir que.
nee·dle·work (nēd'l-wûrk') s. costura, labor *f* ♦ **the n.** los pobres.
need·y (nē'dē) adj. -i- necesitado, indigente ♦ **the n.** los pobres.
ne'er-do-well (nâr'dŏŏ-wĕl') s. inútil *mf.*
ne·far·i·ous (nə-fâr'ē-əs) adj. infame, nefario.
ne·gate (nĭ-gāt') tr. *(to deny)* negar; *(to nullify)* anular.
ne·ga·tion (nĭ-gā'shən) s. negación *f.*
neg·a·tive (nĕg'ə-tĭv) I. adj. negativo II. s. negativa; GRAM. negación *f;* FOTOG. negativo; MAT. término negativo.
ne·glect (nĭ-glĕkt') I. tr. descuidar ♦ **to n. one's duty** faltar al deber de uno • **to n. to** olvidarse de II. s. descuido, negligencia ♦ **out of** o **through n.** por negligencia.
ne·glect·ful (:fəl) adj. negligente.
neg·li·gee (nĕg'lĭ-zhā') s. negligé *m.*
neg·li·gence (nĕg'lĭ-jəns) s. negligencia.
neg·li·gent (:jənt) adj. negligente, descuidado.
neg·li·gi·ble (:jə-bəl) adj. insignificante.
ne·go·tia·ble (nĭ-gō'shə-bəl) adj. negociable.
ne·go·ti·ate (:shē-āt') intr. negociar —tr. negociar; *(obstacle)* franquear.
ne·go·ti·a·tion (-shē-ā'shən) s. negociación *f.*
ne·go·ti·a·tor (-'-ā'tər) s. negociador *m.*
Ne·gro (nē'grō) adj. & s. [pl. **es**] negro.
neigh (nā) I. s. relincho II. intr. relinchar.
neigh·bor (nā'bər) I. s. vecino; *(fellow human)* prójimo II. intr. estar contiguo, lindar.

neigh·bor·hood (:hŏŏd') s. barrio; *(people)* vecindario ♦ **in the n. of** FAM. cerca de, casi.
neigh·bor·ing (:ĭng) adj. vecino.
neigh·bor·ly (:lē) adj. *(relations)* de buena vecindad; *(person, action)* amable.
nei·ther (nē'thər, nī'-) I. adj. ninguno (de los dos) II. pron. ninguno (de dos), ni uno ni otro III. conj. & adv. (ni . . .) tampoco <*she doesn't like winter and n. do I* a ella no le gusta el invierno, ni a mí tampoco> ♦ **n. . . . nor** ni . . . ni <*n. you nor I* ni tú ni yo>.
nem·e·sis (nĕm'ĭ-sĭs) s. [pl. **-ses**] nemesis *f.*
ne·o·clas·sic/si·cal (nē'ō-klăs'ĭk) adj. neoclásico.
ne·ol·o·gism (nē-ŏl'ə-jĭz'əm) s. neologismo.
ne·ol·o·gist (:jĭst) s. neólogo.
ne·on (nē'ŏn') s. neón *m.*
ne·o·phyte (nē'ə-fīt') s. neófito.
nep·o·tism (nĕp'ə-tĭz'əm) s. nepotismo.
nerve (nûrv) I. s. nervio; *(courage)* valor *m;* FAM. *(boldness)* descaro, tupé *m* ♦ **n. center** centro nervioso • **n. gas** gas neurotóxico • **to get on one's nerves** crispar los nervios a uno • **to lose one's n.** acobardarse ♦ pl. nerviosidad II. tr. animar, dar ánimos a.
nerve·less ('lĭs) adj. sin nervios.
nerve·rack·ing (:răk'ĭng) adj. que crispa los nervios, exasperante.
nerv·ous (nûr'vəs) adj. nervioso; *(high-strung)* irritable, excitable ♦ **n. breakdown** depresión nerviosa • **n. about** tener miedo a.
nerv·ous·ness (:nĭs) s. nerviosidad *f.*
nerv·y (nûr'vē) adj. -i- *(brazen)* descarado; *(daring)* audaz; G.B. *(nervous)* nervioso.
nest (nĕst) I. s. nido; *(of hens)* nidal *m; (of wasps)* avispero ♦ **n. egg** ahorros, economías • **to leave the n.** irse a vivir por su cuenta II. intr. anidar; *(boxes)* encajar —tr. encajar.
nes·tle (nĕs'əl) tr. ♦ **to be nestled among** estar situado en • **to be nestled in** *(a place)* estar al abrigo de, *(someone's arms)* acurrucarse en —intr. acurrucarse.
net[1] (nĕt) I. s. red *f; (fabric)* tul *m* II. tr. -tt- coger o atrapar con una red.
net[2] I. adj. *(after deductions)* neto; *(final)* final II. s. *(profit)* ganancia neta; *(weight)* peso neto III. tr. -tt- *(to yield)* producir; *(to clear)* ganar neto.
neth·er (nĕth'ər) adj. inferior.
neth·er·world (:wûrld') s. infierno.
net·ting (nĕt'ĭng) s. red *f.*
net·tle (nĕt'l) I. s. ortiga II. tr. irritar.
net·tle·some (:səm) adj. irritante, molesto.
net·work (nĕt'wûrk') s. red *f.*
neu·ral (nŏŏr'əl) adj. de los nervios.
neu·ral·gia (nŏŏ-răl'jə) s. neuralgia.
neu·ral·gic (:jĭk) adj. neurálgico.
neu·ri·tis (nŏŏ-rī'tĭs) s. neuritis *f.*
neu·rol·o·gist (nŏŏ-rŏl'ə-jĭst) s. neurólogo.
neu·rol·o·gy (:jē) s. neurología.
neu·ron(e) (nŏŏr'ŏn'/ŏn') s. neurona.
neu·ro·sis (nŏŏ-rō'sĭs) s. [pl. **-ses**] neurosis *f.*
neu·ro·sur·ger·y (nŏŏr'ō-sûr'jə-rē) s. neurocirujía.
neu·rot·ic (nŏŏ-rŏt'ĭk) adj. & s. neurótico.
neu·ter (nŏŏ'tər) I. adj. neutro II. s. GRAM. neutro; VET. animal castrado III. tr. castrar.
neu·tral (nŏŏ'trəl) I. adj. neutral; FÍS., QUÍM. neutro II. s. neutral *mf;* AUTO. punto muerto.
neu·tral·i·ty (-trăl'ĭ-tē) s. neutralidad *f.*
neu·tral·ize ('trə-līz') tr. neutralizar.

neu·tral·iz·er (:lǐ'zər) s. neutralizador *m*.
neu·tron (nōō'trōn') s. neutrón *m*.
nev·er (nĕv'ər) adv. nunca, jamás ♦ **n. again** nunca más • **n. ever** nunca jamás • **n. mind** no importa.
nev·er·more ('-môr') adv. nunca más.
nev·er·the·less (:thə-lĕs') adv. sin embargo, no obstante.
new (nōō) **I.** adj. nuevo; *(recent)* reciente; *(modern)* moderno; *(additional)* distinto ♦ **what's n.?** ¿qué hay de nuevo? **II.** adv. recién.
new·born ('bôrn') **I.** adj. recién nacido; FIG. renacido **II.** s. niño recién nacido.
new·com·er (:kŭm'ər) s. recién llegado.
new·el (nōō'əl) s. nabo (de una escalera).
new·fan·gled (:fâng'gəld) adj. novedoso.
new·ly·wed (:lē-wĕd') s. recién casado.
news (nōōz) s. noticia <*that's good n.* es una buena noticia>; *(current events)* noticias, actualidades *f*; *(broadcast)* noticiario ♦ **n. item** noticia • **that's n. to me!** ¡eso para mí es una novedad! • **to break the n.** dar una noticia a.
news·boy ('boi') s. muchacho vendedor de periódicos.
news·cast (:kăst') s. noticiario.
news·cast·er (:kăs'tər) s. locutor *m*.
news·let·ter (:lĕt'ər) s. hoja informativa.
news·man (:măn') s. [pl. **-men**] periodista *mf*.
news·pa·per (:pā'pər) s. periódico, diario.
news·print (:prĭnt') s. papel *m* de periódico.
news·reel (:rēl') s. noticiario cinematográfico.
news·room (:rōōm') s. sala de redacción.
news·stand (:stănd') s. quiosco (de periódicos).
news·wor·thy (:wûr'*th*ē) adj. de interés periodístico.
news·y (nōō'zē) adj. **-i-** FAM. informativo.
newt (nōōt) s. tritón *m*.
new·ton (nōōt'n) s. newton *m*, neutonio.
next (nĕkst) **I.** adj. *(in time)* que viene, próximo; *(adjacent)* de al lado; *(following)* siguiente <*the n. day* el día siguiente> ♦ **to be n.** ser el siguiente • **what n.!** ¡y ahora, qué! **II.** adv. después, luego ♦ **n. door** al lado • **n. to** *(beside)* junto a, al lado de; *(almost)* casi <*n. to nothing* casi nada> • **to come n.** seguir, venir después.
next-door ('dôr') adj. de al lado.
nex·us (nĕk'səs) s. [pl. inv. *o* **es**] nexo.
ni·a·cin (nī'ə-sĭn) s. ácido nicotínico.
nib (nĭb) s. plumilla (de estilográfica).
nib·ble (nĭb'əl) **I.** tr. mordiscar; *(bait)* morder —intr. comisquear ♦ **to n. at** morder **II.** s. *(bite)* mordisco; *(morsel)* bocadito; FIG. *(offer)* oferta.
nice (nīs) adj. *(friendly)* amable, bueno; *(pleasant)* agradable; *(attractive)* bonito, lindo; *(well-done)* bien hecho <*n. job* trabajo bien hecho>; *(virtuous)* decente, *(considerate)* delicado ♦ **n.** and FAM. muy, bien <*n. and warm* bien calentito> • **to be n. to** ser amable con • **to have a n. time** pasarlo bien.
ni·ce·ty (nī'sĭ-tē) s. *(exactness)* precisión *f*; *(subtle detail)* sutileza; *(refinement)* delicadeza.
niche (nĭch, nĕsh) s. ARQ. hornacina, nicho; FIG. *(place)* colocación *f*, lugar *m*.
nick (nĭk) **I.** s. mella, muesca; *(wound)* rasguño ♦ **in the n. of time** en el momento crucial **II.** tr. mellar, hacer muescas en; *(the skin)* cortar.
nick·el (nĭk'əl) s. QUÍM. níquel *m*; *(U.S. coin)* moneda de cinco centavos.
nick·el-and-dime ('-ən-dīm') adj. FAM. de

poco dinero; *(small-time)* de poca monta.
nick·name (nĭk'nām') **I.** s. apodo **II.** tr. apodar.
nic·o·tine (nĭk'ə-tēn') s. nicotina.
niece (nēs) s. sobrina.
nif·ty (nĭf'tē) adj. **-i-** JER. formidable.
nig·gard·ly (nĭg'ərd-lē) adj. *(stingy)* tacaño, avaro; *(meager)* escaso.
nig·gle (nĭg'əl) intr. pararse en pequeñeces.
nig·gling (:lĭng) adj. demasiado meticuloso.
nigh (nī) **I.** adv. cerca **II.** adj. próximo **III.** prep. cerca de.
night (nīt) **I.** s. noche *f*; *(nightfall)* anochecer *m* ♦ **at** *o* **by n.** de noche • **good n.!** ¡buenas noches! • **last n.** anoche, ayer por la noche • **the n. before** la noche anterior • **the n. before last** anteanoche • **to make a n. of it** FAM. pasarse la noche de juerga • **to say good n. (to someone)** dar las buenas noches (a alguien) • **to stay out all n.** trasnochar • **to work nights** trabajar de noche **II.** adj. nocturno, de la noche ♦ **n. owl** FIG. trasnochador • **n. school** escuela nocturna • **n. shift** turno de noche.
night·cap ('kăp') s. *(cap)* gorro de dormir; FAM. *(drink)* bebida tomada antes de acostarse.
night·club (:klŭb') s. club nocturno.
night·fall (:fôl') s. anochecer *m*.
night·gown (:goun') s. camisa de dormir, camisón *m*.
night·hawk (:hôk') s. ORNIT. chotacabras *m*; FIG., FAM. noctámbulo.
night·ie (nī'tē) s. FAM. camisón *m*.
night·in·gale (nīt'n-gāl') s. ruiseñor *m*.
night·life (nīt'līf') s. vida nocturna.
night·light (:līt') s. lamparilla.
night·ly (:lē) **I.** adj. nocturno, de noche; *(every night)* de todas las noches **II.** adv. por la noche; *(every night)* todas las noches.
night·mare (:mâr') s. pesadilla.
night·stick (:stĭk') s. porra de policía.
night·time (:tīm') s. noche *f* ♦ **in the n.** de noche.
ni·hil·ist (nī'ə-lĭst, nē'-) s. nihilista *mf*.
ni·hil·is·tic ('-lĭs'tĭk) adj. nihilista.
nil (nĭl) s. nada; *(zero)* cero.
nim·ble (nĭm'bəl) adj. **-er, -est** ágil.
nim·bus (nĭm'bəs) s. [pl. **es** *o* **-bi**] nimbo.
nin·com·poop (nĭn'kəm-pōōp') s. bobo, necio.
nine (nīn) s. & adj. nueve *m* ♦ **n. hundred** novecientos • **n. o'clock** las nueve.
nine·pins ('pĭnz') s. bolos (juego).
nine·teen (nīn-tēn') s. & adj. diecinueve *m*.
nine·teenth (:tēnth') s. & adj. decimonoveno.
nine·ti·eth (nīn'tē-ĭth) s. & adj. nonagésimo.
nine·ty (nīn'tē) s. & adj. noventa.
nin·ny (nĭn'ē) s. simplón *m*, tonto.
ninth (nīnth) s. & adj. noveno.
nip (nĭp) **I.** tr. **-pp-** *(to pinch)* pellizcar; *(to bite)* morder; *(to chill)* helar; JER. *(to steal)* birlar ♦ **to n. in the bud** cortar de raíz • **to n. off** cortar **II.** s. *(pinch)* pellizco; *(bite)* mordedura; *(sip)* traguito ♦ **n. and tuck** reñido • **there's a n. in the air** hace fresco.
nip·ple (nĭp'əl) s. pezón *m*; *(on bottle)* tetilla.
nip·py (nĭp'ē) adj. **-i-** frío.
nit (nĭt) s. liendre *f*.
ni·ter (nī'tər) s. nitro.
nit-pick (nĭt'pĭk') intr. FAM. fijarse en pequeñeces.
ni·trate (nī'trāt') s. nitrato; *(fertilizer)* nitrato de potasio *o* de sodio.
ni·tric (nī'trĭk) adj. nítrico.

ni·trite (nī′trīt′) s. nitrito.
ni·tro·gen (nī′trə-jən) s. nitrógeno.
ni·tro·glyc·er·in(e) (nī′trō-glĭs′ər-ĭn) s. nitroglicerina.
ni·trous (nī′trəs) adj. nitroso.
nit·ty-grit·ty (nĭt′ē-grĭt′ē) s. JER. esencia, meollo.
nit·wit (nĭt′wĭt′) s. FAM. bobalicón m.
nix (nĭks) FAM. I. s. nada II. adv. no III. tr. prohibir ♦ n. it! ¡no lo hagas!
no (nō) I. adv. no ♦ no longer ya no • no more ya no . . . más <I want no more ya no quiero más>; (not any) no más <there's no more wine no queda más vino> • to say no decir que no II. adj. no; (not one) no . . . ninguno <she has no hope no tiene ninguna esperanza>; (not at all) ninguno <she is no actress no es ninguna actriz> ♦ by no means de ninguna manera • in no time en un abrir y cerrar de ojos • no admittance prohibida la entrada • no matter! ¡no importa! • no more, no less ni más, ni menos • no other más <I see no other way out no veo más solución> • no smoking prohibido fumar • no way! ¡nunca!, ¡jamás! • with no sin <with no chance of sin la oportunidad de> III. s. [pl. es] no ♦ pl. votos en contra.
no-ac·count (nō′ə-kount′) adj. FAM. inútil.
no·bil·i·ty (nō-bĭl′ĭ-tē) s. nobleza.
no·ble (nō′bəl) adj. & s. -er, -est noble mf.
no·ble·man (:mən) s. [pl. -men] noble m.
no·ble·wom·an (:wŏŏm′ən) s. [pl. -women] noble f.
no·bod·y (nō′bŏd′ē) I. pron. nadie ♦ to be n.'s fool no ser tomado por tonto II. s. don nadie m, nadie m.
noc·tur·nal (nŏk-tûr′nəl) adj. nocturno.
nod (nŏd) I. intr. -dd- balancearse, inclinarse; (sleepily) dar cabezadas; (in agreement) asentir con la cabeza; (in greeting) saludar con la cabeza ♦ to n. off dormirse —tr. inclinar (la cabeza) ♦ to n. hello saludar con la cabeza II. s. inclinación f de cabeza ♦ to get the n. obtener la aprobación • to give the n. asentir, aprobar.
nod·al (nōd′l) adj. nodal.
node (nōd) s. protuberancia; BOT. nudo; ANAT., FÍS. nodo.
nod·u·lar (nŏj′ə-lər) adj. nodular.
nod·ule (:ōōl) s. nódulo.
no-fault (nō′fôlt′) adj. sin responsabilidad.
nog·gin (nŏg′ĭn) s. JER. cabeza, coco.
no-go (nō′gō′) adj. JER. que no está listo.
no-good (nō′gŏŏd′) adj. inútil; (vile) vil.
noise (noiz) s. ruido; FÍS. interferencia ♦ to make a lot of n. about quejarse de.
noise·less (′lĭs) adj. silencioso, sin ruido.
noise·mak·er (:mā′kər) s. matraca.
noi·some (noi′səm) adj. nocivo.
nois·y (noi′zē) adj. -i- ruidoso.
no-load (nō′lōd′) adj. sin comisión de ventas.
no·mad (nō′măd′) s. nómada mf.
no·mad·ic (-′ĭk) adj. nómada.
no man's land s. tierra de nadie.
no·men·cla·ture (nō′mən-klā′chər) s. nomenclatura.
nom·i·nal (nŏm′ə-nəl) adj. nominal; (of shares) nominativo; (trifling) insignificante.
nom·i·nate (:nāt′) tr. nombrar; (as a candidate) proponer.
nom·i·na·tion (′-nā′shən) s. nombramiento.
nom·i·na·tive (′-nə-tĭv) adj. & s. nominativo.
nom·i·nee (′-nē′) s. candidato.
non·ag·gres·sion (nŏn′ə-grĕsh′ən) s. no agresión f.

non·a·ligned (:ə-līnd′) adj. no alineado.
non·at·ten·dance (:ə-tĕn′dəns) s. ausencia.
non·break·a·ble (-brā′kə-bəl) adj. irrompible.
non·cha·lance (nŏn′shə-läns′) s. imperturbabilidad f.
non·cha·lant (:länt′) adj. imperturbable.
non·com·bat·ant (nŏn′kəm-băt′nt) s. & adj. no combatiente mf.
non·com·bus·ti·ble (:kəm-bŭs′tə-bəl) adj. incombustible.
non·com·mit·tal (:kə-mĭt′l) adj. evasivo.
non·com·pli·ance (:kəm-plī′əns) s. incumplimiento.
non·con·duc·tor (:kən-dŭk′tər) s. aislante m.
non·con·form·ist (:kən-fôr′mĭst) adj. & s. no conformista mf, disidente mf.
non·con·form·i·ty (:kən-fôr′mĭ-tē) s. no conformidad f, disidencia f.
non·de·nom·i·na·tion·al (:dĭ-nŏm′ə-nā′shə-nəl) adj. no sectario.
non·de·script (:dĭ-skrĭpt′) adj. de poco o ningún carácter.
non·dis·crim·i·na·tion (:dĭ-skrĭm′ə-nā′shən) s. ausencia de discriminación.
non·drink·er (-drĭng′kər) s. no bebedor m.
none (nŭn) I. pron. (nobody) nadie, ninguno; (not one) ninguno <n. of them ninguno de ellos>; (not any) nada ♦ n. but solamente • n. other than nada o nada menos que II. adv. no <he is n. too happy él no está muy contento>.
non·en·ti·ty (nŏn-ĕn′tĭ-tē) s. nulidad f.
non·es·sen·tial (′-ĭ-sĕn′shəl) adj. no esencial.
none·such (nŭn′sŭch′) s. cosa sin par.
none·the·less (′thə-lĕs′) adv. sin embargo.
non·ex·is·tent (nŏn′ĭg-zĭs′tənt) adj. inexistente.
non·fat (′făt′) adj. sin grasa.
non·fea·sance (-fē′zəns) s. incumplimiento.
non·fic·tion (:fĭk′shən) s. literatura no novelesca.
non·flam·ma·ble (:flăm′ə-bəl) adj. no inflamable.
non·in·ter·ven·tion (:′ĭn′tər-vĕn′shən) s. no intervención f.
non·ne·go·tia·ble (′nĭ-gō′shə-bəl) adj. no negociable.
no-no (nō′nō′) s. [pl. 's] FAM. algo prohibido o inadmisible.
non-non·sense (nō′nŏn′sĕns′) adj. práctico.
non·pa·reil (nŏn′pə-rĕl′) adj. & s. (persona) sin igual, (cosa) sin par.
non·par·ti·san (:-pär′tĭ-zən) adj. independiente.
non·pay·ment (:pā′mənt) s. falta de pago.
non·per·for·mance (:pər-fôr′məns) s. incumplimiento.
non·plus (′plŭs′) tr. desconcertar.
non·pro·duc·tive (′prə-dŭk′tĭv) adj. improductivo.
non·pro·fes·sion·al (:prə-fĕsh′ə-nəl) adj. & s. no profesional mf.
non·prof·it (-prŏf′ĭt) adj. sin fin lucrativo.
non·res·i·dent (:rĕz′ĭ-dənt) adj. & s. no residente mf, transeúnte mf.
non·re·stric·tive (:rĭ-strĭk′tĭv) adj. sin restricción.
non·re·turn·a·ble (:rĭ-tûr′nə-bəl) adj. sin devolución.
non·sched·uled (:skĕj′ōōld) adj. no regular.
non·sec·tar·i·an (′sĕk-târ′ē-ən) adj. no sectario.

non·sense (nŏn'sĕns') s. disparate(s) *m* ♦ n.! tonterías • **to talk n.** decir tonterías.
non·sen·si·cal (-sĕn'sĭ-kəl) adj. disparatado.
non·stan·dard (nŏn-stăn'dərd) adj. no reglamentario.
non·stop ('stŏp') I. adv. sin parar II. adj. *(train)* directo; *(plane)* sin escalas.
non·sup·port ('sə-pôrt') s. falta de pago de la pensión alimenticia.
non·tax·a·ble (-tăk'sə-bəl) adj. no imponible.
non·trans·fer·a·ble ('trăns-fûr'ə-bəl) adj. intransferible.
non·un·ion (-yōōn'yən) adj. *(labor)* no sindicado; *(shop)* que no emplea miembros de un sindicato.
non·vi·a·ble (:vī'ə-bəl) adj. no viable.
non·vi·o·lence (:vī'ə-ləns) s. no violencia.
noo·dle (nōōd'l) s. CUL. tallarín *m*, fideo; JER. *(head)* coco.
nook (nōōk) s. rincón *m*.
noon (nōōn) I. s. mediodía *m* ♦ **at high n.** a mediodía II. adj. de mediodía.
noon·day ('dā') adj. & s. (de) mediodía *m*.
no one *o* **no-one** (nō'wŭn') pron. nadie, ninguno.
noon·time (nōōn'tīm') s. mediodía *m*.
noose (nōōs) s. *(knot)* nudo corredizo; *(hangman's rope)* dogal *m*.
nor (nôr) conj. ni <*he was neither willing n. able* ni quería ni podía>; ni tampoco <*n. do I want to go* ni tampoco quiero ir>.
norm (nôrm) s. norma.
nor·mal (nôr'məl) I. adj. normal II. s. normalidad ♦ **to return to n.** volver a la normalidad.
nor·mal·i·ty (-măl'ĭ-tē) s. normalidad *f*.
nor·mal·ize ('mə-līz') tr. normalizar.
nor·ma·tive (:mə-tĭv) adj. normativo.
north (nôrth) I. s. norte *m* ♦ **N.** región septentrional II. adj. del norte III. adv. hacia el norte.
north·bound ('bound') adj. con rumbo al norte.
north·east (-ēst') I. s. nordeste *m* II. adj. del nordeste III. adv. hacia el nordeste.
north·east·ern (:ē'stərn) adj. del nordeste.
north·er·ly (nôr'thər-lē) I. adj. (del) norte II. adv. hacia el norte.
north·ern (:thərn) adj. septentrional, del norte ♦ **n. lights** aurora boreal.
north·ern·er (:thər-nər) s. norteño.
north·land (nôrth'lănd') s. región del norte *f*.
north·ward (:wərd) adv. & adj. hacia el norte.
north·west (-wĕst') I. s. noroeste *m* II. adj. del noroeste III. adv. hacia el noroeste.
north·west·ern (:wĕs'tərn) adj. del noroeste.
nose (nōz) I. s. nariz *f*; *(snout)* hocico; *(sense of smell)* olfato; *(knack)* olfato ♦ **as plain as the n. on one's face** más claro que el agua • **n. cone** morro • **on the n.** exacto • **right under one's n.** delante de las narices • **to blow one's n.** sonarse la nariz • **to follow one's n.** seguir recto • **to lead by the n.** manejar al antojo de uno • **to look down one's n. at** FAM. mirar por encima del hombro a • **to pay through the n.** FAM. pagar un dineral • **to poke** *o* **stick one's n. into** FAM. meter la nariz en • **to turn up one's n. at** FAM. despreciar, desdeñar II. tr. empujar con el hocico —intr. husmear ♦ **to n. forward** avanzar con cuidado • **to n. around** husmear.
nose·bleed ('blēd') s. hemorragia nasal.
nosedive (:dīv') s. picado.
nose·gay (:gā') s. ramillete *m* de flores.

nos·tal·gia (nə-stăl'jə) s. nostalgia.
nos·tal·gic (:jĭk) adj. nostálgico.
nos·tril (nŏs'trəl) s. ventana ♦ pl. narices.
nos·trum (nŏs'trəm) s. panacea.
nos·y (nō'zē) adj. **-i-** entrometido.
not (nŏt) adv. no <*I will n. go* no iré> ♦ **certainly n.!** ¡de ninguna manera! • **n. even** ni siquiera • **n. to mention** por no mencionar • **n. yet** ya no, todavía no.
no·ta·bil·i·ty (nō'tə-bĭl'ĭ-tē) s. notabilidad *f*.
no·ta·ble (nō'tə-bəl) adj. & s. notable *m*.
no·ta·rize (nō'tə-rīz') tr. hacer certificar por notario.
no·ta·ry (:rē) s. notario ♦ **n. public** notario.
no·ta·tion (nō-tā'shən) s. MAT., MÚS. notación *f*; *(brief note)* nota, anotación *f*.
notch (nŏch) I. s. *(cut)* muesca, corte *m*; GEOG. desfiladero; FAM. *(level)* grado ♦ **to take someone down a n.** FAM. bajar los humos a alguien II. tr. hacer una muesca en, cortar.
note (nōt) I. s. nota; FIN. billete *m*; *(bird call)* trino; *(mention)* mención *f*; *(I.O.U.)* pagaré *m* ♦ **of n.** *(renowned)* de renombre; *(important)* de importanca • **to make a n. of** tomar nota de • **to strike a false n.** desentonar ♦ pl. notas, apuntes • **to compare n.** cambiar impresiones II. tr. *(to notice)* notar, advertir; *(to mention)* señalar; *(to observe)* fijarse en.
note·book ('bŏŏk') s. cuaderno.
not·ed (nō'tĭd) adj. notable, eminente.
note·pa·per (nōt'pā'pər) s. papel *m* de escribir.
note·wor·thy (:wûr'thē) adj. notable.
noth·ing (nŭth'ĭng) I. pron. nada; *(not anything)* no . . . nada <*he believes in n.* no cree en nada> ♦ **for n.** *(for free)* por nada; *(in vain)* para nada; *(for no reason)* sin motivo • **n. at all** nada de nada • **n. but** sólo • **n. doing!** FAM. ¡ni hablar! • **there's n. to it** es sencillísimo • **to come to n.** quedar en nada • **to have n. to do with** no tener nada que ver con • **to make n. of** no dar importancia a • **to say n. of** por no hablar de • **to think n. of** no suponer nada (para uno) II. s. nada, nadería; *(person)* cero a la izquierda III. adv. ♦ **n. less than** nada menos que • **n. like** nada <*she is n. like her mother* no se parece nada a su madre>.
no·tice (nō'tĭs) I. s. *(attention)* atención *f*; *(warning)* aviso, notificación *f* <*without prior n.* sin previo aviso>; *(announcement)* anuncio; *(review)* crítica, reseña; *(sign)* letrero ♦ **at a moment's n.** sin previo aviso • **on (such) short n.** en tan poco tiempo • **to be on n.** estar avisado • **to escape one's n.** escapársele a uno • **to give n.** *(to resign)* renunciar a (un empleo); *(to fire)* despedir; *(to inform)* avisar • **to put on** *o* **serve n.** advertir, avisar • **to take n. of** *(someone)* hacer caso a; *(something)* hacer caso de, prestar atención a • **until further n.** hasta nuevo aviso II. tr. *(to note)* observar; *(to see)* fijarse en; *(to realize)* darse cuenta de, advertir.
no·tice·a·ble (nō'tĭ-sə-bəl) adj. notable, sensible; *(obvious)* evidente ♦ **it is barely n.** casi no se nota.
no·ti·fi·ca·tion (nō'tə-fĭ-kā'shən) s. notificación *f*, aviso.
no·ti·fy (nō'tə-fī') tr. notificar, avisar.
no·tion (nō'shən) s. noción *f*, idea; *(opinion)* opinión *f* ♦ **to have no n.** no tener la más mínima idea • **to have a n.** to estar dispuesto a ♦ pl. artículos de mercería.
no·to·ri·e·ty (nō'tə-rī'ĭ-tē) s. notoriedad *f*.
no·to·ri·ous (nō-tôr'ē-əs) adj. de mala fama.

not·with·stand·ing (nŏt'wĭth-stăn'dĭng) prep. & conj. a pesar de (que).

nou·gat (nōō'gət) s. turrón *m* de almendras.

noun (noun) s. sustantivo, nombre *m*.

nour·ish (nûr'ĭsh) tr. nutrir, alimentar; *(to promote)* fomentar; *(hopes)* abrigar.

nour·ish·ment (:mənt) s. alimento.

no·va (nō'və) s. [pl. **s** *o* **-ae**] nova.

nov·el (nŏv'əl) I. s. novela II. adj. nuevo, original.

nov·el·ist (:ə-lĭst) s. novelista *mf*.

nov·el·is·tic ('-lĭs'tĭk) adj. novelístico.

no·vel·la (nō-vĕl'ə) s. cuento, novela corta.

nov·el·ty (nŏv'əl-tē) s. novedad *f*, innovación *f* ♦ pl. chucherías, baratijas.

No·vem·ber (nō-vĕm'bər) s. noviembre *m*.

nov·ice (nŏv'ĭs) s. novato; RELIG. novicio.

no·vi·ti·ate (nō-vĭsh'ē-ĭt) s. noviciado.

now (nou) I. adv. ahora; *(immediately)* ahora mismo; *(at last)* ya; *(as things are)* ahora ya <*n.* we won't be able to stay ahora ya no podemos quedarnos> ♦ **just n.** *(at present)* ahora mismo; *(recently)* hace un momento • **n. . . . n.** ya . . . ya • **n., n.** vamos, vamos • **n. and again** *o* **n. and then** de vez en cuando • **n. then** ahora bien • **right n.!** ¡ahora mismo! II. conj. ♦ **n. that** ya que, ahora que III. s. ♦ **by n.** ya • **for n.** por ahora • **from n. on** de ahora en adelante • **not n.** ahora no • **until** *o* **up to n.** hasta ahora.

now·a·days (:ə-dāz') adv. hoy (en) día.

no·way(s) (nō'wā[z]') adv. de ningún modo.

no·where (nō'hwâr') I. adv. *(location)* en *o* por ninguna parte; *(direction)* a ninguna parte • **n. near** muy lejos *o* • **n. near** as ni mucho menos tan • **to get n.** no conseguir nada II. s. ♦ **in the middle of n.** en el quinto pino • **out of n.** de la nada.

no-win (nō'wĭn') adj. que no se puede ganar.

nox·ious (nŏk'shəs) adj. nocivo, dañino.

noz·zle (nŏz'əl) s. boquilla.

nth (ĕnth) adj. enésimo.

nu·ance (nōō-äns') s. matiz *m*.

nub (nŭb) s. protuberancia; *(core)* esencia.

nu·bile (nōō'bəl, :bīl') adj. núbil.

nuclear (nōō'klē-ər) adj. nuclear.

nu·cle·us (:əs) s. [pl. **es** *o* **-lei**] s. núcleo.

nude (nōōd) s. & adj. desnudo ♦ **in the n.** al desnudo.

nudge (nŭj) I. s. codazo II. tr. dar un codazo a.

nud·ist (nōō'dĭst) s. & adj. nudista *mf*.

nu·di·ty (:dĭ-tē) s. desnudez *f*.

nug·get (nŭg'ĭt) s. pepita.

nul·sance (nōō'səns) s. *(person)* pesado; *(thing)* fastidio, molestia ♦ **to make a n. of oneself** molestar, dar la lata.

null (nŭl) I. adj. nulo ♦ **n. and void** nulo y sin valor II. s. cero.

nul·li·fy (:ə-fī') tr. anular.

nul·li·ty (:ĭ-tē) s. nulidad *f*.

numb (nŭm) I. adj. entumecido; *(with fear)* paralizado II. tr. entumecer; *(with fear)* paralizar.

num·ber (nŭm'bər) I. s. número ♦ **a n. of** *(several)* varios; *(a lot)* muchos • **any n. of** muchos • **beyond n.** innumerable • **by the numbers** *(mechanically)* mecánicamente; *(strictly)* de uno en uno • **to do a n. on** FAM. dañar, arruinar • **to have someone's n.** tener a alguien calado • **your n. is up** FAM. te llegó la hora ♦ pl. *(many)* muchos; MAT. números • **n. game** lotería ilegal II. tr. numerar, po-

ner número a; *(to include, restrict)* contar *(to have)* tener ♦ **to n. among** contar entre —intr. ser <*we* numbered twenty éramos veinte> ♦ **to n. in** contarse (por).

num·ber·ing (:ĭng) s. recuento, enumeración *f*; *(of pages)* numeración *f*.

num·ber·less (:lĭs) adj. innumerable.

numb·ness (nŭm'nĭs) s. entumecimiento.

nu·men (nōō'mən) s. [pl. **-mina**] numen *f*.

nu·mer·a·ble (nōō'mər-ə-bəl) adj. numerable.

nu·mer·al (:əl) s. número ♦ **Arabic, Roman n.** número arábigo, romano.

nu·mer·ate (nōō'mə-rāt') tr. enumerar, contar.

nu·mer·a·tion ('-rā'shən) s. numeración *f*.

nu·mer·a·tor ('-tər) s. numerador *m*.

nu·mer·ic/i·cal (nōō-mĕr'ĭk) adj. numérico.

nu·mer·ol·o·gy ('mə-rŏl'ə-jē) s. numerología.

nu·mer·ous (-mər-əs) adj. numeroso.

nu·mis·mat·ic (nōō'mĭz-măt'ĭk) adj. numismático ♦ **numismatics** s.sg. numismática.

num·skull (nŭm'skŭl') s. tonto, mentecato.

nun (nŭn) s. monja, religiosa.

nun·ner·y ('ə-rē) s. convento de monjas.

nup·tial (nŭp'shəl) I. adj. nupcial II. s. ♦ pl. nupcias.

nurse (nûrs) I. s. enfermero; *(wet nurse)* nodriza; *(nursemaid)* niñera II. tr. *(infant)* criar; *(patient)* cuidar; *(grudge)* guardar; *(drink)* beber lentamente — intr. *(mother)* dar de mamar; *(infant)* mamar.

nurse·maid (:mād') s. niñera.

nurs·er·y (nûr'sə-rē) s. cuarto de los niños; *(center)* guardería infantil; AGR. vivero • **n. rhyme** poesía infantil • **n. school** escuela de párvulos.

nurs·ing (:sĭng) s. profesión *f* de enfermero; *(suckling)* lactancia ♦ **n. home** hogar de ancianos.

nur·ture (nûr'chər) I. s. *(feeding)* alimentación *f*; *(rearing)* crianza, educación *f* II. tr. *(to nourish)* alimentar; *(children)* criar; FIG. cultivar.

nut (nŭt) s. fruto seco, nuez *f*; JER. *(odd person)* estrafalario; *(crazy person)* chiflado; *(fan)* entusiasta *mf*; *(head)* coco; MEC. *(for bolts)* tuerca ♦ **a hard n. to crack** un hueso duro de roer.

nut·crack·er (krăk'ər) s. cascanueces *m*.

nut·meg (nŭt'mĕg') s. nuez moscada.

nu·tri·ent (nōō'trē-ənt) adj. & s. *(alimento)* nutritivo.

nu·tri·ment (:trə-mənt) s. alimento nutritivo.

nu·tri·tion (nōō-trĭsh'ən) s. nutrición *f*.

nu·tri·tion·al (:ə-nəl) adj. nutritivo.

nu·tri·tion·ist (:ə-nĭst) s. especialista *mf* en problemas de nutrición.

nu·tri·tious (:əs) adj. nutritivo.

nu·tri·tive (nōō'trĭ-tĭv) adj. nutritivo.

nuts (nŭts) FAM. I. adj. chalado, chiflado *(about por)* • **to drive someone n.** volver loco a alguien • **to go n.** volverse loco *(over por)* II. interj. ¡cuernos!

nut·shell (nŭt'shĕl') s. cáscara de nuez ♦ **in a n.** en pocas palabras.

nut·ty (nŭt'ē) adj. & adv. **-i-** *(flavor)* con sabor a nuez; JER. *(crazy)* loco, chiflado.

nuz·zle (nŭz'əl) tr. & intr. hocicar.

ny·lon (nī'lŏn') s. nilón *m* ♦ pl. medias de nilón.

nymph (nĭmf) s. ninfa.

nym·pho·ma·ni·a (nĭm'fə-mā'nē-ə) s. ninfomanía.

O

o, O (ō) s. *(letter)* decimoquinta letra del alfabeto inglés; *(zero)* cero.

oaf (ōf) s. zoquete *m*, patán *m*.

oak (ōk) s. roble *m*.

oak·en (ō′kən) adj. de roble.

oar (ōr) s. remo.

o·a·sis (ō-ā′sĭs) s. [pl. **-ses**] oasis *m*.

oat (ōt) s. avena ♦ **to feel one's oats** FAM. estar lleno de vigor.

oath (ōth) s. juramento.

oat·meal (ōt′mēl′) s. *(uncooked)* copas de avena; *(porridge)* gachas de avena.

ob·du·ra·cy (ŏb′dŏŏ-rə-sē) s. obstinación *f*.

ob·du·rate (:rĭt) adj. *(hardhearted)* insensible; *(obstinate)* obstinado, inflexible.

o·be·di·ence (ō-bē′dē-əns) s. obediencia.

o·be·di·ent (:ənt) adj. obediente.

ob·e·lisk (ŏb′ə-lĭsk) s. obelisco.

o·bese (ō-bēs′) adj. obeso.

o·be·si·ty (ō-bē′sĭ-tē) s. obesidad *f*.

o·bey (ō-bā′) tr. obedecer; *(the law)* respetar; *(orders)* cumplir, acatar —intr. ser obediente.

ob·fus·cate (ŏb′fə-skāt′) tr. ofuscar.

ob·fus·ca·tion (′-skā′shən) s. ofuscación *f*.

o·bit·u·ar·y (ō-bĭch′ōō-ěr′ē) s. obituario.

ob·ject¹ (əb-jěkt′) intr. hacer objeciones; *(to disapprove)* desaprobar • **to o.** objetar.

ob·ject² (ŏb′jĭkt) s. objeto; *(purpose)* propósito; *(goal)* fin *m*; GRAM. complemento ♦ **price is no o.** no importa el precio.

ob·jec·tion (əb-jěk′shən) s. objeción *f*, reparo; DER. protesta; *(disapproval)* inconveniente *m* <*there's no o. to her going* no hay inconveniente en que ella vaya> ♦ **if there are no objections** si no hay nada que objetar • **to raise an o.** poner un reparo.

ob·jec·tion·a·ble (:sha-nə-bəl) adj. *(behavior)* reprobable; *(language)* ofensivo.

ob·jec·tive (:tĭv) I. adj. objetivo; GRAM. complementario ♦ **to be o. about** considerar objetivamente II. s. objetivo.

ob·jec·tiv·i·ty (ŏb′jĕk-tĭv′ĭ-tē) s. objetividad *f*.

ob·jec·tor (əb-jěk′tər) s. objetor *m*.

ob·li·gate (ŏb′lĭ-gāt′) tr. obligar ♦ **to be obligated to** tener la obligación de.

ob·li·ga·tion (′-gā′shən) s. obligación *f*; *(duty)* deber *m*; *(commitment)* compromiso ♦ **to be under an o. to** *(do something)* tener la obligación de; *(someone)* estarle reconocido a • **to feel an o. to** sentirse obligado a.

o·blig·a·to·ry (ə-blĭg′ə-tôr′ē) adj. obligatorio.

o·blige (ə-blīj′) tr. obligar <*she is not obliged to do it* nada le obliga a hacerlo>; *(to do a favor for)* hacer un favor a; *(to humor)* complacer ♦ **much obliged** muy agradecido • **to be obliged to** *(do something)* verse obligado a; *(someone)* estarle reconocido a.

o·blig·ing (ə-blī′jĭng) adj. complaciente.

o·blique (ə-blēk′) I. adj. oblicuo; *(evasive)* indirecto II. s. línea oblicua.

o·blit·er·ate (ə-blĭt′ə-rāt′) tr. *(to erase)* borrar; *(to annihilate)* arrasar, aniquilar.

o·bliv·i·on (ə-blĭv′ē-ən) s. olvido.

o·bliv·i·ous (:əs) adj. *(forgetful)* olvidadizo; *(unmindful)* inconsciente *(to, of* de).

ob·long (ŏb′lông′) I. adj. oblongo, rectangular II. s. rectángulo.

ob·nox·ious (ŏb-nŏk′shəs) adj. desagradable, repugnante; *(person)* insoportable.

o·boe (ō′bō) s. oboe *m*.

ob·scene (əb-sēn′) adj. obsceno; *(gesture)* grosero; *(loathsome)* repugnante, soez.

ob·scen·i·ty (əb-sēn′ĭ-tē) s. obscenidad *f*.

ob·scure (əb-skyōōr′) I. adj. **-er, -est** oscuro; *(faint)* indistinto; *(inconspicuous)* imperceptible; *(meaning)* oculto II. tr. oscurecer; *(to hide)* ocultar; *(to complicate)* enredar ♦ **to o. someone's view** tapar la vista a alguien.

ob·scu·ri·ty (:ĭ-tē) s. oscuridad *f*.

ob·se·qui·ous (əb-sē′kwē-əs) adj. servil.

ob·serv·ance (əb-zûr′vəns) s. *(of law, rule)* observancia, cumplimiento; *(of a holiday)* celebración *f*; *(observation)* observación *f*.

ob·serv·ant (:vənt) adj. observador ♦ **to be o. of** *(the law)* respetar; *(one's duty)* cumplir con.

ob·ser·va·tion (ŏb′zər-vā′shən) s. observación *f* ♦ **to be under o.** estar en observación • **to escape o.** pasar desapercibido.

ob·serv·a·to·ry (əb-zûr′və-tôr′ē) s. observatorio.

ob·serve (əb-zûrv′) tr. observar; *(to remark)* decir; *(a contract, duty)* cumplir con; *(law)* acatar; *(silence, a feast)* guardar; *(a holiday)* celebrar.

ob·serv·er (əb-zûr′vər) s. observador *m*.

ob·sess (əb-sěs′) tr. obsesionar.

ob·ses·sion (əb-sěsh′ən) s. obsesión *f*.

ob·ses·sive (əb-sěs′ĭv) adj. obsesivo.

ob·so·les·cence (ŏb′sə-lěs′əns) s. obsolencia.

ob·so·les·cent (:ənt) adj. en desuso.

ob·so·lete (ŏb′sə-lēt′) adj. obsoleto; *(outmoded)* anticuado.

ob·sta·cle (ŏb′stə-kəl) s. obstáculo.

ob·ste·tri·cian (ŏb′stĭ-trĭsh′ən) s. obstetra *mf*.

ob·stet·ric/ri·cal (ŏb-stět′rĭk) adj. obstétrico ♦ **obstetrics** s.sg. obstetricia.

ob·sti·na·cy (ŏb′stə-nə-sē) s. obstinación *f*.

ob·sti·nate (:nĭt) adj. obstinado.

ob·strep·er·ous (əb-strěp′ər-əs) adj. *(noisy)* estrepitoso, ruidoso; *(rebellious)* revoltoso.

ob·struct (əb-strŭkt′) tr. obstruir; *(to hinder)* dificultar; *(view)* tapar.

ob·struc·tion (əb-strŭk′shən) s. obstrucción *f*; *(obstacle)* estorbo, impedimento.

ob·struc·tion·ist (:shə-nĭst) s. obstruccionista *mf*.

ob·tain (əb-tān′) tr. obtener, lograr; *(to acquire)* adquirir —intr. prevalecer.

ob·trude (əb-trōōd′) tr. imponer, introducir a la fuerza —intr. manifestarse.

ob·tru·sion (əb-trōō′zhən) s. intrusión *f*.

ob·tru·sive (:sĭv) adj. llamativo, que se nota.

ob·tuse (əb-tōōs′) adj. obtuso.

ob·verse (ŏb′vûrs′) adj. (del) anverso.

ob·vi·ate (ŏb′vē-āt′) tr. obviar.

ob·vi·ous (ŏb′vē-əs) adj. obvio, patente.

ob·vi·ous·ly (:lē) adv. evidentemente; *(of course)* claro.

oc·ca·sion (ə-kā′zhən) I. s. ocasión *f*; *(event)* acontecimiento; *(reason)* motivo ♦ **as the o. requires** según el caso • **on o.** ocasionalmente • **to rise to the o.** estar a la altura de las circunstancias II. tr. ocasionar, provocar.

oc·ca·sion·al (:zhə-nəl) adj. ocasional.

oc·ci·dent (ŏk′sə-děnt′) s. occidente *m*.

oc·clude (ə-klōōd′) tr. MED. ocluir; *(to obstruct)* obstruir, tapar.

oc·cult (ə-kŭlt′) I. adj. oculto II. s. ciencias ocultas, magia.

oc·cu·pan·cy (ŏk′yə-pən-sē) s. ocupación *f*; *(of house)* residencia; *(of hotel)* estancia.

oc·cu·pant (:pənt) s. *(tenant)* inquilino; *(guest)* huésped *mf*; *(passenger)* pasajero.

oc·cu·pa·tion (ŏk'yə-pā'shən) s. ocupación *f*; *(job)* trabajo; *(pastime)* tarea, pasatiempo.

oc·cu·pa·tion·al (:shə-nəl) adj. ocupacional.

oc·cu·pied (ŏk'yə pīd') adj. ocupado.

oc·cu·py (:pī') tr. *(space)* ocupar; *(time)* emplear ♦ **to o. oneself with** *(to engage in)* ponerse a; *(to busy oneself in)* entretenerse con.

oc·cur (ə-kûr') intr. **-rr-** ocurrir, suceder; *(in special cases)* darse; *(to be found)* encontrarse ♦ **it occurs to me that** se me ocurre que.

oc·cur·rence (:əns) s. *(incident)* suceso; *(instance)* caso; *(presence)* presencia ♦ **to be an unusual o.** no darse a menudo.

o·cean (ō'shən) s. océano ♦ **o. liner** transatlántico ♦ **oceans of** FIG. la mar de.

o·ce·an·ic (ō'shē-ăn'ĭk) adj. oceánico.

o·cean·og·ra·phy (ō'shə-nŏg'rə-fē) s. oceanografía.

o·cher *o* **o·chre** (ō'kər) s. ocre *m*.

o·clock (ə-klŏk') adv. ♦ **one o.** la una • **it's ten o.** son las diez.

oc·ta·gon (ŏk'tə-gŏn') s. octágono, octógono.

oc·tag·o·nal (ŏk-tăg'ə-nəl) adj. octagonal.

oc·tane (ŏk'tān') s. octano.

oc·tave (ŏk'tĭv, ŏk'tāv') s. octava.

Oc·to·ber (ŏk-tō'bər) s. octubre *m*.

oc·to·ge·nar·i·an (ŏk'tə-jə-nâr'ē-ən) adj. & s. octogenario.

oc·to·pus (ŏk'tə-pəs) s. [pl. **es** *o* **-pi**] pulpo.

oc·tu·ple (ŏk'tə-pəl, ŏk-tōō'pəl) adj. óctuplo.

oc·u·lar (ŏk'yə-lər) adj. ocular.

oc·u·list (:lĭst) s. oculista *mf*.

OD (ō-dē') JER. **I.** s. dosis excesiva de drogas **II.** intr. **'d, 'ing** darse una dosis excesiva (on de).

odd (ŏd) adj. *(unusual)* raro, extraño; *(strange)* curioso; *(in excess of)* y pico; *(remaining)* de sobra; *(shoe, glove)* suelto; MAT. impar, non ♦ **at o. intervals** de rato en rato • **o. jobs** chapuces • **o. or even?** ¿pares o nones? • **the o. man out** la excepción.

odd·ball (ŏd'bôl') s. FAM. tipo raro, excéntrico.

odd·i·ty (ŏd'ĭ-tē) s. rareza, singularidad *f*.

odds (ŏdz) s.pl. *(advantage)* ventaja; *(chances)* probabilidades *f* ♦ **o. and ends** retazos • **the o. are against it** no es muy probable • **the o. are that** lo más probable es que • **to be at o. with** *(facts)* no concordar con; *(someone)* estar en punta con.

ode (ōd) s. oda.

o·di·ous (ō'dē-əs) adj. odioso.

o·di·um (:əm) s. odio, rencor *m*.

o·dom·e·ter (ō-dŏm'ĭ-tər) s. odómetro.

o·don·tol·o·gy (ō'dŏn-tŏl'ə-jē) s. odontología.

o·dor (ō'dər) s. olor *m*.

o·dor·less (ō'dər lĭs) adj. inodoro.

o·dor·ous (:əs) adj. *(fragrant)* fragante; *(malodorous)* maloliente, pestilente.

o·dour (ō'dər) G.B. var. de **odor**.

od·ys·sey (ŏd'ĭ-sē) s. odisea.

oe·nol·o·gy (ē-nŏl'ə-jē) s. enología.

of (ŏv, ŭv, əv) prep. de; *(time)* menos, para *‹it is ten minutes of four* las cuatro menos diez›; *(source)* de . . . parte *‹it is very kind of you* es muy gentil de su parte› ♦ **a friend of mine** un amigo mío • **all of them** todos ellos.

off (ôf) **I.** adv. *(distant)* lejos, a distancia; *(away)* a *‹a place five miles o.* un lugar a cinco millas (de distancia)› ♦ **o. and on** de vez en cuando • **o. with you!** ¡lárgate! • **ten per cent o.** diez por ciento de descuento • **to be o.** irse • **to be (two days) o.** faltar (dos días) para **II.** adj. *(lights, appliances)* apagado; *(not operating)* desconectado; *(canceled)* cancelado; *(productivity)* más bajo; *(quality, performance)* inferior; *(incorrect)* equivocado ♦ **in the o. position** en posición de cerrado • **o. chance** posibilidad remota • **to be o.** *(mistaken)* estar equivocado, *(from work)* estar libre • **to have an o. day** tener un día malo **III.** prep. *(from)* de *‹take your feet o. my desk* quita los pies de mi escritorio›; *(branching from)* de; *(near)* frente a, a la altura de *‹o. the coast* frente a la costa›; *(away from)* fuera, lejos de; *(down from)* desde, por *‹to fall o. a cliff* caer por un precipicio›; *(by means of)* gracias a, de *‹he lives o. his pension* vive de su pensión›.

of·fal (ô'fəl) s. *(entrails)* menudos; *(refuse)* desperdicios, desecho.

off·beat (ôf'bēt') **I.** s. MÚS. tiempo débil **II.** adj. JER. excéntrico, raro.

off·col·or (ôf'kŭl'ər) adj. *(improper)* de mal gusto; G.B. *(in bad spirits)* indispuesto.

of·fence (ə-fĕns') G.B. var. de **offense**.

of·fend (ə-fĕnd') tr. ofender ♦ **to be offended at** *o* **by** ofenderse por —intr. ser ofensivo.

of·fend·er (ə-fĕn'dər) s. infractor *m*.

of·fense (ə-fĕns') s. ofensa; *(crime)* delito; *(attack)* ofensiva; DEP. (ŏf'ĕns') equipo con la pelota ♦ **minor o.** delito leve • **no o. (intended)** sin intención de ofender • **second o.** reincidencia • **to give o.** ofender • **to take o. at** ofenderse por.

of·fen·sive (ə-fĕn'sĭv) **I.** adj. ofensivo; *(obscene)* grosero; *(unpleasant)* desagradable **II.** s. ofensiva ♦ **on the o.** a la ofensiva.

of·fer (ô'fər) **I.** tr. ofrecer; *(to propose)* proponer; *(for sale)* vender; *(resistance)* oponer; *(to provide)* proporcionar; *(to present)* presentar —intr. *(to volunteer)* ofrecerse (a); *(opportunity)* presentarse **II.** s. oferta.

of·fer·ing (:ĭng) s. oferta, ofrecimiento; *(donation)* donativo; RELIG. oblación *f*, ofrenda.

off·hand (ôf'hănd') **I.** adv. sin pensarlo ♦ **I can't recall o.** no recuerdo en este momento **II.** adj. improvisado; *(manner)* desenvuelto.

of·fice (ô'fĭs) s. oficina; *(room)* despacho; *(of a doctor)* consultorio; *(of a lawyer)* bufete *m*; *(department)* sección *f*, *(task)* oficio, deber *m*; POL. *(position)* cargo (público); *(Department)* ministerio ♦ **o. clerk** *o* **worker** oficinista • **o. hours** horario de oficina *o* consulta • **to be in o.** hold o. ocupar un cargo.

of·fice·hold·er (:hōl'dər) s. funcionario.

of·fi·cer (ô'fĭ-sər) s. oficial *m*, funcionario; *(in a company)* dirigente *m*; MARÍT., MIL. oficial *m*; *(policeman)* agente *m* de policía.

of·fi·cial (ə-fĭsh'əl) **I.** adj. oficial **II.** s. oficial *m*, funcionario; *(in a company)* dirigente *mf*; *(referee)* árbitro.

of·fi·cial·ese (-'ē-lēz') s. lenguaje burocrático.

of·fi·ci·ate (-'ē-āt') intr. RELIG. oficiar; *(to serve as)* hacer las veces de; DEP. arbitrar.

of·fi·cious (:əs) adj. oficioso.

off·ing (ô'fĭng) s. ♦ **in the o.** a la vista.

off·key (ôf'kē') adj. desafinado; FIG. fuera de tono.

off·lim·its (ôf'lĭm'ĭts) adj. prohibida la entrada.

off·line (ôf'līn') adj. que no se encuentra bajo el control de una computadora central.

off·sea·son (ôf'sē'zən) s. baja estación.

off·set I. tr. (ôf-sĕt') **-set, -tting** compensar; *(to*

counteract) contrarrestar **II.** s. ('') compensación *f;* IMPR. offset *m* ♦ **o. press** ófset.
off·shoot (ŏf'shōōt') s. ramal *m; (descendant)* vástago; BOT. retoño.
off·shore (ŏf'shôr') **I.** adj. de mar adentro; *(coastal)* costanero **II.** adv. mar adentro.
off·side *o* **off side** (ŏf'sīd') adj. fuera de juego.
off·spring (ŏf'sprĭng') s.inv. progenie *f,* prole *f.*
off-the-rack (ŏf'thə-răk') adj. de confección.
off-the-wall (ŏf'thə-wôl') adj. FAM. extraño.
off-white (ŏf'hwīt') adj. & s. (de) color crudo.
oft (ŏft) adv. frecuentemente, a menudo.
of·ten (ŏ'fən) adv. frecuentemente, a menudo ♦ **as o. as** no pocas veces • **every so o.** alguna que otra vez • **how o.?** ¿cuántas veces? • **more o. than not** la mayoría de las veces • **not very o.** pocas veces • **too o.** con demasiada frecuencia.
of·ten·times (:tīmz') adv. frecuentemente.
off-the-rec·ord (ŏf'thə-rĕk'ərd) adj. *(unofficial)* extraoficial; *(confidential)* confidencial.
o·gle (ŏ'gəl) tr. mirar con avidez.
o·gre (ŏ'gər) s. ogro.
oh (ō) interj. *(surprise)* ¡oh!; *(pain)* ¡ay!; *(understanding)* ¡ah! ‹*oh, I see* ¡ah, ya veo!›.
oil (oil) **I.** s. aceite *m; (fuel)* petróleo; *(lubricant)* aceite lubricante; ARTE. óleo ♦ **o. field, well** yacimiento, pozo petrolífero ♦ **o. paint** pintura al óleo **II.** tr. lubricar, aceitar.
oil·can (:kăn') s. aceitera, alcuza.
oil·cloth (:klôth') s. hule *m,* encerado.
oiled (oild) adj. lubricado, aceitado; JER. *(drunk)* borracho.
oil·skin (oil'skĭn') s. *(fabric)* hule *m; (garment)* impermeable *m.*
oil·y (oi'lē) adj. **-i- -i-** aceitoso, grasoso; FIG., FAM. *(unctuous)* untuoso.
oink (oingk) s. gruñido del cerdo.
oint·ment (oint'mənt) s. ungüento, pomada.
O.K. *o* **OK** *o* **o·kay** (ō-kā') **I.** s. [pl. **'s**] autorización *f* **II.** tr. **'d,** **'ing** aprobar, autorizar **III.** interj. ¡muy bien!, ¡de acuerdo!
o·kra (ō'krə) s. quingombó.
old (ōld) **I.** adj. viejo; *(elderly)* mayor, anciano; *(looking old)* envejecido; *(ancient, former)* antiguo ♦ **any o. thing** cualquier cosa • **any o. way** de cualquier manera • **older** mayor • **oldest** (el) mayor • **o. hat** pasado de moda • **o. maid** solterona • **o. wive's tale** cuento de viejas • **to be (ten years)** o. tener (diez años) de edad **II.** s. ♦ **of o.** de la antigüedad • **the o.** *(something)* lo viejo; *(people)* los ancianos.
old·en (ōl'dən) adj. antiguo, pasado.
old-fash·ioned (ōld'făsh'ənd) adj. anticuado; *(person)* chapado a la antigua.
old-line (:līn') adj. conservador, tradicional.
old·ster (:stər) s. FAM. viejo, anciano.
old-time (:tīm') adj. de antaño.
old-tim·er (:tī'mər) s. FAM. viejo, anciano.
old-world (:wûrld') adj. del viejo mundo.
o·le·o (ō'lē-ō') s. margarina.
o·le·o·mar·ga·rine ('--mär'jə-rĭn) s. oleomargarina.
ol·fac·to·ry (ŏl-făk'tə-rē) adj. olfativo.
ol·i·garch (ŏl'ĭgärk') s. oligarca *mf.*
ol·i·gar·chy (:gär'kē) s. oligarquía.
ol·ive (ŏl'ĭv) s. oliva, aceituna; *(color)* verde *m* olivo ♦ **o. oil** aceite de oliva • **o. tree** olivo.
O·lym·pic (ō-lĭm'pĭk) **I.** adj. olímpico **II.** s. ♦ pl. juegos olímpicos.
om·buds·man (ŏm'bŭdz'mən) s. [pl. **-men**] mediador *m* en asuntos de interés público.

om·e·let(te) (ŏm'ə-lĭt) s. tortilla.
o·men (ō'mən) s. presagio, agüero.
om·i·nous (ŏm'ə-nəs) adj. ominoso.
o·mis·sion (ō-mĭsh'ən) s. omisión *f; (error)* descuido.
o·mit (ō-mĭt') tr. **-tt-** omitir.
om·ni·bus (ŏm'nĭ-bŭs') **I.** s. ómnibus *m* **II.** adj. que incluye varias cosas.
om·nip·o·tence (ŏm-nĭp'ə-tns) s. omnipotencia.
om·nip·o·tent (:tnt) adj. omnipotente.
om·nis·cient (ŏm-nĭsh'ənt) adj. omnisciente.
on (ŏn) **I.** prep. *(general)* en; *(on top of)* sobre; *(to, onto)* a, sobre; *(upon)* al ‹*on entering the room* al entrar al cuarto›; *(against)* contra; *(according to)* según; *(for)* por ‹*to travel on business* viajar por negocios›; *(about)* en, sobre ♦ **on July third** el tres de julio • **on my authority** bajo mi autoridad **II.** adv. puesto ‹*with the lid on* con la tapa puesta› ♦ **on and off** de vez en cuando • **on and on** sin parar **III.** adj. *(appliance, lights)* prendido, encendido; *(gas, electricity)* encendido; *(faucet)* abierto; *(brakes, alarms)* puesto; *(planned)* planeado; *(in progress)* empezado, comenzado.
once (wŭns) **I.** adv. *(one time)* una vez; *(formerly)* en otro tiempo; antes; *(before)* hace tiempo ♦ **at o.** *(immediately)* inmediatamente; *(at the same time)* al mismo tiempo • **o. again** otra vez • **o. and for all** de una vez para siempre • **o. in a while** de vez en cuando • **o. more** otra vez • **o. upon a time** érase una vez **II.** s. una vez ♦ **for o.** una vez siquiera **III.** conj. una vez que, tan pronto como.
once-o·ver ('ō'vər) s. JER. revisada a la ligera.
on·col·o·gy (ŏn-kŏl'ə-jē) s. oncología.
on·com·ing (ŏn'kŭm'ĭng) adj. que viene.
one (wŭn) **I.** adj. un, uno; *(sole, only)* solo, único; *(the same)* mismo ♦ **o. and the same** el mismo • **o. hundred** cien • **the o. and only** el incomparable **II.** s. uno; *(unit)* unidad *f* ♦ **all in o.** de una sola pieza • **o'clock** la una • **to be o. up** tener la ventaja **III.** pron. dem. ♦ **that o.** aquél • **this o.** éste • **which o.?** ¿cuál? **IV.** pron. indef. uno; se ‹*o. doesn't do such things* esas cosas no se hacen› ♦ **I, for** o. yo, por lo menos • **o. and all** todos • **o.'s** de uno, su.
one-di·men·sion·al ('dĭ-mĕn'shə-nəl) adj. unidimensional.
one-man (:măn') adj. que consiste de un solo miembro; *(for, by one person)* para *o* de una sola persona.
one-piece (:pēs') adj. enterizo.
on·er·ous (ŏn'ər-əs, ō'nər-) adj. oneroso.
one·self (wŭn-sĕlf') pron. sí (mismo), uno (mismo); *(reflexively)* se ‹*to brace o. for something* prepararse para algo›; *(emphatically)* uno mismo ♦ **by o.** solo • **to come to o.** volver en sí.
one-shot (:shŏt') adj. único, que no se repite.
one-sid·ed (:sī'dĭd) adj. *(biased)* parcial; *(unequal)* desigual.
one·time (:tīm') adj. antiguo.
one-time (:tīm') adj. de una sola vez.
one-to-one (:tə-wŭn') adj. MAT. exacto.
one-track (:trăk') adj. ♦ **to have a o. mind** no poder pensar más que en una sola cosa.
one-up·man·ship (-ŭp'mən-shĭp') s. FAM. arte *m* de superar a competidores.
one-way (:wā') adj. *(street)* de sentido único; *(ticket)* de ida solamente.

on·go·ing (ŏn'gō'ĭng) adj. *(current)* actual; *(in progress)* en marcha.

on·ion (ŭn'yən) s. cebolla.

on·ion-skin (:skĭn') s. papel *m* cebolla.

on·line (ŏn'līn') adj. bajo el control de una computadora central.

on·look·er (ŏn'lŏŏk'ər) s. espectador *m*.

on·ly (ōn'lē) I. adj. *(sole)* único, solo; *(best)* mejor II. adv. *(merely)* sólo; *(simply)* simplemente; *(solely)* únicamente; para luego <they received a raise o. to be laid off recibieron un aumento para luego ser despedidos> ♦ it o. ojalá ♦ not o....but also no sólo...sino también ♦ o. too muy III. conj. *(except that)* sólo que; *(but)* pero <you may go, o. be careful puedes ir, pero ten cuidado>.

on·rush (ŏn'rŭsh') s. arremetida, embestida.

on·shore (ŏn'shŏr') adj. & adv. *(que se dirige)* hacia la costa o a la tierra.

on·slaught (ŏn'slôt') s. ataque violento.

on·to (ŏn'tŏŏ) prep. *(upon)* sobre, encima de; FAM. *(aware of)* al tanto de, al corriente de.

o·nus (ō'nəs) s. carga, obligación *f*.

on·ward (ŏn'wərd) adj. & adv. hacia adelante.

on·wards (ŏn'wərdz) adv. hacia adelante.

on·yx (ŏn'ĭks) s. ónix *m*.

oo·dles (ōōd'lz) s.pl. FAM. montones *m*.

oomph (ŏŏmf) s. JER. vitalidad *f*, energía.

oops (ōōps, ŏŏps) interj. usado para expresar sorpresa o consternación.

ooze[1] (ōōz) tr. rezumar, supurar; *(confidence, charm)* rebozar de —intr. rezumarse, fluir.

ooze[2] s. *(soft mud)* cieno, lama.

o·pal (ō'pəl) s. ópalo.

o·pal·es·cence (ō'pə-lĕs'əns) s. opalescencia.

o·paque (ō-pāk') adj. opaco; *(obtuse)* obtuso.

o·pen (ō'pən) I. adj. abierto; *(fields)* descampado; *(view)* libre, despejado; *(without covering)* descubierto; *(without top)* destapado; *(meeting, court)* público; *(unrestricted)* sin restricción; *(job, post)* vacante, libre; *(question)* pendiente; *(frank)* franco, sincero; *(mind)* sin prejuicios; *(port)* libre, franco ♦ for business abierto al público ♦ o. house recepción general ♦ o. secret secreto a voces ♦ o. sesame! ¡ábrete sésamo! ♦ to be o. to *(ideas, criticism)* estar dispuesto a recibir; *(doubt, interpretation)* admitir, permitir; *(to be vulnerable to)* estar expuesto a II. tr. abrir; *(to unfasten)* desatar; *(way, path)* despejar; *(to unblock)* desatascar; *(to uncover)* destapar; *(to unwrap)* desempaquetar; *(to unfold)* desplegar; *(to begin)* iniciar; *(a business)* establecer ♦ to o. out ensanchar ♦ to o. up *(to make available)* hacer accesible; *(to explore)* explorar —intr. abrirse; *(to come undone)* desatarse; *(halfway)* entreabrirse; *(to unfold)* desplegarse; *(a business)* establecerse; *(to begin)* empezar, comenzar <we opened with a list of complaints comenzamos con una lista de quejas>; TEAT. estrenarse ♦ to o. into dar a ♦ to o. on(to) dar a ♦ to o. out *(to unfold)* desplegar(se); *(to extend)* extenderse ♦ to o. up *(to spread out)* extenderse; *(to begin)* empezar; *(to speak freely)* desplegarse III. s. claro, lugar abierto ♦ in the o. *(outdoors)* al aire libre; *(in the country)* en el campo; *(in a clear space)* a campo abierto; *(revealed)* descubierto ♦ to bring, come into the o. sacar, salir a la luz.

o·pen-air ('-âr') adj. al aire libre.

o·pen-and-shut (:ən-shŭt') adj. simple.

o·pen-end·ed (:-ĕn'dĭd) adj. abierto, ilimitado.

o·pen·er (ō'pə-nər) s. abridor *m*; TEAT. primer

acto ♦ for openers para comenzar.

o·pen·hand·ed (ō'pən-hăn'dĭd) adj. maniabierto.

o·pen·ing (ō'pə-nĭng) s. *(aperture)* abertura, orificio; *(breach)* grieta; *(clearing)* claro; *(beginning)* apertura, comienzo; *(of a movie, play)* estreno; *(of a store, exhibition)* inauguración *f*, *(chance)* oportunidad *f*; *(job)* puesto, vacante *f*; POL. apertura ♦ o. ceremonies actos de inauguración ♦ o. night noche de estreno.

o·pen-mind·ed (ō'pən-mīn'dĭd) adj. receptivo.

op·er·a (ŏp'ər-ə) s. ópera ♦ o. glasses gemelos de teatro ♦ o. house ópera.

op·er·a·ble (ŏp'ər-ə-bəl) s. operable; *(functional)* que funciona.

op·er·ate (ŏp'ə-rāt') intr. *(to work)* funcionar; *(to have an effect)* actuar; CIR., MIL. operar; COM. efectuar operaciones —tr. *(to drive)* manejar; *(tool)* usar; *(machinery)* trabajar en, ocuparse de; *(appliance, device)* hacer funcionar, accionar; *(business)* manejar, administrar ♦ operated by que funciona con.

op·er·at·ing (ŏp'ə-rā'tĭng) adj. *(operational)* que funciona; *(profit, expenses)* de explotación; *(costs)* de mantenimiento ♦ o. room sala de operaciones.

op·er·a·tion (ŏp'ə-rā'shən) s. operación *f*; *(condition)* funcionamiento; *(of vehicles, tools)* manejo; *(management)* administración *f*; *(effect)* acción *f*, efecto; *(undertaking)* maniobra ♦ method of o. procedimiento ♦ to be in o. estar funcionando.

op·er·a·tion·al (:shə-nəl) adj. de operación; *(in working order)* en condiciones de servicio; *(functioning)* en funcionamiento.

op·er·a·tive (ŏp'ər-ə-tĭv') I. adj. *(effective)* operativo, operante; *(functioning)* en condiciones de servicio; *(law)* en vigor; CIR. operatorio II. s. *(worker)* operario; *(agent)* agente secreto.

op·er·a·tor (ŏp'ə-rā'tər) s. *(of a machine)* operario; TEL. telefonista *mf*; *(of a vehicle)* conductor *m*; *(manager)* administrador *m*; *(dealer)* agente *m*; FAM. *(clever person)* maquinador *m*.

op·er·et·ta (ŏp'ə-rĕt'ə) s. opereta.

oph·thal·mol·o·gist (ŏf'thăl-mŏl'ə-jĭst, ŏp'-) s. oftalmólogo.

oph·thal·mol·o·gy (:jē) s. oftalmología.

o·pi·ate (ō'pē-ĭt) s. opiato.

o·pine (ō-pīn') tr. opinar.

o·pin·ion (ə-pĭn'yən) s. opinión *f* ♦ in my o. a mi juicio ♦ in the o. of según.

o·pin·ion·at·ed (:yə-nā'tĭd) adj. obstinado.

o·pi·um (ō'pē-əm) s. opio.

o·pos·sum (ə-pŏs'əm) s. [pl. inv. o s] ZOOL. zarigüeya.

op·po·nent (ə-pō'nənt) s. adversario.

op·por·tune (ŏp'ər-tŏŏn') adj. oportuno.

op·por·tun·ist (:tŏŏ'nĭst) s. oportunista *mf*.

op·por·tu·ni·ty (:nĭ-tē) s. oportunidad *f*.

op·pose (ə-pōz') tr. oponerse a; *(to combat)* hacer frente a; *(to set against)* contraponer.

op·po·site (ŏp'ə-zĭt) I. adj. opuesto; *(direction)* contrario; *(across from)* de enfrente; *(opinions)* contrario ♦ on the o. side of del otro lado de II. s. contrario ♦ it is just the o. es todo lo contrario III. adv. enfrente ♦ to be directly o. estar frente a IV. prep. enfrente de, frente a.

op·po·si·tion (:-zĭsh'ən) s. oposición *f*; *(resistance)* resistencia; POL. *(partido de la)* oposición ♦ to act in o. to obrar en contra de ♦ to be in o. to estar en contra de.

op·press (ə-prĕs') tr. *(to subjugate)* oprimir;

(mind, spirit) deprimir; FIG. agobiar.

op·pres·sion (ǝ-prĕsh'ǝn) s. opresión *f.*

op·pres·sive (ǝ-prĕs'ĭv) adj. opresivo; *(tyrannical)* tiránico; *(feeling)* agobiador.

op·pres·sor (:ǝr) s. opresor *m.*

op·pro·bri·um (ǝ-prō'brē-ǝm) s. oprobio.

opt (ŏpt) intr. optar *(for, to* por).

op·tic (ŏp'tĭk) adj. óptico ♦ **optics** s.sg. óptica.

op·ti·cal (ŏp'tĭ-kǝl) adj. óptico.

op·ti·cian (ŏp-tĭsh'ǝn) s. óptico.

op·ti·mism (ŏp'tǝ-mĭz'ǝm) s. optimismo.

op·ti·mist (:mĭst) s. optimista *mf.*

op·ti·mis·tic ('-mĭs'tĭk) adj. optimista ♦ **to feel o.** tener optimismo.

op·ti·mize ('-mīz') tr. mejorar en todo lo posible; *(results)* hacer rendir lo más posible.

op·ti·mum (:mǝm) **I.** s. ♦ **the o.** lo óptimo **II.** adj. óptimo.

op·tion (ŏp'shǝn) s. opción *f.*

op·tion·al (ŏp'shǝ-nǝl) adj. opcional.

op·tom·e·trist (ŏp-tŏm'ĭ-trĭst) s. optómetra *mf.*

op·tom·e·try (:trē) s. optometría.

op·u·lence (ŏp'yǝ-lǝns) s. opulencia.

op·u·lent (:lǝnt) adj. opulento.

o·pus (ō'pǝs) s. [pl. **es** *o* **opera**] MÚS. opus *m;* LIT. obra.

or (ôr) conj. o; *[before* (h)o] u; *[after negative]* ni <*I don't drink or smoke* ni tomo ni fumo>.

or·a·cle (ôr'ǝ-kǝl) s. oráculo.

o·rac·u·lar (ǝ-rãk'yǝ-lǝr) adj. profético.

o·ral (ôr'ǝl) **I.** adj. oral ♦ **o. hygiene** higiene bucal **II.** s. examen *m* oral.

or·ange (ôr'ĭnj) **I.** s. naranja; *(tree)* naranjo ♦ **o. blossom** azahar • **o. grove** naranjal **II.** adj. anaranjado.

o·rang·u·tan (ǝ-răng'ǝ-tǎn') s. orangután *m.*

o·rate (ô-rāt') intr. declamar.

o·ra·tion (ô-rā'shǝn) s. oración *f.*

or·a·tor (ôr'ǝ-tǝr) s. orador *m.*

or·a·tor·i·cal ('-tôr'ĭ-kǝl) adj. oratorio.

or·a·to·ry¹ (ôr'ǝ-tôr'ē) s. *(rhetoric)* oratoria.

or·a·to·ry² s. *(chapel)* oratorio.

orb (ôrb) s. orbe *m.*

or·bit (ôr'bĭt) **I.** s. órbita ♦ **to go into o.** entrar en órbita **II.** tr. girar alrededor de; *(a satellite)* poner en órbita —intr. *(to revolve)* girar, dar vueltas; *(to be in orbit)* estar en órbita.

or·bit·al (ôr'bĭ-tl) adj. orbital.

or·chard (ôr'chǝrd) s. huerto.

or·ches·tra (ôr'kĭ-strǝ) s. orquesta ♦ **o. seats** butacas de platea.

or·ches·tral (ôr-kĕs'trǝl) adj. orquestal.

or·ches·trate (ôr'kĭ-strāt') tr. MÚS. orquestar; *(to organize)* organizar.

or·ches·tra·tion ('-strā'shǝn) s. orquestación *f.*

or·chid (ôr'kĭd) s. orquídea; *(color)* malva *m.*

or·dain (ôr-dān') tr. ordenar; *(to predestine)* disponer, predestinar.

or·deal (ôr-dēl') s. *(trial)* prueba dura; *(torment)* sufrimiento.

or·der (ôr'dǝr) **I.** s. orden *m;* *(arrangement)* disposición *f;* *(procedure)* regla; *(decree, command)* orden *f;* COM. pedido <*to place an o. for* hacer un pedido de>; *(goods)* mercancía; *(of food)* porción *f;* *(organization)* orden *f,* sociedad *f;* *(kind)* tipo, índole *f;* *(rank)* categoría; DER. mandamiento, orden *f* del juez; RELIG. orden *f;* MAT. grado ♦ **in bad o.** desordenado • **in good o.** en buen estado • **in o.** *(in place)* en orden; *(in good condition)* en buenas condiciones; *(in a meeting)* aceptable; *(appropriate)*

pertinente • **in o. that** a fin de que, para que • **in o. to** a fin de, para • **in short o.** pronto • **out of o.** *(out of place)* en desorden; *(not working)* descompuesto; *(in a meeting)* inaceptable; *(inappropriate)* impertinente • **pay to the o. of** páguese a la orden de **II.** tr. *(to command, arrange)* ordenar; *(to request)* pedir —intr. *(command)* dar una orden; *(request)* hacer un pedido.

or·der·ly (:lē) **I.** adj. *(neat)* ordenado, en orden; *(conduct)* pacífico **II.** s. MED. ayudante *m;* MIL. ordenanza *m* **III.** adv. sistemáticamente.

or·di·nal (ôr'dn-ǝl) adj. & s. (número) ordinal.

or·di·nance (ôr'dn-ǝns) s. *(order)* ordenanza; *(statute)* estatuto.

or·di·nar·y (ôr'dn-ĕr'ē) adj. ordinario; *(plain)* corriente, cualquiera; *(average)* medio ♦ **out of the o.** fuera de lo común, extraordinario.

or·di·nate (:ĭt) s. ordenada.

or·di·na·tion ('-ā'shǝn) s. ordenación *f.*

ord·nance (ôrd'nǝns) s. armamentos, equipos de guerra; *(artillery)* artillería.

ore (ôr) s. mineral *m,* mena.

o·reg·a·no (ǝ-rĕg'ǝ-nō') s. orégano.

or·gan (ôr'gǝn) s. órgano; *(agency)* organismo.

or·gan·dy/die (ôr'gǝn-dē) s. organdí *m.*

or·gan·ic (ôr-gǎn'ĭk) adj. orgánico.

or·gan·ism (ôr'gǝ-nĭz'ǝm) s. organismo.

or·gan·ist (ôr'gǝ-nĭst) s. organista *mf.*

or·gan·i·za·tion (ôr'gǝ-nĭ-zā'shǝn) s. organización *f;* *(group)* organismo.

or·gan·i·za·tion·al (:shǝ-nǝl) adj. de una organización.

or·gan·ize (ôr'gǝ-nīz') tr. organizar; *(to arrange)* arreglar, ordenar —intr. organizarse.

or·gan·iz·er (:nī'zǝr) s. organizador *m.*

or·gan·za (ôr-gǎn'zǝ) s. organdí *m.*

or·gasm (ôr'gǎz'ǝm) s. orgasmo.

or·gi·as·tic (ôr'jē-ǎs'tĭk) adj. orgiástico.

or·gy (ôr'jē) s. orgía.

o·ri·ent (ôr'ē-ǝnt) **I.** s. oriente *m* **II.** tr. (:ĕnt') orientar ♦ **to o. oneself** orientarse.

o·ri·en·tal ('-ĕn'tl) adj. & s. oriental *mf.*

o·ri·en·tate (ôr'ē-ĕn-tāt') tr. orientar.

o·ri·en·ta·tion ('-tā'shǝn) s. orientación *f.*

or·i·fice (ôr'ǝ-fĭs) s. orificio.

or·i·gin (ôr'ǝ-jĭn) s. origen *m;* *(of a flight, object)* procedencia ♦ **to have its origins in** originarse.

o·rig·i·nal (ǝ-rĭj'ǝ-nǝl) **I.** adj. original; *(first)* primero; *(authentic)* legítimo; *(inventive)* creativo **II.** s. persona *o* modelo original; ARTE. original *m.*

o·rig·i·nal·i·ty ('-nǎl'ĭ-tē) s. originalidad *f.*

o·rig·i·nate ('-nāt') tr. *(to introduce)* crear —intr. *(to invent)* crear —intr. *(to start)* originarse, surgir; *(family)* ser originario *u* oriundo de.

o·rig·i·na·tion ('-nā'shǝn) s. origen *m.*

o·rig·i·na·tor ('-'tǝr) s. autor *m,* creador *m.*

o·ri·ole (ôr'ē-ōl') s. oriol *m.*

or·na·ment (ôr'nǝ-mǝnt) **I.** s. ornamento **II.** tr. ornamentar.

or·na·men·tal ('-mĕn'tl) adj. ornamental.

or·na·men·ta·tion (:mĕn-tā'shǝn) s. ornamentación *f;* *(decoration)* ornamento.

or·nate (ôr-nāt') adj. recargado.

or·ner·y (ôr'nǝ-rē) adj. -i- FAM. terco.

or·ni·thol·o·gy (ôr'nǝ-thŏl'ǝ-jē) s. ornitología.

or·phan (ôr'fǝn) **I.** s. & adj. huérfano **II.** tr. dejar huérfano.

or·phan·age (ôr'fǝ-nĭj) s. orfanato, orfelinato.

or·tho·don·tics (ôr'thə·dŏn'tĭks) s.sg. ortodoncia.

or·tho·dox (ôr'thə·dŏks') adj. ortodoxo.

or·tho·dox·y (:dŏk'sē) s. ortodoxia.

or·tho·graph·ic ('-grăf'ĭk) adj. ortográfico.

or·thog·ra·phy (ôr·thŏg'rə·fē) s. ortografía.

or·tho·p(a)e·dic (ôr'thə·pē'dĭk) adj. ortopédico ♦ orthop(a)edics s.sg. ortopedia.

os·cil·late (ŏs'ə·lāt') intr. oscilar.

os·cil·la·tion ('-lā'shən) s. oscilación f.

os·mo·sis (ŏz·mō'sĭs) s. ósmosis f.

os·si·fy (ŏs'ə·fī') tr. & intr. osificar(se).

os·su·ar·y (ŏsh'o͞o·ĕr'ē) s. osario.

os·ten·si·ble (ŏ·stĕn'sə·bəl) adj. ostensible.

os·ten·ta·tion (ŏs'tĕn·tā'shən) s. ostentación f.

os·ten·ta·tious (:shəs) s. ostentoso.

os·te·o·path (ŏs'tē·ə·păth') osteópata mf.

os·te·op·a·thy ('-ŏp'ə·thē) s. osteopatía.

os·tra·cism (ŏs'trə·sĭz'əm) s. ostracismo.

os·tra·cize (:sīz') tr. condenar al ostracismo.

os·trich (ŏs'trĭch) s. [pl. inv. o **es**] avestruz m.

oth·er (ŭth'ər) I. adj. otro; (additional) demás; (different) distinto ♦ o. people otros II. s. otro ♦ no o. ningún otro • no o. than nadie más que III. pron. otro <something or o. una cosa u otra> ♦ sometime or o. cualquier día IV. adv. ♦ o. than (differently to of otro modo); (anything but) otra cosa que.

oth·er·wise (:wīz') I. adv. (differently to of otro modo; (under other circumstances) de lo contrario, si no <o. I would have gone de lo contrario habría ido>; (in other respects) por lo demás, a no ser por eso II. adj. diferente, otro.

ot·ter (ŏt'ər) s. [pl. inv. o **s**] nutria.

ot·to·man (ŏt'ə·mən) s. otomana.

ouch (ouch) interj. ¡ay!

ought (ôt) aux. (to be obliged) deber; (to be wise) convenir, ser conveniente <you o. to wear a raincoat conviene que lleves una gabardina>; (to be desirable) tener que; (to be likely) deber de.

ounce (ouns) s. onza; FIG. pizca, poquito.

our (our) adj. pos. nuestro.

ours (ourz) pron. pos. (el) nuestro.

our·selves (:sĕlvz') pron. nos <we should wash o. debemos lavarnos>; nosotros (mismos) <we did it o. lo hicimos nosotros mismos>.

oust (oust) tr. expulsar.

oust·er (ou'stər) s. expulsión f.

out (out) I. adv. (away from) fuera <o. of the office fuera de la oficina>, (outside) afuera; hasta el final <to argue it o. discutirlo hasta el final>; (on strike) en huelga ♦ all o, con tesón • o. and o. completamente • o. for empeñado en • to be o. (not at home) no estar en casa; (sun, moon) haber salido; (eliminated) quedar excluido; POL. estar fuera del poder II. adj. (exterior) exterior; (absent) ausente; (used up) agotado; (extinguished) apagado; (impossible) impossible <that's o. eso es imposible>; (not in fashion) fuera de moda III. prep. (through) por; (beyond) fuera de, al otro lado de ♦ o. of de <to take o. of sacar de>; (without) sin <o. of money sin dinero>; (because of) por <o. of curiosity por curiosidad>; (from among) de cada IV. s. FAM. (way out) salida; (excuse) excusa ♦ on the outs FAM. enemistado V. intr. descubrirse VI. interj. ¡fuera!

out·age (ou'tĭj) s. corte m de electricidad.

out-and-out (out'n-out') adj. completo, total.

out·bid (-bĭd') tr. -bid, -bid(den), -dd- superar a, ofrecer más que.

out·board ('bôrd') adj. fuera de borda.

out·bound (:bound') adj. de salida, que sale.

out·break (:brāk') s. brote m.

out·burst (:bûrst') s. arranque m, estallido.

out·cast (:kăst') s. paria mf.

out·class (-klăs') tr. ser muy superior a.

out·come ('kum') s. resultado, consecuencia.

out·crop (:krŏp') s. afloramiento

out·cry (:krī') s. protesta; (clamor) alboroto.

out·dat·ed (-dā'tĭd) adj. obsoleto, anticuado.

out·dis·tance (:dĭs'təns) tr. dejar atrás.

out·do (:do͞o') tr. -did, -done superar.

out·door ('dôr') adj. al aire libre.

out·doors (-dôrz') I. adv. al aire libre, (outside) (a)fuera II. s. el aire libre.

out·doors·man (:mən) s. [pl. -men] hombre m que gusta del aire libre, la pesca o la caza.

out·er (ou'tər) adj. exterior, externo ♦ o. ear oído externo • o. space espacio exterior.

out·er·most (:mōst') adj. más alejado.

out·fit (out'fĭt') I. s. (clothing) conjunto; FAM. (military unit) unidad f; (business) empresa II. tr. -tt- equipar.

out·flank (-flăngk') tr. desbordar el flanco de; (to outwit) aventajar tácticamente.

out·flow (:flō') s. flujo.

out·fox (-fŏks') tr. ganar en astucia, burlar.

out·go·ing ('gō'ĭng) adj. de salida, que sale; (retiring) saliente; (friendly) sociable.

out·grow (-grō') tr. -grew, -grown crecer más que; (interests, ideas) perder ♦ to o. one's clothes quedarle la ropa chica a uno.

out·growth ('grōth') s. brote m; FIG. resultado.

out·guess (-gĕs') tr. anticipar.

out·house ('hous') s. excusado, retrete m.

out·ing (:ĭng) s. excursión f.

out·land·ish (-lăn'dĭsh) adj. extravagante.

out·last (:lăst') tr. durar más que.

out·law ('lô') I. s. malhechor m, criminal m; (fugitive) forajido II. tr. prohibir.

out·lay (out'lā') s. desembolso, gastos.

out·let ('lĕt') s. salida; (socket) tomacorriente m; (for feelings) forma de desahogar; (for energies) forma de descargar; COM. (market) salida; (store) distribuidor m.

out·line (:līn') I. s. (contour) contorno; (profile) perfil m; (shape) silueta; (summary) resumen m; ARTE. bosquejo; TEC. trazado ♦ in broad o. en líneas generales II. tr. trazar las líneas o los contornos de; (to profile) perfilar; (to describe) trazar a grandes rasgos; (to summarize) resumir; (to sketch) bosquejar.

out·live (liv') tr. sobrevivir.

out·look ('lo͝ok') s. punto de vista; (attitude) actitud f; (prospect) posibilidades f.

out·ly·ing (:lī'ĭng) adj. alejado del centro ♦ the o. suburbs las afueras de la ciudad.

out·ma·neu·ver ('mə·no͞o'vər) tr. ganar en astucia; AUTO. moverse mejor que.

out·mod·ed (-mō'dĭd) adj. anticuado.

out·num·ber (:nŭm'bər) tr. superar en número.

out-of-date ('əv·dāt') adj. (outmoded) anticuado; (expired) caducado.

out-of-the-way (:thə·wā') adj. (remote) apartado; (secluded) solitario; (unusual) insólito.

out·pa·tient (out'pā'shənt) s. paciente mf que no está hospitalizado.

out·post (:pōst') s. MIL. puesto avanzado; (settlement) puesto fronterizo.

out·pour·ing (:pôr'ĭng) s. efusión f.

out·put (:pŏōt´) s. producción f; (energy) potencia; (yield) rendimiento; COMPUT. salida.

out·rage (:rāj´) I. s. ultraje m; (destructive act) atropello; (anger) indignación f ♦ **an o. against** un atentado contra II. tr. indignar.

out·ra·geous (-rā´jəs) adj. ultrajante; (flagrant) flagrante; (infuriating) indignante; (exorbitant) excesivo.

out·rank (-răngk´) tr. tener un rango superior a; (to surpass) ser superior a.

out·reach (´rēch´) s. servicio especial de asistencia pública.

out·right (:rīt´) I. adv. (frankly) sin reservas; (obviously) patentemente; (utterly) absolutamente; (straightaway) en el acto II. adj. (unqualified) sin reservas; (obvious) patente; (outandout) absoluto <o. viciousness maldad absoluta>.

out·run (-rŭn´) tr. **-ran, -run, -nn-** (to outstrip) dejar rezagado; (to escape) librarse de.

out·sell (:sĕl´) tr. **-sold** vender más que o mejor que; (a product) venderse mejor que.

out·set (´sĕt´) s. principio, inicio.

out·shine (-shīn´) tr. **-shone** brillar más que; FIG. superar.

out·side (out-sīd´) I. s. exterior m; (appearance) superficie f ♦ **at the o.** como mucho o máximo ♦ **from, on the o.** desde, por fuera II. adj. exterior <o. assistance ayuda exterior>; (estimate) máximo; (influence) de afuera; (chance) remoto III. adv. (a)fuera <to stay o. ir afuera>; (outdoors) en o a la calle IV. prep. fuera de ♦ **o.** of fuera de; (except) excepto.

out·sid·er (-sī´dər) s. forastero.

out·skirts (´skûrts´) s.pl. afueras.

out·smart (-smärt´) tr. ser más astuto que.

out·spend (spĕnd´) tr. **-spent** gastar más que.

out·spo·ken (:-spō´kən) adj. abierto, franco ♦ **to be o.** no tener pelos en la lengua.

out·spread (-sprĕd´) I. tr. extender, desplegar II. adj. extendido, desplegado.

out·stand·ing (´stăn´dĭng) adj. sobresaliente; (prominent) destacado; (superior) excelente; (not resolved) pendiente.

out·stretched (:strĕcht´) adj. extendido.

out·strip (:strĭp´) tr. **-pp-** (to leave behind) dejar atrás; (to exceed) sobrepasar.

out·take (´tāk´) s. CINEM. toma de película no utilizada.

out·ward (:wərd) I. adj. exterior, externo; (direction) hacia afuera; (superficial) superficial; (journey) de ida II. adv. o **-wards** hacia afuera.

out·weigh (-wā´) tr. pesar más que.

out·wit (:wĭt´) tr. **-tt-** ser más vivo que, burlar.

o·val (ō´vəl) I. adj. ovalado, oval II. s. óvalo.

o·va·ry (ō´və-rē) s. ovario.

o·va·tion (ō-vā´shən) s. ovación f.

ov·en (ŭv´ən) s. horno.

o·ver (ō´vər) I. prep. sobre; (above) encima de; (across, on, higher than) por encima de <to jump o. the fence saltar por encima de la valla>; (on the other side of) al otro lado de; (throughout) por todo, a través de; (so as to cover or close) para tapar o cerrar; (during) durante <o. the past two years durante los dos últimos años>; (more than) más de o que; (in preference to) antes que; (by means of) por medio de <o. the telephone por teléfono> II. adv. (above) (por) encima; (across) al otro lado, enfrente; allá <o. in Europe allá en Europa>; (again) otra vez, de nuevo; (more) más <ten times o. diez veces más> ♦ **o. again** otra vez, de nuevo ♦ **o. and**

above además de ♦ **o. and o.** una y otra vez ♦ **o. here, there** aquí, allá ♦ **o. with** FAM. acabado III. adj. terminado, acabado.

o·ver·a·bun·dance (´-ə-bŭn´dəns) s. exceso.

o·ver·act (:ăkt´) tr. & intr. exagerar.

o·ver·all o **o·ver·all** (:ōl´) I. adj. total II. adv. en general, generalmente.

o·ver·alls (´-ôlz´) s.pl. mono, overol m.

o·ver·bear·ing (´-bâr´ĭng) adj. (overwhelming) avasallador; (arrogant) arrogante.

o·ver·bid (´-bĭd´) s. oferta mayor.

o·ver·bite (:bīt´) s. oclusión defectuosa.

o·ver·blown (´-blōn´) adj. inflado, pomposo.

o·ver·board (´-bôrd´) adv. por la borda ♦ **man o.!** ¡hombre al agua! ♦ **to go o.** FAM. irse la mano.

o·ver·book (´-bŏŏk´) tr. & intr. vender más localidades de las que hay disponibles (en).

o·ver·bur·den (:bûr´dn) tr. sobrecargar.

o·ver·cast (´kăst´) adj. nublado.

o·ver·cau·tious (´-kô´shəs) adj. demasiado cauteloso.

o·ver·charge I. tr. & intr. (´-chärj´) cobrar demasiado II. s. (´-´) precio excesivo.

o·ver·coat (´-kōt´) s. sobretodo, abrigo.

o·ver·come (´-kŭm´) tr. **-came, -come** (to defeat) derrotar, conquistar; (to overwhelm) abrumar; (obstacle, difficulty) superar ♦ **to be o. by** estar afectado profundamente o.

o·ver·com·pen·sate (´-kŏm´pən-sāt´) tr. & intr. sobrecompensar.

o·ver·con·fi·dent (:kŏn´fĭ-dnt) adj. demasiado confiado.

o·ver·do (:dōō´) tr. **-did, -done** hacer demasiado; (diet, exercise) exagerar; (food) cocinar demasiado —intr. hacer demasiado.

o·ver·dose I. s. (´dōs´) dosis excesiva II. tr. & intr. (´-´) dar(se) una dosis excesiva (on de).

o·ver·draft (´-drăft´) s. giro en descubierto.

o·ver·draw (´-drô´) tr. **-drew, -drawn** girar en descubierto.

o·ver·drawn (:-drôn´) adj. al descubierto.

o·ver·dress (:drĕs´) intr. vestirse con más lujo de lo necesario.

o·ver·drive (´-drīv´) s. sobremarcha.

o·ver·due (:-dōō´) adj. (unpaid) vencido (en el pago); (delayed) retrasado.

o·ver·eat (:ēt´) intr. **-ate, -eaten** comer demasiado.

o·ver·em·pha·size (:ĕm´fə-sīz´) tr. & intr. dar demasiado énfasis (a).

o·ver·es·ti·mate (:ĕs´tə-māt´) tr. sobreestimar.

o·ver·ex·pose (:ĭk-spōz´) tr. exponer demasiado; FOTOG. sobreexponer.

o·ver·ex·po·sure (:ĭk-spō´zhər) s. (publicity) publicidad excesiva; FOTOG. sobreexposición f.

o·ver·ex·tend (:ĭk-stĕnd´) tr. extender o ampliar demasiado.

o·ver·flow I. intr. (´-flō´) desbordarse ♦ **to o. with** rebosar de —tr. desbordar, salirse de; (to flood) inundar II. s. (´-´) (flood) inundación f; (excess) exceso; (outlet) desagüe m.

o·ver·grown (´-grōn´) adj. cubierto (with de).

o·ver·hang I. tr. (´-hăng´) -hung sobresalir o colgar por encima de II. s. (´-´) saliente m.

o·ver·haul I. tr. (´-hôl´) hacer una reparación general de II. s. (´-´) reparación f general.

o·ver·head (´-hĕd´) I. adj. de arriba; (light) del techo; (railway) elevado; (wire) aéreo; COM. general II. s. COM. gastos generales III. adv. (above) arriba; (up) para o hacia arriba.

o·ver·hear ('-hîr') tr. **-heard** oír por casualidad.
o·ver·heat ('-hēt') tr. & intr. recalentar(se).
o·ver·in·dulge (:ĭn-dŭlj') tr. *(child)* consentir; *(appetite)* saciar —intr. ♦ **to o. in** abusar de.
o·ver·in·dul·gence (:ĭn-dŭl'jəns) s. *(permissiveness)* consentimiento excesivo; *(gratification)* exceso, falta de control.
o·ver·joyed (:joid') adj. loco de contento.
o·ver·kill s. ('-kĭl') s. MIL. capacidad excesiva de represalia nuclear; FIG. medidas excesivas.
o·ver·lap ('-lăp') tr. & intr. **-pp-** superponerse (a); *(in time, function)* coincidir en parte (con).
o·ver·lay I. tr. ('-lā') **-laid** cubrir, extender sobre; ARTE. revestir II. s. ('-') revestimiento.
o·ver·load I. tr. ('-lōd') sobrecargar II. s. sobrecarga.
o·ver·look ('-lŏŏk') I. tr. mirar desde lo alto; *(to rise above)* dominar; *(view, window)* dar a, tener vista a; *(to disregard)* pasar por alto; *(to supervise)* supervisar II. s. mirador *m.*
o·ver·ly (:lē) adv. demasiado.
o·ver·much ('-mŭch') I. adj. demasiado, excesivo II. adv. excesivamente.
o·ver·night (:nīt') I. adj. *(guests)* por la noche; *(sudden)* repentino, inesperado ♦ **o. bag** maletín de viaje II. adv. durante o por la noche; *(suddenly)* de la noche a la mañana ♦ **to stay o.** pasar la noche.
o·ver·pass ('-păs') s. paso superior, puente *m.*
o·ver·pay ('-pā') tr. **-paid** pagar demasiado (por).
o·ver·play (:plā') tr. exagerar.
o·ver·pop·u·la·tion (:pŏp'yə-lā'shən) s. superpoblación *f.*
o·ver·pow·er (:pou'ər) tr. abrumar.
o·ver·pow·er·ing (:ĭng) adj. *(overwhelming)* abrumador; *(irresistible)* irresistible.
o·ver·price (:prīs') tr. poner un precio demasiado alto a.
o·ver·pro·duc·tion (:prə-dŭk'shən) s. superproducción *f,* sobreproducción *f.*
o·ver·qual·i·fied (:kwŏl'ə-fīd') adj. excesivamente capacitado.
o·ver·rate (:rāt') tr. sobrestimar ♦ **to be overrated** tener demasiada fama.
o·ver·reach (:rēch') tr. extralimitarse en.
o·ver·re·act (:rē-ăkt') intr. reaccionar de modo exagerado.
o·ver·ride ('-rīd') tr. **-rode, -ridden** *(to prevail over)* imponerse a; *(to nullify)* anular.
o·ver·rule ('-rōōl') tr. *(to rule against)* decidir en contra de; *(to declare null)* anular.
o·ver·run I. tr. (:rŭn') **-ran, -run, -nn-** *(to defeat)* destruir; *(to invade)* invadir; *(limit)* pasarse de II. s. ('-') costo por sobre el presupuesto.
o·ver·seas ('-sēz') I. adv. en el o al extranjero II. adj. extranjero; *(trade)* exterior.
o·ver·see (:sē') tr. **-saw, -seen** supervisar.
o·ver·se·er ('-sē'ər) s. capataz *m.*
o·ver·sen·si·tive (:sĕn'sĭ-tĭv) adj. hipersensible.
o·ver·shad·ow (:shăd'ō) tr. oscurecer.
o·ver·shoe ('-shōō') s. chanclo.
o·ver·shoot ('-shōōt') tr. **-shot** *(to miss)* irse por encima de; *(a runway, goal)* pasarse de.
o·ver·sight ('-sīt') s. *(omission)* descuido, omisión *f; (watchful care)* vigilancia.
o·ver·size(d) (:sīz[d]') adj. demasiado grande; *(clothes)* de talla especial.
o·ver·sleep ('-slēp') intr. **-slept** quedarse dormido.

o·ver·state (:stāt') tr. exagerar.
o·ver·state·ment (:mənt) s. exageración *f.*
o·ver·stay (ō'vər-stā') tr. ♦ **to o. one's welcome** prolongar demasiado la visita.
o·ver·step (:stĕp') tr. **-pp-** traspasar, pasar de ♦ **to o. one's limits** extralimitarse.
o·ver·stock (:stŏk') tr. tener existencias excesivas de, almacenar en exceso.
o·ver·stuff (:stŭf') tr. rellenar abundantemente.
o·ver·sup·ply I. s. ('-sə-plī') suministro excesivo ♦ **an o.** of un exceso de II. tr. ('-') suministrar en exceso.
o·vert (ō-vûrt') adj. abierto, público.
o·ver·take (ō'vər-tāk') tr. **-took, -taken** *(to catch up with)* alcanzar; *(to pass)* pasar.
o·ver·tax (:tăks') tr. oprimir con impuestos; FIG. agotar.
o·ver·the·coun·ter (:thə-koun'tər) adj. *(stock)* que se vende fuera de la bolsa; *(drug)* que se despacha sin receta médica.
o·ver·throw I. tr. ('-thrō') **-threw, -thrown** *(to oust)* derrocar; *(to dethrone)* destronar II. s. ('-') derrocamiento; *(downfall)* caída.
o·ver·time ('-tīm') s. & adv. horas extras.
o·ver·tone (:tōn') s. *(hint)* sugestión *f,* MÚS. armónico ♦ **an o. o** overtones of una nota de.
o·ver·ture (:chōōr') s. *(proposal)* oferta, propuesta; MÚS. obertura.
o·ver·turn (:tûrn') tr. volcar; *(to upset)* trastornar; *(to revoke)* revocar —intr. volcarse; *(a vehicle)* dar una vuelta.
o·ver·use (:yōōs') s. uso excesivo, abuso.
o·ver·val·ue (:văl'yōō) tr. sobrestimar.
o·ver·view ('-vyōō') s. repaso, resumen *m.*
o·ver·weight ('-wāt') adj. pasado de peso; *(obese)* obeso, gordo.
o·ver·whelm (:hwĕlm') tr. *(to defeat)* aplastar; *(to overcome)* abrumar; *(with requests)* acosar ♦ **to be overwhelmed** *(with joy)* rebosar (de contento); *(by grief)* estar abrumado (de dolor).
o·ver·whelm·ing (:hwĕl'mĭng) adj. *(staggering)* abrumador; *(victory)* arrollador; *(majority)* inmenso; *(passion)* irresistible.
o·ver·work (:wûrk') tr. hacer trabajar demasiado; *(an idea)* abusar de —intr. trabajar demasiado.
o·ver·wrought (:rôt') adj. *(agitated)* muy alterado, sobrexcitado; *(ornate)* recargado.
o·vi·duct (ō'vĭ-dŭkt') s. oviducto.
o·void (ō'void') adj. ovoide.
o·vu·late (ō'vyə-lāt', ŏv'yə-) intr. ovular.
o·vule (ō'vyōōl, ŏv'yōōl) s. óvulo.
o·vum (ō'vəm) s. [pl. **ova**] óvulo.
owe (ō) tr. deber ♦ **to o. it to oneself** merecérselo ♦ **to o. someone for** deber a alguien.
ow·ing (ō'ĭng) adj. por pagarse ♦ **o. to** debido a.
owl (oul) s. lechuza, búho.
own (ōn) I. adj. propio ♦ **by their o. admission** según ellos mismos lo reconocieron • **he buys his o. clothes** él mismo se compra la ropa • **it's my o. money** es mi dinero II. pron. el mío, lo tuyo, lo suyo, lo nuestro, lo vuestro ♦ **it's my o.** *(belonging to oneself)* propio; *(peculiar to oneself)* de uno; *(for use by oneself)* para uno • **on one's o.** *(unaided)* sin ayuda de nadie; *(independently)* por cuenta propia • **to be on one's o.** arreglárselas por cuenta propia • **come into one's o.** lograr el éxito merecido • **to get one's o. back** tomar revancha III. tr. ser dueño de, tener ♦ **to o. up to** confesar • **who owns this scarf?** ¿de quién es esta bufanda?

—intr. ♦ **to o. up** confesar.
own·er (ō′nər) s. dueño, propietario.
own·er·ship (:ship′) s. *(state)* posesión *f*; *(legal right)* propiedad *f*.
ox (ŏks) s. [pl. **-en**] buey *m*.
ox·i·dant (ŏk′sĭ-dnt) s. oxidante *m*.
ox·i·da·tion (′-dā′shən) s. oxidación *f*.
ox·ide (ŏk′sīd′) s. óxido.
ox·i·dize (ŏk′sĭ-dīz′) tr. & intr. oxidar(se).
ox·y·gen (ŏk′sĭ-jən) s. oxígeno.
ox·y·gen·ate (ŏk′sĭ-jə-nāt′) tr. oxigenar.
oys·ter (oi′stər) s. ostra.
o·zone (ō′zōn′) s. ozono ♦ **o. layer** ozonosfera.

P

p, P (pē) s. decimosexta letra del alfabeto inglés ♦ **to mind one's p's and q's** tener cuidado con lo que uno hace.
pa (pä) s. FAM. papá *m*.
pace (pās) I. s. paso; *(speed)* ritmo, tren *m* ♦ **at a snail's p.** a paso de tortuga • **to keep p. with** avanzar al mismo paso que; *(to keep abreast of)* mantenerse al corriente de • **to set the p.** fijar el paso, establecer el ritmo • **to put someone through his paces** poner a alguien a prueba II. tr. ir y venir por, pasearse por; *(to measure)* medir a pasos; *(to set the speed)* fijar el paso de ♦ **to p. off** medir a pasos • **to p. oneself** coger el ritmo de uno —intr. pasear.
pace·mak·er (′mā′kər) s. corredor *m* que toma la delantera; MED. marcapaso(s).
pace·set·ter (:sĕt′ər) s. el que da la pauta.
pach·y·derm (păk′ĭ-dûrm′) s. paquidermo.
pa·cif·ic (pə-sĭf′ĭk) adj. pacífico.
pac·i·fi·ca·tion (păs′ə-fĭ-kā′shən) s. pacificación *f*.
pac·i·fi·er (′-fī′ər) s. pacificador *m*; *(for a baby)* chupete *m*.
pac·i·fist (:fĭst) s. pacifista *mf*.
pac·i·fy (:fī′) tr. pacificar, apaciguar.
pack (păk) I. s. paquete *m*; *(knapsack)* mochila; *(batch)* lote *m*; *(heap)* montón *m*; *(of cigarettes)* cajetilla; *(of matches)* cajita; *(of cards)* baraja; *(of dogs)* jauría; *(of wolves)* manada; *(of people)* banda ♦ **p. of lies** una sarta de mentiras • **p. animal** animal de carga II. tr. *(to wrap up)* envolver; *(to fill up)* llenar; *(for traveling)* hacer, preparar; *(for shipping)* embalar; *(to put)* poner; *(to package)* empacar, empaquetar; *(to cram)* apiñar, apretar; *(to compact)* comprimir; *(a panel)* llenar de partidarios; MED. envolver en paños ♦ **to p. a pistol** FAM. llevar una pistola • **to p. down** prensar, comprimir • **to p. someone off** despachar a alguien para • **to send someone packing** FAM. mandar a alguien a paseo —intr. *(for traveling)* hacer las maletas; *(people)* apiñarse, apretarse.
pack·age (păk′ĭj) I. s. paquete *m* ♦ **p. store** tienda de vinos y licores II. tr. empaquetar.
pack·ag·ing (:ĭ-jĭng) s. embalaje *m*.
packed (păkt) adj. *(crowded)* lleno, atestado; *(compressed)* apiñado; *(filled with)* lleno de.
pack·et (păk′ĭt) s. paquete pequeño; *(boat)* paquebote *m*.
pack·horse (:hôrs′) s. caballo de carga.
pack·ing (:ĭng) s. embalaje *m*, envase *m*.
pact (păkt) s. pacto, convenio.
pad¹ (păd) I. s. *(cushion)* almohadilla, cojín *m*; *(stuffing)* relleno; *(of paper)* bloc *m*; *(leaf)*

hoja grande; *(of animals)* pulpejo; *(apartment)* nido ♦ **launch p.** pista de lanzamiento II. tr. **-dd-** *(to stuff)* rellenar; *(to line)* forrar; FAM. *(speech, report)* hinchar.
pad² *intr.* **-dd-** *(to walk)* pisar suavemente.
pad·ded (′ĭd) adj. con una almohadilla; *(upholstered)* relleno; *(shoulders)* con hombreras; *(account)* hinchado, aumentado.
pad·ding (:ĭng) s. relleno.
pad·dle¹ (păd′l) I. s. pagaya, canalete *m*; *(of waterwheel)* paleta, álabe *m* ♦ **p. boat** vapor de ruedas, hidropedal II. intr. remar con pagaya —tr. *(to propel)* hacer avanzar con pagaya; *(to stir)* mover con una paleta; *(to spank)* azotar.
pad·dle² intr. *(to splash)* chapotear; *(to toddle)* hacer pinitos, andar a gatas.
pad·dock (păd′ək) s. potrero, dehesa.
pad·dy (păd′ē) s. arrozal *m*.
pad·lock (păd′lŏk′) I. s. candado II. tr. cerrar con candado.
pa·gan (pā′gən) s. & adj. pagano.
page¹ (pāj) I. s. paje *m*; *(in hotel)* botones *m* II. tr. llamar.
page² I. s. página II. tr. *(to number)* paginar; *(to order)* compaginar —intr. hojear.
pag·eant (păj′ənt) s. espectáculo; *(procession)* desfile histórico.
pag·eant·ry (:ən-trē) s. espectáculo; *(pomp)* pompa.
pag·i·nate (păj′ə-nāt′) tr. paginar.
pag·i·na·tion (′-nā′shən) s. paginación *f*.
paid (pād) cf. **pay**.
pail (pāl) s. cubo, balde *m*.
pain (pān) I. s. dolor *m*; *(distress)* pena, sufrimiento ♦ **on** *o* **under p. of** so pena de, bajo pena de • **to be a p. in the neck** FAM. *(somebody)* ser un pesado; *(something)* dar lata • **to be in p.** tener dolores, sufrir • **to take pains** *(efforts)* hacer esfuerzos, empeñarse; *(care)* esmerarse II. tr. & intr. doler.
pain·ful (′fəl) adj. doloroso; *(difficult)* difícil, penoso; *(pitiful)* lastimoso.
pain·kill·er (:kĭl′ər) s. calmante *m*.
pain·less (:lĭs) adj. indoloro, sin dolor.
pains·tak·ing (pānz′tā′kĭng) adj. esmerado, cuidadoso.
paint (pānt) I. s. pintura II. tr. & intr. pintar ♦ **to p. the town red** JER. irse de juerga.
paint·brush (′brŭsh′) s. brocha; ARTE. pincel *m*.
paint·er (pān′tər) s. pintor *m*.
paint·ing (:ĭng) s. pintura.
pair (pâr) I. s. [pl. inv. *o* **s**] par *m*; *(persons, animals)* pareja; *(of horses, oxen)* yunta; *(in cards)* par ♦ **in pairs** de dos en dos II. tr. *(to match up)* parear, casar; *(to group)* juntar, emparejar; *(to mate)* aparear —intr. hacer pareja ♦ **to p. off** *o* **up** formar parejas.
pa·ja·mas (pə-jä′məz, -jăm′əz) s.pl. piyama *m*.
pal (păl) I. s. FAM. amigote *m*, compinche *m* II. intr. **-ll-** ♦ **to p. around with** ser amigo de.
pal·ace (păl′ĭs) s. palacio.
pal·at·a·ble (păl′ə-tə-bəl) adj. sabroso, apetitoso; *(agreeable)* aceptable.
pal·ate (păl′ĭt) s. paladar *m*.
pa·la·tial (pə-lā′shəl) adj. palaciego; *(splendid)* espléndido, magnífico.
pa·la·ver (pə-lăv′ər) s. palabrería.
pale¹ (pāl) s. *(stake)* estaca; *(wooden fence)* empalizada; *(boundary)* límite *m*, margen *m* ♦ **to be beyond the p.** FIG. no ser aceptable.
pale² I. adj. *(complexion)* pálido; *(color)* claro;

(dim) tenue, sin brillo **II.** tr. poner pálido —intr. palidecer.

pa·le·og·ra·phy (pā'lē-ŏg'rə-fē) s. paleografía.

pa·le·on·tol·o·gy (:ŏn-tŏl'ə-jē) s. paleontología.

pal·ette (păl'ĭt) s. paleta; *(colors)* gama de colores.

pal·i·sade (păl'ĭ-sād') s. *(fence)* estacada, cerca; *(stake)* estaca ♦ pl. acantilado, risco.

pall¹ (pôl) s. *(of a coffin)* paño mortuorio; *(coffin)* ataúd m, *(covering)* capa, cortina ♦ to cast a p. over producir un efecto deprimente en.

pall² intr. *(to become boring)* perder su sabor; *(to become satiated)* saciarse, cansarse.

pall·bear·er ('bâr'ər) s. portador m del ataúd.

pal·let¹ (păl'ĭt) s. *(platform)* paleta.

pal·let² s. *(pad)* jergón m.

pal·li·ate (păl'ē-āt') tr. paliar, mitigar.

pal·li·a·tive (-ā'tĭv) adj. & s. paliativo.

pal·lid (păl'ĭd) adj. pálido.

pal·lor (:ər) s. palidez f.

palm¹ (päm) **I.** s. *(of a hand)* palma; *(measure)* palmo; *(of an oar)* pala ♦ to grease o cross someone's p. untar la mano a alguien **II.** tr. escamotear ♦ to p. off encajar, clavar.

palm² s. palma, palmera; *(emblem)* palma.

palm·is·try (pä'mĭ-strē) s. quiromancia.

pal·pa·ble (păl'nə-bəl) adj. palpable.

pal·pate (păl'pāt') tr. palpar.

pal·pi·tate (păl'pĭ-tāt') intr. palpitar.

pal·pi·ta·tion ('-tā'shən) s. palpitación f.

pal·sied (pôl'zēd) adj. MED. paralítico; *(trembling)* temblante.

pal·sy (:zē) s. parálisis f, perlesía.

pal·try (pôl'trē) adj. -i- *(petty)* miserable; *(trivial)* insignificante; *(worthless)* despreciable.

pam·per (păm'pər) tr. mimar, consentir.

pam·phlet (păm'flĭt) s. folleto.

pan¹ (păn) **I.** s. cacerola; *(frying pan)* sartén f; *(on a scale)* platillo **II.** tr. -nn- MIN. lavar en una batea; *(to criticize)* poner por los suelos —intr. ♦ to p. out FAM. salir bien.

pan² intr. -nn- CINEM. girar la cámara para hacer una toma panorámica.

pan·a·ce·a (păn'ə-sē'ə) s. panacea.

pa·nache (pə-năsh') s. *(plume)* penacho; *(dash)* brio, garbo.

Pan·a·ma hat (păn'ə-mä) s. jipijapa m.

Pan-A·mer·i·can (păn'ə-mĕr'ĭ-kən) adj. panamericano.

pan·cake (păn'kāk') s. panqueque m.

pan·cre·as (păng'krē-əs) s. páncreas m.

... ...·ic (păn-dĕm'ĭk) ...

pan·de·mo·ni·um (păn'də-mō'nē-əm) s. pandemónium m.

pan·der (păn'dər) **I.** s. alcahuete m, proxeneta mf **II.** intr. alcahuetear ♦ to p. to satisfacer.

pane (pān) s. hoja de vidrio; *(glass)* vidrio.

pan·el (păn'əl) **I.** s. panel m; *(of a wall)* entrepaño; *(of a dress)* tabla, paño; *(jury)* jurado; *(group)* grupo **II.** tr. *(a door, wall)* poner paneles en; *(a jury)* elegir.

pan·el·ing (:ə-lĭng) s. revestimiento de madera.

pan·el·ist (:lĭst) s. miembro de un grupo de discusión.

pang (păng) s. *(of pain)* punzada, dolor agudo; *(of conscience)* remordimiento.

pan·han·dle¹ (păn'hăn'dl) s. mango de sartén.

pan·han·dle² tr. & intr. FAM. mendigar.

pan·han·dler (:dlər) s. FAM. mendigo.

pan·ic (păn'ĭk) **I.** s. pánico; JER. persona chistosa **II.** tr. & intr. -ck- aterrar(se), asustar(se).

pan·ick·y (:ĭ-kē) adj. lleno de pánico.

pan·ic-strick·en ('ĭk-strĭk'ən) adj. lleno de pánico.

pan·o·ram·a (păn'ə-răm'ə) s. panorama m.

pan·o·ram·ic (:ĭk) adj. panorámico.

pan·sy (păn'zē) s. BOT. pensamiento.

pant (pănt) **I.** intr. jadear **II.** s. jadeo.

pan·the·on (păn'thē-ŏn') s. panteón m.

pan·ther (păn'thər) s. pantera.

pant·ies (păn'tēz) s.pl. bragas, bombachas.

pant·ing (păn'tĭng) **I.** s. jadeo **II.** adj. jadeante.

pan·to·mime (păn'tə-mīm') **I.** s. pantomima; *(actor)* mimo **II.** tr. representar por gestos —intr. expresarse por medio de gestos.

pan·try (păn'trē) s. despensa.

pants (pănts) s.pl. pantalones m; *(underpants)* calzoncillos m ♦ to be caught with one's p. down FAM. ser sorprendido en una posición embarazosa.

pant·y hose (păn'tē-hōz') s. media pantalón.

pap (păp) s. *(food)* papilla, *(something insubstantial)* tonterías.

pa·pa (pä'pə, pə-pä') s. papá m.

pa·pa·cy (pä'pə-sē) s. papado.

pa·pal (pä'pəl) adj. papal.

pa·pa·ya (pə-pī'ə) s. papaya; *(tree)* papayo.

pa·per (pä'pər) **I.** s. papel m; *(document)* documento; *(essay)* ensayo; *(composition)* trabajo escrito; *(in a symposium)* ponencia, *(newspaper)* periódico ♦ blotting p. papel secante • brown p. papel de empaquetar • drawing p. papel de dibujo • on p. *(in writing)* por escrito; *(in theory)* sobre el papel ♦ p. clip sujetapapeles, presilla • tissue p. papel de seda • tracing p. papel de calcar • wax(ed) p. papel encerado • wrapping p. papel de envolver ♦ pl. papeles; *(ship's papers)* patente de navegación **II.** tr. empapelar **III.** adj. de papel; *(theoretical)* teórico, por realizar ♦ p. cup vaso de cartón.

pa·per·back (:băk') s. libro de bolsillo.

pa·per·board (:bôrd') s. cartón m.

pa·per·weight (:wāt') s. pisapapeles m.

pa·per·work (:wûrk') s. papeleo.

pa·pier-mâ·ché (pāp'yä-mä-shā') s. cartón m piedra, papel m maché.

pa·pist (pā'pĭst) s. papista mf.

pap·py (păp'ē) s. papá m, papi m.

pa·pri·ka (pə-prē'kə) s. paprika, pimentón m.

pa·py·rus (pə-pī'rəs) s. [pl. es o ri] papiro.

par (pär) **I.** s. *(average)* promedio; *(equivalence)* igualdad f, paridad f; *(in golf)* par m; *(face value)* valor m nominal; *(parity)* par, paridad ♦ to be on a p. with estar en un pie de igualdad con **II.** adj. normal, regular; *(nominal)* nominal; *(at parity)* al o a la par.

par·a·ble (păr'ə-bəl) s. parábola.

pa·rab·o·la (pə-răb'ə-lə) s. parábola.

par·a·bol·ic (păr'ə-bŏl'ĭk) adj. parabólico.

par·a·chute (păr'ə-shōt') **I.** s. paracaídas m **II.** tr. lanzar en paracaídas —intr. saltar en paracaídas.

par·a·chut·ist (:shōō'tĭst) s. paracaidista mf.

pa·rade (pə-rād') **I.** s. desfile m; *(pompous display)* ostentación f, alarde m; MIL. desfile de tropas **II.** tr. *(to march)* hacer desfilar; *(to flaunt)* hacer alarde de —intr. desfilar; MIL. formar en parada ♦ to p. around FAM. pasearse.

par·a·digm (păr'ə-dĭm') s. paradigma m.

par·a·dise (păr'ə-dīs') s. *(heaven)* cielo, gloria; *(delight)* paraíso.

par·a·dox (păr'ə-dŏks') s. paradoja.

par·a·dox·i·cal ('-dŏk'sĭ-kəl) adj. paradójico.
par·af·fin (păr'ə-fĭn) s. parafina; G.B. *(fuel)* petróleo, queroseno.
par·a·gon (păr'ə-gŏn') s. dechado, modelo.
par·a·graph (păr'ə-grăf') s. párrafo.
par·a·keet (păr'ə-kēt') s. perico, periquito.
par·al·lel (păr'ə-lĕl') **I.** adj. paralelo; *(corresponding)* correspondiente **II.** s. GEOM. paralela; *(match)* igual *m*; *(comparison)* paralelo, analogía; GEOG. paralelo **III.** tr. extenderse en línea paralela a; *(to match)* ser igual a; *(to compare with)* ser análogo a.
par·al·lel·ism (:ĭz'əm) s. paralelismo.
par·al·lel·o·gram ('-ə-grăm') s. paralelogramo.
pa·ral·y·sis (pə-răl'ĭ-sĭs) s. [pl. **-ses**] parálisis *f*; *(stoppage)* paralización *f*, estancamiento.
par·a·lyt·ic (păr'ə-lĭt'ĭk) adj. & s. paralítico.
par·a·lyze (păr'ə-līz') tr. paralizar.
par·a·med·ic (păr'ə-mĕd'ĭk) s. integrante *mf* de la profesión paramédica.
pa·ram·e·ter (pə-răm'ĭ-tər) s. parámetro; FIG. límite *m*.
par·a·mil·i·tar·y (păr'ə-mĭl'ĭ-tĕr'ē) adj. paramilitar.
par·a·mount (păr'ə-mount') adj. principal.
par·a·mour (păr'ə-mōor') s. amante *mf*.
par·a·noi·a (păr'ə-noi'ə) s. paranoia.
par·a·noi·ac (:ăk') s. & adj. paranoico.
par·a·noid (păr'ə-noid') adj. & s. paranoico.
par·a·pet (păr'ə-pĭt) s. baranda, antepecho; MIL. parapeto.
par·a·pher·na·lia (păr'ə-fər-nāl'yə) s.pl. *(belongings)* avíos; *(equipment)* conjunto de aparatos, accesorios.
par·a·phrase (păr'ə-frāz') **I.** s. paráfrasis *f* **II.** tr. & intr. parafrasear.
par·a·ple·gi·a (păr'ə-plē'jē-ə) s. paraplejía.
par·a·ple·gic (:jĭk) adj. & s. parapléjico.
par·a·pro·fes·sion·al (păr'ə-prə-fĕsh'ə-nəl) s. ayudante *mf* auxiliar de un profesional.
par·a·site (păr'ə-sīt') s. parásito.
par·a·sit·ic ('-sĭt'ĭk) adj. parasítico.
par·a·sol (păr'ə-sŏl') s. parasol, sombrilla.
par·a·troop·er (păr'ə-trōo'pər) s. soldado paracaidista.
par·a·troops (:trōops') s.pl. tropas paracaidistas.
par·boil (păr'boil') tr. sancochar.
par·cel (păr'səl) **I.** s. paquete *m*, fardo; *(of land)* parcela; *(of things)* partida, lote *m* **♦ p. post** servicio de encomienda postal **II.** tr. empaquetar **♦ to p. out** repartir en lotes.
parch (pärch) tr. resecar; *(to roast)* tostar —intr. resecarse.
parch·ment (pärch'mənt) s. pergamino.
par·don (pär'dn) **I.** tr. perdonar; *(an offense)* disculpar; *(to excuse)* excusar **♦ p. me** perdóneme **II.** s. perdón *m*; *(exemption)* indulto **♦ I beg your p.?** ¿cómo?, ¿cómo dijo?
par·don·a·ble (:ə-bəl) adj. perdonable.
pare (pâr) tr. mondar, pelar; *(to clip)* recortar **♦ to p. down** disminuir, reducir.
par·e·gor·ic (păr'ə-gŏr'ĭk) s. elixir paregórico.
par·ent (păr'ənt) s. *(father)* padre *m*; *(mother)* madre *f*; *(forefather)* antepasado; *(cause)* causa, origen *m* **♦ p. company** casa matriz **♦ pl.** padres.
par·ent·age (:ən-tĭj) s. linaje *m*.
pa·ren·tal (pə-rĕn'tl) adj. de los padres.
pa·ren·the·sis (pə-rĕn'thĭ-sĭs) s. [pl. **-ses**] paréntesis *m*.

par·en·thet·ic/i·cal (păr'ən-thĕt'ĭk) adj. entre paréntesis.
par·ent·hood (păr'ənt-hŏod') s. *(father)* paternidad *f*; *(mother)* maternidad *f*.
pa·ri·ah (pə-rī'ə) s. paria *mf*.
pa·ri·e·tal (pə-rī'ĭ-tl) adj. & s. parietal *m* **♦ s.pl.** reglas de conducta en residencias universitarias.
par·ing (pâr'ĭng) s. *(skin)* cáscara; *(peeling)* peladura, mondadura; *(trimming)* recorte *m* **♦ p. knife** cuchillo para mondar.
par·ish (păr'ĭsh) s. parroquia.
pa·rish·ion·er (pə-rĭsh'ə-nər) s. feligrés *m*.
par·i·ty (păr'ĭ-tē) s. paridad *f*.
park (pärk) **I.** s. parque *m*; *(stadium)* estadio; *(preserve)* coto **♦ car p.** G.B. aparcamiento **II.** tr. *(a vehicle)* estacionar; FAM. *(to place)* plantar —intr. estacionarse, parquearse.
park·ing (pär'kĭng) s. aparcamiento, estacionamiento **♦ p. lot** aparcamiento, playa de estacionamiento **• p. meter** parquímetro **• p. place** o **space** plaza de estacionamiento.
park·way (pärk'wā') s. avenida, bulevar *m*.
par·lance (pär'ləns) s. lenguaje *m*, habla *m* **♦ in common p.** en lenguaje corriente.
par·lay (pär'lā') **I.** tr. apostar en un pároli **II.** s. pároli *m*.
par·ley (pär'lē) **I.** s. parlamento, negociaciones *f* **II.** intr. parlamentar.
par·lia·ment (pär'lə-mənt) s. parlamento.
par·lia·men·tar·i·an ('-mĕn-târ'ē-ən) s. parlamentario.
par·lia·men·ta·ry ('-'tə-rē) adj. parlamentario.
par·lor (pär'lər) s. sala de recibo; *(for business)* salón *m* **♦ funeral p.** funeraria **• ice-cream p.** heladería.
pa·ro·chi·al (pə-rō'kē-əl) adj. parroquial; *(provincial)* provincial.
par·o·dy (păr'ə-dē) **I.** s. parodia **II.** tr. parodiar.
pa·role (pə-rōl') **I.** s. libertad *f* bajo palabra; *(word of honor)* palabra de honor **II.** tr. poner en libertad bajo palabra.
pa·rol·ee (pə-rō'lē') s. convicto en libertad condicional.
par·ox·ysm (păr'ək-sĭz'əm) s. paroxismo.
par·quet (pär-kā') **I.** s. parqué *m*, entarimado **II.** tr. poner parqué, entarimar.
par·ri·cide (păr'ĭ-sīd') s. *(person)* parricida *mf*; *(act)* parricidio.
par·rot (păr'ət) **I.** s. papagayo, loro; *(person)* cotorra, lorito **II.** tr. repetir como un loro.
par·ry (păr'ē) **I.** *(in fencing)* parar, esquivar; *(to evade)* evadir, ludir ... *(ing)* parada, quite *m*; *(evasion)* evasión ...
par·si·mo·ni·ous (păr'sə-mō'nē-əs) adj. parsimonioso.
par·si·mo·ny ('-nē) s. parsimonia.
pars·ley (pär'slē) s. perejil *m*.
par·son (pär'sən) s. pastor *m* protestante.
par·son·age (:sə-nĭj) s. rectoría.
part (pärt) **I.** s. parte *f*; *(of a machine)* pieza; *(role)* papel *m*; *(of the hair)* raya del pelo **♦ for the most p.** generalmente, por lo general **• p. and parcel** parte integrante **• the best p.** lo mejor **• the greater p.** la mayor parte **• to be p.** of formar parte de **• to do one's p.** hacer lo que le corresponde a uno **• to have no p. in** no tener nada que ver con **• to look the p.** parecerlo, venirle bien el papel a uno **♦ in these p.** en estas regiones **• private p.** partes pudendas **II.** tr. *(to divide)* dividir; *(to break)* partir, romper; *(to come between)* apartar **♦ to**

p. company with romper relaciones con • **to p. with** *(to get rid of)* deshacerse de; *(to spend)* soltar, gastar —intr. separarse, apartarse; *(to leave)* irse **III.** adv. en parte, parcialmente **IV.** adj. parcial.

par·take (pär tāk') intr. **-took, -taken** participar, tomar parte — **to p. in** participar de, tomar parte en • **to p. of** compartir.

par·tial (pär'shǝl) adj. parcial • **p. to** partidario de, aficionado a

par·ti·al·i·ty (' shē ǎl'ĭ-tē) s. parcialidad *f.*

par·tic·i·pant (pär-tĭs'ǝ-pǝnt) s. & adj. participante *mf,* partícipe *mf.*

par·tic·i·pate ('pāt') intr. participar,

par·tic·i·pa·tion ('-pǎ'shǝn) s. participación *f.*

par·tic·i·pa·to·ry ('-pǝ-tôr'ē) adj. partícipe.

par·ti·ci·ple (pär'tĭ-sǐp'ǝl) s. participio.

par·ti·cle (pär'tĭ-kǝl) s. partícula.

par·tic·u·lar (pǝr-tĭk'yǝ lǝr) **I.** adj. particular; *(fussy)* exigente, minucioso • **in p.** especialmente, en particular **II.** s. particularidad *f,* detalle *m* • pl. pormenores.

par·tic·u·lar·i·ty ('-lär'ĭ-tē) s. particularidad *f.*

par·tic·u·lar·ly ('-lar-lē) adv. *(especially)* especialmente; *(specifically)* específicamente, en particular; *(individually)* particularmente.

part·ing (pär'tĭng) **I.** s. separación *f.* *(departure)* partida, despedida • **p. of the ways** punto de separación **II.** adj. de partida, de despedida.

par·ti·san (pär'tĭ-zǝn) **I.** s. partidario, prosélito **II.** adj. *(of a party)* partidista; *(of a supporter)* partidario; *(biased)* parcial.

par·tite (pär'tīt') adj. partido, dividido.

par·ti·tion (pär-tĭsh'ǝn) **I.** s. partición *f;* *(wall)* tabique *m,* mampara **II.** tr. dividir, repartir • **to p. off** separar con un tabique.

part·ner (pärt'nǝr) s. socio; *(spouse)* cónyuge *mf* *(in a dance, games)* pareja; *(in crime)* cómplice *mf.*

part·ner·ship (':ship') s. sociedad *f.*

par·took (pär-tŏŏk') cf. **partake.**

par·tridge (pär'trĭj) s. [pl. inv. o **s**] perdiz *f.*

part-time (pärt'tīm') adj. & adv. por horas.

par·tu·ri·tion (pär'tyŏŏ-rĭsh'ǝn) s. parto.

part·way (pärt'wā') adv. FAM. hasta cierto punto, en parte.

par·ty (pär'tē) **I.** s. *(gathering)* fiesta; POL. partido; *(group)* grupo; *(team)* equipo; DER. parte *f* • **p. line** *(telephone)* línea colectiva; POL. línea política • **to be a p. to** *(accessory)* ser cómplice en; *(participant)* participar en, tener algo que ver con **II.** intr. FAM. parrandear.

par·ve·nu (pär'vǝ-nōō') s. advenedizo.

pass (păs) **I.** intr. pasar; *(to cross)* cruzarse; *(to be transferred)* ser traspasado; *(to happen)* acontecer; *(in examination, course)* aprobar • **in passing** de paso • **to be passing through** estar de paso • **to come to p.** suceder • **to p. away** o **on** fallecer • **to p. out** desmayarse —tr. pasar; *(to go past)* pasar por delante de; *(to come across)* cruzarse con; *(to exceed)* sobrepasar, superar; *(an examination, student)* aprobar; *(to adopt)* adoptar; *(to approve)* aprobar; DER. votar; FISIOL. evacuar • **to p. off** *(to palm off)* pasar, colar; *(to present)* hacer pasar • **to p. oneself off as** hacerse pasar por • **to p. on** pasar, transmitir • **to p. out** repartir, distribuir • **to p. over** pasar por alto • **to p. up** *(opportunity)* dejar pasar, desperdiciar; *(offer)* rechazar **II.** s. paso; *(written permit)* pase *m;* *(authorization)* permiso, licencia; *(safe-conduct)* salvoconducto; *(free ticket)* pase (gratis); *(in a table game)* pase; DEP., TAUR. pase • **to make a p. at** hacer insinuaciones amorosas a.

pass·a·ble ('ǝ-bǝl) adj. *(road)* transitable; *(work)* aceptable; *(satisfactory)* pasable.

pas·sage (păs'ĭj) s. paso; POL. *(of a bill)* aprobación *f,* promulgación *f;* *(journey)* pasaje *m,* travesía; *(ticket)* pasaje; *(path)* pasaje, pasadizo; *(corridor)* corredor *m,* pasillo; LIT., MÚS. pasaje.

pas·sage·way (:wā') s. *(alley)* callejón *m;* *(corridor)* corredor *m.*

pass·book (păs'bŏŏk') s. *(bankbook)* libreta de banco; COM. libro de cuenta y razón.

pas·sé (pǎ-sā') adj. *(out-of-date)* anticuado, pasado de moda; *(aged)* en decadencia.

pas·sel (păs'ǝl) s. FAM. montón *m.*

pas·sen·ger (păs'ǝn-jǝr) s. pasajero, viajero.

pas·ser·by ('ǝr-bī') s. [pl. **passers-**] transeúnte *mf.*

pass·ing (păs'ĭng) **I.** adj. pasante, que pasa; *(transitory)* pasajero, transitorio; *(casual)* casual, de pasada • **p. grade** EDUC. calificación aprobatoria **II.** s. pasada, transcurso; *(death)* fallecimiento.

pas·sion (păsh'ǝn) s. pasión *f.*

pas·sion·ate (:ǝ-nĭt) adj. apasionado; *(ardent)* ardiente, fervoroso.

pas·sive (păs'ĭv) **I.** adj. pasivo; *(inert)* inerte, inactivo; COM. que no devenga intereses **II.** s. GRAM. voz pasiva.

pas·siv·i·ty (pǎ-sĭv'ĭ-tē) s. pasividad *f.*

pass·key (păs'kē') s. llave maestra.

Pass·o·ver (păs'ō'vǝr) s. Pascua.

pass·port (păs'pôrt') s. pasaporte *m.*

pass·word (:wûrd') s. contraseña, santo y seña.

past (păst) **I.** adj. pasado; *(former)* anterior, último; GRAM. pretérito, pasado • **p. master** experto, perito **II.** s. pasado; *(background)* historia; GRAM. pretérito, pasado **III.** adv. al pasar **IV.** prep. *(by)* por delante de; *(on the far side of)* más allá de; *(older than)* más de; *(beyond)* ya no; *(plus)* y <It's ten p. two son las dos y diez> • **I wouldn't put it p. him** no me extrañaría de su parte.

pas·ta (pä'stǝ) s. masa de harina de trigo; *(dish)* plato de pastas.

paste[1] (pāst) s. engrudo; *(dough)* pasta, masa; *(clay)* barro; JOY. *(glass)* estrás *m;* *(artificial gem)* imitación *f* **II.** tr. *(to stick)* pegar; *(to cover)* engrudar.

paste[2] tr. JER. *(to punch)* pegar.

paste·board ('bôrd') s. cartón *m.*

pas·tel (pǎ-stěl') s. pastel *m.*

paste-up (pāst'ŭp') s. montaje *m,* collage *m;* IMPR. maqueta.

pas·teur·ize (păs'chǝ-rīz') tr. paste(u)rizar.

pas·time (păs'tīm') s. pasatiempo.

pas·tor (păs'tǝr) s. pastor *m.*

pas·tor·al (:ǝl) adj. & s. pastoral *f.*

pas·try (pā'strē) s. *(paste)* pasta; *(cakes)* pasteles *m.*

pas·tur·age (păs'chǝr-ĭj) s. pastura.

pas·ture (păs'chǝr) **I.** s. pastura • **to put out to p.** *(to graze)* apacentar, pastorear; *(to retire)* jubilar, retirar **II.** tr. pastorear, apacentar —intr. pastar, pacer.

past·y[1] (pā'stē) adj. **-i-** *(like paste)* pastoso; *(pale)* pálido.

pas·ty[2] (pă'stē) s. pastel *m,* empanada.

pat (păt) **I.** tr. **-tt-** *(to tap)* dar palmaditas o golpecitos a; *(to stroke)* acariciar; *(to mold)* moldear a palmaditas ♦ **to p. (oneself) on the back** congratular(se) **II. s.** *(with hand)* palmadita; *(with object)* golpecito; *(sound)* ruido ligero; *(small mass)* porción *f* **III. adj.** *(exactly right)* preciso; *(contrived)* preparado, pronto **IV. adv.** ♦ **to have something down p.** FAM. saberse algo al dedillo • **to stand p.** mantenerse firme.

patch (păch) **I. s.** parche *m*; *(in patchwork)* retazo; *(field)* siembra, bancal *m* **II. tr.** poner un parche a; *(to repair poorly)* remendar *o* arreglar mal ♦ **to p. up a quarrel** hacer las paces.

patch·work ('wûrk') **s.** *(needlework)* labor hecha con retazos; *(jumble)* mezcolanza.

patch·y (:ē) **adj. -i-** de remiendos, remendado; *(uneven)* desigual, irregular.

pate (pāt) **s.** FAM. cabeza, coronilla.

pâ·té (pä-tā') **s.** pasta de carne; *(pastry)* pastel *m*, empanada.

pa·ten·cy (păt'n-sē, pāt'n-) **s.** evidencia.

pat·ent (păt'nt) **I. s.** patente *f* **II. adj.** *(obvious)* patente, evidente; *(of patents)* de patentes ♦ **p. leather** charol **III. tr.** patentar.

pat·ent·ly (:lē) **adv.** patentemente.

pa·ter·nal (pə-tûr'nəl) **adj.** *(fatherly)* paternal; *(on the father's side)* paterno.

pa·ter·nal·is·tic ('-'nə-lĭs'tĭk) **adj.** paternalista.

pa·ter·ni·ty (-'nĭ-tē) **s.** paternidad *f*.

path (păth) **s. [pl. s]** *(trail)* sendero, senda; *(track)* camino, pista; *(course)* curso; FIG. camino, senda ♦ **to cross someone's p.** cruzarse con alguien.

pa·thet·ic (pə-thĕt'ĭk) **adj.** patético.

path·find·er (păth'fīn'dər) **s.** explorador *m*.

path·o·gen(e) (păth'ə-jən) **s.** agente *m o* microbio patógeno.

path·o·log·ic/i·cal (păth'ə-lŏj'ĭk) **adj.** patológico.

pa·thol·o·gist (pə-thŏl'ə-jĭst) **s.** patólogo.

pa·thol·o·gy (:jē) **s.** patología.

pa·thos (pā'thŏs') **s.** pathos *m*, patetismo.

path·way (păth'wā') **s.** *(trail)* sendero, senda; *(track)* camino, pista.

pa·tience (pā'shəns) **s.** paciencia; G.B. solitario.

pa·tient (pā'shənt) **adj. & s.** paciente *mf*.

pat·i·na (păt'n-ə, pə-tē'nə) **s.** pátina.

pat·i·o (păt'ē-ō', păt'ē-ō') **s.** patio, terraza.

pat·ois (pă'wä') **s.** inv. dialecto regional.

pa·tri·arch (pā'trē-ärk') **s.** patriarca *m*.

pa·tri·ar·chal ('-är'kəl) **adj.** patriarcal.

pa·tri·ar·chy ('-'kē) **s.** patriarcado.

pa·tri·cian (pə-trĭsh'ən) **s.** patricio.

pat·ri·cide (păt'rĭ-sīd') **s.** *(act)* parricidio; *(person)* parricida *mf*.

pat·ri·mo·ny (:mō'nē) **s.** patrimonio.

pa·tri·ot (pā'trē-ət) **s.** patriota *mf*.

pa·tri·ot·ic ('-ŏt'ĭk) **adj.** patriótico.

pa·tri·ot·ism ('-'-tĭz'əm) **s.** patriotismo.

pa·trol (pə-trōl') **I. s.** *(action)* ronda, patrulla; *(group)* patrulla **II. tr. & intr. -ll-** rondar.

pa·trol·man (:mən) **s. [pl. -men]** policía *mf*, guardia *mf*.

pa·tron (pā'trən) **s.** benefactor *m*, patrocinador *m*; *(customer)* cliente *m*; *(protector)* protector *m*, defensor *m* ♦ **p. saint** santo patrón.

pa·tron·age (pā'trə-nĭj, păt'rə-) **s.** patrocinio; *(clientele)* clientela; POL. influencia política.

pa·tron·ize (:nīz') **tr.** patrocinar, auspiciar; *(a business)* ser cliente de, frecuentar; *(to condescend to)* tratar con condescendencia.

pat·sy (păt'sē) **s.** JER. pelele *mf*, simplón *m*.

pat·ter¹ (păt'ər) **I. intr.** golpetear, tamborilear **II. s.** golpeteo, tamborileo.

pat·ter² **I. intr.** charlar, parlotear —**tr.** farfullar, balbucir **II. s.** parloteo, palique *m*.

pat·tern (păt'ərn) **I. s.** modelo, ejemplo; *(for sewing)* patrón *m*, molde *m*; *(design)* diseño, dibujo; *(on fabrics)* estampado, *(actions)* patrón, norma; *(regularity)* regularidad *f* **II. tr.** adornar con diseños; *(fabrics)* estampar ♦ **to p. after** *o* **on** imitar el ejemplo de.

pat·ty (păt'ē) **s.** croqueta de carne picada *o* pescado; *(candy)* caramelo.

pau·ci·ty (pô'sĭ-tē) **s.** *(small number)* número pequeño; *(scarcity)* escasez *f*.

paunch (pônch) **s.** barriga, vientre *m*.

paunch·y (pôn'chē) **adj. -i-** panzón, barrigón.

pau·per (pô'pər) **s.** pobre *mf*, indigente *mf*; *(beggar)* mendigo.

pause (pôz) **I. intr.** *(mentally)* hacer una pausa; *(physically)* pararse, detenerse; *(to hesitate)* vacilar **II. s.** pausa; *(rest)* descanso ♦ **to give p.** hacer preocupar.

pave (pāv) **tr.** *(with blocks)* adoquinar; *(with asphalt, concrete)* pavimentar; *(with bricks)* enladrillar; *(with cobblestones)* empedrar ♦ **to p. the way for** preparar el camino para.

pave·ment ('mənt) **s.** pavimento; G.B. acera.

pa·vil·ion (pə-vĭl'yən) **s.** pabellón *m*.

pav·ing (pā'vĭng) **s.** pavimentación *f*; *(material)* pavimento.

paw (pô) **I. s.** pata; FAM. *(hand)* manaza, manota **II. tr.** *(to strike)* dar zarpazos a; *(to handle)* manosear, toquetear ♦ **to p. at** manosear.

pawn¹ (pôn) **I. s.** *(object)* prenda; *(act)* empeño, pignoración *f*; *(hostage)* rehén *m* **II. tr.** empeñar, pignorar; *(to risk)* arriesgar.

pawn² **s.** peón *m*; FIG. pelele *m*, juguete *m*.

pawn·bro·ker ('brō'kər) **s.** prestamista *mf*.

pawn·shop (:shŏp') **s.** casa de empeños.

pay (pā) **I. tr. paid** pagar; *(to yield)* dar, producir; *(to profit)* compensar; *(visit, compliment)* hacer; *(respects)* presentar; *(attention)* prestar ♦ **to p. back** *(money)* devolver, reembolsar; *(someone)* pagar; *(to take revenge on)* vengarse de • **to p. off** *(debts)* saldar, liquidar; *(creditor)* reembolsar; *(mortgage)* redimir; *(employee)* pagar y despedir; *(to bribe)* sobornar • **to p. out** *(money)* desembolsar; *(rope, cable)* arriar, soltar • **to p. over** pagar • **to p. the piper** pagar las consecuencias • **to p. up** pagar —**intr.** pagar; *(debt)* saldar una deuda; *(to be profitable)* ser rentable; *(to be worthwhile)* compensar ♦ **it pays** vale la pena • **to p. for it** pagarlas • **to p. off** merecer la pena • **to p. up** pagar una deuda **II. s.** paga, pago; *(of employee)* paga, sueldo; *(of day worker)* jornal *m*; *(of workman)* salario ♦ **to be in the p. of** estar al servicio de **III. adj.** de pago ♦ **p. telephone** teléfono público.

pay·a·ble (pā'ə-bəl) **adj.** pagadero ♦ **accounts p.** cuentas a pagar • **p. to** a favor de.

pay·check (pā'chĕk') **s.** cheque *m* de pago de sueldo.

pay·day (pā'dā') **s.** día *m* de pago.

pay·ee (pā-ē') **s.** *(of a check)* beneficiario; *(of a draft)* tenedor de una letra.

pay·er (pā'ər) **s.** pagador *m*.

pay·ing (pā'ĭng) **I. adj.** que paga; *(profitable)* provechoso, rentable **II. s.** pago.

pay·load (pā'lōd') **s.** carga útil *o* de pago; MIL. carga explosiva.

pay·mas·ter (pā'măs'tər) s. pagador m, cajero.

pay·ment (pā'mənt) s. pago; *(reward)* recompensa, pago ♦ **down p.** desembolso inicial.

pay·off (pā'ôf') s. pago; FAM. *(end result)* resultado final; *(bribe)* soborno, coima.

pay·o·la (pā-ō'lə) s. JER. soborno, coima.

pay·roll (pā'rōl') s. nómina o planilla de pagos; *(total)* suma de dinero para pago de sueldos.

pea (pē) s. guisante m, arveja ♦ **like two peas in a pod** parecidos como dos gotas de agua.

peace (pēs) s. paz f; *(harmony)* armonía; *(law and order)* orden público; *(serenity)* paz, tranquilidad f ♦ **at p.** *(serene)* en calma, tranquilo; *(free from strife)* en paz ♦ **to hold** o **to keep one's p.** guardar silencio ♦ **to keep the p.** mantener el orden ♦ **to make p.** hacer las paces.

peace·a·ble (pē'sə-bəl) adj. pacífico.

peace·ful (pēs'fəl) adj. pacífico; *(tranquil)* apacible, tranquilo.

peace-lov·ing (:lŭv'ĭng) adj. pacífico.

peace·mak·er (:mā'kər) s. pacificador m; *(mediator)* árbitro.

peach (pēch) s. *(tree)* melocotonero, duraznero; *(fruit)* melocotón m, durazno; *(color)* color melocotón m; FIG. monada.

pea·cock (pē'kŏk') s. pavo real.

peak (pēk) I. s. punta; *(of a mountain)* cima, cumbre f; *(mountain)* pico; *(of a cap)* visera; *(climax)* punto culminante, *(maximum)* tope m, máximo II. tr. hacer culminar, traer al máximo —intr. formar un pico; *(to climax)* culminar, llegar al punto culminante; *(to achieve)* llegar al tope o al máximo III. adj. máximo.

peaked (pēkt, pē'kĭd) adj. puntiagudo.

peak·ed² (pē'kĭd) adj. demacrado, consumido.

peal (pēl) I. s. repiqueteo, repique m ♦ **peals of laughter** carcajadas II. intr. repiquetear, repicar —tr. hacer resonar, tañer.

pea·nut (pē'nət) I. s. cacahuate m, maní m ♦ pl. *(cash)* nada II. adj. de maní.

pear (pâr) s. *(tree)* peral m; *(fruit)* pera.

pearl (pûrl) I. s. perla, aljófar m; *(mother-of-pearl)* madreperla, nácar m; FIG. perla, joya II. adj. perlado, de perlas.

pearl·y (pûr'lē) adj. -i- *(in color)* perlino; *(with pearls)* perlado, perlificado ♦ **p. whites** FAM. los dientes.

peas·ant (pĕz'ənt) s. campesino; FIG. patán m.

pea·shoot·er (pē'shōō'tər) s. cerbatana.

peat (pēt) s. turba ♦ **p. moss** BOT. musgo de pantano; AGR. turba.

peb·ble (pĕb'əl) I. s. guijarro, canto rodado II. tr. pavimentar con guijas.

pe·can (pĭ-kän', -kăn') s. pacana.

pec·ca·dil·lo (pĕk'ə-dĭl'ō) s. [pl. (e)s] pecadillo, falta leve.

peck¹ (pĕk) I. tr. *(bird)* picotear; *(to pick up)* recoger con el pico; *(to kiss)* besar —intr. picotear ♦ **pecking order** FIG. jerarquía II. s. *(of a bird)* picotazo, picotada; *(kiss)* beso.

peck² s. *(measure)* celemín m; FAM. *(large quantity)* montón m, sinnúmero.

pec·tin (pĕk'tĭn) s. pectina.

pec·to·ral (pĕk'tər-əl) adj. & s. *(músculo)* pectoral.

pe·cu·liar (pĭ-kyōōl'yər) adj. peculiar; *(odd)* raro, extraño; *(special)* especial, singular.

pe·cu·li·ar·i·ty (pĭ-kyōō'lē-ăr'ĭ-tē) s. peculiaridad f; *(eccentricity)* excentricidad f.

pe·cu·ni·ar·y (pĭ-kyōō'nē-ĕr'ē) adj. pecuniario.

ped·a·gog·ic/i·cal (pĕd'ə-gŏj'ĭk) adj. pedagógico.

ped·a·gogue ('-gŏg') s. pedagogo.

ped·a·go·gy (:gō'jē, :gŏj'ē) s. pedagogía.

ped·al (pĕd'l) I. s. pedal m II. adj. del pie, del pedal III. intr. pedalear.

ped·ant (pĕd'nt) s. pedante mf.

pe·dan·tic (pə-dăn'tĭk) adj. pedante.

ped·ant·ry (pĕd'n-trē) s. pedantería.

ped·dle (pĕd'l) tr. *(to sell)* ir vendiendo de puerta en puerta; *(to disseminate)* difundir, diseminar —intr. vender de puerta en puerta.

ped·dler (:lər) s. vendedor m ambulante.

ped·er·ast (pĕd'ə-răst') s. pederasta m.

ped·es·tal (pĕd'ĭ-stəl) s. pedestal m.

pe·des·tri·an (pə-dĕs'trē-ən) I. s. peatón m, caminante mf II. adj. pedestre.

pe·di·at·ric (pē'dē-ăt'rĭk) adj. pediátrico ♦ **pe·di·at·rics** s.sg. pediatría.

pe·di·a·tri·cian (:ə-trĭsh'ən) s. pediatra mf.

ped·i·cure (pĕd'ĭ-kyōōr') s. pedicura.

ped·i·gree (pĕd'ĭ-grē') s. *(lineage)* linaje m, ascendencia; *(animal's)* pedigrí m.

pe·dom·e·ter (pĭ-dŏm'ĭ-tər) s. pedómetro.

peek (pēk) I. intr. *(to glance)* echar una ojeada; *(to look furtively)* atisbar, mirar a hurtadillas II. s. atisbo, ojeada.

peek·a·boo (pē'kə-bōō') s. escondite m, cucú m.

peel (pēl) I. s. cáscara, mondadura II. tr. *(to pare)* pelar, mondar; *(to unpaste)* despegar; *(to strip away)* quitar —intr. descascararse; *(to shed skin)* despellejarse; *(to lose bark)* descortezarse; *(to become unpasted)* despegarse.

peel·er (pē'lər) s. pelador m.

peel·ing (pē'lĭng) s. peladura, mondadura.

peep¹ (pēp) I. intr. pipiar, piar II. s. pío, piada ♦ **I don't want to hear a p. out of you!** FAM. ¡no digas ni pío!

peep² I. intr. *(to glance)* echar una ojeada; *(to peer from behind)* mirar a hurtadillas II. s. *(glance)* ojeada; *(furtive look)* atisbo.

peep·er¹ (pē'pər) s. *(frog)* rubeta rana; *(bird)* pájaro.

peep·er² s. *(person)* mirón m; JER. *(eye)* ojo.

peep·hole (pēp'hōl') s. mirilla.

peer¹ intr. *(to look)* mirar curiosamente, mirar con atención; *(to peep out)* aparecer, asomar.

peer² s. *(equal)* semejante mf; *(nobleman)* par m; G.B. noble m inglés.

peer·age ('ĭj) s. rango de par.

peer·less (:lĭs) adj. sin par, sin igual.

peeve (pēv) I. tr. irritar II. s. *(vexation)* queja; *(bad mood)* malhumor m, enojo ♦ **pet p.** motivo de enojo.

pee·vish (pē'vĭsh) adj. irritable, picajoso; *(ill-tempered)* malhumorado.

peg (pĕg) I. s. *(plug, spike)* clavija; *(wooden stake)* estaca; *(clothes hook)* percha, gancho; *(degree)* grado, escalón m; *(pretext)* pretexto; MÚS. clavija ♦ **to take down a p.** bajar los humos II. tr. -gg- *(to fasten)* sujetar con una clavija; *(to plug)* tapar con una clavija; *(to mark)* marcar con clavijas ♦ **to have someone pegged** FAM. conocer el juego de alguien —intr. ♦ **to p. away at** machacar, afanarse por.

peg·board ('bôrd') s. tabla de madera prensada perforada.

pe·jo·ra·tive (pĭ-jôr'ə-tĭv) adj. peyorativo.

pel·i·can (pĕl'ĭ-kən) s. pelícano, pelicano.

pel·let (pĕl'ĭt) s. *(small ball)* bolita, pelotilla; *(pill)* píldora; *(bullet)* bala; *(shot)* perdigón m.

pell-mell o **pell·mell** (pĕl'mĕl') adv. *(helter-skelter)* desordenadamente; *(headlong)* atropelladamente.

pelt¹ (pĕlt) s. *(skin)* piel *f*, pellejo.
pelt² I. tr. *(to bombard)* lanzar, arrojar; *(to strike)* apedrear —intr. golpear con fuerza repetidamente II. s. golpe *m*.
pel·vic (pĕl'vĭk) adj. pélvico, pelviano.
pel·vis (:vĭs) s. [pl. **es** *o* **-ves**] pelvis *f*.
pen¹ (pĕn) I. s. pluma; *(ball-point)* boligrafo ♦ **p. name** seudónimo de autor • **p. pal** amigo epistolar II. tr. **-nn-** escribir, redactar.
pen² I. s. *(corral)* corral *m*; *(coop)* gallinero; *(sty)* pocilga II. tr. **-nn-** acorralar, encerrar.
pen³ s. JER. *(jail)* chirona, prisión *f*.
pe·nal (pē'nəl) adj. penal.
pe·nal·ize (pē'nə-līz', pĕn'ə-) tr. penalizar.
pen·al·ty (pĕn'əl-tē) s. pena; *(fine)* multa; *(consequences)* consecuencias; FIN. descuento; DEP. castigo, penalty *m* ♦ **on** *o* **under p.** of so pena de, bajo pena de.
pen·ance (pĕn'əns) s. penitencia.
pen·chant (pĕn'chənt) s. propensión *f*.
pen·cil (pĕn'səl) I. s. lápiz *m* ♦ **p. sharpener** sacapuntas II. tr. escribir con un lápiz; *(to sketch)* esbozar a lápiz ♦ **to p. someone in** FAM. hacer planes tentativos con alguien.
pen·dant/dent (pĕn'dənt) I. s. colgante *m*, *(earring)* pendiente *m* II. adj. pendiente, colgante.
pend·ing (pĕn'dĭng) I. adj. pendiente II. prep. *(during)* durante; *(until)* hasta.
pen·du·lar (pĕn'jə-lər) adj. pendular.
pen·du·lous (:ləs) adj. colgante, pendiente.
pen·du·lum (:ləm) s. péndulo.
pen·e·tra·bil·i·ty (pĕn'ĭ-trə-bĭl'ĭ-tē) s. penetrabilidad *f*.
pen·e·tra·ble ('--bəl) adj. penetrable.
pen·e·trant (pĕn'ĭ-trənt) adj. penetrante.
pen·e·trate (:trāt') tr. penetrar; *(to understand)* entender, descubrir; *(to affect deeply)* conmover —intr. penetrar.
pen·e·trat·ing (:trā'tĭng) adj. penetrante.
pen·e·tra·tion ('-'shən) s. penetración *f*.
pen·guin (pĕng'gwĭn) s. pingüino.
pen·i·cil·lin (pĕn'ĭ-sĭl'ĭn) s. penicilina.
pen·in·su·la (pə-nĭn'syə-lə) s. península.
pe·nis (pē'nĭs) s. [pl. **es** *o* **-nes**] pene *m*.
pen·i·tence (pĕn'ĭ-təns) s. penitencia.
pen·i·tent (:tənt) adj. & s. penitente.
pen·i·ten·tial ('-tĕn'shəl) adj. penitencial.
pen·i·ten·tia·ry (:shə-rē) s. penitenciaria.
pen·knife (pĕn'nīf') s. [pl. **-ves**] navaja, cortaplumas *m*.
pen·man·ship (pĕn'mən-shĭp') s. caligrafía.
pen·nant (pĕn'ənt) s. pendón *m*, gallardete *m*.
pen·ni·less (pĕn'ĭ-lĭs) adj. sin dinero.
pen·ny (pĕn'ē) s. G.B. penique *m*; *(cent)* centavo ♦ **p. pincher** FAM. tacaño, mezquino • **to cost a pretty p.** costar un ojo de la cara.
pen·ny-wise (:wīz') adj. ♦ **to be p. and pound-foolish** hacer economías de chicha y nabo.
pe·nol·o·gy (pē-nŏl'ə-jē) s. penología.
pen·sion (pĕn'shən) I. s. pensión *f*, jubilación *f* II. tr. pensionar ♦ **to p. off** jubilar.
pen·sion·er (:shə-nər) s. pensionado.
pen·sive (pĕn'sĭv) adj. pensativo.
pen·ta·gon (pĕn'tə-gŏn') s. pentágono.
Pen·te·cost (pĕn'tĭ-kôst') s. Pentecostés *m*.
pent·house (pĕnt'hous') s. ático.
pent-up (pĕnt'ŭp') adj. reprimido, contenido.
pe·nul·ti·mate (pĭ-nŭl'tə-mĭt) adj. & s. penúltimo.
pe·num·bra (pĭ-nŭm'brə) s. [pl. **s** *o* **-ae**] penumbra.

pe·nu·ri·ous (pə-nŏŏr'ē-əs) adj. *(stingy)* tacaño, avaro; *(needy)* pobre, indigente.
pen·u·ry (pĕn'yə-rē) s. penuria.
pe·on (pē'ŏn') s. peón *m*; *(servant)* criado.
pe·o·ny (pē'ə-nē) s. peonía.
peo·ple (pē'pəl) I. s.pl. gente *f*; *(nation)* pueblo; *(in definite numbers)* personas <ten p. diez personas>; *(family)* familia; *(ancestors)* antepasados; *(human beings)* personas, seres humanos —s.sg. [pl. **s**] pueblo ♦ **p.'s republic** república popular • **the (common) p.** el pueblo, la gente común y corriente II. tr. poblar.
pep (pĕp) FAM. I. s. ánimo, empuje *m* ♦ **p. pill** JER. píldora de anfetamina • **p. talk** exhortación II. tr. **-pp-** ♦ **to p. up** animar, vigorizar.
pep·per (pĕp'ər) I. s. *(plant)* pimentero; *(condiment)* pimienta; *(fruit)* pimiento II. tr. sazonar con pimienta; *(to pelt)* acribillar; *(to enliven)* salpicar.
pep·per·corn (:kôrn') s. grano de pimienta.
pep·per·mint (:mĭnt') s. *(plant)* hierbabuena, menta; *(candy)* pastilla de menta.
pep·per·y (pĕp'ə-rē) adj. picante.
pep·py (pĕp'ē) adj. **-i-** FAM. lleno de vida, vivaz.
pep·tic (pĕp'tĭk) adj. péptico.
per (pûr) prep. por; *(according to)* según ♦ **as p. usual** como de costumbre • **p. capita** por cabeza • **p. se** por sí mismo.
per·am·bu·la·tor (pə-răm'byə-lā'tər) s. G.B. cochecito de niño.
per·cale (pər-kāl') s. percal *m*.
per·ceive (pər-sēv') tr. percibir; *(to notice)* notar, percatarse de; *(to understand)* comprender.
per cent *o* **per·cent** (pər-sĕnt') I. adv. por ciento II. s.inv. por ciento; *(percentage)* tanto por ciento, porcentaje *m*.
per·cent·age (:sĕn'tĭj) s. porcentaje *m*; FAM. *(gain)* provecho, ventaja.
per·cen·tile (:tīl') s. percentil *m*.
per·cept (pûr'sĕpt') s. percepción *f*.
per·cep·ti·ble (pər-sĕp'tə-bəl) adj. perceptible.
per·cep·tion (:shən) s. percepción *f*.
per·cep·tive (:tĭv) adj. perceptivo.
per·cep·tu·al (:chŏŏ-əl) adj. de percepción.
perch¹ (pûrch) I. s. percha; *(high place)* posición *f*, sitio II. intr. *(to roost)* posarse; *(to balance)* balancearse en un sitio elevado —tr. situar en un sitio elevado.
perch² s. [pl. inv. *o* **es**] ICT. perca.
per·chance (pər-chăns') adv. *(perhaps)* quizás, acaso; *(by chance)* por casualidad.
per·cip·i·ent (pər-sĭp'ē-ənt) adj. perceptor.
per·co·late (pûr'kə-lāt') tr. & intr. filtrar(se).
per·co·la·tor (:lā'tər) s. cafetera de filtro.
per·cuss (pər-kŭs') tr. MED. percutir.
per·cus·sion (:kŭsh'ən) s. percusión *f*.
per·cus·sion·ist (:ə-nĭst) s. músico que toca instrumentos de percusión.
per·cus·sive (pər-kŭs'ĭv) adj. de percusión.
per di·em (pər dē'əm) I. adv. diariamente II. s. dieta III. adj. diario.
per·di·tion (pər-dĭsh'ən) s. perdición *f*.
per·emp·to·ry (pə-rĕmp'tə-rē) adj. perentorio; *(dictatorial)* dictatorial.
per·en·ni·al (pə-rĕn'ē-əl) adj. & s. *(planta)* perenne.
per·fect (pûr'fĭkt) I. adj. perfecto; *(ideal)* ideal II. (pər-fĕkt') tr. perfeccionar.
per·fec·tion (pər-fĕk'shən) s. perfección *f*; *(perfecting)* perfeccionamiento ♦ **to p.** a la perfección.
per·fec·tion·ism (:shə-nĭz'əm) s. perfeccio-

nismo.

per·fec·tion·ist (:nĭst) s. perfeccionista *mf.*

per·fect·ly (pûr′fĭkt-lē) adv. perfectamente; *(completely)* completamente; *(utterly)* absolutamente.

per·fid·i·ous (pər-fĭd′ē-əs) adj. pérfido.

per·fi·dy (pûr′fĭ-dē) s. perfidia.

per·fo·rate (pûr′fə-rāt′) tr. perforar, agujerear.

per·fo·rat·ed (:rā′tĭd) adj. perforado.

per·fo·ra·tion (′-rā′shən) s. perforación *f.*

per·force (pər-fôrs′) adv. por fuerza.

per·form (pər-fôrm′) tr. *(to do)* ejecutar, hacer; *(a function)* desempeñar; TEAT. *(a role)* interpretar; *(a play)* representar; MÚS. ejecutar intr. *(to function)* funcionar, trabajar; *(to fulfill an obligation)* cumplir; TEAT. *(to act)* actuar; *(to do tricks)* hacer trucos; *(to sing)* cantar.

per·form·ance (pər-fôr′məns) s. *(doing)* ejecución *f; (of a function)* ejecución, desempeño; *(of a play)* representación *f; (of a role, musical composition)* interpretación *f; (in a competition)* actuación *f; (functioning)* funcionamiento; *(of an engine)* rendimiento; *(show)* función *f.*

per·form·er (:mər) s. *(actor)* artista *m; (musician)* músico; *(dancer)* bailarín *m.*

per·fume I. s. (pûr′fyōōm′, pər-fyōōm′) perfume II. tr. (pər-fyōōm′) perfumar.

per·func·to·ry (pər-fŭngk′tə-rē) adj. rutinario.

per·fuse (pər-fyōōz′) tr. *(to suffuse)* inundar, bañar; *(to diffuse)* introducir, hacer penetrar.

per·fu·sion (:fyōō′zhən) s. perfusión *f.*

per·haps (pər-hăps′) adv. quizá(s).

per·il (pĕr′əl) s. peligro.

per·il·ous (:ə-ləs) adj. peligroso, arriesgado.

pe·rim·e·ter (pə-rĭm′ĭ-tər) s. perímetro.

pe·ri·od (pîr′ē-əd) s. período, periodo; *(term)* plazo; *(age, stage)* época; *(class)* hora, clase *f; (playing time)* tiempo; *(menstruation)* período, regla; *(punctuation mark)* punto.

pe·ri·od·ic (′-ŏd′ĭk) adj. periódico.

pe·ri·od·i·cal (:ĭ-kəl) I. adj. periódico; *(of a journal)* de revistas II. s. publicación periódica, revista.

per·i·o·don·tal (pĕr′ē-ō-dŏn′tl) adj. periodontal.

pe·riph·er·al (pə-rĭf′ər-əl) adj. periférico.

pe·riph·er·y (:ə-rē) s. periferia.

per·i·scope (pĕr′ĭ-skōp′) s. periscopio.

per·ish (pĕr′ĭsh) intr. perecer; *(to spoil)* echarse a perder.

per·ish·a·ble (′ĭ-shə-bəl) I. adj. perecedero II. s. ‡ pl. artículos de fácil deterioro.

per·i·to·ni·tis (pĕr′ĭ-tn-ī′tĭs) s. peritonitis *f.*

per·jure (pûr′jər) tr. perjurar.

per·ju·ri·ous (pər-jŏŏr′ē-əs) adj. perjurador.

per·ju·ry (pûr′jə-rē) s. perjurio.

perk[1] (pûrk) intr. proyectarse, sobresalir ♦ **to p. up** animarse, reanimarse —tr. alzar, levantar ♦ **to p. up** *(to cheer up)* animar, reanimar; *(to spruce up)* adornar, engalanar; *(to improve)* ir mejor, ir mejorando ♦ **to p. up one's ears** aguzar el oído.

perk[2] s. FAM. *(privilege)* privilegio que corresponde a ciertos puestos.

perk·y (pûr′kē) adj. -i- animado, vivaz.

perm (pûrm) I. s. permanente *f* II. tr. & intr. hacer(se) una permanente.

per·ma·nence (pûr′mə-nəns) s. permanencia.

per·ma·nen·cy (:nən-sē) s. permanencia.

per·ma·nent (:nənt) I. adj. permanente II. s. permanente *f.*

per·me·a·bil·i·ty (pûr′mē-ə-bĭl′ĭ-tē) s. permeabilidad *f.*

per·me·a·ble (′--bəl) adj. permeable.

per·me·ate (pûr′mē-āt′) tr. & intr. penetrar, infiltrar(se).

per·mis·si·ble (pər-mĭs′ə-bəl) adj. permisible.

per·mis·sion (:mĭsh′ən) s. permiso

per·mis·sive (:ĭv) adj. permisivo; *(indulgent)* indulgente.

per·mit I. tr. (pər-mĭt′) **-tt-** permitir; *(to give consent to)* dar permiso a, dejar II. s. (pûr′mĭt) permiso.

per·mu·ta·tion (pûr′myōō-tā′shən) s. permutación *f.*

per·mute (pər-myōōt′) tr. permutar.

per·ni·cious (pər-nĭsh′əs) adj. pernicioso.

per·o·rate (pĕr′ə-rāt′) intr. perorar.

per·o·ra·tion (′-rā′shən) s. peroración *f.*

per·ox·ide (pə-rŏk′sīd′) I. s. peróxido; *(hydrogen peroxide)* peróxido de hidrógeno II. tr. *(to treat)* tratar con peróxido; *(to bleach)* aclarar con peróxido de hidrógeno.

per·pen·dic·u·lar (pûr′pən-dĭk′yə-lər) I. adj. perpendicular; *(vertical)* vertical II. s. perpendicular *f.*

per·pe·trate (pûr′pĭ-trāt′) tr. perpetrar.

per·pe·tra·tion (′-trā′shən) s. perpetración *f.*

per·pe·tra·tor (′-′tər) s. perpetrador *m.*

per·pet·u·al (pər-pĕch′ōō-əl) adj. perpetuo; *(constant)* constante; *(eternal)* eterno.

per·pet·u·ate (:āt′) tr. perpetuar.

per·pet·u·a·tion (′-ā′shən) s. perpetuación *f.*

per·pe·tu·i·ty (pûr′pĭ-tōō′ĭ-tē) s. perpetuidad *f.*

per·plex (pər-plĕks′) tr. desconcertar.

per·plexed (:plĕkst′) adj. perplejo, confuso.

per·plex·i·ty (:plĕk′sĭ-tē) s. perplejidad *f.*

per·qui·site (pûr′kwĭ-zĭt) s. ganancia extra.

per·se·cute (pûr′sĭ-kyōōt′) tr. perseguir; *(to harass)* acosar, atormentar

per·se·cu·tion (′-kyōō′shən) s. persecución *f.*

per·se·cu·tor (′-′tər) s. perseguidor *m.*

per·se·ver·ance (pûr′sə-vîr′əns) s. perseverancia.

per·se·vere (:vîr′) intr. perseverar.

per·sim·mon (pər-sĭm′ən) s. caqui *m.*

per·sist (pər-sĭst′) intr. persistir.

per·sist·ence/en·cy (:sĭs′təns) s. persistencia, empeño.

per·sist·ent (:tənt) adj. persistente.

per·snick·e·ty (pər-snĭk′ĭ-tē) adj. puntilloso, quisquilloso.

per·son (pûr′sən) s. persona.

per·son·a·ble (:sə-nə-bəl) adj. agradable.

per·son·age (:nĭj) s. personaje *m.*

per·son·al (pûr′sə-nəl) adj. personal; *(private)* particular; *(in person)* en persona; *(for one's use)* de uso personal ♦ **p. property** bienes muebles • **to get p.** hacer comentarios de carácter personal.

per·son·al·i·ty (′-năl′ĭ-tē) s. personalidad *f; (celebrity)* personaje *m*, figura.

per·son·al·ize (′-nə-līz′) tr. personalizar.

per·son·i·fi·ca·tion (pər-sŏn′ə-fĭ-kā′shən) s. personificación *f.*

per·son·i·fy (′-fī′) tr. personificar.

per·son·nel (pûr′sə-nĕl′) s. personal *m.*

per·spec·tive (pər-spĕk′tĭv) s. perspectiva ♦ **to put things in p.** apreciar las cosas en su justo valor.

per·spi·ca·cious (pûr′spĭ-kā′shəs) adj. perspicaz.

per·spi·cac·i·ty (:kăs′ĭ-tē) s. perspicacia.

per·spic·u·ous (pər-spĭk′yŏŏ-əs) adj. perspicuo.

per·spi·ra·tion (pûr′spə-rā′shən) s. sudor *m*, transpiración *f*.

per·spire (pər-spīr′) tr. & intr. sudar, transpirar.

per·suade (pər-swād′) tr. persuadir.

per·sua·sion (:swā′zhən) s. persuasión *f*, persuasiva; *(conviction)* convicción *f*, creencia.

per·sua·sive (:sĭv) adj. persuasivo.

per·sua·sive·ness (:nĭs) s. persuasión *f*.

pert (pûrt) adj. *(saucy)* impertinente; *(lively)* vivaz; *(jaunty)* alegre, gracioso.

per·tain (pər-tān′) intr. pertenecer; *(to relate to)* concernir.

per·ti·na·cious (pûr′tn-ā′shəs) adj. pertinaz; *(obstinate)* porfiado, obstinado.

per·ti·nence/nen·cy (′-əns) s. pertinencia.

per·ti·nent (:ənt) adj. pertinente.

per·turb (pər-tûrb′) tr. perturbar.

per·tur·ba·tion (pûr′tər-bā′shən) s. perturbación *f*.

per·tus·sis (pər-tŭs′ĭs) s. tos ferina.

pe·rus·al (pə-rŏŏ′zəl) s. lectura cuidadosa.

pe·ruse (pə-rŏŏz′) tr. leer cuidadosamente.

per·vade (pər-vād′) tr. penetrar, impregnar.

per·va·sive (:vā′sĭv) adj. penetrante.

per·verse (pər-vûrs′) adj. perverso; *(willful)* terco.

per·ver·sion (:vûr′zhən) s. perversión *f*.

per·ver·si·ty (:sĭ-tē) s. *(perversion)* perversión *f*; *(willfulness)* terquedad *f*.

per·vert I. tr. (pər-vûrt′) pervertir; *(to misuse)* abusar de II. s. (pûr′vûrt′) pervertido.

per·vert·ed (pər-vûr′tĭd) adj. pervertido.

pes·ky (pĕs′kē) adj. -i- FAM. molesto.

pes·si·mism (pĕs′ə-mĭz′əm) s. pesimismo.

pes·si·mist (:mĭst) s. pesimista *mf*.

pes·si·mis·tic (′-mĭs′tĭk) adj. pesimista.

pest (pĕst) s. *(insect)* insecto; *(person)* pelmazo, persona molesta; *(plant, animal)* plaga, peste *f*.

pes·ter (pĕs′tər) tr. molestar, fastidiar.

pes·ti·cide (pĕs′tĭ-sīd′) s. pesticida, insecticida.

pes·tif·er·ous (pĕ-stĭf′ər-əs) adj. pestífero.

pes·ti·lence (pĕs′tə-ləns) s. pestilencia, peste *f*.

pes·ti·lent/len·tial (pĕs′tə-lənt/lĕn′shəl) adj. pestilente; *(annoying)* molesto.

pes·tle (pĕs′əl, pĕs′təl) mano *f* (de mortero).

pet (pĕt) I. s. animal domesticado; *(person)* favorito, preferido II. adj. domesticado; *(favorite)* favorito III. tr. -tt- *(to caress)* acariciar; *(to pamper)* mimar.

pet·al (pĕt′l) s. pétalo.

pe·ter (pē′tər) intr. ♦ **to p. out** disminuir.

pe·tite (pə-tēt′) adj. pequeña, chiquita.

pe·ti·tion (pə-tĭsh′ən) I. s. petición *f* II. tr. suplicar, pedir a.

pe·ti·tion·er (:ə-nər) s. peticionario.

pet·ri·fy (pĕt′rə-fī′) tr. & intr. petrificar(se).

pet·ro·chem·i·cal (pĕt′rō-kĕm′ĭ-kəl) s. producto petroquímico.

pet·rol (pĕt′rəl) s. G.B. gasolina.

pe·tro·le·um (pə-trō′lē-əm) s. petróleo ♦ **p. jelly** petrolato.

pet·ti·coat (pĕt′ē-kōt′) I. s. enaguas II. adj. femenino, de mujeres.

pet·ti·ness (pĕt′ē-nĭs) s. *(smallness)* pequeñez *f*; *(behavior)* mezquindad *f*.

pet·ting (pĕt′ĭng) s. FAM. besuqueo.

pet·ty (pĕt′ē) adj. -i- *(insignificant)* insignificante, trivial; *(narrow-minded)* mezquino; *(spiteful)* rencoroso ♦ **p. cash** caja chica • **p.**

---

lar·ce·ny hurto menor, ratería.

pet·u·lance (pĕch′ə-ləns) s. malhumor *m*.

pet·u·lant (:lənt) adj. malhumorado.

pe·tu·nia (pĭ-tŏŏn′yə) s. petunia.

pew (pyŏŏ) s. banco de iglesia.

pew·ter (pyŏŏ′tər) s. & adj. (de) peltre *m*.

pha·lanx (fā′lăngks′) s. [pl. **es** o **-ges**] falange *f*.

phal·lic (făl′ĭk) adj. fálico.

phal·lus (:əs) s. [pl. **es** o **-li**] falo.

phan·tasm (făn′tăz′əm) s. fantasma *m*.

phan·tom (:təm) I. s. fantasma *m* II. adj. fantasmal.

phar·aoh (fâr′ō) s. faraón *m*.

phar·i·see (fâr′ĭ-sē) s. fariseo.

phar·ma·ceu·ti·cal (fär′mə-sŏŏ′tĭ-kəl) adj. & s. farmacéutico ♦ **pharmaceutics** s.sg. farmacia.

phar·ma·cist (′sĭst) s. farmacéutico.

phar·ma·col·o·gy (′-kŏl′ə-jē) s. farmacología.

phar·ma·co·poe·ia (:kə-pē′ə) s. farmacopea.

phar·ma·cy (fär′mə-sē) s. farmacia.

phar·ynx (fär′ĭngks) s. [pl. **es** o **-ges**] faringe *f*.

phase (fāz) I. s. fase ♦ **in p.** en fase, sincronizado • **out of p.** desfasado II. tr. *(to plan)* planear por fases, escalonar; ELEC., FÍS. poner en fase ♦ **to p. in** introducir progresivamente • **to p. out** eliminar progresivamente.

phase·out (′out′) s. eliminación *f* gradual.

pheas·ant (fĕz′ənt) s. [pl. inv. o **s**] faisán *m*.

phe·nom·e·na (fĭ-nŏm′ə-nə) cf. **phenomenon**.

phe·nom·e·nal (:nəl) adj. fenomenal.

phe·nom·e·non (fĭ-nŏm′ə-nŏn′) s. [pl. **s** o **-na**] fenómeno.

phew (fyŏŏ) interj. ¡uy!, ¡puf!

phi·al (fī′əl) s. frasco pequeño.

phi·lan·der (fĭ-lăn′dər) intr. galantear.

phi·lan·der·er (:ər) s. galanteador *m*, tenorio.

phil·an·throp·ic/i·cal (fĭl′ən-thrŏp′ĭk) adj. filantrópico.

phi·lan·thro·pist (fĭ-lăn′thrə-pĭst) s. filántropo.

phi·lan·thro·py (:pē) s. filantropía.

phi·lat·e·ly (fĭ-lăt′l-ē) s. filatelia.

phil·har·mon·ic (fĭl′här-mŏn′ĭk) adj. & s. (orquesta) filarmónica.

Phil·is·tine (fĭl′ĭ-stēn) s. filisteo.

phil·o·den·dron (fĭl′ə-dĕn′drən) s. [pl. **s** o **-dra**] filodendro.

phi·lol·o·gy (fĭ-lŏl′ə-jē) s. filología.

phi·los·o·pher (fĭ-lŏs′ə-fər) s. filósofo.

phil·o·soph·ic/i·cal (fĭl′ə-sŏf′ĭk) adj. filosófico.

phi·los·o·phize (fĭ-lŏs′ə-fīz′) intr. filosofar.

phi·los·o·phy (:fē) s. filosofía.

phil·ter (fĭl′tər) s. filtro, poción *f*.

phle·bi·tis (flĭ-bī′tĭs) s. flebitis *f*.

phle·bot·o·my (:bŏt′ə-mē) s. flebotomía.

phlegm (flĕm) s. flema.

phleg·mat·ic (flĕg-măt′ĭk) adj. flemático.

pho·bi·a (fō′bē-ə) s. fobia.

phoe·nix (fē′nĭks) s. fénix *m*.

phone (fōn) FAM. I. s. teléfono II. tr. & intr. telefonear, llamar por teléfono.

pho·neme (fō′nēm′) s. fonema *m*.

pho·net·ic (fə-nĕt′ĭk) adj. fonético ♦ **phonetics** s.sg. fonética.

pho·ne·ti·cian/net·i·cist (fō′nĭ-tĭsh′ən/fə-nĕt′ĭ-sĭst) s. fonetista *mf*.

phon·ic (fŏn′ĭk) adj. fónico ♦ **phonics** s.sg. fonética.

pho·no·graph (fō′nə-grăf′) s. fonógrafo.

pho·nog·ra·phy (fə-nŏg′rə-fē) s. fonografía.

pho·nol·o·gy (fə-nŏl′ə-jē) s. fonología.

pho·ny (fō′nē) FAM. I. adj. -i- falso; *(fake)*

postizo II. s. *(object)* camelo; *(person)* farsante *mf*, camelista *mf*.

phoo·ey (fōō'ē) interj. ¡puf!

phos·phate (fŏs'fāt') s. fosfato.

phos·phor (:fər) s. substancia fosforescente.

phos·pho·res·cent ('fə-rĕs'ənt) adj. fosforescente.

phos·phor·ic (-fôr'ĭk) adj. fosfórico.

phos·pho·rus (:fər-əs) s. fósforo.

pho·to (fō'tō) s. foto, fotografía.

pho·to·cell (:sĕl') s. fotocélula.

pho·to·cop·i·er (fō'tə-kŏp'ē-ər) s. fotocopiadora.

pho·to·cop·y (:ē) I. tr. fotocopiar II. s. fotocopia.

pho·to·e·lec·tric/tri·cal (fō'tō-ĭ-lĕk'trĭk) adj. fotoeléctrico.

pho·to·en·grave (:ĕn-grāv') tr. fotograbar.

pho·to·gen·ic (fō'tə-jĕn'ĭk) adj. fotogénico.

pho·to·graph (fō'tə-grăf') I. s. fotografía, foto *f* II. tr. fotografiar, sacar una fotografía —intr. ♦ **to p. well** salir bien en las fotografías.

pho·tog·ra·pher (fə-tŏg'rə-phər) s. fotógrafo.

pho·to·graph·ic (fō'tə-grăf'ĭk) adj. fotográfico.

pho·tog·ra·phy (fə-tŏg'rə-fē) s. fotografía.

pho·ton (fō'tŏn') s. fotón *m*.

pho·to·sen·si·tive (fō'tō-sĕn'sĭ-tĭv) adj. fotosensible.

pho·to·stat (fō'tə-stăt') s fotostato

pho·to·syn·the·sis (fō'tō-sĭn'thĭ-sĭs) s. fotosíntesis *f*.

phrase (frāz) I. s. frase *f* ♦ **p. book** diccionario de expresiones ♦ **set p.** frase hecha II. tr. *(in speaking)* expresar; *(in writing)* redactar.

phra·se·ol·o·gy (frā'zē-ŏl'ə-jē) s. fraseología.

phras·ing (frā'zĭng) s. *(wording)* estilo, lenguaje *m*; *(phraseology)* fraseología.

phre·nol·o·gy (frĭ-nŏl'ə-jē) s. frenología.

phy·lum (fī'ləm) s. [pl. **-la**] filum *m*.

phys·ic (fĭz'ĭk) s. catártico.

phys·i·cal (fĭz'ĭ-kəl) I. adj. físico II. s. reconocimiento médico, chequeó.

phy·si·cian (fĭ-zĭsh'ən) s. médico, facultativo.

phys·i·cist (fĭz'ĭ-sĭst) s. físico.

phys·ics (fĭz'ĭks) s.sg. física.

phys·i·o·log·ic/i·cal (fĭz'ē-ə-lŏj'ĭk) adj. fisiológico.

phys·i·ol·o·gist (:ŏl'ə-jĭst) s. fisiólogo.

phys·i·ol·o·gy (:jē) s. fisiología.

phys·i·o·ther·a·py (fĭz'ē-ō-thĕr'ə-pē) s. fisioterapia.

phy·sique (fĭ-zēk') s. físico.

pi·an·ist (pē-ăn'ĭst, pē'ə-nĭst) s. pianista *mf*.

pi·an·o (pē-ăn'ō) s. piano.

pi·az·za (pē-ăz'ə, -ä'zə) s. [pl. **s** *o* **-ze**] plaza; *(verandah)* galería, terraza.

pi·ca (pī'kə) s. IMPR. pica.

pic·a·resque (pĭk'ə-rĕsk') adj. picaresco.

pic·a·yune (pĭk'ē-yōōn') adj. *(paltry)* insignificante; *(petty)* mezquino.

pic·co·lo (pĭk'ə-lō') s. flautín *m*.

pick¹ (pĭk) I. tr. escoger, elegir; *(to gather)* recoger; *(to strip clean)* mondar; *(to pluck)* desplumar; *(to tear off)* sacar, arrancar; *(to break up)* cavar; *(to open)* abrir; *(to peck)* picar, picotear ♦ **to p. a fight** buscar bronca ♦ **to p. apart** *(to tear)* destrozar, despedazar; *(to refute)* echar por tierra ♦ **to p. off** matar de un solo tiro ♦ **to p. oneself up** levantarse ♦ **to p. one's nose** hurgarse la nariz ♦ **to p. one's teeth** mondarse los dientes ♦ **to p. out** *(to choose)* escoger, seleccionar; *(to distinguish)* distinguir ♦ **to p. over**

inspeccionar ♦ **to p. someone's brains** FIG. explotar los conocimientos de alguien ♦ **to p. someone's pocket** robar algo del bolsillo de alguien ♦ **to p. up** *(to lift)* coger; *(fallen object)* recoger; *(to tidy)* recoger; *(to stop for)* recoger; FAM. *(to buy)* comprar; *(to learn)* aprender; *(to notice)* encontrar; *(a habit)* coger, adquirir; *(to pay)* pagar; *(a disease)* coger, pescar; RAD., TELEV. coger, captar; *(speed)* cobrar; JER. *(to arrest)* pescar, coger; *(to continue)* reanudar, proseguir ♦ **to p. up on** darse cuenta de —intr. picar; *(to decide)* decidir cuidadosamente ♦ **to p. at** *(food)* picar, picotear; FAM. *(to nag)* cogerla con ♦ **to p. on** *(to tease)* atormentar; *(to bully)* abusar de ♦ **to p. up** *(to resume)* continuar; FAM. *(to improve)* mejorar II. s. elección *f*, selección *f* ♦ **the p. of the crop** *o* **of the litter** la flor y nata.

pick² s. *(tool)* piqueta, pico; *(picklock)* ganzúa; MÚS. plectro, púa.

pick·a·back (pĭk'ə-băk') I. adv. a cuestas, sobre los hombros II. s. paseo a cuestas.

pick·ax(e) (pĭk'ăks') s. piqueta, zapapico.

picked (pĭkt) adj. escogido, selecto.

pick·et (pĭk'ĭt) I. s. estaca; MIL. piquete *m*; *(strikers)* piquete II. tr. *(to enclose)* cercar con estacas; *(to guard)* guardar *o* vigilar con piquetes —intr. vigilar, estar de guardia.

pick·ing (pĭk'ĭng) s. *(harvest)* recogida, recolección *f*; *(choice)* selección *f* ♦ pl. sobras, restos.

pick·le (pĭk'əl) I. s. *(food)* encurtido; *(solution)* salmuera, escabeche *m*; FAM. *(plight)* lío II. tr. encurtir.

pick·led (:əld) adj. *(food)* en salmuera *o* escabeche; *(person)* borracho, bebido.

pick·pock·et (pĭk'pŏk'ĭt) s. carterista *mf*.

pick·up (pĭk'ŭp') s. *(collection)* recogida; *(acceleration)* poder *m* de aceleración; *(truck)* camioneta; *(increase)* aumento; *(improvement)* mejora; FAM. *(casual acquaintance)* ligue *m*.

pick·y (pĭk'ē) adj. -i- quisquilloso.

pic·nic (pĭk'nĭk) I. s. picnic *m* ♦ **to be no p.** FAM. no ser fácil II. intr. -ck- comer al aire libre.

pic·to·ri·al (pĭk-tôr'ē-əl) adj. pictórico.

pic·ture (pĭk'chər) I. s. *(painting)* cuadro, pintura; *(illustration)* ilustración *f*; *(photograph)* fotografía; *(portrait)* retrato; *(mental image)* imagen *f*, idea; *(description)* descripción *f*, cuadro; *(physical image)* retrato, imagen; *(film)* película, filme *m*; *(television)* imagen ♦ **p. book** libro ilustrado ♦ **p. tube** TELEV. pantalla ♦ **p. window** ventanal ♦ **pretty as a p.** una monada ♦ **to be out of the p.** quedar fuera del juego ♦ **to come into the p.** aparecer ♦ **to give somebody the general p.** dar a alguien una idea general II. tr. *(to paint)* pintar; *(to draw)* dibujar; *(to visualize)* imaginar; *(to describe)* pintar.

pic·tur·esque (pĭk'chə-rĕsk') adj. pintoresco.

pid·dling (pĭd'lĭng) adj. insignificante, trivial.

pid·gin (pĭj'ĭn) s. lengua franca.

pie (pī) s. *(with meat)* empanada; *(with fruit)* pastel *m* ♦ **as easy as p.** FAM. muy fácil ♦ **p. in the sky** ilusiones ♦ **to have a finger in the p.** estar metido en el asunto.

piece (pēs) I. s. pedazo; *(in a set)* pieza; *(specimen)* muestra; *(firearm)* arma; *(distance)* tramo; LIT., MÚS. obra ♦ **in one p.** *(object)* en buen estado; *(person)* sano y salvo ♦ **to give someone a p. of one's mind** FAM. cantar a alguien las cuarenta ♦ **to say one's p.** decir lo que uno piensa ♦ pl. **in p.** *(unassembled)* de sarmado; *(shattered)* hecho añicos • **to go to p.** FAM. no poderse dominar II. tr. ♦ **to p. together** *(to put together)* armar; *(to rearrange)* rehacer; *(to figure out)* llegar a entender.

piece·meal (':mēl') adv. *(bit by bit)* a trozos; *(gradually)* poco a poco.

piece·work (:wûrk') s. trabajo a destajo.

pier (pîr) s. muelle *m*, embarcadero; *(of a bridge)* pila; *(of an arch)* pilar *m*; *(between windows)* entreventana; *(buttress)* contrafuerte *m*.

pierce (pîrs) tr. *(to puncture)* traspasar; *(to perforate)* perforar; *(to penetrate)* atravesar, abrirse paso por ♦ **to have o get one's ears pierced** hacerse agujeros en las orejas.

pierc·ing (pîr'sĭng) adj. *(sharp)* agudo; *(look)* penetrante; *(wind)* cortante.

pi·e·ty (pī'ĭ-tē) s. piedad *f*.

pig (pĭg) I. s. cerdo, puerco; *(pork)* lechón *m*; FAM. *(glutton)* tragón, glotón *m*; *(slob)* cochino, puerco; METAL. lingote *m* ♦ **a p. in a poke** *(pig comprado)* sin saber exactamente qué es • **p. iron** hierro en lingotes II. intr. **-pp-** ♦ **to p. out** comer como un puerco.

pi·geon (pĭj'ən) s. paloma; *(dupe)* tonto.

pi·geon·hole (:hōl') I. s. *(cubbyhole)* casilla; *(category)* clasificación *f* II. tr. *(to file)* archivar; *(to categorize)* clasificar; *(to shelve)* dar carpetazo a.

pi·geon-toed (:tōd') adj. de pies que apuntan hacia adentro.

pig·gish (pĭg'ĭsh) adj. *(greedy)* glotón; *(pigheaded)* testarudo.

pig·gy (:ē) s. cerdito ♦ **p. bank** alcancía.

pig·gy·back (:băk') I. adv. a cuestas; *(in transportation)* en vagón plataforma II. adj. ♦ **p. ride** paseo a cuestas.

pig·head·ed (pĭg'hĕd'ĭd) adj. testarudo, terco.

pig·let (:lĭt) s. cochinillo, lechón *m*.

pig·ment (pĭg'mənt) s. pigmento.

pig·men·ta·tion ('mən-tā'shən) s. pigmentación *f*.

pig·pen (pĭg'pĕn') s. pocilga.

pig·skin (:skĭn') s. piel *f* o cuero de cerdo; *(football)* pelota.

pig·sty (:stī') s. pocilga.

pig·tail (:tāl') s. coleta, trenza.

pike¹ (pīk) s. *(spear)* pica.

pike² s. [pl. inv. o **s**] *(fish)* lucio.

pike³ s. *(turnpike)* carretera de peaje.

pike⁴ s. *(sharp point)* punta.

pile¹ (pīl) I. s. pila, montón *m*; *(funeral pyre)* pira funeraria; JER. *(fortune)* fortuna; FÍS. pila atómica II. tr. apilar, amontar; *(to fill)* llenar ♦ **to p. it on** exagerar • **to p. up** apilar, amontonar —intr. amontonarse ♦ **to p. in** entrar en tropel • **to p. up** acumularse.

pile² (pīl) s. *(furry surface)* pelo.

piles (pīlz) s.pl. hemorroides *f*, almorranas.

pile-up (pīl'ŭp') s. accidente *m* entre varios vehículos.

pil·fer (pĭl'fər) tr. & intr. robar.

pil·fer·age (:ĭj) s. robo.

pil·grim (pĭl'grĭm) s. *(devotee)* peregrino; *(traveler)* viajante *mf*.

pil·grim·age (:grə-mĭj) s. peregrinación *f*.

pil·ing (pī'lĭng) s. *(foundation)* cimentación *f* con pilotes; *(piles)* pilotaje *m*.

pill (pĭl) I. s. píldora; *(contraceptive)* píldora anticonceptiva; *(person)* pelmazo II. intr. formar pelotillas o bolitas.

pil·lage (pĭl'ĭj) I. tr. & intr. pillar, saquear II. s. pillaje *m*, saqueo.

pil·lag·er (:ĭ-jər) s. pillador *m*, saqueador *m*.

pil·lar (pĭl'ər) s. pilar *m* ♦ **from p. to post** de la Ceca a la Meca.

pill·box (pĭl'bŏks') s. cajita para píldoras; *(hat)* pequeño sombrero sin ala; MIL. fortín *m*.

pil·lo·ry (pĭl'ə-rē) I. s. picota II. tr. poner en la picota.

pil·low (pĭl'ō) I. s. almohada; *(for decoration)* almohadón *m* II. tr. *(to rest)* hacer descansar sobre una almohada; *(to support)* servir de almohada.

pil·low·case (:kās') s. funda de almohada.

pi·lot (pī'lət) I. s. AVIA. piloto; MARÍT. *(in a port)* práctico del puerto; *(helmsman)* piloto, timonel *m*; *(leader)* guía *mf*, director *m*; TELEV. programa *m* de introducción de una serie ♦ **p. light** llama piloto II. tr. pilotear III. adj. *(trial)* piloto, experimental; *(guiding)* modelo.

pi·men·to (pĭ-mĕn'tō) s. pimiento, ají *m*.

pi·mien·to (pĭ-mĕn'tō, -myĕn'-) s. pimiento morrón.

pimp (pĭmp) I. s. alcahuete *m* II. intr. alcahuetear.

pim·ple (pĭm'pəl) s. grano.

pim·ply (:plē) adj. granujiento, espinilloso.

pin (pĭn) I. s. alfiler *m*; *(badge)* insignia; *(brooch)* broche *m*; *(cotter)* pasador *m*, chaveta; *(bolt)* perno; *(peg)* clavija; *(in bowling)* bolo ♦ **to hear a p. drop** oír el vuelo de una mosca II. tr. **-nn-** prender con alfileres; *(in wrestling)* sujetar ♦ **to p. down** sujetar, asegurar; *(to immobilize)* inmovilizar; *(to establish)* determinar, precisar; *(to force to be specific)* hacer que (alguien) sea más preciso • **to p. on** prender en; *(hopes)* cifrar en; *(to blame)* echar la culpa a • **to p. up** *(hair)* sujetar con horquillas; *(a notice)* clavar con chinchetas.

pin·a·fore (pĭn'ə-fôr') s. delantal *m*.

pin·ball (pĭn'bôl') s. billar romano.

pince-nez (păns'nā', pĭns'-) s.inv. quevedos *m*.

pin·cer (pĭn'sər) s. pinza ♦ **p.** pl. pinzas, tenazas.

pinch (pĭnch) I. tr. pellizcar; *(to catch)* cogerse, pillarse; *(shoes)* apretar; *(to cause hardship)* poner en aprietos a; JER. *(to steal)* ratear, mangar; *(to arrest)* pescar, prender ♦ **to p. pennies** andar con tacañerías, escatimar gastos —intr. *(shoes)* apretar; *(to economize)* escatimar gastos II. s. pellizco; *(of seasoning)* pizca; *(of snuff)* pulgarada ♦ **in a p.** en caso de apuro o de necesidad • **to feel the p.** pasar apuros, verse apretado.

pin·cush·ion (pĭn'kŏosh'ən) s. alfiletero.

pine¹ (pīn) s. pino ♦ **p. cone** piña.

pine² intr. ♦ **to p. away** consumirse, languidecer • **to p. for** suspirar por, anhelar.

pine·ap·ple (pīn'ăp'əl) s. piña, ananás *m*.

ping (pĭng) I. s. sonido metálico II. intr. producir un sonido metálico.

pin·head (pĭn'hĕd') s. cabeza de alfiler; *(stupid person)* tonto, bobo.

pink¹ (pĭngk) I. s. clavel *m*; *(color)* rosado, rosa ♦ **in the p.** rebosante de salud • **in the p. of** en perfecto estado de II. adj. rosado, rosa.

pink² tr. *(to decorate)* festonear; *(to perforate)* picar ♦ **pinking shears** tijeras dentadas.

pink·eye o **pink eye** (:'ī') s. conjuntivitis aguda.

pink·ie (pĭng'kē) s. FAM. dedo meñique.

pink·ish (pĭng'kĭsh) adj. rosáceo.

pink·o (:kō) s. JER. rojillo, comunacho.

pink·y (pĭng'kē) s. FAM. dedo meñique.

pin·na·cle (pĭn'ə-kəl) s. ARQ. pináculo; *(peak)* pico, cima; FIG. cumbre *f*.

pi·noc(h)·le (pē'nŭk'əl) s. juego de naipes.
pin·point (pin'point') I. s. punta de alfiler II. tr. localizar con precisión III. adj. exacto.
pin·prick (:prik') s. alfilerazo; *(minor annoyance)* molestia.
pin·stripe (:strip') I. s. raya fina II. adj. de rayas finas.
pint (pīnt) s. pinta.
pint-size(d) ('sīz[d]') adj. FAM. pequeño.
pin·up (pin'ŭp') s. *(picture)* fotografía de una mujer atractiva; *(woman)* mujer atractiva.
pin·wheel (:hwēl') s. molinillo; *(fireworks)* girándula.
pi·o·neer (pī'ə-nîr') I. s. pionero II. adj. *(innovating)* innovador; *(of settlers)* de pionero III. tr. *(lo explore)* iniciar la exploración de; *(to open up)* marcar nuevos rumbos en; *(to settle)* colonizar.
pi·ous (pī'əs) adj. piadoso; *(hypocritical)* beato; *(commendable)* digno de alabanza.
pip (pip) s. *(seed)* pepita.
pipe (pīp) I. s. *(for liquids, gas)* tubería, cañería; *(for tobacco)* pipa ♦ **exhaust p.** tubo de escape • **p. cleaner** limpiapipas • **p. dream** ilusión, castillos en el aire • **p. wrench** llave para tubos • **put that in your p. and smoke it!** FAM. ¡chúpate ésa! II. tr. *(tubes)* tubería, cañería; *(bagpipe)* gaita II. tr. *(liquids, gas)* conducir por tuberías; *(to provide with pipes)* instalar tuberías o cañerías en —intr. MÚS. tocar; *(to screech)* chillar; *(bird)* cantar ♦ **to p. down** JER. cerrar el pico, callarse la boca • **to p.** prorrumpir chillando.
pipe·line (:līn') s. *(gas)* gasoducto; *(oil)* oleoducto; *(information)* conducto; *(supply)* línea.
pip·er (pī'pər) s. *(flutist)* flautista *mf; (bagpiper)* gaitero.
pi·pet(te) (pī-pĕt') s. pipeta, probeta.
pip·ing (pī'pĭng) I. s. *(pipes)* tubería, cañería; *(on clothing)* ribete *m* II. adj. ♦ **p. hot** muy caliente.
pip·squeak (pĭp'skwēk') s. cero a la izquierda.
pi·quant (pē'kənt) adj. *(spicy)* picante; *(provocative)* provocativo.
pique (pēk) I. s. pique *m* ♦ **in a fit of p.** por resentimiento II. tr. *(to vex)* picar, molestar; *(interest)* despertar.
pi·ra·cy (pī'rə-sē) s. piratería.
pi·rate (pī'rĭt) I. s. pirata *m; (thief)* persona que comete fraudes II. tr. *(to rob)* robar, pillar; *(books, records)* hacer una edición pirata de.
pir·ou·ette (pĭr'õo-ĕt') I. s. pirueta, cabriola II. intr. piruetear, hacer cabriolas.
pis·ta·chi·o (pĭ-stăsh'ē-õ') s. *(tree)* pistachero, alfóncigo; *(nut)* pistacho, alfóncigo.
pis·tol (pĭs'təl) s. pistola.
pis·ton (pĭs'tən) s. pistón *m*.
pit¹ (pĭt) I. s. *(hole)* hoyo, pozo; *(for cockfights)* reñidero; *(pockmark)* picadura de viruela; *(on a stock exchange)* sección *f* de la bolsa dedicada a una sola transacción; *(for a mechanic)* foso; *(at a racecourse)* puesto ♦ **in the p. of one's stomach** en la boca del estómago • **orchestra p.** foso de la orquesta • **the pits** JER. lo peor de lo peor II. tr. **-tt-** *(to make holes in)* llenar de hoyos; *(by a disease)* llenar de picaduras ♦ **to p. against** oponer —intr. *(surface)* llenarse de hoyos; *(skin)* llenarse de picaduras o de marcas.
pit² I. s. hueso (de frutas) II. tr. **-tt-** deshuesar.
pit·a·pat (pĭt'ə-păt') I. intr. **-tt-** *(to move)* moverse con paso ligero; *(to beat)* latir rápidamente II. s. *(steps)* paso ligero; *(beats)* latido,

palpitación *f* III. adv. ♦ **to go p.** latir rápidamente.
pitch¹ (pĭch) I. s. *(sticky substance)* pez *f; (bitumen)* alquitrán *m*, brea; *(resin)* resina II. tr. embrear, embetunar.
pitch² I. tr. *(to throw)* lanzar, tirar; *(hay)* echar; *(tent)* montar, armar; *(speech)* ajustar; *(a product)* pregonar las virtudes de; *(to incline)* inclinar ♦ **to p. camp** acampar —intr. *(to fall)* caer(se); *(to lurch)* tambalearse, dar tumbos; *(plane, ship)* cabecear; *(to slope)* inclinarse ♦ **to p. in** FAM. dar una mano II. s. *(throw)* lanzamiento, tiro; *(intensity)* grado; *(of a ship)* cabeceo; *(slope)* inclinación *f; (of a roof)* pendiente *f*, JER. *(talk)* charlatanería; MÚS. tono ♦ **p. pipe** diapasón.
pitch-black ('blăk') adj. *(dark)* oscuro como boca de lobo; *(black)* negro como el carbón.
pitch-dark (:dark') adj. oscuro como boca de lobo.
pitch·er¹ (pĭch'ər) s. DEP. lanzador *m*.
pitch·er² s. jarra, cántaro.
pitch·fork (pĭch'fôrk') s. horquilla, horca.
pit·e·ous (pĭt'ē-əs) adj. lastimoso, lastimero; *(pathetic)* patético.
pit·fall (pĭt'fôl') s. *(trap)* trampa; *(difficulty)* dificultad *f*.
pith (pĭth) s. BOT. médula; *(essence)* meollo.
pith·y (pĭth'ē) adj. **-i-** meduloso, medular; *(substantial)* substancial.
pit·i·a·ble (pĭt'ē-ə-bəl) adj. lastimoso.
pit·i·ful (pĭt'ĭ-fəl) adj. lastimoso; *(contemptible)* despreciable.
pit·i·less (:lĭs) adj. despiadado.
pit·tance (pĭt'ns) s. miseria.
pit·ter-pat·ter (pĭt'ər-păt'ər) I. s. *(tapping)* golpeteo; *(of rain)* tamborileo II. intr. *(to tap)* golpetear; *(to rain)* tamborilear.
pi·tu·i·tar·y (pī-tōo'ĭ-tĕr'ē) s. & adj (glándula) pituitaria.
pit·y (pĭt'ē) I. s. piedad *f; (regrettable fact)* lástima, pena II. intr. & tr. compadecer(se) de.
piv·ot (pĭv'ət) I. s. *(shaft)* pivote *m; (center)* eje *m; (turn)* pivote II. tr. hacer girar ♦ **to p. on** *(to turn)* girar sobre; *(to depend on)* depender de —intr. girar sobre un eje.
piv·o·tal ('ə-tl) adj. *(turning)* giratorio, de giro; *(essential)* fundamental, cardinal.
pix·y/ie (pĭk'sē) s. duendecillo, hada traviesa.
piz·za (pēt'sə) s. pizza.
plac·ard (plăk'ärd') I. s. cartel *m*, letrero II. tr. *(to announce)* anunciar por medio de carteles; *(to post)* poner carteles.
pla·cate (plā'kāt', plăk'āt') tr. apaciguar.
place (plās) I. s. lugar *m; (locale)* sitio, local *m; (house)* casa; *(seat)* asiento; *(place setting)* cubierto; *(in a book)* página por donde uno va; *(function)* función *f, (rank)* posición *f* social; *(in a line)* puesto ♦ **all over the p.** por todas partes • **any p.** en o a dondequiera • **if I were in your p.** yo que tú • **in high places** en las altas esferas • **in p.** en orden • **in p. of** en lugar de, en vez de • **not to be one's p.** no corresponderle a uno • **out of p.** fuera de lugar • **p. mat** mantelito individual • **p. setting** cubierto • **to go places** FAM. llegar lejos • **to know one's p.** saber guardar las distancias • **to put someone in his p.** poner a alguien en su lugar • **to take p.** *(to happen)* tener lugar; *(to be held)* celebrarse • **to take the p. of** sustituir II. tr. colocar, poner; *(to situate)* situar, ubicar; *(to estimate)* calcular; *(to bet)* hacer; *(to call)* pedir ♦ **to be**

able to p. saber dónde uno ha visto • **to p. an order** hacer un pedido —intr. clasificarse entre los tres primeros.

pla·ce·bo (plə-sē'bō) s. [pl. **(e)s**] placebo.

place·ment (plās'mənt) s. colocación f.

pla·cen·ta (plə-sĕn'tə) s. [pl. **s** o **-ae**] placenta.

plac·id (plăs'ĭd) adj. tranquilo, apacible.

pla·gia·rism (plā'jə-rĭz'əm) s. plagio.

pla·gia·rize (:rīz') tr. & intr. plagiar.

plague (plāg) I. s. (disease) peste f; (nuisance) molestia, fastidio; (outbreak) plaga II. tr. atormentar.

plaid (plăd) s. tela a cuadros; (pattern) diseño a cuadros.

plain (plān) I. adj. (obvious) claro, evidente; (simple) sencillo; (straightforward) claro, sin rodeos; (unmixed) puro, solo; (unaffected) llano, corriente; (unpatterned) sin adornos; (unattractive) nada atractivo; (utter) puro, absoluto • **in p. sight** a la vista de todos • **the p. truth** la pura verdad II. s. llanura, llano • pl. praderas III. adv. (bluntly) claro; (utterly) absolutamente.

plain·song ('sông') s. canto llano.

plaint (plānt) s. (complaint) queja; (lamentation) lamento, quejido.

plain·tiff (plānt'ĭf) s. demandante mf.

plain·tive (:tĭv) adj. quejumbroso.

plait (plāt, plăt) I. s. (hair) trenza; (pleat) pliegue m II. tr. trenzar.

plan (plăn) I. s. plan m; (schedule) programa m; (intention) intención f; (project) proyecto; (outline) esquema m; (diagram) plano II. tr. **-nn-** planear, proyectar; (to project) planificar; (to draw) hacer el plano de; (to design) diseñar • **to p. to** pensar • **to p. for** esperar —intr. hacer planes • **to p. on** (to count on) contar con, hacerse la idea de; (to intend to) pensar; (to expect) esperar.

plane (plān) I. s. MAT. plano f; (surface) superficie plana; (level) nivel m; (airplane) avión m; CARP. cepillo II. tr. CARP. cepillar.

plan·et (plăn'ĭt) s. planeta m.

plan·e·tar·i·um (:ĭ-târ'ē-əm) s. [pl. **s** o **-ia**] planetario.

plan·e·tar·y ('-tĕr'ē) adj. planetario.

plank (plăngk) I. s. tablón m; POL. punto II. tr. (to cover) entablar; (to broil) cocinar a la plancha • **to p. down** FAM. (to lay down) tirar con violencia; (to pay out) desembolsar.

plank·ton (plăngk'tən) s. plancton m.

plan·ning (plăn'ĭng) I. s. planificación f II. adj. planificador.

plant (plănt) I. s. planta; (factory) fábrica; (installation) instalación f; (spy) espía mf II. tr. plantar; (to found) fundar; (to implant) infundir, inculcar; (spies) apostar; (a blow) asestar.

plan·tain[1] (plăn'tən) s. plantaina.

plan·tain[2] s. (plant) plátano; (fruit) banano.

plan·ta·tion (plăn-tā'shən) s. plantación f; (estate) hacienda.

plant·er (plăn'tər) s. plantador m; (pot) tiesto; (machine) sembradora.

plaque (plăk) s. placa.

plas·ma (plăz'mə) s. plasma m.

plas·ter (plăs'tər) s. yeso; (of a cast) escayola; (poultice) emplasto, cataplasma ♦ **p. cast** ESCULT. vaciado en yeso; MED. enyesado • **p. of Paris** sulfato de cal, yeso mate II. tr. enyesar, enlucir; (to repair) tapar con yeso; FIG. (to cover) llenar; (a limb) escayolar; (to smear) untar; FAM. (to inflict damage on) hacer daño a.

plas·ter·board (:bôrd') s. cartón m de yeso.

plas·tered (plăs'tərd) s. JER. borracho.

plas·ter·ing (:tər-ĭng) s. enyesado.

plas·tic (plăs'tĭk) I. adj. plástico; (artificial) artificial ♦ **p. surgery** cirugía plástica o estética II. s. plástico; JER. (credit card) tarjeta de crédito.

plas·tic·i·ty (plă-stĭs'ĭ-tē) s. plasticidad f.

plat (plăt) I. s. tr. **-tt-** entrelazar II. s. trenza.

plate (plāt) I. s. (dish) plato; (service and food) cubierto; (tableware) vajilla; (plaque) placa; (of metal) plancha, lámina; (coating) revestimiento; (illustration) grabado, lámina; ARM. plancha de blindaje; FOTOG. placa; (of teeth) dentadura postiza; (in baseball) base f del bateador ♦ **p. glass** vidrio cilindrado, luna II. tr. (with metal) chapar; (with gold) dorar; (with silver) platear; (to armor) blindar.

pla·teau (plă-tō') s. [pl. **s** o **-x**] meseta, altiplanicie f.

plat·ed (plā'tĭd) adj. (coated) enchapado; (armored) blindado.

plate·let (plāt'lĭt) s. plaqueta.

plat·form (plăt'fôrm') s. plataforma; (railroad) andén m; POL. programa político.

plat·ing (plā'tĭng) s. enchapado; (of gold) dorado; (of silver) plateado; (armor plate) blindaje m.

plat·i·num (plăt'n-əm) s. platino.

pla·ton·ic (plə-tŏn'ĭk) adj. platónico.

plat·ter (plăt'ər) s. fuente f; (record) disco.

plau·dits (plô'dĭts) s.pl. aplausos.

plau·si·bil·i·ty (plô'zə-bĭl'ĭ-tē) s. plausibilidad f.

plau·si·ble (plô'zə-bəl) adj. plausible.

play (plā) I. intr. jugar; (to jest) bromear; (to pretend to be) fingirse; (to be performed) poner, dar; MÚS. tocar; (light) bailar ♦ **to p. along** cooperar • **to p. around** (to joke) bromear, tomar el pelo; (to flirt) flirtear, coquetear; (to have fun) retozar, juguetear • **to p. fair** jugar limpio • **to p. for** (money) jugar por; (a team) jugar con • **to p. on** aprovecharse de • **to p. up to** FAM. adular, halagar • **to p. with** (to fiddle with) jugar con; (to consider) darle vueltas en la cabeza —tr. jugar (a); TEAT. (a role) desempeñar; (to act as) hacer de; (to give performances in) representar obras en, actuar en; (to compete against) jugar contra; (a card) jugar; (game piece) mover; (to bet) jugarse, apostar; (water, light) dirigir; MÚS. tocar ♦ **to p. back** volver a poner (algo grabado) • **to p. both ends against the middle** meter discordia entre los rivales • **to p. down** quitar importancia a • **to p. hardball** FIG. jugar duro • **to p. havoc** causar estragos (with con, en) • **to p. out** (to exhaust) agotar; (to finish) acabar • **to p. possum** hacerse el muerto • **to p. the field** FIG. salir o andar con más de una persona • **to p. the fool** hacerse el tonto • **to p. up** resaltar II. s. juego; (drama) obra, pieza; (performance) teatro, representación f; (move) jugada; (turn) turno; (dealings) jugada ♦ **to bring into p.** poner en juego • **to come into p.** entrar en el juego • **in p.** (in jest) en broma; DEP. en juego • **p. on words** juego de palabras • **to make a p. for** FAM. hacer proposiciones a.

play·act ('ăkt') intr. (to act) desempeñar un papel, actuar; (to pretend) fingir; (to overreact) hacer la comedia.

play·back (:băk') s. (of a tape) reproducción f; (sound) sonido pregrabado.

play·bill (:ˈbil') s. *(poster)* cartel *m; (program)* programa *m.*

play·boy (:boi') s. hombre *m* de mundo.

play·er (:ər) s. jugador *m; (actor)* actor *m; (actress)* actriz *f; (musician)* ejecutante *mf,* músico ♦ **p. piano** pianola, piano mecánico.

play·ful (:fəl) adj. juguetón; *(humorous)* humorístico.

play·go·er (:gō'ər) s. aficionado al teatro.

play·ground (:ground') s. jardín *m* para jugar.

play·house (:hous') s. *(theater)* teatro; *(for children)* casita para juego de niños.

play·mate (plā'māt') s. compañero de juego.

play·off (:ôf') s. DEP. partido de desempate.

play·pen (:pen') s. corralito para niños.

play·room (:rōōm') s. cuarto de jugar.

play·thing (:thǐng') s. juguete *m.*

play·time (:tīm') s. recreo.

play·wright (:rīt') s. dramaturgo.

pla·za (plä'zə, plăz'ə) s. plaza.

plea (plē) s. súplica; *(excuse)* pretexto; DER. alegato ♦ **to cop a p.** FAM. declararse culpable de un delito menos grave a cambio de no ser acusado de otro más serio.

plead (plēd) intr. **-ed** *o* **pled** suplicar, implorar; *(to argue for)* abogar, interceder; DER. *(to enter a plea)* contestar a los cargos; *(to address a court)* hacer un alegato ♦ **to p. guilty** declararse culpable ♦ **to p. not guilty** declararse inocente —tr. alegar; *(a case, cause)* defender.

pleas·ant (plěz'ənt) adj. agradable.

pleas·ant·ry (:ən trē) s. gracia, chiste *m* ♦ pl. conversación amena.

please (plēz) tr. agradar, gustar; *(to satisfy)* contentar, complacer ♦ **hard to p.** muy exigente • **p.** *(polite)* por favor; *(formal)* se ruega; *(yes)* por supuesto • **to be pleased** alegrarse de que • **to be pleased to** tener mucho gusto en • **to be pleased with** estar contento con • **to p. oneself** hacer uno lo que quiere —intr. agradar, gustar; *(to wish)* querer ♦ **if you p.** *(if you will)* por favor, haga el favor de, *(if you can imagine)* ¡figúrate!

pleas·ing (plē'zǐng) adj. agradable.

pleas·ur·a·ble (plězh'ər ə bəl) adj. agradable.

pleas·ure (plězh'ər) s. placer *m,* gusto; *(wish)* voluntad *f* ♦ **p. cruise** crucero de excursión • **take p. in** gustarle a uno • **with p.** con gusto.

pleat (plēt) I. s. pliegue *m* II. tr. plisar.

ple·be·ian (plǐ-bē'ən) adj. & s. plebeyo.

pleb·i·scite (plěb'ǐ-sīt') s. plebiscito.

pled (plěd) cf. **plead**.

pledge (plěj) I. s. promesa; *(obligation)* compromiso, obligación *f; (pawn)* prenda; *(as security)* entrega de prenda ♦ **p. of allegiance** voto de lealtad • **to take** *o* **make a p. to** FAM. comprometerse a II. tr. prometer; *(to vow)* hacer voto de; *(to bind)* exigir; *(to pawn)* dar en prenda, empeñar —intr. hacer una promesa.

ple·na·ry (plē'nə-rē, plěn'ə-) adj. plenario.

plen·i·po·ten·ti·ar·y (plěn'ə-pə-těn'shē-ěr'ē) adj. & s. plenipotenciario.

plen·i·tude (plěn'ǐ-tōōd') s. plenitud *f.*

plen·te·ous (:tē-əs) adj. abundante, copioso.

plen·ti·ful (:tǐ-fəl) adj. abundante, copioso.

plen·ty (plěn'tē) I. s. abundancia; *(affluence)* afluencia II. adj. abundante; *(sufficient)* suficiente, bastante ♦ **p. of** bastante; *(more than enough)* de sobra III. adv. FAM. muy.

pleth·o·ra (plěth'ər-ə) s. plétora.

pleu·ri·sy (plŏŏr'ǐ-sē) s. pleuresía.

pli·a·ble (plī'ə-bəl) adj. flexible.

pli·ant (:ənt) adj. flexible.

pli·ers (plī'ərz) s. alicates *m,* tenazas.

plight¹ (plīt) s. apuro, situación *f* difícil.

plight² tr. ♦ **to p. one's troth** dar palabra de matrimonio.

plod (plŏd) intr. **-dd-** ♦ **to p. (along)** *(to walk)* andar trabajosamente; *(to work)* trabajar lentamente • **to p. away at** perseverar en.

plop (plŏp) I. s. ¡plum! **-pp-** ♦ **to p. down** caerse de golpe, desplomarse —tr. dejar caer con ruido apagado II. s. ruido apagado.

plot (plŏt) I. s. *(of land)* parcela; *(patch)* cuadro; *(story line)* trama, argumento; *(conspiracy)* complot *m* II. tr. **-tt-** *(to chart)* trazar; *(to scheme)* tramar; MAT. marcar, trazar —intr. conspirar.

plot·ter (:ər) s. intrigante *mf,* conspirador *m.*

plow (plou) I. s. arado; *(snowplow)* quitanieves *m* II. tr. *(a field)* arar; *(to clear)* abrir ♦ **to p. through** *(a crowd)* abrirse paso a través de, *(to read)* leer con dificultad • **to p. under** *(to overwhelm)* agobiar, abrumar; *(to bury)* enterrar • **to p. up** arar, roturar —intr. arar la tierra ♦ **to p. into** FAM. *(to strike)* arremeter *o* precipitarse contra; *(to undertake)* acometer • **to p. through** *(a crowd)* abrirse paso a través de; *(to read)* leer con dificultad.

plow·share (:shâr') s. reja del arado.

ploy (ploi) s. truco, estratagema.

pluck (plŭk) I. tr. *(to pick)* coger; *(eyebrows)* pelar; *(a chicken)* desplumar; *(to pull out)* arrancar; MÚS. pulsar, puntear ♦ **to p. up one's courage** armarse de valor II. s. tirón *m; (courage)* valor *m,* arrojo.

pluck·y (:ē) adj. **-i-** resuelto, valeroso.

plug (plŭg) I. s. tapón *m;* ELEC. enchufe *m; (spark plug)* bujía; *(fireplug)* boca de incendio; *(publicity)* propaganda, publicidad *f; (gunshot)* balazo II. tr. **-gg-** tapar; JER. *(to shoot)* pegar un tiro a; *(to publicize)* hacer propaganda de ♦ **to p. in** enchufar • **to p. up** tapar —intr. ♦ **to p. away** FAM. trabajar obstinadamente • **to p. away at** perseverar en • **to p. for** afanarse por.

plum (plŭm) I. s. *(tree)* ciruelo; *(fruit)* ciruela; *(color)* color *m* ciruela; FIG. breva, chollo II. adj. de color ciruela.

plum·age (plōō'mǐj) s. plumaje *m.*

plumb (plŭm) I. s. plomada II. adj. *(vertical)* a plomo, vertical; *(utter)* completo III. adv. a plomo; *(utterly)* completamente IV. tr. MARIT. sondar; CONSTR. aplomar.

plumb·er (:ər) s. plomero.

plumb·ing (:ǐng) s. *(pipes)* cañería, tubería; *(trade)* plomería.

plume (plōōm) I. s. pluma; *(on a helmet)* penacho; *(of smoke)* penacho II. tr. *(to adorn)* emplumar; *(to preen)* arreglarse las plumas.

plum·met (plŭm'ǐt) intr. *(object)* caer a plomo; *(plane)* caer en picado.

plump¹ (plŭmp) I. adj. rechoncho, regordete II. tr. engordar —intr. ponerse regordete.

plump² I. intr. caer *o* dejarse caer pesadamente —tr. dejar caer pesadamente II. s. *(fall)* caída pesada; *(sound)* ruido sordo III. adv. *(with an impact)* con un ruido sordo; *(straight down)* a plomo; *(directly)* rotundamente, sin rodeos.

plun·der (plŭn'dər) I. tr. saquear —intr. robar II. s. *(booty)* botín *m; (plundering)* saqueo.

plun·der·er (:ər) s. saqueador *m.*

plunge (plŭnj) I. tr. hundir —intr. hundirse; *(to dive)* zambullirse; *(into an activity)* meterse de cabeza *(into en); (to rush)* precipitarse; *(to

descend) bajar vertiginosamente; *(to take a chance)* jugarse el todo por el todo ♦ **to p. ahead** *o* **forward** precipitarse a II. s. *(dive)* zambullida; *(fall)* caída; *(in prices)* baja vertiginosa; *(swim)* chapuzón *m*, baño ♦ **to take a p.** bajar vertiginosamente • **to take the p.** dar el paso decisivo.

plung·er (plŭn′jər) s. *(piston)* émbolo; *(for pipes, drains)* desatascador *m*.

plunk (plŭngk) I. tr. MÚS. puntear ♦ **to p.** *o* **p. down** dejar caer pesadamente —intr. hacer un ruido sordo II. s. *(twang)* rasgueo, punteo; *(hollow sound)* ruido sordo.

plu·ral (plŏŏr′əl) adj. & s. plural *m*.

plu·ral·ism (:ə-lĭz′əm) s. pluralismo.

plu·ral·i·ty (plŏŏ-răl′ĭ-tē) s. pluralidad *f*; *(large part)* mayor parte *f*, mayoría.

plus (plŭs) I. prep. más; *(besides)* además de II. adj. positivo; *(extra)* adicional, extra; FAM. *(and more)* extraordinario III. s. [pl. **-(s)es**] ventaja IV. conj. y además.

plush (plŭsh) I. s. felpa II. adj. afelpado, de felpa; *(luxurious)* lujoso.

plu·toc·ra·cy (plŏŏ-tŏk′rə-sē) s. plutocracia.

plu·to·crat (′tə-krăt′) s. plutócrata *mf*.

plu·to·ni·um (plŏŏ-tō′nē-əm) s. plutonio.

plu·vi·al (plŏŏ′vē-əl) adj. pluvial.

ply¹ (plī) I. tr. *(to twist)* enrollar; *(to fold)* doblar II. s. *(of cloth)* capa; *(of wool)* cabo; *(of wood)* chapa; *(of paper)* pliego.

ply² tr. *(to wield)* manejar; *(to practice)* ejercer; *(to traverse)* hacer el trayecto de.

ply·wood (plī′wŏŏd′) s. madera terciada.

pneu·mat·ic (nŏŏ-măt′ĭk) adj. neumático ♦ **pneumatics** s.sg. neumática.

pneu·mo·ni·a (nŏŏ-mōn′yə) s. pulmonía.

poach¹ (pōch) tr. cocer a fuego lento, escalfar.

poach² intr. cazar o pescar en vedado.

poach·er (pō′chər) s. cazador o pescador furtivo.

pock (pŏk) I. s. pústula; *(pockmark)* cicatriz *f* de viruela II. tr. picar de viruelas.

pock·et (pŏk′ĭt) I. s. bolsillo; *(pouch)* bolsa pequeña; *(of a pool table)* tronera; *(area, group)* foco; *(of air)* bache *m*; *(of gas, oil)* bolsa; *(of ore)* filón *m* ♦ **p. edition** edición de bolsillo • **p. money** dinero para gastos personales • **to line one's pockets** forrarse de dinero II. adj. de bolsillo III. tr. meterse en el bolsillo; *(to steal)* robarse.

pock·et·book (:bŏŏk′) s. *(billfold)* billetera; *(purse)* cartera de mano, monedero; *(financial resources)* recursos; *(book)* libro de bolsillo.

pock·et·knife (:nīf′) s. [pl. **-ves**] navaja, cortaplumas *m*.

pock·et·size(d) (:sīz[d]′) adj. de bolsillo.

pock·mark (pŏk′märk′) I. s. cicatriz *f* de viruela II. tr. picar de viruelas.

pod (pŏd) s. vaina.

po·di·a·trist (pə-dī′ə-trĭst) s. podíatra *m*.

po·di·a·try (:trē) s. podiatría.

po·di·um (pō′dē-əm) s. [pl. **s** o **-ia**] podio.

po·em (pō′əm) s. poema *m*.

po·et (pō′ĭt) s. poeta *mf*.

po·et·ess (pō′ĭ-tĭs) s. poetisa.

po·et·ic (pō-ĕt′ĭk) adj. poético.

po·et·ry (pō′ĭ-trē) s. poesía.

poign·ance/an·cy (poin′yəns) s. patetismo.

poign·ant (:yənt) adj. *(painful)* agudo, intenso; *(sad)* patético; *(touching)* conmovedor.

poin·set·ti·a (poin-sĕt′ē-ə) s. flor *f* de Pascua.

point (point) I. s. punto; *(sharp tip)* punta;

(spot) lugar *m*; *(subject)* tema *m* <stick to the p. no te salgas del tema>; *(reason)* motivo, razón *f*; DEP. punto, tanto; FIN. entero; GEOG. punta; MAT. coma <one p. five uno coma cinco>; ELEC. contacto ♦ **at the p. of** a punto de • **at this p.** a estas alturas • **in p. of fact** en realidad • **p. of order** cuestión de orden • **that's just the p.!** ¡eso es! • **that's not the p.** eso no tiene nada que ver • **to come to the p.** ir al grano • **to make one's p.** salirse con la suya • **to make a p. of** poner empeño en • **to miss the p.** no comprender • **to reach the p. of no return** no poder volver atrás • **to stretch the p.** ir más allá del límite • **to the p.** pertinente • **what's the p.?** ¿para qué? II. tr. *(to aim)* apuntar; *(to show)* indicar; *(to sharpen)* sacar punta a, afilar; *(a dog)* parar; CONSTR. unir con mortero, rellenar ♦ **to p. out** señalar • **to p. up** poner de relieve —intr. apuntar; *(dogs)* pararse; *(ships)* navegar de bolina ♦ **to p. at** señalar (con el dedo) • **to p. to** *(to show)* señalar; *(to suggest)* indicar que.

point-blank (′blăngk′) I. adj. directo; *(at a close range)* a quemarropa; *(blunt)* categórico II. adv. directamente, a quemarropa; *(without hesitation)* sin rodeos.

point·ed (poin′tĭd) adj. *(sharp)* puntiagudo, afilado; *(critical)* mordaz; *(intended)* intencional; *(conspicuous)* evidente, obvio.

point·er (:tər) s. indicador *m*; *(of a scale)* fiel *m*; *(of a watch)* manecilla; *(stick)* puntero; *(dog)* perro de muestra; FAM. *(tip)* consejo útil.

point·less (point′lĭs) adj. *(meaningless)* sin sentido; *(useless)* inútil.

point·y (poin′tē) adj. **-i-** puntiagudo.

poise (poiz) I. tr. poner en equilibrio —intr. estar en equilibrio II. s. equilibrio; *(composure)* aplomo, serenidad *f*; *(bearing)* porte *m*.

poi·son (poi′zən) I. s. veneno, ponzoña; *(insecticide)* insecticida ♦ **p. ivy** zumaque venenoso II. tr. envenenar; *(to pollute)* contaminar III. adj. venenoso, envenenado.

poi·son·ing (poi′zə-nĭng) s. envenenamiento.

poi·son·ous (:nəs) adj. venenoso.

poke (pōk) I. tr. *(to jab)* pinchar, aguijonear; *(with elbow)* dar codazo; *(with finger)* dar con la punta del dedo; *(to thrust)* meter ♦ **to p. a hole** hacer un hueco • **to p. out** *(to gouge)* sacar; *(to stick out)* sacar —intr. meterse ♦ **to p. along** caminar lentamente • **to p. around** *(to search)* hurgar; *(to look around)* curiosear • **to p. at** *(an animal)* pinchar, aguijonear; *(a fire)* atizar • **to p. out** asomar II. s. *(jab)* pinchazo; *(with elbow)* codazo; *(dawdler)* vago.

pok·er¹ (pō′kər) s. atizador *m*, hurgón *m*.

pok·er² s. póker *m*, póquer *m*.

po·key (pō′kē) s. JER. prisión *f*, cárcel *f*.

pok(e)·y (pō′kē) FAM. adj. **-i-** lerdo.

po·lar (pō′lər) adj. polar; *(opposite)* opuesto ♦ **p. bear** oso blanco.

po·lar·i·ty (pō-lăr′ĭ-tē) s. polaridad *f*.

po·lar·ize (pō′lə-rīz′) tr. polarizar.

pole¹ (pōl) s. *(axis)* polo ♦ **North, South P.** polo ártico, antártico.

pole² (pōl) I. s. *(post)* poste *m*, palo II. tr. empujar con una pértiga.

pole·cat (:kăt′) s. zorrillo.

po·lem·ic (pə-lĕm′ĭk) s. polémica ♦ **polemics** s.sg. polémica II. adj. /i·cal polémico.

po·lem·i·cist (:ĭ-sĭst) s. polemista *mf*.

pole·star (pōl′stär′) s. estrella polar; FIG. principio orientador.

pole-vault (pōl'vōlt') I. s. salto con garrocha II. intr. saltar con garrocha.

po·lice (pə-lēs') I. s.inv. policía; MIL. limpieza ✦ **p. force** fuerza pública • **p. officer** agente de policía • **p. record** antecedentes penales • **p. state** estado policial • **p. station** jefatura de policía II. tr. (to patrol) patrullar; (to keep in order) mantener el orden en; MIL. limpiar.

po·lice·man (:mən) s. [pl. -men] policía m.

po·lice·wom·an (:wŏm'ən) s. [pl. -women] mujer f policía.

pol·i·cy¹ (pŏl'ĭ-sē) s. (of a government) política; (of a business) norma; (course of action) sistema m, táctica.

pol·i·cy² s. (written contract) póliza.

pol'i·cy·hold·er (:hōl'dər) s. asegurado.

po·li·o (pō'lē-ō') s. polio f, poliomielitis f.

pol·ish (pŏl'ĭsh) I. tr. (to wax) encerar; (to shine) limpiar; (metals) bruñir; (nails) esmaltar, pintar; (to refine) pulir ✦ **to p. off** FAM. despachar —intr. pulirse II. s. (shininess) brillo, lustre m; (wax) cera; (for metals) líquido de bruñir; (for nails) esmalte m; (act) pulimento; (manners) refinamiento ✦ **shoe p.** betún.

pol·ished (:ĭsht) adj. pulido; (shoes) brilloso, lustroso; (metals) bruñido; (refined) refinado.

pol·ish·er (:ĭ-shər) s. pulidor m.

po·lite (pə-līt') adj. -er, -est (courteous) cortés; (refined) educado, fino.

po·lite·ness (:nĭs) s. cortesía.

pol·i·tic (pŏl'ĭ-tĭk) adj. (artful) diplomático; (clever) astuto.

po·lit·i·cal (pə-lĭt'ĭ-kəl) adj. político.

pol·i·ti·cian (pŏl'ĭ-tĭsh'ən) s. político.

po·lit·i·cize (pə-lĭt'ĭ-sīz') tr. politizar.

po·lit·ick (pŏl'ĭ-tĭk') intr. politiquear.

po·lit·i·co (pə-lĭt'ĭ-kō') s. politiquero.

pol·i·tics (pŏl'ĭ-tĭks) s.sg. política.

pol·ka (pōl'kə) I. s. polca ✦ **p. dots** lunares II. intr. bailar la polca.

poll (pōl) I. s. (votes) votación f; (survey) encuesta; (head) coronilla ✦ pl. urnas, centro electoral ✦ **to go to the p.** ir a las urnas, votar II. tr. (to get votes) obtener, recibir; (to register) registrar los votos de; (to question) hacer una encuesta de; (hair, horns) cortar.

pol·len (pŏl'ən) s. polen m.

pol·li·nate (:ə-nāt') tr. polinizar.

pol·li·na·tion ('-nā'shən) s. polinización f.

poll·ing (pō'lĭng) s. votación f.

pol·li·wog (pŏl'ē-wŏg') s. renacuajo.

poll·ster (pōl'stər) s. encuestador m.

pol·lut·ant (pə-lōōt'nt) s. agente m contaminador.

pol·lute (pə-lōōt') tr. (to corrupt) corromper; (to contaminate) contaminar.

pol·lu·tion (pə-lōō'shən) s. contaminación f.

po·lo (pō'lō) s. polo ✦ **p. shirt** polo.

pol·ter·geist (pōl'tər-gīst') s. duende m.

pol·y·es·ter (pŏl'ē-ĕs'tər) s. poliéster m.

pol·y·eth·yl·ene ('-ĕth'ə-lēn') s. polietileno.

po·lyg·a·mist (pə-lĭg'ə-mĭst) s. polígamo.

po·lyg·a·mous (:məs) adj. polígamo.

po·lyg·a·my (:mē) s. poligamia.

pol·y·gon (pŏl'ē-gŏn') s. polígono.

pol·y·graph (:grăf') s. polígrafo.

pol·y·mer (pŏl'ə-mər) s. polímero.

pol·y·no·mi·al (pŏl'ē-nō'mē-əl) I. adj. polinómico II. s. polinomio.

pol·yp (pŏl'ĭp) s. pólipo.

pol·y·tech·nic (pŏl'ē-tĕk'nĭk) I. adj. politécnico II. s. instituto politécnico.

pol·y·un·sat·u·rat·ed (:ŭn-săch'ə-rā'tĭd) adj. que contiene muchos enlaces no saturados.

pol·y·u·re·thane (:yŏŏr'ə-thān') s. poliuretano.

po·made (pō-mād') s. pomada.

po·man·der (pō'măn'dər) s. (bag) almohadilla perfumada; (box) cajita de perfumes.

pome·gran·ate (pŏm'grăn'ĭt) s. (tree) granado; (fruit) granada.

pom·mel (pŭm'əl, pŏm'-) I. s. (of a weapon) pomo; (of a saddle) perilla II. tr. aporrear.

pomp (pŏmp) s. pompa.

pom·pa·dour (pŏm'pə-dôr') s. copete.

pom·pom/pon (pŏm'pom'/pon') s. borla.

pom·pos·i·ty (pŏm-pŏs'ĭ-tē) s. pomposidad f.

pom·pous (pŏm'pəs) adj. pomposo; (pretentious) presumido; (ceremonious) ceremonioso.

pond (pŏnd) s. charca, estanque m.

pon·der (pŏn'dər) tr. examinar, sopesar —intr. meditar.

pon·der·ous (:əs) adj. voluminoso; (heavy) pesado; (labored) laborioso.

pon·tiff (pŏn'tĭf) s. pontífice m.

pon·tif·i·cal (-tĭf'ĭ-kəl) adj. & s. pontifical m.

pon·tif·i·cate I. s. (:kĭt) pontificado II. intr. (:kāt') pontificar.

pon·toon (pŏn-tōōn') s. pontón m.

po·ny (pō'nē) s. poney m, jaca.

po·ny·tail (:tāl') s. cola de caballo.

pooch (pōōch) s. JER. perro.

poo·dle (pōōd'l) s. perro de lanas, caniche m.

pooh (pōō) interj. ¡bah!

pooh-pooh (pōō'pōō') tr. FAM. desdeñar.

pool¹ (pōōl) s. (small pond) charca; (puddle) charco; (for swimming) piscina.

pool² I. s. (betting fund) banco, bolsa; (team) equipo; (of vehicles) parque m móvil; (common fund) fondos comunes; (billiards) billar americano II. tr. & intr. reunir(se), juntar(se).

poop¹ (pōōp) s. (stern) popa; (deck) toldilla.

poop² tr. dejar sin resuello ✦ **to be pooped** FAM. estar exhausto.

poop³ s. JER. información f.

poor (pŏŏr) adj. pobre; (mediocre) malo, mediocre; (scarce) escaso; (judgment) escaso, poco ✦ **p. thing!** ¡pobrecito! • **to be in p. health** no estar bien de salud • **to be p. at** no ser bueno en.

poor·house ('hous') s. casa de beneficencia, asilo para los pobres.

poor·ly (:lē) adv. pobremente ✦ **to be feeling p.** FAM. estar indispuesto.

pop¹ (pŏp) I. intr. -pp- estallar; (cork) saltar; (eyes) abrirse; (firearm) disparar ✦ **to p. in** entrar de sopetón • **to p. off** (to leave) salir disparado; (to speak) vociferar • **to p. out** (cork, eyes) saltar; (to step out) salir un momento; (to spring) salir de sopetón • **to p. up** (to appear) aparecer de repente; (to come up) surgir, suscitarse —tr. (balloon) hacer estallar; (cork) hacer saltar; (corn) hacer; (to put) meter; (to hit) pegar ✦ **to p. open** abrir haciendo saltar • **to p. out** asomar • **to p. the question** FAM. pedir la mano II. s. estallido; (of a cork) taponazo; (of a firearm) tiro, disparo; (soda pop) gaseosa III. adj. con un estallido; (abruptly) de súbito, de repente ✦ **to go p.** explotar.

pop² s. FAM. papi m, papá m.

pop³ adj. FAM. popular.

pop·corn ('kôrn') s. rosetas de maíz.

pope o **Pope** (pōp) s. papa m.

pop·gun (pŏp'gŭn') s. pistola de aire comprimido.

pop·in·jay (pŏp'ĭn-jā') s. pedante mf.

pop·lar (pŏp'lər) s. álamo.

pop·lin (pŏp'lĭn) s. popelín m, popelina.

pop·pa (pä'pə) s. papá m.

pop·py (pŏp'ē) s. amapola.

pop·py·cock (pŏp'ē-kŏk') s. tonterías.

pop·u·lace (pŏp'yə-lĭs) s. (the masses) populacho; (population) población f.

pop·u·lar (pŏp'yə-lər) adj. popular; (election) democrático; (in vogue) de moda; (prevalent) generalizado, común.

pop·u·lar·i·ty ('-lăr'ĭ-tē) s. popularidad f.

pop·u·lar·ize ('-lə-rīz') tr. popularizar.

pop·u·late (:lāt') tr. (to people) poblar; (to inhabit) habitar.

pop·u·la·tion ('-lā'shən) s. polación f; (neighborhood) vecindario.

pop·u·lism ('-lĭz'əm) s. populismo.

pop·u·list (:lĭst) s. & adj. populista mf.

pop·u·lous (:ləs) adj. populoso.

por·ce·lain (pôr'sə-lĭn) s. porcelana.

porch (pôrch) s. porche m.

por·cine (pôr'sīn') adj. porcino.

por·cu·pine (pôr'kyə-pīn') s. puercoespín m.

pore¹ (pôr) intr. ♦ **to p. over** examinar detenidamente; (to ponder) meditar sobre.

pore² s. ANAT. poro.

pork (pôrk) s. cerdo, carne f de cerdo.

por·no (pôr'nō) o **porn** (pôrn) s. JER. pornografía.

por·nog·ra·pher (pôr-nŏg'rə-fər) s. pornógrafo.

por·no·graph·ic ('nə-grăf'ĭk) adj. pornográfico.

por·nog·ra·phy (-nŏg'rə-fē) s. pornografía.

po·rous (pôr'əs) adj. poroso.

por·poise (pôr'pəs) s. [pl. inv. o s] marsopa.

por·ridge (pôr'ĭj) s. gachas de avena.

port¹ (pôrt) I. s. puerto ♦ **p. of call** puerto de escala II. adj. portuario.

port² I. s. MARÍT. babor m II. adj. a o de babor III. tr. girar a babor.

port³ s. (porthole) portilla; (opening) orificio.

port⁴ s. (wine) oporto.

por·ta·ble (pôr'tə-bəl) adj. & s. (máquina) portátil.

por·tage (:tĭj) I. s. porteo, transporte m; (route) ruta de porteo II. tr. transportar.

por·tal (pôr'tl) s. portal m.

por·tend (pôr-tĕnd') tr. presagiar; (to indicate) indicar.

por·tent (pôr'tĕnt') s. (omen) augurio; (significance) significado; (prodigy) portento.

por·ten·tous (-tĕn'təs) adj. (foreboding) de mal agüero; (prodigious) portentoso.

por·ter¹ (pôr'tər) s. mozo.

por·ter² s. G.B. (doorman) portero.

por·ter³ s. (beer) cerveza negra.

port·fo·li·o (pôrt-fō'lē-ō') s. cartera; (folder) carpeta.

port·hole (pôrt'hōl') s. portilla.

por·ti·co (pôr'tĭ-kō') s. [pl. (e)s] pórtico.

por·tion (pôr'shən) I. s. (part) porción f, parte f; (dowry) dote f; (fate) suerte f, destino II. tr. dividir ♦ **to p. out** repartir, distribuir.

port·ly (pôrt'lē) adj. -i- (stout) corpulento.

por·trait (pôr'trĭt) s. retrato.

por·trai·ture (pôr'trĭ-chŏr') s. pintura de retratos.

por·tray (pôr-trā') tr. (to represent) retratar; (to depict) describir; TEAT. representar.

por·tray·al (:əl) s. (portrait) retrato; (description) descripción f; TEAT. representación f.

pose (pōz) I. intr. posar; (to affect an attitude) asumir una pose ♦ **to p. as** hacerse pasar por —tr. posar, colocar; (question) plantear; (threat) representar II. s. pose f.

posh (pŏsh) adj. FAM. (fashionable) elegante; (luxurious) de lujo; (exclusive) selecto.

pos·it (pŏz'ĭt) tr. proponer, postular.

po·si·tion (pə-zĭsh'ən) I. s. posición f; (place) lugar m, sitio; (job) posición f; (point of view) postura, actitud f; (status) posición social; (job) puesto II. tr. colocar, poner ♦ **to p. oneself** ponerse en un lugar favorable.

pos·i·tive (pŏz'ĭ-tĭv) I. adj. positivo; (emphatic) tajante; (express) explícito, expreso; (irrefutable) categórico, rotundo; (sure) seguro, cierto II. s. positivo; ELEC. polo positivo; FOTOG. positiva.

pos·sess (pə-zĕs') tr. poseer; (to control) dominar; (to obsess) obsesionar; (to drive) impulsar <what possessed him to do it? ¿qué lo impulsó a hacerlo?>.

pos·sessed (pə-zĕst') adj. poseído, poseso; (by an idea) obsesionado; (calm) dueño de sí mismo ♦ **to be p. of** (to own) poseer, tener; (to be blessed with) estar dotado de.

pos·ses·sion (pə-zĕsh'ən) s. posesión f; (holding) tenencia; (self-control) dominio de sí mismo ♦ **in one's p.** en manos de uno • **to be in full p. of one's faculties** tener pleno dominio de sus facultades • **to be in p. of** poseer • **to come into p. of** adquirir • **to get** o **take p. of** apoderarse de ♦ pl. posesiones.

pos·ses·sive (pə-zĕs'ĭv) I. adj. posesivo; (jealous) celoso II. s. GRAM. posesivo.

pos·ses·sor (:ər) s. poseedor m, dueño.

pos·si·bil·i·ty (pŏs'ə-bĭl'ĭ-tē) s. posibilidad f ♦ **to have possibilities** ser prometedor • **within the realm of p.** dentro de lo posible.

pos·si·ble (pŏs'ə-bəl) adj. posible ♦ **as much as p.** todo lo posible • **as soon as p.** lo antes posible • **if p.** si es posible.

pos·sum (pŏs'əm) var. de **opossum**.

post¹ (pōst) I. s. (pole) poste m; (stake) palo, estaca; (starting line) línea de salida II. tr. (to fasten up) pegar, fijar; (to announce) anunciar.

post² I. s. MIL. (base) base f; (position) puesto; (job) puesto, cargo III. tr. (a guard) apostar; (an officer) enviar, destinar; (bail) dar.

post³ I. s. G.B. (mail) correo; (delivery) reparto; (collection) recogida ♦ **p. card** tarjeta postal • **p. office** (oficina de) correos II. intr. viajar de prisa —tr. (to mail) echar al correo; (to inform) poner al corriente ♦ **to keep someone posted** tener a alguien al corriente.

post·age (pō'stĭj) s. franqueo ♦ **p. stamp** sello (postal), estampilla.

post·al (pō'stəl) adj. & s. postal f ♦ **p. service** servicio de correos.

post·date (pōst-dāt') tr. posfechar.

post·er (pō'stər) s. cartel m, afiche m.

pos·te·ri·or (pŏ-stîr'ē-ər) I. adj. posterior II. s. FAM. trasero.

pos·ter·i·ty (pŏ-stĕr'ĭ-tē) s. posteridad f.

post·grad·u·ate (pōst-grăj'ōō-ĭt) adj. & s. postgraduado.

post·haste (pōst'hāst') adv. a toda prisa.

post·hu·mous (pŏs'chə-məs) adj. póstumo.

post·man (pōst'mən) s. [pl. -men] cartero.

post·mark (:märk') I. s. matasellos II. tr. matasellar.

post·mas·ter (:măs'tər) s. administrador m de correos ♦ **p. general** director general de correos.

post·mis·tress (pōst'mĭs'trĭs) s. administradora de correos.

post·mor·tem (pōst-môr'təm) I. adj. postmórtem II. s. autopsia.

post·na·sal (:nā'zəl) adj. postnasal.

post·na·tal (·nāt'l) adj. postnatal.

post·op·er·a·tive (:ŏp'ər-ə-tĭv) adj. postoperatorio.

post·paid (pōst'pād') adj. con franqueo pagado.

post·par·tum (pōst-pär'təm) adj. de después del parto.

post·pone (pōst-pōn') tr. (to delay) posponer; (to put off) diferir, aplazar.

post·pone·ment (:mənt) s. aplazamiento.

post·script (pōst'skrĭpt') s. posdata.

pos·tu·late (pŏs'chə-lāt') I. tr. postular II. s. postulado.

pos·tu·la·tion (·-lā'shən) s. postulación f.

pos·ture (pŏs'chər) I. s. postura II. intr. posar, asumir una pose ♦ **to p. as** darse tono de.

post·war (pōst'wôr') adj. de la postguerra.

po·sy (pō'zē) s. flor f; (bunch) ramillete m de flores.

pot (pŏt) I. s. (for cooking) cazuela, olla; (flowerpot) maceta, tiesto; (in cards) platillo, puesta; FAM. (common fund) fondo común; (potbelly) panza; (marijuana) yerba ♦ **pots and pans** batería de cocina • **p. shot** (shot) tiro al azar; (criticism) crítica gratuita • **to go to p.** FAM. echarse a perder II. tr. -tt- plantar en una maceta.

po·ta·ble (pō'tə-bəl) adj. potable.

pot·ash (pŏt'ăsh') s. potasa.

po·tas·si·um (pə-tăs'ē-əm) s. potasio.

po·ta·to (pə-tā'tō) s. [pl. **es**] patata, papa ♦ **p. chips** papas fritas.

pot·bel·ly (pŏt'bĕl'ē) s. panza, barriga; (stove) salamandra.

pot·boil·er (:boi'lər) s. obra artística de calidad mediocre hecha con fin de lucro.

po·ten·cy (pōt'n-sē) s. potencia.

po·tent (:nt) adj. potente.

po·ten·tate (:n-tāt') s. potentado.

po·ten·tial (pə-tĕn'shəl) I. adj. potencial, posible II. s. posibilidad f; FÍS., GRAM., MAT. potencial m; ELEC. voltaje m.

pot·hold·er (pŏt'hōl'dər) s. agarrador m para utensilios calientes.

pot·hole (:hōl') s. bache m.

po·tion (pō'shən) s. poción f.

pot·pour·ri (pō'poo-rē') s. popurrí m; (sachet) pebete m.

pot·tage (pŏt'ĭj) s. sopa, potaje m.

pot·ted (pŏt'ĭd) adj. (plant) en maceta; JER. (drunk) borracho; (stoned) drogado.

pot·ter (pŏt'ər) s. alfarero ♦ **p.'s field** fosa común • **p.'s wheel** rueda o torno de alfarero.

pot·ter·y (:ə-rē) s. alfarería.

pot·ty¹ (pŏt'ē) G.B. adj. **-i-** (trivial) trivial; (intoxicated) levemente borracho; (silly) chiflado.

pot·ty² s. FAM. orinal m para niños.

pouch (pouch) s. bolsa pequeña, valija; (for game) morral m; (for ammunition) cartuchera; (for tobacco) petaca; ZOOL. bolsa.

poul·tice (pōl'tĭs) s. cataplasma.

poul·try (pōl'trē) s. aves f de corral

pounce (pouns) I. intr. (to spring) saltar sobre; (to attack) abalanzarse sobre —tr. ♦ **to p. on** (to attack) saltar sobre; (an opportunity) no perder II. s. ataque repentino; (jump) salto re-

pentino.

pound¹ (pound) s. [pl. inv o **s**] FIN., FÍS. libra.

pound² I. tr. golpear; (to grind) moler; (to crush) machacar; FIG. inculcar —intr. dar golpes; (to move heavily) andar con paso pesado; (the heart) palpitar, latir violentamente; (waves) batir II. s. golpe m; (sound) ruido de golpes.

pound³ s. (for dogs) perrera; (for cats, property) depósito.

pound·age (poun'dĭj) s. peso.

pour (pôr) tr. echar; (to serve) servir; (to spill) verter, derramar ♦ **to p. out** (a liquid) verter, echar; (feelings) dar rienda suelta a • **to p. one's heart out to someone** abrirse a alguien —intr. (to flow) manar, correr; (to gush) salir a chorros; (to rain) llover a cántaros; (to serve) servir bebidas ♦ **to p. in** (people) entrar en tropel; (letters) llegar en abundancia • **to p. out** (liquid) salir a chorros; (people) salir en tropel.

pout (pout) intr. hacer pucheros; (to sulk) poner mala cara.

pov·er·ty (pŏv'ər-tē) s. pobreza; (deficiency) carencia, escasez f.

pov·er·ty-strick·en (:strĭk'ən) adj. indigente, muy pobre.

pow·der (pou'dər) I. s. polvo; (cosmetic, medicinal) polvos; (gunpowder) pólvora; (snow) nieve seca ♦ **p. keg** (cask) tonel, cuñete de pólvora; (situation) polvorín • **p. puff** mota, borla • **p. room** tocador, servicios II. tr. hacer polvo, pulverizar; (to sprinkle) espolvorear ♦ **to p. one's face** ponerse polvos.

pow·er (pou'ər) I. s. poder m; (capacity) capacidad f; (strength) fuerza; (person) fuerza, influencia; (nation) potencia; (energy) energía; (electricity) electricidad f, corriente f; FIG., ÓPT. potencia ♦ **p. brake** servofreno • **p. drill** taladro eléctrico • **p. line** línea de transmisión eléctrica • **p. of attorney** poder (legal) • **p. steering** servodirección • **p. tool** herramienta eléctrica • **the powers that be** las autoridades ♦ **to come to p.** subir al poder ♦ pl. poder, capacidad II. tr. TEC. suministrar energía a ♦ **to be powered by** funcionar con.

pow·er·boat (:bōt') s. bote m a motor.

pow·er·ful (:fəl) adj. poderoso; (potent) potente; (strong) fuerte; (convincing) convincente.

pow·er·house (:hous') s. central f de energía eléctrica f; (person) persona de mucha energía.

pow·er·less (:lĭs) adj. impotente; (helpless) indefenso; (ineffectual) inútil; (lacking authority) sin autoridad.

pox (pŏks) s. (smallpox) viruela; (chicken pox) varicela; (syphilis) sífilis f.

prac·ti·cal (prăk'tĭ-kəl) adj. práctico ♦ **for all p. purposes** prácticamente, a fin de cuentas • **p. joke** broma pesada.

prac·ti·cal·i·ty ('-kăl'ĭ-tē) s. carácter práctico.

prac·ti·cal·ly (prăk'tĭk-lē) adv. de modo práctico; (almost) prácticamente, casi.

prac·tice (prăk'tĭs) I. tr. practicar; (to train in) ejercitarse o entrenarse en; (to use) ejercer, proceder con; (a profession) ejercer ♦ **to p. what one preaches** actuar según la doctrina de uno —intr. hacer prácticas; (to train) ejercitarse, entrenarse; (a professional) ejercer II. s. práctica; (training) ejercicios; (custom) costumbre f; (of a profession) ejercicio; (of a doctor) clientela; (of a lawyer) bufete m • **to be out of p.** no estar en forma • **to make a p. of** tener por costumbre • **to set up a p.** *(as a doctor)* poner un consultorio; *(as a lawyer)* poner un bufete ♦ pl. procedimientos.

prac·ticed (:tĭst) adj. experimentado, experto.

prac·tic·ing (:tĭ-sĭng) adj. *(professional)* que ejerce; RELIG. practicante, devoto.

prac·ti·tion·er (-tĭsh′ə-nər) s. profesional *mf* ♦ **general p.** médico general.

prag·mat·ic/i·cal (prăg-măt′ĭk) adj. pragmático.

prag·ma·tism ('mə-tĭz′əm) s. pragmatismo.

prag·ma·tist (:tĭst) s. pragmatista *mf*.

prai·rie (prâr′ē) s. llanura, planicie *f* ♦ **p. dog** marmota de las praderas.

praise (prāz) I. s. alabanza ♦ **to sing the praises of** cantar las alabanzas de II. tr. alabar ♦ **to p. to the skies** poner por las nubes.

praise·wor·thy (:wûr′thē) adj. elogiable.

pram (prăm) s. G.B. cochecito de niño.

prance (prăns) intr. EQUIT. cabriolar; FIG. pavonearse.

prank (prăngk) s. jugarreta, travesura; *(joke)* broma.

prank·ster (:stər) s. bromista *mf*.

prate (prāt) I. intr. parlotear II. s. parloteo.

prat·tle (prăt′l) I. intr. parlotear II. s. parloteo.

prawn (prôn) s. camarón *m*, gamba.

pray (prā) intr. rezar, orar; *(to plead)* rogar, suplicar —tr. rogar ♦ **praying mantis** mantis religiosa.

prayer (prâr) s. oración *f*; *(request)* ruego.

preach (prēch) tr. predicar; *(to exhort)* exhortar; *(to deliver)* pronunciar —intr. predicar ♦ **to p. at** sermonear a.

preach·er (prē′chər) s. RELIG. pastor *m*; *(one who preaches)* predicador *m*.

pre·ad·o·les·cence (prē′ăd′l-ĕs′əns) s. preadolescencia.

pre·am·ble (prē′ăm′bəl) s. preámbulo.

pre·ar·range (prē′ə-rānj′) tr. preparar de antemano.

pre·as·signed (:ə-sīnd′) adj. asignado de antemano.

pre·car·i·ous (prĭ-kâr′ē-əs) adj. precario.

pre·cau·tion (prĭ-kô′shən) s. precaución *f*.

pre·cau·tion·ar·y (:sha-nĕr′ē) adj. preventivo.

pre·cau·tious (:shəs) adj. precavido.

pre·cede (prĭ-sēd′) tr. & intr. preceder.

prec·e·dence (prĕs′ĭ-dns, prĭ-sēd′ns) s. precedencia; *(priority)* prioridad *f* ♦ **to take p. over** tener prioridad sobre.

prec·e·dent (:dnt) adj & s. precedente *m*.

pre·ced·ing (prĭ-sē′dĭng) adj. *(antecedent)* precedente; *(previous)* previo.

pre·cept (prē′sĕpt′) s. precepto.

pre·cep·tor (prĭ-sĕp′tər) s. preceptor *m*.

pre·ces·sion (prē-sĕsh′ən) s. precedencia.

pre·cinct (prē′sĭngkt′) s. *(police district)* zona de patrulla; *(police station)* jefatura de policía, comisaría; *(election district)* distrito electoral; *(area)* recinto ♦ pl. *(area)* recinto; *(boundary)* límites; FIG. campo, esfera.

pre·cious (prĕsh′əs) I. adj. precioso; *(cherished)* valioso, preciado; *(beloved)* querido II. adv. muy.

prec·i·pice (prĕs′ə-pĭs) s. precipicio.

pre·cip·i·tant (prĭ-sĭp′ĭ-tnt) I. adj. precipitado; *(sudden)* repentino II. s. QUÍM. precipitado.

pre·cip·i·tate (prĭ-sĭp′ĭ-tāt′) I. tr. *(to bring on)* provocar; *(to hurl)* precipitar; QUÍM. precipitar —intr. METEOR. condensarse; *(to fall)* precipitarse II. adj. (:tĭt) precipitado III. s. (:tāt′,

:tĭt) QUÍM. precipitado.

pre·cip·i·ta·tion (-′-tā′shən) s. precipitación *f*.

pre·cip·i·tous (-′-təs) adj. *(steep)* escarpado; *(hasty)* precipitado.

pré·cis (prā-sē′) s.inv. resumen *m*.

pre·cise (prĭ-sīs′) adj. preciso.

pre·ci·sion (:sĭzh′ən) s. precisión *f*.

pre·clude (prĭ-klōōd′) tr. *(to exclude)* excluir; *(to avoid)* evitar; *(to prevent)* prevenir.

pre·clu·sion (:klōō′zhən) s. *(exclusion)* exclusión *f*; *(prevention)* prevención *f*.

pre·co·cious (prĭ-kō′shəs) adj. precoz.

pre·coc·i·ty (:kŏs′ĭ-tē) s. precosidad *f*.

pre·cog·ni·tion (prē′kŏg-nĭsh′ən) s. precognición *f*.

pre·Co·lum·bi·an (:kə-lŭm′bē-ən) adj. precolombino.

pre·con·ceive (:kən-sēv′) tr. preconcebir.

pre·con·cep·tion (:kən-sĕp′shən) s. preconcepción *f*; *(prejudice)* prejuicio.

pre·con·di·tion (:kən-dĭsh′ən) s. condición previa; *(requisite)* requisito previo.

pre·cook (-kōōk′) tr. precocer.

pre·cur·sor (prĭ-kûr′sər) s. precursor *m*.

pre·cur·so·ry (:sə-rē) adj. precursor.

pre·date (prē-dāt′) tr. preceder; *(to give prior date to)* poner una fecha anterior a.

pred·a·tor (prĕd′ə-tər) s. predator *m*.

pred·a·to·ry (:tôr′ē) adj. *(predacious)* de rapiña; *(plundering)* depradador.

pre·de·cease (prē′dĭ-sēs′) tr. morir antes que.

pred·e·ces·sor (prĕd′ĭ-sĕs′ər) s. predecesor *m*; *(ancestor)* antepasado.

pre·des·ti·na·tion (prē-dĕs′tə-nā′shən) s. *(act, condition)* predestinación *f*; *(destiny)* destino.

pre·des·tine (:tĭn) tr. predestinar.

pre·de·ter·mine (prē′dĭ-tûr′mĭn) tr. predeterminar.

pre·dic·a·ment (prĭ-dĭk′ə-mənt) s. apuro.

pred·i·cate (prĕd′ĭ-kāt′) I. tr. fundar, basar; *(to affirm)* afirmar II. s. (:kĭt) GRAM. predicado III. adj. (:kĭt) GRAM. predicativo.

pred·i·ca·tion (-′kā′shən) s. afirmación *f*.

pre·dict (prĭ-dĭkt′) tr. predecir; *(to forecast)* pronosticar.

pre·dict·a·bil·i·ty (-dĭk′tə-bĭl′ĭ-tē) s. carácter *m* previsible

pre·dict·a·ble (-′-bəl) adj. previsible; *(behavior)* invariable, constante.

pre·dic·tion (prĭ-dĭk′shən) s. predicción *f*; *(forecast)* pronóstico.

pre·dic·tor (:tər) s. pronosticador *m*.

pred·i·lec·tion (prĕd′l-ĕk′shən, prēd′-) s. predilección *f*.

pre·dis·pose (prē′dĭ-spōz′) tr. predisponer.

pre·dis·po·si·tion (:dĭs′pə-zĭsh′ən) s. predisposición *f*; *(tendency)* tendencia.

pre·dom·i·nance (prĭ-dŏm′ə-nəns) s. predominio; *(preponderance)* preponderancia.

pre·dom·i·nant (:nənt) adj. predominante.

pre·dom·i·nate (:nāt′) intr. predominar; *(to prevail)* prevalecer —tr. predominar sobre; *(to prevail over)* prevalecer sobre.

pre·em·i·nence *o* **pre·em·i·nence** (prē-ĕm′ə-nəns) s. preeminencia.

pre·em·i·nent *o* **pre·em·i·nent** (:nənt) adj. preeminente.

pre·empt *o* **pre·empt** (prē-ĕmpt′) tr. *(to displace)* supeditar; *(to appropriate)* apropiarse de; TELEV. substituir.

pre·emp·tive *o* **pre·emp·tive** (:ĕmp′tĭv) adj. MIL. preventivo.

preen (prēn) tr. arreglar, limpiar ♦ **to p. one-self** pavonearse —intr. pavonearse.

pre·ex·ist o **pre·ex·ist** (prē'ĭg-zĭst') tr. existir antes que —intr. preexistir.

pre·fab·ri·cate (-fāb'rĭ-kāt') tr. prefabricar.

pref·ace (prĕf'ĭs) I. s. prefacio, prólogo II. tr. prologar; (remarks) servir de prólogo a.

pref·a·to·ry (:ǝ-tôr'ē) adj. introductorio.

pre·fect (prē'fĕkt') s. prefecto.

pre·fer (prĭ-fûr') tr. **-rr-** preferir.

pref·er·a·ble (prĕf'ǝr-ǝ-bǝl) adj. preferible.

pref·er·ence (:ǝns) s. preferencia ♦ **to have no p.** serle igual.

pref·er·en·tial (prĕf'ǝ-rĕn'shǝl) adj. preferente.

pre·fer·ment (prĭ-fûr'mǝnt) s. (advancement) adelanto; (promotion) ascenso.

pre·fig·ure (prē-fĭg'yǝr) tr. prefigurar; (to imagine) figurarse de antemano.

pre·fix (prē'fĭks') I. tr. anteponer II. s. prefijo.

preg·na·ble (prĕg'nǝ-bǝl) adj. MIL. expugnable.

preg·nan·cy (prĕg'nǝn-sē) s. embarazo.

preg·nant (:nǝnt) adj. encinta, embarazada; (animal) preñada; (meaningful) significativo.

pre·heat (prē-hēt') tr. precalentar.

pre·hen·sile (prē-hĕn'sǝl, :sīl') adj. prensil.

pre·his·tor·ic/i·cal (prē'hĭ-stôr'ĭk) adj. prehistórico.

pre·judge (prē-jŭj') tr. prejuzgar.

prej·u·dice (prĕj'ǝdĭs) I. s. prejuicio II. tr. crear prejuicios a; (to injure) perjudicar.

prej·u·di·cial ('-dĭsh'ǝl) adj. perjudicial.

prej·u·di·cious (:ǝs) adj. perjudicial.

prel·ate (prĕl'ĭt) s. prelado.

pre·lim·i·nar·y (prĭ-lĭm'ǝ-nĕr'ē) adj. & s. preliminar m.

prel·ude (prĕl'yōōd, prā'lōōd') s. preludio.

pre·mar·i·tal (prē-măr'ĭ-tl) adj. premarital.

pre·ma·ture (prē'mǝ-chŏŏr') adj. prematuro.

pre·med (prē'mĕd') FAM. I. adj. preparatorio para el ingreso a la facultad de medicina II. s. estudiante mf que se prepara para el ingreso a la facultad de medicina.

pre·med·i·tate (prē-mĕd'ĭ-tāt') tr. premeditar.

pre·med·i·tat·ed (:tā'tĭd) adj. premeditado.

pre·med·i·ta·tion ('-'shǝn) s. premeditación f.

pre·men·stru·al (prē-mĕn'strōō-ǝl) adj. premenstrual.

pre·mi·er (prē'mē-ǝr, prĭ-mîr') I. adj. (first) primero; (chief) principal II. s. primer ministro; (Canadian) presidente m.

pre·mière (prĭ-mîr', prĭm-yâr') I. s. estreno II. tr. & intr. estrenar III. adj. primero.

prem·ise (prĕm'ĭs) I. s. premisa ♦ pl. (site) local; (building) edificio II. tr. sentar como premisa —intr. formular una premisa.

pre·mi·um (prē'mē-ǝm) s. (prize) premio, recompensa; (fee) prima; (installment) prima (de un seguro) ♦ **to be at a p.** (to cost more) costar más; (in demand) tener mucha demanda • **to put a p. on** valorar mucho.

pre·mo·ni·tion (prē'mǝ-nĭsh'ǝn, prĕm'ǝ-) s. premonición f.

pre·na·tal (prē-nāt'l) adj. prenatal.

pre·oc·cu·pa·tion (prē-ŏk'yǝ-pā'shǝn) s. preocupación f.

pre·oc·cu·pied (-'-pīd') adj. preocupado; (absorbed) absorto.

pre·oc·cu·py (:pī') tr. preocupar; (to engross) absorber.

pre·or·dain (prē'ôr-dān') tr. preordinar.

prep (prĕp) FAM. I. adj. preparatorio ♦ **p. school** escuela secundaria privada II. tr. & intr. preparar(se).

pre·pack·age (prē-pāk'ĭj) tr. preempaquetar.

pre·paid (:pād') I. cf. **prepay** II. adj. pagado por adelantado; (letter) franqueado.

prep·a·ra·tion (prĕp'ǝ-rā'shǝn) s. preparación f; (medicine) preparado ♦ pl. preparativos.

pre·par·a·to·ry (prĭ-pâr'ǝ-tôr'ē) adj. preparatorio.

pre·pare (prĭ-pâr') tr. & intr. preparar(se) ♦ **to be prepared for** estar preparado para. • **to be prepared to** estar dispuesto a.

pre·par·ed·ness (:ĭd nĭs) s. estado de preparación.

pre·pay (prē-pā') tr. **-paid** pagar por adelantado.

pre·pay·ment (:mǝnt) s. pago adelantado.

pre·pon·der·ance (prĭ-pŏn'dǝr-ǝns) s. preponderancia.

pre·pon·der·ant (:ǝnt) adj. preponderante.

prep·o·si·tion (prĕp'ǝ-zĭsh'ǝn) s. preposición f.

pre·pos·sess (prē'pǝ-zĕs') tr. (to influence) predisponer (a favor); (to impress) impresionar (favorablemente).

pre·pos·sess·ing (:ĭng) adj. agradable.

pre·pos·ter·ous (prĭ-pŏs'tǝr-ǝs) adj. absurdo.

prep·pie/py (prĕp'ē) s. FAM. alumno de una escuela preparatoria.

pre·pu·bes·cence (prē'pyōō-bĕs'ǝns) s. prepubescencia.

pre·puce (prē'pyōōs') s. prepucio.

pre·req·ui·site (prē-rĕk'wĭ-zĭt) I. s. condición previa II. adj. requerido de antemano.

pre·rog·a·tive (prĭ-rŏg'ǝ-tĭv) s. prerrogativa.

pres·age (prĕs'ĭj) I. s. presagio II. tr. presagiar.

pre·school (prē'skōōl') I. adj. preescolar II. s. jardín m de infantes.

pre·science (prē'shǝns, prĕsh'ǝns) s. presciencia.

pre·scient (:shǝnt) adj. presciente.

pre·scribe (prĭ-skrīb') tr. prescribir; MED. (a drug) recetar; (treatment) mandar —intr. establecer, dictar; MED. hacer recetas.

pre·scrip·tion (:skrĭp'shǝn) s. prescripción f; MED. receta; (medicine) remedio.

pre·scrip·tive (:tĭv) adj. establecido; (establishing rules) preceptivo.

pres·ence (prĕz'ǝns) s. presencia; (bearing) porte m, talle m; (confidence) seguridad f ♦ **p. of mind** presencia de ánimo.

pres·ent¹ (prĕz'ǝnt) I. s. presente m ♦ **for the p.** por ahora II. adj. presente; (month) corriente; (year) en curso ♦ **at the p. time** en este momento • **to be p.** asistir • **to be p. at** (to be) haber en, (to witness) presenciar.

pre·sent² (prĭ-zĕnt') I. tr. (prĭ-zĕnt') presentar; (to give) regalar, obsequiar; (a case) exponer; (a problem) plantear; (an invoice) pasar; (arms) presentar; (charges) formular II. s. (prĕz'ǝnt) presente m, regalo.

pre·sent·a·ble (prĭ-zĕn'tǝ-bǝl) adj. presentable.

pres·en·ta·tion (prĕz'ǝn-tā'shǝn) s. presentación f; (of a play) representación f; (of a case, argument) exposición f.

pres·ent-day (prĕz'ǝnt-dā') adj. actual.

pre·sen·ti·ment (prĭ-zĕn'tǝ-mǝnt) s. presentimiento.

pres·ent·ly (prĕz'ǝnt-lē) adv. (soon) dentro de poco; (now) actualmente.

pres·er·va·tion (prĕz'ǝr-vā'shǝn) s. preservación f; (of customs, food) conservación f.

pre·ser·va·tive (prǐ-zûr′və-tǐv) **I.** adj. preservativo **II.** s. conservante *m*, preservador *m*.

pre·serve (prǐ-zûrv′) **I.** tr. preservar; *(to maintain)* conservar; *(food)* conservar; *(game)* proteger **II.** s. coto, vedado; FIG. terreno ♦ pl. confitura.

pre·serv·er (:zûr′vər) s. preservador *m*.

pre·side (prǐ-zīd′) intr. presidir.

pres·i·den·cy (prĕz′ǐ-dən-sē) s. presidencia.

pres·i·dent (:dənt) s. presidente *m*.

pres·i·dent-e·lect (′-ǐ-lĕkt′) s. presidente electo.

pres·i·den·tial (prĕz′ǐ-dĕn′shəl) adj. presidencial.

pre·sid·i·um (prǐ-sǐd′ē-əm) s. [pl. **s** *o* **-ia**] presidium *m*.

pre·sort (prē-sôrt′) tr. clasificar en zonas postales antes de llevarlas al correo.

press (prĕs) **I.** tr. *(to bear down on)* apretar; *(to squeeze)* prensar; *(to compress)* comprimir; *(to iron)* planchar; *(to entreat)* instar; *(to harass)* hostigar, acosar; *(to hurry)* apremiar; *(to insist on)* insistir en ♦ **to be pressed for** estar con apuros de • **to p. one's luck** forzar la suerte —intr. apretar, ejercer presión; *(to trouble)* pesar, abrumar; *(to be urgent)* apremiar; *(to crowd)* apiñarse ♦ **to p. ahead** *o* **forward** avanzar con determinación • **to p. for** pedir con insistencia • **to p. on** seguir adelante **II.** s. prensa; *(for printing)* imprenta; *(journalists)* prensa; *(urgency)* urgencia.

press·ing (′ǐng) adj. urgente.

press·room (:rōōm′) s. taller *m* de imprenta.

press·run (:rŭn′) s. tirada.

pres·sure (prĕsh′ər) **I.** s. presión *f*; *(compression)* compresión *f* ♦ **blood p.** presión arterial • **p. cooker** *(pot)* olla de presión; FIG. situación en atmósfera de apremio y urgencia • **to bring p. to bear on** *o* **to put p. on** ejercer presión sobre **II.** tr. ejercer presión sobre.

pres·sur·ize (:ə-rīz′) tr. presurizar.

pres·ti·dig·i·ta·tion (prĕs′tǐ-dǐj′ǐ-tā′shən) s. prestidigitación *f*.

pres·tige (prĕ-stēzh′, -stēj′) s. prestigio.

pres·ti·gious (prĕ-stē′jəs, -stǐj′əs) adj. prestigioso.

pre·sum·a·ble (prǐ-zōō′mə-bəl) adj. presumible.

pre·sume (prǐ-zōōm′) tr. suponer; *(to dare)* tener el atrevimiento de; *(to pretend)* pretender, creerse —intr. presumir ♦ **to p. on** abusar de.

pre·sum·ing (-zōō′mǐng) adj. presumido.

pre·sump·tion (:zŭmp′shən) s. presunción *f*, suposición *f*; *(effrontery)* osadía.

pre·sump·tive (:tǐv) adj. presuntivo; *(presumed)* presunto.

pre·sump·tu·ous (:chōō-əs) adj. presuntuoso; *(rash)* atrevido, osado.

pre·sup·pose (prē′sə-pōz′) tr. presuponer.

pre·tend (prǐ-tĕnd′) tr. *(to feign)* fingir; *(illness, deafness)* hacerse; *(to oneself)* imaginarse; *(to claim)* pretender —intr. *(to feign)* fingir; *(to dissemble)* disimular ♦ **to p. to the throne** pretender al trono.

pre·tend·er (:tĕn′dər) s. fingidor *m*; *(claimant)* pretendiente *mf*.

pre·tense (prǐ-tĕns′, prī-tĕns′) s. fingimiento; *(pretext)* pretexto; *(claim)* pretensión *f*; *(affectation)* ostentación *f*; *(pretentiousness)* presunción *f* ♦ **to make no p.** no pretender • **under false pretenses** por fraude • **under the p. of** con el pretexto de.

pre·ten·tious (prǐ-tĕn′shəs) adj. pretencioso.

pre·ter·nat·u·ral (prē′tər-nách′ər-əl) adj. preternatural; *(supernatural)* sobrenatural.

pre·test (prē′tĕst′) s. prueba preliminar.

pre·text (prē′tĕkst′) s. pretexto.

pret·ty (prǐt′ē) **I.** adj. **-i-** lindo; FAM. considerable ♦ **a p. penny** mucho dinero **II.** adv. bastante ♦ **p. much** más o menos • **to be sitting p.** FAM. tener una buena posición.

pre·vail (prǐ-vāl′) intr. prevalecer; *(to win)* triunfar; *(to predominate)* predominar ♦ **to p. on** *o* **upon** convencer a.

pre·vail·ing (:vā′lǐng) adj. prevaleciente; *(predominant)* predominante; *(current)* corriente; *(widespread)* común.

prev·a·lence (prĕv′ə-ləns) s. predominio.

prev·a·lent (:lənt) adj. común; *(general)* generalizado.

pre·var·i·cate (prǐ-vâr′ǐ-kāt′) intr. *(to twist)* tergiversar; *(to lie)* mentir.

pre·vent (prǐ-vĕnt′) tr. *(to avoid)* evitar; *(to impede)* impedir.

pre·vent·a·ble (:vĕn′tə-bəl) adj. evitable.

pre·ven·ta·tive (:tǐv) var. de preventive.

pre·ven·tion (prǐ-vĕn′shən) s. prevención *f*.

pre·ven·tive (:tǐv) adj. preventivo.

pre·view (prē′vyōō′) **I.** s. exhibición *f* preliminar; CINEM. avance *m* **II.** tr. *(to view)* ver antes que otros; *(to show)* exhibir previamente.

pre·vi·ous (prē′vē-əs) adj. previo ♦ **p. to** antes de.

prey (prā) **I.** s. presa; FIG. víctima **II.** tr. ♦ **to p. on** *(to hunt)* cazar; *(to victimize)* hacer víctima de; *(to weigh)* abrumar.

price (prīs) **I.** s. precio; FIN. cotización *f* ♦ **full p.** precio sin descuento • **list p.** precio de lista • **opening p.** cotización inicial • **p. tag** *(tag)* etiqueta de precio; *(cost)* costo • **to pay a high** *o* **heavy p.** pagar caro **II.** tr. *(to establish)* poner precio a; *(to find out)* averiguar el precio de.

price·less (′lǐs) adj. sin precio, de gran valor; *(amusing)* muy divertido.

prick (prǐk) **I.** s. pinchazo; *(of an insect)* picadura; *(of jealousy, curiosity)* punzada, aguijón *m*; *(pointed object)* aguijón, pincho **II.** tr. pinchar; *(conscience)* remorder; *(jealousy, curiosity)* picar ♦ **to p. up one's ears** *(a dog)* erguir las orejas; FIG. aguzar el oído —intr. *(to hurt)* picar; *(ears)* erguirse.

prick·er (′ər) s. punzón *m*, púa.

prick·le (:əl) **I.** s. *(thorn)* espina; *(spine)* pincho; *(sensation)* picazón *f* **II.** tr. *(to prick)* pinchar; *(to tingle)* picar —intr. sentir picazón.

prick·ly (:lē) adj. **-i-** *(with prickles)* espinoso; *(stinging)* que causa picazón; *(vexatious)* erizado; *(irritable)* quisquilloso ♦ **p. heat** sarpullido causado por el calor.

pride (prīd) **I.** s. orgullo; *(self-respect)* amor propio; *(best)* flor *f*; *(of lions)* manada de leones ♦ **to take p. in** estar orgulloso de **II.** tr. ♦ **to p. oneself on** estar orgulloso de.

priest (prēst) s. sacerdote *m*, cura *m*; *(minister)* presbítero, pastor *m*.

priest·ess (prē′stǐs) s. sacerdotisa.

priest·hood (prēst′hōōd′) s. sacerdocio; *(clergy)* clerecía, clero.

prig (prǐg) s. mojigato.

prim (prǐm) adj. **-mm-** estirado, remilgado.

pri·ma·cy (prī′mə-sē) s. primacía.

pri·mal (:məl) adj. original; *(fundamental)* fundamental; *(primary)* primario.

pri·mar·i·ly (prī-mâr′ə-lē) adv. principalmente.
pri·mar·y (prī′měr′ē, :mə-rē) I. adj. primario; *(primitive)* primitivo; *(foremost)* fundamental II. s. *(in order)* lo primero; *(in importance)* lo principal; *(election)* elección primaria.
pri·mate (prī′māt′) s. RELIG. primado; ZOOL. primate m.
prime (prīm) I. adj. primero; *(main)* fundamental; *(choice)* de primera (calidad); MAT. primo ♦ **p. importance** de la mayor importancia II. s. *(dawn)* alba; *(spring)* primavera; *(age)* flor f de la vida, plenitud f; *(pick)* flor y nata, lo mejor; MAT. número primo ♦ **p. meridian** primer meridiano • **p. minister** primer ministro • **p. mover** fuerza motriz • **p. rate** tasa preferida III. tr. preparar; *(gun, motor)* cebar, cargar; *(walls)* dar una primera mano de pintura ♦ **to p. the pump** FAM. estimular.
prim·er¹ (prĭm′ər) s. texto elemental; *(manual)* manual m.
prim·er² (prī′mər) s. cebador m; *(detonator)* detonador m; PINT. primera mano.
pri·me·val (prī-mē′vəl) adj. primordial.
prim·i·tive (prĭm′ĭ-tĭv) adj. & s. primitivo.
pri·mo·gen·i·tor (prī′mō-jĕn′ĭ-tər) s. primogenitor m.
pri·mo·gen·i·ture (:chŏr′) s. primogenitura.
pri·mor·di·al (prī-môr′dē-əl) adj. primordial.
primp (prĭmp) tr. & intr. emperejilar(se).
prim·rose (prĭm′rōz′) s. primavera, prímula.
prince (prĭns) s. príncipe m ♦ **crown p.** príncipe heredero ♦ **p. charming** el príncipe azul.
prin·cess (prĭn′sĭs) s. princesa.
prin·ci·pal (prĭn′sə-pəl) I. adj. principal II. s. *(of a school)* director m; *(performer)* primera figura; COM., FIN. principal m.
prin·ci·pal·i·ty (prĭn′sə-păl′ĭ-tē) s. principado.
prin·ci·ple (prĭn′sə-pəl) s. principio ♦ **a matter of p.** una cuestión de principios ♦ **in p.** en principio • **on p.** por principio.
prin·ci·pled (:pəld) adj. de principios.
print (prĭnt) I. s. *(impression)* impresión f, huella; *(stamp, seal)* estampa, cuño; *(letters)* letra, tipo; FOTOG. copia; *(engraving)* grabado, estampa; *(fabric)* estampado ♦ **in p.** impreso, publicado • **out of p.** agotado II. tr. imprimir; *(edition)* tirar, hacer una tirada; *(to publish)* publicar; FOTOG. copiar; *(to write)* escribir con letras de imprenta o de molde —intr. *(to be a printer)* trabajar como impresor; *(to write plainly)* escribir con letras de imprenta o de molde; *(book, publication)* imprimirse.
print·er (prĭn′tər) s. *(person)* impresor m; *(machine)* impresora.
print·ing (:tĭng) s. *(art, business)* imprenta; *(act, quality of run)* impresión f; *(run)* tiraje m; *(written characters)* letra de imprenta; *(layout)* tipografía ♦ **p. press** prensa.
print·out (prĭnt′out′) s. salida impresa.
pri·or¹ (prī′ər) adj. previo ♦ **p. to** antes de.
pri·or² s. RELIG. prior m.
pri·or·ess (:ĭs) s. RELIG. priora.
pri·or·i·ty (prī-ôr′ĭ-tē) s. prioridad f; *(time precedence)* anterioridad f.
prism (prĭz′əm) s. prisma m.
pris·on (prĭz′ən) s. cárcel f, prisión f ♦ **to put in o send to p.** encarcelar.
pris·on·er (:ə-nər) s. prisionero, preso; *(under arrest)* detenido; *(accused)* acusado.
pris·sy (prĭs′ē) adj. -i- remilgado.
pris·tine (prĭs′tēn′) adj. prístino; *(pure)* puro.
pri·va·cy (prī′və-sē) s. *(seclusion)* intimidad f,

(isolation) aislamiento; *(secrecy)* secreto.
pri·vate (prī′vĭt) I. adj. privado; *(not public)* particular; *(secluded)* solitario ♦ **p. citizen** particular • **p. enterprise** *(sector)* sector privado; *(business)* empresa particular II. s. soldado raso.
pri·va·tion (prī-vā′shən) s. privación f.
priv·i·lege (prĭv′ə-lĭj) s. privilegio ♦ **to have the p. of** tener el honor de.
priv·i·leged (:lĭjd) adj. privilegiado ♦ **p. communication** comunicación confidencial • **to be p. to** tener el privilegio de.
priv·y (prĭv′ē) I. adj. privado ♦ **p. seal** G.B. sello real • **to be p. to** estar enterado de II. s. excusado, retrete rústico.
prize¹ (prīz) I. s. premio II. adj. de premio; *(given a prize)* premiado; *(outstanding)* de primera categoría III. tr. valorar.
prize² s. MARÍT. presa.
prize³ I. tr. ♦ **to p. open** o **up** abrir o levantar con una palanca II. s. *(leverage)* apalancamiento; *(lever)* palanca.
prize·fight (′fīt′) s. pelea profesional de boxeo.
prize·fight·er (:fī′tər) s. boxeador m profesional.
pro¹ (prō) I. s. ♦ **the pros and cons** el pro y el contra II. adv. a favor III. prep. a favor de IV. adj. partidario.
pro² s. & adj. FAM. profesional mf.
prob·a·bil·i·ty (prŏb′ə-bĭl′ĭ-tē) s. probabilidad f.
prob·a·ble (prŏb′ə-bəl) adj. probable; *(plausible)* verosímil ♦ **p. cause** motivo presunto.
pro·bate (prō′bāt′) DER. I. s. legalización f (de un testamento); **p. court** tribunal sucesorio II. tr. legalizar.
pro·ba·tion (-bā′shən) s. periodo de prueba; *(freedom)* libertad f condicional ♦ **on p.** a prueba.
probe (prōb) I. s. *(device)* sonda; *(exploration)* sondeo; *(investigation)* investigación f II. tr. *(to explore)* sondar; *(to investigate)* investigar —intr. indagar.
pro·bi·ty (prō′bĭ-tē) s. probidad f.
prob·lem (prŏb′ləm) I. s. problema m II. adj. difícil.
prob·lem·at·ic/·i·cal (prŏb′lə-mắt′ĭk) adj. problemático.
pro·bos·cis (prō-bŏs′ĭs) s. [pl. es o -cides] ZOOL. trompa; ENTOM. proboscide f.
pro·ce·dur·al (prə-sē′jər-əl) adj. de procedimiento.
pro·ce·dure (′jər) s. procedimiento.
pro·ceed (prə-sēd′) intr. proceder; *(to continue)* proseguir, continuar; *(to go forward)* avanzar; *(to move along)* ir, desarrollar.
pro·ceed·ing (:sē′dĭng) s. procedimiento, acción f ♦ pl. acontecimientos; *(minutes)* actas; DER. proceso.
pro·ceeds (prō′sēdz′) s.pl. ganancias.
proc·ess (prŏs′ĕs′, :ĭs′) I. s. *(treatment)* procedimiento; *(method)* proceso; DER. proceso; *(summons)* citación f; BIOL. apéndice m ♦ **in p.** en marcha • **in the p.** al hacerlo • **to be in (the) p. of** estar en vías de II. tr. *(an application)* tramitar; *(to treat)* tratar; *(to convert)* transformar; FOTOG. revelar; COMPUT., DER. procesar.
proc·ess·ing (:ĭng) s. *(of food)* tratamiento; *(of raw materials)* transformación f; FOTOG. revelado; COMPUT. procesamiento ♦ **data p.** procesamiento de datos; *(science)* informática.

pro·ces·sion (prə-sĕsh'ən) s. procesión *f*, desfile *m*; *(orderly course)* progresión *f*.

pro·ces·sion·al (:ə-nəl) **I.** adj. procesional **II.** s. *(book)* procesionario; *(hymn)* himno procesionario.

pro·claim (prō-klām') tr. proclamar.

proc·la·ma·tion (prŏk'lə-mā'shən) s. proclamación *f*; *(announcement)* proclama.

pro·cliv·i·ty (prō-klĭv'ĭ-tē) s. propensión *f*.

pro·cras·ti·nate (prō-krăs'tə-nāt') intr. aplazar una decisión —tr. aplazar, postergar.

pro·cras·ti·na·tion (-'-nā'shən) s. dilación *f*, retraso.

pro·cras·ti·na·tor (-'-'tər) s. persona dada a la postergación.

pro·cre·ate (prō'krē-āt') tr. & intr. procrear.

pro·cre·a·tion ('-ā'shən) s. procreación *f*.

pro·cre·a·tive ('-'tĭv) adj. procreador.

proc·tol·o·gy (prŏk-tŏl'ə-jē) s. proctología.

proc·tor (prŏk'tər) **I.** s. vigilante *mf* **II.** tr. vigilar.

proc·u·ra·tor (prŏk'yə-rā'tər) s. procurador *m*.

pro·cure (prō-kyŏŏr') tr. obtener; *(a woman)* alcahuetear —intr. dedicarse al proxenetismo.

pro·cure·ment (:mənt) s. obtención *f*, logro.

pro·cur·er (:ər) s. alcahuete *m*.

prod (prŏd) tr. **-dd-** pinchar; *(to goad)* estimular.

prod·i·gal (prŏd'ĭ-gəl) adj. & s. pródigo.

pro·di·gious (prə-dĭj'əs) adj. enorme; *(marvelous)* prodigioso.

prod·i·gy (prŏd'ə-jē) s. prodigio.

pro·duce I. tr. (prə-dōōs') producir; *(to manufacture)* fabricar; *(to give rise to)* causar; *(to show)* exhibir, mostrar —intr. producir **II.** s. (prŏd'ōōs, prō'dōōs) producto.

pro·duc·er (prə-dō'ʊ̄sər) s. productor *m*.

prod·uct (prŏd'əkt) s. producto.

pro·duc·tion (prə-dŭk'shən) s. producción *f*.

pro·duc·tive (:tĭv) adj. productivo.

pro·duc·tiv·i·ty (prŏd'dŭk-tĭv'ĭ-tē, prōd'ək-) s. productividad *f*.

prof (prŏf) s. FAM. profe *m*, profesor *m*.

pro·fane (prə-fān') **I.** adj. profano; *(vulgar)* vulgar **II.** tr. profanar.

pro·fan·i·ty (:fǎn'ĭ-tē) s. profanidad *f*; *(language)* lenguaje obsceno.

pro·fess (prə-fĕs') tr. *(to affirm)* declarar, proclamar; *(to pretend)* pretender; RELIG. profesar.

pro·fessed (:fĕst') adj. declarado; *(pretended)* supuesto; RELIG. profeso.

pro·fes·sion (:fĕsh'ən) s. profesión *f*.

pro·fes·sion·al (:ə-nəl) adj. & s. profesional *mf*; *(expert)* perito, experto.

pro·fes·sor (prə-fĕs'ər) s. profesor *m*; *(university)* catedrático.

pro·fes·sor·ship (:shĭp') s. profesorado, cátedra.

prof·fer (prŏf'ər) tr. ofrecer, proponer.

pro·fi·cien·cy (prə-fĭsh'ən-sē) s. competencia.

pro·fi·cient (:ənt) adj. capaz, competente.

pro·file (prō'fīl') **I.** s. perfil *m*; *(biography)* retrato; *(description)* descripción *f* ♦ **to keep a low p.** no llamar la atención **II.** tr. perfilar.

prof·it (prŏf'ĭt) **I.** s. beneficio ♦ **p. sharing** participación en los beneficios ♦ **to make a p.** *(person)* ganar dinero; *(business)* rendir ganancias ♦ **to show a p.** ganar dinero ♦ **to turn something to p.** sacar provecho de algo ♦ pl. *(from investments)* rentas; *(gains)* ganancias, utilidades **II.** intr. servir ♦ **to p. by** *o* **from** COM. sacar dinero de; *(to benefit from)* sacar provecho de.

prof·it·a·bil·i·ty ('ĭ-tə-bĭl'ĭ-tē) s. COM. carácter lucrativo.

prof·it·a·ble ('--bəl) adj. beneficioso, provechoso; COM. lucrativo.

prof·i·teer (prŏf'ĭ-tîr') **I.** s. aprovechón *m* **II.** intr. aprovecharse.

prof·li·gate (prŏf'lĭ-gĭt) adj. disoluto; *(wasteful)* derrochador.

pro·found (prə-found') adj. **-er, -est** profundo.

pro·fun·di·ty (:fŭn'dĭ-tē) s. profundidad *f*.

pro·fuse (prə-fyōōs') adj. profuso; *(extravagant)* pródigo.

pro·fu·sion (:fyōō'zhən) s. profusión *f*.

pro·gen·i·tor (prō-jĕn'ĭ-tər) s. *(ancestor)* antepasado; *(parent)* progenitor *m*.

prog·e·ny (prŏj'ə-nē) s. progenie *m*.

pro·ges·ter·one (prō-jĕs'tə-rōn') s. progesterona.

prog·no·sis (prŏg-nō'sĭs) s. [pl. **-ses**] pronóstico.

prog·nos·tic (:nŏs'tĭk) augurio, presagio.

prog·nos·ti·cate (:tĭ-kāt') tr. pronosticar.

prog·nos·ti·ca·tion (-'-kā'shən) s. pronosticación *f*; *(forecast)* pronóstico.

pro·gram (prō'grăm', :grəm) **I.** s. programa *m* **II.** tr. programar.

pro·gram·(m)er (:ər) s. programador *m*.

pro·gram·(m)ing (:ĭng) s. programación *f*.

prog·ress I. s. (prŏg'rĕs', prō'grĕs') progreso; *(development)* desarrollo; *(of events)* marcha, curso ♦ **in p.** en curso ▪ **to make p.** progresar; *(to improve)* mejorar **II.** intr. (prə-grĕs') progresar; *(to improve)* mejorar.

pro·gres·sion (prə-grĕsh'ən) s. progreso; MAT., MÚS. progresión *f*.

pro·gres·sive (:grĕs'ĭv) **I.** adj. progresivo; POL. progresista **II.** s. POL. progresista *mf*.

pro·hib·it (prō-hĭb'ĭt) tr. prohibir.

pro·hi·bi·tion (prō'ə-bĭsh'ən) s. prohibición *f*.

pro·hib·i·tive/to·ry (:ĭ-tĭv/tôr'ē) adj. prohibitivo.

proj·ect I. s. (prŏj'ĕkt') proyecto **II.** tr. (prə-jĕkt') *(to protrude)* hacer sobresalir, sacar; *(missile, image)* proyectar; *(to convey)* sugerir; *(to plan)* proyectar, planear —intr. *(to protrude)* sobresalir, salir; *(to speak)* hablar claramente.

pro·jec·tile (prə-jĕk'təl, :tĭl') s. proyectil *m*.

pro·jec·tion (:shən) s. proyección *f*; *(of a mood)* sugestión *f*; *(protuberance)* saliente *m*, punta; *(estimate)* cálculo, pronóstico.

pro·jec·tion·ist (:shə-nĭst) s. operador *m* de cine que proyecta las películas.

pro·jec·tor (:tər) s. proyector *m*.

pro·le·tar·i·an (prō'lĭ-târ'ē-ən) adj. & s. proletario.

pro·le·tar·i·at (:ĭt) s. proletariado.

pro·lif·er·ate (prə-lĭf'ə-rāt') intr. proliferar —tr. hacer crecer *o* aumentar.

pro·lif·er·a·tion (-'-rā'shən) s. proliferación *f*.

pro·lif·ic (prə-lĭf'ĭk) adj. prolífico.

pro·log(ue) (prō'lŏg') s. prólogo.

pro·long (prə-lŏng') tr. prolongar.

pro·lon·gate (:gāt') tr. prolongar.

pro·lon·ga·tion ('-gā'shən) s. prolongación *f*.

prom·e·nade (prŏm'ə-nād', :näd') **I.** s. paseo **II.** intr. pasearse —tr. pasear.

prom·i·nence (prŏm'ə-nəns) s. prominencia.

prom·i·nent (:nənt) adj. prominente; *(eminent)* notable.

prom·is·cu·i·ty (prŏm'ĭ-skyōō'ĭ-tē) s. promiscuidad *f*.

prom·is·cu·ous (prə-mĭs'kyōō-əs) adj. promiscuo.

prom·ise (prŏm'ĭs) **I.** s. promesa **♦ to break one's p.** faltar a su palabra **• to keep one's p.** cumplir su promesa **• to show p.** ser prometedor **II.** tr. prometer —intr. hacer una promesa.

prom·is·ing (:ĭ sĭng) adj. prometedor.

prom·is·so·ry (:sôr'ē) adj. promisorio **♦ p. note** pagaré.

prom·on·to·ry (prŏm'ən-tôr'ē) s. promontorio.

pro·mote (prə-mōt') tr. (employee, officer) ascender; (student) adelantar de año; (to further) promover, fomentar; (to advocate) apoyar; (to advertise) promocionar; (to finance) financiar.

pro·mot·er (:mō'tər) s. promotor m.

pro·mo·tion (:shən) s. ascenso; (furtherance) fomento.

prompt (prŏmpt) **I.** adj. puntual; (without delay) pronto, rápido **II.** tr. (to incite) incitar; (to inspire) inspirar; TEAT. apuntar.

prompt·er (prŏmp'tər) s TEAT apuntador m.

prompt·ness (prŏmpt'nĭs) s. prontitud f.

prom·ul·gate (prŏm'əl-gāt', prō'məl-) tr. promulgar.

prom·ul·ga·tion (:gā'shən) s. promulgación f.

prom·ul·ga·tor ('-tər) s. promulgador m.

prone (prōn) adj. & adv. boca abajo **♦ to be p. to** ser propenso a.

prong (prŏng) s. punta. (of a fork) diente m.

pro·noun (prō'noun') s. pronombre m.

pro·nounce (prə-nouns') tr. pronunciar; (to declare) declarar —intr. pronunciarse.

pro·nounced (:nounst') adj. pronunciado.

pro·nounce·ment (:nouns'mənt) s. declaración f.

pro·nun·ci·a·tion (prə-nŭn'sē-ā'shən) s. pronunciación f; FONÉT. transcripción fonética.

proof (prōōf) **I.** s. prueba; (alcoholic content) grado **II.** tr. (to proofread) corregir las pruebas de; (to make resistant to) hacer resistente a.

proof·read ('rēd') tr. -read corregir —intr. corregir pruebas.

proof·read·er (:rē'dər) s. corrector m de pruebas.

prop¹ (prŏp) **I.** s. puntal m; FIG. sostén m **II.** tr. -pp- **♦ to p. open** mantener abierto **• to p. up** apuntalar.

prop² s. FAM. accesorio.

prop³ s. FAM. hélice f.

prop·a·gan·da (prŏp'ə-găn'də) s. propaganda.

prop·a·gan·dist (:dĭst) s. propagandista mf

prop·a·gan·dize (:dīz') tr. & intr. hacer propaganda (de).

prop·a·gate (prŏp'ə-gāt') tr. & intr. propagar(se).

prop·a·ga·tion ('-gā'shən) s. propagación f.

pro·pane (prō'pān') s. propano.

pro·pel (prə-pĕl') tr. -ll- propulsar, impeler.

pro·pel·ler/lor (:ər) s. hélice f.

pro·pen·si·ty (prə-pĕn'sĭ-tē) s. propensión f.

prop·er (prŏp'ər) adj. apropiado; (right) debido; (itself) propio, mismo; (correct) correcto; (characteristic) característico; GRAM., MAT. propio.

prop·er·ly (:lē) adv. apropiadamente; (strictly) propiamente; (correctly) correctamente.

prop·er·ty (prŏp'ər-tē) s. propiedad f; (possessions) bienes m; TEAT. accesorio **♦ personal p.** bienes muebles.

proph·e·cy (prŏf'ĭ-sē) s. profecía.

proph·e·sy (:sī') tr. & intr. profetizar.

proph·et (prŏf'ĭt) s. profeta m

proph·et·ess (:ĭ-tĭs) s. profetisa.

pro·phet·ic/i·cal (prə-fĕt'ĭk) adj. profético.

pro·phy·lac·tic (prō'fə-lăk'tĭk) adj. & s. profiláctico.

pro·phy·lax·is (:sĭs) s. [pl. -xes] profilaxis f.

pro·pin·qui·ty (prə-pĭng'kwĭ-tē) s. proximidad f; (kinship) parentesco.

pro·pi·ti·ate (prə-pĭsh'ē-āt') tr. propiciar.

pro·pi·tious (:əs) adj. propicio.

pro·po·nent (prə-pō'nənt) s. proponente mf.

pro·por·tion (prə-pôr'shən) s. proporción f; (part) parte f, porción f **♦ in p.** proporcionado **• out of p.** desproporcionado **♦ pl.** dimensiones, tamaño **II.** tr. proporcionar.

pro·por·tion·al (:sha-nəl) adj. proporcional.

pro·por·tion·ate (:nĭt) adj. proporcional.

pro·pos·al (prə-pō'zəl) s. propuesta; (of marriage) propuesta matrimonial.

pro·pose (prə-pōz') tr. proponer; (to intend) tener intención de —intr. proponerse; (marriage) ofrecer matrimonio.

prop·o·si·tion (prŏp'ə-zĭsh'ən) **I.** s. proposición f; FAM. (matter) asunto, problema m; (immoral) proposición deshonesta **II.** tr. FAM. hacer una propuesta deshonesta a.

pro·pound (prə-pound') tr. proponer.

pro·pri·e·tar·y (prə-prī'ĭ-tĕr'ē) adj. propietario; (patented) patentado.

pro·pri·e·tor (:tər) s. propietario.

pro·pri·e·tor·ship (:ship') s. (derecho de) propiedad f.

pro·pri·e·tress (prə-prī'ĭ-trĭs) s. propietaria

pro·pri·e·ty (:tē) s. conveniencia; (decency) decencia **♦ pl.** convenciones.

pro·pul·sion (prə-pŭl'shən) s. propulsión f.

pro·rate (prō-rāt') tr. prorratear.

pro·sa·ic (prō-zā'ĭk) adj. prosaico.

pro·sce·ni·um (prō-sē'nē-əm) s. proscenio.

pro·scribe (prō-skrīb') tr. proscribir.

pro·scrip·tion (:skrĭp'shən) s. proscripción f.

prose (prōz) s. prosa.

pros·e·cute (prŏs'ĭ-kyōōt') tr. proseguir; DER. (a person) procesar; (claim, case) entablar —intr. entablar una acción judicial.

pros·e·cu·tion ('-kyōō'shən) s. procesamiento; (trial) proceso; (attorney) fiscal mf.

pros·e·cu·tor ('-tər) s. fiscal mf.

pros·e·ly·tize (prŏs'ə-lĭ-tīz') intr. ganar prosélitos —tr. convertir.

pros·o·dy (prŏs'ə-dē) s. (study) métrica; (system) prosodia f.

pros·pect (prŏs'pĕkt') **I.** s. perspectiva; (expectation) expectativa; (customer) cliente m probable; (candidate) candidato probable, (exposure) orientación f; (view) vista **♦ pl.** perspectivas **II.** tr. prospectar **♦ to p. for** buscar.

pro·spec·tive (prə-spĕk'tĭv) adj. (expected) esperado; (likely to be) presunto.

pros·pec·tor (prŏs'pĕk'tər) s. buscador m.

pro·spec·tus (prə-spĕk'təs) s. prospecto.

pros·per (prŏs'pər) intr. prosperar.

pros·per·i·ty (prŏ-spĕr'ĭ-tē) s. prosperidad f.

pros·per·ous (prŏs'pər-əs) adj. próspero; (favorable) favorable.

pros·tate (prŏs'tāt') s. próstata.

pros·the·sis (prŏs-thē'sĭs) s. [pl. -ses] prótesis f.

pros·ti·tute (prŏs'tĭ-tōōt') **I.** s. prostituta **II.** tr. prostituir **♦ to p. oneself** prostituirse.

pros·ti·tu·tion ('-tōō'shən) s. prostitución f.

pros·trate (prŏs'trāt') **I.** tr. postrar **II.** adj. postrado.

pros·tra·tion (prŏ-strā′shən) s. postración f.
pro·tag·o·nist (prŏ-tăg′ə-nĭst) s. protagonista mf.
pro·te·an (prŏ′tē-ən) adj. proteico.
pro·tect (prə-tĕkt′) tr. proteger.
pro·tect·er (:tĕk′tər) s. protector m.
pro·tec·tion (:shən) s. protección f.
pro·tec·tion·ist (:shə-nĭst) s. proteccionista mf.
pro·tec·tive (:tĭv) adj. & s. protector m.
pro·tec·tor (:tər) s. protector m.
pro·tec·tor·ate (:ĭt) s. protectorado.
pro·té·gé (prŏ′tə-zhā′) s. protegido.
pro·tein (prŏ′tēn) s. proteína.
pro·test I. tr. (prə-tĕst′) protestar contra; (to affirm) protestar de —intr. protestar II. s. (prŏ′tĕst′) protesta; (statement) protesto ♦ under p. contra su voluntad.
Prot·es·tant (prŏt′ĭ-stənt) s. & adj. protestante mf.
prot·es·ta·tion (prŏt′ĭ-stā′shən) s. protesta f.
pro·test·er (prə-tĕs′tər) s. persona que protesta; (demonstrator) manifestante mf.
pro·to·col (prŏ′tə-kôl′) s. protocolo.
pro·ton (prŏ′tŏn′) s. protón m.
pro·to·type (prŏ′tə-tīp′) s. prototipo.
pro·tract (prŏ-trăkt′) tr. prolongar.
pro·trac·tion (:trăk′shən) s. prolongación f.
pro·trac·tor (:tər) s. transportador m.
pro·trude (prŏ-trōōd′) tr. sacar —intr. sobresalir, resaltar.
pro·tru·sion (:trōō′zhən) s. acción f de sacar; (state) prominencia; (projection) saliente m.
pro·tru·sive (:trōō′sĭv) adj. sobresaliente.
pro·tu·ber·ance (prŏ-tōō′bər-əns) s. protuberancia.
pro·tu·ber·ant (:ənt) adj. protuberante.
proud (proud) adj. orgulloso; (of oneself) satisfecho; (memorable) memorable; (arrogant) soberbio; (honorable) honorable; (spirited) animoso ♦ to be p. to tener el honor de.
prove (prōōv) tr. **-d, -d** o **-n** probar; (to test) poner a prueba ♦ proving ground campo de pruebas —intr. salir, resultar.
prov·en (prōō′vən) I. cf. **prove** II. adj. probado.
prov·e·nance (prŏv′ə-nəns) s. origen m.
prov·en·der (prŏv′ən-dər) s. (fodder) forraje m; (food) comida.
prov·erb (prŏv′ûrb′) s. proverbio.
pro·ver·bi·al (prə-vûr′bē-əl) adj. proverbial.
pro·vide (prə-vīd′) tr. (to supply) suministrar; (to make available) proveer; (to stipulate) estipular —intr. proveer ♦ provided o providing that con tal que.
prov·i·dence (prŏv′ĭ-dəns) s. providencia.
prov·i·dent (:dənt) adj. providente; (economical) económico.
prov·i·den·tial (′-dĕn′shəl) adj. providencial.
pro·vid·er (prə-vī′dər) s. proveedor m.
prov·ince (prŏv′ĭns) s. provincia; (field) esfera, campo; (jurisdiction) competencia.
pro·vin·cial (prə-vĭn′shəl) I. adj. provincial; (unsophisticated) provinciano; (narrow) de miras estrechas II. s. provinciano.
pro·vi·sion (prə-vĭzh′ən) s. provisión f; (stipulation) estipulación f ♦ to make provisions for (the future) prever; (family) mantener II. tr. proveer.
pro·vi·sion·al (:ə-nəl) adj. provisional.
pro·vi·so (prə-vī′zō) s. pl. **(e)s** condición f.
pro·vi·so·ry (:zə-rē) adj. condicional.
pro·vo·ca·teur (prŏ-vŏk′ə-tûr′) s. agente m

provocador.
prov·o·ca·tion (prŏv′ə-kā′shən) s. provocación f.
pro·voc·a·tive (prə-vŏk′ə-tĭv) adj. provocativo.
pro·voke (prə-vŏk′) tr. provocar.
prow (prou) s. proa.
prow·ess (prou′ĭs) s. (skill) habilidad f, destreza; (courage) valor m.
prowl (proul) I. tr. & intr. merodear, rondar II. s. merodeo, ronda ♦ on the p. buscando algo.
prox·i·mate (prŏk′sə-mĭt) adj. próximo.
prox·im·i·ty (-sĭm′ĭ-tē) s. proximidad f.
prox·y (prŏk′sē) s. (person) apoderado; (authority) poder m ♦ by p. por poder.
prude (prōōd) s. mojigato, gazmoño.
pru·dence (prōōd′ns) s. prudencia.
pru·dent (:nt) adj. prudente.
pru·den·tial (prōō-dĕn′shəl) adj. prudencial.
prune[1] (prōōn) s. (fruit) ciruela pasa.
prune[2] tr. & intr. (to trim) podar; (to remove) cortar, cercenar; (to reduce) reducir.
pru·ri·ent (prŏŏr′ē-ənt) adj. lascivo, libidinoso.
pry[1] (prī) intr. fisgar, curiosear.
pry[2] tr. ♦ **to p. open** abrir con una palanca • **to p. out of** arrancar.
pry·ing (:ĭng) adj. fisgón, entremetido.
psalm (säm) s. salmo.
pseu·do·nym (sōōd′n-ĭm′) s. seudónimo.
pso·ri·a·sis (sə-rī′ə-sĭs) s. psoriasis f.
psy·che (sī′kē) s. psique f.
psy·che·del·ic (sī′kĭ-dĕl′ĭk) adj. psicodélico.
psy·chi·at·ric (sī′kē-ăt′rĭk) adj. psiquiátrico.
psy·chi·a·trist (sī-kī′ə-trĭst, sī-) s. psiquiatra mf.
psy·chi·a·try (:trē) s. psiquiatría f.
psy·chic (sī′kĭk) I. adj. psíquico II. s. medium m.
psy·cho·a·nal·y·sis (sī′kō-ə-năl′ĭ-sĭs) s. psicoanálisis m.
psy·cho·an·a·lyze (:ăn′ə-līz′) tr. psicoanalizar.
psy·cho·log·i·cal (sī′kə-lŏj′ĭ-kəl) adj. psicológico.
psy·chol·o·gist (sī-kŏl′ə-jĭst) s. psicólogo.
psy·chol·o·gy (:jē) s. psicología.
psy·cho·path (sī′kə-păth′) s. psicópata mf.
psy·cho·pa·thy (sī-kŏp′ə-thē) s. psicopatía.
psy·cho·sis (sī-kō′sĭs) s. [pl. **-ses**] psicosis f.
psy·cho·so·mat·ic (sī′kə-sō-măt′ĭk) adj. & s. psicosomático.
psy·cho·ther·a·py (sī′kō-thĕr′ə-pē) s. psicoterapia.
psy·chot·ic (sī-kŏt′ĭk) I. s. psicópata mf II. adj. psicopático.
pto·maine poisoning (tō′mān′) s. envenamiento por tomaínas.
pub (pŭb) s. taberna, cantina.
pu·ber·ty (pyōō′bər-tē) s. pubertad f.
pu·bes·cence (:bĕs′əns) s. pubescencia.
pu·bes·cent (:ənt) adj. pubescente.
pu·bic (pyōō′bĭk) adj. pubiano, público.
pu·bis (:bĭs) s. [pl. **-bes**] pubis m.
pub·lic (pŭb′lĭk) adj. & s. público ♦ **p. defender** defensor de oficio **in • p. school** (U.S.) escuela pública; (G.B.) colegio particular • **p. servant** funcionario • **p. television** televisión no comercial • **p. utility** empresa de servicio público • **to make p.** publicar.
pub·li·ca·tion (pŭb′lĭ-kā′shən) s. publicación f.
pub·li·cist (:sĭst) s. publicista mf.
pub·lic·i·ty (pŭ-blĭs′ĭ-tē) s. publicidad f.
pub·li·cize (pŭb′lĭ-sīz′) tr. publicar.

pub·lic-spir·it·ed (pŭb'lĭk-spĭr'ĭ-tĭd) adj. de espíritu cívico.

pub·lish (pŭb'lĭsh) tr. & intr. publicar.

pub·lish·er (:ĭ-shər) s. editor m.

puck (pŭk) s. disco.

puck·er (pŭk'ər) I. tr. fruncir —intr. ♦ **to p. up** arrugarse II. s. arruga, fruncido.

pud·ding (pŏŏd'ĭng) s. budín m.

pud·dle (pŭd'l) s. charco.

pudg·y (pŭj'ē) adj. -i- regordete.

pu·er·ile (pyōō'ər-əl) adj. pueril.

puff (pŭf) I. s. (of breath) resoplido; (of air) soplo; (of wind) soplido; (of smoke, steam) bocanada; (on a cigarette) fumada; (swelling) hinchazón f; (pastry) buñuelo; (for powder) borla; (flattery) bombo II. intr. (to blow) soplar; (to breathe) resoplar, resollar; (to emit smoke) echar bocanadas; (to smoke) fumar ♦ **to p. up** (to swell) hincharse; (to become vain) engreírse —tr. (to blow) soplar; (to smoke) fumar; (to praise) dar bombo a ♦ **to p. up** (to swell) hinchar; (to make vain) engreír.

puffed-up (pŭft'ŭp') adj. engreído.

puf·fin (pŭf'ĭn) s. frailecillo.

puff·y (pŭf'ē) adj. -i- hinchado.

pu·gil·ism (pyōō'jə-lĭz'əm) s. pugilismo.

pu·gil·ist (:lĭst) s. pugilista m.

pug·na·cious (pŭg-nā'shəs) adj. belicoso.

pug·nac·i·ty (:năs'ĭ-tē) s. belicosidad f.

pug-nosed (pŭg'nōzd') adj. braco.

puke (pyōōk) JER. I. intr. & tr. vomitar II. s. vómito.

pull (pŏŏl) I. tr. (to move) tirar de; (to extract) sacar, extraer; (to tug at) tirar de, tirar de; (trigger) apretar; (to stretch) estirar; (muscle) torcerse; FAM. (to attract) traer; (to do) hacer; (gun) sacar ♦ **to p. apart** (to rend) desgarrar, rasgar; (to criticize) criticar ♦ **to p. down** (to demolish) echar abajo, derribar; (to lower) bajar; (to reduce) rebajar; FAM. (salary) cobrar ♦ **to p. for** (to cheer) animar, (to support) apoyar ♦ **to p. in** (to restrain) contener; FAM. (to arrest) detener; (to attract) atraer ♦ **to p. off** (to take off) quitar; (to carry out) llevar a cabo ♦ **to p. on** (clothes) ponerse; (to tug at) tirar de ♦ **to p. punches** (boxer) no pegar a fondo; (to hold back) andarse con rodeos ♦ **to p. oneself together** componerse, dominarse ♦ **to p. strings** conseguir algo por influencias ♦ **to p. the rug out from under someone** dejar a alguien en la estacada ♦ **to p. the wool over someone's eyes** engañar a alguien ♦ **to p. up** (socks) subirse; (a chair) acercar —intr. (to tug) tirar; (to row) remar ♦ **to p. ahead** destacarse ♦ **to p. away** dejar atrás ♦ **to p. in** (train) entrar en la estación; (to arrive) llegar ♦ **to p. out** (to depart) salir; (to withdraw) retirarse ♦ **to p. over** AUTO. parar ♦ **to p. through** (to survive) salir de una enfermedad o apuro ♦ **to p. together** aunar los esfuerzos ♦ **to p. up** pararse, detenerse II. s. (tug) tirón m; (effort) esfuerzo; (knob, cord) tirador m; (inhalation) chupada; JER. (influence) enchufe m, palanca; FAM. (appeal) atracción f.

pull·back ('băk') s. retirada (de tropas).

pul·let (pŏŏl'ĭt) s. pollo, polla.

pul·ley (pŏŏl'ē) s. polea, roldana.

pull·out (pŏŏl'out') s. retirada.

pull·o·ver (:ō'vər) s. jersey m, suéter m.

pul·mo·nar·y (pŏŏl'mə-nĕr'ē) adj. pulmonar.

pulp (pŭlp) s. pulpa; BOT. médula.

pul·pit (pŏŏl'pĭt, pŭl'-) s. púlpito.

pul·sar (pŭl'sär') s. púlsar m.

pul·sate (:sāt') intr. pulsar.

pul·sa·tion (-sā'shən) s. pulsación f.

pulse (pŭls) I. s. pulso; (amplification) pulsación f II. intr. pulsar.

pul·ver·ize (pŭl'və-rīz') tr. & intr. pulverizar(se).

pu·ma (pyōō'mə, pōō'-) s. puma m.

pum·ice (pŭm'ĭs) s. piedra pómez.

pum·mel (pŭm'əl) tr. aporrear, apuñear.

pump¹ (pŭmp) I. s. MEC. bomba; AUTO. surtidor m II. tr. bombear; (blood) impulsar; (to move up and down) mover de arriba abajo ♦ **to p. for information** sonsacar información.

pump² s. (shoe) escarpín m.

pump·kin (pŭmp'kĭn) s. calabaza.

pun (pŭn) I. s. juego de palabras II. intr. -nn- hacer juegos de palabras.

punch¹ (pŭnch) I. s. punzón m; (for paper) perforadora; (for tickets) máquina de picar billetes ♦ **p. card** tarjeta perforada II. tr. (tickets) picar; (metal, leather) taladrar ♦ **to p. in, out** marcar la hora de llegada, salida del trabajo.

punch² I. tr. dar un puñetazo II. s. puñetazo; (in boxing) pegada; (vigor) vigor m, fuerza ♦ **p. line** gracia de un chiste.

punch³ s. (beverage) ponche m ♦ **p. bowl** ponchera.

punch-drunk ('drŭngk') adj. aturdido; (in boxing) aturdido por los golpes.

punch·y (pŭn'chē) adj. -i- aturdido.

punc·til·i·ous (pŭngk-tĭl'ē-əs) adj. puntilloso.

punc·tu·al (pŭngk'chōō-əl) adj. puntual.

punc·tu·al·i·ty (:-āl'ĭ-tē) s. puntualidad f.

punc·tu·ate ('-āt') tr. puntuar; (to interrupt) interrumpir; (to stress) acentuar.

punc·tu·a·tion (:-ā'shən) s. puntuación f.

punc·ture (pŭngk'chər) I. tr. perforar; (a tire) pinchar; (to deflate) rebajar II. s. perforación f; (in a tire) pinchazo.

pun·dit (pŭn'dĭt) s. (in India) pandit m; (learned person) erudito; (authority) experto.

pun·gent (pŭn'jənt) adj. acre; (piquant) picante; FIG. mordaz.

pun·ish (pŭn'ĭsh) tr. castigar; (to injure) maltratar —intr. imponer castigo.

pun·ish·a·ble (:ĭ-shə-bəl) adj. castigable.

pun·ish·ment (:ĭsh-mənt) s. castigo; (mistreatment) maltrato.

pu·ni·tive (pyōō'nĭ-tĭv) adj. punitivo.

punk¹ (pŭngk) s. (tinder) yesca.

punk² JER. I. s. joven mf sin experiencia II. adj. sin mérito.

pun·ster (pŭn'stər) s. aficionado a los juegos de palabras.

punt¹ (pŭnt) I. s. batea II. tr. impeler una batea.

punt² DEP. I. s. patada II. tr. & intr. dar una patada (a).

pu·ny (pyōō'nē) adj. -i- débil, enclenque.

pup (pŭp) s. (puppy) cachorro; (young animal) cría; (youth) mocoso ♦ **p. tent** pequeña tienda de campaña.

pu·pa (pyōō'pə) s. [pl. s o -ae] crisálida.

pu·pil¹ (pyōō'pəl) s. (student) alumno.

pu·pil² s. ANAT. pupila.

pup·pet (pŭp'ĭt) s. marioneta, títere m; FIG. títere, pelele m.

pup·pet·eer (:ĭ-tîr') s. titiritero.

pup·pet·ry ('-trē) s. arte m del titiritero.

pup·py (pŭp'ē) s. cachorro; (youth) joven inexperto ♦ **p. love** amor juvenil.

pur·chase (pûr'chĭs) I. tr. comprar II. s.

compra ♦ **p. order** orden de compra.
pur·chas·er (:chĭ-sər) s. comprador m.
pure (pyŏŏr) adj. puro; *(clean)* limpio; *(chaste)* casto, virgen.
pure·blood(·ed) ('blŭd'[ĭd]) adj. de pura sangre o raza.
pure·bred ('brĕd) I. adj. de pura sangre II. s. animal m de pura sangre.
pu·rée (pyŏŏ-rā') I. tr. **-réed, -réeing** hacer un puré de II. s. puré m.
pur·ga·tion (pûr-gā'shən) s. purgación f.
pur·ga·tive ('gə-tĭv) adj. & s. purgante m.
pur·ga·to·ry (:tôr'ē) s. purgatorio.
purge (pûrj) I. tr. purgar II. s. purga.
pu·ri·fi·er (pyŏŏr'ə-fī'ər) s. purificador m; TEC. depurador m.
pu·ri·fy (:fī') tr. purificar; *(to refine)* refinar —intr. purificarse.
pur·ist (pyŏŏr'ĭst) s. purista mf.
Pu·ri·tan (:ĭ-tn) s. & adj. puritano.
pu·ri·tan·i·cal ('ĭ-tăn'ĭ-kəl) adj. puritano.
pu·ri·ty (:tē) s. pureza.
purl¹ (pûrl) I. intr. *(to murmur)* susurrar, murmurar II. s. susurro, murmullo.
purl² I. tr. hacer un revés —intr. hacer con puntos al revés II. s. punto al revés.
pur·ple (pûr'pəl) I. s. violeta, morado; *(cloth)* púrpura II. adj. purpúreo, morado; *(royal)* imperial.
pur·port I. tr. (pər-pôrt') pretender II. s. (pûr'pôrt') lo que parece significar.
pur·port·ed (pər-pôr'tĭd) adj. supuesto.
pur·pose (pûr'pəs) I. s. objetivo, *(intention)* propósito f ♦ **for all intents and purposes** para todos los efectos • **for the p. of** con el objeto de • **on p.** a propósito, adrede • **to no p.** para nada II. tr. tener intención de.
pur·pose·ful (:fəl) adj. *(person)* resuelto; *(activity)* útil.
pur·pose·less (:lĭs) adj. sin propósito; *(pointless)* inútil.
pur·pose·ly (:lē) adv. adrede, a propósito.
purr (pûr) I. s. ronroneo; *(of an engine)* zumbido II. intr. ronronear; *(an engine)* zumbar.
purse (pûrs) I. s. *(moneybag)* portamonedas m; *(handbag)* bolso; *(money)* bolsa; *(prize)* premio II. tr. apretar.
purs·er (pûr'sər) s. MARÍT. contador m.
pur·su·ant (pər-sŏō'ənt) adj. ♦ **p. to** según.
pur·sue (pər-sŏō') tr. perseguir; *(to strive for)* aspirar a; *(to follow)* seguir, continuar; *(to devote oneself to)* dedicarse a.
pur·suit (:sŏōt') s. persecución f; *(striving)* búsqueda; *(activity)* pasatiempo ♦ **in p. of** en búsqueda de.
pu·ru·lent (pyŏŏr'ə-lənt) adj. purulento.
pur·vey (pər-vā') tr. proveer, abastecer.
pur·vey·or (:ər) s. proveedor m, abastecedor m; *(distributor)* distribuidor m.
pur·view (pûr'vyŏō') s. *(scope)* alcance m, esfera; *(outlook)* perspectiva.
pus (pŭs) s. pus m.
push (pŏŏsh) I. tr. empujar; *(to urge forward)* hacer adelantar; *(to press)* ejercer presión; *(to extend)* extender; JER. *(to sell)* vender; *(to promote)* promover; *(to recommend)* recomendar ♦ **to p. around** FAM. intimidar • **to p. aside** o **away** apartar • **to p. back** empujar; *(to repel)* hacer retroceder • **to p. down** apretar; *(someone)* hacer caer • **to p. over** *(something)* volcar; *(someone)* hacer caer • **to p. through** pasar por, sacar por; *(to carry out)* llevar a cabo; *(a*

bill)* hacer aceptar • **to p. up** *(to lift)* levantar; *(prices)* hacer subir —intr. empujar; *(to put pressure on)* ejercer presión; *(to advance)* abrirse paso a empujones; *(to expend great effort)* esforzarse ♦ **p. ahead** avanzar • **to p. back** retroceder • **to p. forward** avanzar • **to p. off** FAM. largarse • **to p. on** seguir adelante, continuar II. s. empujón m; *(drive)* empuje m; *(effort)* empujón; MIL. ofensiva ♦ **p. button** pulsador, botón de contacto.
push·cart ('kärt') s. carretilla de mano.
push·er (:ər) s. empujador m; *(ambitious person)* arribista mf; JER. *(of drugs)* vendedor m de drogas.
push·o·ver (:ō'vər) s. *(easy thing)* ganga; *(dupe)* pelele m.
push·up (:ŭp') s. plancha.
push·y (:ē) adj. **-i-** FAM. insistente.
pu·sil·lan·i·mous (pyŏŏ'sə-lăn'ə-məs) adj. pusilánime.
puss¹ (pŏŏs) s. FAM. *(cat)* minino, gatito.
puss² s. JER. *(mouth)* hocico; *(face)* jeta.
puss·y ('ē) s. gatito ♦ **p. willow** sauce común.
puss·y·cat (:kăt') gato; FAM. *(amiable person)* persona afable.
puss·y·foot (:fŏŏt') intr. andar cautelosamente; FIG. andarse con tiento.
pus·tu·lar (pŭs'chə-lər) adj. pustuloso.
pus·tule (:chōōl) s. pústula.
put (pŏŏt) I. tr. put, **-tting** poner; *(to insert)* meter; *(to add)* echar; *(question)* formular, hacer; *(to subject)* someter; *(to attribute)* dar; *(blame)* echar; *(to estimate)* calcular; *(to impose)* gravar con; *(to bet, invest)* poner; *(to say)* decir; *(to hurl)* lanzar, tirar ♦ **to p. across** hacer comprender • **to p. aside** poner a un lado; *(to save)* guardar • **to p. away** FAM. *(to imprison)* encarcelar; *(to institutionalize)* meter en un manicomio; *(to consume)* zamparse • **to p. back** volver a poner en su sitio • **to p. before** *(to submit)* someter a; *(to place before)* anteponer a • **to p. down** *(to let go of)* soltar; *(to suppress)* reprimir; *(to write down)* apuntar; *(to include)* poner en la lista; *(to criticize)* poner por los suelos; *(to attribute)* achacar; *(down payment)* hacer un desembolso inicial de • **to p. forth** *(to sprout)* brotar; *(to offer)* presentar, proponer • **to p. in** meter; *(to install)* poner • **to p. in a good word for** hablar por o en favor de • **to p. into words** expresar • **to p. it mildly** sin exagerar • **to p. off** *(to postpone)* aplazar, diferir; *(to offend)* dar asco, asquear; *(to make wait)* hacer esperar • **to p. on** TEAT. poner en escena; *(clothes)* ponerse; *(to affect)* afectar; *(to turn on)* encender • **to p. on the brakes** echar el freno • **to p. one over on** engañar • **to p. one's house in order** arreglar uno sus asuntos • **to p. out** *(to extinguish)* apagar; *(to inconvenience)* molestar; *(to publish)* publicar; *(to display)* sacar, mostrar • **to p. through** *(to accomplish)* llevar a cabo; *(to enact)* hacer aprobar; *(to cause)* hacer pasar; TEL. poner con • **to p. together** atar cabos • **to p. up** *(to build)* levantar, construir; *(to can)* envasar; *(to nominate)* proponer; *(to provide)* poner, adelantar; *(to offer)* poner; *(to lodge)* hospedar, alojar; *(to hang up)* colgar • **to p. up to** incitar a • **to p. upon** abusar de —intr. • **to p. in** MARÍT. hacer escala en un puerto • **to p. up or shut up** FAM. aguantar • **to p. up with** aguantar II. s. tiro, lanzamiento III. adj. ♦ **to be hard p.** to serle a uno difícil • **to stay p.** quedarse en su sitio.

put-down ('doun') s. JER. desdén *m*.
put-on (:ŏn') I. adj. fingido II. s. JER. engaño.
pu·tre·fac·tion (pyōō'trə-făk'shən) s. putrefacción *f*; *(condition)* podredumbre *f*.
pu·tre·fy ('fī') tr. & intr. pudrir(se).
pu·trid (pyōō'trĭd) adj. pútrido; *(rotten)* podrido; MED. gangrenoso; *(vile)* asqueroso.
putt (pŭt) DEP. I. s. tiro al hoyo II. tr. & intr. tirar al hoyo.
put·ter (pŭt'ər) intr. no hacer nada de particular —tr. ♦ **to p. away** perder.
put·ty (pŭt'ē) s. masilla.
puz·zle (pŭz'əl) I. tr. desconcertar, dejar perplejo ♦ **to p. out** resolver, descifrar —intr. ♦ **to p. over** reflexionar, meditar II. s. enigma *m*, misterio; *(riddle)* acertijo; *(bewilderment)* perplejidad *f* ♦ **crossword p.** crucigrama • **jigsaw p.** rompecabezas.
puz·zle·ment (:mənt) s. perplejidad *f*.
pyg·my (pĭg'mē) adj. & s. pigmeo.
py·ja·mas (pə-jä'məz) G.B. var. de **pajamas**.
py·lon (pī'lŏn') s. *(gateway)* pilón *m*; AVIA. torre marcadora del curso del vuelo; ELEC. poste *m*.
py·or·rhe·a (pī'ə-rē'ə) s. piorrea.
pyr·a·mid (pĭr'ə-mĭd') s. pirámide *f*.
pyre (pīr) s. pira, hoguera.
py·rite (pī'rīt') s. pirita (de hierro).
py·ro·ma·ni·a (pī'rō-mā'nē-ə) s. piromanía.
py·ro·ma·ni·ac (:ăk) s. & adj. pirómano.
py·ro·tech·nic (pī'rə-tĕk'nĭk) adj. pirotécnico ♦ **pyrotechnics** s.sg. pirotecnia.
Pyr·rhic victory (pĭr'ĭk) s. victoria pírrica.
py·thon (pī'thŏn') s. pitón *m*.

Q

q, Q (kyōō) s. decimoséptima letra del alfabeto inglés.
q.t. (kyōō'tē') s. ♦ **on the q.t.** JER. calladamente.
quack¹ (kwăk) I. s. graznido II. intr. graznar.
quack² s. *(doctor)* curandero.
quack·er·y ('ə-rē) s. curandería, charlatanería.
quad¹ (kwŏd) s. ARQ. patio cuadrangular.
quad² s. *(quadruplet)* cuatrillizo.
quad·ran·gle ('răng'gəl) s. cuadrángulo; ARQ. plaza, patio (de una universidad).
quad·rant (:rənt) s. cuadrante *m*.
quad·rate (:rāt') adj. & s. cuadrado.
quad·rat·ic (kwŏ-drăt'ĭk) adj. cuadrático.
quad·ri·ceps (kwŏd'rĭ-sĕps') s. cuadríceps *m*.
quad·ri·lat·er·al ('rə-lăt'ər-əl) s. & adj. cuadrilátero.
qua·drille (kwə-drĭl') s. cuadrilla.
quad·ri·ple·gi·a (kwŏd'rə-plē'jē-ə) s. cuadriplejía.
quad·ri·ple·gic (:jĭk) adj. & s. cuadripléjico.
quad·roon (kwŏ-drōōn') s. cuarterón *m*.
quad·ru·ped (kwŏd'rə-pĕd') s. cuadrúpedo.
quad·ru·ple (kwŏ-drōō'pəl) I. adj. cuádruple II. tr. & intr. cuadruplicar(se).
quad·ru·plet (:plĭt) s. *(group of four)* cuádruplo; *(offspring)* cuatrillizo.
quad·ru·pli·cate (:pli-kĭt) adj. & s. cuádruplo ♦ **in q.** por cuadruplicado.
quaff (kwŏf) tr. & intr. beber a grandes tragos.
quag·gy (kwăg'ē) adj. -i- pantanoso.
quag·mire (:mīr') s. pantano.
quail¹ (kwāl) s. [pl. inv. o s] codorniz *f*.
quail² intr. acobardarse.
quaint (kwānt) adj. pintoresco.

quaint·ness ('nĭs) s. carácter pintoresco.
quake (kwāk) I. intr. temblar; *(with fear)* estremecerse II. s. temblor *m*.
qual·i·fi·ca·tion (kwŏl'ə-fĭ-kā'shən) s. calificación *m*; *(requirement)* requisito; *(restriction)* reserva ♦ pl. credenciales.
qual·i·fied (kwŏl'ə-fīd') adj. *(competent)* capacitado; *(certified)* acreditado; *(restricted)* con reservas.
qual·i·fi·er (:fī'ər) s. calificativo.
qual·i·fy (:fī') tr. calificar, caracterizar; *(to train)* capacitar; *(to entitle)* dar derecho a; *(to certify)* acreditar; *(to moderate)* atenuar; GRAM. modificar —intr. *(for a position)* tener las capacidades necesarias; DEP. clasificarse ♦ **to q. as** merecer el título de.
qual·i·fy·ing (:ĭng) adj. eliminatorio.
qual·i·ta·tive (kwŏl'ĭ-tā'tĭv) adj. cualitativo.
qual·i·ty (kwŏl'ĭ-tē) s. *(nature, excellence)* calidad *f*; *(property)* característica; *(attribute)* cualidad *f*; *(high status)* categoría.
qualm (kwäm, kwŏm) s. *(doubt)* duda; *(scruple)* remordimiento ♦ **to have no qualms about** no vacilar en.
quan·da·ry (kwŏn'də-rē) s. dilema *m*.
quan·ti·fy (kwŏn'tĭ-fī') tr. determinar la cantidad de.
quan·ti·ta·tive (:tā'tĭv) adj. cuantitativo.
quan·ti·ty (kwŏn'tĭ-tē) s. cantidad *f* ♦ **in q. en** grandes cantidades • **unknown q.** incógnita *f*.
quan·tum (kwŏn'təm) s. [pl. -ta] FÍS. cuanto, quantum *m* ♦ **q. jump** FÍS. transición cuántica, FIG. desviación repentina • **q. mechanics,** theory mecánica, teoría cuántica.
quar·an·tine (kwŏr'ən-tēn') I. s. cuarentena II. tr. poner en cuarentena.
quark (kwôrk) s. quark *m*.
quar·rel (kwôr'əl) I. s. pelea, discusión *f* ♦ **to have no q. with** no tener nada en contra de II. intr. *(to argue)* pelear, discutir; *(with an issue)* estar en desacuerdo ♦ **to q. over** discutir.
quar·rel·er (:ə-lər) s. pendenciero.
quar·rel·ing (:ə-lĭng) s. disputas *f*.
quar·rel·some (:əl-səm) adj. pendenciero.
quar·ry¹ (kwôr'ē) s. *(prey)* presa.
quar·ry² s. *(pit)* cantera II. tr. *(stone)* sacar de una cantera; *(land)* excavar.
quart (kwôrt) s. cuarto (de galón).
quar·ter (kwôr'tər) I. s. *(fourth part)* cuarto, cuarta parte; *(of a dollar)* veinticinco centavos; *(of an hour, mile)* cuarto, *(of a year)* trimestre *m*; *(direction)* dirección *f*; *(neighborhood)* barrio; GEOM. cuadrante *m*; DEP. *(period)* tiempo ♦ **(a) q. past** y cuarto • **(a) q. to** o **of** menos cuarto • **q. note** negra ♦ pl. *(residence)* residencia; *(barracks)* cuartel • **at close q.** *(at close range)* de cerca; *(fighting)* cuerpo a cuerpo • **from all q.** de todas partes II. tr. dividir en cuartos, cuartear; *(to lodge)* alojar; MIL. acuartelar ♦ **to draw and q.** descuartizar —intr. *(troops)* acuartelarse; *(to lodge)* alojarse III. adj. cuarto de <*a q. inch* un cuarto de pulgada>.
quar·ter·back (:băk') I. s. jugador *m* que dirige la jugada II. tr. dirigir.
quar·ter·deck (:dĕk') s. alcázar *m*.
quar·ter·fi·nal ('-fī'nəl) s. cuarto de final.
quar·ter·hour (:our') s. cuarto de hora.
quar·ter·ly (:-lē) I. s. & adj. *(publication* *f)* trimestral II. adv. trimestralmente, cada tres meses.
quar·ter·mas·ter (:măs'tər) s. MIL. oficial *m* de

intendencia; MARÍT. cabo de mar.
quar·ter·staff (:stăf´) s. [pl. **-ves**] vara.
quar·tet(te) (kwôr-tĕt´, s. cuarteto.
quar·to (´tō) s. [pl. **-tos**] libro en cuarto.
quartz (kwôrts) s. cuarzo.
quartz·ite (kwôrt´sīt´) s. cuarcita.
qua·sar (kwā´zär´) s. cuásar m.
quash (kwŏsh) tr. *(to annul)* anular; *(uprising, feeling)* sofocar.
qua·si (kwā´zī´, kwā´zē) adj. cuasi, casi.
quat·rain (kwŏt´rān´) s. cuarteto.
qua·ver (kwā´vər) I. intr. temblar; *(to trill)* trinar —tr. decir con voz trémula II. s. *(of voice)* temblor m; *(trill)* trino.
quay (kē, kā) s. muelle m.
quay·age (kē´ĭj, kā´-) s. derechos de muelle.
quea·si·ness (kwē´zē-nĭs) s. náusea.
quea·sy (kwē´zē) adj. **-i-** *(nauseous)* con náuseas; *(stomach)* débil; *(uneasy)* inquieto.
queen (kwēn) s. reina; *(in cards, chess)* dama ♦ **q. mother** reina madre.
queen·ly (´lē) adj. **-i-** de reina, majestuoso.
queen-size (:sīz´) adj. muy grande.
queer (kwîr) I. adj. *(strange)* raro; *(odd)* curioso; *(eccentric)* estrafalario; *(suspicious)* sospechoso ♦ **to feel q.** no sentirse bien II. tr. JER. arruinar.
queer·ness (´nĭs) s. rareza, extrañeza.
quell (kwĕl) tr. *(a riot)* sofocar; *(emotions)* dominar.
quench (kwĕnch) tr. *(fire)* apagar; *(enthusiasm, thirst)* matar; *(metals)* templar.
quench·a·ble (kwĕn´chə-bəl) adj. apagable.
quer·u·lous (kwĕr´ə-ləs) adj. quejumbroso.
que·ry (kwîr´ē) I. s. pregunta; *(doubt)* duda; *(mark)* signo de interrogación II. tr. poner en duda; *(to question)* preguntar.
quest (kwĕst) s. búsqueda.
ques·tion (kwĕs´chən) I. s. pregunta; *(issue)* cuestión f; *(problem)* problema m; *(proposition)* moción f; *(doubt)* duda <there is no q. about no hay duda alguna de> ♦ **beyond q.** fuera de duda • **in q.** en cuestión • **q. mark** signo de interrogación • **to be out of the q.** ser imposible • **to call into q.** poner en tela de juicio • **to raise the q. of** plantear la cuestión de II. tr. preguntar, hacer una pregunta a; DER. interrogar; *(to dispute)* poner en tela de juicio.
ques·tion·a·ble (:chə-nə-bəl) adj. *(debatable)* cuestionable; *(dubious)* dudoso.
ques·tion·er (:nər) s. interrogador m.
ques·tion·ing (:nĭng) I. s. interrogación f II. adj. interrogatorio; *(inquisitive)* inquisitivo.
ques·tion·naire (´-nâr´) s. cuestionario.
queue (kyōō) I. s. cola, fila II. intr. ♦ **to q. up** hacer cola.
quib·ble (kwĭb´əl) I. intr. andar con sutilezas II. s. sutileza.
quiche (kēsh) s. pastel m de queso y huevos.
quick (kwĭk) I. adj. *(fast)* rápido; *(bright)* listo; *(mind)* despierto; *(temper)* irascible ♦ **to be q. about** hacer rápidamente • **to be q. to act** obrar sin perder tiempo • **to be q. to take offense** ofenderse por nada II. s. médula ♦ **the q. and the dead** los vivos y los muertos • **to cut to the q.** herir en lo más vivo III. adv. rápido, rápidamente.
quick-and-dir·ty (´ən-dûr´tē) adj. de mala calidad.
quick·en (´ən) tr. *(pace)* apresurar, acelerar; *(pulse)* acelerar; *(appetite, interest)* reavivar —intr. apresurarse, acelerarse; *(to revive)* re-

sucitar.
quick-freeze (:wĭk´frēz´) tr. **-froze, -frozen** congelar rápidamente.
quick·ie (:ē) s. FAM. cosa hecha rápidamente.
quick·ness (:nĭs) s. rapidez f; *(of mind)* viveza.
quick·sand (:sănd´) s. arena movediza.
quick·sil·ver (:sĭl´vər) I. s. mercurio, azogue m II. adj. caprichoso.
quick·step (:stĕp´) s. marcha militar.
quick-tem·pered (:tĕm´pərd) adj. irascible.
quick-wit·ted (:wĭt´ĭd) adj. listo, agudo.
quid¹ (kwĭd) s. mascada (de tabaco).
quid² s. [pl. inv. *o* **s**] JER., G.B. libra esterlina.
quid·di·ty (kwĭd´ĭ-tē) s. quid m, esencia.
qui·es·cent (kwī-ĕs´ənt) adj. quieto.
qui·et (kwī´ĭt) I. adj. **-er, -est** *(silent)* callado, silencioso; *(calm)* tranquilo; *(not showy)* discreto ♦ **be q.!** ¡cállate! • **to be q.** *(not noisy)* no hacer ruido; *(to stop talking)* callarse II. s. *(calm)* quietud f; *(silence)* silencio; *(rest)* reposo III. tr. *(to silence)* hacer callar; *(to calm)* tranquilizar —intr. ♦ **to q. down** calmarse.
qui·et·ness (:nĭs) s. silencio; *(calmness)* tranquilidad f, quietud f.
qui·e·tude (kwī´ĭ-tōōd´) s. quid m, quietud f.
qui·e·tus (kwī-ē´təs) s. muerte f; *(of a debt)* finiquito.
quill (kwĭl) s. *(feather, pen)* pluma; *(stem)* cañón m (de una pluma); *(of a porcupine)* púa.
quilt (kwĭlt) I. s. colcha II. tr. acolchar.
quilt·ing (kwĭl´tĭng) s. acolchado.
quince (kwĭns) s. membrillo.
qui·nine (kwī´nīn´) s. quinina ♦ **q. water** agua de quina.
quin·sy (kwĭn´zē) s. amigdalitis f.
quint (kwĭnt) s. quintillizo.
quin·tes·sence (kwĭn-tĕs´əns) s. quintaesencia.
quin·tet(te) (:tĕt´) s. quinteto.
quin·tu·plet (:tŭp´lĭt) s. *(group of five)* quíntuplo; *(offspring)* quintillizo.
quip (kwĭp) I. s. ocurrencia II. intr. **-pp-** decir sarcásticamente; *(to gibe)* tirar pullas.
quip·ster (´stər) s. persona ocurrente.
quire (kwīr) s. mano f (de papel).
quirk (kwûrk) s. *(twist)* vuelta; *(idiosyncracy)* peculiaridad f; *(vagary)* capricho.
quirk·y (kwûr´kē) adj. **-i-** *(peculiar)* peculiar, singular; *(capricious)* caprichoso.
quirt (kwûrt) s. cuarta, fusta.
quis·ling (kwĭz´lĭng) s. colaboracionista mf.
quit (kwĭt) I. tr. **quit(ted), -tting** *(to leave)* salir de <to q. work at five salir del empleo a las cinco>; *(a school, job)* abandonar, dejar; *(to stop)* dejar de <to q. smoking dejar de fumar> —intr. *(to stop)* parar <I q. at five paro a las cinco>; *(to give up)* desistir; *(to resign)* renunciar II. adj. ♦ **to be q. of** estar libre de.
quit-claim (kwĭt´klām´) s. renuncia.
quite (kwīt) adv. totalmente <we are q. satisfied estamos totalmente satisfechos>; *(altogether)* del todo <it is not q. finished no está del todo terminado>; *(absolutely)* absolutamente; *(exactly)* exactamente; *(rather)* bastante <q. long bastante largo>; FAM. *(very)* muy, bastante ♦ **q. a bit** bastante • **q. a while** un buen rato • **q. so!** ¡así es! • **to be q. a** ser un gran.
quits (kwĭts) adj. ♦ **to be q.** estar iguales *o* en paz • **to call it q.** dejarlo así.
quit·tance (kwĭt´ns) s. quita.

quit·ter (:ər) s. ♦ **to be a q.** darse por vencido fácilmente.

quiv·er[1] (kwĭv′ər) I. intr. temblar, estremecerse II. s. temblor m, estremecimiento.

quiv·er[2] s. (for arrows) aljaba.

quix·ot·ic (kwĭk-sŏt′ĭk) adj. quijotesco.

quiz (kwĭz) I. tr. **-zz-** interrogar; (to test) examinar II. s. interrogatorio; (test) prueba, examen m ♦ **q. show** concurso de televisión.

quiz·zi·cal (kwĭz′ĭ-kəl) adj. perplejo.

quoin (koin, kwoin) s. piedra angular.

quo·rum (kwôr′əm) s. quórum m.

quo·ta (kwō′tə) s. cuota.

quot·a·ble (kwō′tə-bəl) adj. digno de citarse.

quo·ta·tion (kwō-tā′shən) s. cita; (of prices) cotización f ♦ **q. marks** comillas.

quote (kwōt) I. tr. (words, source) citar; (example, price) dar; FIN. cotizar — intr. hacer una cita ♦ **and I q.** y cito sus palabras II. s. FAM. cita; (mark) comilla <in quotes entre comillas> ♦ **q. unquote** entre comillas.

quo·tid·i·an (kwō-tĭd′ē-ən) adj. (daily) diario, cotidiano; (commonplace) común.

quo·tient (kwō′shənt) s. MAT. cociente m.

R

r, R (är) s. decimoctava letra del alfabeto inglés.

rab·bi (răb′ī) s. rabino.

rab·bit (răb′ĭt) s. [pl. inv. o **s**] conejo.

rab·ble (răb′əl) s. gentío, chusma.

rab·ble-rous·er (:rou′zər) s. demagogo.

rab·id (răb′ĭd) adj. rabioso; (fanatic) fanático.

ra·bies (rā′bēz) s. rabia.

rac·coon (ră-kōōn′) s. [pl. inv. o **s**] mapache m.

race[1] (rās) s. (people) raza.

race[2] I. s. (contest) carrera; (of water) corriente f ♦ **r. car** coche de carreras • **r. car driver** corredor II. intr. correr; (to compete) competir; (engine) embalarse ♦ **to r. around** ajetrearse —tr. competir con, correr contra; (engine) acelerar al máximo ♦ **I'll r. you** te echo una carrera • **to r. after** perseguir.

race·course (:kôrs′) s. (horse) hipódromo; (auto) autódromo.

race·horse (:hôrs′) s. caballo de carreras.

rac·er (rā′sər) s. corredor m.

race·track (rās′trăk′) s. pista; (horse) hipódromo.

ra·cial (rā′shəl) adj. racial.

rac·ism (rā′sĭz′əm) s. racismo.

rac·ist (rā′sĭst) adj. & s. racista mf.

rack[1] (răk) I. s. (in a train, car) portaequipajes m; (for hats, coats) percha; (for feed) comedero; (for torture) potro; (of pain) tormento ♦ **r. and pinion steering** engranaje de cremallera y piñón • **to be on the r.** FAM. estar atormentado • **to go to r. and ruin** venirse abajo II. tr. hacer sufrir ♦ **to be racked by o with** estar atormentado por • **to r. up** FAM. acumular.

rack·et[1] (răk′ĭt) s. DEP. raqueta.

rack·et[2] s. (uproar) alboroto; (illegal business) negocio ilegal; (fraud) timo, estafa.

rack·et·eer (răk′ĭ-tîr′) s. persona que hace negocios deshonestos.

rack·et·eer·ing (:ĭng) s. negocio ilegal; (bribery) soborno; (blackmail) chantaje m.

rac·on·teur (răk′ŏn-tûr′) s. cuentista mf.

rac·y (rā′sē) adj. **-i-** (joke) picante; (lively) animado.

ra·dar (rā′där) s. radar m.

ra·di·al (rā′dē-əl) I. adj. radial II. s. (radius) radio; (tire) neumático radial.

ra·di·ance/an·cy (rā′dē-əns) s. resplandor m.

ra·di·ant (:ənt) adj. radiante.

ra·di·ate (:āt′) intr. (to shine) brillar; (to spread out) radiar; FÍS. irradiar, emitir —tr. (ir)radiar.

ra·di·a·tion (′-ā′shən) s. radiación f.

ra·di·a·tor (′-′tər) s. radiador m.

rad·i·cal (răd′ĭ-kəl) adj. & s. radical m.

rad·i·cle (răd′ĭ-kəl) s. radícula.

ra·di·o (rā′dē-ō′) I. s. radio f ♦ **r. network** red de emisoras • **r. station** emisora II. tr. & intr. transmitir (un mensaje) por radio.

ra·di·o·ac·tive (′-ăk′tĭv) adj. radiactivo.

ra·di·o·ac·tiv·i·ty (:ăk-tĭv′ĭ-tē) s. radiactividad f.

ra·di·o·broad·cast (:brŏd′kăst′) o **ra·di·o·cast** (:kăst′) tr. & intr. **-cast(ed)** radiar.

ra·di·o·gram (:grăm′) s. radiograma m.

ra·di·o·graph (:grăf′) I. s. radiografía II. tr. radiografiar.

ra·di·ol·o·gist (rā′dē-ŏl′ə-jĭst) s. radiólogo.

ra·di·ol·o·gy (:jē) s. radiología.

ra·di·om·e·try (rā′dē-ŏm′ĭ-trē) s. radiometría.

ra·di·o·ther·a·py (:ŏ-thĕr′ə-pē) s. radioterapia.

rad·ish (răd′ĭsh) s. rábano.

ra·di·um (rā′dē-əm) s. radio.

ra·di·us (rā′dē-əs) s. [pl. **es** o **-dii**] radio.

ra·don (rā′dŏn′) s. radón m.

raff·ish (răf′ĭsh) adj. vulgar; (showy) ostentoso.

raf·fle (răf′əl) I. s. rifa II. tr. & intr. rifar.

raft[1] (răft) I. s. balsa II. intr. ♦ **to go rafting** ir en balsa.

raft[2] s. FAM. (great number) montón m.

raft·er (răf′tər) s. par m (de un techo).

rag[1] (răg) s. (cloth) trapo; JER. (newspaper) periodicucho ♦ **in rags** harapos.

rag[2] tr. **-gg-** (to scold) regañar; JER. (to tease) tomar el pelo a.

rag·a·muf·fin (răg′ə-mŭf′ĭn) s. golfo.

rage (rāj) I. s. furia ♦ **to be all the r.** estar en boga • **to fly into a r.** enfurecerse II. intr. (storm) bramar; (plague, fire) propagarse.

rag·ged (răg′ĭd) adj. (beggar) andrajoso; (sleeve) raído; (edge) mellado; (performance) desigual.

rag·time (răg′tīm′) s. jazz m de ritmo sincopado.

rag·weed (răg′wēd′) s. ambrosía.

rah (rä) interj. ¡hurra!

raid (rād) I. s. MIL. incursión f, ataque sorpresivo; (by police) redada II. tr. atacar por sorpresa; (police) hacer una redada en.

raid·er (rā′dər) s. invasor m.

rail[1] (rāl) s. (banister) barandilla; (at racetrack) cerca; F.C. riel m ♦ **by r.** por ferrocarril ♦ pl. ferrocarriles.

rail[2] s. ORNIT. rascón m.

rail[3] intr. ♦ **to r. against** denostar contra.

rail·ing (rā′lĭng) s. (of balcony) baranda; (of stairs) pasamanos.

rail·road (rāl′rōd′) I. s. ferrocarril m ♦ **r. car** vagón • **r. crossing** cruce de ferrocarril • **r. station** estación ferroviaria II. tr. transportar por ferrocarril; FAM. (bill, law) hacer votar apresuradamente; (person) encarcelar falsamente.

rail·way (:wā′) s. ferrocarril m; (track) vía.

rain (rān) I. s. lluvia ♦ **(come) r. or shine** pase lo que pase • **in the r.** bajo la lluvia • **r. forest**

selva tropical II. intr. llover ♦ **it never rains but it pours** las desgracias nunca vienen solas —tr. ♦ **to r. cats and dogs** llover a cántaros.

rain·bow ('bō') s. arco iris.

rain·coat (:kōt') s. impermeable *m.*

rain·drop (:drōp') s. gota de lluvia.

rain·fall (:fôl') s. *(shower)* aguacero; *(precipitation)* precipitación *f.*

rain·storm (:stôrm') s. tempestad *f* de lluvia.

rain·wa·ter (:wô' tər) s. agua de lluvia.

rain·wear (:wâr') s. ropa impermeable.

rain·y (rā'nē) adj. **-i-** lluvioso.

raise (rāz) I. tr. levantar; *(window, prices)* subir; *(land)* divisar; *(flag)* izar; *(a ship)* sacar a flote; *(welt, blister)* producir; *(the dead)* resucitar; *(voice)* alzar; *(rank, level)* ascender; *(children, animals)* criar; *(crop)* cultivar; *(point)* hacer, formular; *(an issue)* plantear; *(doubts)* suscitar; *(to arouse)* sublevar; *(money)* recaudar; *(an army)* reclutar; MARÍT. levar; CUL. hacer subir; MAT. elevar ♦ **to be raised** criarse II. s. aumento.

raised (rāzd) adj. *(in relief)* en relieve; *(embossed)* repujado.

rai·sin (rā'zīn) s. pasa (de uva).

rake¹ (rāk) I. s. *(tool)* rastrillo II. tr. rastrillar; *(leaves)* recoger con el rastrillo; *(to sweep)* rastrear; *(with gunfire)* ametrallar ♦ **to r. in** ganar mucho • **to r. over the coals** censurar duramente • **to r. up** *(gossip)* sacar a relucir; *(money)* reunir.

rake² s. libertino, Don Juan.

ral·ly (răl'ē) I. tr. *(to assemble)* reunir; *(to revive)* recobrar —intr. reunirse; *(to recover)* recuperarse ♦ **to r. round** *o* **to** dar apoyo a, adherirse a II. s. reunión *f;* COM., MED. recuperación *f;* AUTO. rally *m.*

ram (răm) I. s. ZOOL. carnero; MAQ., MEC. pisón *m;* MIL. ariete *m;* MARÍT. espolón *m* II. tr. **-mm-** *(to stuff)* meter a la fuerza; *(to crash into)* chocar con.

ram·ble (răm'bəl) I. intr. *(to walk)* pasear; *(to digress)* divagar II. s. paseo.

ram·bler (:blər) s. vagabundo.

ram·bling (:blĭng) adj. sin orden ni concierto.

ram·bunc·tious (răm-bŭngk'shəs) adj. alborotador.

ram·i·fi·ca·tion (răm'ə-fĭ-kā'shən) s. ramificación *f.*

ramp (rămp) s. rampa.

ram·page (răm'pāj') s. alboroto ♦ **to go on a r.** andar como loco, ir destrozándolo todo.

ram·pant (răm'pənt) adj. desenfrenado.

ram·part (răm'pärt') I. s. muralla; FIG. amparo II. tr. amurallar.

ram·rod (răm'rŏd') s. *(loading)* taco; *(cleaning)* baqueta.

ram·shack·le (răm'shăk' əl) adj. desvencijado.

ran (răn) cf. **run.**

ranch (rănch) I. s. hacienda ♦ **r. house** casa de una sola planta II. intr. llevar una hacienda.

ranch·er (rănch'ər) s. estanciero, hacendado.

ran·cid (răn'sĭd) adj. rancio.

ran·cor (răng'kər) s. rencor *m.*

ran·cor·ous (:əs) adj. rencoroso.

ran·dom (răn'dəm) adj. hecho al azar, fortuito ♦ **at r.** al azar.

rang (răng) cf. **ring².**

range (rānj) I. s. *(reach)* alcance *m; (scope)* extensión *f; (variety)* gama; *(stove)* cocina; *(of merchandise)* surtido; AER. radio de acción; *(firing range)* campo de tiro; *(for livestock)* te-

rreno de pasto; *(habitat)* hábitat *m;* GEOG. cordillera, cadena; MÚS. registro; MIL. distancia *(del blanco)* ♦ **at close r.** de cerca, a quemarropa • **r. of vision** campo visual • **within firing r. a tiro** II. tr. *(in rows)* alinear; *(to classify)* ordenar, clasificar; *(to traverse)* recorrer; *(livestock)* apacentar —intr. extenderse; *(to explore)* recorrer ♦ **to r. from . . . to** ir de . . . a.

rang·er (rān'jər) s. *(of a forest)* guardabosques *m; (mounted policeman)* policía *m.*

rang·y (:jē) adj. **-i-** alto y delgado.

rank¹ (răngk) I. s. *(row)* fila; *(in society)* clase *f; (high status)* rango; *(quality)* categoría; MIL. grado ♦ **r. and file** MIL. soldados rasos; *(ordinary people)* gente común; *(of a union)* miembros ♦ pl. filas • **to break r.** romper filas • **to close (the) r.** cerrar las filas • **to join the r. of** unirse con II. tr. *(in rows)* alinear; *(in order)* clasificar ♦ **to r. above** ser superior a • **to r. among** figurar entre —intr. clasificarse ♦ **to r. high** ocupar una alta posición.

rank² adj. *(growth)* tupido; *(smell)* rancio.

rank·ing (răng'kĭng) adj. superior.

ran·kle (răng'kəl) intr. doler, enconarse.

ran·sack (răn'săk') tr. *(to search)* registrar; *(to plunder)* saquear.

ran·som (răn'səm) I. s. rescate *m* II. tr. rescatar, liberar.

rant (rănt) tr. & intr. vociferar.

rap¹ (răp) I. s. golpe seco ♦ **to beat the r.** JER. librarse de una condena • **to take the r.** JER. cargar con la culpa *(of)* II. tr. **-pp-** *(to strike)* golpear; *(to criticize)* criticar —intr. ♦ **to r. on** *(door)* llamar a; *(table)* golpear.

rap² JER. I. intr. **-pp-** conversar II. s. conversación *f.*

ra·pa·cious (rə-pā'shəs) adj. rapaz.

ra·pac·i·ty (rə-păs'ĭ-tē) s. rapacidad *f.*

rape¹ (rāp) I. s. violación *f; (abduction)* rapto II. tr. violar.

rape² s. BOT. colza.

rap·id (răp'ĭd) I. adj. rápido ♦ **r. transit** sistema de transporte urbano II. s. ♦ pl. rápidos.

ra·pid·i·ty (rə-pĭd'ĭ-tē) s. rapidez *f.*

rap·ine (răp'ĭn) s. rapiña, saqueo.

rap·ist (rā'pĭst) s. violador *m.*

rap·port (ră-pôr') s. relación *f.*

rap·proche·ment (ră'prŏsh-mä') s. acercamiento.

rapt (răpt) adj. *(enraptured)* extasiado; *(engrossed)* absorto.

rap·ture (răp'chər) s. éxtasis *m.*

rap·tur·ous (:əs) adj. extasiado.

rare¹ (râr) adj. raro; *(special)* poco común.

rare² adj. CUL. jugoso, poco hecho.

rar·e·fied (râr'ə-fīd') adj. esotérico, refinado.

rar·e·fy (:fī') tr. & intr. enrarecer(se).

rar·ing (râr'ĭng) adj. FAM. impaciente.

rar·i·ty (râr'ĭ-tē) s. rareza.

ras·cal (răs'kəl) s. tunante *m,* bribón *m.*

rash¹ (răsh) adj. *(act)* precipitado; *(person)* impetuoso.

rash² s. MED. sarpullido; FIG. ola.

rash·er (răsh'ər) s. lonja de jamón, tocino.

rasp (răsp) I. tr. escofinar II. s. escofina; *(sound)* chirrido.

rasp·ber·ry (răz'bĕr'ē) s. *(plant)* frambueso; *(fruit)* frambuesa; JER. abucheo.

rasp·y (răs'pē) adj. **-i-** áspero.

rat (răt) I. s. rata; JER. canalla *m,* traidor *m* ♦ **to smell a r.** FAM. sospechar algo II. intr. **-tt-** ♦ **to r. on** JER. delatar a.

ratch·et (răch'ĭt) s. MEC. trinquete *m*, uña.

rate¹ (rāt) I. s. *(speed)* velocidad *f*; *(of change)* coeficiente *m*; *(of occurence)* índice *m*; *(percentage)* porcentaje *m*; *(of pay)* tipo; FIN. interés *m* ♦ **at any r.** de todos modos ♦ **at this r.** a este paso • **postal r.** tarifa postal • **r. of exchange** cambio II. tr. *(to estimate)* estimar; *(to value)* valorar; *(to classify)* clasificar; *(to deserve)* merecer —intr. ♦ **to be rated (as)** ser considerado como • **to r. high** ocupar una alta posición.

rate² tr. & intr. *(to berate)* regañar.

rath·er (răth'ər) adv. *(more exactly)* mejor dicho, *(quite)* bastante; *(somewhat)* un poco ♦ **but r.** sino (que) • **I would r.** preferiría • **I would r. not** mejor no • **r. than** en vez de.

rat·i·fy (răt'ə-fī') tr. ratificar.

rat·ing (rā'tĭng) s. *(standing)* clasificación *f*; *(credit rating)* solvencia; TELEV. popularidad *f*.

ra·tio (rā'shō) s. proporción *f*; MAT. razón *f*.

ra·ti·oc·i·nate (răsh'ē-ŏs'ə-nāt') tr. raciocinar.

ra·tion (răsh'ən, rā'shən) I. s. ración *f*, porción *f* ♦ pl. MIL. provisiones II. tr. racionar.

ra·tion·al (răsh'ə-nəl) adj. racional; *(sensible)* razonable.

ra·tion·ale ('-năl') s. *(reason)* razón *f* fundamental; *(explanation)* explicación *f*.

ra·tion·al·i·ty (-năl'ĭ-tē) s. racionalidad *f*.

ra·tion·al·i·za·tion (-zā'shən) s. racionalización *f*.

ra·tion·al·ize ('-līz') tr. racionalizar.

ra·tion·ing (răsh'ə-nĭng) s. racionamiento.

rat·tan (ră-tăn') s. rota, junco de Indias.

rat·tle (răt'l) I. intr. *(vehicle)* traquetear; *(window, door)* golpetear; *(teeth)* castañetear ♦ **to r. on** seguir parloteando —tr. *(to shake)* sacudir; FAM. *(to unnerve)* poner nervioso ♦ **to r. off** decir rápidamente II. s. traqueteo; *(of door, window)* golpe *m*; *(of teeth)* castañeteo; *(of baby)* sonajero.

rat·tler ('lər) s. serpiente *f* de cascabel.

rat·tle·snake (:l-snāk') s. serpiente *f* de cascabel.

rat·tle·trap (:trăp') s. cacharro *(vehículo)*.

rat·trap (răt'trăp') s. ratonera; FIG. pocilga.

rat·ty (răt'ē) adj. -i- ratonil; JER. *(dilapidated)* destartalado; *(shabby)* andrajoso.

rau·cous (rô'kəs) adj. ronco, estridente.

raun·chy (rôn'chē) adj. -i- JER. *(grimy)* sucio; *(obscene)* vulgar.

rav·age (răv'ĭj) I. tr. destrozar; *(by army)* saquear II. s. destrozo ♦ pl. estragos.

rave (rāv) I. intr. delirar, desvariar ♦ **to r. about** estar loco por II. s. ♦ **to get r. reviews** FAM. recibir críticas entusiastas.

rav·el (răv'əl) tr. & intr. deshilar(se).

ra·ven (rā'vən) I. s. cuervo II. adj. negro.

rav·en·ous (răv'ə-nəs) adj. hambriento; *(voracious)* voraz.

ra·vine (rə-vēn') s. barranco.

rav·ing (rā'vĭng) I. adj. FAM. extraordinario ♦ **to be r. mad** estar loco de atar II. s. ♦ pl. desvaríos.

rav·ish (răv'ĭsh) tr. *(to seize)* raptar; *(to rape)* violar.

rav·ish·ing (:ĭ-shĭng) adj. encantador.

raw (rô) adj. crudo; *(not refined)* bruto; *(weather)* frío y húmedo; *(inexperienced)* novato; *(socially coarse)* tosco; *(of metal)* inflamado; *(wound)* en carne viva ♦ **in the r.** FAM. desnudo • **r. material** materia prima • **to get a r. deal** JER. recibir un tratamiento injusto.

raw·hide (rô'hīd') s. cuero sin curtir.

ray¹ (rā) s. rayo; MAT., BOT. radio.

ray² s. ICT. raya.

ray·on (rā'ŏn') s. rayón *m*.

raze (rāz) tr. arrasar, demoler.

ra·zor (rā'zər) s. navaja de afeitar ♦ **r. blade** cuchilla *u* hoja de afeitar.

razz (răz) tr. JER. tomar el pelo a, burlarse de.

reach (rēch) I. tr. alcanzar; *(as far as)* llegar hasta; *(to arrive at)* llegar a; *(on the phone)* comunicarse con; *(to get through to)* impresionar; *(in length, height)* llegar a, extenderse hasta; *(in age)* cumplir; FAM. *(to pass an object)* pasar, llegar ♦ **to r. out** extender, alargar —intr. llegar ♦ **to r. down** inclinarse, agacharse • **to r. for** tratar de coger *o* agarrar • **to r. for the stars** aspirar a lo inalcanzable • **to r. in(to)** meter la mano (en) • **to r. out** extender la mano • **to r. up** alzar la mano II. s. alcance *m*; *(comprehension)* comprensión *f*; *(of cord, arm)* extensión *f* ♦ **within r.** *(of the hand)* al alcance de la mano; *(by transportation)* cerca.

re·act (rē-ăkt') intr. reaccionar.

re·ac·tion (rē-ăk'shən) s. reacción *f*.

re·ac·tion·ar·y (:shə-nĕr'ē) adj. & s. reaccionario.

re·ac·ti·vate (:tə-vāt') tr. reactivar.

re·ac·tive (:tĭv) adj. reactivo.

re·ac·tor (:tər) s. QUÍM. reactivo; ELEC., FÍS. reactor *m*.

read (rēd) I. tr. read leer; *(thoughts, the future)* adivinar; G.B. *(to study)* cursar, estudiar; RAD. oír; TEC. *(an instrument)* marcar ‹the dial reads 32°› la esfera marca 32°> ♦ **to r. into** atribuir (a) • **to r. out** leer en voz alta • **to r. over** (to go over) repasar; *(to reread)* releer • **to r. someone like a book** saber lo que alguien está pensando • **to r. up on** informarse acerca de —intr. leer; *(to be worded)* rezar, decir ♦ **to r. between the lines** leer entre líneas II. s. lectura III. adj. ♦ **well-read** *(book)* muy leído; *(person)* instruido.

read·a·ble (rē'də-bəl) adj. *(legible)* legible; *(interesting)* interesante.

read·er (rē'dər) s. lector *m*; *(schoolbook)* libro de lecturas; *(anthology)* antología.

read·i·ly (rĕd'l-ē) adv. *(willingly)* de buena gana; *(easily)* con facilidad.

read·i·ness (:ē nĭs) s. buena disposición *f*.

read·ing (rē'dĭng) s. lectura *f*; *(of a situation)* interpretación *f*; *(of a text)* versión *f*; TEC. indicación *f*; COMPUT. transferencia ♦ **r. room** sala de lectura • **the r. public** el público lector • **to take a r.** TEC. medir.

re·ad·just (rē'ə-jŭst') tr. reajustar, readaptar.

re·ad·just·ment (:mənt) s. reajuste *m*.

read-out (rēd'out') s. información impresa.

read·y (rĕd'ē) I. adj. -i- listo; *(willing)* dispuesto; *(about to)* a punto de; *(clever)* agudo, vivo; *(answer)* rápido; *(available)* disponible ♦ **r. cash** *o* **money** dinero contante • **to get r.** *(to prepare)* preparar(se); *(to fix up)* arreglar(se) II. tr. preparar.

read·y-made (rĕd'ē-mād') adj. hecho.

read·y-to-wear (:tə-wâr') I. adj. hecho, confeccionado II. s. ropa hecha.

re·af·firm (rē'ə-fûrm') tr. reafirmar.

re·al (rē'əl) I. adj. real; *(true)* verdadero; *(objective)* cierto; *(serious)* de verdad ♦ **for r.** FAM. de verdad • **r. estate** bienes inmuebles *o* raíces II. adv. FAM. muy, mucho.

re·a·lign (rē'ə-līn') tr. *(tires)* realinear; *(people)* reagrupar.

re·al·ism (rē'ə-lĭz'əm) s. realismo.
re·al·ist (:lĭst) s. realista mf.
re·al·is·tic ('-lĭs'tĭc) adj. realista.
re·al·i·ty (rē-ăl'ĭ-tē) s. realidad f; (fact) hecho.
re·al·i·za·tion (rē'ə-lĭ-zā'shən) s. (understanding) comprensión f; (fulfillment) realización f.
re·al·ize (rē'ə-lĭz') tr. (to comprehend) darse cuenta de; (to attain) realizar, hacer realidad; (a profit) obtener.
re·al·ly (rē'ə-lē, rē'lē) adv. (in reality) en realidad; (truly) verdaderamente; (very) muy ♦ r.! ¡hay que ver! ♦ r.? ¿de veras?
realm (rĕlm) s. reino.
re·al·tor (rē'əl-tər) s. corredor m de bienes raíces.
re·al·ty (:tē) s. bienes m raíces.
ream¹ (rēm) s. resma ♦ pl. FIG. montones.
ream² tr. (to enlarge) agrandar; (to squeeze) exprimir.
reap (rēp) tr. & intr. cosechar; (to cut) segar.
reap·er (rē'pər) s. (person) segador m; (machine) segadora f.
re·ap·pear (rē'ə-pîr') intr. reaparecer.
re·ap·pear·ance (:əns) s. reaparición f.
re·ap·point (rē'ə-point') tr. nombrar de nuevo.
re·ap·point·ment (:mənt) s. nuevo nombramiento.
re·ap·por·tion (rē'ə-pôr'shən) tr. repartir de nuevo.
re·ap·por·tion·ment (:mənt) s. nueva distribución.
re·ap·prais·al (rē'ə-prā'zəl) s. revaluación f.
rear¹ (rîr) I. s. parte trasera; (of a house) fondo; FAM. (buttocks) nalgas ♦ at the r. of detrás de II. adj. trasero, de atrás ♦ r. guard retaguardia.
rear² tr. (animals) criar; (children) cuidar, educar —intr. (horse) encabritarse.
rear·ing ('ĭng) s. crianza, cría.
re·arm (rē-ärm') tr. & intr. rearmar(se).
re·ar·ma·ment (rē-är'mə-mənt) s. rearme m.
re·ar·range (rē'ə-rānj') tr. volver a arreglar, disponer de otro modo; (plans) cambiar.
re·ar·range·ment (:mənt) s. nuevo arreglo, nueva disposición.
rear·view mirror (rîr'vyōō') s. retrovisor m.
rea·son (rē'zən) I. s. razón f ♦ all the more r. (to) razón de más (para) ♦ by r. of en virtud de ♦ for no r. sin ningún motivo ♦ the r. why el porqué ♦ to be within r. ser razonable ♦ to have r. to tener motivos para ♦ to listen to r. avenirse a razones ♦ to stand to r. ser evidente II. tr. & intr. razonar ♦ to r. out resolver.
rea·son·a·ble (rē'zə-nə-bəl) adj. razonable.
rea·son·ing (:nĭng) s. razonamiento.
re·as·sess (rē'ə-sĕs') tr. valorar de nuevo.
re·as·sur·ance (rē'ə-shŏŏr'əns) s. (confidence) confianza; (promise) promesa.
re·as·sure (rē'ə-shŏŏr') tr. dar confianza.
re·bate (rē'bāt') I. s. rebaja; (repayment) reembolso II. tr. rebajar, reembolsar.
reb·el (rĕb'əl) I. intr. (rĭ-bĕl') -ll- rebelarse II. s. (rĕb'əl) rebelde mf.
re·bel·lion (rĭ-bĕl'yən) s. rebelión f.
re·bel·lious (:yəs) adj. rebelde.
re·birth (rē-bûrth') s. renacimiento.
re·bound I. intr. (rē-bound') rebotar; FIG. recuperarse II. s. ('') rebote m ♦ to marry on the r. casarse por despecho.
re·buff (rĭ-bŭf') I. s. (refusal) rechazo; (snub) desaire m II. tr. rechazar, desairar.
re·build (rē-bĭld') tr. & intr. -built reconstruir.

re·buke (rĭ-byōōk') I. tr. reprender II. s. reprimenda.
re·but (rĭ-bŭt') tr. & intr. -tt- refutar.
re·but·tal (:l) s. refutación f.
re·cal·ci·trant (rĭ-kăl'sĭ-trənt) adj. recalcitrante.
re·call I. tr. (rĭ-kôl') (to remember) recordar, acordarse de; (workers) hacer volver; (diplomat) retirar; (product) retirar del mercado II. s. (rē'kôl') (withdrawal) retiro; (recollection) recuerdo.
re·cant (rĭ-kănt') tr. & intr. retractar(se).
re·cap (rē'kăp') FAM. I. tr. -pp- recapitular II. s. recapitulación f.
re·ca·pit·u·late (rē'kə-pĭch'ə-lāt') tr. recapitular —intr. resumir.
re·ca·pit·u·la·tion ('-'-lā'shən) s. recapitulación f.
re·cap·ture (rē-kăp'chər) I. s. reconquista II. tr. (the past) hacer revivir; (prisoner) volver a capturar; MIL. reconquistar.
re·cede (rĭ-sēd') intr. retroceder; (to become distant) alejarse.
re·ceipt (rĭ-sēt') s. recibo ♦ on r. of al recibir ♦ pl. ingresos.
re·ceiv·a·ble (rĭ-sē'və-bəl) adj. a cobrar.
re·ceive (rĭ-sēv') tr. recibir; (salary) percibir, cobrar; (members) aceptar; (to shelter) acoger ♦ receiving line fila de recepción ♦ intr. recibir ♦ to be well received recibir una buena acogida.
re·ceiv·er (rĭ-sē'vər) s. receptor m; DER. síndico; TEL. auricular m.
re·cent (rē'sənt) adj. reciente.
re·cep·ta·cle (rĭ-sĕp'tə-kəl) s. receptáculo; ELEC. enchufe m hembra.
re·cep·tion (rĭ-sĕp'shən) s. recepción f.
re·cep·tion·ist (:shə-nĭst) s. recepcionista mf.
re·cep·tive (:tĭv) adj. receptivo.
re·cep·tor (:tər) s. receptor m.
re·cess (rē'sĕs', rĭ-sĕs') I. s. (in school) recreo; (in meeting) interrupción f; (in wall) hueco, nicho ♦ to be in r. (Congress) estar clausurado; (school) estar cerrada por vacaciones II. tr. hacer un hueco en —intr. (Congress) suspender; (school) cerrar.
re·ces·sion (rĭ-sĕsh'ən) s. retirada; ECON. recesión f.
re·ces·sive (rĭ-sĕs'ĭv) adj. BIOL. recesivo.
re·charge (rē-chärj') tr. recargar.
re·cid·i·vism (rĭ-sĭd'ə-vĭz'əm) s. reincidencia.
rec·i·pe (rĕs'ə-pē) s. receta f.
re·cip·i·ent (rĭ-sĭp'ē-ənt) adj. & s. receptor m.
re·cip·ro·cal (rĭ-sĭp'rə-kəl) adj. recíproco.
re·cip·ro·cate (:kāt') tr. corresponder a; (to exchange) intercambiar —intr. corresponder.
rec·i·proc·i·ty (rĕs'ə-prŏs'ĭ-tē) s. reciprocidad f.
re·cit·al (rĭ-sīt'l) s. recital m.
rec·i·ta·tion (rĕs'ĭ-tā'shən) s. recitación f; (narration) narración f, relato.
re·cite (rĭ-sīt') tr. & intr. (poem) recitar; (story) narrar; (list) enumerar.
reck·less (rĕk'lĭs) adj. (careless) imprudente; (rash) precipitado.
reck·on (rĕk'ən) tr. calcular; (to regard) considerar; FAM. (to assume) suponer ♦ to r. on contar con —intr. calcular ♦ to r. with tener en cuenta.
reck·on·ing (:ə-nĭng) s. cálculo ♦ day of r. día de ajuste de cuentas.
re·claim (rĭ-klām') tr. (land) recobrar; (swamp) sanear; (from waste) recuperar.

re·cline (rĭ-klīn') tr. & intr. reclinar(se).

re·cluse (rĕk'lōōs', rĭ-klōōs') s. solitario.

re·clu·sive (rĭ-klōō'sĭv) adj. solitario.

rec·og·ni·tion (rĕk'əg-nĭsh'ən) s. reconocimiento.

rec·og·niz·a·ble ('-nī'zə-bəl) adj. reconocible.

rec·og·nize (rĕk'əg-nīz') tr. reconocer; *(speaker)* dar la palabra a.

re·coil I. intr. (rĭ-koil') *(firearm)* dar un culatazo; *(cannon)* retroceder ♦ to r. at *(in fear)* tener horror a; *(in disgust)* tener asco a II. s. (rē'koil') *(of firearm)* culatazo; *(of cannon)* retroceso.

rec·ol·lect (rĕk'ə-lĕkt') tr. & intr. acordarse (de).

rec·ol·lec·tion (:lĕk'shən) s. recuerdo.

rec·om·mend (rĕk'ə-mĕnd') tr. recomendar.

rec·om·men·da·tion (:mĕn-dā'shən) s. recomendación f.

rec·om·pense (rĕk'əm-pĕns') I. tr. recompensar II. s. recompensa.

rec·on·cil·a·ble (rĕk'ən-sī'lə-bəl) adj. reconciliable; *(compatible)* compatible.

rec·on·cile ('-sīl') tr. *(people)* reconciliar; *(differences)* conciliar ♦ to r. oneself to resignarse a.

rec·on·cil·i·a·tion ('-sĭl'ē-ā'shən) s. reconciliación f; *(settlement)* conciliación f.

re·con·di·tion (rē'kən-dĭsh'ən) tr. arreglar.

re·con·firm (rē'kən-fûrm') tr. reconfirmar.

re·con·nais·sance (rĭ-kŏn'ə-səns) s. reconocimiento.

re·con·noi·ter (rē'kə-noi'tər, rĕk'ə-) tr. reconocer —intr. hacer un reconocimiento.

re·con·sid·er (rē'kən-sĭd'ər) tr. & intr. reconsiderar.

re·con·sti·tute (rē-kŏn'stĭ-tōōt') tr. reconstituir; CUL. hidratar.

re·con·struct (rē'kən-strŭkt') tr. reconstruir.

re·con·vene (rē'kən-vēn') tr. convocar de nuevo —intr. reunirse de nuevo.

re·cord I. tr. (rĭ-kôrd') *(facts, data)* registrar; *(impression, idea)* apuntar, anotar; *(to tally)* consignar, llevar cuenta de; *(instrument)* indicar; TEC. grabar —intr. grabar II. s. (rĕk'ərd) *(evidence)* constancia; *(account)* relación f; *(tally)* cuenta; *(testimony)* testimonio; *(of conduct, health)* historial m; *(dossier)* expediente m; *(of an employee)* hoja de servicios; *(of a criminal)* antecedentes m; *(best performance)* récord m; *(for a phonograph)* disco; *(recording)* grabación f ♦ for the r. para que así conste ▪ in r. time en un tiempo récord ▪ in r. numbers en cantidades sin precedentes ▪ r. player tocadiscos ▪ to be off the r. ser extraoficial ▪ to break the r. batir el récord ▪ to go on r. hacer constar ▪ to have a clean r. no tener antecedentes penales ♦ pl. archivos.

re·cord·er (rĭ-kôr'dər) s. *(device)* grabadora; MÚS. flauta dulce.

re·cord·ing (:dĭng) s. grabación f.

re·count (rĭ-kount') tr. relatar.

re·count I. tr. (rē-kount') volver a contar II. s. ('') recuento.

re·coup (rĭ-kōōp') tr. recuperar.

re·course (rē'kôrs', rĭ-kôrs') s. recurso ♦ to have r. to recurrir a.

re·cov·er (rĭ-kŭv'ər) tr. *(to regain)* recuperar; *(damages)* cobrar —intr. recuperarse.

re·cov·er·y (:ə-rē) s. recuperación f.

re·cre·ate (rē'krē-āt') tr. recrear.

rec·re·a·tion (rĕk'rē-ā'shən) s. recreo.

rec·re·a·tion·al (:shə-nəl) adj. recreativo.

re·crim·i·nate (rĭ-krĭm'ə-nāt') tr. recriminar.

re·crim·i·na·tion (-'-nā'shən) s. recriminación f.

re·cruit (rĭ-krōōt') I. tr. *(workers)* contratar; MIL. reclutar —intr. MIL. reclutar II. s. recluta m; *(new member)* socio nuevo

re·cruit·er (rĭ-krōō'tər) s. reclutador m.

re·cruit·ment (:mənt) s. reclutamiento.

rec·tal (rĕk'təl) adj. rectal.

rec·tan·gle (rĕk'tăng'gəl) s. rectángulo.

rec·tan·gu·lar ('-gyə-lər) adj. rectangular.

rec·ti·fy (rĕk'tə-fī') tr. rectificar.

rec·ti·tude (rĕk'tĭ-tōōd') s. rectitud f.

rec·tor (rĕk'tər) s. *(of a parish)* cura párroco; *(of a school)* director m; *(of a university)* rector m.

rec·to·ry (:tə-rē) s. rectoría.

rec·tum (rĕk'təm) s. [pl. **s** o **-ta**] recto.

re·cum·bent (rĭ-kŭm'bənt) adj. recostado.

re·cu·per·ate (rĭ-kōō'pə-rāt') tr. & intr. recuperar(se).

re·cu·per·a·tion (-'-rā'shən) s. recuperación f.

re·cu·per·a·tive ('-'-tĭv) adj. recuperativo.

re·cur (rĭ-kûr') intr. **-rr-** repetirse; *(symptom)* reaparecer ♦ to r. to recurrir a.

re·cur·rence (:əns) s. repetición f, reaparición f; *(return)* vuelta.

re·cur·rent (:ənt) adj. que se repite; *(periodic)* periódico; ANAT. MAT. recurrente.

re·cur·ring (:ĭng) adj. periódico.

re·cy·cle (rē-sī'kəl) tr. reciclar.

red I. s. rojo, colorado ♦ R. POL. rojo ▪ to be in the r. tener pérdidas ▪ to see r. ponerse furioso II. adj. **-dd-** rojo, colorado; *(wine)* tinto ♦ r. tape trámites, papeleo.

re·dact (rĭ-dăkt') tr. redactar.

red-blood·ed (rĕd'blŭd'ĭd) adj. vigoroso.

red·cap (:kăp') s. mozo de equipajes.

red·den (:n) intr. enrojecer; *(a person)* ruborizarse.

red·dish (:ĭsh) adj. rojizo.

re·deem (rĭ-dēm') tr. redimir; *(situation)* salvar; *(to make up for)* compensar.

re·deem·a·ble (rĭ-dē'mə-bəl) adj. redimible.

re·deem·er (:mər) s. redentor m.

re·demp·tion (rĭ-dĕmp'shən) s. redención f; *(of a mortgage)* cancelación f.

red-hand·ed (rĕd'hăn'dĭd) adj. & adv. con las manos en la masa.

red·head (:hĕd') s. pelirrojo.

red-hot (:hŏt') adj. *(very hot)* candente; *(excited)* animado; *(new)* muy reciente.

re·di·rect (rē'dĭ-rĕkt') tr. *(letter)* mandar a otra dirección; *(to reroute)* mostrar otro camino.

re·dis·cov·er (rē'dĭ-skŭv'ər) tr. redescubrir.

re·dis·trib·ute (rē'dĭ-strĭb'yōōt) tr. redistribuir.

red-let·ter (rĕd'lĕt'ər) adj. memorable.

red-light district (.līt') s. barrio de burdeles.

re·do (rē-dōō') tr. **-did, -done** volver a hacer, rehacer; *(to redecorate)* decorar de nuevo.

red·o·lent (rĕd'l-ənt) adj. *(aromatic)* fragante, oloroso; *(suggestive)* evocador.

re·dou·ble (rē-dŭb'əl) tr. & intr. redoblar.

re·doubt·a·ble (rĭ-dou'tə-bəl) adj. formidable.

re·dound (rĭ-dound') intr. redundar (to en).

re·dress (rĭ-drĕs') I. tr. *(to remedy)* reparar; *(to rectify)* rectificar II. s. reparación f, enmienda.

re·duce (rĭ-dōōs') tr. reducir; COM. rebajar —intr. disminuir, reducirse; *(to lose weight)* adelgazar.

re·duc·tion (rĭ-dŭk'shən) s. reducción f, disminución f; *(discount)* descuento.

re·dun·dant (rĭ-dŭn'dənt) s. superfluo; GRAM. redundante.

red·wood (rĕd'wŏŏd') s. secoya.

reed (rēd) s. *(plant, stalk)* caña; MÚS. (instrumento de) lengüeta.

re·ed·u·cate (rē-ĕj'ə-kāt') tr. reeducar.

reef¹ (rēf) s. GEOL. arrecife *m,* escollo.

reef² MARÍT. I. s. rizo (de vela) II. tr. arrizar.

reef·er (rē'fər) s. JER. cigarrillo de marihuana.

reek (rēk) I. intr. *(to stink)* apestar; *(to smell)* oler *(of a)* II. s. olor *m.*

reel¹ (rēl) I. s. *(spool)* carrete *m;* CINEM., FOTOG. rollo II. tr. enrollar en un carrete ♦ **to r. off** recitar de un tirón.

reel² intr. *(to stagger)* tambalear(se); *(to feel dizzy)* tener vértigo.

re·e·lect (rē'ĭ-lĕkt') tr. reelegir.

re·en·act (rē'ĕn-ăkt') tr. *(law)* aprobar de nuevo; *(play)* volver a representar.

re·en·list (rē'ĕn-lĭst') intr. reengancharse.

re·en·try (rē-ĕn'trē) s. reingreso; *(space vehicle)* reentrada.

re·es·tab·lish (rē'ĭ-stăb'lĭsh) tr. restablecer.

re·ex·am·ine (rē'ĭg-zăm'ĭn) tr. reexaminar.

re·fec·to·ry (rĭ-fĕk'tə-rē) s. comedor *m.*

re·fer (rĭ-fûr') tr. **-rr-** *(to direct to)* remitir; *(to send to)* enviar; *(to submit to)* someter a —intr. referirse; *(to apply)* aplicarse.

ref·er·ee (rĕf'ə-rē') I. s. árbitro II. tr. & intr. arbitrar.

ref·er·ence (rĕf'ər-əns) s. referencia; *(allusion)* alusión *f,* mención *f; (person)* fiador *m* ♦ **r. book** libro de consulta • **r. mark** llamada • **with r. to** *(a letter)* con relación a; *(as regards)* en cuanto a.

ref·er·en·dum (rĕf'ə-rĕn'dəm) s. [pl. **s** o **-da**] referéndum *m,* plebiscito.

re·fer·ral (rĭ-fûr'əl) s. referencia.

re·fill I. tr. (rē-fĭl') rellenar II. s. ('') recambio.

re·fine (rĭ-fīn') tr. refinar.

re·fined (rĭ-fīnd') adj. *(pure)* refinado; *(elegant)* fino.

re·fine·ment (rĭ-fīn'mənt) s. *(oil, sugar)* refinación *f; (person)* refinamiento.

re·fin·er·y (rĭ-fī'nə-rē) s. refinería.

re·flect (rĭ-flĕkt') tr. reflejar; *(to manifest)* revelar —intr. reflejarse; *(to think)* reflexionar, meditar ♦ **to r. on** pensar (sobre).

re·flec·tion (rĭ-flĕk'shən) s. *(image)* reflejo; *(contemplation)* reflexión *f* ♦ **on r.** pensándolo bien.

re·flec·tive (:tĭv) adj. que refleja; *(meditative)* pensativo.

re·flec·tor (:tər) s. reflector *m.*

re·flex (rē'flĕks') adj. & s. reflejo.

re·flex·ive (rĭ-flĕk'sĭv) adj. reflexivo.

re·form (rĭ-fôrm') I. tr. & intr. reformar(se) II. s. reforma ♦ **r. school** reformatorio.

ref·or·ma·tion (rĕf'ər-mā'shən) s. reforma.

re·for·ma·to·ry (rĭ-fôr'mə-tôr'ē) s. reformatorio.

re·formed (rĭ-fôrmd') adj. reformado.

re·form·er (rĭ-fôr'mər) s. reformador *m.*

re·form·ist (:mĭst) s. reformista *mf.*

re·fract (rĭ-frăkt') tr. refractar.

re·frac·tion (rĭ-frăk'shən) s. refracción *f.*

re·frac·to·ry (:tə-rē) adj. obstinado, indócil; FÍS. refractario; MED. resistente.

re·frain¹ (rĭ-frān') intr. abstenerse *(from* de).

re·frain² s. MÚS., POET. estribillo.

re·fresh (rĭ-frĕsh') tr. & intr. refrescar(se).

re·fresh·er course (:ər) s. curso de repaso.

re·fresh·ing (:ĭng) adj. refrescante; *(restorative)* reparador; *(pleasant)* placentero.

re·fresh·ment (:mənt) s. refresco ♦ pl. refrigerio, colación.

re·frig·er·ant (rĭ-frĭj'ər-ənt) s. refrigerante *m.*

re·frig·er·ate (:ə-rāt') tr. refrigerar.

re·frig·er·a·tion (-'-rā'shən) s. refrigeración *f.*

re·frig·er·a·tor (-'-tər) s. nevera, frigorífico.

re·fu·el (rē-fyōō'əl) tr. echar gasolina a *o* en —intr. reabastecerse (de gasolina).

ref·uge (rĕf'yōōj) s. refugio ♦ **to take r. in** refugiarse en.

ref·u·gee ('yōō-jē') s. refugiado.

re·ful·gent (rĭ-fŏŏl'jənt) adj. refulgente.

re·fund I. tr. (rĭ-fŭnd') reembolsar II. s. (rē'fŭnd') reembolso.

re·fund·a·ble (rĭ-fŭn'də-bəl) adj. reembolsable.

re·fur·bish (rē-fûr'bĭsh) tr. restaurar.

re·fur·nish (rē-fûr'nĭsh) tr. amueblar de nuevo.

re·fus·al (rĭ-fyōō'zəl) s. negativa.

re·fuse¹ (rĭ-fyōōz') tr. *(offer)* no aceptar; *(permission)* negar —intr. negarse *(to* a).

ref·use² (rĕf'yōōs) s. desperdicios, basura.

ref·u·ta·tion (rĕf'yōō-tā'shən) s. refutación *f.*

re·fute (rĭ-fyōōt') tr. refutar.

re·gain (rē-gān') tr. recuperar, recobrar.

re·gal (rē'gəl) adj. real, regio.

re·gale (rĭ-gāl') tr. agasajar, entretener.

re·ga·lia (rĭ-gāl'yə) s.pl. *(of royalty)* insignias reales; *(finery)* adornos.

re·gard (rĭ-gärd') I. tr. *(to watch)* observar, mirar; *(to consider)* considerar; *(to concern)* apreciar; *(to concern)* referirse a, concernir ♦ **as regards** con respecto a II. s. *(gaze)* mirada; *(attention)* consideración *f; (esteem)* aprecio ♦ **in** o **with r. to** con respecto a • **in (this, that) r.** por lo que a (esto, eso) se refiere • **to send one's regards** dar recuerdos a alguien • **to have r. for** respetar • **with best regards** saludos cordiales de • **without r. to** sin tomar en consideración.

re·gard·ing (rĭ-gär'dĭng) prep. con respecto a.

re·gard·less (rĭ-gärd'lĭs) adv. *(anyway)* a pesar de todo; *(come what may)* pase lo que pase ♦ **r. of** *(without regard to)* sin tener en cuenta; *(in spite of)* a pesar de.

re·gat·ta (rĭ-gät'ə, -gät'ə) s. regata.

re·gen·cy (rē'jən-sē) s. regencia.

re·gen·er·ate (rĭ-jĕn'ə-rāt') I. tr. & intr. regenerar(se) II. adj. (:ər-ĭt) renovado.

re·gen·er·a·tion (-'-rā'shən) s. regeneración *f.*

re·gen·er·a·tive (-'-tĭv) adj. regenerador.

re·gent (rē'jənt) s. regente *mf* ♦ **board of regents** EDUC. junta directiva.

re·gime o **ré·gime** (rä-zhēm') s. régimen *m.*

reg·i·men (rĕj'ə-mən) s. régimen *m.*

reg·i·ment (:mənt) I. s. regimiento II. tr. regimentar.

reg·i·men·ta·tion ('-mĕn-tā'shən) s. reglamentación estricta.

re·gion (rē'jən) s. región *f.*

re·gion·al (rē'jə-nəl) adj. regional.

reg·is·ter (rĕj'ĭ-stər) I. s. registro; *(cash register)* registradora; *(meter)* contador *m; (for heat)* regulador *m* II. tr. registrar; *(a birth, death)* declarar; *(students)* matricular; *(vehicle)* sacar la matrícula de; *(complaint)* presentar; *(on a scale)* marcar; *(emotion)* manifestar, expresar; *(mail)* certificar —intr. *(at the polls, hotel)* inscribirse; *(at school)* matricularse.

reg·is·tered (:stərd) adj. *(trademark)* registrado; *(student, vehicle)* matriculado; *(certified)* titulado ♦ **r. mail** correo certificado.

reg·is·trar (:strär′) s. *(registry)* jefe *m* de registros civiles; *(university)* secretario general.

reg·is·tra·tion (′-strā′shən) s. *(of voters)* inscripción *f*; *(of students, cars)* matrícula; *(for the draft)* alistamiento.

reg·is·try (′-strē) s. registro.

re·gress I. intr. (rĭ-grĕs′) retroceder II. s. (rē′grĕs′) retroceso.

re·gres·sion (rĭ-grĕsh′ən) s. retroceso.

re·gres·sive (rĭ-grĕs′ĭv) adj. regresivo.

re·gret (rĭ-grĕt′) I. tr. **-tt-** *(to be sorry for)* arrepentirse de; *(to be sorry about)* lamentar II. s. *(sorrow)* pena; *(remorse)* arrepentimiento **♦ to have no regrets** no arrepentirse de nada **♦** pl. excusas.

re·gret·ful·ly (:fə-lē) adv. sentidamente.

re·gret·ta·ble (:ə-bəl) adj. lamentable.

re·gret·ta·bly (:ə-blē) adv. desafortunadamente.

re·group (rē-grōōp′) tr. & intr. reagrupar(se).

reg·u·lar (rĕg′yə-lər) I. adj. regular; *(usual)* normal <during r. office hours durante las horas normales de oficina>; *(customary)* habitual, de costumbre; *(work)* fijo; *(customer)* habitual, fijo; FAM. *(nice)* decente, bueno **♦ to make r. use of** emplear con regularidad II. s. MIL. regular *m*; FAM. cliente fijo.

reg·u·lar·i·ty (′-lăr′ĭ-tē) s. regularidad *f*.

reg·u·lar·ize (′-lə-rīz′) tr. regularizar.

reg·u·late (:lāt′) tr. *(to control)* reglamentar; *(to adjust)* regular.

reg·u·la·tion (′-lā′shən) s. *(act)* regulación *f*; *(rule)* regla **♦** pl. reglamento.

reg·u·la·tor (′-lā′tər) s. regulador *m*.

reg·u·la·to·ry (:lə-tôr′ē) adj. regulador.

re·gur·gi·tate (rē-gûr′jĭ-tāt′) intr. regurgitar — tr. vomitar.

re·ha·bil·i·tate (rē′hə-bĭl′ĭ-tāt′) tr. rehabilitar; *(building, neighborhood)* restaurar.

re·ha·bil·i·ta·tion (′-′-tā′shən) s. rehabilitación *f*; *(restoration)* restauración *f*.

re·hash I. tr. (rē-hăsh′) volver a repetir, machacar II. s. (′′) repetición *f*.

re·hears·al (rĭ-hûr′səl) s. ensayo.

re·hearse (rĭ-hûrs′) tr. & intr. ensayar.

reign (rān) I. s. reinado; *(dominance)* dominio **♦ r. of terror** régimen de terror II. intr. reinar.

re·im·burse (rē′ĭm-bûrs′) tr. reembolsar.

re·im·burse·ment (:mənt) s. reembolso.

rein (rān) I. s. rienda **♦ to give free r.** to dar rienda suelta a **• to keep a tight r. on** atar corto a II. tr. poner rienda a **♦ to r. in** refrenar.

rein·deer (rān′dîr′) s. [pl. inv. o s] reno.

re·in·car·nate (rē′ĭn-kär′nāt′) tr. reencarnar.

re·in·car·na·tion (′-nā′shən) s. reencarnación *f*.

re·in·force (rē′ĭn-fôrs′) tr. reforzar **♦ reinforced concrete** concreto armado.

re·in·force·ment (:mənt) s. *(strengthening)* refuerzo **♦** pl. MIL. refuerzos.

re·in·state (rē′ĭn-stāt′) tr. *(to restore to office)* restituir, reintegrar; *(to reestablish)* restablecer.

re·in·sure (rē′-ĭn-shŏŏr′) tr. reasegurar.

re·in·vest (rē′ĭn-vĕst′) tr. reinvertir.

re·in·vest·ment (:mənt) s. reinversión *f*.

re·is·sue (rē-ĭsh′ōō) I. tr. reeditar II. s. reedición *f*.

re·it·er·ate (rē-ĭt′ə-rāt′) tr. reiterar.

re·it·er·a·tion (′-rā′shən) s. reiteración *f*.

re·ject I. tr. (rĭ-jĕkt′) *(to refuse)* rechazar, rehusar; *(to discard)* desechar II. s. (rē′jĕkt′) *(thing)* desecho; *(person)* persona rechazada.

re·jec·tion (rĭ-jĕk′shən) s. rechazo.

re·joice (rĭ-jois′) tr. & intr. regocijar(se).

re·joic·ing (rĭ-joi′sĭng) s. regocijo.

re·join (rē-join′) tr. & intr. responder, replicar.

re·join (rē-join′) tr. & intr. juntar(se) de nuevo.

re·join·der (rĭ-join′dər) s. respuesta.

re·ju·ve·nate (rĭ-jōō′və-nāt′) tr. rejuvenecer.

re·ju·ve·na·tion (′-nā′shən) s. rejuvenecimiento.

re·kin·dle (rē-kĭn′dl) tr. volver a encender.

re·lapse I. intr. (rĭ-lăps′) recaer II. (rē′lăps′) recaída.

re·late (rĭ-lāt′) tr. *(to tell)* relatar, contar; *(to associate)* relacionar, asociar — intr. estar relacionado *(to con)*; *(to interact)* relacionarse *(with,* to con).

re·lat·ed (rĭ-lā′tĭd) adj. relacionado *(to* con); *(by blood, marriage)* emparentado.

re·la·tion (rĭ-lā′shən) s. relación *f*, *(kinship)* parentesco; *(relative)* pariente *mf* **♦ in r.** to en relación a.

re·la·tion·ship (:shĭp′) s. relación *f*; *(kinship)* parentesco; *(tie)* vínculo.

rel·a·tive (rĕl′ə-tĭv) I. adj. relativo II. s. pariente *mf*.

rel·a·tiv·i·ty (′-′ĭ-tē) s. relatividad *f*.

re·lax (rĭ-lăks′) tr. & intr. relajar(se) **♦ r.!** ¡cálmate!

re·lax·a·tion (rē′lăk-sā′shən) s. relajación *f*; *(of efforts)* disminución *f*; *(state)* descanso, reposo; *(recreation)* distracción *f*.

re·laxed (rĭ-lăkst′) adj. relajado; *(calm)* tranquilo.

re·lay (rē′lā′) I. s. relevo; *(of messages)* transmisión *f*; *(of news)* difusión *f*; ELEC. relevador *m* **♦ r. race** carrera de relevos II. tr. transmitir, difundir; RAD., TELEV. retransmitir.

re·lease (rĭ-lēs′) I. tr. *(from captivity)* poner en libertad; *(from one's grip)* soltar; *(from debt, promise)* descargar; *(for sale)* poner en venta; *(film)* estrenar; *(record)* sacar II. s. liberación *f*; *(of film)* estreno; *(record)* disco, grabación *f*; *(communique)* anuncio.

rel·e·gate (rĕl′ĭ gāt′) tr. relegar.

re·lent (rĭ-lĕnt′) intr. ceder.

re·lent·less (:lĭs) adj. *(without pity)* implacable; *(persistent)* incesante.

rel·e·vance/van·cy (rĕl′ə-vəns) s. pertinencia.

rel·e·vant (:vənt) adj. pertinente.

re·li·a·bil·i·ty (rĭ-lī′ə-bĭl′ĭ-tē) s. fiabilidad *f*.

re·li·a·ble (rĭ-lī′ə-bəl) adj. *(person)* de confianza; *(machine)* fiable; *(data, source)* fidedigno.

re·li·ance (:əns) s. confianza.

re·li·ant (:ənt) adj. confiado.

rel·ic (rĕl′ĭk) s. reliquia **♦** pl. restos mortales.

re·lief (rĭ-lēf′) s. alivio; *(assistance)* ayuda; *(replacement)* relevo, ARTE., GEOG. relieve *m* **♦ in r.** en relieve **♦ what a r.!** ¡qué alivio!

re·lieve (rĭ-lēv′) tr. *(to alleviate)* aliviar; *(to aid)* auxiliar; *(from worry)* liberar; *(of duties)* destituir; *(to replace)* reemplazar; *(boredom)* disipar.

re·li·gion (rĭ-lĭj′ən) s. religión *f*.

re·li·gious (:əs) adj. religioso; *(pious)* devoto.

re·lin·quish (rĭ-lĭng′kwĭsh) tr. abandonar; *(to renounce)* renunciar a; *(to release)* soltar.

rel·ish (rĕl′ĭsh) I. s. *(liking)* gusto, afición *f*; *(pleasure)* placer *m*; CUL. condimento II. tr. gustar, encantar.

re·live (rē-lĭv′) tr. volver a vivir, recordar.

re·load (rē-lōd′) tr. & intr. recargar.

re·lo·cate (rē-lō′kāt′) tr. & intr. establecer(se) en un nuevo lugar.

re·lo·ca·tion (′-kā′shən) s. ubicación nueva.

re·luc·tance/tan·cy (rī-lŭk′təns) s. desgana.

re·luc·tant (:tənt) adj. (reticent) reacio; (unwilling) poco dispuesto.

re·ly (rī-lī′) intr. ♦ **to r. (up)on** (to depend) depender de; (to trust) contar con.

re·main (rī-mān′) intr. (to keep being) seguir; (to stay) permanecer, quedarse; (to be left) quedar ♦ **to r. to be (seen)** quedar por (ver).

re·main·der (:dər) s. resto, residuo.

re·main·ing (rī-mā′nĭng) adj. restante.

re·mains (rī-mānz′) s.pl. restos; (corpse) restos mortales.

re·make (rē-māk′) I. tr. **-made** rehacer, hacer de nuevo II. s. (′′) nueva versión.

re·mand (rī-mānd′) tr. (to prison) encarcelar; (to a lower court) remitir al tribunal inferior.

re·mark (rī-märk′) I. tr. & intr. (to comment) comentar (on sobre); (to notice) observar II. s. comentario, observación f.

re·mark·a·ble (rī-mär′kə-bəl) adj. notable; (admirable) extraordinario, admirable.

re·mar·ry (rī-măr′ē) intr. volver a casarse.

re·me·di·al (rī-mē′dē-əl) adj. MED. correctivo; (class, studies) de estudiantes atrasados.

rem·e·dy (rĕm′ĭ-dē) I. s. remedio II. tr. remediar.

re·mem·ber (rī-mĕm′bər) tr. (to recall) acordarse de, recordar; (to bear in mind) tener en cuenta; (in greeting) dar recuerdos o saludos de —intr. acordarse.

re·mem·brance (:brəns) s. recuerdo ♦ **in r. of** en conmemoración de.

re·mind (rī-mīnd′) tr. recordar ♦ **that reminds me!** ¡a propósito!

re·mind·er (rī-mīn′dər) s. (of a date) recordatorio; (notice) aviso, notificación f.

rem·i·nisce (rĕm′ə-nĭs′) intr. recordar el pasado.

rem·i·nis·cent (:ənt) adj. evocador.

re·miss (rī-mĭs′) adj. negligente, descuidado.

re·mis·sion (rī-mĭsh′ən) s. remisión f.

re·mit (rī-mĭt′) tr. **-tt-** (money) remitir; (obligation) rescindir.

re·mit·tal (:l) s. remisión f.

re·mit·tance (:ns) s. remesa, envío.

rem·nant (rĕm′nənt) s. (remainder) resto; (of fabric) retazo; (trace) vestigio.

re·mod·el (rē-mŏd′l) tr. reconstruir, reformar.

re·mon·strate (rī-mŏn′strāt′) intr. protestar.

re·morse (rī-môrs′) s. remordimiento.

re·mote (rī-mōt′) adj. remoto; (relative) lejano ♦ **r. control** control a distancia.

re·mov·al (rī-mōō′vəl) s. (elimination) eliminación f; (transfer) traslado; (from a job) despido; MED. extirpación f.

re·move (rī-mōōv′) I. tr. (to take off, away) quitar(se); (to eliminate) eliminar; (from a job) despedir; CIR. extirpar —intr. mudarse, trasladarse II. s. distancia.

re·moved (rī-mōōvd′) adj. distante ♦ **first cousin once r.** primo segundo.

re·mu·ner·ate (rī-myōō′nə-rāt′) tr. remunerar.

re·mu·ner·a·tion (′-rā′shən) s. remuneración f.

ren·ais·sance (rĕn′ə-säns′) I. s. renacimiento II. adj. renacentista.

re·nal (rē′nəl) adj. renal.

rend (rĕnd) tr. **-ed** o **rent** desgarrar.

ren·der (rĕn′dər) tr. (help) dar; (homage) rendir; (to depict) representar; (to perform) interpretar; (to translate) traducir; (verdict) pronunciar; (to cause to become) dejar; CUL. derretir ♦ **for services rendered** por servicios prestados.

ren·dez·vous (rän′dā-vōō′) I. s.inv. (place) lugar m de reunión; (meeting) cita II. intr. reunirse.

ren·di·tion (rĕn-dĭsh′ən) s. presentación f; (translation) versión f; MÚS. interpretación f.

ren·e·gade (rĕn′ĭ-gād′) s. renegado.

re·nege (rī-nĭg′, -nĕg′) intr. volverse atrás; (in cards) renunciar ♦ **to r. on** no cumplir.

re·new (rī-nōō′) tr. renovar; (to resume) reanudar; (to replenish) volver a llenar.

re·new·al (:əl) s. renovación f; (of negotiations) reanudación f.

re·nounce (rī-nouns′) tr. & intr. renunciar (a).

ren·o·vate (rĕn′ə-vāt′) tr. renovar, restaurar.

ren·o·va·tion (′-vā′shən) s. renovación f; (restoration) restauración f.

re·nown (rī-noun′) s. renombre m.

re·nowned (rī-nound′) adj. renombrado.

rent¹ (rĕnt) I. s. alquiler m <one month's r. un mes de alquiler> ♦ **for r.** se alquila II. tr. & intr. alquilar(se).

rent² I. cf. **rend** II. s. rasgadura.

rent·al (rĕn′tl) I. s. (amount) alquiler m; (property) propiedad alquilada II. adj. de alquiler.

rent·er (:tər) s. inquilino.

re·nun·ci·a·tion (rī-nŭn′sē-ā′shən) s. renuncia.

re·or·gan·i·za·tion (rē-ôr′gə-nī-zā′shən) s. reorganización f.

re·or·gan·ize (′-nīz′) tr. & intr. reorganizar(se).

rep (rĕp) s. FAM. representante mf.

re·pair¹ (rī-pâr′) I. tr. reparar; (clothes) remendar II. s. reparación f ♦ **closed for repairs** cerrado por reformas • **in bad r.** en mal estado • **to be beyond r.** no tener arreglo.

re·pair² intr. (to go) ir, acudir.

re·pair·man (:măn′) s. [pl. **-men**] reparador m.

rep·a·ra·ble (rĕp′ər-ə-bəl) adj. reparable.

rep·a·ra·tion (rĕp′ə-rā′shən) s. reparación f ♦ pl. indemnización.

rep·ar·tee (rĕp′ər-tē′) s. conversación f con réplicas agudas.

re·past (rī-păst′) s. comida.

re·pa·tri·ate (rē-pā′trē-āt′) I. tr. repatriar II. s. (:īt) repatriado.

re·pay (rē-pā′) tr. **-paid** (loan) pagar; (favor) devolver; (to compensate) compensar ♦ **to r. in kind** pagar con la misma moneda.

re·pay·ment (:mənt) s. pago, reembolso; (reward) recompensa.

re·peal (rī-pēl′) I. tr. (to revoke) revocar; (to annul) anular II. s. revocación f, anulación f.

re·peat (rī-pēt′) I. tr. & intr. repetir ♦ **to r. oneself** repetirse II. s. repetición f; RAD., TELEV. segunda difusión f.

re·peat·ed (rī-pē′tĭd) adj. repetido.

re·peat·ing (:tĭng) adj. de repetición.

re·pel (rī-pĕl′) tr. **-ll-** repeler; (advances) rechazar ♦ **to r. each other** repelerse.

re·pel·lent (:ənt) I. adj. repelente; (repulsive) repugnante II. s. ♦ **insect r.** producto contra los insectos.

re·pent (rī-pĕnt′) intr. & tr. arrepentirse (de).

re·pen·tance (rī-pĕn′təns) s. arrepentimiento.

re·pen·tant (:tənt) adj. arrepentido.

re·per·cus·sion (rē′pər-kŭsh′ən, rĕp′ər-) s. repercusión f.

rep·er·toire (rĕp'ər-twär') s. repertorio.
rep·er·to·ry (:tôr'ē) s. repertorio; (theater) teatro de repertorio; (repository) depósito.
rep·e·ti·tion (rĕp'ĭ-tĭsh'ən) s. repetición f.
rep·e·ti·tious (:əs) adj. repetitivo.
re·pet·i·tivo (rĭ-pĕt'ĭ-tĭv) adj. repetitivo.
re·place (rĭ-plās') tr. (to put back) reponer; (to substitute) reemplazar, suplir.
re·place·ment (:mənt) s. reposición f. (substitution) reemplazo; (person) relevo ♦ r. part repuesto.
re·play I. tr. (rē-plā') (game) volver a jugar; (videotape) volver a poner; (to repeat) repetir II. s. (") repetición f.
re·plen·ish (rĭ-plĕn'ĭsh) tr. volver a llenar; (to restore) llenar, restaurar.
re·plete (rĭ-plēt') adj. repleto.
rep·li·ca (rĕp'lĭ-kə) s. copia.
rep·li·cate (:kāt') tr. & intr. duplicar(se).
re·ply (rĭ-plī') I. tr. & intr. contestar, responder II. s. respuesta, contestación f.
re·port (rĭ-pôrt') I. s. (account) relato; (official account) informe m; (of news) reportaje m; (rumor) rumor m; (noise) detonación f ♦ r. card boletín de notas • **weather r.** boletín meteorológico II. tr. (to recount) relatar; (to tell of) informar; (to denounce) denunciar ♦ **it is reported that se dice que** —intr. presentar un informe ♦ **to r. for** (military duty) incorporarse a; (work) presentarse a • **to r. on** hacer un informe sobre; (news) escribir una crónica de.
re·port·ed·ly (rĭ-pôr'tĭd-lē) adv. según se dice.
re·port·er (rĭ-pôr'tər) s. reportero, periodista mf.
re·pose¹ (rĭ-pōz') I. s. (rest) reposo; (sleep) sueño; (calm) tranquilidad f II. intr. & tr. descansar.
re·pose² tr. depositar (confianza).
re·pos·i·to·ry (rĭ-pŏz'ĭ-tôr'ē) s. depósito.
re·pos·sess (rē'pə-zĕs') tr. recuperar.
re·pre·hend (rĕp'rĭ-hĕnd') tr. reprender.
re·pre·hen·si·ble (:hĕn'sə-bəl) adj. reprensible.
re·pre·hen·sion (:shən) s. reprensión f.
rep·re·sent (rĕp'rĭ-zĕnt') tr. representar.
rep·re·sen·ta·tion (:zĕn-tā'shən) s. representación f; DER. declaración f; POL. delegación f.
rep·re·sen·ta·tive ('-'tə-tĭv) I. s. representante mf II. adj. representativo; (typical) típico.
re·press (rĭ-prĕs') tr. & intr. reprimir.
re·pres·sion (rĭ-prĕsh'ən) s. represión f.
re·pres·sive (rĭ-prĕs'ĭv) adj. represivo.
re·prieve (rĭ-prēv') I. tr. (execution) suspender la ejecución de; (sentence) conmutar la pena de II. s. alivio temporal; (of an execution) suspensión f; (of a sentence) conmutación f.
rep·ri·mand (rĕp'rə-mănd') I. tr. reprender II. s. reprimenda.
re·print I. s. (rē'prĭnt') (of book) reimpresión f; (of article) tirada aparte II. tr. (-') reimprimir.
re·pri·sal (rĭ-prī'zəl) s. represalia.
re·prise (rĭ-prēz') s. repetición f.
re·proach (rĭ-prōch') I. tr. reprochar II. s. reproche m ♦ **to be beyond r.** ser intachable.
rep·ro·bate (rĕp'rə-bāt') s. & adj. réprobo.
re·proc·ess (rē-prŏs'ĕs', -prŏ'sĕs') tr. someter de nuevo a algún procedimiento.
re·pro·duce (rē'prə-dōs') tr. & intr. reproducir(se).
re·pro·duc·tion (:dŭk'shən) s. reproducción f.
re·pro·duc·tive (:tĭv) adj. reproductivo.
re·proof (rĭ-prōof') s. reprobación f.

re·prove (rĭ-prōv') tr. reprobar.
rep·tile (rĕp'təl, :tīl') s. reptil m; FIG. rastrero.
rep·til·i·an (rĕp-tĭl'ē-ən) adj. & s. reptil m.
re·pub·lic (rĭ-pŭb'lĭk) s. república.
re·pub·li·can (:lĭ-kən) adj. & s. republicano.
re·pu·di·ate (rĭ-pyōō'dē-āt') tr. repudiar.
re·pug·nance (rĭ-pŭg'nəns) s. repugnancia.
re·pug·nant (:nənt) adj. repugnante.
re·pulse (rĭ-pŭls') I. tr. repeler, rechazar II. s. (act) repulsión f; (rejection) rechazo.
re·pul·sion (rĭ-pŭl'shən) s. repulsión f; (aversion) repugnancia, aversión f.
re·pul·sive (:sĭv) adj. repulsivo.
rep·u·ta·ble (rĕp'yə-tə-bəl) adj. respetable.
rep·u·ta·tion ('-tā'shən) s. reputación f.
re·pute (rĭ-pyōōt') I. tr. ♦ **to be reputed to be** tener fama de II. s. reputación f, fama.
re·put·ed (rĭ-pyōō'tĭd) adj. supuesto.
re·quest (rĭ-kwĕst') I. tr. solicitar II. s. solicitud f ♦ **available on r.** disponible a petición.
re·quire (rĭ-kwīr') tr. (to need) requerir, necesitar; (to demand) exigir.
re·quire·ment (:mənt) s. (prerequisite) requisito; (need) necesidad f.
req·ui·site (rĕk'wĭ-zĭt) I. adj. necesario, indispensable II. s. requisito.
req·ui·si·tion (' :zĭsh'ən) I. s. solicitud f; MIL. requisa II. tr. requisar.
req·ui·tal (rĭ-kwī't'l) s. compensación f.
re·run (rē'rŭn') s. CINEM., TELEV. reestreno, FIG. repetición f.
re·sale (rē'sāl') s. reventa.
re·sched·ule (rē-skĕj'ōōl) tr. (event) volver a programar; (debt) reestructurar.
re·scind (rĭ-sĭnd') tr. rescindir, anular.
re·scis·sion (rĭ-sĭzh'ən) s. rescisión f.
res·cue (rĕs'kyōō) I. tr. rescatar, salvar II. s. rescate m, salvamento ♦ **to come to someone's r.** acudir en auxilio de alguien.
re·search (rĭ-sûrch', rē'sûrch') I. s. investigación f II. tr. & intr. hacer una investigación (sobre).
re·search·er (:ər) s. investigador m.
re·sell (rē-sĕl') tr. **-sold** revender.
re·sem·blance (rĭ-zĕm'bləns) s. parecido.
re·sem·ble (:bəl) tr. parecerse a.
re·sent (rĭ-zĕnt') tr. resentirse por.
re·sent·ful (:fəl) adj. resentido.
re·sent·ment (:mənt) s. resentimiento.
res·er·va·tion (rĕz'ər-vā'shən) s. (of room, table) reservación f; (condition, land) reserva.
re·serve (rĭ-zûrv') I. tr. reservar II. s. reserva ♦ **in r.** de reserva ♦ pl. MIL. reserva • **cash r.** reservas en metálico III. adj. de reserva.
re·served (rĭ-zûrvd') adj. reservado.
res·er·voir (rĕz'ər-vwär') s. embalse m; FIG. fondo.
re·shape (rē-shāp') tr. rehacer, reformar.
re·side (rĭ-zīd') intr. residir.
res·i·dence (rĕz'ĭ-dəns) s. residencia ♦ **in r.** residente.
res·i·den·cy (:dən-sē) s. residencia.
res·i·dent (:dənt) I. s. residente mf; MED. interno II. adj. (residing) residente; (permanent) fijo ♦ **r. alien** extranjero residente.
res·i·den·tial ('-dĕn'shəl) adj. residencial.
re·sid·u·al (rĭ-zĭj'ōō-əl) I. adj. residual II. s. residuo.
res·i·due (rĕz'ĭ-dōō') s. residuo.
re·sign (rĭ-zīn') tr. renunciar, dimitir ♦ **to r. oneself** to resignarse a —intr. dimitir.
res·ig·na·tion (rĕz'ĭg-nā'shən) s. (act) renun-

cia; *(acceptance)* resignación *f.*

re·signed (rĭ-zīnd') adj. resignado.

re·sil·ience/ien·cy (rĭ-zĭl'yəns) s. elasticidad *f*; MEC. resiliencia.

re·sil·ient (:yənt) adj. flexible.

res·in (rĕz'ĭn) I. s. resina II. tr. untar con resina.

res·in·ous (rĕz'ə-nəs) adj. resinoso.

re·sist (rĭ-zĭst') I. tr. & intr. resistir.

re·sis·tance (rĭ-zĭs'təns) s. resistencia.

re·sis·tant (:tənt) adj. resistente.

re·sist·i·ble (:tə-bəl) adj. resistible.

re·sis·tor (:tər) s. resistor *m.*

res·o·lute (rĕz'ə-lōōt') adj. resuelto.

res·o·lu·tion ('-lōō'shən) s. resolución *f* ♦ **to show r.** mostrarse resuelto.

re·solve (rĭ-zŏlv') I. tr. resolver —intr. decidir II. s. resolución *f.*

re·solved (rĭ-zŏlvd') adj. resuelto.

res·o·nance (rĕz'ə-nəns) s. resonancia.

res·o·nant (:nənt) adj. resonante.

res·o·nate (:nāt') tr. & intr. (hacer) resonar.

re·sort (rĭ-zôrt') I. intr. ♦ **to r.** to recurrir a II. s. lugar *m* de temporada ♦ **as a last r.** como último recurso.

re·sound (rĭ-zound') intr. *(sound)* resonar; *(fame)* tener resonancia.

re·sound·ing (rĭ-zoun'dĭng) adj. resonante.

re·source (rē'sôrs', rĭ-sôrs') s. recurso, medio.

re·source·ful (rĭ-sôrs'fəl) adj. listo, ingenioso.

re·spect (rĭ-spĕkt') I. tr. *(to esteem)* respetar; *(to concern)* referirse a II. s. respeto ♦ **in all respects** por lo demás • **in every r.** en todos los aspectos • **in that r.** en cuanto a eso • **out of r. for** por respeto a • **to command r.** hacerse respetar • **to pay one's respects** presentar los respetos • **with r.** to, con relación a.

re·spect·a·ble (rĭ-spĕk'tə-bəl) adj. respetable; *(sum)* considerable; *(clothes)* presentable.

re·spect·ful (rĭ-spĕkt'fəl) adj. respetuoso.

re·spect·ing (rĭ-spĕk'tĭng) prep. respecto a.

re·spec·tive (:tĭv) adj. respectivo.

res·pi·ra·tion (rĕs'pə-rā'shən) s. respiración *f.*

res·pi·ra·tor ('-tər) s. respirador *m.*

res·pi·ra·to·ry (rĕs'pər-ə-tôr'ē) adj. respiratorio.

re·spire (rĭ-spīr') tr. & intr. respirar.

res·pite (rĕs'pĭt) s. respiro; DER. suspensión *f.*

re·splen·dent (rĭ-splĕn'dənt) adj. resplandeciente, reluciente.

re·spond (rĭ-spŏnd') intr. responder.

re·spon·dent (rĭ-spŏn'dənt) I. adj. respondedor II. s. respondedor *m*; DER. demandado.

re·sponse (rĭ-spŏns') s. respuesta; *(to a proposal)* acogida; *(to a stimulus)* reacción *f.*

re·spon·si·bil·i·ty (rĭ-spŏn'sə-bĭl'ĭ-tē) s. responsabilidad *f* ♦ **on one's own r.** bajo su propia responsabilidad • **that is not my r.** eso no es asunto mío.

re·spon·si·ble ('-bəl) adj. responsable *(for de, to ante); (position)* de responsabilidad; *(person)* digno de confianza.

re·spon·sive (rĭ-spŏn'sĭv) adj. sensible (to a).

rest¹ (rĕst) I. s. descanso; *(peace)* tranquilidad *f*; *(sleep)* sueño; *(death)* paz *f*; *(respite)* respiro; *(support)* soporte *m*; MÚS. pausa ♦ **at r.** *(asleep)* dormido; *(quiet)* tranquilo; *(motionless)* quieto • **r. home** *(for sick people)* sanatorio; *(for the aged)* asilo de ancianos • **r. room** baño • **to come to r.** pararse • **to lay to r.** enterrar • **to put to r.** olvidarse de • **to take a r.** descansar un rato II. intr. descansar; *(to re-*

main) quedarse; *(to stop)* pararse ♦ **let it r.** déjalo estar • **may he r. in peace** que en paz descanse • **to r. on** *(a support)* apoyarse en; *(to depend)* depender de —tr. dejar descansar; *(to place, lean)* apoyar, descansar *(on, against* en); *(hopes)* poner; *(defense)* basar ♦ **God r. his soul** que Dios le tenga en su gloria • **to r. one's case** DER. terminar el alegato.

rest² I. s. ♦ **the r.** *(remainder)* el resto; *(others)* los demás II. intr. quedarse *<you can r. assured* puedes quedarte tranquilo>.

res·tau·rant (rĕs'tə-ränt') s. restaurante *m.*

res·tau·ra·teur (rĕs'tər-ə-tûr') s. dueño de un restaurante.

rest·ful (rĕst'fəl) adj. quieto, sosegado.

res·ti·tute (rĕs'tĭ-tōōt') tr. restituir.

res·ti·tu·tion ('-tōō'shən) s. restitución *f*; *(compensation)* indemnización *f.*

res·tive (rĕs'tĭv) adj. *(uneasy)* inquieto; *(unruly)* indócil.

rest·less (rĕst'lĭs) adj. inquieto, agitado.

res·to·ra·tion (rĕs'tə-rā'shən) s. restauración *f*; *(of order, relations)* reintegro.

re·stor·a·tive (rĭ-stôr'ə-tĭv) adj. & s. reconstituyente *m*, fortificante *m.*

re·store (rĭ-stôr') tr. *(order, relations)* restablecer; *(painting, monarch)* restaurar.

re·strain (rĭ-strān') tr. *(to repress)* reprimir; *(to limit)* restringir; *(to confine)* encerrar.

re·strained (rĭ-strānd') adj. *(restricted)* restringido; *(reserved)* reservado, discreto.

re·straint (rĭ-strānt') s. *(limitation)* restricción *f*; *(moderation)* moderación *f*; *(self-control)* dominio (de uno mismo).

re·strict (rĭ-strĭkt') tr. restringir, limitar.

re·strict·ed (rĭ-strĭk'tĭd) adj. *(limited)* restringido, limitado; *(access)* prohibido.

re·stric·tion (:shən) s. restricción *f.*

re·stric·tive (:tĭv) adj. restrictivo.

re·sult (rĭ-zŭlt') I. intr. ♦ **to r. from**, in resultar de, en II. s. resultado ♦ **as a r. of** a causa de.

re·sul·tant (rĭ-zŭl'tənt) adj. & s. resultante *f.*

re·sume (rĭ-zōōm') tr. *(talking)* reanudar; *(working)* reasumir ♦ **to r. one's seat** volver a sentarse —intr. *(working)* reanudar; *(talking)* proseguir.

rés·u·mé (rĕz'ə-mā') s. curriculum vitae *m.*

re·sump·tion (rĭ-zŭmp'shən) s. reanudación *f*; *(continuation)* continuación *f.*

re·sur·gence (rĭ-sûr'jəns) s. resurgimiento.

re·sur·gent (:jənt) adj. renaciente.

res·ur·rect (rĕz'ə-rĕkt') tr. & intr. resucitar.

res·ur·rec·tion (:rĕk'shən) s. *(revival)* restablecimiento; RELIG. resurrección *f.*

re·sus·ci·tate (rĭ-sŭs'ĭ-tāt') tr. resucitar.

re·sus·ci·ta·tion ('-tā'shən) s. *(revival)* renacimiento; MED. resucitación *f.*

re·tail (rē'tāl') COM. I. s. venta al por menor *o* al detalle II. adj. & adv. al por menor, al detalle III. tr. & intr. vender(se) al por menor.

re·tail·er (:ər) s. minorista *mf*, detallista *mf.*

re·tail·ing (:lĭng) s. venta al por menor.

re·tain (rĭ-tān') tr. retener; *(lawyer)* contratar; *(sense of humor)* conservar.

re·tain·er (rĭ-tā'nər) s. *(servant)* criado; *(employee)* empleado; *(fee)* anticipo.

re·tal·i·ate (rĭ-tăl'ē-āt') intr. tomar represalias.

re·tal·i·a·tion (-'-ā'shən) s. venganza.

re·tal·i·a·to·ry (rĭ-tăl'ē-ə tôr'ē) adj. vengativo.

re·tard (rĭ-tärd') tr. retardar, retrasar.

re·tard·ant (rĭ-tär'dənt) adj. que retarda.

re·tar·da·tion (rē'tär-dā'shən) s. atraso, retraso; MED. atraso mental.

re·tard·ed (rĭ-tär′dĭd) adj. atrasado.

retch (rĕch) intr. tener náuseas —tr. vomitar.

re·ten·tion (rĭ-tĕn′shən) s. retención f.

re·ten·tive (:tĭv) adj. retentivo.

ret·i·cence (rĕt′ĭ-səns) s. reserva, reticencia.

ret·i·cent (.sənt) adj. reservado, reticente.

ret·i·cle (rĕt′ĭ-kəl) s. retículo.

ret·i·na (rĕt′n-ə) s. [pl. **s** o **-ae**] retina.

ret·i·nue (rĕt′n-ōō′) s. séquito.

re·tire (rĭ-tīr′) I. tr. (to go to bed) acostarse; (to stop working) jubilarse; (to retreat) retirarse —tr. retirar; (employee) jubilar.

re·tired (rĭ-tīrd′) adj. jubilado.

re·tir·ee (ri-tīr′ē′) s. jubilado.

re·tire·ment (rĭ-tīr′mənt) s. jubilación f ◆ **to go into r.** (worker) jubilarse; (artist) retirarse.

re·tir·ing (:ĭng) adj. timido, retraído.

re·tort¹ (rĭ-tôrt′) I. tr. replicar II. s. réplica.

re·tort² s. QUIM. retorta.

re·touch I. tr. (rē-tŭch′) retocar —intr. hacer retoques II. s. (′) retoque m.

re·trace (rē-trās′) tr. trazar de nuevo ◆ **to r. one's steps** volver sobre los pasos.

re·tract (rĭ-trăkt′) tr. & intr. (to disavow) retractar(se); (to draw back) retraer(se).

re·tract·a·ble/·i·ble (rĭ-trăk′tə-bəl) adj. (remark) retractable; (part) retráctil.

re·trac·tion (:shən) s. (disavowal) retractación f; (drawing back) retracción f.

re·tread I. tr. (rē-trĕd′) recauchutar II. s. (′) neumático recauchutado.

re·treat (rĭ-trēt′) I. s. retirada; (signal) retreta; (refuge) refugio; RELIG. retiro ◆ **to beat a hasty r.** FAM. batirse en retirada II. intr. retirarse.

re·trench (rĭ-trĕnch′) intr. hacer economías.

re·tri·al (rē-trī′əl) s. nuevo juicio.

ret·ri·bu·tion (rĕt′rə-byōō′shən) s. castigo.

re·triev·al (rĭ-trē′vəl) s. recuperación f; (in hunting) cobranza ◆ **beyond r.** irreparable.

re·trieve (rĭ-trēv′) tr. recuperar; (damage) reparar; (thought) recordar; (in hunting) cobrar.

re·triev·er (rĭ-trē′vər) s. perro cobrador.

ret·ro·ac·tive (rĕt′rō-ăk′tĭv) adj. retroactivo.

ret·ro·cede (:sēd′) intr. retroceder.

ret·ro·grade (rĕt′rə-grād′) adj. retrógrado.

ret·ro·gress (:grĕs′) intr. degenerar.

ret·ro·gres·sion (:grĕsh′ən) s. regresión f.

ret·ro·rock·et (rĕt′rō-rŏk′ĭt) s. retrocohete m.

ret·ro·spect (rĕt′rə-spĕkt′) s. ◆ **in r.** retrospectivamente.

ret·ro·spec·tion (′-spĕk′shən) s. retrospección f.

ret·ro·spec·tive (:tĭv) adj. retrospectivo.

re·turn (rĭ-tûrn′) I. intr. volver, regresar; (to respond) responder; (to revert) revertir —tr. devolver; (to put back) volver a colocar; (profits, interest) producir; (love, kindness) corresponder; (lost, stolen property) restituir II. s. (coming back) regreso; (giving back) devolución f; (repayment) pago; (response) respuesta; (profits) ganancia; (of income tax) declaración f ◆ **by r. mail** a vuelta de correo • **in r. (for)** (as a reward) en pago; (in exchange) a cambio • **many happy returns** que cumpla(s) muchos años más • **r. address** dirección del remitente • **r. ticket** billete de ida y vuelta • **r. trip** viaje de regreso ◆ pl. (income) ingresos; (in an election) resultados.

re·un·ion (rē-yōōn′yən) s. reunión f.

re·u·nite (rē′yōō nīt′) tr. & intr. reunir(se)

re·us·a·ble (rē-yōō′zə-bəl) adj. que puede volverse a usar.

re·use tr. (rē-yōōz′) volver a usar.

rev (rĕv) FAM. I. s. revolución f (de un motor) II. tr. **-vv-** ◆ **to r. up** acelerar —intr. ◆ **to r. up** (engine) embalarse.

re·val·u·ate (rē-văl′ym̄-āt′) tr. revalorizar.

re·val·ue (:yōō) tr. revalorizar.

re·vamp (rē-vămp′) tr. renovar, modernizar.

re·veal (rĭ-vēl′) tr. revelar.

rev·eil·le (rĕv′ə-lē) s. MIL. diana.

rev·el (rĕv′əl) I. intr. jaranear ◆ **to r. in** gozar de II. s. ◆ pl. jarana, juerga.

rev·e·la·tion (rĕv′ə-lā′shən) s. revelación f.

rev·el·ry (rĕv′əl-rē) s. jarana, juerga.

re·venge (rĭ-vĕnj′) I. tr. vengar, vengarse de II. s. venganza ◆ **to take r.** vengarse (on de).

rev·e·nue (rĕv′ə-nōō′) s. ingreso, renta; (of a government) rentas públicas.

re·ver·ber·ate (rĭ-vûr′bə-rāt′) intr. resonar.

re·ver·ber·a·tion (-′-rā′shən) s. eco.

re·vere (rĭ-vîr′) tr. reverenciar, venerar.

rev·er·ence (rĕv′ər-əns) I. s. reverencia ◆ **to hold in r.** reverenciar II. tr. reverenciar.

rev·er·end (:ənd) adj. & s. reverendo.

rev·er·ent (:ənt) adj. reverente.

rev·er·en·tial (rĕv′ə-rĕn′shəl) adj. reverencial.

rev·er·ie (rĕv′ə-rē) s. ensueño.

re·ver·sal (rĭ-vûr′səl) s. (of direction, opinion) cambio; (setback) revés m; DER. revocación f.

re·verse (rĭ-vûrs′) I. adj. (opposite) opuesto, contrario, (inverse) inverso <in r. order en orden inverso> ◆ **the r. side** (of cloth) revés, vuelta; (of a form) dorso; (of a page, coin) reverso II. s. (opposite) lo opuesto, lo contrario; (setback) revés m; AUTO. marcha atrás ◆ **just the r.** todo lo contrario • **to put in(to) r.** poner en marcha atrás III. tr. (order) invertir; (to turn inside out) volver al revés; (to transpose) transponer; (policy, direction) cambiar; DER. revocar —intr. AUTO. dar marcha atrás.

re·vers·i·bil·i·ty (′-vûr′sə-bĭl′ĭ-tē) s. reversibilidad f.

re·vers·i·ble (rĭ-vûr′sə-bəl) adj. reversible.

re·ver·sion (rĭ-vûr′zhən) s. reversión f.

re·vert (rĭ-vûrt′) intr. ◆ **to r. to** (to return to) volver a; DER. revertir a.

re·view (rĭ-vyōō′) I. tr. (volver a) examinar; (lesson, text) repasar; (film, book) reseñar, criticar; DER. revisar; MIL. pasar revista a —intr. (to study) repasar (for para); (to write reviews) escribir críticas II. s. examen m; (of lesson) repaso; (critique) crítica; (report) análisis m; MIL., PERIOD. revista; DER. revisión f.

re·view·er (:ər) s. crítico.

re·vile (rĭ-vīl′) tr. injuriar, insultar.

re·vise (rĭ-vīz′) tr. (to correct) revisar, corregir; (to modify) modificar.

re·vi·sion (rĭ-vĭzh′ən) s. corrección f; (modification) modificación f; (of views) revisión f.

re·vi·sion·ist (:ə-nĭst) s. revisionista mf.

re·vis·it (rē-vĭz′ĭt) tr. visitar de nuevo.

re·vi·tal·ize (rē-vīt′l-īz′) tr. revitalizar.

re·viv·al (rĭ-vī′vəl) s. resurgimiento f; ECON. reactivación f; (of interest) renacimiento f; TEAT. reposición f ◆ **r. meeting** asamblea evangelista.

re·vive (rĭ-vīv′) tr. resucitar; (spirits) reanimar; (custom) restablecer; (interest) renovar; (economy) reactivar; (hopes) despertar; (play) reponer —intr. resucitar; (to feel better) reanimarse, volver en sí.

rev·o·ca·ble (rĕv′ə-kə-bəl) adj. revocable.

re·voke (rĭ-vōk′) tr. revocar.

re·volt (rĭ-vōlt') I. intr. rebelarse —tr.. repugnar II. s. rebelión *f* ♦ **in r.** en rebeldía.

re·volt·ing (rĭ-vōl'tĭng) adj. repugnante.

rev·o·lu·tion (rĕv'ə-lōō'shən) s. revolución *f*; *(around axis)* rotación *f*.

rev·o·lu·tion·ar·y (:sha-nĕr'ē) adj. & s. revolucionario.

rev·o·lu·tion·ize (:nīz') tr. revolucionar.

re·volve (rĭ-vōlv') tr. hacer girar —intr. girar ♦ **to r. around** girar alrededor de • **to r. on** girar sobre.

re·volv·er (rĭ-vōl'vər) s. revólver *m*.

re·vue (rĭ-vyōō') s. TEAT. revista.

re·vul·sion (rĭ-vŭl'shən) s. repugnancia, asco.

re·ward (rĭ-wôrd') I. s. recompensa, premio II. tr. recompensar, premiar.

re·ward·ing (rĭ-wôr'dĭng) adj. *(remunerative)* remunerador; *(useful)* provechoso, útil.

re·wind (rē-wīnd') tr. **-wound** rebobinar.

re·word (rē-wûrd') tr. expresar con otras palabras.

re·work (rē-wûrk') tr. revisar (discurso, obra).

re·write I. tr. (rē-rīt') **-wrote, -written** escribir de nuevo II. s. (' ') ♦ **to do a r.** escribir de nuevo.

rhap·so·dize (răp'sə-dīz') intr. ♦ **to r. about** *o* **over** poner por las nubes.

rhap·so·dy (:dē) s. rapsodia ♦ **to go into rhapsodies over** *o* **about** poner por las nubes.

rhet·o·ric (rĕt'ər-ĭk) s. retórica.

rhe·tor·i·cal (rĭ-tôr'ĭ-kəl) adj. retórico.

rheum (rōōm) s. lagaña.

rheu·mat·ic (rōō-mát'ĭk) adj. & s. reumático ♦ **r. fever** fiebre reumática.

rheu·ma·tism (rōō'mə-tĭz'əm) s. reumatismo.

rheu·ma·toid arthritis (:toid') s. reúma *m* articular.

rhine·stone (rīn'stōn') s. diamante falso.

rhi·noc·er·os (rī-nŏs'ər-əs) s. [pl. inv. *o* **es**] rinoceronte *m*.

rho·do·den·dron (rō'də-dĕn'drən) s. rododendro.

rhom·bus (rŏm'bəs) s. [pl. **es** *o* **-bi**] rombo.

rhu·barb (rōō'bärb') s. BOT. ruibarbo; JER. *(quarrel)* riña.

rhyme (rīm) I. s. rima ♦ **without r. or reason** a tontas y a locas II. intr. & tr. rimar.

rhythm (rĭth'əm) s. ritmo.

rhyth·mic/mi·cal (rĭth'mĭk) adj. rítmico.

rib (rĭb) I. s. costilla; BOT. nervio; *(of an umbrella)* varilla; *(in fabric)* cordoncillo II. tr. **-bb-** proveer de costillas; JER. *(to tease)* tomar el pelo a.

rib·ald (rĭb'əld) adj. verde, obsceno.

rib·bing (rĭb'ĭng) s. JER. tomadura de pelo.

rib·bon (rĭb'ən) s. cinta; MIL. galón *m* ♦ **to tear to ribbons** hacer jirones.

rice (rīs) s. arroz *m* ♦ **r. field** *o* **paddy** arrozal.

rich (rĭch) adj. rico; *(food)* con mucha (materia) grasa; *(voice)* potente; *(color)* vivo; FAM. *(amusing)* gracioso ♦ **to be r. in** abundar en • **to get r.** hacerse rico.

rich·es ('ĭz) s.pl. riquezas.

rick·et·y (rĭk'ĭ-tē) adj. **-i-** *(shaky)* desvencijado; MED. raquítico.

ric·o·chet (rĭk'ə-shā') I. intr. rebotar II. s. rebote *m*.

rid (rĭd) tr. **rid(ded), -dding** librar ♦ **to be r. of** estar libre de • **to r. oneself of** librarse de.

rid·dance (:ns) s. liberación *f* ♦ **good r.!** ¡al fin me lo quité de encima!

rid·dle¹ (rĭd'l) tr. acribillar; FIG. llenar.

rid·dle² s. *(puzzle)* acertijo; *(mystery)* enigma *m* ♦ **to talk in riddles** hablar en clave.

ride (rīd) I. intr. **rode, ridden** montar; *(to move)* andar; *(to travel)* ir, viajar; *(in a car)* pasearse; *(to float)* flotar ♦ **to be riding high** estar en plena forma • **to let r.** dejar tranquilo • **to r. on** depender de • **to r. up** *(clothing)* subirse —tr. *(a horse)* montar a; *(a bicycle)* montar en; *(to travel over)* recorrer; *(to tease)* ridiculizar ♦ **to r. out** aguantar, soportar II. s. *(on horse, car)* paseo; *(trip)* viaje *m*; *(tour)* vuelta; *(means for transportation)* medio de transporte ♦ **to go for a r.** dar un paseo • **to take for a r.** JER. dar gato por liebre.

rid·er (rī'dər) s. *(horse)* jinete *m*; *(bicycle)* ciclista *mf*; *(passenger)* viajero; DER. *(clause)* añadida.

ridge (rĭj) s. *(of earth)* lomo; *(of hill)* cresta; *(of hills)* cordillera; *(of roof)* caballete *m*.

rid·i·cule (rĭd'ĭ-kyōōl') I. s. ridículo ♦ **object of r.** blanco de burlas II. tr. ridiculizar, poner en ridículo.

ri·dic·u·lous (rĭ-dĭk'yə-ləs) adj. ridículo.

rife (rīf) adj. corriente ♦ **r. with** repleto de.

riff·raff (rĭf'răf') s. gentuza, chusma.

ri·fle¹ (rī'fəl) I. s. rifle *m*; MIL. fusil *m* ♦ **r. range** campo de tiro ♦ **to rayar.

ri·fle² tr. *(to ransack)* saquear.

rift (rĭft) s. *(in a friendship)* ruptura; *(in a political party)* escisión *f*; GEOL. falla.

rig (rĭg) I. tr. **-gg-** *(to equip)* equipar; *(an election)* amañar; *(a contest)* arreglar; MARÍT. aparejar ♦ **the fight was rigged** hubo tongo en el combate • **to be rigged out as,** in vestirse de, con • **to r. up** preparar rápidamente II. s. *(gear)* equipo; FAM. *(truck)* camión *m*; *(outfit)* traje *m*; MARÍT. aparejo ♦ **oil r.** torre de perforación.

rig·ging (:ĭng) s. MARÍT. aparejo, jarcia.

right (rīt) I. adj. *(just, fair)* justo; *(ethical)* bueno, correcto; *(correct)* correcto; *(exact)* exacto (palabra, hora); *(appropriate)* más indicado; *(ideal)* ideal; *(proper)* debido <**in its r. place** en su debido sitio>; *(conditions)* bueno, favorable; *(in order)* en orden; *(opposite the left)* derecho; POL. de derecha, derechista; GEOM. recto ♦ **all r.** *(fine)* bastante bien; *(reliable)* de confianza; *(well)* bien <**are you all r.?** ¿te encuentras bien?> • **all r.?** ¿está bien? • **all r.!** ¡perfecto! • **is that r.?** ¿de verdad? • **it's all r. by** *o* **with me** estoy de acuerdo • **it's just not r.!** ¡no hay derecho! • **r.!** *o* **that's r.!** ¡eso es! • **r. angle** ángulo recto • **r. wing** POL. derecha • **to be r.** tener razón • **to feel r.** *(well)* sentirse bien; *(pleasurable)* dar gusto (a uno) • **to put r.** arreglar • **to turn out all r.** salir bien II. s. *(justice)* justicia; *(good)* (lo) bueno, bien *m*; *(side, hand)* derecha; *(in boxing)* derechazo; *(claim)* derecho <**the r. to vote** el derecho al voto>; POL. derecha ♦ **by rights** de derecho • **in its own r.** de por sí • **in one's own r.** por derecho propio • **r. of way** derecho de paso • **to be in the r.** tener razón • **to be within one's rights** estar uno en su derecho • **to have a r.** to tener derecho a • **to make a r.** doblar a la derecha III. adv. *(directly)* derecho, directamente <**they came r. home** vinieron derecho a casa>; *(well, correctly)* bien <**it doesn't work r.** no funciona bien>; *(exactly)* exactamente, justo <**r. at the end** justo al final>; *(squarely)* en pleno; *(to the

right) a la derecha; FAM. *(very)* muy, bien ♦ **go r. ahead** siga, continúe • **if I remember r.** si mal no recuerdo • **r. and left** a diestra y siniestra • **r. behind** justo detrás • **r. face!** ¡derecha! • **r. off** inmediatamente • **r. now** ahora mismo • **r. (over) here, there** aquí, ahí mismo • **r. through** *(continuously)* sin parar; *(from side to side)* de lado a lado • **to do r. by** portarse bien con • **to get r.** *(to do)* hacer bien; *(to understand)* entender bien; *(to answer)* contestar bien • **to go r. on . . .** seguir . . . como si nada IV. tr. & intr. enderezar(se).

right·eous (rī′chəs) adj. *(morally right)* recto; *(honest)* honrado; *(just)* justo.

right·ful (rīt′fəl) adj. legítimo.

right-hand (:hănd′) adj. a la derecha ♦ **on the r. side** al lado derecho • **r. man** brazo derecho.

right-hand·ed (:hăn′dĭd) adj. que usa la mano derecha; *(tool)* para la mano derecha.

right·ly (:lē) adv. correctamente; *(properly)* con derecho • **r. so** con razón • **r. or wrongly** con razón o sin ella, mal que bien.

rig·id (rĭj′ĭd) adj. rígido.

ri·gid·i·ty (rĭ-jĭd′ĭ-tē) s. rigidez *f.*

rig·ma·role (rĭg′mə-rōl′) s. galimatías *m.*

rig·or (rĭg′ər) s. rigor *m.*

rig·or·ous (:əs) adj. riguroso.

rile (rīl) tr. irritar.

rim (rĭm) I. s. borde *m;* *(coin)* canto; *(barrel)* aro; *(wheel)* llanta II. tr. **-mm-** bordear.

rind (rīnd) s. *(fruits)* cáscara; *(cheese)* corteza.

ring¹ (rĭng) I. s. anillo; *(hoop)* aro, argolla; *(circle)* círculo; *(on finger)* anillo, sortija; *(at circus)* pista; *(for bullfights)* ruedo; *(in boxing)* ring *m,* cuadrilátero; *(of criminals)* organización *f;* *(of spies)* red *f;* MEC. aro; QUÍM. cadena ♦ **key r.** llavero II. tr. *(to encircle)* rodear; *(to shape)* anillar.

ing¹ I. intr. **rang, rung** *(bells)* sonar, repicar; *(telephone, doorbell)* sonar; *(to jingle)* tintinear; *(to resound)* resonar; *(ears)* zumbar • **to r. false, true** sonar a falso, cierto • **to r. out** oírse —tr. *(a bell, buzzer)* tocar; *(to telephone)* llamar, telefonear; *(the hour)* dar ♦ **to r. up** G.B. telefonear II. s. *(sound)* sonido *(metálico);* *(of telephone, buzzer, voice)* timbre *m;* *(of bell)* tañido; *(tinkle)* tintineo; *(telephone call)* telefonazo; *(quality)* tono *<a suspicious r.* un tono sospechoso> ♦ **it has a familiar r.** me suena.

ring·ing (:ĭng) I. adj. sonoro, resonante II. s. *(of bells)* tañido; *(of buzzer, alarm)* toque *m;* *(of phone)* timbre *m;* *(in the ears)* zumbido.

ring·lead·er (:lē′dər) s. cabecilla *m.*

ring·let (:lĭt) s. bucle *m,* rizo.

ring·mas·ter (:măs′tər) s. maestro de ceremonias.

ring·worm (:wûrm′) s. tiña.

rink (rĭngk) s. pista ♦ **ice-skating, roller-skating r.** pista de hielo, patinaje.

rinse (rĭns) I. tr. enjuagar II. s. enjuague *m.*

ri·ot (rī′ət) I. s. *(disturbance)* disturbio, tumulto; *(insurrection)* motín *m,* alboroto; *(profusion)* derroche *m* ♦ **r. act** ley de orden público • **r. police** guardia de asalto • **to r.** FAM. ser divertidísima II. intr. alborotarse, amotinarse.

ri·ot·er (rī′ə-tər) s. alborotador *m.*

ri·ot·ous (:əs) adj. *(living)* desenfrenado; *(crowd)* alborotador; *(growth)* exuberante.

rip (rĭp) I. tr. **-pp-** rasgar, desgarrar ♦ **to r. apart** desgarrar • **to r. off** arrancar, quitar; JER.

(to rob) robar, limpiar • **to r. open** abrir de un tirón • **to r. out** arrancar; *(a seam)* descoser • **to r. up** desgarrar, destrozar —intr. rasgarse, desgarrarse; *(seam)* descoserse ♦ **to r. by** ir volando • **to r. into** regañar II. s. *(tear)* rasgón *m,* desgarrón *m;* *(split seam)* descosido ♦ **r. tide** corriente turbulenta.

rip·cord (:kôrd′) s. cuerda de apertura.

ripe (rīp) adj. maduro; *(cheese)* hecho; *(age)* avanzado ♦ **r. for** listo para • **the time is r. for** ha llegado el momento de.

rip·en (rī′pən) tr. & intr. madurar.

rip-off (rĭp′ôf′) s. FAM. *(swindle)* timo; *(imitation)* imitación *f* • **r. artist** engañador.

rip·ple (rĭp′əl) I. tr. & intr. *(water)* rizarse; *(wheat)* ondular II. s. *(small wave)* rizo, onda; *(of laughter)* carcajada general.

rise (rīz) I. intr. **rose, risen** *(person, wind, dough)* levantarse; *(buildings, hills, spirits)* elevarse; *(temperature, prices, land)* subir; *(in rank, position)* ascender; *(water level)* crecer; *(voice)* alzarse; *(sun)* salir; *(pressure)* aumentar; *(stock market)* estar en alza; *(from the dead)* resucitar; *(in rebellion)* sublevarse ♦ **to r. above** *(to overcome)* sobreponerse a; *(to loom over)* surgir • **to r. to one's feet** ponerse de pie • **to r. to power** subir al poder • **to r. to the surface** salir a la superficie II. s. *(ascension)* subida, ascensión *f;* *(elevation)* elevación *f;* *(of prices, temperature, land)* subida; *(in water level)* crecida; *(of value, salary)* aumento; *(in rank)* ascenso; *(in pressure, rate, pitch)* elevación; *(of sun, moon)* salida; COM. alza *f* ♦ **r. and fall** MARÍT. flujo y reflujo; HIST. grandeza y decadencia • **to give r. to** ocasionar, dar lugar a.

ris·er (rī′zər) s. ♦ **early r.** madrugador • **late r.** dormilón.

ris·ing (rī′zĭng) adj. ascendente; *(tide, anger)* creciente; *(promising)* prometedor; *(sun, moon)* naciente; *(prices, temperature)* que sube.

risk (rĭsk) I. s. riesgo II. tr. arriesgarse a.

risk·y (rĭs′kē) adj. arriesgado.

ris·qué (rĭ-skā′) adj. escabroso.

rite (rīt) s. rito ♦ **funeral rites** exequias • **last rites** extremaunción.

rit·u·al (rĭch′ōo-əl) s. ritual *m.*

rit·u·al·is·tic (′-ə-lĭs′tĭk) adj. ritualista.

ritz·y (rĭt′sē) adj. JER. lujoso.

ri·val (rī′vəl) I. adj. & s. rival *m* II. tr. rivalizar con.

ri·val·ry (:rē) s. rivalidad *f.*

riv·er (rĭv′ər) s. río.

riv·er·bank (:băngk′) s. ribera, orilla.

riv·er·bed (:bĕd′) s. cauce *m.*

riv·er·boat (:bōt′) s. barco, embarcación *f* de río.

riv·er·side (:sīd′) s. ribera, orilla.

riv·et (rĭv′ĭt) I. s. roblón *m* II. tr. *(attention)* cautivar; *(eyes)* fijar; MAQ. remachar.

roach¹ (rōch) s. [pl. inv. o **es**] ICT. gobio.

roach² s. ENTOM. cucaracha.

road (rōd) s. *(highway)* carretera; *(route, path)* camino; *(way, track)* vía ♦ **r. map** mapa de carreteras • **to be on the r.** TEAT. estar de gira • **to hit the r.** FAM. largarse.

road·bed (:bĕd′) s. F.C. terraplén *m.*

road·block (:blŏk′) s. *(by police, military)* barricada; FIG. obstáculo, impedimento.

road·house (:hous′) s. taberna.

road·side (:sīd′) s. borde *m* de la carretera.

road·way (:wā′) s. carretera.

roam (rōm) intr. & tr. vagar (por).

roan (rōn) adj. & s. (caballo) ruano.

roar (rōr) I. intr. (people) vociferar; (lion) rugir; (bull, wind) bramar ♦ **to r. by** o **past** pasar zumbando • **to r. with laughter** reírse a carcajadas —tr. decir a gritos, vociferar II. s. rugido, bramido; (of traffic) estruendo; (of the crowd) clamor m; (of laughter) carcajada.

roast (rōst) I. tr. (meat) asar; (coffee, nuts) tostar; FAM. (to criticize) poner por los suelos —intr. asarse, tostarse; (to feel hot) asarse II. s. asado; (cut) carne f para asar III. adj. asado ♦ **r. beef** rosbif.

roast·er (rō′stər) s. asador m.

rob (rŏb) tr. & intr. **-bb-** robar ♦ **to r. of** (reputation) quitar, robar; (strength) dejar sin.

rob·ber (:ər) s. (thief) ladrón m; (highwayman) salteador m; (bandit) bandido.

rob·ber·y (:ə-rē) s. robo.

robe (rōb) s. (judge) toga; (priest) sotana; (bathrobe) bata ♦ pl. vestiduras.

rob·in (rŏb′ĭn) s. tordo norteamericano; (Old World) petirrojo.

ro·bot (rō′bət, :bŏt′) s. robot m, autómata m.

ro·bot·ics (rō-bŏt′ĭks) s. técnica de los robots.

ro·bust (rō-bŭst′) adj. robusto, fuerte.

rock[1] (rŏk) s. roca; (stone) piedra; (cliff, crag) peñasco, peña; FIG. base f, soporte m; JER. diamante m ♦ **on the rocks** FAM. con hielo • **bottom** fondo • **r. salt** sal gema • **to be on the rocks** FAM. andar mal.

rock[2] I. intr. (to sway) balancearse; (to shake) estremecerse —tr. (baby, cradle) mecer; (to shake) sacudir; (to upset) dejar estupefacto ♦ **don't r. the boat** JER. deja las cosas como están • **to r. to sleep** mecer II. s. balanceo; MÚS. rock 'n' roll m.

rock·er (′ər) s. (chair) mecedora; (curved piece) arco ♦ **to be off one's r.** JER. estar chalado.

rock·et (rŏk′ĭt) I. s. cohete m; (weapon) proyectil m II. intr. subir rápidamente.

rock·et·ry (:ĭ-trē) s. técnica de los cohetes.

rock·ing (rŏk′ĭng) I. adj. ♦ **r. chair** mecedora • **r. horse** caballito de balancín II. s. balanceo.

rock 'n' roll (rŏk′ən-rōl′) s. rock 'n' roll m.

rock·y[1] (rŏk′ē) adj. **-i-** (stony) rocoso; FIG. difícil.

rock·y[2] adj. **-i-** (shaky) bamboleante, débil.

rod (rŏd) s. (stick) vara; (staff) bastón m; MEC. barra; JER. (pistol) pistolón m ♦ **divining r.** varita adivinatoria • **piston r.** biela.

rode (rōd) cf. **ride.**

ro·dent (rōd′nt) adj. & s. roedor m.

ro·de·o (rō′dē-ō′, rō-dā′ō) s. rodeo.

roe[1] (rō) s. (fish eggs) hueva.

roe[2] s. (deer) corzo.

rogue (rōg) s. pícaro.

role o **rôle** (rōl) s. papel m.

roll (rōl) I. intr. rodar; (to wallow) revolcarse; (prairie, hills) ondular; (thunder) retumbar; (drum) redoblar; AVIA., MARÍT. balancearse ♦ **to get rolling** FAM. ponerse en marcha • **to r. by** o **on** pasar —tr. **to r. down** (tears) correr por; (ball) rodar por, bajar rodando por • **to r. in** llegar en abundancia • **to r. off** caerse rodando • **to r. over** dar una vuelta —tr. (hacer) rodar; (to wheel) empujar; (a cigarette) liar; CINEM. rodar ♦ **rolling pin** rodillo • **to r. back** bajar, reducir • **to r. down** (to push) empujar por; (car windows) bajar • **to r. into** envolver en • **to r. out** (a map, scroll) desenrollar; (dough) extender con el rodillo • **to r. over** (object) voltear; (to destroy) derribar • **to r. up** (paper, rug) enrollar; (sleeves) arremangar II. s. (of paper, film) rollo; (of plane, boat) balanceo; (of the ocean) oleaje m; (of thunder) retumbo; (of money) fajo; (bread) bollo, panecillo ♦ **drum r.** redoble • **r. call** acto de pasar lista • **to call the r.** pasar lista ♦ pl. (records) archivos; (register) listas.

roll·er (rō′lər) s. (cylinder) rodillo; (small wheel) ruedecilla; (for the hair) rulo ♦ **r. coaster** montaña rusa • **r. skate** patín de ruedas.

rol·lick·ing (rŏl′ĭ-kĭng) adj. animado.

ro·ly·po·ly (rō′lē-pō′lē) adj. rechoncho.

Ro·man numeral (rō′mən) s. número romano.

Roman Catholic adj. & s. católico romano.

ro·mance (rō-măns′, ′′) I. s. romance m; (novel) novela romántica; (spirit) lo romántico; (love affair) amores m; (adventure) aventura II. tr. & intr. FAM. galantear.

ro·man·tic (rō-măn′tĭk) adj. & s. romántico.

ro·man·ti·cize (:ǐ-sīz′) tr. hacer romántico —intr. tener ideas románticas.

romp (rŏmp) I. intr. juguetear, retozar II. s. (play) retozo; (victory) triunfo fácil.

roof (rōōf, rŏŏf) I. s. techo, tejado; (of the mouth) paladar m ♦ **to hit the r.** poner el grito en el cielo II. tr. techar.

roof·top (′tŏp′) s. tejado.

rook[1] (rŏŏk) I. s. ORNIT. grajo II. tr. JER. timar.

rook[2] s. (chess) torre f.

rook·ie (rŏŏk′ē) s. JER. (recruit) recluta mf; (in sports, police) novato.

room (rōōm, rŏŏm) I. s. habitación f, cuarto; (for meetings) sala; (space, a spot) sitio ♦ **r. and board** pensión completa • **to make r. for** hacer sitio para • **to take up r.** ocupar sitio ♦ pl. alojamiento II. intr. alojarse ♦ **to r. together** o **with** compartir la habitación (con) • **rooming house** pensión.

room·er (′ər) s. huésped m.

room·mate (:māt′) s. compañero de cuarto.

room·y (:ē) adj. **-i-** espacioso, amplio.

roost (rōōst) I. s. (perch) percha, palo; (coop) gallinero II. intr. posarse para dormir ♦ **to rule the r.** llevar la voz cantante.

roost·er (rōō′stər) s. gallo.

root[1] (rōōt, rŏŏt) I. s. raíz f ♦ **r. canal** ODONT. empaste de la raíz • **r. cellar** bodega en la que se guardan legumbres • **to be at the r. of** ser la raíz de • **to put down roots** radicarse • **to take r.** echar raíces II. intr. echar raíces —tr. arraigar ♦ **to r. out** extirpar.

root[2] tr. (to dig) hocicar —intr. (to rummage) rebuscar.

root[3] intr. ♦ **to r. for** animar a.

rope (rōp) I. s. soga, cuerda; (lasso) lazo ♦ **at the end of one's r.** en un aprieto • **to know the ropes** estar al tanto (de las cosas) • **to learn the ropes** ponerse al tanto II. tr. (to tie) amarrar, atar; (to lasso) coger con lazo ♦ **to r. in** embaucar • **to r. off** acordonar.

rose[1] (rōz) I. s. rosa ♦ **r. garden** rosaleda • **r. water** agua de rosas • **to come up roses** salir bien II. adj. (de color) rosa.

rose[2] (rōz) cf. **rise.**

ro·sé (rō-zā′) s. rosado, clarete m.

rose·bud (rōz′bŭd′) s. capullo.

rose·bush (:bŏŏsh′) s. rosal m.

rose·mar·y (:mĕr′ē) s. romero.

ro·sette (rō-zĕt′) s. rosa, rosetón m.

rose·wood (rōz′wŏŏd′) s. palisandro.

ros·in (rŏz′ĭn) s. colofonia.

ros·ter (rŏs′tər) s. lista, registro.

ros·trum (rŏs′trəm) s. [pl. **s** o **-tra**] estrado.

ros·y (rō'zē) adj. **-i-** *(pink)* rosado; *(skin)* sonrosado; *(future)* prometedor; *(view)* optimista.

rot (rŏt) I. tr. & intr. **-tt-** pudrir(se) II. s. putrefacción f; *(substance)* podredumbre f; *(nonsense)* tontería.

ro·ta·ry (rō'tə-rē) I. adj. rotatorio II. s. *(device)* rotativa; *(traffic circle)* glorieta circular.

ro·tate (rō'tāt') tr. & intr. (hacer) girar, *(crops, wheels)* alternar; *(workers)* turnarse.

ro·ta·tion (rō-tā'shən) s. *(turning)* giro, rotación f; *(turn)* revolución f.

rote (rōt) s. rutina ♦ **by r.** por repetición.

ro·tis·ser·ie (rō-tĭs'ə-rē) s. CUL. asador m.

ro·tor (rō'tər) s. rotor m.

rot·ten (rŏt'n) adj. **-er, -est** *(meat, fruit)* estropeado; *(wood)* carcomido; *(smell, egg)* podrido; *(trick)* malo; *(weather)* pésimo.

ro·tund (rō-tŭnd') adj. rotundo.

ro·tun·da (rō-tŭn'də) s. rotonda.

rou·ble (rū'bəl) s. FIN. rublo.

rouge (rōōzh) s. colorete m.

rough (rŭf) I. adj. *(not smooth)* áspero; *(terrain)* accidentado; *(coarse)* basto, burdo; *(seas)* agitado; *(stormy)* tempestuoso; *(trying)* difícil, malo; *(rowdy)* alborotador; *(rude)* tosco; *(work)* duro; *(idea, guess)* aproximado ♦ **r draft** borrador ♦ **r. sketch** boceto ♦ **to be r. on** *(person)* tratar con dureza; *(situation)* ser una mala suerte para II. s. terreno accidentado ♦ **in the r.** JOY. en bruto III. tr. poner áspero ♦ **to r. it** vivir sin comodidades ♦ **to r. out** bosquejar ♦ **to r. up** *(hair, feathers)* erizar, arrugar; *(someone)* darle una paliza a IV. adv. rudamente, toscamente ♦ **to play r.** jugar duro.

rough·age (:ĭj) s. alimento difícil de digerir que contribuye al movimiento peristáltico.

rough·en (:ən) tr. & intr. poner áspero.

rough·house (:hous') intr. armar una trifulca.

rou·lette (rōō-lĕt') s. ruleta.

round (round) I. adj. redondo; *(complete)* completo, bueno; *(sum)* considerable; *(voice, tone)* sonoro; *(plump)* regordete ♦ **r. trip** viaje de ida y vuelta II. s. *(circle)* círculo; *(of a ladder)* peldaño; *(series)* serie f; *(of talks, drinks)* ronda; *(of applause)* salva; ARM. descarga f; DEP. *(of golf)* partido; *(in boxing)* asalto ♦ **to make one's rounds** *(police, patrol)* hacer la ronda, *(salesperson)* hacer el recorrido, *(doctor)* hacer las visitas III. tr. redondear; *(corner)* doblar, dar la vuelta a ♦ **to r. off** *(object, number)* redondear; *(to finish off)* rematar ♦ **to r. out** completar ♦ **to r. up** *(animals)* acorralar, rodear; *(people)* reunir IV. adv. *(around)* alrededor, *(everywhere)* por todas partes; *(here and there)* aquí y allá ♦ **all r.** para todos ♦ **all year r.** durante todo el año ♦ **r. about** a eso de ♦ **r. and r.** dando vueltas a la redonda V. prep. *(the world)* alrededor de; *(the corner)* a la vuelta de.

round·a·bout (round'ə-bout') adj. indirecto, con rodeos ♦ **to take a r. route** dar un rodeo.

round·ed (:ĭd) adj. redondo, esférico.

round·up (round'ŭp') s. *(of cattle)* rodeo; *(by the police)* redada; *(of news)* resumen m.

rouse (rouz) tr. & intr. despertar(se).

rous·ing (rou'zĭng) adj. conmovedor, animado.

roust (roust) tr. despertar, suscitar.

rout¹ (rout) I. s. *(retreat)* desbandada; *(defeat)* derrota completa II. tr. derrotar.

rout² tr. ♦ **to r. out** *(from hiding)* hacer salir; *(to dig up)* hocicar; *(to uncover)* descubrir.

route (rōōt, rout) I. s. *(course)* ruta, vía; *(road)* carretera; *(for delivery)* recorrido; *(means)* ca-

mino II. tr. mandar, encaminar.

rou·tine (rōō-tēn') I. s. rutina; TEAT. número II. adj. rutinario, habitual.

rove (rōv) intr. vagar, errar.

rov·er (rō'vər) s. vagabundo.

row¹ (rō) s. línea, fila ♦ **in a r.** *(in succession)* seguidos; *(in a line)* en fila ♦ **in rows** en filas ♦ **r. house** casa en hilera.

row² (rō) intr. remar —tr. *(a boat)* conducir remando; *(passengers)* llevar.

row³ (rou) s. *(quarrel)* pelea; *(noise)* jaleo.

row·boat (rō'bōt') s. bote m de remos.

row·dy (rou'dē) I. s. camorrista mf, pendenciero II. adj. **-i-** pendenciero, camorrista.

roy·al (roi'əl) adj. real.

roy·al·ist (:ə-lĭst) s. monárquico, realista mf.

roy·al·ty (:əl-tē) s. familia real; *(rank, power)* realeza; *(payment)* derechos de autor.

rub (rŭb) I. tr. **-bb-** frotar *(against* contra); *(to massage)* friccionar, dar friegas; *(one's hands)* frotarse; *(to irritate)* irritar; *(to chafe)* rozar; *(to polish)* limpiar frotando; *(to scour)* fregar ♦ **to r. down** friccionar ♦ **to r. elbows with** codearse con ♦ **to r. in u on** frotar con ♦ **to r. it in** FAM. machacar ♦ **to r. off** quitar frotando ♦ **to r. off on** *(good qualities)* transmitírsele a uno; *(bad qualities)* pegársele a uno ♦ **to r. the wrong way** irritar, molestar —intr. rozar ♦ **to r, off** quitarse frotando ♦ **to r. (up) against** rozar contra II. s. *(rubbing)* frotamiento; *(massage)* fricción f; *(difficulty)* dificultad f.

rub·ber (rŭb'ər) s. caucho; *(synthetic)* goma; *(eraser)* goma de borrar ♦ **r. band** goma ♦ **r. stamp** sello de goma; *(approval)* aprobación automática.

rub·ber·ize (:ə-rīz') tr. cauchutar.

rub·ber·neck (rŭb'ər-nĕk') intr. curiosear.

rub·ber·stamp ('-stămp') tr. aprobar automáticamente.

rub·ber·y (rŭb'ə-rē) adj. elástico.

rub·bish (rŭb'ĭsh) s. basura; *(nonsense)* tonterías.

rub·ble (rŭb'əl) s. escombros.

rub·down (rŭb'doun') s. masaje m.

rube (rōōb) s. JER. patán m, palurdo.

ru·bel·la (rōō-bĕl'ə) s. rubéola.

ru·bric (rōō'brĭk) s. rúbrica.

ru·by (rōō'bē) s. rubí m.

ruck·sack (rŭk'sāk') s. mochila.

ruck·us (rŭk'əs) s. FAM. trifulca, jaleo.

rud·der (rŭd'ər) s. timón m.

rud·dy (rŭd'ē) adj. **-i-** *(healthy)* rubicundo; G.B., FAM. maldito.

rude (rōōd) adj. *(crude)* crudo, rudo; *(humble)* humilde; *(discourteous)* grosero, descortés.

ru·di·ment (rōō'də-mənt) s. rudimento.

ru·di·men·ta·ry ('-mĕn'tə-rē) adj. rudimentario.

rue¹ (rōō) tr. arrepentirse de, lamentar.

rue² s. BOT. ruda.

rue·ful (:fəl) adj. pesaroso.

ruff (rŭf) s. *(collar)* gola; ZOOL. collar m.

ruf·fi·an (rŭf'ē-ən) s. rufián m.

ruf·fle (rŭf'əl) I. s. volante m, frunce m II. tr. *(to disturb)* agitar; *(cloth)* plegar; *(feathers)* erizar; *(a person)* aturdir ♦ **to get ruffled** fastidiarse.

rug (rŭg) s. alfombra.

rug·ged (rŭg'ĭd) adj. *(terrain)* escabroso; *(mountains)* escarpado; *(features)* duro; *(climate)* riguroso; *(hardy)* robusto.

ru·in (rōō'ĭn) I. s. ruina ♦ **to go to r.** caer en ruinas II. tr. arruinar; *(crops, party)* estropear; *(plans)* echar abajo; *(morally)* deshonrar.

ru·in·a·tion ('ɔ-nā'shɔn) s. ruina.

ru·in·ous ('ɔ-nɔs) adj. ruinoso.

rule (rōōl) I. s. regla; *(control)* dominio, mando <*under foreign r.* bajo dominio extranjero>; *(power)* poder m; *(reign)* reinado ♦ **as a (general) r.** por lo regular ♦ **as a r. of thumb** de forma práctica ♦ **to be the r.** ser normal ♦ **to make it a r.** to ser un deber para uno ♦ **to play by the rules** obrar como es debido ♦ pl. reglamento ♦ **r. of the road** reglamento del tránsito II. tr. *(to govern)* gobernar; *(to control)* dominar; *(to decree)* decretar; *(to decide)* decidir; *(to declare)* declarar; *(with lines)* rayar ♦ **to r. out** *(to exclude)* excluir, descartar; *(to make impossible)* hacer imposible —intr. gobernar, mandar; *(to decide)* decidir; DER. fallar ♦ **to r. against** DER. fallar en contra • **to r. over** gobernar.

rul·er (rōō'lɔr) s. gobernante m; *(strip)* regla.

rul·ing (:lĭng) I. adj. *(class, party)* gobernante; *(passion)* (pre)dominante II. s. DER. decisión f, fallo.

rum[1] (rŭm) s. ron m.

rum[2] adj. -mm- G.B. raro, extraño.

rum·ble (rŭm'bɔl) I. intr. *(vehicle)* rodar con estrépito; *(gunfire, thunder)* retumbar II. s. retumbo; *(of protest)* rumor m; JER. *(fight)* pelea callejera.

ru·mi·nant (rōō'mɔ-nɔnt) adj. & s. rumiante m.

ru·mi·nate (:nāt') tr. & intr. rumiar.

ru·mi·na·tion ('nā'shɔn) s. rumia; *(meditation)* reflexión f.

rum·mage (rŭm'ĭj) I. tr. & intr. revolver, hurgar II. s. búsqueda desordenada ♦ **r. sale** venta benéfica.

rum·my[1] (rŭm'ē) s. *(game)* rami f.

rum·my[2] s. JER. *(drunkard)* borracho.

ru·mor (rōō'mɔr) I. s. rumor m II. tr. ♦ **to be rumored** rumorearse.

rump (rŭmp) s. *(of an animal)* ancas, grupa; *(of beef)* cuarto trasero; *(of a person)* nalgas.

rum·ple (rŭm'pɔl) tr. & intr. arrugar(se).

rum·pus (rŭm'pɔs) s. jaleo ♦ **r. room** cuarto de juegos.

run (rŭn) I. intr. **ran, run, -nn-** correr; *(to flee)* echar a correr, huir; *(to extend)* extenderse; *(to keep company)* andar *(with* con); *(to function)* andar, marchar; *(to be in operation)* estar en marcha, andar; *(to be in service)* circular, estar en servicio; *(wound)* supurar; *(nose)* moquear; *(eyes)* llorar; *(to melt)* derretirse; *(to spread)* correrse (color, tinta); *(stockings)* correrse; *(contract)* ser válido; *(to last)* durar; *(to stretch)* estar colocado <*shelves ran along the walls* los estantes estaban colocados a lo largo de las paredes>; POL. presentarse como candidato; *(to tend)* inclinarse; ZOOL. *(to migrate)* emigrar ♦ **to come** *o* **go running** to acudir a ♦ **to r. along!** *(tvete!>* • **to r. around** *(to roam)* andar; *(to rush)* ajetrearse; *(to be unfaithful)* ser infiel • **to r. around** *(shouting, singing)* ir (gritando, cantando) • **to r. away** *(to flee)* fugarse; *(from home)* abandonar el hogar ♦ **to r. down** parar • **to r. in the family** venir de familia ♦ **to r. loose** andar suelto • **to r. low (on)** *o* **short (of)** andar escaso (de), quedar poco ♦ **to r. off** *(to flee)* fugarse; *(liquid)* irse ♦ **to r. on** *(to chatter)* hablar sin cesar; *(to elapse)* pasar (el tiempo) • **to r. out** *(to be exhausted)* acabarse,

agotarse; *(to expire)* expirar • **to r. over** *(to overflow)* rebosar; *(to go beyond)* durar más de lo previsto • **to r. smoothly** ir sobre ruedas, ir bien • **to r. up** *o* **over** acercarse corriendo — tr. *(race, risk)* correr; *(distance)* recorrer, cubrir; *(errand, experiment)* hacer; *(as candidate)* presentar de candidato; *(to operate)* hacer funcionar; *(to transport)* llevar; *(to smuggle)* pasar de contrabando; *(blockade)* romper; *(tap water)* dejar correr *o* salir; *(film)* dar, poner; *(to publish)* publicar; *(business, campaign)* dirigir; *(household)* llevar; *(to follow)* seguir <*to r. its course* seguir su curso> ♦ **to r. a red light** pasar con la luz roja ♦ **to r. a temperature** *o* **fever** tener fiebre • **to r. after** perseguir, ir detrás de • **to r. against** ir en contra de • **to r. around with** andar con • **to r. away with** llevarse ♦ **to r. down** *(to knock down)* atropellar; *(to capture)* dar con, encontrar; *(to disparage)* poner por los suelos; *(to exhaust)* agotar; *(to review)* repasar • **to r. into** *(to meet by chance)* encontrarse con; *(to collide with)* chocar contra; *(difficulties)* tropezar con; *(to amount to)* llegar a • **to r. off** *(to print)* tirar; *(to force off)* echar de <*he ran us off the road* no echó de la carretera>.• **to r. off with** *(to steal)* llevarse; *(to elope)* fugarse con • **to r. out of** acabársele a uno, quedarse uno sin • **to r. out on** abandonar, dejar • **to r. over** atropellar • **to r. the length of** correr de un extremo a otro de • **to r. through** *(to stab)* traspasar (con arma blanca); *(to squander)* despilfarrar; *(to rehearse)* ensayar • **to r. up** *(prices)* hacer subir; *(charges)* dejar que se acumulen; *(flag)* izar • **to r. up against** tropezar con II. s. *(route)* recorrido, trayecto; *(race)* carrera; *(quick trip)* visita <*a r. into town* una visita a la ciudad>; *(printing)* tirada; *(sudden demand)* gran demanda *(on* de); *(flow)* flujo; *(duration)* duración f; *(stream)* arroyo; *(enclosure)* corral m; *(in stockings)* carrera; *(series)* serie f; *(of luck)* racha; *(in cards)* escalera; *(trend)* dirección f, curso; DEP. *(slope)* pista; MÚS. carrerilla; MIN. veta, filón m; ICT. migración f ♦ **at a r.** corriendo • **on the r.** *(hurrying)* corriendo; *(fleeing)* huyendo; *(without pausing)* a la carrera • **to give someone the r. of the house** poner la casa a disposición de alguien • **to give someone a r. for his money** *(competition)* hacer competencia a alguien; *(satisfaction)* dar satisfacción a alguien • **to have a long r.** permanecer mucho tiempo en el cartel • **to have the r. of a place** tener libre acceso a un lugar • **to make a r. for it** correr.

run-a·round ('ɔ-round') s. evasiva ♦ **to give someone the r.** FAM. dar excusas.

run·a·way (:ɔ-wā') I. s. *(slave)* fugitivo; *(child)* niño desertor II. adj. fugitivo; *(horse)* desbocado; *(child)* desertor; *(victory)* fácil, abrumador; *(inflation)* galopante.

run-down (:doun') I. s. informe detallado II. adj. en estado de deterioro; *(person)* agotado.

rung[1] (rŭng) s. *(step)* peldaño; *(crosspiece)* barrote m.

rung[2] (rŭng) cf. **ring**[2].

run-in (rŭn'ĭn') s. riña.

run·ner (rŭn'ɔr) s. *(racer)* corredor m; *(messenger)* mensajero; *(of a skate)* cuchilla; *(of a sled)* patín m; *(of sliding door)* guía; *(cloth)* tapete m; *(carpet)* alfombra; BOT. planta trepadora.

run·ner-up ('-ŭp') s. segundo.

run·ning (rŭn'ĭng) I. s. *(of a business)* dirección

f; (of a machine, household) manejo ♦ **to be in the r.** tener posibilidades de ganar • **to be out of the r.** no tener ninguna posibilidad de ganar II. adj. *(water)* corriente; *(knot)* corredizo; *(sore)* que supura ♦ **r. start** salida lanzada III. adv. seguido.

run·ny (:ē) adj. -**i-** líquido; *(nose)* que gotea.

run-off (:ôf´) s. *(overflow)* derrame *m*; *(competition)* carrera de desempate.

run-of-the-mill (rŭn´əv-thə-mĭl´) adj. corriente y moliente.

runt (rŭnt) s. *(animal)* animal pequeño; DESPEC. *(person)* enano, renacuajo.

run-through (rŭn´thrōō´) s. ensayo.

run·way (:wā´) s. *(ramp)* rampa; AVIA. pista.

rup·ture (rŭp´chər) I. s. ruptura; *(hernia)* hernia II. tr. & intr. romper; *(an organ)* reventar(se).

ru·ral (rŏŏr´əl) adj. rural.

ruse (rōōs, rōōz) s. artimaña, treta.

rush¹ (rŭsh) I. intr. *(to run)* ir de prisa; *(to hurry)* apresurarse, darse prisa; *(to flow)* correr ♦ **to r.** acudir ajetrearse ♦ **to r. in,** off entrar, marcharse corriendo • **to r. (right) over** acudir, ir corriendo • **to r. through** hacer de prisa —tr. *(a person)* dar prisa, apurar; *(a job)* hacer de prisa; *(an order)* ejecutar urgentemente; *(a package, to the hospital)* llevar de prisa o con urgencia; *(to attack)* atacar ♦ **to r. things** precipitar las cosas II. s. *(of activity)* gran demanda; *(haste)* prisa; *(attack)* acometida; *(onslaught)* fiebre *f* <the gold r. la fiebre del oro>; *(bustle)* bullicio, ajetreo; *(of wind)* ráfaga; *(of water)* torrente *m*; *(of emotion)* arrebato; *(narcotic high)* sensación eufórica ♦ **in a mad r.** precipitadamente • **there's no r.** no corre prisa • **there was a (mad) r.** to la gente se apresuró a • **to be in a r.** andar con prisa III. adj. urgente.

rush² s. BOT. junco.

rus·set (rŭs´ĭt) adj. & s. *(color m)* rojizo.

rust (rŭst) I. s. herrumbre *f*; *(on plants)* tizón *m* II. tr. & intr. oxidar(se), enmohecer(se).

rus·tic (rŭs´tĭk) adj. & s. rústico.

rus·tle (rŭs´əl) I. tr. & intr. *(leaves)* (hacer) susurrar; *(paper, fabric)* (hacer) crujir; *(cattle)* robar (ganado) II. s. susurro.

rust·y (rŭs´tē) adj. -**i-** oxidado, mohoso; *(color)* rojizo ♦ **to be r.** *(person)* estar falto de práctica.

rut¹ (rŭt) I. s. carril *m*; FIG. rutina <to be in a r. ser esclavo de la rutina> II. tr. **-tt-** surcar.

rut² s. ZOOL. *(heat)* celo.

ru·ta·ba·ga (rōō´tə-bā´gə) s. nabo sueco.

ruth·less (rōōth´lĭs) adj. despiadado, cruel.

rye (rī) s. centeno; *(whiskey)* whisky *m* de centeno.

S

s, S (ĕs) s. decimonovena letra del alfabeto inglés.
Sab·bath (săb´əth) s. *(Jewish)* sábado; *(Christian)* domingo.
sab·bat·i·cal (sə-băt´ĭ-kəl) s. licencia sabática.
sa·ber (sā´bər) s. sable *m*.
sa·ble (sā´bəl) s. marta cebellina.
sab·o·tage (săb´ə-täzh´) I. s. sabotaje *m* II. tr. sabotear.
sab·o·teur (´ tûr´) s. saboteador *m*.
sac (săk) s. saco.

sac·cha·rin (săk´ər-ĭn) s. sacarina.
sac·cha·rine (:ĭn) adj. empalagoso; QUÍM. sacarino.
sa·chet (să-shā´) s. almohadilla perfumada.
sack¹ (săk) I. s. *(bag)* saco; JER. *(bed)* cama ♦ **to get the s.** JER. ser despedido II. tr. ensacar; *(to fire)* despedir.
sack² I. tr. *(to loot)* saquear II. s. saqueo.
sack·cloth (săk´klôth´) s. tela de arpillera.
sac·ra·ment (săk´rə-mənt) s. sacramento.
sa·cred (sā´krĭd) adj. sacro, sagrado; *(venerable)* venerable; *(holy)* consagrado ♦ **nothing is s.** no se respeta nada • **s. to** consagrado a.
sac·ri·fice (săk´rə-fīs´) I. s. sacrificio • **at s.** COM. con pérdida • **to make a s.** to ofrecer un sacrificio a II. tr. sacrificar; COM. vender con pérdida —intr. ofrecer un sacrificio.
sac·ri·fi·cial (´-fĭsh´əl) adj. de sacrificio.
sac·ri·lege (săk´rə-lĭj) s. sacrilegio.
sac·ri·le·gious (´ -lĭj´əs, -lē´jəs) adj. sacrílego.
sac·ro·il·i·ac (săk´rō-ĭl´ē-ăk´, sā´krō-) I. adj. sacroiliaco II. s. región sacroiliaca.
sac·ro·sanct (săk´rō-săngkt´) adj. sacrosanto.
sa·crum (sā´krəm) s. [pl. -**cra**] sacro.
sad (săd) adj. -**dd-** triste; *(regrettable)* lamentable ♦ **s. to say** that la triste verdad es que.
sad·den (săd´n) tr. entristecer.
sad·dle (săd´l) I. s. silla de montar; *(of bicycle)* sillín *m*; *(cut of meat)* cuarto trasero II. tr. ensillar ♦ **to s. with** cargar con —intr. ♦ **to s. up** montar en la silla.
sad·dle·bag (´băg´) s. alforja
saddle horse s. caballo de silla.
sa·dism (sā´dĭz´əm, săd´ĭz´-) s. sadismo.
sa·dist (sā´dĭst, săd´ĭst) s. sádico.
sa·dis·tic (sə-dĭs´tĭk) adj. sádico.
sad·ness (săd´nĭs) s. tristeza.
safe (sāf) I. adj. seguro ♦ **have a s. trip!** ¡ten cuidado! • **is it s.?** ¿no es peligroso? • **it is s. to** say that se puede decir con seguridad que • **s. and sound** sano y salvo • **s. in a salvo de** • **to be on the s. side** para mayor seguridad • **to be s.** estar a salvo • **to play it s.** actuar con precaución II. s. caja de caudales.
safe-con·duct (kŏn´dŭkt) s. salvoconducto.
safe-crack·er (:krăk´ər) s. ladrón m de cajas fuertes.
safe·de·pos·it box (´dĭ-pŏz´ĭt) s. caja de seguridad.
safe·guard (´gärd´) I. s. salvaguarda ♦ **to be a s. against** proteger contra II. tr. salvaguardar.
safe·keep·ing (:kē´pĭng) s. *(act)* depósito; *(state)* protección *f*.
safe·ly (:lē) adv. *(without harm)* sin accidente; *(driving)* con cuidado.
safe·ty (:tē) s. seguridad *f*; ARM. seguro ♦ **s. belt, valve** cinturón, válvula de seguridad • **s. pin** imperdible • **to get to s.** ponerse a salvo.
saf·flow·er (săf´lou´ər) s. alazor *m*.
saf·fron (săf´rən) s. azafrán *m*; *(color)* color *m* azafrán.
sag (săg) I. intr. -**gg-** *(skin, clothes)* colgar; *(plank)* combarse; *(clothesline)* aflojarse; *(production, sales)* decaer; *(prices)* bajar II. s. *(decline)* caída; *(in board)* comba.
sa·ga (sä´gə) s. saga.
sa·ga·cious (sə-gā´shəs) adj. sagaz.
sa·gac·i·ty (sə-găs´ĭ-tē) s. sagacidad *f*.
sage¹ (sāj) s. & adj. sabio.
sage² s. BOT. salvia.
sage·brush (´brŭsh´) s. artemisa.
sag·ging (săg´ĭng) adj. *(sunken)* hundido; *(de-*

clining) decreciente.
said (sĕd) I. cf. **say** II. adj. (ante)dicho.
sail (sāl) I. s. vela; *(trip)* viaje *m* en barco; *(of windmill)* brazo ♦ **to make s.** desplegar las velas • **to set s.** hacerse a la vela • **under full s.** a toda vela • **under s.** con las velas alzadas II. intr. navegar; *(to travel)* ir en barco; *(to set out)* zarpar —tr. *(an ocean)* atravesar; *(one's boat)* botar ♦ **to s. around** *(a cape)* doblar; *(the world)* dar la vuelta a • **to s. the seas** surcar los mares • **to s. through** pasar fácil y rápidamente por.
sail·boat ('bōt') s. barco de vela.
sail·cloth (:klōth') s. lona para velas.
sail·fish (:fĭsh') s. [pl. inv. *o* **es**] pez *m* vela.
sail·ing (sā'lĭng) s. navegación *f*; *(sport)* vela; *(departure)* salida ♦ **to be smooth s.** ser fácil.
sail·or (sā'lər) s. marinero.
saint (sānt) I. s. santo II. tr. canonizar.
saint·ed (sān'tĭd) adj. santo.
saint·hood (sānt'hŏŏd') s. santidad *f.*
saint·ly (:lē) adj. **-i-** santo.
sake[1] (sāk) s. ♦ **for God's** *o* **goodness' heaven's s.!** ¡por (el amor de) Dios! • **for one's own s.** por el propio bien de uno • **for the s. of** por.
sa·ke[2] *o* **sa·ki** (sä'kē, :kē) s. sake *m*, saki *m.*
sal·a·ble (sā'lə-bəl) adj. vendible.
sa·la·cious (sə-lā'shəs) adj. salaz.
sal·ad (sāl'əd) s. ensalada ♦ **s. dressing** aderezo.
sal·a·man·der (săl'ə-măn'dər) s. salamandra.
sal·a·ried (săl'ə-rēd) adj. *(person)* salariado; *(work)* a sueldo.
sal·a·ry (săl'ə-rē) s. salario.
sale (sāl) s. venta; *(clearance)* liquidación *f* ♦ **for s.** se vende • **on s.** *(available)* en venta; *(reduced)* en liquidación • **s. price** precio de saldo • **to have a s.** estar de liquidación • **to put up for s.** poner en venta ♦ pl. venta • **s. tax** impuesto a las ventas.
sales·clerk (sālz'klûrk') s. dependiente *m.*
sales·girl (:gûrl') s. vendedora.
sales·man (:mən) s. [pl. **-men**] vendedor *m.*
sales·man·ship (:shĭp') s. arte *m* de vender.
sales·per·son (sālz'pûr'sən) s. vendedor, -a.
sales·wom·an ('wŏŏm'ən) s. [pl. **-women**] vendedora.
sa·li·ent (sā'lē-ənt) adj. *(projecting)* saliente; *(prominent)* sobresaliente.
sa·line (sā'lēn', :lĭn') adj. salino.
sa·li·va (sə-lī'və) s. saliva.
sal·i·var·y (săl'ə-vĕr'ē) adj. salival.
sal·i·vate (:vāt') intr. salivar.
sal·low (săl'ō) adj. **-er, -est** cetrino.
sal·ly (săl'ē) I. intr. ♦ **to s. forth** salir II. s. salida; *(outburst)* arranque; *(jaunt)* paseo.
salm·on (săm'ən, :mən) s. [pl. inv. *o* **s**] salmón *m*; *(color)* color *m* salmón.
sal·mo·nel·la (săl'mə-nĕl'ə) s. [pl. inv. *o* **s** *o* **-ae**] salmonela.
sa·lon (sə-lŏn') s. salón *m.*
sa·loon (sə-lōōn') s. taberna; *(hall, lounge)* salón *m.*
salt (sôlt) I. s. sal *f* ♦ **not to be worth one's s.** no valer gran cosa • **old s.** viejo lobo de mar • **s. water** agua salada II. tr. echar sal a; *(to preserve)* salar; *(writing)* salpicar.
salt·pe·ter (sôlt'pē'tər) s. nitrato de sodio *o* potasio.
salt·shak·er (:shā'kər) s. salero.
salt-wa·ter (:wô'tər) adj. de agua salada.
salt·y (sôl'tē) adj. **-i-** *(saline)* salino; *(with salt)*

salado; *(witty)* agudo; *(lively)* picante.
sa·lu·bri·ous (sə-lōō'brē-əs) adj. salubre.
sal·u·tar·y (săl'yə-tĕr'ē) adj. saludable; *(beneficial)* benéfico.
sal·u·ta·tion (săl'yə-tā'shən) s. saludo.
sa·lu·ta·to·ry (sə-lōō'tə-tôr'ē) adj. de saludo.
sa·lute (sə-lōōt') I. tr. saludar —intr. hacer un saludo II. s. saludo.
sal·vage (săl'vĭj) I. s. MARÍT. salvamento; *(things)* objetos salvados; *(compensation)* prima de salvamento II. tr. salvar.
sal·vage·a·ble (:vī-jə-bəl) adj. salvable.
sal·va·tion (săl-vā'shən) s. salvación *f.*
salve (săv, säv) I. s. ungüento; FIG. bálsamo II. tr. apaciguar.
sal·ver (săl'vər) s. bandeja.
sal·vo (săl'vō) s. [pl. **(e)s**] salva.
same (sām) I. adj. mismo; *(similar)* igual ♦ **at the s. time** sin embargo • **s. difference** *o* **thing** FAM. lo mismo • **the s. old story** la historia de siempre • **to be of the s. mind** pensar igual II. adv. igual III. pron. el mismo; *(thing)* lo mismo ♦ **all the s.** sin embargo • **everything is the s.** todo sigue igual • **it's all the s. to me** me da igual *o* lo mismo • **the s. to you!** ¡igualmente!; *(in anger)* ¡te deseo lo mismo!
same·ness ('nĭs) s. igualdad *f*; *(monotony)* monotonía.
sam·ple (săm'pəl) I. s. muestra; CIENT. espécimen *m* II. tr. tomar una muestra de; CUL. catar.
sam·pler (:plər) s. COST. dechado.
sam·pling (:plĭng) s. muestra.
san·a·tive (săn'ə-tĭv) adj. sanativo.
san·a·to·ri·um (săn'ə-tôr'ē-əm) s. [pl. **s** *o* **-ia**] sanatorio.
sanc·ti·fy (săngk'tə-fī') tr. santificar.
sanc·ti·mo·ni·ous (:'mō'nē-əs) adj. santurrón.
sanc·tion (săngk'shən) I. s. sanción *f* II. tr. sancionar.
sanc·ti·ty (săngk'tĭ-tē) s. santidad *f.*
sanc·tu·ar·y (:chōō-ĕr'ē) s. santuario; *(refuge)* asilo; *(game preserve)* coto.
sand (sănd) I. s. arena ♦ **s. dune** médano ♦ pl. *(land)* arenales; FIG. *(of time)* tiempo II. tr. & intr. *(road)* enarenar; *(wood)* lijar.
san·dal (săn'dl) s. sandalia.
san·dal·wood (:wŏŏd') s. sándalo.
sand·bag (sănd'băg') I. s. saco de arena II. tr. **-gg-** proteger con sacos de arena.
sand·bank (:băngk') s. banco de arena.
sand·bar (:bär') s. arrecife *m* de arena.
sand·blast (:blăst') I. s. chorro de arena II. tr. limpiar con chorro de arena.
sand·box (:bŏks') s. cajón *m* de arena.
sand·er (săn'dər) s. persona *o* aparato que esparce arena; *(tool)* lijadora.
sand·lot (sănd'lŏt') s. solar *m*, baldío.
sand·pa·per (:pā'pər) I. s. papel *m* de lija II. tr. lijar.
sand·pi·per (:pī'pər) s. aguzanieves *f.*
sand·stone (:stōn') s. arenisca.
sand·storm (:stôrm') s. tempestad *f* de arena.
sand·wich (:wĭch) s. emparedado, sandwich *m.*
sand·y (săn'dē) adj. **-i-** *(of color)* rubio; *(terrain)* **-i-** arenoso.
sane (sān) adj. cuerdo; *(reasonable)* razonable.
sang (săng) cf. **sing.**
san·guine (săng'gwĭn) adj. sanguíneo; *(optimistic)* optimista.
san·i·tar·i·um (săn'ĭ-târ'ē-əm) s. [pl. **s** *o* **-ia**] sanatorio.
san·i·tar·y (săn'ĭ-tĕr'ē) adj. sanitario ♦ **s. nap-**

kin paño higiénico.
san·i·ta·tion ('-tā'shən) s. saneamiento.
san·i·tize ('-tīz') tr. sanear.
san·i·ty (săn'ĭ-tē) s. cordura; *(sense)* sensatez *f.*
sank (săngk) cf. **sink**.
sap¹ (săp) s. BOT. savia; *(vitality)* vitalidad *f;* JER. *(dupe)* bobo.
sap² tr. **-pp-** *(to deplete)* agotar; *(to undermine)* socavar.
sa·pi·ent (sā'pē-ənt) adj. sapiente.
sap·ling (săp'lĭng) s. árbol *m* joven.
sap·phire (săf'īr') s. zafiro; *(color)* color *m* zafiro.
sap·py (săp'ē) adj. **-i-** lleno de savia; *(foolish)* tontuelo.
sar·casm (săr'căz'əm) s. sarcasmo.
sar·cas·tic (săr-kăs'tĭk) adj. sarcástico.
sar·dine (săr-dēn') s. sardina.
sar·don·ic (săr-dŏn'ĭk) adj. sardónico.
sash¹ (săsh) s. *(band)* fajín *m.*
sash² *(frame)* marco.
sa·shay (să-shā') intr. FAM. pavonearse.
sass (săs) FAM. I. s. impertinencia II. tr. hablar con insolencia a.
sas·sa·fras (săs'ə-frăs') s. sasafrás *m.*
sas·sy (săs'ē) adj. **-i-** descarado.
sat (săt) cf. **sit**.
sa·tan·ic/i·cal (sā-tăn'ĭk) adj. satánico.
satch·el (săch'əl) s. cartapacio.
sate (sāt) tr. saciar; *(to glut)* hartar.
sat·el·lite (săt'l-īt') s. satélite *m.*
sa·tia·ble (sā'shə-bəl) adj. saciable.
sa·ti·ate (sā'shē-āt') tr. saciar; *(to glut)* hartar.
sa·ti·a·tion ('-ā'shən) s. saciedad *f.*
sa·ti·e·ty (sə-tī'ĭ-tē) s. hartura.
sat·in (săt'n) s. raso, satén *m.*
sat·ire (săt'īr') s. sátira.
sa·tir·ic/i·cal (sə-tĭr'ĭk) adj. satírico.
sat·i·rist (săt'ər-ĭst) s. *(escritor)* satírico.
sat·i·rize (-ə-rīz') tr. satirizar.
sat·is·fac·tion (săt'ĭs-făk'shən) s. satisfacción *f; (compensation)* compensación *f.*
sat·is·fac·to·ry ('-tə-rē) adj. satisfactorio.
sat·is·fy (săt'ĭs-fī') tr. satisfacer; *(requirements)* cumplir con; *(to content)* contentar se; *(to assure)* convencer —intr. dar satisfacción.
sat·is·fy·ing (-īng) adj. satisfactorio; *(experience)* agradable; *(food)* sustancioso.
sat·u·rate (săch'ə rāt') tr. saturar.
sat·u·rat·ed (-'rā'tĭd) adj. saturado.
sat·u·ra·tion ('-shən) s. saturación *f.*
Sat·ur·day (săt'ər dē) s. sábado.
sauce (sôs) I. s. salsa; *(compote)* compota; *(impudence)* descaro II. tr. echar salsa a; FAM. insolentarse con.
sauce·pan (sôs'păn') s. cacerola.
sau·cer (sô'sər) s. platillo.
sau·cy (sô'sē) adj. **-i-** descarado.
sau·na (sô'nə) s. sauna.
saun·ter (sôn'tər) I. intr. pasearse II. s. paseo.
sau·sage (sô'sĭj) s. embutido; *(pork)* salchicha.
sau·té (sō-tā', sô-) tr. **-(e)d** saltear.
sav·age (săv'ĭj) I. adj. salvaje; *(ferocious)* feroz; *(cruel)* cruel II. s. salvaje *mf.*
sav·age·ry (-rē) s. salvajismo.
sa·van·na(h) (sə-văn'ə) s. sabana.
sa·vant (sə-vänt') s. sabio.
save¹ (sāv) I. tr. *(to rescue)* salvar; *(to keep)* guardar; *(to conserve)* ahorrar ♦ **to s. one's breath** ahorrar saliva • **to s. oneself the trouble** ahorrarse la molestia • **to s. the day** salvar

la situación —intr. ahorrar II. s. DEP. parada.
save² I. prep. salvo II. conj. a no ser que ♦ **s. for** salvo por • **s. that** si no fuera porque.
sav·er (sā'vər) s. salvador *m; (of money)* ahorrador *m.*
sav·ing (sā'vĭng) s. salvamento; *(economy)* ahorro ♦ pl. ahorros • **s. account, bank** cuenta, caja de ahorros.
sav·ior (sāv'yər) s. salvador.
sa·vor (sā'vər) I. s. sabor *m* II. intr. ♦ **to s. of** saber a —tr. gozar del sabor de.
sa·vor·y (sā'və rē) adj. sabroso; *(piquant)* picante.
sav·vy (săv'ē) JER. I. intr. entender II. s. sentido común.
saw¹ (sô) I. s. *(handsaw)* serrucho; *(machine)* sierra II. tr. **-ed, -ed** o **-n** (a)serrar.
saw² s. proverbio ♦ **old s.** viejo dicho.
saw³ cf. **see¹**.
saw·dust (sô'dŭst') s. (a)serrín *m.*
saw·horse (sô'hôrs') s. CARP. burro.
saw·mill (sô'mĭl') s. aserradero, serrería.
sax (săks) s. FAM. saxo, saxófono.
sax·o·phone (săk'sə-fōn') s. saxófono.
say (sā) I. tr. **said** decir; *(prayer)* rezar; *(to indicate)* marcar; *(to suppose)* suponer ♦ **enough said!** ¡basta! • **I'll s.!** ¡ya lo creo! • **it goes without saying** huelga decir • **easier said than done** más fácil decirlo que hacerlo • **it is said** se dice • **let us s.** digamos • **no sooner said than done** dicho y hecho • **not to s.** por no decir • **s.!** ¡olga! • **s. no more!** ¡no me digas más! • **that is to s.** o sea, es decir • **to s. nothing of** por no hablar de • **to s. again** volver a decir • **to s. the least** por lo menos • **to s. the word** dar la orden • **to s. to oneself** decir para sí • **what do you s.?** ¿qué te parece? • **when all is said and done** al fin y al cabo • **you can s. that again!** ¡ya lo creo! • **you don't s.!** ¡no me digas! • **you said it!** ¡dímelo a mí! II. s. *(opinion)* voz *f; (turn to speak)* uso de la palabra.
say·ing (sā'ĭng) s. dicho.
say·so (sā'sō') s. FAM. afirmación *f; (authority)* autoridad *f.*
scab (skăb) I. s. postilla; BOT. escabro; FAM. *(strikebreaker)* esquirol *m* II. intr. **-bb-** formar costra; FAM. *(to take a job)* sustituir a un huelguista.
scab·bard (skăb'ərd) s. vaina (de una espada).
scab·by (skăb'ē) adj. **-i-** costroso; VET. roñoso.
sca·bies (skā'bēz') s.inv. sarna.
scab·rous (skăb'rəs, skā'brəs) adj. escabroso.
scads (skădz) s.pl. FAM. montones *m.*
scaf·fold (skăf'əld) s. andamio; *(for executions)* patíbulo.
scaf·fold·ing (-əl-dĭng) s. andamiaje *m.*
scal·a·wag (skăl'ə-wăg') s. FAM. bribón *m.*
scald (skôld) I. tr. escaldar; *(milk)* calentar casi hasta el hervor II. s. escaldadura.
scald·ing (skôl'dĭng) adj. hirviente.
scale¹ (skāl) I. s. *(flake)* escama; *(of pipe)* incrustaciones *f* II. tr. escamar —intr. ♦ **to s. off** *(skin)* pelarse; *(paint)* descascararse.
scale² I. s. escala II. tr. *(to climb)* escalar; *(to adjust)* adaptar ♦ **to s. down, up** reducir, aumentar a escala.
scale³ s. *(balance)* báscula; *(tray)* platillo (de balanza).
scal·lion (skăl'yən) s. cebollino.
scal·lop (skŏl'əp, skăl'-) I. s. ZOOL. vieira; *(shell)* venera; *(border)* festón *m*, onda II. tr. COST. ondular; CUL. guisar al gratén.

scalp (skǎlp) I. s. *(trophy)* escalpe *m*; ANAT. cuero cabelludo II. tr. escalpar; FAM. *(tickets)* revender.

scal·pel (skǎl'pəl) s. escalpelo.

scalp·er (skǎl'pər) s. revendedor *m*.

scal·y (skā'lē) adj. -i- escamoso.

scam (skǎm) s. JER. estafa.

scam·per (skǎm'pər) I. intr. corretear II. s. correteo.

scan (skǎn) I. tr. -nn- *(to examine)* escudriñar; *(to look around)* recorrer con la mirada; *(to glance at)* echar un vistazo a; *(verse)* escandir; ELECTRÓN. registrar, explorar —intr. ELECTRÓN. registrar, explorar; POÉT. escandir II. s. escudriñamiento.

scan·dal (skǎn'dl) s. escándalo; *(gossip)* chismorreo.

scan·dal·ize (:īz') tr. escandalizar.

scan·dal·ous (:əs) adj. escandaloso; *(defamatory)* difamatorio.

scan·ner (skǎn'ər) s. ELECTRÓN. dispositivo explorador; MED. tomógrafo.

scant (skǎnt) I. adj. escaso II. tr. escatimar.

scant·y (skǎn'tē) adj. -i- escaso.

scape·goat (skāp'gōt') s. cabeza de turco.

scar (skär) I. s. cicatriz *f* II. tr. -rr- *(to mark)* señalar; *(the skin)* dejar una cicatriz en —intr. cicatrizar(se).

scar·ab (skär'əb) s. escarabajo.

scarce (skärs) adj. raro; *(insufficient)* escaso ♦ to become s. escasear.

scarce·ly (:lē) adv. apenas; *(hardly)* casi no; *(surely not)* seguramente no.

scar·ci·ty (skär'sĭ-tē) s. escasez *f*.

scare (skâr) I. tr. & intr. asustar(se) ♦ to be scared of asustarse de • to be scared stiff *o* to death estar muerto de miedo • to s. away *o* off ahuyentar • to s. to death dar un miedo espantoso II. s. susto.

scare·crow ('krō') s. espantapájaros *m*.

scarf (skärf) s. [pl. **s** *o* **-ves**] bufanda; *(kerchief)* pañuelo; *(runner)* tapete *m*.

scar·let (skär'lĭt) s. & adj. escarlata ♦ s. fever escarlatina • s. woman mujer de mala vida.

scar·y (skâr'ē) adj. -i- asustador.

scath·ing (skā'*th*ĭng) adj. severísimo.

sca·tol·o·gy (skə-tŏl'ə-jē) s. escatología.

scat·ter (skǎt'ər) I. tr. dispersar; *(to strew)* esparcir —intr. dispersarse.

scat·ter·brain (:brān') s. cabeza de chorlito.

scat·ter·brained (:brānd') adj. ligero de cascos.

scat·ter·ing (:ĭng) s. dispersión *f*.

scav·enge (skǎv'ənj) tr. encontrar entre la basura —intr. buscar en la basura.

scav·en·ger (skǎv'ən-jər) s. trapero; ZOOL. animal *m* que se alimenta de carroña.

sce·nar·i·o (sĭ-nâr'ē-ō') s. TEAT. argumento; CINEM. guión *m*; *(events)* situación *f*.

scene (sēn) s. escena; *(place)* lugar *m*; JER. *(sphere)* mundo; *(situation)* situación *f* ♦ behind the scenes *(backstage)* entre bastidores; *(in private)* en privado • to come on the s. aparecer.

scen·er·y (sē'nə-rē) s. *(landscape)* paisaje *m*; TEAT. decorado.

sce·nic (sē'nĭk) adj. del paisaje; *(picturesque)* pintoresco; TEAT. escénico.

scent (sĕnt) I. s. *(smell)* olor *m*; *(trail)* pista *f* ♦ to pick up the s. encontrar la pista • to throw off the s. despistar II. tr. olfatear; *(to perfume)* perfumar.

scep·ter (sĕp'tər) s. cetro.

sched·ule (skĕj'ōōl) I. s. *(timetable)* horario; *(agenda)* calendario; *(plan)* plan *m*; *(list)* inventario ♦ to be behind s. *(plane)* llevar retraso; *(work)* estar atrasado • to go according to s. desarrollarse como estaba previsto • on s. a la hora II. tr. *(train)* fijar el horario de; *(meeting)* programar ♦ to be scheduled estar previsto.

sche·mat·ic (skē-mǎt'ĭk) adj. esquemático.

scheme (skēm) I. s. *(plan)* proyecto; *(plot)* ardid *m*; *(arrangement)* combinación *f* II. tr. tramar —intr. conspirar.

schem·er (skē'mər) s. intrigante *mf*.

schism (sĭz'əm, skĭz'-) s. escisión *f*; RELIG. cisma *m*.

schiz·oid (skĭt'soid') adj. & s. esquizofrénico.

schiz·o·phre·ni·a (skĭt'sə-frē'nē-ə) s. esquizofrenia.

schol·ar (skŏl'ər) s. erudito; *(specialist)* especialista *mf*; *(student)* estudiante *mf*.

schol·ar·ly (:lē) adj. erudito.

schol·ar·ship (:shĭp') s. erudición *f*; *(financial aid)* beca.

scho·las·tic (skə-lǎs'tĭk) adj. escolar.

school[1] (skōōl) I. s. escuela; *(for teens)* colegio; *(department)* facultad *f*; *(class)* clase *f*; *(students)* alumnado, estudiantado ♦ driving s. escuela para aprender a conducir • military s. academia militar • night s. escuela nocturna • s. of thought escuela filosófica • secretarial s. escuela de secretariado • summer s. curso(s) de verano • Sunday s. RELIG. escuela dominical • to teach s. ser maestro II. tr. educar; *(to train)* disciplinar.

school[2] s. *(fish)* cardumen *m*.

school·book (skōōl'bōōk') s. libro de texto.

school·boy (:boi') s. alumno.

school·girl (:gûrl') s. alumna.

school·house (:hous') s. colegio, escuela.

school·ing (skōō'lĭng) s. instrucción *f*; *(training)* entrenamiento.

school·mas·ter (skōōl'mǎs'tər) s. maestro.

school·mate (:māt') s. compañero de escuela.

school·mis·tress (:mĭs'trĭs) s. maestra.

school·room (:rōōm') s. sala de clase.

school·teach·er (:tē'chər) s. maestro, -a.

schoo·ner (skōō'nər) s. goleta.

sci·at·i·ca (sī-ǎt'ĭ-kə) s. ciática.

sci·ence (sī'əns) s. ciencia ♦ s. fiction ciencia ficción.

sci·en·tif·ic (sī'ən-tĭf'ĭk) adj. científico.

sci·en·tist ('-tĭst) s. científico.

scin·til·late (sĭn'tl-āt') intr. chispear; *(to twinkle)* centellear.

sci·on (sī'ən) s. vástago; BOT. púa.

scis·sors (sĭz'ərz) s.pl. tijeras *f* ♦ a pair of s. tijeras • s. hold DEP. tijereta.

scle·ro·sis (sklĭ-rō'sĭs) s. esclerosis *f*.

scoff (skŏf) intr. mofarse *(at* de).

scoff·law ('lô') s. persona que burla la ley.

scold (skōld) I. intr. & tr. regañar II. s. regañón *m*.

scold·ing (skōl'dĭng) s. regaño ♦ to give a s. regañar.

scone (skōn, skŏn) s. bizcocho, galleta.

scoop (skōōp) I. s. *(ladle)* cucharón *m*; *(amount)* cucharadas; PERIOD. noticia exclusiva; MAQ. *(of shovel)* cuchara; *(of dredge)* cangilón *m* II. tr. ♦ to s. into meter en • to s. out excavar • to s. up *(by hand)* coger; *(with spoon)* sacar.

scoot (skōot) intr. andar rápidamente.

scoot·er (skōo′tər) s. *(child's)* monopatín *m*, patineta; *(motor vehicle)* motoneta.

scope (skōp) s. *(range)* ámbito; *(extent)* amplitud *f*; *(reach)* alcance *m*; *(freedom)* libertad *f*.

scorch (skôrch) I. tr. & intr. quemar(se) II. s. quemadura.

scorch·er (skôr′chər) s. FAM. día *m* abrasador.

score (skôr) I. s. *(notch)* muesca; *(line)* raya; *(twenty)* veintena; DEP. tanteo; EDUC. calificación *f*; MÚS. partitura ♦ **final s.** DEP. resultado ● **on that s.** en cuanto a eso ● **to keep s.** apuntar los tantos ● **to know the score** conocer el percal ● **to settle a s.** ajustar cuentas II. tr. *(to mark off)* apuntar (mediante rayas) en; *(to scratch)* rayar; DEP. marcar; *(to count as)* valer; *(to win)* lograr; FAM. *(to get)* conseguir; EDUC. sacar; MÚS. orquestar —intr. FAM. tener éxito; DEP. marcar un tanto; *(to keep score)* tantear.

score·board (-bôrd′) s. marcador *m*.

scor·er (-ər) s. tanteador *m*; *(player)* jugador *m* que marca tantos; *(in soccer)* goleador *m*.

scorn (skôrn) I. s. desprecio II. tr. despreciar ♦ **to s.** to no dignarse.

scorn·ful (skôrn′fəl) adj. desdeñoso.

scor·pi·on (skôr′pē-ən) s. escorpión *m*.

scotch (kŏch) tr. poner fin a.

scot-free (skŏt′frē′) adj. sin pagos e castigo.

scoun·drel (skoun′drəl) s. canalla *m*.

scour[1] (skour) tr. fregar, restregar.

scour[2] tr. *(to search)* batir; *(to range over)* recorrer —intr. *(to run)* correr.

scourge (skûrj) I. s. azote *m* II. tr. azotar.

scout[1] (skout) I. s. explorar; *(talent)* evaluar —intr. buscar ♦ **to s. around for** hacer una batida por II. s. FAM. *(fellow)* sujeto; MIL. explorador *m* ♦ **Boy Scout** niño explorador ● **s. plane** avión de reconocimiento.

scout[2] tr. rechazar con desprecio, desdeñar

scowl (skoul) I. intr. fruncir el ceño II. s. ceño.

scrag·gly (skrăg′lē) adj. -i- *(unkempt)* desaseado; *(sparse)* ralo.

scram (skrăm) intr. -mm- FAM. largarse.

scram·ble (skrăm′bəl) I. intr. gatear; *(struggle)* pelearse ♦ **to s. out** salir a gatas ● **to s. up** trepar —tr. revolver; ELECTRÓN. perturbar ♦ **scrambled eggs** huevos revueltos ● **to s. into one's clothes** vestirse rápidamente ● **s. together** mezclar II. s. lucha.

scram·bler (-blər) s. aparato para perturbar las emisiones radiofónicas.

scrap[1] (skrăp) I. s. *(of paper)* pedazo; *(of evidence)* pizca; *(metal)* chatarra; *(waste)* desperdicios; *(of fabric)* retazo ♦ pl. *(of food)* restos; *(waste)* desechos II. tr. -pp- desechar; *(ships)* desguazar; *(machines)* desmontar.

scrap[2] JER. I. intr. -pp- pelearse II. s. pelea.

scrap·book (skrăp′book′) s. álbum *m* de recortes.

scrape (skrāp) I. tr. raspar ♦ **to s. off** *o* out quitar (raspando) ● **to s. together** *o* up lograr reunir —intr. *(to graze)* rozar; *(to scrimp)* hacer economías ♦ **to s. by** ir tirando ● **to s.** raspado; *(sound)* chirrido; *(on skin)* rasguño.

scrap·er (skrā′pər) s. rascador *m*, raspador *m*.

scrap·py (skrăp′ē) adj. -i- peleador.

scratch (skrăch) I. tr. rayar(se); *(to claw)* arañar; *(to rub)* rascarse ♦ **to s. out** tachar ● **to s. the surface** no profundizar mucho II. s. raya; *(on skin)* arañazo; *(sound)* chirrido ♦ **from s.** de la nada ● **to come up to s.** satisfa-

cer los requisitos III. adj. al azar ♦ **s. paper** papel (de) borrador.

scratch·pad (-păd′) s. bloc *m* para apuntes; COMPUT. memoria auxiliar.

scratch·y (:ē) adj. -i- *(surface)* rayado; *(fabric)* que pica; *(sound)* chirriante; *(pen)* que raspea.

scrawl (skrôl) I. tr. & intr. garabatear II. s. garabateo.

scraw·ny (skrô′nē) adj. -i- flacucho.

scream (skrēm) I. intr. chillar ♦ **it's enough to make you s.** es para pegarse un tiro ● **to s. in pain** gritar de dolor II. s. chillido ♦ **to be a s.** ser divertidísimo.

scream·er (skrē′mər) s. chillón *m*.

scream·ing (:ing) I. s. grito(s) II. adj. chillón; *(funny)* divertidísimo.

screech (skrēch) I. intr. *(to scream)* chillar; *(to make a shrill noise)* chirriar II. s. chillido.

screen (skrēn) I. s. pantalla; *(for privacy)* biombo; *(for windows)* alambrera; *(for sifting)* criba; *(of troops)* cobertura; *(of planes)* protección *f* ♦ **s. door** puerta de tela metálica II. tr. *(to hide)* ocultar; *(to protect)* resguardar; *(to sift)* cribar; *(a porch)* poner una alambrera a; *(applicants)* pasar por el tamiz; CINEM. proyectar ♦ **to s. out** descartar.

screen·play ('plā') s. guión *m*.

screen·writ·er (:rī′tər) s. guionista *mf*.

screw (skrōō) I. s. CARP. tornillo ♦ **to have a s. loose** tener flojos los tornillos ● **to put the screws to someone** apretarle las clavijas a alguien II. tr. atar; JER. *(to cheat)* estafar ♦ **to have one's head screwed on right** FAM. tener la cabeza bien puesta ● **to s. down** *o* on CARP. atornillar en ● **to s. on** tapar ● **to s. open** *o* off destapar ● **to s. up** FAM. arruinar, desbaratar.

screw·ball ('bôl') s. adj. & s. JER. estrafalario.

screw·driv·er (:drī′vər) s. destornillador *m*.

screwed-up (skrōōd′ŭp′) adj. JER. desbaratado.

screw-up (skrōō′ŭp′) s. JER. metedura de pata.

screw·y (:ē) adj. -i- JER. *(crazy)* chiflado; *(amiss)* errado.

scrib·ble (skrĭb′əl) I. tr. & intr. garabatear II. s. garabato.

scribe (skrīb) s. FAM. *(writer)* escritorzuelo; HIST. *(clerk, copyist)* escribiente *m*.

scrim·mage (skrĭm′ĭj) I. s. DEP. entrenamiento II. intr. entrenarse.

scrimp (skrĭmp) intr. hacer economías ♦ **to s. and save** apretarse el cinturón.

scrip[1] (skrĭp) s. *(money)* vale *m*.

scrip[2] s. título provisional de propiedad.

script (skrĭpt) s. letra cursiva; CINEM. guión *m*.

scrip·tur·al (skrĭp′chər-əl) adj. bíblico.

scrod (skrŏd) s. bacalao inmaduro.

scroll (skrōl) s. rollo de pergamino.

scro·tum (skrō′təm) s. [pl. s *o* -ta] escroto.

scrounge (skrounj) I. tr. juntar ♦ **to s. up** conseguir de gorra —intr. gorronear ♦ **to s. around for** juntar.

scrub[1] (skrŭb) I. tr. -bb- fregar; *(clothes)* restregar; JER. *(mission)* cancelar —intr. fregar II. s. fregado ♦ **s. brush** cepillo.

scrub[2] s. *(shrub)* árbol achaparrado; *(thicket)* matorral *m*, FAM. animal pequeño; *(nobody)* don *m* nadie; DEP. jugador *m* suplente.

scrub·bing (skrŭb′ĭng) s. fregado.

scrub·by (skrŭb′ē) adj. -i- cubierto de maleza; *(stunted)* desarreglado.

scrub·wom·an (skrŭb′wŏŏm′ən) s. [pl. -women] fregona.

scruff (skrŭf) s. cogote *m*.
scruf·fy (skrŭf′ē) adj. -i- desaliñado.
scrump·tious (skrŭmp′shəs) adj. FAM. de rechupete.
scru·ple (skrōō′pəl) s. escrúpulo; *(bit)* pizca.
scru·pu·lous (:pyə-ləs) adj. escrupuloso.
scru·ti·nize (skrōōt′n-īz′) tr. escudriñar.
scru·ti·ny (:ē) s. escrutinio.
scu·ba (skōō′bə) s. escafandra autónoma.
scuff (skŭf) I. intr. estropear —tr. *(feet)* arrastrar; *(shoes, floor)* estropear II. s. arrastre *m* de los pies; *(slipper)* chancleta.
scuf·fle (skŭf′əl) I. intr. pelearse; *(to scuff)* arrastrar los pies II. s. refriega.
scull (skŭl) I. s. *(long oar)* espadilla; *(oar)* remo; *(boat)* bote *m* de remo II. tr. impulsar con remo o espadilla —intr. remar.
scul·ler·y (skŭl′ə-rē) s. trascocina.
sculpt (skŭlpt) tr. esculpir.
sculp·tor (skŭlp′tər) s. escultor *m*.
sculp·tress (:trĭs) s. escultora.
sculp·tur·al (:chər-əl) adj. escultural.
sculp·ture (skŭlp′chər) I. s. escultura II. tr. esculpir.
scum (skŭm) s. *(on pond)* verdín *m*; *(on liquids)* telilla; *(on milk)* nata; *(on metal)* escoria; JER. *(people)* escoria.
scurf (skûrf) s. caspa; *(scab)* costra.
scur·ri·lous (skûr′ə-ləs) adj. grosero.
scur·ry (skûr′ē) intr. correr.
scur·vy (skûr′vē) I. s. escorbuto II. adj. -i- vil.
scut·tle[1] (skŭt′l) I. s. trampilla; MARÍT. escotilla II. tr. FAM. desechar; MARÍT. barrenar.
scut·tle[2] s. *(for coal)* balde *m*.
scut·tle[3] intr. *(to run)* correr.
scythe (sīth) I. s. guadaña II. tr. guadañar.
sea (sē) I. s. mar *mf* ♦ **at s.** en el mar • **by the s.** a (la) orilla del mar • **heavy s.** marejada • **on the high seas** en alta mar • **s. gull** gaviota • **s. urchin** erizo de mar • **s. wall** rompeolas II. adj. marino; *(saltwater)* del mar.
sea·bed (sē′bĕd′) s. fondo del mar.
sea·board (sē′bôrd′) s. litoral *m*.
sea·coast (sē′kōst′) s. litoral *m*.
sea·dog (sē′dôg′) s. FAM. lobo de mar.
sea·far·er (sē′fâr′ər) s. marinero.
sea·far·ing (:ĭng) I. s. marinería II. adj. marinero.
sea·food (sē′fōōd′) s. mariscos; *(fish)* pescado.
sea·go·ing (sē′gō′ĭng) adj. de mar; *(people)* marinero.
seal[1] (sēl) I. s. sello; *(pledge)* garantía; *(sticker)* precinto; *(closure)* cierre *m* II. tr. sellar; *(with wax)* lacrar; *(envelope)* cerrar; *(fate)* determinar ♦ **sealing wax** lacre • **to s.** in encerrar • **to s. off** *(area)* acordonar; *(pipe)* cerrar • **to s. up** *(hole)* tapar; *(envelope)* cerrar.
seal[2] I. s. ZOOL. foca; *(pelt)* piel *f* de foca II. intr. cazar focas.
seal·ant (sē′lənt) s. sellador *m*.
seal·er[1] (sē′lər) s. pintura o barniz utilizado para sellar una superficie.
seal·er[2] s. cazador *m* de focas.
seal·skin (sēl′skĭn′) s. piel *f* de foca.
seam (sēm) I. s. costura; *(crease)* arruga; MIN. veta ♦ **to be bursting at the seams** *(with feelings)* rebosar de; *(with people)* rebosar de gente II. tr. unir; *(to line)* marcar.
sea·man (sē′mən) s. [pl. -men] marinero.
sea·man·ship (:shĭp′) s. pericia náutica.
seam·stress (sēm′strĭs) s. costurera.

seam·y (sē′mē) adj. -i- sórdido.
sé·ance (sā′äns′) s. sesión *f* de espiritismo.
sea·plane (sē′plān′) s. hidroavión *m*.
sea·port (sē′pôrt′) s. puerto marítimo.
sear (sîr) tr. & intr. marchitar(se).
search (sûrch) I. tr. & intr. registrar; *(conscience)* examinar ♦ **s. me!** FAM. ¡yo qué sé! • **to s. for** buscar • **to s. out** descubrir II. s. búsqueda; *(by police)* registro; *(of person)* cacheo; *(of ship)* visita ♦ **in s. of** en busca de la • **s. party** partida de buscadores • **s. warrant** mandamiento de registro.
search·er (sûr′chər) s. buscador *m*.
search·light (sûrch′līt′) s. reflector *m*.
sea·scape (sē′skāp′) s. *(vista)* marina.
sea·shell (sē′shĕl′) s. concha marina.
sea·shore (sē′shôr′) s. *(beach)* orilla del mar; *(coast)* litoral *m*.
sea·sick (sē′sĭk′) adj. mareado ♦ **to get s.** marearse.
sea·sick·ness (:nĭs) s. mareo.
sea·side (sē′sīd′) s. *(beach)* playa; *(coast)* litoral *m* ♦ **s. resort** estación balnearia.
sea·son (sē′zən) I. s. *(of year)* estación *f*; *(time)* temporada; *(of animals)* época ♦ **in s.** *(produce)* en sazón; *(animals)* en celo • **off s.** temporada baja • **s. ticket** abono II. tr. *(food)* sazonar; *(to enliven)* amenizar; *(wood)* secar; *(to accustom)* habituar —intr. *(wood)* secarse.
sea·son·a·ble (sē′zə-nə-bəl) adj. propio de la estación; *(timely)* a su tiempo.
sea·son·al (sē′zə-nəl) adj. estacional; *(unemployment)* temporal; *(worker)* temporero.
sea·son·ing (:nĭng) s. aderezo.
seat (sēt) I. s. asiento; *(for an event)* localidad *f*; *(of trousers)* fondillos; *(of bicycle)* sillín *m*; *(of government)* sede *f*; *(of learning)* centro; POL. escaño; *(buttocks)* trasero ♦ **by the s. of one's pants** FAM. por los pelos • **s. belt** cinturón de seguridad II. tr. sentar; *(to accommodate)* tener sitio para ♦ **be seated** siéntense.
seat·ing (sē′tĭng) s. *(places)* asientos; *(placement)* colocación *f*.
sea·ward (sē′wərd) I. adj. que da al mar II. adv. hacia el mar.
sea·way (sē′wā′) s. ruta marítima.
sea·weed (sē′wēd′) s. alga.
sea·wor·thy (sē′wûr′thē) adj. -i- en condiciones de navegar.
se·cede (sĭ-sēd′) intr. separarse.
se·ces·sion (sĭ-sĕsh′ən) s. secesión *f*.
se·clude (sĭ-klōōd′) tr. recluir ♦ **to s. oneself** apartarse.
se·clud·ed (sĭ-klōō′dĭd) adj. aislado.
se·clu·sion (:zhən) s. reclusión *f* ♦ **in s.** apartado.
sec·ond[1] (sĕk′ənd) s. *(time unit)* segundo; FAM. momento ♦ **s. hand** segundero.
sec·ond[2] I. adj. segundo; *(another)* otro ♦ **every s.** (uno de) cada dos • **on s. thought** pensándolo bien • **s. floor** primer piso (en países hispánicos) • **s. nature** costumbre arraigada • **s. sight** clarividencia • **s. thoughts** dudas • **to be s. to none** no tener igual • **to get one's s. wind** recobrar las fuerzas II. s. segundo; *(in duel)* padrino; MEC. segunda ♦ pl. *(food)* una porción más; COM. artículos con pequeños desperfectos III. tr. *(to attend)* secundar; *(motion)* apoyar IV. adv. en segundo lugar.
sec·ond·ar·y (sĕk′ən-dĕr′ē) adj. secundario ♦ **s. education** enseñanza media.
sec·ond-best (sĕk′ənd-bĕst′) adj. segundo.

sec·ond-class (:kläs′) **I.** adj. de segunda clase **II.** adv. en segunda (clase).
sec·ond-gen·er·a·tion (′-jĕn′ə-rā′shən) adj. de segunda generación.
sec·ond-guess (:gĕs′) tr. *(to criticize)* criticar; *(to anticipate)* anticiparse a.
sec·ond-hand (:hănd′) adj. & adv. de segunda mano.
sec·ond-rate (:rāt′) adj. de segunda categoría.
se·cre·cy (sē′krĭ-sē) s. secreto.
se·cret (sē′krĭt) **I.** adj. secreto; *(secluded)* oculto **II.** s. secreto ♦ **as a s.** confidencialmente ♦ **to keep a s.** guardar un secreto.
sec·re·tar·i·al (sĕk′rĭ-târ′ē-əl) adj. de secretario.
sec·re·tar·i·at (:ĭt) s. secretariado.
sec·re·tar·y (sĕk′rĭ-tĕr′ē) s. secretario; *(desk)* secreter m; *(minister)* ministro.
sec·re·tar·y-gen·er·al (′-jĕn′ər-əl) s. [pl. -taries-] secretario general.
se·crete[1] (sĭ-krēt′) tr. FISIOL. secretar.
se·crete[2] tr. *(to hide)* esconder.
se·cre·tion (sĭ-krē′shən) s. secreción f.
se·cre·tive (sē′krĭ-tĭv) adj. sigiloso.
sect (sĕkt) s. secta.
sec·tar·i·an (sĕk-târ′ē-ən) s. & adj. sectario.
sec·tion (sĕk′shən) **I.** s. sección f, parte f; *(of orange)* gajo; *(of track)* tramo; *(of town)* barrio; DER. aparte m **II.** tr. dividir en secciones.
sec·tion·al (:shə-nəl) adj. *(local)* regional; *(furniture)* desmontable.
sec·tor (sĕk′tər) s. sector m.
sec·u·lar (sĕk′yə-lər) adj. mundano; *(music)* profano; *(school)* laico; *(clergy)* secular.
sec·u·lar·ism (:lə-rĭz′əm) s. laicismo.
sec·u·lar·ize (:rīz′) tr. secularizar.
se·cure (sĭ-kyŏŏr′) **I.** adj. -er, -est seguro; *(stable)* asegurado ♦ **s. from** protegido contra **II.** tr. asegurar; *(to obtain)* conseguir; *(boat)* amarrar ♦ **s. from** proteger contra.
se·cu·ri·ty (:ĭ-tē) s. seguridad f; *(of loan)* garantía ♦ **s. guard** guardia d pl. FIN. valores.
se·dan (sĭ-dăn′) s. *(automobile)* sedán m; *(chair)* silla de manos.
se·date[1] (sĭ-dāt′) adj. sosegado.
se·date[2] tr. MED. administrar calmantes.
se·da·tion (sĭ-dā′shən) s. sedación f.
sed·a·tive (sĕd′ə-tĭv) s. & adj. sedante m.
sed·en·tar·y (sĕd′n-tĕr′ē) adj. sedentario.
sedge (sĕj) s. juncia.
sed·i·ment (sĕd′ə-mənt) s. sedimento.
sed·i·men·tar·y (′-mĕn′tə-rē) adj. sedimentario.
sed·i·men·ta·tion (:mən-tā′shən) s. sedimentación f.
se·di·tion (sĭ-dĭsh′ən) s. sedición f.
se·di·tious (:əs) adj. sedicioso.
se·duce (sĭ-dōōs′) tr. seducir.
se·duc·er (sĭ-dōō′sər) s. seductor m.
se·duc·tion (sĭ-dŭk′shən) s. seducción f.
se·duc·tive (:tĭv) adj. seductivo, seductor.
se·duc·tress (:trĭs) s. seductora.
sed·u·lous (sĕj′ə-ləs) adj. asiduo.
see[1] (sē) tr. **saw, seen** ver; *(to understand)* entender; *(to ensure)* asegurarse de; *(to visit with)* encontrarse con; *(to date)* salir con; *(to socialize with)* verse; *(to consult)* consultar; *(to attend)* recibir; *(to escort)* acompañar; *(to experience)* conocer ♦ **as I s.** it por lo que veo yo • **I saw it in his eyes** se lo vi en la cara • **it is worth seeing** merece la pena verse • **seeing is**

believing ver para creer • **s. you later!** ¡hasta luego! • **s. you (on) Saturday!** ¡hasta el sábado! • **that remains to be seen** eso está por verse • **there's nothing to s.** no hay nada que merezca la pena verse • **to go (and) s.** ir a ver • **to s. off** ir a despedirse de • **to s. red** echar chispas • **to s. the light** comprender • **to s. through** *(person)* ayudar a pasar por; *(task)* llevar a cabo • **to s. things** ver visiones • **to s. to** atender a —intr. ver; *(to understand)* comprender ♦ **as far as the eye can s.** hasta donde alcanza la vista • **let's s.** a ver, veamos • **s.?** ¿ves? • **s. for yourself!** ¡vea usted mismo! • **s. here!** ¡mire! • **s. if I care!** ¡a mí no me importa! • **seeing that . . .** ya que . . . • **to s. fit** creer conveniente • **to s. through someone** calar a alguien • **to wait and s. ver • you s. . . .** es que . . . • **you'll s.!** ¡ya verás! • **we'll s. about that!** ¡ya (lo) veremos!
see[2] s. RELIG. sede f ♦ **Holy S.** Santa Sede.
seed (sēd) **I.** s. [pl. inv. o -s] semilla; *(source)* germen m; *(pip)* pepita; *(progeny)* descendencia; *(sperm)* semen m ♦ **to go to s.** BOT. ir a granar; FIG. echarse a perder **II.** tr. sembrar; *(fruit)* despepitar.
seed·bed (′bĕd′) s. semillero.
seed·ling (:lĭng) s. plantón m.
seed·y (sē′dē) adj. -i- *(clothing)* raído; *(place)* sórdido; BOT. granado.
see·ing (sē′ĭng) conj. ♦ **s. that** visto que.
seek (sēk) tr. **sought** buscar; *(fame)* anhelar, *(advice)* solicitar ♦ **to be (highly) sought after** *(person)* ser (muy) solicitado; *(things)* ser (muy) cotizado ♦ **to s. out** ir en busca de • **to s. to** tratar de —intr. buscar.
seek·er (sē′kər) s. buscador m.
seem (sēm) intr. parecer ♦ **incredible as it may s.** aunque parezca increíble • **it hardly seems possible that** parece mentira que • **what seems to be the trouble?** ¿pasa algo?
seem·ing (sē′mĭng) adj. aparente.
seem·ly (sēm′lē) adj. -i- apropiado.
seen (sēn) cf. **see**[1].
seep (sēp) intr. rezumarse.
seep·age (sē′pĭj) s. filtración f.
seer (sîr, sē′ər) s. vidente mf.
seer·suck·er (sîr′sŭk′ər) s. tejido rayado en relieve.
see·saw (sē′sô′) **I.** s. subibaja m; *(movement)* vaivén m **II.** intr. columpiarse; *(to oscillate)* oscilar.
seethe (sēth) intr. hervir; *(person)* estar agitado ♦ **seething with anger** ardiendo de cólera.
see-through (sē′thrōō′) adj. transparente.
seg·ment (sĕg′mənt) **I.** s. segmento **II.** tr. & intr. (-mĕnt′) segmentar(se).
seg·men·ta·tion (′-mən-tā′shən) s. segmentación f.
seg·ment·ed (sĕg′mĕn′tĭd) adj. dividido en segmentos.
seg·re·gate (sĕg′rĭ-gāt′) tr. & intr. segregar(se).
seg·re·ga·tion (′-gā′shən) s. segregación f.
seine (sān) s. tr. & intr. (pescar con) jábega.
seis·mic (sīz′mĭk) adj. sísmico.
seis·mo·graph (:mə-grăf′) s. sismógrafo.
seis·mol·o·gy (-mŏl′ə-jē) s. sismología.
seize (sēz) tr. agarrar; *(to possess)* apoderarse de; *(to arrest)* detener; *(to confiscate)* incautarse de; *(opportunity)* aprovechar ♦ **to be seized by, with** *(fear)* estar sobrecogido por; *(desire)* entrarle a uno • **to s. upon** aprovecharse de —intr. ♦ **to s. (up)** MEC. agarrotarse.

sei·zure (sē′zhər) s. detención *f*; *(of goods)* embargo; *(of power)* toma; MED. ataque *m*.

sel·dom (sĕl′dəm) adv. rara vez.

se·lect (sĭ-lĕkt′) I. tr. & intr. escoger; DEP. seleccionar II. adj. selecto; *(club)* exclusivo; *(merchandise)* de primera calidad.

se·lec·tion (sĭ-lĕk′shən) s. selección *f*; *(collection)* surtido.

se·lec·tive (:tĭv) adj. selectivo.

se·lec·tiv·i·ty (-′′ĭ-tē) s. selectividad *f*.

se·lect·man (sĭ-lĕkt′măn′) s. [pl. **-men**] concejal *m*.

self (sĕlf) s. [pl. **-ves**] uno mismo; *(ego)* ego ♦ **to be back to one's old s.** volver a ser el mismo de siempre.

self-ad·dressed (′ə-drĕst′) adj. con la dirección del remitente.

self-ag·gran·dize·ment (:ə-grăn′dĭz-mənt) s. exaltación *f* de sí mismo.

self-ap·point·ed (:ə-poin′tĭd) adj. nombrado por sí mismo.

self-as·ser·tive (:ə-sûr′tĭv) adj. agresivo.

self-as·sured (:ə-shŏŏrd′) adj. seguro de sí mismo.

self-cen·tered (′sĕn′tərd) adj. egocéntrico.

self-com·posed (′kəm-pōzd′) adj. dueño de sí mismo.

self-con·fessed (′kən-fĕst′) adj. reconocido por uno mismo.

self-con·fi·dence (′kŏn′fĭ-dəns) s. confianza en sí mismo.

self-con·scious (:kŏn′shəs) adj. cohibido.

self-con·tained (′kən-tānd′) adj. *(self-sufficient)* autónomo; *(reserved)* reservado.

self-con·trol (:kən-trōl′) s. dominio de sí mismo ♦ **to lose one's s.** perder la calma.

self-de·feat·ing (:dĭ-fē′tĭng) adj. contraproducente.

self-de·fense (:dĭ-fĕns′) s. autodefensa; DER. legítima defensa ♦ **in s.** en defensa propia.

self-de·ni·al (:dĭ-nī′al) s. abnegación *f*.

self-de·struct (:dĭ-strŭkt′) intr. autodestruirse.

self-de·struc·tion (:dĭ-strŭk′shən) s. autodestrucción *f*.

self-de·ter·mi·na·tion (:dĭ-tûr′mə-nā′shən) s. autodeterminación *f*.

self-dis·ci·pline (′dĭs′ə-plĭn) s. autodisciplina.

self-doubt (:dout′) s. desconfianza en sí mismo.

self-ed·u·cat·ed (:ĕj′ə-kā′tĭd) adj. autodidacta.

self-ef·fac·ing (′ĭ-fā′sĭng) adj. humilde.

self-em·ployed (:ĕm-ploid′) adj. que trabaja por cuenta propia.

self-es·teem (:ĭ-stēm′) s. amor propio.

self-ev·i·dent (′ĕv′ĭ-dənt) adj. evidente.

self-ex·plan·a·to·ry (′ĭk-splăn′ə-tôr′ē) adj. obvio.

self-ex·pres·sion (:ĭk-sprĕsh′ən) s. expresión *f* de la propia personalidad.

self-ful·fill·ing (:fŏŏl-fĭl′ĭng) adj. que llega a cumplirse.

self-gov·ern·ment (′gŭv′ərn-mənt) s. autonomía.

self-grat·i·fi·ca·tion (′grăt′ə-fĭ-kā′shən) s. satisfacción *f* de los deseos propios.

self-help (′hĕlp′) s. esfuerzo propio.

self-im·age (:ĭm′ĭj) s. representación *f* de sí mismo.

self-im·por·tance (′ĭm-pôr′tns) s. presunción *f*.

self-im·posed (:ĭm-pōzd′) adj. que uno se impone a sí mismo.

self-im·prove·ment (:ĭm-prŏŏv′mənt) s. superación propia.

self-in·crim·i·na·tion (:ĭn-krĭm′ə-nā′shən) s. autoincriminación *f*.

self-in·duced (:ĭn-dōōst′) adj. que uno se hace a sí mismo.

self-in·dul·gence (:ĭn-dŭl′jəns) s. desenfreno.

self-in·flict·ed (:ĭn-flĭk′tĭd) adj. que uno se inflige a sí mismo.

self-in·ter·est (′ĭn′trĭst) s. interés propio; *(selfishness)* egoísmo.

self-in·volved (′ĭn-vŏlvd′) adj. que piensa en su propio interés.

self·ish (sĕl′fĭsh) adj. egoísta.

self·ish·ness (:nĭs) s. egoísmo.

self·less (sĕl′lĭs) adj. desinteresado.

self-love (:lŭv′) s. egoísmo; PSIC. narcisismo.

self-made (:mād′) adj. logrado por propio esfuerzo.

self-pit·y (:pĭt′ē) s. compasión *f* de sí mismo.

self-por·trait (:pôr′trĭt) s. autorretrato.

self-pres·er·va·tion (:prĕz′ər-vā′shən) s. instinto de la propia conservación.

self-pro·claimed (:prō-klāmd′) adj. supuesto.

self-re·gard (:rĭ-gärd′) s. amor propio; *(self-respect)* dignidad *f*.

self-re·li·ance (:rĭ-lī′əns) s. confianza en sí mismo.

self-re·spect (:rĭ-spĕkt′) s. dignidad *f*.

self-re·straint (:rĭ-strānt′) s. control *m*, dominio de sí mismo.

self-right·eous (′rī′chəs) adj. santurrón.

self-ris·ing (:rī′zĭng) adj. que no necesita levadura.

self-rule (:rōōl′) s. autonomía.

self-sac·ri·fice (:săk′rə-fīs′) s. sacrificio de sí mismo.

self·same (:sām′) adj. mismísimo.

self-seek·ing (:kĭng′) I. adj. egoísta II. s. egoísmo.

self-serv·ice (:sûr′vĭs) adj. de autoservicio.

self-serv·ing (:sûr′vĭng) adj. egoísta.

self-suf·fi·cient (:sə-fĭsh′ənt) adj. autosuficiente.

self-sup·port (:sə-pôrt′) s. independencia económica.

self-sus·tain·ing (:sə-stā′nĭng) adj. que se mantiene por sus propios medios.

self-taught (:tôt′) adj. autodidacta.

sell (sĕl) I. tr. **sold** vender ♦ **to be sold on** estar convencido de • **to s. off** COM. liquidar • **to s. short** subestimar —intr. venderse ♦ **to be sold out** estar agotado • **to s. like hot cakes** venderse como pan caliente • **to s. out** liquidar todo; *(cause)* venderse II. s. ♦ **hard, soft s.** publicidad agresiva, discreta.

sell·er (′ər) s. vendedor *m*; *(dealer)* comerciante *mf* ♦ **quick s.** artículo que se vende fácilmente • **s.'s market** mercado favorable al vendedor.

sell-out (:out′) s. COM. liquidación *f* total; TEAT. lleno; FAM. *(traitor)* traidor *m*.

selt·zer (sĕlt′sər) s. agua de seltz.

sel·vage/vedge (sĕl′vĭj) orilla.

se·man·tic (sĭ-măn′tĭk) adj. semántico ♦ **semantics** s.sg. semántica.

sem·a·phore (sĕm′ə-fôr′) I. s. semáforo II. tr. transmitir por semáforo.

sem·blance (sĕm′bləns) s. apariencia; *(copy)* copia.

se·men (sē′mən) s. semen *m*.

se·mes·ter (sə-mĕs′tər) s. semestre *m*.

sem·i·an·nu·al (sĕm'ē-ǎn'yōō-əl) adj. semestral.

sem·i·au·to·mat·ic (:ō'tə-mǎt'ĭk) adj. semiautomático.

sem·i·cir·cle (sĕm'ĭ-sûr'kəl) s. semicírculo.

sem·i·cir·cu·lar ('-'kyə-lər) adj. semicircular.

sem·i·co·lon (sĕm'ĭ-kō'lən) s. punto y coma.

sem·i·con·duc·tor ('ē-kən-dŭk'tər) s. semiconductor m.

sem·i·fi·nal DEP. I. s. (sĕm'ē-fī'nəl) semifinal ♦ II. adj. ('-'nəl) semifinalista.

sem·i·month·ly (sĕm'ē-mŭnth'lē) I. adj. bimensual II. adv. dos veces al mes III. s. publicación f bimensual.

sem·i·nal (sĕm'ə-nəl) adj. seminal; (creative) creativo.

sem·i·nar (sĕm'ə-när') s. seminario; (conference) reunión f.

sem·i·nar·y ('-nĕr'ē) s. seminario.

sem·i·pre·cious (sĕm'ē-prĕsh'əs) adj. semiprecioso ♦ s. stone piedra fina.

sem·i·pri·vate (:prī'vĭt) adj. para dos o tres personas.

sem·i·skilled (:skĭld') adj. poco entrenado.

sem·i·week·ly (:wēk'lē) I. s. & adj. (publicación f) bisemanal II. adv. dos veces por semana.

sem·i·year·ly (:yîr'lē) I. s. & adj. (publicación f) semestral II. adv. dos veces al año.

sen·ate (sĕn'ĭt) s. senado.

sen·a·tor (sĕn'ə-tər) s. senador m.

sen·a·to·ri·al ('-tôr'ē-əl) adj. senatorial.

send (sĕnd) tr. **sent** mandar; (letter) enviar; (to propel) hacer <the blow sent him staggering el golpe lo hizo tambalear>; RAD. transmitir ♦ **to s. away** echar • **to s. away for** ordenar por correo • **to s. back** (person) hacer regresar; (object) devolver • **to s. chills down one's spine** darle a uno escalofríos • **to s. down** hacer bajar • **to s. in** (an entry) mandar; (a person) hacer pasar • **to s. into** lanzar • **to s. off** (letter) echar al buzón; (person) ir a despedir • **to s. on** reexpedir • **to s. out** (invitations) enviar; (leaves) echar; (heat) emitir • **to s. (out) for** enviar a alguien a buscar • **to s. up** (to jail) meter en la cárcel; (prices) hacer subir; (spacecraft) lanzar —intr. enviar.

send·er (sĕn'dər) s. remitente mf.

send-off (sĕnd'ôf') s. despedida afectuosa.

send-up (sĕnd'ŭp') s. FAM. imitación graciosa.

se·nes·cent (sĭ-nĕs'ənt) adj. senescente.

se·nile (sē'nīl', sĕn'īl') adj. senil.

se·nil·i·ty (sĭ-nĭl'ĭ-tē) s. senectud f.

sen·ior (sēn'yər) I. adj. (father) padre; (partner) principal; (senator) más antiguo; (officer) superior; (in school) del último año ♦ s. citizen anciano II. s. anciano; (student) estudiante mf del último año ♦ **to be someone's s.** ser mayor que alguien • **to be five years someone's s.** llevarle cinco años a alguien.

sen·ior·i·ty (sēn-yôr'ĭ-tē) s. antigüedad f; (priority) precedencia.

sen·sa·tion (sĕn-sā'shən) s. sensación f.

sen·sa·tion·al (:shə-nəl) adj. sensacional.

sen·sa·tion·al·ism (:nə-lĭz'əm) s. sensacionalismo.

sen·sa·tion·al·ize (:līz') tr. exagerar.

sense (sĕns) I. s. sentido; (feeling) sensación f; (consciousness) sentimiento; (judgment) sentido común ♦ good s. sentido común • in a s. en cierto sentido • **to come to one's senses** recobrar el juicio • **to have the s. to** tener la

cordura de • **to make s.** tener sentido • **to make s. of** comprender el sentido de • **to talk s.** hablar con sentido común II. tr. (to perceive) darse cuenta de; (to detect) detectar.

sense·less ('lĭs) adj. sin sentido; (foolish) insensato; (unconscious) inconsciente.

sen·si·bil·i·ty (sĕn'sə-bĭl'ĭ-tē) s. sensibilidad f.

sen·si·ble (sĕn'sə-bəl) adj. sensato; (perceptible) sensible ♦ **to be s. of** darse cuenta de.

sen·si·tive (:sĭ-tĭv) adj. sensible; (delicate) delicado ♦ **to be s. to** o **about** ser susceptible a.

sen·si·tiv·i·ty ('-tĭv'ĭ-tē) s. sensibilidad f; (susceptibility) susceptibilidad f.

sen·si·tize ('-tīz') tr. & intr. sensibilizar(se).

sen·sor (sĕn'sər, :sôr') s. sensor m.

sen·so·ry (:sə-rē) adj. sensorio.

sen·su·al (:shōō-əl) adj. sensual.

sen·su·al·i·ty ('-ăl'ĭ-tē) s. sensualidad f.

sen·su·ous ('-əs) adj. sensual.

sent (sĕnt) cf. **send**.

sen·tence (sĕn'tns) I. s. GRAM. oración f, frase f; DER. sentencia ♦ **death s.** pena de muerte • **life s.** condena perpetua • **to be under s. of death** estar condenado a muerte • **to pass s. on** sentenciar • **to serve out one's s.** cumplir la sentencia II. tr. sentenciar.

sen·ten·tious (sĕn-tĕn'shəs) adj. sentencioso.

sen·tient (sĕn'shənt) adj. consciente.

sen·ti·ment (sĕn'tə-mənt) s. sentimiento; (sentimentality) sentimentalismo; (view) opinión f.

sen·ti·men·tal ('-mĕn'tl) adj. sentimental.

sen·ti·men·tal·i·ty (:-tăl'ĭ-tē) s. sentimentalismo.

sen·ti·men·tal·ize ('-tl-īz') tr. hablar con sentimentalismo de —intr. ponerse sentimental.

sen·ti·nel (sĕn'tə-nəl) s. centinela m.

sen·try (sĕn'trē) s. centinela m ♦ **to stand s.** estar de guardia.

sep·a·rate I. tr. & intr. (sĕp'ə-rāt') separar(se) ♦ **to s. from** separar(se); (to distinguish) distinguir(se) entre • **to s. into** dividir(se) en II. adj. (:ər-ĭt) (detached) separado; (loose) suelto; (different) distinto; (another) otro III. s. (:ər-ĭt) ♦ pl. prendas de vestir que se compran por separado.

sep·a·ra·tion ('-rā'shən) s. separación f.

sep·a·ra·tist (sĕp'ər-ə-tĭst) s. separatista mf.

Sep·tem·ber (sĕp-tĕm'bər) s. septiembre m.

sep·tic (sĕp'tĭk) adj. séptico ♦ s. tank fosa séptica, pozo séptico.

sep·ul·cher (sĕp'əl-kər) s. sepulcro.

se·pul·chral (sə-pŭl'krəl) adj. sepulcral.

se·quel (sē'kwəl) s. continuación f; (consequence) consecuencia, resultado.

se·quence (sē'kwəns) s. sucesión f; (arrangement) orden m; (series) serie f.

se·quent (sē'kwənt) adj. subsiguiente; (consequent) consecuente.

se·quen·tial (sĭ-kwĕn'shəl) adj. consecutivo.

se·ques·ter (sĭ-kwĕs'tər) tr. secuestrar; (jury) aislar ♦ **to s. oneself** retirarse.

se·quin (sē'kwĭn) s. lentejuela.

sere (sîr) adj. marchito.

ser·e·nade (sĕr'ə-nād') I. s. serenata II. tr. dar una serenata a.

ser·en·dip·i·ty (sĕr'ən-dĭp'ĭ-tē) s. hallazgo afortunado.

se·rene (sə-rēn') adj. sereno ♦ **His S. Highness** Su Alteza Serenísima.

se·ren·i·ty (sə-rĕn'ĭ-tē) s. serenidad f.

serf (sûrf) s. siervo.

serge (sûrj) s. sarga.

ser·geant (sär'jənt) s. sargento ♦ **s. at arms** ujier.

se·ri·al (... -əl) I. adj. *(program)* seriado; *(novel, story)* ... or capítulos; *(order)* consecutivo ♦ **s. numbe**... número de serie II. s. serial *m.*

se·ri·al·ize (:ə-līz') tr. publicar por capítulos.

se·ries (sîr'ēz) s.inv. serie *f.*

se·ri·ous (sîr'ē-əs) adj. serio; *(illness)* grave ♦ **are you s.?** ¿en serio? • **to be s. about** tomar en serio.

se·ri·ous-mind·ed ('-mīn'dĭd) adj. serio.

se·ri·ous·ness ('-nĭs) s. seriedad *f.*

ser·mon (sûr'mən) s. sermón *m.*

ser·mon·ize (:mə-nīz') tr. & intr. sermonear.

ser·pent (sûr'pənt) s. serpiente *f.*

ser·pen·tine (:pən-tēn', :tīn') adj. serpentino.

ser·rate/rat·ed (sĕr'āt'/ā'tĭd) adj. serrado.

se·rum (sîr'əm) s. [pl. **s** o **-ra**] suero.

ser·vant (sûr'vənt) s. sirviente *m*; *(public)* funcionario.

serve (sûrv) I. tr. servir; *(in a store)* atender; *(Mass)* ayudar a; *(to aid)* ser útil a ♦ **if (my) memory serves me** si la memoria no me falla • **it serves you right!** ¡lo tienes bien merecido! • **to s. as o for** servir de • **to s. no purpose** no servir para nada • **to s. on** ser miembro de —intr. servir; *(to carry out duties)* desempeñar los deberes; *(to satisfy)* ser suficiente II. s. DEP. saque *m.*

serv·ice (sûr'vĭs) I. s. servicio; *(benefit)* utilidad *f*; *(to customers)* atención *f*; *(set)* juego; DEP. saque *m* ♦ **at your s.** a sus órdenes • **diplomatic s.** cuerpo diplomático • **in s.** funcionando • **s. charge** recargo por servicios • **to be of s. (to)** servir (a) • **to be out of s.** no funcionar • **to take into one's s.** emplear II. adj. de servicio; *(military)* militar III. tr. *(to maintain)* mantener; *(to repair)* reparar.

serv·ice·a·ble (:vĭ-sə-bəl) adj. servible.

serv·ice·man (:vĭs-măn') s. [pl. **-men**] militar *m*; *(repairman)* mecánico.

ser·vile (:vəl, :vīl') adj. servil.

serv·ing (sûr'vĭng) s. CUL. porción *f.*

ser·vil·i·ty (sər-vĭl'ĭ-tē) s. servilismo.

ser·vi·tude (:vĭ-tōōd') s. servidumbre *f.*

ses·a·me (sĕs'ə-mē) s. sésamo, ajonjolí *m.*

ses·sion (sĕsh'ən) s. sesión *f*; *(of legislature)* reunión *f* ♦ **summer s.** EDUC. curso(s) de verano • **to be in s.** estar en reunión.

set¹ (sĕt) I. tr. set, -tting poner; *(to locate)* situar; *(bone)* encajar; *(watch)* poner en hora; *(type)* componer; *(stage)* montar; *(precedent)* sentar; *(date, price)* fijar; *(record)* establecer; *(example)* dar; *(pearl)* montar ♦ **to be s. back from** estar a cierta distancia de • **to be s. in** TEAT. desarrollarse en • **to be s. about** ponerse a • **to s. above** anteponer • **to s. against** *(to pit)* enfrentar con; *(to compare)* contraponer a • **to s. apart** separar • **to s. aside** hacer a un lado; *(for future use)* guardar; *(one's feelings)* dejar de lado; *(decision)* anular • **to s. at** fijar en • **to s. at liberty** poner en libertad • **to s. back** atrasar; FAM. costar • **to s. down** poner en el suelo; *(to record)* poner por escrito; *(to attribute)* achacar; *(to establish)* fijar • **to s. forth** exponer • **to s. free** liberar • **to s. off** *(reaction)* iniciar; *(bomb)* hacer estallar; *(alarm)* hacer sonar; *(to distinguish)* hacer sobresalir; *(to accentuate)* hacer resaltar • **to s. oneself up** darselas de • **to s. one's house in order** arreglar los asuntos de uno • **to s. out** *(to lay out)* disponer; *(to*

display) desplegar • **to s. out** to proponerse • **to s. to (work)** ponerse a (trabajar) • **to s. (to) thinking** dar que pensar a • **to s. up** *(to raise, set upright)* levantar; *(machine)* montar; *(in power)* instaurar; *(to trick)* engañar • **to s. up in** ayudar a establecerse en (un negocio) • **to s. upon** acometer —intr. *(sun)* ponerse; *(hen)* empollar; *(cement)* endurecerse; *(bone)* encajarse; *(gelatin)* cuajar; *(dye)* fijarse; FAM. *(to sit)* sentarse • **to s. down** AVIA. aterrizar • **to s. forth** o **off** o **out** salir, encaminarse • **to s. in** *(winter, night)* caer; *(rains)* llegar; *(discontent)* arraigar • **to s. up** establecerse II. adj. *(agreed upon)* señalado; *(price)* fijo; *(procedure)* reglamentario; *(customs)* arraigado; *(opinion)* firme; *(face)* inmóvil; *(determined)* resuelto; *(ready)* listo ♦ **all s.** listo • **dead s. against** resueltamente en contra de • **get ready, get s., go** preparados, listos, ya • **to be s. in one's ways** tener costumbres muy arraigadas • **to be s. on** *(doing something)* estar empeñado en; *(idea)* estar aferrado a • **to get s.** prepararse III. s. *(of shoulders)* postura, porte *m*; *(hardening)* endurecimiento.

set² s. *(of items)* juego; *(of rules)* serie *f*; *(clothes)* muda; *(people)* grupo; *(works)* colección *f*; TEAT. decorado; RAD. aparato; MAT. conjunto; DEP. set *m* ♦ **generating s.** grupo electrógeno • **s. of dishes** vajilla • **s. of teeth** FAM. dentadura • **television s.** televisor • **the smart s.** la gente elegante.

set·back (sĕt'băk') s. revés *m.*

set·tee (sĕ-tē') s. sofá *m.*

set·ter (sĕt'ər) s. perro de muestra.

set·ting (sĕt'ĭng) s. *(place)* marco; *(of action)* escenario; *(scenery)* decorado; *(of gem)* engastadura.

set·tle (sĕt'l) tr. *(affairs)* arreglar; *(claim)* satisfacer; *(debt)* saldar; *(problem)* resolver; *(person)* instalar; *(territory)* colonizar; *(in business)* establecer; *(nerves)* calmar; *(stomach)* asentar; DER. asignar ♦ **that settles it!** ¡no hay más que hablar! • **to s. accounts** ajustar cuentas • **to s. for** contentarse con • **to s. (up)on** decidirse por —intr. *(bird, gaze)* posarse; *(dust)* asentarse; *(in a city)* establecerse; *(disease)* localizarse; *(in dispute)* arreglarse ♦ **to s. down** normalizarse; *(a child)* calmarse; *(conditions)* normalizarse; *(in marriage)* casarse • **to s. down** to ponerse a • **to s. in** instalarse; *(at a job)* acostumbrarse • **to s. up** ajustar cuentas.

set·tled (:ld) adj. *(established)* arraigado; *(stabilized)* estable; *(paid)* pagado.

set·tle·ment (:l-mənt) s. *(of dispute)* arreglo; *(of problem)* solución *f*; *(agreement)* acuerdo; *(colony)* poblado.

set·tler (:lər) s. poblador *m.*

set-to (:tōō') s. disputa; *(fight)* refriega.

set-up (:ŭp') s. *(organization)* organización *f*; *(plan)* plan *m*; JER. combate amañado.

sev·en (sĕv'ən) s. & adj. siete ♦ **s. hundred** setecientos • **s. o'clock** las siete.

sev·en·teen (' tēn') s. & adj. diecisiete *m.*

sev·en·teenth (:tēnth') I. s. *(place)* diecisiete *m*; *(part)* diecisieteava parte II. adj. *(place)* decimoséptimo; *(part)* diecisieteavo.

sev·enth (sĕv'ənth) s. & adj. séptimo.

sev·en·ti·eth (:ən-tē-ĭth) I. s. *(place)* setenta *m*; *(part)* setentava parte II. adj. septuagésimo.

sev·en·ty (sĕv'ən-tē) s. & adj. setenta *m.*

sev·er (sĕv'ər) tr. cortar; *(ties)* romper ♦ **to s.**

from separar de.
sev·er·al (sěv'ər-əl) I. adj. varios; *(distinct)* distintos II. s. varios.
sev·er·ance (sěv'ər-əns) s. separación *f; (breakup)* ruptura ♦ **s. pay** indemnización por despido.
se·vere (sə-vîr') adj. **-er, -est** severo; *(harsh)* riguroso; *(intense)* intenso.
se·ver·i·ty (sə-věr'ĭ-tē) s. severidad *f.*
sew (sō) tr. & intr. **-ed, -ed** *o* **-n** coser ♦ **to s. up** *(deal)* cerrar; *(market)* monopolizar.
sew·age (sōō'ĭj) s. aguas cloacales.
sew·er (sōō'ər) s. alcantarilla, cloaca.
sew·er·age (:ĭj) s. *(system)* alcantarillado; *(sewage)* aguas cloacales *o* residuales.
sew·ing (sō'ĭng) s. costura ♦ **s. circle** grupo de costureras ♦ **s. machine** máquina de coser.
sewn (sōn) cf. **sew.**
sex (sěks) s. sexo ♦ **s. life** vida sexual • **to have s.** tener relaciones sexuales.
sex·ist (sěk'sĭst) adj. & s. (persona) que tiene prejuicios sexuales.
sex·less (sěks'lĭs) adj. asexual, asexuado.
sex·tant (sěk'stənt) s. sextante *m.*
sex·u·al (sěk'shōō-əl) adj. sexual ♦ **s. intercourse** coito.
sex·u·al·i·ty ('-ǎl'ĭ-tē) s. sexualidad *f.*
sex·y (sěk'sē) adj. **-i-** *excitante; (erotic)* erótico.
sh! (sh) interj. ¡chitón!
shab·bi·ness (shǎb'ē-nĭs) s. aspecto andrajoso.
shab·by (shǎb'ē) adj. **-i-** *(clothing, upholstery)* raído; *(beggar)* andrajoso; *(house, neighborhood)* derruido; *(treatment)* malo, mezquino.
shack (shǎk) s. choza.
shack·le (shǎk'əl) I. s. grillete *m* II. tr. poner grilletes a.
shad (shǎd) s. [pl. inv. *o* **s**] sábalo.
shade (shād) I. s. sombra; *(for lamp)* pantalla; *(for window)* persiana; *(hue)* tono; *(of meaning)* matiz *m; (bit)* pizca ♦ **s. tree** árbol que da sombra ♦ pl. JER. anteojos de sol II. tr. *(from light)* resguardar; *(to obscure)* dar sombra a; *(a picture)* sombrear; *(a meaning)* matizar.
shad·ing (shā'dĭng) s. DIB., PINT. *(of darkness)* sombreado; *(of color)* degradación *f.*
shad·ow (shǎd'ō) I. s. sombra ♦ **beyond the s. of a doubt** sin lugar a dudas • **to cast a s. (on)** hacer sombra (sobre) • **to cast a s. over** ensombrecer ♦ pl. oscuridad II. tr. sombrear; *(to trail)* seguir (la pista de) ♦ **to s. forth** *o* **out** presentir III. adj. POL. fantasma.
shad·ow·y (:ē) adj. **-i-** *(dark)* obscuro; *(vague)* vago.
shad·y (shā'dē) adj. **-i-** sombreado; *(person)* sospechoso.
shaft (shǎft) I. s. *(of spear)* asta; *(of arrow)* astil *m; (arrow)* flecha; *(of light)* rayo; *(of tool)* mango; *(of vehicle)* varal *m; (mine)* pozo; *(elevator)* hueco; MEC. eje *m* ♦ **to get the s.** JER. salir perjudicado II. tr. JER. perjudicar.
shag·gy (shǎg'ē) adj. **-i-** *(hairy)* peludo; *(woolly)* lanudo; *(unkempt)* desgreñado.
shake (shāk) I. tr. **shook, -n** sacudir; *(house)* hacer temblar; *(bottle)* agitar; *(faith)* hacer vacilar; *(habit)* librarse de ♦ **to s. down** FAM. sacar dinero a; *(to search)* registrar • **to s. hands** darse la mano • **to s. hands with** dar la mano • **to s. off** librarse de • **to s. one's head** negar con la cabeza • **to s. out** sacudir • **to s. up** *(bottle)* agitar; *(person)* sacudir; *(organization)* reorganizar —intr. temblar ♦ **to s. with** *(fear,*

cold)* temblar de *(miedo, frío)* II. s. sacudida; *(tremble)* temblor *m; (beverage)* batido ♦ **to be no great shakes JER. no valer gran cosa • **to have the shakes** FAM. tener escalofríos.
shake·down ('doun') I. s. prueba; FAM. extorsión *f; (search)* registro II. adj. de prueba.
shak·er (shā'kər) s. *(for cocktails)* coctelera; *(for salt)* salero; *(for pepper)* pimentero.
shake·up (shāk'ŭp') s. reorganización *f.*
shak·y (shā'kē) adj. **-i-** tembloroso; *(unstable)* inestable; *(dubious)* discutible ♦ **to feel s.** sentirse débil.
shale (shāl) s. esquisto.
shall (shăl) aux. [pret. **should**] <I s. be 28 tomorrow cumpliré 28 años mañana> <the penalty s. not exceed two years in prison el castigo no excederá más de dos años de cárcel> <shall I call? ¿quiere que llame por teléfono?>.
shal·lot (shə-lŏt', shăl'ət) s. chalote *m.*
shal·low (shăl'ō) I. adj. poco profundo; *(dish)* llano; FIG. superficial II. s. ♦ pl. MARÍT. bajíos.
sham (shăm) I. s. falsificación *f; (fraud)* farsa; *(impostor)* impostor *m* II. adj. falso; *(feigned)* fingido III. tr. & intr. **-mm-** fingir.
sham·bles (shăm'bəlz) s. caos *m* ♦ **to make a s. of** convertir en caos.
shame (shām) I. s. vergüenza; *(pity)* lástima ♦ **a crying s.** una verdadera lástima • **s. on you!** ¡qué vergüenza! • **to bring s. on** deshonrar a ♦ **to put to shame** avergonzar II. tr. avergonzar; *(to dishonor)* deshonrar.
shame·ful ('fəl) adj. vergonzoso ♦ **how s.!** ¡qué vergüenza!
shame·less (:lĭs) adj. *(person)* descarado, sinvergüenza; *(behavior)* vergonzoso.
sham·poo (shăm-pōō') I. s. champú *m* II. tr. dar un champú a —intr. lavarse la cabeza con champú.
sham·rock (shăm'rŏk') s. trébol *m.*
shang·hai (shăng-hī') tr. obligar a hacer algo por la fuerza.
shank (shăngk) s. *(lower leg)* espinilla; *(of horse)* caña; *(of meat)* pierna; *(of pin)* tija.
shan·ty (shăn'tē) s. choza.
shan·ty·town (:toun') s. villa miseria.
shape (shāp) I. s. forma; *(body)* figura; *(guise)* aspecto; *(condition)* estado ♦ **to be in no s. to** no estar en condiciones de *o* para • **to be out of s.** DEP. no estar en forma • **to knock out of s.** deformar • **to take s.** formarse II. tr. formar; *(object)* dar forma a; *(idea)* concebir; *(one's life)* adaptar ♦ **shaped** en forma de <mushroom-shaped en forma de hongo> • **to s. into** dar forma a —intr. ♦ **to s. up** FAM. ponerse en condiciones.
shape·less ('lĭs) adj. informe; *(misshapen)* deforme.
shape·ly (:lē) adj. **-i-** bien proporcionado.
shard (shärd) s. fragmento; *(pottery)* casco.
share[1] (shâr) I. s. parte *f; (of stock)* acción *f* ♦ **to go shares** in ir a partes iguales en II. tr. compartir ♦ **to s. and s. alike** compartir por partes iguales • **to s. in** tener parte en • **to s. out** repartir.
share[2] s. AGR. reja de arado.
share·crop·per (shâr'krŏp'ər) s. aparcero.
share·hold·er (:hōl'dər) s. accionista *mf.*
shark (shärk) s. tiburón *m;* JER. usurero.
sharp (shärp) I. adj. *(cutting)* afilado; *(pointed)* puntiagudo; *(image)* nítido; *(feature)* anguloso; *(contrast)* marcado; *(abrupt)* repentino;

(curve) cerrado; *(acute)* agudo; *(alert)* atento; *(biting)* mordaz; *(tongue)* de víbora; *(tone)* áspero; *(strong)* fuerte; *(pungent)* acre; MÚS. sostenido; JER. *(stylish)* elegante ♦ **to be s. at** ser un hacha en • **to have a s. temper** enojarse fácilmente II. adv. en punto ♦ **to look s.** estar atento III. s. FAM. *(cheater)* fullero; MÚS. sostenido.

sharp·en (shär'pən) tr. afilar; *(pencil)* sacar punta a; *(senses, appetite)* aguzar.

sharp·en·er (:pə-nər) s. *(for pencil)* sacapuntas m; *(machine)* afiladora.

sharp-eyed (sharp'īd') adj. que tiene ojos de lince; *(observant)* observador.

sharp·ness (:nĭs) s. *(of knife)* filo; *(of cliff)* lo puntiagudo; *(of increase)* brusquedad f; *(of image)* nitidez f; *(of acuteness)* agudeza f; *(of tone)* aspereza; *(of criticism)* mordacidad f; *(of curve)* lo cerrado; *(of taste)* acritud f.

sharp·shoot·er (:sho͞o'tər) s. tirador m de primera.

sharp-sight·ed (:sī'tĭd) adj. que tiene ojos de lince; *(observant)* observador.

sharp-wit·ted (:wĭt'ĭd) adj. perspicaz.

shat·ter (shăt'ər) tr. & intr. hacer(se) añicos.

shat·ter·proof (:pro͞of') adj. inastillable.

shave (shāv) I. tr. **-ed, -ed** o **-n** afeitar; *(hair)* rapar; *(wood)* cepillar; *(cheese)* cortar en tajadas finas —intr. afeitarse II. s. afeitado ♦ **to get a s.** afeitarse • **to have a close s.** librarse por los pelos.

shav·er (shā'vər) s. afeitadora; FAM. *(boy)* mozalbete m.

shav·ing (:vĭng) s. afeitado; *(sliver)* viruta; TEC. cepillado ♦ **s. cream** crema de afeitar.

shawl (shôl) s. chal m.

she (shē) I. pron. ella II. s. hembra.

sheaf (shēf) s. [pl. **-ves**] fajo.

shear (shĭr) tr. **-ed, -ed** o **shorn** *(sheep)* esquilar; *(fabric)* tundir; *(metal)* cizallar; *(hedge)* cortar con tijeras ♦ **to s. of** despojar de • **to s. off** cortar —intr. ♦ **to s. off** TEC. romperse por cizallamiento.

shears (shĭrz) s.pl. tijeras; *(for metal)* cizalla.

sheath (shēth) s. vaina.

sheathe (shēth) tr. *(knife)* enfundar; *(sword)* envainar; *(claws)* retraer; *(cable)* forrar.

shed¹ (shĕd) tr. **shed, -dding** *(tears)* derramar; *(water)* verter; *(skin)* mudar; *(leaves)* despojarse de ♦ **to s. light on** iluminar —intr. mudar.

shed² s. cobertizo.

sheen (shēn) s. brillo; *(of silk)* viso.

sheep (shēp) s.inv. oveja ♦ **s. dog** perro pastor.

sheep·ish (shē'pĭsh) adj. tímido; *(bashful)* vergonzoso.

sheep·skin (shēp'skĭn') s. piel f de carnero; *(leather)* badana; *(parchment)* pergamino.

sheer¹ (shĭr) intr. desviarse.

sheer² I. adj. *(fabric)* transparente; *(drop)* vertical; *(utter)* puro II. adv. perpendicularmente.

sheet¹ (shēt) s. *(for bed)* sábana; *(paper)* hoja; *(glass)* lámina; *(ice)* capa ♦ **s. metal** metal en chapa.

sheet² s. escota ♦ pl. espacios en la proa y popa de un bote • **three s. to the wind** FAM. borracho.

shelf (shĕlf) s. [pl. **-ves**] *(in closet)* tabla, anaquel m; *(shelving)* estante m; GEOL. arrecife m ♦ **on the s.** arrinconado.

shell (shĕl) I. s. concha; *(of crustaceans)* caparazón m; *(of nuts, eggs)* cáscara; *(of peas)*

vaina; MARIT. bote m para regatas; ARM. proyectil m; *(for firearm)* casquillo ♦ **s. shock** trauma psicológico causado por la guerra II. tr. *(peas)* desvainar; *(nuts)* descascarar; MIL. bombardear ♦ **to s. out** FAM. soltar, pagar.

shel·lac (shə-lăk') I. s. laca II. tr. **-ck-** laquear; JER. *(to defeat)* derrotar completamente.

shell·fire (shĕl'fīr') s. cañoneo.

shell·fish (shĕl'fĭsh') s. [pl. inv. o **es**] molusco; *(crustacean)* crustáceo; CUL. mariscos.

shel·ter (shĕl'tər) I. s. cobertizo; *(refuge)* refugio ♦ **to take s.** ponerse a cubierto II. tr. proteger; *(to harbor)* acoger —intr. refugiarse.

shel·tered (:tərd) adj. protegido.

shelve (shĕlv) tr. poner en un estante; *(to put aside)* dar carpetazo a —intr. estar en declive.

shelv·ing (shĕl'vĭng) s. estantería.

she·nan·i·gan (shə-năn'ĭ-gən) s. FAM. engaño ♦ pl. travesuras.

shep·herd (shĕp'ərd) I. s. pastor m II. tr. cuidar.

shep·herd·ess (:ər-dĭs) s. pastora.

sher·bet (shûr'bĭt) s. sorbete m.

sher·iff (shĕr'ĭf) s. sheriff m.

sher·ry (shĕr'ē) s. jerez m.

shield (shēld) I. s. escudo II. tr. escudar; *(to conceal)* tapar.

shift (shĭft) I. tr. *(load)* pasar; *(to switch)* cambiar de —intr. cambiar; *(person)* moverse; AUTO. cambiar de velocidad II. s. cambio; *(of workers)* turno; *(dress)* traje recto ♦ **in shifts** por turnos.

shift·less (shĭft'lĭs) adj. perezoso.

shift·y (shĭf'tē) adj. **-i-** evasivo.

shill (shĭl) s. JER. cómplice m.

shil·ly-shal·ly (shĭl'ē-shăl'ē) intr. titubear.

shim·mer (shĭm'ər) I. intr. destellar II. s. destello.

shim·mer·ing (:ĭng) adj. *(light)* destellante; *(tint)* tornasolado.

shim·my (shĭm'ē) I. s. shimmy m; AUTO. trepidación f oscilante II. intr. AUTO. oscilar.

shin (shĭn) s. espinilla.

shin·bone ('bōn') s. tibia.

shin·dig (shĭn'dĭg') s. JER. fiesta.

shine (shīn) I. intr. **-d** o **shone** brillar ♦ **to s. on** iluminar —tr. *(to polish)* sacar brillo a; *(light)* dirigir II. s. brillo; *(shoeshine)* brillo de zapatos ♦ **rain or s.** llueva o truene.

shin·er (shī'nər) s. JER. ojo a la funerala.

shin·gle¹ (shĭng'gəl) I. s. CONSTR. tablilla ♦ **to hang out one's s.** FAM. establecerse II. tr. cubrir con tablillas.

shin·gle² s. *(beach)* playa de guijarros; *(gravel)* cascajo.

shin·gles (shĭng'gəlz) s.inv. MED. herpes mf.

shin·ny (shĭn'ē) intr. trepar.

shin·y (shī'nē) adj. **-i-** brillante; *(glossy)* lustroso.

ship (shĭp) I. s. barco m; *(boat)* buque m; *(crew)* tripulación f; *(aircraft)* aeronave f II. tr. **-pp-** *(goods)* enviar; *(oars)* desarmar; *(water)* hacer agua ♦ **to s. off** to enviar a —intr. ♦ **to s. (out) as** enrolarse de.

ship·build·er ('bĭl'dər) s. constructor m naval.

ship·build·ing (:dĭng) s. construcción f naval.

ship·ment (shĭp'mənt) s. embarque m; *(cargo)* cargamento.

ship·per (:ər) s. expedidor m.

ship·ping (:ĭng) s. embarque m; *(ships)* barcos.

ship·shape (:shāp') adj. en orden.

ship·wreck (:rĕk′) **I.** s. naufragio **II.** tr. hacer naufragar; FIG. hundir ♦ **to be shipwrecked** naufragar.

ship·yard (:yärd′) s. MARÍT. astillero.

shirk (shûrk) tr. & intr. esquivar.

shirt (shûrt) s. camisa ♦ **stuffed s.** FAM. persona estirada ♦ **to keep one's s. on** JER. no sulfurarse ♦ **to lose one's s.** JER. perder hasta la camisa.

shirt·tail (shûrt′tāl′) s. faldón *m* de camisa.

shiv·er¹ (shĭv′ər) **I.** intr. tiritar **II.** s. escalofrío.

shiv·er² intr. & tr. *(to break)* hacer(se) astillas.

shiv·er·y (shĭv′ə-rē) adj. tembloroso.

shoal¹ (shōl) **I.** s. bajío **II.** intr. hacerse menos profundo **III.** adj. poco profundo.

shoal² **I.** s. *(of fish)* banco **II.** intr. ir en bancos.

shock¹ (shŏk) **I.** s. choque *m*; *(mental)* golpe *m*; *(of earthquake)* sacudida ♦ **s.** absorber amortiguador **II.** tr. & intr. chocar ♦ **to be shocked at** escandalizarse por.

shock² *(of hair)* greña; AGR. tresnal *m*.

shock·er (shŏk′ər) s. cosa horrible.

shock·ing (:ĭng) adj. *(disturbing)* horroroso; *(offensive)* indecente.

shod (shŏd) cf. **shoe.**

shod·dy (shŏd′ē) **I.** s. *(cloth)* lana regenerada; *(goods)* mercancía de mala calidad **II.** adj. regenerado; *(goods)* de mala calidad.

shoe (shōō) **I.** s. zapato; *(for horses)* herradura; *(of brake)* zapata; *(of tire)* cubierta ♦ **s.** **leather** suela de zapato ♦ **s. polish** betún ♦ **s. store** zapatería ♦ **to be in another's shoes** estar en el lugar de otro ♦ **to fill someone's shoes** ocupar el lugar de otro **II.** tr. shod *(person)* calzar; *(horse)* herrar.

shoe·horn (:hôrn′) s. calzador *m*.

shoe·lace (:lās′) s. cordón *m*.

shoe·mak·er (:mā′kər) s. zapatero.

shoe·string (:strĭng′) s. cordón *m* ♦ **on a s.** con poco dinero.

shoe·tree (:trē′) s. horma.

shone (shōn) cf. **shine.**

shoo (shōō) interj. ¡fuera!

shook (shŏŏk) cf. **shake.**

shook-up (:ŭp′) adj. JER. perturbado.

shoot (shōōt) **I.** tr. shot *(a weapon)* disparar; *(to wound)* herir; *(to kill)* matar a tiros; *(to hit)* pegar un tiro; *(to execute)* fusilar; *(to send)* lanzar; *(to film)* rodar; *(to photograph)* fotografiar ♦ **to s. down** derribar ♦ **to s. forth** BOT. echar ♦ **to s. out** resolverlo a tiros ♦ **to s. off** disparar ♦ **to s. the breeze** *o* **bull** FAM. charlar ♦ **to s. the works** FAM. jugarse el todo por el todo ♦ **to s. dead** *o* **to death** matar a tiros ♦ **to s. up** JER. inyectar (drogas) —intr. *(to fire)* disparar; *(to hunt)* cazar, DEP. tirar ♦ **to s. across, through** pasar rápidamente *o* a través de ♦ **to s. ahead** tomar rápidamente la delantera ♦ **to s. at** tirar a ♦ **to s. for** tratar de lograr ♦ **to s. from the hip** hablar a tontas y a locas ♦ **to s. in** entrar como un torbellino ♦ **to s. off** *o* **out** salir disparando ♦ **to s. off one's mouth** hablar demasiado ♦ **to s. out** *(projection)* sobresalir ♦ **to s. past** *o* **by** pasar como un rayo ♦ **to s. up** *(to grow)* espigar; *(prices)* subir de repente; *(sparks)* brotar; *(pain)* inyectar drogas **II.** s. BOT. retoño; *(contest)* tiro **III.** interj. ¡miércoles!

shoot·er (shōō′tər) s. tirador *m*; DEP. goleador *m*.

shoot·ing (:tĭng) **I.** s. *(firing)* tiro; *(shoot-out)*

tiroteo; *(execution)* fusilamiento; *(killing)* matanza; *(murder)* asesinato; *(filming)* rodaje *m* **II.** adj. ♦ **s. pain** dolor punzante.

shoot-out *o* **shoot·out** (shōōt′out′) s. tiroteo.

shop (shŏp) **I.** s. tienda; *(workshop)* taller *m* ♦ **s. window** escaparate ♦ **to set up s.** poner un negocio ♦ **to talk s.** hablar del trabajo **II.** intr. -pp- ir de compras ♦ **to s. around** (for) buscar ♦ **to s. for** ir a comprar.

shop·keep·er (′kē′pər) s. tendero.

shop·lift·er (:lĭf′tər) s. ratero de tiendas.

shop·per (:ər) s. comprador *m*.

shop·ping (:ĭng) s. compras ♦ **s. bag** bolsa ♦ **s. center** centro comercial ♦ **to go s.** ir de compras.

shop·talk (:tôk′) s. conversación *f* sobre el trabajo.

shop·worn (:wôrn′) adj. gastado.

shore¹ (shôr) s. *(coast)* orilla; *(beach)* playa ♦ pl. tierra.

shore² tr. ♦ **to s. up** apuntalar.

shore·line (shôr′lĭn′) s. ribera.

shor·ing (shôr′ĭng) s. puntales *m*.

shorn (shôrn) cf. **shear.**

short (shôrt) **I.** adj. corto; *(in height)* bajo; *(in amount)* poco; *(brusque)* seco; GRAM. breve; FIN. al descubierto; CUL. crujiente ♦ **a s. distance from** a poca distancia de ♦ **s. way off** a corta distancia ♦ **in s.** order sin demora ♦ **s. supply** escaso ♦ **s. and sweet** FAM. corto y bueno ♦ **s. circuit** ELEC. cortocircuito ♦ **s. story** cuento ♦ **to be (a dollar) s.** faltarle a uno (un dólar) ♦ **to be s. of** *(money)* andar escaso de; *(breath)* faltarle a uno ♦ **to be s. on** tener poco ♦ **to be (a foot) too s.** tener (un pie) de menos ♦ **to get the s. end (of the stick)** llevar la peor parte ♦ **to have a s. memory** fallarle a uno la memoria ♦ **to have a s. temper** *o* **fuse** enojarse fácilmente ♦ **to run s. of** agotársele a (uno) **II.** adv. *(abruptly)* en seco; *(near)* cerca ♦ **nothing s.**, of nada menos que ♦ **to catch s.** cogerle a uno desprevenido ♦ **to come up s.** quedarse corto ♦ **to cut s.** *(to cut off)* cortar en seco; *(to abbreviate)* acortar ♦ **to fall s. (of)** no alcanzar ♦ **to sell s.** *(commodities)* vender al descubierto; *(person)* subestimar **III.** s. cortocircuito ♦ **for s.** de mote ♦ **in s.** en resumen ♦ pl. pantalones cortos; *(underpants)* calzoncillos **IV.** tr. & intr. ♦ **to s. out** poner(se) en cortocircuito.

short·age (shôr′tĭj) s. falta.

short·change (short′chänj′) tr. dar de menos en el cambio.

short-cir·cuit (:sûr′kĭt) tr. & intr. poner(se) en cortocircuito.

short·com·ing (:kŭm′ĭng) s. defecto.

short·cut (:kŭt′) s. atajo.

short·en (shôr′ən) tr. & intr. acortar(se).

short·en·ing (:ĭng) s. CUL. materia grasa; *(abbreviation)* acortamiento.

short·fall (shôrt′fôl′) s. déficit *m*.

short·hand (:händ′) s. taquigrafía.

short·hand·ed (:hän′dĭd) adj. falto de mano de obra.

short-lived (:lĭvd′, :līvd′) adj. de breve duración.

short·ly (:lē) adv. dentro de poco; *(succinctly)* brevemente.

short·ness (:nĭs) s. cortedad *f*; *(in height)* pequeñez *f*; *(in duration)* brevedad *f*; *(of breath)* falta; *(of manner)* sequedad *f*.

short-range (:rānj′) adj. de alcance reducido.

short·sight·ed (:sī′tĭd) adj. corto de vista.

short-tem·pered (:těm′pərd) adj. que se enoja fácilmente.
short-term (:tûrm′) adj. a corto plazo.
short-wave (:wāv′) adj. de onda corta.
short-wind·ed (:wĭn′dĭd) adj. corto de resuello.
shot¹ (shŏt) s. disparo; *(marksman)* tirador m; *(drink)* trago; DEP. *(ball)* peso; *(try)* tiro; *(in pool)* golpe m; CINEM. escena f; FOTOG. foto f; MED. inyección f; *(pellets)* perdigones m ♦ **like a s.** como una bala • **not by a long s.** ni mucho menos • **s. in the arm** estímulo • **s. in the dark** conjetura • **to call the shots** llevar la voz cantante • **to take a s.** at tratar de (hacer algo) • **without firing a s.** sin pegar un tiro.
shot² adj. FAM. *(day)* perdido; *(clothes)* gastado ♦ **her nerves are s.** tiene los nervios destrozados.
shot³ cf. **shoot**.
shot·gun (shŏt′gŭn′) s. escopeta.
shot-put (:pŏŏt′) s. lanzamiento de peso.
should (shŏŏd) aux. [pret. de **shall**] *(obligation)* deber; *(expectation)* deber de; *(conditional)* <*if he s. fall, so would I* si él se cayera, me caería yo también> ♦ **how s. I know?** ¿cómo iba yo a saber?
shoul·der (shōl′dər) I. s. hombro; *(of meat)* paletilla; *(of road)* orilla ♦ **s. bag** bolsa de bandolera • **s. blade** omóplato • **s. strap** tirantes • **s. to s.** hombro con hombro • **to give the cold s.** tratar con frialdad • **to shrug one's shoulders** encogerse de hombros II. tr. echarse al hombro; *(blame)* cargar con.
shout (shout) I. s. grito II. tr. & intr. gritar.
shove (shŭv) I. tr. empujar a —intr. dar empujones ♦ **to s. off** JER. largarse II. s. empujón m.
shov·el (shŭv′əl) I. s. pala; *(shovelful)* palada II. tr. *(snow)* quitar con la pala; *(steps)* limpiar con la pala ♦ **to s. food into one's mouth** FAM. zamparse la comida.
show (shō) I. tr. **-ed**, **-ed** o **-n** mostrar; *(to guide)* llevar; *(to present)* presentar; *(to grant)* conceder; *(to prove)* demostrar; *(to manifest)* manifestar; *(to point out)* indicar; *(to exhibit)* exponer ♦ **to have nothing to s. for something** no sacar ningún beneficio • **to s. around** mostrar • **to s. how** to enseñar • **to s. in** hacer entrar • **to s. off** hacer alarde de • **to s. one's hand** poner las cartas boca arriba • **to s. oneself** dejarse ver • **to s. out** acompañar a la puerta • **to s. someone the door** echar de la casa • **to s. up** revelar —intr. verse; FAM. *(to come)* aparecer ♦ **it just goes to s.** sirve para demostrar • **to s. off** alardear • **to s. up** aparecer • **to s. up (against)** destacarse II. s. demostración f; *(pretense)* alarde m; TELEV. programa m; TEAT. espectáculo ♦ **by a s. of hands** a mano alzada • **fashion s.** desfile de modelos • **for s.** para impresionar a los demás • **horse s.** concurso hípico • **one-man s.** exposición individual • **s. business** mundo del espectáculo • **s. room** sala de exposición • **to put on, make a s. of** hacer gala o alarde de • **to run the s.** llevar la voz cantante • **to steal the s.** llevarse todos los aplausos.
show·case (′kās′) I. s. vitrina II. tr. poner bien a la vista.
show·down (:doun′) s. momento decisivo; *(confrontation)* confrontación f.
show·er (shou′ər) I. s. *(rain)* chaparrón m; *(snow)* nevada; *(outpouring)* avalancha; *(party)*

fiesta a la que se llevan regalos; *(bath)* ducha II. tr. *(to sprinkle)* salpicar; *(to pour)* derramar —intr. ducharse.
show·ing (shō′ĭng) s. exposición f; *(performance)* actuación f.
show·man (:mən) s. [pl. **-men**] TEAT. comediante m.
show·man·ship (:shĭp′) s. teatralidad f.
show·off (shō′ôf′) s. FAM. presumido.
show·piece (:pēs′) s. obra maestra.
show·y (:ē) adj. **-i-** llamativo.
shrank (shrăngk) cf. **shrink**.
shrap·nel (shrăp′nəl) s.inv. *(shell)* granada de metralla; *(fragments)* metralla.
shred (shrěd) I. s. jirón m; *(particle)* fragmento ♦ **to rip** o **tear to shreds** hacer trizas II. tr. **-dd-** hacer trizas.
shred·der (′ər) s. desfibradora.
shrew (shrōō) s. *(rodent)* musaraña; FAM. mujer regañona.
shrewd (shrōōd) adj. astuto.
shrew·ish (shrōō′ĭsh) adj. regañón.
shriek (shrēk) I. s. chillido II. intr. chillar ♦ **to s. with laughter** reírse a carcajadas.
shrill (shrĭl) I. adj. chillón II. intr. chillar.
shrimp (shrĭmp) s. [pl. inv. o **s**] camarón m; JER. *(small fry)* renacuajo.
shrine (shrīn) s. relicario; *(tomb)* sepulcro; *(site)* lugar santo.
shrink (shrĭngk) I. intr. **shrank** o **shrunk**, **shrunk(en)** encoger(se); *(to dwindle)* mermar; *(to recoil)* retroceder ♦ **to s. away, back** echarse atrás —tr. encoger II. s. JER. psiquiatra mf.
shrink·age (shrĭng′kĭj) s. encogimiento; *(reduction)* disminución f; *(loss)* merma f.
shriv·el (shrĭv′əl) tr. & intr. *(to shrink)* encoger(se); *(to wrinkle)* arrugar(se); *(to lose vitality)* marchitar(se); *(to waste away)* consumir(se).
shroud (shroud) I. s. sudario; *(veil)* velo; MARÍT. obenque m II. tr. tapar.
shrub (shrŭb) s. matorral m.
shrub·ber·y (′ə-rē) s. matorrales m.
shrug (shrŭg) I. intr. **-gg-** encogerse de hombros —tr. ♦ **to s.** *(to minimize)* no hacer caso de; *(to get rid of)* echar de lado con una sacudida II. s. encogimiento de hombros.
shrunk (shrŭngk), **shrunk·en** (shrŭng′kən) cf. **shrink**.
shuck (shŭk) I. s. *(of nuts)* cáscara; *(of corn)* espata II. tr. *(nuts)* pelar; *(corn)* quitar la espata de; *(peas)* desvainar III. interj. ♦ **shucks** ¡diablos!
shud·der (shŭd′ər) I. intr. estremecerse II. s. estremecimiento.
shuf·fle (shŭf′əl) I. tr. *(to move)* cambiar de sitio; *(to stir)* mezclar; *(cards)* barajar —intr. ♦ **to s. along** arrastrar los pies • **to s. off** irse II. s. arrastramiento de los pies; *(of cards)* barajada.
shun (shŭn) tr. **-nn-** rehuir.
shunt (shŭnt) I. s. desviación f; F.C. maniobras II. tr. & intr. desviar(se); F.C. cambiar de vía.
shush (shŭsh, shŏŏsh) interj. ¡chitón!
shut (shŭt) tr. & intr. **shut**, **-tting** cerrar(se) ♦ **to s. away** guardar bajo llave; *(to imprison)* encerrar • **to s. in** encerrar • **to s. off** *(to isolate)* aislar; *(to turn off)* desconectar • **to s. out** no admitir • **to s. up** encerrar; *(to silence)* hacer callar; *(to be silent)* callarse la boca.
shut·down (′doun′) s. cierre m.
shut·eye (:ī′) s. JER. sueño.

shut·ter (:ər) s. contraventana; FOTOG. obturador *m*.

shut·tle (shŭt'l) I. s. lanzadera; *(vehicle)* vehículo que hace trayectos cortos entre dos puntos ♦ **space s.** transbordador espacial II. intr. hacer trayectos cortos y regulares

shut·tle·cock (:kŏk') s. volante *m*.

shy (shī) I. adj. **-er, -est** o **-i-** tímido; *(bashful)* vergonzoso; *(wary)* cauteloso; FAM. *(lacking)* escaso ♦ **s. of** falto de • **to be s. of** desconfiar de II. intr. sobresaltarse; *(to draw back)* echarse atrás asustado ♦ **to s. away** espantarse • **to s. away (from)** huir de.

shy·lock (shī'lŏk') s. usurero.

shy·ness (shī'nĭs) s. timidez *f*; *(caution)* cautela.

shy·ster (shī'stər) s. JER. picapleitos *m*.

sib·ling (sĭb'lĭng) s. hermano, -a.

sick (sĭk) adj. enfermo; *(disturbed)* trastornado; *(morbid)* morboso; *(disgusted)* asqueado; *(tired)* cansado; *(longing)* anhelante ♦ **s. leave** baja por enfermedad • **to be s.** vomitar • **to be s. and tired of** estar harto de • **to feel s.** tener náuseas • **to feel s. at heart** estar desesperado • **to get s.** *(seasick)* marearse; *(to take sick)* ponerse enfermo • **to make s.** dar asco a.

sick bay (bā') s. enfermería.

sick·bed (:bĕd') s. lecho de enfermo.

sick·en (:ən) tr. & intr. enfermar(se).

sick·en·ing (:ə-nĭng) adj. nauseabundo; *(distressing)* deprimente.

sick·le (sĭk'əl) s. hoz *f*.

sick·ly (sĭk'lē) adj. **-i-** enfermizo; *(weak)* enclenque; *(unhealthy)* malsano.

sick·ness (sĭk'nĭs) s. enfermedad *f*; *(nausea)* náusea.

side (sīd) I. s. lado; *(of hill)* ladera; *(of boat)* costado; *(of coin)* cara; *(edge)* borde *m*; *(lineage)* parte *f*; *(team)* facción *f* ♦ **by the s. of** al lado de • **from all sides** de todas partes • **on all, both sides** por todas, ambas partes • **on either s.** de cada lado • **on every s.** por todas partes • **on one's side** de costado • **on the s.** aparte de la ocupación habitual • **on this s.** por este lado • **s. by s.** juntos • **the other s. of** the coin el reverso de la medalla • **the right s.** el derecho; *(correct)* el lado bueno; *(right-hand)* la derecha • **to be on the safe s.** para estar tranquilo • **to change sides** cambiar de partido • **to get on the right o good s. of** granjearse la simpatía de • **to have on one's s.** tener de parte de uno • **to keep on the right s. of the law** mantenerse dentro de la ley • **to move to one s.** apartarse • **to take sides** tomar partido • **to take sides with** ponerse de parte de • **to turn over on its s.** volcar • **wrong s. out** al o del revés II. adj. lateral; *(indirect)* indirecto; *(supplementary)* adicional ♦ **s. arm** arma de mano • **s. effect** efecto secundario • **s. view** vista de perfil III. intr. ♦ **to s. with** ponerse del lado de.

side·board ('bôrd') s. aparador *m*.

side·burns (:bûrnz') s.pl. patillas.

side·car (:kär') s. sidecar *m*.

side·kick (:kĭk') s. JER. amigo, compañero.

side·line (:līn') s. actividad suplementaria; DEP. línea de banda.

side·long (:lông') I. adj. lateral; *(sideways)* de soslayo II. adv. *(obliquely)* oblicuamente.

side·sad·dle (:săd'l) I. s. silla de amazona II. adv. a la amazona.

side·show (:shō') s. atracción secundaria.

side·split·ting (:splĭt'ĭng) adj. divertidísimo.

side·step (:stĕp') tr. **-pp-** esquivar, evitar; *(to evade)* eludir —intr. dar un paso lateral.

side·swipe (:swīp') I. tr. chocar de refilón contra II. s. golpe *m* de refilón.

side·track (:trăk') I. tr. desviar; *(an issue)* dejar de lado II. s. desvío.

side·walk (:wôk') s. acera.

side·ways (:wāz') I. adv. de lado; *(to step)* hacia un lado II. adj. lateral, de lado.

sid·ing (sī'dĭng) s. F.C. apartadero; CONSTR. tablas de forro.

si·dle (sīd'l) tr. & intr. mover(se) furtiva y lateralmente.

siege (sēj) s. MIL. sitio; FIG. calvario.

sieve (sĭv) I. s. tamiz *m* II. tr. tamizar.

sift (sĭft) tr. cerner; *(to separate)* separar; *(to examine)* examinar.

sift·er (sĭf'tər) s. cedazo.

sigh (sī) intr. suspirar.

sight (sīt) I. s. vista; *(vision)* visión *f*; *(thing to see)* lugar *m* de interés; *(of device)* mira; *(quantity)* gran cantidad ♦ **a s. for sore eyes** FAM. persona grata • **on s.** a primera vista • **s. draft** COM. letra a la vista • **s. unseen** sin haberlo visto • **to be (with)in s. of** estar a la vista de • **to catch s. of** vislumbrar • **to come into s.** aparecer, asomar • **to lose s. of** perder de vista ♦ pl. meta • **to set one's s. on** tener el ojo puesto en II. tr. ver; *(to aim)* apuntar.

sight·ed (sī'tĭd) adj. de vista normal.

sight·less (sīt'lĭs) adj. ciego.

sight·ly (:lē) adj. **-i-** agradable a la vista.

sight·see (:sē') intr. **-saw, -seen** visitar lugares de interés.

sight·see·ing (:ĭng) s. visita a lugares de interés.

sight·se·er (:ər) s. turista *mf*.

sign (sīn) I. s. signo; *(gesture)* gesto; *(poster)* letrero; *(symbol)* símbolo; *(trace)* huella; *(presage)* presagio ♦ **s. language** lenguaje por señas • **to make no s.** no dar señales • **to show signs of** dar muestras de II. tr. firmar; *(to express)* indicar ♦ **to s. away** o over ceder • **to s. on** o up contratar —intr. hacer señas; *(to write)* firmar ♦ **to s. in** inscribirse • **to s. on** o up alistarse • **to s. off** acabar el programa • **to s. out** firmar y salir.

sig·nal (sĭg'nəl) I. s. señal *f* ♦ **s. flare** bengala de señales II. adj. señalado III. tr. dar la señal de o para; *(to make known)* indicar —intr. hacer señales.

sig·na·to·ry (:nə-tôr'ē) adj. & s. signatario.

sig·na·ture (:chər) s. firma; *(act)* signatura; MÚS. armadura.

sign·er (sī'nər) s. firmante *mf*.

sig·net (sĭg'nĭt) s. sello ♦ **s. ring** sortija de sello.

sig·nif·i·cance (sĭg-nĭf'ĭ-kəns) s. significación *f*.

sig·nif·i·cant (:kənt) adj. significativo.

sig·ni·fy (sĭg'nə-fī') tr. significar; *(to intimate)* expresar —intr. significar.

sign·post (sīn'pōst') s. poste *m* indicador.

si·lage (sī'lĭj) s. ensilaje *m*.

si·lence (sī'ləns) I. s. silencio II. tr. hacer callar; *(to suppress)* reprimir.

si·lenc·er (sī'lən-sər) s. silenciador *m*.

si·lent (sī'lənt) adj. silencioso; *(mute)* mudo; *(tacit)* tácito ♦ **s. partner** COM. socio comanditario • **to be s.** callar.

sil·hou·ette (sĭl'ōō-ĕt') I. s. silueta II. tr. siluetear.

sil·i·con (sĭl'ĭ-kŏn') s. silicio.

sil·i·cone (sĭl'ĭ-kōn') s. silicona.

silk (sĭlk) s. seda ◆ **s. cotton** seda vegetal • **s. hat** sombrero de copa • **s. screen** serigrafía.

silk·en (sĭl'kən) adj. de seda.

silk·worm (sĭlk'wûrm') s. gusano de seda.

silk·y (sĭl'kē) adj. **-i-** sedoso; (suave) suave.

sill (sĭl) s. (door) umbral m; (window) alféizar m.

sil·li·ness (sĭl'ē-nĭs) s. tontería.

sil·ly (sĭl'ē) adj. **-i-** tonto, bobo; (ridiculous) ridículo.

si·lo (sī'lō) s. silo.

silt (sĭlt) I. s. cieno II. tr. & intr. enarenar(se); (canal) encenagar(se).

sil·ver (sĭl'vər) I. s. plata; (coins) monedas de plata; (color) plateado II. adj. de plata; (like silver) plateado; (melodious) argentino ◆ **s. plate** platería ◆ **s. screen** CINEM. pantalla • **s. tongue** pico de oro III. tr. platear.

sil·ver·smith (:smĭth') s. platero.

sil·ver·ware (:wâr') s. (vajilla de) plata.

sim·i·an (sĭm'ē-ən) I. adj. símico II. s. simio.

sim·i·lar (sĭm'ə-lər) adj. similar.

sim·i·lar·i·ty ('-lăr'ĭ-tē) s. similitud f.

sim·mer (sĭm'ər) intr. hervir a fuego lento; (to seethe) fermentar ◆ **to s. down** sosegarse —tr. hervir a fuego lento.

sim·per (sĭm'pər) I. intr. sonreír tontamente o con afectación II. s. sonrisa tonta.

sim·ple (sĭm'pəl) adj. **-er, -est** simple; (not elaborate) sencillo; (sincere) sincero.

sim·ple·mind·ed ('-mīn'dĭd) adj. (artless) ingenuo; (silly) tonto; (stupid) simple.

sim·ple·ton ('-tn) s. simplón m.

sim·plic·i·ty (sĭm-plĭs'ĭ-tē) s. sencillez f; (foolishness) simpleza.

sim·pli·fi·ca·tion ('plə-fĭ-kā'shən) s. simplificación f.

sim·pli·fy ('-fī') tr. simplificar.

sim·ply (sĭm'plē) adv. simplemente, sencillamente; (really) absolutamente.

sim·u·late (sĭm'yə-lāt') tr. simular.

sim·u·la·tion ('-lā'shən) s. simulación f.

sim·u·la·tor ('-'tər) s. TEC. simulador m.

si·mul·cast (sī'məl-kăst', sĭm'əl-) s. transmisión simultánea por radio y televisión.

si·mul·ta·ne·ous ('-tā'nē-əs) adj. simultáneo.

sin (sĭn) I. s. pecado II. intr. **-nn-** pecar.

since (sĭns) I. adv. desde entonces; (ago) hace <five days s. hace cinco días> ◆ **ever s.** desde entonces | **how long s.?** ¿cuánto tiempo hace? • **long s.** hace mucho tiempo • **s. when?** ¿desde cuándo? II. prep. desde ◆ **s. that time** desde entonces III. conj. desde que; (inasmuch as) ya que ◆ **ever s.** desde que.

sin·cere (sĭn-sîr') adj. **-er, -est** sincero.

sin·cer·i·ty (sĭn-sĕr'ĭ-tē) s. sinceridad f.

si·ne·cure (sī'nĭ-kyŏŏr', sĭn'ĭ-) s. sinecura.

sin·ew (sĭn'yōō) s. tendón m; FIG. vigor m.

sin·ew·y (:ē) adj. nervudo; (strong) fuerte.

sin·ful (sĭn'fəl) adj. (deed) pecaminoso; (person) pecador.

sing (sĭng) intr. **sang, sung** cantar ◆ **to s. to sleep** arrullar • **to s. a different tune** cambiar de tono.

singe (sĭnj) tr. chamuscar.

sing·er (sĭng'ər) s. cantante mf.

sin·gle (sĭng'gəl) I. adj. solo; (for one) individual; (unmarried) soltero ◆ **every s. one** todos •

---

not a s. one ni uno • **s. bed** cama para una persona • **s. file** hilera II. s. (person) individuo; (accommodation) alojamiento individual; (unmarried person) soltero, -a; (bill) billete m de un dólar ◆ pl. DEP. individual, simple (tenis) III. tr. ◆ **to s. out** (to choose) escoger; (to distinguish) distinguir.

sin·gle-hand·ed ('-hăn'dĭd) adj. solo, sin ayuda.

sin·gle-mind·ed (:mīn'dĭd) adj. resuelto.

sing·song (sĭng'sŏng') s. tono monótono.

sin·gu·lar (sĭng'gyə-lər) adj. & s. singular m.

sin·gu·lar·i·ty ('-lăr'ĭ-tē) s. singularidad f.

sin·is·ter (sĭn'ĭ-stər) adj. siniestro.

sink (sĭngk) I. intr. **sank** o **sunk, sunk** descender; (to incline) inclinarse; (to submerge) hundirse; FIG. debilitarse ◆ **his heart sank** se le cayó el alma a los pies • **to s. in** penetrar • **to s. into** caer en • **to s. or swim** triunfar o fracasar —tr. hundir; (to force down) echar al fondo; (into the ground) echar raíces; COM. (to invest) invertir ◆ **to be sunk** in estar sumido en II. s. (bathroom) lavabo; (kitchen) fregadero; (cesspool) pozo negro.

sink·er (sĭng'kər) s. plomo.

sink·ing (:kĭng) s. hundimiento.

sin·ner (sĭn'ər) s. pecador m.

sin·u·ous (sĭn'yōō-əs) adj. sinuoso.

si·nus (sī'nəs) s. seno.

sip (sĭp) I. tr. & intr. **-pp-** sorber II. s. sorbo.

si·phon (sī'fən) I. s. sifón m II. tr. sacar con sifón.

sir (sûr) s. señor m, caballero ◆ **Dear S.** muy señor mío • **S.** sir (título).

sire (sīr) s. padre m; (animal) semental m; ANT. progenitor m; (title) mi Señor.

si·ren (sī'rən) s. sirena.

sir·loin (sûr'loin') s. solomillo.

sis·sy (sĭs'ē) s. mariquita m; (timid person) timorato.

sis·ter (sĭs'tər) s. hermana; G.B. (nurse) enfermera ◆ **s. ships** buques gemelos.

sis·ter·hood (:hŏŏd') s. hermandad f; RELIG. comunidad f de monjas.

sis·ter-in-law ('-ĭn-lô') s. [pl. **sisters-**] (spouse's sister, brother's wife) cuñada, hermana política; (spouse's brother's wife) concuñada.

sis·ter·ly (:lē) adj. de hermana.

sit (sĭt) intr. **sat** sentarse; (to be at rest) estar sentado; (to perch) posarse (pájaro); (to brood) empollar; (to lie) estar situado; (to pose) posar; (to convene) reunirse; (to be inactive) quedarse; (to babysit) cuidar a niños ◆ **to be sitting pretty** FAM. estar en posición ventajosa • **to s. back** sentarse cómodamente • **to s. down** sentarse • **to s. in** participar; (to protest) tomar parte en una sentada • **to s. for an examination** G.B. presentarse a un examen • **to s. in for** reemplazar • **to s. on** ser miembro de • **to s. on one's hands** no hacer nada • **to s. still** no moverse • **to s. tight** FAM. no moverse • **to s. up** incorporarse; (to stay up) quedarse levantado; (to become alert) prestar atención —tr. sentar; (to ride) montar (un caballo) ◆ **to s. out** o **through** quedarse hasta el final; (to remain seated) quedarse sentado durante (baile).

site (sīt) I. s. sitio; (location) ubicación f II. tr. situar.

sit·ter (sĭt'ər) s. persona que cuida niños.

sit·ting (:ĭng) s. asentada; (session) sesión f ◆ **s. duck** víctima fácil • **s. room** sala de estar.

sit·u·ate (sĭch'ōō-āt') tr. ubicar.

sit·u·a·tion ('-ā'shən) s. situación *f; (position)* puesto.
six (sīks) s. & adj. seis *m* ♦ **at sixes and sevens** en desorden • **s. hundred** seiscientos • **s. o'clock** las seis.
six-gun ('gŭn') s. revólver *m* de seis tiros.
six-pack (:păk') s. caja de seis botellas *o* latas.
six-shoot·er (:shōō'tər) s. FAM. revólver *m* de seis tiros.
six·teen (sĭk-stēn') s. & adj. dieciséis *m.*
six·teenth (:stēnth') I. s. *(place)* dieciséis *m; (part)* dieciseisavo II. adj. *(place)* decimosexto; *(part)* dieciseisavo.
sixth (sĭksth) s. & adj. sexto.
six·ti·eth (sĭk'stē-ĭth) I. s. *(place)* sesenta *m; (part)* sesentavo II. adj. sexagésimo.
six·ty (sĭk'stē) s. & adj. sesenta *m.*
siz·a·ble (sī'zə-bəl) adj. considerable.
size[1] (sīz) I. s. tamaño *f; (of shoes)* número; *(of persons, garments)* talla; *(magnitude)* magnitud *f* ♦ **that's about the s. of it** es más o menos eso • **to cut down to s.** bajarle los humos a • **to cut to s.** cortar algo del tamaño que se necesita • **to try on for s.** probar II. tr. clasificar según el tamaño ♦ **to s. up** evaluar.
size[2] I. s. *(paste)* cola II. tr. encolar.
siz·ing (sī'zĭng) s. apresto, cola.
siz·zle (sĭz'əl) I. intr. chisporrotear, FIG. *(to be furious)* hervir II. s. chisporroteo.
skate[1] (skāt) I. s. patín *m* II. intr. patinar.
skate[2] s. ICT. raya.
skate·board (skāt'bôrd') s. tabla de patinar sobre ruedas.
skat·er (skā'tər) s. patinador *m.*
skein (skān) s. madeja.
skel·e·tal (skĕl'ĭ-tl) adj. esquelético.
skel·e·ton (skĕl'ĭ-tn) s. esqueleto; *(outline)* bosquejo.
skep·tic (skĕp'tĭk) s. escéptico.
skep·ti·cal (:tĭ-kəl) adj. escéptico.
skep·ti·cism (:tĭ-sĭz'əm) s. escepticismo.
sketch (skĕch) I. s. esbozo; *(outline)* bosquejo; LIT. obra corta; MÚS. pieza corta II. tr. esbozar —intr. hacer un croquis.
sketch·book ('bŏŏk') s. bloc *m* de dibujo.
sketch·y (:ē) adj. -i- sin detalles; *(superficial)* superficial.
skew (skyōō) I. intr. torcerse —tr. *(to cut)* sesgar; *(to distort)* tergiversar II. s. sesgo.
skew·er (skyōō'ər) I. s. brocheta II. tr. ensartar.
ski (skē) I. s. esquí *m* ♦ **s. jump** salto con esquís • **s. lift** telesquí • **ski run** *o* **slope** pista de esquí II. intr. & tr. esquiar.
skid (skĭd) I. s. patinazo; *(chock)* calzo; *(ramp)* rampa de descarga; AVIA. patín *m* ♦ **s. row** barrio bajo ♦ pl. MARÍT. varadera • **to be on** *o* **hit the s.** estar de capa caída II. intr. -dd- patinar, resbalar *(rueda, automóvil).*
ski·er (skē'ər) s. esquiador *m.*
ski·ing (:ĭng) s. esquí *m* (deporte).
skill (skĭl) s. maña; *(art)* técnica; *(experience)* experiencia; *(trade)* oficio.
skilled (skĭld) adj. mañoso; *(qualified)* especializado.
skil·let (skĭl'ĭt) s. sartén *f.*
skill·ful (skĭl'fəl) adj. hábil, mañoso.
skill·ful·ness (:nĭs) s. habilidad *f,* maña.
skim (skĭm) I. tr. -mm- *(liquid)* espumar; *(milk)* desnatar; *(to brush)* rozar; *(book)* hojear ♦ **to s. along** volar a ras de ♦ **to s. over** pasar rozando; *(a subject)* tratar superficial-

mente • **to s. through** echar una ojeada a —intr. hojear (libro) II. s. ♦ **s. milk** leche desnatada.
skimp (skĭmp) tr. escatimar —intr. economizar.
skimp·y (skĭm'pē) adj. -i- *(scanty)* escaso; *(small)* pequeño.
skin (skĭn) I. s. piel *f* ♦ **by the s. of one's teeth** por los pelos • **he is nothing but s. and bones** está en los huesos • **it's no s. off my nose** esto no es asunto mío • **s. diving** buceo • **to get under one's s.** irritarle a uno; *(obsession)* ser una obsesión • **to have a thick s.** ser insensible • **to jump out of one's s.** llevarse un susto tremendo • **to save one's s.** salvar el pellejo • **under the s.** en el fondo II. tr. -nn- despellejar; *(to peel)* pelar; *(to scrape)* desollar ♦ **to s. alive** desollar vivo a; *(to scold)* regañar mucho.
skin-deep ('dēp') I. adj. superficial II. adv. superficialmente.
skin-dive (:dīv') intr. bucear.
skin-flint (:flĭnt') s. tacaño.
skin·ny (:ē) adj. -i- flaco.
skin·ny-dip (:dĭp') intr. -pp- FAM. nadar desnudo.
skin·tight (skĭn'tīt') adj. ceñido.
skip (skĭp) I. intr. -pp- saltar; *(engine)* fallar; EDUC. saltar un curso ♦ **to s. out** FAM. desaparecer —tr. saltar; *(class, meeting)* dejar de ir a ♦ **s. it!** ¡olvídalo! • **to s. over** saltar por encima de • **to s. town** FAM. largarse II. s. salto.
skip·per (skĭp'ər) s. MARÍT. capitán *m.*
skir·mish (skûr'mĭsh) I. s. escaramuza; *(dispute)* pelea II. intr. escaramuzar.
skirt (skûrt) I. s. falda II. tr. & intr. bordear; *(to pass around)* faldear; *(to elude)* eludir.
skit (skĭt) s. TEAT. escena satírica.
skit·ter (skĭt'ər) intr. pasar rozando el agua.
skit·tish (skĭt'ĭsh) adj. asustadizo; *(undependable)* caprichoso.
skiv·vy (skĭv'ē) FAM. ♦ pl. calzoncillo y camiseta • **in one's s.** en paños menores.
skulk (skŭlk) intr. *(to lurk)* esconderse; *(to steal)* pasar furtivamente.
skull (skŭl) s. cráneo ♦ **s. and crossbones** calavera • **to be out of one's s.** FAM. estar loco.
skull·dug·ger·y (skŭl-dŭg'ə-rē) s. engaños.
skunk (skŭngk) I. s. ZOOL. mofeta; JER. *(person)* canalla *m* II. tr. JER. derrotar.
sky (skī) s. cielo ♦ **out of the clear blue s.** en el momento menos pensado • **to praise to the skies** poner las nubes.
sky·cap ('kăp') s. changador *m* de un aeropuerto.
sky·dive (:dīv') intr. lanzarse en paracaídas.
sky·jack (:jăk') tr. secuestrar en vuelo.
sky·light (:līt') s. claraboya.
sky·line (:līn') s. horizonte *m; (of city)* perfil *m.*
sky·rock·et (:rŏk'ĭt) I. s. cohete *m* II. tr. & intr. subir rápidamente.
sky·scrap·er (:skrā'pər) s. rascacielos *m.*
sky·ward (:wərd) I. adj. dirigido hacia el cielo II. adv. hacia el cielo.
slab (slăb) s. *(piece)* trozo; *(of stone)* losa; *(of cake)* porción *f; (of wood)* costero.
slack (slăk) I. adj. *(sluggish)* lento; *(not busy)* de poca actividad; *(loose)* flojo; *(negligent)* negligente II. tr. aflojar; *(to slake)* apagar —intr. aflojarse; *(to be remiss)* ser negligente ♦ **to s. off** disminuir III. s. *(loose part)* parte

floja; *(lull)* período de poca actividad ♦ **there is a lot of s. in the rope** la cuerda está muy floja • **to take up the s. in a rope** tensar una cuerda ♦ pl. pantalones.

slack·en ('ən) tr. *(to slow)* aminorar; *(to loosen)* aflojar —intr. *(to slow down)* amainar; *(to loosen)* aflojarse.

slack·er (:ɔr) s. haragán *m.*

slag (slăg) s. escoria.

slain (slān) cf. **slay.**

slake (slāk) tr. aplacar; *(lime)* apagar.

slam¹ (slăm) I. tr. **-mm-** *(to shut)* cerrar de golpe; *(to move)* hacer golpear; *(to hit)* golpear con estrépito ♦ **to s. something down on** poner algo violentamente en • **to s. the door** dar un portazo • **to s. the door on** cerrar la puerta a —intr. cerrarse de golpe; *(to crash)* chocar II. s. golpe *m* fuerte; *(of door)* portazo.

slam² *(in bridge)* slam *m.*

slan·der (slăn'dər) I. s. calumnia; DER. difamación *f* II. tr. calumniar; DER. difamar.

slan·der·ous (:əs) adj. calumnioso; DER. difamador.

slang (slăng) s. jerga.

slang·y (slăng'ē) adj. **-i-** vulgar.

slant (slănt) I. tr. inclinar; *(a problem)* enfocar de modo parcial —intr. inclinarse II. s. inclinación *f; (point of view)* parecer *m.*

slap (slăp) I. s. palmada; *(on face)* bofetada; *(on head)* cachetada ♦ **a s. in the face** FIG. un insulto • **a s. on the back** un espaldazo II. tr. **-pp-** *(to strike)* dar una palmada; *(the face)* abofetar; *(the head)* dar una cachetada; FIG. insultar ♦ **to s. down** prohibir.

slap·hap·py ('hăp'ē) adj. **-i-** JER. aturdido.

slash (slăsh) I. tr. acuchillar; *(to hack)* dar un tajo a; *(prices)* rebajar —intr. tirar *o* dar tajos II. s. tajo; *(slit)* cuchillada; *(virgule)* vírgula.

slat (slăt) s. tablilla.

slate (slāt) I. s. pizarra; *(list)* lista de candidatos elegibles ♦ **to clear the s.** borrar los antecedentes • **to have a clean s.** no tener antecedentes II. tr. empizarrar; *(to appoint)* designar.

slath·er (slăth'ər) tr. FAM. extender en gran cantidad.

slaugh·ter (slô'tər) I. s. matanza II. tr. *(animals)* matar; *(to kill brutally)* matar brutalmente.

slaugh·ter·house (:hous') s. matadero.

slave (slāv) I. s. esclavo ♦ **s. labor** trabajo de esclavo II. intr. trabajar como esclavo.

slav·er¹ (slăv'ər) I. intr. babear II. s. baba.

slav·er² (slā'vər) s. *(ship)* buque *m* traficante de esclavos; *(person)* traficante *m* de esclavos.

slav·er·y (:və-rē, slăv'rē) s. esclavitud *f* ♦ **white s.** trata de blancas.

slay (slā) tr. **slew, slain** matar.

slea·zy (slē'zē) adj. **-i-** ligero; *(cheap)* de mala calidad; *(vulgar)* vulgar.

sled (slĕd) I. s. trineo II. tr. **-dd-** llevar en trineo —intr. ir en trineo.

sled·ding ('ĭng) s. transporte por trineo.

sledge (slĕj) s. trineo.

sledge·ham·mer (slĕj'hăm'ər) s. almádena.

sleek (slēk) adj. suave y brillante; *(well-groomed)* elegante.

sleep (slēp) I. s. sueño ♦ **in one's s.** durante el sueño • **to drop off to s.** quedarse dormido • **to go to s.** dormirse • **to put to s.** *(animal)* sacrificar • **to walk in one's s.** ser sonámbulo II. intr. **slept** dormir ♦ **to s. in** dormir hasta tarde • **to s. like a log** dormir como un tronco

—tr. pasar durmiendo; *(to accommodate)* tener cabida para ♦ **not to s. a wink** no pegar ojo • **to s. off** dormir hasta que pase (dolor de cabeza, borrachera) • **to s. on it** consultar con la almohada.

sleep·er (slē'pər) s. persona que duerme; *(sleeping car)* coche *m* cama; FAM. *(success)* éxito inesperado ♦ **to be a heavy, light s.** tener el sueño pesado, ligero.

sleep·ing (:pĭng) adj. dormido, durmiendo ♦ **s. bag** saco de dormir • **s. car** coche cama • **s. pill** somnífero.

sleep·less (slēp'lĭs) adj. en blanco.

sleep·walk·ing (:wô'kĭng) s. sonambulismo.

sleep·y (slē'pē) adj. **-i-** soñoliento.

sleep·y·head (:hĕd') s. FAM. dormilón *m.*

sleet (slēt) I. s. aguanieve *f* II. intr. cellisquear.

sleeve (slēv) s. manga; *(of record)* funda ♦ **up one's s.** FAM. escondido.

sleeve·less ('lĭs) adj. sin mangas.

sleigh (slā) I. s. trineo II. intr. ir en trineo.

sleight (slīt) s. habilidad *f; (stratagem)* estratagema ♦ **s. of hand** juego de manos.

slen·der (slĕn'dər) adj. **-er, -est** delgado; *(svelte)* esbelto; *(meager)* escaso.

slen·der·ize (:də-rīz') intr. & tr. adelgazar.

slept (slĕpt) cf. **sleep.**

sleuth (slōōth) I. s. FAM. detective *m* II. intr. hacer de detective.

slew¹ (slōō) s. FAM. montón *m.*

slew² cf. **slay.**

slice (slīs) I. s. *(of meat)* tajada; *(of bread)* rebanada; *(of ham)* lonja; *(of fish)* raja; *(share)* parte *f;* DEP. golpe *m* que da efecto a la pelota II. tr. cortar, tajar; *(bread)* rebanar; DEP. golpear con efecto ♦ **to s. off** cortar.

slic·er (slī'sər) s. máquina de cortar.

slick (slĭk) I. adj. resbaladizo; *(adroit)* diestro; *(wily)* astuto II. s. superficie resbaladiza; *(tool)* herramienta para alisar ♦ **oil s.** capa de petróleo III. tr. alisar.

slick·er (:ər) s. impermeable *m;* FAM. *(swindler)* estafador *m.*

slide (slīd) I. intr. **slid** resbalar; *(to coast)* deslizarse; *(to glide)* pasar suavemente ♦ **to let things s.** dejar que las cosas sin hacer nada • **to s. down** bajar deslizándose por —tr. hacer resbalar ♦ **to s. over** pasar por alto II. s. deslizamiento, desliz *m; (surface)* superficie resbaladiza; *(playground)* tobogán *m; (track)* resbaladero; *(microscope)* portaobjeto; *(avalanche)* desprendimiento; FOTOG. diapositiva ♦ **s. rule** regla de cálculo.

slight (slīt) I. adj. escaso; *(trifling)* insignificante; *(slender)* delgado II. tr. menospreciar; *(to shirk)* desatender III. s. desaire *m.*

slim (slĭm) I. adj. **-mm-** delgado; *(scant)* escaso II. tr. & intr. **-mm-** adelgazar.

slime (slīm) s. *(mud)* limo; *(animal substance)* babaza.

slim·y (slī'mē) adj. **-i-** viscoso; *(mucous)* baboso.

sling (slĭng) I. s. *(weapon)* honda; *(for rifle)* portafusil *m;* MED. cabestrillo; MARÍT. eslinga II. tr. **slung** *(to throw)* arrojar; *(to hang)* colgar ♦ **to s. hash** JER. trabajar en un restaurante barato.

sling·shot ('shŏt') s. tirador *m.*

slink (slĭngk) intr. **slunk** escabullirse.

slink·y (slĭng'kē) adj. **-i-** *(stealthy)* sigiloso; FAM. sinuoso.

slip¹ (slĭp) I. intr. **-pp-** deslizarse; *(to steal)* es-

cabullirse; *(to lose one's balance)* resbalar; *(to escape)* soltarse; *(to fall behind)* retrasarse; *(to make a mistake)* equivocarse; FAM. *(to fall off)* empeorar ♦ **my foot slipped** se me fue el pie • **to let an opportunity slip by** dejar pasar una oportunidad • **to let s.** decir sin querer • **to s. away** escabullirse; *(time)* correr • **to s. by** *(time)* correr; *(unnoticed)* pasar inadvertido • **to s. down** dejarse caer • **to s. in** introducirse • **to s. off** escabullirse • **to s. out** salir inadvertido; *(to become known)* saberse • **to s. through** escabullirse por • **to s. through one's fingers** escapársele de las manos • **to s. up** FAM. equivocarse —tr. librarse *(from de)* ♦ **to s. in** introducir • **to s. into** *(to don)* ponerse; *(to enter)* entrar • **to s. on** quitarse (ropa) • **to s. on** ponerse (ropa) • **to s. one over on** FAM. pegársela a • **to s. one's mind** írsele de la memoria a uno
II. s. resbalón *m;* *(false step)* paso en falso; *(error)* equivocación *f;* *(lapse)* desliz *m;* *(undergarment)* combinación *f;* *(pillowcase)* funda; MARÍT. *(pier)* muelle *m;* *(slipway)* grada ♦ **s. of the tongue** lapsus linguae.
slip² s. *(cutting)* esqueje *m;* *(of paper)* papeleta ♦ **a s. of a girl** una chiquilla.
slip·cov·er ('kŭv'ər) s. funda.
slip·knot (:nŏt') s. nudo corredizo.
slip page (ĭj) s. resbalamiento; MEC. pérdida de fuerza de transmisión.
slip·per (:ər) s. zapatilla.
slip·per·y (:ə-rē) adj. -i- resbaladizo; *(evasive)* evasivo.
slip·shod (:shŏd') adj. descuidado.
slip·stream (:strēm') s. estela.
slip-up (:ŭp') s. FAM. error *m.*
slit (slĭt) I. s. corte *m* II. tr. **slit, -tting** hender ♦ **to s. someone's throat** degollar a alguien.
slith·er (slĭth'ər) I. intr. resbalar; *(to crawl)* deslizarse, culebrear II. s. deslizamiento.
sliv·er (slĭv'ər) I. s. *(splinter)* astilla; *(slice)* tajada II. tr. cortar en rodajas —intr. astillarse.
slob (slŏb) s. DESPEC., FAM. palurdo.
slob·ber (slŏb'ər) I. intr. babear II. s. baboseo.
slog (slŏg) tr. **-gg-** golpear —intr. *(to plod)* andar pesadamente; *(to work)* trabajar como un burro.
slo·gan (slō'gən) s. lema *m;* *(in advertising)* slogan *m.*
sloop (slōōp) s. balandro.
slop (slŏp) I. s. *(mud)* fango; *(food)* aguachirle *f* ♦ pl. *(swill)* bazofia II. intr. & tr. **-pp-** *(to splash)* salpicar; *(to spill)* derramar(se).
slope (slōp) I. tr. & intr. inclinar(se) ♦ **to s. down** bajar • **to s. up** subir II. s. *(incline)* cuesta; *(of roof)* vertiente *f;* *(inclination)* inclinación *f* ♦ **on a s.** en declive.
slop·pi·ness (slŏp'ē-nĭs) s. falta de cuidado.
slop·py (slŏp'ē) adj. -i- FAM. *(messy)* desordenado; *(careless)* chapucero.
slosh (slŏsh) tr. salpicar —intr. chapotear.
slot (slŏt) s. *(groove)* ranura; *(on roster)* puesto en el escalafón; FAM. *(niche)* rincón *m* ♦ **s. machine** máquina tragaperras.
sloth (slŏth, slôth) s. indolencia; ZOOL. perezoso.
sloth·ful (:fəl) adj. perezoso, indolente.
slouch (slouch) I. intr. *(to sit)* repantigarse; *(to stand)* tener una postura desgarbada ♦ **to s. around** gandulear —tr. echar hacia adelante II. s. postura desgarbada; *(person)* perezoso ♦ **to walk with a s.** caminar con los hombros cal-

dos.
slough¹ (slōō, slou) s. fangal *m;* *(state of despair)* estado de abatimiento.
slough² (slŭf) I. s. ZOOL. camisa II. intr. caerse; MED. desprenderse (costra) —tr. abandonar *(hábito)* ♦ **to s. off** deshacerse de.
slov·en (slŭv'ən) s. persona desaseada.
slov·en·ly (:lē) adj. desaseado.
slow (slō) I. adj. lento; *(clock)* atrasado; *(tardy)* atrasado; *(dense)* torpe; FAM. *(boring)* aburrido ♦ **business is s.** hay poca actividad • **my watch is five minutes s.** mi reloj tiene cinco minutos de retraso • **s. motion** cámara lenta • **to be s.** to tardar en II. adv. lentamente, despacio III. tr. *(to make slow)* reducir la marcha de; *(to retard)* retrasar —intr. ir más despacio ♦ **s. down!** ¡más despacio!
slow-down ('doun') s. retraso.
slow·ness (:nĭs) s. lentitud *f;* *(boredom)* pesadez *f;* *(stupidity)* torpeza.
slow-poke (:pōk') s. FAM. tortuga (persona).
slow-wit·ted (:wit'ĭd) adj. lento, torpe.
sludge (slŭj) s. cieno; *(sewage)* fango de alcantarillado; *(sediment)* sedimento.
slug¹ (slŭg) s. *(bullet)* bala; *(metal disk)* ficha; *(lump of metal)* trozo de metal; FAM. *(drink)* trago.
slug² s. ZOOL. babosa.
slug³ tr. **-gg-** pegar un porrazo II. s. porrazo.
slug·gish (slŭg'ĭsh) adj. *(slow)* lento; *(lazy)* perezoso; *(inactive)* flojo.
sluice (slōōs) I. s. canal *m;* *(gate)* esclusa II. tr. *(to flush)* regar; *(to send down)* transportar por un canal.
slum (slŭm) I. s. barrio bajo II. intr. **-mm-** ♦ **to go slumming** visitar los barrios bajos.
slum·ber (slŭm'bər) I. intr. dormir; *(to doze)* dormitar II. s. sueño; *(dormancy)* sopor *m.*
slum·ber·ous/brous (:bar-as/brəs) adj. *(asleep)* dormido; *(quiet)* tranquilo.
slump (slŭmp) I. intr. desplomarse; *(to slouch)* repantigarse II. s. disminución brusca; *(depression)* depresión *f.*
slung (slŭng) cf. sling.
slunk (slŭngk) cf. slink.
slur (slûr) I. tr. **-rr-** *(to treat lightly)* hacer poco caso de; *(to pronounce indistinctly)* pronunciar mal; *(to slander)* difamar; MÚS. ligar II. s. *(aspersion)* difamación *f;* MÚS. ligado.
slurp (slûrp) tr. & intr. *(to eat)* comer haciendo ruido; *(to drink)* beber haciendo ruido.
slush (slŭsh) s. *(melted snow)* aguanieve *f;* *(mud)* lodo.
slut (slŭt) s. mujerzuela.
sly (slī) adj. -er, -est o -i- *(cunning)* astuto; *(deceitful)* malicioso; *(roguish)* travieso.
smack¹ (smăk) I. tr. hacer un chasquido con los labios; *(to kiss)* besar sonoramente; *(to strike)* dar un palmada —intr. chasquear; *(to kiss)* dar un beso sonoro II. s. chasquido; *(kiss)* beso sonoro; *(blow)* golpe *m* III. adv. de lleno.
smack² I. s. *(flavor)* sabor *m;* *(trace)* indicio II. intr. saber ♦ **to s. of** oler a.
small (smôl) I. adj. pequeño; *(minor)* insignificante; *(petty)* mezquino; *(humiliated)* humillado ♦ **in a s. way** en pequeña escala • **s. fry** gente menuda • **s. letters** minúsculas • **s. talk** charloteo • **to feel s.** sentir vergüenza II. s. parte pequeña ♦ **the s. of the back** la región lumbar.

small·pox ('pŏks') s. viruela.
smart (smärt) I. adj. *(intelligent)* listo; *(witty)* ingenioso; *(impertinent)* impertinente; *(quick)* rápido; *(fashionable)* de moda II. intr. *(to sting)* escocer.
smart·en (smär'tn) intr. despabilarse.
smash (smăsh) I. tr. romper; *(to shatter)* destrozar; *(to throw)* estrellar; *(to crush)* aplastar —intr. romperse; *(to crash)* estrellarse; *(to be crushed)* hacerse pedazos II. s. *(breakage)* rotura; *(sound)* estrépito; *(collision)* choque *m*; FAM. *(hit)* éxito III. adj. ♦ **a s. hit** un gran éxito.
smash·up ('ŭp') s. choque *m*.
smat·ter·ing (smăt'ər-ĭng) s. conocimiento superficial.
smear (smîr) I. tr. untar; *(to dirty)* embadurnar; *(to vilify)* difamar II. s. mancha.
smell (smĕl) I. tr. **-ed** o **smelt**, **-lling** oler; *(to detect)* olfatear ♦ **I s. a rat** FAM. hay gato encerrado ♦ **to s. out** olfatear —intr. oler; *(to stink)* apestar ♦ **smelling salts** sales aromáticas II. s. *(act)* olfato; *(sense)* olfato; *(odor)* olor *m*.
smell·y ('ē) adj. **-i-** FAM. maloliente.
smelt[1] (smĕlt) tr. & intr. fundir.
smelt[2] s. [pl. inv. o *s*] ICT. eperlano.
smid·gen/gin (smĭj'ən) s. FAM. pizca.
smile (smīl) I. s. sonrisa II. intr. sonreír(se) —tr. expresar con una sonrisa ♦ **to s.** on favorecer.
smirch (smûrch) tr. manchar.
smirk (smûrk) I. intr. sonreír con afectación II. s. sonrisa afectada.
smite (smīt) tr. **smote**, **smitten** o **smote** golpear; *(to destroy)* destruir ♦ **to be smitten with** *(a girl)* estar encaprichado por.
smith (smĭth) s. herrero.
smith·y ('ē, smĭth'ē) s. herrería.
smock (smŏk) I. s. guardapolvo II. tr. COST. fruncir.
smog (smŏg) s. mezcla de humo y niebla.
smog·gy ('ē) adj. **-i-** lleno de humo y niebla.
smoke (smōk) I. s. humo; FAM. *(cigarette)* pitillo ♦ **s. bomb** bomba de humo ♦ **s. detector** ahumadero ♦ **s. screen** cortina de humo ♦ **to go up in s.** irse en humo ♦ **where there's there's fire** cuando el río suena, agua lleva II. intr. humear; *(tobacco)* fumar —tr. fumar; *(to preserve)* ahumar ♦ **to s. out** desalojar con humo; *(to reveal)* descubrir.
smoke·stack ('stăk') s. chimenea.
smok·y (smō'kē) adj. **-i-** *(fire)* humeante; *(room)* lleno de humo; *(color, taste)* ahumado.
smol·der (smōl'dər) I. intr. arder (sin llama); FIG. estar latente II. s. humo espeso.
smooch (smōōch) JER. I. s. beso II. intr. besuquearse.
smooth (smōōth) I. adj. *(fine)* liso; *(soft)* suave; *(calm)* tranquilo; *(fluid)* fluido; *(uneventful)* sin novedad; *(ingratiating)* meloso; *(refined)* refinado; *(unwrinkled)* sin arrugas ♦ **s. talk** zalamerías II. tr. *(to level)* alisar; *(to polish)* pulir; *(to soothe)* aliviar ♦ **to s. the way for** preparar el terreno para ♦ **to s. things over** limar asperezas —intr. alisarse.
smooth-tongued ('tŭngd') adj. zalamero.
smote (smōt) cf. **smite**.
smoth·er (smŭth'ər) I. tr. sofocar; *(to conceal)* enterrar; *(to cover)* cubrir —intr. asfixiarse.
smoul·der (smōl'dər) var. de **smolder**.
smudge (smŭj) I. tr. *(to dirty)* manchar; *(to*

blur) emborronar —intr. manchar(se) II. s. mancha; *(against insects)* humo para fumigar.
smug (smŭg) adj. **-gg-** presumido.
smug·gle (smŭg'əl) tr. pasar de contrabando —intr. contrabandear.
smug·gler (:lər) s. contrabandista *mf.*
smug·gling (:lĭng) s. contrabando.
smug·ness (smŭg'nĭs) s. presunción *f.*
smut (smŭt) s. *(particle)* hollín *m*; *(smudge)* mancha de tizne; *(obscenity)* obscenidad *f.*
smut·ty ('ē) adj. **-i-** *(dirty)* manchado; *(obscene)* obsceno.
snack (snăk) I. s. bocado ♦ **s. bar** cafetería II. intr. tomar(se) un bocado.
snag (snăg) I. s. protuberancia; *(submerged tree)* tronco sumergido; *(obstacle)* tropiezo II. tr. **-gg-** *(to tear)* rasgar; FAM. *(to catch)* agarrar —intr. rasgarse.
snail (snāl) s. caracol *m.*
snake (snāk) I. s. serpiente *f*; FIG. traidor *m* ♦ **s. in the grass** traidor II. tr. & intr. serpentear.
snake·skin ('skĭn') s. piel *f* de serpiente.
snap (snăp) I. intr. **-pp-** *(to click)* chasquear; *(to break)* quebrarse; *(to bite)* morder ♦ **s. out of it!** ¡anímate! ♦ **to s. at** *(dog)* intentar morder; *(to speak harshly to)* hablar con brusquedad a ♦ **to s. off** desprenderse ♦ **to s. open, shut** abrirse, cerrarse de golpe —tr. *(to break)* quebrar; *(to utter)* decir bruscamente; *(fingers, whip)* chasquear ♦ **to s. up** llevarse II. s. *(sound)* chasquido; *(breaking)* rotura; *(of fingers)* castañeteo; *(clasp)* broche *m* de presión; *(cookie)* galleta; *(brief spell)* ola (de frío); *(effortless task)* cosa fácil ♦ **put some s. into it!** ¡muévase! III. adj. rápido.
snap·per ('ər) s. [pl. inv. o *s*] cubera.
snap·py (:ē) adj. **-i-** FAM. *(brisk)* vivo, animado; *(smart)* elegante.
snap·shot (:shŏt') s. instantánea.
snare[1] (snâr) I. s. trampa II. tr. tender trampas; *(to trap)* cazar con trampa.
snare[2] s. MÚS. cuerda ♦ **s. drum** tambor.
snarl[1] (snärl) I. intr. gruñir; *(to speak angrily)* refunfuñar II. s. gruñido; *(hostile utterance)* refunfuño.
snarl[2] I. s. *(tangle)* maraña; *(predicament)* enredo II. tr. & intr. enredar(se).
snatch (snăch) I. tr. agarrar, arrebatar; *(illicitly)* secuestrar —intr. arrebatar II. s. arrebatamiento; *(fragment)* pedacito ♦ **in snatches** a ratos.
snaz·zy (snăz'ē) adj. **-i-** JER. llamativo.
sneak (snēk) I. intr. andar a hurtadillas —tr. hacer furtivamente II. s. persona cobarde; *(exit)* salida disimulada ♦ **s. thief** ratero.
sneak·er (snē'kər) s. zapato de lona.
sneak·y (:kē) adj. **-i-** furtivo; *(surreptitious)* solapado.
sneer (snîr) I. s. gesto de desprecio II. intr. hacer un gesto de desprecio.
sneeze (snēz) I. intr. estornudar II. s. estornudo.
sneez·ing (snē'zĭng) s. estornudo.
snick·er (snĭk'ər) I. intr. reírse disimuladamente II. s. risita.
snide (snīd) adj. sarcástico.
sniff (snĭf) I. intr. aspirar por la nariz; *(in contempt)* despreciar —tr. *(odor)* olfatear; *(drug)* inhalar II. s. aspiración *f*; *(smelling)* olfateo.
snif·fle (:əl) I. intr. resollar; *(to whimper)* lloriquear II. s. resuello; *(whimper)* lloriqueo ♦ pl.

FAM. resfriado.

snif·ter (snĭf'tər) s. copa para coñac.

snig·ger (snĭg'ər) I. s. risa disimulada II. intr. reir disimuladamente.

snip (snĭp) I. tr. & intr. **-pp-** tijeretear II. s. *(action)* tijeretazo; *(piece)* recorte m.

snipe (snīp) I. s. [pl. inv. o **s**] agachadiza II. intr. *(shots)* tirar desde una posición emboscada; *(remarks)* atacar solapadamente.

snip·er (snī'pər) s. francotirador m.

snip·pet (snĭp'ĭt) s. recorte m.

snip·py (snĭp'ē) adj. **-i-** FAM. impertinente.

snit (snĭt) JER. s. arranque m de cólera ♦ **to be in a s.** estar enfadado.

snitch (snĭch) JER. I. tr. birlar —intr. soplar II. s. soplón m.

sniv·el (snĭv'əl) intr. gimotear; *(to run at the nose)* moquear.

snob (snŏb) s. snob m.

snob·ber·y ('ə-rē) s. snobismo.

snob·bish (:ĭsh) adj. como un snob.

snood (snōōd) s. redecilla.

snoop (snōōp) FAM. I. intr. entrometerse ♦ **to s. around** husmear II. s. curioso, entrometido.

snoop·y (snōō'pē) adj. **-i-** FAM. entrometido.

snoot (snōōt) s. JER. *(snout)* hocico; *(nose)* nariz f; *(snob)* snob m.

snoot·y (snōō'tē) adj. **-i-** JER. altanero.

snooze (snōōz) FAM. I. intr. dormitar II. s. sueño ligero.

snore (snôr) I. intr. roncar II. s. ronquido.

snor·kel (snôr'kəl) I. s. tubo de respiración II. intr. bucear con tubo de respiración.

snort (snôrt) I. s. bufido; JER. *(a drink)* trago II. intr. bufar —tr. JER. *(drugs)* inhalar.

snot (snŏt) s. JER. moco; *(person)* mocoso.

snot·ty (snŏt'ē) adj. **-i-** FAM. mocoso; *(angry)* de mal humor.

snout (snout) s. hocico; JER. *(nose)* nariz f.

snow (snō) I. s. nieve f, *(snowfall)* nevada ♦ s. job engaño ♦ s. tire neumático para nieve II. intr. nevar —tr. *(to cover)* cubrir con nieve; JER. *(to flatter)* adular; *(to deceive)* embaucar ♦ **to s. under** abrumar.

snow·ball ('bôl') I. s. bola de nieve II. intr. aumentar rápidamente.

snow·bank (:băngk') s. montón m de nieve.

snow·drift (:drĭft') s. ventisquero.

snow·fall (:fôl') s. nevada.

snow·man (:măn') s. [pl. **-men**] muñeco de nieve.

snow·mo·bile (:mō-bēl') s. vehículo automotor para ir por la nieve.

snow·plow (:plou') s. quitanieves m.

snow·shoe (:shōō') I. s. raqueta II. intr. caminar sobre la nieve con raquetas.

snow·storm (:stôrm') s. tormenta de nieve.

snow·suit (:sōōt') s. traje m que usan los niños en la nieve.

snow·y (:ē) adj. **-i-** nevado; *(subject to snow)* nevoso; *(white)* blanco como la nieve.

snub (snŭb) I. tr. **-bb-** *(to slight)* desairar; *(to stop)* parar bruscamente II. s. desaire m; *(stop)* parada brusca.

snub-nosed ('nōzd') adj. de nariz chata.

snuff¹ (snŭf) tr. & intr. aspirar; *(to sniff)* oler.

snuff² I. s. *(of candle)* pabilo II. tr. despabilar; *(to extinguish)* apagar ♦ **to s. out** destruir.

snuff³ s. *(tobacco)* rapé ♦ **to be up to s.** FAM. ser satisfactorio.

snuff·box ('bŏks') s. caja de rapé.

snuf·fle (snŭf'əl) I. intr. resollar II. s. resuello

♦ pl. FAM. resfrío.

snug (snŭg) adj. **-gg-** *(cozy)* cómodo; *(warm)* calentito; *(tight)* ajustado ♦ **to be as s. as a bug in a rug** estar muy cómodo.

snug·gle (snŭg'əl) tr. & intr. acurrucar(se).

so (sō) I. adv. *(thus)* así, de esta manera; *(to such an extent)* de tal manera, tan; *(consequently)* por eso; *(approximately)* así de <the wound was so wide la herida era así de ancha>; *(likewise)* también <you were on time and so was I tú llegaste a tiempo y yo también>; *(so much)* tanto, *(then)* así que ♦ **and so on and so forth** y así sucesivamente ♦ **how so?** ¿cómo es eso? ♦ **if so** si es así ♦ **I hope so** eso espero, espero que sí ♦ **is that so?** ¿es verdad?, ¿ah, sí? ♦ **I think so** creo que sí ♦ **I told you so** ya te lo dije! ♦ **it just so happens that** pues resulta que ♦ **just so** ni más ni menos ♦ **not so** no es así ♦ **not so much as** ni siquiera ♦ **so more or less** de menos ♦ **so as to** a fin de ♦ **so far** hasta aquí; *(point)* hasta cierto punto ♦ **so far as** hasta donde ♦ **so far as I'm concerned** por lo que a mí respecta ♦ **so far as I know** que yo sepa ♦ **so far so good** por ahora, bien ♦ **so it is!** ¡así es! ♦ **so long** tanto *(tiempo)*; *(good-bye)* hasta luego ♦ **so long as** mientras que ♦ **so many** tantos ♦ **so much** para vaya ♦ **so so** así, así ♦ **so that** de manera que ♦ **so much that** así que ♦ **so to speak** por decirlo así ♦ **so what?** ¡y qué? ♦ **to be so kind as to** tener la bondad de II. adj. así III. conj. así que ♦ **so that** para que, a fin de que IV. pron. lo mismo.

soak (sōk) I. tr. empapar; *(to immerse)* remojar; *(to absorb)* absorber; JER. *(to overcharge)* cobrar demasiado ♦ **to s. to the skin** calar hasta los huesos —intr. remojarse; *(to penetrate)* infiltrarse ♦ **to s. through** penetrar; *(to drench)* calar II. s. remojo.

soak·ing (sō'kĭng) I. s. remojón m II. adj. empapado ♦ **s. wet** calado hasta los huesos.

so-and-so (sō'ən-sō') s. Fulano de Tal.

soap (sōp) I. s. jabón m ♦ **s. opera** serial m II. tr. (en)jabonar.

soap·stone ('stōn') s. esteatita.

soap·y (sō'pē) adj. **-i-** jabonoso.

soar (sôr) intr. *(to rise)* remontarse; *(to ascend)* elevarse súbitamente; AER. planear.

sob (sŏb) I. intr. **-bb-** sollozar II. s. sollozo.

so·ber (sō'bər) I. adj. **-er, -est** sobrio; *(serious)* grave; *(reasonable)* cuerdo ♦ **to s. up** desembriagar —intr. ♦ **to s. up** pasársele a uno la embriaguez.

so·bri·e·ty (sō-brī'ĭ-tē) s. sobriedad f; *(serious-ness)* seriedad f.

so·bri·quet (sō'brĭ-kā') s. apodo.

so-called (sō'kôld') adj. llamado.

soc·cer (sŏk'ər) s. fútbol m.

so·cia·ble (sō'shə-bəl) adj. sociable, *(friendly)* amistoso.

so·cial (sō'shəl) I. adj. social; *(sociable)* sociable ♦ **s. climber** arribista ♦ **s. column** ecos de sociedad ♦ **s. disease** enfermedad venérea ♦ **s. services** programa de asistencia social ♦ **s. work** asistencia social II. s. reunión f.

so·cial·ist (sō'shə-lĭst) s. & adj. socialista mf.

so·cial·is·tic ('-lĭs'tĭk) adj. socialista.

so·cial·ite ('-līt') s. persona de alta sociedad.

so·cial·ize (:līz') tr. & intr. *(to make sociable)* volver sociable ♦ **socialized medicine** medicina estatal —intr. alternar.

so·ci·e·tal (sə-sī'ĭ-tl) adj. social.

so·ci·e·ty (sə-sī'ĭ-tē) s. sociedad f; *(upper class)*

alta sociedad; *(companionship)* compañía ♦ **high s.** alta sociedad ♦ **s. page** noticias de la sociedad ♦ **to go into s.** ser presentada en sociedad.

so·ci·o·ec·o·nom·ic (sō'sē-ō-ěk'ə-nŏm'ĭk) adj. socioeconómico.

so·ci·o·log·i·cal (:ə-lŏj'ĭ-kəl) adj. sociológico.

so·ci·ol·o·gist (:ŏl'ə-jĭst) s. sociólogo.

so·ci·ol·o·gy (:jē) s. sociología.

so·ci·o·path (sō'sē-ə-păth') s. persona antisocial.

so·ci·o·po·lit·i·cal ('-ō-pə-lĭt'ĭ-kəl) adj. sociopolítico.

sock¹ (sŏk) I. s. [pl. **s** o **sox**] calcetín *m* II. tr. ♦ **to s. away** FAM. guardar (dinero).

sock² JER. I. tr. golpear II. s. puñetazo.

sock·et (sŏk'ĭt) s. hueco; *(of bulb)* casquillo; *(connection)* enchufe *m* (hembra); *(eye)* cuenca.

sod (sŏd) I. s. *(lawn)* césped *m*; *(piece)* tepe *m* II. tr. **-dd-** cubrir de césped.

so·da (sō'də) s. carbonato de sodio; *(sodium oxide)* sosa; *(water)* gaseosa; *(refreshment)* soda ♦ **s. fountain** mostrador en el que se despachan bebidas gaseosas y helados • **s. pop** FAM. soda, gaseosa.

so·dal·i·ty (sō-dăl'ĭ-tē) s. RELIG. cofradía; *(fellowship)* asociación *f*.

sod·den (sŏd'n) adj. *(wet)* empapado; *(food, mind)* pesado.

so·di·um (sō'dē-əm) s. sodio ♦ **s. bicarbonate, chloride** bicarbonato, cloruro de sodio.

sod·om·y (sŏd'ə-mē) s. sodomía.

so·fa (sō'fə) s. sofá *m*.

soft (sŏft) adj. *(not hard)* blando; *(not loud)* bajo; *(gentle, smooth)* suave; *(tender)* tierno; *(lenient)* indulgente; *(weak)* débil; FAM. *(easy)* fácil <a s. job un trabajo fácil> ♦ **s. drink** gaseosa • **s. in the head** estúpido • **to be s. on** ser indulgente con.

soft-boiled ('boild') adj. *(egg)* pasado por agua; FAM. *(sentimental)* sensiblero.

soft·en (sŏ'fən) tr. & intr. ablandar(se).

soft-heart·ed (sŏft'här'tĭd) adj. compasivo.

soft·ness (:nĭs) s. suavidad *f*, blandura; *(weakness)* debilidad *f*; *(tenderness)* dulzura.

soft-spo·ken (:spō'kən) adj. de voz suave; *(genial)* afable.

soft·ware (:wâr') s. software *m*, logicial *m*.

sog·gy (sŏg'ē) adj. **-i-** empapado.

soil¹ (soil) s. *(land)* tierra.

soil² I. tr. *(to dirty)* ensuciar; *(to disgrace)* manchar II. s. *(dirtiness)* suciedad *f*; *(stain)* mancha; *(excrement)* excremento.

soiled (soild) adj. sucio, manchado.

so·journ (sō'jûrn') I. intr. residir temporalmente II. s. residencia temporal, estada.

sol·ace (sŏl'ĭs) I. s. consuelo II. tr. consolar.

so·lar (sō'lər) adj. solar.

so·lar·i·um (sō-lâr'ē-əm) s. [pl. **s** o **-ia**] solana.

sold (sōld) cf. **sell.**

sol·der (sŏd'ər) I. s. soldadura II. tr. soldar.

sol·dier (sōl'jər) I. s. soldado ♦ **s. of fortune** mercenario II. intr. servir como soldado.

sold-out (sōld'out') adj. agotado.

sole¹ (sōl) s. *(of foot)* planta; *(of shoe)* suela II. tr. poner suela a (zapato, bota).

sole² adj. *(single)* único <his s. aim su único propósito>; *(rights, ownership)* exclusivo.

sole³ s. [pl. inv. o **s**] ICT. lenguado.

sol·emn (sŏl'əm) adj. solemne; *(sacred)* sagrado.

so·lem·ni·ty (sə-lěm'nĭ-tē) s. solemnidad *f*.

so·lic·it (sə-lĭs'ĭt) tr. solicitar; *(prostitute)* abordar —intr. hacer una petición.

so·lic·i·ta·tion (-'ĭ-tā'shən) s. solicitación *f*.

so·lic·i·tor (-'ĭ-tər) s. *(chief law officer)* procurador *m*; G.B. *(lawyer)* abogado.

so·lic·i·tous (:təs) adj. solícito, atento.

so·lic·i·tude (:tōōd') s. solicitud *f*, cuidado.

sol·id (sŏl'ĭd) I. adj. sólido; *(not hollow)* macizo <s. gold de oro macizo>; *(line)* continuo; *(fact)* seguro; *(citizen)* modelo; *(unanimous)* unánime; *(of color)* uniforme ♦ **s. as a rock** firme como una roca II. s. sólido.

sol·i·dar·i·ty (sŏl'ĭ-dăr'ĭ-tē) s. solidaridad *f*.

so·lid·i·fy (sə-lĭd'ə-fī') tr. & intr. solidificar(se).

so·lid·i·ty (:ĭ-tē) s. solidez *f*.

sol·id·ly (sŏl'ĭd-lē) adv. sólidamente; *(unanimously)* unánimemente; *(non-stop)* sin parar.

so·lil·o·quy (sə-lĭl'ə-kwē) s. soliloquio.

sol·i·taire (sŏl'ĭ-târ') s. solitario.

sol·i·tar·y (sŏl'ĭ-těr'ē) I. adj. solitario; *(single)* solo ♦ **s. confinement** incomunicación II. s. solitario; FAM. *(prison)* incomunicación *f*.

sol·i·tude (:tōōd') s. soledad *f*.

so·lo (sō'lō) I. adj. & s. solo II. adv. a solas III. intr. volar solo.

so·lo·ist (:ĭst) s. solista *mf*.

sol·stice (sŏl'stĭs) s. solsticio.

sol·u·ble (sŏl'yə-bəl) adj. soluble.

sol·ute (:yōōt') s. soluto, substancia disuelta.

so·lu·tion (sə-lōō'shən) s. solución *f*.

solv·a·ble (sŏl'və-bəl) adj. soluble.

solve (sŏlv) tr. resolver, solucionar.

sol·ven·cy (sŏl'vən-sē) s. solvencia.

sol·vent (:vənt) I. adj. COM. solvente; QUÍM. disolvente II. s. solvente *m*, disolvente *m*.

som·ber (sŏm'bər) adj. sombrío.

some (sŭm) I. adj. alguno(s) <s. people algunas personas>; *(a little)* algo de, un poco de; cierto <after s. time después de cierto tiempo>; unos (cuantos), varios <s. days ago hace varios días>; IRÓN. menudo <s. advice! ¡menudo consejo!>; *(remarkable)* extraordinario <s. luck! ¡vaya suerte! • **s. other time** otro día, otro momento • **s. way or other** de una manera u otra II. pron. *(several)* algunos; *(a little)* un poco, algo ♦ **and then s.** y más todavía III. adv. unos <s. forty people unas cuarenta personas>; FAM. *(somewhat)* un poco, algo.

some·bod·y ('bŏd'ē) I. pron. alguien II. s. FAM. alguien *m*, personaje *m* <he thinks he's s. se cree alguien>.

some·day (:dā') adv. algún día, un día de éstos.

some·how (:hou') adv. de algún modo, de alguna manera; *(for some reason)* por alguna razón.

some·one (:wŭn') cf. **somebody.**

some·place (:plās') adv. en o a alguna parte.

som·er·sault (sŭm'ər-sôlt') I. s. salto mortal, FIG. cambio total (de opinion) II. intr. dar un salto mortal.

some·thing (sŭm'thĭng) I. pron. algo ♦ **or s.** o algo por el estilo • **s. or other** una cosa u otra • **to be quite s.** ser algo extraordinario • **to be s.** ser de alguna importancia • **to be s. of a . . .** tener algo de . . . • **to have a certain s.** tener un no sé qué II. adv. *(somewhat)* algo; *(extremely)* sumamente.

some·time (:tīm') I. adv. alguna vez, algún día ♦ **s. soon** pronto II. adj. *(former)* ex, antiguo.

some·times (:ūmz') adv. de vez en cuando, a veces.

some·way (:wā') adv. de alguna manera.

some·what (:hwŏt') adv. algo.

some·where (:hwâr') adv. en *o* a alguna parte; *(approximately)* más o menos, entre ♦ **s. near here** por aquí • **s. or other** en alguna parte.

som·nam·bu·list (sŏm-năm'byə-lĭst) s. sonámbulo.

som·no·lence (sŏm'nə-ləns) s. somnolencia.

som·no·lent (:lənt) adj. soñoliento.

son (sŭn) s. hijo.

so·nar (sō'när') s. sonar *m.*

song (sŏng) s. canción *f; (act)* canto, cantar *m; (poetry)* canto ♦ **for a s.** por poca cosa • **same old s.** FAM. (la misma) cantilena • **to give someone a s. and dance** FAM. contarle a alguien toda una historia.

song·bird ('bûrd') s. cantor *m,* ave canora.

song·ster (:stər) s. cantante *mf.*

song·wrlt·er (:rī'tər) s. compositor *m.*

son·ic (sŏn'ĭk) adj. sónico, acústico ♦ **s. boom** estampido supersónico.

son-in-law (sŭn'ĭn-lô') s. [pl. **sons-**] yerno, hijo político.

son·net (sŏn'ĭt) s. soneto.

son·ny (sŭn'ē) s. FAM. hijito.

so·nor·i·ty (sə-nôr'ĭ-tē) s. sonoridad *f.*

so·no·rous (sə-nôr'əs, sŏn'ər-) adj. sonoro.

soon (sōōn) adv. pronto; *(early)* temprano <back so s.? ¿de vuelta tan temprano?> ♦ **as s.** as en cuanto, tan pronto como • **had sooner** preferiría • **how s.?** ¿cuándo a (más tardar)? • **no sooner said than done** dicho y hecho • **s. after** poco después • **the sooner the better** cuanto más pronto, mejor • **sooner or later** tarde o temprano.

soot (sŏŏt) s. hollín *m,* tizne *m.*

soothe (sōōth) tr. calmar, tranquilizar, *(pain)* aliviar.

sooth·ing (sōō'thĭng) adj. tranquilizador.

sooth·say·er (sōōth'sā'ər) s. adivino.

soot·y (sŏŏt'ē) adj. -i- tiznado, *(dark)* ennegrecido.

sop (sŏp) I. s. & intr. **-pp-** remojar(se) ♦ **to s. up** absorber II. s. dádiva (para apaciguar).

so·phis·ti·cate (sə-fĭs'tĭ-kĭt) s. persona sofisticada.

so·phis·ti·cat·ed (,kā'tĭd) adj. sofisticado, *(complicated)* complejo.

so·phis·ti·ca·tion ('-'shən) s. sofisticación *f.*

soph·is·try (sŏf'ĭ-strē) s. sofistería.

soph·o·more (sŏf'ə-môr') s. estudiante *mf* de segundo año.

soph·o·mor·ic ('-'ĭk) adj. inmaduro.

sop·o·rif·ic (sŏp'ə-rĭf'ĭk) adj. & s. soporífico.

sop·ping (sŏp'ĭng) I. adj. empapado II. adv. ♦ **s. wet** *(thing)* empapado; *(person)* calado hasta los huesos.

so·pran·o (sə-prăn'ō) s. soprano *mf.*

sor·cer·er (sôr'sər-ər) s. hechicero, brujo.

sor·cer·ess (:ĭs) s. hechicera, bruja.

sor·cer·y (sôr'sə-rē) s. hechicería, brujería.

sor·did (sôr'dĭd) adj. sórdido.

sore (sôr) I. adj. dolorido; FAM. *(offended)* molesto ♦ **s. point** asunto delicado • **s. throat** dolor de garganta • **to be s.** doler <my throat is s. me duele la garganta>; FAM. *(mad)* estar enfadado *(at* con) • **to get s.** ofenderse II. s. *(wound)* llaga; *(pain)* dolor *m.*

sore·ly ('lē) adv. *(a lot)* mucho; *(very)* muy.

sor·ghum (sôr'gəm) s. sorgo.

so·ror·i·ty (sə-rôr'ĭ-tē) s. asociación estudiantil femenina.

sor·rel¹ (sôr'əl) s. BOT. acedera.

sor·rel² s. *(color, horse)* alazán *m.*

sor·row (sôr'ō) I. s. *(sadness)* pesar *m,* dolor *m; (grieving)* duelo II. intr. sentir pena.

sor·row·ful (sôr'ə-fəl) adj. *(person)* pesaroso; *(news)* doloroso.

sor·ry (sôr'ē) I. adj. -i- *(sad)* triste; *(wretched)* infeliz; *(paltry)* insignificante • **I'm s.** lo siento • **to be s.** sentir <I'm s. to be late siento llegar tarde> • **to be s. for** compadecer • **to feel s. for oneself** sentirse desgraciado • **you'll be s.!** ¡te arrepentirás! II. interj. ¡perdón!

sort (sôrt) I. s. *(class)* clase *f,* tipo; *(type)* especie *f; (person)* tipo ♦ **after a s.** de mala manera • **it's s. of big** es más bien grande • **nothing of the s.!** ¡nada de eso! • **of sorts** una especie de • **out of sorts** de mal humor • **something of the s.** algo por el estilo II. tr. *(to classify)* clasificar; *(to put in order)* ordenar ♦ **to s. out** *(to separate)* separar; *(problems)* resolver.

sor·tie (sôr'tē) s. MIL. salida.

so-so (sō'sō') adj. & adv. regular.

sot (sŏt) s. borracho.

sought (sôt) cf. **seek.**

soul (sōl) s. alma; personificación *f* <the s. of honor la personificación del honor> ♦ **poor s.** pobre • **to search one's s.** examinar la conciencia.

soul·ful ('fəl) adj. sentimental.

soul-search·ing (:sûr'chĭng) s. examen *m* de conciencia.

sound¹ (sound) I. s. sonido ♦ **from the s. of it** al parecer • **I don't like the s. of it** no me huele bien • **to the s. of** al son de • **s. barrier** barrera del sonido • **s. effects** efectos sonoros • **s. stage** estudio para filmar con sonido II. intr. sonar; *(to seem)* parecer ♦ **to s. off** MIL. marcar el paso; *(to protest)* protestar a voz en grito • **to s.** *(instrument)* tocar; *(alarm)* dar; MED. auscultar.

sound² adj. en buenas condiciones; *(healthy)* sano; *(firm)* firme; *(economy)* fuerte; *(reason)* válido; *(knowledge)* completo; *(sleep)* profundo; *(defeat)* total; *(trustworthy)* de confianza; *(advice)* razonable; DER. válido ♦ **to be s. of mind** estar uno en su sano juicio.

sound³ s. MARÍT. estrecho, brazo de mar.

sound⁴ tr. *(to fathom)* sondar ♦ **s. out** sondear —intr. sondear; *(whale)* sumergirse.

sound·ing¹ (soun'dĭng) s. GEOL., MARÍT. sondeo.

sound·ing² adj. resonante ♦ **s. board** MÚS. tabla de armonía; *(spokesman)* portavoz.

sound·less (sound'lĭs) adj. silencioso, mudo.

sound·ly (·lē) adv. *(solidly)* sólidamente; *(deeply)* profundamente; *(thoroughly)* del todo.

sound·ness (:nĭs) s. *(solidity)* solidez *f; (validity)* validez *f; (good sense)* sensatez *f.*

sound·proof (:prōōf') I. adj. insonoro, a prueba de sonido II. tr. insonorizar.

sound·track (:trăk') s. pista o banda sonora.

soup (sōōp) s. sopa ♦ **from s. to nuts** de cabo a rabo • **s. kitchen** comedor de beneficencia • **to be in the s.** JER. estar en un apuro • **to s. up** AUTO. aumentar la potencia de.

soup·spoon (:spōōn') s. cuchara de sopa.

soup·y (sōō'pē) adj. -i- *(liquid)* espeso; *(foggy)* con niebla espesa.

sour (sour) I. adj. agrio; *(milk)* cortado; *(smell)* acre ♦ **to turn** *o* **go s.** *(wine, mood)* agriarse; *(milk)* cortarse; *(deal)* fracasar **II.** tr. & intr. *(wine, mood)* agriar(se); *(milk)* cortar(se); *(person)* amargar(se).

source (sòrs) s. origen *m*; *(of river)* manantial *m*; *(of supply, information)* fuente *f*.

sour·dough (sour′dō′) s. *(leaven)* levadura; JER. *(prospector)* cateador *m*.

souse (sous) **I.** tr. *(to drench)* empapar; JER. *(to make drunk)* emborrachar **II.** s. CUL. carne conservada en vinagre; JER. *(drunkard)* borracho.

south (south) **I.** s. sur *m* **II.** adj. del sur, austral **III.** adv. hacia el sur.

south·bound (′bound′) adj. con rumbo al sur.

south·east (-ēst′) **I.** s. sudeste *m* **II.** adj. del sudeste **III.** adv. hacia el sudeste.

south·east·ern (:ē′stərn) adj. del sudeste.

south·er·ly (sŭth′ər-lē) adj. del sur.

south·ern (:ərn) adj. del sur.

south·ern·er (:ər-nər) s. habitante *mf* del sur, sureño; HIST. sudista *mf*.

south·paw (south′pô′) s. JER. zurdo.

south·ward (:wərd) adv. hacia el sur.

south·west (-wĕst′) **I.** s. suroeste *m*, sudoeste *m* **II.** adj. del sudoeste **III.** adv. hacia el sudoeste.

south·west·ern (:wĕs′tərn) adj. del sudoeste.

sou·ve·nir (sōō′və-nîr′) s. recuerdo.

sov·er·eign (sŏv′ər-ĭn) adj. & s. soberano.

sov·er·eign·ty (:tē) s. soberanía.

sow¹ (sō) tr. **-ed, -ed** *o* **-n** sembrar.

sow² (sou) s. *(female hog)* cerda.

soy (soi) s. soja ♦ **s. sauce** salsa de soja.

soy·a (′ə) s. soja *(semilla)*.

soy·bean (:bēn′) s. soja.

spa (spä) s. *(mineral spring)* manantial *m* de agua mineral; *(resort)* balneario.

space (spās) **I.** s. espacio; *(blank)* espacio en blanco; *(place)* sitio, lugar *m* <*it takes up too much s.* ocupa demasiado sitio> ♦ **outer s.** espacio exterior ♦ **s. age, suit** era, traje espacial • **s. bar** espaciador • **s. shuttle** transbordador espacial • **to stare into s.** tener la mirada perdida **II.** tr. espaciar, distanciar ♦ **to s. out** separar, distanciar —intr. ♦ **to s. out** JER. abstraerse.

space·craft (′krăft′) s.inv. astronave *f*.

space·flight (:flīt′) s. vuelo espacial.

space·man (:măn′) s. [pl. **-men**] astronauta *mf*.

space·ship (:shĭp′) s. nave *f* espacial.

spac·ing (spā′sĭng) s. espaciamiento.

spa·cious (:shəs) adj. espacioso, amplio.

spa·cy (:ē) adj. **-i-** JER. *(vacant)* vago, abstraído; *(weird)* extraño.

spade¹ (spād) **I.** s. *(digging tool)* pala ♦ **to call a s. a s.** llamar al pan pan y al vino vino **II.** tr. remover con pala.

spade² s. *(cards)* espada, pico.

spa·ghet·ti (spə-gĕt′ē) s. espagueti *m*.

span¹ (spăn) **I.** s. *(breadth)* anchura; *(of wings)* envergadura; *(of bridge)* ojo; *(arched support)* arcada; *(of hand)* palmo; *(period of time)* duración *f* **II.** tr. **-nn-** *(to extend across)* cruzar, atravesar; *(to measure by hand)* medir en palmos; *(in time)* durar.

span² pareja (de caballos o bueyes).

span·gle (spăng′gəl) s. lentejuela.

span·gled (:gəld) adj. *(costume)* adornado con lentejuelas; *(star-studded)* estrellado.

span·iel (spăn′yəl) s. perro de aguas.

Span·ish-speak·ing (spăn′ĭsh-spē′kĭng) adj. hispanoparlante, hispanohablante.

spank (spăngk) **I.** tr. dar una zurra, zurrar —intr. ir de prisa **II.** s. zurra.

spank·ing (spăng′kĭng) **I.** adj. FAM. *(breeze)* fresco **II.** s. zurra.

spar¹ (spär) s. MARÍT. palo.

spar² intr. **-rr-** *(in boxing)* entrenarse; *(to dispute)* discutir, pelear.

spare (spâr) **I.** tr. *(expenses, efforts)* escatimar; *(strength)* reservar; *(to avoid)* evitar <*they spared him the trouble* le evitaron la molestia de hacerlo>; *(not to destroy)* perdonar; *(to save)* salvar; *(to do without)* prescindir de; *(to afford)* dar, dedicar <*I can't s. the time* no puedo dedicar el tiempo>; *(feelings)* no herir ♦ **to s.** de sobra • **to s. oneself** ahorrarse trabajos **II.** adj. *(part)* de repuesto, de recambio; *(extra)* sobrante, de sobra <*s. cash* dinero sobrante>; *(unoccupied)* libre <*in my s. time* en mis ratos libres>; *(thin)* delgado, enjuto ♦ **s. room** cuarto en desuso **III.** s. pieza de repuesto.

spare·ribs (′rĭbz′) s.pl. costillas de cerdo.

spar·ing (:ĭng) adj. *(frugal)* frugal, económico; *(scarce)* parco; *(lenient)* indulgente.

spark¹ (spärk) **I.** s. chispa ♦ **to give off sparks** echar chispas **II.** intr. echar chispas, chispear —tr. provocar ♦ **to s. off** provocar.

spark² **I.** s. *(dandy)* petimetre *m*, pisaverde *m*; *(gallant)* galán *m* **II.** tr. & intr. galantear.

spar·kle (spär′kəl) **I.** intr. *(to glitter)* centellear, brillar; *(with wit)* chispear; *(to effervesce)* burbujear **II.** s. *(glitter)* centelleo, destello; *(vivacity)* viveza, burbujeo.

spar·kler (:klər) s. cohete chispero.

spark·plug (spärk′plŭg′) s. AUTO. bujía.

spar·row (spăr′ō) s. gorrión *m*.

sparse (spärs) adj. disperso, infrecuente.

spasm (spăz′əm) s. espasmo; FIG. arrebato.

spas·mod·ic (spăz-mŏd′ĭk) adj. espasmódico.

spas·tic (spăs′tĭk) adj. & s. espástico.

spat¹ (spăt) cf. **spit¹**.

spat² s. *(gaiter)* polaina ♦ pl. polainas.

spat³ **I.** s. *(quarrel)* riña, pelea **II.** intr. **-tt-** reñir, pelear.

spa·tial (spā′shəl) adj. espacial.

spat·ter (spăt′ər) **I.** tr. & intr. salpicar **II.** s. salpicadura.

spat·u·la (spăch′ə-lə) s. espátula.

spawn (spôn) **I.** s. *(of fish)* freza, hueva; *(outcome)* resultado; *(offspring)* engendro **II.** intr. ICT. frezar —tr. FIG. engendrar, producir.

spay (spā) tr. VET. quitar los ovarios.

speak (spēk) intr. **spoke, spoken** hablar; *(to express oneself)* expresarse; *(in assembly)* tomar la palabra; FIG. decir, expresar <*facts s. more than words* los hechos dicen más que las palabras> ♦ **so to s.** por así decirlo • **to be on speaking terms** hablarse, tener buenas relaciones • **to s. of** mencionar <*there is nothing to s. of* no hay nada que mencionar> • **to s. out** hablar claro • **to s. up** *(louder)* hablar más fuerte; *(to be heard)* decir lo que uno piensa —tr. *(to tell)* decir <*I s. the truth* digo la verdad>; *(a language)* hablar; *(to reveal)* revelar, expresar ♦ **to s. for** *(to recommend)* hablar en favor de; *(on behalf of)* hablar en nombre de • **to s. for itself** ser evidente • **to s. well, ill of** hablar bien, mal de.

speak·er (spē′kər) s. persona que habla; *(spokesperson)* portavoz *m*; *(orator)* orador *m*; *(lecturer)* conferenciante *mf*, conferencista *mf*; *(loudspeaker)* altoparlante *m*, altavoz *m*.

spear (spîr) **I.** s. lanza; *(for fishing)* arpón *m*; BOT. brizna **II.** tr. traspasar, atravesar (con

una lanza); *(fish)* arponear.
spear·head ('hĕd') I. s. punta de lanza; MIL., FIG. vanguardia II. tr. encabezar.
spear·mint (:mĭnt') s. hierbabuena.
spe·cial (spĕsh'əl) I. adj. especial; *(in particular)* de particular <*nothing s.* nada de particular>; *(superior)* especial; *(friend)* íntimo; *(edition, flight)* extraordinario ♦ **s. delivery** entrega inmediata II. s. TELEV. programa *m* especial.
spe·cial·ist (:ə-lĭst) s. especialista *mf.*
spe·ci·al·i·ty ('ē-ăl'ĭ-tē) s. especialidad *f.*
spe·cial·i·za·tion (:ə-lĭ-zā'shən) s. especialización *f.*
spe·cial·ize (spĕsh'ə-līz') intr. especializarse; BIOL. diferenciarse.
spe·cial·ly (:ə-lē) adv. especialmente, en particular.
spe·cial·ty (:əl-tē) s. especialidad *f.*
spe·cie (spē'shē, :sē) s. metálico, efectivo.
spe·cies (spē'shēz, :sēz) s.inv. especie *f.*
spe·cif·ic (spĭ-sĭf'ĭk) I. adj. específico ♦ **s. gravity** peso específico II. s. cualidad específica.
spec·i·fi·ca·tion (spĕs'ə-fĭ-kā'shən) s. especificación *f.*
spec·i·fy (spĕs'ə-fī') tr. especificar.
spec·i·men (spĕs'ə-mən) s. *(sample)* muestra, ejemplar *m*; BIOL. espécimen *m.*
spe·cious (spē'shəs) adj. especioso.
speck (spĕk) I. s. *(small spot)* mancha, mota; *(particle)* partícula II. tr. motear.
speck·le (spĕk'əl) I. s. *(speck)* mancha, mota; *(freckle)* peca II. tr. motear, salpicar de manchas.
speck·led (:əld) adj. *(spotted)* moteado, salpicado de manchas; *(freckled)* pecoso.
specs (spĕks) s.pl. FAM. *(eyeglasses)* gafas; *(specifications)* especificaciones *f.*
spec·ta·cle (spĕk'tə-kəl) s. espectáculo ♦ **to make a s. of oneself** ponerse en ridículo ♦ pl. gafas.
spec·tac·u·lar (-tăk'yə-lər) I. adj. espectacular, grandioso II. s. TEAT. espectáculo.
spec·ta·tor (spĕk'tā'tər) s. espectador *m.*
spec·ter (spĕk'tər) s. espectro.
spec·tral (:trəl) adj. espectral.
spec·tro·graph (:trə-grăf') s. espectrógrafo.
spec·u·late (spĕk'yə-lāt') intr. especular.
spec·u·la·tion ('-lā'shən) s. especulación *f.*
spec·u·la·tive (:'-lə-tĭv) adj. especulativo.
spec·u·la·tor (:lā'tər) s. especulador *m.*
spec·u·lum (spĕk'yə-ləm) s. [pl. **s** o **-la**] ÓPT. espejo; CIR., ZOOL. espéculo.
sped (spĕd) cf. **speed.**
speech (spēch) s. habla; *(conversation)* conversación *f*; *(address)* discurso; *(language)* lenguaje *m* ♦ **free s.** libertad de expresión • **s. impediment** defecto de pronunciación • **to deliver** *o* **make a s.** pronunciar un discurso.
speech·less ('lĭs) adj. mudo, sin habla ♦ **to be** *o* **be left s.** quedarse mudo.
speech·mak·er (:mā'kər) s. orador *m.*
speed (spēd) I. s. velocidad *f*; JER. *(drug)* anfetamina.♦ **at full** *o* **top s.** a toda velocidad ♦ **s. limit** velocidad máxima • **to pick up s.** acelerar II. intr. *(to speed)* ir de prisa, ir corriendo; *(to drive fast)* conducir con exceso de velocidad ♦ **to s. along** ir a gran velocidad; *(to hurry)* apresurarse —tr. ♦ **to s. up** acelerar.
speed·boat ('bōt') s. lancha motora.
speed·ing (spē'dĭng) I. adj. veloz, rápido II. s.

AUTO. exceso de velocidad.
speed·om·e·ter (spĭ-dŏm'ĭ-tər) s. velocímetro.
speed·y (spē'dē) adj. rápido, veloz; *(prompt)* pronto.
spell[1] (spĕl) tr. **-ed** *o* **spelt** *(with letters)* deletrear; *(to write)* escribir <*how do you s. his name?* ¿cómo se escribe su nombre?>; FIG. significar ♦ **to s. out** deletrear; *(to explain)* explicar —intr. escribir.
spell[2] s. *(trance)* sortilegio; FIG. fascinación *f*, encanto ♦ **to be under a s.** estar hechizado • **to cast a s. on** hechizar.
spell[3] I. s. *(of time)* temporada; *(of work)* turno; FAM. *(of weather)* racha; *(of illness)* ataque *m* II. tr. *(to relieve)* relevar, reemplazar.
spell·bind·ing ('bīnd'-ĭng) adj. hechizante.
spell·bound (:bound') adj. hechizado.
spell·er (:ər) s. *(person)* deletreador *m*; *(book)* abecedario.
spell·ing (:ĭng) s. *(orthography)* ortografía; *(action)* deletreo.
spe·lunk·er (spĭ-lŭng'kər) s. espeleólogo.
spend (spĕnd) tr. **spent** *(money)* gastar; *(time)* pasar, dedicar; *(force, anger)* agotar, consumir; *(to use)* emplear —intr. gastar dinero.
spend·ing (spĕn'dĭng) I. s. gasto ♦ **s. money** dinero para gastos menudos II. adj. para gastar.
spend·thrift (spĕnd'thrĭft') s. & adj. derrochador *m*, manirroto.
spent (spĕnt) I. cf. **spend** II. adj. *(consumed)* gastado; *(passed)* acabado; *(exhausted)* agotado.
sperm[1] (spûrm) s. [pl. inv. *o* **s**] BIOL. esperma.
sperm[2] s. *(whale oil)* esperma de ballena ♦ **s. whale** cachalote.
spew (spyoō) tr. & intr. vomitar; *(to eject)* arrojar; *(words)* soltar.
sphere (sfîr) s. esfera.
spher·i·cal ('ĭ-kəl) adj. esférico.
sphinc·ter (sfĭngk'tər) s. esfínter *m.*
sphinx (sfĭngks) s. esfinge *f.*
spice (spīs) I. s. especia; FIG. sabor *m*, interés *m* II. tr. sazonar; FIG. salpimentar.
spick-and-span (spĭk'ən-spăn') adj. *(spotless)* inmaculado; *(brand-new)* flamante.
spic·y (spī'sē) adj. picante.
spi·der (spī'dər) s. araña.
spiel (spēl) JER. I. s. rollo, perorata II. intr. *o* tr. perorar.
spig·ot (spĭg'ət) s. *(faucet)* grifo; *(tap)* espita.
spike[1] (spīk) I. s. *(nail)* clavo, estaca; *(spur)* púa; *(sharp point)* punta ♦ **s. heel** tacón alto y puntiagudo II. tr. *(to impale)* empalar, perforar; *(to nail)* clavar; *(to block)* impedir, frustrar; *(a drink)* echar licor a.
spike[2] s. *(ear of grain)* espiga.
spike·nard (spīk'närd') s. nardo.
spill (spĭl) I. tr. **-ed** *o* **spilt** *(liquid)* derramar, verter; *(blood)* derramar; *(a container)* volcar; *(to divulge)* revelar ♦ **to s. the beans** descubrir el pastel —intr. *(liquid)* derramarse, verterse; *(rider)* caerse ♦ **to s. out** salir, desbordar ♦ **to s. over** salirse II. s. *(of liquid)* derrame *m*; *(fall)* caída.
spill·age ('ĭj) s. *(amount)* derrame *m.*
spill·way (:wā') s. derramadero, aliviadero.
spin (spĭn) I. tr. **spun** *(thread)* hilar; *(web)* tejer; *(to twirl)* hacer girar, dar vueltas a; *(story)* contar; *(a ball)* dar efecto a ♦ **to s. off** derivar • **to s. out** alargar, prolongar —intr. *(to make thread)* hilar; *(to whirl)* girar, dar vueltas; *(to*

reel) tener vértigo; *(wheels)* patinar ♦ **my head was spinning** me daba vueltas la cabeza • **to s. along** ir volando II. s. *(motion)* giro, vuelta; *(on a ball)* efecto; FAM. *(short drive)* vuelta, paseo ♦ **to be in a s.** estar aturdido • **to go for a s.** dar una vueltecita (en coche) • **to go into a s.** AVIA. entrar en barrena; FIG. aturdirse.
spin·ach (spǐn´ǐch) s. espinaca.
spi·nal (spī´nəl) I. adj. espinal, vertebral ♦ **s. column** columna vertebral • **s. cord** médula espinal II. s. anestesia por conducto vertebral.
spin·dle (spǐn´dl) s. TEJ. huso; MEC. eje *m.*
spin·dly (spǐn´dlē) adj. -i- FAM. larguirucho.
spine (spīn) s. ANAT. espina dorsal; *(of a book)* lomo; BOT., ZOOL. espina, púa.
spine·less (´lǐs) adj. invertebrado; *(without will power)* blando, débil.
spin·ner (spǐn´ər) s. *(person)* hilador *m*; *(needle)* aguja giratoria.
spin·ner·et (´ə-rĕt´) s. hilera.
spin·ning (´ǐng) s. *(act)* hilado; *(art)* hilandería ♦ **s. wheel** rueca, torno de hilar.
spin-off (:ôf´) s. subproducto, derivado.
spi·nose (spī´nōs´) adj. espinoso.
spin·ster (spǐn´stər) s. solterona.
spin·y (spī´nē) adj. -i- espinoso.
spi·ral (spī´rəl) I. s. espiral *f* II. adj. espiral ♦ **s. staircase** escalera de caracol III. intr. moverse en espiral.
spire[1] (spīr) s. *(pinnacle)* cúspide *f*, cima; *(steeple)* aguja.
spire[2] s. *(whorl)* vuelta, rosca.
spir·it (spǐr´ǐt) I. s. espíritu *m*; *(soul)* alma; *(mood)* humor *m*; *(courage)* ánimo; QUÍM. alcohol *m* ♦ **in a friendly s.** de manera amistosa • **in s.** para sus adentros • **s. lamp** lámpara de alcohol ♦ pl. *(mood)* humor; *(alcohol)* alcohol, licor • **in high** *o* **good s.** de buen humor • **in poor** *o* **low s.** desanimado • **to keep up one's s.** no perder el ánimo • **to raise someone's s.** animar a alguien II. tr. alentar, animar ♦ **to s. away** *o* **off** llevarse, hacer desaparecer.
spir·it·ed (:ǐ-tǐd) adj. *(animated)* animado; *(vigorous)* enérgico; *(horse)* brioso.
spir·i·tu·al (:ǐ-chōō-əl) adj. & s. espiritual *m.*
spir·i·tu·al·ist (:ə-lǐst) s. *(medium)* espiritista *mf*; FILOS., RELIG. espiritualista *mf.*
spit[1] (spǐt) I. s. saliva; *(act)* escupitajo; ENTOM. espuma II. tr. **spat** *o* **spit**, **-tting** escupir —intr. escupir; *(to sputter)* chisporrotear; *(to rain)* chispear ♦ **to s. at** despreciar.
spit[2] I. s. *(pointed rod)* espetón *m*; GEOG. punta; *(of sand)* banco II. tr. **-tt-** espetar.
spite (spīt) I. s. rencor *m*, ojeriza ♦ **in s. of** a pesar de, no obstante • **out of s.** por despecho II. tr. fastidiar, despechar.
spite·ful (´fəl) adj. rencoroso.
spite·fire (spǐt´fīr´) s. persona colérica.
spit·tle (spǐt´l) s. saliva; ENTOM. espuma.
spit·toon (spǐ-tōōn´) s. escupidera.
splash (splăsh) I. tr. *(to spatter)* salpicar *(with de)*; *(to wet)* chapotear —intr. salpicar; *(in or through water)* chapotear ♦ **s. about** chapotear • **to s. down** amerizar II. s. salpicadura; *(sound)* chapoteo; *(of light, color)* mancha ♦ **to make a s.** causar sensación.
splash·down (´doun´) s. amerizaje *m.*
splash·y (:ē) adj. -i- llamativo.
splat (splăt) s. ruido sordo.
splat·ter (splăt´ər) I. tr. & intr. salpicar II. s. salpicadura.
splay (splā) tr. & intr. extender(se).

spleen (splēn) s. ANAT. bazo; *(ill temper)* mal humor *m.*
splen·did (splĕn´dǐd) adj. espléndido.
splen·dor (:dər) s. esplendor *m.*
splice (splīs) I. tr. empalmar II. s. empalme *m.*
splint (splǐnt) s. tablilla.
splin·ter (splǐn´tər) I. s. astilla; *(of bone)* esquirla ♦ **s. group** grupo disidente II. tr. & intr. astillar.
split (splǐt) I. tr. **split**, **-tting** *(in two)* partir, dividir; *(to crack)* hender; *(to rip)* desgarrar; *(to share)* compartir; QUÍM. descomponer; FÍS. desintegrar ♦ **splitting headache** dolor de cabeza fuertísimo • **to s. off** separar • **to s. one's sides laughing** partirse de risa • **to s. up** *(to divide)* dividir, repartir; *(to separate)* separar —intr. *(in two)* partirse; *(to crack)* henderse; *(cloth)* desgarrarse; JER. *(to leave)* largarse ♦ **to s. off** *o* **up** separarse II. s. *(crack)* grieta; *(tear)* desgarrón *m*; *(in a group)* ruptura III. adj. partido; *(cracked)* agrietado; *(torn)* desgarrado ♦ **s. personality** personalidad doble • **s. second** fracción de segundo.
splotch (splŏch) I. s. manchón *m*, borrón *m* II. tr. manchar.
splotch·y (:ē) adj. -i- manchado.
splurge (splûrj) I. tr. & intr. derrochar II. s. derroche *m.*
splut·ter (splŭt´ər) I. intr. & tr. farfullar II. s. farfulla.
spoil (spoil) I. tr. **-led** *o* **-t** *(to damage)* estropear; *(to impair)* dañar; *(appearance)* afear; *(child)* mimar ♦ **to s. someone's fun** aguarle la fiesta a alguien —intr. estropearse II. s. ♦ pl. *(of war)* botín; *(of political party)* prebendas.
spoil·age (spoi´lǐj) s. putrefacción *f.*
spoil·sport (spoil´spôrt´) s. aguafiestas *mf.*
spoke[1] (spōk) s. *(of a wheel)* radio; *(rung)* peldaño.
spoke[2] (spōk) cf. **speak.**
spo·ken (spō´kən) I. cf. **speak** II. adj. hablado.
spokes·man (spōks´mən) s. [pl. **-men**] portavoz *m*, vocero.
spokes·per·son (:pûr´sən) s. portavoz *mf.*
spokes·wom·an (:wŭm´ən) s. [pl. **-women**] vocera, portavoz *f.*
spo·li·a·tion (spō´lē-ā´shən) s. saqueo.
sponge (spŭnj) I. s. esponja; FIG. *(person)* gorrón *m* ♦ **s. bath** lavado con esponja *o* toalla • **s. cake** bizcocho • **to throw in the s.** FAM. darse por vencido II. tr. limpiar con esponja —intr. FIG. *(to obtain free)* gorronear ♦ **to s. up** absorber —intr. *(to borrow money)* sablear ♦ **to s. off** *o* **on** vivir a costa de.
spong·er (spŭn´jər) s. gorrón *m.*
spong·y (:jē) adj. -i- esponjoso.
spon·sor (spŏn´sər) I. s. patrocinador *m*; *(godparent)* padrino, madrina II. tr. patrocinar; *(as godparent)* apadrinar, amadrinar.
spon·sor·ship (:shǐp´) s. patrocinio ♦ **under the s.** of patrocinado por.
spon·ta·ne·i·ty (spŏn´tə-nē´ǐ-tē, :nā´-) s. espontaneidad *f.*
spon·ta·ne·ous (spŏn-tā´nē-əs) adj. espontáneo ♦ **s. combustion** combustión espontánea.
spoof (spōōf) I. s. *(hoax)* engaño; *(parody)* broma II. tr. engañar, bromear.
spook (spōōk) FAM. I. s. *(specter)* espectro; *(spy)* espía *mf* II. tr. asustar.
spook·y (spōō´kē) adj. -i- FAM. *(eerie)* espectral; *(skittish)* asustadizo.

spool (spōol) I. s. carrete *m*, bobina II. tr. encanillar, enrollar.

spoon (spōon) I. s. cuchara; *(spoonful)* cucharada II. tr. sacar con cuchara —intr. FAM. acariciarse, besuquearse.

spoor (spŏŏr) s. rastro.

spo·rad·ic (spə-răd'ĭk) adj. esporádico.

spore (spŏr) s. espora.

sport (spŏrt) I. s. deporte *m*; *(active pastime)* juego; *(hunting)* caza; *(jest)* broma, burla ♦ **athletic sports** atletismo • **in s.** en broma • **to be a good s.** *(about losing)* ser buen perdedor; *(to be a good person)* ser buena persona • **to make s. of** burlarse de II. intr. jugar, divertirse —tr. lucir <*she is sporting a new dress* luce un nuevo vestido> III. adj. de sport.

sport·ing (spŏr'tĭng) adj. deportivo; *(gambling-related)* jugador.

spor·tive (:tĭv) adj. juguetón.

sports (spŏrts) adj. de sport <*s. jacket* chaqueta de sport> ♦ **s. car** automóvil deportivo.

sports·cast ('kăst') s. programa deportivo.

sports·man (:mən) s. [pl. -men] deportista *m*; *(gentleman)* jugador *m* que se conforma con las reglas.

sports·man·ship (:shĭp') s. deportividad *f*.

sports·wom·an (spŏrts'wŏm'ən) s. [pl. -women] deportista *f*.

sports·writ·er (:rī'tər) s. cronista *mf* deportivo.

sport·y (spŏr'tē) adj. -i- FAM. casual; *(for sport)* deportivo.

spot (spŏt) I. s. lugar *m*; *(stain)* mancha; *(dot)* lunar *m*; TELEV. anuncio ♦ **beauty s.** lunar • **black s.** mancha (en la reputación) • **in a bad o tight s.** en apuros • **in spots** de vez en cuando • **night s.** sala de fiestas • **on the s.** allí mismo; *(pressed)* en situación precaria • **s. price** precio actual en el mercado • **s. remover** quitamanchas • **tender o sore s.** punto sensible • **to hit the s.** FAM. venirle muy bien a uno • **to put on the s.** poner en un aprieto • **to touch a sore s.** poner el dedo en la llaga II. tr. -tt- manchar; *(to detect)* notar —intr. mancharse III. adj. *(random)* al azar; COM., FIN. *(paid immediately)* contante; *(delivered immediately)* para entrega inmediata.

spot-check ('chĕk') tr. & intr. inspeccionar al azar.

spot·less (:lĭs) adj. inmaculado; *(irreproachable)* intachable.

spot·light (:līt') I. s. foco; *(attention)* atención pública II. tr. -ed o -lit iluminar; *(to focus attention on)* destacar.

spot·ty (:tē) adj. -i- irregular.

spou·sals (spou'zəlz) s.pl. desposorios.

spouse (spous, spouz) s. esposo, -a.

spout (spout) I. intr. chorrear; *(whale)* resoplar ♦ **to s. off** FAM. perorar —tr. *(to gush)* echar, arrojar; *(nonsense)* soltar II. s. *(for pouring)* pico; *(tube)* caño; *(stream)* chorro.

sprain (sprān) I. s. torcedura II. tr. torcer.

sprang (sprăng) cf. **spring**.

sprawl (sprôl) I. intr. *(to sit)* repantigarse; *(to spread out)* extenderse II. s. postura desgarbada; *(disorderly growth)* extensión *f* ♦ **urban s.** urbanización desordenada.

spray[1] (sprā) I. s. *(of liquid)* rociada; *(atomizer)* vaporizador *m*; MARIT. espuma ♦ **s. paint** pintura para atomizar • **s. can** lata de atomizado • **s. gun** pistola para pulverizar II. tr. rociar —intr. vaporizarse.

spray[2] s. *(bouquet)* ramo, ramillete *m*.

spray·er (sprā'ər) s. vaporizador *m*.

spread (sprĕd) I. tr. **spread** extender; *(to move apart)* separar; *(butter)* untar; *(religion)* propagar; *(to sow)* sembrar; *(table)* poner ♦ **to s. oneself thin** dedicarse a muchas actividades • **to s. out** esparcir —intr. esparcirse; *(to extend)* extenderse; *(to propagate)* propagarse; *(to become known)* difundirse; *(to move apart)* separarse ♦ **to s. out** extenderse; *(to get wider)* ensancharse II. s. difusión *f*; *(expanse)* extensión *f*; *(ranch)* rancho; *(bedspread)* colcha; *(food)* comida (para untar); FAM. *(meal)* comida (sobre la mesa); IMPR. artículo a dos o más columnas; *(difference)* diferencia.

spread·er ('ər) s. *(for butter)* untador *m*; *(farm implement)* esparcidora; *(beam)* viga cepo.

spree (sprē) s. borrachera; *(party)* parranda ♦ **to go on a shopping o spending s.** hacer muchas compras.

sprig (sprĭg) s. ramito.

spright·ly (sprīt'lē) adj. -i- vivo.

spring (sprĭng) I. intr. **sprang, sprung** *(to jump)* saltar; *(to emerge)* brotar; *(to arise)* surgir; *(to warp)* alabearse ♦ **to s. back** volver a su posición original • **to s. forth** brotar • **to s. open, shut** abrirse, cerrarse de un golpe • **to s. to one's feet** levantarse de un salto • **to s. up** levantarse; *(to grow)* espigarse; *(to emerge)* surgir ♦ **to s. at** lanzarse sobre —tr. *(trap)* hacer funcionar; *(to jump)* saltar; *(to release)* soltar; *(a surprise)* echar ♦ **to s. a leak** empezar a hacer agua II. s. *(coil)* resorte *m*; *(resilience)* elasticidad *f*; *(jump)* salto; *(season)* primavera; *(source)* fuente *f* ♦ **s. cleaning** limpieza general • **s. fever** desasosiego ocasionado por la llegada de la primavera.

spring·board ('bôrd') s. trampolín *m*.

spring·time (:tīm') s. primavera.

spring·y (:ē) adj. -i- elástico.

sprin·kle (sprĭng'kəl) I. tr. rociar —intr. rociar; *(to drizzle)* lloviznar II. s. rociada; *(drizzle)* llovizna; *(small amount)* pizca.

sprin·kler (:klər) s. regadera; *(fire extinguisher)* extintor *m*.

sprin·kling (:klĭng) s. *(spray)* aspersión *f*; *(small amount)* pizca.

sprint (sprĭnt) I. s. sprint *m* II. intr. sprintar.

sprint·er (sprĭn'tər) s. sprinter *m*.

sprite (sprīt) s. duende *m*; *(specter)* espectro.

sprock·et (sprŏk'ĭt) s. diente *m*.

sprout (sprout) I. intr. brotar; *(to burgeon)* crecer rápidamente —tr. hacer crecer II. s. brote *m*.

spruce[1] (sprōōs) s. BOT. picea.

spruce[2] I. adj. ordenado II. tr. & intr. ♦ **to s. up** acicalar(se).

sprung (sprŭng) cf. **spring**.

spry (sprī) adj. -er, -est o -i- activo.

spud (spŭd) s. *(tool)* escarda; JER. *(potato)* papa.

spume (spyōom) s. espuma.

spun (spŭn) cf. **spin**.

spunk (spŭngk) s. yesca; FAM. *(pluck)* valor *m*.

spunk·y (spŭng'kē) adj. -i- valiente.

spur (spûr) I. s. espuela; *(incentive)* incentivo; ORNIT. espolón *m*; F.C. vía muerta ♦ **on the s. of the moment** sin pensarlo II. tr. -rr- espolear.

spu·ri·ous (spyŏr'ē-əs) adj. espurio.

spurn (spûrn) tr. rechazar (con desdén).

spurt (spûrt) I. s. chorro; *(outbreak)* arrebato II. intr. salir a chorros —tr. echar.

sput·ter (spŭt'ər) I. intr. chisporrotear; *(to stammer)* farfullar —tr. farfullar II. s. farfulla; *(of particles)* chisporroteo.
sput·ter·ing (:ĭng) s. chisporroteo.
spu·tum (spyōō'təm) s. [pl. **-ta**] esputo.
spy (spī) I. s. espía *mf* II. tr. *(to watch)* espiar; *(to see)* divisar —intr. **♦ to s. (on)** espiar.
spy·glass ('glăs') s. catalejo **♦** pl. prismáticos.
spy·ing (:ĭng) s. espionaje *m*.
squab (skwŏb) s. pichón *m* implume.
squab·ble (skwŏb'əl) I. intr. pelearse II. s. riña.
squad (skwŏd) s. cuadrilla; *(team)* equipo; MIL. pelotón *m* **♦ s. car** coche patrulla.
squad·ron ('rən) s. MARÍT. escuadra; MIL. escuadrón *m*; AER. escuadrilla.
squal·id (skwŏl'ĭd) adj. escuálido; *(repulsive)* asqueroso; *(sordid)* sórdido.
squall¹ (skwôl) I. s. chillido II. intr. chillar.
squall² (skwôl) s. racha.
squal·or (skwŏl'ər) s. escualidez *f*.
squan·der (skwŏn'dər) tr. derrochar; *(time)* desperdiciar.
square (skwâr) I. s. cuadrado; *(design)* cuadro; *(tool)* escuadra; *(in town)* plaza; JER. *(fogy)* convencionalista *mf* II. adj. cuadrado; *(in a right angle)* a escuadra; *(just)* equitativo; *(paid-up)* saldado; JER. *(old-fashioned)* convencional **♦ s. dance** baile de figuras • **s. deal** FAM. trato justo • **s. knot** nudo de enverga o de rizo • **s. meal** comida completa III. tr. cuadrar; *(to adapt)* ajustar; *(to settle)* saldar **♦ to s. accounts with** ajustar las cuentas a • **to s. away** dejar en orden —intr. cuadrar **♦ to s. off** ponerse de guardia (para pelear).
square·ly ('lē) adv. a escuadra; *(firmly)* firmemente; *(face to face)* de frente; *(honestly)* honradamente; *(exactly)* justo, exactamente.
squash¹ (skwŏsh, skwôsh) s. BOT. calabaza.
squash² I. tr. & intr. *(to crush)* aplastar(se); *(to squeeze)* apretar(se) II. s. DEP. juego de pelota.
squat (skwŏt) I. intr. **-tt-** ponerse en cuclillas; *(to settle)* ocupar ilegalmente un lugar II. adj. **-tt-** regordete III. s. posición *f* en cuclillas.
squat·ter (:ər) s. persona que ocupa ilegalmente un lugar.
squaw (skwô) s. india norteamericana.
squawk (skwôk) I. intr. graznar; *(to complain)* quejar(se) II. s. graznido; *(protest)* protesta.
squeak (skwēk) I. intr. chirriar **♦ to s. through** *o* **by** pasar dificultosamente II. s. chirrido **♦ a narrow s.** un escape apenas.
squeak·y (skwē'kē) adj. **-i-** chirriante.
squeal (skwēl) I. intr. chirriar; JER. *(to betray)* chivatear II. s. chillido.
squeal·er (skwē'lər) s. FAM. chivato.
squea·mish (skwē'mĭsh) adj. *(easily offended)* delicado; *(prudish)* pudibundo; *(oversensitive)* remilgado **♦ to feel s.** sentir náuseas.
squeeze (skwēz) I. tr. *(to compress)* apretar; *(to crush)* exprimir; *(to extract)* extraer; *(to extort)* sonsacar; *(to cram)* forzar **♦ to s. out** sacar; *(to exclude)* excluir —intr. **♦ to s. in, out** meterse, salir con dificultad • **to s. by** pasar a duras penas • **to s. together** apretujarse II. s. presión *f*; *(embrace)* abrazo; *(shortage)* escasez *f*.
squelch (skwĕlch) I. tr. despachurrar II. s. *(sound)* chapoteo; *(answer)* réplica.
squid (skwĭd) s. [pl. inv. *o* **s**] calamar *m*.
squig·gle (skwĭg'əl) I. s. garabato II. intr. re-

torcerse.
squint (skwĭnt) I. intr. entrecerrar los ojos; *(to glance)* mirar de reojo; OFTAL. bizquear II. s. mirada bizca; *(side-glance)* mirada de reojo; OFTAL. estrabismo.
squire (skwīr) I. s. HIST. escudero; G.B. *(country gentleman)* terrateniente *m*; *(dignitary)* señor *m*; *(gallant)* galán *m* II. tr. acompañar.
squirm (skwûrm) I. intr. retorcerse; *(to feel humiliation)* avergonzarse II. s. retorcimiento.
squir·rel (skwûr'əl) s. ardilla.
squirt (skwûrt) I. intr. salir a chorros —tr. dejar salir a chorros; *(to wet)* echar agua a II. s. chorro; *(device)* jeringa; FAM. *(brat)* mequetrefe *m*.
stab (stăb) I. tr. **-bb-** apuñalar; *(to wound)* herir con un cuchillo **♦ to s. to death** matar a puñaladas II. s. puñalada; *(wound)* herida **♦ to take a s. at** intentar.
stab·bing ('ĭng) I. s. puñalada, asesinato a puñaladas II. adj. punzante (dolor).
sta·bil·i·ty (stə-bĭl'ĭ-tē) s. estabilidad *f*; *(steadfastness)* firmeza.
sta·bi·li·za·tion (stā'bə-lĭ-zā'shən) s. estabilización *f*.
sta·bi·lize ('-līz') tr. & intr. estabilizar(se).
sta·bi·liz·ing (:līz'ĭng) adj. estabilizador.
sta·ble¹ (stā'bəl) adj. **-er, -est** estable; *(enduring)* duradero; *(balanced)* equilibrado.
sta·ble² I. s. *(building)* establo; *(horses)* cuadra II. tr. poner en un establo.
stack (stăk) I. s. *(pile)* pila, hacina; *(smokestack)* chimenea; FAM. montón *m* **♦ to blow one's s.** reventar de ira **♦** pl. estantes II. tr. amontonar, hacinar **♦ to s. the deck** hacer trampas **• to s. up** amontonar; FIG. comparar.
sta·di·um (stā'dē-əm) s. [pl. **s** *o* **-ia**] estadio.
staff (stăf) I. s. [pl. **s**] *(personnel)* personal *m*; *(aides)* cuerpo de administración; [pl. **s** *o* **-ves**] *(walking stick)* bastón *m*; *(cudgel)* garrote *m*; *(flagpole)* asta; MÚS. pentagrama **♦ editorial s.** redacción **• s. of life** alimento básico **• teaching s.** cuerpo docente **• to be on the s.** estar en plantilla II. tr. proveer de personal.
staff·er ('ər) s. FAM. empleado.
stag (stăg) I. s. ciervo II. adj. **♦ s. party** reunión de hombres solos III. adv. solo (sin compañera).
stage (stāj) I. s. plataforma; *(setting)* escena, escenario; *(phase)* etapa; *(stagecoach)* diligencia; TEAT. escena; *(boards)* tablas; FIG. teatro; ASTRONAUT. cuerpo **♦ by stages** progresivamente **• in stages** por etapas **• s. door** entrada de artistas **• s. fright** miedo al público **• s. manager** regidor de escena **• to go on the s.** dedicarse al teatro II. tr. TEAT. representar; *(to arrange)* organizar.
stage·hand ('hănd') s. tramoyista *mf*.
stage-struck (:strŭk') adj. apasionado por el teatro.
stag·ger (stăg'ər) I. intr. tambalearse —tr. hacer tambalearse; *(to overwhelm)* asombrar; *(to alternate)* escalonar II. s. tambaleo.
stag·ger·ing (:ĭng) adj. tambaleante; *(overwhelming)* asombroso.
stag·ing (stā'jĭng) s. TEAT. puesta en escena.
stag·nant (stăg'nənt) adj. estancado; *(foul)* rancio; *(sluggish)* inactivo.
stag·nate (:nāt') intr. estancarse.
stag·na·tion (:nā'shən) s. estancamiento.
staid (stād) adj. serio.
stain (stān) I. tr. manchar; *(to dye)* teñir; *(to*

taint) mancillar ♦ **stained glass** vidrio con dibujos coloreados —intr. mancharse **II.** s. mancha; *(dye)* tinte *m.*

stain·less ('līs) adj. limpio; *(corrosion-resistant)* inoxidable, *(unblemished)* inmaculado.

stair (stâr) s. escalón *m* ♦ pl. escalera.

stair·case ('kâs') s. escalera.

stair·way ('wā') s. escalera.

stair·well (wěl') s. caja de la escalera.

stake (stāk) **I.** s. *(stick)* estaca; *(post)* poste *m*; *(interest)* intereses *m*; *(for burning)* hoguera ♦ **at s.** en juego • **to pull up stakes** irse ♦ pl. *(bet)* apuesta, *(prize)* premio **II.** tr. *(to secure)* estacar; *(to tether)* amarrar a un poste, *(a plant)* rodrigar; *(to gamble)* apostar; *(to risk)* jugarse; *(to finance)* financiar ♦ **to s. a claim** delimitar una propiedad con estacas.

stake·out ('out') s. vigilancia.

sta·lac·tite (stə-lăk'tīt') s. estalactita.

sta·lag·mite (stə-lăg'mīt') s. estalagmita.

stale (stāl) **I.** adj. *(food)* rancio; *(bread)* duro; *(wine)* picado; *(news)* viejo; *(trite)* trillado; *(run-down)* decaído **II.** intr. echarse a perder.

stale·mate ('māt') **I.** s. *(deadlock)* estancamiento; *(chess)* ahogado **II.** tr. estancar; *(chess)* ahogar.

stale·ness ('nĭs) s. ranciedad *f*, rancidez *f*.

stalk[1] (stôk) s. *(plant stem)* tallo, *(flower stem)* pedúnculo; *(leaf stem)* pecíolo.

stalk[2] intr. *(to walk)* caminar con paso impresionante —tr. *(to pursue)* acechar.

stall (stôl) **I.** s. *(in barn)* pesebre *m*; *(booth)* caseta; *(pew)* banco de iglesia; *(delaying tactic)* evasiva; *(seat)* butaca; MEC. calado (de motor) **II.** tr. *(to delay)* demorar; AUTO. calar —intr. *(to delay)* andar con rodeos; AUTO. calarse.

stal·lion (stăl'yən) s. semental *m.*

stal·wart (stôl'wərt) **I.** adj. robusto; *(uncompromising)* firme **II.** s. persona fuerte.

sta·men (stā'mən) s. estambre *m.*

stam·i·na (stăm'ə-nə) s. aguante *m.*

stam·mer (stăm'ər) **I.** intr. tartamudear **II.** s. tartamudez *f*, tartamudeo.

stam·mer·ing (·ĭng) s. tartamudeo.

stamp (stămp) **I.** tr. *(to crush)* pisotear; *(to imprint)* estampar; *(to affix stamp)* poner un sello a; *(to impress)* marcar ♦ **to s. on** pisar ♦ **to s. one's feet** patear ♦ **to s. out** *(fire)* apagar con el pie; *(rebellion)* acabar con, sofocar —intr. patear; *(to walk)* caminar con pasos pesados **II.** s. sello; *(postage)* sello, estampilla; *(official)* timbre *m*; TEC. *(die)* cuño ♦ **s. collector** filatelista • **trading s.** cupón.

stam·pede (stăm-pēd') **I.** s. espantada **II.** tr. espantar *(animales)* —intr. abalanzarse.

stance (stăns) s. postura.

stanch[1] (stônch, stănch) tr. restañar *(sangre).*

stanch[2] var. de **staunch**[1].

stan·chion (stăn'chən, ·shən) s. poste *m.*

stand (stănd) **I.** intr. stood estar de pie; *(to rise)* ponerse de pie; *(to place oneself)* ponerse; *(to remain valid)* tener vigencia; *(to be committed)* mantenerse; *(to be situated)* erguirse; *(to rank)* ser ♦ **to s. alone** ser el único • **to s. aside** retirarse • **to s. at attention** cuadrarse • **to s. back** retroceder • **to s. by** estar listo; *(to look on)* mirar y no hacer nada • **to s. down** retirarse del estrado • **to s. fast** no cejar • **to s. in** *o* **on line** hacer cola • **to s. in the way** (of) estorbar • **to s. off** apartarse • **to s. on end** *(hair)* erizarse; *(thing)* ponerse de punta • **to s.**

out resaltar • **to s. still** estarse quieto • **to s. to reason** ser lógico • **to s. to** (win, lose) tener la probabilidad de (ganar, perder) • **to s. together** mantenerse unidos • **to s. up** ponerse de pie • **where do you s.?** ¿qué opinión tienes? —tr. poner de pie; *(to place)* colocar; *(to withstand)* tolerar; *(to resist)* resistir ♦ **to s. against** hacer frente a • **to s. by** permanecer fiel a • **to s. for** representar; *(to support)* abogar por; *(to tolerate)* soportar • **to s. in for** reemplazar • **to s. on end** poner derecho • **to s. one's ground** mantenerse firme • **to s. the test** pasar por la prueba • **to s. up** FAM. dejar plantado a • **to s. up for** sacar la cara por • **to s. up to** hacer frente a; *(to last)* resistir **II.** s. *(halt)* parada; *(dais)* estrado; *(booth)* quiosco; *(counter)* mostrador *m*; *(pedestal)* pie *m*; *(for coats, hats)* perchero; *(for umbrellas)* paragüero ♦ **to make a s. against** oponerse a • **to take a s. for** declararse a favor de • **to take a** (firm) **s.** adoptar una actitud (firme) • **to take the** (witness) **s.** DER. subir a la barra de los testigos ♦ pl. graderías.

stan·dard (stăn'dərd) **I.** s. *(flag)* estandarte *m*; *(criterion)* criterio; *(model)* patrón *m*; *(level)* nivel *m* ♦ **s. of living** nivel de vida ♦ pl. normas **II.** adj. standard; *(accepted)* normal, corriente; *(trite)* trillado ♦ **s. time** hora civil.

stan·dard-bear·er ('băr'ər) s. abanderado.

stan·dard·ize (stăn'dər-dīz') tr. estandardizar.

stand·by (stănd'bī') s. [pl. -bys] *(dependable person)* persona de confianza; *(substitute)* sustituto ♦ **s. list** lista de espera • **s. passenger** pasajero que está en la lista de espera.

stand-in (·ĭn') s. TEAT. suplente *mf*; CINEM. doble *m*; *(substitute)* sustituto.

stand·ing (stăn'dĭng) **I.** s. *(reputation)* reputación *f*; *(length of time)* antigüedad *f* **II.** adj. de pie, parado; *(permanent)* permanente; *(stationary)* fijo, *(stagnant)* estancado ♦ **s. room** sitio donde la gente permanece de pie.

stand·off (stănd'ôf') s. empate *m.*

stand·off·ish (-ô'fĭsh) adj. distante, reservado.

stand·point ('point') s. punto de vista.

stand·still (·stĭl') s. parada.

stank (stăngk) cf. **stink.**

stan·za (stăn'zə) s. estrofa, estancia.

staph·y·lo·coc·cus (stăf'ə-lō-kŏk'əs) s. [pl. -ci] estafilococo.

sta·ple[1] (stā'pəl) s. *(commodity)* producto básico (de una región); *(trade item)* producto principal; *(feature)* elemento básico; *(raw material)* materia prima, *(fiber)* fibra.

sta·ple[2] s. *(metal fastener)* grapa **II.** tr. sujetar con una grapa.

sta·pler (stā'plər) s. grapador *m.*

star (stär) **I.** s. estrella; *(asterisk)* asterisco ♦ **shooting s.** estrella fugaz • **to thank one's lucky stars** dar las gracias a Dios ♦ pl. ASTROL. astros **II.** tr. **-rr-** *(to adorn)* estrellar; *(with asterisk)* poner un asterisco en; *(a feature)* presentar como protagonista —intr. protagonizar; *(to perform well)* destacarse **III.** adj. estelar ♦ **s. sapphire** zafiro estrellado.

star·board (stär'bərd) **I.** s. estribor *m* **II.** adj. de estribor **III.** adv. a estribor.

starch (stärch) **I.** s. *(foodstuff)* fécula; *(stiffener)* almidón *m* **II.** tr. almidonar.

starch·y (stär'chē) adj. -i- feculento; *(like starch)* almidonado.

star·dom (stär'dəm) s. estrellato.

stare (stâr) **I.** intr. mirar fijamente ♦ **to s.**

down hacer bajar la vista a II. s. mirada fija.
star·fish (stär'físh') s. [pl. inv. o **es**] estrella de mar.
star·gaze (:gāz') intr. mirar las estrellas; *(to daydream)* mirar a las telarañas.
stark (stärk) I. adj. *(bleak)* desolado; *(truth, facts)* desnudo; *(complete)* total II. adv. totalmente.
stark·ness ('nĭs) s. *(bleakness)* desolación f; *(bareness)* austeridad f.
star·let (stär'lĭt) s. actriz f joven.
star·light (:lĭt') s. luz f de las estrellas.
star·ling (stär'lĭng) s. estornino.
star·lit (stär'lĭt') adj. iluminado por las estrellas.
star·ry (:ē) adj. -i- estrellado.
star·ry-eyed (:īd') adj. soñador.
start (stärt) I. intr. empezar; *(to set out)* salir; *(motor)* arrancar; *(to jerk)* sobresaltarse ♦ **to s. back** emprender el regreso • **to s. in** o **off** o **out** empezar • **to s. up** arrancar • **to s. with** para comenzar —tr. empezar; *(car, machine)* poner en marcha; *(to initiate)* iniciar; *(to found)* establecer II. s. *(beginning)* principio; *(startle)* sobresalto; *(place)* salida, punto de partida ♦ **flying s.** salida lanzada • **to get off to a good s.** empezar bien • **to give someone a s.** *(to help)* ayudar a alguien • *(to startle)* dar un susto a alguien • **to make a fresh s.** empezar de nuevo • **with a s.** sobresaltando.
start·er (stär'tar) s. iniciador m; AUTO. arranque m; DEP. *(official)* juez m de salida.
star·tle (stär'tl) I. tr. & intr. sobresaltar(se) II. s. sobresalto.
start-up (stärt'ŭp') s. puesta en marcha; *(beginning)* principio.
star·va·tion (stär-vā'shən) s. hambre f; MED. inanición f ♦ **s. wages** sueldos de hambre.
starve (stärv) intr. *(to be hungry)* pasar hambre; *(to die)* morirse de hambre —tr. no dar de comer; *(to kill)* matar de hambre ♦ **to be starved** o **starving for** *(to need)* carecer de; *(to desire)* anhelar.
starv·ing (stär'vĭng) adj. hambriento.
stash (stăsh) FAM. I. tr. esconder II. s. *(cache)* escondrijo; *(hidden thing)* cosa escondida.
sta·sis (stā'sĭs) s. [pl. **-ses**] estasis f.
state (stāt) I. s. estado; *(social position)* rango; *(pomp)* pompa ♦ **the s. of the art** últimos adelantos • **the States** los Estados Unidos • **to be in a s.** agitarse • **to lie in s.** estar en capilla ardiente II. tr. declarar III. adj. estatal; *(ceremonious)* solemne; *(official)* oficial.
state·li·ness ('lē-nĭs) s. majestuosidad f.
state·ly (:lē) adj. -i- majestuoso.
state·ment (stāt'mənt) s. declaración f; COM. *(bill)* cuenta; *(report)* estado de cuenta.
states·man (stāts'mən) s. [pl. **-men**] estadista m.
states·man·ship (:shĭp') s. arte m de gobernar.
state·wide (stāt'wīd') adj. por todo el estado.
stat·ic (stāt'ĭk) I. adj. estático II. s. RAD. parásitos; JER. *(back talk)* insolencias.
sta·tion (stā'shən) I. s. estación f; *(post)* puesto; *(social position)* rango ♦ **military s.** guarnición • **police s.** comisaría • **service s.** estación de servicio • **s. wagon** camioneta II. tr. estacionar; *(to post)* apostar.
sta·tion·ar·y (:shə-něr'ē) adj. estacionario; *(fixed)* fijo.
sta·tion·er (stā'shə-nər) s. papelero.

sta·tion·er·y (:něr'ē) s. papel y sobres m; *(office supplies)* objetos de escritorio; *(store)* papelería.
sta·tion·mas·ter (stā'shən-măs'tər) s. jefe m de estación.
sta·tis·tic (stə-tĭs'tĭk) s. estadística ♦ **statistics** sg. *(science)* estadística.
sta·tis·ti·cal (:tĭ-kəl) adj. estadístico.
stat·is·ti·cian (stăt'ĭ-stĭsh'ən) s. estadístico.
stat·u·ar·y (stăch'ōō-ĕr'ē) s. estatuas; *(art)* estatuaria.
stat·ue (stăch'ōō) s. estatua.
stat·u·esque ('-ĕsk') adj. escultural.
stat·u·ette (:ĕt') s. estatuilla.
stat·ure (stăch'ər) s. estatura; FIG. categoría.
sta·tus (stā'təs, stăt'əs) s. DER. estado; *(position)* posición social f; *(situation)* situación f.
stat·ute (stăch'ōōt) s. estatuto ♦ **s. mile** milla terrestre • **s. of limitations** ley de prescripción.
stat·u·to·ry (:ə-tôr'ē) adj. estatutario.
staunch¹ (stônch, stänch) adj. *(steadfast)* constante; *(true)* fiel; *(strong)* fuerte.
staunch² var. de **stanch¹**.
stave (stāv) I. s. *(of barrel)* duela; *(stanza)* estrofa ♦ pl. cf. **staff** II. tr. **-d** o **stove** ♦ **to s. in** desfondar • **to s. off** rechazar.
stay¹ (stā) I. intr. quedarse; *(to sojourn)* alojarse; *(to stop)* detenerse; *(to wait)* esperar; *(to last)* durar; *(to keep up)* mantenerse, seguir ♦ **it is here to s.** se ha establecido • **to s. away** ausentarse • **to s. away from** evitar • **to s. in** quedarse en casa • **to s. in bed** guardar cama • **to s. on** quedarse • **to s. over** pasar la noche • **to s. out** no entrar; *(all night)* no venir a casa • **to s. put** no moverse • **to s. up** quedarse levantado • **to s. up late** acostarse tarde —tr. detener; *(to postpone)* aplazar; *(to appease)* apaciguar ♦ **to s. the course** continuar hasta el final II. s. *(halt)* parada f; *(visit)* estancia; DER. aplazamiento.
stay² s. *(support)* apoyo; *(of corset)* ballena.
stay³ s. MARÍT. estay m.
stead (stĕd) s. lugar m ♦ **in someone's, something's s.** en lugar de alguien, algo • **to stand someone in good s.** serle útil a alguien.
stead·fast (stĕd'făst') adj. *(fixed)* fijo; *(unchanging)* constante; *(loyal)* leal.
stead·i·ness (stĕd'ē-nĭs) s. estabilidad f; *(firmness)* firmeza.
stead·y (stĕd'ē) I. adj. -i- firme; *(stable)* estable; *(sure)* seguro; *(continuous)* constante; *(calm)* tranquilo; *(reliable)* seguro II. tr. & intr. estabilizar(se); *(to calm)* calmar(se).
steak (stāk) s. bistec m; *(fish)* filete m.
steal (stēl) I. tr. & intr. **stole, stolen** robar ♦ **to s. away** escabullirse • **to s. in, out** entrar, salir furtivamente II. s. robo; JER. *(bargain)* ganga.
steal·ing (stē'lĭng) s. robo.
stealth (stĕlth) s. sigilo ♦ **by s.** furtivamente.
stealth·y (stĕl'thē) adj. -i- *(person)* cauteloso; *(action)* furtivo.
steam (stēm) I. s. vapor m; *(mist)* vaho, humo; *(heating)* calefacción f; *(energy)* energía ♦ **s. engine** máquina a vapor • **s. shovel** pala mecánica • **to let off s.** descargar vapor; FIG. desahogarse II. intr. echar vapor; *(to rise)* humear; *(ship)* avanzar; *(to fog up)* empañarse; FAM. *(to fume)* echar humo —tr. *(to fog)* empañar; CUL. cocer al vapor.
steam·boat ('bōt') s. vapor m.
steam·er (stē'mər) s. *(ship)* vapor m; CUL. olla de vapor ♦ **s. trunk** baúl (de camarote).
steam·roll·er (:rō'lər) I. s. apisonadora II. tr.

apisonar; FIG. aplastar.
steam·ship (:shĭp') s. vapor *m*.
steam·y (stē'mē) adj. -i- vaporoso; JER. *(erotic)* apasionado.
steed (stēd) s. corcel *m*.
steel (stēl) I. s. acero II. adj. de acero ♦ **s. industry** la industria siderúrgica • **s. mill** acería III. tr. acerar ♦ **to s. one's heart** volverse insensible • **to s. oneself** endurecerse.
steel·y (stē'lē) adj. -i- *(of steel)* de acero; *(like steel)* acerado ♦ **s. eyes** mirada penetrante.
steel·yard (stēl'yärd') s. romana.
steep¹ (stēp) adj. *(high)* empinado; *(precipitous)* escarpado; *(price)* excesivo.
steep² tr. remojar —intr. estar en remojo.
stee·ple (stē'pəl) s. torrecilla; *(spire)* aguja.
stee·ple·chase (:chās') s. carrera de obstáculos.
steer¹ (stîr) tr. *(boat)* gobernar; *(car)* conducir; FIG. dirigir, guiar —intr. gobernar, conducir; *(to handle)* conducirse ♦ **steering wheel** volante • **to s. clear of** evitar • **to s. for** poner rumbo a.
steer² s. *(ox)* novillo.
steer·age (stîr'ĭj) s. MARÍT. gobierno; *(accommodation)* entrepuente *m*.
stein (stīn) s. jarra (de cerveza).
stel·lar (stĕl'ər) adj. estelar.
stem¹ (stĕm) I. s. *(trunk)* tronco; *(stalk)* tallo; *(of goblet)* pie *m*; *(of pipe)* cañón *m*; FILOL. radical *m* ♦ **from s. to stern** de proa a popa II. intr. -mm- ♦ **to s. from** ser el resultado de.
stem² tr. -mm- *(to hold back)* contener.
stench (stĕnch) s. hedor *m*.
sten·cil (stĕn'səl) I. s. estarcido II. tr. estarcir.
ste·nog·ra·pher (stə-nŏg'rə-fər) s. estenógrafo.
ste·nog·ra·phy (:fē) s. estenografía.
sten·to·ri·an (stĕn-tôr'ē-ən) adj. estentóreo.
step (stĕp) I. s. paso; *(sound)* pisada; *(of stairs)* escalón *m*; *(measure)* medida; *(degree)* escalón ♦ **in s. with** de acuerdo con • **in s. with** en desacuerdo con • **s. by s.** paso a paso • **to keep in s.** llevar el paso • **to take a s.** dar un paso • **watch your step!** ¡vaya con cuidado! ♦ pl. *(staircase)* escaleras II. intr. -pp- *(to take a step)* dar un paso ♦ **s. this way!** ¡pase por aquí! • **to s. aside** hacerse a un lado • **to s. back** retroceder • **to s. down** bajar; *(to resign)* renunciar • **to s. forward** o up avanzar • **to s. in** entrar; *(to intervene)* intervenir • **to s. out** salir, *(of vehicle)* apearse • **to s. up** subir —tr. ♦ **s. on it!** ¡dáte prisa! • **to s. on** pisar • **to s. up** acelerar; *(to increase)* aumentar.
step·broth·er (:brŭth'ər) s. hermanastro.
step·child (:chīld') s. [pl. -**dren**] hijastro.
step·daugh·ter (:dô'tər) s. hijastra.
step·fa·ther (:fä'thər) s. padrastro.
step·lad·der (stĕp'lăd'ər) s. escalera de tijera.
step·moth·er (stĕp'mŭth'ər) s. madrastra.
step·par·ent (:pâr'ənt) s. padrastro, madrastra.
steppe (stĕp) s. estepa.
step·ping-stone (stĕp'ĭng-stōn') s. pasadera; FIG. *(springboard)* trampolín *m*.
step·sis·ter (stĕp'sĭs'tər) s. hermanastra.
step·son (:sŭn') s. hijastro.
step-up (stĕp'ŭp') s. *(acceleration)* aceleración *f*; *(increase)* aumento.
ster·e·o (stĕr'ē-ō') I. s. equipo estereofónico; *(sound)* sonido estereofónico II. adj. estéreo.
ster·e·o·phon·ic ('--fŏn'ĭk) adj. estereofónico.
ster·e·o·type (stĕr'ē-ə-tīp') I. s. estereotipo

II. tr. estereotipar.
ster·ile (stĕr'əl, :īl') adj. estéril.
ste·ril·i·ty (stə-rĭl'ĭ-tē) s. esterilidad *f*.
ster·il·i·za·tion (stĕr'ə-lĭ-zā'shən) s. esterilización *f*.
ster·il·ize (stĕr'ə-līz') tr. esterilizar.
ster·ling (stûr'lĭng) I. s. FIN. libra esterlina; *(tableware)* plata II. adj. FIN. de la libra esterlina; *(silver)* de plata de ley; FIG. de primera calidad ♦ **s. silver** (artículos de) plata de ley.
stern¹ (stûrn) adj. firme; *(severe)* severo; *(gloomy)* sombrío; *(relentless)* implacable.
stern² s. MARÍT. popa.
ster·num (stûr'nəm) s. [pl. **s** o -**na**] esternón *m*.
ster·oid (stîr'oid', stĕr'-) s. esteroide *m*.
steth·o·scope (stĕth'ə-skōp') s. estetoscopio.
ste·ve·dore (stē'və-dôr') s. estibador *m*.
stew (stōō) I. tr. guisar —intr. cocerse; FAM. *(to worry)* agitarse II. s. guiso; FAM. agitación *f* ♦ **in a s.** agitado.
stew·ard (stōō'ərd) s. administrador *m*; *(household manager)* mayordomo; MARÍT. *(attendant)* camarero; *(officer)* despensero ♦ **shop s.** enlace sindical.
stew·ard·ess (:ər-dĭs) s. azafata.
stew·ard·ship (:ərd-shĭp') s. gerencia.
stewed (stōōd) adj. CUL. guisado; JER. *(drunk)* borracho.
stick (stĭk) I. s. vara; *(twig)* ramita; *(walking stick)* bastón *m*; *(wand)* varilla; *(of dynamite)* cartucho; *(of chocolate)* barra; *(adhesiveness)* adhesión *f*; AVIA. palanca de mando ♦ **s. shift** AUTO. cambio manual • **the sticks** región apartada II. tr. **stuck** *(to push into)* introducir, meter; *(to pin)* prender (con alfileres), *(to glue)* pegar; *(to impale)* clavar • **to s. by** ser fiel a • **to s. down** pegar • **to s. it out** aguantar hasta el fin • **to s. out** *(tongue)* mostrar; *(head)* asomar • **to s. up** atracar • **to s. up for** defender —intr. *(nail, pin)* clavarse; *(to cling)* pegarse; *(to persevere)* persistir; *(to jam)* atascarse ♦ **to s. around** quedarse • **to s. close** mantenerse juntos • **to s. out** sobresalir • **to s. to** *(promise)* cumplir; *(friend)* ser fiel a; *(facts)* ceñirse a • **to s. to business** dejarse de rodeos • **to s. to it** perseverar • **to s. to one's guns** mantenerse uno en sus treces • **to s. together** mantenerse unidos.
stick·er ('ər) s. *(label)* etiqueta adhesiva; *(prickle)* espina.
stick-in-the-mud ('ĭn-thə-mŭd') s. FAM. persona sin iniciativa.
stick·ler (stĭk'lər) s. persona rigorista.
stick·pin (stĭk'pĭn') s. alfiler *m* de corbata.
stick·up (:ŭp') s. JER. atraco.
stick·y (stĭk'ē) adj. -i- pegajoso; *(muggy)* húmedo; FAM. *(difficult)* difícil.
stiff (stĭf) I. adj. rígido; *(not limber)* tieso; *(joint)* anquilosado; *(taut)* tenso; *(formal)* formal; *(thick)* espeso; *(unyielding)* inflexible; *(drink)* fuerte; *(difficult)* difícil; *(punishment)* duro; *(prices)* excesivo II. adv. ♦ **to be bored s.** estar muy aburrido • **to be scared s.** estar muerto de miedo III. s. JER. *(corpse)* fiambre *m*; *(drunk)* borracho.
stiff·en ('ən) tr. & intr. poner(se) rígido.
stiff·ness (stĭf'nĭs) s. rigidez *f*, inflexibilidad *f*; *(toughness)* dureza; *(drink)* consistencia; *(of drink)* fuerza; *(of knee)* anquilosamiento; *(of muscle)* agarrotamiento.
sti·fle¹ (stī'fəl) s. & intr. sofocar(se).
sti·fle² s. ZOOL. babilla.

stig·ma (stĭg′mə) s. [pl. **s** o **-mata**] estigma m.

stig·ma·tize (:tīz′) tr. estigmatizar.

sti·let·to (stə-lĕt′ō) s. [pl. **(e)s**] estilete m.

still[1] (stĭl) I. adj. (silent) silencioso; (at rest) inmóvil; (tranquil) sosegado; (waters) mansa; FOTOG. fija ♦ s. life naturaleza muerta II. s. silencio; FOTOG. foto fija III. adv. (motionlessly) quieto; (yet) todavía, aún; (even) aun; (nevertheless) sin embargo IV. tr. tranquilizar; (to silence) (hacer) callar; (to stop) detener; (to calm) calmar.

still[2] s. alambique m; (distillery) destilería.

still·born (:bôrn′) adj. nacido muerto.

stilt (stĭlt) s. zanco; (support) pilote m.

stilt·ed (stĭl′tĭd) adj. afectado.

stim·u·lant (stĭm′yə-lənt) s. (drug) estimulante m; (stimulus) estímulo.

stim·u·late (:lāt′) tr. estimular.

stim·u·lus (′-ləs) s. [pl. **-li**] estímulo.

sting (stĭng) I. tr. stung picar; (to hurt) escocer; FIG. herir —intr. (to prick) picar; (to cause pain) hacer escocer II. s. picadura; (pain) escozor m; ZOOL. aguijón m.

sting·er (′ər) s. aguijón m.

stin·gy (stĭn′jē) adj. **-i-** tacaño; (scant) escaso.

stink (stĭngk) I. intr. **stank** o **stunk, stunk** heder, apestar; FIG. (person, policy) tener mala fama; (performance) estar fatal ♦ **to s. of money** estar podrido de dinero ♦ **to s. up** dar mal olor II. s. hedor m ♦ **to make** o **raise a s.** armar un escándalo.

stink·er (stĭng′kər) s. JER. canalla mf.

stink·ing (:ĭng) adj. hediondo, apestoso.

stint (stĭnt) I. tr. restringir, limitar ♦ **to s. on** escatimar II. s. faena, trabajo.

sti·pend (stī′pĕnd′) s. estipendio.

stip·ple (stĭp′əl) I. tr. puntear II. s. punteado.

stip·u·late (stĭp′yə-lāt′) tr. & intr. estipular.

stip·u·la·tion (′-lā′shən) s. estipulación f.

stir (stûr) I. tr. **-rr-** (to mix) revolver; (to move) agitar; (liquid, memory) remover; (fire) atizar; (to incite) incitar; (to affect) conmover ♦ **to s. up** (to revive) despertar; (trouble) provocar —intr. moverse II. s. movimiento; (disturbance) conmoción f; (flurry) sensación f.

stir·rer (stûr′ər) s. agitador m.

stir·ring (:ĭng) adj. (rousing) bullicioso; (moving) conmovedor; (lively) animado.

stir·rup (stûr′əp) s. estribo.

stitch (stĭch) I. s. COST. puntada; (decorative) punto; MED. punzada ♦ **a s. in time saves nine** más vale prevenir que curar • **to be in stitches** estar muerto de risa • **without a s. on** en cueros II. tr. coser; (to bind) encuadernar.

stock (stŏk) I. s. (inventory) existencias, stock m; (supply) surtido; (livestock) ganado; (shares) acciones f; (lineage) linaje m; (broth) caldo; (of rifle) culata; (repertoire) repertorio ♦ **in s.** en existencia • **out of s.** agotado • **surplus s.** excedentes • **to put s. in** darle importancia a • **to take s. of** evaluar ♦ pl. (pillory) cepo II. tr. (to supply) surtir; (to keep in supply) tener existencias de ♦ **to s. up on** abastecerse de III. adj. en existencia, de surtido; (standard) trillado ♦ **s. certificate** título de acciones • **s. company** sociedad anónima • **s. exchange** o **market** bolsa.

stock·ade (stŏ-kād′). empalizada.

stock·bro·ker (stŏk′brō′kər) s. corredor m de bolsa.

stock·hold·er (:hōl′dər) s. accionista mf.

stock·ing (stŏk′ĭng) s. media.

stock·pile (stŏk′pīl′) I. s. reservas II. tr. acumular.

stock-still (stŏk′stĭl′) adj. completamente inmóvil.

stock·y (stŏk′ē) adj. **-i-** (solid) fuerte, robusto; (plump) rechoncho.

stock·yard (stŏk′yärd′) s. corral m de ganado.

stodg·y (stŏj′ē) adj. **-i-** (dull) aburrido; (pompous) pomposo.

sto·ic/·i·cal (stō′ĭk) adj. & s. estoico.

sto·i·cism (:ĭ-sĭz′əm) s. estoicismo.

stoke (stōk) tr. & intr. echar combustible a.

stok·er (stō′kər) s. fogonero; (device) cargador mecánico.

stole[1] (stōl) s. estola.

stole[2], **sto·len** (stōl, stō′lən) cf. **steal.**

stol·id (stŏl′ĭd) adj. impasible.

stom·ach (stŭm′ək) I. s. estómago; (abdomen) vientre m; (appetite) apetito II. tr. aguantar.

stom·ach·ache (:āk′) s. dolor m de estómago.

stomp (stŏmp) tr. & intr. pisotear.

stone (stōn) I. s. piedra; (pebble) guijarro; (gem) piedra preciosa; G.B. (weight unit) peso que equivale a 6,350 kg; (pit) hueso; MED. cálculo ♦ **within a s.'s throw** a dos pasos • **to leave no s. unturned** remover Roma con Santiago II. tr. apedrear, lapidar.

stoned (stōnd) adj. JER. (drunk) borracho; (drugged) drogado, intoxicado.

stone-deaf (stōn′dĕf′) adj. sordo como una tapia.

stone·ware (:wâr′) s. gres m.

stone·work (:wûrk′) s. cantería.

ston·y (stō′nē) adj. **-i-** pedregoso; (like stone) pétreo; (unemotional) frío.

stood (stŏŏd) cf. **stand.**

stooge (stōōj) s. (follower) secuaz mf; TEAT. actor m que da pie a un cómico.

stool (stōōl) s. taburete m; (footrest) escabel m; (toilet bowl) taza; FISIOL. deposiciones f ♦ **s. pigeon** JER. soplón.

stoop[1] (stōōp) I. intr. (to bend) encorvarse; (to lower oneself) rebajarse; (to condescend) condescender II. s. inclinación f de hombros.

stoop[2] s. (porch) pórtico.

stop (stŏp) I. tr. **-pp-** (to halt) parar, detener; (to cease) dejar de; (to end) acabar; (to prevent) impedir; (to plug) tapar; (to obstruct) bloquear; (to staunch) restañar; (a check) cancelar ♦ **s. it!** ¡basta! • **to s. one's ears** taparse los oídos • **to s. up** taponar —intr. detenerse; (to cease) cesar; (to visit) hacer alto ♦ **to s. at nothing** no pararse en barras • **to s. by** o **in** hacer una visita corta • **to s. dead** o **short** pararse en seco • **to s. off** pararse • **to s. over** alojarse II. s. (act) detención f; (cessation) cesación f; (finish) término; (stay) estancia; (place) parada; (en route) parada; (plug) tapón m; (on check) orden f de suspensión de pago; MÚS. (organ) registro ♦ **full s.** punto • **s. sign** señal de alto • **to come to a s.** pararse • **to pull out all the stops** tocar todos los registros • **to put a s. to** poner fin a.

stop·gap (′găp′) s. substituto.

stop·light (:līt′) s. (traffic signal) semáforo; (brake light) luz f de frenado.

stop·o·ver (:ō′vər) s. AVIA., MARÍT. escala; (place) lugar visitado.

stop·page (:ĭj) s. (stop) parada, detención f; (work halt) paro; (blockage) obstrucción f.

stop·per (:ər) s. tapón m.

stop·watch (:wŏch′) s. cronómetro.

stor·age (stôr′ĭj) s. almacenamiento; *(space)* almacén *m*; *(fee)* almacenaje *m*; ELEC. acumulación *f* ✦ **s. battery** *o* **cell** acumulador.

store (stôr) I. s. *(shop)* tienda; *(supply)* surtido; *(warehouse)* almacén *m*; *(abundance)* acopio ✦ **department s.** gran almacén • **to be in s. for one** esperarle a uno • **to have in s.** tener guardado • **to set s. by** dar importancia a ✦ pl. MIL. *(equipment)* pertrechos; *(supplies)* provisiones II. tr. almacenar ✦ **to s. away** guardar • **to s. up** acumular.

store·house (′hous′) s. almacén *m*, depósito.

store·keep·er (:kē′pər) s. *(shopkeeper)* tendero.

store·room (:rōōm′) s. despensa, bodega.

sto·ried (stôr′ēd) adj. celebrado por la historia.

stork (stôrk) s. cigüeña.

storm (stôrm) I. s. *(storm)* tormenta, *(wind)* vendaval *m*; *(outburst)* arrebato; *(attack)* asalto; *(of protest)* lluvia ✦ **s. cellar** refugio contra los ciclones • **s. cloud** nubarrón • **s. door** contrapuerta • **s. trooper** miliciano nazi • **s. window** contraventana • **to ride out** *o* **weather a s.** capear el temporal II. intr. haber tormenta; *(to rant)* vociferar ✦ **to s. in, out** entrar, salir violentamente —tr. tomar por asalto.

storm·y (stôr′mē) adj. **-i-** tempestuoso; *(violent)* turbulento.

sto·ry¹ (stôr′ē) s. cuento, relato; *(plot)* trama; *(version)* versión *f*; *(article)* artículo; *(anecdote)* anécdota; *(lie)* mentira.

sto·ry² s. *(of a building)* piso.

sto·ry·book (:bŏŏk′) s. libro de cuentos.

sto·ry·tell·er (:tĕl′ər) s. *(author)* cuentista *mf*; *(narrator)* narrador *m*; FAM. *(liar)* mentiroso.

stout (stout) I. adj. *(bulky)* corpulento; *(determined)* resuelto; *(brave)* valiente; *(sturdy)* fornido; *(substantial)* sólido; *(powerful)* enérgico; *(staunch)* firme II. s. cerveza de malta.

stout·heart·ed (′här′tĭd) adj. valiente.

stove¹ (stōv) s. cocina; *(heater)* estufa.

stove² cf. **stave.**

stow (stō) tr. guardar ✦ **to s. away** *(to put away)* guardar; *(on board)* viajar de polizón.

stow·a·way (′ə-wā′) s. polizón *m*.

strad·dle (străd′l) I. tr. sentarse a horcajadas sobre *o* en; *(an issue)* no tomar ningún partido en ✦ **to s. the fence** nadar entre dos aguas II. s. posición *f* a horcajadas.

strafe (strāf) tr. bombardear.

strag·gle (străg′əl) intr. *(to fall behind)* rezagarse; *(to spread out)* desparramarse.

strag·gly (:lē) adj. desordenado.

straight (strāt) I. adj. *(line)* recto; *(upright, not bent)* derecho; *(frank)* franco; *(uninterrupted)* seguido, *(orderly)* arreglado; *(in sequence)* en orden; *(undiluted)* puro; *(honorable)* honrado; JER. *(conventional)* convencional; *(sober)* sobrio; *(not gay)* heterosexual ✦ **s. face** cara seria • **s. hair** pelo lacio • **s. razor** navaja de afeitar • **s. talk** lenguaje franco • **to keep a s. face** mantenerse impávido II. adv. en línea recta; *(erect)* derecho; *(without delay)* directamente; *(candidly)* sinceramente; *(continuously)* continuamente ✦ **s. ahead** en frente; *(forward)* todo seguido • **s. away** *o* **off** sin interrupción • **to get** *o* **put s.** poner en claro • **to go s.** enmendarse • **to look someone s. in the eye** mirar a alguien a los ojos • **to read s. through** leer de un tirón • **to set s.** corregir; *(to set right)* poner bien • **to tell something s.** decirle algo sin rodeos III. s. *(straight part)* recta; *(card sequence)* escalera ✦ **the s. and narrow** el buen camino.

straight·a·way (′ə-wā′) s. recta.

straight·edge (:ĕj′) s. regla (recta).

straight·en (:n) tr. & intr. enderezar(se) ✦ **to s. out** *(to put in order)* ordenar; *(to solve)* resolver; *(to rectify)* rectificar.

straight·for·ward (-fôr′wərd) adj. *(direct)* directo; *(honest)* sincero.

straight·way (strāt′wā′) adv. en seguida.

strain¹ (strān) I. tr. *(to stretch)* estirar; *(nerves)* agotar; *(limb)* torcer; *(to sieve)* colar; TEC. deformar ✦ **to s. one's eyes** cansar la vista —intr. *(to strive)* esforzarse; *(to stretch)* tenderse; *(to filter)* filtrarse ✦ **to s. under** soportar con gran esfuerzo II. s. *(effort)* esfuerzo; *(stress)* tensión *f*; *(burden)* peso; *(twisting)* torcedura; TEC. deformación *f*.

strain² s. *(race)* raza; *(descent)* cepa; *(tendency)* tendencia; *(tenor)* sentido; *(tune)* melodía.

strained (strānd) adj. colado; *(forced)* forzado; *(relations)* tirante.

strain·er (strā′nər) s. filtro; *(colander)* colador *m*; *(sieve)* cedazo.

strait (strāt) s. estrecho ✦ pl. *(narrows)* estrecho; *(jam)* aprieto.

strait·jack·et (′jăk′ĭt) s. camisa de fuerza.

strait-laced (:lāst′) adj. puritano.

strand¹ (strănd) I. s. playa II. tr. & intr. *(to run aground)* encallar; *(to abandon)* dejar desamparado.

strand² s. *(of rope)* ramal *m*; *(single thread)* hebra; *(of pearls)* sarta.

strange (strānj) adj. *(unfamiliar)* desconocido; *(odd)* extraño, raro; *(peculiar)* peculiar; *(exotic)* exótico; *(uncommon)* desacostumbrado ✦ **strangest of all** lo más extraño del caso es que.

strang·er (strān′jər) s. *(unknown person)* desconocido; *(foreigner)* extranjero; *(outsider)* forastero ✦ **to be no s.** conocer muy bien.

stran·gle (străng′gəl) tr. estrangular; *(to smother)* sofocar; FIG. sofocar, limitar.

stran·gu·late (:gyə-lāt′) tr. & intr. estrangular(se).

stran·gu·la·tion (′-lā′shən) s. estrangulación *f*.

strap (străp) I. s. *(strip)* tira, correa; *(band)* banda; *(of a dress)* tirante *m* II. tr. **-pp-** *(to fasten)* atar; *(to whip)* azotar; *(razor)* suavizar.

strap·less (′lĭs) adj. sin tiras, *(dress)* sin tirantes.

strapped (străpt) adj. FAM. sin un centavo.

strap·ping (străp′ĭng) adj. fornido.

stra·ta (strā′tə, străt′ə) cf. **stratum.**

strat·a·gem (străt′ə-jəm) s. estratagema.

stra·te·gic (strə-tē′jĭk) adj. estratégico.

strat·e·gist (străt′ə-jĭst) s. estratega *m*.

strat·e·gy (străt′ə-jē) s. estrategia.

strat·i·fi·ca·tion (străt′ə-fĭ-kā′shən) s. estratificación *f*.

strat·i·fy (′-fī′) tr. & intr. estratificar(se).

strat·o·sphere (străt′ə-sfîr′) s. estratósfera.

stra·tum (strā′təm) s. [pl. **s** *o* **-ta**] estrato.

straw (strô) I. s. BOT. paja; *(trifle)* comino ✦ **a s. in the wind** un indicio • **the last s.** la última gota • **to grasp at straws** agarrarse a un pelo • **to draw straws** echar suertes II. adj. de paja; *(color)* pajizo; FIG. insignificante.

straw·ber·ry (strô′bĕr′ē) s. fresa.

stray (strā) I. intr. *(to roam)* errar; *(to go astray)* descarriarse II. s. animal *m* callejero III. adj. *(lost)* perdido <s. *bullet* bala perdida>; *(lone)* aislado; *(scattered)* dispersos.

streak (strēk) I. s. *(stripe)* raya; *(trait)* fondo; *(of luck)* racha; *(of lightning)* rayo II. tr. rayar —intr. pasar como un rayo.

streak·y (strē'kē) adj. **-i-** *(streaked)* rayado; *(veined)* veteado.

stream (strēm) I. s. arroyo; *(flow)* chorro; *(of insults)* sarta; *(of tears)* torrente m; *(of people)* oleada ♦ **against the s.** contra la corriente ♦ **to go with the s.** seguir la corriente II. intr. correr; *(to wave)* ondear ♦ **to s. in** entrar a raudales ♦ **to s. out** *(people)* salir en tropel; *(liquid)* salir a torrentes.

stream·er (strē'mər) s. *(pennant)* gallardete m; *(long strip)* serpentina; *(headline)* titular m.

stream·line (strēm'līn') tr. construir en forma aerodinámica; *(to modernize)* modernizar.

stream·lined (:līnd') s. aerodinámico, FIG. modernizado.

street (strēt) s. calle f.

street·car ('kär') s. tranvía m.

street·walk·er (:wô'kər) s. prostituta.

strength (strĕngkth) s. fuerza; *(of material)* resistencia; *(vigor)* fortaleza; *(solidity)* solidez f; *(intensity)* intensidad f; *(validity)* validez f; *(efficacy)* eficacia; *(potency)* potencia ♦ **by sheer s.** a fuerza viva ♦ **on the s. of** en virtud de ♦ **s. of character** entereza ♦ **to be present in great s.** estar en gran número.

strength·en (strĕngk'thən) tr. *(to reinforce)* reforzar; *(physically)* fortalecer; *(ties)* estrechar; *(relations)* intensificar —intr. fortalecerse, intensificarse.

stren·u·ous (strĕn'y o͞o-əs) adj. *(active)* vigoroso; *(energetic)* enérgico.

strep·to·coc·cus (strĕp'tə-kŏk'əs) s. [pl. **-ci**] estreptococo.

stress (strĕs) I. s. *(significance)* hincapié m; *(tension)* tensión f; MED. fatiga nerviosa; GRAM. énfasis m; MEC. fatiga ♦ **to lay s. on** insistir en II. tr. hacer hincapié en; MEC. someter a un esfuerzo; GRAM. acentuar.

stretch (strĕch) I. tr. estirar; *(to reach)* extender; *(wings)* desplegar; *(wire)* tender; *(shoes)* ensanchar ♦ **to a point** excederse ♦ **to s. it** exagerar ♦ **to s. oneself** desperezarse ♦ **to s. the rules** hacer una excepción —intr. estirarse; *(shoes)* ensancharse ♦ **to s. out** *(to lie down)* tumbarse II. s. *(lengthening)* alargamiento; *(elasticity)* elasticidad f; *(of road)* tramo; *(of track)* recta; *(of time)* período; *(of imagination)* esfuerzo ♦ **at a s.** seguido • **home s.** última etapa.

stretch·er ('ər) s. *(litter)* camilla; *(for canvas)* bastidor m.

stretch·er-bear·er (:bâr'ər) s. camillero.

strew (stro͞o) tr. **-ed, -ed** *o* **-n** *(to scatter)* esparcir, desparramar; *(to cover)* cubrir (with de).

stri·a·tion (strī-ā'shən) s. estriación f.

strick·en (strĭk'ən) I. cf. **strike** II. adj. afligido.

strict (strĭkt) adj. estricto.

strict·ly ('lē) adv. estrictamente; *(severely)* severamente ♦ **s. speaking** en realidad.

stric·ture (strĭk'chər) s. censura; MED. estrechez f.

stride (strīd) I. intr. **strode, stridden** caminar a grandes pasos II. s. zancada ♦ **to take in one's s.** tomarse con calma ♦ pl. progreso • **to make great s.** progresar a grandes pasos.

stri·dent (strīd'nt) adj. estridente.

strife (strīf) s. disensión f; *(conflict)* conflicto.

strike (strīk) I. tr. **struck, struck** *o* **stricken** golpear; *(to inflict)* asestar; *(to crash into)* cho-

car con; *(to attack)* atacar; *(coins)* acuñar; *(lightning)* caer en; *(hour)* dar; *(match)* encender; *(to expunge)* tachar; *(oil)* hallar; *(terror)* infundir; *(a pose)* adoptar; *(camp)* desmontar; *(employer)* declararse en huelga contra ♦ **to s. a jury** elegir jurado ♦ **to s. an average** encontrar el término medio ♦ **to s. blind** cegar ♦ **to s. down** derribar; *(disease)* abatir ♦ **to s. off** *(to expunge)* sacar; *(to cross out)* tachar; *(to deduct)* deducir ♦ **to s. one as** dar la impresión de ♦ **to s. out** tachar ♦ **to s. roots** echar raíces ♦ **to s. through** atravesar • **to s. up** *(friendship)* trabar; *(music)* empezar a tocar; *(conversation)* entablar ♦ **to s. upon** ocurrírsele a uno ♦ **to s. with admiration** llenar de admiración ♦ **to s. with terror** sobrecoger de terror —intr. golpear, dar golpes; *(to attack)* atacar; *(bell)* sonar; *(to set out)* dirigirse hacia; *(to stop work)* declararse en huelga ♦ **to s. back** devolver golpe por golpe ♦ **to s. home** dar en el blanco ♦ **to s. out** *(to hit out)* pegar; *(to start out)* tomar una resolución; *(to fail)* fallar • **to s. out (for)** ponerse en marcha (hacia) ♦ **to s. up** MÚS. empezar a tocar II. s. *(act)* golpe m; *(attack)* ataque m; *(labor)* huelga ⟨*on s. en huelga*⟩; *(discovery)* descubrimiento ♦ **a lucky s.** FAM. un golpe de suerte ♦ **to go on s.** declararse en huelga ♦ **to have two strikes against one** FAM. estar uno en posición desventajosa.

strike·break·er ('brā'kər) s. rompehuelgas *mf*.

strik·er (strī'kər) s. huelguista *mf*.

strik·ing (:kĭng) adj. notable.

string (strĭng) I. s. cuerda; *(row)* hilera; *(series)* serie f ♦ **s. beans** CUL. judía verde • **s. of beads** rosario; *(necklace)* collar • **s. orchestra, quartet** orquesta, cuarteto de cuerdas ♦ **to have on a s.** tener a uno en un puño ♦ pl. MÚS. instrumentos de cuerda; *(conditions)* estipulaciones II. tr. **strung** *(to fit with strings)* encordar; *(to thread)* ensartar; *(to fasten)* atar con una cuerda; *(to stretch)* tender ♦ **high strung** muy nervioso • **to s. along with** acompañar a • **to s. someone along** dejar a alguien pendiente; *(to deceive)* engañar.

strin·gen·cy (strĭn'jən-sē) s. *(severity)* rigor m; *(scarcity)* escasez f.

strin·gent (:jənt) adj. riguroso; *(strict)* estricto; *(pressing)* apurado.

string·y (strĭng'ē) adj. **-i-** fibroso; *(with strings)* lleno de fibras.

strip¹ (strĭp) tr. **-pp-** *(to undress)* desnudar; *(bed)* deshacer; *(fruit)* pelar; *(tree)* descortezar; *(to dismantle)* desmantelar; *(gear)* estropear ♦ **to s. down** *(paint)* raspar; *(motor)* desmontar • **s. mine** mina a cielo abierto • **to s. of** despojar de ♦ **to s. off** quitar —intr. desvestirse ♦ **to s. off** desnudarse.

strip² s. faja; AER. pista de aterrizaje.

stripe (strīp) I. s. raya; *(chevron)* galón m; *(kind)* calaña II. tr. rayar.

striped (strīpt, strī'pĭd) adj. a rayas, rayado.

strip·ling (strĭp'lĭng) s. mozalbete m.

strip-mine (:mīn') tr. explotar una mina a cielo abierto.

strip·per (:ər) s. bailarina (de strip-tease).

strive (strīv) intr. **-ed** *o* **strove, -ed** *o* **-n** esforzarse; *(to struggle)* luchar.

strobe (strōb) s. FOTOG. estroboscopio; *(light)* luz estroboscópica ♦ **s. light** luz estroboscópica.

strode (strōd) cf. **stride.**

stroke (strōk) I. s. golpe m; *(of bell)* campanada; *(apoplexy)* apoplejía; *(in rowing)* palada; *(in swimming)* brazada; *(with brush)* pincelada; *(with pen)* trazo ♦ **at the s. of . . .** al dar las . . . • **finishing s.** golpe de gracia • **s. of luck** suerte • **s. of genius** idea genial • **with one s.** de un plumazo II. tr. acariciar.

stroll (strōl) I. intr. pasearse II. s. paseo.

stroll·er (strō′lər) s. paseante *mf*; *(pram)* cochecito de niño.

strong (strông) adj. fuerte; *(powerful)* poderoso; *(persuasive)* persuasivo; *(language)* subido de tono *or* color ♦ **s. point** fuerte • **to be going s.** FAM. marchar bien • **to be s. in numbers** ser numeroso • **to have a s. character** tener mucho carácter • **to have a s. stomach** tener un buen estómago • **to have s. feelings about** tener ideas muy firmes sobre.

strong-arm (′ärm′) FAM. I. adj. de mano dura ♦ **s. tactics** fuerza II. tr. intimidar.

strong·box (:böks′) s. caja fuerte.

strong·hold (:hōld′) s. fortaleza.

strong-mind·ed (.mīn′dĭd) adj. determinado.

strop (strŏp) I. s. suavizador *m* (de navajas) II. tr. **-pp-** suavizar.

strove (strōv) cf. **strive**.

struck (strŭk) I. cf. **strike** II. adj. cerrado (por huelga).

struc·tur·al (strŭk′chər əl) adj. estructural.

struc·ture (strŭk′chər) I. s. estructura II. tr. estructurar.

struc·tured (:chərd) adj. estructurado.

strug·gle (strŭg′əl) I. intr. luchar II. s. lucha; *(effort)* esfuerzo.

strug·gling (:lĭng) adj. que lucha.

strum (strŭm) MÚS. I. tr. & intr. **-mm-** rasguear II. s. rasgueo.

strung (strŭng) cf. **string**.

strut (strŭt) I. intr. **-tt-** pavonearse II. s. *(gait)* pavoneo; *(rod)* puntal *m*.

strych·nine (strĭk′nīn′) s. estricnina.

stub (stŭb) I. s. tocón *m*; *(check)* talón *m*; *(ticket)* resguardo II. tr. **-bb-** *(toe)* tropezar con; *(cigarette)* apagar.

stub·ble (′əl) s. rastrojo; *(beard)* barba incipiente ♦ **s. field** campo de rastrojos.

stub·born (stŭb′ərn) adj. testarudo; *(persistent)* tenaz; *(resistant)* duro.

stub·born·ness (:nĭs) s. testarudez *f*.

stub·by (stŭb′ē) adj. **-i-** rechoncho.

stuc·co (stŭk′ō) I. s. [pl. **(e)s**] estuco II. tr. estucar.

stuck (stŭk) cf. **stick**.

stuck-up (′ŭp′) adj. FAM. engreído.

stud¹ (stŭd) I. s. ARQ. montante *m*; *(ornament)* tachón *m*; *(brace)* travesaño; *(spindle)* espiga II. tr. **-dd-** tachonar; *(to strew)* salpicar.

stud² s. semental *m* ♦ **at s.** de cría.

stu·dent (stōō′dnt) s. estudiante *mf*; *(observer)* observador *m* ♦ **s. body** estudiantado.

stud·ied (stŭd′ēd) adj. afectado.

stu·di·o (stōō′dē-ō′) s. estudio; *(of artist)* taller *m* ♦ **s. apartment** departamento de una habitación, baño y cocina.

stu·di·ous (:əs) adj. estudioso; *(diligent)* aplicado.

stud·y (stŭd′ē) I. s. estudio II. tr. & intr. estudiar ♦ **to s. a part** aprender un papel • **to s. to be** estudiar para • **to s. under** ser alumno de.

stuff (stŭf) I. s. material *m*; FAM. *(belongings)* cosas; *(nonsense)* disparates; *(junk)* porquería; *(capability)* pasta; G.B. *(fabric)* género ♦ **do your s.!** ¡muestra-lo que sabes! • **same old s.**

lo mismo de siempre • **to be hot s.** ser fenomenal • **to know one's s.** conocer el percal II. tr. rellenar; *(to plug)* tapar; *(to gorge)* atiborrar ♦ **s. it** FAM. vete a paseo • **to s. oneself** atiborrarse.

stuffed (stŭft) adj. relleno.

stuff·ing (stŭf′ĭng) s. relleno.

stuff·y (stŭf′ē) adj. **-i-** sofocante, mal ventilado; *(congested)* tupido; FAM. pomposo.

stul·ti·fy (stŭl′tə-fī′) tr. *(to dispirit)* desanimar; *(to disable)* anular; *(to ridicule)* ridiculizar.

stum·ble (stŭm′bəl) I. intr. *(to trip)* tropezar; *(to flounder)* balbucear; *(to blunder)* cometer un desliz ♦ **to s. across** *o* **upon** tropezar con • **stumbling block** tropezó II. s. *(act)* tropiezo, traspié *m*; *(mistake)* desliz *m*.

stump (stŭmp) I. s. *(of tree)* tocón *m*; *(limb)* muñón *m*; *(tooth)* raigón *m*; *(place)* tribuna política ♦ **up a s.** perplejo II. tr. FAM. dejar perplejo —intr. POL. hacer giras políticas.

stump·y (stŭm′pē) adj. **-i-** *(person)* rechoncho; *(land)* lleno de tocones.

stun (stŭn) tr. **-nn-** dejar sin sentido; *(to astound)* dejar estupefacto II. s. choque *m*.

stung (stŭng) cf. **sting**.

stunk (stŭngk) cf. **stink**.

stun·ning (stŭn′ĭng) adj. imponente.

stunt¹ (stŭnt) tr. impedir el crecimiento de.

stunt² s. *(feat)* proeza; *(publicity trick)* truco publicitario.

stu·pe·fac·tion (stōō′pə-făk′shən) s. estupefacción *f*.

stu·pe·fy (′fī′) tr. *(to dull)* atontar; *(to amaze)* dejar estupefacto.

stu·pen·dous (stōō-pěn′dəs) adj. estupendo; *(amazing)* asombroso.

stu·pid (stōō′pĭd) adj. **-er**, **-est** estúpido, tonto.

stu·pid·i·ty (-′ĭ-tē) s. estupidez *f*, tontería.

stu·por (stōō′pər) s. estupor *m*; *(daze)* atontamiento.

stur·di·ness (stûr′dē-nĭs) s. *(firmness)* firmeza; *(strength)* robustez *f*.

stur·dy (stûr′dē) adj. robusto; *(firm)* firme.

stur·geon (stûr′jən) s. esturión *m*.

stut·ter (stŭt′ər) I. intr. tartamudear II. s. tartamudeo.

stut·ter·er (:ər) s. tartamudo.

stut·ter·ing (:ĭng) I. s. tartamudeo II. adj. tartamudo.

sty¹ (stī) s. *(for swine)* pocilga.

sty² s. MED. orzuelo.

style (stīl) I. s. estilo; *(vogue)* moda; *(cut)* hechura; *(type)* modelo, tipo; *(title)* tratamiento; *(stylus)* aguja ♦ **in s.** con estilo, *(in vogue)* de moda II. tr. *(to stylize)* estilizar; *(to design)* diseñar; *(to designate)* titular.

styl·ish (stī′lĭsh) adj. a la moda.

styl·ist (:lĭst) s. diseñador *m*; *(hairdresser)* peluquero; LIT. estilista *mf*.

sty·lis·tic (-lĭs′tĭk) adj. estilístico.

styl·ize (′līz′) tr. estilizar.

sty·lus (stī′ləs) s. [pl. **es** *o* **-li**] estilo; *(needle)* aguja (de fonógrafo); *(tool)* punzón *m*.

sty·mie (stī′mē) tr. obstaculizar.

styp·tic (stĭp′tĭk) adj. astringente.

suave (swäv) adj. afable.

sub (sŭb) FAM. I. s. *(submarine)* submarino; *(substitute)* substituto; *(sandwich)* emparedado grande II. intr. **-bb-** substituir.

sub·a·tom·ic (sŭb′ə-tŏm′ĭk) adj. subatómico.

sub·com·mit·tee (′kə-mĭt′ē) s. subcomité *m*.

sub·com·pact (-kăm′păkt′) s. automóvil pe-

sub·con·scious ('kŏn'shəs) adj. & s. subconsciente *m.*

sub·con·ti·nent (:kŏn'tə-nənt) s. subcontinente *m.*

sub·con·tract (-kŏn'trăkt') I. s. subcontrato II. tr. ('kən-trăkt') subcontratar.

sub·cu·ta·ne·ous (:kyŏ-tā'nē-əs) adj. subcutáneo.

sub·di·vide (:dĭ-vīd') tr. & intr. subdividir(se).

sub·di·vi·sion ('vĭzh'ən) subdivisión *f.*

sub·due (səb-dŏ') tr. sojuzgar; *(to make tractable)* amansar; *(to tone down)* suavizar.

sub·group (sŭb'grŏp') s. subgrupo.

sub·hu·man (-hyŏ'mən) adj. infrahumano.

sub·ject (sŭb'jĭkt) I. adj. dominado ♦ **s. matter** materia • **s. to** *(prone to)* propenso a; *(exposed to)* expuesto a; *(dependent on)* sujeto a II. s. sujeto; *(of country)* súbdito; *(theme)* tema; *(course)* asignatura ♦ **on the s.** of a propósito de • **to keep off a s.** no tocar el tema III. tr. (səb-jĕkt') someter ♦ **to s.** to exponer a; *(to make dependent on)* supeditar a.

sub·jec·tion (səb-jĕk'shən) s. sujeción *f.*

sub·jec·tive (:tĭv) adj. subjetivo.

sub·jec·tiv·i·ty (sŭb'jĕk-tĭv'ĭ-tē) s. subjetividad *f.*

sub·ju·gate (sŭb'jə-gāt') tr. subyugar.

sub·ju·ga·tion ('-gā'shən) s. dominación *f.*

sub·lease (sŭb-lēs') I. tr. subarrendar II. s. ('lēs') subarrendamiento.

sub·let (:lĕt') I. tr. **let, -tting** subalquilar II. s. ('lĕt') FAM. subarrendamiento.

sub·li·mate (sŭb'lə-māt') tr. sublimar.

sub·li·ma·tion ('-mā'shən) s. sublimación *f.*

sub·lime (sə-blīm') I. adj. sublime II. tr. & intr. sublimar(se).

sub·lim·i·nal (sə-blīm'ə-nəl) adj. subconsciente.

sub·ma·chine gun (sŭb'mə-shēn') s. pistola ametralladora, metralleta.

sub·ma·rine (sŭb'mə-rēn') I. adj. submarino II. s. submarino; JER. sandwich *m* grande.

sub·merge (səb-mûrj') tr. sumergir.

sub·mer·gence (:mûr'jəns) s. sumersión *f.*

sub·merse (:mûrs') tr. sumergir.

sub·mis·sion (:mĭsh'ən) s. *(act)* sometimiento; *(meekness)* sumisión *f*; *(proposal)* proposición *f.*

sub·mis·sive (:mĭs'ĭv) adj. sumiso.

sub·mit (səb-mĭt') tr. someter; *(evidence)* presentar; *(to propose)* proponer; *(to suggest)* sugerir —intr. *(to give in)* someterse; *(meekly)* conformarse.

sub·nor·mal (sŭb-nôr'məl) adj. subnormal.

sub·or·di·nate (sə-bôr'dn-ĭt) I. adj. & s. subordinado II. tr. (:āt') subordinar.

sub·or·di·na·tion ('-ā'shən) s. subordinación *f.*

sub·orn (sə-bôrn') tr. sobornar.

sub·poe·na (sə-pē'nə) DER. I. s. citación *f* II. tr. citar.

sub·scribe (səb-scrīb') tr. subscribir —intr. subscribirse; *(to magazines)* abonarse.

sub·scrib·er (:skrī'bər) s. subscriptor *m.*

sub·scrip·tion (:skrĭp'shən) s. firma; *(purchase)* subscripción *f*, abono.

sub·se·quent (sŭb'sĭ-kwĕnt') adj. subsiguiente.

sub·ser·vi·ent (səb-sûr'vē-ənt) adj. subordinado; *(servile)* servil.

sub·side (səb-sīd') intr. *(to sink)* hundirse; *(to settle)* asentarse; *(to abate)* apaciguarse.

sub·sid·i·ar·y (səb-sĭd'ē-ĕr'ē) I. adj. auxiliar; *(secondary)* secundario; *(of subsidy)* subsidiario II. s. *(company)* sucursal *f.*

sub·si·dize (sŭb'sĭ-dīz') tr. subvencionar.

sub·si·dy (:dē) s. subsidio; *(monetary aid)* subvención *f.*

sub·sist (səb-sĭst') intr. subsistir; *(to maintain life)* sustentarse *(on con, de).*

sub·sis·tence (-sĭs'təns) s. subsistencia; *(sustenance)* sustento.

sub·soil (sŭb'soil') s. subsuelo.

sub·stance (sŭb'stəns) s. substancia; *(essence)* esencia; *(solidity)* solidez *f*; *(body)* cuerpo; *(goods)* caudal *m* ♦ **man of s.** hombre acaudalado.

sub·stan·dard (sŭb-stăn'dərd) adj. inferior a lo normal.

sub·stan·tial (səb-stăn'shəl) adj. material; *(real)* verdadero; *(strong)* sólido; *(meal)* sustancioso; *(important)* sustancial; *(considerable)* considerable; *(well-to-do)* adinerado.

sub·stan·ti·ate (:shē-āt') tr. establecer.

sub·stan·ti·a·tion ('-ā'shən) s. justificación *f.*

sub·stan·tive (sŭb'stən-tĭv) I. adj. real; *(essential)* esencial II. s. GRAM. sustantivo.

sub·sti·tute (sŭb'stĭ-tŏt') I. s. substituto II. tr. & intr. substituir.

sub·sti·tu·tion ('-tŏ'shən) s. substitución *f.*

sub·sume (səb-sŏm') tr. incluir en una categoría.

sub·ter·fuge (sŭb'tər-fyŏj') s. subterfugio.

sub·ter·ra·ne·an (sŭb'tə-rā'nē-ən) adj. subterráneo.

sub·ti·tle (sŭb'tīt'l) I. s. subtítulo II. tr. subtitular.

sub·tle (sŭt'l) adj. **-er, -est** *(elusive)* sutil; *(keen)* agudo; *(clever)* astuto; *(devious)* taimado.

sub·tle·ty (:tē) s. *(cleverness)* astucia; *(distinction)* sutileza.

sub·to·tal (sŭb'tōt'l) I. s. subtotal *m* II. tr. ('-'l) sumar parte de una serie de números.

sub·tract (səb-trăkt') tr. sustraer.

sub·trac·tion (:trăk'shən) s. sustracción *f.*

sub·urb (sŭb'ûrb') s. suburbio ♦ **pl.** afueras.

sub·ur·ban (sə-bûr'bən) adj. suburbano.

sub·ur·ban·ite (:bə-nīt') s. habitante *mf* de las afueras.

sub·ur·bi·a (:bē-ə) s. afueras, cercanías.

sub·ven·tion (səb-vĕn'shən) s. subvención *f.*

sub·ver·sion (səb-vûr'zhən) s. subversión *f.*

sub·ver·sive (:sĭv) adj. subversivo.

sub·vert (səb-vûrt') tr. *(to corrupt)* corromper; *(to overthrow)* derrocar.

sub·way (sŭb'wā') s. subterráneo, metro; *(passage)* paso subterráneo.

suc·ceed (sək-sēd') intr. tener éxito; *(to turn out well)* salir bien; *(to follow)* suceder ♦ **to s. to the throne** heredar el trono —tr. suceder a; *(to follow)* seguir.

suc·cess (:sĕs') s. éxito; *(person)* persona que tiene éxito.

suc·cess·ful (:fəl) adj. de éxito, exitoso.

suc·ces·sion (sək-sĕsh'ən) s. sucesión *f* ♦ **in s.** seguido • **in s. to** como sucesor de.

suc·ces·sive (:sĕs'ĭv) adj. sucesivo; *(consecutive)* consecutivo.

suc·ces·sor (:ər) s. sucesor *m.*

suc·cinct (sək-sĭngkt') adj. sucinto.

suc·cor (sŭk'ər) I. s. socorro II. tr. socorrer.

suc·cu·lence (sŭk'yə-ləns) s. suculencia.

suc·cu·lent (:lənt) I. adj. suculento; BOT. carnoso II. s. planta carnosa.

suc·cumb (sə-kŭm′) intr. sucumbir; *(to die)* morir.

such (sŭch) **I.** adj. *(of this nature)* tal, semejante; *(of this kind)* de este tipo; *(so extreme)* tanto, semejante; *(so big)* tan, tan grande; *(so much)* tanto ◆ **one s.** un tal • **s. and s.** tal y cual • **s. as it is** tal cual es **II.** adv. tan **III.** pron. los que; *(so great)* tal; *(the like)* cosas por el estilo ◆ **as s.** *(of itself)* en sí; *(as what one is)* como tal • **s. is life** así es la vida.

such·like (′līk′) **I.** adj. de esta clase, de este tipo **II.** pron. cosas *or* personas semejantes.

suck (sŭk) **I.** tr. chupar; *(a liquid)* sorber; *(air)* aspirar ◆ **to s.** dar chupadas **II.** s. chupada.

suck·er (′ər) **I.** s. chupador *m;* FAM. *(dupe)* primo, incauto; *(lollipop)* piruli *m;* *(mouth part)* ventosa; BOT. chupón *m.*

suck·le (sŭk′əl) tr. amamantar; *(to rear)* criar —intr. tomar el pecho.

suck·ling (sŭk′lĭng) s. mamón *m.*

su·crose (sōō′krōs′) s. sucrosa.

suc·tion (sŭk′shən) s. succión *f;* *(aspiration)* aspiración ◆ **s. pump** bomba aspirante.

sud·den (sŭd′n) adj. *(unforeseen)* imprevisto; *(abrupt)* brusco; *(swift)* súbito, repentino ◆ **all of a s.** de repente.

sud·den·ly (:lē) adv. de repente.

suds (sŭdz) s.pl. *(soapy water)* jabonaduras; *(lather)* espuma, FAM. *(beer)* cerveza.

sue (sōō) tr. suplicar; DER. demandar ◆ **to s. for divorce** presentar demanda de divorcio —intr. entablar acción judicial.

suede *o* **suède** (swād) s. gamuza, ante *m.*

su·et (sōō′ĭt) s. sebo.

suf·fer (sŭf′ər) intr. ser dañado —tr. sufrir ◆ **to s. from** adolecer de.

suf·fer·ance (əns) s. tolerancia; *(tacit assent)* consentimiento tácito.

suf·fice (sə-fīs′) intr. bastar ◆ **s. it to say** basta *(con)* decir.

suf·fi·cien·cy (sə-fĭsh′ən-sē) s. suficiencia.

suf·fi·cient (:ənt) adj. bastante, suficiente.

suf·fi·cient·ly (:lē) adv. bastante.

suf·fix (sŭf′ĭks′) s. sufijo.

suf·fo·cate (sŭf′ə-kāt′) tr. & intr. sofocar(se); *(to stifle)* reprimir(se).

suf·fo·ca·tion (′-kā′shən) s. asfixia.

suf·frage (sŭf′rĭj) s. sufragio; *(right)* derecho al voto.

suf·fuse (sə-fyōōz′) tr. extenderse por.

suf·fu·sion (sə-fyōō′zhən) s. difusión *f.*

sug·ar (shŏŏg′ər) **I.** s. azúcar *mf* ◆ **s. bowl** azucarero • **s. cane** caña de azúcar • **s. loaf** pan de azúcar • **s. mill** ingenio **II.** tr. azucarar ◆ **to s. the pill** FIG. dorar la píldora.

sug·ar-coat (:kōt′) tr. endulzar.

sug·ar·y (shŏŏg′ə-rē) adj. -**i-** azucarado; *(tasting like sugar)* dulzón; FAM. *(cloyingly)* meloso.

sug·gest (səg-jěst′) tr. sugerir; *(to evoke)* hacer pensar en; *(to imply)* insinuar.

sug·ges·tion (:jěs′chən) s. sugerencia; *(hint)* indicación *f;* PSIC. sugestión *f.*

sug·ges·tive (:tĭv) adj. sugestivo; *(indicative)* evocador; *(insinuating)* insinuante.

su·i·cid·al (sōō′ĭ-sīd′l) adj. suicida.

su·i·cide (sōō′ĭ-sīd′) s. suicidio; *(person)* suicida *mf* ◆ **to commit s.** suicidarse.

suit (sōōt) **I.** s. traje *m;* *(set)* conjunto; *(cards)* palo; *(legal)* pleito; *(courtship)* galanteo ◆ **to bring s.** entablar un pleito • **to follow s.** *(in cards)* jugar el mismo palo; FIG. seguir el ejemplo **II.** tr. satisfacer; *(to look good)* quedar bien

◆ **to s. oneself** hacer lo que uno quiere • **to s. to** adaptar a.

suit·a·bil·i·ty (sōō′tə-bĭl′ĭ-tē) s. conveniencia.

suit·a·ble (′-bəl) adj. conveniente; *(compatible)* compatible.

suit·case (sōōt′kās′) s. maleta.

suite (swēt) s. *(retinue)* séquito; *(apartment)* suite *f;* *(furniture)* juego; MÚS. suite.

suit·or (sōō′tər) s. peticionario; *(wooer)* pretendiente *m.*

sul·fate (sŭl′fāt′) s. sulfato.

sul·fide (:fīd′) s. sulfuro.

sul·fite (:fīt′) s. sulfito.

sulfur (:fər) s. azufre *m* ◆ **s. dioxide** dióxido de azufre.

sul·fu·ric (-fyŏŏr′ĭk) adj. sulfúrico.

sul·fur·ous (′fər-əs) adj. sulfuroso; *(from burning sulfur)* azufroso.

sulk (sŭlk) **I.** intr. estar de malhumor **II.** s. mal humor *m.*

sulk·y¹ (sŭl′kē) adj. -**i-** malhumorado.

sulk·y² s. *(vehicle)* tílburi *m*, sulky *m.*

sul·len (sŭl′ən) adj. -**er,** -**est** *(ill-humored)* resentido; *(gloomy)* sombrío.

sul·ly (sŭl′ē) tr. manchar.

sul·phur¹ (sŭl′fər) s. mariposa anaranjada *o* amarilla.

sul·phur² var. de **sulfur.**

sul·tan (sŭl′tən) s. sultán *m.*

sul·try (sŭl′trē) adj. -**i-** bochornoso; *(torrid)* tórrido; *(voluptuous)* voluptuoso.

sum (sŭm) **I.** s. suma; *(total)* total *m;* *(of money)* cantidad *f* ◆ **in s.** en resumen ◆ pl. aritmética **II.** tr. -**mm-** sumar ◆ **to s. up** resumir.

su·mac(h) (sōō′mǎk′) s. zumaque *m.*

sum·ma·rize (sŭm′ə-rīz′) tr. resumir.

sum·ma·ry (:rē) **I.** adj. sumario; *(fast)* rápido **II.** s. resumen *m.*

sum·ma·tion (sə-mā′shən) s. recapitulación *f.*

sum·mer (sŭm′ər) **I.** s. verano ◆ **s. squash** calabaza **II.** intr. veranear *(at, in* en).

sum·mer·house (:hous′) s. cenador *m.*

sum·mer·time (:tīm′) s. verano, estío.

sum·mit (sŭm′ĭt) s. cúspide *f.*

sum·mon (sŭm′ən) tr. convocar; *(to send for)* llamar; DER. citar ◆ **to s. up** armarse de.

sum·mons (sŭm′ənz) **I.** s. [pl. **es**] notificación *f;* DER. *(to defendant)* citación *f* judicial; *(to jury)* requerimiento judicial **II.** tr. citar ante la justicia.

sump·tu·ous (sŭmp′chōō-əs) adj. suntuoso.

sun (sŭn) **I.** s. sol *m* ◆ **in the s.** al sol • **a place in the s.** una buena situación • **s. lamp** lámpara de rayos ultravioletas • **under the s.** en el mundo **II.** tr. & intr. -**nn-** asolear(se).

sun·bathe (′bāth′) intr. tomar el sol.

sun·bon·net (′bŏn′ĭt) s. cofia, papalina.

sun·burn (′bûrn′) **I.** quemadura de sol **II.** tr. & intr. -**ed** *o* -**burnt** quemar(se) al sol.

sun·burst (:bûrst′) s. sol *m* resplandeciente.

sun·dae (sŭn′dē) s. helado con frutas, nueces y almíbar.

Sun·day (sŭn′dē) s. domingo.

sun·der (sŭn′dər) tr. & intr. separar(se).

sun·di·al (sŭn′dī′əl) s. reloj *m* de sol.

sun·down (:doun′) s. ocaso.

sun·dries (sŭn′drēz) s.pl. artículos diversos.

sun·dry (sŭn′drē) adj. diversos.

sun·fish (sŭn′fĭsh′) s. [pl. inv. *o* **es**] pez *m* luna.

sun·flow·er (:flou′ər) s. girasol *m.*

sung (sŭng) cf. **sing.**

sun·glass·es (sŭn'glăs'ĭz) s.pl. gafas de sol.
sunk (sŭngk) cf. **sink.**
sunk·en (sŭng'kən) adj. hundido.
sun·less (sŭn'lĭs) adj. sin sol; *(gloomy)* sombrío.
sun·light (:līt') s. luz *f* del sol.
sun·lit (:lĭt') adj. iluminado por el sol.
sun·ny (:ē) adj. **-i-** soleado; *(cheerful)* risueño.
sun·rise (:rīz') s. amanecer *m.*
sun·roof (:rōōf') s. capota.
sun·set (:sĕt') s. ocaso.
sun·shine (:shīn') s. luz *f* del sol; *(happiness)* alegría.
sun·spot (:spŏt') s. mancha solar.
sun·stroke (:strōk') s. insolación *f.*
sun·tan (:tăn') s. bronceado.
sun·up (:ŭp') s. salida del sol.
sup (sŭp) intr. **-pp-** cenar.
su·per (sōō'pər) FAM. I. s. conserje *m* II. adj. estupendo.
su·per·a·ble (sōō'pər-ə-bəl) adj. superable.
su·per·an·nu·at·ed (sōō'pər-ăn'yōō-ā'tĭd) adj. *(retired)* jubilado; *(obsolete)* anticuado.
su·perb (sōō-pûrb') adj. excelente, soberbio.
su·per·cil·i·ous (sōō'pər-sĭl'ē-əs) adj. desdeñoso.
su·per·fi·cial (sōō'pər-fĭsh'əl) adj. superficial.
su·per·fi·ci·al·i·ty ('-ē-ăl'ĭ-tē) s. superficialidad *f.*
su·per·flu·ous (sōō-pûr'flōō-əs) adj. superfluo.
su·per·high·way (sōō'pər-hī'wā') s. autopista.
su·per·hu·man (:hyōō'mən) adj. sobrehumano.
su·per·im·pose (:ĭm-pōz') tr. sobreponer.
su·per·in·tend (:ĭn-tĕnd') tr. supervisar.
su·per·in·ten·dent (:ĭn-tĕn'dənt) s. superintendente *m; (of building)* conserje *m.*
su·pe·ri·or (sōō-pîr'ē-ər) adj. & s. superior *m.*
su·pe·ri·or·i·ty ('-ôr'ĭ-tē) s. superioridad *f.*
su·per·la·tive (sōō-pûr'lə-tĭv) adj. & s. superlativo.
su·per·man (sōō'pər-măn') s. [pl. **-men**] superhombre *m.*
su·per·mar·ket (:mär'kĭt) s. supermercado.
su·per·nat·u·ral ('-năch'ər-əl) adj. sobrenatural.
su·per·nu·mer·a·ry (:nōō'mə-rĕr'ē) I. adj. supernumerario II. s. supernumerario; TEAT. figurante *m.*
su·per·pow·er ('-pou'ər) s. superpotencia.
su·per·sat·u·rate ('-săch'ə-rāt') tr. supersaturar.
su·per·script ('-skrĭpt') I. adj. sobrescrito II. s. signo o índice sobrescrito.
su·per·sede ('-sēd') tr. suplantar.
su·per·sen·si·tive (:sĕn'sĭ-tĭv) adj. hipersensible.
su·per·son·ic (:sŏn'ĭk) adj. supersónico.
su·per·star ('-stär') s. gran estrella.
su·per·sti·tion (sōō'pər-stĭsh'ən) s. superstición *f.*
su·per·sti·tious (:əs) adj. supersticioso.
su·per·struc·ture (sōō'pər-strŭk'chər) s. superestructura.
su·per·vene ('-vēn') intr. sobrevenir.
su·per·vise ('-vīz') tr. supervisar.
su·per·vi·sion ('-vĭzh'ən) s. supervisión *f.*
su·per·vi·sor ('-vī'zər) s. supervisor *m.*
su·per·vi·so·ry ('-'zə-rē) adj. de supervisión, de supervisor.
su·pine (sōō-pīn') adj. supino; *(passive)* indolente.

sup·per (sŭp'ər) s. cena ♦ **to have s.** cenar.
sup·plant (sə-plănt') tr. suplantar.
sup·ple (sŭp'əl) adj. **-er, -est** flexible.
sup·ple·ment (sŭp'lə-mənt) I. s. suplemento II. tr. suplir; *(to add to)* aumentar.
sup·ple·men·ta·ry/tal ('-mĕn'tə-rē/tl) adj. suplementario.
sup·pli·cant (sŭp'lĭ-kənt) s. & adj. suplicante *m.*
sup·pli·cate (:kāt') tr. & intr. suplicar.
sup·pli·ca·tion ('-kā'shən) s. súplica.
sup·pli·er (sə-plī'ər) s. suministrador *m.*
sup·ply (sə-plī') I. tr. suministrar; *(to satisfy)* satisfacer II. s. suministro; *(stock)* surtido; ECON. oferta ♦ **in short s.** escaso ♦ pl. provisiones; MIL. pertrechos • **office s.** artículos de oficina.
sup·port (sə-pôrt') s. tr. sostener; *(to bear)* soportar; *(doubts)* confirmar; *(a child)* mantener; *(with money)* ayudar ♦ **to s. oneself** ganarse la vida II. s. apoyo; ARQ., TEC. soporte *m; (maintenance)* mantenimiento.
sup·port·er (sə-pôr'tər) s. soporte *m; (advocate)* partidario.
sup·por·tive (:tĭv) adj. sustentador.
sup·pose (sə-pōz') tr. suponer; *(to believe)* creer ♦ **s. we dine together** ¿qué tal si cenamos juntos? —intr. imaginarse.
sup·posed (sə-pōzd', -pō'zĭd) adj. *(presumed)* presunto; *(required)* supuesto.
sup·pos·ing (sə-pō'zing) conj. en el supuesto de que.
sup·po·si·tion (sŭp'ə-zĭsh'ən) s. suposición *f.*
sup·pos·i·to·ry (sə-pŏz'ĭ-tôr'ē) s. supositorio.
sup·press (sə-prĕs') tr. suprimir; *(to prohibit)* prohibir; *(to restrain)* contener.
sup·pres·sion (sə-prĕsh'ən) s. supresión *f; (repression)* represión *f.*
sup·pres·sive (sə-prĕs'ĭv) adj. represivo.
sup·pu·rate (sŭp'yə-rāt') intr. supurar.
sup·pu·ra·tion ('-rā'shən) s. supuración *f.*
su·prem·a·cy (sōō-prĕm'ə-sē) s. supremacía.
su·preme (sōō-prēm') adj. supremo ♦ **s. court** corte supremo.
sur·charge (sûr'chärj') I. s. sobrecarga; *(overcharge)* recargo II. s. sobrecargar, recargar.
sure (shōōr) I. adj. seguro; *(infallible)* certero; *(hand)* firme ♦ **for s.!** ¡claro! • **to be s.** sin duda • **to make s.** asegurarse II. adv. seguramente; *(of course)* claro ♦ **for s.** con toda seguridad • **s. enough** efectivamente.
sure-fire (fīr') adj. FAM. de éxito seguro.
sure-foot·ed (:fŏŏt'ĭd) adj. de pie firme.
sure·ty (:ĭ-tē) s. seguridad *f; (pledge)* garantía; *(person)* garante *mf.*
surf (sûrf) I. s. oleaje *m* II. intr. hacer surfing.
sur·face (sûr'fəs) I. s. superficie *f* ♦ **on the s.** en apariencia II. adj. superficial III. intr. salir a la superficie.
surf·board (sûrf'bôrd') s. tabla hawaiana.
sur·feit (sûr'fĭt) I. tr. hartar II. s. hartura; *(indigestion)* empacho; *(excess)* exceso.
surf·ing (sûr'fĭng) s. surfing *m,* deporte *m* de la tabla hawaiana.
surge (sûrj) I. intr. *(the sea)* encresparse; *(energy, enthusiasm)* subir súbitamente II. s. *(of waves)* oleada; *(billow)* mar *mf* de fondo; *(onrush)* arranque *m;* ELEC. sobretensión *f.*
sur·geon (sûr'jən) s. cirujano.
sur·ger·y (:jə-rē) s. intervención quirúrgica; *(room)* quirófano; *(work)* cirugía.
sur·gi·cal (:jĭ-kəl) adj. quirúrgico.

sur·ly (sûr′lē) adj. **-i-** malhumorado.

sur·mise (sər-mīz′) I. tr. conjeturar II. s. conjetura.

sur·mount (sar-mount′) tr. superar; (to climb) escalar.

sur·name (sûr′nām′) s. apellido.

sur·pass (sər-pās′) tr. sobrepasar; (to exceed) superar.

sur·pass·ing (:ing) adj. incomparable.

sur·plice (sûr′plĭs) s. sobrepelliz f.

sur·plus (sûr′pləs) I. adj. excedente II. s. excedente m; COM. superávit m.

sur·prise (sər-prīz′) I. tr. sorprender ♦ to be surprised at sorprenderse de o con II. s. sorpresa ♦ s. attack ataque por sorpresa • s. visit visita inesperada • to take by s. coger desprevenido.

sur·pris·ing (:prī′zĭng) adj. sorprendente.

sur·re·al (sə-rē′əl) adj. surrealista.

sur·re·al·is·tic (-′ə-lĭs′tĭk) adj. surrealista.

sur·ren·der (sə-rĕn′dər) I. tr. entregar; (to give up) ceder; (to abandon) abandonar ♦ to s. oneself entregarse —intr. rendirse II. s. rendición f; (abandonment) abandono.

sur·rep·ti·tious (sûr′əp-tĭsh′əs) adj. subrepticio.

sur·ro·gate (sûr′ə-gĭt, :gāt′) I. s. substituto; DER. juez m de instrumentación II. adj. substituto.

sur·round (sə-round′) tr. rodear.

sur·round·ings (sə-roun′dĭngz) s.pl. alrededores m.

sur·tax (sûr′tăks′) s. recargo.

sur·veil·lance (sər-vā′ləns) s. vigilancia.

sur·vey (sər-vā′) I. tr. examinar; (to inspect) inspeccionar; (to measure) medir —intr. hacer una encuesta II. s. (sûr′vā′) inspección f; (review) repaso; (measurement) medición f; (map) mapa topográfico.

sur·vey·ing (sər-vā′-ĭng) s. agrimensura.

sur·vey·or (:ər) s. agrimensor m; (inspector) inspector m.

sur·viv·al (sər-vī′vəl) s. supervivencia.

sur·vive (sər-vīv′) tr. & intr. sobrevivir ♦ to s. on subsistir con.

sur·vi·vor (sər-vī′vər) s. sobreviviente mf.

sus·cep·ti·bil·i·ty (sə-sĕp′tə-bĭl′ĭ-tē) s. susceptibilidad f; (sensitivity) sensibilidad f.

sus·cep·ti·ble (-′-bəl) adj. susceptible; (sensitive) sensible ♦ to be s. of permitir • to be s. to ser propenso a.

sus·pect (sə-spĕkt′) I. tr. sospechar II. s. & adj. (sŭs′pĕkt′) sospechoso.

sus·pend (sə-spĕnd′) tr. & intr. suspender.

sus·pend·ers (sə-spĕn′dərz) s.pl. tirantes m.

sus·pense (sə-spĕns′) s. suspensión f; (doubt) incertidumbre f; CINEM. suspenso.

sus·pen·sion (sə-spĕn′shən) s. suspensión f ♦ s. bridge puente colgante.

sus·pi·cion (sə-spĭsh′ən) s. sospecha; (pinch) pizca ♦ above s. fuera de toda sospecha • on s. como sospechoso • to come under s. of ser sospechado de.

sus·pi·cious (:əs) adj. sospechoso.

sus·pi·cious·ness (:nĭs) s. suspicacia.

sus·tain (sə-stān′) tr. sostener; (to encourage) animar; (to maintain) mantener; (an idea) apoyar; (to suffer) sufrir.

sus·tain·a·ble (sə-stā′nə-bəl) adj. sostenible.

sus·tain·ment (sə-stān′mənt) s. sostenimiento.

sus·te·nance (sŭs′tə-nəns) s. sustento; (nourishment) alimento; (livelihood) medios de subsistencia.

su·ture (sōō′chər) I. s. sutura II. tr. suturar.

svelte (svĕlt) adj. esbelto.

swab (swŏb) I. s. tapón m; (mop) estropajo; JER. (sailor) marinero II. tr. **-bb-** limpiar con tapón; (to mop) fregar con estropajo.

swad·dle (swŏd′l) tr. envolver; (to diaper) poner los pañales a.

swag (swăg) s. JER. (loot) botín m.

swag·ger (swăg′ər) I. intr. pavonearse; (to boast) vanagloriarse II. s. (strut) pavoneo; (manner) jactancia.

swain (swān) s. (country youth) zagal m; (suitor) pretendiente m.

swal·low¹ (swŏl′ō) I. tr. tragar, FIG. (insults, pride) tragarse; (feelings) reprimir ♦ to s. one's words comerse sus palabras • to s. up destruir —intr. tragar II. s. deglución f; (of drink) trago; (of food) bocado ♦ at o with one s. de un trago.

swal·low² s. ORNIT. golondrina.

swam (swăm) cf. **swim**.

swamp (swŏmp, swômp) I. s. pantano II. tr. (to inundate) inundar, anegar; (to sink) hundir; FIG. (to overwhelm) sumergir.

swamp·land (′lănd′) s. ciénaga.

swamp·y (swŏm′pē, swôm′-) adj. **-i-** pantanoso.

swan (swŏn) s. cisne m ♦ s. dive salto del ángel • s. song canto del cisne.

swank (swăngk) I. adj. lujoso; (ostentatious) ostentoso II. s. elegancia.

swap (swŏp) FAM. I. tr. & intr. **-pp-** canjear II. s. canje m.

swarm (swôrm) I. s. enjambre m; (of people) muchedumbre f II. intr. pulular, hormiguear; (bees) salir en enjambre —tr. inundar ♦ to s. with bullir de.

swar·thy (swôr′thē) adj. **-i-** prieto.

swash (swŏsh, swôsh) I. s. chapoteo II. intr. chapotear.

swas·ti·ka (swŏs′tĭ-kə) s. esvástica.

swat (swŏt) I. tr. **-tt-** aplastar II. s. golpe repentino.

swatch (swŏch) s. muestra (de un tejido).

swath (swŏth, swôth) s. golpe m de guadaña; (path) ringlera ♦ to cut a wide s. hacer un gran papel.

swathe (swŏth, swôth) tr. vendar.

swat·ter (swŏt′ər) s. matamoscas m.

sway (swā) I. tr. hacer oscilar; (to influence) ejercer influencia en ♦ to s. somebody from apartar a alguien de —intr. balancearse; (to move unsteadily) tambalearse II. s. oscilación f; (power) dominio ♦ to be under the s. of estar dominado por • to hold s. over dominar.

sway·back (′băk′) s. lomo hundido.

swear (swâr) tr. & intr. **swore, sworn** jurar ♦ to s. at maldecir • to s. in investir de un cargo bajo juramento • to s. off FAM. prometer renunciar a • to s. someone to secrecy hacer que alguien jure guardar un secreto • to s. to afirmar bajo juramento • to s. up and down FAM. jurar y perjurar.

swear·word (′wûrd′) s. palabrota.

sweat (swĕt) I. intr. **sweat(ed)** sudar; (to exude) rezumar —tr. sudar; (to cause to perspire) hacer sudar; (to overwork) explotar (obreros) ♦ to s. it out JER. pasar un mal rato II. s. sudor m; (moisture) humedad f ♦ no s. no es ningún problema • s. shirt jersey • s. suit chandel • to be in a s. estar angustiado.

sweat·er (swĕt′ər) s. suéter m.

sweat·shop (:shŏp′) s. fábrica en la que se explota al obrero.

sweat·y (swĕt′ē) adj. -i- sudoroso; *(laborious)* agotador.

sweep (swēp) I. tr. **swept** barrer; *(to remove)* llevarse; *(to traverse)* recorrer ♦ **to s. a constituency** llevarse la mayoría de los votos • **to s. off one's feet** hacerle perder la cabeza a uno • **to s. the board** FAM. llevarse todo • **to s. up** recoger —intr. barrer; *(to flow)* pasar rápidamente; *(to trail)* arrastrarse; *(to extend)* extenderse ♦ **to s. along** andar rápidamente II. s. *(sweeping)* barrido; *(motion)* movimiento amplio; *(reach)* alcance *m*; *(curve)* curva; *(chimney sweep)* deshollinador *m*; *(victory)* victoria aplastante ♦ **at one s.** de una vez • **to make a clean s.** hacer tabla rasa.

sweep·er (swē′pər) s. barrendero; *(machine)* barredora; *(for streets)* barredera.

sweep·ing (:pĭng) I. adj. extenso; *(dramatic)* dramático; *(gesture)* amplio II. s. ♦ pl. basura.

sweep·stake(s) (swēp′stāk[s]) s. lotería.

sweet (swēt) I. adj. dulce; *(gratifying)* agradable; *(lovable)* encantador; *(fresh)* fresco; *(potable)* potable ♦ **s. oil** aceite de oliva • **s. one** querido • **s. pepper** pimiento morrón • **s. potato** batata, boniato • **s. sixteen** quince abriles • **s. talk** lisonjas • **s. tooth** gusto por la confitura • **to be s. on** estar enamorado de • **to take one's own s. time** no darse prisa • **to taste s.** estar dulce II. s. dulce *m*; *(person)* cariño.

sweet·bread (′brĕd′) s. mollejas.

sweet·en (:n) tr. & intr. endulzar(se).

sweet·en·er (:ər) s. dulcificante *m*.

sweet·en·ing (:ĭng) s. endulzamiento; *(sweetener)* dulcificante *m*.

sweet·heart (swēt′härt′) s. enamorado; *(lovable person)* persona adorable.

sweet·meat (:mēt′) s. dulce *m*, confitura.

sweet·ness (:nĭs) s. dulzura.

swell (swĕl) I. intr. -ed, -ed *o* **swollen** hincharse; *(to increase)* aumentar; *(with emotion)* hincharse ♦ **to s. out** *o* **up** hincharse —tr. hinchar; *(increase)* hacer aumentar ♦ **to get a swollen head** FAM. engreírse II. s. *(act)* inflamiento; *(wave)* oleada; FAM. *(handsome person)* guapo III. adj. FAM. *(stylish)* elegante; *(fine)* fenomenal.

swell·ing (′ĭng) s. inflamiento; *(swollen part)* hinchazón *f*.

swel·ter (swĕl′tər) intr. sofocarse de calor.

swel·ter·ing (:ĭng) adj. *(day)* abrasador; *(person)* sudando a mares.

swept (swĕpt) cf. **sweep.**

swerve (swûrv) I. tr. & intr. desviar(se) II. s. desviación *f*.

swift (swĭft) I. adj. veloz; *(quick)* rápido II. s. ORNIT. vencejo.

swift·ness (′nĭs) s. rapidez *f*, velocidad *f*.

swig (swĭg) FAM. I. s. trago II. tr. & intr. -gg- beber a tragos.

swill (swĭl) I. tr. *(to drink)* beber a tragos; *(to flood)* empapar II. s. bazofia; *(refuse)* basura.

swim (swĭm) I. intr. **swam, swum** nadar; *(to glide)* deslizarse; *(to float)* flotar; *(to be immersed)* estar cubierto; *(to whirl)* dar vueltas ♦ **swimming pool** piscina • **to s. with the tide** seguir la corriente —tr. nadar; *(to swim across)* atravesar a nado ♦ **swimming in** lleno de II. s. natación *f*; *(period of swimming)* baño ♦ **to go for** *o* **to take a s.** ir a nadar.

swim·ming·ly (′ĭng-lē) adv. espléndidamente.

swim·suit (:sōōt′) s. traje *m* de baño.

swin·dle (swĭn′dl) I. tr. & intr. timar II. s. timo.

swin·dler (swĭnd′lər) s. timador *m*.

swine (swīn) s.inv. cerdo.

swine·herd (′hûrd′) s. porquerizo.

swing (swĭng) I. intr. **swung** oscilar; *(on a swing)* columpiarse; *(on hinges)* girar; JER. *(to be up to date)* estar al día; MÚS. tocar con ritmo ♦ **to s. clear** dar un viraje para evitar un choque • **to s. to** cerrarse • **to s. to and fro** balancearse —tr. hacer girar; *(on swing)* hacer balancear; JER. *(to manage)* lograr ♦ **to s. an election** ganar una elección • **to s. around a corner** AUTO. doblar una esquina • **to s. at** dirigir un golpe a II. s. oscilación *f*; *(swoop)* descenso rápido; *(for children)* columpio; MÚS. ritmo.

swing·er (′ər) s. oscilador *m*; JER. *(person)* persona a la última moda y sin inhibiciones.

swing·ing (:ĭng) JER. I. s. libertinaje *m* II. adj. muy moderno; *(spirited)* alegre; MÚS. rítmico.

swin·ish (swī′nĭsh) adj. cochino.

swipe (swīp) I. s. golpetazo II. tr. *(to hit)* dar un tortazo; JER. *(to steal)* robar, birlar.

swirl (swûrl) I. intr. dar vueltas —tr. girar II. s. giro; *(whorl)* espiral *m*.

swish (swĭsh) I. intr. *(cane, whip)* silbar; *(fabric)* crujir —tr. *(tail)* menear II. s. silbido; *(rustle)* crujido.

switch (swĭch) I. s. ELEC. interruptor *m*; *(rod)* látigo; *(lashing)* latigazo; *(shift)* cambio; *(fake hair)* trenza postiza; F.C. cambio (de vías) II. tr. *(to whip)* azotar; *(to shift)* cambiar de; *(to exchange)* intercambiar; F.C. desviar ♦ **to s. off** desconectar; *(lights)* apagar • **to s. on** conectar; *(lights)* encender —intr. cambiar.

switch·blade (′blād′) s. navaja de muelle.

switch·board (:bôrd′) s. ELEC. tablero de distribución; TEL. centralita de teléfonos ♦ **s. operator** telefonista *mf*.

switch·man (:mən) s. [pl. -men] guardagujas *m*.

swiv·el (swĭv′əl) I. s. *(link)* eslabón giratorio; *(pivot)* pivote *m* II. intr. & tr. (hacer) girar.

swiz·zle stick (swĭz′əl) s. varilla de cóctel.

swol·len (swō′lən) cf. **swell.**

swoon (swōōn) I. intr. desmayarse II. s. desmayo.

swoop (swōōp) I. intr. abalanzarse II. s. calada ♦ **in one fell s.** de un solo golpe.

sword (sôrd) s. espada; *(instrument)* arma; *(power)* poder *m* militar ♦ **to be at s.'s points** estar a punto de matarse • **to cross swords with** habérselas con alguien • **to put to the s.** pasar a cuchillo.

sword·fish (′fĭsh′) s. [pl. inv. *o* **s**] pez *m* espada.

sword·play (:plā′) s. esgrima.

swords·man (sôrdz′mən) s. [pl. -men] *(fencer)* esgrimista *mf*; *(fighter)* espadachín *m*.

swore (swôr), **sworn** (swôrn) cf. **swear.**

swum (swŭm) cf. **swim.**

swung (swŭng) cf. **swing.**

syb·a·rite (sĭb′ə-rīt′) s. sibarita *mf*.

syc·a·more (sĭk′ə-môr′) s. sicómoro.

syc·o·phant (sĭk′ə-fənt) s. adulón *m*.

syl·lab·ic (sĭ-lăb′ĭk) adj. silábico.

syl·lab·i·cate (:ĭ-kāt′) tr. silabear.

syl·lab·i·ca·tion (′-kā′shən) s. silabeo.

syl·lab·i·fy (-′-fī′) tr. silabear.

syl·la·ble (sĭl′ə-bəl) s. sílaba.

syl·la·bus (sĭl′ə-bəs) s. [pl. **es** *o* **-bi**] programa

m de estudios; *(summary)* resumen *m.*
syl·lo·gism (sĭl′ə-jĭz′əm) s. silogismo.
syl·lo·gis·tic (′-jĭs′tĭk) adj. silogístico.
syl·van (sĭl′vən) adj. silvestre.
sym·bi·o·sis (sĭm′bē-ō′sĭs) s. simbiosis *f.*
sym·bi·ot·ic (:ŏt′ĭk) adj. simbiótico.
sym·bol (sĭm′bəl) s. símbolo.
sym·bol·ic/i·cal (-bŏl′ĭk) adj. simbólico.
sym·bol·ism (′bə-lĭz′əm) s. simbolismo.
sym·bol·ize (:līz′) tr. simbolizar.
sym·met·ric/ri·cal (sĭ mĕt′rĭk) simétrico.
sym·me·try (sĭm′ĭ-trē) s. simetría.
sym·pa·thet·ic (sĭm′pə-thĕt′ĭk) adj. *(compassionate)* compasivo; *(favorable)* favorable; *(supporting)* simpatizante; ANAT. simpático.
sym·pa·thize (′-thīz′) intr. compadecerse; *(to understand)* comprender.
sym·pa·thiz·er (:thī′zər) s. simpatizante *mf.*
sym·pa·thy (sĭm′pə-thē) s. simpatía; *(compatibility)* compatibilidad *f.; (understanding)* comprensión *f.; (expression of sorrow)* pésame *m.; (compassion)* compasión *f* ♦ **her sympathies lie with** simpatiza con • **message of s.** pésame • **to be in s. with** estar de acuerdo con.
sym·phon·ic (sĭm-fŏn′ĭk) adj. sinfónico.
sym·pho·ny (sĭm′fə-nē) s. MÚS. sinfonía; *(orchestra)* orquesta sinfónica; *(harmony)* armonía.
sym·po·si·um (sĭm-pō′zē-əm) s. [pl. **s** o **-la**] simposio; *(collection)* colección *f.*
symp·tom (sĭmp′təm) s. *(indication)* indicio; MED. síntoma *m.*
symp·to·mat·ic (′ tə-măt′ĭk) adj. sintomático.
syn·a·gog(ue) (sĭn′ə-gŏg′) s. sinagoga.
syn·apse (sĭn′ăps′) s. sinapsis *f.*
sync(h) (sĭngk) FAM. **I.** s. sincronización *f* ♦ **to be out of s.** no estar sincronizado **II.** tr. sincronizar.
syn·chro·ni·za·tion (sĭng′krə-nĭ-zā′shən) s. sincronización *f.*
syn·chro·nize (′-nīz′) intr. coincidir; *(to operate in unison)* ser sincrónico —tr. sincronizar.
syn·chro·niz·er (:nī′zər) s. sincronizador *m.*
syn·chro·nous (:nəs) adj. sincrónico; MEC. síncrono.
syn·co·pa·tion (sĭng′kə-pā′shən) s. síncopa.
syn·di·cate (sĭn′dĭ-kĭt) **I.** s. sindicato; *(of newspapers)* cadena de periódicos **II.** tr. (:kāt′) sindicar; PERIOD. vender a través de una agencia —intr. sindicarse.
syn·di·ca·tion (′-kā′shən) s. sindicalización *f.*
syn·drome (sĭn′drōm′) s. síndrome *m.*
syn·er·gism/gy (sĭn′ər-jĭz′əm/jē) sinergia.
syn·od (sĭn′əd) s. sínodo.
syn·o·nym (sĭn′ə-nĭm′) s. sinónimo.
syn·on·y·mous (sĭ-nŏn′ə-məs) adj. sinónimo.
syn·on·y·my (:mē) s. sinonimia.
syn·op·sis (sĭ-nŏp′sĭs) s. [pl. **-ses**] sinopsis *f.*
syn·tac·tic/ti·cal (sĭn-tăk′tĭk) adj. sintáctico.
syn·tax (sĭn′tăks′) s. sintaxis *f.*
syn·the·sis (sĭn′thĭ-sĭs) s. [pl. **-ses**] síntesis *f.*
syn·the·size (:sīz′) tr. sintetizar.
syn·the·siz·er (:sī′zər) s. sintetizador *m.*
syn·thet·ic (sĭn-thĕt′ĭk) adj. & s. *(material)* sintético.
syph·i·lis (sĭf′ə-lĭs) s. sífilis *f.*
syph·i·lit·ic (′-lĭt′ĭk) adj. & s. sifilítico.
sy·ringe (sə-rĭnj′, sĭr′ĭnj) s. jeringa.
syr·up (sĭr′əp) s. CUL. almíbar *m.*
sys·tem (sĭs′təm) s. sistema *m; (human body)* organismo; ANAT. aparato.
sys·tem·at·ic (′tə-măt′ĭk) adj. sistemático.

sys·tem·a·tize (′-mə-tīz′) tr. sistematizar.
sys·tem·ic (sĭ-stĕm′ĭk) adj. sistemático; *(of the body)* que afecta al organismo.
sys·tem·ize (sĭs′tə-mīz′) tr. sistematizar.
sys·to·le (sĭs′tə-lē) s. sístole *f.*

T

t, T (tē) s. vigésima letra del alfabeto inglés ♦ **to a T** a la perfección.
tab (tăb) s. lengüeta; *(at a restaurant)* cuenta; *(of a typewriter)* tabulador *m* ♦ **to keep tabs on** observar detalladamente.
tab·by (tăb′ē). *(striped)* gato atigrado; *(female cat)* gata.
tab·er·na·cle (tăb′ər-năk′əl) s. tabernáculo.
ta·ble (tā′bəl) **I.** s. mesa; *(data)* tabla, cuadro ♦ **t. of contents** índice • **to turn the tables on someone** volver las tornas a alguien • **under the t.** *(covertly)* bajo la mesa; *(drunk)* completamente borracho **II.** tr. *(to place)* poner sobre una mesa; *(to shelve)* dar carpetazo a; *(to tabulate)* tabular; FIG. *(to present)* presentar.
tab·leau (tăb′lō′, tă-blō′) s. [pl. **s** o **-x**] cuadro ♦ **t. vivant** TEAT. cuadro vivo.
ta·ble·cloth (tā′bəl-klŏth′) s. mantel *m.*
ta·ble·land (′-lănd′) s. meseta.
ta·ble·spoon (:spōn′) s. cuchara de sopa; *(quantity)* cucharada.
tab·let (tăb′lĭt) s. tableta, tablilla; *(writing pad)* taco, bloc *m; (pill)* pastilla.
ta·ble·ware (tā′bəl-wâr′) s. servicio de mesa.
tab·loid (tăb′loid′) s. periódico de formato reducido.
ta·boo (tă-bōō′) s. & adj. tabú *m.*
tab·u·lar (tăb′yə-lər) adj. tabular.
tab·u·late (:lāt′) tr. tabular.
tab·u·la·tion (′-lā′shən) s. tabulación *f.*
tab·u·la·tor (′-lā′tər) s. *(person, key)* tabulador *m; (machine)* tabulador *m.*
tac·it (tăs′ĭt) adj. tácito; *(implicit)* implícito.
tac·i·turn (′-tûrn′) adj. taciturno.
tack (tăk) **I.** s. tachuela; *(direction)* dirección *f,* línea; COST. hilván *m;* MARIT. puño de la amura ♦ **to get down to brass tacks** ir al grano **II.** tr. clavar con tachuelas; *(to stitch)* hilvanar; MARIT. virar por avante ♦ **to t. on** añadir, agregar —intr. MARIT. cambiar de bordada.
tack·le (tăk′əl) **I.** s. *(gear)* equipo, avíos *m; (harness)* arreos; MARIT. aparejo, jarcias **II.** tr. atacar, abordar; DEP. agarrar.
tack·y¹ (tăk′ē) adj. -i- *(sticky)* pegajoso.
tack·y² adj. -i- FAM. *(shabby)* descuidado; *(lacking style)* cursi; *(vulgar)* vulgar.
tact (tăkt) s. tacto.
tact·ful (′fəl) adj. discreto.
tac·tic (tăk′tĭk) s. táctica ♦ **tactics** s.sg. táctica.
tac·ti·cal (:tĭ-kəl) adj. táctico.
tac·ti·cian (-tĭsh′ən) s. táctico.
tac·tile (tăk′təl, :tīl′) adj. táctil.
tact·less (tăkt′lĭs) adj. falto de tacto.
tad·pole (tăd′pōl′) s. renacuajo.
taf·fy (tăf′ē) s. melcocha.
tag¹ (tăg) **I.** s. *(label)* etiqueta; *(aglet)* herrete *m; (cliché)* cliché *m; (characterization)* etiqueta, epíteto ♦ **t. line** TEAT. gracia, tono; *(slogan)* slogan **II.** tr. **-gg-** etiquetar; *(to identify)* identificar; *(to characterize)* denominar; *(to follow)* seguir de cerca —intr. ♦ **to t. along** seguir, acompañar

tag² s. *(game)* mancha, pillarse *m*.
tag·a·long ('ə-lông') s. persona que sigue a otra persistentemente.
tail (tāl) I. s. cola; *(backside)* trasero; *(of a shirt)* faldón *m*; FAM. *(spy)* espía *mf* ♦ **from head to t.** de pies a cabeza ♦ **t. end** *(rear)* parte trasera; *(end)* fin, final ♦ **t. pipe** MEC. tubo de escape ♦ **t. wind** viento de cola ♦ **to be on someone's t.** *(to trail)* seguirle el rastro a alguien ♦ pl. *(of a coin)* cruz, reverso; *(tailcoat)* frac II. tr. FAM. *(to follow)* seguir de cerca, espiar —intr. ♦ **to t. away** *o* **off** ir disminuyendo.
tail·gate ('gāt') I. s. compuerta de cola II. tr. & intr. seguir demasiado cerca a (otro vehículo).
tail·light (:līt') s. luz trasera *o* de cola.
tai·lor (tā'lər) I. s. sastre *m* II. tr. hacer a la medida; *(to adapt)* adaptar.
tai·lored (tā'lərd) adj. *(trim)* de corte prolijo; *(custom-made)* hecho a medida.
tai·lor-made (tā'lər-mād') adj. hecho a medida; *(perfect)* perfecto.
tail·piece (tāl'pēs') s. pieza de cola.
tail·spin (:spĭn') s. *(collapse)* colapso emocional; AER. barrena.
taint (tānt) I. tr. manchar; *(to spoil)* contaminar; *(to corrupt)* corromper —intr. mancharse; *(to rot)* corromperse II. s. *(moral defect)* mácula, defecto; *(influence)* mala influencia.
take (tāk) I. tr. **took, taken** tomar; *(to confiscate, steal)* apoderarse de; *(to capture)* capturar; *(to win)* ganar; *(to buy)* comprar; *(to cost)* costar; *(to swindle)* engañar; *(to carry along)* llevarse; *(to captivate)* cautivar, encantar; *(to admit)* recibir; *(to accept)* aceptar; *(to withstand)* aguantar, soportar; *(film, clothing)* usar; *(in shoes)* calzar; *(to study)* estudiar; *(in chess, checkers)* comerse, capturar; *(to remove)* sacar; *(to subtract)* sustraer ♦ **as I t. it** a mi entender ♦ **t. it from me!** ¡créame! ♦ **to t. a bow** agradecer el aplauso ♦ **to t. along** llevar consigo, llevarse ♦ **to t. amiss** tomar mal ♦ **to t. an oath** prestar juramento ♦ **to t. apart** *(to disassemble)* desarmar, desmontar; *(to analyze)* analizar; *(to wreck)* hacer pedazos ♦ **to t. a trip** hacer un viaje ♦ **to t. away** *(to remove)* quitar, sacar; *(to subtract)* restar; *(to carry away)* llevarse ♦ **to t. back** *(to return)* devolver; *(to receive back)* recoger de vuelta; *(person)* volver a recibir; *(former employee)* volver a emplear; *(to retract)* retractar; *(to bring to mind)* hacer recordar, hacer pensar en ♦ **to t. chances** arriesgarse ♦ **to t. down** *(to write down)* anotar; *(to bring down)* bajar; *(to disassemble)* desarmar; *(to knock down)* derribar ♦ **to t. hold of** agarrar ♦ **to t. in** *(to accept)* aceptar; *(to lodge)* alojar; *(to understand)* comprender; *(to include)* incluir; *(to realize)* percatarse de; *(to deceive)* engañar; *(to earn)* ganar; *(a seam)* embeber, meter; *(a dress)* achicar ♦ **to t. it out on** desahogarse con ♦ **to t. it that** suponer que, inferir que ♦ **to t. notes** hacer apuntes ♦ **to t. off** quitar; *(clothes, hat)* quitarse; *(time)* tomarse; *(to deduct)* rebajar ♦ **to t. on** *(characteristic, attitude)* asumir, tomar; *(responsibility)* encargarse de; *(employee)* contratar; *(passengers)* recibir a bordo; *(bet, challenge)* aceptar; *(adversary)* enfrentarse a; *(client, patient)* aceptar ♦ **to t. out** llevar afuera, poner afuera; *(to remove)* sacar; *(license, policy)* sacar; *(stain, spot)* quitar, extraer; *(tooth)* extraer ♦ **to t. over** hacerse cargo

de ♦ **to t. pity on** tener lástima de ♦ **to t. up** *(to raise)* llevar arriba; *(to pick up)* levantar, alzar; *(time, space)* ocupar, llenar; *(challenge, bet)* aceptar; *(career, profession)* dedicarse a; *(study)* empezar; *(residence)* establecer; COST. acortar ♦ **to t. upon oneself** encargarse de ♦ **to t. up with** asociarse con —intr. *(to stick)* adherirse; *(to succeed)* tener éxito; *(to set)* cuajar; *(plants)* arraigar; *(vaccination)* prender ♦ **to t. after** parecerse a ♦ **to t. off** *(to leave)* irse, partir; *(aircraft)* despegar ♦ **to t. over** asumir la autoridad ♦ **to t. to** empezar a ♦ **to t. to someone** tomarle simpatía a alguien ♦ **to t. to something** aficionarse a algo II. s. *(receipts)* entrada, ingresos; *(in hunting)* presa; *(in fishing)* pesca; *(in chess, checkers)* captura, toma; CINEM. toma.
take-home pay ('hōm') s. sueldo neto.
take-off (:ôf') s. AVIA. despegue *m*; FAM. *(imitation)* caricatura.
take-o·ver (:ō'vər) s. toma de poder.
tak·ing (tā'kĭng) I. adj. atractivo II. s. toma; *(catch)* presa, pesca ♦ pl. ingresos.
talc (tălk) I. s. talco II. tr. **-ck(k)-** poner talco a.
tal·cum (tăl'kəm) s. talco; *(powder)* polvos de talco.
tale (tāl) s. cuento; *(lie)* mentira; *(gossip)* chisme *m* ♦ **old wives' t.** cuento de viejas.
tal·ent (tăl'ənt) s. talento; *(aptitude)* aptitud *f*, don *m*; *(persons)* talento.
tal·ent·ed (:ən-tĭd) adj. talentoso.
tal·is·man (tăl'ĭs-mən) s. talismán *m*.
talk (tôk) I. tr. hablar; *(to speak)* decir ♦ **to t. a blue streak** FAM. hablar por los codos ♦ **to t. sense** hablar sensatamente ♦ **to t. into** persuadir a ♦ **to t. out of** disuadir a ♦ **to t. turkey** no andarse con rodeos —intr. hablar; *(to chatter)* charlar ♦ **look who's talking!** ¡mira quién habla! ♦ **now you're talking!** ¡así se habla! ♦ **to t. away** hablar sin parar ♦ **to t. back** replicar ♦ **to t. behind someone's back** hablar (mal) de alguien a sus espaldas ♦ **to t. down to** hablar con altivez a II. s. conversación *f*; *(speech)* discurso; *(jargon)* habla; *(rumor)* rumor *m*; *(subject of conversation)* chisme *m*, comidilla; *(empty speech)* palabrería ♦ pl. negociaciones.
talk·a·tive (tô'kə-tĭv) adj. hablador, locuaz.
talk·er (tô'kər) s. hablador *m*.
talk·ing (tô'kĭng) adj. parlante, que habla; *(movie)* sonora.
talk·ing-to (:-tōō') s. FAM. bronca.
tall (tôl) I. adj. alto; *(of certain height)* de alto, de altura; FAM. *(tale)* exagerado; *(difficult)* difícil ♦ **how t. are you?** ¿cuánto mide usted? II. adv. ♦ **to walk t.** caminar con porte altivo.
tal·low (tăl'ō) s. sebo.
tal·ly (tăl'ē) I. s. *(stick)* tarja, tara; *(score)* cuenta; *(receipt)* talón *m*; COM. lista II. tr. *(to record)* tarjar; *(to score)* llevar la cuenta; *(to cause to agree)* hacer cuadrar —intr. cuadrar.
tal·on (tăl'ən) s. garra.
ta·lus (tā'ləs) s. [pl. **-li**] astrágalo.
tam·bour (tăm'bŏŏr') s. tambor *m*.
tam·bou·rine (tăm'bə-rēn') s. pandereta.
tame (tām) I. adj. domesticado; *(gentle)* manso; *(docile)* dócil; FAM. insípido II. tr. domesticar; *(to break)* domar; *(to subdue)* dominar; *(to soften)* suavizar.
tam-o'-shan·ter (tăm'ə-shăn'tər) s. boina escocesa.
tamp (tămp) tr. apisonar, pisonear.
tam·per (tăm'pər) intr. ♦ **to t. with** interferir en; *(to meddle)* entrometerse en.

tam·pon (tăm'pŏn') s. tapón m, tampón m.

tan (tăn) I. tr. -nn- (leather) curtir; (skin) broncear; FAM. (to beat) zurrar —intr. broncearse, tostarse II. s. & adj. (color) tostado o bronceado.

tan·dem (tăn'dəm) s. & adv. (en) tándem m.

tang (tăng) s. (flavor) gusto fuerte, (odor) olor m penetrante; (of a tool) cola.

tan·gent (tăn'jənt). adj. & s. tangente f.

tan·gen·tial (-jĕn'shəl) adj. tangencial.

tan·ger·ine (tăn'jə-rēn') s. (color) anaranjado rojizo; (tree) mandarino; (fruit) mandarina.

tan·gi·ble (tăn'jə-bəl) adj. tangible; (real) real.

tan·gle (tăng'gəl) I. tr. & intr. (to snarl) enredar(se), enmarañar(se), (to entangle) embrollar(se) ♦ to t. with meterse con II. s. enredo, embrollo; (confusion) confusión f.

tan·gled (-gəld) adj. enredado, embrollado.

tan·go (tăng'gō) I. s. tango II. intr. bailar el tango.

tang·y (tăng'ē) adj. -i- fuerte, penetrante.

tank (tăngk) s. tanque m; JER. (jail) cárcel f.

tank·ard (tăng'kərd) s. jarra de cerveza.

tank·er (tăng'kər) s. buque m tanque; (truck) camión m tanque; (plane) avión m tanque.

tan·ner (tăn'ər) s. curtidor m.

tan·ner·y (:ə-rē) s. curtiduría, curtiembre f.

tan·nic (tăn'ĭk) adj. tánico.

tan·nin (tăn'ĭn) s. tanino.

tan·ning (tăn'ĭng) s. (leather) curtimiento; (skin bronzing) bronceado; FAM. (beating) zurra.

tan·ta·lize (tăn'tə-līz') tr. tentar.

tan·ta·liz·ing (:ĭng) adj. tentador.

tan·ta·mount (tăn'tə-mount') adj. ♦ t. to equivalente a.

tan·trum (tăn'trəm) s. rabieta, pataleta.

tap¹ (tăp) I. tr. -pp- golpear ligeramente; (to rap) dar golpecitos con; (shoes) poner tapas a —intr. dar golpes ligeros; (with the fingers) tamborilear; (with the feet) zapatear II. s. golpe ligero; (sole) media suela; (metal tip) chapa ♦ t. dance zapateado americano.

tap² I. s. (faucet) grifo; (spigot) canilla, espita; (beer) cerveza de barril; MED. drenaje m, MEC. macho de roscar; ELEC. toma de corriente II. tr. -pp- (to put a tap on) espitar; (to pierce) horadar; (tree) sangrar; (to draw) sacar de un barril; (to make use of) utilizar; (to connect) hacer una conexión en; (to wiretap) interceptar; ELEC. desviar; MEC. roscar; MED. drenar.

tap-dance ('dăns') intr. zapatear.

tape (tāp) I. s. (strip) cinta; (adhesive) cinta adhesiva; (magnetic) cinta magnética; (measure) cinta métrica; (recording) grabación f en cinta magnética; DEP. cinta de llegada ♦ red t. papeleo ♦ t. player grabadora ♦ t. recorder grabadora magnetofónica ♦ t. recording cinta grabada II. tr. (to fasten) asegurar con cinta; (to glue) pegar con cinta adhesiva; (to measure) medir; (to record) grabar.

ta·per (tā'pər) I. s. vela delgada; (gradual decrease) ahusamiento II. tr. & intr. ♦ to t. off disminuir.

tape-re·cord (tāp'rĭ-kôrd') tr. grabar en cinta magnetofónica.

tap·es·try (tăp'ĭ-strē) s. tapiz m.

tape·worm (tāp'wûrm') s. tenia, solitaria.

tap·i·o·ca (tăp'ē-ō'kə) s. tapioca.

ta·pir (tā'pər) s. tapir m.

tap·room (tăp'rōōm') s. bar m.

taps (tăps) s. MIL. toque m de queda.

tar¹ (tär) I. s. alquitrán m II. tr. -rr- alquitra-

nar.

tar² s. FAM. (sailor) marinero.

ta·ran·tu·la (tə-răn'cho-lə) s. tarántula.

tar·dy (tär'dē) adj. -i- (late) tardío; (delayed) demorado; (slow) lento ♦ to be t. llegar tarde.

tar·get (tär'gĭt) I. s. blanco; (goal) meta ♦ to be on t. dar en el blanco II. tr. fijar como objetivo.

tar·iff (tăr'ĭf) s. tarifa.

tar·mac (tär'măk') s. asfalto; (runway) pista.

tar·na·tion (tär-nā'shən) s. & interj. FAM. maldición f.

tar·nish (tär'nĭsh) I. tr. & intr. empañar(se), descolorar(se); (to spoil) estropear(se) II. s. empañamiento, deslustre m; (besmirchment) mancha.

tar·ot (tär'ō) s. naipe m de dibujos alegóricos que se usa en la adivinación.

tar·pa·per (tär'pā'pər) s. papel alquitranado.

tar·pau·lin (tär-pô'lĭn, tär'pə-) s. alquitranado.

tar·ra·gon (tăr'ə-gŏn') s. estragón m.

tar·ry¹ (tăr'ē) intr. (to delay) demorar; (to linger) rezagarse.

tar·ry² (tär'ē) adj. -i- alquitranado.

tar·sal (tär'səl) adj. tarsal.

tar·sus (tär'səs) s. tarso.

tart¹ (tärt) adj. (taste) acre; (tone) hiriente.

tart² s. (pie) pastelillo; (prostitute) prostituta.

tar·tan (tär'tn) s. tartán m.

tar·tar (tär'tər) s. QUÍM. tártaro; ODONT. sarro ♦ t. sauce salsa tártara.

task (tăsk) I. s. tarea; (difficult undertaking) faena ♦ t. force fuerza operante • to take to t. reprender II. tr. agobiar con tareas.

task·mas·ter ('măs'tər) s. capataz m exigente.

tas·sel (tăs'əl) s. borla.

taste (tāst) I. tr. probar; (to discern flavors) notar un sabor a; (to sample) catar; (to experience) experimentar —intr. (to distinguish flavors) sentir sabor; (to have a flavor) tener sabor II. s. gusto; (small portion) pizca; (experience) experiencia ♦ in good t. de buen gusto • t. bud papila del gusto.

taste·ful ('fəl) adj. de buen gusto.

taste·less (:lĭs) adj. (flat) sin sabor; (insipid) insípido; (tacky) cursi.

tast·y (tā'stē) adj. -i- sabroso.

tat (tăt) tr. -tt- hacer encaje de frivolité —intr. tejer.

tat·ter (tăt'ər) I. s. andrajo, jirón m ♦ pl. harapos II. tr. convertir en harapos —intr. deshilacharse.

tat·tered (:ərd) adj. andrajoso.

tat·ting (tăt'ĭng) s. encaje m de hilo.

tat·tle (tăt'l) intr. (to gossip) chismear, comadrear; (to prattle) charlar, cotorrear.

tat·tler (:lər) s. (gossip) chismoso; (prattler) parlanchín m.

tat·tle·tale (:l-tāl') s. (gossip) chismoso; (informer) acusón m.

tat·too¹ (tă-tōō') s. MIL. (parade) desfile m militar; (drumming) tamboreo.

tat·too² I. s. tatuaje m II. tr. tatuar.

taught (tôt) cf. **teach.**

taunt (tônt) I. tr. mofarse de, burlarse de II. s. burla.

taupe (tōp) s. gris pardo.

taut (tôt) adj. (tight) tirante; (strained) tenso; (trim) aseado, prolijo.

taut·en ('n) intr. & tr. tensar(se).

tav·ern (tăv'ərn) s. taberna; (inn) posada.

taw·dry (tô'drē) adj. -i- charro.

taw·ny (tô′nē) adj. **-i-** pardo.

tax (tăks) I. s. impuesto; *(strain)* carga II. tr. *(to charge)* gravar; *(to make demands on)* agotar.

tax·a·ble (tăk′sə-bəl) adj. gravable.

tax·a·tion (-sā′shən) s. fijación f de impuestos.

tax-de·duct·i·ble (tăks′dĭ-dŭk′tə-bəl) adj. que se puede deducir como gasto.

tax-ex·empt (:ĭg-zĕmpt′) adj. libre de impuestos.

tax-free (′frē′) adj. libre de impuestos.

tax·i (tăk′sē) I. s. [pl. **(e)s**] taxi m ♦ **t. driver** taxista II. intr. **-iing** o **-ying** ir en taxi; *(airplane)* carretear.

tax·i·cab (:kăb′) s. taxi m.

tax·i·der·my (tăk′sī-dûr′mē) s. taxidermia.

tax·ing (tăk′sĭng) adj. pesado.

tax·pay·er (tăks′pā′ər) s. contribuyente mf.

tea (tē) s. *(drink)* té m; *(gathering)* reunión f social en la cual se sirve té.

teach (tēch) tr. **taught** enseñar; *(students)* dar clases a; *(a subject)* dar clases de —intr. ser maestro.

teach·er (tē′chər) s. maestro, profesor m.

teach·ing (:chĭng) s. enseñanza.

tea·cup (tē′kŭp′) s. taza de té.

teak (tēk) s. *(tree, wood)* teca.

tea·ket·tle (tē′kĕt′l) s. caldero, hervidor m.

teak·wood (tēk′wŏŏd′) s. madera de teca.

teal (tēl) s. [pl. inv. o **s**] *(duck)* cerceta; *(color)* verde azuloso.

team (tēm) I. s. equipo; *(of animals)* yunta II. tr. enyugar ♦ **t. up with** unir fuerzas con.

team·mate (′māt′) s. compañero de equipo.

team·ster (:star) s. carretero; *(truck driver)* camionero profesional.

team·work (′wûrk′) s. trabajo de equipo.

tea·pot (tē′pŏt′) s. tetera.

tear¹ (târ) I. tr. **tore, torn** *(to rend)* desgarrar, rasgar; *(to rip)* despedazar; *(to pull)* arrancar; *(to wound)* herir; *(to wrench)* distender; *(to distress)* angustiar ♦ **to t. apart** *(to rip)* romper; *(to disunite)* dividir ♦ **to t. off** o **out** arrancar ♦ **to t. down** *(to demolish)* demoler; *(to denigrate)* denigrar ♦ **to t. in** o **into** o **to pieces** despedazar ♦ **to t. up** hacer pedazos; *(to uproot)* desarraigar —intr. desgarrarse, rasgarse ♦ **to t. around** correr como un loco ♦ **to t. into** acometer II. s. desgarradura, rasgadura.

tear² (tĭr) I. s. lágrima; *(drop)* gota ♦ **t. gas** gas lacrimógeno ♦ pl. lágrimas, llanto • **in t.** llorando • **to be bored to t.** aburrirse como una ostra • **to move to t.** hacer llorar • **to shed t.** llorar II. intr. llenarse de lágrimas.

tear·drop (tĭr′drŏp′) s. lágrima.

tear·ful (:fəl) adj. lacrimoso.

tear-jerk·er (:jûr′kər) s. JER. drama m sentimentaloide.

tea·room (tē′rŏŏm′) s. salón m de té.

tease (tēz) I. tr. *(to annoy)* fastidiar; *(to make fun of)* tomar el pelo a; *(to tantalize)* tentar; *(wool)* cardar II. s. bromista mf.

teas·er (tē′zər) s. *(joker)* bromista mf; *(puzzle)* rompecabezas m.

tea·spoon (tē′spŏŏn′) s. cucharita de té; *(content)* cucharadita.

teat (tēt, tĭt) s. teta.

tech·ni·cal (tĕk′nĭ-kəl) adj. técnico; *(specialized)* especializado; *(scientific)* científico; *(technological)* tecnológico; *(theoretical)* teórico.

tech·ni·cal·i·ty (′-kăl′ĭ-tē) s. tecnicidad f; *(ex-*

pression) expresión técnica.

tech·ni·cian (tĕk-nĭsh′ən) s. técnico.

tech·nique (:nēk′) s. técnica.

tech·no·log·ic/i·cal (′nə-lŏj′ĭk) adj. tecnológico.

tech·nol·o·gist (-nŏl′ə-jĭst) s. tecnólogo.

tech·nol·o·gy (:jē) s. tecnología.

ted·dy bear (tĕd′ē) s. osito de juguete.

te·di·ous (tē′dē-əs) adj. tedioso.

te·di·um (:əm) s. tedio.

tee¹ (tē) DEP. I. s. tee m II. tr. colocar sobre un tee ♦ **to t. off** *(to hit)* pegarle a la pelota desde el tee; *(to start)* comenzar.

tee² s. meta ♦ **to a t.** a la perfección.

teem (tēm) intr. hervir, abundar.

teen (tēn) adj. & s. adolescente mf, joven mf.

teen-age(d) (′āj[d]′) adj. adolescente.

teen-ag·er (:ā′jər) s. joven mf, adolescente mf.

teens (tēnz) s.pl. *(numbers)* números entre 13 y 19; *(age)* adolescencia.

tee·ny (tē′nē) o **teen·sy** (tēn′sē) adj. **-i-** pequeñito.

tee·ter (tē′tər) intr. FAM. bambolearse; *(to vacillate)* vacilar.

tee·ter-tot·ter (:tŏt′ər) s. columpio, subibaja m.

teeth (tēth) cf. **tooth**.

teethe (tēth) intr. echar los dientes.

tee·to·tal·(l)er (tē′tŏt′l-ər) s. abstemio.

tel·e·cast (tĕl′ĭ-kăst′) I. tr. & intr. **-cast(ed)** televisar II. s. transmisión f de televisión.

tel·e·com·mu·ni·ca·tion (′-kə-myŏŏ′nĭ-kā′shən) s. telecomunicación f ♦ **telecommunications** s.sg. la ciencia de telecomunicaciones.

tel·e·gram (′-grăm′) s. telegrama m.

tel·e·graph (:grăf′) I. s. telégrafo; *(telegram)* telegrama m II. tr. telegrafiar —intr. mandar un telegrama.

tel·e·graph·ic (′-grăf′ĭk) adj. telegráfico.

te·leg·ra·phy (tə-lĕg′rə-fē) s. telegrafía.

tel·e·ki·ne·sis (tĕl′ĭ-ki-nē′sĭs) s. telequinesis f.

tel·e·me·ter (′ə-mē′tər) s. telémetro.

te·lem·e·try (tə-lĕm′ĭ-trē) s. telemetría.

tel·e·pa·thy (tə-lĕp′ə-thē) s. telepatía.

tel·e·phone (tĕl′ə-fōn′) I. s. teléfono II. tr. telefonear, llamar por teléfono —intr. comunicarse por teléfono.

tel·e·pho·to (′-fō′tō) adj. telefotográfico.

tel·e·pho·to·graph (:tə-grăf′) I. s. telefotografía II. tr. fotografiar con una lente telefotográfica.

tel·e·print·er (tĕl′ə-prĭn′tər) s. teletipo.

tel·e·proc·ess·ing (′-prŏs′ĕs′ĭng) s. teleproceso.

tel·e·scope (tĕl′ĭ-skōp′) I. s. telescopio II. tr. extender; *(to compress)* comprimir —intr. extenderse.

tel·e·scop·ic (′-skŏp′ĭk) adj. telescópico.

tel·e·thon (′-thŏn′) s. programa m de televisión destinado para recaudar fondos.

tel·e·vise (:-vīz′) tr. & intr. televisar.

tel·e·vi·sion (:vĭzh′ən) s. televisión f; *(set)* televisor m.

tel·ex (tĕl′ĕks′) I. s. télex m II. intr. enviar un télex.

tell (tĕl) tr. **told** decir; *(to inform)* comunicar; *(to reveal)* revelar; *(to discriminate)* distinguir; *(to assure)* asegurar; *(to know)* adivinar, saber; *(to explain)* explicar ♦ **all told** en total • **I t. you what** se me ocurre una idea • **I told you so!** ¡te lo dije! • **to t. off** FAM. cantar las cuarenta —intr. relatar, contar; *(to have an effect)* producir efecto.

tell·er (′ər) s. narrador m; *(bank employee)* cajero.

tell·ing (:ĭng) adj. *(effective)* efectivo; *(significant)* significante.

tell·tale (:tāl') s. *(informer)* soplón m; *(gossip)* chismoso.

te·mer·i·ty (tə-mĕr'ĭ-tē) s. temeridad f.

tem·per (tĕm'pər) I. tr. & intr. templar(se) II. s. *(disposition)* temperamento; *(composure)* compostura; *(tendency toward anger)* mal genio; *(anger)* ira; *(of metal)* temple m ♦ **to keep one's t.** dominarse • **to lose one's t.** enfadarse.

tem·per·a·ment (:prə-mənt) s. temperamento.

tem·per·a·men·tal ('-mĕn'tl) adj. temperamental; *(moody)* caprichoso; *(unpredictable)* impredecible.

tem·per·ance (tĕm'pər-əns) s. templanza; *(abstinence)* abstinencia

tem·per·ate (:ĭt) adj. moderado; *(tempered)* templado; *(weather)* templado.

tem·per·a·ture (:ə-chŏor') s. temperatura.

tem·pered (tĕm'pərd) adj. *(disposed)* dispuesto; *(moderated)* moderado; METAL., MÚS. templado.

tem·pest (tĕm'pĭst) s. tempestad f; FIG. alboroto.

tem·pes·tu·ous (-pĕs'chŏo-əs) adj. tempestuoso; FIG. turbulento.

tem·plate (tĕm'plĭt) s. plantilla, patrón m

tem·ple¹ (tĕm'pəl) s. templo; *(synagogue)* sinagoga

tem·ple² s. ANAT. sien f.

tem·po (tĕm'pō) s. [pl. **s** o **-pi**] ritmo; MÚS. tempo.

tem·po·ral¹ (tĕm'pər-əl) adj. temporal; *(secular)* secular.

tem·po·ral² adj. ANAT. temporal.

tem·po·rar·y (tĕm'pə-rĕr'ē) I. adj. transitorio; *(worker)* temporero, temporario; *(position)* interino II. s. temporero.

tempt (tĕmpt) tr. tentar; *(to seduce)* seducir; *(to provoke)* provocar.

temp·ta·tion (tĕmp-tā'shən) s. tentación f.

tempt·ing (:tĭng) adj. tentador.

ten (tĕn) s. & adj. diez m ♦ **t. o'clock** las diez.

ten·a·ble (tĕn'ə-bəl) adj. sostenible, defensible.

te·na·cious (tə-nā'shəs) adj. tenaz; *(adhesive)* adhesivo; *(retentive)* retentivo.

te·nac·i·ty (tə-năs'ĭ-tē) s. tenacidad f.

ten·an·cy (tĕn'ən-sē) s. tenencia legal; *(time period)* tiempo de posesión.

ten·ant (tĕn'ənt) s. inquilino.

tend¹ (tĕnd) intr. *(to head)* dirigirse; *(to be likely)* tender; *(to be inclined)* propender a.

tend² tr. *(to look after)* cuidar, atender; *(to serve)* servir —intr. *(to serve)* atender; FAM. *(to pay attention)* prestar atención a.

ten·den·cy (tĕn'dən-sē) s. tendencia.

ten·der¹ (tĕn'dər) adj. **-er, -est** frágil; *(soft)* tierno; *(delicate)* delicado; *(young)* joven; *(sensitive)* sensible; *(painful)* dolorido; *(affectionate)* cariñoso.

ten·der² I. s. *(offer)* oferta de pago; *(bid)* propuesta ♦ **legal t.** dinero II. tr. ofrecer.

ten·der·heart·ed ('-här'tĭd) adj. compasivo.

ten·der·ize (tĕn'də-rīz') tr. ablandar.

ten·der·iz·er (:rī'zər) s. condimento ablandador de carne.

ten·der·loin (tĕn'dər-loin') s. lomo, filete m.

ten·der·ness (:nĭs) s. ternura.

ten·don (tĕn'dən) s. tendón m.

ten·dril (tĕn'drəl) s. zarcillo.

ten·e·ment (tĕn'ə-mənt) s. residencia con departamentos de alquiler; *(rundown building)* conventillo; G.B. *(apartment)* departamento.

ten·et (tĕn'ĭt) s. principio.

ten·fold (tĕn'fōld') I. adj. décuplo II. adv. diez veces.

ten·nis (tĕn'ĭs) s. tenis m.

ten·on (tĕn'ən) s. CARP. espiga, barbilla.

ten·or (tĕn'ər) s. sentido, tono; MÚS. tenor m.

ten·pin (tĕn'pĭn') s. bolo ♦ pl. bolos.

tense¹ (tĕns) I. adj. *(stretched)* estirado; *(taut)* tirante; *(strained)* tenso II. tr. tensar —intr. ponerse tenso.

tense² s. GRAM. tiempo.

ten·sile (tĕn'səl, :sīl') adj. tensivo; *(extensible)* extensible.

ten·sion (tĕn'shən) s. tensión f.

ten·sor (tĕn'sər, :sôr') s. tensor m.

tent (tĕnt) s. tienda.

ten·ta·cle (tĕn'tə-kəl) s. tentáculo.

ten·ta·tive (tĕn'tə-tĭv) adj. *(experimental)* experimental; *(provisional)* provisorio; *(uncertain)* indeciso.

ten·ter·hook (tĕn'tər-hŏok') s. gancho de bastidor ♦ **to be on tenterhooks** estar en ascuas.

tenth (tĕnth) s. & adj. décimo.

ten·u·ous (tĕn'yŏo-əs) adj. tenue; *(slender)* delgado; *(weak)* débil.

ten·ure (tĕn'yər) s. *(occupation)* ocupación f, ejercicio; *(term)* condiciones f, *(period)* riodo; *(permanence)* permanencia.

tep·id (tĕp'ĭd) adj. tibio.

te·qui·la (tə-kē'lə) s. tequila mf.

term (tûrm) I. s. *(time period)* periodo, plazo; *(school year)* periodo académico; *(deadline)* término, fin m; *(of an official)* mandato; *(court session)* periodo de sesión; GRAM. voz f, vocablo; LÓG., MAT. término ♦ **in no uncertain terms** muy claramente • **in terms of** en cuanto a • **in the long t.** a la larga ♦ pl. *(conditions)* condiciones; *(terminology)* términos, *(relations)* relaciones • **to bring to t.** hacer ceder, obligar a convenir • **to come to t.** *(to agree)* llegar a un arreglo; *(to accept)* aceptar II. tr. calificar de, llamar.

ter·mi·nal (tûr'mə-nəl) I. adj. *(fatal)* fatal; *(final)* final; *(periodic)* periódico, recurrente II. s. *(end point)* término; *(station)* terminal f; ELEC., COMPUT. terminal.

ter·mi·nate (:nāt') tr. terminar; *(employment)* dejar cesante —intr. terminar ♦ **to t. in** tener como resultado.

ter·mi·na·tion (:nā'shən) s. terminación f; *(end)* final m.

ter·mi·nol·o·gy (tûr'mə-nŏl'ə-jē) s. terminología.

ter·mi·nus (tûr'mə-nəs) s. [pl. **es** o **-ni**] *(end)* fin m, final m; *(terminal)* estación f terminal.

ter·mite (tûr'mīt') s. termita, comején m.

tern (tûrn) s. golondrina de mar.

ter·race (tĕr'ĭs) I. s. terraza; *(balcony)* balcón m; *(roof)* azotea; *(embankment)* bancal m II. tr. terraplenar.

ter·ra cot·ta (tĕr'ə kŏt'ə) s. terracota.

ter·rain (tə-rān') s. terreno.

ter·rar·i·um (tə-râr'ē-əm) s. [pl. **s** o **-ia**] terrario.

ter·res·tri·al (tə-rĕs'trē-əl) adj. terrestre; *(mundane)* mundano.

ter·ri·ble (tĕr'ə-bəl) s. terrible; *(tremendous)* tremendo; *(disagreeable)* desagradable.

ter·ri·er (tĕr'ē-ər) s. terrier m.

ter·rif·ic (tə-rĭf'ĭk) adj. terrorífico; *(extraor-*

dinary) extraordinario.
ter·ri·fy (tĕr′ə-fī′) tr. aterrorizar.
ter·ri·to·ri·al (tĕr′ĭ-tôr′ē-əl) adj. territorial.
ter·ri·to·ri·al·i·ty ('·'·āl′ĭ-tē) s. territorialidad f.
ter·ri·to·ry (tĕr′ĭ-tôr′ē) s. (region) región f; (jurisdiction) territorio; (sphere) esfera, sector m.
ter·ror (tĕr′ər) s. terror ♦ t. o holy t. FAM. niño travieso.
ter·ror·ism (:ə-rĭz′əm) s. terrorismo.
ter·ror·ist (:rĭst) s. terrorista mf.
ter·ror·is·tic (:rĭs′tĭk) adj. terrorista.
ter·ror·ize (:rīz′) tr. aterrorizar.
ter·ry (tĕr′ē) s. ♦ t. cloth tela de toalla.
terse (tûrs) adj. conciso.
ter·ti·a·ry (tûr′shē-ĕr′ē) adj. & s. tercero; CIENT., ORNIT., RELIG. terciario.
test (tĕst) I. s. examen m, prueba; (criterion) criterio ♦ t. case DER. caso prueba • t. flight vuelo de prueba • t. tube tubo de ensayo, probeta • to put to the t. poner a prueba • to stand the t. of time resistir al paso del tiempo II. tr. examinar; (to subject to a test) someter a prueba.
tes·ta·cy (tĕs′tə-sē) s. la condición de haber hecho testamento antes de morir.
tes·ta·ment (:mənt) s. credo; DER. testamento; RELIG. convenio entre el hombre y Dios ♦ Old, New T. Antiguo, Nuevo Testamento.
tes·tate (tĕs′tāt′) adj. testado.
test·er (tĕs′tər) s. probador m, ensayador m.
tes·ti·cle (tĕs′tĭ-kəl) s. testículo.
tes·ti·fy (tĕs′tə-fī′) intr. ser testigo; DER. atestiguar bajo juramento —tr. testimoniar, revelar; DER. atestiguar bajo juramento ♦ to t. to evidenciar.
tes·ti·mo·ni·al ('-mō′nē-əl) I. s. testimonio; (recommendation) recomendación f; (tribute) homenaje m II. adj. testimonial.
tes·ti·mo·ny (tĕs′tə-mō′nē) s. evidencia, prueba; DER., RELIG. testimonio.
tes·tis (tĕs′tĭs) s. [pl. -tes] teste m, testículo.
tes·tos·ter·one (tĕ-stŏs′tə-rōn′) s. testosterona.
tes·ty (tĕs′tē) adj. -i- irritable.
tet·a·nus (tĕt′n-əs) s. tétano(s).
teth·er (tĕth′ər) I. s. tralla, correa ♦ at the end of one's t. (financially) en las últimas; (patience) harto II. tr. atar.
tet·ra·cy·cline (tĕt′rə-sī′klēn′) s. tetraciclina.
text (tĕkst) s. texto; (theme) tema m.
text·book (′bŏŏk′) s. libro de texto.
tex·tile (tĕk′stīl′, :stəl) s. & adj. textil m.
tex·tu·al (tĕks′chōō-əl) adj. textual.
tex·tur·al (tĕks′chər-əl) adj. de textura.
tex·ture (tĕks′chər) s. textura.
tex·tured (:chərd) adj. de textura.
thal·a·mus (thăl′ə-məs) s. [pl. -mi] tálamo.
tha·lid·o·mide (thə-lĭd′ə-mīd′) s. talidomida.
than (thăn, thən) conj. que <she is a better athlete t. I ella es mejor atleta que yo>; de <more t. half más de la mitad>; del que, de lo que <more complex t. I had anticipated más complejo de lo que había previsto> ♦ other t. aparte de, fuera de • rather t. antes que.
thank (thăngk) tr. agradecer, dar las gracias a ♦ t. you (for) gracias (por).
thank·ful (′fəl) adj. agradecido.
thank·less (:lĭs) adj. (ungrateful) desagradecido; (not appreciated) ingrato.
thanks (thăngks) s.pl. gracias; (acknowledgment) reconocimiento; (gratitude) gratitud f ♦ no t. to a pesar de • t. to gracias a.
thanks·giv·ing (:gĭv′ĭng) s. acción f de gracias.

that (thăt, thət) I. adj. dem. [pl. those] (near) ese; (distant) aquel ♦ t. one (near) ése; (distant) aquél • t. way (direction) por aquel camino; (manner) de ese modo II. pron. dem. [pl. those] (near) ése; (distant) aquél; (neuter) eso, aquello ♦ and t.'s that! ¡eso es todo! • like t. así • t.'s it! ¡eso es! III. pron. rel. [pl. that] que <the house t. I sold la casa que vendí>; quien <the person t. you've heard from la persona de quien recibiste noticias>; el que, la que <the closet t. you keep your clothes in el armario en el que guardas tu ropa>; lo que <all t. they knew todo lo que ellos sabían> ♦ at t. (without further elaboration) así, sin más; (nevertheless) sin embargo; (furthermore) todavía • for all t. a pesar de eso IV. adv. (so) tan; así de <the steps were t. high los escalones eran así de alto> ♦ t. many tantos • t. much tanto V. conj. que • t. is por cuanto • oh, t. . . .! ¡ojalá (que) . . .! • so t. para que.
thatch (thăch) I. s. paja II. tr. cubrir con paja.
thaw (thô) I. intr. derretirse; (to become warm) ponerse tibio; (to relax) relajarse —tr. ♦ to t. out (food) descongelar; (snow) derretir II. s. derretimiento; (warm period) tiempo tibio.
the (the antes de vocal, thə antes de consonante) I. art. def. el, la, lo, las, los II. adv. ♦ t. less . . . t. better cuanto menos . . . mejor • t. more . . . t. more cuanto más . . . más • t. sooner t. better cuanto antes mejor.
the·a·ter/tre (thē′ə-tər) s. teatro; (auditorium) auditorio; (setting) local m; MIL. teatro ♦ operating t. quirófano.
the·at·ri·cal (-ăt′rĭ-kəl) adj. teatral.
the·at·rics (:rĭks) s.sg. arte escénico —s.pl. (effects) efectos teatrales.
thee (thē) pron. ANT., POÉT. te, ti.
theft (thĕft) s. robo.
their (thâr) pron. pos. su, suyo, suya, de ellos, de ellas.
theirs (thârz) pron. pos. (el) suyo, (la) suya, (los) suyos, (las) suyas, de ellos, de ellas.
them (thĕm, thəm) pron. (as direct object) los, las; (as indirect object) les; (as object of preposition) ellos, ellas.
the·mat·ic (thĭ-măt′ĭk) adj. temático.
theme (thēm) s. tema m; (composition) ensayo.
them·selves (thĕm-sĕlvz′, thəm-) pron. (object) se <they prepared t. ellos se prepararon>; (subject) mismos, mismas; (object of preposition) sí mismos, sí mismas <they are always bragging about t. están siempre haciendo alarde de sí mismos> ♦ among t. entre ellos.
then (thĕn) I. adv. (at that time) entonces; (afterward) después; (in that case) entonces; (in addition) además; (consequently) en consecuencia ♦ t. and there ahí mismo II. s. entonces m ♦ from t. on desde entonces • since t. desde entonces • until t. hasta entonces III. adj. entonces, de entonces.
the·oc·ra·cy (thē-ŏk′rə-sē) s. teocracia.
the·o·lo·gian (thē-ə-lō′jən) s. teólogo.
the·o·log·i·cal (:lŏj′ĭ-kəl) adj. teológico.
the·ol·o·gy (thē-ŏl′ə-jē) s. teología.
the·o·rem (thē′ər-əm) s. teorema m.
the·o·ret·ic/i·cal ('ə-rĕtĭk) adj. teórico.
the·o·re·ti·cian (:ər-ə-tĭsh′ən) s. teórico.
the·o·rist (′-ĭst) s. teórico.
the·o·rize (thē′ə-rīz′) intr. teorizar.
the·o·ry (:rē) s. teoría.
ther·a·peu·tic/ti·cal (thĕr′ə-pyōō′tĭk) adj. tera-

péutico ♦ **therapeutics** s.sg. terapéutica.
ther·a·pist ('-pĭst) s. terapeuta *mf.*
ther·a·py (thĕr'ə-pē) s. MED. terapia; PSIC. psicoterapia.
there (thâr) I. adv. allí, allá, ahí; *(in that matter)* en eso ♦ **here and t.** aquí y allá II. pron. ♦ **t. are** hay • **t. is** hay • **t. was** había, hubo • **t. were** habían, hubo • **t. will be** habrá III. interj. ¡vaya! ♦ **t. now!** ¡ya está! • **t., t.** ya, ya.
there·a·bout(s) ('ə-bout[s]) adv. aproximadamente.
there·af·ter (-ăf'tər) adv. de allí en adelante.
there·by (:-bī') adv. *(by that means)* por medio de eso; *(in a specified connection)* por eso.
there·fore ('fōr') adv. por lo tanto.
there·in (-ĭn') adv. *(in that place)* allí dentro; *(in that circumstance)* en eso.
there·of (:ŭv'; :ŏv') adv. de eso.
there·on (:ŏn') adv. *(on that)* sobre eso; *(thereupon)* inmediatamente después.
there·to·fore ('tə-fōr') adv. hasta entonces.
there·up·on (:ə-pŏn') adv. *(upon this)* sobre eso; *(directly following)* luego; *(therefore)* en consecuencia.
there·with (-wĭth') adv. *(with that)* con eso; *(thereafter)* inmediatamente después.
ther·mal (thûr'məl) adj. termal.
ther·mo·dy·nam·ic ('mō-dī-năm'ĭk) adj. termodinámico ♦ **thermodynamics** s.sg. termodinámica.
ther·mo·e·lec·tric/tri·cal (:ĭ-lĕk'trĭk) adj. termoeléctrico.
ther·mom·e·ter (thər-mŏm'ĭ-tər) s. termómetro.
ther·mom·e·try (:trē) s. termometría.
ther·mo·nu·cle·ar (thûr'mō-nōō'klē-ər) adj. termonuclear.
ther·mo·plas·tic (:mə-plăs'tĭk) adj. termoplástico.
ther·mo·stat ('-stăt') s. termostato.
the·sau·rus (thĭ-sôr'əs) s. [pl. **-es** o **-ri**] *(dictionary)* diccionario; *(book of synonyms)* libro de sinónimos.
these (thēz) cf. **this.**
the·sis (the'sĭs') s. [pl. **-ses**] tesis *f.*
they (thā) pron. ellos, ellas ♦ **t. say** se dice.
thi·a·min(e) (thī'ə-mĭn, :mēn') s. tiamina.
thick (thĭk) I. adj. grueso; *(not watery)* espeso; *(in thickness)* de grosor; *(stuffy)* sofocante; *(full of)* atestado *(with* de); *(clouds)* impenetrable; *(indistinct)* poco claro, confuso; *(accent)* fuerte; *(crowd)* denso; *(beard)* tupido; *(lips)* grueso; FAM. *(stupid)* bruto, *(intimate)* íntimos II. adv. grueso ♦ **t. as thieves** inseparables • **to lay it on t.** exagerar al dar cumplidos III. s. ♦ **in the t.** en lo más reñido de • **through t. and thin** contra viento y marea.
thick·en ('ən) tr. & intr. espesar(se); *(to complicate)* complicar(se).
thick·en·ing (:ə-nĭng) s. espesamiento.
thick·et (thĭk'ĭt) s. bosquecillo.
thick·head·ed (thĭk'hĕd'əd) adj. torpe.
thick·ness (:nĭs) s. grosor *m*, espesor *m.*
thick·set (:sĕt') adj. corpulento.
thick·skinned (:skĭnd') adj. de piel gruesa; *(not easily offended)* de mucho estómago; *(insensitive)* insensible.
thief (thēf) s. [pl. **-ves**] ladrón *m.*
thieve (thēv) tr. & intr. robar, hurtar.
thiev·er·y (thē'və-rē) s. robo, hurto.
thigh (thī) s. muslo.
thigh·bone ('bōn') s. fémur *m.*

thim·ble (thĭm'bəl) s. dedal *m.*
thin (thĭn) I. adj. **-nn-** delgado; *(fine)* fino; *(sparse)* escaso; *(hair)* ralo; *(air)* enrarecido; *(soup)* aguado; *(weak)* débil ♦ **to be as t. as a rail** estar en los huesos • **to disappear into t. air** hacerse humo II. adv. débilmente, escasamente III. tr. **-nn-** hacer adelgazar; *(to dilute)* diluir, aguar; *(to cut away)* entresacar; *(to reduce)* reducir —intr. adelgazar; *(to diminish)* reducirse; *(to fade)* disiparse.
thine (thīn) pron. ANT. tuyo.
thing (thĭng) s. cosa; *(object)* objeto; *(creature)* criatura; *(commodity)* artículo; *(obsession)* obsesión *f*; *(situation)* asunto, cuestión *f*; *(dislike)* manía ♦ **a t. or two** unas cuantas cosas • **first t.** a primera hora • **first things first** cada cosa a su debido tiempo • **for another t.** además • **for one t.** en primer lugar • **it's a good t. that** menos mal que • **sure t.!** ¡seguro! • **the latest t.** *(fashions)* el último grito; *(latest development)* la última palabra • **to do one's own t.** JER. hacer lo que uno quiere ♦ pl. *(stuff, conditions)* cosas; *(equipment)* equipo.
thing·a·ma·jig ('ə-mə-jĭg') s. FAM. cómo se llama *m.*
think (thĭngk) tr. thought pensar (en); *(to regard)* creer, parecerle a uno; *(to remember)* recordar; *(to imagine)* imaginarse ♦ **come to t. of it** pensándolo bien • **to be well thought of** *(person)* ser tenido en mucho; *(actions)* ser visto con buenos ojos • **to t. about** pensar (en) • **to t. nothing of it** molestarle nada a uno • **to t. of** pensar; *(to recall)* recordar; *(to have regard for)* pensar en • **to t. of oneself as** creerse • **to t. out** pensar bien; *(a theory, plan)* elaborar; *(a problem)* resolver; *(a solution)* encontrar • **to t. over** *o* **through** pensar bien • **to t. up** inventar —intr. pensar; *(to believe)* creer, parecerle a uno ♦ **just t.!** ¡imagínese!, ¡figúrese! • **not to know what to t.** no saber a qué atenerse • **not to t. much of** *(a thing)* no parecerle a uno gran cosa; *(a person)* no tener un gran concepto de • **to make one t.** dar que pensar a uno • **to t. again** *o* **twice** pensarlo bien, reconsiderar • **to t. back** recordar • **to t. better of it** cambiar de parecer • **to t. of** *(to conceive of)* ocurrírsele a uno; *(to believe)* parecerle a uno; *(to imagine)* imaginarse, figurarse.
think·er (thĭng'kər) s. pensador *m.*
think·ing (:kĭng) I. s. *(thought)* pensamiento; *(judgment)* juicio, opinión *f* II. adj. pensante, racional.
thin-skinned (thĭn'skĭnd') adj. susceptible.
third (thûrd) I. s. tercero; *(part)* tercio, tercera parte; MÚS., AUTO. tercera; ASTRON., GEOM. tercero II. adj. tercero.
third-class ('klăs') I. adj. de tercera clase, de tercera II. adv. en tercera clase, en tercera.
thirst (thûrst) I. s. sed *f*; FIG. deseo ardiente, ansia II. intr. tener sed ♦ **to t. after** *o* **for** ansiar.
thirst·y (thûr'stē) adj. **-i-** sediento; *(arid)* seco ♦ **to be t.** tener sed • **to make t.** dar sed.
thir·teen (thûr-tēn') s. & adj. trece *m.*
thir·teenth (:tēnth') I. s. trece *m*; *(part)* trezavo, decimotercera parte II. adj. decimotercero; *(part)* trezavo.
thir·ti·eth (thûr'tē-ĭth) I. s. *(place)* treinta *m*; *(part)* treintavo, trigésima parte II. adj. *(place)* trigésimo; *(part)* treintavo.
thir·ty (thûr'tē) adj. & s. treinta *m.*
this (thĭs) I. pron. [pl. **these**] I. pron. éste, ésta, esto II. adj. este, esta ♦ **t. way** *(direction)* por aquí,

por acá; *(manner)* de este modo, así **III**. adv.
(so) tan; así de <*it was t. long* era así de largo>
♦ **t. much** tanto.
this·tle (thĭs'əl) s. cardo.
this·tle·down (:doun') s. vilano del cardo.
thong (thông) s. *(strip)* tira de cuero, correa;
(sandal) sandalia de tiras.
tho·rac·ic (thə-răs'ĭk) adj. torácico.
tho·rax (thôr'ăks') s. [pl. **es** *o* **-ces**] tórax *m*.
thorn (thôrn) s. espina; *(plant)* espino, en-
drino; FIG. espina.
thorn·y (thôr'nē) adj. **-i-** espinoso.
thor·ough (thûr'ō) adj. completo; *(detailed)*
detallado, minucioso; *(total)* total.
thor·ough·bred (:ə-brĕd') **I**. s. *(animal)* pura
sangre *mf*; *(person)* persona bien nacida
II. adj. de pura sangre.
thor·ough·fare (:fâr') s. *(highway)* carretera,
camino principal; *(street)* calle *f*, vía pública.
thor·ough·go·ing (:gō'ĭng) adj. *(complete)* cabal, completo; *(unmitigated)* rematado.
thor·ough·ness ('-nĭs) s. minuciosidad *f*.
those (thōz) cf. **that.**
thou¹ (thou) pron. ANT., POÉT. tú.
thou² (thou) s. JER. mil *m* (dólares).
though (thō) **I**. conj. aunque ♦ **as t.** como si ♦
even t. aunque **II**. adv. sin embargo, no obstante.
thought (thôt) **I**. cf. **think II**. s. pensamiento;
(idea) idea; *(philosophy)* filosofía; *(consideration)* consideración *f*; *(intention, purpose)* intención *f*, propósito; *(opinion)* opinión *f*, punto
de vista ♦ **at the t. of** al pensar en • **on second
t.** pensándolo bien • **that's a t.!** ¡buena idea! •
the mere t. of it sólo en pensarlo • **to be lost in
t.** estar absorto en meditación • **to collect
one's thoughts** pensar, concentrarse • **to give
t. to** considerar.
thought·ful ('fəl) adj. pensativo; *(well thought
out)* bien pensado; *(considerate)* atento, solícito.
thought·less (:lĭs) adj. *(unthinking)* irreflexivo,
imprudente; *(careless)* descuidado; *(inconsiderate)* falto de consideración.
thou·sand (thou'zənd) **I**. s. mil *m* ♦ **by the t.**
por millar • **in** *o* **by the thousands** a millares
II. adj. mil.
thou·sandth (:zəndth) **I**. s. mil *m*; *(part)* milésimo, milésima parte **II**. adj. milésimo.
thrall (thrôl) s. *(slave)* esclavo, siervo; *(slavery)*
esclavitud *f*, servidumbre.
thrash (thrăsh) tr. *(to flog)* azotar; *(to flail)* agi-
tar; *(to vanquish)* derrotar, AGR. trillar ♦ **t. out** discutir a fondo —intr. agitarse.
thrash·ing ('ĭng) s. *(flogging)* azotaina; AGR.
trilla.
thread (thrĕd) **I**. s. hilo; *(fiber)* fibra; *(strand)*
hebra; *(of light)* rayo; MEC. filete *m*, rosca ♦
to be hanging by a t. estar pendiente de un hilo •
to lose the t. perder el hilo • **to pick up the t.
again** coger el hilo ♦ pl. JER. ropa, trapos
II. tr. *(a needle)* ensartar, enhebrar; *(beads)* ensartar; *(film, tape)* cargar con; *(screw, nut)* file-
tear, roscar ♦ **to t. one's way through** abrirse
paso por.
thread·bare ('bâr') adj. *(cloth)* raído, gastado;
(trite) trillado.
threat (thrĕt) s. amenaza.
threat·en ('n) tr. & intr. amenazar.
three (thrē) s. & adj. tres *m* ♦ **t. hundred** trescientos • **t. o'clock** las tres.
three-di·men·sion·al ('dĭ-mĕn'shə-nəl) adj.

tridimensional.
three·fold ('fōld') **I**. adj. triple **II**. adv. tres
veces.
three-piece (:pēs') adj. de tres piezas.
three-quar·ter (:kwôr'tər) adj. de tres cuartos.
three-ring circus (:rĭng') s. circo de tres arenas; FIG. confusión *f*, caos *m*.
three·some (:səm) **I**. adj. triple **II**. s. trío.
thresh (thrĕsh) tr. trillar.
thresh·old (thrĕsh'ōld', :hōld') s. umbral *m*.
threw (thrōō) cf. **throw.**
thrice (thrīs) adv. tres veces.
thrift (thrĭft) s. economía, ahorro ♦ **t. shop**
tienda de gangas.
thrift·less ('lĭs) adj. despilfarrador.
thrift·y (:tē) adj. **-i-** económico, ahorrativo.
thrill (thrĭl) **I**. tr. *(to excite)* excitar, emocionar;
(to delight) encantar, deleitar —intr. estremecerse, temblar **II**. s. emoción *f*; *(quiver)* temblor *m*, estremecimiento; MED. tremor *m*.
thrill·er ('ər) s. FAM. novela *o* película de
aventuras excitantes.
thrive (thrīv) intr. **-d** *o* **throve, -d** *o* **-n** *(to prosper)* prosperar, medrar; *(to flourish)* crecer.
throat (thrōt) s. garganta; *(neck)* cuello ♦ **to
clear one's t.** aclararse la voz • **to cut one's
own t.** arruinarse a sí mismo • **to ram down
someone's t.** meterle a alguien por las narices.
throat·y (thrō'tē) adj. **-i-** gutural, ronco.
throb (thrŏb) **I**. intr. **-bb-** *(to beat)* latir, palpitar; *(with pain)* dar punzadas; *(motors)* vibrar;
(engines) zumbar **II**. s. *(beat)* latido, palpitación *f*; *(of pain)* punzada; *(of engines)* zumbido; *(vibration)* vibración *f*.
throe (thrō) s. espasmo, punzada ♦ pl. *(of
death)* agonía; *(of childbirth)* dolores • **in the
t. of** en los dolores *o* suplicio de.
throne (thrōn) s. trono.
throng (thrông) **I**. s. gentío, muchedumbre *f*
II. tr. *(to crowd into)* atestar, llenar; *(to press in
on)* apretar, aplastar —intr. *(to gather)* amontonarse, apiñarse; *(to flock)* afluir.
throt·tle¹ (thrŏt'l) s. *(windpipe)* tráquea; TEC.
válvula de admisión *o* de estrangulación.
throt·tle² tr. FAM. *(to choke)* estrangular, ahogar; *(to suppress)* suprimir; TEC. estrangular,
obturar ♦ **to t. back** reducir la velocidad de.
through (thrōō) **I**. prep. por; *(among)* a través
de; *(by the agency of)* por medio de, a través de;
(during) durante; *(between)* entre; de... a,
desde... hasta <*open Monday t. Friday* abierto
de lunes a viernes>; *(thanks to)* gracias a ♦ **to
have been t. it all** haberlas pasado **II**. adv.
(from one end to another) de un lado al otro;
(from beginning to end) hasta el final; *(completely)* completamente ♦ **t. and t.** *(completely)*
completamente; *(throughout)* hasta los tuétanos
• **to carry something t.** llevar algo a cabo • **to
fall t.** fracasar **III**. adj. directo; *(street)* de
paso libre, de vía libre; *(washed-up)* acabado ♦
to be t. *(to have finished)* haber terminado; *(not
to be able to take it)* no poder más • **to be t.
with** *(to have finished)* haber terminado con; *(to
be fed up with)* no querer ver más a.
through·out (:out') **I**. prep. por todo, en todo;
(during every part of) durante todo **II**. adv.
por todas partes; *(completely)* completamente;
(during the entire time) todo el tiempo.
throve (thrōv) cf. **thrive.**
throw (thrō) **I**. tr. **threw, thrown** tirar, arrojar;
(punches, jabs) dar, asestar; *(to the ground,
floor)* desmontar, echar por tierra; *(opponent)*

derribar, tumbar; (pottery) modelar; (dice) tirar, echar; (glance) echar, dirigir; (party) dar; (switch) echar, conectar; FAM. (to lose a contest) perder adrede ♦ to t. a fit enfurecerse • to t. aside echar a un lado, desechar • to t. away (to waste) malgastar; (to miss) desaprovechar; (to discard) tirar, desechar • to t. back (to return) devolver; (to delay) retrasar • to t. down echar por tierra, derribar • to t. in añadir • to t. off (to reject) desechar, deshacerse de; (to emit) despedir; (to mislead) engañar; (to disconcert) desconcertar • to t. on echarse encima, ponerse rápidamente • to t. oneself at lanzarse sobre • to t. oneself into lanzarse en • to t. out (to reject) rechazar; (to throw away) tirar • to t. over (to abandon) abandonar; (to overthrow) derrocar • to t. up (to raise) alzar; (hands) echarse a la cabeza; (building) construir rápidamente —intr. arrojar, lanzar ♦ to t. up vomitar, devolver II. s. lanzamiento, tiro; (of dice) lance m; (coverlet) colcha, cobertor m; (rug) alfombra pequeña.

throw·a·way ('ə-wā') adj. desechable.

throw·back (:băk') s. retroceso.

thrown (thrōn) cf. throw.

thru (thrōō) FAM. cf. through.

thrush (thrŭsh) s. tordo, zorzal m.

thrust (thrŭst) I. tr. **thrust** (to push) meter con fuerza; (to stab) clavar; (to put in) meter; (to force oneself into) meterse en • to t. at asestar un golpe a • to t. upon imponer —intr. (to push) empujar; (to stab) dar una puñalada; (to force one's way) abrirse paso II. s. empujón m, embestida; (stab) puñalada, estocada; (direction) dirección f; (impetus) ímpetu m, energía; ASTRONÁUT., FÍS. empuje m.

thru·way (thrōō'wā') s. autopista.

thud (thŭd) I. s. (sound) ruido sordo; (blow) batacazo II. intr. **-dd-** dar un batacazo.

thug (thŭg) s. malhechor m, matón m.

thumb (thŭm) I. s. pulgar m ♦ t. index uñeros • thumbs up! FAM. ¡buena suerte! • to be all thumbs ser torpe o desmañado II. tr. manosear; FAM. (a ride) hacer dedo a —intr. hacer autostop ♦ to t. one's nose hacer un palmo de narices • to t. through hojear.

thumb·nail ('nāl') I. s. uña del pulgar II. adj. (small) pequeño; (brief) breve ♦ t. sketch cuadro conciso.

thumb·screw (:skrōō') s. tornillo de mariposa.

thumb·tack (:tăk') s. chinche f, chincheta.

thump (thŭmp) I. s. puñetazo, porrazo; (noise) ruido sordo, baque m II. tr. golpear, aporrear —intr. golpear, aporrear; (to throb) latir violentamente.

thun·der (thŭn'dər) I. s. trueno; (roar) estruendo, estrépito II. intr. tronar; (to vociferate) vociferar, tronar —tr. vociferar.

thun·der·bolt (:bōlt') s. rayo.

thun·der·cloud (:kloud') s. nubarrón m.

thun·der·head (:hĕd') s. masa de nubes.

thun·der·ous (:əs) adj. que truena; (loud) atronador; (deafening) ensordecedor.

thun·der·show·er (:shou'ər) s. borrasca con truenos y lluvia.

thun·der·storm (:stôrm') s. tormenta.

thun·der·struck (:strŭk') adj. atónito.

Thurs·day (thûrz'dē) s. jueves m.

thus (thŭs) adv. así, de esta manera; (therefore) así que, por eso ♦ t. far hasta ahora.

thwack (thwăk) I. tr. golpear, aporrear II. s. golpe fuerte y sonoro.

thwart (thwôrt) tr. frustrar.

thy (thī) adj. pos. ANT. tu.

thyme (tīm) s. tomillo.

thy·mus (thī'məs) s. timo.

thy·roid (thī'roid') adj. & s. tiroides f.

thy·self (thī-sĕlf') pron. reflex. ANT. (yourself) te; (emphatic) tú mismo, ti mismo.

ti·ar·a (tē-ăr'ə, -ä'rə) s. (papal crown) tiara; (woman's headdress) diadema.

tib·i·a (tĭb'ē-ə) s. [pl. **s** o **-iae**] tibia.

tic (tĭk) s. tic m.

tick¹ (tĭk) I. s. (sound) tictac m; (mark) marca, señal f; G.B. (moment) instante m II. intr. hacer tictac ♦ to t. away transcurrir —tr. contar, registrar ♦ to t. off (item) marcar; JER. (person) enojar, irritar.

tick² ENTOM. s. garrapata.

tick³ s. (case) funda; (ticking) cotí m.

tick·er (:ər) s. TELEG. teletipo, teleimpresor m; FAM. (watch) reloj m, JER. (heart) corazón m ♦ t. tape cinta de teleimpresor.

tick·et (tĭk'ĭt) I. s. (for transport) billete m, boleto; (for movies, theater) entrada, boleto; (permit) pase m; (price) etiqueta; (summons) boleta <speeding t. boleta por exceso de veloci­dad>; (coupon) cupón m ♦ one-way t. boleto de ida • round-trip t. boleto de ida y vuelta • that's the t.! ¡eso es! • t. agent (travel agent) agente de viajes; (seller) taquillero • t. office • t. window taquilla II. tr. vender billete a; (to label) etiquetar; (a motorist) darle una boleta a.

tick·ing (tĭk'ĭng) s. cotí m.

tick·le (tĭk'əl) I. tr. hacer cosquillas, cosquillear; (to titillate) excitar agradablemente; (to delight) deleitar ♦ tickled pink o to death FAM. contentísimo, encantado —intr. sentir cosquillas II. s. cosquilleo.

tick·lish (:lĭsh) adj. cosquilloso; FIG. (touchy) quisquilloso; (situation) delicado.

tick·tack·toe (tĭk'tăk'tō') s. tres en raya m.

tick·tock (:tŏk') s. tictac m.

tid·al (tīd'l) adj. de marea ♦ t. wave marejada.

tid·bit (tĭd'bĭt') s. bocado; (gossip) chisme m.

tide (tīd) I. s. marea; (current) corriente f, flujo; (wave) ola, corriente; (season) estación f II. tr. ♦ to t. one over bastarle a uno.

tide·land ('lănd') s. marisma.

tide·wa·ter ('wô'tər) s. agua de marea; (land) tierras bajas del litoral.

tid·ings (tī'dĭngz) s.pl. nuevas, noticias.

ti·dy (tī'dē) I. adj. **-i-** (neat) ordenado, arreglado; (clean) limpio; (substantial) considerable II. tr. & intr. ♦ to t. up ordenar.

tie (tī) I. tr. tying atar; (to knot) anudar; (to link) ligar; (a contest) empatar ♦ to t. down atar, sujetar • to t. in conectar, relacionar • to t. up atar; (to confine) restringir, limitar; (traffic) obstruir; (boat) amarrar; (capital) invertir —intr. atarse; (contestants) empatar ♦ to t. in (with) relacionarse (con) II. s. (cord) cuerda, atadura; (necktie) corbata; (rail support) traviesa; (draw) empate m; (tie beam) tirante m; FIG. (bond) lazo, vínculo; (attachment) atadura.

tie-in (tī'ĭn') s. relación f, conexión f.

tie·pin (tī'pĭn') s. alfiler m de corbata.

tier (tîr) I. s. fila, hilera; (at a theater) fila de palcos; (of a cake) piso II. tr. disponer en filas.

tie-up (tī'ŭp') s. interrupción f.

tiff (tĭf) s. (irritation) pique m; (quarrel) riña.

ti·ger (tī'gər) s. tigre m ♦ t. lily lirio de tigre.

tight (tīt) I. adj. (screw, knot) apretado; (sealed)

hermético; *(faucet, lid)* bien cerrado; *(clothes, shoes)* ajustado; *(opening)* estrecho; *(rope, situation)* tenso; *(strict)* estricto; *(stingy)* tacaño; *(money, credit)* escaso; *(closely contested)* reñido, disputado ♦ **as t. as a drum** muy tirante • **to be in a t. spot** estar en un aprieto • **to be t.** JER. estar borracho • **to be t.** JER. emborracharse II. adv. *(firmly)* bien, fuertemente; *(soundly)* profundamente ♦ **hold t.!** ¡agárrense bien! • **to sit t.** cruzarse de brazos.

tight·en ('n) tr. apretar; *(a cord)* tensar; *(bonds)* estrechar ♦ **to t. one's belt** FIG. apretarse el cinturón —intr. apretarse.

tight·fist·ed (:fĭs'tĭd) adj. FAM. tacaño, avaro.

tight·lipped (:lĭpt') adj. con los labios apretados; *(reticent)* callado.

tight·rope (:rōp') s. cuerda floja.

tights (tīts) s.pl. malla.

tight·wad (tīt'wŏd') s. JER. tacaño, avaro.

ti·gress (tī'grĭs) s. tigresa.

tile (tīl) I. s. *(of a roof)* teja; *(of a floor)* losa, baldosa; *(of a wall)* azulejo; *(tiling)* enlosado; *(of a game)* pieza II. tr. *(a roof)* tejar; *(a floor)* embaldosar; *(a wall)* azulejar.

till[1] I. tr. AGR. labrar, cultivar.

till[2] I. prep. hasta (donde) II. conj. hasta que.

till[3] s. *(for money)* caja, cajón m.

tilt (tĭlt) I. tr. inclinar —intr. inclinarse; HIST. *(to joust)* participar en una justa ♦ **to t. over** *(to lean)* inclinarse; *(to fall)* volcarse, caer II. s. inclinación f; *(joust)* torneo, justa ♦ **(at) full t. a** toda velocidad • **on o at a t.** inclinado.

tim·ber (tĭm'bər) I. s. árboles m maderables; *(lumber)* maderamen m; *(beam)* viga; MARÍT. cuaderna m II. tr. enmaderar.

tim·ber·land (:lănd') s. bosque m maderable.

tim·ber·line (:līn') s. altitud f límite de la vegetación arbórea.

tim·bre (tăm'bər, tĭm'-) s. timbre m.

time (tīm) I. s. tiempo m; *(moment)* momento m; *(instant)* instante m; *(period)* período; *(season)* estación f, temporada; *(era)* era, época; *(a specified time)* hora; *(occasion)* ocasión f; *(instance)* vez f; *(lifetime)* vida; *(prison sentence)* condena; MÚS. tiempo; *(tempo)* compás m; *(duration)* duración f; GRAM. tiempo ♦ **all in good t.** todo a su tiempo • **all the t.** *(every moment)* todo el tiempo; *(always)* siempre • **a long t. ago** hace mucho tiempo • **(at) any t.** en cualquier momento • **a short t.** un rato • **at all times** en todo momento • **at a t.** a la vez • **at no t.** nunca • **at one time** en cierta época • **at the present t.** en la actualidad • **at the same t.** a la vez, al mismo tiempo • **at times** a veces • **behind the times** anticuado • **by that t.** para entonces • **each o every t.** cada vez • **for the t. being** por el momento • **from this t. on** desde ahora en adelante • **from t. to t.** de vez en cuando • **hard t.** mal rato • **hard times** tiempos difíciles • **have a good t.!** ¡diviértanse! • **in a short t.** dentro de poco • **in due t.** en su día • **in no t. (at all)** en un abrir y cerrar de ojos • **in t.** *(on time)* a tiempo; MÚS. al compás • **many a time o many times** muchas veces • **on t.** a tiempo • **t. and t. again** repetidas veces • **t. off** tiempo libre • **time's up!** ¡es la hora! • **to keep good t.** andar bien (un reloj) • **to keep t.** *(clock)* marcar la hora; MÚS. llevar el compás • **to keep up with the times** estar al tanto de las cosas • **to make t.** ganar tiempo • **to pass the t.** pasar el tiempo • **to pass o while the t. away** matar el tiempo • **to serve o do t.** cumplir una condena

• **to take one's t.** tomarse tiempo • **to waste t.** perder el tiempo • **what t. is it?** ¿qué hora es? II. adj. del tiempo; *(on installment)* a plazos ♦ **t. clock** reloj registrador • **t. zone** huso horario III. tr. fijar la hora o el tiempo de; *(to record)* cronometrar.

time·card ('kärd') s. tarjeta de marcar.

timed (tīmd) adj. de duración limitada.

time-hon·ored (tīm'ŏn'ərd) adj. tradicional.

time·keep·er (:kē'pər) s. *(timepiece)* cronómetro, reloj m; DEP. cronometrador m.

time-lapse (:lăps') adj. FOTOG. a intervalos.

time·less (:lĭs) adj. *(eternal)* eterno; *(ageless)* sin limitación de tiempo.

time·li·ness (:lē-nĭs) s. *(punctuality)* puntualidad f; *(fitness of time)* oportunidad f.

time·ly (:lē) I. adj. **-i-** *(opportune)* oportuno; *(punctual)* puntual II. adv. oportunamente.

time-out o **time out** (:out') s. DEP. interrupción f temporal; *(break)* descanso.

time·piece (:pēs') s. reloj m, cronómetro.

tim·er (tī'mər) s. *(timekeeper)* cronometrador m; *(timepiece)* cronómetro, cronógrafo; TEC., ELEC. regulador eléctrico; AUTO. distribuidor m del encendido.

times (tīmz) prep. multiplicado (por).

time·sav·ing (tīm'sā'vĭng) adj. que ahorra tiempo.

time-shar·ing (:shâr'ĭng) s. COMPUT. tiempo compartido.

time·ta·ble (:tā'bəl) s. horario.

time·worn (:wôrn') adj. *(used)* usado, gastado; *(trite)* trillado.

tim·id (tĭm'ĭd) adj. **-er, -est** *(hesitant)* temeroso; *(shy)* tímido.

ti·mid·i·ty (tĭ-mĭd'ĭ-tē) s. timidez f.

tim·ing (tī'mĭng) s. oportunidad f; MÚS. compás m; DEP. coordinación f; TEC., AUTO. regulación f de tiempo.

tim·or·ous (tĭm'ər-əs) adj. timorato.

tin (tĭn) I. s. estaño; *(container)* lata; *(for baking)* molde m II. tr. **-nn-** estañar; G.B. *(to can)* enlatar.

tinc·ture (tĭngk'chər) I. s. colorante m, pigmento; *(hue)* tinte m; *(trace)* vestigio; QUÍM., FARM. tintura II. tr. teñir.

tin·der (tĭn'dər) s. yesca, mecha.

tin·der·box (:bŏks') s. yesquero, FIG. polvorín m.

tine (tīn) s. *(of a pitchfork)* punta; *(of a fork)* diente m.

tin·foil o **tin foil** (tĭn'foil') s. papel m de estaño.

ting (tĭng) I. s. tintineo II. intr. tintinear.

tinge (tĭnj) I. tr. **-(e)ing** matizar, teñir II. s. matiz m, tinte m; *(trace)* vestigio.

tin·gle (tĭng'gəl) I. intr. sentir picazón —tr. picar, causar picazón a II. s. picazón f; *(quiver)* estremecimiento.

tin·ker (tĭng'kər) I. s. calderero remendón; *(bungler)* chapucero ♦ **it's not worth a t.'s damn** JER. no vale un comino II. intr. remendar como calderero; *(to play)* entretenerse ♦ **to t. with** jugar con, juguetear.

tin·kle (tĭng'kəl) I. intr. tintinear —tr. hacer tintinear II. s. tintineo.

tin·kling (:klĭng) s. tintineo.

tin·ny (tĭn'ē) adj. **-i-** *(sound)* metálico; *(flimsy)* frágil.

tin·plate (:plāt') tr. estañar.

tin·sel (tĭn'səl) I. s. oropel m II. adj. de oropel.

tin·smith (tĭn'smĭth') s. estañero.

tint (tĭnt) I. s. tinte m; *(hue)* matiz m; *(trace)*

huella; ARTE. media tinta II. tr. matizar.

ti·ny (tī'nē) adj. **-i-** minúsculo.

tip¹ (tĭp) s. *(end)* punta, cabo; *(extremity)* extremidad *f; (apex)* ápice *m; (of a cigarette)* filtro ♦ **from t. to toe** de pies a cabeza • **to have it on the t. of one's tongue** tenerlo en la punta de la lengua.

tip² I. tr. **-pp-** volcar, derribar; *(to tilt)* inclinar ♦ **to t. one's hat to** saludar (con el sombrero) a • **to t. over** volcar, derribar —intr. volcar, derribar; *(to lean)* inclinarse ♦ **to t. off** caerse • **to t. over** volcarse II. s. inclinación *f.*

tip³ I. tr. **-pp-** golpear ligeramente II. s. golpe ligero

tip⁴ I. s. *(gratuity)* propina, *(information)* información *f; (advice)* consejo II. tr. **-pp-** *(with money)* dar una propina; *(with information)* dar una información ♦ **to t. off** dar una información • **to t. one's hand** revelar uno sus verdaderas intenciones —intr. dar propinas.

tip-off ('ôf') s. FAM. información *f,* soplo.

tip·ple (tĭp'əl) intr. FAM. empinar el codo.

tip·pler (:lər) s. FAM. borrachín *m.*

tip·sy (tĭp'sē) adj. **-i-** *(slightly drunk)* achispado; *(unsteady)* tambalcante.

tip·toe (tĭp'tō') I. intr. andar de puntillas; *(stealthily)* andar sigilosamente II. s. punta del pie III. adj. & adv. de puntillas.

tip top ('tŏp') I. s. cumbre *f,* cima; *(highest quality)* calidad *f* superior II. adj. de calidad superior III. adv. perfectamente.

ti·rade (tī'rād') s. perorata.

tire¹ (tīr) tr. & intr. cansar(se); *(to bore)* aburrir(se).

tire² s. AUTO. llanta, neumático.

tired (tīrd) adj. cansado; *(bored)* aburrido; *(hackneyed)* trillado.

tire·less (tīr'lĭs) adj. incansable.

tire·some (:səm) adj. cansado, tedioso.

tis·sue (tĭsh'ōō) s. BIOL. tejido; *(disposable towel)* pañuelo de papel; *(web)* red *f* ♦ **t. paper** papel de seda.

tit¹ (tĭt) s. ORNIT. paro.

tit² s. teta; *(nipple)* pezón *m* ♦ **to give t. for tat** FIG. pagar con la misma moneda.

ti·tan·ic (tī-tăn'ĭk) adj. gigantesco, colosal; *(powerful)* poderoso.

tithe (tīth) I. s. RELIG. diezmo; *(tenth part)* décima parte II. tr. diezmar —intr. pagar el diezmo.

tit·il·late (tĭt'l-āt') tr. *(to tickle)* cosquillear; *(to stimulate)* estimular.

ti·tle (tīt'l) I. s. título; CINEM. subtítulo; DEP. campeonato ♦ **t. page** portada • **t. role** papel principal II. tr. conferir título a; *(to entitle)* titular.

ti·tled (:ld) adj. titulado; *(person)* con título.

ti·tle·hold·er (:l-hōl'dər) s. titular *mf; (champion)* campeón *m.*

tit·mouse (tĭt'mous') s. [pl. **-mice**] paro.

tit·ter (tĭt'ər) I. intr. reír entre dientes II. s. risa entre dientes.

tit·tle (tĭt'l) s. pizca, ápice *m.*

tit·tle-tat·tle (tĭt'l-tăt'l) I. s. chismorreo, chismes II. intr. chismear.

tit·u·lar (tĭch'ə-lər) adj. titular; *(nominal)* nominal.

tit·u·lar·y (:lĕr'ē) s. titular *mf.*

tiz·zy (tĭz'ē) s. JER. agitación *f.*

to (tōō, tə) prep. a; *(direction)* hacia; *(as far as)* hasta; *(against)* contra; *(of, for)* de, para; *(constituting)* por; *(in accord with)* según, de

acuerdo con; *(as compared with)* comparado a; *(before)* menos, para; *(until)* hasta; *(for the purpose of)* para, en; *(in honor of)* por, en honor a; *(with the result)* para, ante; *(toward)* con; *(not translated)* <tell him if you want to díselo si quieres>.

load (lōd) s. sapo, FIG. persona repulsiva.

toad·stool ('stōōl') s. hongo venenoso.

toad·y (tō'dē) I. s. adulador *m,* cobista *mf* II. tr. & intr. adular (a).

toast¹ (tōst) I. tr. tostar; *(body, hands)* calentar —intr. tostarse II. s. tostada.

toast² I. s. *(drink)* brindis *m* ♦ **the t. of the town** el héroe de la ciudad • **to drink a t. to** brindar por II. tr. & intr. brindar (a).

toast·er (tō'stər) s. tostadora.

toast·mas·ter (tōst'măs'tər) s. maestro de ceremonias en un banquete.

to·bac·co (tə-băk'ō) s. [pl. (e)s] tabaco.

to-be (tōō-bē') adj. futuro.

to·bog·gan (tə-bŏg'ən) s. tobogán *m.*

to·day o **to-day** (tə-dā') I. adv. hoy; *(at the present time)* actualmente II. s. hoy *m; (the present time)* hoy (en) día.

tod·dle (tŏd'l) I. intr. hacer pinitos II. s. pino, pinito.

tod·dler (:lər) s. niño que empieza a andar.

tod·dy (tŏd'ē) s. ponche *m.*

to do (tə-dōō') s. FAM. alboroto, jaleo.

toe (tō) I. s. dedo del pie; *(of a shoe, sock)* puntera ♦ **from head to t.** de pies a cabeza • **to be on one's toes** estar alerta • **to step on someone's toes** herir los sentimientos de alguien II. tr. tocar con la punta del pie ♦ **to t. the line** *o* **mark** conformarse —intr. ♦ **to t. in, out** andar con los pies hacia adentro, hacia afuera.

toed (tōd) adj. ZOOL. de ... dedos en el pie; CARP. metido oblicuamente.

toe·hold (tō'hōld') s. hendidura para apoyar la punta del pie; FIG. asidero.

toe·nail (tō'nāl') s. uña del dedo del pie.

tof·fee (tô'ē) s. melcocha, arropía.

tog (tŏg) FAM. I. s. *(jacket)* chaqueta; *(cloak)* capa ♦ pl. ropa II. tr. **-gg-** vestir.

to·ga (tō'gə) s. toga.

to·geth·er (tə-gĕth'ər) adv. juntos; *(in total)* en total, todos (juntos) ♦ **getting along t.** llevándose bien • **to bring t.** *(to reunite)* reunir; *(to reconcile)* reconciliar • **to come t.** FIG. tener buen éxito • **to get t.** juntarse, reunirse • **to go t.** *(to go out)* salir juntos; *(colors, flavors)* armonizar.

to·geth·er·ness (:nĭs) s. solidaridad *f,* unión *f.*

tog·gle (tŏg'əl) s. MARIT. cabilla; MEC. *(pin)* fiador atravesado; *(joint)* rótula; *(button)* alamar *m* ♦ **t. switch** interruptor eléctrico.

toil¹ (toil) I. intr. trabajar duro; *(to move)* moverse con dificultad II. s. esfuerzo, trabajo.

toil² s. *(net)* red *f* ♦ pl. FIG. red, trampa.

toi·let (toi'lĭt) s. retrete *m,* lavabo; *(toilette)* arreglo, aseo ♦ **t. paper** papel higiénico • **t. water** agua de tocador.

toi·let·ry (toi'lĭ-trē) s. artículo de tocador.

toi·lette (twä-lĕt') s. arreglo, aseo.

to·ken (tō'kən) I. s. señal *f,* prueba; *(symbol)* símbolo; *(souvenir)* recuerdo; *(chip)* ficha ♦ **by the same t.** igualmente II. adj. simbólico.

told (tōld) cf. **tell.**

tol·er·a·ble (tŏl'ər-ə-bəl) adj. tolerable; *(passable)* mediano, pasable.

tol·er·ance (:əns) s. *(acceptance)* tolerancia;

(patience) paciencia.
tol·er·ant (:ənt) adj. tolerante.
tol·er·ate (tŏl'ə-rāt') tr. tolerar; *(suffering, pain)* sufrir, aguantar.
tol·er·a·tion ('-rā'shən) s. tolerancia.
toll¹ (tōl) s. peaje m; *(on a phone call)* tasa, recargo; *(loss)* bajas, número de víctimas.
toll² I. tr. & intr. *(to ring)* tañer, tocar II. s. tañido.
toll·booth ('bōōth') s. caseta de peaje.
toll·gate (:gāt') s. barrera de peaje.
toll·house (:hous') s. garita de peaje.
tom (tŏm) s. macho.
tom·a·hawk (tŏm'ə-hôk') s. hacha de guerra de los indios norteamericanos.
to·ma·to (tə-mā'tō, -mä'-) s. [pl. **es**] tomate m ♦ **t. plant** tomatera.
tomb (tōōm) s. tumba; *(place)* sepultura.
tom·boy (tŏm'boi') s. FAM. marimacho.
tomb·stone (tōōm'stōn') s. lápida.
tom·cat (tŏm'kăt') s. gato macho.
tome (tōm) s. tomo; *(huge book)* librraco.
tom·fool·er·y (tŏm-fōō'lə-rē) s. tonterías, disparate m.
tom·my·rot (tŏm'ē-rŏt') s. JER. disparate m.
to·mor·row (tə-môr'ō) I. s. mañana ♦ **the day after t.** pasado mañana II. adv. mañana.
tom-tom (tŏm'tŏm') s. tantán m, tamtam m.
ton (tŭn) s. tonelada ♦ pl. FAM. montones.
to·nal (tō'nəl) adj. tonal.
to·nal·i·ty (tō-năl'ĭ-tē) tonalidad f.
tone (tōn) I. s. tono II. tr. dar tono a, modificar el tono de; *(colors)* matizar ♦ **to t. down** bajar, suavizar ♦ **to t. up** *(color)* intensificar; *(muscle)* tonificar.
tone·less ('lĭs) adj. apagado.
tongs (tôngz) s.pl. tenacillas; *(fire tool)* tenazas.
tongue (tŭng) I. s. lengua; *(language)* idioma m; *(of a shoe)* lengüeta; *(of a bell)* badajo ♦ **to hold** o **bite one's t.** morderse la lengua, callarse ♦ **to stick out one's t.** sacar la lengua ♦ **t. twister** trabalenguas II. tr. lamer; CARP. ensamblar, machihembrar.
tongue-in-cheek ('in-chēk') adj. irónico.
tongue-lash·ing ('lăsh'ĭng) s. FAM. reprimenda, regaño.
tongue-tied (:tīd') adj. con la lengua atada.
ton·ic (tŏn'ĭk) s. tónico; MÚS., FONÉT. tónica; *(quinine water)* agua tónica.
to·night (tə-nīt') adv. & s. esta noche.
ton·nage (tŭn'ĭj) s. tonelaje m.
ton·sil (tŏn'səl) s. amígdala.
ton·sil·lec·to·my ('sə-lĕk'tə-mē) s. tonsilectomía, amigdalectomía.
ton·sil·li·tis (:lī'tĭs) s. amigdalitis f.
ton·so·ri·al (tŏn-sôr'ē-əl) adj. barberil.
ton·sure (tŏn'shər) s. tonsura.
too (tōō) adv. *(also)* también; *(as well as)* además; *(excessively)* demasiado; *(very)* muy ♦ **not t.** FAM. no muy, nada ♦ **to be t. much** ser demasiado ♦ **t. little** *(amount)* demasiado poco; *(size)* muy pequeño ♦ **t. many** demasiados.
took (tōōk) cf. **take.**
tool (tōōl) I. s. herramienta; *(utensil)* utensilio, útil m; FIG. instrumento II. tr. *(to shape)* labrar; *(to equip)* equipar con herramientas —intr. ♦ **to t. around** FAM. pasear (en coche).
tool·box ('bŏks') s. caja de herramientas.
toot (tōōt) I. intr. sonar, emitir sonidos —tr. tocar, hacer sonar ♦ **to t. one's own horn** FAM. echarse flores II. s. pitazo, bocinazo.

tooth (tōōth) s. [pl. **teeth**] diente m; *(molar)* muela; *(of a saw)* diente; *(of a comb)* púa ♦ **by the skin of one's teeth** por poco, por un pelo ♦ **to cut one's teeth on** iniciarse en • **to fight t. and nail** luchar a brazo partido ♦ **to get one's teeth into** meterse bien en • **to have a sweet t.** ser goloso • **to show one's teeth** mostrar los dientes • **wisdom t.** muela del juicio.
tooth·ache ('āk') s. dolor m de muelas.
tooth·brush (:brŭsh') s. cepillo de dientes.
toothed (tōōtht, tōōthd) adj. dentado; de dientes <*saw-toothed* de dientes aserrados>.
tooth·less (tōōth'lĭs) adj. sin dientes, desdentado; *(ineffectual)* ineficaz.
tooth·paste (:pāst') s. pasta dentífrica.
tooth·pick (:pĭk') s. mondadientes m.
tooth·pow·der (:pou'dər) s. polvo dentífrico.
tooth·some (:səm) adj. sabroso, apetitoso; *(attractive)* atractivo.
tooth·y (tōō'thē) adj. -i- dentudo.
top¹ (tŏp) I. s. parte f superior o de arriba; *(of the head)* coronilla; *(of a container)* borde m; *(of a mountain)* cumbre f; *(of a house)* techo; *(of a tree, hat)* copa; *(of a bottle, pan)* tapa; *(of a page)* cabeza; *(of liquids)* superficie f; *(of plants)* tallo; *(blouse)* blusa; *(jacket)* chaqueta; *(of a bikini)* sostén m; *(peak)* cumbre f ♦ **at the t. of** a la cabeza de • **at the t. of one's form** en plena forma • **from t. to bottom** de arriba abajo • **on t.** encima • **on t. of** además de • **on t. of it all** para colmo de males • **to come out on t.** salir ganando • **to blow one's t.** FAM. salirse de sus casillas II. adj. de arriba; *(topmost)* último; *(highest)* más alto; *(great)* de categoría; *(best)* mejor; *(maximum)* máximo ♦ **t. hat** sombrero de copa III. tr. **-pp-** *(to form a top of)* coronar, rematar; *(to reach a top)* llegar a la cumbre de; *(to cover)* cubrir; *(to surpass)* superar; *(to be at the head of)* estar a la cabeza de; *(to be bigger than)* medir más que, ser más alto que; *(trees)* desmochar ♦ **to t. it all off** por si fuera poco • **to t. off** rematar, coronar.
top² s. *(toy)* peonza, trompo.
to·paz (tō'păz') s. topacio.
top·coat (tŏp'kōt') s. abrigo, sobretodo.
top-drawer (:drôr') FAM. adj. *(first-class)* de la más alta categoría; *(people)* de la alta sociedad.
top-flight (:flīt') adj. de primera categoría.
top-heav·y (:hĕv'ē) adj. más pesado arriba que abajo.
to·pi·ar·y (tō'pē-ĕr'ē) s. *(art)* jardinería; *(garden)* jardín m ornamental.
top·ic (tŏp'ĭk) s. tópico, tema m.
top·i·cal (:ĭ-kəl) adj. tópico; *(contemporary)* corriente, actual; MED. tópico.
top·knot (tŏp'nŏt') s. *(of hair)* moño alto; *(of feathers, bows)* copete m.
top·less (:lĭs) adj. sin la parte superior; *(woman)* con el busto desnudo.
top·most (:mōst') adj. *(highest)* más alto, más elevado; *(uppermost)* máximo.
top-notch (:nŏch') adj. FAM. de primera clase.
to·pog·ra·phy (tə-pŏg'rə-fē) s. topografía.
to·pol·o·gy (tə-pŏl'ə-jē) s. topología.
top·ping (tŏp'ĭng) s. *(sauce)* salsa; *(frosting)* cobertura, garapiña; *(garnish)* aderezo.
top·ple (tŏp'əl) tr. derribar; *(government)* volcar —intr. *(to fall)* volcarse; *(to totter)* tambalearse.
tops (tŏps) adj. JER. fantástico, buenísimo.
top-se·cret (tŏp'sē'krĭt) adj. absolutamente se-

creto.

top·soil (:soil') s. tierra, capa superficial del suelo.

top·sy·tur·vy (tŏp'sē-tûr'vē) **I.** adv. patas arriba, al revés; *(in disorder)* en desorden **II.** adj. desordenado.

torch (tôrch) s. antorcha; *(for welding)* soplete *m*; G.B. *(flashlight)* linterna ♦ **to carry a t.** for **someone** estar enamorado de alguien sin ser correspondido ♦ **t. song** canción de amor.

torch·bear·er (:bâr'ər) s. abanderado.

tore (tôr) cf. **tear¹**.

tor·e·a·dor (tôr'ē-ə-dôr') s. toreador *m*.

tor·ment I. s. (tôr'mĕnt') tormento; *(torture)* tortura **II.** tr. (-') atormentar; *(to torture)* torturar; *(to pester)* molestar.

tor·men·tor/·ment·er (tôr-mĕn'tər) s. atormentador *m*, torturador *m*.

torn (tôrn) cf. **tear¹**.

tor·na·do (tôr-nā'dō) s. [pl. **(e)s**] tornado.

tor·pe·do (tôr-pē'dō) **I.** s. [pl. **es**] torpedo **II.** tr. torpedear.

tor·pid (tôr'pĭd) adj. tórpido; *(lethargic)* letárgico; *(apathetic)* apático.

tor·por (:pər) s. *(dullness)* torpor *m*; *(apathy)* apatía.

torque (tôrk) s. momento o fuerza de torsión, par *m* de torsión.

tor·rent (tôr'ənt) s. torrente *m*.

tor·ren·tial (tô-rĕn'shəl) adj. torrencial.

tor·rid (tôr'ĭd) adj. tórrido; *(scorching)* abrasado; FIG. ardiente.

tor·sion (tôr'shən) s. torsión *f*.

tor·so (tôr'sō) s. [pl. **s** o **-si**] torso *m*.

tort (tôrt) s. DER. agravio.

tor·ti·lla (tôr-tē'yə) s. tortilla (de maíz).

tor·toise (tôr'tĭs) s. tortuga de tierra.

tor·toise·shell (:shĕl') s. concha de carey.

tor·tu·ous (tôr'chōō-əs) adj. tortuoso; *(complex)* complicado.

tor·ture (tôr'chər) **I.** s. tortura **II.** tr. torturar.

tor·tur·er (:ər) s. torturador *m*.

tor·tur·ous (:əs) adj. atormentador.

toss (tôs) **I.** tr. tirar, lanzar; *(one's head, hair)* echar hacia atrás; *(rider)* dejar caer; *(salads)* revolver; *(coin)* echar a cara o cruz ♦ **to add** echar a un lado ♦ **to t. down** beber de un trago ♦ **to t. off** hacer fácilmente ♦ **to t. out** desechar —intr. *(to be flung to and fro)* ser agitado, revolverse; *(to flip a coin)* echar una moneda a cara o cruz ♦ **to t. and turn** dar vueltas en la cama **II.** s. lanzamiento, tiro; *(rapid movement)* sacudida; *(fall)* caída ♦ **to win the t.** ganar a cara o cruz.

toss·up ('ŭp') FAM. s. lanzamiento de una moneda a cara o cruz; *(odds)* probabilidad pareja.

tot¹ (tŏt) s. *(child)* nene *m*; *(drop)* trago.

tot² tr. **-tt-** ♦ **to t. up** sumar.

to·tal (tōt'l) **I.** s. total *m*; *(entirety)* totalidad *f* **II.** adj. total **III.** tr. & intr. ascender a ♦ **to t. up** to ascender a.

to·tal·i·tar·i·an (tō-tăl'ĭ-târ'ē-ən) adj. totalitario.

to·tal·i·ty (-'-tē) s. totalidad *f*.

tote (tōt) **I.** tr. llevar **II.** s. carga, peso ♦ **t. bag** bolsa grande.

to·tem (tō'təm) s. tótem *m* ♦ **t. pole** poste de un tótem.

tot·ter (tŏt'ər) intr. tambalearse.

tot·ter·ing (:ĭng) adj. tambaleante.

tou·can (tōō'kăn', :kän) s. tucán *m*.

touch (tŭch) **I.** tr. tocar; *(to taste)* probar, to

car; *(to disturb)* toquetear, manosear; *(to border)* lindar con; *(to equal)* igualarse a; *(to mention)* referirse a; *(to concern)* concernir a; *(to move* conmover ♦ **to t. bottom** tocar fondo ♦ **to t. off** desencadenar, provocar ♦ **to t. up** *(to add touches to)* corregir, retocar; *(to finish off)* dar los últimos toques a —intr. tocarse; *(to be in contact)* estar en contacto ♦ **to t. down** AVIA. aterrizar **II.** s. toque *m*; *(sense)* tacto; *(mild attack)* ataque ligero; *(dash)* pizca, poquito; *(facility)* mano <to lose one's t. perder la mano>; *(contact)* contacto, comunicación *f*; JER. *(approach for a loan)* sablazo ♦ **by t.** al tacto • **final** o **finishing t.** último toque • **to be out of t. with** *(people)* haber perdido el contacto con; *(things)* no estar al corriente o al tanto de • **to keep in t.** mantenerse en contacto.

touch-and-go ('ən-gō') adj. arriesgado.

touch·down ('doun') s. AER. aterrizaje *m*; DEP. tanto, gol *m*.

touched (tŭcht) adj. *(moved)* conmovido; FAM. *(mentally unbalanced)* tocado de la cabeza.

touch·ing (tŭch'ĭng) adj. conmovedor.

touch·stone ('stōn') s. piedra de toque; *(criterion)* criterio de prueba.

touch-type (:tīp') intr. mecanografiar al tacto.

touch·up (:ŭp') s. retoque *m*.

touch·y (:ē) adj. **-i-** *(oversensitive)* susceptible, quisquilloso; *(requiring tact)* delicado.

tough (tŭf) **I.** adj. duro; *(physically hardy)* fuerte, robusto; *(harsh)* severo, áspero; *(aggressive)* agresivo; *(difficult)* difícil; *(resolute)* decidido; *(rough)* tosco, bruto; *(unyielding)* inflexible ♦ **t.!** o **t. luck!** FAM. ¡mala suerte! **II.** s. matón *m*.

tough·en ('ən) tr. & intr. endurecer(se).

tough-mind·ed (:mīn'dĭd) adj. duro (de carácter).

tou·pee (tōō-pā') s. pcluquín *m*.

tour (tŏor) **I.** s. excursión *f*, viaje *m*; *(visit)* visita; TEAT. gira **II.** tr. recorrer, hacer un viaje por; TEAT. presentar en gira —intr. ir de viaje.

tour·ing ('ĭng) **I.** s. turismo **II.** adj. de turismo; *(theatrical company)* que está de gira.

tour·ism (:ĭz'əm) s. turismo.

tour·ist (:ĭst) **I.** s. turista *m/f* **II.** adj. de turista.

tour·na·ment (tôr'nə-mənt) s. torneo.

tour·ney (:nē) **I.** intr. tornear **II.** s. torneo.

tour·ni·quet (:nĭ-kĭt) s. torniquete *m*.

tou·sle (tou'zəl) tr. *(hair)* desordenar; *(clothes)* arrugar, desarreglar.

tout (tout) FAM. **I.** s. vendedor *m* de informaciones sobre caballos de carrera **II.** tr. *(to recommend)* recomendar; *(to solicit)* solicitar; *(to importune)* importunar.

tow¹ (tō) **I.** tr. remolcar **II.** s. remolque *m*; *(tow truck)* camión *m* remolcador; *(tugboat)* remolcador *m*; *(rope, cable)* remolque, sirga.

tow² s. *(fiber)* estopa.

tow·age (tō'ĭj) s. remolque *m*; *(fee)* derechos de remolque.

to·ward(s) (tôrd[z], tə-wôrd[z]') prep. hacia; *(facing)* próximo a; *(for)* para; *(with)* con, para con; *(near in time)* alrededor de.

tow·el (tou'əl) **I.** s. toalla, paño ♦ **to throw in the t.** DEP. tirar la esponja; FIG. darse por vencido **II.** tr. & intr. secar(se) o frotar(se) con una toalla.

tow·er (tou'ər) **I.** s. torre *f*; *(fortress)* torreón *m*, fortaleza; *(watch tower)* atalaya; AER. torre de control **II.** intr. elevarse ♦ **to t. over** o **above** dominar, destacarse sobre.

tow·er·ing (:ĭng) adj. *(very high)* altísimo; *(outstanding)* sobresaliente; *(intense)* intenso.

tow·head (tō′hĕd′) s. persona rubia.

tow·line (tō′lĭn′) s. remolque *m*, sirga.

town (toun) **I.** s. *(city)* ciudad *f*; *(village)* pueblo; *(commercial center)* centro; *(residents)* gente *f*, pueblo ♦ **to be out of t.** estar fuera, estar de viaje • **to go out on the t.** FAM. salir a divertirse • **to go to t. on** FAM. hacer con toda el alma • **to paint the t. red** JER. ir de juerga **II.** adj. urbano ♦ **t. crier** pregonero • **t. hall** ayuntamiento, municipalidad

town·ship (′shĭp′) s. municipio.

towns·peo·ple (tounz′pē′pəl) s.pl. habitantes *mf* de una ciudad.

tow·rope (tō′rōp′) s. remolque *m*, sirga.

tox·e·mi·a (tŏk-sē′mē-ə) s. toxemia.

tox·ic (tŏk′sĭk) s. tóxico.

tox·i·cant (:ĭ-kənt) s. & adj. tóxico.

tox·ic·i·ty (-sĭs′ĭ-tē) s. toxicidad *f*.

tox·i·col·o·gist (′sĭ-kŏl′ə-jĭst) s. toxicólogo.

tox·i·col·o·gy (:jē) s. toxicología.

tox·in (tŏk′sĭn) s. toxina.

toy (toi) **I.** s. juguete *m*; *(trifle)* nadería; *(bauble)* chuchería, baratija **II.** adj. de juguete ♦ **t. poodle** perro de lanas enano • **t. soldier** soldadito de plomo **III.** intr. jugar, juguetear ♦ **to t. with** *(to play with)* jugar con; *(an idea)* dar vueltas a.

trace¹ (trās) **I.** s. *(mark)* pista; *(footprint)* huella, rastro; *(sign)* señal *f*, indicio; *(bit)* pizca **II.** tr. *(to sketch)* dibujar, trazar; *(to follow a trail)* seguir; *(to locate)* localizar.

trace² s. *(strap)* tirante *m*, tiradera.

trace·a·ble (trā′sə-bəl) adj. fácil de seguir.

trac·er (:sər) s. *(investigator)* investigador *m*; *(instrument)* tiralíneas *m*; COST. patrón *m*; *(bullet)* bala trazadora; QUÍM. indicador *m*.

tra·che·a (trā′kē-ə) s. [pl. **s** *o* **-ae**] tráquea.

tra·che·ot·o·my (′-ŏt′ə-mē) s. traqueotomía.

track (trăk) **I.** s. *(path)* camino, senda; *(footprint)* huella; *(of a person)* pista; *(of things)* vestigio, rastro; *(of a tape recorder)* pista; *(of a bullet)* trayectoria; *(railway)* vía (férrea); DEP. *(for running)* pista; *(sport)* atletismo en pista ♦ **in one's tracks** allí mismo • **to be off the t.** *(train)* estar descarrilado; *(person)* estar despistado • **to be on the right t.** ir por buen camino • **to be on somebody's t.** estar sobre la pista de alguien • **to cover one's tracks** no dejar rastro • **to keep t. of** *(to stay informed about)* seguir con atención, estar al día con; *(to follow)* vigilar de cerca • **to lose t. of** *(people)* perder de vista; *(time)* perder la noción de; *(thought, conversation)* perder el hilo de • **to make tracks** JER. irse, marcharse • **t. meet** concurso de atletismo **II.** tr. *(to trail)* seguir, rastrear; *(to observe)* seguir ♦ **to t. down** localizar —intr. seguir una huella.

track·er (′ər) s. *(person)* perseguidor *m*; *(dog)* rastreador *m*.

track·ing (:ĭng) s. localización *f* ♦ **t. station** estación de seguimiento.

track·suit (:sōōt′) s. chándal *m*.

tract¹ (trăkt) s. tracto; ANAT. sistema.

tract² s. *(pamphlet)* folleto, opúsculo.

trac·ta·ble (trăk′tə-bəl) adj. tratable, dócil; *(malleable)* maleable, dúctil.

trac·tile (:təl, :tīl′) adj. dúctil, maleable.

trac·tion (:shən) s. tracción *f*.

trac·tor (:tər) s. tractor *m*.

trade (trād) **I.** s. ocupación *f*; *(commerce)* co-

mercio, negocio; *(industry)* industria; *(transaction)* transacción *f*; *(exchange)* cambio; *(businessmen)* comerciantes *m*; *(customers)* clientela ♦ **by t.** de profesión • **t. name** nombre comercial • **t. school** escuela vocacional • **t. union** sindicato, gremio **II.** intr. comerciar, negociar; *(to be a customer)* ser cliente ♦ **to t. on** aprovecharse de —tr. cambiar, trocar ♦ **to t. in** dar un artículo usado como pago inicial por otro nuevo • **to t. off** trocar.

trade-in (′ĭn′) s. artículo entregado como pago parcial de una compra.

trade·mark (:märk′) s. marca registrada *o* de fábrica; FIG. sello distintivo.

trade·off *o* **trade-off** (:ôf′) s. trueque *m*.

trad·er (trā′dər) s. comerciante *mf*; *(ship)* buque *m* mercante; FIN. bolsista *mf*.

trades·man (trādz′mən) s. [pl. **-men**] comerciante *mf*.

trad·ing (trā′dĭng) **I.** s. comercio **II.** adj. comercial.

tra·di·tion (trə-dĭsh′ən) s. tradición *f*.

tra·di·tion·al (:ə-nəl) adj. tradicional.

tra·di·tion·al·ist (:nə-lĭst) s. & adj. tradicionalista *mf*.

tra·duce (trə-dōōs′) tr. calumniar, difamar.

traf·fic (trăf′ĭk) **I.** s. tráfico; COM. *(trade)* comercio, negocio; *(exchange)* cambio; *(of ideas)* intercambio ♦ **t. jam** embotellamiento **II.** intr. **-ck-** traficar.

traf·fick·er (:ĭ-kər) s. negociante *mf*; *(of drugs)* traficante *mf*.

tra·ge·di·an (trə-jē′dē-ən) s. trágico.

tra·ge·di·enne (:ĕn′) s. trágica.

trag·e·dy (trăj′ĭ-dē) s. tragedia.

trag·ic (′ĭk) adj. trágico.

trag·i·com·e·dy (′ĭ-kŏm′ĭ-dē) s. tragicomedia.

trag·i·com·ic (:ĭk) adj. tragicómico.

trail (trāl) **I.** tr. *(to drag)* arrastrar; *(to track)* rastrear; *(to follow)* seguir; *(to lag behind)* rezagar —intr. arrastrarse; *(a plant)* trepar ♦ **to t. behind** quedarse a la zaga • **to t. off** desvanecerse **II.** s. *(trace)* huella, rastro; *(of a person)* pista; *(of smoke)* estela; *(path)* camino, sendero; FIG. estela ♦ **to be on the t. of** seguir la pista de • **to lose, to pick up the t.** perder, encontrar la pista.

trail·blaz·er (′blā′zər) s. pionero.

trail·er (trā′lər) s. *(person)* rastreador *m*; *(vehicle)* remolque *m*; *(furnished van)* casa-remolque *m* ♦ **t. truck** camión de remolque.

train (trān) **I.** s. tren *m*; *(succession)* sucesión *f*, serie *f*; *(of people)* séquito, cortejo; *(of a dress)* cola ♦ **to lose one's t. of thought** perder el hilo de lo que uno iba a decir **II.** tr. *(a person)* enseñar; *(a child)* disciplinar, educar; *(an animal)* domar, amaestrar; *(an athlete)* entrenar; *(a plant)* guiar —intr. prepararse, formarse; *(an athlete)* entrenarse.

trained (trānd) adj. *(educated)* entrenado; *(physically)* preparado; *(animals)* amaestrado ♦ **to have a t. eye** tener un ojo experto.

train·ee (trā-nē′) s. aprendiz *mf*.

train·er (′nər) s. DEP. entrenador *m*; *(of horses)* preparador *m*; *(of animals)* amaestrador *m*.

train·ing (:nĭng) s. instrucción *f*, enseñanza; *(apprenticeship)* aprendizaje *m*; *(of animals)* amaestramiento; DEP. entrenamiento.

train·man (trān′mən) s. [pl. **-men**] ferroviario.

traipse (trāps) intr. FAM. andar.

trait (trāt) s. rasgo distintivo, característica.

trai·tor (trā′tər) s. traidor *m*.

trai·tor·ous (:əs) adj. traidor, traicionero.
tra·jec·to·ry (trə-jĕk′tə-rē) s. trayectoria.
tram (trăm) s. G.B. *(streetcar)* tranvía *m*; *(tramway)* rieles *m*, carriles *m*; *(cable car)* teleférico; *(small wagon)* vagoneta.
tram·car (:′kär′) s. G.B. *(streetcar)* tranvía *m*; *(coal car)* vagoneta.
tram·mel (trăm′əl) I. s. traba ♦ pl. trabas, obstáculos II. tr. poner trabas a.
tramp (trămp) I. intr. *(to trudge)* andar con pasos pesados; *(to hike)* caminar, ir a pie; *(to wander)* vagar, errar —tr. pisotear con fuerza II. s. *(footfall)* ruido; *(hike)* caminata, paseo largo; *(vagrant)* vagabundo; JER. *(prostitute)* fulana, ramera.
tram·ple (trăm′pəl) I. tr. pisotear ♦ **to t. on** pisotear —intr. pisar rudamente II. s. pisoteo; *(sound)* ruido de pisadas.
tram·po·line (trăm′pə-lēn′) s. trampolín *m*.
trance (trăns) s. trance *m*.
tran·quil (trăng′kwəl) adj. tranquilo.
tran·quil·(l)ize (:kwə-līz′) tr. & intr. tranquilizar(se).
tran·quil·iz·er (:ər) s. tranquilizante *m*.
tran·quil·(l)i·ty (trăng-kwĭl′ĭ-tē) s. tranquilidad *f*.
trans·act (trăns-săkt′) tr. llevar a cabo, ejecutar.
trans·ac·tion (:săk′shən) s. *(act)* negociación *f*; *(deal)* transacción *f* ♦ pl. actas.
trans·ac·tion·al (:shən-əl) adj. de transacción.
trans·ac·tor (:tər) s. negociante *mf*.
trans·at·lan·tic (trăns′ət-lăn′tĭk) adj. transatlántico.
trans·ceiv·er (trăn-sē′vər) s. transceptor *m*.
trans·cend (trăn-sĕnd′) tr. trascender; *(to surpass)* sobrepasar —intr. trascender.
tran·scen·dence/den·cy (trăn-sĕn′dəns) s. trascendencia.
tran·scen·dent (:dənt) adj. trascendente.
tran·scen·den·tal (′-dĕn′tl) adj. trascendental.
trans·con·ti·nen·tal (trăns′kŏn-tə-nĕn′tl) adj. transcontinental.
tran·scribe (trăn-skrīb′) tr. transcribir; MÚS. adaptar, arreglar.
tran·scrib·er (-skrī′bər) s. transcriptor *m*.
tran·script (trăn′skrĭpt′) s. transcripción *f*.
tran·scrip·tion (-skrĭp′shən) s. transcripción *f*; *(recording)* grabación *f*; RAD., TELEV. emisión diferida.
trans·duc·er (trăns-dōō′sər) s. transductor *m*.
tran·sect (trăn-sĕkt′) tr. cortar transversalmente.
trans·fer (trăns-fûr′) I. tr. -rr- *(to convey)* trasladar; *(to shift)* transferir —intr. *(to move)* trasladarse; *(to change carrier)* transbordar II. s. *(′fər)* *(ticket)* boleto de transbordo; *(of money)* transferencia; *(of power)* transmisión *f*.
trans·fer·a·ble (:ə-bəl) adj. transferible.
trans·fer·al (:əl) s. transferencia.
trans·fer·ence (:əns) s. transferencia.
trans·fig·u·ra·tion (trăns-fĭg′yə-rā′shən) s. transfiguración *f*.
trans·fig·ure (-′yər) tr. *(to alter radically)* transfigurar; *(to exalt)* exaltar, glorificar.
trans·fix (trăns-fĭks′) tr. traspasar, atravesar; FIG. paralizar, inmovilizar.
trans·form (trăns-fôrm′) tr. transformar.
trans·for·ma·tion (′fər-mā′shən) s. transformación *f*.
trans·form·er (-fôr′mər) s. transformador *m*.
trans·fuse (trăns-fyōōz′) tr. *(to transfer)* transvasar, trasegar; *(to permeate)* impregnar; MED.

hacer una transfusión de *o* a.
trans·fu·sion (:fyōō′zhən) s. trasiego; MED. transfusión *f*.
trans·gress (trăns-grĕs′) tr. *(a limit)* traspasar; *(the law)* infringir —intr. *(to sin)* pecar; *(to break the law)* cometer una infracción.
trans·gres·sion (:grĕsh′ən) s. *(of a law)* infracción *f*; *(of a rule)* transgresión *f*; *(of limits)* traspaso; *(sin)* pecado.
trans·gres·sor (:grĕs′ər) s. *(offender)* transgresor *m*; *(sinner)* pecador *m*.
tran·sience (trăn′shəns) transitoriedad *f*.
tran·sient (:shənt) I. adj. transitorio; *(passing through)* transeúnte II. s. transeúnte *mf*.
tran·sis·tor (trăn-zĭs′tər) s. transistor *m*.
tran·sis·tor·ize (:tə-rīz′) tr. equipar con transistores a.
tran·sit (trăn′sĭt) s. tránsito; *(transport)* transporte *m*; *(transition)* transición *f*.
tran·si·tion (trăn zĭsh′ən) s. transición *f*.
tran·si·tion·al (:ə-nəl) adj. de transición.
tran·si·tive (trăn′sĭ-tĭv) adj. transitivo.
tran·si·to·ry (trăn′sĭ-tôr′ē) adj. transitorio.
trans·late (trăns-lāt′, ′′) tr. traducir; *(to explain)* explicar; *(to convert)* convertir.
trans·la·tion (-lā′shən) s. traducción *f*.
trans·la·tor (:lā′tər) s. traductor *m*.
trans·lit·er·ate (trăns-lĭt′ə-rāt′) tr. traducir de un alfabeto a otro.
trans·lu·cent (trăns-lōō′sənt) adj. translúcido.
trans·lu·cid (:sĭd) adj. translúcido.
trans·mi·grate (trăns-mī′grāt′) intr. transmigrar.
trans·mi·gra·tion (′-grā′shən) s. transmigración *f*.
trans·mis·sion (trăns-mĭsh′ən) s. transmisión *f* ♦ **automatic t.** AUTO. cambio automático.
trans·mit (trăns-mĭt′) tr. & intr. -tt- transmitir.
trans·mit·tal (:l) s. transmisión *f*.
trans·mit·ter (:ər) s. *(apparatus)* transmisor *m*; *(station)* emisora.
trans·mu·ta·tion (trăns′myōō-tā′shən) s. transmutación *f*.
trans·mute (trăns-myōōt′) tr. transmutar.
trans·o·ce·an·ic (trăns′ō-shē-ăn′ĭk) adj. transoceánico.
tran·som (trăn′səm) s. *(window)* montante *m*, listón *m*; *(crosspiece)* travesaño.
tran·son·ic (trăn-sŏn′ĭk) adj. transónico.
trans·par·ence (trăns-pâr′əns) s. transparencia.
trans·par·en·cy (:ən-sē) s. transparencia; *(slide)* diapositiva.
trans·par·ent (:ənt) adj. transparente.
trans·pi·ra·tion (trăn′spə-rā′shən) adj. transpiración *f*.
tran·spire (trăn-spīr′) tr. transpirar —intr. *(to exude)* transpirar; *(to reveal)* revelarse; *(to happen)* acontecer.
trans·plant I. tr. (trăns-plănt′) trasplantar II. s. (′′) trasplante *m*.
trans·port I. tr. (trăns-pôrt′) transportar; *(to enrapture)* embelesar II. s. (′′) transporte *m*; *(rapture)* embeleso; *(ship)* buque *m* de transporte; *(aircraft)* avión *m* de transporte.
trans·por·ta·tion (trăns′pər-tā′shən) s. transportación *f*; *(state)* transporte *m*.
trans·pose (trăns-pōz′) tr. transponer; *(to transform)* transformar.
trans·po·si·tion (′pə-zĭsh′ən) s. transposición *f*; MÚS. transporte *m*.
trans·ship (trăns-shĭp′) tr. -pp- transbordar.

tran·sub·stan·ti·ate (trăn'səb-stăn'shē-āt') tr. transubstanciar.

trans·ver·sal (trăns-vûr'səl) adj. & s. transversal *f.*

trans·verse (:vûrs') adj. & s. transversal *f.*

trap (trăp) I. s. trampa; TEC. sifón *m*, bombillo; DEP. lanzaplatos; *(in golf)* hoyo de arena ♦ **shut your t.!** JER. ¡cierra el pico! ♦ **t. door** escotillón ♦ **t. rock** basalto II. tr. **-pp-** *(to ensnare)* coger en una trampa; *(to catch)* atrapar; *(to seal off)* detener —intr. poner trampas.

tra·peze (tră-pēz') s. trapecio ♦ **t. artist** trapecista.

trap·per (trăp'ər) s. trampero.

trap·ping (trăp'ĭng) s. ♦ pl. adornos, atavíos; *(for a horse)* jaeces, arreos.

trap·shoot·ing (trăp'shōō'tĭng) s. tiro al plato.

trash (trăsh) I. s. desechos, desperdicios; *(people)* gentuza II. tr. *(to discard)* desechar; JER. *(to smash)* destrozar.

trash·y ('ē) adj. **-i-** malo.

trau·ma (trô'mə) s. [pl. **s** *o* **-ata**] trauma *m.*

trau·mat·ic (-măt'ĭk) adj. traumático.

trau·ma·tize ('mə-tīz') tr. traumatizar.

tra·vail (trə-vāl') s. *(weariness)* fatiga; *(anguish)* congoja; *(childbirth)* dolores *m* de parto.

trav·el (trăv'əl) I. intr. viajar; *(to be a salesman)* ser viajante; *(light, sound)* propagarse; *(to spread)* extenderse; *(to associate)* frecuentar ♦ **to t. light** viajar con poco equipaje ♦ **traveling salesman** viajante de comercio —tr. viajar por II. s. viaje *m*; *(traffic)* tráfico ♦ pl. viajes.

trav·el(l)ed (:əld) adj. que ha viajado mucho; *(frequented)* frecuentado.

trav·el·(l)er (:ə-lər) s. viajero; G.B. *(salesman)* viajante *m* ♦ **t.'s check** cheque de viajero.

trav·e·log(ue) (:ə-lôg') s. documental *m o* conferencia ilustrada sobre un viaje.

tra·ver·sal (trə-vûr'səl) s. travesía.

tra·verse (trə-vûrs') I. tr. cruzar; *(to move along)* recorrer —intr. cruzar II. s. (trăv'ərs) travesía; *(route)* ruta sinuosa; *(crosspiece)* travesaño III. adj. (trăv'ərs, trə-vûrs') transversal.

trav·es·ty (trăv'ĭ-stē) I. s. parodia II. tr. parodiar.

trawl (trôl) MARÍT. I. s. red barredera II. tr. & intr. pescar con red barredera.

trawl·er (trô'lər) s. *(boat)* jábega; *(fisherman)* jabeguero.

tray (trā) s. bandeja.

treach·er·ous (trĕch'ər-əs) adj. traicionero; *(dangerous)* peligroso.

treach·er·y (:ə-rē) s. traición *f.*

trea·cle (trē'kəl) s. melaza.

tread (trĕd) I. tr. **trod, trod(den)** pisar; *(to trample)* pisotear; *(to crush)* aplastar ♦ **to t. water** pedalear en el agua ♦ **well-trodden path** camino trillado —intr. pisar; *(to walk)* andar, caminar ♦ **to t. lightly** andar con tiento II. s. pisada; *(horizontal step)* huella (de un escalón); *(of a tire)* banda de rodadura.

tread·le ('l) I. s. pedal *m* II. intr. pedalear.

tread·mill (:mĭl') s. rueda de andar; *(routine)* rutina.

trea·son (trē'zən) s. traición *f.*

trea·son·a·ble (:zə-nə-bəl) adj. traicionero.

trea·son·ous (:nəs) adj. traicionero.

treas·ure (trĕzh'ər) I. s. tesoro II. tr. *(to accumulate)* atesorar; *(to appreciate)* estimar.

treas·ur·er (:ər) s. tesorero.

treas·ure-trove (trōv') s. tesoro hallado; *(discovery)* hallazgo.

treas·ur·y (trĕzh'ə-rē) s. *(office)* tesorería; *(public funds)* erario público.

treat (trēt) I. tr. tratar; *(to invite)* convidar, invitar; *(to consider)* tomar ♦ **to t. oneself to** darse el lujo de —intr. invitar, convidar II. s. *(present)* regalo; *(invitation)* invitación *f*; *(delight)* placer *m.*

treat·a·ble (trē'tə-bəl) adj. tratable.

trea·tise (trē'tĭs) s. tratado.

treat·ment (trēt'mənt) s. tratamiento.

trea·ty (trē'tē) s. convenio, tratado.

tre·ble (trĕb'əl) I. adj. MAT. triple; MÚS. de soprano, de tiple II. s. MÚS. soprano, tiple *m* III. tr. & intr. triplicar(se).

tree (trē) I. s. árbol *m*; *(for shoes)* horma; *(post)* poste *m* ♦ **to bark up the wrong t.** equivocarse ♦ **to be up a t.** estar en un aprieto II. tr. *(animal)* hacer refugiarse en un árbol; FIG. poner en un aprieto.

tree·top ('tŏp') s. copa.

tre·foil (trē'foil', trĕf'oil) s. trébol *m.*

trek (trĕk) I. s. viaje largo y difícil II. intr. **-kk-** hacer un viaje largo.

trel·lis (trĕl'ĭs) s. *(frame)* enrejado; *(arbor)* parra.

trem·ble (trĕm'bəl) I. intr. temblar II. s. temblor *m.*

tre·men·dous (trĭ-mĕn'dəs) adj. terrible; *(enormous)* tremendo; *(marvelous)* extraordinario.

trem·or (trĕm'ər) s. temblor *m.*

trem·u·lous (trĕm'yə-ləs) adj. trémulo, tembloroso; *(timid)* tímido.

trench (trĕnch) s. *(furrow)* zanja; *(ditch)* cuneta, foso; MIL. trinchera ♦ **t. coat** impermeable ♦ **t. mouth** inflamación de las encías.

trench·ant (trĕn'chənt) adj. vigoroso; *(incisive)* mordaz.

trend (trĕnd) I. s. *(direction)* dirección *f*; *(tendency)* tendencia; *(fashion)* moda II. intr. tender a, inclinarse a.

trend·set·ter ('sĕt'ər) s. persona que dicta una moda.

trend·y (trĕn'dē) adj. **-i-** FAM. que sigue la última moda.

trep·i·da·tion (trĕp'ĭ-dā'shən) s. aprensión *f.*

tres·pass (trĕs'pəs, :păs') I. intr. *(to infringe upon)* infringir; *(to enter)* entrar ilegalmente; RELIG. pecar II. s. violación *f*; DER. transgresión *f* ♦ **no trespassing** prohibido el paso ♦ pl. RELIG. pecados.

tres·pass·er (trĕs'pə-sər) s. intruso; DER. infractor *m*; RELIG. pecador *m.*

tress (trĕs) s. mechón *f* ♦ pl. cabellera.

tres·tle (trĕs'əl) s. caballete *m.*

tri·ad (trī'ăd') s. tríada.

tri·al (trī'əl) I. s. *(testing)* prueba, ensayo; *(experiment)* experimento; *(attempt)* tentativa; *(hardship)* dificultad *f*; *(test)* prueba; DER. proceso, juicio ♦ **on t.** *(being judged)* enjuiciado, procesado; *(being tested)* a título de prueba ♦ **to bring to t.** encausar, enjuiciar ♦ **to do something by t. and error** hacer algo por un método de tanteos ♦ **to go on t.** ser procesado II. adj. DER. procesal; *(testing)* de prueba ♦ **t. run** experimento.

tri·an·gle (trī'ăng'gəl) s. triángulo.

tri·an·gu·lar (-'gyə-lər) adj. triangular.

tri·an·gu·late (:lāt') I. tr. triangular II. adj. triangulado.

trib·al (trī'bəl) adj. tribal.

tribe (trīb) s. tribu *f*; FAM. familia numerosa.

tribes·man (trībz'mən) s. [pl. **-men**] miembro

de una tribu.

trib·u·la·tion (trĭb'yə-lā'shən) s. tribulación f.

tri·bu·nal (trī-byōō'nəl) s. tribunal m.

trib·une (trĭb'yōōn') s. HIST. tribuno; *(protector)* defensor m de los derechos.

trib·u·tar·y (trĭb'yə-tĕr'ē) I. adj. tributario II. s. *(river)* afluente m; *(person)* tributario.

trib·ute (trĭb'yōōt) s. tributo; *(gift)* ofrenda.

trice (trīs) s. instante m ♦ **in a t.** en un abrir y cerrar de ojos.

tri·cen·ten·ni·al (trī'sĕn-tĕn'ē-əl) I. adj. de trescientos años II. s. tricentenario.

tri·ceps (trī'sĕps') s. [pl. inv. o **es**] triceps m.

trich·i·no·sis (trĭk'ə-nō'sĭs) s. triquinosis f.

trick (trĭk) I. s. truco; *(swindle)* estafa; *(prank)* travesura; *(special skill)* maña; *(of cards)* baza ♦ **a dirty t.** una trastada • **not to miss a t.** no perder una • **to be up to one's old tricks** volver a las andadas • **to do the t.** resolver el problema, surtir efecto II. tr. engañar, burlar; *(to swindle)* estafar III. adj. de truco ♦ **t. photography** trucaje • **t. question** pregunta de pega.

trick·er·y ('ə-rē) s. engaño.

trick·le (trĭk'əl) I. intr. gotear ♦ **to t.** in llegar en pequeñas cantidades II. s. goteo; *(small amount)* gota.

trick·ster (trĭk'stər) s. burlador m.

trick·y (-ē) adj. -i- *(wily)* astuto; *(situation, problem)* delicado.

tri·col·or (trī'kŭl'ər) s. bandera tricolor.

tri·corn(e) (:kôrn') s. tricornio.

tri·cot (trē'kō) s. tricot m.

tri·cy·cle (trī'sĭ-kəl) s. triciclo.

tri·dent (trīd'nt) s. tridente m.

tried (trīd) I. cf. try II. adj. probado.

tried-and-true ('n-trōō') adj. seguro.

tri·fle (trī'fəl) I. s. nadería; *(small amount)* poquito; *(dessert)* bizcocho borracho ♦ **a t.** un poquito, algo II. intr. *(to jest)* bromear; *(to play)* jugar *(with con).*

tri·fling (:lĭng) adj. insignificante, frívolo.

trig (trĭg) adj. acicalado.

trig·ger (trĭg'ər) I. s. *(of a firearm)* gatillo; *(of a mechanism)* disparador m; *(provocation)* provocación f II. tr. poner en funcionamiento.

trig·ger-hap·py (:hăp'ē) adj. pronto a disparar; JER. impulsivo.

trig·o·nom·e·try (trĭg'ə-nŏm'ĭ-trē) s. trigonometría.

trike (trīk) s. FAM. triciclo.

tri·lat·er·al (trī-lăt'ər-əl) s. trilátero.

trill (trĭl) s. gorjeo; MÚS. trino.

tril·lion (trĭl'yən) s. billón m; G.B. trillón m.

tril·o·gy (trĭl'ə-jē) s. trilogía.

trim (trĭm) I. tr. **-mm-** *(to make tidy)* ordenar; *(hair, nails)* recortar; *(branches)* podar; *(to ornament)* decorar; *(to reduce)* reducir; *(sails)* orientar; AVIA., MARÍT. *(to balance)* equilibrar —intr. estar equilibrado II. s. condición f; *(ornamentation)* adorno; *(cuttings)* recorte m; *(of a ship)* asiento; *(of sails)* orientación f; AVIA. equilibrio ♦ **in good t.** en forma • **out of t.** *(person)* en baja forma; *(boat)* mal estibado III. adj. **-mm-** *(in good order)* arreglado; *(elegant)* elegante; *(looking well)* bien parecido.

tri·mes·ter (trī-mĕs'tər) s. trimestre m.

trim·ming (trĭm'ĭng) s. adorno; FAM. *(beating)* paliza, zurra ♦ **t.** *(accesories)* accesorios; CUL. guarnición; *(scraps)* recortes.

trin·i·ty (trĭn'ĭ-tē) s. trío.

trin·ket (trĭng'kĭt) s. *(ornament)* dije m; *(trifle)* chuchería.

tri·o (trē'ō) s. trío.

trip (trĭp) I. s. viaje m; *(excursion)* excursión f; *(stumble)* tropezón m, traspié m; *(mistake)* error m ♦ **round t.** viaje de ida y vuelta II. intr. **-pp-** *(to stumble)* dar un traspié; *(to move nimbly)* andar con paso ligero; *(to make a mistake)* equivocarse —tr. *(a person)* hacer tropezar o caer; *(an alarm)* hacer sonar; *(a catch, spring)* soltar, disparar ♦ **t. up** hacer confundir.

tripe (trīp) s. CUL. callos; FAM. tonterías.

tri·ple (trĭp'əl) I. adj. & s. triple m II. tr. & intr. triplicar(se).

tri·ple-space ('-spās') tr. & intr. escribir a máquina dejando dos líneas en blanco.

tri·plet (trĭp'lĭt) s. trío; *(baby)* trillizo.

tri·pod (trī'pŏd') s. trípode m.

tri·sect (trī'sĕkt') tr. trisecar.

tri·sec·tion (-sĕk'shən) s. trisección f.

trite (trīt) adj. trillado.

tri·umph (trī'əmf) I. intr. triunfar; *(to exult)* regocijarse II. s. triunfo; *(exultation)* regocijo.

tri·um·phal (-ŭm'fəl) adj. triunfal.

tri·um·phant (:fənt) adj. triunfante.

tri·um·vi·rate (tī-ŭm'vər-ĭt) s. triunvirato.

triv·et (trĭv'ĭt) s. *(for cooking)* trébedes m; *(for the table)* salvamantel m.

triv·i·a (trĭv'ē-ə) s.pl. trivialidades f.

triv·i·al (:əl) adj. insignificante, trivial.

triv·i·al·i·ty ('-ăl'ĭ-tē) s. trivialidad f.

trod (trŏd), **trod·den** (trŏd'n) cf. **tread**.

troll[1] (trōl) I. tr. *(to fish)* pescar con cebo de cuchara; *(to sing)* cantar en canon II. s. *(lure)* cebo de cuchara; MÚS. canon m.

troll[2] s. *(creature)* duende m, gnomo.

trol·ley (trŏl'ē) s. tranvía m; *(carriage)* carretilla; *(electric device)* colector m de corriente.

trol·lop (trŏl'əp) s. *(slattern)* mujer sucia; *(prostitute)* prostituta.

trom·bone (trŏm-bōn') s. trombón m.

troop (trōōp) I. s. *(group)* grupo; *(of animals)* manada; *(of soldiers)* escuadrón m; *(scouts)* grupo ♦ **o].** troops II. intr. ir en grupo.

troop·er (:pər) s. *(cavalryman)* soldado de caballería; *(horse)* caballo; *(policeman)* policía montado; *(state police)* patrullero ♦ **to be a t.** FAM. ser un profesional.

tro·phy (trō'fē) s. trofeo.

trop·ic (trŏp'ĭk) I. s. trópico II. adj. tropical.

trop·i·cal (:ĭ-kəl) adj. tropical.

trot (trŏt) I. s. *(gait)* trote m; *(jog)* paso corto; FAM. *(translation)* traducción f literal II. intr. **-tt-** *(to move)* trotar; *(to hurry)* apurarse —tr. hacer trotar ♦ **t. out** FAM. *(to bring out)* sacar a relucir; *(to show off)* hacer alarde de.

troth (trŏth, trōth) s. *(fidelity)* fidelidad f; *(betrothal)* compromiso ♦ **to plight one's t.** dar palabra de matrimonio.

trot·ter (trŏt'ər) s. trotón m.

trou·ba·dour (trōō'ba-dôr') s. trovador m.

trou·ble (trŭb'əl) I. s. *(affliction)* pena; *(misfortune)* desgracia; *(distress)* apuro, aprieto; *(worry)* preocupación f; *(annoyance)* disgusto; *(difficulty)* dificultad f; *(hindrance)* estorbo; *(bother)* molestia; *(effort)* esfuerzo; *(dispute)* conflicto; *(disturbance)* disturbios ♦ **no t. at all** con mucho gusto • **to ask o look for t.** FAM. buscarse líos • **to be in t.** estar en un aprieto • **to be worth the t.** valer la pena • **to get into t.** meterse en líos • **to start t.** dar problemas • **to stay out of t.** no meterse en líos • **to take the t. to** tomarse la molestia de • **what's the t.?** ¿cuál es el problema? II. tr. *(to disturb)* agitar, turbar; *(to affect)* afligir; *(to worry)* preocupar; *(to afflict)* afligir; *(to bother)* molestar —intr. *(to be worried)* preocuparse; *(to take pains)* molestarse.

trou·ble·mak·er (:mā′kər) s. perturbador *m*.

trou·ble·shoot·er (:shō̄′tər) s. mediador *m*.

trou·ble·some (:səm) adj. *(worrisome)* inquietante; *(difficult)* dificultoso.

trough (trôf) s. *(for drinking)* abrevadero; *(for feeding)* pesebre *m*; *(gutter)* canalón *m*; *(depression)* depresión *f*; *(low point)* mínimo; METEOR. zona de presiones bajas.

trounce (trouns) tr. zurrar; *(to defeat)* derrotar rotundamente.

troupe (trōōp) s. TEAT. compañía.

troup·er (trōō′pər) s. TEAT. actor *m*.

trou·sers (trou′zərz) s.pl. pantalones *m*.

trous·seau (trōō′sō) s. [pl. **s** *o* **-x**] ajuar *m*.

trout (trout) s. [pl. inv. *o* **s**] trucha.

trove (trōv) s. hallazgo.

trow·el (trou′əl) s. *(for leveling)* palustre *m*; *(for digging)* desplantador *m*.

troy (troi) adj. troy.

tru·an·cy (trōō′ən-sē) s. falta a clase.

tru·ant (:ənt) s. & adj. (persona) que hace novillos.

truce (trōōs) s. tregua.

truck¹ (trŭk) I. s. camión *m*; *(barrow)* carretilla; G.B., F.C. vagón raso II. tr. transportar en camión —intr. conducir un camión.

truck² I. tr. *(to barter)* trocar; *(to peddle)* vender de puerta en puerta —intr. comerciar II. s. *(garden produce)* hortalizas; *(exchange)* trueque *m*; FAM. *(business)* comercio ♦ **t. farm** huerto, huerta.

truck·age (′ij) s. transporte *m* por camión.

truck·er (:ər) s. camionero.

truck·ing (:ĭng) s. transporte *m* por camión.

truc·u·lent (trŭk′yə-lənt) adj. *(fierce)* feroz; *(pugnacious)* belicoso.

trudge (trŭj) I. intr. caminar con dificultad II. s. caminata larga y penosa.

true (trōō) I. adj. verdadero; *(loyal)* leal; *(legitimate)* legítimo; *(accurate)* exacto ♦ **to come t.** realizarse, cumplirse ♦ **t. to life** conforme a la realidad II. adv. verdaderamente; *(exactly)* exactamente III. s. verdad *f* ♦ **to be out of t.** estar desalineado IV. tr. rectificar, corregir.

true-blue (′blōō′) s. & adj. (persona) leal.

true-love (:lŭv′) s. amor *m*.

truf·fle (trŭf′əl) s. trufa.

tru·ism (trōō′ĭz′əm) s. perogrullada.

tru·ly (:lē) adv. verdaderamente; *(sincerely)* sinceramente; *(properly)* propiamente ♦ **yours t.** suyo atentamente, su seguro servidor.

trump (trŭmp) I. s. triunfo II. tr. matar con un triunfo —intr. ♦ **to t. up** inventar.

trum·pet (trŭm′pĭt) I. s. MÚS. trompeta; *(sound)* trompetilla II. intr. tocar la trompeta —tr. pregonar.

trun·cate (trŭng′kāt′) tr. truncar.

trun·cat·ed (:kā′tĭd) adj. truncado.

trun·cheon (trŭn′chən) s. cachiporra, porra.

trun·dle (trŭn′dl) I. s. carriola II. intr. rodar.

trunk (trŭngk) s. tronco; *(of an elephant)* trompa; *(luggage)* baúl *m*; *(of a car)* portaequipaje *m*, maletera ♦ pl. pantalones cortos ♦ **swimming t.** traje de baño.

truss (trŭs) I. s. MED. braguero; *(framework)* armazón *mf* II. tr. *(to tie up)* atar; *(to support)* apuntalar.

trust (trŭst) I. s. confianza; *(charge)* custodia;

(duty) deber *m*; *(hope)* fe *f*, esperanza; *(credit)* crédito; DER. fideicomiso; COM., FIN. trust *m*, consorcio ♦ **in t.** DER. en depósito • **to take on t.** creer a ojos cerrados • **t. fund** fondo fiduciario II. intr. *(to rely)* depender; *(to hope)* esperar, confiar —tr. tener confianza en, fiarse de; *(to believe)* creer; *(to hope)* esperar; *(to entrust)* confiar; COM., FIN. dar crédito a.

trus·tee (trŭs-tē′) s. *(administrator)* fideicomisario; *(member of a board)* síndico ♦ **board of trustees** consejo de administración

trus·tee·ship (:shĭp′) s. *(position)* cargo de síndico; *(territory)* fideicomiso.

trust·ful (trŭst′fəl) adj. confiado.

trust·ing (trŭs′tĭng) adj. confiado.

trust·wor·thy (trŭst′wûr′thē) adj. **-i-** de confianza.

trust·y (trŭs′tē) adj. **-i-** de confianza.

truth (trōōth) s. [pl. **s**] verdad *f*; *(exactitude)* exactitud *f*; *(reality)* realidad *f*; *(veracity)* veracidad *f*; *(sincerity)* sinceridad *f*.

truth·ful (′fəl) adj. *(honest)* sincero; *(true)* verídico.

truth·ful·ness (:nĭs) s. veracidad *f*.

try (trī) I. tr. *(to test, taste)* probar; *(to make an effort at)* tratar <to t. to ski tratar de esquiar>; DER. *(a case)* someter a juicio; *(a person)* juzgar, procesar ♦ **to t. on** probarse • **t. one's best** hacer todo lo posible • **to t. one's hand at** probar uno su habilidad en • **to t. out** probar —intr. esforzarse II. s. tentativa, intento.

try·ing (′ĭng) adj. irritante, molesto.

try·out (:out′) s. prueba de aptitud; *(audition)* audición *f*.

tryst (trīst) s. *(date)* cita; *(place)* lugar *m* de cita.

tsar (tsär) s. var. de **czar**.

tset·se fly (tsĕt′sē, tsĕt′-) s. mosca tse-tsé.

T-shirt (tē′shûrt′) s. camiseta.

T-square (tē′skwâr′) s. escuadra en T, regla T.

tub (tŭb) s. *(vessel)* tonel *m*; *(bathtub)* bañera; FAM. *(bath)* baño; *(ship)* carraca.

tu·ba (tōō′bə) s. tuba.

tu·bal (tōō′bəl) adj. tubárico, tubario.

tub·by (tŭb′ē) adj. **-i-** rechoncho.

tube (tōōb) s. tubo; ANAT. trompa; FAM. *(television)* tele *f*; G.B. *(subway)* metro.

tu·ber (tōō′bər) s. tubérculo.

tu·ber·cle (:kəl) s. tubérculo.

tu·ber·cu·lar (tōō-bûr′kyə-lər) adj. & s. tuberculoso.

tu·ber·cu·lin (:lĭn) s. tuberculina.

tu·ber·cu·lo·sis (-′-lō′sĭs) s. tuberculosis *f*.

tu·ber·cu·lous (-′-ləs) adj. tuberculoso.

tube·rose (tōōb′rōz′) s. tuberosa.

tu·ber·ous (tōō′bər-əs) adj. tuberoso.

tub·ing (tōō′bĭng) s. tubería.

tu·bu·lar (:byə-lər) adj. tubular.

tu·bule (:byōōl) s. tubo pequeño.

tuck (tŭk) I. tr. plegar ♦ **to t. away** esconder • **to t. in** *(to put in)* meter; *(in bed)* arropar —intr. hacer pliegues II. s. pliegue *m*.

tuck·er (tŭk′ər) tr. FAM. agotar.

Tues·day (tōōz′dē) s. martes *m*.

tuft (tŭft) s. mechón *m*; *(crest)* copete *m*.

tug (tŭg) I. tr. **-gg-** *(to pull)* tirar de; *(to drag)* arrastrar; *(to tow)* remolcar —intr. tirar fuerte II. s. tirón *m*; *(tugboat)* remolcador *m* ♦ **t. of war** DEP. juego de la cuerda; FIG. lucha.

tug·boat (′bōt′) s. remolcador *m*.

tu·i·tion (tōō-ĭsh′ən) s. matrícula; *(instruction)* enseñanza.

tu·lip (tōo′lĭp) s. tulipán m.

tulle (tōol) s. tul m.

tum·ble (tŭm′bəl) I. intr. (to roll) rodar; (to fall) caerse; (to collapse) derrumbarse ♦ to t. down derrumbarse • to t. out salir a montones —tr. (to knock down) derribar; (a government) derrocar ♦ to t. on dar con II. s. (fall) caída; (somersault) voltereta ♦ to take a t. caerse.

tum·ble-down (:doun′) adj. destartalado.

tum·bler (tŭm′blər) s. (acrobat) volatinero; (glass) vaso; (of a lock) seguro, guarda.

tum·ble·weed (:bəl-wēd′) s. planta rodadora.

tum·bling (:blĭng) s. acrobacia.

tu·me·fac·tion (tōo-mə-făk′shən) s. tumefacción f.

tu·mes·cence (tōo-mĕs′əns) s. tumescencia.

tu·mid (tōo′mĭd) adj. hinchado.

tum·my (tŭm′ē) s. FAM. barriga.

tum·my·ache (:āk′) s. FAM. dolor m de estómago.

tu·mor (tōo′mər) s. tumor m.

tu·mult (tōo′mŭlt′) s. (crowd) tumulto; (agitation) agitación f; (riot) motín m.

tu·mul·tu·ous (-mŭl′chōo-əs) adj. tumultuoso.

tu·na (tōo′nə) s. [pl. inv. o -s] atún m.

tun·dra (tŭn′drə) s. tundra.

tune (tōon) I. s. (melody) melodía; (pitch) tono; FIG. armonía ♦ in t. afinado • in t. with FIG. de acuerdo con • out of t. desafinado • to carry a t. cantar afinado • to change one's t. FIG. cambiar de tono • to the t. of FIG. por la cantidad de II. tr. MÚS. afinar; MEC. poner a punto ♦ to t. in RAD., TELEV. sintonizar • to t. out JER. (to ignore) no prestar atención a • to t. up MÚS. afinar; MEC. poner a punto —intr. ♦ to t. up afinar los instrumentos.

tune·ful (′fəl) adj. melodioso.

tun·er (tōo′nər) s. (person) afinador m; (device) sintonizador m.

tune-up (tōon′ŭp′) s. puesta a punto.

tung·sten (tŭng′stən) s. tungsteno.

tu·nic (tōo′nĭk) s. túnica.

tun·nel (tŭn′əl) I. s. túnel m II. tr. construir un túnel m; (to dig) cavar —intr. hacer un túnel.

tun·ny (tŭn′ē) s. [pl. inv. o -ies] atún m.

tur·ban (tûr′bən) s. turbante m.

tur·bid (tûr′bĭd) adj. (muddy) turbio; (dense) espeso; (confused) confuso.

tur·bine (tûr′bĭn′) s. turbina.

tur·bo·charg·er (tûr′bō-chär′jər) s. turbocompresor m.

tur·bo·jet (:jĕt′) s. turborreactor m.

tur·bo·prop (:prŏp′) s. turbopropulsor m.

tur·bot (tûr′bət) s. [pl. inv. o -s] rodaballo.

tur·bu·lence (tûr′byə-ləns) s. turbulencia.

tur·bu·lent (:lənt) adj. turbulento.

tu·reen (tōo-rēn′) s. sopera.

turf (tûrf) s. (sod) césped m; (piece of earth) tepe m; (peat) turba; JER. (territory) territorio; DEP. (track) hipódromo; (sport) hipismo.

tur·gid (tûr′jĭd) adj. MED. hinchado; FIG. ampuloso.

tur·key (tûr′kē) s. pavo; (failure) fracaso; (person) fracasado.

tur·mer·ic (tûr′mər-ĭk) s. cúrcuma.

tur·moil (tûr′moil′) s. confusión f.

turn (tûrn) I. tr. (to revolve) dar vueltas a; (to flip) pasar, volver; (to rotate) girar; (corner) dar la vuelta a, doblar; (to shape) tornear; (a phrase) construir; (to twist) torcer; (stomach) revolver; (to deflect) desviar, (to direct) dirigir; (age) cumplir; (to change color) cambiar el color de; (to transform) convertir, transformar ♦ to t. against volverse en contra de • to t. a profit producir una ganancia • to t. around (words) tergiversar, desvirtuar; (to turn over) dar vuelta a • to t. aside desviar • to t. away (to send away) negar la entrada a; (to deflect) rechazar; (head) volver; (eyes) desviar • to t. back hacer retroceder; (the clock) retrasar • to t. down (to diminish) bajar; (to reject) rechazar; (to fold) doblar, plegar • to t. in (to give over) entregar; (to betray) entregar a la policía; (to produce) hacer • to t. inside out poner al revés • to t. into volverse • to t. loose soltar • to t. off (radio, light) apagar; (tap, gas) cerrar; (electricity, water) cortar; (an engine) parar; JER. (to disgust) disgustar • to t. on (water, gas) abrir la llave; (radio) poner; (light) encender; (an engine) poner en marcha; (a tap) abrir; (stove, fire) encender, prender; (electrical current) conectar; (to become hostile) volverse en contra de; JER. (to excite) excitar • to t. one's back on volver la espalda a • to t. out (light) apagar; (to shut off) cerrar; (to manufacture) producir; (to evict) expulsar • to t. over (to reverse in position) invertir, volcar; (to think about) considerar; (to transfer) entregar • to t. over to (to transfer) traspasar; (to entrust) dejar a cargo de • to t. the tide of cambiar el curso o el rumbo de • to t. up (to find) encontrar, (radio, television) subir, poner más fuerte; (the collar) alzar • to t. upside down poner patas arriba —intr. (to rotate) girar; (to change direction) dar la vuelta; (to change) cambiar; (to become oneself) dedicarse; (to become transformed) transformarse, convertirse en; (to change color) cambiar de color; (to become) ponerse, volverse; (to curdle) cortarse; (to ferment) avinagrarse; (to sour) ponerse rancio ♦ to t. around darse vuelta • to t. aside desviarse • to t. away (to begin to leave) alejarse; (to turn one's back) volver la cara o la espalda • to t. back retroceder • to t. in FAM (to go to bed) acostarse; (to point inward) estar vuelto hacia adentro • to t. off desviarse • to t. out (to be found to be) resultar; (to point outward) estar vuelto hacia afuera • to t. over (car, truck) volcar; (to shift position) voltearse • to t. to recurrir a <who can I t. to? ¿a quién puedo recurrir?>; (to begin) empezar • to t. up aparecer II. s. vuelta; (rotation) rotación f; (change) cambio; (opportunity) oportunidad f; (adeptness) aptitud f; (inclination) inclinación f; (deed) proceder m; (advantage) provecho; (twist in shape) torcedura; (shock) susto, sobresalto ♦ at every t. a cada instante • at the t. of the century al final del siglo pasado • to take a t. for the better, worse mejorarse, empeorarse • to take turns at turnarse.

turn·a·bout (tûrn′ə-bout′) s. cambio radical.

turn·a·round (:ə-round′) s. vuelta.

turn·buck·le (:bŭk′əl) s. tensor m.

turn·coat (:kōt′) s. traidor m.

turn·down (:doun′) s. rechazo.

turned-up (tûrnd′ŭp′) adj. (nose) respingada; (folded up) doblado hacia arriba; (collar) alto.

turn·ing (tûr′nĭng) s. viraje m ♦ t. point momento crucial.

tur·nip (tûr′nĭp) s. nabo.

turn·key (tûrn′kē′) s. carcelero.

turn·off (:ôf′) s. desvío; JER. (disappointment) decepción f.

turn·out (:out′) s. (attendance) concurrencia;

(spectators) entrada; *(outfit)* atuendo.

turn·o·ver (:ō' vər) s. *(upset)* vuelco; *(reversal)* cambio brusco; *(pastry)* empanada; COM. *(of stock)* movimiento de mercancías; *(of business)* volumen de negocios; *(of sales)* volumen de ventas; *(of staff)* cambio de personal.

turn·pike (:pīk') s. autopista de peaje.

turn·screw (:skrōō') s. destornillador *m.*

turn·stile (:stīl') s. torniquete *m.*

turn·ta·ble (:tā' bəl) s. *(platform)* plataforma giratoria; *(of a phonograph)* plato.

tur·pen·tine (tûr' pən-tīn') s. trementina.

tur·pi·tude (tûr'pĭ-tōōd') s. bajeza.

tur·quoise (tûr'kwoiz', :koiz') adj. & s. turquesa.

tur·ret (tûr'ĭt) s. torreón *m*; MIL. torre blindada.

tur·tle (tûr'tl) s. tortuga.

tur·tle·dove (tûr'tl-dŭv') s. tórtola.

tur·tle·neck (tûr'tl-nĕk') s. cuello vuelto *o* alto; *(sweater)* suéter *m* con cuello vuelto.

tusk (tŭsk) s. colmillo grande.

tus·sle (tŭs'əl) I. intr. forcejear II. s. forcejeo.

tut (tŭt) interj. ¡vaya!, ¡basta!

tu·te·lage (tōōt'l-ĭj) s. tutela.

tu·te·lar·y·iar (tōōt' ē/ ər) adj. tutelar.

tu·tor (tōō' tər) I. s. profesor *m* particular; *(in a family)* ayo; *(in universities)* tutor *m* II. tr. dar clases particulares a —intr. ser tutor.

tu·to·ri·al (-tôr'ē-əl) I. adj. de tutor II. clase *f* particular

tu·tu (tōō'tōō) s. tutú *m.*

tu·xe·do (tŭk-sē'dō) s. [pl. **(e)s** smoking *m.*

TV (tē'vē') s. [pl. **(')s** televisión *f*; *(set)* televisor *m..*

twad·dle (twŏd'l) s. tonterías.

twang (twăng) I. intr. *(string)* vibrar; *(voice)* ganguear —tr. hacer vibrar II. s. sonido vibrante; *(of guitar)* tañido; *(voice)* gangueo.

twang·y (' ē) adj. gangoso.

tweak (twēk) s. I. tr. pellizcar II. s. pellizco.

tweed (twēd) s. tejido de lana ♦ pl. traje de lana.

tweed·y (twē'dē) adj. -i- parecido a la lana; *(wearing tweeds)* que viste con traje de lana.

tweet (twēt) I. intr. piar II. s. pío pío.

tweeze (twēz) tr. sacar con pinzas.

tweez·ers (twē'zərz) s.pl. pinzas.

twelfth (twĕlfth) I. s. doce *m*; *(part)* doceavo II. adj. *(place)* duodécimo; *(part)* doceava.

twelve (twĕlv) s. & adj. doce *m* ♦ **t. o'clock** las doce.

twen·ti·eth (twĕn'tē-ĭth) I. s. veinte *m*; *(part)* vigésimo II. adj. vigésimo.

twen·ty (twĕn'tē) adj. & s. veinte *m.*

twerp (twûrp) s. JER. imbécil *mf*, idiota *mf.*

twice (twīs) adv. dos veces, el doble.

twid·dle (twĭd'l) tr. hacer girar —intr. ♦ **to t. one's thumbs** matar el tiempo.

twig (twĭg) s. ramita.

twi·light (twī'līt') I. s. *(time)* crepúsculo; *(light)* media luz; *(decline)* ocaso II. adj. crepuscular.

twill (twĭl) s. tela asargada.

twin (twĭn) I. s. gemelo; *(counterpart)* doble *m* ♦ **Siamese twins** hermanos siameses II. adj. gemelo ♦ **t. bed** cama separada *o* gemela.

twine (twīn) I. s. cordel *m*, bramante *m* II. tr. *(to intertwine)* trenzar; *(to encircle)* ceñir —intr. enroscarse.

twinge (twĭnj) I. s. *(pain)* punzada; *(remorse)* remordimiento II. tr. & intr. dar punzadas.

twin·kle (twĭng'kəl) I. intr. centellear, parpadear; *(eyes)* brillar II. s. centelleo,

parpadeo; *(of eyes)* brillo.

twin·kling (:klĭng) s. centelleo; FIG. instante *m.*

twin-screw (twĭn'skrōō') adj. de dos hélices.

twin-size (:sīz') adj. de cama gemela.

twirl (twûrl) tr. girar —intr. *(to spin around)* dar vueltas; *(to whirl)* girar en redondo.

twist (twĭst) I. tr. torcer; *(to twine)* enrollar; *(a cork, jar top)* dar vueltas a; *(meanings)* tergiversar, desvirtuar ♦ **to t. off** romper retorciendo —intr. torcerse, retorcerse; *(to coil)* enrollarse; *(to meander)* dar vueltas ♦ **to t. and turn** *(road)* serpentear; *(in bed)* dar vueltas II. s. torcimiento; *(of wire)* vuelta; *(of a road, river)* vuelta, recodo; *(of an ankle)* torcedura; *(unexpected change)* giro imprevisto.

twist·er (twĭs'tər) s. ciclón *m*, tornado.

twit (twĭt) I. tr. **-tt-** burlarse de II. s. burla; JER. imbécil *mf.*

twitch (twĭch) I. tr. tirar bruscamente de —intr. crisparse II. s. tic *m*; *(tug)* tirón *m.*

twit·ter (twĭt'ər) I. intr. *(to chirp)* gorjear; *(to chatter)* parlotear II. s. *(chirp)* gorjeo; *(flutter)* agitación *f.*

two (tōō) s. & adj. dos *m* ♦ **to be t. of a kind** ser tal para cual ♦ **to put t. and t. together** atar cabos ♦ **t. cents worth** FAM. opinión ♦ **t. hundred** doscientos ♦ **t. o'clock** las dos.

two-bit ('bĭt') adj. JER. de poca monta.

two-by-four (:bī-fôr') s. madera de dos por cuatro pulgadas.

two-di·men·sion·al ('dĭ-mĕn'shə-nəl, 'dī-) adj. de dos dimensiones.

two-edged ('ĕjd') adj. de doble filo.

two-faced (:fāst') adj. de dos caras; *(false)* falso.

two-fist·ed (:fĭs'tĭd) adj. FAM. viril.

two·fold (:fōld') I. adj. doble II. adv. dos veces.

two·pence (tŭp'əns) s. [pl. inv. *o* **s**] G.B. dos peniques *m*; FIG. comino.

two·pen·ny (tŭp'ə-nē, tōō'pĕn'ē) adj. de dos peniques; *(cheap)* barato.

two-piece (tōō'pēs') adj. de dos piezas.

two·some (:səm) s. pareja.

two-time (:tīm') tr. JER. engañar.

two-tim·er (:tīm'ər) s. JER. traidor *m.*

two-way (:wā') adj. de doble dirección; TEL. emisor y receptor.

ty·coon (tī-kōōn') s. magnate *m.*

tyke (tīk) s. FAM. chiquillo travieso; *(dog)* perro que no es de raza.

tym·pan (tĭm'pən) s. tímpano.

tym·pa·nist (:pə-nĭst) s. timbalero.

tym·pa·num (:nəm) s. [pl. **s** *o* **-na**] tímpano.

tym·pa·ny (:nē) s. tímpanos.

type (tīp) I. s. tipo II. tr. *(with a typewriter)* escribir a máquina; *(blood)* determinar el grupo sanguíneo de; *(to classify)* clasificar —intr. escribir a máquina.

type·cast ('kăst') tr. **-cast** TEAT. encasillar.

type·face (:fās') s. tipografía.

type·script (:skrĭpt') s. texto mecanografiado.

type·set (:sĕt') tr. **-set, -tting** componer.

type·set·ter (:sĕt'ər) s. tipógrafo.

type·set·ting (:sĕt'ĭng) s. composición *f.*

type·write (:rīt') tr. **-wrote, -written** mecanografiar —intr. escribir a máquina.

type·writ·er (tīp'rī'tər) s. máquina de escribir.

type·writ·ing (:tĭng) s. mecanografía.

ty·phoid (tī'foid') adj. tifoideo.

ty·phoon (tī-fōōn') s. tifón *m.*

ty·phus (tī'fəs) s. tifus *m.*

typ·i·cal (tĭp'ĭ-kəl) adj. típico.

typ·i·fy (:fī') tr. *(to embody)* representar el tipo de; *(to symbolize)* simbolizar.

typ·ing (tī'pĭng) s. mecanografía.

typ·ist (tī'pĭst) s. mecanógrafo.

ty·po (tī'pō) s. FAM. error tipográfico.

ly·pog·ra·pher (tī-pŏg'rə-fər) s. tipógrafo.

ty·pog·ra·phy (:fē) s. tipografía.

ty·pol·o·gy (tī-pŏl'ə-jē) s. tipología.

ty·ran·ni·cal (tĭ-răn'ĭ-kəl) adj. tiránico.

tyr·an·nize (tĭr'ə-nīz') tr. tiranizar.

tyr·an·nous (:nəs) adj. tiránico.

tyr·an·ny (:nē) s. tiranía.

ty·rant (tī'rənt) s. tirano.

ty·ro (tī'rō) s. aprendiz *m*. principiante *mf*.

tzar (tsär) var. de **czar.**

tza·ri·na (tsä-rē'nə) var. de **czarina.**

U

u, U (yōō) s. vigésima primera letra del alfabeto inglés.

u·biq·ui·tous (yōō-bĭk'wĭ-təs) adj. ubicuo.

u·biq·ui·ty (:tē) s. ubicuidad *f.*

U-boat (yōō'bōt') s. submarino alemán.

ud·der (ŭd'ər) s. ubre *f.*

UFO (yōō'ěf-ō') s. [pl. **('**)**s**] AER. ovni.

ugh (ŭg, ŭk) interj. ¡uf!

ug·li·ness (ŭg'lē-nĭs) s. fealdad *f.*

ug·ly (ŭg'lē) adj. -**i**- feo; *(unpleasant)* desagradable; *(bad)* malo; *(sky)* amenazante.

uh-huh (ŭ-hŭ') interj. FAM. sí, ajá.

u·ku·le·le (yōō'kə-lā'lē) s. ukelele *m.*

ul·cer (ŭl'sər) s. úlcera; FIG. cáncer *m.*

ul·cer·ate (ŭl'sə-rāt') tr. & intr. ulcerar(se).

ul·cer·ous (ŭl'sər-əs) adj. ulceroso.

ul·na (ŭl'nə) s. [pl. **-ae** *o* -**as**] ANAT. cúbito.

ul·ster (ŭl'stər) s. abrigo amplio y largo.

ul·te·ri·or (ŭl-tîr'ē-ər) adj. ulterior ♦ **u. motive** motivo oculto.

ul·ti·mate (ŭl'tə-mĭt) I. adj. último; *(final)* final; *(fundamental)* fundamental; *(maximum)* máximo II. s. lo último.

ul·ti·ma·tum ('-mā'təm) s. [pl. **s** *o* -**ta**] ultimátum *m.*

ul·tra (ŭl'trə) adj. excesivo, extremado.

ul·tra·con·ser·va·tive ('-kən-sûr'və-tĭv) adj. & s. ultraconservador *m.*

ul·tra·ma·rine (:mə-rēn') I. s. azul ultramarino II. adj. de color azul ultramarino; *(beyond the sea)* ultramarino.

ul·tra·mod·ern (:mŏd'ərn) adj. ultramoderno.

ul·tra·son·ic (:sŏn'ĭk) adj. ultrasónico.

ul·tra·sound ('-sound') s. ultrasonido.

ul·tra·vi·o·let ('-vī'ə-lĭt) I. adj. ultravioleta II. s. luz *f* ultravioleta.

u·lu·late (ŭl'yə-lāt') intr. ulular.

um·bil·i·cal (ŭm-bĭl'ĭ-kəl) I. adj. umbilical ♦ **u. cord** cordón umbilical II. s. ASTRONÁUT. línea de abastecimiento.

um·bil·i·cus (:kəs) s. [pl. **-ci**] ombligo.

um·brage (ŭm'brĭj) s. ofensa ♦ **to take u. at** ofenderse por.

um·brel·la (ŭm-brĕl'ə) s. paraguas *m* ♦ **u. organization** POL. cuerpo coordinador.

um·pire (ŭm'pīr') I. s. árbitro II. tr. arbitrar.

ump·teen (ŭmp'tēn') adj. FAM. innumerables.

ump·teenth (-tēnth') adj. enésimo.

un·a·bat·ed (ŭn'ə-bā'tĭd) adj. no disminuido.

un·a·ble (ŭn-ā'bəl) adj. incapaz

un·a·bridged (ŭn'ə-brĭjd') adj. no abreviado.

un·ac·cent·ed (ŭn-ăk'sĕn-tĭd) adj. sin acento.

un·ac·cept·a·ble (ŭn'ăk-sĕp'tə-bəl) adj. inaceptable.

un·ac·com·pa·nied (ŭn'ə-kŭm'pə-nēd) adj. solo.

un·ac·com·plished (ŭn'ə-kŏm'plĭsht) adj. falto de aptitudes *o* cualidades.

un·ac·count·a·ble (ŭn'ə-koun'tə-bəl) adj. inexplicable; *(not responsible)* no responsable.

un·ac·count·ed (ŭn'ə-koun'tĭd) adj. ♦ **u. for** desaparecido; *(unexplained)* inexplicado.

un·ac·cus·tomed (ŭn'ə-kŭs'təmd) adj. no acostumbrado; *(unusual)* insólito.

un·ac·knowl·edged (ŭn'ăk-nŏl'ĭjd) adj. no reconocido; *(unanswered)* no contestado.

un·ac·quaint·ed (ŭn'ə-kwān'tĭd) adj. ♦ **u. with** ignorante de.

un·a·dorned (ŭn'ə-dôrnd') adj. sin adorno.

un·a·dul·ter·at·ed (ŭn'ə-dŭl'tə-rā'tĭd) adj. no adulterado.

un·ad·vised (ŭn'əd-vīzd') adj. no informado; *(imprudent)* irreflexivo.

un·af·fect·ed (ŭn'ə-fĕk'tĭd) adj. no afectado; *(natural)* sin afectación.

un·a·fraid (ŭn'ə-frād') adj. sin temor.

un·aid·ed (ŭn-ā'dĭd) adj. sin ayuda.

un·al·loyed (ŭn'ə-loid') adj. no mezclado.

un·am·big·u·ous (ŭn'ăm-bĭg'yōō-əs) adj. sin ambigüedad.

u·na·nim·i·ty (yōō'nə-nĭm'ĭ-tē) s. unanimidad *f.*

u·nan·i·mous (yōō-năn'ə-məs) adj. unánime.

un·an·nounced (ŭn'ə-nounst') adj. sin ser anunciado.

un·an·swer·a·ble (ŭn-ăn'sər-ə-bəl) adj. incontestable.

un·ap·pe·tiz·ing (ŭn-ăp'ĭ-tī'zĭng) adj. poco apetitoso; *(not interesting)* poco apetecible.

un·ap·proach·a·ble (ŭn'ə-prō'chə-bəl) adj. inaccesible.

un·armed (ŭn-ärmd') adj. desarmado; *(defenseless)* indefenso.

un·asked (ŭn-ăskt') adj. no solicitado; *(question)* sin formular; *(guest)* no convidado.

un·as·sail·a·ble (ŭn'ə-sā'lə-bəl) adj. inexpugnable.

un·as·sist·ed (ŭn'ə-sĭs'tĭd) adj. sin ayuda.

un·as·sum·ing (ŭn'ə-sōō'mĭng) adj. modesto.

un·at·tached (ŭn'ə-tăcht') adj. suelto; *(not married)* soltero.

un·at·tain·a·ble (ŭn'ə-tā'nə-bəl) adj. inalcanzable.

un·at·tend·ed (ŭn'ə-tĕn'dĭd) adj. desatendido.

un·at·test·ed (ŭn'ə-tĕs'tĭd) adj. no atestiguado.

un·at·trac·tive (ŭn'ə-trăk'tĭv) adj. inatractivo.

un·au·thor·ized (ŭn-ô'thə-rīzd') adj. desautorizado, sin autorización.

un·a·vail·a·ble (ŭn'ə-vā'lə-bəl) adj. *(not available)* no disponible; *(busy)* ocupado.

un·a·vail·ing (ŭn'ə-vā'lĭng) adj. ineficaz.

un·a·void·a·ble (ŭn'ə-voi'də-bəl) adj. inevitable.

un·a·ware (ŭn'ə-wâr') I. adj. ignorante ♦ **to be u. of** no darse cuenta de ● **to be u. that** ignorar que II. adv. de improviso.

un·a·wares (ŭn'ə-wârz') adv. desprevenido.

un·bal·anced (ŭn-băl'ənst) adj. desequilibrado.

un·bar (ŭn-bär') tr. -**rr**- desatrancar; FIG. abrir.

un·bear·a·ble (ŭn-bâr'ə-bəl) adj. insoportable.

un·beat·a·ble (ŭn-bē'tə-bəl) adj. invencible.

un·beat·en (ŭn-bēt'n) adj. invicto.

un·be·com·ing (ŭn'bǐ-kŭm'ǐng) adj. indecoroso.

un·be·known(st) (ŭn'bǐ-nōn[st]') adj. ♦ u. to me sin saberlo yo.

un·be·lief (ŭn'bǐ-lēf') s. incredulidad f.

un·be·liev·a·ble (:lē'və-bəl) adj. increíble.

un·be·liev·er (:vər) s. no creyente mf.

un·be·liev·ing (:vǐng) adj. incrédulo.

un·bend (ŭn-bĕnd') tr. & intr. **-bent** desencorvar(se); (to relax) relajar(se).

un·bend·ing (ŭn-bĕn'dǐng) adj. inflexible.

un·bi·as(s)ed (ŭn-bī'əst) adj. imparcial.

un·bid('den) (ŭn-bǐd'[n]) adj. no pedido.

un·bind (ŭn-bīnd') tr. **-bound** desatar.

un·blink·ing (ŭn-blǐng'kǐng) adj. sin pestañear; (unmoved) impasible; (rigorous) riguroso.

un·blush·ing (ŭn-blŭsh'ǐng) adj. que no se ruboriza; (shameless) desvergonzado.

un·bolt (ŭn-bōlt') tr. desatrancar.

un·born (ŭn-bôrn') adj. no nacido aún; (future) venidero.

un·bound·ed (ŭn-boun'dǐd) adj. ilimitado.

un·bowed (ŭn-boud') adj. recto; FIG. (not subdued) no sometido.

un·break·a·ble (ŭn-brā'kə-bəl) adj. irrompible.

un·breath·a·ble (ŭn-brē'thə-bəl) adj. irrespirable.

un·bri·dled (ŭn-brīd'ld) adj. desembridado; (unrestrained) desenfrenado.

un·bro·ken (ŭn-brō'kən) adj. sin romper; (inviolate) inviolado; (uninterrupted) ininterrumpido; (untamed) no domado.

un·buck·le (ŭn-bŭk'əl) tr. deshebillar.

un·bur·den (ŭn-bûr'dn) tr. descargar; FIG. desahogar.

un·but·ton (ŭn-bŭt'n) tr. & intr. desabotonar(se).

un·caged (ŭn-kājd') adj. libre, suelto.

un·called-for (ŭn-kôld'fôr') adj. (undeserved) inmerecido; (out of place) inapropiado.

un·can·ny (ŭn-kăn'ē) adj. **-i-** inexplicable.

un·cap (ŭn-kăp') tr. **-pp-** destapar.

un·ceas·ing (ŭn-sē'sǐng) adj. incesante.

un·cer·e·mo·ni·ous (ŭn-sĕr'ə-mō'nē-əs) adj. informal; (abrupt) brusco.

un·cer·tain (ŭn-sûr'tn) adj. incierto, dudoso; (undecided) indeciso; (variable) cambiable.

un·cer·tain·ty (ŭn-sûr'tn-tē) s. incertidumbre f.

un·chain (ŭn-chān') tr. desencadenar.

un·change·a·ble (ŭn-chān'jə-bəl) adj. invariable, inalterable.

un·changed (ŭn-chānjd') adj. inalterado.

un·chang·ing (ŭn-chān'jǐng) adj. invariable.

un·char·i·ta·ble (ŭn-chăr'ǐ-tə-bəl) adj. severo.

un·chart·ed (ŭn-chär'tǐd) adj. inexplorado; (unknown) desconocido.

un·chaste (ŭn-chāst') adj. impúdico.

un·cir·cum·cised (ŭn-sûr'kəm-sīzd') adj. no circuncidado.

un·civ·il (ŭn-sǐv'əl) adj. incivil.

un·civ·i·lized (ŭn-sǐv'ə-līzd') adj. incivilizado.

un·clad (ŭn-klăd') adj. desnudo.

un·claimed (ŭn-klāmd') adj. no reclamado.

un·clasp (ŭn-klăsp') tr. desabrochar; (hands, embrace) separar.

un·clas·si·fied (ŭn-klăs'ə-fīd') adj. sin clasificar.

un·cle (ŭng'kəl) s. tío ♦ cry u.! ¡ríndete!

un·clean (ŭn-klēn') adj. **-er, -est** sucio.

un·clean·li·ness (ŭn-klĕn'lē-nǐs) s. suciedad f.

un·clean·ly (ŭn-klĕn'lē) adj. **-i-** sucio.

un·clear (ŭn-klîr') adj. **-er, -est** confuso.

un·clench (ŭn-klĕnch') tr. & intr. relajar(se).

un·cloak (ŭn-klōk') tr. desencapotar; FIG. desenmascarar.

un·clog (ŭn-klôg') tr. **-gg-** desatascar.

un·close (ŭn-klōz') tr. & intr. abrir(se).

un·clothe (ŭn-klōth') tr. desvestir.

un·coil (ŭn-koil') tr. & intr. desenrollar(se).

un·col·lect·ed (ŭn'kə-lĕk'tǐd) adj. no cobrado.

un·com·fort·a·ble (ŭn-kŭm'fər-tə-bəl) adj. incómodo; (disquieting) inquietante.

un·com·mit·ted (ŭn'kə-mǐt'ǐd) adj. no comprometido.

un·com·mon (ŭn-kŏm'ən) adj. **-er, -est** poco común, raro; (remarkable) excepcional.

un·com·mu·ni·ca·tive (ŭn'kə-myōo'nǐ-kā'tǐv, :kə-tǐv) adj. taciturno, reservado.

un·com·plain·ing (ŭn'kəm-plā'nǐng) adj. que no protesta, resignado.

un·com·pli·cat·ed (ŭn-kŏm'plǐ-kā'tǐd) adj. sencillo, simple.

un·com·pli·men·ta·ry (ŭn-kŏm'plə-mĕn'tə-rē) adj. despectivo.

un·com·pro·mis·ing (ŭn-kŏm'prə-mī'zǐng) adj. intransigente.

un·con·cern (ŭn'kən-sûrn') s. indiferencia; (lack of worry) despreocupación f.

un·con·cerned (:sûrnd') adj. despreocupado.

un·con·di·tion·al (:kən-dĭsh'ə-nəl) adj. incondicional.

un·con·di·tioned (:dǐsh'ənd) adj. incondicional; PSIC. no condicionado.

un·con·fined (ŭn'kən-fīnd') adj. libre.

un·con·firmed (:kən-fûrmd') adj. no confirmado.

un·con·nect·ed (ŭn'kə-nĕk'tǐd) adj. inconexo.

un·con·quer·a·ble (ŭn-kŏng'kər-ə-bəl) adj. inconquistable.

un·con·scion·a·ble (ŭn-kŏn'shə-nə-bəl) adj. sin consciencia; (unscrupulous) inescrupuloso.

un·con·scious (:shəs) **I.** adj. inconsciente; MED. sin sentido **II.** s. inconsciente m.

un·con·sid·ered (ŭn'kən-sǐd'ərd) adj. inconsiderado; (rash) irreflexivo.

un·con·sti·tu·tion·al (ŭn-kŏn'stǐ-tōo'shə-nəl) adj. inconstitucional.

un·con·trol·la·ble (ŭn'kən-trō'lə-bəl) adj. incontrolable.

un·con·trolled (:trōld') adj. desenfrenado.

un·con·ven·tion·al (:vĕn'shə-nəl) adj. poco convencional, desacostumbrado.

un·con·vinc·ing (:vǐn'sǐng) adj. poco convincente.

un·cooked (ŭn-kŏŏkt') adj. crudo.

un·cork (ŭn-kôrk') tr. descorchar; (to let out) dar rienda suelta a.

un·cor·rupt·ed (ŭn'kə-rŭp'tǐd) adj. incorrupto.

un·count·ed (ŭn-koun'tǐd) adj. innumerable.

un·cou·ple (ŭn-kŭp'əl) tr. desacoplar.

un·couth (ŭn-kōōth') adj. tosco.

un·cov·er (ŭn-kŭv'ər) tr. destapar; FIG. revelar.

un·cov·ered (ŭn-kŭv'ərd) adj. destapado.

un·cross (ŭn-krôs') tr. descruzar.

unc·tion (ŭngk'shən) s. unción f; (ointment) ungüento; (balm) bálsamo; FIG. untuosidad f.

unc·tu·ous (ŭngk'chōō-əs) adj. (greasy) untuoso; (syrupy) meloso.

un·cul·ti·vat·ed (ŭn-kŭl'tə-vā'tǐd) adj. (land) sin cultivar; (person) inculto.

un·cut (ŭn-kŭt') adj. sin cortar; (stones) en bruto; (pages) intonso; (unabridged) entero.

un·dam·aged (ŭn-dăm'ĭjd) adj. libre de daño.

un·daunt·ed (ŭn-dôn'tĭd) adj. impávido.

un·de·ceive (ŭn'dĭ-sēv') tr. desengañar.

un·de·cid·ed (ŭn'dĭ-sī'dĭd) adj. *(not settled)* no resuelto; *(uncommitted)* no comprometido.

un·de·feat·ed (ŭn'dĭ-fē'tĭd) adj. invicto.

un·de·mon·stra·tive (ŭn'dĭ-mŏn'strə-tĭv) adj. poco expresivo, reservado.

un·de·ni·a·ble (ŭn'dĭ-nī'ə-bəl) adj. innegable.

un·der (ŭn'dər) I. prep. (por) debajo de); *(beneath)* bajo; *(less than)* menos de; *(during)* durante el reinado de; *(with)* con ♦ **u. repair** en reparación • **u. the care of** al cuidado de • **u. the circumstances** dadas las circunstancias II. adv. bajo, debajo; *(less)* menos III. adj. bajo; *(subordinate)* subalterno.

un·der·a·chieve ('-ə-chēv') intr. rendir o lograr menos de lo que se espera de uno.

un·der·age (:āj') adj. menor de edad.

un·der·arm ('-ärm') s. axila.

un·der·bel·ly (:bĕl'ē) s. bajo vientre; FIG. parte *f* vulnerable.

un·der·bid ('-bĭd') tr. **-bid, -dding** COM. ofrecer menos que —intr. rebajar innecesariamente.

un·der·brush ('-brŭsh') s. maleza.

un·der·car·riage (:kăr'ĭj) s. AUTO. chasis *m*; AVIA. tren *m* de aterrizaje.

un·der·charge ('-chärj') tr. COM. cobrar menos de lo debido.

un·der·class·man (:klăs'mən) s. [pl. -men] estudiante *mf* de primer o segundo año.

un·der·clothes ('-klōthz') s.pl. ropa interior.

un·der·cloth·ing (:klō'thĭng) s. ropa interior.

un·der·coat (:kōt') I. s. *(jacket)* chaqueta interior; *(paint)* primera capa; AUTO. capa anticorrosiva II. tr. aplicar una primera capa a.

un·der·cov·er ('-kŭv'ər) adj. clandestino.

un·der·cur·rent ('-kûr'ənt) s. corriente submarina; FIG. fondo.

un·der·cut (ŭn'dər-kŭt') tr. **-cut, -tting** socavar; *(to sell)* vender más barato que.

un·der·de·vel·oped ('-dĭ-vĕl'əpt) adj. insuficientemente desarrollado; ECON. subdesarrollado.

un·der·dog ('-dôg') s. el que no es favorito.

un·der·done ('-dŭn') adj. poco hecho.

un·der·dressed (:drĕst') adj. vestido de forma inapropiada.

un·der·em·ployed (:ĕm-ploid') adj. que no utiliza toda la capacidad obrera.

un·der·es·ti·mate (:ĕs'tə-māt') I. tr. subestimar II. s. (:-mĭt) subestimación *f*.

un·der·es·ti·ma·tion ('-ĕs'tə-mā'-shən) s. subestimación *f*.

un·der·ex·pose (:ĭk-spōz') tr. subexponer.

un·der·ex·po·sure (:ĭk-spō'zhər) s. subexposición *f*.

un·der·foot (:fŏŏt') adv. bajo los pies; *(in the way)* en el camino.

un·der·gar·ment ('-gär'mənt) s. prenda interior.

un·der·go ('-gō') tr. **-went, -gone** *(to experience)* experimentar; *(to endure)* sufrir.

un·der·grad·u·ate (:grăj'ōō-ĭt) s. & adj. (de o para) estudiante universitario no graduado.

un·der·ground ('-ground') I. adj. subterráneo; *(clandestine)* clandestino; *(avant-garde)* de vanguardia II. s. movimiento clandestino; *(resistance)* resistencia; G.B. *(subway)* subterráneo III. adv. bajo tierra.

un·der·growth ('-grōth') s. maleza.

un·der·hand·ed ('-hăn'dĭd) adj. solapado.

un·der·lie (:līʹ) tr. **-lay, -lain, lying** estar o extenderse debajo de; FIG. ser la base de.

un·der·line ('-līn') I. tr. subrayar II. s. raya.

un·der·ling (:lĭng) s. subalterno.

un·der·ly·ing ('-līʹĭng) adj. subyacente; *(basic)* fundamental.

un·der·mine ('-mīn') tr. socavar.

un·der·most ('-mōst') adj. más bajo, último.

un·der·neath (:nēth') I. adv. (por) debajo; *(on the lower part)* en la parte inferior II. prep. hajo, debajo de III. s. parte *f* inferior.

un·der·nour·ish (:nûr'ĭsh) tr. desnutrir.

un·der·nour·ish·ment (:mĭnt) s. desnutrición *f*.

un·der·paid (ŭn'dər-pād') adj. mal pagado.

un·der·pants ('-pănts') s.pl. calzoncillos.

un·der·pass ('-păs') s. paso por debajo.

un·der·pay ('-pā') tr. **-paid** pagar poco.

un·der·pin (:pĭn') tr. **-nn-** apuntalar.

un·der·pin·ning ('-pĭn'ĭng) s. apuntalamiento ♦ pl. base; FAM. *(the legs)* las piernas.

un·der·play ('-plā') tr. & intr. minimizar.

un·der·priv·i·leged (:prĭv'ə-lĭjd) adj. desamparado.

un·der·pro·duc·tion ('-prə-dŭk'shən) s. producción baja o insuficiente.

un·der·rate (:rāt') tr. subestimar.

un·der·score ('-skôr') tr. subrayar.

un·der·sea ('-sē') I. adj. submarino II. adv. bajo la superficie del mar.

un·der·sec·re·tar·y ('-sĕk'rĭ-tĕr'ē) s. subsecretario.

un·der·sell (:sĕl') tr. **-sold** vender más barato que.

un·der·shirt ('-shûrt') s. camiseta.

un·der·shorts ('-shôrts') s.pl. calzoncillos.

un·der·side (:sīd') s. parte *f* de abajo.

un·der·signed (:sīnd') s.inv. ♦ **the u.** el suscrito, el abajo firmante.

un·der·size(d) ('-sīz[d]') adj. *(person)* de talla baja, *(small)* pequeño.

un·der·skirt ('-skûrt') s. enagua.

un·der·stand ('-stănd') I. tr. & intr. **-stood** entender, comprender; *(to infer)* sobreentender.

un·der·stand·a·ble (:stăn'də-bəl) adj. comprensible.

un·der·stand·ing (:dĭng) I. s. comprensión *f*; *(intelligence)* entendimiento *m*; *(opinion)* opinión *f*; *(agreement)* acuerdo II. adj. comprensivo.

un·der·state (ŭn'dər-stāt') tr. subestimar.

un·der·state·ment (:mənt) s. exposición exageradamente modesta.

un·der·stood (ŭn'dər-stŏŏd') I. cf. **understand** II. adj. entendido; *(implied)* sobreentendido ♦ **to make oneself u.** hacerse comprender.

un·der·stud·y ('-stŭd'ē) s. suplente *mf*.

un·der·take ('-tāk') tr. **-took, -taken** *(task)* emprender; *(duty)* encargarse de; *(to promise)* prometer.

un·der·tak·er ('-tā'kər) s. agente funerario.

un·der·tak·ing (:tā'kĭng) s. empresa; *(promise)* promesa; *(trade)* pompas fúnebres.

un·der-the-count·er ('-thə-koun'tər) adj. ilegal.

un·der·tone ('-tōn') s. voz baja; *(color)* color apagado de fondo; *(underlying meaning)* fondo.

un·der·tow ('-tō') s. resaca.

un·der·val·ue ('-văl'yōō) tr. apreciar en menos; *(to underrate)* desapreciar.

un·der·wa·ter ('-wô'tər) adj. subacuático.

un·der·wear ('-wâr') s. ropa interior.

un·der·weight (:wāt') adj. de peso insuficiente

o menor que el normal.

un·der·world ('·wûrld') s. el otro mundo; *(criminal world)* hampa *m.*

un·der·write (:rīt') tr. **-wrote, -written** subscribir; *(to finance)* financiar; *(to insure)* asegurar.

un·der·writ·er (:rī'tər) s. asegurador *m.*

un·de·served (ŭn'dĭ-zûrvd') adj. inmerecido.

un·de·sir·a·ble (ŭn'dĭ-zīr'ə-bəl) adj. & s. (persona) indeseable.

un·dies (ŭn'dēz) s. FAM. ropa interior.

un·dig·ni·fied (ŭn-dĭg'nə-fīd') adj. indecoroso.

un·di·rect·ed (ŭn'dĭ-rĕk'tĭd, -dī-) adj. no dirigido.

un·dis·ci·plined (ŭn-dĭs'ə-plĭnd) adj. indisciplinado.

un·dis·cov·ered (ŭn'dĭ-skŭv'ərd) adj. no descubierto; *(unknown)* desconocido.

un·dis·guised (ŭn'dĭs-gīzd') adj. sincero.

un·dis·put·ed (ŭn'dĭ-spyōō'tĭd) adj. indisputable.

un·dis·tin·guished (:gwĭsht) adj. ordinario.

un·dis·turbed (ŭn'dĭ-stûrbd') adj. tranquilo; *(untouched)* sin tocar.

un·do (ŭn-dōō') tr. **-did, -done** anular; *(to untie)* desatar; *(to open)* desenvolver; *(to destroy)* arruinar; *(to unsettle)* trastornar.

un·do·ing (:ĭng) s. *(of damage)* reparación *f; (loosening)* aflojamiento; *(downfall)* ruina.

un·done (ŭn-dŭn') I. cf. **undo** II. adj. no hecho; *(untied)* desatado; *(emotionally)* deshecho ♦ **to leave u.** dejar sin hacer.

un·doubt·ed (ŭn-dou'tĭd) adj. indudable.

un·dress (ŭn-drĕs') I. tr. & intr. desvestir(se) II. s. desnudez *f.*

un·dressed (ŭn-drĕst') adj. desnudo.

un·due (ŭn-dōō') adj. indebido; *(improper)* impropio.

un·du·lant (ŭn'jə-lənt) adj. ondulante.

un·du·late (:lāt') intr. ondular; *(in form)* ser ondulado.

un·du·la·tion ('-lā'shən) s. ondulación *f.*

un·du·ly (ŭn-dōō'lē) adv. indebidamente; *(improperly)* impropiamente.

un·dy·ing (ŭn-dī'ĭng) adj. eterno.

un·earned (ŭn-ûrnd') adj. *(undeserved)* inmerecido; COM. no devengado.

un·earth (ŭn-ûrth') tr. desenterrar; FIG. descubrir.

un·earth·ly (:lē) adj. -i- extraterreno; *(terrifying)* aterrador; *(absurd)* absurdo.

un·eas·i·ness (ŭn-ē'zē-nĭs) s. inquietud *f.*

un·eas·y (:zē) adj. -i- inquieto; *(worried)* ansioso; *(awkward)* incómodo.

un·ed·u·cat·ed (ŭn-ĕj'ə-kā'tĭd) adj. inculto.

un·em·ployed (ŭn'ĕm-ploid') adj. desempleado; *(idle)* no usado.

un·em·ploy·ment (:ploi'mənt) s. desempleo.

un·en·cum·bered (ŭn'ĕn-kŭm'bərd) adj. ♦ **u. by** sin las trabas de.

un·end·ing (ŭn-ĕn'dĭng) adj. sin fin.

un·e·qual (ŭn-ē'kwəl) adj. desigual; *(asymmetric)* asimétrico; *(fluctuating)* fluctuante; *(inadequate)* inadecuado.

un·e·qualed (ŭn-ē'kwəld) adj. sin igual.

un·e·quiv·o·cal (ŭn'ĭ-kwĭv'ə-kəl) adj. inequívoco.

un·err·ing (ŭn-ûr'ĭng) adj. infalible.

un·es·sen·tial (ŭn'ĭ-sĕn'shəl) adj. no esencial.

un·e·ven (ŭn-ē'vən) adj. **-er, -est** desigual.

un·e·ven·ness (:nĭs) s. desigualdad *f.*

un·e·vent·ful (ŭn'ĭ-vĕnt'fəl) adj. sin novedad.

un·ex·cep·tion·al (ŭn'ĭk-sĕp'shə-nəl) adj.

usual.

un·ex·pect·ed (ŭn'ĭk-spĕk'tĭd) adj. inesperado.

un·ex·plored (ŭn'ĭk-splôrd') adj. inexplorado.

un·ex·posed (ŭn'ĭk-spōzd') adj. no expuesto.

un·ex·pres·sive (ŭn'ĭk-sprĕs'ĭv) adj. inexpresivo.

un·fail·ing (ŭn-fā'lĭng) adj. constante; *(inexhaustible)* inagotable; *(infallible)* infalible.

un·fair (ŭn-fâr') adj. **-er, -est** injusto.

un·fair·ness (:nĭs) s. injusticia.

un·faith·ful (ŭn-fāth'fəl) adj. infiel; *(adulterous)* adúltero; *(inaccurate)* inexacto.

un·faith·ful·ness (:nĭs) s. infidelidad *f.*

un·fa·mil·iar (ŭn'fə-mĭl'yər) adj. desconocido ♦ **u. with** no familiarizado con.

un·fa·mil·iar·i·ty ('--yär'ĭ-tē) s. falta de familiaridad.

un·fash·ion·a·ble (ŭn-fāsh'ə-nə-bəl) adj. fuera de moda; *(not elegant)* poco elegante.

un·fas·ten (ŭn-fās'ən) tr. & intr. desatar(se).

un·fath·om·a·ble (ŭn-fāth'ə-mə-bəl) adj. insondable.

un·fa·vor·a·ble (ŭn-fā'vər-ə-bəl) adj. desfavorable; *(negative)* negativo.

un·feel·ing (ŭn-fē'lĭng) adj. *(numb)* insensible; *(callous)* duro de corazón.

un·fet·ter (ŭn-fĕt'ər) tr. destrabar; FIG. libertar.

un·fin·ished (ŭn-fĭn'ĭsht) adj. incompleto.

un·fit (ŭn-fĭt') adj. incapaz (for, to de); *(unsuitable)* inadecuado; *(unqualified)* incompetente.

un·flag·ging (ŭn-flāg'ĭng) adj. incansable.

un·flap·pa·ble (ŭn-flāp'ə-bəl) adj. impasible.

un·flat·ter·ing (ŭn-flāt'ər-ĭng) adj. poco halagüeño.

un·fledged (ŭn-flĕjd') adj. ORNIT. sin plumas; FIG. inmaduro.

un·flinch·ing (ŭn-flĭn'chĭng) adj. resuelto.

un·fo·cus(s)ed (ŭn-fō'kəst) adj. sin enfocar.

un·fold (ŭn-fōld') tr. & intr. desdoblar(se); *(plot)* desarrollar(se); *(to open out)* abrir(se).

un·fore·seen (ŭn'fər-sēn') adj. imprevisto.

un·for·get·ta·ble (ŭn'fər-gĕt'ə-bəl) adj. inolvidable.

un·for·giv·a·ble (ŭn'fər-gĭv'ə-bəl) adj. imperdonable.

un·formed (ŭn-fôrmd') adj. *(shapeless)* informe; *(uncreated)* no formado aún.

un·for·tu·nate (ŭn-fôr'chə-nĭt) I. adj. desafortunado; *(disastrous)* desastroso; *(regrettable)* lamentable II. s. desgraciado.

un·found·ed (ŭn-foun'dĭd) adj. infundado.

un·friend·li·ness (ŭn-frĕnd'lē-nĭs) s. hostilidad *f.*

un·friend·ly (:lē) adj. -i- hostil.

un·fruit·ful (ŭn-frōōt'fəl) adj. infructuoso.

un·furl (ŭn-fûrl') tr. & intr. desplegar(se).

un·fur·nished (ŭn-fûr'nĭsht) adj. desamueblado.

un·gain·ly (ŭn-gān'lē) adj. -i- desmañado.

un·glued (ŭn-glōōd') adj. JER. trastornado.

un·god·ly (ŭn-gŏd'lē) adj. -i- impío; *(wicked)* perverso; FAM. *(outrageous)* atroz.

un·gov·ern·a·ble (ŭn-gŭv'ər-nə-bəl) adj. ingobernable.

un·gra·cious (ŭn-grā'shəs) adj. brusco.

un·grate·ful (ŭn-grāt'fəl) adj. desagradecido.

un·ground·ed (ŭn-groun'dĭd) adj. infundado.

un·guard·ed (ŭn-gär'dĭd) adj. sin defensa; *(incautious)* incauto.

un·guent (ŭng'gwənt) s. ungüento.

un·gu·late (ŭng'gyə-lĭt) adj. & s. ungulado.

un·hand (ŭn-hānd') tr. desasir.

un·hap·pi·ness (ŭn-hăp'ē-nĭs) s. desgracia.

un·hap·py (ŭn-hăp'ē) adj. -i- infeliz; *(unlucky)* desafortunado; *(inappropriate)* impropio.

un·health·y (ŭn-hĕl'thē) adj. -i- enfermizo; *(unwholesome)* insalubre; *(corruptive)* malsano.

un·heard (ŭn-hûrd') adj. no oído; *(not considered)* desatendido.

un·heard-of (-:ŭv', :ŏv') adj. inaudito.

un·hinge (ŭn-hĭnj') tr. desgoznar; *(the mind)* desquiciar.

un·hitch (ŭn-hĭch') tr. desenganchar.

un·ho·ly (ŭn hō'lē) adj. profano; *(wicked)* impío; FAM. infernal.

un·hook (ŭn-hŏŏk') tr. desenganchar.

u·ni·corn (yōō'nĭ-kôrn') s. unicornio.

u·ni·cy·cle (:sī'kəl) s. monociclo.

un·i·den·ti·fied flying object (ŭn'ī-dĕn'tə-fīd') s. objeto volador no identificado (ovni).

u·ni·fi·ca·tion (yōō'nə-fĭ-kā'shən) s. unificación *f.*

u·ni·form (yōō'nə-fôrm') adj. & s. uniforme *m.*

u·ni·for·mi·ty ('-fôr'mĭ-tē) s. uniformidad *f.*

u·ni·fy (-fī') tr. & intr. unificar(se).

u·ni·lat·er·al ('-lăt'ər-əl) adj. unilateral.

un·i·mag·i·na·ble (ŭn'ĭ-măj'ə-nə-bəl) adj. inimaginable.

un·im·peach·a·ble (ŭn'ĭm-pē'chə-bəl) adv. i-rreprochable; *(unquestionable)* irrecusable.

un·im·por·tant (ŭn'ĭm-pôr'tnt) adj. poco importante.

un·in·form·a·tive (ŭn'ĭn-fôr'mə-tĭv) adj. nada informativo.

un·in·formed (:fôrmd') adj. mal informado.

un·in·hab·it·a·ble (:hăb'ĭ-tə-bəl) adj. inhabitable.

un·in·hab·it·ed (:tĭd) adj. inhabitado.

un·in·hib·it·ed (ŭn'ĭn-hĭb'ĭ-tĭd) adj. sin inhibiciones.

un·in·jured (ŭn-ĭn'jərd) adj. indemne.

un·in·spired (ŭn'ĭn-spīrd') adj. sin inspiración.

un·in·sured (ŭn'ĭn-shŏŏrd') adj. no asegurado.

un·in·tel·li·gent (ŭn'ĭn-tĕl'ə-jənt) adj. poco inteligente.

un·in·tel·li·gi·ble (:jə bəl) adj. ininteligible.

un·in·ter·est·ed (ŭn-ĭn'trĭs-tĭd) adj. desinteresado; *(indifferent)* apático.

un·in·ter·est·ing (:trĭ-stĭng) adj. falto de interés.

un·in·ter·rupt·ed (ŭn-ĭn'tə-rŭp'tĭd) adj. ininterrumpido.

un·ion (yōōn'yən) s. unión *f; (labor)* gremio, sindicato ♦ **student u.** centro estudiantil • **u. jack** bandera.

un·ion·ist (:yə-nĭst) s. sindicalista *mf.*

un·ion·ize (:nīz') tr. & intr. sindicar(se).

u·nique (yōō-nēk') adj. único en su género; *(unparalleled)* sin igual.

u·ni·sex (yōō'nĭ-sĕks') adj. unisexo.

u·ni·sex·u·al ('-sĕk'shŏŏ-əl) adj. unisexual.

u·ni·son (yōō'nĭ-sən) s. unísono; *(agreement)* armonía ♦ **in u.** al unísono.

u·nit (yōō'nĭt) s. unidad *f; (part)* parte *f; (device)* aparato.

u·ni·tar·y (:nĭ-tĕr'ē) adj. unitario; *(whole)* íntegro.

u·nite (yōō-nīt') tr. & intr. unir(se); *(to combine)* combinar(se).

u·ni·ty (yōō'nĭ-tē) s. unidad *f; (unification)* unificación *f; (continuity)* continuidad *f.*

u·ni·va·lent (-vā'lənt) adj. univalente.

u·ni·valve ('-vălv') adj. univalvo.

u·ni·ver·sal (yōō'nə-vûr'səl) adj. universal.

u·ni·ver·sal·i·ty (:vər-săl'ĭ-tē) s. universalidad *f.*

u·ni·verse ('-vûrs') s. universo.

u·ni·ver·si·ty ('-vûr'sĭ-tē) s. universidad *f.*

un·just (ŭn-jŭst') adj. injusto.

un·jus·ti·fi·a·ble (ŭn-jŭs'tə-fī'ə-bəl) adj. injustificable.

un·kempt (ŭn-kĕmpt') adj. despeinado; *(messy)* desarreglado.

un·kind (ŭn-kīnd') adj. **-er, -est** poco amable.

un·know·ing (ŭn-nō'ĭng) adj. ignorante.

un·known (ŭn-nōn') I. adj. desconocido II. s. desconocido; MAT. incógnita.

un·lace (ŭn-lās') tr. desenlazar.

un·lade (ŭn-lād') tr. & intr. descargar.

un·la·dy·like (ŭn-lā'dē-līk') adj. impropio de una dama.

un·lash (ŭn-lăsh') tr. desamarrar.

un·latch (ŭn-lăch') tr. abrir levantando el picaporte.

un·law·ful (ŭn-lô'fəl) adj. ilegal.

un·lead·ed (ŭn-lĕd'ĭd) adj. sin plomo.

un·learn·ed (ŭn-lûr'nĭd) adj. inculto.

un·leash (ŭn-lēsh') tr. soltar; FIG. desencadenar.

un·leav·ened (ŭn-lĕv'ənd) adj. ázimo.

un·less (ŭn-lĕs') conj. a menos que.

un·let·tered (ŭn-lĕt'ərd) adj. analfabeto.

un·like (ŭn'līk') I. adj. *(not alike)* nada parecido; *(not equal)* desigual II. prep. diferente de; *(not typical of)* no característico de.

un·like·li·hood (-'lē-lē-hŏŏd') s. improbabilidad *f.*

un·like·ly (ŭn-līk'lē) adj. -i- improbable; *(likely to fail)* poco prometedor.

un·lim·ber (ŭn-lĭm'bər) tr. & intr. alistar(se) para la acción.

un·list·ed (ŭn-lĭs'tĭd) adj. *(not on a list)* que no figura en la lista; FIN. no cotizado.

un·load (ŭn-lōd') tr. descargar; FIG. desahogar; *(to dispose of)* deshacerse de —intr. descargar.

un·lock (ŭn lŏk') tr. & intr. abrir(se).

un·loos·en (ŭn-lōō'sən) tr. soltar.

un·luck·y (ŭn-lŭk'ē) adj. -i- desgraciado; *(inauspicious)* aciago ♦ **to be u.** tener mala suerte.

un·make (ŭn-māk') tr. **-made** deshacer.

un·man·age·a·ble (ŭn-măn'ĭ-jə-bəl) adj. inmanejable.

un·man·ly (ŭn-măn'lē) adj. -i- *(cowardly)* cobarde; *(effeminate)* afeminado.

un·manned (ŭn-mănd') adj. sin tripulación.

un·man·nered (ŭn-măn'ərd) adj. descortés.

un·man·ner·ly (:ər-lē) adj. grosero.

un·marked (ŭn-märkt') adj. sin marcar.

un·mar·ket·a·ble (ŭn-mär'kĭ-tə-bəl) adj. no comerciable.

un·mar·ried (ŭn-măr'ēd) adj. soltero.

un·mask (ŭn-măsk') tr. desenmascarar; *(to expose)* descubrir —intr. quitarse la máscara.

un·matched (ŭn-măcht') adj. sin par.

un·meant (ŭn-mĕnt') adj. involuntario.

un·men·tion·a·ble (ŭn-mĕn'shə-nə-bəl) I. adj. que no debe mencionarse II. s. ♦ pl. FAM. ropa interior.

un·mer·ci·ful (ŭn-mûr'sĭ-fəl) adj. despiadado; *(excessive)* excesivo.

un·mind·ful (ŭn-mīnd'fəl) adj. olvidadizo ♦ **u.** of descuidoso.

un·mis·tak·a·ble (ŭn'mĭ-stā'kə-bəl) adj. evidente.

un·mit·i·gat·ed (ŭn-mĭt'ĭ-gā'tĭd) adj. implacable; *(absolute)* absoluto.

un·mor·al (ŭn-môr'əl) adj. amoral.
un·named (ŭn-nāmd') adj. anónimo.
un·nat·u·ral (ŭn-năch'ər-əl) adj. no natural.
un·nec·es·sar·y (ŭn-nĕs'ĭ-sĕr'ē) adj. innecesario.
un·nerve (ŭn-nûrv') tr. amilanar.
un·no·tice·a·ble (ŭn-nō'tĭ-sə-bəl) adj. imperceptible.
un·no·ticed (:tĭst) adj. inadvertido.
un·num·bered (ŭn-nŭm'bərd) adj. innumerable; *(lacking a number)* sin número.
un·ob·served (ŭn'əb-zûrvd') adj. desapercibido.
un·ob·tain·a·ble (:tā'nə-bəl) adj. inasequible.
un·ob·tru·sive (:trōō'sĭv) adj. discreto.
un·oc·cu·pied (ŭn-ŏk'yə-pīd') adj. *(vacant)* desocupado; *(idle)* desempleado.
un·of·fi·cial (ŭn'ə-fĭsh'əl) adj. extraoficial.
un·or·gan·ized (ŭn-ôr'gə-nīzd') adj. no organizado; *(not unionized)* sin sindicar.
un·or·tho·dox (ŭn-ôr'thə-dŏks') adj. poco ortodoxo.
un·pack (ŭn-păk') tr. desempacar; *(to unload)* descargar —intr. deshacer las maletas.
un·paid (ŭn-pād') adj. no remunerado.
un·par·al·leled (ŭn-păr'ə-lĕld') adj. sin igual.
un·par·don·a·ble (ŭn-pär'dn-ə-bəl) adj. imperdonable.
un·pa·tri·ot·ic (ŭn-pā'trē-ŏt'ĭk) adj. antipatriótico.
un·pleas·ant (ŭn-plĕz'ənt) adj. desagradable.
un·pleas·ant·ness (ŭn-plĕz'ənt-nĭs) s. desagrado, disgusto.
un·plug (ŭn-plŭg') tr. **-gg-** destapar; ELEC. desenchufar.
un·pol·ished (ŭn-pŏl'ĭsht) adj. FIG. rudo.
un·pol·lut·ed (ŭn'pə-lōō'tĭd) adj. no contaminado.
un·pop·u·lar (ŭn-pŏp'yə-lər) adj. impopular.
un·pop·u·lar·i·ty (-'-lăr'ĭ-tē) s. impopularidad *f.*
un·prac·ticed (ŭn-prăk'tĭst) adj. inexperto.
un·prec·e·dent·ed (ŭn-prĕs'ĭ-dĕn'tĭd) adj. sin precedente.
un·pre·dict·a·ble (ŭn'prĭ-dĭk'tə-bəl) adj. que no se puede predecir *o* pronosticar.
un·prej·u·diced (ŭn-prĕj'ə-dĭst) adj. imparcial.
un·pre·pared (ŭn'prĭ-pârd') adj. desprevenido.
un·pre·pos·sess·ing (ŭn-prē'pə-zĕs'ĭng) adj. poco impresionante.
un·pre·ten·tious (ŭn'prĭ-tĕn'shəs) adj. sin pretenciones.
un·prin·ci·pled (ŭn-prĭn'sə-pəld) adj. falto de principios, sin escrúpulos.
un·print·a·ble (ŭn-prĭn'tə-bəl) adj. impublicable.
un·pro·duc·tive (ŭn'prə-dŭk'tĭv) adj. improductivo; *(attempt)* infructuoso.
un·pro·fes·sion·al (ŭn'prə-fĕsh'ə-nəl) adj. no profesional.
un·prof·it·a·ble (ŭn-prŏf'ĭ-tə-bəl) adj. improductivo; *(useless)* infructuoso.
un·pro·voked (ŭn'prə-vōkt') adj. no provocado.
un·qual·i·fied (ŭn-kwŏl'ə-fīd') adj. incompetente; *(without reservations)* incondicional.
un·ques·tion·a·ble (ŭn-kwĕs'chə-nə-bəl) adj. incuestionable.
un·ques·tioned (ŭn-kwĕs'chənd) adj. incuestionable.
un·qui·et (ŭn-kwī'ĭt) adj. **-er, -est** inquieto.
un·quote (ŭn-kwōt') interj. fin de la cita.

un·rav·el (ŭn-răv'əl) tr. & intr. desenredar(se), desenmarañar(se).
un·read (ŭn-rĕd') adj. no leído; *(ignorant)* poco leído, inculto.
un·read·a·ble (ŭn-rē'də-bəl) adj. ilegible.
un·re·al (ŭn-rē'əl) adj. irreal.
un·re·al·is·tic (ŭn-rē'ə-lĭs'tĭk) adj. no realista.
un·re·al·i·ty (ŭn'rē-ăl'ĭ-tē) s. irrealidad *f.*
un·rea·son·a·ble (ŭn-rē'zə-nə-bəl) adj. irrazonable; *(excessive)* excesivo.
un·rea·son·ing (ŭn-rē'zə-nĭng) adj. irracional.
un·rec·og·niz·a·ble (ŭn-rĕk'əg-nī'zə-bəl) adj. irreconocible.
un·re·gen·er·ate (ŭn'rĭ-jĕn'ər-ĭt) adj. incorregible.
un·re·hearsed (ŭn'rĭ-hûrst') adj. improvisado.
un·re·lat·ed (ŭn'rĭ-lā'tĭd) adj. inconexo ♦ **to be u.** no ser de la misma familia.
un·re·lent·ing (ŭn'rĭ-lĕn'tĭng) adj. implacable.
un·re·li·a·ble (ŭn'rĭ-lī'ə-bəl) adj. que no es de fiar.
un·re·mark·a·ble (ŭn'rĭ-mär'kə-bəl) adj. ordinario.
un·re·mit·ting (ŭn'rĭ-mĭt'ĭng) adj. incesante.
un·re·served (ŭn'rĭ-zûrvd') adj. libre; *(unqualified)* sin reservas; *(candid)* franco.
un·re·spon·sive (ŭn'rĭ-spŏn'sĭv) adj. insensible.
un·rest (ŭn-rĕst') s. desasosiego.
un·re·strained (ŭn'rĭ-strānd') adj. suelto.
un·re·strict·ed (ŭn'rĭ-strĭk'tĭd) adj. libre.
un·ripe (ŭn-rīp') adj. inmaduro; BOT. verde.
un·ri·valed (ŭn-rī'vəld) adj. sin rival.
un·roll (ŭn-rōl') tr. & intr. desenrollar(se).
un·ru·ly (ŭn-rōō'lē) adj. **-i-** indócil.
un·sad·dle (ŭn-săd'l) tr. desensillar.
un·safe (ŭn-sāf') adj. peligroso.
un·said (ŭn-sĕd') adj. sin decir.
un·sal(e)·a·ble (ŭn-sā'lə-bəl) adj. invendible.
un·san·i·tar·y (ŭn-săn'ĭ-tĕr'ē) adj. antihigiénico.
un·sat·is·fac·to·ry (ŭn-săt'ĭs-făk'tə-rē) adj. insatisfactorio.
un·sat·u·rat·ed (ŭn-săch'ə-rā'tĭd) adj. sin grasas saturadas.
un·sa·vor·y (ŭn-sā'və-rē) adj. *(insipid)* soso; *(distasteful)* desabrido; *(offensive)* ofensivo.
un·scathed (ŭn-skāthd') adj. ileso.
un·schooled (ŭn-skōōld') adj. sin instrucción.
un·sci·en·tif·ic (ŭn-sī'ən-tĭf'ĭk) adj. poco científico.
un·scram·ble (ŭn-skrăm'bəl) tr. *(to straighten out)* arreglar; *(to decipher)* descifrar.
un·screw (ŭn-skrōō') tr. destornillar; *(to loosen)* desenroscar —intr. destornillarse.
un·scru·pu·lous (ŭn-skrōō'pyə-ləs) adj. sin escrúpulos, inescrupuloso.
un·seal (ŭn-sēl') tr. romper el sello de.
un·sea·son·a·ble (ŭn-sē'zə-nə-bəl) adj. fuera de temporada *o* tiempo.
un·seat (ŭn-sēt') tr. *(from horse)* derribar; *(from office)* destituir.
un·seem·ly (ŭn-sēm'lē) adj. **-i-** indecoroso.
un·seen (ŭn-sēn') adj. invisible.
un·sel·fish (ŭn-sĕl'fĭsh) adj. generoso.
un·set·tle (ŭn-sĕt'l) tr. trastornar.
un·set·tled (ŭn-sĕt'ld) adj. inestable; *(not resolved)* pendiente; *(not paid)* sin liquidar; *(region)* despoblado; *(not fixed)* inconstante.
un·shack·le (ŭn-shăk'əl) tr. quitar los grillos.
un·shak·a·ble (ŭn-shā'kə-bəl) adj. inquebran-

table.

un·shak·en (ŭn-shā′kən) adj. inconmovible.

un·shaped (ŭn-shāpt′) adj. sin forma.

un·shape·ly (ŭn-shāp′lē) adj. -i- desproporcionado.

un·shav·en (ŭn-shā′vən) adj. sin afeitar.

un·sheathe (ŭn-shēth′) tr. desenvainar.

un·sight·ly (ŭn-sīt′lē) adj. -i- feo.

un·skilled (ŭn-skĭld′) adj. inexperto, sin entrenamiento; *(work)* no especializado; *(worker)* no cualificado.

un·snap (ŭn-snăp′) tr. -pp- desabrochar.

un·snarl (ŭn-snärl′) tr. desenredar.

un·so·cia·ble (ŭn-sō′shə-bəl) adj. insociable.

un·sold (ŭn-sōld′) adj. sin vender.

un·so·lic·it·ed (ŭn-sə-lĭs′ĭ-tĭd) adj. sin solicitar.

un·solved (ŭn-sŏlvd′) adj. sin resolver.

un·so·phis·ti·cat·ed (ŭn′sə-fĭs′tĭ-kā′tĭd) adj. ingenuo.

un·sound (ŭn-sound′) adj. -er, -est poco firme; *(defective)* defectuoso; *(unhealthy)* enfermizo.

un·spar·ing (ŭn-spâr′ĭng) adj. generoso; *(cruel)* despiadado.

un·speak·a·ble (ŭn-spē′kə-bəl) adj. indescriptible; *(atrocious)* abominable.

un·spent (ŭn-spĕnt′) adj. sin gastar.

un·spo·ken (ŭn-spō′kən) adj. tácito.

un·spot·ted (ŭn-spŏt′ĭd) adj. inmaculado.

un·sta·ble (ŭn-stā′bəl) adj. inestable.

un·stead·i·ness (ŭn-stĕd′ē-nĭs) s. inestabilidad *f*; *(inconstancy)* inconstancia.

un·stead·y (ŭn-stĕd′ē) adj. -i- inestable; *(hands)* tembloroso; *(variable)* variable.

un·stick (ŭn-stĭk′) tr. -stuck despegar.

un·stint·ing (ŭn-stĭn′tĭng) adj. generoso.

un·stop (ŭn-stŏp′) tr. -pp- destapar.

un·stop·pa·ble (-ə-bəl) adj. irrefrenable.

un·strap (ŭn-străp′) tr. -pp- aflojar las correas a.

un·stressed (ŭn-strĕst′) adj. sin acento; *(not emphasized)* sin énfasis.

un·struc·tured (ŭn-strŭk′chərd) adj. falto de estructura.

un·strung (ŭn-strŭng′) adj. desatado; *(unnerved)* trastornado.

un·stud·ied (ŭn-stŭd′ēd) adj. sin afectación.

un·sub·stan·tial (ŭn′səb-stăn′shəl) adj. insubstancial; *(flimsy)* ligero.

un·suc·cess·ful (ŭn′sək-sĕs′fəl) adj. fracasado; *(futile)* infructuoso ♦ **to be u.** no tener éxito.

un·suit·a·ble (ŭn-sōō′tə-bəl) adj. inadecuado; *(inconvenient)* inconveniente; *(unbecoming)* inapropiado.

un·sung (ŭn-sŭng′) adj. no cantado; *(uncelebrated)* no celebrado, olvidado.

un·sus·pect·ed (ŭn′sə-spĕk′tĭd) adj. insospechado.

un·sus·pect·ing (:tĭng) adj. confiado.

un·sym·pa·thet·ic (ŭn-sĭm′pə-thĕt′ĭk) adj. indiferente; *(hostile)* hostil.

un·sys·tem·at·ic (ŭn-sĭs′tə-măt′ĭk) adj. poco metódico.

un·tamed (ŭn-tāmd′) adj. indomado.

un·tan·gle (ŭn-tăng′gəl) tr. desenredar.

un·tapped (ŭn-tăpt′) adj. sin explotar.

un·taught (ŭn-tôt′) adj. sin instrucción; *(natural)* natural.

un·ten·a·ble (ŭn-tĕn′ə-bəl) adj. indefensible.

un·thank·ful (ŭn-thăngk′fəl) adj. ingrato.

un·think·a·ble (ŭn-thĭng′kə-bəl) adj. impensable.

un·think·ing (:kĭng) adj. irreflexivo.

un·ti·di·ness (ŭn-tī′dē-nĭs) s. desorden *m*.

un·ti·dy (ŭn-tī′dē) adj. -i- desordenado.

un·tie (ŭn-tī′) tr. -tying desatar; *(to free)* soltar —intr. desatarse.

un·til (ŭn-tĭl′) prep. & conj. hasta (que).

un·time·ly (ŭn-tīm′lē) adj. -i- inoportuno.

un·tir·ing (ŭn-tīr′ĭng) adj. incansable.

un·to (ŭn′tōō) prep. a.

un·told (ŭn-tōld′) adj. nunca antes dicho; *(beyond measure)* incalculable.

un·touch·a·ble (ŭn-tŭch′ə-bəl) adj. & s. intocable *m*.

un·to·ward (ŭn-tôrd′, ŭn-tə-wôrd′) adj. desfavorable; *(obstinate)* obstinado.

un·trav·eled (ŭn-trăv′əld) adj. poco frecuentado; *(person)* que no ha viajado.

un·tried (ŭn-trīd′) adj. no probado.

un·trod·den (ŭn-trŏd′n) adj. no hollado.

un·true (ŭn-trōō′) adj. -er, -est falso; *(inaccurate)* inexacto; *(unfaithful)* desleal.

un·trust·wor·thy (ŭn-trŭst′wûr′thē) adj. -i- indigno de confianza.

un·truth (ŭn-trōōth′) s. falsedad *f*.

un·truth·ful (:fəl) adj. falso; *(lying)* mendaz.

un·tu·tored (ŭn-tōō′tərd) adj. sin instrucción.

un·twist (ŭn-twĭst′) tr. & intr. desenrollar(se).

un·used (ŭn-yōōzd′) adj. sin usar; *(new)* nuevo ♦ **u. to** (ŭn-yōōst′) no acostumbrado a.

un·u·su·al (ŭn-yōō′zhōō-əl) adj. fuera de lo común; *(exceptional)* extraordinario.

un·ut·ter·a·ble (ŭn-ŭt′ər-ə-bəl) adj. inexpresable.

un·var·nished (ŭn-vär′nĭsht) adj. sin barnizar; FIG. puro.

un·veil (ŭn-vāl′) tr. quitar el velo; *(to reveal)* revelar —intr. descubrirse.

un·voiced (ŭn-voist′) adj. no expresado.

un·want·ed (ŭn-wŏn′tĭd) adj. no deseado.

un·war·rant·ed (ŭn-wôr′ən-tĭd) adj. injustificado.

un·war·y (ŭn-wâr′ē) adj. -i- incauto.

un·washed (ŭn-wŏsht′) adj. desaseado.

un·wed (ŭn-wĕd′) adj. soltero.

un·wel·come (ŭn-wĕl′kəm) adj. inoportuno; *(news)* desagradable.

un·well (ŭn-wĕl′) adj. enfermo, indispuesto.

un·whole·some (ŭn-hōl′səm) adj. malsano; *(harmful)* nocivo.

un·wield·y (ŭn-wēl′dē) adj. -i- difícil de manejar.

un·will·ing (ŭn-wĭl′ĭng) adj. no dispuesto.

un·will·ing·ness (:nĭs) s. desgana, desgano.

un·wind (ŭn-wīnd′) tr. -wound desenrollar —intr. desenrollarse; *(to relax)* relajarse.

un·wise (ŭn-wīz′) adj. -er, -est desaconsejado.

un·wit·ting (ŭn-wĭt′ĭng) adj. *(unaware)* inconsciente; *(unintentional)* sin intención.

un·wont·ed (ŭn-wŏn′tĭd) adj. inusitado.

un·world·ly (ŭn-wûrld′lē) adj. -i- espiritual; *(naive)* ingenuo.

un·wor·thy (ŭn-wûr′thē) adj. -i- despreciable ♦ **u. of** no digno de.

un·wound·ed (ŭn-wōōn′dĭd) adj. ileso.

un·wrap (ŭn-răp′) tr. -pp- desenvolver.

un·writ·ten (ŭn-rĭt′n) adj. no escrito; *(traditional)* tradicional.

un·yield·ing (ŭn-yēl′dĭng) adj. inflexible.

un·yoke (ŭn-yōk′) tr. desuncir.

un·zip (ŭn-zĭp′) tr. -pp- bajar la cremallera de.

up (ŭp) I. adv. hacia arriba, en lo alto; arriba <*I put it u. there* lo puse allí arriba>; para arriba

<from ten dollars up de diez dólares para arriba> ♦ **close up** cerca • **high up** muy arriba • **to be u.** haberse levantado (de la cama); *(to be finished)* estar terminado, acabarse • **to be up all night** no acostarse en toda la noche • **to come** *o* **go up to** acercarse a • **to feel up to** sentirse capaz de • **to get up** levantarse • **up!** *o* **get up!** ¡arriba! • **up above** arriba • **up against** junto a • **up and down** de arriba abajo • **up north** hacia *o* en el norte • **up to** hasta • **up to date** al día II. adj. *(moving upward)* que va hacia arriba; *(out of bed)* levantado ♦ **it is up to you** decídelo tú • **to be up against** tener que hacer frente a • **to be up against it** estar en apuros • **to be up for** *(office)* ser candidato a; *(to feel like)* tener ganas de • **to be up on** estar bien enterado sobre • **to be up to standard** satisfacer los requisitos • **to be up to something** estar tramando algo • **up for trial** ante el tribunal • **up in arms** furioso • **up to** hasta; *(capable of)* capacitado para • **what are you up to?** ¿en qué andas? • **what's up?** ¿qué pasa? III. prep. arriba IV. s. ♦ **on the up and up** honesto, legal • **to be on an up** FAM. estar eufórico • **to be on the up** COM. estar en subida • **ups and downs** altibajos V. tr. **-pp-** *(to increase)* aumentar; *(to raise)* elevar —intr. levantarse.

up-and-com·ing (ŭp'ən-kŭm'ĭng) adj. prometedor.

up-and-down (:doun') adj. variante; *(vertical)* vertical.

up·beat (ŭp'bēt') adj. FAM. optimista.

up·braid (ŭp-brād') tr. reprochar.

up·bring·ing (ŭp'brĭng'ĭng) s. crianza.

up·com·ing (ŭp'kŭm'ĭng) adj. futuro.

up·coun·try (ŭp'kŭn'trē) I. s. interior *m* II. adj. del interior III. adv. hacia el interior.

up·date (ŭp-dāt') I. tr. poner al día II. s. (ˈˈ) información actualizada.

up·draft (ŭp'drăft') s. corriente *f* ascendente.

up·end (ŭp-ĕnd') tr. poner de punta; *(to overturn)* derribar.

up·front (ŭp'frŭnt') adj. franco; *(in advance)* por adelantado.

up·grade (ŭp'grād') I. tr. mejorar la calidad de; *(to promote)* ascender II. s. cuesta.

up·heav·al (ŭp-hē'vəl) s. levantamiento; *(disruption)* trastorno; GEOL. solevantamiento.

up·hill (ŭp'hĭl') I. adj. ascendente; *(difficult)* arduo II. s. cuesta III. adv. cuesta arriba.

up·hold (ŭp-hōld') tr. **-held** levantar; *(to support)* sostener; *(to sustain)* defender.

up·hol·ster (ŭp-hōl'stər) tr. tapizar.

up·hol·ster·y (:stə-rē) s. tapicería.

up·keep (ŭp'kēp') s. mantenimiento; *(cost)* gastos de mantenimiento.

up·land (ŭp'lənd) s. altiplanicie *f*.

up·lift I. tr. (ŭp-lĭft') alzar; *(to elevate)* elevar II. s. (ˈˈ) alzamiento.

up·most (ŭp'mōst') adj. más alto.

up·on (ə-pŏn') prep. sobre.

up·per (ŭp'ər) I. adj. superior ♦ **to have the u. hand** llevar ventaja • **u. case** mayúsculas • **u. crust** FAM. la flor y nata II. s. *(of a shoe)* pala; JER. *(drug)* pepa (anfetamina).

up·per·case (ˈ-kās') adj. en mayúsculas.

up·per-class (:klăs') adj. de la clase alta.

up·per·class·man (:'mən) s. [pl. **-men**] estudiante *mf* del tercer *o* cuarto año.

up·per·cut (ŭp'ər-kŭt') s. gancho (en boxeo).

up·per·most (:mōst') I. adj. más alto II. adv. en primer lugar.

up·pi·ty (ŭp'ĭtē) adj. FAM. presumido.

up·raise (ŭp-rāz') tr. levantar.

up·right (ŭp'rīt') I. adj. vertical; *(honorable)* recto II. adv. verticalmente III. s. montante *m*.

up·ris·ing (ŭp'rī'zĭng) s. insurrección *f*.

up·riv·er (ŭp'rĭv'ər) adj. & adv. río arriba.

up·roar (ŭp'rôr') s. alboroto.

up·roar·i·ous (-'ē-əs) adj. tumultuoso; *(boisterous)* ruidoso; *(hilarious)* hilarante.

up·root (ŭp-rōōt') tr. arrancar; FIG. desarraigar.

up·set (ŭp-sĕt') I. tr. **-set, -tting** *(to tip over)* volcar; *(to throw into disorder)* desordenar; *(to trouble)* afectar; *(physically, mentally)* perturbar; *(the stomach)* caer mal a; *(an opponent)* vencer inesperadamente II. s. (ˈˈ) vuelco; *(trouble)* molestia; *(defeat)* derrota inesperada III. adj. *(disordered)* desordenado; *(worried)* preocupado ♦ **don't be u.** *(worried)* no te preocupes; *(angry)* no te enojes • **to have an u. stomach** estar descompuesto del estómago.

up·shot (ŭp'shŏt') s. resultado.

up·side-down (ŭp'sĭd-doun') adv. al revés; FIG. patas arriba ♦ **to turn u.** volcar(se); FIG. trastornar(se).

up·stage (ŭp'stāj') I. adv. en *o* hacia el fondo del escenario II. tr. TEAT. robar la escena; FAM. eclipsar.

up·stairs (ŭp'stârz') I. adv. arriba; *(on upper floor)* en el piso superior II. adj. del piso superior III. s.inv. piso de arriba.

up·stand·ing (ŭp-stăn'dĭng) adj. erguido; *(honest)* recto.

up·start (ŭp'stärt') s. advenedizo.

up·state (ŭp'stāt') adv. hacia la parte norte del estado.

up·stream (ŭp'strēm') adv. aguas arriba.

up·surge (ŭp-sûrj') I. intr. subir repentinamente II. s (ˈˈ) subida repentina.

up·swing (ŭp'swĭng') s. alza.

up·take (ŭp'tāk') s. canal *m* de salida de la chimenea ♦ **quick on the u.** que comprende muy rápidamente.

up·tight (ŭp'tīt') adj. JER. tenso.

up-to-date (ŭp'tə-dāt') adj. al día; *(keeping up)* al tanto.

up-to-the-min·ute (:thə-mĭn'ĭt) adj. de última hora.

up·town (ŭp'toun') adv. & s. (hacia) la parte alta de una ciudad.

up·turn (ŭp'tûrn') s. alza.

up·ward (ŭp'wərd) I. adj. ascendente II. adv. *o* **-wards** hacia *o* para arriba ♦ **u. of** en exceso de, más de.

up·wind (ŭp'wĭnd') adj. contra el viento.

u·ra·ni·um (yōō-rā'nē-əm) s. uranio.

ur·ban (ûr'bən) adj. urbano.

ur·bane (ûr-bān') adj. urbano, cortés.

ur·ban·ite (ûr'bə-nīt') s. habitante *mf* de una ciudad.

ur·ban·i·ty (ûr-băn'ĭ-tē) s. finura.

ur·ban·ize (ûr'bə-nīz') tr. urbanizar.

ur·chin (ûr'chĭn) s. golfillo.

u·re·a (yōō-rē'ə) s. urea.

u·re·mi·a (:mē-ə) s. uremia.

u·re·ter (yōō-rē'ĭ-tər) s. uréter *m*.

u·re·thra (yōō-rē'thrə) s. [pl. **s** *o* **-ae**] uretra.

urge (ûrj) I. tr. *(to impel)* incitar; *(to exhort)* exhortar; *(to advocate)* propugnar II. s. im-

pulso; *(desire)* deseo.
ur·gen·cy (ûr'jən-sē) s. urgencia.
ur·gent (ûr'jənt) adj. urgente.
u·ric (yŏŏr'ĭk) adj. úrico.
u·ri·nal (yŏŏr'ə-nəl) s. *(fixture)* urinal *m*, urinario *m*; *(receptacle)* orinal *m*.
u·ri·nal·y·sis ('-năl'ĭ-sĭs) s. [pl. **-ses**] análisis *m* de orina.
u·ri·nar·y ('-nĕr'ē) adj. urinario.
u·ri·nate ('-nāt') intr. orinar.
u·rine (yŏŏr'ĭn) s. orina.
urn (ûrn) s. urna; *(for tea, coffee)* recipiente *m* grande.
u·ro·gen·i·tal (yŏŏr'ō-jĕn'ĭ-tl) adj. urogenital.
u·rol·o·gy (yŏŏ-rŏl'ə-jē) s. urología.
us (ŭs) pron. nos *<the movie impressed us* la película nos impresionó>; nosotros, nosotras *<to us* a nosotros>.
us·a·ble (yŏŏ'zə-bəl) adj. utilizable.
us·age (yŏŏ'sĭj) s. uso; *(customary practice)* usanza; *(parlance)* lenguaje *m*.
use (yŏŏz) I. tr. usar; *(to treat)* tratar; *(drugs)* tomar ♦ **to be used as, for** servir de, para ♦ **to u. up** agotar —intr. [ú. solamente en la forma imperfecta **used** *<I used to go to Florida every winter* yo solía ir a la Florida todos los inviernos>]. ♦ **to get used to** acostumbrarse a II. s. (yŏŏs) uso; *(usefulness)* utilidad *f* ♦ **it's no u.** es inútil ♦ **to be of no u.** no servir para nada ♦ **to have no u. for** no necesitar; *(to dislike)* no gustarle a uno ♦ **to have the u. of** tener uno a su disposición ♦ **to put to good u.** sacar partido de ♦ **what's the u.!** ¡para qué!
used (yŏŏzd) adj. usado.
use·ful (yŏŏs'fəl) adj. útil.
use·ful·ness (:nĭs) s. utilidad *f*.
use·less (yŏŏs'lĭs) adj. ineficaz; *(futile)* inútil.
use·less·ness (:nĭs) s. inutilidad *f*.
us·er (yŏŏ'zər) s. usuario; *(addict)* adicto.
ush·er (ŭsh'ər) I. s. acomodador *m*; *(doorkeeper)* ujier *m* II. tr. acomodar; *(to escort)* acompañar ♦ **to u. in** anunciar.
ush·er·ette ('ə-rĕt') s. acomodadora.
u·su·al (yŏŏ'zhŏŏ-əl) adj. usual; *(customary)* acostumbrado ♦ **as u.** como de costumbre ♦ **the u. thing** lo de siempre.
u·su·rer (yŏŏ'zhər-ər) s. usurero.
u·su·ri·ous (-zhŏŏr'ē-əs) adj. usurario.
u·surp (yŏŏ-sûrp') tr. & intr. usurpar.
u·sur·pa·tion ('sûr-pā'shən) s. usurpación *f*.
u·sur·per (:'pər) s. usurpador *m*.
u·su·ry (yŏŏ'zhə-rē) s. usura.
u·ten·sil (yŏŏ-tĕn'səl) s. utensilio.
u·ter·ine (yŏŏ'tər-ĭn) adj. uterino.
u·ter·us (:əs) s. útero.
u·til·i·tar·i·an (yŏŏ-tĭl'ĭ-târ'ē-ən) I. adj. utilitario; FILOS. utilitarista II. s. utilitarista *mf*.
u·til·i·ty (yŏŏ-tĭl'ĭ-tē) s. utilidad *f*; *(service)* servicio público.
u·til·iz·a·ble (yŏŏt'l-ī'zə-bəl) adj. utilizable.
u·til·i·za·tion ('-ī-zā'shən) s. utilización *f*.
u·til·ize (yŏŏt'l-īz') tr. utilizar.
ut·most (ŭt'mōst') I. adj. máximo; *(farthest)* más lejano II. s. máximo ♦ **to do one's u.** hacer todo lo posible ♦ **to the u.** hasta más no poder.
u·to·pi·a (yŏŏ-tō'pē-ə) s. utopía.
u·to·pi·an (:ən) adj. utópico II. s. utopista *mf*.
ut·ter¹ (ŭt'ər) tr. decir; *(to pronounce)* pronunciar; *(sigh, cry)* dar.
ut·ter² adj. total, absoluto.

ut·ter·a·ble (ŭt'ər-ə-bəl) adj. decible.
ut·ter·ance (:əns) s. pronunciación *f*; *(expression)* expresión *f*; *(of a sound)* emisión *f*.
ut·ter·ly (ŭt'ər-lē) adv. totalmente.
ut·ter·most (:mōst') adj. extremo.
U-turn (yŏŏ'tûrn') s. AUTO. media vuelta.
u·vu·la (yŏŏ'vyə-lə) s. úvula, campanilla.
ux·o·ri·ous (ŭk-sôr'ē-əs) adj. perdidamente enamorado de la esposa.

V

v, V (vē) s. vigésima segunda letra del alfabeto inglés.
va·can·cy (vā'kən-sē) s. vacío; *(unfilled position)* vacante *f*; *(in a hotel)* habitación *f* libre.
va·cant (vā'kənt) adj. *(empty)* vacío; *(not occupied)* libre; *(position)* vacante; *(look, stare)* inexpresivo, vago.
va·cate (vā'kāt') tr. dejar vacante; *(house)* desocupar; DER. anular —intr. irse, marcharse.
va·ca·tion (vā-kā'shən) I. s. vacaciones *f* *<on v. de vacaciones>* II. intr. tomar las vacaciones.
vac·ci·nate (văk'sə-nāt') tr. & intr. vacunar.
vac·ci·na·tion ('-nā'shən) s. vacunación *f*.
vac·cine (văk-sēn', '') s. vacuna.
vac·il·late (văs'ə-lāt') intr. vacilar.
vac·il·la·tion ('-lā'shən) s. vacilación *f*.
va·cu·i·ty (vă-kyŏŏ'ĭ-tē) s. vacuidad *f*; *(remark)* vaciedad *f*.
vac·u·ous (văk'yŏŏ-əs) adj. *(empty)* vacío; *(inane)* vacuo; *(look)* vago, perdido.
vac·u·um (văk'yŏŏm) I. s. [pl. **-s** o **-ua**] vacío; *(isolation)* aislamiento ♦ **v. cleaner** aspiradora II. tr. & intr. pasar la aspiradora (por).
vac·u·um-packed ('-păkt') adj. envasado al vacío.
vag·a·bond (văg'ə-bŏnd') s. & adj. vagabundo.
va·ga·ry (vā'gə-rē) s. capricho.
va·gi·na (və-jī'nə) s. [pl. **-s** o **-ae**] vagina.
vag·i·nal (văj'ə-nəl) adj. vaginal.
va·gran·cy (vā'grən-sē) s. vagancia.
va·grant (vā'grənt) I. s. *(vagabond)* vagabundo; *(bum)* vago II. adj. vagabundo.
vague (văg) adj. vago; *(reply)* ambiguo; *(shape, idea)* impreciso.
vain (vān) adj. *(fruitless)* vano, inútil; *(conceited)* vanidoso ♦ **in v.** en vano, vanamente.
vain·glo·ri·ous (-glôr'ē-əs) adj. vanaglorioso.
vain·glo·ry (:ē) s. vanagloria.
val·ance (văl'əns) s. doselera.
vale (vāl) s. valle *m*.
val·e·dic·to·ri·an (văl'ĭ-dĭk-tôr'ē-ən) s. alumno que da el discurso de fin de curso.
val·e·dic·to·ry ('-'tə-rē) adj. & s. (discurso de) despedida.
va·lence/len·cy (vā'ləns) s. valencia.
val·en·tine (văl'ən-tīn') s. tarjeta del día de los enamorados; *(sweetheart)* novio, -ia.
val·et (văl'ĭt, vă-lā') s. ayuda de cámara.
val·iance (văl'yəns) s. valentía, bravura.
val·iant (:yənt) adj. & s. valiente *mf*.
val·id (văl'ĭd) adj. válido; DER. *(in effect)* vigente ♦ **to be no longer v.** haber caducado.
val·i·date (:ĭ-dāt') tr. validar; *(to verify)* verificar.
val·i·da·tion ('-dā'shən) s. validación *f*; *(verification)* verificación *f*.
va·lid·i·ty (və-lĭd'ĭ-tē) s. validez *f*.
va·lise (və-lēs') s. maleta, valija.

val·ley (văl'ē) s. valle *m.*

val·or (văl'ər) s. valor *m.*, valentía.

val·or·ous (văl'ər-əs) adj. valeroso, valiente.

val·u·a·ble (văl'yॵ-ə-bəl) I. adj. valioso, de valor; *(information, assistance)* importante, de valor ♦ **to be v.** valer mucho II. s. ♦ pl. objetos de valor.

val·u·ate (:āt') tr. valorar, tasar.

val·u·a·tion ('-ā'shən) s. valoración *f*, tasación *f*; *(value)* valor estimado.

val·ue (văl'yॵ) I. s. valor *m*; *(importance)* importancia ♦ **market o commercial v.** valor comercial • **to attach little v. to** dar poco valor a • **to be of (no) v.** (no) tener valor • **to lose v.** desvalorizarse • **to set a v. on** estimar, valuar II. tr. *(to appraise)* valorizar, tasar; *(to rate)* estimar, valorar; *(to esteem)* estimar, apreciar.

val·ued (:yॵd) adj. estimado, apreciado.

valve (vălv) s. ANAT., TEC. válvula; MÚS. llave *f.*

val·vu·lar (văl'vyə-lər) adj. valvular.

va·moose (vă-mōōs') intr. JER. largarse.

vamp¹ (vămp) s. *(shoe part)* empeine *m*; MÚS. acompañamiento improvisado.

vamp² s. vampiresa, seductora.

vam·pire (văm'pīr') s. vampiro.

van¹ (văn) s. *(truck)* camioneta, furgoneta; G.B., F.C. vagón *m* de carga.

van² s. vanguardia.

van·dal·ism (văn'dl-ĭz'əm) s. vandalismo.

van·dal·ize (:īz') tr. destrozar, destruir.

vane (vān) s. *(weathercock)* veleta; *(of a propeller)* paleta; *(of a windmill)* aspa; *(of a rocket)* estabilizador *m.*

van·guard (văn'gärd') s. vanguardia.

va·nil·la (və-nĭl'ə) s. *(extract)* de vainilla.

van·ish (văn'ĭsh) intr. desaparecer; *(to fade)* desvanecerse ♦ **to v. into thin air** esfumarse.

van·i·ty (văn'ĭ-tē) s. vanidad *f*; *(conceit)* presunción *f*; *(table)* tocador *m* ♦ **v. case** neceser.

van·quish (văng'kwĭsh) tr. derrotar, vencer.

van·tage (văn'tĭj) s. ventaja ♦ **v. point** posición de ventaja, lugar ventajoso.

vap·id (văp'ĭd, vā'pĭd) adj. insípido, soso.

va·por (vā'pər) s. vapor *m*; *(mist)* niebla, bruma; *(fumes)* humo, vapor.

va·por·ize (vā'pə-rīz') tr. & intr. vaporizar(se).

va·por·iz·er (:rī'zər) s. vaporizador *m.*

va·por·ous (vā'pər-əs) adj. vaporoso.

var·i·a·bil·i·ty (vâr'ē-ə-bĭl'ĭ-tē) s. variabilidad *f.*

var·i·a·ble (vâr'ē-ə-bəl) I. adj. variable; *(fickle)* inconstante II. s. variable *f.*

var·i·ance (:əns) s. *(act)* variación *f*; *(deviation)* desviación *f* ♦ **at v.** en desacuerdo.

var·i·ant (:ənt) I. adj. *(differing)* variante, diferente; *(variable)* variable II. s. variante *f.*

var·i·a·tion ('-ā'shən) s. variación *f.*

var·i·cose (văr'ĭ-kōs') adj. varicoso.

var·ied (vâr'ēd) adj. variado.

var·i·e·gat·ed (vâr'ē-ĭ-gā'tĭd) adj. *(varicolored)* abigarrado, jaspeado; *(diversified)* variado.

va·ri·e·ty (və-rī'ĭ-tē) s. variedad *f*; *(assortment)* surtido ♦ **in a v. of** en varios • **v. show** espectáculo de variedades.

var·i·ous (vâr'ē-əs) adj. *(several)* varios; *(varied)* vario; *(different)* diferente.

var·mint (vär'mĭnt) s. FAM. sabandija.

var·nish (vär'nĭsh) I. s. barniz *m*; *(coating)* capa de barniz ♦ **v. remover** quitaesmalte II. tr. barnizar; *(the truth)* embellecer.

var·si·ty (vär'sĭ-tē) s. equipo universitario; G.B. universidad *f.*

var·y (vâr'ē) tr. variar —intr. variar, cambiar;

(to differ) diferir; *(to deviate)* desviarse.

var·y·ing (:ĭng) adj. variante, variable.

vas·cu·lar (văs'kyə-lər) adj. vascular.

vase (vās, vāz, väz) s. jarrón *m*, florero.

va·sec·to·my (və-sĕk'tə-mē) s. vasectomía.

vas·sal (văs'əl) s. vasallo.

vast (văst) adj. vasto, inmenso ♦ **by a v. majority** por una abrumadora mayoría.

vast·ness (:nĭs) s. vastedad *f*, inmensidad *f.*

vat (văt) s. cuba.

va·tic·i·na·tion (və-tĭs'ə-nā'shən) s. vaticinio.

vaude·ville (vôd'vĭl') s. vodevil *m.*

vault¹ (vôlt) I. s. ARQ. bóveda; *(cellar)* sótano; *(of a bank)* cámara acorazada; *(burial chamber)* cripta II. tr. abovedar.

vault² I. tr. & intr. saltar II. s. salto.

vault·ing¹ (vôl'tĭng) s. ARQ. bóveda.

vault·ing² adj. saltador; *(ambition, pride)* desmesurado.

vaunt (vônt) I. tr. & intr. jactarse (de) II. s. alarde *m*, jactancia.

veal (vēl) s. *(carne f* de) ternera.

vec·tor (vĕk'tər) s. vector *m.*

veep (vēp) s. FAM. vicepresidente *m.*

veer (vîr) I. intr. *(to swerve)* desviarse; *(the wind)* cambiar; *(a boat)* virar —tr. desviar; *(a boat)* virar II. s. desvío, viraje *m.*

veg·e·ta·ble (vĕj'tə-bəl) I. s. verdura, legumbre *f*; *(inactive person)* vegetal *m* II. adj. vegetal ♦ **v. oil** aceite vegetal.

veg·e·tal (:ĭ-tl) adj. vegetal.

veg·e·tar·i·an ('-târ'ē-) I. s. vegetariano.

veg·e·tate ('-tāt') intr. vegetar.

veg·e·ta·tion ('-tā'shən) s. vegetación *f.*

ve·he·mence (vē'ə-məns) s. vehemencia.

ve·he·ment (:mənt) adj. vehemente.

ve·hi·cle (vē'ĭ-kəl) s. vehículo.

ve·hic·u·lar (vē-hĭk'yə-lər) adj. de *o* para vehículos.

veil (vāl) I. s. velo; FIG. velo, capa ♦ **under a v. of secrecy** en secreto II. tr. velar.

vein (vān) I. s. vena; BOT., ENTOM. nervio; GEOL., MIN. vena, filón *m*; *(in wood, marble)* vena, veta ♦ **in the same v.** del mismo estilo II. tr. vetear.

veined (vānd) adj. venoso; *(streaked)* veteado.

vel·lum (vĕl'əm) s. vitela, pergamino.

ve·loc·i·ty (və-lŏs'ĭ-tē) s. velocidad *f.*

ve·lour(s) (və-lŏŏr') s. veludillo.

ve·lum (vē'ləm) s. [pl. **-la**] velo del paladar.

vel·vet (vĕl'vĭt) I. s. terciopelo; *(on antlers)* vello II. adj. de terciopelo; *(velvety)* aterciopelado.

vel·vet·een (vĕl'vĭ-tēn') s. veludillo, velludo.

vel·vet·y ('-tē) adj. aterciopelado.

ve·nal (vē'nəl) adj. venal.

ve·nal·i·ty (vē-nǎl'ĭ-tē) s. venalidad *f.*

vend (vĕnd) tr. vender ♦ **vending machine** distribuidor automático, máquina vendedora.

vend·er (vĕn'dər) s. vendedor *m.*

ven·det·ta (vĕn-dĕt'ə) s. vendetta, venganza.

vend·i·ble (vĕn'də-bəl) s. artículo vendible.

ve·neer (və-nîr') I. s. chapa, enchapado; FIG. apariencia, barniz *m* II. tr. chapear, enchapar.

ven·er·a·ble (vĕn'ər-ə-bəl) adj. venerable.

ven·er·ate (vĕn'ə-rāt') tr. venerar.

ven·er·a·tion ('-rā'shən) s. veneración *f.*

ve·ne·re·al (və-nîr'ē-əl) adj. venéreo ♦ **v. disease** enfermedad venérea.

Ve·ne·tian blind (və-nē'shən) s. persiana veneciana, celosías.

ven·geance (vĕn'jəns) s. venganza, vindicta ♦

to take v. on vengarse de • **with a v.** *(furiously)* con violencia; *(excessively)* con creces.

venge·ful (vĕnj′fəl) adj. vengativo.

ve·ni·al (vē′nē-əl) adj. venial.

ven·i·son (vĕn′ĭ-sən) s. *(carne f de)* venado.

ven·om (vĕn′əm) s. veneno.

ven·om·ous (:ə-məs) adj. venenoso.

vent (vĕnt) I. s. *(for air)* respiradero; *(outlet)* salida; *(hole)* agujero, abertura ♦ **to give v. to** dar rienda suelta a II. tr. abrir un agujero en; *(to discharge)* dar salida a, descargar; *(feelings, words)* desahogar, dar rienda suelta a.

ven·ti·late (vĕn′tl-āt′) tr. ventilar.

ven·ti·la·tion (′-ā′shən) s. *(system)* ventilación f; *(air circulation)* aeración f.

ven·ti·la·tor (′-ā′tər) s. ventilador m.

ven·tral (vĕn′trəl) adj. ventral, abdominal.

ven·tri·cle (vĕn′trĭ-kəl) s. ventrículo.

ven·tril·o·quism (vĕn-trĭl′ə-kwĭz′əm) s. ventriloquia.

ven·tril·o·quist (:kwĭst) s. ventrílocuo.

ven·ture (vĕn′chər) I. s. *(undertaking)* aventura; *(stake)* riesgo; COM. empresa o negocio arriesgado ♦ **at a v.** a la (buena) ventura • **v. capital** capital de inversión II. tr. *(money, opinion)* aventurar; *(to dare)* atreverse a ♦ **nothing ventured nothing gained** el que no arriesga no gana —intr. *(to dare)* atreverse; *(to go)* ir ♦ **to v. forth** ir, salir.

ven·ture·some (:səm) adj. aventurado, arriesgado; *(enterprising)* emprendedor.

ven·tur·ous (:əs) adj. valiente, arrojado.

ven·ue (vĕn′yōō) s. *(of a crime)* lugar m; DER. jurisdicción f.

ve·ra·cious (və-rā′shəs) adj. veraz, verídico.

ve·rac·i·ty (və-răs′ĭ-tē) s. veracidad f; *(accuracy)* exactitud f.

ve·ran·da(h) (və-răn′də) s. terraza, veranda.

verb (vûrb) s. verbo.

ver·bal (vûr′bəl) adj. verbal.

ver·bal·ize (:bə-līz′) tr. expresar con palabras.

ver·ba·tim (vər-bā′tĭm) I. adj. literal II. adv. palabra por palabra, literalmente.

ver·bi·age (vûr′bē-ĭj) s. palabrería, verborrea.

ver·bose (vər-bōs′) adj. verboso.

ver·bos·i·ty (:bŏs′ĭ-tē) s. verbosidad f.

ver·dant (vûr′dnt) adj. verde.

ver·dict (vûr′dĭkt) s. veredicto; *(judgment)* dictamen m.

verge¹ (vûrj) I. s. *(edge, rim)* borde m, margen m; *(boundary)* límite m; *(staff)* cetro ♦ **to be on the v. of** estar a punto de II. intr. ♦ **to v. (up)on** *(to come near)* rayar en; *(to tend towards)* estar al borde de.

verge² intr. ♦ **to v. into** o **on** *(to pass into)* rayar en, acercarse a.

ver·i·fi·ca·tion (vĕr′ə-fĭ-kā′shən) s. verificación f.

ver·i·fi·er (′-fī′ər) s. verificador m.

ver·i·fy (vĕr′ə-fī′) tr. verificar.

ver·i·ly (vĕr′ə-lē) adv. verdaderamente.

ver·i·si·mil·i·tude (vĕr′ə-sĭ-mĭl′ĭ-tōōd′) s. verosimilitud f.

ver·i·ta·ble (vĕr′ĭ-tə-bəl) adj. verdadero.

ver·i·ty (vĕr′ĭ-tē) s. verdad f.

ver·mi·cel·li (vûr′mə-chĕl′ē, :sĕl′ē) s. fideos delgados.

ver·mi·cide (vûr′mĭ-sīd′) s. vermicida m.

ver·mi·form (vûr′mə-fôrm′) adj. vermiforme ♦ **v. appendix** apéndice vermiforme.

ver·mi·fuge (:fyōōj′) s. & adj. vermífugo.

ver·mil·(l)ion (vər-mĭl′yən) I. s. bermellón m

II. adj. bermejo.

ver·min (vûr′mĭn) s.inv. *(pest)* bicho(s), sabandija(s); *(person)* sabandija.

ver·mouth (vər-mōōth′) s. vermut m.

ver·nac·u·lar (vər-năk′yə-lər) I. s. *(language)* lengua vernácula; *(popular speech)* lenguaje m popular; *(jargon)* jerga ♦ **to put in the v.** expresar en lenguaje popular II. adj. vernáculo.

ver·nal (vûr′nəl) adj. vernal.

ver·sa·tile (vûr′sə-tl) adj. *(person)* de talentos variados; *(object)* de muchos usos.

ver·sa·til·i·ty (′-tĭl′ĭ-tē) s. *(of an object)* varios usos; *(of a person)* varios talentos.

verse¹ (vûrs) s. *(poetry)* verso; *(stanza)* estrofa; *(of a song)* cuplé m; BIBL. versículo.

verse² tr. familiarizarse con ♦ **to be versed in** estar familiarizado con.

versed (vûrst) adj. versado.

ver·si·fy (vûr′sə-fī′) tr. & intr. versificar.

ver·sion (vûr′zhən) s. versión f; *(adaptation)* adaptación f.

ver·sus (vûr′səs) prep. contra <*conjecture v. evidence* la conjetura contra la evidencia>.

ver·te·bra (vûr′tə-brə) s. [pl. **s** o **-ae**] vértebra.

ver·te·bral (:brəl) adj. vertebral.

ver·te·brate (:brāt′) adj. & s. vertebrado.

ver·tex (vûr′tĕks′) s. [pl. **es** o **-tices**] *(apex)* ápice m; ANAT., GEOM. vértice m.

ver·ti·cal (vûr′tĭ-kəl) adj. & s. vertical f.

ver·ti·go (vûr′tĭ-gō′) s. [pl. **es**] vértigo.

verve (vûrv) s. brío, ánimo.

ver·y (vĕr′ē) I. adv. muy; *(truly)* de veras <*it's the v. best* es de veras mejor>; *(indeed)* mucho <*are you tired?* ¿estás cansado? mucho>; *(precisely)* precisamente, exactamente <*the v. same one* exactamente el mismo>; *(as an intensive)* muy, tan <*he is so v. poor* es tan pobre> ♦ **at the v. latest** a más tardar • **at the v. least** como mínimo • **at the v. most** a lo más, a lo sumo • **not v.** poco <*it was not v. interesting* fue poco interesante> • **the v. best** lo mejor • **v. much (so)** muchísimo II. adj. ♦ **absolute** puro <*the v. truth* la verdad absoluta>; *(selfsame, exact)* mismo <*at that v. moment* en ese mismo momento>; *(mere)* mero, simple <*the v. thought frightens us* el mero pensamiento nos espanta> ♦ **at the v. end** al final de todo • **the v. idea!** ¡vaya idea! • **the v. image of** ser el vivo retrato de • **to shudder at the v. thought of it** temblar con sólo pensarlo.

ves·pers (vĕs′pərz) s.pl. vísperas.

ves·sel (vĕs′əl) s. *(container)* vaso, vasija; MARÍT. nave f, embarcación f; ANAT., BOT. vaso.

vest (vĕst) s. chaleco; G.B. *(undershirt)* camiseta II. tr. ♦ **to v. in** *(rights, property)* conceder, conferir; *(authority, power)* investir.

ves·tal (vĕs′təl) adj. & s. vestal f.

vest·ed (vĕs′tĭd) adj. DER. concedido, establecido ♦ **v. interests** intereses creados.

ves·ti·bule (vĕs′tə-byōōl′) s. vestíbulo, zaguán m.

ves·tige (vĕs′tĭj) s. vestigio.

ves·tig·i·al (vĕ-stĭj′ē-əl) adj. rudimentario.

vest·ment (vĕst′mənt) s. vestidura; *(robe)* toga; RELIG. vestimenta.

ves·try (vĕs′trē) s. sacristía, vestuario.

vet (vĕt) s. FAM. *(veterinarian)* veterinario; *(veteran)* veterano.

vet·er·an (vĕt′ər-ən) adj. & s. veterano.

vet·er·i·nar·i·an (vĕt′ər-ə-nâr′ē-ən) s. veterinario.

vet·er·i·nar·y (′-nĕr′ē) adj. & s. veterinario.

ve·to (vē'tō) I. s. [pl. **es**] veto II. tr. vetar; *(to prohibit)* prohibir.

vex *(to bother)* fastidiar, molestar; *(to baffle)* confundir.

vex·a·tion (věk-sā'shən) s. fastidio, molestia.

vex·a·tious (:shəs) adj. fastidioso, molesto.

vexed (věkst) adj. *(person)* enfadado, irritado; *(question, matter)* controvertido.

vi·a (vī'ə, vē'ə) prep. vía ♦ **v. air mail** por vía aérea.

vi·a·bil·i·ty (vī'ə-bĭl'ĭ-tē) s. viabilidad *f*.

vi·a·ble (vī'ə-bəl) adj. viable.

vi·a·duct (vī'ə-dŭkt') s. viaducto.

vi·al (vī'əl) s. frasco.

vi·and (vī'ənd) s. vianda ♦ pl. provisiones.

vibes (vībz) s. FAM. *(vibraphone)* vibráfono; JER. *(vibrations)* vibraciones *f*.

vi·bran·cy (vī'brən-sē) s. viveza, animación *f*.

vi·brant (vī'brənt) adj. vibrante; *(energetic)* enérgico, animado.

vi·bra·phone (vī'brə-fōn') s. vibráfono.

vi·brate (vī'brāt') intr. vibrar; *(to resonate)* resonar; *(to thrill)* estremecerse —tr. vibrar.

vi·bra·tion (vī-brā'shən) s. vibración *f*; *(quiver)* temblor *m*, estremecimiento ♦ pl. JER. vibraciones.

vi·bra·tor ('-tər) s. vibrador *m*.

vic·ar (vĭk'ər) s. vicario.

vic·ar·age (:ĭj) s. vicaría.

vi·car·i·ous (vī-kâr'ē-əs) adj. *(punishment)* sufrido por otro; *(pleasure)* indirecto.

vice¹ (vīs) s. vicio ♦ **v. squad** dependencia policial que combate al vicio.

vice² var. de **vise**.

vice³ I. s. *(used as a prefix)* vice ♦ **v. chancellor** vicecanciller • **v. president** vice presidente II. prep. en lugar de ♦ **v. versa** viceversa.

vice·roy (vīs'roi') s. virrey *m*.

vice·roy·al·ty (:'ol-tē) s. virreinato.

vi·cin·i·ty (vī-sĭn'ĭ-tē) s. proximidad *f*, *(area)* vecindad *f* ♦ **in the v. of** aproximadamente.

vi·cious (vĭsh'əs) adj. *(addicted to vice)* vicioso; *(malicious)* malicioso, rencoroso; *(storm, attack)* violento, fuerte; *(animal, crime)* salvaje, atroz ♦ **v. circle** círculo vicioso.

vi·cis·si·tude (vī-sĭs'ĭ-tōd') s. vicisitud *f*.

vic·tim (vĭk'tĭm) s. víctima ♦ **to fall (a) v.** to sucumbir a.

vic·tim·ize (:tə-mīz') tr. hacer víctima; *(to swindle)* estafar, embaucar.

vic·tor (vĭk'tər) s. vencedor *m*, triunfador *m*.

Vic·to·ri·an (vĭk-tôr'ē-ən) adj. & s. victoriano.

vic·to·ri·ous (vĭk-tôr'ē-əs) adj. triunfante, vencedor.

vic·to·ry (vĭk'tə-rē) s. victoria, triunfo.

vic·tuals (vĭt'lz) s.pl. vituallas.

vid·e·o (vĭd'ē-ō') adj. & s. vídeo.

vid·e·o·cas·sette ('--kə-sět') s. videocasete *mf*.

vid·e·o·con·fer·ence (:kŏn'fər-əns) s. teleconferencia.

vid·e·o·disc/disk ('--dĭsk') s. videodisco.

vid·e·o·tape (:tāp') I. s. videocinta II. tr. grabar en videocinta.

vie (vī) intr. **vying** competir, contender.

view (vyōō) I. s. *(sight, vista)* vista; *(examination)* examinación *f*, inspección *f*; *(systematic survey)* panorama *m*; *(opinion)* opinión *f*; *(approach)* enfoque *m* <*our v. of the problem* nuestro enfoque del problema>; *(intention)* propósito <*with a v. to doing something* con el propósito de hacer algo>; *(chance)* posibilidad *f*, perspectiva ♦ **in v. of** en vista de, conside-

rando • **point of v.** punto de vista • **to be on v.** estar a la vista • **to come into v.** aparecer • **to have in v.** *(a project)* tener a la vista; *(to keep in mind)* tener presente • **to keep in v.** no perder de vista • **to take a dim v. of** ver con malos ojos • **to take the v. that** pensar que • **v. finder** visor II. tr. ver, mirar; *(to examine)* examinar; *(to consider)* considerar, enfocar.

view·er ('ər) s. espectador *m*; *(television viewer)* televidente *mf*; FOTOG. visor *m*.

view·point (:'point') s. punto de vista.

vig·il (vĭj'əl) s. vigilia ♦ **to keep v.** velar.

vig·i·lance (:ə-ləns) s. vigilancia.

vig·i·lant (:lənt) adj. vigilante, alerto.

vig·i·lan·te (vĭj'ə-lăn'tē) s. vigilante *mf*, miembro de una junta que actúa como policía.

vi·gnette (vĭn-yět') s. IMPR. viñeta; FOTOG. retrato con bordes esfumados; LIT. bosquejo corto; CINEM. escena corta.

vig·or (vĭg'ər) s. vigor *m*.

vig·or·ous (:əs) adj. *(strong)* vigoroso, fuerte; *(energetic)* enérgico.

vig·our (vĭg'ər) G.B. var. de **vigor**.

vile (vīl) adj. *(despicable)* vil, ruin; *(loathsome)* odioso; *(food)* desagradable; *(weather)* pésimo.

vil·i·fy (vĭl'ə-fī') tr. difamar, denigrar.

vil·la (vĭl'ə) s. villa, quinta; G.B. *(residence)* chalet *m*.

vil·lage (vĭl'ĭj) s. *(hamlet)* aldea; *(town)* pueblo; *(inhabitants)* población *f*.

vil·lag·er (:ĭ-jər) s. aldeano.

vil·lain (vĭl'ən) s. villano, canalla *m*; FIG. causa.

vil·lain·ous (:ə-nəs) adj. *(vile)* vil; *(wicked)* villano, malvado.

vil·lain·y (:ə-nē) s. villanía, vileza.

vim (vĭm) s. energía, brío.

vin·ai·grette (vĭn'ĭ-grět') s. *(container)* vinagrera; *(sauce)* vinagreta.

vin·di·cate (vĭn'dĭ-kāt') tr. vindicar, exculpar; *(to justify)* justificar.

vin·di·ca·tion ('-kā'shən) s. vindicación *f*.

vin·dic·tive (vĭn-dĭk'tĭv) adj. vengativo.

vine (vīn) s. enredadera; *(grapevine)* parra, vid *f* ♦ **clinging v.** persona pegajosa.

vin·e·gar (vĭn'ĭ-gər) s. vinagre *m*.

vine·stock (vīn'stŏk') s. cepa (de la vid).

vine·yard (vĭn'yərd) s. viñedo, viña.

vin·tage (vĭn'tĭj) I. s. *(season)* vendimia; *(crop, year)* cosecha II. adj. *(wine)* añejo, de calidad; *(classic)* clásico; *(of the best)* excelente <*a v. year for us un año* excelente para nosotros>.

vint·ner (vĭnt'nər) s. vinatero.

vi·nyl (vī'nəl) s. vinilo.

vi·ol (vī'əl) s. viola.

vi·o·la¹ (vē-ō'lə) s. MÚS. viola.

vi·o·la² (vī-ō'lə, vī'ə-lə) s. BOT. viola, violeta.

vi·o·la·ble (vī'ə-lə-bəl) adj. violable.

vi·o·late (vī'ə-lāt') tr. violar.

vi·o·la·tion ('-lā'shən) s. violación *f*.

vi·o·la·tor ('-lā'tər) s. violador *m*.

vi·o·lence (vī'ə-ləns) s. violencia ♦ **to do v. to** violar, ir en contra de.

vi·o·lent (:lənt) adj. violento; *(pain)* intenso; *(feeling)* profundo ♦ **to become v.** mostrarse violento.

vi·o·let (vī'ə-lĭt) I. s. *(plant)* violeta; *(color)* violeta II. adj. violado, violeta.

vi·o·lin (vī'ə-lĭn') s. violín *m*.

vi·o·lin·ist (:ĭst) s. violinista *mf*.

vi·o·lon·cel·lo (vē'ə-lən-chĕl'ō) s. violoncelo.

VIP (vē'ī-pē') s. FAM. personalidad *f* (impor-

tante).
vi·per (vī′pər) s. víbora.
vi·ral (vī′rəl) s. causado por un virus, virulento.
vir·gin (vûr′jǐn) **I.** s. virgen f ♦ **The V.** la Virgen
María **II.** adj. virgen; *(inttiul)* inicial, primero;
(unsullied) puro, intacto.
vir·gin·al¹ (vûr′jə-nəl) adj. virginal.
vir·gin·al² s. MÚS. espineta.
vir·gin·i·ty (vər-jǐn′ǐ-tē) s. virginidad f.
vir·gule (vûr′gyōol) s. vírgula.
vir·ile (vǐr′əl, :ǐl′) adj. viril, varonil.
vi·ril·i·ty (və-rǐl′ǐ-tē) s. virilidad f.
vi·rol·o·gy (vī-rōl′ə-jē) s. virología.
vir·tu·al (vûr′chōo-əl) adj. virtual.
vir·tu·al·ly (:ə-lē) adv. prácticamente, casi *‹it is
v. impossible* es casi imposible›.
vir·tue (vûr′chōo) s. virtud f; *(chastity)* castidad f, honra; *(advantage)* ventaja ♦ **by** *o* **in v. of**
en virtud de ♦ **of easy v.** fácil.
vir·tu·os·i·ty (vûr′chōo-ŏs′ǐ-tē) s. virtuosismo.
vir·tu·o·so (:ō′sō) s. [pl. **s** *o* **-si**] virtuoso.
vir·tu·ous (vûr′chōo-əs) adj. *(righteous)* virtuoso; *(chaste)* casto, puro.
vir·u·lence (vǐr′yə-ləns) s. virulencia.
vir·u·lent (:lənt) adj. virulento.
vi·rus (vī′rəs) s. virus *m.*
vi·sa (vē′zə) s. visa, visado.
♦**la uga** (:la′ij) n pare semblante *m.*
vis-à-vis (vē′zə-vē′) **I.** adv. frente a frente, cara
a cara **II.** prep. *(opposite to)* frente a, enfrente
de; *(compared with)* comparado con, con relación a.
vis·cer·a (vǐs′ər-ə) s.pl. vísceras.
vis·cer·al (:əl) adj. ANAT. visceral; *(profound)*
profundo, íntimo; *(instinctive)* instintivo.
vis·cos·i·ty (vǐ-skŏs′ǐ-tē) s. viscosidad f.
vis·count (vī′kount′) s. vizconde m.
vis·count·ess (vī′koun′tǐs) s. vizcondesa.
vis·cous (vǐs′kəs) adj. viscoso.
vise (vīs) s. tornillo de banco.
vis·i·bil·i·ty (vǐz′ə-bǐl′ǐ-tē) s. visibilidad f.
vis·i·ble (′-bəl) adj. visible; *(apparent)* manifiesto; *(evident)* evidente.
vi·sion (vǐzh′ən) **I.** s. *(sight)* vista, visión f;
(foresight) clarividencia, previsión f; *(mental
image)* visión, fantasía ♦ **a person** *o* **of v.** una
persona clarividente.
vi·sion·ar·y (:ə-nĕr′ē) **I.** adj. *(foresighted)* visionario; *(dreamy)* de ensueño; *(utopian)* utópico
II. s. visionario.
vis·it (vǐz′ǐt) **I.** tr. visitar; *(as a guest)* pasar
una temporada en; *(punishment, misfortune)* infligir, enviar —intr. hacer una visita, ir de visita; FAM. *(to chat)* charlar **II.** s. visita; *(stay)*
estadía (como invitado) ♦ **to be on a v.** estar
de visita en ♦ **to pay a v.** visitar a.
vis·i·tant (:ǐ-tnt) s. *(guest)* invitado; *(ghost)*
aparecido.
vis·i·ta·tion (′-tā′shən) s. visita; *(calamity)* desgracia, calamidad f ♦ **v. rights** derecho de visita
(a hijos después de divorcio).
vis·it·ing (′-tǐng) adj. *(card, hours)* de visita;
(person) visitante.
vis·i·tor (vǐz′ǐ-tər) s. visitante mf, visita; *(tourist)* turista mf.
vi·sor (vī′zər) s. visera.
vis·ta (vǐs′tə) s. vista, perspectiva.
vi·su·al (vǐzh′ōo-əl) adj. visual; *(inspection,
proof)* ocular ♦ **v. aids** medios visuales.
vi·su·al·ize (vǐzh′ōo-ə-līz′) tr. & intr. visualiza
vi·tal (vīt′l) adj. vital ♦ **v. statistics** esta 'ica
demográfica.

vi·tal·i·ty (vī-tăl′ǐ-tē) s. vitalidad f.
vi·tal·ize (vīt′l-īz′) tr. vitalizar.
vi·tals (vīt′lz) s.pl. órganos vitales; FIG. partes
f esenciales.
vi·ta·min (vī′tə-mǐn) s. vitamina.
vi·ti·ate (vǐsh′ē-āt′) tr. viciar.
vit·i·cul·ture (vǐt′ǐ-kŭl′chər) s. viticultura.
vit·re·ous (vǐt′rē-əs) adj. vítreo.
vit·ri·fy (vǐt′rə-fī′) tr. & intr. vitrificar(se).
vit·ri·ol (vǐt′rē-əl) s. vitriolo; FIG. virulencia,
veneno.
vit·ri·ol·ic (′-ŏl′ǐk) adj. vitriólico; FIG. mordaz.
vi·tu·per·ate (vī-tōo′pə-rāt′) tr. vituperar.
vi·tu·per·a·tion (-pə-rā′shən) s. vituperación f.
vi·tu·per·a·tive (-′pər-ə-tǐv) adj. vituperante.
vi·va·cious (vǐ-vā′shəs, vī-) adj. vivaz.
vi·vac·i·ty (vǐ-văs′ǐ-tē, vī-) s. vivacidad f.
viv·id (vǐv′ǐd) adj. vívido; *(memory)* vivo.
viv·i·fy (vǐv′ə-fī′) tr. vivificar; FIG. animar.
viv·i·sect (vǐv′-sĕkt′) tr. hacer la vivisección
de.
viv·i·sec·tion (′-sĕk′shən) s. vivisección f.
vix·en (vǐk′sən) s. zorra; FIG. arpía.
vo·cab·u·lar·y (vō-kăb′yə-lĕr′ē) s. vocabulario.
vo·cal (vō′kəl) adj. vocal; *(clamorous)* ruidoso;
(outspoken) que dice lo que piensa ♦ **v. cords**
cuerdas vocales.
vo·cal·ist (vō′kə-lǐst) s. vocalista mf.
vo·cal·ize (:līz′) tr. articular —intr. vocalizar.
vo·ca·tion (vō-kā′shən) s. vocación f.
vo·ca·tion·al (:shə-nəl) adj. vocacional ♦ **v.
school** escuela vocacional.
vo·cif·er·ate (vō-sǐf′ə-rāt′) tr. & intr. vociferar.
vo·cif·er·ous (:ər-əs) adj. vociferador.
vogue (vōg) s. moda, boga ♦ **in v.** en boga.
voice (vois) **I.** s. voz f; *(timbre)* tono *‹a gentle
v.* un tono dulce› ♦ **at the top of one's v.** a voz
en cuello ♦ **in a loud, low v.** en voz alta, baja ♦
to give v. to expresar ♦ **to have a v. in** tener
voz en ♦ **to lose, raise one's v.** perder, alzar la
voz ♦ **v. box** laringe **II.** tr. *(to utter)* expresar;
FONÉT. sonorizar.
voice·less (′-lǐs) adj. mudo; FONÉT. sordo.
voice-o·ver (′-ō′vər) s. CINEM. voz f del comen-
tador *o* narrador que no aparece en la imagen.
void (void) **I.** adj. *(empty)* vacío; *(vacant)* vacante; DER. nulo, inválido ♦ **v. of** desprovisto
de **II.** s. vacío **III.** tr. *(to invalidate)* invalidar,
anular; *(to empty)* vaciar; FISIOL. evacuar.
vol·a·tile (vōl′ə-tl, :tǐl′) adj. volátil; FIG. inestable, explosivo.
vol·a·til·i·ty (′-tǐl′ǐ-tē) s. volatilidad f.
vol·can·ic (vŏl-kăn′ǐk) adj. volcánico.
vol·ca·no (vŏl-kā′nō) s. [pl. **(e)s**] volcán m.
vo·li·tion (və-lǐsh′ən) s. volición f, voluntad f.
vol·ley (vŏl′ē) **I.** s. *(of missiles, bullets)* descarga, andanada; *(of stones)* lluvia; *(of oaths,
insults)* torrente m; *(in tennis)* voleo **II.** tr.
MIL. lanzar —intr. DEP. volear.
vol·ley·ball (:bôl′) s. balonvolea m, voleibol
m; *(ball)* balón m.
volt¹ (vōlt) s. ELEC. voltio.
volt² s. EQUIT. vuelta; ESGR. esquiva.
volt·age (vōl′tǐj) s. voltaje m, tensión f.
vol·ta·ic (-tā′ǐk) adj. voltaico.
vol·u·ble (vŏl′yə-bəl) adj. locuaz.
vol·ume (vŏl′yōom) s. volumen m ♦ **v. control**
control del volumen ♦ pl. montones.
vo·lu·mi·nous (və-lōo′mə-nəs) adj. voluminoso; *(information, data)* abundante.
vol·un·tar·y (vŏl′ən-tĕr′ē) adj. voluntario;
(spontaneous) espontáneo

vol·un·teer (' -tîr') I. s. voluntario II. adj. voluntario; *(police, army)* de voluntarios III. tr. & intr. ofrecer(se) voluntariamente; MIL. alistar(se) como voluntario.

vo·lup·tu·ous (və-lŭp'chō͞o-əs) adj. voluptuoso, sensual.

vom·it (vŏm'ĭt) I. tr. & intr. vomitar II. s. vómito.

voo·doo (vō͞o'dō͞o) s. vodú, vudú *f.*

vo·ra·cious (vô-rā'shəs) adj. voraz.

vor·tex (vôr'tĕks') s. [pl. es *o* -tices] vórtice *m*; FIG. vorágine *f.*

vo·ta·ry (vō'tə-rē) s. devoto.

vote (vōt) I. s. voto; *(act, result)* votación *f; (right)* derecho de voto; *(bloc)* votos <the labor v. los votos de los obreros> ♦ **by a majority v.** por una mayoría de votos ♦ **popular, secret v.** votación popular, secreta ♦ **to take a v. on** poner *o* someter a votación ♦ **to put to the v.** poner *o* someter a votación ♦ **unanimous v.** votación por unanimidad ♦ **v. of confidence** voto de confianza II. intr. votar —tr. votar; *(to select)* elegir; FAM. *(to suggest)* sugerir, proponer ♦ **to v. down** votar en contra de, rechazar ♦ **to v. in** elegir (por votación).

vot·er (vō'tər) s. votante *mf*, elector *m.*

vot·ing (vō'tĭng) I. s. votación *f* II. adj. *(person, public)* votante; *(campaign)* electoral.

vo·tive (vō'tĭv) adj. votivo.

vouch (vouch) tr. verificar, comprobar —intr. ♦ **to v. for** avalar, responder por.

vouch·er (vou'chər) s. *(person)* fiador *m; (document)* comprobante *m*, vale *m.*

vouch·safe (vouch-sāf') tr. dignarse a dar.

vow (vou) I. s. promesa; RELIG. voto ♦ **to take vows** hacer votos monásticos II. tr. *(to pledge)* jurar; *(to promise)* prometer.

vow·el (vou'əl) s. vocal *f.*

voy·age (voi'ĭj) I. s. viaje *m*, travesía II. intr. hacer un viaje, viajar.

vul·ca·nize (vŭl'kə-nīz') tr. vulcanizar.

vul·gar (vŭl'gər) adj. vulgar; *(joke, story)* indecente, verde; *(rude)* grosero; *(taste)* vulgar.

vul·gar·i·an (-gâr'ē-ən) s. persona vulgar.

vul·gar·ism ('-gə-rĭz'əm) s. vulgarismo.

vul·gar·i·ty (-găr'ĭ-tē) s. vulgaridad *f*, grosería.

vul·gar·ize ('gə-rīz') tr. vulgarizar.

vul·gate ('gāt') s. lenguaje *m* popular ♦ V. Vulgata.

vul·ner·a·bil·i·ty (vŭl'nər-ə-bĭl'ĭ-tē) s. vulnerabilidad *f.*

vul·ner·a·ble ('--bəl) adj. vulnerable ♦ **to be v.** to ser susceptible a.

vul·ture (vŭl'chər) s. buitre *m*, gallinazo.

vul·va (vŭl'və) s. [pl. -ae] vulva.

W

w, W (dŭb'əl-yō͞o) s. vigésima tercera letra del alfabeto inglés.

wack·y (wăk'ē) adj. -i- JER. loco.

wad (wŏd) s. taco, fajo; *(of papers)* lío; FAM. dineral *m.*

wad·ding ('ĭng) s. taco, fajo.

wad·dle (wŏd'l) I. intr. contonearse II. s. contoneo.

wade (wād) intr. caminar en; *(to struggle)* avanzar con dificultad —tr. vadear.

wad·er (wā'dər) s. vadeador *m*; ORNIT. ave zancuda ♦ pl. botas altas de vadeo.

wa·fer (wā'fər) s. barquillo; RELIG. hostia.

waf·fle¹ (wŏf'əl) s. panqueque *m* al estilo de barquillo.

waf·fle² FAM. intr. *(to waver)* vacilar.

waft (wăft, wäft) I. tr. llevar por el aire *o* sobre el agua —intr. flotar II. s. soplo.

wag¹ (wăg) I. intr. **-gg-** agitarse —tr. menear II. s. meneo; *(of a tail)* coleo.

wag² s. *(joker)* bromista *mf.*

wage (wāj) I. s. pago, sueldo ♦ pl. *(pay)* salario; FIG. fruto II. tr. *(war)* hacer; *(a campaign)* emprender.

wa·ger (wā'jər) I. s. apuesta II. tr. & intr. apostar.

wag·ger·y (wăg'ə-rē) s. broma.

wag·gle (wăg'əl) tr. menear rápidamente —intr. agitarse.

wag·on (wăg'ən) s. *(vehicle)* carro; *(railway car)* vagón *m; (station wagon)* furgoneta ♦ **to be** *o* **to go on the w.** JER. no beber, dejar de beber.

waif (wāf) s. *(child)* expósito; *(animal)* animal abandonado.

wail (wāl) I. intr. lamentarse; *(to howl)* aullar II. s. *(cry)* lamento; *(howl)* aullido.

wain·scot (wān'skət, :skŏt') I. s. revestimiento de madera II. tr. revestir con madera.

wain·wright (wān'rīt') s. carretero.

waist (wāst) s. cintura; *(of garment)* talle *m.*

waist·band ('bănd') s. cinturón *m.*

waist·coat (wĕs'kĭt, wāst'kōt') s. G.B. chaleco.

waist·line (wāst'līn') s. cintura, talle *m.*

wait (wāt) I. intr. esperar ♦ **to w. up** esperar sin acostarse ♦ **waiting list, room** lista, sala de espera —tr. esperar; *(to delay)* retrasar ♦ **to w. for** esperar ♦ **to w. on** *(tables)* servir, atender II. s. espera ♦ **to lie in w.** estar al acecho.

wait·er (wā'tər) s. camarero.

wait·ress (wā'trĭs) s. camarera.

waive (wāv) tr. *(to relinquish)* renunciar a; *(to dispense with)* suspender; *(to put off)* postergar.

waiv·er (wā'vər) s. DER. renuncia.

wake¹ (wāk) I. intr. **-ed** *o* **woke, -ed** *o* **woken** despertarse; *(to be awake)* estar despierto —tr. despertar; *(to alert)* alertar; *(to revive)* resucitar ♦ **to w. up** despertar II. s. velatorio.

wake² s. *(track)* huella; *(of a ship)* estela ♦ **in the w. of** inmediatamente después de.

wake·ful ('fəl) adj. desvelado; *(alert)* alerta.

wak·en (wā'kən) tr. & intr. despertar(se).

wale (wāl) s. verdugón *m.*

walk (wôk) I. intr. caminar, andar; *(to go on foot)* ir a pie; *(to stroll)* pasear ♦ **to w. around** pasear(se) ♦ **to w. away** *o* **off** irse ♦ **to w. in** entrar ♦ **to w. out** *(on strike)* declararse en huelga; *(to leave)* irse ♦ **walking papers** FAM. nota de despido —tr. caminar por; *(a distance)* caminar, andar; *(a horse)* llevar al paso; *(to escort)* acompañar ♦ **to w. away from** alejarse de; *(problems)* evitar; *(accident)* salir ileso de ♦ **to w. away** *o* **off with** llevarse ♦ **to w. in on** aparecérsele inesperadamente a ♦ **to w. into** entrar en; *(wall)* chocar contra; *(trap)* caer en ♦ **to w. out on** FAM. dejar abandonado II. s. paseo; *(hike)* caminata; *(pace)* paso ♦ **people from all walks of life** todo tipo de gente ♦ **to go for** *o* **to take a w.** dar un paseo.

walk·a·way (wô'kə-wā') s. victoria fácil.

walk·er (wô'kər) s. *(pedestrian)* peatón *m; (stroller)* paseante *mf; (for infants)* andador *m.*

walk·ie-talk·ie (wô'kē-tô'kē) s. radioteléfono portátil.

walk-in (wôk'ĭn') adj. tan grande que uno

puede entrar en él; *(services)* que no requiere cita previa.

walk·out (:out') s. *(strike)* huelga; *(quitting)* renuncia.

walk·o·ver (:ō'vər) s. victoria fácil.

walk·up *o* **walk-up** (:ŭp') s. *(building)* edificio sin ascensor; *(apartment)* departamento en un edificio sin ascensor.

walk·way (:wā') s. pasillo.

wall (wôl) I. s. pared *f*; *(around a house)* muro; *(of city)* muralla; *(of garden)* tapia; *(obstacle)* barrera ♦ **to drive up the w.** FAM. volver loco II. tr. poner un muro *o* una pared a ♦ **to w. in** *o* **up** *(house, town)* amurallar; *(garden)* tapiar ♦ **to w. off** separar con una pared III. adj. de pared, mural.

wall·board ('bôrd') s. madera prensada.

wal·let (wŏl'ĭt) s. billetera, cartera.

wall·eye (wôl'ī') s. ojo albino.

wall·flow·er (:flou'ər) s. *(flower)* alhelí *m*; *(person)* persona que no participa.

wal·lop (wŏl'əp) I. tr. pegar con fuerza II. s. *(blow)* golpe *m* fuerte; *(force)* fuerza, impacto.

wal·lop·ing (:ə-pĭng) FAM. I. adj. enorme; *(impressive)* impresionante II. s. paliza.

wal·low (wŏl'ō) I. intr. revolcarse II. s. *(act)* revuelco; *(of animals)* bañadero.

wall·pa·per (wôl'pā'pər) I. s. papel *m* de empapelar II. tr. *e* intr. empapelar.

wall-to-wall (:tə-wôl') adj. de pared a pared; *(all-inclusive)* total.

wal·nut (wôl'nŭt) s. nuez *f*; *(tree, wood)* nogal *m*.

wal·rus (wôl'rəs) s. [pl. inv. *o* **es**] morsa.

waltz (wôlts) I. s. vals *m* II. intr. bailar el vals ♦ **to w. through** FAM. pasar como si tal cosa.

wan (wŏn) adj. **-nn-** pálido; *(weary)* pesaroso.

wand (wŏnd) s. varita mágica; *(rod)* vara.

wan·der (wŏn'dər) intr. *(to roam)* vagar; *(to go astray)* desviarse —tr. vagar por.

wan·der·er (:ər) s. vagabundo.

wan·der·ing (:ĭng) I. adj. nómada II. s. vagabundeo.

wan·der·lust (:lŭst') s. deseos de viajar.

wane (wān) I. intr. disminuir; *(to decline)* declinar; ASTRON. menguar II. s. disminución *f*; ASTRON. cuarto menguante.

wan·gle (wăng'gəl) FAM. tr. conseguir tramposamente —intr. hacer trampa.

wan·ing (wā'nĭng) s. mengua, disminución *f*.

want (wŏnt, wônt) I. tr. querer; *(to desire)* desear; *(to lack)* carecer de; *(to need)* necesitar ♦ **to w. out** FAM. querer irse • **wanted** se busca; *(by an employer)* necesítase —intr. querer ♦ **to w. for** carecer de II. s. *(lack)* falta; *(poverty)* pobreza; *(wish)* deseo.

want·ing (wŏn'tĭng, wôn'-) I. adj. ausente; *(deficient)* deficiente II. prep. *(without)* sin; *(minus)* menos.

wan·ton (wŏn'tən) adj. *(lewd)* sensual; *(unjust)* sin piedad; *(unrestrained)* desenfrenado; *(excessive)* excesivo; *(playful)* juguetón.

war (wôr) I. s. guerra II. adj. de guerra III. intr. **-rr-** guerrear.

war·ble (wôr'bəl) I. intr. trinar II. s. trino.

war·bler (:blər) s. sílvido; *(European)* curruca.

ward (wôrd) I. s. distrito, barrio; *(of hospital)* sala; *(of jail)* pabellón *m*; *(minor)* pupilo; *(custody)* tutela II. tr. ♦ **to w. off** prevenir.

war·den (wôr'dn) s. *(prison official)* director *m*; *(custodian)* guardián *m*.

ward·er (wôr'dər) s. guardia.

ward·robe (wôr'drōb') s. armario; *(garments)* vestuario.

ward·room (wôrd'rōm') s. MARÍT. comedor *m* de oficiales.

ware (wâr) s. *(articles)* artículos; *(ceramics)* cerámica ♦ pl. mercancías.

ware·house ('hous') I. s. almacén *n* II. tr. almacenar.

war·fare (wôr'fâr') s. guerra.

war·head (:hĕd') s. ojiva de proyectil.

war·horse (:hôrs') s. caballo de guerra; FAM. veterano.

war·like (:līk') adj. belicoso; *(of war)* guerrero.

war·lock (wôr'lŏk') s. brujo.

war·lord (wôr'lôrd') s. jefe *m* militar.

warm (wôrm) I. adj. tibio, caliente; *(weather)* cálido, caluroso; *(clothing)* que mantiene abrigado; *(enthusiastic)* entusiasta; *(cordial)* cordial; *(loving)* cariñoso; *(fresh)* fresco; FAM. *(dangerous)* peligroso ♦ **to be w.** *(weather)* hacer calor; *(person)* tener calor; *(thing)* estar caliente II. tr. calentar; *(to cheer)* alegrar ♦ **to w. up** *(food)* recalentar; *(body)* hacer entrar en calor; *(debate)* avivar —intr. calentarse.

warm-blood·ed (:blŭd'ĭd) adj. de sangre caliente; FIG. ardiente.

warm-heart·ed (:här'tĭd) adj. cariñoso.

war·mon·ger (wôr'mŭng'gər) s. belicista *mf*.

warmth (wôrmth) s. calor *m*; *(affection)* afecto; *(ardor)* ardor *m*.

warm-up (wôrm'ŭp') s. DEP. calentamiento.

warn (wôrn) tr. *e* intr. advertir.

warn·ing (wôr'nĭng) I. s. advertencia; *(signal)* señal *f*; *(advice)* aviso ♦ **without w.** de repente II. adj. de advertencia; *(device)* de alarma.

warp (wôrp) I. tr. alabear, deformar; *(to pervert)* pervertir; *(to twist)* torcer —intr. deformarse, torcerse; *(to deviate)* pervertirse II. s. alabeo, deformación *f*; *(perversion)* perversión *f*; TEJ. urdimbre *f*.

war·path (wôr'păth') s. ♦ **to be on the w.** estar propenso a pelear.

war·plane (:plān') s. avión *m* de guerra.

war·rant (wôr'ənt) I. s. autorización *f*; *(guarantee)* garantía, *(grounds)* justificación *f*; *(search, arrest)* orden *f* judicial II. tr. garantizar; *(to justify)* justificar; *(to authorize)* autorizar.

war·ran·tor (:ən-tər, :tôr') s. garante *mf*.

war·ran·ty (:tē) s. garantía; *(grounds)* justificación *f*; *(authorization)* autorización *f*.

war·ren (wôr'ən) s. conejera.

war·ri·or (wôr'ē-ər) s. guerrero.

war·ship (wôr'shĭp') s. buque *m* de guerra.

wart (wôrt) s. verruga ♦ **w. hog** jabalí verrugoso.

war·time (wôr'tīm') s. época de guerra.

war·y (wâr'ē) adj. **-i-** *(guarded)* cauteloso; *(watchful)* cuidadoso.

was (wŏz, wŭz, wəz) pret. de **be.**

wash (wŏsh) I. tr. lavar; *(to moisten)* mojar; *(to lap)* bañar; *(wound, eyes)* bañar; *(to erode)* erosionar ♦ **to w. away** *o* **out** *(grease, stains)* quitar; *(to carry away)* llevarse • **to w. down** limpiar; *(to gulp down)* tragar; *(with wine, beer)* rociar ♦ **to w. off** quitar —intr. lavarse; *(clothes)* lavar ropa ♦ **to w. away** derrumbarse • **to w. off** salir en el lavado ♦ **to w. out** *(colors)* desteñirse; *(to fail)* fracasar ♦ **to w. up** lavarse; *(the dishes)* lavar los platos II. s. *(action)* lavado; *(clothes)* ropa para lavar; *(waste liquid)* desperdicio; *(coating)* baño; *(rush of water)* golpe *m*

de agua; *(sound of water)* rumor *m* ♦ **it will all come out in the w.** al final todo se arreglará.
wash·a·ble (:'ə-bəl) adj. lavable.
wash-and-wear (:ən-wâr') adj. que no se plancha.
wash·ba·sin (:bā'sĭn) s. lavabo.
wash·board (:bôrd') s. tabla de lavar.
wash·bowl (:bōl') s. lavabo.
wash·cloth (:klŏth') s. [pl. **s**] toallita para lavarse.
wash·day (:dā') s. día *m* para lavar.
washed-out (wŏsht'out') adj. descolorido; *(exhausted)* agotado.
washed-up (:ŭp') adj. acabado.
wash·er (wŏsh'ər) s. lavador *m;* *(disc)* arandela; *(machine)* máquina de lavar.
wash·er·wom·an (:wŏm'ən) s. [pl. **-women**] lavandera.
wash·ing (wŏsh'ĭng) s. lavado; *(clothes to be done)* ropa para lavar; *(residue)* residuo.
wash·out (:out') s. derrubio; *(failure)* fracaso.
wash·room (:rōōm') s. baño.
wash·stand (:stănd') s. lavabo.
wash·tub (:tŭb') s. tina de lavar.
wasp (wŏsp) s. avispa.
wasp·ish (wŏs'pĭsh) adj. irascible.
was·sail (wŏs'əl) s. brindis m
wast·age (wā'stĭj) s. desperdicio.
waste (wāst) I. tr. *(money)* despilfarrar; *(time)* perder; *(talent)* desperdiciar; *(to exhaust)* agotar; JER. *(to kill)* matar —intr. *(goods)* desperdiciarse; *(time)* perderse; *(strength, vigor)* debilitarse ♦ **to w. away** consumirse II. s. despilfarro; *(wastage)* desperdicios; *(of time, energy)* pérdida; *(residue)* residuos; *(garbage)* basura ♦ **to go to w.** desperdiciarse III. adj. desperdiciado; *(residual)* residual.
waste·bas·ket ('băs'kĭt) s. cesto de papeles.
wast·ed (wā'stĭd) adj. desperdiciado; *(superfluous)* innecesario; JER. *(stoned)* drogado.
waste·ful (wāst'fəl) adj. despilfarrador.
waste·land (:lănd') s. páramo.
wast·rel (wā'strəl) s. derrochador *m;* *(idler)* vagabundo.
watch (wŏch) I. tr. mirar; *(to keep vigil)* vigilar ♦ **to w. out** tener cuidado —tr. mirar; *(to see)* ver; *(to pay attention to)* fijarse en; *(to guard)* vigilar; *(to take care of)* cuidar; *(to stand vigil over)* velar; *(to be careful with)* tener cuidado con ♦ **to w. for** esperar • **to w. one's step** tener cuidado • **to w. over** vigilar II. s. *(timepiece)* reloj *m;* *(act)* vigilia, vela; *(group of persons)* ronda, guardia; MIL. centinela *m;* *(lookout)* vigía *m* ♦ **to keep w.** estar de guardia.
watch·dog (:dôg') s. perro guardián; FIG. guardián *m.*
watch·ful (:fəl) adj. alerta, vigilante.
watch·mak·er (:mā'kər) s. relojero.
watch·man (:mən) s. [pl. **-men**] sereno.
watch·tow·er (:tou'ər) s. atalaya, garita.
watch·word (:wûrd') s. contraseña.
wa·ter (wŏ'tər) I. s. agua; *(urine)* orina; *(of a fabric)* aguas ♦ **like w.** en gran abundancia • **to be in deep** ○ **hot w.** estar en un gran aprieto • **to hold w.** ser lógico • **to keep one's head above w.** mantenerse a flote • **to pass w.** orinar • **to throw cold w.** on echar un jarro de agua fría sobre • **w. bed** cama con colchón de agua • **w. buffalo** búfalo de India • **w. closet** inodoro, wáter • **w. color** acuarela • **w. cooler** refrigerador de agua • **w. hole** charco • **w. lily**

ninfea II. tr. *(a garden)* regar; *(animals)* abrevar; *(to make wet)* mojar; *(to dilute)* diluir ♦ **to w. down** *(a drink)* aguar; FIG. suavizar, moderar —intr. *(eyes)* llorar ♦ **to make one's mouth w.** hacérsele agua la boca a uno.
wa·ter·borne (:bôrn') adj. flotante.
wa·ter·col·or (:kŭl'ər) adj. & s. (de) acuarela.
wa·ter·course (:kôrs') s. vía navegable; *(channel)* canal *m.*
wa·ter·cress (:krĕs') s. berro, mastuerzo.
wa·ter·fall (:fôl') s. catarata, cascada.
wa·ter·fowl (:foul') s. [pl. inv. ○ **s**] ave acuática.
wa·ter·front (:frŭnt') s. *(land)* costanera; *(dock zone)* muelles *m.*
wa·ter·ing (:ĭng) I. s. riego II. adj. de riego; *(eyes)* lloroso ♦ **w. can** regadera • **w. hole** *(hole)* charco; *(bar)* bar.
wa·ter·logged (:lôgd') adj. saturado de agua.
wa·ter·loo (wŏ'tər-lōō') s. ♦ **to meet one's w.** sufrir una derrota terminante.
wa·ter·mark (wŏ'tər-märk') s. marca de nivel de agua; *(in paper)* marca de agua.
wa·ter·mel·on (:mĕl'ən) s. sandía.
wa·ter·pow·er (:pou'ər) s. energía hidráulica.
wa·ter·proof (:prōōf') I. adj. impermeable II. tr. impermeabilizar.
wa·ter·re·pel·lent (:rĭ-pĕl'ənt) adj. que repele el agua.
wa·ter·re·sis·tant (:rĭ-zĭs'tənt) adj. resistente al agua.
wa·ter·shed (:shĕd') s. línea divisoria; *(area)* cuenca; *(critical point)* momento crítico.
wa·ter·side (:sīd') s. costa, ribera.
wa·ter·ski (:skē') I. intr. hacer esquí acua II. s. [pl. inv. ○ **s**] esquí acuático.
wa·ter·spout (:spout') s. *(tornado)* tromba n. rina; *(pipe)* boquilla (de surtidor).
wa·ter·tight (:tīt') adj. a prueba de agua; *(irrefutable)* irrefutable.
wa·ter·way (:wā') s. vía fluvial.
wa·ter·works (:wûrks') s.inv. sistema *m* de abastecimiento de agua; JER. *(tears)* lágrimas.
wa·ter·y (wŏ'tə-rē) adj. -i- acuoso; *(liquid)* líquido; *(diluted)* aguado; *(without force)* sin fuerza.
watt (wŏt) s. vatio, watt *m.*
watt·age ('ĭj) s. potencia en vatios.
wat·tle (wŏt'l) s. *(branches)* zarzo, estera; ZOOL. carnosidad *f.*
wave (wāv) I. intr. ondear; *(with the hand)* agitar la mano —tr. agitar; *(hair)* ondular ♦ **to w. good-bye** decir adiós II. s. ola; *(on a surface, hair)* ondulación *f;* *(of a hand)* movimiento; *(gesture)* gesto, ademán *m;* *(series)* serie *f;* *(of people)* oleadas; FÍS., RAD. onda.
wave·band (:bănd') s. banda de ondas.
wave·length (:lĕngth') s. longitud *f* de onda ♦ **to be on the same w.** estar en la misma onda.
wa·ver (wā'vər) I. intr. oscilar; *(to vacillate)* vacilar II. s. oscilación *f;* *(vacillation)* vacilación *f.*
wav·y (wā'vē) adj. -i- ondulante, onduloso; *(curly)* ondulado.
wax¹ (wăks) I. s. cera ♦ **w. paper** papel encerado II. tr. encerar.
wax² intr. *(to increase)* crecer.
wax·en (wăk'sən) adj. céreo, ceroso.
wax·work (wăks'wûrk') s. figura de cera ♦ pl. museo de cera.
wax·y (wăk'sē) adj. -i- ceroso; *(made of wax)* céreo.
way (wā) I. s. *(street)* camino; *(passage)* pasaje

m; *(direction)* dirección f; *(method)* manera, modo; *(means)* método; *(mode)* estilo; *(aspect)* aspecto; *(talent)* facilidad f; *(condition)* situación f; *(behavior)* manera de ser ♦ **all the w.** hasta el final; *(completely)* en todo • **by the w.** a propósito • **by w. of** pasando por; *(as a means of)* a manera de • **in a big, small w.** en gran, pequeña escala • **in a w.** en cierto modo • **in every w.** en todos los aspectos • **in my own w.** a mi manera • **(in) no w.** de ninguna manera • **on the w.** en camino • **out of the w.** lejano • **right of w.** derecho de paso • **that w.** por allí; *(manner)* así • **the other w. around** al contrario • **this w.** por aquí; *(thus)* así • **to be in the w.** estar en el camino • **to be set in one's ways** estar acostumbrado a la forma de uno • **to clear the w.** despejar el camino • **to come one's w.** FAM. caerle a uno • **to feel one's w.** tantear el camino • **to get one's w.** salirse con la suya • **to get out of the w.** quitar(se) de en medio • **to get under w.** *(in progress)* progresar; *(to set out)* ponerse en camino; *(to weigh anchor)* zarpar • **to give w. to** *(to be replaced by)* ceder el paso a; *(to give in to)* ceder ante; *(despair)* entregarse a • **to go out of one's w.** tomarse la molestia de • **to have a w. with** tener el don de • **to lead the w.** enseñar el camino • **to look the other w.** hacer la vista gorda • **to make one's w.** abrirse paso • **to mend one's ways** cambiar de vida • **to pave the w. for** preparar el terreno para • **to stand in the w. of** obstaculizar • **to take the easy w. out** tomar el camino más fácil • **w. down** bajada • **w. in** entrada • **w. out** salida; *(escape)* escapatoria • **w. up** subida • **ways and means** medios y arbitrios • **which w.?** ¿por dónde? II. adv. allá.

way·bill s. COM. itinerario.

way·far·er (wā'fâr'ər) s. caminante m.

way·lay (wā'lā') tr. **-laid** *(to lie in wait)* acechar; *(to accost)* abordar; *(to delay)* demorar.

way·side (wā'sīd') s. borde m del camino.

way·ward (wā'wərd) adj. *(naughty)* desobediente; *(unpredictable)* caprichoso.

we (wē) pron. nosotros, nosotras.

weak (wēk) adj. débil; *(fragile)* frágil; *(lacking skill)* flojo; *(unconvincing)* poco convincente.

weak·en (wē'kən) tr. & intr. debilitar(se).

weak-kneed (wēk'nēd') adj. tímido.

weak·ling (·lĭng) s. enclenque m; FIG. tímido.

weak·ly (·lē) adj. -i- enclenque.

weak·ness (:nĭs) s. debilidad f.

weal¹ (wēl) s. *(welfare)* bienestar m general.

weal² s. *(welt)* cardenal f, roncha.

wealth (wēlth) s. *(riches)* riqueza; *(profusion)* abundancia; ECON. caudal m.

wealth·y (wēl'thē) adj. -i- rico.

wean (wēn) tr. destetar ♦ **to w. oneself of** dejar de.

weap·on (wēp'ən) s. arma f.

weap·on·ry (:rē) s. armamento, armas.

wear (wâr) I. tr. **wore, worn** llevar; *(to damage)* deteriorar; *(to exhaust)* agotar ♦ **to w. away** desgastar • **to w. down** *(to damage)* desgastar; *(to exhaust)* agotar • **to w. off** gastar • **to w. out** *(to consume)* consumir; *(to tire)* cansar —intr. *(to last)* durar; *(to deteriorate)* desgastarse ♦ **to w. off** disiparse • **to w. thin** disminuir • **to w. out** gastarse II. s. uso; *(clothing)* ropa; *(damage)* desgaste m; *(durability)* durabilidad f ♦ **w. and tear** deterioro.

wea·ried (wîr'ēd) adj. fatigado.

wea·ri·some (:ē-səm) adj. tedioso.

wea·ry (wîr'ē) I. adj. -i- fatigado II. tr. & intr. fatigar(se); *(to annoy)* fastidiar(se).

wea·sel (wē'zəl) I. s. ZOOL. comadreja; JER. chivato II. intr. ser evasivo.

weath·er (wĕth'ər) I. s. tiempo; *(bad)* mal tiempo ♦ **under the w.** FAM. indispuesto; *(drunk)* borracho II. tr. *(to expose)* exponer a la intemperie; *(to outride)* aguantar —intr. deteriorarse; *(the skin)* curtirse; *(wood)* curarse; *(to resist)* resistir III. adj. meteorológico ♦ **w. stripping** burlete • **w. vane** veleta.

weath·er-beat·en (:bēt'n) adj. deteriorado por la intemperie.

weath·ered (wĕth'ərd) adj. curtido por la intemperie.

weath·er·man (:ər-măn') s. [pl. **-men**] FAM. meteorólogo.

weath·er·proof (:prōōf') I. adj. impermeable II. tr. impermeabilizar.

weave (wēv) I. tr. **wove, woven** tejer; *(to interlace)* entrelazar —intr. tejer; *(to become interlaced)* entrelazarse; *(through traffic)* zigzaguear II. s. tejido.

weav·er (wē'vər) s. tejedor m.

web (wĕb) s. tejido, tela; *(of a spider)* telaraña; *(net)* red f; *(of lies)* sarta; ANAT. membrana.

webbed (wĕbd) o **web-foot·ed** (wĕb'fŏŏt'ĭd) adj. palmeado.

wed (wĕd) tr. **-dded, wed(ded), -dd-** casarse con; FIG. unir —intr. casarse.

wed·ding (:ĭng) I. s. boda, casamiento; *(anniversary)* bodas; FIG. enlace m, unión f II. adj. de boda, nupcial.

wedge (wĕj) I. s. cuña; *(slice)* trozo; *(for securing)* calce m II. tr. *(to split)* partir; *(to fix in place)* calzar; FIG. *(to crowd)* apretar.

wed·lock (wĕd'lŏk') s. matrimonio ♦ **out of w.** ilegítimo.

Wednes·day (wĕnz'dē) s. miércoles m.

wee (wē) adj. pequeñito.

weed¹ (wēd) I. s. mala hierba, maleza II. tr. decherbar ♦ **to w. out** extirpar, eliminar —intr. arrancar la maleza.

weed² s. ♦ pl. ropa de luto de una viuda.

week (wēk) s. semana.

week·day ('dā') s. día m de trabajo.

week·end (:ĕnd') I. s. fin m de semana II. intr. pasar el fin de semana.

week·ly (:lē) I. adj. & adv. semanal(mente) II. s. semanario.

weep (wēp) I. tr. **wept** llorar; *(to lament)* lamentar —intr. llorar; *(to grieve)* dolerse; *(to drip)* gotear II. s. ♦ pl. llanto.

weep·ing (wē'pĭng) adj. lloroso ♦ **w. willow** sauce llorón.

wee·vil (wē'vəl) s. gorgojo, mordihuí m.

weft (wĕft) s. trama; *(fabric)* tela tejida.

weigh (wā) tr. pesar; *(anchor)* levar ♦ **to w. down** sobrecargar; *(to oppress)* abrumar —intr. pesar.

weight (wāt) I. s. peso; *(measured heaviness)* pesa; *(authority)* autoridad f ♦ **to gain** o **or put on w.** engordar • **to lose w.** adelgazar • **to pull one's w.** hacer su parte • **to throw one's w. around** darse importancia II. tr. añadir peso a; *(to hold down)* sujetar con un peso; *(to burden)* cargar; *(statistically)* ponderar.

weight·less ('lĭs) adj. sin peso, ingrávido.

weight·lift·ing (:lĭf'tĭng) s. levantamiento de pesas.

weight·y (wā'tē) adj. -i- *(heavy)* pesado; *(burdensome)* gravoso.

weird (wîrd) adj. misterioso.
weird·o (wîr′dō) s. [pl. **es**] JER. persona estrafalaria.
wel·come (wĕl′kəm) I. adj. bienvenido; *(agreeable)* agradable ♦ **you're w.!** ¡no hay de qué!, ¡de nada! • **you are w. to it** está a su disposición II. s. saludo de bienvenida III. tr. dar la bienvenida a; *(to accept)* aceptar con beneplácito IV. interj. ¡bienvenido!
weld (wĕld) I. tr. soldar; FIG. unir, juntar —intr. soldarse II. s. soldadura.
weld·er (wĕl′dər) s. soldador *m.*
wel·fare (wĕl′fâr′) s. bienestar *m*; *(benefits)* asistencia social.
well¹ (wĕl) I. s. pozo; *(spring)* fuente *f*; *(for stairs)* caja II. intr. manar —tr. verter.
well² (wĕl) **better, best** I. adv. bien ♦ **as w.** también • **as w. as** además de; *(just as)* así como • **that is just as w.** es mejor así • **to do w.** prosperar • **to do w. by** tratar bien • **w. done!** ¡bien hecho! II. adj. bien ♦ **to get w.** mejorar • **w. and good** tanto mejor III. interj. ¡bueno!
well-ap·point·ed (:ə-poin′tĭd) adj. bien amueblado.
well-bal·anced (:băl′ənst) adj. bien equilibrado.
well-be·haved (:bĭ-hāvd′) adj. bien educado.
well-be·ing (:bē′ĭng) s. bienestar *m.*
well-born (′bôrn′) adj. bien nacido.
well-bred (:brĕd′) adj. bien criado.
well-de·fined (′dĭ-fīnd′) adj. bien definido.
well-dis·posed (:dĭ-spōzd′) adj. bien dispuesto.
well-done (′dŭn′) adj. bien hecho; *(cooked)* bien cocido.
well-fixed (:fĭkst′) adj. FAM. acomodado.
well-found·ed (:foun′dĭd) adj. bien fundado.
well-groomed (:grōōmd′) adj. bien arreglado.
well-ground·ed (:groun′dĭd) adj. bien fundado.
well-head (wĕl′hĕd′) s. manantial *m.*
well-heeled (wĕl′hēld′) adj. JER. rico.
well-in·ten·tioned (′ĭn-tĕn′shənd) adj. bien intencionado.
well-known (′nōn′) adj. bien conocido.
well-man·nered (:măn′ərd) adj. de buenos modales.
well-mean·ing (:mē′nĭng) adj. bien intencionado.
well-meant (:mĕnt′) adj. honesto.
well-off (:ôf′) adj. acomodado.
well-read (:rĕd′) adj. leído, ilustrado.
well-round·ed (:roun′dĭd) adj. acabado.
well-spo·ken (:spō′kən) adj. bien hablado.
well-spring (wĕl′sprĭng′) s. fuente *f.*
well-thought-of (wĕl-thôt′ŭv′) adj. de buena reputación.
well-timed (′tīmd′) adj. oportuno.
well-to-do (′tə-dōō′) adj. próspero.
well-turned (′tûrnd′) adj. bien torneado; *(sentence)* bien construido.
well-wish·er (:wĭsh′ər) s. persona que desea el bien de otra.
well-worn (:wôrn′) adj. *(worn-out)* desgastado; *(hackneyed)* trillado.
welsh (wĕlsh, wĕlch) intr. ♦ **to w. on** JER. estafar.
welt (wĕlt) I. s. *(of a shoe)* vira; *(cord)* ribete *m*; *(injury)* verdugón *m*, roncha II. tr. levantar un verdugón en; COST. ribetear.
wel·ter (wĕl′tər) I. intr. revolcarse; *(the sea)* hincharse II. s. confusión *f.*

wel·ter·weight (:wāt′) s. welter *m.*
wench (wĕnch) s. *(girl)* moza; *(servant)* criada; *(prostitute)* prostituta.
wend (wĕnd) tr. ♦ **to w. one's way** dirigirse a.
went (wĕnt) cf. **go.**
wept (wĕpt) cf. **weep.**
were (wûr) pret. de **be.**
were·wolf (wîr′wŏŏlf′) s. [pl. **-ves**] hombre lobo.
west (wĕst) I. s. oeste *m*, occidente *m* II. adj. del oeste, occidental III. adv. al oeste.
west·bound (′bound′) adj. con rumbo al oeste.
west·ern (wĕs′tərn) I. adj. occidental, del oeste II. s. película del oeste.
west·ern·er (:tər-nər) s. habitante *m* del oeste.
west·ern·ize (:nīz′) tr. occidentalizar.
west·ward (wĕst′wərd) adv. hacia el oeste.
wet (wĕt) I. adj. **-tt-** mojado; *(rainy)* lluvioso; *(paint)* fresco ♦ **all w.** JER. totalmente equivocado • **soaking w.** calado hasta los huesos • **to be w. behind the ears** ser un imberbe • **w. blanket** FAM. aguafiestas • **w. nurse** nodriza II. s. mojadura III. tr. **wet(ted), -tting** mojar ♦ **to w. one's whistle** FAM. beber un trago —intr. mojarse.
wet·land (′lănd′) s. tierra húmeda.
whack (hwăk) FAM. I. tr. pegar II. s. golpe *m* fuerte; *(attempt)* intento ♦ **out of w.** averiado.
whale¹ (hwāl) s. ZOOL. ballena.
whale² tr. zurrar —intr. vapulear.
whale·boat (′bōt′) s. bote ballenero.
whale·bone (:bōn′) s. barba de ballena.
whal·er (hwā′lər) s. ballenero.
wham (hwăm) I. s. *(blow)* golpe *m* fuerte; *(thud)* ruido sordo II. tr. **-mm-** golpear con fuerza resonante.
wham·my (hwăm′ē) s. FAM. hechizo.
wharf (hwôrf) s. [pl. **s** o **-ves**] muelle *m.*
wharf·age (hwôr′fĭj) s. muellaje *m.*
what (hwŏt, hwŭt, hwət) I. pron. interrog. qué; *(which)* cuál ♦ **so w.?** ¿y qué? • **w. for?** ¿para qué? • **w. of it?** ¿y eso qué importa? II. pron. rel. el que • **to know what's w.** estar bien enterado • **w. is more** más aún • **w. it takes** lo que es necesario III. adj. interrog. qué; *(which)* cuál IV. adj. rel. que V. adv. cuánto, cómo VI. interj. ¡cómo!
what·ev·er (-ĕv′ər) I. pron. *(anything that)* lo que; *(all of what)* todo lo que; *(no matter what)* cualquier cosa; FAM. qué <**w. does he mean?** ¿qué quiere decir?> II. adj. *(any)* cualquiera que; *(of any kind at all)* de ninguna clase.
what·not (′nŏt′) s. cualquier cosa.
what·so·ev·er (′sō-ĕv′ər) var. de **whatever.**
wheat (hwēt) s. trigo.
whee·dle (hwēd′l) tr. engatusar —intr. lisonjear.
wheel (hwēl) I. s. rueda; *(steering)* volante *m*; *(of ship)* timón *m*; *(of potter)* torno; FAM. bicicleta; *(act of turning)* vuelta ♦ **fifth w.** persona superflua • **to be behind** *o* **at the w.** manejar el coche; *(in charge)* dirigir • **to grease the wheels** FAM. dar coimas ♦ pl. TÉC. engranaje; JER. *(car)* automóvil; *(forces)* mecanismos II. tr. *(to carry)* llevar sobre ruedas; *(to rotate)* hacer rodar —intr. *(to rotate)* girar; *(to roll)* rodar; *(to pivot)* dar una vuelta.
wheel·bar·row (′băr′ō) s. carretilla.
wheel·chair (hwēl′châr′) s. silla de ruedas.
wheeled (hwēld) adj. que tiene ruedas.
wheel·er-deal·er (hwē′lər-dē′lər) s. FAM. persona que anda en tramoyas.

wheeze (hwēz) I. intr. respirar con dificultad II. s. resuello ronco.

wheez·y (hwē′zē) adj. -i- jadeante.

whelp (hwĕlp) I. s. ZOOL. cachorro; FIG. granuja II. tr. & intr. parir.

when (hwĕn) I. adv. cuándo II. conj. cuando; *(as soon as)* al, en cuanto; *(if)* si III. pron. cuándo IV. s. fecha, momento.

whence (hwĕns) I. adv. de dónde II. conj. de donde, de lo cual.

when·ev·er (hwĕn-ĕv′ər) adv. & conj. cuando quiera (que); *(when)* cuando; *(every time that)* siempre que.

where (hwâr) I. adv. dónde; *(from where)* de dónde; *(to where)* adónde II. conj. donde, en donde; *(to where)* a donde III. s. lugar *m.*

where·a·bouts (′ə-bouts′) I. adv. dónde, por dónde II. s. paradero, ubicación *f.*

where·as (-ăz′) conj. *(since)* visto que; *(while)* mientras (que).

where·at (:ăt′) conj. a lo cual, con lo cual.

where·by (:bī′) conj. por o según el cual.

where·fore (′fôr′) I. adv. por qué II. s. porqué *m.*

where·in (-ĭn′) I. adv. en dónde II. conj. donde, en que.

where·of (:ŏv′) conj. *(of what)* de que, de lo que; *(of which, whom)* del que.

where·to (′tō′) I. adv. adónde II. conj. a lo que.

where·up·on (:ə-pŏn′) conj. con lo cual.

wher·ev·er (′ĕv′ər) I. adv. dondequiera que; FAM. dónde diablos II. conj. dondequiera que.

where·with (′wĭth′) conj. con que, con lo cual.

where·with·al (:wĭth-ôl′) s. recursos.

whet (hwĕt) tr. -tt- *(to sharpen)* afilar; *(appetite)* abrir; *(curiosity)* estimular.

wheth·er (hwĕth′ər) conj. *(if)* si; *(for alternatives)* sea . . . o ♦ **w. or not** de todos modos.

whet·stone (hwĕt′stōn′) s. piedra de afilar.

whew (hwōō, hyōō) interj. ¡vaya!

whey (hwā) s. suero de la leche.

which (hwĭch) I. pron. interrog. cuál II. pron. rel. que *<take those w. are yours* toma aquellos que son tuyos>; el cual *<my house, w. is small and old* mi casa, la cual es pequeña y vieja>; lo cual, lo que *<he acted very rudely, w. did not surprise me* se portó muy groseramente, lo que no me sorprendió>; el que, el cual *<the subject on w. he spoke* el tema sobre el cual él habló> III. adj. interrog. qué, cuál ♦ **w. one(s)?** ¿cnál(es)? ♦ **w. way?** ¿por dónde? IV. adj. rel. cuyo; *(any)* cualquier.

which·ev·er (′ĕv′ər) I. pron. cualquiera; *(any one)* el que, lo que II. adj. cualquier, cualquiera que sea.

whiff (hwĭf) I. s. soplo; *(smell)* olor *m*; *(of smoke)* bocanada II. intr. soplar —tr. exhalar.

while (hwīl) I. s. rato, tiempo ♦ **once in a w.** de vez en cuando ♦ **to be worth (one's) w.** valer la pena II. conj. *(as long as)* mientras (que); *(although)* aunque, si bien III. tr. pasar.

whim (hwĭm) s. capricho, antojo.

whim·per (hwĭm′pər) I. intr. lloriquear II. s. gemido, quejido.

whim·si·cal (:zĭ-kəl) adj. *(capricious)* caprichoso; *(fanciful)* extravagante.

whim·s(e)y (:zē) s. capricho.

whine (hwīn) I. intr. gimotear; *(to complain)* quejarse II. s. gimoteo; *(complaint)* quejido.

whin·ny (hwĭn′ē) I. intr. relinchar II. s. relin-

cho.

whip (hwĭp) I. tr. -t o -pped, -pping azotar; *(cream, eggs)* batir; FAM. *(to outdo)* dar una paliza a ♦ **to w. out** sacar de repente • **to w. up** estimular; FAM. preparar rápidamente —intr. *(to dart)* precipitarse, *(to snap about)* restallar II. s. azote *m*; *(dessert)* batido.

whip·lash (′lăsh′) s. latigazo.

whip·per·snap·per (hwĭp′ər-snăp′ər) s. mequetrefe *m.*

whip·pet (hwĭp′ĭt) s. lebrel *m.*

whip·poor·will (hwĭp′ər-wĭl′) s. chotacabras *m.*

whir (hwûr) I. intr. -rr- zumbar II. s. zumbido.

whirl (hwûrl) I. intr. *(to spin)* dar vueltas; *(to turn)* dar una vuelta; *(dust, water)* arremolinarse —tr. hacer girar II. s. giro; *(of dust, water)* remolino; *(tumult)* tumulto; *(of events)* torbellino; *(dizziness)* vértigo ♦ **to give it a w.** FAM. intentar hacerlo.

whirl·i·gig (′lĭ-gĭg′) s. *(toy)* molinete *m*; *(carousel)* tiovivo; *(spinning thing)* torbellino.

whirl·pool (hwûrl′pōōl′) s. remolino.

whirl·wind (:wĭnd′) I. s. torbellino, remolino II. adj. intenso y rápido.

whirl·y·bird (:lē-bûrd′) s. JER. helicóptero.

whisk (hwĭsk) I. tr. sacudir; CUL. batir —intr. moverse rápidamente ♦ **to w. past** pasar a toda velocidad II. s. movimiento rápido; *(whisk-broom)* cepillo de ropa; CUL. batidor *m.*

whisk·broom (′brōōm′) s. cepillo de ropa.

whisk·er (hwĭs′kər) s. pelo ♦ pl. *(of man)* barbas; *(of animal)* bigotes.

whis·k(e)y (hwĭs′kē) s. whisky *m.*

whis·per (hwĭs′pər) I. s. susurro II. intr. susurrar —tr. decir en secreto.

whis·tle (hwĭs′əl) I. intr. silbar; *(with a device)* pitar; *(birds)* piar ♦ **to w. in the dark** intentar cobrar ánimo —tr. silbar II. s. *(instrument)* pito, silbato; *(act, sound)* silbido, pitido.

whit (hwĭt) s. pizca.

white (hwīt) I. s. blanco; *(of an egg)* clara II. adj. blanco; *(pale)* pálido; *(pure)* puro ♦ **as w. as a sheet** o ghost blanco como el papel • **w. lie** mentirilla • **w. water** agua espumosa.

white-col·lar (′kŏl′ər) adj. de oficina.

white·fish (′fĭsh′) s. [pl. inv. o **es**] pescado blanco.

white-hot (:hŏt′) adj. *(fervid)* candente; FIS. al rojo blanco.

whit·en (′n) tr. & intr. blanquear(se)

white·wall tire (:wôl′) s. AUTO. neumático de banda blanca.

white·wash (:wŏsh′) I. s. cal *f*; *(concealing)* encubrimiento II. tr. enjalbegar; FIG. encubrir.

whith·er (hwĭth′ər) adv. *(where)* adónde; *(to which)* adonde; *(wherever)* dondequiera.

whit·tle (hwĭt′l) tr. *(to carve)* tallar; *(to reduce)* reducir —intr. tallar.

whiz(z) (hwĭz) I. intr. -zz- zumbar II. s. [pl. -zes] zumbido ♦ **to be a w.** FAM. ser un as.

who (hōō) I. pron. interrog. quién II. pron. rel. quien; que *<the man w. came to see you* el hombre que vino a verte>; el cual *<my parents, w. built this business* mis padres, los cuales establecieron este negocio>.

whoa (hwō) interj. ¡jo!, ¡cho!

who·dun·it (hōō-dŭn′ĭt) s. FAM. novela o película policial.

who·ev·er (hōō-ĕv′ər) pron. quienquiera que; *(the one who)* el que, quien; FAM. ¿quién diablos?

whole (hōl) **I.** adj. entero, todo; *(total)* total; *(healthy)* sano; *(undamaged)* intacto ♦ **a w. lot of** muchísimo • **w. note** redonda **II.** s. todo, totalidad *f; (complete entity)* suma ♦ **as a w.** en conjunto • **on the w.** en general **III.** adv. FAM. completamente.

whole·heart·ed ('här'tĭd) adj. incondicional.

whole·ness (:nĭs) s. integridad *f.*

whole·sale (:sāl') **I.** s. venta al por mayor **II.** adj. al por mayor; *(general)* general **III.** adv. al por mayor; *(extensively)* en general **IV.** tr. & intr. vender(se) al por mayor.

whole·some (:səm) adj. sano.

whole·wheat (:hwēt') adj. de trigo entero.

whom (hōōm) **I.** pron. interrog. **a quién** <*w. did you see?* ¿a quién viste?>; de quién <*from w. did you get it?* ¿de quién lo recibiste?> **II.** pron. rel. que, quien.

whom·ev·er (-ĕv'ər) pron. a quienquiera.

whom·so·ev·er ('sō-ĕv'ər) var. de **whomever**.

whoop (hōōp, hwōōp) **I.** s. *(shout)* grito; *(bird's cry)* graznido; *(cough)* estertor *m* de la tos ferina ♦ **whooping cough** tos ferina *o* convulsa • **whooping crane** grulla blanca **II.** intr. gritar; *(to hoot)* graznar; *(to cough)* toser ahogándose ♦ **to w. it up** armar jaleo.

whoops (hwōōps, hwōōps) interj. ¡epa!

whoosh (hwōōsh, hwōōsh) **I.** intr. pasar como un silbido **II.** s. silbido.

whop (hwŏp) **I.** tr. **-pp-** derrotar **II.** s. golpe *m.*

whop·per ('ər) s. *(something big)* cosa enorme; *(lie)* mentira colosal.

whop·ping (:ĭng) adj. FAM. enorme.

whore (hôr) s. prostituta.

whore·house ('hous') s. prostíbulo.

whorl (hwôrl, hwûrl) s. espiral *f;* BOT. verticilo.

whose (hōōz) **I.** pron. & adj. interrog. de quién **II.** pron. rel. cuyo.

why (hwī) **I.** adv. por qué, para qué **II.** conj. por que, por lo que **III.** s. [pl. **s**] (la) causa, (el) porqué **IV.** interj. ¡vaya!, ¡toma!

wick (wĭk) s. mecha.

wick·ed (wĭk'ĭd) adj. malvado; *(mischievous)* travieso; *(offensive)* desagradable.

wick·ed·ness (:nĭs) s. maldad *f.*

wick·er (wĭk'ər) **I.** s. mimbre *m; (wickerwork)* artículos de mimbre **II.** adj. de mimbre.

wick·et (wĭk'ĭt) s. *(small gate)* portillo; *(small window)* ventanilla.

wide (wīd) **I.** adj. ancho; *(in width)* de ancho; *(extensive)* extenso; *(large)* amplio; *(eyes)* muy abiertos ♦ **w. of the mark** lejos del blanco **II.** adv. *(completely)* de par en par; *(to the full extent)* bien abierto ♦ **far and w.** por todas partes • **w. open** de par en par.

wide-an·gle lens ('ăng'gəl) s. objetivo gran angular.

wide-a·wake ('ə-wāk') adj. despierto.

wide-eyed ('īd') adj. con los ojos muy abiertos; *(innocent)* inocente.

wide·ly (:lē) adv. *(very)* muy; *(much)* mucho; *(extensively)* extensamente.

wid·en (:n) tr. & intr. ensanchar(se).

wide-o·pen (:ō'pən) adj. abierto de par en par.

wide·spread (:sprĕd') adj. extendido; *(prevalent)* general.

wid·ow (wĭd'ō) **I.** s. viuda **II.** tr. dejar viuda ♦ **to be widowed** quedar viuda.

wid·ow·er (:ər) s. viudo.

width (wĭdth) s. anchura, ancho.

wield (wēld) tr. *(weapon)* blandir; *(tool)* mane-

jar; *(influence)* ejercer.

wie·ner (wē'nər) s. salchicha de Viena.

wife (wīf) s. [pl. **-ves**] esposa, mujer *f.*

wig (wĭg) s. peluca.

wig·gle (wĭg'əl) **I.** intr. & tr. menear(se) **II.** s. meneo.

wild (wīld) **I.** adj. salvaje; *(plant)* silvestre; *(unruly)* desordenado; *(crazy)* loco, extraviado; *(frenzied)* frenético; *(extravagant)* extravagante; *(stormy)* tormentoso; *(guess)* al azar ♦ **to be w. about** FAM. estar loco por • **to run w.** propagarse desmesuradamente • **to sow one's w. oats** correr sus mocedades • **wild-goose chase** búsqueda inútil **II.** s. región *f* salvaje ♦ **in the w.** en estado natural • **the wilds** región inexplorada **III.** adv. alocadamente; *(without being planted)* sin cultivo.

wild·cat ('kăt') **I.** s. fiera; ZOOL. gato montés; TEC. sondeo de exploración **II.** adj. arriesgado ♦ **w. strike** huelga no aprobada por el sindicato.

wil·de·beest (wĭl'də-bēst', vĭl'-) s. ñú *m.*

wil·der·ness (wĭl'dər-nĭs) s. región *f* sin cultivar.

wild-eyed (wīld'īd') adj. de mirada furiosa.

wild·fire (:fīr') s. incendio descontrolado ♦ **to spread like w.** propagarse rapidamente.

wild·flow·er (:flou'ər) s. flor *f* silvestre.

wild·fowl (:foul') s. [pl. inv. *o* **s**] ave *f* silvestre.

wild·life (:līf') s. fauna.

wile (wīl) **I.** s. ardid *m; (cunning)* astucia **II.** tr. atraer ♦ **to w. away the time** pasar el tiempo.

will¹ (wĭl) **I.** s. voluntad *f;* DER. testamento ♦ **good, ill w.** buena, mala voluntad • **last w. and testament** última voluntad • **of one's own free w.** por voluntad propia • **w. power** fuerza de voluntad **II.** tr. querer; *(to order)* ordenar; DER. legar.

will² **I.** aux. [pret. **would**] *(simple futurity)* <*they w. come later* vendrán más tarde>; *(likelihood, certainty)* ir a <*you w. regret this* lo vas a lamentar>; *(willingness)* querer; *(requirement, command)* deber; *(habitual action)* soler <*she would spend hours in the kitchen* solía pasar horas en la cocina>; *(emphasis)* <*I w. do it!* ¡sí, lo haré!> **II.** tr. & intr. querer.

will·ful (wĭl'fəl) adj. *(deliberate)* deliberado; *(obstinate)* obstinado.

wil·lies (wĭl'ēz) s.pl. escalofrío, pelos de punta.

will·ing (wĭl'ĭng) adj. de buena voluntad.

will·ing·ness (:nĭs) s. buena voluntad.

will-o'-the-wisp (wĭl'ə-thə-wĭsp') s. fuego fatuo; *(delusive goal)* quimera.

wil·low (wĭl'ō) s. sauce *m.*

wil·low·y (:ē) adj. -**i**- esbelto.

wil·ly-nil·ly (wĭl'ē-nĭl'ē) adv. de grado o por fuerza.

wilt (wĭlt) intr. & tr. marchitar(se); *(to weaken)* debilitar(se).

wil·y (wī'lē) adj. -**i**- astuto.

wimp (wĭmp) s. JER. mentecato.

wim·ple (wĭm'pəl) s. griñón *m.*

win (wĭn) **I.** adj. **won**, **-nning** ganar, triunfar ♦ **to w. out** salir victorioso • **to w.** ganar; *(to obtain)* conseguir; *(to gain)* alcanzar; *(affection, sympathy)* conquistar ♦ **to w. over** ganarse el apoyo de **II.** s. victoria, triunfo.

wince (wĭns) **I.** intr. respingar **II.** s. respingo.

winch (wĭnch) s. *(hoist)* torno, cabrestante *m; (crank)* manivela, cigüeña.

wind¹ (wĭnd) **I.** s. viento; *(air)* aire *m; (ver-*

biage) palabrería; *(breath)* respiración *f; (flatulence)* flatulencia ♦ **head w.** viento en contra • **there's something in the w.** algo flota en el aire • **to break w.** FAM. ventosear • **to get w. of** enterarse de • **to have the w. knocked out of one** quedar sin aliento ♦ pl. MÚS. instrumentos de viento **II.** tr. dejar sin aliento.

wind² (wīnd) **I.** tr. **wound** envolver; *(to entwine)* enrollar; *(wool, cotton)* devanar; *(to bend)* torcer; *(a watch)* dar cuerda a; *(to lift)* levantar con cabrestante ♦ **to be wound up** estar muy nervioso • **to w. down** disminuir • **to w. up** enrollar; FAM. concluir, terminar —intr. *(road)* serpentear; *(rope)* enrollarse; *(to twist)* torcerse; *(to bend)* encorvarse **II.** s. vuelta.

wind·bag (wīnd'băg') s. JER. charlatán *m.*

wind·break (:brāk') s. protección *f* contra el viento.

wind·ed (wīn'dĭd) adj. jadeante.

wind·fall (wīnd'fôl') s. suerte inesperada.

wind·flow·er (:flou'ər) s. anémona.

wind·ing (wīn'dĭng) **I.** s. enrollamiento; ELEC. bobinado **II.** adj. sinuoso; *(spiral)* en espiral.

wind·jam·mer (wīnd'jăm'ər) s. *(ship)* velero; *(sailor)* marinero.

wind·lass (wīnd'ləs) s. torno, molinete *m.*

wind·mill (wīnd'mĭl') s. molino de viento.

win·dow (wĭn'dō) s. ventana; *(small)* ventanilla; *(pane of glass)* cristal *m; (of a shop)* escaparate *m.*

win·dow-pane (:pān') s. cristal *m* de ventana.

win·dow-shop (:shŏp') intr. **-pp-** comprar con los ojos.

win·dow·sill (:sĭl') s. alféizar *m.*

wind·pipe (wĭnd'pīp') s. tráquea.

wind·shield (:shēld') s. parabrisas *m* ♦ **w. wiper** limpiaparabrisas.

wind·sock (:sŏk') s. manga de aire.

wind·storm (:stôrm') s. vendaval *m.*

wind·swept (:swĕpt') adj. barrido por el viento.

wind-up (wīnd'ŭp') s. conclusión *f*, final *m.*

wind·ward (wīnd'wərd) s. & adj. (de) barlovento.

wind·y (wĭn'dē) adj. **-i-** ventoso; *(unsheltered)* expuesto al viento; *(verbose)* verboso.

wine (wīn) **I.** s. vino **II.** tr. ♦ **to w. and dine** agasajar.

wine·glass ('glăs') s. copa para vino.

wine·grow·er (:grō'ər) s. vinicultor *m.*

wine·press (:prĕs') s. trujal *m*, lagar *m.*

win·er·y (wī'nə-rē) s. vinería, lagar *m.*

wine·skin (wīn'skĭn') s. odre *m*, pellejo de vino.

wing (wĭng) **I.** s. ala; *(of a chair)* oreja; FAM. *(arm)* brazo ♦ **on the w.** volando ♦ pl. TEAT. bastidores **II.** intr. volar —tr. *(to empower)* dar alas a; *(to speed along)* atravesar volando; *(to wound)* herir ♦ **to w. it** FAM. improvisar.

wing·ding (wĭng'dĭng') s. FAM. fiesta animada.

winged (wĭngd, wĭng'ĭd) adj. alado; *(flying)* volador; *(sublime)* sublime.

wing·span/spread (wĭng'spăn'/:sprĕd') s. envergadura.

wink (wĭngk) **I.** intr. pestañear; *(lights)* parpadear; *(stars)* centellear ♦ **to w. at** guiñar el ojo a; FIG. hacer la vista gorda a **II.** s. *(blink)* pestañeo; *(hint)* guiño; *(of light)* parpadeo ♦ **in a w.** en un abrir y cerrar de ojos • **not to sleep a w.** no pegar los ojos, pasar la noche en blanco • **to get forty winks** FAM. echarse un sueñecito.

win·ner (wĭn'ər) s. ganador *m*; IRÓN. *(loser)* perdedor *m.*

win·ning (:ĭng) **I.** adj. victorioso, *(book, ticket)* premiado; *(charming)* encantador **II.** s. victoria ♦ pl. ganancias.

win·now (wĭn'ō) tr. *(grain)* aventar; FIG. *(to separate)* separar; *(to select)* seleccionar.

win·some (wĭn'səm) adj. simpático.

win·ter (wĭn'tər) **I.** s. invierno **II.** intr. invernar.

win·ter·green (:grēn') s. gaultería.

win·ter·ize (wĭn'tə-rīz') tr. preparar para el invierno.

win·ter·time (:tər-tīm') s. invierno.

win·try/ter·y (:trē/tə-rē) adj. **-i-** invernal; FIG. helado.

wipe (wīp) **I.** tr. limpiar; *(to dry)* secar ♦ **to w. away** o **off** quitar • **to w. the slate clean** hacer borrón y cuenta nueva • **to w. out** destruir; *(a debt)* cancelar; FAM. asesinar **II.** s. limpieza.

wire (wīr) **I.** s. alambre *m*, hilo; *(finish line)* línea de llegada; ELEC. cable *m; (telegraph)* telegrafía; *(telegram)* telegrama *m* ♦ **under the w.** al último momento **II.** tr. alambrar; *(a house)* instalar el alambrado de; TELEG. telegrafiar —intr. poner un telegrama.

wired (wīrd) adj. ELEC. con instalación de alambres; JER. nervioso.

wire·less (wīr'lĭs) **I.** adj. sin alambres **II.** s. radio *mf.*

wire·tap (:tăp') TEL. **I.** s. dispositivo interceptor **II.** tr. & intr. **-pp-** interceptar.

wir·ing (:ĭng) s. instalación eléctrica.

wir·y (:ē) adj. **-i-** *(kinky)* ensortijado, crespo; *(lean)* enjuto y fuerte.

wis·dom (wĭz'dəm) s. *(knowledge)* sabiduría; *(common sense)* cordura; *(learning)* erudición *f* ♦ **w. tooth** muela del juicio.

wise¹ (wīz) **I.** adj. sabio; *(judicious)* juicioso; *(sensible)* sensato • **to get w.** JER. *(to understand)* caer en el chiste; *(to become insolent)* ponerse impertinente • **w. guy** FAM. sabelotodo **II.** tr. & intr. ♦ **to w. up** JER. poner(se) al tanto.

wise² s. manera, modo.

wise·a·cre (wīz'ā'kər) s. FAM. sabelotodo *mf.*

wise·crack (:krăk') s. JER. ocurrencia.

wish (wĭsh) **I.** s. deseo **II.** tr. querer, desear; *(to like to)* gustar; *(to bid)* dar.

wish·bone ('bōn') s. espoleta.

wish·ful (:fəl) adj. deseoso ♦ **w. thinking** ilusiones.

wish·y-wash·y (wĭsh'ē-wŏsh'ē) adj. FAM. **-i-** ni fu ni fa.

wisp (wĭsp) s. *(small bunch)* manojo, hacecillo; *(hair)* mechón *m; (trace)* vestigio.

wis·ter·i·a/tar·i·a (wĭ-stîr'ē-ə/-stâr'-) s. glicina.

wist·ful (wĭst'fəl) adj. nostálgico.

wit¹ (wĭt) s. inteligencia; *(good sense)* juicio; *(imagination)* imaginación *f; (cleverness)* ingenio; *(person)* persona ingeniosa ♦ **to be at w.'s end** no saber qué hacer ♦ pl. juicio; *(ingenuity)* ingenio • **to collect one's w.** serenarse • **to keep one's w. about one** no perder la cabeza • **to live by one's w.** vivir uno de su ingenio.

wit² intr. ♦ **to w.** es decir, a saber.

witch (wĭch) s. bruja; FAM. *(young woman)* hechicera ♦ **w. hazel** agua de hamamelis.

witch·craft (:krăft') s. brujería.

witch·er·y (:ə-rē) s. brujería.

witch-hunt (:hunt') s. persecución *f* de brujas; POL. investigación falsa para sacar ventaja.

witch·ing (:ĭng) adj. hechicero, mágico.

with (wĭth, wĭth) prep. con; *(next to)* junto a; *(in the employ of)* en, para; *(according to)* de

with·al (:ôl′) adv. además, también.

with·draw (:drô′) tr. **-drew, -n** sacar, quitar; *(to retract)* retractar —intr. *(to retreat)* retraerse; *(to draw away)* apartarse.

with·draw·al (:drô′əl) s. *(retreat)* retiro; *(removal)* retirada; *(termination)* abandono; FISIOL. síntomas m de reajuste.

with·drawn (:drôn′) adj. remoto; *(shy)* tímido.

with·er (wĭth′ər) intr. secarse; *(to droop)* marchitarse —tr. marchitar; *(to stun)* fulminar.

with·hold (wĭth-hōld′, wĭth-) tr. **-held** *(to restrain)* retener, contener; *(to refuse)* rehusar ♦ **withholding tax** impuesto retenido.

with·in (:ĭn′) I. adv. dentro; *(indoors)* adentro; *(inwardly)* internamente II. prep. dentro de; *(distance)* a menos de; *(time)* antes de; *(not beyond)* dentro de los límites de III. s. adentro.

with-it (wĭth′ĭt) adj. FAM. moderno, al día.

with·out (-out′) I. adv. fuera II. prep. sin; *(on the outside of)* (a)fuera de ♦ **it goes w. saying** se sobreentiende • **to do w.** pasar(se) sin.

with·stand (wĭth-stănd′, wĭth-) tr. **-stood** resistir a —intr. resistirse.

wit·less (wĭt′lĭs) adj. tonto.

wit·ness (:nĭs) I. s. *(person)* testigo; *(act)* testimonio ♦ **to bear false w.** perjurarse • **to bear w.** atestiguar II. tr. atestiguar; *(to provide evidence of)* dar prueba de —intr. atestiguar.

wit·ti·cism (:ĭ-sĭz′əm) s. salida graciosa.

wit·ty (:ē) adj. **-i-** *(clever)* ingenioso; *(humorous)* gracioso.

wiz·ard (wĭz′ərd) s. hechicero; FIG. as m.

wiz·ard·ry (:ər-drē) s. magia, hechicería.

wiz·ened (wĭz′ənd) adj. arrugado.

wob·ble (wŏb′əl) intr. bambolearse; *(to shake)* temblar; *(to waver)* vacilar.

wob·bly (:lē) adj. **-i-** *(shaky)* bamboleante; *(unsteady)* tembloroso; *(uncertain)* vacilante.

woe (wō) I. s. pesar m; *(misfortune)* infortunio II. interj. ♦ **w. is me** ¡ay de mí!

woe·be·gone (wō′bĭ-gôn′) adj. triste.

wo(e)·ful (wō′fəl) adj. *(mournful)* apenado; *(pitiful)* lamentable.

woke (wōk), **wo·ken** (wō′kən) cf. **wake¹**.

wolf (wŏŏlf) I. s. **[pl. -ves]** lobo; FIG. persona rapaz y feroz; JER. don Juan m ♦ **lone w.** persona solitaria • **to cry w.** dar la alarma sin causa • **w. in sheep's clothing** hipócrita II. tr. ♦ **to w. down** comer vorazmente.

wolf·hound (′hound′) s. galgo ruso.

wol·ver·ine (wŏŏl′və-rēn′) s. ZOOL. glotón m.

wom·an (wŏŏm′ən) s. **[pi. women]** mujer f; *(servant)* criada.

wom·an·hood (:hŏŏd′) s. femineidad f.

wom·an·ish (wŏŏm′ə-nĭsh) adj. femenino; *(effeminate)* afeminado.

wom·an·kind (:ən-kīnd′) s. las mujeres.

wom·an·ly (:lē) adj. femenino.

womb (wŏŏm) s. matriz f; FIG. cuna.

wom·bat (wŏm′băt′) s. oso australiano.

wom·en (wĭm′ĭn) cf. **woman**.

wom·en·folk(s) (:fōk[s]′) s.pl. las mujeres.

won (wŭn) cf. **win**.

won·der (wŭn′dər) I. s. maravilla; *(miracle)* milagro; *(astonishment)* asombro ♦ **no o small w.** no es de extrañar • **to do o to work wonders** hacer milagros • **w. child** niño prodigio • **w.**

drug medicamento milagroso II. intr. *(to ponder)* pensar; *(to be doubtful)* dudar ♦ **to w. at** asombrarse de —tr. preguntarse.

won·der·ful (:fəl) adj. *(astonishing)* asombroso; *(excellent)* maravilloso.

won·der·land (:lănd′) s. *(imaginary)* país m de las maravillas; *(real)* lugar bellísimo.

won·der·ment (:mənt) s. *(astonishment)* asombro; *(marvel)* maravilla.

won·drous (wŭn′drəs) adj. maravilloso.

wont (wônt, wōnt) I. adj. acostumbrado; *(apt)* propenso II. s. costumbre f.

wont·ed (wôn′tĭd, wōn′-) adj. habitual.

woo (wŏŏ) tr. cortejar, galantear; *(to seek)* buscar; *(to solicit)* solicitar —intr. cortejar.

wood (wŏŏd) I. s. madera; *(firewood)* leña ♦ pl. bosque II. tr. *(to fuel)* alimentar con leña; *(to forest)* poblar con árboles.

wood·block (′blŏk′) s. grabado en madera.

wood·chuck (:chŭk′) s. marmota de Norteamérica.

wood·cock (:kŏk′) s. **[pl. inv. o s]** coalla.

wood·craft (:krăft′) s. artesanía en madera.

wood·cut (:kŭt′) s. grabado en madera.

wood·cut·ter (:kŭt′ər) s. leñador m.

wood·ed (:ĭd) adj. arbolado, boscoso.

wood·en (:n) adj. de madera; *(leg)* de palo; *(stiff)* tieso; *(expressionless)* sin expresión.

wood·land (:lənd, :lănd′) s. bosque m.

wood·peck·er (:pĕk′ər) s. pájaro carpintero.

wood·pile (:pīl′) s. montón m de leña.

wood·shed (:shĕd′) s. leñera.

woods·man (wŏŏdz′mən) s. **[pl. -men]** habitante m de los bosques.

woods·y (wŏŏd′zē) adj. **-i-** boscoso.

wood·wind (wŏŏd′wĭnd′) s. instrumento de viento de madera.

wood·work (:wûrk′) s. maderaje m.

wood·worm (:wûrm′) s. carcoma.

wood·y (:ē) adj. **-i-** leñoso; *(smell, taste)* a madera; *(land)* arbolado.

woof¹ (wŏŏf, wŏŏf) s. trama; *(texture)* tejido.

woof² (wŏŏf) s. *(bark)* ladrido.

wool (wŏŏl) s. lana ♦ **steel w.** lana de acero.

wool·en (′ən) I. adj. de lana II. s. ♦ pl. prendas de lana.

wool·gath·er·ing (:găth′ər-ĭng) s. distracción f.

wool·ly (:ē) adj. **-i-** de lana; *(fleecy)* lanoso, lanudo; *(unclear)* borroso.

woo·zy (wŏŏ′zē, wŏŏz′ē) adj. **-i-** *(dazed)* aturdido; *(dizzy)* mareado.

word (wûrd) s. palabra; *(order)* orden f; *(password)* santo y seña; *(news)* información f ♦ **by w. of mouth** verbalmente • **in other words** mejor dicho • **mark my words** tome nota de lo que digo • **my w.!** ¡válgame Dios! • **on my w.** bajo mi palabra • **play on words** juego de palabras • **take my w. for it** se lo aseguro • **to eat one's words** retractarse • **to have the last w.** decir la última palabra • **to have o exchange words with someone** reñir de palabra con alguien • **to keep one's w.** cumplir la palabra • **to leave w. that** dejar dicho que • **to put in a good w. for** decir unas palabras en favor de • **to take the words out of someone's mouth** quitar a alguien la palabra de la boca • **w. processing** procesamiento de palabras • **w. processor** procesador de palabras ♦ pl. *(speech)* discurso; *(quarrel)* disputa; MÚS. letra.

word·ing (wûr′dĭng) s. redacción f.

word·y (:dē) adj. **-i-** verboso.

wore (wôr) cf. **wear**.

work (wûrk) I. s. trabajo; *(job)* empleo; *(result, deed)* obra ♦ **let's get to w.!** ¡manos a la obra! • **the works** JER. todo, de todo • **to make short w. of** terminar rápidamente • **w. force** mano de obra ♦ pl. *(output)* obra; *(factory)* taller; *(mechanism)* mecanismo II. intr. trabajar; *(to be employed)* tener trabajo; *(to operate)* funcionar; *(to be effectual)* surtir efecto; *(to contort)* torcerse • **to w. out** *(to go well)* salir bien; *(to do exercises)* hacer gimnasia —tr. producir; *(to handle)* manejar; *(metal)* forjar; *(to solve)* resolver; *(to arrange)* arreglárselas; *(to cultivate)* cultivar; *(to drive)* hacer trabajar; *(to persuade)* influir en ♦ **to w. at** ocuparse de • **to w. in** introducir • **to w. out** resolver, solucionar • **to w. over** alterar • **to w. up** *(to excite)* estimular; *(to develop)* desarrollar.
work·a·ble (wûr'kə-bəl) adj. factible.
work·a·day (:kə-dā') adj. laborable; *(everyday)* cotidiano.
work·a·hol·ic (:hô'lĭk) s. trabajador compulsivo.
work·bench (wûrk'bĕnch') s. mesa de trabajo.
work·book (:bŏŏk') s. cuaderno de ejercicios; *(manual)* manual m de instrucciones.
work·day (:dā') s. día m laborable.
work·er (wûr'kər) s. trabajador m.
work·horse (wûrk'hôrs') s. caballo de tiro; *(person)* persona muy trabajadora.
work·house (:hous') s. correccional m.
work·ing (wûr'kĭng) I. adj. que trabaja; *(class)* obrero; *(hours)* de trabajo; *(expenses)* de explotación; *(day)* laborable; *(knowledge)* básico; *(model)* operativo; MEC. móvil ♦ **to be in w. order** estar funcionando • **w. capital** capital activo II. s. trabajo; *(operation)* funcionamiento; *(of metals, land)* labrado; *(of a mine)* explotación f.
work·ing·man (:măn') s. [pl. -men] trabajador m, obrero.
work·load (wûrk'lōd') s. carga de trabajo.
work·man (:mən) s. [pl. -men] trabajador m.
work·man·like (:līk) adj. hecho a conciencia.
work·man·ship (:shĭp') s. destreza.
work·out (wûrk'out') s. ejercicio.
work·room (:rŏŏm') s. taller m.
work·shop (:shŏp') s. taller m.
work·ta·ble (:tā'bəl) s. mesa de trabajo.
work·week (:wĕk') s. semana laboral.
world (wûrld) s. mundo ♦ **a w. of** la mar de • **for all the w.** ni más ni menos • **not to be long for this w.** quedarle poco a uno • **on top of the w.** FAM. en el séptimo cielo • **out of this w.** FAM. increíble • **to bring into the w.** traer al mundo • **to come down in the w.** venir a menos • **to come into the w.** venir al mundo • **to have the best of both worlds** tenerlo todo al mismo tiempo • **to move up in the w.** prosperar • **to see the w.** ver mundo • **to think the w. of** poner por las nubes a • **where, what in the w.?** ¿dónde, qué diablos? • **w. war** guerra mundial.
world·ly ('lē) adj. -i- secular; *(worldly-wise)* sofisticado; *(material)* material.
world·ly-wise (:wīz') adj. sofisticado.
world·wide (wûrld'wīd') adj. mundial.
worm (wûrm) I. s. gusano; *(parasite)* helminto; *(tormenting force)* gusanillo; *(vile person)* canalla m ♦ pl. MED. helmintiasis II. tr. *(to make way)* colarse, *(to elicit)* sacar; *(to cure)* librar de gusanos —intr. arrastrarse.
worm-eat·en ('ēt'n) adj. agusanado; *(decayed)* podrido; *(antiquated)* anticuado.

worm·wood (:wŏŏd') s. amargura; BOT. absintio, ajenjo.
worm·y (wûr'mē) adj. -i- agusanado; *(worm-eaten)* carcomido.
worn (wôrn) I. cf. **wear** II. adj. *(used)* gastado; *(exhausted)* agotado; *(trite)* trillado.
worn-out ('out') adj. *(used)* gastado; *(exhausted)* agotado.
wor·ri·er (wûr'ē-ər) s. aprensivo.
wor·ri·ment (:mənt) s. preocupación f.
wor·ri·some (:səm) adj. inquietante.
wor·ry (wûr'ē) I. intr. preocupar —tr. *(to distress)* preocupar; *(to bother)* molestar; *(to toy with)* jugar con II. s. preocupación f.
wor·ry·wart (:wôrt') s. persona aprensiva.
worse (wûrs) I. adj. [comp. de **bad, ill**] peor; *(more severe)* más fuerte ♦ **to get w. and w.** ir de mal en peor • **to get w.** empeorar • **to make matters w.** para empeorar las cosas II. s. **and w. y cosas peores** • **to take a turn for the w.** empeorar • **so much the w.** tanto peor • **to be none the w. for it** no perjudicarle a uno • **to think none the w. of** no tener en menos III. adv. peor; *(more severely)* más ♦ **to be w. off** estar peor.
wors·en (wûr'sən) tr. & intr. empeorar(se).
wor·ship (wûr'shĭp) I. s. adoración f; *(devotion)* devoción f II. tr. RELIG. venerar; FIG. adorar —intr. venerar.
wor·ship·(p)er (:shĭ-pər) s. devoto, adorador m; RELIG. fiel mf.
wor·ship·ful (:shĭp-fəl) adj. reverente; *(adoring)* adorador.
worst (wûrst) I. adj. [superl. de **bad, ill**] peor; *(most severe)* más fuerte ♦ **in the w. way** FAM. de mala manera II. adv. peor; *(most severely)* más ♦ **w. of all** peor aún III. tr. derrotar, vencer IV. s. ♦ **at w.** o **if w. comes to w.** en el peor de los casos.
wor·sted (wŏŏs'tĭd, wûr'stĭd) s. *(yarn)* estambre m; *(fabric)* tela de estambre.
worth (wûrth) I. s. valor m, *(wealth)* fortuna; *(merit)* mérito ♦ **to get one's money's w.** sacar provecho de lo pagado II. adj. que vale ♦ **for what it is w.** por si sirve de algo • **to be w.** valer; *(in value)* tener un valor de; *(to be the equivalent of)* valer por • **to be w. it** valer la pena.
worth·less ('lĭs) adj. sin valor; *(contemptible)* despreciable.
worth·while ('hwīl') adj. que vale la pena.
wor·thy (wûr'thē) I. adj. -i- meritorio; *(useful)* útil; *(deserving)* digno II. s. persona ilustre.
would (wŏŏd) cf. **will²**.
would-be ('bē') adj. aspirante.
wound¹ (wŏŏnd) I. s. herida II. tr. & intr. herir.
wound² (wound) cf. **wind²**.
wove (wōv), **wo·ven** (wō'vən) cf. **weave**.
wow (wou) FAM. I. interj. ¡increíble!, ¡cáspita! II. s. gran éxito III. tr. entusiasmar.
wrack (răk) s. despojo, ruina ♦ **to go to w. and ruin** echarse a perder.
wraith (rāth) s. fantasma m, espectro.
wran·gle (răng'gəl) I. intr. pelear —tr. obtener arguyendo II. s. pelea.
wran·gler (:glər) s. *(quarreler)* pendenciero; *(cowboy)* vaquero.
wrap (răp) I. tr. -t o -pped, -pping envolver; *(rope, chain)* enrollar ♦ **to be wrapped up in** estar absorto en • **to w. up** *(to end)* cerrar; *(to summarize)* resumir —intr. enrollarse II. s.

(cloak) manto; *(wrapper)* envoltura ♦ **to keep under wraps** mantener en secreto.

wrap·a·round ('ə-round') s. manto.

wrap·per (:ər) s. *(person)* empaquetador *m*; *(wrap)* envoltura; *(robe)* bata.

wrap·ping (:ĭng) s. envoltura.

wrap·up ('ŭp') s. resumen *m*.

wrath (răth, räth) s. *(anger)* ira; *(fury)* furia.

wrath·ful ('fəl) adj. furioso.

wreak (rēk) tr. infligir; *(anger)* descargar ♦ **to w. havoc** hacer estragos.

wreath (rēth) s. [pl. **s**] guirnalda; *(spiral)* espiral *m*.

wreathe (rēth) tr. hacer una guirnalda de; *(to crown)* coronar con guirnalda; *(to surround)* rodear —intr. *(to curl)* enroscarse.

wreck (rĕk) I. s. destrucción *f*; *(crash)* choque *m*; *(shipwreck)* naufragio; *(collision remains)* destrozos; *(heap)* cascajo ♦ **to be a w.** estar hecho un cascajo II. tr. destrozar; *(to tear down)* derrumbar; *(to ruin)* arruinar —intr. destrozarse.

wreck·age ('ĭj) s. restos, despojos.

wreck·er (:ər) s. destructor *m*; *(demolition expert)* demoledor *m*; *(truck)* grúa.

wren (rĕn) s. reyezuelo, abadejo.

wrench (rĕnch) I. s. *(injury)* torcedura; MEC. llave *f* II. tr. torcer; *(to grieve)* doler.

wrest (rĕst) I. tr. arrebatar; *(to extract)* arrancar II. s. torción violenta.

wres·tle (rĕs'əl) intr. & tr. luchar (con *o* contra).

wres·tler (:lər) s. luchador *m*.

wres·tling (:lĭng) s. lucha.

wretch (rĕch) s. *(unhappy person)* desgraciado; *(base person)* canalla *m*.

wretch·ed ('ĭd) adj. desgraciado, miserable.

wrig·gle (rĭg'əl) I. intr. *(to squirm)* menearse; *(to proceed)* culebrear; *(to get out)* escabullirse; *(to get into)* insinuarse II. s. meneo, culebreo.

wring (rĭng) tr. **wrung** escurrir; *(to wrench)* torcer.

wring·er ('ər) s. escurridor *m*.

wrin·kle (rĭng'kəl) I. s. arruga; FAM. método nuevo II. tr. arrugar; *(brow)* fruncir —intr. arrugarse.

wrist (rĭst) s. puño; ANAT. muñeca ♦ **w. watch** reloj de pulsera.

wrist·band ('bănd') s. muñequera.

writ (rĭt) s. DER. mandato, orden *f*.

write (rīt) tr. **wrote, written** escribir; *(a will, contract)* redactar; *(a check)* extender, hacer; *(insurance)* preparar ♦ **to w. down** poner por escrito; *(to make a note of)* anotar • **to w. off** *(a person)* dar por perdido; *(to depreciate)* amortizar; *(a debt)* cancelar • **to w. out** poner por escrito; *(in full)* escribir con todas las letras —intr. escribir ♦ **to be nothing to w. home about** no ser nada del otro mundo.

write-in ('ĭn') s. candidato no oficial.

writ·er ('ĭtər) s. escritor *m*.

write-up (rīt'ŭp') s. crítica.

writhe (rīth) intr. retorcerse.

writ·ing (rī'tĭng) s. escritura; *(inscription)* inscripción *f*; *(handwriting)* letra; *(written work)* escrito ♦ **in w.** por escrito • **to see the w. on the wall** vérsela venir.

writ·ten (rĭt'n) cf. **write**.

wrong (rông) I. adj. malo; *(unfair)* injusto; *(incorrect)* erróneo; *(mistaken)* equivocado; *(not suitable)* inadecuado ♦ **to be w.** hacer mal; *(to be mistaken)* equivocarse; *(to be amiss)* andar mal • **to get up on the w. side of the bed**

levantarse con el pie izquierdo II. adv. mal ♦ **to do someone w.** ser injusto con • **to do, get w.** hacer, tener mal • **to go w.** *(morally)* ir por mal camino; *(to act mistakenly)* fallar; *(to go amiss)* salir mal • **to have it all w.** estar totalmente equivocado • **you can't go w.** FAM. no hay forma de equivocarse III. s. mal *m*; *(unjust act)* injusticia; *(bad deed)* maldad *f*; *(fault)* error *m* ♦ **to be in the w.** no tener razón • **to right a w.** deshacer un entuerto IV. tr. ser injusto con; *(to treat dishonorably)* agraviar; *(to malign)* calumniar.

wrong·do·er ('dōō'ər) s. maleante *mf*.

wrong·do·ing (:dōō'ĭng) s. mal *m*.

wrong·ful (:fəl) adj. injusto.

wrong-head·ed (:hĕd'ĭd) adj. obstinado.

wrote (rōt) cf. **write**.

wrought (rôt) adj. armado; *(shaped)* formado; *(elaborate)* labrado ♦ **w. iron** hierro forjado • **w. up** agitado.

wrung (rŭng) cf. **wring**.

wry (rī) adj. **-er, -est** *o* **-i-** *(crooked)* torcido; *(twisted)* forzado; *(ironical)* irónico.

wurst (wûrst, wŏŏrst) s. salchicha, embutido.

X

x, X (ĕks) s. vigésima cuarta letra del alfabeto inglés; MAT. incógnita ♦ **x amount of** una cantidad equis de • **to x out** tachar.

x-ax·is ('ăk'sĭs) s. [pl. **-es**] eje *m* horizontal.

X-chro·mo·some (:krō'mə-sōm') s. cromosoma *m* X.

xen·o·phile (zĕn'ə-fīl', zē'nə-) s. xenófilo.

xen·o·phil·i·a ('-fĭl'ē-ə) s. afición *f* a lo extranjero.

xen·o·phobe ('-fōb') s. xenófobo.

xen·o·pho·bi·a ('-fō'bē-ə) s. xenofobia.

xen·o·pho·bic (:bĭk) adj. xenófobo.

Xe·rox (zĭr'ŏks') I. s. marca registrada de un proceso rápido de reproducción; *(copy)* xerocopia II. tr. xerografiar.

X·mas (krĭs'məs, ĕks'məs) s. FAM. Navidad *f*.

x-ra·di·a·tion (ĕks'rā'dē-ā'shən) s. MED. tratamiento con rayos X; FÍS. radiación *f* de rayos X.

X-rat·ed (:rā'tĭd) adj. no apto para menores de 16 años.

x-ray *o* **X-ray** (:rā') I. s. radiografía; FÍS. rayo X II. tr. examinar con rayos X; *(to radiograph)* radiografiar.

xy·lo·phone (zī'lə-fōn') s. xilófono.

Y

y, Y (wī) s. vigésima quinta letra del alfabeto inglés.

yacht (yät) s. yate *m*.

yacht·ing (tä'tĭng) s. navegación *f* (en yate).

ya·hoo (yä'hōō) s. FAM. bruto, bestia.

yak¹ (yăk) s. ZOOL. yac *m*.

yak² intr. **-kk-** JER. parlotear, cotorrear.

yam (yăm) s. *(root)* ñame *f*; *(sweet potato)* batata.

yam·mer (yăm'ər) intr. *(to whimper)* lloriquear; *(to talk)* parlotear.

yank (yăngk) I. tr. & intr. tironear (de), dar un tirón (a) II. s. tirón *m*.

Yan·kee (yăng'kē) adj. & s. yanqui *mf*.

yap (yăp) **I.** intr. **-pp-** ladrar; JER. *(to jabber)* cotorrear **II.** s. ladrido; JER. *(jabber)* cháchara; *(mouth)* hocico.

yard[1] (yärd) s. *(measure)* yarda; MARÍT. verga ♦ **y. goods** tela vendida por yardas, géneros.

yard[2] s. *(enclosed grounds)* patio; *(surrounding grounds)* jardín m, *(work area)* depósito, taller m; *(corral)* corral m; F.C. estación f de depósito.

yard·age (yär′dĭj) s. medida en yardas; *(cloth)* tela.

yard·stick (yärd′stĭk′) s. vara de una yarda de largo; *(standard)* patrón m, norma.

yarn (yärn) s. hilo; FAM. *(story)* cuento, historia.

yaw (yô) **I.** intr. *(a ship)* guiñar; AER. desviarse **II.** s. guiñada, desvío.

yawl (yôl) s. yola.

yawn (yôn) **I.** intr. bostezar; *(cave, chasm)* abrirse **II.** s. bostezo.

yawn·ing (yô′nĭng) adj. abierto, cavernoso.

y-ax·is (wī′ăk′sĭs) s. [pl. **-es**] eje m vertical.

Y-chro·mo·some (wī′krō′mə-sōm′) s. cromosoma m Y.

ye (yē) pron. pers. ANT. vosotros, ustedes.

yea (yā) adv. & s. sí m.

yeah (yĕ′ə, yă′ə) adv. FAM. sí.

year (yĭr) s. año ♦ **a y.** por año, anualmente ♦ **financial** o **fiscal y.** año económico ♦ **from y. to y. año tras año ♦ once o y una vez al año ♦ school y.** año escolar ♦ **y. in y. out** año tras año ♦ pl. *(age)* edad <*she feels her y.* ya siente su edad>; *(long period)* una eternidad.

year·book (′bŏŏk′) s. anuario.

year-end o **year·end** (:ĕnd′) adj. & s. (de) fin m de año económico.

year·ling (:lĭng) s. animal m de un año de edad.

year·long (:lông′) adj. de un año de duración.

year·ly (:lē) **I.** adj. anual **II.** adv. anualmente **III.** s. anuario (revista, libro).

yearn (yûrn) intr. añorar; *(to feel compassion)* sentir compasión ♦ **to y. to** añorar.

yearn·ing (yûr′nĭng) s. anhelo, añoranza.

year-round (yĭr′round′) adj. de todo el año.

yeast (yēst) s. levadura; *(froth)* espuma, *(ferment)* fermento.

yell (yĕl) **I.** tr. & intr. gritar ♦ **to y. for help** pedir auxilio a gritos **II.** s. grito.

yel·low (yĕl′ō) **I.** s. amarillo; *(yolk)* yema ♦ pl. ictericia **II.** adj. *(color)* amarillo; *(hair)* rubio; JER. *(cowardly)* cobarde ♦ **to turn y.** amarillear • **y. jacket** avispa **III.** tr. & intr. volver(se) amarillo.

yel·low-bel·lied (:bĕl′ēd) adj. JER. cobarde.

yel·low·ish (:ĭsh) adj. amarillento.

yelp (yĕlp) **I.** intr. gañir **II.** s. gañido.

yen[1] (yĕn) **I.** intr. **-nn-** anhelar **II.** s. anhelo ♦ **to have a y.** desear • **to have a y. to** tener ganas de.

yen[2] (yĕn) s.inv. FIN. yen m.

yeo·man (yō′mən) **I.** s. [pl. **-men**] MARÍT. oficial m oficinista; G.B. *(landholder)* pequeño terrateniente **II.** adj. *(workmanlike)* sólido.

yeo·man·ry (:rē) s. terratenientes pequeños.

yep (yĕp) adv. FAM. sí.

yes (yĕs) **I.** adv. sí ♦ **to say y.** dar el sí • **y. indeed** claro que sí • **y. of course!** ¡por supuesto! **II.** s. [pl. **-es**] sí m ♦ **y. man** FAM. subordinado servil.

yes·ter·day (yĕs′tər-dā′) **I.** adv. ayer ♦ **I wasn't born y.** no soy tonto • **late y.** ayer a última hora **II.** s. *(the day)* de ayer m ♦ **the day before y.** anteayer ♦ pl. pasado.

yes·ter·year (:yĭr′) s. el año pasado; *(yore)* antaño.

yet (yĕt) **I.** adv. todavía, aún; *(thus far)* ya; *(still more)* aún màs; *(eventually)* probablemente ♦ **as (of) y.** hasta ahora • **not y.** todavía no • **y. again** una vez más • **y. more** aún más **II.** conj. *(nevertheless)* sin embargo; *(but)* pero.

yield (yēld) **I.** tr. dar, producir; *(profit)* rendir; *(to give up)* ceder ♦ **to y. up** entregar; *(secret)* revelar —intr. rendirse; *(in traffic)* ceder el paso ♦ **to y. to** ceder a **II.** s. INDUS. rendimiento; AGR. cosecha; COM. *(profit)* beneficio.

yield·ing (yēl′dĭng) adj. flexible; *(docile)* dócil.

yip (yĭp) **I.** s. ladrido agudo **II.** intr. **-pp-** ladrar.

yip·pee (yĭp′ē) interj. ¡yupi!, ¡huja!

yo·del (yōd′l) **I.** tr. & intr. cantar a la tirolesa **II.** s. canto tirolés.

yo·ga (yō′gə) s. yoga m.

yo·gurt (yō′gərt) s. yogur m.

yoke (yōk) **I.** s. yugo; *(pair of oxen)* yunta; *(carried by a person)* balancín m; *(clamp)* brida; *(of garment)* canesú m ♦ **to throw off the y.** sacudir el yugo **II.** tr. *(to join)* uncir; *(to bind)* unir.

yo·kel (yō′kəl) s. paleto.

yolk (yōk) s. yema.

yon·der (yŏn′dər) **I.** adj. aquel **II.** adv. allá **III.** pron. aquél.

yoo-hoo (yōō′hōō) interj. ¡eh!, ¡hola!

yore (yôr) s. antaño.

you (yōō) pron. pers. [sujeto] *(familiar)* tú, vosotros, vosotras; *(formal)* usted, ustedes; [complemento] *(familiar, direct and indirect)* te, os <*I'll call you later* os llamo más tarde> <*I handed it to you* te lo di>; *(formal, direct)* lo, la, los, las <*I'll see you tomorrow* la veo mañana> <*they invited you* los invitaron>; *(formal, indirect)* le, les, se <*I give you the book* te doy el libro> <*I give it to you* se lo doy>; [después de preposición] *(familiar)* ti, vosotros, vosotras <*the book is for you* el libro es para ti> <*he'll go with you* irá con vosotras>; *(formal)* usted, ustedes <*the book is for you* el libro es para usted> <*he'll go with you* irá con ustedes> ♦ **all of y.** todos vosotros, todos ustedes • **between y. and me** entre tú y yo • **if I were y.** yo que tú • **with y.** contigo, con usted(es), con vosotros • **y. can't do that** eso no se permite • **y. never know** uno nunca sabe.

you-all (yōō-ôl′) pron. FAM. vosotros.

young (yŭng) **I.** adj. joven; *(early life)* de juventud ♦ **in my younger days** en mi juventud • **y. lady** señorita • **y. man, woman** joven **II.** s.pl. jóvenes mf; *(offspring)* cría (de animal) ♦ **with y.** preñada.

young·ish (′ĭsh) adj. bastante joven.

young·ster (yŭng′stər) s. jovencito.

your (yŏr, yər) adj. pos. *(familiar, sg.)* tu(s); *(formal, sg.)* su(s), de usted; *(familiar, pl.)* vuestro(s), vuestra(s); *(formal, pl.)* su(s), de ustedes.

yours (yŏrz) pron. pers. *(familiar, sg.)* tuyo, (la) tuya; *(formal, sg.)* (el o la) de usted, el suyo, la suya; *(familiar, pl.)* (el) vuestro, (la) vuestra; *(formal, pl.)* (el o la) de ustedes, (el) suyo, (la) suya.

your·self (yŏr-sĕlf′, yər-) **I.** pron. pers. *(familiar)* tú (mismo, misma) <*write it down y.* es críbelo tú mismo>; *(formal)* usted (mismo, misma) <*you said it y.* usted misma lo dijo> II. pron. reflex. *(familiar)* te <*please, don't hurt y.* por favor, no te hagas daño>; *(formal)* se <*prepárese ahora* prepare yourself now>.

your·selves (:sĕlvz´) I. pron. pers. *(familiar)* vosotros (mismos), vosotras (mismas) <*you y. wanted it* vosotras mismas lo quisisteis>; *(formal)* ustedes (mismos, mismas) <*you did it to y.* se lo buscaron ustedes mismos> II. pron. reflex. *(familiar)* os <*have you dressed y. yet?* ¿os habéis vestido ya?>; *(formal)* se <*give y. plenty of time* dense suficiente tiempo>.

youth (yōth) s. [pl. **s**] juventud *f*; *(young person)* joven *mf*.

youth·ful (´fəl) adj. joven, juvenil.

yowl (youl) I. intr. dar aullidos, aullar II. s. aullido.

yo-yo (yō´yō´) I. s. *(toy)* yoyó; JER. *(dope)* tonto, patán *m* II. intr. vacilar.

yuc·ca (yŭk´ə) s. yuca.

yum·my (yŭm´ē) adj. **-i-** FAM. delicioso, rico.

Z

z, Z (zē) s. vigésima sexta letra del alfabeto inglés.

za·ny (zā´nē) I. s. persona cómica y estrafalaria; TEAT. bufón *m* II. adj. **-i-** *(comical)* estrafalario; *(clownish)* bufo.

zap (zăp) JER. I. tr. **-pp-** *(to kill)* matar; *(to destroy)* destruir II. interj. ¡zas!

zeal (zēl) s. celo, ahínco.

zeal·ot·ry (zĕl´ə-trē) s. fanatismo.

zeal·ous (:əs) adj. celoso, fervoroso.

ze·bra (zē´brə) s. cebra.

ze·nith (zē´nĭth) s. cenit *m*.

zeph·yr (zĕf´ər) s. brisa; TEJ. céfiro.

zep·pe·lin (zĕp´ə-lĭn) s. zepelín *m*.

ze·ro (zîr´ō) I. s. [pl. **(e)s**] cero; *(nothing)* nada; METEOR. cero grado II. adj. nulo III. tr. & intr. ♦ **to z. in on** afinar la puntería hacia; *(to*

close in) apuntar hacia.

ze·ro-base(d) (:bãs[t]´) que justifica los gastos en términos de necesidad o costo.

zest (zĕst) s. gusto, sabor *m*; *(enjoyment)* brío; *(rind)* cáscara.

zest·ful (´fəl) adj. sabroso; *(spirited)* lleno de vida.

zig·zag (zĭg´zăg´) I. s. zigzag *m* II. adj. en zigzag III. adv. zigzagueando IV. intr. **-gg-** ir zigzagueando —tr. poner en zigzag.

zilch (zĭlch) s. JER. nada, cero.

zil·lion (zĭl´yən) s. FAM. número astronómico.

zinc (zĭngk) s. cinc *m*.

zing (zĭng) I. s. zumbido II. intr. FAM. zumbar.

zing·er (´ər) s. observación *f* mordaz.

zin·ni·a (zĭn´ē-ə) s. cinnia.

zip (zĭp) I. s. silbido; *(energy)* vigor *m* II. intr. **-pp-** zumbar ♦ **to z. by** pasar como una bala • **to z. up** subir o cerrar la cremallera —tr. cerrar la cremallera de.

zip·per (´ər) s. cremallera.

zip·py (:ē) adj. **-i-** vivaz, enérgico.

zir·con (zûr´kŏn´) s. circón *m*.

zith·er (zĭth´ər, zĭth´-) s. cítara.

zo·di·ac (zō´dē-ăk´) s. zodiaco.

zom·bi(e) (zŏm´bē) s. cadáver resucitado; FIG. autómata *m*.

zo·nal (zō´nəl) adj. zonal.

zone (zōn) I. s. zona II. tr. dividir en zonas.

zon·ing (zō´nĭng) s. restricciones *f* para edificar en un barrio de una ciudad.

zonked (zŏngkt) adj. JER. mamado.

zoo (zō) s. zoo; FIG. confusión *f*.

zo·o·log·i·cal (zō´ə-lŏj´ĭ-kəl) adj. zoológico.

zo·ol·o·gist (zō-ŏl´ə-jĭst) s. zoólogo.

zo·ol·o·gy (:jē) s. zoología.

zoom (zōm) I. intr. *(to buzz)* zumbar; AVIA. subir verticalmente; FOTOG. *(in)* acercarse; *(out)* alejarse ♦ **to z. away** salir zumbando II. s. *(sound)* zumbido; AVIA. subida vertical.

zounds (zoundz) interj. ¡cáspita!

zuc·chi·ni (zō-kē´nē) s.inv. zapallito italiano.

zwie·back (swē´bãk´, swī´-) s. tostada de pan ligeramente azucarada.